Tax Formula for Individuals

Income (broadly defined)........	$xx,xxx
Less: Exclusions........	(x,xxx)
Gross income........	$xx,xxx
Less: Deductions *for* adjusted gross income........	(x,xxx)
Adjusted gross income........	$xx,xxx
Less: The greater of— Total itemized deductions *or* standard deduction........	(x,xxx)
Less: Personal and dependency exemptions*........	(x,xxx)
Deduction for qualified business income**........	(x,xxx)
Taxable income........	$xx,xxx
Tax on taxable income........	$ x,xxx
Less: Tax credits (including Federal income tax withheld and prepaid)........	(xxx)
Tax due (or refund)........	$ xxx

*Exemption deductions are not allowed from 2018 through 2025.
**Only applies from 2018 through 2025.

Basic Standard Deduction Amounts

Filing Status	2022	2023
Single	$12,950	$13,850
Married, filing jointly	25,900	27,700
Surviving spouse	25,900	27,700
Head of household	19,400	20,800
Married, filing separately	12,950	13,850

Amount of Each Additional Standard Deduction

Filing Status	2022	2023
Single	$1,750	$1,850
Married, filing jointly	1,400	1,500
Surviving spouse	1,400	1,500
Head of household	1,750	1,850
Married, filing separately	1,400	1,500

Personal and Dependency Exemption

2022	2023
$4,400	$4,700

Note: Exemption deductions have been suspended from 2018 through 2025. However, the personal and dependency exemption amount is used for other purposes (including determining whether a "qualifying relative" is a taxpayer's dependent).

IT'S NOT JUST AN EXAM, IT'S YOUR FUTURE

A legacy of learning for a lifetime of success

As the industry's leading partner in CPA Exam preparation, we work harder (and smarter) to help you get Exam Day Ready(SM). Becker CPA Exam Review is as close as you can get to the real thing. It follows the AICPA blueprint and includes a user-interface that mirrors the exam, so you're already familiar come exam day.

Personalized learning

No two people learn exactly the same way. That's why our proprietary **Adapt2U Technology** makes learning more personal – and more dynamic. Powered by award-winning artificial intelligence, it constantly assesses your knowledge, building upon weaknesses and reinforcing strengths, for a truly personal experience, helping you to becom Exam Day Ready(SM).

1 million +
Candidates have prepared with Becker

90% +
Of Watt Sells award winners (2005–2021) have prepared with Becker

The top 100
Accounting firms rely on Becker for their staff's exam preparation

2,900 +
Accounting firms, corporations, alliances, government agencies and universities choose Becker

94% + Pass rate
Becker's Exam Day Ready(SM) Students report

becker.com     

Becker

SOUTH-WESTERN FEDERAL TAXATION

COMPREHENSIVE VOLUME 2024

General Editors

James C. Young
Ph.D., CPA

Mark B. Persellin
Ph.D., CPA, CFP®

Annette Nellen
J.D., CPA, CGMA

David M. Maloney
Ph.D., CPA

Andrew D. Cuccia
Ph.D., CPA

Sharon S. Lassar
Ph.D., CPA

Bradrick M. Cripe
Ph.D., CPA

Contributing Authors

James H. Boyd
Ph.D., CPA
Arizona State University

Bradrick M. Cripe
Ph.D., CPA
Northern Illinois University

D. Larry Crumbley
Ph.D., CPA
Texas A&M University – Corpus Christi

Andrew D. Cuccia
Ph.D., CPA
University of Oklahoma

Steven C. Dilley
J.D., Ph.D., CPA
Michigan State University

Sharon S. Lassar
Ph.D., CPA
University of Denver

David M. Maloney
Ph.D., CPA
University of Virginia

Annette Nellen
J.D., CPA, CGMA
San Jose State University

Mark B. Persellin
Ph.D., CPA, CFP®
St. Mary's University

William A. Raabe
Ph.D., CPA
Philadelphia, Pennsylvania

Toby Stock
Ph.D., CPA
Ohio University

James C. Young
Ph.D., CPA
Northern Illinois University

Kristina Zvinakis
Ph.D.
The University of Texas at Austin

Australia • Brazil • Canada • Mexico • Singapore • United Kingdom • United States

***Southern-Western Federal Taxation: Comprehensive Volume*, 2024 Edition**

James C. Young, Mark B. Persellin, Annette Nellen, David M. Maloney, Andrew D. Cuccia, Sharon S. Lassar, Bradrick M. Cripe

SVP, Product: Cheryl Costantini

VP, Product: Thais Alencar

Portfolio Product Director: Joe Sabatino

Portfolio Product Manager: Jonathan Gross

Product Assistant: Flannery Cowan

Learning Designer: MariCarmen Constable

Content Manager: Laura Hampton

Digital Project Manager: Steven McMillan

Director, Product Marketing: Danae April

Product Marketing Manager: Jason Sakos

Content Acquisition Analyst: Nichole Nalenz

Production Service: LEAP Publishing Services, Inc. & Straive

Designer: Chris Doughman

Cover Image Source: Pgiam/E+/Getty Images

Interior Image Source:
Concept Summary: iStock.com/enot-poloskun
Global Tax Issues: Enot-Poloskun/E+/Getty Images
Ethics & Equity: iStock.com/LdF
Comprehensive Tax Return Problems: iStock.com/peepo
Financial Disclosure Insights: Vyaseleva Elena/Shutterstock.com
Framework 1040: Concept Photo/Shutterstock.com

For product information and technology assistance, contact us at **Cengage Customer & Sales Support, 1-800-354-9706** or **support.cengage.com.**

For permission to use material from this text or product, submit all requests online at **www.cengage.com/permissions.**

ISSN: 0741-5184
2024 Annual Edition

Student Edition ISBN: 978-0-357-90041-3
Looseleaf Edition ISBN: 978-0-357-90042-0

Cengage
200 Pier 4 Boulevard
Boston, MA 02210
USA

Cengage is a leading provider of customized learning solutions. Our employees reside in nearly 40 different countries and serve digital learners in 165 countries around the world. Find your local representative at **www.cengage.com**.

To learn more about Cengage platforms and services, register or access your online learning solution, or purchase materials for your course, visit **www.cengage.com.**

Printed in the United States of America
Print Number: 01 Print Year: 2023

Preface

Committed to Educational Success

South-Western Federal Taxation (SWFT) is the most trusted and best-selling taxation series used by colleges and universities. We are focused exclusively on providing the most useful, comprehensive, and up-to-date texts, online study aids, tax preparation tools, and research tools to help instructors and students succeed in their tax courses and beyond.

SWFT is a comprehensive package of teaching and learning materials, significantly enhanced with each edition to meet instructor and student needs and to add overall value to learning taxation.

Comprehensive Volume, 2024 Edition provides a dynamic learning experience inside and outside of the classroom. Built with resources and tools that have been identified as the most important, our complete learning system provides pathways for students to achieve success in their tax courses, as well as the CPA and Enrolled Agent exams.

In addition, *Comprehensive Volume,* 2024 Edition provides accessible, comprehensive, and authoritative coverage of the relevant tax code and regulations as they pertain to the individual and business taxpayer, as well as coverage of all major developments in Federal income taxation.

In revising the 2024 Edition, we focused on:

- ***Accessibility. Clarity. Substance.*** The authors and editors made this their focus as they revised the 2024 edition. Coverage has been streamlined to make it more accessible to students, and difficult concepts have been clarified, all without losing the substance that makes up the *South-Western Federal Taxation* series.
- ***Developing professional skills.*** SWFT excels in bringing students to a professional level in their tax knowledge and skills, to prepare them for immediate success in their careers. We include development of written and verbal communication skills, the use of tax preparation and tax research software, orientation toward success on the CPA exam (including the 2024 changes to the exam), exposure to tax policy and tax law development, consideration of the time value of money in the tax planning process, and experience with advanced spreadsheet applications and data analytics.
- ***CNOWv2 as a complete learning system.*** Cengage Learning understands that digital learning solutions are central to the classroom. Through sustained research, we continually refine our learning solutions in CNOWv2 to meet evolving student and instructor needs. CNOWv2 fulfills learning and course management needs by offering a personalized study plan, video lectures, auto-graded homework, auto-graded tests, and a full eBook with features and advantages that address common challenges.

Learning Tools and Features to Help Students Make the Connection

Full-Color Design: We understand that students struggle with learning difficult tax law concepts and applying them to real-world scenarios. The 2024 edition uses color to bring the text to life, capture student attention, and present the tax law in an understandable and logical format.

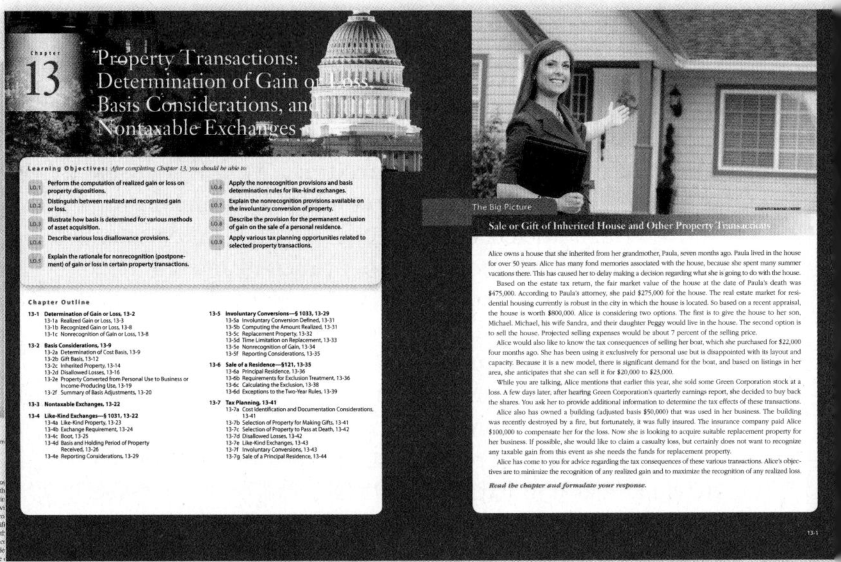

- Selected **content is streamlined** to guide students in focusing on the most important concepts for the CPA exam while still providing in-depth coverage of topics.

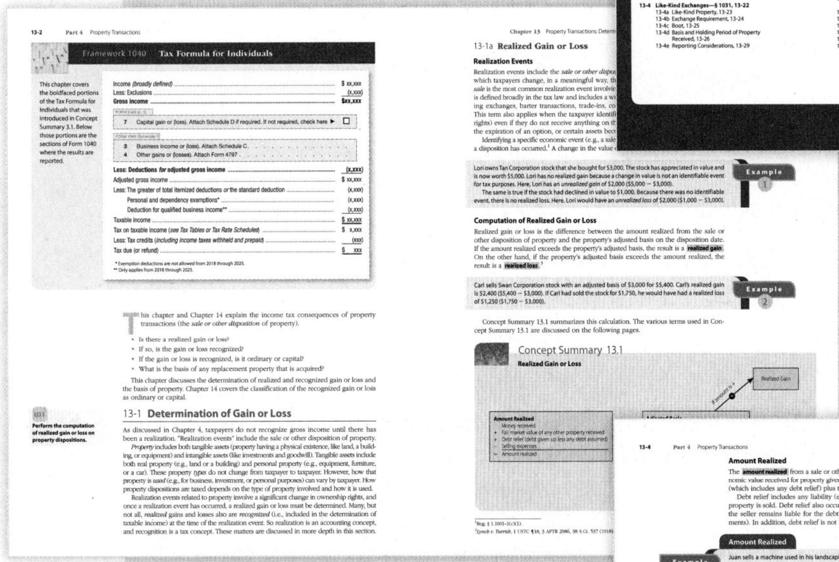

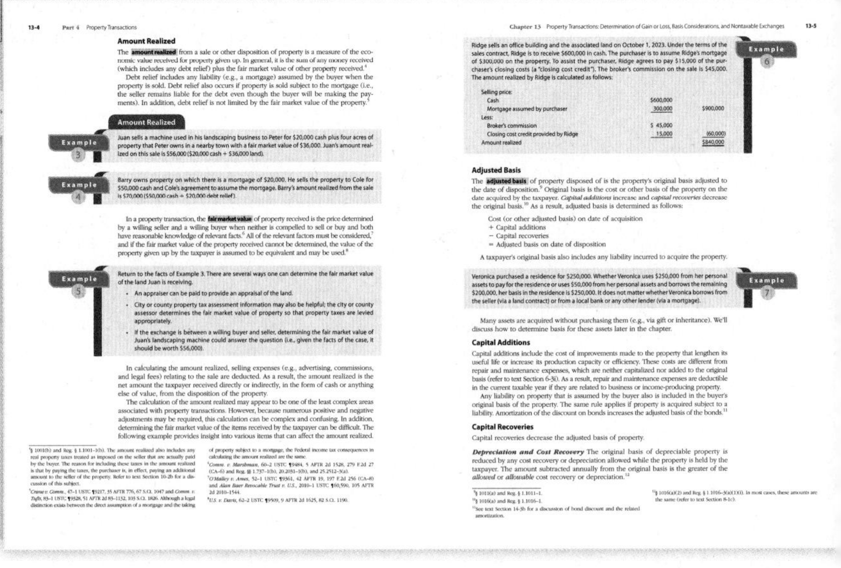

- Examples are clearly labeled and directly follow concepts to assist with student application. An **average of over 40 examples in each chapter** use realistic situations to illustrate the complexities of the tax law and allow students to integrate chapter concepts with illustrations and examples.

Computational Exercises: Students need to learn to apply the rules and concepts covered in each chapter to truly understand them. These exercises, many of which mirror text examples, allow students to practice and apply what they are learning.

- ❑ Found in the end-of-chapter sections of the textbook
- ❑ CNOWv2 provides algorithmic versions of these problems

Computational Exercises

26. LO.1 Sally owns real property for which the annual property taxes are $9,000. She sells the property to Kate on March 9, 2023, for $550,000. Kate pays the real property taxes for the entire year on October 1, 2023.
    a. How much of the property taxes can be deducted by Sally and how much by Kate?
    b. What effect does the property tax apportionment have on Kate's adjusted basis in the property?
    c. What effect does the apportionment have on Sally's amount realized from the sale?
    d. How would the answers in parts (b) and (c) differ if Sally paid the taxes?

Research and Data Analytics Problems:

- ❑ Research Problems provide students with vital practice in an increasingly demanded skill area. These end-of-chapter items ask students to find and analyze tax documents and/or tax data, helping them to understand the application of this information in various scenarios. These essential features prepare students for professional tax environments.

Becker Professional Education Review Questions: End-of-chapter CPA Review Questions from Becker PREPARE STUDENTS FOR SUCCESS. Students review key concepts using proven questions from Becker Professional Education®—one of the industry's most effective tools to prepare for the CPA exam.

- ❑ Located in select end-of-chapter sections
- ❑ Tagged by concept in CNOWv2
- ❑ Questions similar to what students would actually find on the CPA exam

Becker

Becker CPA Review Questions

Becker

1. Jasmin purchased 100 shares of Pinkstey Corporation (publicly traded company) on January 1 of year 1 for $5,000. The FMV of the shares at the end of year 1 was $6,000. On January 1 of year 4, Pinkstey Corporation declared a 2-for-1 stock split when the fair market value of the stock was $65 per share. On January 1 of year 5, Jasmin sold all of her Pinkstey Corporation stock when the fair market value was $40 per share. Which of the following statements is true?
   a. Jasmin reports $6,500 in gross income for the 2-for-1 stock split in year 4.
   b. Jasmin's basis in the Pinkstey Corporation stock at the end of year 4 is $65 per share.
   c. Jasmin has no taxable income for the Pinkstey Corporation stock in year 4.
   d. Jasmin owns 100 shares in Pinkstey Corporation stock at the end of year 4.
2. Alice gifted stock to her son, Bob, in year 5. Alice bought the stock in year 1 for $8,300. The value of the stock on the date of gift was $6,400. Bob sold the stock in year 7 for $15,800. What is Bob's recognized gain or loss on the sale in year 7?
   a. $0
   b. $7,500 gain
   c. $9,400 gain
   d. $15,800 gain

See how the SWFT series helps students understand the big picture and the relevancy behind what they are learning.

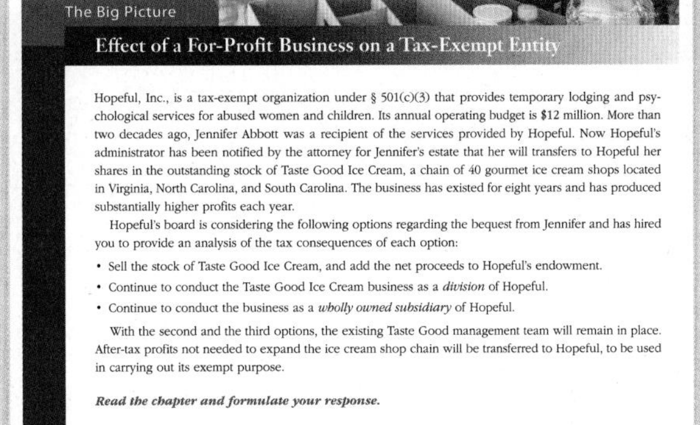

The Big Picture

Effect of a For-Profit Business on a Tax-Exempt Entity

Hopeful, Inc., is a tax-exempt organization under § 501(c)(3) that provides temporary lodging and psychological services for abused women and children. Its annual operating budget is $12 million. More than two decades ago, Jennifer Abbott was a recipient of the services provided by Hopeful. Now Hopeful's administrator has been notified by the attorney for Jennifer's estate that her will transfers to Hopeful her shares in the outstanding stock of Taste Good Ice Cream, a chain of 40 gourmet ice cream shops located in Virginia, North Carolina, and South Carolina. The business has existed for eight years and has produced substantially higher profits each year.

Hopeful's board is considering the following options regarding the bequest from Jennifer and has hired you to provide an analysis of the tax consequences of each option:

- Sell the stock of Taste Good Ice Cream, and add the net proceeds to Hopeful's endowment.
- Continue to conduct the Taste Good Ice Cream business as a *division* of Hopeful.
- Continue to conduct the business as a *wholly owned subsidiary* of Hopeful.

With the second and the third options, the existing Taste Good management team will remain in place. After-tax profits not needed to expand the ice cream shop chain will be transferred to Hopeful, to be used in carrying out its exempt purpose.

Read the chapter and formulate your response.

The Big Picture: Tax Applications for the Real World. Taxation comes alive at the start of each chapter as The Big Picture examples provide a glimpse into the lives, families, careers, and tax situations of typical taxpayers. Students will follow a family, individual, or other taxpayer throughout the chapter, to discover how the concepts they are learning apply in the real world.

Finally, to solidify student comprehension, each chapter concludes with a **Refocus on The Big Picture** summary and tax planning scenario. These scenarios re-emphasize the concepts and topics from the chapter and allow students to confirm their understanding of the material.

Framework 1040: Fitting It All Together. This chapter-opening feature demonstrates how individual income tax topics fit together, using the Income Tax Formula for Individuals as the framework. The framework helps students organize their understanding of the chapters and topics to see how they relate to the basic tax formula and then identify where these items are reported on the Form 1040. Framework 1040 helps students navigate topics by explaining how tax concepts are organized.

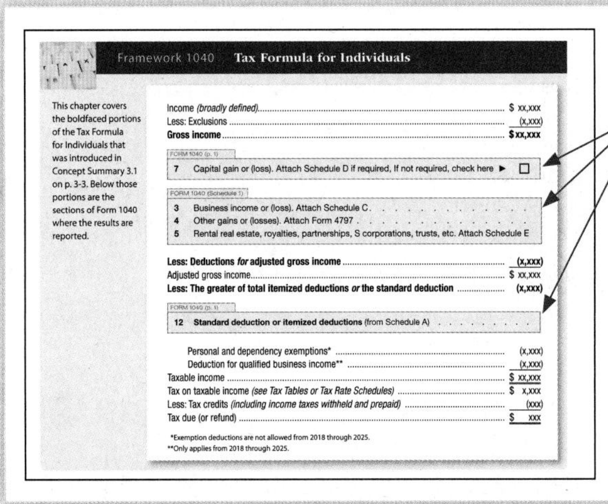

Framework 1040 **Tax Formula for Individuals**

This chapter covers the boldfaced portions of the Tax Formula for Individuals that was introduced in Concept Summary 3.1 on p. 3-3. Below those portions are the sections of Form 1040 where the results are reported.

Income *(broadly defined)*	$ xx,xxx
Less: Exclusions	(x,xxx)
Gross income	**$ xx,xxx**

FORM 1040 (p. 1)
7 Capital gain or (loss). Attach Schedule D if required. If not required, check here ▶ ☐

FORM 1040 (Schedule 1)
3 Business income or (loss). Attach Schedule C
4 Other gains or (losses). Attach Form 4797
5 Rental real estate, royalties, partnerships, S corporations, trusts, etc. Attach Schedule E

Less: Deductions *for* adjusted gross income	**(x,xxx)**
Adjusted gross income	$ xx,xxx
Less: The greater of total itemized deductions *or* the standard deduction	**(x,xxx)**

FORM 1040 (p. 1)
12 **Standard deduction or itemized deductions** (from Schedule A)

Personal and dependency exemptions*	(x,xxx)
Deduction for qualified business income**	(x,xxx)
Taxable income	$ xx,xxx
Tax on taxable income *(see Tax Tables or Tax Rate Schedules)*	$ x,xxx
Less: Tax credits *(including income taxes withheld and prepaid)*	(xxx)
Tax due (or refund)	$ xxx

*Exemption deductions are not allowed from 2018 through 2025.
**Only applies from 2018 through 2025.

Use this chapter-opening **Framework 1040,** which shows the topics as they appear in the individual tax formula, to understand where on Form 1040 these chapter topics appear.

Financial Disclosure Insights: Tax professionals need to understand how taxes affect the financial statements. **Financial Disclosure Insights**, appearing throughout the text, use current information about existing taxpayers to highlight book-tax reporting differences, effective tax rates, and trends in reporting conventions.

> **Financial Disclosure Insights — Tax and Book Depreciation**
>
> A common book-tax difference relates to the depreciation amounts that are reported for GAAP and Federal income tax purposes. Typically, tax depreciation deductions are accelerated; that is, they are claimed in earlier reporting periods than is the case for financial accounting purposes.
>
> Almost every tax law change since 1980 has included depreciation provisions that accelerate the related deductions relative to the expenses allowed under GAAP. Accelerated cost recovery deductions represent a means by which the taxing jurisdiction infuses the business with cash flow created by the reduction in the year's tax liabilities.
>
> For instance, recently, about one-quarter of General Electric's deferred tax liabilities related to depreciation differences. Ford's depreciation differences amounted to about one-third of its deferred tax liabilities. And for the trucking firm Ryder Systems, depreciation differences accounted for virtually all of the deferred tax liabilities.

> **Ethics & Equity — Punching the Time Clock at Year-End**
>
> As the end of the tax year approaches, Julie, a successful full-time real estate developer and investor, recognizes that her income tax situation for the year could be bleak. Unless she and her spouse, Ralph, are able to generate more hours of participation in one of her real estate rental activities, they will not reach the material participation threshold. Consequently, the tax losses from the venture will not be deductible. To ensure deductibility, Julie suggests the following plan:
>
> - She will document the time she spends "thinking" about her rental activities.
> - During the week, Ralph will visit the apartment building to oversee (in a management role) the operations of the rentals.
> - On weekends, she and Ralph will visit the same units to further evaluate the operations.
> - Also on the weekends, they will be on the lookout for other rental properties to buy and visit open houses of homes they find on the market. Julie plans to count both her and Ralph's weekend hours toward the tally of total participation.
>
> Julie contends that the law clearly allows the efforts of one's spouse to count for purposes of the material participation tests. Likewise, nothing in the tax law requires taxpayers to be efficient in their hours of participation. How do you react?

Ethics & Equity: These features will spark critical thinking and invite classroom discussion, enticing students to evaluate their own value system. Suggested responses to Ethics & Equity scenarios appear in the Solutions Manual.

Tax Planning: Chapters include a separate section calling attention to how taxpayers can use the law to reach financial and other goals. Tax planning applications and suggestions appear throughout each chapter, as pertinent topics are discussed.

> **29-5 Tax Planning**
>
> **29-5a The Federal Gift Tax**
>
> For gifts that generate a tax, consideration must be given to the present value to the donor of the gift taxes paid. Because the donor loses the use of these funds, the expected interval between a gift (the imposition of the gift tax) and death (the imposition of the estate tax) may make the gift less attractive from an economic standpoint.

> **Global Tax Issues — Filing a Joint Return**
>
> John is a U.S. citizen and resident, but he spends much of his time in London, where his employer sends him on frequent assignments. John is married to Victoria, a citizen and resident of the United Kingdom.
>
> Can John and Victoria file a joint return for U.S. Federal income tax purposes? Although § 6013(a)(1) specifically precludes the filing of a joint return if one spouse is a nonresident alien, another Code provision permits an exception. Under § 6013(g), the parties can elect to treat the nonqualifying spouse as a "resident" of the United States. This election would allow John and Victoria to file jointly.
>
> But should John and Victoria make this election? If Victoria has considerable income of her own (from non-U.S. sources), the election could be ill-advised. As a nonresident alien, Victoria's non-U.S. source income *would not* be subject to the U.S. income tax. If she is treated as a U.S. resident, however, her non-U.S. source income *will be subject to U.S. tax*. Under the U.S. global approach to taxation, all income (regardless of where earned) of anyone who is a *resident* or *citizen* of the United States is subject to tax.

Global Tax Issues: This feature gives insight into the ways in which taxation is affected by international concerns and illustrates the effects of various events on tax liabilities across the globe.

Take your students from Motivation to Mastery with CNOWv2

CNOWv2 is a powerful course management tool and online homework resource that elevates student thinking by providing superior content designed with the entire student workflow in mind.

- ❑ **Motivation:** engage students and better prepare them for class
- ❑ **Application:** help students learn problem-solving behavior and skills to guide them to complete taxation problems on their own
- ❑ **Mastery:** help students make the leap from memorizing concepts to actual critical thinking

Motivation —

To help with student engagement and preparedness, CNOWv2 for SWFT offers:

- ❑ **"Tax Drills" test students on key concepts and applications.** With three to five questions per learning objective, these "quick-hit" questions help students prepare for class lectures or review prior to an exam.

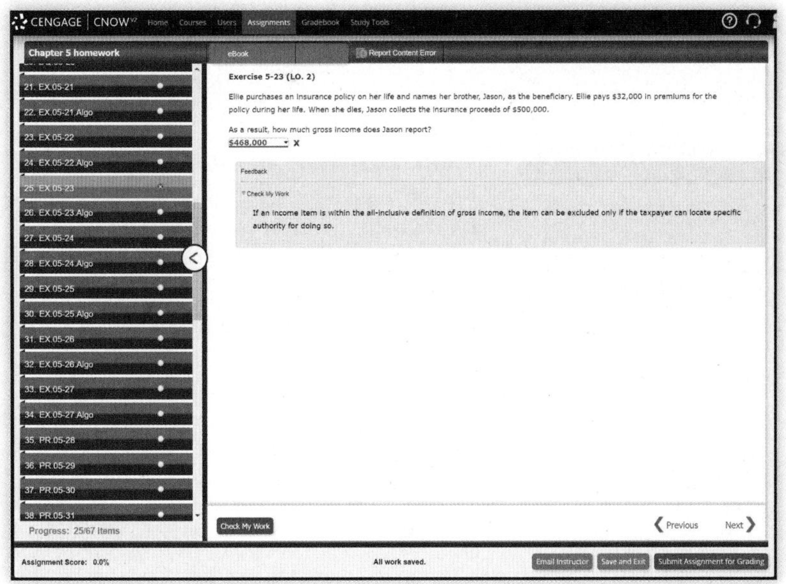

Application —

Students need to learn problem-solving behavior and skills, to guide them to complete taxation problems on their own. However, as students try to work through homework problems, sometimes they need extra help. To reinforce concepts and keep students on the right track, CNOWv2 for SWFT offers the following:

- ❑ **End-of-chapter homework from the text** is expanded and enhanced to follow the workflow a professional would use to solve various client scenarios. These enhancements better engage students and encourage them to think like a tax professional.

- ❑ **Algorithmic versions** of end-of-chapter homework are available for computational exercises and at least 15 problems per chapter.
- ❑ **"Check My Work" Feedback.** Homework questions include immediate feedback so students can learn as they go. Levels of feedback include an option for "check my work" prior to submission of an assignment.
- ❑ **Post-Submission Feedback.** After submitting an assignment, students receive even more extensive feedback explaining why their answers were incorrect. Instructors can decide how much feedback their students receive and when, including the full solution.
- ❑ **Built-in Test Bank** for online assessment.

Mastery —

- ❑ **Tax Form Problems** give students the option to complete the Cumulative Intuit ProConnect Tax problems and other homework items found in the end-of-chapter manually or in a digital environment.
- ❑ **An Adaptive Study Plan** comes complete with an eBook, practice quizzes, glossary, and flashcards. It is designed to help give students additional support and prepare them for the exam.

CNOWv2 Instant Access Code ISBN:
978-0-357-90045-1 (two-semester access)

Contact your Cengage Learning Consultant about different bundle options.

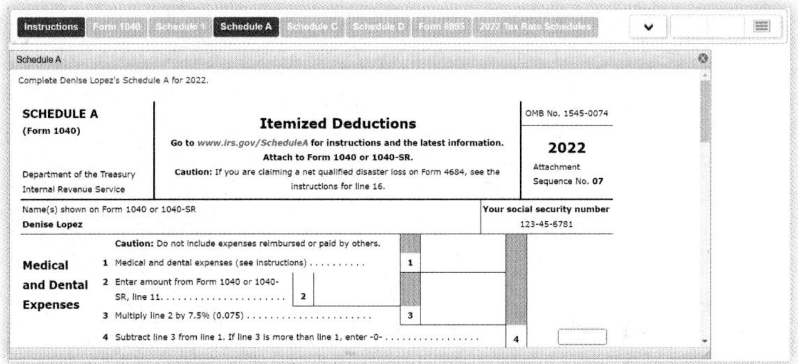

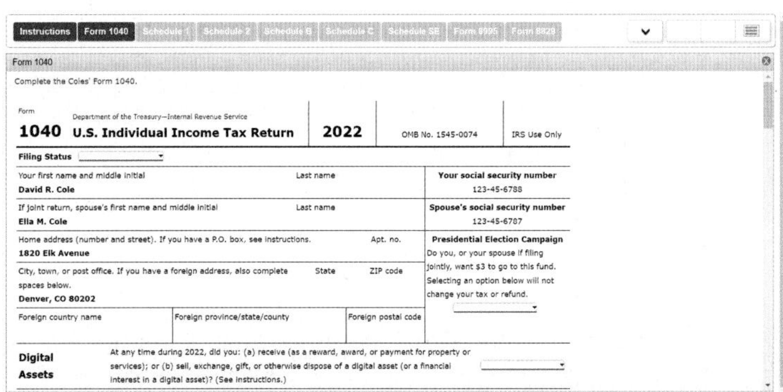

Extensively Revised. Definitively Up to Date.

Each year the ***South-Western Federal Taxation*** series is updated with thousands of changes to each text. Some of these changes result from the feedback we receive from instructors and students in the form of reviews, focus groups, web surveys, and personal e-mail correspondence to our authors and team members. Other changes come from our careful analysis of the evolving tax environment. **We make sure that every tax law change relevant to the introductory taxation course was considered, summarized, and fully integrated into the revision of text and supplementary materials.**

Based on our use of the ***South-Western Federal Taxation*** *Comprehensive Volume* and feedback from adopters, the 2024 edition has been expanded from 28 to 30 chapters. Partnership taxation is now covered in two chapters, rather than just one. Chapter 21 discusses partnership formation, operation, and basis issues. Chapter 22 explores partnership distributions, transfers of interests, and terminations. We have also added a chapter on accounting for income taxes. Chapter 24 covers the basics of income tax accounting that should be relevant for accounting professionals who must interpret the income tax expense reported in financial statements.

With these additions, the chapter numbering for the 2024 edition has changed:

Comprehensive Volume 2024 Edition	***Comprehensive Volume 2023 Edition***
Chapters 1 through 21	Chapters 1 through 21
Chapter 22	
Chapter 23	Chapter 22
Chapter 24	
Chapter 25	Chapter 23
Chapter 26	Chapter 24
Chapter 27	Chapter 25
Chapter 28	Chapter 26
Chapter 29	Chapter 27
Chapter 30	Chapter 28

The ***South-Western Federal Taxation*** authors have made every effort to keep all materials up to date and accurate. All chapters contain the following general changes for the 2024 edition:

- Updated materials to reflect changes made by the Inflation Reduction Act of 2022 and the SECURE 2.0 Act of 2022.
- Updated materials to reflect changes made through other legislative action, new administrative rulings, and court decisions.
- Streamlined chapter content (where applicable) to clarify material and make it easier for students to understand.
- Revised materials as the result of changes caused by indexing of statutory amounts.
- Revised Discussion Questions, Computational Exercises, and Problems; updated Becker CPA Review Questions.
- Updated Chapter Outlines to provide an overview of the material and to make it easier to locate specific topics.
- Revised *Financial Disclosure Insights* and *Global Tax Issues* for current developments.

In addition, the following materials are available online at the Instructor Companion Website (**www.cengage.com/login**):

- An appendix that helps instructors broaden and customize coverage of important tax provisions of the Affordable Care Act.
- An appendix that covers depreciation and the Accelerated Cost Recovery System (ACRS).
- An appendix that has comprehensive tax return problems for the 2022 tax filing year (Appendix F).

A list of other *significant changes* to text chapters follows (chapters not identified have been fully updated and revised as indicated above).

Chapter 1

- Added brief references to the Inflation Reduction Act of 2022, including the stock buy-back excise tax and increased funding for the IRS.
- Added a brief explanation of Circular 230.
- Changed Discussion Question 15 to address another way to categorize taxes (income, consumption, and wealth/valuation).
- Modified Research Problem 5 on the Gramm-Leach-Bliley Safeguards Rule to also focus on the 2022 release by the IRS of templates for the security plan tax practitioners are required to have in place.
- Added Research Problem 6 to consider the Circular 230 competence rule on whether a CPA firm can accept a new client with far more virtual currency transactions than the firm has dealt with before.
- Added two Becker CPA Review Questions on the AICPA Statements on Standards for Tax Services and Circular 230.

Chapter 2

- Added materials on changes to the CPA exam in 2024 and related licensing requirements.
- Added two new Problems (one on the U.S. court system in general and one on differences in Tax Court opinions).
- Added new Research Problem 7 asking students to determine what tax research services are available to them on campus.

Chapter 3

- Added new material on amended tax returns and superseding returns (text Section 3-7e) and added an example illustrating due dates when the amended return results in a tax refund.
- Revised and expanded the discussion of virtual currency (text Section 3-9e) to reflect changes implemented in the Infrastructure Investment and Jobs Act of 2021 (including the definition of a "digital asset" and enhanced reporting requirements for digital asset transactions).

Chapter 4

- Removed discussion of alimony recapture as it is no longer applicable.
- Added table with common income reporting forms and the type of income involved.
- Clarified text to help explain the logic of the formula for determining how much Social Security benefits are taxable.

Chapter 5

- Expanded discussion of exclusions for injuries and sickness to cover some disaster relief payments and added an example about some COVID-19 payments to households (text Section 5-5e).
- Added a Discussion Question on crowdfunding and whether the amounts raised are gifts.

Chapter 6

- Updated Exhibit 6.4 to reflect revised IRS Audit Guide.

Chapter 7

- Deleted text materials related to COVID-19 losses and updated other chapter materials as needed.
- Added new Research Problem 5, asking students to find Rev. Proc. 2018-8 and identify the various safe harbors that are available to taxpayers in calculating casualty losses in Federal disaster areas and provide an illustration of the "estimated repair cost method" safe harbor.

Chapter 8

- Updated chapter materials to reflect changes in additional first-year depreciation in 2023 (the percentage falls from 100% in 2022 to 80% in 2023).
- Updated chapter materials to reflect release of 2023 luxury auto limitations.

Chapter 9

- Added information about the Department of Labor proposed regulations on worker classification (29 CFR § 795.110).
- Added new Research Problem 4 asking students to research name, likeness, and image (NIL) issues for college athletes and create a "frequently asked questions" summary.
- Updated chapter materials and expanded discussion of some retirement plan options (including SECURE 2.0 Act provisions where appropriate).

Chapter 11

- Updated Concept Summary 11.3 to show that the § 461(l) excess business loss limitation has been extended through 2028.

Chapter 12

- Added discussion of the new corporate AMT.
- Added basic coverage of the business energy credits added, or modified, by the Inflation Reduction Act of 2022.
- Added basic coverage of the energy tax credits for individuals added, or modified by the Inflation Reduction Act of 2022 (§§ 25C, 25D, 30D, and 25E).
- Added Computational Exercises related to individual energy credits.

Chapter 13

- Added material on the unforeseen circumstances "facts and circumstances" test for a partial § 121 exclusion (based on IRS private letter rulings).

Chapter 15

- Based on adopter requests, expanded discussion of organizational form by adding two new text sections: 15-1 (Organizational Forms in Which Business May be Conducted) and 15-2 (Nontax Factors). Balance of chapter outline revised based on these additions.

Chapter 16

- Added an explanation of the 2½ month rule for deferred compensation for accrual method taxpayers.
- Updated for inflation and the latest revenue procedure listing automatic method changes.

Chapter 17

- Revised discussion and related examples of business interest expense limitation to reflect changes effective in 2023.
- Added new Learning Objective 4 addressing the new corporate AMT; renumbered subsequent learning objectives.
- Added discussion of the new corporate AMT (based on book income), including a new example.
- Added a Discussion Question and a Problem addressing the new corporate AMT.
- Added a Research Problem asking students to research the new corporate AMT.

Chapter 18

- Rearranged order of topics to improve comprehension and document flow.

Chapter 19

- Added discussion of the new excise tax on stock repurchases, including a new example.
- Added a Discussion Question and a Problem addressing the new excise tax on stock repurchases.

Chapter 20

- Added Financial Disclosure Insights feature titled Digital Transformation Drives M&A Activity.

Chapter 21

- A revised chapter based primarily on text Sections 21-1 through 21-5 of the 2023 edition.
- Added Example 1, dealing with two individuals who combine resources to mine cryptocurrency.
- Added references to state law when calculating a partner's tax basis capital account for state K-1 purposes.
- Added new Research Problem 4 on decentralized autonomous organizations (DAOs) and the entity implications for such groups.
- Moved topics previously discussed in text Sections 21-6 through 21-8 of the 2023 edition to new Chapter 22.

Chapter 22

- A new chapter that includes topics previously discussed in text Sections 21-6 through 21-8 of the 2023 edition.
- Materials have been expanded to include disproportionate distributions, liquidating distributions to retiring or deceased partners (§ 736), optional adjustments to property basis (§ 754), family partnerships, and partnership terminations.

Chapter 23 (formerly Chapter 22)

- Added new Learning Objective 11 regarding other tax issues applicable to S corporations; renumbered remaining learning objective.
- Updated statistics on business entity choices (Exhibit 23.1).
- Added discussion of Form 7203, S Corporation Shareholder Stock and Debt Basis Limitations, including when the form must be filed by shareholders.
- Added Tax Planning considerations regarding Form 7203.
- Added discussion of SALT cap workarounds.
- Added discussion of an LLC electing S corporation status.

Chapter 24

- A new chapter covering accounting for income taxes including materials on common book-tax differences, the basic principles of ASC 740, tax disclosures in the financial statements, and benchmarking.

Chapter 25 (formerly Chapter 23)

- Made a minor modification to Learning Objective 7.
- Revised outline of text Sections 25-3 and 25-5; revised title of text Section 25-3.
- Reorganized text Section 25-3 on excise taxes; streamlined some materials and added new materials and an example.

Chapter 26 (formerly Chapter 24)

- Added new Research Problem 6 requiring students to search for a recent state tax update.

Chapter 27 (formerly Chapter 25)

- Added a Global Tax Issues feature titled Meet Your Fast-Food Restaurant Cashier—From 2,500 Miles Away.
- Revised text Section 27-7 (Reporting Requirements) to provide an overview of the purpose of Forms 5471, 5472, 8858, and 8865 and added an end-of-chapter Discussion Question asking students to identify who is responsible for filing Forms 5471 and 5472.
- Updated Research Problem 6 asking students to argue in favor of or against a U.S. corporate minimum tax on global profits.

Chapter 28 (formerly Chapter 26)

- Revised The Big Picture scenario at the beginning of the chapter.
- Added new Exhibit 28.1 on the organizational structure of the IRS.
- Updated chapter materials related to tax administration, the tax gap, organization of the IRS, the audit process, and the role of informants.
- Added several key terms: information returns, installment agreement, John Doe summons, and Notice CP 2000.

Chapter 29 (formerly Chapter 27)

- Added key term and related discussion: deceased spousal unused exclusion (DSUE) election.
- Added Research Problem 2 on estate inclusions.

Tax Law Outlook

From your SWFT Series Editors:
With the House of Representatives and the Senate controlled by different political parties in 2023, it is unlikely that any significant tax legislation will occur during the year. In August 2022, Congress passed the Inflation Reduction Act which contains a number of new and revised energy tax credits, a new corporate alternative minimum tax, an excise tax on stock buybacks, and increased funding for the IRS. In December 2022, as part of a larger appropriations bill, Congress passed the bipartisan SECURE 2.0 Act which made a number of prospective changes affecting retirement plans. Our texts have been updated for both of these Acts.

Although discussed, Congress did not act on a number of tax provisions that expired at the end of 2021 and 2022. Nor did Congress act on three provisions that had been attracting much attention: an extension of the ability to expense research and experimentation expenditures under § 174, maintaining the 100 percent bonus depreciation allowance past 2022, and continuing to allow depreciation to be used as part of the calculation limiting business interest expense. We expect that Congress will revisit all of these provisions at some point during 2023. Annually, the Joint Committee on Taxation publishes a report of all expired and expiring provisions in the tax law. Almost 50 provisions expired in 2021 or 2022, or will expire in 2023 (see **jct.gov/publications/2022/jcx-1-22/** and **jct.gov/publications/2023/jcx-1-23**).

Taxpayers and their advisers will need to evaluate how these changes affect their financial planning strategies and adjust their plans appropriately. The SWFT editors will be monitoring guidance from the IRS and the Treasury Department related to recent law changes, tracking any legislative activities (including extender legislation), and providing updates to adopters as needed.

Supplements Support Students and Instructors

Built around the areas students and instructors have identified as the most important, our integrated supplements package offers more flexibility than ever before to suit the way instructors teach and students learn.

Online and Digital Resources for Students

Cengage CNOWv2

CNOWv2 is a powerful course management and online homework tool that provides robust instructor control and customization to optimize the student learning experience and meet desired outcomes.

CNOWv2 Instant Access Code ISBN:
978-0-357-90045-1 (two-semester access)

Contact your Cengage Learning Consultant about different bundle options.

the answer company™ THOMSON REUTERS®

Thomson Reuters Checkpoint™ is the leading online tax research database used by professionals. Checkpoint™ helps introduce students to tax research in three simple ways:

- Intuitive web-based design makes it fast and simple to find what you need.
- Checkpoint™ provides a comprehensive collection of primary tax law, cases, and rulings along with analytical insight you simply can't find anywhere else.
- Checkpoint™ has built-in productivity tools such as calculators to make research more efficient—a resource more tax pros use than any other.

Six months' access to Checkpoint™ (after activation) is packaged automatically with every NEW copy of the textbook.*

ProConnect™ Tax

More than software: Put the experience of ProConnect™ Tax on your side.

- Get returns done right the first time with access to all the forms you need, backed by industry-leading calculations and diagnostics.
- Save time with logical data-entry worksheets instead of traditional forms-based methods.
- It's all online, so there's nothing to install or maintain.

Online access to ProConnect™ Tax software is offered with each NEW copy of the textbook—at no additional cost to students.*

www.cengage.com Students can use **www.cengage.com** to select this textbook and access Cengage Learning content, empowering them to choose the most suitable format and giving them a better chance of success in the course. Buy printed materials, eBooks, and digital resources directly through Cengage Learning and save at **www.cengage.com.**

Online Student Resources

Students can go to **www.cengage.com** for free resources to help them study as well as the opportunity to purchase additional study aids. These valuable free study resources will help students earn a better grade:

- Flashcards use chapter terms and definitions to aid students in learning tax terminology for each chapter.
- Online glossary for each chapter provides terms and definitions from the text in alphabetical order for easy reference.
- Learning objectives can be downloaded for each chapter to help keep students on track.
- Tax tables used in the textbook are downloadable for reference.

Cengage Unlimited

The first-of-its-kind digital subscription designed specially to lower costs.

Students get total access to everything Cengage has to offer on demand—in one place. That's 20,000 eBooks, 2,300 digital learning products, and dozens of study tools across 70 disciplines and over 675 courses. **www.cengage.com/unlimited**

Printed Resources for Students

Looseleaf Edition (978-0-357-90042-0)

This version provides all the pages of the text in an unbound, three-hole-punched format for portability and ease of use. Online access to ProConnect™ Tax software is included with every NEW textbook as well as Checkpoint™ from Thomson Reuters.*

*NEW printed copies of the textbook are automatically packaged with access to Checkpoint™ and ProConnect™ Tax software. If students purchase the eBook, they will not automatically receive access to Checkpoint™ and ProConnect™ Tax software.

Comprehensive Supplements Support Instructors' Needs

Cengage
CNOWv2

CNOWv2 is a powerful course management and online homework tool that provides robust instructor control and customization to optimize the student learning experience and meet desired outcomes. In addition to the features and benefits mentioned earlier for students, CNOWv2 includes these features for instructors.

- **Learning Outcomes Reporting** and the ability to analyze student work from the gradebook. Each exercise and problem is tagged by topic, learning objective, level of difficulty, estimated completion time, and business program standards to allow greater guidance in developing assessments and evaluating student progress.
- **Built-in Test Bank for online assessment.** The Test Bank files are included in CNOWv2 so that they may be used as additional homework or tests.

Solutions Manual

Written by the ***South-Western Federal Taxation*** editors and authors, the Solutions Manual features solutions arranged in accordance with the sequence of chapter material.

Solutions to all homework items are tagged with their Estimated Time to Complete, Level of Difficulty, and Learning Objective(s), as well as the AACSB's and AICPA's core competencies—giving instructors more control than ever in selecting homework to match the topics covered. The Solutions Manual also contains the solutions to Appendix F: Practice Set Assignments—Comprehensive Tax Return Problems and answers with explanations to the end-of-chapter Becker CPA Review Questions. **Available on the Instructor Companion Website at www.cengage.com/login.**

PowerPoint® Lectures with Notes

The Instructor PowerPoint® Lectures contain more than 30 slides per chapter, including outlines and instructor guides, concept definitions, and key points. **Available on the Instructor Companion Website at www.cengage.com/login.**

Test Bank

Written by the ***South-Western Federal Taxation*** editors and authors, the Test Bank contains approximately 2,200 items and solutions arranged in accordance with the sequence of chapter material.

Each test item is tagged with its Estimated Time to Complete, Level of Difficulty, and Learning Objective(s), as well as the AACSB's and AICPA's core competencies—for easier instructor planning and test item selection. The 2024 Test Bank is available in Cengage's test generator software, Cognero.

Cengage Learning Testing Powered by Cognero is a flexible, online system that allows you to:

- author, edit, and manage Test Bank content from multiple Cengage Learning solutions
- create multiple test versions in an instant
- deliver tests from your LMS, your classroom, or wherever you want
- create tests from school, home, the coffee shop—anywhere with Internet access (No special installs or downloads needed.)

Test Bank files in Word format as well as versions to import into your LMS are available on the Instructor Companion Website. **Cognero Test Banks are available via single sign-on (SSO) account at www.cengage.com/login.**

Other Instructor Resources

All of the following instructor course materials are available online at www.cengage.com/login. Once logged into the site, instructors should select this textbook to access the online Instructor Resources.

- Instructor Guide
- Edition-to-edition correlation grids by chapter
- CPA Evolution Learning Objective Mapping Grid
- An appendix that helps instructors broaden and customize coverage of important tax provisions of the Affordable Care Act
- Depreciation and the Accelerated Cost Recovery System (ACRS) appendix
- Comprehensive Tax Return Problems appendix

Custom Solutions

Cengage Learning Custom Solutions develops personalized solutions to meet your taxation education needs. Consider the following for your adoption of ***South-Western Federal Taxation 2024 Edition***.

- Remove chapters you do not cover or rearrange their order to create a streamlined and efficient text.
- Add your own material to cover additional topics or information.
- Add relevance by including sections from Sawyers/Gill's *Federal Tax Research* or your state's tax laws and regulations.

Acknowledgments

We want to thank all the adopters and others who participated in numerous online surveys as well as the following individuals who provided content reviews and feedback in the development of the ***South-Western Federal Taxation 2024 titles***.

James C. Young / Mark B. Persellin / Annette Nellen / David M. Maloney / Andrew D. Cuccia / Sharon S. Lassar / Bradrick M. Cripe

Ken Abramowicz, *University of Alaska Fairbanks*
Lindsay G. Acker, *University of Wisconsin – Madison*
Deborah S. Adkins, *Nperspective, LLC*
Mark P. Altieri, *Kent State University*
Terry W. Bechtel, *Texas A&M University – Texarkana*
Tamara Berges, *UCLA*
Ellen Best, *University of North Georgia*
Tim Biggart, *Berry College*
Rachel Birkey, *Illinois State University*
Israel Blumenfrecht, *Queens College*
Patrick M. Borja, *Citrus College / California State University, Los Angeles*
Dianne H. Boseman, *Nash Community College*
Cathalene Bowler, *University of Northern Iowa*
Madeline Brogan, *Lone Star College – Montgomery*
Timothy G. Bryan, *Marshall University*
Ryan L. Burger, *Concordia University Nebraska*
Lisa Busto, *William Rainey Harper College*
Julia M. Camp, *Providence College*
Al Case, *Southern Oregon University*
Machiavelli W. Chao, *Merage School of Business, University of California, Irvine*
Eric Chen, *University of Saint Joseph*
Christine Cheng, *University of Mississippi*
James Milton Christianson, *Southwestern University and Austin Community College*
James M. DeSimpelare, *Ross School of Business at the University of Michigan*
John Dexter, *PennWest University Edinboro*
James Doering, *University of Wisconsin – Green Bay*
Michael P. Donohoe, *University of Illinois at Urbana Champaign*
Deborah A. Doonan, *Johnson & Wales University*
Monique O. Durant, *Central Connecticut State University*
Wayne L. Edmunds, *Virginia Commonwealth University*
Rafi Efrat, *California State University, Northridge*
Frank J. Faber, *St. Joseph's University*
John Forsythe, *Eagle Gate College*
Carolyn Galantine, *Pepperdine University*
Sheri Geddes, *Hope College*
Alexander Gelardi, *University of St. Thomas*
Daniel J. Gibbons, *Waubonsee Community College*
Marina Grau, *Houston Community College – Houston, TX*
Jeffrey S. Haig, *Santa Monica College*
Kenneth W. Hodges, *Sinclair Community College*
Susanne Holloway, *Salisbury University*
Jeffrey L. Hoopes, *University of North Carolina*
Marsha M. Huber, *Youngstown State University*
Carol Hughes, *Asheville-Buncombe Technical Community College*
Helen Hurwitz, *Saint Louis University*
Janeé M. Johnson, *University of Arizona*
Brad Van Kalsbeek, *University of Sioux Falls*
Carl Keller, *Missouri State University*
Gordon Klein, *UCLA Anderson School*
Taylor Klett, *Sam Houston State University*
Aaron P. Knape, *University of Nebraska at Omaha*
Cedric Knott, *Colorado State University – Global Campus*
Ausher M. B. Kofsky, *Western New England University*
Emil Koren, *Saint Leo University*
Adena LeJeune, *Louisiana State University – Alexandria*
Gene Levitt, *Mayville State University*
Teresa Lightner, *Oklahoma State University*
Roger Lirely, *The University of Texas at Tyler*
Jane Livingstone, *Western Carolina University*
Anne M. Magro, *George Mason University*
Harold J. Manasa, *Winthrop University*
Barry R. Marks, *University of Houston – Clear Lake*
Norman Massel, *Loyola University Chicago*
Bruce W. McClain, *Cleveland State University*
Jeff McGowan, *Trine University*
Allison M. McLeod, *University of North Texas*
Robert H. Meyers, *University of Wisconsin – Whitewater*
Tracie L. Miller, *Franklin University*
Jonathan G. Mitchell, *Stark State College*
Richard Mole, *Hiram College*
Lisa Nash, *University of North Georgia*
Al Oddo, *Niagara University*
Vivian J. Paige, *Old Dominion University*
Ronald Pearson, *Bay College*
Thomas Pearson, *University of Hawaii at Manoa*
Nichole L. Pendleton, *Friends University*
Chuck Pier, *Angelo State University*
Lincoln M. Pinto, *DeVry University*
Sonja Pippin, *University of Nevada – Reno*
Steve Platau, *The University of Tampa*
Elizabeth Plummer, *TCU*
Walfyette Powell, *Strayer University*
Darlene Pulliam, *West Texas A&M University*
Thomas J. Purcell, *Creighton University*
John S. Repsis, *University of Texas at Arlington*
Jennifer Hardwick Robinson, *Trident Technical College*
Shani N. Robinson, *Sam Houston State University*
Donald Roth, *Dordt College*
Richard L. Russell, *Jackson State University*
Robert L. Salyer, *Northern Kentucky University*
Rhoda Sautner, *University of Mary*
Bunney L. Schmidt, *Utah Valley University*
Allen Schuldenfrei, *Towson University*
Eric D. Schwartz, *LaRoche College*
Tony L. Scott, *Norwalk Community College*
Wayne Shaw, *Southern Methodist University*
Georgi Smatrakalev, *Florida Atlantic University*
Randy Smit, *Dordt College*

Leslie S. Sobol, *California State University Northridge*
Eric J. Sommermeyer, *Wartburg College*
Marc Spiegel, *University of California, Irvine*
Teresa Stephenson, *University of Alaska Anchorage*
Beth Stetson, *Oklahoma City University*
Debra Stone, *Eastern New Mexico University*
Julie Straus, *Culver – Stockton College*
James Sundberg, *Eastern Michigan University*
Randall R. Thomas, *Iowa Wesleyan University*
Ronald R. Tidd, *Central Washington University*
MaryBeth Tobin, *Bridgewater State University*
James P. Trebby, *Marquette University*
Heidi Tribunella, *University of Rochester*
Stanley Veliotis, *Fordham University*
Terri Walsh, *Stetson University*
Natasha R. Ware, *Southeastern University*
Mark Washburn, *Sam Houston State University*
Kent Williams, *Indiana Wesleyan University*
Candace Witherspoon, *Valdosta State University*
Sheila Woods, *Alvin Community College*
Xinmei Xie, *California State University Stanislaus*

Special Thanks

We are grateful to the faculty members who have diligently worked through the problems and test questions to ensure the accuracy of the ***South-Western Federal Taxation*** homework, solutions manuals, test banks, and comprehensive tax form problems. Their comments and corrections helped us focus on clarity as well as accuracy and tax law currency. We also thank Thomson Reuters for its permission to use Checkpoint™ with the text.

Sandra A. Augustine, (retired) *Hilbert College*
Robyn Dawn Jarnagin, *University of Arkansas*
Kate Mantzke, *Northern Illinois University*
Ray Rodriguez, *Murray State University*
Miles Romney, *Florida State University*
George R. Starbuck, *McMurry University*
Donald R. Trippeer, *State University of New York College at Oneonta*
Raymond Wacker, *Southern Illinois University, Carbondale*
Michael Weissenfluh, *Tillamook Bay Community College*
Marvin Williams, *University of Houston – Downtown*

The South-Western Federal Taxation Series

To find out more about these books, go to www.cengage.com.

Individual Income Taxes, 2024 Edition

(Young, Nellen, Persellin, Lassar, Cuccia, Cripe, Editors) provides accessible, comprehensive, and authoritative coverage of the relevant tax code and regulations as they pertain to the individual taxpayer, as well as coverage of all major developments in Federal taxation.

(ISBN 978-0-357-90055-0)

Corporations, Partnerships, Estates & Trusts, 2024 Edition

(Raabe, Nellen, Young, Cripe, Lassar, Persellin, Cuccia, Editors) covers tax concepts as they affect corporations, partnerships, estates, and trusts. The authors provide accessible, comprehensive, and authoritative coverage of relevant tax code and regulations, as well as all major developments in Federal income taxation. This market-leading text is intended for students who have had at least a previous course in tax.

(ISBN 978-0-357-90067-3)

Comprehensive Volume, 2024 Edition

(Young, Persellin, Nellen, Maloney, Cuccia, Lassar, Cripe, Editors) Combining the number one individual tax text with the number one tax entities text, *Comprehensive Volume, 2024 Edition* is a true winner. An edited version of the first two ***South-Western Federal Taxation*** textbooks, this book is ideal for undergraduate or graduate levels. This text works for either a one-semester course in which an instructor wants to integrate coverage of individual and corporate taxation or for a two-semester sequence in which the use of only one book is desired.

(ISBN 978-0-357-90041-3)

Essentials of Taxation: Individuals and Business Entities, 2024 Edition

(Nellen, Cuccia, Persellin, Young, Editors) emphasizes tax planning and the multidisciplinary aspects of taxation. This text is designed with the AICPA Model Tax Curriculum in mind, presenting the introductory Federal taxation course from a business entity perspective. Its **Tax Planning Framework** helps users fit tax planning strategies into an innovative pedagogical framework. The text is an ideal fit for programs that offer only one course in taxation where users need to be exposed to individual taxation, as well as corporate and other business entity taxation. This text assumes no prior course in taxation has been taken.

(ISBN 978-0-357-90079-6)

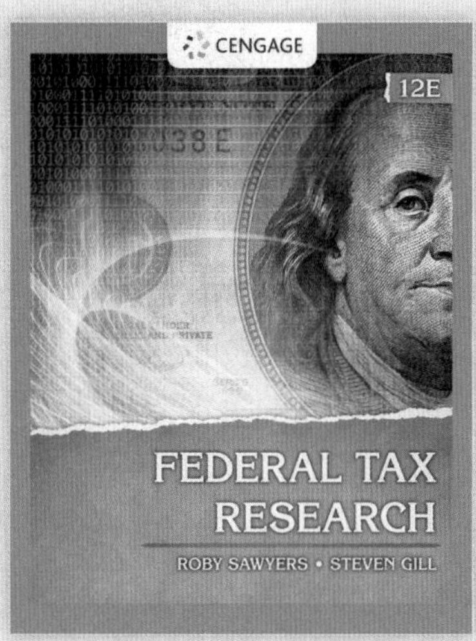

Federal Tax Research, 12E

(Sawyers and Gill) *Federal Tax Research*, Twelfth Edition, offers hands-on tax research analysis and fully covers computer-oriented tax research tools. Also included in this edition is coverage on international tax research, a review of tax ethics, and many new real-life cases to help foster a true understanding of Federal tax law.

(ISBN 978-0-357-36638-7)

About the Editors

James C. Young is the PwC Professor of Accountancy Emeritus at Northern Illinois University. A graduate of Ferris State University (B.S.) and Michigan State University (M.B.A. and Ph.D.), Jim's research focuses on taxpayer responses to the income tax using archival data. His dissertation received the PricewaterhouseCoopers/American Taxation Association Dissertation Award, and his subsequent research has received funding from a number of organizations, including the Ernst & Young Foundation Tax Research Grant Program. His work has been published in a variety of academic and professional journals, including the *National Tax Journal, The Journal of the American Taxation Association*, and *Tax Notes*. Jim is a Northern Illinois University Distinguished Professor, received the Illinois CPA Society Outstanding Accounting Educator Award in 2012, and has received university teaching awards from Northern Illinois University, George Mason University, and Michigan State University.

Mark B. Persellin, Ph.D., CPA, CFP®, is the Ray and Dorothy Berend Professor of Accounting at St. Mary's University. He is a graduate of the University of Arizona (B.S.), the University of Texas at Austin (M.P.A. in Taxation), and the University of Houston (Ph.D.). He teaches Personal Income Tax, Business Income Tax, and Research in Federal Taxation. Prior to joining St. Mary's University in 1991, Professor Persellin taught at Florida Atlantic University and Southwest Texas University (Texas State University) and worked on the tax staff of a Big 4 firm. His research has been published in numerous academic and professional journals including *The Journal of the American Taxation Association, The Accounting Educators' Journal, The Tax Adviser, The CPA Journal, Journal of Taxation, Corporate Taxation, The Tax Executive, TAXES—The Tax Magazine, Journal of International Taxation,* and *Practical Tax Strategies*. In 2003, Professor Persellin established the St. Mary's University Volunteer Income Tax Assistance (VITA) site, and he continues to serve as a trainer and reviewer at the site.

Annette Nellen, J.D., CPA, CGMA, directs San José State University's graduate tax program (MST) and teaches courses in tax research, tax fundamentals, accounting methods, property transactions, employment tax, ethics, leadership, and tax policy. Professor Nellen is a graduate of CSU Northridge, Pepperdine (MBA), and Loyola Law School. Prior to joining SJSU in 1990, she was with a Big 4 firm and the IRS. At SJSU, Professor Nellen is a recipient of the Outstanding Professor and Distinguished Service Awards. Professor Nellen is an active member of the tax sections of the AICPA and American Bar Association, including chairing the AICPA Virtual Currency Task Force. In 2013, she received the AICPA Arthur J. Dixon Memorial Award, the highest award given by the accounting profession in the area of taxation. Professor Nellen is the author of BloombergBNA Tax Portfolio, *Amortization of Intangibles*. She has published numerous articles in the *AICPA Tax Insider, Tax Adviser, Tax Notes State*, and *The Journal of Accountancy*. She is a research fellow with the Silicon Valley Institute for Regional Studies. Professor Nellen has testified before the House Ways & Means and Senate Finance Committees and other committees on Federal and state tax reform. Professor Nellen maintains the 21st Century Taxation Website and blog (21stcenturytaxation.com) as well as Websites on tax policy and reform, virtual currency, and state tax issues (sjsu.edu/people/annette.nellen/).

David M. Maloney, Ph.D., CPA, is the Carman G. Blough Professor of Accounting Emeritus at the University of Virginia's McIntire School of Commerce. He completed his undergraduate work at the University of Richmond and his graduate work at the University of Illinois at Urbana-Champaign. Upon joining the Virginia faculty in January 1984, Dr. Maloney taught Federal taxation in the graduate and undergraduate programs and was a recipient of major research grants from the Ernst & Young and KPMG Foundations. Dr. Maloney has published work in numerous professional journals, including *Journal of Taxation, The Tax Adviser, Tax Notes, Corporate Taxation, Accounting Horizons, Journal of Taxation of Investments,* and *Journal of Accountancy.*

Andrew D. Cuccia, Ph.D., CPA, is the Steed Professor of Accounting at the University of Oklahoma. He is a graduate of Loyola University, New Orleans (B.B.A.), and the University of Florida (Ph.D.). Prior to entering academia, Andy practiced as a CPA with a Big 4 accounting firm. Before joining the University of Oklahoma, he was on the faculty at Louisiana State University and the University of Illinois. His research focuses on taxpayer and tax professional judgment and decision making and has been published in several journals including *The Accounting Review, The Journal of Accounting Research, The Journal of the American Taxation Association,* and *Tax Notes*. He has taught undergraduate and graduate courses in income tax fundamentals as well as graduate courses in corporate tax, tax policy, and tax research. Andy is a past president of the American Taxation Association and a member of the American Accounting Association and the AICPA.

Sharon S. Lassar, Ph.D., CPA (Florida), is the John J. Gilbert Professor and Director of the School of Accountancy at The University of Denver. Dr. Lassar earned her Ph.D. at the University of Southern California, her Master of Taxation at Bentley University, and her Bachelor's in Accounting from West Virginia University. Prior to joining the University of Denver, Dr. Lassar was the Director of the School of Accounting at Florida International University and previously served on the faculties of Florida Atlantic University and the University of Arizona. She began her career with a Big 4 firm. Dr. Lassar has served the profession in many ways, most recently as a member of the AICPA Council. Dr. Lassar is a past president of the Accounting Programs Leadership Group and Past Chair of the Colorado Society of CPAs. Dr. Lassar also served on the Accounting Accreditation Task Force of AACSB International whose work resulted in new standards for accreditation, the hallmark of them being fully engaging practitioners in the accreditation process.

Bradrick M. Cripe, Ph.D., CPA, is a Presidential Teaching Professor and the Donald E. Kieso Endowed Chair of Accountancy at Northern Illinois University. He is a graduate of New Mexico State University (B.A., B.C.J., and M.Acc.) and the University of Nebraska–Lincoln (Ph.D.). Prior to receiving his Ph.D. in 2006, he worked on the tax staff of a Big 4 accounting firm. Professor Cripe teaches courses in taxation and business strategy, corporate taxation, international taxation, and advanced issues in taxation. He has published in *The Accounting Review, Issues in Accounting Education, Journal of Accountancy, Tax Notes,* and other academic and practitioner journals.

Brief Contents

Part 1: Introduction and Basic Tax Model

Part 2: Gross Income

Part 3: Deductions and Credits

Part 4: Property Transactions

Part 5: Special Tax Computations and Accounting Periods and Methods

Part 6: Corporations

Part 7: Flow-Through Entities

Part 8: Advanced Tax Practice Considerations

Part 9: Family Tax Planning

Contents

Part 1: Introduction and Basic Tax Model

Part 3: Deductions and Credits

Chapter 6 Deductions and Losses: In General 6-1

Chapter 7 Deductions and Losses: Certain Business Expenses and Losses 7-1

Part 4: Property Transactions

Part 6: Corporations

Part 8: Advanced Tax Practice Considerations

Part 9: Family Tax Planning

Appendices

Online Appendices

Introduction and Basic Tax Model

Part 1 provides an introduction to taxation in the United States. Although this text focuses on income taxation, other types of taxes also are briefly discussed. The purposes of the Federal tax law are examined, and the legislative, administrative, and judicial sources of Federal tax law, including their application to the tax research process, are analyzed. Part 1 concludes by introducing the basic tax model for the individual taxpayer (the tax formula), discussing tax determination, and providing an overview of property transactions.

Chapter 1

An Introduction to Taxation and Understanding the Federal Tax Law

Learning Objectives: *After completing Chapter 1, you should be able to:*

LO.1 Explain the importance of taxation and apply methods for studying this topic.

LO.2 Describe some of the history and trends of the Federal income tax.

LO.3 Apply principles of good tax policy relevant to the design of a tax system.

LO.4 Identify the different taxes imposed in the United States at the Federal, state, and local levels.

LO.5 Explain the administration of the tax law, including the audit process utilized by the IRS.

LO.6 Evaluate some of the ethical guidelines involved in tax practice.

LO.7 Classify tax rules based on their possible economic, social, equity, and political reasons for inclusion in a particular tax system.

LO.8 Explain the role played by the IRS and the courts in the evolution of the Federal tax system.

Chapter Outline

The Big Picture

Family and Taxes—A Typical Year

Travis and Amy Carter are married and live in a state that imposes both a sales tax and an income tax. They have two children, April (age 17) and Martin (age 18). Travis is a mining engineer who specializes in land reclamation. After several years with a mining corporation, Travis established a consulting practice that involves a considerable amount of travel due to work he performs in other states. Amy is a registered nurse who, until recently, was a homemaker. In November of this year, she decided to reenter the job market and accepted a position with a medical clinic. The Carters live only a few blocks from Ernest and Mary Walker, Amy Carter's parents. The Walkers are retired and live on interest, dividends, and Social Security benefits.

Activities during the year with possible tax ramifications are summarized below:

- The ad valorem property taxes on the Carters' residence are increased, whereas those on the Walkers' residence are lowered.
- When Travis registers an automobile purchased last year in another state, he is required to pay a sales tax to his home state.
- As an anniversary present, the Carters gave the Walkers a new recreational vehicle (RV).
- Travis employs his children to draft blueprints and prepare scale models for use in his work. Both April and Martin have had training in drafting and topography.
- Early in the year, the Carters are audited by the state on an income tax return filed a few years ago. Later in the year, they are audited by the IRS on a Form 1040 they filed for the same year. In each case, the Carters met with a state or IRS examiner (employee) to discuss their tax return and provide requested documentation. The Carters were assessed additional taxes and interest on both tax returns.
- The Walkers are audited by the IRS. Unlike the Carters, they did not have to deal directly with an IRS examiner but settled the matter by mail.

Explain these developments, and resolve the issues raised.

Read the chapter and formulate your response.

This chapter provides an introduction to our Federal tax system to set a foundation for what you'll learn in subsequent chapters. Among the topics discussed are:

- The importance and relevance of taxation and how to study taxation.
- A brief history of the Federal income tax.
- The types of taxes imposed at the Federal, state, and local levels.
- Some highlights of tax law administration.
- Tax concepts that help explain the reasons for various tax provisions.
- The influence the Internal Revenue Service (IRS) and the courts have had in the evolution of current tax law.

1-1 Approaching the Study of Taxation

LO.1

Explain the importance of taxation and apply methods for studying this topic.

1-1a What Is Taxation?

"Taxes are what we pay for civilized society."

This is a famous quote from U.S. Supreme Court Justice Oliver Wendell Holmes, Jr. (1841 to 1935).[1] It is engraved above the entrance to the government building at 1111 Constitution Avenue in Washington, D.C.—headquarters of the Internal Revenue Service (IRS). This quote eloquently sums up the primary purpose of taxation—to raise revenue for government operations. Governments at all levels—national, state, and local—require funds for defense, protection (police and fire), education, roads, the court system, social services, and more. Various types of taxes provide the resources to pay for government services.

In addition, taxation is often used as a tool to influence the behavior of individuals and businesses. For example, an income tax credit (which reduces a taxpayer's tax bill) may be designed to *encourage* people to purchase a fuel-efficient car. A tobacco excise tax may *discourage* individuals from smoking by increasing the cost of tobacco products. The tax system can also be used to provide direct benefits to taxpayers (e.g., to help pay for health insurance) and indirect benefits (in the form of exclusions, deductions, and credits that reduce a taxpayer's tax liability).

1-1b Taxation in Our Lives

"Nothing is certain, except death and taxes."

Most people attribute this quote to Benjamin Franklin (1706–1790). Taxes permeate our society. Various types of taxes, such as income, sales, property, and excise taxes (discussed in text Section 1-4), come into play in many of the activities of individuals, businesses, nonprofit entities (e.g., charitable organizations), and even governments.

Most directly, individuals are affected by taxes by paying them. Taxes may be paid directly or indirectly. A direct tax is paid to the government by the person who pays the tax. Examples include the personal income tax, which is paid by filing a personal income tax return (Form 1040 at the Federal level), and property taxes on one's home (paid to the local government). Individuals also pay many taxes indirectly. For example, most states impose sales tax on the purchase of tangible goods such as clothes. While this tax is collected and remitted to the government by the seller, the buyer is charged the tax along with the purchase price of the goods or services. Taxes can also be imposed indirectly when embedded in the prices charged by the seller. For example, when you buy gasoline for your car, the price you pay likely includes some of the income taxes and the gasoline excise taxes owed by the oil company. And a renter indirectly pays property taxes assessed on the landlord (who will consider that cost when determining how much rent to charge).

Ultimately, all taxes are paid by individuals. The corporate income tax, for example, is paid directly by the corporation but is really paid indirectly by individuals in their capacity as customers, investors (owners), or employees. Economists and others often study

[1] *Compania General De Tabacos De Filipinas v. Collector of Internal Revenue*, 275 U.S. 87, 100 (1927), dissenting opinion.

this topic to estimate the percentage of the corporate income tax borne by individuals in these different capacities. It is not easy to measure, but it is known that taxes are passed along to individuals through higher prices, lower dividends, and/or lower wages.

Taxes also affect the lives of individuals via the ballot box. Federal, state, and local elections often include initiatives that deal with taxation, such as whether state income taxes should be raised (or lowered), whether a new tax should be imposed on soda, or whether the sales tax rate should be changed. Candidates running for office often have positions on tax changes they would like to make if elected.

Given the pervasiveness of taxation—in our roles as both direct and indirect payers of taxes as well as citizens/voters—it is important that we understand how the tax system operates.

1-1c The Relevance of Taxation to Accounting and Finance Professionals

The U.S. corporate income tax rate is 21 percent. State income taxes can easily constitute, on average, an additional 5 percent. So a large corporation such as a Fortune 500 company may have to devote 26 percent or more of its net income to pay income taxes. In addition, businesses are subject to employment taxes, property taxes, sales taxes, and various excise taxes. Corporations with international operations are subject to taxation in other countries. Small businesses are also subject to a variety of taxes that affect profits and cash flows.

Given its significance, taxation is a crucial topic for accounting and finance professionals (whether serving individuals or businesses or working in an organization). Those assisting businesses must understand the various types of taxes to assist effectively with the following:

- *Compliance:* Ensure that the business files all tax returns and makes all tax payments on time. Mistakes and missed due dates will lead to penalty and interest expenses.
- *Planning:* Help a business apply favorable tax rules, such as income deferral and tax credits, to minimize tax liability (and maximize owner wealth). The time value of money concept is also important here, as is coordinating tax planning with other business goals to maximize earnings per share.[2]
- *Financial reporting:* Financial statements include a variety of tax information, including income tax expense on the income statement and deferred tax assets and liabilities on the balance sheet. Footnotes to the financial statements report various tax details including the company's effective tax rate. Computation and proper reporting of this information require knowledge of both tax and financial reporting rules [including the Financial Accounting Standards Board's Accounting Standards Codification (ASC) 740, *Income Taxes*].
- *Environmental, Social, and Governance (ESG) reporting:* A growing trend in corporate reporting is to address various business sustainability and responsibility matters and to report environmental, social, and governance activities and impact. Standard frameworks might be used that include tax metrics such as the Global Reporting Initiative (GRI) Standards or ones generated by the World Economic Forum.[3] This reporting can include taxes paid in each country (part of "country-by-country reporting"), reconciliation between taxes paid and the statutory tax rate on financial statement profits, financial assistance received from governments via tax deductions and credits, and an explanation of the corporation's tax policy and strategy.[4] Tax professionals assist businesses in identifying relevant and possibly required ESG reporting and help verify that the information is accurate and clearly explained.

[2]A corporate tax director or vice president of tax is typically involved in the strategic planning and growth of the company due to the significance of tax liabilities and planning opportunities to the business. For example, a 2021 position announcement for a Tax Director at Roblox stated that the director would lead initiatives to support global growth of the company.

[3]For example, see World Economic Forum, *Toward Common Metrics and Consistent Reporting of Sustainable Value Creation,* Jan. 2020; **www3.weforum.org/docs/WEF_IBC_ESG_Metrics_Discussion_Paper.pdf**.

[4]For examples, see Intel's 2021–22 Corporate Responsibility Report; **csrreportbuilder.intel.com/pdfbuilder/pdfs/CSR-2021-22-Full-Report.pdf**; and The Walt Disney Company's 2021 Corporate Social Responsibility Report; **impact.disney.com/app/uploads/2022/02/2021-CSR-Report.pdf**.

- *Controversy:* This term refers to an interaction a taxpayer may have with a tax agency such as the IRS. The IRS and state and local tax agencies regularly audit tax returns that have been filed to verify that taxes were properly computed and paid.
- *Cash management:* Taxes must be paid on time to avoid penalties and interest. Income and self-employment taxes must be estimated and paid quarterly and reconciled on the annual return. Other taxes may be due weekly, monthly, or semiannually. Businesses must be sure they have the funds ready when the taxes are due and have procedures to track due dates.
- *Data analysis:* With a majority, if not all, of a company's records maintained in digital form, there are opportunities to use this information to enhance profits, better understand the customer base, and improve and understand the information from a tax perspective. Tax practitioners often need skills in data analysis and visualization to identify samples for both internal and external audits, find ways to identify the products and services subject to sales tax in different states, and extract tax data to help inform other business functions such as where to locate a new sales office.
- *Tax advocacy:* Taxpayers and tax practitioners can add tremendous value to the improvement and evolution of our tax laws by sharing their knowledge, experiences, and ideas with lawmakers and tax agencies. Some of this work is performed by professional organizations such as the American Institute of CPAs (AICPA), industry associations, and various policy organizations. This input might take the form of comment letters, testimony before legislative committees (delivered in person or submitted for the record), or individual correspondence and meetings.[5]

These tasks are also relevant to professionals such as CPAs who advise businesses and individual clients.

The level and depth of tax knowledge needed for any accounting or tax professional depends on the specific job. The vice president of tax for a company clearly needs thorough knowledge in all areas of taxation; the same is true of a partner in a CPA firm. In contrast, the corporate treasurer likely focuses more on cash management, while working closely with the company's tax advisers. A person in any accounting or finance role must have sufficient tax knowledge to converse with tax advisers and understand their company's tax obligations.

Ultimately, much of taxation is transaction-based. How a transaction is structured (e.g., as a sale or a lease) has varying tax consequences that must be considered. Even the purchase of a home can result in significant change—the new mortgage interest and property tax deductions may mean that an individual itemizes their deductions (using Schedule A of Form 1040) rather than using the standard deduction. And life events such as marriage (and divorce) will change an individual's tax situation. Similar "life events" can also affect a corporation (e.g., acquiring a corporation or spinning off a subsidiary).

It is essential in working with taxation to maintain a balanced perspective. A corporation that is deciding where to locate a new factory does not automatically select the city or state that offers the most generous tax benefits. Nor does the person who is retiring to a warmer climate pick Belize over Arizona because the former has no income tax but the latter does. Tax considerations should not control decisions, but they remain one of many factors to be considered (and often one of the most significant).

1-1d **How to Study Taxation**

The goal of studying taxation is to be able to recognize issues (or transactions) that have tax implications and, when possible, try to understand the justification for them. Suppose, for example, that you come upon a situation that involves a discharge of indebtedness. If you know that forgiveness of debt results in income but that there are exceptions to this

[5]For examples of such advocacy, see formal letters submitted by the AICPA (**aicpa.org/advocacy/tax.html**); testimony delivered at tax reform hearings in Congress (**sjsu.edu/people/annette.nellen/website/117th-hearings.htm**); and tax policy activities and reports of various industry and policy organizations such as the U.S. Chamber of Commerce (**uschamber.com/taxes**) and the Center on Budget and Policy Priorities (**cbpp.org/research/topics/federal-tax**).

rule, you're doing well. The issue has been identified, and the outcome (i.e., when an exception applies) can be resolved through research. A variety of commercial and free tools and resources are available to help you research and reach a conclusion.

You may have heard that tax is a difficult subject because of the many rules, exceptions, and definitions, as well as frequent changes to tax rules. You may even have heard that taxation is boring. Taxation is a challenging topic, but it is certainly not boring. Taxation is an important and exciting topic due to constant change by the three branches of our Federal government (as well as changes by state and local governments), the significance of taxes to the bottom line of a company and an individual's finances, and the impact on our economy and society.

Tax professionals tend to find enjoyment in their chosen field due to the intellectual challenge of dealing with tax rules for compliance and planning purposes, the opportunity to interact with colleagues or clients to help them understand the effect of taxes, and the knowledge that their work affects the financial well-being of individuals and businesses.

In studying taxation, focus on understanding the rules and the why(s) behind them (rather than memorizing the many rules and terms). The rules become more meaningful by thinking about why they exist for the particular type of tax. For example, why does the Federal income tax allow for a casualty loss deduction in certain situations? Why is tax depreciation different from that used for financial reporting? Also consider how the rules apply to different types of taxpayers (like employees, sole proprietors, corporations, investors, children, and retirees). Also think about how the rules apply to taxpayers of varying income levels and sophistication of transactions (a homeowner versus someone who owns assets in several countries). Aiming for understanding rather than memorization will make your journey into the world of taxation interesting and meaningful and will prepare you well for dealing with taxation in your accounting or finance career.

For tax professionals, the study of taxation is an ongoing and intriguing process. When Congress changes the tax law, tax professionals must review the new rules in order to understand how they affect clients or their employer. In addition, decisions rendered by the courts in tax disputes and guidance issued by the Treasury Department and Internal Revenue Service must be understood to ensure correct compliance with the law as well as identification of updated and proper tax planning ideas.

Concept Summary 1.1 illustrates the various ways that individuals deal with, and are affected by, taxes.

1-2 A Brief History of U.S. Taxation

LO.2

Describe some of the history and trends of the Federal income tax.

1-2a Early Periods

An income tax was first enacted in 1634 by the English colonists in the Massachusetts Bay Colony, but the Federal government did not adopt an income tax until 1861. In fact, both the Federal Union and the Confederate States of America used the income tax to raise funds to finance the Civil War.

When the Civil War ended, the need for additional revenue disappeared, and the income tax was repealed. Once again the Federal government was able to finance its operations almost exclusively from customs duties (tariffs).

When a new Federal income tax on individuals was enacted in 1894, its opponents were prepared to successfully challenge its constitutionality. In *Pollock v. Farmers' Loan and Trust Co.*, the U.S. Supreme Court found that taxes on the income of real and personal property were the legal equivalent of a tax on the property involved and, therefore, required apportionment based on the population of the United States, as required by Article I, Section 8 of the Constitution.[6]

[6]3 AFTR 2602, 15 S.Ct. 912 (USSC, 1895). See Chapter 2 for an explanation of the citations of judicial decisions.

Concept Summary 1.1

Individuals and Taxes

The diagram to the right illustrates the many ways individuals interact with taxes. For example, as shown in the outer circle, individuals pay taxes and file tax returns (tax compliance). They also engage in tax planning as part of their desire to maximize after-tax wealth. If their tax return is audited or they do not pay their taxes, taxpayers will deal with the IRS or their state tax agency (tax controversy). Individuals deal with tax rules and planning in their roles as consumers, employees, investors, and business owners. Tax law is designed around these various taxpayer activities. Finally, as shown by the inner circle, individuals have a personal responsibility to comply with tax laws and pay any taxes due. Individuals also have a civic responsibility to understand taxes in their role as citizens and voters. And individuals need to understand how taxes affect their personal cash flows, consumption, and savings.

Use this diagram as you study the materials in this text, considering where in the circle various rules fit.

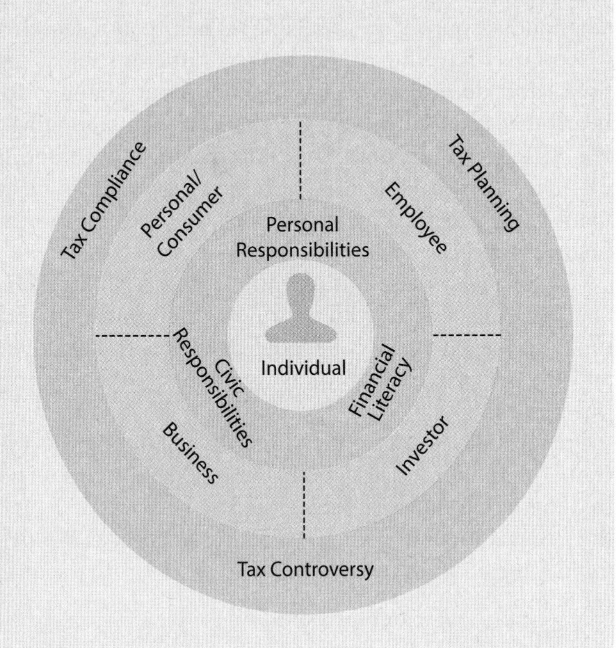

A Federal corporate income tax, enacted by Congress in 1909, fared better in the judicial system. The U.S. Supreme Court found this tax to be constitutional because it was treated as an excise tax.[7] In essence, it was a tax on the right to do business in the corporate form. So it was viewed as a form of the franchise tax.[8] Since the corporate form of doing business had been developed in the late nineteenth century, it was unknown to the framers of the U.S. Constitution. Because a corporation is an entity created under law, jurisdictions possess the right to tax its creation and operation. Using this rationale, many states still impose franchise taxes on corporations.

The ratification of the Sixteenth Amendment to the U.S. Constitution in 1913 sanctioned both the Federal individual and corporate income taxes and, as a consequence, neutralized the continuing effect of the *Pollock* decision.

1-2b **Revenue Acts**

After the Sixteenth Amendment was ratified by the states, Congress enacted the Revenue Act of 1913. Under this Act, the first Form 1040 was due on March 1, 1914. The law allowed various deductions and personal exemptions of $3,000 for a single individual and $4,000 for married taxpayers. These large exemptions excluded all but the more wealthy taxpayers from the new income tax.[9] Rates ranged from a low of 1 percent to a high of 6 percent. The 6 percent rate applied only to taxable income in excess of $500,000.[10]

Various revenue acts were passed between 1913 and 1939. In 1939, all of these revenue laws were codified (arranged in a systematic manner) into the Internal Revenue Code of 1939. In 1954, a similar codification took place. The Internal Revenue Code of 1986, which largely carries over the provisions of the 1954 Code, is our current law. Tax law changes occur almost every year (how this happens is discussed in Chapter 2).

[7] *Flint v. Stone Tracy Co.*, 3 AFTR 2834, 31 S.Ct. 342 (USSC, 1911).

[8] See the discussion of state franchise taxes later in text Section 1-4g.

[9] A $3,000 exemption in 1913 would be about $90,000 today, while a $4,000 exemption would be about $121,000.

[10] This should be contrasted with the highest 2023 tax rate of 37%, which applies once taxable income exceeds $578,125 for single taxpayers and $693,750 for married taxpayers filing a joint return.

1-2c **Trends**

The income tax is a major source of revenue for the Federal government. Exhibit 1.1 shows the tax revenue sources[11] and the importance of the income tax. Income tax collections from individuals and corporations amount to 60 percent of the total receipts. One revenue source missing from the Exhibit 1.1 pie chart is borrowing to cover the deficit, which in recent years has represented between 10 to 40 percent of total government revenues.

The need for revenues to finance the war effort during World War II converted the income tax from one that applied mostly to high-income individuals to a *mass tax*. In 1939, less than 6 percent of the U.S. population was subject to the Federal income tax. By 1945, more than 74 percent of the population was subject to the Federal income tax.[12]

Certain tax law changes are important to understand. In 1943, Congress passed the Current Tax Payment Act, which provided for a pay-as-you-go tax system. A pay-as-you-go income tax system requires employers to withhold a specified portion of an employee's wages and remit them to the government to cover the worker's income taxes. Persons with income from other than wages may have to make quarterly payments to the IRS for estimated taxes due for the year.

The increasing complexity of the Federal income tax laws causes concern among many, including lawmakers, taxpayers, and tax practitioners. Congress has added to this complexity by frequently changing the tax laws (e.g., by adding or deleting deductions or tax credits). This complexity forces many taxpayers to seek assistance in preparing their income tax returns. According to estimates, more than one-half of individual taxpayers who file a return pay a preparer, and most of these returns are prepared using tax software.[13] The IRS estimates that the average time spent by individuals to prepare and file their tax returns and engage in necessary recordkeeping is 13 hours

New ways of doing business and living often require changes and/or clarifications to the tax law. For example, increased longevity requires a need for more revenues from Social Security taxes (and/or an increase in retirement age). Increased global business activity means modifying a country's tax system to be more in line with other countries to make sure businesses are not impeded when entering the global marketplace. New types of digital assets [e.g., virtual currency (or cryptocurrency) and non-fungible tokens (NFTs)] often require lawmakers or the IRS to clarify how existing tax rules apply to the new assets and related transactions. Ideally, lawmakers should review tax systems periodically to ensure that they continue to be efficient in light of changes in how businesses and individuals function.

Exhibit 1.1 **Federal Tax Revenues (Estimated) in 2023**

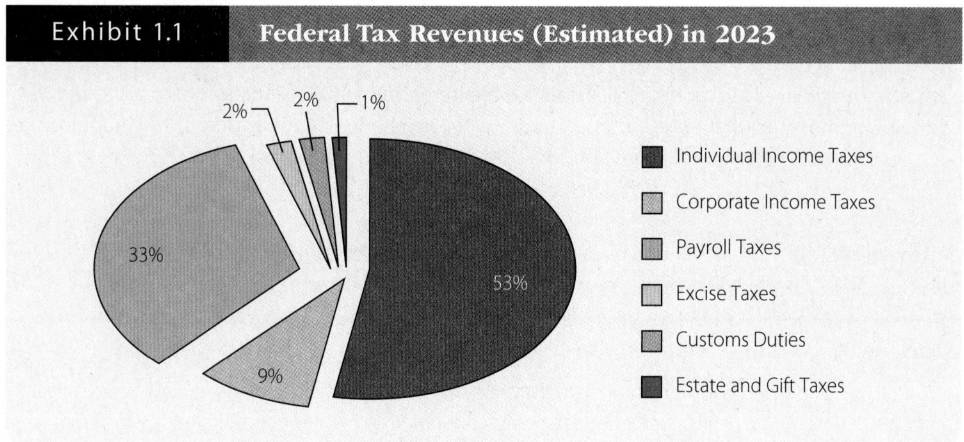

[11]Revenue data can be found at **irs.gov/statistics**, **cbo.gov**, and **whitehouse.gov/omb**. The instruction booklet for Form 1040 includes a revenue pie chart that includes borrowing to cover the deficit, as well as a pie chart that shows government spending in broad categories.

[12]Richard Goode, *The Individual Income Tax* (Washington, D.C.: The Brookings Institution, 1964), pp. 2–4.

[13]Most IRS instructions for forms and schedules include an estimate of the time needed to prepare the form or schedule.

Apply principles of good tax policy relevant to the design of a tax system.

1-3 Tax System Design

1-3a Legal Foundation

Article I, Section 8 of the U.S. Constitution states in part: "The Congress shall have power to lay and collect taxes." The Constitution also provided some limits on this taxing power, which led to the enactment of the Sixteenth Amendment to allow for an income tax (discussed in text Section 1-2a). This history lesson is important for a legislature or an electorate that wants to change a tax system. The jurisdiction's underlying governing documents (whether a country, state, or city) must be reviewed to determine whether they impose any restrictions relevant to taxation.

For example, the California Constitution (Article 13A) states that the maximum tax rate for real property taxation is 1 percent. The Florida Constitution (Section 5) specifies limits on the imposition of income taxes on natural persons. Also, state law may impose limitations on the types or amounts of taxes that cities and counties can impose.

Thus, the governing documents of a jurisdiction must be considered as part of any effort to modify that jurisdiction's tax system to make sure the change is permissible. If a change is not permissible but desired, then the governing document must be amended, as was done with the addition of the Sixteenth Amendment to the U.S. Constitution.

1-3b The Basic Tax Formula

The basic formula for any tax is:

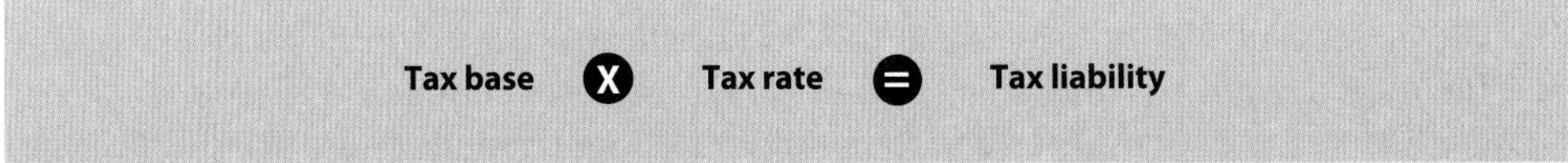

Tax Base

A tax base is the amount to which the tax rate is applied. In the case of the Federal income tax, the tax base is *taxable income*. As noted later in the chapter (Exhibit 1.3), taxable income is gross income reduced by certain deductions (both business and personal).

Tax Rates

Tax rates are applied to the tax base to determine a taxpayer's liability. Some taxes, like the sales tax and the gasoline excise tax, apply a fixed tax rate to all transactions.

Kansas applies a sales tax rate of 6.5% to all taxable items. In contrast, Illinois applies a sales tax rate of 6.25% for most taxable items but applies a rate of 1% when the tax base consists of food or prescription drugs.

Alternatively, for some taxes, tax rates may vary depending on the details of the tax base. Income taxes tend to use a *progressive* tax rate structure where a higher rate of tax applies as the tax base increases.

Bill and Chris, a married couple filing jointly, have taxable income of $15,000. Their Federal income tax rate for 2023 is 10%, which is the rate that applies to the first $22,000 of taxable income for a married couple filing jointly. Their tax liability is $1,500.

If, however, their taxable income is $95,000, their Federal income tax rates progress from 10% to 12% to 22% as their taxable income increases. In this case, their 2023 Federal income tax liability is $11,515. The Federal income tax uses a *progressive* rate structure that applies higher rates to taxable income (the tax base) as that income increases (see Appendix A to confirm these calculations, and note how progressivity is built into the rate structure of the Federal income tax).

The basic tax formula (shown above) is relevant for both computing taxes and planning, as well as for reforming a tax system. For example, if a legislator wants to lower tax rates but generate the same amount of tax revenues, the tax base must be increased. However, if she wants to increase tax revenues, the tax base can be increased *or* tax rates can be increased (or both can be increased). Changes to the tax base will depend on how it is constructed. For example, the income tax base is taxable income (income minus income exclusions minus deductions). To increase this tax base, income exclusions or deductions could be limited or eliminated. The details of the income tax base are discussed in later chapters. Tax system changes also involve canons (or principles) of taxation, discussed next.

1-3c **Tax Principles**

In the late 1700s, Adam Smith identified the following *principles of taxation*, which are still considered today when evaluating a particular tax structure:[14]

- *Equity*: Each taxpayer enjoys fair or equitable treatment by paying taxes in proportion to his or her income level. Ability to pay a tax is one of the measures of how equitably a tax is distributed among taxpayers.
- *Certainty*: A tax should be certain rather than arbitrary. Taxpayers need to be able to understand how tax rules work so that they understand the effect of the rules on various transactions and can comply.
- *Convenience of payment*: Taxes should be imposed in a manner that involves a convenient time for payment. An advantage of the existing withholding system (pay-as-you-go) is its convenience for taxpayers.
- *Economy in collection*: A *good* tax system involves only nominal collection costs by the government and minimal compliance costs on the part of the taxpayer.

The American Institute of Certified Public Accountants (AICPA) has issued suggestions to guide tax reform and policy activities. Titled *Guiding Principles of Good Tax Policy: A Framework for Evaluating Tax Proposals*, the monograph identifies 12 principles that are commonly used as indicators of desirable tax policy. The first four principles are adapted from Adam Smith's *The Wealth of Nations*. The complete list is as follows:[15]

1. *Equity and Fairness*: Similarly situated taxpayers should be taxed in a similar manner.
2. *Certainty*: Taxpayers should have certainty rather than ambiguity as to when and how a tax is paid, as well as how to calculate it.
3. *Convenience of Payment*: A tax should be due at a time and manner that is most convenient for the taxpayer.
4. *Effective Tax Administration*: Tax compliance and administrative costs should be kept to a minimum.
5. *Information Security*: Taxpayer information must be protected from improper disclosure.
6. *Simplicity*: Tax rules should be simple so that taxpayers understand them and can follow them in a cost-efficient manner.
7. *Neutrality*: The effect of tax rules on taxpayer decision making should be kept to a minimum.
8. *Economic Growth and Efficiency*: The tax system should not harm economic growth or distort economic effects among different activities and investments.
9. *Transparency and Visibility*: Taxpayers should know that a tax exists and how and when it applies to them.
10. *Minimum Tax Gap*: A tax should be structured to minimize noncompliance.
11. *Accountability to Taxpayers*: Taxpayers should have access to information on taxes, as well as proposed law changes and their rationale.
12. *Appropriate Government Revenues*: Tax rules should enable the government to predict the amount and timing of revenue production.

[14] *The Wealth of Nations* (New York: Dutton, 1910), Book V, Chapter II, Part II.

[15] AICPA, *Guiding Principles of Good Tax Policy: A Framework for Evaluating Tax Proposals*, 2017. Similarly, see GAO, *Understanding the Tax Reform Debate: Background, Criteria, & Questions*, 2005. As "long-standing criteria," the GAO lists "equity; economic efficiency; and a combination of simplicity, transparency, and administrability."

Exhibit 1.2 provides an application of these principles to a proposed tax law change.

Exhibit 1.2 Application of the *Guiding Principles of Good Tax Policy*

The *Guiding Principles of Good Tax Policy* can be applied to evaluate an existing tax rule or a proposed change. Here is an example of how the principles apply to a state's proposal to exempt college textbooks from sales tax.

Principle	Application	Result
Equity and fairness	Although all college students would pay no sales tax on their textbooks, the effect varies among students based on their ability to pay. This proposal provides tax savings not only to lower-income students but also to higher-income students who may not need the tax break to cover school costs. Also, higher-income students might buy full-price new books rather than lower-cost used books, resulting in larger tax savings.	Not fully met
Certainty	College textbooks can be identified, such as by looking at what is listed on a course syllabus.	Met
Convenience of payment	A sales tax exemption generally means that the tax is not owed at the time of purchase. If, instead, the exemption is structured for the student to pay the sales tax and apply for a refund later, convenience of payment would not be met.	Met
Effective tax administration	Sellers will have additional record keeping and reporting requirements to separate tax-exempt textbook sales from taxable sales. Some type of system is needed to prove that the buyer is a student purchasing a book for a college class. The state tax agency will incur additional time and costs in writing rules, modifying tax forms, and auditing compliance with the new rule.	Not met
Information security	If obtaining the exemption requires that students show proof to retailers that they are a student, there should be no need to provide a Social Security number. If students are required to claim the exemption with the state tax agency after purchasing the textbooks, the agency might request a student's Social Security number, which could increase the risk of identity theft.	Likely met
Simplicity	"Textbook" needs to be defined. The intent of the exemption is to benefit students. The seller needs to verify that the book is for use by a student for a class. For example, both students and nonstudents might buy a copy of *Romeo and Juliet*. Only the student purchasing it for a college class is entitled to the sales tax exemption. Complexity exists in the procedures needed to ensure that the exemption is used properly.	Not met
Neutrality	Students purchase textbooks because they are needed for class. The exemption is unlikely to change a student's behavior.	Met
Economic growth and efficiency	The exemption will reduce costs of attending college by a small amount. As a result, the change is unlikely to result in a greater number of college graduates (which might benefit the economy). Savings from not paying sales tax might be spent on other consumables. The impact on the economy is likely minor.	Met
Transparency and visibility	Students and textbook sellers are likely to be aware of the exemption because colleges will promote it as a reduction in the cost of attending college.	Met
Minimum tax gap	Students may abuse the rule by using the exemption for books that are not for class use. Nonstudents may abuse this rule by claiming they are college students.	Not met
Accountability to taxpayers	Were students and universities, particularly those funded by the state, aware of the textbook sales tax exemption proposal? Students and universities could provide information to legislators on whether there is a need for a sales tax exemption or if other financial support would be more helpful. Bookstores would want an opportunity to provide information on the compliance costs and challenges of the exemption.	More information needed
Appropriate government revenue	Existing data on how many textbooks are purchased enable the government to estimate how much tax revenues will decrease due to the new exemption.	Met

***Conclusion*:** Although the majority of the principles are met, the ones that are not met (effective tax administration, simplicity, and minimum tax gap) are significant. If lawmakers believe this tax exemption is necessary to help lower costs for college students, then they should consider alternative means of achieving the goal that are less complex. For example, grants could be offered or increased for college students in need of financial assistance.

1-4 **Types of Taxes**

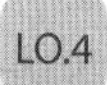

Identify the different taxes imposed in the United States at the Federal, state, and local levels.

While this text focuses on the Federal income tax, there are other types of Federal taxes. In addition, state and local governments also impose taxes. A simple example illustrates the importance of state and local taxes, as well as taxes that are not imposed on income.

Rick is employed by Flamingo Corporation in San Antonio, Texas, at a salary of $74,000. Rick's employer offers him a chance to transfer to its New York City office at a salary of $94,000.

Although Rick must consider many nontax factors before he decides on a job change, he should also evaluate the tax climate. How do state and local taxes compare? For example, neither Texas nor San Antonio imposes an income tax, but New York State and New York City do. A quick computation indicates that the additional income taxes (Federal, state, and local) involve approximately $12,000. If Rick owns a home, he should also consider how property taxes differ between Texas and New York. In addition, there are likely differences in sales taxes (both the rate and what items are subject to the tax).

What appears to be a $20,000 pay increase is actually only about $8,000 when the additional $12,000 of income taxes are taken into account. Other taxes and costs (e.g., property taxes, sales taxes, food, utilities, transportation) must also be factored into Rick's decision.

1-4a **Property Taxes**

Correctly referred to as **ad valorem taxes** because they are based on value, property taxes are a tax on wealth, or capital. As a result, they have much in common with estate taxes and gift taxes discussed later in the chapter. Although property taxes do not tax income, the income actually derived from the property (or the potential for any income) may be relevant if it affects the value of the property being taxed.

Property taxes fall into *two* categories: those imposed on real property (land and buildings) and those imposed on personal property (assets other than land and buildings). Both have added importance because they often generate a deduction for Federal income tax purposes (see Chapter 10).

Ad Valorem Taxes on Real Property

Property taxes on real property are used exclusively by states and their local subdivisions (such as cities, counties, and school districts). They represent a major source of revenue for *local* governments (and school districts).

How real property is defined can have an important bearing on which assets are subject to tax. This is especially true in jurisdictions that do not impose ad valorem taxes on personal property. Real property, or **realty**, generally includes real estate and any fixtures. A *fixture* is something so permanently attached to the real estate that its removal will cause irreparable damage. A built-in bookcase is likely a fixture, whereas a movable bookcase is not. Electrical wiring and plumbing become realty when they are installed in a building.

Here are some of the characteristics of ad valorem taxes on real property:

- Property owned by the Federal government is exempt from tax. In general, the same is true for property owned by state and local governments and by charitable organizations.
- Some states provide for lower valuations on property used for agriculture or other special uses (e.g., wildlife sanctuaries).
- States may have a homestead exemption, which makes some portion of the value of a personal residence exempt from tax.
- Lower taxes may apply to a residence owned by a taxpayer aged 65 or older.
- When non-income-producing property (e.g., a personal residence) is converted to income-producing property (e.g., a rental house), the appraised value may be increased.

The Big Picture

Example 4

Return to the facts of *The Big Picture* on p. 1-1. Why did the Walkers' property taxes decrease but those of the Carters increase?

A likely explanation is that one (or both) of the Walkers achieved senior citizen status, leading to a reduction of their property taxes. In the case of the Carters, the assessed value of their property might have increased due to property values increasing in their location. Or perhaps they made significant home improvements (e.g., kitchen/bathroom renovation or addition of a deck) that increased the value (tax base) of the home.

Ad Valorem Taxes on Personal Property

Personal property, or **personalty**, can be defined as all property that is not realty. There is a difference between how property is *classified* (realty or personalty) and how it is *used*. Both realty and personalty can be either business use or personal use property. Examples include a residence (realty that is for personal use), an office building (realty that is for business use), surgical instruments (personalty that is for business use), and home furniture (personalty that is for personal use).[16]

Personal property can also be classified as tangible property or intangible property. For ad valorem tax purposes, intangible personalty includes stocks, bonds, and various other securities (e.g., bank shares).

Here are some general rules related to ad valorem taxes on personal property:

- Generally, for individuals, vehicles (e.g., cars and boats) are the only non-realty personal use assets subject to property tax. The value of a vehicle is typically established by a schedule based on its age and make/model (a high-priced car versus a low-priced car). Usually, any vehicle property tax is assessed and collected along with vehicle license or registration fees.
- Generally, businesses are assessed property taxes on equipment and other tangible property, although many states do not tax inventory.
- A few states levy an ad valorem tax on intangibles such as stocks and bonds.

1-4b Transaction Taxes

Transaction taxes, imposed at the manufacturer's, wholesaler's, or retailer's level, cover a wide range of transfers. Transaction taxes can be assessed by any taxing authority (Federal, state, or local government). As the description implies, these taxes cover transfers of property and normally are determined by multiplying the value by a percentage rate.

Federal Excise Taxes

In general, Federal **excise taxes** cover fewer items than in the past. Congress has focused (and substantially increased) the Federal excise taxes on items such as tobacco products, fuel and gasoline sales, and air travel. Other Federal excise taxes include:

- Manufacturers' excise taxes on trucks, trailers, tires, firearms, sporting equipment, and coal and the gas guzzler tax on automobiles.[17]
- A 1 percent excise tax imposed on a corporation buying back its stock. The tax is assessed on the fair market value of the stock when repurchased.[18]

[16] The distinction, important for ad valorem and for Federal income tax purposes, often becomes confusing when personalty is referred to as "personal" property to distinguish it from "real" property. This designation does not give a complete picture of what is involved. The description "personal" residence, however, is clearer, because a residence can be identified as being realty. What is meant in this case is realty that is personal use property.

[17] The gas guzzler tax is imposed on the manufacturers of automobiles (both domestic and foreign) with fuel economy under 22.5 miles per gallon (mpg). For example, a 2022 Rolls-Royce Dawn gets about 14 mpg in combined city/highway driving and costs about $428,000. The gas guzzler tax on this vehicle is $5,400. The highest gas guzzler tax is $7,700, and the lowest is $1,000. § 4064.

[18] § 4501, added by the Inflation Reduction Act of 2022 (P.L. 117–169; August 16, 2022). Exceptions are provided for repurchases of $1 million or less, if the repurchase was part of a reorganization, and if the repurchased stock is contributed to an employer-sponsored retirement plan.

- Alcohol taxes.
- Miscellaneous taxes (e.g., the tax on wagering and the tax on investment income of certain private colleges and universities).

When reviewing the list of both Federal and state excise taxes, recognize that these taxes may be trying to influence social or economic behavior. For example, the gas guzzler tax is intended as an incentive for an individual to buy (and for the automobile companies to build) fuel-efficient cars.

State and Local Excise Taxes

Many state and local excise taxes parallel the Federal version. For example, all states tax the sale of gasoline, liquor, and tobacco products. However, the rates vary significantly. For gasoline products, for example, compare the 58.7 cents per gallon imposed by the Commonwealth of Pennsylvania with the 19.0 cents per gallon levied by the state of Arizona. For tobacco sales, contrast the 17.0 cents per pack of 20 cigarettes in effect in Missouri with the $4.35 per pack in the state of New York.

Other excise taxes found at some state and local levels include those on admission to amusement facilities, on the sale of playing cards, and on prepared foods. Some counties impose a transaction tax on the transfer of property that requires the recording of documents (e.g., real estate sales).

Over the last few years, two types of excise taxes imposed at the local level have become increasingly popular: the hotel occupancy tax and the rental car "surcharge." The hotel occupancy tax is called a transient occupancy tax (TOT) in some areas. This tax also can apply to short-term rentals of one's home or a room in the home (such as via Airbnb). Because they tax the visitor who cannot vote, they are a political windfall and are often used to finance special projects that generate civic pride (e.g., convention centers and state-of-the-art sports arenas). These levies can be significant, as demonstrated by Houston's hotel tax of 17 percent [6 percent (state) + 7 percent (city) + 2 percent (county) + 2 percent (sports authority)].

General Sales Taxes

The distinction between an excise tax and a general **sales tax** is easy to make. One is restricted to a particular transaction (e.g., the 18.4 cents per gallon Federal excise tax on the sale of gasoline), whereas the other covers a multitude of transactions (e.g., a 5 percent tax on *all* retail sales). In actual practice, however, the distinction is not always that clear. Some states exempt certain items from the general sales taxes (e.g., groceries, medicines, and drugs). Also, sales tax rates can vary. Many states, for example, allow lower rates for the sale of agricultural equipment or prescription drugs or apply different rates (either higher or lower than the general rate) to the sale of automobiles.

A **use tax** is a complement to the sales tax and is assessed at the same rate as the sales tax. A use tax is owed on property purchased outside the state but used in the state. The purpose of a use tax is to prevent the avoidance of a sales tax. For example, if you purchase clothes online and are not charged sales tax but clothes are subject to sales tax in your state, you owe use tax on the purchase. State rules vary on how use tax is collected. Many states allow individuals to pay it along with their state income tax. Alaska, Delaware, Montana, New Hampshire, and Oregon do not impose sales or use taxes. There is no Federal general sales or use tax.

The Big Picture

Example 5

Return to the facts of *The Big Picture* on p. 1-1. The payment Travis made when he registered the car is probably a use tax.

When the car was purchased in another state, likely no (or a lesser) sales tax was levied. The current payment makes up for the amount of sales tax he would have paid had the car been purchased in his home state.

Ethics & Equity **Making Good Use of Out-of-State Relatives**

Marcus, a resident of Austin, Texas, has found the ideal gift for his spouse in celebration of their upcoming wedding anniversary—a $22,000 gold watch. However, Marcus is appalled at the prospect of paying the state and local sales tax of $1,815 (combined rate of 8.25 percent). So, he asks his aunt, a resident of Montana, to purchase the watch. The jewelry store lists the aunt as the buyer and ships the watch to her, with no sales tax owed on the transaction. Prior to the anniversary, Marcus receives the watch from his aunt. Is Marcus able to save $1,815 on the present for his spouse? What can go wrong?

Local general sales taxes, over and above state sales taxes, are common. It is not unusual to find taxpayers living in the same state but paying different general sales taxes due to the location of their residence.

Pete and Sam both live in a state that has a general sales tax of 3%. Sam, however, resides in a city that imposes an additional general sales tax of 2%. Even though Pete and Sam live in the same state, one is subject to a rate of 3%, whereas the other pays a tax of 5%.

For various reasons, some jurisdictions will suspend the application of a general sales tax for a specified, brief time period. For example, a state may have a "sales tax holiday" in late summer for back-to-school clothing and supplies. Some states use sales tax holidays to encourage the purchase of energy-conserving appliances and hurricane preparedness items.

Severance Taxes

Severance taxes are transaction taxes that are based on the notion that the state has an interest in its natural resources (e.g., oil, gas, iron ore, or coal). Therefore, a tax is imposed when the natural resources are extracted. For some states, severance taxes can be a significant source of revenue.

1-4c Taxes on Transfers at Death

The right to transfer property or to receive property upon the death of the owner may be subject to estate and/or inheritance taxes. Consequently, such taxes fall into the category of excise taxes. An **estate tax** is levied on the estate of the decedent (it is a tax on the right to pass property at death). An **inheritance tax** is levied on the person receiving the property (the heir). The value of the property transferred provides the base for determining the amount of the tax.

The Federal government imposes only an estate tax. Some state governments, however, levy inheritance taxes, estate taxes, or both. Some states (e.g., Florida and Texas) levy neither tax.

At the time of her death, Cari lived in a state that imposes an inheritance tax but not an estate tax. Amy, one of Cari's heirs, lives in the same state. Cari's estate is subject to the Federal estate tax, and Amy is subject to the state inheritance tax.

The Federal Estate Tax

The Revenue Act of 1916 incorporated the estate tax into the tax law. The tax was originally intended to prevent large concentrations of wealth from being kept in a family for many generations. Whether this objective has been accomplished is debatable. Like the income tax, estate taxes can be reduced through various planning procedures.

The gross estate includes property the decedent owned at the time of death.[19] It also includes property interests, such as life insurance proceeds paid to the estate. All property included in the gross estate is valued as of the date of death or, if the alternate valuation date is elected, six months later.[20]

Deductions from the gross estate in arriving at the taxable estate include funeral and administration expenses; certain taxes; debts of the decedent; casualty losses[21] incurred during the administration of the estate; transfers to charitable organizations; and, in some cases, the marital deduction. The *marital deduction* is available for amounts actually passing to a surviving spouse (a widow or widower).

Once the taxable estate has been determined and certain taxable gifts made by the decedent during life have been added to it, the estate tax can be computed. From this amount, various credits are subtracted to arrive at the tax, if any, that is due.[22] The most significant credit is the *unified transfer tax credit*. The main reason for this credit is to eliminate or reduce the estate tax liability for certain estates. For 2023, the credit exempts a tax base of up to $12,920,000, meaning that the vast majority of estates pass tax-free to the heirs.

Jason made no taxable gifts before his death in 2023. If Jason's taxable estate amounts to $12,920,000 or less, no Federal estate tax is due because of the application of the unified transfer tax credit.

State Taxes on Transfers at Death

As noted earlier, some states levy an inheritance tax, an estate tax, or both. Typically, a state inheritance tax divides the heirs into classes based on their relationship to the decedent. The more closely related the heir, the lower the rates imposed and/or the greater the exemption allowed. Some states allow amounts passing to a surviving spouse to escape taxation.

1-4d Gift Taxes

Like taxes on transfers at death, a **gift tax** is an excise tax levied on property transfers made during the owner's life and not at death. If the recipient pays the donor for the property (but at an amount less than its fair market value), the difference is a gift.

Carl sells property worth $50,000 to his daughter for $1,000. Although property worth $50,000 has been transferred, only $49,000 represents a gift because this is the portion that was not paid for.

The Federal Gift Tax

First enacted in 1932, the Federal gift tax was intended to complement the estate tax. If lifetime transfers by gift were not taxed, it would be possible to avoid the estate tax and escape taxation entirely.

[19]For further information on these matters, see Chapter 29.

[20]See the discussion of the alternate valuation date in Chapter 13.

[21]For a definition of *casualty losses*, see the Glossary in Appendix C.

[22]For tax purposes, it is crucial to appreciate the difference between a deduction and a credit. A *credit* is a dollar-for-dollar reduction of tax liability. A *deduction*, however, provides a benefit only to the extent of the taxpayer's tax bracket. A taxpayer in a 50% tax bracket, for example, would need $2 of deductions to eliminate $1 of tax liability. In contrast, $1 of credit eliminates $1 of tax liability.

Only taxable gifts are subject to the gift tax. For this purpose, a taxable gift is measured by the fair market value of the property on the date of transfer less the *annual exclusion per donee* and, in some cases, less the *marital deduction*, which allows tax-free transfers between spouses. In 2023, each donor is allowed an annual exclusion of $17,000 for each donee ($16,000 in 2022).[23]

On December 31, 2023, Yasmin (a widow) gives $17,000 to each of her four married children, their spouses, and her eight grandchildren. On January 2, 2024, she repeats the procedure.

Due to the annual exclusion, Yasmin has not made a taxable gift, although she transferred $272,000 [$17,000 (annual exclusion) × 16 (donees)] in 2023 and another $272,000 in 2024, for a total of $544,000 ($272,000 + $272,000).

A married couple may make a special election that allows one-half of the gift made by the donor-spouse to a third party to be treated as being made by the non-donor-spouse. This *gift splitting* effectively allows the annual exclusion to double.

The Big Picture

Return to the facts of *The Big Picture* on p. 1-1. Although the value of the RV is not stated, it is likely to exceed the annual exclusion allowed of $68,000 [$17,000 (annual exclusion) × two donees (the Walkers) × two donors (the Carters)].

As a result, a taxable gift results, and a Form 709 (Gift Tax Return) must be filed. Whether any gift tax is due depends on what past taxable gifts the Carters have made and how much of their unified transfer tax credit (see the following discussion) is still available.

The gift tax and estate tax rate schedules are the same. The schedule is commonly referred to as the *unified transfer tax rate schedule*.

The Federal gift tax is *cumulative* in effect. What this means is that the tax base for current taxable gifts includes past taxable gifts. Although a credit is allowed for prior gift taxes, the result of adding past taxable gifts to current taxable gifts could force the donor into a higher tax bracket.[24] Like the Federal estate tax rates, the Federal gift tax rates are progressive (see Example 2 earlier in this chapter).

The unified transfer tax credit is available for all taxable gifts. As was the case with the Federal estate tax, the credit for 2023 is $5,113,800 (which covers taxable gifts up to $12,920,000) and for 2022 is $4,769,800 (which covers taxable gifts up to $12,060,000). There is, however, only one unified transfer tax credit, and it applies to both taxable gifts and the Federal estate tax. Once the unified transfer tax credit has been used up for Federal gift tax purposes, any transfers at death will be subject to the Federal estate tax.

Making lifetime gifts of property carries several tax advantages over passing the property at death. If income-producing property is involved (e.g., marketable securities and rental real estate), a gift may shift subsequent income to donees in a lower income tax bracket. If the gift involves property that is expected to appreciate in value (e.g., life insurance policies, real estate, and artwork), future increases in value will be assigned to the donee and will not be included in the donor's estate. And due to the annual exclusion ($17,000 per donee in 2023; $16,000 per donee in 2022), some of the gift can escape tax (with gift splitting, married donors can double the annual exclusion).

Neither the actual receipt of a gift nor an inheritance will cause income tax consequences to the donee or heir.

[23]The purpose of the annual exclusion is to avoid the need to report and pay a tax on *modest* gifts. Without the exclusion, the IRS could face a real problem of taxpayer noncompliance. The annual exclusion is indexed as the level of inflation warrants. The exclusion was $15,000 from 2018 to 2021, $14,000 from 2013 to 2017, and $13,000 from 2009 through 2012.

[24]For further information on the Federal gift tax, see Chapter 29.

1-4e **Income Taxes**

Income taxes are levied by the Federal government, most states, and some local governments. Income taxes generally are imposed on individuals, corporations, and certain fiduciaries (estates and trusts). Most jurisdictions attempt to ensure the collection of income taxes by requiring pay-as-you-go procedures, including withholding requirements for employees and estimated tax payments for all taxpayers.

Federal Income Taxes

Exhibit 1.3 illustrates the formula for the Federal income tax imposed on individuals. This formula provides a framework for part of the text. Beginning with Chapter 3, each component of the formula is illustrated and explained.

Unlike its individual counterpart, the Federal corporate income tax is not progressive, but instead uses a flat tax rate of 21 percent.[25] Also, it does not include the computation of adjusted gross income (AGI) and does not provide for the standard deduction or the deduction for qualified business income. As a result, a corporation's taxable income is the difference between gross income and deductions. Chapter 17 discusses the rules relating to the determination of the Federal income tax on corporations.[26]

Exhibit 1.3 Formula for Federal Income Tax on Individuals

Income (broadly defined)	$xx,xxx
Less: Exclusions (income that is not subject to tax)	(x,xxx)
Gross income (income that is subject to tax)	$xx,xxx
Less: Certain deductions (usually referred to as deductions *for* adjusted gross income)	(x,xxx)
Adjusted gross income (AGI)	$xx,xxx
Less: The greater of:	
Certain personal and investment deductions (referred to as *itemized deductions*)	
or	
The standard deduction (including any additional standard deduction)	(x,xxx)
Less: Personal and dependency exemptions*	(x,xxx)
Deduction for qualified business income**	(x,xxx)
Taxable income	$xx,xxx
Tax on taxable income (see the Tax Tables and Tax Rate Schedules in Appendix A)	$ x,xxx
Less: Tax credits (including Federal income tax withheld and other prepayments of Federal income taxes)	(xxx)
Tax due (or refund)	$ xxx

*Exemption deductions are not allowed from 2018 through 2025.
**Only applies from 2018 through 2025.

[25]Starting in 2023, some very large corporations (in general, those with over $1 billion of financial statement income) may be subject to an alternative minimum tax of 15%, if it is greater than their regular tax liability. Congress' Joint Committee on Taxation expects that only about 150 corporations (about 30% of the Fortune 500) could be subject to this tax each year.

[26]For an in-depth treatment of the Federal income tax as it affects corporations, partnerships, estates, and trusts, and owners or beneficiaries of these entities as well as sole proprietors, see Chapters 17 through 23 and 30. See Chapters 6 and 15 for additional discussion of the deduction for qualified business income.

State Income Taxes

Almost all states impose an income tax on individuals.[27]

Here are some of the characteristics of state income taxes:

- With few exceptions, all states require some form of withholding procedures.
- Most states use as the tax base the income determination made for Federal income tax purposes. This is often referred to as the piggyback approach to state income taxation. Although the term *piggyback* does not lend itself to a precise definition, in this context it means making use, for state income tax purposes, of what was done for Federal income tax purposes.
- Some states "decouple" from selected Federal tax changes passed by Congress. The purpose of the decoupling is to retain state revenue that would otherwise be lost. For example, some states do not allow "bonus depreciation" allowed for Federal tax purposes.
- Because of the tie-ins to the Federal return, a state may be notified of any changes made by the IRS upon audit of a Federal return (or vice versa).
- Most states allow a deduction for personal and dependency exemptions. Some states substitute a tax credit for a deduction.
- Many state income tax returns provide checkoff boxes for donations to various causes. Many are dedicated to medical research and wildlife programs, but special projects are not uncommon. For example, Wisconsin uses one for maintenance and operating costs of Lambeau Field (home of the Green Bay Packers). These checkoff boxes have been criticized as adding complexity to the returns and misleading taxpayers.[28]
- The objective of most states is to tax the income of residents and those who conduct business in the state (e.g., employees sent to the state to help a client or a professional athlete playing a game in the state).
- Most states allow their residents some form of tax credit for income taxes paid to other states.

The Big Picture

Example 12

Return to the facts of *The Big Picture* on p. 1-1. Travis will need to review the state income tax laws in each state he has clients to determine if he is subject to that state's tax on his consulting income earned in that state. If the income is subject to tax in another state as well as his home state, the home state might provide a credit to negate the double taxation.

- The due date for filing generally is the same as for the Federal income tax (for individuals, the fifteenth day of the fourth month following the close of the tax year; usually April 15 for calendar year taxpayers).
- Some states have occasionally instituted amnesty programs that allow taxpayers to pay back taxes (and interest) on unreported income with no (or reduced) penalty. In many cases, the tax amnesty has generated enough revenue to warrant the authorization of follow-up programs covering future years.[29] Amnesties usually include other taxes as well (e.g., sales, franchise, and severance).

[27]Alaska, Florida, Nevada, South Dakota, Tennessee, Texas, Washington, and Wyoming do not have an individual income tax. New Hampshire imposes an individual income tax only on interest and dividends.

[28]Many taxpayers do not realize they are paying for the checkoff donation (usually with some of their income tax refund). Unlike the presidential election campaign fund available for Federal income tax purposes ($3 in this case), the contribution is *not made* by the government.

[29]Although the suggestion has been made, no comparable amnesty program has been offered for the Federal income tax. The IRS has, however, offered an exemption from certain penalties for taxpayers who disclosed offshore bank accounts or participated in certain tax shelters.

- Because many consumers do not pay state and local sales taxes on out-of-state purchases, state income tax returns, in some states, include a separate line for reporting any use tax that is due. As a result, the income tax return serves as a means of collecting use taxes.

Nearly all states have an income tax applicable to corporations. Other states have a franchise tax (discussed later in the chapter) that can be based in part on corporate income.

Local Income Taxes

Cities imposing an income tax include Baltimore, Cincinnati, Cleveland, Detroit, Kansas City (Missouri), New York, Philadelphia, and St. Louis. The application of a city income tax is not limited to local residents.

1-4f Employment Taxes

Employment taxes are a type of income tax imposed on employers and employees. We concentrate on the two major employment taxes: FICA (Federal Insurance Contributions Act—commonly referred to as the Social Security tax) and FUTA (Federal Unemployment Tax Act). Both taxes can be justified by social and public welfare considerations: FICA offers some measure of retirement security, and FUTA provides a modest source of income in the event of loss of employment.

These employment taxes come into play for employees (*not self-employed* individuals) if the particular work is covered under FICA or FUTA or both.[30]

FICA Taxes

The **FICA tax** rates and wage base have increased steadily over the years. It is difficult to imagine that the initial rate in 1937 was only 1 percent of the first $3,000 of covered wages. Thus, the maximum tax due was only $30.

The FICA tax has two components: Social Security tax (old age, survivors, and disability insurance) *and* Medicare tax (hospital insurance). The Social Security tax rate is 6.2 percent and generally does not change. The base amount usually increases each year. For 2023, the base amount is $160,200 ($147,000 for 2022).

The Medicare portion of FICA is applied at a rate of 1.45 percent and, unlike Social Security, is not subject to any dollar limitation. The Affordable Care Act (ObamaCare) imposes an additional 0.9 percent tax on earned income (including self-employment income) *above* $200,000 (single filers) or $250,000 (married filing jointly). Unlike the Social Security tax of 6.2 percent and the regular Medicare portion of 1.45 percent, an employer does not have to match the employees' 0.9 percent tax.

A spouse employed by another spouse is subject to FICA. However, children under the age of 18 who are employed in a parent's unincorporated trade or business are exempted.

The Big Picture

Example 13

Return to the facts of *The Big Picture* on p. 1-1. Presuming that April and Martin perform meaningful services for Travis (which the facts seem to imply), they are legitimate employees. April is not subject to Social Security tax because she is under the age of 18. However, Martin is 18 and needs to be covered. Furthermore, recall that Amy Carter is now working at a medical clinic and will likewise be subject to Social Security tax. Travis, as an independent contractor, is subject to self-employment tax.

Taxes Related to FICA Taxes

Self-employed individuals are subject to tax at the combined employer and employee FICA rate of 15.3%. Also, as part of the Affordable Care Act, Congress created a new tax on the investment income of high income individuals that uses the combined employer and employee Medicare tax rate plus the additional 0.9 rate for a rate of 3.8%. These two taxes are discussed briefly below and explained in detail in Chapter 12.

---

[30]Chapter 12 includes additional coverage of employment taxes for employees, employers, and self-employed persons. See also Circular E, *Employer's Tax Guide*, issued by the IRS as Publication 15.

Self-Employment Tax Taxpayers who are not employees (e.g., sole proprietors and independent contractors) may also be subject to Social Security taxes. Known as the self-employment tax, the rates are 12.4 percent for Social Security and 2.9 percent for Medicare, or twice that applicable to an employee. The additional 0.9 percent Medicare tax also covers situations involving high net income from self-employment. The Social Security tax is imposed on net self-employment income up to the annual base amount ($160,200 for 2023; $147,000 for 2022). The Medicare portion of the self-employment tax is not subject to any dollar limitation.

Net Investment Income Tax (NIIT) To help cover the government's cost of medical care, Congress enacted a special tax on investment income.[31] For this purpose, "investment income" is often referred to as "unearned income" because it is not generated by the performance of services. A tax of 3.8 percent is imposed on net investment income when a taxpayer's modified adjusted gross income (MAGI) exceeds certain threshold amounts.[32] The threshold amounts are $250,000 for married taxpayers and $200,000 for single taxpayers. Investment income generally includes passive-type income (e.g., rents, taxable interest, dividends, and capital gains). For further discussion, see Chapter 12 and the online appendix on the Affordable Care Act.

FUTA Taxes

The purpose of the **FUTA tax** is to provide funds the states can use to administer unemployment benefits. This leads to the somewhat unusual situation of one tax being handled by both Federal and state governments. This joint administration means that the employer must observe two sets of rules. State and Federal returns must be filed and payments made to both governmental units.

In 2023, FUTA is 6 percent on the first $7,000 of covered wages paid during the year to each employee. The Federal government allows a credit for FUTA paid (or allowed under a merit rating system) to the state. The credit cannot exceed 5.4 percent of the covered wages. Thus, the amount required to be paid to the Federal government could be as low as 0.6 percent (6.0% − 5.4%).

States reduce the unemployment tax on employers who experience stable employment, since the state pays less unemployment benefits. Thus, an employer with little or no employee turnover might find that the state rate drops to as low as 0.1 percent or, in some states, even to zero.

FUTA, unlike FICA, is paid entirely by the employer. A few states, however, levy a special tax on employees to provide either disability benefits or supplemental unemployment compensation or both.

1-4g **Other U.S. Taxes**

To complete the overview of the U.S. tax system, some missing links need to be covered that do not fit into the classifications discussed elsewhere in this chapter.

Federal Customs Duties

The tariff on imported goods,[33] also known as customs duties, together with excise taxes, provided most of the revenues needed by the Federal government during the nineteenth century. In view of present times, it is remarkable that tariffs and excise taxes alone paid off the national debt in 1835 and enabled the U.S. Treasury to pay a surplus of $28 million to the states.

In recent years, tariffs have served both as an instrument for carrying out protectionist policies and for generating revenue. By imposing customs duties on the importation of foreign goods that can be sold at lower prices, protectionists contend that the tariff thereby neutralizes the competitive edge held by the producer of the foreign goods. However, history shows that tariffs often lead to retaliatory action on the part of the nation or nations affected.

[31]Enacted as part of the Health Care and Education Reconciliation Act of 2010.

[32]MAGI is adjusted gross income (see Exhibit 1.3 and page 1 of Form 1040) plus any foreign income or excluded foreign housing costs. An online appendix covers the net investment income tax (NIIT) and other Affordable Care Act tax provisions.

[33]Less-developed countries that rely principally on one or more major commodities (e.g., oil or coffee) are prone to favor *export* duties.

Miscellaneous State and Local Taxes

Most states impose a **franchise tax** on corporations for the right to do business in the state.[34] The tax base used varies from state to state but most often is based on the capitalization of the corporation (either with or without certain long-term indebtedness).

Similar to the franchise tax are **occupational fees** that apply to various trades or businesses (e.g., a liquor store license; a taxicab permit; or a fee to practice a profession such as law, medicine, or accounting). Most of these are not significant revenue producers, and the fees are used to fund the costs of regulating the business or profession in the interest of the public good.

The Big Picture

Return to the facts of *The Big Picture* on p. 1-1. Although the facts do not mention the matter, both Travis and Amy might owe occupation or license fees—Travis for engineering and Amy for nursing.

Concept Summary 1.2 provides an overview of the major taxes existing in the United States and specifies which political jurisdiction imposes them.

Concept Summary 1.2

Overview of Taxes in the United States

	Imposed by Jurisdiction		
Type of Tax	**Federal**	**State**	**Local**
Property taxes:			
Ad valorem on realty	No	Yes	Yes
Ad valorem on personalty	No	Yes	Yes
Transaction taxes:			
Excise	Yes	Yes	Few*
General sales	No	Most	Some
Severance	Yes**	Most	No
Estate	Yes	Some	No
Inheritance	No	Some	No
Gift	Yes	Few	No
Income taxes:			
Corporations	Yes	Most	Few
Individuals	Yes	Most	Few
Employment taxes:			
FICA	Yes	No	No
FUTA	Yes	Yes	No
Customs duties	Yes	No	No
Franchise taxes	No	Yes	No
Occupational taxes or fees***	Yes	Yes	Yes

* An example of a local excise tax is a tax on hotel occupancy, typically referred to as a transient occupancy tax (TOT).
** For Federal public lands and continental-shelf areas.
*** An example is a fee to operate a beauty salon or barbershop.

[34] Only five states do not impose a franchise tax (Michigan, Nevada, South Dakota, Washington, and Wyoming).

1-4h Proposed U.S. Taxes

The last two major reforms to the U.S. tax system were in 2017 [the Tax Cuts and Jobs Act (TCJA) of 2017] and in 1986 (the Tax Reform Act of 1986). Tax reform discussions over the past few decades also have included use of a consumption tax to replace all or a portion of the income tax or as a new additional tax. Consumption taxes considered include the flat tax, a national sales tax, and a value added tax. Federal tax reform discussions have also included adding a carbon tax or a financial transactions tax. A brief description of these types of taxes follows.

Flat Tax

The **flat tax**, as introduced in 1981 by economists Robert Hall and Alvin Rabushka of the Hoover Institution, is a form of a consumption tax. Their proposal achieves some of the administrative advantages of a value added tax (VAT) relative to a sales tax while also partially addressing concerns that consumption taxes impose a relatively heavier tax burden on lower-income taxpayers. It assesses a "flat" 19 percent tax on all businesses (corporate or otherwise)—identical to the VAT, except that wages, pension contributions, materials costs, and capital investments are deducted from the tax base. Individuals (or households) are assessed a 19 percent flat-rate tax on wages and pension benefits above an exemption of $25,500 for a family of four. No other income is taxable, and no other deductions are allowed. Over the past 35 years, the Hall-Rabushka proposal has served as the blueprint for a number of proposals to reform the Federal tax system.[35]

National Sales Tax

A **national sales tax** would operate similarly to most state sales taxes although the tax base would be larger. The rate would also be higher to generate the revenues needed to replace the Federal income tax.

A frequent proposal for a national sales tax, called the "Fair Tax," would tax all purchases—including food and medicine, real property, and many types of services—at approximately 23 percent. Exempt items include business expenses, used goods, and the costs of education. The Fair Tax would replace the income tax (both individual and corporate), payroll taxes (including the self-employment tax), and the gift and estate taxes. To help address the regressivity of the tax, many individuals would receive a monthly rebate to offset a portion of sales tax paid.

Value Added Tax

A **value added tax (VAT)** is imposed on the value added by each party in a production cycle. For example, a furniture maker is charged VAT on wood purchased to make the furniture. Customers are charged VAT when they buy the furniture. A system of credits results in the VAT ultimately only being paid by the final consumer. This form of VAT—a credit invoice VAT—is similar to a sales tax. It is viewed as more efficient than a sales tax because assessment throughout the production process better ensures collection of the tax. The credit invoice VAT is widely used throughout the world.

A VAT has been considered in the United States various times since the 1960s. In 1984, the Treasury Department released a three-volume tax reform report, with one volume devoted to the VAT.[36] In 2016, Congressman James Renacci (R-OH) introduced a proposal to replace the corporate income tax with a credit invoice VAT as part of his Simplifying America's Tax System (SATS) proposal.[37]

[35] Usually, the tax bill carries the number H.R. 1040. See R. E. Hall and A. Rabushka, *The Flat Tax*, Hoover Institution (2007).

[36] U.S. Treasury Department, *Tax Reform for Fairness, Simplicity, and Economic Growth: The Treasury Department Report to the President*, Volume 3, 1984.

[37] Tax Foundation, *Details and Analysis of Rep. Jim Renacci's Tax Reform Proposal*, July 14, 2016.

Global Tax Issues **VAT in USA?**

The United States is the only country in the OECD (Organization of Economic Cooperation and Development) that does not have a value added tax (VAT). Over 140 countries around the world use a VAT, with rates ranging from 5 percent to 27 percent.

Is the United States out of sync with most other countries by not having a VAT? One advantage of a VAT is that it provides a significant revenue source, allowing for lower individual and corporate income tax rates. Also, unlike the income tax, a VAT is "border-adjustable," meaning that a country can impose it on imports but not exports. These are some considerations for U.S. lawmakers in evaluating the economic effects of the U.S. tax system and tax reform options in a global perspective.

One challenge of implementing a VAT in the United States is that it is a regressive tax (it has a greater impact on lower-income taxpayers relative to higher-income taxpayers). As a result, adjustments need to be implemented to protect lower-income taxpayers (e.g., expanding the earned income tax credit and/or child tax credit; both occur in the SATS proposal). Another challenge is that the Treasury Department (and IRS) will have to learn how to implement and enforce the VAT.

Carbon Tax

A **carbon tax** aims to help reduce carbon emissions (i.e., greenhouse gases). The tax could be applied to fossil fuels based on their level of greenhouse gas emissions. Because a significant fossil fuel is gasoline, some people suggest a higher gasoline excise tax as a simple form of a carbon tax.

Financial Transaction Tax

A **financial transaction tax** can take many forms. For example, it could be imposed on the value of financial instruments purchased (e.g., stocks and bonds). It could be restricted in some way (e.g., only applying to high-frequency trading). It could be imposed on the value of bank assets. Because the tax base is quite large, the tax rate would likely be low, perhaps even less than 1 percent. The primary concern with this type of tax is the possible adverse effects on financial markets.

Space Flight Excise Tax

With the growth of commercial space flight activity and Sir Richard Branson and Jeff Bezos riding on rockets their companies (Virgin Galactic and Blue Origin, respectively) recently launched into space, Congress is evaluating whether to assess specific taxes on these commercial ventures. Just as there is already an excise tax on airline tickets, many think the same should apply to tickets for space flights. In 2021, Congressman Blumenauer (D-OR) announced the Securing Protections Against Carbon Emissions (SPACE) Tax Act proposal. This tax is also intended to help address the externalities of the emissions resulting from rocket launches.

1-5 Tax Administration

LO.5

Explain the administration of the tax law, including the audit process utilized by the IRS.

1-5a Internal Revenue Service

The responsibility for administering the Federal tax laws rests with the Treasury Department. The IRS is part of the Department of the Treasury and is responsible for enforcing the tax laws. The Commissioner of Internal Revenue is appointed by the President with the advice and consent of the Senate. The Commissioner is responsible for establishing policy and supervising the activities of the IRS. Here is the mission statement of the IRS:

> *Provide America's taxpayers top quality service by helping them understand and meet their tax responsibilities and enforce the law with integrity and fairness to all.*

1-5b The Audit Process

Selection of Returns for Audit

Only a small number of tax returns are audited each year. The overall audit rate for individuals is 0.2 percent. The audit rate for corporations is 0.3 percent. Keep in mind, however, that the probability for audit increases for higher-income taxpayers.[38] Additional funding provided to the IRS by the Inflation Reduction Act of 2022 is expected to enable the IRS to increase overall audit rates to at least 1 percent of taxpayers. The additional resources will also allow the IRS to investigate higher income taxpayers (who employ sophisticated tax strategies).

Tax returns are selected for audit in different ways. A common technique for individuals is called information matching. For example, the IRS compares information returns it receives (e.g., a Form 1099 interest income statement from a bank related to an individual) to an individual's tax return. If the information is not reported correctly, the IRS sends a notice to the taxpayer indicating the problem and the additional tax owed. Another approach is done through computer scoring. This approach uses mathematical formulas and statistical sampling techniques to select tax returns that are most likely to contain errors and to provide significant amounts of additional tax revenues when audited. The mathematical formula produces what is called a Discriminant Function (DIF) score. It is the DIF score given to a particular return that may lead to its selection for audit. Periodically, the IRS updates the DIF components by auditing a random cross section of returns to determine the most likely areas of taxpayer noncompliance.

Although the IRS does not openly disclose the details of all of its audit selection techniques, here are some general comments about audit selection:

- Certain groups of taxpayers are subject to audit much more frequently than others. These groups include individuals with large amounts of gross income, self-employed individuals with substantial deductions, and taxpayers with prior tax deficiencies. The same is true for businesses that receive a large proportion of their receipts in cash (e.g., cafés and small service businesses) and thus have a high potential for tax avoidance.

Jack owns and operates a liquor store on a cash-and-carry basis. Because all of Jack's sales are for cash, he might be a prime candidate for an audit by the IRS. Cash transactions are easier to conceal than those made on credit.

- If information returns (e.g., Form 1099 or Form W–2) are not in substantial agreement with reported income, an audit can be anticipated.
- If an individual's itemized deductions are in excess of averages established for various income levels, the probability of an audit is increased.
- Filing of a refund claim by the taxpayer may prompt an audit of the return.
- Information obtained from other sources (e.g., informants and news items) may lead to an audit.

The IRS pays rewards to persons who provide information leading to the discovery and punishment of those who violate the tax laws. The rewards may not exceed 30 percent of the taxes, fines, and penalties recovered.

Information Leading to an IRS Audit

After 15 years of service, Rita is discharged by her employer, Dr. Benjamin Smith. Shortly thereafter, the IRS receives an anonymous letter stating that Dr. Smith keeps two separate sets of books and that the one used for tax reporting substantially understates his cash receipts.

[38] Internal Revenue Service, *Data Book 2021*, Table 17. Examination Coverage and Recommended Additional Tax After Examination, by Type and Size of Return, Tax Year 2019.

Information Leading to an IRS Audit

Example 17

During a divorce proceeding, it is revealed that Leo, a public official, kept large amounts of cash in a shoe box at home. This information is widely disseminated by the news media and comes to the attention of the IRS. Needless to say, the IRS is interested in knowing whether these funds originated from a taxable source and, if so, whether they were reported on Leo's income tax returns.

Types of Audits

Once a return is selected for audit, the taxpayer is notified by mail. If the issue involved is minor, the matter often can be resolved simply by correspondence (a **correspondence audit**) between the IRS and the taxpayer. For fiscal year 2021, approximately 78 percent of audits were handled via correspondence.[39]

Other examinations are generally classified as either office audits or field audits. An **office audit** usually is restricted in scope and is conducted in IRS offices. In contrast, a **field audit** involves an examination of numerous items reported on the return and is conducted at the taxpayer's location (or that of the taxpayer's representative).

The Big Picture

Example 18

Return to the facts of *The Big Picture* on p. 1-1. The audit of the Walkers by the IRS obviously was a correspondence type. The reason for the audit was probably triggered by a minor oversight by the Walkers, such as the omission of some interest or dividend income. The audit of the Carters, however, was more serious—probably a field or office type. Because the Federal audit followed a state audit that was productive (i.e., led to the assessment of a deficiency), there may have been an exchange of information between the two taxing authorities—see p. 1-16 in this chapter.

At the end of an audit, the examining agent issues a Revenue Agent's Report (RAR) that summarizes the findings. The RAR will result in a refund (the tax was overpaid), a deficiency (the tax was underpaid), or a no change (the tax was correct) finding. If, during the course of an audit, a special agent accompanies (or takes over from) the regular auditor, the IRS suspects fraud. In this case, the taxpayer should retain competent legal counsel.

Settlement Procedures

If an audit results in an assessment of additional tax and no settlement is reached with the IRS agent, the taxpayer may request an appeal within the IRS. The Independent Office of Appeals of the IRS is authorized to settle all disputes based on the *hazards of litigation* (the probability of favorable resolution of the disputed issue or issues, if litigated). In some cases, a taxpayer may be able to obtain an overall reduction of the assessment or a favorable settlement of one or more disputed issues.

If a satisfactory settlement is not reached within the IRS, the taxpayer can litigate the case in the Tax Court, a Federal District Court, or the Court of Federal Claims. However, litigation is normally discouraged because of the legal costs involved and the uncertainty of the final outcome. Tax litigation considerations are discussed more fully in Chapter 2.

1-5c **Statute of Limitations**

A **statute of limitations** is a provision that requires any lawsuit to be brought within a reasonable period of time. Found at the state and Federal levels, such statutes cover a multitude of suits, both civil and criminal.

For the Federal income tax, two categories are involved, which cover time limits on the assessment of additional tax deficiencies by the IRS and time limits related to refund claims by taxpayers.

[39]Internal Revenue Service, *Data Book, 2021*, p. 34.

Assessment by the IRS

In general, the IRS may assess an additional tax liability against a taxpayer within *three years* of the filing of the income tax return. If the return is filed early, the three-year period begins to run from the due date of the return (usually April 15 for a calendar year individual taxpayer). If the taxpayer files the return late (i.e., beyond the due date), the three-year period begins to run on the date filed.

If a taxpayer omits an amount of gross income in excess of 25 percent of the gross income reported on the return, the statute of limitations is increased to six years.

For 2023, Amin, a calendar year taxpayer, reported gross income of $400,000 on a timely filed income tax return. If Amin omitted more than $100,000 (25% × $400,000), the six-year statute of limitations would apply to the 2023 tax year.

The six-year provision on assessments by the IRS applies only to the omission of income; it does not cover other factors that might lead to an understatement of tax liability, such as overstatement of deductions and credits.

There is *no* statute of limitations on assessments of tax if *no return* is filed or if a *fraudulent* return is filed.

Limitations on Refunds

If a taxpayer believes that an overpayment of Federal income tax was made, a claim for refund should be filed with the IRS. A *claim for refund* is a request to the IRS that it return a tax overpayment to the taxpayer.[40]

A claim for refund generally must be filed within *three years* from the date the return was filed *or* within *two years* from the date the tax was paid, whichever is later. Income tax returns that are filed early are deemed to have been filed on the date the return was due.

1-5d Interest and Penalties

Interest rates are determined quarterly by the IRS based on the existing Federal short-term rate. Currently, the rates for tax refunds (overpayments) for individual taxpayers are the same as those applicable to assessments (underpayments). For the first quarter (January 1–March 31) of 2023, the rates were 7 percent for refunds and assessments.[41]

For assessments of additional taxes, the interest begins running on the unextended due date of the return. With refunds, however, no interest is allowed if the overpayment is refunded to the taxpayer within 45 days of the date the return is filed. For this purpose, returns filed early are deemed to have been filed on the due date.

In addition to interest, the tax law provides various penalties for lack of compliance by taxpayers. Some of these penalties are summarized as follows:

- For *failure to file* a tax return by the due date (including extension—see Chapter 3), a penalty of 5 percent per month up to a maximum of 25 percent is imposed on the amount of tax shown as due on the return. Any fraction of a month counts as a full month.
- A penalty for *failure to pay* the tax due as shown on the return is imposed in the amount of 0.5 percent per month up to a maximum of 25 percent. Again, any fraction of a month counts as a full month. During any month in which both the failure to file penalty and the failure to pay penalty apply, the failure to file penalty is reduced by the amount of the failure to pay penalty.

---

[40] Generally, an individual filing a claim for refund should use Form 1040X (Amended U.S. Individual Income Tax Return).

[41] Rev.Rul. 2022–23; the rates for the remainder of 2023 were not available when the text went to press.

Global Tax Issues — Outsourcing of Tax Return Preparation

The use of foreign nationals to carry out certain job assignments for U.S. businesses is an increasingly popular practice. Outsourcing activities such as telemarketing to India, for example, can produce the same satisfactory result as having the work done in the United States but at a lower cost.

Outsourcing is also being applied to the preparation of tax returns. This practice not only can be expected to continue but also is likely to increase in volume. Outsourcing tax return preparation does not violate Federal law and is compatible with accounting ethical guidelines as long as three safeguards are followed: First, the practitioner must make sure client confidentiality is maintained. Second, the practitioner must verify the accuracy of the work that has been outsourced. Third, the practitioner must inform clients, preferably in writing, when any third-party contractor is used to provide professional services.

Practitioners justify outsourcing as a means of conserving time and effort that can be applied toward more meaningful tax planning on behalf of their clients.

Example 20

Adam files his tax return 18 days after the due date of the return. Along with the return, he remits a check for $1,000, which is the balance of the tax he owed. Disregarding the interest element, Adam's total penalties are as follows:

Failure to pay penalty (0.5% × $1,000)		$ 5
Plus:		
Failure to file penalty (5% × $1,000)	$50	
Less failure to pay penalty for the same period	(5)	
Failure to file penalty		45
Total penalties		$50

Note that the penalties for one full month are imposed even though Adam was delinquent by only 18 days. Unlike the method used to compute interest, any part of a month is treated as a whole month.

- A *negligence* penalty of 20 percent is imposed if any of the underpayment was for intentional disregard of rules and Regulations without intent to defraud. The penalty applies to just that portion attributable to the negligence.

Cindy underpaid her taxes in the amount of $20,000, of which $15,000 is attributable to negligence. Cindy's negligence penalty is $3,000 (20% × $15,000).

- Various penalties may be imposed in the case of *fraud*. Fraud involves specific intent on the part of the taxpayer to evade a tax. In the case of *civil* fraud, the penalty is 75 percent of the underpayment attributable to fraud. In the case of *criminal* fraud, the penalties can include large fines as well as prison sentences. The difference between civil and criminal fraud is one of degree. Criminal fraud involves the presence of willfulness on the part of the taxpayer. Also, the burden of proof, which is on the IRS in both situations, is more stringent for criminal fraud than for civil fraud. The negligence penalty is not imposed when the fraud penalty applies. For possible fraud situations, refer to Examples 16 and 17.

1-5e **Tax Practice**

A practitioner who is a member of a profession (e.g., public accounting or law) must abide by certain ethical standards. Furthermore, the Internal Revenue Code imposes penalties on Federal tax return preparers who violate identified acts and procedures.

LO.6

Evaluate some of the ethical guidelines involved in tax practice.

Ethical Guidelines

Circular 230 Generally, CPAs, attorneys, and **Enrolled Agents (EAs)**[42] are subject to additional rules of conduct to be allowed to practice before the IRS. **Circular 230** ("Regulations Governing Practice before the Internal Revenue Service") issued by the Treasury Department contains rules governing practitioner competence, due diligence in tax work, making clients aware of errors on their returns, prohibiting use of contingent fees with limited exceptions, restricting against representing clients who have a conflict of interest between them, and more.

Circular 230 is administered by the IRS Office of Professional Responsibility (OPR). Among other duties, the OPR carries out disciplinary hearings and issues penalties, such as fines and licensing restrictions and retractions, relative to tax preparers. Information about Circular 230 violations is published in the weekly Internal Revenue Bulletin. A Circular 230 violation could lead to the loss or suspension of a CPA's license at the state level as well.

Statements on Standards for Tax Services (STSS) The American Institute of CPAs has issued its **Statements on Standards for Tax Services (SSTS)**, dealing with CPAs engaged in tax practice. These pronouncements are *enforceable* as part of its Code of Professional Conduct. They include the following summarized provisions:

- Do not take questionable positions on a client's tax return in the hope the return will not be selected for audit by the IRS. Any positions taken should be supported by a good-faith belief that they have a realistic possibility of being sustained if challenged. The client should be fully advised of the risks involved and of the penalties that will result if the position taken is not successful.
- A practitioner can use a client's estimates if they are reasonable under the circumstances. If the tax law requires receipts or other verification, the client should be so advised. In no event should an estimate be given the appearance of greater accuracy than is the case. For example, an estimate of $1,000 should not be deducted on a return as $999.
- Every effort should be made to answer questions appearing on tax returns. A question need not be answered if the information requested is not readily available, the answer is voluminous, or the question's meaning is uncertain. The failure to answer a question on a return cannot be justified on the grounds that the answer could prove disadvantageous to the taxpayer.
- Upon learning of an error on a past tax return, advise the client to correct it. Do not, however, inform the IRS of the error. If the error is material and the client refuses to correct it, consider withdrawing from the engagement. This will be necessary if the error has a carryover effect and prevents the current year's tax liability from being determined correctly.

Statutory Penalties Imposed on Tax Return Preparers

In addition to ethical constraints, a tax return preparer may be subject to specific penalties, including the following:

- Penalty for understatement of a tax liability based on a position that lacks substantial authority. If the position has a reasonable basis, the penalty can be avoided by disclosing it on the return.
- Penalty for any willful attempt to understate taxes. This usually results when a preparer disregards or makes no effort to obtain pertinent information from a client.
- Penalty for failure to exercise due diligence in determining eligibility for, or the amount of, an earned income tax credit, the child tax credit, or the American opportunity tax credit.

[42] An Enrolled Agent has passed an IRS-administered exam and agrees to be subject to the rules of Circular 230 (described above).

- Various penalties involving procedural matters. Examples include failing to furnish the taxpayer with a copy of the return, endorsing a taxpayer's refund check, failing to sign the return as a preparer, failing to furnish one's identification number, and failing to keep copies of returns or maintain a client list. The identification number required of preparers of most Federal tax returns is the **Preparer Tax Identification Number (PTIN)**. A PTIN is required by all persons who are paid for preparing or assisting in preparing all or substantially all of a Federal tax return.[43]

In a few months, Jaden, an accounting major at State University, will start an internship at Nguyen & Associates, CPAs. He will assist other employees by organizing and analyzing client data for completeness, entering client information into the tax preparation software program used by the firm, and comparing results to the prior year's return. Jaden will not sign any tax returns.

Jaden will need to obtain a PTIN from the IRS because he is assisting in the preparation of the returns. If, instead, Jaden were only entering data provided by his colleagues and making copies and not exercising any discretion or independent judgment regarding client tax information, he would not need a PTIN.[44]

1-6 Understanding the Federal Tax Law

LO.7

Classify tax rules based on their possible economic, social, equity, and political reasons for inclusion in a particular tax system.

The Federal tax law reflects the three branches of our Federal government. It is a mixture of laws passed by Congress, explanations provided by the Treasury Department and the Internal Revenue Service (IRS), and interpretation of the law by the courts. Anyone who has attempted to work with this vast amount of information is familiar with its complexity. For the person who has to sift through this information to find the solution to a tax problem, it is good to know that there are reasons behind the law. Knowing these reasons is the first step toward understanding the Federal tax law.

The *primary objective* of any tax system is to raise the revenue needed to fund government operations. Although the fiscal needs of the government are important, other considerations (economic, social, equity, and political factors) also play a significant role. The Treasury Department, the IRS, and the courts also have significant impacts on the evolution of Federal tax law. The remainder of the chapter focuses on these topics. While the discussion focuses on the Federal tax system, it also applies to any level of government that imposes taxes.

1-6a Revenue Needs

Raising revenues to fund the cost of government operations is the key factor in structuring a tax system. In a perfect world, taxes raised by the government would equal the expenses incurred by government operations. However, this goal is rarely achieved by the U.S. government but is typically achieved by state and local governments that may face restrictions on borrowing.

When enacting tax legislation, a deficit-conscious Congress often has been guided by the concept of **revenue neutrality** so that changes neither increase nor decrease the net revenues received by the government. With revenue-neutral legislation, there are likely to be both "winners" (taxpayers who see a reduction in taxes paid) and "losers" (taxpayers who see an increase in taxes paid).

[43] § 6109(a)(4). Also see IRS website on PTINs that includes an online tool to obtain or annually renew a PTIN (**rpr.irs.gov/ptin**).

[44] § 6109(a)(4) and Reg. §§ 1.6109–2(d) and (g).

In addition to making revenue-neutral changes in the tax law, several other procedures can be taken to mitigate any revenue loss. When tax reductions are involved, the full impact of the legislation can be phased in over a period of years. Or, as an alternative, the tax reduction can be limited to a period of years. When the period expires, the prior law is reinstated through a **sunset provision**. For example, at times, Congress has allowed more rapid depreciation treatment for a specified number of years. These sunset (or temporary) provisions move legislation toward revenue neutrality (even though it is not fully achieved).

1-6b Economic Considerations

Sometimes tax legislation is designed to help control the economy or encourage certain activities and businesses.

Control of the Economy

Congress has used the tax depreciation rules as a means of controlling the economy. Theoretically, shorter asset lives and accelerated methods should encourage additional investment in depreciable property acquired for business use. On the other hand, longer asset lives and use of straight-line depreciation should discourage capital outlays. Congress also uses incentives such as bonus depreciation to stimulate the economy when needed.

A change in tax rates has a more immediate impact on the economy. With lower tax rates, taxpayers retain money that can be used for other purposes (e.g., purchases or savings). If, however, Congress is using the concept of revenue neutrality, these rate reductions may be offset by a reduction or elimination of deductions or credits. As a result, lower tax rates do not always mean lower taxes.

Encouragement of Certain Activities

Congress uses the tax law to encourage certain types of economic activity or segments of the economy. For example, certain research and development expenditures may generate a tax credit that reduces the taxpayer's tax liability. Inventions are also encouraged by tax law. Under certain conditions, the sale of a patent results in long-term capital gain treatment.

Part of the tax law addresses the nation's energy policy—in terms of both our reliance on carbon-based fuels and the need to ease the problem of climate change. For example, tax credits are available for installation of solar and small wind energy equipment, as well as for the purchase of clean energy vehicles. Residential energy credits are available for home improvements that conserve energy or make its use more efficient (e.g., solar water heaters). Ecological considerations explain why pollution control facilities can be amortized over 60 months (rather than over the 39-year period for most buildings).

Is saving desirable for the economy? Saving can lead to capital formation, making funds available to finance home construction and industrial expansion. The tax law encourages saving by giving private retirement plans preferential treatment. Besides contributions to certain Individual Retirement Accounts (IRAs) and Keogh (H.R. 10) plans being deductible, income from the contributions accumulates tax-free until it is withdrawn.

Encouragement of Certain Industries

Historically, agricultural activities have been favored under Federal tax law. Among the benefits are the election to expense rather than capitalize certain soil and water conservation expenditures and fertilizers and the election to defer the recognition of gain on the receipt of crop insurance proceeds.

The tax law favors the development of natural resources by permitting the use of percentage depletion and a write-off (rather than a capitalization) of certain exploration costs. The railroad and banking industries also receive special tax treatment under Federal tax law. To encourage the manufacture of semiconductors in the United States, the Advanced Manufacturing Investment Credit provides a credit equal to 25 percent of the basis of qualified property used for this purpose.[45]

Encouragement of Small Business

Small business development is also encouraged under the tax law. For example, the shareholders of a small business corporation can make an election that allows the profits (or losses) of the corporation to flow through to its shareholders, avoiding the corporate income tax.[46] Another provision allows non-corporate shareholders of certain small corporations to exclude from income their gain from the sale of the stock if held over five years.

1-6c **Social Considerations**

Some provisions of the Federal tax law, particularly those dealing with individuals, can be explained by social considerations. Here are some notable examples:

- Certain benefits provided to employees through accident and health plans financed by employers are nontaxable to employees. It is socially desirable to encourage these plans because they provide medical benefits in the event of an employee's illness or injury. In addition, insurance companies are paying for these benefits (rather than the government).
- Most premiums paid by an employer for group term insurance covering the life of the employee are nontaxable to the employee. Life insurance proceeds (which are also nontaxable) provide funds to help the family unit adjust to the loss of wages caused by the employee's death.
- A contribution made by an employer to a qualified pension or profit sharing plan for an employee may receive special treatment. The contribution and any income it generates are not taxed to the employee until the funds are distributed. This arrangement also benefits the employer by allowing a tax deduction for the contribution to the qualified plan. Private retirement plans are encouraged to supplement any Social Security payments.[47]
- A deduction is allowed for contributions to qualified charities. The deduction shifts some of the financial and administrative burden of socially desirable programs from the public (the government) to the private sector.
- A tax credit is allowed for amounts spent to furnish care for dependents to enable the taxpayer to work. A credit for employers who incur certain child care expenses assists employees indirectly.
- To encourage taxpayers to join the workforce even though their wages may be low, an earned income tax credit can be claimed. The credit varies depending on the number of qualifying children and the level of wages earned.
- Certain credits are made available to individuals aged 65 and older and those with disabilities. Credits also are allowed to businesses that incur expenditures to make their facilities more accessible to the disabled.

[45]§ 48D, added by the Creating Helpful Incentives to Produce Semiconductors (CHIPS) Act (P.L. 117–167, August 9, 2022).

[46]Known as the S election, it is discussed in Chapter 23.

[47]The same rationale explains the availability of similar arrangements for self-employed persons (e.g., the H.R. 10, or Keogh, plan).

- Various tax credits, deductions, and exclusions are designed to encourage taxpayers to obtain additional education.[48]
- A tax deduction is not allowed for certain expenses deemed to be contrary to public policy. Expenses not allowed include fines, penalties, illegal kickbacks, bribes to government officials, and gambling losses in excess of gains. In addition, any business expense (including attorney fees) related to sexual harassment or abuse is not deductible if the settlement or payment is subject to a nondisclosure agreement.

1-6d Equity Considerations

The concept of equity (or fairness) is relative. One measure of equity is whether a tax is *regressive* or *progressive*. The determination is made by calculating the percentage of a taxpayer's income that is used to pay a tax. As noted earlier, the Federal income tax is progressive. In contrast, the gasoline excise tax is regressive.

Hanna and Lori are single taxpayers living in the same state. Hanna has income of $100,000, and Lori has income of $10,000. Assume that Hanna pays $5,000 in state income taxes while Lori pays only $100. The state income tax represents 5% of Hanna's income but only 1% of Lori's income. Because the higher-income taxpayer (Hanna) devotes a larger percentage of her income to pay the tax relative to a lower-income taxpayer (Lori), this state income tax is *progressive* in its effect on taxpayers.

Alternatively, assume that Hanna and Lori each purchase the same quantity of gasoline during the year and each pays a gasoline excise tax of $200. This tax represents less than 0.1% of Hanna's income but 2% of Lori's income. Because the lower-income taxpayer (Lori) devotes a larger percentage of her income to pay the tax relative to a higher-income taxpayer (Hanna), the gasoline excise tax is *regressive* in its effect on taxpayers.

Lawmakers and others often consider whether a tax change is progressive or regressive to understand its impact on taxpayers and whether the change should be made. If a tax represents the same percentage of the income of all taxpayers, it is a *proportional* tax.

Eduardo and Sanjay are single taxpayers living in the same state. Eduardo has income of $50,000 and pays $1,500 in state taxes. Sanjay has income of $20,000 and pays $600 in state taxes. In this case, Eduardo and Sanjay are devoting the same percentage of their income to the state tax (3%), making the tax *proportional* in terms of the effect it has on taxpayers.

The concept of equity also appears in tax provisions that alleviate the effect of multiple taxation and postpone the recognition of gain when the taxpayer lacks the ability or wherewithal to pay the tax. Provisions that mitigate the effect of the application of the annual accounting period concept and help taxpayers cope with the eroding results of inflation also reflect equity considerations.

Alleviating the Effect of Multiple Taxation

Equity considerations can explain the Federal tax treatment of certain income from foreign sources. Because double taxation results when the same income is subject to both foreign and U.S. income taxes, the tax law permits the taxpayer to choose between a credit and a deduction for the foreign taxes paid.

[48]These provisions can also be justified under the category of economic considerations because a better-educated workforce carries a positive economic impact.

The Wherewithal to Pay Concept

The **wherewithal to pay** concept recognizes the inequity of taxing a transaction when the taxpayer lacks the means (i.e., funds) to pay the tax. This concept is typically applied to transactions where the taxpayer's economic position has not changed significantly.

An illustration of the wherewithal to pay concept is the tax treatment of an involuntary conversion. An involuntary conversion occurs when property is destroyed by a casualty (e.g., a fire or hurricane) or taken by a public authority through condemnation (e.g., taking land to build a new road). If gain results from the conversion, it is deferred if the taxpayer replaces the property within a specified period of time.

Some of the pasture land belonging to Ron, a rancher, is condemned by the state for use as a game preserve. The condemned pasture land cost Ron $120,000, but the state pays him $150,000 (its fair market value). Shortly thereafter, Ron buys more pasture land for $150,000.

In Example 25, Ron has a realized gain of $30,000 [$150,000 (condemnation award) − $120,000 (cost of land)]. It would be inequitable to force Ron to pay a tax on this gain for two reasons. First, without selling the property acquired (the new land), Ron does not have the funds to pay the tax. Second, his economic position has not changed (i.e., he still owns pasture land worth $150,000). If, however, the taxpayer's economic position changes in any way, tax consequences may result.

Assume the same facts as in Example 25, except that Ron reinvests only $140,000 of the award in new pasture land. Now Ron has a taxable gain of $10,000. Instead of ending up with only replacement property, Ron has $10,000 in cash.

Mitigating the Effect of the Annual Accounting Period Concept

All taxpayers must report their taxable income to the Federal government at regular intervals. The accounting period used to report taxable income (and settle any tax liability) is one year. Referred to as the annual accounting period concept, its effect is to divide each taxpayer's life, for tax purposes, into equal annual intervals.

The annual accounting period concept can lead to different tax treatment for taxpayers who are in the same economic position. Consider the following example.

José and Alicia, both sole proprietors, showed the following results during the past three years:

	Profit (or Loss)	
Year	**José**	**Alicia**
2021	$50,000	$150,000
2022	60,000	60,000
2023	60,000	(40,000)

Although José and Alicia have the same total profit of $170,000 over the three-year period, the annual accounting period concept places Alicia at a definite disadvantage for tax purposes. The net operating loss (NOL) deduction offers Alicia some relief by allowing her to carry forward (but not back) some or all of her 2023 loss to future years. With a net operating loss carryforward, Alicia may apply her 2023 loss to future years' profits (with certain limitations; see Chapter 7).

The reasoning used to support the net operating loss deduction can also explain the special treatment the tax law accords to excess capital losses and excess charitable contributions.[49] Carryback and carryover procedures help mitigate the effect of limiting a loss or a deduction to the accounting period in which it was realized. Using these procedures, a taxpayer can salvage a loss or a deduction that might otherwise be lost.

The installment method of recognizing gain on the sale of property allows a taxpayer to spread tax consequences over the payout period.[50] The installment method is supported by the wherewithal to pay concept; recognition of gain corresponds to the collection of the cash received from the sale of the property. The tax consequences match the seller's ability to pay the tax.

Coping with Inflation

Because of the progressive nature of the income tax, a wage adjustment to compensate for inflation could place the employee in a higher income tax bracket. Known as *bracket creep*, its overall impact is an erosion of purchasing power. Congress recognizes this problem and adjusts various income tax components, such as tax brackets, standard deduction amounts, and a wide variety of other items, through an indexation procedure. **Indexation** is based on the change in the chained consumer price index over the prior year.

1-6e Political Considerations

A large segment of the Federal tax law is made up of statutory provisions. Because these statutes are enacted by Congress, political considerations often influence tax law. The effect of political considerations on the tax law includes special interest legislation, political expediency situations, and state and local government influences.

Special Interest Legislation

There is no doubt that certain provisions of the tax law can largely be explained by the political influence some groups have had on Congress. For example, prepaid subscription and dues income is not taxed until earned, whereas prepaid rents are taxed to the landlord in the year received. This exception was created because certain organizations (e.g., the American Automobile Association) convinced Congress that special tax treatment was needed for multi-year dues and subscriptions.

Another provision, sponsored by a senator from Georgia, suspended the import duties on ceiling fans. The nation's largest seller of ceiling fans is Atlanta-based Home Depot.

Although some special interest legislation can be justified on economic or social grounds, in most cases it cannot. It is, however, an inevitable product of our political system.

Political Expediency Situations

Various tax changes can be tied to the shifting moods of the American public. That Congress is sensitive to popular feelings is an accepted fact. As a result, certain provisions of the tax law can be explained by the political climate at the time they were enacted.

Measures that deter more affluent taxpayers from obtaining so-called preferential tax treatment have always had popular appeal and, consequently, the support of Congress. Tax provisions like the imputed interest rules and the limitations on the deductibility of interest on investment indebtedness affect affluent taxpayers directly. More subtle are

---

[49] The tax treatment of these items is discussed in Chapters 7, 10, and 14.

[50] Under the installment method, each payment received by the seller represents both a recovery of capital (the nontaxable portion) and profit from the sale (the taxable portion). The tax rules governing the installment method are discussed in Chapter 16.

provisions that phase out tax breaks as income rises. These phaseouts are often called *stealth taxes* because the effects are *indirect* (and the taxpayer might not be aware of them). The tax law contains several of these phaseout rules. Examples include the phaseout of the child tax credit and education tax credits.

State and Local Government Influences

Political considerations played a major role in the nontaxability of interest received on state and local obligations. Somewhat less apparent has been the influence state law has had in shaping our present Federal tax law. Such was the case with community property systems. The nine states with community property systems are Arizona, California, Idaho, Louisiana, Nevada, New Mexico, Texas, Washington, and Wisconsin. The rest of the states are common law jurisdictions.[51] The difference between common law and community property systems centers around the property rights possessed by married persons. In a common law system, each spouse owns whatever each earns. Under a community property system, one-half of the earnings of each spouse is considered owned by the other spouse.

Adam and Fran are married, and their only income is the $80,000 annual salary Adam receives. If they live in New Jersey (a common law state), the $80,000 salary belongs to Adam. If, however, they live in Arizona (a community property state), the $80,000 is divided equally, in terms of ownership, between Adam and Fran.

At one time, the tax position of the residents of community property states was so advantageous that many common law states adopted community property systems. Needless to say, the political pressure placed on Congress to correct the disparity in tax treatment was considerable. To a large extent, this was accomplished in the Revenue Act of 1948, which extended many of the community property tax advantages to residents of common law jurisdictions.

Congress accomplished this by allowing married taxpayers to file joint returns and compute their tax liability as if one-half of the income had been earned by each spouse. This result is automatic in a community property state because half of the income earned by one spouse belongs to the other spouse. The income-splitting benefits of a joint return are now incorporated as part of the tax rates applicable to married taxpayers. See Chapter 3.

1-6f Influence of the Internal Revenue Service

LO.8

Explain the role played by the IRS and the courts in the evolution of the Federal tax system.

The IRS has exerted its influence in many areas of the tax law. As the protector of the national revenue, the IRS has been instrumental in securing the passage of legislation designed to curtail aggressive tax avoidance practices (i.e., closing *tax loopholes*). In addition, the IRS has sought and obtained law changes to make its job easier (to attain administrative feasibility).

The IRS as Protector of the Revenue

Many provisions in the tax law resulted from the direct efforts of the IRS to prevent taxpayers from exploiting a tax loophole. Working within the letter of existing laws, ingenious taxpayers and their advisers devise techniques that accomplish indirectly what cannot be accomplished directly. As a result, Congress passes laws to close the loopholes that taxpayers have located and exploited.

In addition, Congress has passed laws that enable the IRS to make adjustments based on the substance of a transaction (rather than the form chosen by the taxpayer). For example, the IRS can make adjustments to a taxpayer's method of accounting when the method used by the taxpayer does not *clearly reflect income*.[52]

[51] In Alaska, spouses can choose to have the community property rules apply. Otherwise, property rights are determined under common law rules.

[52] See Chapter 16.

Tran owns and operates a clothing distribution business with over $29,000,000 of annual gross receipts. The merchandise acquired is charged to the purchases account and written off (expensed) for tax purposes in the year of acquisition. Since this procedure does not clearly reflect income, it would be appropriate for the IRS to require that Tran establish and maintain an ending inventory account.

Administrative Feasibility

Some tax laws are created to simplify the task of the IRS in collecting the revenue and administering the law. As to collecting revenue, the IRS long ago realized the importance of placing taxpayers on a pay-as-you-go basis. Withholding procedures apply to wages, but the tax on other types of income may have to be paid via quarterly estimated payments. The IRS has been instrumental in convincing the courts that accrual basis taxpayers should, in most cases, pay taxes on prepaid income in the year received and not when earned. The approach may be contrary to generally accepted accounting principles, but prepayment is consistent with the wherewithal to pay concept.

To help the IRS collect revenues when due, Congress has passed many provisions that impose interest and penalties on taxpayers if they don't comply with the tax law. Provisions such as the penalties for failure to pay a tax or to file a return that is due, the negligence penalty for intentional disregard of rules and Regulations, and various penalties for civil and criminal fraud are intended to encourage taxpayers to comply with the tax law.

The audit process conducted by the IRS is key to an effective administration of our tax system. To carry out this function, the IRS is aided by provisions that reduce the chance of taxpayer error or manipulation, thus simplifying the audit effort. For example, by increasing the standard deduction amount, the audit function is simplified because fewer returns with itemized deductions need to be checked.[53]

1-6g Influence of the Courts

In addition to interpreting statutory provisions and the administrative pronouncements issued by the Treasury Department and the IRS, the Federal courts have influenced tax law in two other ways.[54] First, the courts have developed a number of judicial concepts and doctrines that help guide how tax provisions are applied. Second, certain key decisions have led to changes in the Internal Revenue Code.

Judicial Concepts and Doctrines Relating to Tax

A leading tax concept developed by the courts deals with the interpretation of statutory tax provisions that operate to benefit taxpayers. The courts have decided that these relief provisions are exceptions to general tax rules so they should be applied narrowly. If a taxpayer wants a relief provision to apply, the taxpayer has the responsibility to meet the provision's requirements (i.e., no exceptions).

The *arm's length* concept is applied in dealings between related parties. Transactions may be tested by asking this question: Would unrelated parties have handled the transaction in the same way?

Matt, the sole shareholder of Silver Corporation, leases property to the corporation for a yearly rent of $60,000. To test whether the corporation should be allowed a rent deduction for this amount, the IRS and the courts will apply the arm's length concept. Would Silver Corporation have paid $60,000 a year in rent if it had leased the same property from an unrelated party (rather than from Matt)?

continued

[53]For a discussion of the standard deduction, see Chapter 3. The same justification was given by the IRS when it proposed to Congress the $100 limitation on personal casualty and theft losses. Imposition of the limitation eliminated many casualty and theft loss deductions and, as a consequence, saved the IRS considerable audit time. Later legislation, in addition to retaining the $100 feature, generally limits deductible losses to those in Federally declared disaster areas. In addition, only losses in excess of 10% of a taxpayer's adjusted gross income are allowed. See Chapter 7.

[54]A great deal of case law is devoted to ascertaining congressional intent. The courts, in effect, ask: What did Congress have in mind when it enacted a particular tax provision?

Suppose it is determined that an unrelated third party would have charged an annual rent for the property of only $50,000. Under these circumstances, Silver Corporation will be allowed a deduction of only $50,000. The other $10,000 it paid for the use of the property represents a nondeductible dividend. Accordingly, Matt will be treated as having received rent income of $50,000 and dividend income of $10,000.

A judicial doctrine that must be considered in some transactions is the *substance over form* doctrine. Here, no matter how a transaction is structured, the actual substance of how the transaction is carried out controls.

Gold Corporation hired Adam to work as its bookkeeper for six months while the regular bookkeeper is on sick leave. This is a full-time position, and Adam reports to Gold's CFO who directs his assignments. Gold gave Adam a contract that states he is not an employee of Gold but is instead an independent contractor. Despite the form saying Adam is not an employee, the substance of what he does and the relationship between Gold and Adam will control Adam's employment designation for tax purposes.

Judicial Influence on Statutory Provisions

Some court decisions have been so important that Congress incorporated them into the Internal Revenue Code. For example, many years ago the courts found that stock dividends distributed to the shareholders of a corporation were not taxable as income. This result was largely accepted by Congress, and the Code was modified to reflect the court's position.

On occasion, however, Congress reacts negatively to judicial interpretations of the tax law.

Example 32

Nora leases unimproved real estate to Wade for 20 years. At a cost of $400,000, Wade erects a building on the land. The building is worth $150,000 when the lease terminates and Nora takes possession of the property.

Does Nora have any income either when the improvements are made or when the lease terminates? In a landmark decision, a court held that Nora must recognize income of $150,000 upon the termination of the lease.

Congress believed that the result reached in Example 32 was not consistent with the wherewithal to pay concept. As a result, the tax law was changed to provide that a landlord does not recognize any income either when the improvements are made (unless made in lieu of rent) or when the lease terminates.[55]

1-6h **Summary**

In addition to raising revenues, other factors have influenced the development of Federal tax law:

- *Economic considerations*: Congress uses the tax law to help regulate the economy and encourage certain activities and types of businesses.
- *Social considerations*: The tax law has been used to encourage (or discourage) certain socially desirable (or undesirable) practices.
- *Equity considerations*: The tax law can be designed to alleviate the effect of multiple taxation, recognize the wherewithal to pay concept, mitigate the effect of the annual accounting period concept, and recognize the eroding effect of inflation.
- *Political considerations*: Some tax law represents special interest legislation, reflects political expediency, or illustrates the effect of state and local law.
- *Influence of the IRS*: Laws are enacted to aid the IRS in the collection of revenue and the administration of the tax law.
- *Influence of the courts*: Court decisions have established a body of judicial concepts relating to tax law and have, on occasion, led Congress to enact laws to either clarify or negate their effect.

These factors help us understand how tax law develops (and why some provisions exist). We also must learn to work with the tax law, which is the subject of Chapter 2.

[55] *M.E. Blatt Co. v. U.S.*, 305 U.S. 267 (1938) and § 109.

Refocus on The Big Picture

Family and Taxes—A Typical Year

CORBIS/SUPERSTOCK

The explanation given for the difference in the ad valorem property taxes—the Carters' increase and the Walkers' decrease—seems reasonable (see Example 4). It is not likely that the Carters' increase was solely due to a *general* upward assessment in valuation because the Walkers' taxes on their residence (located nearby) dropped. More business use of the Carters' residence (presuming that Travis conducts his consulting practice from his home) might be responsible for the increase, but capital improvements appear to be a more likely cause.

The imposition of the use tax when Travis registered the new automobile illustrates one of the means by which a state can preclude the avoidance of its sales tax (see Example 5).

When gifts between family members are material in amount (e.g., an RV) and exceed the annual exclusion, a gift tax return needs to be filed (see Example 11). Even though no gift tax may be due because of the availability of the unified transfer tax credit, the filing of a return starts the running of the statute of limitations.

The Carters must recognize that some of their income is subject to income taxes in more than one state and take advantage of whatever relief is available to mitigate the result of double taxation (see Example 12).

Employment within and by the family group (e.g., children, other relatives, and domestics) has become a priority item in the enforcement of Social Security tax and income tax withholdings. Thus, the Carters must be aware of the need to cover their son, Martin (see Example 13).

Because of the double audit (i.e., both state and Federal) and the deficiency assessed, the Carters need to make sure that future returns do not contain similar errors (see Example 18). As the text suggests, taxpayers with prior deficiencies are among those whose returns may be selected for audit.

Key Terms

Ad valorem taxes, 1-11
Carbon tax, 1-23
Circular 230, 1-28
Correspondence audit, 1-25
Employment taxes, 1-19
Enrolled Agents (EAs), 1-28
Estate tax, 1-14
Excise taxes, 1-12
FICA tax, 1-19
Field audit, 1-25
Financial transaction tax, 1-23
Flat tax, 1-22
Franchise tax, 1-21
FUTA tax, 1-20
Gift tax, 1-15
Indexation, 1-34
Inheritance tax, 1-14
National sales tax, 1-22
Occupational fees, 1-21
Office audit, 1-25
Personalty, 1-12
Preparer tax identification number (PTIN), 1-29
Realty, 1-11
Revenue neutrality, 1-29
Sales tax, 1-13
Severance taxes, 1-14
Statements on Standards for Tax Services (SSTS), 1-28
Statute of limitations, 1-25
Sunset provision, 1-30
Use tax, 1-13
Value added tax (VAT), 1-22
Wherewithal to pay, 1-33

Discussion Questions

1. **LO.1** This textbook includes many features beyond the text materials in each chapter. For example, a glossary is included in the appendices and the end of each chapter contains a list of key terms. Skim through the chapters, appendices, and any other supplemental materials required for your course, and identify two special features. For each, explain what it is and how it can help you understand taxation in this tax course.

2. **LO.1, 4** In the following independent situations, is the tax position of the taxpayer likely to change? Explain why or why not.
   a. John started renting out a spare room in his home.
   b. Theresa quit her job as a staff accountant and established her own practice as a CPA.
   c. Paul's employer transferred him from its California office to an office in Florida.

3. **LO.1, 4** Marvin is the executor and sole heir of his aunt's estate. The estate includes her furnished home, which Marvin is considering converting to rental property to generate additional cash flow. What are some of the tax considerations Marvin may confront? Critical Thinking

4. **LO.2** World War II converted the Federal income tax into a *mass tax*. Explain.

5. **LO.2** How does the pay-as-you-go procedure apply to wage earners? To persons who have income from sources other than wages?

6. **LO.3** Jane, a tax practitioner, has reviewed the law on how a certain state's income tax applies to a client's web-based consulting business but is unable to reach a conclusion for which she has a high level of confidence. Assuming that Jane is a knowledgeable and experienced tax professional, which *Guiding Principles of Good Tax Policy* might not be followed by this state?

7. **LO.3** Distinguish between taxes that are *regressive* and those that are *progressive*.

8. **LO.4** Several years ago Ethan purchased the former parsonage of St. James Church to use as a personal residence. To date, Ethan has not received any ad valorem property tax bills from either the city or the county tax authorities. Critical Thinking
   a. What is a reasonable explanation for this oversight?
   b. What should Ethan do?

9. **LO.4** The Adams Independent School District wants to sell a parcel of unimproved land that it does not need. Its three best offers are as follows: from the state's Department of Public Safety (DPS), $2,300,000; from the Second Baptist Church, $2,200,000; and from Baker Motors, $2,100,000. DPS would use the property for a new state highway patrol barracks, Second Baptist would start a church school, and Baker would open a car dealership. If you are the financial adviser for the school district, which offer would you prefer? Why? Critical Thinking

10. **LO.4** The commissioners for Walker County are actively negotiating with Falcon Industries regarding the location of a new manufacturing plant in the area. Since Falcon is considering several other sites, a "generous tax holiday" may be needed to influence the final choice. The local school district is opposed to any "generous tax holiday."
    a. What would probably be involved in a generous tax holiday?
    b. Why would the school district be opposed?

11. **LO.4** Sophia lives several blocks from her parents in the same residential subdivision. Sophia is surprised to learn that her ad valorem property taxes for the year were raised but those of her parents were lowered. What is a possible explanation for the difference?

12. **LO.4** The Agarwal family lives in Massachusetts. They moor their sailboat in Rhode Island. What might be a plausible reason for this?

13. **LO.4** Is the breadth and number of Federal excise taxes increasing or decreasing? Explain.

14. **LO.4** After her first business trip to a major city, Jayla is alarmed when she reviews her credit card receipts. Both the hotel bill and the car rental charge are in

excess of the price she was quoted. Was Jayla overcharged, or is there an explanation for the excess amounts?

15. **LO.4** The types of taxes described in text Section 1-4 can also be categorized as (1) income taxes, (2) consumption taxes, or (3) wealth (or valuation) taxes. Categorize the taxes described in text Section 1-4 into these three categories and briefly explain your rationale for the placement of each tax.

16. **LO.4** The Garcías live in Clay County, which is adjacent to Jackson County. Although the retail stores in both counties are comparable, the Garcías usually drive a few extra miles to shop in Jackson County. As to why the Garcías might do this, consider the following:
    a. Clay County is in a different state than Jackson County.
    b. Clay County and Jackson County are in the same state.

Critical Thinking

17. **LO.4** During a social event, Muriel and Caleb are discussing the home computer each recently purchased. Although the computers are identical makes and models, Muriel is surprised to learn that she paid a sales tax but Caleb did not. Comment as to why this could happen.

18. **LO.4** Distinguish between an estate tax and an inheritance tax.
    a. Do some states impose both? Neither?
    b. Which, if either, does the Federal government impose?

19. **LO.4** Jake (age 72) and Jessica (age 28) were recently married. To avoid any transfer taxes, Jake has promised to leave Jessica all of his wealth when he dies. Is Jake under some misconception about the operation of the Federal gift and estate taxes? Explain.

20. **LO.4** Address the following issues:
    a. What is the purpose of the unified transfer tax credit?
    b. Is the same amount available for both the Federal gift tax and the estate tax? Explain.
    c. Does the use of the credit for a gift affect the amount of credit available for the estate tax? Explain.

21. **LO.4** Elijah and Anastasia are married and have five married children and nine minor grandchildren. For 2023, what is the maximum amount they can give to their family (including the sons- and daughters-in-law) without using any of their unified transfer tax credit?

22. **LO.4** What is the difference between the Federal income tax on individuals and that imposed on corporations?

23. **LO.4** As to those states that impose an income tax, comment on the following:
    a. "Piggyback" approach and possible "decoupling" from this approach.
    b. Use of IRS audit results as part of a state tax audit.
    c. Credit for taxes paid to other states.

24. **LO.4** In May 2023, Hernando, a resident of California, has his 2021 Federal income tax return audited by the IRS. An assessment of additional tax is made because he inadvertently omitted some rental income. In October 2023, California audits his state return for the same year. Explain the coincidence.

Critical Thinking

25. **LO.4** Mike was an outstanding football player in college and expects to be drafted by the NFL in the first few rounds. Mike has let it be known that he would prefer to sign with a club located in Florida, Texas, or Washington. Mike sees no reason why he should have to pay state income tax on his player's salary. Is Mike's rationale correct? Explain.

26. **LO.4, 5** A question on a state income tax return asks the taxpayer if any out-of-state internet or mail-order catalog purchases were made during the year. The question requires a yes or no answer, and if the taxpayer answers yes, the total dollar amount of these purchases is to be provided. Critical Thinking
    a. Does this inquiry have any relevance to the state income tax? If not, why is it being asked?
    b. Your client, Hannah, wants to leave the question unanswered. As the preparer of her return, how do you respond?

27. **LO.4** Many state income tax returns contain checkoff boxes that allow taxpayers to make donations to a multitude of local charitable causes. On what grounds has this procedure been criticized?

28. **LO.4** Many states have occasionally adopted amnesty programs that allow taxpayers to pay back taxes with reduced penalties.
    a. Besides the revenue generated, how are these programs advantageous?
    b. Could an amnesty program be used by a state that does not levy an income tax?
    c. Does the IRS utilize this approach?

29. **LO.4** Contrast FICA and FUTA as to the following:
    a. Purpose of the tax.
    b. Upon whom imposed.
    c. Governmental administration of the tax.
    d. Reduction of tax based on a merit rating system.

30. **LO.4** In connection with the Medicare component of FICA, comment on the following:
    a. Any dollar limitation imposed.
    b. The applicability of the 0.9% increase in the 1.45% regular tax rate.

31. **LO.4** One of the tax advantages of hiring family members to work in your business is that FICA taxes are avoided. Do you agree with this statement? Explain.

32. **LO.4** Describe the nature and purpose of the following taxes:
    a. Severance taxes.
    b. Franchise taxes.
    c. Occupational fees.
    d. Customs duties.
    e. Export duties.

33. **LO.4** Regarding the value added tax (VAT), comment on the following:
    a. Popularity of this type of tax.
    b. Nature of the tax.
    c. Effect on government spending.

34. **LO.4** Both a value added tax (VAT) and a national sales tax have been criticized as *regressive* in their effect.
    a. Explain.
    b. How could this shortcoming be remedied?

35. **LO.4, 5** Serena operates a gift shop. To reduce costs of credit card transactions, she offers customers a discount if they pay in cash. For the holiday rush, she hires some short-term workers but pays them cash and does not add them to the payroll.
    a. What are some of the tax problems Serena might have?
    b. Assess Serena's chances of audit by the IRS.

36. LO.5 With regard to the IRS audit process, comment on the following:
    a. The audit is resolved by mail.
    b. The audit is conducted at the office of the IRS.
    c. A "no change" RAR results.
    d. A special agent joins the audit team.

37. LO.5 Deven has just been audited by the IRS. He does not agree with the agent's findings but believes that he has only two choices: pay the proposed deficiency or resort to the courts. Do you agree with Deven's conclusion? Why or why not?

38. LO.5 What purpose is served by a statute of limitations? How is it relevant in the case of tax controversies?

39. LO.5 Regarding the statute of limitations on additional assessments of tax by the IRS, determine the applicable period in each of the following situations. Assume a calendar year individual with no fraud or substantial omission involved.
    a. The income tax return for 2022 was filed on February 19, 2023.
    b. The income tax return for 2022 was filed on June 25, 2023.
    c. The income tax return for 2022 was prepared on April 4, 2023, but was never filed. Through some misunderstanding between the preparer and the taxpayer, each expected the other to file the return.
    d. The income tax return for 2022 was never filed because the taxpayer thought no additional tax was due.

40. LO.5 Naya, a calendar year taxpayer, files her income tax return for 2022 on February 3, 2023. Although she makes repeated inquiries, she does not receive her refund from the IRS until May 28, 2023. Is Naya entitled to interest on the refund? Explain.

41. LO.5, 6 On a Federal income tax return filed five years ago, Andy inadvertently omitted a large amount of gross income.
    a. Andy seeks your advice as to whether the IRS is barred from assessing additional income tax in the event he is audited. What is your advice?
    b. Would your advice differ if you were the person who prepared the return in question? Explain.
    c. Suppose Andy asks you to prepare his current year's return. Would you do so? Explain.

42. LO.5 Rita files her income tax return 35 days after the due date of the return without obtaining an extension from the IRS. Along with the return, she remits a check for $40,000, which is the balance of the tax she owes. Disregarding the interest element, what are Rita's penalties for failure to file and for failure to pay?

43. LO.5 For tax year 2021, the IRS assesses a deficiency against David for $500,000. Disregarding the interest component, what is David's penalty if the deficiency is attributable to:
    a. Negligence?
    b. Fraud?

44. LO.5, 6 In March 2023, Kuni asks you to prepare his Federal income tax returns for tax years 2020, 2021, and 2022. In discussing this matter with him, you discover that he also has not filed for tax year 2019. When you mention this fact, Kuni tells you that the statute of limitations precludes the IRS from taking any action as to this year.

a. Is Kuni correct about the application of the statute of limitations? Why or why not?

b. If Kuni refuses to file for 2019, should you prepare returns for 2020 through 2022? Explain.

45. **LO.5, 6** The Benson CPA firm is considering utilizing an offshore service provider to prepare many of its tax returns. In this regard, what ethical considerations must be taken into account?

46. **LO.7** In terms of tax policy, what do the following mean?

a. Revenue neutrality.

b. Sunset provision.

c. Indexation.

47. **LO.7** Some tax rules can be justified on multiple grounds (e.g., economic and social). In this connection, comment on the possible justification for the rules governing the following, and also describe any reasons why these tax rules might not be justified:

a. Pension plans.

b. Education.

c. Home ownership.

48. **LO.7, 8** Discuss the probable justification for each of the following aspects of the tax law. Be sure to use concepts and terminology covered in this chapter. Critical Thinking

a. A tax credit is allowed for amounts spent to furnish care for minor children while the parent works.

b. Deductions for interest on home mortgage and property taxes on a personal residence.

c. The income-splitting benefits of filing a joint return.

d. Fines and penalties are not deductible.

e. Net operating losses of a current year can be carried forward to profitable years.

f. A taxpayer who sells property on an installment basis can recognize gain on the sale over the period the payments are received.

g. The exclusion from Federal tax of certain interest income from state and local bonds.

h. Prepaid income is taxed to the recipient in the year received and not in the year earned.

49. **LO.7** Mia owns a warehouse that has a cost basis to her of $80,000. The city condemns the warehouse to make room for a new fire station. It pays Mia $400,000 for the property, its agreed-to fair market value. Shortly after the condemnation, Mia purchases another warehouse as a replacement. What is her recognized gain if the new property cost:

a. $280,000?

b. $444,000?

c. $80,000?

d. What, if any, is the justification for deferring the recognition of gain on the involuntary conversion?

50. **LO.8** A mother sells a valuable collection of antiques to her son for $1,000. What judicial concept might the IRS invoke to question this transaction?

Research Problems

Use internet tax resources to address the following questions. Look for reliable websites and blogs of the IRS and other government agencies, media outlets, businesses, tax professionals, academics, think tanks, and political outlets.

Research Problem 1. Using information from this chapter as well as information from the tax agency in your state (likely called the Department of Revenue) and your local government, find all of the taxes to which a sole proprietor is subject. Create a table that lists all of these taxes, the rate(s), and the level(s) of government that imposes each tax.

Critical Thinking

Research Problem 2. Use **congress.gov** or another reliable website to find a proposal for a carbon tax or a financial transactions tax. Draft a summary of the tax, and analyze it against five of the AICPA's principles of good tax policy.

Critical Thinking

Research Problem 3. Find a Federal or state proposal for a soda tax or sweetened beverage tax. Provide the bill number and a brief explanation. Also apply the AICPA's principles of good tax policy to support your recommendation for or against the bill.

Communications
Data Analytics

Research Problem 4. Visit the websites of a few public accounting firms to learn how they are using data analytics and visualization in the tax function. In an e-mail to your instructor, explain what you found, provide the source(s) you used, and explain how you think the data analysis helps businesses engage in tax compliance and planning.

Communications

Research Problem 5. Use the IRS website to find Form W–12 (IRS Paid Preparer Tax Identification Number (PTIN) Application and Renewal) and its instructions. Review these documents and focus specifically on Question 11 (related to the data security responsibilities of the paid preparer). One purpose of this question is to remind preparers of their obligations to comply with the "Safeguards Rule" overseen by the Federal Trade Commission. Use IRS Publication 4557, *Safeguarding Taxpayer Data*, to find information on this rule. Also review the data security plan resources described by the IRS in IR–2022–147 (August 9, 2022); **irs.gov/newsroom/security-summit-releases-new-data-security-plan-to-help-tax-professionals-new-wisp-simplifies-complex-area**. Prepare an e-mail to your instructor that briefly describes this rule, and identifies three key items that should be in a data security plan.

Communications

Research Problem 6. Find Circular 230 posted on the IRS website (**irs.gov**). Skim Circular 230 to find § 10.35 on Competence and answer the following question: A new client has approached your CPA firm for compliance and planning assistance. In the past year, they engaged in over 2,500 trades involving virtual currency. Your firm has not had a client with more than 50 virtual currency transactions in a year. Based on the Competence rule in Circular 230, write a memo to your manager on whether your CPA firm can accept this client.

Becker CPA Review Questions

Becker

1. Treasury Department Circular 230 provides guidance for doing which of the following activities?
   a. Practicing before the IRS.
   b. Practicing before the U.S. Tax Court.
   c. Presenting before state boards of accountancy.
   d. Reporting income taxes in financial statements.
2. Which of the following is *not* required conduct for a preparer of an income tax return, under AICPA Tax Standards?
   a. Abide by the tax Code and legally minimize the taxpayer's tax liability.
   b. Verify that the information the client provides is correct.
   c. Notify the client if the preparer becomes aware of an error in a tax return.
   d. Inform the taxpayer about how to correct the situation of the taxpayer's failure to file an income tax return.

Chapter 2

Working with the Tax Law

Learning Objectives: *After completing Chapter 2, you should be able to:*

- **LO.1** Distinguish between the statutory, administrative, and judicial sources of the tax law and understand the purpose of each source.
- **LO.2** Locate and work with the appropriate tax law sources.
- **LO.3** Develop an awareness of tax research tools.
- **LO.4** Describe the tax research process.
- **LO.5** Communicate the results of the tax research process in a client letter and a tax file memorandum.
- **LO.6** Apply tax research techniques and planning procedures.
- **LO.7** Be aware of taxation on the CPA examination.

Chapter Outline

The Big Picture

Importance of Tax Research

Early in November 2023, Fred and Megan Martel scheduled a meeting with you to discuss a potential tax problem. Fred and Megan purchased a 40-acre parcel of property in 2018 for $195,000. On it, they built their "dream home" in 2019. In March 2023, while walking on a remote part of their property, they spotted something shiny on the ground. They started digging and eventually unearthed eight metal cans containing more than 1,400 rare gold coins in $5, $10, and $20 denominations dated from 1846 to 1895. The face value of the gold coins is about $28,000, and many of the coins are in mint condition. Their delay in coming to you for tax advice was due to a state law that required their discovery to be turned over to the state for disposition. The state, for a period of six months, was required to publicize the find and ask if anyone could prove ownership. When no one came forward, the coins were returned to the Martels in October 2023. Since they are now the rightful owners of the coins, they want to know the tax implications (if any) of their discovery.

Read the chapter and formulate your responses.

Federal tax law reflects the three branches of our Federal government. It is a mixture of laws passed by Congress, explanations provided by the Treasury Department and the Internal Revenue Service (IRS), and court decisions. Anyone who has attempted to work with this vast amount of information is familiar with its complexity. The tax research process allows us to understand, evaluate, and apply these sources of tax law to questions that are raised by taxpayers and tax practitioners.

In addition to being able to locate, interpret, and apply tax law, a tax professional also must understand the relative *weight of authority* that each source carries. The tax law is of little significance, however, until it is applied to a set of facts and circumstances. This chapter introduces the statutory, administrative, and judicial sources of tax law and explains how the law is applied to individual and business transactions. It also explains how to apply tax research techniques and use planning procedures effectively. A large part of tax research focuses on determining the intent of Congress.

Frequently, uncertainty in the tax law causes disputes between the Internal Revenue Service (IRS) and taxpayers. Due to these *gray areas* and the complexity of the tax law, a taxpayer may have more than one alternative for structuring a financial transaction. In structuring financial transactions and engaging in other tax planning activities, the tax adviser must be cognizant that the objective of tax planning is not necessarily to minimize the tax liability. Instead, a taxpayer's after-tax wealth should be maximized, which may include maximizing nontax as well as noneconomic benefits.

LO.1

Distinguish between the statutory, administrative, and judicial sources of the tax law and understand the purpose of each source.

2-1 Tax Law Sources

Understanding taxation requires a strong understanding of the sources of tax law. These sources include laws passed by Congress, which are contained in the Internal Revenue Code and congressional Committee Reports, Treasury Department Regulations, other Treasury Department and IRS pronouncements, and court decisions. As a result, the *primary sources* of tax law include information from all three branches of government: legislative (or statutory), executive, and judicial.[1]

2-1a Statutory Sources of the Tax Law

Statutory sources of law include the Constitution (Article I, Sections 7, 8, and 10), the Internal Revenue Code, and tax treaties (agreements between countries to mitigate the double taxation of taxpayers subject to the tax laws of those countries). The Constitution grants Congress the power to impose and collect taxes and authorizes the creation of treaties with other countries. The power of Congress to implement and collect taxes is reflected in the Internal Revenue Code, the official title of U.S. tax law, and the Code is the basis for arriving at solutions to all tax questions.

Origin of the Internal Revenue Code

Before 1939, the statutory provisions relating to Federal taxation were contained in the individual revenue acts enacted by Congress. Because dealing with many separate acts was inconvenient and confusing, Congress codified all of the Federal tax laws in 1939. Known as the Internal Revenue Code of 1939, the codification arranged all Federal tax provisions in a logical sequence and placed them in a separate part of the Federal statutes. A further rearrangement took place in 1954 and resulted in the Internal Revenue Code of 1954, which continued in effect until 1986 when it was replaced by the Internal Revenue Code of 1986. Although Congress did not recodify the law in the Tax Reform Act (TRA) of 1986, the magnitude of the changes made by TRA of 1986 did provide some rationale for renaming the Federal tax law the Internal Revenue Code of 1986.[2]

[1] *Secondary sources* also are used by tax practitioners to help understand the tax law and find primary sources. Secondary sources include items like tax articles from professional tax journals, newsletters, and textbooks. Commentary contained in various tax research services (such as Thomson Reuters *Checkpoint*) also are secondary sources.

[2] This point is important in assessing judicial decisions interpreting provisions of the Internal Revenue Code of 1939 and the Internal Revenue Code of 1954. If a provision from the 1939 or 1954 Code was included in the Internal Revenue Code of 1986 and has not been subsequently amended, the provision and the related judicial decisions have continuing validity.

The Legislative Process

Exhibit 2.1 illustrates the legislative process for enacting changes to the Internal Revenue Code of 1986. Federal tax legislation generally originates in the House of Representatives, where it is first considered by the House Ways and Means Committee.[3] Once approved by the House Ways and Means Committee, the proposed bill is referred to the entire House of Representatives for approval or disapproval. Approved bills are sent to the Senate, where they are considered by the Senate Finance Committee.[4]

After approval by the Senate Finance Committee, the bill is sent to the entire Senate. Assuming no disagreement between the House and Senate, passage by the Senate results in referral to the President for approval or veto. If the bill is approved or if the President's veto is overridden, the bill becomes law and part of the Internal Revenue Code of 1986.

Exhibit 2.1 Legislative Process for Tax Bills

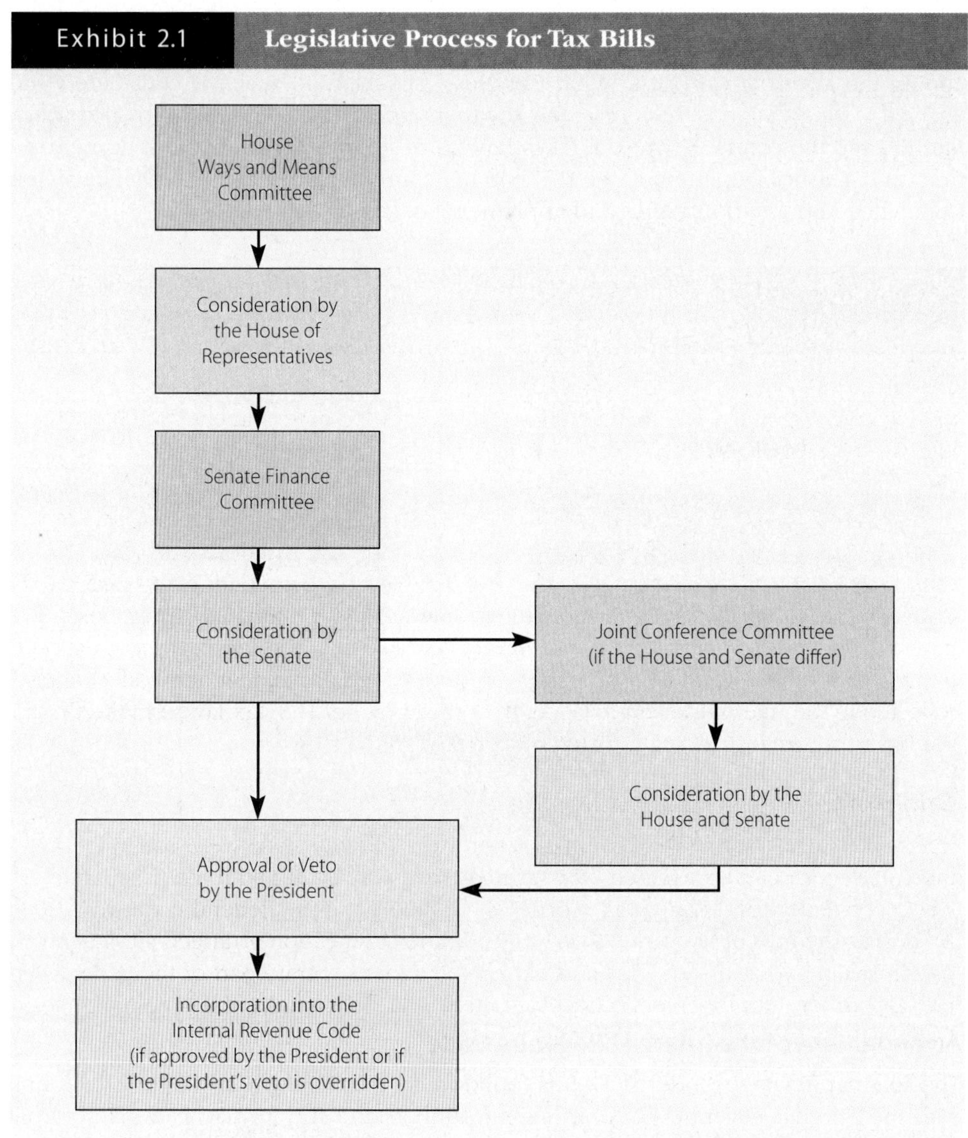

[3]Congress enacts tax legislation virtually every year, and each piece of legislation contains changes to the Internal Revenue Code of 1986.

[4]Although rare, a tax bill can originate in the Senate when it is attached as a rider to a different legislative proposal. The Tax Equity and Fiscal Responsibility Act of 1982 originated in the Senate, and its constitutionality was upheld by the courts.

House and Senate versions of major tax bills frequently differ. One reason bills are often changed in the Senate is that each senator has considerable latitude to make amendments when the Senate as a whole is voting on a bill referred to it by the Senate Finance Committee.[5] In contrast, the entire House of Representatives either accepts or rejects what is proposed by the House Ways and Means Committee, and changes from the floor are rare. When the Senate version of the bill differs from that passed by the House, the Joint Conference Committee, which includes members of both the House Ways and Means Committee and the Senate Finance Committee, resolves the differences. The deliberations of the Joint Conference Committee usually produce a compromise between the two versions, which is then voted on by both the House and the Senate. If both bodies accept the bill, it is referred to the President for approval or veto.

The role of the Joint Conference Committee indicates the importance of compromise in the legislative process. Exhibit 2.2 illustrates what happened with amendments to the child tax credit in the Tax Cuts and Jobs Act (TCJA) of 2017.

The House Ways and Means Committee, the Senate Finance Committee, and the Joint Conference Committee each produce a Committee Report. These Committee Reports explain the provisions of the proposed legislation and are a valuable source for ascertaining the *intent of Congress*. What Congress had in mind when it considered and enacted tax legislation is, of course, the key to interpreting the legislation by taxpayers, the IRS, and the courts. Because it takes time to develop other primary authority (e.g., from the Treasury Department, the IRS, and the courts), tax researchers rely heavily on Committee Reports to interpret and apply new tax laws.

Exhibit 2.2 **Example of Compromise in the Joint Conference Committee**

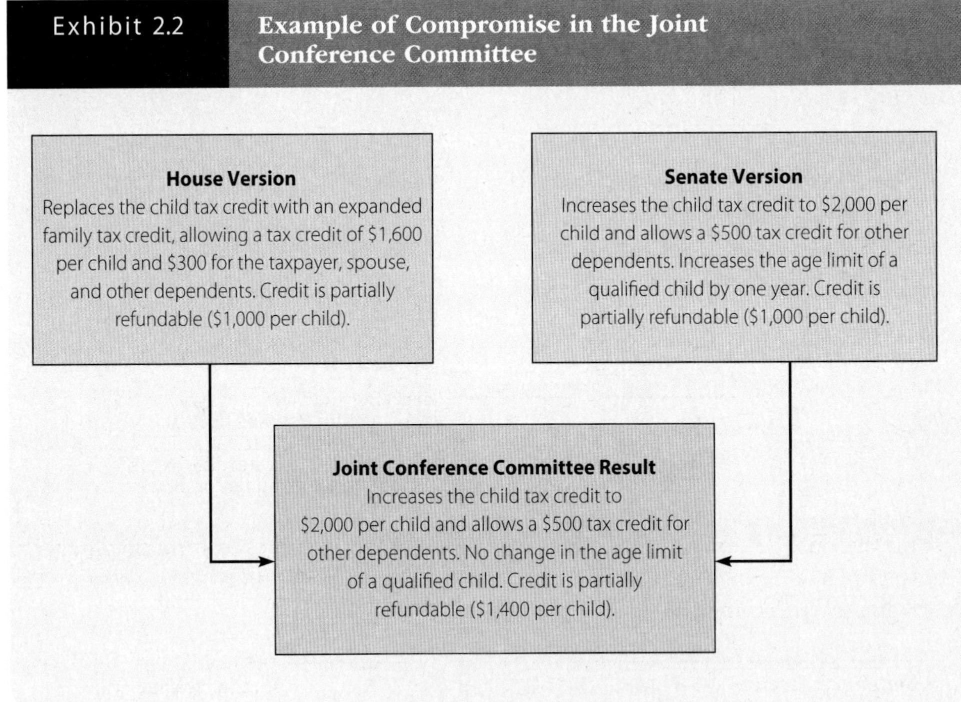

Arrangement of the Internal Revenue Code

The Internal Revenue Code of 1986 is found in Title 26 of the U.S. Code. In working with the Internal Revenue Code, it helps to understand the format. Here is a partial table of contents:

Subtitle A. Income Taxes
  Chapter 11. Normal Taxes and Surtaxes

[5]During the passage of the Tax Reform Act of 1986, Senate leaders tried to make the bill *amendment proof* to avoid the normal amendment process.

Subchapter A. Determination of Tax Liability
Part I. Tax on Individuals
Sections 1–5
Part II. Tax on Corporations
Sections 11–12

In referring to a provision of the Code, the *key* is usually the Section number. In citing a Section number, identifying the related Subtitle, Chapter, Subchapter, and Part is not necessary. Merely mentioning the Section is sufficient because the Section numbers run consecutively and do not begin again with each new Subtitle, Chapter, Subchapter, or Part.[6]

Tax researchers often refer to specific areas of income tax law by their Subchapters. Some of the more common Subchapter designations include Subchapter C ("Corporate Distributions and Adjustments"), Subchapter K ("Partners and Partnerships"), and Subchapter S ("Tax Treatment of S Corporations and Their Shareholders").

Citing the Code

Code Sections often are broken down into subparts.[7] Code § 2(a)(1)(A) serves as an example.

Broken down by content, § 2(a)(1)(A) becomes:

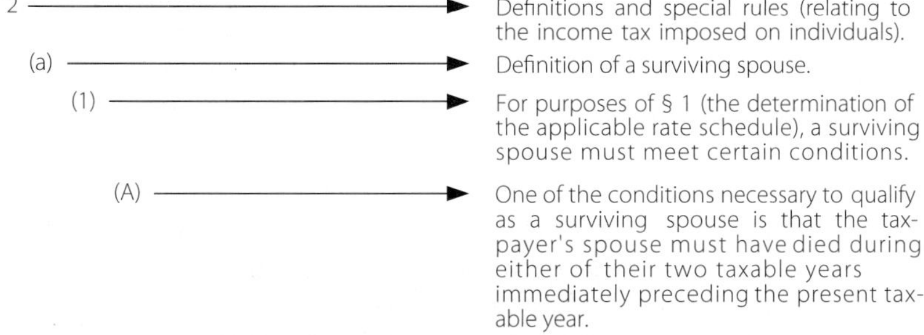

Throughout the text, references to the Code Sections are in the form given above. The symbols "§" and "§§" are used in place of "Section" and "Sections," respectively. The following table summarizes the format that we use:

Complete Reference	Text Reference
Section 2(a)(1)(A) of the Internal Revenue Code of 1986	§ 2(a)(1)(A)
Sections 1 and 2 of the Internal Revenue Code of 1986	§§ 1 and 2
Section 2 of the Internal Revenue Code of 1954	§ 2 of the Internal Revenue Code of 1954
Section 12(d) of the Internal Revenue Code of 1939[9]	§ 12(d) of the Internal Revenue Code of 1939

[6]When the 1954 Code was drafted, some Section numbers were intentionally omitted so that later changes could be incorporated into the Code without disrupting its organization. When Congress does not leave enough space, subsequent Code Sections are given A, B, C, etc., designations. A good example is the treatment of §§ 280A through 280H.

[7]Some Code Sections do not require subparts. See, for example, §§ 211 and 241.

[8]Some Code Sections omit the subsection designation and use the paragraph designation as the first subpart. See, for example, §§ 212(1) and 1222(1).

[9]Code § 12(d) of the Internal Revenue Code of 1939 is the predecessor to § 2 of the Internal Revenue Code of 1954 and the Internal Revenue Code of 1986. Keep in mind that the 1954 Code superseded the 1939 Code and the 1986 Code superseded the 1954 Code. Footnote 2 explains why references to the 1939 or 1954 Code are included.

2-1b Administrative Sources of the Tax Law

The administrative sources of the Federal tax law include Treasury Department Regulations, Revenue Rulings and Revenue Procedures, and various other administrative pronouncements (see Exhibit 2.3). All are issued by either the U.S. Treasury Department or the IRS.

Treasury Department Regulations

Regulations are issued by the U.S. Treasury Department under authority granted by Congress.[10] Interpretive by nature, they provide taxpayers with considerable guidance on the meaning and application of the Code. Regulations, which carry considerable authority as the official interpretation of tax law, may be issued in *proposed*, *temporary*, or *final* form.

Because Regulations interpret the Code, they are arranged in the same sequence as the Code. A number is added at the beginning, however, to indicate the type of tax or administrative, procedural, or definitional matter to which they relate.[11] For example, the prefix 1 designates the Regulations under the income tax law. As a result, the Regulations under Code § 2 are cited as Reg. § 1.2, with subparts added for further identification. The numbering patterns of these subparts often have no correlation with the Code subsections.

Exhibit 2.3 Administrative Sources

Source	Location	Authority
Regulations	*Federal Register*	Force and effect of law.
Temporary Regulations	*Federal Register* *Internal Revenue Bulletin (IRB)* *Cumulative Bulletin**	May be cited as a precedent.
Proposed Regulations	*Federal Register* *Internal Revenue Bulletin* *Cumulative Bulletin**	Preview of Final Regulations. Not yet a precedent.
Revenue Rulings	*Internal Revenue Bulletin* *Cumulative Bulletin**	IRS interpretation only. Items published in the IRB are binding on the IRS. Taxpayers can rely on these items.** Weak precedent.
Revenue Procedures Notices	*Internal Revenue Bulletin* *Cumulative Bulletin**	
Chief Counsel Advice Technical Advice Memoranda Actions on Decisions	Tax Analysts' *Tax Notes;* Thomson Reuters *Checkpoint****; CCH *IntelliConnect;* IRS website	May not be cited as a precedent.
Letter Rulings	Tax services from Thomson Reuters, CCH Wolters Kluwer, and Bloomberg Law; IRS website	Applicable only to taxpayer addressed. May not be cited as precedent by others but can be used as authority to avoid certain tax penalties on audit.
Frequently Asked Questions (FAQs)	IRS website****	FAQs have no precedential value. However, if relied upon in good faith, a taxpayer will have a "reasonable cause" defense against any negligence penalty or accuracy-related penalty.

Note: All Administrative Sources can be accessed electronically through Thomson Reuters *Checkpoint* (and other commercial tax services).

*Through 2008, the contents of Internal Revenue Bulletins were consolidated semiannually into a Cumulative Bulletin. The IRS no longer produces a Cumulative Bulletin because Internal Revenue Bulletins from mid-2003 are available electronically on the IRS website (**irs.gov/irb**).

**Internal Revenue Manual (IRM) 4.10.7.2.4 (01-10-2018).

***Thomson Reuters *Checkpoint* includes a wide variety of tax resources. The most significant are materials produced by the Research Institute of America (RIA), including the *Federal Tax Coordinator 2d.*

****Starting after October 15, 2021, FAQs on newly enacted tax legislation are announced in a news release and posted on the IRS website as a Fact Sheet. FAQs on other topics are posted on the website and not announced in a news release (IR-2021-202).

[10] § 7805.

[11] The prefix 20 designates estate tax Regulations, 25 covers gift tax Regulations, 31 relates to employment taxes, and 301 refers to procedure and administration.

Ethics & Equity **Reporting Tax Fraud**

Maybe someone in your extended family is driving a luxury car and comments that only fools pay all of their taxes. Or maybe a contractor demands payment in cash. Or perhaps someone at work is not reporting all of their income. If cheating on taxes bothers you, the IRS wants to hear from you (and may make it worthwhile). The IRS has two whistleblower programs. The small-awards program is for situations involving less than $2 million of tax, and the award can be as high as 15% of collections, although it often is less. The large-awards program covers situations involving $2 million or more of tax. Here the reward can go as high as 30%. The IRS no longer takes tax law violations over the phone, but the appropriate form to report tax fraud is Form 3949–A (Information Referral). Form 211, Application for Award for Original Information, is required to claim an award. Would you turn in someone?

New Regulations and changes to existing Regulations are usually issued in proposed form before they are finalized. The interval between the proposal of a Regulation and its finalization permits taxpayers and other interested parties to comment on the propriety of the proposal. **Proposed Regulations** under Code § 2, for example, are cited as Prop.Reg. § 1.2. The Tax Court indicates that Proposed Regulations carry little weight in the litigation process.[12] **Final Regulations** have the force and effect of law.

Sometimes the Treasury Department issues **Temporary Regulations** where immediate guidance is important. These Regulations are issued without the comment period required for Proposed Regulations. Temporary Regulations, cited as Temp.Reg. §, have the same authoritative value as Final Regulations and may be cited as precedents. However, Temporary Regulations also must be issued as Proposed Regulations and automatically expire within three years after the date of issuance.[13]

Proposed, Temporary, and Final Regulations are published in the *Federal Register*, in the *Internal Revenue Bulletin* (I.R.B.), and by major tax services. Final Regulations are issued as Treasury Decisions (TDs).

Regulations also may be classified as *legislative, interpretive*, or *procedural*. These classifications are discussed in text Section 2-3d (Assessing the Validity of Tax Law Sources) later in the chapter.

Revenue Rulings, Revenue Procedures, and Notices

Revenue Rulings are official pronouncements of the National Office of the IRS.[14] They typically provide one or more examples of how the IRS would apply a law to *specific fact situations*. Like Regulations, Revenue Rulings are designed to provide interpretation of the tax law. Although they do not carry the same legal force and effect as Regulations because they are focused on a specific fact pattern, they provide a more detailed analysis of the law.

Although letter rulings (discussed below) are not the same as Revenue Rulings, a Revenue Ruling often results from a specific taxpayer's request for a letter ruling. If the IRS believes that a letter ruling request has widespread impact, the letter ruling will be converted into a Revenue Ruling and issued. Revenue Rulings also can be issued in response to technical advice to District Offices of the IRS, court decisions, and suggestions from tax practitioner groups.

Revenue Procedures deal with the internal management practices and procedures of the IRS. For example, Rev.Proc. 2023–1 provides general instructions for taxpayers requesting letter rulings or determination letters from the IRS. A taxpayer's failure to follow a Revenue Procedure can result in unnecessary delay or, in a discretionary situation, can cause the IRS to decline to act.

Notices are issued when immediate guidance is needed by taxpayers and tax practitioners. Typically, this guidance is transitional while the IRS works on permanent

---

[12] *F. W. Woolworth Co.*, 54 T.C. 1233 (1970); *Harris M. Miller*, 70 T.C. 448 (1978); and *James O. Tomerlin Trust*, 87 T.C. 876 (1986).

[13] § 7805(e).

[14] § 7805(a).

guidance on the particular topic. For example, Notice 2022–6 sets a floor interest rate of 5 percent for calculating tax-deferred retirement account payments.

Revenue Rulings, Revenue Procedures, and Notices serve an important function by providing *guidance* to IRS personnel and taxpayers in handling routine tax matters. Revenue Rulings and Revenue Procedures generally apply retroactively and are binding on the IRS until revoked or modified by subsequent rulings or procedures, Regulations, legislation, or court decisions.

Revenue Rulings, Revenue Procedures, and Notices are published weekly by the U.S. Government in the *Internal Revenue Bulletin* (I.R.B.).

The proper form for citing Revenue Rulings is shown below. Revenue Procedures and Notices are cited in the same manner, except that "Rev.Proc." or "Notice" is substituted for "Rev.Rul."

Rev.Rul. 2022–10, 2022–23 I.R.B. 1157.

Explanation: Revenue Ruling Number 10, appearing on page 1157 of the 23rd weekly issue of the *Internal Revenue Bulletin* for 2022.

Internal Revenue Bulletins can be found at the IRS website: **irs.gov/irb**.[15]

Letter Rulings

Letter rulings are issued for a fee upon a taxpayer's request and describe how the IRS will treat a *proposed* transaction for tax purposes. Issued by the National Office of the IRS, they apply only to the taxpayer who asks for and obtains the ruling.[16] Letter rulings can be useful to taxpayers who want to be certain of how a transaction will be taxed before proceeding with it. Letter rulings also allow taxpayers to avoid unexpected tax costs and may be the most effective way to carry out tax planning. However, the IRS limits the issuance of individual rulings to restricted, preannounced areas of taxation.[17] The IRS issues more than 2,500 letter rulings each year.

The IRS must make individual rulings available for public inspection after identifying details are deleted.[18] Published digests of private letter rulings can be found in a variety of sources, including *IRS Letter Rulings Reports* (published by CCH), Bloomberg BNA's *Daily Tax Reports*, Tax Analysts' *Tax Notes*, and electronic (online) tax research services (such as Thomson Reuters *Checkpoint*).

Letter rulings are issued multi-digit file numbers that indicate the year and week of issuance as well as the number of the ruling during that week. For example, Ltr.Rul. 202228002 granted a taxpayer an extension of time to make an election to deduct additional first-year depreciation.

2022	28	002
Year 2022	28th week of 2022	2nd ruling issued during the 28th week

Other Administrative Pronouncements

Treasury Decisions (TDs) are issued by the Treasury Department to announce new Regulations, amend or change existing Regulations, or announce the position of the

[15]Commercial sources for Revenue Rulings and Revenue Procedures are available, usually requiring a subscription fee. Older Revenue Rulings and Revenue Procedures are often cited as being published in the *Cumulative Bulletin* (C.B.) rather than in the *Internal Revenue Bulletin* (I.R.B.).

[16]Letter rulings differ from Revenue Rulings, which are applicable to *all* taxpayers. A letter ruling may later lead to the issuance of a Revenue Ruling if the holding affects many taxpayers. In its Internal Revenue Manual, the IRS indicates that letter rulings may be used as a guide with other research materials in formulating a District Office position on an issue. The IRS is required to charge a taxpayer a fee for letter rulings, determination letters, etc.

[17]Rev.Proc. 2023–3 contains a list of areas in which the IRS will not issue advance rulings. According to the IRS, the main reason it will not rule in certain areas is that specific fact-oriented situations are involved. As a result, a ruling may not be obtained on many of the problems that are particularly troublesome for taxpayers.

[18]§ 6110.

Government on selected court decisions. Like Revenue Rulings and Revenue Procedures, TDs are published in the *Internal Revenue Bulletin*.

The IRS also publishes other administrative communications on its website, including Announcements, IRs (News Releases), Internal Legal Memoranda (ILMs), Chief Counsel Advice (CCA), Chief Counsel Notices (CCN), and Frequently Asked Questions (FAQs).

Like letter rulings, **determination letters** are issued at the request of taxpayers and provide guidance on the application of the tax law. They differ from letter rulings in that the issuing source is an IRS Area Director (rather than the National Office of the IRS). Also, determination letters usually involve *completed* (as opposed to proposed) transactions. Determination letters are not published and are made known only to the party making the request.

The following examples illustrate the distinction between letter rulings and determination letters.

Difference between Letter Rulings and Determination Letters

The shareholders of Red Corporation and Green Corporation want assurance that the consolidation of the corporations into Blue Corporation will be a nontaxable reorganization. The proper approach is to request that the National Office of the IRS issue a letter ruling concerning the income tax effect of the proposed transaction.

Chris operates a barbershop in which he employs eight barbers. To comply with the rules governing income tax and payroll tax withholdings, Chris wants to know whether the barbers working for him are employees or independent contractors. The proper procedure is to request a determination letter on their status from the IRS.

A variety of internal memoranda that constitute the working law of the IRS also are released. These Chief Counsel Advice (CCAs), Technical Advice Memoranda (TAMs), and Internal Legal Memoranda (ILMs) are not officially published, and the IRS indicates that they may not be cited as precedents by taxpayers.[19] However, these working documents do explain the IRS's position on various issues. In addition, the "Law" section of these documents refers to primary authority (e.g., the Code, Regulations, and court cases) that is being relied on in developing the conclusion(s).

The National Office of the IRS releases **Technical Advice Memoranda (TAMs)** weekly. TAMs resemble letter rulings in that they give the IRS's determination of an issue. However, they differ in several respects. Letter rulings deal with proposed transactions and are issued to taxpayers at their request. In contrast, TAMs deal with completed (rather than proposed) transactions. TAMs are issued by the National Office of the IRS in response to questions raised by taxpayers or IRS field personnel during audits. TAMs are not officially published and may not be cited or used as precedent.[20] They are assigned file numbers according to the same procedure used for letter rulings. For example, TAM 202229036 refers to the 36th TAM issued during the 29th week of 2022.

The Office of Chief Counsel prepares Chief Counsel Advice (CCAs) and Chief Counsel Notices (CCNs) to help IRS employees. These are issued in response to requests for advice, guidance, and analysis on difficult or significant tax issues and are not binding on either the taxpayer to whom they pertain or the IRS. Another form of field guidance are Technical Expedited Advice Memoranda (TEAMs). The purpose of TEAMs is to expedite legal guidance to field agents as disputes are developing.[21]

---

[19] These are made available by the publishers listed in Exhibit 2.3.

[20] § 6110(k)(3). PLRs and TAMs may be authority for purposes of avoiding the accuracy-related penalty. Reg. § 1.6662–4(d)(3).

[21] A TEAM guidance differs from a TAM in several ways, including a mandatory presubmission conference involving the taxpayer. In the event of a tentatively adverse conclusion for the taxpayer or the field agent, a conference of right is offered to the taxpayer and to the field agent; once the conference of right is held, no further conferences are offered.

2-1c **Judicial Sources of the Tax Law**

Five Federal courts have jurisdiction over tax disputes between the IRS and taxpayers: the U.S. Tax Court, the U.S. District Court, the U.S. Court of Federal Claims, the U.S. Court of Appeals, and the U.S. Supreme Court.

The Judicial Process in General

Once a taxpayer has exhausted the remedies available within the IRS (i.e., no satisfactory settlement has been reached at the agent or at the Independent Office of Appeals level), the dispute can be taken to the Federal courts. The trial and appellate court system for Federal tax litigation is illustrated in Exhibit 2.4.

A trial court, also known as a **court of original jurisdiction**, initially hears the case. Appeals (either by the taxpayer or the IRS) are heard by the appropriate appellate court. A taxpayer has a choice of *three trial courts:* a **U.S. District Court**, the **U.S. Court of Federal Claims**, or the **U.S. Tax Court**.

The U.S. Tax Court contains a **Small Cases Division** that only hears cases involving amounts of $50,000 or less. The ruling of the judge is final (no appeal is available), and these rulings are not precedent for any other cases (i.e., they are not primary authority and are not citable as substantial authority). Proceedings of the Small Cases Division are informal, and, because there is no requirement that a taxpayer be represented by an attorney, they can be less costly for a taxpayer (the filing fee is only $60). The typical small case lasts one to two hours, and the taxpayer only needs to tell the judge their story and present any supporting evidence. Special trial judges, rather than Tax Court judges, often preside over these hearings. Some of these cases can be found on the U.S. Tax Court website.

American law, following English law, is frequently *created* by judicial decisions. Under the doctrine of *stare decisis* ("let the decision stand"), each case has precedential value for future cases with the same set of facts. Judges are not required to follow judicial precedent beyond their own jurisdiction. For example, the decisions of an appellate court are binding only on the trial courts within its jurisdiction and not on other trial courts. Different appellate courts may reach different opinions about the same issue. Further, the doctrine of *precedential authority* requires a court to follow prior cases only when the issues and material facts of the current case are essentially the same as those involved in the prior decisions.

Exhibit 2.4 **Federal Judicial System**

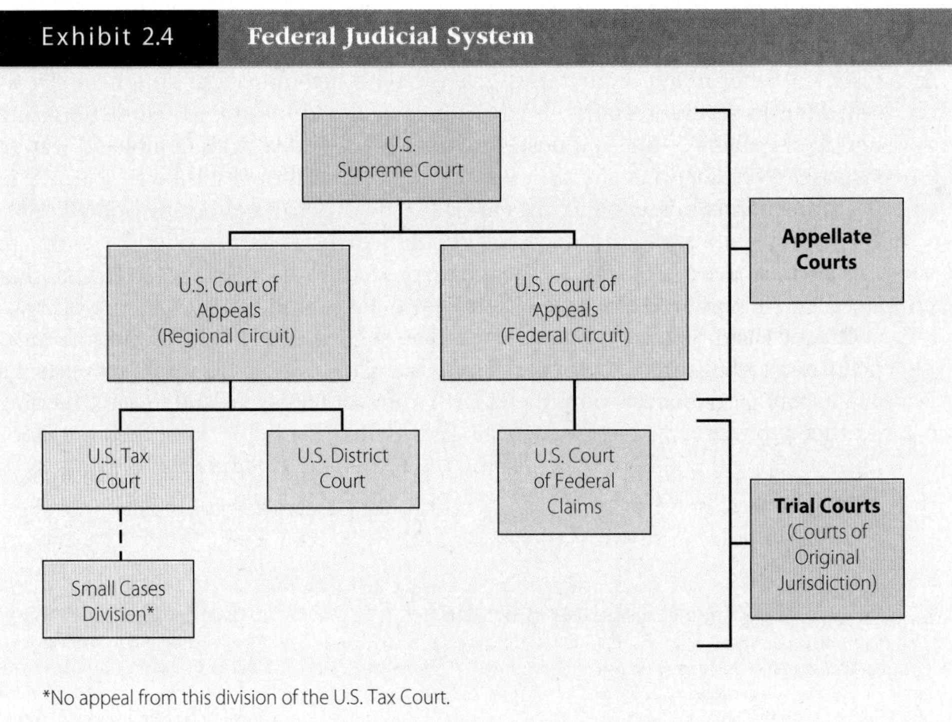

Most Federal and state appellate court decisions and some decisions of trial courts are published. Published court decisions are organized by jurisdiction (Federal or state) and level of court (trial or appellate).[22]

Several other terms are important to understand. The *plaintiff* is the party requesting a hearing, and the *defendant* is the party being challenged. Sometimes a court uses the terms *petitioner* and *respondent* (rather than *plaintiff* and *defendant*). At the trial court level, a taxpayer is normally the plaintiff (or petitioner), and the Government is the defendant (or respondent). If the taxpayer wins and the Government appeals, the Government becomes the petitioner (or appellant), and the taxpayer becomes the respondent.

Trial Courts

Here are some differences between the various trial courts (courts of original jurisdiction):

- *Number of courts*: There is only one Court of Federal Claims and only one Tax Court, but there are many U.S. District Courts. District Courts hear cases based on where the taxpayer lives (so a taxpayer in Atlanta would have her case heard by the Atlanta U.S. District Court).
- *Number of judges*: District Courts have a number of judges, but only one judge hears a case. The Court of Federal Claims has 16 judges, and the Tax Court has up to 19 regular judges. Typically, Tax Court cases are heard and decided by only one of the 19 regular judges. However, if the case is viewed as important or novel tax issues are raised, the entire Tax Court might hear the case. If a case is reviewed by the full Tax Court, such an *en banc* decision has compelling authority.
- *Location*: The Court of Federal Claims meets most often in Washington, D.C. Each state has at least one District Court, and the more populous states have more than one. Although the Tax Court is officially based in Washington, D.C., its judges travel to different parts of the country and hear cases at predetermined locations and dates.
- *Jurisdiction of the Tax Court and District Courts*: The Tax Court hears only Federal tax cases and is the most frequently used forum for tax cases since its judges have more tax expertise; many had careers in the IRS or Treasury Department before being appointed to the Tax Court. The District Courts hear a wide variety of nontax cases as well as tax cases. As a result, District Court judges are viewed as generalists (rather than specialists) in tax law.
- *Jurisdiction of the Court of Federal Claims*: The Court of Federal Claims has jurisdiction over any claim against the United States. As a result, the Court of Federal Claims hears nontax litigation as well as tax cases. Court of Federal Claims judges are tax law generalists. This court is viewed as a stronger option when equity is an issue (as opposed to purely technical issues) or when the case requires extensive discovery of evidence. It is considered by some to have a pro-business orientation.[23]
- *Jury trial*: A jury trial is available only in a District Court. However, because juries can decide only questions of fact (and not questions of law), taxpayers who choose a District Court often do not request a jury trial. In that event, the judge decides all issues in a bench trial. A District Court decision carries precedential value only in its district.
- *Payment of deficiency*: Before the Court of Federal Claims or a District Court will hear a case, the taxpayer must pay any taxes assessed by the IRS and sue for a refund. This is not the case with the Tax Court. Here, a taxpayer may request a hearing without making any payments to the IRS. As a result, whether to pay the

[22]A decision of a particular court is called its holding. Sometimes a decision includes *dicta*, or incidental opinions beyond the current facts. Such passing remarks, illustrations, or analogies are not essential to the current holding. Although the holding has precedential value under *stare decisis*, dicta are not binding on a future court.

[23]T. D. Peyser, "The Case for Selecting the Claims Court to Litigate a Federal Tax Liability," *Tax Executive* (Winter 1988): 149.

tax in advance (and limit further interest and penalties) or wait to pay the tax (and risk additional interest and penalties) becomes part of the decision-making process of selecting a trial court.

- *Appeals*: Appeals from a District Court or a Tax Court decision go to the U.S. Court of Appeals for the circuit where the taxpayer lives. Appeals from the Court of Federal Claims go to the Court of Appeals for the Federal Circuit.
- *Bankruptcy*: When a taxpayer files a bankruptcy petition, the IRS, like other creditors, is prevented from taking action against the taxpayer. Sometimes a bankruptcy court may settle a tax claim.
- *Gray areas*: Because there are "gray areas" in the tax laws, courts may disagree as to the proper tax treatment of an item. With these differences in judicial authority, a taxpayer must consider how a specific court might rule when choosing the most favorable forum to hear the case.

See Concept Summary 2.1 for a summary of various attributes of the Federal trial courts.

Concept Summary 2.1

Federal Judicial System: Trial Courts

Issue	U.S. Tax Court	U.S. District Court	U.S. Court of Federal Claims
Number of judges per court	19*	Varies	16
Payment of deficiency before trial	No	Yes	Yes
Jury trial available	No	Yes	No
Types of disputes	Tax cases only	Most criminal and civil issues	Claims against the United States
Jurisdiction	Nationwide	Location of taxpayer	Nationwide
IRS acquiescence policy	Yes	Yes	Yes
Appeal route	U.S. Court of Appeals	U.S. Court of Appeals	U.S. Court of Appeals for the Federal Circuit

*Some positions may be unfilled at any time. Senior judges and special trial judges may be used to manage the caseload.

Appellate Courts

A trial court decision can be appealed to the appropriate **Circuit Court of Appeals** by the losing party. The 11 geographic circuits, the circuit for the District of Columbia, and the Federal Circuit[24] appear in Exhibit 2.5. Generally, a three-judge panel hears a Court of Appeals case; occasionally, the *full* court decides more controversial cases.

If the Government loses at the trial court level (District Court, Tax Court, or Court of Federal Claims), it may decide not to appeal. However, the fact that the IRS does not appeal does not mean that the IRS agrees with the result (and it may litigate similar issues in the future).

The IRS may decide not to appeal for a number of reasons. First, the IRS may decide that available personnel should be assigned to other more important cases. Second, the IRS may decide that the taxpayer has a sympathetic position or the facts are particularly strong in their favor. In that event, the IRS may wait to test the legal issues with a different taxpayer (who might have a weaker case). Third, the Court of Appeals jurisdiction might matter. Based on past experience and precedent, the IRS may decide that the chance for success on a particular issue might be more promising in a different Court of Appeals.

The Federal Circuit provides the taxpayer with an alternative forum. When a particular Circuit Court of Appeals has issued an adverse decision in a similar case, the taxpayer may prefer the Court of Federal Claims route because any appeal is to the Federal Circuit.

[24]The Court of Appeals for the Federal Circuit was created effective October 1, 1982, by P.L. 97–64 (4/2/82) to hear decisions appealed from the Claims Court (now the Court of Federal Claims).

Exhibit 2.5 **The Federal Courts of Appeals**

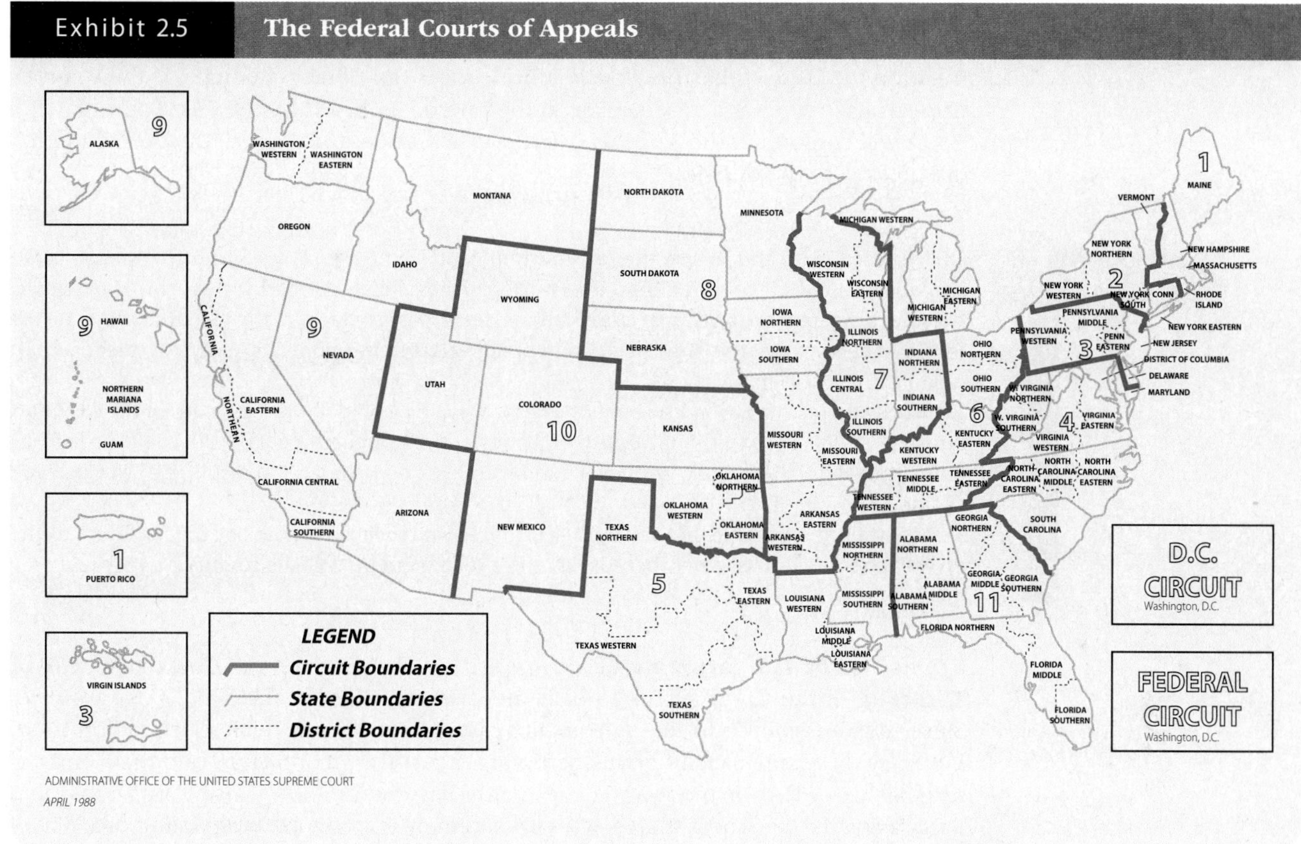

ADMINISTRATIVE OFFICE OF THE UNITED STATES SUPREME COURT
APRIL 1988

The Appellate Process

The *role* of the appellate court usually is limited to a review of whether the trial court applied the proper law in arriving at its decision. Rarely does an appellate court question a lower court's fact-finding determination. Both the Code and the Supreme Court indicate that Federal appellate courts are bound by findings of facts unless they are clearly erroneous.[25]

An appeal can have a number of possible outcomes. The appellate court may approve (affirm) or disapprove (reverse) the lower court's finding, or it may send the case back to the trial court for further consideration (remand). When many issues are involved, a mixed result is not unusual. As a result, the lower court may be affirmed (*aff'd*) on Issue A and reversed (*rev'd*) on Issue B, and Issue C is remanded (*rem'd*) for additional fact finding.

When more than one judge is involved in the decision-making process, disagreements are common. In addition to the majority view, one or more judges may concur (agree with the result reached but not with some or all of the reasoning) or dissent (disagree with the result). In any decision, of course, the majority controls. But concurring and dissenting views can have an influence on future cases or other courts.

Appellate Precedents and the Tax Court District Courts, the Tax Court, and the Court of Federal Claims must abide by the **precedents** set by a Court of Appeals jurisdiction. A particular Court of Appeals need not follow the decisions of another Court of Appeals. All courts, however, must follow the decisions of the **U.S. Supreme Court**.

This pattern of appellate precedents raises an issue for the Tax Court. Because the Tax Court is a national court, it decides cases from all parts of the country. Under a

[25] §§ 7482(a) and (c). *Comm. v. Duberstein*, 60–2 USTC ¶9515, 5 AFTR 2d 1626, 80 S.Ct. 1190 (USSC, 1960). See Rule 52(a) of the Federal Rules of Civil Procedure.

policy known as the *Golsen* rule, the Tax Court decides a case as it believes the law should be applied *only* if the Court of Appeals of appropriate jurisdiction has not yet ruled on the issue or has previously affirmed the Tax Court's rationale. If the Court of Appeals has ruled on a case similar to the one being heard by the Tax Court, the Tax Court will conform to the Appeals Court decision under the *Golsen* rule even though it disagrees with the decision.[26]

Emily lives in Texas and sues in the Tax Court on Issue A. The Fifth Circuit Court of Appeals is the appropriate appellate court for Texas. The Fifth Circuit has already decided, in a case involving similar facts but a different taxpayer, that Issue A should be resolved in favor of the taxpayer. Although the Tax Court believes that the Fifth Circuit Court of Appeals is wrong, under its *Golsen* rule the trial court will rule in favor of Emily.

Shortly thereafter, Rashad, a resident of New York, in a comparable case, sues in the Tax Court on Issue A. The Second Circuit Court of Appeals, the appellate court that would hear a Tax Court appeal from New York, has never expressed itself on Issue A. As a result, the Tax Court will decide against Rashad.

As a result, it is possible for two taxpayers, both having their cases heard by the Tax Court, to end up with opposite results merely because they live in different parts of the country.

Appeal to the U.S. Supreme Court Appeal to the U.S. Supreme Court is by **Writ of Certiorari**. If the Court agrees to hear the case, it will grant the Writ (*Cert. granted*). Since the Supreme Court rarely hears tax cases, most often it denies jurisdiction (*Cert. denied*). The Court usually grants certiorari to resolve a conflict among the Courts of Appeals (e.g., two or more appellate courts have assumed opposing positions on a particular issue) or where the tax issue is extremely important. The granting of a Writ of Certiorari indicates that at least four of the nine members of the Supreme Court believe that the issue is of sufficient importance to be heard by the full Court.

LO.2

Locate and work with the appropriate tax law sources.

Judicial Citations

Court decisions are an important source of tax law, and the ability to cite and locate a case is a critical skill when working with the tax law. Judicial citations usually follow a standard pattern: case name, volume number, reporter series, page or paragraph number, court (where necessary), and year of the decision (see Concept Summary 2.2). These conventions are based on the legacy of publishing court decisions in books, but they carry on even in today's electronic research environment.

Judicial Citations—The U.S. Tax Court The U.S. Tax Court issues two types of decisions: Regular and Memorandum, based on the Chief Judge's determination. They differ in both substance and form. In terms of substance, *Memorandum* decisions deal with cases that involve only the application of established principles of law. *Regular* decisions involve novel issues not previously resolved by the Tax Court. In actual practice, however, both *Regular* and *Memorandum* represent the position of the Tax Court and, as such, can be relied on.[27]

The Regular and Memorandum decisions issued by the Tax Court also differ in form. Regular decisions are published by the U.S. Government in a series entitled *Tax Court of the United States Reports* (T.C.). Each volume of these *Reports* covers a six-month period (January 1 through June 30 and July 1 through December 31) and is given a succeeding volume number. Usually there is a time lag between the date a decision is rendered and the date it is published. A temporary citation may be necessary to help the researcher locate a recent Regular decision. Consider, for example, the temporary and permanent citations for *TBL Licensing LLC*, a decision filed on January 31, 2022.

[26]*Jack E. Golsen*, 54 T.C. 742 (1970).

[27]In contrast, U.S. Tax Court Small Cases Division Summary Opinions carry no precedential value. Summary Opinions issued after January 9, 2001, are available on the U.S. Tax Court website.

Concept Summary 2.2

Judicial Sources

Court	Location	Authority
U.S. Supreme Court	S.Ct. Series (West)	Highest authority
	U.S. Series (U.S. Gov't.)	
	L.Ed.2d (Lawyer's Co-op.)	
	AFTR (RIA)	
	USTC (CCH)	
U.S. Courts of Appeal	Federal 3d (West)	Next highest appellate court
	AFTR (RIA)	
	USTC (CCH)	
Tax Court (Regular decisions)	U.S. Gov't. Printing Office	Highest trial court*
	RIA/CCH separate services	
Tax Court (Memorandum decisions)	RIA T.C.Memo. (RIA)	Less authority than Regular T.C. decision
	TCM (CCH)	
U.S. Court of Federal Claims**	Federal Claims Reporter (West)	Similar authority as Tax Court
	AFTR (RIA)	
	USTC (CCH)	
U.S. District Courts	F.Supp.2d Series (West)	Lowest trial court
	AFTR (RIA)	
	USTC (CCH)	
Small Cases Division of Tax Court	U.S. Tax Court website***	No precedent value

Note: All Judicial Sources can be accessed electronically through Thomson Reuters *Checkpoint* (and other commercial tax services).

*Theoretically, the Tax Court, Court of Federal Claims, and District Courts are on the same level of authority. But some people believe that, because the Tax Court hears and decides tax cases from all parts of the country (i.e., a national court), its decisions may be more authoritative than a Court of Federal Claims or District Court decision.

**Before October 29, 1992, the U.S. Claims Court.

***Starting in 2001.

Temporary Citation	*TBL Licensing LLC*, 158 T.C. _____, No. 1 (2022). *Explanation:* Page number left blank because not yet known.
Permanent Citation	*TBL Licensing LLC*, 158 T.C. 1 (2022). *Explanation:* Page number now available.

Both citations tell us that the case will ultimately appear in Volume 158 of the *Tax Court of the United States Reports*. But, until this volume is made available, the page number must be left blank. Instead, the temporary citation identifies the decision as being the first Regular decision issued by the Tax Court since Volume 157 ended. With this information, the decision can easily be located in the special Tax Court services published by Commerce Clearing House (CCH) and Research Institute of America (RIA). Once Volume 158 is released, the permanent citation can be substituted and the number of the case dropped. Starting in 1995, both Regular decisions and Memorandum decisions are published on the U.S. Tax Court website (**ustaxcourt.gov**). Memorandum decisions, although available on the U.S. Tax Court website, are not published by the U.S. Government.

Before 1943, the Tax Court was called the Board of Tax Appeals, and its decisions were published as the *United States Board of Tax Appeals Reports* (B.T.A.). These 47 volumes cover the period from 1924 to 1942. For example, the citation *Karl Pauli*, 11 B.T.A. 784 (1928), refers to the 11th volume of the *Board of Tax Appeals Reports*, page 784, issued in 1928.

Memorandum decisions are published by both CCH and RIA. Consider, for example, the three different ways the *Nick R. Hughes* case can be cited:

Nick R. Hughes, T.C.Memo. 2009–94
Explanation: The 94th Memorandum decision issued by the Tax Court in 2009.

Nick R. Hughes, 97 TCM 1488
Explanation: Page 1488 of Vol. 97 of the CCH *Tax Court Memorandum Decisions.*

Nick R. Hughes, 2009 RIA T.C.Memo. ¶2009,094
Explanation: Paragraph 2009,094 of the RIA *T.C. Memorandum Decisions.*

Note that the third citation contains the same information as the first. Thus, ¶2009,094 indicates both the year and decision number of the case.[28]

U.S. Tax Court Summary Opinions relate to decisions of the Tax Court's Small Cases Division.[29] These opinions may not be treated as precedent for any other case. For example, *Sharon A. Struble*, decision entered on January 6, 2022, is cited as follows:

Sharon A. Struble, T.C. Summary Opinion 2022–1.

If the IRS loses a decision, it may indicate whether it agrees or disagrees with the results reached by the court by publishing an **acquiescence** ("A" or "*Acq.*") or **nonacquiescence** ("NA" or "*Nonacq.*"), respectively. The acquiescence or nonacquiescence is published in the *Internal Revenue Bulletin* (and an *Action on Decision* is issued). The IRS can revoke an acquiescence or a nonacquiescence retroactively.

Most often, the IRS issues nonacquiescences to adverse decisions that are not appealed. In this manner, the Government indicates that it disagrees with the result reached, despite its decision not to seek review of the matter in an appellate court. A nonacquiescence provides a warning to taxpayers that a similar case cannot be settled administratively. A taxpayer will incur fees and expenses while the case moves through the IRS even though the IRS may be unwilling to litigate a fact pattern similar to a nonacquiescence decision.[30]

Judicial Citations—The U.S. District Court, Court of Federal Claims, and Courts of Appeals District Court, Court of Federal Claims, Court of Appeals, and Supreme Court decisions dealing with Federal tax matters are reported in both the CCH *U.S. Tax Cases* (USTC) and the RIA *American Federal Tax Reports* (AFTR) series. U.S. District Court decisions, dealing with *both* tax and nontax issues, also are published by West in its *Federal Supplement Second Series* (F.Supp.2d).[31] The following examples illustrate three different ways of citing a District Court case:

Turner v. U.S., 2004–1 USTC ¶60,478 (D.Ct. Tex., 2004).
Explanation: Reported in the first volume of the *U.S. Tax Cases*, published by Commerce Clearing House, for calendar year 2004 (2004–1) and located at paragraph 60,478 (¶60,478).

Turner v. U.S., 93 AFTR 2d 2004–686 (D.Ct. Tex., 2004).
Explanation: Reported in the 93rd volume of the second series of the *American Federal Tax Reports* (AFTR 2d), published by RIA, and beginning on page 686.

Turner v. U.S., 306 F.Supp.2d 668 (D.Ct. Tex., 2004).
Explanation: Reported in the 306th volume of the *Federal Supplement Second Series* (F.Supp.2d), published by West, and beginning on page 668.

The case name, the reference to the U.S. District Court of Texas (D.Ct. Tex.), and the year the decision was rendered (2004) appear in each of the citations.[32]

[28] In this text, the RIA citation for Memorandum decisions of the U.S. Tax Court is omitted. As a result, *Nick R. Hughes* is cited as 97 TCM 1488, T.C. Memo. 2009–94.

[29] In 2005, the U.S. Supreme Court held that decisions of the Small Cases Division must be made public.

[30] G. W. Carter, "Nonacquiescence: Winning by Losing," *Tax Notes* (September 19, 1988): 1301–1307.

[31] Cases prior to 1999 are found in West's *Federal Supplement Series* (F.Supp.).

[32] In this text, the case is cited in the following form: *Turner v. U.S.*, 2004–1 USTC ¶60,478, 93 AFTR 2d 2004–686, 306 F.Supp.2d 668 (D.Ct. Tex., 2004).

Decisions of the Court of Federal Claims[33] and the Courts of Appeals are published in the USTCs, the AFTRs, and two West reporters. The *Federal Third Series* (F.3d) reports Courts of Appeals decisions, whereas the *Federal Claims Reporter* (abbreviated as Fed.Cl.) reports Court of Federal Claims decisions.[34] The following examples illustrate the different forms:

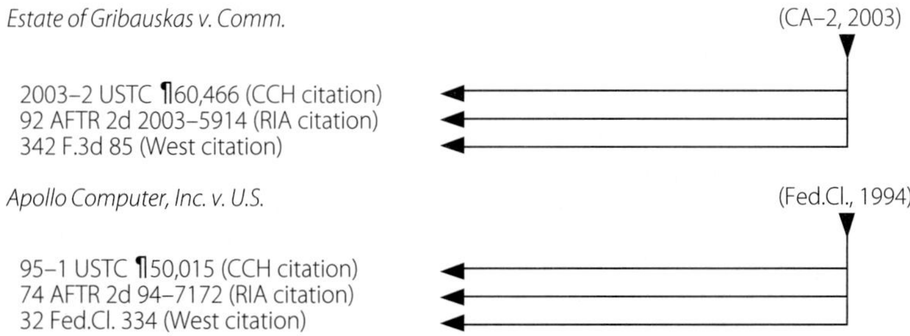

Estate of Gribauskas v. Comm. is a decision rendered by the Second Circuit Court of Appeals in 2003 (CA–2, 2003), and *Apollo Computer, Inc.*, was issued by the Court of Federal Claims in 1994 (Fed.Cl., 1994).

Judicial Citations—The U.S. Supreme Court Supreme Court decisions are published by CCH in the USTCs and by RIA in the AFTRs. The U.S. Government Printing Office also publishes these decisions in the *United States Supreme Court Reports* (U.S.), as does West in its *Supreme Court Reporter* (S.Ct.), and the Lawyer's Co-operative Publishing Company in its *United States Reports, Lawyer's Edition* (L.Ed.). The following illustrates the different ways the same decision can be cited:

The parenthetical reference (USSC, 1969) identifies the decision as having been rendered by the U.S. Supreme Court in 1969. In this text, Supreme Court decision citations are limited to the CCH (USTC), RIA (AFTR), and West (S.Ct.) versions.

2-1d **Other Sources of the Tax Law**

Other sources of tax information that a tax professional may need to consult include tax treaties and tax periodicals.

Tax Treaties

The United States signs certain tax treaties (sometimes called tax conventions) with foreign countries to assist in tax enforcement and to avoid double taxation. These treaties affect transactions involving U.S. persons and entities operating or investing in a foreign country, as well as persons and entities of a foreign country operating or investing in the United States. Although these bilateral agreements are not codified in any one source, they are available from the IRS at **tinyurl.com/taxtreaties**, as well as in various commercial tax services.

Neither a tax law nor a tax treaty automatically takes legal precedence. When there is a direct conflict between the Code and a treaty, the most recent item takes precedence. A taxpayer must disclose on the tax return any position where a treaty overrides a tax law.[35]

[33]Before October 29, 1992, the Court of Federal Claims was called the Claims Court. Before October 1, 1982, the Court of Federal Claims was called the Court of Claims.

[34]West's *Federal Second Series* (F.2d) contains cases prior to 1994. Beginning in October 1982, the Court of Federal Claims decisions were published in a different West reporter called the *Claims Court Reporter* (abbreviated Cl.Ct.).

[35]§ 7852(d); there is a $1,000 penalty per failure to disclose for individuals and a $10,000 per failure penalty for corporations. See Reg. §§ 301.6114–1, 301.6712–1, and 301.7701(b)(7).

Tax Periodicals

The use of tax periodicals can often shorten the research time needed to resolve a tax issue. An article relevant to the issue at hand may provide the references needed to locate the primary sources of the tax law that apply (e.g., citations to judicial decisions, Regulations, and other IRS pronouncements).

Several indexes are available for locating tax articles, including CCH's *Federal Tax Articles* (which includes a subject index, a Code Section number index, and an author's index) and the *Index to Federal Tax Articles* (published by Thomson Reuters). Both of these indexes are available by subscription.

Here are some of the more useful tax periodicals:

Journal of Taxation
Journal of International Taxation
Practical Tax Strategies
Estate Planning
Corporate Taxation
Business Entities
Taxation of Exempts
Real Estate Taxation
store.tax.thomsonreuters.com

The Tax Executive
tei.org

The Tax Adviser (AICPA)
thetaxadviser.com

Tax Law Review
law.nyu.edu/tax/taxlawreview/

Journal of the American Taxation Association
aaajournals.org/loi/atax

The ATA Journal of Legal Tax Research
aaajournals.org/loi/jltr

Oil, Gas & Energy Quarterly
faculty.tamucc.edu/dcrumbley/index.html

Trusts & Estates
wealthmanagement.com/trusts-estates

Journal of Passthrough Entities
TAXES—The Tax Magazine
taxna.wolterskluwer.com

Tax Notes
Tax Notes State
Tax Notes International
taxnotes.com

LO.3

Develop an awareness of tax research tools.

2-2 Working with the Tax Law—Tax Research Tools

Tax law consists of a body of legislative (e.g., Code Sections and tax treaties), administrative (e.g., Regulations and Rulings), and judicial (e.g., court cases) pronouncements. Working with the tax law requires being able to locate and use these sources effectively. A major consideration is the time required to find relevant information related to the issues identified.

Unless the problem is simple (e.g., the Code Section is known, and there is a Regulation on point), the research process begins with a tax service.

2-2a Commercial Tax Services

In the past, commercial tax services could be classified as *annotated* (i.e., organized by Internal Revenue Code) or *topical* (i.e., organized by major topics). However, as tax research has become electronic, this classification system is no longer appropriate. For example, Thomson Reuters *Checkpoint* includes both the *Federal Tax Coordinator 2d* (topical) and the *United States Tax Reporter* (annotated).

Here is a partial list of the available commercial tax services:

- *CCH IntelliConnect* and CCH *AnswerConnect*, CCH/Wolters Kluwer. Includes the *Standard Federal Tax Reporter* (along with other CCH materials).
- Thomson Reuters *Checkpoint*, Research Institute of America. Includes RIA's *Federal Tax Coordinator 2d* and *United States Tax Reporter*.

- *Practical Tax Expert*, CCH/Wolters Kluwer.
- *Tax Management Portfolios*, Bloomberg BNA.
- *Parker Tax Pro Library*.
- *Mertens Law of Federal Income Taxation*, Thomson Reuters.
- Thomson Reuters *Westlaw* and *WestlawNext*—compilations include access to *Tax Management Portfolios, Federal Tax Coordinator 2d*, and *Mertens*.
- LexisNexis *TaxCenter*—a compilation of primary sources and various materials taken from CCH, Matthew Bender, Kleinrock, and Bloomberg BNA.

2-2b **Using Electronic (Online) Tax Services**

A competent tax professional must become familiar and proficient with electronic research services and be able to use them to complete research projects efficiently. Following certain general procedures can simplify the research process. The following suggestions may be helpful:[36]

- Carefully choose keywords for the search, and put quotation marks around the terms. Words with a broad usage, such as *income*, are of limited value. If the researcher is interested in a specific type of dividend income, the search phrase *dividend income* is too broad because it finds a variety of topics including stock dividends, constructive dividends, and liquidating dividends (drawing about 2,000 hits in Thomson Reuters *Checkpoint*). Searching for *qualified dividend income, stock dividend income, cash dividend income*, or *property dividend income* narrows the number of items found.
- Take advantage of *connectors* such as "+" and quotation marks to place parameters on the search and further restrict the output. Although each tax service has its own set of connectors, many are similar. Enclosing words in quotation marks means "exact phrase" in both Thomson Reuters *Checkpoint* and CCH *IntelliConnect* (e.g., "personal service corporation").
- Be selective in choosing the data to search. For example, if the research project does not involve case law, do not include judicial decisions in the search.
- Use a table of contents, an index, or a citation when appropriate. Although the keyword approach is used most frequently, electronic databases can be searched in other ways. Using the table of contents or index may narrow the information that needs to be examined. Tax law (including annotations) also can be accessed by a citation: statutory (e.g., Code Section), administrative (e.g., Rev.Rul.), or judicial (e.g., Tax Court).
- Always check for current developments. Tax services are updated several times a day, and tax newsletters often feature highlights of recent tax law developments. In addition, there is no substitute for the original source. Do not base a conclusion solely on a tax service's commentary. If a Code Section, Regulation, or case is vital to the research, read it.

2-2c **Noncommercial Electronic (Online) Tax Services**

The internet provides a wealth of tax information in several popular forms, sometimes at no cost to the researcher. A tax professional can access a significant amount of information that can assist in the research process.

---

[36] For a more complete discussion of the use of Thomson Reuters *Checkpoint* and CCH *IntelliConnect* and internet research in taxation, see Sawyer and Gill, *Federal Tax Research*, 12th ed. (Cengage Learning, 2021), Chapters 6 and 7.

- *Websites* are provided by accounting and consulting firms, publishers, tax academics, libraries, and governmental bodies as a means of making information widely available. One of the best sites available to the tax professional is the Internal Revenue Service's home page, illustrated in Exhibit 2.6. This site offers downloadable forms and instructions, interpretations of Regulations, and news update items. Exhibit 2.7 lists some of the websites that may be most useful to tax researchers.
- *Blogs and RSS sites* provide a means by which information related to the tax law can be exchanged among taxpayers, tax professionals, and others who subscribe to the group's services. Individuals can read the exchanges and offer replies and suggestions to inquiries. Discussions address the interpretation and application of existing law, analysis of proposals and new pronouncements, and reviews of tax software.

Although tax information on the internet is plentiful, information in the public domain should not be relied upon without referring to other sources. Anyone can set up a website, and the quality of the information can be difficult for a tax professional to ascertain.

LO.4

Describe the tax research process.

2-3 Working with the Tax Law—Tax Research

Tax research is the process of finding a competent and professional conclusion to a tax problem. The problem may originate from completed or proposed transactions. In the case of a completed transaction, the objective of the research is to determine the tax result of what has already taken place. For example, is a taxpayer expense deductible? When dealing with proposed transactions, tax research has a different objective: effective tax planning by determining the tax consequences of various alternatives. A large part of a tax professional's career is spent on this type of tax research.

Exhibit 2.6 **The IRS's Home Page**

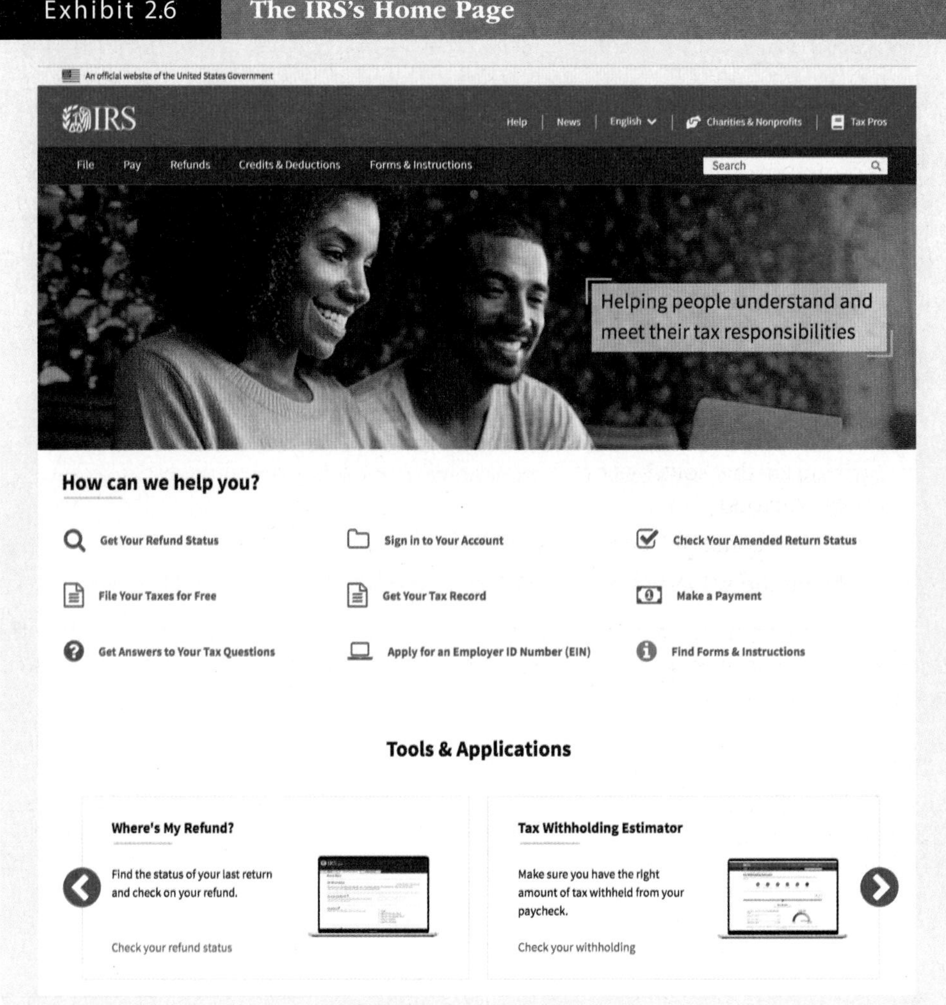

IRS-Internal Revenue Service

Exhibit 2.7 Tax-Related Websites

Website	Web Address	Description
Accounting firms and professional organizations	For instance, the AICPA's page is at **aicpa.org**, Ernst & Young is at **ey.com**, Deloitte is at **deloitte.com**, KPMG is at **kpmg.com**, and PricewaterhouseCoopers is at **pwc.com**	Tax planning newsletters, descriptions of services offered and career opportunities, and exchange of data with clients and subscribers
Cengage Learning	**cengage.com**	Informational updates, newsletters, support materials for students and adopters, and continuing education
Commercial tax publishers	For instance, **taxnotes.com**, **taxna.wolterskluwer.com**, **tax.thomsonreuters.com**, and **pro.bloombergtax.com**	Information about products and services available for subscription and newsletter excerpts
Court opinions	The site at **law.justia.com** covers state, Federal, and Supreme Court decisions (but not Tax Court)	A synopsis of result reached by the court
Federal Register	**federalregister.gov**	Releases from the IRS (e.g., Regulations)
Internal Revenue Service	**irs.gov**	News releases, downloadable forms and instructions, tables, Circular 230, and e-mail
Tax Almanac	**taxalmanac.org**	Smorgasbord of tax research resources
Tax Analysts	**taxnotes.com**	Policy-oriented readings on the tax law and proposals to change it and articles on various tax subjects
	taxnotes.com/research/federal	Tax-related laws, regulations, rulings, procedures, and other documents
Tax Foundation	**taxfoundation.org**	Nonprofit educational organization that promotes sound tax policy and measures tax burdens
Tax laws online	Regulations are at **law.cornell.edu/cfr**, and the Code is at **uscode.house.gov**	
U.S. Tax Court decisions	**ustaxcourt.gov**	Recent U.S. Tax Court decisions

Caution: Web addresses change frequently.

Tax research involves the following steps:

- Identifying and refining the problem.
- Locating the appropriate tax law sources.
- Assessing the validity of the tax law sources.
- Arriving at the solution or at alternative solutions (including consideration of nontax factors).
- Effectively communicating the solution to the taxpayer.
- Updating the solution (where appropriate) in light of new developments.

The tax research process is illustrated in Exhibit 2.8. The broken lines reflect the steps of particular interest when tax research is directed toward proposed, rather than completed, transactions.

2-3a Identifying the Problem

Problem identification starts by documenting the relevant facts involved with the issue.[37] *All* of the facts that may have a bearing on the problem must be gathered; if any facts are omitted, the solution provided will likely change. To illustrate, return to the facts of

[37]For an excellent discussion of the critical role of facts in carrying out tax research, see Gardner, Stewart, and Worsham, *Tax Research Techniques*, 10th ed. (New York: The American Institute of Certified Public Accountants, 2017), Chapter 2.

Exhibit 2.8 Tax Research Process

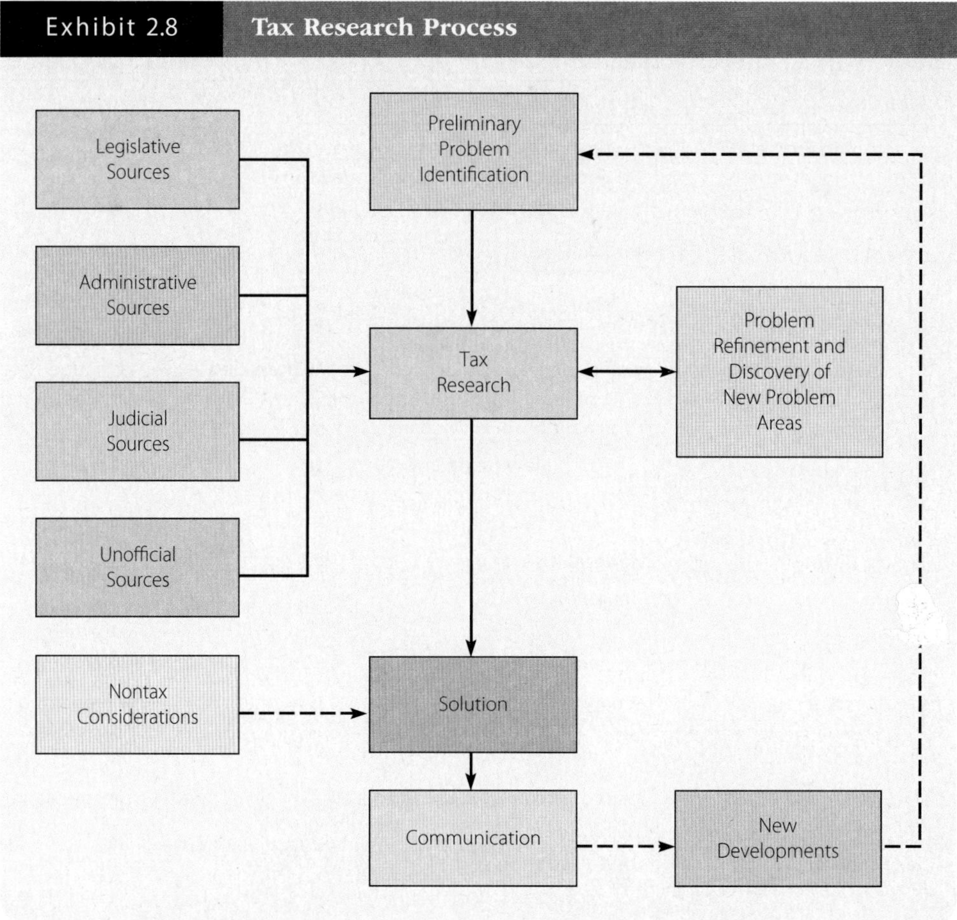

The Big Picture on p. 2-1 and consider the tax implications of the gold coins discovered by Fred and Megan Martel.

2-3b Refining the Problem

In the facts of *The Big Picture* on p. 2-1, the question of the tax implications of the Martels' discovery can be determined with some basic research. Internal Revenue Code § 61 defines gross income as "all income from whatever source derived."[38] Further, Treasury Regulation § 1.61–14(a) states that "a treasure trove, to the extent of its value in United States currency, constitutes gross income for the taxable year in which it is reduced to undisputed possession."

Given that the Martels discovered the coins on their property in March 2023 and the state returned the coins to them in October 2023 ("undisputed possession"), their gross income in 2023 will include the "value in United States currency" of the coins. The question of "value" is key to the Martels' situation.

2-3c Locating the Appropriate Tax Law Sources

Once a problem is clearly defined, what is the next step? Although the next step is a matter of individual judgment, most tax research begins with a keyword search using an electronic tax service. If the problem is not complex, the researcher may turn directly to the Internal Revenue Code and Treasury Regulations. The Code and Regulations are accessible electronically (and also available in print from a number of publishers).[39]

[38]See the related discussion in Chapter 4.

[39]The Internal Revenue Service provides a gateway to the Internal Revenue Code, Treasury Department Regulations, and other items at **irs.gov/tax-professionals/tax-code-regulations-and-official-guidance**.

2-3d **Assessing the Validity of Tax Law Sources**

Once a source has been located, the next step is to assess it in light of the problem at hand. Proper assessment involves careful interpretation of the tax law with consideration given to its relevance and validity. In connection with validity, an important step is to check for recent changes in the tax law.

Interpreting the Internal Revenue Code

The language of the Code can be extremely difficult to comprehend. Some of this difficulty is due to its structure (the Code follows the structure of all U.S. law), so getting used to reading (and interpreting) the Code can take time.

The Code must be read carefully for restrictive language such as "*at least* 80 percent" and "*more than* 80 percent" or "*less than* 50 percent" and "*exceeds* 50 percent." Whether two or more clauses are connected by *or* or by *and* makes a great deal of difference.

Sometimes the Code directs the researcher elsewhere for the answer. For example, § 162(c) refers to the Foreign Corrupt Practices Act for purposes of determining when payments to foreign officials are deductible.

Definitions vary from one Code Section to another. For example, § 267 disallows losses between related parties. Brothers and sisters are included in this definition of related parties. This is not the case with § 318, which deals with the definition of related parties for certain stock redemptions. Research has shown that in one-third of the conflicts reaching the Tax Court, the court could not discern the intent of Congress by simply reading the statute (the Court had to look to Committee Reports to understand intent).[40]

If an answer is not in the Code, it may be necessary to look to other tax law, including Regulations and judicial decisions.

Assessing the Validity of a Treasury Regulation

Treasury Regulations are the official interpretation of the Code and are entitled to great deference. Occasionally, however, a court invalidates a Regulation (or a portion of it) because the Regulation is contrary to the intent of Congress. Usually, courts do not question the validity of Regulations. Courts believe that "the first administrative interpretation of a provision as it appears in a new act often expresses the general understanding of the times or the actual understanding of those who played an important part when the statute was drafted."[41]

Keep the following things in mind when you assess the validity of a Regulation:

- IRS agents must give the Code and any related Regulations equal weight when dealing with taxpayers and their representatives.
- Proposed Regulations provide a preview of future Final Regulations, but they are not binding on the IRS or taxpayers.
- Taxpayers have the burden of proof to show that a Regulation varies from the language of the statute and is not supported by the related Committee Reports.
- If the taxpayer challenges a Regulation and loses, a 20 percent accuracy-related penalty may apply.[42]

[40] T. L. Kirkpatrick and W. B. Pollard, "Reliance by the Tax Court on the Legislative Intent of Congress," *The Tax Executive* (Summer 1986): 358–359.

[41] *Augustus v. Comm.*, 41–1 USTC ¶9255, 26 AFTR 612, 118 F.2d 38 (CA–6, 1941).

[42] §§ 6662(a) and (b)(1). This accuracy-related penalty applies to any failure to make a reasonable attempt to comply with the tax law and any disregard of rules and Regulations [§ 6662(c)]. The term *reasonable* is not defined in the Code; the IRS looks at all of the facts and circumstances surrounding the effort of the taxpayer to report the correct tax liability.

- Final Regulations can be classified as procedural, interpretive, or legislative. **Procedural Regulations** are *housekeeping-type instructions* indicating information that taxpayers should provide the IRS, as well as information about the internal management and conduct of the IRS itself.
- Some **interpretive Regulations** rephrase or elaborate what Congress stated in the Committee Reports that were issued when the tax legislation was enacted. These Regulations are almost impossible to overturn because they clearly reflect the intent of Congress. Historically, an interpretive Regulation has been given less deference than a legislative Regulation.[43] The Supreme Court has told lower courts to analyze Treasury Regulations carefully before accepting the Treasury's interpretation.[44]
- In some Code Sections, Congress has given the *Treasury Secretary or his delegate* the authority to prescribe Regulations to carry out the details of administration or to otherwise complete the operating rules. In these cases, Congress is delegating its legislative powers to the Treasury Department. Regulations issued under this type of authority possess the force and effect of law and are often called **legislative Regulations**.
- Courts tend to apply a legislative reenactment doctrine. A particular Regulation is assumed to have received congressional approval if the Regulation was finalized many years earlier and Congress has not amended the related Code Section.

Assessing the Validity of Other Administrative Sources of the Tax Law

Revenue Rulings issued by the IRS carry less weight than Treasury Department Regulations. Revenue Rulings are important, however, in that they reflect the position of the IRS on tax matters. IRS agents will follow the results reached in a Revenue Ruling that relates to the research question (or the tax return). A 1986 Tax Court decision, however, indicated that Revenue Rulings "typically do not constitute substantive authority for a position."[45] Most Revenue Rulings apply retroactively unless the ruling indicates otherwise.[46]

Actions on Decisions document the IRS's reaction to certain court decisions. The IRS follows a practice of either acquiescing (agreeing) or nonacquiescing (not agreeing) with selected judicial decisions.

Assessing the Validity of Judicial Sources of the Tax Law

How much reliance can be placed on a particular decision depends on the following variables:

- *The level of court*: A decision rendered by a trial court (e.g., a U.S. District Court) carries less weight than one issued by an appellate court (e.g., the Fifth Circuit Court of Appeals). Unless Congress changes the Code, decisions by the U.S. Supreme Court represent the last word on any tax issue.
- *Residence of the taxpayer*: A decision of the appellate court in the taxpayer's circuit carries more weight than one rendered by an appellate court in a different circuit. If, for example, a taxpayer lives in Texas, a decision of the Fifth Circuit Court of Appeals (which would hear an appeal from a Texas trial court) means more than one rendered by the Second Circuit Court of Appeals.[47]

---

[43]However, see *Mayo Foundation for Medical Education and Research*, 2011–1 USTC ¶50,143, 107 AFTR 2d 2011–341, 103 S.Ct. 704 (USSC, 2011), where the Supreme Court provided greater deference to interpretive Regulations (and appeared to blur the line between legislative and interpretive Regulations).

[44]*U.S. v. Vogel Fertilizer Co.*, 82–1 USTC ¶9134, 49 AFTR 2d 82–491, 102 S.Ct. 821 (USSC, 1982); *National Muffler Dealers Assn., Inc.*, 79–1 USTC ¶9264, 43 AFTR 2d 79–828, 99 S.Ct. 1304 (USSC, 1979).

[45]*Nelda C. Stark*, 86 T.C. 243 (1986). See also *Ann R. Neuhoff*, 75 T.C. 36 (1980). For a different opinion, however, see *Industrial Valley Bank & Trust Co.*, 66 T.C. 272 (1976).

[46]Rev.Proc. 87–1.

[47]Before October 1, 1982, an appeal from the then-named U.S. Court of Claims (the other trial court) was directly to the U.S. Supreme Court.

- *Regular or Memorandum decision*: A Tax Court Regular decision carries more weight than a Memorandum decision because the Tax Court does not consider Memorandum decisions to be binding precedents.[48] A Tax Court *reviewed* decision (where *all* of the Tax Court judges participate) carries even more weight.
- *Circuit Court decision*: A Circuit Court decision heard *en banc* (all of the judges participate) carries more weight than a normal Circuit Court case.
- *Other courts' support*: A decision that is supported by cases from other courts carries more weight than a decision that is not supported by other cases.
- *Status on appeal*: The weight of a decision also can be affected by its status on appeal. For example, was the decision affirmed or overruled?

In connection with the last three variables, the use of a citator is invaluable to tax research.[49] A **citator** provides the history of a case, including the authority relied on (e.g., other judicial decisions) in reaching the result. Reviewing the references listed in the citator discloses whether the decision was appealed and, if so, with what result (e.g., affirmed, reversed, or remanded). The Thomson Reuters *Checkpoint* citator also shows other cases with the same or similar issues and how they were decided. As a result, a citator reflects on the validity of a case and may lead to other relevant judicial material.[50] If one intends to rely on a judicial decision, "citating" the case is imperative.

Assessing the Validity of Other Sources

Primary sources of tax law include the Constitution, legislative history materials, statutes, treaties, Treasury Regulations, IRS pronouncements, and judicial decisions. The IRS considers only primary sources to constitute substantial authority. However, reference to *secondary sources* such as legal periodicals, treatises, legal opinions, IRS publications, and other materials can be useful. In general, secondary sources are not authority.

Although the statement that the IRS regards only primary sources as substantial authority generally is true, there is one exception. For purposes of the accuracy-related penalty in § 6662, the IRS expands the list of substantial authority to include a number of nonprimary sources (e.g., letter rulings, Chief Counsel Advice, and the Bluebook).[51] "Authority" does not include conclusions reached in treatises, legal periodicals, and opinions rendered by tax professionals.

A letter ruling or determination letter is substantial authority *only* for the taxpayer to whom it is issued, except for the accuracy-related penalty.

Once major tax legislation is completed, the staff of the Joint Committee on Taxation (in consultation with the staffs of the House Ways and Means and Senate Finance Committees) often prepares a General Explanation of the Act, commonly known as the Bluebook (because of the color of its cover). The IRS and the courts do not accept this detailed explanation as having legal effect. The Bluebook does, however, provide valuable guidance to tax advisers and taxpayers until Regulations are issued.

2-3e **Arriving at the Solution or at Alternative Solutions**

The Big Picture on p. 2-1 raises the question of how a "treasure trove" should be taxed. Based on Reg. § 1.61–14(a), the Martels must include in their gross income the "value in United States currency" of the coins once they have "undisputed possession" of the coins.

Does it make any difference that the couple paid $195,000 for the land where the coins were buried? Since the taxpayers found the gold coins on their own property, they could argue that they purchased the coins when they purchased the land. This argument is similar to an individual discovering oil or natural gas on her property. And with

[48] *Severino R. Nico, Jr.*, 67 T.C. 647 (1977).

[49] The major citators are published by CCH, RIA, Westlaw, and Shepard's.

[50] The CCH citator is available online through the CCH *IntelliConnect* service; RIA's citator can be found in Thomson Reuters *Checkpoint*. Westlaw's citator (KeyCite) is part of its online service. Shepard's citator is part of LexisNexis.

[51] Reg. § 1.6661–3(b)(2).

Financial Disclosure Insights — Where Does GAAP Come From?

Tax law is developed by many entities, including Congress and the legislators of other countries, the courts, and the IRS. Accounting principles also have many sources. Consequently, in reconciling the tax and financial accounting reporting of a transaction, the tax professional needs to know the hierarchy of authority of accounting principles—in particular, the level of importance to assign to a specific GAAP document. The diagram below presents the sources of GAAP arranged in a general order of authority from highest to lowest.

Professional research is conducted to find and analyze the sources of accounting reporting standards in much the same way a tax professional conducts research on an open tax question. In fact, many of the publishers that provide tax research materials also can be used to find GAAP and International Financial Reporting Standards (IFRS) documents. The Financial Accounting Standards Board (FASB) also makes its standards and interpretations available by subscription.

Highest Authority

- Financial Accounting Standards and Interpretations of the FASB.
- Pronouncements of bodies that preceded the FASB, such as the Accounting Principles Board (APB).

- FASB Technical Bulletins.
- Audit and Accounting Guides, prepared by the American Institute of CPAs (AICPA) and cleared by the FASB.
- Practice Bulletins, prepared by the American Institute of CPAs (AICPA) and cleared by the FASB.

- Interpretation Guides of the FASB Staff.
- Accounting Interpretations of the AICPA.
- IASB Accounting Standards.
- FASB Concepts Standards.
- Widely accepted accounting practices, professional journals, accounting textbooks, and treatises.

natural resources, there must be a realization event (e.g., a sale or exchange) before there is income. Would this notion work for this couple? Unfortunately, no. A decision affirmed by the Sixth Circuit Court of Appeals indicates that the *entire value* of the couple's discovery would be included in their income in the year of discovery.[52] In *Cesarini*, the taxpayer purchased a piano that happened to conceal cash. The courts allocated the entire purchase price to the piano, so the "windfall" currency was wholly taxable in the year of discovery. Although the Martels might want to argue that there is no "income" until the coins are sold (i.e., the coins have a zero basis on discovery), Reg. § 1.61–14(a) and *Cesarini* indicate that the treasure trove's value should be included in gross income as soon as the couple has "undisputed possession."

Finally, the "value" is *not* the $28,000 face value of the coins. Rather, it is the *fair market* value of the coins. But how does one *value* the coins? Valuation will likely depend on the appraisal of the coins (and, as you might suspect, there could be differences in appraisals). If the Martels sell any of the coins, they could argue that the best "value" would be the sales price of the coins. But an appraisal will be required to determine the fair market value of the coins, and this amount must be included in the Martels' 2023 gross income.[53]

LO.5

Communicate the results of the tax research process in a client letter and a tax file memorandum.

2-3f Communicating Tax Research

Once the research process has been completed (including checking for any new developments; see Exhibit 2.8), the researcher will need to prepare a memo, a letter, or an oral presentation. The form of communication depends on a number of factors. For example, most firms document the results of a tax research project in a memorandum. Although the

[52] *Cesarini v. U.S.*, 69–1 USTC ¶9270, 23 AFTR 2d 69–997, 296 F.Supp. 3 (D.Ct. N.Oh., 1969), *aff'd* 70–2 USTC ¶9509, 26 AFTR 2d 70–5107, 428 F.2d 812 (CA–6, 1970).

[53] This *Big Picture* example is based on a 2013 discovery made in California; see **en.wikipedia.org/wiki/Saddle_Ridge_Hoard**. For more detail on the tax implications of this discovery, see M. Morris, C. Cheng, and D. L. Crumbley, "The Saddle Ridge Gold Coin Discovery: How the U.S. Should Tax U.S. Currency Under the Treasure Trove Regulations," *Houston Business and Tax Law Journal*, Vol. 17, Issue 2 (2017), pp. 120–145.

format of this memorandum can vary, certain elements appear in all memos. In addition, virtually all memos are reviewed by senior tax professionals to ensure accuracy.

How are results communicated to the client (does the client receive the tax research memo, a letter, or some other form of communication)? If an oral presentation is required, who will be the audience? Whatever form it takes, the following elements will be part of the communication:

- A clear statement of the issue.
- In more complex situations, a short review of the facts that raised the issue.
- A review of the relevant tax law sources (e.g., Code, Regulations, Revenue Rulings, Revenue Procedures, Notices, and judicial authority).
- Any assumptions made in arriving at the solution.
- The solution recommended and the logic or reasoning supporting it.
- The references consulted in the research process.

A good tax research communication should tell the reader what was researched, the results of that research, and the justification for any recommendations.[54]

Exhibits 2.9 and 2.10 present the tax file memorandum (internal to the firm) and the client letter associated with the facts of *The Big Picture*.

Exhibit 2.9 **Tax File Memorandum**

November 10, 2023

TAX FILE MEMORANDUM

FROM: John J. Jones
SUBJECT: Fred and Megan Martel
Income from Coin Discovery

Today I met with Fred and Megan Martel related to a request for tax assistance. In 2018, the Martels purchased 40 acres of land for $195,000; they built their current residence on the property in 2019. In March 2023, while walking on a remote part of their property, they spotted something shiny on the ground. They started digging and eventually unearthed eight metal cans containing more than 1,400 rare gold coins in $5, $10, and $20 denominations dated from 1846 to 1895. The face value of the gold coins is about $28,000, and the coins are in mint condition. As required by state law, the Martels turned over the coins to the state for disposition. For a period of six months, the state was required to publicize the find and ask if anyone could prove ownership. When no one came forward, the coins were returned to the Martels in October 2023.

ISSUE: What are the tax implications of the Martels' coin discovery?

FINDINGS: Internal Revenue Code § 61 defines gross income as "all income from whatever source derived." Further, Treasury Regulation § 1.61–14(a) states that "a treasure trove, to the extent of its value in United States currency, constitutes gross income for the taxable year in which it is reduced to undisputed possession." The fact that the state returned the coins to the Martels in October 2023 appears to indicate "undisputed possession" as required by Reg. § 1.61–14(a). As a result, their gross income will include "value in United States currency" of the coins. The question of "value" is key to the Martels' situation.

Since the Martels found the gold coins on their own property, the taxpayers could argue that they purchased the coins when they purchased the land. This argument is similar to an individual discovering oil or natural gas on her property. With natural resources, there must be a realization event (e.g., a sale or exchange) before there is income.

Given the findings in *Cesarini* [70–2 USTC ¶9509, 26 AFTR 2d 70–5107, 428 F.2d 812 (CA–6, 1970)], this notion would not appear to work for the Martels. In *Cesarini*, the taxpayer purchased a piano that happened to conceal cash. The court allocated the entire purchase price to the piano, so the "windfall" currency was wholly taxable in the year of discovery. As a result, this decision by the Sixth Circuit Court of Appeals would indicate that the *entire value* of the couple's discovery is to be included in their income in the year of discovery.

Although the Martels might want to argue that there is no "income" until the coins are sold (i.e., the coins have a zero basis on discovery), Reg. § 1.61–14(a) and *Cesarini* indicate that the treasure trove's value should be included in gross income as soon as the couple has "undisputed possession."

Finally, the "value" is *not* the $28,000 face value of the coins. Rather, it is the *fair market value* of the coins. The Martels should engage a qualified appraiser (or appraisers) to value the coins appropriately. Then the appraised value of the coins will be included in their 2023 gross income.

[54] See Gardner, Stewart, and Worsham, *Tax Research Techniques*, 10th ed. (New York: The American Institute of Certified Public Accountants, 2017), Chapter 7. For oral presentations, see W. A. Raabe and G. E. Whittenburg, "Talking Tax: How to Make a Tax Presentation," *Tax Adviser* (March 1997): 179–182.

Exhibit 2.10 Client Letter

SWFT, LLP
5191 Natorp Boulevard
Mason, OH 45040

November 17, 2023

Mr. and Mrs. Fred Martel
111 Saddle Ridge Road
Williamsburg, VA 23185

Dear Mr. and Mrs. Martel:

This letter is in response to your request for advice related to your discovery of gold coins on your property in March 2023. Our conclusions are based on the facts discussed during our meeting with you on November 11, 2023. Any change in the facts may affect our conclusions.

In general, the fair market value of the coins you discovered must be included in your 2023 gross income. This conclusion is based on your "undisputed possession" of the coins (as of October 2023) and opinions expressed in U.S. Treasury Department Regulations and court cases (including one from the Sixth Circuit Court of Appeals).

Given the potential value of your discovery, I would encourage you to seek a competent appraiser (or appraisers) to assess the value of the coins. Once a determination of value is made, we can work on a plan to pay the related Federal and state income taxes.

Should you need more information or want to clarify our conclusions, do not hesitate to contact me.

Sincerely yours,

John J. Jones, CPA
Partner

LO.6

Apply tax research techniques and planning procedures.

2-4 Working with the Tax Law—Tax Planning

Tax research and tax planning are inseparable. The *primary* purpose of effective *tax planning* is to maximize the taxpayer's after-tax wealth. The course of action selected might not produce the lowest possible tax under the circumstances. The minimization of tax liability must be considered in context with the nontax goals of the taxpayer.

A *secondary* objective of effective tax planning is to reduce or defer the tax in the current tax year. Specifically, this objective aims to accomplish one or more of the following:

- Eliminating the tax entirely.
- Eliminating the tax in the current year.
- Deferring the receipt of income.
- Converting ordinary income into capital gains.
- Converting active income to passive activity income.
- Converting passive activity expense to active expense.
- Increasing the number of taxpayers (i.e., forming partnerships and corporations or making lifetime gifts to family members).
- Avoiding double taxation.
- Avoiding ordinary income.
- Creating, increasing, or accelerating deductions.

However, this objective should be approached with caution. For example, a tax election in one year may reduce taxes currently but cause future years to have disadvantageous tax positions.

2-4a **Nontax Considerations**

There is a danger that tax considerations may impair the exercise of sound financial planning or business judgment by the taxpayer. As a result, the tax planning process can lead to ends that are economically (or socially) incorrect. Unfortunately, a tendency exists for planning to move toward the opposing extremes of placing either too little or too much emphasis on tax considerations. The goal should be a balance that recognizes the significance of taxes but not beyond the point where planning detracts from the exercise of good business judgment. In general, if the only reason for pursuing a specific course of action is because of the tax benefits, then one should rethink that decision.

2-4b **Components of Tax Planning**

The popular perception of tax planning often is restricted to the adage "defer income and accelerate deductions." Although this timing approach does hold true and is important, meaningful tax planning involves considerably more.

Preferable to deferring taxable income is complete *avoidance* of taxation. Consider, for example, the employee who chooses nontaxable fringe benefits (e.g., group term life insurance and health insurance coverage) over a fully taxable future pay increase.[55] Complete avoidance of gain recognition also occurs when the owner of appreciated property transfers it by death. Here, the "step-up" (appreciation) in basis to fair market value completely escapes the income tax.[56]

If the recognition of income cannot be avoided, its deferral will postpone income tax consequences. A tax paid in the future costs less than a tax paid today because of the time value of money. *Deferral* of income can take many forms. Besides like-kind exchanges and involuntary conversions, most retirement plans postpone income tax consequences until the benefits are paid. Deferral of gain recognition also can occur when appreciated property is transferred to a newly formed corporation or partnership.[57]

A corollary to the deferral of income is the acceleration of deductions. For example, if an accrual basis, calendar year corporation authorizes a charitable contribution in 2023 and pays it on or before the due date of its tax return in 2024, the deduction can be claimed for 2023.[58] Taxes also can be saved by *shifting* income to lower-bracket taxpayers. Gifts of appreciated property to lower-bracket family members can reduce the related capital gain tax rate on a later sale by 15 percentage points (from 15 percent to 0 percent).[59] For certain high-income taxpayers, the reduction is 20 percentage points.

If income cannot be avoided, deferred, or shifted, the nature of the gain can be *converted*. By changing the classification of property, income taxes can be reduced. As a result, a taxpayer who transfers appreciated inventory to a controlled corporation has converted ordinary income property (the inventory) to a capital asset (stock in the corporation). When the taxpayer's stock is later sold, preferential capital gain rates apply.

The conversion approach also can work in tax planning for losses. Properly structured, a loan to a corporation that becomes worthless can be an ordinary loss rather than a capital loss. Likewise, via § 1244, an investor in qualified small business stock can convert what would be a capital loss into an ordinary loss.[60]

Effective tax planning requires that careful consideration be given to the *choice of entity* used for conducting a business. The corporate form results in double taxation but permits shareholder-employees to be covered by fringe benefit programs. Partnerships and S corporations allow a pass-through of losses and other tax attributes, but transferring ownership interests as gifts to family members may be difficult.[61]

Although the substance of a transaction rather than its form generally controls, this rule is not always the case with tax planning. *Preserving formalities*, with particularly

[55]See text Sections 5-6 and 5-8.

[56]See text Section 13-2c.

[57]See Chapters 18 and 21.

[58]See text Section 17-1h.

[59]See text Section 13-7b.

[60]See text Section 14-3a.

[61]See Chapters 21 and 22.

clear documentation, often is crucial to the result. Is an advance to a corporation a loan or a contribution to capital? The answer may depend on the existence of a note.

Along with preserving formalities, the taxpayer should keep records that support how a transaction is treated. Returning to the issue of loan versus contribution to capital, how is the advance listed on the books of the borrower? What do the corporate minutes say about the advance?

Finally, effective tax planning requires *consistency* on the part of taxpayers. A shareholder who treats a corporate distribution as a return of capital cannot later avoid a stock basis adjustment by contending that the distribution was really a dividend.

In summary, the key components of tax planning include the following:

- *Avoid* the recognition of income (usually by resorting to a nontaxable source or nontaxable event).
- *Defer* the recognition of income (or accelerate deductions).
- *Convert* the classification of income (or deductions) to a more advantageous form (e.g., ordinary income into capital gain).
- *Choose* the business *entity* with the desired tax attributes.
- Preserve *formalities* by generating and maintaining supporting documentation.
- Act in a manner *consistent* with the intended objective.

2-4c **Tax Avoidance and Tax Evasion**

A fine line exists between legal tax planning and illegal tax planning—tax avoidance versus tax evasion. **Tax avoidance** is merely tax minimization through legal techniques, which is the proper objective of all tax planning. Tax evasion, although also aimed at the elimination or reduction of taxes, connotes the use of subterfuge and fraud as a means to an end. Popular usage—probably because of the common goals involved—has so linked these two concepts that many individuals are no longer aware of the true distinctions between them. Consequently, some taxpayers may not take advantage of planning possibilities. The now classic words of Judge Learned Hand in *Commissioner v. Newman* reflect the true values the taxpayer should have:

> Over and over again courts have said that there is nothing sinister in so arranging one's affairs as to keep taxes as low as possible. Everybody does so, rich or poor; and all do right, for nobody owes any public duty to pay more than the law demands: taxes are enforced extractions, not voluntary contributions. To demand more in the name of morals is mere cant.[62]

As Denis Healy, a former British Chancellor, once said, "The difference between tax avoidance and tax evasion is the thickness of a prison wall."

The National Taxpayers Union estimates that the annual economic tax compliance costs to taxpayers were $339 billion in 2021, with over 6.5 billion hours spent on Federal tax compliance.[63] The Tax Foundation estimates that these compliance costs equate to about 1.4 percent of GDP.[64] For example, the Treasury Department's Final Regulations related to the qualified business income deduction are 248 pages long, and the IRS estimates that they could increase compliance costs by $1.3 billion over the next 10 years. Of course, additional time is spent filing state tax returns each year.

2-4d **Follow-Up Procedures**

Because tax planning usually involves a proposed (rather than a completed) transaction, being aware of if or when the law changes is critical to the tax planning process. A change in the tax law (legislative, administrative, or judicial) could alter the original conclusion. Additional research may be necessary to test the solution in light of current developments (refer to the broken lines at the right in Exhibit 2.8).

[62] *Comm. v. Newman*, 47–1 USTC ¶9175, 35 AFTR 857, 159 F.2d 848 (CA–2, 1947).

[63] Demian Brady, "Increasing Complexity Brings Back Bigger Compliance Burdens," National Taxpayers Union Foundation, April 18, 2022.

[64] Scott A. Hodge, "The Tax Compliance Costs of IRS Regulations," Tax Foundation, August 23, 2022.

2-4e **Tax Planning**

Throughout this text, each chapter concludes with observations on Tax Planning. These observations are not all-inclusive, but they are intended to illustrate some of the ways in which the material covered in the chapter can be effectively utilized to minimize taxes.

2-5 **Taxation on the CPA Examination**

LO.7

Be aware of taxation on the CPA examination.

The CPA exam continues to test in the familiar four sections—Auditing and Attestation (AUD), Business Environment and Concepts (BEC), Financial Accounting and Reporting (FAR), and Regulation (REG). However, the exam continues to evolve, placing less emphasis on remembering-and-understanding skills and greater focus on higher-level analysis and evaluation skills.

- Task-based simulations, a highly effective way to assess higher-order skills, are part of each section of the CPA exam. Four task-based simulations appear on the BEC section, and eight task-based simulations appear on the AUD, FAR, and REG sections.
- Total testing time is 16 hours (4 hours per section).
- Multiple-choice questions and task-based simulations each contribute about 50 percent toward the candidate's score in the AUD, FAR, and REG sections. In the BEC section, multiple-choice questions contribute about 50 percent of the scoring, with 35 percent coming from task-based simulations and 15 percent from written communication.
- Using Bloom's taxonomy, the CPA exam tests remembering and understanding, application, analysis, and evaluation. In prior years, the CPA exam only tested for the first two of these items.

2-5a **Preparation Blueprints**

To prepare for the CPA exam, candidates are able to use AICPA-developed Blueprints that replaced the Content Specification Outline (CSO) and Skill Specification Outline (SSO).[65]

The Blueprints provide candidates with more detail about what to expect on the exam. They contain about 570 representative tasks, which are aligned with the skills required of newly licensed CPAs, across the four exam sections. The Blueprints are designed to provide candidates with clearer information on the material the exam tests and show educators what knowledge and skills candidates need as newly licensed CPAs. In addition, the Blueprints provide candidates with sample tasks that align with both the content and skill level at which the content will be tested.

2-5b **Regulation Section**

Taxation continues to be tested within the REG section of the CPA exam. Testing within REG is administered in five blocks called testlets, which feature multiple-choice questions (MCQs) and task-based simulations (TBSs). Candidates receive at least one research question (research-oriented TBS) that requires the candidate to search the applicable authoritative literature and find an appropriate reference.

Each of the five topics in REG includes one or more representative tasks that are not necessarily questions on the exam. For example, the exam does not specifically ask

[65]Both the July 1, 2021 and January 1, 2024 Blueprints can be accessed at **aicpa.org/resources/download/learn-what-is-tested-on-the-cpa-exam**; the Practice Analysis Final Report that details the changes reflected in the January 1, 2024 Blueprints also is available on this website.

a candidate to "Calculate taxpayer penalties relating to Federal tax returns." However, identifying *situations* where a taxpayer penalty might apply would be appropriate. In addition, tasks are to be inclusive, not exclusive, of exam content. For example, the task "Calculate tax depreciation for a tangible business property..." could include the calculation of additional first-year (bonus) depreciation.

Task-based simulations are case studies that allow candidates to demonstrate their knowledge and skills by generating responses to questions rather than simply selecting an answer. They typically require candidates to use spreadsheets and/or to research authoritative literature provided in the CPA exam (e.g., Internal Revenue Code, Treasury Department Regulations, IRS publications, and Federal tax forms).

There are five content areas in the REG section of the CPA exam:

- Area 1: Ethics, professional responsibilities, and Federal tax procedures (weight: 10 to 20 percent).
- Area 2: Business law (weight: 10 to 20 percent).
- Area 3: Federal taxation of property transactions (weight: 12 to 22 percent).
- Area 4: Federal taxation of individuals (weight: 15 to 25 percent).
- Area 5: Federal taxation of entities (weight: 28 to 38 percent).

Area 1 covers ethics and responsibilities in tax practice, licensing and disciplinary systems, Federal tax procedures, and legal duties and responsibilities of a CPA.

Area 3 covers Federal taxation of property transactions and Federal estate and gift taxation.

Area 4 covers the Federal income taxation of individuals from both a tax preparation and tax planning perspective (e.g., income, exclusions, deductions, and retirement plans).

Area 5 covers the Federal income taxation of entities, including sole proprietorships, partnerships, limited liability companies, C corporations, S corporations, joint ventures, trusts, estates, and tax-exempt organizations from both a tax preparation and tax planning perspective.

Accounting methods and periods and tax elections are included in Areas 3, 4, and 5. Only Area 2 does not involve taxation.

Remembering-and-understanding skills are tested mainly in Areas 1 and 2. Application and analysis skills are tested primarily in Areas 3, 4, and 5. These three areas contain more of the day-to-day tasks that newly licensed CPAs are expected to perform. As a result, they are tested at the higher end of the skill level continuum. Overall, the REG section tests skills in the following way: remembering and learning (25 to 35 percent), application (35 to 45 percent), and analysis (25 to 35 percent). The REG section does not test any content at the evaluation skill level since newly licensed CPAs are not expected to demonstrate that level of skill in regard to the REG content.

Topical coverage in the REG section of the CPA exam is reviewed and updated regularly. For example, beginning in July 2021, the alternative minimum tax, estate taxation, and certain tax-exempt organization topics (obtaining and maintaining tax-exempt status) are no longer covered. In addition, net operating loss and capital loss limitations, unrelated business income of tax-exempt organizations, and bankruptcy and insolvency are being tested on a more simplified level.

The REG section has 76 multiple-choice questions and 8 task-based simulations (TBSs). The TBSs are used by the AICPA to assess the candidate's higher-order skills. In addition, TBSs on the CPA exam provide increased background material and data that require candidates to determine what information is or is not relevant to the question. The scoring weight of multiple-choice questions and TBSs is about 50 percent each on the REG section of the CPA exam.

Depending on the skill level being assessed, well-prepared candidates likely will spend 15 to 20 minutes for each TBS. Certain analysis and/or evaluation-level TBSs could take a well-prepared candidate up to 30 minutes to complete. Several illustrations of task-based simulations are shown in the examples that follow.

CPA Exam Simulation Examples

The *tax citation type* simulation requires the candidate to research the Internal Revenue Code and enter a Code Section and subsection.

For example, Amber Company is considering using the simplified dollar-value method of pricing its inventory for purposes of the LIFO method that is available to certain small businesses. What Code Section is the relevant authority in the Internal Revenue Code you should use to determine whether the taxpayer is eligible to use this method? To be successful, the candidate must find § 474.

Example 5

A *tax form completion* simulation requires the candidate to fill out a portion of a tax form. For example, Red Company is a limited liability company (LLC) for tax purposes. Complete the income section of Form 1065 for Red Company using the values found and calculated on previous tabs along with the following data:

Ordinary income from other partnerships	$ 5,200
Net gain (loss) from Form 4797	2,400
Management fee income	12,000

The candidate is provided with page 1 of Form 1065 on which to record the appropriate amounts.

Any field that requires an entry is a shaded rectangular cell. Some white rectangular cells will automatically calculate based on the entries in the shaded cells.

Candidates can learn more about the CPA examination at **aicpa.org/resources/toolkit/cpa-exam**. In addition to accessing the Uniform CPA Examination Blueprints, candidates will find tutorials related to the exam, have the ability to take sample exams, learn how the exam is graded, and discover the requirements needed to sit for the CPA exam in each licensing jurisdiction.

2-5c The 2024 CPA Exam

Beginning in January 2024, a new CPA licensure process and CPA Exam will be implemented (see **evolutionofcpa.org**). The transformation of the CPA Exam is being implemented in recognition of the rapidly changing skills and competencies practice requires today and will require in the future. It is a joint effort of the National Association of State Boards of Accountancy (NASBA) and the American Institute of Certified Public Accountants (AICPA).

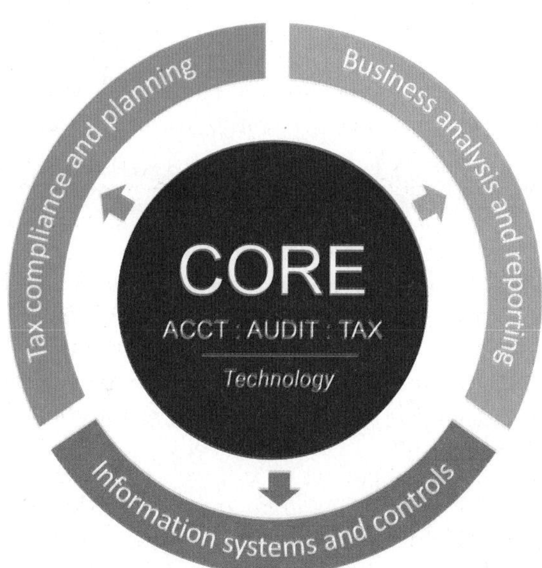

The new CPA licensure and CPA Exam model is a Core + Discipline model. Candidates must first pass three core exam sections in financial accounting and reporting (FAR), auditing and attestation (AUD), and taxation and regulation (REG).

Then, each candidate must choose a Discipline section in which to demonstrate greater skills and knowledge. The new Disciplines are:

- Business analysis and reporting (BAR).
- Information systems and controls (ISC).
- Tax compliance and planning (TCP).

Technology knowledge and skills will be tested in all sections as it pertains to each section. Regardless of a candidate's chosen discipline, this model leads to a full CPA license, with rights and privileges consistent with any other CPA. The Discipline section selected for testing does not mean the CPA is limited to that practice area.

Candidates who bridge from the current CPA exam to the 2024 CPA exam are covered by a transition policy. Under this policy, candidates who have credit for AUD, FAR, or REG on the current CPA Exam will not need to take the corresponding new core section of AUD, FAR, or REG on the 2024 CPA Exam. Candidates who have credit for BEC on the current CPA Exam will not need to take any of the three Discipline sections.

2-5d **Foundational Competencies Framework for Aspiring CPAs**

In November 2022, the AICPA released its Foundational Competencies Framework for Aspiring CPAs to help students acquire the knowledge and develop the skills and abilities that will lead to success in the accounting profession.[66] The framework categorizes these competencies into three areas:

- Technical competencies (risk assessment, analysis and decision-making, measurement and reporting, research, and technology, systems, and process management).
- Organizational competencies (strategic management, performance management, resource management, and environment, social, and governance management).
- Leadership competencies (ethical behavior, critical thinking, collaboration, self-management, and communication).

Developed by a working group of educators and practicing professionals, these competencies are relevant regardless of a student's career path (public, industry, government, or not-for-profit) or the specific services they will perform.

[66] **thiswaytocpa.com/collectedmedia/files/foundational-competencies-framework-pdf.pdf**.

Key Terms

Acquiescence, 2-16
Circuit Court of Appeals, 2-12
Citator, 2-25
Court of original jurisdiction, 2-10
Determination letters, 2-9
Final Regulations, 2-7
Interpretive Regulations, 2-24
Legislative Regulations, 2-24
Letter rulings, 2-8
Nonacquiescence, 2-16
Notices, 2-7
Precedents, 2-13
Procedural Regulations, 2-24
Proposed Regulations, 2-7
Revenue Procedures, 2-7
Revenue Rulings, 2-7
Small Cases Division, 2-10
Tax avoidance, 2-30
Tax research, 2-20
Technical Advice Memoranda (TAMs), 2-9
Temporary Regulations, 2-7
U.S. Court of Federal Claims, 2-10
U.S. District Court, 2-10
U.S. Supreme Court, 2-13
U.S. Tax Court, 2-10
Writ of Certiorari, 2-14

Discussion Questions

Note: Relevant documents for the end-of-chapter materials can be found by using the Thomson Reuters Checkpoint™ online tax research database (which accompanies this textbook), Tax Notes (taxnotes.com/research/federal), or the IRS website (including irs.gov/irb).

1. **LO.1** A large part of tax research consists of determining what?

2. **LO.1** Why do taxpayers often have more than one alternative for structuring a business transaction?

3. **LO.1** Where does Federal tax legislation generally originate?

4. **LO.2, 5** Sonja Bishop operates a small international firm named Tile, Inc. A new treaty between the United States and Spain conflicts with a Section of the Internal Revenue Code. Sonja asks you for advice. If she follows the treaty position, does she need to disclose this on her tax return? If she is required to disclose, are there any penalties for failure to disclose? Prepare a letter in which you respond to Sonja. Tile's address is 100 International Drive, Tampa, FL 33620. Communications

5. **LO.1, 2** Interpret this Regulation citation: Reg. § 1.163–10(a)(2).

6. **LO.1** A client who is a small independent oil and gas producer asks you to determine whether the business qualifies for percentage depletion. The client is worried that it may be classified as a refiner. Look up and read Code § 613A(d)(4), and prepare a response to your client. Critical Thinking

7. **LO.1, 4** Rank the following items from the lowest to highest authority in the Federal tax law system:
   a. Interpretive Regulation.
   b. Legislative Regulation.
   c. Letter ruling.
   d. Revenue Ruling.
   e. Internal Revenue Code.
   f. Proposed Regulation.

8. **LO.1** Interpret each of the following citations:
   a. Temp.Reg. § 1.956–2T.
   b. Rev.Rul. 2012–15, 2012–23 I.R.B. 975.
   c. Ltr.Rul. 200204051.

9. **LO.1, 5** Sally Andrews calls you on the phone. She says that she has found a 2015 letter ruling that agrees with a position she wants to take on her tax return. She asks you about the precedential value of a letter ruling. Draft a memo for the tax files, outlining what you told Sally. Communications

10. **LO.1** Sri is considering writing the IRS to find out whether a possible stock redemption would be a qualified stock redemption. Outline some relevant tax issues Sri faces in determining whether to request a letter ruling. Critical Thinking

11. **LO.1** Where may private letter rulings be found?

12. **LO.1** What are the differences between Technical Advice Memoranda (TAMs) and Technical Expedited Advice Memoranda (TEAMs)?

13. **LO.1** Sanjay receives a settlement letter from the IRS after his discussion with an IRS appeals officer. He is not satisfied with the $101,000 settlement offer. Identify the relevant issues facing Sanjay if he chooses to contest the settlement offer. Critical Thinking

14. **LO.1** List an advantage and a disadvantage of using the U.S. Court of Federal Claims as the trial court for Federal tax litigation.

Communications
Planning

15. **LO.1, 5** Edmund Falls is considering litigating a tax deficiency of approximately $229,030 in the court system. He asks you to provide him with a short description of his alternatives, indicating the advantages and disadvantages of each. Prepare your response to Edmund in the form of a letter. His address is 200 Mesa Drive, Tucson, AZ 85714.

16. **LO.1** List an advantage and a disadvantage of using the U.S. Tax Court as the trial court for Federal tax litigation.

17. **LO.1** A taxpayer lives in Michigan. In a controversy with the IRS, the taxpayer loses at the trial court level. Describe the appeal procedure under the following different assumptions:
    a. The trial court was the Small Cases Division of the U.S. Tax Court.
    b. The trial court was the U.S. Tax Court.
    c. The trial court was a U.S. District Court.
    d. The trial court was the U.S. Court of Federal Claims.

18. **LO.1** What is meant by the term *petitioner*?

19. **LO.1** An appellate court will often become involved in fact-finding determination. Discuss the validity of this statement.

20. **LO.1** For the U.S. Tax Court, U.S. District Court, and U.S. Court of Federal Claims, indicate the following:
    a. Number of regular judges per court.
    b. Availability of a jury trial.
    c. Whether the deficiency must be paid before the trial.

21. **LO.1** A taxpayer living in the following states would appeal a decision of the U.S. District Court to which Court of Appeals?
    a. Wyoming.
    b. Nebraska.
    c. Idaho.
    d. Louisiana.
    e. Illinois.

22. **LO.1** What precedents must each of these courts follow?
    a. U.S. Tax Court.
    b. U.S. Court of Federal Claims.
    c. U.S. District Court.

23. **LO.1** What determines the appropriate Circuit Court of Appeals for a particular taxpayer?

24. **LO.1, 2, 4** In assessing the validity of a prior court decision, discuss the significance of the following on the taxpayer's issue:
    a. The decision was rendered by the U.S. District Court of Wyoming. Taxpayer lives in Wyoming.
    b. The decision was rendered by the U.S. Court of Federal Claims. Taxpayer lives in Wyoming.
    c. The decision was rendered by the Second Circuit Court of Appeals. Taxpayer lives in California.
    d. The decision was rendered by the U.S. Supreme Court.
    e. The decision was rendered by the U.S. Tax Court. The IRS has acquiesced in the result.
    f. Same as part (e), except that the IRS has issued a nonacquiescence as to the result.

25. **LO.2** In the citation *Schuster's Express, Inc.*, 66 T.C. 588 (1976), *aff'd* 562 F.2d 39 (CA–2, 1977), *nonacq.*, to what do the 66, 39, and *nonacq.* refer?

26. **LO.1** Is there an automatic right to appeal to the U.S. Supreme Court? If so, what is the process?

27. **LO.2** Referring to the citation only, determine which court issued these decisions.
    a. 716 F.2d 693 (CA–9, 1983).
    b. 20 T.C. 734 (1953).
    c. 348 U.S. 426 (1955).
    d. 3 B.T.A. 1042 (1926).
    e. T.C.Memo. 1957–169.
    f. 50 AFTR2d 92–6000 (Ct. Cl., 1992).
    g. Ltr.Rul. 9046036.
    h. 111 F.Supp.2d 1294 (S.D.N.Y., 2000).
    i. 98–50, 1998–1 C.B. 10.

28. **LO.2** Interpret each of the following citations:
    a. 14 T.C. 74 (1950).
    b. 592 F.2d 1251 (CA–5, 1979).
    c. 95–1 USTC ¶50,104 (CA–6, 1995).
    d. 75 AFTR2d 95–110 (CA–6, 1995).
    e. 223 F.Supp. 663 (W.D. Tex., 1963).
    f. 491 F.3d 53 (CA–1, 2007).
    g. 775 F.Supp.2d 765 (D.Ct. V.I., 2011).

29. **LO.2** Give the Commerce Clearing House citation for the following courts:
    a. Small Cases Division of the Tax Court.
    b. U.S. District Court.
    c. U.S. Supreme Court.
    d. U.S. Court of Federal Claims.
    e. Tax Court Memorandum decision.

30. **LO.2** Where can you locate a published decision of the U.S. Court of Federal Claims?

31. **LO.1, 2** Which of the following items probably can be found in the *Internal Revenue Bulletin*?
    a. Action on Decision.
    b. Small Cases Division of the U.S. Tax Court decision.
    c. Letter ruling.
    d. Revenue Procedure.
    e. Finalized Regulation.
    f. U.S. Court of Federal Claims decision.
    g. Acquiescences to Tax Court decisions.
    h. U.S. Circuit Court of Appeals decision.

32. **LO.3** For her tax class, Yvonne must prepare a research paper discussing the tax aspects of qualified stock options. Explain to Yvonne how she can research this topic using various tax research resources. Critical Thinking

33. **LO.4** Where can a researcher find the current Internal Revenue Code of 1986?

Critical Thinking
Decision Making

34. LO.2, 3, 4 You inherit a tax problem that was researched five months ago. You believe the answer is correct, but you are unfamiliar with the general area. How would you find recent articles dealing with the subject area? How do you evaluate the reliability of the authority cited in the research report? How do you determine the latest developments pertaining to the research problem?

35. LO.6 What is the primary purpose of effective tax planning? Explain.

36. LO.7 Describe the task-based simulations that are part of the CPA exam.

Problems

37. LO.1 In which Subchapter of the Internal Revenue Code would one find information about corporate distributions?
   a. Subchapter S.
   b. Subchapter C.
   c. Subchapter P.
   d. Subchapter K.
   e. Subchapter M.

38. LO.1, 2 Identify the general contents of each of the following Internal Revenue Code sections:
   a. § 1.
   b. § 11.
   c. § 61.
   d. § 62.
   e. § 162.
   f. § 212.
   g. § 262.

39. LO.1, 2 Log on to **waysandmeans.house.gov** (the website for the House Ways and Means Committee of the U.S. House of Representatives) and answer the following questions:
   a. Who is the Chair of the committee? What district does he or she represent?
   b. What is the total number of members on the committee? How many are representatives of each party (Democratic and Republican)?
   c. Locate and summarize the history of the committee.
   d. The Ways and Means Committee has several subcommittees. Identify three of these subcommittees.

40. LO.1 To locate an IRS Revenue Procedure that was issued during the past month, which source would you consult?
   a. *Federal Register*.
   b. *Internal Revenue Bulletin*.
   c. Internal Revenue Code.
   d. Some other source.

41. LO.1 Which of the following items can be found in the *Federal Register*?
   a. Letter Ruling.
   b. Action on Decision.
   c. Revenue Procedure.
   d. Temporary Regulation.
   e. Technical Advice Memorandum.

42. LO.1, 4 Rank the items below from most reliable to least reliable. Decision Making
   a. Letter Ruling.
   b. Legislative Regulation.
   c. Code Section.
   d. Revenue Ruling.
   e. Proposed Regulation.
   f. Interpretive Regulation.
   g. Recent Temporary Regulation.

43. LO.1, 2 Locate each of the following revenue rulings. What is the subject of each ruling?
   a. Rev.Rul. 2021–1.
   b. Rev.Rul. 2014–17.
   c. Rev.Rul. 77–323.
   d. Rev.Rul. 2005–47.

44. LO.1, 2 Locate each of the following revenue procedures. What is the subject of each procedure?
   a. Rev.Proc. 2015–48.
   b. Rev.Proc. 2021–31.
   c. Rev.Proc. 2017–60.
   d. Rev.Proc. 86–14.

45. LO.1, 2 Locate, read, and summarize Announcement 2020-1.

46. LO.1, 2 Locate, read, and summarize PLR 201450001.

47. LO.1, 2 Locate the pronouncement at 2019–14 I.R.B. 931.
   a. Identify the pronouncement.
   b. What issue is addressed by the pronouncement?
   c. What is the holding of the pronouncement?

48. LO.1 Using the legend provided, classify each of the following statements (more than one answer per statement may be appropriate):

Legend
D = Applies to the District Court
T = Applies to the Tax Court
C = Applies to the Court of Federal Claims
A = Applies to the Circuit Court of Appeals
U = Applies to the Supreme Court
N = Applies to none of the above

   a. Decides only Federal tax matters.
   b. Decisions are reported in the F.3d Series.
   c. Decisions are reported in the USTCs.
   d. Decisions are reported in the AFTRs.
   e. Appeal is by *Writ of Certiorari.*
   f. Court meets most often in Washington, D.C.
   g. Offers the choice of a jury trial.
   h. Is a trial court.
   i. Is an appellate court.

j. Allows appeal to the Court of Appeals for the Federal Circuit and bypasses the taxpayer's own Circuit Court of Appeals.

k. Has a Small Cases Division.

l. Is the only trial court where the taxpayer does not have to first pay the tax assessed by the IRS.

49. **LO.1** What is the difference between a Regular decision, a Memorandum decision, and a Summary Opinion of the U.S. Tax Court?

Critical Thinking

50. **LO.1, 2** Sonja and Evan are homeowners with an adjustable rate mortgage. In 2021, they claimed an itemized deduction for interest paid. In 2023, due to an error noted by their mortgage servicer, they receive a refund of a portion of the interest they paid in 2021. Are Sonja and Evan required to include the refund as gross income? Locate and read Announcement 92–172 and formulate a response.

Critical Thinking

51. **LO.1, 2** Leland and Amy are buying their first home. They are considering paying "points" to reduce the interest rate on a Veteran Affairs (VA) or Federal Housing Administration (FHA) loan. If they do this, they would like to know whether this expense can be deducted in the year a house is purchased. Locate Rev. Proc. 92–12 and Rev. Proc. 94–27 and formulate a response.

Critical Thinking
Decision Making

52. **LO.2** A client contacts you and asks if an exchange of different cryptocurrencies qualifies for like-kind exchange treatment (e.g., an exchange of bitcoin for ethereum). In addition, she mines cryptocurrency and would like to know if her activities result in self-employment income. Research these questions in preparation for a meeting with your client.

Critical Thinking

53. **LO.2** A client contacts you and indicates that she would like to obtain a private letter ruling from the IRS. You are not familiar with the process. How do you determine what is required to obtain a private letter ruling?

Critical Thinking
Decision Making

54. **LO.2** Alejandra invites Zach, a business client, to a college football game. Alejandra purchases both tickets and buys Zach's lunch in the alumni tent before the game. The lunch is purchased separately from the tickets. Substantive business discussions occur during lunch and at various times during the football game. Consult § 274, Reg. §§ 1.274–12 and 1.274–11(b)(1), and Notice 2018–76 to determine which of these expenses are deductible (if any).

55. **LO.2, 4** Using the legend provided, classify each of the following tax sources:

Legend
P = Primary tax source
S = Secondary tax source
B = Both
N = Neither

a. Sixteenth Amendment to the U.S. Constitution.

b. Tax treaty between the United States and India.

c. Revenue Procedure.

d. An IRS publication.

e. U.S. District Court decision.

f. *Yale Law Journal* article.

g. Temporary Regulations (issued 2019).

h. U.S. Tax Court Memorandum decision.
i. Small Cases Division of the U.S. Tax Court decision.
j. House Ways and Means Committee report.
k. Notice.

56. **LO.1, 2** Using the legend provided, classify each of the following citations as to publisher:

Legend
RIA = Research Institute of America
CCH = Commerce Clearing House
W = West
U.S. = U.S. Government
O = Others

a. 83–2 USTC ¶9600.
b. 52 AFTR 2d 83–5954.
c. 67 T.C. 293 (1976).
d. 39 TCM 32 (1979).
e. 416 U.S. 938.
f. RIA T.C. Memo. ¶80,582.
g. 89 S.Ct. 501.
h. 40 Fed.Cl. 172.
i. 415 F.2d 488.
j. 592 F.Supp. 18.
k. 77–37, 1977–2 C.B. 568.
l. S. Rep. No. 1622, 83rd Cong., 2d Sess. 42 (1954).

57. **LO.1, 2** Locate the court case *Commissioner v. Glenshaw Glass Co.*, 348 U.S. 486. Read the case and answer the following questions: Critical Thinking
a. Which court heard this case?
b. In what year was the case decided?
c. What was the issue (or issues) involved in the case? What was the court's ruling?

58. **LO.1, 2** Locate the court case *David H. Hoffman, et ux. v. Commissioner*, T.C. Memo. 2016–69. Use the headnotes to the case to answer the following questions: Critical Thinking
a. What issue (or issues) did the court address?
b. What was the court's ruling?

59. **LO.1, 2** Locate the court decision with the following citation: 144 T.C. 279. Critical Thinking
a. What is the name of the case?
b. Which court heard this case?
c. In what year was the case decided?
d. What was the issue (or issues) involved in the case? What was the court's ruling?

60. **LO.6** Using the legend provided, classify each of the following statements:

Legend
A = Tax avoidance
E = Tax evasion
N = Neither

a. Sue writes a $707 check for a charitable contribution on December 26, 2023, but does not mail the check to the charitable organization until January 10, 2024. She takes a deduction in 2023.

b. Sam decides not to report interest income from a bank because the amount is only $19.75.

c. Harry pays property taxes on his home in December 2023 rather than waiting until February 2024.

d. Variet switches her investments from taxable corporate bonds to tax-exempt municipal bonds.

e. Mel encourages his mother to save most of her Social Security benefits so that he will be able to claim her as a dependent.

Research Problems

Note: Solutions to the Research Problems can be prepared by using the Thomson Reuters Checkpoint™ online tax research database, which accompanies this textbook. Solutions can also be prepared by using research materials found in a typical tax library.

Research Problem 1. Determine the missing data in these court decisions and rulings.

a. *Higgens v. Comm.*, 312 U.S. ______ (1941).
b. *Talen v. U.S.*, 355 F.Supp.2d 22 (D.Ct. D.C., ______).
c. Rev.Rul. 2008–18, 2008–13 I.R.B. ______.
d. *Pahl v. Comm.*, 150 F.3d 1124 (CA–9, ______).
e. *Veterinary Surgical Consultants PC*, 117 T.C. ______ (2001).
f. *Yeagle Drywall Co.*, T.C.Memo. 2001______.

Research Problem 2. Can a Tax Court Small Case Decision be treated as a precedent for other cases? Explain.

Partial list of research aids:
IRC § 7463(b).
Maria Antionette Walton Mitchell, T.C. Summ. 2004–160.

Decision Making **Research Problem 3.** When Oprah gave away new cars to her TV audience, was the value of the cars taxable? Several years ago, World Furniture Mall in Plano, Illinois, gave away $275,000 of furniture because the Chicago Bears shut out the Green Bay Packers in the team's football season opener at Lambeau Field in Green Bay. Was the free furniture in the form of a discount or rebate taxable, or should the furniture company have handed the customers a Form 1099–MISC?

Decision Making **Research Problem 4.** You are interviewing a client before preparing his tax return. He indicates that he did not list as income $96,000 received as a recovery for false imprisonment. What should you do with respect to this significant recovery?

Partial list of research aids:
CCA 200809001.
Daniel and Brenda Stadnyk, T.C.Memo. 2008–289.
Rev.Rul. 2007–14.
§ 104.

Use internet tax resources to address the following questions. Look for reliable websites and blogs of the IRS and other government agencies, media outlets, businesses, tax professionals, academics, think tanks, and political outlets.

Research Problem 5. (1) Use an internet search engine (e.g., Google) to find Internal Revenue Code § 61(a). What is defined in this Code Section? Is the definition broad or narrow? (2) Go to the U.S. Tax Court website (**ustaxcourt.gov**), and find the U.S Tax Court case in which Mark Spitz, the former Olympic gold medalist, is the petitioner. Answer the following questions about the case:

a. What tax years are at issue in the case?
b. In what year was the case decided?
c. Did the court decide in favor of Mr. Spitz or the IRS?
d. Were any penalties imposed on Mr. Spitz? Why or why not?

Research Problem 6. Go to the U.S. Tax Court website (**ustaxcourt.gov**). Communications

a. What different types of cases can be found on the site?
b. What is a Summary Opinion? Find one (and record its citation).
c. What is a Memorandum Opinion? Find one (and record its citation).
d. Find the "Rules of Practice and Procedure." Summarize one (and its citation).
e. Communicate your findings in an e-mail to your instructor. Is the website reader-friendly? If not, e-mail the Tax Court (and copy your instructor).

Research Problem 7. Determine if your campus has any of the following tax research services available for student use. If a service is available, describe how you would gain access to that service. Communications

- Thomson Reuters *Checkpoint*.
- Thomson Reuters *Westlaw* or *WestlawNext*.
- CCH *IntelliConnect* or CCH *AnswerConnect*.
- LexisNexis *Tax Center*.
- Bloomberg BNA *Tax Management Portfolios*.

Summarize your findings in a memorandum and e-mail it to your instructor.

Chapter 3

Tax Formula and Tax Determination; An Overview of Property Transactions

Learning Objectives: *After completing Chapter 3, you should be able to:*

- **LO.1** Identify and apply the components of the Federal income tax formula.
- **LO.2** Explain the standard deduction and evaluate its choice in arriving at taxable income.
- **LO.3** Describe the current status of the exemption deduction.
- **LO.4** Explain the rules for determining whether someone is a dependent.
- **LO.5** Choose the proper filing status and identify the related filing requirements.
- **LO.6** Demonstrate the proper procedures for determining the tax liability.
- **LO.7** Identify and report the unearned income of dependent children (the kiddie tax).
- **LO.8** Explain the fundamentals of property transactions.
- **LO.9** Evaluate tax planning opportunities associated with the individual tax formula.

Chapter Outline

The Big Picture

A Divided Household

Aleha maintains a household in which she lives with her unemployed husband (Trevor), stepdaughter (Paige), and a family friend (Terrah). She provides more than half of the support for both Paige and Terrah. Terrah was fatally injured in an automobile accident in February, and Aleha paid for her hospitalization and funeral expenses. Paige, an accomplished gymnast, graduated from high school last year. Paige has a part-time job but spends most of her time training and looking for an athletic scholarship to the "right" college. In March, Trevor left for parts unknown and has not been seen or heard from since. Aleha was more surprised than distressed over Trevor's unexpected departure. One reaction, however, was to sell her wedding rings to a cousin who was getting married. The rings cost $11,800 and were sold for their approximate value of $9,000.

Based on these facts, what are Aleha's income tax concerns for the current year?

Read the chapter and formulate your response.

Framework 1040 **Tax Formula for Individuals**

This chapter covers the boldfaced portions of the Tax Formula for Individuals that is introduced in Concept Summary 3.1 on p. 3-3. Below those portions are the sections of Form 1040 where the results are reported.

Income *(broadly defined)*	$ xx,xxx
Less: Exclusions	(x,xxx)
Gross income	**$xx,xxx**
Less: Deductions *for* adjusted gross income	**(x,xxx)**
Adjusted gross income	$ xx,xxx

FORM 1040 (p. 1)

Filing Status Check only one box. ☐ Single ☐ Married filing jointly ☐ Married filing separately (MFS) ☐ Head of household (HOH) ☐ Qualifying surviving spouse (QSS)

If you checked the MFS box, enter the name of your spouse. If you checked the HOH or QSS box, enter the child's name if the qualifying person is a child but not your dependent:

FORM 1040 (p. 1)

Standard Deduction **Someone can claim:** ☐ You as a dependent ☐ Your spouse as a dependent
☐ Spouse itemizes on a separate return or you were a dual-status alien

Age/Blindness **You:** ☐ Were born before January 2, 1958 ☐ Are blind **Spouse:** ☐ Was born before January 2, 1958 ☐ Is blind

Dependents (see instructions):

If more than four dependents, see instructions and check here . . ☐

(1) First name	Last name	(2) Social security number	(3) Relationship to you	(4) Check the box if qualifies for (see instructions): Child tax credit	Credit for other dependents
				☐	☐
				☐	☐
				☐	☐
				☐	☐

FORM 1040 (p. 1)

12 Standard deduction or itemized deductions (from Schedule A) . . . .

13 Qualified business income deduction from Form 8995 or Form 8995-A.** . . . . . .

Personal and dependency exemptions*	(x,xxx)
Taxable income	**$ xx,xxx**
Tax on taxable income *(see Tax Tables or Tax Rate Schedules)*	**$ x,xxx**
Less: Tax credits *(including income taxes withheld and prepaid)*	(xxx)
Tax due (or refund)	$ xxx

* Exemption deductions are not allowed from 2018 through 2025.
** Only applies from 2018 through 2025.

The tax formula provides a framework for applying the Federal income tax to individuals. It is an integral part of our U.S. tax system (i.e., local, state, and Federal). Chapter 3 presents a summary of its components while providing a detailed discussion of several of its key components—the standard deduction, determination of whether someone is a dependent, and tax determination. In addition, the tax formula establishes the framework for much of the text; its relationship to the chapters that follow are reflected in Concept Summary 3.1.

Chapter 3 also provides an overview of property transactions. When property is sold, a gain or loss results, and this can affect the determination of taxable income. Chapters 13 and 14 discuss property transactions in detail. But understanding the basic rules will help in applying other materials in the text. In addition, we discuss two concepts unique to the income tax: the difference between realized and recognized gain or loss and the classification of gain or loss (as ordinary or capital).

LO.1

Identify and apply the components of the Federal income tax formula.

3-1 Tax Formula

We begin by reviewing the various components of the income tax formula. Then we explore several components in more depth: the standard deduction, exemptions, filing status, and tax determination. The structure of the individual income tax return parallels the tax formula. The 2022 Form 1040 is included on pages 3-9 and 3-10; three schedules to Form 1040 (Schedules 1, 2, and 3) appear on pages 3-11 through 3-16. Review these as you read about the tax formula.

Concept Summary 3.1

Tax Formula for Individuals (Components Integrated into the Text)

		Text Discussion
Income (broadly defined)	$xx,xxx	Chs. 3, 4
Less: **Exclusions**	(x,xxx)	Ch. 5
Gross income	$xx,xxx	Chs. 4, 13, 14
Less: **Deductions *for*** adjusted gross income	(x,xxx)	Chs. 6–9, 11, 13, 14
Adjusted gross income	$xx,xxx	
Less: The greater of—		
Total **itemized deductions** *or* **standard deduction**	(x,xxx)	Chs. 6, 9, 10, 11 Ch. 3
Less: **Personal** and **dependency exemptions***	(x,xxx)	Ch. 3
Less: **Deduction for qualified business income****	(x,xxx)	Chs. 6, 15
Taxable income	$xx,xxx	Chs. 3, 12
Tax on taxable income	$ x,xxx	Chs. 3, 12
Less: **Taxes withheld/Tax credits**	(xxx)	Ch. 12
Tax due (or refund)	$ xxx	Chs. 3, 12

*Exemption deductions are not allowed from 2018 through 2025.
**Only applies from 2018 through 2025.

3-1a **Components of the Tax Formula**

Income (Broadly Defined)

In the tax formula, *income* is broadly defined and includes all of the taxpayer's income, both taxable and nontaxable. In general, the courts have defined *income* as "any increase in wealth."[1] As a result, it does not include a return of capital or borrowed funds.

Dan decides to quit renting and buy a new house. The owner of the apartment building returns to Dan the $600 damage deposit he previously made. To make a down payment on the house, Dan sells stock for $50,000 (original cost of $28,000) and borrows $200,000 from a bank.

Only the $22,000 gain from the sale of the stock is income to Dan. The $600 damage deposit and the $28,000 cost of the stock are a return of capital. The $200,000 bank loan is not income since Dan has an obligation to repay that amount (and it does not increase his wealth).

Exclusions

For various reasons, Congress has chosen to exclude certain types of income from the income tax base. A partial list of these exclusions is shown in Exhibit 3.1. Income exclusions are covered in Chapter 5.

Gross Income

The Internal Revenue Code defines gross income broadly as "except as otherwise provided ..., all income from whatever source derived."[2] The "except as otherwise provided" phrase refers to exclusions. A partial list of items included in gross income

[1] *Comm. v. Glenshaw Glass Co.*, 55–1 USTC ¶9308, 47 AFTR 162, 75 S.Ct. 473.   [2] § 61(a).

Exhibit 3.1 Partial List of Exclusions from Gross Income

Accident insurance proceeds	Life insurance paid at death
Alimony (divorces after 2018)	Meals and lodging (if furnished for employer's convenience)
Annuities (cost element)	Military allowances
Bequests	Minister's dwelling rental value allowance
Child support payments	Railroad retirement benefits (to a limited extent)
Cost-of-living allowance (for military)	Scholarship grants (to a limited extent)
Damages for personal injury or sickness	Social Security benefits (to a limited extent)
Gifts received	Veterans' benefits
Group term life insurance, premium paid by employer (for coverage up to $50,000)	Welfare payments
Inheritances	Workers' compensation benefits
Interest from state and local (i.e., municipal) bonds	

Example 2

Beth received the following amounts during the year:

Salary	$30,000
Interest on savings account	900
Gift from her aunt	10,000
Prize won in state lottery	1,000
Alimony from ex-spouse (divorce finalized in 2015)	12,000
Child support from ex-spouse	6,000
Damages for injury in auto accident	25,000
Ten $50 bills in an unmarked envelope found in an airport lounge (airport authorities could not locate anyone who claimed ownership)	500
Federal income tax refund for last year's tax overpayment	120
Increase in the value of stock held for investment	5,000

Review Exhibits 3.1 and 3.2 to determine the amount Beth must include in the computation of taxable income and the amount she may exclude.[3]

appears in Exhibit 3.2. Gross income does not include *unrealized* gains (e.g., stock that has appreciated in value but has not been sold). Gross income is discussed in Chapters 4 and 5.

Deductions *for* Adjusted Gross Income

Individual taxpayers have two categories of deductions: (1) deductions *for* adjusted gross income (deductions from gross income to arrive at adjusted gross income) and (2) deductions *from* adjusted gross income.

Deductions *for* adjusted gross income (AGI) are sometimes called *above-the-line* deductions because on the tax return, they are taken before the "line" designating AGI. Deductions *for* AGI include, but are not limited to, the following:[4]

- Trade or business expenses.
- Part of the self-employment tax.
- Contributions to traditional Individual Retirement Accounts (IRAs) and other retirement plans.

[3] Beth must include $44,400 in computing taxable income ($30,000 salary + $900 interest + $1,000 lottery prize + $12,000 alimony + $500 found property). She can exclude $41,000 ($10,000 gift from aunt + $6,000 child support + $25,000 damages). The $120 Federal income tax refund is excluded because it represents an adjustment (i.e., overpayment) of a nondeductible expenditure made in the previous year. The unrealized gain on the stock held for investment also is not included in gross income.

[4] § 62(a); many of these deductions are limited in some way. And some of these deductions appear on supporting schedules or forms. For example, the business expenses of a sole proprietor appear on Schedule C (Form 1040).

Exhibit 3.2 Partial List of Gross Income Items

- Alimony (divorces before 2019)
- Annuities (income element)
- Awards
- Back pay
- Bargain purchase from employer
- Bonuses
- Breach of contract damages
- Business income
- Clergy fees
- Commissions
- Compensation for services
- Death benefits
- Debts forgiven
- Director's fees
- Dividends
- Embezzled funds
- Employee awards (in certain cases)
- Employee benefits (except certain fringe benefits)
- Estate and trust income
- Farm income
- Fees
- Gains from illegal activities
- Gains from sale of property
- Gambling winnings
- Group term life insurance, premium paid by employer (for coverage over $50,000)
- Hobby income
- Interest
- Jury duty fees
- Living quarters, meals (unless furnished for employer's convenience)
- Mileage allowance (in certain cases)
- Military pay (unless combat pay)
- Notary fees
- Partnership income
- Pension distributions
- Prizes
- Professional fees
- Punitive damages
- Rents
- Rewards
- Royalties
- Salaries
- Severance pay
- Strike and lockout benefits
- Supplemental unemployment benefits
- Tips and gratuities
- Travel allowance (in certain cases)
- Treasure trove (found property)
- Wages

- Contributions to Health Savings Accounts (HSAs).
- Interest on student loans.
- Excess capital losses.
- Certain alimony payments.

The following example illustrates how deductions *for* AGI affect the computation of AGI.

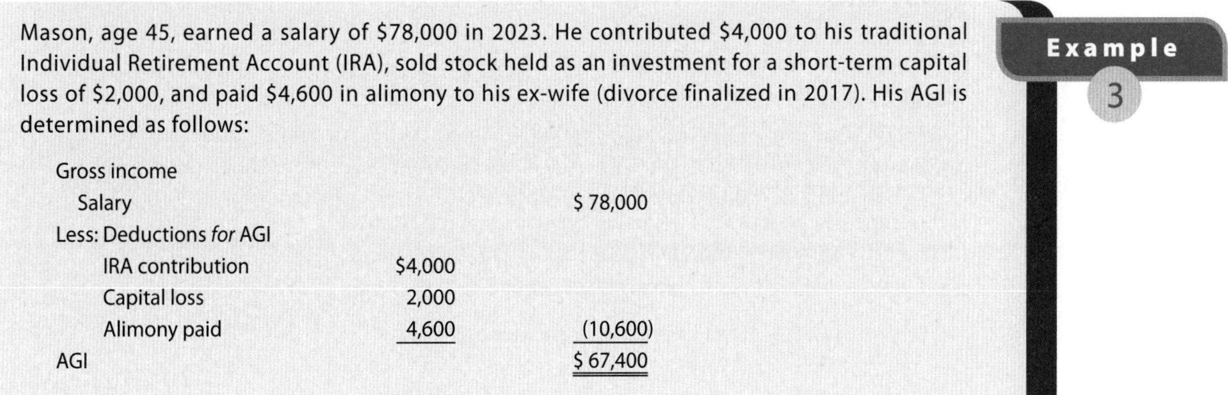

Example 3

Mason, age 45, earned a salary of $78,000 in 2023. He contributed $4,000 to his traditional Individual Retirement Account (IRA), sold stock held as an investment for a short-term capital loss of $2,000, and paid $4,600 in alimony to his ex-wife (divorce finalized in 2017). His AGI is determined as follows:

Gross income		
Salary		$ 78,000
Less: Deductions *for* AGI		
IRA contribution	$4,000	
Capital loss	2,000	
Alimony paid	4,600	(10,600)
AGI		$ 67,400

The principal deductions *for* AGI are discussed in Chapters 6, 7, 8, 9, 11, 13, and 14.

Deductions *from* Adjusted Gross Income

As a general rule, personal expenses are not allowed as deductions in computing taxable income. However, Congress allows some personal expenses as deductions *from* AGI (commonly referred to as **itemized deductions**); see Exhibit 3.3 for a partial list of these deductions.

AGI is an important calculation since it is used to limit certain itemized deductions (e.g., medical expenses, charitable contributions, and casualty losses). For example, medical expenses are deductible only to the extent they exceed 7.5 percent of AGI, and charitable contribution deductions may not exceed 50 percent of AGI (60 percent for cash contributions to public charities). These limitations can be described as a *floor* under the medical expense deduction and a *ceiling* on the charitable contribution deduction.

Assume the same facts as in Example 3, and assume that Mason had medical expenses of $8,000. Medical expenses are included in itemized deductions to the extent they exceed 7.5% of AGI. In computing his itemized deductions, Mason includes medical expenses of $2,945 [$8,000 medical expenses − $5,055 (7.5% × $67,400 AGI)].

In addition, taxpayers are allowed itemized deductions for expenses related to (1) the production or collection of income and (2) the management of property held for the production of income.[5] These expenses, sometimes referred to as *nonbusiness expenses*, are expenses incurred in connection with an income-producing activity that does *not* qualify as a trade or business. The deductions for many of these expenses are suspended from 2018 through 2025.

Leo is the owner and operator of a small package delivery service. All allowable expenses that he incurs in connection with the delivery business are deductions *for* AGI. In addition, Leo has an extensive portfolio of stocks and bonds.

Leo's investment activity is not treated as a trade or business. Any allowable expenses that Leo incurs in connection with these investments (e.g., subscriptions to investment publications, financial planning fees, safety deposit box rental) are itemized deductions. These are "miscellaneous itemized deductions" and are not deductible from 2018 through 2025.

Itemized deductions are discussed in Chapters 9 and 10.

Exhibit 3.3 Partial List of Itemized Deductions

Medical expenses in excess of 7.5% of AGI
State and local income or sales taxes*
Real estate taxes*
Personal property taxes*
Interest on home mortgage (subject to certain limitations)
Investment interest (up to the amount of net investment income)
Charitable contributions (within specified percentage limitations)
Casualty and theft losses in excess of 10% of AGI

*Only $10,000 of combined state and local taxes is deductible.

[5] § 212.

Nondeductible Expenses

Many expenses are not deductible and, therefore, provide no tax benefit. Here are some examples:

- Personal living expenses.
- Employee business expenses (unless reimbursed by employer).*
- Most investment expenses (e.g., investment counsel fees, safe deposit box rental, and publications).*
- Tax return preparation fees.*
- Losses on the sale of personal use property (e.g., the furniture you own).
- Hobby expenses.*
- Life insurance premiums.
- Gambling losses (in excess of gains).
- Child support payments.
- Fines and penalties.
- Political contributions.
- Funeral expenses.
- Capital expenditures.

*Prior to 2018, these "miscellaneous itemized deductions" were allowed as *from* AGI deductions, subject to a 2%-of-AGI floor. These deductions are not allowed from 2018 through 2025.

Many of these items are discussed in Chapters 6, 9, and 10.

Standard Deduction

Instead of claiming itemized deductions, taxpayers can use the **standard deduction**. As discussed later in the chapter, the standard deduction varies depending on filing status, age, and blindness. The standard deduction is adjusted each year for inflation.

Personal and Dependency Exemptions

Prior to 2018, exemption deductions were allowed for the taxpayer, the taxpayer's spouse, and each dependent of the taxpayer. Exemption deductions are suspended from 2018 through 2025.

Deduction for Qualified Business Income

From 2018 through 2025, a deduction for qualified business income is allowed. In general, this deduction relates to business income generated by *noncorporate* businesses (e.g., proprietorships, S corporations, partnerships, and LLCs). In general, the deduction allowed is the *lesser* of (1) 20 percent of qualified business income or (2) 20 percent of modified taxable income. This deduction is introduced in Chapter 6 and discussed extensively in Chapter 15.

Taxable Income

The determination of taxable income is illustrated in Example 6.

Grace, age 25, is not married and has her disabled and dependent mother living with her during 2023. This qualifies Grace for head-of-household filing status and a standard deduction of $20,800. In 2023, Grace earned a $54,000 salary as a high school teacher. Her other income consisted of $1,100 interest on a certificate of deposit (CD) and $500 interest on nontaxable municipal bonds that she had received as a graduation gift in 2016. During 2023, she sold stock that resulted in a $1,000 deductible capital loss. Her itemized deductions are $11,000. Grace's taxable income for the year is computed as follows:

Income (broadly defined)	
Salary	$ 54,000
Interest on a CD	1,100
Interest on municipal bonds	500
	$ 55,600
Less: Exclusion—Interest on municipal bonds	(500)
Gross income	$ 55,100
Less: Deduction *for* adjusted gross income—capital loss	(1,000)
Adjusted gross income	$ 54,100
Less: The greater of total itemized deductions ($11,000) *or* the standard deduction for head of household ($20,800)	(20,800)
Less: Deduction for qualified business income	(–0–)
Taxable income	$ 33,300

The exclusion of $500 (i.e., interest from municipal bonds) is subtracted in determining gross income, and the capital loss of $1,000 is classified as a deduction *for* AGI. Grace chose to use the standard deduction as her *from* AGI deduction since it exceeded her total itemized deductions. We will determine Grace's income tax liability later in the chapter (in Example 51).

Tax Due (or Refund)

The last step in applying the tax formula is the determination of tax due (or refund). Tax rates (which differ based on filing status) are applied to taxable income to determine the tax liability.[6] Once the tax is computed, this amount is reduced by any taxes withheld and tax credits allowed to arrive at the additional tax due or overpayment (i.e., refund). Filing status and the tax computation are discussed later in this chapter; tax credits are the subject of Chapter 12.

3-1b Tax Formula—Correlation with Form 1040

Now that you understand the definitions used in the tax formula, review the Form 1040 (and related Schedules 1, 2, and 3) included on the following pages. The 2022 Form 1040 is included in the text because the 2023 Form 1040 was not available when we went to press. As you can see, the structure of the individual income tax return parallels the tax formula in Concept Summary 3.1. In arriving at gross income (referred to as *total income*), *most* exclusions are *not* reported on the tax return. Form 1040 (page 1) includes the most common gross income items (e.g., wages, interest, dividends, retirement distributions, and Social Security benefits). Less common income items (including net income from sole proprietorships and rental activities and gains and losses from property transactions) are reported on Schedule 1 (Form 1040); the total of these amounts is reported on line 8 of Form 1040. Deductions *for* AGI also are summarized on (Schedule 1) Form 1040 and used to determine the taxpayer's AGI (see line 11 of Form 1040).

A taxpayer's "itemized deductions" (a *from* AGI deduction) are carried over from Schedule A (Form 1040) to page 1, line 12 of Form 1040, where the choice between the standard deduction and itemized deductions is made. This is followed by the deduction for qualified business income to arrive at taxable income. Page 2 of Form 1040 contains the tax computation and reductions for tax credits and withholdings. The format of Form 1040 and its connections to the various supporting schedules containing tax formula information is illustrated in Exhibit 6.2 of Chapter 6.

[6] § 1. Tax Rate Schedules can be found in Appendix A. Tax Tables, developed by the IRS, are used if taxable income is less than $100,000 (the 2022 Tax Tables can be found in Appendix A; 2023 Tax Tables are available on the IRS website).

Form **1040** Department of the Treasury—Internal Revenue Service
U.S. Individual Income Tax Return **2022** OMB No. 1545-0074 IRS Use Only—Do not write or staple in this space.

Filing Status ☐ Single ☐ Married filing jointly ☐ Married filing separately (MFS) ☐ Head of household (HOH) ☐ Qualifying surviving spouse (QSS)

Check only one box.

If you checked the MFS box, enter the name of your spouse. If you checked the HOH or QSS box, enter the child's name if the qualifying person is a child but not your dependent:

Your first name and middle initial	Last name			**Your social security number**
If joint return, spouse's first name and middle initial	Last name			**Spouse's social security number**
Home address (number and street). If you have a P.O. box, see instructions.			Apt. no.	**Presidential Election Campaign** Check here if you, or your spouse if filing jointly, want $3 to go to this fund. Checking a box below will not change your tax or refund. ☐ **You** ☐ **Spouse**
City, town, or post office. If you have a foreign address, also complete spaces below.		State	ZIP code	
Foreign country name	Foreign province/state/county		Foreign postal code	

Digital Assets At any time during 2022, did you: (a) receive (as a reward, award, or payment for property or services); or (b) sell, exchange, gift, or otherwise dispose of a digital asset (or a financial interest in a digital asset)? (See instructions.) ☐ **Yes** ☐ **No**

Standard Deduction **Someone can claim:** ☐ You as a dependent ☐ Your spouse as a dependent
☐ Spouse itemizes on a separate return or you were a dual-status alien

Age/Blindness **You:** ☐ Were born before January 2, 1958 ☐ Are blind **Spouse:** ☐ Was born before January 2, 1958 ☐ Is blind

Dependents (see instructions):

If more than four dependents, see instructions and check here . . ☐

(1) First name	Last name	(2) Social security number	(3) Relationship to you	(4) Check the box if qualifies for (see instructions): Child tax credit	Credit for other dependents
				☐	☐
				☐	☐
				☐	☐
				☐	☐

Income

Attach Form(s) W-2 here. Also attach Forms W-2G and 1099-R if tax was withheld.

If you did not get a Form W-2, see instructions.

Attach Sch. B if required.

Standard Deduction for—
- Single or Married filing separately, $12,950
- Married filing jointly or Qualifying surviving spouse, $25,900
- Head of household, $19,400
- If you checked any box under *Standard Deduction,* see instructions.

1a	Total amount from Form(s) W-2, box 1 (see instructions)			1a	
b	Household employee wages not reported on Form(s) W-2			1b	
c	Tip income not reported on line 1a (see instructions)			1c	
d	Medicaid waiver payments not reported on Form(s) W-2 (see instructions)			1d	
e	Taxable dependent care benefits from Form 2441, line 26			1e	
f	Employer-provided adoption benefits from Form 8839, line 29			1f	
g	Wages from Form 8919, line 6			1g	
h	Other earned income (see instructions)			1h	
i	Nontaxable combat pay election (see instructions)	1i			
z	Add lines 1a through 1h			1z	
2a	Tax-exempt interest	2a	**b** Taxable interest	2b	
3a	Qualified dividends	3a	**b** Ordinary dividends	3b	
4a	IRA distributions	4a	**b** Taxable amount	4b	
5a	Pensions and annuities	5a	**b** Taxable amount	5b	
6a	Social security benefits	6a	**b** Taxable amount	6b	
c	If you elect to use the lump-sum election method, check here (see instructions) ☐				
7	Capital gain or (loss). Attach Schedule D if required. If not required, check here ☐			7	
8	Other income from Schedule 1, line 10			8	
9	Add lines 1z, 2b, 3b, 4b, 5b, 6b, 7, and 8. This is your **total income**			9	
10	Adjustments to income from Schedule 1, line 26			10	
11	Subtract line 10 from line 9. This is your **adjusted gross income**			11	
12	**Standard deduction or itemized deductions** (from Schedule A)			12	
13	Qualified business income deduction from Form 8995 or Form 8995-A			13	
14	Add lines 12 and 13			14	
15	Subtract line 14 from line 11. If zero or less, enter -0-. This is your **taxable income**			15	

For Disclosure, Privacy Act, and Paperwork Reduction Act Notice, see separate instructions. Cat. No. 11320B Form **1040** (2022)

Form 1040 (2022) Page **2**

Tax and Credits	16	**Tax** (see instructions). Check if any from Form(s): **1** ☐ 8814 **2** ☐ 4972 **3** ☐ ______		16	
	17	Amount from Schedule 2, line 3		17	
	18	Add lines 16 and 17		18	
	19	Child tax credit or credit for other dependents from Schedule 8812		19	
	20	Amount from Schedule 3, line 8		20	
	21	Add lines 19 and 20		21	
	22	Subtract line 21 from line 18. If zero or less, enter -0-		22	
	23	Other taxes, including self-employment tax, from Schedule 2, line 21		23	
	24	Add lines 22 and 23. This is your **total tax**		24	
Payments	25	Federal income tax withheld from:			
	a	Form(s) W-2	25a		
	b	Form(s) 1099	25b		
	c	Other forms (see instructions)	25c		
	d	Add lines 25a through 25c		25d	
If you have a qualifying child, attach Sch. EIC.	26	2022 estimated tax payments and amount applied from 2021 return		26	
	27	Earned income credit (EIC)	27		
	28	Additional child tax credit from Schedule 8812	28		
	29	American opportunity credit from Form 8863, line 8	29		
	30	Reserved for future use	30		
	31	Amount from Schedule 3, line 15	31		
	32	Add lines 27, 28, 29, and 31. These are your **total other payments and refundable credits**		32	
	33	Add lines 25d, 26, and 32. These are your **total payments**		33	
Refund	34	If line 33 is more than line 24, subtract line 24 from line 33. This is the amount you **overpaid**		34	
	35a	Amount of line 34 you want **refunded to you**. If Form 8888 is attached, check here ☐		35a	
Direct deposit? See instructions.	b	Routing number ☐☐☐☐☐☐☐☐☐ **c** Type: ☐ Checking ☐ Savings			
	d	Account number ☐☐☐☐☐☐☐☐☐☐☐☐☐☐☐☐☐			
	36	Amount of line 34 you want **applied to your 2023 estimated tax**	36		
Amount You Owe	37	Subtract line 33 from line 24. This is the **amount you owe**. For details on how to pay, go to *www.irs.gov/Payments* or see instructions		37	
	38	Estimated tax penalty (see instructions)	38		

Third Party Designee — Do you want to allow another person to discuss this return with the IRS? See instructions ☐ **Yes.** Complete below. ☐ **No**

Designee's name | Phone no. | Personal identification number (PIN) ☐☐☐☐☐

Sign Here

Under penalties of perjury, I declare that I have examined this return and accompanying schedules and statements, and to the best of my knowledge and belief, they are true, correct, and complete. Declaration of preparer (other than taxpayer) is based on all information of which preparer has any knowledge.

Your signature	Date	Your occupation	If the IRS sent you an Identity Protection PIN, enter it here (see inst.) ☐☐☐☐☐☐
Spouse's signature. If a joint return, **both** must sign.	Date	Spouse's occupation	If the IRS sent your spouse an Identity Protection PIN, enter it here (see inst.) ☐☐☐☐☐☐
Phone no.	Email address		

Joint return? See instructions. Keep a copy for your records.

Paid Preparer Use Only

Preparer's name	Preparer's signature	Date	PTIN	Check if: ☐ Self-employed
Firm's name				Phone no.
Firm's address				Firm's EIN

Go to *www.irs.gov/Form1040* for instructions and the latest information. Form **1040** (2022)

SCHEDULE 1 (Form 1040)

Department of the Treasury
Internal Revenue Service

Additional Income and Adjustments to Income

Attach to Form 1040, 1040-SR, or 1040-NR.
Go to *www.irs.gov/Form1040* for instructions and the latest information.

OMB No. 1545-0074
2022
Attachment Sequence No. 01

Name(s) shown on Form 1040, 1040-SR, or 1040-NR	**Your social security number**

Part I Additional Income

1	Taxable refunds, credits, or offsets of state and local income taxes			**1**	
2a	Alimony received			**2a**	
b	Date of original divorce or separation agreement (see instructions): ________				
3	Business income or (loss). Attach Schedule C			**3**	
4	Other gains or (losses). Attach Form 4797			**4**	
5	Rental real estate, royalties, partnerships, S corporations, trusts, etc. Attach Schedule E			**5**	
6	Farm income or (loss). Attach Schedule F			**6**	
7	Unemployment compensation			**7**	
8	Other income:				
a	Net operating loss	**8a**	( )		
b	Gambling	**8b**			
c	Cancellation of debt	**8c**			
d	Foreign earned income exclusion from Form 2555	**8d**	( )		
e	Income from Form 8853	**8e**			
f	Income from Form 8889	**8f**			
g	Alaska Permanent Fund dividends	**8g**			
h	Jury duty pay	**8h**			
i	Prizes and awards	**8i**			
j	Activity not engaged in for profit income	**8j**			
k	Stock options	**8k**			
l	Income from the rental of personal property if you engaged in the rental for profit but were not in the business of renting such property	**8l**			
m	Olympic and Paralympic medals and USOC prize money (see instructions)	**8m**			
n	Section 951(a) inclusion (see instructions)	**8n**			
o	Section 951A(a) inclusion (see instructions)	**8o**			
p	Section 461(l) excess business loss adjustment	**8p**			
q	Taxable distributions from an ABLE account (see instructions)	**8q**			
r	Scholarship and fellowship grants not reported on Form W-2	**8r**			
s	Nontaxable amount of Medicaid waiver payments included on Form 1040, line 1a or 1d	**8s**	( )		
t	Pension or annuity from a nonqualifed deferred compensation plan or a nongovernmental section 457 plan	**8t**			
u	Wages earned while incarcerated	**8u**			
z	Other income. List type and amount: ________	**8z**			
9	Total other income. Add lines 8a through 8z			**9**	
10	Combine lines 1 through 7 and 9. Enter here and on Form 1040, 1040-SR, or 1040-NR, line 8			**10**	

For Paperwork Reduction Act Notice, see your tax return instructions. Cat. No. 71479F **Schedule 1 (Form 1040) 2022**

Schedule 1 (Form 1040) 2022 Page **2**

Part II Adjustments to Income

11	Educator expenses	**11**	
12	Certain business expenses of reservists, performing artists, and fee-basis government officials. Attach Form 2106	**12**	
13	Health savings account deduction. Attach Form 8889	**13**	
14	Moving expenses for members of the Armed Forces. Attach Form 3903	**14**	
15	Deductible part of self-employment tax. Attach Schedule SE	**15**	
16	Self-employed SEP, SIMPLE, and qualified plans	**16**	
17	Self-employed health insurance deduction	**17**	
18	Penalty on early withdrawal of savings	**18**	
19a	Alimony paid	**19a**	
b	Recipient's SSN		
c	Date of original divorce or separation agreement (see instructions):		
20	IRA deduction	**20**	
21	Student loan interest deduction	**21**	
22	Reserved for future use	**22**	
23	Archer MSA deduction	**23**	
24	Other adjustments:		
a	Jury duty pay (see instructions) **24a**		
b	Deductible expenses related to income reported on line 8l from the rental of personal property engaged in for profit **24b**		
c	Nontaxable amount of the value of Olympic and Paralympic medals and USOC prize money reported on line 8m **24c**		
d	Reforestation amortization and expenses **24d**		
e	Repayment of supplemental unemployment benefits under the Trade Act of 1974 **24e**		
f	Contributions to section 501(c)(18)(D) pension plans **24f**		
g	Contributions by certain chaplains to section 403(b) plans **24g**		
h	Attorney fees and court costs for actions involving certain unlawful discrimination claims (see instructions) **24h**		
i	Attorney fees and court costs you paid in connection with an award from the IRS for information you provided that helped the IRS detect tax law violations **24i**		
j	Housing deduction from Form 2555 **24j**		
k	Excess deductions of section 67(e) expenses from Schedule K-1 (Form 1041) **24k**		
z	Other adjustments. List type and amount: **24z**		
25	Total other adjustments. Add lines 24a through 24z	**25**	
26	Add lines 11 through 23 and 25. These are your **adjustments to income**. Enter here and on Form 1040 or 1040-SR, line 10, or Form 1040-NR, line 10a	**26**	

Schedule 1 (Form 1040) 2022

SCHEDULE 2 (Form 1040)

Department of the Treasury
Internal Revenue Service

Additional Taxes

Attach to Form 1040, 1040-SR, or 1040-NR.
Go to *www.irs.gov/Form1040* for instructions and the latest information.

OMB No. 1545-0074

2022

Attachment Sequence No. 02

Name(s) shown on Form 1040, 1040-SR, or 1040-NR	**Your social security number**

Part I Tax

1	Alternative minimum tax. Attach Form 6251			1	
2	Excess advance premium tax credit repayment. Attach Form 8962			2	
3	Add lines 1 and 2. Enter here and on Form 1040, 1040-SR, or 1040-NR, line 17			3	

Part II Other Taxes

4	Self-employment tax. Attach Schedule SE			4	
5	Social security and Medicare tax on unreported tip income. Attach Form 4137	5			
6	Uncollected social security and Medicare tax on wages. Attach Form 8919	6			
7	Total additional social security and Medicare tax. Add lines 5 and 6			7	
8	Additional tax on IRAs or other tax-favored accounts. Attach Form 5329 if required. If not required, check here ☐			8	
9	Household employment taxes. Attach Schedule H			9	
10	Repayment of first-time homebuyer credit. Attach Form 5405 if required			10	
11	Additional Medicare Tax. Attach Form 8959			11	
12	Net investment income tax. Attach Form 8960			12	
13	Uncollected social security and Medicare or RRTA tax on tips or group-term life insurance from Form W-2, box 12			13	
14	Interest on tax due on installment income from the sale of certain residential lots and timeshares			14	
15	Interest on the deferred tax on gain from certain installment sales with a sales price over $150,000			15	
16	Recapture of low-income housing credit. Attach Form 8611			16	

(continued on page 2)

Schedule 2 (Form 1040) 2022 Page **2**

Part II Other Taxes *(continued)*

17	Other additional taxes:		
a	Recapture of other credits. List type, form number, and amount: ______	**17a**	
b	Recapture of federal mortgage subsidy, if you sold your home see instructions	**17b**	
c	Additional tax on HSA distributions. Attach Form 8889	**17c**	
d	Additional tax on an HSA because you didn't remain an eligible individual. Attach Form 8889	**17d**	
e	Additional tax on Archer MSA distributions. Attach Form 8853 .	**17e**	
f	Additional tax on Medicare Advantage MSA distributions. Attach Form 8853	**17f**	
g	Recapture of a charitable contribution deduction related to a fractional interest in tangible personal property	**17g**	
h	Income you received from a nonqualified deferred compensation plan that fails to meet the requirements of section 409A . . .	**17h**	
i	Compensation you received from a nonqualified deferred compensation plan described in section 457A	**17i**	
j	Section 72(m)(5) excess benefits tax	**17j**	
k	Golden parachute payments	**17k**	
l	Tax on accumulation distribution of trusts	**17l**	
m	Excise tax on insider stock compensation from an expatriated corporation	**17m**	
n	Look-back interest under section 167(g) or 460(b) from Form 8697 or 8866	**17n**	
o	Tax on non-effectively connected income for any part of the year you were a nonresident alien from Form 1040-NR	**17o**	
p	Any interest from Form 8621, line 16f, relating to distributions from, and dispositions of, stock of a section 1291 fund	**17p**	
q	Any interest from Form 8621, line 24	**17q**	
z	Any other taxes. List type and amount: ______	**17z**	

18	Total additional taxes. Add lines 17a through 17z	**18**	
19	Reserved for future use	**19**	
20	Section 965 net tax liability installment from Form 965-A . . . **20**		
21	Add lines 4, 7 through 16, and 18. These are your **total other taxes**. Enter here and on Form 1040 or 1040-SR, line 23, or Form 1040-NR, line 23b	**21**	

Schedule 2 (Form 1040) 2022

SCHEDULE 3 (Form 1040)

Department of the Treasury
Internal Revenue Service

Additional Credits and Payments

Attach to Form 1040, 1040-SR, or 1040-NR.
Go to *www.irs.gov/Form1040* for instructions and the latest information.

OMB No. 1545-0074
2022
Attachment Sequence No. **03**

Name(s) shown on Form 1040, 1040-SR, or 1040-NR	**Your social security number**

Part I Nonrefundable Credits

1	Foreign tax credit. Attach Form 1116 if required			1	
2	Credit for child and dependent care expenses from Form 2441, line 11. Attach Form 2441			2	
3	Education credits from Form 8863, line 19			3	
4	Retirement savings contributions credit. Attach Form 8880			4	
5	Residential energy credits. Attach Form 5695			5	
6	Other nonrefundable credits:				
a	General business credit. Attach Form 3800	6a			
b	Credit for prior year minimum tax. Attach Form 8801	6b			
c	Adoption credit. Attach Form 8839	6c			
d	Credit for the elderly or disabled. Attach Schedule R	6d			
e	Alternative motor vehicle credit. Attach Form 8910	6e			
f	Qualified plug-in motor vehicle credit. Attach Form 8936 . . .	6f			
g	Mortgage interest credit. Attach Form 8396	6g			
h	District of Columbia first-time homebuyer credit. Attach Form 8859	6h			
i	Qualified electric vehicle credit. Attach Form 8834	6i			
j	Alternative fuel vehicle refueling property credit. Attach Form 8911	6j			
k	Credit to holders of tax credit bonds. Attach Form 8912 . . .	6k			
l	Amount on Form 8978, line 14. See instructions	6l			
z	Other nonrefundable credits. List type and amount: ____________	6z			
7	Total other nonrefundable credits. Add lines 6a through 6z			7	
8	Add lines 1 through 5 and 7. Enter here and on Form 1040, 1040-SR, or 1040-NR, line 20			8	

(continued on page 2)

Schedule 3 (Form 1040) 2022 Page 2

Part II Other Payments and Refundable Credits

9	Net premium tax credit. Attach Form 8962	9	
10	Amount paid with request for extension to file (see instructions)	10	
11	Excess social security and tier 1 RRTA tax withheld	11	
12	Credit for federal tax on fuels. Attach Form 4136	12	
13	Other payments or refundable credits:		
a	Form 2439	13a	
b	Credit for qualified sick and family leave wages paid in 2022 from Schedule(s) H for leave taken before April 1, 2021	13b	
c	Reserved for future use	13c	
d	Credit for repayment of amounts included in income from earlier years	13d	
e	Reserved for future use	13e	
f	Deferred amount of net 965 tax liability (see instructions)	13f	
g	Reserved for future use	13g	
h	Credit for qualified sick and family leave wages paid in 2022 from Schedule(s) H for leave taken after March 31, 2021, and before October 1, 2021	13h	
z	Other payments or refundable credits. List type and amount:	13z	
14	Total other payments or refundable credits. Add lines 13a through 13z	14	
15	Add lines 9 through 12 and 14. Enter here and on Form 1040, 1040-SR, or 1040-NR, line 31	15	

Schedule 3 (Form 1040) 2022

3-2 Standard Deduction

LO.2

Explain the standard deduction and evaluate its choice in arriving at taxable income.

The effect of the standard deduction is to exempt part of a taxpayer's income from Federal income tax liability. Congress has indicated that the standard deduction, when coupled with the child tax credit and dependent tax credit, should be roughly equal to the poverty level.[7]

3-2a Basic and Additional Standard Deduction

The standard deduction is the sum of two components: the *basic* standard deduction and the *additional* standard deduction.[8] Exhibit 3.4 lists the basic standard deduction allowed for taxpayers in each filing status. Certain taxpayers, however, are not allowed to claim *any* standard deduction, and the standard deduction is *limited* for others.

A taxpayer who is age 65 or over *or* blind in 2023 qualifies for an *additional standard deduction* of $1,500 or $1,850, depending on filing status (see amounts in Exhibit 3.5). Two additional standard deductions are allowed for a taxpayer who is age 65 or over *and* blind. The additional standard deduction provisions also apply for a qualifying spouse who is age 65 or over or blind but not for a dependent.

To determine whether to itemize, the taxpayer compares the *total* standard deduction (the sum of the basic standard deduction and any additional standard deductions) with total itemized deductions. Taxpayers are allowed to deduct the *greater* of itemized deductions or the standard deduction. The choice is elective each year. For example, a taxpayer who buys a home may change from using the standard deduction to itemizing

Exhibit 3.4 **Basic Standard Deduction Amounts**

	Standard Deduction Amount	
Filing Status	**2022**	**2023**
Single	$12,950	$13,850
Married, filing jointly	25,900	27,700
Surviving spouse	25,900	27,700
Head of household	19,400	20,800
Married, filing separately	12,950	13,850

Exhibit 3.5 **Additional Standard Deduction Amounts**

Filing Status	**2022**	**2023**
Single	$1,750	$1,850
Married, filing jointly	1,400	1,500
Surviving spouse	1,400	1,500
Head of household	1,750	1,850
Married, filing separately	1,400	1,500

[7] S.Rep. No. 92-437, 92nd Cong., 1st Sess., 1971, p. 54, discusses the combination of the standard deduction and exemption deductions. Congress expanded the child tax credit and added a dependent tax credit to offset the suspension of the dependency exemption deductions from 2018 through 2025. Another purpose of the standard deduction, discussed in Chapter 1, is to reduce the number of taxpayers who itemize their deductions. Reducing the number of taxpayers who itemize also reduces the audit effort required from the IRS.

[8] § 63(c)(1).

deductions (because of mortgage interest and property tax deductions). The taxpayer's age also can make a difference. In recent years, between 85 and 90 percent of individual tax returns filed use the standard deduction (rather than itemized deductions).

Using Itemized Deductions or Standard Deduction

Juan and Lisa, married taxpayers filing a joint return, have been renting an apartment while saving money for a down payment on a house. Early in 2023, they purchased a house. Interest paid on their home mortgage in 2023 amounted to $11,200, and they paid property taxes of $5,500. In addition, they had charitable contributions of $8,600 and paid state income taxes of $4,000.

In total, their itemized deductions amount to $29,300, and they will compute their taxable income using this amount rather than the $27,700 standard deduction.

Prior to 2023, Sara, who is single, had always chosen to itemize. In 2023, however, she reaches age 65. Her itemized deductions for 2023 are $14,800, but her total standard deduction is $15,700 [$13,850 (basic standard deduction) + $1,850 (additional standard deduction)].

Sara should compute her taxable income for 2023 using the standard deduction ($15,700) because it exceeds her itemized deductions ($14,800).

3-2b Individuals Not Eligible for the Standard Deduction

Some individuals are not allowed to use the standard deduction. The following individual taxpayers must itemize their deductions:[9]

- A married individual filing a separate return where either spouse itemizes deductions.
- An individual who is neither a U.S. citizen nor a U.S. resident (the Internal Revenue Code refers to these individuals as "nonresident aliens").

If an individual dies during a year, a full standard deduction is available for the final tax return; the deduction is not reduced because the return only covers a portion of the calendar year.

Sandy (age 80 and single) died on January 14, 2023. Her itemized deductions for 2023 amounted to $2,400. On her final income tax return, covering the period from January 1 to January 14, 2023, a standard deduction of $15,700 can be claimed (the $13,850 basic standard deduction plus the $1,850 age-related standard deduction).

3-2c Special Limitations on the Standard Deduction for Dependents

Special rules apply to the standard deduction of an individual who can be claimed as a dependent on another person's tax return.

When a dependent files a tax return, the *dependent's* basic standard deduction in 2023 is limited to the greater of $1,250 or the sum of the individual's earned income for the year plus $400.[10] However, if the sum of the individual's earned income plus $400 exceeds the basic standard deduction, the basic standard deduction is used (see Exhibit 3.4). A dependent who is 65 or over or blind or both also is allowed the additional standard deduction amount on his or her return (refer to Exhibit 3.5). These provisions are illustrated in Examples 10 through 13.

[9] § 63(c)(6); also ineligible is an individual filing a return for a period of less than 12 months because of a change in the annual accounting period.

[10] § 63(c)(5). Both amounts are subject to adjustment for inflation each year. In 2022, the amounts were $1,150 and $400.

Dependent Standard Deduction

Gabrielle, who is 17 years old and single, is a dependent of her parents. During 2023, she received $1,200 interest (unearned income) on a savings account. She also earned $450 from a part-time job. When Gabrielle files her own tax return, her standard deduction is $1,250 [the greater of $1,250 or $850 (the sum of earned income of $450 plus $400)].

Assume the same facts as in Example 10, except that Gabrielle is 67 years old and is a dependent of her son. In this case, when Gabrielle files her own tax return, her standard deduction is $3,100 [$1,250 (see Example 10) + $1,850 (the additional standard deduction allowed because Gabrielle is 65 or older)].

Aleshia, who is 16 years old and single, earned $950 from a summer job and had no unearned income during 2023. She is a dependent of her parents. Her standard deduction is $1,350 [the greater of $1,250 or $1,350 (the sum of $950 earned income plus $400)].

Javier, a 20-year-old, single, full-time college student, is a dependent of his parents. He worked as a musician during the summer of 2023, earning $13,750. Javier's standard deduction is $13,850 [the greater of $1,250 or $14,150 (the sum of $13,750 earned income plus $400, but limited to the $13,850 basic standard deduction for a single taxpayer)].

3-3 Exemptions

LO.3

Describe the current status of the exemption deduction.

Historically, the use of exemptions in the tax system has been based in part on the idea that a taxpayer with a small amount of income should be exempt from income taxation. Two types of exemptions have been allowed— **personal exemptions** and **dependency exemptions**. Beginning in 2018, however, Congress suspended the deduction for exemptions through 2025 (and increased the standard deduction amount for taxpayers).

Even though the exemption deduction has been suspended through 2025, understanding the definitions and the exemption amount remains important. For example, the *exemption amount* is used to determine whether certain taxpayers are dependents. In addition, the *definition of a "dependent"* is used for a variety of purposes in the Internal Revenue Code. Personal exemptions are granted to the taxpayer and spouse. Dependency exemptions are allowed for a qualifying child or a qualifying relative. The exemption amount in 2023 is $4,700 (it was $4,400 in 2022). Dependent status is discussed in the following section.

3-4 Dependents

LO.4

Explain the rules for determining whether someone is a dependent.

Under the Internal Revenue Code, there are two types of dependents—a *qualifying child* and a *qualifying relative*. Unique tests apply to each type of dependent; these tests are discussed next.

3-4a Qualifying Child

Congress has adopted a uniform definition of a qualifying child. The definition applies to the following tax provisions:

- Head-of-household filing status.
- Earned income tax credit.
- Child tax credit.
- Credit for child and dependent care expenses.

A **qualifying child** must meet the relationship, residence, age, and support tests (discussed below). A qualifying child must *also* satisfy the joint return test and the citizenship or residency test (discussed later).

Relationship Test

The relationship test includes a taxpayer's child (son or daughter), adopted child, stepchild, eligible foster child, brother, sister, half brother, half sister, stepbrother, stepsister, or a *descendant* of any of these parties (e.g., grandchild, nephew, niece). *Ancestors* of any of these parties (e.g., uncles and aunts) and in-laws (e.g., son-in-law and brother-in-law) *are not included.*

An adopted child includes a child placed with the taxpayer even though the adoption is not final. An eligible foster child is a child who is placed with the taxpayer by an authorized placement agency or by a court order.

Maureen's household includes her mother, grandson, stepbrother, stepbrother's daughter, uncle, and sister. All meet the relationship test for a qualifying child *except* the mother and uncle.

Residence Test

A qualifying child must live with the taxpayer for more than half of the year. Temporary absences (e.g., school, vacation, medical care, military service, detention in a juvenile facility) are ignored. Special rules apply in the case of certain kidnapped children.[11]

Age Test

A qualifying child must, by the end of the tax year, be (1) under age 19 or (2) under age 24 *and* a full-time student. A full-time student is a child who was in school during any part of five months of the year.[12] The age test does not apply to a child who is disabled during any part of the year.[13] Also, a qualifying child must be younger than the taxpayer claiming the child (e.g., a brother cannot claim his older sister as a qualifying child).

The Big Picture

Return to the facts of *The Big Picture* on p. 3-1. Does Paige meet the requirements of a qualifying child as to Aleha? Paige satisfies the relationship and residence tests, but the answer to the age test remains unclear. Because she is not a full-time student or disabled, she must be under 19 to meet the age test.

Support Test

To be a qualifying child, the individual must not be self-supporting (i.e., provide more than half of the individual's own support). Support includes food, shelter, clothing, medical and dental care, education, recreation/toys, transportation, and similar items.[14] In the case of a child who is a full-time student, scholarships are not considered to be support.[15]

---

[11] § 152(f)(6).

[12] §§ 152(c)(3)(A) and (f)(2).

[13] § 152(c)(3)(B). Within the meaning of § 22(e)(3). Concept Summary 12.1 contains a brief discussion of the elderly and disabled tax credit.

[14] A worksheet for determining support is provided in IRS Publication 501 (*Dependents, Standard Deduction, and Filing Information*).

[15] § 152(f)(5).

Shawn, age 23, is a full-time student and lives with his parents and an older cousin. During 2023, Shawn receives his support from the following sources: 30% from a part-time job, 30% from a scholarship, 20% from his parents, and 20% from the cousin.

Shawn is not self-supporting and is a dependent of his parents even though they contribute only 20% of his support. (Note: Shawn cannot be his cousin's qualifying child due to the relationship test.)

Tiebreaker Rules

In some situations, a child may be a qualifying child to more than one person. In this event, the tax law specifies which person has priority in claiming the child as a dependent.[16] Called "tiebreaker rules," these rules are summarized in Concept Summary 3.2 and are illustrated in the examples that follow.

Concept Summary 3.2

Tiebreaker Rules for Claiming Qualified Child

Persons Eligible to Claim Qualified Child as Dependent	Person Prevailing
One of the persons is the parent.	Parent
Both persons are the parents, and the child lives longer with one parent.	Parent with the longer period of residence
Both persons are the parents, and the child lives with each the same period of time.	Parent with the higher adjusted gross income (AGI)
None of the persons is the parent.	Person with highest AGI

Qualified Child—Tiebreaker Rules

Tim, age 15, lives in the same household with his mother and grandmother. As the parent, the mother has priority to claim Tim as a dependent.

Jennifer, age 17, lives in the same household with her parents during the entire year. If her parents file separate returns, the one with the higher AGI has priority to claim Jennifer as a dependent.

Assume the same facts as in Example 18, except that the father moves into an apartment in November (Jennifer remains with her mother). The mother has priority to claim Jennifer as a dependent (see Concept Summary 3.2).

3-4b Qualifying Relative

In addition to a qualifying child, a **qualifying relative** can be a dependent. A qualifying relative must meet the relationship, gross income, and support tests.[17]

[16] § 152(c)(4).

[17] § 152(d).

Relationship Test

The relationship test for a qualifying relative is more expansive than for a qualifying child. Also included are the following relatives:

- Lineal ascendants (e.g., parents and grandparents).
- Collateral ascendants (e.g., uncles and aunts).
- Certain in-laws (e.g., son-, daughter-, father-, mother-, brother-, and sister-in-law).[18]

Children who do not satisfy the qualifying child definition (e.g., a 25-year-old daughter) may meet the qualifying relative criteria.

The relationship test also includes individuals who are "members of the household" (i.e., live with the taxpayer for the *entire year*). These individuals can be related or unrelated. For example, cousins are not "qualifying relatives" (cousins are not included in the list above). But a cousin can meet the relationship test if the cousin is a "member of the household." Member-of-the-household status is not available for anyone who was a spouse during any part of the year.[19] However, an ex-spouse can qualify as a member of the household in a year following the year of the divorce.

As the relationship test indicates, the category designation of "qualifying relative" is somewhat misleading, since persons *other than relatives* can qualify as dependents. And not all relatives will qualify (although relatives who are not listed could be a "member of the household").

The Big Picture

Example 20

Return to the facts of *The Big Picture* on p. 3-1. Although Terrah is unrelated to Aleha, she qualifies as Aleha's dependent by being a member of the household. Because Terrah is a dependent, Aleha also can claim the medical expenses she paid on Terrah's behalf. The funeral expenses are not deductible.

Gross Income Test

A dependent's gross income must be *less* than the exemption amount—$4,700 in 2023 ($4,400 in 2022). Gross income is determined by any income that is taxable. In the case of scholarships, for example, include the taxable portion (e.g., amounts received for room and board) and exclude the nontaxable portion (e.g., amounts received for books and tuition).

Gross Income Test

Haylie provides more than half of the support of her son, Tom, who does not live with her. Tom, age 26, is a full-time student in medical school, earns $3,000 from a part-time job, and receives a $12,000 scholarship covering his tuition.

Tom is Haylie's dependent because he meets the gross income test and is a qualifying relative. (Note: Tom is *not* a qualifying child; he fails both the residence and age tests.)

Aaron provides more than half of the support of his widowed aunt, Myrtle, who does not live with him. Myrtle's income for the year is as follows: dividend income of $1,100, earnings from pet sitting of $2,350, nontaxable Social Security benefits of $6,000, and nontaxable interest from City of Milwaukee bonds of $8,000.

Because Myrtle's gross income is only $3,450 ($1,100 + $2,350), she meets the gross income test and is Aaron's dependent.

[18]Reg. § 1.152–2(d). Once established by marriage, in-law status continues to exist and survives divorce.

[19]§§ 152(d)(2)(H) and (f)(3); also excluded is anyone whose relationship to the taxpayer violates local law.

Return to the facts of *The Big Picture* on p. 3-1. Assuming that Paige is not a qualifying child (see Example 15), can she be a qualifying relative? She meets the relationship and support tests, but what about the gross income test?

If her income from her part-time job is less than $4,700 (the 2023 exemption amount), she does qualify and would be Aleha's dependent.

Support Test

The taxpayer must furnish over half of the qualifying relative's support. As with a qualifying child, support includes food, shelter, clothing, medical and dental care, education, recreation, transportation, and similar items. If a child is being evaluated as a qualifying relative (and is a full-time student), a scholarship received by the child is *not included* for purposes of computing whether the taxpayer furnished more than half of the child's support. Any other relative being evaluated must include a scholarship as support in making this determination.

Waleed contributed $3,400 (consisting of food, clothing, and medical care) toward the support of his nephew, Aroosa, who lives with him. Aroosa earned $1,300 from a part-time job and received $2,000 from a student loan to attend a local university. Assuming that the other dependency tests are met, Waleed can claim Aroosa as a dependent because he contributed more than half of Aroosa's support.

If the individual does not spend funds that have been received from any source, the unexpended amounts are *not* counted for purposes of the support test.

Emily contributed $3,000 to her father's support during the year. In addition, her father received $2,400 in Social Security benefits, $200 of interest, and wages of $600. Her father deposited the Social Security benefits, interest, and wages in his own savings account and did not use any of the funds for his support. Thus, the Social Security benefits, interest, and wages are not considered as support provided by Emily's father. Emily's father is her dependent if the other tests are met.

An individual's own funds, however, must be taken into account if applied toward support. The source of the funds is not relevant.

Dominic contributes $8,000 toward his parents' total support of $20,000. The parents, who do not live with Dominic, obtain the other $12,000 from savings and a home equity loan on their residence. Although the parents have no income, their use of savings and borrowed funds are counted as part of their support. Because Dominic does not satisfy the support test, he cannot claim his parents as dependents.

Capital expenditures for items like furniture, appliances, and automobiles are included in total support if the item does, in fact, constitute support.

Tebin purchased a television set costing $950 and gave it to his mother who lives with him. The television set was placed in his mother's bedroom and was used exclusively by her. Tebin should include the cost of the television set in determining the support of his mother.

Multiple Support Agreements An exception to the support test involves a **multiple support agreement**. A multiple support agreement allows a group of taxpayers—none of whom provide more than 50 percent of the support of a taxpayer—to designate one member of the group to claim the individual as a dependent. All taxpayers in the group must satisfy the other dependency requirements (e.g., the relationship test), and, collectively, the group must provide more than 50 percent of the support. Any taxpayer in the group who contributed *more than 10 percent* of the support is entitled to claim the individual as a dependent. This provision is often used by the children of aged dependent parents when none of the children meet the support test.

Wanda, who resides with her son, Adam, received $12,000 from various sources during the year. This constituted her entire support for the year. She received support from the following:

	Amount	Percentage of Total
Adam, a son	$ 5,760	48%
Bob, a son	1,200	10
Carol, a daughter	3,600	30
Diane, a friend	1,440	12
	$12,000	100%

If Adam and Carol file a multiple support agreement, either may claim Wanda as a dependent. Bob may not claim Wanda because he did not contribute *more than 10%* of her support. Bob's consent is not required for Adam and Carol to file a multiple support agreement. Diane does not meet the relationship or member-of-the-household test and cannot be a party to the agreement. The decision as to who claims Wanda rests with Adam and Carol. It is possible for Carol to claim Wanda even though Adam furnished more of Wanda's support.

Form 2120 (Multiple Support Declaration) must be completed and filed by the individual claiming the dependent. In addition, every other person who qualifies under the more-than-10% rule must provide a signed statement agreeing not to claim the individual as a dependent.

Children of Divorced or Separated Parents Another exception to the support test applies when parents with children are divorced or separated. Unmarried parents living apart for the last six months of the year also are covered by these rules. This exception applies if the parents meet the following conditions:

- They would have been entitled to claim the individual(s) as a dependent had they been married and filed a joint return.
- They have custody (either jointly or singly) of the child (or children) for more than half of the year.

In general, the parent having custody of the child (children) for the greater part of the year (i.e., the custodial parent) is entitled to claim the dependent(s).[20] However, the custodial parent can sign a waiver that allows the noncustodial parent to claim the child as a dependent.[21]

The waiver, Form 8332 (Release/Revocation of Release of Claim to Exemption for Child by Custodial Parent), can apply to a single year, a number of specified years, or all future years. Form 8332 must be attached to the noncustodial parent's tax return.

[20] Reg. § 1.152–4; the general rule does not apply if a multiple support agreement is in effect.

[21] § 152(e)(2).

3-4c **Other Rules for Determining Dependents**

In addition to fitting into either the qualifying child or the qualifying relative category, a dependent must meet the joint return and citizenship tests.

Joint Return Test

In general, a taxpayer cannot claim as a dependent a married individual who files a joint return with his or her spouse.[22] The joint return rule does not apply, however, if the reason for filing is to claim a refund for tax withheld (and no tax liability exists).[23]

Paul provides over half of the support of his son, Quinn. He also provides over half of the support of Vera, who is Quinn's wife. During the year, both Quinn and Vera had part-time jobs. To recover the taxes withheld, they file a joint return. If Quinn and Vera are not required to file a return, both are dependents of Paul.

Citizenship Test

To be a dependent, the individual must be a U.S. citizen, a U.S. resident, or a resident of Canada or Mexico for some part of the calendar year in which the taxpayer's tax year begins. However, from 2018 through 2025, a taxpayer may not claim a dependent tax credit unless the individual is a U.S. citizen or a U.S. resident.[24]

Under an exception, an adopted child need not be a citizen or resident of the United States (or a contiguous country) as long as the child's principal residence is with a U.S. citizen.

Alexis is a U.S. citizen who lives and works in Spain. She has adopted Benito, a four-year-old Italian national, who lives with her and is a member of her household.

Although Benito does not meet the citizenship test, he is covered by the exception. Benito is a qualifying child and a dependent of Alexis.

3-4d **Comparison of Dependent Categories**

Concept Summary 3.3 identifies the tests for the two categories of dependents. In contrasting the two categories, here are some observations:

- As to the relationship tests, the qualifying relative category is considerably more expansive. In addition to including those identified under the qualifying child grouping, other relatives are added. Nonrelated persons who are members of the household also are included.
- The support tests are entirely different. In the case of a qualifying child, the key is that the child is *not* self-supporting.
- The qualifying child category has no gross income limitation; the qualifying relative category has no age restriction.

---

[22] § 152(b)(2).

[23] Prop.Reg. § 1.152–1(a)(2)(ii) and Rev.Rul. 54–567.

[24] §§ 152(b)(3) and 24(h)(4)(B). See text Section 3-4e.

Concept Summary 3.3

Tests for Dependents

Test	Qualifying Child	Qualifying Relative
Relationship:		
• Children (natural, step, or adopted) and their *descendants*, and siblings and stepsiblings and their *descendants*.	X	
• Children (natural, step, or adopted) and their *descendants*, siblings and their children, parents and their *ascendants*, uncles and aunts, stepparents and stepsiblings, and certain in-laws.		X
• Member of the household (live with taxpayer for *entire* year; relative or non-relative)		X
Residence	X	
Age	X	
Support:		
• Not self-supporting ("child" furnishes half or less of his or her support)	X	
• Taxpayer furnishes over half of the support of potential dependent		X
Gross income less than the exemption amount		X
Joint return (potential dependent cannot file joint return)	X	X
Citizenship (potential dependent must meet test)	X	X

Ethics & Equity **Whose Qualifying Child Is He?**

The Rands are successful professionals and have combined AGI of approximately $450,000. Their household includes two children: Henry (age 16) and Belinda (age 22). Belinda is not a student and has a job where she earns $15,000 a year. After a short family meeting in early April 2023, the parties decide that Belinda should claim Henry as her qualifying child. As a result, Belinda is able to claim a child tax credit and an earned income tax credit yielding significant tax savings (more than $4,600, much of which is refundable). Had the Rands claimed Henry as their dependent, no child tax credit or earned income credit would have been available (these credits are phased out for higher-income taxpayers). Has the Rand family acted properly?

3-4e Child and Dependent Tax Credits

The **child tax credit** and **dependent tax credit** are provided to individual taxpayers based on the *number* of their qualifying children and dependents. With the suspension of the exemption deductions from 2018 through 2025, Congress increased the amount of the child tax credit, expanded its scope, and made it available to more taxpayers during the same time frame.[25] Congress also created a dependent tax credit.

A $2,000 child tax credit is allowed for each qualifying child (including stepchildren and foster children). To be eligible for the credit, the child must be under age 17 at the end of the year, must be a U.S. citizen, and must be a dependent of the taxpayer.[26] A Social Security number must be provided for any qualifying child.[27]

[25] § 24(h).

[26] §§ 24(c) and 24(i)(2).

[27] § 24(h)(4)(7).

Due to the COVID-19 pandemic, Congress provided a temporary increase in the child tax credit. For 2021, the amount of the child tax credit was increased to $3,000 ($3,600 for a qualifying child under age 6 at the end of the year) and the IRS provided a portion of the credit in advance via monthly payments.[28]

In addition, a $500 tax credit is allowed for each dependent of the taxpayer (other than a qualifying child).[29] Examples of qualifying relatives for purposes of the dependent tax credit include children over age 16 (including full-time students under age 24), children without a Social Security number, parents of the taxpayer, and "members of the household" (see text Section 3-4b). For purposes of the dependent tax credit, these qualifying relatives must be a U.S. citizen, a U.S. national, or a U.S. resident.[30]

The child tax credit and the dependent tax credit are subject to specific phaseout rules based on a taxpayer's adjusted gross income.

Child and Dependent Tax Credits Phaseout

The available $2,000 child tax credit and $500 dependent tax credit both begin to phase out when AGI reaches $400,000 for married taxpayers filing jointly ($200,000 for all other taxpayers). These credits are phased out by $50 for each $1,000 (or part thereof) of AGI above the $400,000 (or $200,000) amount.[31] Because the maximum credit amount depends on the *number* of qualifying children and dependents, the income level at which these credits are phased out completely also depends on the *number* of qualifying children and dependents.

If married taxpayers filing a joint return have one qualifying child, the child tax credit is completely phased out if their AGI exceeds $439,000. If those taxpayers have two qualifying children, the child tax credit is completely phased out if their AGI exceeds $479,000. For all other taxpayers, these amounts would be $239,000 and $279,000, respectively. The allowed tax credit can be determined using the following steps:

1. AGI − Threshold amount = Excess amount.
2. Excess amount ÷ $1,000 = Reduction factor (round up to next whole number; for example, 18.2 = 19).
3. Reduction factor × $50 = Child and dependent tax credit reduction.
4. Maximum child and dependent tax credit amount − Child and dependent tax credit reduction = Child and dependent tax credit allowed.

Child and Dependent Tax Credit and Phaseout

In 2023, Juanita and Alberto are married and file a joint tax return. They have two dependent children, ages 4 and 7. Their AGI is $85,400. Juanita and Alberto's maximum child tax credit is $4,000 ($2,000 × 2).

Because Juanita and Alberto's AGI is less than the $400,000 threshold, they will be allowed a child tax credit of $4,000.

[28] § 24(i)(3). To address the issue of child poverty, a number of proposals have been made to modify the child tax credit (including having the IRS pay any credit in advance on a monthly basis). See, for example, The Family Security Act of 2022 (**romney.senate.gov/wp-content/uploads/2021/02/family-security-act_one-pager.pdf**).

[29] § 24(h)(4)(A).

[30] § 24(h)(4)(B).

[31] § 24(b), as modified by § 24(h)(3). AGI is modified for this purpose; the threshold amounts are *not* indexed for inflation.

Child and Dependent Tax Credit and Phaseout

Assume the same facts as Example 31, except that Juanita and Alberto's 2023 AGI is $412,400. Since their AGI is over the $400,000 threshold, the maximum child tax credit ($4,000) must be reduced by $50 for every $1,000 (or portion of $1,000) above the $400,000 threshold. The child tax credit allowed is $3,350, computed as follows:

1. $412,400 (AGI) − $400,000 (Threshold amount) = $12,400 (Excess amount).
2. $12,400 (Excess amount) ÷ $1,000 = Reduction factor (12.4, rounded up to 13).
3. 13 (Reduction factor) × $50 = $650 (Child and dependent tax credit reduction).
4. $4,000 (Maximum child and dependent tax credit amount) − $650 (Child and dependent tax credit reduction) = $3,350 (Child and dependent tax credit allowed).

Assume the same facts as Example 32, but also assume that Juanita's mother (age 88) is living with Juanita and Alberto and is a qualifying relative.

Since Juanita's mother is a qualifying relative, Juanita and Alberto will receive a $500 dependent tax credit. Their maximum combined child and dependent tax credit is $4,500 ($4,000 child tax credit + $500 dependent tax credit). This maximum amount is reduced by $650 (the child and dependent tax credit reduction; see Example 32). So their allowed child and dependent tax credit is $3,850 ($4,500 − $650).

Refundable Portion of Child Tax Credit

In 2023, any child tax credit is refundable to the extent of the *lesser* of:[32]

1. $1,600 of the child tax credit for each qualifying child, or
2. 15 percent of the taxpayer's earned income in excess of $2,500.

The $1,600 amount is adjusted for inflation each year (it was $1,500 in 2022 and may increase in 2024); the $2,500 amount is not inflation-adjusted. The $500 dependent tax credit is *nonrefundable*.

Return to the facts of Example 31. In 2023, assume that Juanita and Alberto have $82,000 of earned income and their taxable income is $57,700. Their child tax credit will be $4,000 ($2,000 × 2 children). The refundable portion of their child tax credit is $3,200, computed as follows:

1. $3,200 (2 qualifying children × $1,600), or
2. $11,925 [15% × ($82,000 – $2,500)].

However, since their 2023 tax liability exceeds $4,000, they will claim the full amount of their child tax credit ($4,000).

Based on the computations in Example 34, one can see that the *refundability* of the child tax credit is aimed at lower-income taxpayers with earned income.

Example 35

In 2023, Tom and Cindy are married (filing jointly) and have two qualifying children. Their AGI is $18,000 (entirely earned income). With their standard deduction, Tom and Cindy will have no taxable income (and no Federal tax liability). Because the child tax credit is partially refundable, Tom and Cindy will receive a refund related to the child tax credit of $2,325, computed as follows:

1. $3,200 (2 qualifying children × $1,600), or
2. $2,325 [15% × ($18,000 – $2,500)]

If a taxpayer has three or more qualifying children, an alternative formula is available to determine the refundable portion.[33] In this case, the refundable portion is equal to the amount by which a taxpayer's Social Security (or self-employment) taxes exceed the earned income tax credit. The earned income tax credit, which also is partially refundable, is discussed in Chapter 12.

[32] §§ 24(d)(1)(A) and (h)(5) and (6).

[33] § 24(d)(1)(B)(ii).

3-5 Filing Status and Filing Requirements

Choose the proper filing status and identify the related filing requirements.

Individuals must know their *filing status* to correctly compute both taxable income and the related income tax liability. In addition, individuals need to understand the tax return filing process. Text Sections 3-5 through 3-7 cover these important tax compliance points:

- Determination of filing status and whether a tax return must be filed (text Section 3-5).
- Computation of tax liability and adjustment for available tax credits (text Section 3-6; also see Concept Summary 3.1 and the tax formula).
- Selection of the appropriate tax form and how to file it with the IRS (text Section 3-7).

3-5a Filing Status

Every year, taxpayers must determine their **filing status**. The taxpayer's filing status is important because it is used to determine:

- The taxpayer's standard deduction (see Exhibits 3.4 and 3.5).
- Whether the taxpayer must file a tax return.
- The taxpayer's tax liability.
- Reductions of itemized deductions and certain tax credits.
- Eligibility for certain provisions (e.g., some credits are not available when the married, filing separately status is used).

There are five filing statuses, and all taxpayers will file a return based on the filing status selected.

- Single.
- Married, filing jointly.
- Married, filing separately.
- Surviving spouse (qualifying widow or widower).
- Head of household.

The amount of tax varies considerably depending on which filing status is used. Consider the following example.

The following amounts of tax are computed using the 2023 Tax Rate Schedules for a taxpayer (or taxpayers in the case of a joint return) with $70,000 of taxable income (see Appendix A).

Filing Status	Amount of Tax
Single	$10,708
Married, filing jointly	7,960
Married, filing separately	10,708
Surviving spouse	7,960
Head of household	9,101

These sample calculations are intended to illustrate the rate schedule differences for these filing statuses. To qualify for head-of-household status, the taxpayer would also have a child or dependent tax credit that would reduce the tax liability.

Single Taxpayers

A taxpayer who is unmarried (including a taxpayer who is legally separated or divorced) and does not qualify for head-of-household status (discussed below) will file as a single taxpayer.

Phil was divorced in March and is unmarried at the end of the year. Phil has no dependents. As a result, Phil's filing status is single.

Global Tax Issues Filing a Joint Return

John is a U.S. citizen and resident, but he spends much of his time in London, where his employer sends him on frequent assignments. John is married to Victoria, a citizen and resident of the United Kingdom.

Can John and Victoria file a joint return for U.S. Federal income tax purposes? Although § 6013(a)(1) specifically precludes the filing of a joint return if one spouse is a nonresident alien, another Code provision permits an exception. Under § 6013(g), the parties can elect to treat the nonqualifying spouse as a "resident" of the United States. This election would allow John and Victoria to file jointly.

But should John and Victoria make this election? If Victoria has considerable income of her own (from non-U.S. sources), the election could be ill-advised. As a nonresident alien, Victoria's non-U.S. source income *would not* be subject to the U.S. income tax. If she is treated as a U.S. resident, however, her non-U.S. source income *will be subject to U.S. tax*. Under the U.S. global approach to taxation, all income (regardless of where earned) of anyone who is a *resident* or *citizen* of the United States is subject to tax.

Married Taxpayers

Married couples can file tax returns together (married, filing jointly) or apart (married, filing separately). In general, marital status is determined on the last day of the year. As mentioned above, when one spouse dies during the year, the surviving spouse is considered to be married to the spouse who died at the end of the year. Most married couples will find it beneficial to file a joint return.

Married, Filing Jointly The joint filing status was originally enacted in 1948 to establish equity between married taxpayers in common law states and those in community property states. Before the joint filing status was established, taxpayers in community property states were in an advantageous position relative to taxpayers in common law states because they could split their income. For instance, in a community property state, if one spouse earned $100,000 and the other spouse was not employed, each spouse could report $50,000 of income. Splitting the income in this manner caused the total income to be subject to lower marginal tax rates; each spouse would start at the bottom of the rate structure.

Taxpayers in common law states did not have this income-splitting option, so their taxable income was subject to higher marginal rates. This inconsistency in treatment was remedied by the joint filing status. The joint return Tax Rate Schedule is constructed based on the assumption that income is earned equally by the two spouses.

A legally married same-sex couple is treated as married for Federal tax purposes no matter where they live. Registered domestic partners, however, are not "spouses" under Federal law. Therefore, they cannot file Federal tax returns using married, filing jointly or married, filing separately status. The same rule applies to same-sex partners in civil unions.[34]

Marital status is determined as of the last day of the tax year, except when a spouse dies during the year. In that case, marital status is determined as of the date of death.

Return to the facts of Example 37. Would things be different if, rather than getting a divorce, Phil's spouse passed away during the year? Yes. In this case, Phil would still be "married" for tax purposes at the end of the year.

What if Phil remarried during the year? In this case, Phil and his new spouse are a married couple (and they would file joint or separate returns). Phil's deceased spouse's filing status is married, filing separately.

Filing a joint return carries the potential disadvantage of joint and several liability.[35] This means that the IRS can pursue the collection of the tax due for that year against either spouse.

---

[34]Reg. § 301.7701–18 and *U.S. v. Windsor*, 2013–2 USTC ¶50,400, 111 AFTR 2d 2013–2385, 133 S.Ct. 2675; **irs.gov/newsroom/Answers-to-Frequently-Asked-Questions-for-Registered-Domestic-Partners-and-Individuals-in-Civil-Unions**.

[35]§ 6013(d)(3).

Once a joint return has been filed and the due date has passed, the spouses cannot switch to separate returns for that year. However, if married persons file separately, they can change later to a joint return.

Married, Filing Separately If married individuals file separate returns, each reports only their own income, deductions, and credits, and each must use the married, filing separately tax rates. In a community property state, each individual must report half of the community property income.[36] Most married couples file a joint return, because the combined amount of tax is lower. However, special circumstances (e.g., significant medical expenses incurred by one spouse subject to the 7.5%-of-AGI limitation) may lead a married couple to file separate returns.

The Internal Revenue Code places some limitations on married persons who file separate returns. Here are some examples:

- If either spouse itemizes deductions, the other spouse also must itemize.
- The earned income credit and the credit for child and dependent care expenses cannot be claimed (see Chapter 12).
- No deduction is allowed for interest paid on qualified education loans (see Chapter 10).
- Only $1,500 of excess capital losses can be claimed by each spouse (see Chapter 14).

Surviving Spouse A special filing status applies for two years following the death of one spouse if the surviving spouse maintains a household for a dependent child. The child must be a son, stepson, daughter, or stepdaughter who qualifies as a dependent of the taxpayer (the gross income and joint return tests are waived for this purpose). This is referred to as **surviving spouse** status.[37] While surviving spouse is a distinct filing status, taxpayers filing as a surviving spouse use the married, filing jointly tax rates and standard deduction amounts.

Dylan dies in 2023, leaving Jennifer with a dependent child. For the year of Dylan's death (2023), Jennifer files a joint return with Dylan. For the next two years (2024 and 2025), Jennifer, as a surviving spouse, may use the married, filing jointly tax rates. Beginning in 2026, Jennifer may use the head-of-household rates if she continues to maintain a household for her dependent child.

Marriage Penalty When Congress enacted the rate structure available to those filing joint returns, it generally favored married taxpayers. In certain situations, however, the parties would incur less tax if they were not married and filed as single taxpayers. The additional tax that a joint return caused, commonly called the **marriage penalty**, usually occurs when *both* spouses have substantial income. Long aware of the inequity of the marriage penalty, Congress reduced its effect on couples by increasing the standard deduction available to married filers to 200 percent of that applicable to single persons and doubling the size of the married filer tax brackets below 35 percent. However, the marriage penalty still exists for couples who itemize their deductions and have substantial amounts of income beyond the 32 percent tax bracket.

Head of Household

Unmarried individuals who maintain a household for a dependent (or dependents) can use the **head-of-household** filing status.[38] The tax liability using the head-of-household rates falls between the tax liabilities for married taxpayers filing jointly and single taxpayers.

To qualify for the head-of-household filing status, a taxpayer must pay more than half the cost of maintaining a household where the taxpayer lives. The household also must be the principal home of a dependent. Except for temporary absences (e.g., school, hospitalization), the dependent must live in the taxpayer's household for over half the year.

A dependent must be either a qualifying child or a qualifying relative who meets the relationship test (other than someone who qualifies under the member-of-the-household test).

[36] Form 8958 (Allocation of Tax Amounts Between Certain Individuals in Community Property States) is used for this purpose.

[37] § 2(a)(1). The IRS term for surviving spouse status is "qualifying widow(er) with dependent child."

[38] § 2(b).

The Big Picture

Example 40

Return to the facts of *The Big Picture* on p. 3-1. Assuming that Aleha can be treated as single (i.e., not married), can Terrah qualify Aleha for head-of-household filing status? The answer is no. Even though Terrah can be claimed as Aleha's dependent (see Example 20), she does not meet the relationship test for head-of-household status (Terrah qualified as a dependent under the member-of-the-household test).

Kohsei, a widow, maintains a household in which she and her aunt live. If the aunt qualifies as a dependent, Kohsei may file as head of household. Note that an aunt meets the relationship test.

A special rule allows taxpayers to avoid having to live with their parents. Head-of-household status is allowed if a taxpayer maintains a *separate home* for the taxpayer's *parent or parents* if at least one parent qualifies as a dependent of the taxpayer.[39]

Melissa, an unmarried individual, lives in New York City and maintains a household in Detroit for her dependent parents. Melissa may use the head-of-household filing status even though her parents do not reside in her New York home.

Head-of-household status is not changed during the year by the death of the dependent. As long as the taxpayer provided more than half of the cost of maintaining the household prior to the dependent's death, head-of-household status is preserved.

Abandoned Spouse Rules

When married persons file separate returns, several unfavorable tax consequences result. For example, the taxpayer must use the married, filing separately tax rates. But what about a taxpayer who is abandoned by his or her spouse? Since the taxpayer is married, absent a special rule, the taxpayer would likely have no choice but to file separately (a harsh result). To mitigate this outcome, Congress enacted the **abandoned spouse** rules. Under these rules, the taxpayer is treated as *not married* and qualifies for head-of-household status if the following conditions are met:[40]

- The taxpayer does not file a joint return.
- The taxpayer paid more than half the cost of maintaining a home for the tax year.
- The taxpayer's spouse did not live in the home during the last six months of the tax year.
- The home was the principal residence of the taxpayer's son, daughter, stepson, stepdaughter, foster child, or adopted child for more than half the year, and the child can be claimed as a dependent.[41]

The Big Picture

Example 43

Return to the facts of *The Big Picture* on p. 3-1. Can Aleha qualify as an abandoned spouse?

Yes, if she can claim Paige as a dependent—either as a qualifying child (see Example 15) or as a qualifying relative (see Example 23). If so, Aleha can use head-of-household filing status. If not, her filing status is married, filing separately.

[39] § 2(b)(1)(B).

[40] § 7703(b).

[41] §§ 7703(b)(1) and 152(e). The dependency requirement does not apply, however, if the taxpayer could have claimed the child as a dependent except for the fact that the child was claimed as a dependent by the noncustodial parent under a written agreement.

Ethics & Equity **Abandoned Spouse?**

Bob and Carol have been in and out of marital counseling for the past few years. Early in 2023, they decide to separate. However, because they are barely able to get by on their current incomes, they cannot afford separate housing or the legal costs of a divorce. So Bob moves out of their house in March and takes up residence in their detached garage (which has an enclosed workshop and bathroom). Carol stays in the house with their two children and pays more than half of the costs of maintaining their residence. Bob does not enter the house for the remainder of the year. Can Carol qualify as an abandoned spouse?

3-5b **Filing Requirements**

General Rules

In general, an individual must file a tax return if gross income equals or exceeds the applicable standard deduction.[42] A married taxpayer filing a separate return is required to file a return if *any* amount of gross income must be reported. Because the standard deduction amounts are subject to an annual inflation adjustment, the gross income amounts for determining whether a tax return must be filed normally change each year.[43] For example, a single taxpayer under age 65 must file a tax return in 2023 if gross income equals or exceeds $13,850 (the amount of the standard deduction). Exhibit 3.6 lists the income levels that require tax returns under the general rule and under certain special rules.

The additional standard deduction for being age 65 or older is considered in determining the gross income filing requirements. For example, the 2023 filing requirement for a single taxpayer age 65 or older is $15,700 ($13,850 basic standard deduction + $1,850

Exhibit 3.6 Filing Requirements for Most Taxpayers

Filing Status	2022 Gross Income	2023 Gross Income
Single		
Under 65	$12,950	$13,850
65 or older	14,700	15,700
Married, filing jointly		
Both spouses under 65	$25,900	$27,700
One spouse 65 or older	27,300	29,200
Both spouses 65 or older	28,700	30,700
Married, filing separately		
All	$ *	$ *
Head of household		
Under 65	$19,400	$20,800
65 or older	21,150	22,650
Qualifying widow(er)		
Under 65	$25,900	$27,700
65 or older	27,300	29,200

*Any amount of gross income will require a return to be filed.

[42] § 6012(f), modifying § 6012(a)(1) from 2018 through 2025; in years prior to 2018, an individual was required to file a return if gross income equaled or exceeded the sum of the exemption amount plus the applicable standard deduction.

[43] See §§ 1(f), 63(c)(4), and 151(d)(3).

additional standard deduction). Except in the case of dependents, the additional standard deduction for blindness is not taken into account in determining whether a taxpayer must file a tax return (see Filing Requirements for Dependents below).

A self-employed individual with net earnings of $400 or more from a business or profession must file a tax return regardless of the amount of gross income.

Even though an individual has gross income below the filing level amounts and therefore does not owe any tax, the individual must file a return to obtain a tax refund of amounts withheld. A return is also necessary to obtain the benefits of the earned income credit (see Chapter 12).

Filing Requirements for Dependents

Computation of the gross income filing requirement for an individual who can be claimed as a dependent on another person's tax return is subject to more complex rules. These rules are tied to the amount of a dependent's standard deduction (see text Section 3-2c). For 2023, a dependent with *any* of the following must file a return:

- Earned income only and gross income that is more than the total standard deduction (including any additional standard deduction).
- Unearned income only and gross income of more than $1,250 plus any additional standard deduction.
- Both earned and unearned income and gross income of more than the larger of $1,250 or the sum of earned income plus $400 (but limited to the basic standard deduction) plus any additional standard deduction.

Dependent Filing Requirements

Example 44

Tom is an unmarried dependent child who works part-time at the neighborhood pool as a lifeguard. During 2023, Tom earns $4,800 and has no other income. He receives a Form W–2 from his employer that reports his $4,800 of wages, Federal income taxes withheld of $422, FICA (Social Security and Medicare) taxes of $367, and no state income taxes. Must Tom file a return?

Answer: No. He had earned income only, and his gross income is less than his standard deduction of $13,850; his taxable income is zero and he has no Federal income tax liability. However, Tom will want to file a return to get a refund of his $422 Federal income taxes withheld.

Martha is a widow, age 68, who lives with her son (and is his dependent). In 2023, her only source of income is interest income from her bank account ($450) and tax-exempt interest income of $200. Must Martha file a return?

Answer: No. She has unearned income only and gross income of only $450 (which is less than $3,100; $1,250 plus her $1,850 additional standard deduction).

Return to the facts of Example 44. Tom also has $150 of interest income from his savings. Must Tom file a return?

Answer: No. He has earned income of $4,800 and gross income of $4,950. His standard deduction is $5,200 (earned income plus $400). As in Example 44, Tom will want to file a return to get a refund of any income taxes withheld.

If Tom had $450 of interest income, he would need to file a return. Now his gross income of $5,250 exceeds his $5,200 standard deduction (earned income plus $400).

3-6 Tax Determination

LO.6

Demonstrate the proper procedures for determining the tax liability.

The computation of income tax due (or refund) involves applying the proper set of tax rates to taxable income and then adjusting for available credits. In certain cases, however, the application of the kiddie tax will change how the tax is determined (see text Section 3-6c).

3-6a Tax Rates

The basic tax rate structure is progressive, with current rates ranging from 10 percent to 37 percent.[44] By way of comparison, the lowest rate structure, which was in effect in 1913–1915, ranged from 1 to 7 percent, and the highest, in effect during 1944–1945, ranged from 23 to 94 percent.

Tax Table Method

The tax liability is computed using either the Tax Table method or the Tax Rate Schedule method. Most taxpayers compute their tax using the **Tax Table**. Eligible taxpayers compute taxable income (as shown in Concept Summary 3.1) and *must* determine their tax by reference to the Tax Table. The following taxpayers, however, may *not* use the Tax Table method:

- Individuals whose taxable income exceeds the maximum (ceiling) amount in the Tax Table. In 2022, the Tax Table applies to taxable income below $100,000 for Form 1040.
- An estate or a trust.

The IRS does not release the Tax Tables until late in the year to which they apply. So the 2023 Tax Tables will be available at the end of 2023. The 2023 Tax Rate Schedules were released at the end of 2022.[45] For purposes of estimating tax liability and making quarterly estimated tax payments, the Tax Rate Schedules normally are used. Because it is available, the 2022 Tax Table is used to illustrate the tax computation using the Tax Table method.

Although the Tax Table is derived from the Tax Rate Schedules (discussed next), the tax calculated using the two methods may vary slightly. This is because the tax for a particular income range in the Tax Table is based on the midpoint amount.

Liang is single and has taxable income of $30,000 for calendar year 2022. To determine Liang's tax using the Tax Table (see Appendix A), find the $30,000 to $30,050 income line. Liang's tax is $3,398. This amount is actually the tax the Tax Rate Schedule for 2022 would yield on taxable income of $30,025 (i.e., the midpoint amount between $30,000 and $30,050).

Tax Rate Schedule Method

Taxpayers who do not use the Tax Tables use the **Tax Rate Schedules**. The 2023 Tax Rate Schedule for single taxpayers is reproduced in Exhibit 3.7.[46] This schedule is used to illustrate the tax computations in Examples 48 and 49.

Pat is single and had $5,810 of taxable income in 2023. His tax, based on the Tax Rate Schedule, is $581 ($5,810 × 10%).

Pat's tax, based on the Tax Table, is $583. This tax is based on taxable income of $5,825 (the midpoint between $5,800 and $5,850). Because his taxable income is less than $100,000, Pat must use the Tax Table.

Several terms are used to describe tax rates. The rates in the Tax Rate Schedules are often referred to as *statutory* (or nominal) rates. The *marginal* rate is the tax rate that would be assessed on the next dollar of income for a particular taxpayer. In Example 48, the statutory rate and the marginal rate are both 10 percent.

[44] Rev.Proc. 2022–38.

[45] The 2022 Tax Tables and the 2023 and 2022 Tax Rate Schedules are reproduced in Appendix A; 2023 Tax Tables will be available on the IRS website in late 2023. For quick reference, the Tax Rate Schedules also are reproduced inside the front cover of this text.

[46] § 1(i), as modified by § 1(j).

Exhibit 3.7 2023 Tax Rate Schedule for Single Taxpayers

If Taxable Income Is			
Over	**But Not Over**	**The Tax Is:**	**Of the Amount Over**
$ -0-	$ 11,000	10%	$ -0-
11,000	44,725	$ 1,100.00 + 12%	11,000
44,725	95,375	5,147.00 + 22%	44,725
95,375	182,100	16,290.00 + 24%	95,375
182,100	231,250	37,104.00 + 32%	182,100
231,250	578,125	52,832.00 + 35%	231,250
578,125		174,238.25 + 37%	578,125

Jocelyn is single and had taxable income of $102,000 in 2023. Her tax is $17,880.00 [$16,290.00 + 24%($102,000 − $95,375)].

The *average* rate is equal to the tax liability divided by taxable income. In Example 49, Jocelyn has statutory rates of 10 percent, 12 percent, 22 percent, and 24 percent. Jocelyn's average rate is 17.53 percent ($17,880 tax liability ÷ $102,000 taxable income); her marginal rate is 24 percent.

A tax is *progressive* (or graduated) if a higher rate of tax applies as the tax base increases. The progressive nature of the Federal income tax on individuals is illustrated by computing the tax in Example 49 using each rate bracket.

Tax on first $11,000 at 10%	$ 1,100.00
Tax on $44,725 − $11,000 at 12%	4,047.00
Tax on $95,375 − $44,725 at 22%	11,143.00
Tax on $102,000 − $95,375 at 24%	1,590.00
Total tax on taxable income of $102,000	$17,880.00

A special computation (see text Section 3-9d) limits the effective tax rate on qualified dividends (see Chapter 4) and net long-term capital gain (see Chapter 14).

3-6b Computation of Net Taxes Payable or Refund Due

The pay-as-you-go feature of the Federal income tax system requires payment of all or part of the taxpayer's income tax liability during the year. These payments take the form of Federal income tax withheld by employers or estimated tax paid by the taxpayer or both.[47] The payments are applied against the tax liability to determine whether the taxpayer will get a refund or pay additional tax.

Employers are required to withhold income tax on compensation paid to their employees and to pay this tax to the government. The employer must provide each employee a Form W–2 (Wage and Tax Statement), which documents wages and taxes withheld (including income, Social Security, and Medicare taxes). An employee should receive a 2023 Form W–2 no later than January 31, 2024.

If taxpayers receive income that is not subject to withholding or income from which not enough tax is withheld, they may have to pay estimated tax. Form 1040–ES (Estimated Tax for Individuals) is used for these payments, and estimates are due quarterly (see Chapter 12 for a thorough discussion).

[47] § 3402 for withholding; § 6654 for estimated payments.

The income tax liability is reduced by any available tax credits (which are different from tax deductions). Tax credits reduce the tax liability dollar for dollar. Tax deductions reduce taxable income on which the tax liability is based.

In 2023, Gail is a single taxpayer in the 24% tax bracket. As a result of incurring $1,000 in child care expenses, she is entitled to a $200 child care credit ($1,000 child care expenses × 20% credit rate; see Chapter 12 for details). She also contributed $1,000 to the American Cancer Society and included this amount in her itemized deductions.

The child care credit results in a $200 reduction of Gail's tax liability for the year. The contribution to the American Cancer Society reduces taxable income by $1,000 and results in a $240 reduction in Gail's tax liability ($1,000 reduction in taxable income × 24% tax rate).

Tax credits (other than the child and dependent tax credits; see text Section 3-4e) are discussed in Chapter 12. Some of the more common credits include:

- Earned income credit.
- Credit for child and dependent care expenses.
- Education tax credits.
- Premium tax credit.

The computation of net taxes payable or refund due can be illustrated by returning to the facts of Example 6.

Example 51

Grace is not married and has her disabled and dependent mother living with her. This qualifies Grace for head-of-household filing status. Recall that Example 6 established that Grace has taxable income of $33,300. In addition, assume that you have the following information: income tax withheld, $3,000; estimated tax payments, $600; and dependent tax credit, $500. Grace's net taxes payable is computed as follows:

Income tax (from 2023 Tax Rate Schedule, for head of household, Appendix A)		$3,682
Less: Tax credits and prepayments—		
Dependent tax credit	$ 500	
Income tax withheld	3,000	
Estimated tax payments	600	(4,100)
Net taxes payable or (refund due)		($ 418)

Grace's tax was computed using the Tax Rate Schedules rather than the Tax Tables because the 2023 Tax Tables were not available when this textbook was published (they are not available until the end of 2023).

3-6c Kiddie Tax—Unearned Income of Dependent Children

LO.7 **Identify and report the unearned income of dependent children (the kiddie tax).**

At one time, a dependent child could claim an exemption deduction (along with a standard deduction) on his or her own return even if claimed as a dependent by the parents. This enabled a parent to shift investment income (like interest and dividends) to a child by transferring income-producing assets. The child would pay no tax on the income to the extent that it was sheltered by the child's exemption and standard deduction amounts. And if the child did pay any tax, that tax was at the child's (lower) rates rather than the parents' (higher) rates.

To reduce the tax savings that result from shifting income from parents to children, the net **unearned income**[48] (commonly called investment income) of certain children is taxed using special rules. This provision, commonly referred to as the **kiddie tax**, applies to any child who is under age 19 (or under age 24 if a full-time student) and has unearned income of more than $2,500 in 2023 ($2,300 in 2022).[49]

[48] Unearned income includes taxable interest, dividends, capital gains, rents, royalties, the taxable portion of scholarships, pension and annuity income, and income (other than earned income) received as the beneficiary of a trust.

[49] § 1(g)(2). The kiddie tax does not apply if the child has earned income that exceeds half of the support received, if the child is married and files a joint return, or if both parents are deceased.

Net Unearned Income

In 2023, net unearned income of a dependent child is computed as follows:[50]

Unearned income
Less: $1,250
Less: The greater of:
- $1,250 of the standard deduction, *or*
- The amount of allowable itemized deductions directly connected with the production of the unearned income

Equals: Net unearned income

If net unearned income is zero (or negative), the child's tax is computed using the appropriate Tax Rate Schedule (likely single). If net unearned income is positive, this amount is taxed at the parents' rate. The child's remaining taxable income (known as nonparental source income) is taxed at the child's rate.

Tax Determination

If a child is subject to the kiddie tax, there are two options for computing the tax on the income. A separate return may be filed for the child, or the parents may elect to report the child's income on their own return.

If a separate return is filed for the child, the tax on net unearned income (referred to as the *allocable parental tax*) is computed as though the income had been included on the parents' return. Form 8615 (Tax for Certain Children Who Have Unearned Income) is used to compute the tax. The steps required in this computation are illustrated in Example 52.

Example 52

Olaf and Olga have a child, Hans (age 10). In 2023, Hans received $3,600 of interest income, paid investment-related fees of $200, and had no earned income. Olaf and Olga had $70,000 of taxable income, not including their child's investment income. The parents have no qualified dividends or capital gains. Olaf and Olga do not make the parental election (discussed below).

1. Determine Hans's net unearned income	
Gross income (unearned)	$ 3,600
Less: $1,250	(1,250)
Less: The greater of	
• $1,250 or	
• Investment expense ($200)	(1,250)
Equals: Net unearned income	$ 1,100
2. Determine allocable parental tax	
Parents' taxable income	$70,000
Plus: Hans's net unearned income	1,100
Equals: Revised taxable income	$71,100
Tax on revised taxable income	$ 8,092
Less: Tax on parents' taxable income	(7,960)
Allocable parental tax	$ 132
3. Determine Hans's nonparental source tax	
Hans's AGI	$ 3,600
Less: Standard deduction	(1,250)
Less: Personal exemption	(–0–)
Equals: Taxable income	$ 2,350
Less: Net unearned income	(1,100)
Nonparental source taxable income	$ 1,250
Nonparental source tax ($1,250 × 10% rate)	$ 125
4. Determine Hans's total tax liability	
Nonparental source tax (Step 3)	$ 125
Allocable parental tax (Step 2)	132
Total tax	$ 257

Without the kiddie tax, Hans's tax liability would have been $235 ($2,350 taxable income × 10% rate); as a result, the kiddie tax results in an increased tax liability of $22 ($257 – $235) for Hans.

[50] The $1,250 amounts in the net unearned income computation are adjusted each year for inflation. The amounts were $1,150 in 2022.

Election to Claim Certain Unearned Income on Parent's Return

A parent may elect to report the child's unearned income that exceeds $2,500 ($2,300 in 2022) on the parent's own tax return if the child meets *all* of the following requirements:

- Gross income is from interest and dividends only.
- Gross income is more than $1,250 but less than $12,500 (for 2022, these amounts are $1,150 and $11,500).
- No estimated tax has been paid in the name and Social Security number of the child, and the child is not subject to backup withholding.

If this election is made, the child is treated as having no gross income and is not required to file a tax return. In this case, Form 8814 (Parents' Election to Report Child's Interest and Dividends) must be filed as part of the parents' tax return. The parent(s) also must pay an additional tax equal to the smaller of $125 or 10 percent of the child's gross income over $1,250.[51]

Other Rules

Here are a few other rules that apply to the kiddie tax:[52]

- If parents have more than one child subject to the tax on net unearned income, the tax for the children is computed as shown in Example 52 and then allocated to the children based on their relative amounts of income.
- For children of divorced parents, the taxable income of the custodial parent is used to determine the allocable parental tax. This parent is the one who may elect to report the child's unearned income.
- For married individuals filing separate returns, the individual with the greater taxable income is the applicable parent.

3-7 Tax Return Filing Procedures

3-7a Selecting the Proper Form

Because the 2023 tax forms had not been released when this text was published, the following comments apply to the 2022 forms.[53]

All taxpayers use Form 1040 as a starting point. Then depending on their various activities (e.g., business, investment, personal), supplemental schedules may be required.

If the taxpayer:	File:
Has additional income to report (e.g., business income or loss, unemployment compensation, prize or award money, or gambling winnings). *OR* Has any deductions *for* AGI to claim (e.g., student loan interest, self-employment tax, individual retirement account contributions, or educator expenses).	Schedule 1 (Form 1040)
Owes the alternative minimum tax or needs to make an excess advance premium tax credit repayment. *OR* Owes other taxes (e.g., the self-employment tax, household employment taxes, or additional taxes on IRAs or other qualified retirement plans and tax-favored accounts).	Schedule 2 (Form 1040)

[51] § 1(g)(7). Parents who have substantial itemized deductions based on AGI (see Chapter 10) may find that making the parental election increases total taxes for the family unit. Taxes should be calculated both with and without the parental election to determine the appropriate choice.

[52] See IRS Publication 17 (*Your Federal Income Tax*) and Form 8615 (Tax for Certain Children Who Have Unearned Income).

[53] Draft tax forms are available from the IRS at **irs.gov/draft-tax-forms**.

If the taxpayer:	File:
Can claim a nonrefundable credit other than the child tax credit or the dependent tax credit (e.g., the foreign tax credit, education credits, or the general business credit). *OR* Can claim a refundable credit other than the earned income credit, American Opportunity credit, or additional child tax credit (e.g., the net premium tax credit, health coverage tax credit, or qualified sick and family leave credits). *OR* Has other payments to report (e.g., an amount paid with an extension to file or excess Social Security tax withheld).	Schedule 3 (Form 1040)

Schedules 1, 2, and 3 are reproduced on pages 3-11 through 3-16. The other schedules are available on the IRS website (**irs.gov**). Other forms and schedules may be needed to supplement Form 1040 and Schedules 1 through 3. For example, a self-employed taxpayer will need to complete Schedule C (Form 1040) as a supplement to Schedule 1 while also computing any self-employment tax liability by completing Schedule SE (Form 1040) as a supplement to Schedule 2. Taxpayers who want to itemize deductions *from* AGI need to complete Schedule A (Form 1040) to document those deductions.

The IRS has developed a tax return (Form 1040-SR) for taxpayers who are age 65 by the last day of the year. Form 1040-SR is very similar to Form 1040.[54]

3-7b The E-File Approach

The **e-file** program is used by the vast majority of individual taxpayers (and is mandatory for most tax return preparers). The required tax information is transmitted to the IRS electronically either directly from the taxpayer (i.e., an "e-file online return") or indirectly through an "Authorized *e-file* Provider." These Providers are tax professionals who have been accepted into the electronic filing program by the IRS. Providers often are the preparers of the return as well.

Taxpayers also can use IRS Free File (with online fillable forms) or use commercial software to file a tax return at no cost. A number of software providers offer free e-filing services. These services are generally available only to taxpayers who have AGI of $73,000 or less. Eligibility requirements and a list of the software providers are available on the IRS website: **irs.gov/filing/e-file-options**.

All taxpayers and tax return preparers must attest to the returns they file. For most taxpayers, this is done through an electronic return signature using a personal identification number (a Self-Select PIN). Or the taxpayer can authorize a tax preparer to generate a PIN by signing Form 8879 (IRS *e-file* Signature Authorization). If certain paper documents must be submitted, a one-page form must be completed and filed when the return is e-filed. Form 8453 (U.S. Individual Income Tax Transmittal for an IRS *e-file* Return) is used to submit required attachments for both self- and practitioner-prepared electronic returns.

The *e-file* approach has two major advantages over paper filing. First, it eliminates many reporting errors. Second, it reduces the time required for processing a refund.

3-7c When and Where to File

Tax returns of individuals are due on or before the fifteenth day of the fourth month following the close of the tax year. For the calendar year taxpayer, the usual filing date is on or before April 15 of the following year.[55] When the due date falls on a Saturday, Sunday, or legal holiday, the filing deadline is the next business day. If the return is mailed to the proper address with sufficient postage and is postmarked on or before the due date, it is deemed timely filed.[56] The return should be sent or delivered to the IRS Regional Service Center listed in the instructions for each type of return or contained in software applications.[57]

[54]Created by Sec. 41106 of P.L. 115–123, the Bipartisan Budget Act of 2018.

[55]§ 6072(a); Rev.Rul. 2015–13 provides filing deadline guidance when there are unique state holidays.

[56]The Code allows the IRS to prescribe rules when taxpayers use FedEx, UPS, or a similar delivery service [§ 7502(f)]. See Notice 2016–30 for the current list of "designated private delivery services" that, if used, will meet the timely filed rules.

[57]The appropriate IRS Regional Service Center address can be found at **irs.gov/filing/where-to-file-addresses-for-taxpayers-and-tax-professionals-filing-form-1040**.

If a taxpayer is unable to file the return by the return's due date, a six-month extension of time can be obtained by filing Form 4868 (Application for Automatic Extension of Time to File U.S. Individual Income Tax Return) by the return's due date. Members of the U.S. Armed Forces also are allowed additional time for filing their Federal income tax returns.[58]

Although an extension provides additional time to file a return, it does not extend the deadline for paying any taxes due. If more tax is owed, it should be paid when the Form 4868 is filed. If a taxpayer does not obtain an extension of time to file and/or pay any tax due, the failure to file and failure to pay penalties can be assessed (these are discussed in Chapter 1).

3-7d **Modes of Payment**

Payments of any taxes due can be made in a variety of ways, including check or money order (with payment made to "United States Treasury"), IRS Direct Pay (electronic funds withdrawal from a bank account), or the Electronic Federal Tax Payment System (EFTPS). In addition, the IRS has approved the use of MasterCard, American Express, Discover, and Visa to pay Federal taxes using a payment processor (fees will apply to these transactions).

3-7e **Amended Tax Returns**

If a taxpayer discovers an error on a previously filed tax return (e.g., a failure to report some income or missed deductions or tax credits), an **amended tax return** should be filed. Form 1040–X (Amended U.S. Individual Income Tax Return) is used for this purpose.

If tax is owed because taxable income on the amended return is greater than originally reported or a tax credit was originally reported that was higher than allowed, interest and penalties will be assessed by the IRS unless the taxpayer provides a reasonable explanation for the changes (see text Section 1-5d).

If the changes result in a refund, the deadline for filing a Form 1040–X and getting the refund is generally the *later* of:[59]

1. Three years after the date the original return was filed, or
2. Two years after the date any taxes were paid with the original return.

Returns filed before the due date (without regard to extensions) are considered filed on the due date, and withholding is deemed to be tax paid on the due date.[60]

Assume that Christina filed her 2022 tax return on March 1, 2023 and paid the taxes due on that date. After filing her return, Christina realizes that she should have itemized her deductions instead of taking the standard deduction; this will result in a tax refund. Based on the three-year rule, Christina has until April 15, 2026 to file an amended 2022 tax return and claim a refund.

On the other hand, assume that Christina filed for an extension of time to file her 2022 tax return to October 15, 2023, and ultimately filed her return on September 1, 2023. In this case, the three-year period for filing an amended 2022 tax return starts running on September 1, 2023.

If a taxpayer files a return before the due date (including before the extended due date) and discovers an error before the due date (or extended due date if an extension was filed), they can fix this by filing another return (not a 1040–X) and this later filed return—referred to as a *superseding return*, is treated as the original return.

[58] Reg. § 1.6081–4. See also IRS Publication 17 (*Your Federal Income Tax*), Chapter 1.

[59] § 6511.

[60] § 6513.

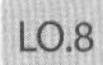

Explain the fundamentals of property transactions.

3-8 Gains and Losses from Property Transactions—In General

Gains and losses from property transactions are discussed in detail in Chapters 13 and 14. But an overview is relevant for topics that are discussed in the intervening chapters.

When property is sold (or otherwise disposed of), a gain or loss results. This gain or loss has a tax effect on the seller when the *realized* gain or loss is *recognized* for tax purposes. Without a transaction generating realized gain or loss, there generally can be no recognized gain or loss. Realized gain or loss is computed as follows:

Amount realized from the sale  **Adjusted basis of the property**  **Realized gain (or loss)**

The amount realized is the selling price of the property less any costs of disposition (e.g., brokerage commissions) incurred by the seller. The adjusted basis of the property is determined as follows:

	Cost (or other original basis) at date of acquisition[61]
Add:	Capital additions
Subtract:	Depreciation (if appropriate) and other capital recoveries (see Chapter 8)
Equals:	Adjusted basis at date of sale or other disposition

In general, all realized gains are recognized (taxable). However, the tax law provides some exceptions (see, for example, Chapter 13 dealing with certain nontaxable exchanges). Realized losses may or may not be recognized (deductible) for tax purposes. For example, losses realized from the sale of personal use property (e.g., a residence, home furnishings, clothing, sports equipment) are not recognized.

During the current year, Ted sells his sailboat (adjusted basis of $4,000) for $5,500. Ted also sells one of his personal automobiles (adjusted basis of $8,000) for $5,000.

Ted's realized gain of $1,500 from the sale of the sailboat is recognized. On the other hand, the $3,000 realized loss on the sale of the automobile is not recognized and will not provide Ted with any deductible tax benefit.

In terms of the tax formula, recognized gains from property transactions are included in gross income. If the gain is deferred (e.g., like-kind exchanges or involuntary conversions—see Chapter 13) or not recognized (e.g., sale of a residence—see Chapter 13), there is no immediate tax effect. Recognized losses from property transactions are treated as deductions *for* adjusted gross income (AGI).

If a property disposition results in a recognized gain or loss, the gain or loss must be *classified* as capital or ordinary. Although ordinary gain is fully taxable and ordinary loss is fully deductible, the same is often not true for capital gains and capital losses.

3-9 Gains and Losses from Property Transactions—Capital Gains and Losses

Capital gains and losses are treated uniquely in the Federal income tax system. Capital gains are included in the determination of taxable income and may be taxed at lower (preferential) tax rates. Capital losses, on the other hand, may not be fully deductible when determining taxable income (if limited, the amount not allowed can be carried over and used in subsequent years).

[61] Cost usually means purchase price plus expenses related to the acquisition of the property and incurred by the purchaser (e.g., brokerage commissions). For the basis of property acquired by gift or inheritance and other basis rules, see Chapter 13.

3-9a **Definition of a Capital Asset**

Capital assets are defined in the Code as any property held by the taxpayer *other than* certain items including inventory, accounts receivable, and depreciable property or real estate used in a business (see Chapter 14 for a complete discussion). As a result, the sale or exchange of these assets normally results in ordinary income or loss (see Chapter 14).

Kelly owns a pizza parlor. During the current year, he sells an automobile that had been used as a delivery car for three years. The sale resulted in a loss of $1,000. Because this automobile is property used in his business, Kelly has an ordinary loss deduction of $1,000 rather than a capital loss deduction.

The principal capital assets held by an individual taxpayer include (1) assets held for personal (rather than business) use (e.g., a personal residence or an automobile) and (2) assets held for investment purposes (e.g., corporate securities or land). Capital assets generally include collectibles, which are subject to somewhat unique tax treatment. **Collectibles** include art, antiques, gems, metals, stamps, some coins and bullion, and alcoholic beverages that are held as investments.

3-9b **Determination of Net Capital Gain**

To arrive at a net capital gain, capital losses must be taken into account. First, capital gains and losses are categorized based on their holding period: *short term* (held for one year or less) and *long term* (held for more than one year). Then gains and losses in each category are netted together. If excess losses result, they are applied to the category carrying the *highest* tax rate. A *net capital gain* occurs if the net long-term capital gain (NLTCG) exceeds the net short-term capital loss (NSTCL).

In the current year, Colin has the following capital transactions and resulting gains (losses):

Penguin Corporation stock (held for 8 months)	$ 1,000
Owl Corporation stock (held for 10 months)	(3,000)
Cardinal Corporation stock (held for 5 years)	2,000
Land (held as an investment for 3 years)	4,000

The Penguin Corporation short-term capital gain (STCG) of $1,000 is offset by the Owl Corporation short-term capital loss (STCL) of $3,000, resulting in a net STCL of $2,000. The Cardinal Corporation long-term capital gain (LTCG) and the land LTCG are combined, resulting in a net LTCG of $6,000. The net STCL offsets the net LTCG, resulting in a net capital gain of $4,000.

3-9c **Treatment of Net Capital Loss**

For individual taxpayers, net capital loss can be used to offset ordinary income of up to $3,000 ($1,500 for married persons filing separate returns). If a taxpayer has both shortand long-term capital losses, short-term losses are used first. Any remaining net capital loss is carried over indefinitely until used up (subject to the annual $3,000 limit). When carried over, the excess capital loss retains its classification as short- or long-term.

In 2023, Tina has a short-term capital loss of $2,000, a long-term capital loss of $2,500, and no capital gains. She can deduct $3,000 ($2,000 short-term + $1,000 long-term) of this amount as an ordinary loss. The remaining $1,500 is carried over to 2024 as a long-term capital loss.

The Big Picture

Example 58

Return to the facts of *The Big Picture* on p. 3-1. Aleha's sale of her wedding rings resulted in a realized capital loss of $2,800 [$9,000 (selling price) − $11,800 (cost basis)]. However, because they were personal use property, Aleha cannot deduct the loss.

3-9d **Taxation of Net Capital Gain**

Net capital gains are classified and taxed as follows:

Classification	Maximum Rate*
Short-term gains (held for one year or less)	37%
Long-term gains (held for more than one year):	
Collectibles	28%
Certain depreciable property used in a trade or business (known as unrecaptured § 1250 gain and discussed in Chapter 14)	25%
All other long-term capital gains	20%, 15%, or 0%

*Does not include additional Medicare taxes on high-income taxpayers.

The special tax rates for long-term capital gains (called the alternative tax computation) are used when the taxpayer's regular tax rate *exceeds* the alternative tax rate. When tax liability is determined, long-term capital gains are taxed last. As a result, the tax rate applied to a long-term capital gain will depend on the taxpayer's regular tax rate on other income and the size of the long-term capital gain (a large long-term capital gain may cross marginal rates brackets and, theoretically, could be taxed at 0%, 15%, and 20% rates). The alternative rates are applied based on the taxpayer's filing status and taxable income (see Exhibit 3.8).[62] Special rates apply to collectibles and certain types of depreciable realty. If losses are used to offset gains, the losses are first used to offset gains with the *highest* tax rates.[63] These special tax rates also apply to qualified dividend income (see Chapter 4). Chapter 14 provides a detailed discussion of these tax computations.

Exhibit 3.8 **2023 Alternative Tax Rates on Net Capital Gains (NCG) (Based on Filing Status and Taxable Income)**

FILING STATUS								
Single		Married, Filing Jointly		Married, Filing Separately		Head of Household		NCG Tax Rate
Taxable Income		Taxable Income		Taxable Income		Taxable Income		
Greater Than	No More Than	Greater Than	No More Than	Greater Than	No More Than	Greater Than	No More Than	
$ -0-	$ 44,625	$ -0-	$ 89,250	$ -0-	$ 44,625	$ -0-	$ 59,750	0%
44,625	492,300	89,250	553,850	44,625	276,900	59,750	523,050	15%
492,300		553,850		276,900		523,050		20%

[62] In 2022, the 0% rate applies when taxable income does not exceed $83,350 (married, filing jointly), $55,800 (head of household), or $41,675 (single and married, filing separately). The 20% rate applies only when the taxpayer's taxable income exceeds $517,200 (married, filing jointly), $258,600 (married, filing separately), $488,500 (head of household), or $459,750 (single).

[63] § 1(h)(1).

Net Capital Gain Tax Computation

Example 59

During 2023, Marco is single, has taxable income of $35,000, and has the following capital gains for the year:

Robin Corporation stock (held for 6 months)	$1,000
Crow Corporation stock (held for 13 months)	1,000

Although both transactions yield a $1,000 capital gain, the tax effects are quite different. Marco pays a tax of $120 ($1,000 × 12%) on the Robin stock gain but $0 ($1,000 × 0%) on the Crow stock gain (his taxable income does not exceed $44,625).

Assume the same facts as in Example 59, except that Marco's taxable income for the year is $140,000 (rather than $35,000). Marco's taxable income puts him in the 24% tax bracket. In addition, his taxable income is above $44,625 (where the 0% rate would apply to long-term capital gains) and does not exceed $492,300 (where the 20% rate would apply to long-term capital gains).

Marco now pays a tax of $240 ($1,000 × 24%) on the Robin stock gain and $150 ($1,000 × 15%) on the Crow stock gain.

Example 61

In 2023, Colin is single, has taxable income of $195,000, and has the following capital transactions and resulting gains (losses):

Penguin Corporation stock (held for 8 months)	$ 1,000
Owl Corporation stock (held for 10 months)	(3,000)
Stamp collection (held for 5 years)	2,000
Land (held as an investment for 3 years)	4,000

The Penguin Corporation short-term capital gain (STCG) of $1,000 is offset by the Owl Corporation short-term capital loss (STCL) of $3,000, resulting in a net STCL of $2,000. This $2,000 net STCL is then applied against the stamp collection gain—a collectible long-term capital gain (LTCG) with the highest tax rate (28%). Because there is no remaining STCL, Colin has a net LTCG of $4,000 from the land sale. Because Colin's taxable income exceeds $44,625 and does not exceed $492,300, the net LTCG is taxed at a 15% rate.

3-9e Taxation of Digital Assets (Including Virtual Currency)

Broadly speaking, a digital asset is anything that is created and stored digitally, is identifiable and discoverable, and has or provides value. Digital assets have become more popular and valuable as technological advances become integrated into our lives. Data, images, video, written content, and other items have long been considered digital assets with ownership rights.

The creation of bitcoin in 2008 and its distributed ledger technology (for bitcoin, it is a blockchain) allowed digital assets to be recorded and tracked using sophisticated technology. This technology allows the rightful owner to be identified and verified (generally only via a code for the asset and not the owner's name); this avoids transferring the digital asset to multiple people. With distributed ledger technology, just about anything that can be tracked in a digital form can be "tokenized" and have value (the same is true of things that exist only in an intangible form). In addition, many digital asset transactions are governed by "smart contracts," where the terms of an agreement are directly written into lines of code in the distributed ledger. This allows actions to take place automatically if the specified conditions occur (that is, these contracts are self-executing).

Cryptocurrency is one example of a digital asset. Over 6,000 types of virtual currency exist. The first and best-known virtual currency is bitcoin, which had its first real-world transaction in 2010 (to purchase two pizzas).[64] Another example of digital assets are non-fungible tokens (NTFs). NFTs are unique, identifiable digital assets (for example, art or music or special rights and privileges) that are often accompanied by a digital certificate of authenticity. Just as an automobile has a title which identifies the owner, an NFT has a token that identifies its owner (and the record of ownership is secured on a distributed ledger).

[64] **en.bitcoinwiki.org/wiki/Bitcoin_history**. Other virtual currencies include Ethereum, Tether, and Binance.

In 2021, Congress added the term "digital asset" to the tax law.[65] A digital asset is defined as "any digital representation of value which is recorded on a cryptographically secured distributed ledger or any similar technology" as specified by the Treasury Department. Virtual currencies, NFTs, and other digital assets that can be tokenized appear to meet this definition.

IRS Guidance on Virtual Currency

In 2014, the IRS issued guidance on the tax treatment of convertible virtual currency used to pay for goods or services.[66] Convertible means that the virtual currency can be exchanged for real (sovereign) currency in that it acts as a substitute for real currency, such as the U.S. dollar. The key point of this IRS guidance is that virtual currency is treated as *property* rather than as a *foreign currency*. As a result, if an employee is paid in bitcoin, her wages are equal to the value of the bitcoin when received. When a holder of virtual currency uses it to acquire goods, services, or a different virtual currency, the transaction is treated as a barter transaction with tax consequences to the holder.

Neha acquired $500 of bitcoin from a virtual currency exchange in 2021 to hold for investment. In 2023, when its value was $1,650, Neha used all of her bitcoin to pay for repairs to her car (the repair business accepted bitcoin from customers).

Neha must report a long-term capital gain of $1,150 ($1,650 fair market value less $500 basis; her holding period is more than one year). She is treated as having sold her bitcoin for $1,650 when she exchanged it for services worth $1,650. Neha will also answer "yes" to the digital asset question on page 1 of her Form 1040 (discussed below).

Reporting of Digital Asset Transactions

Given that virtual currency is treated as property for tax purposes, the IRS asked Congress to expand the information reporting requirements for these assets. The Infrastructure Investment and Jobs Act of 2021 includes several provisions relating to tax information reporting of digital assets. Digital asset brokers (including cryptocurrency exchanges) will be required to report a summary of any customer's digital asset transactions to the IRS on a Form 1099–DA ("DA" for "digital assets"). The form is expected to be like the form currently used by brokers to report transactions involving stocks, bonds, or other investment securities (Form 1099–B).[67] Currently, businesses are required to report the receipt of more than $10,000 in *cash* to the IRS. Beginning in 2024, this requirement is expanded to include the receipt of more than $10,000 in digital assets.[68]

The 2022 Form 1040 includes a specific question about digital assets (see the last line in the partial Form 1040 presented below).

Form **1040** Department of the Treasury—Internal Revenue Service
U.S. Individual Income Tax Return **2022** OMB No. 1545-0074 IRS Use Only—Do not write or staple in this space.

Filing Status ☐ Single ☐ Married filing jointly ☐ Married filing separately (MFS) ☐ Head of household (HOH) ☐ Qualifying surviving spouse (QSS)
Check only one box.
If you checked the MFS box, enter the name of your spouse. If you checked the HOH or QSS box, enter the child's name if the qualifying person is a child but not your dependent:

Your first name and middle initial	Last name			**Your social security number**
If joint return, spouse's first name and middle initial	Last name			**Spouse's social security number**
Home address (number and street). If you have a P.O. box, see instructions.			Apt. no.	**Presidential Election Campaign** Check here if you, or your spouse if filing jointly, want $3 to go to this fund. Checking a box below will not change your tax or refund. ☐ **You** ☐ **Spouse**
City, town, or post office. If you have a foreign address, also complete spaces below.		State	ZIP code	
Foreign country name	Foreign province/state/county		Foreign postal code	

Digital Assets At any time during 2022, did you: (a) receive (as a reward, award, or payment for property or services); or (b) sell, exchange, gift, or otherwise dispose of a digital asset (or a financial interest in a digital asset)? (See instructions.) ☐ **Yes** ☐ **No**

[65] § 6045(g)(3)(D), added by the Infrastructure and Jobs Act of 2021 (P.L. 117–58).

[66] Notice 2014–21.

[67] §§ 6045(c)(1)(D) and (g)(3)(B) and (C). In Announcement 2023–2, the IRS delayed broker reporting of digital asset transactions until final regulations under § 6045 are issued.

[68] § 6050I(d)(3). The Form 8300 used for this reporting is due from the business to the IRS within 15 days of the transaction.

Since most individuals do not own digital assets (including virtual currency), most Form 1040 filers will answer "no." The purpose of the question is to remind taxpayers about the need to report taxable digital asset transactions, like the sale of virtual currency for cash or other virtual currency, the receipt of virtual currency for performance of services, or the use of virtual currency to buy goods or services. According to the IRS, receiving (or disposing) of a digital asset in exchange for property or services provided, selling a digital asset, or transferring a digital asset as a gift all require a "yes" response. However, taxpayers can answer "no" if their activities were limited to the purchase of a digital asset with cash, the holding of a digital asset in a wallet or an account, or the transfer of a digital asset from one wallet or account to another (owned by the same taxpayer).[69] To assist taxpayers in complying with these rules, the IRS maintains a set of "*frequently asked questions*" along with a short summary of digital assets and related tax implications on its website.[70]

3-10 Tax Planning

LO.9

Evaluate tax planning opportunities associated with the individual tax formula.

3-10a Maximizing the Use of the Standard Deduction

In some cases, the difference between using the standard deduction and itemizing may not be a significant amount. Here, taxes might be saved by alternating between the two options. The taxpayer does this by using the cash method to concentrate multiple years' deductions in a single year (e.g., church pledges for several years can be paid in one year). Then the standard deduction is used in alternate years.

3-10b Dependents

The Joint Return Test

A married person can be claimed as a dependent only if that individual does not file a joint return with his or her spouse. If a joint return has been filed, the damage may be undone if separate returns are substituted on or before the due date of the return.

Example 63

While preparing a client's 2022 income tax return on April 3, 2023, the tax professional discovered that the client's daughter had filed a joint return with her spouse in late January 2023. Presuming that the daughter otherwise qualifies as the client's dependent, her dependency status is not lost if she and her spouse file separate returns on or before April 15, 2023.

If the daughter and her spouse attempt to file separate returns after April 15, 2023, the returns will not be accepted (the joint return election is binding).[71]

Keep in mind that the filing of a joint return will not affect dependency status if the parties are filing solely to recover all income tax withholdings and no tax liability exists.

Support Considerations

The support of a qualifying child becomes relevant only if the child is self-supporting. In cases where the child has an independent source of funds, planning could help prevent an undesirable result. When a qualifying relative is involved, meeting the support test is essential.

Example 64

In 2023, Cheryl maintains a household that she shares with her son and mother. The son, Barry, is 23 years old and a full-time student in law school. The mother, Gladys, is 68 years old and active in charitable causes. Barry works part-time for a local law firm, and Gladys has income from

continued

[69] See IR–2023–12 (January 24, 2023).

[70] **irs.gov/individuals/international-taxpayers/frequently-asked-questions-on-virtual-currency-transactions** and **irs.gov/businesses/small-businesses-self-employed/digital-assets**.

[71] Reg. § 1.6013–1(a)(1).

investments. In resolving the support issue (or self-support in the case of Barry), Cheryl's contribution must be compared with that made by Barry and Gladys.[72]

What Barry and Gladys do with their funds becomes crucial. Funds that are used for nonsupport purposes (e.g., purchase of investments) or not used at all (e.g., deposited in a bank) are not considered. Limiting how much Barry and Gladys contribute to their own support enhances Cheryl's chances of claiming them as dependents. Records should be maintained showing the amount of support and its source.

Example 64 does not mention the possible application of the gross income test. Presuming that Barry is a qualifying child, the amount he earns does not matter, since the gross income test does not apply. Gladys, however, comes under the qualifying relative category, where the gross income test applies. In 2023, for her to be claimed as a dependent, her gross income must be less than $4,700.

Community Property Ramifications

In certain cases, state law can have an effect on dependent status.

Dependents: State Law Implications

During the year, Mitch provides more than half of the support of his son, Ross, and daughter-in-law, Connie, who live with him. Ross, age 22, is a full-time student, and Connie earns $5,000 from a part-time job. Ross and Connie do not file a joint return. All parties live in New York, a common law state. Mitch can claim Ross as a dependent since he is a qualifying child. Connie is not a dependent because she does not meet the gross income test under the qualifying relative category.

Example 66

Assume the same facts as in Example 65, except that all parties live in Arizona, a community property state. Now Connie also qualifies as a dependent. Because Connie's gross income is only $2,500 (half of the community income), she satisfies the gross income test.

3-10c Taking Advantage of Tax Rate Differentials

It is natural for taxpayers to be concerned about the taxes they are paying. How does a tax professional communicate information about tax rates to clients? There are several possibilities.

The *marginal rate* (refer to Examples 48 and 49) provides information that can help a taxpayer evaluate a particular course of action or structure a transaction in the most advantageous manner. For example, a taxpayer who is in the 12 percent bracket this year and expects to be in the 24 percent bracket next year should, if possible, defer payment of deductible expenses until next year to maximize the tax benefit of the deduction.

However, Congress understands these tax planning possibilities and has enacted many provisions to limit them. Some income-shifting limitations are discussed in Chapters 4, 5, and 16. Limitations that affect a taxpayer's ability to shift deductions are discussed in Chapters 6 through 11 and in Chapter 16.

A taxpayer's *effective rate* can be an informative measure of the effectiveness of tax planning. The effective rate is computed by dividing the taxpayer's tax liability by the total amount of income. A low effective rate can be considered an indication of effective tax planning.

[72]As part of her support contribution to Barry and Gladys, Cheryl can count the fair market value of the meals and lodging she provides.

One way of lowering the effective rate is to exclude income from the tax base. For example, a taxpayer might consider investing in tax-free municipal bonds rather than taxable corporate bonds. Although pretax income from corporate bonds is usually higher, after-tax income may be higher if the taxpayer invests in tax-free municipals.[73]

Another way of lowering the effective rate is to make sure the taxpayer's expenses and losses are deductible. For example, losses on investments in passive activities may not be deductible (see Chapter 11). Therefore, a taxpayer who plans to invest in an activity that will produce a loss in the early years should take steps to ensure that the business is treated as active rather than passive. Active losses are deductible, but passive activity losses are not.

3-10d **Income of Certain Children**

Taxpayers can use several strategies to avoid or minimize the effect of the rules that tax the unearned income of certain children. Parents should consider giving a younger child assets that defer taxable income until the child reaches 19 (or 24 for full-time students). For example, U.S. government Series EE savings bonds can be used to defer income until the bonds are cashed in (see Chapter 4).

Growth stocks, which typically pay little in the way of dividends, are another option. If the child holds the stock and then sells it at a profit once the child reaches a safe age, the profit is taxed at the child's low rates.

Taxpayers who own a business can employ their children. The child's earned income is sheltered by the standard deduction, and the parents' business is allowed a deduction for the wages.

Refocus on The Big Picture

A Divided Household

ISTOCK.COM/ATNOYDUR

Of major concern to Aleha is her filing status. If she qualifies as an abandoned spouse, she is entitled to file as head of household. If not, she is considered to be a married person filing separately. Moreover, to be an abandoned spouse, Aleha must be able to claim Paige as a dependent. To be a dependent, Paige must meet the requirements of a qualifying child *or* a qualifying relative.

For qualifying child purposes, Paige must meet either the age (i.e., under age 19) or the full-time student (under age 24) test. (A disabled child exception seems highly unlikely.) Because Paige currently is not a full-time student, is she under age 19? If so, she is a qualifying child (see Example 15). If Paige is not a qualifying child, is she a qualifying relative? Here, the answer depends on meeting the gross income test (see Example 23). How much did Paige earn from her part-time job? If her earnings are under $4,700, she satisfies the gross income test. As a result, if Paige can be claimed as a dependent under either the qualifying child or the qualifying relative category, Aleha is an abandoned spouse entitled to head-of-household filing status (see Example 43). If not, she is a married person filing separately.

Terrah can be claimed as Aleha's dependent because she is a member of the household. It does not matter that she died in February. Because Terrah is her dependent,

continued

[73]Investment in tax-free bonds also will reduce the net investment income tax (§ 1411) if the individual is subject to this additional tax (see Chapter 12).

Aleha can claim the medical expenses she paid on Terrah's behalf. The funeral expenses, however, are not deductible (see Example 20).

Does Terrah qualify Aleha for head-of-household filing status? No—although she is a dependent, Terrah does not meet the relationship test (see Example 40).

The sale of the wedding rings results in a capital loss of $2,800 ($9,000 – $11,800). Because the loss is for personal use property, it cannot be claimed for tax purposes (see Example 58).

What If?

Assume that Trevor left for parts unknown in *August* (not March). Now Aleha cannot qualify as an abandoned spouse. Her spouse lived in the home during part of the last six months of the year. Since Aleha is married, she cannot qualify for head-of-household filing status. She must file as a married person filing separately. The change in when Trevor left will not affect the dependency issue regarding Paige, however.

Key Terms

Abandoned spouse, 3-32
Amended tax return, 3-41
Child tax credit, 3-26
Collectibles, 3-43
Dependency exemptions, 3-19
Dependent tax credit, 3-26
E-file, 3-40
Filing status, 3-29
Head-of-household, 3-31
Itemized deductions, 3-6
Kiddie tax, 3-37
Marriage penalty, 3-31
Multiple support agreement, 3-24
Personal exemptions, 3-19
Qualifying child, 3-20
Qualifying relative, 3-21
Standard deduction, 3-7
Surviving spouse, 3-31
Tax Rate Schedules, 3-35
Tax Table, 3-35
Unearned income, 3-37

Discussion Questions

Critical Thinking

1. **LO.1, 5, 8, 9** During the year, Addison is involved in the following transactions:
   a. Lost money gambling on a recent trip to a casino.
   b. Helped pay for her neighbor's dental bills. The neighbor is a good friend who is unemployed.
   c. Received from the IRS a tax refund due to Addison's overpayment of last year's Federal income taxes.
   d. Paid a traffic ticket received while double parking to attend a business meeting.
   e. Contributed to the mayor's reelection campaign. The mayor had promised Addison to have some of her land rezoned. The mayor was reelected and got Addison's land rezoned.
   f. Borrowed money from a bank to make a down payment on an automobile.
   g. Sold a houseboat and a camper on eBay. Both were personal use items, and the gain from one offset the loss from the other.
   h. Paid for dependent grandfather's funeral expenses.
   i. Paid premiums on her dependent son's life insurance policy.

   What are the possible income tax ramifications of these transactions?

2. **LO.1** Which of the following items are *inclusions* in gross income?
   a. During the year, stock that the taxpayer purchased as an investment doubled in value.
   b. Amount an off-duty motorcycle police officer received for escorting a funeral procession.
   c. While his mother was in the hospital, the taxpayer sold some of her jewelry to help pay for the hospital bills.
   d. Child support payments received.
   e. A damage deposit the taxpayer recovered when he vacated the apartment he had rented.
   f. Interest received by the taxpayer on an investment in general purpose bonds issued by IBM.
   g. Amounts received by the taxpayer, a baseball "Hall of Famer," for autographing sports equipment (e.g., balls and gloves).
   h. Tips received by a bartender from patrons. (Taxpayer is paid a regular salary by the cocktail lounge that employs him.)
   i. Taxpayer sells his Super Bowl tickets for three times what he paid for them.
   j. Taxpayer receives a new BMW from his grandmother when he passes the CPA exam.

3. **LO.1** Which of the following items are *exclusions* from gross income?
   a. Alimony payments received (relates to a divorce settlement in 2016).
   b. Damages award received by the taxpayer for personal physical injury—none were for punitive damages.
   c. A new golf cart won in a church raffle.
   d. Amount collected on a loan previously made to a college friend.
   e. Insurance proceeds paid to the taxpayer on the death of her uncle—she was the designated beneficiary under the policy.
   f. Interest income on City of Chicago bonds.
   g. Jury duty fees.
   h. Stolen funds the taxpayer had collected for a local food bank drive.
   i. Reward paid by the IRS for information provided that led to the conviction of the taxpayer's former employer for tax evasion.
   j. An envelope containing $8,000 found (and unclaimed) by the taxpayer in a bus station.

4. **LO.1, 8, 9** In late 2023, the Polks come to you for tax advice. They are considering selling some stock investments for a loss and making a contribution to a traditional IRA. In reviewing their situation, you note that they have large medical expenses and a casualty loss (in a Federally declared disaster area), neither of which is covered by insurance. What advice would you give the Polks?

   Critical Thinking
   Decision Making
   Planning

5. **LO.2** In choosing between taking the standard deduction and itemizing deductions *from* AGI, what effect, if any, does each of the following have?

   Critical Thinking

   a. The age of the taxpayer(s).
   b. The health (i.e., physical condition) of the taxpayer.
   c. Whether taxpayers rent or own their residence.
   d. Taxpayer's filing status (e.g., single, married, filing jointly).
   e. Whether married taxpayers decide to file separate returns.
   f. The taxpayer's uninsured personal residence that was recently destroyed by a wildfire (the region was declared a disaster area by the Federal government).
   g. The number of dependents the taxpayer can claim.

6. **LO.2, 3, 5** In 2023, David is age 78, is a widower, and is being claimed as a dependent by his son. How does this situation affect the following?
   a. David's own individual filing requirement.
   b. The standard deduction allowed to David.
   c. The availability of any additional standard deduction.

Critical Thinking

7. **LO.4** Magda maintains a household that includes a son (age 30) and a cousin (age 28). She can claim the cousin as a dependent but not her son. Explain.

8. **LO.4** Heather, age 12, lives in the same household with her mother, grandmother, and uncle.
   a. Who can claim Heather as a dependent?
   b. Who takes precedence?

9. **LO.4** Caden and Lily are divorced on March 3, 2022. For financial reasons, however, Lily continues to live in Caden's apartment and receives her support from him. Caden does not claim Lily as a dependent on his 2022 Federal income tax return but does so on his 2023 return. Explain.

10. **LO.4** Isabella, Emma, and Jacob share equally in the support of their parents. Jacob tells each of his sisters to claim one of their parents as a dependent. Explain what Jacob means.

Critical Thinking

11. **LO.4** Mark and Lisa were divorced in 2022. In 2023, Mark has custody of their children, but Lisa provides nearly all of their support. Who is entitled to claim the children as dependents?

Critical Thinking

12. **LO.4** Mario, who is single, is a U.S. citizen and resident. He provides almost all of the support of his parents and two aunts, who are citizens and residents of Guatemala. Mario's parents and aunts are seriously considering moving to and becoming residents of Mexico. Would such a move have any impact on Mario? Why or why not?

13. **LO.5** Casey is a U.S. citizen employed by a multinational corporation at its London office. Casey is married to Michael, a British citizen, and they reside in England. Michael receives substantial rent income from real estate he owns in western Europe.
    a. Must Casey file a U.S. income tax return?
    b. Under what circumstances might Michael be considered a resident of the United States? Would such a classification be advantageous? Disadvantageous? Explain.

14. **LO.4, 5** Comment on the availability of head-of-household filing status for 2023 in each of the following independent situations:
    a. Taxpayer lives alone but maintains the household of his parents. In July 2023, the parents use their savings to purchase a new BMW for $62,000.
    b. Taxpayer maintains a home in which she and her dependent father live. The father enters a nursing facility for treatment of a mental disorder.
    c. Taxpayer, a single parent, maintains a home in which she and her unmarried son live. The son, age 18, earns $5,000 from a part-time job.
    d. Assume the same facts as in part (c), except that the son is age 19 (not 18), is not a full-time student, and is not disabled.
    e. Taxpayer is married and maintains a household in which he and his dependent stepson live.
    f. Taxpayer lives alone but maintains the household where her dependent daughter lives.
    g. Taxpayer maintains a household that includes an unrelated friend who qualifies as his dependent.

15. **LO.5** In many cases, a surviving spouse ultimately becomes a head of household for filing status purposes. Explain this statement.

16. **LO.6** Jayden calculates his 2023 income tax by using both the Tax Tables and the Tax Rate Schedules. Because the Tax Rate Schedules yield a slightly lower tax liability, he plans to pay this amount.
    a. Why is there a difference?
    b. Is Jayden's approach permissible? Why or why not?

17. **LO.7** In connection with the application of the kiddie tax, comment on the following:
    a. The child has only earned income.
    b. The child has a modest amount of unearned income.
    c. The child is age 20, is not a student, and is not disabled.
    d. The child is married.
    e. Effect of the parental election.
    f. The result when the parental election is made and the married parents file separate returns.

18. **LO.8** During the year, Hernando has the following transactions:

    - Gain on the sale of stock held as an investment for 10 months.
    - Gain on the sale of land held as an investment for 4 years.
    - Gain on the sale of a houseboat owned for 2 years and used for family vacations.
    - Loss on the sale of a reconditioned motorcycle owned for 3 years and used for recreational purposes.

    How should Hernando treat these transactions for income tax purposes?

19. **LO.8** During the year, Brandi had the following transactions: a long-term capital gain from the sale of land, a short-term capital loss from the sale of stock, and a long-term capital gain from the sale of a gun collection.
    a. How are these transactions treated for income tax purposes?
    b. Does this treatment favor the taxpayer or the IRS? Explain.

Computational Exercises

20. **LO.2** Brett and Abby are dependents of their parents, and each has income of $2,100 for the year. Brett's standard deduction for the year is $1,250, and Abby's is $2,500. Because their income is the same, what causes the difference in the amount of the standard deduction? Critical Thinking

21. **LO.2** Compute the 2023 standard deduction for the following taxpayers.
    a. Ellie is 15 and claimed as a dependent by her parents. She has $800 in dividend income and $1,400 in wages from a part-time job.
    b. Ruby and Woody are married and file a joint tax return. Ruby is age 66, and Woody is 69. Their taxable retirement income is $10,000.
    c. Shonda is age 68 and single. She is claimed by her daughter as a dependent. Her earned income is $500, and her interest income is $125.
    d. Frazier, age 55, is married but is filing a separate return. His wife itemizes her deductions.

22. **LO.5, 9** Paul and Sonja, who are married, had itemized deductions of $14,000 and $500, respectively, during 2023. Paul suggests that they file separately—he will itemize his deductions *from* AGI, and she will claim the standard deduction. Critical Thinking
    a. Evaluate Paul's suggestion.
    b. What should they do?

23. **LO.6** Compute the 2023 tax liability and the marginal and average tax rates for the following taxpayers (use the 2023 Tax Rate Schedules in Appendix A for this purpose):
    a. Chandler, who files as a single taxpayer, has taxable income of $98,700.
    b. Lazare, who files as a head of household, has taxable income of $61,100.

24. **LO.7** In 2023, Jack, age 12, has interest income of $4,900 on funds he inherited from his aunt and no earned income. He has no investment expenses. Christian and Danielle (his parents) have taxable income of $88,150 and file a joint return. Assume that no parental election is made. Determine Jack's net unearned income, allocable parental tax, and total tax liability.

25. **LO.8** Madeline sells her personal scooter for $550. She purchased the scooter for $700 three years ago. She also sells a painting for $1,200 that she acquired five years ago for $900. What are the tax implications of these sales?

26. **LO.8** During the year, Tamara had capital transactions resulting in gains (losses) as follows:

Sold stock in ABC Company (acquired two years ago)	($1,500)
Sold collectible coins (held for more than one year)	2,000
Sold stock in XYZ Company (acquired six months ago)	(4,100)
Sold stock in LMN Company (acquired three years ago)	500

Determine Tamara's net capital gain or loss as a result of these transactions.

Problems

27. **LO.1** Compute the taxable income for 2023 in each of the following independent situations:
    a. Aaron and Michele, ages 40 and 41, respectively, are married and file a joint return. In addition to four dependent children, they have AGI of $125,000 and itemized deductions of $29,000.
    b. Sybil, age 40, is single and supports her dependent parents who live with her, as well as her grandfather who is in a nursing home. She has AGI of $80,000 and itemized deductions of $8,000.
    c. Scott, age 49, is a surviving spouse. His household includes two unmarried stepsons who qualify as his dependents. He has AGI of $76,800 and itemized deductions of $10,100.
    d. Amelia, age 33, is an abandoned spouse who maintains a household for her three dependent children. She has AGI of $58,000 and itemized deductions of $10,650.
    e. Chang, age 42, is divorced but maintains the home in which he and Lei, his daughter, live. Lei is single and qualifies as Chang's dependent. Chang has AGI of $65,400 and itemized deductions of $14,200.

Note: Problems 28 and 29 can be solved by referring to Concept Summary 3.1, Exhibits 3.1 through 3.5, *and the discussion under* Deductions *for* Adjusted Gross Income *in this chapter.*

28. **LO.1, 8** Compute the taxable income for 2023 for Emily on the basis of the following information. Her filing status is single.

Salary	$85,000
Interest income from bonds issued by Xerox	1,100
Alimony payments received (divorce occurred in 2014)	6,000
Contribution to traditional IRA	6,500
Gift from parents	25,000
Short-term capital gain from stock investment	2,500
Amount lost in football office pool	500
Age	40

29. **LO.1** Compute the taxable income for 2023 for Aiden on the basis of the following information. Aiden is married but has not seen or heard from his wife since 2021.

Salary	$ 80,000
Interest on bonds issued by City of Boston	3,000
Interest on CD issued by Wells Fargo Bank	2,000
Cash dividend received on Chevron common stock	2,200
Life insurance proceeds paid at death of aunt (Aiden was the designated beneficiary of the policy)	200,000
Inheritance received at death of aunt	100,000
Jackson (a cousin) repaid a loan Aiden made to him in 2017 (no interest was provided for)	5,000
Itemized deductions (state income tax, property taxes on residence, interest on home mortgage, and charitable contributions)	15,200
Number of dependents (children, ages 17 and 18, and mother-in-law, age 70)	3
Age	43

30. **LO.2** Determine the amount of the standard deduction allowed for 2023 in the following independent situations. In each case, assume that the taxpayer is claimed as another person's dependent.
    a. Curtis, age 18, has income as follows: $700 interest from a certificate of deposit and $13,600 from repairing cars.
    b. Mattie, age 18, has income as follows: $600 cash dividends from investing in stock and $4,700 from working as a lifeguard at a local pool.
    c. Jason, age 16, has income as follows: $675 interest on a bank savings account and $1,000 for painting a neighbor's fence.
    d. Ayla, age 15, has income as follows: $400 cash dividends from a stock investment and $500 from grooming pets.
    e. Sarah, age 67 and a widow, has income as follows: $500 from a bank savings account and $3,200 from babysitting.

31. **LO.4** Analyze each of the characteristics in considering the indicated test for dependency as a qualifying child or qualifying relative. In the last two columns, after each listed test (e.g., Gross income), state whether the particular test is Met, Not Met, or Not Applicable (NA).

	Characteristic	**Qualifying Child Test**	**Qualifying Relative Test**
a.	Taxpayer's son has gross income of $7,000.	Gross income	Gross income
b.	Taxpayer's niece has gross income of $3,000.	Gross income	Gross income
c.	Taxpayer's uncle lives with him.	Relationship	Relationship
d.	Taxpayer's daughter is 25 and disabled.	Age	Age
e.	Taxpayer's daughter is age 18, has gross income of $8,000, and does not live with him.	Residence Gross income	Gross income
f.	Taxpayer's cousin does not live with her.	Relationship Residence	Relationship
g.	Taxpayer's brother does not live with her.	Residence	Relationship
h.	Taxpayer's sister has dropped out of school, is age 17, and lives with him.	Relationship Residence Age	Relationship
i.	Taxpayer's older nephew is age 23 and a full-time student.	Relationship Age	Relationship
j.	Taxpayer's grandson lives with her and has gross income of $7,000.	Relationship Residence	Relationship Gross income

32. **LO.3, 4** For tax year 2023, determine the number of dependents in each of the following independent situations:

   a. Ben and Molly (ages 48 and 46, respectively) are married and furnish more than 50% of the support of their two children, Libby (age 18) and Sam (age 24). During the year, Libby earns $4,500 providing transportation for older persons with disabilities, and Sam receives a $5,000 scholarship for tuition at the law school he attends.

   b. Audry (age 45) was divorced this year. She maintains a household in which she, her ex-husband (Clint), and his mother (Olive) live and furnishes more than 50% of their support. Olive is age 91 and blind.

   c. Crystal, age 45, furnishes more than 50% of the support of her married son, Andy (age 18), and his wife, Paige (age 19), who live with her. During the year, Andy earned $9,600 from a part-time job. All parties live in Iowa (a common law state).

   d. Assume the same facts as in part (c), except that all parties live in Washington (a community property state).

33. **LO.3, 4** Determine the number of dependents in each of the following independent situations:

   a. Reginald, a U.S. citizen and resident, contributes 100% of the support of his parents who are citizens of Canada and live there.

   b. Pablo, a U.S. citizen and resident, contributes 100% of the support of his parents, who are citizens of Panama. Pablo's father is a resident of Panama, and his mother is a legal resident of the United States.

   c. Gretchen, a U.S. citizen and resident, contributes 100% of the support of her parents, who are U.S. citizens but residents of Germany.

   d. Elena is a U.S. citizen and a resident of Italy. Her household includes Carlos, a four-year-old adopted son who is a citizen of Spain.

34. **LO.3, 4** Determine the number of dependents in each of the following independent situations, and identify whether the dependent is a qualifying child or a qualifying relative.

   a. Andy maintains a household that includes a cousin (age 12), a niece (age 18), and a son (age 26). All are full-time students. Andy furnishes all of their support, and all are "members of the household."

   b. Mandeep provides all of the support of a family friend's son (age 20) who lives with her. She also furnishes most of the support of her stepmother, who does not live with her.

   c. Raul, a U.S. citizen, lives in Costa Rica. Raul's household includes a friend, Mariana, who is age 19 and a citizen of Costa Rica. Raul provides all of Mariana's support.

   d. Karen maintains a household that includes her ex-spouse, her mother-in-law, and her brother-in-law (age 23 and not a full-time student). Karen provides more than half of all of their support; all meet the gross income test. Karen is single and was divorced last year.

35. **LO.4** During 2023, Jenny, age 14, lives in a household with her father, uncle, and grandmother. The household is maintained by the uncle. The parties, all of whom file separate returns, have AGI as follows: father ($30,000), uncle ($50,000), and grandmother ($40,000).

   a. Who is eligible to claim Jenny as a dependent?

   b. Who has precedence to claim Jenny as a dependent?

36. **LO.4, 9** Wesley and Camilla (ages 90 and 88, respectively) live in an assisted care facility and for 2022 and 2023 received their support from the following sources:

	Percentage of Support
Social Security benefits	16%
Son	20
Niece	29
Cousin	12
Brother	11
Family friend (not related)	12

a. Which persons are eligible to claim Wesley and Camilla as dependents under a multiple support agreement?
b. Must Wesley and Camilla be claimed as dependents by the same person(s) for both 2022 and 2023? Explain.
c. Who, if anyone, can claim their medical expenses?

37. **LO.3, 7** Taylor, age 18, is claimed as a dependent by her parents. For 2023, she has the following income: $6,250 wages from a summer job, $800 interest from a money market account, and $300 interest from City of Chicago bonds.
a. What is Taylor's taxable income for 2023?
b. What is Taylor's tax for 2023? [Her parents file a joint return and have taxable income of $135,000 (no dividends or capital gains).]

38. **LO.4, 9** Walter and Nancy provide 60% of the support of their daughter (age 18) and son-in-law (age 22). The son-in-law (John) is a full-time student at a local university, and the daughter (Stella) holds various part-time jobs from which she earns $11,000. Walter and Nancy engage you to prepare their tax return for 2023. During a meeting with them in late March 2024, you learn that John and Stella have filed a joint return. What tax advice would you give based on the following assumptions?

Critical Thinking
Decision Making

a. All parties live in Louisiana (a community property state).
b. All parties live in New Jersey (a common law state).

39. **LO.1, 2, 3, 4, 5, 6** Charlotte (age 40) is a surviving spouse and provides all of the support of her four minor children (ages 4, 8, 11, and 14) who live with her. She also maintains the household in which her parents live and furnished 60% of their support. Charlotte's father earned $2,400 from a part-time job and received $5,500 of municipal bond interest. Charlotte has a salary of $81,800, a short-term capital loss of $2,000, a cash prize of $4,000 from a church raffle, and itemized deductions of $10,500. Using the Tax Rate Schedules, compute Charlotte's 2023 tax liability and any available child and dependent tax credits.

40. **LO.1, 2, 3, 4, 5, 6** Morgan (age 45) is single and provides more than 50% of the support of Tammy (a family friend), Jen (a niece, age 18), and Jerold (a nephew, age 18). Both Tammy and Jen live with Morgan, but Jerold (a French citizen) lives in Canada. Morgan earns a salary of $96,000, contributes $6,500 to a traditional IRA, and receives sales proceeds of $15,000 for an RV that cost $60,000 and was used for vacations. She has $8,200 in itemized deductions. Using the Tax Rate Schedules, compute Morgan's 2023 tax liability and any available child and dependent tax credits.

41. **LO.5** Which of the following individuals are required to file a tax return for 2023? Should any of these individuals file a return even if filing is not required? Why or why not?

a. Patricia, age 19, is a self-employed single individual with gross income of $5,200 from an unincorporated business. Business expenses amounted to $4,900.

b. Mike is single and is 67 years old. His gross income from wages was $14,150.

c. Ronald is a dependent child under age 19 who received $6,800 in wages from a part-time job.

d. Sam is married and files a joint return with his spouse, Lana. Both Sam and Lana are 67 years old. Their combined gross income was $26,250.

e. Quinn, age 20, is a full-time college student who is claimed as a dependent by his parents. For 2023, Quinn has taxable interest and dividends of $2,600.

Critical Thinking
Decision Making

42. **LO.5, 6, 9** Sarah and Brandi are engaged and plan to get married. During 2023, Sarah is a full-time student and earns $11,000 from a part-time job. With this income, student loans, savings, and nontaxable scholarships, she is self-supporting. For the year, Brandi is employed and has wages of $62,000. How much income tax, if any, can Brandi save if she and Sarah marry in 2023 and file a joint return?

43. **LO.5** In each of the following independent situations, determine Winston's filing status for 2023. Winston is not married.

a. Winston lives alone, but he maintains a household in which his parents live. The mother qualifies as Winston's dependent, but the father does not.

b. Winston lives alone but maintains a household in which his married daughter, Karin, lives. Both Karin and her husband (Winston's son-in-law) qualify as Winston's dependents.

c. Winston maintains a household in which he and a family friend, Ward, live. Ward qualifies as Winston's dependent.

d. Winston maintains a household in which he and his mother-in-law live. Winston's wife died in 2022.

e. Same as part (d), except that Winston's wife disappeared (i.e., she did not die) in 2021.

44. **LO.4, 5** Christopher died in 2021 and is survived by his spouse, Becca, and their 18-year-old son, Dylan. Becca is the executor of Christopher's estate and maintains the household in which she and Dylan live. All of their support is furnished by Becca, and Dylan saves his earnings. Dylan's earnings and student status for 2021 to 2023 are as follows:

Year	Earnings	Student Status
2021	$5,000	Yes
2022	7,000	No
2023	6,000	Yes

What is Becca's filing status for:

a. 2021?

b. 2022?

c. 2023?

45. **LO.3, 4, 5** Nadia died in 2022 and is survived by her husband, Jerold (age 44); her married son, Travis (age 22); and her daughter-in-law, Macy (age 18). Jerold is the executor of his wife's estate. He maintains the household where he, Travis, and Macy live and furnishes all of their support. During 2022 and 2023, Travis is a full-time student, and Macy earns $7,000 each year from a part-time job. Travis and Macy do not file jointly during either year. What is Jerold's filing status for 2022 and 2023 if all parties reside in:
    a. Idaho (a community property state)?
    b. Kansas (a common law state)?

46. **LO.1, 3, 7** Paige, age 17, is a dependent of her parents. Her parents report taxable income of $120,000 on their joint return (no qualified dividends or capital gains). During 2023, Paige earned $3,900 pet sitting and $4,500 in interest on a savings account. What are Paige's taxable income and tax liability for 2023?

47. **LO.1, 3, 7** Terri, age 16, is a dependent of her parents. During 2023, Terri earned $5,200 in interest income and $3,000 from part-time jobs.
    a. What is Terri's taxable income?
    b. How much of Terri's income is taxed at her rate? At her parent's rate?
    c. Can the parental election be made? Why or why not?

48. **LO.8** During 2023, Inez (a single taxpayer) had the following transactions involving capital assets:

Gain on the sale of unimproved land (held as an investment for 3 years)	$ 6,000
Loss on the sale of a camper (purchased 2 years ago and used for family vacations)	(5,000)
Gain on the sale of ADM stock (purchased 9 months ago as an investment)	2,450
Gain on the sale of a fishing boat and trailer (acquired 18 months ago at an auction and used for recreational purposes)	1,000

How much income tax results from these capital asset transactions if:
    a. Inez has taxable income of $188,450?
    b. Inez has taxable income of $32,250?

49. **LO.8** During 2023, Chester (a married taxpayer filing a joint return) had the following transactions involving capital assets:

Gain on the sale of an arrowhead collection (acquired as an investment at different times but all pieces have been held for more than 1 year)	$ 6,000
Loss on the sale of IBM Corporation stock (purchased 11 months ago as an investment)	(3,500)
Gain on the sale of a city lot (acquired 5 years ago as an investment)	2,000

How much income tax results from these capital asset transactions if:
    a. Chester has taxable income of $378,400?
    b. Chester has taxable income of $74,125?

50. **LO.9** Each year, Tom and Cindy Bates normally have itemized deductions of $24,000 (which includes a $4,000 pledge payment to their church). On the advice of a friend, they do the following: in early January 2023, they pay their pledge for 2022; during 2023, they pay their pledge for 2023; and in late December 2023, they prepay their pledge for 2024.

Communications
Critical Thinking
Decision Making
Planning

    a. Explain what the Bateses are trying to accomplish.
    b. What will be the tax savings if their marginal tax bracket is 24% for all three years? (Assume that the standard deduction amounts for 2023 and 2024 are the same.)
    c. Write a letter to Tom and Cindy Bates (8212 Bridle Court, Reston, VA 20194) summarizing your analysis.

Tax Return Problems

Tax Forms Problem

ProConnect™ Tax

51. Lance H. and Wanda B. Dean are married and live at 431 Yucca Drive, Santa Fe, NM 87501. Lance works for the convention bureau of the local Chamber of Commerce, and Wanda is employed part-time as a paralegal for a law firm.

During 2022, the Deans had the following receipts:

Salaries ($60,000 for Lance, $42,500 for Wanda)		$102,500
Interest income—		
City of Albuquerque general purpose bonds	$1,000	
Ford Motor company bonds	1,100	
Ally Bank certificate of deposit	400	2,500
Child support payments from John Allen		7,200
Annual gifts from parents		26,000
Settlement from Roadrunner Touring Company		90,000
Lottery winnings		600
Federal income tax refund (for tax year 2021)		400

Wanda was previously married to John Allen. When they divorced several years ago, Wanda was awarded custody of their two children, Penny and Kyle. (Note: Wanda has never issued a Form 8332 waiver.) Under the divorce decree, John was obligated to pay alimony and child support—the alimony payments were to terminate if Wanda remarried.

In July, while going to lunch in downtown Santa Fe, Wanda was injured by a tour bus. Because the driver was clearly at fault, the owner of the bus, Roadrunner Touring Company, paid her medical expenses (including a one-week stay in a hospital). To avoid a lawsuit, Roadrunner also transferred $90,000 to her in settlement of the personal injuries she sustained.

The Deans had the following expenditures for 2022:

Medical expenses (not covered by insurance)		$7,200
Taxes—		
Property taxes on personal residence	$3,600	
State of New Mexico income tax (includes amount withheld from wages during 2022)	4,200	7,800
Interest on home mortgage (First National Bank)		6,000
Charitable contributions (cash)		3,600
Life insurance premiums (policy on Lance's life)		1,200
Contribution to traditional IRA (on Wanda's behalf)		6,000
Traffic fines		300
Contribution to the reelection campaign fund of the mayor of Santa Fe		500
Funeral expenses for Wayne Boyle		6,300

The life insurance policy was taken out by Lance several years ago and designates Wanda as the beneficiary. As a part-time employee, Wanda is excluded from coverage under her employer's pension plan. Consequently, she provides for her own retirement with a traditional IRA obtained at a local trust company. Because the mayor is a member of the local Chamber of Commerce, Lance felt compelled to make the political contribution.

The Deans' household includes the following, for whom they provide more than half of the support:

	Social Security Number	Birth Date
Lance Dean (age 42)	123-45-6786	12/16/1980
Wanda Dean (age 40)	123-45-6787	08/08/1982
Penny Allen (age 19)	123-45-6788	10/09/2003
Kyle Allen (age 16)	123-45-6780	05/03/2006
Wayne Boyle (age 75)	123-45-6785	06/15/1947

Penny graduated from high school on May 9, 2022, and is undecided about college. During 2022, she earned $8,500 (placed in a savings account) playing a harp in the lobby of a local hotel. Wayne is Wanda's widower father who died on December 20, 2022. For the past few years, Wayne qualified as a dependent of the Deans.

Federal income tax withheld is $3,900 (Lance) and $1,600 (Wanda). The proper amount of Social Security and Medicare tax was withheld.

Determine the Federal income tax for 2022 for the Deans on a joint return by completing the appropriate forms. They do not own and did not use any digital assets during the year, and they do not want to contribute to the Presidential Election Campaign Fund. If an overpayment results, it is to be refunded to them. Suggested software: ProConnect Tax.

52. Logan B. Taylor is a widower whose spouse, Sara, died on June 6, 2020. He lives at 4680 Dogwood Lane, Springfield, MO 65801. He is employed as a paralegal by a local law firm. During 2022, he had the following receipts:

Communications
Decision Making
Planning
Tax Forms Problem

ProConnect™ Tax

Salary		$ 80,000
Interest income—		
Money market account at Omni Bank	$ 300	
Savings account at Boone State Bank	1,100	
City of Springfield general purpose bonds	3,000	4,400
Inheritance from Daniel		60,000
Life insurance proceeds		200,000
Amount from sale of St. Louis lot		80,000
Proceeds from estate sale		9,000
Federal income tax refund (for 2021 tax overpayment)		700

Logan inherited securities worth $60,000 from his uncle, Daniel, who died in 2022. Logan also was the designated beneficiary of an insurance policy on Daniel's life with a maturity value of $200,000. The lot in St. Louis was purchased on May 2, 2017, for $85,000 and held as an investment. Because the neighborhood has deteriorated, Logan decided to cut his losses and sold the lot on January 5, 2022, for $80,000. The estate sale consisted largely of items belonging to Sara and Daniel (e.g., camper, boat, furniture, and fishing and hunting equipment). Logan estimates that the property sold originally cost at least twice the $9,000 he received and has declined or stayed the same in value since Sara and Daniel died.

Logan's expenditures for 2022 include the following:

Medical expenses (including $10,500 for dental)		$13,500
Taxes—		
State of Missouri income tax (includes withholdings during 2022)	$4,200	
Property taxes on personal residence	4,500	8,700
Interest on home mortgage (Boone State Bank)		5,600
Contribution to church (paid pledges for 2022 and 2023)		4,800

While Logan and his dependents are covered by his employer's health insurance policy, he is subject to a deductible, and dental care is not included. The $10,500 dental charge was for Helen's implants. Helen is Logan's widowed mother, who lives with him (see below). Logan normally pledges $2,400 ($200 per month) each year to his church. On December 5, 2022, on the advice of his pastor, he prepaid his pledge for 2023.

Logan's household, all of whom he supports, includes the following:

	Social Security Number	Birth Date
Logan Taylor (age 48)	123-45-6787	08/30/1974
Helen Taylor (age 70)	123-45-6780	01/13/1952
Asher Taylor (age 23)	123-45-6783	02/18/1999
Mia Taylor (age 22)	123-45-6784	07/16/2000

Helen receives a modest Social Security benefit. Asher, a son, is a full-time student in dental school and earns $4,500 as a part-time dental assistant. Mia, a daughter, does not work and is engaged to be married.

Part 1—Tax Computation

Using the appropriate forms and schedules, compute Logan's income tax for 2022. Federal income tax of $4,200 was withheld from his wages. If Logan has any overpayment on his income tax, he wants the refund sent to him. Assume that the proper amounts of Social Security and Medicare taxes were withheld. Logan received the appropriate coronavirus recovery rebates (economic impact payments); related questions in ProConnect Tax should be ignored. Logan does not own and did not use any virtual currency during the year, and he does not want to contribute to the Presidential Election Campaign Fund. Suggested software: ProConnect Tax.

Part 2—Follow-Up Advice

In early 2023, the following take place:

- Helen decides that she wants to live with one of her daughters and moves to Arizona.
- Asher graduates from dental school and joins an existing practice in St. Louis.
- Mia marries, and she and her spouse move in with his parents.
- Using the insurance proceeds he received on Daniel's death, Logan pays off the mortgage on his personal residence.

Logan believes that these events may have an effect on his tax position for 2023. Therefore, he requests your advice.

Write a letter to Logan explaining in general terms the changes that will occur for tax purposes. Assume that Logan's salary and other factors not mentioned (e.g., property and state income taxes) will remain the same.

Research Problems

Note: Solutions to the Research Problems can be prepared by using the Thomson Reuters Checkpoint™ online tax research database, which accompanies this textbook. Solutions can also be prepared by using research materials found in a typical tax library.

Communications

Research Problem 1. Kathy and Brett Ouray married in 2005. They began to experience marital difficulties in 2019 and, in the current year, although they are not legally separated, consider themselves completely estranged. They have contemplated getting a divorce. However, because of financial concerns and because they both want to remain involved in the lives of their three sons, they have not yet filed for divorce. In addition, their financial difficulties have meant that Kathy and Brett cannot afford to live in separate residences. So although they consider themselves emotionally estranged, they and their three sons all reside in a single-family home in Chicago, Illinois.

Although Brett earns significantly more than Kathy, both contribute financially to maintaining their home and supporting their teenage sons. In one of their few and brief conversations this year, they determined that Brett had contributed far more than Kathy to the maintenance of their home and the support of their sons. Thus, Brett has decided that for the current tax year, they will file separate Federal income tax returns and that he will claim head-of-household filing status. Although they live under the same roof, Brett believes that he and Kathy should maintain separate households. Given this fact and the fact that he provides significantly more for the support of their sons, he believes that he is eligible for head-of-household filing status. Advise Brett on which filing status is most appropriate for him in the current year. His address is 16 Lahinch, Chicago, IL 60608.

Research Problem 2. John and Janet Baker are married and maintain a household in which the following persons live: Calvin and Florence Carter and Darin, Andrea, and Morgan Baker.

Decision Making

- Calvin and Florence are Janet's parents, who are retired. During the year, they receive $19,000 in nontaxable funds (e.g., disability income, interest on municipal bonds, and Social Security benefits). Of this amount, $8,000 is spent equally between them for clothing, transportation, and recreation (e.g., vacation) and the balance of $11,000 is invested in tax-exempt securities. Janet paid $1,000 for her mother's dental work and the $1,200 premium on an insurance policy her father owned on his own life. Calvin also had medical expenses, but he insisted on paying for them with his own funds.
- Darin is the Bakers' 18-year-old son, who is not a student but operates a pool-cleaning service on a part-time basis. During the year, he earns $14,000 from the business, which he places in a savings account for later college expenses.
- Andrea is the Bakers' 19-year-old daughter, who does not work or go to school. Tired of the inconvenience of borrowing and sharing the family car, during the year, she purchased a Camaro for $21,000. Andrea used funds from a savings account she had established several years ago with an inheritance from her paternal grandfather.
- Morgan is the Bakers' 23-year-old daughter. To attend graduate school at a local university, she applied for and obtained a student loan of $20,000. She uses the full amount to pay her college tuition.

The Bakers' fair rental value of their residence, including utilities, is $14,000, and their total food expense for the household is $10,500.

a. How many dependents are the Bakers entitled to claim for the year? Explain your answer.

b. From a planning standpoint, how might the Bakers have improved the tax result?

Partial list of research aids:
Reg. §§ 1.152–1(a) and –1(c).
IRS Publication 17 (*Your Federal Income Tax*), Chapter 3.

Use internet tax resources to address the following questions. Look for reliable websites and blogs of the IRS and other government agencies, media outlets, businesses, tax professionals, academics, think tanks, and political outlets.

Research Problem 3. How do U.S. individuals generate their income? Does it vary by size of income (AGI)? Go to the IRS tax statistics website (**irs.gov/statistics**), and download a recent tax year's information on "sources of income." Compare the following types of income by size of AGI: (1) wages, (2) capital gain distributions,

Communications
Data Analytics

(3) sales of capital assets, and (4) sales of property other than capital assets. Cluster the data into no more than six AGI categories. Present your findings in a visual (e.g., bar chart), and summarize your findings in a one-page memo to your instructor.

Research Problem 4. Locate IRS Form 2120 (at **irs.gov**), and answer the following questions:

a. Who must sign the form?

b. Who must file the form?

c. Can it be used for someone who is not related to the taxpayer? Explain.

Research Problem 5. What purpose is served by Form 8857? Read the directions for the form, and see IRS Publication 971 for additional information.

Research Problem 6. A nonresident alien earns money in the United States that is subject to Federal income tax. What guidance does the IRS provide about what tax form needs to be used and when it should be filed? In terms of the proper filing date, does it matter whether the earnings were subject to income tax withholding? Explain.

Research Problem 7. Research the following questions regarding virtual currency, and write your answers in the form of a set of "frequently asked questions" (FAQs) suitable for the website of your CPA firm. As part of your research, consider the IRS's FAQs on virtual currency transactions (**irs.gov/individuals/international-taxpayers/frequently-asked-questions-on-virtual-currency-transactions**) and Rev.Rul. 2019–24.

a. Since taxpayers want to easily track virtual currency and use it to acquire goods and services, how do taxpayers typically "hold" their virtual currency?

b. Janice acquired bitcoin in 2019 and 2021. This year, she used a portion of her bitcoin holdings to acquire 100 litecoin. What are the tax implications of this transaction? What do you recommend Janice do to help track her acquisition and use of virtual currency (in order to have records readily available about these investments and their tax consequences)?

c. Rajiv acquired $20 worth of bitcoin in 2018 using an automatic teller machine that converted cash to bitcoin. He has never used any of this currency. How should Rajiv answer the digital asset question on Form 1040 this year? Why? Consider the possibility that there was a "hard fork" or an "airdrop" associated with Rajiv's bitcoin (also explain these terms in your FAQs).

Becker CPA Review Questions

Becker

1. Bob provides more than half of his mother's support. His mother earns $6,000 per year as a hairdresser. She lives in an apartment across town. Bob is unmarried and has no children. What is Bob's most advantageous filing status?

   a. Single

   b. Head of household

   c. Qualifying single

   d. Supporting single

2. Jane is 20 years old and is a sophomore at Lake University. She is a full-time student and does not have any gross income. Jane spends the holidays and summers at home with her parents. Her total support for the current tax year is $30,000, including a scholarship for $5,000 to cover her tuition. Jane used $12,000 of her savings, and her grandparents provided $13,000. Which of the following statements regarding the dependency rules for Jane is true?

   a. If Jane's parents (rather than her grandparents) provided the $13,000, then they would not be able to claim Jane as a dependent because Jane provided more than half of her own support.

b. Jane's grandparents can claim her as a dependent because Jane did not provide more than half of her own support.

c. Jane's grandparents cannot claim her as a dependent because Jane provided more than half of her own support.

d. Jane does not qualify as a dependent for either her parents or grandparents.

3. In the current tax year, Blake Smith provided more than half of the support for his cousin, his niece, and a close family friend. Blake lives alone and sends a monthly support check to each person. None of the individuals whom Blake supports has any income or files a tax return. All three individuals are U.S. citizens. Which of the three people Blake supports can he claim as a dependent on his tax return?

   a. Cousin
   b. Niece
   c. Family friend
   d. None

4. Jeff and Rhonda are married and have two children, Max and Jen. Max is 20, attends college in the Los Angeles area full-time, and works as a stunt double for a television show while he is in school. Max earns $15,000 per year as a stunt double and lives at home when school is not in session. Jeff and Rhonda pay for Max's tuition and all of his living expenses. Jen, who lives at home, is 18 years old and makes $18,000 per year working full-time as an office administrator. Jeff and Rhonda pay for 65% of Jen's living expenses. In addition, Rhonda's mother, Joanne (a widow), resides with the family, earns $3,000 per year in taxable interest and dividends from her investments, and receives $9,000 per year in nontaxable Social Security benefits. Jeff and Rhonda receive no rent from Joanne and provide all the support she needs for the year. Everyone mentioned is a U.S. citizen. How many people qualify as dependents for Jeff and Rhonda's income tax return?

   a. Two
   b. Three
   c. Four
   d. Five

5. Katherine and Bill Grant have two children. Kelly is 22 years old and is a full-time student. She lives on campus at an out-of-state university but will return home for the summer. Kelly earns $5,000 a year working part-time. Her parents provide her with $15,000 of support, and her grandparents provide her with $15,000 of support. Jake is 15 years old and lives at home. He is fully supported by his parents. Jake's friend Luke also lives with the Grants. Luke is 15 years old and moved into the Grant home in April. The Grants pay all of Luke's support. How many total dependents may Katherine and Bill Grant claim for the current year?

   a. One
   b. Three
   c. Two
   d. Zero

6. Bill and Anne Chambers are married and file a joint return. They have no children. Their college friend, Ryan, lived with them for the entire current tax year. Ryan is 40 years old and earned $2,000 at a part-time job and received $25,000 in municipal bond interest. Ryan is a citizen of the United States and is unmarried. Which of the following statements is true regarding claiming Ryan as a dependent on the Chambers' tax return?

   a. If Ryan earns $15,000 in self-employment income in addition to the part-time job and municipal bond interest, he will qualify as a dependent on the Chambers' tax return.

   b. Ryan qualifies as a dependent for the Chambers under the qualifying child rules.

   c. As long as Ryan does not provide more than half of his own support, he qualifies as a dependent for the Chambers under the qualifying relative rules because he lived with them for the entire year.

   d. As long as the Chambers provide more than half of Ryan's support, he qualifies as a dependent for the Chambers under the qualifying relative rules.

7. Susie, John, Luke, and Will provide support for their 80-year-old mother, Joyce. Joyce lives by herself in an apartment in Miami, Florida. Joyce earned $5,000 this year working at her church. Joyce provides 5% of her own support. Susie provides 30% of Joyce's support, John provides 10% of Joyce's support, Luke provides 15% of Joyce's support, and Will provides 40% of Joyce's support. Under a multiple support agreement, who may claim Joyce as a dependent?
   a. Susie, Luke, John, and Will
   b. Susie, Luke, and Will
   c. Susie and Will
   d. Will

8. Heather is single and has one son, Rhett, who is 19 years old. Rhett lived at home for four months of the current tax year before moving away to take a full-time job in another city. Heather provided more than half of Rhett's support for the taxable year. Rhett earned $20,000 in gross income and is unmarried. Which of the following statements regarding the dependency rules for Rhett is true?
   a. Heather may claim Rhett as a dependent because he is a qualifying child.
   b. Heather may claim Rhett as a dependent because he is a qualifying relative.
   c. Rhett fails the age limit test for a qualifying child.
   d. Rhett must live with Heather for the entire year to meet the qualifying relative test.

9. Jonathan Jones is a 19-year-old full-time college student at the local community college. He lives in an apartment near campus during the school year and returns home for the summer break and holidays. Jonathan earned $5,000 this year working at the campus bookstore. His parents gave him $20,000 and his grandparents gave him $10,000 this year in support. Which of the following statements is true?
   a. Jonathan does not qualify as a dependent for his parents because his gross income is too high.
   b. Jonathan does not meet the residency test for a qualifying child.
   c. Jonathan's grandparents can claim him as a dependent.
   d. Jonathan's parents can claim him as a dependent.

10. In 2023, Madison and Nick Koz have two children, ages 8 and 10. Both children meet the definition of qualifying child. The Koz family has adjusted gross income of $300,000. What is the amount of the child tax credit on the couple's income tax return?
   a. $1,000
   b. $2,000
   c. $3,000
   d. $4,000

11. The Tiller family has an adjusted gross income of $200,000 in 2023. The Tillers have two children, ages 12 and 13, who qualify as dependents. All of the Tillers' income is from wages. What is the Tillers' child tax credit, and what portion of their child tax credit is refundable?

	Child Tax Credit	Refundable Portion
a.	$4,000	$0
b.	$4,000	$3,200
c.	$2,000	$1,600
d.	$2,000	$0

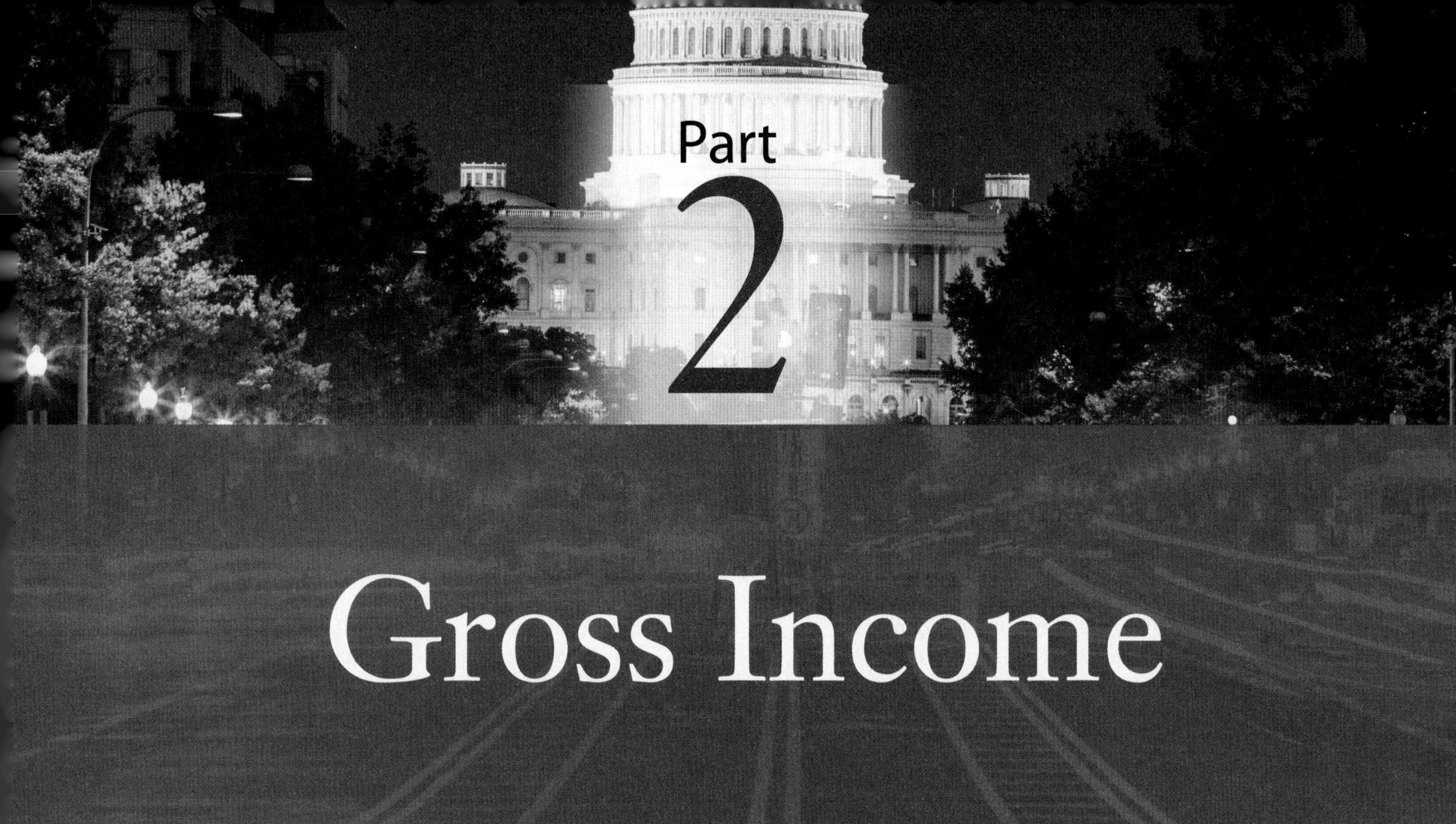

Part 2

Gross Income

Chapter 4
Gross Income: Concepts and Inclusions

Chapter 5
Gross Income: Exclusions

Part 2 presents information related to the income component of the basic tax model. The determination of what is income and the statutory exclusions that are permitted in calculating gross income are discussed. Because the taxpayer's accounting method and accounting period affect when income is reported, a basic discussion of these topics is also provided.

Chapter 4

Gross Income: Concepts and Inclusions

Learning Objectives: *After completing Chapter 4, you should be able to:*

- **LO.1** **Explain the differences between the economic, accounting, and tax concepts of gross income.**
- **LO.2** **Describe the taxable years and tax accounting methods generally available to taxpayers and other tax reporting entities.**
- **LO.3** **Identify the general sources of gross income and to whom they are taxed.**
- **LO.4** **Recognize and apply the special tax rules related to alimony, loans made at below-market interest rates, annuities, prizes and awards, unemployment compensation, Social Security benefits, and foreign bank accounts.**
- **LO.5** **Identify tax planning strategies for minimizing gross income and the present value of the related tax.**

Chapter Outline

Bob Daemmrich/Alamy Stock Photo

Calculation of Gross Income

In 2023, Dr. Cliff Payne, age 27, opened his dental practice as a sole proprietorship with a December 31 year-end. By the beginning of February, construction on his medical building was completed. He also leased a separate office building and entered into a contract to make improvements to it. In addition, early in the year, he invested $12,000 in the stock of an unrelated corporation.

The following financial information shows the results of Dr. Payne's first year of operation:

Revenues (amounts billed patients for dental services throughout the year)	$385,000
Accounts receivable: January 1	–0–
Accounts receivable: December 31	52,000

During the year, Sam Jones, a contractor who owed Dr. Payne $4,000 for dental services, satisfied his account by installing solar panels on the roof of Dr. Payne's new medical building.

As an undergraduate student, Dr. Payne took an accounting course in which he learned that the accrual method of accounting provides a good measure of the income and expenses of a business. Based on this knowledge and the above financial information, Dr. Payne concludes that the gross income for Federal income tax purposes is the $385,000 he billed his patients for the dental services rendered.

Has Dr. Payne correctly calculated the gross income of his dental practice in its first year of operations? Is there an alternative method of accounting that would result in less taxable income in this first year?

Read the chapter and formulate your response.

Framework 1040 **Tax Formula for Individuals**

This chapter covers the boldfaced portions of the Tax Formula for Individuals that was introduced in Concept Summary 3.1 on p. 3-3. Below those portions are the sections of Form 1040 where the results are reported.

Income *(broadly defined)*	$xx,xxx
Less: Exclusions	(x,xxx)
Gross income	$xx,xxx

FORM 1040 (p. 1)

1a	Total amount from Form(s) W-2, box 1 (see instructions)				1	
2a	Tax-exempt interest	2a		b Taxable interest	2b	
3a	Qualified dividends	3a		b Ordinary dividends	3b	
4a	IRA distributions	4a		b Taxable amount	4b	
5a	Pensions and annuities	5a		b Taxable amount	5b	
6a	Social security benefits	6a		b Taxable amount	6b	

FORM 1040 (Schedule 1)

2a	Alimony received
b	Date of original divorce or separation agreement (see instructions) ▶
3	Business income or (loss). Attach Schedule C
8	Other income:

Less: Deductions *for* adjusted gross income	(x,xxx)
Adjusted gross income	$xx,xxx
Less: The greater of total itemized deductions *or* the standard deduction	(x,xxx)
Personal and dependency exemptions*	(x,xxx)
Deduction for qualified business income**	(x,xxx)
Taxable income	$xx,xxx
Tax on taxable income *(see Tax Tables or Tax Rate Schedules)*	$ x,xxx
Less: Tax credits *(including income taxes withheld and prepaid)*	(xxx)
Tax due (or refund)	$ xxx

* Exemption deductions are not allowed from 2018 through 2025.
** Only applies from 2018 through 2025.

This chapter addresses the first step in the computation of taxable income—the determination of gross income. Questions that are addressed include the following:

- What is gross income?
- When is gross income recognized?
- To whom is gross income taxable?

As you will see, the Code starts with a comprehensive definition of gross income that includes all income regardless of its source or type. However, as discussed in Chapter 5, the Code goes on to identify a variety of income sources and types that are specifically excluded from gross income (called exclusions). When gross income is recognized, or taxable, is determined by the tax accounting periods and methods used by the taxpayer. Finally, income is generally recognized by the taxpayer who has the legal right to the income, although exceptions and special rules sometimes apply. These issues are addressed in more depth below.

4-1 Gross Income

LO.1

Explain the differences between the economic, accounting, and tax concepts of gross income.

4-1a Definition

Code § 61(a) of the Internal Revenue Code defines the term **gross income** as follows:

> Except as otherwise provided in this subtitle, gross income means all income from whatever source derived.

This definition, taken from the Sixteenth Amendment to the Constitution, provides perhaps the broadest definition of gross income possible. It clearly requires that all income be included in a taxpayer's gross income unless it is explicitly excluded elsewhere in the Code. However, neither the Sixteenth Amendment nor the Code provide a definition of income itself. As a result, it became the responsibility of the judicial and administrative branches to specifically determine the meaning of *income*. Some of the most important issues related to the meaning of income are discussed below.

4-1b The Recovery of Capital Doctrine

Although gross income is clearly defined to include all income, the Supreme Court has held that gross income is not synonymous with gross receipts. One important example is that a taxpayer does not have income until recovering any amount of capital invested in an item that is sold.[1] This concept, known as the **recovery of capital doctrine**, prevents income from being taxed more than once. The rationale is that "capital" is the accumulation of previously taxed income.

In its simplest application, this doctrine means that sellers can reduce their gross receipts on the sale of assets (the selling price) by the adjusted basis of the property sold in determining their gross income.[2] Generally, the adjusted basis of property is its cost adjusted for any allowable depreciation. Other issues in determining adjusted basis are discussed in Chapter 13.

The Big Picture

Return to the facts of *The Big Picture* on p. 4-1. Assume that Dr. Payne receives $15,000 when he sells the common stock he had purchased for $12,000. Although he has $15,000 of gross receipts, $12,000 represents a recovery of his capital invested in the stock, leaving him with $3,000 of gross income.

Global Tax Issues — From "All Sources" Is a Broad Definition

When § 61 refers to "income from whatever source derived," the law is reaching far beyond the borders of the United States. Although one interpretation of "source" in this context is type of income (e.g., wages and interest), a broader interpretation revolves around the place where the income is generated. Citizens and residents of the United States are subject to taxation on income earned from sources both inside and outside the country. This "worldwide income" tax base can cause potential double taxation problems, with other countries also taxing income earned within their borders. However, mechanisms such as the foreign earned income exclusion and the foreign tax credit can alleviate double taxation.

Even without double taxation, a world-wide tax system may result in a country's citizens paying more tax on income they earn in countries with lower tax rates than they would if they were a citizen of a country with a lower rate. Over the years, a number of individuals have relocated to other countries and renounced their U.S. citizenship to avoid high U.S. tax rates. Others who have already relocated may renounce their U.S. citizenship to avoid complicated filing and reporting requirements. After hitting a record high of 6,707 in 2020, the number of expatriations declined to 2,426 in 2021, perhaps due to additional practical challenges in completing the expatriation process caused by the COVID-19 pandemic. Once per quarter, the Department of State publishes the names of U.S. citizens who have renounced their citizenship. Some of these individuals may owe Federal taxes as a result of renouncing. See § 877A.

See "Does Renouncing U.S. Citizenship Make Sense for the Average American Abroad?" at **forbes.com/sites/kathleenpeddicord/2022/07/28/does-renouncing-us-citizenship-make-sense-for-the-average-american-abroad/**.

[1] *Doyle v. Mitchell Bros. Co.*, 1 USTC ¶17, 3 AFTR 2979, 38 S.Ct. 467 (USSC, 1916).

[2] Reg. § 1.61–3.

4-1c The Economic and Accounting Concepts of Income

Even after clarifying that **income** did not include recoveries of capital, the courts were nonetheless required to interpret "the commonly understood meaning of the term [income] which must have been in the minds of the people when they adopted the Sixteenth Amendment to the Constitution."[3] Early in the development of the income tax law, a choice had to be made between two competing models: economic income and accounting income.

Economists measure income (**economic income**) as the sum of (1) the value of goods and services consumed during a period and (2) the change in the value of net assets (assets minus liabilities) from the beginning to the end of the period. Importantly, the change in the value of net assets is not dependent on the sale or exchange of those assets: economic income is derived by a mere change in the value of assets held. Similarly, economic income includes in consumption the imputed value of personally provided items such as the rental value of an owner-occupied home and the value of food grown for personal consumption.[4]

Example 2

Sharon has economic income as follows:

Consumption			
Food, clothing, and other personal expenditures	$ 25,000		
Imputed rental value of the home Sharon owns and occupies	12,000		
Total consumption			$37,000
Fair market value of Sharon's assets on December 31, 2023	$220,000		
Less liabilities on December 31, 2023	(40,000)		
Net worth on December 31, 2023		$180,000	
Fair market value of Sharon's assets on January 1, 2023	$200,000		
Less liabilities on January 1, 2023	(80,000)		
Net worth on January 1, 2023		(120,000)	
Increase in net worth			60,000
Economic income for 2023			$97,000

The need to value assets annually would make compliance with the tax law burdensome and would cause numerous controversies between the taxpayer and the IRS over valuation. In addition, including changes in the value of assets in income for tax purposes could result in liquidity problems. Although a taxpayer's assets may increase in value, they may not be readily convertible into the cash needed to pay the tax (e.g., commercial real estate). For these reasons, the courts have rejected the economic concept of income as impractical.[5]

In contrast, the accounting concept of income (**accounting income**) is founded on the realization principle: no income is recognized until it is realized.[6] Realization requires (1) an exchange of goods or services to take place between the accounting entity and some independent, external party and (2) the accounting entity to receive in the exchange something that is capable of being objectively valued. For example, income is not recognized merely due to the appreciation of assets held by the taxpayer or when an individual or a business creates an asset for its own use. Income is realized, however, whenever a taxpayer enters into any transaction that results in an accession to wealth.[7]

[3] *Merchants Loan and Trust Co. v. Smietanka*, 1 USTC ¶42, 3 AFTR 3102, 41 S.Ct. 386 (USSC, 1921).

[4] See Henry C. Simons, *Personal Income Taxation* (Chicago: University of Chicago Press, 1933), Chapters 2–3.

[5] *Eisner v. Macomber*, 1 USTC ¶32, 3 AFTR 3020, 40 S.Ct. 189 (USSC, 1920).

[6] See the American Accounting Association Committee Report on the "Realization Concept," *The Accounting Review* (April 1965): 312–322.

[7] *Glenshaw Glass Co.*, 348 U.S. 426, 429–430, 75 S.Ct. 473, 99 L.Ed. 483 (1955); Reg. § 1.61–14.

4-1d **Financial Accounting Income versus Taxable Income**

As discussed above, the measurement of taxable income is much closer to accounting income than it is to economic income. However, due to the different purposes they serve, several differences exist between accounting and taxable income.

The purpose of financial reporting is to provide information to investors and creditors relevant to predicting a business's future cash flows. To better predict future cash flows, financial accounting income will sometimes stray from the realization principle, valuing assets at their net realizable value with any appreciation recognized as income. For example, an increase in the value of marketable securities is recognized as income for financial accounting purposes.

Conversely, taxable income is primarily intended to capture taxpayers' relative abilities to pay tax. As a result, the determination of taxable income seldom strays from the realization principle. For example, the same appreciation of marketable securities that leads to the recognition of income for financial reporting purposes will not result in taxable income. Similarly, to better predict future cash flows and to better match expenses with the revenues they generate, financial accounting is amenable to the use of estimates. For example, estimates of receivables that will not be collected and future costs that will be incurred to honor warranties on products sold during the current period reduce financial accounting income but have no impact on taxable income.

The Supreme Court, in a decision involving inventory and bad debt adjustments, provided an explanation for some of the variations between accounting and taxable income:

> The primary goal of financial accounting is to provide useful information to management, shareholders, creditors, and others properly interested; the major responsibility of the accountant is to protect these parties from being misled. The primary goal of the income tax system, in contrast, is the equitable collection of revenue.... Consistently with its goals and responsibilities, financial accounting has as its foundation the principle of conservatism, with its corollary that "possible errors in measurement [should] be in the direction of understatement rather than overstatement of net income and net assets." In view of the Treasury's markedly different goals and responsibilities, understatement of income is not destined to be its guiding light.
>
> ... Financial accounting, in short, is hospitable to estimates, probabilities, and reasonable certainties; the tax law, with its mandate to preserve the revenue, can give no quarter to uncertainty.[8]

Finally, because the tax law is used by the government to achieve several social and economic goals, taxable income is impacted by several things that do not impact accounting income and vice versa. For example, although income earned by foreign subsidiaries, the appreciation of property donated to charity, and the payment of fines and penalties all impact financial accounting income, none are included in the determination of taxable income. Conversely, although taxable income may be reduced for a portion of income earned on sales to customers in foreign countries, there is no corresponding reduction of financial accounting income. For these reasons, the taxable income reported by corporations in their financial statements may differ significantly from their taxable income (see text Section 17-3c). Many of these differences between accounting and taxable income will be discussed in greater detail throughout this text.

[8] *Thor Power Tool Co. v. Comm.*, 79–1 USTC ¶9139, 43 AFTR 2d 79–362, 99 S.Ct. 773 (USSC).

4-1e **Form of Receipt**

As discussed above, income is not taxable until it is realized. Realization, however, does not require the receipt of cash. "Gross income includes income realized in any form, whether in money, property, or services. Income may be realized [and recognized], therefore, on the receipt of services, meals, accommodations, stock or other property, as well as in cash."[9]

Form of Receipt

Ostrich Corporation allows Bill, an employee, to use a company car for his vacation. Bill realizes income equal to the rental value of the car.

Khalil owes $10,000 on a mortgage. The creditor accepts $8,000 in full satisfaction of the debt. Khalil realizes income of $2,000 from retiring the debt, the amount of the debt that is forgiven.[10]

Sam, a practicing attorney, owns a personal residence in need of repairs. Sam decided to list his services on a barter exchange. He offered to provide legal services in exchange for home repairs.

A qualified carpenter performed the repairs in eight hours. The carpenter normally charges $50 an hour. Sam agreed to form a corporation for the carpenter in exchange for the carpenter's services. Sam realized $400 (8 hours × $50) in gross income for his services.

LO.2

Describe the taxable years and tax accounting methods generally available to taxpayers and other tax reporting entities.

4-2 **The Timing of Income Recognition**

4-2a **Taxable Year**

As in financial reporting, taxable income must be measured and reported on a periodic basis. The annual accounting period, or **taxable year**, is a basic component of our tax system. As a general rule, a taxpayer may use as a taxable year either a calendar year or a fiscal year (a period of 12 months ending on the last day of any month other than December) as long as adequate books and records based on that year are maintained.[11] Although it is not required, most individuals use a calendar year as their taxable year. As discussed in Chapter 16, the fiscal year option generally is not available to partnerships, S corporations, and personal service corporations.[12]

It is important that income be recognized in the proper year for several reasons. For example, a taxpayer's tax rate may vary across years. This may occur for one or more of the following reasons:

- Given the progressive rates applicable to individual taxpayers, a taxpayer's marginal tax rate can change from year to year.
- Congress may change the tax rates.
- The rates that apply to a specific taxpayer may change because of a change in the taxpayer's status (e.g., a person may marry, or a business may be incorporated).

Even when the rates do not change between tax years, deferring the recognition of income and, therefore, the payment of tax to a future tax year reduces the present value of the tax. Finally, several provisions in the Code are dependent on the taxpayer's gross

[9] Reg. § 1.61–1(a).

[10] Reg. § 1.61–12. See *U.S. v. Kirby Lumber Co.*, 2 USTC ¶814, 10 AFTR 458, 52 S.Ct. 4 (USSC, 1931). Exceptions to this general rule are discussed in Chapter 5.

[11] § 441.

[12] §§ 441(i), 706, and 1378.

income for the year (e.g., a deduction or credit might not be available if the taxpayer's income exceeds a specified amount). Therefore, the proper determination of several items of income and deduction will depend on other items being recognized in the proper year.

4-2b Accounting Methods

The year an item of gross income is recognized depends on which acceptable **accounting method** the taxpayer regularly employs.[13] The two primary methods of accounting allowed are (1) the cash receipts and disbursements method and (2) the accrual method. Most individuals and many small businesses may use either of these allowable methods, although most choose to use the cash method. In general, large corporations are required to use the accrual method. Generally, the tax law also requires larger taxpayers to use the accrual method for determining sales and the cost of goods sold when inventory is an income-producing factor.[14] However, taxpayers may also use a hybrid method that is a combination of the cash and accrual methods of accounting (e.g., the accrual method for sales and cost of goods sold and the cash method for all other items of income and expenses).

In addition to these overall accounting methods, taxpayers may be allowed or required to use special accounting methods in specific situations. For example, a taxpayer may choose to spread the gain from a sale of eligible property over the collection period by using the *installment method* of income recognition. Taxpayers who are parties to certain long-term contracts may either spread the profits from the contract over the periods in which the work is done (the *percentage of completion method*) or defer all profit until the year in which the project is completed (the *completed contract method*).[15]

The availability of any accounting method is dependent on its ability to clearly reflect the taxpayer's income. Code § 446(b) grants the IRS broad powers to determine whether a taxpayer's accounting method *clearly reflects income*:

> If no method of accounting has been regularly used by the taxpayer, or *if the method used does not clearly reflect income, the computation of taxable income shall be made under such method as, in the opinion of the Secretary ... does clearly reflect income.*

Unless a taxpayer is required to use a particular accounting method, an accounting method generally is selected by a taxpayer simply by using it the first time income is calculated and reported. A change in accounting method, however, generally requires the advance consent of the IRS.[16]

Cash Method

Under the **cash method**, income is recognized in the year it is actually or constructively received by the taxpayer or the taxpayer's agent, regardless of whether the income was earned in that year.[17] Further, in spite of the method's name, the taxpayer need not receive cash to be required to recognize income under the cash method. Rather, the receipt of anything that can be valued in terms of money, or that has a cash equivalent, is includible in income under the cash method.[18] As a result, a cash basis taxpayer who receives a note in payment for services has income equal to the value of the note in the year the note is received. However, a creditor's mere promise to pay (e.g., an account receivable), with no supporting note, usually is not considered to have a fair market value and, therefore, is not a cash equivalent.[19] As a result, a cash basis taxpayer who receives an account receivable in return for goods or services defers income recognition until the receivable is collected.

---

[13] See Accounting Methods in Chapter 16.

[14] Reg. § 1.446–1(c)(2)(i) and § 471(c). Other circumstances in which the accrual method must be used are presented in Chapter 16.

[15] §§ 453 and 460. See Chapter 16 for limitations on the use of the installment method and the completed contract method. See Appendix C for definitions of *installment method* and *completed contract method*.

[16] § 446(e).

[17] *Julia A. Strauss*, 2 B.T.A. 598 (1925). See the Glossary in Appendix C for a discussion of the terms *cash equivalent doctrine* and *constructive receipt*.

[18] Reg. §§ 1.446–1(a)(3) and (c)(1)(i).

[19] *Bedell v. Comm.*, 1 USTC ¶359, 7 AFTR 8469, 30 F.2d 622 (CA–2, 1929).

Dana, an accountant, reports her income using the cash method. In 2023, she performed an audit for Orange Corporation and billed the client for $5,000, which was collected in 2024. In 2023, Dana also performed an audit for Blue Corporation. Because of Blue's precarious financial position, Dana required Blue to issue an $8,000 secured negotiable note in payment of the fee. The note had a fair market value of $6,000. Dana collected $8,000 on the note in 2024. Dana's gross income for the two years is as follows:

	2023	2024
Fair market value of note received from Blue	$6,000	
Cash received		
From Orange on account receivable		$ 5,000
From Blue on note receivable		8,000
Less: Recovery of capital (Blue's note receivable)		(6,000)
Total gross income	$6,000	$ 7,000

Generally, a check is considered a cash equivalent and must be recognized as income when received by a cash basis taxpayer. An exception to this rule applies if the person paying with the check requests that the check not be cashed until a subsequent date. In this case, the income is deferred until that later date.[20]

The tax law restricts the availability of the cash method for several reasons. For example, the cash method could distort taxable income as income and expenses from the same activity may be recognized in different tax years. Moreover, a taxpayer using the cash method has some degree of control over when income is recognized (e.g., by delaying the sending of invoices to customers). One important restriction requires most corporations with average annual gross receipts greater than $29 million over the preceding three-year period to use the accrual method. Other businesses with average annual gross receipts in excess of $29 million, whether or not they are corporations, are required to account for their inventory under the accrual method.[21]

Accrual Method

Under the **accrual method**, income is generally included in gross income in the year in which it is earned, regardless of when it is collected. Income is earned when (1) all events have occurred that fix the right to receive such income (the **all events test**), and (2) the amount to be received can be determined with reasonable accuracy.

Generally, a taxpayer's right to income accrues when title to property being sold passes to the buyer or services are performed for the customer or client.[22] If the rights to the income have accrued but are subject to a potential refund claim (e.g., under a product warranty), the income is reported in the year of sale and a deduction is allowed in subsequent years when actual claims accrue.[23]

Where a taxpayer's right to income is contested (e.g., when a customer claims that a contractor has failed to meet the specifications of a construction contract), the year in which the income is subject to tax depends on whether payment has been received. If payment has not been received, no income is recognized until the claim is settled. Only then is the right to the income established.[24] However, if the payment is received before the dispute is settled, the **claim of right doctrine** requires the taxpayer to recognize the income in the year of receipt.[25]

[20] *Charles F. Kahler*, 18 T.C. 31 (1952); *Bright v. U.S.*, 91–1 USTC ¶50,142, 67 AFTR 2d 91–673, 926 F.2d 383 (CA–5); *M. Fischer*, 14 T.C. 792 (1950).

[21] §§ 448, 471(c), and 263A(i). Code § 448, which requires certain taxpayers to use the accrual method, does not apply to individuals, partnerships without a C corporation partner, S corporations, estates, and trusts. In general, these types of taxpayers may use the cash receipts method regardless of their gross receipts level (unless the entity is a tax shelter per § 448(d)(3)). Additional analysis as to accounting methods is required if these taxpayers have inventory as well as gross receipts above the $29 million threshold. The $29 million threshold applicable in 2023 is adjusted annually for inflation. See further discussion in Chapter 16.

[22] *Lucas v. North Texas Lumber Co.*, 2 USTC ¶484, 8 AFTR 10276, 50 S.Ct. 184 (USSC, 1930). See also Rev.Rul. 84–31, 1984–1 C.B. 127.

[23] *Brown v. Helvering*, 4 USTC ¶1222, 13 AFTR 851, 54 S.Ct. 356 (USSC, 1933).

[24] *Burnet v. Sanford and Brooks*, 2 USTC ¶636, 9 AFTR 603, 51 S.Ct. 150 (USSC, 1931).

[25] *North American Oil Consolidated Co. v. Burnet*, 3 USTC ¶943, 11 AFTR 16, 52 S.Ct. 613 (USSC, 1932).

The Big Picture

Return to the facts of *The Big Picture* on p. 4-1. Assume that, on completing the construction improvements to Dr. Payne's medical office building in 2023, the contractor, who uses the accrual method, submitted a bill. Dr. Payne refused to pay the bill, however, claiming that the contractor had not met specifications. The contractor did not reach a settlement with Dr. Payne until 2024. No income is taxable to the contractor until 2024. If Dr. Payne had paid for the work and then filed suit for damages, the contractor could not defer the income (the income would be taxable in 2023).

Under the accrual method, the amount of income that must be included in gross income is the amount the taxpayer has earned and, therefore, has the right to receive. Unlike the cash basis, the value of a customer's obligation is irrelevant in measuring accrual basis income. The ability to defer income that is earned but not yet received is a distinct advantage of the cash method over the accrual method. However, as discussed above, most larger corporations are required to use the accrual method.[26]

Assume the same facts as in Example 6, except that Dana is an accrual basis taxpayer. Dana must recognize $13,000 ($8,000 + $5,000) of gross income in 2023, the year her rights to the income accrued.

Hybrid Method

The **hybrid method** is a combination of the accrual method and the cash method. Generally, a taxpayer using the hybrid method is in the business of buying and selling inventory but not otherwise required to use the accrual method. As a result, a taxpayer using the hybrid method would account for the sale of goods and cost of goods sold using the accrual method and use the cash method for other income and expense items (e.g., services and interest income). Because most small businesses can use the cash method for sales and cost of goods sold, the hybrid method is not commonly used.

4-2c Special Rules Applicable to Cash Basis Taxpayers

Constructive Receipt

In general, a cash basis taxpayer does not recognize income until it is received. Income that has not actually been received by the taxpayer is nonetheless taxed as though it had been received—the income is considered constructively received—if the amount is made readily available to the taxpayer and not subject to substantial limitations or restrictions.[27] The purpose of the **constructive receipt** doctrine is to prevent a cash basis taxpayer from deferring the recognition of income over which they have practical control. For instance, a taxpayer is not permitted to defer income earned in December simply by refusing to accept payment until January. Conversely, if an employee receives a paycheck on December 31 that is dated for January 8, the constructive receipt doctrine would allow the employee to defer recognizing the income until January. Whether income is *readily available* and whether *substantial limitations or restrictions exist* is determined by all the facts and circumstances surrounding a situation.[28] Following are some examples of the application of the constructive receipt doctrine.

[26] §§ 448(c) and 471(c) and Reg. § 1.446–1(c)(2).

[27] Reg. § 1.451–2(a).

[28] *Baxter v. Comm.*, 87–1 USTC ¶9315, 59 AFTR 2d 87–1068, 816 F.2d 493 (CA–9).

Constructive Receipt

Ted is a member of a barter club. In 2023, Ted performed services for other club members and earned 1,000 points. Each point entitles him to $1 in goods and services provided by other members of the club; the points can be used at any time. In 2024, Ted exchanged his points for a new high-definition TV. Ted must recognize $1,000 gross income in 2023 when the 1,000 points were credited to his account.[29]

Example 10

Brianna has a savings account with Eagle Savings and Loan Association. Under the terms of the account, interest accrues monthly and the depositor can withdraw the funds (including accrued interest) at any time. The interest accrued during the year is constructively received by Brianna even though she does not withdraw the funds.[30]

The Big Picture

Example 11

Return to the facts of *The Big Picture* on p. 4-1. On December 31, Dr. Payne has $10,000 in patients' checks that have not been deposited. They include a check for $3,000 from a patient who asked Dr. Payne not to deposit the check until after January 4 of next year because her account did not contain sufficient funds to pay the debt.

Under the cash method, Dr. Payne must recognize $7,000 of income from the $7,000 in checks on hand in the current year because the checks are a cash equivalent that is actually received. The income from the $3,000 check is neither actually nor constructively received in the current year because an insufficient account means that the funds are not available.[31]

The constructive receipt doctrine does not apply to income the taxpayer is not yet entitled to receive even though the taxpayer could have contracted to receive the income at an earlier date.[32]

The Big Picture

Example 12

Return to the facts of *The Big Picture*. Assume that Dr. Payne adopted the cash basis of accounting. On December 15, Dr. Payne sees a new patient in need of extensive dental work at a cost of $2,000. The patient indicates she may be willing to pay for the services before they are performed if they are scheduled before the end of the year. However, before the services are performed, the parties agree to a payment plan that requires payment to be made within 30 days after services are performed. The services are performed on December 28, and the patient pays on January 15.

Dr. Payne is not in constructive receipt of the $2,000 at the end of the year. Although Dr. Payne could have collected the fee prior to year-end, he was not yet entitled to the fee when he contracted to receive payment at a later date.[33]

Even income set apart or made available to the taxpayer is not constructively received if the ultimate right to it is subject to *substantial restrictions*. For example, employees sometimes receive from their employers property subject to substantial restrictions, such as stock or stock options. Generally, no income is recognized until the restrictions lapse.[34]

[29] Rev.Rul. 80–52.

[30] Reg. § 1.451–2(a).

[31] *L. M. Fischer*, 14 T.C. 792 (1950).

[32] *Baxter v. Comm.*, 816 F.2d 493, 59 AFTR 2d 87–1068, 87–1 USTC ¶9315 (CA–9, 1997).

[33] *Cowden v. Comm.*, 61–1 USTC ¶9382, 7 AFTR 2d 1160, 289 F.2d 20 (CA–5).

[34] § 83(a).

Carlos is a key employee of Red, Inc. The corporation gives stock with a value of $10,000 to Carlos. The stock cannot be sold, however, for five years. Carlos is not required to recognize income until the restrictions lapse at the end of five years.

The life insurance industry has used substantial restrictions as a cornerstone for designing life insurance contracts with favorable tax features. Ordinary life insurance policies provide (1) current protection—an amount payable in the event of death—and (2) a savings feature—a cash surrender value payable to the policyholder if the policy is terminated during the policyholder's life. The annual increase in cash surrender value is not taxable because the policyholder must cancel the policy to actually receive the increase in value. Because the cancellation requirement is a substantial restriction, the policyholder does not constructively receive the annual increase in cash surrender value.[35]

Income Received by an Agent

Income received by the taxpayer's agent is considered to be received by the taxpayer. Therefore, a cash basis principal must recognize the income at the time it is received by the agent.[36]

Jack, a cash basis taxpayer, delivered cattle to the auction barn in late December. The auctioneer, acting as Jack's agent, sold the cattle and collected the proceeds in December. The auctioneer did not pay Jack until the following January. Jack must include the sales proceeds in his gross income for the year the auctioneer received the funds.

Original Issue Discount

Lenders frequently make loans that require a payment at maturity of more than the amount of the original loan. The difference between the original amount of the loan and the amount due at maturity, or the **original issue discount**, is actually interest. In such an arrangement, the original issue discount must be reported as it accrues, regardless of the taxpayer's accounting method.[37] The accrued interest is calculated using the effective interest rate method.

On January 1, 2023, Mark, a cash basis taxpayer, pays $90,703 to a bank for a 24-month certificate of deposit (i.e., Mark loaned $90,703 to the bank). The certificate is priced to yield 5% (the effective interest rate) with interest compounded annually. No interest is paid until maturity, when Mark receives $100,000.

As a result, Mark's gross income from the certificate is $9,297 ($100,000 − $90,703). Mark's income earned each year is calculated as follows:

2023 (5% × $90,703)	$4,535
2024 [5% × ($90,703 + $4,535)]	4,762
	$9,297

The original issue discount rules do not apply to U.S. savings bonds (discussed in the following paragraphs) or to obligations with a maturity date of one year or less from the date of issue.[38] See Chapter 14 for additional discussion of the tax treatment of original issue discount.

Series E and Series EE Bonds

Certain U.S. government savings bonds (Series E before 1980 and Series EE after 1979) are issued at a discount. No interest payments are actually made. Instead, the difference between the purchase price and the amount received on redemption is the bondholder's interest income from the investment.

[35] *Theodore H. Cohen*, 39 T.C. 1055 (1963).

[36] Rev.Rul. 79–379.

[37] §§ 1272(a)(3) and 1273(a).

[38] § 1272(a)(2).

As mentioned above, although these bonds are issued at a discount, they are not subject to the rules generally applicable to original issue discount. Instead, the income from these savings bonds is generally deferred until the bonds are redeemed or mature. As a result, U.S. savings bonds have attractive income deferral features not available with corporate bonds and certificates of deposit issued by financial institutions.

Of course, the deferral feature of government bonds issued at a discount is not an advantage if the investor has insufficient income to be subject to tax as the income accrues. In fact, the deferral may work to the investor's disadvantage if the investor will face a higher tax rate at the time of redemption than they do as the income accrues or if the bunching of the bond interest into one tax year moves the investor to a higher tax bracket than they would otherwise be in. To avoid this possibility, a cash basis taxpayer may elect to include in gross income the interest on Series E and EE bonds annually as it accrues.[39] This election can be especially valuable for a child whose current income is below the available standard deduction but anticipates higher income when the bond is redeemed.

Kate purchases Series EE U.S. savings bonds for $500 (face value of $1,000) on January 2 of the current year. If the bonds are redeemed during the first six months, no interest is paid. At December 31, the redemption value is $519.60.

If Kate makes no election, she will report no interest income for the current year. However, she may elect to report the interest income annually, requiring her to report income of $19.60 in the current year.

When the bond matures, Kate may receive a Form 1099 indicating that she should include as income all of the interest that accrued over the life of the bond. If she elects to report the income as it accrues, she should keep good records to prove that she did so.

An election to report the income from the bonds annually must apply to all such bonds the taxpayer owns at the time of the election and to all such bonds acquired subsequent to the election. A change in the method of reporting the income from the bonds requires permission from the IRS.

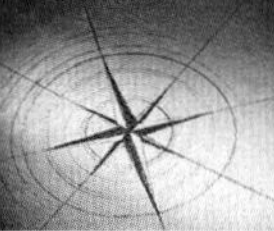

Ethics & Equity — Should the Tax Treatment of Government Bonds and Corporate Bonds Be Different?

Taxpayers are permitted to defer the original issue discount earned on U.S. Government Series EE bonds until the bonds mature, but the original issue discount on a corporate bond must be taken into gross income each year the bond is held. Is this difference in the tax treatment of income earned on government and corporate bonds defensible in terms of equity? Why or why not?

Amounts Received under an Obligation to Repay

The receipt of funds with an obligation to repay those funds in the future is the essence of borrowing. Because the taxpayer's assets and liabilities increase by the same amount, no income is realized when the borrowed funds are received. This same concept extends to the receipt by a taxpayer of any funds that carry an obligation for repayment.

A landlord receives a damage deposit from a tenant when the tenant first signs a lease. The landlord does not recognize income unless and until the deposit is forfeited because the landlord has an obligation to repay the deposit if no damage occurs.[40] However, if the amount paid at signing is the prepayment of the final month's rent, it is taxed in the year of receipt.

[39] § 454(a).

[40] *John Mantell*, 17 T.C. 1143 (1952) and *Indianapolis Power & Light Co.*, 90–1 USTC ¶50,007, 65 AFTR2d 90–394, 110 S.Ct. 589 (USSC).

4-2d **Special Rules Applicable to Accrual Basis Taxpayers**

The All Events Test and Financial Reporting

Under the accrual method of accounting, income generally is not included in gross income until all the events have occurred that fix the taxpayer's right to that income. Conversely, for financial reporting purposes, income is recognized as an entity performs those obligations that are necessary to earn the income, even if all the obligations necessary to fix the entity's right to the income have not been met.

E&I Company contracts with a customer to install new equipment so that it is integrated efficiently into the customer's production process. The contract calls for E&I to bill the customer after the installation and integration are complete. As of the end of E&I's year, it has completed the installation but not the integration.

E&I must provide certified GAAP financial statements to its bank for credit purposes. For financial reporting purposes, E&I has met one of its obligations under its contract with the customer and, therefore, recognizes the income from the installation of the equipment but not the system integration.

Under the **financial statement income inclusion rule**, if an accrual method taxpayer issues certified GAAP financial statements (referred to as a type of *applicable financial statement*), the all events test is generally considered satisfied no later than when the income is included in those financial statements.[41] However, an important exception to this rule prevents a taxpayer from having to recognize additional gross income based on their financial statements if the taxpayer does not have an enforceable right to the income by the end of the year. Whether such a right exists is determined by the terms of the contract between the taxpayer and their customer or client.[42]

Return to the facts of Example 18. Because E&I has not legally met all the requirements necessary to be entitled to the income from its contract with the customer by the end of the year, the all events test would generally not be considered met, and the company would recognize no gross income for tax purposes. However, because E&I is issuing certified financial statements, the financial statement inclusion rule must be considered. Assume that E&I has an enforceable right to the income from the installation (e.g., it would be contractually entitled to the revenue if the customer were to cancel the contract before the integration). In this case, the all events test would be considered met and E&I would be required to recognize in its gross income the revenue related to the installation and included in its financial statements. If, however, E&I did not have an enforceable right to the income (e.g., it would receive no income if it did not complete the integration), no gross income would be recognized related to the installation regardless of it being reported in the financial statements.

If E&I did not issue GAAP certified financial statements, it would not recognize any income for tax purposes until the all events test was met (i.e., it both delivered the equipment and completed the system integration as required by the contract).

Unearned Income

For financial reporting purposes, advance payments received from customers are initially reflected in the financial statements of the seller as a liability and recognized as income over the period in which the income is earned. However, for tax purposes, even accrual basis taxpayers generally must include unearned income in their gross income in the year of receipt.

In December 2023, a tenant pays his January 2024 rent of $1,000. The accrual basis landlord must include the $1,000 in her 2023 gross income for tax purposes, although the unearned rent income is reported as a liability on the landlord's December 31, 2023 financial accounting balance sheet.

However, accrual basis taxpayers who receive advance payments for goods or services may elect to include in gross income in the year of receipt only the amount that would be recognized as income in their financial statements with the remaining amount

[41] § 451(b).

[42] § 1.451–3(b).

recognized in the subsequent year.[43] The special deferral rule for accrual method taxpayers is a method of accounting that must be properly adopted (discussed further in Chapter 16). This special method will continue to result in differences in the timing of the reporting of revenue when financial reporting rules require the revenue to be reported over three or more years, as illustrated in the following example.

Example 21

Yellow Corporation, an accrual basis calendar year taxpayer, sells its services under 12-month, 24-month, and 36-month contracts. The corporation provides services to each customer every month. On May 1, 2023, Yellow Corporation sold the following customer contracts:

Length of Contract	Total Proceeds
12 months	$3,000
24 months	4,800
36 months	6,300

For tax purposes, Yellow may defer until 2024 all of the income that will be earned after 2023.

	Income Reported in 2023	Income Reported in 2024	
Length of Contract	Financial Reporting and Taxable Gross Income	Financial Reporting	Taxable Gross Income
12 months	$2,000 ($3,000 × 8/12)	$1,000 ($3,000 × 4/12)	$1,000 ($3,000 − $2,000 reported in 2023)
24 months	$1,600 ($4,800 × 8/24)	$2,400 ($4,800 × 12/24)	$3,200 ($4,800 − $1,600 reported in 2023)
36 months	$1,400 ($6,300 × 8/36)	$2,100 ($6,300 × 12/36)	$4,900 ($6,300 − $1,400 reported in 2023)

Although all income is recognized for tax purposes in 2023 and 2024, financial reporting will recognize the income over four years (2023 through 2026) with $2,900 income reported in 2025 and $700 income reported in 2026.

The special election generally is available for advance payments for goods and services. It is not available, however, for unearned rent, interest, insurance premiums, and certain other advance payments. Advance payments for these items are taxed in the year of receipt.

LO.3

Identify the general sources of gross income and to whom they are taxed.

4-3 General Sources of Gross Income and to Whom They Are Taxed

Gross income is often described as including that coming from labor (i.e., personal services) and capital (i.e., property). This section examines several issues generally related to income from personal services and property, including when and to whom this income is taxable.

4-3a Personal Services

It is a well-established principle of taxation that income from personal services must be included in the gross income of the person who performs the services. This principle was first established in a Supreme Court decision, *Lucas v. Earl*.[44] Mr. Earl entered into a binding agreement with his wife under which Mrs. Earl was to receive one-half of Mr. Earl's salary. Justice Holmes used the celebrated **fruit and tree metaphor** to explain that the fruit (income) must be attributed to the tree from which it came (Mr. Earl). A mere **assignment of income** does not shift the liability for the tax.

Services of an Employee

As discussed above, the income from personal services generally is taxable to the person performing the services. However, services performed by an employee for an employer's customers or clients are considered performed by the employer. So the employer is

[43] § 451(c).

[44] 2 USTC ¶496, 8 AFTR 10287, 50 S.Ct. 241 (USSC, 1930).

taxed on the income from the services provided, and the employee is taxed on any compensation received from the employer.[45]

The Big Picture

Example 22

Return to the facts of *The Big Picture* on p. 4-1. Assume that instead of operating his dental practice as a sole proprietorship, Dr. Payne incorporated his dental practice in an attempt to limit his liability. He entered into an employment contract with his corporation and was to receive a salary. All patients contract to receive their services from the corporation, and those services are provided by the corporation's employee, Dr. Payne.

As a result, the corporation earned the income from Dr. Payne's services and must include the patients' fees in its gross income. Dr. Payne must include his salary in his gross income. The corporation is allowed a deduction for the reasonable salary paid to Dr. Payne. (See the discussion of unreasonable compensation in Chapters 6 and 19.)

Services of a Child

In the case of a child, the Code specifically provides that amounts earned from personal services must be included in the child's gross income. This result applies even though the income may be paid to other persons (e.g., the child's parents).[46]

4-3b Income from Property

The courts have used the fruit and tree metaphor also to determine who should pay the tax on the income from property. In this context, the "tree" is the property and income is its "fruit." The owner of the tree has control over the fruit; therefore, the owner of the property should pay tax on the income the property produces. For example, if a father gives his daughter the right to collect the rent from his rental property, the father must nonetheless include the rent in his own gross income because he retains ownership of the property.[47] The fact that he can grant the right to the income to his daughter is evidence that he has control over the income. On the other hand, if a father gives his daughter the property, she is taxed on all the income earned after ownership of the property is transferred to her.

Interest

Because income from property is taxable to the owner of the property when the income is generated, it is important to determine when that income is deemed generated, especially when ownership of the property may be transferred during the year. Interest is considered to accrue daily regardless of when it is paid. Therefore, the interest income on an obligation for the period that includes a transfer of ownership is allocated between the transferor and transferee based on the number of days during the period that each owned the obligation.

Floyd, a cash basis taxpayer, gave his son, Ethan, corporate bonds with a face amount of $12,000 and a 5% stated annual interest rate, with interest paid on the last day of each calendar quarter. The gift was made on February 28, 2023. Floyd must recognize $100 of interest income (5% × $12,000 × 2/12) accrued at the time of the gift.

When interest income must be recognized depends on the accounting method and the manner in which the property was transferred. In the case of a gift of income-producing property, the transferor must recognize their share of the accrued income at the time it would have been recognized had the property not been transferred.[48]

Return to the facts of Example 23. Floyd will recognize the $100 of interest income as of March 31, the date he would have received the interest had he retained ownership of the bonds.

[45] *Sargent v. Comm.*, 91–1 USTC ¶50,168, 67 AFTR 2d 91–718, 929 F.2d 1252 (CA–8).

[46] § 73. For treatment of the child's unearned income, see Kiddie Tax—Unearned Income of Dependent Children in text Section 3-6c.

[47] *Galt v. Comm.*, 54–2 USTC ¶9457, 46 AFTR 633, 216 F.2d 41 (CA–7); *Helvering v. Horst*, 40–2 USTC ¶9787, 24 AFTR 1058, 61 S.Ct. 144 (USSC).

[48] Rev.Rul. 72–312.

If the property transfer is the result of a sale, the sale proceeds must include any income accrued prior to the sale. Because the transferor has indirectly received the income, the accrued income is recognized immediately on the sale of the property.

Mia purchased a corporate bond at its face amount of $10,000 on July 1, 2023. The bond pays 5% interest on each June 30. On September 30, 2023, Mia sold the bond for $10,600. Mia must recognize $125 of interest income in 2023 (5% × $10,000 × 3 / 12). She must also recognize a $475 capital gain from the sale of the bond:

Amount received from sale	$ 10,600
Less accrued interest income	(125)
Selling price of bond excluding interest	$ 10,475
Less cost of the bond	(10,000)
Capital gain on sale	$ 475

Dividends

As a separate taxable entity, a corporation is taxed on its earnings with those earnings taxed again as dividends when distributed to shareholders. Therefore, corporate earnings distributed as dividends are subject to double taxation. Partial relief from this double taxation is provided by taxing qualified dividends received by individuals at the same rate as capital gains ranging from 0 to 20 percent based on the taxpayer's taxable income (see text Section 3-9d).[49]

To be eligible for the special rates, stock must have been held for more than 60 days during the 121-day period beginning 60 days before the ex-dividend date.[50] The purpose of this requirement is to prevent taxpayers from buying stock shortly before a dividend is paid, receiving the preferentially-taxed dividend, and then selling the stock at a loss (a short-term capital loss) after the stock goes ex-dividend (a stock's price often declines after the stock goes ex-dividend).

Note that qualified dividends are *not* capital gains; as a result, they cannot be used to recognize capital losses. Qualified dividend income is merely taxed at the rates that would apply to taxpayers if they had an excess of net long-term capital gain over net short-term capital loss.

Stock Holding Period

In June 2023, Green Corporation pays a dividend of $1.50 on each share of its common stock. Madison and Daniel, two unrelated shareholders, each own 1,000 shares of the stock. Consequently, each receives a dividend of $1,500 (1,000 shares × $1.50). Assume that Daniel satisfies the 60/121-day holding period rule but Madison does not.

The $1,500 that Daniel receives is subject to preferential 0%/15%/20% treatment in 2023. The $1,500 that Madison receives, however, is not. Because Madison did not comply with the holding period rule, her dividend is not a *qualified dividend* and is taxed at ordinary income rates.

Assume that both Madison and Daniel in Example 26 are in the 32% tax bracket. Consequently, Madison's tax liability will increase by $480 (32% × $1,500) as a result of her dividend, whereas Daniel's tax will increase by $225 (15% × $1,500) as a result of his. The $255 savings that Daniel enjoys underscores the advantages of qualified dividend treatment.

Unlike individuals, corporations are not granted special tax rates for capital gains or dividends. However, corporations are permitted a dividends received deduction ranging from 50 percent to 100 percent of the dividends received from another domestic corporation. This deduction is discussed in text Section 17-1k.

[49] §§ 1(h)(11) and (j).

[50] The ex-dividend date is the date before the record date on which the corporation finalizes the list of shareholders who will receive the dividends.

Although interest generally accrues on a daily basis, dividends do not because the declaration of a dividend is at the discretion of the corporation's board of directors. Generally, dividends are taxed to the person who is entitled to receive them—the shareholder on the record date.[51] As a result, if a taxpayer sells stock after a dividend has been declared but before the record date, the dividend generally will be taxed to the purchaser.

This rule differs in the case of a gift of stock. If a donor makes a gift of stock to someone (e.g., a family member) after the declaration date but before the record date, the Tax Court has held that the dividend must be included in the gross income of the donor, not the donee. The *fruit* has sufficiently ripened as of the declaration date to tax the dividend income to the donor of the stock.[52] However, where a taxpayer gave stock to a qualified charity (a charitable contribution) after the declaration date and before the record date, the Fifth Circuit Court of Appeals concluded that the dividend income should be included in the gross income of the donee (the owner at the record date). As a result, dividends declared on stock gifted to a charity and stock gifted to family members are treated differently.[53]

Example 28

On June 20, the board of directors of Black Corporation declares a $10 per share dividend. The dividend is payable on June 30 to shareholders of record on June 25. As of June 20, Maria owned 200 shares of Black Corporation's stock. On June 21, Maria sold 100 of the shares to Norm for their fair market value and gave 100 of the shares to Sam (her son). Both Norm and Sam are shareholders of record as of June 25.

Norm (the purchaser) will be taxed on $1,000 because he is entitled to receive the dividend. However, Maria (the donor) will be taxed on the $1,000 received by Sam (the donee) because the gift was made after the declaration date but before the record date of the dividend.

Some payments are frequently referred to as dividends but are *not* considered dividends for tax purposes, although they are included in gross income:

- Dividends received on deposits with savings and loan associations, credit unions, and banks are actually interest (an amount paid for the use of money).
- Patronage dividends paid by cooperatives (e.g., for farmers) are rebates made to the users and are considered reductions in the cost of items purchased from the association. The rebates usually are made after year-end (after the cooperative has determined whether it has met its expenses) and are apportioned among members on the basis of their purchases.
- Mutual insurance companies pay dividends on unmatured life insurance policies that are considered rebates of premiums.
- Shareholders in a mutual investment fund are allowed to report as capital gains their proportionate share of the fund's gains realized and distributed. The capital gain and ordinary income portions are reported on the Form 1099 that the fund supplies to its shareholders each year.

4-3c Income from Partnerships, S Corporations, Trusts, and Estates

Unlike a corporation, a **partnership** is not a separate taxpaying entity for Federal income tax purposes. Rather, the income of a partnership is included in the taxable income of its partners. A partnership merely files an information return (Form 1065) that serves to provide the data necessary for determining the amount and character of each partner's distributive share of the partnership's income and deductions. Partners must each report their distributive share of the partnership's income and deductions for the partnership's tax year ending in or with the partner's tax year. The income must be reported by each

[51] Reg. § 1.61–9(c). The record date is the cutoff for determining the shareholders who are entitled to receive the dividend.

[52] *M. G. Anton*, 34 T.C. 842 (1960).

[53] *Caruth Corp. v. U.S.*, 89–1 USTC ¶9172, 63 AFTR 2d 89–716, 865 F.2d 644 (CA–5).

partner in the year it is recognized by the partnership, even if such amounts are not actually distributed to the partners. Because a partner pays tax on partnership income as the partnership earns it, a distribution by the partnership to the partner generally is treated as a tax-free recovery of capital.[54]

Example 29

Tara owns a one-half interest in the capital and profits of T & S Company (a calendar year partnership). For tax year 2023, the partnership earned revenue of $150,000 and had operating expenses of $80,000. During the year, Tara withdrew $2,500 per month from her capital account (for a total of $30,000).

For 2023, Tara must report $35,000 as her share of the partnership's profits [½ × ($150,000 − $80,000)] even though she received distributions of only $30,000. The $30,000 distribution is a recovery of capital and has no impact on Tara's taxable income.

Contrary to the general rule that a corporation must pay tax on its income, a *small business corporation* may elect to be taxed, under Subchapter S of the Internal Revenue Code, similarly to a partnership. As a result, the shareholders rather than the corporation pay the tax on the corporation's income.[55] The electing corporation is commonly referred to as an **S corporation**. Similar to partners in a partnership, the shareholders report their proportionate shares of the corporation's income and deductions for the year, regardless of whether the corporation actually makes any distributions to the shareholders.

Unlike partnerships and S corporations, estates and trusts generally are not business entities. Rather, they are intended to care for assets on behalf of their beneficiaries until those assets are distributed. However, because those assets are often income-generating (e.g., investments), estates and trusts often earn income while caring for and administering their assets. The *beneficiaries of estates and trusts* generally are taxed on the income earned by the estates or trusts that is actually distributed or required to be distributed to them.[56] Any income not taxed to the beneficiaries is taxable to the estate or trust.

The taxation of income and distributions of partnerships, S corporations, and estates and trusts is compared in Concept Summary 4.1.

Concept Summary 4.1

Taxation of Income and Distributions from Partnerships, S Corporations, Trusts, and Estates

	Partnership	S Corporation	Estate or Trust
Share of the income for the year	Taxable to partner when earned by the partnership.	Taxable to stockholder when earned by the S corporation.	Undistributed income taxed to the estate or trust.
Distributions	Recovery of capital, which reduces basis in the partnership.	Recovery of capital, which reduces basis in the stock.	Taxable to beneficiary when distributed.

4-3d Income in Community Property States

General

State law in Arizona, California, Idaho, Louisiana, Nevada, New Mexico, Texas, Washington, and Wisconsin is based on a community property system. In Alaska, spouses can choose to have the community property rules apply. All other states have a common law property system. The basic difference between common law and community property systems centers around the property rights of married persons. Questions about the taxation of income from community property most frequently arise when spouses file separate returns.

Under a **community property** system, all property owned by a married individual is deemed either to be separately owned by one spouse or to belong to the marital community. Property may be owned separately by a spouse if it was acquired before marriage or received by gift or inheritance following marriage. Otherwise, property is deemed to be community property.

[54] § 706(a) and Reg. § 1.706–1(a)(1). For further discussion, see Chapter 22.

[55] §§ 1361(a) and 1366. For further discussion, see Chapter 23.

[56] §§ 652(a) and 662(a). For further discussion of the taxation of income from partnerships, S corporations, trusts, and estates, see Chapters 21, 22, 23, and 29.

The Federal income taxation of income generated by property in community property states generally is based on who has the right to the income. Any income generated by community property is taxable equally to each spouse. The taxation of income from separate property, however, differs across community property states. The laws of Idaho, Louisiana, Texas, and Wisconsin distinguish between separate property and the income it produces. In these states, the income from separate property belongs to the community. As a result, for Federal income tax purposes, each spouse is taxed on one-half of the income. In the remaining community property states, separate property produces separate income that the owner-spouse must report on his or her Federal income tax return.

What appears to be income, however, may really represent a recovery of capital. A recovery of capital and gain realized on separate property retain their identity as separate property. Items such as nontaxable stock dividends, royalties from mineral interests, and gains and losses from the sale of property take on the same classification as the assets to which they relate.

Bob and Jane are married and reside in California. Among other transactions during the year, the following occurred:

- A nontaxable stock dividend was received by Jane on stock that was given to her by her mother after Jane's marriage.
- A gain of $10,000 was realized on the sale of unimproved land purchased by Bob before the marriage.
- Oil royalties of $15,000 were received from a lease Jane acquired with her separate funds after the marriage.

Because the stock dividend was distributed on stock held by Jane as separate property, it also is her separate property. The same result occurs for the oil royalties Jane receives. All of the proceeds from the sale of the unimproved land (including the gain of $10,000) are Bob's separate property.

In all community property states, income from personal services (e.g., salaries, wages, and income from a professional partnership) is generally treated as if one-half is earned by each spouse.

Fred and Wilma are married but file separate returns. Fred received $25,000 of salary and $300 of taxable interest on a savings account he established in his name. All deposits to the savings account were made from Fred's salary that he earned since the marriage. Wilma collected $2,000 taxable dividends on stock she inherited from her father.

Wilma's gross income is computed as follows under three assumptions as to the state of residency of the couple:

	California	Texas	Common Law States
Dividends	$ 2,000	$ 1,000	$2,000
Salary	12,500	12,500	-0-
Interest	150	150	-0-
	$14,650	$13,650	$2,000

Note that the savings account is a community asset because it was created with community funds (i.e., Fred's salary).

Because they have community property income and are filing separately, both Fred and Wilma must include Form 8958, Allocation of Tax Amounts Between Certain Individuals in Community Property States, with their Form 1040.

Community property should not be confused with jointly owned property. There are several differences between the two. For example:

- Jointly owned property (i.e., property owned by tenants in common or joint tenants) is not limited to married couples.
- More than two owners can own property jointly. For example, three siblings or two or more unrelated individuals can be joint owners of a tract of land.
- Ownership interests in jointly owned property need not be equal. For example, one sibling can hold a one-half interest while two others own a one-quarter interest each.

Community Property Spouses Living Apart

The general rules for taxing the income from services performed by residents of community property states can create complications and even inequities for spouses who are living apart.

Mason and Lily, a married couple, have always lived in a community property state. After a bitter argument in December 2022, Lily moves in with her parents, where she remains for all of 2023. During 2023, Lily receives none of Mason's income. Nor is she sure how much income Mason earned. When Lily files her separate return for 2023, must she include one-half of Mason's salary?

Congress has developed a simple solution to this problem. A spouse (or former spouse) is taxed only on his or her actual earnings from personal services if all of the following conditions are met:[57]

- The spouses (or former spouses) live apart for the entire year.
- They do not file a joint return with each other.
- No portion of the earned income is transferred between the individuals.

As a result, in the prior example, Lily will not include any of Mason's salary in her gross income for the year.

LO.4

Recognize and apply the special tax rules related to alimony, loans made at below-market interest rates, annuities, prizes and awards, unemployment compensation, Social Security benefits, and foreign bank accounts.

4-4 Special Rules Related to Certain Items Included in Gross Income

Although § 61 makes it clear that all income is taxable unless explicitly excluded, Congress has deemed it necessary to clarify and provide specific rules for several types of income. Some of these special rules appear in §§ 71–91 of the Code.

4-4a Alimony and Separate Maintenance Payments

There are several financial consequences that result when a married couple divorce or become legally separated. For example, when a divorce occurs, state law generally requires a division of the property accumulated during the marriage. In addition, one spouse may have a legal obligation to support the other spouse. The Code has treated property divisions and support payments (alimony or separate maintenance) differently from each other with those differences changing over time. Because the tax treatment of a divorce arrangement and any subsequent payments are generally determined as of the date of the divorce, the current tax treatment of divorced couples will differ depending on when they were divorced.

Property Settlements

A transfer of property owned prior to divorce to a former spouse under a divorce decree or agreement is not a taxable event. The transferor is not entitled to a deduction and does not recognize gain or loss on the transfer. The transferee does not recognize income and has a basis equal to the transferor's basis.[58]

[57] § 66. See Form 8958.

[58] § 1041, added to the Code in 1984 to repeal the rule of *U.S. v. Davis*, 62–2 USTC ¶9509, 9 AFTR 2d 1625, 82 S.Ct. 1190 (USSC). Under the *Davis* rule, which applied to pre-1985 divorces, a property transfer incident to divorce was a taxable event.

Paul transfers stock to Rob as part of a divorce settlement. The cost of the stock to Paul is $12,000, and the stock's value at the time of the transfer is $15,000. Rob later sells the stock for $16,000. Neither Paul nor Rob recognizes any gain or income from the transfer of the stock to Rob. Rob has a realized and recognized gain of $4,000 ($16,000 − $12,000) when he sells the stock.

Support Payments

Alimony and separate maintenance payments made under a divorce agreement executed after 2018 are neither taxable to the recipient nor deductible by the payor.[59] Payments made under an agreement entered into on or before December 31, 2018, are *includible* in the gross income of the party receiving the payments and *deductible for* AGI by the party making the payments. For payments related to these pre-2019 agreements, income is shifted from the income earner to the income beneficiary, who has a legal right to the income and is better able to pay the tax on the amount received.

Pete and Tina were divorced in 2018. Pete is required to pay Tina $15,000 of alimony each year. Pete earns $61,000 a year. Tina has the ultimate legal right to the $15,000 and is better able than Pete to pay the tax on it. Therefore, Tina must include the $15,000 in her gross income. Pete is required to include the $61,000 in his gross income but is allowed to deduct $15,000 from his gross income.

If the divorce occurred in 2023, Tina would not be required to include the alimony in her income, and Pete would not be allowed a deduction for the alimony paid.

Requirements for Alimony

Because a payor may face a higher marginal tax rate than a payee, parties entering into divorce agreements before 2019 may have had an incentive to have payments treated as support obligation (alimony) rather than as part of a property settlement. To clarify the appropriate treatment of payments between former spouses subsequent to a divorce, Congress developed the following objective rules. Payments made under pre-2019 agreements and decrees are *classified as alimony* only if the following conditions are satisfied:

- The agreement or decree does not specify that the payments are not alimony. (This allows the parties to determine by agreement whether the payments will be alimony.)
- The payments are in cash. (Payments other than cash are likely to be part of a property division.)
- There is no liability to make the payments for any period after the death of the payee. (Payments due after death would be a property interest that could be transferred to the heirs.)
- The payor and payee are not members of the same household at the time the payments are made. (This ensures that the payments are for maintaining two households.)

Child Support

As the consequence of a divorce, one former spouse also may be required to make payments to the other with the express purpose of supporting a child. A taxpayer does not realize income from the receipt of child support payments since the money received must be used for the child's benefit. Similarly, the payor is not allowed to deduct the child support payments because the payments are made to satisfy the payor's legal obligation to support the child.

[59] §§ 71 and 215.

In many cases, it may be difficult to determine whether payments subject to pre-2019 agreements are intended to be alimony or child support. The tax law generally treats any payments that would be reduced on the happening of a contingency related to a child (e.g., the child attains age 21 or dies) as child support. In addition, if the total payments actually made during the year are less than legally required, the payments that are made are considered first to cover the required child support with any excess treated as the required alimony payments. These rules are applied even though the divorce agreement specifies other amounts for the support of the child.[60]

Under a divorce agreement entered into in 2017, Matt is required to make periodic payments of $500 per month to Grace. However, when Matt and Grace's child reaches age 21, marries, or dies (whichever occurs first), the payments will be reduced to $300 per month. Grace has custody of the child. Because the required payments will be reduced by $200 per month once the child reaches age 21, $200 of the monthly payments will be considered child support for Federal tax purposes regardless of how they are labeled in the agreement. Only $300 of the monthly payment will be considered alimony.

If Matt makes payments of only $350 per month, $200 is treated as child support with the remaining $150 considered to be alimony.

Ethics & Equity The Taxation of Alimony and the Alimony Tax Gap

Prior to 2019, alimony payments were deductible by payors and taxable to recipients. This was consistent with the assignment of income doctrine, the idea that income is taxable to the party who has the right to that income. To ensure that recipients properly reported alimony payments as income, payors were required to report the Social Security numbers of the recipient on their tax returns. For divorce agreements reached after 2018, alimony is no longer deductible by payors, nor taxable to recipients, leaving those who earn but are legally obligated to transfer income subject to tax on amounts they directly receive but have no right to keep.

Of course, assuming the recipient of alimony is generally in a lower tax bracket than is the payor, placing the tax burden of amounts transferred as alimony on recipients lowers overall tax revenues. However, transferring the burden to recipients may lower tax revenues for other reasons as well. A 2019 examination of 2016 individual tax returns found that the amount by which total deductions for alimony exceeded the amount reported by recipients had grown to more than $3.2 billion, a 38% increase over the amount determined in 2010. Approximately half of the 2016 discrepancy related to differences in the amounts reported by payors and the recipients whose identity had been reported, resulting in $248 million of unpaid taxes. Nearly half of the discrepancy related to amounts reported by payors for which the corresponding recipient's tax return could not be identified. Nearly $40 million related to amounts claimed by payors who reported invalid Social Security numbers. Of the nearly 285,000 tax returns resulting in a reporting discrepancy, nearly half of all returns reporting alimony deductions, the IRS previously had selected only 7,500 for audit.

Should those who are legally required to transfer their income in the form of alimony to another party be required to pay tax on that income? What role, if any, should the potential loss in tax revenue, whether due to the differences in the tax rates of payors and recipients or the potential overreporting of alimony by payors, play in the decision? Are there other factors that should be considered?

Data source: Treasury Inspector General for Tax Administration (TIGTA) Report 2019-40-048 at **treasury.gov/tigta/auditreports/2019reports/201940048fr.pdf.**

[60]§§ 71(c)(2) and (3), and *Allen H. Johnson*, 107 TCM 1358, T.C.Memo. 2014–67.

The tax rules relating to divorce settlements are reviewed in Concept Summary 4.2.

Concept Summary 4.2

Tax Treatment of Payments and Transfers Pursuant to Divorce Agreements and Decrees

	Payor	Recipient
Property settlement	No income or deduction.	No income or deduction; basis for the property is the same as the transferor's basis.
Alimony pursuant to divorce after 2018	Not deductible.	Not taxable.
Alimony pursuant to a divorce prior to 2019	Deductible *for* AGI in year paid.	Included in gross income in year received.
Child support	Not deductible.	Not taxable.

4-4b **Imputed Interest on Below-Market Loans**

The overall tax on income can be reduced if the taxation of the income can be shifted to a taxpayer in a lower tax bracket. As discussed above, shifting the taxation of income from services is difficult given the assignment of income doctrine. Although shifting the taxation of the income from property can be accomplished by shifting the ownership of the property, this might be a high price to pay. However, lending income-producing property to another taxpayer without charging interest on the loan, as illustrated in the following example, could allow such shifting without requiring the taxpayer to give up ownership of the income-producing property.

Example 36

Kareem is in the 50% (combined Federal and state) marginal tax bracket, while his daughter, Veneia, is in the 20% marginal tax bracket. Kareem has $400,000 available to invest. He plans to use the income from the investment to help support Veneia. Rather than invest the money himself, Kareem decides to loan the money to Veneia in exchange for a non-interest-bearing demand note. Veneia could invest the cash, and the resulting income would be taxed at her 20% tax rate. In addition, Kareem retains control over the principal because he could demand payment on the note at any time.

Although this was a common tax planning technique at one time, the imputed interest rules now reduce the benefits of the income shifting illustrated in the example. Even when no interest is charged on a loan, the lender and borrower may be required to calculate their income as if it had been. If the rules are applicable, lenders are treated as if they had earned interest on the loan and are required to recognize this **imputed interest** in their gross income. Likewise, borrowers are treated as if they had incurred interest expense, although whether the interest expense is deductible will depend on several factors (see Chapters 10 and 11).[61]

Example 37

Returning to Example 36, Kareem would be treated as if he had earned interest on the loan and be required to recognize the imputed interest in his gross income. Veneia would be treated as if she had incurred interest expense. Veneia's interest may be deductible as investment interest if she itemizes her deductions.

Imputed interest is calculated using the rate the Federal government pays on new borrowings, compounded semiannually. This Federal rate is adjusted monthly and is published by the IRS.[62] There are three Federal rates: short-term (applicable to loans not over three years, including demand loans), mid-term (applicable to loans over three years but not over nine years), and long-term (applicable to loans over nine years).[63]

[61] § 7872(a)(1).

[62] §§ 7872(b)(2) and (f)(2).

[63] § 1274(d).

Assume that the Federal rate applicable to the loan in Example 36 is 3.5% through June 30 and 4% from July 1 through December 31. Kareem makes the loan on January 1, and the loan is still outstanding on December 31. Kareem must recognize interest income of $15,140, and Veneia has interest expense of $15,140.

Imputed interest calculations:	
January 1–June 30: 3.5% × $400,000 × ½ year	$ 7,000
July 1–December 31: 4% × ($400,000 + $7,000) × ½ year	8,140
	$15,140

If interest is charged on the loan at less than the Federal rate, the imputed interest is the difference between the amount that would have been charged at the Federal rate and the amount actually charged.

Assume the same facts as in Example 38, except that Kareem charged 3% interest, compounded annually.

Interest at the Federal rate	$ 15,140
Less interest charged (3% × $400,000)	(12,000)
Imputed interest	$ 3,140

Although a lender may be required to recognize imputed interest as income for tax purposes, the lender nonetheless has realized no economic benefit. To better capture the economic positions of the parties involved, the lender is deemed to transfer back to the borrower an amount of money equal to the imputed interest. The nature of this transfer (and its Federal tax consequences) is determined by the relation of the parties to each other.

Return to Example 38. Kareem is deemed to transfer back to Veneia $15,140, the same amount he is deemed to have received in interest. Assuming that Kareem's only relation to Veneia is as a family member, the transfer from Kareem to Veneia is deemed to be a gift. Since gifts are not subject to income taxes (see Chapter 5), this transfer has no income tax consequences for either Kareem or Veneia. However, it may have gift tax consequences for Kareem (see Chapters 1 and 28).

The imputed interest rules apply to most below-market rate loans including the following:[64]

- Gift loans (loans made out of love, affection, or generosity, as in Example 36).
- Compensation-related loans (loans made by an employer to an employee).
- Corporation-shareholder loans (loans made by a corporation to a shareholder).

The effects of these loans on the borrower and lender are summarized in Concept Summary 4.3.

Concept Summary 4.3

Effect of Certain Below-Market Loans on the Lender and Borrower

Type of Loan	Lender	Borrower
Gift loans	Interest income Gift made	Interest expense Gift received
Compensation-related loans	Interest income Compensation expense	Interest expense Compensation income
Corporation to shareholder loans	Interest income Dividend paid	Interest expense Dividend income

[64] § 7872(c).

Exceptions and Limitations

An important exception to the imputed interest rules may apply to loans on which the imputed interest would be negligible. No interest is imputed on total outstanding *gift loans* of $10,000 or less between individuals unless the loan proceeds are used to purchase income-producing property.[65] This exception eliminates loans that do not result in material shifts of income. However, if total gift loans between individuals exceed $10,000 or the proceeds of such a loan are used to purchase income-producing property, this exception does not apply.

A limitation on the amount of interest that must be imputed may apply when the borrower has little investment income and, therefore, income shifting was likely not a motivation for the loan. On gift loans of $100,000 or less between individuals, the interest that must be imputed is limited to the borrower's net investment income for the year (gross income from all investments less the related expenses).[66] In addition, if the borrower's net investment income for the year does not exceed $1,000, no interest is imputed. However, these limitations for loans of $100,000 or less do not apply if a principal purpose of a loan is tax avoidance.[67]

Example 41

Vicki made interest-free gift loans as follows:

Borrower	Amount	Borrower's Net Investment Income	Purpose
Susan	$ 8,000	$ -0-	Education
Dan	9,000	500	Purchase of stock
Bonnie	25,000	-0-	Purchase of a business
Megan	90,000	15,000	Purchase of a residence
Olaf	120,000	-0-	Purchase of a residence

Assume that tax avoidance is not a principal purpose of any of the loans. The loan to Susan is not subject to the imputed interest rules because the $10,000 exception applies. The $10,000 exception does not apply to the loan to Dan because the proceeds were used to purchase income-producing assets. However, under the $100,000 exception, the imputed interest is limited to Dan's investment income ($500). Because the $1,000 threshold also applies to this loan, no interest is imputed.

No interest is imputed on the loan to Bonnie because the gift loan is less than $100,000, and Bonnie has no investment income. The $100,000 exception also applies to the loan made to Megan. Although interest must be imputed, the amount imputed will be no more than Megan's investment income. None of the exceptions apply to the loan to Olaf because the loan was for more than $100,000.

Assume that the relevant Federal rate is 5% and that the loans were outstanding for the entire year. Vicki would recognize interest income, compounded semiannually, as follows:

Loan to Megan:	
First 6 months (5% × $90,000 × ½ year)	$ 2,250
Second 6 months (5% × $92,250 × ½ year)	2,306
	$ 4,556
Loan to Olaf:	
First 6 months (5% × $120,000 × ½ year)	$ 3,000
Second 6 months (5% × $123,000 × ½ year)	3,075
	$ 6,075
Total imputed interest ($4,556 + $6,075)	$10,631

As with gift loans, there is a $10,000 exemption for *compensation-related loans* and *corporation-shareholder loans*. However, the $10,000 exception does not apply to compensation-related or corporation-shareholder loans if tax avoidance is one of the principal purposes of the loan.[68] This vague tax avoidance standard makes practically all compensation-related and corporation-shareholder loans suspect. Nevertheless, the $10,000 exception should apply when an employee's borrowing was necessitated by personal needs (e.g., to meet unexpected expenses) rather than tax considerations.

[65] § 7872(c)(2).

[66] § 7872(d).

[67] *Deficit Reduction Tax Act of 1984: Explanation of the Senate Finance Committee* (April 2, 1984), p. 484.

[68] § 7872(c)(3).

These exceptions to the imputed interest rules are summarized in Concept Summary 4.4.

Concept Summary 4.4

Exceptions to the Imputed Interest Rules for Below-Market Loans

Exception	Eligible Loans	Ineligible Loans and Limitations
De minimis—aggregate loans of $10,000 or less	Gift loans	Proceeds are used to purchase income-producing assets.
	Employer-employee	Principal purpose is tax avoidance.
	Corporation-shareholder	Principal purpose is tax avoidance.
Aggregate loans of $100,000 or less	Gift loans	Principal purpose is tax avoidance. For all other loans, interest is imputed to the extent of the borrower's net investment income if that income exceeds $1,000.

Ethics & Equity Taxing "Phantom" Income

Under the imputed interest rules, a taxpayer who makes a below-market loan may be required to recognize income not actually received. For example, assume that Christiana loans $200,000 to Max, her son, to start a business.

Christiana does not charge interest because Max needs the funds to operate a struggling startup business. Why should Christiana be required to pay tax on interest she did not collect? On one hand, she received no interest income. On the other hand, interest would have been charged by Christiana in an arm's length loan made to any other borrower or by any other lender on a loan to Max. Christiana's choice not to charge interest is really an indirect gift to Max. Should Christiana be able to avoid tax on the income she assigned to Max? This type of income is sometimes referred to as "phantom" income.

4-4c Income from Annuities

Annuity contracts generally involve a purchaser (the annuitant) paying a fixed amount for the right to receive a future stream of payments. Typically, the issuer of the contract is an insurance company. The insurance company invests the amounts received from the annuitant, and the income earned serves to increase the cash value of the annuity. If the annuitant cancels the contract early, the issuer will pay the annuitant the cash value of the annuity.

Generally, the increase in the cash value of the contract is not immediately taxable because it is subject to substantial restrictions (the contract must be canceled to realize the benefit). However, if the contract is canceled early, the amount received over the cost of the contract must be recognized as income.

Jean, age 50, pays $30,000 for an annuity contract that is to pay her $500 per month beginning when she reaches age 65 and continuing until her death. A year after purchasing the contract, its cash value increases to $30,200. If Jean should cancel the policy after one year, she would include $200 ($30,200 − $30,000) in her gross income. However, if she does not cancel the policy, the $200 increase in value is not includible in her gross income.

The tax accounting problem associated with receiving periodic payments under an annuity contract is one of apportioning the amounts received between recovery of capital (the original investment in the contract) and income.

Computing the Exclusion Amount

The annuitant can exclude from income the portion of each payment that represents a recovery of capital. The *exclusion amount* is calculated as follows:

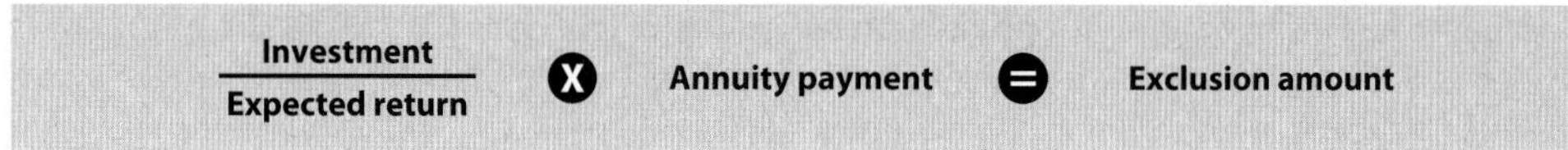

The taxpayer's *investment* in the annuity contract is the total amount paid by the taxpayer for the annuity. The *expected return* is the annual amount to be paid to the annuitant multiplied by the number of years the payments will be received. The payment period may be fixed (a *term certain*) or may be for the life of one or more individuals. When payments are for life, the taxpayer generally must use an annuity table published by the IRS to determine the expected return (see Exhibit 4.1).[69] The expected return is calculated by multiplying the appropriate multiple (life expectancy) by the annual payment.

Exhibit 4.1 Ordinary Life Annuities: One Life—Expected Return Multiples

Age	Multiple	Age	Multiple	Age	Multiple
5	76.6	42	40.6	79	10.0
6	75.6	43	39.6	80	9.5
7	74.7	44	38.7	81	8.9
8	73.7	45	37.7	82	8.4
9	72.7	46	36.8	83	7.9
10	71.7	47	35.9	84	7.4
11	70.7	48	34.9	85	6.9
12	69.7	49	34.0	86	6.5
13	68.8	50	33.1	87	6.1
14	67.8	51	32.2	88	5.7
15	66.8	52	31.3	89	5.3
16	65.8	53	30.4	90	5.0
17	64.8	54	29.5	91	4.7
18	63.9	55	28.6	92	4.4
19	62.9	56	27.7	93	4.1
20	61.9	57	26.8	94	3.9
21	60.9	58	25.9	95	3.7
22	59.9	59	25.0	96	3.4
23	59.0	60	24.2	97	3.2
24	58.0	61	23.3	98	3.0
25	57.0	62	22.5	99	2.8
26	56.0	63	21.6	100	2.7
27	55.1	64	20.8	101	2.5
28	54.1	65	20.0	102	2.3
29	53.1	66	19.2	103	2.1
30	52.2	67	18.4	104	1.9
31	51.2	68	17.6	105	1.8
32	50.2	69	16.8	106	1.6
33	49.3	70	16.0	107	1.4
34	48.3	71	15.3	108	1.3
35	47.3	72	14.6	109	1.1
36	46.4	73	13.9	110	1.0
37	45.4	74	13.2	111	0.9
38	44.4	75	12.5	112	0.8
39	43.5	76	11.9	113	0.7
40	42.5	77	11.2	114	0.6
41	41.5	78	10.6	115	0.5

[69]The life expectancies in Exhibit 4.1 apply for annuity investments made on or after July 1, 1986. See *General Rules for Pensions and Annuities*, IRS Publication 939 (Rev. Dec. 2018), p. 26. See also *Pension and Annuity Income*, IRS Publication 575.

A taxpayer, age 60, purchases an annuity from an insurance company for $90,000. In return, she is to receive $500 per month for life. Her life expectancy (from Exhibit 4.1) is 24.2 years from the annuity starting date. As a result, her expected return is $500 × 12 × 24.2 = $145,200, and the exclusion amount is $3,719 [($90,000 investment ÷ $145,200 expected return) × $6,000 annual payment]. On an annual basis, $3,719 is treated as a nontaxable return of capital and $2,281 ($6,000 − $3,719) is included in gross income.

The *exclusion ratio* (investment ÷ expected return) applies until the annuitant has recovered their entire investment in the contract. Once the investment is recovered, the entire amount of subsequent payments is taxable. If the annuitant dies before recovering the investment, the unrecovered cost (adjusted basis) is deductible in the year the payments cease (usually the year of death).[70]

Assume that the taxpayer in Example 43 receives annuity payments for 25.2 years (302 months). For the last 12 months [302 − (12 × 24.2) = 12], the taxpayer will include $500 (the total amount received) each month in gross income. If instead the taxpayer dies after 36 months, she is eligible for a $78,843 deduction on her final tax return.

Cost of the contract	$ 90,000
Cost previously recovered [$90,000 ÷ $145,200 × 36($500)]	(11,157)
Deduction	$ 78,843

Simplified Method for Annuity Distributions from Qualified Retirement Plans

A simplified method is required for allocating basis to the annuity payments received under a qualified retirement plan. The portion of each annuity payment that is excluded as a return of capital is the employee's investment in the contract, if any, divided by the number of anticipated monthly payments determined in accordance with Exhibit 4.2 rather than the annuity table illustrated in Exhibit 4.1.[71]

Andrea, age 62, receives an annuity distribution of $500 per month for life from her qualified retirement plan beginning in January 2020. Her investment in the contract is $100,100. The excludible amount of each payment is $385 ($100,100 investment ÷ 260 monthly payments). As a result, $115 ($500 − $385) of each annuity payment is included in Andrea's gross income.

The rules for annuity payments received after the basis has been recovered by the annuitant and for the annuitant who dies before the basis is recovered are the same as under the exclusion ratio method discussed earlier.

Exhibit 4.2 Number of Anticipated Monthly Annuity Payments under the Simplified Method

Age	Number of Anticipated Monthly Payments
55 and under	360
56–60	310
61–65	260
66–70	210
71 and over	160

[70] § 72(b).

[71] § 72(d).

4-4d **Prizes and Awards**

Gross income includes the fair market value of any prizes and awards (other than scholarships exempted under § 117; see text Section 5-4) received by a taxpayer.[72] For example, TV giveaway prizes, magazine publisher prizes, door prizes, and awards from an employer to an employee in recognition of performance are fully taxable to the recipient.

A narrow exception permits a prize or an award to be excluded from gross income if *all* of the following requirements are satisfied:

- The prize or award is received in recognition of religious, charitable, scientific, educational, artistic, literary, or civic achievement (e.g., Nobel Prize, Pulitzer Prize, or faculty teaching award).
- The recipient was selected without any action on his or her part to enter the contest or proceeding.
- The recipient transfers the prize or award to a qualified governmental unit or nonprofit organization.
- The recipient is not required to render substantial future services as a condition for receiving the prize or award.[73]

The transfer of the property to a qualified governmental unit or nonprofit organization ordinarily would be a deductible charitable contribution (an itemized deduction as explained in Chapter 10). The exclusion produces beneficial tax consequences in the following situations:

- The taxpayer does not itemize deductions and so would receive no tax benefit from the charitable contribution.
- The taxpayer's charitable contributions exceed the annual statutory ceiling on the deduction.
- Including the prize or award in gross income would reduce the amount of deductions for which the taxpayer would otherwise qualify because of gross income limitations (e.g., the adjusted gross income limitation in calculating the medical expense deduction).

Another exception allows an exclusion for certain *employee achievement awards* made in the form of tangible personal property (e.g., a gold watch) but not cash or cash equivalents (e.g., gift certificates, meals, lodging, or tickets to theater or sporting events). To qualify for the exclusion, the award must be made in recognition of an employee's length of service or safety achievement. Generally, the ceiling on the excludible amount for an employee is $400 per taxable year. However, if the award is made as a part of a tax qualified plan, the ceiling on the exclusion is $1,600 per taxable year.[74]

A third exception allows certain participants in the Olympic and Paralympic Games to exclude the value of any medal and cash award received. The exclusion is only available to those with income of $1 million or less. The rationale offered for this tax preference is that the athletes "perform a valuable patriotic service."[75]

Finally, a taxpayer also can avoid including prizes and awards in gross income by simply refusing to accept the prize or award.[76]

4-4e **Unemployment Compensation**

The unemployment compensation program is sponsored and operated by the states and Federal government to provide a source of income for people who have been employed and are temporarily (hopefully) out of work. In a series of rulings over a period of 40 years, the IRS had exempted unemployment benefits from tax. These payments were considered social benefit programs for the promotion of the general welfare. After experiencing dissatisfaction with the IRS's treatment of unemployment compensation, Congress amended the Code to make the benefits taxable.[77]

---

[72] § 74.

[73] § 74(b).

[74] § 74(c). Qualified plan awards are defined in § 274(j) and explained in *Business Expenses*, Chapter 2 (IRS Publication 535).

[75] P.L. 114-239 (10/7/16), adding § 74(d) effective for awards received after 2015. Also see H.R. Rep. No. 114–762 (9/20/16).

[76] See Rev.Rul. 57–374 and Rev.Proc. 87–54.

[77] § 85.

Ethics & Equity Tax Treatment of Unemployment Compensation

The unemployment insurance program is a joint Federal-state program designed to replace a portion of wages for workers who have lost their jobs. Prior to the COVID-19 pandemic, those who left a job voluntarily were not covered. Nor were the self-employed, including independent contractors and gig workers. Although eligibility requirements and benefits differed by state, most states required workers to have a minimum amount of time worked or earnings to qualify. Qualified workers generally were eligible for coverage for up to 26 weeks. On average, benefits replaced half of a worker's previous earnings or $387 per week. Any benefits received were taxable, as was the income they replaced.

In response to the COVID-19 pandemic and the resulting recession, the 2020 Coronavirus Aid and Economic Security (CARES) Act made several temporary changes to the unemployment system. It eliminated prior work requirements and extended coverage to part-time workers, independent contractors, and the self-employed through the end of 2020. Along with the pandemic itself, this significantly increased the number of taxpayers receiving unemployment benefits. The Act also extended benefits an additional 13 weeks and initially increased payments by $600 per week over existing benefits.

Estimates suggest that the enhanced benefits resulted in covered individuals receiving, on average, 90 percent of their previous earnings with approximately two-thirds making more than they did when employed and 20 percent receiving more than twice their prior earnings. Although most agreed that it was appropriate to adjust unemployment benefits in response to the pandemic, some believed it was inconsistent to require some of the economic assistance to be repaid through income taxes. Conversely, some worried that the increased benefits would discourage people from returning to work when able, hindering any economic recovery.

The American Rescue Plan Act of 2021 extended Federal unemployment benefits through August 2021 at a reduced rate of $300 per week. It also allowed households with AGI less than $150,000 to exclude up to $10,200 of unemployment compensation received during 2020.

However, fearing the increased benefits were preventing people from reentering the workforce, many states discontinued the benefits early. Do you think unemployment compensation should be taxable? Why or why not?

More information may be found at **taxfoundation.org/unemployment-compensation-taxable-income/** and **usatoday.com/story/money/2021/07/09/unemployment-benefits-jobs-worker-shortage/7826616002/**.

4-4f Social Security Benefits

The amount of Social Security benefits included in a taxpayer's gross income is based on two factors: (1) the taxpayer's ability to pay and (2) the amount of benefits considered to be a recovery of the taxpayer's contributions, or a recovery of capital. In this context, ability to pay is based on *modified adjusted gross income* (MAGI). MAGI is equal to the taxpayer's adjusted gross income from all sources other than Social Security benefits, increased by any tax-exempt income including the foreign earned income exclusion.

If a taxpayer's MAGI plus 50 percent of Social Security benefits received, often referred to as *provisional income*, does *not exceed* a threshold amount ($32,000 for married taxpayers filing a joint return or $25,000 for single taxpayers), the taxpayer need not include any Social Security benefits in gross income. If provisional income *exceeds* this threshold, the taxpayer must include a portion of the Social Security benefits in gross income, determined as follows:

1. The amount included in gross income is equal to 50 percent of the amount by which the provisional income exceeds the threshold, limited to 50 percent of the benefits themselves.
2. If the taxpayer's provisional income also exceeds a second threshold ($44,000 for a married couple filing a joint return or $34,000 for a single taxpayer), the amount included in gross income is equal to 85 percent of the amount that provisional income exceeds the higher threshold, plus the *lesser* of the following:
   - The amount determined in 1, above.
   - Fifty percent of the difference between the two threshold amounts (i.e., $6,000 for a married taxpayer filing jointly or $4,500 for a single taxpayer).

In general, the threshold amounts for married taxpayers filing separately are set at zero.

Regardless of a taxpayer's MAGI, or ability to pay, the total amount included in gross income is limited to 85 percent of the benefits themselves.[78] A summary of the rules covering the taxation of Social Security benefits is illustrated in Exhibit 4.3.

[78] § 86. On average, 15% of recipients' Social Security benefits is a recovery of their initial contributions to the program. The remaining 85% is funded by employer contributions and interest earned by the Social Security trust fund.

Exhibit 4.3 Inclusion of Social Security Benefits in Gross Income

Social Security Inclusion Rate	On Provisional Income of: Single Taxpayers	Married Taxpayers Filing Jointly	Limited to
0%	\$0–\$25,000	\$0–\$32,000	
50%	\$25,000–\$34,000	\$32,000–\$44,000	50% of benefits received
85%	Over \$34,000	Over \$44,000	

In no case will taxable benefits exceed 85% of the benefits received.

Taxation of Social Security Benefits

Example 46

A married couple with adjusted gross income of \$30,000 before Social Security benefits, no tax-exempt income, and \$13,000 of Social Security benefits who file jointly must include \$2,500 of the benefits in gross income. This is determined as follows:

Modified Adjusted Gross Income (MAGI)	\$30,000
Social Security benefits (\$13,000 × ½)	6,500
Provisional income	36,500
Threshold amount	(32,000)
	4,500
	× 50%
Tentative taxable benefits	\$ 2,500
Limited to	
Social Security benefits	\$13,000
	× 50%
	\$ 6,500

If instead the couple had adjusted gross income of \$15,000, none of the benefits would be taxable because provisional income [\$15,000 + (50% × \$11,000)] does not exceed \$32,000.

Example 47

A married couple who file jointly have adjusted gross income of \$72,000 before Social Security benefits, no tax-exempt income, and \$13,000 of Social Security benefits. Their includible Social Security benefits are \$11,050, determined as follows:

	Provisional Income Above Second (85%) Threshold	Provisional Income Above First (50%) Threshold			Total Taxable Benefits
	(1)	(2a)	(2b)	(2c)	(1) + Lesser of (2a), (2b), or (2c)
Modified Adjusted Gross Income (MAGI)	\$72,000	\$72,000			
Social Security benefits (\$13,000 × ½)	6,500	6,500			
Provisional income	78,500	78,500			
Threshold amount	(44,000)	(32,000)	13,000*	12,000**	
Inclusion base	34,500	46,500			
Inclusion percentage	× 85%	× 50%	× 50%	× 50%	
	\$29,410	\$23,250	\$ 6,500	\$ 6,000	\$35,410
Limited to					
Social Security benefits					\$13,000
					× 85%
					\$11,050

* Social Security benefits received.
** Range of 50% inclusion rate.

Because 85% of the Social Security benefits received is less than \$35,410 (\$29,410 + \$6,000), \$11,050 is included in the couple's gross income.[79]

[79] To help taxpayers compute taxable benefits, a worksheet is provided in the instructions to Form 1040, as well as in *Social Security and Equivalent Railroad Retirement Benefits* (IRS Publication 915).

4-4g Income Earned from Foreign Bank and Financial Accounts and FBAR Rules

Given the broad definition of gross income, income earned outside the United States by a U.S. taxpayer generally is included in gross income (although limited exclusions are available, as discussed in Chapter 5). However, because it has historically been difficult for the IRS to get information regarding this income and its sources from international payers, taxpayers with a foreign bank account, brokerage account, or similar financial account generally are required to file an annual report with the Treasury Department. If the aggregate value of their foreign accounts exceeds $10,000 at any time during the calendar year, FinCEN Form 114, **Report of Foreign Bank and Financial Accounts (FBAR)**, must be filed electronically with the Treasury Department. This form is due by April 15 (with an automatic extension until October 15) for the preceding tax year. The form is filed separately from the account holder's income tax return. Schedule B of Form 1040 includes questions that also must be answered for individuals with foreign accounts. The penalty for failure to comply with the FBAR reporting requirements can be substantial: as much as 50 percent of the value of the foreign accounts.[80]

Jane, an employee of Maple Corporation, travels frequently for her work. She learned that it is easier to handle rent and other payments while working abroad if she has banking arrangements in these countries. In June and July of this year, during her trips, she opened an account in Canada and an account in France. Each started with a deposit of $6,000. Because on at least one day this year Jane had over $10,000 in foreign financial accounts, she must file FinCEN Form 114 (FBAR) to report the accounts. In addition, any interest earned on the accounts is included in calculating her Federal income tax liability.

The tax law requires that many forms of income paid to individual taxpayers be reported to the taxpayer, as well as the IRS, by the party making the payments. Of course, the taxability of income does not depend on whether it is required to be reported. For example, wages and interest are taxable even if the amount earned or received is less than the reporting threshold. In addition, if the party who is required to issue the reporting form fails to do so, the recipient of the income must still report that income on their tax return. A summary of reporting requirements for some of the most common types of income received by individuals is presented in Exhibit 4.4.

Exhibit 4.4 Third-Party Reporting Requirements

Type of Income	Reported on Form	Comments
Wages	W–2	Generally required for payments or $600 or more.
Business Income	1099–NEC	Generally required for payments of $600 or more made in the course of a payer's trade or business.
Interest	1099–INT	Generally required for payments of $10 or more.
Dividends	1099–DIV	Generally required for payments of $10 or more.
Property transactions	1099–B	Required of brokers for taxpayers for whom they sold stocks, securities, other financial instruments, or commodities. Taxpayer must generally determine the basis of the assets sold.
	1099–S	Reportable by party responsible for closing real estate transactions of $600 or more. Sales of a taxpayer's residence for $250,000 or less are exempt.
Income from partnerships, S corporations, estates, and trusts	K–1	Includes taxpayer's distributive share of each type of income earned by the entity; these items are included in the calculation of the taxpayer's own taxable income.
Alimony (for divorces finalized prior to 2019)		Taxpayers deducting alimony must report the Social Security number of the recipient on their tax return. The amount is not reported directly to the recipient.
Prizes and Awards	1099–MISC	Generally required for payments of $600 or more.
Social Security benefits	SSA–1099	All benefits are reported. Taxpayers must determine the amount that is taxable.
Distributions from pensions	1099–R	Generally required for payments of $10 or more.

[80]See **fincen.gov/resources/filing-information**. FinCEN is the Financial Crimes Enforcement Network and is part of the U.S. Department of the Treasury.

4-5 Tax Planning

LO.5

Identify tax planning strategies for minimizing gross income and the present value of the related tax.

The topics covered in this chapter have focused on the following questions:

- What is gross income?
- When is gross income recognized?
- To whom is gross income taxable?

Planning strategies suggested by these questions include the following:

- Minimize the economic benefits that are included in gross income.
- Defer the recognition of gross income.
- Shift the taxability of income to taxpayers who are in a lower marginal tax bracket.

Some specific techniques for accomplishing these strategies are discussed in the following paragraphs.

4-5a Minimizing Income Included in Gross Income

Given the broad definition of gross income included in the Code, most items of income are included in gross income. However, a taxpayer may be able to restructure a transaction so that an item is not considered income. For example, a lessor may be able to structure a lease such that some advance payments received under the contract are considered deposits. Given the requirement that the amount be repaid under certain circumstances, the receipt would not be considered income.[81] Of course, this could also result in the taxpayer forfeiting their right to the amount that is reclassified. Conversely, in situations in which more than one taxpayer is involved, taxpayers may find it advantageous to have transfers between the parties considered income. For example, before 2019, it was often advantageous to structure divorce agreements such that payments between former spouses would qualify as taxable alimony rather than child support or a property settlement. Assuming that the payor was in a higher tax bracket than the recipient, alimony payments could reduce the joint tax liability of the parties. Similarly, taxpayers may prefer to have some items treated as taxable receipts (rather than gifts) if the taxable payments might be deductible by the payor.

In spite of the broad general definition of gross income, several types of income are specifically excluded from gross income. Several of these are discussed in Chapter 5.

4-5b Deferring Income Recognition

General

Because deferring the recognition of income and the payment of the related tax reduces the net present value of the tax liability, the deferral of taxes is a primary goal of the tax planner. In fact, a significant amount of tax planning deals with when taxes are owed rather than how much is owed. As discussed in text Section 4-2, the timing of income recognition generally is determined by the taxpayer's accounting method. The cash method provides the taxpayer with more deferral opportunities than does the accrual method. For example, under the cash method, income derived from services can be deferred until it is collected rather than recognized when the services are provided as required under the accrual method. Although taxpayers are somewhat constrained by the constructive receipt doctrine (they cannot turn their backs on income), seldom will customers and clients offer to pay before they are asked. The usual lag between billings and collections (e.g., December's billings collected in January) will result in a continuous deferral of some income until the last year of operations.

Regardless of a taxpayer's method of accounting, no income is recognized and no tax is due on a property transaction until a gain has been realized. Therefore, the law favors investments that appreciate in value over ones that provide regular cash payments.

[81] See *Commissioner v. Indianapolis Power and Light*, 90–1 USTC ¶50,007, 65 AFTR 2d 90–394, 110 S.Ct. 589 (USSC).

Example 49

Vera can buy a corporate bond or an acre of land for $10,000. The bond pays $500 of interest (5%) each year, and Vera expects the land to increase in value 5% each year for the next 10 years. She is in the 40% (combined Federal and state) tax bracket. Assuming that the bond would mature or the land would be sold in 10 years and Vera would reinvest the interest at a 5% before-tax return, she would accumulate the following amount at the end of 10 years:

		Bond	Land
Original investment		$10,000	$10,000
Annual income	$ 500		
Less tax	(200)		
	$ 300		
Compound amount reinvested for 10 years at after-tax return of 3% [5% × (1 − 0.4)]	× 11.46	3,438	
		$13,438	
Compound amount, 10 years at 5%			× 1.63
			$16,300
Less tax on sale:			
40%($16,300 − $10,000)			(2,520)
			$13,780

Therefore, the value of the deferral that results from investing in the land rather than in the bond is $342 ($13,780 − $13,438). The advantage of investing in the land may be increased further by the availability of the lower rates applicable to long-term capital gains.

Of course, a taxpayer can often defer the recognition of income from appreciated property by postponing the event triggering realization (the final closing on a sale or exchange of property). If the taxpayer needs cash, obtaining a loan by using the appreciated property as collateral may be a less costly alternative than selling the property. The need to sell an appreciated asset to purchase a new investment will practically increase the return required on the new asset necessary to make it preferable to the old (commonly referred to as the "lock-in" effect).

Example 50

Ira owns 100 shares of Pigeon Company common stock with a cost of $20,000 and a fair market value of $50,000. Although the stock's value has increased substantially in the past three years, Ira thinks future appreciation will be much less. Ira is considering selling the Pigeon stock and investing the proceeds from the sale in other common stock. Assuming that Ira's marginal tax rate on the sale is 15%, he will have only $45,500 [$50,000 − 15%($50,000 − $20,000)] to reinvest. Therefore, if considered as competing alternatives, Ira will have to earn approximately 10% more ($50,000 ÷ $45,500) on a new investment to make it as profitable as his current investment in the Pigeon stock.

As discussed in text Section 4-2c, Series EE bonds offer taxpayers the unusual opportunity of long-term deferral of interest income until the maturity of the bond. In situations where the taxpayer's goal is merely to shift income one year into the future, bank certificates of deposit are useful tools. If the maturity period is one year or less, all interest is reported in the year of maturity. Bank certificates of deposit are especially useful for taxpayers who find themselves in an unusually high tax bracket in one year (perhaps due to a nonrecurring gain on the sale of property) but expect their gross income to be less the following year.

Generally, the timing of income recognition under the accrual method is not impacted by when cash is received. However, even accrual basis taxpayers may be able to defer the recognition of income by deferring when payment is received. Recall that an accrual basis taxpayer who receives unearned income need only recognize for tax purposes in the year of receipt what is recognized in their financial statements but cannot defer recognition of the remainder beyond the year following the year of receipt. In some cases, deferring receipt from a year prior to when income would first be recognized to a subsequent year may result in a valuable tax deferral.

Example 51

NerdSquad, Inc., sells three-year computer service agreements for $15,000, requiring the customer to prepay for the service when a contract is signed. In December 2023, NerdSquad will sell several three-year contracts covering the period from January 2024 to December 2026. It is considering whether to require customers to pay in December 2023 or January 2024. As illustrated below, Nerd-Squad will recognize in its financial statements $5,000 of income from each contract in each year from 2024 through 2026. However, by deferring receipt of the revenue for only a short period, the company will defer the tax on a significant portion of it.

		Taxable Income	
	Financial Statement Income	If payments are received December 30, 2023	If payments are received January 2, 2024
2023	$ -0-	$ -0-	$ -0-
2024	5,000	15,000	5,000
2025	5,000		10,000
2026	5,000		

Of course, the tax planner must also consider the tax rates for the years the income is shifted from and to. For example, a one-year deferral of income from a year in which the taxpayer's tax rate is 24 percent to a year in which the tax rate will be 35 percent would not be advisable unless the taxpayer could earn an after-tax return of approximately 45 percent on the deferred tax.

4-5c Shifting Income to Other Taxpayers

The benefits of income are often shared among multiple individuals regardless of who earns it. For example, the earnings of one family member may be used to support his or her spouse, children, and parents. The tax liability of a family who may be directly or indirectly sharing income can be minimized by shifting the taxability of that income from higher- to lower-bracket family members. This can be accomplished through gifts of income-producing property. Furthermore, in many cases, income can be shifted with no negative effect on the family's spending or investment plans.

Income Shifting

Example 52

Adam, who is in the 24% tax bracket, helps support his father, Mike, who is a widower. Mike's main source of income is Social Security. Rather than simply transferring part of his income to Mike, Adam could transfer to Mike income-producing property. Some of the income would be offset by Mike's standard deduction with the rest subject to tax at Mike's tax rate, which is likely lower than Adam's.

Example 53

Adam, from Example 52, also would like to save for his children's education. All of his children are under 19 years of age and are dependents of Adam. Adam could transfer income-producing properties to the children as well. However, in this case, the kiddie tax may negate the benefits of shifting more than $1,100 of income to each child (see text Section 3-6c).

The Uniform Gifts to Minors Act, a model law adopted by all states (but with some variations among the states), facilitates such income shifting. Under the Act, a gift of intangibles (e.g., bank accounts, stocks, bonds, and life insurance contracts) can be made to a minor but with an adult serving as custodian. Usually, the parent who makes the gift is also named as custodian. State laws allow the custodian to sell or redeem and reinvest the principal and to accumulate or distribute the income, practically at the custodian's discretion provided there is no commingling of the child's income with the parent's property. By giving appreciated securities to the child, and having the donor custodian sell the securities and reinvest the proceeds, the parent shifts both the gain and the annual income to the child. Such planning is limited by the kiddie tax (refer to text Section 3-6c).

U.S. savings bonds provide another opportunity for income shifting. As discussed above, taxpayers may defer the interest (original issue discount) earned on U.S. government (Series EE) bonds. However, if and when this income is shifted to children, it may be beneficial to elect to recognize the interest early while the child has little or no other income. When this is done, the children generally should file a return and elect to report the income on the accrual basis.

Abby pays $7,500 for Series EE bonds in 2023 and registers them in her son's name. Her son, Wade, will enter college the year of original maturity of the bonds. The bonds have a maturity value of $10,000. Wade elects to report the annual increment in redemption value as income for each year the bonds are held. The first year the increase is $250, and Wade includes that amount in his gross income. If Wade has no other income, no tax will be due on the $250 bond interest because such an amount will be more than offset by his available standard deduction. The following year the increment is $260, and Wade includes this amount in income. As a result, over the life of the bonds, Wade will include $2,500 in income ($10,000 − $7,500), none of which will result in a tax liability, assuming that he has no other income.

However, if the election had not been made, Wade would have been required to include $2,500 in income on the bonds in the year of original maturity if they had been redeemed as planned. This amount of income might result in a tax liability.

Refocus on The Big Picture

Calculation of Gross Income

Bob Daemmrich/Alamy Stock Photo

Dr. Cliff Payne has correctly calculated the gross income of his sole proprietorship based on the accrual method of accounting. He will report $385,000, including the $4,000 he received in the form of the solar panels, on his tax return (Schedule C of Form 1040).

What If?

From a tax planning perspective, what can Dr. Payne do to decrease his gross income from the first year of operating his dental practice and thereby produce better financial results for him?

Rather than adopt the accrual method of accounting, Dr. Payne could instead adopt the cash method of accounting. His gross income for Federal income tax purposes under the cash method is calculated as follows:

Revenues	$385,000
Plus: Accounts receivable: January 1	–0–
Less: Accounts receivable: December 31	(52,000)
Gross income	$333,000

The cash method of accounting enables Dr. Payne to defer paying Federal income taxes on the accounts receivable he has yet to collect. Furthermore, each year that Dr. Payne has accounts receivable at the end of the tax year, that income is continuously deferred. As a result, if his accounts receivable remain at $52,000 at the end of each tax year, by using the cash method of accounting rather than the accrual method, he will effectively defer that amount of income until he terminates his practice.

Key Terms

Accounting income, 4-4
Accounting method, 4-7
Accrual method, 4-8
Alimony and separate maintenance payments, 4-21
All events test, 4-8
Annuity, 4-26
Assignment of income, 4-14
Cash method, 4-7
Claim of right doctrine, 4-8
Community property, 4-18
Constructive receipt, 4-9
Economic income, 4-4
Financial statement income inclusion rule, 4-13
Fruit and tree metaphor, 4-14
Gross income, 4-3
Hybrid method, 4-9
Imputed interest, 4-23
Income, 4-4
Original issue discount, 4-11
Partnership, 4-17
Recovery of capital doctrine, 4-3
Report of Foreign Bank and Financial Accounts (FBAR), 4-32
S corporation, 4-18
Taxable year, 4-6

Discussion Questions

1. **LO.1** According to the Supreme Court, would it be good tax policy to use income as computed by financial accounting principles as the correct measure of income for Federal income tax purposes? Explain.

2. **LO.1** Compare and contrast the economist's concept of income with the concept employed in measuring taxable income.

3. **LO.1** Allen visits Reno, Nevada, once a year to gamble. This year his gambling loss was $25,000. He commented to you, "At least I didn't have to pay for my airfare and hotel room. The casino paid that because I am such a good customer. That was worth at least $3,000." What are the relevant tax issues for Allen? *Critical Thinking*

4. **LO.1, 4** Hana lost her job in 2023 when her employer moved its plant. During the year, she collected unemployment benefits for three months, a total of $1,800. While she was waiting to hear from prospective employers, she painted her house. If Hana had paid someone else to paint her house, the cost would have been $3,000. The cost of the paint Hana used was $800. What is Hana's 2023 gross income for tax purposes from the above events?

5. **LO.1** Howard buys wrecked cars and stores them on his property. Recently, he purchased a 1991 Ford Taurus for $400. If he can sell all of the usable parts, his total proceeds from the Taurus will be over $2,500. As of the end of the year, he has sold only the radio for $75 and he does not know how many, if any, of the remaining parts will ever be sold. What are Howard's income recognition issues? *Critical Thinking*

6. **LO.2** On December 29, 2023, an employee received a $5,000 check from her employer's client. The check was payable to the employer. The employee did not remit the funds to the employer until December 30, 2023. The employer deposited the check on December 31, 2023, but the bank did not credit the employer's bank account until January 2, 2024. When is the cash basis employer required to include the $5,000 in gross income?

7. **LO.2** What is the purpose of the constructive receipt doctrine?

8. **LO.2** A taxpayer is considering two alternative investments. A Series EE U.S. government savings bond accrues 3.5% interest each year. The bond matures in three years, at which time the principal and interest will be paid. Alternatively, a bank will pay the taxpayer a 3.5% interest rate each year if he agrees to leave money on deposit for three years. What tax advantage does the Series EE bond offer that is not available with the bank deposit? *Planning*

9. **LO.2** A taxpayer performs services for customers with payment due within 30 days. All customers pay within the time limit. What would be the benefit to the taxpayer using the cash method of accounting rather than the accrual method? *Planning*

10. **LO.3, 5** Wade paid $7,000 for an automobile that needed substantial repairs. He worked nights and weekends to restore the car and spent $2,400 on parts for it. He knows that he can sell the car for $13,000, but he is very wealthy and does not need the money. On the other hand, his daughter, who has very little income, needs money to make the down payment on a house.

    a. Would it matter, after taxes, whether Wade sells the car and gives the money to his daughter or whether he gives the car to his daughter and she sells it for $13,000? Explain.

    b. Assume that Wade gave the car to his daughter after he had arranged for another person to buy it from his daughter. The daughter then transferred the car to the buyer and received $13,000. Who is taxed on the gain?

11. **LO.3** Anita, a cash basis taxpayer, sued her former employer for wage discrimination. Her attorney agreed to pursue the case on a contingent fee basis—the attorney would receive one-third of any settlement or court award. The parties reached a settlement, and the attorney for Anita's former employer wrote a check payable to Anita for $320,000 and a check payable to her attorney for $160,000. Anita reasons that she and the attorney were partners in the lawsuit who shared profits two-thirds and one-third, respectively. Therefore, she includes $320,000 in her gross income. Is Anita's analysis correct? Explain.

12. **LO.3** Rex purchased a 30% interest in a partnership for $200,000. In 2023, the partnership generated $400,000 of taxable income and Rex withdrew $100,000. In 2024, the partnership earned $600,000 of taxable income and Rex withdrew $200,000. What is Rex's gross income from the partnership in 2023 and 2024?

13. **LO.4** A divorce agreement entered into in 2017 requires Alice to pay her former spouse $50,000 a year for the next 10 years. Will the payments qualify as alimony? Why or why not?

Critical Thinking

14. **LO.4, 5** William and Abigail, who live in San Francisco, have been experiencing problems with their marriage. They have a three-year-old daughter, April, who stays with William's parents during the day because both William and Abigail are employed. Abigail worked to support William while he attended medical school, and now she has been accepted by a medical school in Mexico. Abigail has decided to divorce William and attend medical school. April will stay in San Francisco because of her strong attachment to her grandparents and because they can provide her with excellent day care. Abigail knows that William will expect her to contribute to the cost of raising April. Abigail also believes that to finance her education, she must receive cash for her share of the property they accumulated during their marriage. In addition, she believes that she should receive some reimbursement for her contribution to William's support while he was in medical school. She expects the divorce proceedings to take several months. Identify the relevant tax issues for Abigail.

Decision Making
Planning

15. **LO.4, 5** Patrick and Eva are planning to divorce in 2023. Patrick has offered to pay Eva $12,000 each year until their 11-year-old daughter reaches age 21. Alternatively, Patrick will transfer to Eva common stock that he owns with a fair market value of $100,000. What factors should Eva and Patrick consider in deciding between these two options?

16. **LO.4** In the current year, Madero Corporation made a $400,000 interest-free loan to Francisco Madero, the corporation's controlling shareholder. Mr. Madero is also the corporation's chief executive officer and receives a salary of $300,000 a year. What are the tax consequences of classifying the loan as a compensation-related loan rather than as a corporation-shareholder loan?

17. **LO.4** Connor purchased an annuity that was to pay him a fixed amount each month for the remainder of his life. He began receiving payments in 2006, when he was 65 years old. In 2023, Connor was killed in an automobile accident. What are the effects of the annuity on Connor's final tax return?

18. **LO.4** Carlos is retired and receives Social Security benefits. During the year, Carlos appeared on a television game show and won $5,000. By how much will the prize increase his gross income? Critical Thinking

19. **LO.4** In January 2023, Sonja deposited $20,000 in a bank in the Bahamas. She earned $500 interest income. She closed the account in December 2023.
    a. Is Sonja subject to the FBAR reporting requirement? Explain.
    b. Is the interest income taxable in the United States? Explain.

Computational Exercises

20. **LO.2** On January 1, 2023, Kunto, a cash basis taxpayer, pays $46,228 for a 24-month certificate of deposit. The certificate is priced to yield 4% (the effective interest rate) with interest compounded annually. No interest is paid until maturity, when Kunto receives $50,000.
    a. Compute Kunto's gross income from the certificate for 2023.
    b. Compute Kunto's gross income from the certificate for 2024.

    Round all calculations to the nearest dollar.

21. **LO.2** Bigham Corporation, an accrual basis calendar year taxpayer, sells its services under 12- and 24-month contracts. The corporation provides services to each customer every month. On July 1, 2023, Bigham sold the following customer contracts:

Length of Contract	Total Proceeds
12 months	$14,000
24 months	$24,000

Determine the income to be recognized in taxable income in 2023 and 2024.

Length of Contract	2023 Income	2024 Income
12 months	a. ______	c. ______
24 months	b. ______	d. ______

22. **LO.3** Simba and Zola are married but file separate returns. Simba received $80,000 of salary and $1,200 of taxable dividends on stock he purchased in his name with the salary he earned since the marriage. Zola collected $900 in taxable interest on a certificate of deposit she inherited from her aunt. Compute Zola's gross income under two assumptions as to the state of residency of the couple. If an amount is zero, enter "$0."

	Idaho (Community Property State)	South Carolina (Common Law State)
Dividends	a. ______	d. ______
Interest	b. ______	e. ______
Salary	c. ______	f. ______

23. **LO.4** Casper and Cecile divorced in 2018. As part of the divorce settlement, Casper transferred stock to Cecile. Casper purchased the stock for $25,000, and it had a market value of $43,000 on the date of the transfer. Cecile sold the stock for $40,000 a month after receiving it. In addition, Casper is required to pay Cecile $1,500 a month in alimony. He made five payments to her during the year.

    By how much will each of the above transfers and transactions impact Casper's AGI? Cecile's AGI?

24. LO.4 Elizabeth made the following interest-free loans during the year. Assume that tax avoidance is not a principal purpose of any of the loans. Assume that the relevant Federal rate is 5% and that the loans were outstanding for the last six months of the year.

Borrower	Amount	Borrower's Net Investment Income	Purpose of Loan
Richard	$ 5,000	$800	Gift
Woody	8,000	600	Purchase stock
Irene	105,000	–0–	Purchase residence

By how much do each of these loans increase Elizabeth's gross income?

a. Richard

b. Woody

c. Irene

25. LO.4 A taxpayer, age 64, purchases an annuity from an insurance company for $50,000. She is to receive $300 per month for life. Her life expectancy is 20.8 years from the annuity starting date. Assuming that she receives $3,600 this year, how much is included in her gross income? Round any percentages to two decimal places. Round the final answer for the income to the nearest dollar.

26. LO.4 Compute the taxable Social Security benefits in each of the following situations:

a. Tyler and Candice are married and file a joint tax return. They have adjusted gross income of $46,000 before considering their Social Security benefits, no tax-exempt interest, and $12,400 of Social Security benefits.

b. Tyler and Candice have adjusted gross income of $12,000 before considering their Social Security benefits, no tax-exempt interest, and $16,000 of Social Security benefits.

c. Tyler and Candice have adjusted gross income of $85,000 before considering their Social Security benefits, no tax-exempt interest, and $15,000 of Social Security benefits.

Problems

27. LO.1 Determine the taxpayer's current-year (1) economic income and (2) gross income for tax purposes from the following events:

a. Ja-ron's employment contract as chief executive of a large corporation was terminated, and he was paid $500,000 not to work for a competitor of the corporation for five years.

b. Elliot, a six-year-old child, was paid $5,000 for appearing in a television commercial. His parents put the funds in a savings account for the child's education.

c. Valery found a suitcase that contained $100,000. She could not determine who the owner was.

d. Winn purchased a lottery ticket for $5 and won $750,000.

e. Larry spent $1,000 to raise vegetables that he and his family consumed. The cost of the vegetables in a store would have been $2,400.

f. Dawn purchased an automobile for $1,500 that was worth $3,500. The seller was in desperate need of cash.

28. **LO.1, 2, 5** Harper is considering three alternative investments of $10,000. Assume that the taxpayer is in the 24% marginal tax bracket for ordinary income and 15% for qualifying capital gains in all tax years. The selected investment will be liquidated at the end of five years. The alternatives are: Decision Making Planning

- A taxable corporate bond yielding 5.333% before tax, and the interest can be reinvested at 5.333% before tax.
- A Series EE bond that will have a maturity value of $12,200 (a 4% before-tax rate of return).
- Land that will increase in value.

The gain on the land is classified and taxed as a long-term capital gain. The income from the bonds is taxed as ordinary income. How much must the land increase in value to yield a greater after-tax return than either of the bonds? For this analysis, ignore the effect of property taxes on the land.

Use the future value tables in Appendix E as needed for your calculations and comparisons. Present your answers using spreadsheet software such as Microsoft Excel.

29. **LO.1** Determine Amos's gross income in each of the following cases:
    a. In the current year, Amos purchased an automobile for $25,000. As part of the transaction, Amos received a $1,500 rebate from the manufacturer.
    b. Amos sold his business. In addition to the selling price of the stock, he received $50,000 for a covenant not to compete—an agreement that he will not compete with his former business for five years.
    c. Amos owned some land he held as an investment. As a result of a change in the zoning rules, the property increased in value by $20,000.

30. **LO.1,2** Determine the taxpayer's gross income for tax purposes in each of the following situations:
    a. Deb, a cash basis taxpayer, traded a corporate bond with accrued interest of $300 for corporate stock with a fair market value of $12,000 at the time of the exchange. Deb's cost of the bond was $10,000. The value of the stock had decreased to $11,000 by the end of the year.
    b. Deb needed $10,000 to make a down payment on her house. She instructed her broker to sell some stock to raise the $10,000. Deb's cost of the stock was $3,000. Based on her broker's advice, instead of selling the stock, she borrowed the $10,000 using the stock as collateral for the debt.
    c. Deb's boss gave her two tickets to the Rabid Rabbits rock concert because she met her sales quota. At the time she received the tickets, each ticket had a face price of $200 and was selling on eBay for $300. On the date of the concert, the tickets were selling for $250 each. Deb and her son attended the concert.

31. **LO.2, 5** Al is a medical doctor who conducts his practice as a sole proprietor. During 2023, he received cash of $280,000 for medical services. Of the amount collected, $40,000 was for services provided in 2022. At the end of 2023, Al had accounts receivable of $60,000, all for services rendered in 2023. In addition, at the end of the year, Al received $12,000 as an advance payment from a health maintenance organization (HMO) for services to be rendered in 2024. Compute Al's gross income for 2023: Decision Making Planning
    a. Using the cash basis of accounting.
    b. Using the accrual basis of accounting.
    c. Advise Al on which method of accounting he should use.

32. **LO.2** Selma operates a contractor's supply store. She maintains her books using the cash method. At the end of 2023, her accountant computes her accrual basis income that is used on her tax return. For 2023, Selma had cash receipts of $1,400,000, which included $200,000 collected on accounts receivable from 2022

sales. It also included the proceeds of a $100,000 bank loan. At the end of 2023, she had $250,000 in accounts receivable from customers, all from 2023 sales.

a. Compute Selma's accrual basis gross revenues for 2023.

b. Selma paid cash for all of the purchases. The total amount paid for merchandise in 2023 was $1,300,000. At the end of 2022, she had merchandise on hand with a cost of $150,000. At the end of 2023, the cost of merchandise on hand was $300,000. Compute Selma's gross income from merchandise sales for 2023.

Communications

33. **LO.2** Trip Garage, Inc. (459 Ellis Avenue, Harrisburg, PA 17111), is an accrual basis taxpayer that repairs automobiles. In late December 2023, the company repaired Samuel Mosley's car and charged him $1,000. Samuel did not think the problem had been fixed and refused to pay; as a result, Trip refused to release the automobile. In early January 2024, Trip made a few adjustments and convinced Samuel that the automobile was working properly. At that time, Samuel agreed to pay only $900 because he did not have the use of the car for a week. Trip said "fine," accepted the $900, and released the automobile to Samuel. An IRS agent thinks Trip, as an accrual basis taxpayer, should report $1,000 of income in 2023, when the work was done, and then deduct a $100 loss in 2024. Prepare a memo to Susan Apple, the treasurer of Trip, with the recommended treatment for the disputed income.

34. **LO.2** Determine the effects of the following on a cash basis taxpayer's gross income for 2023 and 2024:

a. On the morning of December 31, 2023, the taxpayer received a $1,500 check from a customer. The taxpayer did not cash the check until January 3, 2024.

b. The same as part (a), except that the customer asked the taxpayer not to cash the check until January 3, 2024, after the customer's salary check could be deposited.

c. The same as part (a), except that the check was not received until after the bank had closed on December 31, 2023.

35. **LO.2, 4** Marlene, a cash basis taxpayer, invests in Series EE U.S. government savings bonds and bank certificates of deposit (CDs). Determine the tax consequences of the following on her 2023 gross income:

a. On September 30, 2023, she cashed in Series EE bonds for $10,000. She purchased the bonds in 2013 for $7,090. The yield to maturity on the bonds was 3.5%.

b. On July 1, 2022, she purchased a 24-month CD for $10,000. The CD matures on June 30, 2024, and will pay $10,816, yielding a 4% annual return.

c. On July 1, 2023, she purchased a 12-month CD for $10,000. The maturity date on the CD was June 30, 2024, when Marlene will receive $10,300.

36. **LO.2** Drake Appliance Company, an accrual basis taxpayer, sells home appliances and service contracts. Determine the effect of each of the following transactions on the company's 2023 gross income assuming that the company uses any available options to defer its taxes.

a. In December 2022, the company received a $1,200 advance payment from a customer for an appliance that Drake special-ordered from the manufacturer. The appliance did not arrive from the manufacturer until January 2023, and Drake immediately delivered it to the customer. The sale was reported in 2023 for financial accounting purposes.

b. In October 2023, the company sold a 6-month service contract for $240. The company also sold a 36-month service contract for $1,260 in July 2023.

c. On December 31, 2023, the company sold an appliance for $1,200. The company received $500 cash and a note from the customer for $700 and $240 interest, to be paid at the rate of $10 a month for 24 months. Because of the customer's poor credit record, the fair market value of the note was only $600. The cost of the appliance was $750.

37. **LO.2** In 2023, Wright's, Inc., signs a contract to design and deliver 100 laptop computers customized to perform certain functions required by a customer. Wright's will be paid $300 per computer but must deliver all 100 laptops to fulfill the contract. At the end of 2023, Wright's has completed and delivered 75 laptops and recognizes $22,500 (75 × $300) in revenues in its audited financial statements.
    a. Assuming Wright's is an accrual basis taxpayer, how much gross income must it recognize in its 2023 taxable income?
    b. (How) would your answer change if the contract allowed the customer to cancel the contract prior to delivery of the 100 computers but required them to pay for any computers completed prior to cancellation?

38. **LO.2, 5** Freda is a cash basis taxpayer. In 2023, she negotiated her salary for 2024. Her employer offered to pay her $21,000 per month in 2024 for a total of $252,000. Freda countered that she would accept $10,000 each month for the 12 months in 2024 and the remaining $132,000 in January 2025. The employer accepted Freda's terms for 2024 and 2025.
    a. Did Freda actually or constructively receive $252,000 in 2024?
    b. What could explain Freda's willingness to spread her salary over a longer period of time?

39. **LO.2, 5** The Bluejay Apartments, a new development, is in the process of structuring its lease agreements. The company would like to set the damage deposits high enough that tenants will keep the apartments in good condition. The company is actually more concerned about damage than about tenants not paying their rent. Decision Making Planning
    a. Discuss the tax effects of the following alternatives:
        - $1,000 damage deposit with no rent prepayment.
        - $500 damage deposit and $500 rent for the final month of the lease.
        - $1,000 rent for the final two months of the lease and no damage deposit.
    b. Which option do you recommend? Why?

40. **LO.1, 2, 3** Rusty has been experiencing serious financial problems. His annual salary was $100,000, but a creditor garnished his salary for $20,000 [i.e., the employer paid the creditor (rather than Rusty) the $20,000]. To prevent creditors from attaching his investments, Rusty gave his investments to his 21-year-old daughter, Rebecca. Rebecca received $5,000 in dividends and interest from the investments during the year. Rusty transferred some cash to a Swiss bank account that paid him $6,000 interest during the year. Rusty did not withdraw the interest from the Swiss bank account. Rusty also hid some of his assets in his wholly owned corporation that received $150,000 rent income but had $160,000 in related expenses, including a $20,000 salary paid to Rusty. Rusty reasons that his gross income should be computed as follows:

Salary received	$ 80,000
Loss from rental property ($150,000 − $160,000)	(10,000)
Gross income	$ 70,000

Determine Rusty's gross income for the year, and explain any differences between your calculation and Rusty's.

41. **LO.2** Troy, a cash basis taxpayer, is employed by Eagle Corporation, also a cash basis taxpayer. Troy receives a salary of $60,000 per year. He also receives a bonus equal to 10% of all collections from clients he serviced during the year. Determine the tax consequences of the following events to the corporation and to Troy:
    a. On December 31, 2023, Troy was visiting a customer. The customer gave Troy a $10,000 check payable to the corporation for appraisal services Troy performed during 2023. Troy did not deliver the check to the corporation until January 2024.
    b. The facts are the same as in part (a), except that the corporation is an accrual basis taxpayer and Troy deposited the check on December 31, but the bank did not add the deposit to the corporation's account until January 2024.

c. The facts are the same as in part (a), except that the customer told Troy to hold the check until January 2024 when the customer could make a bank deposit that would cover the check.

42. **LO.3** Faye, Gary, and Heidi each have a one-third interest in the FGH Partnership. The following information is available with respect to the partnership for the year and the amount allocable to each partner.

	Faye	Gary	Heidi	Total
Withdrawals	(20,000)	(35,000)	(10,000)	(65,000)
Additional contributions	–0–	–0–	5,000	5,000
Allocable share of profits	90,000	90,000	90,000	270,000

Compute each partner's gross income from the partnership for the tax year.

43. **LO.3, 5** During the year, Alva received dividends on her stocks as follows:

Amur Corporation (a French corporation whose stock is traded on an established U.S. securities market)	$60,000
Blaze, Inc., a Delaware corporation	40,000
Grape, Inc., a Virginia corporation	22,000

a. Alva purchased the Grape stock three years ago, and she purchased the Amur stock two years ago. She purchased the Blaze stock 18 days before it went ex-dividend and sold it 20 days later at a $5,000 loss. Alva had no other capital gains and losses for the year. She is in the 32% marginal tax bracket. Compute Alva's tax on her dividend income for the year.

b. Alva's daughter, who is 25 and not Alva's dependent, had taxable income of $6,000, which included $1,000 of dividends on Grape, Inc. stock. The daughter had purchased the stock two years ago. Compute the daughter's tax liability on the dividends.

c. Alva can earn 4.5% before-tax interest on a corporate bond or a 4% dividend on a preferred stock. Assuming that the appreciation in value is the same, which investment produces the greater after-tax income?

d. The same as part (c), except that Alva's daughter is to make the investment.

44. **LO.3** Imani and Doug were divorced on December 31, 2023, after 10 years of marriage. Their current year's income received before the divorce was as follows:

Doug's salary	$41,000
Imani's salary	55,000
Rent on apartments purchased by Imani 15 years ago	8,000
Dividends on stock Doug inherited from his mother 4 years ago	1,900
Interest on a savings account in Imani's name funded with her salary	2,400

Determine Imani's and Doug's separate gross incomes assuming that they live in:

a. California.

b. Texas.

45. **LO.4** Nell and Kirby are in the process of negotiating their divorce agreement, to be finalized in 2023. What should be the tax consequences to Nell and Kirby if the following, considered individually, became part of the agreement?

a. In consideration for her one-half interest in their personal residence, Kirby will transfer to Nell stock with a value of $200,000 and $50,000 of cash. Kirby's cost of the stock was $150,000, and the value of the personal residence is $500,000. They purchased the residence three years ago for $300,000.

b. Nell will receive $1,000 per month for 120 months. If she dies before receiving all 120 payments, the remaining payments will be made to her estate.

c. Nell is to have custody of their 12-year-old son, Bobby. She is to receive $1,200 per month until Bobby (1) dies or (2) attains age 21 (whichever occurs first). After either of these events occurs, Nell will receive only $300 per month for the remainder of her life.

d. How would the answer to part (b) change if the divorce had been finalized in 2017?

46. **LO.4** Alicia and Rafel are in the process of negotiating a divorce agreement to be finalized in 2023. They both worked during the marriage and contributed an equal amount to the marital assets. They own a home with a fair market value of $400,000 (cost of $300,000) that is subject to a mortgage of $250,000. They have lived in the home for 12 years. They also have investment assets, all held more than one year, with a cost of $160,000 and a fair market value of $410,000. As a result, the net worth of the couple is $560,000 ($400,000 − $250,000 + $410,000). Alicia would like to continue to live in the house. Therefore, she has proposed that she receive the residence subject to the mortgage, a net value of $150,000. In addition, she would receive $17,600 each year for the next 10 years, which has a present value (at 6% interest) of $130,000. Rafel would receive the investment assets. If Rafel accepts this plan, he must sell one-half of the investments so that he can purchase a home. Assume that you are counseling Alicia. Explain to Alicia whether the proposed agreement would be "fair" on an after-tax basis. Decision Making

47. **LO.4, 5** Roy decides to buy a personal residence and goes to the bank for a $150,000 loan. The bank tells him that he can borrow the funds at 4% if his father will guarantee the debt. Roy's father, Hal, owns a $150,000 CD currently yielding 3.5%. The Federal rate is 3%. Hal agrees to either of the following: Decision Making

- Roy borrows from the bank with Hal's guarantee to the bank.
- Hal cashes in the CD (with no penalty) and lends Roy the funds at 2% interest.

Hal is in the 32% marginal tax bracket. Roy, whose only source of income is his salary, is in the 12% marginal tax bracket. The interest Roy pays on the mortgage will be deductible by him. Which option will maximize the family's after-tax wealth?

48. **LO.4** Your client, Aldridge, is a generous individual. During the year, he made interest-free loans to various family members when the Federal rate was 3%. What impact, if any, will each of the following loans have on Aldridge's gross income?

a. On June 30, 2023, Aldridge loaned $12,000 to his cousin, Jim, to buy a used truck. Jim's only source of income was his wages on various construction jobs during the year.

b. On August 1, 2023, Aldridge loaned $8,000 to his niece, Sonja. The loan was to enable her to pay her college tuition. Sonja had $1,200 interest income from CDs her parents had given her.

c. On September 1, 2023, Aldridge loaned $25,000 to his brother, Al, to start a business. Al had $220 of dividends and interest for the year.

d. On September 30, 2023, Aldridge loaned $150,000 to his mother so that she could enter a nursing home. His mother's only income was $9,000 of Social Security benefits and $500 of interest income.

49. **LO.4** For each of the following situations, determine whether the imputed interest rules should apply and, if so, how much interest must be imputed. Assume that all of the loans were made at the beginning of the tax year unless otherwise indicated.

a. Mike loaned his sister $90,000 to buy a new home. Mike did not charge interest on the loan. The Federal rate was 5%. Mike's sister had $900 of investment income for the year.

b. Nico's employer maintains an emergency loan fund for its employees. During the year, Nico's wife was very ill and he incurred unusually large medical expenses. He borrowed $8,500 from his employer's emergency loan fund for six months. The Federal rate was 5.5%. Nico and his wife had no investment income for the year.

c. Jody borrowed $25,000 from her controlled corporation for six months. She used the funds to pay her daughter's college tuition. The corporation charged Jody 4% interest. The Federal rate was 5%. Jody had $3,500 of investment income for the year.

d. Kait loaned her son, Jake, $60,000 for six months. Jake used the $60,000 to pay off college loans. The Federal rate was 5%, and Kait did not charge Jake any interest. Jake had dividend and interest income of $2,100 for the tax year.

50. **LO.4** Vito is the sole shareholder of Vito, Inc. He also is employed by the corporation. On June 30, 2023, Vito borrowed $8,000 from Vito, Inc., and on July 1, 2024, he borrowed an additional $10,000. Both loans were due on demand. No interest was charged on the loans, and the Federal rate was 4% for all relevant dates. Vito used the money to purchase a boat, and he had $2,500 of investment income. Determine all of the tax consequences to Vito and Vito, Inc., in each of the following situations:

a. The loans are considered employer-employee loans.

b. The loans are considered corporation-shareholder loans.

51. **LO.4** Pam retires after 28 years of service with her employer. She is 66 years old and has contributed $42,000 to her employer's qualified pension fund, all of which was taxable when earned. She elects to receive her retirement benefits as an annuity of $3,000 per month for the remainder of her life.

a. Assume that Pam retired in June 2022 and collected six annuity payments that year. What is her gross income from the annuity payments in the first year?

b. Assume that Pam lives 25 years after retiring. What is her gross income from the annuity payments in the twenty-fourth year?

c. Assume that Pam dies after collecting 160 payments. She collected eight payments in the year of her death. What are Pam's gross income and deductions, if any, from the annuity contract in the year of her death?

52. **LO.4** For each of the following, determine the amount that should be included in gross income:

a. Peyton was selected the most valuable player in the Super Bowl. In recognition of this, he was awarded an automobile with a value of $60,000. Peyton did not need the automobile, so he asked that the title be put in his parents' names.

b. Jacob was awarded the Nobel Peace Prize. When he was presented the check for $1,400,000, Jacob said, "I do not need the money. Give it to the United Nations to use toward the goal of world peace."

c. Linda appeared on a television game show during the year, winning $6,000 of cash and $4,000 of furniture and appliances.

53. **LO.2, 3, 4** Herbert was employed for the first six months of 2023 and earned $90,000 in salary. During the next six months, he collected $8,800 of unemployment compensation, borrowed $12,000 (using his personal residence as collateral), and withdrew $2,000 from his savings account (including $60 of interest). He received dividends of $550. His luck was not all bad; in December, he won $1,500 in the lottery on a $5 ticket. Calculate Herbert's gross income.

54. **LO.4, 5** Linda and Don are married and file a joint return. In 2023, they received $12,000 in Social Security benefits and $35,000 in taxable pension benefits and interest.

Decision Making
Planning

a. Compute the couple's adjusted gross income on a joint return.
b. Don would like to know whether they should sell for $100,000 (at no gain or loss) a corporate bond that pays 8% in interest each year and use the proceeds to buy a $100,000 nontaxable State of Virginia bond that will pay $6,000 in interest each year. Assume that their marginal tax rate is 12%.
c. If Linda in part (a) works part-time and earns $30,000, how much will Linda and Don's adjusted gross income increase?

55. **LO.3, 4, 5** Donna does not think she has an income tax problem but would like to discuss her situation with you just to make sure there is no unexpected tax liability. Base your suggestions on the following relevant financial information:

a. Donna's share of the SAT Partnership income is $150,000, but none of the income can be distributed because the partnership needs the cash for operations.
b. Donna's Social Security benefits totaled $8,400, but Donna loaned the cash received to her nephew.
c. Donna assigned to a creditor the right to collect $1,200 of interest on some bonds she owned.
d. Donna and her husband lived together in California until September, when they separated. Donna has heard rumors that her husband had substantial gambling winnings since they separated.

Tax Return Problems

56. Daniel B. Butler and his spouse Freida C. Butler file a joint return. The Butlers live at 625 Oak Street in Corbin, KY 40701. Dan's Social Security number is 111-11-1112, and Freida's is 123-45-6780. Dan was born on January 15, 1971, and Freida was born on August 20, 1971.

Communications
Decision Making
Tax Forms Problem

ProConnect™ Tax

During 2022, Dan and Freida furnished over half of the total support of each of the following individuals, all of whom still live at home:

a. Gina, their daughter, age 22, a full-time student, who married on December 21, has no income of her own and did not file a joint return with her husband, Casey, who earned $10,600 during 2022. Gina's Social Security number is 123-45-6788.
b. Willie, their son, age 19, graduated high school in May 2022. He is taking a leap year and will not begin college until 2023. He had gross income of $6,300 in 2022. Willie's Social Security number is 123-45-6787.
c. Ben, their oldest son, age 26, is a full-time graduate student with gross income of $5,200. Ben's Social Security number is 123-45-6786.

Dan was employed as a manager by WJJJ, Inc. (employer identification number 11-1111111, 604 Franklin Street, Corbin, KY 40702), and Freida was employed as a salesperson for Corbin Realty, Inc. (employer identification number 98-7654321, 899 Central Street, Corbin, KY 40701). Selected information from the W–2 forms provided by the employers is presented below. Dan and Freida use the cash method.

Line	Description	Dan	Freida
1	Wages, tips, other compensation	$74,000	$86,000
2	Federal income tax withheld	11,000	12,400
17	State income tax withheld	2,960	3,440

Freida sold a house on December 30, 2022, and will be paid a commission of $3,100 (not included in the $86,000 reported on the W–2) on the January 10, 2023, closing date.

Other income (as reported on 1099 forms) for 2022 consisted of the following:

Dividends on CSX stock (qualified)	$4,200
Interest on savings at Second Bank	1,600
Interest on City of Corbin bonds	900
Interest on First Bank CD	382

The $382 from First Bank was an original issue discount. Dan and Freida collected $16,000 on the First Bank CD that matured on September 30, 2022. The CD was purchased on October 1, 2019, for $14,995, and the yield to maturity was 3.3%. Dan participated on a game show and won a cash prize of $7,000.

In addition to the above information, Dan and Freida's itemized deductions included the following:

Paid on 2022 Kentucky income tax	$ 700
Personal property tax paid	600
Real estate taxes paid	1,800
Interest on home mortgage (Corbin S&L)	4,900

Sales tax from the sales tax table is $1,860. Dan and Freida made Federal estimated tax payments of $6,000. They have never owned or used any digital assets, and they do not wish to contribute to the Presidential Election Campaign. The Kentucky income tax rate is 4%.

Compute Dan and Freida's 2022 Federal income tax payable (or refund due), and complete their 2022 tax return using the appropriate forms and schedules. Suggested software: ProConnect Tax.

Tax Computation Problem

57. Cecil C. Seymour is a 64-year-old widower. He had income for 2023 as follows:

Pension from former employer	$39,850
Interest income from Alto National Bank	5,500
Interest income on City of Alto bonds	4,500
Dividends received from IBM stock held for over one year	2,000
Collections on annuity contract he purchased from Great Life Insurance	5,400
Social Security benefits	14,000
Rent income on townhouse	9,000

The cost of the annuity was $46,800, and Cecil was expected to receive a total of 260 monthly payments of $450. Cecil has received 22 payments through 2023.

Cecil's 40-year-old daughter, Sarah C. Seymour, borrowed $60,000 from Cecil on January 2, 2023. She used the money to start a new business. Cecil does not charge her interest because she cannot afford to pay it, but he does expect to collect the principal eventually. Sarah is living with Cecil until the business becomes profitable. Except for housing, Sarah provides her own support from her business and $1,600 in dividends on stocks that she inherited from her mother.

Other relevant information is presented below.

- Expenses on rental townhouse:

Utilities	$2,800
Maintenance	1,000
Depreciation	2,000
Real estate taxes	750
Insurance	700

- State income taxes paid: $3,800
- County personal property taxes paid: $3,100
- Payments on estimated 2023 Federal income tax: $5,900
- Charitable contributions of cash to Alto Baptist Church: $7,400
- Federal interest rate: 4%
- Sales taxes paid: $912

Compute Cecil's 2023 Federal income tax payable (or refund due).

Research Problems

Note: Solutions to the Research Problems can be prepared by using the Thomson Reuters Checkpoint™ online tax research database, which accompanies this textbook. Solutions can also be prepared by using research materials found in a typical tax library.

Communications

Research Problem 1. Tranquility Funeral Home, Inc., your client, is an accrual basis taxpayer that sells preneed funeral contracts. Under these contracts, the customer pays in advance for goods and services to be provided at the contract beneficiary's death. These payments are refundable at the contract purchaser's request, pursuant to state law, anytime until the goods and services are furnished. Tranquility, consistent with its financial accounting reporting, includes the payments in income for the year the funeral service is provided. The IRS agent insists that the payments be prepaid income subject to tax in the year of receipt. Your client believes that the amounts involved are customer deposits. Write a letter to Tranquility that contains your advice about how the issue should be resolved. The client's address is 400 Rock Street, Memphis, TN 38152.

Research Problem 2. Your client was the beneficiary of an annuity contract purchased by her stepmother. When the stepmother died, the insurance company paid the client $400,000 and sent her a Form 1099 indicating that the taxable portion (i.e., the amount in excess of the investment in the contract) was $50,000. However, according to the client, her father fraudulently convinced her that he was the intended beneficiary. She gave her father a check equal to the amount she had received from the insurance company. She did not report any of the annuity proceeds in her income tax return. She later discovered the fraud and filed a lawsuit to collect from her father. The IRS has examined your client's return and has taken the position that she must include the $50,000 in her gross income.

Evaluate the IRS's position.

Research Problem 3. Your client owns a life insurance policy on his life. He has paid $6,800 in premiums, and the cash surrender value of the policy is $30,000. He borrowed $30,000 from the insurance company, using the cash surrender value as collateral. He is considering canceling the policy in payment of the loan. He would like to know the tax consequences of canceling his policy.

Research Problem 4. Your client is a new retailer who often issues store gift (debit) cards to customers in lieu of a cash refund. You recall that a special rule allows accrual method taxpayers to defer all or a portion of advance payments received. Conduct research to determine if this rule applies to the gift cards issued as refunds for product returns.

Use internet tax resources to address the following questions. Look for reliable websites and blogs of the IRS and other government agencies, media outlets, businesses, tax professionals, academics, think tanks, and political outlets.

Research Problem 5. Lottery winnings are taxable for Federal income tax purposes. What many lottery hopefuls forget to factor into their tax considerations are that lottery winnings are also taxable in many states. Search the internet to see if you can determine whether lottery winnings are taxable for California residents.

Communications

Research Problem 6. Go to the web page of a consulting firm that offers counseling services to individuals as they negotiate the terms of a divorce. What specific tax-related services do these firms offer? Suggest a new tax-related service the consulting firm could offer.

Becker CPA Review Questions

Becker

1. Which of the following statements is true regarding the taxation of Social Security benefits?
   a. 85% is the maximum amount of taxable Social Security benefits.
   b. 50% is the maximum amount of taxable Social Security benefits.
   c. If a taxpayer's only source of income is $10,000 of Social Security benefits, then 50% of the benefits are taxable.
   d. If a taxpayer's only source of income is $10,000 of Social Security benefits, then 85% of the benefits are taxable.

2. Fred and Wilma were divorced in year 1 (before 2019). Fred is required to pay Wilma $12,000 of alimony each year until their child turns 18. At that time, the payment will be reduced to $10,000 per year. In year 3, in accordance with the divorce agreement, Fred paid $6,000 directly to Wilma and $6,000 directly to the law school Wilma is attending. What amount of the payments received in year 3 is income to Wilma?
   a. $6,000
   b. $10,000
   c. $12,000
   d. $0

3. Bill and Jane Jones were divorced on January 1, 2018. They have no children. In accordance with the divorce decree, Bill transferred the title of their house over to Jane. The home had a fair market value of $250,000 and was subject to a $100,000 mortgage. Under the divorce agreement, Bill is to make $1,000 monthly mortgage payments on the home for the remainder of the mortgage. In the current year, Bill made 12 mortgage payments. What amount is taxable to Jane in the current year?
   a. $12,000
   b. $250,000
   c. $100,000
   d. $0

4. Jake pays the following amounts to his former spouse during the current year:

Regular alimony payments	$ 12,000
Child support	10,000
Residence as part of a property settlement	115,000

   What amount can Jake deduct as alimony for the current year? Assume that the divorce occurred before 2019.
   a. $0
   b. $12,000
   c. $22,000
   d. $137,000

5. Mary purchased an annuity that pays her $500 per month for the rest of her life. She paid $70,000 for the annuity. Based on IRS annuity tables, Mary's life expectancy is 16 years. How much of the first $500 payment will Mary include in her gross income (round to two decimals)?

   a. $0
   b. $135.42
   c. $364.58
   d. $500.00

6. Which of the following is taxable as gross income?

   a. Child support received based on a divorce agreement executed in 2015.
   b. Alimony received based on a divorce agreement executed in 2015.
   c. Child support received based on a divorce agreement executed in 2019.
   d. Alimony received based on a divorce agreement executed in 2019.

7. Parents lend $2,000,000 to their child to start a business. The loan is interest-free and is payable on demand. The imputed interest is subject to:

   a. The gift tax only in the year the parents lend the money.
   b. The gift tax only in the year the loan is repaid.
   c. The gift tax each year the loan is outstanding.
   d. An excise tax.

Chapter 5 Gross Income: Exclusions

Learning Objectives: *After completing Chapter 5, you should be able to:*

LO.1 **Explain the difference between exclusions and items that are not income.**

LO.2 **Discuss commonly encountered income exclusions.**

LO.3 **Determine the extent to which receipts can be excluded under the tax benefit rule.**

LO.4 **Identify tax planning strategies for obtaining the maximum benefit from exclusions.**

Chapter Outline

VM/E+/GETTY IMAGES

The Big Picture

Exclusions

Paul is a graduate student in the last semester of the accounting program at State University. This past summer he was an intern with a CPA firm, working in the compliance area. Paul was paid well enough for his work as an intern that he was able to pay for his meals and lodging and to save some for school. The CPA firm was so pleased with Paul's work that, at the conclusion of his internship, he was given a bonus of $1,500 more than the firm had agreed to pay him. The extra amount was intended to help with his graduate school expenses. The CPA firm offered him a full-time job after he completes his graduate program in December.

Because of his excellent academic record, the university awarded Paul a graduate assistantship that waives his tuition of $6,000 per semester and pays him $400 per month. Paul is required to teach a principles of accounting course each semester. Paul has used the $400 per month for books and for room and board.

In November, Paul was crossing a street in the pedestrian crosswalk when a delivery van struck him. The driver of the truck was found to be driving while under the influence of alcohol. Paul suffered a severe injury to his right arm that delayed his starting date for work by three months. The delivery company's insurance company settled the case by paying the following damages:

Compensatory damages:	
Medical expenses	$ 30,000
Injury to Paul's right arm	100,000
Pain and suffering	50,000
Loss of income	15,000
Legal fees	25,000
Punitive damages	160,000
	$380,000

Paul's mother was with him in the crosswalk. Fortunately, the van did not hit her, and she was not physically injured. But she did suffer emotional distress and received $25,000 in the settlement.

Besides being Paul's friend, you are also a senior accounting major and have a keen interest in taxation. You tell Paul that you will look into the tax consequences of the payments made by the insurance company.

Read the chapter and formulate your response.

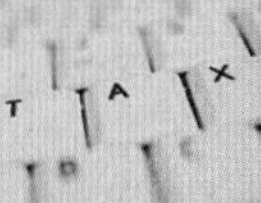

Framework 1040 **Tax Formula for Individuals**

This chapter covers the boldfaced portions of the Tax Formula for Individuals that was introduced in Concept Summary 3.1 on p. 3-3. Below those portions are the sections of Form 1040 where the results are reported.

Income *(broadly defined)*	$xx,xxx
Less: Exclusions	**(x,xxx)**

FORM 1040 (p. 1)

2a Tax-exempt interest . . . **2a** | **b** Taxable interest . . . **2b**

Gross income	**$xx,xxx**

FORM 1040 (Schedule 1)

1 Taxable refunds, credits, or offsets of state and local income taxes

7 Unemployment compensation

8 Other income: ▶

Less: Deductions *for* adjusted gross income	(x,xxx)
Adjusted gross income	$xx,xxx
Less: The greater of total itemized deductions *or* the standard deduction	(x,xxx)
Personal and dependency exemptions*	(x,xxx)
Deduction for qualified business income**	(x,xxx)
Taxable income	$xx,xxx
Tax on taxable income *(see Tax Tables or Tax Rate Schedules)*	$ x,xxx
Less: Tax credits *(including income taxes withheld and prepaid)*	(xxx)
Tax due (or refund)	$ xxx

* Exemption deductions are not allowed from 2018 through 2025.
** Only applies from 2018 through 2025.

Chapter 4 discussed the concepts and judicial doctrines that affect the determination of gross income. If an income item is within the all-inclusive definition of gross income, the item can be excluded only if the taxpayer can locate specific authority for doing so. Chapter 5 focuses on the exclusions Congress has authorized. The chapter begins by defining exclusions and distinguishing them from items that are not income.

LO.1

Explain the difference between exclusions and items that are not income.

5-1 Income Exclusions

5-1a Exclusion Defined

Code §§ 101 through 140 provide the authority for excluding specific items from gross income. Exclusion means that something that should be in the tax base is removed per provisions in the tax law. Each exclusion has its own reason for enactment.

Some exclusions are intended as tax relief measures, such as the exclusion on up to $500,000 of gain from sale of a principal residence.[1] Others are to encourage and support certain activities, such as higher education. Some exclusions relate to design of the income tax. For example, damages received for physical injury are excluded under the premise that they are restoring damage to one's body rather than increasing one's personal wealth.[2]

At times, Congress responds to specific events. For example, in 2001, Congress enacted § 139, Disaster Relief Payment, to ensure that victims of a *qualified disaster* (disaster resulting from a terrorist attack, Presidentially declared disaster, or common carrier accident of a catastrophic nature) could exclude from gross income payments received for living expenses, funeral expenses, and property damage resulting from the disaster.

[1] § 121. See Chapter 13.

[2] Other examples include § 117 on certain scholarships and § 104 on physical injury; each is discussed in more detail later in this chapter.

For some types of transactions, the IRS does not tax what is in fact income because the revenue involved is not worth the collection effort or it is too difficult to measure the income. For example, the IRS has decided that it will not attempt to tax the value of frequent flier miles earned on airline tickets purchased for business use.

5-1b **Exclusions versus Non-Income Items**

Exclusions apply to specified income items. That is, the item must constitute income to possibly warrant an exclusion. For example, a gift you receive from your grandmother is *income* because it is a realized increase in your wealth. However, you'll learn in this chapter that a statutory *exclusion* exists for gifts—making gifts nontaxable for income tax purposes. A gift is income, but it is excluded (and not part of gross income).

In contrast, when a business borrows money from the bank, that money is not income because there is an offsetting liability to repay the amount. Here, there is no increase in wealth. No exclusion is needed because the loan proceeds are not income in the first place. A return of capital (e.g., a specific type of distribution a shareholder receives from a corporation) is another example of something that is not income.

Corporate Distributions

Corporate distributions are payments to shareholders with respect to their stock (see Chapter 4).

- Distributions are taxed as dividends to shareholders only to the extent the payments are made from *either* the corporation's *current earnings and profits* (similar to net income per books) or its *accumulated earnings and profits* (similar to retained earnings per books).[3]
- Distributions that exceed earnings and profits are treated as a nontaxable recovery of capital and reduce the shareholder's basis in the stock. These distributions are not considered income.
- Once the shareholder's basis is reduced to zero, any subsequent distributions are taxed as capital gains (see Chapters 13 and 19).[4]

When a corporation issues a simple stock dividend (e.g., common stock issued to common shareholders), the shareholder has received additional shares but maintains the same total investment. As a result, the shareholder does not realize income; instead, the per share basis is reduced.[5]

However, if the shareholder has the *option* of receiving either cash or stock in the corporation, the individual realizes gross income whether they receive stock or cash.[6] A taxpayer who elects to receive the stock values the stock dividend by determining the value of the stock received (which could be different from the cash rejected).[7] See Chapter 19 for a discussion of stock dividends.

5-2 **Gifts and Inheritances**

LO.2

Discuss commonly encountered income exclusions.

5-2a **Legislative Intent**

From the beginning of the Federal income tax in 1913, Congress has allowed the recipient of a gift to exclude its value from gross income. The exclusion applies to gifts made during the life of the donor (*inter vivos* gifts) and transfers that take effect upon the death of the donor (bequests and inheritances).[8] However, as discussed in Chapter 4, when income-producing property is gifted, the recipient is subject to tax on the income subsequently earned from the property. Also, as discussed in Chapter 1, gift or estate taxes on the transfer might apply.

In many cases, gifts are made in a business setting. For example, a salesperson gives a purchasing agent free samples, an employer gives cash to an employee on retirement,

[3] § 316(a). Refer to the discussion of the beneficial tax rates for qualified dividends in Chapter 4.

[4] § 301(c). See Chapter 19 for a detailed discussion of corporate distributions.

[5] *Eisner v. Macomber*, 1 USTC ¶32, 3 AFTR 3020, 40 S.Ct. 189 (1920); § 305(a).

[6] § 305(b).

[7] Refer to the discussion of constructive receipt in Chapter 4.

[8] § 102.

or a corporation makes payments to employees who were victims of a natural disaster. In these and similar instances, it is frequently unclear whether the payment was a gift or represents compensation for past, present, or future services.

The courts have defined a gift as "a voluntary transfer of property by one to another without adequate [valuable] consideration or compensation therefrom."[9] If the payment is intended to be for services rendered, it is *not* a gift, even though the payment is made without legal or moral obligation, and the payor receives no economic benefit from the transfer. To qualify as a gift, the payment must be made "out of affection, respect, admiration, charity, or like impulses."[10] As a result, these cases have been decided by looking at the donor's intent.

In a landmark case, *Comm. v. Duberstein*,[11] the taxpayer (Duberstein) received a Cadillac from a business acquaintance. Duberstein had supplied the businessman with the names of potential customers with no expectation of compensation. The Supreme Court concluded:

> ... despite the characterization of the transfer of the Cadillac by the parties [as a gift] and the absence of any obligation, even of a moral nature, to make it, it was at the bottom a recompense for Duberstein's past service, or an inducement for him to be of further service in the future.

As a result, Duberstein was required to include the fair market value of the car in gross income.

5-2b **Employer Payments to Employees**

In the case of cash or other property *received by an employee* from an employer, Congress has eliminated any ambiguity. Transfers from an employer to an employee cannot be excluded as a gift.[12]

The Big Picture

Example 1

Return to the facts of *The Big Picture* on p. 5-1. The $1,500 bonus paid to Paul by his summer employer was compensation for his services rather than a gift, even though the employer had not contracted to pay this additional amount. This results because the payment was most likely not motivated by the employer's generosity but, rather, was made as a result of business considerations. Even if the payment had been made out of generosity, because the payment was received from his employer, Paul could not exclude the "gift."

5-2c **Employee Death Benefits**

An employer may make payments (**death benefits**) to a deceased employee's surviving spouse, children, or other beneficiaries. If the decedent had a nonforfeitable right to the payments (e.g., the decedent's accrued salary), the amounts are generally taxable to the recipient as if the employee had lived and collected the payments. Many employers provide group term life insurance for employees in order to provide assistance to the deceased employee's family. If the employer makes voluntary payments (not accrued wages, a late paid bonus, or life insurance proceeds) to the family of the deceased employee, the facts and circumstances must be evaluated to determine if the payments are a nontaxable gift or additional compensation attributable to the deceased employee.[13]

---

[9] *Estate of D. R. Daly*, 3 B.T.A. 1042 (1926).

[10] *Robertson v. U.S.*, 52–1 USTC ¶9343, 41 AFTR 1053, 72 S.Ct. 994.

[11] 60–2 USTC ¶9515, 5 AFTR 2d 1626, 80 S.Ct. 1190.

[12] § 102(c). But see § 139 for qualified disaster situations.

[13] Rev.Rul. 62–102, *Estate of Sydney J. Carter v. Comm.*, 72–1 USTC ¶9129, 29 AFTR 2d 332, 453 F.2d 61 (CA–2), and *Simpson v. U.S.*, 58–2 USTC ¶9923, 2 AFTR 2d 6036, 261 F.2d 497 (CA–7), *cert. denied* 79 S.Ct. 724 (1959).

Income earned by an employee that was not received by the employee prior to their death is not an employee death benefit. These earnings are referred to as "income in respect of a decedent"[14] and are generally taxable income to the decedent's beneficiary. This is another rare instance where the beneficiary of the income, rather than the person who earned the income, is subject to tax.

5-3 Life Insurance Proceeds

5-3a General Rule

Life insurance proceeds paid to the beneficiary because of the death of the insured are excluded from gross income.[15]

Linda purchases an insurance policy on her life and names her husband, Tyler, as the beneficiary. Linda pays $45,000 in premiums. When she dies, Tyler collects the insurance proceeds of $200,000. The $200,000 is excluded from Tyler's gross income (and exempt from Federal income tax).

Congress believed it was good tax policy to exclude life insurance proceeds for the following reasons:

- For family members, life insurance proceeds serve much the same purpose as a nontaxable inheritance.
- In a business context (as well as in a family situation), life insurance proceeds replace an economic loss suffered by the business.

Gold Corporation purchases a life insurance policy to cover its CEO (a key employee). If the proceeds were taxable, the corporation would require more insurance coverage to pay the tax as well as to cover the economic loss of the employee.

5-3b Accelerated Death Benefits

Generally, if the owner of a life insurance policy cancels the policy and receives the cash surrender value, the taxpayer must recognize gain equal to the excess of the amount received over premiums paid on the policy (a loss is not deductible). The gain is recognized because the proceeds were *not* paid on the death of the insured. If the taxpayer cancels the policy and receives the cash surrender value, the life insurance policy is treated as an investment by the insured.

In a limited circumstance, however, the insured is permitted to receive the benefits of the life insurance contract without having to include the gain in gross income. Under the **accelerated death benefits** rules, an exclusion is available for insured taxpayers who are either terminally ill or chronically ill.[16] A terminally ill taxpayer can collect the cash surrender value of the policy from the insurance company or assign the policy proceeds to a qualified third party. The resulting gain, if any, is excluded from the insured's gross income. A person is *terminally ill* if a medical doctor certifies that death is likely to occur within 24 months.

In the case of a chronically ill patient, no gain is recognized if the proceeds of the policy are used for the patient's long-term care. A person is *chronically ill* if they are

[14] § 691.

[15] § 101(a).

[16] § 101(g); reporting may be required per § 6050Y.

certified as needing assistance to perform certain activities of daily living. These exclusions for the terminally ill and the chronically ill are available only to the insured. A person who purchases a life insurance policy from the insured does not qualify.

Accelerated Death Benefits

Tom owned a term life insurance policy at the time he was diagnosed as having a terminal illness. After paying $5,200 in premiums, he sold the policy to Amber Benefits, Inc., a company that is authorized by the state of Virginia to purchase such policies (such a company is referred to as a viatical settlement provider). Amber paid Tom $50,000. When Tom died six months later, Amber collected the face amount of the policy, $75,000. Tom is not required to include the $44,800 gain ($50,000 − $5,200) on the sale of the policy in his gross income.

Assume that Amber Benefits, Inc., in Example 4 paid additional premiums of $4,000 during the six months it owned the policy. When Amber collects the life insurance proceeds of $75,000, it must include the $21,000 gain [$75,000 proceeds − ($50,000 cost + $4,000 additional premiums paid)] in gross income.

Ethics & Equity Should the Terminally Ill Pay Social Security Taxes?

The rationale for excluding accelerated death benefits from the gross income of the terminally ill is that they often use the funds to pay medical expenses and other costs associated with dying and do not have the ability to pay tax on the gain from the accelerated receipt of the life insurance proceeds. Yet the wages of a terminally ill person who is employed (or profits of a self-employed person) are subject to Social Security taxes. The Social Security taxes are intended to pay for retirement benefits, but a terminally ill person is unlikely to collect any Social Security benefits.

Bills have been introduced in Congress to exempt the terminally ill from the Social Security tax. Evaluate the equity of the current tax treatment versus that in the proposed legislation.

5-3c Transfer for Valuable Consideration

A life insurance policy (other than one associated with accelerated death benefits) may be transferred after it is issued by the insurance company. If the policy is *transferred for valuable consideration*, the insurance proceeds are includible in the gross income of the purchaser to the extent the proceeds received exceed the amount paid for the policy plus any subsequent premiums paid.

Adam pays premiums of $4,000 for an insurance policy that has a face amount of $10,000 on the life of Brianna and subsequently transfers the policy to Carol for $6,000. Upon Brianna's death, Carol receives the proceeds of $10,000.

The amount Carol can exclude from gross income is limited to $6,000 plus any premiums she paid subsequent to the transfer.

The Code, however, provides five exceptions to the rule illustrated in Example 6. Exclusion treatment is allowed for transfers to the following:

1. The insured under the policy.
2. A partner of the insured.
3. A partnership in which the insured is a partner.
4. A corporation in which the insured is an officer or a shareholder.
5. A transferee whose basis in the policy is determined by reference to the transferor's basis.

The fifth exception applies to policies that were transferred in a tax-free exchange or were received by gift.[17]

[17] § 101(a)(2). See the discussion of gifts in Chapter 13 and tax-free exchanges in Chapters 13, 18, and 21. In the case of a gift, the donor's basis becomes the donee's basis.

Example 7

When Logan's daughter Emily was born, he purchased an insurance policy on her life. Twenty-four years later after Emily graduated from college and married, Logan sold her the policy for its fair value. When Emily dies, the transfer for consideration rules will not apply.

Because the transfer was to the insured, the policy proceeds paid to Emily's beneficiaries will be excluded from the recipient's gross income. The results would be the same if Logan gave (rather than sold) the policy to Emily.

Investment earnings arising from the reinvestment of life insurance proceeds are generally subject to income tax. Often the beneficiary will elect to collect the insurance proceeds in installments. The annuity rules (discussed in text Section 4-4c) are used to apportion the installment payment between the principal element (excludible) and the interest element (includible).[18]

5-4 **Scholarships**

5-4a **General Information**

Payments or benefits received by a student at an educational institution may be (1) compensation for services, (2) a gift, or (3) a scholarship. If the payments or benefits are received as compensation for services (past or present), the fact that the recipient is a student generally does not render the amounts received nontaxable.[19] A university teaching or research assistant is generally considered an employee, and a stipend is taxable compensation. On the other hand, athletic scholarships generally are nontaxable when the individual is expected (but not required) to participate in the sport.[20] Unless received from family members, amounts received for educational purposes cannot be excluded as gifts because conditions usually attached to the funds mean that the payments were not made out of "detached generosity."

The **scholarship** rules are intended to provide exclusion treatment for education-related benefits that cannot qualify as gifts but are not compensation for services. To be excluded from income, the scholarship must be used for qualified tuition and related expenses (e.g., books and supplies).[21] The recipient must be a candidate for a degree at an educational institution.[22]

Aliyah enters a contest sponsored by a local newspaper. Each contestant is required to submit an essay on local environmental issues. The prize is one year's tuition at State University. Aliyah wins the contest. The newspaper has a legal obligation to Aliyah (as contest winner). As a result, the benefits are not a gift. However, because the tuition payment aids Aliyah in pursuing her studies, the payment is a scholarship.

If a nonprofit educational institution provides tuition reductions for its employees, the employees can exclude these amounts from their gross income. The exclusion also applies to tuition reductions granted to the employee's spouse and the employee's dependent children. In general, the exclusion applies only to education below the graduate level. However, tuition reductions for graduate students who are engaged in teaching or research activities at the educational institution also qualify for the exclusion.[23]

The Big Picture

Return to the facts of *The Big Picture* on p. 5-1. Paul was paid $400 a month by the university for teaching. This is reasonable compensation for his services. Although he received the assistantship because of his excellent academic record, the monthly payment of $400 must be included in his gross income because it is compensation for his services. However, the $6,000 graduate tuition reduction can be excluded from gross income.

[18] Reg. §§ 1.72–7(c)(1) and 1.101–7.

[19] Reg. § 1.117–2(a). See *C. P. Bhalla*, 35 T.C. 13 (1960), for a discussion of the distinction between a scholarship and compensation. See also *Bingler v. Johnson*, 69–1 USTC ¶9348, 23 AFTR 2d 1212, 89 S.Ct. 1439. For potential exclusion treatment, see the subsequent discussion of qualified tuition reductions.

[20] Rev.Rul. 77–263.

[21] § 117(b).

[22] § 117(a).

[23] § 117(d).

The exclusion for qualified scholarships does not apply to room and board.[24] The NCAA allows athletic scholarships to include a "cost of attendance" amount. In addition to tuition, fees, books, and room and board, an athletic scholarship can include expenses like academic-related supplies, transportation, and other similar items. The value of these benefits may differ from campus to campus. However, only the amounts received for tuition, books, and supplies can be excluded from gross income.[25]

Kelly received an athletic scholarship from State University. The scholarship pays her tuition of $9,000 and books and supplies of $2,400. She also receives $4,500 a year for costs of attendance, which she uses to pay for housing, food, laundry, and transportation.

The tuition and the cost of books and supplies are excluded from gross income as a qualified scholarship. The $4,500 received as costs of attendance does not qualify for the scholarship exclusion, and Kelly must include that amount in her gross income.

Some employers make scholarships available solely to the children of key employees. The tax objective of these plans is to provide a nontaxable fringe benefit to the executives by making the payment to the child in the form of an excludible scholarship. However, the IRS has ruled that the payments are generally includible in the gross income of the parent-employee.[26]

5-4b **Timing Issues**

Frequently, the scholarship recipient is a cash basis taxpayer who receives the money in one tax year but pays the educational expenses in a subsequent year. The amount eligible for exclusion may not be known at the time the money is received. In that case, the transaction is held *open* until the educational expenses are paid.[27]

In August 2023, Sanjay received a $10,000 scholarship for the 2023–2024 academic year. Sanjay's expenditures for tuition, books, and supplies were as follows:

August–December 2023	$3,000
January–May 2024	4,500
	$7,500

Sanjay's gross income for 2024 includes $2,500 ($10,000 − $7,500) that is not excludible as a scholarship. None of the scholarship is included in his gross income in 2023.

5-5 Compensation for Injuries, Sickness, and Disaster Relief

5-5a **Damages**

A person who suffers harm caused by another is often entitled to compensatory damages. The tax consequences of the damages awarded depend on the type of harm the taxpayer experienced. The taxpayer may seek recovery for (1) a loss of income, (2) expenses incurred, (3) property destroyed, or (4) personal injury.

Generally, reimbursement for a loss of income is taxed the same as the income replaced (see the exception under Personal Injury below). The recovery of an expense is not income unless the expense was deducted; if the expense was deducted, the damages generally are taxable under the tax benefit rule, discussed later in this chapter.

A payment for damaged or destroyed property is treated as an amount received in a sale or exchange of the property. As a result, the taxpayer has a realized gain if the damages received exceed the property's basis. Damages for personal injuries receive special treatment under the Code.

[24] § 117(b). See also **irs.gov/newsroom/tax-benefits-for-education-information-center**.

[25] Student-athletes might also receive "Alston payments" allowed after a 2021 U.S. Supreme Court decision [*NCAA v. Alston*, 141 S.Ct. 2141 (2021)]. These payments are taxable unless they satisfy the exclusion for scholarships. Student-athletes receiving payments for "name, image or likeness," (or NIL) payments have taxable income for services (these payments are from non-university sources).

[26] Rev.Rul. 75–448; *Richard T. Armantrout*, 67 T.C. 996 (1977).

[27] Prop.Reg. § 1.117–6(b)(2).

Personal Injury

The legal theory of personal injury damages is that the amount received is intended "to make the plaintiff [the injured party] whole as before the injury."[28] It follows that if the damages payments received were subject to tax, the after-tax amount received would be less than the actual damages incurred, and the injured party would not be "whole as before the injury." In terms of personal injury damages, a distinction is made between compensatory damages and punitive damages.

Ethics & Equity Tax Treatment of Damages Not Related to Physical Personal Injury

An individual who prevails in a personal injury claim for something other than a physical injury or sickness must include the amount of the award or settlement in gross income. In contrast, an award or a settlement for a physical personal injury or sickness can be excluded (except for punitive damages) from gross income. Should damages awarded for a physical personal injury or sickness be treated more favorably than damages awarded for emotional distress or other nonphysical personal injuries such as age and sex discrimination?

Compensatory damages are intended to compensate the taxpayer for the damages incurred. Only those compensatory damages received for *physical personal injury or physical sickness* can be excluded from gross income.[29] This includes amounts received for loss of income associated with the physical personal injury or physical sickness.[30] Compensatory damages awarded for emotional distress cannot be excluded (except to the extent of any amount received for medical care) from gross income. Likewise, any amounts received for age discrimination or injury to one's reputation cannot be excluded.

Punitive damages are amounts the person who caused the harm must pay to the victim as punishment for the bad conduct. Punitive damages are not intended to compensate the victim but, rather, to punish the party who caused the harm. So, amounts received as punitive damages may actually place the victim in a better economic position than before the harm was experienced. As a result, punitive damages are included in gross income.

These rules are summarized in Concept Summary 5.1.

Concept Summary 5.1
Taxation of Damages

Type of Claim	Taxation of Award or Settlement
Breach of contract (generally loss of income)	Taxable.
Property damages	Gain to the extent damages received exceed basis. A loss is deductible for business property and investment property to the extent of basis over the amount realized. In certain cases, a loss may be deductible for personal use property (see discussion of casualty losses in Chapter 7).
Personal injury	
Physical	All compensatory amounts are excluded unless previously deducted (e.g., medical expenses). Amounts received as punitive damages are included in gross income.
Nonphysical	Compensatory damages and punitive damages are included in gross income.

[28] *C. A. Hawkins*, 6 B.T.A. 1023 (1927).

[29] § 104(a)(2).

[30] Rev.Rul. 85–97.

The Big Picture

Return to the facts of *The Big Picture* on p. 5-1. The amounts Paul received were compensatory damages awarded as a result of the physical personal injury he suffered. As a result, all of the compensatory damages are excluded from Paul's income (including the compensation for the loss of income of $15,000). The punitive damages, however, must be included in Paul's gross income.

Paul's mother did not suffer a personal physical injury or sickness. So, the $25,000 she received must be included in her gross income.

Ethics & Equity Classifying the Amount of the Claim

Lee was injured in an automobile accident caused by a negligent driver of a commercial vehicle. Lee threatened to file a lawsuit against the company for $100,000 in damages for his physical injury and $100,000 for punitive damages. The company's insurer would not pay punitive damages. As a result, the company advised Lee to revise his claim for $150,000 in physical damages and no punitive damages. Should Lee accept the offer?

5-5b Wrongful Incarceration

Code § 139F exempts amounts received as damages for being wrongfully incarcerated. The exclusion applies to an individual convicted of a Federal or state crime who is later exonerated.

5-5c Workers' Compensation

State workers' compensation laws require the employer to pay fixed amounts for specific job-related injuries. The state laws were enacted to allow the employee to recover the damages without suing the employer. Although the payments are intended, in part, to compensate for a loss of future income, Congress has specifically excluded workers' compensation benefits from gross income.[31]

5-5d Accident and Health Insurance Benefits

The income tax treatment of accident and health insurance benefits depends on whether the policy providing the benefits was purchased by the taxpayer or the taxpayer's employer. Benefits collected under an accident and health insurance policy *purchased by the taxpayer* are excludible even though the payments are a substitute for income.[32]

Tax-Exempt Benefits

Quynh purchases a medical and disability insurance policy. The insurance company pays Quynh $1,000 per week to replace wages she loses while in the hospital. Although the payments serve as a substitute for income, the amounts received are tax-exempt benefits collected under Quynh's insurance policy.

Joe's injury results in a partial paralysis of his left foot. He receives $20,000 for the injury from his accident insurance company under a policy he had purchased. The $20,000 accident insurance proceeds are tax-exempt.

A different set of rules applies if the accident and health insurance protection was *purchased by the individual's employer*, as discussed in text Section 5-6.

5-5e Disaster Relief Benefits

Certain tax rules address the treatment of payments received due to a disaster. For example, § 139 provides an exclusion for payments an individual receives as a *qualified disaster relief payment*. Such payments include those to pay or reimburse an individual

[31] § 104(a)(1).

[32] § 104(a)(3).

for reasonable and necessary personal, family, living, or funeral expenses that arise due to a Federally declared disaster. This exclusion also applies to payments for repair or rehabilitation of a personal residence or its damaged contents.

The Watson family, like other households, were required to shelter in place for much of 2020 because of the COVID-19 pandemic. The Watson's two school-age children attended school online using laptop computers. Their parents worked from home. During this time, their city provided payments to families to cover extra costs of in-home schooling, and the parents' employers provided reimbursement for various computer and online resources to improve internet connectivity in employee homes and help parents have additional activities for children while they were at home all day. Their state government provided $300 to each household to cover increased food costs.

Because the COVID-19 pandemic was a Federally declared disaster, the payments the Watsons received from their employers and state and local governments are excluded from income under § 139.

Code § 123 provides an exclusion for insurance payments received by an individual for living expenses when the individual is not able to use their principal residence due to damage or destruction related to a casualty or threat of a casualty.

5-6 Employer-Sponsored Accident and Health Plans

Congress encourages employers to provide employees, retired former employees, and their dependents with **accident and health benefits**, disability insurance, and long-term care plans. The *premiums* are deductible by the employer and excluded from the employee's income.[33] Although § 105(a) provides the general rule that the employee has includible income when they collect the insurance *benefits*, two exceptions are provided.

Code § 105(b) generally excludes payments received for medical care of the employee, spouse, and dependents. However, if the payments are for expenses that do not meet the Code's definition of medical care,[34] the amount received must be included in gross income. In addition, the taxpayer must include in gross income any amounts received for medical expenses that were deducted by the taxpayer on a prior return.

In 2023, Branden's employer-sponsored health insurance plan pays $4,000 for hair transplants that do not meet the Code's definition of medical care. Branden must include the $4,000 in his gross income for 2023.

Code § 105(c) excludes payments for the permanent loss or the loss of the use of a member or function of the body or the permanent disfigurement of the employee, the spouse, or a dependent. Payments that are a substitute for salary (e.g., related to the period of time absent) are includible.

Jill loses an eye in an automobile accident unrelated to her work. As a result of the accident, Jill incurs $2,000 of medical expenses, which she deducts on her return. She collects $100,000 from an accident insurance policy carried by her employer. The benefits are paid according to a schedule of amounts that vary with the part of the body injured (e.g., $100,000 for loss of an eye and $150,000 for loss of a hand).

Because the payment is for loss of a *member or function of the body*, the $100,000 is excluded from gross income. Jill is absent from work for several weeks as a result of the accident. Her employer provides her with insurance for the loss of income due to illness or injury. Jill collects $7,500, and this amount is includible in her gross income.

[33] § 106, Reg. § 1.106–1, and Rev.Rul. 82–196.

[34] See the discussion of medical care in Chapter 10.

5-6a Medical Reimbursement Plans

As discussed above, amounts received through the insurance coverage (insured plan benefits) are excluded from income under § 105 or § 106. Instead of providing the employee with insurance coverage for hospital and medical expenses, the employer may agree to reimburse the employee for these expenses (a self-insured arrangement). Generally, the benefits received under a self-insured plan can be excluded from the employee's income if the plan does not discriminate in favor of highly compensated employees.[35]

There is also an alternative means of accomplishing a medical reimbursement plan. The employer can purchase a medical insurance plan with a high deductible (e.g., the employee is responsible for the first $3,000 of the family's medical expenses) and then make contributions to the employee's **Health Savings Account (HSA)**.[36] The employer can make contributions each month up to the maximum contribution of 100 percent of the deductible amount. The monthly deductible amount is limited to one-twelfth of $3,850 under a high-deductible plan for self-only coverage. The monthly amount for an individual who has family coverage is limited to one-twelfth of $7,750 under a high-deductible plan. Withdrawals from the HSA must be used to reimburse the employee for the medical expenses paid by the employee that are not covered under the high-deductible plan. The employee is not taxed on the employer's contributions to the HSA, the earnings on the funds in the account, or the withdrawals made for medical expenses.[37]

5-6b Long-Term Care Insurance Benefits

Generally, **long-term care insurance**, which covers expenses such as the cost of care in a nursing home, is treated the same as accident and health insurance benefits. As a result, the employee does not recognize income when the employer pays the premiums. Also, the individual who purchases his or her own policy can exclude the benefits from gross income. However, the Code specifies limits (annually indexed for inflation) for the following amounts:

- Premiums paid by the employer.
- Benefits collected under the employer's plan.
- Benefits collected from the individual's policy.

The employer or insurance company generally provides the employee with information on the amount of his or her taxable benefits. The maximum amount excluded must be reduced by any amount received from third parties (e.g., Medicare, Medicaid).[38]

Hazel, who suffers from Alzheimer's disease, is a patient in a nursing home for the last 30 days of 2023. While in the nursing home, she incurs total costs of $9,400. Medicare pays $3,800 of the costs. Hazel receives $9,400 from her long-term care insurance policy, which pays benefits while she is in the nursing home. In 2023, $420 per day of long-term care benefits is excludible from gross income.

The amount Hazel may exclude is calculated as follows:

Greater of:		
Daily excludible amount in 2023 ($420 × 30 days)	$12,600	
Actual cost of the care	9,400	$12,600
Less: Amount received from Medicare		(3,800)
Available exclusion amount		$ 8,800

As a result, Hazel must include $600 ($9,400 − $8,800) of the long-term care benefits received in her gross income.

The exclusion for long-term care insurance is not available if it is provided as part of a cafeteria plan or a flexible spending plan (explained later in the chapter).

[35] § 105(h). Also see § 106 and Rev.Rul. 61–146. Employers should make sure such reimbursement plans fall within the requirements of the Affordable Care Act to avoid an excise tax. See § 4980D, Notice 2013–54 and Notice 2015–17. Also see rules on Qualified Small Employer Health Reimbursement Arrangements (QSEHRA) at § 9831(d) and Notice 2017–67.

[36] §§ 106(d) and 223. See additional coverage in Chapter 10.

[37] §§ 106(d), 223(b), and 223(d). The 2023 inflation-adjusted amounts are published in Rev.Proc. 2022–24. The amounts for 2022 were $3,650 and $7,300.

[38] §§ 7702B and 213(d)(10). See IRS Publication 525 for the taxable and nontaxable amounts that the employer is required to report on the employee's W–2.

5-7 Meals and Lodging

5-7a General Rules for the Exclusion

As discussed in Chapter 4, income can take any form, including meals and lodging. However, § 119 excludes from income the value of meals and lodging provided to the employee and the employee's spouse and dependents under the following conditions:[39]

- The meals and/or lodging are *furnished* by the employer on the employer's *business premises* for the *convenience of the employer*. From 2018 through 2025, the employer may only deduct 50 percent of the cost of the meals provided.[40] After 2025, employers may not claim any deduction for these meals. If the employer continues to provide such meals, their value remains as an exclusion for the employees.
- In the case of lodging, the *employee is required* to accept the lodging as a condition of employment.

The courts have interpreted these requirements strictly.

Furnished by the Employer

The following two questions have been raised with regard to the *furnished by the employer* requirement:

- Who is considered an *employee*?
- What is meant by *furnished*?

The IRS and some courts have reasoned that because a partner is not an employee, the exclusion does not apply to a partner. However, the Tax Court and the Fifth Circuit Court of Appeals disagree with this conclusion.[41]

The Supreme Court held that a cash meal allowance was ineligible for the exclusion because the employer did not actually furnish the meals. Similarly, one court denied the exclusion where the employer paid for the food and supplied the cooking facilities but the employee prepared the meal.[42]

On the Employer's Business Premises

The *on the employer's business premises* requirement, applicable to both meals and lodging, has resulted in much litigation. The Regulations define business premises as simply "the place of employment of the employee."[43] The Sixth Circuit Court of Appeals held that a residence, owned by the employer and occupied by an employee, two blocks from the motel that the employee managed was *not* part of the business premises.[44] However, the Tax Court considered an employer-owned house across the street from the hotel that was managed by the taxpayer to be on the business premises of the employer.[45] Apparently, the closer the lodging is to the business operations, the more likely the convenience of the employer is served.

---

[39] § 119(a). The value of the meals and lodging is also excluded from FICA and FUTA tax. *Rowan Companies, Inc. v. U.S.*, 81–1 USTC ¶9479, 48 AFTR 2d 81–5115, 101 S.Ct. 2288.

[40] For 2021 and 2022, taxpayers can deduct 100% of meals provided by a restaurant. § 274(n)(2)(D).

[41] Rev.Rul. 80; *Comm. v. Doak*, 56–2 USTC ¶9708, 49 AFTR 1491, 234 F.2d 704 (CA–4); but see *G. A. Papineau*, 16 T.C. 130 (1951); *Armstrong v. Phinney*, 68–1 USTC ¶9355, 21 AFTR 2d 1260, 394 F.2d 661 (CA–5).

[42] *Comm. v. Kowalski*, 77–2 USTC ¶9748, 40 AFTR 2d 6128, 98 S.Ct. 315; *Tougher v. Comm.*, 71–1 USTC ¶9398, 27 AFTR 2d 1301, 441 F.2d 1148 (CA–9).

[43] Reg. § 1.119–1(c)(1).

[44] *Comm. v. Anderson*, 67–1 USTC ¶9136, 19 AFTR 2d 318, 371 F.2d 59 (CA–6, 1966).

[45] *J. B. Lindeman*, 60 T.C. 609 (1973).

For the Convenience of the Employer

The *convenience of the employer* test is intended to focus on the employer's motivation for furnishing the meals and lodging rather than on the benefits received by the employee. If the employer furnishes the meals and lodging primarily to enable the employee to perform any required duties properly, the "convenience" test is met.

The Regulations give the following examples where the "convenience" test is met:[46]

- A restaurant requires its service staff to eat their meals on the premises during the busy lunch and breakfast hours.
- A bank furnishes meals on the premises for its tellers to limit the time the employees are away from their booths during the busy hours.
- A worker is employed at a construction site in a remote part of Alaska. The employer must furnish meals and lodging due to the inaccessibility of other facilities.

Required as a Condition of Employment

The *required as a condition of employment* test applies only to lodging. If the employee's use of the housing would serve the convenience of the employer, but the employee is not required to use the housing, the exclusion is not available.

Khalid is the manager of a large apartment complex. The employer requires Khalid to live on the premises but does not charge him rent. The rental value of his apartment is $9,600 a year. Although Khalid considers the rent-free housing a significant benefit, he is not required to include the value of the housing in his gross income.

5-7b Other Housing Exclusions

An employee of an educational institution may be able to exclude the value of campus housing provided by the employer. If the employee pays annual rents equal to or greater than 5 percent of the appraised value of the facility, the housing benefit may be excluded. If the rent payments are less than 5 percent of the value of the facility, the deficiency must be included in gross income.[47]

Ministers of the gospel and other religious leaders can exclude (1) the rental value of a home furnished as compensation; (2) a rental allowance paid to them as compensation, to the extent the allowance is used to rent, buy, or provide a home; or (3) the rental value of a home owned by the minister.[48] The housing or housing allowance must be provided as compensation for the conduct of religious worship, the administration and maintenance of religious organizations, or the performance of teaching and administrative duties at theological seminaries.

Military personnel are allowed housing exclusions under various circumstances. Authority for these exclusions generally is found in Federal laws that are not part of the Internal Revenue Code.[49]

5-8 Employee Fringe Benefits

Benefits other than wages and salary that are provided to employees by the employer are often referred to as **fringe benefits**. Generally, Congress decided that the availability of these benefits serves social goals. In addition, providing an income tax

[46] Reg. § 1.119–1(f).

[47] § 119(d).

[48] § 107 and Reg. § 1.107–1.

[49] H. Rep. No. 99–841, 99th Cong., 2d Sess., p. 548 (1986). See § 134 and *Armed Forces Tax Guide* (IRS Publication 3).

exclusion provides an incentive for employees to bargain for these nontaxable fringe benefits instead of taxable compensation. For example, if the employee is in the 22 percent marginal tax bracket, $100 of nontaxable fringe benefits is equivalent to $128 [$\$100 \div (1 - 0.22) = \$128$] in taxable compensation. From the employer's perspective then, it costs only $100 to provide $128 in value to that employee in the form of a tax-favored fringe benefit.

In Chapter 4 and earlier in this chapter, various fringe benefits were discussed (e.g., accident and health insurance and meals and lodging). Other employee benefits are discussed below.

5-8a **Specific Benefits**

Congress has dealt specifically with some other fringe benefits, which are summarized below.

- An employee does not have to include in gross income the value of child and dependent care services paid for by the employer and incurred to enable the employee to work. The exclusion cannot exceed $5,000 per year ($2,500 if married and filing separately). For a married couple, the annual exclusion cannot exceed the earned income of the spouse with the smaller amount of earned income. For an unmarried taxpayer, the exclusion cannot exceed the taxpayer's earned income.[50]
- The value of the use of a gymnasium or other athletic facilities by employees, their spouses, and their dependent children may be excluded from an employee's gross income. The facilities must be on the employer's premises, and substantially all of the use of the facilities must be by employees and their family members.[51]
- Qualified employer-provided educational assistance (tuition, fees, books, and supplies) at the undergraduate and graduate levels is excludible from gross income. Through 2025, eligible assistance includes principal and interest on a student loan. An employee can exclude a maximum of $5,250 per year.[52] The exclusion does not cover meals, lodging, and transportation costs. In addition, it does not cover educational payments for courses involving sports, games, or hobbies.
- If an employer has a qualified adoption assistance program, an employee can exclude up to $15,950 of adoption expenses that are paid or reimbursed by the employer.[53] If the child has special needs (is not physically or mentally capable of caring for themselves), the $15,950 exclusion from gross income applies even if the actual adoption expenses are less than that amount. For 2023, the exclusion is phased out as adjusted gross income increases from $239,230 to $279,230.

5-8b **Cafeteria Plans**

Generally, if an employee is offered a choice between cash and some other form of compensation, the employee is deemed to have constructively received the cash even when the noncash option is elected. As a result, the employee has gross income regardless of the option chosen.

An exception to this constructive receipt treatment is provided under the **cafeteria plan** rules. Under these plans, the employee can choose between cash and nontaxable benefits (e.g., group term life insurance, health and accident protection, child care). If the employee chooses nontaxable benefits, the cafeteria plan rules enable the benefits

[50] § 129. The exclusion applies to the same types of expenses that, if paid by the employee (and not reimbursed by the employer), would be eligible for the credit for child and dependent care expense discussed in Chapter 12.

[51] § 132(j)(4).

[52] § 127.

[53] § 137. A credit is also available under § 23, as discussed in Chapter 12.

to remain nontaxable.[54] Cafeteria plans provide tremendous flexibility in tailoring the employee pay package to fit individual needs. Some employees (usually younger employees) prefer cash, while others (usually older employees) will opt for the fringe benefit program.

Hawk Corporation offers its employees (on a nondiscriminatory basis) a choice of any one or all of the following benefits:

Benefit	Cost
Group term life insurance	$ 200
Hospitalization insurance for family members	2,400
Child care payments	1,800
	$4,400

If a benefit is not selected, the employee receives cash equal to the cost of the benefit. Kay, an employee, has a spouse who works for another employer that provides hospitalization insurance but no child care payments. Kay elects to receive the group term life insurance, the child care payments, and $2,400 of cash. Only the $2,400 must be included in Kay's gross income.

5-8c Flexible Spending Plans

Flexible spending plans (often referred to as flexible benefit plans) operate much like cafeteria plans. Under these plans, the employee accepts lower cash compensation in return for the employer agreeing to pay certain costs that would normally be excludible from the employee's income. An annual inflation-adjusted cap applies to these plans ($3,050 in 2023).

For example, assume that the employer's health insurance policy does not cover dental expenses. Under a flexible spending plan, an employee estimates any dental expenses for the upcoming year and agrees to a salary reduction equal to the estimated dental expenses. The employer then pays or reimburses the employee for the actual dental expenses incurred, with a ceiling of the amount of the salary reduction. If the employee's actual dental expenses are less than the reduction in cash compensation, the employee cannot recover the difference. As a result, these plans are often called *use or lose* plans. To avoid the loss of unpaid amounts, the IRS allows a payment until two and a half months after the end of the plan year to count (March 15 for calendar year plans). Flexible spending plans cannot be used to pay long-term care insurance premiums (this is also the case for cafeteria plans).

5-8d General Classes of Excluded Benefits

An employer can provide many forms and types of economic benefits to employees. Under the all-inclusive concept of income, the benefits are taxable unless the Code specifically excludes the item from gross income. The amount of the income is the fair market value of the benefit.

Ryan is employed in New York as a ticket clerk for Trans National Airlines. He has a sick mother in Miami, Florida but has no money for plane tickets. Trans National has daily flights from New York to Miami that often leave with empty seats. The cost of a round-trip ticket is $400.

In general, if Trans National allows Ryan to fly without charge to Miami, Ryan has income equal to the value of a ticket ($400). However, as discussed below, this is one of several classes of excluded benefits allowed under the tax law.

[54] § 125.

Because Congress believed that taxing fringe benefits often yielded harsh results, § 132 was enacted to provide gross income exclusions for eight broad classes of employee benefits:[55]

- No-additional-cost services.
- Qualified employee discounts.
- Working condition fringes.
- *De minimis* fringes.
- Qualified transportation fringes.
- Qualified moving expense reimbursements.
- Qualified retirement planning services.
- Qualified military base realignment and closure fringes.

No-Additional-Cost Services

The value of the services that the employer provides its employees is nontaxable under certain circumstances. Example 21 above illustrates the reason for the **no-additional-cost service** type of fringe benefit. The services are excludible from the employee's gross income if all of the following conditions are satisfied:

- The employee receives services, as opposed to property.
- The employer does not incur substantial additional cost, including forgone revenue, in providing the services to the employee.
- The services are offered to customers in the ordinary course of the business in which the employee works.[56]

In Example 21, although the airplane may burn slightly more fuel because Ryan is on board and he may receive the same snacks as paying customers, the additional costs to the airline are *not* substantial. As a result, the flight qualifies as a no-additional-cost service, and the value of Ryan's flight is excluded from his gross income.

The no-additional-cost exclusion extends to the employee's spouse and dependent children and to retired and disabled former employees.[57] However, the exclusion is not allowed to highly compensated employees unless the benefit is available on a nondiscriminatory basis.

Qualified Employee Discounts

When the employer sells goods or services (other than no-additional-cost benefits just discussed) to the employee for a price that is less than the price charged regular customers, the employee realizes income equal to the discount. However, the discount, referred to as a **qualified employee discount**, can be excluded from the employee's gross income, subject to the following conditions and limitations:

- The exclusion is not available for real property (e.g., a house) or for personal property commonly held for investment (e.g., common stock).
- The property or services must be from the same line of business in which the employee works.
- In the case of *property*, the exclusion is limited to the *gross profit component* of the customer price.
- In the case of *services*, the exclusion is limited to 20 percent of the customer price.

---

[55]See, generally, § 132.

[56]§ 132(b) and Reg. § 1.132–2.

[57]§ 132(h) and Reg. § 1.132–1(b).

Silver Corporation, which operates a department store, sells a television to a store employee for $300. The regular customer price is $500, and the gross profit rate is 25%. The corporation also sells the employee a service contract for $120; the regular customer price for the contract is $150. The employee must include $75 in gross income ($75 for the television; $0 for the service contract).

Customer price for property (television)	$ 500
Less: Gross profit (25%)	(125)
	$ 375
Employee price	(300)
Income	$ 75
Customer price for service contract	$ 150
Less: 20% (maximum exclusion)	(30)
	$ 120
Employee price	(120)
Income	$ –0–

As in the case of no-additional-cost benefits, the exclusion applies to employees (including service partners), employees' spouses and dependent children, and former employees who left due to retirement or disability.

Working Condition Fringes

Generally, an employee is not required to include in gross income the cost of property or services provided by the employer if the employee could deduct the cost of those items if they had actually paid for them. These benefits are called **working condition fringes**.

Jaden is a CPA employed by an accounting firm. The employer pays Jaden's annual dues to professional organizations. Jaden is not required to include the payment of the dues in gross income because it is an allowable business expense to Jaden (as discussed in text Section 9-10).[58]

Unlike the other fringe benefits discussed previously, working condition fringes can be made available on a discriminatory basis and still qualify for the exclusion.

De Minimis Fringes

As the term suggests, ***de minimis* fringe** benefits are so small that accounting for them is impractical. The House Report contains the following examples of *de minimis* fringes:

- Occasional personal use of a company copying machine, occasional company cocktail parties or picnics for employees, occasional supper money or taxi fare for employees because of overtime work, and certain holiday gifts of property with a low fair market value are excluded.
- Subsidized eating facilities (e.g., an employees' cafeteria) operated by the employer are excluded if located on or near the employer's business premises, if revenue equals or exceeds direct operating costs, and if nondiscrimination requirements are met. This exclusion applies regardless of whether the employer can deduct any of the facility's costs.

When taxpayers venture beyond the specific examples contained in the House Report and the Regulations, there can be room for disagreement as to what is *de minimis*. According to the IRS, cash or gift cards are not considered *de minimis*.[59]

The value of a cell phone can be excluded if it is provided for business reasons (e.g., to enable the employee to be in contact with clients when the employee is away from the office). When the primary purpose test is satisfied, any personal use of the employer-provided cell phone will be excluded as a *de minimis* fringe benefit.[60]

[58]In many cases, this exclusion merely avoids reporting income and using an off-setting deduction. However, the deduction for unreimbursed employee business expenses is suspended from 2018 through 2025. So if Jaden paid the dues on his own, he could not deduct them. IRS Publication 15B, *Employer's Tax Guide to Fringe Benefits*, states that the payment continues to be a nontaxable fringe benefit for the employee.

[59]TAM 200437030 (9/10/04) and IRS Publication 15B, *Employer's Tax Guide to Fringe Benefits*.

[60]Notice 2011–72.

Qualified Transportation Fringes

The exclusion for **qualified transportation fringes** is intended to encourage the use of mass transit for commuting to and from work. Qualified transportation fringes include the following benefits provided by the employer to the employee:

1. Transportation in a commuter highway vehicle between the employee's residence and the place of employment.
2. A transit pass.
3. Qualified parking.

These exclusions have annual limits. For 2023, the inflation adjusted limit is $300 per month ($280 in 2022).[61]

A *commuter highway vehicle* is any highway vehicle with a seating capacity of at least six adults (excluding the driver). In addition, at least 80 percent of the vehicle's use must be for transporting employees between their residences and place of employment.

Qualified parking includes the following:

- Parking provided to an employee on or near the employer's business premises.
- Parking provided to an employee on or near a location from which the employee commutes to work via mass transit, in a commuter highway vehicle, or in a carpool.

Qualified transportation fringes may be provided directly by the employer or may be in the form of cash reimbursements.

Gray Corporation's offices are located in the center of a large city. The company pays for parking spaces to be used by the company officers. Steve, a vice president, receives $320 of such benefits each month during 2023. The parking space rental qualifies as a qualified transportation fringe. Of the $320 benefit Steve received each month, $300 is excludible from gross income. The balance of $20 is included in his gross income. The same result would occur if Steve paid for the parking and was reimbursed by his employer.

In general, employers are prohibited from *deducting* their expenses of qualified transportation fringe benefits provided to employees [§ 274(a)(4)]. If the employer provides the benefit, though, the employee may exclude it from income within the limits stated above.

Qualified Moving Expense Reimbursements

Prior to 2018, qualified moving expenses reimbursed or paid by the employer were excludible from gross income. A qualified moving expense would be deductible under § 217. For 2018 through 2025, the exclusion only applies to members of the Armed Forces on active duty. See the discussion of moving expenses in text Section 9-6b.

Qualified Retirement Planning Services

Qualified retirement planning services include any retirement planning advice or information that an employer who maintains a qualified retirement plan provides to an employee or the employee's spouse. Congress decided to exclude the value of these services from gross income because they are a key part of retirement income planning and they may serve as motivation for more employers to provide retirement planning services to their employees.

Qualified Military Base Realignment and Closure Fringe

Payments made under the Demonstration Cities and Metropolitan Development Act of 1966 are generally excluded from income.

[61]Prior to 2018, qualified transportation fringes included qualified bicycle commuting reimbursement up to $20 per month. For 2018 through 2025, this benefit is not treated as a qualified transportation fringe benefit. As a result, if an employer provides this benefit, it is taxable to the employee and deductible by the employer as wages.

Ethics & Equity **Fringe Benefits**

The Tax Cuts and Jobs Act of 2017 changed the tax treatment of certain fringe benefits to better tie an employer's deduction for employee compensation with the amount employees report as wage income. The approach taken, such as for meals provided for the convenience of the employer and qualified transportation fringe benefits, was to retain the exclusion for the employee receiving these benefits but to repeal or reduce the deduction for the employer (denial of a deduction effectively makes the expenditure taxable to the payor entity). Did Congress take the right approach? Or should Congress instead have allowed employers to deduct the cost of the benefits provided to employees with the employees including the benefits in wage income? How can equity motivate changes in the tax law to be sure such fringe benefits provided by tax-exempt employers (like charitable organizations) are also taxed?

Nondiscrimination Provisions

For no-additional-cost services, qualified employee discounts, and qualified retirement planning services that are discriminatory in favor of highly compensated employees, exclusion treatment is denied. However, for the discriminatory plans, the exclusion treatment for non-highly compensated employees remains.[62]

Example 26

Dove Company's officers are allowed to purchase goods from the company at a 25% discount. All other employees are allowed only a 15% discount. The company's gross profit margin on these goods is 30%. Because the officers receive more favorable discounts, the plan is discriminatory in favor of the officers. In regard to all other employees, the discount is "qualified" because it is available to all employees (other than the officers who receive a more favorable discount) and the discount is less than the company's gross profit.

Peggy, an officer in the company, purchased goods from the company for $750 when the price charged to customers was $1,000. Peggy must include $250 in gross income because the plan is discriminatory.

Mason, an employee of the company who is not an officer, purchased goods for $850 when the customer price was $1,000. Mason is not required to recognize gross income because he received a qualified employee discount.

De minimis (except in the case of subsidized eating facilities) and working condition fringe benefits can be provided on a discriminatory basis. The *de minimis* benefits are not subject to tax because the accounting problems that would be created are out of proportion to the amount of additional tax that would result.

A review of employee fringe benefits is provided in Concept Summary 5.2.

5-8e Group Term Life Insurance

For many years, the IRS did not attempt to tax the value of life insurance protection provided to an employee or former employee by the employer. Some companies took undue advantage of the exclusion by providing large amounts of insurance protection for executives. As a result, Congress enacted § 79, which created a limited exclusion for **group term life insurance**. The premiums on the first $50,000 of group term life insurance protection are excludible from the employee's and former employee's gross income.

The benefits of this exclusion are available only to employees. Proprietors and partners are not considered employees. The Regulations generally require broad-scale coverage of employees to satisfy the *group* requirement (e.g., shareholder-employees would not constitute a qualified group). The exclusion applies only to term insurance (protection for a period of time but with no cash surrender value) and not to ordinary life insurance (lifetime protection plus a cash surrender value that can be drawn upon before death).

As mentioned, the exclusion applies to the first $50,000 of group term life insurance protection. For each $1,000 of coverage in excess of $50,000, the employee must include the amounts indicated in Exhibit 5.1 in gross income.[63]

[62] §§ 132(j)(1) and (m)(2).

[63] Reg. § 1.79–3(d)(2).

Exhibit 5.1 **Uniform Premiums for $1,000 of Group Term Life Insurance Protection**

Attained Age on Last Day of Employee's Tax Year	Cost per $1,000 of Protection for One-Month Period*
Under 25	$0.05
25–29	0.06
30–34	0.08
35–39	0.09
40–44	0.10
45–49	0.15
50–54	0.23
55–59	0.43
60–64	0.66
65–69	1.27
70 and above	2.06

*Reg. § 1.79–3, effective for coverage after June 30, 1999.

Finch Corporation has a group term life insurance policy with coverage equal to the employee's annual salary. Keith, age 52, is president of the corporation and receives an annual salary of $350,000. Keith must include $828 in gross income from the insurance protection for the year.

$$\frac{\$350{,}000 - \$50{,}000}{\$1{,}000} \times \$0.23 \times 12 \text{ months} = \$828$$

Generally, the amount that must be included in gross income, computed from Exhibit 5.1, is much less than the price an individual would pay an insurance company for the same amount of protection. As a result, even the excess coverage provides some tax-favored income for employees when group term life insurance coverage exceeds $50,000.

If the plan discriminates in favor of certain key employees (e.g., officers), the key employees are not eligible for the exclusion. In such a case, the key employees must include in gross income the *greater* of actual premiums paid by the employer or the amount calculated from the Uniform Premiums in Exhibit 5.1. The other employees are still eligible for the $50,000 exclusion and continue to use the Uniform Premiums table to compute the income from excess insurance protection.[64]

5-9 Foreign Earned Income

For individuals, the United States uses a global (or citizen-based) tax system as opposed to a territorial system. Under this global system, U.S. citizens generally are subject to tax on their income regardless of its economic origin. Some other countries use a territorial system; that is, a person's income is taxed only in the country in which the income was earned. Under a global system, a U.S. citizen who earns income in another country could experience double taxation—the same income would be taxed in the United States and in the foreign country. Out of a sense of fairness and to encourage U.S. citizens to work abroad (so that exports might be increased), Congress has provided alternative forms of relief from taxes on foreign earned income. Taxpayers can elect *either* (1) to include the foreign earned income in their taxable income and then claim a credit for foreign taxes paid or (2) to exclude up to $120,000 of foreign earned income from their U.S. gross income (the **foreign earned income exclusion**).[65] As will be apparent from the following discussion, most taxpayers choose the exclusion.

[64] § 79(d).

[65] § 911(a). The exclusion for 2022 was $112,000.

Concept Summary 5.2

Employee Fringe Benefits

Type of Benefit	Exclusion
Group term life insurance (§ 79)	Premiums on up to $50,000 of protection
Employee achievement awards (§ 74)	Up to $1,600 in a year
Accident, health, and long-term care insurance and medical reimbursement (§§ 105 and 106)	Insurance premiums paid by the employer and benefits collected
High-deductible health insurance and contributions to employee's Health Savings Account (§§ 106 and 223)	Employer premiums on high-deductible medical insurance plus contributions to Health Savings Account (statutory limits, indexed for inflation)
Meals and lodging furnished for the convenience of the employer (§ 119)	Value of meals and lodging on the employer's premises
Child care provided by the employer or reimbursement for employee's cost (§ 129)	Services provided or reimbursement of expenses up to $5,000 a year
Athletic facilities on the employer's premises (§ 132)	Value of services
Educational assistance for tuition, fees, books, and supplies (§ 127)	Limited to $5,250 per year
No-additional-cost services [e.g., use of employer's facilities (§ 132)]	Value of the use
Employee discount on purchase of goods from employer at employer's cost (§ 132)	Employer's normal profit margin
Employee discount for purchases of employer's services (§ 132)	Maximum of 20% of employer's normal price
Working condition fringes [e.g., a mechanic's tools (§ 132)]	Employer's cost
De minimis items so small that the accounting effort is not warranted [e.g., use of employer telephone (§ 132)]	Value of the goods or services
Qualified transportation [e.g., transit passes and parking (§ 132)]	Statutory amounts, adjusted for inflation
Moving expense reimbursement for members of the Armed Forces on active duty (§ 132)	Reimbursement to the extent otherwise deductible by employee
Retirement planning services (§ 132)	Reasonable cost of services

Foreign earned income consists of the earnings from the individual's personal services rendered in a foreign country (other than as an employee of the U.S. government). To qualify for the exclusion, the taxpayer must have a tax home in a foreign country and be either:

- A bona fide resident of the foreign country (or countries) for an uninterrupted period which includes an entire tax year, or
- Present in a foreign country (or countries) for at least 330 days during any 12 consecutive months.[66]

The following rules apply in calculating the exclusion and tax owed:

- The exclusion must be computed on a daily basis when the exclusion period straddles two years.
- The tax on the income in excess of the excluded amount is taxed at the marginal rate that would apply without the exclusion (i.e., as though the excluded income were included in taxable income).

Global Tax Issues — Benefits of the Earned Income Exclusion Are Questioned

The foreign earned income exclusion is intended to be a means to increase exports. But a GAO study questioned whether the $6 billion of lost revenue is money well spent. The report was inconclusive. It is clear that repealing the exclusion would make it more costly for U.S. companies to send their employees abroad, but there is no evidence that the benefits to the United States, in general, are worth the cost.

Source: Economic Benefits of Income Exclusion for U.S. Citizens Working Abroad Are Uncertain GAO-14-387: Published: May 20, 2014, available at **gao.gov/products/GAO-14-387**.

[66] § 911(d). For the definition of *resident*, see Reg. § 1.871–2(b). Under the Regulations, a taxpayer is not a resident if they are there for a definite period (e.g., until completion of a construction contract).

Calculating the Exclusion and Tax

Sandra's time spent in a foreign country in connection with her work were as follows:

Arrived in Foreign Country	Returned to United States
March 11, 2022	February 16, 2023

During the 12 consecutive months ending on March 11, 2023, Sandra was present in the foreign country for at least 330 days (365 days less the 12 days remaining in February 2023 and 11 days in March 2023 equals 342 days). As a result, assuming Sandra's tax home is in the foreign country (rather than in the U.S.), the income earned in the foreign country through March 11, 2023, is eligible for the exclusion.

Keith qualifies for the foreign earned income exclusion. He was present in France for all of 2023. Keith's salary for 2023 is $140,000. Because all of the days in 2023 are qualifying days, Keith can exclude $120,000 of his $140,000 salary.

Assume instead that only 342 days were qualifying days. Then, Keith's exclusion is limited to $112,438, computed as follows:

$$\$120{,}000 \times \frac{342 \text{ days in foreign country}}{365 \text{ days in the year}} = \$112{,}438$$

In 2023, Alejandra, who is not married, had taxable income of $30,000 after excluding $120,000 of foreign earned income. Without the benefit of the exclusion, Alejandra's taxable income would have been $150,000 ($30,000 + $120,000). The tax on the taxable income of $30,000 is calculated using the marginal rate applicable to income between $120,000 and $150,000, which is 24%. As a result, Alejandra's tax liability is $7,200 ($30,000 × 24%).

As previously mentioned, the taxpayer may elect to include the foreign earned income in gross income and claim a credit (an offset against U.S. tax) for the foreign tax paid. The credit alternative may be advantageous if the individual's foreign earned income exceeds the excludible amount so that the foreign taxes paid exceed the U.S. tax on the amount excluded. However, once an election is made, it applies to all subsequent years unless affirmatively revoked. A revocation is effective for the year of the change and the four subsequent years.

In addition to the foreign earned income exclusion, the employee also can exclude or deduct a foreign housing amount if certain requirements are met. To qualify, the employer must pay for all or a portion of the housing costs (either paid directly by the employer or paid by the employee using their wages).[67]

5-10 Interest on Certain State and Local Government Obligations

At the time the Sixteenth Amendment was ratified by the states, there was some question as to whether the Federal government possessed the constitutional authority to tax interest on state and local government obligations. Taxing this interest was thought to violate the doctrine of intergovernmental immunity in that the tax would impair the state and local governments' ability to finance their operations.[68] As a result, interest on state and local government obligations was specifically exempted from Federal income

[67] § 911 and Reg. § 1.911–4(d).

[68] *Pollock v. Farmer's Loan & Trust Co.*, 3 AFTR 2602, 15 S.Ct. 912 (1895).

taxation.[69] However, the Supreme Court concluded that there is no constitutional prohibition against levying a nondiscriminatory Federal income tax on state and local government obligations.[70] Congress, however, has shown no inclination to eliminate this exclusion.

Obviously, the exclusion of the interest reduces the cost of borrowing for state and local governments. A taxpayer in the 35 percent tax bracket requires only a 3.9 percent yield on a tax-exempt bond to obtain the same after-tax income as a taxable bond paying 6 percent interest [$3.9\% \div (1-0.35) = 6\%$].

The current exempt status applies solely to state and local government bonds. Income received from the accrual of interest on a condemnation award or an overpayment of state income tax is fully taxable.[71] In addition, the exemption does not apply to gains on the sale of tax-exempt securities.

Megan purchases State of Virginia bonds for $10,000 on July 1, 2022. The bonds pay $300 interest each June 30 and December 31. On March 31, 2023, Megan sells the bonds for $10,500 plus $150 for accrued interest. Megan must recognize a $500 gain ($10,500 − $10,000), but the $150 accrued interest is exempt from taxation.

Although the Internal Revenue Code excludes from Federal gross income the interest on state and local government bonds, the interest on U.S. government bonds is *not* excluded from the Federal tax base. Congress decided, however, that if the Federal government does not tax state and local bond interest, state and local governments should not tax interest on U.S. government bonds.[72] However, state and local governments are free to tax each other's obligations. As a result, some states exempt the interest on the bonds they issue but tax the interest on bonds issued by other states.[73]

5-11 **Educational Savings Bonds**

The cost of a college education has risen dramatically during the past few decades. According to U.S. Department of Education estimates, the cost of attending a publicly supported university for four years now commonly exceeds $60,000. For a private university, the cost often exceeds $200,000. As a result, Congress has passed a variety of legislation to assist low- to middle-income parents in paying for their children's college education.

One of the ways the Federal government assists these families is through an interest income exclusion on **educational savings bonds**.[74] The interest on Series EE U.S. government savings bonds may be excluded from gross income if the bond proceeds are used to pay qualified higher education expenses. The bonds must be issued to a taxpayer age 24 or older.

[69] § 103(a).

[70] *South Carolina v. Baker III*, 88–1 USTC ¶9284, 61 AFTR 2d 88–995, 108 S.Ct. 1355.

[71] *Kieselbach v. Comm.*, 43–1 USTC ¶9220, 30 AFTR 370, 63 S.Ct. 303; *U.S. Trust Co. of New York v. Anderson*, 3 USTC ¶1125, 12 AFTR 836, 65 F.2d 575 (CA–2, 1933).

[72] 31 U.S.C.A. § 742.

[73] The practice of a state exempting interest on its bonds from tax but taxing the interest on bonds issued by other states has been upheld by the Supreme Court. See *Department of Revenue of Kentucky v. Davis*, 128 S.Ct. 1801 (2008).

[74] § 135.

Qualified higher education expenses consist of tuition and fees paid to an eligible educational institution for the taxpayer, spouse, or dependent. If the redemption proceeds (both principal and interest) exceed the qualified higher education expenses, only a pro rata portion of the interest will qualify for exclusion treatment.

Tracy's redemption proceeds from qualified savings bonds during the taxable year are $6,000 (principal of $4,000 and interest of $2,000). Tracy's qualified higher education expenses are $5,000. Because the redemption proceeds exceed the qualified higher education expenses, only $1,667 [($5,000 ÷ $6,000) × $2,000] of the interest is excludible.

Once a taxpayer's modified adjusted gross income exceeds a threshold amount, the exclusion is phased out. *Modified adjusted gross income (MAGI)* is adjusted gross income prior to the foreign earned income exclusion and the educational savings bond exclusion. The threshold amounts are adjusted for inflation each year. For 2023, the phaseout begins at $91,850 ($137,800 on a joint return).[75] The phaseout is completed when MAGI exceeds the threshold amount by more than $15,000 ($30,000 on a joint return). The otherwise excludible interest is reduced by the amount calculated as follows:

$$\frac{\text{MAGI} - \$91{,}850}{\$15{,}000} \times \text{Excludible interest before phaseout} = \text{Reduction in excludible interest}$$

On a joint return, $137,800 is substituted for $91,850 (in 2023), and $30,000 is substituted for $15,000.

Assume the same facts as in Example 32, except that Tracy's MAGI for 2023 is $97,000. The phaseout results in Tracy's interest exclusion being reduced by $572 {[($97,000 − $91,850) ÷ $15,000] × $1,667}. As a result, Tracy's exclusion is $1,095 ($1,667 − $572).

5-12 Education Savings Programs (§ 529 and § 530 Plans)

The Federal tax law provides two types of programs to help individuals and families save for education costs. These savings programs are referred to as the qualified tuition program (§ 529 plans) and Coverdell education savings accounts (§ 530 plans). Earnings in these accounts are not taxable if distributions are used for qualified education expenses. Also, rules govern the type of account that can be used for these savings programs, and specific rules exist regarding contributions, distributions, rollovers, and other transfers. In addition, the benefits of these plans must be coordinated with other educational tax provisions, such as nontaxable scholarships. Distributions from these accounts are reported on Form 1099–Q, Payments from Qualified Education Programs. Taxable distributions (generally those not used for qualified purposes) may be subject to an additional 10 percent tax [reported on Form 5329, Additional Taxes on Qualified Plans (Including IRAs) and Other Tax-Favored Accounts].

There are income limits on contributions to Coverdell accounts as well as a dollar limit on the annual contribution per beneficiary. A beneficiary may have both § 529 and § 530 plans.

[75]The indexed amounts for 2022 were $85,800 and $128,650.

5-12a **Qualified Tuition Program**

Nearly all states have created programs whereby parents can in effect prepay their child's college tuition. The prepayment serves as a hedge against future increases in tuition. Generally, if the child does not attend college, the parents are refunded their payments plus interest. Although these prepaid tuition programs resemble the below-market loans (discussed in text Section 4-4b), Congress has created an exclusion provision for these programs.

Under a **qualified tuition program (§ 529 plan)**, the amounts contributed must be used for qualified higher education expenses. These expenses include tuition, fees, books, supplies, room and board, and equipment required for enrollment or attendance at a college, a university, or certain vocational schools. Allowable expenses also include computers and peripheral equipment, software, and internet access used primarily by the beneficiary while enrolled at an eligible educational institution. Qualified higher education expenses also include the expenses for special needs services that are incurred in connection with the enrollment and attendance of special needs students. Tuition paid to public, private, and religious K–12 schools, as well as certain apprenticeship programs, are also allowable expenses. In addition, a lifetime maximum of $10,000 of funds in a § 529 account may be used to pay principal or interest on a qualified education loan.

The earnings of the contributed funds, including the discount on tuition charged to participants, are not included in Federal gross income provided the contributions and earnings are used for qualified higher education expenses. Some states also exclude these educational benefits from state gross income.

Angie paid $20,000 into a qualified tuition program to be used for her son's college tuition. When her son graduated from high school, the fund balance had increased to $30,000 as a result of interest credited to the account. The interest was not included in Angie's gross income. During the current year, $7,500 of the balance in the fund was used to pay the son's tuition and fees. None of this amount is included in either Angie's or the son's gross income.

If the parent receives a refund (e.g., child does not attend college), the excess of the amount refunded over the amount contributed by the parent is included in the parent's gross income. A special rule applies to refunded amounts recontributed to a qualified tuition program of the beneficiary.

5-12b **Coverdell Education Savings Account**

A **Coverdell education savings account (§ 530 plan)** may be used to save for K–12 education as well as postsecondary education expenses. The contributions to the plan are limited to $2,000 in any year, and the beneficiary must be under 18 or must be a special needs beneficiary in the year the contribution is made. As with the § 529 plan, contributions are nondeductible, but the income to the beneficiary is nontaxable provided the funds are used for qualified education expenses.

5-13 **Qualified ABLE Programs (§ 529A Plans)**

The **qualified ABLE program** was created to assist individuals who become blind or disabled before age 26. The program allows for § 529A plans, or ABLE (Achieving a Better Life Experience) plans, similar in concept to § 529 plans described earlier. The program must be established by a state. The ABLE account must be for the benefit of a designated beneficiary's disability expenses, and the beneficiary must have a disability certification from the government.

Contributions to the account must be in cash and may not, in total, exceed the annual gift tax exclusion for the year ($17,000 for 2023; $16,000 for 2022). Contributions to the account are not deductible. The tax benefit of an ABLE account is that its earnings are not taxable. Distributions from the account also are not taxable provided they do not exceed the qualified disability expenses of the designated beneficiary. Certain rollovers from a § 529 account to an ABLE account are permitted for 2018 through 2025.

5-14 Income from Discharge of Indebtedness

When a person is relieved of a debt for less than the amount owed, the debtor's net worth increases. This increase in net worth must be included in gross income unless one of the exceptions discussed below applies.[76]

Kayla is unable to make her credit card payments and has negotiated a settlement with the credit card issuer. Her $40,000 debt will be settled for $25,000. Kayla must recognize income of $15,000 from the discharge of debt.

When property serves as security for debt, the creditor may foreclose on the property. The foreclosure is treated as a sale.[77]

Juan owns land that serves as security for a $60,000 mortgage held by State Bank. Juan does not have personal liability for the mortgage (it is nonrecourse debt). When Juan's basis in the land is $20,000, and the land's fair market value is $50,000, the bank forecloses on the loan and takes title to the land. Juan must recognize a $40,000 gain on the foreclosure, as though he sold the land for $60,000 (the amount of the nonrecourse debt). No income from discharge of indebtedness is generated in this transaction.

If property serves as security for the debt and the taxpayer is personally liable for the difference between the value of the property and the amount of the debt (i.e., the debt is "with recourse"), the taxpayer may have income from the discharge of the debt in addition to gain or loss from the foreclosure.

Assume the same facts in Example 36, except that Juan's debt is recourse. Juan is treated as selling the property for its fair market value ($50,000) resulting in a gain or loss. His gain is $30,000 ($50,000 sales price − $20,000 basis). In addition, Juan has $10,000 of income from discharge of indebtedness because the lender accepted the $50,000 sales price in discharging the $60,000 debt. Juan will want to determine whether any exclusion applies to his income from discharge of indebtedness (discussed next).

[76] § 61(a)(11) and Reg. § 1.1001–2(a).

[77] *Estate of Delman*, 73 T.C. 15 (1979).

The following discharge of indebtedness situations are subject to special exclusion treatment:[78]

1. Creditors' gifts.
2. Discharges under Federal bankruptcy law.
3. Discharges that occur when the debtor is insolvent (the exclusion is limited to the amount of insolvency).
4. Discharge of the farm debt of a solvent taxpayer.
5. Discharge of **qualified real property business indebtedness**.
6. A seller's cancellation of the buyer's indebtedness.
7. A shareholder's cancellation of the corporation's indebtedness.
8. Forgiveness of certain loans to students.
9. Discharge of indebtedness on the taxpayer's principal residence that occurs between January 1, 2007 and January 1, 2026 and is the result of the financial condition of the debtor.[79]

If the creditor reduces the debt as an act of *love, affection*, or *generosity*, the debtor has simply received a nontaxable gift (situation 1). Rarely will a gift be found to have occurred in a business context. A businessperson may settle a debt for less than the amount due but as a matter of business expediency (e.g., high collection costs or disputes as to contract terms) rather than generosity.[80]

In situations 2, 3, 4, 5, and 9, the Code allows the debtor to reduce the related asset's basis by the realized income from the discharge.[81] As a result, the realized income is merely deferred until the assets are sold (or depreciated). Similarly, in situation 6 (a price reduction), the debtor reduces the basis in the specific assets financed by the seller.[82]

A shareholder's cancellation of the corporation's indebtedness to them (situation 7) usually is considered a tax-free contribution of capital to the corporation by the shareholder. As a result, the corporation's paid-in capital is increased, and its liabilities are decreased by the same amount.[83]

Many states make loans to students on the condition that the loan will be forgiven if students practice a profession in the state upon completing their studies. The amount of the loan that is forgiven (situation 8) is excluded from gross income.[84] In addition, any portion of a student loan forgiven after December 31, 2020 and before January 1, 2026 is excludible from gross income. This exclusion applies to all loans made by the Federal or state governments, as well as loans made by private lenders and educational institutions. However, the exclusion does not apply to debt forgiven in exchange for services rendered by the student to the lending organization.[85]

LO.3

Determine the extent to which receipts can be excluded under the tax benefit rule.

5-15 Tax Benefit Rule

Often a person will incur a cost or an expense in one year but receive a refund or recovery in a subsequent year. Effectively, this refund or recovery reduces the original cost. For example, the taxpayer may purchase an item from a retailer and then receive a rebate from the manufacturer. The rebate is generally a purchase price adjustment. If the item purchased did not result in a tax deduction (e.g., the purchase of a personal automobile), the rebate does not affect taxable income. However, if the original payment resulted in a tax deduction in one year, and the rebate is received in a subsequent year,

[78]§ 108. See Rev.Proc. 2020–11 for special debt discharge exclusions under the U.S. Department of Education's "Defense to Repayment" program.

[79]When Congress extended this exclusion for 2021 through 2025, it lowered the maximum exclusion from $2,000,000 to $750,000 to match the debt limit for the home mortgage interest deduction (see text Section 10-3); Consolidated Appropriations Act of 2021 (P.L. 116–260).

[80]*Comm. v. Jacobson*, 49–1 USTC ¶9133, 37 AFTR 516, 69 S.Ct. 358.

[81]§§ 108(a), (c), (e), and (g). Note that § 108(b) provides that other tax attributes (e.g., net operating loss) will be reduced by the realized gain from the debt discharge prior to the basis adjustment unless the taxpayer elects to apply the basis adjustment first. See § 1017 for the basis reduction rules.

[82]§ 108(e)(5).

[83]§ 108(e)(6).

[84]§ 108(f).

[85]§ 108(f)(5), as modified by the American Rescue Plan Act of 2021 (P.L. 117–2).

the tax benefit rule will apply. Generally, if a taxpayer claims a deduction for an item in one year and, in a later year, recovers all or a portion of the prior deduction, the recovery is included in gross income in the year received.[86]

An accrual basis taxpayer deducted as a loss a $1,000 receivable from a customer when it appeared the amount would never be collected. The following year, the customer paid $800 on the receivable. The taxpayer must report the $800 as gross income in the year it is received.

However, the § 111 **tax benefit rule** provides that no income is recognized upon the recovery of a deduction, or the portion of a deduction, that did not yield a tax benefit in the year it was taken. If the taxpayer in Example 38 had no tax liability in the year of the deduction (e.g., itemized deductions exceeded adjusted gross income), the recovery would be partially or totally excluded from gross income in the year of the recovery.[87]

A common situation that leads to consideration of the tax benefit rule occurs when individuals who itemize their deductions (on Schedule A of Form 1040) get part of their state income tax back as a refund the next year. The TCJA of 2017 added a new wrinkle to this situation. For 2018 through 2025, individuals may only deduct up to $10,000 of state and local taxes as part of their itemized deductions. This is often referred to as the "SALT" deduction. This new limitation raises the question of how the tax benefit rule works when individuals who itemize their deductions (1) paid state and local taxes (SALT) greater than the $10,000 allowable deduction and (2) receive a state income tax refund the next year.

The IRS has issued guidance on how the tax benefit rule applies to state income tax refunds in light of the $10,000 SALT cap.[88] Basically, taxpayers need to determine what their tax return would have looked like if they had known the actual state income tax amount when the return was prepared (factoring in the later refund). This analysis leads to one of the following:

1. *All or part of the refund is taxable:* If the amount of the refund causes the actual SALT amount for the year to drop below $10,000, then the individual obtained a tax benefit from the SALT deduction, and all or part of that refund is taxable under the tax benefit rule. The individual also must determine if the refund results in total itemized deductions totaling less than the standard deduction amount. See Example 39.
2. *The refund is not taxable:* If the individual had a SALT amount greater than $10,000, and the SALT amount equals or exceeds $10,000 even when considering the refund, then no income results under the tax benefit rule. See Example 40.

Tax Benefit Rule and the SALT Cap

Example 39

Ali filed his 2022 income tax return as a single individual. His AGI for 2022 was $78,000. He had $13,500 in itemized deductions, including $6,200 in state income tax and no other state or local taxes. In 2023, he received a $700 refund of the state income taxes that he paid in 2022.

continued

[86]§ 111(a).

[87]Itemized deductions are discussed in Chapter 10.

[88]Rev.Rul. 2019–11.

Because the standard deduction in 2022 was $12,950, Ali's $6,200 of state income tax deduction in 2022 yielded a tax benefit of only $550 ($13,500 itemized deductions − $12,950 standard deduction). Under the tax benefit rule, only $550 of the state income tax refund is included in gross income in 2023.

Julie filed her 2022 return as a single individual. Her AGI for 2022 was $170,000, and she reported $22,000 of itemized deductions. In 2022, Julie paid property taxes on her home of $8,000 and state income taxes of $15,000, for total SALT of $23,000. Due to the SALT cap, she could only deduct $10,000 of this amount on her 2022 return.

After filing her 2022 state income tax return in early 2023, Julie received a state income tax refund of $1,250. Under the tax benefit rule and IRS guidance on the TCJA of 2017, none of this refund is includible in Julie's 2023 gross income; even if the refund was received in 2022, Julie would still be subject to the SALT cap of $10,000. As a result, she received no tax benefit from the $1,250 state income taxes paid in 2022 that were refunded to her in 2023.

Identify tax planning strategies for obtaining the maximum benefit from exclusions.

5-16 Tax Planning

The present law excludes certain types of economic gains from taxation. As a result, taxpayers may find tax planning techniques helpful in obtaining the maximum benefits from the exclusion of such gains. Following are some of the tax planning opportunities made available by the exclusions described in this chapter.

5-16a Life Insurance

Life insurance offers several favorable tax attributes. As discussed in Chapter 4, the annual increase in the cash surrender value of the policy is not taxable (because no income has been actually or constructively received). By borrowing on the policy's cash surrender value, the owner can actually receive the policy's increase in value in cash without recognizing income.

5-16b Employee Fringe Benefits

Generally, employees view accident and health insurance, as well as life insurance, as necessities. Employees can obtain group coverage at much lower rates than individuals would have to pay for the same protection. Premiums paid by the employer can be excluded from the employees' gross income. Because of the exclusion, employees will have a greater after-tax and after-insurance income if the employer pays a lower salary but also pays the insurance premiums.

Pat receives a salary of $30,000. The company has group insurance benefits, but Pat is required to pay his own premiums as follows:

Hospitalization and medical insurance	$1,400
Term life insurance ($30,000 coverage)	200
Disability insurance	400
	$2,000

To simplify the analysis, assume that Pat's tax rate on income is 24%. After paying taxes of $7,200 ($30,000 × 24%) and $2,000 for insurance, Pat has $20,800 remaining ($30,000 − $7,200 − $2,000) for his other living needs.

continued

If Pat's employer reduced Pat's salary by $2,000 (to $28,000) but paid his insurance premiums, Pat's tax liability would be only $6,720 ($28,000 × 24%). As a result, Pat would have $21,280 ($28,000 − $6,720) to meet his other living needs. The change in the compensation plan would save Pat $480 ($21,280 − $20,800).

Similarly, employees often incur expenses for child care and parking. The employee can have more income for other uses if the employer pays these costs but reduces the employee's salary by the cost of the benefits.

The use of cafeteria plans has increased dramatically in recent years. These plans allow employees to tailor their benefits to meet their individual situations. As a result, where both spouses are working, duplication of benefits can be avoided and other needed benefits can often be added. If less than all of the employee's allowance is spent, the employee can receive cash.

The meals and lodging exclusion enables employees to receive from their employer what they ordinarily must purchase with after-tax dollars. Although the employee must live on the employer's premises in order to exclude the value of the lodging, the exclusion is an important factor in the employee's compensation in certain situations (e.g., hotels, motels, restaurants, farms, and ranches). The meals and lodging are clearly a benefit to the employee but are also for the convenience of the employer; as a result, they are excluded from income.

The employees' discount provision is especially important for manufacturers and wholesalers. Employees of manufacturers can avoid tax on the manufacturer's, wholesaler's, and retailer's markups. The wholesaler's employees can avoid tax on an amount equal to the wholesale and retail markups.

The exclusion of benefits is generally available only to employees. Proprietors and partners must pay tax on the same benefits their employees receive tax-free. By incorporating and becoming an employee of the corporation, the former proprietor or partner also can receive these tax-exempt benefits. As a result, the availability of employee benefits is a consideration in the decision to incorporate.

5-16c **Investment Income**

Tax-exempt state and local government bonds are logical investments for high-income taxpayers, who may be subject to a 37 percent regular tax rate plus a 3.8 percent rate on their net investment income. To realize the maximum benefit from the exemption, the investor can purchase zero-coupon bonds. Like Series EE U.S. government savings bonds, these investments pay interest only at maturity. The advantage of the zero-coupon feature for a tax-exempt bond is that the investor can earn tax-exempt interest on the accumulated principal and interest. If the investor purchases a bond that pays the interest each year, the interest received may be such a small amount that an additional tax-exempt investment cannot be made. In addition, reinvesting the interest may entail transaction costs (brokers' fees). The zero-coupon feature avoids these problems.

Series EE U.S. government savings bonds can earn tax-exempt interest if the bond proceeds are used for qualified higher education expenses. Many taxpayers can foresee these expenditures being made for their children's educations. In deciding whether to invest in the bonds, however, the investor must take into account the income limitations for excluding the interest from gross income.

Refocus on The Big Picture

Exclusions

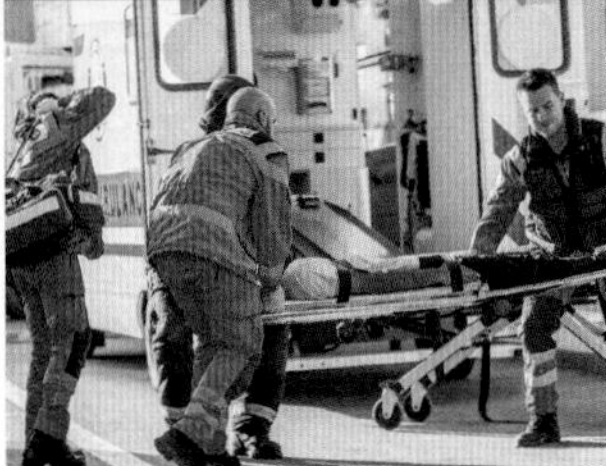
VM/E+/GETTY IMAGES

You have looked into Paul's tax situation and have the following information for him:

- *Compensation.* The amount Paul was paid for his internship is compensation for services rendered and must be included in his gross income. This includes both his base pay and the $1,500 bonus (Example 1).
- *Graduate assistantship.* The tuition waiver of $6,000 is excluded from Paul's gross income. The related payments of $400 per month are intended as a form of compensation. So, Paul must include the $400 per month in his gross income (Example 9).
- *Damages.* Damages awards that relate to personal physical injury or sickness can be excluded from gross income if the payments are for compensatory damages. So all of the compensatory damages of $220,000 can be excluded from gross income. The punitive damages of $160,000 must be included in Paul's gross income. Likewise, the compensatory damages of $25,000 received by Paul's mother must be included in her gross income because emotional distress does not qualify as personal physical injury or sickness (Example 12).

What If?

From a tax planning perspective, can Paul do anything to reduce the amount of the punitive damages settlement that he must include in his gross income?

As things now stand (i.e., a completed settlement), Paul cannot reduce the $160,000 punitive damages amount he must include in gross income. However, proper tax planning might have enabled Paul to reduce the amount includible in gross income. Note that both the amount of the damages and the labels attached to the damages are negotiated. If a larger portion of the settlement had been assigned to compensatory damages rather than punitive damages, Paul could have reduced the amount he must include in his gross income.

Key Terms

Accelerated death benefits, 5-5
Accident and health benefits, 5-11
Cafeteria plan, 5-15
Compensatory damages, 5-9
Coverdell education savings account (§ 530 plan), 5-26
De minimis fringe, 5-18
Death benefits, 5-4
Educational savings bonds, 5-24
Flexible spending plans, 5-16
Foreign earned income exclusion, 5-21
Fringe benefits, 5-14
Group term life insurance, 5-20
Health Savings Account (HSA), 5-12
Life insurance proceeds, 5-5
Long-term care insurance, 5-12
No-additional-cost service, 5-17
Punitive damages, 5-9
Qualified ABLE program, 5-26
Qualified employee discount, 5-17
Qualified real property business indebtedness, 5-28
Qualified transportation fringes, 5-19
Qualified tuition program (§ 529 plan), 5-26
Scholarship, 5-7
Tax benefit rule, 5-29
Working condition fringes, 5-18

Discussion Questions

1. **LO.1, 2** Fred specified in his will that his nephew John should serve as executor of Fred's estate. John received $10,000 for serving as executor. John inherited $100,000 of cash from his uncle as well. He also borrowed $5,000 when he bought a new car this year. Classify each of the amounts received by John using terminology covered in this chapter. Explain the rationale for each classification.

2. **LO.2** Leonard's home was damaged by a fire. He also had to be absent from work for several days to make his home habitable. Leonard's employer paid Leonard his regular salary, $2,500, while he was absent from work. In Leonard's pay envelope was the following note from the employer: To help you in your time of need. Leonard's fellow employees also took up a collection and gave him $900. Leonard spent over $4,000 repairing the fire damage.

   Based on the above information, how much is Leonard required to include in his gross income?

3. **LO.2** Megan is a college student who works as a part-time server in a restaurant. Her usual tip is 20% of the price of the meal. A customer ordered a piece of pie and said that he would appreciate prompt service. Megan abided by the customer's request. The customer's bill was $8, but the customer left a $100 bill on the table and did not ask for a receipt. Megan gave the cashier $8 and pocketed the $100 bill (so Megan ends up with $92). Megan concludes that the customer thought that he had left a $10 bill, although the customer did not return to correct the apparent mistake. The customer had commented about how much he appreciated Megan's prompt service. Megan thinks that a $2 tip would be sufficient and that the excess is like "found money." How much should Megan include in her gross income?

4. **LO.2** Carey is a waiter at a restaurant that pays a small hourly amount plus tips. Customers are not required to tip the waiter. Carey is especially attentive and friendly, and her tips average 25% of the restaurant charges. Is Carey required to include any of her tips in gross income when the customer has no legal obligation to make the payment? Explain the basis for your conclusion.

5. **LO.2** Lime Finance Company requires its customers to purchase a credit life insurance policy associated with the loans it makes. Lime is the beneficiary of the policy to the extent of the remaining balance on the loan at the time of the customer's death. In 2022, Lime wrote off as uncollectible a $5,000 account receivable from Wally, which included $1,500 of accrued interest. When Wally died in 2023, the life insurance policy was still in force, and Lime received $3,500. Is the $3,500 of life insurance proceeds received by Lime included in its gross income? Explain.

6. **LO.2** Billy fell off a bar stool and hurt his back. As a result, he was unable to work for three months. He sued the bar owner and collected $100,000 for the physical injury and $50,000 for the loss of income. Billy also collected $15,000 from an income replacement insurance policy he purchased. Amber was away from work for three months following heart bypass surgery. Amber collected $30,000 under an income replacement insurance policy purchased by her employer. Are the amounts received by Billy and Amber treated the same under the tax law? Explain.

7. **LO.2** Wes was a major league baseball pitcher who earned $10,000,000 for his 20 wins this year. Sam was also a major league baseball pitcher before a career-ending injury caused by a negligent driver. Sam sued the driver and collected $6,000,000 as compensation for lost estimated future income as a pitcher and $4,000,000 as punitive damages. Do the amounts that Wes and Sam receive have the same effect on their gross income? Explain.

8. **LO.2** Holly was injured while working in a factory and received $12,000 as workers' compensation while she was unable to work because of the injury. Jill, who was self-employed, was also injured and unable to work. Jill collected $12,000 on an

insurance policy she had purchased to replace her loss of income while she was unable to work. How much are Holly and Jill each required to include in their gross income?

Decision Making

9. **LO.2, 4** Casey is in the 12% marginal tax bracket, and Mei is in the 35% marginal tax bracket. Their employer is experiencing financial difficulties and cannot continue to pay for the company's health insurance plan. The annual premiums are approximately $8,000 per employee. The employer has proposed to either (1) require the employee to pay the premiums or (2) reduce each employee's pay by $10,000 per year with the employer paying the premium. Which option is less objectionable to Casey, and which is less objectionable to Mei?

10. **LO.2** Anh suffered injuries when she fell out of her bed while hospitalized. She sued the hospital for $90,000 (for her physical injuries). She lost the case and brought a lawsuit against the lawyer who represented her in the hospital litigation, alleging malpractice. Anh won a judgment of $100,000 from the law firm. What is the tax treatment of this $100,000 judgment for Anh?

11. **LO.2** Ted works for Azure Motors, an automobile dealership. All employees can buy a car at the company's cost plus 2%. The company does not charge employees the $300 dealer preparation fee that nonemployees must pay. Ted purchased an automobile for $29,580 ($29,000 + $580). The company's cost was $29,000. The price for a nonemployee would have been $33,900 ($33,600 + $300 preparation fee). What is Ted's gross income from the purchase of the automobile?

Planning

12. **LO.2, 4** Wilbur has been offered a job at a salary that would put him in the 24% marginal tax bracket. In addition to his salary, he would receive health insurance coverage. Another potential employer does not offer health insurance but has agreed to match the first offer on an after-tax and insurance basis. The cost of health insurance comparable to that provided by the other potential employer is $9,000 per year. How much more in salary must the second potential employer pay so that Wilbur's financial status will be the same under both offers?

13. **LO.2, 4** Eagle Life Insurance Company pays its employees $0.30 per mile for driving their personal automobiles to and from work. The company reimburses each employee who rides the bus $100 a month for the cost of a pass. Tom collected $100 for his automobile mileage, and Mason received $100 as reimbursement for the cost of a bus pass.

    a. What are the effects of the above on Tom's and Mason's gross income?
    b. Assume that Tom and Mason are in the 24% marginal tax bracket and the actual before-tax cost for Tom to drive to and from work is $0.30 per mile. What are Tom's and Mason's after-tax costs of commuting to and from work?

Critical Thinking

14. **LO.2** Several of Egret Company's employees have asked the company to create a hiking trail that employees could use during their lunch hours. The company owns vacant land that is being held for future expansion but would have to spend approximately $50,000 if it were to make a trail. Nonemployees would be allowed to use the facility as part of the company's effort to build strong community support. What are the relevant tax issues for the employees?

15. **LO.2** The Sage Company has the opportunity to purchase a building located next to its office. Sage would use the building as a day care center for the children of its employees and an exercise facility for the employees. Occasionally, portions of the building could be used for employees' family events such as reunions, birthday parties, and anniversaries. The company would like to know if the planned uses of the building would fit into a beneficially taxed employee compensation plan.

Decision Making
Planning

16. **LO.2, 4** Katie, a resident of Virginia, is considering purchasing a North Carolina bond that yields 4.6% before tax. She is in the 35% Federal marginal tax bracket and the 5% state marginal tax bracket. She is aware that State of Virginia bonds of comparable risk are yielding 4.5%. However, the Virginia bonds are exempt from Virginia tax, but the North Carolina bond interest is taxable in Virginia. Which of the two options will provide the greater after-tax return to Katie? Katie can deduct

any state taxes paid on her Federal income tax return. In your analysis, assume that the bond amount is $100,000.

17. **LO.2** Andrea entered into a § 529 qualified tuition program for the benefit of her daughter, Joanna. Andrea contributed $15,000 to the fund. The fund balance had accumulated to $25,000 by the time Joanna was ready to enter college. However, Joanna received a scholarship that paid for her tuition, fees, books, supplies, and room and board. So Andrea withdrew the funds from the § 529 plan and bought Joanna a new car.
    a. What are the tax consequences to Andrea of withdrawing the funds?
    b. Assume instead that Joanna's scholarship did not cover her room and board, which cost $7,500 per academic year. During the current year, $7,500 of the fund balance was used to pay for Joanna's room and board. The remaining amount was left in the § 529 plan to cover her room and board for future academic years. What are the tax consequences to Andrea and to Joanna of using the $7,500 to pay for the room and board?

18. **LO.2** Ralph has experienced financial difficulties as a result of his struggling business. He has been behind on his mortgage payments for the last six months. The mortgage holder, who is a friend of Ralph's, has offered to accept $80,000 in full payment of the $100,000 owed on the mortgage and payable over the next 10 years. The interest rate of the mortgage is 7%, and the market rate is now 8%. What tax issues are raised by the creditor's offer? Critical Thinking

19. **LO.2** Pooja's sister (Kiara) became quite ill earlier this year and had extensive medical bills which she could not cover. Kiara's financial problems were made worse as she had to take a 10-month leave of absence from work. Pooja set up a crowdfunding website to help her sister and raised $80,000; Kiara gave these funds to the hospital to help cover her medical bills. What is the tax treatment of the $80,000 to Kiara? Explain. Critical Thinking

20. **LO.3** Dolly is a cash basis taxpayer. In 2023, she filed her 2022 South Carolina income tax return and received a $2,200 refund. Dolly took the standard deduction on her 2022 Federal income tax return but will itemize her deductions in 2023. Molly, a cash basis taxpayer, also filed her 2022 South Carolina income tax return in 2023 and received a $600 refund. She deducted no other state or local taxes. Molly had $16,000 in itemized deductions on her 2022 Federal income tax return but will take the standard deduction in 2023. How does the tax benefit rule apply to Dolly's and Molly's situations? Explain.

Computational Exercises

21. **LO.2** Valentino is a patient in a nursing home for 45 days of 2023. While in the nursing home, he incurs total costs of $13,500. Medicare pays $8,000 of the costs. Valentino receives $15,000 from his long-term care insurance policy, which pays while he is in the facility. Assume that the Federal daily excludible amount for Valentino is $420.
    Of the $15,000, what amount may Valentino exclude from his gross income?

22. **LO.2** Mio was transferred from New York to Germany. He lived and worked in Germany for 340 days in 2023 and can show that his tax home is now Germany. Mio's salary for 2023 is $190,000. In your computation, round any division to four decimal places before converting to a percentage. For example, 0.473938 would be rounded to 47.39%.
    What is Mio's foreign earned income exclusion?

23. **LO.2** Ellie purchases an insurance policy on her life and names her brother, Jason, as the beneficiary. Ellie pays $32,000 in premiums for the policy during her life. When she dies, Jason collects the insurance proceeds of $500,000.
    As a result, how much gross income does Jason report?

24. **LO.2** Alfred owned a term life insurance policy at the time he was diagnosed with a terminal illness. After paying $18,300 in premiums, he sold the policy to a company that is authorized by the state of South Carolina to purchase such policies. The company paid Alfred $125,000. When Alfred died 18 months later, the company collected the face amount of the policy, $150,000.

    As a result of the sale of the policy, how much is Alfred required to include in his gross income?

25. **LO.1, 2** Leland pays premiums of $5,000 for an insurance policy in the face amount of $25,000 upon the life of Caleb and subsequently transfers the policy to Tyler for $7,500. Over the years, Tyler pays subsequent premiums of $1,500 on the policy. Upon Caleb's death, Tyler receives the proceeds of $25,000.

    As a result, what amount is Tyler required to include in his gross income?

26. **LO.1, 2** Jarrod receives a scholarship of $18,500 from East State University to be used to pursue a bachelor's degree. He spends $12,000 on tuition, $1,500 on books and supplies, $4,000 for room and board, and $1,000 for personal expenses.

    How much may Jarrod exclude from his gross income?

27. **LO.3** Apply the tax benefit rule to determine the amount of the state income tax refund included in gross income in 2023.
    a. Myrna and Geoffrey filed a joint tax return in 2022. Their AGI was $85,000, and itemized deductions were $26,600, which included $7,000 in state income tax and no other state or local taxes. In 2023, they received a $1,800 refund of the state income taxes they paid in 2022. The standard deduction for married filing jointly in 2022 was $25,900.
    b. Veronica filed as a single taxpayer in 2022. Her AGI was $230,000, and itemized deductions were $42,000. Her local property taxes were $13,000, and her state income taxes were $17,000. In 2023, Veronica received a $2,100 refund of the state income taxes she paid in 2022. The standard deduction for single filers in 2022 was $12,950.

Problems

28. **LO.2** Ed, an employee of the Natural Color Company, suffered from a rare disease that was very expensive to treat. The local media ran several stories about Ed's problems, and the family created a website that generated more than $10,000 in gifts from individuals to help pay the medical bills. Ed's employer provided hospital and medical insurance for its employees, but the policy did not cover Ed's illness. When it became apparent that Ed could not pay all of his medical expenses, the hospital canceled the $25,000 Ed owed at the time of his death. After Ed's death, his former employer paid Ed's widow $12,000 in "her time of need." Ed's widow also collected $50,000 on a group term life insurance policy paid for by Ed's employer. What are Ed's and his widow's gross income?

29. **LO.2** Determine the gross income of the beneficiaries in the following cases:
    a. Justin's employer was downsizing and offered employees an amount equal to one year's salary if the employee would voluntarily retire.
    b. Trina contracted a disease and was unable to work for six months. Because of her dire circumstances, her employer paid her one-half of her regular salary while she was away from work.
    c. Coral Corporation collected $1,000,000 on a key person life insurance policy when its chief executive died. The corporation had paid the premiums on the policy of $77,000, which were not deductible by the corporation.
    d. Juan collected $40,000 on a life insurance policy when his husband, Leon, died in 2023. The insurance policy was provided by Leon's employer, and the premiums were excluded from Leon's gross income as group term life insurance. In 2023, Juan also collected the $3,500 accrued salary owed to Leon at the time of his death.

30. **LO.2, 4** As a result of a cancer diagnosis in early 2023, Laura has begun chemotherapy treatments. A cancer specialist has stated that Laura has less than one year to live. She has incurred many medical bills and other general living expenses and is in need of cash. So she is considering selling stock that cost $35,000 and has a fair market value of $50,000. This amount would be sufficient to pay her medical bills. However, she has read about a company (the Vital Benefits Company) that would purchase her life insurance policy for $50,000. She has paid $30,000 in premiums on the policy.

Decision Making
Planning

a. Considering only the tax effects, would selling the stock or selling the life insurance policy result in more beneficial tax treatment?

b. Assume that Laura is a dependent child and that her mother owns the stock and the life insurance policy, which is on the mother's life. Which of the alternative means of raising the cash would result in more beneficial tax treatment?

31. **LO.2** What is the taxpayer's gross income in each of the following situations?

a. Darrin received a salary of $50,000 from his employer, Green Construction.

b. In July, Green gave Darrin an all-expenses-paid trip to Las Vegas (value of $3,000) for exceeding his sales quota.

c. Marta received $10,000 from her employer to help her pay medical expenses not covered by insurance.

d. Blake received $15,000 from his deceased spouse's employer as compensation for a bonus earned prior to death.

e. Clint collected $50,000 as the beneficiary of a group term life insurance policy when his wife died. The premiums on the policy were paid by his deceased wife's employer.

32. **LO.2** Donald was killed in an accident while he was on the job. Darlene, Donald's wife, received several payments as a result of Donald's death. What is Darlene's gross income from the items listed below?

a. Donald's employer paid Darlene an amount equal to Donald's three months' salary ($60,000), which is what the employer does for all widows and widowers of deceased employees.

b. Donald had $20,000 in accrued salary that was paid to Darlene.

c. Donald's employer had provided Donald with group term life insurance of $480,000 (twice his annual salary), which was payable to his widow in a lump sum. Premiums on this policy totaling $12,500 had been included in Donald's gross income under § 79.

d. Donald had purchased a life insurance policy (premiums totaled $250,000) that paid $600,000 in the event of accidental death. The proceeds were payable to Darlene, who elected to receive installment payments as an annuity of $30,000 each year for a 25-year period. She received her first installment this year.

33. **LO.2** Ray and Carin are partners in an accounting firm. The partners have entered into an arm's length agreement requiring Ray to purchase Carin's partnership interest from Carin's estate if she dies before Ray. The price is set at 120% of the book value of Carin's partnership interest at the time of her death. Ray purchased an insurance policy on Carin's life to fund this agreement. After Ray had paid $45,000 in premiums, Carin was killed in an automobile accident and Ray collected $800,000 of life insurance proceeds. Ray used the life insurance proceeds to purchase Carin's partnership interest.

a. What amount should Ray include in his gross income from receiving the life insurance proceeds?

b. The insurance company paid Ray $16,000 interest on the life insurance proceeds during the period Carin's estate was in administration. During this period, Ray had left the insurance proceeds with the insurance company. Is this interest taxable?

c. When Ray paid $800,000 for Carin's partnership interest, priced as specified in the agreement, the fair market value of Carin's interest was $1,000,000. How much should Ray include in his gross income from this bargain purchase?

34. **LO.2** Sally was an all-state soccer player during her junior and senior years in high school. She accepted an athletic scholarship from State University. The scholarship provided the following:

Tuition and fees	$15,000
Housing and meals	6,000
Books and supplies	1,500
Transportation	1,200

a. Determine the effect of the scholarship on Sally's gross income.

b. Sally's brother, Willy, was not a gifted athlete, but he received $8,000 from their father's employer as a scholarship during the year. The employer grants the children of all executives a scholarship equal to one-half of annual tuition, fees, books, and supplies. Willy also received a $6,000 scholarship (to be used for tuition) as the winner of an essay contest related to bioengineering, his intended field of study. Determine the effect of the scholarships on Willy's and his father's gross income.

35. **LO.2** Adrian was awarded an academic scholarship to State University for the 2023–2024 academic year. He received $6,500 in August and $7,200 in December 2023. Adrian had enough personal savings to pay all expenses as they came due. Adrian's expenditures for the relevant period were as follows:

Tuition, August 2023	$3,700
Tuition, January 2024	3,750
Room and board	
August–December 2023	2,800
January–May 2024	2,500
Books and educational supplies	
August–December 2023	1,000
January–May 2024	1,200

Determine the effect on Adrian's gross income for 2023 and 2024.

36. **LO.2** Leigh sued an overzealous bill collector and received the following settlement:

Damage to her automobile that the collector attempted to repossess	$ 3,300
Physical damage to her arm caused by the collector	15,000
Loss of income while her arm was healing	6,000
Punitive damages	80,000

a. What effect does the settlement have on Leigh's gross income?

b. Assume that Leigh also collected $25,000 of damages for slander to her personal reputation caused by the bill collector misrepresenting the facts to Leigh's employer and other creditors. Is this $25,000 included in Leigh's gross income? Explain.

37. **LO.2** Determine the effect on gross income in each of the following cases:

a. Eloise received $150,000 in settlement of a sex discrimination case against her former employer.

b. Nell received $10,000 for damages to her personal reputation. She also received $40,000 in punitive damages.

c. Orange Corporation, an accrual basis taxpayer, received $50,000 from a lawsuit filed against its auditor who overcharged for services rendered in a previous year.

d. Beth received $10,000 in compensatory damages and $30,000 in punitive damages in a lawsuit she filed against a tanning parlor for severe burns she received from using its tanning equipment.

e. Joanne received compensatory damages of $75,000 and punitive damages of $300,000 from a cosmetic surgeon who botched her nose job.

38. **LO.2** Rex, age 55, is an officer of Blue Company, which provides him with the following nondiscriminatory fringe benefits in 2023:

- Hospitalization insurance premiums for Rex and his dependents. The cost of the coverage for Rex is $2,900 per year, and the additional cost for his dependents is $3,800 per year. The plan has a $3,000 deductible, but his employer contributed $1,500 to Rex's Health Savings Account (HSA). Rex withdrew only $800 from the HSA, and the account earned $50 of interest during the year.
- Insurance premiums of $840 for salary continuation payments. Under the plan, Rex will receive his regular salary in the event he is unable to work due to illness. Rex collected $4,500 on the policy to replace lost wages while he was ill during the year.
- Rex is a part-time student working on his bachelor's degree in engineering. His employer reimbursed his $5,200 tuition under a plan available to all full-time employees.

Determine the amount Rex must include in gross income.

39. **LO.2** The UVW Union and HON Corporation are negotiating contract terms. Assume that the union members are in the 24% marginal tax bracket and that all benefits are provided on a nondiscriminatory basis. Write a letter to the UVW Union members, explaining the tax consequences of the options discussed below. The union's address is 905 Spruce Street, Washington, DC 20227. Communications Planning

   a. The company would eliminate the $250 deductible on medical insurance benefits. Most employees incur more than $250 each year in medical expenses.
   b. Employees would get an additional paid holiday with the same annual income (the same pay but less work).
   c. An employee who did not need health insurance (because the employee's spouse works and receives family coverage) would be allowed to receive the cash value of the coverage.

40. **LO.2, 4** Mauve Corporation has a group hospitalization insurance plan that has a $200 deductible amount for hospital visits and a $15 deductible for doctor visits and prescriptions. The deductible portion paid by employees who have children has become substantial for some employees. The company is considering adopting a medical reimbursement plan or a flexible benefits plan to cover the deductible amounts. Either of these plans can be tailored to meet the needs of the employees. What are the cost considerations to the employer that should be considered in choosing between these plans? Decision Making

41. **LO.2** Belinda spent the last 60 days of 2023 in a nursing home. The cost of the services provided to her was $18,000 ($300 per day). Medicare paid $8,500 toward the cost of her stay. Belinda also received $7,500 of benefits under a long-term care insurance policy she purchased. Assume that the Federal daily excludible amount is $420. What is the effect on Belinda's gross income?

42. **LO.2** Tim is the vice president of western operations for Maroon Oil Company and is stationed in San Francisco. He is required to live in an employer-owned home, which is three blocks from his company office. The company-provided home is equipped with high-speed internet access and several telephone lines. Tim receives telephone calls and e-mails that require immediate attention any time of day or night because the company's business is spread all over the world. A full-time administrative assistant resides in the house to assist Tim with the urgent business matters. Tim often uses the home for entertaining customers, suppliers, and employees. The fair market value of comparable housing is $9,000 per month. Tim is also provided with free parking at his company's office. The value of the parking is $370 per month. Calculate the amount associated with the company-provided housing and free parking that Tim must include in his gross income for 2023.

43. LO.2 Does the taxpayer recognize gross income in the following situations?

a. Ava is a filing clerk at a large insurance company. She is permitted to leave the premises for lunch, but she usually eats in the company's cafeteria because it is quick, and she is on a tight schedule. On average, she pays $2 for a lunch that would cost $12 at a restaurant and it cost her employer $10 to prepare. However, if the prices in the cafeteria were not so low and the food was not so delicious, she would probably bring her lunch at a cost of $3 per day.

b. Scott is an executive for an international corporation located in New York City. Often he works late, taking telephone calls from the company's European branch. Scott often stays in a company-owned condominium when he has a late-night work session. The condominium is across the street from the company office and has the technology needed to communicate with employees and customers throughout the world.

c. Ira recently moved to take a job. For the first month on the new job, Ira was searching for a home to purchase or rent. During this time, his employer permitted Ira to live in an apartment the company maintains for customers during the buying season. The month that Ira occupied the apartment was not during the buying season, and the apartment would not otherwise have been occupied.

Decision Making
Planning

44. LO.2, 4 Bertha is considering taking an early retirement offered by her employer. She would receive $3,000 per month, indexed for inflation. However, she would no longer be able to use the company's health facilities, and she would be required to pay her hospitalization insurance premiums of $8,000 each year. Bertha and her husband will file a joint return and take the standard deduction. She currently receives a salary of $55,000 a year. If she retires, she will spend approximately $300 less each month for commuting and clothing. Bertha and her husband have other sources of income and are in and will remain in the 22% marginal tax bracket. Her income tax for the current year was $8,875. She currently pays Social Security and Medicare taxes of 7.65% on her salary, but her retirement pay would not be subject to this tax. According to Bertha, she and her husband could live well if her after-tax retirement income was at least 50% of her current income. Provide Bertha with information she will need to make her decision.

Communications

45. LO.2, 4 Finch Construction Company provides the carpenters it employs with all of the required tools. However, the company believes that this practice has led to some employees not taking care of the tools and to the mysterious disappearance of some tools. The company is considering requiring all of its employees to provide their own tools. Each employee's salary would be increased by $1,500 to compensate for the additional cost. Write a letter to Finch's management explaining the tax consequences of this plan to the carpenters. Finch's address is 300 Harbor Drive, Vermillion, SD 57069.

Critical Thinking
Planning

46. LO.2, 4 Bluebird, Inc., does not provide its employees with any tax-exempt fringe benefits. The company is considering adopting a hospital and medical benefits insurance plan that will cost approximately $9,000 per employee. To adopt this plan, the company may have to reduce salaries and/or lower future salary increases. Bluebird is in the 25% (combined Federal and state rates) bracket. Bluebird is also responsible for matching the Social Security and Medicare taxes withheld on employees' salaries (at the full 7.65% rate). The hospital and medical benefits insurance plan will not be subject to the Social Security and Medicare taxes, and the company is not eligible for the small business credit for health insurance. The employees generally fall into two marginal tax rate groups:

Income Tax	Social Security and Medicare Tax	Total
12%	7.65%	19.65%
24%	1.45%	25.45%

The company has asked you to assist in its financial planning for the hospital and medical benefits insurance plan by computing the following:

a. How much taxable compensation is the equivalent of $9,000 of exempt compensation for each of the two classes of employees?

b. What is the company's after-tax cost of the taxable compensation computed in part (a)?

c. What is the company's after-tax cost of providing the employee the taxable compensation equivalent of $9,000 exempt compensation?

d. Briefly explain your conclusions from the preceding analysis.

47. **LO.2, 4** Rosa's employer has instituted a flexible benefits program. Rosa will use the plan to pay for her daughter's dental expenses and other medical expenses that are not covered by health insurance. Rosa is in the 24% marginal tax bracket and estimates that the medical and dental expenses not covered by health insurance will be within the range of $2,000 to $3,000. Her employer's plan permits her to set aside as much as $3,050 in the flexible benefits account. Rosa does not itemize her deductions. Decision Making

a. Rosa puts $2,050 into her flexible benefits account, and her actual expenses are $3,050. What is her cost of underestimating the expenses?

b. Rosa puts $3,050 into her flexible benefits account, and her actual expenses are only $2,050. What is her cost of overestimating her expenses?

c. What is Rosa's cost of underfunding as compared with the cost of overfunding the flexible benefits account?

d. Does your answer in part (c) suggest that Rosa should fund the account closer to the low end or to the high end of her estimates?

48. **LO.2** Sparrow Corporation would like you to review its employee fringe benefits program with regard to the tax consequences of the plan for the company's president (Polly), who is also the majority shareholder.

a. The company has a qualified retirement plan. The company pays the cost of employees attending a retirement planning seminar. The employee must be within 10 years of retirement, and the cost of the seminar is $1,500 per attendee.

b. The company owns a parking garage that is used by customers, employees, and the general public but primarily by the employees. Only the general public is required to pay for parking. The charge to the general public for Polly's parking for the year would have been $4,200 (a $350 monthly rate).

c. All employees are allowed to use the company's fixed charge long-distance telephone services, as long as the privilege is not abused. Although no one has kept track of the actual calls, Polly's use of the telephone had a value (what she would have paid on her personal telephone) of approximately $600.

d. The company owns a condominium at the beach, which it uses to entertain customers. Employees are allowed to use the facility without charge when the company has no scheduled events. Polly used the facility 10 days during the year. Her use had a rental value of $1,000.

e. The company is in the household moving business. Employees are allowed to ship goods without charge whenever there is excess space on a truck. Polly purchased a dining room suite for her daughter. Company trucks delivered the furniture to the daughter. Normal freight charges would have been $750.

f. The company has a storage facility for household goods. Officers are allowed a 20% discount on charges for storing their goods. All other employees are allowed a 10% discount. Polly's discounts for the year totaled $900.

49. **LO.2** George is a U.S. citizen who is employed by Hawk Enterprises, a global company. Beginning on June 1, 2023, George began working in London. He worked there until January 31, 2024, when he transferred to Paris. He worked in Paris the remainder of 2024. His salary for the first five months of 2023 was

$100,000, and it was earned in the United States. His salary for the remainder of 2023 was $175,000, and it was earned in London. George's 2024 salary from Hawk was $300,000, with part being earned in London and part being earned in Paris. What is George's gross income in 2023 and 2024? (Assume that the foreign earned income exclusion amount is the same in both 2023 and 2024.)

50. **LO.2, 3** Determine Hazel's gross income from the following receipts for the year:

Gain on sale of Augusta County bonds	$800
Interest on U.S. government savings bonds	400
Interest on state income tax refund	200
Interest on Augusta County bonds	700
Patronage dividend from Potato Growers Cooperative	350

The patronage dividend was received in March of the current year for amounts paid for her (nondeductible) garden and lawn supplies.

51. **LO.1** In January 2023, Ezra purchased 2,000 shares of Gold Utility Mutual Fund for $20,000. In June, Ezra received an additional 100 shares as a dividend, in lieu of receiving $1,000 in cash dividends. In December, the company declared a two-for-one stock split. Ezra received an additional 2,100 shares, but there was no option to receive cash. At the time of the stock dividend in December and at the end of the year, the fund shares were trading for $5 per share. Also, at the end of the year, the fund offered to buy outstanding shares for $4.50. Ezra did not sell any shares during the year.
    a. What is Ezra's gross income from the 100 shares received in June?
    b. What is Ezra's gross income from the receipt of the 2,100 shares as a two-for-one stock split in December?
    c. Should Ezra be required to recognize gross income in 2023 even though the fair market value of his investment at the end of the year was less than the fair market value at the beginning of the year? Explain.

Decision Making
Planning

52. **LO.2** Tonya, who lives in California, inherited a $100,000 State of California bond in 2023. Her marginal Federal tax rate is 35%, she itemizes deductions on her Federal tax return, and her marginal state tax rate is 5%. The California bond pays 3.3% interest, which is not subject to California income tax. She can purchase a corporate bond of comparable risk that will yield 5.2% or a U.S. government bond that pays 4.6% interest. Which investment will provide the greatest after-tax yield?

Communications
Decision Making
Planning

53. **LO.2** Lynn Swartz's husband died three years ago. Her parents have income of over $200,000 a year and want to ensure that funds will be available for the education of Lynn's eight-year-old son, Eric. Lynn is currently earning $45,000 a year. Lynn's parents have suggested that they start a savings account for Eric. They have calculated that if they invest $4,000 a year for the next 8 years, at the end of 10 years, sufficient funds will be available for Eric's college expenses. Lynn realizes that the tax treatment of the investments could significantly affect the amount of funds available for Eric's education. She asked you to write a letter to her advising about options available to her parents and to her for Eric's college education. Lynn's address is 100 Myrtle Cove, Fairfield, CT 06824.

54. **LO.2** Starting in 2012 Chuck and Luane have been purchasing Series EE bonds in their name to use for the higher education of their daughter Susie, who currently is age 18. During the year, they cash in $12,000 of the bonds to use for freshman year tuition, fees, and room and board. Of this amount, $5,000 represents interest. Of the $12,000, $8,000 is used for tuition and fees, and $4,000 is used for room and board. Chuck and Luane's AGI, before the educational savings bond exclusion, is $142,200. Review § 135, and answer the following questions.
    a. Determine the tax consequences for Chuck and Luane, who will file a joint return, and for Susie.
    b. Assume that Chuck and Luane purchased the bonds in Susie's name. Determine the tax consequences for Chuck and Luane and for Susie.

55. **LO.2** Albert established a qualified tuition program for each of his twins, Kim and Jim. He started each fund with $20,000 when the children were five years old. Albert made no further contributions to his children's plans. Thirteen years later, both children have graduated from high school. Kim's fund has accumulated to $45,000, and Jim's has accumulated to $42,000. Kim decides to attend a state university, which will cost $60,000 for four years (tuition, fees, room and board, and books). Jim decides to go to work instead of going to college. During the current year, $7,500 is used from Kim's plan to pay the cost of her first semester in college. Because Jim is not going to college now or in the future, Albert withdraws the $42,000 plan balance and gives it to Jim to start his new life after high school.

    a. During the period since the plans were established, should Albert or the twins have been including the annual plan earnings in gross income? Explain.
    b. What are the tax consequences to Kim and Albert of the $7,500 being used for the first semester's higher education costs?
    c. Because of her participation in the qualified tuition program, Kim received a 10% reduction in tuition charges; so less than $7,500 was withdrawn from her account. Is either Albert or Kim required to include the value of this discount in gross income? Explain.
    d. What are the tax consequences to Albert and Jim of Jim's qualified tuition program being closed?

56. **LO.3** How does the tax benefit rule apply in the following cases?

    a. In 2021, the Orange Furniture Store, an accrual method sole proprietorship, sold furniture on credit for $1,000 to Sammy. The cost of the furniture was $600. In 2022, Orange took a bad debt deduction for the $1,000. In 2023, Sammy inherited some money and paid Orange the $1,000 he owed. Orange's owner was in the 35% marginal tax bracket in 2021, the 12% marginal tax bracket in 2022, and the 35% marginal tax bracket in 2023.
    b. In 2022, Marvin, a cash basis taxpayer, took a $2,000 itemized deduction for state income taxes paid; the deduction was not limited by the SALT cap. This increased his itemized deductions to a total that was $800 more than the standard deduction. In 2023, Marvin received a $1,500 refund when he filed his 2022 state income tax return. Marvin was in the 12% marginal tax bracket in 2022 but was in the 35% marginal tax bracket in 2023.
    c. In 2022, Barb, a cash basis taxpayer, was in an accident and incurred $8,000 in medical expenses, which she claimed as an itemized deduction for medical expenses. Because of the 7.5%-of-AGI reduction, the expense reduced her taxable income by only $3,000. In 2023, Barb successfully sued the person who caused the physical injury and collected $8,000 to reimburse her for the cost of her medical expenses. Barb was in the 22% marginal tax bracket in 2022, 12% in 2023.

57. **LO.2** Vic, who was experiencing financial difficulties, was able to adjust his debts as follows:

    a. Vic is an attorney. Vic owed his uncle $25,000. The uncle told Vic that if he serves as the executor of the uncle's estate, Vic's debt will be canceled in the uncle's will.
    b. Vic borrowed $80,000 from First Bank. The debt was secured by land that Vic purchased for $100,000. Vic was unable to pay, and the bank foreclosed when the liability was $80,000, which was also the fair market value of the property.
    c. The Land Company, which had sold land to Vic for $80,000, reduced the mortgage on the land by $12,000.

    Determine the tax consequences to Vic.

Tax Return Problems

Critical Thinking
Decision Making
Tax Forms Problem
ProConnect™ Tax

58. Alfred E. Old and Beulah A. Crane, each age 42, married on September 7, 2020. Alfred and Beulah will file a joint return for 2022. Alfred's Social Security number is 111-11-1109. Beulah's Social Security number is 123-45-6780, and she has chosen to use "Old" as her married name. They live at 211 Brickstone Drive, Atlanta, GA 30304.

    Alfred was divorced from Sarah Old in March 2017. Under the divorce agreement, Alfred is to pay Sarah $1,250 per month for the next 10 years or until Sarah's death, whichever occurs first. Alfred paid Sarah $15,000 in 2022. In addition, in January 2022, Alfred paid Sarah $50,000, which is designated as being for her share of the marital property. Also, Alfred is responsible for all prior years' income taxes. Sarah's Social Security number is 123-45-6788.

    Alfred's salary for 2022 is $150,000. He is an executive working for Cherry, Inc. (Federal I.D. No. 98-7654321). As part of his compensation package, Cherry provides him with group term life insurance equal to twice his annual salary. His employer withheld $22,800 for Federal income taxes and $8,000 for state income taxes. The proper amounts were withheld for FICA taxes.

    Beulah recently graduated from law school and is employed by Legal Aid Society, Inc. (Federal I.D. No. 11-1111111), as a public defender. She received a salary of $42,000 in 2022. Her employer withheld $6,300 for Federal income taxes and $2,400 for state income taxes. The proper amounts were withheld for FICA taxes.

    Alfred and Beulah received taxable interest income of $500. They received a $1,900 refund on their 2021 state income taxes; they claimed the standard deduction on their 2021 Federal income tax return. Alfred and Beulah paid $4,500 interest and $1,450 property taxes on their personal residence in 2022. They paid sales taxes of $1,400, for which they maintain the receipts. Alfred and Beulah have never owned or used any digital assets, and they do not want to contribute to the Presidential Election Campaign.

    Compute the Olds' net tax payable (or refund due) for 2022. Suggested software: ProConnect Tax.

Communications
Decision Making
Planning
Tax Computation Problem

59. Martin S. Albert (Social Security number 111-11-1111) is 39 years old and is married to Michele R. Albert (Social Security number 123-45-6789). The Alberts live at 512 Ferry Road, Newport News, VA 23601. They file a joint return and have two dependent children, Charlene, age 16, and Jordan, age 18. Charlene's Social Security number is 123-45-6788, and Jordan's Social Security number is 123-45-6787. In 2023, Martin and Michele had the following transactions:

    a. Michele received $130,000 in salary from Red Steel Corporation, where she is a construction engineer. Withholding for Federal income tax was $10,750. The amounts withheld for FICA taxes were as follows: $7,440 ($120,000 × 6.2%) for Social Security and $1,740 ($120,000 × 1.45%) for Medicare. Michele worked in Mexico from January 1, 2022, until February 15, 2023. Her $120,000 salary for 2023 includes $18,000 she earned for January and one-half of February 2023 while working in Mexico.
    b. Martin and Michele received $400 interest on Montgomery County (Virginia) school bonds.
    c. Martin received $2,300 interest from a Bahamian bank account.
    d. Michele received 50 shares of Applegate Corporation common stock as a stock dividend. The shares had a fair market value of $2,500 at the time Michele received them, and she did not have the option of receiving cash.
    e. Martin and Michele received a $1,200 refund on their 2022 Virginia income taxes. Their itemized deductions in 2022 totaled $34,000 and included state taxes of $7,400.
    f. Michele paid $6,600 alimony to her former husband, Benjamin P. Morgan (Social Security number 123-45-6786). The divorce was finalized in March 2016.

g. Martin and Michele kept the receipts for their sales taxes paid of $1,100.

h. Martin and Michele's itemized deductions were as follows:
   - State income tax paid and withheld totaled $5,100.
   - Real estate taxes on their principal residence were $3,700.
   - Mortgage interest on their principal residence was $2,500.

Part 1—Tax Computation
Compute the Alberts' net tax payable (or refund due) for 2023.

Part 2—Tax Planning
The Alberts are considering buying another house. Their house mortgage payments would increase by $500 (to $1,500) per month, which includes a $250 increase in interest and a $100 increase in property tax. The Alberts would like to know how much the mortgage payments would increase net of any change in their income tax. Write a letter to the Alberts that contains your advice.

Research Problems

Note: Solutions to the Research Problems can be prepared by using the Thomson Reuters Checkpoint™ online tax research database, which accompanies this textbook. Solutions can also be prepared by using research materials found in a typical tax library.

Research Problem 1. Your client Murray reported to the Environmental Protection Agency that his employer was illegally dumping chemicals into a river. His charges were true, and Murray's employer was fined. In retaliation, Murray's employer fired him and made deliberate efforts to prevent Murray from obtaining other employment. Murray sued the employer, claiming that his reputation had been damaged. Murray won his lawsuit and received an award for "damages to his personal and professional reputation and for his mental suffering." Murray has asked you whether the award is taxable. He argues that he was awarded damages as a recovery of his human capital and that a recovery of capital is not income. Is Murray's logic correct?

Research Problem 2. The employees of the city of Greenville must make mandatory contributions to the city's postretirement health benefit plan. The employees' contributions are placed in a trust and are used exclusively for the employees' benefits. The employees believe that because they are required to make the contributions from their base salaries, the result should be the same as if the employer made the contribution and had reduced their salaries by the amount of the contributions. As a result, the employees believe they should be permitted to exclude the payments from gross income. The employees have asked you to research the issue.

Research Problem 3. Your client, Simon Che, is an avid Texas Rangers fan. Last March at the Rangers' home opener, as a result of a random drawing of those in attendance at the game, Simon won 300 Shipley Do-Nut coupons. Each coupon entitled him to a cup of coffee and a free doughnut or a dozen doughnut holes.

Simon used some of the coupons (approximately 20), but he found that eating so many doughnuts directly conflicted with his goal of losing weight. The unused coupons expired on January 1, 2024. As a result, Simon was surprised when he received a Form 1099 in February 2024 that valued his prize at $900. Simon would like to know whether the value of the doughnut coupons should be included in income and asks you to research his question. If you conclude that their value should be included in income, Simon also would like to know if he can reduce his gross income by including in income only the value of the coupons that he used. He has the unused coupons as documentation that neither he nor anyone else used them.

Research Problem 4. Aubrey Brown is a decorated veteran. As a result of a significant injury sustained in combat, Aubrey is unable to work. He received $12,000 of Social Security disability payments in the current year. He reasons that the payments should be excluded from his gross income because the payments are compensation for the physical injury he suffered as a result of his service in the armed forces. Is Aubrey correct? Explain.

Partial list of research aids:
Rev.Rul. 77–318.
Reimels v. Comm., 2006–1 USTC ¶50,147, 97 AFTR 2d 2006–820, 436 F.3d 344 (CA–2).

Use internet tax resources to address the following questions. Look for reliable websites and blogs of the IRS and other government agencies, media outlets, businesses, tax professionals, academics, think tanks, and political outlets.

Communications
Data Analytics

Research Problem 5. Use information about individual income tax returns available at the IRS Tax Stats website (**irs.gov/statistics/soi-tax-stats-individual-income-tax-returns**) to find data on the number of individuals who report tax-exempt interest income on their tax return and the amount of that exempt income. The data you find should show this information for individuals at different ranges of adjusted gross income (AGI). Use the data to create pie charts (or similar visuals) of the percent of AGI represented by the tax-exempt interest income exclusion as well as the number of individuals claiming this exclusion at different AGI levels. Analyze the IRS data, draw conclusions from it, and summarize your findings in a two- to three-paragraph e-mail sent to your instructor. Be sure your conclusions are explained and supported by the data.

Research Problem 6. Employers often use the internet as a means of attracting applications from potential employees. Locate an internet site offering employment opportunities, ideally one provided by a well-known corporation. How does the employer promote its fringe benefit and cafeteria plan packages? Compare and contrast three such sites.

Research Problem 7. One income exclusion that some states allow but the Federal government does not is for lottery winnings. Does your state have an exclusion for lottery winnings? If so, how does it work? Why do you think a state might allow winnings from its own state lottery to be excluded from state income taxes?

Becker CPA Review Questions

Becker

1. Stephen is a graduate student at West University. He works part-time at the campus coffee shop earning $5,000 this year. Stephen also receives a $25,000 scholarship that pays for his tuition, fees, and books. What amount does Stephen include in his gross income?

   a. $25,000
   b. $5,000
   c. $30,000
   d. $0

2. Jeffrey Dean, a Master's Degree candidate at North State Central University, was awarded a $15,000 scholarship from North State Central in the current year. During the current year, he paid the following expenses:

Tuition	$12,000
Books	1,000
Fees	500
Room and board	1,500

   In addition, he received $6,000 for teaching two undergraduate accounting courses. What amount must be included in Dean's gross income?

   a. $0
   b. $6,000
   c. $7,500
   d. $21,000

3. Linda is an employee of JRH Corporation. Which of the following would be included in Linda's gross income?
   a. Premiums paid by JRH Corporation for a group term life insurance policy for $50,000 of coverage for Linda.
   b. $1,000 of tuition paid by JRH Corporation to State University for Linda's master's degree program.
   c. A $2,000 trip given to Linda by JRH Corporation for meeting sales goals.
   d. $1,200 paid by JRH Corporation for an annual parking pass for Linda.

4. Kim was seriously injured at her job. As a result of her injury, she received the following payments:
   - $5,000 reimbursement from employer-provided health insurance for medical expenses paid by Kim. The premiums this year paid by Kim's employer totaled $6,000.
   - $15,000 disability pay. Kim has disability insurance provided by her employer as a nontaxable fringe benefit. Kim's employer paid $6,000 in disability premiums this year on behalf of Kim.
   - $10,000 received for damages for personal physical injury.
   - $200,000 for punitive damages.

   What amount is taxable to Kim?

   a. $215,000
   b. $225,000
   c. $236,000
   d. $0

5. Danny received the following interest and dividend payments this year. What amount should Danny include in his gross income?

Source Amount	
City of Atlanta bond interest	$1,200
U.S. Treasury bond interest	500
State of Georgia bond interest	1,000
Ellis Company common stock dividend	400
Row Corporation bond interest	600

   a. $2,500
   b. $1,500
   c. $3,700
   d. $2,200

6. Elizabeth received the following sources of income in the current year:

U.S. Treasury bond certificates interest	$500
Interest on state tax refund (paid by state government for late payment of tax refund to Elizabeth)	200
Corporate bond interest	600
Amount received for opening a new savings account at a local bank	50
Puerto Rico bond interest	350

   What amount must Elizabeth include in gross income on her Federal income tax return?

   a. $650
   b. $1,150
   c. $1,350
   d. $1,700

Part 3

Deductions and Credits

Part 3 presents information related to the deduction component of the basic tax model. Deductions are classified as business versus nonbusiness, "for" AGI versus "from" AGI, employee versus employer, active versus passive, and reimbursed versus unreimbursed. The effect of each of these classifications is analyzed. The deduction for qualified business income, deduction limitations, and deduction disallowances are also covered. A separate chapter examines the special tax treatment affecting losses from investment activities. Part 3 concludes with an examination of the general procedures related to the determination and payment of tax liability, including a discussion of tax credits and additional taxes.

Chapter 6

Deductions and Losses: In General

Learning Objectives: *After completing Chapter 6, you should be able to:*

LO.1 Differentiate between deductions *for* and *from* adjusted gross income and describe the relevance of the differentiation.

LO.2 Describe the cash and accrual methods of accounting with emphasis on the deduction aspects.

LO.3 Apply some of the most common Internal Revenue Code deduction disallowance provisions.

LO.4 Identify tax planning opportunities for maximizing deductions and minimizing the disallowance of deductions.

Chapter Outline

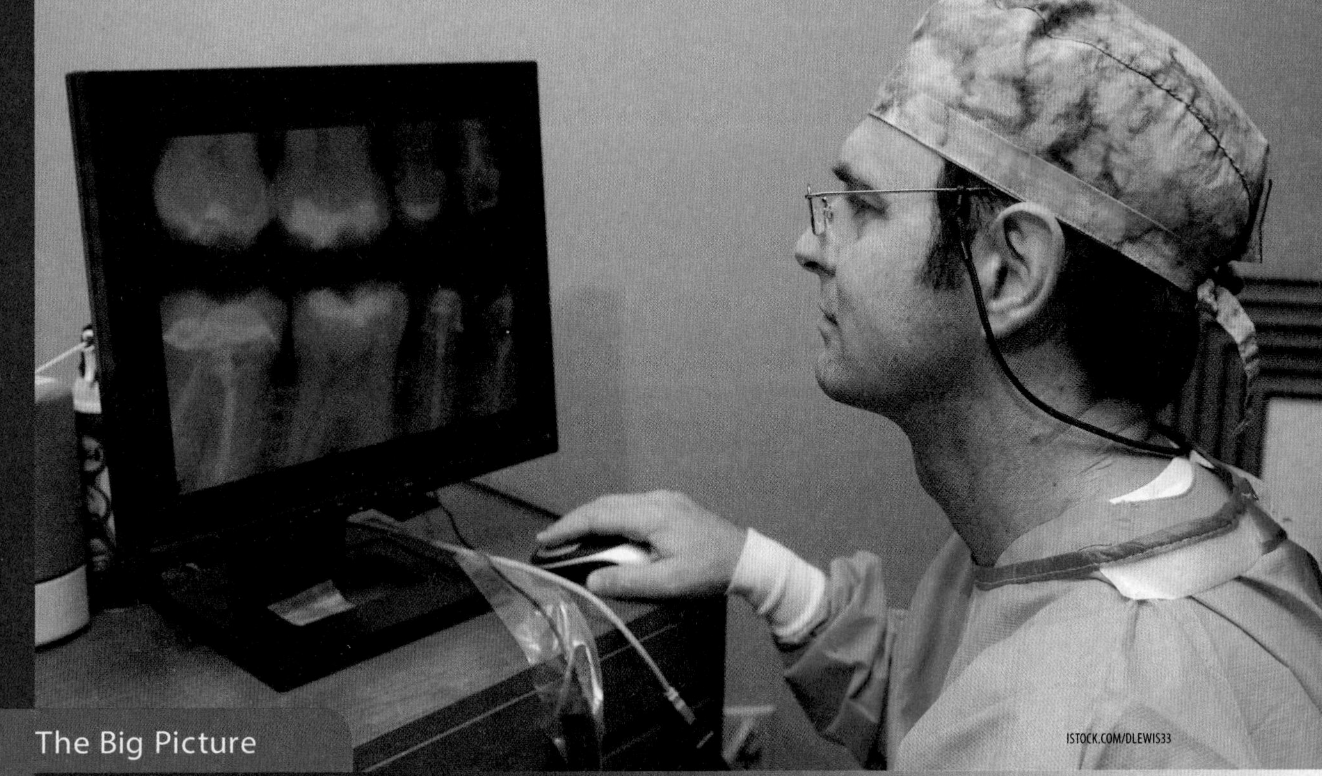

ISTOCK.COM/DLEWIS33

Calculation of Deductible Expenses

Dr. Cliff Payne determines that the deductible expenses associated with his dental practice (a sole proprietorship) are as follows:

Salaries including FICA ($5,000 are unpaid at year-end)	$120,000
Building rent	24,000
Depreciation of dental equipment and office furnishings and equipment	52,000
Insurance (malpractice, dental equipment, and office furnishings and equipment)	22,000
Dental supplies	16,000
Office supplies	3,000
Investigation expenses	6,000
Contribution to the State Senate campaign fund of Tom Smith	1,000
Contribution to the State Senate campaign fund of Virginia White	1,000
Legal expenses associated with patient lawsuit	4,000
Fine imposed by city for improper disposal of medical waste	3,000
Dues paid to The Dental Society	10,000
Draw by Dr. Payne for living expenses ($5,000 monthly)	60,000

Has Dr. Payne correctly calculated the deductible business expenses for his dental practice?

Read the chapter and formulate your response.

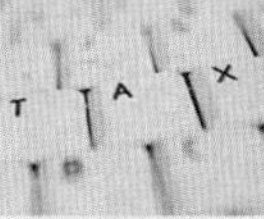

Framework 1040 **Tax Formula for Individuals**

This chapter covers the boldfaced portions of the Tax Formula for Individuals that was introduced in Concept Summary 3.1 on p. 3-3. Below those portions are the sections of Form 1040 where the results are reported.

Income *(broadly defined)*	$ xx,xxx
Less: Exclusions	(x,xxx)
Gross income	**$xx,xxx**
Less: Deductions *for* adjusted gross income	**(x,xxx)**

FORM 1040 (Schedule 1)

3	Business income or (loss). Attach Schedule C . . . .

Adjusted gross income	$ xx,xxx
Less: The greater of total itemized deductions *or* the standard deduction	(x,xxx)

FORM 1040 (p. 1)

12	**Standard deduction or itemized deductions** (from Schedule A) . . . .

Personal and dependency exemptions*	(x,xxx)
Deduction for qualified business income**	(x,xxx)
Taxable income	$ xx,xxx
Tax on taxable income *(see Tax Tables or Tax Rate Schedules)*	$ x,xxx
Less: Tax credits *(including income taxes withheld and prepaid)*	(xxx)
Tax due (or refund)	$ xxx

* Exemption deductions are not allowed from 2018 through 2025.
** Only applies from 2018 through 2025.

The tax law has an all-inclusive definition of income; that is, income from whatever source derived is includible in gross income. Income cannot be excluded unless there is a specific statement to that effect in the tax law.

The opposite approach is used for deductions. A deduction is allowed only if there is a specific provision in the tax law that permits it. The inclusive definition of income and the exclusive definition of deductions may not seem fair to taxpayers, but it is the structure of the tax law. The courts agree with this structure, holding that any exclusions from income and all deductions are gifts from Congress.[1]

LO.1

Differentiate between deductions *for* and *from* adjusted gross income and describe the relevance of the differentiation.

6-1 Classification of Deductible Expenses

It is important to classify deductible expenses as **deductions *for* adjusted gross income** (AGI) or **deductions *from* adjusted gross income**. Deductions *for* AGI can be claimed whether or not the taxpayer itemizes. With the exception of the deduction for qualified business income, deductions *from* AGI result in a tax benefit only if, collectively, they exceed the taxpayer's standard deduction. If itemized deductions (*from* AGI) are less than the standard deduction, they provide no tax benefit. As Example 1 illustrates, whether a deduction is classified as *for* AGI or *from* AGI can affect the benefit the taxpayer receives from the deduction.

[1]The courts refer to this as "legislative grace"; see *New Colonial Ice Co. v. Helvering*, 4 USTC ¶1292, 13 AFTR 1180, 54 S.Ct. 788 (1934).

Example 1

Steve is a self-employed CPA. Ralph is one of Steve's employees. During the year, Steve and Ralph incur the following expenses:

	Steve	Ralph
Dues to American Institute of CPAs and State Society of CPAs	$ 400	$ 300
Subscriptions to professional journals	500	200
Registration fees for tax conferences	800	800
	$1,700	$1,300

Steve does not reimburse any of his employees for dues, subscriptions, or educational programs.

Steve's expenses are classified as deductions *for* AGI because they are business expenses of a sole proprietor. As a result, he can deduct the $1,700 on his Federal income tax return. Ralph's unreimbursed employee business expenses are classified as deductions *from* AGI. However, these expenses are miscellaneous itemized deductions and, from 2018 through 2025, are not deductible.

Deductions *for* AGI may affect the *amount* of itemized deductions directly because some itemized deductions are limited to amounts in excess of specified percentages of AGI. Itemized deductions that have AGI limitations include medical expenses (7.5% of AGI) and personal casualty losses (10% of AGI).

Example 2

Tina, age 36, earns a salary of $90,000 and has no other income. She itemizes her deductions during 2023. Unreimbursed medical expenses for the year are $12,000. Tina's medical expense deduction is $5,250, as computed below.

Alternatively, assume that Tina receives a $10,000 bonus from her employer in 2023. Her AGI would then be $100,000 ($90,000 + $10,000), and her medical expense is reduced by $750 to $4,500.

	Without Bonus	With Bonus
Qualified medical expenses	$12,000	$12,000
Reduction: AGI × 7.5%	(6,750)	(7,500)
Deductible medical expenses	$ 5,250	$ 4,500

When Tina's income increased by $10,000, this reduced her medical expense deduction by $750; so the total effect on taxable income is an increase of $10,750.[2]

6-1a Classifying Deductions

Two key issues must be resolved for any potential deduction. First, it must be determined whether the item is deductible, as discussed in text Section 6-1b. If the item is deductible, then the second issue is to determine if the deduction is classified as *for* AGI or *from* AGI. Deductions *for* AGI are listed in § 62. If a deduction is not listed in § 62, it is an itemized deduction. Exhibit 6.1 provides a partial list of the items classified as deductions *for* AGI.

6-1b Authority for Deductions

The specific authority for deductions is provided in many different Code sections. However, two of the most important are § 212 and § 162. To determine the proper authority

[2]See Chapter 10 for additional discussion of medical expenses.

Exhibit 6.1 Common Deductions *for* Adjusted Gross Income

Deduction	Chapter
Alimony payments (divorce decrees before 2019)	4
Expenses attributable to property held for the production of rents and royalties	6
Expenses attributable to a trade or business	9
Employee business expenses (reimbursed)	9
Professional development and supplies (up to $300) for elementary and secondary school teachers	9
Student loan interest	9 and 10
Contributions to retirement plans	9
Medical insurance premiums paid by a self-employed taxpayer	10
Self-employment taxes	12
Losses on the sale or exchange of property	13 and 14
Penalty on premature withdrawal of funds from time savings accounts	

for claiming a deduction, first determine what type of activity the expenditure relates to. All activities can be divided into one of the following mutually exclusive categories:

1. Investment/production of income (§ 212).
2. Trade or business (§ 162).
3. Personal (various Code sections).

For example, are legal expenses deductible? To make that determination, first determine whether the legal expense relates to an investment, a trade or business, or a personal activity.

Darryl pays $400 to an attorney for her advice. If this payment relates to his business, it is a § 162 business expense. If the payment relates to the purchase of land that he intends to hold for profit, it is a § 212 investment/production of income expense. If the payment relates to the development of an estate plan, it is a nondeductible personal expense (§ 262).

Section 212 Expenses

Code § 212 allows deductions for ordinary and necessary expenses paid or incurred for:

- The production or collection of income.
- The management, conservation, or maintenance of property held for the production of income.
- Expenses paid in connection with the determination, collection, or refund of any tax.

Expenses related to rent and royalty income (reported on Schedule E) are § 212 expenses, and these expenses are deductible *for* AGI. All other § 212 expenses are itemized deductions (deductions *from* AGI). For example, investment interest expense and investment-related state and local taxes are deductible *from* AGI (but subject to specific limitations discussed in Chapters 10 and 11). Any remaining § 212 expenses (e.g., safe deposit box rentals and investment advisory fees) are miscellaneous itemized deductions and, from 2018 through 2025, are not deductible.[3]

Section 162 Trade or Business Expenses

Code § 162(a) permits a deduction for all ordinary and necessary expenses paid or incurred in carrying on a trade or business. These include reasonable salaries paid for services, expenses for the use of business property, and one-half of self-employment taxes paid (see Chapters 9 and 12). These expenses are deducted *for* AGI.

[3] § 62(a)(4) and Reg. § 1.212–1(g).

It is sometimes difficult to determine whether an expense is deductible as a trade or business expense. The term *trade or business* is not defined in the Code or Regulations, and the courts have not provided a satisfactory definition. One key determination is to ensure that the activity is not a hobby. If the taxpayer's operations are not extensive enough to indicate that a trade or business exists, expenses related to the activity are deductible only to the extent of the activity's income (see text Section 6-3e).

Code § 162 *excludes* the following items from classification as trade or business expenses:

- Charitable contributions or gifts.
- Illegal bribes and kickbacks and certain treble damage payments.
- Fines and penalties.

6-1c **Deduction Criteria for § 162 and § 212**

Expenses under § 162 and § 212 must be **ordinary and necessary** to be deductible. In addition, compensation for services must be "reasonable" in amount.

An expense is *necessary* if a prudent businessperson would incur the same expense and the expense is expected to be appropriate and helpful in the taxpayer's business.[4] An expense is *ordinary* if it is normal, usual, or customary in the type of business conducted by the taxpayer and is not capital in nature.[5] However, an expense need not be recurring to be deductible as ordinary. For example, a business may be in a situation that is a very rare occurrence and incur an expense. If other businesses in a similar situation are likely to incur a similar expense, then the expense can be ordinary even though it is not recurring.

Nisha engaged in a mail-order business. The post office judged that her advertisements were false and misleading. Under a fraud order, the post office stamped "fraudulent" on all letters addressed to Nisha's business and returned them to the senders. Nisha spent $30,000 on legal fees in an unsuccessful attempt to force the post office to stop.

The legal fees (although not recurring) were ordinary business expenses because they were normal, usual, or customary in the circumstances.[6]

To be deductible, an expense must be both ordinary *and* necessary.

Pat purchased a business that had just been adjudged bankrupt. Because the business had a poor financial rating, Pat wanted to restore its financial reputation. Consequently, he paid off some of the debts owed by the former owners that had been canceled by the bankruptcy court.

Because Pat had no legal obligation to make these payments, the U.S. Supreme Court found that he was trying to generate goodwill. Although the payments were necessary (i.e., appropriate and helpful), they were *not* ordinary and their deduction *was not* allowed.[7]

The Code refers to **reasonableness** solely with respect to salaries and other compensation for services.[8] But the courts have held that for any business expense to be ordinary and necessary, it also must be reasonable in amount.[9] Example 6 illustrates the reasonableness concept for an investment expense.

Danielle is a retired pilot who owns a small portfolio of investments, including 10 shares of Robin, Inc., a publicly traded company, worth $1,000. She incurred $350 in travel expenses to attend the annual shareholders' meeting where she voted her 10 shares against the current management group.

No deduction is permitted because a 10-share investment is insignificant in value in relation to the travel expenses incurred.[10]

What constitutes reasonableness is a question of fact. If an expense is unreasonable, the excess amount is not allowed as a deduction.

[4] *Welch v. Helvering*, 3 USTC ¶1164, 12 AFTR 1456, 54 S.Ct. 8 (1933).

[5] *Deputy v. DuPont*, 40–1 USTC ¶9161, 23 AFTR 808, 60 S.Ct. 363.

[6] *Comm. v. Heininger*, 44–1 USTC ¶9109, 31 AFTR 783, 64 S.Ct. 249 (1943).

[7] *Welch v. Helvering*, cited in Footnote 4.

[8] § 162(a)(1).

[9] *Comm. v. Lincoln Electric Co.*, 49–2 USTC ¶9388, 38 AFTR 411, 176 F.2d 815 (CA–6).

[10] *J. Raymond Dyer*, 36 T.C. 456 (1961).

The question of reasonableness generally arises with respect to closely held corporations since there is no separation of ownership and management. Transactions between the shareholders and the closely held company may result in the disallowance of deductions for excessive salaries and rent expense paid by the corporation to the shareholders. An unusually large salary will often be challenged by the IRS, but the courts may conclude that it is reasonable given the facts that surround a particular business.[11] If excessive payments for salaries and rents are closely related to the percentage of stock owned by the recipients, the payments are generally treated as dividends.[12] Because dividends are not deductible by the corporation, the disallowance results in an increase in the corporate taxable income.

Example 7

Sparrow Corporation, a closely held corporation, is owned equally by Lupe, Carlos, and Ramon. The company has been highly profitable for several years and has not paid dividends. Lupe, Carlos, and Ramon are key officers of the company, and each receives a salary of $300,000. Salaries for similar positions in comparable companies average only $200,000.

Amounts paid to the owners in excess of $200,000 may be deemed unreasonable; if so, a total of $300,000 in salary deductions by Sparrow is disallowed. The disallowed amounts are treated as dividends rather than salary to Lupe, Carlos, and Ramon because the payments are proportional to stock ownership. Salaries are deductible by the corporation, but dividends are not.

Note that the shareholders may benefit from this reclassification. Salaries would be taxed at ordinary income rates and are subject to payroll taxes. However, dividend income would be taxed at long-term capital gains rates if qualified and would not be subject to payroll taxes.

6-1d **Personal Expenses**

Expenditures incurred in one's personal life are deductible only if a specific Code section authorizes the deduction. These expenses are usually deductions *from* AGI (and also referred to as "itemized deductions"). Some of the more common deductions in this category include:

- Contributions to qualified charitable organizations.
- Mortgage interest expense.
- State and local taxes.
- Medical expenses.
- Personal casualty losses.

Many of these deductions are limited in some way. For example, only those medical expenses and casualty losses in excess of a specific percentage of AGI are deductible. Charitable contributions made in cash are limited to a maximum of 60 percent of a taxpayer's AGI. The deduction for state and local taxes is capped at $10,000. Casualty losses are discussed in Chapter 7; the other itemized deductions are discussed in Chapter 10.

Yolanda paid her doctor $650 for a medical procedure this year. She also made a charitable contribution to the United Way for $1,000. She spent $400 on uniforms for her children to wear to school.

The Code specifically provides for deducting medical expenses and qualified charitable contributions, so these are deductible. Since the Code does not provide a deduction for clothing worn for personal use, the uniforms are not deductible.

6-1e **Business and Nonbusiness Losses**

Code § 165 provides for a deduction for losses not compensated for by insurance. As a general rule, deductible losses of individual taxpayers are limited to those incurred in a trade or business or in a transaction entered into for profit. Individuals also are allowed to deduct losses that are the result of a casualty, but only if the casualty occurs in a Federally declared disaster area. Casualty losses include, but are not limited to, those caused by fire, storm, shipwreck, and theft (see Chapter 7). A deductible personal casualty loss is an itemized deduction (i.e., *from* AGI).

[11] *Kennedy, Jr. v. Comm.*, 82–1 USTC ¶9186, 49 AFTR 2d 82–628, 671 F.2d 167 (CA–6).

[12] Reg. § 1.162–8.

During the current year, Kareem encountered a series of unfortunate events. A tornado hit his personal residence in March, and he incurred a loss of $30,000; due to the widespread damage, his county was declared a Federal disaster area. In June, he sold his car to generate cash to pay his bills. The loss on the car sale was $3,500. In October, he sold 100 shares of stock in MMM Company at a loss of $2,000.

Since the tornado is a casualty that occurred in a Federal disaster area, the $30,000 loss is potentially deductible on Schedule A (but subject to limitations). The car is a personal use asset, and the loss was not caused by a casualty, so the $3,500 loss is not deductible. The $2,000 stock loss is from an investment activity, so this is deductible as a capital loss.

6-1f Deduction for Qualified Business Income

An individual can deduct up to 20 percent of **qualified business income (QBI)** from a sole proprietorship, a partnership, or an S corporation. This *from* AGI deduction reduces the tax on income from proprietorships and flow-through businesses.[13] The deduction does *not* reduce self-employment income. The QBI deduction is discussed in detail in Chapter 15; a brief overview is provided here.

In general, the deduction for QBI is the *lesser of* 20 percent of:

1. Qualified business income.
2. Modified taxable income (taxable income before the QBI deduction, reduced by any net capital gain).[14]

Qualified business income is defined as the ordinary income less ordinary deductions a taxpayer earns from a "qualified trade or business" (e.g., from a sole proprietorship, an S corporation, or a partnership). QBI does not include any wages earned as an employee, any capital gains or losses, any dividend income, or any interest income. In determining QBI, all deductions attributable to a trade or business are taken into account. Relevant deductions include the self-employment tax deduction [§ 164(f)], the self-employed health insurance deduction [§ 162(l)], and any deduction for contributions to qualified retirement plans [§ 404].[15] If a taxpayer has a qualified business loss in one year, no QBI deduction is allowed and the loss is carried over to the next year to reduce QBI (but not below zero).

Trevor, a single taxpayer, has modified taxable income of $150,000. His sole proprietorship reports $108,000 of net income [on Schedule C (Form 1040)]. As a result, Trevor's self-employment tax liability is $15,260 ($108,000 × 0.9235 × 15.3%). He is allowed a *for* AGI deduction for one-half of his self-employment tax liability ($7,630; $15,260 × 1/2). Trevor's QBI is $100,370 ($108,000 − $7,630).

Since Trevor's QBI is less than his modified taxable income, his QBI deduction is $20,074 ($100,370 × 20%).

Limit on the QBI Deduction Based on Wages and Capital Investment

In 2023, if taxable income before the QBI deduction is greater than $364,200 (married, filing jointly) or $182,100 (all other taxpayers), the QBI deduction cannot exceed (i.e., is limited to) the *greater of*:[16]

1. 50 percent of the W–2 wages relating to the qualified trade or business.
2. The sum of:
   a. 25 percent of the W–2 wages relating to the qualified trade or business.
   b. 2.5 percent of the unadjusted basis (immediately after acquisition) of all qualified property.

This limit is phased in over $100,000 (married, filing jointly) or $50,000 (all other taxpayers) of taxable income. Once a married couple has taxable income in 2023 over $464,200 ($232,100 for all other taxpayers), the W–2 wages and capital investment limitation will be completely in play. Exhibit 6.2 summarizes the limitations that may reduce or eliminate the QBI deduction.

[13] § 199A.

[14] § 199A(a).

[15] § 199A(c) and Reg. § 1.199A–3(b)(1)(vi).

[16] In 2022, the threshold amounts were $340,100 (married taxpayers filing a joint return) and $170,050 (all other taxpayers).

Exhibit 6.2 2023 QBI Limitations

Filing Status*	Taxable Income Before the QBI Deduction		
Married, Filing Jointly	$364,200 or less	More than $364,200 and less than $464,200	$464,200 or more
Single and Head of Household	$182,100 or less	More than $182,100 and less than $232,100	$232,100 or more
Wage/Asset Limitation	Does not apply	Limitation phased in	Limitation applies in full
Specified Services Limitation	Does not apply	QBI deduction partially allowed	QBI deduction not allowed
Does 20% of Modified Taxable Income Limitation Apply?	Yes	Yes	Yes

* In 2023, married taxpayers filing separately have a threshold amount of $182,100.

QBI Deduction Limitation

Example 11

Simone, a married taxpayer, operates a business as a sole proprietor. The business has one employee, who is paid $80,000 during 2023. Assume that the business has no significant assets. During 2023, Simone reports qualified business income of $500,000 and taxable income before the QBI deduction of $600,000. Because Simone's taxable income before the QBI deduction exceeds $464,200, her QBI deduction is $40,000, the lower of:

- $100,000 (20% × $500,000).
- $40,000 (50% of W–2 wages of $80,000).

Example 12

Assume the same facts as in Example 11, except that Simone's taxable income before the QBI deduction is $404,200.

Because Simone's taxable income before the QBI deduction exceeds $364,200 but is less than $464,200, the W–2 limit is partially phased in. Her taxable income before the QBI deduction exceeds $364,200 by $40,000. So Simone must reduce her "normal" QBI deduction ($100,000) by 40% ($40,000 ÷ $100,000) of the difference between the "normal" QBI deduction and the "limited" QBI deduction (based on W–2 wages; $40,000). As a result, Simone's QBI deduction is $76,000, computed as follows:

Normal QBI deduction	$100,000
Less: 40% × $60,000 ($100,000 – $40,000)	(24,000)
QBI deduction	$ 76,000

Qualified Trade or Business

A qualified trade or business means any trade or business *other than* a "specified service trade or business."[17] Specified services include the following:

- Health.
- Law.
- Accounting.
- Actuarial Science.
- Performing Arts.
- Consulting.
- Athletics.
- Financial Services.
- Brokerage Services.

Special rules apply to specified service businesses. In general, a trade or business is *not* a specified service trade or business if the trade or business has gross receipts of

[17] §§ 199A(d)(1) and (2).

$25 million or less in a taxable year and *less than 10 percent* of its gross receipts relates to a "specified service." For a trade or business with gross receipts greater than $25 million in a taxable year, the test is *less than 5 percent* (rather than less than 10 percent).[18] And if taxable income is below the thresholds identified, a taxpayer is still allowed a partial (or full) QBI deduction. These rules are discussed in more depth in Chapter 15.

6-1g **Reporting Procedures**

All deductions *for* AGI are ultimately reported on Schedule 1 (Form 1040). Most of the deductions *for* AGI originate on supporting schedules. Examples include business expenses (Schedule C); rent, royalty, partnership, and fiduciary deductions (Schedule E); and farming expenses (Schedule F). Other deductions *for* AGI, such as contributions to traditional IRAs and Keogh retirement plans and alimony payments, are entered directly on Schedule 1 (Form 1040).

Adjusted gross income appears on page 1 of Form 1040. Deductions *from* AGI (itemized deductions) are reported on Schedule A (Form 1040). The total of all itemized deductions is subtracted *from* AGI (unless the standard deduction is greater). Then the qualified business income deduction is subtracted to arrive at taxable income.

Exhibit 6.3 summarizes the reporting and flow of deductions on the taxpayer's return (Form 1040). See Concept Summary 6.4 later in the chapter for the classification of deductions as *for* AGI or *from* AGI.

Exhibit 6.3 Format of Form 1040

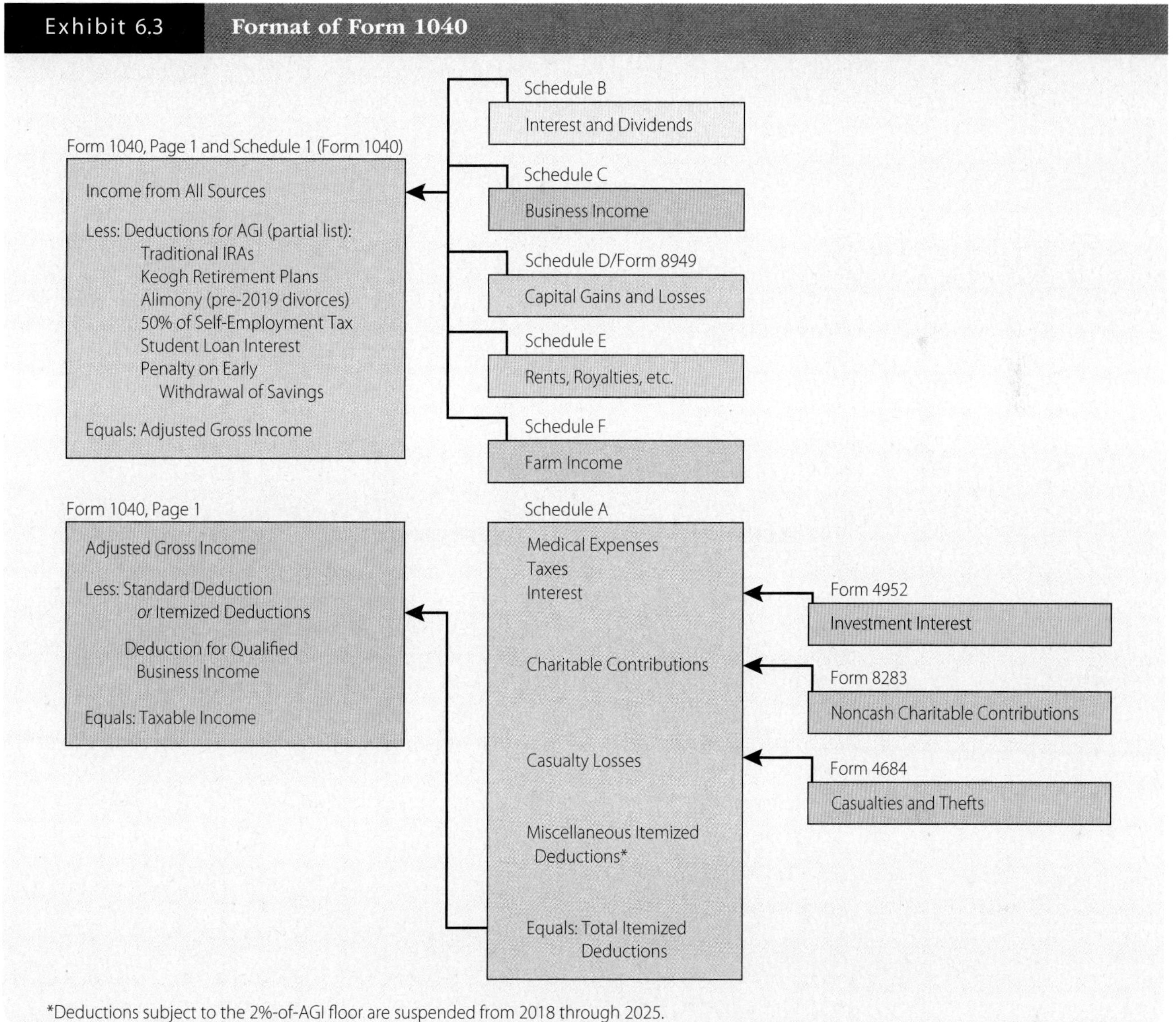

*Deductions subject to the 2%-of-AGI floor are suspended from 2018 through 2025.

[18] Reg. § 1.199A–5(c)(1).

Describe the cash and accrual methods of accounting with emphasis on the deduction aspects.

6-2 Deductions and Losses—Timing of Expense Recognition

6-2a Importance of Taxpayer's Method of Accounting

A taxpayer's **accounting method** is a major factor in determining taxable income. The method used determines when an item is includible in income and when an item is deductible on the tax return. Usually, the taxpayer's normal method of record keeping is used for income tax purposes.[19] The taxing authorities require that the method used clearly reflect income and that items be handled consistently.[20] The most common methods of accounting are the cash method and the accrual method. If a taxpayer owns multiple businesses, it may be possible to use the cash method for some and the accrual method for others.

Throughout the portions of the Code dealing with deductions, the phrase *paid or incurred* is used. *Paid* refers to the cash basis taxpayer who gets a deduction only in the year of payment. *Incurred* concerns the accrual basis taxpayer who obtains the deduction in the year in which the liability for the expense becomes certain (refer to Chapter 4).

6-2b Cash Method Requirements

The expenses of cash basis taxpayers are deductible only when they are actually paid with cash or other property. Promising to pay or issuing a note does *not* satisfy the actually paid requirement.[21] However, the payment can be made with borrowed funds. At the time taxpayers charge expenses on their credit cards, they are allowed to claim the deduction. They borrowed money from the credit card issuer and simultaneously paid the expenses.[22]

A current deduction is not allowed for capital expenditures except through amortization, depletion, or depreciation over the life of the asset. An expenditure that creates an asset having a useful life that extends substantially beyond the end of the tax year must be capitalized.[23]

As Chapter 16 explains, not all taxpayers are allowed to use the cash method.[24] For example, in some cases, the taxpayer is required to use the accrual method for sales and cost of goods sold if inventories are an income-producing factor of the business. In 2023, corporations can use the cash method if average gross receipts for the prior three years do not exceed $29 million ($27 million in 2022). Exceptions to the inventory reporting rules also are provided for taxpayers meeting the average gross receipts test.

6-2c Accrual Method Requirements

The period in which an accrual basis taxpayer can deduct an expense is determined by applying the *all events test* and the *economic performance test*. That is, a deduction cannot be claimed until (1) all of the events have occurred to create the taxpayer's liability, and (2) the amount of the liability can be determined with reasonable accuracy. Once these requirements are satisfied, the deduction is permitted only if economic performance has occurred. The economic performance test is met only when the service, property, or use of property giving rise to the liability is actually performed for, provided to, or used by the taxpayer.[25]

[19]§ 446(a).

[20]§§ 446(b) and (e); Reg. § 1.446–1(a)(2).

[21]*Page v. Rhode Island Trust Co., Exr.*, 37–1 USTC ¶9138, 19 AFTR 105, 88 F.2d 192 (CA–1).

[22]Rev.Rul. 78–39. See also Rev.Rul. 80–335, which applies to pay-by-phone arrangements.

[23]Reg. § 1.461–1(a).

[24]§ 448.

[25]§ 461(h).

Greg's entertainment business sponsored a jazz festival in a rented auditorium at a local college. His business is responsible for cleaning up after the festival, which took place on December 22, 2023, and reinstalling the auditorium seats. Because the college is closed over the Christmas holidays, the company hired by Greg to perform the work did not begin these activities until January 3, 2024. Greg's business cannot deduct the related costs until 2024, when the services are performed.

An exception to the economic performance requirements allows certain *recurring items* to be deducted immediately if all of the following conditions are met:

- The item is recurring in nature and is treated consistently by the taxpayer.
- Either the accrued item is not material or accruing it in the current period results in better matching of income and expenses.
- All of the events have occurred that determine the existence of the liability, and the amount of the liability can be determined with reasonable accuracy.
- Economic performance occurs within a reasonable period (but not later than 8½ months after the close of the taxable year).[26]

The Third Circuit Court of Appeals has ruled that accrual basis taxpayers who award points to customers to use for future purchases can deduct the value of the points when awarded to the customers.[27] The IRS and Tax Court had taken the position that the deduction could not be recorded until the points were redeemed and used. In addition, the Third Circuit noted that the points are recurring items and can qualify for this exception to the economic performance test if the requirements listed above have been met.

Exceptions to Economic Performance Rules

Marco, an accrual basis, calendar year taxpayer, entered into a monthly maintenance contract during the year. He makes a monthly accrual at the end of every month for this service and pays the fee sometime between the first and fifteenth of the following month when services are performed. The amount involved is immaterial, and all of the other tests are met.

The December 2023 accrual is deductible in 2023 even though the service is performed on January 12, 2024.

Rita, an accrual basis, calendar year taxpayer, shipped merchandise sold on December 30, 2023, via Greyhound Van Lines on January 3, 2024, and paid the freight charges at that time.

Because Rita reported the sale of the merchandise in 2023, the shipping charge also should be deductible in 2023. This procedure results in a better matching of income and expenses.

Reserves for estimated expenses such as warranties and bad debts are often deducted for financial accounting purposes before the specific expense is identified. Generally, these reserves are not allowed for tax purposes because the economic performance test cannot be satisfied.

Blackbird Airlines is required by Federal law to test its engines after 3,000 flying hours. Aircraft cannot return to flight until the tests have been conducted. An unrelated aircraft maintenance company does all of the company's tests for $1,500 per engine.

For financial reporting purposes, the company accrues an expense based upon $0.50 per hour of flight and credits an allowance account. The actual amounts paid for maintenance are offset against the allowance account.

For tax purposes, the economic performance test is not satisfied until the work has been done. Therefore, the reserve method cannot be used for tax purposes.

---

[26]§ 461(h)(3)(A).

[27]*Giant Eagle, Inc.*, 2016–1 USTC ¶50,274, 117 AFTR 2d 2016–1476, 822 F.3d 666 (CA–3). Also see IRS Action on Decision 2016–03.

6-2d Prepaid Expenses—The "12-Month Rule"

A taxpayer doesn't have to capitalize amounts paid to create a benefit that doesn't extend beyond the earlier of (1) 12 months after the first date on which the taxpayer realized the benefit or (2) the end of the tax year following the tax year in which the payment was made (the "12-month rule").[28] Although this rule applies to both cash and accrual method taxpayers, accrual method taxpayers cannot claim a deduction unless economic performance has occurred.[29]

"12-Month Rule"

Example 17

On November 1, 2023, Nada, a calendar year and cash basis taxpayer, pays $6,000 for a one-year premium on a catastrophic liability policy that takes effect December 15, 2023. Nada will receive a benefit from this policy from December 15, 2023, through December 14, 2024. Her benefit does not extend beyond 12 months after the benefit begins on December 15. It also does not extend beyond the end of 2024. Therefore, this payment satisfies the requirements of the 12-month rule and Nada can deduct the $6,000 in 2023.

Example 18

Assume the same facts as in Example 17, except that the benefit from the policy runs from February 1, 2024, through January 31, 2025. Nada's benefit now extends beyond the end of the tax year following the tax year in which the payment was made (December 31, 2024), so the 12-month rule requirements are not met. Nada must capitalize the $6,000 payment in 2023 and amortize it over the benefit period.

6-2e Time Value of Tax Deductions

Both the time value of money and marginal tax rate changes must be considered when an expense can be paid and deducted in either of two years. Cash basis taxpayers often have the choice to pay expenses at the end of the current year or at the beginning of the following year. In view of the time value of money, a tax deduction this year may be worth more than the same deduction next year. However, accelerating the payment may not be advantageous if the taxpayer's marginal tax rate is higher in the following year. Before accelerating a payment, the taxpayer also needs to forecast future cash flow to ensure that an early payment makes sense.

Example 19

Rita pledged $50,000 to her church's special building fund. She can make the contribution on December 31, 2023, or January 1, 2024. Rita is in the 24% tax bracket in 2023 and in the 35% bracket in 2024. She itemizes her deductions in both years. Assume that Rita's discount rate is 5%. If she takes the deduction in 2024, she saves $4,667 ($16,667 − $12,000). Even though the tax savings from a January 1, 2024 contribution won't be realized until her 2024 tax return is filed, the increase in her deduction due to her increased marginal tax rates overcomes the time value of money consequences. See Table E-2 in Appendix E.

	2023	2024
Contribution	$50,000	$50,000
Tax bracket	× 0.24	× 0.35
Tax savings	$12,000	$17,500
Discounted @ 5%	×1.0000	×0.9524
Savings in present value	$12,000	$16,667

If tax rates are changing between two years, there are several areas in which taxpayers may have discretion as to which year to make a payment to achieve tax savings. Examples include certain alimony payments (see Chapter 4), assets purchased and expensed under § 179 or additional first-year (bonus) depreciation (see Chapter 8), home mortgage interest, and charitable contributions (see Chapter 10). Always remember to consider the time value of money in the analysis.

[28] Reg. § 1.263(a)–4(f).

[29] Reg. § 1.263(a)–4(f)(6).

6-3 **Disallowance Possibilities**

LO.3

Apply some of the most common Internal Revenue Code deduction disallowance provisions.

Certain types of expenses are disallowed by the tax law. Without these restrictions, taxpayers might attempt to deduct items that, in reality, are personal expenditures. For example, specific tax rules are provided to determine whether an expense is for trade or business purposes or is related to a personal hobby.

6-3a **Public Policy Limitation**

Payments considered to be in violation of public policy are not deductible. In addition, any payment to a governmental entity is not deductible. This provision does not apply to payments that are restitution for damage caused by the taxpayer or payments for taxes paid.[30]

Justification for Denying Deductions

The courts developed the principle that a payment in violation of public policy is not a necessary expense and is not deductible.[31] Allowing a deduction would, in effect, be indirectly subsidizing a taxpayer's wrongdoing. The following expenses, which are considered contrary to public policy, are not deductible:

- Bribes and kickbacks, including those associated with Medicare or Medicaid (in the case of foreign bribes and kickbacks, only if the payments violate the U.S. Foreign Corrupt Practices Act of 1977).
- Fines and penalties paid to a government for violation of law.
- Two-thirds of the treble damage payments made to claimants resulting from violation of the antitrust law.[32]

The Big Picture

Refer to the facts of *The Big Picture* on p. 6-1. Dr. Payne had not instituted proper procedures for disposing of medical waste from his laboratory. During the current tax year, he was fined $3,000 by the city. Dr. Payne believes the fine should be deducted as an ordinary business expense.

However, because the fine was due to a violation of public policy, the $3,000 is not deductible.

To be disallowed, a bribe or kickback must be illegal under either Federal or state law and also must subject the payor to a criminal penalty or the loss of a license or privilege to engage in a trade or business. For a bribe or kickback that is illegal under state law, a deduction is denied if the state law is generally enforced.

During the year, Jean-Paul, an insurance salesperson, paid $5,000 to Karen, a real estate broker. The payment represented 20% of the commissions Jean-Paul earned from customers referred by Karen. Under state law, the splitting of commissions by an insurance salesperson is an act of misconduct that could warrant a revocation of the salesperson's license.

Jean-Paul's $5,000 payments to Karen are not deductible if the state law is generally enforced.

Legal Expenses Incurred in Defense of Civil or Criminal Penalties

To deduct legal expenses, the taxpayer must be able to show that the origin and character of the claim are related directly to (1) a trade or business or (2) an income-producing activity. Personal legal expenses are not deductible. As a result, legal fees incurred in connection with a criminal defense are deductible only if the crime is associated with the taxpayer's trade or business or income-producing activity.[33]

---

[30] § 162(f)(1).

[31] *Tank Truck Rentals, Inc. v. Comm.*, 58–1 USTC ¶9366, 1 AFTR 2d 1154, 78 S.Ct. 507.

[32] §§ 162(c), (f), and (g).

[33] *Comm. v. Tellier*, 66–1 USTC ¶9319, 17 AFTR 2d 633, 86 S.Ct. 1118.

Global Tax Issues — Overseas Gun Sales Result in Large Fines

The Foreign Corrupt Practices Act (FCPA) is intended to punish taxpayers who make illegal payments to foreign officials to obtain economic advantages. Besides such payments (usually improperly recorded as business expenses) being nondeductible for income tax purposes, serious and consistent violations can lead to the imposition of fines. Severe consequences can result from violating the bribery provisions of the FCPA, as Smith & Wesson discovered.

Smith & Wesson is a Massachusetts-based firearms manufacturer that wanted to begin selling firearms in India, Pakistan, and other foreign countries. As a small player in this international market, company officials decided to provide gifts to government officials in these countries to encourage them to do business with Smith & Wesson. This turned out to be a costly mistake. Smith & Wesson had profits of only $100,000 from this scheme before it was uncovered, and in 2014, it agreed to pay the Securities and Exchange Commission fines of more than $2 million. Of course, the fines are not deductible because they are a violation of public policy [§ 162(f)].

Source: **sec.gov/news/press-release/2014-148.**

Debra, a financial officer of Blue Corporation, incurs legal expenses in connection with her defense in a criminal indictment for evasion of Blue's income taxes.

Debra's legal expenses relate to her role as an employee because she is deemed to be in the trade or business of being an executive. The legal action impairs her ability to conduct this business activity.[34] However, since these legal expenses are employee business expenses, they are classified as a miscellaneous itemized deduction (and not deductible from 2018 through 2025).

The following legal expenses are deductible *for* AGI:

- Ordinary and necessary expenses incurred in connection with a trade or business.
- Ordinary and necessary expenses incurred in conjunction with rental or royalty property held for the production of income.

Legal expenses for tax advice relative to the preparation of an individual's income tax return are a miscellaneous itemized deduction (and not deductible from 2018 through 2025). On the other hand, legal fees for tax advice relative to the preparation of the portion of the tax return for a sole proprietor's trade or business (Schedule C) or an individual's rental or royalty income (Schedule E) are a *for* AGI deduction.

Example 23

Gabriela received an invoice from MJY LLC (a law firm) for $5,000 for the following services performed in 2023:

- $1,200 (advising on a lawsuit filed against her sole proprietorship).
- $800 (advising on a dispute with a tenant who lives in a duplex she owns and rents).
- $1,300 (fees related to preparing and filing her Form 1040).
- $1,700 (fees for preparing a will).

The $1,700 in fees for preparing her will is a personal expense and is not deductible. The $1,300 for preparing and filing her Form 1040 is a miscellaneous itemized deduction (and currently is not deductible). The balance of the legal fees ($2,000) is deductible when paid.

The $1,200 for the sole proprietorship is deducted on Schedule C (Form 1040) as a *for* AGI deduction. The $800 related to the duplex is a rental expense and is deducted on Schedule E as a *for* AGI deduction.

Expenses Relating to an Illegal Business

The ordinary and necessary expenses of operating an illegal business (e.g., a gambling operation) are deductible.[35] Although allowing deductions for illegal activity may seem inappropriate, this is necessary because the law taxes net income from a business

[34]Rev.Rul. 68–662.

[35]*Comm. v. Sullivan*, 58–1 USTC ¶9368, 1 AFTR 2d 1158, 78 S.Ct. 512.

operation, not gross revenue. However, § 162 disallows a deduction for fines, bribes to public officials, illegal kickbacks, and other illegal payments whether these payments are part of a legal or illegal business.

Example 24

Sam owns and operates an illegal gambling establishment. In connection with this activity, he has the following expenses during the year:

Rent	$ 60,000
Payoffs to the police	40,000
Depreciation on equipment	100,000
Wages	140,000
Interest	30,000
Criminal fines	50,000
Illegal kickbacks	10,000
Total	$430,000

All of the usual expenses (rent, depreciation, wages, and interest) are deductible; payoffs, fines, and kickbacks are not deductible. Of the $430,000 spent, $330,000 is deductible and $100,000 is not.

An exception applies to expenses incurred in illegal trafficking in drugs.[36] *Drug dealers* are not allowed a deduction for ordinary and necessary business expenses incurred in their business, except for cost of goods sold.[37]

Assume in Example 24 that instead of an illegal gambling business, Sam was operating an illegal drug business. Also assume that the $100,000 was not for depreciation, but for the cost of the drugs sold.

Of the $430,000 spent, only $100,000 (the cost of goods sold) is deductible. Also note that to claim the cost of goods sold as a deduction, Sam will need documentation supporting the purchases.

Ethics & Equity **State Allowed Marijuana Activity: Do Regular Business Deduction Rules Apply (or Those for Drug Dealers)?**

Cole England operates Herbal Center in Sacramento, California, as a sole proprietorship. The distribution of marijuana for medical purposes as well as nonmedical use by adults is legal in California.

This is Cole's first year of business operations, and he reports the following tax information:

Revenues	$200,000
Cost of goods sold	120,000
Other business expenses	50,000

Cole reported $30,000 of net income on Schedule C this year for Herbal Center. Is this reporting appropriate?

6-3b **Political Contributions and Lobbying Activities**

Generally, no business deduction is allowed for direct or indirect payments for political purposes.[38] The government has been reluctant to allow these deductions since it might encourage abuses and enable businesses to have undue influence on the political process.

[36] § 280E.

[37] Reg. § 1.61–3(a). Gross income is defined as sales minus cost of goods sold. Thus, although § 280E prohibits any deductions for drug dealers, it does not modify the normal definition of gross income.

[38] § 276.

The Big Picture

Example 26

Refer to the facts of *The Big Picture* on p. 6-1. Dr. Payne had made political contributions to the State Senate campaigns of Tom Smith and Virginia White. Dr. Payne made these contributions to encourage these senators to support a new bill that is beneficial to the state's dental profession. Therefore, he assumed that these would be deductible business expenses.

However, political contributions are not deductible, so he will receive no tax benefit from them.

Lobbying expenses incurred in attempting to influence local, state, or Federal legislation or the actions of certain high-ranking public officials are not deductible.[39] The disallowance also applies to a pro rata portion of the membership dues of trade associations and other groups that are involved in lobbying activities.

The Big Picture

Example 27

Refer to the facts of *The Big Picture* on p. 6-1. Dr. Payne had made contributions to The Dental Society, a trade association for dentists. The trade association estimates that 70% of its dues are allocated to lobbying activities. As a result, his deduction on Schedule C is limited to $3,000 ($10,000 × 30%).

There are two exceptions to the disallowance of lobbying expenses. First, the disallowance provision does not apply to activities devoted solely to monitoring legislation. Second, a *de minimis* exception is provided for annual in-house expenditures (lobbying expenses other than those paid to professional lobbyists or any portion of dues used by associations for lobbying) if such expenditures do not exceed $2,000. If the in-house expenditures exceed $2,000, none of the in-house expenditures can be deducted.

Example 28

The city of Florence, Tennessee, is considering spending $1,000,000 to build a sports complex that will host youth baseball and softball tournaments. Julie, who owns a local hotel, spends $1,500 on lobbying (not paid to a professional lobbyist) to persuade the five members of the Florence City Council to support the project.

The $1,500 is deductible as a lobbying expense since it meets the *de minimis* exception.

6-3c Excessive Executive Compensation

The deduction of executive compensation normally is subject to two limitations. As discussed earlier, the compensation of shareholder-employees of closely held corporations is subject to the reasonableness requirement. The second limitation, known as the millionaires' provision, applies to publicly held corporations, including foreign corporations traded on U.S. exchanges.

The millionaires' provision does not limit the amount of compensation that can be paid to an employee. Instead, it limits the amount the employer can deduct for the taxable compensation of a covered executive to $1 million annually. Covered employees are anyone serving as the chief executive officer (CEO) or the chief financial officer (CFO) during the year and the next three most highly compensated executives. Designation as a covered employee is permanent even if the employee takes a different position in the company. As a result, the compensation deduction for any of these covered employees will be permanently capped at $1 million per year.[40]

In general, the $1 million maximum applies to compensation, commissions based on individual performance, and performance-based compensation tied to overall company performance. Before 2018, the $1 million limit *excluded* commissions and performance-based compensation. Contracts in place on November 2, 2017, are grandfathered into pre-2018 law as long as there are no material changes to the contract.

[39] § 162(e).

[40] § 162(m). For taxable years beginning after December 31, 2026, this provision will also apply to a second group of employees: the five highest compensated employees that are not included in the first group of covered employees. This second group of covered employees—not limited to officers—does not permanently retain this status in subsequent tax years.

Example 29

Yvette became CEO of Lowe's Depot, a home supply store and a publicly traded corporation on May 1, 2023 (the date her contract was signed by Yvette and the Board of Lowe's Depot). For 2023, her compensation package consists of the following:

Cash compensation	$1,800,000
Taxable fringe benefits	100,000
Bonus from a qualified bonus plan tied to company performance	5,000,000

Lowe's Depot can deduct only $1,000,000 of her compensation.

6-3d **Investigation of a Business**

Investigation expenses are expenses paid or incurred to determine the feasibility of entering a new business or expanding an existing business. They include such costs as travel, engineering and architectural surveys, marketing reports, and various legal and accounting services. How such expenses are treated for tax purposes depends on a number of variables, including the following:

- The current business, if any, of the taxpayer.
- The nature of the business being investigated.
- The extent to which the investigation has proceeded.
- Whether the acquisition actually takes place.

If the taxpayer is in a business that is the *same as or similar to* that being investigated, all investigation expenses are deductible in the year paid or incurred. The tax result is the same whether or not the taxpayer acquires the business being investigated.[41]

The Big Picture

Refer to the facts of *The Big Picture* on p. 6-1. Dr. Payne believes that his administrative and business skills can be used to turn around dental practices whose revenues have been declining. He investigates Teeth Restoration LLC, a local dental practice that is for sale. Expenses paid to consultants and accountants as part of this investigation totaled $6,000. He determined that Teeth Restoration would not be a good investment, so he did not buy it.

The $6,000 spent to investigate this business is deductible as a business expense because Dr. Payne is already in the dental business. Expenses incurred to investigate new business opportunities in one's current trade or business are deductible as ordinary and necessary business expenses.

When the taxpayer is *not* in a business that is the same as or similar to the one being investigated, the tax result depends on whether the new business is acquired. If the business is not acquired, all investigation expenses generally are nondeductible.[42]

Example 31

Lynn, a retired merchant, incurs expenses in traveling from Rochester, New York, to California to investigate the feasibility of acquiring several auto care centers.

If no acquisition takes place, none of the expenses are deductible.

If the taxpayer is *not* in a business that is the same as or similar to the one being investigated and actually acquires the new business, the expenses must be capitalized as **startup expenditures**. Startup expenses are not deductible under § 162 because they are incurred *before* a business begins rather than in the course of carrying on a trade or business. The first $5,000 of the expenses is immediately deducted. Any excess over $5,000 is amortized over a period of 180 months (15 years). In arriving at the $5,000

[41] *York v. Comm.*, 58–2 USTC ¶9952, 2 AFTR 2d 6178, 261 F.2d 421 (CA–4).

[42] Rev.Rul. 57–418; *Morton Frank*, 20 T.C. 511 (1953); and *Dwight A. Ward*, 20 T.C. 332 (1953).

immediate deduction allowed, a dollar-for-dollar reduction must be made for those expenses in excess of $50,000.[43] An election can be made by the taxpayer not to deduct or amortize any portion of the startup costs. In that case, this intangible asset will remain on the balance sheet until the business is sold.

Dasha owns and operates 10 restaurants located in various cities throughout the Southeast. She travels to Atlanta to discuss the acquisition of an auto dealership. In addition, she incurs legal and accounting costs associated with the potential acquisition. After incurring total investigation costs of $52,000, she acquires the auto dealership on October 1, 2023.

Dasha may immediately deduct $3,000 [$5,000 − ($52,000 − $50,000)] and amortize the balance of $49,000 ($52,000 − $3,000) over a period of 180 months. For calendar year 2023, therefore, Dasha can deduct $3,817 [$3,000 + ($49,000 × 3/180)].

Concept Summary 6.1 depicts the tax rules related to the costs involved in investigating a business.

Concept Summary 6.1

Costs of Investigating a Business

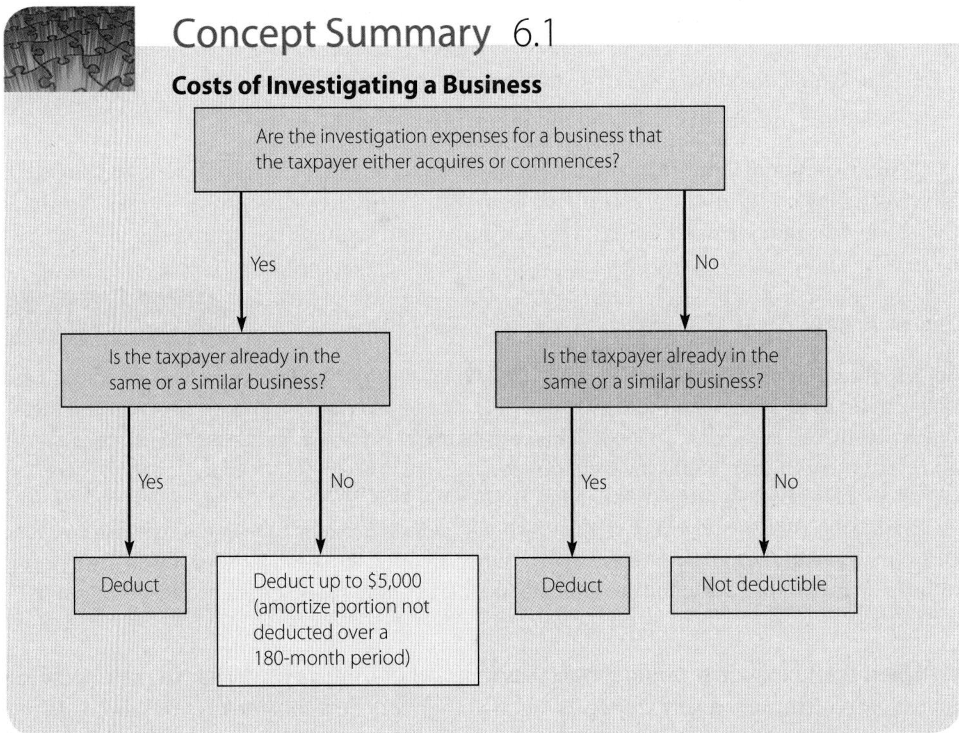

6-3e **Hobby Losses**

Business or investment expenses are deductible only if the taxpayer can show that the activity was entered into for the purpose of making a profit. Certain activities can have attributes that make it difficult to determine if the primary motivation for the activity is to make a profit or is for personal pleasure. Examples include raising horses and operating a farm used as a weekend residence.

Although personal losses are not deductible, losses attributable to profit-seeking activities may be deducted and used to offset a taxpayer's other income. Activities that have both personal and profit-seeking motives are classified as hobbies, and the tax law limits the deductibility of **hobby losses**.

The income and deductions from a hobby are reported separately on the tax return. The revenue for the hobby is always reported as other income [line 8j of Schedule 1 (Form 1040)]. The deductions (and how they are reported) are discussed in more detail below.

[43] § 195(b).

General Rules

If an individual can show that an activity has been conducted with the intent to earn a profit, losses from the activity are fully deductible (and reported, along with any income, on Schedule C). The hobby loss rules apply only if the activity is *not* engaged in for profit. Hobby expenses are deductible only to the extent of hobby income.[44]

The Regulations indicate that the following nine factors should be considered in determining whether an activity is profit-seeking or is a hobby:[45]

- Whether the activity is conducted in a businesslike manner.
- The expertise of the taxpayers or their advisers.
- The time and effort expended.
- The expectation that the assets of the activity will appreciate in value.
- The taxpayer's previous success in conducting similar activities.
- The history of income or losses from the activity.
- The relationship of profits earned to losses incurred.
- The financial status of the taxpayer (e.g., if the taxpayer does not have substantial amounts of other income, this may indicate that the activity is engaged in for profit).
- Elements of personal pleasure or recreation in the activity.

Whether an activity is profit-seeking or a hobby does not depend on the presence or absence of one of these factors. Rather, the decision is a subjective one that is based on an analysis of all of the facts and circumstances. Exhibit 6.4 provides a list of the activities that have been treated as hobbies. Concept Summary 6.2 provides more details on the nature of the nine factors identified in the Regulations.

Presumptive Rule of § 183

The Code provides a rebuttable presumption that an activity is profit-seeking if the activity shows a profit in at least three of the previous five tax years.[46] If the activity involves horses, a profit in at least two of the previous seven tax years meets the presumptive rule. If these profitability tests are met, the activity is presumed to be a trade or business rather than a personal hobby. If this is the case, the IRS must prove that the activity is personal rather than trade- or business-related. In all circumstances, the history of profits and losses is just one of the factors used in determining whether the activity is a hobby or business.

Example 33

Camille and Walter are married taxpayers who enjoy a busy lifestyle. Camille, who is an executive for a large corporation, is paid a salary of $800,000. Walter is a collector of antiques. Several years ago he opened an antique shop in a local shopping center and spends most of his time buying and selling antiques. He occasionally earns a small profit from this activity but more frequently incurs substantial losses. If Walter's losses are business-related, they are fully deductible against Camille's salary income on a joint return. In resolving this issue, consider the following:

- Initially determine whether Walter's antique activity has met the three-out-of-five years profit test.
- If the presumption is not met, the activity may nevertheless qualify as a business if Walter can show that the intent is to engage in a profit-seeking activity. It is not necessary to show actual profits.
- Determine if the operation is for profit, using the nine factors identified in the Regulations.

[44] § 183(b)(2).

[45] Reg. §§ 1.183–2(b)(1) through (9).

[46] § 183(d).

Exhibit 6.4 Activities That Have Been Classified as Hobbies

Acting	Dog Breeding	Operating a Bed & Breakfast
Aircraft Rentals	Farming	Operating a Talent Agency
Amway Distributorships	Fishing	Practicing Law
Art Work	Golfing	Sound Recordings
Auto Racing	Gunsmithing	Tax Shelters
Boat Chartering	Horse Breeding	Used Car Sales
Boat Racing	Making Movies and Videos	Venture Capitalization
Cattle Ranching	Mining and Drilling	Writing

Source: Internal Revenue Service Publication 5558: Activities Not Engaged in for Profit Audit Technique Guide (September 2021).

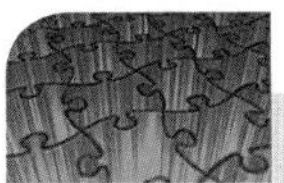

Concept Summary 6.2

Common Questions from the IRS Concerning Hobbies/Businesses with Losses

Whether the activity is conducted in a businesslike manner.

- Is there a written business plan?
- Is there business insurance? Is it covered in the company name?
- Are books and records maintained for the business?
- Is there a business license to operate?

The expertise of the taxpayers or their advisers.

- Does the taxpayer have any relevant education?
- Did the taxpayer prepare for the activity by conducting research or an extensive study of its accepted business, economic, and scientific practices?

The time and effort expended.

- How many hours are spent on this activity per week? Per month? Per year? Per season?
- Who is involved with the day-to-day business operations?

The expectation that the assets of the activity will appreciate in value.

- Were the assets held prior to starting the business?
- Has anyone ever offered to buy any of the assets?

The taxpayer's previous success in conducting similar activities.

- In what other activities has the taxpayer had previous success?
- Was the business ultimately profitable?

The history of income or losses from the activity.

- Is there a trend toward profitability?
- Did the taxpayer change operating methods, adopt new techniques, or abandon nonprofitable methods in a manner consistent with intent to improve profitability?

The relationship of profits earned to losses incurred.

- Is this a highly speculative business?
- What amount of investment has the taxpayer made in the business?

The financial status of the taxpayer.

- Does the taxpayer have substantial income or capital (e.g., investments) from other sources?
- Are there other economic reasons for the taxpayer to be engaged in the activity (e.g., reduced property taxes for farmland, low-interest loans, or federal grants)?

Elements of personal pleasure or recreation in the activity.

- Are elements of fun or recreation generally associated with it by the taxpayer, by members of the taxpayer's family, or by the taxpayer's friends?
- If there are any personal benefits to being in this business, are they substantial?

Source: Internal Revenue Service Publication 5558: Activities Not Engaged in For Profit Audit Technique Guide (September 2021).

Determining the Amount of the Deduction

If an activity is a hobby, any gross income (sales less cost of goods sold) generated is taxable. Other expenses are deductible only to the extent of the gross income from the hobby. These expenses must be deducted in the following order:

1. Amounts deductible under other Code sections without regard to the nature of the activity, such as property taxes and home mortgage interest.

2. Amounts deductible under other Code sections if the activity had been engaged in for profit, but only if those amounts do not affect adjusted basis (e.g., maintenance and utilities).
3. Amounts for depreciation, amortization, and depletion.[47]

Expenses included in items 2 and 3 are miscellaneous itemized deductions. From 2018 through 2025, *miscellaneous itemized deductions are not deductible*. Since property taxes and mortgage interest are deductible without the hobby revenue, the net effect is that the taxpayer is taxed on all of the gross income from the hobby.

Example 34

Stefan, the vice president of an oil company, has AGI of $180,000. He decides to pursue painting in his spare time. He uses a home studio exclusively for his painting; it comprises 10% of the home's square footage. During the current year, Stefan incurs the following expenses:

Frames	$ 2,800
Art supplies	900
Home studio expenses:	
Total home property taxes	2,000
Total home mortgage interest	10,000
Total home maintenance and utilities	4,600
Calculated depreciation on 10% of home	500

During the year, Stefan sold paintings for a total of $5,660. His cost of goods sold is $3,700 (the cost of the frames and art supplies) and his gross income is $1,960. If the activity is held to be a hobby, Stefan would determine his potential deductions under the hobby loss rules as follows:

Gross income	$ 1,960
Deduct: Property taxes and mortgage interest (10% of $12,000)	(1,200)
Remainder	$ 760
Deduct: Maintenance and utilities (10%)	(460)
Remainder	$ 300
Deduct: Depreciation ($500, but limited to $300)	(300)
Net income	$ -0-

Outcome: Stefan includes the $1,960 of gross income in AGI, making his AGI $181,960. The taxes and interest are itemized deductions, deductible in full. The remaining $760 of expenses are *miscellaneous itemized deductions and currently not deductible.*

Because the property taxes and home mortgage interest are deductible even without the hobby and no deduction is allowed for the other expenses, Stefan is taxed on his $1,960 of gross income.

6-3f Rental of Vacation Homes

Restrictions on the deductions allowed for part-year rentals of personal **vacation homes** prevent taxpayers from deducting essentially personal expenses as rental losses. Many taxpayers who own vacation homes use the property for personal use during a portion of the year and rent the property at other times. For example, assume that a summer cabin is rented for two months per year, used for a family vacation for one month, and left vacant the rest of the year. The issue is how to treat expenses during the nine months the cabin is vacant. If these expenses are allowed as rental expenses, a rental loss is likely to result (personal expenses have been converted to rental expenses). Code § 280A eliminates

[47]Reg. § 1.183–1(b)(1).

this treatment by not allowing a loss for property that is not used primarily for rental purposes. Deductions are only allowed to the extent of income received.

There are three possible tax treatments for residences used for both personal and rental purposes. The treatment depends upon the *relative time* the residence is used for personal purposes versus rental use. These rules are summarized in Concept Summary 6.3.

Primarily Personal Use

If the residence is *rented* for *fewer than 15 days* in a year, it is treated as a personal residence. The rent income is excluded from gross income, and mortgage interest and real estate taxes are allowed as itemized deductions, as with any personal residence.[48] No other expenses (e.g., depreciation, utilities, and maintenance) are deductible.

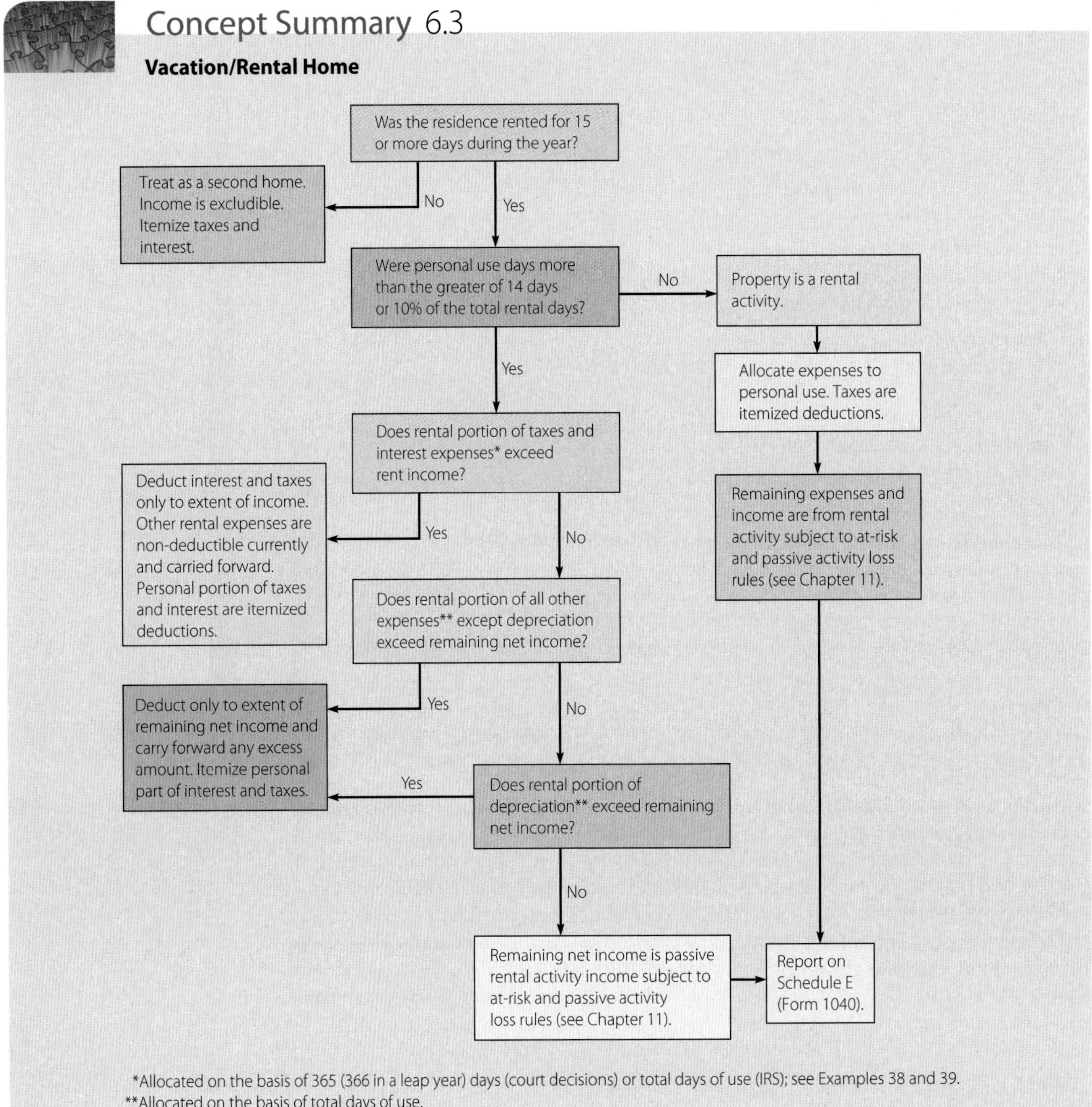

---

48 § 280A(g).

Example 35

Catherine owns a vacation cottage on the lake. During the current year, she rented it for $1,600 for two weeks, lived in it two months, and left it vacant the remainder of the year. The year's expenses amounted to $6,000 mortgage interest expense, $500 property taxes, $1,500 utilities and maintenance, and $2,400 depreciation.

Because the property was not rented for at least 15 days, the income is excluded, the mortgage interest and property tax expenses are itemized deductions, and the remaining expenses are nondeductible personal expenses.

Primarily Rental Use

If the residence is *rented* for 15 days or more in a year and is *not used* for personal purposes for more than the greater of (1) 14 days or (2) 10 percent of the total days rented, the residence is treated as rental property.[49] The expenses must be allocated between personal and rental days if there are any personal use days during the year. The real estate taxes allocated to the personal days are deductible as an itemized deduction. However, the mortgage interest allocated to the personal days cannot be deducted because the property is not a qualified residence. The deduction of the expenses allocated to rental days can exceed rent income and result in a rental loss. The loss may be deductible, subject to the at-risk and passive activity loss rules (discussed in Chapter 11).

Example 36

Assume instead that Catherine in Example 35 used the cottage for 12 days and rented it for 48 days for $4,800. The threshold for personal use is 14 days—the greater of (1) 14 days or (2) 4.8 days (10% × 48 rental days). Because she rented the cottage for 15 days or more but did not use it for more than 14 days, the cottage is treated as rental property. The expenses must be allocated between personal and rental days.

	Percentage of Use	
	Rental 80%	**Personal 20%**
Income	$4,800	$ -0-
Expenses		
Mortgage interest ($6,000)	($4,800)	($1,200)
Property taxes ($500)	(400)	(100)
Utilities and maintenance ($1,500)	(1,200)	(300)
Depreciation ($2,400)	(1,920)	(480)
Total expenses	($8,320)	($2,080)
Rental loss	($3,520)	$ -0-

Catherine deducts the $3,520 rental loss *for* AGI on Schedule E (assuming that she satisfies the at-risk and passive activity loss rules, discussed in Chapter 11). She also has an itemized deduction for property taxes of $100 associated with the personal use. The mortgage interest of $1,200 associated with the personal use is not deductible as an itemized deduction because the cottage is not a qualified residence (qualified residence interest) for this purpose (see Chapter 10). The portion of utilities and maintenance and depreciation attributable to personal use is not deductible.

Personal/Rental Use

If the residence is rented for 15 days or more in a year *and* is used for personal purposes for more than the greater of (1) 14 days or (2) 10 percent of the total days rented, it is treated as a personal/rental use residence. The expenses must be allocated between personal days and rental days. Expenses are allowed only to the extent of rent income.[50]

[49] § 280A(d) and Prop.Reg. § 1.280A–3(c).

[50] A related issue is whether a taxpayer's primary residence is subject to the preceding rules if it is converted to rental property. If the vacation home rules apply, a taxpayer who converts a personal residence to rental property during the tax year, without any tax-avoidance motive, could have the allowable deductions limited to the rent income. To prevent this from occurring, the personal use days will not cause the property to be treated as personal/rental if once the rental period begins, the property is rented for at least 12 consecutive months at a fair rental price (a qualified rental period).

Example 37

Assume instead that Catherine in Example 35 rented the property for 30 days and lived in it for 30 days. The threshold for personal use is 14 days—the greater of (1) 14 days or (2) 3 days (10% × 30 rental days).

The residence is classified as personal/rental use property because she used it more than 14 days and rented it for 15 days or more. The expenses must be allocated between rental use and personal use, and the rental expenses are allowed only to the extent of rent income.

If a residence is classified as personal/rental use property, the expenses that are deductible anyway (e.g., real estate taxes and mortgage interest) must be deducted first. If a positive net income results, expenses, other than depreciation, that are deductible for rental property (e.g., maintenance, utilities, and insurance) are allowed next. Finally, if any positive balance remains, depreciation is allowed. Any disallowed expenses allocable to rental use are carried forward and used in future years subject to the same limitations. Note that these ordering rules for deductions are the same as for hobby expenses.

Expenses must be allocated between personal and rental days before the limits are applied. The courts have held that real estate taxes and mortgage interest, which accrue ratably over the year, are allocated on the basis of 365 days (366 days in a leap year).[51] The IRS, however, disagrees and allocates real estate taxes and mortgage interest on the basis of total days of use.[52] Other expenses (e.g., utilities, maintenance, depreciation) are allocated on the basis of total days used.

Personal/Rental: IRS vs. Courts

Example 38

Jason rents his vacation home for 60 days and lives in the home for 30 days. The property is classified as personal/rental because it is rented for 15 days or more, and personal use (30 days) is greater than 14 [greater of 14 days or 6 days (10% × 60 rental days)]. Jason's gross rent income is $10,000. For the entire year, the real estate taxes are $2,190, his mortgage interest expense is $10,220, utilities and maintenance expense equals $2,400, and depreciation is $9,000.

Using the IRS approach, these amounts are deductible in this specific order:

Gross income	$10,000
Deduct: Taxes and interest ($^{60}/_{90}$ × $12,410)	(8,273)
Remainder to apply to rental operating expenses and depreciation	$ 1,727
Deduct: Utilities and maintenance ($^{60}/_{90}$ × $2,400)	(1,600)
Balance	$ 127
Deduct: Depreciation ($^{60}/_{90}$ × $9,000 = $6,000 but limited to above balance)	(127)
Net rent income	$ -0-

The nonrental use portion of real estate taxes and mortgage interest ($4,137 in this case) is deductible if the taxpayer elects to itemize (see Chapter 10). The personal use portion of utilities, maintenance, and depreciation is not deductible in any case.

Jason has a carryover of $5,873 ($6,000 − $127) of the unused depreciation, which he may be able to deduct in future years. Also note that the basis of the property is only reduced by the $127 depreciation allowed because of the above limitation. (See text Section 8-1c for a discussion of the reduction in basis for depreciation allowed or allowable.)

[51] *Bolton v. Comm.*, 82–2 USTC ¶9699, 51 AFTR 2d 83–305, 694 F.2d 556 (CA–9).

[52] Prop.Reg. § 1.280A–3(d)(4).

Personal/Rental: IRS vs. Courts

Example 39

Using the court's approach in allocating real estate taxes and mortgage interest, Jason, in Example 38, would have this result:

Gross income	$10,000
Deduct: Taxes and interest ($^{60}/_{365}$ × $12,410)	(2,040)
Remainder to apply to rental operating expenses and depreciation	$ 7,960
Deduct: Utilities and maintenance ($^{60}/_{90}$ × $2,400)	(1,600)
Balance	$ 6,360
Deduct: Depreciation ($^{60}/_{90}$ × $9,000 but limited to above balance)	(6,000)
Net rent income	$ 360

Jason can deduct $10,370 ($12,410 paid − $2,040 deducted as expense in computing net rent income) of personal use mortgage interest and real estate taxes as itemized deductions.

Note the contrasting results in Examples 38 and 39. The IRS's approach (Example 38) results in no rental gain or loss and an itemized deduction for real estate taxes and mortgage interest of $4,137. In Example 39, Jason has net rent income of $360 and $10,370 of itemized deductions. The court's approach decreases his taxable income by $10,010 ($10,370 itemized deductions less $360 net rent income). The IRS's approach reduces his taxable income by only $4,137.

6-3g **Expenditures Incurred for Taxpayer's Benefit or Taxpayer's Obligation**

To be deductible, an expense must be incurred for the taxpayer's benefit or arise from the taxpayer's obligation. An individual cannot claim a tax deduction for the payment of the expenses of another individual.

Example 40

During the current year, Carlos pays the property taxes on his son Jayden's home. Neither Carlos nor Jayden can take a deduction for the amount paid for Jayden's property taxes. Carlos is not entitled to a deduction because the property taxes are not his obligation. Jayden cannot claim a deduction because he did not pay the property taxes.

The tax result would have been more favorable had Carlos made a cash gift to Jayden and let him pay the property taxes. Then Jayden could have deducted the property taxes.

One exception to this disallowance rule is the payment of medical expenses for a dependent. These expenses are deductible by the payor subject to the normal rules that limit the deductibility of medical expenses (see Chapters 3 and 10).[53] The Tax Court has provided a different exception to this disallowance rule in the case of a mother who paid medical expenses and property taxes for her adult daughter, who was not her dependent.[54] The mother, who was not legally obligated to do so, paid medical providers and the city government directly on behalf of her daughter. The Tax Court ruled that the mother had, in substance, made a gift to her daughter in the amounts of the payments and deemed that the daughter had then paid the related medical expenses and property taxes. As a result, the daughter was permitted to take a deduction for these expenses on her return. Although this case provides substantial authority for these deductions, when planning with taxpayers, it is better to have the donor make the gift directly to the donee and then have the donee pay the expenses.

[53] § 213(a).

[54] *Judith F. Lang*, 100 TCM 603, T.C.Memo. 2010–286.

6-3h Disallowance of Personal Expenditures

In general, no deduction is allowed for personal, living, or family expenses.[55] To justify a deduction, an individual must be able to identify a particular section of the Code that permits the deduction (e.g., charitable contributions and medical expenses).

Ethics & Equity **Personal or Business Expenses?**

For the last eight years, Jaynice and her family have lived in a large Victorian house in New England. In the current year, Jaynice and her husband decide to convert the home into a bed-and-breakfast. The family (including the two children and the dog) moves into the basement, which accounts for 30 percent of the square footage of the house. The basement has two bedrooms, two baths, a den, and a small kitchen. The upper two floors of the house are used for the bed-and-breakfast, which is operated as a sole proprietorship.

Jaynice hires two employees to help her run the business. Total expenses for the first year of operation are as follows:

Mortgage interest	$18,000
Real estate taxes	3,000
Salaries for two employees	40,000
Groceries for breakfast and snacks	7,000
Depreciation	10,000

For breakfast, all of the family members eat the same food that is prepared for the guests. They usually also share in the homemade cookies and cakes in the evening.

On Jaynice's Schedule C for the business, she deducts $78,000 of expenses for the current tax year. Discuss whether these deductions are appropriate.

6-3i Disallowance of Deductions for Capital Expenditures

A deduction is not allowed for amounts paid for new buildings or for permanent improvements or betterments that increase the value of any property.[56] Incidental repairs and maintenance of the property are not capital expenditures and can be deducted as ordinary and necessary business expenses. Repairing a roof is a deductible expense, but replacing a roof is a capital expenditure subject to depreciation deductions over its recovery period. The tune-up of a delivery truck is an expense; a complete engine overhaul probably is a capital expenditure. Adding new gravel to a gravel parking lot is a repair, but paving the parking lot is a capital expenditure because this is doing more than restoring the asset to its original condition.

All costs incurred in acquiring or producing a unit of property (UOP) are included in its cost, except for employee compensation and overhead costs. The taxpayer can elect to capitalize employee compensation and overhead costs (can elect separately or both). The cost includes all related expenditures incurred before the date the asset is placed in service, even if these expenditures would be repairs if incurred after the asset was placed in service. The cost of a UOP includes costs incurred to obtain a clean title and investigation costs.[57] Material or supplies that cost $200 or less can generally be deducted in the first tax year they are used or consumed.[58]

Example 41

Capitalize or Expense

In year 1, Corporation Biz purchases 100 cell phones for its employees to use, each phone costing $130. Each cell phone is considered to be a unit of property. During year 1, 60 of the phones are put into use. The remaining phones are not used until year 2.

Since the cell phones cost less than $200, they are considered to be material and supplies. As a result, 60 of the phones can be expensed in year 1 ($7,800). The remaining 40 phones cannot be expensed until they are put into use in year 2.

[55] § 262.
[56] § 263(a)(1).
[57] Reg. § 1.263(a)–3(e)(1).
[58] Reg. § 1.162–3(a)(1).

Capitalize or Expense

Example 42

Jared owns a building that has 10 apartments. During the current year, one of the apartments needed a new stove. Jared paid $800 for the stove, including $75 of sales tax. He also paid $50 for the stove to be delivered and an extra $60 for it to be installed.

The stove is considered to be a unit of property, and all of these costs are included in its basis. Therefore, $910 ($800 + $50 + $60) is capitalized for the stove and this amount will be depreciated.

A single UOP includes all components that are functionally interdependent. Thus, a building includes, for example, the walls, floors, ceilings, roof, windows, doors, electrical systems, plumbing, and heating and air systems. The major exception to this rule is that if a component is treated separately for depreciation purposes, it will not be grouped into another UOP.[59]

Taxpayers can elect under the *de minimis* safe harbor election to expense outlays for lower-cost items. The election is irrevocable. This safe harbor applies if the taxpayer:

- Has written procedures in place at the beginning of the tax year that provide for the expensing of amounts below a specified dollar amount or that have a useful life of 12 months or less.
- Also expenses the items for its accounting/book records.
- Ensures that items costing more than $5,000 are capitalized [$2,500 if the company does not have applicable (generally meaning audited) financial statements].

The *de minimis* safe harbor election cannot be made for inventory, land, and certain types of spare parts.[60]

Freight Car Unlimited builds railroad cars and has adopted a written policy providing that any item purchased for $5,000 or less will be expensed for both financial reporting and tax purposes. Freight Car has audited financial statements.

During the current tax year, Freight Car purchases 120 laptop computers that cost $2,700 each. These computers do not have to be capitalized and will be expensed in Freight Car's current-year tax return.

Routine maintenance to keep UOPs operating efficiently is expensed, such as testing, cleaning, inspecting, and replacing parts. To be routine, the expectation is that the expenditure will be needed more than once during the asset's life. An expense cannot be treated as routine maintenance if it improves a UOP (treated as a betterment). A cost is treated as a betterment if it:

- Enlarges or increases the capacity of a UOP.
- Materially increases the productivity, efficiency, or quality of the UOP.[61]

Qualifying small taxpayers (those with $10 million or less of average annual gross receipts in the three preceding tax years) can deduct improvements made to an eligible building property (one with an unadjusted basis of $1 million or less). The safe harbor election applies only if the total amount paid during the tax year for repairs, maintenance, improvements, and similar activities performed on the eligible building does not exceed the lesser of $10,000 or 2 percent of the building's unadjusted basis.[62]

Capitalization versus Expense

When an expenditure is for a tangible asset that has an ascertainable life, it is capitalized and may be deducted as depreciation (or cost recovery) over its depreciable life. Land is not subject to depreciation (or cost recovery) because it does not have an ascertainable life. [See Chapter 8 for a discussion of depreciation (cost recovery).]

[59]Reg. § 1.263(a)–3(e).

[60]Reg. § 1.263(a)–1(f)(1).

[61]Reg. § 1.263(a)–3(i)(1).

[62]Reg. § 1.263(a)–3(h)(1) and Rev.Proc. 2015–14.

Stan purchased a prime piece of land located in an apartment-zoned area. Stan paid $500,000 for the property, which had an old but usable apartment building on it. He immediately had the building demolished at a cost of $100,000.

The $500,000 purchase price and the $100,000 demolition costs must be capitalized, and the basis of the land is $600,000. Because land is a nondepreciable asset, no deduction is allowed.

If the expenditure is for an intangible asset (e.g., copyright, patent, covenant not to compete, and goodwill), the capitalized expenditure can be amortized regardless of whether the intangible asset has an ascertainable life. Intangible assets, referred to as § 197 intangibles, are amortized over a 15-year statutory period using the straight-line method. See Chapter 8 for additional discussion of the amortization of intangibles.

Elite Fireworks purchased all of the assets of Interstate Fireworks for $2,000,000. The fair market value of Interstate's assets is $1,400,000.

The additional $600,000 paid is allocated to goodwill. The goodwill is a § 197 intangible asset and will be amortized over 15 years.

6-3j Transactions between Related Parties

The Code places restrictions on the recognition of losses from **related-party transactions**. Without these restrictions, relationships created by birth, marriage, and business would provide endless possibilities for engaging in financial transactions that produce tax savings with no real economic substance or change. For example, to create an artificial loss, a wife could sell investment property to her husband at a loss and deduct the loss on their joint return. Her husband could then hold the asset indefinitely, and the family would sustain no real economic loss. A complex set of rules has been designed to eliminate these possibilities.

Relationships and Constructive Ownership

Before reviewing the tax consequences of related-party sales, it is important to know the individuals and business entities that are considered to be related parties. *Related parties* include the following:

- Brothers and sisters (whether whole, half, or adopted), spouse, ancestors (parents and grandparents), and lineal descendants (children and grandchildren) of the taxpayer.
- A corporation that is owned more than 50 percent (directly or indirectly) by the taxpayer.
- Two corporations that are members of a controlled group.
- A series of other complex relationships between trusts, corporations, partnerships, and individual taxpayers.

Constructive ownership provisions are applied to determine whether the taxpayers are related. Under these provisions, stock owned by certain relatives or related entities is *deemed* to be owned by the taxpayer for purposes of applying the loss disallowance provisions. For example, a taxpayer is deemed to own not only his or her stock but also the stock owned by lineal descendants, ancestors, brothers and sisters or half-brothers and half-sisters, and spouse.

The stock of Sparrow Corporation is owned 20% by Ted, 30% by Ted's father, 30% by Ted's mother, and 20% by Ted's sister. Although Ted actually owns only 20% of Sparrow Corporation, he is *deemed* to own the stock owned by his father (30%), mother (30%), and sister (20%).

As a result, Ted directly and indirectly owns 100% of Sparrow Corporation, and Ted and Sparrow are related parties. The same outcome (100% direct and indirect ownership) results for all of the shareholders in this example.

Losses

Losses are disallowed from sales or exchanges of property between related parties.[63] A right of offset is created equal to the disallowed loss. When the property is subsequently sold to a nonrelated party, any gain recognized is reduced by the right of offset. However, the right of offset cannot create or increase a loss. Any right of offset is permanently lost if it is not used by the related-party buyer to offset some or all of the recognized gain on a subsequent sale or exchange to an unrelated party.

Use of Right of Offset

Example 47

Ming sells common stock with a basis of $10,000 to her son, Jin, for its fair market value of $8,000. The $2,000 realized loss is not recognized, which creates a $2,000 right of offset. Jin sells the stock several years later for $11,000.

Ming's $2,000 loss is disallowed on the sale to Jin, and only $1,000 of gain ($11,000 selling price − $8,000 basis − $2,000 right of offset) is recognized by Jin on the subsequent sale.

Assume the same facts as in Example 47, except that Jin sells the stock for $9,500. Jin's gain of $1,500 ($9,500 selling price − $8,000 basis) is not recognized because of the right of offset of $2,000 from Ming's sale. The remaining $500 right of offset is permanently lost.

Note that the offset may result in only partial tax benefit on the subsequent sale (as in this case). If Ming had sold the stock to an unrelated party rather than to Jin, she could have recognized a $2,000 loss. However, as a family unit, Ming and Jin recognized only $1,500 of loss.

6-3k **Substantiation Requirements**

The tax law is built on a voluntary compliance system. Taxpayers file their tax returns, report income and take deductions to which they are entitled, and pay their taxes through withholding or estimated tax payments during the year. The taxpayer has the burden of proof for substantiating expenses deducted on the returns and must retain adequate records. Upon audit, the IRS can disallow any undocumented or unsubstantiated deductions. These requirements have resulted in numerous conflicts between taxpayers and the IRS.

For example, *specific* and *more stringent* rules apply for deducting travel, entertainment, and gift expenses, which are discussed in Chapter 9. Certain mixed-use (both personal and business use) assets also are subject to more stringent documentation rules (see Chapter 8).

Substantiation is also important for establishing the basis of an asset (see Chapter 13). An asset's basis includes all costs incurred to place an asset in service, which includes transportation, sales tax, setup, testing, unpaid property taxes of the previous owner, and other purchase costs. Basis is used to determine gain or loss on a sale of the asset and to compute depreciation for depreciable assets. The taxpayer must document all expenses included in basis.

6-3l **Expenses and Interest Relating to Tax-Exempt Income**

Certain income, such as interest on municipal bonds, is tax-exempt.[64] The law also allows the taxpayer to deduct expenses incurred for the production of income.[65] However, expenses related to the production of tax-exempt income are not deductible.[66] Interest on debt used to purchase or hold tax-exempt financial instruments also is disallowed.

[63] § 267(a)(1).

[64] § 103.

[65] § 212.

[66] § 265.

Expenses Related to Tax-Exempt Income

Example 49

Sandy, a taxpayer in the 35% bracket, purchased $100,000 of 6% municipal bonds. At the same time, she used the bonds as collateral on a bank loan of $100,000 at 8% interest. A positive cash flow would result from the tax benefit as follows:

Cash paid for interest expense on loan	($8,000)
Cash received as interest income from bonds	6,000
Net negative cash flow	($2,000)

Had the deduction of $8,000 been allowed for interest expense, this would have resulted in a tax benefit of $2,800 (35% × $8,000). In that case, a positive cash flow of $800 ($6,000 + $2,800 − $8,000) would have resulted.

In January of the current year, Alan borrowed $100,000 at 8% interest. He used the loan proceeds to purchase 5,000 shares of stock in White Corporation. In July, he sold the stock for $120,000 and reinvested the proceeds in City of Denver bonds, the income from which is tax-exempt.

Assuming that the $100,000 loan remained outstanding throughout the entire year, Alan cannot deduct the interest attributable to the period in which he held the tax-exempt bonds.

6-3m **Other Disallowances**

The following expenditures also are disallowed:

- Settlements or payments, including attorney's fees, related to sexual harassment or sexual abuse if subject to a nondisclosure disagreement.[67]
- Payments for qualified transportation fringe benefits, including mass transit and qualified parking.[68]
- Net interest expense, which is limited to business interest income plus 30 percent of adjusted taxable income. Any disallowed interest is carried forward indefinitely. The limitation does not apply to businesses that have annual average gross receipts of $29 million or less during the prior three taxable years.[69]

For 2023, Corporation NFL has $50,000,000 of adjusted taxable income, $1,000,000 of business interest income, and $20,000,000 of business interest expense. Interest expense is limited to $16,000,000, the sum of its $1,000,000 of business interest income plus 30% of its adjusted taxable income (30% × $50,000,000 = $15,000,000). The $4,000,000 of disallowed interest expense is carried forward to future tax years.

The classification of various expenses in terms of their deductibility and nondeductibility is reflected in Concept Summary 6.4.

LO.4

Identify tax planning opportunities for maximizing deductions and minimizing the disallowance of deductions.

6-4 Tax Planning

6-4a **Vacation Homes**

As discussed previously in this chapter, homes that are used for both personal and rental use can fall into one of three categories, all of which have different tax consequences. Therefore, careful tax planning often ensures that the home is classified into the category that provides the optimal tax result. For example, if a taxpayer is

[67] § 162(q).

[68] § 274(a)(4).

[69] §§ 163(j) and 448(c).

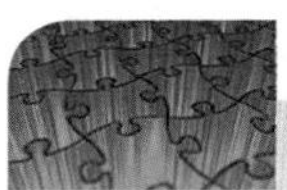

Concept Summary 6.4

Classification of Expenses

Expense Item	Deductible		Not Deductible	Applicable Code Section
	For AGI	From AGI		
Business				
Employee				
Reimbursed expenses[1]	X			§§ 162(a) and 62(a)(2)(A)
Teacher professional development and supplies	X			§ 62(a)(2)(D)
Commuting expenses			X	§ 262
Moving expenses			X	§ 217(k)
Meals and entertainment[1]			X[2]	§ 162(a)
Travel and transportation[1]			X[2]	§ 162(a)(2)
All other employee expenses[1]			X[2]	§ 162(a)
Self employed				
Entertainment			X	§ 274(a)(1)(A)
Meals[3]	X			§ 274(n)
Taxes	X			§§ 162, 164, and 62(a)(1)
Interest	X			§§ 162, 163, and 62(a)(1)
Bad debt	X			§§ 166 and 62(a)(1) or (3)
Casualty losses	X			§ 165(c)(1)
Rent	X			§§ 162 and 62(a)(1) or (4)
Other	X			§§ 162 and 62(a)(1)
Qualified Business Income (QBI) deduction		X		§ 199A
Investigation of a business	X			§§ 195, 162, and 62(a)(1)
Certain expenses of performing artists	X			§ 62(a)(2)(B)
Personal				
Medical		X		§ 213
Taxes				
Real property		X		§ 164(a)(1)
Personal property		X		§ 164(a)(2)
State and local income *or* sales tax		X		§§ 164(a)(3) and (b)(5)
Interest				
Qualified residence		X		§ 163(h)(3)
Student loan	X			§ 221
Other			X	§ 163(h)(1)
Qualified tuition and related expenses	X			§§ 62(a)(18) and 222
Charitable contributions		X		§ 170
Casualty losses		X		§ 165(c)(3)
All other personal expenses			X	§ 262
Investment/Production of Income				
Rent and royalty producing property investment expenses	X			§§ 212 and 62(a)(4)
Other income producing investment expenses				
Interest		X		§§ 212 and 163(d)(3)
Taxes		X		§§ 212 and 164
All other investment expenses			X[2]	§ 212

[1]Deduction for AGI if reimbursed, an adequate accounting is made, and employee is required to repay excess reimbursements.
[2]From 2018 through 2025, miscellaneous itemized deductions are not deductible.
[3]50% of meals related to business related activities are deductible. A 100% deduction was allowed for food and beverages provided by a restaurant in calendar years 2021 and 2022.

Note: A number of expenses listed above are subject to limitations that are discussed in subsequent chapters.

planning to rent a home for 15 or more days, this will subject the net income from the rental activity to taxation. If the homeowner could rent the home for 14 days or less (possibly just one less day), then all of the rental income received would escape taxation. This strategy is particularly attractive to individuals who live in areas where major sporting or entertainment events are held if there is a lack of hotel accommodations in the area.

In addition, assume that a taxpayer intends to use a home for 150 rental days and 16 personal days. Because the personal days exceed 15 (the greater of 14 days or 10% × the number of rental days), the property will be classified as *rental/personal* and a rental loss will not be allowed. However, if the owner can reduce the personal use days by only one day to 15, then the property will be classified as *rental*, and a rental loss can be allowed (subject to the passive activity loss rules).

6-4b **Hobby Losses**

To demonstrate that an activity has been entered into for the purpose of making a profit, a taxpayer should treat the activity as a business. The business should engage in advertising, use business letterhead stationery, and maintain a business phone.

If a taxpayer's activity earns a profit in three out of five consecutive years, the presumption is that the activity is engaged in for profit. It may be possible for a cash basis taxpayer to meet these requirements by timing the payment of expenses or the receipt of revenues. The payment of certain expenses incurred before the end of the year might be made in the following year. The billing of year-end sales might be delayed so that collections are received in the following year.

Keep in mind that the three-out-of-five-years rule under § 183 is not absolute. All it does is shift the burden of proof. If a profit is not made in three out of five years, the losses still may be allowed if the taxpayer can show that they are due to the nature of the business. For example, success in artistic or literary endeavors can take a long time, so losses for several years in a row could occur even for a legitimate business. Also, depending on the state of the economy, full-time farmers and ranchers may have losses for several consecutive years.

Merely satisfying the three-out-of-five-years rule does not guarantee that a taxpayer is automatically home free. If the three years of profits are insignificant relative to the losses of other years, or if the profits are not from the ordinary operation of the business, the taxpayer is vulnerable. The IRS may still be able to establish that the taxpayer is not engaged in an activity for profit.

Example 52

Ashley had the following gains and losses in an artistic endeavor:

2019	($50,000)
2020	(65,000)
2021	400
2022	200
2023	125

Under these circumstances, the IRS might try to overcome the presumption that this is a business because it has profits in three of the last five years. To do this, the IRS would focus on the nine factors from the Regulations discussed in text Section 6-3e.

On the other hand, if Ashley could show conformity with the factors enumerated in the Regulations or could show evidence of business hardships (e.g., injury, death, or illness), the government might have difficulty overriding the presumption.[70]

[70] *Faulconer, Sr. v. Comm.*, 84–2 USTC ¶9955, 55 AFTR 2d 85–302, 748 F.2d 890 (CA–4).

6-4c Do Deduction Limits Affect Executive Compensation?

Only $1 million of compensation can be deducted for the CEO, the CFO, and the three other highest compensated executives of publicly traded companies. However, this limitation did not apply to performance-based compensation before 2018. This exception was removed because it was broad enough to allow publicly traded companies to pay substantial compensation to executives and still receive a tax deduction.

For example, in 2014, the CEO of Microsoft received a base salary of $918,917, which was just under the $1 million limitation. However, he received bonuses and stock incentives of over $80 million, which qualified to be deducted under the performance-based exception.

The *Wall Street Journal* recently reported that the median pay for the CEOs of 425 major companies in 2021 exceeded $14 million, setting a sixth-straight annual record. Roughly two-thirds of CEO compensation is in the form of stock or stock-option awards. The median salary, bonus, and other cash compensation was $4.1 million.[71] The removal of the exception for performance-based compensation seems to have had no effect on the amount and type of executive compensation.

Refocus on The Big Picture

Calculation of Deductible Business Expenses and Tax Planning

Of the expenses incurred by Dr. Payne, several comments need to be made. Being personal in nature, none of the $5,000 monthly draw is deductible. Nor is the amount involved subject to the reasonableness test (see Example 7). Dr. Payne is a sole proprietor and not in an employment relationship. The fine paid for violating waste control rules comes under the public policy limitations (see Example 20) and is specifically made nondeductible by § 162(f). Along the same line, the political contributions (Example 26) are made nondeductible by § 162(e). However, Dr. Payne's investigation of the practice of another dental firm (Example 30) appears reasonable and the expense incurred is deductible. The dues paid to The Dental Society are not 100 percent deductible because 70 percent of the Society's efforts relate to lobbying activities (Example 27). Although not specifically discussed in the text, his legal fees incurred in connection with a lawsuit filed by a patient appear related to his practice (Example 22). As a result, they are deductible because they are ordinary and necessary to his trade or business.

What If?

From a tax planning perspective, should Dr. Payne calculate his deductible business expenses using the accrual method of accounting or the cash method?

In Chapter 4, we concluded that Dr. Payne could minimize his Federal income tax liability if he used the cash method of accounting. If the cash method is used for reporting the gross income of a Schedule C business, the cash method also must be used for reporting the deductible business expenses that will appear on Schedule C of Form 1040.

[71]Theo Francis, "Pay Packages for CEOs Rise to Record Level," *Wall Street Journal*, May 16, 2022, page B1.

Key Terms

Accounting method, 6-10
Deductions *for* adjusted gross income, 6-2
Deductions *from* adjusted gross income, 6-2
Hobby losses, 6-18
Ordinary and necessary, 6-5
Qualified business income (QBI), 6-7
Reasonableness, 6-5
Related-party transactions, 6-28
Startup expenditures, 6-17
Vacation homes, 6-21

Discussion Questions

1. **LO.1** "All income must be reported, and all deductions are allowed unless specifically disallowed in the Code." Discuss.

2. **LO.1** Michael earned $20,000 at the K-M Resort Golf Club during the summer prior to his senior year in college. He wants to make a contribution to a traditional IRA, but the amount is dependent on whether it reduces his taxable income. If Michael is going to claim the standard deduction, will a contribution to a traditional IRA reduce his taxable income? Explain.

3. **LO.1** Classify each of the following expenditures paid in 2023 as a deduction *for* AGI, a deduction *from* AGI, or not deductible:
   a. Roberto gives cash to his father as a birthday gift.
   b. Sandra gives cash to her church.
   c. Albert pays Dr. Dafashy for medical services rendered.
   d. Mia pays alimony to Bill according to a divorce decree entered last year.
   e. Rex, who is self-employed, contributes to his pension plan.
   f. Bonita pays expenses associated with her rental property.

4. **LO.1** Classify each of the following expenditures paid in 2023 as a deduction *for* AGI, a deduction *from* AGI, or not deductible:
   a. Barak contributes to his H.R. 10 plan (i.e., a retirement plan for a self-employed individual).
   b. Keith pays child support to his former wife, Renee, for the support of their son, Chris.
   c. Judy pays professional dues that are *not* reimbursed by her employer.
   d. Ted pays $500 as the monthly mortgage payment on his personal residence. Of this amount, $100 represents a payment on principal and $400 represents an interest payment.
   e. Oni pays a moving company for moving her household goods to Detroit, where she is starting a new job. She is not reimbursed by her employer.
   f. Ralph pays $6,000 of property taxes on his personal residence and $5,000 of state income taxes.

Critical Thinking

5. **LO.1** In 2023, Larry and Susan each invest $10,000 in separate investment activities. They each incur deductible expenses of $800 associated with their respective investments. Explain why Larry's expenses might not be deductible and Susan's expenses might be appropriately classified as deductions *for* AGI.

6. **LO.1** Nanette, a single taxpayer, is a first-grade teacher. Potential deductions are charitable contributions of $800, personal property taxes on her car of $240,

and various supplies purchased for use in her classroom of $225 (none reimbursed by her school). How will these items affect Nanette's Federal income tax return for 2023?

7. **LO.1** In the determination of whether a business expense is deductible, the reasonableness requirement applies only to salaries. Evaluate this statement.

8. **LO.1** Dave uses the second floor of a building for his residence and the first floor for his business. The uninsured building is destroyed by fire. Are the tax consequences the same for each part of the building? Explain. Critical Thinking

9. **LO.1** Monique owns a building that she leases to an individual who operates a grocery store. Rent income is $10,000, and rental expenses are $6,000. On what Form 1040 schedule or schedules are the income and expenses reported?

10. **LO.2** What is the "actually paid" requirement for the deduction of an expense by a cash basis taxpayer? Does actual payment ensure a deduction? Explain.

11. **LO.2** Aubry, a cash basis and calendar year taxpayer, decides to reduce his taxable income for the current year by buying $65,000 worth of supplies for his business on December 27, 2023. Aubry thinks it will take more than a year to use up the supplies.
    a. Can Aubry deduct the expenditure for 2023? Explain.
    b. Would your answer in part (a) change if Aubry bought the supplies because the seller was going out of business and offered a large discount on the price? Explain.

12. **LO.3** Clear, Inc., is a bottled water distributor. Clear's delivery trucks frequently are required to park in no-parking zones to make their deliveries. If the trucks are occasionally ticketed, can Clear deduct the fines that it pays? Explain.

13. **LO.3** Angelo, an agent for an airline manufacturer, is negotiating a sale with a representative of the U.S. government and with a representative of a developing country. Angelo's company has sufficient capacity to handle only one of the orders. Both orders will have the same contract price. Angelo believes that if his employer authorizes a $500,000 payment to the representative of the foreign country, he can guarantee the sale. He is not sure that he can obtain the same result with the U.S. government. Identify the relevant tax issues for Angelo. Critical Thinking

14. **LO.3** Stuart, an insurance salesperson, is arrested for allegedly robbing a convenience store. He hires an attorney who is successful in getting the charges dropped. Is the attorney's fee deductible? Explain.

15. **LO.3** Linda operates an illegal gambling operation. Which of the following expenses that she incurs can reduce taxable income?
    a. Bribes paid to city employees.
    b. Salaries to employees.
    c. Security cameras.
    d. Kickbacks to police.
    e. Rent on an office.
    f. Depreciation on office furniture and equipment.
    g. Tenant's casualty insurance.
    h. Utilities.

16. **LO.3** Gordon anticipates that being positively perceived by the individual who is elected mayor will be beneficial for his business. Therefore, he contributes to the campaigns of both the Democratic and Republican candidates. The Republican candidate is elected mayor. Can Gordon deduct any of the political contributions he made?

Critical Thinking

17. **LO.3** Melissa, the owner of a sole proprietorship, does not provide health insurance for her 20 employees. She plans to spend $1,500 lobbying in opposition to legislation that would require her to provide such insurance. Discuss the tax advantages and disadvantages of paying the $1,500 to a professional lobbyist rather than spending the $1,500 on in-house lobbying expenditures.

18. **LO.3** What limits exist on the deductibility of executive compensation? Do the limits apply to all types of business entities? Are there any exceptions to the limitations? Explain.

Critical Thinking

19. **LO.3** Blaze operates a restaurant in Cleveland. He travels to Columbus to investigate acquiring a business. He incurs expenses as follows: $1,500 for travel, $2,000 for legal advice, and $3,500 for a market analysis. Based on the different tax consequences listed below, describe the circumstances that were involved in Blaze's investigation of the business.
    a. Blaze deducts the $7,000 of expenses.
    b. Blaze cannot deduct any of the $7,000 of expenses.
    c. Blaze deducts $5,000 of the expenses and amortizes the $2,000 balance over a period of 180 months.

Critical Thinking
Planning

20. **LO.3** Karen and Andy own a beach house. They have an agreement with a rental agent to rent it up to 200 days per year. For the past three years, the agent has been successful in renting it for 200 days. Karen and Andy use the beach house for one week during the summer and one week during Thanksgiving. Their daughter, Sarah, a college student, has asked if she and some friends can use the beach house for the week of spring break. Advise Karen and Andy on how they should respond, and identify any relevant tax issues.

21. **LO.3** Hank was transferred from Arizona to North Dakota on March 1 of the current year. He immediately put his home in Phoenix up for rent. The home was rented May 1 to November 30 and was vacant during the month of December. It was rented again on January 1 for six months. What expenses related to the home, if any, can Hank deduct on his return? Which deductions are *for* AGI, and which ones are *from* AGI?

Critical Thinking
Decision Making
Planning

22. **LO.3** Ray loses his job as a result of a corporate downsizing. Consequently, he falls behind on the mortgage payments on his personal residence. His friend Sahar would like to make the delinquent mortgage payments for him.
    a. Could the payments be structured so that Ray can deduct the mortgage interest?
    b. Could the payment arrangement deny both Ray and Sahar a mortgage interest deduction?
    c. Could the payments be structured so that Sahar can deduct the mortgage interest?

Critical Thinking
Planning

23. **LO.3** Ella owns 60% of the stock of Peach, Inc. The stock has declined in value since she purchased it five years ago. She is going to sell 5% of the stock to a relative. Ella also is going to make a gift of 10% of the stock to another relative. Identify the relevant tax issues for Ella.

24. **LO.3** Jarret owns City of Charleston bonds with an adjusted basis of $190,000. During the year, he receives interest payments of $3,800. Jarret partially financed the purchase of the bonds by borrowing $100,000 at 5% interest. Jarret's interest payments on the loan this year are $4,900, and his principal payments are $1,100.
    a. What is Jarret's gross income from the interest income this year? Explain.
    b. Can Jarret deduct any interest expense this year? Explain.

25. **LO.3** In 2023, Blair Corporation paid its CEO base compensation of $700,000 and a performance bonus of $500,000; the CEO was hired in January 2021. How much of the compensation can Blair deduct? Discuss.

Computational Exercises

26. **LO.2** Shanna, a calendar year and cash basis taxpayer, rents property to be used in her business from Janice. As part of the rental agreement, Shanna pays $8,400 rent on April 1, 2023, for the 12 months ending March 31, 2024.
    a. How much is Shanna's deduction for rent expense in 2023?
    b. Assume the same facts, except that the $8,400 is for 24 months' rent ending March 31, 2025. How much is Shanna's deduction for rent expense in 2023?

27. **LO.2** Falcon, Inc., paid salaries of $500,000 to its employees during its first year of operations. At the end of the year, Falcon had unpaid salaries of $45,000.
    a. Calculate the salary deduction if Falcon is a cash basis taxpayer.
    b. Calculate the salary deduction if Falcon is an accrual basis taxpayer.

28. **LO.2** Meghan, a calendar year taxpayer, is the owner of a sole proprietorship that uses the cash method. On February 1, 2023, she leases an office building to use in her business for $120,000 for an 18-month period. To obtain this favorable lease rate, she pays the $120,000 at the inception of the lease. How much rent expense may Meghan deduct on her 2023 tax return?

29. **LO.3** Vella owns and operates an illegal gambling establishment. In connection with this activity, he has the following expenses during the year:

Rent	$ 24,000
Bribes	40,000
Travel expenses	4,000
Utilities	18,000
Wages	230,000
Payroll taxes	13,800
Property insurance	1,600
Illegal kickbacks	22,000

What are Vella's total deductible expenses for tax purposes?

30. **LO.3** Printer Company pays a $25,000 annual membership fee to a trade association for paper wholesalers. The trade association estimates that 60% of its dues are allocated to lobbying activities.
    a. What are Printer's total deductible expenses for tax purposes?
    b. Assume the same facts as above, except that the $25,000 was incurred for in-house lobbying expenses. What are Printer's total deductible expenses for tax purposes?

31. **LO.3** Stanford owns and operates two dry cleaning businesses. He travels to Boston to discuss acquiring a restaurant. Later in the month, he travels to New York to discuss acquiring a bakery. Stanford does not acquire the restaurant but does purchase the bakery on November 1, 2023.

    Stanford incurred the following expenses:

Total investigation costs related to the restaurant	$28,000
Total investigation costs related to the bakery	51,000

What is the maximum amount Stanford can deduct in 2023 for investigation expenses?

32. **LO.3** Tobias has a brokerage account and buys on the margin, which resulted in an interest expense of $20,000 during the year. Income generated through the brokerage account was as follows:

Municipal interest	$ 50,000
Taxable dividends and interest	350,000

How much investment interest can Tobias deduct?

Problems

33. LO.1 Amos is a self-employed tax attorney. He and Monica, his employee, attend a tax conference in Dallas sponsored by the American Institute of CPAs. The following expenses are incurred during the trip:

	Amos	Monica
Conference registration	$ 900	$900
Airfare	1,200	700
Taxi fares	100	-0-
Lodging in Dallas	750	300

a. Amos pays for all of these expenses. Calculate the effect of these expenses on Amos's AGI.

b. Would your answer to part (a) change if the American Bar Association had sponsored the conference? Explain.

Critical Thinking
Decision Making

34. LO.1 Daniel, age 38, is single and has the following income and expenses in 2023:

Salary income	$65,000
Net rent income	6,000
Dividend income	3,500
Payment of alimony (divorce finalized in March 2021)	12,000
Mortgage interest on residence	9,900
Property tax on residence	1,200
Contribution to traditional IRA	6,000
Contribution to United Church	2,100
Loss on the sale of real estate (held for investment)	2,000
Medical expenses	3,250
State income tax	2,300
Federal income tax	5,800

a. Calculate Daniel's AGI.

b. Should Daniel itemize his deductions *from* AGI or take the standard deduction? Explain.

Critical Thinking
Planning

35. LO.1 María, age 32, earns $60,000 working in 2023. She has no other income. Her medical expenses for the year total $6,000. During the year, she suffers a casualty loss of $9,500 when her apartment is damaged by flood waters (part of a Federally declared disaster area). María contributes $6,000 to her church and pays $4,000 of state income taxes. On the advice of her friend, María is trying to decide whether to contribute $5,000 to a traditional IRA. What effect would the IRA contribution have on María's itemized deductions?

36. LO.1 A list of the items that Faith sold and the losses she incurred during the current tax year is as follows:

Yellow, Inc. stock	$ 1,600
Faith's personal use SUV	8,000
Faith's personal residence	10,000
City of Newburyport bonds	900

She also had a theft loss of $1,500 on her uninsured business use car. Calculate Faith's deductible losses.

37. LO.1 Suzanne, a single taxpayer, operates a printing business as a sole proprietor. The business has two employees who are paid a total of $90,000 during 2023.

Assume that the business has no significant assets. During 2023, the business generates $150,000 of income and Suzanne's taxable income before the QBI deduction is $155,000.

a. What is Suzanne's qualified business income deduction?

b. What is Suzanne's qualified business income deduction if the facts are the same except that the business income is $250,000 and Suzanne's taxable income before the QBI deduction is $270,000?

38. **LO.2** Duck, an accrual basis corporation, sponsored a rock concert on December 29, 2023. Gross receipts were $300,000. The following expenses were incurred and paid as indicated: Critical Thinking Planning

Expense		Payment Date
Rental of coliseum	$ 25,000	December 21, 2023
Cost of goods sold:		
Food	30,000	December 30, 2023
Souvenirs	60,000	December 30, 2023
Performers	100,000	January 5, 2024
Cleaning of coliseum	10,000	February 1, 2024

Because the coliseum was not scheduled to be used again until January 15, the company with which Duck had contracted did not perform the cleanup until January 8–10, 2024.

a. Calculate Duck's net income from the concert for tax purposes for 2023.

b. Using the present value tables in Appendix E, what is the true cost to Duck if it had to defer the $100,000 deduction for the performers until 2024? Assume a 5% discount rate and a 21% marginal tax rate in 2023 and 2024.

39. **LO.3** Fynn incurred and paid the following expenses during 2023:

- $150 for a ticket for running a red light while he was commuting to work.
- $500 for a ticket for parking in a handicapped parking space.
- $300 to an attorney to represent him in traffic court as to the two tickets.
- $500 to an attorney to draft an agreement with a tenant for a one-year lease on an apartment that Fynn owns.
- $1,000 to an attorney to negotiate a reduction in his child support payments.
- $2,500 to an attorney to negotiate a reduction in his alimony payments to a former spouse.

Calculate the amount of Fynn's deductible expenses.

40. **LO.3** Trevor, a friend of yours from high school, works as a server at the ST Café. He asks you to help him prepare his Federal income tax return. When you inquire about why his bank deposits substantially exceed his tip income, he confides to you that he is a bookie on the side. Trevor then provides you with the following documented income and expenses for the year:

Tip income	$16,000
Gambling income	52,000
Gambling expenses	
Payouts to winners	29,000
Employee compensation	8,000
Bribe to police officer who is aware of Trevor's bookie activity	7,500

a. How will these items affect Trevor's AGI (ignore the impact of self-employment taxes)?

b. His taxable income (ignore the impact of self-employment taxes)?

Communications
Critical Thinking
Decision Making
Planning

41. **LO.3, 4** Ascend, a publicly held corporation, hired its current president, Lasya Lasisi, in September 2017 at a base salary of $1,000,000 plus a bonus that is contingent upon meeting certain performance targets. Every year since she was hired, Lasya has earned a substantial bonus. Her bonus in 2023 is expected to be $1,200,000, bringing her total compensation to $2,200,000. Ascend's Board of Directors is considering renegotiating Lasya's employment contract to provide a base salary of $2,000,000 with a new performance-based bonus that specifies new targets. Prepare a letter to Ascend's Board of Directors that identifies the amount of compensation that will be deductible by Ascend in 2023 and identifies any issues associated with changing the president's compensation and bonus plans. Address the letter to the board chairperson, Angela Riddle, whose address is 150 Erieview Tower, Cleveland, OH 44106.

42. **LO.3** Henrietta, the owner of a very successful hotel chain in the Southeast, is exploring the possibility of expanding the chain into a city in the Northeast. She incurs $35,000 of expenses associated with this investigation. Based on the regulatory environment for hotels in the city, she decides not to expand. During the year, she also investigates opening a restaurant that will be part of a national restaurant chain. Her expenses for this are $53,000. She proceeds with opening the restaurant, and it begins operations on September 1. Determine the amount that Henrietta can deduct in the current year for investigating these two businesses.

43. **LO.3** Terry traveled to a neighboring state to investigate the purchase of two hardware stores. His expenses included travel, legal, accounting, and miscellaneous expenses. The total was $52,000. He incurred the expenses in June and July 2023. Under the following circumstances, what can Terry deduct in 2023?

a. Terry was in the hardware store business and did not acquire the two hardware stores.

b. Terry was in the hardware store business and acquired the two hardware stores and began operating them on October 1, 2023.

c. Terry did not acquire the two hardware stores and was not in the hardware store business.

d. Terry acquired the two hardware stores but was not in the hardware store business when he acquired them. Operations began on October 1, 2023.

44. **LO.3** Jamari Peters (Social Security number 123-45-6789) operates a business with the following results in 2023:

Revenue	$20,000
Depreciation on car	3,960
Operating expenses of car	3,100
Rent	6,000
Wages	8,200
Amortization of intangibles	680

Jamari estimates that due to a depressed real estate market, the value of land owned by the business declined by $5,200.

a. Calculate the effect of Jamari's business on his AGI.

b. How would your answer in part (a) change if the activity was a hobby?

45. **LO.3** Alex, who is single, conducts an activity in the current year that is appropriately classified as a hobby. The activity produces the following revenues and expenses:

Revenue	$18,000
Property taxes	3,000
Materials and supplies	4,500
Utilities	2,000
Advertising	5,000
Insurance	750
Depreciation	4,000

Without regard to this activity, Alex's AGI is $62,000. Determine the amount of income Alex must report and the amount of the expenses he is permitted to deduct.

46. **LO.3** Piper owns a vacation cabin in the Tennessee mountains. Without considering the cabin, she has gross income of $65,000. During the year, she rents the cabin for two weeks for $2,500 and uses it herself for four weeks. The total expenses for the year are $10,000 mortgage interest; $1,500 property tax; $2,000 utilities, insurance, and maintenance; and $3,200 depreciation.

   a. What effect does the rental of the vacation cabin have on Piper's AGI?

   b. What expenses can Piper deduct, and how are they classified (i.e., *for* or *from* AGI)?

47. **LO.3** Adelene, who lives in a winter resort area, rented her personal residence for 14 days while she was visiting Brussels. Rent income was $5,000. Related expenses for the year were as follows:

Real property taxes	$ 3,800
Mortgage interest	7,500
Utilities	3,700
Insurance	2,500
Repairs	2,100
Depreciation	15,000

Determine the effect on Adelene's AGI.

48. **LO.3** During the year (not a leap year), Anna rented her vacation home for 30 days, used it personally for 20 days, and left it vacant for 315 days. She had the following income and expenses:

Rent income	$ 7,000
Expenses	
Real estate taxes	2,500
Interest on mortgage	9,000
Utilities	2,400
Repairs	1,000
Roof replacement (a capital expenditure)	12,000
Depreciation	7,500

   a. Compute Anna's net rent income or loss and the amounts she can itemize on her tax return, using the court's approach to allocating property taxes and interest.

   b. How would your answer in part (a) differ using the IRS's method of allocating property taxes and interest?

49. **LO.3** How would your answer to Problem 48 differ if Anna had rented the house for 87 days and had used it personally for 13 days? Use the IRS's method of allocating property taxes and interest.

50. **LO.1, 3** Chee, single, age 40, had the following income and expenses during 2023: Critical Thinking

Income	
Salary	$43,000
Rental of vacation home (rented 60 days, used personally 60 days, vacant 245 days)	4,000
Municipal bond interest	2,000
Dividend from General Electric	400
Expenses	
Interest on home mortgage	8,400
Interest on vacation home	4,758
Interest on loan used to buy municipal bonds	3,100
Property tax on home	2,200
Property tax on vacation home	1,098

State income tax	$3,300
State sales tax	900
Charitable contributions	1,100
Tax return preparation fee	300
Utilities and maintenance on vacation home	2,600
Depreciation on rental portion of vacation home	3,500

Calculate Chee's taxable income for the year. If Chee has any options, choose the method that maximizes his deductions.

Critical Thinking
Decision Making

51. LO.1, 3, 4 Elisa and Clyde operate a retail sports memorabilia shop. For the current year, sales revenue is $75,000 and expenses are as follows:

Cost of goods sold	$30,000
Advertising	1,000
Utilities	2,000
Rent	4,500
Insurance	1,500
Wages to Boyd	9,000

Elisa and Clyde pay $9,000 in wages to Boyd, a part-time employee. Because this amount is $1,000 below the minimum wage, Boyd threatens to file a complaint with the appropriate Federal agency. Although Elisa and Clyde pay no attention to Boyd's threat, Chelsea (Elisa's mother) gives Boyd a check for $1,000 for the disputed wages. The retail shop is the only source of income for Elisa and Clyde.

a. Calculate Elisa and Clyde's AGI.

b. Can Chelsea deduct the $1,000 payment on her tax return? Explain.

c. How could the tax position of the parties be improved?

Communications
Decision Making
Planning

52. LO.3, 4 Brittany Callihan sold stock (basis of $184,000) to her son, Ridge, for $160,000, the fair market value.

a. What are the tax consequences to Brittany?

b. What are the tax consequences to Ridge if he later sells the stock for $190,000? For $152,000? For $174,000?

c. Prepare your solution using spreadsheet software such as Microsoft Excel. The spreadsheet should compute the gain or loss for Ridge for all scenarios. Use the IF function to compute the right of offset.

d. Write a letter to Brittany in which you inform her of the tax consequences if she sells the stock to Ridge for $160,000. Explain how a sales transaction could be structured that would produce better tax consequences for her. Brittany's address is 32 Country Lane, Lawrence, KS 66045.

53. LO.3 For each of the following independent transactions, calculate the recognized gain or loss to the seller and the adjusted basis to the buyer.

a. Kiera sells Parchment, Inc. stock (adjusted basis $17,000) to Phillip, her brother, for its fair market value of $12,000.

b. Darnell sells land (adjusted basis $85,000) to his nephew, Boyd, for its fair market value of $70,000.

c. Susan sells a tax-exempt bond (adjusted basis $20,000) to her wholly owned corporation for its fair market value of $19,000.

d. Sinbad sells a business truck (adjusted basis $20,000) that he uses in his sole proprietorship to his cousin, Agnes, for its fair market value of $18,500.

e. Martha sells her partnership interest (adjusted basis $175,000) in Pearl Partnership to her adult daughter, Kim, for $220,000.

54. **LO.1, 3, 4** During the current year, Robert pays the following amounts associated with his own residence:

Communications
Critical Thinking
Decision Making
Planning

Property taxes	$ 3,000
Mortgage interest	8,000
Repairs	1,200
Utilities	2,700
Replacement of roof	14,000

In addition, Robert paid $1,500 of property taxes on the home that is owned and used by Anne, his daughter.

a. Which of these expenses can Robert deduct?

b. Can Anne deduct the $1,500 of property taxes?

c. Are the deductions *for* AGI or *from* AGI (itemized)?

d. How could the tax consequences be improved? Summarize your recommendation in an e-mail, and send it to your instructor.

55. **LO.3** For 2023, MSU Corporation has $500,000 of adjusted taxable income, $22,000 of business interest income, and $120,000 of business interest expense. It has average annual gross receipts of more than $29,000,000 over the prior three taxable years.

a. What is MSU's interest expense deduction?

b. How much interest expense can be deducted if MSU's adjusted taxable income is $300,000?

Tax Return Problems

Tax Forms Problem

ProConnect™ Tax

56. Roberta Santos, age 41, is single and lives at 120 Sanborne Avenue, Springfield, IL 62701. Her Social Security number is 123-45-6780. Roberta has been divorced from her former husband, Wayne, for two years. She has a son, Jason, who is 16, and a daughter, June, who is 18. Jason's Social Security number is 111-11-1112, and June's is 123-45-6788. Roberta has never owned or used a digital asset. She does not want to contribute $3 to the Presidential Election Campaign Fund.

Roberta, an advertising executive, earned a salary from ABC Advertising of $136,000 in 2022. Her employer withheld $16,000 in Federal income tax and $4,400 in state income tax.

Roberta has legal custody of Jason and June. The divorce decree provides that Roberta is to receive the dependency deductions for the children. Jason lives with his father during summer vacation. Wayne indicates that his expenses for Jason are $5,500. Roberta can document that she spent $8,500 for Jason's support during 2022. In prior years, Roberta gave a signed Form 8332 to Wayne regarding Jason. For 2022, she has decided not to do so. Roberta provides all of June's support.

Roberta's mother died on January 7, 2022. Roberta inherited assets worth $625,000 from her mother. As the sole beneficiary of her mother's life insurance policy, Roberta received insurance proceeds of $300,000. Her mother's cost basis for the life insurance policy was $120,000. Roberta's favorite aunt gave her $15,000 for her birthday in October.

On November 8, 2022, Roberta sells for $22,000 Amber stock that she had purchased for $24,000 from her first cousin, Walt, on December 5, 2017. Walt's cost basis for the stock was $26,000. On December 1, 2022, Roberta sold Falcon stock for $13,500. She had acquired the stock on July 2, 2018, for $8,000.

An examination of Roberta's records reveals that she received the following:

- Interest income of $2,500 from First Savings Bank.
- Groceries valued at $750 from Kroger Groceries for being the 100,000th customer.
- Qualified dividend income of $1,800 from Amber.
- Interest income of $3,750 on City of Springfield school bonds.
- Alimony of $16,000 from Wayne; divorce finalized in May 2020.
- Distribution of $4,800 from ST Partnership (Employer Identification Number: 46-4567893). Her distributive share of the partnership passive taxable income was $5,300. She had no prior passive activity losses. Assume that the qualified business income deduction applies and the W–2 wage limitation does not.

From her checkbook records, she determines that she made the following payments during 2022:

- Charitable contributions of $4,500 to First Presbyterian Church and $1,500 to the American Red Cross (proper receipts obtained).
- Payment of $5,000 to ECM Hospital for the medical expenses of a friend from work.
- Mortgage interest on her residence of $7,800 to Peoples Bank.
- Property taxes of $3,200 on her residence and $1,100 (ad valorem) on her car.
- $800 for landscaping expenses for residence.
- Estimated Federal income taxes of $2,800 and estimated state income taxes of $1,000.
- Medical expenses of $5,000 for her and $800 for Jason. In December, her medical insurance policy reimbursed $1,500 of her medical expenses.
- A $1,000 ticket for parking in a handicapped space.
- Attorney's fees of $500 associated with unsuccessfully contesting the parking ticket.
- Contribution of $250 to the campaign of a candidate for governor.

Because she did not maintain records of the sales tax she paid, she calculates the amount from the sales tax table to be $1,808.

Calculate Roberta's net tax payable or refund due for 2022. Use the appropriate forms and schedules. Suggested software: ProConnect Tax.

Communications
Critical Thinking
Decision Making
Planning
Tax Computation Problem

57. John and Mary Jane Diaz are married, filing jointly. Their address is 204 Shoe Lane, Blacksburg, VA 24061. John is age 35, and Mary Jane is age 30. They are expecting their first child in early 2024. John's salary in 2023 was $125,000, from which $22,800 of Federal income tax and $5,700 of state income tax were withheld. Mary Jane made $62,000 and had $5,600 of Federal income tax and $3,100 of state income tax withheld. The appropriate amounts of FICA tax and Medicare tax were withheld for John and for Mary Jane. John's Social Security number is 111-11-1111, and Mary Jane's Social Security number is 123-45-6789.

Both John and Mary Jane are offered medical insurance by their employers with 80% of the premiums being paid by the employers. Mary Jane declines coverage by her employer. The premium paid by John's employer for the family plan he receives is $21,350. Mary Jane received medical benefits of $7,300 under the plan. John was not ill during 2023. Mary Jane paid noncovered medical expenses of $1,300.

John makes child support payments of $15,000 for his son, Rod, who lives with Jill, John's former spouse, except for two months in the summer when he visits John and Mary Jane. At the time of the divorce, John worked for a Fortune 500 company and received a salary of $225,000. As a result of corporate downsizing, he lost his job.

Mary Jane's father lived with them until his death in November. His only sources of income were salary of $3,800, unemployment compensation benefits of $3,500, and Social Security benefits of $4,100. Of this amount, he deposited $6,000 in a savings account. The remainder of his support of $11,000, which included funeral expenses of $4,500, was provided by John and Mary Jane.

Other income received by the Diazes was as follows:

Interest on certificates of deposit	$3,500
Share of S corporation taxable income (distributions from the S corporation to Mary Jane were $1,100; assume no wage limitation for qualified business income deduction)	4,500
Award received by Mary Jane from employer for an outstanding suggestion for cutting costs	4,000

John has always wanted to operate his own business. In October 2023, he incurred expenses of $15,000 in investigating the establishment of a retail computer franchise. With the birth of their child expected next year, however, he decides to forgo self-employment for at least a couple of years.

John and Mary Jane made charitable contributions of $8,700 during the year and paid an additional $1,800 in state income taxes in 2023 upon filing their 2022 state income tax return. Their deductible home mortgage interest was $9,800, and their property taxes came to $4,800. They paid sales taxes of $2,000, for which they have receipts. They paid a ticket of $150 that Mary Jane received for running a red light (detected by a red light camera).

Part 1—Tax Computation
Calculate John and Mary Jane's tax (or refund) due for 2023.

Part 2—Tax Planning
Assume that the Diazes come to you for advice in December 2023. John has learned that he will receive a $40,000 bonus. He wants to know if he should take it in December 2023 or in January 2024. Mary Jane will quit work on December 31 to stay home with the baby. Their itemized deductions will decrease by $3,100 because Mary Jane will not have state income taxes withheld. Mary Jane will not receive the employee award in 2024. She expects the medical benefits received to be $9,000. The Diazes expect all of their other income items to remain the same in 2024. Write a letter to John and Mary Jane that contains your advice, and prepare a memo for the tax files.

Research Problems

Note: Solutions to the Research Problems can be prepared by using the Thomson Reuters Checkpoint™ online tax research database, which accompanies this textbook. Solutions can also be prepared by using research materials found in a typical tax library.

Communications
Critical Thinking

Research Problem 1. Gray Chemical Company manufactured pesticides that were toxic. Over the course of several years, the toxic waste contaminated the air and water around the company's plant. Several employees suffered toxic poisoning, and the Environmental Protection Agency cited the company for violations. In court, the judge found Gray guilty and imposed fines of $15 million. The company voluntarily set up a charitable fund for the purpose of bettering the environment and funded it with $8 million. The company incurred legal expenses in setting up the foundation and defending itself in court. The court reduced the fine from $15 million to $7 million.

Gray Chemical Company deducted the $8 million paid to the foundation and the legal expenses incurred. The IRS disallowed both deductions on the grounds that the payment was, in fact, a fine and in violation of public policy.

Gray's president, Ted Jones, has contacted you regarding the deductibility of the $7 million fine, the $8 million payment to the foundation, and the legal fees. Write a letter to Mr. Jones that contains your advice, and prepare a memo for the tax files. Gray's address is 200 Lincoln Center, Omaha, NE 68182.

Partial list of research aids:
§§ 162(a) and (f).
Reg. § 1.162–21(b).

Critical Thinking

Research Problem 2. Rex and Agnes Harrell purchased a beach house at Duck, North Carolina, in early 2023. Although they intended to use the beach house occasionally for recreational purposes, to help pay the mortgage payments, property taxes, and maintenance costs, they also planned to rent it through the realty agency that had handled the purchase. Rex is a surgeon, and Agnes is a counselor.

The beach house was in need of substantial repairs. Rather than hiring a contractor, Rex and Agnes decided they would make the repairs themselves. During both high school and college, Rex had worked summers in construction. In addition, he had taken an advanced course in woodworking and related subjects from a local community college several years ago.

During 2023, according to a log maintained by the Harrells, they occupied the beach house 38 days and rented it 49 days. The log also indicated that on 24 of the 38 days they occupied the beach house, one or both of them were engaged in work on the beach house. Their two teenage children were with them on all of these days but did not help with the work being done. On their 2023 income tax return, Rex and Agnes, who filed a joint return, treated the beach house as a rental property and deducted a pro rata share of the property taxes, mortgage interest, utilities, maintenance and repairs, and depreciation in determining their net loss from the beach home. In the current year, after examining their return, an IRS agent has limited the deductions to the rent income. He contends that the 14-day personal use provision was exceeded and that many of the alleged repairs were capital expenditures. Advise the Harrells on how they should respond to the IRS.

Critical Thinking

Research Problem 3. Mona viewed herself as a creative individual who had chosen to go to law school for economic reasons. Mona's undergraduate majors were creative writing and American Indian studies.

Mona was very successful as an attorney and eventually was admitted to partnership in her law firm, having an expertise in negotiating settlements involving Indian water rights.

While practicing law, Mona continued her interest in the arts. She had directed plays in high school and maintained her involvement in the theater, even during law school. She belonged to local theater organizations while she practiced law. She took several courses in filmmaking and read extensively in the area. She even took several months off from her legal practice to enroll in NYU's filmmaking program. Her enrollment in the program provided her with hands-on experience and taught her about the technical aspects of filmmaking and allowed her to meet individuals who would later work with her on her documentary.

When she discovered that her husband had similar interests, she decided to create a documentary about Way to Sing America. After acquiring the rights to all of the archival footage of Way to Sing America, she hired a video production company to film interviews that she conducted with Way to Sing America alumni (over 400 hours of such interviews). She spent weekends and nights over a three-year period working on the documentary.

Once the documentary was completed, Mona began marketing it at film festivals. At some of these festivals, her documentary received awards. At the same time, she developed a business plan, hired a bookkeeper to manage the finances, and hired an accounting firm to provide tax advice.

During this three-year period, she reported the following losses:

2020	$ 30,000
2021	400,000
2022	200,000

On her tax returns for the three-year period, in each year, she offset these amounts against her law firm income of approximately $1,000,000.

Upon audit by the IRS, the agent concluded that her filmmaking activity is a hobby and therefore the losses cannot be deducted except to the extent of the income generated.

Who is correct? Explain.

Use internet tax resources to address the following questions. Look for reliable websites and blogs of the IRS and other government agencies, media outlets, businesses, tax professionals, academics, think tanks, and political outlets.

Research Problem 4. Isabelle was contemplating making a contribution to her traditional IRA in 2023. She determined that she would contribute $6,000 in December 2023, but forgot about making the contribution until she was preparing her 2023 tax return in February 2024. Use the website of any well-known IRA provider (e.g., Fidelity, Vanguard, T. Rowe Price) to determine if Isabelle can make a 2023 contribution to her IRA after the tax year has ended.

Research Problem 5. The $1 million maximum compensation deduction does not seem to have deterred large corporations from remunerating their executives at very high levels. Do companies report their inability to deduct executive compensation to their shareholders? What might companies be trying to achieve with their compensation plans?

Research Problem 6. A qualified expense is not deductible unless there is appropriate substantiation to document it. Find two websites and/or articles that provide (1) guidance on the types of substantiation required for business expenses and (2) suggestions for taxpayers on how to collect this information and organize it.

Becker CPA Review Questions

Becker

1. Which of the following is a deduction *for* AGI?
   a. Charitable contributions of property.
   b. Bar Association dues paid by self-employed attorney.
   c. State income taxes.
   d. Mortgage interest paid on your primary residence.

2. Which of the following is *not* a deduction *for* AGI?
   a. Retirement contributions by a self-employed individual.
   b. Business rent on a self-employed business.
   c. Property taxes paid on your primary residence.
   d. One half of self-employment tax.

3. David is a CPA and enjoys playing the lottery. This year David won $10,000 in lottery scratch-off tickets. He spent $200 purchasing the tickets. Which statement is true regarding David's winnings?
   a. David must include $9,800 in gross income.
   b. David must include the $10,000 in gross income and can deduct $200 as an itemized deduction.
   c. David must include $10,000 in gross income and can deduct $200 as an adjustment to AGI.
   d. David's winnings are not taxable.

4. Bob is a farmer and is required to use the accrual method. At the beginning of the year, Bob has inventory, including livestock held for resale, amounting to $10,000. During the year, Bob purchased livestock totaling $3,000. Bob's ending inventory was $4,000. Bob's net sales for the year totaled $17,000. What is Bob's gross profit for the current year?

   a. $9,000
   b. $17,000
   c. $8,000
   d. $13,000

5. The Griffins own a mountain cabin that is used for both personal and rental purposes. In the current year, the Griffins rented the cabin out for 150 days and used it personally for 50 days. Assume that the Griffins itemize their deductions. Which of the following statements regarding the treatment of the mountain cabin on the Griffins' tax return is true?

   a. 100% of the utilities for the mountain cabin for the entire year are deductible.
   b. Depreciation is deductible under all rental circumstances.
   c. Real estate taxes are deductible under all rental circumstances.
   d. The rental income received is not included in gross income.

6. The Groves own a beach house as a second home. This year, the Groves used the beach house personally for four months. For 14 days during the summer, the Groves rented out their beach house for $5,000 total to friends. Which statement is true regarding the taxability of the Groves' beach house?

   a. $5,000 is included in gross income.
   b. Mortgage interest paid on the beach house is deductible.
   c. All repair expenses on the beach house are deductible.
   d. Depreciation expense on the beach house is deductible.

Chapter 7

Deductions and Losses: Certain Business Expenses and Losses

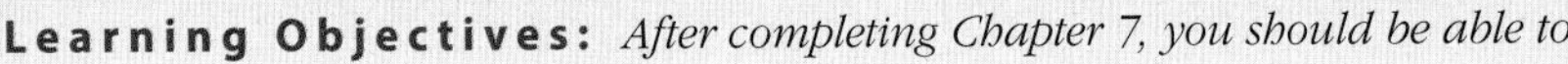

Learning Objectives: *After completing Chapter 7, you should be able to:*

- **LO.1** Determine the amount, classification, and timing of the bad debt deduction.
- **LO.2** Illustrate the tax treatment of worthless securities, including § 1244 stock.
- **LO.3** Distinguish between deductible and nondeductible losses of individuals.
- **LO.4** Identify a casualty and determine the amount, classification, and timing of casualty and theft losses.
- **LO.5** Apply the alternative tax treatments for research and experimental expenditures.
- **LO.6** Apply the excess business loss limitation rules.
- **LO.7** Determine the amount of the net operating loss, and review the effect of the carryover provisions on previous and subsequent years' taxable income.
- **LO.8** Identify tax planning opportunities in deducting certain business expenses, business losses, and personal losses.

Chapter Outline

TETRA IMAGES/GETTY IMAGES

Losses

Martha, a cash basis and calendar year taxpayer, is nearing the end of a year she would like to forget. Several years ago she loaned $25,000 to her friend Janice to enable her to start a business. Janice had made scheduled payments of $7,000 ($1,000 of this was interest) when she unexpectedly died in January. At the time of her death, Janice was insolvent. Martha's attempts to collect on the debt were fruitless.

On October 1, 2022, Martha invested $50,000 in the stock of a pharmaceutical company that previously had been profitable. However, as a result of losing a patent infringement suit, the company declared bankruptcy on May 31, 2023. The bankruptcy trustee has informed shareholders that they should not expect to receive anything from the company.

Martha has owned and operated a bookstore as a sole proprietorship for the past 10 years. The bookstore previously produced annual profits of about $75,000. Due to the continued growth of online vendors and e-books, Martha's bookstore sustained a net loss of $180,000 this year.

On September 28, 2023, a hurricane caused a large oak tree to blow over onto Martha's house. In the aftermath of the hurricane, Martha's county was designated a Federal disaster area by the President. The cost of removing the tree and making repairs was $32,000. Martha received a check for $25,000 from her insurance company in final settlement of the claim. Her adjusted basis for the house was $280,000.

On March 8, 2022, Martha purchased what she believed to be "small business stock" (§ 1244 stock) from her friend Peter for $20,000. The stock's value began to decline significantly soon after its purchase. On November 2, 2023, Martha sold the stock for $12,000.

Can you help relieve Martha's feeling of despair by making her aware of beneficial loss provisions in the tax law?

Read the chapter and formulate your response.

Framework 1040 **Tax Formula for Individuals**

This chapter covers the boldfaced portions of the Tax Formula for Individuals that was introduced in Concept Summary 3.1 on p. 3-3. Below those portions are the sections of Form 1040 where the results are reported.

Income *(broadly defined)*	$ xx,xxx
Less: Exclusions	(x,xxx)
Gross income	$ xx,xxx
Less: Deductions *for* adjusted gross income	**(x,xxx)**
FORM 1040 (Schedule 1) — 3 Business income or (loss). Attach Schedule C	
Adjusted gross income	$ xx,xxx
Less: The greater of total itemized deductions *or* the standard deduction	**(x,xxx)**
FORM 1040 (p. 1) — 12 **Standard deduction or itemized deductions** (from Schedule A)	
Personal and dependency exemptions*	(x,xxx)
Deduction for qualified business income**	(x,xxx)
Taxable income	$ xx,xxx
Tax on taxable income *(see Tax Tables or Tax Rate Schedules)*	$ x,xxx
Less: Tax credits *(including income taxes withheld and prepaid)*	(xxx)
Tax due (or refund)	$ xxx

* Exemption deductions are not allowed from 2018 through 2025.
** Only applies from 2018 through 2025.

Individual deductions must be properly classified as either *for* adjusted gross income (AGI) or *from* AGI (e.g., itemized deductions). Business expenses and losses, along with expenses and losses related to rent and royalty activities (entered into for profit), are deducted *for* AGI. Most other investment expenses are deducted *from* AGI. The determination of the taxpayer's activity (i.e., whether the taxpayer is engaged in a trade or business, an investment, or a personal activity) is crucial in this classification process.[1]

Deductible losses on personal use property are deductions *from* AGI (as itemized deductions). Casualty and theft losses on personal use property are discussed in this chapter; other itemized deductions are discussed in Chapter 10.

In determining the amount and timing of the deduction for bad debts, proper classification is again important. A business bad debt is classified as a deduction *for* AGI, and a nonbusiness bad debt is classified as a short-term capital loss.

Other topics discussed in Chapter 7 are research and experimental expenditures, the limitation on excess business losses, and the net operating loss deduction.

LO.1

Determine the amount, classification, and timing of the bad debt deduction.

7-1 Bad Debts

If a taxpayer sells goods or provides services on credit and, later, the account receivable becomes worthless, a **bad debt** deduction is allowed only if the income related to the account receivable was previously included in income.[2] No deduction is allowed, for example, for a bad debt related to the sale of a product or service when the taxpayer is on the cash basis because no income is reported until the cash has been collected.

[1] See, for example, *Groetzinger v. Comm.*, 85–2 USTC ¶9622, 56 AFTR 2d 85–5683, 771 F.2d 269 (CA–7), *aff'd* in 87–1 USTC ¶9191, 59 AFTR 2d 87–532, 107 S.Ct. 980.

[2] Reg. § 1.166–1(e).

Daniela, a sole proprietor, operates a business named Executive Accounting and Tax Services. Last year Pat hired Daniela to help him with the accounting for his small business. Daniela also prepared the S corporation income tax return for the business and Pat's personal income tax return. Daniela billed Pat $8,000 for the services she performed. Pat has never paid the bill, his business no longer exists, and his whereabouts are unknown.

If Daniela is an *accrual basis taxpayer*, she includes the $8,000 in income when the services are performed. When she determines that Pat's account will not be collected, she deducts the $8,000 as a bad debt expense.

If Daniela is a *cash basis taxpayer*, she does not include the $8,000 in income until payment is received. When she determines that Pat's account will not be collected, she cannot deduct the $8,000 as a bad debt expense because it was never recognized as income.

The Big Picture

Example 2

Return to the facts of *The Big Picture* on p. 7-1. Because Martha is a cash basis taxpayer, she cannot take a bad debt deduction for any unpaid accrued interest on the loan to Janice (her friend) because the interest was never recognized as income.

A bad debt also can result from the nonrepayment of a loan made by the taxpayer or from purchased debt instruments.

7-1a Specific Charge-Off Method

In general, the **specific charge-off method** must be used for tax purposes when accounting for bad debts. Certain financial institutions are allowed to use the **reserve method** for computing deductions for bad debts.

A taxpayer using the specific charge-off method may claim a deduction in the year when a specific business debt becomes either partially or wholly worthless. A nonbusiness debt must be wholly worthless to claim a deduction.[3] The taxpayer must be able to document the fact that the debt is either partially or completely worthless. This is one of the more difficult tasks facing a taxpayer. Legal proceedings against the debtor are not required as long as the taxpayer can demonstrate that collection is unlikely.

In the case of a business debt, partial worthlessness can result in a deduction. If, in a later year, the balance of the debt is deemed uncollectible, it can be deducted. In the case of a nonbusiness debt, a deduction is only allowed in the year the debt becomes completely worthless.

In 2021, Ross loaned $1,000 to Josh, who agreed to repay the loan in two years. In 2023, Josh disappeared after the note became delinquent. If a reasonable investigation by Ross indicates that he cannot find Josh or that a suit against Josh would not result in collection, Ross can deduct the $1,000 in 2023.

Bankruptcy is generally an indication of at least partial worthlessness of a debt. Bankruptcy may create worthlessness before the settlement date. If this is the case, the deduction may be taken in the year of worthlessness.

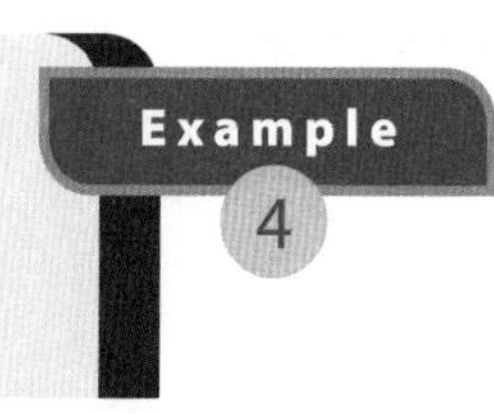

In Example 3, assume that Josh filed for personal bankruptcy in 2022 and that the debt is a business debt. At that time, Ross learned that unsecured creditors (including Ross) were ultimately expected to receive 20 cents on the dollar.

In 2023, settlement is made, and Ross receives only $150. He should deduct $800 ($1,000 loan − $200 expected settlement) in 2022 and $50 in 2023 ($200 balance − $150 proceeds).

[3] §§ 166(a) and (d).

If a receivable is written off (deducted) as uncollectible and then collected in a later tax year, income will result if the deduction yielded a tax benefit in the year it was taken. See the discussion and examples in text Section 5-15.

Concept Summary 7.1 provides a summary of the tax treatment of bad debts using the specific charge-off method.

Concept Summary 7.1

The Tax Treatment of Bad Debts Using the Specific Charge-Off Method

	Business Bad Debts	Nonbusiness Bad Debts
Timing of deduction	A deduction is allowed when the debt becomes either partially or wholly worthless.	A deduction is allowed *only* when the debt becomes wholly worthless.
Character of deduction	The bad debt is deducted as an ordinary loss.	The bad debt is classified as a short-term capital loss, subject to the $3,000 net capital loss limitation for individuals.
Recovery of amounts previously deducted	If the account recovered was written off during the current tax year, the write-off entry is reversed. If the account was written off in a previous tax year, income is created subject to the tax benefit rule.	If the account recovered was written off during the current tax year, the write-off entry is reversed. If the account was written off in a previous tax year, income is created subject to the tax benefit rule.

7-1b **Business versus Nonbusiness Bad Debts**

Whether a debt is business or nonbusiness depends on the role of the lender. How the borrower uses the funds is of no consequence. A **nonbusiness bad debt** is unrelated to the lender's trade or business either when it was created or when it became worthless. Loans to relatives or friends are the most common type of nonbusiness bad debt.

The Big Picture

Example 5

Return to the facts of *The Big Picture* on p. 7-1. Martha loaned her friend Janice $25,000. Janice used the money to start a business, which subsequently failed. When Janice died, after having made payments of $7,000 on the loan, she was insolvent.

Even though the proceeds of the loan were used in a business, the loan is a nonbusiness bad debt because the business was Janice's, not Martha's, and Martha is not in the business of lending money.

The distinction between a business bad debt and a nonbusiness bad debt is important. A **business bad debt** is treated as an ordinary deduction in the year incurred. In contrast, a nonbusiness bad debt is always treated as a short-term capital loss. Since net capital loss deductions are limited to no more than $3,000 per year, a taxpayer's nonbusiness bad debt deduction could have a limited benefit (see Chapter 14 for a detailed discussion). It is assumed that any loans made by a business are related to its trade or business. Credit sales to customers are a common example. Any bad debts that occur from these transactions are business bad debts.

The following example is an illustration of business bad debts adapted from the Regulations.[4]

Example 6

In 2022, Leif sold his business but retained a claim (note or account receivable) against Bob. The claim became worthless in 2023.

Leif's loss is treated as a business bad debt because the debt was created in the conduct of his former trade or business. Leif is accorded business bad debt treatment even though he was holding the note as an investor and was no longer in a trade or business when the claim became worthless.

[4] Reg. § 1.166–5(d).

7-1c Loans between Related Parties

Loans between related parties (especially family members) raise the issue of whether the transaction was a *bona fide* loan or a gift. The Regulations indicate that individual circumstances must be examined to determine whether advances between related parties are gifts or loans. Some considerations are these:

- Was a note properly executed?
- Was there a reasonable rate of interest?
- Was collateral provided?
- What collection efforts were made?
- What was the intent of the parties?

Lana loans $2,000 to her widowed mother for an operation. Lana's mother owns no property and is not employed, and her only income consists of Social Security benefits. No note is issued for the loan, no provision for interest is made, and no repayment date is mentioned. In the current year, Lana's mother dies, leaving no estate.

Assuming that the loan is not repaid, Lana cannot take a deduction for a nonbusiness bad debt because the facts indicate that no debtor-creditor relationship existed.

See Concept Summary 7.2 for a review of the bad debt deduction rules.

Concept Summary 7.2

Bad Debt Deductions

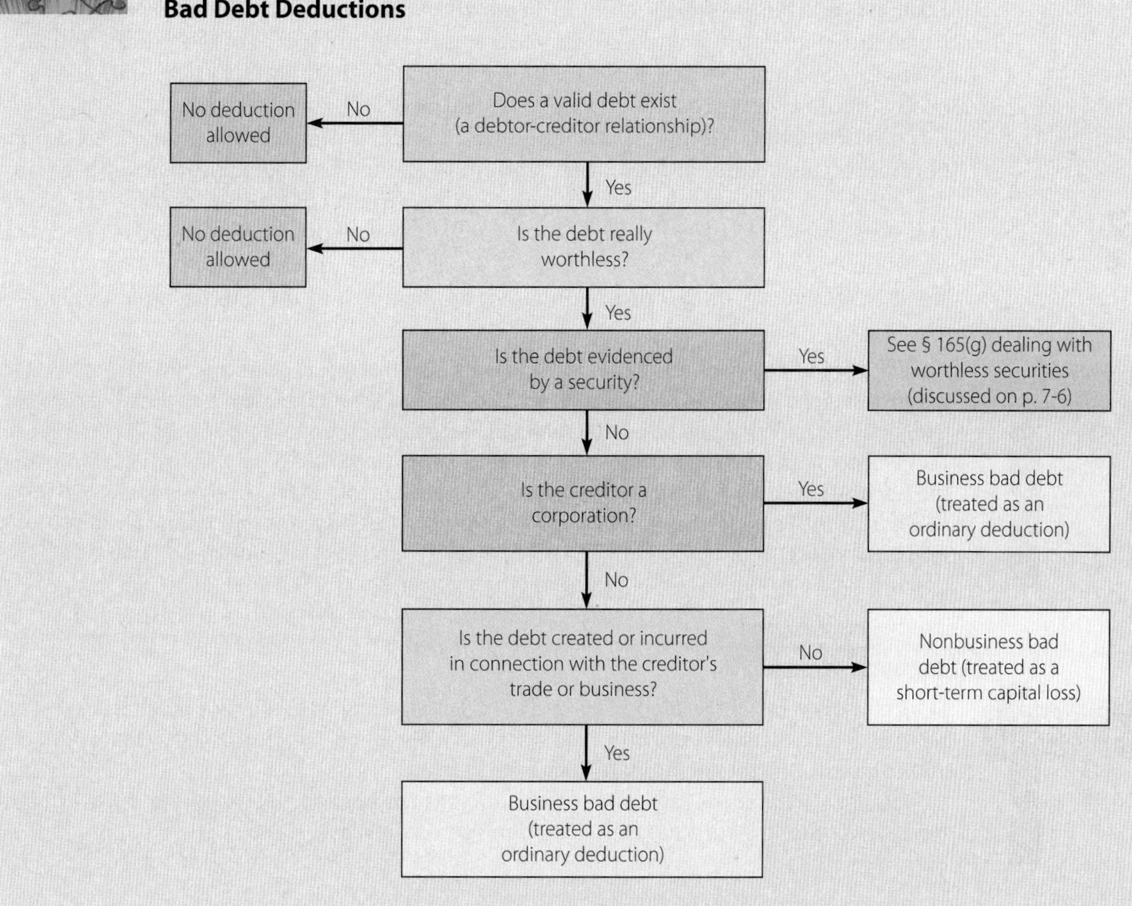

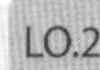

LO.2

Illustrate the tax treatment of worthless securities, including § 1244 stock.

7-2 Worthless Securities and Small Business Stock Losses

7-2a Worthless Securities

A loss is allowed for securities that become *completely* worthless during the year (**worthless securities**).[5] Securities covered by this rule include shares of stock, bonds, notes, or other evidence of indebtedness issued by a corporation or government. The losses generated are treated as capital losses deemed to have occurred on the *last day* of the taxable year. By treating the loss as having occurred on the last day of the taxable year, a loss that would otherwise have been classified as short term (if the date of worthlessness was used) may be classified as a long-term capital loss. Capital losses may be of limited benefit due to the $3,000 net capital loss limitation.[6]

The Big Picture

Example 8

Return to the facts of *The Big Picture* on p. 7-1. Martha owned stock in a pharmaceutical company that she acquired as an investment on October 1, 2022, at a cost of $50,000. On May 31, 2023, the stock became worthless when the company declared bankruptcy.

Because the stock is deemed to have become worthless as of December 31, 2023, Martha has a capital loss from an asset held for 15 months (a long-term capital loss).

7-2b Small Business Stock (§ 1244 Stock) Losses

In general, shareholders receive capital gain or loss treatment when they sell stock. However, it is possible to receive an ordinary loss deduction if the loss relates to **small business stock (§ 1244 stock)**. Only *individuals*[7] who acquired the stock *from* the corporation are eligible to receive ordinary loss treatment under § 1244. The ordinary loss is limited to $50,000 ($100,000 for married individuals filing jointly) per year. Losses in excess of these limits receive capital loss treatment.

The corporation issuing the stock must be a "small business corporation."[8] A corporation meets this definition if the total amount of money and other property received by the corporation for stock as a contribution to capital (or paid-in surplus) does not exceed $1 million. The $1 million test is made at the time the stock is issued. Code § 1244 stock can be common or preferred stock. Code § 1244 applies only to losses. If § 1244 stock is sold at a gain, the provision is not applicable and the gain is capital gain.

Example 9

Paulina, a single individual, was looking for an investment that would give some diversity to her stock portfolio. A friend suggested that she acquire some stock in Eagle Corporation, a new startup company. On July 1, 2021, Paulina purchased 100 shares of Eagle Corporation for $100,000. At the time Paulina acquired her stock from Eagle Corporation, the corporation had $700,000 of paid-in capital. As a result, the stock qualified as § 1244 stock. On June 20, 2023, Paulina sold all of her Eagle stock for $20,000.

Because the Eagle stock is § 1244 stock, Paulina has a $50,000 ordinary loss and a $30,000 long-term capital loss.

The Big Picture

Example 10

Return to the facts of *The Big Picture* on p. 7-1. On March 8, 2023, Martha purchases what she believes is "small business stock" (§ 1244 stock) from her friend Peter for $20,000. On November 2, 2023, she sells the stock in the marketplace for $12,000.

Because Martha did not acquire the stock from the corporation, the stock is *not* § 1244 stock to Martha. As a result, Martha has an $8,000 short-term capital loss.

[5] § 165(g); see *MCM Investment Management, LLC* (118 TCM 437, T.C.Memo. 2019–158) where the Tax Court provides a comprehensive overview of the law in many different contexts (e.g., worthless stock, partnership interests, and other assets).

[6] § 1211(b).

[7] The term *individuals* for this purpose does not include a trust or an estate (but could include a partnership or an LLC). §§ 1244(a) and (d)(4).

[8] § 1244(c)(3).

7-3 **Losses of Individuals**

Distinguish between deductible and nondeductible losses of individuals.

An individual may deduct the following losses under § 165(c):

- Losses incurred in a trade or business (e.g., business loss of a sole proprietor or sale of a business asset at a loss).
- Losses incurred in a transaction entered into for profit (e.g., sale of an asset used in a rental activity at a loss).
- Losses caused by fire, storm, shipwreck, or other casualty or by theft (e.g., a residence damaged in a hurricane).

Although the terms *fire*, *storm*, *shipwreck*, and *theft* are easy to understand, what is meant by *other casualty*? First, it means that events similar to a fire, storm, or shipwreck qualify. In addition, accidental losses also qualify.

Overall, the loss must result from an event that is (1) identifiable; (2) damaging to property; and (3) sudden, unexpected, and unusual in nature.[9] Examples include auto accidents, mine cave-ins, sonic booms, and vandalism. Weather that causes damage (e.g., drought) must be unusual and severe for the particular region. Damage must be to the taxpayer's property to qualify as a **casualty loss**.

In general, losses on personal use property (e.g., a car, furniture, or a residence) are not deductible. The casualty loss rules are an exception. However, from 2018 through 2025, a taxpayer can take a deduction for a *personal* casualty or theft loss only if the loss occurs in a Federally declared disaster area.[10]

In May 2023, due to significant rainstorms, the river behind Jiawen's house overflows its banks and floods the basement. After receiving an insurance settlement, Jiawen's remaining loss is $10,000. Although this event results in a casualty loss, Jiawen's loss will not be deductible unless the event is part of a Federally declared disaster.

Assume instead that the flooding affects a rental home owned by Jiawen. Because the rental home is *not* a personal use asset, the loss is deductible.

See text Section 7-3e for an exception to this rule when there are personal casualty gains during the year.

7-3a **Events That Are Not Casualties**

LO.4 **Identify a casualty and determine the amount, classification, and timing of casualty and theft losses.**

Not all acts of nature are treated as casualty losses for income tax purposes. Because a casualty must be sudden, unexpected, and unusual, progressive deterioration (e.g., erosion due to wind or rain) is not a casualty because it does not meet the suddenness test.

Examples of nonsudden events that generally do not qualify as casualties include disease and insect damage. When the damage was caused by termites over a period of several years, some courts have disallowed a casualty loss deduction.[11] Other examples of events that are not casualties are losses resulting from a decline in value rather than an actual loss of the property. No loss was allowed where the taxpayer's home declined in value as a result of a landslide that destroyed neighboring homes but did no actual damage to the taxpayer's home.[12] Similarly, a taxpayer was allowed a loss for the actual flood damage to his property but not for the decline in market value due to the property being flood-prone.[13]

---

[9] Rev.Rul. 72–592.

[10] § 165(h)(5). A Federally declared disaster is a disaster determined by the President of the United States to warrant assistance by the Federal government under the Stafford Disaster Relief and Emergency Assistance Act [§ 165(i)(5)].

[11] *Fay v. Helvering*, 41–2 USTC ¶9494, 27 AFTR 432, 120 F.2d 253 (CA–2); *U.S. v. Rogers*, 41–1 USTC ¶9442, 27 AFTR 423, 120 F.2d 244 (CA–9). The current position of the IRS is that termite damage is not deductible (Rev.Rul. 63–232).

[12] *H. Pulvers v. Comm.*, 69–1 USTC ¶9222, 23 AFTR 2d 69–678, 407 F.2d 838 (CA–9).

[13] *S. L. Solomon*, 39 TCM 1282, T.C.Memo. 1980–87.

7-3b Theft Losses

Theft includes, but is not necessarily limited to, larceny, embezzlement, and robbery.[14] Theft does not include misplaced items.[15]

Theft losses are deducted in the year of *discovery*, which may not be the same as the year of the theft. If an insurance claim exists and there is a reasonable expectation of recovering the adjusted basis of the asset from the insurance company, no deduction is permitted.[16] If in the year of settlement the recovery is less than the asset's adjusted basis, a partial deduction may be available. If the recovery is greater than the asset's adjusted basis, gain may be recognized.

Keith's new sailboat, which he uses for business purposes, was stolen from the storage marina in May 2023. He discovered the loss on June 3, 2023, and filed a claim with his insurance company that was settled on January 30, 2024.

Assuming that there is a reasonable expectation of full recovery, no deduction is allowed in 2023 (the year of discovery). A partial deduction may be available in 2024 if the actual insurance proceeds are less than the lower of the fair market value or the adjusted basis of the asset.

If Keith used his sailboat personally (i.e., not for business), no deduction would be allowed. In general, only personal casualty losses in Federally declared disaster areas are deductible.

7-3c When to Deduct Casualty Losses

General Rule

Generally, a casualty loss is deducted in the year the loss occurs. However, no casualty loss is permitted if an insurance claim with a *reasonable prospect of full recovery* exists.[17] If the taxpayer has a partial claim, only part of the loss can be claimed in the year of the casualty, and the remainder is deducted in the year the claim is settled.

Brian's new fishing boat, which he uses in his charter fishing business, was completely destroyed by fire in 2023. Its cost and fair market value were $15,000. Brian's only claim against the insurance company was on a $10,000 policy, which was not settled by year-end. The following year, 2024, Brian settled with the insurance company for $8,000.

Brian is entitled to a $5,000 deduction in 2023 ($10,000 − $15,000) and a $2,000 deduction in 2024.

If a taxpayer receives reimbursement for a casualty loss sustained and deducted in a previous year, an amended return is *not* filed. Instead, the taxpayer includes the reimbursement in gross income when it is received to the extent the previous deduction resulted in a tax benefit.

Selena had a deductible casualty loss of $4,000 on her 2022 tax return. Selena's taxable income for 2022 was $60,000. In June 2023, Selena is reimbursed $2,750 for the prior year's casualty loss.

Selena includes the entire $2,750 in gross income for 2023 because the deduction in 2022 produced a tax benefit.

[14] Reg. § 1.165–8(d).

[15] *Mary Francis Allen*, 16 T.C. 163 (1951).

[16] Reg. §§ 1.165–1(d)(2) and 1.165–8(a)(2).

[17] Reg. § 1.165–1(d)(2)(i).

Disaster Area Losses

An exception to the general rule for the time of deduction is allowed for **disaster area losses**, which are casualties sustained in an area designated as a disaster area by the President of the United States.[18] In these cases, a taxpayer may *elect* to treat the loss as having occurred in the taxable year immediately *preceding* the taxable year in which the disaster actually occurred. The rationale for this exception is to provide immediate relief to disaster victims by accelerating the tax refunds related to the loss.

The Big Picture

Example 15

Return to the facts of *The Big Picture* on p. 7-1. On September 28, 2023, Martha's personal residence was damaged when a hurricane caused an oak tree to fall onto the house. The amount of her uninsured loss was $7,000 ($25,000 insurance settlement − $32,000 damages incurred). Because of the extent of the damage in the area, the President of the United States designated the area a disaster area.

Because Martha's loss is a disaster area loss, she may elect to file an amended return for 2022 and take the loss in that year. Alternatively, she may take the loss on her 2023 income tax return.

7-3d Measuring the Amount of Loss

Amount of Loss

The rules for determining the amount of a loss depend in part on whether business use, income-producing use, or personal use property was involved. Another factor that must be considered is whether the property was partially or completely destroyed.

If business or rental property is *completely destroyed*, the loss is equal to the adjusted basis of the property at the time of destruction.

Zoë's business equipment was destroyed by flood. Zoë had no flood insurance on her business. The fair market value of the equipment was $9,000 at the time of the flood, and its adjusted basis was $10,000.

Zoë is allowed a loss deduction of $10,000 (the basis of the equipment). The $10,000 loss is a deduction *for* AGI.

A different measurement rule applies for *partial destruction* of business or rental property and for *partial* or *complete destruction* of personal use property. In these situations, the loss is the *lesser* of the following:

- The adjusted basis of the property.
- The difference between the fair market value of the property before the event and the fair market value immediately after the event.

[18] § 165(i) refers to Federally declared disasters. Disaster loss treatment also applies if a residence has been rendered unsafe as the result of a disaster within 120 days of the disaster loss designation [§ 165(k)].

Example 17

Wan's uninsured automobile, which was used only for business purposes, was damaged in an accident. On the date of the accident, the fair market value of the automobile was $12,000, and its adjusted basis was $9,000. After the accident, the automobile was appraised at $4,000.

Wan's loss deduction is $8,000 (the lesser of the adjusted basis or the decrease in fair market value). The $8,000 loss is a deduction *for* AGI.

If the property is used for both personal and business/rental use, the loss deduction must be computed separately for the business portion and the personal portion. If a taxpayer has insurance coverage on *personal use* property, an insurance claim must be filed to claim a casualty loss.[19]

Generally, an appraisal before and after the casualty is needed to measure the amount of the loss. However, the *cost of repairs* can be used if the following criteria are met:

- The repairs are necessary to restore the property to its condition immediately before the casualty.
- The amount spent for repairs is not excessive.
- The repairs do not extend beyond the damage suffered.
- The value of the property after the repairs does not, as a result of the repairs, exceed the value of the property immediately before the casualty.[20]

Ethics & Equity **Is Policy Cancellation an Escape Hatch?**

Noah's house is flooded for the third time, and he knows that if he files a claim, the insurance company will cancel his homeowner's policy or impose a prohibitive premium. Noah does not file a claim, yet he deducts the loss on his tax return. Is his loss allowed?

Personal Use Loss Reductions: The $100-per-Event and 10%-of-AGI Floors

The amount of the allowed loss for *personal use* property must be further reduced by a $100-*per-event* floor and a 10%-of-AGI *aggregate* floor.[21] The $100 floor applies separately to each casualty and applies to the entire loss from each casualty (e.g., if a storm damages both a taxpayer's residence and automobile, only $100 is subtracted from the total amount of the loss). The losses are then added together, and the total is reduced by 10 percent of the taxpayer's AGI. The resulting loss is the taxpayer's itemized deduction for casualty and theft losses.

Example 18

Nick, who had AGI of $30,000, lost all the furniture in his apartment as a result of a flood in a Federally declared disaster area in 2023. His furniture had a fair market value of $12,000 and an adjusted basis of $9,000 and was completely destroyed. He received $5,000 from his insurance company.

Nick's casualty loss deduction is $900 [$9,000 basis − $5,000 insurance recovery − $100 floor − $3,000 (10% × $30,000 AGI)]. The $900 casualty loss is an itemized deduction (*from* AGI).

---

[19] § 165(h)(4)(E).

[20] Reg. § 1.165–7(a)(2)(ii).

[21] § 165(h).

When a personal casualty loss is spread between two taxable years because of an outstanding insurance claim, the loss in the second year is not reduced by the $100 floor (the "$100-per-event" reduction occurred in the first year). However, the loss in the second year is still subject to the 10 percent floor based upon the taxpayer's second-year AGI. For taxpayers who suffer qualified disaster area losses, the 10%-of-AGI floor is determined by using the AGI of the year the deduction is claimed.[22]

Brian's new *personal use* sailboat was completely destroyed by a hurricane in 2023 (a Federally declared disaster area). The boat had a $15,000 cost and fair market value, but Brian only had $10,000 of insurance coverage for the boat. He filed an insurance claim and settled with the insurance company in 2024 for $8,000.

Brian is entitled to a $5,000 deduction in 2023 ($10,000 − $15,000) and a $2,000 deduction in 2024. Brian's $5,000 casualty loss deduction in 2023 is reduced first by $100 and then by 10% of his 2023 AGI. The $2,000 deduction in 2024 is reduced by 10% of his 2024 AGI.

Multiple Losses

The rules for computing loss deductions where multiple losses have occurred are explained in Examples 20 and 21.

Multiple Casualty Losses

Example 20

During the year, Kien had the following casualty losses related to assets used in his business:

		Fair Market Value of Asset		
Asset	**Adjusted Basis**	**Before the Casualty**	**After the Casualty**	**Insurance Recovery**
A	$900	$600	$−0−	$400
B	300	800	250	100

The following losses are allowed:

Asset A: $500. The complete destruction of a business asset results in a deduction of the adjusted basis of the property (reduced by any insurance recovery), regardless of the asset's fair market value.

Asset B: $200. The partial destruction of a business (or personal use) asset results in a deduction equal to the lesser of the adjusted basis ($300) or the decline in value ($550), reduced by any insurance recovery ($100).

Both Asset A and Asset B losses are deductions *for* AGI. The $100 floor and the 10%-of-AGI floor do not apply because the assets are business assets.

Example 21

During the year, Emily had AGI of $20,000 and the following personal casualty losses related to a flood in a Federally declared disaster area:

		Fair Market Value of Asset		
Asset	**Adjusted Basis**	**Before the Casualty**	**After the Casualty**	**Insurance Recovery**
A	$1,900	$1,400	$ −0−	$200
B	2,500	4,000	1,000	−0−
C	800	400	100	250

continued

[22] § 165(i).

The loss for each asset is computed as follows:

Asset A:	$1,200. The lesser of the adjusted basis of $1,900 or the $1,400 decline in value, reduced by the insurance recovery of $200.
Asset B:	$2,500. The lesser of the adjusted basis of $2,500 or the $3,000 decline in value.
Asset C:	$50. The lesser of the adjusted basis of $800 or the $300 decline in value, reduced by the insurance recovery of $250.

Since the losses all related to a single casualty, Emily must reduce the sum of the losses by $100 and then apply the 10%-of-AGI floor. Emily's itemized casualty loss deduction for the year is $1,650:

Asset A loss	$ 1,200
Asset B loss	2,500
Asset C loss	50
Total loss	$ 3,750
Less: $100-per-event reduction	(100)
Less: 10% of AGI (10% × $20,000)	(2,000)
Itemized casualty loss deduction	$ 1,650

7-3e **Personal Casualty Gains and Losses**

If a taxpayer has personal casualty and theft gains as well as losses, a special set of rules applies for determining the tax consequences. Here, an exception to the rule that disallows a deduction for personal casualty losses other than those in Federally declared disaster areas applies.[23] In this case, the taxpayer may use a personal casualty loss (or losses) *not* attributable to a Federally declared disaster to offset any personal casualty gains. After this netting process, if any loss remains, it is not deductible (since it relates to a non-Federally declared disaster area casualty). If, however, a net personal casualty gain remains, it is offset by any Federally declared disaster area casualty losses.

Calculating Personal Casualty Gains and Losses

Example 22

During 2023, Emmanuel has AGI of $50,000 and the following personal casualty gains and losses (after deducting the $100 floor):

Asset	Item	Gain or (Loss)
A	Personal casualty gain	$ 2,500
B	Personal casualty loss (non-Federally declared disaster area)	(2,000)
C	Personal casualty loss (Federally declared disaster area)	(9,000)

Emmanuel first offsets the non-Federally declared disaster area losses against the personal casualty gain, resulting in an excess personal casualty gain of $500, computed as follows:

Personal casualty gain	$ 2,500
Personal casualty loss (non-Federally declared disaster area)	(2,000)
Excess personal casualty gain	$ 500

Next, the excess personal casualty gain offsets the Federally declared disaster area loss. Emmanuel's overall net personal casualty loss is $8,500, computed as follows:

Personal casualty loss (Federally declared disaster area)	($ 9,000)
Less: Excess personal casualty gain	500
Overall net personal casualty loss	($ 8,500)

After this second netting process, because a net personal casualty loss remains, it will be deductible to the extent of the 10%-of-AGI floor. Emmanuel's itemized deduction for casualty losses is $3,500, computed as follows:

Net personal casualty loss	$ 8,500
Less: 10% of AGI (10% × $50,000)	(5,000)
Itemized deduction for casualty loss	$ 3,500

[23] § 165(h)(5)(B); personal casualty gains and losses are defined at § 165(h)(3).

Calculating Personal Casualty Gains and Losses

Example 23

Refer back to the facts of Example 22. How would your answer change if the casualty loss related to Asset B was $4,000 (rather than $2,000)?

Emmanuel would begin by offsetting the non-Federally declared disaster area losses against the personal casualty gain, resulting in an excess personal casualty loss of $1,500, computed as follows:

Personal casualty gain	$ 2,500
Personal casualty loss (non-Federally declared disaster area)	(4,000)
Excess personal casualty loss	($ 1,500)

Since this net loss relates to a non-Federally declared disaster area, the loss is *not* deductible. Emmanuel's itemized deduction for casualty losses is $4,000, computed as follows:

Personal casualty loss (Federally declared disaster area)	$ 9,000
Less: 10% of AGI (10% × $50,000)	(5,000)
Itemized deduction for casualty loss	$ 4,000

One further complication exists—determining the character of the casualty gains and losses. If the gains exceed the losses, the gains and losses are treated as gains and losses from the sale of capital assets.[24] The capital gains and losses are short term or long term, depending on how long the taxpayer held each of the assets (assets held more than one year are long term). In the netting process, personal casualty and theft gains and losses are not netted with the gains and losses on business and income-producing property.

Example 24

During the year, Cliff had the following personal casualty gains and losses (after deducting the $100 floor):

Asset	Holding Period	Gain or (Loss)
A	Three months	($ 300)
B	Three years	(2,400)
C	Two years	3,200

Cliff computes the tax consequences as follows:

Personal casualty gain	$ 3,200
Personal casualty loss ($300 + $2,400)	(2,700)
Net personal casualty gain	$ 500

Cliff treats all of the gains and losses as capital gains and losses:

Short-term capital loss (Asset A)	$ 300
Long-term capital loss (Asset B)	2,400
Long-term capital gain (Asset C)	3,200

If personal casualty losses exceed personal casualty gains, all gains and losses are treated as ordinary items. The gains—and the losses to the extent of gains—are treated as ordinary income and ordinary loss in computing AGI. Losses in excess of gains are deducted as itemized deductions and are deductible only if related to a Federally declared disaster.[25]

[24] § 165(h)(2)(B).

[25] § 165(h).

During the year, Hazel had AGI of $20,000 and the following personal casualty gain and loss (after deducting the $100 floor). Neither are related to a Federally declared disaster:

Asset	Holding Period	Gain or (Loss)
A	Three years	($2,700)
B	Four months	200

Hazel computes the tax consequences as follows:

Personal casualty loss	($2,700)
Personal casualty gain	200
Net personal casualty loss	($2,500)

Hazel treats the gain and the loss as ordinary items. The $200 gain and $200 of the loss are included in computing AGI. The remaining net personal casualty loss is not deductible (it is not related to a Federally declared disaster area).

See Concept Summary 7.3 for a review of the tax treatment of casualty gains and losses.

Concept Summary 7.3

Casualty Gains and Losses

	Business Use or Income-Producing Property	Personal Use Property*
Event creating the loss	Any event.	Casualty or theft.
Amount	The lesser of the decline in fair market value or the adjusted basis, but always the adjusted basis if the property is totally destroyed.	The lesser of the decline in fair market value or the adjusted basis.
Insurance	Insurance proceeds received reduce the amount of the loss.	Insurance proceeds received (or for which there is an unfiled claim) reduce the amount of the loss.
$100 floor	Not applicable.	Applicable per event.
Gains and losses	Gains and losses are netted (see detailed discussion in Chapter 14).	Personal casualty and theft gains and losses are netted.
Gains exceeding losses	See Chapter 14.	The gains and losses are treated as gains and losses from the sale of capital assets.
Losses exceeding gains	See Chapter 14.	The gains—and the losses to the extent of gains—are treated as ordinary items in computing AGI. The losses in excess of gains, to the extent they exceed 10% of AGI, are itemized deductions.

*In general, from 2018 through 2025, losses are allowed only if the event is related to a Federally declared disaster; if there are both casualty gains and losses, non-Federally declared casualty losses can be used to offset casualty gains.

7-3f Statutory Framework for Deducting Losses of Individuals

Concept Summary 7.4 provides a summary of the statutory framework of deducting losses of individuals.

Concept Summary 7.4

Statutory Framework for Deducting Losses of Individuals

	Personal Casualty/Theft Losses*		Employee Casualty/Theft Losses		
	$100-per-Event Rule	**10%-of-AGI Rule**	**Reimbursed Expenses and 2%-of-AGI Rule**	**Production of Income Casualty/Theft Losses**	**Trade or Business Casualty/Theft Losses**
General Application	Reduce each casualty or theft loss by $100 when figuring the potential casualty loss deduction. Apply this rule to personal use property after the amount of the loss has been determined.	Reduce the *total* casualty or theft loss by 10% of adjusted gross income. Apply this rule to personal use property after each loss is reduced by $100 (the "$100-per-event rule").	Casualty and theft losses incurred by an employee in connection with a trade or business are deductible *for* AGI if the loss is reimbursed by the employer (with the net loss being deductible). If the loss is *not* reimbursed, the loss is deductible *from* AGI as an employee business expense (a miscellaneous itemized deduction). Although these losses are not subject to the $100-per-event rule or the 10%-of-AGI rule, miscellaneous itemized deductions are currently not deductible.[26]	Casualty and theft losses incurred by an individual in a transaction entered into for profit are not subject to the $100-per-event and the 10%-of-AGI limitations. If these losses are attributable to rents or royalties, the deduction is *for* AGI.[27] If not, they are deductions *from* AGI (and are *not* a miscellaneous itemized deduction).[28]	Casualty and theft losses incurred by an individual in connection with a trade or business are deductible *for* AGI.[29] These losses are not subject to the $100-per-event and the 10%-of-AGI limitations.
Single Event	Apply this rule only once to each casualty or theft event, even if many pieces of property are affected by the event.	Apply this rule only once, even if many pieces of property are affected.	Apply this rule only once, even if many pieces of property are affected.		
More Than One Event	Apply to the loss from each event.	Apply to the total of all losses from all events.	Apply to the total of all losses from all events.		

*From 2018 through 2025, only personal casualty or theft losses occurring in Federally declared disaster areas are allowed.

7-4 Research and Experimental Expenditures

LO.5

Apply the alternative tax treatments for research and experimental expenditures.

Code § 174 covers the treatment of research and experimental expenditures. The Regulations define **research and experimental expenditures** as follows:

> all such costs incident to the development or improvement of a product (including an experimental or pilot model, a plant process, a product, a formula, an invention, or similar property). The term includes the costs of obtaining a patent, such as attorneys' fees expended in making

[26] § 67(b)(3). See Chapter 10; no deduction is allowed for miscellaneous itemized deductions from 2018 through 2025.

[27] § 62(a)(4).

[28] § 67(b)(3).

[29] § 62(a)(1).

> and perfecting a patent application. Expenditures represent research and development costs in the experimental or laboratory sense if they are for activities intended to discover information that would eliminate uncertainty concerning the development or improvement of a product. The term does not include expenditures such as those for the ordinary testing or inspection of materials or products for quality control or those for efficiency surveys, management studies, consumer surveys, advertising, or promotions.[30]

Currently, the law permits *two options* for the handling of research and experimental expenditures. These expenditures can either be:[31]

- Capitalized, or
- Capitalized and amortized.

7-4a **Capitalization**

If the research and experimentation costs are capitalized, a deduction may not be available until the research project is abandoned or is deemed worthless. Because many products resulting from research activities do not have a definite and limited useful life, most taxpayers choose to capitalize and amortize these expenditures.[32]

7-4b **Capitalization and Amortization Method**

Taxable Years Beginning after December 31, 2021

Research and experimental expenditures paid or incurred in taxable years beginning after December 31, 2021 can be capitalized and amortized. Amortization begins at the midpoint of the year the expenses are paid or incurred and the expenditures are amortized ratably over a five-year period (15 years for foreign research expenditures). If a research project is abandoned, any unamortized expenditures are deducted over the remaining amortization period.[33]

Gold Corporation, a calendar year corporation, decides to develop a new line of adhesives. The project begins in 2022. Gold incurs the following expenses in 2022 and 2023 in connection with the project:

	2022	2023
Salaries	$25,000	$18,000
Materials	8,000	2,000
Depreciation on machinery	6,500	5,700

The benefits from the project are realized starting in March 2024.

Gold's research and experimental expenditures total $39,500 in 2022 and $25,700 in 2023. Gold will amortize both sets of expenditures over a five-year period beginning at the mid-point of the year the expenditures are incurred (in this case, July 1 of 2022 or 2023); the year benefits will be

continued

[30] Reg. §§ 1.174–2(a)(1), (2), and (3). Expenses in connection with the acquisition or improvement of land or depreciable property are not research and experimental expenditures. Rather, they increase the basis of the land or depreciable property. However, depreciation on an asset used for research may be a research and experimental expense.

[31] § 174 as amended by P.L. 115–97. In taxable years beginning before January 1, 2022, taxpayers could immediately expense all of the research and experimental expenditures incurred, provided this method was adopted for the first taxable year in which these expenditures were paid or incurred. Most taxpayers used this option. If this option were still the law after 2021, in Example 26, Gold would have deducted $39,500 in 2022 rather than only $3,950 (with the balance deductible over the next five years).

[32] A credit for increasing research expenditures is also available; § 41. See Chapter 12 for a more detailed discussion of this credit.

[33] In taxable years beginning before January 1, 2022, a taxpayer could elect to capitalize and amortize research and experimental expenditures ratably over a period of not less than 60 months. Amortization started with the month in which the taxpayer first realized benefits from the research and experimental expenditures.

realized does not matter. Gold's deduction for research and experimental expenditures in 2022 and 2023 is computed as follows:

2022 Taxable Year	
2022 expenditures [($39,500 ÷ 5 years) × ½ year]	$ 3,950
2023 Taxable Year	
2022 expenditures ($39,500 ÷ 5 years)	$ 7,900
2023 expenditures [($25,700 ÷ 5 years) × ½ year]	2,570
Total research and experimental expenditures deduction	$10,470

7-5 Excess Business Losses

LO.6

Apply the excess business loss limitation rules.

If a noncorporate taxpayer has an **excess business loss** for the year, it is not allowed.[34] Instead, it is carried forward and treated as part of the taxpayer's net operating loss (NOL) carryforward in subsequent years (NOLs are discussed in text Section 7-6).

7-5a Excess Business Loss Defined

An *excess business loss* is defined as:[35]

	The aggregate deductions for the year attributable to the taxpayer's businesses
Less:	The sum of aggregate gross income or gains of the taxpayer
Less:	A threshold amount (in 2023, $578,000 for married taxpayers filing a joint return; $289,000 for all other taxpayers)

The threshold amounts are adjusted for inflation each year.[36]

At its core, the purpose of the excess business loss limitation is to limit the amount of nonbusiness income (e.g., salaries, interest, dividends, and capital gains) that can be "sheltered" from tax as a result of business losses.

Calculating an Excess Business Loss

Example 27

In 2023, Tonya, a single taxpayer, operates a sole proprietorship in which she materially participates. Her proprietorship generates gross income of $326,000 and deductions of $630,000, resulting in a loss of $304,000. The large deductions are due to the acquisition of equipment and the use of immediate expense and additional first-year depreciation to deduct all of the costs associated with the acquisitions. Tonya's excess business loss is $15,000, computed as follows:

Aggregate business deductions	$ 630,000
Less: Aggregate business gross income and gains	(326,000)
Less: Threshold amount	(289,000)
Excess business loss	$ 15,000

So of Tonya's $304,000 proprietorship loss, $289,000 can be used to offset nonbusiness income. The $15,000 excess business loss is treated as part of Tonya's net operating loss carryforward in subsequent years.

[34] § 461(l). The provision applies to taxable years beginning after December 31, 2020, and before January 1, 2029.

[35] § 461(l)(3).

[36] In 2022, the threshold amounts were $540,000 and $270,000, respectively.

Assume the same facts as Example 27, except that Tonya is married and files a joint return. In this case, Tonya does not have an excess business loss due to the increased threshold amount.

Aggregate business deductions	$ 630,000
Less: Aggregate business gross income and gains	(326,000)
Less: Threshold amount	(578,000)
Excess business loss	$ None

As a result, Tonya's $304,000 sole proprietorship loss is fully deductible and can be used to offset nonbusiness income (e.g., her spouse's wages and their interest and dividend income).

The excess business loss limitation applies to the aggregate gross income and deductions from all of a taxpayer's trades or businesses.[37] So if a married couple files a joint return, information from all of the couple's trades or businesses must be consolidated. Further, as noted in Example 28, if married taxpayers file a joint return, the losses of one spouse can be used to offset the other spouse's nonbusiness income (up to the $578,000 limit in 2023).

7-5b **Losses from Partnerships or S Corporations**

For a partnership or an S corporation, the excess business loss limitation applies at the partner or shareholder level.[38] Each partner's or S corporation shareholder's share of items of income, gain, deduction, or loss of the partnership or S corporation is taken into account in applying the limitation for the tax year of the partner or S corporation shareholder.

Jayson, a single taxpayer, is an S corporation shareholder and materially participates in the grocery store business. During 2023, the store had a large depreciation deduction causing a substantial loss. Jayson has a flow-through loss of $345,000 from the S corporation. He also received a $78,000 salary from the corporation. At the beginning of the year, Jayson had a $520,000 basis in his S corporation shares—enough to absorb the S corporation loss. Because he materially participates in the business, it is not a passive activity (see Chapter 11 for a discussion of passive activity losses).

However, Jayson's flow-through loss exceeds the $289,000 excess business loss threshold by $56,000 ($345,000 − $289,000). So Jayson can deduct $289,000 (and use it to offset his salary and other nonbusiness income). The $56,000 excess is not deductible in 2023 but carries forward as a net operating loss.

Assume that in 2024, the grocery store business generates a profit and flows through $210,000 of income to Jayson. Jayson can deduct the 2023 excess business loss of $56,000 against this flow-through income.

The excess business loss rules also treat similarly situated owners differently (based on their filing status).

Maggie leaves her job in 2023 to pursue her dream, a technology startup. Maggie is single and invests $500,000 of capital, as does her business partner Julita, who is married. Together they form TechStart LLC (which reports as a partnership for Federal tax purposes); both materially participate in the business. In 2023, the LLC reports a net loss of $700,000. Each LLC member receives a Schedule K–1 from the LLC indicating a $350,000 ordinary loss; each will report this loss on her 2023 individual income tax return [on Form 1040 (Schedule E)].

Maggie has an excess business loss of $61,000 ($350,000 minus the $289,000 threshold for single taxpayers). This excess business loss is an NOL carryforward for Maggie.[39] Julita can use the full $350,000 loss in 2023 since it is less than the $578,000 threshold that applies to married taxpayers who file jointly.

[37] § 461(l)(3)(A).

[38] § 461(l)(4)(A).

[39] Prior to 2021, NOLs could be carried back to prior tax years and used to offset income in those years (a five-year carryback for losses incurred in 2018, 2019, and 2020; a two-year carryback for losses incurred prior to 2018). This carryback allowed taxpayers to immediately "monetize" an NOL by using the NOL to generate an income tax refund in those years. Beginning in 2021, NOL carrybacks are no longer allowed; NOLs can only be carried forward. As a result, in addition to treating similarly situated owners differently based on filing status, the inability to carry back these losses also is detrimental to business owners.

7-5c **Other Rules**

The excess business loss limitation is applied *after* the application of the § 469 passive activity loss rules (see Chapter 11 for a discussion of these rules).[40] Given this requirement, losses from *passive* trades or businesses (e.g., a business in which the taxpayer does not materially participate) are limited first by the § 469 passive activity loss rules, and once the losses are allowed under § 469, they are subject to these rules.

The Treasury Department and IRS are to specify reporting requirements necessary to implement these rules.[41] Form 461 (Limitation on Business Losses) is used to calculate and report the loss limitation.

7-6 **Net Operating Losses**

LO.7

Determine the amount of the net operating loss, and review the effect of the carryover provisions on previous and subsequent years' taxable income.

The requirement that every taxpayer file an annual income tax return may result in inequities for taxpayers who experience income fluctuations (and losses in certain tax years) versus taxpayers with stable income levels. A loss in a particular tax year would produce no tax benefit if the Code did not provide for the use of these losses in profitable years.

Example 31

Juanita has a business and realizes $300,000 of taxable income or loss over a five-year period as follows: year 1, $50,000; year 2, ($30,000); year 3, $100,000; year 4, ($200,000); and year 5, $380,000. She is married and files a joint return. Sean also has a business and has a taxable income pattern of $60,000 every year ($300,000 over the five-year period). He, too, is married and files a joint return. Assuming that there is no provision for carryback or carryover of net operating losses (NOLs), Juanita and Sean would pay the following taxes over the five-year period:

Year	Juanita's Tax	Sean's Tax
1	$ 5,560	$ 6,760
2	-0-	6,760
3	12,615	6,760
4	-0-	6,760
5	79,264	6,760
	$97,439	$33,800

Note: The 2023 Tax Rate Schedules are used to compute the tax.

Even though Juanita and Sean realized the same total taxable income over the five-year period, Juanita had to pay taxes of $97,439, while Sean paid taxes of only $33,800.

To provide partial relief from this inequitable tax treatment, a **net operating loss (NOL)** deduction is allowed.[42] NOLs for any one year can be offset against taxable income of other years. In general, only losses from the operation of a trade or business and casualty and theft losses can create an NOL.

[40]§ 461(l)(6).

[41]§ 461(l)(5).

[42]§ 172(a).

7-6a **General Rules**

Carryforward Only (with Certain Exceptions)

For taxable years beginning after December 31, 2020, an NOL can be carried forward indefinitely (and cannot be carried back).[43] As a result, taxpayers must wait at least one year to receive a tax benefit from the loss.[44]

For 2023, the taxpayer and spouse have an NOL of $50,000. The NOL can be carried forward indefinitely (beginning with 2024).

NOL Deduction Limit

For taxable years beginning after December 31, 2020, an NOL deduction is limited to 80 percent of taxable income, determined without regard to the NOL deduction itself.[45] If the NOL carryover is less than the computed limitation, the entire carryover is allowed as a deduction. As a result, the 80 percent of taxable income limit may extend the time over which an NOL is used, making taxpayers wait longer to receive a tax benefit from the NOL (and reducing the present value of the related tax benefit).

For 2023, a married couple have an NOL of $25,000 (and no other NOL carryovers exist). The NOL is carried forward to 2024. In 2024, the taxpayers have taxable income of $80,000 before considering the 2023 NOL carryover. The taxpayers' 2024 NOL deduction can be no more than $64,000 ($80,000 × 80%). Since the NOL carryover from 2023 is only $25,000, the entire 2023 NOL carryover can be used to reduce their 2024 taxable income. As a result, their 2024 taxable income is $55,000 ($80,000 − $25,000).

If, instead, the taxpayers had taxable income of $30,000 before considering the 2023 NOL carryover, only $24,000 ($30,000 × 80%) of the carryover could be used. In this case, their 2024 taxable income would be $6,000 ($30,000 − $24,000), and the remaining $1,000 of the 2023 NOL carryover would be carried forward to 2025.

NOLs and the Deduction for Qualified Business Income

The deduction for qualified business income will not create or increase a net operating loss.[46] Losses from qualified businesses are carried over separately and will offset future income from qualified businesses, reducing the related deduction for qualified business income.[47]

NOLs and Self-Employment Taxes

An NOL *cannot* be used to reduce self-employment income. As a result, a taxpayer's self-employment tax liability will not change as the result of an NOL deduction.[48]

7-6b **Computation of the Net Operating Loss**

Because the NOL provisions apply solely to business-related and casualty losses, individual taxpayers must make adjustments to their taxable income since nonbusiness deductions are allowed (e.g, itemized deductions). To arrive at the NOL for an individual, taxable income must be adjusted as follows:[49]

1. No deduction is allowed for personal and dependency exemptions. From 2018 through 2025, the exemption deduction amount is zero, so there will be no add-back during these years for these amounts.
2. The NOL carryover from another year is not allowed in the computation of the current year's NOL.

---

[43] § 172(b)(1)(A).

[44] A two-year carryback period is available for any NOL resulting from a farming business; § 172(b)(1)(B)(i).

[45] § 172(a)(2).

[46] § 172(d)(8).

[47] § 199A(c)(2).

[48] § 1402(a).

[49] § 172(d); Reg. § 1.172-3(a). Also see *Net Operating Losses (NOLs) for Individuals* (IRS Publication 536).

3. The qualified business income deduction (§ 199A) is not allowed.
4. Capital losses and nonbusiness deductions are limited in determining the current year's NOL. These limits are as follows:
   a. The excess of nonbusiness capital losses over nonbusiness capital gains must be added back.
   b. The excess of nonbusiness deductions over the sum of nonbusiness income and *net* nonbusiness capital gains must be added back. *Net nonbusiness capital gains* are the excess of nonbusiness capital gains over nonbusiness capital losses. *Nonbusiness income* is income that is not related to a taxpayer's trade or business (e.g., dividends, investment interest, alimony received, and Social Security income). *Nonbusiness deductions* are those deductions that are not related to a taxpayer's trade or business [e.g., Individual Retirement Account (IRA) deductions, alimony paid deductions, and most itemized deductions]. Personal casualty and theft losses, losses incurred in a transaction entered into for profit, and employee business expense deductions are allowed.

      A taxpayer who does not itemize deductions computes the excess of nonbusiness deductions over nonbusiness income by substituting the standard deduction for total itemized deductions.
   c. The excess of business capital losses over the sum of business capital gains and the excess of nonbusiness income and net nonbusiness capital gains over nonbusiness deductions must be added back.
   d. The add-back for net nonbusiness capital losses and excess business capital losses does not include net capital losses not included in the current-year computation of taxable income because of the capital loss limitation provisions (discussed in text Section 14-5d).

For a review of the computation of the net operating loss for individuals, see Concept Summary 7.5.

Concept Summary 7.5

Computation of Net Operating Loss

Taxable income shown on the return

Add back:

1. Personal and dependency exemptions (suspended from 2018 through 2025).
2. Net operating loss carryover from another year.
3. The qualified business income deduction (§ 199A).
4. The excess of nonbusiness capital losses over nonbusiness capital gains.
5. The excess of nonbusiness deductions over the sum of nonbusiness income plus *net* nonbusiness capital gains.
6. The excess of business capital losses over the sum of business capital gains plus the excess of nonbusiness income and *net* nonbusiness capital gains over nonbusiness deductions.

Note: The add-back from the total of items 4 and 6 will not exceed $3,000 because of the capital loss limitation rules.

Equals: The net operating loss

The capital loss and nonbusiness deduction limits are illustrated in Examples 34 through 37.

Capital Loss and Nonbusiness Deduction Limits

Example 34

For 2023, taxpayer and spouse have $6,000 of nonbusiness capital losses and $4,000 of nonbusiness capital gains.

They must add back $2,000 to taxable income ($6,000 − $4,000), which is the excess of nonbusiness capital losses over nonbusiness capital gains.

Capital Loss and Nonbusiness Deduction Limits

Example 35

For 2023, taxpayer and spouse have $2,600 of nonbusiness capital gains, $1,000 of nonbusiness capital losses, $2,000 of interest income, and no itemized deductions.

They must add back $24,100 to taxable income {$27,700 standard deduction − [$2,000 interest income + $1,600 ($2,600 − $1,000) net nonbusiness capital gains]}.

Note that, in this example, there is no excess of nonbusiness capital losses over nonbusiness capital gains.

Example 36

For 2023, taxpayer and spouse have $2,600 of nonbusiness capital gains, $1,000 of nonbusiness capital losses, $30,000 of interest income, $29,000 of itemized deductions (none of which are personal casualty and theft losses), $4,000 of business capital losses, and $1,000 of business capital gains.

They must add back $400 to taxable income {$4,000 business capital losses − [$1,000 business capital gains + ($30,000 nonbusiness income + $1,600 net nonbusiness capital gains − $29,000 nonbusiness deductions)]}.

Note that, in this example, there is no excess of nonbusiness capital losses over nonbusiness capital gains, nor is there an excess of nonbusiness deductions over the sum of nonbusiness income and net nonbusiness capital gains.

Example 37

For 2023, taxpayer and spouse have $2,600 of nonbusiness capital gains, $3,000 of nonbusiness capital losses, $28,000 of interest income, $30,000 of itemized deductions (none of which are personal casualty and theft losses), $8,000 of business capital losses, and $4,000 of business capital gains.

They must add back $5,000 to taxable income:

(1) $2,000 ($30,000 − $28,000), which is the excess of nonbusiness deductions over nonbusiness income.

(2) $3,000, the excess of combined capital losses is $4,400, but the capital loss limitation caps the loss at $3,000 in computing taxable income for the year.

Example 38 illustrates the computation of an NOL.

Example 38

James opened a retail store in 2022 and experienced an NOL of $2,000 for that year. James is married, has no dependents, and files a joint return. For 2023, James and his spouse have the following taxable income:

Gross income from the business	$ 67,000	
Less: Business expenses	(73,000)	($ 6,000)
Salary from a part-time job		875
Interest on savings account		525
Nonbusiness long-term capital gain		1,000
NOL carryover from 2022		(2,000)
Net loss on rental property (managed by James)		(100)
Adjusted gross income		($ 5,700)
Less: Itemized deductions		
Interest expense on home mortgage	$ 4,600	
Taxes	7,300	
Casualty loss	2,000	
Total itemized deductions	$ 13,900	
Standard deduction (greater than itemized deductions)		(27,700)
Deduction for qualified business income*		(–0–)
Taxable income		($33,400)

*James has no qualified business income in 2023; the retail store generated a loss of $6,000, and the rental property he manages generated a loss of $100. These losses carry forward to future years and will reduce any qualified business income in those years.

continued

James's 2023 NOL is computed as follows:

Taxable income				($33,400)
Add:				
Net operating loss from 2022			$ 2,000	
Excess of nonbusiness deductions over nonbusiness income				
Standard deduction		$27,700		
Less: Interest income	$ 525			
Less: Long-term capital gain	1,000	(1,525)	26,175	28,175
Net operating loss				($ 5,225)

Effectively, the 2023 NOL is made up of the following amounts:

Business loss	($ 6,000)
Rental loss	(100)
Salary income	875
Net operating loss	($ 5,225)

7-6c Computation of Taxable Income for Year to Which Net Operating Loss Is Carried

When an NOL is carried to a nonloss year, the taxable income for the year is determined by including the NOL as a deduction *for* AGI. Several deductions (such as medical expenses and charitable contributions) are based on the amount of AGI. These deductions must be determined on the basis of the AGI after the NOL has been applied.

Example 39

Continue with the facts from Example 38. Assume that in 2024, James and his spouse report the following information:

Gross income from the business	$ 98,000	
Less: Business expenses	(74,000)	$24,000
Salary (spouse)		32,000
Interest on savings account		310
Net income on rental property (managed by James)		750

In addition, assume that James and his spouse will use the standard deduction. Determine their taxable income for the year and any NOL carryforward to 2025.

Solution: Due to the 80% of taxable income limitation on NOL carryforwards, a multistep process is required: (1) determine taxable income before application of the NOL, (2) determine the NOL deduction, and (3) determine final taxable income.

(1) Determine taxable income before application of the NOL:

Gross income from the business	$ 98,000	
Less: Business expenses	(74,000)	$ 24,000
Salary (spouse)		32,000
Interest on savings account		310
Net income on rental property		750
Adjusted gross income		$ 57,060
Less: Standard deduction*		(27,700)
Less: Deduction for qualified business income:**		
Store [$24,000 − $2,000 (2022 loss) − $6,000 (2023 loss)] × 20%	$ 3,200	
Rental [$750 − $100 (2023 loss)] × 20%	130	(3,330)
Taxable income		$ 26,030

* Because the 2024 standard deduction amount will not be released by the IRS until late 2023, the 2023 standard deduction amount is used.

** According to § 199A, the deduction for qualified business income must be determined separately for each trade or business. This example assumes that a managed rental property qualifies for the deduction. The § 199A(b)(1) "combined qualified business income amount" is $3,330. Taxable income before the QBI deduction is $29,360 ($57,060 − $27,700); this is also modified taxable income. So the QBI deduction is not limited by the overall taxable income limitation (modified taxable income × 20%).

continued

(2) Determine the NOL deduction:

The NOL deduction is limited to the lesser of:

1. The NOL carryforward ($7,225; $2,000 from 2022 and $5,225 from 2023), or
2. 80% of taxable income computed in step 1: $20,824 ($26,030 × 80%).

Because the NOL carryforward is less than the 80% limitation, the entire NOL carryover is allowed as a *for* AGI deduction in 2024.

(3) Determine final taxable income:

Gross income from the business	$ 98,000	
Less: Business expenses	(74,000)	$ 24,000
Salary (spouse)		32,000
Interest on savings account		310
Net income on rental property		750
NOL deduction		(7,225)
Adjusted gross income		$ 49,835
Less: Standard deduction		(27,700)
Less: Deduction for qualified business income:*		
Store [$24,000 − $2,000 (2022 loss) − $6,000 (2023 loss)] × 20%	$ 3,200	
Rental [$750 − $100 (2023 loss)] × 20%	130	(3,330)
Taxable income		$ 18,805

Note: The NOL deduction is a *for* AGI deduction. As a result, if the taxpayers were itemizing their deductions, this recomputation of AGI could have an impact on their itemized deductions (e.g., medical, contributions, or casualty loss).

*Taxable income before the QBI deduction is $22,135 ($49,835 − $27,700); this is also modified taxable income. So the QBI deduction is not limited by the overall taxable income limitation (modified taxable income × 20%).

(4) Determine any NOL carryforward to 2025:

As the 2022 and 2023 NOL carryforwards were entirely used in 2024, there is no NOL carry forward to 2025.

7-6d **Calculation of the Remaining Net Operating Loss**

After computing taxable income for the initial carryforward year, it is then necessary to determine the extent to which any NOL remains to carry over to future years.[50] The amount of this carryover loss is the excess of the NOL over the taxable income of the year to which the loss is being applied. However, the taxable income of the year to which the loss is being applied must be determined with the following *modifications*:

- No deduction is allowed for excess capital losses over capital gains.
- No deduction is allowed for an NOL that is being carried back. However, deductions are allowed for NOLs occurring before the loss year.
- Any deductions claimed that are based on or limited by AGI must be determined after making the preceding adjustments. However, charitable contributions do not take into account any NOL carryback.
- The qualified business income deduction is not allowed.
- No deduction is allowed for personal and dependency exemptions; from 2018 through 2025, the exemption amount is zero.

Although this computation is somewhat similar to the calculations discussed previously, additional nuances exist, including determining the implications of recent legislative changes to the NOL carryforward computation (e.g., the 80 percent of taxable income limitation on NOLs and the qualified business income deduction). The resulting complexities and lack of current guidance from the Treasury Department and the IRS make this computation challenging (and beyond the scope of this text).

[50]Taxpayers with an NOL carryover must keep records to track its use in carryforward years.

7-7 Tax Planning

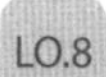

Identify tax planning opportunities in deducting certain business expenses, business losses, and personal losses.

7-7a Small Business Stock (§ 1244 Stock) Losses

Because § 1244 limits the amount of loss classified as ordinary loss on a yearly basis, a taxpayer might maximize the benefits of § 1244 by selling the stock in more than one taxable year. The result could be that the losses in any one taxable year would not exceed the § 1244 limits on ordinary loss.

Mitch, a single individual, purchased small business stock in 2021 for $150,000 (150 shares at $1,000 per share). On December 20, 2023, the stock is worth $60,000 (150 shares at $400 per share). Mitch wants to sell the stock at this time. Mitch earns a salary of $80,000 a year, has no other capital transactions, and does not expect any in the future.

If Mitch sells all of the small business stock in 2023, his recognized loss will be $90,000 ($60,000 − $150,000). The loss will be characterized as a $50,000 ordinary loss and a $40,000 long-term capital loss. In computing taxable income for 2023, Mitch could deduct the $50,000 ordinary loss but could deduct only $3,000 of the capital loss. The remainder of the capital loss could be carried over and used in future years subject to the $3,000 limitation if Mitch has no capital gains.

Instead, if Mitch sells 82 shares in 2023, he will recognize an ordinary loss of $49,200 [82 × ($1,000 − $400)]. If Mitch then sells the remainder of the shares in 2024, he will recognize an ordinary loss of $40,800 [68 × ($1,000 − $400)]. Mitch could deduct the $49,200 ordinary loss in computing 2023 taxable income and the $40,800 ordinary loss in computing 2024 taxable income.

7-7b Casualty Losses

A special election is available for taxpayers who sustain casualty losses in an area designated by the President as a disaster area. This election affects only the *timing*, not the calculation, of the deduction. The benefit, of course, is a faster refund (or reduction in tax). It will also be advantageous to carry the loss back if the taxpayer's tax rate in the carryback year is higher than the tax rate in the year of the loss.

To find out if an event qualifies as a disaster area loss, one can look in any of the major tax services, the Compilation of Presidential Documents (released by the U.S. Government Publishing Office), or the *Internal Revenue Bulletin*.

Refocus on The Big Picture

Losses

TETRA IMAGES/GETTY IMAGES

Martha can receive tax benefits associated with her unfortunate occurrences during the current tax year. Some of the losses, however, will provide a greater tax benefit than others as a result of different tax provisions governing the amount and the classification of the losses.

Bad Debt

Based on the facts provided, it appears that Martha's loan to her friend Janice was a bona fide debt. Otherwise, nothing would be deductible. The amount of the deduction is the unpaid principal balance of $19,000 ($25,000 − $6,000). Unfortunately, because the bad debt is a nonbusiness bad debt, it is classified as a short-term capital loss (see Example 5).

continued

Investment Losses

The $50,000 loss from the pharmaceutical company stock is deductible. However, it appears that the loss should be classified as a long-term capital loss rather than as a short-term capital loss. Although the actual holding period was not greater than one year (October through May), the disposal date for the stock (which qualifies as a worthless security) is deemed to be the last day of the tax year (October of last year through end of December of the current year). Further, the loss does not appear to qualify for ordinary loss treatment under § 1244 (see Example 8).

The stock she purchased from her friend Peter results in an $8,000 short-term capital loss (and does not qualify under § 1244; see Example 10).

Loss from Bookstore

The $180,000 loss from Martha's sole proprietorship (her bookstore) is reported on Schedule C of Form 1040. It is an ordinary loss, and it qualifies for NOL treatment. Martha can carry forward any net loss and offset it against future taxable income. However, the NOL carryforward will be limited (each year) to the lesser of the NOL or 80 percent of taxable income (computed without regard to the NOL carryforward).

Casualty Loss

The loss from the damage to Martha's personal residence is classified as a personal casualty loss. Using the cost of repairs method, the amount of the casualty loss is $7,000 ($25,000 − $32,000). However, this amount must be reduced by the $100-per-event floor and the 10%-of-AGI floor.

Because the President classified the county in which Martha's house is located as a Federal disaster area, Martha has the option of deducting the casualty loss on the prior year's tax return (see Example 15).

Key Terms

Bad debt, 7-2
Business bad debt, 7-4
Casualty loss, 7-7
Disaster area losses, 7-9
Excess business loss, 7-17
Net operating loss (NOL), 7-19
Nonbusiness bad debt, 7-4
Research and experimental expenditures, 7-15
Reserve method, 7-3
Small business stock (§ 1244 stock), 7-6
Specific charge-off method, 7-3
Theft losses, 7-8
Worthless securities, 7-6

Discussion Questions

1. **LO.1** Explain how an account receivable can give rise to a bad debt deduction.
2. **LO.1** Ron, a cash basis taxpayer, sells his business accounts receivable of $100,000 to Felicia for $70,000 (70% of the actual accounts receivable). Discuss the amount and classification of Ron's bad debt deduction.
3. **LO.1** Discuss when a bad debt deduction can be taken for a nonbusiness debt.
4. **LO.1** Discuss the treatment of a business bad debt when the business also has long-term capital gains.

5. **LO.1, 2, 3, 4, 7** Many years ago, Jack purchased 400 shares of Canary stock. During the current year, the stock became worthless. It was determined that the company "went under" because several corporate officers embezzled a large amount of company funds. Identify the relevant tax issues for Jack. Critical Thinking

6. **LO.1, 2** Sean is in the business of buying and selling stocks and bonds. He has a bond of Green Corporation for which he paid $200,000. The bond is currently worth only $50,000. Discuss whether Sean can take a $150,000 loss for a business bad debt or for a worthless security.

7. **LO.2** Discuss the tax treatment of the sale of § 1244 stock at a gain.

8. **LO.3, 4** Jim discovers that his residence has extensive termite damage. Discuss whether he may take a deduction for the damage to his residence.

9. **LO.3, 4** The value of Terrah's personal residence has declined significantly because of a recent forest fire in the area where she lives. The fire was a Federally declared disaster. Terrah's house suffered no actual damage during the fire, but because much of the surrounding area was destroyed, the value of all of the homes in the area declined substantially. Discuss whether Terrah can take a casualty loss for the decline in value of her residence caused by the fire.

10. **LO.4** Discuss at what point in time a theft loss generally is recognized.

11. **LO.4** Discuss the circumstances under which the cost of repairs to the damaged property can be used to measure the amount of a casualty loss.

12. **LO.4** In 2023, Kelsey sustained a loss on the theft of a painting. She had paid $20,000 for the painting, but it was worth $40,000 at the time of the theft. Evaluate the tax consequences of treating the painting as investment property or as personal use property.

13. **LO.2, 4** Kelly decided to invest in Lime, Inc. common stock after reviewing Lime's public disclosures, including recent financial statements and a number of press releases issued by Lime. On August 7, 2021, Kelly purchased 60,000 shares of Lime for $210,000. In May 2022, Lime entered into a joint venture with Cherry, Inc. In November 2022, the joint venture failed, and Lime's stock began to decline in value. In December 2022, Cherry filed a lawsuit against Lime for theft of corporate opportunity and breach of fiduciary responsibility. In February 2023, Lime filed a countersuit against Cherry for fraud and misappropriation of funds. At the end of December 2023, Kelly's stock in Lime was worth $15,000. Identify the relevant tax issues for Kelly. Critical Thinking

14. **LO.3, 4** In 2020, John opened an investment account with Randy Hansen, who held himself out to the public as an investment adviser and securities broker. John contributed $200,000 to the account in 2020. John provided Randy with a power of attorney to use the $200,000 to purchase and sell securities on John's behalf. John instructed Randy to reinvest any gains and income earned. In 2020, 2021, and 2022, John received statements of the amount of income earned by his account and included these amounts in his gross income for these years. In 2023, it was discovered that Randy's purported investment advisory and brokerage activity was in fact a fraudulent investment arrangement known as a Ponzi scheme. In reality, John's account balance was zero, the money having been used by Randy in his scheme. Identify the relevant tax issues for John. Critical Thinking

15. **LO.5** Discuss under what circumstances a company would elect to amortize research and experimental expenditures rather than use the expense method.

Critical Thinking

16. **LO.6, 7** Amos began a business, Silver LLC (a single-member LLC), on July 1, 2020. The business extracts and processes silver ore. During 2023, as a result of a decline in demand for silver ore, Amos expects to generate a large loss. Identify the relevant tax issues for Amos.

17. **LO.6** Discuss the rationale behind the excess business loss provision.

18. **LO.7** Discuss whether unreimbursed employee business expenses can create an NOL for an individual taxpayer.

19. **LO.7** Discuss whether deductions *for* AGI can be treated as nonbusiness deductions in computing an individual's NOL.

Critical Thinking

20. **LO.7** Thomas believes that he has an NOL for the current year and plans to carry it forward, offsetting it against future income. In determining his NOL, Thomas offset his business income by alimony payments he made to his ex-wife and contributions he made to his traditional Individual Retirement Account (IRA). His reason for using these items in the NOL computation is that each item is a deduction *for* AGI. Identify the relevant tax issues for Thomas.

Computational Exercises

21. **LO.1** Last year Aleshia identified $15,000 as a nonbusiness bad debt. In that tax year, before considering the tax implications of the nonbusiness bad debt, Aleshia had $100,000 of taxable income, of which $12,000 consisted of short-term capital gains. This year Aleshia collected $8,000 of the amount she had previously identified as a bad debt. Determine Aleshia's tax treatment of the $8,000 received in the current tax year.

22. **LO.1** Bob owns a collection agency. He purchases uncollected accounts receivable from other businesses at 60% of their face value and then attempts to collect these accounts. During the current year, Bob collected $60,000 on an account with a face value of $80,000. Determine the amount of Bob's bad debt deduction.

23. **LO.2** On May 9, 2021, Calvin acquired 250 shares of stock in Hobbes Corporation, a new startup company, for $68,750. Calvin acquired the stock directly from Hobbes, and it is classified as § 1244 stock (at the time Calvin acquired his stock, the corporation had $900,000 of paid-in capital). On January 15, 2023, Calvin sold all of his Hobbes stock for $7,000. Assuming that Calvin is single, determine his tax consequences as a result of this sale.

24. **LO.4** Determine the treatment of a loss on rental property under the following facts:

Basis	$650,000
FMV before the loss	800,000
FMV after the loss	200,000

25. **LO.4** Belinda was involved in a boating accident in 2023. Her speedboat, which was used only for personal use and had a fair market value of $30,000 and an adjusted basis of $14,000, was completely destroyed. She received $10,000 from her insurance company. Her AGI for 2023 is $37,000. What is Belinda's casualty loss deduction (after any limitations)?

26. **LO.4** During the current year, Tucker had the following personal casualty gains and losses (after deducting the $100 floor):

Asset	Holding Period	Gain or (Loss)
Asset 1	18 months	($1,200)
Asset 2	2 months	750
Asset 3	3 years	1,500

What are the tax consequences of these items to Tucker?

27. **LO.5** Sandstorm Corporation decides to develop a new line of paints. The project begins in 2023 in the U.S. Sandstorm incurs the following expenses in 2023 in connection with the project:

Salaries	$85,000
Materials	30,000
Depreciation on equipment	12,500

The benefits from the project will be realized starting in July 2024. Sandstorm Corporation capitalizes and amortizes its research and experimental expenditures. What are its related deductions in 2023 and 2024?

28. **LO.6** Tim, a single taxpayer, operates a business as a single-member LLC. In 2023, his LLC reports business income of $225,000 and business deductions of $595,000, resulting in a loss of $370,000. What are the implications of this business loss? Can this business loss be used to offset other income that Tim reports? If so, how much? If not, what happens to the loss?

29. **LO.7** Valeria and Trey are married and file a joint tax return. For 2023, they have $4,800 of nonbusiness capital gains, $2,300 of nonbusiness capital losses, $500 of interest income, and no itemized deductions. The standard deduction for married filing jointly is $27,700.

Based on these transactions, to arrive at the NOL, Valeria and Trey's taxable income must be adjusted by what amount?

30. **LO.7** Emily, who is single, sustains an NOL of $7,800 in 2023. The loss is carried forward to 2024. For 2024, Emily's income tax information before taking into account the 2023 NOL is as follows:

Adjusted gross income		$ 48,200
Itemized deductions*:		
Medical [$3,650 − (7.5% × $48,200)]	$ 35	
Taxes	6,100	
Interest expense on home mortgage	11,000	(17,135)
Taxable income		$ 31,065

*The 2023 single standard deduction is $13,850; Emily's itemized deductions will exceed the 2024 single standard deduction (after adjustment for inflation).

How much of the NOL carryforward can Emily use in 2024, and what is her adjusted gross income and her taxable income?

Problems

Communications

31. **LO.1** Several years ago Amy Westbrook, who is in the lending business, loaned Sara Stuart $30,000 to purchase an automobile to be used for personal purposes. In August of the current year, Sara filed for bankruptcy, after paying back $1,000 of the loan to Amy. Amy was notified by the bankruptcy court that she could not expect to receive more than an additional $4,000. Amy has contacted you about the possibility of taking a bad debt deduction for the current year.

    Write a letter to Amy that contains your advice as to whether she can claim a bad debt deduction for the current year. Also prepare a memo for the tax files. Amy's address is 100 Tyler Lane, Erie, PA 16563.

32. **LO.1** Monty loaned his friend Ned $20,000 three years ago. Ned signed a note and made payments on the loan. Last year, when the remaining balance was $11,000, Ned filed for bankruptcy and notified Monty that he would be unable to pay the balance on the loan. Monty treated the $11,000 as a nonbusiness bad debt. Last year, before considering the tax implications of the nonbusiness bad debt, Monty had capital gains of $9,000 and taxable income of $45,000. During the current year, Ned paid Monty $10,000 in satisfaction of the debt. Determine Monty's tax treatment for the $10,000 received in the current year.

33. **LO.1** Sally is in the business of purchasing accounts receivable. Last year Sally purchased an account receivable with a face value of $80,000 for $60,000. During the current year, Sally settled the account, receiving $65,000. Determine the maximum amount of the bad debt deduction for Sally for the current year.

34. **LO.1, 2** Jocelyn and Esteban file a joint return. For the current year, they had the following items:

Salaries	$120,000
Loss on sale of § 1244 stock acquired two years ago	105,000
Gain on sale of § 1244 stock acquired six months ago	20,000
Nonbusiness bad debt	19,000

    Determine their AGI for the current year.

Critical Thinking
Decision Making
Planning

35. **LO.2, 8** Abby, a single taxpayer, purchased 10,000 shares of § 1244 stock several years ago at a cost of $20 per share. In November of the current year, Abby received an offer to sell the stock for $12 per share. She has the option of either selling all of the stock now or selling half of the stock now and half of the stock in January of next year. Abby will receive a salary of $80,000 for the current year and $90,000 next year. Abby will have long-term capital gains of $8,000 for the current year and $10,000 next year. If Abby's goal is to minimize her AGI for the two years, determine whether she should sell all of her stock this year or half of her stock this year and half next year.

Critical Thinking
Decision Making
Planning

36. **LO.3, 4, 8** Olaf lives in the state of Minnesota. In May 2023, a tornado hit the area and damaged his home and automobile. Applicable information is as follows:

Item	Adjusted Basis	FMV before	FMV after	Insurance Proceeds
Home	$350,000	$500,000	$100,000	$280,000
Auto	60,000	40,000	10,000	20,000

    Because of the extensive damage caused by the tornado, the President designated the area a Federal disaster area.

    Olaf and his wife, Anna, always file a joint return. Their 2022 tax return shows AGI of $180,000 and taxable income of $150,000. In 2023, their return shows AGI of $300,000 and taxable income (exclusive of the casualty loss deduction) of $245,000.

    Determine the amount of Olaf and Anna's loss and the year in which they should take the loss.

37. **LO.3, 4** Heather owns a two-story building. The building is used 40% for business use and 60% for personal use. During 2023, a fire caused major damage to the building and its contents. Heather purchased the building for $800,000 and has taken depreciation of $100,000 on the business portion. At the time of the fire, the building had a fair market value of $900,000. Immediately after the fire, the fair market value was $200,000. The insurance recovery on the building was $600,000. The contents of the building were insured for any loss at fair market value. The business assets had an adjusted basis of $220,000 and a fair market value of $175,000. These assets were totally destroyed. The personal use assets had an adjusted basis of $50,000 and a fair market value of $65,000. These assets were also totally destroyed. If Heather's AGI is $100,000 before considering the effects of the fire, determine her itemized deduction as a result of the fire. Also determine Heather's AGI.

38. **LO.3, 4** On February 20, 2024, Trevor Pickard was involved in an accident with his business use automobile. Trevor had purchased the car for $30,000. The automobile had a fair market value of $20,000 before the accident and $8,000 immediately after the accident. Trevor has taken $20,000 of depreciation on the car. The car is insured for the fair market value of any loss. Because of Trevor's history, he is afraid that if he submits a claim, his policy will be canceled. As a result, he is considering not filing a claim and has come to you for advice. Trevor believes that the tax loss deduction will help mitigate the loss of the insurance reimbursement. Trevor's current marginal tax rate is 35%.

Communications
Decision Making
Planning

Write a letter to Trevor that contains your advice with respect to the tax and cash-flow consequences of filing versus not filing a claim for the insurance reimbursement for the damage to his car. Also prepare a memo for the tax files. Trevor's address is 450 Colonel's Way, Warrensburg, MO 64093.

39. **LO.5** Blue Corporation, a manufacturing company, decided to develop a new line of merchandise. The project began in 2022. Blue had the following expenditures in connection with the project, all incurred in the U.S.:

	2022	2023
Salaries	$500,000	$600,000
Materials	90,000	70,000
Insurance	8,000	11,000
Utilities	6,000	8,000
Cost of inspection of materials for quality control	7,000	6,000
Promotion expenses	11,000	18,000
Advertising	–0–	20,000
Equipment depreciation	15,000	14,000
Cost of market survey	8,000	–0–

The new product will be introduced for sale beginning in April 2024.

a. Determine Blue Corporation's research and experimental expenditures for 2022 and 2023.

b. Determine Blue Corporation's deduction for research and experimental expenditures for 2022 and 2023.

40. **LO.6** During 2023, Leisel, a single taxpayer, operates a sole proprietorship in which she materially participates. Her proprietorship generates gross income of $142,000 and deductions of $460,000, resulting in a loss of $318,000. The large deductions are due to the acquisition of equipment and the use of immediate expense and additional first-year depreciation to deduct all of the acquisitions. Can Leisel use all of this loss to offset other income she has? Explain.

41. **LO.6** Timothy Gates and Prada Singh decide to form a new company, TGPS LLC (a multimember LLC that will report its operations as a partnership). Timothy is married, and Prada is single. Each contributes $400,000 of capital to begin the business, and both materially participate in the business. In 2023, TGPS reports a net loss of $610,000. What are the implications of this loss for Timothy and Prada?

42. **LO.7** Mario, a single taxpayer with two dependent children, has the following items of income and expense during 2023:

Gross receipts from business	$144,000
Business expenses	180,000
Net capital gain	22,000
Interest income	3,000
Itemized deductions (state taxes, residence interest, and contributions)	24,000

a. Determine Mario's taxable income for 2023.

b. Determine Mario's NOL for 2023.

43. **LO.7** Xinran, who is married and files a joint return, owns a grocery store. In 2023, his gross sales were $276,000 and operating expenses were $320,000. Other items on his 2023 return were as follows:

Nonbusiness capital gains (short term)	$20,000
Nonbusiness capital losses (long term)	9,000
Itemized deductions	18,000
Ordinary nonbusiness income	8,000
Salary from part-time job (spouse)	10,000

In 2024, Xinran provides the following information:

Net business income		$60,000
Salary (spouse)		25,000
Interest income		2,000
Adjusted gross income		$87,000
Itemized deductions*		
Charitable contributions (cash)	$35,000	
Medical expenses of $6,925 [limited to the amount in excess of 7.5% of AGI ($6,925 – $6,525)]	400	
Total itemized deductions		$35,400

*The 2023 married filing jointly standard deduction is $27,700; Xinran's itemized deductions will exceed the 2024 standard deduction (after adjustment for inflation).

a. What is Xinran's 2023 NOL?

b. Determine Xinran's taxable income for 2024.

44. **LO.7** During 2023, Rick and his wife, Sara, had the following items of income and expense to report:

Gross receipts from business	$400,000
Business expenses	525,000
Interest income from bank savings accounts	8,000
Sara's salary	50,000
Long-term capital gain on stock held as an investment	4,000
Itemized deductions	15,000

a. Assuming that Rick and Sara file a joint return, what is their taxable income for 2023?

b. What is the amount of Rick and Sara's NOL for 2023?

c. To what years can Rick and Sara's NOL be carried?

d. Based on your computations, identify the components of their NOL. What is the rationale for excluding the items that do not affect the NOL computation?

45. **LO.1, 2, 3, 4, 7** Jed, age 55, is married with no children. During 2023, Jed had the following income and expense items:

a. Three years ago, Jed loaned a friend $10,000 to help him purchase a new car. In June of the current year, Jed learned that his friend had been declared bankrupt and had left the country. There is no possibility that Jed will ever collect any of the $10,000.

b. In April 2021, Jed purchased some stock for $5,000. In March 2023, the company was declared bankrupt and Jed was notified that his shares of stock were worthless.

c. Several years ago Jed purchased some § 1244 stock for $120,000. This year he sold the stock for $30,000.

d. In July of this year, Jed sold some land that he had held for two years for $60,000. He had originally paid $42,000 for the land.

e. Jed received $40,000 of interest income from State of Minnesota bonds.

f. In September, Jed's home was damaged by an earthquake; Jed's county was declared a Federal disaster area by the President. Jed's basis in his home was $430,000. The value of the home immediately before the earthquake was $610,000. After the earthquake, the home was worth $540,000. Because earthquake damage was an exclusion on Jed's homeowner's insurance policy, he received no insurance recovery.

g. Jed received a salary of $80,000.

h. Jed paid home mortgage interest of $14,000.

If Jed files a joint return for 2023, determine his NOL for the year.

Tax Return Problems

46. Denise Lopez, age 40, is single and has no dependents. She is employed as a legal secretary by Legal Services, Inc. She owns and operates Typing Services located near the campus of Florida Atlantic University at 1986 Campus Drive, Boca Raton, FL 33434. Denise is a material participant in the business, she is a cash basis taxpayer, and her Social Security number is 123-45-6781. Denise lives at 2020 Oakcrest Road, Boca Raton, FL 33431. Denise wants to designate $3 to the Presidential Election Campaign Fund. She has never owned or used any virtual currency. During 2022, Denise had the following income and expense items:

Communications
Critical Thinking
Decision Making
Planning
Tax Forms Problem
ProConnect™ Tax

a. $100,000 salary from Legal Services, Inc.

b. $20,000 gross receipts from her typing services business.

c. $700 interest income from Third National Bank.

d. $1,000 Christmas bonus from Legal Services, Inc.

e. $60,000 life insurance proceeds on the death of her sister.

f. $5,000 check given to her by her wealthy aunt.

g. $100 won in a bingo game.

h. Expenses connected with Typing Services:

Office rent	$7,000
Supplies	4,400
Utilities and telephone	4,680
Wages to part-time typists	5,000
Payroll taxes	500
Equipment rentals	3,000

i. $9,500 interest expense on a home mortgage (paid to Boca Raton Savings and Loan).

j. $15,000 fair market value of silverware stolen from her home by a burglar on October 12, 2022. Denise had paid $14,000 for the silverware on July 1, 2012. She was reimbursed $10,000 by her insurance company.

k. Denise had loaned $2,100 to a friend, Joan Jensen, on June 3, 2018. Joan declared bankruptcy on August 14, 2022, and was unable to repay the loan. Assume that the loan is a bona fide debt.

l. Legal Services, Inc., withheld Federal income tax of $14,000 and the appropriate amount of FICA tax from her wages.

m. Alimony of $10,000 received from her former husband, Omar Guzman; divorce was finalized on December 2, 2013, and no changes have been made to the divorce decree since that time.

n. Interest income of $800 on City of Boca Raton bonds.

o. Denise made estimated Federal tax payments of $2,000.

p. Sales taxes from the sales tax table of $953.

q. Property taxes on her residence of $3,200.

r. Charitable contribution of $2,500 to her alma mater, Citrus State College.

s. On November 1, 2022, Denise was involved in an automobile accident. At the time of the accident, her automobile's FMV was $45,000. After the accident, the automobile's FMV was $38,000. Denise acquired the car on May 2, 2021, at a cost of $52,000. Denise's car was covered by insurance, but, because the policy had a $5,000 deduction clause, Denise decided not to file a claim for the damage.

Part 1—Tax Computation

Compute Denise Lopez's 2022 Federal income tax payable (or refund due), and complete her 2022 Federal tax return using appropriate forms and schedules. Suggested software: ProConnect Tax.

Part 2—Tax Planning

In 2023, Denise plans to continue her job with Legal Services, Inc. As a result, items a, d, and l will recur in 2023. Denise plans to continue her typing services business (refer to item b) and expects gross receipts of $34,000. She projects that all business expenses (refer to item h) will increase by 10%, except for office rent, which, under the terms of her lease, will remain the same as in 2022. Items e, f, g, j, k, and s will not recur in 2023. Items c, i, m, n, p, q, and r will be approximately the same as in 2022.

Based on this information, Denise would like you to provide a tentative computation of her 2023 taxable income. Prepare a memo for her tax files that details this computation.

Tax Computation Problem

47. Mason Phillips, age 45, and his wife, Alyssa, live at 230 Wood Lane, Salt Lake City, UT 84101. Mason's Social Security number is 111-11-1111. Alyssa's Social Security number is 123-45-6789. Mason and Alyssa are cash basis taxpayers and report the following items for 2023:

- Salary of $140,000.
- Collection of unpaid rent from a prior year of $6,000.

- Rental income of $60,000 (not including prior year unpaid rent; the rental property is managed by the Phillips).
- Rental expenses of $33,000.
- Uncollected rent (bad debts) of $4,000.
- Casualty loss on rental property of $10,000.
- Sale of § 1244 stock resulting in a loss of $105,000. The stock was acquired eight months ago.
- Personal casualty loss (from one event) of $3,000; not in a Federally declared disaster area.
- Theft loss of $8,000 on a painting held for investment.
- Other itemized deductions of $21,000.
- Federal income tax withheld of $3,000.

Compute Mason and Alyssa's 2023 Federal income tax payable (or refund due).

Research Problems

Note: Solutions to the Research Problems can be prepared by using the Thomson Reuters Checkpoint™ online tax research database, which accompanies this textbook. Solutions can also be prepared by using research materials found in a typical tax library.

Research Problem 1. During 2023, your client, Kendra Adams, was the chief executive officer and a shareholder of Maze, Inc. She owned 60% of the outstanding stock of Maze. In 2020, Kendra and Maze, as co-borrowers, obtained a $100,000 loan from United National Bank. This loan was secured by Kendra's personal residence. Although Maze was listed as a co-borrower, Kendra repaid the loan in full in 2023. On Maze's Form 1120 tax returns, no loans from shareholders were reported. Discuss whether Kendra is entitled to a bad debt deduction for the amount of the payment on the loan.

Partial list of research aids:
U.S. v. Generes, 92 S.Ct. 827 (1972).
Dale H. Sundby, T.C.Memo. 2003–204.
Arrigoni v. Comm., 73 T.C. 792 (1980).
Estate of Herbert M. Rapoport, T.C.Memo. 1982–584.
Clifford L. Brody and Barbara J. DeClerk, T.C. Summary Opinion, 2004–149.

Research Problem 2. Esther owns a large home on the Southeast Coast. Her home is surrounded by large, mature oak trees that significantly increase the value of her home. In September 2023, a hurricane damaged many of the trees surrounding her home; her region was declared a Federal disaster area as a result of the hurricane's damage. In October 2023, Esther engaged a local arborist to evaluate and treat the trees, but five of the largest trees were seriously weakened by the storm. These trees died from disease in 2024. Esther has ascertained that the amount of the casualty loss from the death of the five trees is $25,000; however, she is uncertain in which year to deduct this loss and has come to you for advice. Discuss whether the casualty loss should be deducted in the calculation of Esther's 2023 or 2024 taxable income. Planning

Partial list of research aids:
Reg. § 1.165–1.
Oregon Mesabi Corporation, 39 B.T.A. 1033 (1939).

Use internet tax resources to address the following questions. Look for reliable websites and blogs of the IRS and other government agencies, media outlets, businesses, tax professionals, academics, think tanks, and political outlets.

Research Problem 3. Find an article that discusses tax planning for casualty losses when a Federal disaster area designation is made. Does the article convey the pertinent tax rules correctly? Then list all of the locations identified by the President as Federal disaster areas in the last two years.

Communications
Data Analytics

Research Problem 4. How many U.S. individuals claim a deduction for casualties? Does it vary by size of income (AGI)? How do casualty loss deductions compare to the amounts of other itemized deductions claimed by taxpayers? Go to the IRS tax statistics website (**irs.gov/statistics**), and download a recent tax year's information on "Individual Income Tax Returns with Itemized Deductions." Cluster the data into no more than six AGI categories. Present your findings in a visual (e.g., a bar chart), and summarize your findings in a one-page memo to your instructor.

Communications

Research Problem 5. Locate Rev. Proc. 2018–8 and identify the various safe harbors that are available to taxpayers in calculating casualty losses in Federal disaster areas. In a memo to your instructor, briefly summarize the safe harbors that are available. As part of your memo, provide an illustration of the "estimated repair cost method" safe harbor.

Communications

Research Problem 6. There is significant debate about the excess business loss deduction. Some believe it should be repealed; others (including the President) believe it should be made permanent. Find several articles that summarize this debate, synthesize the articles into a one-page memo, and share the memo with your instructor.

Becker CPA Review Questions

Becker

1. Mark and Lucy owned two stocks, Tinker Inc., and Chance Inc., that became worthless during year 8. The adjusted basis in Tinker was $300,000. Tinker was incorporated in year 2, and Mark and Lucy purchased their stock in year 4. Their adjusted basis in Chance was $200,000. Chance was incorporated in year 2, and Mark and Lucy were original stockholders. Both stocks were purchased for cash, and each corporation had total capital of $500,000. How much ordinary loss can Mark and Lucy deduct on their joint year 8 tax return as a result of these transactions?

   a. $0
   b. $100,000
   c. $200,000
   d. $300,000

2. Mark and Lucy owned two stocks, Tinker Inc., and Chance Inc., that became worthless during year 8. The adjusted basis in Tinker was $80,000. Tinker was incorporated in year 2, and Mark and Lucy purchased their stock in year 4. Their adjusted basis in Chance was $20,000. Chance was incorporated in year 2, and Mark and Lucy were original stockholders. Both stocks were purchased for cash, and each corporation had total capital of $500,000. How much ordinary loss can Mark and Lucy deduct on their joint year 8 tax return as a result of these transactions?

   a. $0
   b. $20,000
   c. $80,000
   d. $100,000

3. Chad owned an office building that was destroyed in a tornado. The area was declared a Federal disaster area. The adjusted basis of the building at the time was $890,000. After the deductible, Chad received an insurance check for $850,000. He used the $850,000 to purchase a new building that same year. How much is Chad's recognized loss, and what is his basis in the new building?

	Recognized Loss	New Basis
a.	$0	$850,000
b.	$0	$890,000
c.	$40,000	$850,000
d.	$40,000	$890,000

4. Which of the following is a true statement regarding the carryback and carryforward of a net operating loss (NOL) arising in a calendar tax year after 2020, assuming that there are no NOL carryforwards from previous years?
   a. The NOL can be carried forward and offset 100 percent of taxable income in the following year.
   b. The NOL can be carried forward and offset 80 percent of taxable income in the following year.
   c. The NOL can be carried back and offset 100 percent of taxable income in the previous year.
   d. The NOL can be carried back and offset 80 percent of taxable income in the previous year.

Chapter 8

Depreciation, Cost Recovery, Amortization, and Depletion

Learning Objectives: *After completing Chapter 8, you should be able to:*

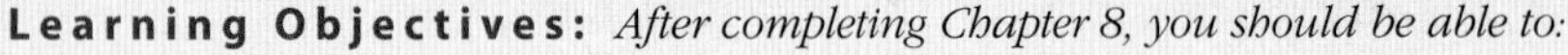

- **LO.1** State the rationale for allowing the cost recovery of an asset.
- **LO.2** Determine the amount of cost recovery under the Modified Accelerated Cost Recovery System (MACRS).
- **LO.3** Recognize when and how to make the § 179 expensing election, use additional first-year depreciation, and calculate the amount of these deductions as part of the MACRS calculation.
- **LO.4** Identify listed property and apply the deduction limitations on listed property and on luxury automobiles.
- **LO.5** Determine when and how to use the alternative depreciation system (ADS).
- **LO.6** Report cost recovery deductions appropriately.
- **LO.7** Identify intangible assets that are eligible for amortization and calculate the amount of the deduction.
- **LO.8** Determine the amount of depletion expense, including being able to apply the alternative tax treatments for intangible drilling and development costs.
- **LO.9** Identify tax planning opportunities for cost recovery, amortization, and depletion.

Chapter Outline

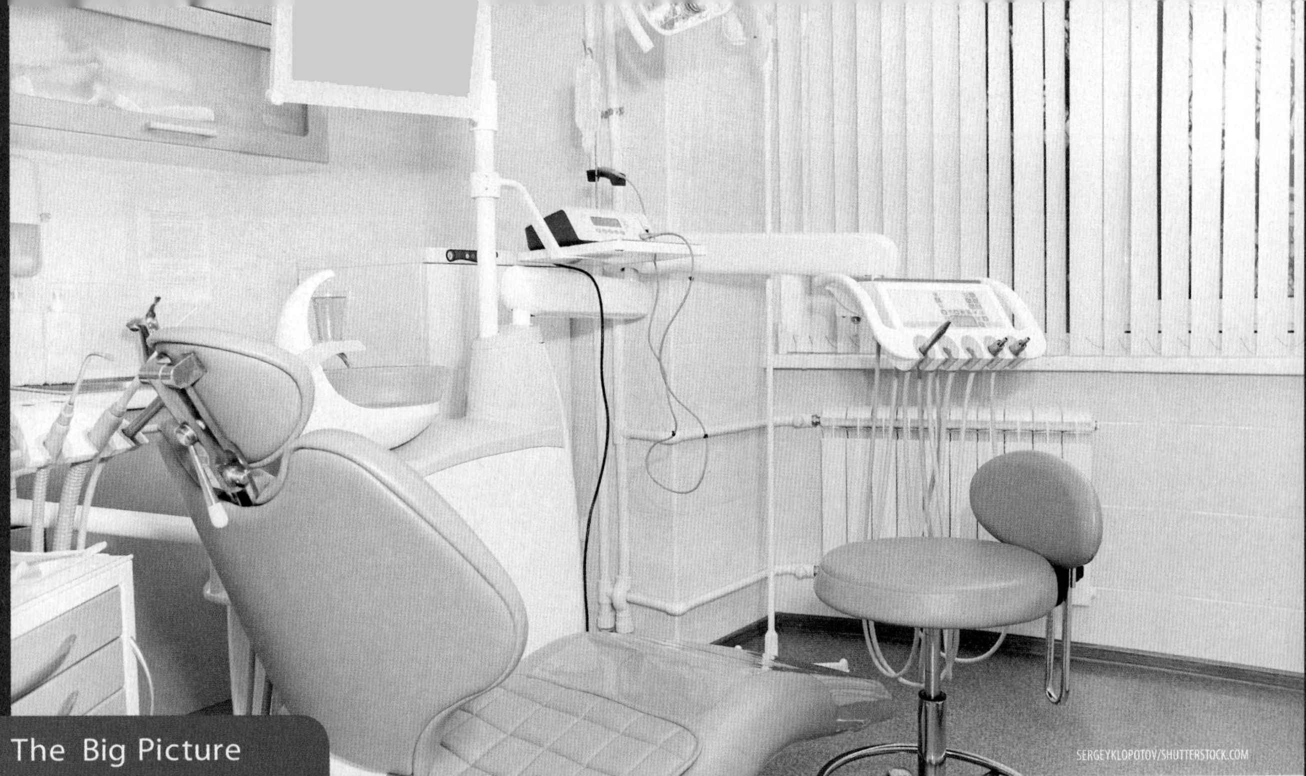

The Big Picture

Calculating Cost Recovery Deductions

Dr. Cliff Payne purchased and placed in service $612,085 of new fixed assets in his dental practice during the current year.

Office furniture and fixtures	$ 70,000
Computers and peripheral equipment	67,085
Dental equipment	475,000

Using his financial reporting system, he concludes that the depreciation expense on Schedule C of Form 1040 is $91,298.

Office furniture and fixtures ($70,000 × 14.29%)	$10,003
Computers and peripheral equipment ($67,085 × 20.00%)	13,417
Dental equipment ($475,000 × 14.29%)	67,878
	$91,298

In addition, this year Dr. Payne purchased a new personal residence for $480,000 and converted his original residence (purchased for $250,000 in 2009) to a rental property.

Has Dr. Payne correctly calculated the depreciation expense for his dental practice? Will he be able to deduct any depreciation expense for his rental property?

Read the chapter and formulate your response.

Framework 1040 **Tax Formula for Individuals**

This chapter covers the boldfaced portions of the Tax Formula for Individuals that was introduced in Concept Summary 3.1 on p. 3-3. Below those portions are the sections of Form 1040 where the results are reported.

Income *(broadly defined)*	$ xx,xxx
Less: Exclusions	(x,xxx)
Gross income	**$xx,xxx**
Less: Deductions *for* adjusted gross income	**(x,xxx)**

FORM 1040 (Schedule 1)

3	Business income or (loss). Attach Schedule C. . . . .

Adjusted gross income	$ xx,xxx
Less: The greater of total itemized deductions *or* the standard deduction	(x,xxx)
Personal and dependency exemptions*	(x,xxx)
Deduction for qualified business income**	(x,xxx)
Taxable income	$ xx,xxx
Tax on taxable income *(see Tax Tables or Tax Rate Schedules)*	$ x,xxx
Less: Tax credits *(including income taxes withheld and prepaid)*	(xxx)
Tax due (or refund)	$ xxx

* Exemption deductions are not allowed from 2018 through 2025.
** Only applies from 2018 through 2025.

The Internal Revenue Code allows a depreciation, cost recovery, amortization, or depletion deduction based on an asset's cost. These deductions reflect the recovery of capital doctrine (see text Section 4-1b). Cost recovery deductions are based on the idea that the asset acquired (or improvement made) benefits more than one accounting period. If not, the expenditure is deducted in the year incurred.[1]

Taxpayers may "write off" (deduct) the cost of certain assets that are used in a trade or business or held for the production of income. The deduction may take the form of depreciation (or cost recovery), depletion, or amortization. Tangible assets, other than natural resources, are *depreciated*. Natural resources, such as oil, gas, coal, and timber, are *depleted*. Intangible assets, such as copyrights and patents, are *amortized*. Generally, a deduction is allowed for an asset only if it has a determinable useful life.

Congress completely revised the tax **depreciation** rules in 1981 by creating the **accelerated cost recovery system (ACRS)**, which shortened depreciable lives and allowed accelerated depreciation methods. In 1986, Congress made substantial modifications to ACRS, which resulted in the **modified accelerated cost recovery system (MACRS)**, which is the focus of this chapter. Although the terms *depreciation* and **cost recovery** often are used interchangeably, the former normally refers to the allocation of costs to the appropriate period for financial reporting purposes whereas the latter refers to an equivalent concept for tax purposes.[2] A brief discussion of the amortization of intangible property and startup expenditures and the depletion of natural resources concludes the chapter.

8-1 Depreciation and Cost Recovery

LO.1

State the rationale for allowing the cost recovery of an asset.

8-1a Nature of Property

Property includes both realty (real property) and personalty (personal property). *Realty* generally includes land and buildings permanently affixed to the land. *Personalty* is

[1]See the discussion of capitalization versus expense in text Section 6-3i.

[2]§ 168. The terms *depreciation* and *cost recovery* are used interchangeably in the text and in § 168. Pre-1986 depreciation rules are covered in the online appendix *Depreciation and the Accelerated Cost Recovery System (ACRS)*.

defined as any asset that is not realty.[3] Personalty includes furniture, machinery, equipment, and any other asset that is movable or not permanently affixed to land. Personalty (or personal property) should not be confused with *personal use* property. Personal use property is any property (realty or personalty) that is held for personal use rather than for use in a trade or business or an income-producing activity. Cost recovery deductions are not allowed for personal use assets.

In summary, both realty and personalty can be either business use/income-producing property or personal use property. Examples include:

- A residence (realty that is personal use).
- An office building (realty that is business use).
- A dump truck (personalty that is business use).
- Common clothing (personalty that is personal use).

It is critical that the distinction between the *classification* of an asset (realty or personalty) and the *use* to which the asset is put (business/income-producing or personal) be understood.

Assets used in a trade or business or for the production of income are eligible for cost recovery if they are subject to wear and tear, decay or decline from natural causes, or obsolescence (e.g., equipment the taxpayer rents to third parties). Assets that do not decline in value on a predictable basis or that do not have a determinable useful life (e.g., land, stock, and antiques) are not eligible for cost recovery.

8-1b **Placed in Service Requirement**

Cost recovery begins on the date an asset is placed in service (ready and available for use), *not* the date of purchase. This distinction is particularly important for an asset that is purchased near the end of the tax year but not placed in service until the following tax year.

8-1c **Cost Recovery Allowed or Allowable**

To prevent the recovery of the same cost more than once (i.e., through periodic cost recovery during the asset's life and via its basis on the sale of the asset), the basis of property is reduced by any cost recovery deducted on a tax return (this is the *allowed* cost recovery). However, the property's basis is reduced by at least the amount of cost recovery that could have been taken using the appropriate cost recovery method (this is the *allowable* cost recovery). As a result, even if the taxpayer does not claim any cost recovery on property during a particular year, the basis of the property still is reduced by the amount of cost recovery that should have been deducted (the allowable cost recovery).

Example 1

On March 15, year 1, Jack purchased a copier, to use in his business, for $10,000. The copier is 5-year property, and Jack elected to use the straight-line method of cost recovery. Jack made the election because the business was a new undertaking, and he reasoned that, in the first few years of the business, a large cost recovery deduction was not needed.

Because the business was doing poorly, Jack did not deduct any cost recovery in years 3 and 4. In years 5 and 6, Jack deducted the proper amount of cost recovery. The *allowed* cost recovery (cost recovery actually deducted) and the *allowable* cost recovery are computed as follows:

	Cost Recovery Allowed	Cost Recovery Allowable
Year 1	$1,000	$1,000
Year 2	2,000	2,000
Year 3	–0–	2,000
Year 4	–0–	2,000
Year 5	2,000	2,000
Year 6	1,000	1,000

continued

[3]Refer to text Section 1-4a for further discussion.

If Jack sold the copier for $800 in year 7, he would recognize an $800 gain ($800 amount realized − $0 adjusted basis); the adjusted basis of the copier is zero ($10,000 cost − $10,000 total *allowable* cost recovery in years 1 through 6).

8-1d **Cost Recovery Basis for Personal Use Assets Converted to Business or Income-Producing Use**

If personal use assets are converted to business or income-producing use, the basis for cost recovery and for loss is the *lower* of the adjusted basis or the fair market value at the time the property was converted. This rule ensures that any decline in value that occurred while the property was a personal use asset is not eligible for cost recovery.

The Big Picture

Example 2

Return to the facts of *The Big Picture* on p. 8-1. In 2009, Dr. Payne purchased a personal residence for $250,000. In the current year, Dr. Payne found a larger home that he acquired for his personal residence. Because of the downturn in the housing market, however, he was not able to sell his original residence and recover his purchase price of $250,000. The residence was appraised at $180,000.

Instead of continuing to try to sell the original residence, Dr. Payne converted it to rental property. The basis for cost recovery of the rental property is $180,000 because the fair market value is less than the adjusted basis. The $70,000 decline in value is deemed to be personal (because it occurred while the property was held for personal use by Dr. Payne) and, therefore, nondeductible.

LO.2

Determine the amount of cost recovery under the Modified Accelerated Cost Recovery System (MACRS).

8-2 **Modified Accelerated Cost Recovery System (MACRS): General Rules**

Under the modified accelerated cost recovery system (MACRS), the cost of an asset is recovered over a time period that generally is shorter than the economic life of an asset. The MACRS rules were designed to encourage investment, improve productivity, and simplify the tax law and its administration.

MACRS provides separate cost recovery systems for realty and personalty. Based on cost recovery periods (called class lives), methods, and conventions specified in the Internal Revenue Code, the IRS provides tables that identify cost recovery allowances for personalty and for realty. Excerpts from the IRS tables are provided in text Section 8-7c.

Concept Summary 8.1 provides an overview of the class lives, methods, conventions, and deductions in the year of disposition that apply to personalty and realty under MACRS.

Concept Summary 8.1

MACRS: Class Lives, Methods, and Conventions

	Personalty (and Certain Realty)	**Realty**
Class lives	3 to 20 years	Residential: 27.5 years Nonresidential: 39 years
Method	200% declining balance for property with class lives less than 15 years 150% declining balance for property with 15- or 20-year class lives	Straight-line
Convention	Half-year or mid-quarter	Mid-month
Cost recovery deduction in the year of disposition*	Half-year for year of sale or half-quarter for quarter of sale	Half-month for month of sale

* A disposition can include a sale, an exchange, abandonment, or retirement. For simplicity, we will assume a sale in this chapter.

8-2a Personalty (and Certain Realty): Recovery Periods and Methods

Classification of Property

MACRS provides that the basis of eligible personalty (and certain realty) is recovered over 3, 5, 7, 10, 15, or 20 years. An asset's MACRS recovery period is determined by identifying its Asset Depreciation Range (ADR) midpoint life (determined by the IRS).[4] See Exhibit 8.1 for examples of assets in each class.[5]

Double declining balance is used for the 3-, 5-, 7-, and 10-year classes, with a switchover to straight-line depreciation when appropriate. Cost recovery for the 15- and 20-year classes is based on the 150 percent declining-balance method, with an appropriate straight-line switchover.[6] These methods and conventions are built into the IRS tables. As a result, it is generally not necessary to make these calculations.

To determine an asset's cost recovery deduction for a year, you identify the asset's MACRS class, find the cost recovery percentage for the year using the appropriate IRS table, and multiply this percentage by the asset's cost. The MACRS percentages for personalty appear in Exhibit 8.3 (see text Section 8-7c).

Exhibit 8.1 Cost Recovery Periods: MACRS Personalty (and Certain Realty)

Property Class	Generally Includes Assets with the Following ADR Lives	Examples
3-year	4 years or less	Tractor units for use over the road
		A racehorse that is more than 2 years old, or any other horse that is more than 12 years old, at the time it is placed in service
		Special tools used in the manufacturing of motor vehicles, such as dies, fixtures, molds, and patterns
5-year	More than 4 years and less than 10 years	Automobiles and taxis
		Light and heavy general-purpose trucks
		Calculators and copiers
		Computers and peripheral equipment
		Rental appliances, furniture, carpets
7-year	10 years or more and less than 16 years	Office furniture, fixtures, and equipment
		Agricultural machinery and equipment
10-year	16 years or more and less than 20 years	Vessels, barges, tugs, and similar water transportation equipment
		Assets used for petroleum refining or for the manufacture of grain and grain mill products, sugar and sugar products, or vegetable oils and vegetable oil products
		Single-purpose agricultural or horticultural structures
15-year	20 years or more and less than 25 years	Land improvements
		Qualified improvement property
		Assets used for industrial steam and electric generation and/or distribution systems
		Assets used in the manufacture of cement
20-year	25 years or more	Farm buildings except single-purpose agricultural and horticultural structures
		Water utilities

[4] Personalty is assigned to recovery classes based on Asset Depreciation Range (ADR) midpoint lives (Rev.Proc. 87–56). ADR lives generally represent estimates of an asset's useful economic life.

[5] § 168(e).

[6] § 168(b).

Financial Disclosure Insights — Tax and Book Depreciation

A common book-tax difference relates to the depreciation amounts that are reported for GAAP and Federal income tax purposes. Typically, tax depreciation deductions are accelerated; that is, they are claimed in earlier reporting periods than is the case for financial accounting purposes.

Almost every tax law change since 1980 has included depreciation provisions that accelerate the related deductions relative to the expenses allowed under GAAP. Accelerated cost recovery deductions represent a means by which the taxing jurisdiction infuses the business with cash flow created by the reduction in the year's tax liabilities.

For instance, recently, about one-quarter of General Electric's deferred tax liabilities related to depreciation differences. Ford's depreciation differences amounted to about one-third of its deferred tax liabilities. And for the trucking firm Ryder Systems, depreciation differences accounted for virtually all of the deferred tax liabilities.

Taxpayers may *elect* the straight-line method to compute cost recovery allowances for each of these classes of property. Certain property is not eligible for accelerated cost recovery and must be depreciated under an alternative depreciation system (ADS). Both the straight-line election and ADS are discussed later in the chapter.

Cost recovery for personalty generally incorporates the **half-year convention**; that is, cost recovery in the year the asset is placed in service, as well as the year it is removed from service, is based on the assumption that the asset was used for exactly one-half of the year, allowing a half-year of cost recovery.[7] For example, the regular MACRS recovery period for property with a life of three years begins in the middle of the year an asset is placed in service and ends three years later, in the fourth taxable year. In practical terms, this means that an asset's cost is actually recovered over 4, 6, 8, 11, 16, or 21 years.

Example 3

MACRS Personalty; Half-Year Convention

Kareem acquires and places in service a 5-year class asset on April 10, 2023, for $30,000. Kareem's cost recovery deduction for 2023 is computed as follows:

MACRS cost recovery [$30,000 × 0.20 (Exhibit 8.3)] $6,000

Example 4

Assume the same facts as in Example 3. Kareem sells the asset on March 5, 2025. Kareem's cost recovery deduction for 2025 is $2,880 [$30,000 × 0.192 (Exhibit 8.3) × ½].

Mid-Quarter Convention

The half-year convention is based on the simplifying presumption that assets generally are acquired at an even pace throughout the tax year. However, Congress was concerned that taxpayers might defeat that presumption by placing large amounts of property in service toward the end of the taxable year (and by doing so, receive a half-year's depreciation on those large end-of-year acquisitions).

[7] § 168(d)(4)(A).

To inhibit this behavior, Congress added the **mid-quarter convention** that applies if more than 40 percent of the cost of property other than real estate (see text Section 8-2b) is placed in service during the last quarter of the year.[8] If the mid-quarter convention applies, property acquisitions are grouped by the quarter of acquisition. Acquisitions made during the first quarter are allowed 10.5 months (three and one-half quarters) of cost recovery in the first year; the second quarter, 7.5 months (two and one-half quarters); the third quarter, 4.5 months (one and one-half quarters); and the fourth quarter, 1.5 months (one-half quarter). The percentages are shown in Exhibit 8.4.

Example 5

Silver Corporation acquires and places in service the following new 5-year class property in 2023.

Property Acquisition Dates	Cost
February 15	$ 200,000
July 10	400,000
December 5	600,000
Total	$1,200,000

Because more than 40% ($600,000 ÷ $1,200,000 = 50%) of the acquisitions are in the last quarter, the mid-quarter convention applies. Silver's cost recovery allowances for the first two years are computed below.

2023

	Mid-Quarter Convention Depreciation (Exhibit 8.4)	Total Depreciation
February 15	$200,000 × 0.35	$ 70,000
July 10	$400,000 × 0.15	60,000
December 5	$600,000 × 0.05	30,000
		$160,000

2024

	Mid-Quarter Convention Depreciation (Exhibit 8.4)	Total Depreciation
February 15	$200,000 × 0.26	$ 52,000
July 10	$400,000 × 0.34	136,000
December 5	$600,000 × 0.38	228,000
		$416,000

Without the mid-quarter convention, Silver's 2023 cost recovery deduction would have been $240,000 [$1,200,000 × 0.20 (Exhibit 8.3)]. As a result, the mid-quarter convention reduces the taxpayer's available cost recovery deductions in the acquisition year (and defers those deductions to later years).

When "mid-quarter" property is sold, the property is treated as though it were sold at the midpoint of the quarter. So, in the quarter when sold, cost recovery is allowed for one-half of the quarter.

[8] § 168(d)(3).

Example 6

Assume the same facts as in Example 5, except that Silver Corporation sells the $400,000 asset on November 30, 2024. The cost recovery deduction for 2024 is computed as follows (using Exhibit 8.4):

February 15	$200,000 × 0.26	$ 52,000
July 10	$400,000 × 0.34 × (3.5/4)	119,000
December 5	$600,000 × 0.38	228,000
Total cost recovery deduction		$399,000

The tax adjusted basis of the $400,000 asset when sold is $221,000 [$400,000 (cost) − $60,000 (2023 cost recovery) − $119,000 (2024 cost recovery)].

The Big Picture

Example 7

Return to the facts of *The Big Picture* on p. 8-1. If the placed-in-service date for the office furniture and fixtures and computers and peripheral equipment is September 29 and the placed-in-service date for the dental equipment is October 3, Dr. Payne's total cost recovery deduction is computed as follows:

Office furniture and fixtures:	
MACRS cost recovery $70,000 × 0.1071 (Exhibit 8.4)	$ 7,497
Computers and peripheral equipment:	
MACRS cost recovery $67,085 × 0.15 (Exhibit 8.4)	10,063
Dental equipment:	
MACRS cost recovery $475,000 × 0.0357 (Exhibit 8.4)	16,958
Total cost recovery deduction	$34,518

Note the implications of the mid-quarter convention. If the dental equipment had been placed in service before October 1 (the beginning of the fourth quarter), the total cost recovery deduction would have been $91,298 (as detailed on p. 8-1).

Qualified Improvement Property

Nonresidential realty has a 39-year life, and any improvements made to this property would normally have a 39-year life. An exception to this general rule is provided for **qualified improvement property**. Qualified improvement property is recovered over a 15-year life using the half-year convention and the straight-line method.[9]

Qualified improvement property is any improvement to an interior portion of nonresidential real property made after the property is placed in service, including leasehold improvements. However, it does not include the costs of an elevator or escalator or improvements that enlarge a building or modify its internal framework.

Example 8

Redbud, Inc., finishes construction of an office building in July 2022. It plans to lease the third floor of the building to a tenant. In January 2023, Crimson Enterprises leases the third floor and immediately builds out the rental space to meet its needs. It spends $50,000 on cubicles, shelving, and other nonpermanent additions. These improvements are qualified improvement property and will be recovered over 15 years using the half-year convention and straight-line method.

In 2023, Crimson's cost recovery deduction is $1,667 ($50,000 × 0.03333; see Exhibit 8.5 for cost recovery percentages).

Straight-Line Election

A taxpayer may *elect* to use the straight-line method for personal property.[10] If elected, the property is depreciated using the MACRS life of the asset with a half-year convention

[9] § 168(e)(6).

[10] § 168(b)(5).

or a mid-quarter convention, whichever applies. The election is available on a class-by-class and year-by-year basis (see Concept Summary 8.2). So, for example, a taxpayer could elect the straight-line method for 5-year MACRS assets placed in service during the current year; 5-year MACRS assets placed in service the following year are not bound by this choice. And the choice of having 5-year MACRS assets on the straight-line method would not apply to other personalty (e.g., the 3-year and 7-year MACRS classes) unless elected by the taxpayer. The percentages for the straight-line election with a half-year convention appear in Exhibit 8.5.

Concept Summary 8.2

Straight-Line Cost Recovery under MACRS (Personalty vs. Realty)

	Personalty	Realty*
Convention	Half-year or mid-quarter	Mid-month
Cost recovery deduction in the year of disposition**	Half-year for year of sale or half-quarter for quarter of sale	Half-month for month of sale
Elective or mandatory	Elective	Mandatory
Breadth of election	Class by class	

*Straight-line method must be used.

**A disposition can include a sale, exchange, abandonment, or retirement. For simplicity, we will assume a sale in this chapter.

The Big Picture

Example 9

Return to the facts of *The Big Picture* on p. 8-1. If Dr. Payne elects the straight-line method of cost recovery, his total cost recovery deduction is computed as follows:

Office furniture and fixtures ($70,000 × 0.0714) (Exhibit 8.5)	$ 4,998
Computers and peripheral equipment ($67,085 × 0.10) (Exhibit 8.5)	6,709
Dental equipment ($475,000 × 0.0714) (Exhibit 8.5)	33,915
Total cost recovery deduction	$45,622

If Dr. Payne does not elect the straight-line cost recovery method, his cost recovery deduction is $91,298 (as detailed on p. 8-1).

The Big Picture

Example 10

Assume the same facts as in Example 9, except that Dr. Payne sells the computers and peripheral equipment on November 21, 2024. His cost recovery deduction for 2024 is $6,709 ($67,085 × 0.20 × ½) (Exhibit 8.5).

8-2b Realty: Recovery Periods and Methods

Under MACRS, the cost of most real property is recovered using the straight-line method. The recovery period for residential rental real estate is 27.5 years. **Residential rental real estate** includes property where 80 percent or more of the gross rental revenues are from residential units (e.g., an apartment building). Hotels, motels, and similar establishments are not residential rental property. Nonresidential real estate is recovered over 39 years.[11]

[11] §§ 168(b), (c), and (e). A 31.5-year life is used for nonresidential real estate placed in service before May 13, 1993.

Some items of real property are not treated as real estate under MACRS. For example, single-purpose agricultural structures are in the 10-year MACRS class. Land improvements are in the 15-year MACRS class.

All MACRS real estate is depreciated using the **mid-month convention**.[12] Under this convention, one-half month's cost recovery is allowed for the month the property is placed in service. So if a calendar year taxpayer places MACRS real estate in service on June 2 of the current tax year, it will be able to deduct six and one-half months of cost recovery (June 15 to December 31). If the property is sold before the end of the recovery period, one-half month's cost recovery is allowed for the month of sale (no matter when the property is sold).

As with personalty, the IRS provides tables to assist taxpayers in computing cost recovery on realty. Cost recovery is computed by multiplying the applicable rate (Exhibit 8.8) by the cost recovery basis.

Real Estate Cost Recovery

Example 11

Alec acquired and placed in service a building on April 1, 2006, for $800,000. If the building is classified as residential rental real estate, the cost recovery deduction for 2023 is $29,088 (0.03636 × $800,000).

If, instead, the building is sold on October 7, 2023, the cost recovery deduction for 2023 is $23,028 [0.03636 (Exhibit 8.8) × (9.5/12) × $800,000].

Marie acquired and placed in service a building on March 2, 1993, for $1,000,000. If the building is classified as nonresidential real estate, the cost recovery deduction for 2023 is $31,740 (0.03174 × $1,000,000).

If, instead, the building is sold on January 5, 2023, the cost recovery deduction for 2023 is $1,323 [0.03174 (Exhibit 8.8) × (0.5/12) × $1,000,000].

Marco acquired and placed in service a building on November 19, 2023, for $1,200,000. If the building is classified as nonresidential real estate, the cost recovery deduction for 2023 is $3,852 [0.00321 (Exhibit 8.8) × 1,200,000]. The cost recovery deduction for 2024 is $30,768 [0.02564 (Exhibit 8.8) × 1,200,000].

If, instead, the building is sold on May 21, 2024, the cost recovery deduction for 2024 is $11,538 [0.02564 (Exhibit 8.8) × (4.5/12) × $1,200,000].

LO.3

Recognize when and how to make the § 179 expensing election, use additional first-year depreciation, and calculate the amount of these deductions as part of the MACRS calculation.

8-3 Modified Accelerated Cost Recovery System (MACRS): Special Rules

A number of special rules apply under MACRS. To encourage investment in capital assets and reduce the related compliance costs, Congress has implemented two rules: immediate expensing (§ 179) and additional first-year depreciation (also called bonus depreciation). To curb potential taxpayer abuses of certain assets—particularly when the assets are used for both business and personal purposes—Congress established specific rules for "listed property." Finally, Congress also created an alternative depreciation system (ADS) that taxpayers can use instead of MACRS. The ADS must be used in certain settings (e.g., for the alternative minimum tax).

8-3a Election to Expense Assets (§ 179)

Code § 179 (Election to Expense Certain Depreciable Business Assets) permits the taxpayer to deduct up to $1,160,000 in 2023 ($1,080,000 in 2022) of the acquisition cost of specific types of *trade or business* property. Amounts that are expensed under § 179 reduce the asset's basis for additional first-year depreciation (see text Section 8-3b) and MACRS cost recovery (see text Section 8-2a).

[12] § 168(d)(1).

The **§ 179 expensing** election (also known as the immediate expense election) applies to the acquisition cost of property placed in service during a year. Property to which § 179 applies includes tangible personal property, computer software, qualified improvement property, and certain real property (roofs; heating, ventilation, and air conditioning units; fire protection and alarm systems; security systems). In general, the immediate expense election is not available for real property or for property used for the production of income.[13]

Any elected § 179 expense is taken *before* additional first-year depreciation is computed (see text Section 8-3b). Any MACRS deduction is calculated on the basis of the asset net of the § 179 expense and any additional first-year depreciation.

§ 179 Election and Basis

Example 14

Allison acquires and places in service business equipment (a 5-year class asset) on February 1, 2023, at a cost of $80,000. It is the only asset she places in service in 2023. If Allison elects § 179, she can deduct the asset's entire cost in 2023. If not, she will use MACRS to recover the asset's cost over six years.

- If Allison elects § 179:

2023	§ 179 deduction	$80,000

- If Allison uses MACRS (see Exhibit 8.3):

2023	$80,000 × 0.20	$16,000
2024	$80,000 × 0.32	25,600
2025	$80,000 × 0.192	15,360
2026	$80,000 × 0.1152	9,216
2027	$80,000 × 0.1152	9,216
2028	$80,000 × 0.0576	4,608
		$80,000

Example 15

Assume the same facts as in Example 14. Allison sells the asset in 2025 for $50,000.

- If Allison elects § 179, the asset's adjusted basis is zero ($80,000 − $80,000) and she has a realized gain of $50,000.
- If Allison uses MACRS, the asset's adjusted basis is $30,720 and she has a realized gain of $19,280.

Selling price			$ 50,000
Cost		$ 80,000	
Less: Cost recovery			
2023 MACRS	$16,000		
2024 MACRS	25,600		
2025 MACRS ($15,360 × ½)	7,680	(49,280)	(30,720)
Realized gain			$ 19,280

Deduction Limitations

The § 179 expense deduction is subject to three limitations, applied in this order.

1. **Ceiling Amount.** A taxpayer's § 179 deduction cannot exceed an annual ceiling amount ($1,160,000 in 2023; $1,080,000 in 2022).
2. **Property Placed in Service Maximum.** The § 179 deduction ceiling amount ($1,160,000 in 2023) is reduced dollar for dollar when § 179 property placed in

[13]The § 179 amount allowed is per taxpayer, per year. On a joint return, the statutory amount applies to the couple. If the taxpayers are married and file separate returns, each spouse is eligible for 50% of the statutory amount.

The annual expense and phaseout amounts in § 179 ($1,000,000 and $2,500,000, respectively) are adjusted for inflation each year and rounded to the nearest $10,000 multiple.

service during the taxable year exceeds a specified maximum amount ($2,890,000 in 2023; $2,700,000 in 2022). In 2023, a taxpayer who places in service $4,050,000 or more of qualifying property ($1,160,000 + $2,890,000) cannot claim a § 179 deduction.

3. **Business Income Limitation.** The § 179 deduction allowed for a taxable year cannot exceed the taxpayer's business income for the year.

Ceiling Amount. A taxpayer can choose to use *all, part, or none* of the annual § 179 amount. If a business expects its marginal tax rate to increase in the future, it may decide *not* to use the § 179 deduction. In such a situation, it may be better to defer deductions to those later years. As discussed below, the business income limitation also may lead a business owner to choose not to expense assets.

In 2023, Sonya places in service $450,000 of 7-year MACRS assets. Although she could immediately expense all of these assets, she would prefer to use § 179 on just $275,000 of the assets. She knows that combining this expense with regular MACRS depreciation effectively reduces her business income to zero, and she wants to defer the remaining deductions to future years when her marginal tax rate will be higher. As a result, Sonya's total cost recovery deduction for 2023 is calculated as follows:

§ 179 expense	$275,000
MACRS cost recovery [($450,000 − $275,000) × 0.1429 (Exhibit 8.3)]	25,008
Total cost recovery deduction	$300,008

Property Placed in Service Maximum. This rule effectively restricts the application of the § 179 deduction to smaller businesses. In 2023, a business that places in service more than $2,890,000 of qualifying property will have its § 179 deduction reduced. A business that places in service $4,050,000 or more of qualifying property will have its § 179 deduction eliminated.

§ 179: Property Placed in Service Maximum

During 2023, Madison places $1,245,000 of § 179 property in service for use in her engineering consultancy. Madison can take a $1,160,000 § 179 expense election; there is no reduction in the § 179 amount; the property placed in service maximum ($2,890,000) was not reached.

During 2023, George places $3,570,000 of § 179 property in service for use in his manufacturing business (all assets are 7-year MACRS assets). Because George placed in service more than the $2,890,000 maximum, he must reduce his § 179 deduction ($3,570,000 − $2,890,000 = $680,000).

As a result, George's maximum § 179 deduction is $480,000 ($1,160,000 − $680,000). This reduction cannot be reclaimed in any way; it is permanently lost. George's total cost recovery deduction for 2023 is calculated as follows:

§ 179 expense	$480,000
MACRS cost recovery [($3,570,000 − $480,000) × 0.1429 (Exhibit 8.3)]	441,561
Total cost recovery deduction	$921,561

George also places in service a $1,500,000 office building during 2023. Will this have any effect on the calculation above? No. The building is MACRS *realty*. Only *§ 179 property* is used to determine whether the § 179 ceiling amount ($1,160,000 in 2023) is reduced.

Note: George also can take additional first-year (bonus) depreciation on the 7-year MACRS assets. We will revisit this example after discussing bonus depreciation.

Business Income Limitation. The §179 deduction allowed for a taxable year cannot exceed the taxpayer's business income for the year. For this purpose, business income is calculated by deducting all business expenses except the § 179 deduction. As a result, a taxpayer's § 179 deduction cannot create (or increase) a net operating loss. A taxpayer's "business income" includes income not only from a sole proprietorship but also from wages and any allocated business income from a partnership or an S corporation.

During 2023, Lance has a sole proprietorship through which he provides accounting and tax services that generated net income of $68,000. In addition, Lance is a 40% shareholder in a management consultancy operated as an S corporation. The S corporation pays Lance a salary of $40,000, and it recorded taxable income of $50,000. In this case, Lance's business income is $128,000 [$68,000 + $40,000 + $20,000 ($50,000 × 40%)].

Any § 179 amount in excess of business income is carried forward to future taxable years and added to other amounts eligible for expensing. Then the various limitations for that carryforward year are applied (i.e., the ceiling amount, the placed in service maximum amount, and the business income limitation).

Jill owns a computer service and operates it as a sole proprietorship. In 2023, taxable income is $138,000 before considering any § 179 deduction. If Jill spends $3,100,000 on new equipment, her § 179 expense deduction for the year is computed as follows:

§ 179 deduction before adjustment	$1,160,000
Less: Dollar limitation reduction ($3,100,000 − $2,890,000)	(210,000)
Remaining § 179 deduction	$ 950,000
Business income limitation	$ 138,000
§ 179 deduction allowed	$ 138,000
§ 179 deduction carryforward ($950,000 − $138,000)	$ 812,000

Additional first-year (bonus) depreciation is *not* limited by a taxpayer's taxable income. Taxpayers who make large capital investments with limited taxable income may choose *not* to make a § 179 election and only take bonus depreciation on these items.

Effect on Basis

The basis of the property for cost recovery purposes is reduced by the § 179 amount after accounting for the current-year amount of property placed in service in excess of the specified maximum amount ($2,890,000 for 2023). This adjusted amount does not reflect any business income limitation.

Assume the same facts as in Example 20. Jill's adjusted basis in the equipment for cost recovery purposes is $2,150,000 ($3,100,000 cost less the $950,000 § 179 expense amount before the business income limitation). If any portion of the $812,000 carryover (due to the business income limitation) is not deducted before the equipment is sold, this amount may be added back to the basis of the equipment in determining its adjusted basis.

Section 179 and the Mid-Quarter Convention

The mid-quarter convention generally results in smaller depreciation deductions in the asset's acquisition year. However, the basis of property used to determine whether the mid-quarter convention applies is derived *after* any § 179 immediate expense election.[14] As a result, a taxpayer may be able to avoid the mid-quarter convention by designating § 179 treatment for assets placed in service during the last quarter of the taxable year.

[14] Reg. § 1.168(d)–1(b)(4).

Example 22

Dimond Manufacturing places the following assets in service during 2023. All are 5-year class assets, and they are the only assets Dimond placed in service during the year.

Asset 1 (April 3, 2023)	$ 873,000
Asset 2 (July 17, 2023)	232,000
Asset 3 (October 22, 2023)	1,185,000
Total	$2,290,000

Since Dimond has placed more than 40% of the assets in service during the last quarter of the taxable year, the mid-quarter convention applies ($1,185,000 ÷ $2,290,000 = 51.7%). As a result, Dimond's cost recovery deduction for the year is computed as follows (see Exhibit 8.4).

Asset 1	$ 873,000 × 0.25	$ 218,250
Asset 2	$ 232,000 × 0.15	34,800
Asset 3	$1,185,000 × 0.05	59,250
Total		$ 312,300

However, if Dimond elects to expense $1,160,000 of the October 22 acquisition under § 179, the mid-quarter convention would not apply.

Asset 1 (April 3, 2023)	$ 873,000
Asset 2 (July 17, 2023)	232,000
Asset 3 (October 22, 2023; $1,185,000 − $1,160,000)	25,000
Total	$1,130,000

Now Dimond has placed only 2.2% ($25,000 ÷ $1,130,000) of the assets in service during the last quarter of the taxable year. As a result, the mid-quarter convention does not apply, and Dimond's cost recovery deduction for the year (including the § 179 expense election) is as follows.

MACRS cost recovery (1,130,000 × 0.20; Exhibit 8.3)	$ 226,000
§ 179 expense (Asset 3)	1,160,000
Total cost recovery deduction	$1,386,000

As a result of its effective use of § 179, Dimond has increased its 2023 cost recovery deduction and simplified its reporting and record keeping related to these assets.

Conversion to Personal Use

Conversion of the expensed property to personal use at any time results in recapture income (see text Section 14-9). A property is converted to personal use if it is not used predominantly in a trade or business.[15]

Ethics & Equity Section 179 Limitation

Joe Moran worked in the construction business throughout most of his career. In June of the current year, he sold his interest in Ajax Enterprises LLC for a profit of $300,000. Shortly thereafter, Joe started his own business, which involves the redevelopment of distressed residential real estate.

In connection with his new business venture, Joe purchased a dump truck at a cost of $70,000. The new business struggled and showed a net operating loss for the year. Joe is considering expensing the $70,000 cost of the truck under § 179 on this year's tax return. Evaluate Joe's plan.

8-3b Additional First-Year Depreciation (Bonus Depreciation)

Congress often uses the tax system to stimulate the economy. An example is **additional first-year depreciation** (also referred to as bonus depreciation). In 2023, taxpayers are allowed to deduct 80 percent cost recovery of any *qualified property* that is placed in service (100 percent in 2022).[16]

[15] See Reg. § 1.179–1(e) and related examples.

[16] § 168(k). Additional first-year depreciation is allowed for qualified property placed in service after 2011 and before 2027. The additional first-year depreciation percentage (100% from 2018 to 2022) decreases to 80% in 2023, 60% in 2024, 40% in 2025, and 20% in 2026. No bonus depreciation is scheduled for tax years after 2026. Different rules applied between 2008 and 2017 (in general, the bonus depreciation percentage was no more than 50%).

The term *qualified property* includes most depreciable assets other than buildings with a recovery period of 20 years or less.[17] Bonus depreciation applies to both new *and* used property.[18]

The additional first-year depreciation is taken in the year in which the qualifying property is placed in service; it is computed after any immediate expense (§ 179) deduction is claimed. After the additional first-year depreciation is determined, the regular MACRS cost recovery deduction is calculated by multiplying the remaining cost recovery basis (original cost recovery basis less § 179 expense and additional first-year depreciation) by the appropriate MACRS percentage. A taxpayer may elect *not* to take additional first-year depreciation.

Example 23

Kelly acquires and places in service equipment (a 5-year class asset) on February 1, 2023, at a cost of $1,345,000 and elects to expense $1,160,000 under § 179. Kelly also chooses to take bonus depreciation. As a result, her total cost recovery deduction for the year is calculated as follows:

§ 179 expense	$1,160,000
Additional first-year depreciation [($1,345,000 − $1,160,000) × 80%]	148,000
MACRS cost recovery [($1,345,000 − $1,160,000 − $148,000) × 0.20 (Exhibit 8.3)]	7,400
Total cost recovery deduction	$1,315,400

Alternatively, Kelly could choose not to elect § 179 on the equipment, deduct 80% of the cost of the equipment using bonus depreciation, and take MACRS cost recovery on the remaining 20% of the equipment's cost:

Additional first-year depreciation ($1,345,000 × 80%)	$1,076,000
MACRS cost recovery [($1,345,000 − $1,076,000) × 0.20 (Exhibit 8.3)]	53,800
Total cost recovery deduction	$1,129,800

8-3c **Using § 179 and Bonus Depreciation Effectively**

Through a combination of § 179 and bonus depreciation, the majority of taxpayers will be able to deduct a large portion of any MACRS personalty. However, there may be times when the taxpayer finds it better to defer some of these deductions to future years. This might be the case if the taxpayer expects marginal tax rates to increase over time. In addition, the limitations on excess business losses (see text Section 7-5) or the 80 percent of taxable income limit on net operating losses (see text Section 7-6) might lead a taxpayer not to use § 179 and/or bonus depreciation. In addition, certain assets might not qualify for § 179 expensing or bonus depreciation. If any of these conditions applies, then other considerations come into play.

Deferring MACRS Deductions to Future Years

Taxpayers may find it better not to use § 179 expensing and/or bonus depreciation to write off asset acquisitions. If taxpayers expect their marginal tax rates to increase over time (and in some instances, remain the same), it might be best, in present value terms, to defer some MACRS deductions to future years.

[17]Bonus depreciation is available for both "qualified film or television productions" and "qualified live theatrical productions." Bonus depreciation is *not* available to (1) any business that has floor-plan financing (e.g., an auto dealer) if the related interest is deducted in full or (2) regulated public utilities. In addition, bonus depreciation is *not* available on any asset that is required to use ADS depreciation.

[18]Effective for property placed in service after September 27, 2017. Used property will qualify as long as it is the taxpayer's first use of the property. § 168(k)(2)(E)(ii)(I).

Priyanka is married and operates a small business in Fairfax, Virginia. During 2023, she purchases $550,000 of equipment (5-year MACRS assets) for use in her business. Priyanka and her spouse report $617,500 of taxable income before considering any cost recovery related to the equipment. Their marginal tax rate is 35%.

Priyanka is confident that her business will grow significantly over the next few years and expects her marginal tax rate to remain at least 35% during that time. As a result, she is wondering whether to use a combination of immediate expensing and bonus depreciation on the entire 2023 purchase or spread her MACRS deductions over the next few years.

If Priyanka takes $550,000 of immediate expense and bonus depreciation in 2023, she and her spouse will have tax savings of $152,254.* However, much of the cost recovery will offset income that would have been taxed at rates lower than 35%.

Another option is to take just enough cost recovery (via a combination of immediate expensing, bonus depreciation, and regular MACRS) to reduce the couple's taxable income from $617,500 to $462,500 (the bottom of the 35% rate bracket in 2023). We can determine this combined amount using the following formula:

§ 179/Bonus depreciation + [($550,000 − § 179/Bonus depreciation) × 20% (first-year MACRS)] = $155,000

Solving for § 179/Bonus depreciation yields $56,250. So we can reduce the couple's taxable income to $462,500 by taking a combination of immediate expense and bonus depreciation of $56,250 and the usual MACRS of $98,750 [($550,000 − $56,250) × 20%].

If we assume a 5% discount rate on future tax savings, Priyanka and her spouse will save $178,386 in taxes by deferring some of the available cost recovery deductions and using it to offset future income that would otherwise be subject to a 35% tax rate.

	2023	2024	2025	2026	2027	2028
Normal MACRS	$493,750	$493,750	$493,750	$493,750	$493,750	$493,750
MACRS factor	× 0.2000	× 0.3200	× 0.1920	× 0.1152	× 0.1152	× 0.0576
MACRS depreciation	$ 98,750	$158,000	$ 94,800	$ 56,880	$ 56,880	$ 28,440
§ 179/Bonus depreciation	56,250	−0−	−0−	−0−	−0−	−0−
Total MACRS deduction	$155,000	$158,000	$ 94,800	$ 56,880	$ 56,880	$ 28,440
Marginal tax rate	× 35%	× 35%	× 35%	× 35%	× 35%	× 35%
Tax savings	$ 54,250	$ 55,300	$ 33,180	$ 19,908	$ 19,908	$ 9,954
PV factors @ 5% (Appendix E)	× 1.0000	× 0.9524	× 0.9070	× 0.8638	× 0.8227	× 0.7835
	$ 54,250	$ 52,668	$ 30,094	$ 17,197	$ 16,378	$ 7,799
Net present value	$178,386					

Overall, the combination of $56,250 immediate expense and bonus depreciation in 2023 plus MACRS cost recovery in 2023 through 2028 provides a better outcome for Priyanka and her spouse, generating $26,132 of tax savings in present value terms over the next six years ($178,386 tax savings by deferring MACRS deductions *less* $152,254 tax savings by using $550,000 of immediate expense and bonus depreciation in 2023).

*Tax on $617,500 = $159,914 {$105,664 + [($617,500 – $462,500) × 35%]}; tax on $67,500 = $7,660 [$2,200 + ($45,500 × 12%)].

Choosing Assets for Immediate Expensing

The § 179 deduction can be allocated to reduce the basis of qualifying assets in any manner the taxpayer chooses. This allows the deduction to be allocated proportionally across all assets acquired during the year or to specific assets identified by the taxpayer. This flexibility is important.

Two general rules might affect this choice. First, taxpayers generally should *not* use the § 179 election on automobiles. Automobiles are subject to special cost recovery rules (and annual limits), which we discuss later in this chapter. Second, given the time value of money, taxpayers should accelerate deductions to the earliest year possible. This is accomplished by expensing the assets with the *longest* MACRS lives first.

Example 25

During 2023, Dexter purchases manufacturing equipment (a 7-year MACRS asset) costing $825,000 and a computer system costing $480,000 (a 5-year MACRS asset). As the total amount of MACRS assets placed in service for the year ($1,305,000; $825,000 + $480,000) is less than $2,890,000, there is no reduction in the $1,160,000 § 179 deduction.

Dexter chooses not to take bonus depreciation. How should Dexter allocate his $1,160,000 § 179 expense election?

Dexter should expense the longest-lived MACRS asset first (the equipment; the 7-year MACRS asset). If he makes this choice, Dexter's total cost recovery deduction in 2023 is $1,189,000, calculated as follows:

Equipment (7-year MACRS asset)	
§ 179 expense	$ 825,000
Computer system (5-year MACRS asset)	
§ 179 expense ($1,160,000 − $825,000)	335,000
MACRS cost recovery [($480,000 − $335,000) × 0.20 (Exhibit 8.3)]	29,000
Total cost recovery deduction	$1,189,000

If Dexter were to allocate the § 179 expense election to the machinery (5-year MACRS asset), his total cost recovery deduction in 2023 would be only $1,180,721, calculated as follows:

Computer system (5-year MACRS asset)	
§ 179 expense	$ 480,000
Equipment (7-year MACRS asset)	
§ 179 expense ($1,160,000 − $480,000)	680,000
MACRS cost recovery [($825,000 − $680,000) × 0.1429 (Exhibit 8.3)]	20,721
Total cost recovery deduction	$1,180,721

No matter which asset is expensed, after using both § 179 and bonus depreciation, $145,000 is subject to MACRS cost recovery. However, if the 7-year MACRS asset is expensed, this $145,000 is cost recovered over six tax years (here, the $145,000 relates to the 5-year MACRS asset). If the 5-year MACRS asset is expensed, the $145,000 will be recovered over eight tax years (here, the $145,000 relates to the 7-year MACRS asset).

Using the § 179 expense election on the longest-lived asset accelerates overall cost recovery deductions to earlier years, gaining a time-value-of-money advantage for the taxpayer.

Using Both § 179 and Bonus Depreciation

In general, in 2023, a business that places in service $1,160,000 or less of qualifying § 179 property will exclusively use § 179 to immediately expense all of those assets, while a business placing in service $4,050,000 or more of qualifying assets (the point at which the § 179 amount is completely phased out; $1,160,000 + $2,890,000) will qualify only for bonus depreciation. Any business placing in service between $1,160,000 and $4,050,000 of qualifying § 179 property will be able to use a combination of both § 179 and bonus depreciation (see Concept Summary 8.3).[19]

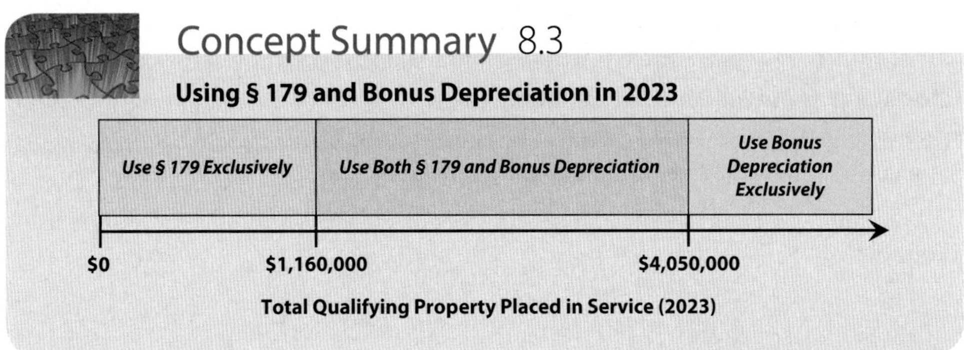

[19]This general rule applies to the vast majority of taxpayers. However, it would not apply if the § 179 taxable income limitation applied or the taxpayer chose to defer deductions to later tax years (e.g., if the taxpayer expects marginal tax rates to increase) to gain a time value of money advantage.

Example 26

Return to the facts of Example 18. Given that George has placed $3,570,000 of 7-year MACRS assets in service during 2023, he can use both § 179 and additional first-year depreciation (see Concept Summary 8.3). If George uses both § 179 and bonus depreciation, his total cost recovery deduction will increase to $3,040,312.

§ 179 expense	$ 480,000
Additional first-year depreciation [($3,570,000 − $480,000) × 80%]	2,472,000
MACRS cost recovery [($3,570,000 − $480,000 − $2,472,000) × 0.1429 (Exhibit 8.3)]	88,312
Total cost recovery deduction	$3,040,312

As discussed above, George might choose to use only a portion of the § 179 election and/or choose not to use bonus depreciation. However, it is possible for George to deduct a significant portion of his 2023 acquisitions immediately.

The Big Picture

Example 27

Return to the facts of *The Big Picture* on p. 8-1 and assume that the tax year is 2023. Dr. Payne has placed $612,085 of assets in service ($70,000 + $67,085 + $475,000). Because this amount is less than $2,890,000, there is no reduction in the $1,160,000 maximum § 179 deduction.

If Dr. Payne has sufficient business income to avoid § 179's business income limitation, he can use § 179 to expense all of the assets placed in service in 2023 ($612,085).

If § 179's business income limitation comes into play, Dr. Payne can elect out of § 179 and deduct $612,085 using additional first-year depreciation (which has no income limitation). In this case, however, other limitations might affect his decision (including the excess business loss limitation; see text Section 7-5). Or he can apply § 179 or additional first-year depreciation to selected assets, reducing his taxable income this year and deferring some deductions to future years.

If Dr. Payne chooses to use neither § 179 nor additional first-year depreciation, his cost recovery deduction will be $91,298 (as detailed on p. 8-1).

LO.4

Identify listed property and apply the deduction limitations on listed property and on luxury automobiles.

8-3d **Business and Personal Use of Automobiles and Other Listed Property**

Limits exist on cost recovery deductions for automobiles and other listed property that are used for both personal and business purposes.[20] If listed property is not *predominantly used* for business purposes when placed in service, it is not eligible for the accelerated methods built into MACRS, the immediate expense election (§ 179), or bonus depreciation.

If not *predominantly used* for business when placed in service, the listed property's cost must be recovered using the *straight-line method* (see Exhibit 8.5). Further, the straight-line method must continue to be used even if, at some later date, the property *is* predominantly used for business.

Listed property includes:

- Any passenger automobile.
- Any other property used as a means of transportation.
- Any property of a type generally used for purposes of entertainment, recreation, or amusement.
- Any other property specified in the Regulations.

A computer or peripheral equipment placed in service after 2017 is not listed property.[21]

[20] § 280F.

[21] § 280F(d)(4)(A). A computer or peripheral equipment placed in service before 2018 is subject to the listed property rules.

Automobiles and Other Listed Property Used Predominantly in Business

For listed property to be *predominantly used in business*, its *business use* must exceed 50 percent.[22] The use of listed property for production of income does not qualify as business use for purposes of the more-than-50% test. However, both production of income and business use percentages are used to compute the cost recovery deduction.

On September 1, 2023, Emma places in service listed property (5-year MACRS property). The property cost $10,000. She elects not to take any available additional first-year depreciation.

If Emma uses the property 40% for business and 25% for the production of income, the property is not considered as predominantly used for business. The cost is recovered using straight-line cost recovery. Emma's cost recovery allowance for the year is $650 ($10,000 × 0.10 × 65%).

If, however, Emma uses the property 60% for business and 25% for the production of income, the property is considered as used predominantly for business. As a result, she may use the regular MACRS method. Emma's cost recovery allowance for the year is $1,700 ($10,000 × 0.20 × 85%).

In determining the percentage of business use of listed property, a mileage-based percentage is used for automobiles. For other listed property, one employs the most appropriate unit of time (e.g., hours) for which the property actually is used (rather than its availability for use).[23]

Limits on Cost Recovery for Automobiles

The law places further limits on the annual cost recovery deductions for passenger automobiles. These dollar limits were imposed because of the belief that the tax system was being used to underwrite automobiles whose cost and luxury far exceeded what was needed for the taxpayer's business use.

A *passenger automobile* is any four-wheeled vehicle manufactured for use on public streets, roads, and highways with an unloaded gross vehicle weight (GVW) rating of 6,000 pounds or less.[24] This definition specifically excludes vehicles used directly in the business of transporting people or property for compensation [e.g., taxicabs (including autos used for Uber or Lyft), ambulances, hearses, and trucks and vans].

The following "luxury auto" depreciation limits apply.[25]

Date Placed in Service	First Year	Second Year	Third Year	Fourth and Later Years
2023*	$12,200	$19,500	$11,700	$6,960
2022	$11,200	$18,000	$10,800	$6,460
2021	$10,200	$16,400	$ 9,800	$5,860
2019–2020	$10,100	$16,100	$ 9,700	$5,760

*2024 indexed amounts will be released by the IRS early in 2024.

In the event a passenger automobile used predominantly for business qualifies for additional first-year depreciation, the first-year recovery limitation is increased by $8,000 for automobiles placed in service before 2027.[26] As a result, for acquisitions made in 2023, the initial-year cost recovery limitation increases from $12,200 to $20,200 ($12,200 + $8,000).[27]

The luxury auto limits must be reduced proportionally for any personal use of the auto. In addition, the limitation in the first year includes any amount the taxpayer elects

[22] § 280F(b)(3).

[23] Reg. § 1.280F–6T(e).

[24] § 280F(d)(5).

[25] § 280F(a)(1); Rev.Proc. 2023–14. Cost recovery limitations for years prior to 2019 are found in IRS Publication 463.

[26] § 168(k)(2)(F)(i).

[27] Different cost recovery limitations apply to trucks and vans and to electric automobiles.

to expense under § 179.[28] If the passenger automobile is used partly for personal use, the personal use percentage is ignored for the purpose of determining the unrecovered cost available for deduction in later years.

Example 29

On July 1, 2023, Dan places in service a new automobile that cost $65,000. He does not elect § 179 expensing, and he elects not to take any available additional first-year depreciation. The car is used 80% for business and 20% for personal use in each tax year. Dan chooses the MACRS 200% declining-balance method of cost recovery (the auto is a 5-year MACRS asset).

The depreciation computation for 2023 through 2028 is summarized in the table below. The cost recovery allowed is the lesser of the MACRS amount or the recovery limitation.

Year	MACRS Amount	Recovery Limitation	Depreciation Allowed
2023	$10,400	$9,760	$ 9,760
	($65,000 × 0.2000 × 80%)	($12,200 × 80%)	
2024	$16,640	$15,600	$15,600
	($65,000 × 0.3200 × 80%)	($19,500 × 80%)	
2025	$9,984	$9,360	$ 9,360
	($65,000 × 0.1920 × 80%)	($11,700 × 80%)	
2026	$5,990	$5,568	$ 5,568
	($65,000 × 0.1152 × 80%)	($6,960 × 80%)	
2027	$5,990	$5,568	$ 5,568
	($65,000 × 0.1152 × 80%)	($6,960 × 80%)	
2028	$2,995	$5,568	$ 2,995
	($65,000 × 0.0576 × 80%)	($6,960 × 80%)	

If Dan continues to use the car after 2028, his cost recovery is limited to the lesser of the recoverable basis or the recovery limitation (i.e., $6,960 × business use percentage). For this purpose, the recoverable basis is computed as if the full recovery limitation was allowed even if it was not. As a result, the recoverable basis as of January 1, 2029, is $3,936 ($65,000 − $12,200 − $19,500 − $11,700 − $6,960 − $6,960 − $3,744*).

If Dan takes additional first-year depreciation in 2023, that amount would be calculated as $41,600 [$65,000 × 80% (2023 bonus depreciation percentage) × 80% (business use)]. He would also be allowed normal MACRS of $2,080 [$13,000 (the car's depreciable basis after taking bonus depreciation) × 0.2000 × 80% (business use)]. However, his MACRS deduction would be limited to $16,160 [($12,200 + $8,000) × 80% business use].

* $65,000 × 0.0576 × 100%; this is the full 2028 MACRS amount (which is less than the $6,960 recovery limitation for the year).

The cost recovery limitations are maximum amounts. If the regular MACRS calculation produces a smaller amount of cost recovery, the smaller amount is used.

Example 30

On April 2, 2023, Gail places in service a used automobile that cost $26,200. The car is used 70% for business and 30% for personal use. The cost recovery allowance for 2023 is $3,668 ($26,200 × 0.20 MACRS table factor × 70%), not $8,540 ($12,200 passenger auto maximum × 70%).

Special Limitation for Sport-Utility Vehicles (SUVs)

Some sport-utility vehicles (SUVs) are not considered passenger automobiles and, therefore, are not subject to the luxury automobile limitations. However, in 2023, a $28,900 limit applies for the § 179 deduction when the luxury auto limits do not apply ($27,000 in 2022). The limit is in effect for SUVs with an unloaded GVW rating of more than 6,000 pounds and not more than 14,000 pounds.[29]

[28] § 280F(d)(1).

[29] § 179(b)(5).

During 2023, Jay acquires and places in service a new SUV that cost $72,600 and has a GVW of 8,000 pounds. Jay uses the vehicle 100% of the time for business use and elects not to use bonus depreciation. The total cost recovery deduction for 2023 with respect to the SUV is computed as follows:

§ 179 expense	$28,900
MACRS cost recovery [($72,600 – $28,900) × 0.20 (Exhibit 8.3)]	8,740
Total cost recovery deduction	$35,740

If Jay chooses to also use additional first-year depreciation on the SUV, then his total cost recovery deduction for 2023 would be $65,608, computed as follows:

§ 179 expense	$28,900
Additional first-year depreciation [($72,600 – $28,900) × 80%]	34,960
MACRS cost recovery [($72,600 – $28,900 – $34,960) × 0.20 (Exhibit 8.3)]	1,748
Total cost recovery deduction	$65,608

Automobiles and Other Listed Property Not Used Predominantly in Business

For automobiles and other listed property not used predominantly in business in the year of acquisition (i.e., 50 percent or less), the straight-line method under the alternative depreciation system is required (see text Section 8-3e).[30] Under this system, the straight-line recovery period for automobiles is five years. However, the cost recovery deduction for any passenger automobile cannot exceed the luxury auto limit.

Auto Not Predominantly Used in Business

On July 27, 2023, Fred places in service an automobile that cost $20,000. The auto is used 40% for business and 60% for personal use. The cost recovery allowance for 2023 is $800 [$20,000 × 0.10 (Exhibit 8.7) × 40%].

Assume the same facts as in Example 32, except that the automobile cost $50,000. The cost recovery allowance for 2023 is $2,000 [$50,000 × 0.10 (Exhibit 8.7) × 40%; $2,000 is less than 40% of the first-year limit].

The straight-line method is used even if, at some later date, the business use of the property increases to more than 50 percent (although the cost recovery allowed will reflect the increase in business use).

Assume the same facts as in Example 32, except that in 2024, Fred uses the automobile 70% for business and 30% for personal use. Fred's cost recovery allowance for 2024 is $2,800 [$20,000 × 0.20 (Exhibit 8.7) × 70%], which is less than 70% of the second-year limit.

Change from Predominantly Business Use

If the business use percentage of listed property falls to 50 percent or less after the year the property is placed in service, the property is subject to *cost recovery recapture*. The amount required to be recaptured and included in the taxpayer's ordinary income is the *excess cost recovery*.

Excess cost recovery is the excess of the cost recovery deduction taken in prior years using the regular MACRS method over the amount that would have been allowed if the straight-line method had been used since the property was placed in service.[31]

[30] § 280F(b)(1).

[31] § 280F(b)(2).

Seth purchased a new car on January 22, 2023, at a cost of $40,000. Business use was 80% in 2023, 70% in 2024, 40% in 2025, and 60% in 2026. Seth elects not to take any available additional first-year depreciation. Seth's excess cost recovery to be recaptured as ordinary income in 2025 is computed as follows:

2023	
MACRS ($40,000 × 0.20 × 80%, limited to $12,200 × 80%)	$ 6,400
Straight-line ($40,000 × 0.10 × 80%, limited to $12,200 × 80%)	(3,200)
Excess	$ 3,200
2024	
MACRS ($40,000 × 0.32 × 70%, limited to $19,500 × 70%)	$ 8,960
Straight-line ($40,000 × 0.20 × 70%, limited to $19,500 × 70%)	(5,600)
Excess	$ 3,360
2025	
2023 excess	$ 3,200
2024 excess	3,360
Ordinary income recapture	$ 6,560

After the business use of the listed property drops below the more-than-50% level, the straight-line method is used for the remaining life of the property.

Assume the same facts as in Example 35. Seth's cost recovery deductions for 2025 and 2026 are:

2025	$3,200 [$40,000 × 0.20 × 40% ($3,200), limited to $11,700 × 40% ($4,680)]
2026	$4,176 [$40,000 × 0.20 × 60% ($4,800), limited to $6,960 × 60% ($4,176)]

Leased Automobiles

Taxpayers who lease rather than purchase a passenger automobile for business purposes are not subject to the luxury auto limits. To prevent taxpayers from circumventing the luxury auto limits by deducting the full amount of rental payments associated with a luxury automobile leased for business, the law requires these taxpayers to report an *inclusion amount* in gross income.

The inclusion amount (determined from an IRS table) is based on the fair market value of the automobile. It must be computed for each taxable year the automobile is leased. Once determined, the inclusion amount is prorated for the number of days the auto is used during the taxable year. The prorated dollar amount then is multiplied by the business and income-producing use percentage.[32] The taxpayer deducts the lease payments, multiplied by the business and income-producing use percentage. In effect, the taxpayer's annual deduction for the lease payment is reduced by the inclusion amount.

[32]Reg. § 1.280F–7(a).

Example 37

On April 1, 2023, Jim leases and places in service a passenger automobile worth $88,600. The lease is to be for a period of five years. During the taxable years 2023 and 2024, Jim uses the automobile 70% for business and 30% for personal use.

Assuming that the dollar amounts from the IRS table for 2023 and 2024 are $172 and $378, respectively, Jim includes in gross income:

2023	$172 × (275/365) × 70% = $91
2024	$378 × (366/366) × 70% = $265

In each year, Jim still can deduct 70% of the lease payments made (i.e., the amount related to his business use of the auto).

Substantiation Requirements

The substantiation requirements of § 274 apply to listed property. A taxpayer must be able to prove for any business use the amount of expense or use, the time and place of use, the business purpose for the use, and the business relationship to the taxpayer of persons using the property.

Substantiation requires adequate records or sufficient evidence corroborating the taxpayer's statement. For example, to document business use of an automobile, it is expected that a taxpayer maintain a contemporaneous record of business miles driven (versus other miles), any expenses incurred (e.g., fuel, repairs, business tolls, parking), and the business reason for the auto's use.[33]

8-3e Alternative Depreciation System (ADS)

LO.5 **Determine when and how to use the alternative depreciation system (ADS).**

The **alternative depreciation system (ADS)** must be used:[34]

- To calculate the portion of depreciation treated as an alternative minimum tax (AMT) adjustment for purposes of the individual AMT (see text Section 12-5d).[35]
- For residential and nonresidential real estate and any qualified improvement property placed in service after 2017 by a "real property trade or business" that opts out of the interest expense limitations of § 163(j). In general, these interest expense limitation rules only apply to businesses with annual gross receipts in excess of $29 million (in 2023; $27 million in 2022).
- To compute depreciation allowances for earnings and profits purposes (see text Section 19-2a).

In general, ADS depreciation is computed using the straight-line method. However, for AMT, depreciation of personal property is computed using the 150 percent declining-balance method with a switch to the straight-line method when appropriate.

The taxpayer must use the half-year or the mid-quarter convention, whichever is applicable, for all property other than real estate. The mid-month convention is used for real estate. Under ADS, personal property (other than qualified improvement property) is depreciated using the appropriate asset class life (e.g., 5- or 7-year) and the 150 percent declining-balance method (see Exhibits 8.6 and 8.7). Under ADS, qualified improvement property has a 20-year life, residential rental real estate has a 30-year life, and nonresidential real estate has a 40-year life; all are depreciated using the straight-line method (see Exhibits 8.5 and 8.9).[36]

[33] §§ 274(d) and (i). These substantiation requirements do not apply to vehicles that, by reason of their nature, are not likely to be used more than a *de minimis* amount for personal purposes.

[34] § 168(g). ADS also must be used to compute cost recovery for property used predominantly outside the United States, by a tax-exempt entity, and in several other situations.

[35] This AMT adjustment applies for real and personal property placed in service before 1999. However, it also applies for personal property placed in service after 1998 if the taxpayer uses the 200% declining-balance method for regular income tax purposes.

[36] Residential rental real estate placed in service before 2018 uses an ADS life of 40 years. The class life for certain properties described in § 168(e)(3) is specially determined under § 168(g)(3)(B).

To simplify reporting, taxpayers may *elect* to use the 150 percent declining-balance method to compute cost recovery for the regular income tax (rather than the 200 percent declining-balance method that is available for personal property). If this election is made, there is no difference between the regular income tax and AMT cost recovery.[37]

On March 1, 2023, Abby acquires and places in service computer-based telephone central office switching equipment for $80,000. Abby elects not to take any available additional first-year depreciation. If Abby uses regular MACRS cost recovery (assuming no § 179 election), her deduction for 2023 is $16,000 [$80,000 × 0.20 (Exhibit 8.3, 5-year class property)].

If Abby elects to use ADS 150% declining-balance cost recovery for the regular income tax (assuming no § 179 election), the cost recovery allowance for 2023 is $12,000 [$80,000 × 0.15 (Exhibit 8.6, 5-year class property)].

Rather than determining depreciation under the regular MACRS method, taxpayers may *elect* straight-line under ADS. One reason for making this election is to defer cost recovery deductions to later years (presuming that marginal tax rates will be higher in those years). Another reason is to simplify record keeping, since the cost recovery deduction will be the same as earnings and profits depreciation.[38]

Palladium, Inc., acquires and places in service an office building on March 17, 2023, for $1,700,000. It takes the maximum cost recovery allowance for determining taxable income. For 2023, Palladium deducts $34,561 [$1,700,000 × 0.02033 (Exhibit 8.8)].

However, Palladium's cost recovery for computing its earnings and profits is only $33,643 [$1,700,000 × 0.01979 (Exhibit 8.9)].

Report cost recovery deductions appropriately.

8-4 **Reporting Procedures**

Sole proprietors engaged in a business file a Schedule C, Profit or Loss from Business, to accompany Form 1040. A 2022 Schedule C is illustrated; the 2023 Schedule C was not available when we published.

The top part of page 1 requests certain key information about the taxpayer (e.g., name, address, Social Security number, principal business activity, and accounting method used). Part I provides for the reporting of items of income. If the business requires the use of inventories and the computation of cost of goods sold (see text Section 16-2 for when this is necessary), Part III must be completed and the cost of goods sold amount transferred to line 4 of Part I.

Part II allows for the reporting of deductions. Some of the deductions discussed in this chapter and their location on the form are depletion (line 12) and depreciation (line 13). Other expenses (line 27a) include those items not already covered (see lines 8 through 26). An example is research and experimental expenditures.

If depreciation is claimed, Form 4562 should be completed. A 2022 Form 4562 is illustrated; the 2023 Form 4562 was not available when we published. The amount reported on line 22 of Form 4562 is transferred to line 13 of Part II of Schedule C.

[37] For personal property placed in service before 1999, taxpayers making the election use the ADS recovery periods in computing cost recovery for the regular income tax. The ADS recovery periods generally are longer than the regular recovery periods under MACRS.

[38] This straight-line election is made on a year-by-year basis. For property other than real estate, the election is made by MACRS class and applies to all assets in that MACRS class. So, for example, the election could be made for 7-year MACRS property and not for 5-year MACRS property placed in service during the same year. For real estate, the election is made on a property-by-property basis.

Thomas Andrews, Social Security number 111-11-1111, was employed as an accountant until May 2022, when he opened his own practice as a CPA (Andrews Accounting Services; business activity code: 541211). His business address is 279 Mountain View, Ogden, UT 84201. Andrews keeps his books on the cash basis and reported the following revenue and business expenses in 2022.

a. Revenue from accounting practice, $192,000.
b. Insurance, $5,000.
c. Office supplies, $4,000.
d. Office rent, $16,000.
e. Copier lease payments, $3,000.
f. Licenses, $2,000.
g. New furniture and fixtures were acquired and placed in service on May 10 for $142,000. Thomas elects § 179 expensing and uses the regular MACRS cost recovery method.

Thomas reports the above information on Schedule C and Form 4562 as illustrated on the following pages.

8-5 **Amortization**

LO.7

Identify intangible assets that are eligible for amortization and calculate the amount of the deduction.

Taxpayers can recover the costs of certain intangible assets through an **amortization** deduction. The amount of the deduction is determined by amortizing the adjusted basis of these intangibles ratably over a 15-year period beginning in the month in which the intangible is acquired.[39]

Code § 197 covers the amortization of most intangibles. *Amortizable § 197 intangibles* include most intangibles acquired after August 10, 1993, and acquired in connection with the acquisition of a business, including goodwill, going-concern value, franchises, trademarks, copyrights, patents, and covenants not to compete. Generally, self-created intangibles are *not* § 197 intangibles.

The 15-year amortization period applies regardless of the actual useful life of an amortizable § 197 intangible. No other depreciation or amortization deduction is permitted for these intangibles.

On June 1, 2023, Neil purchased and began operating the Falcon Café. Of the purchase price, $90,000 is allocated to goodwill. The 2023 § 197 amortization deduction is $3,500 [($90,000 ÷ 15) × (7/12)].

Startup expenditures are partially amortizable by election.[40] A taxpayer must make this election no later than the due date of the return for the taxable year in which the trade or business begins.[41] If no election is made, the startup expenditures are capitalized.[42]

The amortization election for startup expenditures allows the taxpayer to deduct the smaller of (1) the startup expenditures related to the trade or business or (2) $5,000. The $5,000 maximum is reduced dollar for dollar by the amount of startup expenditures in excess of $50,000. As a result, if startup expenditures equal or exceed $55,000, no immediate deduction is allowed. Any startup expenditures not deducted are amortized ratably over a 180-month period, beginning in the month in which the trade or business begins.[43]

[39] § 197(a).
[40] §§ 195(a) and (b).
[41] § 195(d).
[42] § 195(a).
[43] §§ 195(b)(1)(A) and (B).

Form **4562**

Department of the Treasury
Internal Revenue Service

Depreciation and Amortization

(Including Information on Listed Property)

Attach to your tax return.

Go to *www.irs.gov/Form4562* for instructions and the latest information.

OMB No. 1545-0172

2022

Attachment Sequence No. **179**

Name(s) shown on return	Business or activity to which this form relates	Identifying number
Thomas Andrews	*Andrews Accounting Services*	*111-11-1111*

Part I **Election To Expense Certain Property Under Section 179**
Note: If you have any listed property, complete Part V before you complete Part I.

1	Maximum amount (see instructions)	1	*1,080,000*
2	Total cost of section 179 property placed in service (see instructions)	2	*142,000*
3	Threshold cost of section 179 property before reduction in limitation (see instructions)	3	*2,700,000*
4	Reduction in limitation. Subtract line 3 from line 2. If zero or less, enter -0-	4	*-0-*
5	Dollar limitation for tax year. Subtract line 4 from line 1. If zero or less, enter -0-. If married filing separately, see instructions	5	*142,000*

6	(a) Description of property	(b) Cost (business use only)	(c) Elected cost
	Furniture and Fixtures	*142,000*	*142,000*

7	Listed property. Enter the amount from line 29	7	
8	Total elected cost of section 179 property. Add amounts in column (c), lines 6 and 7	8	*142,000*
9	Tentative deduction. Enter the **smaller** of line 5 or line 8	9	*142,000*
10	Carryover of disallowed deduction from line 13 of your 2021 Form 4562	10	*-0-*
11	Business income limitation. Enter the smaller of business income (not less than zero) or line 5. See instructions	11	*142,000*
12	Section 179 expense deduction. Add lines 9 and 10, but don't enter more than line 11	12	*142,000*
13	Carryover of disallowed deduction to 2023. Add lines 9 and 10, less line 12	13	

Note: Don't use Part II or Part III below for listed property. Instead, use Part V.

Part II **Special Depreciation Allowance and Other Depreciation (Don't** include listed property. See instructions.**)**

14	Special depreciation allowance for qualified property (other than listed property) placed in service during the tax year. See instructions	14	
15	Property subject to section 168(f)(1) election	15	
16	Other depreciation (including ACRS)	16	

Part III **MACRS Depreciation (Don't** include listed property. See instructions.**)**

Section A

17	MACRS deductions for assets placed in service in tax years beginning before 2022	17	
18	If you are electing to group any assets placed in service during the tax year into one or more general asset accounts, check here ☐		

Section B—Assets Placed in Service During 2022 Tax Year Using the General Depreciation System

(a) Classification of property	(b) Month and year placed in service	(c) Basis for depreciation (business/investment use only—see instructions)	(d) Recovery period	(e) Convention	(f) Method	(g) Depreciation deduction
19a 3-year property						
b 5-year property						
c 7-year property						
d 10-year property						
e 15-year property						
f 20-year property						
g 25-year property			25 yrs.		S/L	
h Residential rental property			27.5 yrs.	MM	S/L	
			27.5 yrs.	MM	S/L	
i Nonresidential real property			39 yrs.	MM	S/L	
				MM	S/L	

Section C—Assets Placed in Service During 2022 Tax Year Using the Alternative Depreciation System

20a Class life					S/L	
b 12-year			12 yrs.		S/L	
c 30-year			30 yrs.	MM	S/L	
d 40-year			40 yrs.	MM	S/L	

Part IV **Summary** (See instructions.)

21	Listed property. Enter amount from line 28	21	
22	**Total.** Add amounts from line 12, lines 14 through 17, lines 19 and 20 in column (g), and line 21. Enter here and on the appropriate lines of your return. Partnerships and S corporations—see instructions	22	*142,000*
23	For assets shown above and placed in service during the current year, enter the portion of the basis attributable to section 263A costs	23	

For Paperwork Reduction Act Notice, see separate instructions. Cat. No. 12906N Form **4562** (2022)

SCHEDULE C (Form 1040)
Department of the Treasury Internal Revenue Service

Profit or Loss From Business
(Sole Proprietorship)

Go to *www.irs.gov/ScheduleC* for instructions and the latest information.
Attach to Form 1040, 1040-SR, 1040-NR, or 1041; partnerships must generally file Form 1065.

OMB No. 1545-0074
2022
Attachment Sequence No. **09**

Name of proprietor	*Thomas Andrews*	**Social security number (SSN)** *111-11-1111*
A	Principal business or profession, including product or service (see instructions) *Certified Public Accountant*	**B Enter code from instructions** *5 4 1 2 1 1*
C	Business name. If no separate business name, leave blank. *Andrews Accounting Services*	**D Employer ID number (EIN)** (see instr.)
E	Business address (including suite or room no.) *279 Mountain View*	
	City, town or post office, state, and ZIP code *Ogden, UT 84201*	

F Accounting method: **(1)** ☑ Cash **(2)** ☐ Accrual **(3)** ☐ Other (specify)

G Did you "materially participate" in the operation of this business during 2022? If "No," see instructions for limit on losses ☑ Yes ☐ No

H If you started or acquired this business during 2022, check here ☐

I Did you make any payments in 2022 that would require you to file Form(s) 1099? See instructions ☐ Yes ☐ No

J If "Yes," did you or will you file required Form(s) 1099? ☐ Yes ☐ No

Part I Income

1	Gross receipts or sales. See instructions for line 1 and check the box if this income was reported to you on Form W-2 and the "Statutory employee" box on that form was checked ☐	1	*192,000*
2	Returns and allowances	2	
3	Subtract line 2 from line 1	3	*192,000*
4	Cost of goods sold (from line 42)	4	
5	**Gross profit.** Subtract line 4 from line 3	5	*192,000*
6	Other income, including federal and state gasoline or fuel tax credit or refund (see instructions)	6	
7	**Gross income.** Add lines 5 and 6	7	*192,000*

Part II **Expenses.** Enter expenses for business use of your home **only** on line 30.

		Line	Amount			Line	Amount
8	Advertising	8		18	Office expense (see instructions)	18	*4,000*
9	Car and truck expenses (see instructions)	9		19	Pension and profit-sharing plans	19	
				20	Rent or lease (see instructions):		
10	Commissions and fees	10		a	Vehicles, machinery, and equipment	20a	*3,000*
11	Contract labor (see instructions)	11		b	Other business property	20b	*16,000*
12	Depletion	12		21	Repairs and maintenance	21	
13	Depreciation and section 179 expense deduction (not included in Part III) (see instructions)	13	*142,000*	22	Supplies (not included in Part III)	22	
				23	Taxes and licenses	23	*2,000*
				24	Travel and meals:		
14	Employee benefit programs (other than on line 19)	14		a	Travel	24a	
15	Insurance (other than health)	15	*5,000*	b	Deductible meals (see instructions)	24b	
16	Interest (see instructions):			25	Utilities	25	
a	Mortgage (paid to banks, etc.)	16a		26	Wages (less employment credits)	26	
b	Other	16b		27a	Other expenses (from line 48)	27a	
17	Legal and professional services	17		b	**Reserved for future use**	27b	

28	**Total expenses** before expenses for business use of home. Add lines 8 through 27a	28	*172,000*
29	Tentative profit or (loss). Subtract line 28 from line 7	29	*20,000*
30	Expenses for business use of your home. Do not report these expenses elsewhere. Attach Form 8829 unless using the simplified method. See instructions. **Simplified method filers only:** Enter the total square footage of (a) your home: ______ and (b) the part of your home used for business: ______. Use the Simplified Method Worksheet in the instructions to figure the amount to enter on line 30	30	
31	**Net profit or (loss).** Subtract line 30 from line 29. • If a profit, enter on both **Schedule 1 (Form 1040), line 3,** and on **Schedule SE, line 2.** (If you checked the box on line 1, see instructions.) Estates and trusts, enter on **Form 1041, line 3.** • If a loss, you **must** go to line 32.	31	*20,000*

32 If you have a loss, check the box that describes your investment in this activity. See instructions.

• If you checked 32a, enter the loss on both **Schedule 1 (Form 1040), line 3,** and on **Schedule SE, line 2.** (If you checked the box on line 1, see the line 31 instructions.) Estates and trusts, enter on **Form 1041, line 3.**

• If you checked 32b, you **must** attach **Form 6198.** Your loss may be limited.

32a ☐ All investment is at risk.
32b ☐ Some investment is not at risk.

Startup Expenditures

Example 42

Green Corporation begins business on August 1, 2023. The corporation incurs startup expenditures of $47,000. If Green elects amortization under § 195, the total startup expenditures that Green may deduct in 2023 are computed as follows:

Deductible amount	$5,000
Amortizable amount {[($47,000 − $5,000) ÷ 180] × 5 months}	1,167
Total deduction	$6,167

Example 43

Assume the same facts as in Example 42, except that the startup expenditures total $53,000. The 2023 deduction is computed as follows:

Deductible amount [$5,000 − ($53,000 − $50,000)]	$2,000
Amortizable amount {[($53,000 − $2,000) ÷ 180] × 5 months}	1,417
Total deduction	$3,417

Amortizable startup expenditures generally must satisfy two requirements.[44] First, the expenses must be paid or incurred in connection with:

- Creating a business.
- Investigating the creation or acquisition of a business.
- Anticipating an activity becoming a business.

Second, the expenses must reflect those that could be deducted in an existing trade or business in the same field (see Investigation of a Business, text Section 6-3d).

The startup costs of creating a new active trade or business could include advertising; salaries and wages; travel and other expenses incurred in lining up prospective distributors, suppliers, or customers; and salaries and fees for executives, consultants, and professional services. Costs that relate to either created or acquired businesses could include expenses incurred for the analysis or survey of potential markets, products, labor supply, transportation facilities, and the like. Startup expenditures do not include allowable deductions for interest, taxes, and research and experimental costs.[45]

Amortization deductions also can be claimed for organizational expenses (see text Section 17-1k) and research and experimental expenditures (see text Section 7-4).

LO.8

Determine the amount of depletion expense, including being able to apply the alternative tax treatments for intangible drilling and development costs.

8-6 Depletion

Natural resources (e.g., oil, gas, coal, gravel, and timber) are subject to **depletion**, a form of cost recovery that applies to natural resources. Land generally cannot be depleted.

Although all natural resources are subject to depletion, oil and gas wells are used as an example in the following paragraphs to illustrate the related costs and issues.

In developing an oil or gas well, the producer typically makes four types of expenditures.

- Natural resource costs.
- Intangible drilling and development costs.
- Tangible asset costs.
- Operating costs.

Natural resources are physically limited, and the costs to acquire them (e.g., oil under the ground) are, therefore, recovered through depletion. Costs incurred in making the

[44] §§ 195(c)(1)(A) and (B).

[45] § 195(c).

property ready for drilling, such as the cost of labor in clearing the property, erecting derricks, and drilling the hole, are **intangible drilling and development costs (IDCs)**. These costs generally have no salvage value and are a lost cost if the well is dry.

Costs for tangible assets such as tools, pipes, and engines are capitalized and recovered through depreciation (cost recovery). Costs incurred after the well is producing are operating costs. These costs include expenditures for such items as labor, fuel, and supplies. Operating costs are deductible as trade or business expenses. Depletable costs and intangible drilling and development costs receive different treatment.

8-6a Intangible Drilling and Development Costs (IDCs)

Intangible drilling and development costs can be handled in one of two ways at the option of the taxpayer. They can be *either* charged off as an expense in the year in which they are incurred *or* capitalized and written off through depletion. The taxpayer makes the election in the first year such expenditures are incurred, either by taking a deduction on the return or by adding them to the depletable basis.

Once made, the election is binding on both the taxpayer and the IRS for all such expenditures in the future. If the taxpayer fails to elect to expense IDCs on the original timely filed return for the first year in which such expenditures are incurred, an irrevocable election to capitalize them has been made.

As a general rule, it is more advantageous to expense IDCs. The obvious benefit of an immediate write-off (as opposed to a deferred write-off through depletion) is not the only advantage. Because a taxpayer can use percentage depletion, which is calculated without reference to basis (see Example 47), the IDCs may be completely lost as a deduction if they are capitalized.

8-6b Depletion Methods

There are two methods of calculating depletion. *Cost depletion* can be used on any wasting asset (and is the only method allowed for timber). *Percentage depletion* is subject to a number of limitations, particularly for oil and gas deposits. Depletion should be calculated both ways, and the method that results in the larger deduction should be used. The choice between cost depletion and percentage depletion is an annual decision; the taxpayer can use cost depletion in one year and percentage depletion in the following year.

Cost Depletion

Cost depletion resembles units-of-production depreciation.[46] The basis is divided by the estimated recoverable units of the asset (e.g., barrels and tons) to arrive at the depletion per unit. This amount then is multiplied by the number of units sold (*not* the units produced) during the year to arrive at the cost depletion allowed.

On January 1, 2023, Pablo purchases the rights to a mineral interest for $1,000,000. At that time, the remaining recoverable units in the mineral interest are estimated to be 200,000. The depletion per unit is $5 ($1,000,000 adjusted basis ÷ 200,000 estimated recoverable units).

If 60,000 units are mined and 25,000 are sold this year, the cost depletion is $125,000 ($5 depletion per unit × 25,000 units sold).

If the taxpayer later discovers that the original estimate was incorrect, the depletion per unit for future calculations is redetermined using the revised estimate.[47]

[46] § 612.

[47] § 611(a).

Example 45

Assume the same facts as in Example 44. In 2024, Pablo realizes that an incorrect estimate was made as to the capacity of the mine. The remaining recoverable units now are determined to be 400,000. Based on this new information, the revised depletion per unit is $2.1875 ($875,000 adjusted basis ÷ 400,000 estimated recoverable units). The $875,000 adjusted basis is the original cost ($1,000,000) reduced by the depletion claimed in 2023 ($125,000).

If 30,000 units are sold in 2024, the depletion for the year is $65,625 ($2.1875 depletion per unit × 30,000 units sold).

Percentage Depletion

Percentage depletion uses a specified percentage provided by the Code. The percentage varies according to the type of mineral interest involved. A sample of these percentages is shown in Exhibit 8.2. The rate is applied to the gross income from the property, but in no event may percentage depletion exceed 50 percent of the taxable income from the property before the allowance for depletion.[48]

Example 46

CarrollCo reports gross income of $100,000 and other property-related expenses of $60,000 and uses a depletion rate of 22%. CarrollCo's depletion allowance is determined as follows.

Gross income	$100,000
Less: Other expenses	(60,000)
Taxable income before depletion	$ 40,000
Depletion allowance [the lesser of $22,000 (22% × $100,000) or $20,000 (50% × $40,000)]	(20,000)
Taxable income after depletion	$ 20,000

The adjusted basis of CarrollCo's property is reduced by $20,000, the depletion deduction allowed. If the other expenses had been only $55,000, the full $22,000 could have been deducted, and the adjusted basis would have been reduced by $22,000.

Exhibit 8.2 Selected Percentage Depletion Rates

22% Depletion		
Cobalt	Nickel	Sulfur
Lead	Platinum	Tin
15% Depletion		
Copper	Iron	Oil shale
Gold	Oil and gas	Silver
14% Depletion		
Borax	Limestone	Potash
Granite	Marble	Slate
10% Depletion		
Coal	Lignite and perlite	Sodium chloride
5% Depletion		
Gravel	Peat	Sand

48 § 613(a). Special rules apply for certain oil and gas wells (e.g., the 50% ceiling is replaced with a 100% ceiling and the percentage depletion may not exceed 65% of the taxpayer's taxable income from all sources before the allowance for depletion). § 613A.

Note that percentage depletion is based on a percentage of the gross income from the property and makes no reference to cost. All other deductions detailed in this chapter are a function of the adjusted basis (cost) of the property. Thus, when percentage depletion is used, it is possible to claim aggregate depletion deductions that exceed the original cost of the property. If percentage depletion is used, however, the adjusted basis of the property (for computing cost depletion in a future tax year) is reduced by any depletion deducted until the basis reaches zero.

Melissa reports the following related to her sulfur mine.

Remaining depletable basis	$ 11,000
Gross income (10,000 units)	100,000
Expenses (other than depletion)	30,000

Because cost depletion is limited to the remaining depletable basis of $11,000, Melissa would choose percentage depletion of $22,000 (a 22% depletion rate is used for sulfur). Her basis in the mine then becomes zero. In future years, however, she can continue to take percentage depletion; percentage depletion is computed without reference to the remaining basis.

8-7 Tax Planning

LO.9

Identify tax planning opportunities for cost recovery, amortization, and depletion.

8-7a Cost Recovery

Cost recovery schedules should be reviewed annually for possible retirements, abandonments, and obsolescence.

An examination of the cost recovery schedule of Eagle Company reveals the following:

- Asset A was abandoned when it was discovered that the cost of repairs would be in excess of the cost of replacement. Asset A had an adjusted basis of $3,000.
- Asset J became obsolete this year, at which point its adjusted basis was $8,000.

Assets A and J should be written off, resulting in deductions of $11,000.

Another consideration when making decisions related to cost recovery is whether faster (or slower) cost recovery will be more beneficial for the taxpayer. If the taxpayer's goal is to recover the cost of fixed assets as quickly as possible, then using § 179 or additional first-year depreciation is preferable.

If, however, a taxpayer has a new business with little income or a business with a net operating loss carryover, the taxpayer's goal may be to slow down cost recovery. In this situation, the taxpayer generally should do the following.

- Elect not to take additional first-year depreciation, if available.
- Choose the straight-line cost recovery method.
- Elect not to expense assets under § 179.
- Defer placing assets in service in the current tax year or postpone capital outlays until future tax years.

8-7b **Amortization**

When a business is purchased, goodwill and covenants not to compete are both subject to an amortization period of 15 years. Given that goodwill and covenants not to compete are treated the same from a tax perspective, bargaining for a covenant should be based on legal rather than tax reasons. The seller, however, may have different motives because goodwill is a capital asset whereas a covenant is an ordinary income asset.

Because the amortization period for both goodwill and a covenant is 15 years, the purchaser may want to assign purchase costs to assets with shorter lives (e.g., inventory, receivables, and personalty). If, however, the purchase price will be assigned to assets with longer recovery periods (e.g., realty) or to assets not eligible for cost recovery (e.g., land), the purchaser would likely prefer costs to be assigned to goodwill or a covenant.

8-7c **Cost Recovery Tables**

Summary of Tables

Exhibit 8.3 Regular MACRS table for personalty.
Depreciation methods: 200 or 150 percent declining-balance switching to straight-line.
Recovery periods: 3, 5, 7, 10, 15, 20 years.
Convention: half-year.

Exhibit 8.4 Regular MACRS table for personalty.
Depreciation method: 200 percent declining-balance switching to straight-line.
Recovery periods: 3, 5, 7 years.
Convention: mid-quarter.

Exhibit 8.5 MACRS optional straight-line table for personalty.
Depreciation method: straight-line.
Recovery periods: 3, 5, 7, 10, 15, 20 years.
Convention: half-year.

Exhibit 8.6 Alternative minimum tax declining-balance table for personalty.
Depreciation method: 150 percent declining-balance switching to straight-line.
Recovery periods: 3, 5, 7, 9.5, 10, 12 years.
Convention: half-year.

Exhibit 8.7 Alternative depreciation system straight-line table for personalty.
Depreciation method: straight-line.
Recovery periods: 5, 10, 12 years.
Convention: half-year.

Exhibit 8.8 Regular MACRS straight-line table for realty.
Depreciation method: straight-line.
Recovery periods: 27.5, 31.5, 39 years.
Convention: mid-month.

Exhibit 8.9 Alternative depreciation system straight-line table for realty.
Depreciation method: straight-line.
Recovery period: 30, 40 years.
Convention: mid-month.

Exhibit 8.3 MACRS Accelerated Depreciation for Personal Property Assuming Half-Year Convention (Percentage Rates)

For Property Placed in Service after December 31, 1986

Recovery Year	3-Year (200% DB)	5-Year (200% DB)	7-Year (200% DB)	10-Year (200% DB)	15-Year (150% DB)	20-Year (150% DB)
1	33.33	20.00	14.29	10.00	5.00	3.750
2	44.45	32.00	24.49	18.00	9.50	7.219
3	14.81*	19.20	17.49	14.40	8.55	6.677
4	7.41	11.52*	12.49	11.52	7.70	6.177
5		11.52	8.93*	9.22	6.93	5.713
6		5.76	8.92	7.37	6.23	5.285
7			8.93	6.55*	5.90*	4.888
8			4.46	6.55	5.90	4.522
9				6.56	5.91	4.462*
10				6.55	5.90	4.461
11				3.28	5.91	4.462
12					5.90	4.461
13					5.91	4.462
14					5.90	4.461
15					5.91	4.462
16					2.95	4.461
17						4.462
18						4.461
19						4.462
20						4.461
21						2.231

*Switchover to straight-line depreciation.

Exhibit 8.4 MACRS Accelerated Depreciation for Personal Property Assuming Mid-Quarter Convention (Percentage Rates)

For Property Placed in Service after December 31, 1986 (Partial Table*)

3-Year

Recovery Year	First Quarter	Second Quarter	Third Quarter	Fourth Quarter
1	58.33	41.67	25.00	8.33
2	27.78	38.89	50.00	61.11

5-Year

Recovery Year	First Quarter	Second Quarter	Third Quarter	Fourth Quarter
1	35.00	25.00	15.00	5.00
2	26.00	30.00	34.00	38.00

7-Year

Recovery Year	First Quarter	Second Quarter	Third Quarter	Fourth Quarter
1	25.00	17.85	10.71	3.57
2	21.43	23.47	25.51	27.55

*The figures in this table are taken from the official tables that appear in Rev.Proc. 87–57. Because of their length, the complete tables are not presented.

Exhibit 8.5 MACRS Straight-Line Depreciation for Personal Property Assuming Half-Year Convention*

For Property Placed in Service after December 31, 1986

		Other Recovery Years		Last Recovery Year	
MACRS Class	**% First Recovery Year**	**Years**	**%**	**Year**	**%**
3-year	16.67	2–3	33.33	4	16.67
5-year	10.00	2–5	20.00	6	10.00
7-year	7.14	2–7	14.29	8	7.14
10-year	5.00	2–10	10.00	11	5.00
15-year	3.33	2–15	6.67	16	3.33
20-year	2.50	2–20	5.00	21	2.50

*The official table contains a separate row for each year. For ease of presentation, certain years are grouped in this table. In some instances, this will produce a difference of .01 for the last digit when compared with the official table.

Note: The last two rows of this table are used for qualified improvement property (15-year normal MACRS; 20-year ADS).

Exhibit 8.6 Alternative Minimum Tax: 150% Declining-Balance Assuming Half-Year Convention (Percentage Rates)

For Property Placed in Service after December 31, 1986 (Partial Table*)

Recovery Year	3-Year 150%	5-Year 150%	7-Year 150%	9.5-Year 150%	10-Year 150%	12-Year 150%
1	25.00	15.00	10.71	7.89	7.50	6.25
2	37.50	25.50	19.13	14.54	13.88	11.72
3	25.00**	17.85	15.03	12.25	11.79	10.25
4	12.50	16.66**	12.25**	10.31	10.02	8.97
5		16.66	12.25	9.17**	8.74**	7.85
6		8.33	12.25	9.17	8.74	7.33**
7			12.25	9.17	8.74	7.33
8			6.13	9.17	8.74	7.33
9				9.17	8.74	7.33
10				9.16	8.74	7.33
11					4.37	7.32
12						7.33
13						3.66

*The figures in this table are taken from the official table that appears in Rev.Proc. 87–57. Because of its length, the complete table is not presented.

**Switchover to straight-line depreciation.

Exhibit 8.7 ADS Straight-Line for Personal Property Assuming Half-Year Convention (Percentage Rates)

For Property Placed in Service after December 31, 1986 (Partial Table)*

Recovery Year	3-Year	5-Year	7-Year	10-Year	12-Year
1	16.67	10.00	7.14	5.00	4.17
2	33.33	20.00	14.29	10.00	8.33
3	33.33	20.00	14.29	10.00	8.33
4	16.67	20.00	14.29	10.00	8.33
5		20.00	14.29	10.00	8.33
6		10.00	14.29	10.00	8.33
7			14.29	10.00	8.34
8			7.14	10.00	8.33
9				10.00	8.34
10				10.00	8.33
11				5.00	8.34
12					8.33
13					4.17

*The figures in this table are taken from the official table that appears in Rev.Proc. 87–57. Because of its length, the complete table is not presented. The tables for the mid-quarter convention also appear in Rev.Proc. 87–57.

Exhibit 8.8 MACRS Straight-Line Depreciation for Real Property Assuming Mid-Month Convention* (Percentage Rates)

For Property Placed in Service after December 31, 1986: 27.5-Year Residential Real Property

Recovery Year(s)	The Applicable Percentage Is (Use the Column for the Month in the First Year the Property Is Placed in Service):											
	1	2	3	4	5	6	7	8	9	10	11	12
1	3.485	3.182	2.879	2.576	2.273	1.970	1.667	1.364	1.061	0.758	0.455	0.152
2–18	3.636	3.636	3.636	3.636	3.636	3.636	3.636	3.636	3.636	3.636	3.636	3.636
19–27	3.637	3.637	3.637	3.637	3.637	3.637	3.637	3.637	3.637	3.637	3.637	3.637
28	1.970	2.273	2.576	2.879	3.182	3.485	3.636	3.636	3.636	3.636	3.636	3.636
29	0.000	0.000	0.000	0.000	0.000	0.000	0.152	0.455	0.758	1.061	1.364	1.667

For Property Placed in Service after December 31, 1986, and before May 13, 1993: 31.5-Year Nonresidential Real Property

Recovery Year(s)	The Applicable Percentage Is (Use the Column for the Month in the First Year the Property Is Placed in Service):											
	1	2	3	4	5	6	7	8	9	10	11	12
1	3.042	2.778	2.513	2.249	1.984	1.720	1.455	1.190	0.926	0.661	0.397	0.132
2–19	3.175	3.175	3.175	3.175	3.175	3.175	3.175	3.175	3.175	3.175	3.175	3.175
20–31	3.174	3.174	3.174	3.174	3.174	3.174	3.174	3.174	3.174	3.174	3.174	3.174
32	1.720	1.984	2.249	2.513	2.778	3.042	3.175	3.175	3.175	3.175	3.175	3.175
33	0.000	0.000	0.000	0.000	0.000	0.000	0.132	0.397	0.661	0.926	1.190	1.455

For Property Placed in Service after May 12, 1993: 39-Year Nonresidential Real Property

Recovery Year(s)	The Applicable Percentage Is (Use the Column for the Month in the First Year the Property Is Placed in Service):											
	1	2	3	4	5	6	7	8	9	10	11	12
1	2.461	2.247	2.033	1.819	1.605	1.391	1.177	0.963	0.749	0.535	0.321	0.107
2–39	2.564	2.564	2.564	2.564	2.564	2.564	2.564	2.564	2.564	2.564	2.564	2.564
40	0.107	0.321	0.535	0.749	0.963	1.177	1.391	1.605	1.819	2.033	2.247	2.461

*The official tables contain a separate row for each year. For ease of presentation, certain years are grouped in these tables. In some instances, this will produce a difference of .001 for the last digit when compared with the official tables.

Exhibit 8.9 **ADS Straight-Line for Real Property Assuming Mid-Month Convention (Percentage Rates)**

For Property Placed in Service after December 31, 2017; 30-Year Residential Rental Property

Recovery Year	Month Placed in Service											
	1	2	3	4	5	6	7	8	9	10	11	12
1	3.194	2.917	2.639	2.361	2.083	1.806	1.528	1.250	0.972	0.694	0.417	0.139
2–30	3.333	3.333	3.333	3.333	3.333	3.333	3.333	3.333	3.333	3.333	3.333	3.333
31	0.139	0.417	0.694	0.972	1.250	1.528	1.806	2.083	2.361	2.639	2.917	3.194

For Property Placed in Service after December 31, 1986; 40-Year Nonresidential Real Property*

Recovery Year	Month Placed in Service											
	1	2	3	4	5	6	7	8	9	10	11	12
1	2.396	2.188	1.979	1.771	1.563	1.354	1.146	0.938	0.729	0.521	0.313	0.104
2–40	2.500	2.500	2.500	2.500	2.500	2.500	2.500	2.500	2.500	2.500	2.500	2.500
41	0.104	0.312	0.521	0.729	0.937	1.146	1.354	1.562	1.771	1.979	2.187	2.396

*Also used for residential rental property placed in service before 2018.

Refocus on The Big Picture

Calculating Cost Recovery Deductions

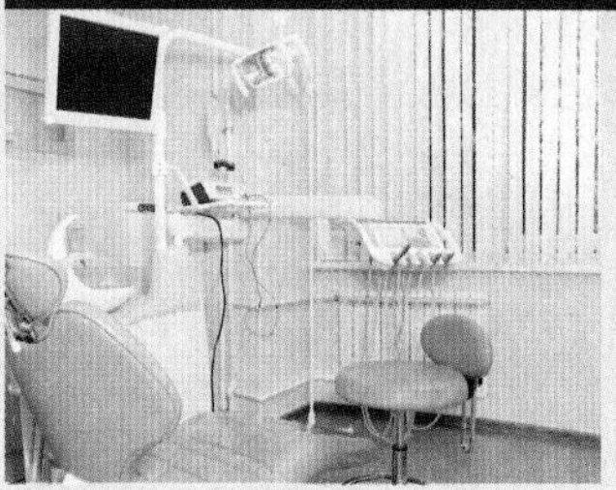

Regardless of whether the accrual or cash method of accounting is used, MACRS must be used to calculate the cost recovery of fixed assets for tax purposes. Evidently, Dr. Payne's financial reporting system uses MACRS because $91,298 is the correct amount of cost recovery. The computers and peripheral equipment are 5-year property. The office furniture and fixtures and the dental equipment are 7-year property.

Based on the IRS cost recovery tables, the following percentages are used in calculating depreciation expense for the first year of each asset's life.

5-year property	20.00%
7-year property	14.29%

Dr. Payne can deduct depreciation on the house he converted from personal use to rental use and on the rental house he purchased.

What If?

From a tax planning perspective, Dr. Payne can increase the cost recovery deductions associated with the purchase of these fixed assets and reduce the amount of the business net income reported on Schedule C of Form 1040 for his dental practice by using the § 179 immediate expense election or additional first-year (bonus) depreciation.

Code § 179 applies to personalty, but does not apply to realty (e.g., buildings). The maximum amount that can be deducted under § 179 is subject to several limitations. First, the total amount deducted cannot exceed $1,160,000. Second, the maximum amount is reduced dollar for dollar for any § 179 assets placed in service in excess of $2,890,000. Finally, the § 179 deduction cannot exceed the taxable income from the business. Additional first-year (bonus) depreciation allows 80 percent of qualified property to be deducted in 2023.

The sequence of calculating the cost recovery deduction is, in order:

1. § 179 immediate expensing.
2. Additional first-year depreciation.
3. Regular MACRS cost recovery.

continued

If Dr. Payne reports sufficient business income to avoid the § 179 business income limitation, he can use § 179 to expense all of the assets placed in service in 2023 ($612,085).

If § 179's business income limitation comes into play, Dr. Payne can elect out of § 179 and deduct $612,085 using additional first-year depreciation (which has no income limitation). In this case, however, other limitations might affect his decision (including the excess business loss limitation; see text Section 7-5). Or he can apply § 179 or additional first-year depreciation to selected assets, reducing his taxable income this year and deferring some deductions to future years.

Key Terms

Accelerated cost recovery system (ACRS), 8-2
Additional first-year depreciation, 8-14
Alternative depreciation system (ADS), 8-23
Amortization, 8-25
Cost depletion, 8-29
Cost recovery, 8-2
Depletion, 8-28
Depreciation, 8-2
Half-year convention, 8-6
Intangible drilling and development costs (IDCs), 8-29
Listed property, 8-18
Mid-month convention, 8-10
Mid-quarter convention, 8-7
Modified accelerated cost recovery system (MACRS), 8-2
Percentage depletion, 8-30
Qualified improvement property, 8-8
Residential rental real estate, 8-9
Section 179 expensing, 8-11
Startup expenditures, 8-25

Discussion Questions

1. **LO.1** Discuss whether property that is classified as personal use is subject to cost recovery.

2. **LO.1** Discuss the difference between personal property and personal use property.

3. **LO.1** Discuss whether land improvements used in a trade or business are eligible for cost recovery.

4. **LO.2** At the beginning of the current year, Henry purchased a ski resort for $10,000,000. Henry does not own the land on which the resort is located. The Federal government owns the land, and Henry has the right to operate the resort on the land pursuant to Special Use Permits, which are terminable at will by the Federal government, and Term Special Use Permits, which allow the land to be used for a fixed number of years. Critical Thinking

   In preparing the income tax return for the current year, Henry properly allocated $2,000,000 of the purchase price to the costs of constructing mountain roads, slopes, and trails. Since the acquisition, Henry has spent an additional $2,000,000 on maintaining the mountain roads, slopes, and trails. Identify the relevant tax issues for Henry.

5. **LO.2** Identify the three factors reflected in the MACRS tables when the amount of cost recovery is determined.

6. **LO.2** Discuss the computation of cost recovery in the year an asset is placed in service when the mid-quarter convention is being used.

7. **LO.2** Discuss the computation of cost recovery in the year of sale of an asset when the mid-quarter convention is being used.

Critical Thinking

8. **LO.2** Robert purchased and placed in service $100,000 of 7-year class assets on August 10 of the current year. He also purchased and placed in service $500,000 of 5-year class assets on November 15 of the current year. He does not claim any available additional first-year depreciation. If Robert elects to use the MACRS straight-line method of cost recovery on the 7-year class assets, discuss the calculation of cost recovery for the 5-year class assets.

9. **LO.3** Discuss when § 179 expense must be recaptured.

10. **LO.3** Explain how the § 179 immediate expensing deduction affects the computation of MACRS cost recovery.

11. **LO.3** Discuss the treatment of a § 179 expensing carryforward.

12. **LO.3** Discuss the definition of *business income* as it is used in limiting the § 179 expensing amount.

Critical Thinking

13. **LO.2, 3** A professional consulting business sells professional tools and equipment and provides associated services, such as repair and maintenance, to its customer base. The company's employees include technicians who are required to provide and maintain their own tools and equipment for performing the repairs and maintenance work. The company will reimburse a technician for amounts spent to purchase tools and equipment eligible for a § 179 deduction up to a set amount each year. Any costs for tools and equipment that exceed the set amount will not be reimbursed.

    Jiaxu is a technician for the company. During the current year, he purchased equipment that qualifies for the § 179 deduction. Jiaxu paid $50,000 for the equipment and was reimbursed the set amount of $40,000. Identify the relevant tax issues for Jiaxu with respect to § 179 and the computation of his taxable income.

14. **LO.4** Discuss how the limits on cost recovery apply to listed property.

15. **LO.4** Discuss the tax consequences if the business use percentage of listed property falls to 50% or lower after the year the property is placed in service.

Critical Thinking

16. **LO.7** Harold and Bart own 75% of the stock of Orange Motors. The other 25% of the stock is owned by Jeb. Orange Motors entered into an agreement with Harold and Bart to acquire all of their Orange stock.

    In addition, Harold and Bart signed a noncompete agreement with Orange Motors. Under the terms of the noncompete agreement, Orange will pay Harold and Bart $15,000 each per year for four years. Identify the relevant tax issues for Orange Motors.

Critical Thinking

17. **LO.4, 7** In May 2023, Gwen began searching for a trade or business to acquire. In anticipation of finding a suitable acquisition, Gwen hired an investment banker to evaluate three potential businesses. She also hired a law firm to begin drafting regulatory approval documents for a target company. Eventually, Gwen decided to purchase all of the assets of Brash Corporation. Brash and Gwen entered into an acquisition agreement on December 1, 2023. Identify the relevant tax issues for Gwen.

18. **LO.8** Discuss how the cost of mineral rights enters into the calculation of cost depletion.

Computational Exercises

19. **LO.2** Euclid places in service a 7-year class asset on May 9, 2023, for $80,000 (the only asset acquired during the year). Euclid does not elect immediate expensing under § 179. She does not claim any available additional first-year depreciation. Calculate Euclid's cost recovery deduction for 2023 and 2024.

20. **LO.2** Hamlet places in service a 7-year class asset on November 23, 2023, for $100,000 (the only asset acquired during the year). Hamlet does not elect immediate expensing under § 179. He does not claim any available additional first-year depreciation. Calculate Hamlet's cost recovery deductions for 2023 and 2024.

21. **LO.2** Lopez acquired and placed in service a building on June 1, 2018, for $1,000,000. Calculate Lopez's cost recovery deduction for 2023 if the building is:
    a. Classified as residential rental real estate.
    b. Classified as nonresidential real estate.

22. **LO.2** Andre acquired and placed in service a computer on March 3, 2023, for $2,800. He elects the straight-line method for cost recovery. Andre does not elect immediate expensing under § 179. He does not claim any available additional first-year depreciation. Calculate Andre's cost recovery deduction for the computer for tax years 2023 and 2024.

23. **LO.2, 3** Diana acquires, for $65,000, and places in service a 5-year class asset on December 19, 2023. It is the only asset that Diana acquires during 2023. Diana does not elect immediate expensing under § 179. She elects additional first-year deprecation. Calculate Diana's total cost recovery deduction for 2023.

24. **LO.3** McKenzie placed in service qualifying equipment (7-year MACRS class) for his business that cost $212,000 in 2023. The taxable income of the business for the year is $5,600 before consideration of any § 179 deduction.
    a. Calculate McKenzie's § 179 expense deduction for 2023 and any carryover to 2024.
    b. How would your answer change if McKenzie decided to use additional first-year (bonus) depreciation on the equipment instead of using § 179 expensing?

25. **LO.4** On April 5, 2023, Kinsey places in service a new automobile that cost $70,000. He does not elect § 179 expensing, and he elects not to take any available additional first-year depreciation. The car is used 75% for business and 25% for personal use in each tax year.

    Kinsey uses the regular MACRS method of cost recovery (the auto is a 5-year asset). Compute the total depreciation allowed for 2023 and 2024.

26. **LO.7** On October 1, 2023, Verónica purchased a business. Of the purchase price, $60,000 is allocated to a patent and $375,000 is allocated to goodwill. Calculate Verónica's 2023 § 197 amortization deduction.

27. **LO.8** On March 25, Parscale Company purchases the rights to a mineral interest for $8,000,000. At that time, the remaining recoverable units in the mineral interest are estimated to be 500,000 tons. If 80,000 tons are mined and 75,000 tons are sold this year, calculate Parscale's cost depletion for the year.

28. **LO.8** Jebali Company reports gross income of $340,000 and other property-related expenses of $229,000 and uses a depletion rate of 14%. Calculate Jebali's depletion allowance for the current year.

Problems

29. **LO.1, 2** On November 4, 2021, Blue Company acquired and placed in service an asset (27.5-year residential real property) for $200,000 for use in its business. In 2021 and 2022, respectively, Blue deducted $642 and $5,128 of cost recovery. These amounts were incorrect; Blue applied the wrong percentages (i.e., those for 39-year rather than 27.5-year assets). Blue should have taken $910 and $7,272 cost recovery in 2021 and 2022, respectively.

    On January 1, 2023, the asset was sold for $180,000. Calculate the gain or loss on the sale of the asset for that year.

30. **LO.1, 2** In 2020, José purchased a house for $325,000 ($300,000 relates to the house; $25,000 relates to the land). He used the house as his personal residence. In March 2023, when the fair market value of the house was $400,000, he converted the house to rental property. What is José's cost recovery for 2023?

31. **LO.2, 3** Orange Corporation acquired and placed in service new office furniture on August 15, 2023, for $130,000. Orange does not elect immediate expensing under § 179. Orange claims any available additional first-year depreciation.
    a. Determine Orange's cost recovery for 2023.
    b. How would your answer change if Orange decided to use $52,000 of immediate expensing and use normal MACRS on the balance of the acquisition cost?

32. **LO.2** Juan places in service a new 5-year class asset on March 14, 2023, for $200,000. This is the only asset Juan acquired during the year. He does not elect immediate expensing under § 179. He does not claim any available additional first-year depreciation. On July 15, 2024, Juan sells the asset.
    a. Determine Juan's cost recovery for 2023.
    b. Determine Juan's cost recovery for 2024.

33. **LO.2** Debra acquired and placed in service the following new assets during 2023.

Date	Asset	Cost
April 11	Furniture	$40,000
July 28	Trucks	40,000
November 3	Computers	70,000

    Determine Debra's cost recovery deductions for the current year. Debra does not elect immediate expensing under § 179. She does not claim any available additional first-year depreciation.

34. **LO.2** On August 2, 2023, Wendy purchased a new office building for $3,800,000. On October 1, 2023, she began to rent out office space in the building. On July 15, 2027, Wendy sold the office building.
    a. Determine Wendy's cost recovery deduction for 2023.
    b. Determine Wendy's cost recovery deduction for 2027.

35. **LO.2** On April 3, 2023, Terry purchased and placed in service a building that cost $2,000,000. An appraisal determined that 25% of the total cost was attributed to the value of the land. The bottom floor of the building is leased to a retail business for $32,000. The other floors of the building are rental apartments with an annual rent of $160,000. Determine Terry's cost recovery deduction for 2023.

36. **LO.2** On May 5, 2023, Christy purchased and placed in service a hotel. The hotel cost $10,800,000, and the land cost $1,200,000 ($12,000,000 in total). Calculate Christy's cost recovery deductions for 2023 and for 2033.

37. **LO.2** Janice acquired and placed in service an apartment building on June 4, 2023, for $1,600,000. The value of the land is $300,000. Janice sold the apartment building on November 29, 2029.
   a. Determine Janice's cost recovery deduction for 2023.
   b. Determine Janice's cost recovery deduction for 2029.

38. **LO.2, 3, 9** Lori, who is single, purchased and placed in service 5-year class property for $200,000 and 7-year class property for $420,000 on May 20, 2023. Lori expects the taxable income derived from her business (before considering any amount expensed under § 179) to be about $550,000. Lori has determined that she should elect immediate § 179 expensing in the amount of $520,000, but she doesn't know which asset she should completely expense under § 179. She does not claim any available additional first-year depreciation.

Communications
Critical Thinking
Decision Making
Planning

   a. Determine Lori's total cost recovery deduction if the § 179 expense is first taken with respect to the 5-year class asset.
   b. Determine Lori's total cost recovery deduction if the § 179 expense is first taken with respect to the 7-year class asset.
   c. What is your advice to Lori?
   d. Assume that Lori is in the 24% marginal tax state and Federal income bracket and that she elects § 179 for the 7-year class asset. Determine the present value of the tax savings from the cost recovery deductions for both assets. See Appendix E for present value factors, and assume a 6% discount rate.
   e. Assume the same facts as in part (d), except that Lori decides not to use § 179 on either asset. Determine the present value of the tax savings under this choice. In addition, determine which option Lori should choose.
   f. Present your solution to parts (d) and (e) of the problem in a spreadsheet using appropriate Microsoft Excel formulas. E-mail your spreadsheet to your instructor with a two-paragraph summary of your findings.

39. **LO.2, 3** Olga is the proprietor of a small business. In 2023, the business's income, before consideration of any cost recovery or § 179 deduction, is $250,000. Olga spends $620,000 on new 7-year class assets and elects to take the § 179 deduction on them. She does not claim any available additional first-year depreciation. Olga's cost recovery deduction for 2023, except for the cost recovery with respect to the new 7-year class assets, is $95,000. Determine Olga's total cost recovery for 2023 with respect to the 7-year class assets and the amount of any § 179 carryforward.

Critical Thinking

40. **LO.2, 3, 9** On June 5, 2022, Javier Sanchez purchased and placed in service a new 7-year class asset costing $560,000 for use in his landscaping business, which he operates as a single member LLC (Sanchez Landscaping LLC). During 2022, his business generated a net income of $945,780 before any § 179 immediate expense election.
   a. Rather than using bonus depreciation, Javier would like to use § 179 to expense $200,000 of this asset and then use regular MACRS to cost recover the remaining cost. Given this information, determine the cost recovery deductions that Javier can claim with respect to this asset in 2022 and 2023.
   b. Complete Javier's Form 4562 (page 1) for 2022. His Social Security number is 123-45-6789.

41. **LO.2, 4** On October 15, 2023, Jon purchased and placed in service a used car that cost $38,000. This was the only business use asset Jon acquired in 2023. He used the car 80% of the time for business and 20% for personal use. Jon does not elect § 179 expensing, and does not claim any available additional first-year depreciation. Calculate the cost recovery deduction Jon may take for 2023 with respect to the car.

42. **LO.4** On June 5, 2022, Leo purchased and placed in service a new car that cost $75,000. The business use percentage for the car is always 100%. Leo does not elect § 179 expensing, and does not claim any available additional first-year depreciation. Compute Leo's cost recovery deductions for 2022 and 2023.

43. **LO.2, 3, 4** On March 15, 2023, Helen purchased and placed in service a new Escalade. The purchase price was $62,000, and the vehicle had a rating of 6,500 GVW. The vehicle was used 100% for business.

   a. Assuming that Helen does not use additional first-year depreciation, calculate the total depreciation deduction that she can take on the vehicle for 2023.

   b. What would your answer be if Helen decided to take additional first-year depreciation?

44. **LO.2, 4** On May 28, 2023, Mary purchased and placed in service a new $68,000 car. The car was used 60% for business, 20% for production of income, and 20% for personal use in 2023. In 2024, the usage changed to 40% for business, 30% for production of income, and 30% for personal use. Mary did not elect immediate expensing under § 179. She did not claim any available additional first-year depreciation. Compute Mary's 2023 and 2024 cost recovery deductions and any cost recovery recapture for 2024.

Decision Making

45. **LO.2, 4, 9** Naya purchased and placed in service a new computer (5-year MACRS property) on June 1, 2023, for $4,000. Naya could use the computer 100% of the time in her business, or she could allow her family to use the computer as well. Naya estimates that if her family uses the computer, the business use will be 45% and the personal use will be 55%.

   Determine the tax cost to Naya, in the year of acquisition, of allowing her family to use the computer. Assume that Naya would not elect § 179 immediate expensing and that her marginal income tax rate is 32%. She does not claim any available additional first-year depreciation.

Communications
Critical Thinking
Decision Making
Planning

46. **LO.2, 4, 9** Dennis Harding is considering acquiring a new automobile that he will use 100% for business. The purchase price of the automobile would be $71,500. If Dennis leased the car for five years, the lease payments would be $945 per month. Dennis will acquire the car on January 1, 2023. Assume that the inclusion dollar amounts from the IRS table for the next five years are $65, $143, $212, $256, and $297.

   Dennis wants to know the effect on his adjusted gross income of purchasing versus leasing the car for the next five years. He does not claim any available additional first-year depreciation. Write a letter to Dennis summarizing your calculations. Then prepare a memo for the tax files containing your analysis. Dennis's address is 150 Avenue I, Memphis, TN 38112.

47. **LO.2, 5** In 2023, Muhammad purchased a new computer for $16,000. The computer is used 100% for business. Muhammad did not make a § 179 election with respect to the computer. He does not claim any available additional first-year depreciation. If Muhammad uses the regular MACRS method, determine his cost recovery deduction for 2023 for computing taxable income and for computing his alternative minimum tax.

Communications
Critical Thinking
Decision Making
Planning

48. **LO.2, 5, 9** Jamie purchased and placed in service $100,000 of new office furniture for her business in June of the current year. Jamie understands that if she elects to use ADS to compute her regular income tax, there will be no difference between the cost recovery for computing the regular income tax and the AMT.

   a. Jamie wants to know the present value of the *tax cost*, after three years, of using ADS rather than MACRS. Assume that Jamie does not elect § 179 expensing, she does not claim any additional first-year depreciation, and her combined state and Federal income marginal tax rate is 32%. See Appendix E for present value factors, and assume a 6% discount rate.

   b. What is the present value of the tax savings/costs that result over the life of the asset if Jamie uses MACRS rather than ADS?

   c. Present your solution to part (b) of the problem in a spreadsheet using appropriate Microsoft Excel formulas. E-mail your spreadsheet to your instructor with a one-paragraph explanation.

49. **LO.2, 7, 9** Mike Saxon is negotiating the purchase of a business. The final purchase price ($2,000,000) has been agreed upon, but the allocation of the purchase price to the assets is still being discussed. Appraisals on a warehouse range from $1,200,000 to $1,500,000. If a value of $1,200,000 is used for the warehouse, the remainder of the purchase price, $800,000, will be allocated to goodwill. If $1,500,000 is allocated to the warehouse, goodwill will be $500,000.

Communications
Critical Thinking
Decision Making
Planning

Mike wants to know what effect each alternative will have on cost recovery and amortization during the first year. Under the agreement, Mike will take over the business on January 1 of next year.

Write a letter to Mike in which you present your calculations and recommendation. Then prepare a memo for the tax files, addressing these matters. Mike's address is 200 Rolling Hills Drive, Shavertown, PA 18708.

50. **LO.7** Oleander Corporation, a calendar year entity, begins business on March 1, 2023. The corporation incurs startup expenditures of $64,000. If Oleander elects § 195 treatment, determine the total amount of startup expenditures that it may deduct for 2023.

51. **LO.7** Martha was considering starting a new business. During her preliminary investigations related to the new venture, she incurred the following expenditures.

Salaries	$22,000
Travel	18,000
Interest on short-term note	4,000
Professional fees	13,000

Martha begins the business on July 1 of the current year. If Martha elects § 195 treatment, determine her startup expenditure deduction for the current year.

52. **LO.8** Wes acquired a mineral interest during the year for $10,000,000. A geological survey estimated that 250,000 tons of the mineral remained in the deposit. During the year, 80,000 tons were mined and 45,000 tons were sold for $12,000,000. Other related expenses amounted to $5,000,000. Assuming that the mineral depletion rate is 22%, calculate Wes's lowest taxable income after any depletion deductions.

53. **LO.2, 9** Build an Excel spreadsheet that calculates annual cost recovery and end-of-year adjusted basis for MACRS 3-, 5-, and 7-year assets. Begin by constructing a table that incorporates the relevant MACRS cost recovery percentages from Exhibit 8.3. Then build a table that links to the MACRS cost recovery table, allowing a user to input three data points: (1) Asset cost, (2) Year of acquisition, and (3) MACRS life. Based on these inputs, your spreadsheet should create a schedule that provides annual MACRS cost recovery and end-of-year adjusted basis for that asset. Once completed, e-mail the spreadsheet to your instructor. *Hint*: Your spreadsheet needs to use "IF" functions to create the MACRS cost recovery/adjusted basis schedule.

Critical Thinking

Tax Return Problems

54. Janice Morgan, age 24, is single and has no dependents. She is a freelance writer. In January 2022, Janice opened her own office located at 2751 Waldham Road, Pleasant Hill, NM 88135. She called her business Writers Anonymous. Janice is a cash basis taxpayer. She lives at 132 Stone Avenue, Pleasant Hill, NM 88135. Her Social Security number is 123-45-6782. Janice's parents continue to provide health insurance for her under their policy. Janice did not engage in any virtual currency transactions during the year and wants to contribute to the Presidential Election Campaign Fund.

Tax Forms Problem
ProConnect™ Tax

During 2022, Janice reported the following income and expense items connected with her business.

Income from sale of articles	$95,000
Rent	16,500
Utilities	7,900
Supplies	1,800
Insurance	5,000
Travel (including restaurant meals of $600)	2,900

Janice purchased and placed in service the following fixed assets for her business. Janice wants to elect immediate expensing under § 179, if possible.

- Furniture and fixtures (new) costing $21,000 on January 10.
- Computer equipment (new) costing $12,400 on July 28.

Janice's itemized deductions include:

State income tax	$2,950
Home mortgage interest paid to First National Bank	8,000
Property taxes on home	2,500
Charitable contribution to her alma mater, State College	1,200

Janice did not keep a record of the sales tax she paid. The amount allowed by the sales tax table is $437.

Janice reports interest income of $4,000 on certificates of deposit at Second National Bank. Janice makes estimated tax payments of $5,000 for 2022.

Compute Janice Morgan's 2022 Federal income tax payable (or refund due), and complete her 2022 tax return using appropriate forms and schedules. Suggested software: ProConnect Tax.

Communications
Decision Making
Planning
Tax Computation Problem

55. John Rivera, age 31, is single and has no dependents. At the beginning of 2023, John started his own excavation business and named it Earth Movers. John lives at 1045 Center Street, Lindon, UT, and his business is located at 381 State Street, Lindon, UT. The Zip Code for both addresses is 84042. John's Social Security number is 111-11-1111, and the business identification number is 11-1111111. John is a cash basis taxpayer. During 2023, John reports the following items in connection with his business.

Fee income for services rendered	$912,000
Building rental expense	36,000
Office furniture and equipment rental expense	9,000
Office supplies	2,500
Utilities	4,000
Salary for secretary	34,000
Salary for equipment operators	42,000
Payroll taxes	7,000
Fuel and oil for the equipment	21,000
Purchase of three new front-end loaders on January 15, 2023	560,000
Purchase of a new dump truck on January 18, 2023	80,000

During 2023, John recorded the following additional items.

Interest income from First National Bank	$10,000
Dividends from ExxonMobil	9,500
Quarterly estimated tax payments	11,500

John wants to maximize his cost recovery deductions (including taking any § 179 expense and any available additional first-year depreciation).

On October 8, 2023, John inherited IBM stock from his Aunt Mildred. John had been her favorite nephew. According to the data provided by the executor of Aunt Mildred's estate, the stock was valued for estate tax purposes at $110,000. John is considering selling the IBM stock for $125,000 on December 29, 2023, and using $75,000 of the proceeds to purchase an Acura ZDX. He would use the car 100% for business. John wants to know what effect these transactions would have on his 2023 adjusted gross income.

Write a letter to John in which you present your calculations. Ignore any Federal self-employment tax implications.

Research Problems

Note: Solutions to the Research Problems can be prepared by using the Thomson Reuters Checkpoint™ online tax research database, which accompanies this textbook. Solutions can also be prepared by using research materials found in a typical tax library.

Research Problem 1. Your client, Dave's Sport Shop, sells sports equipment and clothing in three retail outlets in New York City. During 2023, the CFO decided that keeping track of inventory using a combination of QuickBooks and spreadsheets was not an efficient way to manage the stores' inventories. So Dave's purchased an inventory management system for $9,000 that allowed the entity to keep track of inventory, as well as automate ordering and purchasing, without replacing QuickBooks for its accounting function. Communications

The CFO would like to know whether the cost of the inventory management program can be expensed in the year of purchase. Write a letter to the CFO, Cassandra Martin, that addresses the tax treatment of purchased software. Cassandra's mailing address is 867 Broadway, New York, NY 10003.

Research Problem 2. In 2019, Jed James began planting a vineyard. The costs of the land preparation, labor, rootstock, and planting were capitalized. The land preparation costs do not include any nondepreciable land costs. In 2023, when the plants became viable, Jed placed the vineyard in service. Jed wants to know whether he can claim a deduction under § 179 on his 2023 income tax return for the 2019 costs for planting the vineyard.

Research Problem 3. Juan owns a business that acquires exotic automobiles that are high-tech, state-of-the-art vehicles with unique design features or equipment. The exotic automobiles are not licensed or set up to be used on the road. Rather, the cars are used exclusively for car shows or related promotional photography. With respect to the exotic automobiles, Juan would like to know whether he can take a cost recovery deduction on his Federal income tax return.

Partial list of research aids:
Bruce Selig, 70 TCM 1125, T.C.Memo. 1995–519.

Use internet tax resources to address the following questions. Look for reliable websites and blogs of the IRS and other government agencies, media outlets, businesses, tax professionals, academics, think tanks, and political outlets.

Research Problem 4. Locate a financial calculator app or program that assesses the wisdom of buying versus leasing a new car. Use it to work through Problem 46 in this chapter.

Research Problem 5. There are significant tax planning opportunities related to fixed asset acquisition (and depreciation). Search out how large public accounting firms are assisting clients in this area. Summarize your findings in an e-mail to your instructor. Communications

Research Problem 6. Do depreciation deductions vary by entity type or by industry? Go to the IRS Tax Statistics page (**irs.gov/statistics**), and review the spreadsheets containing data for corporations, partnerships, and nonfarm proprietorships by sector or industry. You can find these in the Business Tax Statistics section of the IRS site. Communications Critical Thinking Data Analytics

Evaluate the depreciation deductions by sector (19 sectors are identified in the IRS spreadsheets) and by entity using Microsoft Excel. E-mail the spreadsheet to your instructor along with a brief summary of your findings.

Becker CPA Review Questions

Becker

1. Michael Sima, a sole proprietor craftsman, purchased an amount of equipment in the current year that exceeded the maximum allowable § 179 depreciation election limit by $20,000. Sima's total purchases of property placed in service in the current year did not exceed the § 179 phaseout threshold. All of the personal property (including the equipment) was purchased in November of the current year. Sima elected the maximum § 179 and elected out of bonus depreciation. The § 179 expense election did not create or increase a loss on Sima's Schedule C for the current year. Which method may Sima use to depreciate the remaining equipment in the current year?
   a. Sima may not depreciate any additional equipment other than the § 179 maximum in the current year and must carry forward the excess amount to use in the following taxable year.
   b. MACRS half-year convention for personal property.
   c. MACRS mid-quarter convention for personal property.
   d. Straight-line, mid-month convention for real property.

2. Cox Construction, a company in its 10th year of business, purchased a piece of equipment on April 1, year 9, for $20,000. Cox has used it for business purposes since the initial purchase date. The company depreciated the equipment using the MACRS half-year table for 5-year assets. For tax purposes, what is the amount of accumulated depreciation for the equipment as of December 31, year 10?
   a. $6,000
   b. $10,400
   c. $11,600
   d. $12,800

3. Stem Corp. bought a machine in February of year 7 for $20,000. Then Stem bought furniture in November of year 7 for $30,000. Both machines were placed in service for business purposes immediately after purchase. No other assets were purchased during year 7. What depreciation convention must Stem use for the machine purchased in February year 7?
   a. Mid-month
   b. Half-year
   c. Mid-quarter
   d. Full-year

4. Data, Inc., purchased and placed in service $5,000 of office furniture on August 24, year 3. This is the only asset purchase during the year. Code § 179 expensing and bonus depreciation were not elected. Using the excerpt of the MACRS half-year convention table below, what is the MACRS depreciation in year 3 for the office furniture?

Recovery Period	5-Year	7-Year	10-Year
1	20%	14.29%	10%
2	32%	24.49%	18%
3	19.2%	17.49%	14.4%

   a. $500
   b. $715
   c. $875
   d. $1,000

5. Which statement below is correct?
   a. Real property is depreciated using the half-year convention.
   b. Residential real estate is depreciated over a 39-year life.
   c. One-half month of depreciation is taken for the month real property is disposed of.
   d. Salvage value is considered in MACRS depreciation.

6. Charlie purchased an apartment building on November 16, year 1, for $1,000,000. Determine the cost recovery for year 20.
   a. $36,360
   b. $32,100
   c. $45,500
   d. $331,850

7. Under which of the following tax cost recovery methods can the amount a taxpayer can deduct each year be limited?
   a. MACRS depreciation.
   b. Straight-line depreciation.
   c. § 179 expense.
   d. First-year bonus depreciation.
8. Which statement below is incorrect about the § 179 deduction?
   a. The § 179 deduction is allowed even if there is a loss.
   b. The § 179 deduction may be reduced based on total purchases.
   c. Real property is generally not eligible for the § 179 deduction.
   d. Corporations may elect to take the § 179 deduction.

Chapter 9

Deductions: Employee and Self-Employed-Related Expenses

Learning Objectives: *After completing Chapter 9, you should be able to:*

- LO.1 Distinguish between employee and self-employed (independent contractor) status.
- LO.2 Recognize deductible transportation expenses.
- LO.3 Describe how travel expenses are treated.
- LO.4 Differentiate between deductible and nondeductible education expenses.
- LO.5 Identify other business expenses.
- LO.6 Compare various deductions for contributions to retirement accounts.
- LO.7 Demonstrate the difference between accountable and nonaccountable employee plans.
- LO.8 Recognize the limitations on miscellaneous itemized deductions.
- LO.9 Identify tax planning ideas related to employee and self-employed business expenses.

Chapter Outline

ISTOCK.COM/SVETIKD

The Big Picture

The First Job

After an extensive search, Morgan, a recent college graduate with a major in child development, has accepted a job with Enrichment Child Care Center (ECCC) in a neighboring state. ECCC is located in the western suburbs of a large metropolitan city, roughly 30 miles from the center of the city. Morgan will be moving into a two-bedroom apartment about two miles from ECCC. At ECCC, Morgan will work with pre-school children Monday to Friday from 7 A.M. to 3 P.M. One of the reasons she accepted the position at ECCC is the flexibility it provides. Because she is eager to pay off her student loans and save to buy a house, she has decided to freelance in the late afternoons and evenings and on weekends—joining the "gig economy."

She finds two ways to freelance: (1) transporting people, packages, and meals for a few companies where she finds work through an "app" (like driving for Uber) and (2) tutoring elementary school students in English and math. Her tutoring can take place online or in person (either in her apartment or at the child's home). She has dedicated the second bedroom in her apartment for freelancing. She has a large table and several chairs in this bedroom that allow her to meet her tutoring students or connect with them via her laptop. She keeps all of her freelancing records in a file cabinet, which she keeps in a closet in the bedroom. She also purchases and keeps various supplies for her tutoring activities in the closet. Although there are some freelance driving options in the suburbs, most often Morgan heads for the city where there are more passengers and higher fares.

What are some of the income tax issues presented by this situation?

Read the chapter and formulate your response.

Framework 1040 **Tax Formula for Individuals**

This chapter covers the boldfaced portions of the Tax Formula for Individuals that was introduced in Concept Summary 3.1 on p. 3-3. Below those portions are the sections of Form 1040 where the results are reported.

Income *(broadly defined)*	$xx,xxx
Less: Exclusions	(x,xxx)
Gross income	$xx,xxx
Less: Deductions *for* adjusted gross income	**(x,xxx)**

FORM 1040 (Schedule 1)

3	Business income or (loss). Attach Schedule C
11	Educator expenses
12	Certain business expenses of reservists, performing artists, and fee-basis government officials. Attach Form 2106
15	Deductible part of self-employment tax. Attach Schedule SE
16	Self-employed SEP, SIMPLE, and qualified plans
17	Self-employed health insurance deduction
20	IRA deduction

Adjusted gross income	$xx,xxx
Less: The greater of total itemized deductions *or* the standard deduction	(x,xxx)

FORM 1040 (p. 1)

12	**Standard deduction or itemized deductions** (from Schedule A)

Personal and dependency exemptions*	(x,xxx)
Deduction for qualified business income**	(x,xxx)
Taxable income	$xx,xxx
Tax on taxable income *(see Tax Tables or Tax Rate Schedules)*	$ x,xxx
Less: Tax credits *(including income taxes withheld and prepaid)*	(xxx)
Tax due (or refund)	$ xxx

* Exemption deductions are not allowed from 2018 through 2025.

** Only applies from 2018 through 2025.

Considering the large number of taxpayers affected, the tax treatment of job-related expenses is somewhat complex. To resolve this complexity, a number of key questions must be asked:

- Is the taxpayer an *employee* or *self-employed*?
- What expenses *qualify* as deductions?
- How are the deductible expenses *classified* for tax purposes (*for* AGI or *from* AGI)?
- To the extent the expenses are classified as deductions *from* AGI, are they subject to any *limitation*?

In addition to answering these questions, the chapter also discusses contributions to retirement accounts and provides some tax planning ideas.

9-1 Employee versus Independent Contractor

LO.1

Distinguish between employee and self-employed (independent contractor) status.

When one person performs services for another, the person performing the service either is an employee or is self-employed (an **independent contractor**). Failure to recognize a person's work status correctly can have serious tax consequences (in addition to Federal and state labor law consequences). Tax deficiencies as well as interest and penalties may result from improper classification.

Unlike employees, self-employed individuals do not have to be included in the employer's various fringe benefit programs (e.g., group term life insurance and retirement plans). Because self-employed individuals are not covered by FICA and FUTA (see Chapter 1), a business also avoids these payroll costs. The IRS is aware of the tendency of some businesses to attempt to classify workers as self-employed rather than as employees.

Employment status also makes a great deal of difference to the person who performs the services. Expenses of self-employed individuals, if deductible, are classified as deductions *for* AGI and are reported on Schedule C (Profit or Loss From Business) of Form 1040.[1] Unless reimbursed under an accountable plan (discussed later in the chapter), employee business expenses are deductions *from* AGI as miscellaneous itemized deductions. However, from 2018 through 2025, the deduction for miscellaneous itemized deductions is suspended. As a result, there is no tax benefit from these deductions during this period.[2]

Most persons classified as employees are common law employees. The common law employee classification originated in the courts and is summarized in various IRS pronouncements.[3] Revenue Ruling 87–41, for example, lists 20 factors to determine whether a worker is a common law employee or an independent contractor (and, thus, self-employed).[4] The IRS has indicated that these 20 factors can be grouped into three broad categories: behavioral control, financial control, and the relationship of the parties.

An employee-employer relationship exists when the employer has the right to control what is to be done and the ways and means by which results are to be attained.[5] In general, this means that a worker is classified as an employee if the employer identifies *what* should be done and *how* it should be done. If an individual is told *what* to do but is allowed to independently determine how to do it, an employee-employer relationship likely does not exist.

If a business provides the following items to a worker, a common law employee-employer relationship likely exists:

- Furnishing tools or equipment and a place to work.
- Providing support services, including the hiring of assistants to help do the work.
- Training the worker for needed job skills.
- Allowing participation in various workplace fringe benefits (e.g., accident and health plans, group life insurance, and retirement plans).
- Paying for services based on time rather than the task performed.

Alternatively, independent contractors are more likely to have unreimbursed business expenses, a significant investment in tools and work facilities, and less permanency in their business relationships. Independent contractors anticipate a profit from their work, make their services available to the relevant marketplace, and are likely to be paid a flat fee on a per-job basis.

In resolving employment status, each case must be tested on its own merits. But the key test is whether the business (service recipient) has the *right to control* the means and methods of accomplishment (both what must be done *and* how it should be done). If this is the case, an employer-employee relationship exists. Concept Summary 9.1 provides an overview of the current IRS position in this area.

Code § 6041(a) requires businesses that pay $600 or more in a calendar year to a contractor to issue Form 1099–NEC (Nonemployee Compensation) to the IRS and the contractor after year-end. While this helps the contractor determine their income tax obligations, it is crucial that this business owner (contractor) maintain proper records of all receipts and expenses to be able to satisfy all of their income and other tax obligations.

[1]In simple situations, a Schedule C–EZ can be used. Also, a Schedule SE (Self-Employment Tax) must be filed.

[2]§ 67(g); added by the Tax Cuts and Jobs Act (TCJA) of 2017.

[3]See, for example, IRS Publication 15–A (*Employer's Supplemental Tax Guide*).

[4]Also see IRS Publication 1779 (*Independent Contractor or Employee*). On October 11, 2022, the Department of Labor released proposed guidance on worker classification (29 CFR § 795.110). Under the proposed regulation, a multi-factor *economic realities* test is used looking at the "totality of the circumstances" to determine if the worker is economically dependent on the employer. The factors to analyze include (1) how much control the worker has over their job duties, (2) the worker's opportunity for profit or loss based on personal initiative or investment, (3) investments by the worker and the employer, (4) the degree of permanence of the working relationship, (5) the extent to which the work performed is an integral part of the employer's business, and (6) the degree of skill and initiative exhibited by the worker. No single factor is determinative and other factors may be considered.

[5]Reg. § 31.3401(c)–(1)(b).

Concept Summary 9.1

Employee versus Independent Contractor

Although the 20 factors identified by the Internal Revenue Service in Revenue Ruling 87–41 remain relevant, the IRS has grouped these factors into three broad categories in order to provide some clarity to a difficult area, while acknowledging that the 20 factors are not all-inclusive.

Behavioral Control

- Does the business control (or have the right to control) what the worker does and how the worker does their job?
- Facts that show whether the business has **behavioral control** include:
  - *Instructions*. An employee is generally told:
    1. When, where, and how to work.
    2. What equipment, tools, or processes to use.
    3. What workers can be hired to assist with the work.
    4. Where to purchase supplies and services.
    5. What work must be performed by a specified individual.
    6. What order or sequence to follow in performing the work.
  - *Training*. An employee normally receives training to perform work in a particular manner.

Financial Control

- Are the business aspects of the worker's job controlled by the payer?
- Facts that show whether the business has **financial control** include:
  - The extent to which the worker has unreimbursed business expenses.
  - The extent of the worker's investment.
  - The extent to which the worker makes services available to a larger market (e.g., is the worker marketing their services to multiple businesses?).
  - How the business pays the worker (is it the same as or different from how employees are paid?).
  - The extent to which the worker can realize a profit or loss.

The Relationship of the Parties

- A variety of facts and documents can show the **relationship of the parties**:
  - Written contracts describing the relationship the parties intended to create.
  - Whether the worker is provided with employee-type fringe benefits.
  - The permanency of the relationship (e.g., is the work for a specified period of time or indefinite?).
  - How integral the services are to the principal activity of the business.

Summary

1. Businesses must weigh all factors when determining whether a worker is an employee or independent contractor. Some factors might indicate that the worker is an employee, and other factors might indicate that the worker is an independent contractor.
2. No set number of factors "makes" the worker an employee or an independent contractor, and no one factor controls in making this determination. Also, factors that are relevant in one setting may not be relevant in a different setting.
3. Overall, one must look at the entirety of the relationship, consider the degree or extent of the right to direct and control, and document each of the factors used in coming to a decision.

Employee *versus* Independent Contractor

Arnold is a lawyer whose major client accounts for 60% of his billings. He does the routine legal work and income tax returns at the client's request. He is paid a monthly retainer in addition to amounts charged for extra work. Arnold is a self-employed individual. Even though most of his income comes from one client, he still has the right to determine how the end result of his work is attained.

Ellen is a lawyer hired by Arnold to assist him in the performance of services for the client mentioned in Example 1. Ellen is under Arnold's supervision; he reviews her work and pays her an hourly fee. Ellen is an employee of Arnold.

When one taxpayer holds multiple jobs, it is possible to have dual status as both an employee and an independent contractor (i.e., self-employed).

Dr. Stephanie Davis, DDS, is a full-time employee at the Robin University Health Center. In the evenings and on weekends, she shares a practice with another dentist who works the Monday through Friday day-time shifts. Dr. Davis is both employed and self-employed.

Certain workers who *are not* common law employees are treated as employees for employment tax purposes. Known as **statutory employees**, this group includes certain drivers (e.g., nondairy beverage distributors and laundry and dry cleaning pickup service), life insurance sales agents, home workers, and other salespersons. These employees are allowed to claim their business-related expenses as deductions *for* AGI by using Schedule C. The wages or commissions paid to statutory employees are not subject to Federal income tax withholding but are subject to Social Security tax.[6]

To avoid the confusion that might otherwise result in their classification, the tax law categorically treats certain categories of workers as independent contractors. Included in this group are licensed real estate agents and direct sellers. These individuals are treated as self-employed for all Federal purposes, including income and employment taxes.[7]

If a taxpayer wants to know whether employee or independent contractor status exists, the IRS will make a determination if the taxpayer files a Form SS–8 (Determination of Worker Status for Purposes of Federal Employment Taxes and Income Tax Withholding).

9-2 Self-Employed and Employee-Related Expenses—In General

Self-employed and employee expenses fall into one of the following categories:

- Transportation.
- Travel.
- Moving.
- Education.
- Entertainment.
- Other (including office in the home and miscellaneous expenses).

Self-employed deductions are allowed *for* AGI; most employee business expenses are miscellaneous itemized deductions (a *from* AGI deduction and subject to a 2%-of-AGI floor). The Tax Cuts and Jobs Act (TCJA) of 2017 made a significant change in this area by suspending the deduction for miscellaneous itemized deductions (including unreimbursed employee business expenses) from 2018 through 2025. As a result, the only employee business expenses that are currently deductible are those that are *reimbursed by an employer* (and these expenses, once reimbursed, have no effect on an employee's taxable income).

Given the TCJA of 2017 changes to the status of employee business expenses, the materials that follow are focused on the self-employed taxpayer. However, employees incurring these expenses in employer-related activities might be able to seek reimbursement for them. In addition, an employee also might have a separate business (e.g., consulting, rentals, etc.) that would allow these business expenses to be deducted in that activity.

9-3 Transportation Expenses

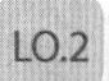

Recognize deductible transportation expenses.

9-3a Qualified Expenses

A deduction is allowed for business transportation expenses. **Transportation expenses** include only the cost of transporting the self-employed taxpayer (or employee) from one place to another in the course of business when the taxpayer is *not in travel status* (discussed in text Section 9-4). Transportation costs include taxi fares, automobile expenses, tolls, and parking.

[6] § 3121(d)(3). See Circular E, *Employer's Tax Guide* (IRS Publication 15), for further discussion of statutory employees.

[7] § 3508. Also see *Employer's Supplemental Tax Guide* (IRS Publication 15–A).

Commuting Expenses

Commuting between home and one's place of employment is a personal, nondeductible expense. The fact that one employee drives 30 miles to work and another employee walks six blocks to work does not matter.

Geraldo is employed by Sparrow Corporation. He drives 22 miles each way to work. The 44 miles he drives each workday are nondeductible commuting expenses.

If a taxpayer has a home office that qualifies as a principal place of business, the transportation costs between home and various work locations are deductible (i.e., the costs are *not* a commuting expense).

The Big Picture

Example 5

Return to the facts of *The Big Picture* on p. 9-1. Because Morgan will have an office in her home for her two freelancing businesses, the apartment will be her principal place of business. As a result, any transportation from her home to freelancing sites (e.g., driving to a child's home for tutoring) is *not* a commuting expense.[8] However, Morgan will have commuting expenses for the mileage between her apartment and her job at Enrichment Child Care Center.

9-3b **Computation of Automobile Expenses**

A taxpayer has two choices in determining automobile expenses: the automatic mileage method and the actual cost method. If an automobile is used for both business and personal purposes (mixed use), only the expenses related to the business use are deductible. The percentage of business use is usually arrived at by comparing the business mileage with total mileage—both business and personal.

Automatic Mileage Method

Also called the standard mileage method, the **automatic mileage method** is convenient in that it simplifies record keeping. The rate allowed per mile takes into account average operating expenses (such as gas and oil, repairs, and depreciation). Consequently, the taxpayer only has to multiply the automatic mileage rate by the business miles driven to compute the deduction.

For 2023, the deduction is based on 65.5 cents per mile for business miles.[9] This represents a seven cent increase from the 58.5 cents per mile rate that applied during the first half of 2022 and a three cent increase from the 62.5 cents per mile rate that applied during the second half of 2022.[10] Although the mileage rate usually remains constant for an entire year, the IRS occasionally makes mid-year changes to the rate, usually when there is a large change in the cost of fuel (as there was in 2022). As a result, it is important that the taxpayer keep records to identify when the driving took place.

Chad drove his car 20,000 miles for business during 2023. To determine his standard mileage deduction, he simply multiplies his business miles by the appropriate standard mileage rate (65.5 cents per mile in 2023). So his total standard mileage deduction for the year is $13,100 (20,000 miles × 65.5 cents per mile).

The automatic mileage rate for deductible education expenses is the same as for business; 22 cents per mile is allowed for medical purposes, and the rate for the charitable contribution deduction is 14 cents a mile (see Chapter 10 for a discussion of medical

[8] *Walter K. Strohmalter*, 113 T.C. 106 (1999).

[9] Notice 2023–3 and Rev.Proc. 2019–46.

[10] Notice 2022–3 and Announcement 2022–13.

expenses and charitable contributions). Parking fees and tolls are allowed in addition to the deduction computed using the automatic mileage method.

Generally, a taxpayer may elect either method for any particular year. However, the following restrictions apply to the standard mileage method:

- The vehicle must be owned or leased by the taxpayer.
- If five or more vehicles are in use (for business purposes) at the *same* time (not alternately), a taxpayer may not use the automatic mileage method.
- A basis adjustment for depreciation is required if the taxpayer changes from the automatic mileage method to the actual operating cost method. The depreciation adjustment for the business miles is determined using the following schedule:

Year	Rate per Mile
2023	28 cents
2022	26 cents
2021	26 cents
2020	27 cents
2019	26 cents

Tim purchased his automobile in 2020 for $36,000. It is used 90% for business purposes. Tim drove the automobile for 10,000 business miles in 2022, 8,500 business miles in 2021, and 6,000 business miles in 2020. At the beginning of 2023, the basis of the business portion of his car is $25,970.

Depreciable basis ($36,000 × 90%)	$32,400
Less depreciation:	
2022 (10,000 miles × 26 cents)	(2,600)
2021 (8,500 miles × 26 cents)	(2,210)
2020 (6,000 miles × 27 cents)	(1,620)
Adjusted business basis 1/1/2023	$25,970

- Use of the automatic mileage method in the first year an auto is placed in service is considered an election to exclude the auto from MACRS cost recovery (discussed in Chapter 8).
- A taxpayer may not switch to the automatic mileage method if the MACRS statutory percentage method or a § 179 expense election has been used.

Actual Cost Method

Under this method, the actual cost of operating the automobile is used to compute the deduction. Actual costs include the following expenses:

- Gas and oil, lubrication.
- Depreciation (or lease payments).
- Insurance.
- Dues to auto clubs.
- Repairs.
- Tires and other parts.
- Licenses and registration fees.
- Parking and tolls.

Example 8

Return to the facts of Example 6. Chad drove his car a total of 25,000 miles in 2023 (20,000 for business and 5,000 for personal use). He incurred the following automobile costs (he has receipts for all of these expenses):

Lease payments ($400 per month)	$ 4,800
Fuel	3,800
Insurance	1,800
Repairs and maintenance	1,500
State registration fee	150
Total expenses	$ 12,050
× Business use percentage (20,000 ÷ 25,000)	× 80%
Actual cost method deduction	$ 9,640

As a result, Chad is better off using the automatic mileage method. Chad's true cost of operating the vehicle is 48.2 cents per mile ($12,050 ÷ 25,000 miles), yet the government is allowing him to deduct 65.5 cents per mile.

As noted in Chapter 8, deductions for depreciation (or lease payments) are subject to limitations when a "mixed use" vehicle is involved (e.g., a vehicle used in both business and personal activities). Interest on a car loan is not deductible if the taxpayer is an employee, but it can qualify as a business expense if the taxpayer is self-employed. Sales taxes paid on the purchase of a car are added to the cost of the car and recovered via the MACRS deduction. In mixed use situations, the portion of the sales tax attributable to personal use may, in some cases, be claimed as a deduction *from* AGI (see Chapter 10 and the choice required between state and local income and sales taxes).

Except for parking and tolls, none of the expenses noted previously can be separately claimed under the automatic mileage method. A deduction for parking tickets and other traffic violations is not allowed under either method because it is a violation of public policy [§ 162(f); see Chapter 6].

The Big Picture

Example 9

Return to the facts of *The Big Picture* on p. 9-1. During Morgan's senior year in college, her parents gave her one of the family cars—a 2019 Toyota Camry. Morgan has no idea as to the car's original cost or the odometer reading at the time the car was registered in her name. She has, however, kept track of the miles driven for business since she accepted her new job. Morgan should use the automatic mileage method in claiming business use of the car.

Which Method Is Best?

Every year the American Automobile Association estimates how much it costs per mile to drive a car in the United States. Its most recent report shows that it costs, on average, anywhere from 54.6 cents to 69.0 cents per mile to drive a sedan for 15,000 miles. Driving a compact SUV for 15,000 miles costs an average of 62.2 cents per mile, and an all-wheel drive SUV costs 75.4 cents per mile.[11]

The difference depends on the size (and cost) of the car and the number of miles driven during the year—the more miles driven, the less one's cost per mile.

In general, taxpayers are better off using the standard mileage rate if they drive a smaller car, particularly if they drive many business miles. And a taxpayer is likely to benefit from using the standard mileage rate if an old or inexpensive car is used. Why? Because the same fixed deduction rate applies no matter how much the car is worth. Because the standard mileage rate factors in depreciation (which does not vary), an inexpensive car might benefit more from using this method than would an expensive vehicle.

[11]American Automobile Association, *Your Driving Costs*, 2022 edition.

The actual cost method will likely provide a larger deduction if the taxpayer drives a more expensive car, an SUV, or a minivan. In addition, the actual cost method will normally result in a larger deduction if fewer business miles are driven.

Yet the only way to know for sure which method is best is to keep careful track of the actual costs and the business mileage driven. Then calculations can be done under both methods, and the larger deduction can be taken.

The Big Picture

Example 10

Return to the facts of *The Big Picture* on p. 9-1. Morgan wants to make sure she documents her business miles appropriately. She knows that the IRS expects her to keep track of her business miles on a regular basis, including where she drove and the business reason for the trip. She wonders whether there are some mobile apps that can help.

Actually, a number of mileage tracking apps are available that would allow Morgan to begin logging miles automatically every time she started a trip. Some use Bluetooth and begin as soon as the car starts moving; others (usually free) require the user to input locations. All of the apps create detailed records of all trips; the user just needs to identify the purpose of the trip. Here are a few apps that are available (with information from the developer's website):

- **MileIQ (mileiq.com)** tracks every trip you take automatically. Then it lets you quickly categorize a trip as business, personal, medical, charity, or a custom category you create. It also lets you log any additional information (like freeway tolls or parking fees). Trip information is backed up automatically using MileIQ's cloud servers, and its data integrates with a number of accounting/tax software programs (including QuickBooks). MileIQ is free if you track fewer than 40 trips per month and about $60 per year with unlimited trip tracking.
- **TripLog (triplogmileage.com)** monitors your mileage via GPS; tracks any parking, tolls, or other expenses; records fuel costs; generates IRS-ready reports; and integrates with QuickBooks. As with MileIQ, you have the option of specifying the nature of the trip (business, charity, medical, etc.), entering notes, and adding any applicable parking or toll costs. TripLog's basic features are free. Advanced features, such as Bluetooth "autostart" and automatic daily cloud backup, cost about $60 per year. You also can use TripLog to estimate your gas mileage and find the best gas prices.
- **QuickBooks Self-Employed (quickbooks.intuit.com/self-employed/)** automatically tracks mileage using your phone's GPS and groups the information into trips (allowing you to categorize them as business or personal). This feature, combined with easy expense categorization (via swiping on the phone) and the ability to organize receipts by taking a picture, lets you easily compare whether you should use the standard mileage or actual cost method. And it integrates seamlessly with TurboTax when it is time to file a tax return. Currently, the app costs $7.50 per month ($12 per month when combined with TurboTax).
- **Stride Drive (stridehealth.com/drive)** is a free mileage and expense tracking app that records your mileage by running in the background as you drive. You can start and stop recording your mileage for each trip by tapping the start button when you leave home, or, in some versions of the app, you can set it up to record automatically. You also can use Stride Drive to log your receipts and expense records, so all your business deductions are in one place at tax time. The app includes preloaded categories and explanations (many geared toward rideshare drivers) that help identify which expenses to log (and what percentage of them you can deduct).

9-4 Travel Expenses

LO.3

Describe how travel expenses are treated.

9-4a Definition of Travel Expenses

A deduction is allowed for business travel expenses. **Travel expenses** include transportation expenses, meals and lodging, and incidental expenses while working away from home. In general, the reason for allowing a travel expense deduction is to alleviate the duplication of living expenses (where the taxpayer incurs expenses while at home and while working away from home).

Transportation expenses (discussed previously) are deductible even if the taxpayer is *not* away from home. Meals cannot be lavish or extravagant. Examples of incidental expenses include laundry, baggage fees and/or tips, and ATM fees. A deduction for travel expenses, however, is only allowed if the taxpayer is away from their tax home.

9-4b **Away-from-Home Requirement**

The crucial test for the deductibility of travel expenses is whether the taxpayer is away from home overnight. "Overnight" need not be a 24-hour period, but it must be a period substantially longer than an ordinary day's work and must require rest, sleep, or a relief-from-work period.[12] A one-day business trip normally does not warrant travel status; therefore, meals and lodging for such a trip are not deductible.

Temporary Assignments

The taxpayer must be away from home for a temporary period. If a taxpayer relocates to a new area for an indefinite period of time, that new location becomes the taxpayer's tax home. *Temporary* indicates that the assignment's termination is expected within a reasonably short period of time. The position of the IRS is that the tax home is the business location of the taxpayer. As a result, travel expenses are not deductible if a taxpayer is reassigned for an indefinite period and does not move their place of residence to the new location.

Temporary Becomes Permanent

Example 11

Malcolm maintains a consulting practice in Los Angeles. Due to new client responsibilities, Malcolm decided to open a new office in San Diego. Malcolm worked out of the new office for three months to train a new manager and to assist in setting up the new office. He tried commuting from his home in Los Angeles for a week and decided that he could not continue driving several hours a day. He rented an apartment in San Diego, where he lived during the week. He spent weekends with his wife and children at their home in Los Angeles.

Malcolm's rent, meals, laundry, incidentals, and automobile expenses in San Diego are deductible. To the extent that Malcolm's transportation expense related to his weekend trips home exceeds what his cost of meals and lodging would have been, the excess is personal and nondeductible.

Assume that Malcolm in Example 11 decided that he was the best person to manage the new office in San Diego and so decided to move there permanently. His wife and children continued to live in Los Angeles until the end of the school year.

Malcolm is no longer "away from home" because the assignment is not temporary. His travel expenses are not deductible.

To curtail controversy in this area, the Code specifies that a taxpayer "*shall not* be treated as *temporarily* away from home during any period of employment if such period exceeds one year."[13]

Determining the Tax Home

In most situations, determining the location of a taxpayer's tax home is not difficult. The tax home is the area in which the taxpayer works.

It is possible for a taxpayer never to be away from their tax home. In other words, the tax home follows the taxpayer. In this situation, all meals and lodging remain personal and are not deductible.

---

[12] *U.S. v. Correll*, 68–1 USTC ¶9101, 20 AFTR 2d 5845, 88 S.Ct. 445 (1967); Rev.Rul. 75–168.

[13] § 162(a).

Jim is single and works full-time as a long-haul truck driver. He lists his mother's home as his address and stays there during holidays. However, he contributes nothing toward its maintenance.

Because Jim has no regular place of duty or place where he regularly lives, his tax home is where he works (i.e., on the road). As an itinerant (transient), he is never away from home, and all of his meals and lodging while on the road are personal and not deductible.

The result reached in Example 13 is justified on the grounds that there is no duplication of living expenses in the case of itinerant taxpayers.[14]

When a taxpayer has more than one place of business or work, the main one is considered to be the tax home. This is determined by considering the time spent, the level of activity involved, and the income earned at each job.

Art, a physical therapist, lives with his family in Lancaster, Pennsylvania. For seven months each year, he is employed by the New Orleans Saints football team at a salary of $150,000. During this period, he rents an apartment in New Orleans. In the off-season, he works for the Lancaster YMCA at a salary of $15,000.

Art's tax home is clearly New Orleans and not Lancaster. Consequently, his living expenses while in New Orleans (i.e., food and lodging) are not deductible.

9-4c Restrictions on Travel Expenses

The possibility always exists that taxpayers will attempt to treat vacation or pleasure travel as deductible business travel. To prevent such practices, the law contains restrictions on certain travel expenses.

Conventions

For travel expenses to be deductible, a convention must be directly related to the taxpayer's trade or business.[15] Compare Examples 15 and 16.

Type of Convention

Dr. Hill, a pathologist who works for a hospital in Ohio, travels to Las Vegas to attend a two-day session on recent developments in estate planning. No deduction is allowed for Dr. Hill's travel expenses.

Assume the same facts as in Example 15, except that the convention deals entirely with recent developments in pathology. Now a travel deduction is allowed.

The taxpayer must attend convention sessions along with other participants in order to claim a deduction. Attendance does not include watching or listening to sessions at a later date that are recorded (e.g., a taxpayer cannot vacation during the convention sessions and watch the videos later). However, a deduction will be allowed for costs (other than travel, meals, and entertainment) of renting or using recorded materials related to business.

[14]Rev.Rul. 73–529 and *James O. Henderson*, 70 TCM 1407, T.C.Memo. 1995–559, *aff'd* by 98–1 USTC ¶50,375, 81 AFTR 2d 98–1748, 143 F.3d 497 (CA–9).

[15]§ 274(h)(1).

A CPA is unable to attend a convention at which current developments in taxation are discussed. She pays $300 to stream the recorded sessions and views them at home later. The $300 is a deduction *for* AGI if the CPA is self-employed. If the CPA is an employee, the $300 is a miscellaneous itemized deduction (and not allowed from 2018 through 2025).

The Code places stringent restrictions on the deductibility of travel expenses of the taxpayer's spouse or dependent.[16] Generally, there must be a business reason for the spouse or dependent to attend, and the expenses must be otherwise deductible.

Assume the same facts as in Example 16 with the additional fact that Dr. Hill is accompanied by her husband, Mr. Hill. Mr. Hill is not employed but possesses secretarial skills and takes notes during the proceedings. No deduction is allowed for Mr. Hill's travel expenses.

If, however, Mr. Hill is a medical professional trained in pathology and is employed by Dr. Hill as her assistant, his travel expenses become deductible.

Education

Travel as a form of education is not deductible.[17] If, however, the education qualifies as a deduction, the travel involved is allowed. Compare Examples 19 and 20.

Education Travel

Example 19

Greta, a German teacher, travels to Germany to maintain general familiarity with the language and culture. No travel expense deduction is allowed.

Jean-Claude, a scholar of French literature, travels to Paris to do specific library research that cannot be done elsewhere and to take courses that are offered only at the Sorbonne. The travel costs are deductible, assuming that the other requirements for deducting education expenses (discussed later in the chapter) are met.

9-4d Combined Business and Pleasure Travel

To be deductible, travel expenses need not be incurred in the performance of specific job functions.

Domestic Travel for Business and Pleasure

In order to limit the possibility of a taxpayer claiming a tax deduction for what is essentially a personal vacation, several rules were created to handle deductions associated with combined business and pleasure trips. If the business/pleasure trip is entirely within the United States, the transportation expenses are deductible only if the trip is *primarily for business*.[18] Meals, lodging, and other expenses are allocated between business and personal days. If the trip is primarily for pleasure, no transportation expenses qualify as a deduction. Compare Examples 21 and 22.

[16] § 274(m)(3).

[17] § 274(m)(2).

[18] Reg. § 1.162–2(b)(1).

Meeting the Primary Business Purpose Requirement

Example 21

In 2023, Hana travels from Seattle to New York primarily for business. She spends five days conducting business and three days sightseeing and attending shows. Her plane and taxi fare amounts to $1,160. Her meals amount to $200 per day, and lodging and incidental expenses are $350 per day.

She can deduct the transportation charges of $1,160 because the trip is primarily for business (five days of business versus three days of sightseeing). Meals are limited to five days and are subject to a 50% reduction (see text Section 9-6c). Her meals deduction will be $500 [5 days × ($200 × 50%)], and other expenses are limited to $1,750 (5 days × $350).

Example 22

Assume that Hana goes to New York for a two-week vacation. While there, she spends several hours renewing acquaintances with people in her company's New York office. Her transportation expenses are not deductible.

Foreign Travel for Business and Pleasure

When the trip is *outside the United States*, different rules apply. Transportation expenses must be allocated between business and personal unless:

1. The taxpayer is away from home for seven days or less.
2. Less than 25 percent of the time was for personal purposes.

No allocation is required if the taxpayer has no substantial control over arrangements for the trip or the desire for a vacation is not a major factor in taking the trip. If the trip is primarily for pleasure, no transportation charges are deductible. Days devoted to travel are considered business days. Weekends, legal holidays, and intervening days are considered business days, provided both the day before and the day after were business days.[19] Compare Examples 23 and 24.

The Amount of Nonbusiness Time Permitted

Example 23

In 2023, Robert takes a trip from New York to Japan primarily for business purposes. He is away from home from June 10 through June 19. He spends three days vacationing and seven days (including two travel days) conducting business. His airfare is $4,000, his meals amount to $200 per day (all at local restaurants), and lodging and incidental expenses are $300 per day. Because Robert is away from home for more than seven days and more than 25% of his time is devoted to personal purposes, only 70% (7 days business/10 days total) of the transportation is deductible. His deductions are as follows:

Transportation (70% × $4,000)		$2,800
Lodging ($300 × 7)		2,100
Meals ($200 × 7)	$1,400	
Less: 50% reduction (see text Section 9-6c)	(700)	700
Total		$5,600

Example 24

Assume the same facts as in Example 23. Robert is gone the same period of time but spends only two days (rather than three) vacationing.

Now no allocation of transportation is required. Because the pleasure portion of the trip is less than 25% of the total, all of the airfare qualifies for the travel deduction.

[19] § 274(c) and Reg. § 1.274–4. For purposes of the seven-days-or-less exception, the departure travel day is not counted.

Record-Keeping Requirements

Distinguishing between business and personal expenses can be difficult (and somewhat subjective). As a result, the tax law includes specific provisions that require the taxpayer to maintain specific, written, contemporaneous records for travel expenses.[20] These records, which assist the IRS and courts in reaching a fair determination of the legitimacy of the expenses, must include the amount, time (or dates), place, and business purpose behind the expenses.

LO.4

Differentiate between deductible and nondeductible education expenses.

9-5 Education Expenses

9-5a General Requirements

In general, a self-employed taxpayer can deduct **education expenses** provided the expenses are:

- To meet the specific legal requirements to keep their job.
- To maintain or improve existing skills required in the present job.

Education expenses are *not* deductible if the education is:

- To meet the minimum educational standards for qualification in the taxpayer's existing job.
- To qualify the taxpayer for a new trade or business.[21]

A deduction is generally allowed for education related to new duties if the new duties involve the same general work. For example, the IRS has ruled that a practicing dentist's education expenses incurred to become an orthodontist are deductible.[22] Fees incurred for professional qualification exams (the bar exam, for example) and fees for review courses (such as a CPA review course) are not deductible.[23] From 2018 through 2025, employees incurring education expenses that are not reimbursed by the employer may not deduct these expenses (they are employee business expenses and miscellaneous itemized deductions).

9-5b Legal Requirements to Keep a Job

Taxpayers can deduct education expenses if the education is required by law. If, however, the required education is the minimum degree required for the job, no deduction is allowed. So a taxpayer classified as a staff accountant who went back to school to obtain a bachelor's degree in accounting was not allowed to deduct the expenses, since a bachelor's degree was the minimum requirement for his job.[24] Education required by law for various professions also qualifies for a deduction.

To satisfy the State Board of Public Accountancy rules for maintaining her CPA license, Nancy takes an auditing course sponsored by a local college. The cost of the education is deductible.

[20] § 274(d). Corroborating evidence (e.g., receipt from a hotel or an airline ticket) also is required. In general, approximations and estimates are not sufficient. If a taxpayer is unable to substantiate expenses, courts use the Cohan rule to estimate the deductible amount [*Cohan v. Commissioner*, 39 F.2d 540 (CA–2, 1930)].

[21] Reg. §§ 1.162–5(b)(2) and (3).

[22] Rev.Rul. 74–78.

[23] Reg. § 1.212–1(f) and Rev.Rul. 69–292.

[24] Reg. § 1.162–5(b)(2)(iii) Example (2); *Collin J. Davidson*, 43 TCM 743, T.C.Memo. 1982–119.

9-5c **Maintaining or Improving Existing Skills**

The "maintaining or improving existing skills" requirement has been difficult for both taxpayers and the courts to interpret. For example, a business consultant may be permitted to deduct the costs of obtaining an advanced degree on the grounds that the advanced management education is undertaken to maintain and improve existing management skills. The consultant also can deduct the costs of specialized, nondegree management courses that maintain or improve existing skills. Expenses incurred by a self-employed accountant to obtain a law degree are not deductible, however, because the education constitutes training for a new trade or business.[25]

The conditions required for the regular education expense deduction are summarized in Concept Summary 9.2.

Concept Summary 9.2

Conditions for Deducting Regular Education Expenses

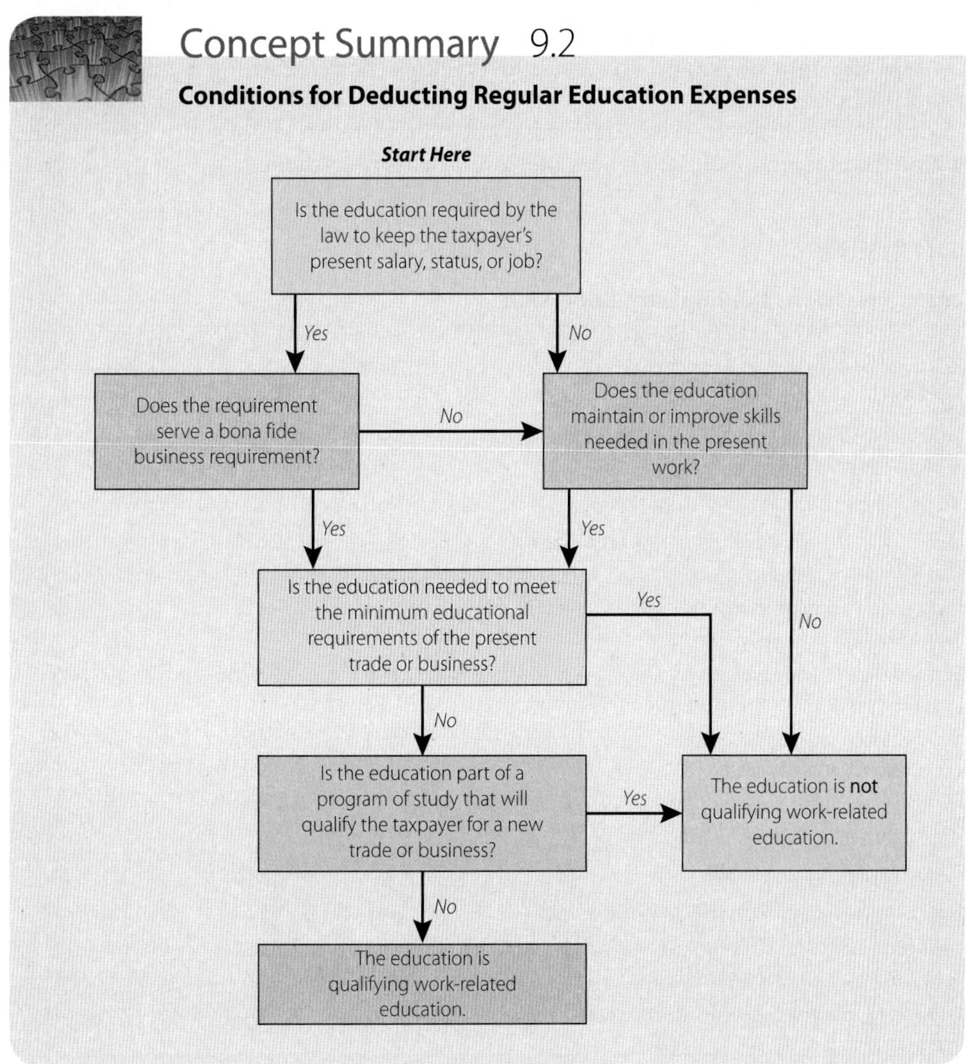

9-5d **What Expenses Are Allowed?**

Education expenses include tuition, books and supplies, and transportation (e.g., from the office to school) and travel (e.g., meals and lodging while away from home at an executive education training program).

[25]Reg. § 1.162–5(b)(3)(ii) Example (1).

The Big Picture

Example 26

Return to the facts of *The Big Picture* on p. 9-1. After starting her new job, Morgan enrolls in the evening master's degree program in child development at a local university and begins attending classes.

Although Morgan believes that the master's degree would be useful, it is not a requirement of ECCC, and it is not needed to maintain or improve existing skills in her current job. As a result, none of her education expenses are deductible.[26] However, the tuition and fees (but not any expenses for books and supplies) will qualify for the lifetime learning credit (see text Section 13-4e).

9-5e Other Provisions Dealing with Education

Although this chapter deals with employment-related expenses, a wide variety of tax provisions deal with education. Because the encouragement of education is a desirable social goal, Congress continues to enact laws that provide tax incentives. The incentives come in the form of income exclusions, deductions (both *for* AGI and *from* AGI), and various credits.

Concept Summary 9.3 reviews the tax consequences of the various provisions dealing with education and indicates where they are discussed in the text.

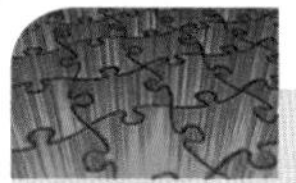

Concept Summary 9.3

Tax Consequences of Provisions Dealing with Education

Provision	Tax Effect	Income Phaseout[a]	Reference	
			Code	Text
Educational savings bonds	*Exclusion* for interest on U.S. Series EE bonds used for higher education	Yes	§ 135	Ch. 5, p. 5-24
Qualified tuition program	No deduction; *exclusion* for distributions	No	§ 529	Ch. 5, p. 5-26
Educational assistance plans	*Exclusion* of up to $5,250 for employer-provided assistance	No[b]	§ 127	Ch. 5, p. 5-15
Scholarships	*Exclusion* allowed for education costs (excluding room and board)	No	§ 117	Ch. 5, p. 5-7
Qualified tuition reduction plan	*Exclusion* as to tuition waivers for employees (and dependents) of nonprofit educational institutions	No[b]	§ 117(d)	Ch. 5, p. 5-7
Coverdell education savings account	No deduction ($2,000 maximum annual contribution); *exclusion* for distributions	Yes[c]	§ 530	Ch. 5, p. 5-26
Early distributions from IRAs	If used for qualified higher education, income recognized but penalty waived	—	§ 72(t)	Ch. 9, p. 9-29
Educator expenses	*Deduction for* AGI; up to $300	No	§ 62(a)(2)(D)	Ch. 9, p. 9-24
Interest on student loans	*Deduction for* AGI; up to $2,500 per year	Yes	§ 221	Ch. 10, p. 10-14
Job-related education expenses	*Deduction for* AGI for self-employed taxpayer; *no deduction* for employees through 2025	No	§ 162	Ch. 9, p. 9-14; p. 9-24; p. 9-35
American Opportunity credit	Allowed for the first four years of postsecondary education; up to $2,500 per year	Yes	§ 25A(i)	Ch. 12, p. 12-17
Lifetime learning credit	20% of qualifying expenses (not to exceed $10,000 per year)	Yes	§ 25(A)(c)	Ch. 12, p. 12-17

[a]The phaseout of benefits occurs when income reaches a certain level. The phaseout amounts vary widely, depend on filing status (i.e., single or married filing jointly), and are based on AGI that is modified in some way (MAGI).
[b]The availability of the benefit cannot be discriminatory (i.e., cannot favor higher-income taxpayers).
[c]The phaseout begins once AGI reaches $190,000 (married taxpayers) or $95,000 (unmarried taxpayers).

[26]*Steven Galligan*, 83 TCM 1859, T.C.Memo. 2002–150.

9-6 Other Business Expenses

LO.5

Identify other business expenses.

9-6a Office in the Home

Most expenses for personal use assets are not deductible. Except for certain expenses (primarily interest and taxes), this is the case with a personal residence. However, self-employed individuals are allowed a deduction for **office in the home expenses** if a portion of the residence is used *exclusively* on a *regular basis* as either:

- The principal place of business for any trade or business of the taxpayer.
- A place of business used by clients, patients, or customers.

From 2018 through 2025, employees are not allowed an office in the home deduction because these expenses are employee business expenses (and miscellaneous itemized deductions).

The term *principal place of business* includes a place of business that satisfies the following requirements:[27]

- The office is used by the taxpayer to conduct administrative or management activities of a trade or business.
- There is no other fixed location of the trade or business where the taxpayer conducts these activities.

Josh Butler is a self-employed anesthesiologist. During the year, he spends 30 to 35 hours per week administering anesthesia and postoperative care to patients in three hospitals, none of which provides him with an office. He also spends two or three hours per day in a room in his home that he uses exclusively as an office. He does not meet patients there, but he performs a variety of tasks related to his medical practice (e.g., contacting surgeons, doing bookkeeping, and reading medical journals).

A deduction will be allowed because Dr. Butler uses the office in the home to conduct administrative or management activities of his trade or business, and there is no other fixed location where these activities can be carried out.

The exclusive use requirement means that part of the home must be used *solely* for business purposes. An exception allows mixed use (both business and personal) of the home if a licensed day-care business is involved.

Exclusive Use Requirement

Trisha is employed by a local law firm, is working remotely from home, and maintains an office in her home for business purposes. The office also is used by her spouse to pay the family bills and by their children to do homework assignments. The exclusive use requirement is not met, and no office in the home deduction is allowed.

What if Trisha's office was not used for any other purpose but her remote work? Although the exclusive use test is now met, Trisha is an employee and her home office expenses are employee business expenses which are not deductible from 2018 to 2025 (since they are miscellaneous itemized deductions subject to the 2%-of-AGI floor).

[27] § 280A(c)(1).

Exclusive Use Requirement

Example 29

Muriel operates a licensed day-care center in her home. The children use the living room as a play area during the day, and Muriel and her family use it for personal purposes in the evening and on weekends. Even though the living room is used for both business and personal purposes, Muriel can claim an office in the home deduction.

The office in the home deduction can be determined in either of two ways: the Regular (actual expense) Method or the Simplified (safe harbor) Method.

Regular Method

When using the Regular Method, relevant expenses must be categorized as direct or indirect. Direct expenses benefit only the business part of the home (e.g., repainting the office) and are deducted in full. Indirect expenses are for maintaining and operating the home (e.g., utilities and insurance). Because indirect expenses benefit both business and personal use, an allocation between the two is necessary. The allocation is made based on the floor space involved, dividing the business area by the total home area to arrive at the business percentage.

The allowable home office expenses cannot exceed the gross income from the business less all other business expenses (i.e., this deduction cannot create a loss). And the home office expenses that are allowed as itemized deductions anyway (e.g., mortgage interest and real estate taxes) must be deducted first.

Home office expenses of a self-employed individual are trade or business expenses and are deductible *for* AGI. Any disallowed home office expenses are *carried forward* and used in future years subject to the same limitations.

Luis is a certified public accountant employed by a regional CPA firm as a tax manager. He operates a separate furniture refinishing business that he operates out of his home. For this business, he uses two rooms in the basement exclusively and regularly. The floor space of the two rooms is 240 square feet, which is 10% of the total floor space of his 2,400-square-foot residence. Gross income from the business totals $8,000. Expenses of the business (other than home office expenses) are $6,500. Luis incurs the following home office expenses:

Real property taxes on residence	$ 4,000
Interest expense on residence	7,500
Operating expenses of residence (including homeowners insurance)	2,000
MACRS cost recovery on residence (based on 10% business use)	350

Luis's deductions are determined as follows:

Business income		$ 8,000
Less: Other business expenses		(6,500)
Net income from the business (before the office in the home deduction)		$ 1,500
Less: Allocable taxes ($4,000 × 10%)	$400	
Allocable interest ($7,500 × 10%)	750	(1,150)
		$ 350
Allocable operating expenses of the residence ($2,000 × 10%)		(200)
		$ 150
Allocable MACRS cost recovery ($350, limited to remaining income)		(150)
		$ -0-

Luis has a carryover of $200 (the unused excess MACRS cost recovery). Because he is self-employed, the allocable taxes and interest ($1,150), the other deductible office expenses ($200 + $150), and $6,500 of other business expenses are deductible *for* AGI.

As noted in Example 30, the office in the home deduction includes an allocable portion of the cost recovery on the personal residence. To arrive at this cost recovery, taxpayers use the MACRS percentage for 39-year nonresidential real property (see Chapter 8). Except for the first and last years (i.e., 1 and 40), the applicable percentage is 2.564 percent—see Exhibit 8.8. Cost recovery for office equipment and furnishings is computed using the MACRS rules for personal property—see Exhibits 8.1 and 8.3. These assets also can be expensed under § 179; bonus depreciation is also available.

An office in the home deduction is also available to those who rent (rather than own) their home. In this case, the business use percentage is applied to the rent being paid.

If the Regular Method is used, the office in the home deduction is claimed using Form 8829 (Expenses for Business Use of Your Home).

Simplified Method

Because of the record keeping and calculations involved in using the Regular Method, the IRS established an optional Simplified Method for the office in the home deduction.[28] If the Simplified Method is used, Form 8829 is not required. Taxpayers using the Simplified Method are allowed a deduction of $5 per square foot of space devoted to the office. However, since no more than 300 square feet can be counted, the maximum deduction is limited to $1,500.

The various rules governing the use of the Simplified Method are summarized below.

- No depreciation on the residence can be claimed.
- Actual expenses of maintaining and operating the home (e.g., qualified residence interest, property taxes, homeowners insurance, utilities) are ignored. Expenses that are deductible elsewhere on the tax return (e.g., qualified residence interest, property taxes) can be claimed in full without any reduction due to a home office deduction being claimed.
- Office in the home deductions in excess of the net income from the business *cannot* be carried over to a future year. An unused Regular Method deduction from a prior year *cannot* be carried to a Simplified Method year.

Taxpayers can choose between the Regular Method and the Simplified Method each year. However, once a choice is made, that choice cannot be changed for that year. Care should be taken in making the choice because the Simplified Method may yield a smaller deduction.

Assume the same facts as in Example 30, except that Luis chooses the Simplified Method. This choice results in the following deduction:

Net income from the business (before the office in the home deduction)	$ 1,500
Simplified Method office in the home deduction ($5 × 240 square feet)	(1,200)
Net income from the business	$ 300

In comparing the results of Examples 30 and 31, note that the use of the Simplified Method left Luis with $500 less in deductions (counting the $200 unused carryover). However, Luis can now use the property taxes ($400) and interest ($750) allocated to the office in the home deduction under the Regular Method as itemized deductions on Schedule A.

[28] Rev.Proc. 2013–13.

Which Method to Use

The availability of the Simplified Method presents an annual decision for the taxpayer. In choosing which method to use, here are some factors to consider:

- Both methods require exclusive and regular use of the home office.
- The Simplified Method requires fewer calculations and less record keeping.
- Because no depreciation is allowed, the Simplified Method will avoid the 25 percent tax on real estate gains when the home is sold (see Chapter 14).
- Even though the Simplified Method frees up certain home-related expenses (e.g., qualified residence interest, property taxes, homeowners insurance, utilities), not all of these expenses are deductible. Some are (property taxes), and some are not (homeowners insurance). But even the expenses that are deductible (property taxes) may be subject to other itemized deduction limitations (see Chapter 10).
- With a maximum deduction of $1,500, the Simplified Method, in most cases, will result in a smaller deduction than the Regular Method.
- Under the Simplified Method, a taxpayer is not allowed to carry over unused deductions.
- Once a taxpayer has made a choice for a year, the choice cannot be changed.

Tyler, a calendar year taxpayer, prepared and filed his own tax return for 2022. Being in a hurry, he decided to use the Simplified Method of computing his home office deduction. In March 2024, Tyler seeks tax advice and learns how much he could have saved by using the Regular Method. Tyler cannot file an amended return for 2022, but he can switch to the Regular Method for 2023.

The Big Picture

Example 33

Return to the facts of *The Big Picture* on p. 9-1. Morgan is using her apartment's second bedroom as a home office. Her apartment has 1,200 square feet; the second bedroom has 200 square feet. Her home office is, therefore, one-sixth of her apartment (200 square feet ÷ 1,200 square feet). During 2023, her apartment expenses include:

Rent ($1,250 per month)	$15,000
Utilities	2,600
Renter's insurance	1,100
Total	$18,700

In addition, she purchases various supplies and software for her tutoring ($700) and freelance driving ($75), as well as office furniture ($100 for a file cabinet to store her business records, $400 for a table, $250 for chairs, and $50 for a lamp; $800 total). The office furniture, which she can expense immediately under § 179, will be allocated to her freelance businesses based on total revenues.

Income from her tutoring amounts to $6,795, and she earned $8,305 from her freelance driving. She also has documented her business mileage for the year (630 for tutoring and 5,400 for freelance driving) and has receipts for freeway tolls of $175 (all related to her freelance driving). Morgan uses the automatic mileage method for her business miles (see Example 9).

continued

Using the Simplified Method, Morgan's home office deduction would be $1,000 (200 square feet × $5 per square foot). Morgan will be better off using the Actual Cost Method, where her deduction will be $3,117 ($18,700 total apartment expenses × ⅙). This deduction will be allocated to her freelance businesses (tutoring and freelance driving), based on total revenues.

	Tutoring	Freelance Driving	Total
Revenues	$ 6,795	$ 8,305	$15,100
Expenses:			
Business mileage:			
630 × $0.655/mile	(413)		(413)
5,400 × $0.655/mile		(3,537)	(3,537)
Business tolls		(175)	(175)
Supplies/Software	(700)	(75)	(775)
Office furniture	(360)	(440)	(800)
Home office	(1,403)	(1,714)	(3,117)
Net income	$ 3,919	$ 2,364	$ 6,283

Note: This example assumes that Morgan meets the "exclusive use" requirement for her home office (see text Section 9-6a and Examples 27, 28, and 29). As discussed there, the "exclusive use" requirement is a significant constraint. What would happen if on *one day* during the year Morgan went into the home office, opened her laptop computer, and spent *one hour* responding to her personal e-mails?

Answer: The "exclusive use" test would not be met, and Morgan would lose the home office deduction. Further, proving a negative is difficult (how does one document that the home office was *never* used for personal purposes?). But Morgan needs to understand the standard and ensure that she complies with it. In our example, that means when she wants to use her laptop for personal purposes, she needs to use it somewhere other than the office.

9-6b **Moving Expenses**

The deduction for moving expenses has been suspended from 2018 through 2025. However, during this period, the moving expense deduction is retained for members of the Armed Forces (or their spouse or dependents) on active duty who move because of a military order that relates to a permanent change of station.[29] The rules providing for exclusions of amounts attributable to in-kind moving and storage expenses (and reimbursements or allowances for these expenses) also remain in place for these individuals.

9-6c **Entertainment and Meal Expenses**

Many businesses incur entertainment and meal expenses. Although such expenses can help build business activity, a personal element also is involved in these activities. As a result, Congress decided to limit these deductions. *No deduction* is allowed with respect to:

1. An activity generally considered to be entertainment, amusement, or recreation.
2. Membership dues with respect to any club organized for business, pleasure, recreation, or other social purposes.
3. A facility (or portion thereof) used in connection with any of the above items.

[29] § 217(k).

However, taxpayers still may deduct some or all of the *food and beverage expenses* associated with operating their trade or business (e.g., a business meal with a current or potential client, or meals consumed by employees on work travel). In general, only *50 percent* of food and beverage expenses can be deducted.[30] However, given the impact of the COVID-19 pandemic on restaurants, Congress provided a temporary 100 percent deduction for meals and beverages provided by a restaurant in 2021 and 2022.[31]

Subsidized Eating Facilities and *De Minimis* Fringe Benefits

Prior to 2018, additional exceptions to the 50% rule applied to meals and entertainment in a subsidized eating facility or where the *de minimis* fringe benefit rule applied to food and beverages provided to employees (see Chapter 5). From 2018 through 2025, the 50 percent limitation is applied to these items.[32] Beginning in 2026, the deduction for these items will be eliminated.

Subsidized Eating Facilities and *De Minimis* Fringe Benefits

Example 34

General Hospital has an employee cafeteria on the premises for its doctors, nurses, and other employees. The cafeteria operates at cost. The 50% rule applies to the employee cafeteria costs of General Hospital.

Canary Corporation provides coffee and sometimes doughnuts to employees in the breakroom. This is a *de minimis* fringe benefit that is not taxable to the employees. Canary may deduct only 50% of the cost of this food.

Exceptions to the 50% Rule

The 50% rule has a number of exceptions.[33] One exception covers the case where the full value of the meals is included in the compensation of the employee (or independent contractor). Expenses directly related to business meetings of employees also are not subject to the 50% rule (and are fully deductible). A similar exception applies to employer-paid recreational or social activities for employees (e.g., the annual holiday party or spring picnic). In addition, businesses that have retreats and/or other off-site training events are generally allowed to deduct 100 percent of the meals provided to participants at those sites.[34]

Myrtle wins an all-expense-paid trip to Europe for selling the most insurance for her company during the year. Her employer treats this trip as additional compensation to Myrtle. The 50% rule does not apply to the employer.

---

[30] § 274; Reg. § 1.274–11.

[31] § 274(n)(2)(D). The expenses must be paid or incurred after December 31, 2020, and before January 1, 2023. The statutory language does not provide a definition of the term *restaurant*. Taxpayers may treat the meal portion of a *per diem* allowance (see text Section 9-9a) as if it were provided by a restaurant (Notice 2021–63).

[32] We do not know whether a subsidized eating facility is a "restaurant" for purposes of the 100% food and beverages deduction in 2021 and 2022.

[33] §§ 274(e) and (n).

[34] *Jacobs*, 148 T.C. 490 (2017); *acq.* 2019-8 I.R.B. 569; A.O.D. 2019-01.

Business Meals

A business meal is deductible only if all of the following conditions are met:[35]

- The expense is reasonable (i.e., not lavish or extravagant).
- The taxpayer (or an employee) is present at the meal.
- The food and beverages are provided to a current or potential business customer or client.
- If combined with entertainment, the meal and beverages cost is separately itemized on the bill or receipt.

Business Meals

During 2023, Lance submits a proposed consulting contract to a local business. He invites the two business owners to dinner at a local restaurant and pays for the meal. During the meal, Lance discusses and answers questions about the proposed contract. Lance can deduct 100% of this qualified business meal.

Assume the same facts as Example 37, except that Lance buys dinner for the two business owners but does not attend the dinner. Since Lance was not present at the meal, no deduction is allowed.

If the taxpayer is in travel status, any meal expenses can be deducted, subject to the 50% rule (100% in 2021 and 2022 for restaurant meals).

During 2023, Liang travels to San Francisco for a business convention. She pays for her meals at local restaurants and is reimbursed by her employer. Liang's employer can deduct 50% of the cost of her meals.

What if Liang's employer reimbursed some (but not all) of her meal expenses? The unreimbursed meal expenses are employee business expenses, which are not deductible from 2018 to 2025 (since they are miscellaneous itemized deductions subject to the 2%-of-AGI floor).

Ethics & Equity **Your Turn or Mine?**

Natalie (a CPA), Mathew (an attorney), Jacob (a banker), and Shanice (an insurance agent) all live and work in the same community. They have been friends since college. Every Friday, they have lunch together and make it a point to discuss some business matters. They take turns paying for the group's lunches, and each deducts the amount they paid for the lunch as an entertainment expense. Presuming that one of the four is audited, do you anticipate any difficulty with the IRS? Explain.

[35] § 274(k); Reg. § 1.274–12.

Business Gifts

Although not subject to the 50 percent limit on meals, business gifts are deductible only to the extent of $25 per donee per year.[36] Incidental costs such as engraving, gift-wrapping, mailing, and delivery also are allowed (in addition to the $25 maximum). Gifts costing $4 or less (e.g., pens with the employee's or company's name on them) or promotional materials are not subject to the $25 limit. Records must be maintained to substantiate business gifts.

Business Gifts

In December, Prism Associates purchases framed prints from a local artist and mails one to each of its clients. Each print costs $70; packaging and shipping costs are $10 per print. Prism may deduct $35 for each print sent ($25 gift maximum plus $10 for packaging and shipping).

Assume the same facts as Example 40. In addition to the framed prints, Prism also encloses a coffee mug imprinted with its name and logo. Each mug costs $3.

The coffee mug is considered a promotional item, and its cost also is allowed as a deduction.

Record-Keeping/Documentation Requirements

Proper documentation of meal expenses is essential because of the strict record-keeping requirements that must be met. For example, documentation that consists solely of credit card receipts and canceled checks may be inadequate to substantiate the business purpose and business relationship.[37] Taxpayers should maintain detailed records of amounts, time, place, business purpose, and business relationships. A credit card receipt details the place, date, and amount of the expense. Noting the names of the person(s) attending, the business relationship, and the topic of discussion on the physical receipt (or creating a digital note on your phone or an e-mail to yourself with this information) should be sufficient.

9-6d Miscellaneous Employee Expenses

Miscellaneous employee expenses include costs that are job-related, not reimbursed by the employer, and not covered elsewhere in the tax law. Expenses related to maintaining job status make up a significant category of miscellaneous expenses. They include union dues; membership dues to professional organizations; subscriptions to trade publications and professional journals; special clothing (e.g., uniforms, protective shoes, and safety glasses); and various license fees paid to government agencies and other regulatory bodies. As mentioned previously, the deduction for miscellaneous itemized deductions (including employee business expenses) has been suspended from 2018 through 2025.

Educator Expenses

Many teachers pay for professional development courses or purchase school supplies for classroom use and are not reimbursed by their employer. These expenses are miscellaneous itemized deductions (i.e., *from* AGI deductions) and are not deductible from 2018 through 2025 (see text Section 9-11a).

Modest relief is provided though for elementary and secondary school educators, allowing them to claim up to $300 (in 2022 and 2023) of these expenses as a deduction *for* AGI.[38] Eligible educators must work at least 900 hours during a school year as a teacher, an instructor, a counselor, a principal, or an aide. Covered costs include unreimbursed expenses for

[36] § 274(b)(1). Multiple gifts to members of the same customer's family are consolidated (so only one $25 deduction will be allowed). Gifts to an employer (or an employee's superior) are not deductible.

[37] *Kenneth W. Guenther*, 54 TCM 382, T.C.Memo. 1987–440.

[38] § 62(a)(2)(D).

professional development courses, books, supplies, computer and other equipment, and supplementary materials used in the classroom. Personal protective equipment, disinfectant, and other supplies used to prevent the spread of COVID-19 also qualify.[39]

Ron is a full-time teacher at Hoover Elementary. During 2023, he spends $1,200 for school supplies for his fourth-grade class. Under an accountable plan (see text Section 9-10a), Hoover reimburses him for $400 of these supplies. As to the $800 balance, Ron may claim $300 as a deduction *for* AGI. The remaining expenses ($500) are miscellaneous itemized deductions (employee business expenses) and not allowed from 2018 through 2025.

9-7 Contributions to Retirement Accounts

LO.6

Compare various deductions for contributions to retirement accounts.

Pension considerations are an essential feature of any compensation arrangement. From a tax policy perspective, providing retirement security for employees can be justified on both economic and social grounds. Because the public sector (i.e., Social Security) will not provide sufficient retirement security for recipients, the private sector must fill the need. Congress has given the private sector the necessary incentive by enacting various measures that provide significant tax advantages for retirement plans. Although amounts that may be deferred under these plans are limited, the tax advantages are substantive and include (1) the deductibility of contributions (individuals are not taxed on these contributions until they are distributed), (2) income earned on the contributions is not subject to tax until distributed (thus growing at a tax-free rate of return), and (3) employer contributions to and benefits payable under qualified plans generally are not subject to FICA and FUTA taxes.

Although a wide variety of retirement plans exist, we will focus on some typical qualified retirement plans: (1) § 401(k) plans (a defined contribution plan[40] typically offered to employees); (2) Individual Retirement Accounts (available to any person who has earned income); and (3) plans available to self-employed individuals, including Keogh plans (also known as H.R. 10 plans), Solo § 401(k) plans, Saving Incentive Match for Employees (SIMPLE) plans, and Simplified Employee Pension (SEP) plans.

9-7a § 401(k) Plans

In General

A **§ 401(k) plan** is offered by many businesses to provide retirement assets for their employees. The plans are popular and make up about 20 percent of all retirement assets, or almost $8 trillion. About 60 million individuals participate in a § 401(k) plan.

Both employers and employees can contribute to a § 401(k) plan. A participant can elect either to receive up to $22,500 in 2023[41] in cash (taxed currently) or to have a contribution made on their behalf to a profit sharing or stock bonus plan. Many employers encourage their personnel to contribute to the § 401(k) plan by providing a full or partial match of any funds contributed by the employee; a match like this increases the employee's total compensation and encourages a long-term investment in their future well-being.

Any employee-elected § 401(k) plan contributions are excluded from gross income in the year of the deferral; they are 100 percent vested on behalf of the employee. Like employer plan contributions, employee contributions are tax-deferred until distributed, as are earnings on those contributions. The qualified plan vesting provisions apply to employer contributions and investment earnings.

[39] Consolidated Appropriations Act, 2021 § 275 (P.L. 116-260). Applies to items purchased after March 12, 2020.

[40] There are two types of qualified pension plans: defined benefit plans and defined contribution plans. A defined benefit plan includes a formula that defines the *benefits* employees are to receive. A defined contribution plan defines the amount of the *contribution* to the plan. The majority of employer pension plans today are defined contribution plans.

[41] §§ 402(g)(1) and (4). This amount was $20,500 in 2022 and $19,500 in 2021 and 2020.

Alejandro participates in a § 401(k) plan of his employer. The plan permits the participants to choose between a full salary or a reduced salary where the reduction becomes a pretax contribution to a retirement plan. Alejandro elects to contribute 10% of his annual compensation of $40,000 to the plan. Current-year income taxes are paid by Alejandro only on $36,000. No income taxes are paid on the $4,000—or on any earnings—until it is distributed from the plan to Alejandro. The main benefit of a § 401(k) plan is that Alejandro can shift a portion of his income to a later taxable year.

There can be traditional § 401(k) plans and Roth § 401(k) plans. A traditional § 401(k) plan reduces the employee's gross income when a contribution is made. With a Roth § 401(k) plan, contributions are made with after-tax dollars (i.e., no deduction is allowed for contributions).

The maximum annual elective contribution to a § 401(k) plan is reduced dollar for dollar by other salary-reduction contributions to tax-sheltered annuities, simplified employee pension plans, and § 401(k) plans. Elective contributions in excess of the maximum limitation are taxable in the year of deferral. These amounts may be refunded from the plan tax-free before April 15 of the following year. Excess amounts not timely distributed will be double-taxed because they will be taxable in the year of distribution, even though they were included in income in the year of deferral. Annual elective contributions are also limited by complicated nondiscrimination requirements designed to encourage participation by non-highly compensated employees and by the general defined contribution plan limitations.

A person who has attained age 50 by the end of 2023 can make catch-up contributions of $7,500.[42]

9-8 Individual Retirement Accounts (IRAs)

9-8a General Rules

Employees not covered by another qualified plan can establish their own tax-deductible **Individual Retirement Accounts (IRAs)**. IRAs are a popular device for retirement savings; 37 percent of U.S. households hold some type of IRA, with about $14 trillion invested in these vehicles.

The investor contributes to the IRA, selecting the dates and amounts of those transfers. For 2023, the annual IRA contribution ceiling is the smaller of $6,500 ($13,000 for spousal IRAs, discussed later) or 100 percent of compensation.[43] The contribution ceiling applies to all types of IRAs (traditional deductible, traditional nondeductible, and Roth). An individual who attains the age of 50 by the end of the tax year can make an additional catch-up IRA contribution of $1,000 for the year.

The amount accumulated in an IRA can be substantial. For example, if each spouse of a married couple contributes just $4,000 annually to an IRA from ages 25–65 and earns an average of 6 percent annually on the investment, the two account balances will approximate $1.4 million at age 65.

If the taxpayer is an *active participant* in another qualified plan, the traditional IRA deduction limitation is phased out *proportionately* between certain AGI ranges, as shown in Exhibit 9.1.[44] If AGI is above the phaseout range, no IRA deduction is allowed. There is a $200 floor on the IRA deduction for individuals whose AGI is not above the phaseout range.

Exhibit 9.1 Phaseout of IRA Deduction of an Active Participant in 2023

Filing Status (AGI Phaseout)	Phaseout Begins*	Phaseout Ends
Single and head of household	$ 73,000	$ 83,000
Married, filing joint return	116,000	136,000
Married, filing separate return	–0–	10,000

*These amounts are indexed annually for inflation.

[42] § 414(v). The catch-up contribution amount is indexed in $500 increments.

[43] §§ 219(b)(1) and (c)(2). The limit is adjusted annually for inflation in $500 increments.

[44] § 219(g).

IRA Deduction Calculation

Dan, who is single and age 45, earns compensation income of $79,000 in 2023 and is an active participant in his employer's qualified retirement plan. Dan contributes $6,500 to a traditional IRA. The deductible amount is reduced by $3,900 because of the phaseout.

$$\frac{\$6{,}000 \text{ amount into phaseout range}}{\$10{,}000 \text{ phaseout range}} \times \$6{,}500 \text{ contribution} = \$3{,}900 \text{ reduction}$$

As a result of the $6,500 contribution, Dan can deduct only $2,600 ($6,500 – $3,900).

Aaron, an unmarried individual who is age 45, is an active participant in his employer's qualified retirement plan in 2023. With AGI of $82,800, he normally would have an IRA deduction limit of $130 ($6,500 – {[($82,800 – $73,000) ÷ $10,000] × $6,500}). However, because of the floor amount, Aaron is allowed a $200 IRA deduction.

An individual is not considered an active participant in a qualified plan merely because the individual's spouse is an active participant in such a plan for any part of a plan year. Thus, even when filing jointly, the nonparticipating individual may take a full $6,500 deduction regardless of the participation status of his or her spouse unless the couple has AGI above $218,000. If their AGI is above $218,000, the phaseout of the deduction begins at $218,000 and ends at $228,000 (phaseout over the $10,000 range) rather than beginning and ending at the phaseout amounts in Exhibit 9.1.[45]

Nell is covered by a qualified employer retirement plan at work. Her husband, Nick, is not an active participant in a qualified plan. If Nell and Nick's combined AGI is $145,000, Nell cannot make a deductible IRA contribution because she exceeds the income threshold for an active participant in Exhibit 9.1.

However, because Nick is not an active participant and their combined AGI does not exceed $218,000, he can make a deductible contribution of $6,500 to his own IRA.

To the extent that an individual is ineligible to make a deductible contribution to an IRA, *nondeductible contributions* can be made to the account.[46] The nondeductible contributions are subject to the same dollar limits as deductible contributions ($6,500 of earned income, $13,000 for a spousal IRA). Income in the account accumulates tax-free until distributed. Only the account earnings are taxed upon distribution; the individual's account basis equals the contributions made.

A taxpayer may be entitled to a nonrefundable credit for contributions to an IRA or elective deferrals for a § 401(k) plan (see text Section 12-4e). Distributions to a traditional IRA holder must begin no later than April 1 of the calendar year following the year in which the IRA holder reaches 73.[47]

Roth IRAs

A **Roth IRA** is a *nondeductible* alternative to the traditional deductible IRA. Earnings inside a Roth IRA are not taxable to the investor, and all qualified distributions from a Roth IRA are tax-free.[48] The maximum allowable annual contribution to a Roth IRA for 2023 is the smaller of $6,500 ($13,000 for spousal IRAs) or 100 percent of the individual's

[45] § 219(g)(7).

[46] § 408(o).

[47] 401(a)(9)(C)(v). In December 2022, as part of the 2023 Consolidated Appropriations Act, Congress passed the SECURE 2.0 Act that made a number of changes to retirement provisions. Although many of these changes are prospective, the Act increased the age by which RMDs must begin from 72 to 73 for individuals who attain age 72 after 2022.

[48] § 408A.

compensation for the year. Contributions to a Roth IRA must be made by the due date (excluding extensions) of the taxpayer's tax return. Roth IRAs are not subject to the minimum distribution rules that apply to traditional IRAs.

A taxpayer can make tax-free withdrawals from a Roth IRA after an initial five-year holding period if any one of the following requirements is satisfied:

- The distribution is made on or after the date on which the participant attains age 59 ½.
- The distribution is made to a beneficiary (or the participant's estate) on or after the participant's death.
- The participant becomes disabled.
- The distribution is used to pay for qualified first-time homebuyer's expenses (statutory ceiling of $10,000).

Amy establishes a Roth IRA at age 42 and contributes $5,000 per year for 20 years. The account is now worth $149,400, consisting of $100,000 of nondeductible contributions and $49,400 in accumulated earnings that have not been taxed. Amy may withdraw the $149,400 tax-free from the Roth IRA because she is over age 59 ½ and has met the five-year holding period requirement.

If the taxpayer receives a distribution from a Roth IRA and does not satisfy the aforementioned requirements, the distribution may be taxable to the extent of the plan's accumulated earnings. Distributions are treated as first made from the individual's contributions (i.e., as a return of capital).

Assume the same facts as in the previous example, except that Amy is age 50 and receives a distribution of $55,000. Because her adjusted basis for the Roth IRA is $100,000 (contributions made), the distribution is tax-free, and her adjusted basis is reduced to $45,000 ($100,000 − $55,000).

Roth IRAs are subject to income limits. In 2023, the maximum annual contribution of $6,500 is phased out beginning at AGI of $138,000 for single taxpayers and $218,000 for married couples who file a joint return. The phaseout range is $10,000 for married filing jointly and $15,000 for single taxpayers. For a married taxpayer filing separately, the phaseout begins with AGI of $0 and is phased out over a $10,000 range.[49]

Ben, a gig worker who is single, would like to contribute $6,500 to his Roth IRA in 2023. However, his AGI is $148,000, so his contribution is limited to $2,167 ($6,500 − $4,333).

$$\frac{\$10{,}000 \text{ amount into phaseout range}}{\$15{,}000 \text{ phaseout range}} \times \$6{,}500 \text{ contribution} = \$4{,}333 \text{ reduction}$$

Spousal IRAs

For a married couple, each spouse may establish an IRA individually and deduct contributions of up to $6,500 if the combined compensation of the spouses is at least equal to the total contributed amount. Thus, if only one spouse is employed or if both are

[49] The income limits for Roth IRA contributions are indexed annually for inflation.

employed but one has compensation of less than $6,500, each of them may contribute a maximum of $6,500 if their combined compensation is at least $13,000.

For the spousal IRA provision to apply, a joint return must be filed.[50] The spousal IRA deduction is reduced proportionately for active participants whose AGI exceeds the above target ranges.

Spousal IRAs

Tony, who is married, is eligible to establish an IRA. He received $130,000 in compensation in 2023, and his spouse Lita does not work outside the home. Tony can contribute up to $13,000 to two IRAs to be divided in any manner between the two spouses, with no more than $6,500 allocated to either spouse.

Assume the same facts as in the previous example, except that Lita has compensation income of $2,200. Without the spousal IRA provision, Tony could contribute $6,500 to his IRA, and Lita could contribute only $2,200 to her IRA. With the spousal IRA provision, they both can contribute $6,500 to their IRAs.

Timing of Contributions

Contributions (both deductible and nondeductible) can be made to an IRA anytime before the due date of the individual's tax return.[51] For example, an individual can establish and contribute to an IRA through April 15, 2024 (the 2023 individual tax return due date), and deduct this amount on his or her 2023 tax return. IRA contributions that are made during a tax return extension period do not satisfy the requirement of being made by the return due date.[52]

9-8b **Taxation of Benefits**

A participant has a zero basis in the *deductible* contributions of a traditional IRA because the contributions were deducted.[53] Therefore, all withdrawals from a deductible IRA are taxed as ordinary income in the year of receipt. They are not eligible for the 10-year averaging allowed for certain lump-sum distributions.

A participant has a basis equal to the contributions made for a *nondeductible* traditional IRA. As a result, only the earnings component of withdrawals is included in gross income. Such amounts are taxed as ordinary income in the year of receipt.

In addition to being included in gross income, payments from IRAs made to a participant before age 59½ are subject to a nondeductible 10 percent penalty tax on such payments.[54] However, an individual may make penalty-free withdrawals to pay for deductible medical expenses, to pay for qualified higher-education expenses, and to pay for qualified first-time homebuyer expenses (up to $10,000). Further, an individual who has received unemployment compensation for at least 12 consecutive weeks may use IRA withdrawals to pay for their own health insurance and for insurance on a spouse or dependent without incurring the 10 percent penalty tax.[55]

[50] § 219(c).

[51] § 219(f)(3).

[52] § 404(h)(1)(B).

[53] § 408(d)(1).

[54] § 72(t). There are limited exceptions to the penalty on early distributions.

[55] §§ 72(t)(2)(B), (D), (E), and (F). There are a variety of other exceptions to the penalty tax including distributions to an individual with a terminal illness expected to result in death within 84 months and distributions up to $22,000 as a result of a Federally declared disaster.

9-8c **Rollovers and Conversions**

An IRA may be the recipient of a rollover from another qualified plan, including another IRA. Such a distribution from a qualified plan is not included in gross income if it is transferred within 60 days of receipt to an IRA or to another qualified plan.

Ruth withdraws $15,000 from a traditional IRA on May 2, 2023 (closing the account). She deposits these funds into a different traditional IRA on June 5, 2023. This situation is a qualified rollover and will not result in any gross income for Ruth during 2023.

Taxpayers are allowed only one traditional IRA rollover per 12-month period regardless of how many IRAs they have.[56] A Roth IRA may be rolled over tax-free into another Roth IRA.[57]

Unlike a traditional IRA, which requires withdrawals at age 73, there are no required withdrawals from a Roth IRA.[58] Such savings can be accumulated over the taxpayer's lifetime and then passed to heirs without incurring Federal income or estate taxes.[59]

Frank has both traditional IRAs and Roth IRAs. A rollover between his traditional IRA to a Roth IRA (a conversion) is not subject to the one-per-year rule. However, a rollover between his Roth IRAs will preclude a separate rollover within the one-year period between his traditional IRAs (including SEP and SIMPLE IRAs) and vice versa.

Concept Summary 9.4 provides a comparison of the key features of IRAs.

Concept Summary 9.4

Comparison of IRAs

	Traditional		
	Deductible IRA	**Nondeductible IRA**	**Roth IRA**
Maximum contribution (per year)	$6,500*	$6,500*	$6,500*
Tax-deductible contribution	Yes	No	No
Tax-free growth of income	Yes	Yes	Yes
Beginning of AGI phaseout for active participant (2023)	$73,000 single, $118,000 joint	N/A	$138,000 single, $218,000 joint
Income tax on distributions	Yes, for entire distribution	Yes, for the earnings portion	No, if satisfy 5-year holding period**
25% excise tax: age 73 insufficient distributions	Yes	Yes	No
10% early withdrawal penalty (before age 59½)	Yes, with exceptions†	Yes, with exceptions†	Yes, with exceptions†

*The total of deductible, nondeductible, and Roth IRA contributions may not exceed $6,500 per year.

**In addition, the distribution must satisfy one of the following: made after age 59½, used for qualified first-time homebuyer expenses, made to participant who is disabled, or made to a beneficiary on or after the participant's death.

†Qualified education and first-time homebuyer costs (up to $10,000) avoid the 10% penalty.

[56] *Bobrow v. Commissioner,* T.C.Memo. 2014–21; IRS Announcements 2014–15 and 2013–32.

[57] § 408A(c)(3)(B).

[58] § 408A(c)(4).

[59] Additional details on traditional and Roth IRAs can be found in IRS Publication 590, *Individual Retirement Accounts (IRAs).*

9-9 Retirement Plans for Self-Employed Individuals

A wide variety of retirement plans are available to self-employed individuals. In addition to Individual Retirement Accounts (discussed previously), self-employed individuals can establish a Keogh plan (also known as an H.R. 10 plan), a Solo § 401(k) plan, a Saving Incentive Match for Employees (SIMPLE) plan, or a Simplified Employee Pension plan (SEP).

9-9a Keogh (H.R. 10) Plans

Keogh plans are the self-employed equivalent of corporate pension plans. A Keogh plan covers the self-employed party, and it can extend to other employees of the business. These plans must be administered by an independent trustee, but if an individual elects to make all investment decisions for the plan, a *self-directed Keogh plan* is established. In such a case, the individual may prefer to invest the funds with a financial institution such as a broker, bank, or mutual fund. Investment in most collectibles is not allowed in a self-directed Keogh plan.

Contribution Limitations

A self-employed individual must consider contribution rules that apply to an employee and deduction rules that apply to an employer. Considering both, a self-employed individual may contribute annually to a *defined contribution* Keogh plan the smaller of $66,000 in 2023 ($61,000 in 2022) or 25 percent of earned income.[60] However, an employer's deduction for contributions is limited under a *defined benefit* Keogh plan. The annual benefit payable to an employee or a self-employed person is limited to the smaller of $265,000 in 2023 ($245,000 in 2022) or 100 percent of the individual's average compensation for the three highest years of employment.[61]

Earned income equals one's net earnings from self-employment[62] (i.e., the gross income derived from a trade or business less appropriate deductions).[63] Earned income is reduced by contributions to a Keogh plan on the individual's behalf and by 50 percent of any self-employment tax.[64]

Pat, a sole proprietor, has earned income of $150,000 in 2023 (after the deduction for one-half of self-employment tax). The maximum contribution Pat may make to a defined contribution Keogh plan is $37,500, the smaller of $37,500 ($150,000 × 25%) or $66,000.

Although a Keogh plan must be established before the end of the year in question, contributions may be made up to the tax return filing date for that year. Self-employed individuals who hire employees may want to choose a different retirement plan, since a Keogh plan must provide retirement benefits to all employees on a nondiscriminatory basis (i.e., the sole proprietor's employees also must be covered by the Keogh plan). This requirement could be a substantial cost to the owner. Thus, a sole proprietor with few or no employees is an ideal candidate for a Keogh plan.

9-9b Solo § 401(k) Plans

A Solo § 401(k) plan is designed for self-employed individuals with no employees (except a spouse). A self-employed person can make elective deferrals up to $22,500 in 2023. Since the employee is also the owner, an additional contribution of 20 percent of net self-employment income can be made. Total contributions cannot exceed $66,000 in 2023.[65]

A Solo § 401(k) plan is required to file an annual report with the IRS when assets exceed $250,000; if an employee is added, nondiscrimination rules apply.

[60] § 415(c)(1).

[61] § 415(b)(1).

[62] § 401(c)(2).

[63] § 1402(a).

[64] §§ 401(c)(2)(A)(v) and 164(f).

[65] See **irs.gov/retirement-plans/one-participant-401k-plans**.

Dan is 35 years old and is a sole proprietor. His net earnings from self-employment in 2023 are $100,000. Dan sets up a Solo § 401(k) plan for his retirement. Dan, as the employer, can contribute $20,000 (20% of $100,000) of non-elective contributions to the plan and make a § 401(k) elective deferral of 100% of compensation up to $22,500 for 2023. As a result, Dan can make a total retirement contribution of $42,500 ($20,000 + 22,500), which is less than the maximum combined amount allowed of $66,000.

9-9c **Savings Incentive Match Plan for Employees (SIMPLE Plans)**

Employers with 100 or fewer employees who do not maintain another qualified retirement plan may establish a *savings incentive match plan for employees* (SIMPLE plan).[66] The plan can be in the form of a § 401(k) plan or an IRA. A SIMPLE § 401(k) plan is not subject to the nondiscrimination rules that usually apply to § 401(k) plans.

All employees who received at least $5,000 in compensation from the employer during any two preceding years and who reasonably expect to receive at least $5,000 in compensation during the current year must be eligible to participate in the plan. The decision to participate is that of the employee.

The contributions made by the employee (a salary-reduction approach) must be expressed as a percentage of compensation, not as a fixed dollar amount. The SIMPLE plan must not permit the SIMPLE elective employee contribution for the year to exceed $15,500 in 2023 ($14,000 in 2022).[67] The SIMPLE elective deferral limit is increased under the catch-up provision for employees age 50 and over. The catch-up amount is $3,500 in 2023 ($3,000 in 2022).[68]

Generally, the employer must either match elective employee contributions up to 3 percent of the employee's compensation or provide nonmatching contributions of 2 percent of compensation.

No other contributions may be made to the plan other than the employee elective contribution and the required employer matching contribution (or nonmatching contribution under the 2 percent rule). All contributions are fully vested on behalf of the employee.

9-9d **Simplified Employee Pension Plans (SEPs)**

Simplified Employee Pensions—referred to as SEPs or SEP-IRAs—are retirement plans that allow the proprietor to deduct up to 20 percent of self-employment income.[69]

As with Keogh and Solo § 401(k) plans, the maximum deduction allowed is $66,000 in 2023 ($61,000 in 2022). SEPs are simple to establish and administer, and costs are minimal. Overall, SEPs are as easy to administer as deductible IRAs but have a higher annual contribution limit.

LO.7

Demonstrate the difference between accountable and nonaccountable employee plans.

9-10 **Classification of Employee Expenses**

The classification of employee expenses depends on whether the expenses are reimbursed by the employer under an accountable plan. If so, neither the reimbursement nor the expense is reported by the employee. In effect, this result is equivalent to treating the expenses as deductions *for* AGI. If the expenses are reimbursed under a nonaccountable plan or are not reimbursed at all, then they are classified as deductions

[66] § 408(p).

[67] The $15,500 statutory amount is indexed for inflation in $500 increments; § 408(p)(2)(E)(i). As a result, the maximum amount that may be contributed to the plan for an employee under age 50 for 2023 is $25,400 [$15,500 employee contributions + $9,900 ($330,000 compensation ceiling × 3%) employer match].

[68] The catch-up amount is indexed for inflation in $500 increments.

[69] § 408; the contribution for employees can be 25% of earned income up to the annual maximum.

from AGI and are classified as miscellaneous itemized deductions.[70] Given that the TCJA of 2017 suspends the deduction of miscellaneous itemized deductions from 2018 through 2025, understanding the difference between accountable and nonaccountable plans is important.

9-10a **Accountable Plans**

An **accountable plan** requires the employee to satisfy these two requirements:

- *Substantiate the Expenses.* An employee provides an *adequate accounting* by submitting a record (e.g., completing an employer-provided travel expense reimbursement form), with receipts and other substantiation, to the employer.[71]
- *Return Any Excess Reimbursement or Allowance.* An "excess reimbursement or allowance" is any amount the employee does not adequately account for as an ordinary and necessary business expense.

Substantiation

No deduction is allowed for any travel, entertainment, business gift, or listed property (e.g., automobiles and computers) expenses unless properly substantiated by adequate records. The records should contain the following information:[72]

- The amount of the expense.
- The time and place of travel or entertainment (or date of gift).
- The business purpose of the expense.
- The business relationship of the taxpayer to the person entertained (or receiving the gift).

As a result, the taxpayer must keep records (e.g., in a calendar or by other means) to document these expenses. Documentary evidence, such as itemized receipts, is required to support any lodging expenses while traveling away from home and for any other expenditure of $75 or more. If a taxpayer fails to keep adequate records, a written or oral statement of the exact details of the expense will be required, along with other corroborating evidence.[73]

Inadequate Substantiation

Ben has travel expenses substantiated only by canceled checks. The checks establish the date, place, and amount of the expenditure. Because neither the business relationship nor the business purpose is established, the deduction is disallowed.[74]

Mohammed has travel and entertainment expenses substantiated by a digital diary showing the time, place, and amount of the expenditure. He is able to provide information about the business relationship and business purpose orally. However, because he has no receipts, any expenditures of $75 or more are disallowed.[75]

---

[70] The employment-related expenses of performing artists are allowed as *for* AGI deductions; § 62(b).

[71] Reg. § 1.162–17(b)(4).

[72] § 274(d).

[73] Reg. § 1.274–5T(c)(3).

[74] *William T. Whitaker*, 56 TCM 47, T.C.Memo. 1988–418.

[75] *W. David Tyler*, 43 TCM 927, T.C.Memo. 1982–160.

Deemed Substantiation

Instead of reimbursing actual expenses for travel away from home, many employers reduce their paperwork by adopting a policy of reimbursing employees with a *per diem* allowance, a flat dollar amount per day of business travel. Of the substantiation requirements listed previously, the *amount* of the expense is proved, or *deemed substantiated*, by using such a per diem allowance or reimbursement procedure. The amount of expenses that is deemed substantiated is equal to the lesser of the per diem allowance or the amount of the Federal per diem rate.

The regular Federal per diem rate is the highest amount the Federal government will pay to its employees for lodging, meals, and incidental expenses[76] while traveling. The rates are different for different locations.[77]

The use of the standard Federal per diem rates for meals and incidental expenses also constitutes an adequate accounting. Employees and self-employed persons can use these standard allowances instead of deducting the actual cost of daily meals and incidental expenses, even if not reimbursed.

Only the amount of the expense is considered substantiated under the deemed substantiated method. Records must be maintained for the other items: place, date, business purpose of the expense, and the business relationship of the parties involved.

9-10b **Nonaccountable Plans**

A **nonaccountable plan** is a plan where an adequate accounting or return of excess amounts, or both, is not required. All expense reimbursements are included as wages on the employee's Form W–2. Any allowable expenses are deductible in the same manner as unreimbursed expenses.

Unreimbursed Employee Expenses

Unreimbursed employee business expenses (including 50 percent of any meals) are treated as miscellaneous itemized deductions and not deductible from 2018 through 2025 (see text Section 9-11). If the employee could have received but did not seek reimbursement for whatever reason, none of the employment-related expenses are deductible.

Failure to Comply with Accountable Plan Requirements

An employer may have an accountable plan and require employees to return excess reimbursements or allowances, but an employee may fail to follow the rules of the plan. In that case, the expenses and reimbursements are subject to nonaccountable plan treatment.

LO.8

Recognize the limitations on miscellaneous itemized deductions.

9-11 **Limitations on Itemized Deductions**

Most itemized deductions (*from* AGI deductions) are restricted in some way. Some are subject to limitations based on a taxpayer's AGI. For example, only those medical expenses in excess of 7.5 percent of AGI are deductible (this is often called a "floor") and charitable contributions made in cash are normally limited to a maximum of 60 percent of a taxpayer's AGI (this is often called a "ceiling"). The deduction for state and

[76]For this purpose, incidental expenses include tips and fees to porters, bellhops, hotel maids, etc. These expenses are expected to be relatively small and typically paid out in cash.

[77]*Per Diem Rates* (IRS Publication 1542) contains the list and amounts for the year. This publication is available only on the internet at **irs.gov**. Links to per diem rates also can be found at **gsa.gov**.

local taxes is limited to $10,000 each year. These limitations are discussed in Chapter 10. Casualty losses (discussed in Chapter 7) are subject to both a minimum floor (more than $100) and a 10%-of-AGI floor.

Miscellaneous itemized deductions (including employee business expenses) are also subject to limitations. From 2018 through 2025, the deduction for miscellaneous itemized deductions subject to the 2%-of-AGI floor has been suspended (these items are discussed in text Section 9-11a). A number of other itemized deductions are not subject to the 2%-of-AGI floor and remain deductible as a *from* AGI deduction (these items are discussed in text Section 9-11b).

9-11a **Miscellaneous Itemized Deductions Subject to the 2%-of-AGI Floor**

Certain miscellaneous itemized deductions, including most *unreimbursed employee business expenses*, are subject to a 2%-of-AGI floor. These expenses, which are listed below, are not deductible from 2018 through 2025.[78]

- All § 212 expenses, except expenses of producing rent and royalty income (see Chapter 6).
- All unreimbursed employee business expenses, after the 50 percent limit for meals, if applicable.
- Professional dues and subscriptions.
- Union dues and work uniforms.
- Employment-related education expenses.
- Expenses of job hunting (including employment agency fees and résumé-writing expenses).
- Home office expenses of an employee or outside salesperson.
- Legal, accounting, and tax return preparation fees.
- Hobby expenses, up to hobby income (see Chapter 6).
- Investment expenses, including investment counsel fees, subscriptions, and safe deposit box rental.
- Custodial fees relating to income-producing property or a traditional IRA or a Keogh plan.
- Appraisal fees paid to determine a casualty loss or charitable contribution.

9-11b **Itemized Deductions Not Subject to the 2%-of-AGI Floor**

Certain itemized deductions, including the following, are *not* subject to the 2%-of-AGI floor and remain deductible *from* AGI:

- Impairment-related work expenses of individuals with a disability.
- Amortizable premium on taxable bonds.
- Losses from Ponzi-type investment schemes.
- Gambling losses to the extent of gambling winnings.
- Unrecovered investment in an annuity.

---

[78]§ 67(g).

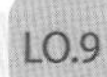

Identify tax planning ideas related to employee and self-employed business expenses.

9-12 Tax Planning

9-12a Employment Status

When considering the merits of employee or independent contractor status, much depends on which party is involved. Earlier in the chapter, we discussed some of the employer implications of this choice. If it is the worker, being self-employed carries the obvious advantage of a deduction *for* AGI category of work-related expenses and the avoidance of the limitations related to employee business expenses.

However, a self-employed individual may have other costs, such as local gross receipts taxes, license fees or taxes, franchise fees, personal property taxes, and occupation taxes. In addition, the record-keeping and filing requirements can be quite burdensome.

One of the most expensive considerations is the Social Security tax versus the self-employment tax. For an employee in 2023, for example, the Social Security tax applies at a rate of 6.2 percent on a base amount of wages of $160,200 ($147,000 in 2022) and the Medicare tax applies at a rate of 1.45 percent with no limit on the base amount. Further, a 0.9 percent additional Medicare tax applies to certain high earners. For self-employed persons, the Social Security and Medicare tax rates *double* (to 12.4 percent and 2.9 percent, respectively). Even though a deduction *for* AGI is allowed for part of the self-employment tax paid, an employee and a self-employed individual are not in the same tax position on equal amounts of earnings. The self-employment tax is explained in Chapter 12. For the applicability of these taxes to employees, see Chapter 1.

9-12b Implications of Misclassifying Workers

The Affordable Care Act (ACA) places specific compliance burdens (both financial and reporting) on employers regarding the provision of health care coverage for their employees. The rules are complex and vary according to the size of the employer (large or small) and the status of the employee (full- or part-time).[79] Because the ACA does not apply to independent contractors and part-time employees, employers may be more likely to misclassify workers. To discourage this from happening, penalties are levied on those employers who wrongfully categorize workers as independent contractors.

There are many reasons to favor classifying workers as independent contractors rather than as employees. Besides avoiding payroll taxes and income tax withholdings, the employer circumvents a myriad of state and local laws. Examples include vacation pay obligations, unemployment tax and workers' compensation requirements, and overtime and minimum wage restrictions. Because complying with these rules is costly and burdensome, some employers are motivated to misclassify their workers as independent contractors.

In the event of misclassification, two remedies are available regarding Federal employment taxes—one legislative and one administrative. The legislative option, known as Section 530 relief, absolves the employer of the employment taxes that

[79] Large employers are those with 50 or more full-time or full-time equivalent employees. Part-time employees work less than 30 hours per week.

should have been paid.[80] To obtain Section 530 relief, *all* three of the following requirements must be met:

1. The employer has a reasonable basis for *not* treating the workers as employees. Reasonable basis means reliance on any of the following:
   - A court case, a published IRS ruling, or IRS technical advice.
   - A past IRS audit that resulted in no employment tax assessment.
   - A long-standing practice of independent contractor status in the same industry.
2. The employer has consistently treated the workers as independent contractors.
3. The employer filed a Form 1099–NEC (Nonemployee Compensation) for each worker (when required).

A Federal administrative remedy for employers who are misclassifying workers is the Voluntary Classification Settlement Program (VCSP).[81] A type of amnesty arrangement, the VCSP allows the applicant to be absolved from all employment taxes that should have been paid plus any interest and penalties that would be due. To be accepted, Form 8952 [Application for Voluntary Classification Settlement Program (VCSP)] must be filed with the IRS and certain conditions met.[82] A major condition is the payment of 10 percent of the employment taxes that are usually due when workers are reclassified.

9-12c **Transportation and Travel Expenses**

Adequate detailed records of all transportation and travel expenses should be kept. Because the automatic (standard) mileage method applies to all automobiles in the same manner, a new, expensive automobile used primarily for business may generate a higher deduction using the actual cost method. Once a method is chosen, a later change may be possible. Switching from the automatic mileage method to the actual cost method is allowed if a basis adjustment is made for depreciation deemed taken (see Example 7). Switching from the actual cost method to the automatic mileage method is possible only if the taxpayer has not used the MACRS statutory percentage method and has not claimed § 179 limited expensing.

If an automobile has mixed use (i.e., both personal and business), maintaining a record of business miles driven is critical. Further, the business use portion should be realistic under the circumstances. Although a 95 percent business use allocation for a one-car family living in the suburbs is possible, the IRS might question this allocation (i.e., does the 5 percent allocated to personal use reasonably account for commuting to work, trips to the grocery store and mall, soccer practice, and dance lessons?).

If a taxpayer wants to sightsee or vacation on a business trip, scheduling business on both the Friday and Monday surrounding the weekend turns the weekend into business days for allocation purposes. It is especially crucial to schedule appropriate business days when foreign travel is involved.

---

[80] This safe harbor for withholding purposes originated in Section 530 of the Revenue Act of 1978. See IRS *Headliner*, vol. 152 (March 27, 2006). Section 530 relief does not absolve an employer of any Affordable Care Act penalties.

[81] Announcement 2011–64.

[82] The conditions to be met are identified in the instructions for Form 8952. Many of these conditions are the same as those required for Section 530 relief.

Refocus on The Big Picture

The First Job

The first issue that might arise as a result of Morgan's new job is the dependency exemption possibility. If Morgan was living at home and accepted the job late in the year, she could qualify as a dependent of her parents. If so, they also might be able to claim the qualified tuition deduction (or the lifetime learning credit). If, however, her employment began early in the year, she could not be a qualifying child (due to the self-supporting limitation) or a qualifying relative (due to the gross income limitation)—see Chapter 3.

Morgan can claim an office in the home deduction because she is using her second bedroom exclusively for her tutoring and freelance driving businesses. She can use either the Regular (actual expense) Method or the Simplified (safe harbor) Method. Under the Regular Method, the deduction would include a portion of the rent, utilities, and insurance paid. The Simplified Method would allow Morgan $5 per square foot for business space, but not more than 300 square feet, or $1,500. Since her second bedroom is 200 square feet, the Simplified Method produces a $1,000 deduction (see Example 33). Under either method, she also would be allowed to deduct other business expenses, including her software, supplies, and depreciation (or expensing) of office equipment and furnishings (e.g., computer, copier, desk, file cabinet). She must be careful, however, not to violate the "exclusive use" restriction (see Examples 28, 30, and 31) regardless of which method she uses. Morgan will use the Regular Method, since it results in a larger deduction ($3,117; see Example 33).

In addition to commuting between her apartment and her job at ECCC, Morgan also will use her car for her freelance businesses (see Example 5). Normally, she would need to make a choice between the automatic mileage method and the actual cost method. However, because she is using a car given to her by her parents (see Example 9), she will use the automatic mileage method.

In addition to her automobile expenses, Morgan should document any meal expenses she incurs while driving for Uber and other companies. However, any meals are subject to the 50 percent limitation. These expenses will be *for* AGI deductions.

Any expenses she incurs related to her job with Enrichment Child Care Center will be classified as employee business expenses. The total of all employment-related expenses is a miscellaneous itemized deduction (a *from* AGI deduction) and not deductible in 2023 (and through 2025).

Morgan must maintain adequate records regarding all of these transactions. Detailed records are particularly important in arriving at her office in the home deduction (if the Regular Method is used) and the business use of her car (for her freelancing jobs).

Key Terms

Discussion Questions

1. **LO.1** Mason performs services for Isabella. In determining whether Mason is an employee or an independent contractor, comment on the relevance of each of the factors listed below.
   a. Mason performs services only for Isabella and does not work for anyone else.
   b. Mason sets his own work schedule.
   c. Mason reports his job-related expenses on a Schedule C.
   d. Mason obtained his job skills from Isabella's training program.
   e. Mason performs the services at Isabella's business location.
   f. Mason is paid based on time worked rather than on task performed.

2. **LO.2** Milton is a resident of Mobile (Alabama) and is employed by Scaup Corporation. Because Scaup closed its Mobile office, Milton no longer has any nondeductible commuting expenses although he continues to work for Scaup. Explain why. Critical Thinking

3. **LO.2** In 2021, Emma purchased an automobile, which she uses for both business and personal purposes. Although Emma does not keep records as to operating expenses (e.g., gas, oil, and repairs), she can prove the percentage of business use and the miles driven each year. In March 2023, Emma seeks your advice as to what income tax benefit, if any, she can derive from the use of her automobile. What would you suggest? Critical Thinking Planning

4. **LO.3** Dr. Werner is a full-time professor of accounting at Pelican University. During the year, he teaches continuing education programs for CPA groups in several cities. He also serves as an expert witness in numerous lawsuits involving accounting fraud. Comment on the possible tax treatment of Dr. Werner's job-related expenses. Critical Thinking

5. **LO.4, 8** Jamie has an undergraduate degree in finance and has an established financial planning practice (a single-member LLC). To expand her knowledge base and serve her clients better, she decides to pursue a master's degree in quantitative finance at a local university. Is the full cost of this education deductible to her?

6. **LO.5** In each of the following situations, indicate whether the 50% reduction for meals applies. Assume the year is 2023.
   a. Each year, the employer awards its top salesperson an all-expense-paid trip to Jamaica.
   b. The employer has a cafeteria for its employees where meals are furnished at cost.
   c. The employer sponsors an annual Labor Day picnic for its employees.
   d. Every Christmas, the employer gives each employee a fruitcake.
   e. The taxpayer gives business gifts to her clients at Christmas.

7. **LO.5** In connection with the office in the home deduction, comment on the following:
   a. The exclusive use requirement.
   b. The distinction between *direct* and *indirect* expenses.
   c. The effect of the taxpayer's work status (i.e., employed or self-employed) on the deduction.
   d. The ownership status of the residence (i.e., owned or rented).
   e. The tax treatment of office furnishings (e.g., desk, chairs, and file cabinets).
   f. The treatment of expenses that exceed the gross income from the business.

Communications 8. **LO.5** Review the advantages and disadvantages of the Simplified Method for determining the office in the home deduction. Create a brief summary of your findings, and e-mail it to your instructor.

9. **LO.6** Regarding the tax implications of various retirement plans, comment on the following:
   a. The difference between Keogh (H.R. 10) and traditional deductible IRA plans.
   b. The difference between traditional IRA and Roth IRA plans.

10. **LO.6** Joey, who is single, is not covered by another qualified retirement plan and earns $140,000 at his job in 2023. How much can he contribute to a traditional IRA in 2023?

11. **LO.7** What tax return reporting procedures must be followed by an employee under the following circumstances?
   a. Expenses and reimbursements are equal under an accountable plan.
   b. Reimbursements at the appropriate Federal per diem rate exceed expenses, and an adequate accounting is made to the employer.
   c. Expenses exceed reimbursements under a nonaccountable plan.

Computational Exercises

12. **LO.2** Lara uses the standard mileage method for determining auto expenses. During 2023, she used her car as follows: 9,000 miles for business, 2,000 miles for personal use, 2,500 miles for a move to a new job, 1,000 miles for charitable purposes, and 500 miles for medical visits. Presuming that all the mileage expenses are allowable (i.e., not subject to percentage limitations), what is Lara's deduction for:
   a. Business?
   b. Charitable?
   c. Medical?

13. **LO.3** Tyler, a self-employed taxpayer, travels from Denver to Miami primarily on business. He spends five days conducting business and two days sightseeing. His expenses are $400 (airfare), $150 per day (meals at local restaurants), and $300 per night (lodging). What are Tyler's deductible expenses if the year is 2022? 2023?

14. **LO.3** In November 2023, Kortney (who is a self-employed management consultant) travels from Chicago to Barcelona (Spain) on business. She is gone 10 days (including two days of travel) during which time she spends five days conducting business and three days sightseeing. Her expenses are $1,500 (airfare), $200 per day (meals at local restaurants), and $400 per night (lodging). Because Kortney stayed with relatives while sightseeing, she only paid for five nights of lodging. What is Kortney's deduction for:
   a. Airfare?
   b. Meals?
   c. Lodging?

15. **LO.4** Samantha was recently employed by an accounting firm. During the year, she spends $2,500 for a CPA exam review course and begins working on a law degree in night school. Her law school expenses were $4,200 for tuition and $450 for books (which are not a requirement for enrollment in the course). Assuming no reimbursement, how much of these expenses can Samantha deduct?

16. **LO.5** In 2023, Robert takes four key clients and their spouses out to dinner at a local restaurant. Business discussions occurred over dinner. Expenses were $700 (drinks and dinner) and $140 (tips to servers). If Robert is self-employed, how much can he deduct for this event?

17. **LO.5** In 2023, the CEO of Crimson, Inc., entertains seven clients at a skybox in Memorial Stadium for a single athletic event during the year. Substantive business discussions occurred at various times during the event. The box costs $2,000 per event and seats 10 people. (The cost of a regular seat at Memorial ranges from $55 to $100.) Refreshments served during the event cost $700. How much of these costs may Crimson deduct?

18. **LO.5** Andrew sends Godiva chocolates to 10 of his key clients at Christmas. The chocolates cost $50 a box not including $4 for gift wrapping and shipping. How much can Andrew deduct?

19. **LO.5** Jayda maintains an office in her home that comprises 8% (200 square feet) of total floor space. Gross income for her business is $42,000, and her residence expenses are as follows:

Real property taxes	$2,400
Interest on mortgage	4,000
Operating expenses	2,200
Depreciation (based on 8% business use)	450

What is Jayda's office in the home deduction based on:

a. The Regular Method?

b. The Simplified Method?

20. **LO.8** In 2023, Ava, an employee, has AGI of $58,000 and the following itemized deductions:

Home office expenses	$1,200
Union dues and work uniforms	350
Unreimbursed employee expenses	415
Gambling losses to the extent of gambling winnings	890

What is Ava's total itemized deduction related to these items?

Problems

21. **LO.2** Jackson, a self-employed taxpayer, uses his automobile 90% for business and during 2023 drove a total of 14,000 business miles. Information regarding his car expenses is listed below.

Business parking	$ 140
Auto insurance	1,300
Auto club dues (includes towing service)	180
Toll road charges (business-related)	200
Oil changes and engine tune-ups	210
Repairs	160
Depreciation allowable	2,850
Fines for traffic violations (incurred during business use)	320
Gasoline purchases	2,800

What is Jackson's deduction in 2023 for the use of his car if he uses:

a. The actual cost method?

b. The automatic mileage method?

c. What records must Jackson maintain?

22. **LO.2** On July 1, 2019, Brent purchases a new automobile for $40,000. He uses the car 80% for business and drives the car for business purposes as follows: 8,000 miles in 2019, 19,000 miles in 2020, 20,000 miles in 2021, and 15,000 miles in 2022. Determine Brent's basis in the business portion of the auto as of January 1, 2023, under the following assumptions:
    a. Brent uses the automatic mileage method.
    b. Brent uses the actual cost method. [Assume that no § 179 expensing is claimed and that 200% declining-balance cost recovery with the half-year convention is used—see Chapter 8. The recovery limitation for an auto placed in service in 2019 is as follows: $10,100 (first year), $16,100 (second year), $9,700 (third year), and $5,760 (fourth year).]

23. **LO.3** Kristen, an independent management consultant, is based in Atlanta. During March and April of 2023, she is contracted by a national hardware chain to help implement revised human resource policies in Jackson (Mississippi) temporarily. During this period, Kristen flies to Jackson on Sunday night, spends the week at the district office, and returns home to Atlanta on Friday afternoon. The cost of returning home is $550, and the cost of spending the weekend in Jackson would have been $490.
    a. Presuming no reimbursement for these expenses, how much, if any, of these weekend expenses may Kristen deduct?
    b. Would your answer in part (a) change if the amounts involved were reversed (i.e., the trip home would have cost $490; staying in Jackson would have been $550)? Explain.

24. **LO.3, 5** In June 2023, Enrique and Denisse Espinosa traveled to Denver to attend a three-day conference sponsored by the American Society of Implant Dentistry. Denisse, a self-employed practicing oral surgeon, participated in scheduled technical sessions dealing with the latest developments in surgical procedures. On two days, Enrique attended group meetings where various aspects of family tax planning were discussed. On the other day, he went sightseeing. Enrique does not work for his wife, but he prepares their tax returns and handles the family investments. Expenses incurred in connection with the conference are summarized below.

Airfare (two tickets)	$2,000
Lodging (single and double occupancy are the same rate—$250 each day)	750
Meals at local restaurants ($200 × 3 days)*	600
Conference registration fee (includes $120 for Family Tax Planning sessions)	620
Car rental	300

*Split equally between Enrique and Denisse Espinosa.

How much, if any, of these expenses can the Espinosas deduct?

25. **LO.1, 3, 5** Kim works for a clothing manufacturer as a dress designer. During 2023, she travels to New York City to attend five days of fashion shows and then spends three days sightseeing. Her expenses are as follows:

Airfare	$1,500
Lodging (8 nights)	1,920
Meals at local restaurants (8 days)	1,440
Airport transportation	120

[Assume that lodging/meals are the same amount for the business and personal portion of the trip ($240 per day for lodging and $180 per day for meals).]
    a. Presuming no reimbursement, how much can Kim deduct as to the trip?
    b. Would the tax treatment of Kim's deduction differ if she was an independent contractor (rather than an employee)? Explain.

26. **LO.3** On Thursday, Justin flies from Baltimore (where the office for his sole proprietorship is located) to Cadiz (Spain). He conducts business on Friday and Tuesday; vacations on Saturday, Sunday, and Monday (a legal holiday in Spain); and returns to Baltimore on Thursday. Justin was scheduled to return home on Wednesday, but all flights were canceled due to bad weather. As a result, he spent Wednesday watching floor shows at a local casino.
    a. For tax purposes, what portion of Justin's trip is regarded as being for business?
    b. Suppose Monday was not a legal holiday. Would this change your answer to part (a)? Explain.
    c. Under either part (a) or (b), how much of Justin's airfare qualifies as a deductible business expense?

27. **LO.3** Monica, a self-employed taxpayer, travels from her office in Boston to Lisbon, Portugal, on business. Her absence of 13 days was spent as follows:

Critical Thinking
Decision Making

Thursday	Depart for and arrive at Lisbon
Friday	Business transacted
Saturday and Sunday	Vacationing
Monday through Friday	Business transacted
Saturday and Sunday	Vacationing
Monday	Business transacted
Tuesday	Depart Lisbon and return to office in Boston

    a. For tax purposes, how many days has Monica spent on business?
    b. What difference does it make?
    c. Could Monica have spent more time than she did vacationing on the trip without loss of existing tax benefits? Explain.

28. **LO.5** During 2023, Stork Associates paid $60,000 for a 20-seat skybox at Veterans Stadium for eight professional football games. Regular seats to these games range from $80 to $250 each. At one game, an employee of Stork entertained 18 clients. Stork furnished food and beverages for the event at a cost of $1,300. The game was preceded by a bona fide business discussion, and all expenses are adequately substantiated. How much may Stork deduct for this event?

29. **LO.5** During 2023, José, a self-employed technology consultant, made gifts in the following amounts:

To Haley (José's personal assistant) at Christmas	$36
To Darryl (a key client)—$3 was for gift wrapping	53
To Darryl's wife (a homemaker) on her birthday	20
To Veronica (José's office manager) at Christmas	30

In addition, on professional assistants' day, José takes Haley to lunch at a local restaurant at a cost of $82. Presuming that José has adequate substantiation, how much can he deduct?

30. **LO.5** Melanie is employed full-time as an accountant for a national hardware chain. She recently started a private consulting practice, which provides tax advice and financial planning to the general public. For this purpose, she maintains an office in her home. Expenses relating to her home for 2023 are as follows:

Real property taxes	$3,600
Interest on home mortgage	3,800
Operating expenses of home	900

Melanie's residence cost $350,000 (excluding land) and has living space of 2,000 square feet, of which 20% (400 square feet) is devoted to business. The office was placed in service in February 2022, and under the Regular Method, Melanie had an unused office in the home deduction of $800 for 2022. Presuming sufficient net income from her consulting practice, what is Melanie's office in the home deduction under the:

a. Regular Method?

b. Simplified Method?

31. **LO.5** Christine is a full-time fourth-grade teacher at Vireo Academy. During 2023, she spends $1,400 for classroom supplies. On the submission of adequate substantiation, Vireo reimburses her for $500 of these expenses—the maximum reimbursement allowed for supplies under school policy. [The reimbursement is not shown as income (Box 1) of Form W–2 given to Christine by Vireo.] What are the income tax consequences of the $1,400 if Christine:

a. Itemizes her deductions *from* AGI?

b. Chooses the standard deduction?

Planning

32. **LO.6** Amber's employer, Lavender, Inc., uses a § 401(k) plan that permits salary deferral elections by its employees. Amber's salary is $99,000, her marginal tax rate is 24%, and she is 42 years old.

a. What is the maximum amount Amber can elect for salary deferral treatment for 2023?

b. If Amber elects salary deferral treatment for the amount in part (a), how much can she save in Federal income taxes?

c. What amount would you recommend that Amber elect for salary deferral treatment for 2023, considering only the Federal income tax effects?

33. **LO.6** Shyam is a participant in a SIMPLE § 401(k) plan. He elects to contribute 4% of his $40,000 compensation to the account, and his employer contributes 3%. What amount will not vest immediately, if any?

34. **LO.6** Harvey is a self-employed accountant with earned income from the business of $320,000 (after the deduction for one-half of his self-employment tax). He uses a defined contribution Keogh plan. What is the maximum amount Harvey can contribute to his retirement plan in 2023?

35. **LO.6** Answer the following independent questions with respect to traditional IRA contributions for 2023.

a. Juan, age 41, earns a salary of $58,000 and is not an active participant in any other qualified plan. His wife, Agnes, generates no earned income. What is the maximum total deductible contribution to their IRAs?

b. Abby, age 29, reports earned income of $45,000, and her husband, Sam, reports earned income of $4,600. They are not active participants in any other qualified plan. What is the maximum contribution to their IRAs?

c. Leo's employer makes a contribution of $3,500 to Leo's simplified employee pension plan. If Leo is single, he reports earned income of $70,000, and his AGI is $55,000, what amount, if any, can he contribute to an IRA?

36. **LO.6** Jimmy establishes a Roth IRA at age 47 and contributes $89,600 over 18 years. The account is now worth $162,000. How much of these funds may Jimmy withdraw tax-free?

37. **LO.6** Carri and Dane, ages 34 and 32, respectively, have been married for 11 years, and both are active participants in employer qualified retirement plans. Their total AGI in 2023 is $231,000, and they earn salaries of $109,000 and $95,000, respectively. What amount may Carri and Dane:

a. Contribute to traditional IRAs?

b. Deduct for their contributions in part (a)?

c. Contribute to Roth IRAs?

d. Deduct for their contributions in part (c)?

38. **LO.5, 7, 8, 9** Ava recently graduated from college and is interviewing for a position in marketing. Gull Corporation has offered her a job as a sales representative that will require extensive travel and entertainment but provide valuable experience. Under the offer, she has two options: she receives a salary of $53,000, and she absorbs all expenses; she receives a salary of $39,000, and Gull reimburses for all expenses. Gull assures Ava that the $14,000 difference in the two options will be adequate to cover the expenses incurred. What issues should have an impact on Ava's choice?

Critical Thinking
Decision Making
Planning

39. **LO.1, 2, 5, 8** Complete the following table by classifying each of the independent expenditures (assume that no reimbursement takes place and that employee business expenses are not deductible).

Expense Item	Deductible *for* AGI	Deductible *from* AGI	Not Deductible
a. Tax return preparation fee incurred by an employed plumber	____	____	____
b. Safety glasses purchased by an employed pipefitter	____	____	____
c. Dues to auto club (e.g., AAA) for taxpayer who uses the automatic mileage method	____	____	____
d. Nursing refresher course for taxpayer who retired from nursing five years ago	____	____	____
e. Gambling loss not in excess of gambling gain by a self-employed architect	____	____	____
f. Contribution to Roth IRA by a self-employed attorney	____	____	____
g. Business travel expenses by a statutory employee	____	____	____
h. Job hunting expense by an elementary school teacher seeking a position as an elementary school principal	____	____	____
i. Cost of bar exam review course taken by a recent law school graduate	____	____	____

Tax Return Problems

40. David R. and Ella M. Cole (ages 39 and 38, respectively) are husband and wife who live at 1820 Elk Avenue, Denver, CO 80202. David is a self-employed consultant specializing in retail management, and Ella is a dental hygienist for a chain of dental clinics.

Communications
Critical Thinking
Tax Forms Problem

ProConnect™ Tax

- David earned consulting fees of $145,000 in 2022. He maintains his own office and pays for all business expenses. The Coles are adequately covered by the medical plan provided by Ella's employer but have chosen not to participate in its § 401(k) retirement plan.

  David's employment-related expenses for 2022 are summarized below.

Airfare	$8,800
Lodging	4,320
Meals from restaurants (during travel status)	2,400
Entertainment	3,600
Ground transportation (e.g., limos, rental cars, and taxis)	800
Business gifts	900
Office supplies (includes postage, overnight delivery, and copying)	1,500

The entertainment involved taking clients to sporting and musical events. The business gifts consisted of $50 gift certificates to a national restaurant. These were sent by David during the Christmas holidays to 18 of his major clients.

During 2022, David drove his 2020 Ford Expedition 11,000 miles for business (5,000 during the first half of 2022) and 3,000 for personal use. He purchased the Expedition on August 15, 2019, and has always used the automatic (standard) mileage method for tax purposes. Parking and tolls relating to business use total $340 in 2022.

- When the Coles purchased their present residence in April 2019, they devoted 450 of the 3,000 square feet of living space to an office for David. The property cost $440,000 ($40,000 of which is attributable to the land) and has since appreciated in value. Expenses relating to the residence in 2022 (except for mortgage interest and property taxes; see below) are as follows:

Insurance	$2,600
Repairs and maintenance	900
Utilities	4,700
Painting office area; area rugs and plants (in the office)	1,800

In terms of depreciation, the Coles use the MACRS percentage tables applicable to 39-year nonresidential real property. As to depreciable property (e.g., office furniture), David tries to avoid capitalization and uses whatever method provides the fastest write-off for tax purposes.

- Ella works at a variety of offices as a substitute when a hygienist is ill or on vacation or when one of the clinics is particularly busy (e.g., prior to the beginning of the school year). Besides her transportation, she must provide and maintain her own uniforms. Her expenses for 2022 appear below.

Uniforms	$690
State and city occupational licenses	380
Professional journals and membership dues in the American Dental Hygiene Association	340
Correspondence study course (taken online) dealing with teeth whitening procedures	420

Ella's salary for the year is $42,000, and her Form W–2 for the year shows income tax withholdings of $4,000 (Federal) and $1,000 (state) and the proper amount of Social Security and Medicare taxes.

- Besides the items already mentioned, the Coles had the following receipts during 2022:

Interest income—		
State of Colorado general purpose bonds	$2,500	
IBM bonds	800	
Wells Fargo Bank	1,200	$ 4,500
Federal income tax refund for year 2021		510
Life insurance proceeds paid by Eagle Assurance Corporation		200,000
Inheritance of savings account from Sarah Cole		50,000
Sales proceeds from two ATVs		9,000

For several years, the Coles' household has included David's divorced mother, Sarah, who has been claimed as their dependent. In late December 2021, Sarah unexpectedly died of a heart attack in her sleep. Unknown to Ella and David, Sarah had a life insurance policy and a savings account (with David as the designated beneficiary of each). In 2021, the Coles purchased two ATVs for $14,000. After several near mishaps, they decided that the sport was too dangerous. In 2022, they sold the ATVs to their neighbor.

- Additional expenditures for 2022 include:

Funeral expenses for Sarah		$ 4,500
Taxes—		
Real property taxes on personal residence	$6,400	
Colorado state income tax due (paid in April 2022 for tax year 2021)	310	6,710
Mortgage interest on personal residence (Rocky Mountain Bank)		6,600
Contributions to traditional IRAs for Ella and David ($6,000 + $6,000)		12,000

In 2022, the Coles made quarterly estimated tax payments of $6,000 (Federal) and $500 (state) for a total of $24,000 (Federal) and $2,000 (state).

Using the appropriate forms and schedules, compute the Coles' Federal income tax for 2022. Disregard the alternative minimum tax (AMT) and various education credits since these items are not discussed until later in the text (Chapter 12). Relevant Social Security numbers are:

David Cole	123-45-6788
Ella Cole	123-45-6787

During the year, the Coles purchased $20,000 of bitcoin. They do not want to contribute to the Presidential Election Campaign Fund. Also, the Coles want any overpayment of tax refunded to them and *not* applied toward next year's tax liability. David will have a self-employment tax liability; refer to Chapter 12 to compute this liability. Suggested software: ProConnect Tax.

41. Saanvi Patel (Social Security number 123-45-6785), single and age 32, lives at 3218 Columbia Drive, Spokane, WA 99210. She is employed as a regional sales manager by VITA Corporation, a manufacturer and distributor of vitamins and food supplements. During 2023, Saanvi is paid an annual salary of $83,000 and a separate travel allowance of $30,000. In order to access the travel allowance, VITA requires adequate accounting by Saanvi. Tax Computation Problem

- Saanvi participates in VITA's contributory health and § 401(k) plans. During 2023, she paid $4,500 for her share of the medical insurance and contributed $11,000 to the § 401(k) retirement plan.
- Saanvi uses her automobile 70% for business and 30% for personal. The automobile, a Toyota Avalon, was purchased new on June 30, 2021, for $37,000 (no trade-in was involved). Depreciation has been claimed using the MACRS 200% declining-balance method, and no § 179 election was made in the year of purchase. (For depreciation information, see text Section 8-3d.) During 2023, Saanvi drove 15,000 miles and incurred and paid the following expenses relating to the automobile:

Gasoline	$3,100
Insurance	2,900
Auto club dues	240
Interest on car loan	1,100
Repairs and maintenance	1,200
Parking (during business use)	600
Traffic fines (during business use)	500

- Because VITA does not have an office in Spokane, the company expects Saanvi to maintain one in her home. Out of 1,500 square feet of living space in her apartment, Saanvi has set aside 300 square feet as an office. Expenses for 2023 that relate to her home office are listed below.

Apartment rent	$18,000
Apartment utilities	4,000
Apartment insurance (renter's casualty and theft coverage)	1,600
Carpet replacement (office area only)	1,200

- Saanvi's employment-related expenses for 2023 (except for the trip to Korea; discussed next) are summarized below.

Airfare	$4,100
Lodging	3,200
Meals (at local restaurants during travel)	2,800
Transportation (taxis and airport limos)	300
Business gifts	540
Continuing education	400
Professional journals	140

Most of Saanvi's business trips involve visits to retail outlets in her region. Store managers and their key employees, as well as some suppliers, were the parties entertained. The business gifts were boxes of candy costing $30 ($25 each plus $5 for wrapping and shipping) sent to 18 store managers at Christmas. The continuing education was a noncredit course dealing with improving management skills that Saanvi took online.

- In July 2023, Saanvi traveled to Korea to investigate a new process that is being developed to convert fish parts to a solid consumable tablet form. She spent one week checking out the process and then took a one-week vacation tour of the country. The round-trip airfare was $3,600, and her expenses relating to business were $2,100 for lodging ($300 each night), $1,470 for meals, and $350 for transportation. Upon returning to the United States, Saanvi sent her findings about the process to her employer. VITA was so pleased with her report that it gave her an employee achievement award of $10,000. The award was sent to Saanvi in January 2024.
- Besides the items already mentioned, Saanvi had the following receipts in 2023:

Interest income—		
City of Tacoma general purpose bonds	$ 350	
Olympia State Bank	400	$ 750
Proceeds from property sales—		
City lot	$13,000	
Sailboat	18,000	31,000
Cash found at airport		5,000

Regarding the city lot (located in Vancouver), Saanvi purchased the property in 2008 for $16,000 and held it as an investment. Unfortunately, the neighborhood where the lot was located deteriorated, and property values declined. In 2023, Saanvi decided to cut her losses and sold the property for $13,000. The sailboat was used for pleasure and was purchased in 2019 for $16,500. Saanvi sold the boat because she purchased a new and larger model (see below). While at the Spokane airport, Saanvi found an unmarked envelope containing $5,000 in $50 bills. Because no mention of any lost funds was noted in the media, Saanvi kept the money.

- Saanvi's expenditures for 2023 (not previously noted) are summarized below.

Medical (not covered by insurance)	$6,000
State and local general sales tax	3,400
Church pledge (2023 and 2024)	6,400
Fee paid for preparation of 2022 income tax return	500
Contribution to mayor's reelection campaign fund	200
Contribution to a Coverdell education savings account (on behalf of a favorite nephew)	2,000

Saanvi keeps careful records regarding sales taxes. In 2023, the sales tax total was unusually high due to the purchase of a new sailboat. In 2023, Saanvi decided to pay her church pledge for both 2023 and 2024. The insurance premium was on a policy covering her father's life. (Saanvi is the designated beneficiary under the policy.)

Saanvi's employer withheld $8,400 for Federal income tax purposes, and she applied her $500 overpayment for 2022 toward the 2023 tax liability.

Compute Saanvi's Federal income tax payable (or refund) for 2023. In making the calculation, use the Tax Rate Schedule and disregard the application of the alternative minimum tax (AMT), which is not discussed until Chapter 12.

Research Problems

Note: Solutions to the Research Problems can be prepared by using the Thomson Reuters Checkpoint™ online tax research database, which accompanies this textbook. Solutions can also be prepared by using research materials found in a typical tax library.

Research Problem 1. Aaron, a resident of Minnesota, has been a driver for Green Delivery Service for the past six years. For this purpose, he leases a truck from Green, and his compensation is based on a percentage of the income resulting from his pickup and delivery services. Green allows its drivers to choose their 10-hour shifts and does not exercise any control on how these services are carried out (e.g., the route to be taken or the order in which parcels are delivered or picked up). Under Green's operating agreement with its drivers, Green can terminate the arrangement after 30 days' notice. In practice, however, Green allows its truckers to quit immediately without giving advance notice. The agreement also identifies the drivers as independent contractors. Green maintains no health or retirement plans for its drivers, and each year it reports their income by issuing Forms 1099–NEC (and not Forms W–2). Green requires its drivers to maintain a commercial driver's license and be in good standing with the state highway law enforcement division.

Citing the employment tax Regulations in §§ 31.3121(d)–1(c)(2) and 31.3306(i)–1(b), an IRS agent contends that Aaron is an independent contractor and, therefore, is subject to the self-employment tax. Based on *Peno Trucking, Inc.* (93 TCM 1027, T.C.Memo. 2007–66), Aaron disagrees and contends that he is an employee (i.e., not self-employed). Who is correct? Why?

Research Problem 2. Your client, a large construction firm organized as a C corporation, allows certain employees (including the president of the corporation) to use its company-owned airplane for nonbusiness flights. The employees include the value of the flights in their income. Your client is uncertain about how to treat the expenses related to these nonbusiness flights. In certain situations, the expenses of operating the plane are more than the income imputed to the employees, and in certain circumstances, the expenses are less. In doing some of its own research, your client found *Sutherland Lumber-Southwest, Inc.* [114 T.C. 197 (2000)], which suggests that as long as the employee imputes income, the full amount of the related expenses can be deducted. [The decision in the case was affirmed on appeal, *Sutherland Lumber-Southwest, Inc. v. Comm.*, 2001–2 USTC ¶50,503, 88 AFTR 2d 2001–5026, 255 F.3d 495 (CA–8).] Should your client follow the approach in *Sutherland*? Explain.

Use internet tax resources to address the following questions. Look for reliable websites and blogs of the IRS and other government agencies, media outlets, businesses, tax professionals, academics, think tanks, and political outlets.

Communications

Research Problem 3. Prepare a blog post for the "Online Tutor Match Company" to explain to its freelancers the tax implications of their work. Topics should include (1) what records to keep (both for income and expenses), (2) what unique situations freelancers face (e.g., home office deductions; self-employment status), and (3) what tax forms must be filed and (briefly) how to prepare those forms [e.g., Schedule C (Form 1040)].

Communications

Research Problem 4. One of your roommates is working part-time for your university's athletic director. Given the implications of "name, image, and likeness" (NIL) payments for college athletes, the athletic director would like to have a "frequently asked questions" (FAQ) developed for the student-athletes. Your roommate suggested that an accounting major could research and draft such a document (and has suggested you do the work).

Research the tax and reporting implications of NIL payments and develop a comprehensive FAQ (two to three pages). At a miniimum, the FAQ should provide information on what constitutes a NIL payment (i.e., provide a definition), whether the student-athlete is an independent contractor, and the tax reporting implications of NIL payments for the student athlete (e.g., what records must be kept, what tax forms are likely to be received, and what tax forms must be filed). Share your FAQ document with your instructor.

Communications

Research Problem 5. Download IRS Form 1099–K and its instructions from the IRS website. What is the purpose of the form, and when is it used? Go to the Square, Inc. website (**squareup.com**), and search for information about this form. Summarize what you discover in an e-mail to your instructor.

Research Problem 6. Download IRS Form 8919 (Uncollected Social Security and Medicare Tax on Wages) from the IRS website. According to the instructions, who should file this form?

Becker CPA Review Questions

Becker

1. In the current year, Barlow moved from Chicago to Miami to start a new job, incurring costs of $1,200 to move household goods and $2,500 in temporary living expenses. Barlow was not reimbursed for any of these expenses. What amount should Barlow deduct as an itemized deduction for moving expense?

   a. $0
   b. $1,200
   c. $2,500
   d. $3,700

2. Bob and Nancy are married and file a joint return in 2022. They are both under age 50 and employed, with wages of $50,000 each. Their total AGI is $117,000. Neither of them is an active participant in a qualified plan. What is the maximum traditional IRA deduction they can take for the current year?

   a. $0
   b. $6,000
   c. $9,600
   d. $12,000

Chapter 10

Deductions and Losses: Certain Itemized Deductions

Learning Objectives: *After completing Chapter 10, you should be able to:*

LO.1 Distinguish between deductible and nondeductible personal expenses.

LO.2 Define medical expenses and compute the medical expense deduction.

LO.3 Contrast deductible taxes with nondeductible fees, licenses, and other charges.

LO.4 Explain the Federal income tax treatment of property taxes, state and local income taxes, and sales taxes.

LO.5 Distinguish between deductible and nondeductible interest, and apply the appropriate limitations to deductible interest.

LO.6 Recognize charitable contributions, and identify their related measurement problems and percentage limitations.

LO.7 List the expenses that are deductible as other itemized deductions.

LO.8 Identify tax planning strategies to maximize the benefit of itemized deductions.

Chapter Outline

ISTOCK.COM/IZUSEK

The Big Picture

Impact of Itemized Deductions on Major Purchases

John and Kiara Williamson, a young professional couple, have been renting an apartment in Atlanta, Georgia, since they were married. Their income has grown as they've become more established in their careers, and they now believe the time has come to purchase their own home. In addition, their desire to buy a home now may be coming at a good time because John's mother, Martha, needs to move in with them due to her declining health, and their current apartment is too small to accommodate her. John and Kiara's current monthly rent is $2,000, but they are willing to spend up to $2,600 per month on an after-tax basis for their first home.

After months of house hunting, they have found the perfect home, but they are concerned it may be too expensive. If they acquire a standard mortgage to finance the purchase of the home, the total cash outlay during the first year of ownership will be $43,000 ($2,000 principal payments, $37,000 interest payments, and $4,000 real estate taxes). Alternatively, if they use their retirement and taxable investments to secure the home financing, they can qualify for a lower interest rate and thereby reduce the interest charge from $37,000 to $35,000. They expect their Federal AGI to be about $200,000 and their taxable income to range between $170,000 and $185,000 for the year. John and Kiara have not itemized their deductions in prior years because the amount of their qualifying expenses has been just below the standard deduction amount. Assume that the Willliamsons face a 6 percent state income tax rate (after any Federal tax benefit).

Can John and Kiara Williamson afford to pursue their dream of home ownership?

Read the chapter and formulate your response.

Framework 1040 **Tax Formula for Individuals**

This chapter covers the boldfaced portions of the Tax Formula for Individuals that was introduced in Concept Summary 3.1 on p. 3-3. Below those portions are the sections of Form 1040 where the results are reported.

Income *(broadly defined)*	$xx,xxx
Less: Exclusions	(x,xxx)
Gross income	$xx,xxx
Less: Deductions *for* adjusted gross income	**(x,xxx)**

FORM 1040 (Schedule 1)

13	Health savings account deduction. Attach Form 8889
17	Self-employed health insurance deduction
21	Student loan interest deduction

Adjusted gross income	$xx,xxx
Less: The greater of total itemized deductions *or* the standard deduction	**(x,xxx)**

FORM 1040 (p. 1)

12	**Standard deduction or itemized deductions** (from Schedule A)

Personal and dependency exemptions*	(x,xxx)
Deduction for qualified business income**	(x,xxx)
Taxable income	$xx,xxx
Tax on taxable income *(see Tax Tables or Tax Rate Schedules)*	$ x,xxx
Less: Tax credits *(including income taxes withheld and prepaid)*	(xxx)
Tax due (or refund)	$ xxx

* Exemption deductions are not allowed from 2018 through 2025.
** Only applies from 2018 through 2025.

LO.1

Distinguish between deductible and nondeductible personal expenses.

As a general rule, personal expenses are not deductible (see § 262 of the Code). However, Congress has chosen to allow certain personal expenses to be deducted as itemized deductions. Personal expenses that are deductible as itemized deductions include medical expenses, certain taxes, mortgage interest, and charitable contributions. These (and other) personal expenses allowed as itemized deductions are covered in this chapter. Although certain exceptions exist (e.g., certain alimony and traditional IRA contributions are deductible *for* AGI), personal expenses not specifically allowed as itemized deductions by the tax law are nondeductible.

Certain business and investment expenses are also deductible, like interest expense on loans to acquire investment assets (e.g., publicly traded securities) and state income taxes on business and investment income. These rules are covered in this chapter and Chapter 11.

Allowable itemized deductions are deductible *from* AGI in arriving at taxable income if the taxpayer *elects* to itemize. A taxpayer will elect to itemize when total itemized deductions exceed the standard deduction based on the taxpayer's filing status.[1]

Itemized deductions are reported on Schedule A (Form 1040) and filed with an individual's Federal income tax return (Form 1040).

The Big Picture

Return to the facts of *The Big Picture* on p. 10-1. John and Kiara Williamson will discover that with the purchase of a home, they will be able to itemize their deductions for the first time instead of claiming the standard deduction. Assuming that the home mortgage interest expense and real estate taxes meet the requirements discussed in this chapter, they can be deducted *from* AGI because their total will exceed the amount of the standard deduction for a married couple filing a joint return. Other qualifying expenses, including up to $10,000 of state and local taxes as well as charitable contributions, also will be deductible as itemized deductions. All of these items provide a tax benefit to the Williamsons.

[1]See §§ 63(c) and (d), respectively, for the definitions of the terms *standard deduction* and *itemized deductions.*

10-1 Medical Expenses

LO.2

Define medical expenses and compute the medical expense deduction.

Medical expenses paid for the care of the taxpayer, spouse, and dependents are allowed as an itemized deduction to the extent the expenses are not reimbursed. The **medical expense** deduction is limited to the amount by which these expenses *exceed* 7.5 percent of the taxpayer's AGI.[2]

The threshold percentage, sometimes referred to as a "floor," is used to restrict deductions, because expenses below the floor are not deductible. Here, the floor is significant. Only medical expenses *in excess* of the "7.5%-of-AGI floor" are deductible. As a result, a medical expense deduction is rare (especially for high-income taxpayers; these taxpayers are also likely to have most of their medical expenses covered by health insurance).

The Big Picture

Example 2

Return to the facts of *The Big Picture* on p. 10-1. If, as expected, the Williamsons' AGI for the year is $200,000, to receive a tax benefit from any unreimbursed medical expenses, they must itemize their deductions and have more than $15,000 ($200,000 × 7.5%) of those expenses.

If they accumulate $27,000 of unreimbursed medical expenses during the year and itemize their deductions, their total itemized deductions will increase by only $12,000 ($27,000 unreimbursed medical expenses − $15,000 AGI floor).

10-1a Medical Expenses Defined

The term *medical care* includes expenses incurred for the "diagnosis, cure, mitigation, treatment, or prevention of disease, or for the purpose of affecting any structure or function of the body."[3] A *partial* list of deductible and nondeductible medical items appears in Exhibit 10.1.

Exhibit 10.1 Examples of Deductible and Nondeductible Medical Expenses Paid by Taxpayer

Deductible	Nondeductible
Medical (including dental, mental, and hospital) care	Funeral, burial, or cremation expenses
Prescription drugs and insulin	Over-the-counter medicines (except insulin)
Personal protective equipment to prevent spread of COVID-19; COVID-19 home testing kit	Bottled water
Special equipment:	Toiletries, cosmetics
• Wheelchairs	Diaper service, maternity clothes
• Crutches	Programs for the *general* improvement of health:
• Artificial limbs	• Weight reduction
• Eyeglasses (including contact lenses)	• Health spas
• Hearing aids	• Social activities (e.g., dancing and swimming lessons)
Transportation for medical care	Unnecessary cosmetic surgery
Medical and hospital insurance premiums	Illegal operations or treatments
Long-term care insurance premiums (subject to limitations)	Non-prescribed controlled substances
Cost of alcohol and drug rehabilitation	
Certain costs to stop smoking	
Weight reduction programs related to obesity	

[2] § 213(a).

[3] § 213(d)(1)(A).

A medical expense does not have to relate to a particular ailment to be deductible. Because the definition of medical care is broad enough to cover preventive measures, the cost of periodic physical and dental exams qualifies even for a taxpayer in good health.

Amounts paid for unnecessary *cosmetic surgery* are not deductible medical expenses. Cosmetic surgery is necessary—and, therefore, deductible—when it improves the effects of (1) a deformity arising from a congenital abnormality, (2) a personal injury, or (3) a disfiguring disease.[4]

Jacob, age 75, paid $21,000 to a plastic surgeon for a face-lift. Jacob merely wanted to improve his appearance. The $21,000 does not qualify as a medical expense because the surgery was unnecessary.

In contrast, Marge's face is disfigured as a result of a serious automobile accident. Here, the cost of restorative cosmetic surgery is deductible as a medical expense.

The cost of care in a *nursing home or home for the aged*, including meals and lodging, is a deductible medical expense if the primary reason for being in the home is to get medical care. If the primary reason for being there is personal, any costs for medical or nursing care are deductible medical expenses, but the cost of meals and lodging must be excluded.[5]

Norman has a chronic heart ailment. In October, his family decides to place Norman in a nursing home equipped to provide medical and nursing care. Total nursing home expenses amount to $80,000 during the year. Of this amount, $50,000 is directly attributable to medical and nursing care.

Because Norman is in need of significant medical and nursing care and is placed in the facility primarily for this purpose, all $80,000 of the nursing home costs are deductible (subject to the AGI floor, explained earlier).

Tuition expenses of a dependent at a special school for a mentally or physically handicapped individual may be deductible as a medical expense. The deduction is allowed if a principal reason for sending the individual to the school is the school's special resources for alleviating the infirmities. In this case, the cost of meals and lodging, in addition to the tuition, are deductible medical expenses.[6]

Jason's daughter Jasmine attended public school through the seventh grade. Because Jasmine was a poor student, she was examined by a psychiatrist who concluded that Jasmine has dyslexia. Acting on the psychiatrist's recommendation, Jason enrolls Jasmine in a private school so that she can receive individual attention. The school specializes in students with learning disabilities and has a program of study designed to help students with dyslexia (including a staff of educational and psychological professionals who have developed the specialized curriculum).

The expense related to Jasmine's attendance is deductible as a medical expense. The cost of any psychiatric care also qualifies as a medical expense.[7]

10-1b **Capital Expenditures for Medical Purposes**

When capital expenditures are incurred for medical purposes, they must be deemed medically necessary by a physician and used primarily by the patient. In addition, their costs must be reasonable. Examples include dust elimination systems,[8] elevators,[9] and vans specially designed for wheelchair-bound taxpayers. Other expenditures that may qualify

[4] § 213(d)(9)(A).

[5] Reg. § 1.213–1(e)(1)(v). In general, medical care is required if a taxpayer is deemed to be chronically ill and under a prescribed plan of care. A taxpayer is chronically ill if he or she cannot perform at least two daily living tasks (dressing, eating, bathing, toileting, moving from one place to another, continence) for 90 days or more [§ 7702B(c)].

[6] Reg. § 1.213–1(e)(1)(v)(a). See *Donald R. Pfeifer*, 37 TCM 816, T.C.Memo. 1978–189, *aff'd* 79–2 USTC ¶9518 (CA–10). Also see Rev.Rul. 78–340. Based on recent rulings, the IRS is allowing a deduction where there is a diagnosis of a neurologically based learning disability or other handicap, leading to a recommendation of and attendance at an institution specially equipped to help the student overcome the handicap.

[7] Ltr.Rul. 200521003.

[8] Ltr.Rul. 7948029.

[9] *Riach v. Frank*, 62–1 USTC ¶9419, 9 AFTR 2d 1263, 302 F.2d 374 (CA–9).

are swimming pools (if the taxpayer does not have access to a neighborhood pool) and air conditioners if they do not become permanent improvements (e.g., window units).[10]

Both a capital expenditure for a permanent improvement and related operating and maintenance costs may qualify as medical expenses. The allowable costs are deductible in the year incurred. Although depreciation is required for most other capital expenditures, it is not required for those qualifying for medical purposes (in other words, the entire cost of a qualifying capital expenditure is immediately deductible).

A permanent capital improvement that ordinarily would not have a medical purpose qualifies as a medical expense if it is directly related to prescribed medical care (e.g., an elevator in a personal residence). Here, the cost is deductible to the extent it *exceeds* the increase in value of the related property. Appraisal costs related to capital improvements are not medical expenses. Instead, these costs are classified as miscellaneous itemized deductions (expenses incurred in the determination of the taxpayer's tax liability).[11] However, the deduction for miscellaneous itemized deductions has been suspended from 2018 through 2025 (see text Section 10-6).

Fred is afflicted with heart disease. His physician advises him to install an elevator in his residence so that he will not be required to climb the stairs. The cost of installing the elevator is $10,000, and the increase in the value of the residence is determined to be only $4,000.

Therefore, $6,000 ($10,000 − $4,000) is treated as a medical expense. Additional utility costs to operate the elevator and maintenance costs are also medical expenses as long as the medical reason for the capital expenditure continues to exist.

The full cost of certain home-related capital expenditures incurred to enable a *physically handicapped* individual to live independently and productively qualifies as a medical expense. Qualifying costs include expenditures for constructing entrance and exit ramps to the residence, widening hallways and doorways to accommodate wheelchairs, installing support bars and railings in bathrooms and other rooms, and adjusting electrical outlets and fixtures.[12] These expenditures are only subject to the AGI floor; the increase in the home's value is deemed to be zero.

10-1c **Medical Expenses Incurred for Spouse and Dependents**

In computing the medical expense deduction, a taxpayer may include medical expenses for a spouse and for a person who was a dependent at the time the expenses were paid or incurred. Of the requirements that normally apply in determining dependency status, neither the gross income nor the joint return test applies in determining dependency status for medical expense deduction purposes.[13]

William (age 22) is married and a full-time student at a university. During the year, William incurred medical expenses that were paid by Sheba (William's mother). She provided more than half of William's support for the year.

Even if William files a joint return with his wife, Sheba may claim the medical expenses she paid for him. Sheba would combine William's expenses with her own before applying the AGI floor.

For *divorced persons* with children, a special rule applies to the noncustodial parent. The noncustodial parent may claim any medical expenses paid even though the children are not the noncustodial parent's dependents.

Sam and Joan were divorced last year, and Joan was awarded custody of their child, Keith. During the current year, Sam pays $2,500 of Keith's medical bills. Together, Sam and Joan provide more than half of Keith's support.

Even though Keith is Joan's dependent, Sam can combine the $2,500 of medical expenses that he pays for Keith with his own when calculating his medical expense deduction.

---

[10] Reg. § 1.213–1(e)(1)(iii).

[11] § 212(3).

[12] For a complete list of the items that qualify, see Rev.Rul. 87–106.

[13] §§ 213(a) and (d)(5). Refer to text Section 3-4 for discussion of the dependency requirements.

10-1d **Transportation, Meal, and Lodging Expenses for Medical Treatment**

Payments for transportation to and from a point of treatment for medical care are deductible as medical expenses (subject to the AGI floor). These costs include bus, taxi, train, or plane fare; charges for ambulance service; and out-of-pocket expenses for the use of an automobile. A mileage allowance of 22 cents per mile for 2023 may be used instead of actual out-of-pocket automobile expenses.[14] Whether the taxpayer chooses to claim out-of-pocket automobile expenses or the 22 cents per mile automatic mileage option, related parking fees and tolls also can be deducted. Also included are transportation expenditures for someone like a family member or nurse who must accompany the patient. The cost of meals while en route to obtain medical care is not deductible.

A deduction is allowable for lodging while away from home for medical care if the following requirements are met:[15]

- The lodging is primarily for and essential to medical care.
- Medical care is provided by a physician in a licensed hospital or a similar medical facility (e.g., a clinic).
- The lodging is not lavish or extravagant.
- There is no significant element of personal pleasure in the travel.

The deduction for lodging expenses cannot exceed $50 *per* night for *each* person. The lodging deduction is allowed not only for the patient but also for anyone who must travel with the patient.

The Big Picture

Example 9

Return to the facts of *The Big Picture* on p. 10-1. John's mother, Martha, eventually moves in with the Williamsons because of her declining health, and she becomes their dependent. Later, John is advised by Martha's physician that she needs specialized treatment for her heart condition. Consequently, John and Martha fly to Cleveland, Ohio, where Martha receives the therapy at a heart clinic on an outpatient basis. Expenses in connection with the trip are as follows:

Round-trip airfare ($250 each)	$500
Lodging in Cleveland for two nights ($120 each per night)	480

Assuming that the Williamsons itemize their deductions (including medical expenses), the medical expense deduction for transportation is $500 and the medical expense deduction for lodging is $200 ($50 per night per person). Because of the severity of Martha's health condition, it is assumed that John's accompanying her is justified.

No deduction is allowed for the cost of meals unless they are part of the medical care and are furnished at a medical facility. If deductible, these meals are not subject to the 50 percent limit applicable to business meals (see text Section 9-6).

10-1e **Amounts Paid for Medical Insurance Premiums**

Medical insurance premiums (including Medicare insurance costs withheld from a Social Security recipient's monthly benefits) are included with other medical expenses subject to the AGI floor. Premiums paid by the taxpayer under a group plan or an individual plan are included as medical expenses. If an employer pays all or part of the taxpayer's medical insurance premiums, the amount paid by the employer is not included in the employee's gross income (and these amounts are not deductible by the employee). However, the medical insurance premiums paid by the employer are deductible as business expenses on the employer's tax return.

[14] This amount is adjusted periodically; see Notice 2023-3. In 2022, the allowance was 18 cents per mile for the first half of the year and 22 cents per mile for the second half of the year.

[15] § 213(d)(2).

If a taxpayer is *self-employed*, insurance premiums paid for medical coverage are deductible as a *business* expense (*for* AGI).[16] The deduction *for* AGI is allowed for premiums paid for the taxpayer, the taxpayer's spouse, and dependents of the taxpayer. However, this deduction is not allowed if the taxpayer (or taxpayer's spouse) is eligible to participate in an employer-provided health plan.

The Big Picture

Return to the facts of *The Big Picture* on p. 10-1. John Williamson is the sole practitioner in his unincorporated accounting practice. During the year, he paid health insurance premiums of $12,000 for his own coverage and $8,000 for coverage for his wife, Kiara. John can deduct $20,000 as a business deduction (*for* AGI) in computing their taxable income.

Taxpayers also may include premiums paid on qualified long-term care insurance contracts in medical expenses, subject to limitations based on the age of the insured. For 2023, the per-person limits range from $480 for taxpayers age 40 and under to $5,960 for taxpayers over age 70.[17]

10-1f **Year of Deduction**

Regardless of a taxpayer's method of accounting, medical expenses are deductible only in the year *paid*. In effect, individual taxpayers are on a cash basis for the medical expense deduction. One exception, however, is allowed for deceased taxpayers. If the medical expenses are paid within one year from the day following the day of death, they can be treated as being paid at the time they were *incurred*. As a result, these expenses may be reported on the final income tax return of the decedent or on earlier returns if incurred before the year of death.

No current deduction is allowed for payment for medical care to be rendered in the future unless the taxpayer is under an obligation to make the payment. Whether an obligation to make the payment exists depends on the policy of the physician or the institution furnishing the medical care.

Upon the recommendation of his regular dentist, in December 2023, Terrell consults Dr. Smith, a prosthodontist, who specializes in crown and bridge work. Dr. Smith tells Terrell that he can do the necessary restorative work for $12,000 and that he requires all new patients to prepay 40% of the total cost of the procedure. Accordingly, Terrell pays $4,800 in December 2023. The balance of $7,200 is paid when the work is completed in January 2024.

Under these circumstances, the qualifying medical expense deductions are $4,800 for 2023 and $7,200 in 2024. The result would be the same even if Terrell prepaid the full $12,000 in 2023.

10-1g **Reimbursements**

If medical expenses are reimbursed in the same year as paid, the reimbursement merely reduces the amount that would otherwise qualify for the medical expense deduction. But what happens if the reimbursement occurs in a later year than the expenditure? In computing casualty losses, any reasonable prospect of recovery must be considered (refer to text Section 7-3). For medical expenses, however, any expected reimbursement is disregarded in measuring the amount of the deduction. Instead, the reimbursement is accounted for separately in the year in which it occurs.

Under the *tax benefit rule*, a taxpayer who receives an insurance reimbursement for medical expenses deducted in a previous year must include the reimbursement in income up to the amount of the deductions that decreased taxable income in the earlier

[16] § 162(l).

[17] The amounts for 2022 were $450 for taxpayers age 40 and under and $5,640 for taxpayers over age 70. See IRS Publication 502, *Medical and Dental Expenses*, for details relating to requirements for deducting costs associated with qualified long-term care insurance contracts.

year. A taxpayer who did not itemize deductions in the year the expenses were paid did not receive a tax benefit and is *not* required to include a reimbursement in gross income.

Daniel had AGI of $45,000 for 2023. He was injured in a car accident and paid $4,300 for hospital expenses and $1,700 for doctor bills. Daniel also incurred medical expenses of $600 for his dependent child. In 2024, Daniel was reimbursed $950 by his insurance company for the medical expenses attributable to the car accident. His deduction for medical expenses in 2023 is computed as follows:

Hospitalization	$ 4,300
Bills for doctor's services	1,700
Medical expenses for dependent	600
Total	$ 6,600
Less: Medical expense floor (7.5% of $45,000)	(3,375)
Medical expense deduction (assuming that Daniel itemizes his deductions)	$ 3,225

Assume that Daniel would have elected to itemize his deductions even if he had no medical expenses in 2023. If the reimbursement for medical care had occurred in 2023, the medical expense deduction would have been only $2,275 [$6,600 (total medical expenses) − $950 (reimbursement) − $3,375 (floor)] and Daniel would have paid more income tax.

Because the reimbursement was made in a subsequent year, Daniel will include $950 in gross income for 2024. If Daniel had not itemized in 2023, he would *not* have included the $950 reimbursement in 2024 gross income because he would have received no tax benefit for the medical expenses in 2023.

10-1h Health Savings Accounts

Qualifying individuals may make deductible contributions to a **Health Savings Account (HSA)**.[18] A taxpayer can use an HSA in conjunction with a high-deductible medical insurance policy to help reduce the overall cost of medical coverage. Converting from a low-deductible to a high-deductible plan generally can save an individual a considerable amount in premiums. The high-deductible policy provides coverage for extraordinary medical expenses (in excess of the deductible), and expenses not covered by the policy can be paid with funds withdrawn tax-free from the HSA.

Antonio, who is married and has three dependent children, carries a high-deductible medical insurance policy with a deductible of $4,400. He establishes an HSA and contributes the maximum allowable amount to the HSA in 2023.

During 2023, Antonio's family incurs medical expenses of $7,000. The high-deductible policy covers $2,600 of the expenses ($7,000 expenses − $4,400 deductible). Antonio may withdraw $4,400 from the HSA to pay the medical expenses not covered by the high-deductible policy.

High-Deductible Plans

High-deductible policies are less expensive than low-deductible policies, so taxpayers with low medical costs can benefit from the lower premiums and use funds from the HSA to pay costs not covered by the high-deductible policy. A plan must meet two requirements to qualify as a high-deductible plan.[19]

1. The annual deductible in 2023 is not less than $1,500 for self-only coverage ($3,000 for family coverage).
2. The annual limit in 2023 on total out-of-pocket costs (excluding premiums) under the plan does not exceed $7,500 for self-only coverage ($15,000 for family coverage).

[18] § 223(a). An HSA is a qualified trust or custodial account administered by a qualified HSA trustee, which can be a bank, an insurance company, or another IRS-approved trustee. § 223(d).

[19] § 223(c)(2) and Rev. Proc. 2022–24. In 2022, the annual deductible limits were $1,400 (self-only coverage) and $2,800 (family coverage), and the annual out-of-pocket cost limits were $7,050 (self-only coverage) and $14,100 (family coverage).

Tax Treatment of HSA Contributions and Distributions

To establish an HSA, a taxpayer contributes funds to a custodial account.[20] As illustrated in the preceding example, funds can be withdrawn from an HSA to pay medical expenses that are not covered by the high-deductible policy. The following general tax rules apply to HSAs:

1. Contributions made by the taxpayer to an HSA are a deduction *for* AGI (i.e., the contributions reduce gross income in arriving at AGI). As a result, the taxpayer does not need to itemize to take the deduction.
2. Earnings on HSAs are not subject to taxation unless distributed, in which case taxability depends on the way the funds are used.[21]

    - Distributions from HSAs are excluded from gross income if they are used to pay for medical expenses not covered by the high-deductible policy.
    - Distributions that are not used to pay for medical expenses are included in gross income and are subject to an additional 20 percent penalty if made before age 65, death, or disability. Any distributions made by reason of death or disability and distributions made after the HSA beneficiary becomes eligible for Medicare are taxed but not penalized.

HSAs have at least two other attractive features. First, an HSA is portable. Taxpayers who switch jobs can take their HSAs with them. Second, anyone under age 65 who has a high-deductible plan and is not covered by another policy that is not a high-deductible plan can establish an HSA.

Deductible Amount

The annual deduction for contributions to an HSA is limited to an amount that depends on whether the taxpayer has self-only coverage or family coverage. The annual limit for an individual who has self-only coverage in 2023 is $3,850, and the annual limit for an individual who has family coverage in 2023 is $7,750. These amounts are subject to annual cost-of-living adjustments.[22] An eligible taxpayer who has attained age 55 by the end of the tax year may make an additional annual contribution in 2023 of up to $1,000. This additional amount is referred to as a *catch-up* contribution. A deduction is not allowed after the individual becomes eligible for Medicare coverage.

Determining the Maximum HSA Contribution Deduction

Liu (age 45), who is married and self-employed, carries a high-deductible medical insurance policy with family coverage and an annual deductible of $4,000. In addition, he has established an HSA. Liu's maximum annual deductible contribution to the HSA in 2023 is $7,750.

During 2023, Adam, who is self-employed, made 12 monthly payments of $1,200 for an HSA contract that provides medical insurance coverage with a $3,600 deductible. The plan covers Adam, his spouse, and two children. Of the $1,200 monthly fee, $675 was for the high-deductible policy and $525 was deposited into an HSA.

Because Adam is *self-employed*, he can deduct $8,100 of the amount paid for the high-deductible policy ($675 per month × 12 months) as a deduction *for* AGI (refer to Example 10 and related discussion). In addition, he can deduct the $6,300 ($525 × 12) paid to the HSA as a deduction *for* AGI. Note that the $6,300 HSA deduction does not exceed the $7,750 annual ceiling.

[20] § 223(d).

[21] § 223(f).

[22] § 223(b)(2). See Rev.Proc. 2022–24. The annual limits were $3,650 and $7,300 in 2022.

10-1i **Affordable Care Act Provisions**

Information about the tax provisions of the Affordable Care Act can be found in an online appendix to the text.

LO.3

Contrast deductible taxes with nondeductible fees, licenses, and other charges.

10-2 **Taxes**

A deduction is allowed for *certain* state and local taxes paid or accrued by a taxpayer.[23]

10-2a **Deductibility as a Tax**

It is important to understand the difference between a tax and a fee, because fees are not deductible unless incurred as a business expense or as an expense in the production of income. Here is the IRS definition of a tax:

> The word *taxes* has been defined as an enforced contribution, exacted pursuant to legislative authority in the exercise of taxing power, and imposed and collected for the purpose of raising revenue to be used for public or governmental purposes and not as payment for some special privilege granted or service rendered.[24]

As a result, fees for dog licenses, automobile inspections, automobile titles and registration, hunting and fishing licenses, bridge and highway tolls, driver's licenses, parking meter deposits, and postage are not taxes.

Not all taxes are deductible. For example, Federal income taxes are not deductible. Other taxes are not deductible by individuals if they relate to personal activities (rather than business activities). An example is excise taxes included in the cost of purchasing gasoline. Deductible and nondeductible taxes are summarized in Exhibit 10.2.

State and Local Taxes—*For* AGI versus *From* AGI

State and local taxes imposed directly on business or rental property are deductible *for* AGI. For example, real property taxes imposed on the buildings or personal property taxes imposed on the equipment used by a sole proprietor are deductible as a business expense [*for* AGI; reported on Schedule C (Form 1040)]. Real property taxes imposed on an individual's rental property are also deductible *for* AGI [reported on Schedule E (Form 1040)].

In contrast, real property taxes imposed on an individual's personal residence are only deductible if the individual itemizes deductions [i.e., *from* AGI; reported on Schedule A (Form 1040)]. Additionally, real property taxes imposed on investment property (e.g., undeveloped land held for investment) are deductible as an itemized deduction (and not subject to the annual cap on state and local taxes discussed below).

Generally, state and local *income* taxes are considered to be only indirectly imposed on an individual's business and investment activity. Consider a sole proprietor with income who is operating in a state that imposes an income tax. This business owner pays state income taxes on this business income. The calculation of this state income tax, though, depends on other income and deductions of the sole proprietor as well as filing status and tax credits. As a result, the income tax is *not* directly imposed on the sole proprietorship business income (unlike property taxes that *are* directly imposed on the property used by the business). Since the income tax is *not* directly imposed on the business income, the state income tax is only deductible *from* AGI.

Changes made by Congress in 2017 make more relevant the distinction between state and local taxes *directly* imposed on a business versus those taxes *indirectly* imposed, as explained next.[25]

[23]Most deductible taxes are listed in § 164, and nondeductible items are included in § 275.

[24]Rev.Rul. 81–191.

[25]Rev.Rul. 58–25 and Rev.Rul. 81–288.

Exhibit 10.2 Deductible and Nondeductible Taxes

Deductible	Nondeductible
State, local, and foreign real property taxes	Federal income taxes
State and local personal property taxes	FICA taxes imposed on employees
State and local income taxes *or* sales/use taxes	Employer FICA taxes paid on domestic household workers
Foreign income taxes	Estate, inheritance, and gift taxes
	Federal, state, and local excise taxes (e.g., gasoline, tobacco, and spirits)
	Foreign income taxes if the taxpayer chooses the foreign tax credit option
	Taxes on real property to the extent these taxes are to be apportioned and treated as imposed on another taxpayer

Overall Limit on State and Local Taxes

From 2018 through 2025, the deduction for state and local taxes (including property taxes and either income taxes or sales taxes) is limited to a maximum of $10,000 per year ($5,000 if married filing separately). This limit applies to the taxes deductible *from* AGI that are *not directly imposed* on business and investment activity or property.[26]

Example 16

Adam owns and operates a dry cleaning business as a sole proprietorship. During 2023, Adam paid $7,000 of real property taxes on the building used in the business and $1,200 of personal property taxes on the equipment used in the business. In calculating and paying estimated state income taxes of $5,600 for 2023, Adam included the profit from his sole proprietorship, his investment income, and his itemized deductions and claimed a state tax credit for solar panels he installed on his home.

The $8,200 of property taxes imposed on his business ($7,000 + $1,200) is deductible *for* AGI [on Schedule C (Form 1040)], but his state income taxes are deductible *from* AGI [on Schedule A (Form 1040)]. Only the $5,600 of state income taxes is subject to the $10,000 limit on state and local taxes, not the $8,200.

Now assume that in addition to his state income taxes, Adam paid $6,000 of property taxes on his personal residence in 2023. His total state and local taxes are $11,600 ($5,600 + $6,000), and his Federal itemized deduction for state and local taxes is limited to $10,000.

10-2b Property Taxes

LO.4

Explain the Federal income tax treatment of property taxes, state and local income taxes, and sales taxes.

State, local, and foreign taxes on real property are generally deductible only by the person upon whom the tax is imposed. Foreign real property taxes are not deductible from 2018 through 2025 unless the taxes relate to an individual's business or investment property. Deductible personal property taxes must be *ad valorem* (assessed in relation to the value of the property). So a motor vehicle tax based on weight, model, year, and horsepower is not deductible. However, a tax based on value and other criteria will be partially deductible.

[26] § 164(b)(6). Foreign income taxes also are included in this limit. This limitation is sometimes referred to as the "SALT cap." SALT is an acronym for *state and local taxes*. Notice 2020–75 provides that if a state imposes an income tax on a partnership or an S corporation, it is treated as an entity-level tax even if the entity's owners receive a partial or full deduction or credit for the tax for state income tax purposes. The benefit to the owners is that the income tax paid by the entity is not subject to the $10,000 SALT cap for the individual owners. Over 20 states impose such a tax.

The Big Picture

Example 17

Return to the facts of *The Big Picture* on p. 10-1. Assuming that the Williamsons proceed with the purchase of a home, the real estate taxes they pay will be deductible *from* AGI (subject to the aggregate $10,000 limit) because they qualify to itemize their deductions. They also should review their annual registration statement for their car because a portion of it may represent personal property tax (if based on the value of the car).

For example, assume that in their state, the government imposes a motor vehicle registration tax on 2% of the value of the vehicle plus 40 cents per hundredweight. The Williamsons own a car having a value of $20,000 and weighing 3,000 pounds. They pay an annual registration fee of $412. Of this amount, $400 (2% × $20,000 of value) is deductible as a personal property tax (subject to the aggregate $10,000 annual limit). The remaining $12, based on the weight of the car, is not deductible. Any other amount included in the annual fee (e.g., processing charges) is not a tax.

Assessments for Local Benefits

As a general rule, real property taxes do not include taxes assessed for local benefits if the assessments increase the value of the property (e.g., special assessments for streets, sidewalks, curbing, and other similar improvements).[27] Instead of being deductible, these assessments are added to the basis of the taxpayer's property. Assessments included for personal benefit (e.g., trash removal and tree trimming) are not deductible and do not affect the basis of the property.

Apportionment of Real Property Taxes between Seller and Purchaser

Real estate taxes for the entire year are apportioned between the buyer and seller on the basis of the number of days the property was held by each during the real property tax year. This apportionment is required whether the tax is paid by the buyer or the seller or is prorated according to the purchase agreement. The apportionment determines who is entitled to deduct the real estate taxes in the year of sale. The required apportionment prevents the shifting of the deduction for real estate taxes from the buyer to the seller or vice versa. In making the apportionment, the assessment date and the lien date are disregarded.[28]

A county's real property tax year runs from January 1 to December 31. Sara, the owner on January 1 of real property located in the county, sells the real property to Bob on June 30. Bob owns the real property from June 30 through December 31. The tax for the real property tax year, January 1 through December 31, is $3,650.

Assuming that this is not a leap year, the portion of the real property tax treated as imposed upon Sara, the seller, is $1,800 [(180/365) × $3,650, January 1 through June 29], and $1,850 of the tax [(185/365) × $3,650, June 30 through December 31] is treated as imposed upon Bob, the buyer.

If the actual real estate taxes are not prorated between the buyer and seller as part of the purchase agreement, adjustments are required. The adjustments are necessary to determine the amount realized by the seller and the basis of the property to the buyer. If the buyer pays the entire amount of the tax, the buyer has, in effect, paid the seller's portion of the real estate tax and has therefore paid more for the property than the

[27] Reg. § 1.164–4(a); see *Erie H. Rose*, 31 TCM 142, T.C.Memo. 1972–39, where a taxpayer was denied a deduction for the cost of a new sidewalk in front of his personal residence, even though the construction was required by the city and the sidewalk may have provided an incidental benefit to public welfare.

[28] For most years, the apportionment is based on a 365-day year. However, in a leap year (i.e., a year that is evenly divisible by 4, like 2024), the taxes are prorated over 366 days. In making the apportionment, the date of sale counts as a day the property is owned by the buyer. § 164(d).

actual purchase price. As a result, the amount of real estate tax that is apportioned to the seller (for Federal income tax purposes) and paid by the buyer is added to the buyer's basis. The seller must increase the amount realized on the sale by the same amount.

Seth sells real estate on October 3 for $400,000. The buyer, Barbara, pays the real estate taxes of $3,650 for the calendar year, which is the real estate property tax year.

Assuming that this is not a leap year, $2,750 (for 275 days) of the real estate taxes is apportioned to and is deductible by the seller, Seth, and $900 (for 90 days) of the taxes is deductible by Barbara.

Barbara has, in effect, paid Seth's real estate taxes of $2,750 and has, therefore, paid $402,750 for the property. Barbara's basis is increased to $402,750, and the amount realized by Seth from the sale is increased to $402,750.

The opposite result occurs if the seller (rather than the buyer) pays the real estate taxes. In this case, the seller reduces the amount realized from the sale by the amount that has been apportioned to the buyer. The buyer is required to reduce the basis by a corresponding amount.

10-2c **State and Local Income Taxes and Sales Taxes**

The position of the IRS is that state and local income taxes imposed upon an individual are deductible only as itemized deductions, even if the taxpayer's sole source of income is from a business, rents, or royalties.

Cash basis taxpayers are entitled to deduct state income taxes in the year *payment is made*. This includes taxes withheld by the employer, amounts paid with the state income tax return when filed, and estimated state income tax payments.[29] If the taxpayer overpays state income taxes, any refund received is included in gross income in the year received to the extent the deduction reduced taxable income in the prior year. See text Section 5-15 for a discussion of how the tax benefit rule applies to state income tax refunds when the overall $10,000 limit on state and local taxes applied in the prior year.

Leona, a cash basis, unmarried taxpayer, had $800 of state income tax withheld from her paychecks during 2023. Also in 2023, Leona paid $100 that was due when she filed her 2022 state income tax return and made estimated payments of $300 toward her 2023 state income tax liability. When Leona files her 2023 Federal income tax return in April 2024, she elects to itemize deductions, which amount to $15,500, including the $1,200 of state income tax payments and withholdings, all of which reduce her taxable income.

As a result of overpaying her 2023 state income tax, Leona receives a refund of $200 early in 2024. She will include this amount in her 2024 gross income in computing her Federal income tax. It does not matter whether Leona received a check from the state for $200 or applied the $200 toward her 2024 state income tax.

Individuals can elect to deduct *either* their state and local income taxes *or* their sales/use taxes paid as an itemized deduction. This election is intended to provide equity to taxpayers living in states that do not impose a state income tax (but do have sales taxes). Taxpayers making this election can deduct either actual sales/use tax payments *or* an amount from an IRS table (available on the IRS website). The IRS table amount can be increased by sales tax paid on the purchase of motor vehicles, boats, and other specified items.

[29]Rev.Rul. 71–190. See also Rev.Rul. 82–208, where a deduction is not allowed when the taxpayer cannot, in good faith, reasonably determine that there is additional state income tax liability.

LO.5

Distinguish between deductible and nondeductible interest, and apply the appropriate limitations to deductible interest.

10-3 Interest

A deduction for interest has been allowed since the income tax law was enacted in 1913. However, despite its long history, the interest deduction has been a controversial area for tax policy. Should all interest be allowed as a deduction? If not, what limits should apply? Should an interest deduction be allowed for only the taxpayer's principal residence (or all residences)? What about interest on credit cards and student loans? Lawmakers and taxpayers continue to raise these questions (and others).

Personal (consumer) interest is not deductible. This includes credit card interest, interest on car loans, and other types of personal interest. However, interest on qualified student loans, qualified residence (home mortgage) interest, and investment interest are deductible, subject to the limits discussed on the following pages.[30]

10-3a Allowed and Disallowed Items

The Supreme Court has defined *interest* as compensation for the use of money.[31] The general rule permits a deduction for interest paid or accrued within the taxable year on indebtedness.

Interest on Qualified Student Loans

Taxpayers who pay interest on a qualified student loan may be able to deduct the interest as a deduction *for* AGI. The deduction is allowed if the proceeds of the loan are used to pay qualified education expenses. These payments must be made to qualified educational institutions.[32]

The maximum annual deduction for qualified student loan interest is $2,500. However, in 2023, the deduction is phased out for taxpayers with modified AGI (MAGI) between $75,000 and $90,000 ($155,000 and $185,000 on joint returns). The interest expense deduction is phased out by applying the following formula:

$$\text{Education interest expense} \times \frac{\text{Modified AGI} - \text{AGI phaseout floor}}{\$15{,}000\ (\$30{,}000 \text{ for married filing jointly})}$$

The deduction is not allowed for taxpayers who are claimed as dependents or for married taxpayers filing separately.[33]

In 2023, Curt and Rita, who are married and file a joint return, paid $3,000 of interest on a qualified student loan. Their MAGI was $162,500. Their maximum potential deduction for qualified student loan interest is $2,500, but it must be reduced by $625 as a result of the phaseout rules.

$$\$2{,}500 \text{ interest} \times \frac{\$162{,}500\ (\text{MAGI}) - \$155{,}000\ (\text{AGI phaseout floor})}{\$30{,}000\ (\text{phaseout range})} = \$625 \text{ reduction}$$

Curt and Rita are allowed a student loan interest deduction of $1,875 ($2,500 maximum deduction − $625 reduction = $1,875 deduction *for* AGI).

Qualified Residence Interest

Qualified residence interest is interest paid or accrued during the taxable year on indebtedness (subject to limitations) *secured* by a qualified residence of the taxpayer. Qualified residence interest falls into two categories: (1) interest on acquisition indebtedness and (2) interest on home equity loans.[34]

[30]As discussed in Chapter 6, interest expense paid or incurred in a trade or business also is deductible (§ 162; a *for* AGI deduction).

[31]*Old Colony Railroad Co. v. Comm.*, 3 USTC ¶880, 10 AFTR 786, 52 S.Ct. 211 (1932).

[32]§§ 62(a)(17) and 221. See IRS Publication 970, *Tax Benefits for Education*, for details.

[33]§§ 221(c) and (e)(2). See § 221(b)(2)(C) for the definition of MAGI. The 2022 MAGI threshold amounts were $70,000 and $85,000 ($145,000 and $175,000 on joint returns).

[34]§ 163(h)(3).

A *qualified residence* includes the taxpayer's principal residence and one other residence of the taxpayer or spouse. The *principal residence* meets the requirement for nonrecognition of gain upon sale under § 121 (see text Section 13-6). The *one other residence*, or second residence, is used as a residence if not rented or, if rented, meets the requirements for a personal residence under the rental of vacation home rules (refer to Chapter 6). A taxpayer who has more than one second residence can choose the qualified second residence each year (i.e., the taxpayer can select a different second residence each year). A residence includes a house, a cooperative apartment, a condominium, and mobile homes and boats that have living quarters (sleeping, bathroom, and cooking facilities).

Although in most cases interest paid on a home mortgage is fully deductible, there are limitations.[35] A deduction is allowed for interest paid or accrued during the tax year on aggregate **acquisition indebtedness**. *Acquisition indebtedness* refers to amounts incurred in acquiring, constructing, or substantially improving the taxpayer's qualified residence that serves as security for that indebtedness. The amount of acquisition indebtedness is limited based on when the debt was incurred. If the debt is incurred after December 15, 2017, and before January 1, 2026, acquisition indebtedness is limited to $750,000 ($375,000 for married taxpayers filing separate returns). Debt incurred on or before December 15, 2017, is limited to $1 million ($500,000 for married taxpayers filing separate returns). These higher debt limits will apply to all homeowners after 2025, regardless of the date of borrowing.

The Big Picture

Example 22

Return to the facts of *The Big Picture* on p. 10-1. Given that John and Kiara Williamson will need to borrow at least a portion of the purchase price of a new home, a standard mortgage likely will qualify as acquisition indebtedness because the borrowed funds are used to acquire a principal residence. However, the interest on the acquisition indebtedness will be fully deductible only if the amount of the mortgage is $750,000 or less (assuming that John and Kiara file a joint return) and the mortgage is secured by the home, which is the typical case.

Recall that the Williamsons also are considering what appears to be a less expensive route of using their retirement and taxable investments to secure the debt. If they choose this alternative, the interest will not be deductible as qualified residence interest because the loan would not be acquisition indebtedness (i.e., the loan would not be secured by the home).

From 2018 through 2025, interest on **home equity loans** is not deductible unless the funds are used to improve the principal residence (and the total acquisition debt and home equity debt is $750,000 or less). Home equity loans utilize the personal residence of the taxpayer as security, typically in the form of a second mortgage. If the funds from home equity loans are used for personal purposes (e.g., auto purchases, vacations, medical expenses), the related interest expense is not deductible.[36]

Example 23

Larry owns a personal residence with a fair market value of $600,000 and an outstanding first mortgage of $420,000. Therefore, his equity in his home is $180,000 ($600,000 − $420,000). Larry borrows $75,000 that is secured by a second mortgage on his home to put an addition on his home.

All of Larry's interest is deductible; both loans are secured by his residence, and the total of the loans ($420,000 + $75,000) does not exceed $750,000 or the value of his residence. If Larry used the home equity loan proceeds to buy a new car and boat, the home equity loan interest would not be deductible.

[35] § 163(h)(3).

[36] § 163(h)(3)(F). Interest on home equity loans prior to 2018 was deductible only on the portion of a home equity loan that did not exceed the lesser of (1) the fair market value of the residence reduced by any acquisition indebtedness or (2) $100,000 ($50,000 for married persons filing separate returns). Proceeds from these home equity loans could be used for any purpose without impairing the interest deductibility. From 2018 through 2025, the treatment of interest expense on an equity debt that was not used to improve the home is determined using the interest tracing rules of Temp. Reg. § 1.163–8T and Reg. § 1.163–15.

In years prior to 2022, mortgage insurance premiums paid by the taxpayer on a qualified residence were deductible (and treated as qualified residence interest). The amount allowed was subject to a phaseout based on AGI.[37]

Interest Paid for Services

Mortgage loan companies commonly charge a fee, often called a loan origination fee, for finding, placing, or processing a mortgage loan. Loan origination fees are typically nondeductible amounts included in the basis of the acquired property. Other fees, sometimes called **points** and expressed as a percentage of the loan amount, are paid to reduce the interest rate charged over the term of the loan. Essentially, the payment of points is a prepayment of interest and is considered compensation to a lender for the use of money.[38]

In general, points are capitalized and are amortized and deductible ratably over the life of the loan. However, the purchaser of a principal residence can deduct qualifying points in the year of payment.This exception also covers points paid to obtain funds for improvements to a principal residence.[39]

Points paid to *refinance* acquisition indebtedness (i.e., an existing home mortgage) must be capitalized and amortized as an interest deduction over the life of the new loan.[40]

Sandra purchased her residence many years ago, obtaining a 30-year mortgage at an annual interest rate of 6%. In the current year, Sandra refinances the mortgage to reduce the interest rate to 4%. To obtain the refinancing, she has to pay points of $2,600.

The $2,600, which is considered prepayment of interest, must be capitalized and amortized over the life of the mortgage.

Points paid by the seller for a buyer are, in effect, treated as an adjustment to the price of the residence, and the buyer is treated as having used cash to pay the points that were paid by the seller. A buyer may deduct seller-paid points in the tax year in which they are paid if certain conditions are met.[41]

Prepayment Penalty

When a mortgage or loan is paid off in full in a lump sum before its term (early), the lending institution may require an additional payment (normally, a specific percentage of the loan balance). This is known as a prepayment penalty and is considered to be interest (e.g., personal, qualified residence, or investment) in the year paid. The general rules for deductibility of interest also apply to prepayment penalties.

Investment Interest

Taxpayers sometimes borrow funds to acquire investment assets (e.g., stock). Congress, however, has limited the deductibility of interest on funds borrowed to purchase or hold investment property. The deduction for investment interest expense is limited to the net investment income for the year and is only deductible if the taxpayer itemizes deductions. A complete discussion of investment interest occurs in text Section 11-4.

Tax-Exempt Securities

No deduction is allowed for interest on debt incurred to purchase or hold tax-exempt securities.[42] Refer to text Section 6-3l for further discussion of this topic.

[37]§§ 163(h)(3)(E). In 2021, the deduction phased out for taxpayers with AGI in excess of $100,000 ($50,000 for married taxpayers filing separately) and is fully phased out when AGI exceeds $109,000 ($54,500 for married taxpayers filing separately).

[38]Rev.Rul. 69–188. To be deductible, points must be in the nature of interest and cannot be a form of service charge or payment for specific services.

[39]§ 461(g)(2).

[40]Rev.Rul. 87–22.

[41]Refer to Rev.Proc. 94–27 for a complete list of these conditions and additional aspects of this arrangement.

[42]§ 265(a)(2).

10-3b **Restrictions on Deductibility and Timing Considerations**

Even if interest expense is deductible (e.g., qualified residence interest), a current deduction still may not be available unless certain additional conditions described below are met.

Taxpayer's Obligation

Allowed interest is deductible if the related debt represents a bona fide obligation of the taxpayer.[43] For interest to be deductible, both the debtor and the creditor must intend for the loan to be repaid. Intent of the parties can be especially crucial between related parties (e.g., family members or a shareholder and a closely held corporation).

In addition, an individual may not deduct interest paid on behalf of another taxpayer. For example, a shareholder may not deduct interest paid by the corporation on the shareholder's behalf.[44] Likewise, a husband may not deduct interest paid on his wife's property if he files a separate return, except in the case of qualified residence interest. If both husband and wife consent in writing, either the husband or the wife may deduct the allowed interest on the principal residence and one other residence.

Time of Deduction

Under the cash method, interest must be paid to secure a deduction. Under the accrual method, interest is deductible ratably over the life of the loan.

On November 1, 2023, Ramon borrows $2,000 to purchase computers for his consulting business. The loan is payable in 90 days at 6% interest. On the due date in late January 2024, Ramon pays the $2,000 note and interest amounting to $30.

Ramon can deduct the accrued portion ($\frac{2}{3} \times \$30 = \$20$) of the interest in 2023 only if he is an accrual basis taxpayer. Otherwise, the entire amount of interest ($30) is deductible in 2024.

Prepaid Interest

The accrual method treatment must be used by cash basis taxpayers for interest prepayments that extend beyond the end of the taxable year.[45] These payments must be allocated to the tax years to which the interest payments relate. This provision prevents cash basis taxpayers from creating tax deductions before the end of the year by prepaying interest.

10-3c **Classification of Interest Expense**

Whether interest is deductible *for* AGI or as an itemized deduction (*from* AGI) depends on whether the indebtedness has a business, investment, or personal purpose. If the debt proceeds are used for a business expense (other than performing services as an employee) or for an expense for an activity for the production of rent or royalty income, the interest is deductible *for* AGI. Business expenses appear on Schedule C of Form 1040, and expenses related to rents or royalties are reported on Schedule E.

If the indebtedness produces qualified residence interest, any deduction allowed is taken *from* AGI and is reported on Schedule A of Form 1040 (the taxpayer must itemize deductions to get any benefit). Recall, however, that interest on a limited amount of student loans is a deduction *for* AGI. If the taxpayer is an employee who incurs debt in relation to the taxpayer's employment, the interest is considered to be personal interest and is not deductible. Debt proceeds used for personal purposes (e.g., to pay for a vacation or personal credit card bills) produce nondeductible personal interest expense.

See Concept Summary 10.1 for a summary of the interest deduction rules.

[43] *Arcade Realty Co.*, 35 T.C. 256 (1960), *acq.* 1961–2 C.B. 3.

[44] *Continental Trust Co.*, 7 B.T.A. 539 (1927).

[45] § 461(g)(1).

Concept Summary 10.1

Deductibility of Personal, Student Loan, Mortgage, and Investment Interest

Type	Deductible	Comments
Personal (consumer) interest	No	Includes any interest that is not qualified residence interest, qualified student loan interest, investment interest, or business interest. Examples include interest on car loans and credit card debt.*
Qualified student loan interest	Yes	Deduction *for* AGI; subject to limitations.
Qualified residence interest (acquisition indebtedness)	Yes	Deductible as an itemized deduction; limited to indebtedness of $750,000 (up to $1 million if incurred on or before December 15, 2017).
Qualified residence interest (home equity indebtedness)	No	In general, not deductible from 2018 through 2025.* Prior to 2018 and after 2025, deductible as an itemized deduction; limited to indebtedness equal to the lesser of $100,000 or the FMV of residence minus acquisition indebtedness.
Investment interest (*not* related to rental or royalty property)	Yes	Itemized deduction; limited to net investment income for the year; disallowed interest can be carried over to future years (see text Section 11-4).*
Investment interest (related to rental or royalty property)	Yes	Deduction *for* AGI; limited to net investment income for the year; disallowed interest can be carried over to future years (see text Section 11-4).*

* The classification rules for interest expense are provided by Temp.Reg. § 1.163–8T, Reg. § 1.163–15, and Notice 89–35.

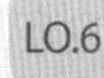

LO.6

Recognize charitable contributions, and identify their related measurement problems and percentage limitations.

10-4 Charitable Contributions

Code § 170 allows individuals and corporations to deduct contributions made to qualified *domestic* organizations. Contributions to qualified charitable organizations serve certain social welfare needs and thus relieve the government of the cost of providing these needed services to the community.

The **charitable contribution** provisions are among the most complex in the tax law. To determine the amount deductible as a charitable contribution, several important questions must be answered:

- What constitutes a charitable contribution?
- Was the contribution made to a qualified organization?
- When is the contribution deductible?
- What record-keeping and reporting requirements apply to charitable contributions?
- How is the value of donated property determined?
- What special rules apply to contributions of property that has increased in value?
- What percentage limitations apply to the charitable contribution deduction?
- What rules apply to amounts in excess of percentage limitations (carryovers)?

These questions are addressed in the sections that follow.

10-4a Criteria for a Gift

A *charitable contribution* is defined as a gift of property made to a qualified organization. The major elements needed to qualify a contribution as a gift are a donative intent, the absence of consideration, and acceptance by the donee. Consequently, the taxpayer has the burden of establishing that the transfer was made from motives of *disinterested generosity* as established by the courts.[46] This test is quite subjective and has led to problems of interpretation (refer to the discussion of gifts in text Section 5-2).

Benefit Received Rule

When a donor derives a benefit from a contribution, the donor cannot deduct the value of the benefit.

[46] *Comm. v. Duberstein*, 60–2 USTC ¶9515, 5 AFTR 2d 1626, 80 S.Ct. 1190.

Jacob purchases a ticket at $100 for a special performance of the local symphony (a qualified charity). If the price of a ticket to a symphony concert is normally $35, Jacob is allowed only $65 as a charitable contribution. Even if Jacob does not attend the concert, the deduction is limited to $65.

If, however, Jacob does *not* accept the ticket from the symphony (or returns it prior to the event), he can deduct the full $100.

Contributions in Exchange for State and Local Tax Credits

Several states provide a state or local tax credit to taxpayers who donate to specified state or local funds or public charities. Primarily due to concerns that state and local governments might expand the availability of these programs to help taxpayers "work around" the $10,000 state and local tax deduction limit, the IRS issued rules limiting the Federal tax benefits of these "contributions." Under these rules, if taxpayers receive a state or local tax credit greater than 15 percent of the payments made, the taxpayers must reduce their charitable contribution deduction by the amount of that credit.[47]

In 2023, Prisha, a resident of State G, donated $5,000 to State G's Scholar Program. This donation provides Prisha with a 60% state income tax credit [$3,000 ($5,000 × 60%)] that can be used to reduce her overall state income tax liability. By making this contribution, Prisha is attempting to convert a state income tax payment (with an overall limit of $10,000 per year) into a charitable contribution (with a 50%-of-AGI limit).

On Prisha's 2023 Federal return, she must reduce this charitable contribution by $3,000 because the credit she received was more than 15% of the payment made. As a result, Prisha's charitable contribution deduction for this $5,000 donation is reduced to only $2,000 ($5,000 payment − $3,000 state income tax credit).

Contribution of Services

No deduction is allowed for a contribution of one's services to a qualified charitable organization. However, unreimbursed expenses related to the services rendered may be deductible. For example, the cost of a uniform (without general utility) that is required to be worn while performing services may be deductible. In addition, deductions are permitted for out-of-pocket transportation costs, reasonable expenses for lodging, and the cost of meals while away from home that are incurred in performing the donated services. In lieu of these out-of-pocket costs for an automobile, a standard mileage rate of 14 cents per mile is allowed.[48] The travel expenses are not deductible if the travel involves a significant element of personal pleasure, recreation, or vacation.[49]

Grace, a delegate representing her church in Miami, Florida, travels to a two-day national meeting in Denver, Colorado, in February. After the meeting, Grace spends two weeks at a nearby ski resort.

Under these circumstances, none of the transportation, meals, or lodging is deductible because the travel involved a significant element of personal pleasure, recreation, or vacation.

Nondeductible Items

In addition to the benefit received rule and the restrictions placed on contributions of services, the following items may *not* be deducted as charitable contributions:

- Dues, fees, or bills paid to country clubs, lodges, fraternal orders, or similar groups.
- Cost of raffle, bingo, or lottery tickets.
- Cost of tuition.
- Payment for the right to purchase tickets for seating at an athletic event in a university stadium.[50]

[47] Reg. § 1.170A–1(h)(3). Reg. § 1.162–15 allows a C corporation making contributions to such funds to treat the portion of the contribution for which a credit is earned as a business expense (§ 162). If the business is a pass-through entity and the credit applies to a tax imposed directly on the business (e.g., a property tax), the payment is treated as a business deduction. Reg. § 1.164–3(j) allows an individual with state and local taxes below the $10,000 cap to treat the disallowed charitable contribution amount as a state tax deduction (but not to exceed the $10,000 cap).

[48] § 170(i).

[49] § 170(j).

[50] § 170(l).

- Value of blood given to a blood bank.
- Donations to homeowners associations.
- Gifts to individuals.
- Rental value of property used by a qualified charity.

10-4b Qualified Organizations

To be deductible, a contribution must be made to one of the following organizations:[51]

- A state or possession of the United States (or any subdivision).
- A corporation, trust, community chest, fund, or foundation located in the United States and organized and operated exclusively for religious, charitable, scientific, literary, or educational purposes or for the prevention of cruelty to children or animals.
- A veterans' organization.
- A fraternal organization operating under the lodge system.
- A cemetery company.

It is commonly understood that contributions to a church, a synagogue, or another religious organization are allowed. But for less well-known recipients, taxpayers can consult an IRS list of organizations that have applied for and received tax-exempt status under § 501 of the Code.[52]

Gifts made to needy individuals are not deductible (e.g., a needy family or a homeless individual). A deduction is allowed only if the gift is made to a qualified organization.

Sarah's neighbor is very ill and has been in the hospital for several weeks. Her insurance won't cover all of her medical bills. A neighborhood friend set up a crowdfunding website, allowing people to contribute money to help Sarah's neighbor with her medical bills. Sarah transfers $700 to this crowdfunding campaign.

Sarah may not treat the $700 as a charitable contribution because it is a nondeductible gift [i.e., for the benefit of an individual rather than a charitable (qualified) organization].

Ethics & Equity An Indirect Route to a Contribution Deduction

In July, a plane crashed into a residential community in Middleboro, destroying and damaging many homes. Chloe's church, a qualified charitable organization, initiated a fund-raising drive to help the Middleboro citizens whose homes had been affected. Chloe donated $50,000 to First Middleboro Church and suggested to the pastor that $25,000 of her contribution should be given to her sister, Rebecca, whose home had suffered extensive damage. The pastor appointed a committee to award funds to needy citizens. The committee solicited applications from the community and awarded Rebecca $15,000. Discuss whether Chloe is justified in deducting $50,000 as a charitable contribution.

10-4c Time of Deduction

A charitable contribution generally is deducted in the year the payment is made. This rule applies to both cash and accrual basis individuals. A contribution ordinarily is deemed to have been made on the delivery of the property to the donee. For example, if a gift of common stock is made to a qualified charitable organization, the gift is considered complete on the day of delivery or mailing. However, if the donor delivers the stock certificate to the bank or broker or to the issuing corporation, the gift is considered complete on the date the stock is transferred on the books of the corporation.

A contribution made by check is considered delivered on the date of mailing. Thus, a check mailed on December 31, 2023, is deductible on the taxpayer's 2023 tax return. If the contribution is charged on a credit card, the date the charge is made determines the year of deduction.

[51]§ 170(c).

[52]Although this *Cumulative List of Organizations*, IRS Publication 78, may be helpful, not all organizations that qualify are listed in this publication. The IRS maintains a searchable database at **irs.gov/charities-non-profits/tax-exempt-organization-search**.

10-4d **Record-Keeping and Valuation Requirements**

Recall that income tax deductions allowed by law are a matter of legislative grace, but a taxpayer still bears the burden of showing that the taxpayer is entitled to claim the deduction. Not surprisingly, the tax law provides specific documentation requirements that must be met to claim a charitable contribution deduction.

Record-Keeping Requirements

In order to claim a charitable contribution deduction, the taxpayer must have appropriate documentation. The specific type of documentation required depends on the amount of the contribution and whether the contribution is made in cash or noncash property.[53] In addition, special rules may apply to gifts of certain types of property (e.g., used cars or boats) where Congress noted taxpayer abuse in the past. In addition, for certain gifts of noncash property, Form 8283 (Noncash Charitable Contributions) must be attached to the taxpayer's return.

The taxpayer must have the required documentation by the date the tax return is filed for the year the contribution is claimed (and no later than the due date, including extensions, of that tax return). Failure to comply with the reporting rules typically results in disallowance of the charitable contribution deduction. In addition, substantial penalties may apply if the taxpayer significantly overvalues any contributed property.

Common documentation and substantiation requirements are summarized in Concept Summary 10.2.

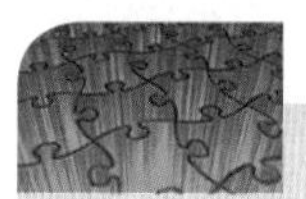

Concept Summary 10.2

Documentation and Substantiation Requirements for Charitable Contributions

Cash gifts	• A deduction is allowed only if the taxpayer has a proper receipt (e.g., a canceled check or written statement from the charity) showing the name of the charitable organization and the date and amount of the contribution. • A written statement from the charity is required if a payment is for more than $75 and is partly a contribution and partly for goods or services. The statement must provide an estimate of the value of the goods and services received by the donor.
Noncash gifts (e.g., household items)	• A receipt from the charity must be kept for any gift of property other than money. Clothes or other household items are deductible if they are in "good used condition or better" at the time of the gift. • If an item is not in good used condition or better, and its value exceeds $500, a deduction is allowed if a "qualified appraisal" is included with the return.
Used cars, boats, or airplanes	• The deduction is generally limited to the amount the charity receives on the sale of the car, boat, or airplane. The taxpayer should obtain a statement from the charity documenting the sales price. Form 1098–C (Contributions of Motor Vehicles, Boats, and Airplanes) must be attached to the return if the taxpayer claims a deduction in excess of $500.
Cash or noncash gifts (including out-of-pocket expenses) of $250 or more	• A contemporaneous written acknowledgment (CWA) from the charity (as well as certain payroll records in the case of gifts made by payroll deductions) is required to deduct a single cash or property contribution of $250 or more. A CWA also is required for a donation of $250 or more of out-of-pocket expenses a donor might incur in providing services to a charity. The CWA must include the amount of money and a description of any other property contributed, whether the charity provided any goods or services in return for the contribution, and a description and estimated value of the goods or services provided. Contemporaneous means that the donor must have the CWA by the earlier of (1) the date the tax return is filed for the year of the donation or (2) the due date (including extensions) for the tax return.
Noncash gifts of more than $500	• Additional substantiation (e.g., how the property was acquired and its basis) is required on the tax return if donated noncash property is valued at more than $500. Qualified appraisals may be required if noncash contributions exceed $5,000 in value.
Antiques, paintings, jewelry, and other "tangible personal property"	• The deduction is equal to the property's appreciated FMV only if the charity puts the property to "a use related to its tax-exempt purpose." Otherwise, the deduction is limited to the property's cost. The taxpayer should obtain a statement from the charity documenting the property's use.

[53]The specific documentation thresholds and requirements are provided in § 170(f).

Global Tax Issues — Choose the Charity Wisely

Eleonora, a U.S. citizen of Italian descent, was distressed by the damage caused by a major earthquake in central Italy. She donated $100,000 to the Earthquake Victims' Relief Fund, an Italian charitable organization that was set up to help victims of the earthquake. Stefano, also a U.S. citizen of Italian descent, donated $100,000 to help with the relief effort. However, Stefano's contribution went to his church, which sent the proceeds of a fund drive to the Earthquake Victims' Relief Fund in Italy. Eleonora's contribution is not deductible, but Stefano's is. Why? Contributions to charitable organizations are not deductible unless the organization is a U.S. charity.

Valuation Requirements

Property donated to a charity is generally valued at fair market value at the time the gift is made. The Code provides very little guidance on the measurement of the fair market value. The Regulations provide this definition:[54] "The fair market value is the price at which the property would change hands between a willing buyer and a willing seller, neither being under any compulsion to buy or sell and both having reasonable knowledge of relevant facts."

Generally, charitable organizations do not provide the fair market value of the donated property. Nevertheless, as noted in Concept Summary 10.2, the taxpayer must obtain written evidence of the donation from the charity and value the donation appropriately.

10-4e Limitations on Charitable Contribution Deduction

The charitable contribution deduction is the total of all donations made during the year, both money and property. However, the charitable contribution deduction is subject to a number of limitations (based on the taxpayer's AGI, the type of property contributed, and the charity receiving the property). In general:

- If the qualifying contributions for the year total 20 percent or less of AGI, they are fully deductible.
- If the qualifying contributions are more than 20 percent of AGI, the deductible amount may be limited to 20 percent, 30 percent, 50 percent, or 60 percent of AGI, depending on the type of property given and the type of organization to which the donation is made.
- In any case, the maximum charitable contribution deduction may not exceed 60 percent of AGI for the tax year.

If a taxpayer's contributions for the year exceed the limitations, the excess contributions may be carried forward and deducted during a five-year carryover period.

To understand the complex rules for computing the amount of a charitable contribution deduction, it is necessary to understand the distinction between ordinary income property and capital gain property. In addition, it is necessary to understand when the various limitations apply. These topics are discussed in the sections that follow.

Ordinary Income Property

Ordinary income property is any property that, if sold, will result in the recognition of ordinary income. The term includes inventory for sale in the taxpayer's trade or business, a work of art created by the donor, and a manuscript prepared by the donor. It also includes, *for purposes of the charitable contribution calculation*, a capital asset held by the donor for a year or less (this is the holding period for short-term capital gain treatment; see text Section 14-4). If a business contributes depreciable property, it is ordinary income property to the extent of any depreciation recapture that would have been recognized had the

[54]Reg. § 1.170A–1(c)(2).

property been sold. Ordinary income property also includes personal use and investment assets that have declined in value (i.e., the fair market value is *less than* the taxpayer's basis). Used clothing contributed to the Salvation Army would fit this description.[55]

If ordinary income property is contributed, the deduction is equal to the fair market value of the property less the amount of ordinary income that would have been reported if the property were sold. In most instances, the deduction is limited to the basis of the property to the donor.

Tim donates stock in White Corporation to a university on May 1, 2023. Tim had purchased the stock for $2,500 on March 3, 2023, and the stock had a value of $3,600 when he made the donation. Because he had not held the property long enough to meet the long-term capital gain requirement, Tim would have recognized a short-term capital gain of $1,100 if he had sold the property.

Because short-term capital gain property is treated as ordinary income property for charitable contribution purposes, Tim's charitable contribution deduction is limited to the property's basis of $2,500 ($3,600 − $1,100).

Assume, instead, that the stock had a fair market value of $2,300 (rather than $3,600) when Tim donated it to the university. Because the fair market value now is less than the basis, the charitable contribution deduction is $2,300.

Capital Gain Property

Capital gain property is any property that would have resulted in the recognition of long-term capital gain or § 1231 gain if the property had been sold by the donor.[56] As a general rule, the deduction for a contribution of capital gain property is equal to the fair market value of the property.

Two common exceptions disallow the deductibility of the appreciation on capital gain property. The first exception relates to the contribution of *tangible personalty*. Tangible personalty is all property that is not realty (land and buildings) and does not include intangible property (e.g., stock or securities). If tangible personalty is contributed to a public charity (e.g., a museum, church, or university) and the property is put to an *unrelated use*, the charitable deduction is limited to the property's basis (rather than its fair market value). The term *unrelated use* means a use that is unrelated to the exempt purpose or function of the charitable organization. For example, artwork donated to the American Red Cross is unlikely to be put to a related use. Instead, the Red Cross would likely sell the art to generate funds that would then be used to support its mission of providing assistance to individuals who have been struck by disasters.

Knowing this, taxpayers usually specify how their contributed property will be used and target donors appropriately (i.e., giving artwork to a museum rather than the Red Cross). As a result, this reduction will not apply if the property is put to a related use or if, at the time of the contribution, it was reasonable to anticipate that the property would not be put to an unrelated use by the donee.[57]

Example 31

Emma contributes a Picasso painting, for which she paid $20,000, to a local museum. She had owned the painting for four years. It had a value of $30,000 at the time of the donation. The museum displays the painting for five years and subsequently sells it for $50,000.

The charitable contribution is $30,000. It is not reduced by the unrealized appreciation because the painting is not put to an unrelated use even though it is later sold by the museum.

The second exception relates to certain private foundations. Private foundations are organizations that traditionally do not receive their funding from the general public (e.g., the Bill and Melinda Gates Foundation). Generally, foundations fall into two categories: operating and nonoperating. A private *operating* foundation spends substantially all of its income in the active conduct of its charitable purposes. Other private foundations are

[55]Depreciation recapture rules are discussed in Chapter 14. For a more complete discussion of the difference between ordinary income and capital gain property, see Chapter 14.

[56]See text Section 14-4 for a discussion of holding periods.

[57]§ 170(e)(1)(B)(i) and Reg. § 1.170A–4(b)(3)(ii)(b).

nonoperating foundations. Often, only the private foundation knows its status (operating or nonoperating) for sure, and the status can change from year to year.

If capital gain property is contributed to a private *nonoperating* foundation, the taxpayer must reduce the contribution by the long-term capital gain that would have been recognized if the property had been sold at its fair market value. The effect of this provision is to limit the deduction to the property's basis.[58]

Ten years ago, Walter purchased land for $8,000 and has held it as an investment since then. This year, when the land is worth $20,000, he donates it to a private *nonoperating* foundation. Walter's charitable contribution is $8,000 ($20,000 − $12,000), the land's basis.

If, instead, Walter had donated the land to either a public charity or a private *operating* foundation, his charitable contribution would have been $20,000, the fair market value of the land.

Fifty Percent Ceiling

Contributions made to public charities may not exceed 50 percent of an individual's AGI for the year. Given that this ceiling is quite high, most taxpayers making contributions never have their charitable contributions limited. The 50 percent ceiling on contributions applies to public charities (e.g., churches; schools; hospitals; and Federal, state, or local governmental units). The 50 percent ceiling also applies to contributions to private operating foundations and certain private nonoperating foundations.

In the remaining discussion of charitable contributions, public charities and private foundations (both operating and nonoperating) that qualify for the 50 percent ceiling will be referred to as *50 percent organizations.*

During the year, Tom and Emma Waters contribute $8,000 to their church, donate $500 to the Salvation Army, and give used clothes to Goodwill Industries (cost of $1,000; fair market value of $200). The clothes are ordinary income property, and the charitable contribution deduction is limited to the fair market value. Their AGI for the year is $125,000.

Tom and Emma's charitable contribution deduction is $8,700 ($8,000 + $500 + $200). Their charitable contribution deduction is not limited, since $8,700 is less than 50% of their AGI ($62,500; $125,000 × 50%).

Temporary Sixty Percent Ceiling

From 2018 through 2025, the deduction limit for *cash donations* to 50 percent organizations is 60 percent of AGI (rather than 50 percent of AGI). Congress was concerned that the combination of the increased standard deduction and the scaling back of many individual itemized deductions during this period would reduce the tax incentive to make charitable contributions. Most policy organizations believe that the increased ceiling will have little, if any, effect on the expected decline in individual donations to charities.

Thirty Percent Ceiling

A 30 percent ceiling applies to contributions of cash and ordinary income property to private nonoperating foundations that are not 50 percent organizations. The 30 percent ceiling also applies to contributions of appreciated capital gain property to 50 percent organizations.[59]

[58] § 170(e)(1)(B)(ii).

[59] Under a special election, a taxpayer may choose to permanently forgo a deduction of the appreciation on capital gain property. Referred to as the reduced deduction election, this enables the taxpayer to move from the 30% limitation to the 50% limitation. See § 170(b)(1)(C)(iii).

In the event the contributions for any one tax year involve both 50 percent and 30 percent property, the allowable deduction comes first from the 50 percent property.

Example 34

During the year, Lisa makes the following donations to her church: cash of $2,000 and unimproved land worth $30,000. Lisa had purchased the land four years ago for $22,000 and held it as an investment. Therefore, it is capital gain property. Lisa's AGI for the year is $60,000. Disregarding percentage limitations, Lisa's potential deduction is $32,000 [$2,000 (cash) + $30,000 (fair market value of land)].

In applying the percentage limitations, however, the *current* deduction for the land is limited to $18,000 [30% (limitation applicable to capital gain property) × $60,000 (AGI)]. Thus, the total current deduction is $20,000 ($2,000 cash + $18,000 land). Note that the total deduction does not exceed $30,000, which is 50% of Lisa's AGI.

Twenty Percent Ceiling

A 20 percent ceiling applies to contributions of appreciated capital gain property to private nonoperating foundations that are not 50 percent organizations.

Concept Summary 10.3 summarizes the limitations on the deductibility of charitable contributions by individuals.

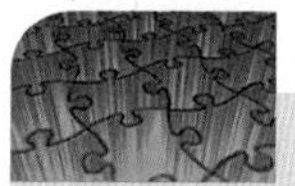

Concept Summary 10.3

Determining the Deduction for Contributions by Individuals

If the Type of Property Contributed Is:	And the Property Is Contributed to:	The Contribution Is Measured by:	But the Deduction Is Limited to:
1. Capital gain property (see Example 34)	A 50% organization	Fair market value of the property	30% of AGI
2. Ordinary income property (see Example 30)	A 50% organization	The basis of the property*	50% of AGI
3. Capital gain property (and the property is tangible personal property put to an unrelated use by the donee; see Example 31)	A 50% organization	The basis of the property*	50% of AGI
4. Capital gain property (see Example 32)	A private nonoperating foundation that is not a 50% organization	The basis of the property*	The lesser of: 1. 20% of AGI 2. 50% of AGI minus other contributions to 50% organizations
5. Cash	A 50% organization	Amount of cash	60% of AGI

*If the fair market value of the property is less than the basis (i.e., the property has declined in value instead of appreciating), the fair market value is used.

Contribution Carryovers

Contributions that exceed the percentage limitations for the current year can be carried over for five years. In the carryover process, these contributions do not lose their identity for limitation purposes. Thus, if the contribution originally involved 30 percent property, the carryover will continue to be classified as 30 percent property in the carryover year.

Example 35

Assume the same facts as in Example 34. Because only $18,000 of the $30,000 value of the land is deducted in the current year, the balance of $12,000 may be carried over to the following year. But the carryover still will be treated as capital gain property and is subject to the 30%-of-AGI limitation in the carryover year.

In applying the percentage limitations, current charitable contributions must be claimed first before any carryovers can be considered. If carryovers involve more than one year, they are utilized in a first-in, first-out order.

10-5 Timing of Payments to Maximize Deductions

Because an individual may use the standard deduction in one year and itemize deductions in another year, maximum benefits can be obtained by shifting itemized deductions from one year to another. For example, if a taxpayer's itemized deductions and the standard deduction are approximately the same for each year of a two-year period, the taxpayer should use the standard deduction in one year and shift itemized deductions (to the extent permitted by law) to the other year. The individual could, for example, prepay a church pledge for a particular year to shift the deduction to the current year or avoid paying end-of-the-year medical expenses to shift the deduction to the following year.

It is sometimes possible to defer or accelerate the payment of certain deductible items (e.g., state taxes and charitable contributions) to maximize deductions when itemized deductions are close to the standard deduction. For instance, the final installment of estimated state income tax is generally due in mid-January (after the end of a given tax year). Accelerating the payment of the final installment to December could result in larger itemized deductions for the current year.

Timing to Maximize Deductions

Example 36

Jenny, who is single, expects to have itemized deductions of $11,600 in 2023 and $8,000 in 2024. She needs to pay $2,900 as the final installment on her 2023 estimated state income tax, which is due on January 15, 2024. The standard deduction for 2023 is $13,850 for single taxpayers. If Jenny pays the final installment of her 2023 state taxes in 2023, she increases her itemized deductions. If instead she pays it in January 2024 when she knows she will be claiming the standard deduction in 2024, she obtains no tax benefit for that payment.

As a result, making the final installment payment in 2023 is good tax planning. If Jenny pays the final installment in December 2023, and assuming that her state and local tax deduction is not limited, her itemized deductions will be $14,500 ($11,600 + $2,900) in 2023 and she will benefit from itemizing.

Example 37

Juan and Lisa Garcia are married and file a joint tax return. Their state income and real estate taxes are greater than $10,000 each year. They do not have a mortgage, and their health insurance typically covers all of their medical expenses. They usually make charitable contributions of about $11,000 each year. With these facts, the Garcias will claim the standard deduction ($27,700 in 2023) rather than itemize their deductions.

If the Garcias change the timing of their charitable contributions to make them every other year (or every third year), they can increase their deductions over that period of time. For example, if they opt to make no charitable contributions in 2023, they will claim the $27,700 standard deduction. If in 2024 they make $22,000 of charitable contributions, representing what they otherwise would have contributed in 2023 and 2024, they will claim itemized deductions of $32,000 (which will likely exceed their 2024 standard deduction). They can repeat this pattern to maximize their *from AGI* deductions over time.

10-6 **Other Itemized Deductions**

LO.7

List the expenses that are deductible as other itemized deductions.

In general, no deduction is allowed for personal, living, or family expenses.[60] However, a number of other expenses and losses are allowed as itemized deductions on Schedule A (Form 1040):

- Gambling losses up to the amount of gambling winnings.
- Impairment-related work expenses of a handicapped person.
- Federal estate tax on income in respect of a decedent.
- Deduction for repayment of amounts under a claim of right (but only if more than $3,000; discussed in text Section 16-1e).
- The unrecovered investment in an annuity contract when the annuity ceases by reason of death, discussed in text Section 4-4c.

Prior to 2018, certain other personal expenses were deductible to the extent, in total, they exceeded 2 percent of the taxpayer's AGI (and only if the taxpayer itemized deductions instead of claiming the standard deduction). These **miscellaneous itemized deductions** included unreimbursed employee business expenses, certain investment expenses, tax return preparation fees (other than for portions of the return related to business), and expenses related to hobby income (refer to text Section 6-3e). From 2018 through 2025, these expenses are not deductible.

10-7 **Comprehensive Example of Schedule A**

Jean Brown is single and had the following transactions for 2022:

Medicines that required a prescription	$ 830
Doctor and dentist bills paid and not reimbursed	3,120
Medical insurance premium payments	9,200
Contact lenses	370
Transportation for medical purposes on March 1, 2022 (344 miles × 18 cents per mile + $10.00 parking)	72
State income tax withheld (This amount exceeds the sales tax from the sales tax table.)	7,900
Real estate taxes	6,580
Interest paid on qualified residence mortgage (acquisition indebtedness)	4,340
Qualifying charitable contributions paid by check; proper documentation exists	2,160
Transportation in performing charitable services (800 miles × 14 cents per mile + $7.00 parking and tolls)	119
Unreimbursed employee expenses	1,870
Tax return preparation	450
Safe deposit box (used for keeping investment documents and tax records)	170

Jean's AGI is $120,000. The total of her itemized deductions is $21,211 (see the completed 2022 Schedule A on the following page). This amount is greater than her standard deduction of $12,950.[61]

[60] § 262.

[61] Jean's unreimbursed employee expenses, tax return preparation fee, and safe deposit box rental cost are miscellaneous itemized deductions. From 2018 through 2025, the deduction for these items has been suspended. In 2026, the total of these expenses ($2,490) will be deductible to the extent they exceed 2% of Jean's AGI.

SCHEDULE A (Form 1040)
Department of the Treasury Internal Revenue Service

Itemized Deductions

Go to *www.irs.gov/ScheduleA* for instructions and the latest information.
Attach to Form 1040 or 1040-SR.
Caution: If you are claiming a net qualified disaster loss on Form 4684, see the instructions for line 16.

OMB No. 1545-0074
2022
Attachment Sequence No. **07**

Name(s) shown on Form 1040 or 1040-SR	Your social security number
Jean Brown	*123-45-6789*

Medical and Dental Expenses		**Caution:** Do not include expenses reimbursed or paid by others.				
	1	Medical and dental expenses (see instructions)	1	*13,592*		
	2	Enter amount from Form 1040 or 1040-SR, line 11 [2] *120,000*				
	3	Multiply line 2 by 7.5% (0.075)	3	*9,000*		
	4	Subtract line 3 from line 1. If line 3 is more than line 1, enter -0-			4	*4,592*
Taxes You Paid	5	State and local taxes.				
	a	State and local income taxes or general sales taxes. You may include either income taxes or general sales taxes on line 5a, but not both. If you elect to include general sales taxes instead of income taxes, check this box ☐	5a	*7,900*		
	b	State and local real estate taxes (see instructions)	5b	*6,580*		
	c	State and local personal property taxes	5c			
	d	Add lines 5a through 5c	5d	*14,480*		
	e	Enter the smaller of line 5d or $10,000 ($5,000 if married filing separately)	5e	*10,000*		
	6	Other taxes. List type and amount:	6			
	7	Add lines 5e and 6			7	*10,000*
Interest You Paid Caution: Your mortgage interest deduction may be limited. See instructions.	8	Home mortgage interest and points. If you didn't use all of your home mortgage loan(s) to buy, build, or improve your home, see instructions and check this box ☐				
	a	Home mortgage interest and points reported to you on Form 1098. See instructions if limited	8a	*4,340*		
	b	Home mortgage interest not reported to you on Form 1098. See instructions if limited. If paid to the person from whom you bought the home, see instructions and show that person's name, identifying no., and address	8b			
	c	Points not reported to you on Form 1098. See instructions for special rules	8c			
	d	Reserved for future use	8d			
	e	Add lines 8a through 8c	8e			
	9	Investment interest. Attach Form 4952 if required. See instructions	9			
	10	Add lines 8e and 9			10	*4,340*
Gifts to Charity Caution: If you made a gift and got a benefit for it, see instructions.	11	Gifts by cash or check. If you made any gift of $250 or more, see instructions	11	*2,160*		
	12	Other than by cash or check. If you made any gift of $250 or more, see instructions. You **must** attach Form 8283 if over $500	12	*119*		
	13	Carryover from prior year	13			
	14	Add lines 11 through 13			14	*2,279*
Casualty and Theft Losses	15	Casualty and theft loss(es) from a federally declared disaster (other than net qualified disaster losses). Attach Form 4684 and enter the amount from line 18 of that form. See instructions			15	
Other Itemized Deductions	16	Other—from list in instructions. List type and amount:			16	
Total Itemized Deductions	17	Add the amounts in the far right column for lines 4 through 16. Also, enter this amount on Form 1040 or 1040-SR, line 12			17	*21,211*
	18	If you elect to itemize deductions even though they are less than your standard deduction, check this box ☐				

10-8 Tax Planning

LO.8

Identify tax planning strategies to maximize the benefit of itemized deductions.

10-8a Maximizing the Medical Deduction

When a taxpayer anticipates that medical expenses will be close to the percentage floor for a year, the taxpayer should consider accelerating other medical expenses into the year. Any of the following techniques can help build a deduction by the end of the year:

- Incur the obligation for needed dental work or have needed work carried out.[62]
- Have elective remedial surgery that may have been postponed from prior years.
- Incur the obligation for capital improvements to the taxpayer's personal residence recommended by a physician (e.g., an air filtration system to alleviate a respiratory disorder).

The use of credit cards is deemed to be payment for purposes of timing the deductibility of charitable and medical expenses.

On December 13, 2023, Mary (a calendar year taxpayer) purchases two pairs of prescription contact lenses and one pair of prescribed orthopedic shoes for a total of $850. These purchases are charged separately to Mary's credit card. On January 6, 2024, Mary receives her statement containing these charges and makes payment shortly thereafter.

The purchases are deductible as medical expenses in the year charged (2023) rather than in the year the account is settled (2024).

Recognizing which expenses qualify for the medical deduction also may be crucial to exceeding the percentage limitations.

Ethan employs Leah (an unrelated party) to care for his incapacitated and dependent mother. Leah is not a trained nurse but spends approximately one-half of the time performing nursing duties (e.g., administering injections and providing physical therapy) and the rest of the time doing household chores. An allocable portion of Leah's wages that Ethan pays (including the employer's portion of FICA taxes) qualifies as a medical expense.

10-8b Ensuring the Charitable Contribution Deduction

For a charitable contribution deduction to be available, the recipient must be a qualified charitable organization. Sometimes the mechanics of how the contribution is carried out can determine whether a deduction results.

Fumiko wants to donate $5,000 to her church's mission in Kobe, Japan. In this regard, she considers three alternatives:

1. Send the money directly to the mission.
2. Give the money to her church in Charlotte with the understanding that it is to be passed on to the mission.
3. Give the money directly to the missionary in charge of the mission who is currently in the United States on a fund-raising trip.

If Fumiko wants to obtain a deduction for the contribution, she should choose alternative 2. A direct donation to the mission (alternative 1) is not deductible because the mission is a foreign charity. A direct gift to the missionary (alternative 3) does not comply because an individual cannot be a qualified charity for income tax purposes.[63]

[62] Prepayment of medical expenses does not generate a current deduction unless the taxpayer is under an obligation to make the payment.

[63] *Thomas E. Lesslie*, 36 TCM 495, T.C.Memo. 1977–111.

When making noncash donations, the type of property chosen can have significant implications in determining the amount, if any, of the deduction.

Sam wants to give $60,000 in value to his church in some form other than cash. In this connection, he considers four alternatives:

1. Stock held for two years as an investment with a basis of $100,000 and a fair market value of $60,000.
2. Stock held for five years as an investment with a basis of $10,000 and a fair market value of $60,000.
3. The rent-free use for a year of a building that normally leases for $5,000 a month.
4. A valuable stamp collection held as an investment and owned for 10 years with a basis of $10,000 and a fair market value of $60,000. The church plans to sell the collection if and when it is donated.

Alternative 1 is ill-advised as the subject of the gift. Even though Sam would obtain a deduction of $60,000, he would forgo the potential loss of $40,000 that would be recognized if the property were sold.[64]

Alternative 2 makes good sense because the deduction still is $60,000 and none of the $50,000 of appreciation that has occurred must be recognized as income.

Alternative 3 yields no deduction at all and is not a wise choice.

Alternative 4 involves tangible personalty that the church plans to sell. As a result, the amount of the deduction is limited to $10,000, the stamp collection's basis.[65]

For property transfers (particularly real estate), the ceiling limitations on the amount of the deduction allowed in any one year (50 percent, 30 percent, or 20 percent of AGI, as the case may be) could be a factor to take into account. With proper planning, donations can be controlled to stay within the limitations and avoid the need for a carryover of unused charitable contributions.

Andrew wants to donate to Eastern University (a qualified charitable organization) a tract of unimproved land held as an investment. The land has been held for six years and has a current fair market value of $300,000 and a basis to Andrew of $50,000. Andrew's AGI for the current year is estimated to be $200,000, and he expects much the same for the next few years. In the current year, he deeds (transfers) an undivided one-fifth interest in the real estate to the university.

What has Andrew in Example 42 accomplished for income tax purposes? In the current year, he will be allowed a charitable contribution deduction of $60,000 ($\frac{1}{5} \times$ $300,000), which will be within the applicable AGI limitation (30% $\times$ $200,000). Presuming no other charitable contributions for the year, Andrew has avoided the possibility of a carryover. In future years, Andrew can follow the same pattern. The only difficulty with this approach is the need to revalue the real estate each year before the donation, because the amount of the deduction is based on the fair market value of the interest contributed at the time of the donation.

The rules on documenting charitable contributions are crucial to the deduction. Thus, it is important for individuals who itemize their deductions to have and retain this documentation.

Karen made several charitable contributions this year. She wrote 10 checks of $500 each to different charitable organizations. In addition, she donated some of her furniture with an estimated value of $1,200.

Karen may claim only the $5,000 of cash donations if she has the canceled checks (or other proof of payment). In addition, because each donation was $250 or more, she must have a contemporaneous written acknowledgment from the charity before she files her return.

continued

[64] *LaVar M. Withers*, 69 T.C. 900 (1978).

[65] No reduction of appreciation is necessary in alternative 2 because stock is intangible property and not tangible personalty.

Because Karen donated noncash items valued at over $500, she must complete a Form 8283, documenting the date each item was acquired, how it was acquired, the basis (generally, cost) and fair market value of each item, and how that value was determined. A contemporaneous written acknowledgment also is required for these items (since the donation was valued at $250 or more).

Karen can only claim a charitable contribution deduction for those items for which she has the required documentation.

10-8c Planning to Avoid Nondeductible Treatment

Many personal expenditures are not deductible (e.g., tax return preparation fees and unreimbursed employee business expenses). Consideration should be given to whether any of these nondeductible items can become deductible with planning and knowledge of the tax law. For example, if an individual has a sole proprietor business, the tax return preparation fees can be split between the nondeductible personal portion and the deductible portion related to the business and reported on Schedule C (Form 1040).[66]

Employees who must incur expenses for work (e.g., continuing education classes and uniform cleaning) should encourage their employer to reimburse them for these expenses. If the employer establishes an accountable plan, the expenses are deductible by the employer and not treated as income to the employee.[67]

Refocus on The Big Picture

Impact of Itemized Deductions on Major Purchases

ISTOCK.COM/IZUSEK

Because the Federal tax law provides that qualified residence interest and real estate taxes are deductible by individual taxpayers, the after-tax cost of a home purchase will be reduced by the tax savings associated with these itemized tax deductions (see Example 1). Given the Williamsons' projected taxable income, they are in the 24 percent Federal income tax bracket and the 6 percent state income tax bracket (i.e., aggregate marginal tax bracket of 30 percent). As a result, the after-tax cost of financing the purchase of the home will be:

Nondeductible principal payments	$ 2,000
Deductible qualified residence interest and real estate taxes [($37,000 + $4,000) × (1 − 0.30)]	28,700
Total	$30,700
After-tax monthly cost ($30,700 ÷ 12)	$ 2,558

Because the Williamsons will be able to itemize their deductions if they purchase a new home and will be able to deduct most of their monthly house payment, the home purchase will be affordable (see Examples 17 and 22).

What If?

What if the Williamsons use the less expensive route to finance the purchase of their home by using their retirement and taxable portfolio as security for the loan? What may at first appear to be a cost-effective approach ends up being more costly when considering the impact of the tax law. With this approach, the interest expense is not deductible because it is not qualified residence interest (see Example 22); further, it is not deductible as investment interest (see text Section 11-4). Therefore, the after-tax cost of financing the home using this approach makes the home more expensive, and perhaps unaffordable, for the Williamsons.

Nondeductible principal and interest payments ($2,000 + $35,000)	$37,000
Deductible real estate taxes [$4,000 × (1 − 0.30)]	2,800
Total	$39,800
After-tax monthly cost ($39,800 ÷ 12)	$ 3,317

66 Rev.Rul. 92–29.

67 Reg. § 1.62–2.

Key Terms

Acquisition indebtedness, 10-15
Capital gain property, 10-23
Charitable contribution, 10-18
Health Savings Account (HSA), 10-8
Home equity loans, 10-15
Medical expense, 10-3
Miscellaneous itemized deductions, 10-27
Ordinary income property, 10-22
Points, 10-16
Qualified residence interest, 10-14

Discussion Questions

1. **LO.1, 2** Dan, a self-employed individual taxpayer, prepared his own income tax return for the past year and has asked you to check it for accuracy. Your review indicates that Dan failed to claim certain business meals expenses. Will the correction of this omission affect the amount of medical expenses Dan can deduct? Explain.

2. **LO.2** Ángel was in an accident and required cosmetic surgery for injuries to his nose. He also had the doctor do additional surgery to reshape his chin, which had not been injured. Will the cosmetic surgery to Ángel's nose qualify as a medical expense? Will the cosmetic surgery to Ángel's chin qualify as a medical expense? Explain.

3. **LO.2, 8** Jerry and Elaine are comparing their tax situations. Both are paying all of the nursing home expenses of their parents. Jerry can include the expenses in computing his medical expense deduction, but Elaine cannot. What explanation can you offer for the difference?

Critical Thinking
Planning

4. **LO.2** Cheryl incurred $8,700 of medical expenses in November 2023. On December 5, the clinic where she was treated mailed her the insurance claim form it had prepared for her with a suggestion that she sign and return the form immediately to receive her reimbursement from the insurance company by December 31. What tax issues should Cheryl consider in deciding whether to sign and return the form in December 2023 or January 2024?

5. **LO.2** David, a sole proprietor of a bookstore, pays a $7,500 premium for medical insurance for him and his family. Joan, an employee of a small firm that doesn't provide her with medical insurance, pays medical insurance premiums of $8,000 for herself. How does the tax treatment differ for David and Joan?

6. **LO.2** Jayden, a calendar year taxpayer, paid $16,000 in medical expenses and sustained a $20,000 casualty loss in 2023 (the loss occurred in a Federally declared disaster area). He expects $12,000 of the medical expenses and $14,000 of the casualty loss to be reimbursed by insurance companies in 2024. Before considering any limitations on these deductions, how much can Jayden include in determining his itemized deductions for 2023?

7. **LO.2** Jacob, a self-employed taxpayer, is married and has two children. He has asked you to explain the tax and nontax advantages of creating a Health Savings Account (HSA) for him and his family.

Critical Thinking
Decision Making
Planning

8. **LO.5, 8** Michaela owns a principal residence in Georgia, a townhouse in San Francisco, and a yacht in Cape Cod. All of the properties have mortgages on which Michaela pays interest. What are the limitations on Michaela's mortgage interest deduction? What strategy should Michaela consider to maximize her mortgage interest deduction?

9. **LO.5, 8** Mason Gregg's car was destroyed by a flood that occurred in a Federally declared disaster area. Unfortunately, his insurance had lapsed two days before he incurred the loss. Mason uses his car for both business and personal use. Mason, who is self-employed, does not have adequate savings to replace the car and must borrow money to purchase a new car. He is considering using his credit card, at a 12% interest rate, to obtain funds for the purchase. Margaret, his wife, would prefer to sell some of their stock in Bluebird, Inc., to raise funds to purchase the new car. Mason does not want to sell the stock because it has declined in value since they purchased it, and he is convinced that its price will increase in the next two years. Mason has suggested that they obtain conventional financing for the purchase from their bank, which charges 7% interest on car loans. Identify the tax issues and planning considerations related to each of the three alternatives for Mason and Margaret. Critical Thinking Planning

10. **LO.5** Commercial Bank has initiated an advertising campaign that encourages customers to take out loans secured by their home to pay for purchases of automobiles. Are there any tax advantages related to this type of borrowing? Explain.

11. **LO.5** Thomas purchased a personal residence from Monique. To sell the residence, Monique agreed to pay $5,500 in points related to Thomas's mortgage. Discuss the deductibility of the points.

12. **LO.6** The city of Lawrence recently was hit by a tornado, leaving many families in need of food, clothing, shelter, and other necessities. Betty contributed $500 to a family whose home was completely destroyed by the tornado. Jack contributed $700 to the family's church, which gave the money to the family. Discuss the deductibility of these contributions.

13. **LO.6** Mike purchased four $100 tickets to a fund-raising dinner and dance sponsored by the public library, a qualified charitable organization. In its advertising for the event, the library indicated that the cost of the tickets would be deductible for Federal income tax purposes. Comment on the library's assertion.

14. **LO.6, 8** William, a high school teacher, earns about $50,000 each year. In December 2023, he won $1,000,000 in the state lottery. William plans to donate $100,000 to his church. He has asked you, his tax adviser, whether he should donate the $100,000 in 2023 or 2024. Identify the tax issues related to William's decision. Critical Thinking Planning

Computational Exercises

15. **LO.2** Barbara incurred the following expenses during 2023: $840 dues at a health club she joined at the suggestion of her physician to improve her general physical condition, $240 for multiple vitamins and antioxidant vitamins, $3,500 for a smoking cessation program, $250 for nonprescription nicotine gum, $2,600 for insulin, and $7,200 for funeral expenses for her mother who passed away in June. Barbara's AGI for 2023 is $54,000. What is Barbara's medical expense deduction for 2023?

16. **LO.3, 4** Tabitha sells real estate on March 2 for $260,000. The buyer, Ramona, pays the real estate taxes of $5,200 for the calendar year, which is the real estate property tax year. Assume that this is *not* a leap year.
    a. Determine the real estate taxes apportioned to and deductible by the seller, Tabitha, and the amount of taxes deductible by Ramona.
    b. Calculate Ramona's basis in the property and the amount realized by Tabitha from the sale.

17. **LO.4** Pierre, a cash basis, unmarried taxpayer, had $1,400 of state income tax withheld during 2023. Also in 2023, Pierre paid $455 that was due when he filed his 2022 state income tax return and made estimated payments of $975 toward his 2023 state income tax liability. When Pierre files his 2023 Federal income tax return in April 2024, he elects to itemize deductions, which amount to $15,650, including the state income tax payments and withholdings, all of which reduce his taxable income.

    a. What is Pierre's 2023 state income tax deduction?

    b. As a result of overpaying his 2023 state income tax, Pierre receives a refund of $630 early in 2024. The standard deduction for single taxpayers for 2023 was $13,850. How much of the $630 will Pierre include in his 2024 gross income?

18. **LO.4** Derek, a cash basis, unmarried taxpayer, had $610 of state income tax withheld during 2023. Also in 2023, Derek paid $50 that was due when he filed his 2022 state income tax return and made estimated payments of $100 toward his 2023 state income tax liability. When Derek files his 2023 Federal income tax return in April 2024, he elects to take the standard deduction, which reduced his taxable income. As a result of overpaying his 2023 state income tax, Derek receives a refund of $435 early in 2024. How much of the $435 will Derek include in his 2024 gross income?

19. **LO.5** Miller owns a personal residence with a fair market value of $195,000 and an outstanding first mortgage of $157,500, which was used entirely to acquire the residence. This year, Miller gets a home equity loan of $10,000 to purchase a new fishing boat for personal use. How much of this mortgage debt is treated as qualified residence indebtedness?

20. **LO.6** Donna donates stock in Chipper Corporation to the American Red Cross on September 10, 2023. She purchased the stock for $18,100 on December 28, 2022, and it had a fair market value of $27,000 when she made the donation.

    a. What is Donna's charitable contribution deduction?

    b. Assume instead that the stock had a fair market value of $15,000 (rather than $27,000) when it was donated to the American Red Cross. What is Donna's charitable contribution deduction?

    c. What documentation should you request from Donna to confirm the amount of her charitable contribution deduction?

21. **LO. 5, 8** The Wilmoths plan to purchase a house but want to determine the after-tax cost of financing its purchase. Given their projected taxable income, the Wilmoths are in the 24% Federal income tax bracket and the 8% state income tax bracket (i.e., an aggregate marginal tax bracket of 32%). Assume that the Wilmoths will benefit from itemizing their deductions for both Federal and state purposes. The total cash outlay during the first year of ownership will be $23,400 ($1,200 principal payments, $22,200 qualified residence interest payments). Determine the initial year after-tax cost of financing the purchase of the home.

Problems

Communications

22. **LO.2** Emma Doyle is employed as a corporate attorney. For calendar year 2023, she had AGI of $75,000 and paid the following medical expenses:

Medical insurance premiums	$3,700
Doctor and dentist bills for Bob and April (Emma's parents)	6,800
Doctor and dentist bills for Emma	5,200
Prescription medicines for Emma	400
Nonprescription insulin for Emma	350

Bob and April would qualify as Emma's dependents except that they file a joint return. Emma's medical insurance policy does not cover them. Emma filed a claim for reimbursement of $2,800 of her own expenses with her insurance company in

December 2023 and received the reimbursement in January 2024. What is Emma's maximum allowable medical expense deduction for 2023? Prepare a memo for your firm's tax files in which you document your conclusions.

23. **LO.2** Reba is a single taxpayer. Lawrence, Reba's 84-year-old dependent grandfather, lived with Reba until this year, when he moved to Lakeside Nursing Home because he needs specialized medical and nursing care. During the year, Reba made the following payments on behalf of Lawrence:

Room at Lakeside	$11,000
Meals for Lawrence at Lakeside	2,200
Doctor and nurse fees at Lakeside	1,700
Cable TV service for Lawrence's room at Lakeside	380
Total	$15,280

Lakeside has medical staff in residence. Disregarding the AGI floor, how much, if any, of these expenses qualifies for a medical expense deduction by Reba?

24. **LO.2** Paul suffers from emphysema and severe allergies and, upon the recommendation of his physician, has a dust elimination system installed in his personal residence. In connection with the system, Paul incurs and pays the following amounts during 2023:

Doctor and hospital bills	$ 4,500
Dust elimination system	10,000
Increase in utility bills due to the system	450
Cost of certified appraisal	300

In addition, Paul pays $750 for prescribed medicines.

The system has an estimated useful life of 20 years. The appraisal was to determine the value of Paul's residence with and without the system. The appraisal states that his residence was worth $350,000 before the system was installed and $356,000 after the installation. Paul's AGI for the year was $50,000. How much is Paul's medical expense deduction in 2023?

25. **LO.2** For calendar year 2023, Giana was a self-employed consultant with no employees. She had $80,000 of net profit from consulting and paid $7,000 in medical insurance premiums on her policy covering 2023. How much of these premiums may Giana deduct as a deduction *for* AGI? How much may she deduct as an itemized deduction (subject to the AGI floor)?

26. **LO.2** During 2023, Susan incurred and paid the following expenses for Beth (her daughter), Ed (her father), and herself:

Surgery for Beth	$4,500
Red River Academy charges for Beth:	
Tuition	5,100
Room, board, and other expenses	4,800
Psychiatric treatment	5,100
Doctor bills for Ed	2,200
Prescription drugs for Susan, Beth, and Ed	780
Insulin for Ed	540
Nonprescription drugs for Susan, Beth, and Ed	570
Charges at Heartland Nursing Home for Ed:	
Medical care	5,000
Lodging	2,700
Meals	2,650

Beth qualifies as Susan's dependent, and Ed also would qualify except that he receives $7,400 of taxable retirement benefits from his former employer. Beth's psychiatrist recommended Red River Academy because of its small classes and specialized psychiatric treatment program that is needed to treat Beth's illness. Ed, who is a paraplegic and diabetic, entered Heartland in October. Heartland offers the type of care that he requires.

Upon the recommendation of a physician, Susan has an air filtration system installed in her personal residence. She suffers from severe allergies. In connection with this equipment, Susan incurs and pays the following amounts during the year:

Filtration system and cost of installation	$6,500
Increase in utility bills due to the system	700
Cost of certified appraisal	360

The system has an estimated useful life of 10 years. The appraisal was to determine the value of Susan's residence with and without the system. The appraisal states that the system increased the value of Susan's residence by $2,200. Ignoring the AGI floor, what is the total of Susan's expenses that qualifies for the medical expense deduction?

Critical Thinking

27. **LO.2** In May, Rebecca's daughter, Isabella, sustained a serious injury that made it impossible for her to continue living alone. Isabella, who is a novelist, moved back into Rebecca's home after the accident. Isabella has begun writing a novel based on her recent experiences. To accommodate Isabella, Rebecca incurred significant remodeling expenses (widening hallways, building a separate bedroom and bathroom, and making kitchen appliances accessible to Isabella). In addition, Rebecca had an indoor swimming pool constructed so that Isabella could do rehabilitation exercises prescribed by her physician.

    In September, Isabella underwent major reconstructive surgery in Denver. The surgery was performed by Dr. Rama Patel, who specializes in treating injuries of the type Isabella sustained. Rebecca drove Isabella from Champaign, Illinois, to Denver, a total of 1,100 miles, in Isabella's specially equipped van. They left Champaign on Tuesday morning and arrived in Denver on Thursday afternoon. Rebecca incurred expenses for gasoline, highway tolls, meals, and lodging while traveling to Denver. Rebecca stayed in a motel near the clinic for eight days while Isabella was hospitalized. Identify the relevant tax issues based on this information, and prepare a list of questions you would need to ask Rebecca and Isabella to advise them as to the resolution of any issues you have identified.

28. **LO.2** In the current year, Roger pays a $3,000 premium for high-deductible medical insurance for him and his family. In addition, he contributed $2,600 to a Health Savings Account.

    a. How much may Roger deduct if he is self-employed? Is the deduction *for* AGI or *from* AGI?

    b. How much may Roger deduct if he is an employee? Is the deduction *for* AGI or *from* AGI?

29. **LO.3, 4** Alicia sold her personal residence to Rick on June 30 for $300,000. Before the sale, Alicia paid the real estate tax of $4,380 for the calendar year. For income tax purposes, the deduction is apportioned as follows: $2,160 to Alicia and $2,220 to Rick. What is Rick's basis in the residence?

30. **LO.4** Nichole, who is single and uses the cash method of accounting, lives in a state that imposes an income tax. In April 2023, she files her state income tax return for 2022 and pays an additional $1,000 in state income taxes. During 2023, her withholdings for state income tax purposes amount to $7,400, and she pays

estimated state income tax of $700. In April 2024, she files her state income tax return for 2023, claiming a refund of $1,800. Nichole receives the refund in August 2024. Nichole has no other state or local tax expenses.

a. Assuming that Nichole itemized deductions in 2023, how much may she claim as a deduction for state income taxes on her Federal return for calendar year 2023 (filed April 2024)?

b. Assuming that Nichole itemized deductions in 2023 (which totaled $20,000), how will the refund of $1,800 that she received in 2024 be treated for Federal income tax purposes?

c. Assume that Nichole itemized deductions in 2023 (which totaled $20,000) and that she elects to have the $1,800 refund applied toward her 2024 state income tax liability. How will the $1,800 be treated for Federal income tax purposes?

d. Assuming that Nichole did not itemize deductions in 2023, how will the refund of $1,800 received in 2024 be treated for Federal income tax purposes?

31. **LO.5** This year, Amy purchased a personal residence at a cost of $1,000,000. She borrowed $800,000 secured by the home to make the purchase. This year, she paid interest expense on this mortgage of $12,000. How much may she deduct?

32. **LO.6** This year, Nadia donates $4,000 to Eastern University's athletic department. The payment guarantees that Nadia will have preferred seating at football games near the 50-yard line. Assume that Nadia subsequently buys four $100 game tickets. How much can she deduct as a charitable contribution to the university's athletic department?

33. **LO.6** Liz had AGI of $130,000 in 2023. She donated Bluebird Corporation stock with a basis of $10,000 to a qualified charitable organization on July 5, 2023.

a. What is the amount of Liz's deduction assuming that she purchased the stock on December 3, 2022, and the stock had a fair market value of $17,000 when she made the donation?

b. Assume the same facts as in part (a), except that Liz purchased the stock on July 1, 2020.

c. Assume the same facts as in part (a), except that the stock had a fair market value of $7,500 (rather than $17,000) when Liz donated it to the charity.

34. **LO.6, 8** Ramon had AGI of $180,000 in 2023. He is considering making a charitable contribution this year to the American Heart Association, a qualified charitable organization. Determine the current allowable charitable contribution deduction in each of the following independent situations, and indicate the treatment for any amount that is not deductible currently. Identify any planning ideas to minimize Ramon's tax liability.

Critical Thinking
Decision Making
Planning

a. A cash gift of $95,000.

b. A gift of OakCo stock worth $95,000 on the contribution date. Ramon had acquired the stock as an investment two years ago at a cost of $84,000.

c. A gift of a painting worth $95,000 that Ramon purchased three years ago for $60,000. The charity has indicated that it would sell the painting to generate cash to fund medical research.

d. Ramon has decided to make a cash gift to the American Heart Association of $113,000. However, he is considering delaying his gift until 2024 when his AGI will increase to $300,000 and he will be in the 32% income tax bracket, an increase from his 2023 income tax bracket of 24%. Ramon asks you to determine the tax savings from the tax deduction in present value terms if he were to make the gift in 2023 rather than delay the gift until 2024. See Appendix E for the present value factors, and assume a 6% discount rate.

35. **LO.6** On December 27, 2023, Roberta purchased four tickets to a charity ball sponsored by the city of San Diego for the benefit of underprivileged children. Each ticket cost $200 and had a fair market value of $35. On the same day as the purchase, Roberta gave the tickets to the minister of her church for personal use by his family. At the time of the gift of the tickets, Roberta pledged $4,000 to the building fund of her church. The pledge was satisfied by a check dated December 31, 2023, but not mailed until January 3, 2024.

   a. Presuming that Roberta is a cash basis and calendar year taxpayer, how much can she deduct as a charitable contribution for 2023?

   b. Would the amount of the deduction be any different if Roberta was an accrual basis taxpayer? Explain.

Communications
Critical Thinking
Planning

36. **LO.6, 8** In December of each year, Eleanor Young contributes 10% of her gross income to the United Way (a 50% organization). Eleanor, who is in the 24% marginal tax bracket, is considering the following alternatives for satisfying the contribution.

	Fair Market Value
(1) Cash donation	$23,000
(2) Unimproved land held for six years ($3,000 basis)	23,000
(3) Blue Corporation stock held for eight months ($3,000 basis)	23,000
(4) Gold Corporation stock held for two years ($28,000 basis)	23,000

Eleanor has asked you to help her decide which of the potential contributions listed above will be most advantageous taxwise. Evaluate the four alternatives, and write a letter to Eleanor to communicate your advice to her. Her address is 2622 Bayshore Drive, Berkeley, CA 94709.

Communications
Critical Thinking
Planning

37. **LO.2, 3, 4, 5, 7, 8** Bart and Elizabeth Forrest are married and have no dependents. They have asked you to advise them whether they should file jointly or separately in 2023. Bart incurred some significant medical expenses during the year related to an unexpected surgery. They present you with the following information:

	Bart	Elizabeth	Joint
Salary (Bart)	$38,000		
Salary (Elizabeth)		$110,000	
Interest income	400	1,200	$2,200
Deductions *for* AGI	2,400	14,000	
Medical expenses	10,427	3,358	
State income tax	900	11,800	
Real estate tax			5,800
Mortgage interest			4,200
Unreimbursed employee expenses	1,200		

If they file separately, Bart and Elizabeth will split the real estate tax and mortgage interest deductions equally. Write Bart and Elizabeth a letter in which you make and explain a recommendation on filing status for 2023. Bart and Elizabeth reside at 2003 Highland Drive, Durham, NC 27707.

38. **LO.2, 3, 4, 5, 6, 7** Evan is single and has AGI of $277,300 in 2023. His potential itemized deductions before any limitations for the year total $52,300 and consist of the following:

Medical expenses (before the 7.5%-of-AGI limitation)	$31,000
Interest on home mortgage	8,700
State income taxes	9,500
Real estate taxes	3,600
Charitable contributions	2,500

After all necessary adjustments are made, what is the amount of itemized deductions Evan may claim?

39. **LO.2, 3, 4, 5, 6, 7** Linda, who files as a single taxpayer, had AGI of $280,000 for 2023. She incurred the following expenses and losses during the year:

Medical expenses (before the 7.5%-of-AGI limitation)	$33,000
State and local income taxes	4,800
State sales tax	1,300
Real estate taxes	6,000
Home mortgage interest	5,000
Automobile loan interest	750
Credit card interest	1,000
Charitable contributions	7,000
Casualty loss (before the 10%-of-AGI limitation but after the $100 floor; not in a Federally declared disaster area)	34,000
Unreimbursed employee business expenses	7,600

Calculate Linda's allowable itemized deductions for the year.

40. **LO.2, 3, 4, 5, 6, 7** For calendar year 2023, Stuart and Pamela Gibson file a joint return reflecting AGI of $350,000. Their itemized deductions are as follows:

Casualty loss in a Federally declared disaster area (not covered by insurance; before the 10%-of-AGI limitation but after the $100 floor)	$48,600
Home mortgage interest (loan qualifies as acquisition indebtedness)	19,000
Credit card interest	800
Property taxes on home	16,300
Charitable contributions	28,700
State income tax	18,000
Tax return preparation fees	1,200

Calculate the amount of itemized deductions the Gibsons may claim for the year.

Tax Return Problems

Decision Making
Planning
Tax Forms Problem
ProConnect™ Tax

41. Alice J. and Bruce M. Byrd are married taxpayers who file a joint return. Their Social Security numbers are 123-45-6784 and 111-11-1113, respectively. Alice's birthday is September 21, 1975, and Bruce's is June 27, 1974. They live at 473 Revere Avenue, Lowell, MA 01850. Alice is the office manager for Lowell Dental Clinic, 433 Broad Street, Lowell, MA 01850 (Employer Identification Number 98-7654321). Bruce is the manager of a Super Burgers fast-food outlet owned and operated by Plymouth Corporation, 1247 Central Avenue, Hauppauge, NY 11788 (Employer Identification Number 11-1111111).

The following information is shown on their Wage and Tax Statements (Form W–2) for 2022.

Line	Description	Alice	Bruce
1	Wages, tips, other compensation	$58,000	$62,100
2	Federal income tax withheld	4,500	5,300
3	Social Security wages	58,000	62,100
4	Social Security tax withheld	3,596	3,850
5	Medicare wages and tips	58,000	62,100
6	Medicare tax withheld	841	900
15	State	Massachusetts	Massachusetts
16	State wages, tips, etc.	58,000	62,100
17	State income tax withheld	2,950	3,100

The Byrds provide over half of the support of their two children, Cynthia (born January 25, 1998, Social Security number 123-45-6788) and John (born February 7, 2002, Social Security number 123-45-6780). Both children are full-time students and live with the Byrds except when they are away at college. Cynthia earned $6,200 from a summer internship in 2022, and John earned $3,800 from a part-time job. Both children received scholarships covering tuition and materials.

During 2022, the Byrds provided 60% of the total support of Bruce's widower father, Sam Byrd (born March 6, 1946, Social Security number 123-45-6787). Sam lived alone and covered the rest of his support with his Social Security benefits. Sam died in November, and Bruce, the beneficiary of a policy on Sam's life, received life insurance proceeds of $1,600,000 on December 28.

The Byrds had the following expenses relating to their personal residence during 2022:

Property taxes	$5,000
Qualified interest on home mortgage (acquisition indebtedness)	8,700
Repairs to roof	5,750
Utilities	4,100
Fire and theft insurance	1,900

The Byrds had the following medical expenses for 2022:

Medical insurance premiums	$4,500
Doctor bill for Sam incurred in 2021 and not paid until 2022	7,600
Operation for Sam	8,500
Prescription medicines for Sam	900
Hospital expenses for Sam	3,500
Reimbursement from insurance company, received in 2022	3,600

The medical expenses for Sam represent most of the 60% that Bruce contributed toward his father's support.

Other relevant information follows:

- When they filed their 2021 state return in 2022, the Byrds paid additional state income tax of $900.
- During 2022, Alice and Bruce attended a dinner dance sponsored by the Lowell Police Disability Association (a qualified charitable organization). The Byrds paid $300 for the tickets. The cost of comparable entertainment would normally be $50.
- The Byrds contributed $5,000 to Lowell Presbyterian Church and gave used clothing (cost of $1,200 and fair market value of $350) to the Salvation Army. All donations are supported by receipts, and the clothing is in very good condition.
- Via a crowdfunding site (gofundme.com), Alice and Bruce made a gift to a needy family who lost their home in a fire ($400). In addition, they made several cash gifts to homeless individuals downtown (estimated to be $65).
- In 2022, the Byrds received interest income of $2,750, which was reported on a Form 1099–INT from Second National Bank, 125 Oak Street, Lowell, MA 01850 (Employer Identification Number 98-7654322).
- The home mortgage interest was reported on Form 1098 by Lowell Commercial Bank, P.O. Box 1000, Lowell, MA 01850 (Employer Identification Number 98-7654323). The mortgage (outstanding balance of $425,000 as of January 1, 2022) was taken out by the Byrds on May 1, 2018.
- Alice's employer requires that all employees wear uniforms to work. During 2022, Alice spent $850 on new uniforms and $566 on laundry charges.

- Bruce paid $400 for an annual subscription to the *Journal of Franchise Management* and $741 for annual membership dues to his professional association.
- Neither Alice's nor Bruce's employer reimburses for employee expenses.
- The Byrds do not keep the receipts for the sales taxes they paid and had no major purchases subject to sales tax.
- This year, the Byrds gave each of their children $2,000, which was then deposited into their Roth IRAs.
- Alice and Bruce paid no estimated Federal income tax, and they did not engage in any digital asset transactions during the year. Neither Alice nor Bruce wants to designate $3 to the Presidential Election Campaign Fund.

Part 1—Tax Computation
Compute net tax payable or refund due for Alice and Bruce Byrd for 2022, and complete their 2022 Federal tax return using appropriate forms and schedules. If they have overpaid their taxes, they want the amount to be refunded to them. Suggested software: ProConnect Tax.

Part 2—Tax Planning
Alice and Bruce are planning some significant changes for 2023. They have provided you with the following information and asked you to project their taxable income and tax liability for 2023.

The Byrds will invest the $1,600,000 of life insurance proceeds in short-term certificates of deposit (CDs) and use the interest for living expenses during 2023. They expect to earn total interest of $32,000 on the CDs.

Bruce has been promoted to regional manager, and his salary for 2023 will be $88,000. He estimates that state income tax withheld will increase by $4,000 and the Social Security tax withheld will be $5,456.

Alice, who has been diagnosed with a serious illness, will take a leave of absence from work during 2023, so she will not receive a salary or incur any work-related expenses during the year. The estimated cost for her medical treatment is $15,400, of which $6,400 will be reimbursed by their insurance company in 2023. Their medical insurance premiums will increase to $9,769. Property taxes on their residence are expected to increase to $5,100. The Byrds' home mortgage interest expense and charitable contributions are expected to be unchanged from 2022.

John will graduate from college in December 2022 and will take a job in New York City in January 2023. His starting salary will be $46,000.

Assume that all of the information reported in 2022 will be the same in 2023 unless other information has been presented above.

42. Paul and Donna Decker are married taxpayers, ages 44 and 42, respectively, who file a joint return for 2023. The Deckers live at 1121 College Avenue, Carmel, IN 46032. Paul is an assistant manager at Carmel Motor Inn, and Donna is a teacher at Carmel Elementary School. They present you with W–2 forms that reflect the following information: Tax Computation Problem

	Paul	Donna
Salary	$68,000	$56,000
Federal tax withheld	5,770	5,630
State income tax withheld	1,400	1,100
FICA (Social Security and Medicare) withheld	5,202	4,284
Social Security numbers	111-11-1112	123-45-6789

Donna is the custodial parent of two children from a previous marriage who reside with the Deckers throughout the school year. The children, Larry and Jane Parker, reside with their father, Bob, during the summer. Relevant information for the children follows:

	Larry	Jane
Age	16	18
Social Security numbers	123-45-6788	123-45-6787
Months spent with Deckers	9	9

Under the divorce decree, Bob pays child support of $150 per month per child during the nine months the children live with the Deckers. Bob says that he spends $200 per month per child during the three summer months they reside with him. Donna and Paul can document that they provide $2,000 support per child per year. The divorce decree is silent as to which parent can claim the exemptions for the children.

In August, Paul and Donna added a suite to their home to provide more comfortable accommodations for Hannah Snyder (123-45-6786), Donna's mother, who had moved in with them in February 2022 after the death of Donna's father. Not wanting to borrow money for this addition, Paul sold 300 shares of Acme Corporation stock for $50 per share on May 3, 2023, and used the proceeds of $15,000 to cover construction costs. The Deckers had purchased the stock on April 29, 2018, for $25 per share. They received dividends of $750 on the jointly owned stock a month before the sale.

Hannah, who is 66 years old, received $7,500 in Social Security benefits during the year, of which she gave the Deckers $2,000 to use toward household expenses and deposited the remainder in her personal savings account. The Deckers determine that they have spent $2,500 of their own money for food, clothing, medical expenses, and other items for Hannah. They do not know what the rental value of Hannah's suite would be, but they estimate it would be at least $300 per month.

Interest paid during the year included the following:

Home mortgage interest (paid to Carmel Federal Savings & Loan)	$7,890
Interest on an automobile loan (paid to Carmel National Bank)	1,660
Interest on Citibank Visa card	620

In July, Paul hit a submerged rock while boating. Fortunately, he was uninjured after being thrown from the boat and landing in deep water. However, the boat, which was uninsured, was destroyed. Paul had paid $25,000 for the boat in June 2022, and its value was appraised at $18,000 on the date of the accident.

The Deckers paid doctor and hospital bills of $12,700 and were reimbursed $2,000 by their insurance company. They spent $640 for prescription drugs and medicines and $5,904 for premiums on their health insurance policy. They have filed additional claims of $1,200 with their insurance company and have been told they will receive payment for that amount in January 2024. Included in the amounts paid for doctor and hospital bills were payments of $380 for Hannah and $850 for the children.

Additional information of potential tax consequence follows:

Real estate taxes paid	$6,850
Sales taxes paid (per table)	1,379
Contributions to church	4,600
Appraised value of books donated to public library	740
Refund of state income tax for 2022 (the Deckers itemized on their 2022 Federal tax return, their total state and local taxes were less than $10,000, and their total itemized deductions exceeded their standard deduction by $5,400)	1,520

Compute net tax payable or refund due for the Deckers for 2023.

Research Problems

Note: Solutions to the Research Problems can be prepared by using the Thomson Reuters Checkpoint™ online tax research database, which accompanies this textbook. Solutions can also be prepared by using research materials found in a typical tax library.

Research Problem 1. Jane suffers from a degenerative spinal disorder. Her physician said that swimming could help prevent the onset of permanent paralysis and recommended the installation of a swimming pool at her residence for her use. Jane's residence had a market value of approximately $500,000 before the swimming pool was installed. The swimming pool was built, and an appraiser estimated that the value of Jane's home increased by $98,000 because of the addition.

The pool cost $194,000, and Jane claimed a medical expense deduction of $96,000 ($194,000 − $98,000) on her tax return. Upon audit of the return, the IRS determined that an adequate pool should have cost $70,000 and would increase the value of her home by only $31,000. Thus, the IRS claims that Jane is entitled to a deduction of only $39,000 ($70,000 − $31,000).

a. Is there any ceiling limitation on the amount deductible as a medical expense? Explain.
b. Can capital expenditures be deductible as medical expenses? Explain.
c. What is the significance of a "minimum adequate facility"? Should aesthetic or architectural qualities be considered in the determination? Why or why not?

Research Problem 2. Ken and Mary Jane Blough, your neighbors, have asked you for advice after receiving correspondence in the mail from the IRS. You learn that the IRS is asking for documentation in support of the itemized deductions the Bloughs claimed on a recent tax return. The Bloughs tell you that their income in the year of question was $75,000. Because their record-keeping habits are poor, they felt justified in claiming itemized deductions equal to the amounts that represent the average claimed by other taxpayers in their income bracket. These averages are calculated and reported by the IRS annually based on actual returns filed in an earlier year. Accordingly, they claimed medical expenses of $7,102, taxes of $6,050, interest of $10,659, and charitable contributions of $2,693. What advice do you give the Bloughs?

Partial list of research aids:
Cheryl L. de Werff, T.C. Summary Opinion, 2011–29.

Research Problem 3. Marcia, a shareholder in a corporation with stores in five states, donated stock with a basis of $10,000 to a qualified charitable organization in 2022. Although the stock of the corporation was not traded on a public stock exchange, many shares had been sold over the past several years. Based on the average selling price for the stock in 2022, Marcia deducted $95,000 on her 2022 tax return. Marcia received a notice from the IRS that the $95,000 deduction had been reduced to $10,000 because she had not obtained a qualified appraisal or attached a summary of her appraisal to her tax return. Marcia has asked you to advise her on this matter. Write a letter containing your conclusions to Ms. Marcia Meyer, 1311 Santos Court, San Bruno, CA 94066. Communications

Partial list of research aids:
Reg. § 1.170A–13(c)(2).

Research Problem 4. On March 5, 2017, the Hortons borrowed $100,000 against the equity in their personal residence with the loan secured by that home. In 2017, they were able to deduct the interest expense on this loan as home equity interest expense [an itemized deduction on Schedule A (Form 1040)]. The Tax Cuts and Jobs Act of 2017 disallows this interest expense deduction for 2018 through 2025. The Hortons'

CPA has asked them to review their financial records for February and March of 2017. They discover that they sold Disney stock on February 20, 2017, and used the proceeds to purchase Microsoft stock. Why is their CPA asking them for this information? How might this stock purchase in March 2017 help them obtain a deduction for all or part of the interest paid in 2018 and later on this home equity loan?

Partial list of research aids:
Temp.Reg. § 1.163–8T and Reg. § 1.163–15.

Use internet tax resources to address the following questions. Look for reliable websites and blogs of the IRS and other government agencies, media outlets, businesses, tax professionals, academics, think tanks, and political outlets.

Research Problem 5. The Federal government incurs a cost for every item that is deductible in the computation of taxable income. These costs, which take the form of forgone tax revenue, are often referred to as "tax expenditures." The Joint Committee on Taxation regularly estimates the current and projected tax expenditures associated with a long list of provisions in the tax law. Locate the Joint Committee on Taxation's most recent analysis, and identify the current tax expenditure associated with the deductions for medical expenses, interest on student loans, mortgage interest, and charitable contributions. How are these costs expected to change over the next five years? How is the concept of tax expenditures helpful to tax policy analysts?

Research Problem 6. Look for reliable data on how many individuals are affected by the $10,000 SALT cap. Use that data to make an argument for or against the cap.

Becker CPA Review Questions

Becker

1. In the current year, Wells paid the following expenses:

Premiums on an insurance policy against loss of earnings due to sickness or accident	$3,000
Physical therapy after spinal surgery	2,000
Premium on an insurance policy that covers reimbursement for the cost of prescription drugs	500

In the current year, Wells recovered $1,500 of the $2,000 that she paid for physical therapy through insurance reimbursement from a group medical policy paid for by her employer. Disregarding the adjusted gross income percentage threshold, what amount could be claimed on Wells's current-year income tax return for medical expenses?

a. $4,000
b. $3,500
c. $1,000
d. $500

2. Jordan Johnson is single and has adjusted gross income of $50,000 in the current year. Additional information is as follows:

State income taxes paid	$2,000
Mortgage interest on her personal residence	9,000
Points paid on purchase of her personal residence	1,000
Deductible contributions to her IRA	3,000
Uninsured realized casualty loss (in a Federal disaster area)	6,000
Tax preparation fees for her prior year income tax return	400

What amount may Jordan claim as itemized deductions on her current-year income tax return?

a. $12,000
b. $12,900
c. $13,300
d. $15,900

3. Sydney, a single taxpayer who itemizes deductions, had $80,000 in adjusted gross income in year 2. During the year, she contributed $15,000 to her church. She also had a $17,000 contribution carryover from her year 1 church contributions. What is the maximum amount of charitable deduction that Sydney may claim on her year 2 income tax return?

a. $40,000
b. $32,000
c. $19,200
d. $15,000

4. Kurstie received an $800 state income tax refund this year. Kurstie deducted $3,000 of state income taxes paid in the prior year as part of her itemized deductions. Which of the following statements regarding the taxability of Kurstie's refund is true?

a. If Kurstie's itemized deductions exceeded the standard deduction by $200, then the $800 refund is included in gross income.
b. If Kurstie's itemized deductions exceeded the standard deduction by $200, then $200 of the refund is included in gross income.
c. If Kurstie claimed the standard deduction instead, then the $800 refund is taxable.
d. Kurstie must include $3,000 in gross income in the current year.

5. Which of the following would preclude a taxpayer from deducting student loan interest expense?

a. The total amount paid is $1,000.
b. The taxpayer is single with AGI of $55,000.
c. The taxpayer is married filing jointly with AGI of $120,000.
d. The taxpayer is a dependent of another taxpayer.

6. Which of the following may *not* be claimed as a deduction by a taxpayer who claims the standard deduction?

a. Interest penalty on early withdrawal of savings
b. Self-employed health insurance
c. State income tax paid
d. IRA contribution

7. Chandler's home was damaged by a hurricane in a Federally declared disaster area. The fair market value of his home before the hurricane was $300,000. After the hurricane, the fair market value of the home dropped to $250,000. Damage to his home was estimated at $75,000. The adjusted basis of Chandler's home before the hurricane was $150,000. Chandler received an insurance payment for the damage in the amount of $30,000. Chandler's AGI is $90,000. What is Chandler's deductible casualty loss?

a. $65,900
b. $49,900
c. $35,900
d. $10,900

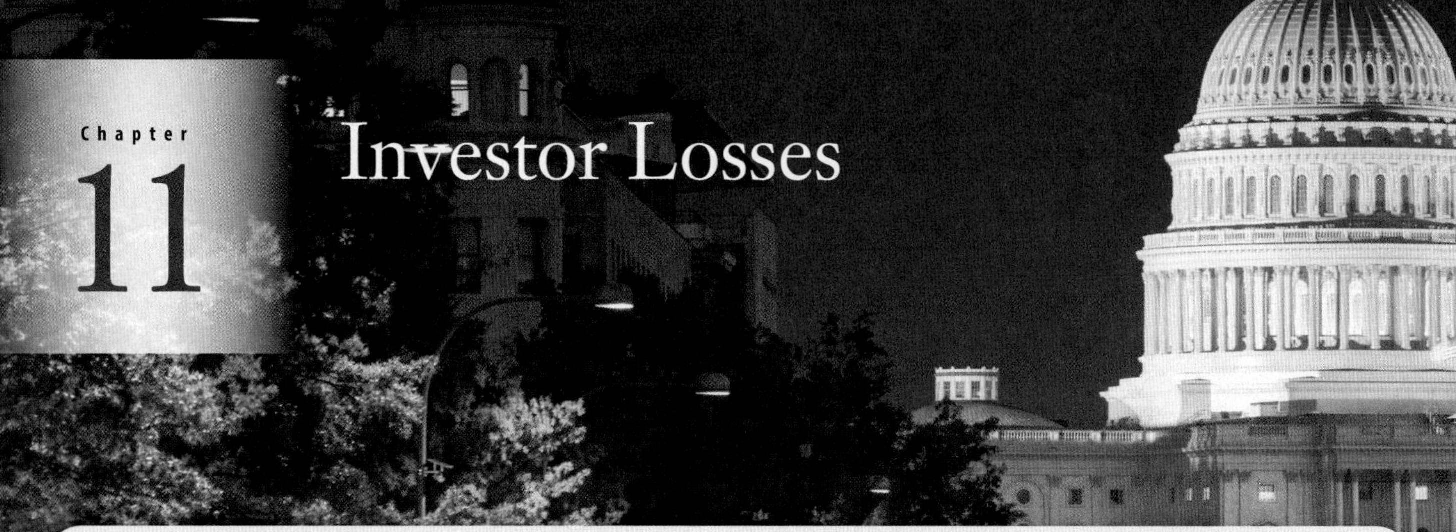

Chapter 11

Investor Losses

Learning Objectives: *After completing Chapter 11, you should be able to:*

LO.1 Explain the tax shelter problem and the reasons for the at-risk and passive activity loss limitations.

LO.2 Explain the at-risk limitation.

LO.3 Describe how the passive activity loss rules limit deductions for losses, and identify the taxpayers subject to these restrictions.

LO.4 Define passive activity, and describe the rules for identifying an activity.

LO.5 Identify the tests for material participation.

LO.6 Describe the classification of rental activities under the passive activity loss rules.

LO.7 Determine the relationship between the at-risk and passive activity loss limitations.

LO.8 Recognize the special treatment available to certain real estate activities.

LO.9 Determine the proper tax treatment for the disposition of a passive activity.

LO.10 Apply restrictions placed on the deductibility of investor losses and deductions, including those that apply to investment interest.

LO.11 Suggest tax planning strategies to minimize the effect of the passive activity loss and investment interest limitations, and recognize the general impact of the additional tax on net investment income.

Chapter Outline

The Big Picture

Investor Loss Limitations Affect the Viability of Certain Investment Opportunities

Ana and Jim Lopez are considering ways to enhance their financial security. In fact, they are willing to borrow a substantial sum so that they can make an appropriate investment.

Currently, Ana and Jim's sole sources of income are their salaries, totaling $180,000, from their full-time jobs. Their most significant asset is their personal residence (fair market value of $500,000 with a mortgage of $350,000). Each has a retirement plan at work; both are fully funding those plans as allowed by the law. The Lopezes' financial planner suggests that they borrow $50,000 at 4 percent and use the proceeds to make *one* of the following investments:

- A high-growth, low-yield portfolio of marketable securities. The portfolio's value is expected to grow 8 percent each year.
- An interest in a limited partnership that owns and operates orange groves in Florida. The limited partnership interest is expected to generate tax losses of $12,000 in each of the next five years, after which profits are expected. Assuming the losses are deductible when incurred, their financial planner predicts that the Lopezes would average an annual 8 percent return over a 10-year period.
- An interest in a local general partnership that owns and rents apartments to college students. This partnership interest also would generate losses of $12,000 per year for five years, after which profits would follow. Assuming the losses are deductible when incurred, these expected profits and losses would produce an average annual total return of 8 percent over a 10-year period.

Ana and Jim want to choose the alternative that produces the best after-tax return over a 10-year planning horizon. They are aware, however, that tax restrictions may limit the advantages of some of these investment options. In this connection, evaluate each option.

Read the chapter and formulate your response.

Framework 1040 **Tax Formula for Individuals**

This chapter covers the boldfaced portions of the Tax Formula for Individuals that was introduced in Concept Summary 3.1 on p. 3-3. Below those portions are the sections of Form 1040 where the results are reported.

Income *(broadly defined)*	$ xx,xxx
Less: Exclusions	(x,xxx)
Gross income	**$xx,xxx**

FORM 1040 (p. 1)

7 Capital gain or (loss). Attach Schedule D if required, If not required, check here ▶ ☐

FORM 1040 (Schedule 1)

3 Business income or (loss). Attach Schedule C
4 Other gains or (losses). Attach Form 4797
5 Rental real estate, royalties, partnerships, S corporations, trusts, etc. Attach Schedule E

Less: Deductions *for* adjusted gross income	**(x,xxx)**
Adjusted gross income	$ xx,xxx
Less: The greater of total itemized deductions *or* the standard deduction	**(x,xxx)**

FORM 1040 (p. 1)

12 **Standard deduction or itemized deductions** (from Schedule A)

Personal and dependency exemptions*	(x,xxx)
Deduction for qualified business income**	(x,xxx)
Taxable income	$ xx,xxx
Tax on taxable income *(see Tax Tables or Tax Rate Schedules)*	$ x,xxx
Less: Tax credits *(including income taxes withheld and prepaid)*	(xxx)
Tax due (or refund)	$ xxx

*Exemption deductions are not allowed from 2018 through 2025.
**Only applies from 2018 through 2025.

As discussed in Chapter 6, a tax deduction for an expense or a loss is not allowed unless specifically permitted by Congress. For example, losses can be recognized and deducted in the case of certain unprofitable investments only because the Code allows them. These losses can arise from the operation of an activity *or* on its sale. For most individual taxpayers, deductible investment losses come within the scope of § 165(c)(2) relating to transactions entered into for profit.[1] But what happens if the investment is mostly motivated by the tax loss it generates? Or what if the investment is expected to generate current expenses that offset ordinary income, but later is expected to produce appreciation taxed at capital gain rates? This chapter addresses these tax minimization strategies and the rules put in place to restrict their use.

LO.1

Explain the tax shelter problem and the reasons for the at-risk and passive activity loss limitations.

11-1 The Tax Shelter Problem

Before Congress passed laws to reduce their effectiveness, **tax shelters** provided a popular way to avoid or defer taxes, since they could generate deductions and other benefits to offset income from other sources. Because of the tax avoidance potential of many tax shelters, they were attractive to wealthy taxpayers in high-income tax brackets. Many tax shelters merely provided an opportunity for "investors" to obtain tax deductions and credits (and some had no profit motive).

[1] If the losses are incurred in connection with a trade or business, § 165(c)(1) applies.

Although it may seem odd that a taxpayer would intentionally invest in an activity designed to produce losses, there is a logical explanation. The typical tax shelter took advantage of accelerated deductions related to an activity (e.g., accelerated cost recovery or depletion). These deductions generated ordinary losses in the activity's early years that could offset the investor's other sources of income (e.g., salary, interest, and dividends) and deferred the recognition of the economic profits (if any) until the activity was sold. Depending on the activity, any gain recognized on the sale might be taxed at lower capital gains rates. In addition, many tax shelters were financed with *nonrecourse debt*, which posed no risk of loss to the investor.[2] This meant that the expenditures generating the deductions were paid with borrowed funds, while the related debt produced interest deductions. Finally, many tax shelters were operated as limited partnerships, attracting multiple investors who were not required (or allowed) to actively participate in the activity (and protected from the risks related to participation). The following example illustrates what was possible *before* Congress stepped in to curb tax shelter abuses in the 1980s.

Example 1

Bob, who earned a salary of $400,000 as a business executive and dividend income of $15,000, invested $20,000 for a 10% interest in a cattle-breeding tax shelter. Through the use of $800,000 of nonrecourse financing and available cash of $200,000, the partnership acquired a herd of an exotic breed of cattle costing $1,000,000. Depreciation, interest, and other deductions related to the activity resulted in a loss of $400,000, of which Bob's share was $40,000. Bob was allowed to deduct the $40,000 loss even though he had invested and stood to lose only $20,000 if the investment became worthless.

The net effect of the $40,000 deduction from the partnership was that a portion of Bob's salary and dividend income was "sheltered" (i.e., offset or neutralized by the deduction), and as a result, he was required to calculate his tax liability on only $375,000 of income [$415,000 (salary and dividends) − $40,000 (deduction)] rather than $415,000. If this deduction were available under current law, and if Bob was in a combined Federal and state income tax bracket of 40%, this deduction would generate a tax savings of $16,000 ($40,000 × 40%) in the first year alone!

A review of Example 1 shows that the taxpayer claimed a *two-for-one* write-off ($40,000 deduction, $20,000 investment). Tax shelter promoters often promised tax deductions for the investor well in excess of the amount invested.

The first major law change aimed at tax shelters was the **at-risk limitation**. Its objective is to limit a taxpayer's deductions to the amount economically "at risk," which is the amount the taxpayer stands to lose if the investment becomes worthless. So in Example 1, the at-risk rule limits Bob's deductible loss to $20,000—the amount he invested.

The second major legislative attack on tax shelters came with the passage of the **passive activity loss** rules. The passive activity loss rules require the taxpayer to segregate all income and losses into three categories: active, portfolio, and passive (these categories are defined in text Section 11-3). In general, these rules disallow the deduction of passive activity losses against *active or portfolio income* even when the taxpayer is at risk to the extent of the loss. In general, passive activity losses can only offset passive activity income.

So in Example 1, the passive activity loss rules disallow a current deduction for any of the loss. The loss from the tax shelter is a passive activity loss because Bob does not "materially participate" in the activity (see text Section 11-3c). As a result, the $20,000 loss that is allowed under the at-risk rules is disallowed under the passive activity loss rules. Why? Because Bob does not report any passive activity income for the year—he reports only active and portfolio income. Consequently, Bob's current-year income only includes his nonpassive activity income of $415,000. As explained later in the chapter, the passive activity loss is suspended and may be deducted in a future year under certain conditions.

The nature of the at-risk limits and the passive activity loss rules and their impact on investors are discussed in the pages that follow. Because of these rules, investors now

[2]Nonrecourse debt is an obligation for which the borrower is not personally liable. An example of nonrecourse debt is a liability on real estate acquired by a partnership without the partnership or any of the partners assuming any liability for the mortgage. The acquired property generally is pledged as collateral for the loan.

focus primarily on the economics of the investment instead of the tax benefits or tax avoidance possibilities that an investment may generate.

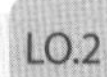

LO.2

Explain the at-risk limitation.

11-2 At-Risk Limits

The at-risk rules limit the deductibility of losses from business and income-producing activities. These rules, which apply only to individuals and closely held corporations, are designed to prevent taxpayers from deducting losses in excess of their actual economic investment in an activity. In the case of activities conducted by an S corporation or a partnership, the at-risk limits apply at the owner level. Under these rules, a taxpayer's deductible loss from an activity for any taxable year is limited to the amount the taxpayer has at risk at the end of the taxable year (the amount the taxpayer could actually lose in the activity).

Although the amount at risk usually changes over time, the initial "at-risk" amount includes the following:[3]

- The amount of cash and the adjusted basis of property contributed to the activity by the taxpayer.
- Any amounts borrowed for use in the activity for which the taxpayer is personally liable or has pledged as security property not used in the activity.

This amount generally is increased each year by the taxpayer's share of income and is decreased by the taxpayer's share of deductible losses and withdrawals from the activity. In addition, because general partners are jointly and severally liable for recourse debts of the partnership, their at-risk amounts are increased when the partnership increases its debt and are decreased when the partnership reduces its debt. However, a taxpayer generally is *not* considered at risk with respect to borrowed amounts if:

- The taxpayer is not personally liable for repayment of the debt (e.g., nonrecourse debt).
- The lender has an interest (other than as a creditor) in the activity.

An important exception provides that in the case of an activity that holds real property, a taxpayer's share of any *qualified nonrecourse financing* that is secured by real property used in the activity is considered at risk.[4]

A taxpayer may deduct a loss as long as the at-risk amount is positive (but the passive activity loss rules still may apply to limit the deduction). However, once the at-risk amount is exhausted, any remaining loss cannot be deducted until a later year. Any losses disallowed for any given taxable year by the at-risk rules may be deducted when there is, and to the extent of, a positive at-risk amount.

The Big Picture

Example 2

Return to the facts of *The Big Picture* on p. 11-1. In 2023, in addition to the three investment options presented to the Lopezes, they invest $20,000 in an oil partnership. In its first year of operation, the partnership incurs a net loss, $30,000 of which is allocable to the Lopezes. Assume that the Lopezes' interest in the partnership is subject to the at-risk limits but is not subject to the passive activity loss limits.

Because the Lopezes have only $20,000 of capital at risk, they cannot deduct more than $20,000 against their other income. Further, they must reduce their at-risk amount to zero ($20,000 at-risk amount − $20,000 loss deducted). The nondeductible loss of $10,000 ($30,000 loss generated − $20,000 loss allowed) can be carried over to 2024.

[3] § 465(b)(1).

[4] *Qualified nonrecourse financing* is defined in § 465(b)(6).

Continue with the facts of the previous example. In 2024, the Lopezes have taxable income of \$15,000 from the oil partnership and invest an additional \$10,000 in the venture. Their at-risk amount is now \$25,000 (\$0 beginning balance + \$15,000 taxable income + \$10,000 additional investment). This enables them to deduct the \$10,000 carryover loss and reduces their at-risk amount to \$15,000 (\$25,000 at-risk amount − \$10,000 carryover loss allowed).

Complicating the at-risk rule is the fact that previously allowed losses must be recaptured to the extent the at-risk amount falls below zero.[5] Under this rule, taxpayers must recognize income to bring the at-risk amount up to zero. Typically, this rule is triggered when the taxpayer receives a distribution or when the status of indebtedness changes from recourse to nonrecourse.

Calculation of at-risk amount is reviewed in Concept Summary 11.1.

Concept Summary 11.1

Calculation of At-Risk Amount

Increases to a taxpayer's at-risk amount:

- Cash and the adjusted basis of property contributed to the activity.
- Amounts borrowed for use in the activity for which the taxpayer is personally liable or has pledged as security property not used in the activity.
- Taxpayer's share of amounts borrowed for use in the activity that are qualified nonrecourse financing.
- Taxpayer's share of the activity's income.

Decreases to a taxpayer's at-risk amount:

- Withdrawals from the activity.
- Taxpayer's share of the activity's deductible loss.
- Taxpayer's share of any reductions of debt for which recourse against the taxpayer exists or any reductions of qualified nonrecourse debt.

11-3 Passive Activity Loss Limits

LO.3

Describe how the passive activity loss rules limit deductions for losses, and identify the taxpayers subject to these restrictions.

This section identifies and explains the key issues that apply to the passive activity loss limits. Here are some key points:

- The limits apply only to passive activity losses incurred by certain types of taxpayers.
- Losses are limited under these rules only if they are generated by a passive activity.
- Special rules exist for interests in real estate activities.
- Any suspended losses are generally allowed when a passive activity is sold.

11-3a Classification and Tax Treatment of Passive Activity Income and Losses

The passive activity loss rules (§ 469) operate by requiring taxpayers to classify their income and losses into three categories: active, portfolio, or passive. Then the rules limit the extent to which losses in the passive category can be used to offset income in the other categories.

[5] § 465(e).

Classification

The passive activity loss rules require income and losses to be classified as active, portfolio, or passive.

Active income includes:

- Wages, salary, commissions, bonuses, and other payments for services rendered by the taxpayer.
- Profit from a trade or business in which the taxpayer is a material participant (material participation is described in text Section 11-3c).
- Gain on the sale or other disposition of assets used in an active trade or business.
- Income from intangible property if the taxpayer's personal efforts significantly contributed to the creation of the property.

Portfolio income includes:

- Interest, dividends, annuities, and royalties not derived in the ordinary course of a trade or business.
- Gain or loss from the disposition of property that produces portfolio income or is held for investment purposes.

Passive activity income or loss arises from activities that are treated as passive, which include:

- Any trade or business or income-producing activity in which the taxpayer does not materially participate.
- Subject to certain exceptions (discussed in text Section 11-3e), all rental activities whether the taxpayer materially participates or not.

General Impact

Losses or expenses generated by passive activities can be deducted only to the extent of income from the taxpayer's passive activities. Any excess passive activity loss may not be used to offset active income or portfolio income. Instead, any unused passive activity losses are suspended and carried forward to future years to offset passive activity income generated in those years. Any remaining suspended losses may be used only when a taxpayer disposes of their *entire interest* in the activity that generated the loss. When that occurs, generally all current and suspended passive activity losses related to the activity may offset active and portfolio income.

The Big Picture

Example 4

Return to the facts of *The Big Picture* on p. 11-1. In addition to their salaries of $180,000 from full-time jobs, assume that the Lopezes receive $5,000 in dividends and interest from various portfolio investments. Further, assume that they decide to invest $50,000 in the orange grove limited partnership, which is a passive activity that produces a $12,000 loss for the Lopezes this year.

Because their at-risk basis in the partnership is $50,000, the current $12,000 loss is not limited by the at-risk rules. However, because the loss is a passive activity loss, it is not deductible against their other income. The loss is suspended and carried over to the future.

If the Lopezes have passive activity income from this investment or from other passive activities in the future, they can offset the suspended loss against that passive activity income. If they do not have passive activity income to offset this suspended loss in the future, they will be allowed to offset the loss against other types of income when they eventually dispose of their investment in the passive activity.

Impact of Suspended Passive Activity Losses

When a taxpayer disposes of the entire interest in a passive activity, the actual economic gain or loss from the investment, including any suspended losses, can finally be determined. As a result, under the passive activity loss rules, when a fully taxable disposition occurs, any overall loss realized from the taxpayer's activity is recognized and can offset any income.

A *fully taxable disposition* generally involves a sale of the property to a third party at arm's length. This would imply that the sales price is equal to the property's fair market value. As presented in the following example, a gain recognized on the sale of a passive activity generally is treated as passive and is first offset by the suspended passive activity losses from that activity.

Chloe sells an apartment building, a passive activity, with an adjusted basis of $500,000 for $580,000. In addition, she has suspended passive activity losses of $60,000 associated with the building. Her total gain, $80,000, and her taxable gain, $20,000, are calculated as follows:

Net sales price	$ 580,000
Less: Adjusted basis	(500,000)
Total gain	$ 80,000
Less: Suspended passive activity losses	(60,000)
Taxable gain (passive)	$ 20,000

As highlighted in Example 5, gain recognized on the sale of a passive activity generally is treated as passive and is first offset by any suspended passive activity losses from that activity. This accomplishes the purpose of determining the true economic gain or loss from the activity.

But what happens if the suspended losses exceed the gain recognized or the sale results in a loss? In this case, the excess loss is allowed to offset other income in the following order:

1. Net passive activity income or gains (if any).
2. Nonpassive income or gains (active or portfolio).

Example 6

Dean sells an apartment building, a passive activity, with an adjusted basis of $600,000 for $650,000. In addition, he has current and suspended passive activity losses of $60,000 associated with the building and has no other passive activities. His total gain of $50,000 and his deductible loss of $10,000 are calculated as follows:

Net sales price	$ 650,000
Less: Adjusted basis	(600,000)
Total gain	$ 50,000
Less: Suspended passive activity losses	(60,000)
Deductible loss (not passive)	($ 10,000)

The $10,000 deductible loss offsets Dean's active and portfolio income.

What would be the outcome if Dean sold the building for $590,000? In this case, there would be a loss on the sale of $10,000 and an overall deductible loss of $70,000. This total loss, including the suspended passive activity losses, is deductible as a nonpassive activity loss.

Carryovers of Suspended Passive Activity Losses

The preceding examples assumed that the taxpayer had an interest in only one passive activity; as a result, the suspended loss was related exclusively to the activity that was sold. However, taxpayers may own interests in more than one activity, in which case any suspended losses must be allocated among those passive activities that generated losses. The allocation to an activity is made by multiplying the disallowed passive activity loss from all activities using the following fraction:

$$\frac{\textbf{Loss from one passive activity}}{\textbf{Sum of losses for taxable year from all passive activities having losses}}$$

Diego has investments in three passive activities with the following income and losses for 2022:

Activity A	($30,000)
Activity B	(20,000)
Activity C	10,000
Net passive activity loss	($40,000)
Net passive activity loss of $40,000 allocated to:	
Activity A [$40,000 × ($30,000 ÷ $50,000)]	($24,000)
Activity B [$40,000 × ($20,000 ÷ $50,000)]	(16,000)
Total suspended passive activity losses	($40,000)

Suspended losses are carried over indefinitely and are offset in the future first against any passive activity income from the activities to which they relate and then against passive activity income from other passive activities.[6] Taxpayers subject to the passive activity loss limitation rule must maintain records to track the suspended losses and the activities to which they belong.

Assume that the facts are the same as in Example 7 and that, in 2023, Activity A produces $10,000 of income. Diego may use $10,000 of Activity A's suspended loss of $24,000 from 2022 to offset the $10,000 income from this activity.

If Diego sells Activity A in early 2024, the remaining $14,000 suspended loss is used to offset any income from the activity reported by Diego in 2024 and to determine his final gain or loss.

Passive Activity Credits

Credits (such as the low-income housing credit and rehabilitation credit—discussed in Chapter 12) that arise from passive activities are limited in much the same way as passive activity losses. Passive activity credits can be used only against regular tax attributable to passive activity income,[7] which is calculated by comparing the tax on all income (including passive activity income) with the tax on income excluding passive activity income.

Sam owes $50,000 of tax, disregarding net passive activity income, and $80,000 of tax, considering both net passive activity and other taxable income (disregarding the credits in both cases). The amount of tax attributable to the passive activity income is $30,000.

In the preceding example, Sam can claim a maximum of $30,000 of passive activity credits; the excess credits are carried over. These passive activity credits can be used only against the *regular* tax attributable to passive activity income. If a taxpayer has a net loss from passive activities during a given year, no credits can be used.

Carryovers of Passive Activity Credits

Tax credits related to passive activities can be carried forward indefinitely much like suspended passive activity losses. Unlike passive activity losses, however, passive activity credits are permanently lost when the activity is disposed of in a taxable transaction where a *loss* is recognized. Credits are allowed on dispositions only when there is sufficient tax on passive activity income to absorb them.

Use of Passive Activity Credits on Disposition of an Activity

Alicia sells a passive activity for a gain of $10,000. The activity had suspended losses of $40,000 and suspended credits of $15,000. The $10,000 gain is offset by $10,000 of the suspended losses, and the remaining $30,000 of suspended losses is deductible against Alicia's active and portfolio income. The suspended credits are permanently lost because the sale of the activity did not generate any tax.

[6] § 469(b).

[7] § 469(d)(2).

Use of Passive Activity Credits on Disposition of an Activity

Example 11

If Alicia in Example 10 had realized a $100,000 gain on the sale of the passive activity, the suspended credits could have been used to the extent of the regular tax related to the net passive activity income.

Gain on sale	$100,000
Less: Suspended passive activity losses	(40,000)
Taxable gain	$ 60,000

If the tax related to the taxable gain of $60,000 is $15,000 or more, the entire $15,000 of suspended credits can be used. If the tax related to the gain is less than $15,000, the excess of the suspended credits over the tax related to the gain is lost.

When a taxpayer has a sufficient regular tax liability from passive activities to trigger the use of suspended credits, the credits lose their character as passive activity credits. They are reclassified as regular tax credits and made subject to the same limits as other credits (discussed in Chapter 12).

Passive Activity Changes to Active

If a passive activity becomes an active one, suspended passive activity losses are allowed to the extent of income from the now active business.[8] If any of the suspended loss remains, it continues to be treated as a loss from a passive activity. The excess suspended loss can be deducted from passive activity income or carried over to the next tax year and deducted to the extent of income from the now active business in the succeeding year(s). The activity must continue to be the same activity.

Example 12

For several years, Rebecca has owned an interest in a passive activity that has produced losses of $80,000 during that period. Because she did not have passive activity income from other sources, she could not deduct any of the activity's passive activity losses.

In the current year, she has become a material participant in the activity (i.e., the passive activity is now an active business), and her share of the business profits total $25,000. As a result, she may use $25,000 of the suspended passive activity loss to offset the current business profits. Rebecca's remaining suspended passive activity loss from the activity is $55,000 ($80,000 − $25,000), which is carried over to future years and used to offset income from the formerly passive activity or income from other passive activities.

11-3b Taxpayers Subject to the Passive Activity Loss Rules

The passive activity loss rules apply to individuals, estates, trusts, personal service corporations, and closely held C corporations.[9] Passive activity income or loss from investments in partnerships or S corporations (see Chapters 21 and 23) flows through to the owners, and the passive activity loss rules are applied at the owner level.

Personal Service Corporations

Application of the passive activity loss limitations to personal service corporations is intended to prevent taxpayers from sheltering personal service income by creating personal service corporations and acquiring passive activities at the corporate level.

Two tax accountants who earn an aggregate of $200,000 a year in their individual practices agree to work together in a newly formed personal service corporation. Shortly after its formation, the corporation invests in a passive activity that produces a $200,000 loss during the year. Because the passive activity loss rules apply to personal service corporations, the corporation may not deduct the $200,000 passive activity loss against the $200,000 of active income.

[8] § 469(f).

[9] § 469(a).

Determination of whether a corporation is a **personal service corporation** is based on rather broad definitions. A personal service corporation is a regular (or C) corporation that meets *both* of the following conditions:

- The principal activity is the performance of personal services.
- Such services are substantially performed by employee-owners.

Generally, personal service corporations include those in the fields of health, law, engineering, architecture, accounting, actuarial science, performing arts, and consulting.[10] A corporation is treated as a personal service corporation if more than 10 percent of the stock (by value) is held by employee-owners.[11] An employee is treated as an employee-owner if the employee owns stock on *any day* during the taxable year.[12] For these purposes, shareholder status and employee status do not have to occur on the same day.

Closely Held C Corporations

Application of the passive activity loss rules to closely held (nonpersonal service) C corporations also is intended to prevent individuals from incorporating to avoid the passive activity loss limitations. A corporation is classified as a **closely held corporation** if at any time during the taxable year more than 50 percent of the value of its outstanding stock is owned, directly or indirectly, by or for five or fewer individuals. Closely held C corporations (other than personal service corporations) may use passive activity losses to offset *active* income but not portfolio income.

Silver Corporation, a closely held (nonpersonal service) C corporation, has $475,000 of passive activity losses from a rental activity, $400,000 of active income, and $100,000 of portfolio income. The corporation may offset $400,000 of the $475,000 passive activity loss against the $400,000 of active business income but may not offset the remainder against the $100,000 of portfolio income. As a result, $75,000 of the passive activity loss is suspended ($475,000 passive activity loss − $400,000 offset against active income).

Applying the passive activity loss limitations to closely held C corporations eliminates a benefit to taxpayers from transferring their portfolio investments (e.g., stocks and bonds) to these corporations.

LO.4

Define passive activity, and describe the rules for identifying an activity.

11-3c Rules for Determining Passive Activities

As noted earlier, the following types of activities are treated as passive:

- Any trade or business or income-producing activity in which the taxpayer does not materially participate.
- All rental activities, subject to certain exceptions pertaining to real estate (discussed in text Section 11-3e).

To understand the meaning of the term *passive activity* and the impact of the rules, one must address the following issues, each of which is the subject of statutory or administrative guidance:

- What constitutes an *activity?*
- What is meant by *material participation?*
- When is an activity a *rental activity?*

Even though guidance is available to help the taxpayer deal with these issues, their resolution is anything but simple.

[10] § 448(d)(2)(A).
[11] § 469(j)(2).
[12] § 269A(b)(2).

Identification of an Activity

Identifying what constitutes an activity is the first step in applying the passive activity loss rules. Taxpayers who are involved in complex business operations need to determine whether a given segment of their overall business operations constitutes a separate activity or is to be treated as part of a larger activity. Proper treatment is necessary to determine whether income or loss from an activity is active or passive.

Treatment as a Component of an Activity or as a Separate Activity

Ben owns a business with two separate departments. Department A generates net income of $120,000, and Department B generates a net loss of $95,000. Ben participates 700 hours in the operations of Department A and 100 hours in Department B. If Ben is allowed to treat the departments as components of a single activity, he can offset the $95,000 loss from Department B against the $120,000 of income from Department A.

Assume the same facts as in the previous example. If Ben is required to treat each department as a separate activity, the tax result is not as favorable. Because he is a material participant in Department A (having devoted 700 hours to it), the $120,000 profit is active income. Assuming that Ben is not considered a material participant in Department B, the $95,000 loss is a passive activity loss. As a result, Ben cannot offset the $95,000 passive activity loss from Department B against the $120,000 of active income from Department A. (A discussion of the material participation rules follows.)

On the disposition of a passive activity, a taxpayer is allowed to offset suspended losses from the activity against other types of income. As illustrated in the next example, identifying what constitutes an activity is of crucial importance for this purpose too.

Jasmine owns a business with two departments. Department A has a net loss of $125,000 in the current year, and Department B has a $70,000 net loss. She sells Department B at the end of the year.

Assuming that Jasmine is allowed to treat the two departments as separate passive activities, she can offset the passive activity loss from Department B against other types of income in the following order: gain from disposition of the passive activity, other passive activity income, and nonpassive activity income. This treatment leaves her with a suspended loss of $125,000 from Department A.

If, however, Departments A and B are treated as components of the same activity, when Department B is sold, its $70,000 net loss would be suspended along with the other $125,000 of suspended loss of the activity (from Department A).

Treasury Regulations provide guidelines for identifying activities subject to the passive activity loss rules.[13] These guidelines indicate, in general, that a taxpayer can treat one or more trade or business activities or rental activities as a single activity if those activities form an *appropriate economic unit* for measuring gain or loss. In making this decision, all of the relevant facts and circumstances must be considered. Taxpayers may use any reasonable method in applying the facts and circumstances. The following example, adapted from the Regulations, illustrates the application of the general rules for grouping activities.[14]

Taj owns a men's clothing store and a brewpub in Chicago. He also owns a men's clothing store and a brewpub in Milwaukee. Reasonable methods of applying the facts and circumstances test may result in any of the following groupings:

- All four activities may be grouped into a single activity because of common ownership and control.

continued

[13] Reg. § 1.469–4.

[14] Reg. § 1.469–4(c)(3).

- The clothing stores may be grouped into an activity, and the brewpubs may be grouped into a separate activity.
- The Chicago activities may be grouped into an activity, and the Milwaukee activities may be grouped into a separate activity.
- Each of the four activities may be treated as a separate activity.

Regrouping of Activities Taxpayers should consider all tax factors carefully when deciding how to group their activities. Once activities have been grouped, they cannot be regrouped unless the original grouping was clearly inappropriate or there has been a material change in the facts and circumstances. The Regulations allow the IRS to regroup activities when *both* of the following conditions exist:[15]

- The taxpayer's grouping fails to reflect one or more appropriate economic units.
- One of the primary purposes of the taxpayer's grouping is to avoid the passive activity loss limitations.

Special Grouping Rules for Rental Activities Two rules deal specifically with the grouping of rental activities. These rules are designed to prevent taxpayers from grouping rental activities, which are generally passive, with other businesses in a way that result in a tax advantage.

First, a rental activity may be grouped with a trade or business activity only if one activity is insubstantial in relation to the other. That is, the rental activity must be insubstantial in relation to the trade or business activity, or the trade or business activity must be insubstantial in relation to the rental activity. The Regulations provide no clear guidelines as to the meaning of "insubstantial."[16]

Example 19

Schemers, a CPA firm, owns a building in Washington, D.C., in which it conducts its public accounting practice. The firm also rents space on the street level of the building to several retail establishments, which generally is considered a passive activity. Of the total revenue generated by the firm, 95% is associated with the public accounting practice and 5% is related to the rental operation.

It is likely that the rental activity would be considered insubstantial relative to the accounting practice and the two ventures could be grouped as one nonrental activity. This grouping could be advantageous to the firm, particularly if the rental operation generates a loss, since the rental loss could be used to offset any income from the public accounting practice.

Alternatively, treating the rental operation as a *separate* activity may be advantageous if this operation produces (passive activity) income. The passive activity income could then be used to absorb otherwise nondeductible passive activity losses.

Second, taxpayers generally may not treat an activity involving the rental of real property and an activity involving the rental of personal property as a single activity.

LO.5

Identify the tests for material participation.

Material Participation

If an individual taxpayer *materially participates* in a nonrental trade or business activity, any loss from that activity is treated as an active loss that can offset active or portfolio income. If a taxpayer does not materially participate, the loss is treated as a passive activity loss, which can offset only passive activity income. As a result, controlling whether a particular activity is treated as active or passive is an important part of the tax strategy of a taxpayer who owns an interest in one or more businesses. Consider the following examples.

[15]Reg. § 1.469–4(f).

[16]Reg. § 1.469–4(d).

Implications of Material Participation Status

Noah, a corporate executive, earns a salary of $600,000 per year. In addition, he owns a separate business in which he participates. The business produces a loss of $100,000 during the year. If Noah materially participates in the business, the $100,000 loss is an active loss that may offset his active income from his corporate employer.

If he does not materially participate, the loss is passive and is suspended unless he has other passive activity income. Noah may use the suspended passive activity loss in the future only when he has passive activity income or disposes of the activity.

Junghee, an attorney, earns $350,000 a year in her law practice. In addition, she owns interests in two activities, A and B, in which she participates. Activity A, in which she does *not* materially participate, produces a loss of $50,000. Activity B produces income of $80,000. However, Junghee has not yet met the material participation standard, described below, for Activity B. But Junghee can meet the material participation standard if she spends an additional 50 hours in Activity B during the year. Should Junghee attempt to meet the material participation standard for Activity B?

If she continues working in Activity B and becomes a material participant, the $80,000 of income from the activity is *active*, and the $50,000 passive activity loss from Activity A must be suspended. A more favorable tax strategy is for Junghee *not to meet* the material participation standard for Activity B, thus making the income from that activity passive. This enables her to offset the $50,000 passive activity loss from Activity A against most of the passive activity income from Activity B.

It is possible to devise numerous scenarios in which the taxpayer could control the tax outcome by increasing or decreasing participation in different activities. Examples 20 and 21 demonstrate some of the possibilities. In most analyses of this type, taxpayers will benefit by having profitable activities classified as passive so that any passive activity losses can be used to offset that passive activity income. If the activity produces a loss, however, the taxpayer will benefit if it is classified as active so that the loss is not subject to the passive activity loss limitations.

A nonrental trade or business in which a taxpayer owns an interest must be treated as a passive activity unless the taxpayer materially participates. A material participant is one who has "a significant nontax economic profit motive" for taking on activities and selects them for their economic value.[17] In contrast, a passive investor mainly seeks a return from a capital investment (including a possible reduction in taxes) as a supplement to an ongoing source of livelihood.

Even if the concept of being a material participant is clear, the precise meaning of the term **material participation** can be vague. As enacted, § 469 requires a taxpayer to participate on a *regular, continuous*, and *substantial* basis to be a material participant. In many situations, however, it is difficult or impossible to gain any assurance that this nebulous standard is met.

In response to this dilemma, Temporary Regulations[18] provide seven tests that serve to determine when material participation is achieved. Material participation is achieved by meeting any *one* of the tests. These tests are listed in Concept Summary 11.2 and can be divided into the following three categories:

- Tests based on current participation.
- Tests based on prior participation.
- Tests based on facts and circumstances.

[17] *General Explanation of the Tax Reform Act of 1986* ("Blue Book"), prepared by The Staff of the Joint Committee on Taxation, May 4, 1987, H.R. 3838, 99th Cong., p. 212.

[18] Temp.Reg. § 1.469–5T(a).

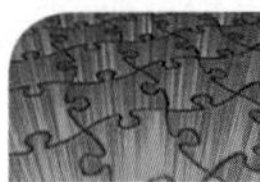

Concept Summary 11.2

Tests to Determine Material Participation

Tests Based on Current Participation

1. The individual participates in the activity for more than 500 hours during the year.
2. The individual's participation in the activity for the taxable year constitutes substantially all of the participation in the activity of all individuals (including nonowner employees) for the year.
3. The individual participates in the activity for more than 100 hours during the year, and this participation is not less than that participation of any other individual (including nonowner employees) for the year.
4. The activity is a **significant participation activity** (where the person's participation *exceeds* 100 hours during the year and no other material participation test is met), and the hours for all significant participation activities during the year is more than 500 hours.

Tests Based on Prior Participation

5. The individual materially participated in the activity for any five taxable years during the 10 taxable years that immediately precede the current taxable year.
6. The activity is a personal service activity, and the individual materially participated in the activity for any three preceding taxable years.

Test Based on Facts and Circumstances

7. Based on all of the facts and circumstances, the individual participates in the activity on a regular, continuous, and substantial basis during the year and such participation for the year exceeds 100 hours.

Participation Defined Participation generally includes any work done by an individual in an activity that the individual owns. Participation does not include work of a type not customarily done by owners *and* if one of the principal purposes for the work is to avoid the disallowance of passive activity losses or credits. Also, work done in an individual's capacity as an investor (e.g., reviewing financial reports in a nonmanagerial capacity) is not counted in applying the material participation tests. Participation by an owner's spouse counts as participation by the owner.[19]

Emma, who is a partner in a CPA firm, owns a computer store that operated at a loss during the year. To offset this loss against the income from her CPA practice, Emma would like to avoid having the computer business classified as a passive activity. During the year, she worked 480 hours in the business participating in management and sales activities and 30 hours doing janitorial chores. In addition, Emma's spouse participated 40 hours as a salesperson.

It is likely that Emma's 480 hours of participation in management and sales activities will count as participation in work customarily done by owners, but the 30 hours spent doing janitorial chores will not. In addition, the 40 hours of participation by her spouse also will count.

Assuming that none of the participation's principal purposes is to avoid the disallowance of passive activity losses or credits, Emma will qualify as a material participant under the more-than-500-hour rule (480 + 40 = 520).

Limited Partners A *limited* partner is a partner whose liability to third-party creditors of the partnership is limited to the amount the partner has invested in the partnership and who has no ability to participate in the management of the partnership. Such a partnership must have at least one *general* partner who is fully liable in an individual capacity for the debts of the partnership to third parties.

Generally, a *limited partner* is not considered a material participant unless the limited partner qualifies under Test 1, 5, or 6 as shown in Concept Summary 11.2. However, a *general partner* may qualify as a material participant by meeting any of the seven tests. If a general partner also owns a limited interest in the same limited partnership, all interests are treated as a general interest.[20]

[19] § 469(h)(5) and Temp.Reg. § 1.469–5T(f)(3).

[20] § 469(h)(2) and Temp.Reg. § 1.469–5T(e)(3)(ii).

Rental Activities

LO.6

Describe the classification of rental activities under the passive activity loss rules.

Subject to certain exceptions, all rental activities are treated as passive activities.[21] A **rental activity** is defined as any activity where payments are received principally for the use of tangible (real or personal) property.[22] Importantly, an activity that is classified as a rental activity is subject to the passive activity loss rules even if the taxpayer involved is a material participant.

Sarah owns a fleet of automobiles that are held for rent, and she spends an average of 60 hours a week in the activity. Assuming that her automobile business is classified as a rental activity, it is *automatically* subject to the passive activity rules even though Sarah spends more than 500 hours a year in its operation.

Certain rentals of real and personal property might be classified under the passive activity loss rules as *nonrental* activities.[23] In these situations, assuming that the activity is a trade or business, the material participation tests shown in Concept Summary 11.2 must be applied to determine whether the activity is a passive activity. Consider the following example.

Arturo owns a bicycle rental business at a nearby resort. Because the average period of customer use is seven days or less, Arturo's business is not treated as a rental activity.

Example 24 illustrates an exception to the definition of a rental activity. This exception is based on the presumption that a person who rents property for seven days or less is generally required to provide significant services to the customer. Providing these services supports a conclusion that the person is engaged in a service business rather than a rental business. Other examples of this exception include most hotels or motels and businesses that rent tools, tuxedos, or cars.[24]

This result, however, does not mean that Arturo's business is a nonpassive activity. Instead, it is treated as a trade or business activity subject to the material participation standards listed in Concept Summary 11.2. If Arturo is a material participant, the business is treated as active. If he is not a material participant, it is treated as a passive activity.

11-3d Interaction of the At-Risk and Passive Activity Loss Limits

Determine the relationship between the at-risk and passive activity loss limitations.

The determination of whether a loss is suspended under the passive activity loss rules is made *after* application of the at-risk rules, as well as other rules relating to the measurement of taxable income. A loss that is not allowed for the year because of the at-risk rules is suspended under those rules, not under the passive activity loss rules. Further, a taxpayer's at-risk basis is reduced by the losses (but not below zero) even if the deductions are not currently usable because of the passive activity loss rules. The following examples illustrate these points.

At-Risk and Passive Activity Loss Interactions

Jack's adjusted basis in a passive activity is $10,000 at the beginning of 2021. His loss from the activity in 2021 is $4,000. Because Jack has no passive activity income, the $4,000 cannot be deducted. At year-end, Jack has an adjusted basis and an at-risk amount of $6,000 in the activity and a suspended passive activity loss of $4,000.

[21] § 469(c)(2).

[22] § 469(j)(8).

[23] Temp.Reg. § 1.469–1T(e)(3).

[24] For additional discussion of the rental exceptions, see IRS Publication 925 (*Passive Activity and At-Risk Rules*).

At-Risk and Passive Activity Loss Interactions

Example 26

Jack in Example 25 has a loss of $9,000 in the activity in 2022. Because the $9,000 exceeds his at-risk amount ($6,000) by $3,000, that $3,000 loss is disallowed by the at-risk rules. If Jack has no passive activity income, the remaining $6,000 is suspended under the passive activity rules. At year-end, he has:

- A $3,000 loss suspended under the at-risk rules.
- $10,000 of suspended passive activity losses ($4,000 from 2021 and $6,000 from 2022).
- An adjusted basis and an at-risk amount in the activity of zero.

Example 27

Jack in Example 26 realizes $1,000 of passive activity income from the activity in 2023. Because the $1,000 increases his at-risk amount, $1,000 of the $3,000 unused loss from 2022 is reclassified as a passive activity loss. If he has no other passive activity income, the $1,000 income is offset by $1,000 of suspended passive activity losses. At the end of 2023, Jack has:

- No taxable passive activity income.
- $2,000 ($3,000 − $1,000) of suspended losses under the at-risk rules.
- $10,000 of (reclassified) suspended passive activity losses ($10,000 + $1,000 of reclassified suspended at-risk losses − $1,000 of passive activity losses offset against passive activity income).
- An adjusted basis and an at-risk amount in the activity of zero.

Example 28

In 2024, Jack has no gain or loss from the activity in Example 27. He contributes $5,000 more to the passive activity. Because the $5,000 increases his at-risk amount, the $2,000 of losses suspended under the at-risk rules is reclassified as passive. Jack gets no passive activity loss deduction in 2024. At year-end, he has:

- No suspended losses under the at-risk rules.
- $12,000 of suspended passive activity losses ($10,000 + $2,000 of reclassified suspended at-risk losses).
- An adjusted basis and an at-risk amount of $3,000 ($5,000 additional investment − $2,000 of reclassified losses).

The Big Picture

Example 29

Return to the facts of *The Big Picture* on p. 11-1. If the Lopezes invest in the orange grove limited partnership, the at-risk rules will not limit the deductibility of the $12,000 losses until after year 4. Sufficient at-risk basis will exist until the close of that year (i.e., the at-risk basis is reduced from $50,000 by $12,000 over each of the first four years of the investment).

However, the passive activity loss rules prohibit deductions for the losses in the first four years of the investment (assuming that the Lopezes do not have passive activity income from other sources). Based on the facts provided, none of the suspended losses would be deductible until year 6, when the orange grove is expected to begin producing profits.

Concept Summary 11.3 illustrates the interactions of the at-risk and passive activity limits.

LO.8

Recognize the special treatment available to certain real estate activities.

11-3e Special Passive Activity Rules for Real Estate Activities

The passive activity loss limits contain two exceptions related to real estate activities. The first exception allows certain rental real estate activities to avoid automatic classification as a passive activity. The second exception allows all or part of real estate rental losses to offset active or portfolio income even though the activity otherwise is defined as a passive activity.

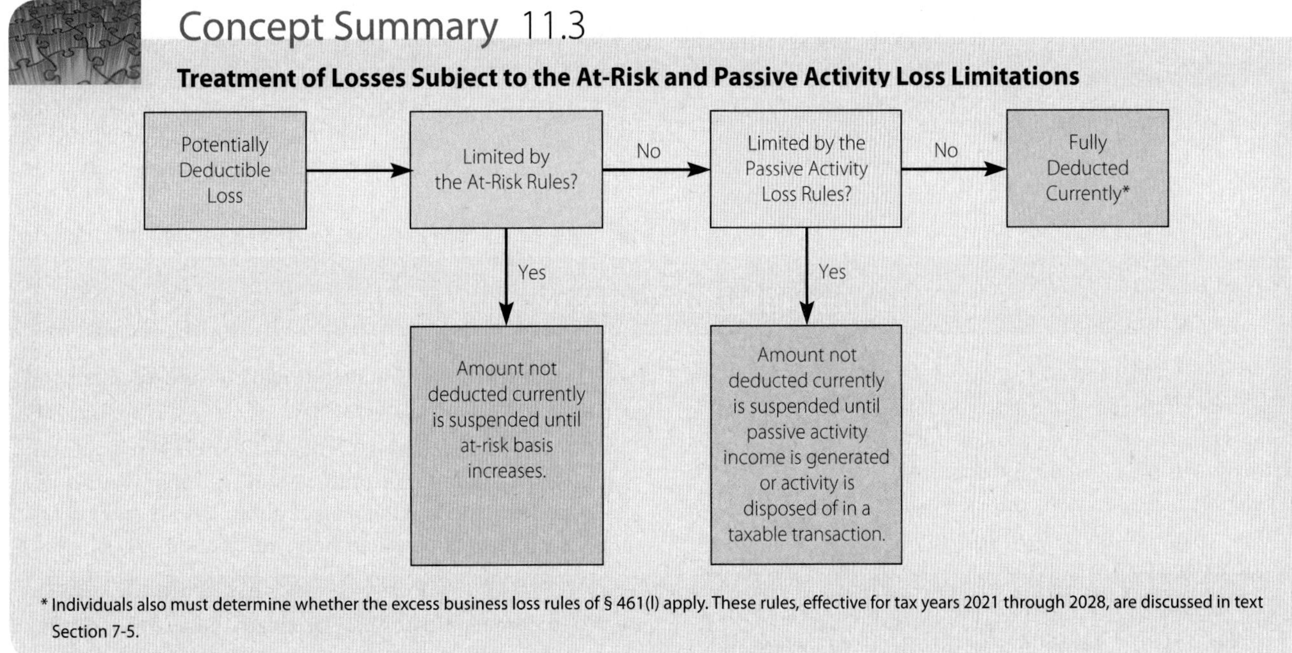

Material Participation in a Real Property Rental Trade or Business

The first exception to the passive activity loss rules provides relief to real estate professionals.[25] Under this exception, taxpayers meeting specific requirements are allowed to apply one of the seven material participation tests to their rental real estate activities (i.e., these *rental activities* are *not* automatically treated as passive activities). To qualify for this exception, a taxpayer must satisfy *both* of the following requirements:

- More than half of the personal services that the taxpayer performs in trades or businesses are performed in real property trades or businesses in which the taxpayer materially participates.
- The taxpayer performs more than 750 hours of services in real property trades or businesses in which the taxpayer materially participates.

Taxpayers who do not satisfy the above requirements must continue to treat income and losses from real estate rental activities as passive activity income and losses.

During the current year, Della performs personal service activities as follows: 900 hours as a personal financial planner, 550 hours in a real estate development business, and 600 hours in a rental real estate activity. Any loss Della incurs in either real estate activity will not be subject to the passive activity loss rules.

- Being a nonrental business, the real estate development business is deemed active under the more-than-500-hour material participation test.
- Della may apply a material participation test to the real estate rental activity because (1) more than 50% of Della's personal services are devoted to real property trades or businesses (i.e., the development and rental businesses) in which she materially participates, *and* (2) she has over 750 hours in real property trades or businesses in which she materially participates.
- As a result, any loss from Della's rental real estate activity can offset active and portfolio sources of income because she meets the over-500-hour material participation test for that rental activity, and she qualifies as a real estate professional. Likewise, any income from this activity would be nonpassive (active) income.

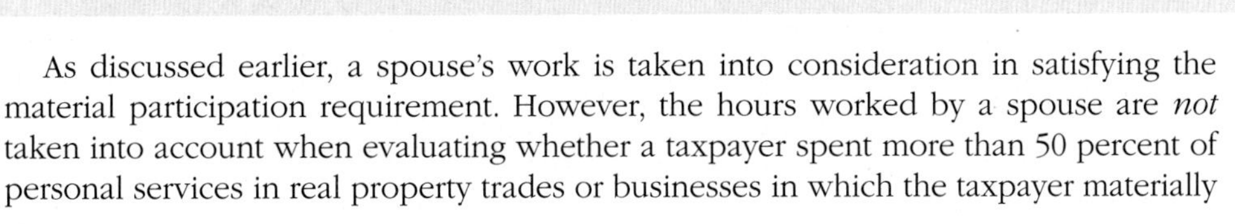

As discussed earlier, a spouse's work is taken into consideration in satisfying the material participation requirement. However, the hours worked by a spouse are *not* taken into account when evaluating whether a taxpayer spent more than 50 percent of personal services in real property trades or businesses in which the taxpayer materially

[25] § 469(c)(7).

participates or has worked for more than 750 hours in these real property trades or businesses during the year.[26] Services performed by an employee are not treated as related to a real property trade or business unless the employee performing the services owns more than a 5 percent interest in the employer. In addition, a closely held C corporation also may qualify for the passive activity loss relief if more than 50 percent of its gross receipts for the year are derived from real property trades or businesses in which it materially participates.

Ethics & Equity **Punching the Time Clock at Year-End**

As the end of the tax year approaches, Julie, a successful full-time real estate developer and investor, recognizes that her income tax situation for the year could be bleak. Unless she and her spouse, Ralph, are able to generate more hours of participation in one of her real estate rental activities, they will not reach the material participation threshold. Consequently, the tax losses from the venture will not be deductible. To ensure deductibility, Julie suggests the following plan:

- She will document the time she spends "thinking" about her rental activities.
- During the week, Ralph will visit the apartment building to oversee (in a management role) the operations of the rentals.
- On weekends, she and Ralph will visit the same units to further evaluate the operations.
- Also on the weekends, they will be on the lookout for other rental properties to buy and visit open houses of homes they find on the market. Julie plans to count both her and Ralph's weekend hours toward the tally of total participation.

Julie contends that the law clearly allows the efforts of one's spouse to count for purposes of the material participation tests. Likewise, nothing in the tax law requires taxpayers to be efficient in their hours of participation. How do you react?

Real Estate Rental Activities with Active Participation

The second exception to the passive activity loss limits is more significant in that it is *not* restricted to real estate professionals. This exception allows individuals to deduct up to $25,000 of losses from real estate rental activities against active and portfolio income each year.[27] The potential annual $25,000 deduction is reduced by 50 percent of the taxpayer's AGI in excess of $100,000. As a result, the entire deduction is phased out at $150,000 of AGI. If married individuals file separately, the $25,000 deduction is reduced to zero unless they lived apart for the entire year. In this case, the loss amount is $12,500 each and the phaseout begins at $50,000 of AGI.[28]

To qualify for the $25,000 exception, a taxpayer must meet *both* of the following requirements:[29]

- *Actively participate* in the real estate rental activity.
- Own 10 percent or more (in value) of all interests in the activity during the entire taxable year (or shorter period during which the taxpayer held an interest in the activity).

The difference between *active participation* and *material participation* is that the active participation threshold can be satisfied *without* regular, continuous, and substantial involvement in operations. The active participation standard is met if the taxpayer participates in making management decisions in a significant and bona fide sense. Approving new tenants, deciding on rental terms, and approving capital or repair expenditures meet this test.

[26] § 469(c)(7)(B) and Reg. § 1.469–9. In *Frank Aragona Trust*, 142 T.C. 165 (2014), the Tax Court found that a trust also could qualify for the real estate professional rule.

[27] § 469(i).

[28] In general, AGI for purposes of the phaseout is calculated without regard to IRA deductions, Social Security benefits, interest deductions on education loans, and net losses from passive activities. See § 469(i)(3)(F). The figures used for this phaseout are not adjusted for inflation.

[29] § 469(i)(6).

The Big Picture

Example 31

Return to the facts of *The Big Picture* on p. 11-1. If the Lopezes invest in the apartment rental partnership, which is a passive activity, a portion (or all) of their $12,000 loss will be deductible under the real estate rental activities exception (the deductible loss will depend on their AGI and the loss phaseout that applies once AGI exceeds $100,000). This also assumes that they actively participate and own at least a 10% interest in the partnership.

The loss will be deductible in each of the first four years of their investment before their at-risk basis has been exhausted even if they do not have passive activity income from other sources (as explained earlier, the Lopezes' original at-risk basis of $50,000 plus their share of the partnership's qualified nonrecourse financing will be reduced to $0 over four years).

The $25,000 allowance is available after all active participation rental losses and gains are netted and applied to other passive activity income. If a taxpayer has a real estate rental loss in excess of the amount that can be deducted under the real estate rental exception, that excess is treated as a passive activity loss, usable in future years.

Example 32

Brad has $90,000 of AGI before considering rental activities. Brad also has $85,000 of losses from a real estate rental activity in which he actively participates. He also actively participates in another real estate rental activity from which he has $30,000 of income. He has other passive activity income of $36,000.

Of the net rental loss of $55,000 ($30,000 − $85,000), $36,000 offsets the passive activity income, leaving $19,000 that can be deducted against active or portfolio income because of the availability of the $25,000 allowance.

The $25,000 allowance is an aggregate of both deductions and the "deduction equivalent" of tax credits. The deduction equivalent of a passive activity credit is the amount of deductions that reduces the tax liability for the taxable year by an amount equal to the credit.[30] A taxpayer with $2,200 of credits and a tax bracket of 22 percent would have a deduction equivalent of $10,000 ($2,200 ÷ 22%).

If the total deduction and deduction equivalent exceed $25,000, the taxpayer must allocate the allowance on a pro rata basis, first among the losses (including real estate rental activity losses suspended in prior years) and then to credits in the following order: (1) credits other than rehabilitation and low-income housing credits, (2) rehabilitation credits, and (3) low-income housing credits.

Deduction Equivalent Considerations

Kevin is an active participant in a real estate rental activity that produces $8,000 of income, $26,000 of deductions, and $1,500 of credits. Kevin is a single taxpayer with $98,000 of AGI before considering this rental activity and is in the 22% tax bracket. As a result, he may deduct the net passive activity loss of $18,000 ($8,000 − $26,000).

After deducting the loss, he has an available deduction equivalent of $7,000 ($25,000 − $18,000 passive activity loss). Because the actual credits produce a $6,818 deduction equivalent ($1,500 ÷ 22% = $6,818) and this amount is less than $7,000, Kevin may claim the entire $1,500 credit.

Example 34

Kelly is an active participant in three separate real estate rental activities. Kelly is a single taxpayer with $92,000 of AGI before considering these rental activities and is in the 22% tax bracket. The relevant tax results for each activity are as follows:

- Activity A: $20,000 of losses.
- Activity B: $10,000 of losses.
- Activity C: $1,100 of credits.

continued

[30] § 469(j)(5).

Kelly's deduction equivalent from the credits is $5,000 ($1,100 ÷ 22%). As a result, the total passive activity losses and deduction equivalents are $35,000 ($20,000 + $10,000 + $5,000), which exceeds the maximum allowable amount of $25,000. Consequently, Kelly must allocate the $25,000 allowance on a pro rata basis, first from among losses and then from among credits. Deductions from losses are limited as follows:

- Activity A {$25,000 × [$20,000 ÷ ($20,000 + $10,000)]} = $16,667
- Activity B {$25,000 × [$10,000 ÷ ($20,000 + $10,000)]} = $8,333

Because the amount of passive activity losses exceeds the $25,000 maximum, the remaining losses of $5,000 and passive activity credits of $1,100 must be carried forward. Kelly's suspended losses and credits by activity are as follows:

		Activity		
	Total	**A**	**B**	**C**
Allocated losses	$ 30,000	$ 20,000	$10,000	$ -0-
Allocated credits	1,100	-0-	-0-	1,100
Utilized losses	(25,000)	(16,667)	(8,333)	-0-
Suspended losses	5,000	3,333	1,667	-0-
Suspended credits	1,100	-0-	-0-	1,100

LO.9

Determine the proper tax treatment for the disposition of a passive activity.

11-3f Dispositions of Passive Activities

If a taxpayer disposes of an entire interest in a passive activity, any suspended losses (and in certain cases, suspended credits) may be used when calculating the final economic gain or loss on the investment. In addition, if there is an overall loss from the disposition, that loss can offset other types of income. However, the tax consequences may be different if the activity is disposed of in transactions that are not fully taxable (e.g., a transfer at death or by gift or an installment sale). The following sections discuss these types of dispositions.

Disposition of a Passive Activity at Death

When a transfer of a taxpayer's interest occurs because of a taxpayer's death, suspended losses are allowed (to the decedent) only to the extent they exceed the amount, if any, of the allowed increase (step-up) in basis.[31] Suspended losses that are equal to or less than the amount of the basis increase are, however, lost. The losses allowed generally are reported on the final return of the deceased taxpayer.

Disposition of Suspended Passive Activity Losses at Death

Alyson dies with passive activity property having an adjusted basis of $40,000, suspended losses of $10,000, and a fair market value at the date of her death of $75,000. The increase (step-up) in basis is $35,000 (fair market value at date of death in excess of adjusted basis).

None of the $10,000 suspended loss is deductible on Alyson's final return or by the beneficiary. The suspended losses ($10,000) are lost because they do not exceed the step-up in basis ($35,000).

Assume the same facts as in the previous example, except that the property's fair market value at the date of Alyson's death is $47,000.

Because the step-up in basis is only $7,000 ($47,000 − $40,000), the suspended losses allowed are limited to $3,000 ($10,000 suspended loss at time of death − $7,000 increase in basis). The $3,000 loss available to Alyson is reported on her final income tax return.

[31] § 469(g)(2); the basis of inherited property is generally the fair market value on the date of death (see Chapter 13).

Disposition of a Passive Activity by Gift

If a taxpayer's interest in a passive activity is transferred by gift, the suspended losses are added to the donee's basis of the property.[32] As a result, the donor will see no benefit from any suspended losses. However, a tax *benefit* may be available to the donee. Due to the increase in the property's basis, greater depreciation deductions can result, and there will be less gain (or more loss) on a subsequent sale of the property. The benefits of increased basis do not materialize if the recipient is a charity, as such organizations generally are not subject to income taxation.

Carlton makes a gift to Maddie of passive activity property having an adjusted basis of $40,000, suspended losses of $10,000, and a fair market value at the date of the gift of $100,000. Carlton cannot deduct the suspended losses in the year of the disposition. However, the suspended losses transfer with the property and are added to the adjusted basis of the property, which becomes $50,000 in Maddie's hands.

Assuming that Maddie is able to sell the property for $105,000 soon after she receives the gift, her taxable gain will be $55,000 ($105,000 − $50,000), which reflects the benefit from the increased basis.

Installment Sale of a Passive Activity

An installment sale of a taxpayer's entire interest in a passive activity triggers recognition of the suspended losses.[33] The losses are allowed each year as payments are received on the installment obligation in the ratio that the gain recognized in each year bears to the total gain on the sale.

Lucas sells his entire interest in a passive activity for $100,000. His adjusted basis in the property is $60,000. If he uses the installment method, his gross profit ratio is 40% ($40,000 gross profit ÷ $100,000 sales proceeds). If Lucas receives a $20,000 down payment, he will recognize a gain of $8,000 (40% of $20,000). If the activity has a suspended loss of $25,000, Lucas will deduct $5,000 [($8,000 ÷ $40,000) × $25,000] of the suspended loss in the first year.

This pattern will continue as Lucas receives installment payments. So, for example, if Lucas receives a $10,000 installment payment in the following year, he will recognize gain of $4,000 and can deduct $2,500 of the suspended loss in that year.

The general rules relating to passive activity losses are reviewed in Concept Summary 11.4.

11-4 Investment Interest Limitation

LO.10

Apply restrictions placed on the deductibility of investor losses and deductions, including those that apply to investment interest.

Another way investors previously used the tax law to increase their wealth involved the interest expense deduction. By borrowing to purchase investments that would appreciate over time, the interest on the debt was claimed as an ordinary deduction when paid. Later, when the asset was sold at a gain, only a capital gains tax was due on the appreciation. In addition to the "mismatch" of ordinary deductions leading to capital gains, the time value of money also played a role in these decisions (current deductions leading to lower taxes today; capital gains at lower rates at some point in the future).

11-4a Limitation Imposed

In response, Congress limited the deductibility of **investment interest** for noncorporate taxpayers. Investment interest is interest paid on debt borrowed for the purpose of

[32] § 469(j)(6).

[33] § 469(g)(3).

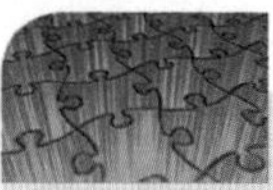

Concept Summary 11.4

Passive Activity Loss Rules: Key Issues and Answers

What is the fundamental passive activity rule?	Passive activity losses may be deducted only against passive activity income and gains. Losses not allowed are suspended and used in future years.
Who is subject to the passive activity rules?	Individuals.
	Estates.
	Trusts.
	Personal service corporations.
	Closely held C corporations.
What is a passive activity?	Trade or business or income-producing activity in which the taxpayer does not materially participate during the year or rental activities, subject to certain exceptions, regardless of the taxpayer's level of participation.
What is an activity?	One or more trade or business or rental activities that comprise an appropriate economic unit.
How is an appropriate economic unit determined?	Based on a reasonable application of the relevant facts and circumstances.
What is material participation?	In general, the taxpayer participates on a regular, continuous, and substantial basis. More specifically, when the taxpayer meets the conditions of one of the seven tests provided in the Regulations.
What is a rental activity?	In general, an activity where payments are received for the use of tangible property. Special rules apply to rental real estate.

purchasing or continuing to hold investment property. The deduction for investment interest allowed during the tax year is limited to the lesser of the investment interest paid or net investment income.[34]

The Big Picture

Example 39

Return to the facts of *The Big Picture* on p. 11-1. If the Lopezes invest in the high-growth, low-yield portfolio of marketable securities, most of the investment return will consist of appreciation, which will not be taxed until the securities are sold. Relatively little of the current return will consist of currently taxable interest and dividend income.

Assume that the interest and dividend income for the year from these securities equals $1,500 and that all of it is treated as investment income. If the investment interest expense on the $100,000 loan is $4,000, only $1,500 of this interest will be deductible this year (i.e., the deduction for the investment interest is limited to the $1,500 of net investment income).

Net Investment Income

Net investment income, which serves as the ceiling on the deductibility of investment interest, is the excess of investment income over investment expenses. **Investment income** includes gross income from interest, annuities, and royalties not derived in the ordinary course of a trade or business.[35] However, investment income does not include any income taken into account when calculating income or loss from a passive activity.

Investment expenses are those deductible expenses directly connected with the production of investment income, such as property taxes on investment holdings. Investment expenses do not include interest expense and, from 2018 through 2025, any expenses that are miscellaneous itemized deductions (e.g., brokerage charges and investment counsel fees).

[34] § 163(d)(1).

[35] § 163(d)(4)(B). Investment income also includes net capital gains and qualified dividends to the extent the taxpayer elects to give up the preferential tax rates that apply to these items; see text Section 11-6b.

11-4b Computation of Allowable Deduction

After net investment income is determined, the allowable deductible investment interest expense is calculated.

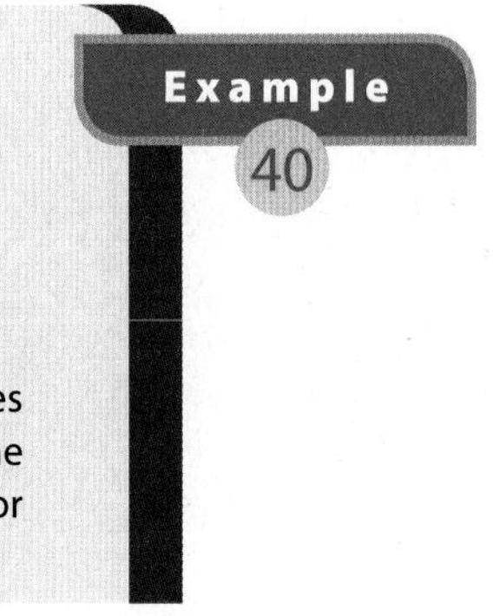

Ethan's financial records for the year reflect the following:

Interest income from bank savings account	$10,000
Taxable annuity receipts	5,500
Local ad valorem property tax on investments	200
Investment interest expense	17,000

Ethan's investment income amounts to $15,500 ($10,000 + $5,500), and investment expenses total $200. As a result, his net investment income is $15,300 ($15,500 − $200). Consequently, the investment interest deduction is limited to $15,300 (the lesser of investment interest expense or net investment income).

The amount of investment interest disallowed is carried over to future years. In Example 40, the amount that is carried over to the following year is $1,700 ($17,000 investment interest expense − $15,300 deduction allowed). No limit is placed on the length of the carryover period.[36] The investment interest expense deduction is determined by completing Form 4952 (Investment Interest Deduction).

11-5 Other Investment Losses

The investment activities summarized below are discussed elsewhere in this text as shown in Concept Summary 11.5.

- Sales of securities held as investments for less than basis result in capital losses. These losses can offset capital gains. In the case of individual taxpayers, excess losses are applied against ordinary income up to $3,000 per year (§ 1211). Any remaining excess capital losses are carried over for use in future years (§ 1212).
- Losses on small business stock (i.e., stock that qualifies under § 1244) are treated as ordinary losses up to a maximum of $100,000. As a result, the limitations placed on capital losses (see above) are avoided.
- Vacation homes that are rented for part of the year may generate investment losses depending on the extent of the rental period as compared to time devoted to personal use (§ 280A). If sufficient rental activity takes place, the vacation home may be treated as rental property. As a result, any losses could be subject to the passive activity loss rules.
- Securities held as an investment that become worthless produce capital losses. The losses are usually long term because they are treated as occurring on the last day of the year in which the securities become worthless [§ 165(g)(1)]. Because the securities must be completely worthless, determining the year this takes place is often difficult.

[36]§ 163(d)(2).

Concept Summary 11.5

Common Investment Loss Limitation Rules

Item	Refer to Chapter	General Nature of Limitation
At-risk rules	11	Losses in excess of the at-risk basis are not deducted in the current year. Losses not deducted are suspended and used in future years when the at-risk basis increases.
Passive activity loss limitations	11	Generally, passive activity losses are deducted only to the extent of passive activity income. Excess passive activity losses are suspended and used in future years.
Investment interest expense	11	The deduction of investment interest is limited to the taxpayer's net investment income. Excess investment interest is deductible in future years.
Vacation homes	6	The deductibility of losses from vacation homes may be limited depending on the relative number of rental use days and personal use days of the property.
Small business (§ 1244) stock	7	Losses from the disposition of small business stock are given ordinary treatment up to a maximum of $100,000 per year.
Worthless securities	7	Losses arising from investment securities that become worthless are treated as occurring on the last day of the tax year.
Wash sales	13	Loss from the sale or other disposition of stock or securities is disallowed if the taxpayer acquires substantially identical stock or securities in the period 30 days before the disposition to 30 days after the disposition.
Losses from the sale or exchange of capital assets	14	Individuals may offset capital gains by capital losses realized. Up to $3,000 of realized net capital losses may offset ordinary income per year. Remaining excess capital losses are carried over to future years.

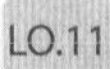

LO.11

Suggest tax planning strategies to minimize the effect of the passive activity loss and investment interest limitations, and recognize the general impact of the additional tax on net investment income.

11-6 Tax Planning

11-6a Minimizing the Impact of the Passive Activity Loss Limits

Perhaps the biggest challenge individuals face with the passive activity loss rules is to recognize the potential impact of the rules and then to structure their affairs to minimize this impact. If a taxpayer does invest in an activity that produces losses subject to the passive activity loss rules, the following discussion describes strategies that may help minimize the loss of current deductions.

Taxpayers who have passive activity losses should adopt a strategy of buying an interest in an activity that is generating passive activity income that can be offset (or sheltered) by the existing passive activity losses. From a tax perspective, it would be foolish to buy a loss-generating passive activity unless (1) the taxpayer has other passive activity income to shelter, (2) the activity is rental real estate that can qualify for the $25,000 exception, or (3) the activity qualifies for the exception available to real estate professionals.

If money is borrowed to finance the purchase of a passive activity, the associated interest expense is generally treated as part of any passive activity loss. Consequently, by using more available (i.e., not borrowed) cash to purchase the passive investment, the investor will need less debt and will incur less interest expense. By incurring less interest expense, a possible suspended passive activity loss deduction is reduced.

As explained earlier, unusable passive activity losses often accumulate and provide no current tax benefit because the taxpayer has no passive activity income. When the taxpayer disposes of the entire interest in a passive activity, however, any suspended losses from that activity are used to reduce the taxable gain. If any taxable gain still remains, it can be offset by losses from other passive activities. As a result, the taxpayer should carefully select the year in which to dispose of a passive activity. It is to the taxpayer's advantage to wait until sufficient passive activity losses have accumulated to offset any gain recognized on the asset's disposition.

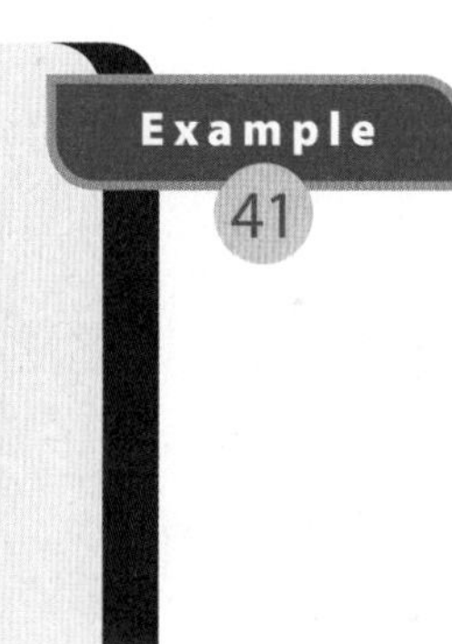

Bill, a calendar year taxpayer, owns interests in two passive activities: Activity A, which he plans to sell in December of this year at a gain of $100,000, and Activity B, which he plans to keep indefinitely. Current and suspended passive activity losses associated with Activity B total $60,000, and Bill expects losses from the activity to be $40,000 next year.

If Bill sells Activity A this year, the $100,000 gain can be offset by the current and suspended losses of $60,000 from Activity B, producing a net taxable gain of $40,000. However, if Bill delays the sale of Activity A until January of next year, the $100,000 gain will be fully offset by the $100,000 of losses generated by Activity B ($60,000 current and prior losses + $40,000 next year's loss). Consequently, by postponing the sale by one month, he could avoid recognizing $40,000 of gain that would otherwise result.

Taxpayers with passive activity losses should consider the level of their involvement in all other trades or businesses in which they have an interest. If they do not materially participate in a profitable activity, the activity becomes a passive activity. Any income generated by the profitable business then could be sheltered by current and suspended passive activity losses. Family partnerships in which certain members do not materially participate would qualify. The silent partner in any general partnership engaged in a trade or business also would qualify.

Example 42

Naya has an investment in a limited partnership that produces annual passive activity losses of approximately $25,000. She also owns a newly acquired interest in a convenience store where she works. Her share of the store's income is $35,000. If she works enough to be classified as a material participant, her $35,000 share of income is treated as active income. This results in $35,000 being subject to tax every year, whereas her $25,000 loss is suspended.

However, if Naya reduces her involvement at the store so that she is not a material participant, the $35,000 of income receives passive activity treatment. Consequently, the $35,000 of passive activity income can be offset by the $25,000 passive activity loss, resulting in only $10,000 being subject to tax. By reducing her involvement, Naya ensures that the income from the profitable trade or business receives passive activity treatment and can then be used to absorb passive activity losses from other passive activities.

The impact of the passive activity loss rules often extends to other seemingly unrelated Code sections. For example, because of the restrictive nature of the passive activity loss rules, it may be advantageous for a taxpayer to use a vacation home enough to convert it to a second residence. This would enable qualified interest and real estate taxes to be deducted (subject to the limitations discussed in Chapter 10). However, this strategy would lead to the loss of other deductions, such as repairs, maintenance, and insurance. See text Section 6-3f for a discussion of the vacation home rental rules.

The passive activity loss rules can have a dramatic effect on a taxpayer's ability to claim passive activity losses currently. As a result, it is important to keep accurate records of all sources of income and losses, particularly any suspended passive activity losses and credits and the activities to which they relate, so that their potential tax benefit will not be lost.

11-6b **Maximizing the Investment Interest Deduction**

The term *investment income* includes net capital gain and qualified dividend income only if the taxpayer *elects* to treat them as such. For this purpose:

- Net capital gain includes gain attributable to property held for investment.
- Qualified dividend income includes dividends that are taxed at the same marginal rate that is applicable to a net capital gain.

By electing to include net capital gain and qualified dividend income as components of investment income, the amount of investment interest deductible for the year likewise increases. Form 4952 is used to make such an election. However, the election comes with a cost and is available only if the taxpayer agrees to reduce amounts qualifying for the preferential tax rates that otherwise apply to net capital gain (see Chapter 14) and qualified dividends (refer to Chapter 4) by an equivalent amount.[37]

Olivia incurred $13,000 of interest expense related to her investments during the year. Her investment income included $4,000 of interest, $2,000 of qualified dividends, and a $5,000 net capital gain on the sale of investment securities.

If Olivia does not make the election to include the net capital gain and qualified dividends in investment income, her investment income for purposes of computing the investment income limitation is $4,000 (interest income). If she does make the election, her investment income is $11,000 ($4,000 interest + $2,000 qualified dividends + $5,000 net capital gain). In that case, $11,000 of her interest expense, rather than $4,000, is deductible currently. However, her net capital gain and qualified dividends will be taxed at ordinary tax rates.

Should Olivia in the previous example make the election to include the additional $7,000 of qualified dividends and net capital gain as investment income? By doing so, the current-year investment interest deduction increases by $7,000, and the investment interest deduction potentially carried forward to future years is reduced by the same amount. That is, the election allows for an acceleration of the investment interest deduction. As Olivia evaluates her decision, she should consider the following points:

- The election would make sense only if her marginal ordinary income tax rate exceeded the applicable capital gains rate.
- Using present value concepts, she should compare the tax cost of postponing the interest deduction to a subsequent year with the impact of losing the benefit from the preferential capital gains rate. In performing this analysis, consideration should be given to the length of the deferral of the investment interest deduction and the current and future years' tax brackets.

11-6c **Effect of the Additional Tax on Net Investment Income**

As if the passive activity loss and investment interest limitations are not complicated enough, individuals, estates, and trusts also are subject to an additional 3.8 percent tax on net investment income.[38] Net investment income *for this purpose* generally includes amounts such as interest, dividends, long- and short-term capital gains, royalties, rents, and income from passive activities.

The tax is levied at the flat 3.8 percent rate on the lesser of the taxpayer's net investment income or the excess of modified AGI over a threshold amount. The threshold amounts for individuals are $250,000 for surviving spouses and taxpayers filing a joint return, $125,000 for married taxpayers filing separate returns, and $200,000 for all other individual taxpayers. As a result, this tax is aimed at higher-income taxpayers and can potentially increase the marginal capital gain tax rate to 23.8 percent (from 20 percent) and the marginal ordinary income tax rate to 40.8 percent (from 37 percent). See text Section 12-5c for a discussion of this tax.

[37] Reg. § 1.163(d)–1.

[38] § 1411.

Refocus on The Big Picture

Investor Loss Limitations Can Affect Investment Returns

The objective for most investors should be to maximize after-tax wealth from among investment alternatives. This requires an understanding of the relevant tax restrictions that apply to certain expenses and losses arising from various investment choices. The after-tax returns from the three alternatives the Lopezes are considering may be affected by the at-risk, passive activity, and investment interest limitations.

The high-growth, low-yield portfolio is expected to generate very little, if any, current interest and dividend income (i.e., investment income). Nonetheless, if the financial planner's prediction is correct, the market value of the securities will grow by approximately 8 percent a year. However, the annual $2,000 of interest expense on the debt incurred to purchase the securities is not deductible as investment interest to the extent there is no investment income. Unless investment income is generated from this or some other source, the interest will not be deductible until the securities are sold (see Example 39). In addition, to the extent that any capital gain from the portfolio's sale is treated as investment income, the gain will not be subject to preferential capital gains rates (see Example 43). As a result, the net after-tax return will be impaired because of the investment interest limitation.

The net returns from the other two investment choices will be diminished by the at-risk and passive activity loss rules in addition to the investment interest limitation. The projected 8 percent return is apparently contingent on the investors being able to use the current tax losses as they arise. These benefits will be deferred because the at-risk and passive activity loss rules delay the timing of the deductions. For example, in the case of the orange grove investment, although the Lopezes are at-risk for $100,000, none of the passive activity losses are deductible until year 6, when the investment is expected to produce passive activity income (see Example 29). In the real estate rental venture, the Lopezes are similarly limited by the at-risk and the passive activity loss rules. The Lopezes cannot deduct the passive activity loss under the exception for rental real estate for the first four years, because their AGI is too high (see Example 31); the at-risk rules would limit any additional losses in year 5 to the at-risk amount. Consequently, because the at-risk and passive activity loss rules limit the tax losses flowing to the Lopezes, the after-tax return will not be nearly as high as their financial planner predicts.

What If?

If the Lopezes decide that the investment in marketable securities is their best option, could they modify their plan so that they avoid the restriction imposed by the investment interest limitation? The Lopezes' net after-tax return would improve if the interest cost of financing their investment could be deducted as incurred. A viable strategy prior to 2018 would have been to finance their investment by borrowing up to $100,000 against the equity in their home. Using this strategy would have made the interest on the home equity loan fully deductible and increased the after-tax return from their investment. Currently, however, home equity loan interest generally is not deductible. As a result, the investment interest limitation continues to negatively impact the after-tax return from an investment in marketable securities.

Key Terms

Active income, 11-6
At-risk limitation, 11-3
Closely held corporation, 11-10
Investment income, 11-22
Investment interest, 11-21
Material participation, 11-13
Net investment income, 11-22
Passive activity loss, 11-3
Personal service corporation, 11-10
Portfolio income, 11-6
Rental activity, 11-15
Significant participation activity, 11-14
Tax shelters, 11-2

Discussion Questions

Communications

1. **LO.1, 2, 3** Identify two rules designed to limit the tax benefits a taxpayer may obtain from a tax shelter investment. In an e-mail to your instructor, describe how these rules reduce or defer the recognition of tax losses.

Planning

2. **LO.2** List some events that increase or decrease an investor's at-risk amount. What are some strategies that a taxpayer can employ to increase the at-risk amount to claim a higher deduction for losses?

3. **LO.2, 3** Roberto invested $18,000 in a chicken production operation. Using nonrecourse notes, the business purchases $120,000 worth of grain to feed the chickens. If Roberto's share of the expense is $26,000, how much can he deduct?

4. **LO.3** Explain the meaning of the terms *active income, portfolio income*, and *passive activity income*.

5. **LO.3** Carlos owns an interest in an activity that produces a $100,000 loss during the year. Would he prefer to have the activity classified as active or passive? Explain.

6. **LO.3** Kim owns an interest in an activity that produces $100,000 of income during the year. Would Kim prefer to have the activity classified as active or passive? Discuss.

7. **LO.3** On a taxable disposition of a passive activity, the taxpayer can use any suspended losses and credits related to that activity. Do you agree? Explain.

8. **LO.3** Discuss whether the passive activity loss rules apply to the following: individuals, closely held C corporations, S corporations, partnerships, and personal service corporations.

9. **LO.3** Bronze Corporation has $100,000 of active income, $55,000 of portfolio income, and a $55,000 passive activity loss. Under what circumstances is Bronze prohibited from deducting the loss? Allowed to deduct the loss?

10. **LO.4** Discuss what constitutes a passive activity.

11. **LO.5** What is the significance of the term *material participation*? Why is the extent of a taxpayer's participation in an activity important in determining whether a loss from the activity is deductible or nondeductible?

12. **LO.5** How many hours must a participant work in a nonrental activity to be guaranteed material participation status?

Decision Making
Planning

13. **LO.5** Suzanne owns interests in a bagel shop, a lawn and garden store, and a convenience store. Several full-time employees work at each of the enterprises. As of the end of November of the current year, Suzanne has worked 150 hours in the bagel shop, 250 hours at the lawn and garden store, and 70 hours at the convenience store. In reviewing her financial records, you learn that she has no passive investments that are generating income and that she expects these three ventures

collectively to produce a loss. What recommendation would you offer Suzanne as she plans her activities for the remainder of the year?

14. **LO.5, 11** Jesse, an engineer, operates a separate business that he acquired eight years ago. If he participates 85 hours in the business and it incurs a loss of $34,000, under what circumstances can Jesse claim an active loss?

15. **LO.2, 3, 5** Rita retired from public accounting after a long and successful career of 45 years. As part of her retirement package, she continues to share in the profits and losses of the firm, albeit at a lower rate than when she was working full-time. Because Rita wants to stay busy during her retirement years, she has invested and works in a local hardware business, operated as a partnership. Unfortunately, the business has recently gone through a slump and has not been generating profits. Identify relevant tax issues for Rita. Critical Thinking

16. **LO.5** Some types of work are counted in applying the material participation standards, and some types are not counted. Discuss and give examples of each type.

17. **LO.5** Last year Alan's accountant informed him that he could not claim any of his passive activity losses on his income tax return because of his lack of material participation. To circumvent the tax problem this year, Alan tells his spouse that she may have to put in some time at the various businesses. Identify the tax issues that Alan faces. Critical Thinking

18. **LO.5** Sean, a limited partner in Ivy Nursery, is informed that his portion of the entity's current loss is $18,000. As a limited partner, can Sean assume that his share of the partnership loss is a passive activity loss? Explain.

19. **LO.6** Explain why some non-real estate rental activities may not be *treated* as such under the passive activity loss rules.

20. **LO.3, 4, 5, 6, 8, 11** Odette owns a beach home that she converted to rental use last year. A company manages the property, and rentals are primarily on weekends. Since the average period of customer use is seven days or less, this is not a rental activity. As a result, Odette cannot use up to $25,000 of losses annually with the special active participation rule. What might Odette do next year to be able to apply this rule given that her income is below the threshold for this special loss provision? Critical Thinking Planning

21. **LO.8** What is a *real estate professional?* Why could qualifying for this status be beneficial under the passive activity loss rules?

22. **LO.8** Caroline owns a real estate rental activity that produces a loss of $65,000 during the current year. Under what circumstances can Caroline treat the entire loss as nonpassive?

23. **LO.8** Since his college days, Charles has developed an entrepreneurial streak. After working in his family's grocery business, he starts several ventures on his own. Even though Charles is independently wealthy, he is looking forward to working in each of the ventures. He plans to "drop in" on the businesses from time to time between personal trips to Europe and the Caribbean. As of the end of the year, he has established computer software stores in Dayton (Ohio), Austin, and Seattle; bagel bakeries in Albany, Athens (Georgia), and Tallahassee; and mountain bike and ski rental shops in small towns in Vermont, West Virginia, Colorado, and California. Identify the tax issues that Charles faces. Critical Thinking

24. **LO.8** Bailey owns a small rental townhouse complex that generates a loss during the year. Under what circumstances can Bailey deduct a loss from the rental activity? What limitations apply? Planning

25. **LO.8** In connection with passive activities, what is a *deduction equivalent* and how is it computed?

26. **LO.10** What is *investment interest expense?* Describe the basic rules that may limit its deductibility.

Computational Exercises

27. **LO.2** In the current year, Ming invests $30,000 in an oil partnership. He has taxable income for the current year of $2,000 from the oil partnership and withdraws $10,000. What is Ming's at-risk amount at the end of the year?

28. **LO.3** Lucy sells her partnership interest, a passive activity, with an adjusted basis of $305,000 for $330,000. In addition, she has current and suspended losses of $28,000 associated with the partnership and has no other passive activities. Calculate Lucy's total gain and her current deductible loss. Describe the type of income that the deductible loss may offset.

29. **LO.4, 5** Zhou owns a nonrental business with two separate departments. Department A generates net income of $70,000, and Department B generates a net loss of $58,000. Zhou participates 800 hours in the operations of Department A and 300 hours in the operations of Department B. If Zhou is allowed to treat the departments as components of a single activity, calculate the amount of the Department B loss that can be offset against the income from Department A in the current year.

30. **LO.7** Rhonda has an adjusted basis and an at-risk amount of $7,500 in a passive activity at the beginning of the year. She also has a suspended passive activity loss of $1,500 carried over from the prior year. During the current year, she has a loss of $12,000 from the passive activity. Rhonda has no passive activity income from other sources this year. Determine the following items relating to Rhonda's passive activity as of the end of the year.
    a. Adjusted basis and at-risk amount in the passive activity.
    b. Loss suspended under the at-risk rules.
    c. Suspended passive activity loss.

31. **LO.8** Noah Yobs, who has $62,000 of AGI (solely from wages) before considering rental activities, has $70,000 of losses from a real estate rental activity in which he actively participates. He also actively participates in another real estate rental activity from which he has $33,000 of income. He has other passive activity income of $20,000.
    a. What amount of rental loss can Noah use to offset active or portfolio income in the current year?
    b. Compute Noah's AGI on Form 1040 [pages 1 and 2; also complete Schedule 1 (Form 1040)] for the current year. His Social Security number is 123-45-6789.

32. **LO.9** Rose dies with passive activity property having an adjusted basis of $65,000, suspended losses of $13,000, and a fair market value at the date of her death of $90,000. Of the $13,000 suspended loss existing at the time of Rose's death, how much is deductible on her final return or by the beneficiary?

33. **LO.10** Troy's financial records for the year reflect the following:

Interest income from bank savings account	$ 900
Taxable annuity receipts	1,800
City ad valorem property tax on investments	125
Investment interest expense	3,200

Calculate Troy's net investment income and his current investment interest deduction. How is a deduction for any potential excess investment interest treated?

Problems

34. LO.2 In 2022, Fred invested $50,000 in a general partnership. Fred's interest is not considered to be a passive activity. If his share of the partnership losses is $35,000 in 2022 and $25,000 in 2023, how much can he deduct in each year?

35. LO.2 In the current year, Bill Parker (54 Oak Drive, St. Paul, MN 55164) is considering making an investment of $60,000 in Best Choice Partnership. If Bill makes the investment, he will participate in the business operated by Best Choice (and will meet one of the material participation tests). As a result, it will not be a passive activity. Bill's share of the entity's loss in the current year will likely be $40,000, whereas his share of the partnership loss next year will probably be $25,000. Write a letter to Bill in which you indicate how the losses would be treated for tax purposes in the current year and the following year. Communications

36. LO.2, 11 Heather wants to invest $40,000 in a relatively safe venture and has discovered two alternatives that would produce the following reportable ordinary income and loss over the next three years: Critical Thinking Decision Making Planning

Year	Alternative 1 Income (Loss)	Alternative 2 Income (Loss)
1	($20,000)	($48,000)
2	(28,000)	32,000
3	72,000	40,000

She is interested in the after-tax effects of these alternatives over a three-year horizon. Assume that Heather's investment portfolio produces sufficient passive activity income to offset any potential passive activity loss that may arise from these alternatives, that her cost of capital is 6%, that she is in the 24% tax bracket, that each investment alternative possesses equal growth potential, and that each alternative exposes her to comparable financial risk. In addition, assume that in the loss years for each alternative, there is no cash flow from or to the investment (i.e., the loss is due to depreciation), whereas in those years when the income is positive, cash flows to Heather equal the amount of the income.

a. Based on these facts, compute the present value of these two investment alternatives and determine which option Heather should choose. Refer to Appendix E for the present value factors.
b. Prepare your solution using spreadsheet software such as Microsoft Excel.

37. LO.1, 3 Dorothy acquired a 100% interest in two passive activities: Activity A in January 2018 and Activity B in 2019. Through 2021, Activity A was profitable, but it produced losses of $200,000 in 2022 and $100,000 in 2023. Dorothy has passive activity income from Activity B of $20,000 in 2022 and $40,000 in 2023. After offsetting passive activity income, how much of the net losses may she deduct?

38. LO.1, 3 A number of years ago, Kayla acquired an interest in a partnership in which she is not a material participant. Kayla's basis in her partnership interest at the beginning of 2022 is $40,000. Kayla's share of the partnership loss is $35,000 in 2022, and her share of the partnership income is $15,000 in 2023. How much may Kayla deduct in 2022 and 2023, assuming that she owns no other passive activities?

39. LO.3 Mike, an attorney, earns $200,000 from his law practice and receives $45,000 in dividends and interest during the year. In addition, he incurs a loss of $50,000 from an investment in a passive activity acquired three years ago. What is Mike's net income for the current year after considering the passive investment?

40. LO.3, 11 Emily has $100,000 that she wants to invest and is considering the following two options: Critical Thinking Decision Making Planning

- Option A: Investment in Redbird Mutual Fund, which is expected to produce interest income of $8,000 per year.

- Option B: Investment in Cardinal Limited Partnership (buys, sells, and operates wine vineyards). Emily's share of the partnership's ordinary income and loss over the next three years will be as follows:

Year	Income (Loss)
1	($ 8,000)
2	(2,000)
3	34,000

Emily is interested in the after-tax effects of these alternatives over a three-year horizon. Assume that Emily's investment portfolio produces ample passive activity income to offset any passive activity losses that may be generated. Her cost of capital is 8%, and she is in the 32% tax bracket. The two investment alternatives possess equal growth potential and comparable financial risk.

a. Based on these facts, compute the present value of these two investment alternatives and determine which option Emily should choose. Refer to Appendix E for the present value factors.

b. Prepare your solution using spreadsheet software such as Microsoft Excel.

41. **LO.3** Seojun acquired an activity several years ago, and in the current year, it generates a loss of $50,000. Seojun has AGI of $140,000 before considering the loss from the activity. If the activity is a bakery and Seojun is not a material participant, what is his AGI?

Decision Making
Planning

42. **LO.3, 9, 11** Jorge owns two passive investments, Activity A and Activity B. He plans to sell Activity A in the current year or next year. Juanita has offered to buy Activity A this year for an amount that would produce a taxable passive activity gain to Jorge of $115,000. However, if the sale, for whatever reason, is not made to Juanita, Jorge believes that he could find a buyer who would pay about $7,000 less than Juanita. Passive activity losses and gains generated (and expected to be generated) by Activity B follow:

Two years ago	($35,000)
Last year	(35,000)
This year	(8,000)
Next year	(30,000)
Future years	Minimal profits

All of Activity B's losses are suspended. Should Jorge close the sale of Activity A with Juanita this year, or should he wait until next year and sell to another buyer? Jorge is in the 32% tax bracket.

43. **LO.3, 9** Sarah has investments in four passive activity partnerships purchased several years ago. Last year the income and losses were as follows:

Activity	Income (Loss)
A	$ 30,000
B	(30,000)
C	(15,000)
D	(5,000)

In the current year, she sold her interest in Activity D for a $10,000 gain. Activity D, which had been profitable until last year, had a current loss of $1,500. How will the sale of Activity D affect Sarah's taxable income in the current year?

44. **LO.3, 9** Leon sells his interest in a passive activity for $100,000. Determine the tax effect of the sale based on each of the following independent facts:

a. Adjusted basis in this investment is $35,000. Losses from prior years that were not deductible due to the passive activity loss restrictions total $40,000.

b. Adjusted basis in this investment is $75,000. Losses from prior years that were not deductible due to the passive activity loss restrictions total $40,000.

c. Adjusted basis in this investment is $75,000. Losses from prior years that were not deductible due to the passive activity loss restrictions total $40,000. In addition, suspended credits total $10,000.

45. **LO.3** Ash, Inc., a closely held personal service corporation, has $100,000 of passive activity losses. In addition, Ash has $80,000 of active business income and $20,000 of portfolio income. How much of the passive activity loss may Ash use to offset the other types of income?

46. **LO.3** In the current year, White, Inc., earns $400,000 from operations and receives $36,000 of interest income from various portfolio investments. White also pays $150,000 to acquire a 20% interest in a passive activity that produces a $200,000 loss.

a. Assuming that White is a personal service corporation, how will these transactions affect its taxable income?

b. Same as part (a), except that White is closely held but not a personal service corporation.

47. **LO.2, 3, 7, 11** Kristin Graf (123 Baskerville Mill Road, Jamison, PA 18929) is trying to decide how to invest a $10,000 inheritance. One option is to make an additional investment in Rocky Road Excursions in which she has an at-risk basis of $0, suspended losses under the at-risk rules of $7,000, and suspended passive activity losses of $1,000. If Kristin makes this investment, her share of the expected profits this year will be $8,000. If her investment stays the same, her share of profits from Rocky Road Excursions will be $1,000. Another option is to invest $10,000 as a limited partner in the Ragged Mountain Winery; this investment will produce passive activity income of $9,000. Write a letter to Kristin to review the tax consequences of each alternative. Kristin is in the 24% tax bracket.

Communications
Critical Thinking
Decision Making
Planning

48. **LO.2, 3, 7, 11** The end of the year is approaching, and Maxine has begun to focus on ways of minimizing her income tax liability. Several years ago she purchased an investment in Teal Limited Partnership, which is subject to the at-risk and the passive activity loss rules. (Last year Maxine sold a different investment that was subject to these rules and that produced passive activity income.) She believes that her investment in Teal has good long-term economic prospects. However, it has been generating tax losses for several years in a row. In fact, when she was discussing last year's income tax return with her tax accountant, he said that unless "things change" with respect to her investments, she would not be able to deduct losses this year.

Decision Making
Planning

a. What was the accountant referring to in his comment?

b. You learn that Maxine's current at-risk basis in her investment is $1,000 and that her share of the current loss is expected to be $13,000. Based on these facts, how will her loss be treated?

c. After reviewing her situation, Maxine's financial adviser suggests that she invest at least an additional $12,000 in Teal to ensure a full loss deduction in the current year. How do you react to his suggestion?

d. What would you suggest Maxine consider as she attempts to maximize her current-year deductible loss?

49. **LO.2, 3, 7** A number of years ago, Lee acquired a 20% interest in the BlueSky Partnership for $60,000. The partnership was profitable through 2022, and Lee's amount at risk in the partnership interest was $120,000 at the beginning of 2023. BlueSky incurred a loss of $400,000 in 2023 and reported income of $200,000 in 2024. Assuming that Lee is not a material participant, how much of his loss from BlueSky Partnership is deductible in 2023 and 2024? Consider the at-risk and passive activity loss rules, and assume that Lee owns no other passive investments.

50. **LO.2, 3, 5, 7** Grace acquired an activity four years ago. The loss from the activity is $50,000 in the current year (at-risk basis of $40,000 as of the beginning of the year). Without considering the loss from the activity, she has gross income of $140,000. If the activity is a convenience store and Grace is a material participant, what is the effect of the activity on her taxable income?

51. **LO.2, 3, 5, 7** Jonathan, a physician, earns $200,000 from his practice. He also receives $18,000 in dividends and interest from various portfolio investments. During the year, he pays $45,000 to acquire a 20% interest in a partnership that operates a retail store and has no debt. The partnership produces a $300,000 loss this year. Compute Jonathan's AGI assuming that:

    a. He does not participate in the operations of the partnership.

    b. He is a material participant in the operations of the partnership.

52. **LO.2, 3, 7** Five years ago Gerald invested $150,000 in a passive activity, his sole investment venture. On January 1, 2022, his amount at risk in the activity was $30,000. His shares of the income and losses were as follows:

Year	Income (Loss)
2022	($40,000)
2023	(30,000)
2024	50,000

Gerald holds no suspended at-risk or passive activity losses at the beginning of 2022. How much can Gerald deduct in 2022 and 2023? What is his taxable income from the activity in 2024? Consider the at-risk rules as well as the passive activity loss rules.

Communications

53. **LO.3, 8** Several years ago Benny Jackson (125 Hill Street, Charleston, WV 25311) acquired an apartment building that currently generates a loss of $60,000. Benny's AGI is $130,000 before considering the loss. The apartment building is in an exclusive part of the city, and Benny is an active participant. Write a letter to Benny explaining what effect the loss will have on his AGI.

54. **LO.3, 5, 8** This year Maria works 1,200 hours as a computer consultant, 320 hours in a real estate development business, and 400 hours in real estate rental activities. Juan, her spouse, works 250 hours in the real estate development business and 180 hours in the real estate rental business. Maria earns $80,000 as a computer consultant, and she and Juan lost $18,000 in the real estate development business and $26,000 in the real estate rental business. How should they treat the losses?

Decision Making
Planning

55. **LO.3, 8, 11** Bonnie and Jake (ages 35 and 36, respectively) are married with no dependents and live in Montana (not a community property state). Because Jake has large medical expenses, they seek your advice about filing separately to save taxes. Their income and expenses for 2023 are as follows:

Bonnie's salary	$ 42,500
Jake's salary	26,000
Interest income (joint)	1,500
Rental loss from actively managed rental property	(23,000)
Jake's unreimbursed medical expenses	8,500
All other itemized deductions:*	
Bonnie	19,000
Jake	6,400

*None subject to limitations

Determine whether Bonnie and Jake should file jointly or separately for 2023.

Decision Making

56. **LO.3, 8, 11** Mary and Charles have owned a beach cottage on the New Jersey shore for several years and have always used it as a family retreat. When they acquired the property, they had no intentions of renting it. Because family

circumstances have changed, they are considering using the cottage for only one week a year and renting it for the remainder of the year. Their AGI approximates $100,000 per year, they are in the 30% tax bracket (combined Federal and state), and their total itemized deductions exceed the standard deduction amount. Interest and real estate taxes total $8,000 per year and are expected to continue at this level in the foreseeable future. If Mary and Charles rent the property, their *incremental* revenue and expenses are projected to be:

Rent income	$ 22,000
Rental commissions	(4,000)
Maintenance expenses	(9,000)
Depreciation expense	(10,000)

If the cottage is converted to rental property, they plan to be actively involved in key rental and maintenance decisions. Given the tax effects of converting the property to rental use, would the cash flow from renting the property be enough to meet the $12,000 annual mortgage payment? Explain.

57. **LO.3, 8** During the current year, Gene, a CPA, performs services as follows: 1,800 hours in his tax practice and 50 hours in an apartment leasing operation in which he has a 15% interest. Because of his oversight duties, Gene is considered to be an active participant. He expects that his share of the loss realized from the apartment leasing operation will be $30,000 and that his tax practice will show a profit of approximately $80,000. Gene is single and has no other income. Discuss the character and treatment of the income and losses generated by these activities.

58. **LO.3, 8** Mandy, who has AGI of $80,000 before considering rental activities, is active in three separate real estate rental activities and is in the 22% tax bracket. She has $12,000 of losses from Activity A, $18,000 of losses from Activity B, and income of $10,000 from Activity C. She also has $2,100 of tax credits from Activity A. Calculate the deductions and credits she is allowed and the suspended losses and credits.

59. **LO.8** Jiu has $105,000 of losses from a real estate rental activity in which she actively participates. She has other rental income of $25,000 and other passive activity income of $32,000. Her AGI before considering these items of income and loss is $95,000. How much rental loss can Jiu deduct against active and portfolio income (ignoring the at-risk rules)? Does she have any suspended losses to carry over? Explain.

60. **LO.9** At death, Francine owns an interest in a passive activity property (adjusted basis of $160,000, suspended losses of $16,000, and fair market value of $170,000). What is deductible on Francine's final income tax return?

61. **LO.9** In the current year, Abe gives an interest in a passive activity to his daughter, Andrea. The value of the interest at the date of the gift is $25,000, and its adjusted basis to Abe is $13,000. During the time that Abe owned the investment, losses of $3,000 could not be deducted because of the passive activity loss limitations. What is the tax treatment of the suspended passive activity losses to Abe and Andrea?

62. **LO.9** Tonya sells a passive activity in the current year for $150,000. Her adjusted basis in the activity is $50,000, and she uses the installment method of reporting the gain. The activity has suspended losses of $12,000. Tonya receives $60,000 in the year of sale. What is her gain? How much of the suspended losses can she deduct?

63. **LO.10, 11** In 2023, Kathleen Tweardy incurs $30,000 of interest expense related to her investments. Her investment income includes $7,500 of interest, $6,000 of qualified dividends, and a $12,000 net capital gain on the sale of securities. Kathleen asks you to compute the amount of her deduction for investment interest, taking into consideration any options she might have. In addition, she wants your

Communications
Decision Making
Planning

suggestions as to any tax planning alternatives that are available. Write a letter to her that contains your advice. Kathleen lives at 11934 Briarpatch Drive, Midlothian, VA 23113.

64. **LO.10** Helen Derby borrowed $150,000 to acquire a parcel of land to be held for investment purposes. During the current year, she reported AGI of $90,000 and paid interest of $12,000 on the loan. Other items related to Helen's investments include the following:

Interest and annuity income	$11,000
Long-term capital gain on sale of stock	3,500
Real estate tax on the investment land	800

a. Determine Helen's investment interest deduction for the current year.

b. Discuss the treatment of the portion of Helen's investment interest that is disallowed for the current year.

c. Complete Helen's Form 4952 for the current year. For this purpose, assume that she chooses not to include the long-term capital gain as investment income. Her Social Security number is 123-45-6789.

Research Problems

Note: Solutions to the Research Problems can be prepared by using the Thomson Reuters Checkpoint™ online tax research database, which accompanies this textbook. Solutions can also be prepared by using research materials found in a typical tax library.

Research Problem 1. Carol is a successful physician who owns 100% of her incorporated medical practice. She and her spouse, Jordan, are considering the purchase of a commercial office building located near the local community hospital. If they purchase the building, Carol will move her medical practice to the new location and rent space for an arm's length price. The rent income Carol and Jordan receive will be available to absorb passive activity losses generated by other passive activities they own. The net effect of this arrangement is a reduction in their income tax liability. Will Carol and Jordan's plan work? Why or why not?

Research Problem 2. Five years ago, Bridget decided to purchase a limited partnership interest in a fast-food restaurant conveniently located near the campus of Southeast State University. The general partner of the restaurant venture promised her that the investment would prove to be a winner. During the process of capitalizing the business, $2,000,000 was borrowed from Northside Bank; however, each of the partners was required to pledge personal assets as collateral to satisfy the bank loan in the event that the restaurant defaulted. Bridget pledged shares of publicly traded stock (worth $200,000, basis of $75,000) to satisfy the bank's requirement.

The restaurant did a good business until just recently, when flagrant health code violations were discovered and widely publicized by the media. As a result, business has declined to a point where the restaurant's continued existence is doubtful. In addition, the $2,000,000 loan is now due for payment. Because the restaurant cannot pay, the bank has called for the collateral provided by the partners to be used to satisfy the debt. Bridget sells the pledged stock for $200,000 and forwards the proceeds to the bank. Bridget believes that her share of the restaurant's current and suspended passive activity losses can offset the $125,000 gain from the stock sale. As a result, after netting the passive activity losses against the gain, none of the gain is subject to tax.

How do you react to Bridget's position?

Research Problem 3. Ida Ross has decided to purchase a new home in a retirement community for $400,000. She has $50,000 in cash for the down payment but needs to borrow the remaining $350,000 to finance the purchase. Her financial adviser, Marc, suggests that rather than seeking a conventional mortgage, she should borrow the funds from State Bank using her portfolio of appreciated securities as collateral. Selling the securities to generate $350,000 in cash would lead to a substantial tax on the capital gain recognized. As a result, a better strategy would be to borrow against her securities and then claim a deduction for the interest paid on the loan. How do you react to the financial adviser's strategy? Planning

Partial list of research aids:
Temp.Reg. § 1.163–8T(c) and Reg. § 1.163–15.

Use internet tax resources to address the following questions. Look for reliable web-sites and blogs of the IRS and other government agencies, media outlets, businesses, tax professionals, academics, think tanks, and political outlets.

Research Problem 4. Since the first bitcoin transaction in 2009, the number of virtual currencies has grown to over 9,000, and some taxpayers trade the currencies multiple times each day (i.e., like a day trader). Find a reliable article on investment strategies for virtual currency and a software tool that can help the investor track the basis, fair market value, and dates of the trades. Send an e-mail to your professor that details your findings (including an investment strategy, the name of a software tool that can help with tax record keeping, and its capability of producing the necessary tax reporting form for the investor and their tax adviser). Communications Planning

Research Problem 5. Oil and gas ventures operating as publicly traded partnerships typically attract sophisticated investors who purchase limited partnership interests. Investments in these types of publicly traded partnerships are subject to a restrictive set of passive activity loss rules. Identify two publicly traded oil and gas partnerships that are currently marketed to investors, describe the benefits the promoters claim will result from such investments, and briefly review the basic nature of the unique passive activity loss restrictions placed on such investments.

Research Problem 6. Investment interest is incurred when taxpayers borrow money that is used to purchase investment property. Using *IRS Tax Statistics* for the most recent year available (**www.irs.gov/statistics**), determine (a) the number of taxpayers who claimed a deduction for investment interest expense, (b) the aggregate amount deducted by all taxpayers, and (c) the amount not deducted because of the net investment income limitation. Also determine the percentage of the total investment interest deduction claimed across various ranges of AGI. Data Analytics

Becker CPA Review Questions

Becker

1. Which of the following statements regarding passive activity losses is true?
   a. A net passive activity loss may be deducted against wages.
   b. Losses on rental property are always considered passive.
   c. A passive activity is one in which the taxpayer does not materially participate.
   d. Expenses related to passive activities may be deducted from passive activity income and portfolio income.

2. Michael owns a rental house that generated a $10,000 loss this year. Michael manages the rental property but does not meet the standards for material participation. Michael is a college professor and has wages of $60,000 and $5,000 in dividend income. How is the $10,000 rental real estate loss treated on Michael's tax return?
   a. $5,000 of the loss is deductible against the passive dividend income.
   b. The rental loss is not deductible because Michael does not have any passive income.
   c. $10,000 loss is not deductible because Michael does not materially participate in the rental activity.
   d. $10,000 loss is deductible under the rental real estate exception because Michael actively participates in the rental activity.
3. What is the correct order of applying the loss limitation rules?
   a. Passive loss limits, tax basis, at-risk amount
   b. Tax basis, at-risk amount, passive loss limits
   c. At-risk amount, tax basis, passive loss limits
   d. Passive loss limits, at-risk amount, tax basis
4. Sam rents his second home. During the current year, he reported a $40,000 net loss from the rental. Assume that Sam actively participates in the rental activity and no phase-out limitations apply. What is the greatest amount of the rental loss that Sam can deduct against ordinary income in the current year?
   a. $0
   b. $5,000
   c. $25,000
   d. $40,000
5. Sally recently invested $10,000 (tax basis) in a limited partnership interest. Her at-risk amount is also $10,000. The partnership lost $6,000 this year, and Sally's share of the loss is $2,000. Sally has $40,000 in wage income and $2,000 of dividend income. In addition, Sally's share of income from a different limited partnership is $1,000. Sally does not meet the tests for material participation for either of her partnership interests. How much of Sally's $2,000 loss from the limited partnership can she deduct this year?
   a. $2,000
   b. $0
   c. $1,000 because she has $2,000 of dividend income
   d. $1,000 because she has $1,000 income from another limited partnership
6. Thomas is an active participant in the rental condominium property he owns. During the year, the property generates a $15,000 loss. If Thomas has $120,000 of salary, $5,000 of long-term capital gains, $6,000 of dividends, and no additional sources of income or deductions, how much loss can Thomas deduct? Assume that Thomas has sufficient tax basis and at-risk basis to absorb the loss.
   a. $25,000
   b. $15,000
   c. $9,500
   d. $0

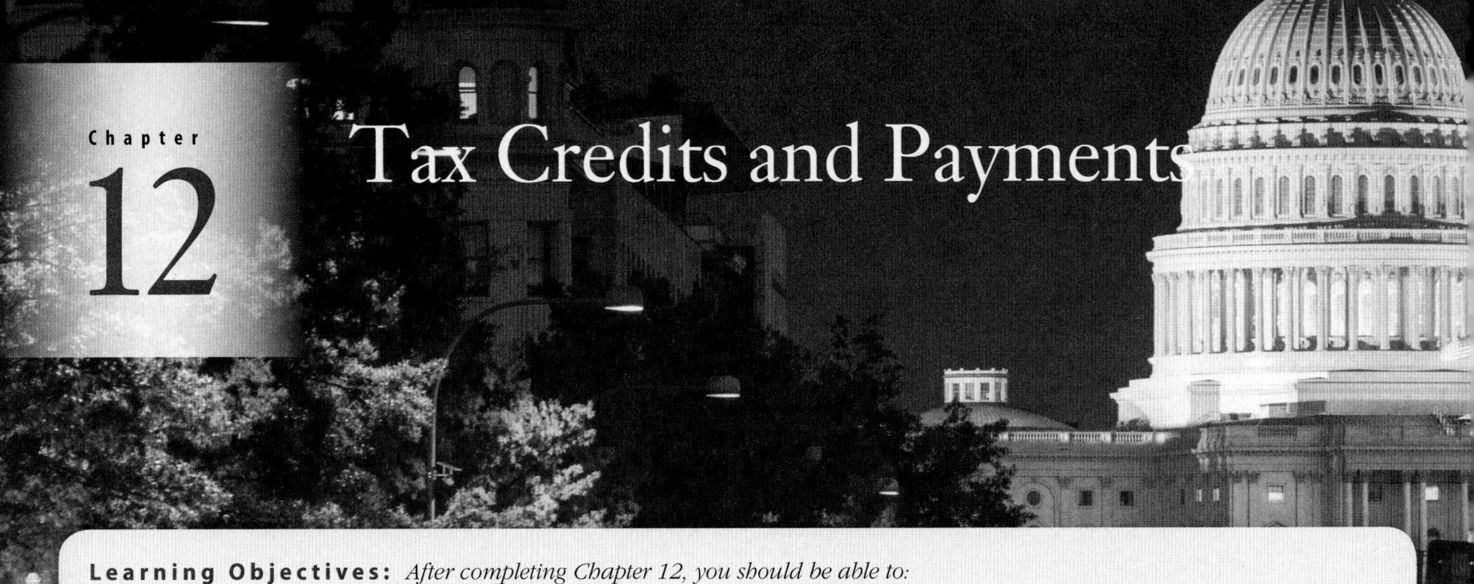

Chapter 12

Tax Credits and Payments

Learning Objectives: *After completing Chapter 12, you should be able to:*

- **LO.1** Explain how tax credits are used to achieve social, economic, or environmental objectives or to promote equity among taxpayers.
- **LO.2** Distinguish between refundable and nonrefundable credits, and understand the order in which they can be used by taxpayers.
- **LO.3** Describe various business-related tax credits.
- **LO.4** Describe the foreign tax credit and various tax credits available to individual taxpayers.
- **LO.5** Describe the tax withholding and payment procedures applicable to employers.
- **LO.6** Explain the payment procedures applicable to self-employed persons.
- **LO.7** Explain the additional Medicare taxes assessed on high-income individuals.
- **LO.8** Explain the purpose and basic computation of the alternative minimum tax (AMT).
- **LO.9** Identify tax planning opportunities related to tax credits and payment procedures.

Chapter Outline

The Big Picture

Education Tax Credits

Tom and Jennifer Snyder have two children in college. Lora is a freshman, and her tuition and required fees in 2023 total $14,000. Lora has a partial scholarship amounting to $6,500, and the Snyders paid the balance of her tuition ($7,500), plus room and board of $8,500. Sam is a junior, and the Snyders paid $8,100 for his tuition, plus $7,200 for his room and board. Both students qualify as Tom and Jennifer's dependents.

The Snyders have AGI of $158,000. They would like to know what tax options are available to them related to these educational expenses. They have heard about education tax credits, but they believe that their income is too high for them to get any benefit. Are they correct?

Read the chapter and formulate your response.

Framework 1040 **Tax Formula for Individuals**

This chapter covers the boldfaced portions of the Tax Formula for Individuals that was introduced in Concept Summary 3.1 on p. 3-3. Below those portions are the sections of Form 1040 where the results are reported.

Income *(broadly defined)*	$xx,xxx
Less: Exclusions	(x,xxx)
Gross income	$xx,xxx
Less: Deductions *for* adjusted gross income	(x,xxx)
Adjusted gross income	$xx,xxx
Less: The greater of total **itemized deductions** *or* the standard deduction	(x,xxx)
Personal and dependency exemptions*	(x,xxx)
Deduction for qualified business income**	(x,xxx)
Taxable income	$xx,xxx
Tax on taxable income *(see Tax Tables or Tax Rate Schedules)*	$ x,xxx
Less: Tax credits *(including income taxes withheld and prepaid)*	(xxx)
Tax due (or refund)	$ xxx

* Exemption deductions are not allowed from 2018 through 2025.
** Only available from 2018 through 2025.

Presentation of Tax and Credits on Form 1040:

FORM 1040 (2022 p. 2)

Tax and Credits	16	**Tax** (see instructions). Check if any from Form(s): 1 ☐ 8814 2 ☐ 4972 3 ☐ ______		16
	17	Amount from Schedule 2, line 3		17
	18	Add lines 16 and 17		18
	19	Child tax credit or credit for other dependents from Schedule 8812		19
	20	Amount from Schedule 3, line 8		20
	21	Add lines 19 and 20		21
	22	Subtract line 21 from line 18. If zero or less, enter -0-		22
	23	Other taxes, including self-employment tax, from Schedule 2, line 21		23
	24	Add lines 22 and 23. This is your **total tax**		24
Payments	25	Federal income tax withheld from:		
	a	Form(s) W-2	25a	
	b	Form(s) 1099	25b	
	c	Other forms (see instructions)	25c	
	d	Add lines 25a through 25c		25d
If you have a qualifying child, attach Sch. EIC.	26	2022 estimated tax payments and amount applied from 2021 return		26
	27	Earned income credit (EIC)	27	
	28	Additional child tax credit from Schedule 8812	28	
	29	American opportunity credit from Form 8863, line 8	29	
	30	Reserved for future use	30	
	31	Amount from Schedule 3, line 15	31	
	32	Add lines 27, 28, 29, and 31. These are your **total other payments and refundable credits**		32
	33	Add lines 25d, 26, and 32. These are your **total payments**		33

As explained in Chapter 1, Federal tax law often serves purposes besides merely raising revenue for the government. Evidence of equity, social, and economic considerations is found throughout the tax law, including in the area of **tax credits**. Consider the following examples.

Example 1

Paul and Peggy, husband and wife, are both employed outside the home. Their combined salaries are $50,000. However, after paying for child care expenses of $2,000 on behalf of their daughter, Polly, the net economic benefit from both spouses working is $48,000. The child care expenses are, in a sense, business-related because they would not have been incurred if both spouses did not work outside the home. If no tax benefits are associated with the child care expenses, $50,000 is subject to tax.

Another couple, Alicia and Diego, also have a child, John. Diego stays home to care for John (the value of those services is $2,000) while Alicia earns a $48,000 salary. Because the value of Diego's services rendered is not subject to tax, only Alicia's earnings of $48,000 are subject to tax.

The *credit for child and dependent care expenses* helps to mitigate the costs incurred by working taxpayers who must pay for child care services to work outside the home.

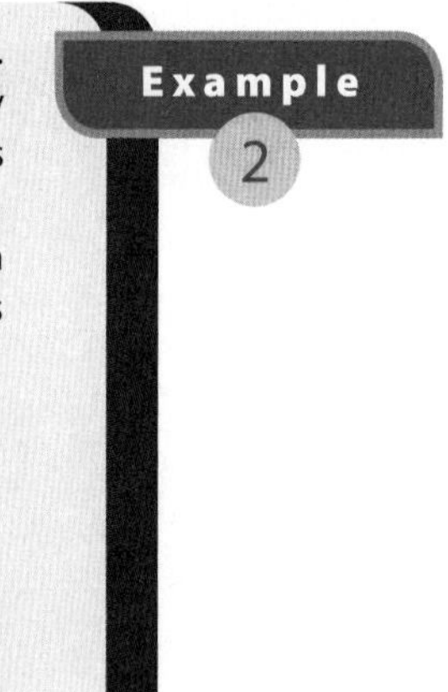

Consider two taxpayers, Graham and Addison, both of whom incur the same economic income in 2023.

Graham, age 66, is a retired taxpayer who receives $18,000 of Social Security benefits as his only source of income. His Social Security benefits are excluded from gross income. As a result, Graham's income tax is $0.

Addison, a single taxpayer 66 years of age, has, as her sole source of income, $18,000 from a pension plan funded by her former employer. Assuming that Addison has no itemized deductions or deductions *for* AGI, her income tax (before credits) is computed as follows:

Pension plan benefits	$18,000
Less: Basic standard deduction	(12,950)
Additional standard deduction	(1,750)
Taxable income	$ 3,300
Income tax (at 10%)	$ 330

The *tax credit for elderly or disabled taxpayers* was enacted to mitigate the perceived inequity of some taxpayers with equal incomes paying different amounts of Federal income tax.

Jane is a single parent who depends on the government's "safety net" for survival—she receives benefits under the Temporary Assistance to Needy Families (TANF) program in the amount of $15,000 per year. Jane wants to work and found a job that will pay $15,500 per year. She has also found an individual to care for her child at no cost. But with the $1,185.75 ($15,500 × 7.65% tax rate) withholding for Social Security and Medicare taxes, the economic benefit from working is less than remaining on TANF benefits ($14,314.25 versus $15,000).

The *earned income credit* helps offset the effect of Social Security and Medicare taxes on wages of the working poor and provides an incentive to work.

The tax credits available to individuals and other taxpayers are a major focus of this chapter. Tax credits are categorized as being either refundable or nonrefundable; this distinction may affect the taxpayer's ability to enjoy a tax benefit from a particular credit. The chapter continues with a discussion of the credits available to businesses and to individual taxpayers, and the ways in which credits enter into the calculation of the tax liability.

The Federal income tax system largely is based on the pay-as-you-go concept. That is, taxpayers or their employers are required to make deposits with the Federal government during the year related to the annual tax liability. These deposits are, in effect, refundable credits. The chapter concludes with a brief discussion of employer withholding procedures; special rules encountered by self-employed persons; penalties imposed on underpayments; and an overview of two tax provisions that are part of the Affordable Care Act—the premium tax credit and additional Medicare taxes on high-income individuals.

12-1 **Tax Policy Considerations**

LO.1

Explain how tax credits are used to achieve social, economic, or environmental objectives or to promote equity among taxpayers.

Congress generally uses tax credits to encourage taxpayers to change their behavior in order to achieve various social or economic objectives. Credits are also used to promote equity across taxpayers. For example, the disabled access credit was enacted to accomplish a social objective: to encourage taxpayers to renovate older buildings to be in compliance with the Americans with Disabilities Act. The research activities credit encourages high-tech and energy research in the United States. The use of tax credits as a policy tool continues to evolve as economic and political circumstances change.

A tax credit is much different from an income tax deduction. Income tax deductions reduce a taxpayer's tax base; tax credits reduce a taxpayer's tax liability. As a result, the tax benefit received from a tax deduction depends on the tax rate; a tax credit is not affected by the tax rate of the taxpayer.

Assume that Congress wants to encourage a certain type of activity. One way to accomplish this objective is to allow a tax credit of 25% for any expenses paid related to this activity. Another way is to allow an itemized deduction for the expenses. Abby's tax rate is 12%, Bill's tax rate is 35%, and they both itemize their deductions. Carmen does not incur enough qualifying expenses to itemize deductions. The following tax benefits are available to each taxpayer for a $1,000 payment:

	Abby	Bill	Carmen
Tax benefit if a 25% credit is allowed	$250	$250	$250
Tax benefit if an itemized deduction is allowed	120	350	–0–

As these results indicate, tax credits provide benefits on a more equitable basis than do tax deductions—all three taxpayers reduce their tax liabilities by the same amount. Equally apparent is that the deduction approach in this case benefits only taxpayers who itemize deductions, while the credit approach benefits all taxpayers who make the specified payments.

LO.2

Distinguish between refundable and nonrefundable credits, and understand the order in which they can be used by taxpayers.

12-2 Overview and Priority of Credits

12-2a Refundable versus Nonrefundable Credits

Exhibit 12.1 identifies some of the more common refundable and nonrefundable credits. **Refundable credits** are paid to the taxpayer even if the amount of the credit (or credits) exceeds the taxpayer's tax liability.

Exhibit 12.1 Partial Listing of Refundable and Nonrefundable Credits

Refundable Credits

Taxes withheld on wages
Child tax credit*
Earned income credit
Affordable Care Act premium tax credit (covered in the online ACA appendix)

Nonrefundable Credits

General business credit, which includes:
- Tax credit for rehabilitation expenditures
- Work opportunity tax credit
- Research activities credit
- Low-income housing credit
- Disabled access credit
- Credit for small employer pension plan startup costs
- Credit for employer-provided child care
- Credit for employer-provided family and medical leave

Credit for elderly and disabled
Foreign tax credit
Adoption expenses credit
Dependent tax credit
Credit for child and dependent care expenses**
Education tax credits***
Energy credits
Credit for certain retirement plan contributions
Small employer health insurance credit

*In 2021, the child tax credit was fully refundable. In 2022, the child tax credit is refundable to the extent of 15% of the taxpayer's earned income in excess of $2,500 (limited to a maximum of $1,500). Parents with three or more qualifying children compute the refundable portion using an alternative method.
**Refundable in 2021.
***Forty percent of the American Opportunity credit is refundable.

Ted, who is single, had taxable income of $22,000 in 2023. His income tax from the 2023 Tax Rate Schedule is $2,420. During 2023, Ted's employer withheld income tax of $3,200. Ted is entitled to a refund of $780, because the credit for tax withheld on wages is a refundable credit.

Nonrefundable credits are not paid if they exceed the taxpayer's tax liability.

Tina is single, age 67, and retired. Her taxable income for 2023 is $1,320, and the tax on this amount is $132. Tina's tax credit for the elderly is $225. This nonrefundable credit can be used to reduce her net tax liability to zero, but it will not result in a refund, even though the credit ($225) exceeds Tina's tax liability ($132).

Some nonrefundable credits, like the general business credit, can be "carried over" to other tax years if they exceed the credit allowed in a given year. Other nonrefundable credits, like the lifetime learning credit, simply are lost if they cannot be used in the tax year. Because some credits are refundable and others are not and because some credits are subject to carryover provisions and others are not, the order in which credits are offset against the tax liability can be important.

12-2b **General Business Credit**

The **general business credit** is composed of a number of other credits, each of which is computed separately under its own set of rules.[1] The general business credit combines these credits into one amount to limit the amount of business credits that can be used to offset a taxpayer's income tax liability.

For any tax year, the general business credit is limited to the taxpayer's *net income tax* reduced by the greater of:[2]

- The *tentative minimum tax*. See text Section 12-5d.
- 25 percent of *net regular tax liability* that exceeds $25,000.[3]

Net regular tax liability is the regular tax liability reduced by certain nonrefundable credits (e.g., credit for child and dependent care expenses and foreign tax credit).

Aleshia's general business credit for the current year is $70,000. Her net income tax is $150,000, tentative minimum tax is $130,000, and net regular tax liability is $150,000. She has no other tax credits. Aleshia's general business credit allowed for the tax year is computed as follows:

Net income tax	$ 150,000
Less: The greater of	
$130,000 (tentative minimum tax)	
$31,250 [25% × ($150,000 − $25,000)]	(130,000)
Amount of general business credit allowed for tax year	$ 20,000

Aleshia then has $50,000 ($70,000 − $20,000) of unused general business credits that may be carried back or forward as discussed below.

Unused general business credits are initially carried back one year and are applied to reduce the tax liability during that year. As a result, the taxpayer may receive a tax refund as a result of the carryback. Any remaining unused credits are then carried forward 20 years.[4]

[1] The separate credits are listed in § 38(b).

[2] § 38(c).

[3] This amount is $12,500 for married taxpayers filing separately unless one of the spouses is not entitled to the general business credit.

[4] § 39(a)(1).

A FIFO method is applied to the carrybacks, carryovers, and utilization of credits earned during a particular year. By using the oldest credits first, the FIFO method minimizes the potential for loss of a general business credit benefit due to the expiration of credit carryovers.

This example illustrates the use of general business credit carryovers.

General business credit carryovers		
2020	$ 4,000	
2021	6,000	
2022	2,000	
Total carryovers	$12,000	
2023 general business credit		$ 40,000
Total credit allowed in 2023 (based on tax liability)	$50,000	
Less: Utilization of carryovers		
2020	(4,000)	
2021	(6,000)	
2022	(2,000)	
Remaining credit allowed in 2023	$38,000	
Applied against		
2023 general business credit		(38,000)
2023 unused amount carried forward to 2024		$ 2,000

LO.3

Describe various business-related tax credits.

12-3 Specific Business-Related Tax Credits

Each component of the general business credit is determined separately under its own set of rules. Some of the more important credits that make up the general business credit are explained here in the order listed in Exhibit 12.1.

12-3a Tax Credit for Rehabilitation Expenditures

The **rehabilitation expenditures credit** is intended to discourage businesses from moving from older, economically distressed areas to newer locations while encouraging the preservation of historic structures. The credit is 20 percent of qualified rehabilitation expenditures related to a certified historic structure (either residential or nonresidential).[5] The 20 percent credit is taken ratably over a five-year period starting with the year the rehabilitated building is placed in service. When taking the credit, the basis of a rehabilitated building must be reduced by the full rehabilitation credit allowed.[6]

In the current year, Juan spent $100,000 to rehabilitate a certified historic structure (adjusted basis of $40,000). He is allowed a $20,000 (20% × $100,000) credit for rehabilitation expenditures. The credit will be spread equally over five years ($4,000 per year). Juan then increases the basis of the building by a net amount of $80,000 [an increase of $100,000 (rehabilitation expenditures) and a decrease of $20,000 (credit allowed)].

To qualify for the credit, *certified historic structures* must be substantially rehabilitated during a 24-month period. A *certified historic structure* is any building listed in the National Register of Historic Places or located in a registered historic district and certified as being of historic significance to the district. A building has been *substantially rehabilitated* if qualified rehabilitation expenditures exceed the greater of:

- The adjusted basis of the property before the rehabilitation expenditures, or
- $5,000.

[5] § 47.

[6] § 50(c).

Qualified rehabilitation expenditures do not include the cost of acquiring a building, the cost of facilities related to a building (such as a parking lot), and the cost of enlarging an existing building.

12-3b Work Opportunity Tax Credit

The **work opportunity tax credit** encourages employers to hire individuals from one or more of a number of targeted and economically disadvantaged groups.[7] Examples include long-term unemployed individuals (those unemployed for at least 27 weeks), qualified ex-felons, high-risk youths, participants in the Federal Supplemental Nutrition Assistance Program (SNAP), veterans, summer youth employees, and long-term family assistance recipients.

Computation of the Work Opportunity Tax Credit: General

The credit is generally equal to 40 percent of the first $6,000 of wages (per eligible employee) for the first 12 months of employment. In general, the credit is not available for any wages paid to an employee after the *first year* of employment. If the employee's first year overlaps two of the employer's tax years, however, the employer may take the credit over two tax years. If the credit is taken, the employer's tax deduction for wages is reduced by the amount of the credit.

For an employer to qualify for the 40 percent credit, the employee must (1) be certified by a designated local agency as being a member of one of the targeted groups and (2) have completed at least 400 hours of service to the employer. If an employee meets the first condition but not the second, the credit rate is reduced to 25 percent provided the employee has completed a minimum of 120 hours of service to the employer.

Work Opportunity Credit Calculation

Example 10

In January 2023, Green Company hires four individuals who are certified to be members of a qualifying targeted group. Each employee works 800 hours and is paid wages of $8,000 during the year. Green Company's work opportunity credit is $9,600 [($6,000 × 40%) × 4 employees].

If the tax credit is taken, Green must reduce its deduction for wages paid by $9,600. No credit is available for wages paid to these employees after their first year of employment.

Example 11

On June 1, 2023, Maria, a calendar year taxpayer, hires Joe, a certified member of a targeted group. During the last seven months of 2023, Joe is paid $3,500 for 500 hours of work. Maria is allowed a credit of $1,400 ($3,500 × 40%) for 2023. Joe continues to work for Maria in 2024 and is paid $7,000 through May 31, 2024.

Because up to $6,000 of first-year wages are eligible for the credit, Maria is allowed a 40% credit on $2,500 [$6,000 − $3,500 (wages paid in 2023)] of wages paid in 2024. The credit is $1,000 ($2,500 × 40%). None of Joe's wages paid after May 31, 2024, the end of the first year of Joe's employment, are eligible for the credit.

12-3c Research Activities Credit

To encourage business-related research and experimentation, also termed research and development (R&D), a credit is allowed for certain qualifying expenditures paid or incurred by a taxpayer. Credit eligible expenditures include wages, supplies, and 65 percent of contract research expenses incurred for qualified research. Qualified research must meet strict requirements including that it is undertaken to discover information that is technological in nature and substantially all of the R&D activities involve a process of experimentation.[8]

[7] § 51. The credit is available for qualifying employees who start work before 2026.

[8] § 41(d).

The research credit is *not* allowed for:[9]

- Research conducted once commercial production begins.
- Surveys and studies such as market research, testing, or routine data collection.
- Research conducted *outside* the United States, Puerto Rico, or U.S. possessions.
- Research in the social sciences, arts, or humanities.

The **research activities credit** is the *sum* of three components: an incremental research activities credit, a basic research credit, and an energy research credit.[10]

Incremental Research Activities Credit

The incremental research activities credit is equal to 20 percent of the *excess* of qualified research expenses for the taxable year over the base amount. Determining the base amount involves historical levels of research activity by the taxpayer. The purpose of using a historic base is to ensure that the credit rewards taxpayers who increase their research over the base level.

Research Activities Credit

Example 12

Javiera incurs the following research expenditures:

In-house wages, supplies	$50,000
Payment to Cutting Edge Scientific (a contractor)	30,000

Javiera's qualified research expenditures are $69,500 [$50,000 + ($30,000 × 65%)].

Example 13

Jack, a calendar year taxpayer, incurred qualified research expenditures of $200,000 in 2023. Assuming that the base amount of qualified expenditures was $100,000, the incremental research activities credit is $20,000 [($200,000 − $100,000) × 20%].

Alternatively, a taxpayer may elect to claim the alternative simplified credit which rewards increased research relative to recent years. The simplified credit equals 14 percent of the qualified research expenses for the year in excess of 50 percent of the average qualified research expenses for the prior three-year period.[11]

To prevent taxpayers from receiving multiple benefits from the same expenditures, taxpayers claiming the research credit may be required to reduce their R&D deduction (if the credit exceeds the deduction) or elect to claim a reduced research activities credit.[12]

Basic Research Credit

Corporations (other than S corporations or personal service corporations) are allowed an additional 20 percent credit for basic research payments made in *excess* of a base amount. *Basic research* is defined generally as any original investigation for the advancement of scientific knowledge not having a specific commercial objective. The basic research credit calculation is complex and is based on expenditures in excess of a specially defined base amount. The portion of the basic research expenditures not in excess of the base amount qualifies for the incremental research activities credit.

Orange Corporation pays $75,000 to a university for basic research. Orange's base amount for the basic research credit is $50,000. The basic research activities credit allowed is $5,000 [($75,000 − $50,000) × 20%].

[9] §§ 41(d), 41(e)(7)(A)(i), and 41(f)(6)(C). See also Reg. §§ 1.41–1 through 1.41–7.

[10] § 41. An eligible small business ($50 million or less in gross receipts) can use the credit to reduce its alternative minimum tax (AMT) liability. In addition, a qualified startup company (less than $5 million in gross receipts) can offset up to $500,000 of the credit against its payroll tax liability.

[11] §§ 41(c)(4) and (5).

[12] § 280C.

Energy Research Credit

This component of the research credit encourages taxpayers to support an exempt organization conducting energy research called an energy research consortium. The credit is equal to 20 percent of payments made to these organizations.

12-3d Low-Income Housing Credit

To encourage the development of affordable housing for low-income individuals, a credit is available to owners of qualified low-income housing projects.[13]

More than any other credit, the **low-income housing credit** is influenced by nontax factors. For example, these credits are distributed nationally to various state and local agencies. So the property must be approved by the appropriate agency authorized to provide low-income housing credits.

The annual credit is determined by multiplying the qualified basis of the project by a credit rate. The qualified basis is the the proportion of the basis in the entire project allocable to use by low-income tenants (those with incomes that do not exceed a specified percentage of the income of those in the local area). The credit rate is determined monthly by the Treasury and is intended to produce over a 10-year period credits with a present value up to 70 percent of the qualified basis.[14]

The credit is claimed over a 10-year period if the property continues to meet the required conditions. Generally, first-year credits are prorated based on the date the project is placed in service. A full year's credit is taken in each of the next nine years, and any remaining first-year credit is claimed in the eleventh year.

Example 15

Sarah spends $1,000,000 to build a qualified low-income housing project that is completed on January 1 of the current year. The entire project is rented to low-income families. Assume that the credit rate for property placed in service during January is 7.25%. Sarah may claim a credit of $72,500 ($1,000,000 × 7.25%) in the current year and in each of the following nine years.

If Sarah only made 75% of the project's units available to low-income families, her credit would be $54,375 [($1,000,000 × 75%) × 7.25%].

Recapture of a portion of the credit may be required if certain events occur (e.g., if the number of low-income tenant units falls below a minimum threshold or if the taxpayer sells the property).

12-3e Disabled Access Credit

The **disabled access credit** encourages eligible small businesses to make their facilities accessible to disabled individuals. The credit is 50 percent of the eligible expenditures that exceed $250 but do not exceed $10,250. As a result, the maximum credit is $5,000 ($10,000 × 50%).[15]

An *eligible small business* is a business that during the previous year either had gross receipts of $1 million or less or had no more than 30 full-time employees. An eligible business can include a sole proprietorship, a partnership, a regular corporation, or an S corporation.

Eligible expenditures include reasonable and necessary amounts that are paid or incurred to make older buildings accessible (only buildings first placed in service before November 6, 1990, qualify). Qualifying projects include installing ramps, widening doorways, and adding raised markings on elevator control buttons. Costs to assist hearing- or visually-impaired employees or customers who interact with the business also qualify. These costs can include both personnel (e.g., an interpreter) or equipment (e.g, audio or visual equipment or modifications to existing equipment).

The property's tax basis is reduced by the amount of the credit.

[13]§ 42.

[14]The qualified basis is the property's cost times the percentage of units made available to low-income tenants; the rate is subject to adjustment every month by the IRS.

[15]§ 44.

This year, Red, Inc., an eligible small business, makes $11,000 of capital improvements to a building that had been placed in service in June 1990. The improvements make Red's business more accessible to disabled individuals and are eligible expenditures for purposes of the disabled access credit.

The amount of the credit is $5,000 [($10,250 − $250) × 50%]. Although $11,000 of eligible expenditures are incurred, only $10,000 qualifies for the credit. The capital improvements have a depreciable basis of $6,000 [$11,000 (cost) − $5,000 (amount of the credit)].

12-3f **Energy Credits**

Businesses, including those conducted as sole proprietorships, may be eligible for a variety of **energy tax credits** that exist to incentivize and reduce costs of using alternative energy (such as solar), reducing carbon emissions, and producing clean fuels. See Exhibit 12.4 for a list of energy credits, categorized by the energy and environmental goals they are intended to encourage.

Most of these credits are temporary and only apply to activities engaged in, or facilities constructed, by the taxpayer during a specific time period. Many were added or modified by the Inflation Reduction Act of 2021 (P.L. 117–169). Common features for some of the energy credit changes made by this act, particularly for credits available to businesses, include:

- A domestic content or production requirement for producing or sourcing materials or activities in the United States.
- A prevailing wage requirement for the taxpayer and any subcontractors to pay wages at the rates for the locality where the facility or production is located, as determined by the Secretary of Labor.[16]
- An apprenticeship requirement for a certain percentage of the work to be performed by qualified apprentices.[17]

For some credits, such as § 30C, Alternative fuel vehicle refueling property credit, the base credit is relatively small but is increased five-fold if the business meets the prevailing wage and apprenticeship requirements. Finally, a few of the energy credits may be transferred or sold to other taxpayers to ensure that taxpayers (including certain tax-exempt entities) who engage in activities that qualify for the credit are able to use them regardless of their income or tax liability for the year.

12-3g **Credit for Small Employer Pension Plan Startup Costs**

Small businesses are entitled to a nonrefundable credit for administrative costs associated with establishing and maintaining certain qualified retirement plans (primarily, plans for non-highly compensated employees).[18] Although these costs (e.g., payroll system changes, retirement-related education programs, and consulting fees)[19] are deductible as ordinary and necessary business expenses, the credit lowers the after-tax cost of establishing a qualified retirement program and encourages eligible employers to offer retirement plans for their employees.

The **credit for small employer pension plan startup costs** is generally 50 percent of qualified startup costs.[20] An eligible employer is one with no more than 100 employees who have earned at least $5,000 of compensation. In general, the maximum credit is the *lesser* of (1) $5,000 or (2) $250 times the number of non-highly compensated employees. However, the minimum credit is $500. The deduction for the startup costs incurred is reduced by the amount of the credit.

[16]See Notice 2022–61 and Dept. of Labor information at **dol.gov/agencies/whd/IRA**.

[17]See Notice 2022–61 also published in the Federal Register for Nov. 30, 2022 (**govinfo.gov/content/pkg/FR-2022-11-30/pdf/2022-26108.pdf**).

[18]§ 45E. A highly compensated employee is one who owns 5% of the business in the current or prior year or in the prior year earned more than $150,000 (if 2023 is the prior year; $135,000 for 2022; see Notice 2022–55). In addition to this credit, a $500 credit is available to small employers who include an automatic enrollment provision in retirement plans they offer (§ 45T).

[19]§§ 45E(c)(1) and (d)(1).

[20]For plans started after 2022, the credit is increased to 100 percent of the qualified startup costs for employers with no more than 50 employees [§ 45E(e)(4)].

Maple Company decides to establish a qualified retirement plan for its non-highly compensated employees. In the process, it pays consulting fees of $21,200 to a firm that will provide educational seminars to Maple's eligible employees and will assist the payroll department in making necessary changes to the payroll system. Maple has 65 non-highly compensated employees who are eligible to participate in the plan.

Maple claims a credit for the pension plan startup costs of $5,000 [the *lesser* of $5,000 or $16,250 ($250 × 65 non-highly compensated employees)]. Its deduction for these expenses is reduced to $16,200 ($21,200 − $5,000).

For plans established after 2022, the credit is increased annually for up to $1,000 of contributions made by the employer on behalf of each employee with less than $100,000 of wages (indexed annually for inflation). The potential increase is reduced 2% for each employee over 50 so that it is totally phased out for employers with 100 or more employees. The credit is reduced by 25% per year for each year after the plan is first established.[21]

Assume Maple Company, from Example 10, contributes $1,200 to the new plan on behalf of each of its 65 employees, none of which earn wages in excess of $100,000. Maple may claim an additional credit of $45,500 {$1,000 × 65 employees × (1 − [0.02 × (65 − 50)])}.

If Maple continues to contribute at least $1,000 on behalf of each of its 65 employees and none earn more than $100,000 annually, it may take a credit of $34,125, $22,750, and $11,375 in the second, third, and fourth year of the plan.

12-3h Credit for Employer-Provided Child Care

An employer's expenses to provide for the care of employee children is a deductible business expense. Alternatively, employers may claim a credit for providing child care facilities to their employees during normal working hours.[22]

The **credit for employer-provided child care**, limited annually to $150,000, is composed of the aggregate of two components: 25 percent of qualified child care expenses and 10 percent of qualified child care resource and referral services. *Qualified child care expenses* include the costs of acquiring, constructing, rehabilitating, expanding, and operating a child care facility. *Child care resource and referral services* include amounts paid or incurred under a contract to provide child care resource and referral services to an employee.

Any qualifying expenses otherwise deductible by the taxpayer are reduced by the amount of the credit. In addition, the taxpayer's basis for any property acquired or constructed and used for qualifying purposes is reduced by the amount of the credit. If within 10 years of being placed in service a child care facility ceases to be used for a qualified use, the taxpayer must recapture a portion of the credit previously claimed.[23]

During the year, Tan Company constructed a child care facility for $400,000. The facility will be used by Tan employees who have preschool-aged children in need of child care services while their parents are at work. In addition, Tan incurred $100,000 of salaries for child care workers and other administrative costs associated with the facility.

As a result, Tan's credit for employer-provided child care is $125,000 [($400,000 + $100,000) × 25%]. Correspondingly, the basis of the facility is reduced to $300,000 ($400,000 − $100,000), and the deduction for salaries and administrative costs is reduced to $75,000 ($100,000 − $25,000).

12-3i Credit for Employer-Provided Family and Medical Leave

Employers can claim a general business credit equal to 12.5 percent of the wages paid to qualifying employees while they are on family and medical leave.[24] To claim the **credit for employer-provided family and medical leave**, employers must pay a minimum of 50 percent of the wages normally paid to an employee during the leave. If the wages paid during the leave *exceed* 50 percent of normal wages, the credit is increased by 0.25 percentage point for each percentage point above 50 percent. For example, if the employer pays 60 percent of the usual wages, then the credit is 15 percent [12.5 percent + (0.25 × 10)].

[21] § 45E(f).

[22] § 45F.

[23] § 45F(d). Such a rule, often referred to as a *clawback*, is an accountability measure to help ensure that tax incentives are used as intended.

[24] § 45S; "family and medical leave" is as defined by the Family and Medical Leave Act of 1993.

The credit is capped at 25 percent of wages paid (this would be allowed if the employer paid 100 percent of the employee's wages during the leave). The credit is limited to 12 weeks of leave per employee during any taxable year.

An employer must have a written policy in place that allows all qualifying full-time employees no less than two weeks of annual paid family and medical leave (non-full-time employees must be offered leave on a pro rata basis). Wages paid as vacation leave, personal leave, or other medical or sick leave are not considered to be family and medical leave. The credit applies to wages paid in taxable years beginning after 2017 and before 2026.

LO.4

Describe the foreign tax credit and various tax credits available to individual taxpayers.

12-4 Foreign Tax Credit and Individual Tax Credits

12-4a Foreign Tax Credit

The **foreign tax credit (FTC)** is designed to mitigate double taxation of income earned by U.S. taxpayers, and subject to tax, in a foreign jurisdiction. Individual taxpayers and corporations may claim the tax credit for foreign income tax paid on income earned and subject to income tax in another country or a U.S. possession.[25] Alternatively, a taxpayer can claim a deduction instead of a credit.[26] In most instances, the foreign tax credit (FTC) is advantageous because it provides a direct offset against the tax liability.

Although the FTC is based on the foreign taxes paid by the taxpayer, it is limited to the U.S. tax attributable the taxpayer's foreign income. This limitation may result in some form of double taxation on income where the applicable U.S. tax rates are lower than those of the countries in which the income is earned.

Computation

The FTC allowed is the lesser of the foreign taxes paid or incurred, or the overall limitation computed as follows.[27]

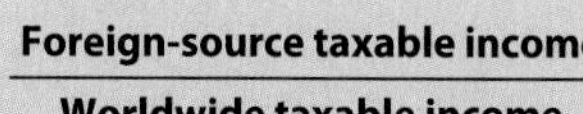

In 2023, Ian, a calendar year taxpayer, records $10,000 of income from Country Y, which imposes a 15% tax, and $20,000 from Country Z, which imposes a 50% tax. He reports taxable income of $60,000 from within the United States and is married filing a joint return. Ian's worldwide taxable income is $90,000 ($10,000 + $20,000 + $60,000). Assume that Ian's U.S. tax before the credit is $11,034. The overall limitation is computed as follows:

$$\frac{\text{Foreign-source taxable income}}{\text{Worldwide taxable income}} \times \frac{\$30,000}{\$90,000} \times \$11,034 = \$3,678$$

In this case, $3,678 is allowed as the FTC because this amount is less than the $11,500 of foreign taxes imposed [$1,500 (Country Y) + $10,000 (Country Z)].

As a result, the overall limitation may result in some of the foreign income being subjected to double taxation. Unused FTCs [e.g., the $7,822 ($11,500 − $3,678) from Example 20] can be carried back 1 year and forward 10 years.[28]

Only income taxes, war profits taxes, and excess profits taxes (or taxes paid in lieu of such taxes) qualify for the credit.[29] Value added taxes (VAT), severance taxes, property taxes, and sales taxes do not qualify for the FTC because they are not taxes on income.

[25]Code § 27 provides for the credit, but the qualifications and calculation procedure for the credit are contained in §§ 901–908.

[26]§ 164.

[27]§ 904. For individual taxpayers, worldwide taxable income is computed before personal and dependence exemptions are deducted. The exemption amount is zero through 2025.

[28]§ 904(c) and Reg. § 1.904–2(g), Example 1.

[29]Reg. § 1.901–1(a)(3)(i).

12-4b Earned Income Credit

The **earned income credit** provides income tax equity to the working poor. In addition, the credit helps to offset other Federal taxes, such as employment taxes and the gasoline tax, that impose a relatively larger burden on low-income taxpayers. Further, the credit encourages economically disadvantaged individuals to become contributing members of the workforce.

The earned income credit is determined by multiplying a maximum amount of earned income by the appropriate credit percentage (see Exhibit 12.2). Generally, earned income includes employee compensation and net earnings from self-employment; it excludes items such as interest, dividends, pension benefits, nontaxable employee compensation, and alimony.[30] If a taxpayer has children, the credit percentage used in the calculation depends on the number of qualifying children.

In 2023, the maximum earned income credit for a taxpayer with one qualifying child is $3,995 ($11,750 × 34%), $6,604 ($16,510 × 40%) for a taxpayer with two qualifying children, and $7,430 ($16,510 × 45%) for a taxpayer with three or more qualifying children. The maximum credit for a taxpayer with no qualifying child is $600. The maximum earned income credit is phased out completely if the taxpayer's earned income or AGI exceeds certain thresholds, as shown in Exhibit 12.2.[31]

To the extent that the greater of earned income or AGI exceeds $28,120 in 2023 for married taxpayers filing a joint return ($21,560 for other taxpayers), the difference, multiplied by the appropriate phaseout percentage, is subtracted from the maximum earned income credit.

Exhibit 12.2 Earned Income Credit and Phaseout Percentages

Tax Year	Number of Qualifying Children	Earned Income Base Amount	Credit Percentage	Maximum Credit	Phaseout Base	Phaseout Percentage	Phaseout Ends at Income of
2023	*Married, Filing Jointly*						
	No children	$ 7,840	15.30	$ 600	$16,370	15.30	$24,210
	One child	11,750	34.00	3,995	28,120	15.98	53,120
	Two children	16,510	40.00	6,604	28,120	21.06	59,478
	Three or more children	16,510	45.00	7,430	28,120	21.06	63,398
	Other Taxpayers						
	No children	$ 7,840	15.30	$ 600	$9,800	15.30	$17,640
	One child	11,750	34.00	3,995	21,560	15.98	46,560
	Two children	16,510	40.00	6,604	21,560	21.06	52,918
	Three or more children	16,510	45.00	7,430	21,560	21.06	56,838
2022	*Married, Filing Joint*						
	No children	$ 7,320	7.65	$ 560	$15,290	7.65	$22,610
	One child	10,980	34.00	3,733	26,260	15.98	49,622
	Two children	15,410	40.00	6,164	26,260	21.06	55,529
	Three or more children	15,410	45.00	6,935	26,260	21.06	59,187
	Other Taxpayers						
	No children	$ 7,320	7.65	$ 560	$ 9,160	7.65	$16,480
	One child	10,980	34.00	3,733	20,130	15.98	43,492
	Two children	15,410	40.00	6,164	20,130	21.06	49,399
	Three or more children	15,410	45.00	6,935	20,130	21.06	53,057

[30] § 32. The earned income credit is not available if the taxpayer's unearned income (e.g., interest and dividends) exceeds $11,000 in 2023 ($10,300 in 2022). See § 32(i).

[31] § 32(a)(2)(B). A married taxpayer filing a separate return (and living apart from his or her spouse for the last six months of the year) can claim the earned income credit provided the taxpayer lives with a qualifying child for more than half of the year.

Grace and her spouse file a joint return. In 2023, the couple, who have one qualifying child, earns a total of $30,000 of wages but has no other income. The couple's 2023 earned income credit is $3,691, their maximum earned income credit of $3,995 ($11,750 × 34%) reduced by $304 [($30,000 − $28,100) × 15.98%].

If, instead, the couple had three or more qualifying children, their earned income credit would be $7,034, their maximum earned income credit of $7,430 ($16,510 × 45%) reduced by $396 [($30,000 − $28,120) × 21.06%].

Earned Income Credit Table and Earned Income Tax Credit Assistant

It is not necessary to compute the credit as shown in Example 21. To simplify the compliance process, the IRS issues an Earned Income Credit Table for the determination of the appropriate amount of the credit. This table and a worksheet are included in IRS Publication 596 at **irs.gov**. In addition, the IRS has created an Earned Income Tax Credit Assistant to help taxpayers compute their credit (**apps.irs.gov/app/eitc/**).

Eligibility Requirements

Eligibility for the credit may depend not only on the taxpayer meeting the earned income and AGI thresholds but also on whether the taxpayer has a qualifying child. The term *qualifying child* generally has the same meaning here as it does for purposes of determining who qualifies as a dependent (see text Section 3-4a).

In addition to being available for taxpayers with qualifying children, the earned income credit also is available to certain *workers without children*. In general, the credit is available only to taxpayers ages 25 through 64 who cannot be claimed as a dependent on another taxpayer's return. As shown in Exhibit 12.2, the credit for 2023 is calculated on a maximum earned income of $7,840 times 7.65 percent and reduced by 7.65 percent of earned income over $9,860 ($16,370 for married taxpayers filing a joint return).

Walt, who is single, is 28 years of age, is a U.S. citizen, and is not claimed as a dependent on anyone else's return, earns $12,000 during 2023. Even though he does not have any qualifying children, he qualifies for the earned income credit. Walt's credit is $432, the maximum earned income credit of $600 ($7,840 × 7.65%) reduced by $168 [($12,000 − $9,800) × 7.65%].

12-4c Child and Dependent Tax Credits

A **child tax credit** and **dependent tax credit** are provided to individual taxpayers based on the *number* of their qualifying children and dependents. These credits are two of several "family-friendly" provisions in the Federal income tax law. To be eligible for the child tax credit, the child must be under age 17 at the end of the year, must be a U.S. citizen, and must be a dependent of the taxpayer. The dependent tax credit is available for each dependent of the taxpayer (other than a qualifying child).

The child tax credit is $2,000 per child, and the dependent tax credit is $500 per non-child dependent. The credits phase out as AGI exceeds $400,000 (married filing jointly) or $200,000 (other taxpayers). These credits are phased out by $50 for each $1,000 (or fraction thereof) of AGI above the $400,000 (or $200,000) amount.

In 2023, the child tax credit is partially refundable (up to $1,600 per child but no more than 15 percent of earned income in excess of $2,500). The dependent tax credit is not refundable. See text Section 3-4e for further discussion of these credits.

12-4d Credit for Child and Dependent Care Expenses

The **credit for child and dependent care expenses** mitigates the costs of child care services incurred by taxpayers to work outside the home.[32] The credit is a specified percentage of child and dependent care expenses. The credit percentage varies based on the taxpayer's AGI, and expenses are capped at a maximum of $6,000.

[32] § 21.

Eligibility

To be eligible for the credit, an individual must have either:

- A dependent under age 13, or
- A dependent or spouse who is physically or mentally incapacitated and who lives with the taxpayer for more than one-half of the year.

Generally, married taxpayers must file a joint return to obtain the credit.

Eligible Employment-Related Expenses

Eligible expenses include amounts paid for household services and care of a qualifying individual that are incurred to enable the taxpayer to be employed. The care can be provided in the home (e.g., by a nanny) or outside the home (e.g., at a day-care center).

Out-of-the-home expenses incurred for an older dependent or spouse who is physically or mentally incapacitated qualify for the credit if that person regularly spends at least eight hours each day in the taxpayer's household. This makes the credit available to taxpayers who keep handicapped older children and relatives who are 65 years and older in the home instead of institutionalizing them.

Child care payments to a relative are eligible for the credit unless the relative is a child (under age 19) of the taxpayer.

Wilma is an employed mother of an 8-year-old child. She pays her mother, Rita, $1,500 per year to care for the child after school. Wilma pays her daughter Eleanor, age 17, $900 for the child's care during the summer. Of these amounts, only the $1,500 paid to Rita qualifies as employment-related child care expenses.

Earned Income Ceiling

Qualifying employment-related expenses are limited to an individual's earned income. For married taxpayers, this limitation applies to the spouse with the *lesser* amount of earned income. Special rules are provided for taxpayers with nonworking spouses who are disabled or are full-time students. Here, the nonworking spouse is *deemed* to have earned income of $250 per month if there is one qualifying individual in the household or $500 per month if there are two or more qualifying individuals in the household. In the case of a student-spouse, only months when the student is enrolled on a full-time basis are counted.[33]

Calculation of the Credit

In general, the credit is equal to a percentage of *unreimbursed* employment-related expenses up to $3,000 for one qualifying individual and $6,000 for two or more individuals. The credit rate starts at 35 percent and decreases to 20 percent as AGI increases; see Exhibit 12.3.

During 2023, Nancy worked full-time while her spouse, Ron, was attending college for 10 months during the year. The couple has two children under age 13. Nancy earned $22,000 and incurred $6,200 of child care expenses. Ron is deemed to have earned $500 for each of the 10 months (or a total of $5,000).

Because Nancy and Ron report AGI of $22,000, they are allowed a credit rate of 31%. Nancy and Ron are limited to $5,000 in qualified child care expenses ($6,000 maximum expenses, limited to Ron's deemed earned income of $5,000). As a result, they are entitled to a child care credit of 1,550 (31% × $5,000; see Exhibit 12.3).

[33] § 21(d).

Exhibit 12.3 Child and Dependent Care Credit Rates

Adjusted Gross Income		
Over	**But Not Over**	**Applicable Rate of Credit**
$ 0	$15,000	35%
15,000	17,000	34%
17,000	19,000	33%
19,000	21,000	32%
21,000	23,000	31%
23,000	25,000	30%
25,000	27,000	29%
27,000	29,000	28%
29,000	31,000	27%
31,000	33,000	26%
33,000	35,000	25%
35,000	37,000	24%
37,000	39,000	23%
39,000	41,000	22%
41,000	43,000	21%
43,000	No limit	20%

Ethics & Equity Is This the Right Way to Use the Credit for Child and Dependent Care Expenses?

During 2024, your friends, Tim and Shia, hired a child care provider (Rebecca) to come into their home while they are at work to care for their two children. Rebecca charges $4,500 for her services for the year. Tim and Shia have discovered that up to $6,000 of qualifying expenses will generate a credit for child and dependent care expenses and that qualifying expenses can include payments for housecleaning services.

As a result, they ask Rebecca whether she would be interested in working several hours more per week, after Tim returns from work, for the sole purpose of cleaning the house. The couple offers to pay Rebecca $1,500 for the additional work. The net cost of the additional services would be only $1,200 [$1,500 − ($1,500 × 20%)] due to the availability of the credit for child and dependent care expenses.

You learn of Tim and Shia's opportunity but think it is unfair. If you hired someone to perform similar housecleaning services at the same price, your net cost would be $1,500, not $1,200, because you do not qualify for the credit. You are troubled by this inequity. Is this the way the income tax law should work? Explain.

Dependent Care Assistance Program

A taxpayer is allowed an exclusion from gross income for a limited amount of employer-reimbursed child or dependent care expenses; see text Section 5-8a. If this occurs, the applicable ceilings for allowable child and dependent care expenses are reduced dollar for dollar by the amount of the employer's reimbursement.[34]

Assume the same facts as in Example 24, except that of the $6,200 paid for child care, Nancy was reimbursed $2,500 by her employer under a qualified dependent care assistance program. Under the employer's plan, the reimbursement is excludable from Nancy's taxable wages. As a result, Nancy and Ron have AGI of $19,500 ($22,000 − $2,500).

In this case, the child care expense ceiling of $6,000 is reduced by the $2,500 reimbursement to $3,500. Their out-of-pocket child care expenses are $3,700 ($6,200 − $2,500), resulting in a credit of $1,120 ($3,500 × 32%).

[34] § 21(c).

12-4e **Education Tax Credits**

The **American Opportunity credit** and the **lifetime learning credit**[35] are available to help qualifying low- and middle-income individuals defray the cost of higher education. The credits are available for qualifying tuition and related expenses incurred by students pursuing undergraduate or graduate degrees or vocational training. Books and other course materials are eligible for the American Opportunity credit (but not the lifetime learning credit) if they are required for the student's coursework.[36] Room and board are ineligible for both credits.

Maximum Credit

The American Opportunity credit permits a maximum credit of $2,500 per year (100 percent of the first $2,000 of tuition expenses plus 25 percent of the next $2,000 of tuition expenses) for the *first four years* of postsecondary education. The lifetime learning credit permits a credit of 20 percent of qualifying expenses (up to $10,000 per year) incurred in a year in which the American Opportunity credit is not claimed. Generally, the lifetime learning credit is used for individuals who are beyond the first four years of postsecondary education.

Eligible Individuals

Both education credits are available for qualified expenses incurred by a taxpayer, taxpayer's spouse, or taxpayer's dependent. The American Opportunity credit is available per eligible student, while the lifetime learning credit is calculated per taxpayer. To be eligible for the American Opportunity credit, a student must take at least one-half the full-time course load for at least one academic term at a qualifying educational institution. No comparable requirement exists for the lifetime learning credit. So taxpayers who are seeking new job skills or maintaining existing skills through graduate training or continuing education are eligible for the lifetime learning credit. Taxpayers who are married must file a joint return to claim either education credit.

Income Limitations and Refundability

Both education credits are phased out beginning when the taxpayer's AGI (modified for this purpose) reaches $80,000 ($160,000 for married taxpayers filing jointly).[37] The credits are reduced proportionally over a $10,000 phaseout range ($20,000 for married taxpayers filing jointly). As a result, each credit is eliminated when modified AGI reaches $90,000 ($180,000 for married taxpayers filing jointly).

Forty percent of the American Opportunity credit is refundable, and it can offset a taxpayer's alternative minimum tax (AMT) liability. The lifetime learning credit is neither refundable nor an AMT liability offset.[38]

The Big Picture

Return to the facts of *The Big Picture* on p. 12-1. Recall that Tom and Jennifer Snyder are married; file a joint tax return; have modified AGI of $158,000; and have two children, Lora and Sam. The Snyders paid $7,500 of tuition and $8,500 for room and board for Lora (a freshman) and $8,100 of tuition plus $7,200 for room and board for Sam (a junior). Both Lora and Sam are full-time students and are Tom and Jennifer's dependents.

Lora's tuition and Sam's tuition are qualified expenses for the American Opportunity credit. For 2023, Tom and Jennifer may claim a $2,500 American Opportunity credit for both Lora's and Sam's expenses [(100% × $2,000) + (25% × $2,000)]; in total, they qualify for a $5,000 American Opportunity credit.

[35] § 25A.

[36] § 25A(i)(3).

[37] These amounts are not adjusted for inflation.

[38] If the credit is claimed for a taxpayer subject to § 1(g) (the "kiddie tax," discussed in text Section 3-6c), the credit is not refundable.

The Big Picture

Example 27

Return to the facts of *The Big Picture* on p. 12-1. Now assume that Tom and Jennifer's 2023 modified AGI is $172,000 instead of $158,000. In this case, Tom and Jennifer can claim a $2,000 American Opportunity credit for 2023 (rather than a $5,000 credit).

The credit is reduced because the taxpayers' modified AGI exceeds the $160,000 limit for married taxpayers. The reduction is the amount by which modified AGI exceeds the limit, expressed as a percentage of the phaseout range. In this case, the reduction is 60%, computed as [($172,000 − $160,000) ÷ $20,000]. Therefore, the maximum available credit for 2023 is $2,000 ($5,000 × 40% allowable portion).

The Big Picture

Example 28

Return to the facts of *The Big Picture* on p. 12-1. Now assume that Tom is going to school on a part-time basis to complete a graduate degree and pays qualifying tuition and fees of $4,000 during 2023.

Tom's qualifying tuition and fees are eligible for the lifetime learning credit. The potential lifetime learning credit of $800 ($4,000 × 20%) is reduced because the Snyders' modified AGI exceeds the $160,000 limit for married taxpayers. As modified AGI exceeds the $160,000 limit by $12,000 and the phaseout range is $20,000, the couple's lifetime learning credit is reduced by 60%.

As a result, the Sndyers' lifetime learning credit for 2023 is $320 ($800 × 40%), and their total education credits are $2,320 ($2,000 American Opportunity credit and $320 lifetime learning credit).

Restrictions on Double Tax Benefit

Taxpayers who claim an education credit may not deduct the expenses (see text Section 9-5), nor may they claim the credit for amounts that are otherwise excluded from gross income (e.g., scholarships and employer-paid educational assistance; see text Sections 5-4 and 5-8a).

12-4f **Residential Energy Credits**

Although most energy credits are aimed at businesses, including sole proprietorships (text Section 12-3f), others exist to incentivize individuals to make their homes more energy efficient. Still others are intended to encourage the purchase of clean energy vehicles (covered in text Section 12-4g). These credits have detailed definitions and qualifications and are reported on special tax forms attached to the individual's Form 1040.

Energy Efficient Home Improvement Credit

Individuals may claim a 30 percent credit each year on the sum of the following expenditures:

1. Qualified energy efficiency improvements installed during the year.
2. Residential energy property expenditures paid during the year.
3. Home energy audit expenditures paid during the year.

Qualified energy efficiency improvements are *building envelope* items that protect a structure from the elements including exterior windows, skylights, and doors as well as insulation material or systems. The maximum annual credit available for windows and skylights is $600 and for doors is $500. Residential energy property expenditures include energy efficient heating and cooling equipment such as air conditions, heaters, heat pumps, and water heaters. The maximum annual credit for most energy property expenditures is $600 and for energy audits is $150. The total maximum annual credit is $1,200. Notwithstanding the overall limit, the credit for certain qualified energy property, including certain heating and cooling systems, may be as high as $2,000.[39] To qualify for the credit, expenditures

[39] Generally, the annual credit limit is $1,200. However, if the taxpayer purchases certain heat pump, heat pump water heaters, biomass stoves or boilers, the annual credit can be a maximum of $3,200. See IRS FAQs on the residential energy credits; **irs.gov/credits-deductions/frequently-asked-questions-about-energy-efficient-home-improvements-and-residential-clean-energy-property-credits**.

in categories (1) and (3) must be made for the taxpayer's primary residence while those in category (2) may be made to any dwelling used by the taxpayer as a residence. The credit is not available for rental property owned by the individual taxpayer.

The credit is neither refundable nor available for carryover. If the allowable credit exceeds the taxpayer's tax liability for the year, the excess amount is lost. This credit expires after 2032.[40]

In 2023, Amy decides to explore how she might reduce the energy costs of her primary residence. In March 2023, she paid $600 to a certified home energy auditor for an examination of her home and utilities usage to learn which improvements would provide the most cost-effective energy efficiency improvements for her home. Later in the year, Amy paid $1,200 to have two windows replaced that met Energy Star certification. In 2024, also based on the results of the energy audit, Amy paid $4,600 to have a central air conditioner installed that met the highest efficiency tier per the Consortium for Energy Efficiency. Amy's tax liability each year exceeds $15,000.

Amy will generate an Energy Efficient Home Improvement Credit for 2023 of $510. This consists of a credit of $150 for the energy audit ($600 × 30% = $180; limited to $150) and $360 for the windows ($1,200 × 30%, which is below the $600 annual maximum for windows).

For 2024, Amy will generate a credit of $600 ($4,600 × 30% = $1,380; limited to $600).

Residential Clean Energy Credit

Individuals also may claim a 30 percent credit for certain alternative energy property, including solar panels and geothermal heat pumps, installed in or on their principal residence.

Unlike the Energy Efficient Home Improvement Credit, if the eligible Residential Clean Energy Credit exceeds the taxpayer's tax liability for the year, the excess amount is carried forward to the next year. This credit drops to 26 percent for 2033 and 22 percent for 2034 after which it is no longer available.[41]

James and Maria, a married couple, want to use as much solar energy as possible to power their primary residence. In 2023, they hire Solar Premiums to install several solar panels on their roof at a cost of $54,000. The couple can claim a residential clean energy credit for 2023 of $16,200 ($54,000 × 30%). If this amount is greater than their income tax liability for 2023, the excess credit will carry forward to be used in 2024 (or later years).

12-4g **Clean Vehicle Credits**

Clean Vehicle Credit

A taxpayer may claim a credit up to $7,500 for the purchase of a *clean vehicle.* This amount consists of a credit of $3,750 if the vehicle's battery has the specified percentage of the value of its critical minerals extracted or processed in the United States or a country with which the United States has a free trade agreement or were recycled in North America. The buyer can claim another $3,750 credit if the battery has the specified percentage of its components manufactured or assembled in North America.

A clean vehicle is a motor vehicle meeting several requirements including the following:

- First use is by the taxpayer (not used).
- Created by a *qualified manufacturer.*
- Gross vehicle weight rating is under 14,000 pounds.
- Is propelled to a significant extent by an electric motor drawing electricity from a battery with a capacity of at least 7 kilowatt hours and that can be recharged from an external source of electricity.
- Final assembly was in North America.

[40] § 25C.

[41] § 25D.

- The seller provides a report to the IRS and buyer with specific information including the vehicle identification number (VIN), battery capacity, that the buyer is the first user of the vehicle, and the credit amount the vehicle qualifies for.
- The manufacturer's suggested retail price (MSRP) does not exceed $80,000 for a van, SUV, or pickup truck; or $55,000 for other vehicles (such as a sedan).

In addition, for either the year of purchase or the preceding year, the buyer's modified adjusted gross income (MAGI) must not exceed the following amounts based on the buyer's filing status:

- Married filing jointly or surviving spouse $300,000
- Head of household $225,000
- Single $150,000

The definitional requirements for this credit, particularly for the critical minerals and battery component specification, are lengthy and detailed.

Starting after 2023, buyers will have the option of transferring their credit to a registered dealer. This will enable the buyer to obtain immediate benefit of their credit when they buy the vehicle rather than waiting until they file their tax return for the year of purchase. This credit expires after 2032.[42]

Anthony is interested in getting a new electric car. His income consists of wages of $110,000 and investment income of about $500. In June 2023, Anthony purchased a new sedan from a car dealer. This car met both the critical minerals and battery components requirements, as well as all other requirements, including having an MSRP of $55,000 or less, to entitle Anthony to claim a clean vehicle credit of $7,500 on his 2023 tax return.

Previously-Owned Clean Vehicle Credit

Individual taxpayers may qualify for a credit for purchasing a used clean vehicle. This credit is 30 percent of the sales price, not to exceed a credit of $4,000. Several qualifications exist for this credit including the following:

- The model year is at least two years earlier than the calendar year of purchase.
- The vehicle was made by a *qualified manufacturer*.
- The vehicle has a gross vehicle weight rating of under 14,000 pounds.
- The VIN must be reported on the tax return for the year of purchase.
- The sale is the first one after August 16, 2022, to a *qualified buyer*.
- The sales price does not exceed $25,000.

The vehicle need not be assembled in North America.

A qualified buyer must not have claimed this credit in the prior three years. Like the clean vehicle credit, the buyer must be at or below specified MAGI thresholds in either the year of purchase or preceding year, as follows based on filing status:

- Married filing jointly or surviving spouse $150,000
- Head of household $112,500
- Single $ 75,000

This credit expires after 2032.[43]

Mary's income consists solely of wages of $70,000. She would like to buy an electric car but cannot afford a new one. In 2023, she finds a dealer selling a 2020 used electric car for $21,000. With information from the dealer, the IRS website, and her tax adviser, Mary buys the car, confident that she will be able to claim the credit for previously-owned clean vehicles. Mary's credit for 2023 is $4,000 ($21,000 × 30% = $6,300 but limited to a maximum credit of $4,000).

[42] § 30D.

[43] § 25E.

12-4h Credit for Certain Retirement Plan Contributions

Taxpayers may claim a nonrefundable **credit for certain retirement plan contributions** based on eligible contributions of up to $2,000 to certain qualified retirement plans, like traditional and Roth IRAs and § 401(k) plans.[44] This credit, sometimes referred to as the "saver's credit," encourages lower- and middle-income taxpayers to contribute to qualified retirement plans. If a taxpayer (and/or spouse) contributes to and receives distributions from a qualifying plan, these amounts must be netted. Distributions in the tax year, in the two prior tax years, and during the period prior to the due date of the return are used in this netting process.

Exhibit 12.4 Partial List of Energy Credits

Source	Description	Availability
For producing clean energy (generally based on the amount of energy produced each year)		
§ 45[1]	For producing electricity from specific renewable resources	For electricity produced in facilities construction of which begins before 2025
§ 45Y[1, 3]	For producing electricity with zero greenhouse gas emissions regardless of technology /power source	Through 2032 for electricity produced in facilities placed in service after 2024
For the production, sale, and use of clean fuels (generally based on the amount of fuel produced each year)		
§ 40A	For the production, sale, or use of biodiesel fuel	Through 2024
§ 40B	For the sale or use of sustainable aviation fuel	Through 2024
§ 45V[1, 2]	For the production of clean hydrogen	For production from facilities construction of which begins before 2034. Available for 10 years after facility is placed in service.
§ 45Z[1]	For the production and sale of low-emissions transportation fuel	Through 2027
For investment in clean energy manufacturing (generally based on a percentage of the cost of property placed in service)		
§ 48	For investment in property that uses specific renewable sources to generate power	For projects constructed before 2025
§ 48E[1, 2, 3]	For investment in energy facilities producing zero greenhouse gas emissions regardless of the technology/power source used.	Through 2032 for projects placed in serve after 2024
§ 48C[1, 2]	For re-equipping or expanding certain facilities, including equipment designed to reduce emissions by at least 20%	Through 2032 for projects placed in serve after 2024
§ 45X[1]	For producing and selling clean energy technology components that use alternative sources to produce energy	Through 2032
For enhancing the energy efficiency of homes		
§ 25C	For energy efficient improvements made by homeowners	Through 2032
§ 25D	For increased use of renewable energy by homeowners	For property placed in service before 2035
§ 45L[2]	For the construction and sale of new energy-efficient homes	Through 2032
For purchasing and facilitating the use of clean vehicles		
§ 30D	For the purchase of new plug-in or fuel cell electric vehicle	Through 2032
§ 25E	For the purchase by individuals of used electric vehicle	Through 2032
§ 45W	For the purchase of commercial use clean vehicles	Through 2032
§ 30C[1, 2]	For building alternative fuel vehicle refueling property including EV recharging stations	For property placed in service before 2033

[1]Transferable per § 6418.
[2]Credit five times greater if prevailing wage and apprenticeship requirements are met.
[3]Taxpayers must choose between the technology-neutral production (§ 45Y) and investment (§ 48E) credits.

[44]§ 25B.

The credit rate applied to the eligible contributions depends on the taxpayer's AGI[45] and filing status as shown in Exhibit 12.5. However, the maximum credit allowed to an individual is $1,000 ($2,000 × 50%). Once AGI exceeds the upper end of the applicable range, no credit is available. To qualify for the credit, the taxpayer must be at least 18 years of age and cannot be a dependent of another taxpayer or a full-time student.

Esau and Mandy, married taxpayers, each contribute $2,500 to § 401(k) plans offered through their employers. AGI reported on their joint return is $45,000. The eligible retirement plan contributions for purposes of the credit are limited to $2,000 for Esau and $2,000 for Mandy.

As a result, Esau and Mandy may claim a $400 retirement plan contributions credit [($2,000 × 2) × 10%]. They would not qualify for the credit if their AGI had exceeded $68,000.

Exhibit 12.5 "Saver's" Credit Rate and AGI Thresholds (2023)

Joint Return		Head of Household		All Others		
Over	**Not Over**	**Over**	**Not Over**	**Over**	**Not Over**	**Applicable Percentage**
$ 0	$43,500	$ 0	$32,625	$ 0	$21,750	50%
43,500	47,500	32,625	35,625	21,750	23,750	20%
47,500	73,000	35,625	54,750	23,750	36,500	10%
73,000		54,750		36,500		0%

Concept Summary 12.1 provides an overview of the tax credits discussed in this chapter.

Concept Summary 12.1

Tax Credits

Credit	Computation	Comments
Tax withheld on wages (§ 31)	Amount is reported to employee on Form W-2.	Refundable credit.
Earned income (§ 32)	Amount is determined by reference to Earned Income Credit Table published by IRS. Computations of underlying amounts in Earned Income Credit Table are illustrated in Example 21.	Refundable credit. A form of negative income tax to assist low-income taxpayers. Earned income and AGI must be less than certain threshold amounts. Generally, one or more qualifying children must reside with the taxpayer.
Child and dependent care (§ 21)	Rate ranges from 50% to 0% depending on AGI in 2021 (35% to 20% in prior and subsequent years). In 2021, maximum base for credit is $8,000 for one qualifying individual, $16,000 for two or more ($3,000 and $6,000 in prior and subsequent years).	Nonrefundable personal credit (fully refundable in 2021). No carryback or carryforward. Benefits taxpayers who incur employment-related child or dependent care expenses in order to work or seek employment. Eligible taxpayers must have a dependent under age 13 or a dependent (any age) or spouse who is physically or mentally incapacitated.

continued

[45]The AGI thresholds are indexed annually for inflation; Notice 2022-55. For purposes of this credit, the AGI thresholds are modified to include certain excluded income items. See § 25B(e).

Tax Credits—(Continued)

Credit	Computation	Comments
Elderly or disabled (§ 22)	15% of sum of base amount minus reductions for (1) Social Security and other nontaxable benefits and (2) AGI in excess of base amount ($5,000 single, $7,500 head of household, $10,000 married filing jointly).	Nonrefundable personal credit. No carryback or carryforward. Provides relief for taxpayers not receiving substantial tax-free retirement benefits.
Adoption expenses (§ 23)	Up to $14,890 of costs incurred to adopt an eligible child qualify for the credit. Taxpayer claims the credit in the year qualified expenses were paid or incurred if they were paid or incurred during or after year in which adoption was finalized. For expenses paid or incurred in a year prior to when adoption was finalized, credit must be claimed in tax year following the tax year during which the expenses are paid or incurred.	Nonrefundable credit. The credit is phased out ratably over a $40,000 range once AGI exceeds $223,410. Unused credit may be carried forward five years. Purpose is to assist taxpayers who incur nonrecurring costs associated with the adoption process.
Child and Dependent (§ 24)	Credit is based on *number* of qualifying children under age 17 (under age 18 in 2021) and dependents. In general, credit is $2,000 per child and $500 per dependent (additional child tax credits were available in 2022 and 2021). Credits are phased out for higher-income taxpayers.	Child tax credit is partially refundable (up to $1,500), but limited to 15% of earned income in excess of $2,500 (the child tax credit was fully refundable in 2021). Dependent tax credit is not refundable. Purpose is to assist families with children or dependents.
Education (§ 25A)	American Opportunity credit is available for qualifying education expenses of students in first four years of postsecondary education. Maximum credit is $2,500 per year per eligible student. Credit is phased out for higher-income taxpayers.	Credit is partially refundable. Credit is designed to help defray costs of first four years of higher education for low- to middle-income families.
	Lifetime learning credit permits a credit of 20% of qualifying expenses (up to $10,000 per year) provided American Opportunity credit is not claimed with respect to those expenses. Credit is calculated per taxpayer, not per student, and is phased out for higher-income taxpayers.	Nonrefundable credit. Credit is designed to help defray costs of higher education beyond first four years and of costs incurred in maintaining or improving existing job skills for low- to middle-income taxpayers.
Credit for certain retirement plan contributions (§ 25B)	Calculation is based on amount of contribution multiplied by a percentage that depends on the taxpayer's filing status and AGI.	Nonrefundable credit. Purpose is to encourage contributions to qualified retirement plans by low- and middle-income taxpayers.
Premium tax credit (PTC) (§ 36B)	Available to individuals who purchase their health insurance from an exchange and are not offered affordable coverage from their employer.	This refundable credit may be obtained in advance of filing with the credit amount given to the health insurance provider to lower the insured's monthly premium payments. The individual must reconcile the credit on their tax return using Form 8962. See the online appendix on Affordable Care Act Provisions for additional information.
Foreign tax credit (for businesses and individuals) (§ 27)	Lesser of (1) the tax paid to the foreign country or (2) the ratable share of U.S. income tax liability related to foreign-source income.	Nonrefundable credit. Taxpayer instead can deduct the taxes paid. Unused credit may be carried back 1 year and then forward 10 years. Purpose is to mitigate the double taxation that may arise when income is taxed in more than one country.

continued

Tax Credits—(Continued)

Credit	Computation	Comments
Energy tax credits (§ 25C, § 25D, § 25E, § 30D for individuals; numerous provisions for businesses)	Energy credits tend to have numerous qualifications and percentage rates.	Nonrefundable credits. Energy tax credits vary as to whether unused amounts can be carried forward, income limitations, and expiration dates. Typically complex requirements exist for eligibility.
General business (§ 38)	May not exceed net income tax minus the greater of tentative minimum tax or 25% of net regular tax liability that exceeds $25,000.	Nonrefundable credit. Components include tax credit for rehabilitation expenditures, work opportunity tax credit, research activities credit, low-income housing credit, disabled access credit, credit for small employer pension plan startup costs, credit for employer-provided child care, and credit for employer-provided medical and family leave. Unused credit may be carried back 1 year and forward 20 years. FIFO method applies to carrybacks, carryovers, and credits earned during current year.
Rehabilitation expenditures (§ 47)	Qualifying expenditures times 20% rate for certified historic structures.	Nonrefundable credit. Part of general business credit and therefore subject to same carryback, carryover, and FIFO rules. Purpose is to discourage businesses from moving from economically distressed areas to newer locations.
Research activities (§ 41)	Incremental credit is 20% of excess of computation year expenditures over the base amount. Basic research credit is allowed to certain corporations for 20% of cash payments to qualified organizations that exceed a specially calculated base amount. Energy research credit also available.	Nonrefundable credit. Part of general business credit and therefore subject to same carryback, carryover, and FIFO rules. Purpose is to encourage high-tech and energy research in the United States.
Low-income housing (§ 42)	Appropriate rate times eligible basis (portion of project attributable to low-income units). Credit is available each year for 10 years. Recapture may apply.	Nonrefundable credit. Part of general business credit and therefore subject to same carryback, carryover, and FIFO rules. Purpose is to encourage construction of housing for low-income individuals.
Disabled access (§ 44)	Credit is 50% of eligible access expenditures that exceed $250 but do not exceed $10,250. Maximum credit is $5,000. Available only to eligible small businesses.	Nonrefundable credit. Part of general business credit and therefore subject to same carryback, carryover, and FIFO rules. Purpose is to encourage small businesses to become more accessible to disabled individuals.
Credit for small employer pension plan startup costs (§ 45E)	Credit equals 50% of qualified startup costs incurred by eligible employers. Maximum annual credit is $500. Deduction for related expenses is reduced by the amount of the credit.	Nonrefundable credit. Part of general business credit and therefore subject to same carryback, carryover, and FIFO rules. Purpose is to encourage small employers to establish qualified retirement plans for their employees.
Credit for employer-provided child care (§ 45F)	Credit is equal to 25% of qualified child care expenses plus 10% of qualified expenses for child care resource and referral services. Maximum credit is $150,000. Deduction for related expenses or basis must be reduced by the amount of the credit.	Nonrefundable credit. Part of general business credit and therefore subject to same carryback, carryover, and FIFO rules. Purpose is to encourage employers to provide child care for their employees' children during normal working hours.

continued

Tax Credits—(Continued)

Credit	Computation	Comments
Credit for employer-provided family and medical leave (§ 45S)	Credit is equal to 12.5% of wages paid to qualifying employees while they are on family and medical leave (limited to 12 weeks per employee per year). Employers must pay a minimum of 50% of the wages normally paid; if wages paid during the leave *exceed* 50% of normal wages, the credit is increased by 0.25% for each percentage point above 50% to a maximum credit of 25%.	Nonrefundable credit. Part of general business credit and therefore subject to same carryback, carryover, and FIFO rules. Purpose is to encourage employers to provide leave to their employees for family and medical purposes (e.g,, birth of a child; care for a sick child, spouse, or parent).
Work opportunity (§ 51)	Credit is limited to 40% of the first $6,000 of wages paid to each eligible employee.	Nonrefundable credit. Part of the general business credit and therefore subject to the same carryback, carryover, and FIFO rules. Purpose is to encourage employment of individuals in specified groups.

12-5 Payment Procedures

The tax law contains elaborate "pay-as-you-go" rules that require the prepayment of various Federal taxes. In addition, these rules carry penalties for any lack of compliance.[46] Prepayment procedures fall into two major categories: those applicable to employers and those applicable to self-employed persons. For employers, both payroll taxes (FICA and FUTA) and income taxes may be involved. With self-employed taxpayers, the focus is on the income tax and the self-employment tax.

12-5a Employers

LO.5

Describe the tax withholding and payment procedures applicable to employers.

Employment taxes include FICA (Federal Insurance Contributions Act; commonly known as Social Security) and FUTA (Federal Unemployment Tax Act). The employer usually is responsible for withholding the employee's share of FICA and appropriate amounts for income taxes. In addition, the employer must match the FICA portion withheld and fully absorb the cost of FUTA. Employers are required to pay these amounts to the IRS on a regular basis (usually weekly or monthly).

The key to employer compliance in this area involves the following:

- Identifying which employees and wages are covered by employment taxes and are subject to withholding for income taxes.
- Determining the amount to be paid and/or withheld.
- Reporting and paying employment taxes and income taxes withheld to the IRS on a timely basis through the use of proper forms and procedures.

IRS Publication 15, *Employer's Tax Guide* (Circular E), is a key resource for employers.

[46]See, for example, § 3403 (employer liable for any taxes withheld and not paid over to the IRS), § 6656 (penalty on amounts withheld and not paid over), and § 6654 (penalty for failure by an individual to pay estimated income taxes).

Amount of FICA Taxes

The FICA tax has two components: Social Security tax (old age, survivors, and disability insurance) *and* Medicare tax (hospital insurance). The tax rates and wage base under FICA have increased substantially over the years. The base amount is adjusted each year for inflation. Exhibit 12.6 shows the base amounts for both the Social Security and Medicare taxes and the related employee tax rates. The employer must match the employee's portion, so the total Social Security tax rate is 12.4 percent and the total Medicare tax rate is 2.9 percent.

Employee withholdings continue until the maximum base amount is reached. In 2023, for example, FICA withholding for the Social Security portion (6.2 percent) ends once the employee has earned $160,200 of wages. However, the employer will continue to withhold Medicare taxes on wages above $160,200 since there is no limit on this portion of the FICA tax.

In 2023, Keshia earned a salary of $165,000 from her employer. As a result, FICA taxes withheld from her salary are $9,932.40 ($160,200 × 6.2%) plus $2,392.50 ($165,000 × 1.45%) for a total of $12,324.90. In addition to paying the amount withheld from Keshia's salary to the Federal government, her employer also must pay $12,324.90.

In at least two situations, changing jobs during the year or having multiple jobs at the same time, it is possible for an employee to have paid excess FICA taxes during a tax year.

Excess FICA Taxes Withheld

Example 35

During 2023, Kevin changed employers in the middle of the year and earned $85,000 (all of which was subject to FICA) from each job. As a result, each employer withheld $5,737.50 [(6.2% × $85,000) + (1.45% × $85,000)] for a total of $13,005.

Although each employer acted properly, Kevin's total FICA tax liability for the year is only $12,397 [(6.2% × $160,200) + (1.45% × $170,000)]. As a result, Kevin has overpaid his share of FICA taxes by $608 [$13,005 (amount paid) − $12,397 (amount of correct liability)]. Kevin can claim this amount as a tax credit when filing his 2023 income tax return.

During 2023, Lori earned $136,000 from her regular job and $35,000 from a part-time job (all of which was subject to FICA). As a result, one employer withheld $10,404 [(6.2% × $136,000) + (1.45% × $136,000)] while the other employer withheld $2,678 [(6.2% × $35,000) + (1.45% × $35,000)], for a total withheld for Lori of $13,082.

Lori's total FICA tax liability for the year is only $12,412 [(6.2% × $160,200) + (1.45% × $171,000)]. As a result, Lori has overpaid her share of FICA taxes by $670 [$13,082 (amount paid) − $12,412 (amount of correct liability)]. Lori can claim this amount as a tax credit when filing her 2023 income tax return.

Exhibit 12.6 FICA Rates and Base

	Social Security Tax				Medicare Tax				
	Percent	×	**Base Amount**	+	**Percent**	×	**Base Amount**	=	**Maximum Tax**
2021	6.20%	×	142,800	+	1.45%**	×	Unlimited	=	Unlimited
2022	6.20%	×	147,000	+	1.45%**	×	Unlimited	=	Unlimited
2023	6.20%	×	160,200	+	1.45%**	×	Unlimited	=	Unlimited
2024	6.20%	×	*	+	1.45%**	×	Unlimited	=	Unlimited

*Not yet determined.
**Does not include the additional Medicare taxes on high-income individuals (see text Section 12-6b).

The FICA tax must be paid for an individual employed by their spouse. No tax is collected for children under the age of 18 who are employed in the parent's trade or business.

Amount of Income Tax Withholding

To ensure that sufficient Federal income taxes are withheld from their wages, employees complete Form W–4, Employee's Withholding Certificate. As part of this process, employees are encouraged to use an IRS-developed application to determine the appropriate amount of withholding (**apps.irs.gov/app/tax-withholding-estimator**). In addition, the employee can provide information about any available child and dependent tax credits. Once completed, the Form W–4 is provided to (and used by) the employer to support the amount of Federal income taxes withheld.[47] The form is retained by the employer as part of its payroll records.

Reporting and Payment Procedures

Employers devote a significant amount of time and expense in complying with the various employment tax and income tax withholding rules. Among the Federal forms that must be filed are the following:

Tax Form	Title
W–2	Wage and Tax Statement
940 or 940 EZ	Employer's Annual Federal Unemployment (FUTA) Tax Return
941	Employer's Quarterly Federal Tax Return

Form W–2 furnishes essential information to employees concerning wages paid, FICA, and income tax withholdings. This form (reporting information for the previous calendar year) must be furnished to an employee not later than January 31. Employees then report the relevant amounts on the appropriate lines of their Form 1040. These amounts also typically are used on the state and/or local tax return.

Form 940 (or Form 940 EZ) is the employer's annual accounting of its FUTA liability. Generally, it is due one month after the end of the calendar year (i.e., no later than January 31, 2024, for the 2023 calendar year) and must include any remaining FUTA due.

Employers make deposits of employment taxes, usually weekly or monthly,[48] and they pay any outstanding amounts at the end of every quarter, using Form 941.

Backup Withholding

Some payments made to individuals by banks or businesses are subject to backup withholding to ensure that income tax is collected on interest income and other payments reported on a Form 1099. Backup withholding is required if the taxpayer does not give their Social Security number to the business or bank when required.[49] If backup withholding applies, the payor withholds 24 percent of the gross amount.

12-5b **Self-Employed Taxpayers**

LO.6

Explain the payment procedures applicable to self-employed persons.

Although the following discussion largely centers on self-employed taxpayers, employed taxpayers may be required to pay estimated tax if they have income other than wages that is not subject to withholding (e.g., investment income, or a second trade or business in a self-employment capacity).

[47]The withholding provisions are contained in §§ 3401 and 3402. IRS Publication 15, *Employer's Tax Guide* (Circular E), contains detailed information about the income tax withholding process.

[48]Deposit requirements are specified in IRS Publication 15, *Employer's Tax Guide* (Circular E).

[49]§ 3406(a). The backup withholding rate is the fourth lowest tax rate for single filers.

Estimated Tax for Individuals

Estimated tax is the amount of tax (including AMT and self-employment tax) an individual expects to owe for the year after subtracting tax credits and income tax withheld. Any individual who has estimated tax of $1,000 or more *and* whose withholding does not equal or exceed the required annual payment (discussed below) must make quarterly payments.[50] If these payments are not made, a penalty may be assessed. No quarterly payments are required (and no penalty will apply) if the taxpayer's estimated tax is under $1,000. In addition, no penalty will apply if the taxpayer had a zero tax liability for the prior tax year, provided the prior tax year was 12 months (i.e., not a short year) *and* the taxpayer was a citizen or resident for that entire year.

The required annual payment must be computed first. This is the *smaller* of the following amounts.

- Ninety percent of the tax shown on the current year's return.
- One hundred percent of the tax shown on the preceding year's return (the return must cover the full 12 months of the preceding year). If the AGI on the preceding year's return exceeds $150,000 ($75,000 if married filing separately), the 100 percent requirement is increased to 110 percent.

In general, one-fourth of this required annual payment is due on April 15, June 15, and September 15 of the tax year and January 15 of the following year.

An equal part of withholding is deemed paid on each due date. So if $10,000 has been withheld during the year, $2,500 is applied to each quarter. If the quarterly estimates are determined to be $3,000, then $500 ($3,000 − $2,500) must be paid each quarter. Payments are submitted with the payment voucher for the appropriate quarter from Form 1040–ES.

Penalty on Underpayments

A nondeductible penalty is imposed on any estimated tax underpayment. The penalty rate is adjusted quarterly to reflect changes in the average prime rate.

An *underpayment* occurs when any installment (the sum of estimated tax paid and income tax withheld) is less than 25 percent of the required annual payment. The penalty is applied to the amount of the underpayment for the period of the underpayment.[51]

Example 37

Marta made the following payments of estimated Federal income tax for 2023. Marta had no Federal income tax withheld.

April 18, 2023	$1,400
June 15, 2023	2,300
September 15, 2023	1,500
January 16, 2024	1,800

Marta's actual tax for 2023 is $8,000, and her tax in 2022 was $10,000. As a result, each installment should have been at least $1,800 [($8,000 × 90%) × 25%]. Of the payment on June 15, $400 will be credited to the unpaid balance of the first quarterly installment due on April 18, effectively stopping the underpayment penalty for the first quarter.[52] Of the remaining $1,900 payment on June 15, $100 is credited to the September 15 payment, resulting in this third quarterly payment being $200 short.

Then $200 of the January 16 payment is credited to the September 15 shortfall, ending the underpayment period for that amount. The January 16, 2024 installment is now underpaid by $200, and a penalty will apply from January 16, 2024, to April 15, 2024 (unless some tax is paid sooner). Marta's estimated tax underpayments for the various periods are as follows:

1st installment	$400 from April 18 to June 15, 2023
2nd installment	Paid in full
3rd installment	$200 from September 15, 2023, to January 16, 2024
4th installment	$200 from January 16, 2024, to April 15, 2024

[50] §§ 6654(c)(1) and 6654(e)(1).

[51] § 6654(b)(2).

[52] Payments are credited to unpaid installments in the order in which the installments are required to be paid. § 6654(b)(3).

If a possible underpayment of estimated tax is indicated, Form 2210 is filed to compute the penalty due or to justify that no penalty applies.

Self-Employment Tax

The tax on self-employment income is levied to provide Social Security and Medicare benefits (old age, survivors, and disability insurance and hospital insurance) for self-employed individuals. Individuals with net earnings of $400 or more from self-employment are subject to the **self-employment tax**.[53] For 2023, the self-employment tax is 15.3 percent of self-employment income up to $160,200 and 2.9 percent of self-employment income in excess of $160,200 (see Exhibit 12.7).

Net earnings from self-employment includes gross income from a trade or business less allowable trade or business deductions, the distributive share of any partnership income or loss derived from a trade or business activity, and net income from rendering personal services as an independent contractor. This amount includes profits from sales of inventory.

Self-employed taxpayers are allowed a deduction from net earnings from self-employment, at one-half of the self-employment rate, for purposes of determining self-employment tax[54] *and* an income tax deduction (normally, one-half of the self-employment tax liability).[55]

Determining the amount of self-employment tax to be paid for 2023 involves completing the steps in Exhibit 12.8. The result of step 3 or 4 is the amount of self-employment tax to be paid. For *income tax purposes*, the amount to be reported is net earnings from self-employment before the deduction for the self-employment tax. Then the taxpayer is allowed a deduction *for* AGI of the appropriate amount of the self-employment tax.

Exhibit 12.7 Self-Employment Tax: Social Security and Medicare Portions

Year		Tax Rate	Ceiling Amount
2023	Social Security portion	12.4%	$160,200
	Medicare portion	2.9%	Unlimited
	Aggregate rate	15.3%	
2022	Social Security portion	12.4%	$147,000
	Medicare portion	2.9%	Unlimited
	Aggregate rate	15.3%	

Exhibit 12.8 2023 Self-Employment Tax Worksheet

1. Net earnings from self-employment. ________
2. Multiply line 1 by 92.35%. ________
3. If the amount on line 2 is $160,200 or less, multiply the line 2 amount by 15.3%. This is the self-employment tax. ________
4. If the amount on line 2 is more than $160,200, multiply line 2 by 2.9% and add $19,865. This is the self-employment tax. ________

Note: $19,865 is the maximum Social Security contribution in 2023 ($160,200 × 12.4%).

[53] § 6017.

[54] § 1402(a)(12).

[55] § 164(f).

Example 38

In 2023, Nathan and Terry report net earnings from self-employment of $55,000 and $185,000, respectively. Using the format in Exhibit 12.8, determine their self-employment tax.

Nathan's Self-Employment Tax Worksheet	
1. Net earnings from self-employment.	$55,000.00
2. Multiply line 1 by 92.35%.	$50,792.50
3. If the amount on line 2 is $160,200 or less, multiply the line 2 amount by 15.3%. This is the self-employment tax.	$ 7,771.25
4. If the amount on line 2 is more than $160,200 multiply line 2 by 2.9% and add $19,865. This is the self-employment tax.	

Terry's Self-Employment Tax Worksheet	
1. Net earnings from self-employment.	$185,000.00
2. Multiply line 1 by 92.35%.	$170,847.50
3. If the amount on line 2 is $160,200 or less, multiply the line 2 amount by 15.3%. This is the self-employment tax.	
4. If the amount on line 2 is more than $160,200, multiply line 2 by 2.9% and add $19,865. This is the self-employment tax.	$ 24,819.58

For income tax purposes, Nathan has net earnings from self-employment of $55,000 and a deduction *for* AGI of $3,885.63 ($7,771.25 × 50%). Terry has net earnings from self-employment of $185,000 and a deduction *for* AGI of $12,409.79 (24,819.58 × 50%).

If an individual also receives wages subject to the FICA tax, the ceiling amount of the Social Security portion on which the self-employment tax is computed is reduced. However, a combination of FICA wages and self-employment earnings will not reduce the Medicare component of the self-employment tax, because there is no ceiling on this component of the tax.

Example 39

In 2023, Kelly reported $86,000 of net earnings from a data imaging services business she owns. During the year, she also received wages of $81,700 as an employee of an accounting firm. The amount of Kelly's self-employment income subject to the Social Security portion (12.4%) is $78,500 ($160,200 − $81,700), producing a tax of $9,734 ($78,500 × 12.4%); her Social Security ceiling amount ($78,500) is less than her net self-employment income ($79,421).

	Social Security Portion
Ceiling amount	$160,200
Less: FICA wages	(81,700)
Net ceiling	$ 78,500
Net self-employment income ($86,000 × 92.35%)	$ 79,421
Lesser of net ceiling or net self-employment income	$ 78,500

Although there is a limit on Social Security taxes ($160,200 maximum base in 2023), no such limit exists for the Medicare portion of the self-employment tax. As a result, all of Kelly's net self-employment income ($86,000 × 0.9235 = $79,421) is subject to the 2.9% Medicare portion of the self-employment tax. The self-employment tax on this portion is $2,303 ($79,421 × 2.9%). In total, Kelly's self-employment tax liability is $12,037 [$9,734 (Social Security) + $2,303 (Medicare)].

If Kelly's wages were only $50,000, then the net ceiling in the table above would be $110,200. Because her net self-employment income ($79,421) is less than this amount, she computes her self-employment tax using the format in Exhibit 12.8.

Exhibit 12.9 **2022 Self-Employment Tax Worksheet**

1. Net earnings from self-employment. ________
2. Multiply line 1 by 92.35%. ________
3. If the amount on line 2 is $147,000 or less, multiply the line 2 amount by 15.3%. This is the self-employment tax. ________
4. If the amount on line 2 is more than $147,000, multiply line 2 by 2.9% and add $18,228. This is the self-employment tax. ________

Note: $18,228 is the maximum Social Security contribution in 2022 ($147,000 × 12.4%).

For 2022, the self-employment tax computations use the 2022 Social Security ceiling amount (see Exhibit 12.9).

12-5c Additional Medicare Taxes on High-Income Individuals

LO.7

Explain the additional Medicare taxes assessed on high-income individuals.

High-income taxpayers are required to pay two types of additional Medicare taxes: (1) an additional 0.9 percent tax on *wages* received in excess of specified amounts and (2) an additional 3.8 percent tax on *unearned income.*

Additional Tax on Wages

An additional 0.9 percent Medicare tax is imposed on wages received in excess of $250,000 for married taxpayers filing a joint return ($125,000 if married filing separately) and $200,000 for all other taxpayers.[56] Unlike the general 1.45 percent Medicare tax on wages, the additional tax on a joint return is based on the *combined* wages of the employee and the employee's spouse. As a result, the Medicare tax rate is:

1. 1.45 percent on the first $200,000 of wages ($125,000 on a married filing separate return; $250,000 of combined wages on a married filing joint return), and
2. 2.35 percent (1.45% + 0.9%) on wages in excess of $200,000 ($125,000 on a married filing separate return; $250,000 of combined wages on a married filing joint return).

Additional Medicare Tax on Wages

Jenna, who is single, earns wages of $500,000 in 2023. Jenna will pay $2,900 of Medicare taxes on the first $200,000 of her wages ($200,000 × 1.45%) and $7,050 of Medicare taxes on her wages in excess of $200,000 ($300,000 × 2.35%). In total, her Medicare tax is $9,950, of which $2,700 ($300,000 × 0.9%) represents Jenna's additional Medicare tax.

Patrick and Paula file a joint return in 2023. During the year, Patrick earns wages of $125,000, and Paula earns wages of $175,000—so their total wages are $300,000. Patrick and Paula will pay total Medicare taxes of $4,800 ($250,000 × 1.45% plus $50,000 × 2.35%), of which $450 ($50,000 × 0.9%) represents Patrick and Paula's additional Medicare tax.

Employers must withhold the additional 0.9 percent Medicare tax on wages paid in excess of $200,000.[57] An employer is not responsible for determining wages earned by an employee's spouse (and the implications of those wages on the total Medicare tax to be paid).

[56] § 3101(b)(2). The base amounts are not indexed for inflation.

[57] § 3102(f).

Example 42

Return to the facts of Example 41. In 2022, neither Patrick's nor Paula's employer will withhold the additional Medicare tax since both wage amounts are less than $200,000. Therefore, Paula will have $2,537.50 of Medicare tax withheld ($175,000 × 1.45%), and Patrick will have $1,812.50 of Medicare tax withheld ($125,000 × 1.45%). Total Medicare tax withheld is $4,350.00 ($2,537.50 + $1,812.50). Patrick and Paula pay an additional $450.00 of Medicare taxes when they file their return.[58]

The additional Medicare tax also applies to self-employed individuals—with net earnings from self-employment being used for the threshold computations. As a result, the tax rate for the Medicare tax on self-employment income will be:

1. 2.9 percent on the first $200,000 of net earnings from self-employment ($125,000 on a married filing separate return; $250,000 on a married filing joint return); and
2. 3.8 percent (2.9% + 0.9%) on net earnings from self-employment in excess of $200,000 ($125,000 on a married filing separate return; $250,000 on a married filing joint return).

For married taxpayers, one of whom has wages and one of whom has self-employment income, the thresholds are reduced (but not below zero) by the amount of wages taken into account in determining the additional 0.9 percent Medicare tax on wages.[59] Although self-employed individuals are allowed an income tax deduction for part of the self-employment tax, this additional 0.9 percent Medicare tax will *not* create a deduction (i.e., the deduction is determined without regard to this additional tax).[60]

Additional Tax on Unearned Income (Net Investment Income Tax)

An additional 3.8 percent Medicare tax is imposed on the unearned income of individuals, estates, and trusts.[61] The net investment income tax (NIIT) is 3.8 percent of the lesser of:[62]

1. Net investment income, or
2. The excess of modified adjusted gross income over $250,000 for married taxpayers filing a joint return ($125,000 if married filing separately) and $200,000 for all other taxpayers.[63]

In general, "net investment income" includes interest, dividends, annuities, royalties, rents, income from passive activities, and net gains from the sale of investment property less deductions allowed in generating that income.[64] Modified adjusted gross income (MAGI) is adjusted gross income (AGI) increased by any foreign earned income exclusion.[65] For individuals who don't incur any excluded foreign earned income, MAGI is the same as AGI.

Additional Medicare Tax on Unearned Income

Example 43

In 2023, Xinran earns net investment income of $50,000 and MAGI of $180,000 and files as a single taxpayer. Since Xinran's MAGI does not exceed $200,000, she need not pay the additional Medicare tax on unearned income.

[58]Couples in this situation might need to make estimated tax payments to account for the additional Medicare taxes.

[59]§ 1401(b)(2)(B).

[60]§ 164(f).

[61]§ 1411.

[62]§ 1411(a)(1).

[63]§ 1411(b). The base amounts are not indexed for inflation.

[64]§ 1411(c). Certain types of income, including qualified retirement plan distributions, tax-exempt income, and untaxed gain from the sale of a principal residence, are excluded from this definition.

[65]§ 1411(d).

Additional Medicare Tax on Unearned Income

Assume the same facts as in Example 43, except that Xinran reports net investment income of $85,000 and MAGI of $220,000.

In this case, she pays a Medicare tax on the lesser of (1) $85,000 (her net investment income) or (2) $20,000 (the amount by which her MAGI exceeds the $200,000 threshold). As a result, Xinran's additional Medicare tax on unearned income is $760 ($20,000 × 3.8%).

Assume the same facts as Example 44, except that Xinran's MAGI is $290,000.

Because her MAGI exceeds the threshold amount by $90,000, she pays a Medicare tax on the entire $85,000 of net investment income. As a result, Xinran's additional Medicare tax on unearned income is $3,230 ($85,000 × 3.8%).

The 3.8 percent additional Medicare tax on unearned income is *in addition to* the additional 0.9 percent Medicare tax on wages or self-employment income. Taxpayers who have both high wages (or self-employment income) *and* high investment income may be subject to both taxes.

Assume the same facts as Example 45, except that Xinran reports MAGI of $325,000 (including $240,000 of wages and $85,000 of net investment income).

In this case, Xinran must pay an additional Medicare tax on wages of $360 ($40,000 × 0.9%, her wages in excess of $200,000). In total, Xinran pays $3,590 in additional Medicare taxes ($3,230 on unearned income and $360 on wages).

12-5d Alternative Minimum Tax

LO.8

Explain the purpose and basic computation of the alternative minimum tax (AMT).

The tax law always has included incentives intended to influence the economic and social behavior of taxpayers. As a result, some taxpayers take advantage of these incentives to significantly minimize or entirely avoid any Federal income tax liability in a particular year. In such circumstances, although taxpayers are legally minimizing their tax liabilities, concerns arise about the inequity that results when taxpayers with substantial economic incomes avoid paying income tax because they can utilize a variety of special tax deductions, exclusions, and credits. The **alternative minimum tax (AMT)** was enacted to address this inequity and help ensure that all taxpayers with more than modest economic incomes pay some minimum amount of tax.[66]

In 2017, approximately 5 million individual taxpayers incurred an AMT liability, resulting in $37.7 billion in revenue for the U.S. Treasury. However, changes made by the Tax Cuts and Jobs Act (TCJA) of 2017, particularly the $10,000 SALT cap (text Section 10-2a), significantly reduced the number of taxpayers subject to the AMT. For instance, IRS data show that only 156,549 individual taxpayers incurred an AMT liability for the 2020 tax year.[67] Currently, the AMT applies to individuals, corporations, trusts, and estates.

The AMT works as an alternative tax calculation, such that all noncorporate taxpayers are required to compute both the regular tax and the AMT, and then to *pay whichever liability is higher*. As most taxpayers now complete their income tax filings by using tax software and/or a tax professional, this typically does not present a compliance burden for the individual. However, additional record keeping and tax planning considerations are required.

The AMT Tax Base

The AMT tax base is designed to allow fewer tax deductions and exclusions, and to make some items available in a manner that is less favorable than applies for the regular tax. Similarly, income items are identified in the AMT base that are included earlier than is the case for regular tax purposes, and a few additional income items are subject to

[66] The tax law governing AMT is provided at § 55 to § 59. A portion of the AMT might generate a minimum tax credit usable in future years (§ 53); the MTC is not covered in this textbook.

[67] **irs.gov/pub/irs-pdf/p1304.pdf#page=6.**

tax only under the AMT rules. The result is a form of income tax with lower rates and a broader tax base. In addition, most tax credits are not allowed to reduce AMT.

Here are some examples of items that are treated differently under the AMT rules, in deriving the tax base that is used to compute the AMT. These are examples of modifications to taxable income to derive alternative minimum taxable income (AMTI).

- Most cost recovery computations allow deductions that are taken over a longer time period. When a depreciable asset is sold, then, the AMT gain typically is smaller than the corresponding regular tax gain, as the AMT basis for the asset is larger.
- For an individual who itemizes deductions on Form 1040, the limited deduction for taxes paid is not allowed for AMT purposes.
- For AMT purposes, only the percentage of completion method of accounting can be used for long-term contracts, and not the completed contract method.
- The AMT includes in the tax base the "spread" related to an incentive stock option (i.e., the excess of the stock's fair market value over the exercise price on the date of the option's exercise). This affects the AMT gain that is recognized when the shares obtained with the option are later sold.
- Percentage depletion deductions can be taken under the AMT only until the basis of the productive property reaches zero.
- Municipal bond interest is included in the AMT tax base if the bond proceeds were used to benefit the "private activity" of a commercial business (e.g., in building a factory).

Individuals who are especially vulnerable to the AMT are those who claim large amounts of accelerated cost recovery deductions. One also might be subject to the AMT in a year when a large volume of profitable incentive stock options is exercised, or when large investments in private activity municipal bonds are made.

Computing and Paying the AMT

After AMTI is computed, an annual exemption is allowed. As the AMT tax base increases, the exemption phases out, potentially to zero, at a rate of 25 cents for each dollar of AMT tax base in the phaseout range.

		Exemption Phaseout	
Taxpayer's Filing Status	**Exemption Amount (2023)**	**Begins at**	**Ends (Exemption is $0) at**
Married, joint	$126,500	$1,156,300	$1,662,300
Single or head of household	81,300	578,150	903,350
Married, separate	63,250	578,150	831,150

Harry, who is single, records AMTI of $680,000 for the year. His $81,300 exemption amount is reduced by $25,463 [($680,000 – $578,150) × 25% phaseout rate]. Harry's AMT exemption is $55,837 ($81,300 exemption – $25,463 reduction).

AMTI less the exemption equals the AMT base. This base amount is multiplied by the tax rate(s) and reduced by any credits that are allowed, resulting in the tentative minimum tax (TMT).

A two-bracket tax schedule is used for AMT (26 percent and 28 percent). In 2023, a 26 percent rate applies to the first $220,700 ($110,350 for married filing separately) of the AMT base and a 28 percent rate applies to any remaining AMT base.[68] Any net capital gain or qualified dividend income included in the AMT base is taxed at the favorable tax rates for such amounts rather than at the AMT rates.

The relationship between the regular tax liability and the TMT is key to the AMT calculation. If the regular tax liability exceeds the TMT, the taxpayer's AMT liability is zero. However, if the TMT exceeds the regular tax liability, the excess is the taxpayer's

[68]The exemption and phaseout threshold amounts are indexed annually for inflation. § 55(d)(4).

AMT liability. Technically, the AMT is a surtax; both tax law and the Form 6251 categorize any excess of TMT over the taxpayer's regular tax liability as the AMT amount. For practical purposes, the taxpayer pays whichever tax liability is greater—that calculated using the regular tax rules or that calculated using the AMT rules.

Example 48

Anna, an unmarried individual, reports regular taxable income of $650,000. She exercised an incentive stock option (ISO) in 2023. Her regular tax liability for 2023 is $200,832. Her AMT in 2023 is calculated as follows.

Taxable income	$650,000
"Spread" on ISO exercised this year	135,000
Equals: AMTI	$785,000
Minus: AMT exemption [$81,300 – 25%($785,000 – $578,150)]	29,587
Equals: AMT base	$755,413
TMT [($220,700 × 26%) + ($755,413 – $220,700) × 28%]	$207,102
Minus: Regular tax liability	200,832
Equals: AMT	$ 6,270

Anna will pay total Federal income tax of $207,102, consisting of her regular tax liability of $200,832 plus AMT of $6,270.

AMT liabilities must be included in the taxpayer's estimated tax payments. Form 6251 is used by individuals to report the tax.

The Corporate AMT

In an effort to ensure that corporations with significant economic income also pay some minimum amount of Federal income tax, a new corporate alternative minimum tax (AMT) was enacted as part of the Inflation Reduction Act of 2022.

Similar to the individual AMT, a corporation has an AMT liability only if its tentative minimum tax exceeds its regular tax liability. However, unlike the calculation of the individual AMT, which begins with taxable income, the calculation of the corporate AMT begins with a corporation's financial statement income. Thus, the corporate AMT could be described as a "book minimum tax."

The corporate AMT applies to any corporation with more than $1 billion in average annual adjusted financial statement income (AFSI) for the three-year period ending with the current tax year. Tentative minimum tax is equal to 15 percent of the AFSI for the year, less any AMT foreign tax credit for year. Due to the $1 billion AFSI threshold, the corporate AMT will impact only a small number of corporate taxpayers.[69]

12-6 **Tax Planning**

LO.9

Identify tax planning opportunities related to tax credits and payment procedures.

12-6a **Credit for Child and Dependent Care Expenses**

A taxpayer may incur employment-related expenses that also qualify as medical expenses (e.g., a nurse is hired to provide in-home care for an incapacitated dependent parent, allowing the adult child to go to work). These expenses may be either deducted as medical expenses (generally subject to the 7.5%-of-AGI limitation) or used in determining the child and dependent care credit. If the child and dependent care credit is chosen and the employment-related expenses exceed the limitation ($3,000, $6,000, or earned income), the excess will qualify as a medical expense. If, however, the taxpayer chooses to deduct qualified employment-related expenses as medical expenses, any portion that is not deductible because of the percentage limitation may not be used in computing the credit for child and dependent care expenses.

[69] §§ 55(a)(2) and (b)(2), 56A, and 59(k). For discussion of the corporate minimum tax, see Chapter 3, *South-Western Federal Taxation: Corporations, Partnerships, Estates & Trusts*.

Alicia reports the following information for 2023:

Adjusted gross income		$60,000
Potential itemized deductions *from* AGI—		
Other than medical expenses	$ 4,500	
Medical expenses	12,900	$17,400

All of Alicia's medical expenses were incurred to provide nursing care for her disabled father while she was working. Alicia's father lives with her and qualifies as her dependent.

What should Alicia do in this situation? One approach would be to use $3,000 of the nursing care expenses to obtain the maximum child and dependent care credit allowed of $600 (20% × $3,000). The remaining expenses should be claimed as medical expenses. After a reduction of 7.5 percent of AGI, this would produce a medical expense deduction of $5,400 [$9,900 (remaining medical expenses) − (7.5% × $60,000)].

Another approach would be to claim the full $12,900 as a medical expense in lieu of any child and dependent care credit. After applying the 7.5%-of-AGI floor of $4,500 (7.5% × $60,000), a deduction of $8,400 remains.

The choice, then, is between a credit of $600 plus a deduction of $5,400 or a credit of $0 plus a deduction of $8,400. The relative tax savings involved then depend on Alicia's marginal tax rate and whether she itemizes her deductions.

One of the traditional goals of *family tax planning* is to minimize the present value of the total tax burden of the family unit. With proper planning and implementation, the child and dependent care credit can be used to help achieve this goal. For example, payments to certain relatives for the care of qualifying dependents and children qualify for the credit if the care provider is *not* a child (under age 19) of the taxpayer. So if the care provider is in a lower tax bracket than the taxpayer, the following benefits result:

- Income is shifted to a lower-bracket family member.
- The taxpayer qualifies for the credit for child and dependent care expenses.

In addition, the goal of minimizing the family income tax liability can be enhanced in some other situations, but only if the credit's limitations are recognized and avoided. For example, tax savings may be enjoyed even if the qualifying expenses incurred by a cash basis taxpayer have reached the annual ceiling ($3,000 or $6,000). To the extent that any additional payments can be shifted into future tax years, the benefit from the credit may be preserved on these excess expenses.

Andre, a calendar year and cash basis taxpayer, has spent $3,000 by December 1 on qualifying child care expenses for his dependent 11-year-old son. The $250 that is due the care provider for child care services rendered in December does not generate a tax credit benefit if the amount is paid in the current year because the $3,000 ceiling has been reached. However, if the payment can be delayed until the next year, the total credit over the two-year period for which Andre is eligible may be increased.

A similar shifting of expenses to the next year may be wise if this nonrefundable credit was limited by the tax liability.

12-6b **Adjustments to Increase Withholding**

The penalty for underpayment of estimated tax by individuals is computed for each quarter of the tax year. A taxpayer can play *catch-up* to a certain extent. Each quarterly payment is credited to the unpaid portion of any previous required installment. As a result, the penalty stops on that portion of the underpayment for the previous quarter. However, because income tax withheld is assumed to have been paid evenly throughout the year and is allocated equally among the four installments in computing any penalty, a taxpayer who otherwise would be subject to a penalty for underpayment should increase withholdings late in the year. This can be done by modifying the Form W–4 or by making a special arrangement with the employer to increase the amount withheld.

12-6c **Adjustments to Avoid Overwithholding**

If a taxpayer has unusually large itemized deductions, deductions *for* AGI, net losses from Schedules C, D, E, and F, or tax credits, the IRS Withholding Calculator (**apps.irs.gov/app/tax-withholding-estimator**) should be used to determine the correct amount of withholding. Net operating loss carryovers also may be considered in the computation. Based on this calculation, the taxpayer can file a revised Form W–4 with the employer.

Refocus on The Big Picture

Education Tax Credits

YELLOW DOG PRODUCTIONS/GETTY IMAGES

The American Opportunity tax credit provides some relief for Tom and Jennifer Snyder.

Lora and Sam qualify for the American Opportunity credit in 2023 because they are both in their first four years of postsecondary education. Lora and Sam both qualify for a $2,500 credit (100 percent of the first $2,000 and 25 percent of the next $2,000 of qualified expenses).

These credits phase out over a range of $20,000 once married taxpayers' AGI exceeds $160,000. Since the Snyders' AGI ($158,000) is less than this amount, the total education credits available to them amount to $5,000, and they may claim this amount as a credit on their 2023 income tax return (see Example 26). In addition, this credit may be used to offset any AMT liability, and 40 percent ($2,000) is refundable to the Snyders.

What If?

What if the Snyders' AGI is $188,000? In 2023, the Snyders would not qualify for any education credits (their income exceeds the limits for both the American Opportunity and the lifetime learning credits).

Key Terms

Alternative minimum tax (AMT), 12-33
American Opportunity credit, 12-17
Child tax credit, 12-14
Credit for certain retirement plan contributions, 12-21
Credit for child and dependent care expenses, 12-14
Credit for employer-provided child care, 12-11
Credit for employer-provided family and medical leave, 12-11
Credit for small employer pension plan startup costs, 12-10
Dependent tax credit, 12-14
Disabled access credit, 12-9
Earned income credit, 12-13
Employment taxes, 12-25
Energy tax credits, 12-10
Estimated tax, 12-28
Foreign tax credit (FTC), 12-12
General business credit, 12-5
Lifetime learning credit, 12-17
Low-income housing credit, 12-9
Nonrefundable credits, 12-5
Refundable credits, 12-4
Rehabilitation expenditures credit, 12-6
Research activities credit, 12-8
Self-employment tax, 12-29
Tax credits, 12-2
Work opportunity tax credit, 12-7

Discussion Questions

1. **LO.1** Would an individual taxpayer receive greater benefit from deducting an expense or from taking a credit equal to 25% of the expense? How would your response change if the item would only be deductible *from* AGI?

Critical Thinking

2. **LO.2** Clint, a self-employed engineering consultant, is contemplating purchasing an old building for renovation. After the work is completed, Clint plans to rent out two-thirds of the floor space to businesses and to live and work in the remaining portion. Identify the relevant tax issues for Clint.

Critical Thinking

3. **LO.3** Sonja is considering the purchase and renovation of an old building. She has heard about the tax credit for rehabilitation expenditures but does not know the specific rules applicable to the credit. Explain the most important and relevant provisions for her.

4. **LO.3** Explain the purpose of the disabled access credit, and identify several examples of the type of structural changes to a building that qualify for the credit.

5. **LO.4** Is the earned income credit a form of negative income tax? Why or why not?

Critical Thinking

6. **LO.4** Tim recently was called into the partner's office and offered a two-year assignment in his public accounting firm's Shanghai office. Realizing that Tim will face incremental expenses while in Shanghai, such as foreign income taxes and rent, the firm will try to make him "whole" from a financial perspective by increasing his salary to help offset the expenses he will incur while living overseas. If Tim takes the assignment, he likely will rent his U.S. personal residence and sell several major tangible assets such as his personal automobile. Identify the relevant Federal income tax issues.

Critical Thinking

7. **LO.4** Mark and Lisa are approaching an exciting time in their lives as their oldest son, Austin, graduates from high school and moves on to college. What are some of the tax issues Mark and Lisa should consider as they think about paying for Austin's college education?

Critical Thinking

8. **LO.4** Maria, a single individual with wage income of $170,000 and no other income, is considering purchasing a new electric car. What are some of the features she should look for to be able to claim the clean vehicle credit?

9. **LO.5** Kathy, a sole proprietor, owns and operates a grocery store. Kathy's spouse and her 16-year-old daughter work in the business and are paid wages. Will her spouse and daughter be subject to FICA? Explain.

10. **LO.6** Describe the exposure (i.e., wage base and tax rate) of a self-employed individual to the self-employment tax for 2023.

11. **LO.7** Describe the two additional Medicare taxes that are assessed on high-income taxpayers.

Computational Exercises

12. **LO.2** Carlson's general business credit for the current year is $84,000. His net income tax is $190,000, tentative minimum tax is $175,000, and net regular tax liability is $185,000. He has no other Federal income tax credits. Determine Carlson's general business credit allowed for the year and any amounts that can be carried back and forward.

13. **LO.3** Emily spent $135,000 to rehabilitate a certified historic building (adjusted basis of $90,000) that originally had been placed in service in 1936. What is Emily's rehabilitation expenditures tax credit?

14. **LO.3** During 2023, Lincoln Company hires seven individuals who are certified to be members of a qualifying targeted group. Each employee works in excess of 600 hours and is paid wages of $7,500 during the year. Determine the amount of Lincoln's work opportunity credit.

15. **LO.3** Alison incurs the following research expenditures:

In-house wages	$60,000
In-house supplies	5,000
Payment to ABC, Inc., for research	80,000

a. Determine the amount of qualified research expenditures.

b. Assuming that the base amount is $60,000, determine Alison's incremental research activities credit.

16. **LO.4** Samuel and Annamaria are married, file a joint return, and have three qualifying children. In 2023, they earn wages of $34,000 and have no other income. Determine the amount of their earned income credit for 2023.

17. **LO.4** In 2023, Henri, a U.S. citizen and calendar year taxpayer, reports $30,000 of income from France, which imposes a 10% income tax, and $50,000 from Italy, which imposes a 40% tax. In addition, Henri reports taxable income of $90,000 from within the United States.

Henri is married filing a joint return, and his U.S. tax before the foreign tax credit is $28,634. Determine the amount of Henri's foreign tax credit.

18. **LO.4** In 2023, Santiago and Amy are married and file a joint tax return. They have three dependent children, ages 12, 14, and 19. All parties are U.S. citizens. The couple's AGI is $140,000. Determine any available child tax credit and dependent tax credit.

19. **LO.4** In 2023, Ivanna, who has three children under age 13, worked full-time while her spouse, Sergio, was attending college for nine months during the year. Ivanna earned $47,000 and incurred $6,400 of child care expenses. Determine Ivanna and Sergio's child and dependent care credit.

20. **LO.4, 9** Ava and her husband, Leo, file a joint return and are in the 24% tax bracket in 2023. Ava's employer offers a child and dependent care reimbursement plan that allows up to $5,000 of qualifying expenses to be reimbursed in exchange for a $5,000 reduction in the employee's salary (Ava's salary is $75,000). Because Ava and Leo have two minor children requiring child care that costs $5,800 each year, Ava is wondering if she should sign up for the program instead of taking advantage of the credit for child and dependent care expenses.

Critical Thinking
Decision Making
Planning

Analyze the effect of the two alternatives. How would your answer differ if Ava's salary was $30,000, their AGI was $25,000, and their marginal tax rate was 10%?

21. **LO.4** Paola and Isidora are married; file a joint tax return; report modified AGI of $148,000; and have one dependent child, Dante. The couple paid $12,000 of tuition and $10,000 for room and board for Dante (a freshman). Dante is a full-time student. Determine the amount of the American Opportunity credit for 2023.

22. **LO.4** Rafael and Lucy, married taxpayers, each contribute $2,900 to their respective § 401(k) plans offered through their employers. The AGI reported on the couple's joint return is $42,000. Determine their credit for retirement plan contributions (the Saver's Credit).

23. **LO.5** In 2023, Bianca earned a salary of $174,000 from her employer. Determine the amount of FICA taxes and Medicare taxes withheld from her salary.

24. **LO.6** In 2023, Miranda records net earnings from self-employment of $168,500. She has no other income. Determine the amount of Miranda's self-employment tax and her *for* AGI income tax deduction.

25. **LO.7** Determine the additional Medicare taxes for these individuals.
    a. Mario, who is single, earns wages of $440,000.
    b. George and Shirley are married and file a joint return. During the year, George earns wages of $138,000, and Shirley earns wages of $210,000.
    c. Simon has net investment income of $38,000 and MAGI of $223,000 and files as a single taxpayer.

Problems

26. **LO.2** Adelyn has a tentative general business credit of $42,000 for the current year. Adelyn's net regular tax liability before the general business credit is $107,000, and her tentative minimum tax is $88,000. Compute Adelyn's allowable general business credit for the year.

27. **LO.2** Oak Corporation has the following general business credit carryovers:

2019	$ 5,000
2020	15,000
2021	6,000
2022	19,000
Total carryovers	$45,000

If the general business credit generated by activities during 2023 equals $36,000 and the total credit allowed during the current year is $60,000 (based on tax liability), what amounts of the current general business credit and carryovers are utilized against the 2023 income tax liability? What is the amount of unused credit carried forward to 2024?

Communications
Critical Thinking
Decision Making
Planning

28. **LO.3, 9** In the current year, Paul Chaing (4522 Fargo Street, Geneva, IL 60134) acquires a qualifying historic structure for $350,000 (excluding the cost of the land) and plans to substantially rehabilitate the structure. He is planning to spend either $320,000 or $380,000 on rehabilitation expenditures.

    Write a letter to Paul and a memo for the tax files explaining, for the two alternative expenditures, (1) the computation that determines the rehabilitation expenditures tax credit available to Paul, (2) the impact of the credit on Paul's adjusted basis in the property, and (3) the cash-flow differences as a result of the tax consequences related to his expenditure choice.

29. **LO.3** Green Corporation hires six individuals on January 4, 2023, all of whom qualify for the work opportunity credit. Three of these individuals receive wages of $8,500 during 2023, and each individual works more than 400 hours during the year. The other three individuals work 300 hours and receive wages of $5,000 during the year.
    a. Calculate the amount of Green's work opportunity credit for 2023.
    b. If Green pays total wages of $140,000 to its employees during the year, how much of this amount is deductible in 2023 assuming that the work opportunity credit is taken?

Decision Making

30. **LO.3, 9** Tom, a calendar year taxpayer, informs you that in 2022, he incurred expenditures of $40,000 that qualify for the incremental research activities credit. In addition, it is determined that his base amount for the year is $32,800. Determine Tom's incremental research activities credit for 2022.

Communications

31. **LO.3** Ahmed Zinna (16 Southside Drive, Charlotte, NC 28204), one of your clients, owns two retail establishments in downtown Charlotte and has come to you seeking advice concerning the tax consequences of complying with the Americans with Disabilities Act. He understands that he needs to install various features at his stores (e.g., ramps, doorways, and restrooms that are accessible) to make them more accessible to disabled individuals. He asks whether any tax credits will be available

to help offset the cost of the necessary changes. He estimates the cost of the planned changes to his facilities as follows:

Location	Projected Cost
Calvin Street	$22,000
Stowe Avenue	8,500

He reminds you that the Calvin Street store was constructed in 2005 and the Stowe Avenue store is in a building that was constructed in 1948. Ahmed operates his business as a sole proprietorship and has approximately eight employees at each location. Write a letter to Ahmed in which you summarize your conclusions concerning the tax consequences of his proposed capital improvements.

32. **LO.4** Which of the following individuals qualifies for the earned income credit for 2023?
    a. Thomas is single, is 21 years of age, and has no qualifying children. His income consists of $9,000 in wages.
    b. Shannon, who is 27 years old, maintains a household for a dependent 11-year-old son and is eligible for head-of-household tax rates. Her income consists of $16,050 of salary and $50 of taxable interest (Shannon's AGI is $16,100).
    c. Keith and Susan, both age 30, are married and file a joint return. Keith and Susan have no dependents. Their combined income consists of $28,500 of salary and $100 of taxable interest (their AGI is $28,600).
    d. Colin is a 26-year-old self-supporting, single taxpayer. He has no qualifying children and generates earnings of $14,000.

33. **LO.4** Jason, a single parent, lives in an apartment with his three minor children, whom he supports. Jason earned $28,400 during 2023 and uses the standard deduction. Calculate the amount, if any, of Jason's earned income credit.

34. **LO.4, 9** Joyce, a single parent, lives in an apartment with her two minor children (ages 8 and 10), whom she supports. Joyce earns $33,000 during 2023. She uses the standard deduction and files as a head of household.

    Critical Thinking
    Decision Making
    Planning

    a. Calculate the amount, if any, of Joyce's earned income credit.
    b. During the year, Joyce is offered a new job that has greater future potential than her current job. If she accepts the job offer, her earnings for the year will be $40,400; however, she is afraid she will not qualify for the earned income credit. Using after-tax cash-flow calculations, determine whether Joyce should accept the new job offer. Since the child tax credit will be the same under either scenario, you can ignore it for purposes of this analysis.

35. **LO.4** Kim, a U.S. citizen and resident, owns and operates a novelty goods business. During 2023, Kim reports taxable income of $115,000: $50,000 from foreign sources and $65,000 from U.S. sources. In calculating taxable income, the standard deduction is used. The income from foreign sources is subject to foreign income taxes of $17,500. For 2023, Kim files a joint return with her spouse.

    Decision Making
    Planning

    a. Assuming that Kim chooses to claim the foreign taxes as an income tax credit, what is her net Federal income tax payable for 2023?
    b. Recently, Kim has become disenchanted with the location of her business and is considering moving her offshore operation to a different country. Based on her research, if she moved her business to her country of choice, all relevant revenues and costs would remain approximately the same, except that the income taxes payable to that country would be only $7,000. Given that any foreign income taxes paid are available to offset the U.S. tax liability (whether she operates in a high-tax or low-tax jurisdiction), what effect will this have on her decision regarding the potential move?

36. **LO.4** Blue Sky, Inc., a U.S. corporation, is a manufacturing concern that sells most of its products in the United States. It also conducts some business in the European Union through various branches. During the current year, Blue Sky reports taxable

income of $700,000, of which $500,000 is U.S.-sourced and $200,000 is foreign-sourced. Foreign income taxes paid amounted to $35,000. Blue Sky's U.S. income tax liability is $147,000. What is its U.S. income tax liability net of the allowable foreign tax credit?

37. **LO.4** In 2023, Joshua and Ellen are married and file a joint return. Three individuals qualify as their dependents: their two children, ages five years and six months, and Ellen's son from a previous marriage, age 19. All parties are U.S. citizens. Joshua and Ellen's combined AGI is $98,000. Compute their child tax credit and dependent tax credit.

38. **LO.4** Paul and Karen Kent are married, and both are employed (Paul earns $44,000 and Karen earns $9,000 during 2023). Paul and Karen have two dependent children, both under the age of 13 (Samuel and Joy). So that they can work, Paul and Karen pay $3,800 ($1,900 for each child) to Sunnyside Day Care Center (422 Sycamore Road, Fort Worth, TX 76028; Employer Identification Number: 11-2345678) to care for their children while they are working. Assuming that Paul and Karen file a joint return, what, if any, is their tax credit for child and dependent care expenses?

39. **LO.4** Jim and Mary Jean are married and have two dependent children under the age of 13. Both parents are gainfully employed and during 2023 earn salaries as follows: $130,000 (Jim) and $5,200 (Mary Jean). To care for their children while they work, they pay Eleanor (Jim's mother) $5,600. Eleanor does not qualify as a dependent of Jim and Mary Jean. Assuming that Jim and Mary Jean file a joint tax return, what, if any, is their credit for child and dependent care expenses?

Communications

40. **LO.4, 9** Jenna, a longtime client of yours, is employed as an architect and is the president of the local Rotary chapter. To keep up to date with developments in her profession, she attends continuing education seminars offered by the architecture school at State University. During 2023, Jenna spends $2,000 on course tuition to attend these seminars. She spends another $400 on architecture books during the year.

Jenna's daughter, Caitlin, is a senior majoring in engineering at the University of the Midwest. During the 2023 calendar year, Caitlin incurs the following expenses: $8,200 for tuition ($4,100 per semester) and $750 for books and course materials. Caitlin, who Jenna claims as a dependent, lives at home while attending school full-time. Jenna is married, files a joint return, and reports a combined AGI with her spouse of $121,000.

a. Calculate the couple's education tax credits for 2023.
b. Calculate the couple's education tax credits if combined AGI was $162,000.
c. In her capacity as president of the local Rotary chapter, Jenna has asked you to prepare a 30- to 45-minute speech outlining the different ways the tax law helps defray (1) the cost of higher education and (2) the cost of continuing education once someone is in the workforce. Prepare an outline of possible topics for presentation. A tentative title for your presentation is "How Can the Tax Law Help Pay for College and Continuing Professional Education?"

41. **LO.4** Kathleen and Glenn decide that this is the year to begin getting serious about saving for their retirement by participating in their employers' § 401(k) plans. As a result, they each have $3,000 of their salary set aside in their qualified plans.

a. Calculate the maximum credit for these retirement plan contributions available to Kathleen and Glenn if the AGI on their joint return is $35,000.
b. Kathleen and Glenn persuade their dependent 15-year-old son, Joel, to put $500 of his part-time earnings into a Roth IRA during the year. What is the credit available to Joel for this contribution? His AGI is $7,000.

42. **LO.4** This year, Jalissa and Jesse, a married couple, made energy-saving improvements to their home. These improvements included $6,300 to replace all windows with Energy Star certified windows and $570 for a home energy audit.

a. Compute this couple's energy efficient home improvement credit, if any.
b. What tax planning advice would you offer this couple as they continue to incur costs to make their home more energy efficient?

43. **LO.4** For each of the following independent situations, calculate the clean vehicle credit for the taxpayer, assuming the vehicle meets the defintion of a

clean vehicle and the battery meets the critical minerals and battery components requirements.

a. Jorge, single, has MAGI of $110,000. He purchased a new electric SUV from a dealer. The MSRP is $72,000.

b. Sam and Jeremy, a married couple who file jointly, have MAGI of $240,000. They purchased a new electric car from a dealer. The MSRP is $62,000.

c. Marion files as head-of-household and has MAGI of $160,000. She purchased an electric car from a dealer, with an MSRP of $52,000. The car had 8,200 miles on the odometer at the time of purchase.

44. **LO.5** In each of the following independent situations, determine the amount of FICA that should be withheld from the employee's 2023 salary by the employer.

a. Harry earns a $50,000 salary and files a joint return.

b. Hazel earns a $115,000 salary and files a joint return.

c. Tracy earns a $190,000 salary and files a joint return.

d. Alicia's 17-year-old son, Carlos, earns $10,000 at the family sole proprietorship.

45. **LO.5** During 2023, Greg Cruz (1401 Orangedale Road, Troy, MI 48084) works for Maple Corporation and Gray Company. He earns $116,000 at Maple Corporation, where he is a full-time employee. Greg also works part-time for Gray Company for wages of $54,000. Communications

a. Did Greg experience an overwithholding of FICA taxes? Write a letter to Greg and a memo for the tax files in which you explain your conclusion.

b. Did Maple Corporation and Gray Company overpay the employer's portion of FICA? Explain.

46. **LO.6** Julie, a self-employed individual, is required to make estimated payments of her tax liability for the year. Her tax liability for 2022 was $25,000, and her AGI was less than $150,000. For 2023, Julie ultimately determines that her income tax liability is $18,000. During the year, however, she made the following payments, totaling $13,000:

April 18, 2023	$ 4,500
June 15, 2023	2,800
September 15, 2023	4,100
January 16, 2024	1,600
Total paid	$13,000

Because Julie prepaid so little of her ultimate income tax liability, she now realizes that she may be subject to the penalty for underpayment of estimated tax.

a. Determine Julie's estimated tax underpayment for each installment period, if any.

b. Instead, assume that Julie's tax liability for 2022 was $15,960.

47. **LO.6** a. In 2023, Maria records self-employed earnings of $135,000. Using the format illustrated in the text, compute Maria's self-employment tax liability and the allowable income tax deduction for the self-employment tax paid.

b. Express the calculation of the 2023 self-employment tax as a Microsoft Excel formula.

48. **LO.8** Arthur Wesson, an unmarried individual who is age 58, reports taxable income of $510,000 in 2023. His AMTI is $625,000, and his regular tax liability in 2023 is $150,395.

a. What is Arthur's AMT?

b. What is the total amount of Arthur's tax liability?

c. Draft an e-mail to Arthur explaining why he must pay tax greater than his regular tax liability. Arthur's e-mail address is AWesson@FederalWest.com.

49. **LO.8** Renee and Sanjeev Patel, who are married, reported taxable income of $1,500,000 for 2023. They incurred positive AMT modifications of $142,500. The couple itemizes their deductions.

a. Compute the Patels' AMTI for 2023.

b. Compute their tentative minimum tax for 2023.

Tax Return Problems

Planning

Tax Forms Problem

ProConnect™ Tax

50. Beth R. Jordan lives at 2322 Skyview Road, Mesa, AZ 85201. She is a tax accountant with Mesa Manufacturing Company, 1203 Western Avenue, Mesa, AZ 85201 (employer identification number 11-1111111). She also writes computer software programs for tax practitioners and has a part-time tax practice. Beth is single and has no dependents. Beth was born on July 4, 1976, and her Social Security number is 123-45-6785. She did not engage in any digital asset transactions during the year, and she wants to contribute $3 to the Presidential Election Campaign Fund.

The following information is shown on Beth's Wage and Tax Statement (Form W–2) for 2022:

Line	Description	Amount
1	Wages, tips, other compensation	$65,000.00
2	Federal income tax withheld	9,500.00
3	Social Security wages	65,000.00
4	Social Security tax withheld	4,030.00
5	Medicare wages and tips	65,000.00
6	Medicare tax withheld	942.50
15	State	Arizona
16	State wages, tips, etc.	65,000.00
17	State income tax withheld	1,954.00

During the year, Beth received interest of $1,300 from Arizona Federal Savings and Loan and $400 from Arizona State Bank. Each financial institution reported the interest income on a Form 1099–INT. She received qualified dividends of $800 from Blue Corporation, $750 from Green Corporation, and $650 from Orange Corporation. Each corporation reported Beth's dividend payments on a Form 1099–DIV.

Beth received a $1,100 income tax refund from the state of Arizona on April 29, 2022. On her 2021 Federal income tax return, she used the standard deduction.

Fees earned from her part-time tax practice in 2022 totaled $3,800. She paid $600 to have the tax returns processed by a computerized tax return service.

On February 8, 2022, Beth bought 500 shares of Gray Corporation common stock for $17.60 a share. On September 12, 2022, Beth sold the stock for $14 a share.

On January 2, 2022, Beth acquired 100 shares of Blue Corporation common stock for $30 a share. She sold the stock on December 19, 2022, for $55 a share. Both stock transactions were reported to Beth on Form 1099–B; basis was not reported to the IRS.

Beth bought a used sport utility vehicle for $6,000 on June 5, 2022. She purchased the vehicle from her brother-in-law, who was unemployed and was in need of cash. On November 2, 2022, she sold the vehicle to a friend for $6,500.

During the year, Beth records revenues of $16,000 from the sale of a software program she developed. Beth incurred the following expenses in connection with her software development business:

Cost of personal computer	$7,000
Cost of printer	2,000
Furniture	3,000
Supplies	650
Fee paid to computer consultant	3,500

Beth elected to expense the maximum portion of the cost of the computer, printer, and furniture allowed under the provisions of § 179. These items were placed in service on January 15, 2022, and used 100% in her business.

Although her employer suggested that Beth attend an in-person conference on current developments in corporate taxation, Beth was not reimbursed for the travel expenses of $1,420 she incurred in attending the meeting. The $1,420 included $200 for the cost of meals.

During the year, Beth paid $300 for prescription medicines and $2,875 for doctor bills and hospital bills. Medical insurance premiums were paid by her employer. Beth paid real property taxes of $1,766 on her home. Interest on her home mortgage (Valley National Bank) was $3,845, and credit card interest was $320. Beth contributed $2,080 in cash to various qualifying charities during the year. Professional dues and subscriptions totaled $350.

Beth paid estimated taxes of $1,000.

Part 1—Tax Computation

Compute Beth Jordan's 2022 Federal income tax payable (or refund due), and complete her 2022 tax return using appropriate forms and schedules. Suggested software: ProConnect Tax.

Part 2—Tax Planning

Beth is anticipating significant changes in her life in 2023, and she has asked you to estimate her taxable income and tax liability for 2023.

Beth just received word that she has been qualified to adopt a two-year-old daughter. Beth expects that the adoption will be finalized in 2023 and that she will incur approximately $2,000 of adoption expenses. In addition, she expects to incur approximately $3,500 of child and dependent care expenses relating to the care of her new daughter, which will enable her to keep her job at Mesa Manufacturing Company. However, with the additional demands on her time because of her daughter, she has decided to discontinue her two part-time jobs (i.e., the part-time tax practice and her software business), and she will cease making estimated income tax payments.

In your computations, assume that all other 2023 income and expenses will be the same as 2022 amounts.

51. Tim and Sarah Lawrence are married and file a joint return. They reside at 100 Olive Lane, Covington, LA 70434. They have two dependent children, Sean and Debra, ages 12 and 16, respectively. Tim is a self-employed businessperson (sole proprietor of an unincorporated business), and Sarah is a corporate executive. Tim has the following income and expenses from his business in 2023: Tax Computation Problem

Gross income	$325,000
Business expenses	201,000

Records related to Sarah's employment provide the following information:

Salary	$130,000
Unreimbursed travel expenses (including $200 of meals)	1,600

Other pertinent information for the tax year includes the following:

Proceeds from sale of stock acquired on July 15, 2023 (cost of $12,000), and sold on August 1, 2023	$ 9,800
Proceeds from sale of stock acquired on September 18, 2022 (cost of $5,000), and sold on October 5, 2023	3,800
Wages paid to full-time domestic worker for housekeeping and child supervision	10,000
Interest income received	7,000
Total itemized deductions (not including any potential deductions above)	28,900
Federal income tax withheld	28,850
Purchase of a clean new vehicle (an SUV with MSRP of $81,000)	87,200
Estimated Federal income tax payments	20,000

Compute the Lawrences' net Federal income tax payable or refund due for 2023.

Research Problems

Note: Solutions to the Research Problems can be prepared by using the Thomson Reuters Checkpoint™ online tax research database, which accompanies this textbook. Solutions can also be prepared by using research materials found in a typical tax library.

Research Problem 1. Ashby and Curtis, married professionals, have a two-year-old son, Jason. Curtis works full-time as an electrical engineer, but Ashby has not worked outside the home since Jason was born. Because Jason is getting older, Ashby thinks that he would benefit from attending nursery school several times a week, which would give her an opportunity to reinvigorate her love of painting at a nearby art studio. Ashby thinks that if she is lucky, the proceeds from the sale of her paintings will pay for the nursery school tuition.

Ashby plans to claim the credit for child and dependent care expenses, because the care provided Jason at the nursery school is required for her to pursue her art career. Can Ashby and Curtis claim the credit for child and dependent care expenses for the nursery school expense? Why or why not?

Critical Thinking

Research Problem 2. During a recent Sunday afternoon excursion, Miriam, an admirer of early twentieth-century architecture, discovers a 1920s-era house in the countryside outside Mobile, Alabama. She wants not only to purchase and renovate the house but also to move the structure into Mobile so that her community can enjoy its architectural features. Being aware of the availability of the tax credit for rehabilitation expenditures, she wants to maximize her use of the provision, if it is available in this case, once the renovation work begins in Mobile.

Miriam informs you that she will pursue the purchase, relocation, and renovation of the house only if the tax credit is available. Comment on Miriam's decision and on whether any renovation expenditures incurred will qualify for the tax credit for rehabilitation expenditures.

Partial list of research aids:
George S. Nalle III v. Comm., 93–2 USTC ¶50,468, 72 AFTR 2d 93–5705, 997 F.2d 1134 (CA–5, 1993).

Communications
Critical Thinking
Data Analytics

Research Problem 3. Which tax credits are most often claimed by individual taxpayers? Do the credits claimed vary by size of income (AGI)? To answer these questions, go to the IRS Tax Statistics page (**irs.gov/statistics**) and download the Microsoft Excel spreadsheet for the most recent tax year that documents tax liability, tax credits, and tax payments. You can find this in the Individual Income Tax Return (Form 1040) Statistics section of the site; click on the "by Size of Adjusted Gross Income" link. Scroll down this page until you find "All Returns: Tax Liability, Tax Credits, and Tax Payments."

Evaluate the credits claimed (both nonrefundable and refundable) by size of AGI. Analyze the data by clustering it into the following AGI classes: $25,000 or less; $25,000 to $50,000; $50,000 to $100,000; $100,000 to $500,000; $500,000 or more. Present your findings in a visual depiction (e.g., bar chart), summarize your findings in a one-page memo, and send your graphic and memo to your instructor.

Communications

Research Problem 4. Taxpayers who purchase health insurance coverage through the Health Insurance Marketplace may be eligible for the premium tax credit under § 36B. Use the IRS website to determine which taxpayers are eligible for the credit. Send a one-page summary of your findings to your instructor.

Communications

Research Problem 5. The IRS provides a web-based tool to help taxpayers determine whether they are eligible for the earned income tax credit. Locate the EITC Assistant at the IRS website. Then apply the facts related to Walt in Example 22 for either 2023 or 2022. Determine whether the earned income credit is available for Walt and save the results as a pdf. In an e-mail to your instructor, report the estimated credit amount and attach your pdf.

Research Problem 6. Find and read Code § 25C, Energy Efficient Home Improvement Credit, to complete the following chart. Place an X in the appropriate box if the individual may claim a credit for the indicated improvement covered by Code § 25C.

Critical Thinking

Type of improvement	Amy owns her principal residence	Ben owns a vacation home	Carmen rents the home she lives in	Deepa rents a vacation home for a few weeks each year
Qualified energy efficiency improvements [§ 25C(c)]				
Residential energy property expenditures [§ 25C(d)]				
Home energy audit [§ 25C(e)]				

Becker CPA Review Questions

Becker

1. Which of the following statements regarding the self-employment tax is true?
   a. Income and expenses from self-employment are reported on Schedule D (Form 1040).
   b. Self-employment income is subject to both Federal income tax and self-employment tax.
   c. One half of self-employment tax is deductible as an itemized deduction.
   d. All self-employment income is subject to both Medicare and Social Security tax.

2. Which of the following credits is considered "refundable"?
   a. Child and dependent care credit
   b. Retirement plan contribution credit
   c. Child tax credit
   d. Credit for the elderly or permanently disabled

3. Jim spent four years earning his undergraduate degree at a local university. He began his first year of law school in January of the current year. Assuming he is under the phaseout limitation, what education tax credit is Jim eligible for in the current year?
   a. American Opportunity credit
   b. Earned income credit
   c. Lifetime learning credit
   d. Professional education and training credit

4. Disregarding any small business exceptions, for the current year, which of the following situations will result in a taxpayer owing a penalty for underpayment of taxes?
   a. A married filing joint taxpayer had AGI of $160,000 and total tax of $35,000 in the prior year. For the current year, AGI is $175,000 and total tax is $40,000. They had no withholding in the current year and paid a total of $35,000 in estimated taxes.
   b. The taxpayer owes $950 in taxes after his withholding was applied to his current year's tax return.

c. The taxpayer had AGI of $75,000 and total tax of $15,000 in the prior year. For the current year, his AGI is $62,000 and total tax is $12,500. He had no withholding in the current year and paid a total of $11,500 in estimated taxes.

d. The taxpayer had AGI of $100,000 and total tax of $20,000 in the prior year. For the current year, his AGI is also $100,000, but his total tax is $15,000. His withholding amounted to $10,000, and he paid $6,000 in estimated taxes.

5. In 2023, Madison and Nick Koz have two children, ages 8 and 10. Both children meet the definition of qualifying child. The Koz family has adjusted gross income of $300,000. What is the amount of the child tax credit on the couple's income tax return?

   a. $1,000
   b. $2,000
   c. $3,000
   d. $4,000

6. Which of the following individual tax credits can result in a carryback and/or carryforward?

   a. Earned income credit
   b. Child and dependent care credit
   c. Credit for the elderly or permanently disabled
   d. Foreign tax credit

Property Transactions

Chapter **13**

Property Transactions: Determination of Gain or Loss, Basis Considerations, and Nontaxable Exchanges

Chapter **14**

Property Transactions: Capital Gains and Losses, § 1231, and Recapture Provisions

Part 4 covers the tax treatment of sales, exchanges, and other dispositions of property. Included here are the rules used to determine the realized gain or loss, whether the realized gain or loss is recognized, and the characterization of any recognized gain or loss as capital or ordinary. The topic of basis is evaluated both in terms of its effect on the calculation of the gain or loss and how the basis of any property acquired as part of the transaction is determined. Part 4 concludes with a discussion of § 1231 which, in general, covers transactions involving depreciable assets and land used by a business (or in rental activities).

Chapter 13

Property Transactions: Determination of Gain or Loss, Basis Considerations, and Nontaxable Exchanges

Learning Objectives: *After completing Chapter 13, you should be able to:*

- **LO.1** **Perform the computation of realized gain or loss on property dispositions.**
- **LO.2** **Distinguish between realized and recognized gain or loss.**
- **LO.3** **Illustrate how basis is determined for various methods of asset acquisition.**
- **LO.4** **Describe various loss disallowance provisions.**
- **LO.5** **Explain the rationale for nonrecognition (postponement) of gain or loss in certain property transactions.**
- **LO.6** **Apply the nonrecognition provisions and basis determination rules for like-kind exchanges.**
- **LO.7** **Explain the nonrecognition provisions available on the involuntary conversion of property.**
- **LO.8** **Describe the provision for the permanent exclusion of gain on the sale of a personal residence.**
- **LO.9** **Apply various tax planning opportunities related to selected property transactions.**

Chapter Outline

The Big Picture

ISTOCKPHOTO.COM/MICHAEL COURTNEY

Sale or Gift of Inherited House and Other Property Transactions

Alice owns a house that she inherited from her grandmother, Paula, seven months ago. Paula lived in the house for over 50 years. Alice has many fond memories associated with the house, because she spent many summer vacations there. This has caused her to delay making a decision regarding what she is going to do with the house.

Based on the estate tax return, the fair market value of the house at the date of Paula's death was $475,000. According to Paula's attorney, she paid $275,000 for the house. The real estate market for residential housing currently is robust in the city in which the house is located. So based on a recent appraisal, the house is worth $800,000. Alice is considering two options. The first is to give the house to her son, Michael. Michael, his wife Sandra, and their daughter Peggy would live in the house. The second option is to sell the house. Projected selling expenses would be about 7 percent of the selling price.

Alice would also like to know the tax consequences of selling her boat, which she purchased for $22,000 four months ago. She has been using it exclusively for personal use but is disappointed with its layout and capacity. Because it is a new model, there is significant demand for the boat, and based on listings in her area, she anticipates that she can sell it for $20,000 to $23,000.

While you are talking, Alice mentions that earlier this year, she sold some Green Corporation stock at a loss. A few days later, after hearing Green Corporation's quarterly earnings report, she decided to buy back the shares. You ask her to provide additional information to determine the tax effects of these transactions.

Alice also has owned a building (adjusted basis $50,000) that was used in her business. The building was recently destroyed by a fire, but fortunately, it was fully insured. The insurance company paid Alice $100,000 to compensate her for the loss. Now she is looking to acquire suitable replacement property for her business. If possible, she would like to claim a casualty loss, but certainly does not want to recognize any taxable gain from this event as she needs the funds for replacement property.

Alice has come to you for advice regarding the tax consequences of these various transactions. Alice's objectives are to minimize the recognition of any realized gain and to maximize the recognition of any realized loss.

Read the chapter and formulate your response.

Framework 1040 Tax Formula for Individuals

This chapter covers the boldfaced portions of the Tax Formula for Individuals that was introduced in Concept Summary 3.1. Below those portions are the sections of Form 1040 where the results are reported.

Income *(broadly defined)*	$ xx,xxx
Less: Exclusions	(x,xxx)
Gross income	**$xx,xxx**

FORM 1040 (p. 1)

7	Capital gain or (loss). Attach Schedule D if required. If not required, check here ▶ ☐

FORM 1040 (Schedule 1)

3	Business income or (loss). Attach Schedule C.
4	Other gains or (losses). Attach Form 4797

Less: Deductions *for* adjusted gross income	**(x,xxx)**
Adjusted gross income	$ xx,xxx
Less: The greater of total itemized deductions *or* the standard deduction	(x,xxx)
Personal and dependency exemptions*	(x,xxx)
Deduction for qualified business income**	(x,xxx)
Taxable income	$ xx,xxx
Tax on taxable income (*see Tax Tables or Tax Rate Schedules*)	$ x,xxx
Less: Tax credits (*including income taxes withheld and prepaid*)	(xxx)
Tax due (or refund)	$ xxx

* Exemption deductions are not allowed from 2018 through 2025.
** Only applies from 2018 through 2025.

This chapter and Chapter 14 explain the income tax consequences of property transactions (the *sale or other disposition* of property).

- Is there a realized gain or loss?
- If so, is the gain or loss recognized?
- If the gain or loss is recognized, is it ordinary or capital?
- What is the basis of any replacement property that is acquired?

This chapter discusses the determination of realized and recognized gain or loss and the basis of property. Chapter 14 covers the classification of the recognized gain or loss as ordinary or capital.

LO.1

Perform the computation of realized gain or loss on property dispositions.

13-1 Determination of Gain or Loss

As discussed in Chapter 4, taxpayers do not recognize gross income until there has been a realization. "Realization events" include the sale or other disposition of property.

Property includes both tangible assets (property having a physical existence, like land, a building, or equipment) and intangible assets (like investments and goodwill). Tangible assets include both real property (e.g., land or a building) and personal property (e.g., equipment, furniture, or a car). These property *types* do not change from taxpayer to taxpayer. However, how that property is *used* (e.g., for business, investment, or personal purposes) can vary by taxpayer. How property dispositions are taxed depends on the type of property involved and how it is used.

Realization events related to property involve a significant change in ownership rights, and once a realization event has occurred, a realized gain or loss must be determined. Many, but not all, *realized* gains and losses also are *recognized* (i.e., included in the determination of taxable income) at the time of the realization event. So realization is an accounting concept, and recognition is a tax concept. These matters are discussed in more depth in this section.

13-1a **Realized Gain or Loss**

Realization Events

Realization events include the *sale or other disposition* of property (i.e., transactions in which taxpayers change, in a meaningful way, their ownership interest in an asset). A *sale* is the most common realization event involving property. The term *other disposition* is defined broadly in the tax law and includes a wide variety of realization events including exchanges, barter transactions, trade-ins, condemnations, and bond retirements. This term also applies when the taxpayer identifies a change in property (or property rights) even if they do not receive anything on the "disposition" (e.g., a casualty, theft, the expiration of an option, or certain assets becoming worthless).

Identifying a specific economic event (e.g., a sale) is a key factor in determining whether a disposition has occurred.[1] A change in the value of the property is *not* sufficient.[2]

Lori owns Tan Corporation stock that she bought for $3,000. The stock has appreciated in value and is now worth $5,000. Lori has no realized gain because a change in value is not an identifiable event for tax purposes. Here, Lori has an *unrealized gain* of $2,000 ($5,000 − $3,000).

The same is true if the stock had declined in value to $1,000. Because there was no identifiable event, there is no realized loss. Here, Lori would have an *unrealized loss* of $2,000 ($1,000 − $3,000).

Computation of Realized Gain or Loss

Realized gain or loss is the difference between the amount realized from the sale or other disposition of property and the property's adjusted basis on the disposition date. If the amount realized exceeds the property's adjusted basis, the result is a **realized gain**. On the other hand, if the property's adjusted basis exceeds the amount realized, the result is a **realized loss**.[3]

Carl sells Swan Corporation stock with an adjusted basis of $3,000 for $5,400. Carl's realized gain is $2,400 ($5,400 − $3,000). If Carl had sold the stock for $1,750, he would have had a realized loss of $1,250 ($1,750 − $3,000).

Concept Summary 13.1 summarizes this calculation. The various terms used in Concept Summary 13.1 are discussed on the following pages.

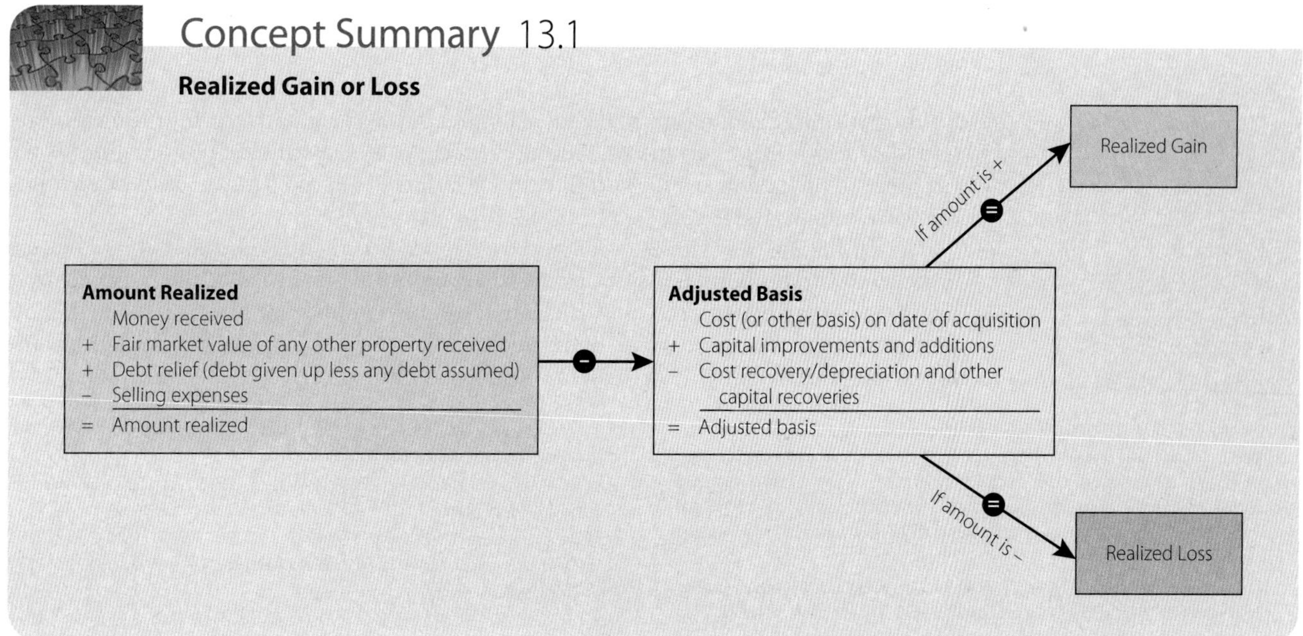

[1] Reg. § 1.1001–1(c)(1).

[2] *Lynch v. Turrish*, 1 USTC ¶18, 3 AFTR 2986, 38 S.Ct. 537 (1918).

[3] § 1001(a) and Reg. § 1.1001–1(a).

Amount Realized

The **amount realized** from a sale or other disposition of property is a measure of the economic value received for property given up. In general, it is the sum of any money received (which includes any debt relief) plus the fair market value of other property received.[4]

Debt relief includes any liability (e.g., a mortgage) assumed by the buyer when the property is sold. Debt relief also occurs if property is sold subject to the mortgage (i.e., the seller remains liable for the debt even though the buyer will be making the payments). In addition, debt relief is not limited by the fair market value of the property.[5]

Amount Realized

Example 3

Juan sells a machine used in his landscaping business to Peter for $20,000 cash plus four acres of property that Peter owns in a nearby town with a fair market value of $36,000. Juan's amount realized on this sale is $56,000 ($20,000 cash + $36,000 land).

Barry owns property on which there is a mortgage of $20,000. He sells the property to Cole for $50,000 cash and Cole's agreement to assume the mortgage. Barry's amount realized from the sale is $70,000 ($50,000 cash + $20,000 debt relief).

In a property transaction, the **fair market value** of property received is the price determined by a willing seller and a willing buyer when neither is compelled to sell or buy and both have reasonable knowledge of relevant facts.[6] All of the relevant factors must be considered,[7] and if the fair market value of the property received cannot be determined, the value of the property given up by the taxpayer is assumed to be equivalent and may be used.[8]

Return to the facts of Example 3. There are several ways one can determine the fair market value of the land Juan is receiving.

- An appraiser can be paid to provide an appraisal of the land.
- City or county property tax assessment information may also be helpful; the city or county assessor determines the fair market value of property so that property taxes are levied appropriately.
- If the exchange is between a willing buyer and seller, determining the fair market value of Juan's landscaping machine could answer the question (i.e., given the facts of the case, it should be worth $56,000).

In calculating the amount realized, selling expenses (e.g., advertising, commissions, and legal fees) relating to the sale are deducted. As a result, the amount realized is the net amount the taxpayer received directly or indirectly, in the form of cash or anything else of value, from the disposition of the property.

The calculation of the amount realized may appear to be one of the least complex areas associated with property transactions. However, because numerous positive and negative adjustments may be required, this calculation can be complex and confusing. In addition, determining the fair market value of the items received by the taxpayer can be difficult. The following example provides insight into various items that can affect the amount realized.

[4] § 1001(b) and Reg. § 1.1001–1(b). The amount realized also includes any real property taxes treated as imposed on the seller that are actually paid by the buyer. The reason for including these taxes in the amount realized is that by paying the taxes, the purchaser is, in effect, paying an additional amount to the seller of the property. Refer to text Section 10-2b for a discussion of this subject.

[5] *Crane v. Comm.*, 47–1 USTC ¶9217, 35 AFTR 776, 67 S.Ct. 1047 and *Comm. v. Tufts*, 83–1 USTC ¶9328, 51 AFTR 2d 83–1132, 103 S.Ct. 1826. Although a legal distinction exists between the direct assumption of a mortgage and the taking of property subject to a mortgage, the Federal income tax consequences in calculating the amount realized are the same.

[6] *Comm. v. Marshman*, 60–2 USTC ¶9484, 5 AFTR 2d 1528, 279 F.2d 27 (CA–6) and Reg. §§ 1.737–1(b), 20.2031–1(b), and 25.2512–3(a).

[7] *O'Malley v. Ames*, 52–1 USTC ¶9361, 42 AFTR 19, 197 F.2d 256 (CA–8) and *Alan Baer Revocable Trust v. U.S.*, 2010–1 USTC ¶60,590, 105 AFTR 2d 2010–1544.

[8] *U.S. v. Davis*, 62–2 USTC ¶9509, 9 AFTR 2d 1625, 82 S.Ct. 1190.

Example 6

Ridge sells an office building and the associated land on October 1, 2023. Under the terms of the sales contract, Ridge is to receive $600,000 in cash. The purchaser is to assume Ridge's mortgage of $300,000 on the property. To assist the purchaser, Ridge agrees to pay $15,000 of the purchaser's closing costs (a "closing cost credit"). The broker's commission on the sale is $45,000. The amount realized by Ridge is calculated as follows:

Selling price:		
Cash	$600,000	
Mortgage assumed by purchaser	300,000	$900,000
Less:		
Broker's commission	$ 45,000	
Closing cost credit provided by Ridge	15,000	(60,000)
Amount realized		$840,000

Adjusted Basis

The **adjusted basis** of property disposed of is the property's original basis adjusted to the date of disposition.[9] Original basis is the cost or other basis of the property on the date acquired by the taxpayer. *Capital additions* increase and *capital recoveries* decrease the original basis.[10] As a result, adjusted basis is determined as follows:

Cost (or other adjusted basis) on date of acquisition
\+ Capital additions
− Capital recoveries
= Adjusted basis on date of disposition

A taxpayer's original basis also includes any liability incurred to acquire the property.

Veronica purchased a residence for $250,000. Whether Veronica uses $250,000 from her personal assets to pay for the residence or uses $50,000 from her personal assets and borrows the remaining $200,000, her basis in the residence is $250,000. It does not matter whether Veronica borrows from the seller (via a land contract) or from a local bank or any other lender (via a mortgage).

Many assets are acquired without purchasing them (e.g., via gift or inheritance). We'll discuss how to determine basis for these assets later in the chapter.

Capital Additions

Capital additions include the cost of improvements made to the property that lengthen its useful life or increase its production capacity or efficiency. These costs are different from repair and maintenance expenses, which are neither capitalized nor added to the original basis (refer to text Section 6-3i). As a result, repair and maintenance expenses are deductible in the current taxable year if they are related to business or income-producing property.

Any liability on property that is assumed by the buyer also is included in the buyer's original basis of the property. The same rule applies if property is acquired subject to a liability. Amortization of the discount on bonds increases the adjusted basis of the bonds.[11]

Capital Recoveries

Capital recoveries decrease the adjusted basis of property.

Depreciation and Cost Recovery The original basis of depreciable property is reduced by any cost recovery or depreciation allowed while the property is held by the taxpayer. The amount subtracted annually from the original basis is the greater of the *allowed* or *allowable* cost recovery or depreciation.[12]

[9] § 1011(a) and Reg. § 1.1011–1.

[10] § 1016(a) and Reg. § 1.1016–1.

[11] See text Section 14-3b for a discussion of bond discount and the related amortization.

[12] § 1016(a)(2) and Reg. § 1.1016–3(a)(1)(i). In most cases, these amounts are the same (refer to text Section 8-1c).

Refer back to Example 3. The machine Juan sold was acquired four years ago for $100,000. It was 7-year MACRS property, and Juan did not take either an immediate expense deduction (§ 179) or bonus depreciation on the property. Juan's adjusted basis is computed as follows:

Original cost		$100,000
Cost recovery:		
Year 1 ($100,000 × 0.1429)	$14,290	
Year 2 ($100,000 × 0.2449)	24,490	
Year 3 ($100,000 × 0.1749)	17,490	
Year 4 ($100,000 × 0.1249 × ½)	6,245	
Total cost recovery		(62,515)
Adjusted basis		$ 37,485

Since Juan's amount realized on the sale was $56,000, his realized gain is $18,515.

Amount realized	$ 56,000
− Adjusted basis	(37,485)
Realized gain (loss)	$ 18,515

Casualties and Thefts A casualty or theft may result in the reduction of the adjusted basis of property.[13] Adjusted basis is reduced by the amount of the *deductible* loss. In addition, adjusted basis is reduced by the amount of insurance proceeds received. However, the receipt of insurance proceeds may result in a recognized gain rather than a deductible loss. The gain increases the adjusted basis of the property.[14]

Capital Recoveries: Casualties and Thefts

An insured truck that Marvin used in his trade or business is destroyed in an accident. At the time of the accident, the adjusted basis of the truck was $8,000, and its fair market value was $6,500. Marvin receives insurance proceeds of $6,500.

The amount of the casualty loss is $1,500 ($6,500 insurance proceeds − $8,000 adjusted basis). The truck's adjusted basis is reduced by the $1,500 casualty loss and the $6,500 of insurance proceeds received ($8,000 basis before casualty − $1,500 casualty loss − $6,500 insurance proceeds = $0 adjusted basis).

How would your answer to Example 9 change if the basis of the truck was $6,000, its fair market value was $9,000, and Marvin received a $9,000 insurance settlement?

Now Marvin has a casualty gain of $3,000 ($9,000 insurance proceeds − $6,000 adjusted basis). The truck's adjusted basis is increased by the $3,000 casualty gain and is reduced by the $9,000 of insurance proceeds received ($6,000 basis before casualty + $3,000 casualty gain − $9,000 insurance proceeds = $0 adjusted basis).

Certain Corporate Distributions A nontaxable corporate distribution is treated as a return of capital, and it reduces the shareholder's stock basis.[15] Corporations typically disclose this information to shareholders. Once the basis of the stock is reduced to zero, the amount of any subsequent distributions is recorded as a capital gain if the stock is a capital asset. These rules are illustrated in text Section 19-2d.

[13]Refer to text Section 7-3 for a discussion of casualties and thefts. In general, personal casualty losses are deductible only if they occur in a Federally declared disaster area; personal thefts are not deductible.

[14]Reg. § 1.1016–6(a).

[15]§ 1016(a)(4) and Reg. § 1.1016–5(a).

Amortizable Bond Premium The basis in a bond purchased at a premium is reduced by the amortizable portion of the bond premium.[16] Investors in taxable bonds may *elect* to amortize the bond premium, with an interest deduction allowed for the amount of the amortized premium.[17] So the election enables the taxpayer to take an annual interest deduction to offset ordinary income in exchange for a larger capital gain or smaller capital loss on the disposition of the bond. The amortization deduction is allowed for taxable bonds because the premium is viewed as a cost of earning the taxable interest from the bonds.

Unlike taxable bonds, the premium on tax-exempt bonds *must be* amortized (and the basis is reduced even though the amortization is not allowed as a deduction). No amortization deduction is permitted on tax-exempt bonds because the interest income is exempt from tax and the amortization of the bond premium merely represents an adjustment of the tax-exempt income earned on the bond.

Antonio purchases Eagle Corporation taxable bonds with a face value of $100,000 for $110,000, thus paying a premium of $10,000. The annual interest rate is 7%, and the bonds mature 10 years from the date of purchase. The annual interest income is $7,000 (7% × $100,000).

If Antonio elects to amortize the bond premium, the $10,000 premium is deducted over the 10-year period. Antonio's basis for the bonds is reduced each year by the amount of the amortization deduction.

If the bonds were tax-exempt, amortization of the bond premium and the basis adjustment would be mandatory. However, no deduction would be allowed for the amortization.

Easements An easement is the legal right to use another's land for a special purpose. Easements typically are used to obtain rights-of-way for utility lines, roads, and pipelines. In recent years, grants of conservation easements have become a popular means of obtaining charitable contribution deductions and reducing the value of real estate for transfer tax (i.e., estate and gift) purposes. For example, a conservation easement on property containing a rare wildlife habitat might prohibit any development; one on a farm might allow continued farming and the building of additional agricultural structures but no other development. Although a conservation easement can be sold, typically it is donated to a charitable organization (like the Nature Conservancy). If donated, the difference between the value of the land with and without the easement would be a charitable contribution. Likewise, scenic easements (granted to protect open spaces or scenic views) are used to reduce the value of land as assessed for property tax purposes.

The amount received for granting an easement is subtracted from the basis of the property. If the taxpayer does not retain any right to the use of the land, all of the basis is assigned to the easement. However, if the use of the land is only partially restricted, an allocation of some of the basis to the easement is appropriate. If, however, it is impossible or impractical to separate the basis of the part of the property on which the easement is granted, the basis of the whole property is reduced by the amount received. If the amount received for the easement exceeds the basis, a taxable gain results.[18]

---

[16]§ 1016(a)(5) and Reg. § 1.1016–5(b). The accounting treatment of bond premium amortization is the same as that for tax purposes. The amortization results in a decrease in the bond investment account.

[17]§ 171(c).

[18]See Rev.Rul. 68–291 and Rev.Rul. 77–414.

LO.2

Distinguish between realized and recognized gain or loss.

13-1b Recognized Gain or Loss

Recognized gain is the amount of the realized gain that is included in the taxpayer's gross income.[19] A **recognized loss**, on the other hand, is the amount of a realized loss that is deductible for tax purposes.[20] As a general rule, the entire amount of a realized gain or loss is recognized.[21]

Concept Summary 13.2 summarizes the realized gain or loss and recognized gain or loss concepts.

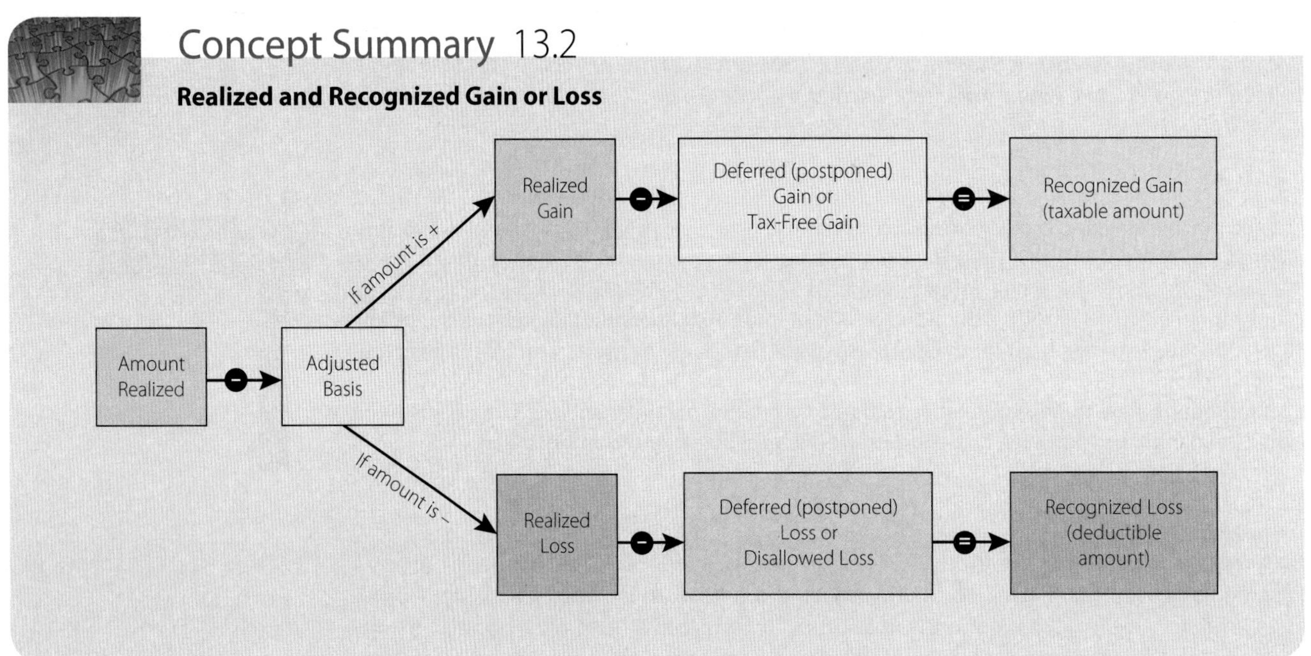

13-1c Nonrecognition of Gain or Loss

In certain cases, a realized gain or loss on a property disposition is not recognized. Like-kind exchanges, covered later in this chapter, are examples of such non-recognition events. Others include losses realized on the sale, exchange, or condemnation of personal use assets (as opposed to business or income-producing property) and gains realized on the sale of a residence. In addition, realized losses from the sale or exchange of business or income-producing property between certain related parties are not recognized.[22]

Sale, Exchange, or Condemnation of Personal Use Assets

A realized loss from the sale, exchange, or condemnation of personal use assets (e.g., a personal residence or an automobile used only for personal purposes) is not recognized for Federal income tax purposes. An exception exists for certain casualty or theft losses from personal use assets (see text Section 7-3). On the other hand, generally gains realized from the sale or other disposition of personal use assets are fully taxable.

[19] § 61(a)(3) and Reg. § 1.61–6(a).

[20] § 165(a) and Reg. § 1.165–1(a).

[21] § 1001(c) and Reg. § 1.1002–1(a).

[22] § 267(a)(1).

Return to the facts of *The Big Picture* on p. 13-1. Assume that Alice sells the boat, which she has held exclusively for personal use, for $23,000. Recall that her adjusted basis for the boat is $22,000. Alice records a realized and recognized gain of $1,000 ($23,000 − $22,000).

Example 12

Return to the facts of *The Big Picture* on p. 13-1. Assume that Alice sells the boat in Example 12 for $20,000. She records a realized loss of $2,000 ($20,000 − $22,000), but the loss is not recognized because the boat is a personal use asset.

Example 13

13-2 Basis Considerations

LO.3

Illustrate how basis is determined for various methods of asset acquisition.

A key element in calculating gain or loss from a property transaction is the asset's basis at the time of the transaction. Various methods for determining basis apply, depending on how the asset was acquired.

13-2a Determination of Cost Basis

As noted earlier, the basis of property generally equals the property's cost. Cost is the amount paid for the property in cash or other property.[23]

A *bargain purchase* of property is an exception to the general rule for determining basis. A bargain purchase results, for instance, when an employer transfers property to an employee at less than the property's fair market value (as compensation), or when a corporation transfers property to a shareholder at less than the property's fair market value (a dividend).

In these cases, the amount included in gross income as either compensation for services or dividend income is the difference between the bargain purchase price and the property's fair market value. The basis of property acquired in a bargain purchase is the property's fair market value.[24] If the basis of the property were not increased by the bargain amount, the taxpayer would be taxed on this amount again at disposition.

Wade buys land from his employer for $10,000 on December 30. The fair market value of the land is $15,000.

Wade must include in his gross income the $5,000 difference between the cost and the fair market value of the land. The bargain element represents additional compensation to Wade. His basis for the land is $15,000, the land's fair market value.

Identification Problems

Cost identification problems are frequently encountered in securities transactions. For example, the Regulations require that the taxpayer identify the particular shares of stock that have been sold (specific identification).[25] A problem arises when the

[23] § 1012 and Reg. § 1.1012–1(a).

[24] Reg. §§ 1.61–2(d)(2)(i) and 1.301–1(j). See text Section 5-8d for a discussion of the circumstances under which what appears to be a taxable bargain purchase is an excludible qualified employee discount.

[25] Reg. § 1.1012–1(c)(1).

taxpayer has purchased separate lots of stock on different dates or at different prices and cannot specifically identify the shares of stock being sold. If that is the case, the stock is presumed to come from the earliest shares purchased (a first-in, first-out presumption).[26] Brokers must provide investors with an annual report on the cost basis of stock sold during the year (this information is included on Form 1099–B and reported to the IRS).

Polly purchases 100 shares of Olive Corporation stock on July 1, 2021, for $5,000 ($50 a share) and another 100 shares of Olive stock on July 1, 2022, for $6,000 ($60 a share). She sells 50 shares of the stock on January 2, 2023.

The cost of the stock sold, assuming that Polly cannot adequately identify the shares, is $50 a share, or $2,500. If Polly was able to specifically identify the shares sold as the shares purchased in 2021, the cost basis would be $60 a share and the holding period (see text Section 14-4) would be short term.

Allocation Problems

When a taxpayer acquires *multiple assets in a lump-sum purchase*, the total cost must be allocated among the individual assets.[27] Allocation is necessary for several reasons.

- Some of the assets acquired may be depreciable (e.g., buildings), but others are not (e.g., land).
- If one of the assets acquired is sold, its basis must be known to compute realized gain or loss.
- Some of the assets may be capital or § 1231 assets that receive special tax treatment when sold in the future.

The lump-sum cost is allocated on the basis of the fair market values of the individual assets acquired.

Harry purchases a building and land for $800,000. Because of the depressed nature of the industry in which the seller was operating, Harry was able to negotiate a favorable purchase price. Appraisals of the individual assets indicate that the fair market value of the building is $600,000, and that of the land is $400,000.

Harry's basis for the building is $480,000[($600,000 ÷ $1,000,000) × $800,000], and his basis for the land is $320,000[($400,000 ÷ $1,000,000) × $800,000].

If a business is purchased and **goodwill** is involved, a special allocation rule applies. Initially, the purchase price is allocated among the assets acquired, other than goodwill, based on their fair market value. Goodwill then is assigned the residual amount of the purchase price. This allocation applies to both the buyer and the seller.[28]

[26] *Kluger Associates, Inc.*, 69 T.C. 925 (1978).

[27] Reg. § 1.61–6(a).

[28] § 1060. The classification of the seller's recognized gain associated with the goodwill is discussed in text Section 14-14b.

Example 17

Kwame sells his business to Renata. An independent appraisal indicates that the business assets, other than goodwill, have the following fair market values:

Inventory	$ 50,000
Customer Lists	50,000
Machinery and Equipment	150,000
Building	400,000
Land	100,000

After negotiations, Kwame and Renata agree on a sales price of $1,000,000. Applying the residual method with respect to goodwill results in the following allocation of the $1,000,000 purchase price:

Inventory	$ 50,000
Customer Lists	50,000
Machinery and Equipment	150,000
Building	400,000
Land	100,000
Goodwill	250,000

The residual method requires that the excess of the purchase price over the fair market value of the assets other than goodwill ($1,000,000 − $750,000 = $250,000) be allocated to goodwill.

In the case of *nontaxable stock dividends*, the allocation depends on whether the dividend is a common stock dividend on common stock or a preferred stock dividend on common stock. If the stock dividend is common stock on common, the cost of the original common shares is allocated to the total shares owned after the dividend.[29]

Example 18

Susan owns 100 shares of Sparrow Corporation common stock for which she paid $1,100. She receives a 10% common stock dividend, giving her a new total of 110 shares. Before the stock dividend, Susan's basis was $11 per share ($1,100 ÷ 100 shares). The basis of each share after the stock dividend is $10 ($1,100 ÷ 110 shares).

If the nontaxable stock dividend is preferred stock on common, the cost of the original common shares is allocated between the common and preferred shares on the basis of their relative fair market values on the date of distribution.[30]

Example 19

Fran owns 100 shares of Cardinal Corporation common stock for which she paid $1,000. She receives a nontaxable stock dividend of 50 shares of preferred stock on her common stock. The fair market values on the date of distribution of the preferred stock dividend are $30 a share for common stock and $40 a share for preferred stock.

Fair market value of common ($30 × 100 shares)	$3,000
Fair market value of preferred ($40 × 50 shares)	2,000
	$5,000
Basis of common: $\frac{3}{5}$ × $1,000	$ 600
Basis of preferred: $\frac{2}{5}$ × $1,000	$ 400

The basis per share for the common stock is $6 ($600 ÷ 100 shares). The basis per share for the preferred stock is $8 ($400 ÷ 50 shares).

[29] §§ 305(a) and 307(a).

[30] Reg. § 1.307–1(a).

The holding period for a nontaxable stock dividend, whether received in the form of common stock or preferred stock, includes the holding period of the original shares.[31] The significance of the holding period for capital assets is discussed in text Section 14-4.

13-2b Gift Basis

When a taxpayer receives property as a gift, the donee (recipient) of the gift has paid nothing to take ownership of the asset. Thus, under the cost basis provision, the donee's basis would be zero. However, this would violate the intent of the law that gifts not be subject to Federal income tax.[32] With a zero basis, if the donee sold the property, all of the amount realized would be treated as realized gain. As a result, a basis is assigned to the property received depending on:

- The date of the gift.
- The basis of the property to the donor.
- The amount of Federal gift tax paid.
- The fair market value of the property.

Gift Basis Rules, in General

The basis rules for gifts of property include the following:

- If the fair market value of the property on the date of the gift exceeds (or is equal to) the donor's basis, then the recipient's (donee's) basis is the same as the donor's (i.e., a carryover basis).[33]

Melissa purchased stock in 2022 for $10,000. In 2023, she gave the stock to her son, Joe, when the fair market value was $15,000. Joe subsequently sells the property for $18,000. Joe's basis is $10,000, and he has a realized gain of $8,000 ($18,000 − $10,000).

If Joe sold the stock for $12,000, he would have a realized gain of $2,000 ($12,000 − $10,000). If Joe sold the stock for $7,000, he would have a realized loss of $3,000 ($7,000 − $10,000).

- If the fair market value of the property on the date of the gift is less than the donor's basis, then special *dual basis* rules apply. Here, the donee has one basis for measuring a gain and a different basis for measuring a loss. This special rule is in place to prevent the shifting of losses (typically among family members) to the individual who would receive the greatest benefit. Under this rule, the donee's *gain basis* is the donor's adjusted basis; the donee's *loss basis* is the fair market value of the property.

Burt purchased stock in 2021 for $10,000. In 2022, he gave the stock to his son, Cliff, when the fair market value was $7,000. Cliff later sells the stock for $6,000.

Cliff's basis is $7,000 (fair market value is less than donor's adjusted basis of $10,000), and the realized loss from the sale is $1,000 ($6,000 amount realized − $7,000 basis).

[31] § 1223(5) and Reg. § 1.1223–1(e).

[32] § 102(a).

[33] § 1015(a) and Reg. § 1.1015–1(a)(1). See Reg. § 1.1015–1(a)(3) for rules where the facts necessary to determine the donor's adjusted basis are unknown. Refer to Example 23 for the effect of depreciation deductions by the donee.

The amount of the loss basis will *differ* from the amount of the gain basis only if, at the date of the gift, the adjusted basis of the property exceeds the property's fair market value. The loss basis rule prevents the donee from receiving a tax benefit from a decline in value that occurred while the donor held the property.

So, in Example 21, Cliff records a loss of only $1,000 rather than a loss of $4,000 ($6,000 − $10,000). The $3,000 difference represents the decline in value that occurred while Burt held the property. In contrast, however, the donee may be subject to income tax on the appreciation that occurred while the donor held the property, as illustrated in Example 20.

If the amount realized from a sale is *between* the donee's loss basis and gain basis, no gain or loss is realized; here, the basis is deemed to be the same as the amount realized.

Assume the same facts as in Example 21, except that Cliff sells the stock for $8,000. Application of the gain basis rule produces a loss of $2,000 ($8,000 − $10,000). Application of the loss basis rule produces a gain of $1,000 ($8,000 − $7,000).

Because the amount realized is between the gain basis and the loss basis, Cliff recognizes neither a gain nor a loss.

Adjustment for Federal Gift Tax Paid

If Federal gift taxes are paid by the donor, the portion of the gift tax paid that is related to any appreciation is taken into account in determining the donee's gain basis.[34]

Holding Period

The **holding period** for property acquired by gift begins on the date the donor acquired the property if the gain basis rule applies.[35] The holding period starts on the date of the gift if the loss basis rule applies.[36]

Basis for Depreciation

The basis for depreciation on depreciable gift property is the donee's gain basis.[37] This rule is applicable even if the donee later sells the property at a loss and uses the loss basis rule in calculating the amount of the realized loss.

Example 23

Vito gave a machine (a MACRS 5-year asset) to Tina in 2023. At that time, the adjusted basis was $32,000 (cost of $40,000 − accumulated depreciation of $8,000), and the fair market value was $26,000. No Federal gift tax was paid. Tina's gain basis at the date of the gift is $32,000, and her loss basis is $26,000. During 2023, Tina deducts depreciation (cost recovery) of $6,400 ($32,000 × 20%). At the end of 2023, Tina's gain basis and loss basis are:

	Gain Basis	Loss Basis
Donor's basis or fair market value	$32,000	$26,000
Less: Depreciation (cost recovery)	(6,400)	(6,400)
	$25,600	$19,600

[34]§ 1015(d)(6) and Reg. § 1.1015–5(c)(2). Examples illustrating these rules can be found in Reg. § 1.1015–5(c)(5) and IRS Publication 551 (*Basis of Assets*), p. 9.

[35]§ 1223(2) and Reg. § 1.1223–1(b).

[36]Rev.Rul. 59–86.

[37]§ 1011 and Reg. §§ 1.1011–1 and 1.167(g)–1.

13-2c Inherited Property

Special basis rules apply for inherited property (property acquired from a decedent). Typically, these rules are favorable to the taxpayer receiving this property.

General Rules

The basis of inherited property almost always is the property's fair market value at the date of death.[38]

The Big Picture

Example 24

Return to the facts of *The Big Picture* on p. 13-1. Alice inherited property from Paula, who died recently. At the date of death, Paula's basis for the property Alice inherited was $275,000. The house's fair market value at the date of death was $475,000.

Alice's basis for income tax purposes is $475,000. This commonly is referred to as a *stepped-up basis.*

The Big Picture

Example 25

Return to the facts of *The Big Picture* on p. 13-1. Assume the same facts as in Example 24, except that the house's fair market value at the date of Paula's death was $260,000.

Alice's basis for income tax purposes is $260,000. This is commonly referred to as a *stepped-down basis.*

An *alternate valuation amount* is available to estates for which a Federal estate tax return must be filed [generally, estates with a valuation in excess of $12.92 million for deaths in 2023 ($12.06 million in 2022)]. If elected by the estate's executor, the property's basis is the fair market value six months after the date of death.[39] The alternate valuation date can be elected *only if*, as a result of the election, both the value of the gross estate and the estate tax liability are lower than they would have been if the primary valuation date had been used.[40]

Income in Respect of a Decedent

Income in respect of a decedent (IRD) usually exists when a cash basis taxpayer dies and, on the date of death, is entitled to some form of income (e.g., compensation, interest, or dividends) but has yet to receive it. IRD includes most post-death distributions from retirement plans, including traditional IRAs and § 401(k) plans.

IRD is included in the estate at its fair market value (on the appropriate valuation date). Because IRD is not subject to the step-up or step-down rules applicable to property passed by death, the income tax basis of the decedent transfers to the estate or heirs.[41] Furthermore, the recipient of IRD must classify it in the same manner (e.g., ordinary income or capital gain) as the decedent would have.[42]

[38] §§ 1014(a) and 1022. See Chapter 29 for additional information.

[39] § 2032(a)(1) and Rev.Rul. 56–60. For any property distributed by the executor during the six-month period preceding the alternate valuation date, the adjusted basis to the beneficiary is the fair market value on the date of distribution.

[40] § 2032(c). This provision prevents the alternate valuation election from being used to increase the basis of the property to the beneficiary for income tax purposes without simultaneously increasing the estate tax liability (because of estate tax deductions or credits).

[41] § 1014(c).

[42] § 691(a)(3).

George, age 58, was entitled to a salary payment of $18,000 and a bonus of $20,000 at the time of his death. In addition, George had been contributing to a traditional IRA for over 20 years. The IRA has a basis of $83,000 (due to some nondeductible contributions over the years) and a current value of $560,000. George's estate collects the salary and bonus payments, and George's wife (Maria, his only beneficiary) cashes in the IRA.

Both the estate and Maria have received income in respect of a decedent (IRD) and must include ordinary income in their computation of taxable income for the year. The estate has IRD of $38,000 (salary of $18,000 + bonus of $20,000), and Maria recognizes IRD of $477,000 ($560,000 proceeds − $83,000 basis).[43]

Survivor's Share of Property

Both the decedent's share and the survivor's share of *community property* have a basis equal to the fair market value on the date of the decedent's death.[44] This occurs because the decedent's share of the community property is included in the estate and assumes a fair market value basis, whereas the surviving spouse's share is treated as if it were received from the decedent at its fair market value.

Example 27

Andrew and LaTonya own, as community property, 200 shares of Biltmore Company stock acquired in 1991 for $100,000. Andrew dies in 2023, when the securities are valued at $300,000. One-half of the Biltmore stock is included in Andrew's estate. If LaTonya inherits Andrew's share of the community property, the basis for gain or loss is $300,000:

LaTonya's one-half of the community property (stepped up from $50,000 to $150,000 due to Andrew's death)	$150,000
Andrew's one-half of the community property (stepped up from $50,000 to $150,000 due to inclusion in his gross estate)	150,000
LaTonya's new basis	$300,000

In a *common law* state, only one-half of jointly held property of spouses (tenants by the entirety or joint tenants with rights of survivorship) is included in the estate.[45] In such a case, no adjustment of the basis is permitted for the surviving spouse's share of the asset.

Example 28

Assume the same facts as in the previous example, except that the property is jointly held by Andrew and La Tonya, who reside in Indiana, a common law state. Andrew purchased the property and made a gift of one-half of the property to LaTonya when the stock was acquired. No Federal gift tax was paid.

Only one-half of the Biltmore stock is included in Andrew's estate. LaTonya's basis for determining gain or loss in the excluded half is not adjusted upward for the increase in value to date of death. As a result, LaTonya's basis is $200,000:

LaTonya's one-half of the jointly held property (carryover basis of $50,000)	$ 50,000
Andrew's one-half of the jointly held property (stepped up from $50,000 to $150,000 due to inclusion in his gross estate)	150,000
LaTonya's new basis	$200,000

[43] See Chapter 29 for additional information.

[44] § 1014(b)(6). The community property states are listed in text Section 4-3d.

[45] § 2040(b).

Holding Period of Inherited Property

The holding period of inherited property is *deemed to be long term* (held for the required long-term holding period). This rule applies regardless of whether the property is disposed of at a gain or at a loss.[46]

LO.4

Describe various loss disallowance provisions.

13-2d Disallowed Losses

In certain situations, realized losses are not recognized. Transactions between related parties and wash sales are two of these situations.

Related Taxpayers

Realized losses from sales or exchanges of property, directly or indirectly, between certain related parties are not recognized. This loss disallowance rule applies to several types of related-party transactions. The most common involve (1) members of a family and (2) an individual and a corporation (where the individual owns, directly or indirectly, more than 50 percent in value of the corporation's outstanding stock).[47]

The loss disallowance rules (1) prevent a taxpayer from directly transferring an unrealized loss to a related taxpayer in a higher tax bracket who could receive a greater tax benefit from recognition of the loss and (2) eliminate a substantial administrative burden on the IRS (there is no need to determine whether the selling price is equal to the asset's fair market value). The rules governing these relationships are discussed in text Section 6-3j.

If income-producing or business property is transferred to a related taxpayer and a loss is disallowed, the related-party buyer's basis is equal to the amount paid (i.e., its cost). However, if the related-party buyer later sells the property and realizes a gain, the gain is reduced by the loss that previously was disallowed.[48] This *right of offset* is not applicable if the original sale involved the sale of a personal use asset (e.g., the sale of a personal residence between related taxpayers). Furthermore, the right of offset is available only to the original transferee (the related-party buyer).[49]

Example 29

Pedro sells business property with an adjusted basis of $50,000 to his daughter, Josefina, for its fair market value of $40,000. Pedro's realized loss of $10,000 ($40,000 − $50,000) is not recognized.

- How much gain does Josefina recognize if she sells the property for $52,000? Josefina recognizes a $2,000 gain. Her realized gain is $12,000 ($52,000 less her basis of $40,000), but she can offset Pedro's $10,000 loss against the gain.
- How much gain does Josefina recognize if she sells the property for $48,000? Josefina recognizes no gain or loss. Her realized gain is $8,000 ($48,000 less her basis of $40,000), but she can offset $8,000 of Pedro's $10,000 loss against the gain. The balance of Pedro's disallowed loss ($2,000) disappears and cannot be used. Note that Pedro's loss can only offset Josefina's gain. It cannot create a loss for Josefina.
- How much loss does Josefina recognize if she sells the property for $38,000? Josefina recognizes a $2,000 loss, the same as her realized loss ($38,000 less $40,000 basis). Pedro's loss does not increase Josefina's loss. His loss only can offset a gain. Because Josefina has no realized gain, Pedro's loss cannot be used and never is recognized. Note that if the property was a personal use asset (not business), her $2,000 loss would be personal and would not be recognized.

The holding period of the buyer for the property is not affected by the holding period of the seller; the *holding period* includes only the period of time the buyer held the property.[50]

Wash Sales

The **wash sale** rules are designed to eliminate the opportunity to sell stock at a loss, recognize the loss for tax purposes, but replace the stock sold by buying back identical shares shortly before or after the sale. If the wash sale rule applies, a realized loss on

[46] § 1223(9).

[47] Code § 707 provides a similar disallowance provision where the related parties are a partner and a partnership in which the partner owns, directly or indirectly, more than 50% of the capital interests or profits interests in the partnership.

[48] § 267(d) and Reg. § 1.267(d)–1(a).

[49] The loss disallowance rules are applicable even when the selling price is equal to the fair market value and can be validated (e.g., listed stocks).

[50] §§ 267(d) and 1223(2) and Reg. § 1.267(d)–1(c)(3).

the sale or exchange of stock or securities is not recognized. Recognition of the loss is disallowed because the taxpayer is considered to be in substantially the same economic position after the sale and repurchase as before the sale and repurchase.

The wash sale rule applies if a taxpayer sells or exchanges stock or securities at a loss and within 30 days before *or* after the date of the sale or exchange acquires substantially identical stock or securities.[51] Concept Summary 13.3 provides an overview of these rules.

Wash sale rules are triggered only when the investor buys a "substantially identical" investment to the one that was sold for a loss. According to the IRS, "stocks or securities of one corporation are not considered substantially identical to stocks or securities of another corporation." [52] However, an option to purchase substantially identical securities is treated the same as actually buying the stock. So, for instance, selling Ford and buying back Ford (or Ford call options) would trigger the wash sale rules, but selling Ford and buying General Motors, or selling Dell and buying Hewlett-Packard (in the same industry, but clearly a different company) would avoid the wash sale rules. Corporate bonds and preferred stock normally are not considered substantially identical to the corporation's common stock.[53]

Although the application of the "substantially identical" rule is fairly settled when dealing with individual stocks or bonds, there is more uncertainty when dealing with mutual funds or exchange-traded funds. For example, Vanguard's Windsor fund and Fidelity's Value Discovery fund have similar investment objectives (both are large cap, value funds). Not surprisingly, there is some overlap in their stock holdings. So, would the "substantially identical" rule apply if 30 percent of their holdings were identical? 50 percent? Unfortunately, there is little authoritative guidance on this issue. The lack of clear direction from the Treasury Department and the courts has led many investment advisers to develop a working list of transactions that are generally considered to be acceptable under the wash sale rules.[54]

For example, a tax-loss swap from one S&P 500 Index fund to another S&P 500 Index fund managed by a different fund company may result in scrutiny from the IRS. However, if the new fund tracks another large capitalization index, such as the Russell 1000, the tax loss should be allowed. These mutual fund transactions generally fall outside of the wash sale rules, despite the lack of a concrete definition of what is a "substantially identical" security.

1. Sell one index fund and buy another index fund, provided that the indexes of the two funds differ (e.g., S&P 500 for the Russell 1000).
2. Sell one actively managed fund and buy a fund at another company with different portfolio managers.
3. Sell an index fund and buy an actively managed fund regardless of the fund company.
4. Sell an actively managed fund and buy an index fund regardless of the fund company.

Attempts to avoid the application of the wash sales rules by having a related taxpayer repurchase the securities have been unsuccessful.[55]

Realized loss that is not recognized under the wash sale rule is added to the *basis* of the substantially identical stock or securities whose acquisition resulted in the nonrecognition of loss.[56] In other words, the basis of the replacement stock or securities is increased by the amount of the unrecognized loss. If the loss were not added to the basis of the newly acquired stock or securities, the taxpayer never would recover the entire basis of the old stock or securities.

The basis of the new stock or securities includes the unrecovered portion of the basis of the formerly held stock or securities. As a result, the *holding period* of the new stock or securities begins on the date of acquisition of the old stock or securities.[57]

[51] § 1091(a) and Reg. §§ 1.1091–1(a) and (f).

[52] IRS Publication 550 (Investment Income and Expenses), p. 56.

[53] Rev.Rul. 56–406. However, if the bonds and preferred stock are convertible into common stock, they may be considered substantially identical.

[54] See, for example, "Keeping Transactions Clean from the Wash Sale Rules," Kevin Trout, *Journal of the American Association of Independent Investors* (December 2014) and "Tax Loss Harvesting: The Re-Balancing Act," Lee C. McGowen, *Journal of Financial Planning* (December 2008).

[55] *McWilliams v. Comm.*, 47–1 USTC ¶9289, 35 AFTR 1184, 67 S.Ct. 1477.

[56] § 1091(d) and Reg. § 1.1091–2(a).

[57] § 1223(3) and Reg. § 1.1223–1(d).

The Big Picture

Example 30

Return to the facts of *The Big Picture* on p. 13-1. Alice owned 100 shares of Green Corporation stock (basis of $20,000). She sold 50 shares for $8,000. Ten days later, she purchased 50 shares of the same stock for $7,000.

Alice's realized loss of $2,000 ($8,000 amount realized − $10,000 basis of 50 shares) is not recognized because it resulted from a wash sale. Alice's basis in the newly acquired stock is $9,000 ($7,000 purchase price + $2,000 unrecognized loss from the wash sale).

A taxpayer may acquire fewer shares than the number sold in a wash sale. In this case, the loss from the sale is prorated between recognized and unrecognized loss on the basis of the ratio of the number of shares acquired to the number of shares sold.[58]

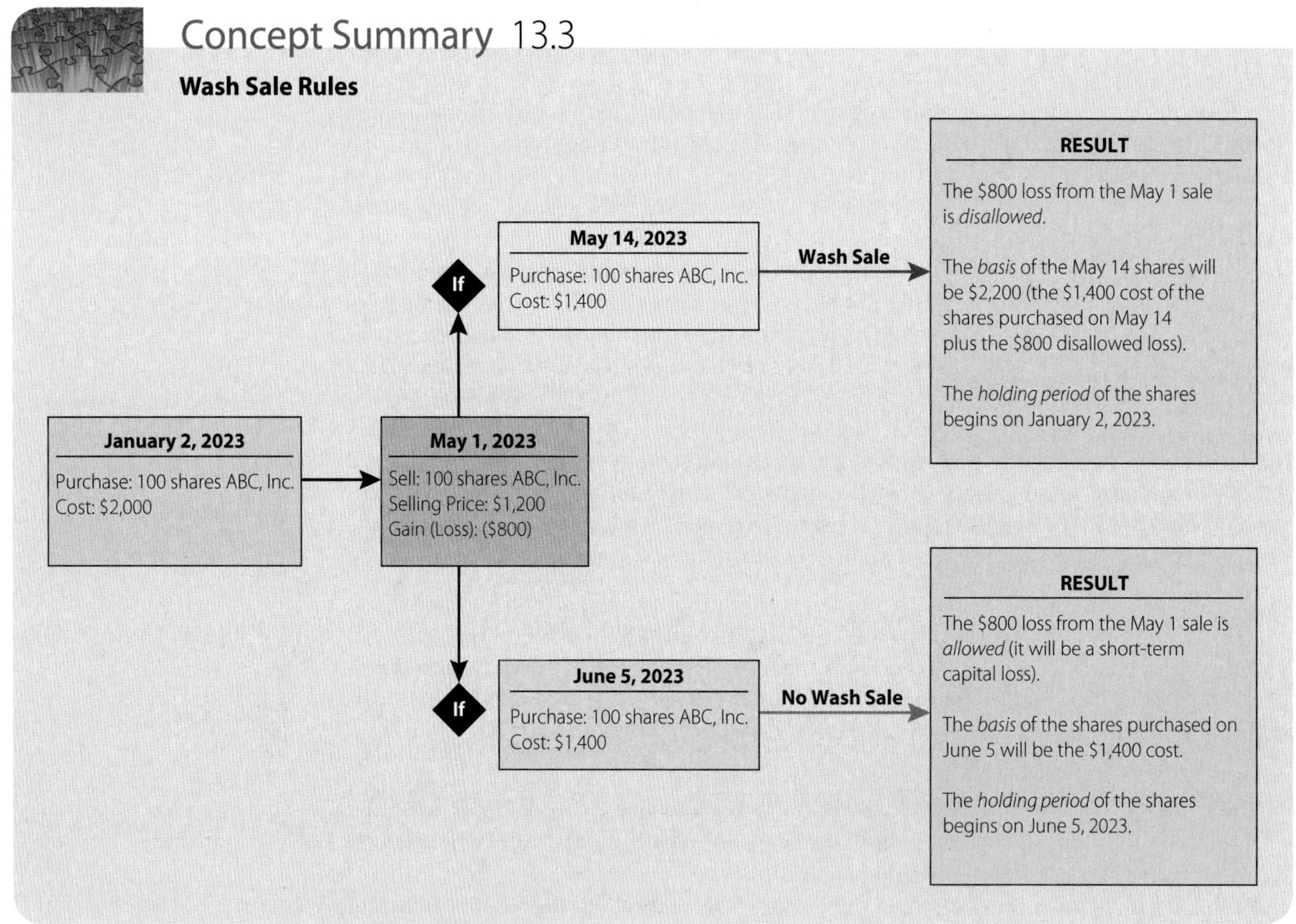

The Big Picture

Example 31

Assume the same facts as Example 30, except that instead of purchasing 50 shares of Green Corporation stock for $7,000 ($140 per share), Alice purchased only 40 shares of the stock for $5,600 (40 shares × $140 per share).

Because Alice replaced only 40 of the 50 shares previously sold at a loss, only 80% (40 ÷ 50) of the $2,000 realized loss is disallowed ($1,600; 80% × $2,000). As a result, Alice will recognize a $400 loss ($2,000 × 20%) and will have a basis of $7,200 in the 40 shares of Green Corporation she purchased ($5,600 purchase price + $1,600 disallowed loss).

[58] § 1091(b) and Reg. § 1.1091–1(c).

Ethics & Equity Washing a Loss Using an IRA

Ajit owns 1,500 shares of Eagle, Inc. stock that he purchased over 10 years ago for $80,000. Although the stock has a current market value of $52,000, Ajit still views the stock as a solid long-term investment. He has sold other stock during the year with overall gains of $30,000, so he would like to sell the Eagle stock and offset the $28,000 loss against these gains, but somehow keep his Eagle investment. He has devised a plan to keep his Eagle investment by using funds in his traditional IRA to purchase 1,500 Eagle shares immediately after selling the shares he currently owns. Evaluate Ajit's treatment of these stock transactions. Can his plan work?

The wash sale rules do *not* apply to taxpayers engaged in the business of buying and selling securities.[59] In addition, the wash sales provisions do *not* apply to gains. As a result, taxpayers with capital losses (or capital loss carryovers from prior years) can sell an appreciated asset and then reacquire it, using the gain to offset the capital losses. Because the basis of the replacement stock will be the purchase price, the taxpayer gets an increased basis for the stock while using the capital gain to offset otherwise nondeductible capital losses.

13-2e Property Converted from Personal Use to Business or Income-Producing Use

As discussed previously, losses from the sale of personal use assets are not recognized for tax purposes, but losses from the sale of business and income-producing assets are deductible. Can a taxpayer convert a personal use asset that has declined in value to business or income-producing use and then sell the asset to recognize a business or income-producing loss?

The tax law prevents this practice by specifying that the *original basis for loss* on personal use assets converted to business or income-producing use is the *lower* of the property's adjusted basis or fair market value on the date of conversion.[60] The *gain basis* for converted property is the property's adjusted basis on the date of conversion. The tax law is not concerned with gains on converted property because gains are recognized regardless of whether property is business, income-producing, or personal use.

Diane's personal residence has an adjusted basis of $175,000 and a fair market value of $160,000. Diane converts the personal residence to rental property. Her basis for loss is $160,000 (lower of $175,000 adjusted basis and fair market value of $160,000). The $15,000 decline in value is a personal loss and never is recognized for tax purposes. Diane's basis for gain is $175,000.

The basis for loss is also the *basis for depreciating* the converted property.[61] This is an exception to the general rule that the basis for depreciation is the gain basis (e.g., property received by gift). This exception prevents the taxpayer from recovering a personal loss indirectly through depreciation of the higher original basis. After the property is converted, both its basis for loss and its basis for gain are adjusted for depreciation deductions from the date of conversion to the date of disposition. These rules apply only if a conversion from personal to business or income-producing use has actually occurred.

At a time when his personal residence (adjusted basis of $140,000) is worth $150,000, Keith converts one-half of it to rental use. The property will be depreciated using the straight-line method, has an estimated useful life of 20 years, and has no salvage value. As a result, annual depreciation will be $3,500 ($70,000 ÷ 20 years).

continued

[59] Reg. § 1.1091–1(a).

[60] Reg. § 1.165–9(b)(2).

[61] Reg. § 1.167(g)–1.

After renting the converted portion for five years, Keith sells the property for $144,000. All amounts relate only to the building; assume that the land has been accounted for separately. Keith has a $2,000 realized gain from the sale of the personal use portion of the residence and a $19,500 realized gain from the sale of the rental portion.

	Personal Use	Rental
Original basis for gain and loss—adjusted basis on date of conversion (fair market value is *greater than* the adjusted basis)	$70,000	$ 70,000
Depreciation—five years	(–0–)	(17,500)
Adjusted basis—date of sale	$70,000	$ 52,500
Amount realized	72,000	72,000
Realized gain	$ 2,000	$ 19,500

Keith may be able to exclude the $2,000 realized gain from the sale of the personal use portion of the residence (see text Section 13-6). If the exclusion applies, only $17,500 (equal to the depreciation deducted) of the $19,500 realized gain from the rental portion is recognized.

Example 34

Assume the same facts as in the previous example, except that the fair market value on the date of conversion is $130,000 and the sales proceeds are $90,000. Keith has a $25,000 realized loss from the sale of the personal use portion of the residence and a $3,750 realized loss from the sale of the rental portion. These losses are computed as follows:

	Personal Use	Rental
Original basis for loss—fair market value on date of conversion (fair market value is *less than* the adjusted basis)	$70,000*	$ 65,000
Depreciation—five years	(–0–)	(16,250)**
Adjusted basis—date of sale	$70,000	$ 48,750
Amount realized	45,000	45,000
Realized loss	($25,000)	($ 3,750)

*Not applicable; use one-half of adjusted basis ($140,000 × 50%).
**($65,000 ÷ 20) × 5.

The $25,000 loss from the sale of the personal use portion of the residence is not recognized. The $3,750 loss from the rental portion is recognized.

13-2f **Summary of Basis Adjustments**

Some of the more common items that either increase or decrease the basis of an asset appear in Concept Summary 13.4.

There are a number of techniques for determining basis for tax purposes, with the method dependent on the manner in which the asset was acquired. In summary, the basis of an asset can be determined by reference to any of the following:

- The asset's cost.
- The basis of another asset.
- The asset's fair market value.
- The basis of the asset to another taxpayer.

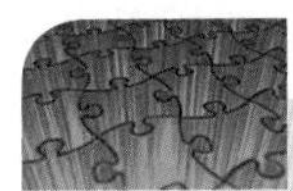

Concept Summary 13.4

Adjustments to Basis

Item	Effect	Refer to Chapter	Explanation
Amortization of bond discount	Increase	14	Amortization is mandatory for certain taxable bonds and elective for tax-exempt bonds.
Amortization of bond premium	Decrease	13	Amortization is mandatory for tax-exempt bonds and elective for taxable bonds.
Amortization of covenant not to compete	Decrease	8	Covenant must be for a definite and limited time period. The amortization period is a statutory period of 15 years.
Amortization of intangibles	Decrease	8	Intangibles are amortized over a 15-year period.
Assessment for local benefits	Increase	10	To the extent not deductible as taxes (e.g., assessment for streets and sidewalks that increase the value of the property versus one for maintenance or repair or for meeting interest charges).
Bad debts	Decrease	7	Only the specific charge-off method is permitted.
Capital additions	Increase	13	Certain items, at the taxpayer's election, can be capitalized or deducted (e.g., selected medical expenses).
Casualty	Decrease	7	For a casualty loss, the amount of the adjustment is the sum of the deductible loss and the insurance proceeds received. For a casualty gain, the amount of the adjustment is the insurance proceeds received reduced by the recognized gain.
Condemnation	Decrease	13	Same as for Casualty.
Cost recovery	Decrease	8	§ 168 is applicable to tangible assets placed in service after 1980 whose useful life is expressed in terms of years; includes additional first-year (bonus) depreciation.
Depletion	Decrease	8	Use the greater of cost or percentage depletion. Percentage depletion can still be deducted when the basis is zero.
Depreciation	Decrease	8	§ 167 is applicable to tangible assets placed in service before 1981 and to tangible assets not depreciated in terms of years.
Easement	Decrease	13	If the taxpayer does not retain any use of the land, all of the basis is allocable to the easement transaction. However, if only part of the land is affected by the easement, only part of the basis is allocable to the easement transaction.
Expensing under § 179	Decrease	8	Occurs only if the taxpayer elects § 179 treatment.
Improvements by lessee to lessor's property	Increase	1	Adjustment occurs only if the lessor is required to include the fair market value of the improvements in gross income under § 109.
Imputed interest	Decrease	16	Amount deducted is not part of the cost of the asset.
Medical capital expenditure permitted as a medical expense	Decrease	10	Adjustment is the amount of the deduction (the effect on basis is to increase it by the amount of the capital expenditure net of the deduction).
Real estate taxes: apportionment between the buyer and seller	Increase or decrease	10	To the extent the buyer pays the seller's pro rata share, the buyer's basis is increased. To the extent the seller pays the buyer's pro rata share, the buyer's basis is decreased.
Rebate from manufacturer	Decrease	5	Because the rebate is treated as an adjustment to the purchase price, it is not included in the buyer's gross income.
Stock dividend	Decrease	13	Adjustment occurs only if the stock dividend is nontaxable. Although the basis per share decreases, the total stock basis does not change.
Stock rights	Decrease	13	Adjustment to stock basis occurs only for nontaxable stock rights and only if the fair market value of the rights is at least 15% of the fair market value of the stock or, if less than 15%, the taxpayer elects to allocate the basis between the stock and the rights.
Theft	Decrease	7	Same as for Casualty.

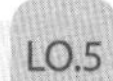

Explain the rationale for nonrecognition (postponement) of gain or loss in certain property transactions.

13-3 Nontaxable Exchanges

A taxpayer who is going to replace a business asset (e.g., land and building) may decide to sell the old asset and purchase a new asset. In this case, any realized gain or loss on the asset sold is recognized and the basis of the new asset is its cost. Alternatively, the taxpayer may be able to trade the old asset (e.g., land and building) for a new asset (e.g., a large parcel of land on which the taxpayer will construct a new manufacturing plant) in an exchange that might qualify for nontaxable exchange treatment.

In certain situations, the tax law allows deferral or avoidance of gain/loss recognition when there is a change in the *form* but not in the *substance* of the taxpayer's relative economic position. Effectively, the replacement property received in the exchange is viewed as a continuation of the old investment.[62] In such an exchange, the taxpayer may have received no cash as part of the exchange. As a result, the taxpayer does not have the *wherewithal to pay* the tax on any realized gain that would be recognized.

In a **nontaxable exchange**, realized gains or losses are not recognized. Instead, the recognition of gain or loss is *postponed* (deferred) until the property received in the nontaxable exchange is subsequently sold in a taxable transaction. This "deferral" is accomplished by assigning a carryover basis to the replacement property.

Debra completes a nontaxable exchange of property with an adjusted basis of $10,000 and a fair market value of $12,000 for property with a fair market value of $12,000.

Debra has a realized gain of $2,000 ($12,000 amount realized − $10,000 adjusted basis). Her recognized gain is $0. Her basis in the replacement property is a carryover basis of $10,000.

Assume that the replacement property is nondepreciable and that Debra subsequently sells it for $12,000. Her realized and recognized gain will be the $2,000 gain that was postponed (deferred) in the nontaxable transaction. If the replacement property is depreciable, the carryover basis of $10,000 is used in calculating depreciation.

In some nontaxable exchanges, only part of the property involved in the transaction qualifies for nonrecognition treatment. If the taxpayer receives cash or other nonqualifying property, part or all of the realized gain from the exchange is recognized; the taxpayer has the wherewithal to pay tax. Here, the basis of the replacement property is adjusted to reflect any deferred gain (gain realized but not recognized).

It is important to distinguish between a nontaxable disposition, as the term is used in the statute, and a tax-free transaction. The term *nontaxable* refers to postponement of recognition via a carryover basis (these transactions may also be referred to as tax-deferred). In a *tax-free* transaction, the nonrecognition is permanent. Here, the basis of any property acquired does not depend on the basis of the property sold by the taxpayer. In this chapter, we discuss two nontaxable transactions (like-kind exchanges and involuntary conversions) and one tax-free transaction (sale of a personal residence).

LO.6

Apply the nonrecognition provisions and basis determination rules for like-kind exchanges.

13-4 Like-Kind Exchanges—§ 1031

Code § 1031 requires nontaxable treatment if the following **like-kind exchange** requirements are satisfied:[63]

- The property is *like-kind* property (only *real property* qualifies).[64]
- The form of the transaction is an *exchange*.
- Both the property given up and the property received are either "used in a trade or business" *or* "held for investment."

[62] Reg. § 1.1002–1(c).

[63] § 1031(a) and Reg. § 1.1031(a)–1(a).

[64] Prior to 2018, business and investment *personalty* also qualified for like-kind exchange treatment. Personalty includes machines, equipment, furniture and fixtures, trucks, and automobiles.

Business and investment personal property (i.e., non-real property), inventory, any property held for personal use, domestic property exchanged for foreign property, and partnership interests (both limited and general) do *not* qualify under the like-kind exchange rules. In addition, transactions involving financial instruments (e.g., stock, bonds, or a note) do *not* qualify for like-kind exchange treatment even though they are held for investment.

If a taxpayer exchanges like-kind property *solely* for like-kind property, gain or loss realized is not recognized (it is deferred), and the basis and holding period from the old property attaches (carries over) to the new property.[65]

During the current year, Andy exchanged 40 acres of unimproved land in Illinois (fair market value $200,000, basis $70,000) for 10 acres of unimproved land in California (fair market value $200,000).

Although Andy has a realized gain of $130,000 on this transaction ($200,000 amount realized − $70,000 basis), none of the gain is recognized; the transaction qualifies as a like-kind exchange. Andy's basis in the new property is $70,000. This carryover basis reflects the realized gain that is deferred ($200,000 California property fair market value − $130,000 gain deferred). The like-kind exchange rules acknowledge that Andy—after the exchange—would not have the wherewithal to pay tax if the realized gain were recognized.

If Andy were to sell the California property for its market value, he would have a realized and recognized gain of $130,000.

The nonrecognition provision for like-kind exchanges is *mandatory* rather than elective. A taxpayer who wants to recognize a realized gain or loss must structure the transaction in a way that fails the like-kind exchange requirements. For example, a taxpayer may want to avoid like-kind treatment so that a realized loss can be recognized, or a taxpayer might want to recognize a gain so that capital loss carryovers can be used. We discuss this more in the Tax Planning section of the chapter.

During the current year, Stephanie exchanged her rental condo in Vail, worth $250,000 (basis of $325,000), plus $80,000 of cash for a rental condo in Malibu worth $330,000. Although Stephanie has a realized loss of $75,000 on this transaction [$330,000 amount realized − ($325,000 basis + $80,000 cash)], none of the loss is recognized since the transaction qualifies as a like-kind exchange.

Stephanie would likely be better off for tax purposes by selling her Vail condo (and recognizing the loss) and then buying the Malibu property.

The like-kind exchange rules are applied independently to each taxpayer in the exchange; one taxpayer may qualify for like-kind treatment, and the other may not.

13-4a **Like-Kind Property**

The term *like-kind* is intended to be interpreted very broadly.[66] *Real property* (or realty) includes rental buildings, office and store buildings, manufacturing plants, warehouses, and land. It is immaterial whether realty is improved or unimproved. As a result, an exchange of unimproved land for an apartment house can involve like-kind property. Real property held primarily for sale (i.e., inventory) does *not* qualify as like-kind property.[67]

[65]Subject to certain exceptions, related parties can engage in tax-free like-kind exchanges, but a two-year holding period applies to both the relinquished property and the replacement property [§ 1031(f)].

[66]Reg. § 1.1031(a)–1(b).

[67]§ 1031(a)(2).

If the exchange transaction involves multiple business assets (e.g., a television station for another television station), the determination of whether the assets qualify as like-kind property are not made at the business level.[68] Instead, the underlying assets are evaluated, and only the real property that is part of the exchange would qualify for like-kind exchange treatment.

13-4b **Exchange Requirement**

The transaction must involve a direct *exchange* of property to qualify as a like-kind exchange. The sale of old property and the purchase of new property, even though like-kind, is not an exchange. However, if the two transactions are mutually dependent, the IRS may treat them as a like-kind exchange.[69]

Time Limitations

Like-kind exchanges of real estate can be complex. Further, it can be extremely difficult to coordinate a simultaneous transaction if the properties being exchanged are located in different counties or states. As a result, delayed (nonsimultaneous) exchanges can qualify, subject to time limits.

In a delayed like-kind exchange (often called a *Starker exchange*[70]), one party does not take immediate title to the new property because it has not yet been identified. The Code provides that the delayed swap—often made with the assistance of a qualified intermediary—will qualify as a like-kind exchange if the following requirements are satisfied (see Concept Summary 13.5):[71]

- *Identification period.* The new property must be identified within 45 days of the date when the old property was transferred to the qualified intermediary.
- *Exchange period.* The new property must be received:[72]
  - Within 180 days of the date when the old property was transferred to the qualified intermediary (usually a bank or broker), or
  - If *earlier*, by the due date (including extensions) for the tax return covering the year of the transfer.

Example 38

Phil owns a store in downtown Plano. Adjacent to his store is a commercial parking lot owned by Sally (fair market value of $175,000). Phil would like to acquire the parking lot, which would allow him to expand his store, but Sally does not want to sell the lot due to the large gain she would recognize (her basis in the lot is only $3,000).

Phil agrees to purchase any "like-kind" property worth $175,000 that is acceptable to Sally if Sally agrees to immediately transfer the parking lot to Phil. Sally agrees to the plan, and the commercial lot is transferred to Phil on October 1 of the current year.

Later that month, Sally identifies a townhouse worth $175,000 and directs Phil to buy it for her. Phil negotiates the sale, which closes on December 12, and transfers the property to Sally.

This is a like-kind exchange since the replacement property was identified within 45 days of the parking lot being transferred to Phil and the townhouse was transferred to Sally within 180 days of the original transfer date. In effect, Sally sold the parking lot to Phil for $175,000 and then reinvested the proceeds in another piece of real estate without having to pay tax on the realized gain. Her basis in the townhouse ($3,000) reflects the realized gain that is deferred.

[68]Reg. § 1.1031(j)–1.

[69]Rev.Rul. 61–119.

[70]*T.J. Starker v. U.S.*, 79–2 USTC ¶9541, 44 AFTR 2d 79–5525, 602 F.2d 1341 (CA–9). This decision first allowed deferred like-kind exchanges.

[71]§ 1031(a)(3).

[72]In general, the IRS allows *no deviation* from either the identification period or the exchange period even when events outside the taxpayer's control preclude strict compliance. However, see Rev.Proc. 2010–14; here, the IRS allowed an exception where the qualified intermediary defaulted due to bankruptcy.

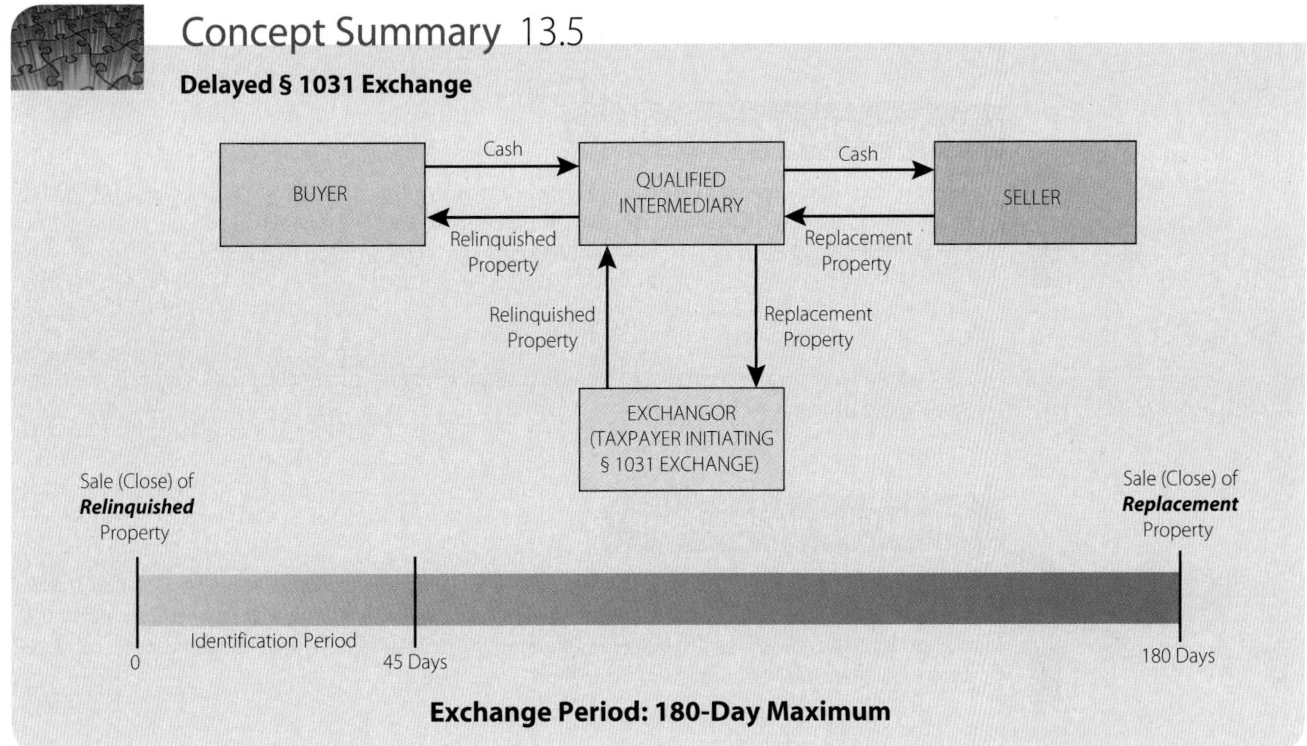

13-4c Boot

It is unusual to find like-kind transactions where the value of the property given up is exactly equal to the value of the property received. In most situations, one party normally provides some other property (e.g., cash) to "even out" the exchange. When a taxpayer in a like-kind exchange gives or receives some property that is *not* like-kind property, gain or loss recognition may occur. Property that is not like-kind, including cash, is referred to as **boot**. Although the term *boot* does not appear in the Code, tax practitioners commonly use it rather than saying "property that is not like-kind property."

The *receipt* of boot will trigger recognition of gain if there is realized gain. The amount of the recognized gain is the *lesser* of the boot received or the realized gain. If a taxpayer recognizes gain in a like-kind exchange, the character of the gain depends on the character of the asset given up (and depreciation recapture rules can apply; see text Section 14-10).

Implications of Boot Received

Emily and Fran exchange land, and the exchange qualifies as like kind. Because Emily's land (adjusted basis of $20,000) is worth $24,000 and Fran's land has a fair market value of $19,000, Fran also gives Emily cash of $5,000.

Emily's recognized gain is $4,000, the lesser of the realized gain ($24,000 amount realized − $20,000 adjusted basis) or the fair market value of the boot received ($5,000).

Assume the same facts as in the previous example, except that Fran's land is worth $21,000 (not $19,000). Under these circumstances, Fran gives Emily cash of $3,000 to make up the difference.

Emily's recognized gain is $3,000, the lesser of the realized gain of $4,000 ($24,000 amount realized − $20,000 adjusted basis) or the fair market value of the boot received of $3,000.

The receipt of boot does not result in recognition if there is realized loss.

Implications of Boot Received

Example 41

Assume the same facts as in Example 39, except that the adjusted basis of Emily's land is $30,000.

Emily's realized loss is $6,000 ($24,000 amount realized − $30,000 adjusted basis). The receipt of the boot of $5,000 does not trigger loss recognition; the recognized loss is $0.

The *giving* of boot usually does not trigger recognition. If the boot given is cash, no realized gain or loss is recognized.

Implications of Boot Given

Example 42

Sarah and Trevon exchange land in a like-kind exchange. Sarah receives land with a fair market value of $75,000 and transfers land worth $63,000 (adjusted basis of $45,000) and cash of $12,000.

Sarah's realized gain is $18,000 ($75,000 amount realized − $45,000 adjusted basis − $12,000 cash). However, none of Sarah's realized gain is recognized.

If, however, the boot given is appreciated or depreciated property, gain or loss is recognized to the extent of the difference between the adjusted basis and the fair market value of the boot. For this purpose, *appreciated or depreciated property* is defined as property whose adjusted basis is not equal to the fair market value.

Implications of Boot Given

Example 43

Assume the same facts as in the previous example, except that Sarah transfers land worth $30,000 (adjusted basis of $36,000) and boot worth $45,000 (adjusted basis of $27,000). Sarah's net gain on this exchange is $12,000 [$75,000 amount realized − adjusted basis of $63,000 ($36,000 + $27,000)]. But she is transferring two pieces of property: land (like-kind property) with a built-in realized loss of $6,000 ($30,000 fair market value − $36,000 adjusted basis) and non-like-kind property (boot) with a built-in realized gain of $18,000 ($45,000 fair market value − $27,000 adjusted basis).

In this case, the $6,000 realized loss on the like-kind property is *deferred* (not recognized) and the $18,000 realized gain on the non-like-kind property is recognized. In other words, the realized loss on the like-kind property *cannot* be used to offset the realized gain on the boot given up as part of the transaction.

13-4d **Basis and Holding Period of Property Received**

The basis of property received in a like-kind exchange must be adjusted to reflect any postponed (deferred) gain or loss. The basis of *like-kind property* received in the exchange is the property's fair market value less postponed gain or plus postponed loss (this is often referred to as the "simplified method"). The basis of any *boot* received is the boot's fair market value.

Basis of Like-Kind Property Received

Jaime exchanges a building (used in his business) with an adjusted basis of $430,000 and a fair market value of $438,000 for land with a fair market value of $438,000. The exchange qualifies as like kind (an exchange of business real property for investment real property) and the $8,000 realized gain is deferred.

The basis of the land is $430,000 (land's fair market value of $438,000 − $8,000 postponed gain on the building). If the land later is sold for its fair market value of $438,000, the $8,000 postponed gain is recognized.

Example 45

Assume the same facts as in the previous example, except that the building has an adjusted basis of $480,000 and a fair market value of only $380,000. Jaime receives land with a fair market value of $380,000, and the $100,000 realized loss is deferred.

The basis in the newly acquired land is $480,000 (fair market value of $380,000 + $100,000 postponed loss on the building). If the land later is sold for its fair market value of $380,000, the $100,000 postponed loss is recognized.

One may use an alternative approach to determine the basis of like-kind property received.

  Adjusted basis of like-kind property surrendered
+ Adjusted basis of boot given
+ Gain recognized
− Fair market value of boot received
− Loss recognized
= *Basis of like-kind property received*

This approach is logical in terms of the recovery of capital doctrine: the unrecovered cost or other basis is increased by additional cost (boot given) or decreased by cost recovered (boot received). Any gain recognized is included in the basis of the new property. The taxpayer has been taxed on this amount and now is entitled to recover it tax-free. Any loss recognized is deducted from the basis of the new property because the taxpayer has received a tax benefit on that amount.

The holding period of the property surrendered in the exchange carries over and *tacks on* to the holding period of the like-kind property received.[73] The holding period for boot received in a like-kind exchange begins with the date of the exchange. See text Section 14-4 for a discussion of the relevance of the holding period.

Depreciation recapture potential carries over to the property received in a like-kind exchange.[74] See text Section 14-11 for a discussion of this topic.

Like-Kind Exchanges: Comprehensive Examples

Example 46

Vicki exchanged a building used in her business for a parcel of unimproved land on which she plans to construct a new building. Her building has a fair market value of $1,200,000 and an adjusted basis of $400,000. The land she acquires has a fair market value of $900,000, and she will receive cash of $300,000 as part of the exchange. What is Vicki's realized and recognized gain or loss, and what is her basis in the land she receives (using both the simplified and alternative methods)?

continued

[73] § 1223(1) and Reg. § 1.1223–1(a). The like-kind property surrendered must have been either a capital asset or § 1231 property.

[74] Reg. §§ 1.1245–2(a)(4) and 1.1250–2(d)(1).

Realized Gain (Loss)		
	Amount realized ($900,000 + $300,000)	$1,200,000
–	Adjusted basis of building	(400,000)
=	Realized gain	$ 800,000
Boot Received		
	Cash	$ 300,000
Recognized Gain		
	Lesser of realized gain or boot received	$ 300,000
Basis of New Land (Simplified Method)		
	Fair market value of property received	$ 900,000
–	Postponed gain ($800,000 – $300,000)	(500,000)
=	Basis of like-kind property received	$ 400,000
Basis of New Land (Alternative Method)		
	Adjusted basis of property given up	$ 400,000
+	Adjusted basis of boot given	–0–
+	Gain recognized	300,000
–	Fair market value of boot received	(300,000)
–	Loss recognized	–0–
=	Basis of like-kind property received	$ 400,000

Example 47

Assume the same facts as Example 46, except that Vicki's building has a fair market value of $300,000 and she provides $600,000 cash to the seller as part of the exchange.

Realized Gain (Loss)		
	Amount realized (FMV of new land)	$ 900,000
–	Adjusted basis ($400,000 building + $600,000 cash)	(1,000,000)
=	Realized loss	($ 100,000)
Boot Received		$ –0–
Recognized Loss		$ –0–
Basis of New Land (Simplified Method)		
	Fair market value of property received	$ 900,000
+	Postponed loss	100,000
=	Basis of like-kind property received	$ 1,000,000
Basis of New Land (Alternative Method)		
	Adjusted basis of property given up	$ 400,000
+	Adjusted basis of boot given	600,000
+	Gain recognized	–0–
–	Fair market value of boot received	–0–
–	Loss recognized	–0–
=	Basis of like-kind property received	$ 1,000,000

If the taxpayer assumes a liability (or takes property subject to a liability) in the exchange, the amount of the liability is treated as boot given. For the taxpayer whose liability is assumed (or whose property is taken subject to the liability), the amount of the liability is treated as boot received.

Example 48

Jill Rodriguez and Rick Thompson exchange real estate investments. Jill gives up property with an adjusted basis of $250,000 (fair market value of $420,000) that is subject to a mortgage of $80,000 (assumed by Rick). In return for this property, Jill receives property with a fair market value of $340,000 (Rick's adjusted basis in the property is $200,000). Jill's and Rick's realized and recognized gains and their basis in the like-kind property received are computed as follows:[75]

		Jill	Rick
Compute Realized Gain (Loss)			
	FMV of like-kind property received	$ 340,000	$ 420,000
+	FMV of other property received		
+	Cash received		
+	Debt relief	80,000	
−	Cash paid		
−	Debt assumed		(80,000)
=	Net consideration received	$ 420,000	$ 340,000
−	Adjusted basis of property given	(250,000)	(200,000)
=	Realized gain (loss)	$ 170,000	$ 140,000
Compute Boot Received			
	Debt relief	$ 80,000	$ –0–
+	Cash received		–0–
+	FMV of other property received		
=	Boot received	$ 80,000	$ –0–
Compute Recognized Gain			
Lesser of realized gain or boot received		$ 80,000	$ –0–
Compute Basis for New Property (Other Than Cash)			
	Adjusted basis of property given	$ 250,000	$ 200,000
+	Boot given (cash paid, debt assumed)	–0–	80,000
+	Gain recognized	80,000	–0–
−	Boot received	(80,000)	–0–
=	Basis of new property	$ 250,000	$ 280,000

13-4e **Reporting Considerations**

Code § 1031 transactions are reported on Form 8824 (Like-Kind Exchanges). Part III of Form 8824 is shown below based on the information provided for Jill Rodriguez's exchange (Example 48).

This form must be filed even if the like-kind exchange transaction results in no recognized gain or loss. It is filed with the regular return for the tax year when the like-kind exchange occurs.

13-5 **Involuntary Conversions—§ 1033**

Explain the nonrecognition provisions available on the involuntary conversion of property.

In most cases, taxpayers sell property (or exchange it) when they need to do so. There are times, however, when the taxpayer *involuntarily* (i.e., outside the taxpayer's control) disposes of property. When this happens, the taxpayer usually receives some sort of compensation (e.g., insurance proceeds or a condemnation award). Code § 1033 provides that a taxpayer who experiences an involuntary conversion of property may postpone recognition of *gain* realized from the conversion. As a result, this provision provides relief to a taxpayer who has experienced an involuntary conversion and does not have the *wherewithal to pay* the tax on any gain realized as a result of the conversion.

[75]Example (2) of Reg. § 1.1031(d)–2 illustrates a special situation where both the buyer and the seller transfer liabilities that are assumed by the other party (or both parties acquire property that is subject to a liability).

Form 8824 (2022) Page **2**

Name(s) shown on tax return. Do not enter name and social security number if shown on other side.	Your social security number
Jill Rodriguez (Example 48)	

Part III Realized Gain or (Loss), Recognized Gain, and Basis of Like-Kind Property Received

Caution: If you transferred **and** received (**a**) more than one group of like-kind properties, or (**b**) cash or other (not like-kind) property, see ***Reporting of multi-asset exchanges*** in the instructions.

Note: Complete lines 12 through 14 **only** if you gave up property that was not like-kind. Otherwise, go to line 15.

Line	Description			Line	Amount
12	Fair market value (FMV) of other property given up. See instructions	12			
13	Adjusted basis of other property given up	13			
14	Gain or (loss) recognized on other property given up. Subtract line 13 from line 12. Report the gain or (loss) in the same manner as if the exchange had been a sale			14	
	Caution: If the property given up was used previously or partly as a home, see ***Property used as home*** in the instructions.				
15	Cash received, FMV of other property received, plus net liabilities assumed by other party, reduced (but not below zero) by any exchange expenses you incurred. See instructions			15	80,000
16	FMV of like-kind property you received			16	340,000
17	Add lines 15 and 16			17	420,000
18	Adjusted basis of like-kind property you gave up, net amounts paid to other party, plus any exchange expenses **not** used on line 15. See instructions			18	250,000
19	**Realized gain or (loss).** Subtract line 18 from line 17			19	170,000
20	Enter the smaller of line 15 or line 19, but not less than zero			20	80,000
21	Ordinary income under recapture rules. Enter here and on Form 4797, line 16. See instructions			21	0
22	Subtract line 21 from line 20. If zero or less, enter -0-. If more than zero, enter here and on Schedule D or Form 4797, unless the installment method applies. See instructions			22	80,000
23	**Recognized gain.** Add lines 21 and 22			23	80,000
24	Deferred gain or (loss). Subtract line 23 from line 19. If a related party exchange, see instructions			24	90,000
25	**Basis of like-kind property received.** Subtract line 15 from the sum of lines 18 and 23. See instructions			25	250,000

Realized gain is postponed to the extent the taxpayer *reinvests* the amount realized (e.g., insurance proceeds) in replacement property. The rules for nonrecognition of gain are as follows:

- If the amount reinvested in replacement property *equals or exceeds* the amount realized, realized gain is *not recognized.*
- If the amount reinvested in replacement property is *less than* the amount realized, realized gain *is recognized* to the extent of the deficiency.

Involuntary Conversions: General Rules

Example 49

Jason operates a charter fishing business in Panama City, Florida, taking customers out in the Gulf of Mexico on daylong fishing trips. Unfortunately, his boat was completely destroyed when Hurricane Bonnie hit the Florida coast. His boat had a basis of $78,000 ($120,000 cost − $42,000 of accumulated depreciation). Fortunately, Jason had marine insurance (which included a replacement cost rider). He filed an insurance claim shortly after his boat was destroyed and received $175,000 in insurance proceeds three weeks later.

Jason has a realized gain of $97,000, computed as follows:

Amount realized (insurance proceeds)	$175,000
Less: Adjusted basis	(78,000)
Realized gain	$ 97,000

Jason can defer the entire realized gain, provided that he uses all of the insurance proceeds to purchase a new boat.

Example 50

Refer to the facts of Example 49, and assume that Jason buys a new boat for $180,000. He uses the entire insurance settlement as part of the purchase.

In this case, Jason's $97,000 realized gain is deferred, and the basis of his new boat must reflect that deferral. As a result, his new boat's basis is $83,000 ($180,000 cost − $97,000 deferred gain).

Involuntary Conversions: General Rules

Continuing with the facts of Example 49, assume that Jason is able to negotiate an excellent price for his new boat. In fact, he is able to replace his old boat for only $168,000 and uses the $7,000 remaining from the insurance settlement to pay for other business expenses.

Jason recognizes a gain of $7,000, the difference between the $175,000 insurance settlement and the amount he paid for the new boat ($168,000; the amount of the insurance proceeds he reinvested in replacement property).

The balance of the realized gain is deferred, and the basis of his new boat must reflect that deferral. As a result, his new boat's basis is $78,000 ($168,000 cost − $90,000 deferred gain).

If an involuntary conversion results in a *loss*, § 1033 does not change the normal loss recognition rules. If a realized loss would otherwise be recognized, § 1033 does not change the result.

Refer to the facts of Example 49, but assume that Jason had only partial coverage on his boat and his insurance settlement is only $50,000. In this case, Jason has a loss of $28,000, computed as follows:

Amount realized (insurance proceeds)	$ 50,000
Less: Adjusted basis	(78,000)
Realized loss	($ 28,000)

No tax deferral applies; Jason's realized loss of $28,000 is recognized.

13-5a Involuntary Conversion Defined

An **involuntary conversion** results from the destruction (complete or partial), theft, seizure, condemnation, or sale or exchange under threat of condemnation (e.g., a city seizing property under its right of eminent domain) of the taxpayer's property.[76] A voluntary act (e.g., a taxpayer destroying the property by arson) is *not* an involuntary conversion.[77]

Government seizures are unique events, and as a result, a unique set of rules has developed. In general, the government entity must have made a decision to acquire the property for public use and the taxpayer must have reasonable grounds to believe the property will be taken.[78]

13-5b Computing the Amount Realized

The amount realized from an involuntary conversion typically includes any insurance proceeds received. In the case of the condemnation of property, the amount realized usually includes only the amount received as compensation for the property.[79]

Any amount received that is designated as severance damages by both the government and the taxpayer is *not* included in the amount realized. *Severance awards* usually occur when only a portion of the property is condemned (e.g., a strip of land is taken to build a highway). Severance damages are awarded because the value of the taxpayer's remaining property has declined as a result of the condemnation. In general, severance damages are a tax-free recovery of capital and reduce the basis of the property.

[76] § 1033(a) and Reg. §§ 1.1033(a)–1(a) and –2(a).

[77] Rev.Rul. 82–74.

[78] Rev.Rul. 63–221 and *Joseph P. Balistrieri*, 38 TCM 526, T.C.Memo. 1979–115.

[79] *Pioneer Real Estate Co.*, 47 B.T.A. 886 (1942), *acq.* 1943 C.B. 18.

The government condemns a portion of Ron's farmland to upgrade a highway for driverless vehicles. Because the project denies his cattle access to a pond and some grazing land, Ron receives severance damages in addition to the condemnation proceeds for the land taken.

Ron must reduce the basis of the property by the amount of the severance damages. If the amount of the severance damages received exceeds the adjusted basis, Ron recognizes gain.

13-5c **Replacement Property**

The requirements for replacement property generally are more restrictive than those for like-kind property. The basic requirement is that the replacement property be *similar or related in service or use* to the involuntarily converted property.[80]

Different interpretations of the phrase *similar or related in service or use* apply depending on whether the involuntarily converted property is held by an *owner-user* (e.g., in a business or by an individual) or by an *owner-investor* (e.g., lessor). For an owner-investor, the *taxpayer use test* applies, and for an owner-user, the *functional use test* applies. In most cases, the functional use test is more restrictive than the taxpayer use test. In addition, a special rule applies in the case of involuntary conversions that result from condemnations.

Taxpayer Use Test

The taxpayer use test for owner-investors provides much more flexibility in terms of what qualifies as replacement property. Essentially, the properties must be used by the owner-investor in similar endeavors. For example, rental property held by an owner-investor qualifies if replaced with other rental property, regardless of the type of rental property involved. For example, the test is met if the owner-investor of a building being rented to a manufacturing business replaces the facility with a building rented to a business using the facility as a grocery warehouse.[81] The replacement of a rental residence with a personal residence does *not* meet the test.[82]

Functional Use Test

The functional use test applies to owner-users. Under this test, the taxpayer's use of the replacement property and of the involuntarily converted property must be the same. A manufacturer whose manufacturing plant is destroyed by fire must replace the plant with another facility of similar functional use. Replacing a manufacturing plant with an office building (both used in the same business) does *not* meet this test. The manufacturing plant would have to be replaced with another manufacturing plant. Replacing a rental residence with a personal residence also does not pass the test.

Special Rule for Condemnations

If business real property or investment real property is *condemned*, the broader replacement rules for like-kind exchanges can be used instead of the narrower involuntary conversion replacement rules. This gives the taxpayer substantially more flexibility in selecting replacement property. For example, improved real property can be replaced with unimproved real property.

---

[80] § 1033(a) and Reg. § 1.1033(a)–1.

[81] *Loco Realty Co. v. Comm.*, 62–2 USTC ¶9657, 10 AFTR 2d 5359, 306 F.2d 207 (CA–8).

[82] Rev.Rul. 70–466.

The rules concerning the nature of replacement property relative to involuntary conversions are illustrated in Concept Summary 13.6.

Concept Summary 13.6

Involuntary Conversions: Replacement Property Tests

Type of Property and User	Taxpayer Use Test	Functional Use Test	Special Rule for Condemnations*
An investor's rented shopping mall is destroyed by fire; the mall may be replaced with other rental properties (e.g., an apartment building).	X		
A manufacturing plant is destroyed by fire; replacement property must consist of another manufacturing plant that is functionally the same as the property converted.		X	
Personal residence of a taxpayer is condemned by a local government authority; replacement property must consist of another personal residence.		X	
Land used by a manufacturing company is condemned by a local government authority.			X
Apartment and land held by an investor are sold due to the threat or imminence of condemnation.			X

*For condemnation of real property held for use in a business or for investment, § 1033(g) allows the use of the like-kind standard in identifying replacement property.

13-5d **Time Limitation on Replacement**

In general, the taxpayer must acquire replacement property within a two-year period after the close of the taxable year in which gain is realized.[83] Typically, gain is realized when insurance proceeds or damages are received.

Example 54

Megan's warehouse is destroyed by fire on December 16, 2022. The adjusted basis is $325,000. Megan receives $400,000 from the insurance company on February 2, 2023. She is a calendar year and cash method taxpayer.

The latest date for replacement is December 31, 2025 (the end of the taxable year in which realized gain occurred plus two years). The critical date is not the date the involuntary conversion occurred, but rather the date of gain realization.

In the case of a condemnation of real property used in a trade or business or held for investment, a three-year period is used.

Example 55

Assume the same facts as in the previous example, except that Megan's warehouse is condemned. Megan receives notification of the future condemnation on November 1, 2022. The condemnation occurs on December 16, 2022, with the condemnation proceeds being received on February 2, 2023.

The latest date for replacement is December 31, 2026 (the end of the taxable year in which realized gain occurred plus three years).

The *earliest date* for replacement typically is the date the involuntary conversion occurs. However, if the property is condemned, it is possible to replace the condemned property before this date. In this case, the earliest date is the date of the threat of condemnation of the property. This rule allows the taxpayer to make an orderly replacement of the condemned property.

[83] §§ 1033(a)(2)(B) and (g)(4) and Reg. § 1.1033(a)–2(c)(3). The two-year period is extended to a four-year period if the property is located in a Federally declared disaster area. The taxpayer can apply for an extension of this time period anytime before its expiration [Reg. § 1.1033(a)–2(c)(3)]. The period for filing the application for extension also can be extended if the taxpayer shows reasonable cause for the delay.

Example 56

Assume the same facts as in Example 55. The earliest date that Megan can replace the warehouse is November 1, 2022, which is the date of an official notice regarding the condemnation of the warehouse.

13-5e **Nonrecognition of Gain**

Nonrecognition of gain can be either mandatory or elective, depending on whether the conversion is direct (into replacement property) or indirect (into money).

Direct Conversion

If the conversion is directly into replacement property rather than into money, nonrecognition of realized gain is *mandatory*. In this case, the basis of the replacement property is the same as the adjusted basis of the converted property. Direct conversion is rare in practice and usually involves condemnations.

Example 57

Lupe's property, with an adjusted basis of $20,000, is condemned by the state. Lupe receives property with a fair market value of $50,000 as compensation for the property taken.

Because the nonrecognition of realized gain is mandatory for direct conversions, Lupe's realized gain of $30,000 is not recognized and the basis of the replacement property is $20,000 (adjusted basis of the condemned property).

Conversion into Money

If the conversion is into money, the realized gain is recognized only to the extent the amount realized from the involuntary conversion exceeds the cost of the qualifying replacement property.[84] This is the usual case, and nonrecognition (postponement) is *elective*. If the election is not made, the realized gain is recognized.

The basis of the replacement property is the property's cost less any postponed (deferred) gain.[85] If the election to postpone gain is made, the holding period of the replacement property includes the holding period of the converted property.

Code § 1033 applies *only to gains* and *not to losses*. Losses from involuntary conversions are recognized if the property is held for business or income-producing purposes. Certain personal casualty losses are recognized (the limitations are discussed in text Section 7-3), but condemnation losses related to personal use assets (e.g., a personal residence) are neither recognized nor postponed.

The Big Picture

Example 58

Return to the facts of *The Big Picture* on p. 13-1. Alice's building (used in her trade or business), with an adjusted basis of $50,000, is destroyed by fire on October 5, 2023. Alice is a calendar year taxpayer. On November 17, 2023, she receives an insurance reimbursement of $100,000 for the loss. Alice invests $80,000 in a new building. Alice uses the other $20,000 of insurance proceeds to pay off credit card debt.

- Alice has until December 31, 2025, to make the new investment and qualify for the nonrecognition election.
- Alice's realized gain is $50,000 ($100,000 insurance proceeds received − $50,000 adjusted basis of old building).
- Assuming that the replacement property qualifies as similar or related in service or use, Alice's recognized gain is $20,000. Because she reinvested $20,000 less than the insurance proceeds received ($100,000 proceeds − $80,000 reinvested), her realized gain is recognized to that extent.
- Alice's basis in the new building is $50,000. This is the building's cost of $80,000 less the postponed gain of $30,000 (realized gain of $50,000 − recognized gain of $20,000).

[84] § 1033(a)(2)(A) and Reg. § 1.1033(a)–2(c)(1).

[85] § 1033(b).

The Big Picture

Return to the facts of *The Big Picture* on p. 13-1. Assume the same facts as in the previous example, except that Alice receives only $45,000 in insurance proceeds. She has a realized and recognized loss of $5,000. The basis of the new building is the building's cost of $80,000.

Example 59

If the destroyed building in Example 59 had been held for personal use, the recognized loss would have been subject to the casualty loss limitations.[86] Personal casualty losses are deductible only if they occur in a Federally declared disaster area. In that case, the loss of $5,000 would have been limited to the decline in fair market value of the property, and the amount of the loss would have been reduced first by $100 and then by 10 percent of adjusted gross income (see text Section 7-3d).

13-5f **Reporting Considerations**

In general, taxpayers are allowed to elect whether to defer any gain realized from an involuntary conversion. Normally, the election is made by not reporting any gain on the tax return. However, the tax return filed for the year of conversion must include detailed information related to the involuntary conversion.[87] This requirement usually is satisfied with a statement attached to the return detailing the involuntary conversion and the replacement property acquired.

What if the taxpayer intends to acquire qualifying replacement property but has not done so by the time the tax return is filed? The taxpayer should elect involuntary conversion treatment and report all the details of the transaction on a statement attached to the return. When the qualifying replacement property is acquired, the taxpayer attaches a statement to the later tax return that contains relevant information for the replacement property.

An amended return must be filed if qualified replacement property is not acquired during the replacement time period. An amended return also is required if the cost of the replacement property is less than the amount realized from the involuntary conversion. In this case, the return would recognize the portion of the realized gain that no longer can be deferred.

13-6 **Sale of a Residence—§ 121**

LO.8

Describe the provision for the permanent exclusion of gain on the sale of a personal residence.

A taxpayer's **personal residence** is a personal use asset. Therefore, a realized loss from the sale of a personal residence is not recognized.[88]

A realized gain from the sale of a personal residence is recognized. However, taxpayers meeting the **§ 121 exclusion** requirements are allowed to exclude up to $250,000 ($500,000 on certain joint returns) of realized gain on the sale of a principal residence.[89] Any gain in excess of this amount normally qualifies as a long-term capital gain (subject to preferential tax rates).

Tom and Eileen Atwood bought their home in 2014 for $525,000 and have used it as their principal residence since that time. In July 2023, they sell their home for $670,000. The Atwoods have a realized gain of $145,000 on the sale ($670,000 − $525,000), and the entire gain is excluded as a result of § 121.

What if the Atwoods sold their home for $500,000? In this case, since their home is a personal use asset, they would have a $25,000 realized loss that would not be recognized.

Example 60

[86] § 165(c)(3) and Reg. § 1.165–7.

[87] Reg. § 1.1033(a)–2(c)(2).

[88] § 165(c).

[89] § 121(b).

13-6a Principal Residence

Whether property is the taxpayer's principal residence "depends upon all of the facts and circumstances in each case." According to the Regulations, the most important factor is where the taxpayer spends most of his or her time.[90] A residence does not have to be a house. For example, a houseboat, a house trailer, or a motor home can qualify.[91] The principal residence includes the land on which a home sits (so any gain on the land also qualifies for exclusion). An adjacent lot can qualify if it is regularly used by the owner as part of the residential property.

Mitch graduates from college and moves to Boston, where he is employed. He decides to rent an apartment in Boston because of its proximity to his office. He purchases a beach condo in the Cape Cod area that he occupies most weekends. Mitch does not intend to live at the beach condo except on weekends. The apartment in Boston is his principal residence.

13-6b Requirements for Exclusion Treatment

To qualify for exclusion treatment, at the date of the sale, the residence must have been *owned* and *used* by the taxpayer as the principal residence for at least two years during the five-year period ending on the date of the sale of a taxpayer's principal residence.[92]

Melissa sells her principal residence on September 18, 2023. She had purchased it on July 5, 2021, and lived in it since then. The sale of Melissa's residence qualifies for the § 121 exclusion.

The ownership and use requirements are *two separate tests*. Although in most situations ownership and use overlap (as in Example 62), there is no requirement that they do so for purposes of § 121. Further, the law does not require that the two-year periods be continuous.[93]

Ownership and Use Tests

Kayla purchased a home in San Diego in May 2008 and lived in it until she took a new job in Los Angeles on January 1, 2019. From January 2019 until she sold the house on July 31, 2023, she only used the home occasionally since she lived in an apartment near her job in downtown Los Angeles. Because the house was sold on July 31, 2023, the five-year window runs from August 1, 2018, to the date of sale.

In determining whether the § 121 exclusion is available, Kayla meets the ownership test because she owned the house for two of the five years prior to its sale. However, she fails the use test. During the five-year window, she used the house as her principal residence for only five months (from August 1, 2018, to December 31, 2018).

[90] Other factors include the address listed on a driver's license and/or voter registration card, the location of the taxpayer's employer and/or bank, and the mailing address used for bills and correspondence. See Reg. § 1.121–1(b)(2).

[91] Reg. § 1.121–1(b)(1); Reg. § 1.1034–1(c)(3)(i).

[92] § 121(a). Code § 121(d)(10) provides that exclusion treatment does not apply if the residence was acquired in a like-kind exchange within the prior five years of the sale of the residence.

[93] According to Reg. § 1.121–1(c)(1), taxpayers must document 730 days (365 × 2) of ownership and use during the five-year period that ends on the sale date.

Ownership and Use Tests

Charles lives in a townhouse that he rents from 2016 through January 17, 2020. On January 18, 2020, he purchases the townhouse. On February 1, 2021, due to a decline in health, Charles moves into his daughter's home. On May 25, 2023, while still living in his daughter's home, Charles sells his townhouse.

The § 121 exclusion applies because Charles *owned* the townhouse for at least two years out of the five years preceding the sale (from January 19, 2020, until May 25, 2023)[94] and he *used* the townhouse as his principal residence for at least two years during the five-year period preceding the sale [from May 25, 2018 (the beginning of the five-year window) until February 1, 2021].

Aaron has owned and used his house as his principal residence since 2006. On January 31, 2020, Aaron moves to another state. Aaron rents his house to tenants from that date until April 18, 2022, when he sells it.

Aaron is eligible for the § 121 exclusion because he has owned and used the house as his principal residence for at least two of the five years preceding the sale.

The five-year window enables the taxpayer to qualify for the § 121 exclusion even though the property is not his or her principal residence at the date of the sale. In applying the use test, short absences (i.e., vacation or other seasonal absence) are counted as periods of use.[95]

Benjamin sells his former principal residence on August 16, 2023. He had purchased it on April 1, 2015, and lived in it until July 1, 2022, when he converted it to rental property.

Even though the property is rental property on August 16, 2023, rather than Benjamin's principal residence, the sale qualifies for the § 121 exclusion.[96] During the five-year period from August 16, 2018, to August 16, 2023, Benjamin owned and used the property as his principal residence for at least two years.

In addition to the ownership and use requirements, § 121 can be used by a taxpayer only once every two years.[97] This rule restricts taxpayers who might be tempted to make liberal use of the § 121 exclusion as a means of speculating when the price of residential housing is rising. Without any time restriction on its use, § 121 would permit the exclusion of realized gain on multiple sales of principal residences.

Miguel sells his principal residence (the first residence) in June 2022 for $150,000 (realized gain of $60,000). He then buys and sells the following (all of which qualify as principal residences):

	Date of Purchase	Date of Sale	Purchase/ Sales Price
Second residence	July 2022		$160,000
Second residence		April 2023	180,000
Third residence	May 2023		200,000

Because multiple sales have taken place within a period of two years, § 121 does not apply to the sale of the second residence. As a result, Miguel's realized gain of $20,000 [$180,000 (selling price) − $160,000 (purchase price)] must be recognized.

[94]As discussed in text Section 14-4a, the holding period begins the day after acquisition date and includes the disposition date.

[95]Reg. § 1.121–1(c)(2)(i).

[96]However, any realized gain on the sale that is attributable to depreciation is not eligible for the § 121 exclusion. See Example 74.

[97]Code § 121(b)(3) denies the application of the § 121 exclusion to sales occurring within two years of its last use.

13-6c Calculating the Exclusion

General Rule

The § 121 exclusion available on the sale of a principal residence is $250,000.[98] If the realized gain does not exceed $250,000, there is no recognized gain.

Realized gain is calculated in the normal manner. The *amount realized* is the selling price less any selling expenses (e.g., real estate broker commissions, advertising expenses, and legal fees). Repairs and maintenance costs to aid in selling the property are personal expenses and not deductible (and they do not increase the home's basis).

The § 121 Exclusion Amount

Example 68

Mandy, who is single, sells her personal residence (adjusted basis of $130,000) for $290,000. She has owned and lived in the residence for three years. Her selling expenses are $18,000. Three weeks prior to the sale, Mandy paid a carpenter and a painter $1,000 to make some repairs and paint two rooms. Her recognized gain is $0.

Amount realized ($290,000 – $18,000)	$ 272,000
Adjusted basis	(130,000)
Realized gain	$ 142,000
§ 121 exclusion	(142,000)
Recognized gain	$ -0-

Since the available § 121 exclusion of $250,000 exceeds Mandy's realized gain of $142,000, her recognized gain is $0.

Assume the same facts as in the previous example, but the selling price is $490,000. Since the realized gain of $342,000 exceeds the § 121 exclusion amount of $250,000, Mandy's recognized gain is $92,000 ($342,000 – $250,000).

Amount realized ($490,000 – $18,000)	$ 472,000
Adjusted basis	(130,000)
Realized gain	$ 342,000
§ 121 exclusion	(250,000)
Recognized gain	$ 92,000

Married Couples

If a married couple files a joint return, the $250,000 amount is increased to $500,000 if the following requirements are met:[99]

- Either spouse meets the at-least-two-years *ownership* requirement.
- Both spouses meet the at-least-two-years *use* requirement.
- Neither spouse sold a principal residence within the prior two years and used the § 121 exclusion.

A surviving spouse can use the $500,000 exclusion amount on the sale of a personal residence for the two years following the year of the deceased spouse's death. If the sale occurs in the year of death, a joint return must be filed by the surviving spouse.

[98] § 121(b)(1).

[99] § 121(b)(2).

Example 70

Margaret sells her personal residence (adjusted basis of $150,000) for $650,000. She has owned and lived in the residence for six years. Her selling expenses are $40,000. Margaret is married to Ted, and they file a joint return. Ted has lived in the residence since they were married two and one-half years ago.

Amount realized ($650,000 – $40,000)	$ 610,000
Adjusted basis	(150,000)
Realized gain	$ 460,000
§ 121 exclusion	(460,000)
Recognized gain	$ -0-

Because the realized gain of $460,000 is less than the available § 121 exclusion amount of $500,000, no gain is recognized.

13-6d **Exceptions to the Two-Year Rules**

The two-year ownership and use requirements and the "only once every two years" rule could create a hardship for taxpayers in certain situations that are beyond their control. As a result, under the following special circumstances, the requirements are waived.[100]

- Change in place of employment,
- Health issues, or
- Other unforeseen circumstances.

Treasury Department guidance on these three exceptions is discussed in the sections that follow.[101] Each of these exceptions provides a *partial* exclusion. The calculation of the partial exclusion is discussed after each of the exceptions is reviewed.

Change in Place of Employment

For this exception to apply, the taxpayer measures the distance (in miles) between (1) the taxpayer's *old residence* and *old job location* and (2) the taxpayer's *old residence* and *new job location*. The exception applies if (2) exceeds (1) by at least 50 miles. The location of the new residence does not matter for this purpose.

In addition, the house being sold must be used as the principal residence of the taxpayer when the employment change happens. The exception applies whether the taxpayer takes a job with a new employer; is transferred by the current employer; or, if self-employed, moves the proprietorship to a new location.

Assume the same facts as in Example 67, except that in March 2023, Mike's employer transfers him to a job in another state that is 400 miles away.

As a result, the sale of the second residence and the purchase of the third residence were due to relocation of employment. Consequently, the § 121 exclusion is partially available on the sale of the second residence.

Health Issues

The health exception uses either a general facts and circumstances approach or a safe harbor established in the Regulations. If a physician recommends a change of location due to health issues (or to obtain specialized care), the safe harbor is met. A sale that is merely beneficial to the general health or well-being of the individual will not qualify.

[100] § 121(c)(2)(B).

[101] See Reg. § 1.121–3 and IRS Publication 523 (*Selling Your Home*) for further details and illustrations.

Unforeseen Circumstances

For unforeseen circumstances, the primary reason for the sale or exchange of the residence must be an event the taxpayer did not anticipate before purchasing and occupying the residence. The Regulations allow a safe harbor approval in any of the following instances:

- Involuntary conversion of the residence.
- Natural or human-made disasters or acts of war or terrorism resulting in a casualty to the residence.
- Death of a qualified individual.
- Cessation of employment resulting in eligibility for unemployment compensation.
- Change in employment or self-employment that results in the taxpayer being unable to pay housing costs and reasonable basic living expenses for the taxpayer's household.
- Divorce or legal separation.
- Multiple births resulting from the same pregnancy.

If none of the above instances apply, the taxpayer can claim that the general facts and circumstances justify the exception. The IRS has ruled that the following circumstances qualify as "unforseen":

- Additional dependents (including an adult child moving back in with parents, an elderly or disabled parent moving in, the creation of a large blended family, the need for a larger home to facilitate an adoption, and the arrival of an additional child without the necessary bedroom space).
- Environmental factors (including an increase in crime in the neighborhood and aircraft noise).
- Job-related circumstances (including a police officer who became a K–9 officer needing to care for and kennel his dog and a narcotics investigator who was threatened by associates of a drug dealer he had arrested).

Maria and Raji are engaged and buy a house (sharing the mortgage payments) and live in it as their personal residence. Eighteen months after the purchase, they cancel their wedding plans, and Raji moves out of the house. Because Maria cannot afford to make the payments alone, they sell the house.

Although the sale does not fit under the safe harbor events, the broken engagement is an unforeseen event; it qualifies under the "facts and circumstances" provision.[102]

Partial § 121 Exclusion

When one of the exceptions applies, a partial § 121 exclusion is allowed. The exclusion amount ($250,000 or $500,000) is multiplied by a fraction, the numerator of which is the number of qualifying months and the denominator of which is 24 months. The resulting amount is the excluded gain.[103]

On October 1, 2022, Rich and Audrey, who file a joint return and live in Chicago, sell their personal residence, which they have owned and lived in for eight years. The realized gain of $325,000 is excluded under § 121. They purchase another personal residence for $525,000 on October 2, 2022. Audrey's employer transfers her to the Denver office in August 2023. Rich and Audrey sell their Chicago residence on August 2, 2023, and they purchase a residence in Denver shortly thereafter. The realized gain on the sale is $300,000.

The $325,000 gain on the first Chicago residence is excluded under § 121. The sale of the second Chicago residence is within the two-year window of the prior sale, but because it resulted from a change in employment, Rich and Audrey can qualify for partial exclusion treatment.

continued

[102] Reg. § 1.121–3(e)(4), Example (6).

[103] § 121(c)(1).

Realized gain	$ 300,000
§ 121 exclusion:	
$\frac{10 \text{ months}}{24 \text{ months}} \times \$500,000$	(208,333)
Recognized gain	$ 91,667

Basis of New Residence

Because § 121 is an exclusion provision (rather than a deferral of gain provision), the basis of a new residence is its cost.[104]

Implications of Renting or Using a Residence as a Home Office

The residence does not have to be the taxpayer's principal residence at the date of sale to qualify for the § 121 exclusion. During part of the five-year period, it could have been rental property (e.g., as a vacation home), or the taxpayer might have used part of the principal residence as a qualifying home office.

In either of these circumstances, the taxpayer may have claimed deductions for the expenses attributable to the rental or business use. What effect, if any, do such deductions have on a later sale of the residence? Will the sales proceeds still qualify for nonrecognition of gain treatment under § 121?

As long as the various § 121 requirements are met, an income exclusion will be available. However, if the taxpayer deducted depreciation, any realized gain is recognized to the extent of the depreciation deductions.[105]

On December 5, 2023, Amanda sells her principal residence, which qualifies for the § 121 exclusion. Her realized gain is $190,000. From January through November 2022, she was temporarily out of town on a job assignment in another city and rented the residence to a college student. For this period, she deducted MACRS cost recovery of $7,000.

Without the depreciation provision, Amanda could exclude the $190,000 realized gain. However, the depreciation taken requires her to recognize $7,000 of the realized gain.

13-7 Tax Planning

LO.9

Apply various tax planning opportunities related to selected property transactions.

13-7a Cost Identification and Documentation Considerations

When multiple assets are acquired in a single transaction, the contract price must be allocated for several reasons. First, some of the assets may be depreciable but others are not. Here, the buyer and the seller may have different tax perspectives that will need to be reconciled. The seller will likely prefer a high allocation for nondepreciable assets (see Chapter 14); the purchaser likely will prefer a high allocation for depreciable assets subject to cost recovery. Second, the seller must be able to characterize gains and losses appropriately as capital or ordinary. Allocating the price among the assets sold allows this to happen. For example, an allocation to goodwill or to a covenant not to compete (see Chapters 8 and 14) produces different tax consequences to the seller. Third, the buyer must identify the adjusted basis of each asset to be able to determine cost recovery, amortization, or depletion (if available), and to calculate the realized gain or loss if an asset is sold.

13-7b Selection of Property for Making Gifts

A donor can achieve several tax advantages by making gifts of appreciated property. The donor avoids income tax on the unrealized gain that would have occurred had the property been sold. And if the donee is in a lower tax bracket than the donor, there will be tax

[104] § 1012.

[105] § 121(d)(6).

savings if the property is sold. Any increase in value after the gift also is taxed at a lower rate. Such gifts of appreciated property can be an effective tool in family tax planning.

Taxpayers generally should not make gifts of property that has decreased in value; the donor does not receive an income tax deduction for the unrealized loss element. In addition, the donee receives no benefit from this unrealized loss upon the subsequent sale of the property because of the loss basis rule. If the donor anticipates that the donee will sell the property upon receiving it, the donor should sell the property and take any loss deduction. The donor can then give the proceeds from the sale to the donee.

13-7c Selection of Property to Pass at Death

A taxpayer generally should distribute appreciated property via his or her will. Doing so enables both the decedent and the heir to avoid income tax on the unrealized gain; the recipient takes a fair market value basis.

A taxpayer generally should not distribute property at death that, if sold, would produce a realized loss; the decedent does not receive an income tax deduction for the unrealized loss. In addition, the heir will receive no benefit from this unrealized loss upon the subsequent sale of the property.

On the date of her death, Marta owned land held for investment purposes. The land had a basis of $130,000 and a fair market value of $100,000. If Marta had sold the property before her death, the recognized loss would have been $30,000.

If instead, Roger inherits the property and later sells it for $90,000, the recognized loss is $10,000 (the decline in value since Marta's death). In addition, regardless of the period of time Roger holds the property, the holding period is long term.

From an income tax perspective, it is better to transfer appreciated property as an inheritance rather than as a gift. Why? Because inherited property receives a step-up in basis but property received by gift has a carryover basis to the donee. However, in making this decision, any nontax and estate tax effects of the inheritance should be weighed against the gift tax results.

13-7d Disallowed Losses

Taxpayers should avoid transactions that trigger the related-party loss disallowance rules. Even with the ability of the related-party buyer to offset their realized gain by the related-party seller's disallowed loss, several inequities exist. First, any tax benefit associated with the disallowed loss is shifted to the related-party buyer (the related-party seller receives no tax benefit). Second, the tax benefit of this offset is delayed until the related-party buyer sells the property. Third, if the property does not appreciate during the time period the related-party buyer holds it, part or all of the disallowed loss is permanently lost. Fourth, the right of offset is available only to the original transferee (the related-party buyer); use of the disallowed loss is eliminated permanently if the original transferee transfers the property by gift or inheritance.

Example 76

Tim sells property with an adjusted basis of $35,000 to Wes, his brother, for $25,000, the fair market value of the property. The $10,000 realized loss to Tim is disallowed by § 267.

If Wes subsequently sells the property to an unrelated party for $37,000, he records a recognized gain of $2,000 (realized gain of $12,000 reduced by disallowed loss of $10,000). As a result, from the perspective of the family unit, the original $10,000 realized loss ultimately is recognized.

However, if Wes sells the property for $29,000, he reports a recognized gain of $0 (realized gain of $4,000 reduced by disallowed loss of $4,000 necessary to offset the realized gain). From the perspective of the family unit, $6,000 of the realized loss of $10,000 is permanently lost ($10,000 realized loss − $4,000 offset permitted).

13-7e **Like-Kind Exchanges**

Because the like-kind exchange provisions are mandatory rather than elective, in certain instances, it may be preferable to avoid qualifying for § 1031 nonrecognition. For example, immediate recognition of gain (which also will result in a higher basis for the newly acquired asset) may be preferable if the taxpayer has unused capital loss carryovers. If so, the taxpayer can structure the transaction so that at least one of the § 1031 like-kind exchange requirements is not met.

Alicia sells land and a building (used in her business) with an adjusted basis of $300,000 for $400,000. She also acquires a new building and land for $900,000. Alicia has a $125,000 capital loss carryover.

If § 1031 applies, the $100,000 realized gain is not recognized and the basis of the new land and building is reduced by $100,000 (from $900,000 to $800,000). Assuming no other capital asset transactions, Alicia can deduct only $3,000 of her capital loss carryover.

If § 1031 does not apply, a $100,000 gain is recognized and can be used to offset her $125,000 capital loss carryover. In addition, the basis of the new land and building is $900,000 rather than $800,000 because the entire gain was recognized (allowing for a larger depreciation deduction on the new building).

The like-kind exchange rules also should be avoided when a realized loss exists (adjusted basis exceeds the fair market value).

Assume the same facts as in the previous example, except that the fair market value of the land and building is $250,000. If § 1031 applies, the $50,000 realized loss is not recognized.

To recognize the loss, Alicia should sell the old land and building and purchase the new one. The purchase and sale transactions should be with different taxpayers.

Tax planning for exchanges must consider the present value of tax deferrals and the possibility of future changes in tax rates. Taxpayers may prefer to pay no more than 20 percent today (the maximum tax rate on long-term capital gains) if they believe that tax rates will go up in the future. Although turning down a tax deferral may sound like a strange strategy, it fits the notion of "pay a tax today to avoid a higher tax tomorrow."

13-7f **Involuntary Conversions**

In certain cases, a taxpayer may prefer to recognize gain from an involuntary conversion. This is a possibility because involuntary conversion treatment generally is an elective provision.

Ahmad has a $40,000 realized gain from the involuntary conversion of an office building. He reinvests the entire proceeds of $450,000 in a new office building. He does not elect to postpone gain under § 1033, however, because a net operating loss carryforward offsets the gain.

Because Ahmad did not elect gain postponement, his basis in the replacement property is the property's cost of $450,000 rather than $410,000 ($450,000 reduced by the $40,000 realized gain).

13-7g Sale of a Principal Residence

Waiving the Exclusion

The § 121 exclusion automatically applies if the taxpayer is eligible (i.e., the taxpayer need not make an election). However, a taxpayer can waive the § 121 exclusion.[106]

George owns two personal residences that satisfy the two-year ownership and use test with respect to the five-year window. The Elm Street residence has appreciated by $25,000, and the Maple Street residence has appreciated by $230,000. He intends to sell both of them and move into a rental property. He sells the Elm Street residence in December 2023 and expects to sell the Maple Street residence early next year.

Unless George elects not to apply the § 121 exclusion to the sale of the Elm Street residence, he will exclude the $25,000 realized gain on that residence in 2023. In 2024, however, he recognizes a gain of $230,000 on the sale of the Maple Street residence.

If George elects to waive the exclusion on the Elm Street residence sale, he will report a recognized gain of $25,000 on this sale in 2023. But by using the § 121 exclusion in 2024, he will eliminate the recognized gain of $230,000 on the sale of the Maple Street residence.

Qualification for § 121 Exclusion

The key requirement for the § 121 exclusion is that the taxpayer must have *owned* and *used* the property as a principal residence for at least two years during the five-year window. As taxpayers advance in age, they frequently make decisions related to their personal residence(s).

- Sell the principal residence and buy a smaller residence or rent a principal residence.
- Sell vacation homes they own.
- Sell homes they are holding as rental property.

These properties may have experienced substantial appreciation while owned by the taxpayers. Proper planning can make it possible for multiple properties to qualify for the exclusion. Although this strategy may require taxpayers to be flexible about where they live, it can result in substantial tax savings.

Eleanor and David, residents of Virginia, are approaching retirement. They have substantial appreciation on their principal residence in Richmond and on a house they own in Virginia Beach (about two hours away). After retirement, they plan to move to Florida. They have owned and lived in the principal residence for 28 years and have owned the beach house for 9 years.

If they sell their principal residence, it qualifies for the § 121 exclusion. At retirement, they could move into their beach house for two years and make it eligible for the exclusion before they relocate to Florida.

If the beach house were close enough to things they needed to do in Richmond currently (e.g., charitable work), they could sell the principal residence now and move into the beach house to start the running of the two-year use period. As noted previously, any realized gain on the beach house attributable to depreciation is not eligible for the § 121 exclusion. In addition, a reduction in the § 121 exclusion for prior use as a vacation home is required.[107]

[106] § 121(f).

[107] Additional information and examples can be found in IRS Publication 523 (*Selling Your Home*).

Refocus on The Big Picture

Sale or Gift of Inherited House and Other Property Transactions

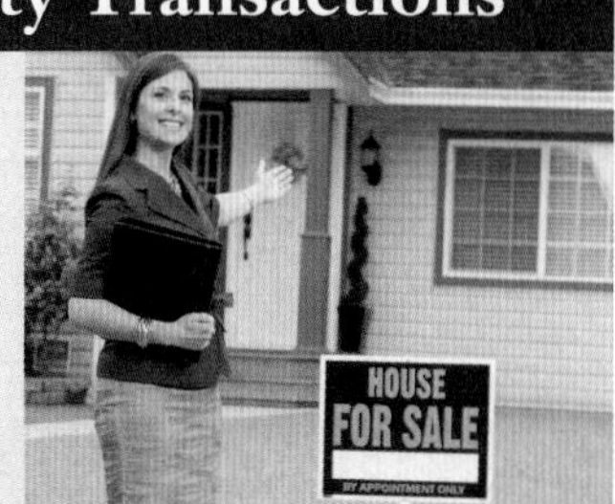

Gift of Inherited House

Based on an inquiry you made of Alice, this is the only gift she would make to Michael this year. She has made no prior gifts to any individual that exceeded the annual per donee exclusion amount (i.e., currently $15,000).

With this information, you inform Alice that no gift tax would be due on the gift of the house to Michael. However, she would use up $585,000 ($600,000 − $15,000) of her lifetime gift tax exemption of $12.06 million. Michael's basis for the house would be a carryover of Alice's basis of $475,000 (i.e., for inherited property, the fair market value at the date of the decedent's death).

Sale of Inherited House

You advise Alice that her adjusted basis for the house in calculating gain or loss on its sale is the $475,000 fair market value on the date of her grandmother's death. If Alice sells the house for $800,000, her projected selling expenses (i.e., real estate agent's commission, attorney's fees, other closing costs) would be $40,000 ($800,000 × 5%). She would have a recognized gain of $285,000 as calculated below. The house is a capital asset, and Alice's holding period is long term because she inherited the house. Thus, the gain would be classified as a long-term capital gain (i.e., subject to the 15 percent or 20 percent tax rate). So the Federal income tax due would be $42,750 ($285,000 × 15%) if the 15 percent rate applies.

Amount realized ($800,000 − $40,000)	$ 760,000
Less: Adjusted basis	(475,000)
Realized gain	$ 285,000
Recognized gain	$ 285,000

Other Issues

See Examples 12 and 13 for the tax consequences associated with Alice's questions regarding selling the boat. See Examples 30 and 31 for the tax consequences associated with Alice's questions regarding the wash sale of the stock.

See Examples 58 and 59 for Alice's tax consequences associated with the involuntary conversion.

What If?

Alice is leaning toward selling the house. However, she knows that her grandmother would not want her to have to pay income taxes on the sale. Alice inquires as to whether there is any way she could reduce the Federal income tax on the sale to $0.

You inform Alice of the exclusion provision under § 121 of the Code. She can qualify for this gain exclusion rule if she satisfies the at least two-out-of-five-years ownership and use requirements. This would necessitate her moving into the house for at least two years and occupying it as her principal residence.

From a tax planning perspective, what could Alice have done so that none of the $50,000 of realized gain in Example 58 from the involuntary conversion was recognized?

To have full postponement of the $50,000 realized gain, Alice would have to reinvest all of the $100,000 of insurance proceeds received in another qualifying building. Under this circumstance, the basis of a replacement building costing $100,000 would be a carryover basis of $50,000 ($100,000 cost − $50,000 deferred gain).

Key Terms

Adjusted basis, 13-5
Amount realized, 13-4
Boot, 13-25
Fair market value, 13-4
Goodwill, 13-10
Holding period, 13-13
Involuntary conversion, 13-31
Like-kind exchange, 13-22
Nontaxable exchange, 13-22
Personal residence, 13-35
Realized gain, 13-3
Realized loss, 13-3
Recognized gain, 13-8
Recognized loss, 13-8
Section 121 exclusion, 13-35
Wash sale, 13-16

Discussion Questions

Critical Thinking

1. **LO.1** Isabelle invests in land, and Grace invests in taxable bonds. The land appreciates by $8,000 each year, and the bonds earn interest of $8,000 each year. After holding the land and bonds for five years, Isabelle and Grace sell them. There is a $40,000 realized gain on the sale of the land and no realized gain or loss on the sale of the bonds. Are the tax consequences to Isabelle and Grace the same for each of the five years? Explain.

2. **LO.1, 2** Suki and Dave each purchase 100 shares of stock of Burgundy, Inc., a publicly owned corporation, in July for $10,000 each. Suki sells her stock on December 31 for $8,000. Because Burgundy's stock is listed on a national exchange, Dave can ascertain that his shares are worth $8,000 on December 31. Does the Federal income tax law treat the decline in value of the stock differently for Suki and Dave? Explain.

3. **LO.1** If a taxpayer sells property for cash, the amount realized consists of the net proceeds from the sale. For each of the following, indicate the effect on the amount realized if:
   a. The property is sold on credit.
   b. A mortgage on the property is assumed by the buyer.
   c. A mortgage on the property is assumed by the seller.
   d. The buyer acquires the property subject to a mortgage of the seller.
   e. Stock that has a basis to the purchaser of $6,000 and a fair market value of $10,000 is received by the seller as part of the consideration.

Decision Making
Planning

4. **LO.1** Taylor is negotiating to buy some land. Under the first option, Taylor will give Ella $150,000 and assume her mortgage on the land for $100,000. Under the second option, Taylor will give Ella $250,000 and she will pay off the mortgage immediately. Taylor wants his basis for the land to be as high as possible. Given this objective, which option should Taylor select? Explain.

5. **LO.1** Lee owns land and a building (held for investment) with an adjusted basis of $75,000 and a fair market value of $250,000. The property is subject to a mortgage of $400,000. Because Lee is in arrears on the mortgage payments, the creditor is willing to accept the property in return for canceling the amount of the mortgage.
   a. How can the adjusted basis of the property be less than the amount of the mortgage?
   b. If the creditor's offer is accepted, what are the effects on the amount realized, the adjusted basis, and the realized gain or loss for Lee?

6. **LO.4** On July 16, 2023, Logan acquires land and a building for $500,000 to use in his sole proprietorship. Of the purchase price, $400,000 is allocated to the building, and $100,000 is allocated to the land. Cost recovery of $4,708 is deducted in 2023 for the building (nonresidential real estate).
   a. What is the adjusted basis for the land and the building at the acquisition date?
   b. What is the adjusted basis for the land and the building at the end of 2023?

7. **LO.1** Auralia owns stock in Orange Corporation and Blue Corporation. She receives a $10,000 distribution from both corporations. Information from Orange states that the $10,000 is a dividend. Blue states that the $10,000 is not a dividend. What could cause the instructions to differ as to the Federal income tax consequences?

8. **LO.1** On July 1, 2023, Katrina purchased tax-exempt bonds (face value of $75,000) for $82,000. The bonds mature in five years, and the annual interest rate is 3%. Discuss the tax reporting implications of this transaction.

9. **LO.2** Wanda is considering selling two personal use assets that she owns. One has appreciated in value by $20,000, and the other has declined in value by $17,000. Wanda believes that she should sell both assets in the same tax year so that the loss of $17,000 can offset the gain of $20,000. Decision Making
   a. Advise Wanda regarding the tax consequences of her plan.
   b. Could Wanda achieve better tax results by selling the assets in different tax years? Explain.

10. **LO.2** Ron sold his sailboat for a $5,000 loss in the current year because he was diagnosed with skin cancer. His spouse wants him to sell his Harley-Davidson motorcycle because her brother broke his leg while riding his motorcycle. Because Ron no longer has anyone to ride with, he is seriously considering his wife's advice. Critical Thinking

    Because the motorcycle is a classic model, Ron has received two offers. Each offer would result in a $5,000 gain. Joe would like to purchase the motorcycle before Christmas, and Jeff would like to purchase it after New Year's. Identify the relevant tax issues Ron faces in making his decision.

11. **LO.1, 2, 3, 9** Simon owns stock that has declined in value since acquired. He will either give the stock to his nephew, Fred, or sell it and give Fred the proceeds. If Fred receives the stock, he then will sell it to obtain the proceeds. Simon is in the 12% Federal income tax bracket, and Fred's bracket is 22%. In either case, the holding period for the stock will be short term. Critical Thinking

    Identify the tax issues relevant to Simon in deciding whether to give the stock or the sale proceeds to Fred.

12. **LO.3** Robin inherits 1,000 shares of Walmart stock from her aunt Julieta in 2023. According to the information received from the executor of Julieta's estate, Robin's adjusted basis for the stock is $55,000. Albert, Robin's fiancé, receives 1,000 shares of Walmart stock from his uncle Roberto as a gift in 2023. Roberto tells Albert that his adjusted basis for the Walmart stock is $7,000. What could cause the substantial difference in the adjusted basis for Robin's and Albert's respective 1,000 shares of Walmart stock?

13. **LO.3** Thelma inherited land from Sadie on June 7, 2023. The land appreciated in value by 100% during the six months Sadie owned it. The value has remained stable during the three months Thelma has owned it, and she expects it to continue to do so in the near future. Although she would like to sell the land now, Thelma has decided to postpone the sale for another three months. The delay is undertaken to enable the recognized gain to qualify for long-term capital gain treatment. Evaluate Thelma's understanding of the tax law.

14. **LO.4** Marilyn owns land that she acquired three years ago as an investment for $250,000. Because the land has not appreciated in value as she anticipated, she sells it to her brother, Amos, for its fair market value of $180,000. Amos sells the land two years later for $240,000.
   a. Explain why Marilyn's realized loss of $70,000 ($180,000 amount realized − $250,000 adjusted basis) is disallowed at the time of the sale to her brother.
   b. Explain why Amos records neither a recognized gain nor a recognized loss on his sale of the land.
   c. How does the related-party disallowance rule affect the total gain or loss recognized by the family unit?
   d. Which party wins and which party loses, in a Federal income tax sense?
   e. How could Marilyn have avoided the loss disallowance on her sale of the land?

15. **LO.4, 5** Comment on the following transactions.
   a. Mort owns 500 shares of Pear, Inc. stock with an adjusted basis of $22,000. On July 28, 2023, he sells 100 shares for $3,000. On August 16, 2023, he purchases another 100 shares for $3,400. Explain why Mort's realized loss of $1,400 ($3,000 − $4,400) on the July 28 sale is not recognized and his adjusted basis for the 100 shares purchased on August 16 is $4,800.
   b. Explain how and why your answer in part (a) would change if Mort purchased the 100 shares on December 27, 2023, rather than on August 16, 2023.

16. **LO.6** Which of the following qualify as like-kind exchanges under § 1031?
   a. Improved for unimproved real estate.
   b. Rental house for personal residence.
   c. Business land for rental house (held for investment).
   d. Warehouse for office building (both used for business).
   e. Truck for computer (both used in business).
   f. Rental house for land (both held for investment).
   g. Office furniture for office equipment (both used in business).
   h. Unimproved land in Jackson, Mississippi, for unimproved land in Toledo, Spain.
   i. General partnership interest for a general partnership interest.

Critical Thinking

17. **LO.6** Ross would like to dispose of some land he acquired five years ago because he believes it will not continue to appreciate. Its value has increased by $50,000 over the five-year period. He also intends to sell stock that has declined in value by $50,000 during the eight-month period he has owned it.

Ross has four offers to acquire the stock and land. Identify the tax issues relevant to Ross in disposing of this land and stock.

Buyer 1:	Exchange land.
Buyer 2:	Purchase land for cash.
Buyer 3:	Exchange stock.
Buyer 4:	Purchase stock for cash.

18. **LO.6** Edith exchanges a building and land used in her business for land and stock of Teal, Inc. If Edith had sold her building and land, she would have had a realized gain. Explain why the new land will have a different holding period than the stock.

19. **LO.6** Mortgaged real estate may be received in a like-kind exchange. If the taxpayer's mortgage is assumed, what effect does the mortgage have on the recognition of realized gain? On the basis of the real estate received?

20. **LO.7** Sheila's appreciated property is involuntarily converted. She receives insurance proceeds equal to the fair market value of the property. What is the minimum amount Sheila must reinvest in qualifying property to defer recognition of realized gain?

21. **LO.7** Vera owns an office building that she leases to tenants. If the building is destroyed by a tornado, is the *functional use test* or the *taxpayer use test* applied as to replacement property? Explain the differences between the two tests.

22. **LO.7** Reba, a calendar year taxpayer, owns an office building that she uses in her business. The building is involuntarily converted on November 15, 2023. On January 5, 2024, Reba receives enough proceeds to produce a realized gain. What is the latest date she can replace the building and qualify for § 1033 postponement treatment if the conversion event is:
    a. A flood?
    b. A condemnation?
    c. A tornado?

23. **LO.7** Bob is notified by the city public housing authority on May 3, 2023, that his apartment building is going to be condemned as part of a commercial development project. On June 1, 2023, Stella offers to buy the building from Bob. Bob sells the building to Stella on June 30, 2023. Condemnation occurs on September 1, 2023, and Stella receives the condemnation proceeds from the city. Both Bob and Stella are calendar year taxpayers.
    a. What is the earliest date on which Bob can dispose of the building and qualify for involuntary conversion treatment?
    b. Does the sale to Stella qualify as an involuntary conversion? Why or why not?
    c. What is the latest date on which Stella can acquire qualifying replacement property and qualify for postponement of the realized gain?
    d. What type of property will be qualifying replacement property?

24. **LO.7** A warehouse owned by Martha and used in her business (i.e., to store inventory) is being condemned by the city to provide a right-of-way for a highway. The warehouse has appreciated by $180,000 based on Martha's estimate of its fair market value. In the negotiations, the city is offering $35,000 less than what Martha believes the property is worth. Critical Thinking

    Alan, a real estate broker, has offered to purchase Martha's property for $20,000 more than the city's offer. Martha plans to invest the proceeds she will receive in an office building she will lease to various tenants.
    a. Identify the relevant tax issues for Martha.
    b. Would the answer in part (a) change if Martha's warehouse was property being held for investment rather than being used in her business? Explain.

25. **LO.8** To qualify for exclusion treatment on the sale of a principal residence, the residence must have been owned and used by the taxpayer for at least two years during the five-year period ending on the date of the sale. Are there any exceptions to this provision? Explain.

Computational Exercises

26. **LO.1** Sally owns real property for which the annual property taxes are $9,000. She sells the property to Kate on March 9, 2023, for $550,000. Kate pays the real property taxes for the entire year on October 1, 2023.
    a. How much of the property taxes can be deducted by Sally and how much by Kate?
    b. What effect does the property tax apportionment have on Kate's adjusted basis in the property?
    c. What effect does the apportionment have on Sally's amount realized from the sale?
    d. How would the answers in parts (b) and (c) differ if Sally paid the taxes?

27. **LO.1** Melba purchases land from Adrian. Melba gives Adrian $225,000 in cash and agrees to pay Adrian an additional $400,000 one year later plus interest at 5%.
    a. What is Melba's adjusted basis for the land at the acquisition date?
    b. What is Melba's adjusted basis for the land one year later?

28. **LO.3** Luciana, a nonshareholder, purchases a condominium from her employer for $85,000. The fair market value of the condominium is $120,000. What is Luciana's basis in the condominium and the amount of any income as a result of this purchase?

29. **LO.3** Sebastian purchases two pieces of equipment for $100,000. Appraisals of the equipment indicate that the fair market value of the first piece of equipment is $72,000 and that of the second piece of equipment is $108,000. What is Sebastian's basis in these two assets?

30. **LO.3** Juliana purchased land three years ago for $50,000. She made a gift of the land to Tom, her brother, in the current year, when the fair market value was $70,000. No Federal gift tax is paid on the transfer. Tom subsequently sells the property for $63,000.
    a. What is Tom's basis in the land? What is his realized gain or loss on the sale?
    b. Assume instead that the land has a fair market value of $45,000 on the date of the gift, and that Tom sold the land for $43,000. Now what is Tom's basis in the land, and what is his realized gain or loss on the sale?

31. **LO.4** Lisa sells business property with an adjusted basis of $130,000 to her son, Alfred, for its fair market value of $100,000.
    a. What is Lisa's realized and recognized gain or loss?
    b. What is Alfred's recognized gain or loss if he subsequently sells the property for $138,000? For $80,000?

32. **LO.4** Arianna's personal residence has an adjusted basis of $230,000 and a fair market value of $210,000. Arianna converts the personal residence to rental property. What is Arianna's gain basis? What is her loss basis?

33. **LO.4** Peyton sells an office building and the associated land on May 1 of the current year. Under the terms of the sales contract, Peyton is to receive $1,600,000 in cash. The purchaser is to assume Peyton's mortgage of $950,000 on the property. To enable the purchaser to obtain adequate financing, Peyton is to pay the $9,000 in points charged by the lender. The broker's commission on the sale is $75,000. What is Peyton's amount realized?

34. **LO.6, 9** Vijay owns land (adjusted basis of $40,000) that he uses in his business. He exchanges the land and $20,000 in cash for a different parcel of land worth $50,000. May Vijay avoid like-kind exchange treatment to recognize his realized loss of $10,000? Explain.

35. **LO.6** In June 2023, Sue exchanges a sport-utility vehicle (adjusted basis of $16,000; fair market value of $19,500) for cash of $2,000 and a pickup truck (fair market value of $17,500). Both vehicles are held for business use. Sue believes that her basis for the truck is $17,500. Is Sue correct? Why or why not? As part of your response, compute Sue's realized gain or loss (and any recognized gain or loss) on the exchange.

36. **LO.6** Logan and Jonathan exchange land, and the exchange qualifies as like kind under § 1031. Because Logan's land (adjusted basis of $85,000) is worth $100,000 and Jonathan's land has a fair market value of $80,000, Jonathan also gives Logan cash of $20,000.
    a. What is Logan's recognized gain?
    b. Assume instead that Jonathan's land is worth $90,000 and he gives Logan $10,000 cash. Now what is Logan's recognized gain?

37. **LO.7** On June 5, 2023, Brown, Inc., a calendar year taxpayer, receives cash of $750,000 from the county upon condemnation of its warehouse building (adjusted basis of $500,000 and fair market value of $750,000).
    a. What must Brown do to qualify for § 1033 postponement of gain treatment?
    b. How would your advice to Brown differ if the adjusted basis was $795,000?

38. **LO.7** Camilo's property, with an adjusted basis of $155,000, is condemned by the state. Camilo receives property with a fair market value of $180,000 as compensation for the property taken.
    a. What is Camilo's realized and recognized gain?
    b. What is the basis of the replacement property?

39. **LO.7** On February 24, 2023, Allison's building, with an adjusted basis of $1,300,000 (and used in her trade or business), is destroyed by fire. On March 31, 2023, she receives an insurance reimbursement of $1,650,000 for the loss. Allison invests $1,550,000 in a new building and buys stock with the balance of insurance proceeds. Allison is a calendar year taxpayer.
    a. By what date must Allison make the new investment to qualify for the nonrecognition election?
    b. Assuming that the replacement property qualifies as similar or related in service or use, what are Allison's realized gain, recognized gain, and basis in the replacement building?

40. **LO.8,9** Gary, who is single, sells his principal residence (owned and occupied by him for seven years) in November 2023 for a realized gain of $148,000. He had purchased a more expensive new residence eight months prior to the sale. He anticipates that he will occupy this new house as his principal residence for only about 18 additional months. He expects it to appreciate substantially while he owns it.

    Gary would like to recognize the realized gain on the 2023 sale to offset a large investment loss from the sale of stock. Can he recognize the realized gain of $148,000 on the sale of his principal residence in 2023? Explain.

41. **LO.8, 9** Constanza, who is single, sells her current personal residence (adjusted basis of $165,000) for $450,000. She has owned and lived in the house for 30 years. Her selling expenses are $22,500. What is Constanza's realized and recognized gain?

42. **LO.8** On August 31, 2022, Nolan and Lei, who file a joint return and live in Charleston, South Carolina, sell their personal residence, which they have owned and lived in for 10 years. The realized gain of $292,000 was excluded under § 121. They purchased another personal residence in Charleston for $480,000 on September 1, 2022.

    In 2023, Nolan's employer transfers him to Houston, Texas. The couple sells the Charleston home on February 28, 2023, and purchases a new home in Houston. The realized gain on the second sale is $180,000. What is Nolan and Lei's recognized gain on the second sale?

Problems

43. **LO.1** Anne sold her home for $290,000 in 2023. Selling expenses were $17,400. She purchased it in 2017 for $200,000. During the period of ownership, Anne had done the following:

- Deducted $50,500 office-in-home expenses, which included $4,500 in depreciation. (Refer to text Section 9-6a.)
- Deducted a casualty loss in 2019 for residential trees destroyed by a hurricane (her county was declared a Federal disaster area). The total loss was $19,000 (after the $100 floor and the 10%-of-AGI floor), and Anne's insurance company reimbursed her for $13,500. (Refer to text Section 7-3.)
- Paid street paving assessment of $7,000 and added sidewalks for $8,000.
- Installed an elevator for medical reasons. The total cost was $20,000, and Anne deducted $13,000 as medical expenses. (Refer to text Section 10-1b.)

What is Anne's realized gain?

44. **LO.1** Kareem bought a rental house in March 2018 for $300,000, of which $50,000 is allocated to the land and $250,000 to the building. Early in 2020, he had a tennis court built in the backyard at a cost of $7,500. Kareem has deducted $30,900 for depreciation on the house and $1,300 for depreciation on the court. In January 2023, he sells the house and tennis court for $330,000 cash.

   a. What is Kareem's realized gain or loss?
   b. If an original mortgage of $80,000 is still outstanding and the buyer assumes the mortgage in addition to the cash payment, what is Kareem's realized gain or loss?
   c. If the buyer takes the property subject to the $80,000 mortgage rather than assuming it, what is Kareem's realized gain or loss?

45. **LO.1** Norm is negotiating the sale of a tract of his land to Pat. Use the following classification scheme to classify each of the items contained in the proposed sales contract.

Legend		
DARN	=	Decreases amount realized by Norm
IARN	=	Increases amount realized by Norm
DABN	=	Decreases adjusted basis to Norm
IABN	=	Increases adjusted basis to Norm
DABP	=	Decreases adjusted basis to Pat
IABP	=	Increases adjusted basis to Pat

   a. Norm is to receive cash of $50,000.
   b. Norm is to receive Pat's note payable for $25,000, payable in three years.
   c. Pat assumes Norm's mortgage of $5,000 on the land.
   d. Pat agrees to pay the realtor's sales commission of $8,000.
   e. Pat agrees to pay the property taxes on the land for the entire year. If each party paid their respective share, Norm's share would be $1,000 and Pat's share would be $3,000.
   f. Pat pays legal fees of $500.
   g. Norm pays legal fees of $750.

46. **LO.1, 2** Liam owns a personal use boat that has a fair market value of $35,000 and an adjusted basis of $45,000. Liam's AGI is $100,000. Calculate the realized and recognized gain or loss if:

   a. Liam sells the boat for $35,000.
   b. Liam exchanges the boat for another boat worth $35,000.

c. The boat is stolen and Liam receives insurance proceeds of $35,000.

d. Would your answer in part (a) change if the fair market value and the selling price of the boat were $48,000? Explain.

47. **LO.1** Zoe purchases Tan, Inc. bonds for $108,000 on January 2, 2023. The face value of the bonds is $100,000; the maturity date is December 31, 2027; and the annual interest rate is 5%. Zoe will amortize the premium only if he is required to do so. Zoe sells the bonds on July 1, 2025, for $106,000.

a. Determine the interest income Zoe should report for 2023.

b. Calculate Zoe's recognized gain or loss on the sale of the bonds in 2025.

48. **LO.1, 2** Which of the following results in a recognized gain or loss?

a. Kay sells her vacation cabin (adjusted basis of $100,000) for $150,000.

b. Hernan sells his personal residence (adjusted basis of $150,000) for $100,000.

c. Carl's personal residence (adjusted basis of $65,000) is condemned by the city. He receives condemnation proceeds of $55,000.

d. Olga's land is worth $40,000 at the end of the year. She had purchased the land six months earlier for $25,000.

e. Vera's personal vehicle (adjusted basis of $22,000) is stolen. She receives $23,000 from the insurance company and does not plan to replace the automobile.

f. Jerry sells used clothing (adjusted basis of $500) to a thrift store for $50.

49. **LO.1, 2** Yancy's personal residence is condemned as part of an urban renewal project. His adjusted basis for the residence is $480,000. He receives condemnation proceeds of $460,000 and invests the proceeds in stocks and bonds.

a. Calculate Yancy's realized and recognized gain or loss.

b. If the condemnation proceeds are $505,000, what are Yancy's realized and recognized gain or loss?

c. What are Yancy's realized and recognized gain or loss in part (a) if the house was rental property?

50. **LO.3** Brent Morgan is a real estate agent for Coastal Estates, a residential real estate development. Because of his outstanding sales performance, Brent is permitted to buy a lot for $300,000 that normally would sell for $500,000. Brent is the only real estate agent for Coastal Estates who is permitted to do so. Communications

a. Does Brent recognize gross income from the transaction? Explain.

b. What is Brent's adjusted basis for the land?

c. Write a letter to Brent informing him of the income tax consequences of his acquisition of the lot. His address is 100 Tower Road, San Diego, CA 92182.

51. **LO.1, 2, 3** Karen Samuels (Social Security number 123-45-6789) makes the following purchases and sales of stock:

Transaction	Date	Number of Shares	Company	Price per Share
Purchase	1-1-2021	300	MDG	$ 75
Purchase	6-1-2021	150	GRU	300
Purchase	11-1-2021	60	MDG	70
Sale	12-3-2021	200	MDG	80
Purchase	3-1-2022	120	GRU	375
Sale	8-1-2022	90	GRU	330
Sale	1-1-2023	150	MDG	90
Sale	2-1-2023	75	GRU	500

Assuming that Karen is unable to identify the specific lots that are sold with the original purchase, determine the recognized gain or loss on each type of stock.

a. As of July 1, 2021.

b. As of December 31, 2021.

c. As of December 31, 2022.

d. As of July 1, 2023.

e. Form 8949 and Schedule D (Form 1040) are used to report sales of capital assets (which include stock sales). Go to the IRS website, and download the most current Form 8949 and Schedule D (Form 1040). Then complete the forms for part (c) of this problem, assuming that the brokerage firm did *not* report Karen's basis to the IRS [complete Schedule D (Form 1040) through line 16].

52. **LO.1, 2, 3** Mahan purchases 1,000 shares of Bluebird Corporation stock on October 3, 2023, for $300,000. On December 12, 2023, Mahan purchases an additional 750 shares of Bluebird stock for $210,000. According to market quotations, Bluebird stock is selling for $285 per share on December 31, 2023. Mahan sells 500 shares of Bluebird stock on March 1, 2024, for $162,500.

a. What is the adjusted basis of Mahan's Bluebird stock on December 31, 2023?

b. What is Mahan's recognized gain or loss from the sale of Bluebird stock on March 1, 2024, assuming that the shares sold are from the shares purchased on December 12, 2023?

c. What is Kevin's recognized gain or loss from the sale of Bluebird stock on March 1, 2024, assuming that Mahan cannot adequately identify the shares sold?

Communications

53. **LO.3** Rod Clooney purchases Kayla Mitchell's sole proprietorship for $990,000 on August 15, 2023. The assets of the business are:

Asset	Agnes's Adjusted Basis	FMV
Accounts receivable	$ 70,000	$ 70,000
Inventory	90,000	100,000
Equipment	150,000	160,000
Furniture and fixtures	95,000	130,000
Building	190,000	250,000
Land	25,000	75,000
Total	$620,000	$785,000

a. Calculate Kayla's realized and recognized gain.

b. Determine Rod's basis for each of the assets.

c. Write a letter to Rod informing him of the tax consequences of the purchase. His address is 300 Riverview Drive, Delaware, OH 43015.

54. **LO.1, 2, 3** Roberto has received various gifts over the years and has decided to dispose of several of these assets. What is the recognized gain or loss from each of the following transactions, assuming that no Federal gift tax was paid when the gifts were made?

a. In 1988, he received land worth $32,000. The donor's adjusted basis was $35,000. Roberto sells the land for $95,000 in 2023.

b. In 1993, he received stock in Gold Company. The donor's adjusted basis was $19,000. The fair market value on the date of the gift was $34,000. Roberto sells the stock for $40,000 in 2023.

c. In 1999, he received land worth $15,000. The donor's adjusted basis was $20,000. Roberto sells the land for $9,000 in 2023.

d. In 2020, he received stock worth $30,000. The donor's adjusted basis was $42,000. Roberto sells the stock for $38,000 in 2023.

e. Build a spreadsheet-based solution that provides the solution to parts (a) through (d) above and uses only the donor's basis, the fair market value at the time of the gift, and the selling price as inputs. You may want to use the IF and AND functions together.

55. **LO.1, 2, 3** Nicky receives a car from Sam as a gift. Sam paid $48,000 for the car. Sam had used it for business purposes and had deducted $10,000 for depreciation up to the time she gave the car to Nicky. The fair market value of the car is $33,000.

a. Assuming that Nicky uses the car for business purposes, what is her basis for depreciation?

b. Assume that Nicky deducts depreciation of $6,500 and then sells the car for $32,500. What is her recognized gain or loss?

c. Assume that Nicky deducts depreciation of $6,500 and then sells the car for $20,000. What is her recognized gain or loss?

56. **LO.3** Margo receives a gift of real estate with an adjusted basis of $175,000 and a fair market value of $100,000. The donor paid gift tax of $15,000 on the transfer. If Margo later sells the property for $110,000, what is her recognized gain or loss?

57. **LO.3** On September 18, 2023, Gerald received land and a building from Luna as a gift. No gift tax was paid on the transfer. Luna's records show the following:

Asset	Adjusted Basis	FMV
Land	$100,000	$212,000
Building	80,000	100,000

a. Determine Gerald's adjusted basis for the land and building.

b. Assume instead that the fair market value of the land was $87,000 and that of the building was $65,000. Determine Gerald's adjusted basis for the land and building.

58. **LO.1, 2, 3, 9** Tyler Meade is planning to make a charitable contribution to the Girl Scouts. He will contribute Crystal, Inc. stock worth $20,000. The stock has an adjusted basis of $15,000. A friend has suggested that Tyler sell the stock and contribute the $20,000 in proceeds rather than contribute the stock.

Communications
Critical Thinking

a. Should Tyler follow the friend's advice? Why or why not?

b. Assume that the fair market value is only $13,000. In this case, should Tyler follow the friend's advice? Why or why not?

c. Rather than make a charitable contribution to the Girl Scouts, Tyler is going to make a gift to Melissa, his niece. Advise Tyler regarding parts (a) and (b).

d. Write a letter to Tyler regarding whether in part (a) he should sell the stock and contribute the cash or contribute the stock. He has informed you that he purchased the stock six years ago. Tyler's address is 500 Ireland Avenue, DeKalb, IL 60115.

59. **LO.3** As sole heir, Nadia receives all of Mary's property (adjusted basis of $11,400,000 and fair market value of $13,820,000). Six months after Mary's death, the fair market value is $13,835,000.

a. Can the executor of Mary's estate elect the alternate valuation date and amount? Explain.

b. What is Nadia's basis for the property?

c. Assume instead that the fair market value six months after Mary's death is $13,800,000. Respond to parts (a) and (b).

60. **LO.3** Dan bought a hotel for $2,600,000 in January 2019. In May 2023, he died and left the hotel to Ed. While Dan owned the hotel, he deducted $289,000 of cost recovery. The fair market value in May 2023 was $2,800,000. The fair market value six months later was $2,850,000. Assume that an estate tax return (Form 706) is not required to be filed.

   a. What is the basis of the property to Ed?

   b. What is the basis of the property to Ed if the fair market value six months later was $2,500,000 (not $2,850,000) and the objective of the executor was to minimize the estate tax liability?

Communications

61. **LO.3** Ella and Emma are twin sisters who live in Louisiana and Mississippi, respectively. Ella is married to Frank, and Pauline is married to Richard. Frank and Richard are killed in an auto accident in 2023 while returning from a sporting event.

   Ella and Frank jointly owned some farmland in Louisiana, a community property state (value of $940,000, cost of $450,000). Emma and Richard jointly owned some farmland in Mississippi, a common law state (value of $940,000, cost of $450,000). Assume that all of Frank's and Richard's property passes to their surviving wives.

   a. Calculate Ella's basis in the land.

   b. Calculate Emma's basis in the land.

   c. What causes the difference? Summarize your answer in a one-paragraph e-mail to your instructor.

Decision Making

62. **LO.3, 4** Sheila sells land to Elaine, her sister, for the fair market value of $40,000. Six months later when the land is worth $45,000, Elaine gives it to Jacob, her son. (No gift tax resulted.) Shortly thereafter, Jacob sells the land for $48,000.

   a. Assuming that Sheila's adjusted basis for the land is $24,000, what are Sheila's and Jacob's recognized gain or loss on the sales?

   b. Assuming that Sheila's adjusted basis for the land is $60,000, what are Sheila's and Jacob's recognized gain or loss on the sales?

63. **LO.1, 2, 3, 4** Louis owns three pieces of land with an adjusted basis as follows: parcel A, $75,000; parcel B, $125,000; and parcel C, $175,000. Louis sells parcel A to his uncle for $50,000, parcel B to his partner for $120,000, and parcel C to his mother for $150,000.

   a. What is the recognized gain or loss from the sale of each parcel?

   b. If Louis's uncle eventually sells his land for $90,000, what is his recognized gain or loss?

   c. If Louis's partner eventually sells his land for $130,000, what is his recognized gain or loss?

   d. If Louis's mother eventually sells her land for $165,000, what is her recognized gain or loss?

Decision Making

64. **LO.1, 2, 3, 4** Thania inherited 1,000 shares of Aqua, Inc. stock from Joe. Joe's basis was $35,000, and the fair market value on July 1, 2023 (the date of death), was $45,000. The shares were distributed to Thania on July 15, 2023. Thania sold the stock on July 29, 2024, for $33,000. After giving the matter more thought, she decides that Aqua is a good investment and purchases 1,000 shares for $30,000 on August 19, 2024.

   a. What is Thania's basis for the 1,000 shares purchased on August 19, 2024?

   b. Could Thania have obtained different tax consequences in part (a) if she had sold the 1,000 shares on December 27, 2023, and purchased the 1,000 shares on January 5, 2024? Explain.

65. **LO.1, 2, 4** Abby's home had a basis of $360,000 ($160,000 attributable to the land) and a fair market value of $340,000 ($155,000 attributable to the land) when she converted 70% of it to business use by opening a bed-and-breakfast. Four

years after the conversion, Abby sells the home for $500,000 ($165,000 attributable to the land).

a. Calculate Abby's basis for gain, loss, and cost recovery for the portion of her personal residence that was converted to business use.

b. Calculate the cost recovery deducted by Abby during the four-year period of business use, assuming that the bed-and-breakfast is opened on January 1 of year 1 and the house is sold on December 31 of year 4.

c. What is Abby's recognized gain or loss on the sale of the business use portion?

66. **LO.4** Surendra's personal residence originally cost $340,000 (ignoring the value of the land). After living in the house for five years, he converts it to rental property. At the date of conversion, the fair market value of the house is $320,000. As to the rental property, calculate Surendra's basis for: Communications Critical Thinking

a. Loss.

b. Depreciation.

c. Gain.

d. Could Surendra have obtained better tax results if he had sold his personal residence for $320,000 and then purchased another house for $320,000 to hold as rental property? Explain.

e. Summarize your answer to this problem in an e-mail to your instructor.

67. **LO.6** Katrina owns undeveloped land with an adjusted basis of $300,000. She exchanges it for other undeveloped land worth $750,000.

a. What are Katrina's realized and recognized gain or loss?

b. What is Katrina's basis in the undeveloped land she receives?

c. Would the answers in parts (a) and (b) change if Katrina exchanged the undeveloped land for land and a building? Explain.

68. **LO.6** Daniela Fletcher owns undeveloped land (adjusted basis of $80,000 and fair market value of $92,000) on the East Coast. On January 4, 2023, she exchanges it with Lisa Martin (an unrelated party) for undeveloped land on the West Coast and $3,000 cash. Lisa has an adjusted basis of $72,000 for her land, and its fair market value is $89,000. Because the real estate market on the East Coast is thriving, on September 1, 2024, Lisa sells the land she acquired for $120,000. Communications Critical Thinking

a. What are Daniela's recognized gain or loss and adjusted basis for the West Coast land on January 4, 2023?

b. What are Lisa's recognized gain or loss and adjusted basis for the East Coast land on January 4, 2023?

c. What is Lisa's recognized gain or loss from the September 1, 2024 sale?

d. What effect does Lisa's 2024 sale have on Daniela?

e. Write a letter to Daniela advising her of the Federal income tax consequences of this exchange. Her address is The Corral, El Paso, TX 79968.

69. **LO.6** Katie exchanges a building and land (used in her business) for Tyler's land and building and some equipment (used in his business). The assets have the following characteristics:

	Adjusted Basis	Fair Market Value
Katie's real property	$120,000	$300,000
Tyler's real property	60,000	220,000
Equipment	50,000	80,000

a. What are Katie's recognized gain or loss and basis for the land and building and equipment acquired from Tyler?

b. What are Tyler's recognized gain or loss and basis for the land and building acquired from Katie?

Critical Thinking
Planning

70. **LO.6, 9** In two unrelated transactions, Laura exchanges property that qualifies for like-kind exchange treatment. In the first exchange, Laura gives up land purchased in May 2021 (adjusted basis of $20,000; fair market value of $17,000) in exchange for a different parcel of land (fair market value of $15,000) and $2,000 cash. In the second exchange, Laura receives a parking garage (to be used in her business) with a fair market value of $50,000 in exchange for a plot of land she had held for investment. The land was purchased in April 2015 for $12,000 and has a current fair market value of $48,000. In addition to transferring the land, Laura pays an additional $2,000 to the other party.
    a. What is Laura's adjusted basis for the new parcel of land?
    b. When does the holding period begin?
    c. What is Laura's adjusted basis for the parking garage?
    d. When does the holding period begin?
    e. How could Laura structure either of the transactions differently to produce better tax consequences?

71. **LO.6** What is the basis of the received property in each of the following exchanges?
    a. Apartment building held for investment (adjusted basis of $145,000) for office building to be held for investment (fair market value of $225,000).
    b. Land and building used as a barbershop (adjusted basis of $190,000) for land and building used as a grocery store (fair market value of $350,000).
    c. Office building (adjusted basis of $45,000) for bulldozer (fair market value of $42,000), both held for business use.
    d. IBM common stock (adjusted basis of $20,000) for ExxonMobil common stock (fair market value of $28,000).
    e. Rental house (adjusted basis of $90,000) for mountain cabin to be held for rental use (fair market value of $225,000).
    f. General partnership interest (adjusted basis of $400,000) for a limited partnership interest (fair market value of $580,000).

72. **LO.6** Suni owns land (adjusted basis of $90,000; fair market value of $125,000) that she uses in her business. She exchanges it for another parcel of land (worth $100,000) and stock (worth $25,000). Determine Suni's:
    a. Realized and recognized gain or loss on the exchange.
    b. Basis in the new land.
    c. Basis in the stock she received.

73. **LO.6** Ed owns investment land with an adjusted basis of $35,000. Polly has offered to purchase the land from Ed for $175,000 for use in a real estate development. The amount offered by Polly is $10,000 in excess of what Ed perceives as the fair market value of the land. Ed would like to dispose of the land to Polly but does not want to incur the tax liability that would result. He identifies an office building with a fair market value of $175,000 that he would like to acquire. Polly purchases the office building and then exchanges the office building for Ed's land.
    a. Calculate Ed's realized and recognized gain on the exchange and his basis for the office building.
    b. Calculate Polly's realized and recognized gain on the exchange and her basis in the land.

Decision Making

74. **LO.6, 9** Steve owns real estate (adjusted basis of $12,000 and fair market value of $15,000), which he uses in his business. Steve sells the real estate for $15,000 to Aubry (a dealer) and then purchases a new parcel of land for $15,000 from Joan (also a dealer). The new parcel of land would normally qualify as like-kind property.
    a. What are Steve's realized and recognized gain on the sale of the land he sold to Aubry?

b. What is Steve's basis for the land he purchased from Joan?

c. What factors would motivate Steve to sell his land to Aubry and purchase the land from Joan rather than exchange one parcel of land for the other?

d. Assume that the adjusted basis of Steve's original parcel of land is $15,000 and the fair market value of both parcels of land is $12,000. Respond to parts (a) through (c).

75. **LO.6, 9** Tom Howard and Frank Pérez are good friends (and former college roommates). Each owns investment property in the other's hometown (Tom lives in Kalamazoo, MI; Frank lives in Austin, TX). To make their lives easier, they decide to exchange the investment properties. Under the terms of the exchange, Frank will transfer realty (20 acres of unimproved land; adjusted basis of $52,000; fair market value of $80,000) and Tom will exchange realty (25 acres of unimproved land; adjusted basis of $60,000; fair market value of $92,000). Tom's property is subject to a mortgage of $12,000 that will be assumed by Frank.

Communications
Critical Thinking
Planning

a. What are Frank's and Tom's recognized gains?

b. What are their adjusted bases?

c. As an alternative, Frank has proposed that, rather than assuming the mortgage, he will transfer cash of $12,000 to Tom. Tom would use the cash to pay off the mortgage. In an e-mail, advise Tom on whether this alternative would be beneficial to him from a tax perspective.

d. Assuming that Tom and Frank proceed with the original exchange [rather than the alternative in part (c)], complete Form 8824 (Parts I and III) for Tom. Assume that the exchange occurs on September 16, 2022 (Tom acquired his 25-acre parcel on February 15, 2013). Tom's Social Security number is 123-45-6789.

76. **LO.6** Determine the realized, recognized, and postponed gain or loss and the new basis for each of the following like-kind exchanges.

Communications
Critical Thinking

	Adjusted Basis of Old Asset	Boot Given	Fair Market Value of New Asset	Boot Received
a.	$ 7,000	$ -0-	$12,000	$4,000
b.	14,000	2,000	15,000	-0-
c.	3,000	7,000	8,000	500
d.	15,000	-0-	29,000	-0-
e.	10,000	-0-	11,000	1,000
f.	17,000	-0-	14,000	-0-

g. Create a spreadsheet that—by entering the fair market value and basis of property given up and the fair market value of property received—will compute (1) realized gain or loss, (2) boot received, (3) boot given, (4) gain (loss) recognized, (5) gain (loss) deferred, and (6) the basis of like-kind property received. In separate tabs, the spreadsheet should apply the "simplified method" and the "alternative method." Ignore the implications of debt and depreciation.

Test your spreadsheet using the data in this problem. E-mail your spreadsheet to your instructor along with a brief summary of how you built the spreadsheet.

77. **LO.7** Quintin's roadside vegetable stand (adjusted basis of $275,000) is destroyed by a tractor-trailer accident. He receives insurance proceeds of $240,000. Quintin immediately uses the proceeds plus additional cash of $45,000 to build another roadside vegetable stand at the same location. What are the Federal income tax consequences to Quintin?

78. **LO.7** Albert owns 100 acres of land on which he grows spruce trees. His adjusted basis for the land is $100,000. He receives condemnation proceeds of $10,000 when the city's new beltway takes 5 acres along the eastern boundary of his property.

He also receives a severance award of $6,000 associated with the possible harmful effects of exhaust fumes on his trees. Albert invests the $16,000 in a growth mutual fund. Determine the tax consequences to Albert of the:

a. Condemnation proceeds.

b. Severance award.

79. **LO.7** Mitchell, a calendar year taxpayer, is the sole proprietor of a fast-food restaurant. His adjusted basis for the building and the related land is $450,000. On March 12, 2023, state authorities notify Mitchell that his property is going to be condemned so that the highway can be widened. On June 20, Mitchell's property is officially condemned, and he receives an award of $625,000. Because Mitchell's business has been successful in the past, he would like to reopen the restaurant in a new location.

a. What is the earliest date Mitchell can acquire a new restaurant and qualify for gain postponement?

b. On June 30, Mitchell purchases land and a building for $610,000. Assuming that he elects the maximum postponement amount, what is his recognized gain?

c. What is Mitchell's adjusted basis for the new land and building?

d. If he does not elect § 1033, what are Mitchell's recognized gain and adjusted basis?

e. Suppose he invests the $625,000 condemnation proceeds in the stock market on June 30. What is Mitchell's recognized gain?

80. **LO.7** Emily's warehouse (adjusted basis of $450,000) is destroyed by a hurricane in October 2023. Emily, a calendar year taxpayer, receives insurance proceeds of $525,000 in January 2024. Calculate Emily's realized gain or loss, recognized gain or loss, and basis for the replacement property if she:

a. Acquires a new warehouse for $550,000 in January 2024.

b. Acquires a new warehouse for $500,000 in January 2024.

c. Does not acquire replacement property.

Critical Thinking
Planning

81. **LO.7, 9** Cabel's warehouse, which has an adjusted basis of $380,000 and a fair market value of $490,000, is condemned by an agency of the Federal government to make way for a highway interchange. The initial condemnation offer is $425,000. After substantial negotiations, the agency agrees to transfer to Cabel a surplus warehouse that is worth $490,000. Cabel is a calendar year taxpayer. The condemnation and related asset transfer occur during September 2023.

a. What are the recognized gain or loss and the basis of the replacement warehouse if Cabel's objective is to recognize as much gain as possible?

b. Advise Cabel regarding what he needs to do by what date to achieve his objective.

82. **LO.7** What are the *maximum* postponed gain or loss and the basis for the replacement property for the following involuntary conversions?

	Property	Type of Conversion	Amount Realized	Adjusted Basis	Amount Reinvested
a.	Drugstore (business)	Casualty	$160,000	$130,000	$110,000
b.	Apartments (investment)	Condemned	100,000	125,000	175,000
c.	Grocery store (business)	Casualty	400,000	300,000	450,000
d.	Residence (personal)	Casualty*	16,000	18,000	17,000
e.	Vacant lot (investment)	Condemned	240,000	160,000	220,000
f.	Residence (personal)	Casualty*	20,000	18,000	19,000
g.	Residence (personal)	Condemned	18,000	20,000	26,000
h.	Apartments (investment)	Condemned	150,000	100,000	200,000

* Casualty occurred in a Federally declared disaster area.

83. **LO.7, 9** Wanda, a calendar year taxpayer, owned a building (adjusted basis of $250,000) in which she operated a bakery that was destroyed by fire in December 2023. She receives insurance proceeds of $290,000 for the building the following March. Wanda is considering two options regarding the investment of the insurance proceeds. First, she could purchase a local building (suitable for a bakery) that is for sale for $275,000. Second, she could buy a new home for $290,000 and go back to college and finish her degree. Decision Making Planning

a. To minimize her tax liability, which of these alternatives should Wanda choose?

b. What is the latest date on which Wanda can replace the involuntarily converted property to qualify for § 1033?

c. What is the latest date on which Wanda can replace the involuntarily converted property to qualify for § 1033 if the involuntary conversion is a condemnation?

84. **LO.8, 9** Karl purchased his residence on January 2, 2022, for $260,000, after having lived in it during 2021 as a tenant under a lease with an option to buy clause. On August 1, 2023, Karl sells the residence for $315,000. On June 13, 2023, Karl purchases a new residence for $367,000. Critical Thinking Planning

a. What is Karl's recognized gain? His basis for the new residence?

b. Assume instead that Karl purchased his original residence on January 2, 2021 (rather than January 2, 2022). What is Karl's recognized gain? His basis for the new residence?

c. In part (a), what could Karl do to minimize his recognized gain?

85. **LO.8** Wesley, who is single, listed his personal residence with a real estate agent on March 3, 2023, at a price of $390,000. He rejected several offers in the $350,000 range during the summer. Finally, on August 16, 2023, he and the purchaser signed a contract to sell for $363,000. The sale (i.e., closing) took place on September 7, 2023. The closing statement showed the following disbursements:

Real estate agent's commission	$ 21,780
Appraisal fee	600
Exterminator's certificate	300
Recording fees	800
Mortgage to First Bank	305,000
Cash to seller	34,520

Wesley's adjusted basis for the house is $200,000. He owned and occupied the house for seven years. On October 1, 2023, Wesley purchases another residence for $325,000.

a. Calculate Wesley's recognized gain on the sale.

b. What is Wesley's adjusted basis for the new residence?

c. Assume instead that the selling price is $800,000. What is Wesley's recognized gain? His adjusted basis for the new residence?

86. **LO.8** Pedro, age 57, is the sole owner of his principal residence, which he has owned and occupied for 10 years. Maria, his spouse, has lived there with Pedro for the full 10 years. He sells the house for a realized gain of $340,000.

a. Can Pedro use the § 121 exclusion if he and Maria file a joint return? If so, what are the available amount of the exclusion and the recognized gain?

b. Can Pedro use the § 121 exclusion if he files a separate return? If so, what are the available amount of the exclusion and the recognized gain?

c. Assume instead that the realized gain is $550,000 and a joint return is filed.

d. Assume instead that the realized gain is $550,000 and separate returns are filed.

e. Assume instead that Maria and Pedro have been married for only 18 months and that she has lived in his house only since their marriage. They file a joint return.

Communications
Planning

87. **LO.8** Nell, Nina, and Nora Potter, who are sisters, sell their principal residence (owned as tenants in common) in which they have lived for the past 25 years. The youngest of the sisters is age 60. The selling price is $960,000, selling expenses and legal fees are $63,000, and the adjusted basis is $120,000 (the fair market value of the residence when inherited from their parents 25 years ago; they made no capital improvements during the time they held the residence). The sisters plan to move into rental housing and not acquire another residence. Nell has contacted you on behalf of the Potters regarding the tax consequences of the sale.

    a. Write a letter to Nell advising her of the tax consequences and how taxes can be minimized. Nell's address is 100 Oak Avenue, Billings, MT 59101.

    b. Prepare a memo for the tax files discussing your approach to the situation.

Critical Thinking

88. **LO.8, 9** Ramesh owns a beach house (four years) and a cabin in the mountains (six years). His adjusted basis is $300,000 in the beach house and $315,000 in the mountain cabin. Ramesh also rents a townhouse in the city where he is employed. During the year, he occupies each of the three residences as follows:

Townhouse	135 days
Beach house	155 days
Mountain cabin	75 days

The beach house is close enough to the city so that he can commute to work during the spring and summer. Although this level of occupancy may vary slightly from year to year, it is representative during the time period that Ramesh has owned the two residences.

Because Ramesh plans to retire in several years, he sells both the beach house and the mountain cabin. The mountain cabin is sold on March 3, 2023, for $540,000 (related selling expenses of $35,000). The beach house is sold on December 10, 2023, for $700,000 (related selling expenses of $42,000).

    a. Calculate Ramesh's least allowable recognized gain on the sale of the two residences.

    b. Assume instead that both residences satisfy the two-year ownership and use tests as Ramesh's principal residence. Because the mountain cabin is sold first, can Ramesh apply the § 121 exclusion to the sale of the beach house? Explain.

Critical Thinking
Planning

89. **LO.8, 9** Missy, age 30, has owned her principal residence (adjusted basis of $225,000) for five years. During the first three years of ownership, she occupied it as her principal residence. During the past two years, she was in graduate school and rented the residence. After graduate school, Missy returned to the same location where she previously worked. At this point, she purchased another residence for $400,000 and listed her old residence for sale at $340,000. Due to a slow real estate market, 11 months later Missy finally receives an offer of $330,000.

    a. What is Missy's recognized gain if she immediately accepts the $330,000 offer (i.e., 11 months after the listing date)? Selling expenses are $20,000.

    b. What is Missy's recognized gain if she rejects the $330,000 offer and accepts another offer of $340,000 three months later (i.e., 14 months after the listing date)? Selling expenses are $20,000.

    c. Advise Missy on which offer she should accept. She is in the 24% Federal income tax bracket).

Tax Return Problems

Tax Forms Problem

ProConnect™ Tax

90. Alton Newman, age 67, is married and files a joint return with his wife, Clair, age 65. Alton and Clair are both retired, and during 2022, they received Social Security benefits of $10,000. Both Alton and Clair are covered by Medicare. Alton's Social Security number is 111-11-1119, and Clair's is 123-45-6786. They reside at 210 College Drive, Columbia, SC 29201.

    Alton, who retired on January 1, 2022, receives benefits from a qualified pension plan of $2,750 a month for life. His total contributions to the plan (none of which were deductible) were $168,250. In January 2022, he received a bonus of $2,000 from his former employer for service performed in 2021. No Federal or state income taxes were withheld on this bonus by his former employer (Amalgamated Industries, Inc.; EIN 12-3456789; 114 Main Street, Columbia, SC 29201). Although Amalgamated Industries, Inc., accrued the bonus in 2021, it was not paid until 2022.

    Clair, who retired on December 31, 2021, started receiving benefits of $1,400 a month on January 1, 2022. Her contributions to the qualified pension plan (none of which were deductible when made) were $74,100.

    On September 27, 2022, Alton and Clair received a pro rata 10% stock dividend on 600 shares of stock they owned. They had bought the stock on March 5, 2015, for $20 a share. On December 16, 2022, they sold the 60 dividend shares for $55 a share.

    On October 10, 2021, Clair sold the car she had used in commuting to and from work for $17,000. She had paid $31,000 for the car in 2016.

    On July 14, 2014, Alton and Clair received a gift of 1,000 shares of stock from their son, Thomas. Thomas's basis in the stock was $35 a share (fair market value at the date of gift was $25). No gift tax was paid on the transfer. Alton and Clair sold the stock on October 8, 2022, for $24 a share.

    On May 1, 2022, Clair's mother died, and Clair inherited her personal residence. In February 2022, her mother had paid the property taxes for 2022 of $2,100. The residence had a fair market value of $235,000 and an adjusted basis to the mother of $160,000 on the date of her death. Clair listed the house with a real estate agent, who estimated it was worth $240,000 as of December 31, 2022.

    Clair received rent income of $6,000 on a beach house she inherited three years ago from her uncle Charles. She had rented the property for one week during the July 4 weekend and one week during the Thanksgiving holiday. Charles's adjusted basis in the beach house was $150,000, and its fair market value on the date of his death was $240,000. Clair and Alton used the beach house for personal purposes for 56 days during the year. Expenses associated with the house were $3,700 for utilities, maintenance, and repairs; $2,200 for property taxes; and $800 for insurance. There are no mortgages on the property.

    Clair and Alton paid estimated Federal income tax of $2,000 and had itemized deductions of $6,800 (excluding any itemized deductions associated with the beach house). They did not engage in any digital asset transactions during the year. If they have overpaid their Federal income tax, they want the amount refunded. Both Clair and Alton want $3 to go to the Presidential Election Campaign Fund.

    Compute their 2022 Federal income tax payable or refund due and complete their 2022 tax return using appropriate forms and schedules. Suggested software: ProConnect Tax.

Tax Forms Problem

ProConnect™ Tax

91. Devon Bishop, age 45, is single. He lives at 1507 Rose Lane, Albuquerque, NM 87131. His Social Security number is 111-11-1117. Devon did not engage in any digital asset transactions during the year, and he does not want $3 to go to the Presidential Election Campaign Fund.

Devon's wife, Ariane, passed away in 2018. Devon's son, Tom, who is age 18, resides with Devon. Tom's Social Security number is 123-45-6788.

Devon owns a sole proprietorship for which he uses the accrual method of accounting and maintains no inventory; the business operates as Devon's Copy Shop, 422 E. Main Street, Albuquerque, NM 87131, IRS business activity code: 453990. His revenues and expenses for 2022 are as follows:

Sales revenue	$740,000
Cost of goods sold (based on purchases for the year)	405,000
Salary expense	88,000
Rent expense	30,000
Utilities	8,000
Telephone	6,500
Advertising	4,000
Bad debts	5,000
Depreciation*	21,000
Health insurance**	26,000
Accounting and legal fees	7,000
Supplies	1,000

*New office equipment ($21,000); Devon uses the immediate expense election.
**$18,000 for employees and $8,000 for Devon.

Other income received by Devon includes the following:

Dividend income (qualified dividends):	
Swan, Inc.	$10,000
Wren, Inc.	2,000
Interest income:	
First National Bank	11,000
Second City Bank	2,500
County of Santa Fe, NM bonds	17,000

During the year, Devon and his sole proprietorship were involved in the following property transactions. Stock transactions were reported to Devon on Form 1099–B; basis was not reported to the IRS.

a. Sold Blue, Inc. stock for $45,000 on March 12, 2022. He had purchased the stock on September 5, 2019, for $50,000.

b. Received an inheritance of $300,000 from his uncle, Henry. Devon used $200,000 to purchase Green, Inc. stock on May 15, 2022, and invested $100,000 in Gold, Inc. stock on May 30, 2022.

c. Received Orange, Inc. stock worth $9,500 as a gift from his aunt, Jane, on June 17, 2022. Her adjusted basis for the stock was $5,000. No gift taxes were paid on the transfer. Jane had purchased the stock on April 1, 2016. Devon sold the stock on July 1, 2022, for $22,000.

d. On July 15, 2022, Devon sold one-half of the Green, Inc. stock for $40,000.

e. Devon was notified on August 1, 2022, that Yellow, Inc. stock he purchased from a colleague on September 1, 2021, for $52,500 had become worthless. Although he understood that investing in Yellow was risky, Devon did not anticipate that the corporation would declare bankruptcy.

f. On August 15, 2022, Devon received a parcel of land in Phoenix worth $220,000 in exchange for a parcel of land he owned in Tucson. Because the Tucson parcel was worth $245,000, he also received $25,000 cash. Devon's adjusted basis for the Tucson parcel was $210,000. He originally purchased it on September 18, 2019.

g. On December 1, 2022-, Devon sold the condominium in which he had been living for the past 20 years (1844 Lighthouse Lane, Albuquerque, NM 87131) and moved into a rented townhouse. The sales price was $480,000, selling expenses were $28,500, and repair expenses related to the sale were $9,400. Devon purchased the condominium for $180,000.

Devon's potential itemized deductions, exclusive of the previous information, are as follows:

Medical expenses (before the 7.5%-of-AGI floor)	$ 9,500
Property taxes on residence	5,800
State income taxes	4,000
Charitable contributions	10,000
Mortgage interest on residence (First National Bank)	9,900
Sales taxes paid	5,000

During the year, Devon makes estimated Federal income tax payments of $35,000.

Compute Devon's Federal income tax payable or refund due for 2022 (assuming that he makes any available elections that will reduce the tax), and complete his tax return using appropriate forms and schedules. Suggested software: ProConnect Tax.

92. Tom and Alice Honeycutt, ages 45 and 46, respectively, live at 101 Glass Road, Delton, MI 49046. Tom is a county employee, and Alice is a self-employed accountant. Tom's Social Security number is 111-11-1111; Alice's Social Security number is 123-45-6789. The income and expenses associated with Alice's accounting practice for 2023 are as follows:

Communications
Critical Thinking
Planning
Tax Computation Problem

Revenues (cash receipts during 2023)	$185,000
Expenses	
Salaries	$ 45,000
Office supplies	3,200
Postage	2,900
Depreciation of equipment	42,000
Telephone	800
	$ 93,900

Because Alice is a cash method taxpayer, she does not record her receivables as revenue until she receives cash payment. At the beginning of 2023, her accounts receivable were $48,000, and the balance had decreased to $8,000 by the end of the year.

Alice used one room in their 10-room house as the office for her accounting practice (400 square feet out of a total square footage of 4,000). They paid the following expenses related to the house during 2023:

Utilities	$4,500
Insurance	2,100
Property taxes	5,200
Repairs	3,500

Tom and Alice purchased the house on September 1, 2022, for $400,000 (exclusive of land cost).

Tom received a salary of $54,000 during 2023. The appropriate amounts of Social Security tax and Medicare tax were withheld. In addition, $4,000 of Federal income taxes and $2,000 of state income taxes were withheld.

Tom and Alice's allowable itemized deductions during 2023, excluding any itemized deductions related to the house, were $24,600. They made estimated Federal income tax payments of $20,000.

Part 1—Tax Computation

Compute Tom and Alice's Federal income tax payable or refund due for 2023.

Part 2—Tax Planning

Tom and Alice own 30 acres of prime farmland that they inherited from Tom's father several years ago. At that time, the fair market value of the land was $150,000 (which became their basis in the land). The Honeycutts have been holding the land as an investment. The property recently was appraised for $190,000, and there is an outstanding mortgage on the land of $28,000. They are considering trading this land for property in the mountains of southern Colorado. The Colorado property owner—who has significant land holdings in the area—has provided two options to Tom and Alice (in both cases, the Colorado property owner would assume the mortgage as part of the exchange).

1. 15 acres of property with a fair market value of $135,000 plus $27,000 of cash or
2. 10 acres of property with a fair market value of $160,000 plus $2,000 of cash

The Honeycutts have come to you for advice, believing either transaction to be a like-kind exchange that will allow them to defer any gain. Assume that Tom and Alice expect their 2024 taxable income to be about the same as in 2023 (with any net capital gain taxed at a 15% rate). Write a letter to Tom and Alice that contains your advice on the proposed transactions.

Research Problems

Note: Solutions to the Research Problems can be prepared by using the Thomson Reuters Checkpoint™ online tax research database, which accompanies this textbook. Solutions can also be prepared by using research materials found in a typical tax library.

Research Problem 1. Terry owns real estate with an adjusted basis of $600,000 and a fair market value of $1,100,000. The amount of the nonrecourse mortgage on the property is $2,500,000. Because of substantial past and projected future losses associated with the real estate development (occupancy rate of only 37% after three years), Terry deeds the property to the creditor.

a. What are the tax consequences to Terry?

b. Assume that the data are the same, except that the fair market value of the property is $2,525,000. As a result, when Terry deeds the property to the creditor, she also receives $25,000 from the creditor. What are the tax consequences to Terry?

Communications

Research Problem 2. Ruth Ames died on January 10, 2023. In filing the estate tax return, her executor, Melvin Sims, elects the primary valuation date and amount (fair market value on the date of death). On March 12, 2023, Melvin invests $30,000 of cash that Ruth had in her money market account in acquiring 1,000 shares of Orange, Inc. ($30 per share). On January 10, 2023, Orange was selling for $29 per share. The stock is distributed to a beneficiary, Annette Rust, on June 1, 2023, when it is selling for $33 per share.

Melvin wants you to determine the amount at which the Orange shares should appear on the estate tax return and the amount of Annette's adjusted basis for the stock. Write a letter to Melvin in which you respond to his inquiry, and prepare a memo for the tax files. His address is 100 Center Lane, Miami, FL 33124.

Critical Thinking

Research Problem 3. Randall owns an office building (adjusted basis of $250,000) that he has been renting to a group of physicians. During negotiations over a new seven-year lease, the physicians offer to purchase the building for $900,000. Randall accepts the offer with the stipulation that the sale be structured as a delayed § 1031 transaction. Consequently, the sales proceeds are paid to a qualified third-party intermediary on the closing date of September 30, 2023.

On October 2, 2023, Randall properly identifies an office building that he would like to acquire. Unfortunately, on November 10, 2023, the property Randall selected is withdrawn from the market. Working with the intermediary, on November 12, 2023, Randall identifies another office building that meets his requirements. The purchase of this property closes on December 15, 2023, and the title is transferred to Randall.

Randall treats the transaction as a like-kind exchange. Even though the original office building identified was not acquired, Randall concludes that in substance, he has satisfied the 45-day rule. He identified the acquired office building as soon as the negotiations ceased on his first choice. Should the IRS accept Randall's attempt to comply? Explain.

Use internet tax resources to address the following questions. Look for reliable websites and blogs of the IRS and other government agencies, media outlets, businesses, tax professionals, academics, think tanks, and political outlets.

Research Problem 4. How are transactions using bitcoin (or another virtual currency) treated under U.S. tax law? Locate the IRS guidance on this question. Some background on bitcoin can be found at **bitcoin.org/en/faq**. In addition, locate the American Institute of CPAs Comment Letters on virtual currency (issued in May 2018 and February 2020). What are the IRS reporting requirements related to cryptocurrency transactions? After reading any relevant materials, provide a one-page written summary to your instructor. Communications

Communications
Data Analytics

Research Problem 5. How do U.S. individuals generate their income? Does it vary by size of income (AGI)? Go to the IRS tax statistics website (**irs.gov/statistics**), and download a recent tax year's information on "sources of income." Compare the following types of income by size of AGI: (1) wages, (2) capital gain distributions, (3) sales of capital assets, and (4) sales of property other than capital assets. Cluster the data into no more than six AGI categories. Present your findings in a visual (e.g., bar chart), and summarize your findings in a one-page memo to your instructor.

Becker CPA Review Questions

Becker

1. Jasmin purchased 100 shares of Pinkstey Corporation (publicly traded company) on January 1 of year 1 for $5,000. The FMV of the shares at the end of year 1 was $6,000. On January 1 of year 4, Pinkstey Corporation declared a 2-for-1 stock split when the fair market value of the stock was $65 per share. On January 1 of year 5, Jasmin sold all of her Pinkstey Corporation stock when the fair market value was $40 per share. Which of the following statements is true?

   a. Jasmin reports $6,500 in gross income for the 2-for-1 stock split in year 4.

   b. Jasmin's basis in the Pinkstey Corporation stock at the end of year 4 is $65 per share.

   c. Jasmin has no taxable income for the Pinkstey Corporation stock in year 4.

   d. Jasmin owns 100 shares in Pinkstey Corporation stock at the end of year 4.

2. Alice gifted stock to her son, Bob, in year 5. Alice bought the stock in year 1 for $8,300. The value of the stock on the date of gift was $6,400. Bob sold the stock in year 7 for $15,800. What is Bob's recognized gain or loss on the sale in year 7?

   a. $0
   b. $7,500 gain
   c. $9,400 gain
   d. $15,800 gain

3. Jerry inherits an asset from his uncle, who purchased the asset five days before he died. Which of the following statements is correct?

   a. If Jerry sells the asset a few days after receiving it, any gain or loss on the sale will be short term.

   b. Jerry's basis in the asset is the carryover basis from his uncle.

   c. Jerry's basis is the FMV on the alternate valuation date or date it is distributed to him.

   d. Jerry's basis is the FMV on his uncle's date of death.

4. Which of the following statements is *not* correct?
   a. The basis of an asset that is purchased must be adjusted for depreciation allowable.
   b. The general rule for the basis of property acquired by gift is a carryover of basis from the donor.
   c. If an asset is acquired by gift and the FMV on the date of gift is lower than the donor's carryover basis, the recipient's basis cannot be determined until the asset is disposed of.
   d. The basis of property acquired from a decedent is always the FMV on the date of death.

5. Rick purchased 100 shares of XYZ stock on April 4, year 4, for $8,600. He sold 50 shares on February 8, year 5, for $3,000. He then bought another 50 shares of XYZ on March 1, year 5, for $3,200. How much loss will Rick realize in year 5?
   a. $0
   b. $1,300
   c. $3,000
   d. $5,600

6. Agnes sold 50 shares of ABC stock to her son, Steve, in year 4 for $42,000. She bought the stock eight years ago for $50,000. Steve sold the stock to an unrelated party in year 6 for $60,000. How much gain will Steve recognize from the sale in year 6?
   a. $0
   b. $10,000
   c. $18,000
   d. $60,000

7. On February 1 of the current year, Duffy learned that he was bequeathed 1,000 shares of common stock under his father's will. Duffy's father had paid $12,500 for the stock 20 years ago. Fair market value of the stock on February 1 of the current year, the date of his father's death, was $14,000 and had increased to $15,500 six months later. The executor of the estate elected the alternative valuation date for estate tax purposes. Duffy sold the stock for $14,500 on June 1 of the current year, the date that the executor distributed the stock to him. How much income should Duffy include in his current-year individual income tax return for the inheritance of the 1,000 shares of stock which he received from his father's estate?
   a. $5,500
   b. $4,000
   c. $2,500
   d. $0

8. On January 25, year 10, Mother Hall gave her daughter, Nadyne, 500 shares of common stock of XYZ, Corp. The fair market value of the stock on January 25 was $2,000. Mother Hall had paid $4,000 for the stock three years earlier. Nadyne decided a month after receiving the stock that she doesn't want to hold it and sold it for $1,000, the fair market value at the time of the sale. How much income (loss) must Nadyne include in her tax return for year 10 in regards to the sale of the stock?
   a. $0
   b. ($1,000)
   c. ($2,000)
   d. ($3,000)

9. In early year 8, Alice sold Tom, her son, 20 shares of common stock for $20,000. Alice had paid $25,000 for the stock in year 2. In late year 8, Tom sold the stock to an unrelated third party for $35,000. How much gain must Tom report in his year 8 tax return for the sale of the stock?
   a. $0
   b. $5,000
   c. $10,000
   d. $15,000

10. Susie purchased her primary residence on March 15, year 4, for $550,000. She sold it on October 15, year 7, for $240,000. What amount of loss from the sale is recognized on her year 7 income tax return?

    a. $0
    b. $60,000
    c. $250,000
    d. $310,000

11. Chad owned an office building that was destroyed in a tornado. The adjusted basis of the building at the time was $890,000. After the deductible, Chad received an insurance check for $850,000. He used the $850,000 to purchase a new building that same year. How much is Chad's recognized loss, and what is his basis in the new building?

	Recognized Loss	New Basis
a.	$0	$850,000
b.	$0	$890,000
c.	$40,000	$850,000
d.	$40,000	$890,000

12. Chad owned an office building that was destroyed in a tornado. The adjusted basis of the building at the time was $890,000. After the deductible, Chad received an insurance check for $950,000. He used $900,000 of the insurance proceeds to purchase a new building that same year. How much is Chad's recognized gain, and what is his basis in the new building?

	Recognized Gain	New Basis
a.	$0	$890,000
b.	$0	$900,000
c.	$50,000	$890,000
d.	$60,000	$900,000

13. Marsha exchanged land in Florida with an FMV of $72,700 and an adjusted basis of $40,000 for land in Iowa with an FMV of $57,700. Marsha also assumed a $5,000 liability on the land received in the transaction and was relieved of a $20,000 liability on the land that was given up. What is Marsha's recognized gain on the transaction?

    a. $0
    b. $15,000
    c. $20,000
    d. $32,700

14. Marsha exchanged land in Florida with an FMV of $52,700 and an adjusted basis of $60,000 for land in Iowa with an FMV of $57,700. Marsha also paid $5,000 cash in the transaction. What is Marsha's basis in the land received?

    a. $55,000
    b. $57,700
    c. $60,000
    d. $65,000

Chapter

14 Property Transactions: Capital Gains and Losses, § 1231, and Recapture Provisions

Learning Objectives: *After completing Chapter 14, you should be able to:*

- **LO.1** Explain the general scheme of taxation for capital gains and losses.
- **LO.2** Distinguish capital assets from ordinary assets.
- **LO.3** Explain the relevance of a sale or exchange to classification as a capital gain or loss and apply the special rules for the capital gain or loss treatment of the retirement of corporate obligations, options, patents, franchises, and lease cancellation payments.
- **LO.4** Determine whether the holding period for a capital asset is long term or short term.
- **LO.5** Describe the beneficial tax treatment for capital gains and the detrimental tax treatment for capital losses for noncorporate taxpayers.
- **LO.6** Describe the tax treatment for capital gains and the detrimental tax treatment for capital losses for corporate taxpayers.
- **LO.7** State and explain the rationale for and the nature and treatment of gains and losses from the disposition of business assets.
- **LO.8** Distinguish § 1231 assets from ordinary assets and capital assets and calculate the § 1231 gain or loss.
- **LO.9** Determine when § 1245 recapture applies and how it is computed.
- **LO.10** Determine when § 1250 recapture applies.
- **LO.11** State and explain considerations common to §§ 1245 and 1250.
- **LO.12** Recognize special recapture provisions that are part of the tax law.
- **LO.13** Describe the reporting procedures for §§ 1231, 1245, and 1250.
- **LO.14** Identify tax planning opportunities arising from the sale or exchange of capital assets and avoid pitfalls associated with the recapture provisions.

Chapter Outline

The Big Picture

Managing Capital Asset Transactions

Maurice has come to you for tax advice regarding his investments. He inherited $750,000 from his uncle, Joe. A financial adviser suggested that he make the following investments, which he did nine months ago.

- $5,000 for 100 shares of Eagle Company stock.
- $50,000 for a 50 percent interest in a patent that Kevin, a college roommate who is an unemployed inventor, obtained for a special battery he developed to power green cars. To date, Kevin has been unable to market the battery to an auto manufacturer or supplier, but he has high hopes of doing so in the future.
- $95,000 to invest in a franchise from Orange, Inc.
- $200,000 in the stock of Purple, Inc., a publicly held bank that follows a policy of occasionally paying dividends. At one time, the stock appreciated to $300,000, but now it is worth only $210,000. Maurice is considering selling this stock.
- $50,000 in tax-exempt bonds. The interest rate on the bonds is only 3 percent. Maurice is considering moving this money into taxable bonds that pay 3.5 percent.
- $100,000 for a 10 percent ownership interest as a limited partner in a real estate development. Lots in the development are selling well.

Maurice read an article that discussed the beneficial tax rates for capital assets and dividends. He really liked the part about "costless" capital gains, although he did not understand it.

Maurice has retained his job as a toll booth supervisor at the municipal airport. His annual compensation is $35,000. He likes the job and has met some interesting people there.

Respond to Maurice's request for tax advice.

Read the chapter and formulate your response.

Framework 1040 **Tax Formula for Individuals**

This chapter covers the boldfaced portions of the Tax Formula for Individuals that was introduced in Concept Summary 3.1. Below those portions are the sections of Form 1040 where the results are reported.

Income *(broadly defined)*	$ xx,xxx
Less: Exclusions	(x,xxx)
Gross income	**$xx,xxx**

FORM 1040 (p. 1)

7	Capital gain or (loss). Attach Schedule D if required. If not required, check here ▶	☐

FORM 1040 (Schedule 1)

3	Business income or (loss). Attach Schedule C
4	Other gains or (losses). Attach Form 4797

Adjusted gross income	$ xx,xxx
Less: The greater of total itemized deductions *or* the standard deduction	(x,xxx)
Personal and dependency exemptions*	(x,xxx)
Deduction for qualified business income**	(x,xxx)
Taxable income	$ xx,xxx
Tax on taxable income *(see Tax Tables or Tax Rate Schedules)*	**$ x,xxx**

FORM 1040 (p. 2)

16	**Tax** (see instructions). Check if any from Form(s): **1** ☐ 8814 **2** ☐ 4972 **3** ☐ ______

Less: Tax credits *(including income taxes withheld and prepaid)*	(xxx)
Tax due (or refund)	$ xxx

* Exemption deductions are not allowed from 2018 through 2025.
** Only applies from 2018 through 2025.

Fourteen years ago, a taxpayer purchased 100 shares of IBM stock for $17 a share. This year the taxpayer sells the shares for $132 a share. Should the $115 per-share gain receive any special tax treatment? The $115 gain has built up over 14 years, so it may not be fair to tax it the same as income that was all earned this year.

What if the stock had been purchased for $132 per share and sold for $17 a share? Should the $115 loss be fully deductible? The tax law has an intricate approach to answering these investment activity-related questions.

Property transactions involve the *disposition* of *assets*. The sale of the IBM stock was the disposition of an investment-related asset. As you study this chapter, keep in mind that how investment-related gains and losses are taxed can dramatically affect whether taxpayers make investments and which investments are made. Except for a brief discussion in Chapter 3, earlier chapters dwelt on how to determine the amount of gain or loss from a property disposition, but did not discuss the classification of gains and losses. This chapter will focus on that topic.

The tax law requires **capital gains** and **capital losses** to be separated from other types of gains and losses. There are two reasons for this treatment. First, long-term capital gains may be taxed at a lower rate than ordinary gains. Second, a net capital loss is subject to deduction limitations. For noncorporate taxpayers, a net capital loss is only deductible up to $3,000 per year. Any excess loss over the annual limit carries over and may be deductible in a future tax year.

For these reasons, capital gains and losses must be distinguished from other types of gains and losses. This chapter describes:

- The intricate rules needed to determine what *type* of gains and losses the taxpayer has,
- How those gains and losses are intermingled among themselves,
- How the result of that intermingling then is integrated with the other items on the taxpayer's tax return, and
- How those gains and losses are taxed as part of the taxpayer's taxable income.

14-1 General Scheme of Taxation

LO.1

Explain the general scheme of taxation for capital gains and losses.

Recognized gains and losses must be properly *classified*. Proper classification depends on three characteristics:

- The tax *status* of the property (capital, § 1231, or ordinary).
- The manner of the property's *disposition* (sale, exchange, worthlessness, casualty, theft, or condemnation).
- The *holding period* of the property (*short-term*: one year or less; *long-term*: more than one year).

A major focus of this chapter is capital gains and losses. But in addition, § 1231 assets and ordinary gains and losses also are discussed.

14-2 Capital Assets

LO.2

Distinguish capital assets from ordinary assets.

Personal use assets and investment assets are the most common capital assets owned by individual taxpayers. Personal use assets usually include things like a residence, furniture, clothing, recreational equipment, and automobiles. Investment assets usually include stocks, bonds, and mutual funds. Remember, however, that losses from the sale or exchange of personal use assets are not recognized.

The crux of capital asset determination hinges on whether the asset is held for personal use (capital asset), investment (capital asset), or business (ordinary asset). How a taxpayer uses the property typically answers this question.

David buys an expensive painting.

- If David purchased the painting for personal use (as a decoration in his home) and it is not of investment quality, it is a capital asset. However, any loss on its sale is not usable, whereas gain from its sale is taxable. Investment quality generally means that the painting is expected to appreciate in value.
- If the painting is used to decorate David's business office and is of investment quality, the painting is not depreciable and, therefore, is a capital asset.
- If David's business is buying and selling paintings, the painting is inventory and, therefore, an ordinary asset.
- If the painting is not of investment quality and the business did not purchase it for investment, the painting is an ordinary asset and it is depreciable even though it serves a decorative purpose in David's office. If David depreciates the painting, that is evidence that the painting is held for use in his business (and *not* being held for investment or as inventory). As a result, it is not a capital asset.

Since capital assets receive preferential tax treatment, taxpayers prefer capital gains rather than ordinary gains. So the definition of a capital asset is critically important. As discussed next, this definition has been the subject of many court cases and rulings.

14-2a **Definition of a Capital Asset (§ 1221)**

Capital assets are not directly defined in the Code. Instead, § 1221(a) defines what is *not* a capital asset. In general, a **capital asset** is property *other than* inventory, accounts and notes receivable, supplies, and most fixed assets of a business.

Specifically, the Code defines a capital asset as property held by the taxpayer (when it is connected with the taxpayer's business) that is *not* any of the following:

- Inventory or property held primarily for sale to customers in the ordinary course of a business.
- Accounts and notes receivable generated from the sale of goods or services in a business.
- Depreciable property or real estate used in a business.
- A patent, invention, model, or design (whether or not patented); a secret formula or process; certain copyrights; literary, musical, or artistic compositions; or letters, memoranda, or similar property created by or for the taxpayer.[1]
- Certain U.S. government publications.
- Supplies used in a business.

Often, the only business asset that is a capital asset is "self-generated" goodwill (purchased goodwill is a § 1231 asset). The following discussion provides further detail on each part of the capital asset definition.

Inventory

What constitutes inventory is determined by the taxpayer's business.

Inventory Determination

Example 2

Green Company buys and sells used cars. Its cars are inventory. Its gains from the sale of the cars are ordinary income.

Soong sells her personal use automobile at a $500 gain. The automobile is a personal use asset and, therefore, a capital asset. The gain is a capital gain.

No asset is inherently capital or ordinary. If Soong (Example 3) sells her "capital asset" automobile to Green Company (Example 2), that same automobile loses its capital asset status, because the automobile is inventory to Green Company. Whether an asset is capital or ordinary, therefore, depends entirely on the relationship of the asset to the taxpayer who sold it. This classification dilemma is but one feature of capital asset treatment that makes this area so confusing and complicated.

Accounts and Notes Receivable

Accounts and notes receivable are often created as part of a business transaction. These assets may be collected by the creditor, be sold by the creditor, or become completely or partially worthless. Also, the creditor may be on the accrual or cash basis of accounting.

Collection of an *accrual basis* account or note receivable does not result in a gain or loss because the amount collected equals the receivable's basis. If sold, an ordinary gain or loss is generated if the receivable is sold for more or less than its basis (the receivable is an ordinary asset). If the receivable is partially or wholly worthless, the creditor has a "bad debt," which may result in an ordinary deduction (see text Section 7-1).

[1] §§ 1221(a)(3) and 1221(b)(3).

Collection of a *cash basis* account or note receivable does not result in a gain or loss because the amount collected is ordinary income. In addition, a cash basis receivable has a zero basis since no revenue is recorded until the receivable is collected. If sold, an ordinary gain is generated (the receivable is an ordinary asset). There is no bad debt deduction for cash basis receivables because they have no basis. See text Section 14-3 for more details on "sale or exchange."

Oriole Company has accounts receivable of $100,000. Because Oriole needs working capital, it sells the receivables for $83,000 to a financial institution.

If Oriole is an *accrual basis taxpayer*, it has a $17,000 ordinary loss. Revenue of $100,000 would have been recorded and a $100,000 basis would have been established when the receivable was created.

If Oriole is a *cash basis taxpayer*, it has $83,000 of ordinary income because it would not have recorded any revenue earlier; as a result, the receivable has no tax basis.

Business Fixed Assets

Depreciable personal property and real estate (both depreciable and nondepreciable) used by a business are *not* capital assets (even though they have been capitalized for accounting purposes). To avoid any confusion, we will refer to these as fixed assets. The tax law related to this property is complex; most of these rules are discussed later in this chapter. Although business fixed assets are not capital assets, a long-term capital gain can sometimes result from their sale. The potential capital gain treatment for business fixed assets under § 1231 is also discussed later in this chapter. Another rule—real property subdivided for sale (§ 1237)—is discussed in text Section 14-2c.

Inventions and Processes

A patent, invention, model, or design (whether or not patented) and a secret formula or process are excluded from being a capital asset. These are *ordinary* assets. The assets may be held either by the taxpayer who created the property or by a taxpayer who received the asset from the taxpayer who created the property. As a result, gains or losses from the sale or exchange of these assets do *not* receive capital gain treatment. In limited circumstances, patents (even though they are not capital assets) may be *treated* as capital assets. Those special rules are discussed in text Section 14-3d.

Abigail invents a multifunctional case for a popular brand of cell phones. She has a manufacturer produce them for her and sells them via the internet. Her cost is $2.30 per case, and she sells each one for $10. To her surprise, she quickly achieves $45,000 in total sales. She has not capitalized any of the costs of developing the invention and has not patented it.

She sells all of her rights to the invention for $350,000 to a company that is in the business of producing cell phone cases. Her profit from sales of the cases is ordinary income because the cases are inventory. The $350,000 gain from selling the rights to the invention is an ordinary gain because the invention is not a capital asset.

Copyrights and Creative Works

Generally, the person whose efforts led to the copyright or creative work has an ordinary asset, not a capital asset. *Creative works* include the works of authors, composers, and artists. Also, the person for whom a letter, a memorandum, or another similar property was created has an ordinary asset. Finally, a person receiving a copyright, a creative work, a letter, a memorandum, or similar property by gift from the creator or the person for whom the work was created has an ordinary asset. A taxpayer may elect to treat the sale or exchange of a musical composition or a copyright of a musical work as the disposition of a capital asset.

Creative Works

Wanda is a part-time music composer. A music publisher purchases one of her songs for $5,000.

Wanda has a $5,000 ordinary gain from the sale of an ordinary asset unless she elects to treat the gain as a capital gain.

Ed received a letter from the President of the United States in 1982. In the current year, Ed sells the letter to a collector for $300.

Ed has a $300 ordinary gain from the sale of an ordinary asset (because the letter was created for Ed).

Isabella gives her son a song she composed. The son sells the song to a music publisher for $5,000.

The son has a $5,000 ordinary gain from the sale of an ordinary asset unless he elects to treat the gain as a capital gain.

If the son inherits the song from Isabella, his basis for the song is its fair market value at Isabella's death. In this situation, the song is a capital asset because the son's basis is not related to Isabella's basis for the song.

Ethics & Equity Sculpture as a Capital Asset

Cynthia is a successful sculptor who created a work that is now worth $400,000 and has no tax basis. Cynthia forms a corporation and contributes the sculpture to it in exchange for the corporation's shares. Fourteen months later, she sells all the stock for $400,000. She wants to treat the sale of the stock as a long-term capital gain. Evaluate the propriety of Cynthia's actions.

U.S. Government Publications

U.S. government publications received from the U.S. government (or its agencies) for a reduced price are *not* capital assets. This prevents a taxpayer from later donating the publications to charity and claiming a charitable contribution deduction equal to the fair market value of the publications. Normally, the charitable contribution of an ordinary asset provides a deduction equal to the asset's basis. If the taxpayer received the property at no cost, its basis is equal to zero. If this property is given to someone else, it retains its ordinary asset status (see text Section 10-4e for more about property contributions).

14-2b Effect of Judicial Action

Because the Code only lists categories of what are *not* capital assets, judicial interpretation is sometimes required to determine whether a specific item fits into one of those categories. The Supreme Court follows a literal interpretation of the categories. For instance, because corporate stock is not mentioned in § 1221, it is *usually* a capital asset. However, what if corporate stock is purchased for resale to customers? Then it is *inventory* (and not a capital asset) because inventory is one of the categories in § 1221.

Intent also matters. What happens when a taxpayer who does not normally acquire stock for resale to customers acquires stock but intends to resell it? The Supreme Court decided that because the stock was not acquired primarily for sale to customers (the taxpayer did not sell the stock to its regular customers), the stock was a capital asset.[2]

[2] *Arkansas Best v. Comm.*, 88–1 USTC ¶9210, 61 AFTR 2d 88–655, 108 S.Ct. 971.

Because of the uncertainty associated with capital asset status, Congress has enacted several Code Sections to clarify its definition. These clarifications are discussed next.

14-2c **Statutory Expansions**

In several instances, Congress has clarified its general definition of what is *not* a capital asset.

Dealers in Securities

As a general rule, securities (stocks, bonds, and other financial instruments) held by a dealer are considered to be inventory and are, therefore, not subject to capital gain or loss treatment. A *dealer in securities* is a merchant (e.g., a brokerage firm) that regularly engages in the purchase and resale of securities to customers.

The dealer must identify any securities being held for investment. Generally, if a dealer clearly identifies certain securities as held for investment purposes by the close of business on the acquisition date, gain from the securities' sale will be capital gain. However, the gain will not be capital gain if the dealer ceases to hold the securities for investment prior to the sale. Losses are capital losses if at any time the securities have been clearly identified by the dealer as held for investment.

Example 9

Tracy is a securities dealer. She purchases 100 shares of Swan stock. If Tracy takes no further action, the stock is inventory and an ordinary asset.

If she designates in her records that the stock is held for investment, the stock is a capital asset. Tracy must designate the investment purpose by the close of business on the acquisition date. If Tracy maintains her investment purpose and later sells the stock, the gain or loss is capital gain or loss.

If Tracy redesignates the stock as held for resale (inventory) and then sells it, any gain is ordinary, but any loss is capital loss.

Real Property Subdivided for Sale (§ 1237)

Substantial real property development activities may result in the owner being considered a dealer for tax purposes. If so, ordinary income will result from any lots sold. However, § 1237 allows real estate investors capital gain treatment if they engage *only* in *limited* development activities. To be eligible for § 1237 treatment, the following requirements must be met:

- The taxpayer may not be a corporation.
- The taxpayer may not be a real estate dealer.
- No substantial improvements may be made to the lots sold. *Substantial* generally means more than a 10 percent increase in the value of a lot. Shopping centers and other commercial or residential buildings are considered substantial improvements, while filling, draining, leveling, and clearing operations are not.
- The taxpayer must have held the lots sold for at least 5 years, except for inherited property. The substantial improvements test is less stringent if the property is held at least 10 years.

If these requirements are met, all gain is capital gain until the tax year in which the *sixth* lot is sold. Sales of contiguous lots to a single buyer in the same transaction count as the sale of one lot. Beginning with the tax year the *sixth* lot is sold, 5 percent of the revenue from lot sales is potential ordinary income. That potential ordinary income is offset by any selling expenses from the lot sales. As sales commissions often are at least 5 percent of the sales price, typically none of the gain is treated as ordinary income.

Code § 1237 does not apply to losses. A loss from the sale of subdivided real property is an ordinary loss unless the property qualifies as a capital asset under § 1221. The following example illustrates the application of § 1237.

Jack owns a large tract of land and subdivides it for sale. Assume that Jack meets all of the requirements of § 1237 and during the tax year sells the first 10 lots to 10 different buyers for $10,000 each. Jack's basis in each lot sold is $3,000, and he incurs total selling expenses of $4,000 ($400 for each lot) on the sales. Jack's gain is computed as follows:

Selling price (10 × $10,000)	$100,000	
Less: Selling expenses (10 × $400)	(4,000)	
Amount realized		$ 96,000
Basis (10 × $3,000)		(30,000)
Realized and recognized gain		$ 66,000
Classification of recognized gain:		
Ordinary income		
Five percent of selling price (5% × $100,000)	$ 5,000	
Less: Selling expenses	(4,000)	
Ordinary gain		(1,000)
Capital gain		$ 65,000

A portion of the gain is given ordinary treatment because the *sixth* lot is sold in the current year.

Nonbusiness Bad Debts

A loan not made in the ordinary course of business is classified as a nonbusiness receivable. In the year the receivable becomes completely worthless, it is a *nonbusiness bad debt*, and the bad debt is treated as a short-term capital loss. Even if the receivable was outstanding for more than one year, the loss is still a short-term capital loss. Chapter 7 discusses nonbusiness bad debts more thoroughly (see text Section 7-1b).

LO.3

Explain the relevance of a sale or exchange to classification as a capital gain or loss and apply the special rules for the capital gain or loss treatment of the retirement of corporate obligations, options, patents, franchises, and lease cancellation payments.

14-3 Sale or Exchange

Recognition of capital gain or loss usually requires a sale or exchange of a capital asset. The Code uses the term **sale or exchange**, but does not define it. Generally, a property *sale* involves the receipt of money by the seller and/or the assumption by the purchaser of the seller's liabilities. An *exchange* involves the transfer of property for other property. So an involuntary conversion (casualty, theft, or condemnation) is not a sale or exchange.

In several situations, Congress has created rules that specifically provide for sale or exchange treatment. For example, assume that the expiration of a right to personal property (other than stock) that would be a capital asset in the hands of the taxpayer results in a recognized gain or loss. This is a capital gain or loss.[3] Several of these special rules are discussed below, including worthless securities, the retirement of corporate obligations, options, patents, franchises, and lease cancellation payments.

14-3a Worthless Securities and § 1244 Stock

Occasionally, securities such as stock and, especially, bonds may become worthless due to the insolvency of their issuer. If such a security is a capital asset, the loss is deemed to have occurred as the result of a sale or exchange on the *last day* of the tax year.[4] This last-day rule may have the effect of converting what otherwise would have been a short-term capital loss into a long-term capital loss. Code § 1244 allows an ordinary deduction on disposition of stock at a loss. The stock must be that of a small business corporation, and the ordinary deduction is limited to $50,000 ($100,000 for married taxpayers filing jointly) per year. See Chapter 7 (and text Sections 7-2a and 7-2b) for a more complete discussion of these rules.

[3] § 1234A.

[4] § 165(g)(1).

14-3b Retirement of Corporate Obligations

A debt obligation (e.g., a bond or note payable) may have a tax basis in excess of or less than its redemption value because it may have been acquired at a premium or discount. Consequently, the collection of the redemption value may result in a loss or gain. Generally, the collection of a debt obligation is *treated* as a sale or exchange.[5] Therefore, any loss or gain can be a capital loss or capital gain because a sale or exchange has taken place.

Fran acquires $1,000 of Osprey Corporation bonds for $980 in the open market. If the bonds are held to maturity, the $20 difference between Fran's collection of the $1,000 redemption value and her cost of $980 is treated as capital gain.

Original Issue Discount (§§ 1272–1288)

The benefit of the sale or exchange exception that allows a capital gain from the collection of certain obligations is reduced when the obligation has original issue discount. **Original issue discount (OID)** arises when the issue price of a debt obligation is less than the maturity value of the obligation. OID must generally be amortized over the life of the debt obligation using the effective interest method. The OID amortization increases the basis of the bond.

Most new publicly traded bond issues do not carry OID because the stated interest rate is set to make the market price on issue the same as the bond's face amount. In addition, even if the issue price is less than the face amount, the difference is not considered to be OID if the difference is less than one-fourth of 1 percent of the redemption price at maturity multiplied by the number of years to maturity.[6]

In the case where OID does exist, it may or may not have to be amortized, depending upon the date the obligation was issued. When OID is amortized, the amount of gain upon collection, sale, or exchange of the obligation is correspondingly reduced. The obligations covered by the OID amortization rules and the method of amortization are presented in §§ 1272–1275. Similar rules for other obligations can be found in §§ 1276–1288.

Jerry purchases $10,000 of newly issued White Corporation bonds for $6,000. The bonds have OID of $4,000. Jerry must amortize the discount over the life of the bonds. The OID amortization *increases* his interest income. (The bonds were selling at a discount because the market rate of interest was greater than the bonds' stated interest rate.) After Jerry has amortized $1,800 of OID, he sells the bonds for $8,000. Jerry has a capital gain of $200 [$8,000 – ($6,000 cost + $1,800 OID amortization)].

The OID amortization rules prevent him from converting ordinary interest income into capital gain. Without the OID amortization, Jerry would have capital gain of $2,000 ($8,000 – $6,000 cost).

14-3c Options

Frequently, a potential buyer of property wants some time to make the purchase decision, but wants to control the sale and/or the sale price in the meantime. **Options** are used to achieve these objectives. The potential purchaser (grantee) pays the property owner (grantor) for an option on the property. The grantee then becomes the option holder. The option, which usually sets a price at which the grantee can buy the property, expires after a specified period of time.

Exercise of Options by Grantee

If the option is exercised, the amount paid for the option is added to the optioned property's selling price. This increases the gain (or reduces the loss) to the grantor resulting from the sale of the property. The grantor's gain or loss is capital or ordinary depending on the tax status of the property. The grantee adds the cost of the option to the basis of the property purchased.

[5] § 1271.

[6] § 1273(a)(3).

Sale of an Option

A grantee may sell or exchange the option rather than exercise it or let it expire. Generally, the grantee's sale or exchange of the option results in capital gain or loss if the option property is (or would be) a capital asset to the grantee.[7]

Rosa wants to buy some vacant land for investment purposes. However, she cannot afford the full purchase price at the present time. Instead, Rosa (grantee) pays the landowner (grantor) $3,000 to obtain an option to buy the land for $100,000 anytime in the next two years. The option is a capital asset for Rosa because if she actually purchased the land, the land would be a capital asset.

Three months after purchasing the option, Rosa sells it for $7,000. She has a $4,000 ($7,000 − $3,000) short-term capital gain on this sale because she held the option for one year or less.

Failure to Exercise Options

If an option holder (grantee) fails to exercise the option, the lapse of the option is considered a sale or exchange on the option expiration date. As a result, the loss is a capital loss if the property subject to the option is (or would be) a capital asset in the hands of the grantee.

The grantor of an option on *stocks, securities, commodities, or commodity futures* receives short-term capital gain treatment upon the expiration of the option. Options on property *other than* stocks, securities, commodities, or commodity futures (for instance, vacant land) result in ordinary income to the grantor when the option expires.

For example, an individual investor who owns certain stock (a capital asset) may sell a call option, entitling the buyer of the option to acquire the stock at a specified price higher than the value at the date the option is granted. The writer of the call receives a premium (e.g., 10 percent) for writing the option. If the price of the stock does not increase during the option period, the option will expire unexercised. When the option expires, the grantor must recognize short-term capital gain (whereas the grantee recognizes a loss, the character of which depends on the underlying asset). These rules do not apply to options held for sale to customers (the inventory of a securities dealer).

The Big Picture

Example 14

Return to the facts of *The Big Picture* on p. 14-1. On February 1, 2023, Maurice purchases 100 shares of Eagle Company stock for $5,000. On April 1, 2023, he writes a call option on the stock, giving the grantee the right to buy the stock for $6,000 during the following six-month period. Maurice (the grantor) receives a call premium of $500 for writing the call.

- If the call is exercised by the grantee on August 1, 2023, Maurice has $1,500 ($6,000 + $500 − $5,000) of short-term capital gain from the sale of the stock. The grantee has a $6,500 ($500 option premium + $6,000 purchase price) basis for the stock.
- Investors sometimes get nervous and want to "lock in" gains or losses.
  - Assume that Maurice, prior to exercise of the grantee's call, decides to sell his stock for $6,000 and enters into a closing transaction by purchasing a call on 100 shares of Eagle Company stock for $5,000.
  - Because the Eagle stock is selling for $6,000, Maurice must pay a call premium of $1,000.
  - He recognizes a $500 short-term capital loss [$500 (call premium received) − $1,000 (call premium paid)] on the closing transaction.

continued

[7] § 1234(a) and Reg. § 1.1234–1(a)(1).

- On the actual sale of the Eagle stock, Maurice has a short-term capital gain of $1,000 [$6,000 (selling price) − $5,000 (cost)].
- The original grantee is not affected by Maurice's closing transaction. The original option is still in existence, and the grantee's tax consequences depend on what action the grantee takes—exercising the option, letting the option expire, or selling the option.

- Assume that the original option expired unexercised. Maurice has a $500 short-term capital gain equal to the call premium received for writing the option. This gain is not recognized until the option expires. The grantee has a loss from expiration of the option. The nature of the loss will depend upon whether the option was a capital asset or an ordinary asset.

Concept Summary 14.1 summarizes the consequences of various transactions involving options to both the grantor and grantee.

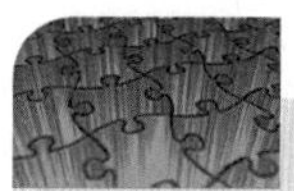

Concept Summary 14.1

Options: Consequences to the Grantor and Grantee

	Effect on	
Event	**Grantor**	**Grantee**
Option is granted.	Receives value and has a contract obligation (a liability).	Pays value and has a contract right (an asset).
Option is exercised.	Amount received for option increases proceeds from sale of the option property.	Amount paid for option becomes part of the basis of the option property purchased.
Option is sold or exchanged by grantee.	Result depends upon whether option later expires or is exercised (see above).	Could have gain or loss (capital gain or loss if option property would have been a capital asset for the grantee).
Option expires.	Has a short-term capital gain if the option property is stocks, securities, commodities, or commodity futures. Otherwise, gain is ordinary income.	Has a loss (capital loss if option property would have been a capital asset for the grantee).

14-3d **Patents**

Transfer of a **patent** is treated as the sale or exchange of a long-term capital asset when *all substantial rights* to the patent are transferred by a *holder*.[8] The transferor/holder may receive payment in virtually any form, including contingent payments based on the transferee/purchaser's productivity, use, or disposition of the patent. If the transfer meets these requirements, any gain or loss is *automatically a long-term* capital gain or loss. Whether the asset was a capital asset for the transferor, whether a sale or exchange occurred, and how long the transferor held the patent are not relevant.

Substantial Rights

To receive favorable capital gain treatment, *all substantial rights* to the patent must be transferred. The sale of a partial interest qualifies if the sale places no restrictions on the use of the patent by the purchaser. All substantial rights have not been transferred when the transfer is limited geographically within the issuing country or when the transfer is for a period less than the remaining life of the patent. All the facts and circumstances of the transaction, not just the language of the transfer document, are examined when making this determination.[9]

[8] § 1235.

[9] Reg. § 1.1235–2(b)(1).

Example 15 illustrates the special treatment for patents.

The Big Picture

Example 15

Return to the facts of *The Big Picture* on p. 14-1. Shortly after your conversation with Maurice, Green Battery Company offers to buy the patent developed by Kevin for $2,000,000 plus $0.50 for each battery sold. Kevin and Maurice agree to sell the patent.

As Maurice transferred all his remaining rights, he automatically has a long-term capital gain from both his 50% share of the lump-sum payment ($1,000,000) and the $0.50 per battery royalty to the extent those proceeds exceed his basis for the patent.

Whether Maurice gets long-term capital gain treatment depends upon whether Maurice is a *holder*. See the following discussion and Example 16.

Holder Defined

The *holder* of a patent must be an *individual*. Usually, this is the invention's creator or an individual who purchases the patent rights from the creator before the patented invention is put into production ("reduced to practice"). So if the creator's employer has all rights to an employee's inventions, the employer is *not* eligible for long-term capital gain treatment. The employer normally will have an ordinary asset because the patent was developed as part of its business.

The Big Picture

Example 16

Return to the facts of *The Big Picture* on p. 14-1. Continuing with the facts of Example 15, Kevin is clearly a holder of the patent because he is the inventor and was not an employee when he invented the battery. When Maurice purchased a 50% interest in the patent nine months ago, he became a *holder* because the patent was not being used to manufacture batteries at the time of the purchase (i.e., it had not been "reduced to practice").

Since Maurice is also a holder, he will have an automatic long-term capital gain or loss if he transfers all substantial rights in his 50% interest to Green Battery Company. Maurice's basis for his share of the patent is $50,000, and the proceeds from Green Battery Company equal $1,000,000 plus $0.50 for each battery sold; Maurice has a long-term capital gain even though he has not held his interest in the patent for more than one year.

Compare the results here to those in Example 5. There, Abigail sold all substantial rights, but she had no patent and the invention had been "reduced to practice" because it was being manufactured and sold.

14-3e Franchises, Trademarks, and Trade Names (§ 1253)

A mode of operation, a widely recognized brand name (trade name), and a widely known business symbol (trademark) are all valuable assets. These assets may be licensed (commonly known as franchising) by their owner for use by other businesses. Many fast-food restaurants (such as McDonald's and Taco Bell) are franchises. The franchisee usually pays the owner (franchisor) an initial fee plus a contingent fee. The contingent fee is often based upon the franchisee's sales volume.

For Federal income tax purposes, a **franchise** is an agreement that gives the franchisee the right to distribute, sell, or provide goods, services, or facilities within a specified area.[10] A franchise transfer includes the grant of a franchise, a transfer by one franchisee to another person, or the renewal of a franchise.

Code § 1253 provides that a transfer of a franchise, trademark, or trade name is not a transfer of a capital asset when the transferor retains any significant power, right, or continuing interest in the property transferred.

[10] § 1253(b)(1).

Significant Power, Right, or Continuing Interest

In most franchising operations, the transferor retains some powers or rights. As a result, the transaction is not a capital asset transfer. *Significant powers, rights, or continuing interests* include control over franchise assignment, quality of products and services, sale or advertising of products or services, the requirement that substantially all supplies and equipment be purchased from the transferor, and the right to terminate the franchise.

In the unusual case where the transferor does not retain any significant power, right, or continuing interest, a capital gain or loss may occur. For capital gain or loss treatment to be available, the asset transferred must qualify as a capital asset.

The Big Picture

Return to the facts of *The Big Picture* on p. 14-1. Maurice sells for $210,000 to Mauve, Inc., the franchise purchased from Orange, Inc., nine months ago. The $210,000 received by Maurice is not contingent, and all significant powers, rights, and continuing interests are transferred.

The $115,000 gain ($210,000 proceeds − $95,000 basis) is a short-term capital gain because Maurice has held the franchise for only nine months.

Franchise Payments

In most franchise settings, when the transferor retains significant power or rights, both contingent (e.g., based on sales) and noncontingent payments occur.

Noncontingent Payments Any noncontingent payments made by the franchisee to the franchisor are ordinary income to the franchisor. The franchisee capitalizes the payments and amortizes them over 15 years. If the franchise is sold, the amortization is subject to recapture under § 1245.[11]

Grey Company signs a 10-year franchise agreement with DOH Donuts. Grey (the franchisee) makes payments of $3,000 per year for the first 8 years of the franchise agreement—a total of $24,000. Grey cannot deduct $3,000 per year as the payments are made. Instead, Grey may amortize the $24,000 total over 15 years. As a result, Grey may deduct $1,600 per year for each of the 15 years of the amortization period.

The same result would occur if Grey made a $24,000 lump-sum payment at the beginning of the franchise period. Assuming that DOH Donuts (the franchisor) retains significant powers, rights, or a continuing interest, it will have ordinary income when it receives the payments from Grey.

Contingent Payments Any contingent franchise payments are ordinary income for the franchisor and an ordinary deduction for the franchisee. Contingent payments must meet the following requirements:

- The payments are made at least annually throughout the term of the transfer agreement.
- The payments are substantially equal in amount or are payable under a fixed formula.

TAK, a spicy chicken franchisor, transfers an eight-year franchise to Phyllis. TAK retains a significant power, right, or continuing interest. Phyllis, the franchisee, agrees to pay TAK 15% of sales. This contingent payment is ordinary income to TAK and a business deduction for Phyllis as the payments are made.

[11]The recapture rules are discussed later in this chapter.

Sports Franchises

Professional sports franchises (e.g., the Detroit Tigers) are subject to § 1253. Player contracts are usually one of the major assets acquired with a sports franchise. These contracts last only for the time stated in the contract. By being classified as § 197 intangibles, the player contracts and other intangible assets acquired in the purchase of the sports franchise are amortized over a statutory 15-year period.[12]

Concept Summary 14.2 reviews the effects of transactions involving franchises on both the franchisor and franchisee.

Concept Summary 14.2

Franchises: Consequences to the Franchisor and Franchisee

	Effect on	
Event	**Franchisor**	**Franchisee**
Franchisor Retains Significant Powers and Rights		
Noncontingent payment	Ordinary income.	Capitalized and amortized over 15 years as an ordinary deduction; if franchise is sold, amortization is subject to recapture under § 1245.
Contingent payment	Ordinary income.	Ordinary deduction.
Franchisor Does *Not* Retain Significant Powers and Rights		
Noncontingent payment	Ordinary income if franchise rights are an ordinary asset; capital gain if franchise rights are a capital asset (unlikely).	Capitalized and amortized over 15 years as an ordinary deduction; if the franchise is sold, amortization is subject to recapture under § 1245.
Contingent payment	Ordinary income.	Ordinary deduction.

14-3f Lease Cancellation Payments

The tax treatment of payments received for canceling a lease depends on whether the recipient is the **lessor** or the **lessee** and whether the lease is a capital asset.

Lessee Treatment

Lease cancellation payments received by a lessee are treated as an exchange.[13] The treatment of these payments depends on the underlying use of the property and how long the lease has existed.[14]

- If the property was used personally (e.g., an apartment used as a residence), the payment results in a capital gain (and long term if the lease existed for more than one year).
- If the property was used for business and the lease existed for one year or less, the payment results in ordinary income.
- If the property was used for business and the lease existed for more than one year, the payment results in a § 1231 gain.

[12]§ 197(a).

[13]§ 1241 and Reg. § 1.1241–1(a).

[14]Reg. § 1.1221–1(b) and PLR 200045019.

Mark owns an apartment building that he is going to convert into an office building. Vicki is one of the apartment tenants and receives $1,000 from Mark to cancel the lease.

Vicki has a capital gain of $1,000 (which is long term or short term depending upon how long she has held the lease). Mark has an ordinary deduction of $1,000.

Lessor Treatment

Payments received by a lessor for a lease cancellation are always ordinary income because they are considered to be in lieu of rental payments.[15]

Darnell owns an apartment building near a university campus. Hui-Fen is one of the tenants. Hui-Fen is graduating early and offers Darnell $800 to cancel the apartment lease. Darnell accepts the offer.

Darnell has ordinary income of $800. Hui-Fen has a nondeductible payment because the apartment was personal use property.

14-4 Holding Period

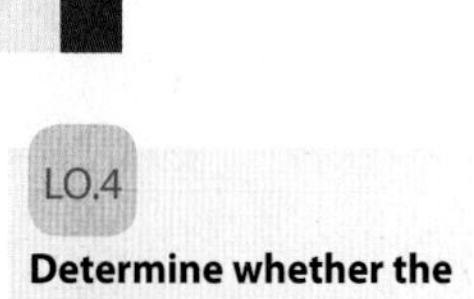

LO.4

Determine whether the holding period for a capital asset is long term or short term.

14-4a General Rules

Property must be held for *more than one year* to qualify for long-term capital gain or loss treatment.[16] Property held for one year or less results in short-term capital gain or loss. To compute the **holding period**, start counting on the day *after* the property was acquired and include the day of disposition.

The Big Picture

Return to the facts of *The Big Picture* on p. 14-1. Assume that Maurice purchased the Purple stock on January 15, 2023. If he sells it on January 16, 2024, Maurice's holding period is more than one year, and therefore, long term.

If, instead, Maurice sells the stock on January 15, 2024, the holding period is exactly one year and the gain or loss is short term.

An asset's holding period is based on calendar months and fractions of calendar months (not the number of days). It does not matter that different months have different numbers of days.[17]

Leo purchases a capital asset on February 28, 2023. If Leo sells the asset on February 28, 2024, the holding period is one year and Leo will have a short-term capital gain or loss.

If Leo sells the asset on February 29, 2024, the holding period is more than one year and he will have a long-term capital gain or loss.

14-4b Special Holding Period Rules

There are several special holding period rules.[18] The application of these rules depends upon the type of asset and how it was acquired.

Nontaxable Exchanges

The holding period of property received in a like-kind exchange includes the holding period of the former asset if the property that has been exchanged is a capital asset or a § 1231 asset. In these settings, the holding period of the former property is *tacked on* to the holding period of the newly acquired property.

[15] Reg. § 1.61–8(b). Also known as the *substitute for income* doctrine; *Hort v. Comm.*, 41–1 USTC ¶9354, 25 AFTR 1207, 61 S.Ct. 757 (USSC).

[16] § 1222.

[17] Rev.Rul. 66–7.

[18] § 1223.

On April 22, 2023, Alejandra exchanges a business building she acquired on March 15, 2020, for another business building in a qualifying like-kind exchange.

The holding period of the replacement building begins March 15, 2020, because the holding period of the building given up in the exchange *tacks* to the holding period of the replacement building.

Gifts

When a gift occurs, if the donor's basis carries over to the recipient, the donor's holding period is *tacked on* to the recipient's holding period. This will occur when the property's fair market value at the date of the gift is greater than the donor's adjusted basis. Transactions of this nature are discussed in Chapter 13.

Carryover Basis

Kareem acquires 100 shares of Robin Corporation stock for $1,000 on December 31, 2019. He transfers the shares by gift to Megan on December 31, 2022, when the stock is worth $2,000. Kareem's basis of $1,000 becomes the basis for determining gain or loss on a subsequent sale by Megan. Megan's holding period begins with the date the stock was acquired by Kareem.

Assume the same facts as in Example 25, except that the fair market value of the shares is only $800 on the date of the gift. The holding period begins on the date of the gift if Megan sells the stock for a loss. The value of the shares on the date of the gift is used in determining her basis for loss. If she sells the shares for $500 on April 1, 2023, Megan has a $300 recognized capital loss and the holding period is from December 31, 2022 to April 1, 2023 (as a result, the loss is short term).

Certain Disallowed Loss Transactions

Under several Code provisions, realized losses are disallowed. When a loss is disallowed, there is no carryover of holding period. Losses can be disallowed under § 267 (sale or exchange between related taxpayers) and § 262 (sale or exchange of personal use assets) as well as other Code Sections. Taxpayers who acquire property in a disallowed loss transaction will have a new holding period begin and will have a basis equal to the purchase price.

Janet sells her personal automobile at a loss. She may not deduct the loss because it arises from the sale of personal use property. Janet purchases a replacement automobile for more than the selling price of her former automobile. Janet has a basis equal to the cost of the replacement automobile, and her holding period begins when she acquires the replacement automobile.

Inherited Property

The holding period for inherited property is treated as long term no matter how long the property is actually held by the heir. The holding period of the decedent or the decedent's estate is not relevant for the heir's holding period.

Shonda inherits Blue Company stock from her father, who died in 2023. She receives the stock on April 1, 2023, and sells it on November 1, 2023. Even though Shonda did not hold the stock more than one year, she receives long-term capital gain or loss treatment on the sale.

14-4c Special Rules for Short Sales

General

The Code provides special holding period rules for short sales.[19] A **short sale** occurs when a taxpayer sells borrowed property and repays the lender with substantially identical property either held on the date of the sale or purchased after the sale (even though they are not capital assets).

[19] § 1233.

Short sales usually involve corporate stock. The seller's objective is to make a profit in anticipation of a decline in the stock's price. If the price declines, the seller in a short sale recognizes a profit equal to the difference between the sales price of the borrowed stock and the price paid for the replacement stock.

Chris does not own any shares of Brown Corporation. However, Chris sells 30 shares of Brown. The shares are borrowed from Chris's broker and must be replaced within 45 days. Chris has a short sale because he was short the shares he sold. He will close the short sale by purchasing Brown shares and delivering them to his broker.

If the original 30 shares were sold for $10,000 and Chris later purchased 30 shares for $8,000, he would have had a gain of $2,000. Chris's hunch that the price of Brown stock would decline was correct. Chris was able to profit from selling high and buying low.

If Chris had to purchase Brown shares for $13,000 to close the short sale, he would have a loss of $3,000. In this case, Chris would have sold low and bought high—not the result he wanted. Chris would be making a short sale against the box if he borrowed shares from his broker to sell and then closed the short sale by delivering other Brown shares he owned at the time he made the short sale.

Concept Summary 14.3 summarizes the short sale rules. These rules are intended to prevent the conversion of short-term capital gains into long-term capital gains and long-term capital losses into short-term capital losses.

In most settings, short sale gain or loss results in a capital gain or loss. The gain or loss is not recognized until the short sale is closed. Generally, the holding period of the short sale property is determined by how long the property used to close the short sale was held. However, when *substantially identical property* (e.g., other shares of the same stock) is held by the taxpayer, the holding period is determined as follows:

- The short sale *gain or loss* is *short term* when, on the short sale date, the substantially identical property has been held *short term* (i.e., for one year or less). (See Examples 30 and 31.)
- The short sale *gain* is *long term* when, on the short sale date, the substantially identical property has been held *long term* (i.e., for more than one year) and is used to close the short sale. If the long-term substantially identical property is not used to close the short sale, the short sale gain is *short term*. (See Example 32.)
- The short sale *loss* is *long term* when, on the short sale date, the substantially identical property has been held *long term* (i.e., for more than one year).
- The short sale *gain or loss* is *short term* if the substantially identical property is acquired *after* the short sale date and on or before the closing date. (See Example 33.)

Disposition Rules for Short Sales against the Box

A short sale against the box occurs when the stock is borrowed from a broker by a seller and the seller already owns substantially identical securities on the short sale date or acquires them before the closing date.[20] To remove the taxpayer's flexibility as to when the short sale gain must be reported, a constructive sale approach is used. If the taxpayer has not closed the short sale by delivering the short sale securities to the broker *before* January 31 of the year following the short sale, the short sale is deemed to have been closed on the *earlier* of two events:

- On the short sale date if the taxpayer owned substantially identical securities at that time.
- On the date during the year of the short sale that the taxpayer acquired substantially identical securities.[21]

[20] The "box" refers to the safe deposit box that stock owners routinely used to keep physical stock certificates safe. Although today shares of stock are typically held electronically (rather than physically), the terminology *short sale against the box* is still used.

[21] § 1259.

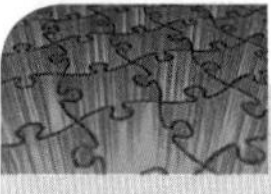

Concept Summary 14.3

Short Sales of Securities

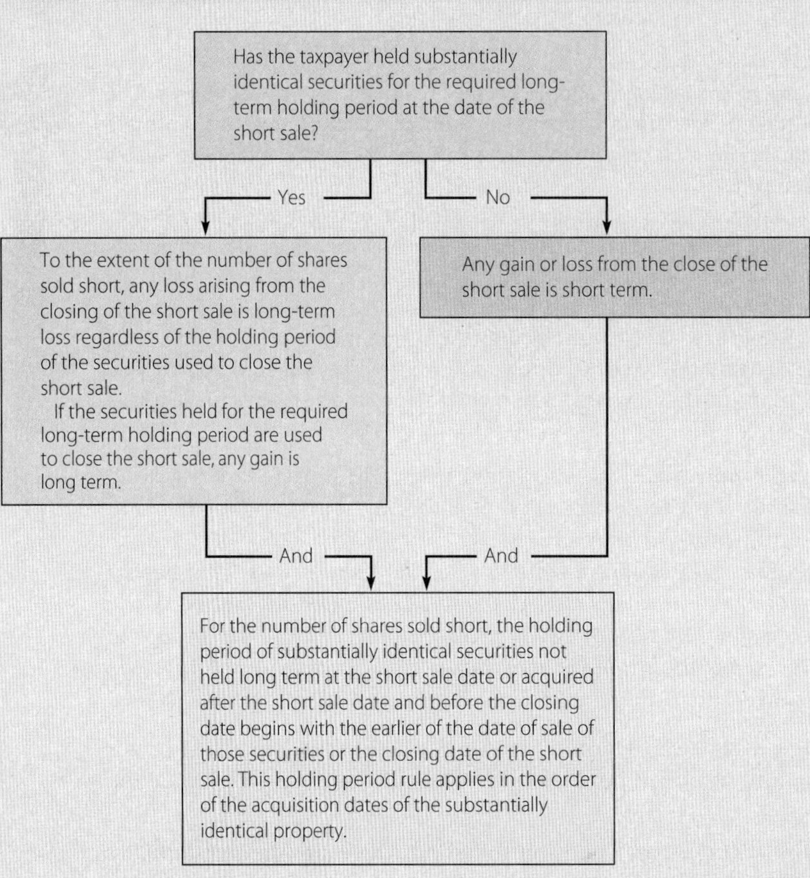

The basis of the shares in the deemed transfer of shares is used to compute the gain or loss on the short sale. As Examples 32 and 33 illustrate, when shares are *actually* transferred to the broker to close the short sale, there may be a gain or loss because the shares transferred will have a basis equal to the short sale date price and the value at the *actual* short sale closing date may be different from the short sale date price.

Illustrations

The following examples illustrate the treatment of short sales and short sales against the box.

Short Sales and Short Sales Against the Box

Example 30

On January 4, 2023, Caden purchases five shares of Osprey Corporation common stock for $100. On April 14, 2023, he engages in a short sale of five shares of the same stock for $150. On August 15, Caden closes the short sale by repaying the borrowed stock with the five shares purchased on January 4. Because his substantially identical shares were held short term as of the short sale date, Caden's $50 capital gain is short term.

Example 31

Assume the same facts as in the previous example, except that Caden closes the short sale on January 28, 2024, by repaying the borrowed stock with five shares purchased on January 27, 2024, for $200. Because Caden's substantially identical property (purchased on January 4, 2023) was short-term property at the April 14, 2023 short sale date, his $50 capital loss ($200 cost of stock purchased on January 27, 2024, and a short sale selling price of $150) is short term.

Short Sales and Short Sales Against the Box

Example 32

On January 18, 2022, Rita purchases 200 shares of Owl Corporation stock for $1,000. On November 11, 2023, she sells short, for $1,300, 200 shares of Owl Corporation stock that she borrows from her broker. On February 10, 2024, Rita closes the short sale by delivering the 200 shares of Owl Corporation stock that she had acquired in 2022. On that date, Owl Corporation stock had a market price of $3 per share.

Because Rita owned substantially identical stock on the date of the short sale and did not close the short sale before January 31, 2024, she is *deemed* to have closed the short sale on November 11, 2022 (the date of the short sale). On her 2023 tax return, she reports a $300 long-term capital gain ($1,300 short sale price − $1,000 basis).

On February 10, 2024, Rita has a $700 short-term capital loss [$600 short sale closing date price (200 shares × $3 per share) − $1,300 basis] because the holding period of the shares used to close the short sale commences with the date of the short sale.

Assume the same facts as in Example 32, except that Rita did not own any Owl Corporation stock on the short sale date and acquired the 200 shares of Owl Corporation stock for $1,000 on December 12, 2023 (after the November 11, 2023 short sale date).

The *deemed* closing of the short sale is December 12, 2023, because Rita held substantially identical shares at the end of 2023 and did not close the short sale before January 31, 2024. Her 2023 short sale gain is a *short-term* gain of $300 ($1,300 short sale price − $1,000 basis), and she still has a short-term capital loss of $700 on February 10, 2024.

14-5 Tax Treatment of Capital Gains and Losses of Noncorporate Taxpayers

LO.5

Describe the beneficial tax treatment for capital gains and the detrimental tax treatment for capital losses for noncorporate taxpayers.

All taxpayers net their capital gains and losses. Short-term gains and losses (if any) are netted against one another, and long-term gains and losses (if any) are netted against one another. The results will be net short-term gain or loss and net long-term gain or loss. If these two net positions are of opposite sign (one is a gain and one is a loss), they are netted against each other.

Six possibilities exist for the result after all possible netting has been completed.

1. A net long-term capital gain (NLTCG).
2. A net short-term capital gain (NSTCG).
3. Both NLTCG and NSTCG.
4. A net long-term capital loss (NLTCL).
5. A net short-term capital loss (NSTCL).
6. Both NLTCL and NSTCL.

Net long-term capital gains of noncorporate taxpayers are eligible for an alternative tax calculation that normally results in a lower tax liability. Neither NLTCLs nor NSTCLs are treated as ordinary losses. Treatment as an ordinary loss generally is preferable to capital loss treatment because ordinary losses are deductible in full while the deductibility of capital losses is subject to certain limitations. An individual taxpayer may deduct a maximum of $3,000 of net capital losses for a taxable year.[22]

14-5a Capital Gain and Loss Netting Process

Net short-term capital gain is not eligible for any special tax rate. It is taxed at the same rate as the taxpayer's other taxable income.

Net long-term capital gain is eligible for one or more of *five* alternative tax rates: 0 percent, 15 percent, 20 percent, 25 percent, and 28 percent. The 25 percent and 28 percent rates are used only in unique circumstances. The net long-term capital gain components are referred to as the *0%/15%/20% gain*, the *25% gain*, and the *28% gain*.

[22]§ 1211(b).

The *25% gain* is called the **unrecaptured § 1250 gain** and is related to gain from disposition of § 1231 assets (discussed later in this chapter). Here, the discussion focuses only on how the *25% gain* is taxed and not how it is determined. The *28% gain* relates to collectibles and qualified small business stock (§ 1202, see discussion in Chapter 18). The definition of collectibles is discussed later in this section. As discussed in text Section 14-5c, the 0%/15%/20% rates are applied at various ranges of taxable income based on the taxpayer's filing status (see also Exhibit 14.1).

When the long-term capital gain exceeds the short-term capital loss, a **net capital gain (NCG)** exists.[23] Net capital gain qualifies for beneficial alternative tax treatment (see the coverage later in the chapter).

Because there are both short- and long-term capital gains and losses and because the long-term capital gains may be taxed at various rates, an *ordering procedure* is required. The ordering procedure, which ensures that any long-term capital gain is taxed at the lowest preferential rate possible, includes the following steps:

Step 1. Group all gains and losses into four groups: short term, and 28%, 25%, and 0%/15%/20% long term.

Step 2. Net the gains and losses within each group.

Step 3. Offset the net 28% and net 25% amounts, if they are of opposite sign.

Step 4. Offset the results after step 3 against the 0%/15%/20% amount, if they are of opposite sign. If the 0%/15%/20% amount is a loss, offset it against the *highest-taxed gain first*. After this step, there is a net long-term capital gain or loss. If there is a net long-term capital gain, it may consist of only *28% gain*, only *25% gain*, only *0%/15%/20% gain*, or some combination of all of these gains. If there is a net long-term capital loss, it is simply a net long-term capital loss.

Step 5. Offset the net short-term amount against the long-term results of step 4, if they are of opposite sign. The netting rules offset net short-term capital loss against the *highest-taxed gain first*. So a net short-term capital loss first offsets any *28% gain*, then any *25% gain*, and finally any *0%/15%/20% gain*.

If the result of step 5 is *only* a short-term capital gain, the taxpayer is not eligible for a reduced tax rate. If the result of step 5 is a loss, the taxpayer may be eligible for a *capital loss deduction* (discussed later in this chapter). If there was no offsetting in step 5 because the short-term and step 4 results were both gains *or* if the result of the offsetting is a long-term gain, a net capital gain exists and the taxpayer may be eligible for a reduced tax rate. The net capital gain may consist of *28% gain, 25% gain*, and/or *0%/15%/20% gain*.

As you might suspect, this *ordering procedure* can produce many different results. The following series of examples illustrates some of these outcomes.

Capital Gain and Loss Netting Process

Example 34

This example shows how a *net short-term capital gain* may result from the netting process.

Step	Short Term	Long-Term Gains and Losses 28%	25%	0%/15%/20%	Comment
1	$13,000	$ 12,000		$ 3,000	
	(2,000)	(20,000)			
2	$11,000	($ 8,000)		$ 3,000	
3					No 28%/25% netting because no opposite sign.
4		3,000	→	(3,000)	Netted because of opposite sign.
		($ 5,000)		$ -0-	
5	(5,000) ←	5,000			The net short-term capital gain is taxed as ordinary income.
	$ 6,000	$ -0-			
	Net short-term capital gain				

[23] § 1222(11).

Capital Gain and Loss Netting Process

Example 35

This example shows how a *net long-term capital gain* may result from the netting process.

Step	Short Term	Long-Term Gains and Losses 28%	25%	0%/15%/20%	Comment
1	$ 3,000	$15,000	$4,000	$ 3,000	
	(5,000)	(7,000)		(8,000)	
2	($ 2,000)	$ 8,000	$4,000	($ 5,000)	
3					No 28%/25% netting because no opposite sign.
4		(5,000)	←	5,000	Netted because of opposite sign. Net 0%/15%/20% loss is netted against *28% gain* first.
		$ 3,000		$ -0-	
5	2,000 →	(2,000)			The net short-term capital loss is netted against *28% gain* first. The net long-term capital gain is $5,000 ($1,000 + $4,000).
	$ -0-	$ 1,000	$4,000		
		Net *28% gain*	Net *25% gain*		

Example 36

This example shows how a *net long-term capital loss* may result from the netting process.

Step	Short Term	Long-Term Gains and Losses 28%	25%	0%/15%/20%	Comment
1	$ 3,000	$ 1,000		$ 3,000	
				(8,000)	
2	$ 3,000	$ 1,000		($ 5,000)	
3					No 28%/25% netting because no opposite sign.
4		(1,000)	→	1,000	Netted because of opposite sign.
		$ -0-		($ 4,000)	
5	(3,000)	→	→	3,000	The net short-term capital gain is netted against the net long-term capital loss, and the remaining loss is eligible for the capital loss deduction.
	$ -0-			($ 1,000)	
				Net long-term capital loss	

Use of Capital Loss Carryovers

A short-term capital loss carryover to the current year retains its character as short term and is combined with the short-term items of the current year. A net long-term capital loss carries over as a long-term capital loss and is combined with the current-year long-term items. The long-term loss carryover is first offset with *28% gain* of the current year, then *25% gain*, and then *0%/15%/20% gain* until it is absorbed.

Example 37

In 2023, Abigail has a $4,000 short-term capital gain, a $36,000 28% long-term capital gain, and a $13,000 0%/15%/20% long-term capital gain. She also has a $3,000 short-term capital loss carryover and a $2,000 long-term capital loss carryover from 2022.

As a result, in 2023, Abigail has a $1,000 net short-term capital gain ($4,000 − $3,000), a $34,000 net 28% long-term capital gain ($36,000 − $2,000), and a $13,000 net 0%/15%/20% long-term capital gain.

Definition of Collectibles

Capital assets that are collectibles, even though they are held long term, are not eligible for the *0%/15%/20%* alternative tax rate. Instead, a 28 percent alternative tax rate applies.

For capital gain or loss purposes, **collectibles** include:[24]

- Any work of art.
- Any rug or antique.
- Any metal or gem.
- Any stamp.
- Any alcoholic beverage.
- Most coins.
- Any historical objects (documents, clothes, etc.).

14-5b **Qualified Dividend Income**

Dividends paid by domestic and certain foreign corporations are eligible to be taxed at the 0%/15%/20% long-term capital gain rates if they are **qualified dividend income (QDI)** (see the discussion of QDI in text Section 4-3b). Here, the discussion focuses on how the qualified dividend income is taxed.

The Big Picture

Example 38

Return to the facts of *The Big Picture* on p. 14-1. After holding the Purple stock for 10 months, Maurice receives $350 of dividends. If Purple is a domestic or qualifying foreign corporation, these are qualified dividends eligible for the 0%/15%/20% tax rate.

After the net capital gain or loss has been determined, the QDI is added to the net long-term capital gain portion of the net capital gain and is taxed as 0%/15%/20% gain. If there is a net capital loss, the net capital loss is still deductible *for* AGI up to $3,000 per year with the remainder of the loss (if any) carrying forward. In this case, the QDI is still eligible to be treated as *0%/15%/20% gain* in the alternative tax calculation (it is *not* offset by the net capital loss).

Example 39

Refer to Example 35, but assume that there is qualified dividend income (QDI) of $2,500 in addition to the items shown. The QDI is not netted against the capital gains and losses. Instead, the taxpayer has $1,000 of *28% gain*, $4,000 of *25% gain*, and $2,500 of QDI taxed at 0%/15%/20%.

Refer to Example 36, but assume that there is QDI of $2,500 in addition to the items shown. The QDI is not netted against the net capital loss. The taxpayer has a $1,000 capital loss deduction and $2,500 of QDI taxed at 0%/15%/20%.

14-5c **Alternative Tax on Net Capital Gain and Qualified Dividend Income**

Code § 1 contains the rules that enable the *net capital gain* to be taxed at special rates (0, 15, 20, 25, and 28 percent). This calculation is referred to as the **alternative tax** on

[24] § 408(m)(2) and Reg. § 1.408–10(b).

net capital gain.[25] The alternative tax applies only if taxable income includes some long-term capital gain (there is net capital gain) and/or qualified dividend income (QDI). Taxable income includes *all* of the net capital gain and/or QDI unless taxable income is less than the net capital gain and/or QDI. In addition, the net capital gain and/or QDI is taxed *last*, after other taxable income (including any short-term capital gain).

The *0%/15%/20%* rates are applied to any net capital gain and qualified dividend income based on the taxpayer's filing status and taxable income (see Exhibit 14.1). The taxable income ranges are adjusted for inflation each year.

Joan, a single taxpayer, has taxable income of $118,000, including a $10,000 net capital gain and $2,000 QDI. The last $12,000 of her $118,000 taxable income is the layer related to the net capital gain and/or QDI. The first $106,000 ($118,000 − $12,000) of her taxable income is her other taxable income and is not subject to any special tax rate, so it is taxed using the regular tax rates.

Because the net capital gain and/or QDI may be made up of various *rate layers*, it is important to know in what order those layers are taxed. (Review the five-step ordering procedure discussed in text Section 14-5a and the related examples.) For *each* of the layers, the taxpayer compares the regular tax rate on that layer of income and the alternative tax rate on that portion of the net capital gain and/or QDI and uses the lower of those rates.

The layers are taxed in the following order:

- Any *25% gain*,
- Any *28% gain*,
- The 0 percent portion of the *0%/15%/20% gain* and/or QDI,
- The 15 percent portion of the *0%/15%/20% gain* and/or QDI, and then
- The 20 percent portion of the *0%/15%/20% gain* and/or QDI.

Exhibit 14.1 Alternative Tax Rates on Net Capital Gains (NCG) (Based on Filing Status and Taxable Income)

2023: FILING STATUS

Single		Married, Filing Jointly		Married, Filing Separately		Head of Household		NCG Tax Rate
Taxable Income		Taxable Income		Taxable Income		Taxable Income		
Greater Than	No More Than	Greater Than	No More Than	Greater Than	No More Than	Greater Than	No More Than	
$ –0–	$ 44,625	$ –0–	$ 89,250	$ –0–	$ 44,625	$ –0–	$ 59,750	0%
44,625	492,300	89,250	553,850	44,625	276,900	59,750	523,050	15%
492,300		553,850		276,900		523,050		20%

2022: FILING STATUS

Single		Married, Filing Jointly		Married, Filing Separately		Head of Household		NCG Tax Rate
Taxable Income		Taxable Income		Taxable Income		Taxable Income		
Greater Than	No More Than	Greater Than	No More Than	Greater Than	No More Than	Greater Than	No More Than	
$ –0–	$ 41,675	$ –0–	$ 83,350	$ –0–	$ 41,675	$ –0–	$ 55,800	0%
41,675	459,750	83,350	517,200	41,675	258,600	55,800	488,500	15%
459,750		517,200		258,600		488,500		20%

[25] § 1(h). Note: Examples 41, 42, and 43 use the 2023 Tax Rate Schedules rather than the 2023 Tax Tables (which are not yet available) to calculate the tax on the non-long-term capital gain portion of taxable income. This approach is used to better illustrate the concepts under discussion. The actual tax on the non-long-term portion of taxable income would be calculated using the Tax Tables because that income is less than $100,000.

As a result of this layering:

- The taxpayer benefits from the 0 percent portion of the net capital gain and/or QDI if the taxpayer is still in the 10 percent or 12 percent regular tax bracket after taxing other taxable income and the 25 percent and 28 percent portions of the net capital gain. Depending on the taxpayer's filing status, however, a portion of income in the taxpayer's 12 percent tax bracket is subject to the 15 percent alternative tax rate. In 2023, the 0 percent alternative tax rate applies only through $89,250 of taxable income for married taxpayers filing jointly or surviving spouses, $44,625 for single taxpayers, $59,750 for heads of household, and $44,625 for married taxpayers filing separately. These "break points" for the alternative tax rates do not correspond with the normal tax bracket "break points" (see the 2023 Tax Rate Schedules in Appendix A and compare the maximum amounts in each of the 12 percent tax brackets to the maximum amounts subject to the 0 percent alternative tax rate). This means that in 2023, the last $200 (married, filing jointly and surviving spouses), $100 (single), $100 (heads of household), and $100 (married, filing separately) in the 12 percent bracket is subject to the 15 percent alternative rate. As the normal tax rate (12 percent) is less than the alternative tax rate (15 percent), this means that for these small ranges, any net capital gain or QDI will be taxed at 12 percent (rather than 15 percent).
- The taxpayer benefits from the 15 percent portion of the net capital gain and/or QDI if the taxpayer is in the 22 percent, 24 percent, and 32 percent brackets or a portion of the 35 percent regular rate bracket after taxing other taxable income and the 25 percent, 28 percent, and 0 percent portions of the net capital gain and/or QDI. In 2023, the 15 percent tax rate applies until taxable income exceeds $553,850 for married taxpayers filing jointly, $492,300 for single taxpayers, $523,050 for heads of household, and $276,900 for married taxpayers filing separately.
- The taxpayer benefits from the 20 percent portion of the net capital gain and/or QDI when taxable income exceeds the maximum taxable income thresholds for the 15 percent alternative tax rate.

Concept Summary 14.4 summarizes the alternative tax computation.

Concept Summary 14.4

Income Layers for Alternative Tax on Capital Gain Computation

Compute tax on:		Other taxable income (including net short-term capital gain) using the regular tax rates.
Compute tax on:		Each of the layers below using the *lower* of the alternative tax rate or the regular tax rate for that layer (or portion of a layer) of taxable income.
	+	25% long-term capital gain (unrecaptured § 1250 gain) portion of taxable income.
	+	28% long-term capital gain.
	+	0% long-term capital gain [portion of *0%/15%/20% gain* and/or qualified dividend income (QDI) that is taxed at 0%; available only if other taxable income plus 25% and 28% capital gain layers do not put the taxpayer above specified thresholds in the 12% regular tax bracket*; 0% rate is no longer available once income, including the portion of the gain and/or QDI taxed at 0%, puts the taxpayer above these thresholds].
	+	15% long-term capital gain (portion of *0%/15%/20% gain* and/or QDI that is taxed at 15%; available only if other taxable income plus the 25%, 28%, and 0% layers put the taxpayer above the 12% regular tax bracket and only until other taxable income plus the 25%, 28%, 0%, and 15% layers put the taxpayer at or below specified thresholds in the 35% regular tax rate bracket)**.
	+	20% long-term capital gain (portion of *0%/15%/20% gain* and/or QDI that is taxed at 20%; available when other taxable income plus the 25%, 28%, 0%, and 15% layers put the taxpayer above the specified thresholds in the 35% regular tax rate bracket).
	=	Alternative tax on taxable income

*See Exhibit 14.1 for the taxable income ranges where the 0%/15%/20% rates apply. In 2023, the last $200 (married filing jointly and surviving spouse), $100 (single), $100 (heads of household), and $100 (married filing separately) of the 12% bracket is subject to the 15% alternative tax rate. As the normal tax rate of 12% is less than the alternative tax rate of 15%, any *0%/15%/20% gain* or QDI in these ranges will be taxed at 12%.

**See Exhibit 14.1 for the taxable income amounts where the 20% rate begins to apply.

Alternative Tax on Net Capital Gain

Example 41

In Example 40, Joan had $118,000 taxable income. Now assume that Joan's $10,000 net capital gain is made up of $7,000 *25% gain* and $3,000 *0%/15%/20% gain*. In addition, she has $2,000 of QDI. Examination of the 2023 tax rates reveals that $106,000 ($118,000 − $12,000) of other taxable income for a single individual puts Joan at a marginal tax rate of 24%. Consequently, she uses the alternative tax on the $7,000 gain, the $3,000 gain, and the $2,000 QDI.

Her alternative tax liability is $21,270:

	$18,840	(tax on $106,000 of other taxable income)
+	1,680	($7,000 × 0.24; 24% rate on *25% gain*)
+	450	($3,000 × 0.15; 15% rate on *0%/15%/20% gain*)
+	300	($2,000 × 0.15; 15% rate on QDI)
=	$21,270	Alternative tax liability

Since her marginal tax rate is still 24% after taxing the $106,000 other taxable income, she uses the 24% regular tax rate rather than the 25% alternative tax rate on the $7,000 *25% gain*. As the combination of the $106,000 other taxable income and her $7,000 *25% gain* puts her above the 12% regular tax bracket, none of the $3,000 *0%/15%/20% gain* or $2,000 QDI is taxed at 0%.

Her regular tax liability on $118,000 is $21,720. As a result, Joan saves $450 ($21,720 − $21,270) by using the alternative tax calculation. Because Joan's taxable income is $492,300 or less, none of her *0%/15%/20% gain* or QDI is taxed at the 20% alternative tax rate.

Example 42

Assume that Joan, a single taxpayer, has 2023 taxable income of $25,000. Of this amount, $11,000 is net capital gain, $1,000 is QDI, and $13,000 is other taxable income. The $11,000 net capital gain is made up of $8,300 of *25% gain* and $2,700 of *0%/15%/20% gain*.

Her alternative tax liability is $2,351:

	$1,355	(tax on $13,000 of other taxable income)
+	996	(tax on $8,300 *25% gain* at 12%)
+	0	(tax on $2,700 *0%/15%/20% gain* at 0%)
+	0	(tax on $1,000 QDI at 0%)
=	$2,351	Alternative tax liability

Because her marginal rate is still 12% after taxing the $13,000 of other taxable income, she uses the 12% regular tax rate rather than the 25% alternative tax rate on the $8,300 *25% gain*. After taxing the $13,000 and the $8,300, a total of $21,300 of the $25,000 taxable income has been taxed. Because her remaining taxable income ($3,700) remains in the 12% tax bracket (and her total taxable income does not exceed $41,675), she uses the 0% alternative rate for the $2,700 of *0%/15%/20% gain* and $1,000 QDI.

Joan's regular tax liability on $25,000 is $2,795. As a result, she saves $444 ($2,795 − $2,351) by using the alternative tax calculation.

The alternative tax computation allows the taxpayer to receive the *lower of* the regular tax or the alternative tax on *each layer* of net capital gain and/or QDI or *portion of each layer* of net capital gain and/or QDI.

Example 43

Assume the same facts as in Example 42, except that Joan's 2023 taxable income is $48,000, consisting of $11,000 of net capital gain (made up of $8,300 of *25% gain* and $2,700 of *0%/15%/20% gain*), $1,000 of QDI, and $36,000 of other taxable income.

Not all of the combined *0%/15%/20% gain* and QDI ($3,700; $2,700 + $1,000) is taxed at 0% because Joan's taxable income exceeds $44,625, taking her out of the 0% alternative tax. Consequently, the last $3,375 ($48,000 − $44,625) of the $3,700 is taxed at 12% and 15% rather than 0%.

continued

Her tax liability using the alternative tax computation is $5,599:

	$4,100	(tax on $36,000 of other taxable income)
+	996	(tax on $8,300 *25% gain* at 12%)
+	0	(tax on $325 of the $3,700 combined *0%/15%/20% gain* and QDI at 0%)
+	12	(tax on $100 of the $3,700 combined *0%/15%/20% gain* and QDI at 12%)
+	491	(tax on $3,275 of the $3,700 combined *0%/15%/20% gain* and QDI at 15%)
=	$5,599	Alternative tax liability

Joan's regular tax liability on $48,000 is $5,868. As a result, she saves $269 ($5,868 − $5,599) by using the alternative tax calculation.

14-5d **Treatment of Net Capital Losses**

Computation of Net Capital Loss

A **net capital loss (NCL)** results if capital losses exceed capital gains for the year. An NCL may be all long term, all short term, or part long and part short term.[26] The characterization of an NCL as long or short term is important in determining the capital loss deduction (discussed next).

Example 44

Three different individuals have the following capital gains and losses during the year:

	Short Term			Long Term			Combined	
Taxpayer	STCG	STCL	Net Short Term	LTCG	LTCL	Net Long Term	Combined Short Term and Long Term	Description of Result
Paulina	$1,000	($ 500)	$ 500	$1,000	($2,800)	($1,800)	($1,300)	NLTCL
Carlos	1,000	(2,800)	(1,800)	1,000	(500)	500	(1,300)	NSTCL
Anibal	500	(1,200)	(700)	400	(1,200)	(800)	(1,500)	NSTCL ($700) NLTCL ($800)

Paulina's NCL of $1,300 is all long term. Carlos's NCL of $1,300 is all short term. Anibal's NCL is $1,500, $700 of which is short term and $800 of which is long term.

Capital Loss Deduction

A net capital loss is deductible *for* AGI, but limited to no more than $3,000 per tax year.[27] So although a net capital gain receives favorable tax treatment, there is *unfavorable* treatment for capital losses due to the $3,000 annual limitation. If the NCL includes both long- and short-term capital loss, the short-term capital loss is counted first toward the $3,000 annual limitation.

Burt has an NCL of $5,500, of which $2,000 is STCL and $3,500 is LTCL. Burt has a capital loss deduction of $3,000 ($2,000 of STCL and $1,000 of LTCL). He has an LTCL carryforward of $2,500 ($3,500 − $1,000).

Carryovers

Taxpayers are allowed to carry over unused capital losses indefinitely. The short-term capital loss (STCL) retains its character as STCL. Likewise, the long-term capital loss retains its character as LTCL.

[26] Code § 1222(10) defines a net capital loss as the net loss after the capital loss deduction. However, that definition confuses the discussion of net capital loss. Therefore, net capital loss is used here to mean the result after netting capital gains and losses and before considering the capital loss deduction.

[27] § 1211(b)(1). Married taxpayers filing separate returns are limited to a $1,500 deduction per tax year. When a taxpayer has both a capital loss deduction and negative taxable income, a special computation of the capital loss carryover is required. See § 1212(b).

In 2023, Jake incurred $1,000 of STCL and $11,000 of LTCL. In 2024, Jake has a $400 LTCG.

- Jake's NCL for 2023 is $12,000. Jake deducts $3,000 ($1,000 STCL and $2,000 LTCL). He has $9,000 of LTCL carried forward to 2023.
- Jake combines the $9,000 LTCL carryforward with the $400 LTCG for 2024. He has an $8,600 NLTCL for 2024. Mark deducts $3,000 of LTCL in 2024 and carries forward $5,600 of LTCL to 2025.

Concept Summary 14.5 summarizes the rules for noncorporate taxpayers' treatment of capital gains and losses.

Concept Summary 14.5

Final Results of the Capital Gain and Loss Netting Process and How They Are Taxed

Result	Maximum Tax Rate	Comments
Net short-term capital loss	—	Eligible for capital loss deduction ($3,000 maximum per year).
Net long-term capital loss	—	Eligible for capital loss deduction ($3,000 maximum per year).
Net short-term capital loss *and* net long-term capital loss	—	Eligible for capital loss deduction ($3,000 maximum per year). Short-term capital losses are counted first toward the deduction.
Net short-term capital gain	10%–37%	Taxed as ordinary income.
Net long-term capital gain	0%–28%	The net long-term capital gain may have as many as five tax rate components: 25%, 28%, and 0%/15%/20%.
• The net long-term capital gain is the *last* portion of taxable income.		The components are taxed in the following order: 25%, 28%, 0%, 15%, 20%. They are taxed *after* the non-long-term capital gain portion of taxable income has been taxed. The 0%/15%/20% component may include qualified dividend income.
• Each net long-term capital gain component of taxable income is taxed at the *lower* of the regular tax on that component or the alternative tax.		The alternative tax on net long-term capital gain can never increase the tax on taxable income, but it can reduce the tax on taxable income.
Net short-term capital gain *and* net long-term capital gain	10%–37% on net short-term capital gain; 0%–28% on net long-term capital gain	The net short-term capital gain is taxed as ordinary income; the net long-term capital gain is taxed as discussed above for just net long-term capital gain.

14-6 Tax Treatment of Capital Gains and Losses of Corporate Taxpayers

Describe the tax treatment for capital gains and the detrimental tax treatment for capital losses for corporate taxpayers.

The treatment of a corporation's net capital gain or loss differs from the rules for individuals. Briefly, the differences are as follows:

- There is no NCG alternative tax rate.
- Capital losses offset only capital gains. No deduction of capital losses is permitted against other taxable income (whereas a $3,000 deduction is allowed to individuals).[28]
- Corporations may carry back net capital losses (whether long term or short term) as short-term capital losses for three years; if losses still remain after the carryback, the remaining losses may be carried forward five years.[29] Individuals may carry forward unused capital losses indefinitely, but there is no carryback.

[28] § 1211(a).

[29] § 1212(a)(1).

Sparrow Corporation has a $15,000 NLTCL for the current year and $57,000 of other taxable income. Sparrow may not offset the $15,000 NLTCL against its other income by taking a capital loss deduction.

The $15,000 NLTCL becomes a $15,000 STCL for carryback and carryover purposes. This amount may be offset against capital gains in the three-year carryback period or, if not absorbed there, offset capital gains in the five-year carryforward period. Any amount remaining after this carryforward period expires is permanently lost.

14-7 Overview of § 1231 and the Recapture Provisions

Generic Manufacturing LLC (a limited liability company) sold machinery, office furniture, and unneeded production plants for $100 million last year. The company's disposition of these assets resulted in $60 million of gains and $13 million of losses. How are these gains and losses treated for tax purposes? Do any special tax rules apply? Could any of the gains and losses receive capital gain or loss treatment?

The remainder of this chapter answers these questions by explaining how to *classify* gains and losses from the disposition of assets that are used in the business rather than held for resale. Chapter 8 discussed how to *depreciate* such assets. Chapter 13 discussed how to determine the *adjusted basis* and the *amount* of gain or loss from their disposition.

A long-term capital gain was defined earlier in this chapter as the recognized gain from the sale or exchange of a capital asset held for the required long-term holding period.[30] Long-term capital assets are capital assets held more than one year.

The remainder of this chapter explains asset classification under § 1231, a fairly complex Code Section, but one that impacts many transactions involving business assets. These transactions generally involve depreciable assets and land. Taxpayers that are affected by § 1231 are those involved in a business (sole proprietors, partnerships, corporations, and some trusts) and taxpayers owning rental property.

In general, § 1231 applies to the sale or exchange of business properties and to certain involuntary conversions. These properties are *not* capital assets because they are depreciable and/or real property used in business or for the production of income.[31] Nonetheless, these business properties may be held for long periods of time and may be sold at a gain.

Congress decided many years ago that § 1231 assets deserved limited capital gain-type treatment. Capital gain treatment sometimes gives too much tax advantage when assets are eligible for depreciation (or cost recovery). As a result, depreciation recapture rules were created to prevent capital gain treatment when gains are realized on § 1231 assets. This chapter also covers the recapture rules that treat a portion (or all) of the gain as ordinary income (even though the gain might otherwise qualify for long-term capital gain treatment).

LO.7

State and explain the rationale for and the nature and treatment of gains and losses from the disposition of business assets.

14-8 Section 1231 Assets

14-8a Relationship to Capital Assets

Because depreciable property and real property used in business are not capital assets, the recognized gains from the disposition of this property would appear to be ordinary income rather than capital gain. Due to § 1231, however, *net gain* from the

[30] § 1222(3).

[31] § 1221(a)(2).

disposition of this property is sometimes *treated* as *long-term capital gain*. In order for this to occur:

- A long-term holding period requirement must be met (held for *more than* a year);
- The disposition must generally be from a sale, exchange, or involuntary conversion; and
- Certain recapture provisions must be satisfied.

Code § 1231 may also apply to involuntary conversions of capital assets even though such a disposition, which is not a sale or exchange, normally would not result in a capital gain.

If the disposition of depreciable property and real property used in business results in a *net loss*, § 1231 *treats* the *loss* as an *ordinary loss* rather than as a capital loss. Ordinary losses are fully deductible *for* adjusted gross income (AGI). Capital losses offset capital gains, and if any loss remains, the loss is deductible to the extent of $3,000 per year for individuals and currently is not deductible at all by regular corporations.

In general, § 1231 provides the *best* of both potential results: net gain may be treated as long-term capital gain, and net loss is treated as ordinary loss; note the results in Examples 48 and 49.

Section 1231 Treatment

Roberto sells a building at a $5,000 gain and equipment at a $3,000 loss. Both properties were § 1231 assets because they were used in Roberto's trade or business and held for the long-term holding period (more than one year).

Roberto's net gain is $2,000, and that net gain *may* (depending on various recapture rules discussed later in this chapter) be treated as a long-term capital gain under § 1231.

Samantha sells business equipment at a $10,000 loss and business land at a $2,000 gain.

Both properties were held for the long-term holding period and, therefore, are § 1231 assets. Samantha's net loss is $8,000, and that net § 1231 loss is an ordinary loss.

The rules regarding § 1231 treatment do *not* apply to *all* business property. Code § 1231 has specific holding period requirements and, in general, requires that the property must be either depreciable property or real estate used in business. As a result, neither inventory nor receivables are § 1231 assets. Nor is § 1231 necessarily limited to business property. Transactions involving certain capital assets may fall into the § 1231 category.

As discussed earlier in this chapter, long-term capital gains receive beneficial tax treatment. Code § 1231 requires netting of **§ 1231 gains and losses**. If the result is a gain, it may be treated as a long-term capital gain. The net gain is added to the "real" long-term capital gains (if any) and netted with capital losses (if any). As a result, the net § 1231 gain may eventually be eligible for beneficial capital gain treatment or help avoid the deduction limitations that apply to a net capital loss. If the § 1231 gain and loss netting results in a loss, it is an ordinary loss. Finally, § 1231 assets are treated the same as capital assets for purposes of the appreciated property charitable contribution provisions (refer to Chapter 10).

14-8b **Property Included**

LO.8

Distinguish § 1231 assets from ordinary assets and capital assets and calculate the § 1231 gain or loss.

Section 1231 property generally includes the following assets if they are held for more than one year:

- Depreciable or real property used in business or for the production of income (principally machinery and equipment, buildings, and land).
- Timber, coal, or domestic iron ore.
- Livestock held for draft, breeding, dairy, or sporting purposes.

- Unharvested crops on land used in business.
- Certain *purchased* intangible assets (such as patents and goodwill) that are eligible for amortization.

These assets are ordinary assets until they have been held for more than one year. Only then do they become § 1231 assets.

14-8c **Property Excluded**

Code § 1231 property generally does *not* include the following:

- Property not held for the long-term holding period.[32]
- Nonpersonal use property where casualty losses exceed casualty gains for the taxable year. If a taxpayer has a net casualty loss, the individual casualty gains and losses are treated as ordinary gains and losses.
- Inventory and property held primarily for sale to customers.
- A patent, invention, model, or design (whether or not patented); a secret formula or process; certain copyrights; literary, musical, or artistic compositions; and certain U.S. government publications.
- Accounts receivable and notes receivable arising in the ordinary course of the trade or business.

14-8d **Section 1231 Assets Disposed of by Casualty or Theft**

When § 1231 assets are disposed of by casualty or theft, a special netting rule is applied. For simplicity, the term *casualty* is used to mean both casualty and theft dispositions. First, the casualty gains and losses from § 1231 assets *and* the casualty gains and losses from **long-term nonpersonal use capital assets** are determined.[33] A nonpersonal use capital asset might be art held as an investment or a baseball card collection held by a nondealer.

Next, the § 1231 asset casualty gains and losses and the nonpersonal use capital asset casualty gains and losses are netted together (see Concept Summary 14.6).

- If the result is a *net loss*, the § 1231 casualty gains and the nonpersonal use capital asset casualty gains are treated as ordinary gains, the § 1231 casualty losses are deductible *for* AGI, and the nonpersonal use capital asset casualty losses are deductible *from* AGI as miscellaneous itemized deductions (which are not deductible from 2018 through 2025).
- If the result of the netting is a *net gain*, the net gain is treated as a § 1231 gain.

As a result, a § 1231 asset disposed of by casualty may or may not get § 1231 treatment, depending on whether the netting process results in a gain or a loss. Also, a nonpersonal use capital asset disposed of by casualty may get § 1231 treatment or ordinary treatment, but will not get capital gain or loss treatment.

Casualties, thefts, and condemnations are *involuntary conversions*. Involuntary conversion gains may be deferred if conversion proceeds are reinvested; involuntary conversion losses are recognized currently (refer to Chapter 13) regardless of whether the conversion proceeds are reinvested. Thus, the special netting process discussed previously for casualties and thefts would not include gains that are not currently recognizable because the insurance proceeds are reinvested.

The special netting process for casualties and thefts also does not include condemnation gains and losses. Consequently, a § 1231 asset disposed of by condemnation will receive § 1231 treatment. This variation between recognized casualty and condemnation gains

[32]Because the benefit of § 1231 is long-term capital gain treatment, the holding period must correspond to the more-than-one-year holding period that applies to capital assets. Livestock must be held at least 12 months (24 months in some cases). Unharvested crops do not have to be held for the required long-term holding period, but the land must be held for the long-term holding period.

[33]*Personal use property casualty* losses (unless they arise in a Federal disaster area) are not usable except to the extent they offset casualty gains. *Personal use property net casualty gains* are treated as long-term capital gains.

Concept Summary 14.6

Section 1231 Netting Procedure (Discussed in text Section 14-8e)

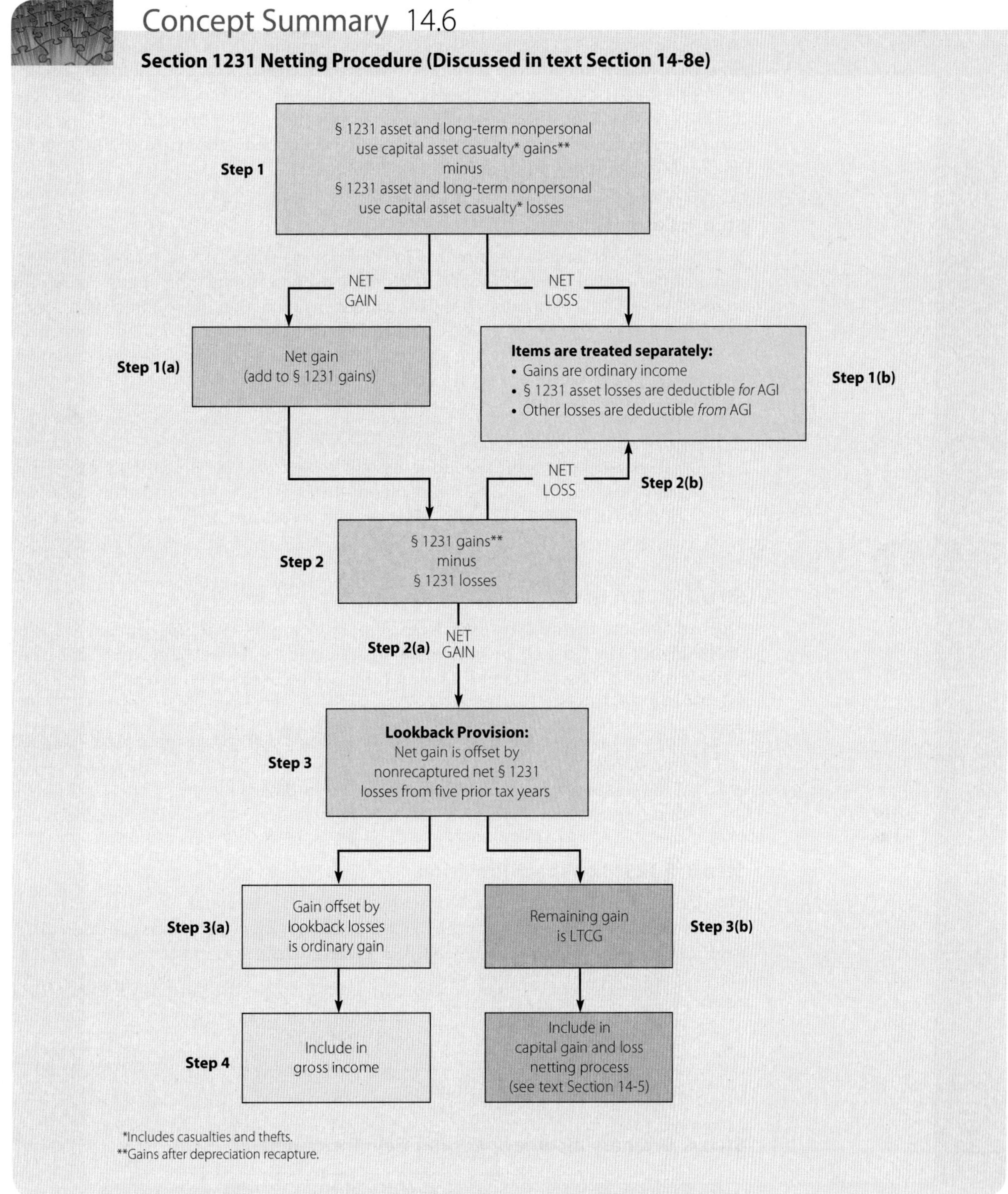

and losses sheds considerable light on what § 1231 is all about. Code § 1231 has no effect on whether *realized* gain or loss is recognized. Instead, § 1231 merely dictates how such *recognized* gain or loss is *classified* (ordinary, capital, or § 1231) under certain conditions.[34]

[34] *Personal use property condemnation* gains and losses are not subject to the § 1231 rules. The gains are capital gains (because personal use property is a capital asset), and the losses are nondeductible because they arise from the disposition of personal use property.

14-8e General Procedure for § 1231 Computation

Most of the time, § 1231 gains and losses result from the sale of business assets. However, as we have already discussed, disposition by casualty and/or theft can also be part of the § 1231 discussion. Consequently, the tax treatment of § 1231 gains and losses depends on the results of a complex *netting* procedure. When there are no casualties and/or thefts (the usual case), step 1 below can be skipped and the procedure is much simpler. Here are the steps that need to be followed:

Step 1: Casualty Netting

Net all recognized long-term gains and losses from casualties of § 1231 assets and nonpersonal use capital assets. Casualty gains result when insurance proceeds exceed the adjusted basis of the property. These are gains remaining after any depreciation recapture (discussed later in text Sections 14-9 and 14-10). This casualty netting is beneficial because if there is a net gain, the gain may receive long-term capital gain treatment. If there is a net loss, it receives ordinary loss treatment.

a. If the casualty gains exceed the casualty losses, add the excess to the other § 1231 gains for the taxable year.
b. If the casualty losses exceed the casualty gains, exclude all casualty losses and gains from further § 1231 computation. If this is the case, all casualty gains are ordinary income. Code § 1231 asset casualty losses are deductible *for* AGI. Other casualty losses may be deductible *from* AGI.

Step 2: § 1231 Netting

After adding any net casualty gain from step 1a to the other § 1231 gains and losses (including recognized § 1231 asset condemnation gains and losses), net all § 1231 gains [gains remaining after any depreciation recapture (discussed later in text Sections 14-9 and 14-10)] and losses.

a. If the gains exceed the losses, the § 1231 "lookback" provision must be applied (see step 3).
b. If the losses exceed the gains, all gains are ordinary income. Code § 1231 asset losses are deductible *for* AGI. Other casualty losses may be deductible *from* AGI.

Step 3: § 1231 Lookback Provision

The net § 1231 gain from step 2a is offset by the nonrecaptured net § 1231 losses for the five preceding taxable years (the **§ 1231 lookback** provision). For transactions in 2023, the lookback years are 2018, 2019, 2020, 2021, and 2022.

a. To the extent of the nonrecaptured net § 1231 loss, the current-year net § 1231 gain is ordinary income. The *nonrecaptured* net § 1231 losses are those that have not already been used to offset net § 1231 gains.
b. Only the net § 1231 gain exceeding this net § 1231 loss carryforward is given long-term capital gain treatment.

Step 4: Ordinary Income or Capital Gain Treatment

a. Include the portion (if any) of step 3a that is an ordinary gain in the taxpayer's gross income.
b. Include the portion (if any) of step 3b that is net § 1231 gain in the capital gain and loss netting process (see text Section 14-5).

Concept Summary 14.6 on p. 14-31 summarizes the § 1231 computational procedure. Examples 50 and 51 illustrate its application without the § 1231 lookback provision. Examples 52 and 53 illustrate its application with the § 1231 lookback provision.

Section 1231 Computations

Example 50

During 2023, Ross had $125,000 of AGI before considering the following recognized gains and losses:

Capital Gains and Losses	
Long-term capital gain	$3,000
Long-term capital loss	(400)
Short-term capital gain	1,000
Short-term capital loss	(200)
Casualties	
Theft of diamond ring (owned four months)	($ 800)*
Fire damage to personal residence (owned 10 years)	(400)*
Gain from insurance recovery on fire loss to business building (owned two years)	200
§ 1231 Gains and Losses from Sale of Depreciable Business Assets Held Long Term	
Asset A	$ 300
Asset B	1,100
Asset C	(500)
Gains and Losses from Sale of Depreciable Business Assets Held Short Term	
Asset D	$ 200
Asset E	(300)

*As adjusted for the $100 floor on personal casualty losses.

Ross had no net § 1231 losses in tax years before 2023.

Ross's gains and losses receive the following tax treatment. [The gains on the business building and Assets A and B are *after* any depreciation recapture (discussed later in the chapter).]

- The diamond ring and the residence are personal use assets. Therefore, these casualties are not § 1231 transactions. The $800 (ring) plus $400 (residence) losses are not deductible because they are not Federal disaster area losses and there are no personal use property casualty gains to offset these losses.
- **Step 1:** Only the business building (a § 1231 asset) casualty gain remains. The netting of the § 1231 asset and nonpersonal use capital asset casualty gains and losses contains only one item—the $200 gain from the business building. Consequently, there is a net gain, and that gain is treated as a § 1231 gain (and added to the § 1231 gains).
- **Steps 1(a) and 2:** The gains from § 1231 transactions (Assets A and B and the § 1231 asset casualty gain) exceed the losses (Asset C) by $1,100 ($1,600 − $500). This excess is a long-term capital gain and is added to Ross's other long-term capital gains.
- **Step 3:** Not applicable since there is no § 1231 lookback loss.
- **Step 4(b):** Ross's net long-term capital gain is $3,700 ($3,000 + $1,100 from § 1231 transactions − $400 long-term capital loss). Ross's net short-term capital gain is $800 ($1,000 − $200). The result is capital gain net income of $4,500. The $3,700 net long-term capital gain portion is eligible for beneficial capital gain treatment [assume that all of the gain is *0%/15%/20% gain* (see the discussion earlier in this chapter)]. The $800 net short-term capital gain is subject to tax as ordinary income.[35]

continued

[35]Ross's taxable income (unless his itemized deductions are extremely large) will put him in at least the 24% bracket. Thus, the alternative tax computation will yield a lower tax. See Example 41.

- Ross treats the gain and loss from Assets D and E (depreciable business assets held for less than the long-term holding period) as ordinary gain and loss.

Results of the Gains and Losses on Ross's Tax Computation	
NLTCG	$ 3,700
NSTCG	800
Ordinary gain from sale of Asset D	200
Ordinary loss from sale of Asset E	(300)
AGI from other sources	125,000
AGI	$129,400

- Ross will have personal use property casualty losses of $1,200 [$800 (diamond ring) + $400 (personal residence)]. The $1,200 is not deductible because the losses are not Federal disaster area losses and there are no personal use property casualty gains to offset these losses.

Example 51

Assume the same facts as in Example 50, except that the loss from Asset C was $1,700 instead of $500.

- The treatment of the casualty losses is the same as in Example 50.
- **Step 1(b):** The losses from § 1231 transactions now exceed the gains by $100 ($1,700 − $1,600). As a result, the gains from Assets A and B and the § 1231 asset casualty gain are ordinary income, and the loss from Asset C is a deduction *for* AGI (a business loss). The same result can be achieved by simply treating the $100 net loss as a deduction *for* AGI.
- **Steps 2 and 3:** Not applicable since there is no net § 1231 gain.
- **Step 4 (b):** Since there is no net § 1231 gains in step 3, the capital gain and loss netting process does not include any such gain. Capital gain net income is $3,400 ($2,600 long term + $800 short term). The $2,600 net long-term capital gain portion is eligible for beneficial capital gain treatment, and the $800 net short-term capital gain is subject to tax as ordinary income.

Results of the Gains and Losses on Ross's Tax Computation	
NLTCG	$ 2,600
NSTCG	800
Net ordinary loss on Assets A, B, and C and § 1231 casualty gain	(100)
Ordinary gain from sale of Asset D	200
Ordinary loss from sale of Asset E	(300)
AGI from other sources	125,000
AGI	$128,200

- The $1,200 of personal casualty losses is not deductible because the losses are not Federal disaster area losses and there are no personal use property casualty gains to offset these losses.

Example 52

Assume the same facts as in Example 50, except that Ross has a $700 nonrecaptured net § 1231 loss from 2022.

- The treatment of the casualty losses is the same as in Example 50.
- **Step 3(a):** The 2023 net § 1231 gain of $1,100 is treated as ordinary income to the extent of the 2022 nonrecaptured § 1231 loss of $700.
- **Step 3(b):** The remaining $400 net § 1231 gain is a long-term capital gain and is added to Ross's other long-term capital gains.

continued

- **Step 4(b):** Ross's net long-term capital gain is $3,000 ($3,000 + $400 from § 1231 transactions − $400 long-term capital loss). Ross's net short-term capital gain is still $800 ($1,000 − $200). The result is capital gain net income of $3,800. The $3,000 net long-term capital gain portion is eligible for beneficial capital gain treatment, and the $800 net short-term capital gain is subject to tax as ordinary income.

Results of the Gains and Losses on Ross's Tax Computation	
NLTCG	$ 3,000
NSTCG	800
Ordinary gain from recapture of § 1231 losses	700
Ordinary gain from sale of Asset D	200
Ordinary loss from sale of Asset E	(300)
AGI from other sources	125,000
AGI	$129,400

- The $1,200 of personal casualty losses is not deductible because the losses are not Federal disaster area losses and there are no personal use property casualty gains to offset these losses.

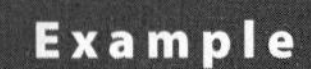

Example 53

Assume the same facts as in Example 50, except that Ross had a net § 1231 loss of $2,700 in 2021 and a net § 1231 gain of $300 in 2022.

- The treatment of the casualty losses is the same as in Example 50.
- **Step 3(a):** The 2021 net § 1231 loss of $2,700 will have carried over to 2022 and been offset against the 2022 net § 1231 gain of $300. Thus, the $300 gain will have been classified as ordinary income, and $2,400 of nonrecaptured 2021 net § 1231 loss will carry over to 2023. The 2023 net § 1231 gain of $1,100 will be offset against this loss, resulting in $1,100 of ordinary income. The nonrecaptured net § 1231 loss of $1,300 ($2,400 − $1,100) carries over to 2024.
- **Step 4(b):** Since there is no net § 1231 gain in step 3, the capital gain and loss netting process does not include any such gain. Capital gain net income is $3,400 ($2,600 net long-term capital gain + $800 net short-term capital gain). The $2,600 net long-term capital gain portion is eligible for beneficial capital gain treatment, and the $800 net short-term capital gain is subject to tax as ordinary income.

Results of the Gains and Losses on Ross's Tax Computation	
NLTCG	$ 2,600
NSTCG	800
Ordinary gain from recapture of § 1231 losses	1,100
Ordinary gain from sale of Asset D	200
Ordinary loss from sale of Asset E	(300)
AGI from other sources	125,000
AGI	$129,400

- The $1,200 of personal casualty losses is not deductible because the losses are not Federal disaster area losses and there are no personal use property casualty gains to offset these losses.

14-9 Section 1245 Recapture

LO.9

Determine when § 1245 recapture applies and how it is computed.

Now that the basic rules of § 1231 have been introduced, it is time to add some additional complications. The Code contains two major *recapture* provisions—§§ 1245 and 1250.[36] These provisions cause *gain* to be treated *initially* as ordinary gain. Thus, what may appear to be a § 1231 gain is ordinary gain instead. This recapture phenomenon applies exclusively to § 1231 gains; § 1231 assets generating losses are unaffected by these recapture provisions.

[36] Due to the passage of time, § 1250 is largely ineffective, but is still important in certain situations.

These recapture provisions may also cause a gain in a nonpersonal use casualty to be *initially* ordinary gain rather than casualty gain. Classifying gains (and losses) properly is important; improper initial classification may lead to incorrect mixing and matching of gains and losses. We begin by discussing the § 1245 recapture rules; the § 1250 recapture rules are discussed in text Section 14-10.

Code § 1245 requires taxpayers to treat all gain as ordinary gain unless the property is disposed of for more than its original cost. This result is accomplished by requiring that all gain be treated as ordinary gain to the extent of the depreciation taken on the property disposed of. The excess of the sales price over the original cost is § 1231 gain. Code § 1245 applies *primarily* to non-real-estate property like machinery, trucks, and office furniture. Code § 1245 does not apply if property is disposed of at a loss. Generally, the loss will be a § 1231 loss unless the form of the disposition is a casualty.

Example 54

Jalissa purchased a $100,000 business machine and deducted $70,000 depreciation before selling it for $80,000. If it were not for § 1245, the $50,000 gain would be § 1231 gain ($80,000 amount realized − $30,000 adjusted basis). Code § 1245 prevents this potentially favorable result by treating as ordinary income (not as § 1231 gain) any gain to the extent of depreciation taken. In this example, the entire $50,000 gain would be ordinary income.

If Jalissa had sold the machine for $120,000, she would have a gain of $90,000 ($120,000 amount realized − $30,000 adjusted basis). The § 1245 gain would be $70,000 (equal to the depreciation taken), and the § 1231 gain would be $20,000 (equal to the excess of the sales price over the original cost).

Section 1245 recapture provides, in general, that the portion of recognized gain from the sale or other disposition of § 1231 property that represents depreciation is *recaptured* as ordinary income.[37] As a result, in Example 54, $50,000 of the $70,000 depreciation taken is recaptured as ordinary income when the business equipment is sold for $80,000. Only $50,000 is recaptured rather than $70,000 because Jalissa is only required to recognize § 1245 recapture ordinary gain equal to the *lower* of the depreciation taken or the gain recognized.

The method of depreciation (e.g., accelerated or straight-line) does not matter. All depreciation taken is potentially subject to recapture. For this reason, § 1245 recapture is often referred to as *full recapture*. Any remaining gain after subtracting the amount recaptured as ordinary income will usually be § 1231 gain.

If the property is disposed of in a casualty event, however, the remaining gain will be casualty gain. If the business machine in Example 54 had been disposed of by casualty and the $80,000 received had been an insurance recovery, Jalissa would still have a gain of $50,000, and the gain would still be recaptured by § 1245 as ordinary gain. The § 1245 recapture rules apply before there is any casualty gain. Because all the $50,000 gain is recaptured, no casualty gain arises from the casualty.

The following examples illustrate the general application of § 1245.

Section 1245 Recapture Computations

Example 55

Partial Ordinary Gain Due to § 1245 Recapture and Partial § 1231 Gain. In the current year, Santiago sold for $13,000 a machine acquired several years ago for $12,000. He had taken $10,000 of depreciation on the machine.

- The recognized gain from the sale is $11,000. This is the amount realized of $13,000 less the adjusted basis of $2,000 ($12,000 cost − $10,000 depreciation taken).
- Depreciation taken is $10,000. Therefore, because § 1245 recapture gain is the lower of depreciation taken or gain recognized, $10,000 of the $11,000 recognized gain is ordinary income, and the remaining $1,000 gain is § 1231 gain.
- The § 1231 gain of $1,000 is also equal to the excess of the sales price over the original cost of the property ($13,000 − $12,000 = $1,000 $1231 gain).

[37]The term *depreciation* includes § 167 depreciation, § 168 cost recovery, § 179 immediate expensing, § 168(k) additional first-year depreciation, and § 197 amortization.

Section 1245 Recapture Computations

Example 56

All Ordinary Gain Due to § 1245 Recapture. Assume the same facts as in the previous example, except that the asset is sold for $9,000 instead of $13,000.

- The recognized gain from the sale is $7,000. This is the amount realized of $9,000 less the adjusted basis of $2,000.
- Depreciation taken is $10,000. Therefore, because the $10,000 depreciation taken exceeds the recognized gain of $7,000, the entire $7,000 recognized gain is ordinary income.
- The § 1231 gain is zero. There is no § 1231 gain because the selling price ($9,000) does not exceed the original purchase price ($12,000).

Example 57

All § 1231 Ordinary Loss. Assume the same facts as in Example 55, except that the asset is sold for $1,500 instead of $13,000.

- The recognized loss from the sale is $500. This is the amount realized of $1,500 less the adjusted basis of $2,000.
- Because there is a loss, there is no depreciation recapture. All of the loss is § 1231 loss.

If § 1231 property that is potentially subject to § 1245 recapture is disposed of in a transaction other than a sale, exchange, or involuntary conversion, the maximum amount recaptured is the excess of the property's fair market value over its adjusted basis. See the discussion under Considerations Common to §§ 1245 and 1250 in text Section 14-11.

14-9a Section 1245 Property

Generally, **§ 1245 property** includes all depreciable personal property (e.g., machinery and equipment), including livestock. Buildings and their structural components generally are not § 1245 property. The following property is *also* subject to § 1245 treatment:

- Amortizable personal property such as goodwill, patents, copyrights, and leaseholds of § 1245 property.
- Professional baseball and football player contracts.
- Certain depreciable tangible real property (other than buildings and their structural components) employed as an integral part of certain activities such as manufacturing and production. For example, a natural gas storage tank where the gas is used in the manufacturing process is § 1245 property.
- Pollution control facilities, railroad grading and tunnel bores, on-the-job training, and child care facilities.
- Single-purpose agricultural and horticultural structures and petroleum storage facilities (e.g., a greenhouse or silo).
- Fifteen-year, 18-year, and 19-year nonresidential real estate for which accelerated cost recovery is used. This property, known as ACRS property, would have been placed in service after 1980 and before 1987.

Example 58

Steve acquired nonresidential real estate on December 1, 1986, for $100,000. He used the required ACRS accelerated method to compute the cost recovery. He sells the asset on January 15, 2023, for $120,000. The amount and nature of Steve's gain are computed as follows:

Amount realized		$120,000
Adjusted basis		
Cost	$ 100,000	
Less cost recovery: 1986–2005	(100,000)	
2006–2023	(–0–)	
January 15, 2023 adjusted basis		(–0–)
Gain realized and recognized		$120,000

continued

The gain of $120,000 is treated as ordinary income to the extent of *all* depreciation taken because the property is 19-year nonresidential real estate for which accelerated depreciation was used. As a result, Steve reports ordinary income of $100,000 and § 1231 gain of $20,000 ($120,000 − $100,000).

14-9b Observations on § 1245

- In most instances, the total depreciation taken will exceed the recognized gain. Therefore, the disposition of § 1245 property usually results in ordinary income rather than § 1231 gain. No § 1231 gain will occur unless the § 1245 property is disposed of for more than its original cost. Refer to Examples 55 and 56.
- Recapture applies to the total amount of depreciation allowed or allowable regardless of the depreciation method used.
- Recapture applies regardless of the holding period of the property. If the property is held for less than the long-term holding period, the entire recognized gain is ordinary income because § 1231 does not apply.
- Code § 1245 does not apply to losses, which receive § 1231 treatment.
- Gains from the disposition of § 1245 assets may also be treated as passive activity gains (see Chapter 11).

LO.10

Determine when § 1250 recapture applies.

14-10 Section 1250 Recapture

Generally, **§ 1250 property** is depreciable real property (principally buildings and their structural components) that is not subject to § 1245.[38] Intangible real property, such as leaseholds of § 1250 property, is also included.

Section 1250 recapture rarely applies because only the amount of *additional depreciation* (depreciation *in excess* of straight-line depreciation) is subject to recapture. Straight-line depreciation is not recaptured (except for property held one year or less). Because the straight-line depreciation method is required for depreciable real property placed in service after 1986, there will usually be *no § 1250 depreciation recapture* on such property. Finally, § 1250 does not apply if the real property is sold at a loss.

Although there is no depreciation recapture on § 1250 property, the gain from this property may be subject to a special 25 percent tax rate. See the discussion of Unrecaptured § 1250 Gain (Real Estate 25% Gain) in text Section 14-10b.

Sanjay acquires a residential rental building on January 1, 2022, for $300,000. He receives an offer of $450,000 for the building in 2023 and sells it on December 23, 2023.

- Sanjay takes $20,909 {($300,000 × 0.03485) + [$300,000 × 0.03636 × (11.5/12)] = $20,909} of total depreciation for 2022 and 2023, and the adjusted basis of the property is $279,091 ($300,000 − $20,909).
- Sanjay's recognized gain is $170,909 ($450,000 − $279,091).
- All of the gain is § 1231 gain.

[38] As noted previously, in one limited circumstance, § 1245 does apply to nonresidential real estate. If the nonresidential real estate was placed in service after 1980 and before 1987 and accelerated depreciation was used, the § 1245 recapture rules would apply (rather than the § 1250 recapture rules).

14-10a **Section 1250 Recapture Situations**

In addition to residential real estate acquired before 1987 and nonresidential real estate acquired before 1981, accelerated depreciation may be taken on other types of real property. The § 1250 recapture rules apply to the following property for which accelerated depreciation was used:

- Any immediate expense deduction (§ 179) and/or additional first-year depreciation [§ 168(k)] exceeding straight-line depreciation taken on leasehold improvements and qualified improvement property.
- Real property used predominantly outside the United States.
- Certain government-financed or low-income housing.[39]

Concept Summary 14.7 compares and contrasts the § 1245 and § 1250 depreciation recapture rules.

Concept Summary 14.7

Comparison of § 1245 and § 1250 Depreciation Recapture

	§ 1245	**§ 1250**
Property affected	All depreciable personal property, but also nonresidential real property acquired after December 31, 1980, and before January 1, 1987, for which accelerated cost recovery was used. Also includes miscellaneous items such as § 179 expense and § 197 amortization of intangibles such as goodwill, patents, and copyrights.	Nonresidential real property acquired after December 31, 1969, and before January 1, 1981, on which accelerated depreciation was taken. Residential rental real property acquired after December 31, 1975, and before January 1, 1987, on which accelerated depreciation was taken.
Depreciation recaptured	Potentially all depreciation taken. If the selling price is greater than or equal to the original cost, all depreciation is recaptured. If the selling price is between the adjusted basis and the original cost, only some depreciation is recaptured.	Normally, there is no depreciation recapture, but in the special situations listed above, there can be § 1250 depreciation recapture of additional depreciation (the excess of accelerated cost recovery over straight-line cost recovery or the excess of accelerated depreciation over straight-line depreciation).
Limit on recapture	Lower of depreciation taken or gain recognized.	Lower of additional depreciation or gain recognized.
Treatment of gain exceeding recapture gain	Usually § 1231 gain.	Usually § 1231 gain.
Treatment of loss	No depreciation recapture; loss is usually § 1231 loss.	No depreciation recapture; loss is usually § 1231 loss.

14-10b **Unrecaptured § 1250 Gain (Real Estate 25% Gain)**

Any unrecaptured § 1250 gain is subject to a 25 percent tax rate. This gain, which relates to the sale of depreciable real estate, is used in the alternative tax computation for net capital gain discussed earlier in this chapter. Unrecaptured § 1250 gain (*25% gain*) is some or all of the § 1231 gain that is treated as long-term capital gain.

The maximum amount of this *25% gain* is the depreciation taken on real property sold at a recognized gain. That maximum amount is computed in one or more of the following ways:

- The recognized gain from disposition is more than the depreciation taken. The *25% gain* is equal to the depreciation taken. Refer to Example 59. The depreciation taken was $20,909, but the recognized gain was $170,909. Consequently, *some* of the recognized gain is potential *25%* § 1231 gain.

[39]Described in § 1250(a)(1)(B).

- The recognized gain from disposition is less than or equal to the depreciation taken. In this case, the *25% gain* is all of the recognized gain. Refer to Example 59, but assume that the building sales price is $285,000. The recognized gain is $5,909 ($285,000 − $279,091), all of this gain is a § 1231 gain, and it is entirely a *25%* § 1231 gain.
- There is § 1245 depreciation recapture because the property is nonresidential real estate acquired in 1981–1986 on which accelerated depreciation was taken. No *25%* § 1231 gain will be left because § 1245 will recapture all of the depreciation or the recognized gain, whichever is less. Refer to Example 58. Depreciation of $100,000 was taken, but all of it was recaptured as ordinary income by § 1245. Thus, there is no remaining potential *25%* § 1231 gain. The entire $20,000 § 1231 gain in Example 58 is potential *0%/15%/20% gain*.
- Code § 1231 loss from disposition of other § 1231 assets held long term reduces the gain from real estate.
- Code § 1231 lookback losses convert some or all of the potential *25%* § 1231 gain to ordinary income.

Special 25% Gain Netting Rules

Where there is a § 1231 gain from real estate and that gain includes both potential *25% gain* and potential *0%/15%/20% gain*, any § 1231 loss from disposition of other § 1231 assets *first offsets* the *0%/15%/20%* portion of the § 1231 gain and then offsets the *25% gain* portion of the § 1231 gain. Also, any § 1231 lookback loss *first recharacterizes* the *25% gain* portion of the § 1231 gain and then recharacterizes the *0%/15%/20%* portion of the § 1231 gain as ordinary income.

Net § 1231 Gain Limitation

The amount of unrecaptured § 1250 gain may not exceed the net § 1231 gain that is eligible to be treated as long-term capital gain. The unrecaptured § 1250 gain is the *lesser of* the unrecaptured § 1250 gain or the net § 1231 gain that is treated as capital gain. Thus, if there is a net § 1231 gain but it is all converted to ordinary income by the five-year § 1231 lookback loss provision, there is no surviving § 1231 gain or unrecaptured § 1250 gain.

Refer to Example 52. There was $200 of § 1231 gain from the building fire that would also be potential *25% gain* if at least $200 of depreciation was taken. The net § 1231 gain was $1,100 including the $200 building gain. (The $500 loss from Asset C would offset the potential *0%/15%/20%* § 1231 gain and not the potential *25% gain*, so all of the potential *25% gain* of $200 is in the $1,100 net § 1231 gain.) However, the $700 of § 1231 lookback losses would *first* absorb the $200 building gain, so the $400 of § 1231 gain that is treated as long-term capital gain includes no *25% gain*.

Section 1250 Property for Purposes of the Unrecaptured § 1250 Gain

Code § 1250 property includes any real property (other than § 1245 property) that is or has been depreciable. Land is *not* § 1250 property because it is not depreciable.

Example 60

Bridget is a single taxpayer with 2023 taxable income of $120,000 composed of:

- $100,000 ordinary taxable income,
- $(3,000) short-term capital loss,
- $15,000 long-term capital gain from sale of stock, and
- $8,000 § 1231 gain that is all unrecaptured § 1250 gain (the actual unrecaptured gain was $11,000, but net § 1231 gain is only $8,000).

Bridget's net capital gain is $20,000 [$15,000 long-term capital gain + $8,000 unrecaptured (§ 1250 gain/net § 1231 gain) − $3,000 short-term capital loss]. The $3,000 short-term capital loss

continued

is offset against the $8,000 unrecaptured § 1250 gain, reducing that gain to $5,000 (see the discussion earlier in the chapter concerning netting of capital losses). Bridget's adjusted net capital gain is $15,000 ($20,000 net capital gain − $5,000 unrecaptured § 1250 gain).

Bridget's total tax (using the alternative tax calculation discussed earlier) is $20,850 [$17,400 (tax on $100,000 other taxable income) + $1,200 ($5,000 unrecaptured § 1250 gain × 24%) + $2,250 ($15,000 adjusted net capital gain × 15%)]. Bridget uses the regular 24% tax rate on the $5,000 unrecaptured § 1250 gain because it is less than the 25% alternative tax rate on the gain.

Ethics & Equity The Sale of a "Cost-Segregated" Building

Many taxpayers have "cost-segregated" their buildings. This means that an engineering study is done to determine whether some of a building's cost can be segregated into tangible personal property (generally a 5-year or 7-year MACRS life with accelerated depreciation) rather than real property (a 27.5-year or 39-year MACRS life with straight-line depreciation). The faster depreciation for the tangible personal property yields significant tax savings.

A CPA is determining the gain or loss from disposition of an office building. A sale document details the selling price of the land and building. However, the building was cost-segregated and the CPA finds records of cost and related depreciation for the tangible personal property that was part of the cost segregation. No mention of this tangible personal property was made in the sale agreement, but the building and all of its contents were sold. What should the CPA do?

14-11 Considerations Common to §§ 1245 and 1250

LO.11

State and explain considerations common to §§ 1245 and 1250.

14-11a Exceptions

Gifts

Depreciation recapture potential carries over to the donee.[40]

Wade gives his daughter, Helen, § 1245 property with an adjusted basis of $1,000. The amount of recapture potential is $700. Helen uses the property in her business and claims further depreciation of $100 before selling it for $1,900.

Helen's recognized gain is $1,000 ($1,900 amount realized − $900 adjusted basis), of which $800 is recaptured as ordinary income ($100 depreciation taken by Helen + $700 recapture potential carried over from Wade). The remaining gain of $200 is § 1231 gain. Even if Helen used the property for personal purposes, the $700 recapture potential would still be carried over.

Death

Although not a very attractive tax planning approach, death eliminates all recapture potential.[41] Any depreciation recapture potential is eliminated when property passes from a decedent to an estate or heir.

Assume the same facts as in Example 61, except that Helen receives the property as a result of Wade's death. The $700 recapture potential from Wade is extinguished. Helen has a basis for the property equal to the property's fair market value at Wade's death (assume that the FMV is $1,700).

Helen will have a $300 gain when the property is sold because the selling price ($1,900) exceeds the property's adjusted basis of $1,600 ($1,700 original basis to Helen − $100 depreciation) by $300. Because of § 1245, $100 is ordinary income. The remaining gain of $200 is § 1231 gain.

[40] §§ 1245(b)(1) and 1250(d)(1) and Reg. §§ 1.1245–4(a)(1) and 1.1250–3(a)(1).

[41] §§ 1245(b)(2) and 1250(d)(2).

Global Tax Issues — Depreciation Recapture in Other Countries

The rules for dispositions of depreciated property are more complex in the United States than in most other countries. Most countries treat the gain or loss from the disposition of business depreciable assets as ordinary income or loss. Consequently, although the U.S. rules are more complex, they can be more beneficial than those of other countries because at least some gains from the disposition of depreciable business property may be taxed at the lower capital gain rates.

Charitable Transfers

If depreciable property is contributed to a charity, the contribution deduction (normally fair market value) must be reduced by any ordinary gain that would have resulted had the property been sold (e.g., from depreciation recapture).[42]

Example 63

Kanisha donates to her church § 1245 property with a fair market value of $10,000 and an adjusted basis of $7,000. Assume that the amount of recapture potential is $2,000 (the amount of recapture that would occur if the property were sold).

Her charitable contribution deduction (subject to the limitations discussed in Chapter 10) is $8,000 ($10,000 fair market value − $2,000 recapture potential).

Certain Nontaxable Transactions

In certain transactions, the transferor's adjusted basis of property carries over to the transferee.[43] If this is the case, any depreciation recapture potential also carries over to the transferee.[44] Included in this category are the following transfers of property:

- Nontaxable incorporations under § 351 (see Chapter 18).
- Certain subsidiary liquidations under § 332 (see Chapter 20).
- Nontaxable contributions to a partnership under § 721 (see Chapter 21).
- Nontaxable reorganizations (see Chapter 20).

Gain may be recognized in these transactions if boot is received. If gain is recognized, it is treated as ordinary income to the extent of the recapture potential or recognized gain, whichever is lower.[45]

Like-Kind Exchanges (§ 1031) and Involuntary Conversions (§ 1033)

Realized gain is recognized to the extent of boot received in a like-kind exchange. Realized gain also will be recognized to the extent the proceeds from an involuntary conversion are not reinvested in similar property. Any recognized gain is subject to recapture as ordinary income under §§ 1245 and 1250. However, since only real property can be the subject of a like-kind exchange, § 1245 recapture is not likely because it generally only applies to tangible personal property. Code § 1250 recapture is also not likely because it infrequently applies to dispositions of real property. On the other hand, unrecaptured § 1250 gain (25% gain) is likely to be present if depreciable real property was the subject of the exchange. The remaining recapture potential, if any, carries over to the property received in the exchange. Realized losses are not recognized in like-kind exchanges, but are recognized in involuntary conversions (see Chapter 13).

---

[42] § 170(e)(1)(A) and Reg. § 1.170A–4(b)(1). In certain circumstances, § 1231 gain also reduces the amount of the charitable contribution. See § 170(e)(1)(B).

[43] §§ 1245(b)(3) and 1250(d)(3) and Reg. §§ 1.1245–4(c) and 1.1250–3(c).

[44] Reg. §§ 1.1245–2(a)(4) and –2(c)(2) and 1.1250–2(d)(1) and (3) and –3(c)(3).

[45] §§ 1245(b)(3) and 1250(d)(3) and Reg. §§ 1.1245–4(c) and 1.1250–3(c).

Example 64

Sometimes, transactions *structured as exchanges* do not qualify as § 1031 like-kind exchanges. For example, exchanges of personalty do not qualify for like-kind treatment (see Chapter 13). Assume that Hazel exchanges equipment (fair market value $128,000, adjusted basis $74,960, and § 1245 depreciation recapture potential $375,040) by "trading it in" on replacement property. If the equipment received in the exchange was worth $150,000, Hazel would have to pay $22,000 of cash ($150,000 − value of the equipment given up in the exchange) to acquire the replacement property. In this situation, Hazel would not have a § 1031 like-kind exchange because this was not an exchange of real property.

Instead, her realized and recognized ordinary gain is $53,040 ($128,000 fair market value of the equipment given up − $74,960 adjusted basis of the equipment given up). All of the gain is recaptured by § 1245 because it is less than the $375,040 depreciation taken.

The remaining recapture potential of $322,000 ($375,040 − $53,040) is extinguished, and the basis of the replacement equipment is its fair market value, $150,000.

14-11b **Other Applications**

The §§ 1245 and 1250 recapture rules *override* all other Code Sections.[46] Special applications include installment sales and property dividends.

Installment Sales

Recapture gain is recognized in the year of the sale regardless of whether gain is otherwise recognized under the installment method.[47] All gain is ordinary income until the recapture potential is fully absorbed. Nonrecapture (§ 1231) gain is recognized under the installment method as cash is received.

Seth sells § 1245 property for $20,000, to be paid in 10 annual installments of $2,000 each plus interest at 6%. Seth realizes a $6,000 gain from the sale, of which $4,000 is attributable to depreciation taken.

If Seth uses the installment method, he recognizes the entire $4,000 of recapture gain as ordinary income in the year of the sale. The $2,000 of nonrecapture (§ 1231) gain will be recognized at the rate of $200 per year for 10 years.

Gain is also recognized on installment sales in the year of the sale in an amount equal to the § 179 (immediate expensing) deduction taken with respect to the property sold, because § 179 immediate expensing is depreciation subject to recapture.

Property Dividends

A corporation generally recognizes gain if it distributes appreciated property as a dividend. Recapture under §§ 1245 and 1250 applies to the extent of the *lower* of the recapture potential or the excess of the property's fair market value over the adjusted basis.[48]

Emerald Corporation distributes § 1245 property as a dividend to its shareholders. The amount of the recapture potential is $300, and the excess of the property's fair market value over the adjusted basis is $800. Emerald recognizes $300 of ordinary income and $500 of § 1231 gain.

Concept Summary 14.8 integrates the depreciation recapture rules with the § 1231 netting process. It is an expanded version of Concept Summary 14.6.

---

[46] §§ 1245(d) and 1250(i).

[47] § 453(i). The installment method of reporting gains on the sale of property is discussed in Chapter 16.

[48] § 311(b) and Reg. §§ 1.1245–1(c) and –6(b) and 1.1250–1(a)(4), –1(b)(4), and –1(c)(2).

Concept Summary 14.8

Depreciation Recapture and § 1231 Netting Procedure

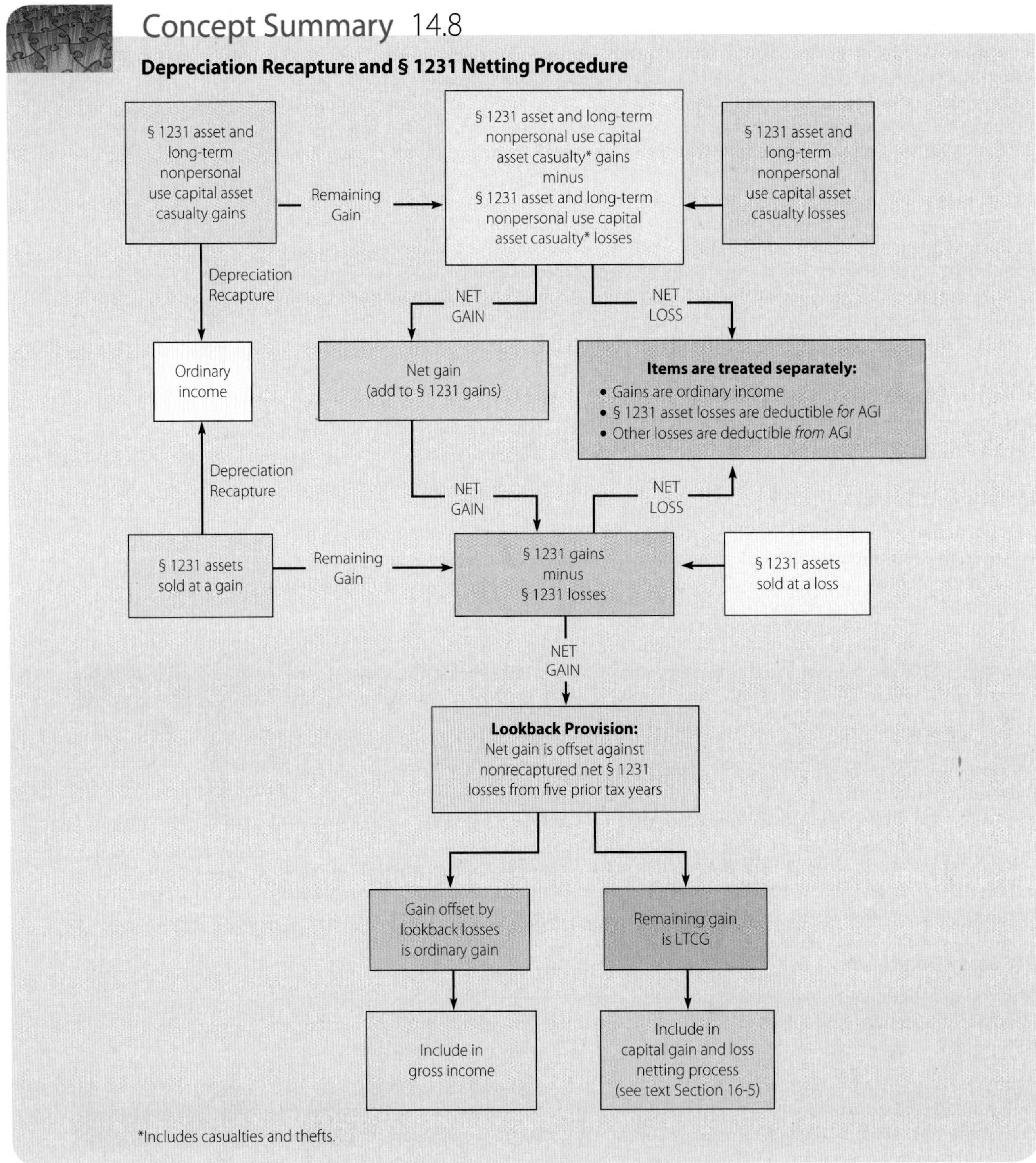

LO.12

Recognize special recapture provisions that are part of the tax law.

14-12 Special Recapture Provisions

14-12a Special Recapture for Corporations

Corporations selling depreciable real estate may have ordinary income in addition to that required by § 1250.[49] Under this provision, corporations selling depreciable real property are required to recapture as ordinary income the smaller of two amounts: (1) 20 percent of the recognized gain or (2) 20 percent of the depreciation taken. See text Section 17-1e for further discussion.

[49] § 291(a)(1).

14-12b **Gain from Sale of Depreciable Property between Certain Related Parties**

If related parties sell or exchange property that is depreciable in the hands of the *transferee* (principally machinery, equipment, and buildings, but not land), any gain recognized by the *transferor* is ordinary income.[50] This rule applies to both direct and indirect sales or exchanges. A **related party** is defined as an individual and his or her controlled corporation or partnership or a taxpayer and any trust in which the taxpayer (or the taxpayer's spouse) is a beneficiary.

Isabella sells a personal use automobile (therefore nondepreciable) to her controlled corporation. The automobile, which was purchased two years ago, originally cost $5,000 and is sold for $7,000. The automobile is to be used in the corporation's business.

If the related-party provision did not exist, Isabella would realize a $2,000 long-term capital gain. The income tax consequences would be favorable because Isabella's controlled corporation is entitled to depreciate the automobile based on the purchase price of $7,000. Under the related-party provision, Isabella's $2,000 gain is ordinary income.

14-12c **Intangible Drilling Costs**

Taxpayers may elect to either *expense or capitalize* intangible drilling and development costs for oil, gas, or geothermal properties.[51] **Intangible drilling and development costs (IDCs)** include operator (one who holds a working or operating interest in any tract or parcel of land) expenditures for wages, fuel, repairs, hauling, and supplies. These expenditures must be incident to and necessary for the drilling of wells and preparation of wells for production. In most instances, taxpayers elect to expense IDCs to maximize tax deductions during drilling.

Intangible drilling and development costs are subject to § 1254 recapture when the property is sold. Any gain realized on the disposition is recognized as ordinary income to the extent of IDCs expensed (but limited to the realized gain).

14-13 **Reporting Procedures**

LO.13

Describe the reporting procedures for §§ 1231, 1245, and 1250.

Noncapital gains and losses are reported on Form 4797 (Sales of Business Property). However, before Form 4797 is filled out, Part B of Form 4684 (Casualties and Thefts) must be completed to determine whether any casualties will enter into the § 1231 computation procedure. Recall that recognized gains from § 1231 asset casualties may be recaptured by § 1245 or § 1250. These gains will not appear on Form 4684. The § 1231 gains and nonpersonal use long-term capital gains are netted against § 1231 losses and nonpersonal use long-term capital losses on Form 4684 to determine if there is a net gain to transfer to Form 4797, Part I.

Ethics & Equity **Incorrect Depreciation and Recognized Gain**

A staff accountant for a large international company is calculating the tax gain from a disposition of business equipment. The equipment was seven-year MACRS property and has been fully depreciated for tax purposes. The staff accountant notices that the equipment was used in Germany, not the United States, although it is listed as an asset of the U.S. company for which the staff accountant works. Because the property was used outside the United States, it should have been depreciated using straight-line over a nine-year life. Consequently, the tax depreciation has been overstated, and the tax basis should be greater than zero, causing a smaller gain. What should the staff accountant do?

---

[50] § 1239.

[51] § 263(c).

LO.14

Identify tax planning opportunities arising from the sale or exchange of capital assets and avoid pitfalls associated with the recapture provisions.

14-14 Tax Planning

14-14a Importance of Capital Asset Status

Why is capital asset status important? Because of the alternative tax on net capital gain. Individuals who receive income in the form of long-term capital gains or qualified dividend income have an advantage over taxpayers who cannot receive income in these forms.

If a net capital loss results, the maximum deduction is $3,000 per year. Consequently, capital gains and losses must be segregated from other types of gains and losses and must be reported separately on Schedule D of Form 1040.

14-14b Planning for Capital Asset Status

Capital asset status often is a question of objective evidence. Property that is not a capital asset to one person may qualify as a capital asset to another person.

Mila, a real estate dealer, transfers by gift a tract of land to Jeff, her son. The land was recorded as part of Mila's inventory (it was held for resale) and was therefore not a capital asset to her. Jeff, however, treats the land as an investment. The land is a capital asset in Jeff's hands, and any later taxable disposition of the property by him will yield a capital gain or loss.

With proper tax planning, even a dealer may obtain long-term capital gain treatment on the sale of property normally held for resale.

Jim, a real estate dealer, segregates Tract A from the real estate he regularly holds for resale and designates the property as being held for investment purposes. The property is not advertised for sale and is disposed of several years later. The negotiations for the subsequent sale were initiated by the purchaser and not by Jim. Under these circumstances, it would appear that any gain or loss from the sale of Tract A should be a capital gain or loss.[52]

When a business is being sold, one of the major decisions usually concerns whether a portion of the sales price is for goodwill. For the seller, goodwill generally represents the disposition of a capital asset. Goodwill has no basis and represents a residual portion of the selling price that cannot be allocated reasonably to the known assets. As a result, the amount of goodwill represents capital gain.

From a legal perspective, the buyer may prefer that the residual portion of the purchase price be allocated to a covenant not to compete (a promise that the seller will not compete against the buyer by conducting a business similar to the one the buyer has purchased). Both purchased goodwill and a covenant not to compete are § 197 intangibles. As a result, both must be capitalized and can be amortized over a 15-year statutory period.

To the seller, a covenant produces ordinary income. So, the seller would prefer that the residual portion of the selling price be allocated to goodwill—a capital asset. If the buyer does not need the legal protection provided by a covenant, the buyer is neutral regarding whether the residual amount is allocated to a covenant or to goodwill. Because the seller would receive a tax advantage from labeling the residual amount as goodwill, the buyer should factor this into the negotiation of the purchase price.

[52] *Toledo, Peoria & Western Railroad Co.*, 35 TCM 1663, T.C.Memo. 1976–366.

Global Tax Issues **Capital Gain Treatment in the United States and Other Countries**

The United States currently requires a complex tax calculation when taxable income includes net long-term capital gain. However, the alternative tax on net long-term capital gain can generate tax savings even when the taxpayer is in the lowest regular tax bracket (10 percent) because there is an alternative tax rate of 0 percent. Many other countries also have an alternative tax rate on long-term capital gains. Consequently, even though the U.S. system is complex, it may be preferable because of the lower tax rates and because the lower rates are available to taxpayers in all tax brackets.

Marcia is buying Jack's dry cleaning proprietorship. An appraisal of the assets indicates that a reasonable purchase price would exceed the value of the known assets by $30,000. If the purchase contract does not specify the nature of the $30,000, the amount will be for goodwill and Jack will have a long-term capital gain of $30,000. Marcia will have a 15-year amortizable $30,000 asset.

If Marcia is paying the extra $30,000 to prevent Jack from operating another dry cleaning business in the area (a covenant not to compete), Jack will have $30,000 of ordinary income. Marcia will have a $30,000 deduction over the statutory 15-year amortization period rather than over the actual life of the covenant (e.g., 5 years).

14-14c **Effect of Capital Asset Status in Transactions Other Than Sales**

The nature of an asset (capital or ordinary) is important in determining the tax consequences that result when a sale or exchange occurs. It may, however, be just as significant in circumstances other than a taxable sale or exchange. When a capital asset is disposed of, the result is not always a capital gain or loss. Rather, in general, the disposition must be a sale or exchange. Collection of a debt instrument having a basis less than the face value results in a capital gain if the debt instrument is a capital asset. The collection is a sale or exchange. Sale of the debt shortly before the due date for collection will produce a capital gain.[53] If selling the debt in such circumstances could produce a capital gain but collecting could not, the consistency of what constitutes a capital gain or loss would be undermined. Another illustration of the sale or exchange principle involves a donation of certain appreciated property to a qualified charity. Recall that in certain circumstances, the measure of the charitable contribution is fair market value when the property, if sold, would have yielded a long-term capital gain (refer to the discussion of contributions of capital gain property in Chapter 10).

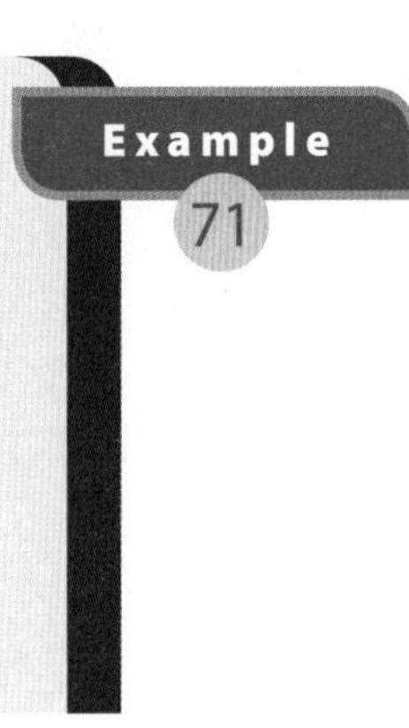

Sharon wants to donate a tract of unimproved land (basis of $40,000 and fair market value of $200,000) held for the required long-term holding period to State University (a qualified charitable organization). However, Sharon currently is under audit by the IRS for capital gains she reported on certain real estate transactions during an earlier tax year. Although Sharon is not a licensed real estate broker, the IRS agent conducting the audit is contending that she has achieved dealer status by virtue of the number and frequency of the real estate transactions she has conducted.

Under these circumstances, Sharon would be well advised to postpone the donation to State University until her status is clarified. If she has achieved dealer status, the unimproved land may be inventory (refer to Example 69 for another possible result) and Sharon's charitable contribution deduction would be limited to $40,000. If not and if the land is held as an investment, Sharon's deduction is $200,000 (the fair market value of the property).

[53] § 1271(b).

14-14d **Stock Sales**

The following rules apply in determining the date of a stock sale:

- The date the sale is executed is the date of the sale. The execution date is the date the broker completes the transaction on the stock exchange.
- The settlement date is the date the cash or other property is paid to the seller of the stock. This date is *not* relevant in determining the date of sale.

Lupè, a cash basis taxpayer, sells stock that results in a gain. The sale was executed on December 29, 2022. The settlement date is January 2, 2023. The date of sale is December 29, 2022 (the execution date). The holding period for the stock sold ends with the execution date.

14-14e **Maximizing Benefits**

Ordinary losses generally are preferable to capital losses because of the limitations imposed on the deductibility of net capital losses and the requirement that capital losses be used to offset capital gains. The taxpayer may be able to convert what would otherwise have been capital loss to ordinary loss. For example, business (but not nonbusiness) bad debts, losses from the sale or exchange of small business investment company stock, and losses from the sale or exchange of small business corporation stock all result in ordinary losses.[54]

Although capital losses can be carried over indefinitely, *indefinite* becomes definite when a taxpayer dies. Any loss carryovers not used by the taxpayer are permanently lost. That is, no tax benefit can be derived from the carryovers subsequent to death.[55] Therefore, the potential benefit of carrying over capital losses diminishes when dealing with older taxpayers.

It is usually beneficial to spread gains over more than one taxable year. In some cases, this can be accomplished through the installment sales method of accounting.

14-14f **Year-End Planning**

The following general rules can be applied for timing the recognition of capital gains and losses near the end of a taxable year:

- If the taxpayer already has recognized more than $3,000 of capital loss, sell assets to generate capital gain equal to the excess of the capital loss over $3,000.

Kevin has already incurred a $7,000 STCL. Kevin should generate $4,000 of capital gain. The gain will be offset by $4,000 of the loss. The remaining loss of $3,000 can be deducted against ordinary income.

- If the taxpayer already has recognized capital gain, sell assets to generate capital loss equal to the capital gain. The gain will not be taxed, and the loss will be fully *deductible* against the gain.
- Generally, if the taxpayer has a choice between recognizing short-term capital gain or long-term capital gain, long-term capital gain should be recognized because it is subject to a lower tax rate.

14-14g **Timing of § 1231 Gain**

Although § 1245 recaptures much of the gain from the disposition of business property, sometimes § 1231 gain is still substantial. For instance, land held as a business asset will generate either § 1231 gain or § 1231 loss. If the taxpayer already has a capital loss for

[54] §§ 166(d), 1242, and 1244. Refer to the discussion in Chapter 7.

[55] Rev.Rul. 74–175.

the year, the sale of land at a gain should be postponed so that the net § 1231 gain is not netted against the capital loss. The capital loss deduction will therefore be maximized for the current tax year, and the capital loss carryforward (if any) may be offset against the gain when the land is sold. If the taxpayer already has a § 1231 loss, § 1231 gains might be postponed to maximize the ordinary loss deduction this year. However, the carryforward of unrecaptured § 1231 losses will make the § 1231 gain next year an ordinary gain.

Section 1231 Planning

Example 74

Mark has a $2,000 net STCL for 2023. He could sell business land held 27 months for a $3,000 § 1231 gain. He will have no other capital gains and losses or § 1231 gains and losses in 2023 or 2024. He has no nonrecaptured § 1231 losses from prior years. Mark is in the 24% tax bracket in 2023 and will be in the 22% bracket in 2024. If he sells the land in 2023, he will have a $1,000 net LTCG ($3,000 § 1231 gain − $2,000 STCL) and will pay a tax of $150 ($1,000 × 15%).

If Mark sells the land in 2024, he will have a 2023 tax savings of $480 ($2,000 capital loss deduction × 24% tax rate on ordinary income). In 2024, he will pay tax of $450 ($3,000 × 15%).

By postponing the sale by a year, Mark gets the use of $630 ($480 + $150) of tax savings until he has to pay $450 in 2024, for a net savings of $180 between the two years without considering the time value of money and other factors.

Example 75

Beth has a $15,000 § 1231 loss in 2023. She could sell business equipment held 30 months for a $20,000 § 1231 gain and a $12,000 § 1245 gain. Beth is in the 24% tax bracket in 2023 and will be in the 22% bracket in 2024. She has no nonrecaptured § 1231 losses from prior years. If she sold the equipment in 2023, she would have a $5,000 net § 1231 gain and $12,000 of ordinary gain. Her tax would be $3,630 [($5,000 § 1231 gain × 15%) + ($12,000 ordinary gain × 24%)].

If Beth postponed the equipment sale until 2024, she would have a 2023 ordinary loss of $15,000 and tax savings of $3,600 ($15,000 × 24%). In 2024, she would have $5,000 of § 1231 gain (the § 1231 lookback rule applies and the 2023 net § 1231 loss recharacterizes $15,000 of the 2024 § 1231 gain as ordinary income). She would also have $27,000 of ordinary gain ($12,000 from depreciation recapture plus $15,000 from the § 1231 lookback rule). Her tax would be $6,690 [($5,000 § 1231 gain × 15%) + ($27,000 ordinary gain × 22%)].

By postponing the sale of the § 1231 property until 2024, Beth gets the use of $7,230 ($3,600 + $3,630) of tax savings until she has to pay $6,690 in 2024, for a net savings of $540 between the two years without considering the time value of money and other factors.

14-14h **Timing of Recapture**

Because recapture is usually not triggered until the property is sold or disposed of, it may be possible to plan for recapture in low tax bracket or loss years. If a taxpayer has net operating loss (NOL) carryovers, the recognition of ordinary income from recapture may be advisable to absorb the loss carryovers.

Ahmad has a $15,000 NOL carryover. He owns a machine that he plans to sell in the early part of next year. The expected gain of $17,000 from the sale of the machine will be recaptured as ordinary income under § 1245. Ahmad sells the machine before the end of this year and uses the $15,000 NOL carryover to offset $15,000 of the ordinary income.

14-14i **Postponing and Shifting Recapture**

It is also possible to postpone recapture or to shift the burden of recapture to others. For example, recapture is postponed and shifted on the exchange of a § 1231 asset if the taxpayer exchanges the property for stock in a § 351 nontaxable incorporation. In this instance, the recapture potential is shifted to the corporation.

Recapture can be shifted to others through the gratuitous transfer of § 1245 or § 1250 property to family members. A subsequent sale of such property by the donee will trigger recapture to the donee rather than the donor (refer to Example 61). This procedure would be advisable only if the donee was in a lower income tax bracket compared with the donor.

14-14j **Avoiding Recapture**

The immediate expensing election (§ 179) and additional first-year (bonus) depreciation [§ 168(k)] are subject to § 1245 recapture. If the elections are not made, the § 1245 recapture potential will accumulate more slowly (refer to Chapter 8). Because using the immediate expense election and/or additional first-year depreciation deduction complicates depreciation and book accounting for the affected asset(s), not taking these deductions may make sense even though the time value of money might indicate that they should be taken.

Refocus on The Big Picture

Managing Capital Asset Transactions

AUREMAR/SHUTTERSTOCK.COM

You explain to Maurice that your area of expertise is tax, so you are providing tax advice and not investment advice. From an overall perspective, he is correct that certain capital gains and dividends are eligible for either a 0 percent, a 15 percent, or a 20 percent tax rate rather than the regular income tax rates that go as high as 37 percent. You then discuss the potential tax consequences of each of his investments.

- *Purple stock and Eagle stock.* To qualify for the beneficial tax rate, the holding period for the stock must be longer than one year. From a tax perspective, Maurice should retain his stock investments for at least an *additional* three months and a day. To be eligible for the "costless" capital gains as a single taxpayer (i.e., taxed at the 0 percent rate), his taxable income should not exceed $44,625 for 2023. The dividends received on the Purple stock are "qualified dividends" eligible for the 0%/15%/20% alternative tax rate.
- *Patent.* Because he is a "holder" of the patent, it will qualify for the beneficial capital gain rate regardless of the holding period if the patent should produce income in excess of his $50,000 investment. However, if he loses money on the investment, he will be able to deduct only $3,000 of the loss per year against his ordinary income (assuming that there are no offsetting capital gains). See Examples 15 and 16.
- *Tax-exempt bonds.* The after-tax return on the taxable bonds would be less than the 3 percent on the tax-exempt bonds. In addition, the interest on the taxable bonds would increase his taxable income, possibly moving it out of the desired 12 percent marginal tax rate into the 22 percent marginal tax rate.
- *Franchise rights.* The franchise rights purchased from Orange, Inc., probably require the payment of a franchise fee based upon the sales in the franchise business. Maurice should either start such a business or sell the franchise rights.
- *Partnership interest.* Whether Maurice receives capital or ordinary treatment associated with his partnership interest depends on whether he is reporting his share of profits or losses (ordinary income or ordinary loss) or is reporting recognized gain or loss from the sale of his partnership interest (capital gain or capital loss).

You conclude your tax advice to Maurice by telling him that whatever he does regarding his investments should make economic sense. There are no 100 percent tax rates. For example, disposing of the bank stock in the current market could be the wise thing to do.

Key Terms

Alternative tax, 14-22
Capital asset, 14-4
Capital gains, 14-2
Capital losses, 14-2
Collectibles, 14-22
Franchise, 14-12
Holding period, 14-15
Intangible drilling and development costs (IDCs), 14-45
Lessee, 14-14
Lessor, 14-14
Long-term nonpersonal use capital assets, 14-30
Net capital gain (NCG), 14-20
Net capital loss (NCL), 14-26
Options, 14-9
Original issue discount (OID), 14-9
Patent, 14-11
Qualified dividend income (QDI), 14-22
Related party, 14-45
Sale or exchange, 14-8
Section 1231 gains and losses, 14-29
Section 1231 lookback, 14-32
Section 1231 property, 14-29
Section 1245 property, 14-37
Section 1245 recapture, 14-36
Section 1250 property, 14-38
Section 1250 recapture, 14-38
Short sale, 14-16
Unrecaptured § 1250 gain, 14-20

Discussion Questions

1. **LO.2, 4, 5** Sheila inherited 300 shares of stock, 100 shares of Magenta and 200 shares of Purple. She has a stockbroker sell the shares for her, uses the proceeds for personal expenses, and thinks nothing further about the transactions. What issues does she face when she prepares her Federal income tax return? Critical Thinking

2. **LO.2** An individual taxpayer sells some used assets at a garage sale. Why are none of the proceeds taxable in most situations? Critical Thinking

3. **LO.2, 4** Alison owns a painting that she received as a gift from her aunt 10 years ago. The aunt created the painting. Alison has displayed the painting in her home and has never attempted to sell it. Recently, a visitor noticed the painting and offered Alison $5,000 for it. If Alison decides to sell the painting, what tax issues does she face? Critical Thinking

4. **LO.2** Is a note receivable that arose in the ordinary course of the taxpayer's retail business a capital asset? Why or why not?

5. **LO.2** Anwar owns vacant land that he purchased many years ago as an investment. After getting approval to subdivide it into 35 lots, he made minimal improvements and then sold the entire property to a real estate developer. Anwar's recognized gain on the sale was $1,200,000. Is this transaction eligible for the "real property subdivided for sale" rules? Why or why not?

6. **LO.3** Hubert purchases all of the rights in a patent from the inventor who developed the patented product. After holding the patent for two years, Hubert sells all of the rights in the patent for a substantial gain. What issues does Hubert face if he wants to treat the gain as a long-term capital gain? Critical Thinking

7. **LO.3** Blue Corporation and Fuchsia Corporation are engaged in a contract negotiation over the use of Blue's trademarked name, DateSiteForSeniors. For a one-time payment of $45,000, Blue licensed Fuchsia to use the name DateSiteForSeniors, and the license requires that Fuchsia pay Blue a royalty every time a new customer signs up on Fuchsia's website. Blue is a developer of "website ideas" that it then licenses to other companies such as Fuchsia. Did Fuchsia purchase a franchise right from Blue, or did Fuchsia purchase the name DateSiteForSeniors from Blue?

8. **LO.4** At the date of a short sale, Sylvia has held substantially identical securities for more than 12 months. What is the nature of any gain or loss from the close of her short sale?

9. **LO.5** After netting all of her short-term and long-term capital gains and losses, Misty has a net short-term capital loss and a net long-term capital loss. Can she net these against each other? Why or why not?

10. **LO.2, 5** Charlie sells his antique farm tractor collection at a loss. He had acquired all of the tractors for his personal pleasure and sold all of them for less than he paid for them. What is the tax status of the tractors? Is his loss a 28% collectibles loss? Explain.

Critical Thinking

11. **LO.7, 8** Hakim's rental building (a § 1231 asset) was not insured when it was destroyed by a hurricane. His adjusted basis for the building was substantial but was less than he had paid for the building in 2018. The building was Hakim's only asset that was damaged by the hurricane. How should Hakim handle this situation?

12. **LO.8** An individual taxpayer had a net § 1231 loss in 2023. Could any of this loss be treated as a long-term capital loss? Why or why not?

Critical Thinking

13. **LO.8** Steven established a sole proprietorship in 2017. He sold § 1231 assets at a loss in 2021 and 2022. He had only sold § 1231 assets at a gain before 2021. In 2023, he could sell a § 1231 asset at a gain and would like to have the gain taxed as a long-term capital gain. What issue is Steven facing?

14. **LO.8** Review Examples 50 and 52 in the text. In both examples, the taxpayer's AGI is $129,400 even though in Example 52 there is $700 of nonrecaptured § 1231 loss from 2022. Explain why the two AGI amounts are the same.

15. **LO.8** A depreciable business dump truck has been owned for four years and is no longer useful to the taxpayer. What would have to be true for the disposition of the dump truck to generate at least some § 1231 loss?

16. **LO.7, 9** If depreciable equipment used in a business is sold at a recognized gain on July 10, 2023, and it was purchased on August 21, 2022, does § 1245 depreciation recapture apply to the asset? Explain.

Communications

17. **LO.9** A retailer's store is destroyed by a tornado but is insured for its replacement cost. Consequently, the retailer has a $40,000 gain after receiving the insurance proceeds. The store is not replaced because the retailer spends the insurance proceeds on additional inventory. What is the nature of the gain if the building originally cost $100,000 three years ago and had an adjusted basis of $82,000 at the time of its destruction? Prepare an e-mail to your supervisor, Sharon Regan, summarizing your answer. E-mail this response to your instructor.

18. **LO.10** In the current year, an individual taxpayer has net long-term capital gain from disposition of capital assets and has unrecaptured § 1250 gain. What would the circumstances have to be for the unrecaptured § 1250 gain to be taxed at 25%?

19. **LO.9, 11** Mary receives tangible personal property as a gift. The property was depreciated by the donor, and Mary will also depreciate it. At the date of the gift, the property was worth more than the donor's adjusted basis. What is the impact of these facts on Mary when she sells the property at a gain several years after she acquired it?

20. **LO.9, 11** Thomas receives tangible personal property as an inheritance from a decedent who died in 2023. The property was depreciated by the deceased, and Thomas will also depreciate it. At the date of the deceased's death, the property was worth more than the deceased's adjusted basis. What is the impact of these facts on Thomas when he sells the property at a gain several years after he acquired it?

21. **LO.9, 11** Dino contributes to charity some tangible personal property that he had used in his business and depreciated. At the date of the donation, the

property has a fair market value greater than its adjusted basis, but less than the original cost. What is the impact of these facts on Dino's charitable contribution?

22. **LO.9, 11** A corporation distributes a truck it has owned for three years to its sole shareholder. The shareholder will use the truck for personal use activity. The truck's fair market value at the time of the distribution is greater than its adjusted basis but less than its original cost. Does the corporation recognize a gain? If so, what is the character of the gain?

23. **LO.12** A corporation distributes a truck it has owned for three years to its sole shareholder. The shareholder will use the truck for business activity. The truck's fair market value at the time of the distribution is greater than its adjusted basis but less than its original cost. Does the corporation recognize a gain? If so, what is the character of the gain?

Computational Exercises

24. **LO.2** Dexter owns a large tract of land and subdivides it for sale. Assume that Dexter meets all of the requirements of § 1237 and during the tax year sells the first eight lots to eight different buyers for $22,000 each. Dexter's basis in each lot sold is $15,000, and he incurs total selling expenses of $900 on each sale. What is the amount of Dexter's capital gain and ordinary income? Formulate your answer by constructing a spreadsheet using a format similar to that found in Example 10.

25. **LO.3** Sheila purchases $50,000 of newly issued Gingo Corporation bonds for $45,000. The bonds have original issue discount (OID) of $5,000. After Sheila amortized $2,300 of OID and held the bonds for four years, she sold the bonds for $48,000. What is the amount and character of her gain or loss?

26. **LO.3** Olivia wants to buy some vacant land for investment purposes. She cannot afford the full purchase price. Instead, Olivia pays the landowner $8,000 to obtain an option to buy the land for $175,000 anytime in the next four years. Fourteen months after purchasing the option, Olivia sells the option for $10,000. What is the amount and character of Olivia's gain or loss?

27. **LO.3** On May 9, 2023, Glenna purchases 500 shares of Ignaz Company stock for $7,500. On June 30, 2023, she writes a call option on the stock, giving the grantee the right to buy the stock for $9,000 during the following 12-month period. Glenna receives a call premium of $750 for writing the call. The call is exercised by the grantee on December 15, 2023.
    a. What is the amount and character of Glenna's gain or loss?
    b. Assume that the original option expired unexercised. What is the amount and character of Glenna's gain or loss?

28. **LO.4** Shen purchased corporate stock for $20,000 on April 10, 2021. On July 14, 2023, when the stock was worth $12,000, Shen died and his son, Mijo, inherited the stock. Mijo sold the stock for $14,200 on November 12, 2023. What is the amount and character of Mijo's gain or loss?

29. **LO.5** Coline has the following capital gain and loss transactions for 2023.

Short-term capital gain	$ 5,000
Short-term capital loss	(2,100)
Long-term capital gain (28%)	6,000
Long-term capital gain (15%)	2,000
Long-term capital loss (28%)	(10,500)

After the capital gain and loss netting process, what is the amount and character of Coline's gain or loss?

30. **LO.5** Elliott has the following capital gain and loss transactions for 2023.

Short-term capital gain	$ 1,500
Short-term capital loss	(3,600)
Long-term capital gain (28%)	12,000
Long-term capital gain (25%)	4,800
Long-term capital gain (15%)	6,000
Long-term capital loss (28%)	(4,500)
Long-term capital loss (15%)	(9,000)

After the capital gain and loss netting process, what is the amount and character of Elliott's gain or loss?

31. **LO.7** Lena is a sole proprietor. In April of this year, she sold equipment purchased four years ago for $26,000 with an adjusted basis of $15,500 for $17,000. Later in the year, Lena sold another piece of equipment purchased two years ago with an adjusted basis of $8,200 for $5,500. What is the amount and character of Lena's gain or loss?

32. **LO.9** Renata Corporation purchased equipment in 2021 for $180,000 and has taken $83,000 of regular MACRS depreciation. Renata Corporation sells the equipment in 2023 for $110,000. What is the amount and character of Renata's gain or loss?

33. **LO.9** Jacob purchased business equipment for $56,000 in 2020 and has taken $35,000 of regular MACRS depreciation. Jacob sells the equipment in 2023 for $26,000. What is the amount and character of Jacob's gain or loss?

34. **LO.7, 8, 9** Shannon owns two items of business equipment. Both were purchased in 2019 for $100,000, both have a 7-year MACRS recovery period, and both have an adjusted basis of $37,490. Shannon is considering selling these assets in 2023. One of them is worth $60,000, and the other is worth $23,000. Because both items were used in her business, Shannon simply assumes that the loss on one will offset the gain from the other and that the net gain or loss will increase or reduce her business income. What is the amount and character of Shannon's gain or loss?

35. **LO.10** An apartment building was acquired in 2014. The depreciation taken on the building was $123,000, and the building was sold for a $34,000 gain. What is the maximum amount of *25% gain*?

36. **LO.10** Enzo is a single taxpayer with the following gains and losses for 2023:
    - $2,100 short-term capital loss.
    - $24,000 long-term capital gain from sale of stock.
    - $14,000 § 1231 gain that is all unrecaptured § 1250 gain.

    What is the amount and character of Enzo's gain or loss?

37. **LO.11** In a § 1031 like-kind exchange, Rafael exchanges a business building that originally cost $200,000. On the date of the exchange, the building given up has an adjusted basis of $85,000 and a fair market value of $110,000. Rafael pays $15,000 and receives a building with a fair market value of $125,000. What is the amount and character of Rafael's gain or loss?

Problems

38. **LO.2** During the year, Eugene had the four property transactions summarized on the next page. Eugene is a collector of antique glassware and occasionally sells a piece to get funds to buy another. What are the amount and nature of the gain or loss from each of these transactions?

Property	Date Acquired	Date Sold	Adjusted Basis	Sales Price
Antique vase	06/18/12	05/23/23	$37,000	$42,000
Blue Growth Fund (100 shares)	12/23/14	11/22/23	22,000	38,000
Orange bonds	02/12/15	04/11/23	34,000	42,000*
Green stock (100 shares)	02/14/23	11/23/23	11,000	13,000

*The sales price included $750 of accrued interest.

39. **LO.2, 5** Rennie owns a video game arcade. He buys vintage video games from estates, often at much less than the retail value of the property. He usually installs the vintage video games in a special section of his video game arcade that appeals to players of "classic" video games. Recently, Rennie sold a classic video game that a customer "just had to have." Rennie paid $11,250 for it, owned it for 14 months, and sold it for $18,000. Rennie had suspected that this particular classic video game would be of interest to collectors; so he had it refurbished, put it on display in his video arcade, and listed it for sale on the internet. No customers in the arcade had played it other than those testing it before considering it for purchase. Rennie would like the gain on the sale of the classic video game to be a long-term capital gain. Did he achieve that objective? Why or why not?

Critical Thinking
Decision Making
Planning

40. **LO.2** George is the owner of numerous classic automobiles. His intention is to hold the automobiles until they increase in value and then sell them. He rents the automobiles for use in various events (e.g., antique automobile shows) while he is holding them. In 2023, he sold a classic automobile for $1,500,000. He had held the automobile for five years, and it had a tax basis of $750,000.

   a. Was the automobile a capital asset? Why or why not?
   b. Assuming a rate of return of 7%, how much would he have had to invest five years ago (instead of putting $750,000 into the car) to have had $1,500,000 this year? See Appendix E for the present value factors.

41. **LO.2, 4** Barbella purchased a wedding ring for $15 at a yard sale in May. She thought the ring was costume jewelry, but it turned out to be a real diamond ring. She is not in the business of buying and selling anything. She researched the ring on the internet and discovered that it was worth at least $1,000. She sold it on an internet auction site for $1,100 in July. Was the ring a capital asset? What were the amount and nature of the gain or loss from its sale by Barbella? Prepare your answer in the form of an e-mail communication between you as a staff person of the Fuchsia CPA Firm LLP and your boss, Maria Hernandez, CPA. Assume that her e-mail address is *mhernandez@fuchsiacpas.com*. Maria referred the situation to you and is aware of the facts and the questions you should answer.

Communications

42. **LO.2** Pebble Securities is a corporation that buys and sells financial assets. It purchases notes receivable from manufacturers that need cash immediately and cannot wait to collect the notes. Pebble pays about 88% of the face value of the receivables and then collects them. Because of the quality of the notes, Pebble collected less than it paid for some of the notes. Does Pebble have a capital loss when it collects the receivables for less than it paid for them? Explain.

43. **LO.2** Faith Godwin is a dealer in securities. She has spotted a fast-rising company and would like to buy and hold its stock for investment. The stock is currently selling for $2 per share, and Faith thinks it will climb to $40 a share within two years. Faith's coworkers have told her that there is "no way" she can get long-term capital gain treatment when she purchases stock because she is a securities dealer. Faith has asked you to calculate her potential gain and tell her whether her coworkers are right. Draft a letter to Faith, responding to her request. Her address is 200 Catamon Drive, Great Falls, MT 59406.

Communications
Planning

44. **LO.2** Maria meets all of the requirements of § 1237 (subdivided realty). In 2023, she begins selling lots and sells four separate lots to four different purchasers. She also sells two contiguous lots to another purchaser. The sales price of each lot is $30,000. Maria's basis for each lot is $15,000. Selling expenses are $500 per lot.

a. What are the realized and recognized gain?

b. Explain the nature of the gain (i.e., ordinary income or capital gain).

c. Would your answers change if, instead, the lots sold to the fifth purchaser were not contiguous? If so, how?

Critical Thinking
Decision Making

45. **LO.2, 3, 5** Melaney has had a bad year with her investments. She lent a friend $8,000; the friend did not repay the loan when it was due and then declared bankruptcy. The loan is totally uncollectible. Melaney also was notified by her broker that the Oak corporate bonds she owned became worthless on October 13, 2023. She had purchased the bonds for $22,000 on November 10, 2022. Melaney also had a $60,000 loss on the disposition of § 1244 corporate stock that she purchased several years ago. Melaney is single.

a. What are the nature and amount of Melaney's losses?

b. What is Melaney's AGI for 2023 assuming that she has $65,000 of ordinary gross income from sources other than those discussed?

c. What are the nature and amount of Melaney's loss carryforwards?

46. **LO.2, 3** Benny purchased $400,000 of Peach Corporation face value bonds for $320,000 on November 13, 2022. The bonds had been issued with $80,000 of original issue discount because Peach was in financial difficulty in 2022. On December 3, 2023, Benny sold the bonds for $283,000 after amortizing $1,000 of the original issue discount. What are the nature and amount of Benny's gain or loss?

Critical Thinking
Decision Making
Planning

47. **LO.3** Fred is an investor in vacant land. When he thinks he has identified property that would be a good investment, he approaches the landowner, pays the landowner for a "right of first refusal" to purchase the land, records this right in the property records, and then waits to see if the land increases in value. The right of first refusal is valid for four years. Fourteen months ago, Fred paid a landowner $9,000 for a right of first refusal. The land was selected as the site of a new shopping center, and the landowner was offered $1,000,000 for the land. In its title search on the land, the buyer discovered Fred's right of first refusal and involved him in the purchase negotiations. Ultimately, the landowner paid Fred $220,000 to give up his right of first refusal; the landowner then sold the land to the buyer for $1,220,000. Fred has a marginal tax rate of 37%.

a. What difference does it make whether or not Fred treats the right of first refusal as an option to purchase the land?

b. What difference does it make whether Fred is a "dealer" in land?

48. **LO.3** Carla was the owner of vacant land that she was holding for investment. She paid $2,000,000 for the land in 2020. Raymond was an investor in vacant land. He thought Carla's land might be the site of an exit ramp from a new freeway. Raymond gave Carla $836,000 for an option on her land in 2021. The option was good for two years and gave Raymond the ability to purchase Carla's land for $4,765,000. The freeway was not approved by the government, and Raymond's option expired in 2023. Does Carla have $836,000 of long-term capital gain upon the expiration of the option? Explain.

49. **LO.2, 3** Hilde purchased all of the rights to a patent on a new garden tool developed by a friend of hers who is an amateur inventor. The inventor obtained the patent rights, set up a manufacturing company to produce and sell the garden tool, and produced substantial quantities of the tool, but he then became discouraged when no large garden company would agree to distribute the tool for him. Hilde purchased the patent rights (but not the manufacturing company) for $120,000 on

October 24, 2022. Hilde had never engaged in such a transaction before, but she is a salesperson in the garden industry and thought she could succeed where her friend had failed. On June 27, 2023, she sold all patent rights to Garden Tool Company for $1,233,000. Garden Tool will manufacture the tool in its own factory and sell it to its customers.What is the nature of Hilde's gain from this transaction?

50. **LO.3, 4, 14** Mac, an inventor, obtained a patent on a chemical process to clean old aluminum siding so that it can be easily repainted. Mac has a $50,000 tax basis in the patent. Mac does not have the capital to begin manufacturing and selling this product, so he has done nothing with the patent since obtaining it two years ago. Now a group of individuals has approached him and offered two alternatives. Under one alternative, they will pay Mac $600,000 (payable evenly over the next 15 years) for the exclusive right to manufacture and sell the product. Under the other, they will form a business and contribute capital to it to begin manufacturing and selling the product; Mac will receive 20% of the company's shares of stock in exchange for all of his patent rights. Discuss which alternative is better for Mac.

Critical Thinking
Decision Making
Planning

51. **LO.3** Freys, Inc., sells a 12-year "stuffed potato" franchise to Reynaldo. The franchise contains many restrictions on how Reynaldo may operate his store. For instance, Reynaldo cannot use less than Grade 10 Idaho potatoes, must bake the potatoes at a constant 410 degrees, must dress store personnel in Freys-approved uniforms, and must have a Freys sign that meets detailed specifications on size, color, and construction. When the franchise contract is signed, Reynaldo makes a noncontingent $160,000 payment to Freys. During the same year, Reynaldo pays Freys $300,000—14% of Reynaldo's sales. How does Freys treat each of these payments? How does Reynaldo treat each of the payments?

52. **LO.3** Angie owns numerous strip malls. A major tenant of one of the strip malls wanted to cancel its lease because it was moving to another city. After lengthy negotiations, the tenant paid Angie $60,000 to cancel its obligations under the lease. If the tenant had fulfilled the lease terms, Angie would have received rent of $700,000. What factors should Angie consider to determine the amount and character of her income from these circumstances?

Critical Thinking

53. **LO.3** Consuela was a tenant in a campus apartment. She is a student at State University. Her lease began on August 1, 2023, and was due to expire on July 31, 2024. However, her landlord sold the building, and the new owner wanted to demolish it to build a retail building. Consuela's landlord paid her $1,000 to cancel the lease. Consuela received the $1,000 on November 30, 2023; moved out; and rented another apartment. How should Consuela treat the $1,000?

54. **LO.4** Roger inherited 100 shares of Periwinkle stock when his mother, Emily, died. Emily had acquired the stock for a total of $60,000 on November 15, 2019. She died on August 10, 2023, and the shares were worth a total of $55,000 at that time. Roger sold the shares for $36,000 on December 22, 2023. How much gain or loss does Roger recognize? What is the nature of that gain or loss?

55. **LO.4** Sarah received a gift of farmland from her father. The land was worth $4,000,000 at the date of the gift, had been farmed by her father for 40 years, and had a tax basis for her father of $30,000. Sarah never farmed the land and sold it eight months after receiving it from her father for $4,200,000. What is Sarah's holding period for the farmland? What is the nature of the gain from its disposition?

56. **LO.4** Dennis sells short 100 shares of ARC stock at $20 per share on January 15, 2023. He buys 200 shares of ARC stock on April 1, 2023, at $25 per share. On May 2, 2023, he closes the short sale by delivering 100 of the shares purchased on April 1.
   a. What are the amount and nature of Dennis's loss upon closing the short sale?
   b. When does the holding period for the remaining 100 shares begin?
   c. If Dennis sells (at $27 per share) the remaining 100 shares on January 20, 2024, what will be the nature of his gain or loss?

Communications

57. **LO.5** Liana Amiri (single with no dependents) has the following transactions in 2023:

AGI (exclusive of capital gains and losses)	$540,000
Long-term capital gain	22,000
Long-term capital loss	(8,000)
Short-term capital gain	19,000
Short-term capital loss	(23,000)

What is Liana's net capital gain or loss? Draft a letter to Liana describing how the net capital gain or loss will be treated on her tax return. Note that Liana's income from other sources puts her in the 37% tax bracket. Liana's address is 300 Ireland Avenue, Shepherdstown, WV 25443.

Communications

58. **LO.3, 5** In 2023, Beth Jarow had a $28,000 loss from the sale of a personal residence. She also purchased a patent on a rubber bonding process from an individual inventor for $7,000 (and resold it in two months for $18,000). The patent had not yet been reduced to practice. Beth purchased the patent as an investment. In addition, she had the following capital gains and losses from stock transactions:

Long-term capital loss	($ 6,000)
Long-term capital loss carryover from 2022	(12,000)
Short-term capital gain	21,000
Short-term capital loss	(7,000)

What is Beth's net capital gain or loss? Draft a letter to Beth explaining the tax treatment of the sale of her personal residence. Assume that Beth's income from other sources puts her in the 24% bracket. Beth's address is 1120 West Street, Ashland, OR 97520.

Critical Thinking
Planning

59. **LO.2, 4, 5, 14** Bridgette is known as the "doll lady." She started collecting dolls as a child, always received one or more dolls as gifts on her birthday, never sold any dolls, and eventually owned 600 dolls. She is retiring and moving to a small apartment and has decided to sell her collection. She lists the dolls on an internet auction site and, to her great surprise, receives an offer from another doll collector of $45,000 for the entire collection. Bridgette sells the entire collection, except for five dolls she purchased during the last year. She had owned all of the dolls sold for more than a year. What tax factors should Bridgette consider in deciding how to report the sale?

60. **LO.5** Phil and Susan Hammond are married taxpayers filing a joint return. The couple have two dependent children. Susan has wages of $34,000 in 2022. Phil does not work due to a disability, but he is a buyer and seller of stocks. He generally buys and holds for long-term gain, but occasionally gets in and out of a stock quickly. The couple's 2021 stock transactions are detailed below. In addition, they have $2,300 of qualifying dividends.

Item	Date Acquired	Date Sold	Cost	Sales Price
Blue stock (10 shares)	11/10/21	03/12/22	$ 3,000	$ 6,000
Purple stock (100 shares)	12/13/20	05/23/22	36,000	32,000
Beige stock (50 shares)	12/14/17	07/14/22	13,000	14,500
Red stock (100 shares)	06/29/21	05/18/22	26,000	27,000
Black stock (100 shares)	05/15/21	10/18/22	67,000	67,800
Gray stock (100 shares)	04/12/20	10/18/22	89,000	88,200

a. What is Phil and Susan's AGI?

b. Complete a 2022 Form 8949 for the Hammonds (Phil's Social Security number is 123-45-6789). Assume that the stock sale information was reported to the Hammonds on a Form 1099–B and that basis information was provided to the IRS.

61. **LO.5** Paul has the following long-term capital gains and losses for 2023: $62,000 28% gain, $21,000 28% loss, $18,000 25% gain, and $64,000 0%/15%/20% gain. He also has a $53,000 short-term loss and a $5,000 short-term gain. What is Paul's AGI from these transactions? If he has a net long-term capital gain, what is its makeup in terms of the alternative tax rates?

62. **LO.5** Helena has the following long-term capital gains and losses for 2023: $65,000 28% gain, $53,000 28% loss, $28,000 25% gain, and $24,000 0%/15%/20% loss. She also has a $33,000 short-term loss and a $65,000 short-term gain. What is Helena's AGI from these transactions? If she has a net long-term capital gain, what is its makeup in terms of the alternative tax rates?

63. **LO.5** For 2023, Maddie has gross income of $38,350 and a $5,000 long-term capital loss. She claims the standard deduction. Maddie is 35 years old and unmarried with two dependent children. How much of Maddie's $5,000 capital loss carries over to 2024?

64. **LO.5** Jane and Blair are married taxpayers filing jointly and have 2023 taxable income of $117,000. The taxable income includes $5,000 of gain from a capital asset held five years, $2,100 of gain from a capital asset held seven months, and $13,000 of gain from a capital asset held four years. All of the capital assets were stock in publicly traded corporations. Jane and Blair also have qualified dividend income of $3,000. What is the couple's tax on taxable income and the related tax savings from the alternative tax computation (if any)?

65. **LO.5** For 2023, Wilma has properly determined taxable income of $36,000, including $3,000 of unrecaptured § 1250 gain and $8,200 of 0%/15%/20% gain. Wilma qualifies for head-of-household filing status. Compute Wilma's tax liability and the tax savings from the alternative tax on net capital gain.

66. **LO.5** Asok's AGI for 2023 is $133,250. Included in this AGI is a $45,000 25% long-term capital gain and a $13,000 0%/15%/20% long-term capital gain. Asok is single and uses the standard deduction. Compute his taxable income, the tax liability, and the tax savings from the alternative tax on net capital gain.

67. **LO.6** Gray, Inc., a C corporation, has taxable income from operations of $1,452,000 for 2023. It also has a net long-term capital loss of $355,000 from the sale of a subsidiary's stock. The year 2023 is the first year in the last 10 years that Gray has not had at least $500,000 per year of net long-term capital gains. What is Gray's 2023 taxable income? What, if anything, can it do with any unused capital losses? Planning

68. **LO.3, 14** Harriet, who is single, is the owner of a sole proprietorship. Two years ago, Harriet developed a process for preserving doughnuts that gives the doughnuts a much longer shelf life. The process is not patented or copyrighted, and only Harriet knows how it works. Harriet has been approached by a company that would like to buy the process. Harriet insists that she receive a long-term employment contract with the acquiring company as well as be paid for the rights to the process. The acquiring company offers Harriet a choice of two options: (1) $650,000 in cash for the process and a 10-year covenant not to compete at $65,000 per year or (2) $650,000 in cash for a 10-year covenant not to compete and $65,000 per year for 10 years in payment for the process. Which option should Harriet accept? What is the tax effect on the acquiring company of each approach? Critical Thinking Decision Making

69. **LO.8** A sculpture that Korliss Kane held for investment was destroyed in a flood. The sculpture was insured, and Korliss had a $60,000 gain from this casualty. He also had a $17,000 loss from an uninsured antique vase that was destroyed by the flood. The vase was also held for investment. Korliss had no other property transactions during Communications

the year and has no nonrecaptured § 1231 losses from prior years. Both the sculpture and the vase had been held more than one year when the flood occurred (i.e., both are long-term nonpersonal use capital assets). Compute Korliss's net gain or loss, and identify how it would be treated. Also write a letter to Korliss, explaining the nature of the gain or loss. Korliss's address is 2367 Meridian Road, Hannibal, MO 63401.

70. **LO.8** Keshara has the following net § 1231 results for each of the years shown. What would be the nature of the net gains in 2022 and 2023?

Tax Year	Net § 1231 Loss	Net § 1231 Gain
2018	$18,000	
2019	33,000	
2020	42,000	
2021		$41,000
2022		30,000
2023		41,000

Critical Thinking
Decision Making

71. **LO.8, 14** Jinjie owns two parcels of business land (§ 1231 assets). One parcel can be sold at a loss of $60,000, and the other parcel can be sold at a gain of $70,000. Jinjie has no nonrecaptured § 1231 losses from prior years. The parcels could be sold at any time because potential purchasers are abundant. Jinjie has a $35,000 short-term capital loss carryover from a prior tax year and no capital assets that could be sold to generate long-term capital gains. Both land parcels have been held more than one year. What should Jinjie do based upon these facts? (Assume that tax rates are constant, and ignore the present value of future cash flow.)

72. **LO.7, 8, 9** Siena Industries (a sole proprietorship) sold three § 1231 assets during 2023. Data on these property dispositions are as follows:

Asset	Cost	Acquired	Accumulated Depreciation	Sold for	Sold on
Rack	$100,000	10/10/19	$62,000	$86,000	10/10/23
Forklift	35,000	10/16/20	23,000	4,000	10/10/23
Bin	87,000	03/12/22	34,000	60,000	10/10/23

a. Determine the amount and the character of the recognized gain or loss from the disposition of each asset.

b. Assuming that Siena has no nonrecaptured net § 1231 losses from prior years, analyze these transactions and determine the amount (if any) that will be treated as a long-term capital gain.

73. **LO.8, 9** Copper Industries (a sole proprietorship) sold three § 1231 assets during 2023. Data on these property dispositions are as follows:

Asset	Cost	Acquired	Accumulated Depreciation	Sold for	Sold on
Rack	$110,000	10/10/20	$70,000	$55,000	10/10/23
Forklift	45,000	10/16/20	21,000	15,000	10/10/23
Bin	97,000	03/12/22	31,000	60,000	10/10/23

a. Determine the amount and the character of the recognized gain or loss from the disposition of each asset.

b. Assuming that Copper has $6,000 nonrecaptured net § 1231 losses from prior years, analyze these transactions and determine the amount (if any) that will be treated as a long-term capital gain.

Communications

74. **LO.8, 9** On December 1, 2021, Lavender Manufacturing Company (a corporation) purchased another company's assets, including a patent. The patent was used

in Lavender's manufacturing operations; $49,500 was allocated to the patent, and it was amortized at the rate of $275 per month. On July 30, 2023, Lavender sold the patent for $95,000. Twenty months of amortization had been taken on the patent. What are the amount and nature of the gain Lavender recognizes on the disposition of the patent? Prepare your solution using Microsoft Excel (or a similar program). Write a letter to Lavender, discussing the treatment of the gain. Lavender's address is 6734 Grover Street, Boothbay Harbor, ME 04538. The letter should be addressed to Bill Cubit, Controller.

75. **LO.8, 10** On June 1, 2019, Skylark Enterprises, a calendar year LLC reporting as a sole proprietorship, acquired a retail store building for $500,000 (with $100,000 being allocated to the land). The store building was 39-year real property, and the straight-line cost recovery method was used. The property was sold on June 21, 2023, for $385,000.

    a. Compute the cost recovery and adjusted basis for the building using Exhibit 8.8 from Chapter 8.

    b. What are the amount and nature of Skylark's gain or loss from disposition of the property? What amount, if any, of the gain is unrecaptured § 1250 gain?

76. **LO.8, 9, 10** On May 2, 1993, Hannah Weather (Social Security number: 111-22-3333) acquired residential real estate for $450,000. Of the cost, $100,000 was allocated to the land and $350,000 to the building. On August 20, 2022, the building, which then had an adjusted basis of $0, was sold for $545,000 and the land for $200,000.

    a. Determine the amount and character of the recognized gain from the sale of the building.

    b. Determine the amount and character of the recognized gain from the sale of the land.

    c. Complete a 2022 Form 4797 for these transactions. Assume that there are no § 1231 lookback losses.

77. **LO.8, 9, 10** Javier is the sole proprietor of a sporting goods business. During 2023, the following transactions occurred:

    - Unimproved land adjacent to Javier's store was condemned by the city on February 1. The condemnation proceeds were $15,000. The land, acquired in 1990, had an allocable basis of $40,000. Javier has additional parking across the street and plans to use the condemnation proceeds to build his inventory.
    - A delivery truck used in Javier's business was sold on January 2 for $3,500. The truck was purchased on January 2, 2019, for $6,000. On the date of sale, the adjusted basis was zero.
    - Javier sold a rowing machine at an auction. Net proceeds were $4,900. The rowing machine was purchased as used equipment 17 years ago for $5,200 and is fully depreciated.
    - Javier sold an apartment building for $300,000 on September 1. The property was purchased on September 1, 2020, for $150,000 and was being depreciated over a 27.5-year life using the straight-line method. At the date of sale, the adjusted basis was $124,783. Javier actively managed the property as a trade or business.
    - Javier's personal yacht was stolen on September 5. The yacht had been purchased in August at a cost of $25,000. The fair market value immediately preceding the theft was $19,600. Javier was insured for 50% of the original cost, and he received $12,500 on December 1.
    - Javier sold a Buick on May 1 for $9,600. The vehicle had been used exclusively for personal purposes. It was purchased on September 1, 2019, for $20,800.
    - A trampoline stretching machine (owned two years and used in Javier's business) was stolen on May 5, but the business's insurance company will not pay any of the machine's value because Javier failed to pay the insurance premium. The machine had a fair market value of $8,000 and an adjusted basis of $6,000 at the time of theft.

- Javier had AGI of $102,000 from sources other than those described above.
- Javier has no nonrecaptured § 1231 lookback losses.

a. For each transaction, what are the amount and nature of recognized gain or loss?

b. What is Javier's 2023 AGI?

Communications
Planning

78. **LO.8, 10** On January 1, 2014, Stephanie Bridges acquired depreciable real property for $50,000. She used straight-line depreciation to compute the asset's cost recovery. The asset was sold for $96,000 on January 3, 2023, when its adjusted basis was $38,000.

a. What are the amount and nature of the gain if the real property is residential?

b. Stephanie is curious about how the recapture rules differ for tangible personal property and for residential rental real estate acquired in 1987 and thereafter. Write a letter to Stephanie, explaining the differences. Her address is 2345 Westridge Street #23, Edna, KS 67342.

Critical Thinking
Decision Making
Planning

79. **LO.8, 9, 11, 14** Hana is in the 24% tax bracket and owns depreciable business equipment that she purchased several years ago for $135,000. She has taken $100,000 of depreciation on the equipment, and it is worth $55,000. Hana's niece, Michelle, is starting a new business and is short of cash. Michelle has asked Hana to gift the equipment to her so that Michelle can use it in her business. Hana no longer needs the equipment. Identify the alternatives available to Hana if she wants to help Michelle and the tax effects of those alternatives. (Assume that all alternatives involve the business equipment in one way or another, and ignore the gift tax.)

80. **LO.8, 9, 11** Anna received tangible personal property with a fair market value of $65,000 as a gift in 2021. The donor had purchased the property for $77,000 and had taken $77,000 of depreciation. Anna used the property in her business. Anna sells the property for $23,000 in 2023. What are the tax status of the property and the nature of the recognized gain when she sells the property?

81. **LO.8, 9, 11** Miguel receives tangible personal property as an inheritance in 2021. The property was depreciated by the deceased (Miguel's father), and Miguel will also depreciate it. At the date of the deceased's death, the property was worth $532,000. The deceased had purchased it for $900,000 and taken $523,000 of depreciation on the property. Miguel takes $223,000 of depreciation on the property before selling it for $482,000 in 2023. What are the tax status of the property and the nature of the recognized gain when Miguel sells the property?

82. **LO.11** David contributes to charity some tangible personal property that he had used in his business and depreciated. At the date of the donation, the property has a fair market value of $233,000 and an adjusted basis of zero; it was originally acquired for $400,000. What is the amount of David's charitable contribution?

83. **LO.8, 9, 11** Dedriea contributes to her wholly owned corporation some tangible personal property she had used in her sole proprietorship business and depreciated. She had acquired the property for $566,000 and had taken $431,000 of depreciation on it before contributing it to the corporation. At the date of the contribution, the property had a fair market value of $289,000. The corporation took $100,000 of depreciation on the property and then sold it for $88,000 in 2023. What are the tax status of the property to the corporation and the nature of the recognized gain or loss when the corporation sells the property?

84. **LO.8, 9, 12** Tan Corporation purchased depreciable tangible personal property for $100,000 in 2021 and immediately expensed the entire cost under § 179. In 2023, when the property was worth $80,000, Tan distributed it as a dividend to the corporation's sole shareholder. What was the tax status of this property for Tan? What is the nature of the recognized gain or loss from the distribution of the property?

85. **LO.7, 8, 10** Jasmine owned rental real estate that she sold to her tenant in an installment sale. Jasmine acquired the property in 2011 for $400,000; took $178,000 of depreciation on it; and sold it for $210,000, receiving $25,000 immediately and the balance (plus interest at a market rate) in equal payments of $18,500 for 10 years.

   a. What is the nature of the recognized gain or loss from this transaction?

   b. Assuming that the interest rate on the installment contract is 5%, what is the present value of the installment payments? See Appendix E for present value factors.

86. **LO.9** Jay sold three items of business equipment for a total of $300,000. None of the equipment was appraised to determine its value. Jay's cost and adjusted basis for the assets are shown below.

Critical Thinking
Decision Making
Planning

Asset	Cost	Adjusted Basis
Skidder	$230,000	$ 40,000
Driller	120,000	60,000
Platform	620,000	–0–
Total	$970,000	$100,000

Jay has been unable to establish the fair market values of the three assets. All he can determine is that combined they were worth $300,000 to the buyer in this arm's length transaction. How should Jay allocate the sales price and figure the gain or loss on the sale of the three assets?

Tax Return Problems

87. Ashley Panda lives at 1310 Meadow Lane, Wayne, OH 43466, and her Social Security number is 123-45-6777. Ashley is single and has a 20-year-old son, Bill. His Social Security number is 111-11-1112. Karl lives with Ashley, and she fully supports him. Bill spent 2022 traveling in Europe and was not a college student. He had gross income of $4,655 in 2022. Bill paid $4,000 of lodging expenses that Ashley reimbursed after they were fully documented. Ashley paid the $4,000 to Bill using a check from her sole proprietorship. That amount is not included in the items listed below. Ashley had substantial health problems during 2022, and many of her expenses were not reimbursed by her health insurance.

Tax Forms Problem

ProConnect™ Tax

Ashley owns Panda Enterprises LLC (98-7654321), a data processing service that she reports as a sole proprietorship. Her business is located at 456 Hill Street, Wayne, OH 43466. The business activity code is 514210. Her 2022 Form 1040, Schedule C for Panda Enterprises shows revenues of $315,000, office expenses of $66,759, employee salary of $63,000, employee payroll taxes of $4,820, business meal expenses of $11,000 (all at restaurants), and rent expense of $34,000. The rent expense includes payments related to renting an office ($30,000) and payments related to renting various equipment ($4,000). There is no depreciation because all depreciable equipment owned has been fully depreciated in previous years. No fringe benefits are provided to the employee. Ashley personally purchases health insurance on herself and Bill. The premiums are $23,000 per year.

Ashley has an extensive stock portfolio and has prepared the following analysis:

Stock	Number of Shares	Date Purchased	Date Sold	Per-Share Cost	Per-Share Selling Price	Total Dividends
Beige	10	10/18/21	10/11/22	$80	$ 74	$30
Garland	30	10/11/15	10/11/22	43	157	70
Peach	15	3/10/22	8/11/22	62	33	45

Note: Ashley received a Form 1099-B from her stockbroker that included the adjusted basis and sales proceeds for each of her stock transactions. The per-share cost includes commissions, and the per-share selling price is net of commissions. Also, the dividends are the actual dividends received in 2022, and these are both ordinary dividends and qualified dividends.

Ashley had $800 of interest income from State of Ohio bonds and $600 of interest income on her Wayne Savings Bank account. She paid $25,000 of alimony to her former husband (divorce finalized in June 2017). His Social Security number is 123-45-6788.

Ashley itemizes her deductions and provides the following information, which may be relevant to her return:

Item	Amount	Comment
Unreimbursed medical expenses for Ashley	$9,748	Does not include health insurance premiums.
State income taxes paid	1,830	
Real property taxes on personal residence	3,230	
Interest paid on home mortgage (Form 1098)	8,137	The loan is secured by the residence and was incurred when the home was purchased.
Charitable contributions	1,399	$940 cash payments to Ashley's church and $459 cash payments made to homeless persons for whom she felt sorry. She can document all the expenditures.
Sales taxes	619	Amount per sales tax table.

Ashley paid $27,000 in estimated Federal income taxes, did not engage in any digital asset transactions during the year, does not want any of her taxes to finance presidential elections, has no foreign bank accounts or trusts, and wants any refund to be applied against her 2023 taxes.

Compute Ashley's net tax payable or refund due for 2022 and complete her 2022 Federal tax return using appropriate forms and schedules. Ashley qualifies for the § 199A deduction for qualified business income. Be sure to include that in your calculations. Suggested software: ProConnect Tax.

Tax Forms Problem

ProConnect™ Tax

88. Justin Stone was an employee of DataCare Services, Inc. His salary was $45,000 through November 10, 2022, when he was laid off. DataCare Services provided medical insurance for Justin and his family during his employment and agreed to continue this coverage through the end of 2022. He received $7,000 of unemployment compensation from November 11, 2022, through December 31, 2022. FICA withholdings were as follows: Social Security of $2,790 ($45,000 × 6.2%) and Medicare of $653 ($45,000 × 1.45%). Justin lives at 112 Green Road, Crown City, OH 45623. His Social Security number is 111-11-1118.

Justin owned an apartment building until November 22, 2022, when he sold it for $200,000 (the apartment building's address is 4826 Orange Street, Crown City, OH 45623). For 2022, he had rent revenue of $33,000. He incurred and paid expenses as follows: $4,568 of repairs, $12,000 of mortgage interest, $10,000 of real estate taxes, and $1,000 of miscellaneous expenses. He purchased the building on January 2, 2016, for $125,000 (the related land was purchased for $10,000). The building generated an operating profit each year that Justin owned it.

Justin received $13,000 in cash as a gift from his mother to help "tide him over" while he was unemployed. He also withdrew $10,000 from his checking account. He "invested" $300 in lottery tickets during the year but had no winnings.

Other relevant tax information for Justin follows:

- On November 22, 2022, Justin sold for $3,500 equipment that had been used for repairing various items in the apartments. The equipment was purchased for $25,000 on July 10, 2015, and was fully depreciated prior to 2022.
- Justin has $3,000 of unrecaptured § 1231 losses from prior years.
- Justin is age 38; is single; is divorced; and has custody of his nine-year-old son, Flint.
- Justin provides more than 50% of Flint's support. Flint's Social Security number is 123-45-6788.
- Justin had $1,000 interest income from Blue Corporation bonds.
- Justin had $1,500 interest income from a State Bank certificate of deposit.

- Justin had a $2,000 0%/15%/20% long-term capital gain distribution from the Brown Stock Investment Fund.
- Justin had the following itemized deductions: $4,600 real estate taxes on his home; $8,900 mortgage interest on his home; $4,760 charitable contributions (all in cash, all properly documented, and no single contribution exceeding $25); $4,300 state income tax withholding during 2022; $2,000 state estimated income tax payments during 2022; $2,600 sales taxes paid.
- Justin does not own or use any digital assets.
- Justin does not want to donate to the Presidential Election Campaign Fund.
- Justin had $10,000 of Federal income tax withholding during 2022 and made total Federal estimated income tax payments of $12,000 during 2022.

Compute Justin's 2022 net tax payable or refund due. Ignore the § 199A deduction for qualified business income (if applicable). Suggested software: ProConnect Tax.

See Appendix F for Comprehensive Tax Return Problems—Form 1040

Research Problems

Note: Solutions to the Research Problems can be prepared by using the Thomson Reuters Checkpoint™ online tax research database, which accompanies this textbook. Solutions can also be prepared by using research materials found in a typical tax library.

Research Problem 1. Siva, a new client of yours, owns various plots of land in Fulton County, Georgia. He acquired the land at various times during the last 20 years. About every fourth year, Siva subdivides into lots one of the properties he owns. He then has water, sewer, natural gas, and electricity hookups put in each lot and paves new streets. Siva has always treated his sales of such lots as sales of capital assets. His previous tax returns were prepared by an accountant whose practice you recently purchased. Has the proper tax treatment been used on the prior tax returns? Explain.

Partial list of research aids:
§§ 1221 and 1237 and *Jesse W. and Betty J. English*, 65 TCM 2160, T.C.Memo. 1993–111.

Research Problem 2. Your long-time tax client, Clyde, has a major "classification" problem he needs help with. Clyde had worked for many years as the chief executive of Red Industries, Inc., and had been a major shareholder. Clyde and the company had a falling out, and Clyde was terminated. Clyde and Red executed a document under which Clyde's stock in Red would be redeemed and Clyde would agree not to compete against Red in its geographic service area. After extensive negotiations between the parties, Clyde agreed to surrender his Red stock in exchange for $600,000. Clyde's basis in his shares was $143,000, and he had held the shares for 17 years. The agreement made no explicit allocation of any of the $600,000 to Clyde's agreement not to compete against Red. How should Clyde treat the $600,000 payment on his 2023 tax return?

Research Problem 3. Your client, Alternate Fuel, Inc. (a regular corporation) has a problem and needs your help. It owns three sandwich shops in the Philadelphia area. In 2020, the year Alternate Fuel incorporated, it acquired land on the outskirts of Philadelphia with the hope of someday farming the land to cultivate humanely harvested meat and grow organic fruits and vegetables to use in its sandwich shops.

In 2022, Alternate Fuel drew up plans for the farm and began consulting with agricultural experts about the best locations for crops and the number of animals that could be sustained on the acreage. After reviewing those plans, Alternate Fuel's CEO decided that the plans are not currently financially feasible and would like to sell the land in 2023. The land has appreciated substantially in value, and the company could use the cash infusion. Given that the land has not been used in the business, will any gain realized be categorized as a § 1231 gain or as a long-term capital gain? Explain.

Research Problem 4. Your supervisor at your CPA firm has questioned whether the depreciation taken on a building under § 168(k) is subject to § 1250 depreciation recapture. Find a discussion in the Form 4797 instructions confirming that this depreciation is subject to § 1250 recapture.

Use internet tax resources to address the following questions. Look for reliable websites and blogs of the IRS and other government agencies, media outlets, businesses, tax professionals, academics, think tanks, and political outlets.

Research Problem 5. Perform a Google search to find information about capital gains tax rates worldwide (and across U.S. states). Try searching for "capital gains rate by country (state)." What jurisdiction has the highest capital gains tax rate? What U.S. states have high capital gains tax rates?

Data Analytics

Research Problem 6. Using the *IRS Tax Statistics* that can be found at **irs.gov/statistics**, based on adjusted gross income for the most recent year available, determine the amount of net long-term capital gain taxpayers reported. Use the search function to look for a table related to "capital gain."

Becker CPA Review Questions

Becker

1. A gain on the sale of which of the following assets will *not* result in a capital gain?
   a. Stock in a public company
   b. A home used as a personal residence
   c. Goodwill of a corporation
   d. Inventory of a corporation

2. Conner purchased 300 shares of Zinco stock for $30,000 in year 1. On May 23, year 6, Conner sold all the stock to his daughter Alice for $20,000, its then fair market value. Conner realized no other gain or loss during year 6. On July 26, year 6, Alice sold the 300 shares of Zinco for $25,000. What was Alice's recognized gain or loss on her sale?
   a. $0
   b. $5,000 long-term gain
   c. $5,000 short-term loss
   d. $5,000 long-term loss

3. Brad and Angie are married and file a joint return. For year 14, they had income from wages in the amount of $100,000 and had the following capital transactions to report on their income tax return:

Carryover of capital losses from year 13	$200,000
Loss on sale of stock purchased in March year 14, sold on October 10, year 14, and repurchased on November 2, year 14	20,000
Gain on the sale of stock purchased 5 years ago and sold on March 14, year 14	15,000
Gain on the sale of their personal residence (all qualifications have been met for the maximum allowable gain exclusion)	675,000
Loss on the sale of their personal automobile	10,000
Gain on the sale of their personal furniture	5,000
Loss on the sale of investment property (land only)	150,000

What is the amount of capital loss carryover to year 15?

a. ($155,000)
c. ($132,000)
b. ($152,000)
d. ($125,000)

4. A piece of depreciable machinery is sold. It has been held for three years and qualifies as § 1231 property. The selling price is greater than the adjusted basis, but less than the original purchase price. Which statement below is correct?
   a. All of the gain will be subject to § 1245 recapture.
   b. Only a portion of the gain will be subject to § 1245 recapture.
   c. None of the gain will be subject to § 1245 recapture.
   d. Section 1245 recapture will not apply because there is a loss on the sale.

5. Jerry uses a building for business purposes. The building was purchased on April 1, year 3, for $124,000. It was sold on October 3, year 6, for $200,000. Accumulated depreciation as of the date of sale was $14,000, $4,000 of which was in excess of straight line. How much of the gain in year 6 is recaptured as ordinary under § 1250?
   a. $4,000
   c. $14,000
   b. $10,000
   d. $100,000

6. Jerry uses a building for business purposes. The building was purchased on April 1, year 3, for $124,000. It was sold on October 3, year 6, for $200,000. Accumulated depreciation as of the date of sale was $14,000, $4,000 of which was in excess of straight line. How much of the gain in year 6 is unrecaptured § 1250 gain?
   a. $4,000
   c. $14,000
   b. $10,000
   d. $100,000

7. Wally, Inc., sold the following three personal property assets in year 6:

Asset	Purchase Date	Cost	Accumulated Depreciation	Selling Price
A	5/1/year 3	$5,000	$3,000	$2,300
B	8/13/year 4	1,200	500	2,000
C	2/18/year 4	3,800	1,800	1,500

   What is Wally's net § 1231 gain or loss in year 6?
   a. $500 loss
   c. $800 gain
   b. $300 gain
   d. $1,600 gain

8. Wally, Inc., sold the following three personal property assets in year 6:

Asset	Purchase Date	Cost	Accumulated Depreciation	Selling Price
A	5/1/year 3	$5,000	$3,000	$1,300
B	8/13/year 4	1,200	500	1,100
C	2/18/year 4	3,800	1,800	1,500

   What is Wally's net § 1231 gain or loss in year 6?
   a. $500 loss
   c. $1,200 loss
   b. $700 loss
   d. $1,200 gain

9. Wally, Inc., sold the following three personal property assets in year 6:

Asset	Purchase Date	Cost	Accumulated Depreciation	Selling Price
A	5/1/year 3	$5,000	$3,000	$2,300
B	8/13/year 4	1,200	500	2,000
C	2/18/year 6	3,800	1,800	1,500

What is Wally's net § 1231 gain or loss in year 6?

a. $500 loss
b. $300 gain
c. $800 gain
d. $1,600 gain

10. Wally, Inc., sold the following three personal property assets in year 6:

Asset	Purchase Date	Cost	Accumulated Depreciation	Selling Price
A	5/1/year 3	$5,000	$3,000	$2,300
B	8/13/year 4	1,200	500	2,000
C	2/18/year 6	3,800	1,800	1,500

What is Wally's § 1245 recapture in year 6?

a. $500 loss
b. $300 gain
c. $800 gain
d. $1,600 gain

11. Net § 1231 losses are:
   a. Deducted as a capital loss against other capital gains and nothing against ordinary income.
   b. Deducted as a capital loss against other capital gains and up to $3,000 against ordinary income.
   c. Not allowed as a deduction.
   d. Deducted as an ordinary loss.

12. Section 1245 recapture applies to which of the following?
   a. Section 1231 real property sold at a gain with accumulated depreciation in excess of straight line.
   b. Section 1231 personal property sold at a gain with accumulated depreciation.
   c. Section 1231 real property sold at a gain with accumulated depreciation equal to straight-line depreciation.
   d. Section 1231 personal property sold at a loss.

13. Section 1250 recapture applies to which of the following?
   a. Section 1231 real property sold at a gain with accumulated depreciation in excess of straight line.
   b. Section 1231 personal property sold at a gain with accumulated depreciation.
   c. Section 1231 real property sold at a gain with accumulated depreciation equal to straight-line depreciation.
   d. Section 1231 personal property sold at a loss.

Special Tax Computations and Accounting Periods and Methods

Chapter **15**

The Deduction for Qualified Business Income for Noncorporate Taxpayers

Chapter **16**

Accounting Periods and Methods

Part 5 begins by discussing the distinctions between various taxpayer entities, including sole proprietorships, partnerships, and corporations. Then the deduction for qualified business income available to *noncorporate* taxpayers is explored. This part also provides a comprehensive exploration of the accounting periods and accounting methods that were introduced in Part 2. A discussion of special accounting methods related to installment sales and long-term contracts is also included.

Chapter 15

The Deduction for Qualified Business Income for Noncorporate Taxpayers

Learning Objectives: *After completing Chapter 15, you should be able to:*

LO.1 **Summarize the tax treatment of various forms of conducting a business.**

LO.2 **Explain the rationale for the deduction for qualified business income.**

LO.3 **Describe the types of taxpayers and activities that potentially generate a deduction for qualified business income.**

LO.4 **Determine a taxpayer's deduction for qualified business income.**

LO.5 **List and evaluate tax planning ideas for choice of entity and the deduction for qualified business income.**

Chapter Outline

JOESAPHOTOS/SHUTTERSTOCK.COM

The Big Picture

Entrepreneurial Pursuits

Amy plans to start at least two different business activities after she graduates from college. She will apply the knowledge gained in her business courses to use various forms of social media to promote her skills and experience as a soccer player to help younger players develop their skills. She plans to generate income from advertising on her social media sites. She also will use her artistic and marketing talents to find work using several web platforms, like Upwork and Freelancer. Although still in college, she has signed a "name, image, and likeness (NIL)" contract with several soccer-related businesses (Amy also plays for U.S.A. Soccer and was a member of the 2021 U.S.A. Olympic team).

Based on what she has read on websites and heard from friends, Amy is wondering if she should form a corporation or a limited liability company for these pursuits or just be a sole proprietor. She is also curious whether, for tax and legal purposes, how many businesses she has.

After reading this chapter, you can help Amy with her questions, including aiding her in better framing the questions should she decide to seek assistance from an attorney on business entity formation matters or a CPA for tax and accounting assistance.

Read the chapter and formulate your response.

For Federal income tax purposes, the distinctions among forms of business organization are important. This chapter begins by discussing the distinctions between sole proprietorships, partnerships, S corporations, and regular corporations. Limited liability companies, which generally are taxed as one of these entity forms, also are introduced.

A key piece of the Tax Cuts and Jobs Act (TCJA) of 2017 was to lower the corporate income tax rate from a progressive tax rate structure (with rates from 15 percent to 35 percent) to a flat tax of 21 percent. To also provide a tax reduction for businesses that do *not* operate as regular corporations, the TCJA of 2017 created a special deduction for noncorporate taxpayers with business income. These changes affect both tax liabilities and tax planning, including the form of business organization.

LO.1

Summarize the tax treatment of various forms of conducting a business.

15-1 Organizational Forms in Which Business May be Conducted

The principal legal forms in which to conduct a business are the sole proprietorship, partnership, limited liability company (LLC), and corporation.[1] The specific legal attributes of each of these organizational forms, including their relations to their owners and nonowners, are determined by the laws of the state in which they are organized.

State law generally uses one of two perspectives when defining the rights and responsibilities of a business entity: the conduit perspective or the entity perspective. In its simplest form, the conduit, or aggregate, perspective treats the business as simply an aggregation of its owners joined together in an agency relationship. Under the strictest interpretation of the **conduit perspective**, the business is viewed merely as an extension of its owners. Conversely, the **entity perspective** considers the business as an entity separate and distinct from its owners, with its own rights and responsibilities.

The rights and responsibilities afforded to corporations consistently reflect the entity perspective. A corporation is recognized as a separate legal entity with the following characteristics:

- *Continuity of life.* A corporation's existence does not depend on the life of its owners. A corporation continues to exist even if its shareholders die or sell their stock.
- *Centralized management.* All management responsibilities of a corporation lie in its board of directors. The board then appoints officers to carry out the corporation's business. Shareholders vote for board members but have no other ability to participate directly in the management of the corporation or its business.
- *Free transferability of interests.* Shares of stock in a corporation are freely transferable without the need of approval of the corporation or other shareholders.
- *Limited liability.* Corporations have the right to contract directly with other parties and are responsible for their own liabilities. The liability of shareholders for the debts of the corporation is limited to the amount paid for their stock.

The entity versus aggregate perspective for partnerships is less consistent. In many respects, partnerships reflect the conduit perspective. For example, general partners have the right to participate directly in the management of a partnership as well as to bind the partnership to contracts. It follows then that general partners are liable for the debts arising from the partnership's activities and contractual obligations. However, partnerships also reflect the entity perspective in several respects. For example, a partnership does not reduce its income for charitable contributions; instead, partners report their share of the contributions on their own income tax returns.

Different types of partnerships are afforded even more characteristics consistent with the entity perspective. For example, limited partners in a **limited partnership (LP)** are treated much like shareholders in a corporation, with no ability to participate in the

[1]A business entity also can be conducted in the form of a trust or an estate. These two forms are not discussed in this chapter. See Chapter 30.

management of the partnership and their liability limited to their investment in the entity. However, limited partnerships must have at least one general partner. A **limited liability partnership (LLP)** provides all partners protection from partnership liabilities, but only those liabilities arising from acts of negligence, fraud, or malpractice committed by other partners. Like general partners in a general partnership, partners in an LLP continue to be liable for the contractual liabilities of the partnership.

As mentioned previously, limited partners have similar liability protection as shareholders in a corporation. This provides limited partnerships much the same ability to raise capital as corporations. In some instances, limited partnerships have registered their interests on established securities exchanges so that they may be publicly traded. Generally, a **publicly traded partnership (PTP)** is treated as a corporation for tax purposes. An important exception allows limited partnerships who derive nearly all of their revenues from investments and natural resources to continue to be treated as partnerships for tax purposes even if their partnership interests are publicly traded.[2]

Similar to shareholders of a corporation, all members of a **limited liability company (LLC)** are shielded from all of the entity's liabilities. However, although LLCs provide the same liability protection of a corporation, they typically lack one or more other corporate characteristics (e.g., centralized management, free transferability of interest, or continuity of life). The combination and extent of these other characteristics afforded LLCs differ depending on the state in which the LLC is organized.

As discussed more fully in text Section 15-3d, most unincorporated business entities, including LLCs, are either disregarded or treated as partnerships for tax purposes depending on the number of owners. For example, an LLC with only one owner is a disregarded entity for tax purposes, treated as a sole proprietorship if the owner is an individual or as a division of a corporate owner. In general, an LLC with more than one owner is taxed as a partnership.

See Exhibit 15.1 for a breakdown of the number and proportion of legal business forms in which businesses have recently been conducted.

Exhibit 15.1 Comparison of the Business Entity Types

Various business entities filed Federal income tax returns for 2019. Included in the partnership category are general and limited partnerships as well as limited liability companies that are taxed as partnerships.

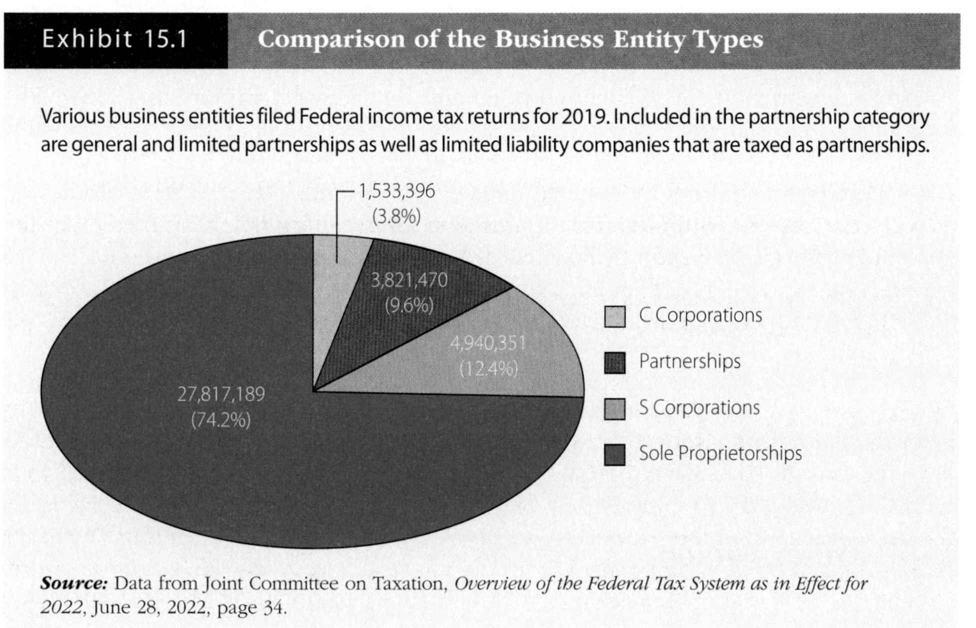

Source: Data from Joint Committee on Taxation, *Overview of the Federal Tax System as in Effect for 2022*, June 28, 2022, page 34.

[2]§ 7704.

15-2 Nontax Factors

Of course, taxes are only one of many factors to consider when making a business decision and often not the most important one. Above all, any business decision must make economic sense. Although the economics of most business decisions are impacted by taxes, often influencing how a business and its owners achieve their goals, tax savings alone are not sufficient to support a business or investment decision.

The importance of both tax and nontax factors extends to the choice of the legal form in which to conduct the business. Although the choice of organizational form can significantly impact the after-tax return available from a business venture, other factors may be just as, or more, important. Some of those factors are briefly discussed next.

15-2a Limited Liability

Perhaps the most important nontax factor affecting a business owner's choice of organizational form is his or her personal exposure to the liabilities of the business. As a separate legal entity, distinct from its shareholders, a corporation is liable for its own debts under state law. A shareholder generally cannot be held liable for the debts or actions of the corporation. Therefore, a shareholder's personal liability resulting from investing in a corporation is limited to his or her investment. This protection from personal liability is perhaps the most valued nontax advantage of the corporate form.

Ed, Fran, and Gabriella each invest $25,000 for all the stock of Brown Corporation. Brown obtains creditor financing of $100,000. Brown is subsequently sued due to an accident involving one of its delivery trucks. The court awards a judgment of $2,500,000 to the plaintiff. The award exceeds Brown's insurance coverage by $1,500,000. Even if the judgment results in Brown's bankruptcy, the shareholders will have no personal liability for the unpaid corporate debts.

It should be noted that limited liability is not available to the shareholders of all corporations. For example, laws in some states do not permit individual professionals (e.g., accountants, attorneys, architects, and physicians) to limit their liability for the performance of professional services by incorporating.

Even if state law provides for limited liability, the benefit may not be practically available for the shareholders of small corporations. Often, such corporations are unable to obtain external financing (e.g., a bank loan) unless the shareholders personally guarantee the loan.

Business owners also may achieve limited liability with LLCs and LLPs if allowed under state law.[3] As with a corporation though, external funding may require owner guarantees, which will expose the owners to liability. Although limited partnerships provide limited liability for their limited partners, limited partnerships must have at least one general partner potentially liable for partnership debts.

Sarah and Juan want to form a bike rental business. Entity forms available to them include corporation, partnership, and LLC. Regardless of which form they choose, when they go to the bank for a loan to help get their business started, the bank likely will require them to guarantee the loan. That means that if the business cannot repay the loan, Sarah and Juan must repay it out of their personal funds.

15-2b Other Factors

Other nontax factors may be significant in selecting an organization form, including the following:

- The estimated life of the business.
- The number of owners and their roles in the management of the business.

[3]See text Section 21-1a for a review of types of partnerships.

- The freedom to choose the methods of transferring ownership interests.
- Organizational formality, including the related cost and extent of government regulation.
- The ease of increasing equity by admitting new owners.

15-2c **Capital Formation**

The combination of liability exposure with other nontax factors may significantly affect a venture's ability to raise capital. For example, a sole proprietorship offers the proprietor no protection against the venture's liabilities and limits its available capital to that which can be provided, or raised, by the proprietor. A partnership has a greater opportunity to raise funds through the pooling of owner resources. However, general partners remain subject to any liabilities generated by the business, making it relatively difficult to attract additional investors.

Adam and Beth form a general partnership, AB, to build and manage an apartment building. Adam contributes cash of $200,000, and Beth contributes land (FMV $200,000; adjusted basis $60,000) on which the apartment building will be constructed. The building will cost $1,000,000.

The partnership is considering borrowing $800,000 to construct the building. Adam and Beth would each be legally responsible for the repayment of the loan as well as for other liabilities the venture generates. Alternatively, Adam and Beth are considering borrowing only $200,000 and seeking additional partners to finance the remaining cost of the building. However, new partners may be concerned about being responsible for the loan as well as other debts of the venture that may arise. Adam and Beth are also concerned about sharing management rights and responsibilities with additional general partners.

The limited partnership offers greater potential to raise capital than the general partnership form because a limited partnership can secure funds from investors (limited partners) without exposing them to the liabilities related to the venture or involving them in the management of the business.

Carol and Dhani form a limited partnership, CD. Carol contributes cash of $200,000, and Dhani contributes land with an adjusted basis of $60,000 and a fair market value of $200,000. The partnership will construct a shopping center at a cost of $5,000,000. Included in this cost is the purchase price of $800,000 for land adjacent to that contributed by Dhani. Thirty limited partnership interests are sold for $100,000 each to raise $3,000,000. CD also pledges the shopping center (including the land) and obtains nonrecourse financing of $2,000,000 from a third party. The limited partners are neither liable for any of the partnership's debts nor able to participate in the management of the partnership.

Both the at-risk and the passive activity loss provisions restrict the tax attractiveness of investments in real estate, particularly in the limited partnership form. In most cases, the tax consequences have a critical effect on the economic results.[4]

Of the different forms of business entities, the corporate form offers the greatest ease and potential for obtaining financing by selling stock to shareholders who assume no liability for the debts of the business. The ultimate examples of this form are the large public companies listed on the stock exchanges.

Marble, Inc., a publicly traded corporation can raise additional capital by issuing new shares of stock. It must follow Federal and state securities laws, but a public offering can be attractive to third-party investors with no other connection to the entity.

[4]See the related discussion in text Section 21-4g.

15-3 Tax Treatment of Various Business Forms

The tax treatment of business forms varies by form type. A sole proprietorship, partnership, and most LLCs are subject to a *single* level of taxation. This occurs because the owner(s) and the entity generally are not considered to be separate persons for income tax purposes. As a result, the income tax liability is levied at the owner level rather than at the entity level.

On the other hand, the corporate form can be subject to double taxation. This frequently is cited as the major disadvantage of the corporate form. Under *double* taxation, the corporation is taxed on its earnings and owners are taxed on distributions from the corporation to the extent that they are made from corporate earnings. The tax treatment of each of these business forms is discussed briefly below.

15-3a Sole Proprietorships

A sole proprietorship is not a separate taxable entity. Rather, its operations are reported as part of the sole proprietor's individual income tax return. The owner of a sole proprietorship reports all business income and expenses of the proprietorship on Schedule C of Form 1040, with the net profit or loss from the proprietorship included in the taxable income of the individual proprietor. The proprietor reports all of the net profit from the business, regardless of any amounts actually withdrawn during the year.

Income and expenses of the proprietorship retain their character when reported by the proprietor. For example, ordinary income of the proprietorship is treated as ordinary income when reported by the proprietor, and capital gain is treated as capital gain. In addition, a deduction for qualified business income (§ 199A, discussed in text Section 15-5) is available for sole proprietors. In general, this deduction is 20 percent of proprietorship net income (or, if less, taxable income before the qualified business income deduction less any net capital gain) and is claimed on the proprietor's Form 1040 in determining taxable income.[5]

The Big Picture

Example 6

Return to the facts of *The Big Picture* on p. 15-1. The easiest business entity for Amy to form is a sole proprietorship. She need not create any legal documents for the proprietorship, although she may need to obtain a business license in her county or city (and pay a tax or fee for it), including filing a statement of business purpose.

She should also set up accounting records (e.g., using QuickBooks) and make her accounting and tax record keeping simpler by having a separate bank account and credit card for business purposes (accounts that are *not* used for personal purchases).

15-3b Partnerships

Partnerships are not subject to a Federal income tax. However, a partnership is required to file Form 1065, which reports the results of the partnership's activities. Business income and expense items are aggregated in computing the ordinary business income (loss) of the partnership on Form 1065. Any remaining income and expense items are reported separately to the partners.[6] Partnerships are discussed in detail in Chapters 21 and 22.

[5]There are limitations on this deduction for higher-income taxpayers. This chapter includes a detailed discussion of the deduction for qualified business income. For treatment of the qualified business income deduction by partnerships and S corporations, see Chapters 21 and 23, respectively.

[6]Some examples of separately reported income items are interest income, dividend income, and long-term capital gain. Examples of separately reported expenses include charitable contributions and expenses related to investment income.

The partnership ordinary business income (loss) and the separately reported items are allocated to the partners according to the partnership's profit and loss sharing agreement. Each partner receives a Schedule K–1 that reports this information. Each partner then reports these items on his or her own tax return. In addition, individual partners can claim the deduction for qualified business income (to the extent available) on their individual tax return (Form 1040).

Sundra and Patel are equal partners in Canary Enterprises, a calendar year partnership. During the year, Canary Enterprises had $500,000 gross income and $350,000 operating expenses. In addition, the partnership sold land that had been held for investment purposes for a long-term capital gain of $60,000. During the year, Sundra withdrew $40,000 from the partnership, and Patel withdrew $45,000.

The partnership's Form 1065 reports ordinary business income of $150,000 ($500,000 income − $350,000 expenses) and long-term capital gain of $60,000 as a separately stated item.

Sundra and Patel each receive a Schedule K–1 reporting ordinary business income of $75,000 and separately stated long-term capital gain of $30,000. Each partner reports ordinary business income of $75,000 and long-term capital gain of $30,000 on his or her own return. Likewise, Sundra and Patel would claim any related deduction for qualified business income on their individual tax returns.

15-3c **Corporations**

Corporations are governed by Subchapter C or Subchapter S of the Internal Revenue Code. Those governed by Subchapter C are referred to as **C corporations** or **regular corporations**. Corporations governed by Subchapter S are referred to as **S corporations**.

S corporations, which generally do not pay Federal income tax, are similar to partnerships in that ordinary business income (loss) flows through to the shareholders to be reported on the shareholder's separate returns. Also like partnerships, certain items flow through from the S corporation to the shareholders and retain their separate character when reported on the shareholders' returns. In general, only individuals can be S corporation shareholders (no such limitation exists for partnerships). The S corporation ordinary business income (loss) and the separately reported items are allocated to the shareholders according to their stock ownership interests. In addition, S corporation shareholders can claim the deduction for qualified business income (to the extent available) on their individual tax return (Form 1040). S corporations are discussed in detail in Chapter 23.

Unlike proprietorships, partnerships, and S corporations, C corporations are subject to an entity-level Federal income tax. This results in what is known as *double taxation*. A C corporation reports its income and expenses on Form 1120 and then computes tax on its taxable income using a flat 21 percent rate.[7] When a corporation distributes its income, the corporation's shareholders report dividend income on their own tax returns; further, no corporate deduction is allowed for the dividends paid (discussed next). As a result, income that has already been taxed at the corporate level is also taxed at the shareholder level.

Taxation of Dividends

Double taxation stems, in part, from the fact that dividend distributions are not deductible by a C corporation. To avoid this, closely held corporation shareholders try to convert dividend distributions into tax-deductible expenses. A common way to do this is to increase compensation to shareholder-employees. However, the IRS scrutinizes compensation and other economic transactions (e.g., loans, leases, and sales) between shareholders and closely held corporations to ensure that payments are reasonable in amount.[8]

[7] § 11. For taxable years prior to 2018, corporations faced tax rates that varied from 15% to 39%. Corporations with taxable income of $18,333,333 or more paid a flat 35% tax rate.

[8] See Chapter 19 for a discussion of constructive dividends.

For individual shareholders, some of the double taxation effect is alleviated because dividends are generally taxed at lower tax rates. Qualified dividend income is taxed at a rate of 15 percent (20 percent for high-income taxpayers; 0 percent for lower-income taxpayers).[9] These rates also apply to long-term capital gains.[10]

The effects of double taxation are illustrated in Examples 8 and 9.

Double Taxation Illustrated

Example 8

Lavender Corporation has taxable income of $100,000 in 2023. It pays corporate tax of $21,000. This leaves $79,000, all of which is distributed as a dividend to Ashley, a 43-year-old single individual and the corporation's sole shareholder. Ashley has no income sources other than Lavender Corporation.

Ashley has taxable income of $65,150 ($79,000 − $13,850 standard deduction). She pays tax at the preferential rate applicable to qualified dividends received by individuals. Her tax is $3,076 [($44,625 × 0%) + ($100 × 12%) + ($20,425 × 15%)].

The combined tax on the corporation's net profit is $24,076 ($21,000 paid by the corporation + $3,076 paid by the shareholder).

Example 9

Assume the same facts as in Example 8, except that the business is organized as a sole proprietorship. Ashley reports the $100,000 profit from the business on her tax return. Ashley pays self-employment taxes of $14,130 ($100,000 × 0.9235 × 15.3%); one-half of this amount ($7,065) is a deduction *for* AGI. She has taxable income of $63,268 {$100,000 − $7,065 SE tax deduction − $13,850 standard deduction − $15,817 deduction for qualified business income [($100,000 − $7,065 − $13,850) × 20%]} and pays tax of $9,226.

As a result, operating the business as a sole proprietorship results in an income tax *savings* of $14,850 in 2023 [$24,076 (from Example 8) − $9,226].

Comparison of Corporations and Other Forms of Doing Business

When comparing C corporations to other business forms, there are a number of factors to consider, including:

- Tax rates,
- Character of business income,
- Business losses,
- Employment taxes, and
- State taxes.

Each of these is discussed below.

Tax Rates As noted earlier, a flat rate of 21 percent applies to corporate taxable income. The marginal rates for individuals range from 10 percent to 37 percent. In many cases, taxes will be greater in the corporate form (as in Example 8). However, the corporate form of doing business presents tax savings opportunities when the applicable corporate marginal rate is *lower* than the applicable individual marginal rate. The flat 21 percent corporate rate that now applies could significantly increase these tax savings opportunities.

[9]The 0% (20%) rate applies if taxable income, including the net capital gain, is below (above) specific thresholds based on filing status. In 2023, below $89,250 (or above $553,850) for married taxpayers filing a joint return; below $44,625 (or above $492,300) for single taxpayers.

[10]§ 1(h). A 3.8% Medicare surtax applies to net investment income in excess of modified adjusted gross income of $200,000 ($250,000 if married filing jointly), thus increasing the double taxation of dividend income for high-income taxpayers. § 1411.

Susanna, an individual taxpayer in the 37% marginal tax rate bracket, can generate $100,000 of additional taxable income in the current year. If the income is taxed to Susanna, the associated tax is $37,000 ($100,000 × 37%).

If, however, Susanna is able to shift the income to a newly created corporation, the corporate tax is $21,000 ($100,000 × 21%). As a result, by taking advantage of the lower corporate marginal tax rates, a tax *savings* of $16,000 ($37,000 − $21,000) is achieved.

Any attempt to take advantage of the difference between the corporate and individual marginal tax rates also must consider the effect of double taxation. When the preferential rate for dividend income is considered, however, tax savings opportunities still exist.

Assume in Example 10 that the corporation distributes all of its after-tax earnings to Susanna as a dividend. The dividend results in income tax of $15,800 [($100,000 − $21,000) × 20%] to Susanna.

As a result, even when the double taxation effect is considered, the combined tax burden of $36,800 ($21,000 paid by the corporation + $15,800 paid by the shareholder) represents an income tax *savings* of $200 when compared to the $37,000 of tax that results when the $100,000 of income is subject to Susanna's 37% marginal rate.

Examples 10 and 11 ignore other tax issues that also must be considered in selecting the proper form of doing business (e.g., the availability of the deduction for qualified business income), but they illustrate the tax savings that can be achieved by taking advantage of rate differentials.

Character of Business Income Unlike other forms of business, the tax attributes of income and expense items of a C corporation do not pass through the corporate entity to the shareholders. As a result, if the business is expected to generate tax-favored income (e.g., tax-exempt income or long-term capital gains), it may be better to choose a different business form.

Pass-Through of Losses C corporation losses are treated differently than losses of other business forms. A loss incurred by a proprietorship may be deductible by the owner, because all income and expense items are reported by the proprietor. Partnership and S corporation losses are passed through the entity and may be deductible by the partners or S corporation shareholders. C corporation losses, however, are retained at the corporate level. If losses are anticipated, it may be better to choose a business form other than a C corporation.

Franco plans to start a business this year. He expects that the business will incur operating losses for the first three years and then become highly profitable. Franco decides to operate as an S corporation during the loss period, because the losses will flow through and be deductible on his personal return. When the business becomes profitable, he intends to switch to C corporation status.

Employment Taxes The net income of a proprietorship is subject to the self-employment tax (15.3 percent), as are some partnership allocations of income to partners. Alternatively, wages paid to a shareholder-employee of a corporation (C or S) are subject to payroll taxes. The combined corporation-employee payroll tax burden must be compared with the self-employment tax in the proprietorship and partnership business forms. This analysis should include the benefit of the deduction available to a corporation for payroll taxes paid, as well as the deduction available to an individual for one-half of the self-employment taxes paid.

State Taxes At the entity level, state corporate income taxes and/or franchise taxes apply to corporations. Some states impose a franchise tax on all business forms (including partnerships and S corporations). If a business will be operating in multiple states, state taxes become more important (Chapter 26 discusses the taxation of multistate corporations). At the owner level, the income of sole proprietorships, S corporations, and partnerships (along with dividend distributions) is subject to state individual income taxation.

The tax attributes of the various forms of business entities are compared in Concept Summary 15.1.[11]

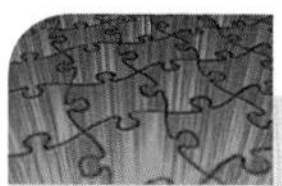

Concept Summary 15.1

Tax Treatment of Business Forms Compared

	Sole Proprietorships	Partnerships	S Corporations	Regular (C) Corporations
Entity tax return	None	Form 1065	Form 1120S	Form 1120
Taxation of entity income	No separate entity-level income tax. Proprietorship's income and expenses are reported on owner's Form 1040 (Schedule C). Character of entity income and expenses retained at owner level. Proprietor eligible for deduction for qualified business income.	No separate entity-level income tax. Partnership's income and expenses are allocated and reported (on Schedule K–1) to partners who report these items on their returns (e.g., Form 1040 for individual partners). Character of entity income and expenses retained at partner level. Individual partners eligible for deduction for qualified business income.	Generally, no separate entity-level income tax. S corporation's income and expenses are allocated and reported (on Schedule K–1) to shareholders who report these items on their returns (e.g., Form 1040 for individual shareholders). Character of entity income and expenses retained at shareholder level. Shareholders eligible for deduction for qualified business income.	Corporate income tax applies. Flat rate of 21% on corporate taxable income.
Taxation of withdrawals/ distributions from entity	Withdrawals by owner are not subject to separate tax.	Distributions to partners are generally not subject to separate tax.	Distributions to shareholders are generally not subject to separate tax.	Character of entity income and expenses not retained at shareholder level. Instead, distributions to shareholders are generally taxed as dividend income. Preferential tax rates (0%/15%/20%) apply to qualified dividends.
Employment taxes	Schedule C income subject to self-employment tax.	Some partnership allocations subject to self-employment tax.	Compensation paid to shareholder/employees subject to payroll taxes. Shareholder's allocated portion of entity income not subject to self-employment tax.	Compensation paid to shareholder/employees subject to payroll taxes.

[11]Text Section 23-6 presents a detailed comparison of the tax attributes of sole proprietorships, partnerships, S corporations, and C corporations as forms of doing business.

Global Tax Issues **U.S. Corporate Taxes and International Business Competitiveness**

In a 2017 study, the Tax Foundation examined the impact of national tax systems on international business competitiveness. In its report, the Tax Foundation ranked the international tax competitiveness of the 35 members of the Organization for Economic Co-operation and Development (OECD) by examining each country's tax policies. The rankings were based on many tax policy factors, including corporate and individual tax rates, consumption taxes, payroll and property taxes, and international tax rules.

In 2017, the United States ranked 30th out of the 35 OECD countries in overall international tax competitiveness, largely due to its comparative rankings on corporate taxes (35th) and international tax rules (33rd). Estonia claimed the top ranking in the report, followed by New Zealand, Switzerland, and Latvia.

One of the primary goals underlying the enactment of the TCJA of 2017 was to increase the international competitiveness of U.S. businesses. The reduction in the corporate tax rate to 21 percent was the centerpiece of that legislation. In the 2022 Tax Foundation rankings, the United States ranked 22nd. An interactive tool allows readers to explore their data in more depth (**tax-competition.org**). It will be interesting to see how the United States ranks in future studies on international tax competitiveness.

Source: **taxfoundation.org/publications/international-tax-competitiveness-index/.**

15-3d **Limited Liability Companies**

The limited liability company (LLC) is a business form that blends some corporate form advantages into a flow-through entity. All 50 states and the District of Columbia have passed laws that allow LLCs, and thousands of companies have chosen LLC status. As with a corporation, operating as an LLC allows its owners (called "members") to avoid unlimited liability exposure, which is a primary *nontax* consideration in choosing a business form. The tax advantage of LLCs is that qualifying businesses may be treated as proprietorships or partnerships for tax purposes, thereby avoiding the problem of double taxation associated with regular corporations.[12]

Entity Classification

Can an organization that is *not* a corporation under state law still be treated as one for Federal income tax purposes? The tax law defines a corporation as including "associations, joint-stock companies, and insurance companies."[13] Unfortunately, the Code contains no definition of what constitutes an *association*, and the issue became the subject of frequent litigation.

It was finally determined that an entity would be treated as a corporation if it had a majority of characteristics common to corporations.

- Continuity of life.
- Centralized management.
- Limited liability.
- Free transferability of interests.

These criteria did not resolve all of the problems that continued to arise over corporate classification. And when the states allowed the creation of LLCs, the IRS was deluged with inquiries regarding its tax status. The Code does not identify LLCs as a business form. And state LLC laws differed (e.g., some allowed centralized management, but others did not). So the question was how these entities would be treated under Federal tax law.

[12]Some states allow an LLC to have centralized management, but not continuity of life or free transferability of interests. Other states allow LLCs to adopt any or all of the corporate characteristics of centralized management, continuity of life, and free transferability of interests.

[13]§ 7701(a)(3).

To ease this problem, the **Check-the-box Regulations** were issued by the Treasury Department.[14] The Regulations enable taxpayers to choose the tax status of a business entity without regard to its corporate (or noncorporate) characteristics. These rules simplified tax administration considerably and eliminated much of the litigation related to association (i.e., corporation) status.

Under the Check-the-box Regulations, an unincorporated entity with *more than one* owner is, by default, classified as a partnership. An unincorporated entity with *only one* owner is, by default, classified as a **disregarded entity** (or DRE). A DRE is treated as a sole proprietorship if it is owned by an individual or as a branch or a division of a corporate owner. If the entity wants to use its default status, it simply files the appropriate tax return. If it wants to use a different status or change its status, it does so by "checking a box" on Form 8832. Thus, an LLC (single or multi-member) can choose to be taxed as a C corporation and, if it otherwise qualifies, even elect S corporation status.[15] Although an LLC does not typically pay Federal income taxes, LLCs are required to report and pay employment and excise taxes.

15-4 The Challenges of Taxing Business Activities: Entity Tax Rates

One goal of U.S. tax policy is to ensure the international competitiveness of U.S. corporations and attract investment in the United States from non-U.S. multinational corporations. Although this can be accomplished by lowering corporate tax rates, other challenges can emerge.

15-4a Challenges of Lowering Tax Rates

As a member of a global economy, other countries are likely to respond to actions taken by the United States. For example, in 1986, the United States lowered the Federal corporate income tax rate from a maximum of 46 percent to 34 percent. This led many other industrialized countries also to lower their corporate tax rate. After many years, most of these countries had lowered their rate below 34 percent. During this time, the United States raised its top corporate rate to 35 percent. In response, the United States lowered its corporate tax rate to 21 percent in 2018. This, however, presented additional challenges.

By lowering tax rates, the Federal government will experience reduced revenues. In response to lowering tax rates, the tax base can be expanded (or broadened; recall that tax liability equals tax base times tax rate). However, broadening the tax base for the corporate tax system is difficult because virtually all business expenses are allowed as deductions in determining taxable income.

Another challenge to lowering the Federal corporate income tax rate is that most businesses in the United States operate in a *noncorporate* form (e.g., sole proprietorships, partnerships, S corporations, or LLCs). These non-C corporation entities are pass-through entities, where the business income is taxed to owners (rather than being subject to double taxation). In addition, the owners of these businesses are likely to have other forms of income. For example, a sole proprietor also is likely to have investment

[14] Reg. §§ 301.7701–1 through –4, and –7.

[15] The "check-the-box" option is not available to entities that are incorporated under state law or to entities that are required to be taxed as corporations under Federal law (e.g., certain publicly traded partnerships). LLCs are not treated as being incorporated under state law, so they default to either partnership or DRE status.

income and wages. As a result, determining how to tax the business income of pass-through entities in a manner comparable to that of a C corporation is challenging, as explained next.

15-4b **Lowering Tax Rates for Different Business Forms**

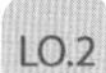

LO.2

Explain the rationale for the deduction for qualified business income.

There is more than one way to lower the tax rate on the business income that noncorporate taxpayers generate from their businesses. For example, similar to the lower income tax rates that apply to the net capital gains and qualified dividends received by noncorporate taxpayers, an alternative rate structure could be applied to business income. Alternatively, noncorporate taxpayers could be allowed a special deduction to reduce the income from their business activities, thereby lowering the tax base (and lowering the taxes due).

Challenges exist in both of these approaches. For example, given the double taxation of corporate profits (via the nondeductibility of dividend payments), what noncorporate tax rate is comparable to the corporate tax rate? In addition, entity differences must be taken into account (e.g., sole proprietors and partnerships do not pay wages to their owners, but S corporations generally do).

Ultimately, to balance the reduced Federal corporate tax rate, Congress selected the business deduction approach and § 199A (Qualified Business Income) was added to the Internal Revenue Code. The qualified business income (QBI) deduction allows up to a 20 percent deduction on the qualified business income of *noncorporate* taxpayers. As a result, this deduction is potentially available to individuals, trusts, and estates. Owners of partnerships and S corporations use relevant information provided to them from the entity (on their Schedule K–1 and related attachments) to calculate the deduction on their tax return (e.g., an individual's Form 1040).

As with most of the noncorporate changes made by Congress in 2017, the deduction for qualified business income is temporary; it is in effect from 2018 through 2025. At some point, Congress will need to revisit § 199A, deciding whether to extend, make permanent, modify, or repeal this deduction. The balance of this chapter explains the QBI deduction and its numerous definitions, limitations, and special rules. Appreciating the purpose of the deduction—to reduce the tax on business income derived outside of the C corporate form—will help in understanding this complex provision.

15-5 **The Deduction for Qualified Business Income**

LO.3

Describe the types of taxpayers and activities that potentially generate a deduction for qualified business income.

With the decision to reduce the top Federal corporate income tax rate, Congress needed to provide a means of reducing the taxes on businesses that operate in different business forms (e.g., sole proprietors, partnerships, and S corporations). Congress accomplished this with the creation of the **deduction for qualified business income** (§ 199A), which applies to *noncorporate taxpayers.*[16]

In general, the deduction for qualified business income is 20 percent of qualified business income (QBI). As you would suspect, however, the deduction is subject to a variety of limitations. We begin by discussing the general rules, defining key terms, and providing some basic examples. Then we turn our attention to the various limitations that apply to higher-income taxpayers, illustrate the reporting requirements related to the qualified business income deduction (**QBI deduction**), and conclude with a discussion of some other rules related to the QBI deduction.

[16] § 199A(a).

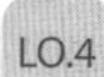

LO.4

Determine a taxpayer's deduction for qualified business income.

15-5a **General Rule**

At its most basic level, § 199A permits an individual to deduct 20 percent of the qualified business income generated through a sole proprietorship, a partnership, or an S corporation.[17] As will quickly become apparent, § 199A uses the word *qualified* to modify many phrases. For example, to determine the "qualified business income deduction," one has to understand the definition of a "qualified trade or business" and "qualified business income." But let's begin with the basics. In general, the deduction for qualified business income is the *lesser of*:[18]

1. 20 percent of qualified business income (QBI),[19] or
2. 20 percent of modified taxable income.[20]

Effectively, the QBI deduction—a *from* AGI deduction—is the last deduction taken in determining taxable income.[21] Further, the deduction is available whether a taxpayer uses the standard deduction or itemizes deductions.[22]

There are *three limitations* on the QBI deduction: an overall limitation (based on modified taxable income), another that applies to high-income taxpayers, and a third that applies to certain types of services businesses. The second and third limitations only apply when taxable income before the QBI deduction exceeds, in 2023, $364,200 (married taxpayers filing a joint return) or $182,100 (single and head-of-household taxpayers).[23] We'll discuss these two limitations later.

15-5b **The Overall Limitation: Modified Taxable Income**

In all cases, the § 199A deduction may not exceed 20 percent of the taxpayer's modified taxable income. Modified taxable income is taxable income *before* the deduction for qualified business income[24] reduced by any net capital gain.[25] In computing modified taxable income, the term *net capital gain* includes both a net capital gain [the excess of a long-term capital gain over a short-term capital loss; § 1222(11)] plus any qualified dividend income.[26]

15-5c **Definition of Qualified Business Income**

Qualified business income[27] (QBI) is defined as the ordinary income less ordinary deductions a taxpayer earns from a "qualified trade or business" conducted in the United States by the taxpayer (e.g., from a sole proprietorship).[28] It also includes the distributive share of these amounts from each partnership or S corporation interest held by the taxpayer.

---

[17]§§ 199A(a), (b)(1)(A), and (b)(2)(A).

[18]§ 199A(a).

[19]If the taxpayer has more than one qualified trade or business, the qualified business income deduction is determined for each business independently [§ 199A(b)(1)(A)]. These are then combined [into the "combined qualified business income amount" of § 199A(a)(1)] and compared to the modified taxable income limitation.

[20]In addition, taxpayers are allowed a deduction for 20% of qualified REIT dividends and 20% of qualified publicly traded partnership income [§ 199A(b)(1)(B)].

[21]See the last sentence of § 62(a) and § 63(b)(3).

[22]§ 63(d)(3).

[23]In 2023, married taxpayers filing separately (MFS) have a threshold amount of $182,100. We have not included MFS taxpayers in the text discussion. In 2022, the threshold amounts were $340,100 (married taxpayers filing a joint return), $170,050 (married taxpayers filing separately), and $170,050 (single and head-of-household taxpayers).

[24]§ 199A(e)(1).

[25]§ 199A(a)(2)(B).

[26]§ 199A(a)(2)(B) and Reg. § 1.199A–1(b)(3); § 199A relies on the definition of "net capital gain" in § 1(h).

[27]§ 199A(c).

[28]§ 199A(c)(3)(A). As a result, foreign trade or business income does not qualify for the deduction. Certain Puerto Rico activities qualify for the deduction.

In determining QBI, all deductions attributable to a trade or business are taken into account.[29] Relevant deductions include the self-employment tax deduction [§ 164(f)], the self-employed health insurance deduction [§ 162(l)], and any deduction for contributions to qualified retirement plans [§ 404].[30]

Vicki Howard's sole proprietorship reports $54,000 of net income [on Schedule C (Form 1040)]. As a result, Vicki's self-employment tax liability is $7,630 ($54,000 × 0.9235 × 15.3%). She is allowed a *for* AGI deduction for one-half of her self-employment tax liability ($3,815; $7,630 × ½). Vicki's QBI is $50,185 ($54,000 − $3,815).

Qualified business income does not include certain types of investment income, such as:[31]

- Capital gains or capital losses (including any net § 1231 gain included in capital gain and loss computations),[32]
- Dividends,
- Interest income (unless "properly allocable" to a trade or business, such as lending), or
- Certain other investment items.

Nor does qualified business income include:[33]

- The "reasonable compensation" paid to the taxpayer with respect to any qualified trade or business, or
- Guaranteed payments made to a partner for services rendered.

As noted above, the § 199A Regulations indicate that a net § 1231 gain for a taxable year that is treated as a long-term capital gain is *excluded* from the computation of qualified business income. The Regulations also note that if the result of § 1231 netting is a *loss*, the ordinary loss will *reduce* qualified business income for that year. The Regulations are silent regarding what to do if there are multiple qualified trades or businesses and each has § 1231 gains and losses.

15-5d **Definition of a Qualified Trade or Business**

For taxpayers who fall below critical taxable income thresholds established under § 199A (in 2023, $364,200 for married taxpayers filing jointly; $182,100 for single and head-of-household taxpayers), the scope of a **qualified trade or business** (QTB) is broad. In general, it includes any trade or business other than providing services as an employee.[34]

As a result, the deduction is available to sole proprietors, independent contractors, and noncorporate owners of S corporations, partnerships, and LLCs. But as discussed below, this otherwise broad application has some considerable restrictions for high-income taxpayers who are engaged in businesses involving the performance of services in certain "specified" fields.

[29] § 199A(c)(3)(A).

[30] Reg. § 1.199A–3(b)(1)(vi).

[31] § 199A(c)(3)(B).

[32] Reg. § 1.199A–3(b)(2)(ii).

[33] § 199A(c)(4).

[34] § 199A(d)(1)(B).

Basic QBI Deduction Computation

Example 14

Sanjay, a married taxpayer, operates a candy store as a sole proprietor. The business has no employees (Sanjay provides all services to customers). During 2023, Sanjay's qualified business income is $210,000 [this is his Schedule C (Form 1040) net income reduced by his self-employment tax deduction]. Sanjay's AGI is $277,700, which includes wages earned by his spouse, but no other income or deductions. He and his spouse claim the standard deduction ($27,700). Sanjay's modified taxable income is $250,000 ($277,700 − $27,700).

Sanjay's QBI deduction is $42,000, the *lesser of:*

1. 20% of qualified business income ($42,000; $210,000 × 20%), or
2. 20% of modified taxable income ($50,000; $250,000 × 20%).

Sanjay's taxable income is $208,000 ($250,000 of taxable income before the QBI deduction less his $42,000 QBI deduction).

Example 15

Assume that Abby is a single taxpayer who does not itemize deductions and operates a sole proprietorship. During 2023, her business generates $140,000 of business income, $40,000 of deductible business expenses (including her self-employment tax deduction), and $3,850 of interest income from her business deposits. She has no other sources of income and no other deductions. Abby's AGI is $103,850.

Abby has $100,000 of qualified business income ($140,000 − $40,000). The interest income does not qualify for the QBI deduction. Her modified taxable income is $90,000 ($103,850 AGI − $13,850 standard deduction).

Abby's QBI deduction is $18,000, the *lesser of:*

1. 20% of qualified business income ($20,000; $100,000 × 20%), or
2. 20% of modified taxable income ($18,000; $90,000 × 20%).

Abby's taxable income is $72,000 ($90,000 of taxable income before the QBI deduction less her $18,000 QBI deduction).

Example 16

Assume the same facts as in Example 15, except that Abby has no interest income, but $3,850 of qualified dividend income. Abby's AGI remains $103,850, and her taxable income before the QBI deduction remains $90,000 ($103,850 AGI – $13,850 standard deduction).

However, Abby's modified taxable income is now $86,150 [$90,000 taxable income before the QBI deduction less $3,850 of "net capital gain" (the qualified dividend income)].

Abby's QBI deduction is $17,230, the *lesser of:*

1. 20% of qualified business income ($20,000; $100,000 × 20%), or
2. 20% of modified taxable income ($17,230; $86,150 × 20%).

Abby's taxable income is $72,770 ($90,000 of taxable income before the QBI deduction less her $17,230 QBI deduction).

"Trade or Business" Under § 199A

What is a "trade or business" for purposes of § 199A? Reg. § 1.199A–1(b)(14) interprets the term *trade or business* by looking at the meaning of this phrase under § 162(a). With no formal definition of that phrase in § 162, the Supreme Court[35] has determined that to be "engaged in a trade or business, the taxpayer must be involved in the activity with continuity and regularity and that the taxpayer's primary purpose for engaging in the activity must be for income or profit." Ultimately, this is a "facts and circumstances" test.[36] The § 199A Regulations acknowledge that multiple businesses might be contained in a single entity, but emphasize that this determination depends on "all the facts and circumstances." At a minimum, for § 199A to apply to each business, separate books and records must be maintained for each business.

[35] *Groetzinger v. Comm.*, 85–2 USTC ¶9622, 56 AFTR 2d 85–5683, 771 F.2d 269 (CA–7), *aff'd* in 87–1 USTC ¶9191, 59 AFTR 2d 87–532, 107 S.Ct. 980. Performing services as an employee is *not* a "trade or business."

[36] *Higgins v. Comm.*, 41–1 USTC ¶9233, 25 AFTR 1160, 61 S.Ct. 475.

The Big Picture

Example 17

How many businesses is Amy operating? Ultimately, it will depend on her ability to meet the trade or business definition adopted by the Supreme Court. Amy will need to document her "regular and continual" involvement in an activity *and* show that her "primary purpose" is to generate a profit.

It seems likely that contracting her artistic and marketing skills as (apparently) an independent contractor could meet this test. The same is possible with her efforts on social media sites. Although she will likely "profit" from the royalties related to her "name, image, and likeness" contract, it will be more challenging for her to demonstrate the "regular and continual" involvement required by the Supreme Court's definition. However, if she is actively and regularly involved in promoting name and image to generate more revenue, such facts will lean toward being in a trade or business. Ultimately, the determination will be based on all the "facts and circumstances" related to these activities. In all cases, it would be wise for Amy to maintain separate accounting records for each activity.

Does a rental activity qualify as a "trade or business"? Only if its activities rise to the level of those seen in a non-rental business. Here, the courts have based their decisions on a variety of factors including the type of property (commercial real property versus a residential condominium versus personal property), the number of properties rented, the nature of the owner's involvement [handling matters directly (or through an agent) versus a triple net lease arrangement], and the rental period (short term versus long term).[37]

Rental Real Estate Safe Harbor A rental real estate activity (or multiple rentals if the taxpayer chooses to combine them) will be treated as a trade or business for purposes of § 199A if the following conditions are met:[38]

- Separate books and records are maintained for each rental activity (or the combined enterprise if grouped together).
- At least 250 hours of "rental services" are performed per year for the activity (or combined enterprise). Rental services include time spent on maintenance, repairs, collecting rent, paying bills, providing services to tenants, supervising contractors and employees, and efforts to rent the property (including advertising and negotiating and executing a lease). The work does not have to be performed by the taxpayer (owner). It also can be performed by employees, agents, or contractors of the property owner.
- The taxpayer maintains contemporaneous records, including time reports or similar documents, supporting the services performed by the taxpayer and others (including hours, dates, description of services, and who performed the services).
- A statement is attached to the timely filed return that indicates the taxpayer is using the safe harbor, describing the properties, and acknowledging that the requirements for the safe harbor are met.

A taxpayer can't use the safe harbor for the rental of any residence that the taxpayer uses as a personal residence for more than 14 days during the year (e.g., a vacation home). In addition, the taxpayer must own the rental property directly (rather than, for example, as a partner in a partnership). Finally, triple net leases are excluded from the safe harbor (these are leases where the landlord passes on the responsibility for paying real estate taxes, insurance, and maintenance to the tenant).

If property owners do not satisfy the safe harbor conditions, they still might find that their real estate rental is a trade or business under § 162 as defined in case law and the specific court cases that have considered whether rental properties constitute a trade or business.

Taxpayers with Multiple Businesses

The deduction for qualified business income must be determined separately for each qualified trade or business.[39] These independent calculations are then aggregated [becoming

[37]See, for example, *Alvary v. U.S.*, 62–1 USTC ¶9493, 9 AFTR 2d 1633, 302 F.2d 790 (CA–2), *Edwin R. Curphey*, 73 T.C. 766 (1980), *Gilford v. Comm.*, 53–1 USTC ¶9201, 43 AFTR 221, 201 F.2d 735 (CA–2), *James B. Murtaugh*, 74 TCM 75, T.C. Memo. 1997–319, and *Victoria Balsamo*, 54 TCM 608, T.C. Memo. 1987–477.

[38]Rev.Proc. 2019–38.

[39]§ 199A(b)(2).

the "combined qualified business income amount" identified in § 199A(a)(1)(A)]. This combined amount is then compared to the overall modified taxable income limit.

15-5e Limitations on the QBI Deduction

The basic application of § 199A becomes more complex once a taxpayer reaches certain taxable income thresholds. These taxable income thresholds—determined without regard to the QBI deduction—are $364,200 for married taxpayers filing jointly and $182,100 for single and head-of-household taxpayers in 2023.[40] In 2022, these amounts were $340,100 and $170,050.

Once these thresholds are reached, § 199A imposes two *independent* limitations.

1. The QBI deduction is capped based on the percentage of the W–2 wages paid by the business (i.e., wages paid to its employees) *or* based on a smaller percentage of W–2 wages paid by the business and a percentage of the cost of its depreciable property used to produce QBI.[41]
2. The QBI deduction generally is *not available* for income earned from "specified service" businesses.[42] "Specified service" businesses include doctors, dentists, lawyers, accountants, consultants, investment advisers, entertainers, and athletes (among others), but not engineers and architects.

These limitations, discussed in more detail below, are fully phased in once taxable income (before the QBI deduction) exceeds $464,200 for married taxpayers filing jointly and $232,100 for single and head-of-household taxpayers. Within the phase-in ranges ($100,000 for married taxpayers filing jointly; $50,000 for all other taxpayers), the limitations are each applied by comparing the amount of taxable income that exceeds the threshold amount to the appropriate phase-in range.[43]

Because the "specified services" limitation can be more complex (due to incorporating the "wages and capital investment" limitation after the "specified services" limitation), the wages and capital investment limitation is discussed first, followed by the "specified services" limitation.

Remember that in all cases, the QBI deduction can never exceed 20 percent of the taxpayer's modified taxable income (taxable income before the QBI deduction reduced by any net capital gain, including qualified dividend income). To help navigate this "thicket," Concept Summary 15.2 provides a flowchart to assist in applying these rules.

15-5f Limitation Based on Wages and Capital Investment

The **W–2 Wages/Capital Investment Limit**, which does not apply to taxpayers below the taxable income thresholds mentioned previously and is phased in as a taxpayer's income exceeds those thresholds, limits the 20 percent QBI deduction to the *greater of*:

1. 50 percent of the "W–2 wages" paid by the QTB, or
2. 25 percent of the "W–2 wages" paid by the QTB *plus* 2.5 percent of the taxpayer's share of the unadjusted basis immediately after acquisition of all tangible depreciable property (including real estate) used in the QTB that has not been fully depreciated prior to the close of the taxable year.

W–2 Wages Limit

"W–2 wages" includes the total amount of wages subject to income tax withholding, compensation paid into qualified retirement accounts, and certain other forms of deferred compensation paid to the employees of the business.[44] For labor-intensive businesses, 50 percent of the W–2 wages paid by the business will likely be the relevant limit on the QBI deduction.

W–2 Wages/Capital Investment Limit

For capital-intensive businesses (e.g., real estate), an alternate limit exists. It begins with 25 percent of W–2 wages paid by the QTB and adds to this amount 2.5 percent of the unadjusted basis (immediately after acquisition) of "qualified property."

---

[40] § 199A(e)(2). Married taxpayers filing separately have a taxable income threshold of $182,100 in 2023 ($170,050 in 2022).

[41] § 199A(b)(2)(B).

[42] § 199A(d)(2).

[43] §§ 199A(b)(3)(B) and (d)(3).

[44] § 199A(b)(4).

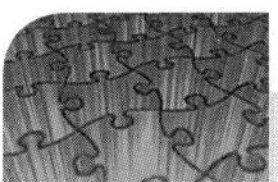

Concept Summary 15.2

An Overview of the 2023 Qualified Business Income Deduction

How to Use the Concept Summary: ***First,*** identify all qualified trades or businesses (QTB) of the taxpayer and the related qualified business income (QBI). ***Then*** for each QTB, move through the flowchart to determine the QBI amount for each QTB. Once this process is complete, combine all of the QBI amounts (this is the "combined qualified business income amount"). ***Finally,*** apply the *overall limitation* (based on modified taxable income). The QBI deduction is the *lesser of:*

1. The combined "qualified business income (QBI) amount," or
2. 20% of modified taxable income.*

* Modified taxable income is taxable income *before* the QBI deduction less any "net capital gain" (including any qualified dividend income).

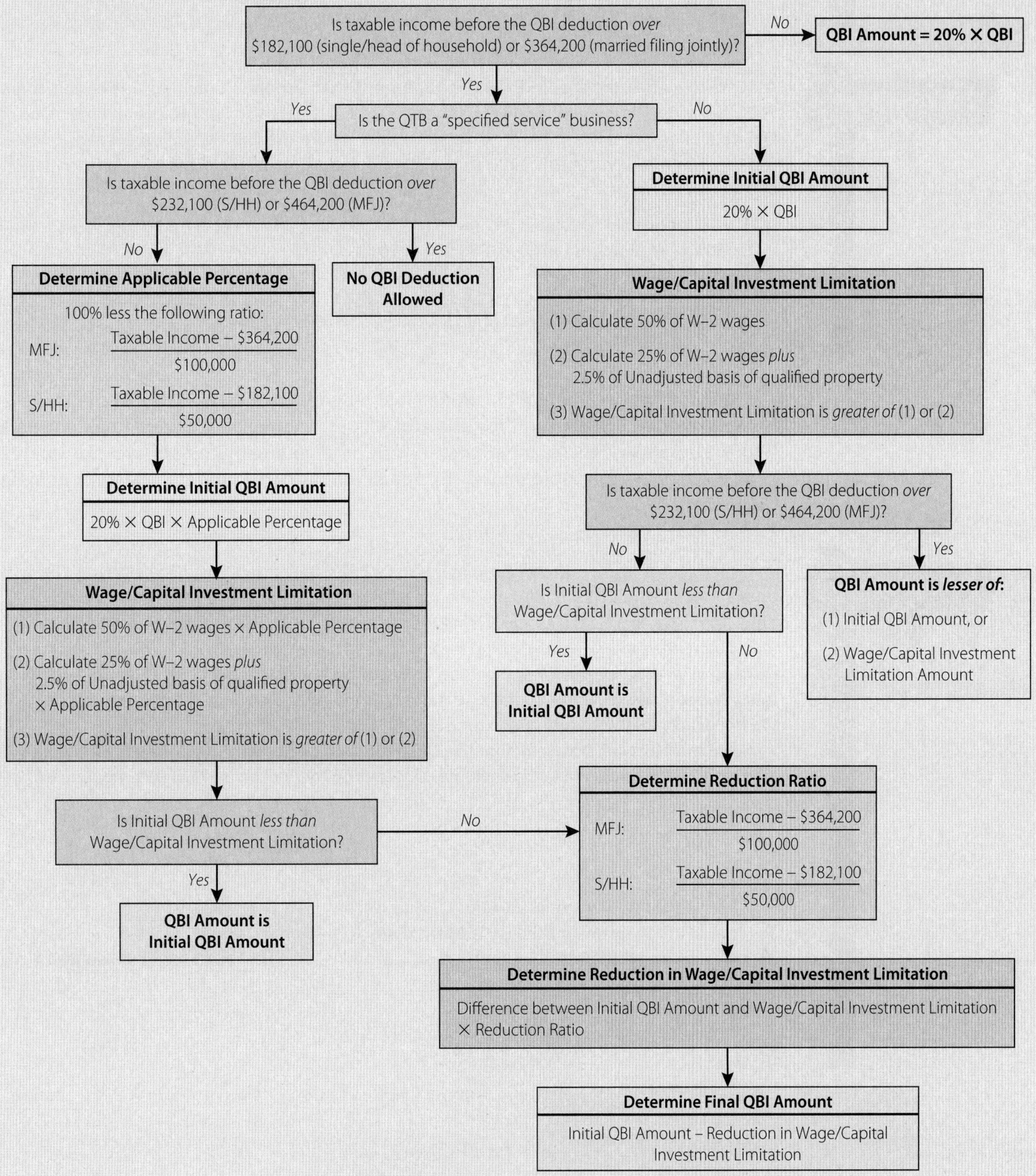

Is taxable income before the QBI deduction *over* $182,100 (single/head of household) or $364,200 (married filing jointly)?

No → **QBI Amount = 20% × QBI**

Yes → Is the QTB a "specified service" business?

Yes (specified service):

Is taxable income before the QBI deduction *over* $232,100 (S/HH) or $464,200 (MFJ)?

Yes → **No QBI Deduction Allowed**

No → **Determine Applicable Percentage**

100% less the following ratio:

MFJ: $\frac{\text{Taxable Income} - \$364{,}200}{\$100{,}000}$

S/HH: $\frac{\text{Taxable Income} - \$182{,}100}{\$50{,}000}$

Determine Initial QBI Amount

20% × QBI × Applicable Percentage

Wage/Capital Investment Limitation

(1) Calculate 50% of W–2 wages × Applicable Percentage

(2) Calculate 25% of W–2 wages *plus* 2.5% of Unadjusted basis of qualified property × Applicable Percentage

(3) Wage/Capital Investment Limitation is *greater of* (1) or (2)

Is Initial QBI Amount *less than* Wage/Capital Investment Limitation?

Yes → **QBI Amount is Initial QBI Amount**

No → Determine Reduction Ratio (below)

No (not a specified service):

Determine Initial QBI Amount

20% × QBI

Wage/Capital Investment Limitation

(1) Calculate 50% of W–2 wages

(2) Calculate 25% of W–2 wages *plus* 2.5% of Unadjusted basis of qualified property

(3) Wage/Capital Investment Limitation is *greater of* (1) or (2)

Is taxable income before the QBI deduction *over* $232,100 (S/HH) or $464,200 (MFJ)?

Yes → **QBI Amount is *lesser of*:**

(1) Initial QBI Amount, or

(2) Wage/Capital Investment Limitation Amount

No → Is Initial QBI Amount *less than* Wage/Capital Investment Limitation?

Yes → **QBI Amount is Initial QBI Amount**

No → Determine Reduction Ratio

Determine Reduction Ratio

MFJ: $\frac{\text{Taxable Income} - \$364{,}200}{\$100{,}000}$

S/HH: $\frac{\text{Taxable Income} - \$182{,}100}{\$50{,}000}$

Determine Reduction in Wage/Capital Investment Limitation

Difference between Initial QBI Amount and Wage/Capital Investment Limitation × Reduction Ratio

Determine Final QBI Amount

Initial QBI Amount – Reduction in Wage/Capital Investment Limitation

W–2 Wages Limit

Example 18

Simone, a married taxpayer, operates a business as a sole proprietor. The business has one employee, who is paid $80,000 during 2023. Assume that the business has no significant assets. During 2023, Simone's qualified business income is $230,000, and her modified taxable income is $250,000 (this is also her taxable income before the QBI deduction).

Since Simone's taxable income before the QBI deduction is below the income threshold for married taxpayers filing a joint return ($364,200), the W–2/Capital Investment Limitation does not apply. As a result, Simone's QBI deduction is $46,000, the *lesser of:*

1. 20% of qualified business income ($46,000; $230,000 × 20%), or
2. 20% of modified taxable income ($50,000; $250,000 × 20%).

Assume the same facts as in Example 18, except that Simone's qualified business income is $500,000 and her modified taxable income is $600,000 (this is also her taxable income before the QBI deduction). Because Simone's taxable income before the QBI deduction exceeds $464,200, the W–2/Capital Investment Limitation fully applies. As a result, Simone's QBI deduction is $40,000, the *lesser of:*

1. 20% of qualified business income ($100,000; $500,000 × 20%), or
2. 50% of W–2 wages ($40,000; $80,000 × 50%).

And *no more than*:

3. 20% of modified taxable income ($120,000; $600,000 × 20%).

Qualified property includes depreciable tangible property—real or personal—that is used by the QTB during the year and whose "depreciable period" has not ended before the end of the taxable year.[45] Land and intangible assets are *not* qualified property. The "depreciable period" for "qualified property" under § 199A is a minimum of 10 years.[46]

Tom and Eileen are married and file a joint return for 2023. Their taxable income before the QBI deduction is $500,000 (this is also their modified taxable income). They have $400,000 in QBI from a restaurant they own (a two-member LLC that reports as a partnership). They employed four individuals (cook, bartender, and wait staff) during the year and paid them $150,000 in W–2 wages. They own the building in which the restaurant is located. They bought the building (and its furniture and fixtures) four years ago for $600,000, and the land was worth $100,000, so the unadjusted acquisition basis of the building (and its furniture and fixtures) is $500,000.

Since their taxable income before the QBI deduction exceeds the $464,200 threshold, the W–2 Wages/Capital Investment Limit comes into play. Their QBI deduction is $75,000, computed as follows:

1. 20% of qualified business income ($400,000 × 20%)		$ 80,000
2. But no more than the *greater of*:		
• 50% of W–2 wages ($150,000 × 50%), or		$ 75,000
• 25% of W–2 wages ($150,000 × 25%) *plus*	$37,500	
• 2.5% of the unadjusted basis of qualified property ($500,000 × 2.5%)	12,500	$ 50,000
And *no more than*:		
3. 20% of modified taxable income ($500,000 × 20%)		$100,000

[45] § 199A(b)(6)(A).

[46] § 199A(b)(6)(B).

Many owners of pass-through businesses, especially landlords, have no employees. As a result, the 25 percent of W–2 wages plus 2.5 percent of the unadjusted basis of qualified property is most likely to affect them.

Example 21

Jiaxiu, a single taxpayer, owns a five-unit apartment building that he purchased five years ago. His unadjusted basis in the building (purchase price minus the value of the land) is $500,000. He has taxable income before the QBI deduction of $250,000 during 2023 (this is also his modified taxable income). He has no employees in his business, and his QBI is $220,000.

Since his taxable income before the QBI deduction exceeds the $232,100 threshold, the W–2 Wages/Capital Investment Limit comes into play. His QBI deduction is $12,500, computed as follows:

1. 20% of qualified business income ($220,000 × 20%)		$44,000
2. But no more than the *greater of*:		
• 50% of W–2 wages ($0 × 50%), or		$ -0-
• 25% of W–2 wages ($0 × 25%) *plus*	$ -0-	
• 2.5% of the unadjusted basis of qualified property ($500,000 × 2.5%)	12,500	$12,500
And *no more than*:		
3. 20% of modified taxable income ($250,000 × 20%)		$50,000

Phase-In of W–2 Wages/Capital Investment Limit

The W–2 Wages/Capital Investment Limit does not apply to taxpayers with taxable income before the QBI deduction less than the threshold amount (in 2023, $364,200 for married taxpayers filing jointly; $182,100 for single and head-of-household taxpayers). And if taxable income before the QBI deduction exceeds the threshold amount by more than $100,000 (married filing jointly) or $50,000 (all other taxpayers), the W–2 Wages/Capital Investment Limit must be used.

If, however, the taxpayer's taxable income before the QBI deduction is between these two amounts *and the W–2 Wages/Capital Investment portion of the QBI deduction is capping the deduction*, then the general 20 percent QBI amount is used, but reduced as follows:

1. Determine difference between the general 20 percent QBI deduction amount and the W–2 Wages/Capital Investment amount.[47]
2. Determine the Reduction Ratio:[48]

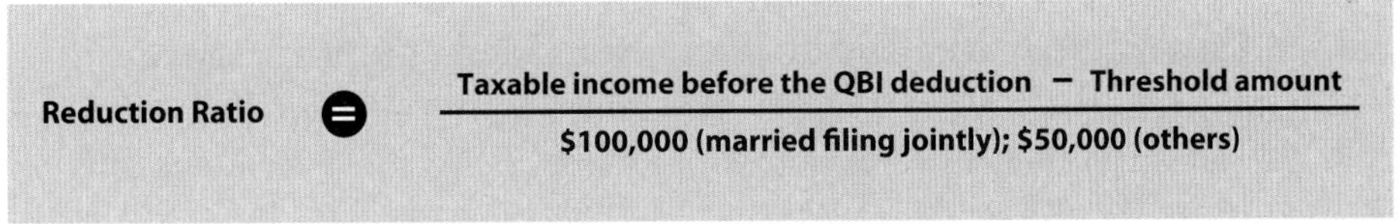

$$\text{Reduction Ratio} = \frac{\text{Taxable income before the QBI deduction} - \text{Threshold amount}}{\$100{,}000 \text{ (married filing jointly); } \$50{,}000 \text{ (others)}}$$

3. Determine the Reduction in the W–2 Wages/Capital Investment Limit:

   Reduction = Difference [from (1)] × Reduction ratio [from (2)]

4. Determine QBI amount:

   20% QBI deduction − Reduction [from (3)]

[47]This is the "excess amount" in § 199A(b)(3)(B)(iii).

[48]§ 199A(b)(3)(B)(ii).

Example 22

Return to the facts of Example 20, but assume that Tom and Eileen's taxable income before the QBI deduction is $404,200 (this is also their modified taxable income), QBI is $320,000, and W–2 wages are $100,000. Their unadjusted property basis remains at $500,000. Tom and Eileen's initial calculation yields a qualified business income amount of $50,000, computed as follows:

1. 20% of qualified business income ($320,000 × 20%)		$ 64,000
2. But no more than the *greater of*:		
• 50% of W–2 wages ($100,000 × 50%), or		$ 50,000
• 25% of W–2 wages ($100,000 × 25%) *plus*	$25,000	
• 2.5% of the unadjusted basis of qualified property ($500,000 × 2.5%)	12,500	$ 37,500
And *no more than*:		
3. 20% of modified taxable income ($404,200 × 20%)		$ 80,840

Since Tom and Eileen's taxable income before the QBI deduction exceeds $364,200 but is less than $464,200 and *the W–2 Wages/Capital Investment portion of the computation is capping the deduction*, the general 20% QBI amount is used, but reduced as follows:

1. Determine the difference between the general 20% QBI deduction amount and the W–2 Wages/Capital Investment amount:

General 20% QBI deduction amount	$ 64,000
Less: The W–2 Wages/Capital Investment Limit	(50,000)
Excess	$ 14,000

2. Determine the Reduction Ratio:

$$\text{Reduction Ratio} = \frac{\$40,000\ (\$404,200 - \$364,200)}{\$100,000} = 40\%$$

3. Determine the Reduction in the W–2 Wages/Capital Investment Limit:

Excess ($14,000) × Reduction ratio (40%) = $5,600

4. Determine Final QBI Amount:

General 20% QBI deduction amount	$64,000
Less: Reduction in the W–2 Wages/Capital Investment Limit	(5,600)
Final QBI amount	$58,400

Since the QBI amount ($58,400) is less than 20% of their modified taxable income ($80,840; $404,200 × 20%), they will be allowed a $58,400 deduction for qualified business income.

15-5g Limitation for "Specified Services" Businesses

For high-income taxpayers (in 2023, $464,200 for married taxpayers filing jointly; $232,100 for single and head-of-household taxpayers), § 199A excludes any "specified service trade or business" from the definition of a qualified trade or business.[49] A **specified service trade or business** includes those involving:[50]

- The performance of services in certain fields, including health, law, accounting, actuarial science, performing arts, consulting, athletics, financial services, and brokerage services;
- Services consisting of investing and investment management, trading or dealing in securities, partnership interests, or commodities; and
- Any trade or business where the business's principal asset is the reputation of one or more of its employees or owners.

Architects and engineers are specifically excluded from this definition.[51]

[49] §§ 199A(d)(1)(A) and (d)(2).

[50] § 199A(d)(2); see also § 1202(e)(3)(A).

[51] § 199A(d)(2)(A).

According to the legislative history of § 199A, the taxable income thresholds where the QBI deduction is phased out for "specified service" businesses were set by Congress "to deter high-income taxpayers from attempting to convert wages or other compensation for personal services to income eligible for the 20 percent deduction under the provision." However, the phaseout rules operate without regard to the taxpayer's specific motivation.

Example 23

In Example 14, Sanjay operated a sole proprietorship that generated QBI of $210,000 and he was able to claim a QBI deduction of $42,000.

But if his spouse had a salary of $300,000 (instead of $64,000), Sanjay would not be able to claim a QBI deduction since their taxable income before the QBI deduction exceeds $464,200 [$210,000 (QBI) + $300,000 (spouse's wages) − $27,700 (standard deduction) = $482,300]. Sanjay did not attempt to "convert wages to . . . income eligible for the (QBI) deduction." The *income of his spouse* triggered the limitation.

Example 23 illustrates a crucial fact. The QBI deduction phaseout for a "specified services" business is based on *taxable income* before the QBI deduction (*not* on QBI). *Any* income that contributes to taxable income can cause the "specified services" QBI deduction to be reduced.

"Specified Services" Under the § 199A Regulations

The § 199A Regulations provide specific guidance for each of the "specified services" fields identified in § 199A.[52] Exhibit 15.2 provides an overview of this guidance.

A series of examples in the Regulations illustrate these concepts.[53]

"Specified Services" Businesses

Example 24

Surgery Centers LLC (SC) operates specialty surgical centers that provide outpatient medical procedures (none of which require the patient to stay overnight). The company owns a number of facilities throughout the country. For each facility, SC ensures compliance with Federal and state laws and manages each facility's operations and performs all administrative functions. SC does not employ physicians, nurses, and medical assistants. Rather, it enters into agreements with medical professionals and other medical organizations to perform the procedures and provide all needed medical care. Patients are billed by SC for the facility costs related to their procedure; they are separately billed by the health care professional (or the medical organization) for the costs of the procedure performed by the physician and medical support team.

SC is *not* engaged in a "specified services" business (health) because it is not providing the medical services (the medical professionals using the centers are operating businesses in the field of health).

Example 25

Abby, a singer, records a song. Abby is paid a mechanical royalty when the song is licensed or streamed. She is also paid a performance royalty when the recorded song is played publicly.

Abby is engaged in a "specified services" business (performing arts).

Example 26

Ravi is a partner in RoundballSports (RS), which owns and operates a professional basketball team. RS employs athletes and sells tickets to the public to attend games in which its basketball team competes.

RS is engaged in a "specified services" business (athletics).

[52] Reg. § 1.199A–5(b)(2).

[53] Reg. § 1.199A–5(b)(3).

Exhibit 15.2 "Specified Services"

Field	"Specified Services"	Not "Specified Services"
Health	Doctors, pharmacists, nurses, dentists, veterinarians, physical therapists, psychologists, and other similar health care professionals.	Those who provide services that may improve the health of the recipient (e.g., the operator of a health club or spa) or the research, testing, and sale of pharmaceuticals or medical devices.
Law	Lawyers, paralegals, legal arbitrators, and mediators.	Those who provide services not unique to law, like printing, stenography, or delivery services.
Accounting	Accountants, enrolled agents, return preparers, financial auditors, bookkeepers, and similar professionals (whether licensed by a state or not).	Businesses that provide payment processing and billing analysis.
Actuarial Science	Actuaries and similar professionals.	Services provided by analysts, economists, mathematicians, and statisticians not engaged in analyzing or assessing the financial costs of risk or uncertainty of events.
Performing Arts	Actors, singers, musicians, entertainers, directors, and similar professionals (including screenwriters and composers) who provide services that lead to the creation of performing arts.	Those who broadcast or disseminate video or audio to the public and those who maintain or operate equipment or facilities used in the performing arts.
Consulting	Those who provide professional advice and counsel to clients to assist in achieving goals and solving problems, including government lobbyists.	Salespeople and those who provide training or educational courses. Services provided in the fields of architecture or engineering.
Athletics	Athletes, coaches, and team managers.	Broadcasters or those who maintain or operate equipment used in an athletic event; services related to the maintenance and operation of equipment or facilities for use in athletic events.
Financial Services	Those who provide financial services to clients, including managing wealth, developing retirement or transition plans, providing advisory services related to mergers and acquisitions (including restructurings, raising capital, underwriting, and other valuation services). In summary, financial advisers, investment bankers, wealth planners, and retirement advisers.	Banking services (e.g., taking deposits or making loans).
Brokerage Services	A broker who arranges *securities* transactions.	Real estate agents and brokers.
Investment Management	Persons who receive fees for providing investing, asset management, or investment management services.	Real estate managers.
Trading	Persons who trade in securities, commodities, or partnership interests.	A farmer or manufacturer who engages in hedging transactions as part of his or her trade or business.
Reputation of One or More Employees or Owners	Any trade or business that consists of any of the following (or any combination of them): (1) Receiving fees, compensation, or other income for endorsing products or services; (2) Licensing or receiving fees, compensation, or other income for the use of an individual's image, likeness, name, signature, voice, trademark, or any other symbols associated with the individual's identity; and (3) Receiving fees, compensation, or other income for appearing at an event or on radio, television, or another media format.	Persons not covered by this narrowly crafted definition (and not in another "specified services" field). Examples include authors and personal trainers.

"Specified Services" Businesses

Christian is in the business of providing services that assist unrelated entities in making their personnel structures more efficient. Christian studies a variety of client organizations and structures and compares each to peers in its industry. He then makes recommendations and provides advice to clients regarding possible changes to their personnel structure, including the use of temporary workers.

Christian is engaged in a "specified services" business (consulting).

Danielle is in the business of licensing software to customers. As part of her business, she evaluates a customer's software needs and discusses alternatives with her customers. She advises the customer on the particular software products her business licenses. Danielle is paid a flat price for the software license. After a customer licenses the software, Danielle helps to implement it.

Danielle is engaged in the trade or business of licensing software and is *not* engaged in a "specified services" business.

Krystal is in the business of providing services to assist clients with their finances. Krystal generally studies a particular client's financial situation, including the client's present income, savings, and investments, and anticipated future economic and financial needs. Based on this study, she then assists the client in making decisions and plans regarding the client's financial activities. This planning includes the design of a personal budget to assist the client in monitoring the client's financial situation, the adoption of investment strategies tailored to the client's needs, and other similar services.

Krystal is engaged in a "specified services" business (financial services).

Emeril is a well-known chef and the sole owner of multiple restaurants, each of which is an LLC. Due to his skill and reputation as a chef, Emeril receives an endorsement fee of $5,000,000 for the use of his name on a line of cooking utensils and cookware.

Emeril is in the trade or business of being a chef and owning restaurants—*neither* is a "specified services" business. However, he is also in the trade or business of receiving endorsement income. This business—consisting of endorsement fees for Emeril's skill and/or reputation—is a "specified services" business.

Jennifer is a well-known actor. Jennifer entered into a partnership with Shoe Company, in which she contributed her likeness and the use of her name to the partnership in exchange for a 50% interest in the partnership and a guaranteed payment.

Jennifer's trade or business consisting of the receipt of the partnership interest and guaranteed payment for use of her likeness and name is a "specified services" business.

De Minimis Rule

The § 199A Regulations contain a *de minimis* rule providing that a trade or business will *not* be considered a "specified services" business merely because it provides a small amount of services in a "specified service" activity.[54]

- If a business has gross receipts of $25 million or less and *less than 10 percent* of its receipts relates to a "specified service," the business will *not* be a "specified services" business.
- If the business has gross receipts greater than $25 million, then the test is *less than 5 percent* (rather than less than 10 percent).

Computer Company has annual revenue of $20,000,000 ($18,500,000 of the revenue is related to the sale of computers and peripheral equipment; the remaining $1,500,000 relates to consulting, installation, and training services).

Because its consulting services revenues are less than 10% of Computer Company's total revenues, those services are ignored for purposes of determining whether Computer Company is a "specified services" business. As a result, Computer Company is *not* a "specified services" business.

[54]Reg. § 1.199A–5(c)(1).

Although the *de minimis* rules offer relief to a business with both service and non-service income, what happens if the "specified services" income is more than *de minimis*? Is the entire business tainted (or just the "specified services" portion of the business)? The § 199A Regulations provide two examples to illustrate the consequences.

"Specified Services" *De Minimis* Rule

Example 33

Landscape LLC sells lawn care and landscaping equipment. It also provides advice and counsel on landscape design for large office parks and residential buildings. The landscape design services include advice on the selection and placement of trees, shrubs, and flowers (these are "consulting services" under § 199A).

Landscape LLC separately invoices for its landscape design services and does not sell the trees, shrubs, or flowers it recommends for use in the landscape design. Landscape LLC maintains one set of books and records and treats the equipment sales and design services as a *single trade or business*. Landscape LLC has gross receipts of $2,000,000; $250,000 of the gross receipts relates to the landscape design services.

Because the gross receipts from the consulting services exceed 10% of Landscape LLC's total gross receipts, the entirety of Landscape LLC's business is considered a "specified services" business.

Example 34

Animal Care LLC provides veterinary services performed by licensed staff. It also develops and sells its own line of organic dog food at its veterinarian clinic and online. The veterinary services are in the field of health (a "specified service"). Animal Care LLC separately invoices for its veterinarian services and the sale of its organic dog food. Animal Care LLC maintains separate books and records for its veterinarian clinic and its development and sale of its dog food. Animal Care LLC also has separate employees who are unaffiliated with the veterinary clinic and who only work on the formulation, marketing, sales, and distribution of the organic dog food products.

Animal Care LLC treats its veterinary practice and the dog food development and sales as *separate trades or businesses*. Animal Care LLC has gross receipts of $3,000,000; $1,000,000 of the gross receipts relates to the veterinary services. Although the gross receipts from the veterinary services exceed 10% of Animal Care LLC's total gross receipts, the dog food development and sales business is *not* considered a "specified services" business. Animal Care LLC has chosen to treat each business separately, so the veterinarian services business is a "specified services" business, while the dog food business is not.

As you can see, two factors led to the favorable result in Example 34. First, the taxpayer keeps separate books and records for each business. Second, each business has separate employees. As discussed previously, it is possible for a single entity to have multiple trades or businesses. However, whether multiple businesses exist depends on "all the facts and circumstances." At a minimum, separate books and records must be maintained; the § 199A Regulations imply (via the outcome in Example 34) that separate employees with separate books and records means separate businesses. But the differing outcomes of Examples 33 and 34 do mean that without separate books and records, multiple businesses in a single entity are not possible. And in that case, if the "specified services" revenue becomes more than *de minimis*, the entire entity is tainted.

Phase-In of the "Specified Services" Limit

In computing the qualified business income with respect to a "specified services" business, the taxpayer takes into account only the "applicable percentage" of QBI *and* the components of the W–2 Wages/Capital Investment Limit.[55]

Applicable percentage  **100%** − $\frac{\textbf{Taxable income before the QBI deduction} - \textbf{Threshold amount}}{\textbf{\$100,000 (married filing jointly); \$50,000 (others)}}$

[55] § 199A(d)(3)(B).

Example 35

In 2023, a single taxpayer has modified taxable income of $212,100, of which $150,000 is attributable to an accounting sole proprietorship that pays wages of $100,000 to employees.

The taxpayer has an applicable percentage of 40%, computed as follows:

$$\text{Applicable percentage} = 100\% - \frac{\$30{,}000\ (\$212{,}100 - \$182{,}100)}{\$50{,}000} = 40\%$$

In determining includible qualified business income, the taxpayer takes into account 40% of $150,000, or $60,000. In determining the includible W–2 wages, the taxpayer takes into account 40% of $100,000, or $40,000.

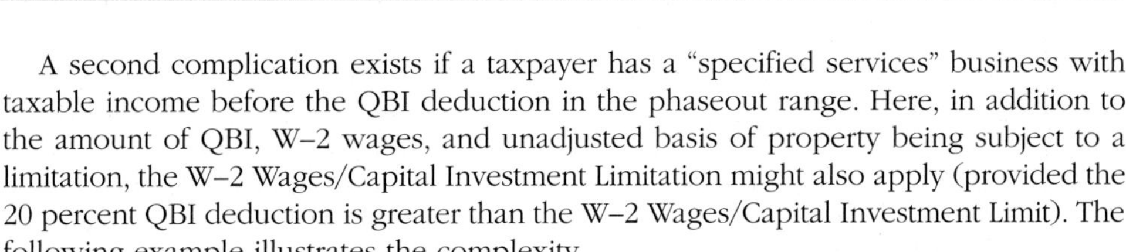

A second complication exists if a taxpayer has a "specified services" business with taxable income before the QBI deduction in the phaseout range. Here, in addition to the amount of QBI, W–2 wages, and unadjusted basis of property being subject to a limitation, the W–2 Wages/Capital Investment Limitation might also apply (provided the 20 percent QBI deduction is greater than the W–2 Wages/Capital Investment Limit). The following example illustrates the complexity.

"Specified Services" Limit

Example 36

In 2023, Jenna and Paul have taxable income before the QBI deduction (and modified taxable income) of $404,200, and Jenna is a part-time financial adviser (a "specified service trade or business") with QBI of $75,000. Jenna pays $20,000 in wages to employees and has qualified business property of $90,000.

Normally, Jenna and Paul would be entitled to a QBI deduction of $15,000 ($75,000 × 20%). But since their taxable income exceeds the threshold for married taxpayers ($364,200), their QBI deduction is limited to $7,800, computed as follows:

1. Determine Applicable Percentage:

$$\text{Applicable percentage} = 100\% - \frac{\$40{,}000\ (\$404{,}200 - \$364{,}200)}{\$100{,}000} = 60\%$$

2. Determine QBI deduction:

a. 20% of qualified business income ($75,000 × 20%)		$15,000
× Applicable percentage		× 60%
		$ 9,000
b. But no more than the *greater of*:		
• 50% of W–2 wages ($20,000 × 50% × 60%), or		$ 6,000
• 25% of W–2 wages ($20,000 × 25% × 60%) *plus*	$3,000	
• 2.5% of the unadjusted basis of qualified property ($90,000 × 2.5% × 60%)	1,350	$ 4,350

Since Jenna and Paul's taxable income before the QBI deduction exceeds $364,200 but is less than $464,200 and *the W–2 Wages/Capital Investment portion of the computation is capping the deduction*, the general 20% QBI amount is used, but reduced as follows:

1. Determine the difference between the general 20% QBI deduction amount and the W–2 Wages/Capital Investment amount:

General 20% QBI deduction amount	$ 9,000
Less: The W–2 Wages/Capital Investment Limit	(6,000)
Excess	$ 3,000

2. Determine the Reduction Ratio:

$$\text{Reduction Ratio} = \frac{\$40{,}000\ (\$404{,}200 - \$364{,}200)}{\$100{,}000} = 40\%$$

continued

3. Determine the Reduction in the W–2 Wages/Capital Investment Limit:

Excess ($3,000) × Reduction Ratio (40%) = $1,200

4. Determine Final QBI Amount:

General 20% QBI deduction amount	$ 9,000
Less: Reduction in the W–2 Wages/Capital Investment Limit	(1,200)
Final QBI amount	$ 7,800

Since the QBI amount ($7,800) is less than 20% of their modified taxable income ($80,840; $404,200 × 20%), they will be allowed a $7,800 deduction for qualified business income.

Example 37

Assume the same facts as Example 36, except that Jenna and Paul's taxable income before the QBI deduction is $480,000.

Because their modified taxable income exceeds the $464,200 threshold for married taxpayers and their only QBI is from a "specified services" business, Jenna and Paul are not allowed a QBI deduction.

Example 38

Now assume the same facts as Example 36, except that Jenna's business is a flower and gift shop (*not* a "specified services" business). As before, Jenna and Paul have modified taxable income of $404,200 and Jenna has QBI of $75,000, pays $20,000 in wages to employees, and has qualified business property of $90,000. Their QBI deduction is $13,000, computed as follows:

1. 20% of qualified business income ($75,000 × 20%)		$15,000
2. But no more than the *greater of*:		
• 50% of W–2 wages ($20,000 × 50%), or		$10,000
• 25% of W–2 wages ($20,000 × 25%) *plus*	$5,000	
• 2.5% of the unadjusted basis of qualified property ($90,000 × 2.5%)	2,250	$ 7,250
And *no more than*:		
3. 20% of modified taxable income ($404,200 x 20%)		$80,840

Since Jenna and Paul's modified taxable income exceeds $364,200 but is less than $464,200 and *the W–2 Wages/Capital Investment portion of the computation is capping the deduction*, the general 20% QBI amount is used, but reduced as follows:

1. Determine the difference between the general 20% QBI deduction amount and the W–2 Wages/Capital Investment amount:

General 20% QBI deduction amount	$ 15,000
Less: The W–2 Wages/Capital Investment Limit	(10,000)
Excess	$ 5,000

2. Determine the Reduction Ratio:

$$\text{Reduction Ratio} = \frac{\$40{,}000\ (\$404{,}200 - \$364{,}200)}{\$100{,}000} = 40\%$$

3. Determine the Reduction in the W–2 Wages/Capital Investment Limit:

Excess ($5,000) × Reduction Ratio (40%) = $2,000

4. Determine Final QBI Amount:

General 20% QBI deduction amount	$ 15,000
Less: Reduction in the W–2 Wages/Capital Investment Limit	(2,000)
Final QBI amount	$ 13,000

Since the QBI amount ($13,000) is less than 20% of their modified taxable income ($80,840; $404,200 × 20%), they will be allowed a $13,000 deduction for qualified business income.

A comparison of Examples 36 and 38 demonstrates the implications (and disadvantages) of having a "specified services" business.

An even more complex setting is having multiple businesses—some "specified services" and others not. Here, a QBI deduction is determined for each business and then combined. This "combined qualified business income amount" is then compared to the overall modified taxable income limitation.

Example 39

Chaz and Abby Klein are involved in two businesses during 2023. Chaz is a management consultant. Chaz's consulting business is an LLC (and a "specified services" business), which he reports as a sole proprietorship. The proprietorship generates qualified business income of $230,000, Chaz pays W–2 wages of $50,000 to an employee, and he has $100,000 of qualified property. Chaz and his wife, Abby, also own and operate rental properties. The couple report $186,900 of net income from their rental real estate (three rental properties that they manage; they meet the rental real estate safe harbor requirements for these rentals). They pay no wages with respect to the rental properties, and they have $450,000 of qualified property. They have no other income or deductions (and will use the standard deduction).

Their modified taxable income is $389,200 (AGI of $416,900 less their $27,700 standard deduction); this is also taxable income before the QBI deduction. The maximum QBI deduction they can claim is $77,840 ($389,200 × 20%). Because their modified taxable income is more than $364,200 and less than $464,200, both of the QBI deduction limitations apply.

Consulting ("Specified Services") Business

1. Determine Applicable Percentage:

$$\text{Applicable percentage} = 100\% - \frac{\$25{,}000\ (\$389{,}200 - \$364{,}200)}{\$100{,}000} = 75\%$$

2. Determine QBI deduction:

a. 20% of qualified business income ($230,000 × 20%)		$46,000
× Applicable percentage		× 75%
		$34,500
b. But no more than the *greater of*:		
• 50% of W–2 wages ($50,000 × 50% × 75%), or		$18,750
• 25% of W–2 wages ($50,000 × 25% × 75%) *plus*	$ 9,375	
• 2.5% of the unadjusted basis of qualified property ($100,000 × 2.5% × 75%)	1,875	$11,250

Since their taxable income before the QBI deduction exceeds $364,200 but is less than $464,200 and *the W–2 Wages/Capital Investment portion of the computation is capping the deduction*, the general 20% QBI amount is used, but reduced as follows:

1. Determine the difference between the general 20% QBI deduction amount and the W–2 Wages/Capital Investment amount:

General 20% QBI deduction amount	$ 34,500
Less: The W–2 Wages/Capital Investment Limit	(18,750)
Excess	$ 15,750

2. Determine the Reduction Ratio:

$$\text{Reduction Ratio} = \frac{\$25{,}000\ (\$389{,}200 - \$364{,}200)}{\$100{,}000} = 25\%$$

3. Determine the Reduction in the W–2 Wages/Capital Investment Limit:

Excess ($15,750) × Reduction Ratio (25%) = $3,938

4. Determine Final QBI Amount:

General 20% QBI deduction amount	$ 34,500
Less: Reduction in the W–2 Wages/Capital Investment Limit	(3,938)
Final QBI amount	$ 30,562

continued

Rentals

1. General QBI Deduction Computation:

a. 20% of qualified business income ($186,900 × 20%)		$37,380
b. But no more than the *greater of*:		
• 50% of W–2 wages ($0 × 50%), or		$ -0-
• 25% of W–2 wages ($0 × 25%) *plus*	$ -0-	
• 2.5% of the unadjusted basis of qualified property ($450,000 × 2.5%)	11,250	$11,250

Since their taxable income before the QBI deduction exceeds $364,200 but is less than $464,200 and *the W–2 Wages/Capital Investment portion of the computation is capping the deduction*, the general 20% QBI amount is used, but reduced as follows:

1. Determine the difference between the general 20% QBI deduction amount and the W–2 Wages/Capital Investment amount:

General 20% QBI deduction amount	$ 37,380
Less: The W–2 Wages/Capital Investment Limit	(11,250)
Excess	$ 26,130

2. Determine the Reduction Ratio:

$$\text{Reduction Ratio} = \frac{\$25{,}000\ (\$389{,}200 - \$364{,}200)}{\$100{,}000} = 25\%$$

3. Determine the Reduction in the W–2 Wages/Capital Investment Limit:

Excess ($26,130) × Reduction Ratio (25%) = $6,533

4. Determine Final QBI Amount:

General 20% QBI deduction amount	$37,380
Less: Reduction in the W–2 Wages/Capital Investment Limit	(6,533)
Final QBI amount	$30,847

So for Chaz and Abby, the "combined qualified income amount" is $61,409, computed as follows:

QBI amount from consulting business	$30,562
+ QBI amount from rental business	30,847
Combined qualified business income amount	$61,409

Since the combined QBI amount ($61,409) is *less than* 20% of their modified taxable income ($77,840; $389,200 × 20%), they will be allowed a $61,409 deduction for qualified business income. Their final taxable income is $327,791 ($389,200 − $61,409).

15-5h **Reporting the Qualified Business Income Deduction**

The IRS has developed a series of forms and schedules to determine and report the QBI deduction.

- **Form 8995 (Qualified Business Income Deduction Simplified Computation)** is used when taxable income before the QBI deduction is below the limitation thresholds for the year (in 2022, $340,100 for married taxpayers filing jointly and $170,050 for single and head-of-household taxpayers; $364,200 and $182,100, respectively, in 2023).

- **Form 8995–A (Qualified Business Income Deduction)** is used by taxpayers whose taxable income before the QBI deduction exceeds the limitation thresholds. A series of schedules supplement the Form 8995–A: Schedule A (Specified Service Trades or Businesses), Schedule B (Aggregation of Business Operations), Schedule C (Loss Netting and Carryforward), and Schedule D (Patrons of Agricultural or Horticultural Cooperatives).

We will use the taxpayers in Example 39 (Chaz and Abby Klein), and their 2022 information, to illustrate Form 8995–A and Schedule A (Form 8995–A).

Example 40

Chaz and Abby Klein (see Example 39) provide you with the following information on their two businesses for 2022. Chaz's proprietorship (Chaz Management Consulting LLC; EIN 32-4567890) generated qualified business income of $230,000, he paid W–2 wages of $50,000 to an employee, and he has $100,000 of qualified property. The couple reported $161,000 of net income from their real estate rentals (Abby/Chaz Real Estate Management; EIN 32-0987654). They own and manage three rental properties (meeting the rental real estate safe harbor), they pay no wages, and they have $450,000 of qualified property.

They have no other income or deductions (and will use the standard deduction). Their modified taxable income is $365,100 (AGI of $391,000 less their $25,900 standard deduction); this is also taxable income before the QBI deduction. The maximum QBI deduction they can claim is $73,020 ($365,100 × 20%). Because their 2022 modified taxable income is more than $340,100 and less than $440,100, both of the QBI deduction limitations apply. Based on the various QBI deduction limitations, their 2022 QBI deduction is $57,524 ($30,562 for Chaz's consulting business and $26,962 from their rental real estate).

Consult the completed Form 8995–A and Schedule A (Form 8995–A) to see how their QBI deduction was determined. Form 8995–A, Part I provides a summary of the Kleins' qualified trades or businesses. As indicated in Part I, taxpayers must complete any appropriate schedules before completing Form 8995–A.

Because Chaz has a "specified service" trade or business, the Kleins must begin by completing Schedule A (Form 8995–A). On Schedule A, the "applicable percentage" for Chaz's business is determined on lines 5 through 10. It is then applied to the business's QBI, W–2 wages, and qualified property. The resulting figures (on lines 11 through 13) are then transferred to Form 8995–A (Part II, Column A, lines 2, 4, and 7).

The determination of their QBI deduction now continues on Form 8995–A. The Kleins' rental real estate information is added in Column B. The remainder of Part II computes the QBI deduction for each business (including, in Part III, the phase-in reductions required because the Kleins' taxable income before the QBI deduction is greater than $340,100 but less than $440,100 in 2022). The Kleins' "combined qualified business income amount" is reported on line 16 of Part II. Part IV completes the QBI deduction determination by applying the overall limitation (based on modified taxable income). Because the Kleins are using the rental real estate safe harbor to treat their rentals as a business for § 199A purposes, they must also attach a statement to their return indicating they are using this safe harbor.

Compare the completed forms to the computational structure of the QBI deduction contained in Example 39 to see how the forms implement these computations.

15-5i Aggregation of Qualified Trades and Businesses Under the § 199A Regulations

In general, each trade or business conducted by an individual or a "relevant pass-through entity" (e.g., a partnership or an S corporation; RPE) is a separate trade or business under § 199A. However, under the § 199A Regulations, taxpayers may aggregate businesses if the following requirements are met:[56]

1. There must be control. The same person or a group of persons must own, directly or indirectly, *50 percent or more* of each business to be aggregated.[57]
    - For S corporations, ownership is measured by reference to the outstanding stock.
    - For partnerships, ownership is measured by reference to the interest in capital or profits in the partnership.
2. Control is met for the "majority" of the tax year (which must include the last day of the tax year).
3. The businesses share the same tax year.

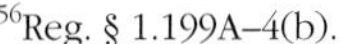

[56] Reg. § 1.199A–4(b).

[57] The § 267(b) or § 707(b) attribution rules are used for this purpose.

Form **8995-A** Department of the Treasury Internal Revenue Service

Qualified Business Income Deduction

Attach to your tax return.

Go to *www.irs.gov/Form8995A* for instructions and the latest information.

OMB No. 1545-2294 **2022** Attachment Sequence No. **55A**

Name(s) shown on return	Your taxpayer identification number
Chaz and Abby Klein	*123-45-6789*

Note: *You can claim the qualified business income deduction **only** if you have qualified business income from a qualified trade or business, real estate investment trust dividends, publicly traded partnership income, or a domestic production activities deduction passed through from an agricultural or horticultural cooperative. See instructions.*

Use this form if your taxable income, before your qualified business income deduction, is above $170,050 ($340,100 if married filing jointly), or you're a patron of an agricultural or horticultural cooperative.

Part I Trade, Business, or Aggregation Information

Complete Schedules A, B, and/or C (Form 8995-A), as applicable, before starting Part I. Attach additional worksheets when needed. See instructions.

1	(a) Trade, business, or aggregation name	(b) Check if specified service	(c) Check if aggregation	(d) Taxpayer identification number	(e) Check if patron
A	*Chaz Management Consulting LLC*	☑	☐	*32-4567890*	☐
B	*Abby/Chaz Real Estate Management*	☐	☐	*32-0987654*	☐
C		☐	☐		☐

Part II Determine Your Adjusted Qualified Business Income

			A	B	C
2	Qualified business income from the trade, business, or aggregation. See instructions	2	*172,500*	*161,000*	
3	Multiply line 2 by 20% (0.20). If your taxable income is $170,050 or less ($340,100 if married filing jointly), skip lines 4 through 12 and enter the amount from line 3 on line 13	3	*34,500*	*32,200*	
4	Allocable share of W-2 wages from the trade, business, or aggregation	4	*37,500*	*-0-*	
5	Multiply line 4 by 50% (0.50)	5	*18,750*	*-0-*	
6	Multiply line 4 by 25% (0.25)	6	*9,375*	*-0-*	
7	Allocable share of the unadjusted basis immediately after acquisition (UBIA) of all qualified property	7	*75,000*	*450,000*	
8	Multiply line 7 by 2.5% (0.025)	8	*1,875*	*11,250*	
9	Add lines 6 and 8	9	*11,250*	*11,250*	
10	Enter the greater of line 5 or line 9	10	*18,750*	*11,250*	
11	W-2 wage and UBIA of qualified property limitation. Enter the smaller of line 3 or line 10	11	*18,750*	*11,250*	
12	Phased-in reduction. Enter the amount from line 26, if any	12	*30,562*	*26,962*	
13	Qualified business income deduction before patron reduction. Enter the greater of line 11 or line 12	13	*30,562*	*26,962*	
14	Patron reduction. Enter the amount from Schedule D (Form 8995-A), line 6, if any. See instructions	14	*-0-*	*-0-*	
15	Qualified business income component. Subtract line 14 from line 13	15	*30,562*	*26,962*	
16	Total qualified business income component. Add all amounts reported on line 15	16	*57,524*		

For Privacy Act and Paperwork Reduction Act Notice, see separate instructions. Cat. No. 71661B Form **8995-A** (2022)

Form 8995-A (2022) Page **2**

Part III Phased-in Reduction

Complete Part III only if your taxable income is more than $170,050 but not $220,050 ($340,100 and $440,100 if married filing jointly) and line 10 is less than line 3. Otherwise, skip Part III.

					A	B	C
17	Enter the amounts from line 3			**17**	*34,500*	*32,200*	
18	Enter the amounts from line 10			**18**	*18,750*	*11,250*	
19	Subtract line 18 from line 17			**19**	*15,750*	*20,950*	
20	Taxable income before qualified business income deduction	**20**	*365,100*				
21	Threshold. Enter $170,050 ($340,100 if married filing jointly)	**21**	*340,200*				
22	Subtract line 21 from line 20	**22**	*25,000*				
23	Phase-in range. Enter $50,000 ($100,000 if married filing jointly)	**23**	*100,000*				
24	Phase-in percentage. Divide line 22 by line 23	**24**	*25%*				
25	Total phase-in reduction. Multiply line 19 by line 24			**25**	*3,938*	*5,238*	
26	Qualified business income after phase-in reduction. Subtract line 25 from line 17. Enter this amount here and on line 12, for the corresponding trade or business			**26**	*30,562*	*26,962*	

Part IV Determine Your Qualified Business Income Deduction

27	Total qualified business income component from all qualified trades, businesses, or aggregations. Enter the amount from line 16	**27**	*57,524*		
28	Qualified REIT dividends and publicly traded partnership (PTP) income or (loss). See instructions	**28**	*-0-*		
29	Qualified REIT dividends and PTP (loss) carryforward from prior years	**29**	( )		
30	Total qualified REIT dividends and PTP income. Combine lines 28 and 29. If less than zero, enter -0-	**30**	*-0-*		
31	REIT and PTP component. Multiply line 30 by 20% (0.20)	**31**	*-0-*		
32	Qualified business income deduction before the income limitation. Add lines 27 and 31			**32**	*57,524*
33	Taxable income before qualified business income deduction	**33**	*365,100*		
34	Net capital gain. See instructions	**34**	*-0-*		
35	Subtract line 34 from line 33. If zero or less, enter -0-			**35**	*365,100*
36	Income limitation. Multiply line 35 by 20% (0.20)			**36**	*73,020*
37	Qualified business income deduction before the domestic production activities deduction (DPAD) under section 199A(g). Enter the smaller of line 32 or line 36			**37**	*57,524*
38	DPAD under section 199A(g) allocated from an agricultural or horticultural cooperative. Don't enter more than line 33 minus line 37			**38**	*-0-*
39	Total qualified business income deduction. Add lines 37 and 38			**39**	*57,524*
40	Total qualified REIT dividends and PTP (loss) carryforward. Combine lines 28 and 29. If zero or greater, enter -0-			**40**	(*-0-*)

Form **8995-A** (2022)

SCHEDULE A (Form 8995-A)

Department of the Treasury
Internal Revenue Service

Specified Service Trades or Businesses

Attach to Form 8995-A.
Go to *www.irs.gov/Form8995A* for instructions and the latest information.

OMB No. 1545-2294
2022
Attachment Sequence No. **55B**

Name(s) shown on return	Your taxpayer identification number
Chaz and Abby Klein	*123-45-6789*

Complete Schedule A only if your trade or business is a specified service trade or business (see instructions) and your taxable income is more than $170,050 but not $220,050 ($340,100 and $440,100 if married filing jointly). If your taxable income isn't more than $170,050 ($340,100 if married filing jointly) and you're not a patron of an agricultural or horticultural cooperative, don't file this form; instead, file Form 8995, Qualified Business Income Deduction Simplified Computation. Otherwise, complete Schedule D (Form 8995-A) before beginning Schedule A. If your taxable income is more than $220,050 ($440,100 if married filing jointly), your specified service trade or business doesn't qualify for the deduction. If you have more than three trades or businesses, attach as many Schedules A as needed. See instructions.

Part I Other Than Publicly Traded Partnerships (PTP)

See instructions before completing Parts I and II.

				A	B	C
1a	Trade or business name		**1a**	*Chaz Management Consulting LLC*		
b	Taxpayer identification number		**1b**	*32-4567890*		
2	Qualified business income or (loss) from the trade or business		**2**	*230,000*		
3	Allocable share of W-2 wages from the trade or business		**3**	*50,000*		
4	Allocable share of the unadjusted basis immediately after acquisition (UBIA) of all qualified property		**4**	*100,000*		
5	Taxable income before qualified business income deduction	**5**	*365,100*			
6	Threshold. Enter $170,050 ($340,100 if married filing jointly)	**6**	*340,100*			
7	Subtract line 6 from line 5	**7**	*25,000*			
8	Phase-in range. Enter $50,000 ($100,000 if married filing jointly)	**8**	*100,000*			
9	Divide line 7 by line 8	**9**	*25%*			
10	Applicable percentage. Subtract line 9 from 100%	**10**	*75%*			
11	Applicable percentage of qualified business income or (loss). Multiply line 2 by line 10. Enter this amount on Schedule C (Form 8995-A) or on Form 8995-A, line 2, for the corresponding trade or business, as appropriate		**11**	*172,500*		
12	Applicable percentage of W-2 wages. Multiply line 3 by line 10. Enter this amount on Form 8995-A, line 4, for the corresponding trade or business, as appropriate		**12**	*37,500*		
13	Applicable percentage of the UBIA of qualified property. Multiply line 4 by line 10. Enter this amount on Form 8995-A, line 7, for the corresponding trade or business, as appropriate		**13**	*75,000*		

Part II Publicly Traded Partnership

			A	B	C
14	Trade or business name	**14**			
15	Taxpayer identification number	**15**			
16	Qualified PTP income or (loss)	**16**			

17	Total PTP specified service trade or business (SSTB) income or (loss). Combine all amounts on line 16	**17**	
18	Taxable income before qualified business income deduction	**18**	
19	Threshold. Enter $170,050 ($340,100 if married filing jointly)	**19**	
20	Subtract line 19 from line 18	**20**	
21	Phase-in range. Enter $50,000 ($100,000 if married filing jointly)	**21**	
22	Divide line 20 by line 21	**22**	
23	Applicable percentage. Subtract line 22 from 100%	**23**	%
24	Applicable percentage of qualified PTP income or (loss). Multiply line 17 by line 23. Include this amount on Form 8995-A, line 28	**24**	

For Privacy Act and Paperwork Reduction Act Notice, see separate instructions. Cat. No. 72681D **Schedule A (Form 8995-A) 2022**

4. None of the businesses are "specified services" businesses.
5. The businesses to be aggregated must satisfy two of the following three factors:
   - They must provide products or services that are the same or customarily offered together.
   - They must share facilities or significant centralized business elements, such as personnel, accounting, legal, manufacturing, purchasing, human resources, or information technology resources.
   - The businesses are operated in coordination with, or reliance upon, one or more of the businesses in the aggregated group.

Aggregation can be done by either an owner or an RPE.[58] If an RPE chooses to aggregate, the owners of the RPE are bound by that aggregation.[59] If an RPE does not aggregate, the RPE owners need not aggregate in the same manner. As a result, one owner may choose to aggregate that business with another business while a second owner may not choose to do so.

Aggregation is optional and generally cannot be changed once businesses are aggregated.[60] An individual (or RPE) may add a newly created (or acquired) business to the aggregation provided all of the requirements (above) are met.[61] If, in a subsequent year, there is a change in facts and circumstances indicating that a prior aggregation is no longer allowed, the aggregation is terminated and the taxpayer must reapply the aggregation rules to see if aggregation is allowed.

If businesses are aggregated, the taxpayer determines his or her share of qualified business income, W–2 wages, and property basis for the aggregated businesses before computing the QBI deduction.

Aggregating QTBs

Example 41

Anita wholly owns and operates a catering business and a restaurant through separate entities. The catering business and the restaurant share centralized purchasing to obtain volume discounts and a centralized accounting office that performs all of the bookkeeping, tracks and issues statements on all of the receivables, and prepares the payroll for each business. Anita maintains a website and print advertising materials that reference both the catering business and the restaurant. She uses the restaurant kitchen to prepare food for the catering business. The catering business employs its own staff and owns equipment and trucks that are not used by the restaurant.

Because the restaurant and catering business are held in separate entities, Anita will be treated as operating each of these businesses directly. Both businesses offer prepared food to customers. The two businesses share the same kitchen facilities in addition to centralized purchasing, marketing, and accounting. As a result, Anita may choose to treat the catering business and restaurant as a single trade or business in determining her QBI deduction.

Example 42

Assume the same facts as in the previous example. However, the catering and restaurant businesses are operated in separate partnerships with Anita, Ben, Carole, and David each owning a 25% interest in the capital and profits of each partnership. The partners are unrelated.

Because Anita, Ben, Carole, and David together own more than 50% of the capital and profits in each of the partnerships, *each* may choose to treat the catering business and the restaurant as a single trade or business in determining their QBI deduction. Further, if Anita chooses to aggregate the businesses, her decision has no effect on what Ben, Carole, and David may (independently) choose to do.

Wanda owns a 75% interest in Sunshine, Inc., (a clothing manufacturer operating as an S corporation) and a 75% interest in PetFriendly (a retail pet food store operating as a partnership). Wanda manages both businesses, but they operate in separate facilities, with no overlap of business operations, and do not coordinate or rely on each other.

As a result, Wanda must treat the two businesses separately for purposes of determining the QBI deduction.

---

[58] Reg. § 1.199A–4(b)(2).

[59] Reg. § 1.199A–4(b)(2)(ii).

[60] Reg. § 1.199A–4(a). According to Reg. §§ 1.199A–4(c)(2) and (4), if aggregation occurs, an individual must attach a statement to his or her income tax return *each year* identifying each aggregated trade or business (an RPE must attach this statement to each owner's Schedule K–1). Failure to disclose this information may result in the IRS not permitting the aggregation.

[61] Reg. §§ 1.199A–4(c)(1) and (3).

Here is a key point: The owner does *not* have to own more than 50 percent of each business directly; rather, the owner must simply establish that a group of persons owns 50 percent or more of all of the entities the owner wants to aggregate.

Frank owns a 75% interest and Geoff owns a 5% interest in each of five partnerships. Helen owns a 10% interest in only two of the partnerships. Each partnership operates a restaurant, each restaurant is a trade or business, and there is centralized management across the restaurants (Geoff is the executive chef of all of the restaurants, and he creates the menus and orders all of the food and related supplies).

Frank may choose to aggregate all five partnerships. Geoff may do the same even though he only owns a 5% interest in each partnership (Geoff can show that Frank owns 50% or more of each of the partnerships; as a result, they are "commonly controlled"). Helen may only aggregate the two partnerships in which she has an interest.

In order to include a business within an aggregated group, the activity must rise to the level of a trade or business under § 162.

Jennifer owns a majority interest in a sailboat racing team; she also owns an interest in JB Marina (a partnership that operates a marina). JB Marina is a trade or business under § 162, but the operations of the sailboat racing team are not sufficient to establish a trade or business under § 162.

As a result, Jennifer has only one trade or business for purposes of § 199A and cannot aggregate her interest in the sailboat racing team with her interest in JB Marina.

15-5j Treatment of Losses

If a taxpayer has a qualified business loss in one year, no QBI deduction is allowed, and the loss is carried over to the next year to reduce QBI (but not below zero).[62] Further, the statute indicates that if a taxpayer has more than one QTB and the net results of all businesses create a loss, the net loss is carried forward to the following year. Here is an example from the TCJA of 2017 Conference Report.

A taxpayer has QBI of $20,000 from qualified business A and a qualified business loss of $50,000 from qualified business B in 2022. The taxpayer is not permitted a deduction for 2022 and has a carryover qualified business loss of $30,000 to 2023.

In 2023, the taxpayer has QBI of $20,000 from qualified business A and QBI of $50,000 from qualified business B. To determine the deduction for 2023, the taxpayer reduces the 20% deductible amount determined for the QBI of $70,000 from qualified businesses A and B by 20% of the $30,000 carryover qualified business loss.

The result is that the taxpayer has a QBI deduction in 2023 of $8,000 [($20,000 + $50,000) − $30,000 = $40,000 × 20% = $8,000].

The statute and Conference Report provided no guidance, however, on what happens when there is a loss from one QTB and net income from another QTB that nets to a *positive amount*. Fortunately, the § 199A Regulations provide the guidance needed.[63] The Regulations begin by restating the general rule of § 199A(c)(2): if the net amount of all positive and negative QBI is a loss, no § 199A deduction is allowed in the current year and the net loss is carried forward to the next year. The Regulations also indicate that the § 199A loss limitation has no effect on the availability of the loss for other purposes (e.g., reducing taxable income and/or creating a net operating loss). The Regulations make clear, however, that no W–2 wages or capital investment amounts carry forward—only the loss.

[62] § 199A(c)(2).

[63] Reg. § 1.199A–1(d)(2)(iii).

Where a taxpayer's netting of all positive and negative QBI is positive, and at least one business produces negative QBI, an "adjusted QBI" is determined by allocating the negative QBI among all of the businesses that produce QBI in proportion to their respective amounts of QBI. Only *after* this allocation and netting takes place are the W–2 wages and capital investment limitations applied, and no part of the W–2 wages or capital investment amounts related to the loss business are used by the businesses with positive QBI.[64] By requiring the allocation of the loss across all of the businesses that generate QBI, the § 199A Regulations prevent taxpayers from selectively allocating the loss to businesses that will have limited (or no) QBI deduction (e.g., taxpayers above the threshold amount with businesses that pay no W–2 wages).

Multiple Businesses and Negative QBI

Example 47

Erica, who is single, operates three sole proprietorships that generate the following information in 2023 (none are "specified services" businesses):

Business	QBI	W–2 Wages	Capital Investment
A	$200,000	$60,000	$ -0-
B	100,000	-0-	-0-
C	20,000	40,000	-0-

Erica chooses not to aggregate the businesses. She also earns $250,000 of wages from an unrelated business, and her modified taxable income (before any QBI deduction) is $520,000.

Because Erica's taxable income is above the threshold amount, her QBI deduction is subject to the W–2 Wages/Capital Investment limitations. These limitations must be applied on a business-by-business basis. None of the businesses own "qualified property." As a result, only the "W–2 Wages" limitation applies.

Because QBI from each business is positive, Erica applies the limitation by determining the lesser of 20% of QBI and 50% of W–2 wages for each business.

Business	QBI × 20%	W–2 Wages × 50%	Lesser
A	$40,000	$30,000	$30,000
B	20,000	-0-	-0-
C	4,000	20,000	4,000

Erica's "combined qualified business income amount" is $34,000 ($30,000 + $0 + $4,000). Since this amount is less than 20% of Erica's modified taxable income ($104,000; $520,000 × 20%), her QBI deduction is $34,000 and her taxable income is $486,000.

Example 48

Assume the same facts as in Example 47, except that Business C generates a loss that results in ($90,000) of negative QBI.

Business	QBI	W–2 Wages	Capital Investment
A	$200,000	$60,000	$ -0-
B	100,000	-0-	-0-
C	(90,000)	40,000	-0-

Erica chooses not to aggregate the businesses. Erica also earns $250,000 of wages from an unrelated business, and her modified taxable income (before any QBI deduction) is $410,000.

Absent the rules provided by the § 199A Regulations, Erica would allocate the Business C negative QBI to Business B. Why? Since Erica's income is over the threshold amount and Business B pays no wages, Business B will not generate a QBI deduction. By offsetting the Business C negative QBI against Business B's positive QBI, Erica maximizes her QBI deduction on Business A.

continued

[64] Reg. § 1.199A–1(d)(2)(iii)(A).

However, under the § 199A Regulations, Erica is not allowed to choose where to allocate Business C's negative QBI. Erica must allocate Business C's negative QBI to Business A and Business B in proportion to their positive QBI amounts ($200,000 for Business A and $100,000 for Business B). As a result, the negative QBI from Business C is apportioned 66.66% to Business A and 33.33% to Business B. So ($60,000) is apportioned to Business A and ($30,000) to Business B.

Business	Adjusted QBI	W–2 Wages	Capital Investment
A	$140,000 ($200,000 − $60,000)	$60,000	$ -0-
B	$70,000 ($100,000 − $30,000)	-0-	-0-
C	$-0- [($90,000) + $90,000]	40,000	-0-

Erica now applies the "W–2 Wages" limitation by determining the lesser of 20% of QBI and 50% of W–2 wages for each business.

Business	QBI × 20%	W–2 Wages × 50%	Lesser
A	$28,000 ($140,000 × 20%)	$30,000	$28,000
B	$14,000 ($70,000 × 20%)	-0-	-0-
C	$ -0-	20,000	-0-

Erica's "combined qualified business income amount" is $28,000 ($28,000 + $0 + $0). Since this amount is less than 20% of Erica's modified taxable income ($82,000; $410,000 × 20%), her QBI deduction is $28,000, and her taxable income is $382,000. There is no carryover of any loss into the following taxable year for purposes of § 199A (the Business C negative QBI was completely used).

Example 49

Assume the same facts as in Example 48, except that Businesses A, B, and C meet the aggregation requirements of Reg. § 1.199A–4 and Erica chooses to aggregate the three businesses.

Because Erica's taxable income is above the threshold amount, her QBI deduction is subject to the W–2 wages and capital investment limitations. Because the businesses are aggregated, these limitations are applied on an *aggregated* basis.

Business	QBI	W–2 Wages	Capital Investment
A	$200,000	$ 60,000	$ -0-
B	100,000	-0-	-0-
C	(90,000)	40,000	-0-
Total	$210,000	$100,000	$ -0-

None of the businesses own "qualified property." As a result, only the "W–2 Wages" limitation applies. Erica's "combined qualified income amount" is $42,000, the lesser of 20% of the QBI from the aggregated businesses ($42,000; $210,000 × 20%), or 50% of W–2 wages from the aggregated businesses ($50,000; $100,000 × 50%).

Erica then applies the overall limitation, comparing her "combined qualified income amount" ($42,000) to 20% of her modified taxable income ($82,000; $410,000 × 20%). Erica's QBI deduction is $42,000 (the lesser of $42,000 or $82,000).

Note that by aggregating her businesses, Erica has increased the amount of her QBI deduction.

15-5k **Coordination with Other Rules**

The deduction for qualified business income operates along with other rules (e.g., how to determine business income). In other cases, Congress specified the treatment. For example, § 199A(f)(3) provides that the QBI deduction is allowed only for *income* taxes. As a result, the QBI deduction does not reduce the tax bases for self-employment taxes or the net investment income tax (NIIT).

Also, in computing an individual's alternative minimum taxable income (AMTI), qualified business income is not changed by any of the AMT's preferences or adjustments (like depreciation) that usually apply in determining AMTI.[65]

[65] § 199A(f)(2). The alternative minimum tax is discussed in text Section 12-5d.

15-5l Considerations for Partnerships and S Corporations

The deduction for qualified business income applies to taxpayers other than corporations. As a result, the QBI deduction is available to individuals, trusts, and estates. As explained earlier, C corporations received a tax benefit via the reduction in income tax rates to 21 percent.

Although the earlier examples involved sole proprietors, the same result would occur if the business income was instead generated by a partnership or an S corporation. These entities will need to report information to their owners (on the Schedule K–1) to enable the owners to compute their QBI deduction. The QBI deduction will vary among owners even if they share equally in the net earnings of the partnership or S corporation because the taxable income of owners will vary.

AB Partnership operates an accounting practice that is equally owned by two CPAs, Ava and Barbara. In 2023, partnership income is $340,000 and no guaranteed payments are made to the partners. Both Ava and Barbara are married and file jointly with their spouses. Ava's spouse has wage income of $80,000, and Barbara's spouse has wage income of $300,000. Assume that each couple has other income equal to their standard deduction amount.

The CPA practice is a "specified services" trade or business. Limitations on the QBI deduction will apply if the taxpayer's taxable income exceeds $364,200 if married filing jointly, and no deduction will be available if the couple's taxable income exceeds $464,200.

Ava and her spouse have taxable income of $250,000 ($170,000 partnership income + $80,000 of wage income). They may claim a QBI deduction. In contrast, Barbara and her spouse have taxable income of $470,000 ($170,000 partnership income + $300,000 of wage income). This couple may *not* claim a QBI deduction.

Unlike sole proprietors, partnerships and S corporations might use a tax year other than a calendar year. Because the QBI deduction is claimed by the individual owner rather than the entity, the information needed for the owner to compute the QBI deduction on his or her calendar year tax return follows the same protocol as all other entity items reported on the Schedule K–1 (see text Section 21-2g).

Grover Partnership is owned by two individuals and a C corporation. The individuals, Jordan and Imani, each own 20%, and Elmer, Inc., owns 60%. Elmer uses a June 30 fiscal year, which also requires Grover to use a June 30 fiscal year (because Elmer is the majority interest partner).

When Jordan and Imani received their Schedule K–1s from Grover for the partnership ended June 30, 2018, all of the information was reported on their 2018 tax returns. And all of this information was included in the calculation of their 2018 QBI deduction even though this partnership information includes six months of activity from 2017 before the QBI deduction was effective.

The QBI deduction is in effect for 2018 through 2025 (eight years). Assuming that there is no change in the tax year of Grover Partnership and Jordan and Imani remain partners, they will obtain eight years of QBI deductions consisting of information from the partnership years ending in 2018 through 2025. They will not receive a QBI deduction for Grover's activity for the year ended June 30, 2026, even though it includes six months of 2025.

15-5m Other Items in the § 199A Regulations

Employee Turned Independent Contractor

The § 199A Regulations indicate that the status of an individual as an employee or independent contractor is determined by common law and statutory rules.[66] However, under the Regulations, an individual who was an employee of an employer and becomes an independent contractor while providing substantially the same services (either directly or indirectly through another entity) is presumed, for a three-year period, still to be an employee.[67] This presumption may be overturned if it can be demonstrated—using common law and statutory rules—that the individual is *not* an employee.

---

[66] See, for example, Rev.Rul. 87–41 and Reg. §§ 31.3121(d)–1, 31.3306(i)–1, and 31.3401(c)–1.

[67] Reg. § 1.199A–5(d)(3).

Example 52

Corbin is an attorney employed as an associate with LegalEagles LLP (LE). Corbin and the other associates in LE have taxable income below the threshold amount. LE terminates its employment relationship with Corbin and its other associates, allowing Corbin and the other former associates to form a new partnership, LegalBeagles LLP (LB). LB then contracts to perform services to LE. Corbin continues to provide substantially the same services to LE and its clients through LB.

The goal, obviously, is for Corbin (and the other associates) to convert wage income into pass-through income from LB that is eligible for the QBI deduction (even though LB is a "specified services" business, Corbin is below the taxable income threshold).

Because Corbin was formerly an employee of LE and continues to provide substantially the same services to LE, Corbin is presumed to be an employee of LE. Unless the presumption is rebutted, Corbin's distributive share of income from LB will be treated like wages for purposes of § 199A for a period of three years and will not be treated as qualified business income.

What if LB, instead, provides contractual services to a *different* law firm? Now the QBI deduction is available (again assuming that Corbin is below the taxable income threshold).

Determination of "W–2 Wages"

In general, the term *W–2 wages* includes the total amount of wages [as defined in § 3401(a)] plus the total amount of elective compensation deferrals (under § 457) plus the amount of designated Roth contributions (§ 402A).[68]

A business can take into account any W–2 wages paid by another business provided that the W–2 wages were paid to "common law employees or officers" of that business.[69] This means that a business using a professional employer organization (PEO) to manage parts of its business (e.g., human resources) or to lease employees can use an allocable portion of the PEO's W–2 wages in determining its total W–2 wages. Of course, this also means that the business that actually paid and reported the W–2 wages must reduce its § 199A wages by the same amount.

Determination of Unadjusted Basis Immediately After Acquisition (UBIA)

For purchased or produced property, UBIA generally will be the property's cost (under § 1012) when the property is placed in service. An addition or improvement to qualified property already placed in service is treated as *separate qualified property* on the date the addition or improvement is placed in service.[70] For purposes of the QBI deduction, property is not qualified property if it is acquired within 60 days of the end of the tax year and disposed of within 120 days without having been used in a trade or business for at least 45 days prior to disposition, unless the taxpayer demonstrates that the principal purpose of the acquisition and disposition was a purpose other than increasing the QBI deduction.[71]

LO.5

List and evaluate tax planning ideas for choice of entity and the deduction for qualified business income.

15-6 Tax Planning

15-6a Corporate versus Noncorporate Forms of Business Organization

The form of business organization is an important tax planning consideration. It affects the application of various tax rules including tax rates, deductions, tax accounting methods, and tax years. The decision on what form to use can change as a business grows. For example, in the early years of a business (when it is more likely to generate losses), a pass-through entity is usually desired so that individual owners can utilize the losses generated by the business. If instead the entity was a C corporation from the beginning, it would not be able to use the losses until later years when it generates taxable income.

[68] Reg. § 1.199A–2(b)(2). Notice 2018–64 and Rev.Proc. 2019–11 provide detailed guidance about calculating "W–2 wages" for purposes of the QBI deduction.

[69] Reg. § 1.199A–2(b)(2)(ii).

[70] Reg. § 1.199A–2(c)(1)(ii).

[71] Reg. § 1.199A–2(c)(1)(iv).

15-6b **Optimizing the Deduction for Qualified Business Income**

As noted in a few of the QBI deduction examples, some planning is possible to increase the deduction or perhaps to avoid losing the deduction.

- For taxpayers with taxable income above the thresholds ($364,200 if married filing jointly and $182,100 for single and head-of-household taxpayers in 2023), consider converting any contractor payments to employee wages to increase the 50 percent of W–2 wages limitation.
- For a married couple who does not reside in a community property state and has "specified services" business income above the thresholds that allow a QBI deduction, determine whether it might be better to file separate tax returns, enabling the spouse with QBI to qualify for the QBI deduction.
- Given the § 199A Regulations, consider how businesses can be combined or separated, including perhaps placing one or more in separate legal entities, to increase the QBI deduction.
- Employees might consider whether they can become self-employed in their field (which would enable the QBI deduction). As part of this consideration, the employee will need to consider whether it is possible to generate greater income tax savings via the QBI deduction (and other business deductions). Also important will be considering the effect of self-employment taxes and the need to provide health insurance and other benefits, as well as potentially incurring additional business expenses.

Refocus on The Big Picture

Entrepreneurial Pursuits

JOESAPHOTOS/SHUTTERSTOCK.COM

The simplest entity for Amy to use is a sole proprietorship. If she generates losses, they can be used to offset other income she might have (e.g., if she also takes on a part-time job until her businesses generate sufficient income to enable Amy to support herself).

If the risks for her business, such as injury to customers, are minimal, she will likely find that forming an LLC or a corporation to reduce her personal risk is not warranted. The additional formation costs, continuing fees, and possible business taxes she might owe in her state of residence can be avoided. And Amy can purchase insurance to reduce the costs of any personal risk.

If Amy wants a more formal structure or a legal structure to reduce her personal risk, an S corporation should work well since it allows her income and losses to flow through to her individual tax return. As Amy's income grows, she might consider converting to a C corporation due to the 21 percent maximum rate, although she must also consider the effect of double taxation.

Amy must also consider the QBI deduction (assuming that she does not operate as a C corporation). Until her income reaches the thresholds for the specified service trade or business, she should obtain a deduction even though her pursuits might be a "specified services" business (i.e., consulting or where the principal business asset is Amy's reputation or skill).

Finally, Amy should consider state and local taxes. She will need to check these laws to determine, for example, if a business license tax is owed. Although her NIL royalties might not create a trade or business, she will be subject to Federal income tax on this income. In addition, she will be subject to state and local income taxes (and these taxes might be assessed on any income allocable to locations where she plays volleyball).

Key Terms

C corporations, 15-7
Check-the-box Regulations, 15-12
Conduit perspective, 15-2
Deduction for qualified business income, 15-13
Disregarded entity, 15-12
Entity perspective, 15-2
Limited liability company (LLC), 15-3
Limited liability partnership (LLP), 15-3
Limited partnership (LP), 15-2
Publicly traded partnership (PTP), 15-3
QBI deduction, 15-13
Qualified business income, 15-14
Qualified trade or business, 15-15
Regular corporations, 15-7
S corporations, 15-7
Specified service trade or business, 15-22
W–2 Wages/Capital Investment Limit, 15-18

Discussion Questions

1. **LO.1** Jennifer and Jamie are starting a business and have asked you for advice about whether they should form a partnership, a corporation, or some other type of entity. Prepare a list of questions you would ask in helping them decide which type of entity they should choose. Explain your reasons for asking each of the questions.

2. **LO.1** Brianna owns 40% of the stock of Cassowary Corporation (a C corporation) and 40% of the stock of Emu Corporation (an S corporation). In the current year, each corporation has operating income of $120,000 and tax-exempt interest income of $8,000. Neither corporation pays any dividends during the year. Discuss how this information will be reported by the corporations and Brianna for the year.

Critical Thinking
Planning

3. **LO.1, 5** Art, an executive with Azure Corporation, plans to start a part-time business selling products on the internet. He will devote about 15 hours each week to running the business. Art's salary from Azure places him in the 35% tax bracket. He projects substantial losses from the new business in each of the first three years and expects sizable profits thereafter. Art plans to leave the profits in the business for several years, sell the business, and then retire. Would you advise Art to incorporate the business or operate it as a sole proprietorship? Why?

4. **LO.1** Can a sole proprietor form as a single member limited liability company (LLC)? If so, how would such an LLC be taxed?

5. **LO.1** In the current year, Juanita and Joseph form a two-member LLC and do not file Form 8832 (Entity Classification Election). As a result, the LLC will be treated as a partnership for Federal income tax purposes. Assess the validity of this statement.

6. **LO.2** Why did Congress decide to provide a deduction for qualified business income?

7. **LO.3** Who can claim the qualified business income (QBI) deduction?

8. **LO.4** What are the general rules surrounding the QBI deduction? How is it computed?

9. **LO.3, 4** Define each of the following terms, and explain how each is used in determining the QBI deduction.
   a. Modified taxable income.
   b. Qualified business income.
   c. Qualified trade or business.
   d. "Specified services" business.

Critical Thinking
Planning

10. **LO.3, 4, 5** Jane and Ben are married and usually file a joint return. They live in a separate property state (rather than a community property state). Jane is a partner in a law firm and typically generates income of $178,000. Ben is a grade school teacher with wage income of $75,000. The couple has investment income that

is less than their standard deduction. With enactment of the deduction for qualified business income, the couple is wondering if they should continue to file as married filing jointly or instead use the married filing separately status. Why do they wonder this, and what advice would you offer them and why?

11. **LO.3, 4** Which of the following taxpayers may claim a deduction for qualified business income?

    a. A driver for Uber or Lyft.

    b. A veterinarian operating as an S corporation. In addition to veterinary services, revenues are also derived from the sale of pet food and supplies and from the boarding of animals.

    c. A CPA operating as an LLC taxed as a sole proprietorship. The CPA is single and has taxable income of $150,000.

    d. Same as part (c), except that the CPA has taxable income of $200,000.

    e. A real estate salesperson.

    f. A pet sitter/dog walker.

    g. A sole proprietor software developer.

    h. An individual wage earner who derives $60,000 of rental income from a duplex she owns.

12. **LO.3, 4** Identify the requirements that must be met in order to aggregate businesses for purposes of the QBI deduction.

13. **LO.3, 4** Paul wholly owns and operates an office supplies business and a printing/shipping business through separate entities. The office supplies business and printing/shipping business share centralized purchasing to obtain volume discounts and also share a centralized accounting office that performs all necessary accounting for both businesses (including preparing financial statements, paying bills, collecting receivables, and preparing payrolls for both businesses). Paul maintains a website that promotes both businesses. The businesses operate in separate spaces in the same building (next to each other) but share an office and a shipping/receiving space at the rear of the building and an opening in the shared inside wall that allows customers to move between the businesses without going outside. Each business owns its own equipment and employs its own staff. May Paul aggregate these businesses for purposes of the QBI deduction? Explain.

14. **LO.2, 4** Why do you think the QBI deduction is limited to earnings from a business conducted in the United States and doesn't also include business income from a foreign business activity?

Computational Exercises

15. **LO.3, 4** In 2023, Meghann, a single taxpayer, has QBI of $110,000 and modified taxable income of $78,000 (this is also her taxable income before the QBI deduction). Given this information, what is Meghann's QBI deduction?

16. **LO.3, 4** Charlotte is a partner in, and sales manager for, CD Partners, a domestic business that is not a "specified services" business. During the tax year, she receives guaranteed payments of $250,000 from CD Partners for her services to the partnership as its sales manager. In addition, her distributive share of CD Partners' ordinary income (its only item of income or loss) was $175,000. What is Charlotte's qualified business income?

Critical Thinking

17. **LO.3, 4** Robert is the sole shareholder and CEO of ABC, Inc., an S corporation that is a qualified trade or business. During the current year, ABC has net income of $325,000 after deducting Robert's $100,000 salary. In addition to his compensation, ABC pays Robert dividends of $250,000.
    a. What is Robert's qualified business income?
    b. Would your answer to part (a) change if you determined that reasonable compensation for someone with Robert's experience and responsibilities is $200,000? Why or why not?

Critical Thinking

18. **LO.3, 4, 5** Maria and Javier are the equal partners in MarJa, a partnership that is a qualified trade or business. In the current year, MarJa had $350,000 of ordinary income after reporting $500,000 in guaranteed payments to Maria and Javier for their services to MarJa ($250,000 each).
    a. What is Maria's and Javier's qualified business income?
    b. How would your answer to part (a) change if MarJa had $550,000 of ordinary income after reporting $300,000 in guaranteed payments to Maria and Javier ($150,000 each)?

19. **LO.3, 4** Thad, a single taxpayer, has taxable income before the QBI deduction of $212,100. Thad, a CPA, operates an accounting practice as a single member LLC (which he reports as a sole proprietorship). During 2023, his proprietorship generates qualified business income of $150,000, W–2 wages of $125,000, and $10,000 of qualified property. What is Thad's qualified business income deduction?

20. **LO.3, 4** Jason and Paula are married. They file a joint return for 2023 on which they report taxable income before the QBI deduction of $200,000. Jason operates a sole proprietorship, and Paula is a partner in the PQRS Partnership. Both are a qualified trade or business, and neither is a "specified services" business. Jason's sole proprietorship generates $150,000 of qualified business income and W–2 wages of $45,000 and has qualified property of $50,000. Paula's partnership reports a loss for the year, and her allocable share of the loss is $40,000. The partnership reports no W–2 wages, and Paula's share of the partnership's qualified property is $20,000. What is their QBI deduction for the year?

21. **LO.3, 4** In 2022, Henry Jones (Social Security number 123-45-6789) works as a freelance driver, finding customers using various platforms like Uber and Grubhub. He is single and has no other sources of income. In 2022, Henry's qualified business income from driving is $61,200.
    a. Compute Henry's QBI deduction and his tax liability for 2022.
    b. Complete Henry's 2022 Form 8995 (Qualified Business Income Deduction Simplified Computation).

Problems

Critical Thinking

22. **LO.1** Ellie and YiLing are equal owners in Otter Enterprises, a calendar year business. During the current year, Otter Enterprises has $320,000 of gross income and $210,000 of operating expenses. In addition, Otter has a long-term capital gain of $15,000 and makes distributions to Ellie and YiLing of $25,000 each. Discuss the impact of this information on the taxable income of Otter, Ellie, and YiLing if Otter is:
    a. A partnership.
    b. An S corporation.
    c. A C corporation.

Critical Thinking

23. **LO.1** In 2023, Purple Company reports $200,000 in net income before deducting any compensation or other payment to its sole owner, Kirsten. Kirsten is single and she claims the $13,850 standard deduction for 2023 (she has no other deductions).

Purple Company is Kirsten's only source of income. Ignoring any employment tax considerations, compute Kirsten's after-tax income if:

a. Purple Company is a proprietorship and Kirsten withdraws $50,000 from the business during the year; Kirsten claims a $37,230 deduction for qualified business income.

b. Purple Company is a C corporation and the corporation pays out all of its after-tax income as a dividend to Kirsten.

c. Purple Company is a C corporation and the corporation pays Kirsten a salary of $158,000.

24. **LO.3, 4** Shelly has $200,000 of QBI from her local jewelry store (a sole proprietorship). Shelly's proprietorship paid $30,000 in W–2 wages and has $20,000 of qualified property. Shelly's spouse earned $77,700 of wages as an employee, they earned $20,000 of interest income during the year and have no other income or deductions. Shelly and her spouse will file jointly and use the standard deduction. What is their QBI deduction for 2023?

25. **LO.3, 4** Peter owns and manages his single member LLC that provides a wide variety of financial services to his clients. He is married and will file a joint tax return with his spouse, Marta. His LLC reports $300,000 of qualified business income, W–2 wages of $120,000, and assets with an unadjusted basis of $75,000. Their taxable income before the QBI deduction is $285,000 (this is also their modified taxable income). Determine their QBI deduction for 2023.

26. **LO.3, 4** Ashley (a single taxpayer) is the owner of ABC LLC. The LLC (which reports as a sole proprietorship) generates QBI of $900,000 and is not a "specified services" business. ABC paid total W–2 wages of $300,000, and the total unadjusted basis of property held by ABC is $30,000. Ashley's taxable income before the QBI deduction is $740,000 (this is also her modified taxable income). What is Ashley's QBI deduction for 2023?

27. **LO.3, 4** Donald (a married taxpayer filing jointly) owns a wide variety of commercial rental properties held in a single member LLC. Donald's LLC reports rental income of $1,500,000. The LLC pays no W–2 wages; rather, it pays a management fee to an S corporation Donald controls. The management company pays W–2 wages but reports no income (or loss). Donald's total unadjusted basis of the commercial rental property is $10,000,000. Donald's taxable income before the QBI deduction (and his modified taxable income) is $2,000,000. What is Donald's QBI deduction for 2023?

28. **LO.3, 4** Scott and Laura are married and will file a joint tax return. Laura has a sole proprietorship (not a "specified services" business) that generates qualified business income of $300,000. The proprietorship pays W–2 wages of $40,000 and holds property with an unadjusted basis of $10,000. Scott is employed by a local school district. Their taxable income before the QBI deduction is $424,200 (this is also their modified taxable income). Critical Thinking

a. Determine Scott and Laura's QBI deduction, taxable income, and tax liability for 2023.

b. After providing you the original information in the problem, Scott finds out that he will be receiving a $6,000 bonus in December 2023 (increasing their taxable income before the QBI deduction by this amount). Redetermine Scott and Laura's QBI deduction, taxable income, and tax liability for 2023.

c. What is the marginal tax rate on Scott's bonus?

29. **LO.3, 4** Stella Watters is a CPA and operates her own accounting firm (Watters CPA LLC). As a single member LLC, Stella reports her accounting firm operations as a sole proprietorship. Stella has QBI from her accounting firm of $540,000, she reports W–2 wages of $156,000, and the unadjusted basis of property used in the LLC is $425,000. Stella is married and will file a joint tax return with her spouse. Their taxable income before the QBI deduction is $475,000, and their modified taxable income is $448,000. Determine Stella's QBI deduction for 2023.

30. **LO.3, 4** Ben and Molly are married and will file jointly. Molly generates $300,000 of qualified business income from her single member LLC (a law firm). She reports her business as a sole proprietorship. Wages paid by the law firm amount to $40,000; the law firm has no significant property. Ben is employed as a tax manager by a local CPA firm. Their modified taxable income is $424,200 (this is also their taxable income before the deduction for qualified business income). Determine their QBI deduction for 2023.

31. **LO.3, 4** Tammy, a single taxpayer, has a part-time job at BigCo, a company in which she has no ownership interest. In addition, she owns and operates LittleCo, a sole proprietorship that is a qualified trade or business. Tammy is paid wages of $40,000 by BigCo and has $100,000 in qualified business income from LittleCo. She has no other items of income or loss and $25,000 of itemized deductions. What is her qualified business income deduction for 2023?

32. **LO.3, 4** Assume the same facts as in Problem 31, except that Tammy does not have a part-time job at BigCo. How does this affect her qualified business income deduction?

33. **LO.3, 4** Kyra, a single taxpayer, owns and operates a bakery (as a sole proprietorship). The business is *not* a "specified services" business. In 2023, the business pays $100,000 in W–2 wages, has $150,000 of qualified property, and generates $350,000 of qualified business income. Kyra has no other items of income, deduction, or loss and will take the standard deduction. What is Kyra's qualified business income deduction?

34. **LO.3, 4** Assume the same facts as in Problem 33, except that Kyra's business generates $150,000 of qualified business income. What is Kyra's QBI deduction?

35. **LO.3, 4** Assume the same facts as in Problem 33, except that Kyra's business pays $60,000 of W–2 wages and generates $200,000 of qualified business income. Kyra also has a part-time job earning wages of $12,200 and receives $3,650 of interest income. What is Kyra's QBI deduction?

Critical Thinking

36. **LO.3, 4** Jennifer is a CPA and a single taxpayer using the standard deduction. In 2023, her CPA practice generates qualified business income of $163,850 and she has no other items of income, deduction, or loss. Jennifer's taxable income before the QBI deduction is $150,000 ($163,850 – $13,850 standard deduction). Jennifer employs an administrative assistant in her practice and pays him $75,000 in wages. The unadjusted basis of depreciable assets employed in the practice totals $30,000.

    a. What is Jennifer's qualified business income deduction?

    b. Determine Jennifer's qualified business income deduction if her CPA practice generates qualified business income of $273,800.

37. **LO.3, 4** Elliot operates his clothing store as a single member LLC (which he reports as a sole proprietorship). In 2023, his proprietorship generates qualified business income of $280,000, he pays W–2 wages of $170,000, and he has qualified business property of $140,000. Elliot's wife, Julie, is an attorney who works for a local law firm and receives wages of $125,000. They have no other items of income, deduction, or loss, will file jointly, and use the standard deduction. What is Elliot's qualified business income deduction?

Critical Thinking

38. **LO.3, 4** Assume the same facts as in Problem 37, except that the business is a "specified services" business (e.g., a consulting firm) owned equally by Elliot and Conrad (an unrelated individual) in a two-member LLC. Assume that each member's share of qualified business income, W–2 wages, and qualified business property is one-half of the information provided in Problem 37. Conrad's wife, Rachel, earned wages during the year of $395,000, and Conrad and Rachel have itemized deductions of $62,000.

    a. What is Elliot's qualified business income deduction?

    b. What is Conrad's qualified business income deduction?

39. **LO.4** Tristan, who is single, operates three sole proprietorships that generate the following information in 2023 (none are "specified services" businesses).

Business	QBI	W–2 Wages	Capital Investment
A	$300,000	$90,000	$ -0-
B	(135,000)	60,000	-0-
C	150,000	-0-	-0-

Tristan chooses not to aggregate the businesses. She also earns $150,000 of wages from an unrelated business, and her modified taxable income (before any QBI deduction) is $380,000.

a. What is Tristan's QBI deduction?

b. Assume that Tristan can aggregate these businesses. Determine her QBI deduction if she decides to aggregate the businesses.

Research Problems

Note: Solutions to the Research Problems can be prepared by using the Thomson Reuters Checkpoint™ online tax research database, which accompanies this textbook. Solutions can also be prepared by using research materials found in a typical tax library.

Research Problem 1. A client has asked you for guidance on selecting the best type of entity for her new business. Using the internet as your sole research source, prepare an outline detailing the advantages and disadvantages of the entity forms available to a sole owner. Include both tax and nontax issues in your analysis. Communications

Research Problem 2. Starting with the website for the Secretary of State's office in your state, find out how to create an LLC and whether your state has any restrictions on the type of business or size. Present your findings using slides suitable for a presentation to your classmates. Communications

Research Problem 3. The deduction for qualified business income received considerable praise and criticism in the press from the time it was introduced in November 2017 to the present. Find reliable articles that explain at least two arguments for and against the QBI deduction. Explain whether you agree with these positions and why.

Research Problem 4. Some states automatically conform to any Federal tax changes, but others require special legislation to conform. Generally, states do not conform to rate changes because state income tax systems have their own rate structure (generally at rates well below the Federal tax rates). Find out if your state conformed to the deduction for qualified business income. Explain why the state did or did not conform. Do you agree? Explain.

Becker CPA Review Questions

Becker

1. Which of the following is considered a specified service trade or business (SSTB) for purposes of the qualified business income deduction?

   a. Accounting firm
   b. Manufacturing company
   c. Engineering firm
   d. Architectural services

2. What is the basic deduction calculation for the qualified business income deduction?

   a. 30% × Qualified business income (QBI)
   b. 20% × W–2 wages
   c. 20% × Qualified business income (QBI)
   d. 30% × W–2 wages

3. Which of the following statements is true regarding taxpayers with taxable income below the taxable income limitations for the qualified business income (QBI) deduction?
   a. QBI deduction is only allowed if a qualified trade or business (QTB).
   b. QBI deduction is a phased-out deduction if a specified service trade or business (SSTB).
   c. QBI deduction is limited to 50 percent of W–2 wages.
   d. A qualified trade or business (QTB) and specified trade or business (SSTB) are treated the same.

4. Which of the following is true about the qualified business income (QBI) deduction for taxpayers with taxable income above the taxable income limitations?
   a. If the taxpayer is a specified service trade or business (SSTB), no QBI deduction is allowed.
   b. If the taxpayer is a qualified trade or business (QTB), W–2 wage and property limitations do not apply.
   c. If the taxpayer is a qualified trade or business (QTB), W–2 wage and property limitations are phased in.
   d. If the taxpayer is a specified service trade or business (SSTB), W–2 wage and property limitations apply.

5. Which of the following is the overall limitation to the qualified business income (QBI) deduction?
   a. Lesser of 50 percent of combined QBI or 20 percent of the taxpayer's taxable income in excess of net capital gain.
   b. Lesser of combined QBI or 20 percent of the taxpayer's taxable income in excess of net capital gain.
   c. Lesser of 50 percent of W–2 wages or 25 percent of W–2 wages plus 2.5 percent of the unadjusted basis of qualified property.
   d. Taxable income limitations based on filing status.

6. Calculate the taxpayer's 2023 qualified business income deduction for a qualified trade or business:

Filing status:	Single
Taxable income:	$100,000
Net capital gains:	$0
Qualified business income (QBI):	$30,000
W–2 wages:	$10,000

   a. $5,000 c. $20,000
   b. $70,000 d. $6,000

7. Calculate the taxpayer's 2023 qualified business income deduction for a qualified trade or business:

Filing status:	Single
Taxable income:	$200,000
Net capital gains:	$0
Qualified business income (QBI):	$80,000
W–2 wages:	$20,000

   a. $16,000 c. $2,700
   b. $10,000 d. $13,852

Chapter 16

Accounting Periods and Methods

Learning Objectives: *After completing Chapter 16, you should be able to:*

- LO.1 Explain the relevance of the accounting period concept, accounting period options, and limitations on their use.
- LO.2 Apply the cash, accrual, and hybrid methods of accounting.
- LO.3 Explain the procedure for changing accounting methods.
- LO.4 Determine when the installment method of accounting applies and its effect on taxable income.
- LO.5 Recognize the methods of accounting for long-term contracts.
- LO.6 Recognize when accounting for inventories must occur and the key tax accounting methods for inventory.
- LO.7 Identify tax planning opportunities related to accounting periods and accounting methods.

Chapter Outline

The Big Picture

Accounting Period and Method

Belinda (an individual), Pearl, Inc. (a C corporation), and Tweety, Inc. (an S corporation) are going to form a partnership (Silver Partnership). The ownership interests and tax years of the partners are as follows:

Partner	Partnership Interest	Tax Year Ends
Belinda	25%	December 31
Pearl, Inc.	35%	November 30
Tweety, Inc.	40%	June 30

The partnership expects to begin business on April 1, 2023. The partners have several issues they would like you to address.

- A potential conflict exists among the partners regarding when the tax year should end for Silver. Belinda and Pearl would like a year-end close to their own year-ends, and Tweety would like to have a June 30 year-end. Is this a decision Tweety can make because it owns more of the partnership than either of the other two partners? Is this a decision Belinda and Pearl can make because collectively they own more of the partnership than Tweety owns?
- Because Silver will begin business on April 1, 2023, will the first tax year be a "short" tax year? Will annualization of the net income of the partnership be required?
- How will the partners know when their share of Silver's net income or net loss should be reported on their respective income tax returns?
- Belinda is a cash basis taxpayer, and the other partners use the accrual method to report their incomes. What accounting method must be used to compute Belinda's share of the partnership income?

Read the chapter and formulate your response.

Framework 1040 **Tax Formula for Individuals**

This chapter covers the boldfaced portions of the Tax Formula for Individuals that was introduced in Concept Summary 3.1 on p. 3-3. Below those portions are the sections of Form 1040 where the results are reported.

Income *(broadly defined)*	$xx,xxx
Less: Exclusions	(x,xxx)
Gross income	**$xx,xxx**

FORM 1040 (Schedule 1)

3	Business income or (loss). Attach Schedule C.

Less: Deductions *for* adjusted gross income	**(x,xxx)**
Adjusted gross income	$xx,xxx
Less: The greater of total itemized deductions *or* the standard deduction	(x,xxx)
Personal and dependency exemptions*	(x,xxx)
Deduction for qualified business income**	(x,xxx)
Taxable income	$xx,xxx
Tax on taxable income *(see Tax Tables or Tax Rate Schedules)*	$ x,xxx
Less: Tax credits *(including income taxes withheld and prepaid)*	(xxx)
Tax due (or refund)	$ xxx

* Exemption deductions are not allowed from 2018 through 2025.
** Only applies from 2018 through 2025.

Tax professionals must determine *when* items of income and expense are recognized as well as *whether* the items are includible in taxable income. Earlier chapters discussed the types of income subject to tax (gross income and exclusions) and allowable deductions (the *whether* issue).[1] This chapter focuses on the related issue of the periods in which income and deductions are reported (the *when* issue).

Generally, a taxpayer's income and deductions must be assigned to identified 12-month periods—calendar years or fiscal years. Accounting methods also are important for determining when costs are part of inventory and cost of sales, as well as the basis of fixed assets.

Income and deductions are placed within tax years through the use of tax accounting methods. The basic tax accounting methods are the cash receipts and disbursements method, the accrual method, and a hybrid method. Other special purpose methods, such as the installment method and the methods used for long-term construction contracts, are available for specific circumstances or types of transactions.

Over the long run, the accounting period and tax accounting methods used by a taxpayer will not affect the aggregate (or lifetime) amount of reported taxable income. However, taxable income for a given tax year may vary significantly due to the use of a particular accounting method. This chapter discusses the taxpayer's alternatives for accounting periods and accounting methods. The focus is on business entities, including sole proprietors, rather than individuals; most individuals report taxable income using a calendar year and use the cash method of accounting.

16-1 Accounting Periods

LO.1

Explain the relevance of the accounting period concept, accounting period options, and limitations on their use.

Generally, an individual or a corporation that keeps adequate books and records may elect a **fiscal year**, a 12-month period ending on the *last day* of a month other than December, for the **accounting period**. Otherwise, a *calendar year* must be used.[2] Frequently, corporations can satisfy the record-keeping and other requirements and

[1] See Chapters 4, 5, and 6.

[2] § 441(c) and Reg. § 1.441–1(b)(1)(ii).

elect to use a fiscal year.[3] Often, the fiscal year conforms to a natural business year (e.g., a summer resort's fiscal year may end on September 30, after the close of the season). Individuals seldom use a fiscal year because they do not maintain the necessary books and records to do so and because common reporting forms they receive, such as Forms W–2 and 1099, report income based on the calendar year.

Generally, a tax year may not exceed 12 calendar months. However, if certain requirements are met, a taxpayer may elect to use an annual period that varies from 52 to 53 weeks.[4] In that case, the year-end must be on the same day of the week (e.g., the Tuesday falling closest to September 30, or the last Tuesday in September). The day of the week selected for ending the tax year may depend upon business considerations. For example, a retail business that is not open on Sundays may end its tax year on a Sunday so that it can take an inventory without interrupting business operations.

Wade, Inc., is in the business of selling farm supplies. Its natural business year terminates at the end of October with the completion of harvesting. At the end of the fiscal year, Wade must take an inventory, which is most easily accomplished on a Friday. Therefore, Wade could adopt a 52- to 53-week tax year ending on the Friday closest to October 31.

If the company selects this approach, the year-end date may fall in the following month if that Friday is closer to October 31, or the beginning date may fall in the same month as the ending date. The tax year ending in 2023 will contain 52 weeks beginning on Saturday, October 29, 2022, and ending on Friday, November 3, 2023. The tax year ending in 2024 will have 52 weeks beginning on Saturday, November 4, 2023, and ending on Friday, November 1, 2024.

16-1a **Specific Provisions for Partnerships, S Corporations, and Personal Service Corporations**

When a partner and the partnership have different tax years, the partner may enjoy a deferral of income. This results because partners report their share of the partnership's income and deductions for the partnership's tax year ending within or with the partner's tax year.[5] For example, if the tax year of the partnership ends on January 31, a calendar year partner will not report partnership profits for the first 11 months of the partnership tax year until the following year (that is, on the partner's tax year that includes the January 31 partnership year-end). To minimize abuse of this arrangement, the tax law provides special tax year requirements.

In general, the partnership tax year must be the same as the tax year of the majority interest partners. The **majority interest partners** are the partners who together own a greater-than-50-percent interest in the partnership capital and profits and share the same tax year-end. If there is no majority interest tax year, the partnership must adopt the same tax year that is shared by all of its principal partners. A **principal partner** is a partner with a 5 percent or more interest in the partnership capital or profits.[6]

Example 2

The RST Partnership is owned equally by Rose Corporation, Sunflower Corporation, and Tom. The partners use the following tax years.

	Partner's Tax Year Ending
Rose Corporation	June 30
Sunflower Corporation	June 30
Tom	December 31

The partnership's tax year must end on June 30 because Rose and Sunflower together have a greater-than-50% interest in the partnership. If Sunflower's and Tom's tax years both end on December 31, the partnership must adopt a calendar year.

[3] Reg. § 1.441–1(e)(2).

[4] § 441(f).

[5] Reg. § 1.706–1(a).

[6] §§ 706(b)(1)(B) and 706(b)(3).

If all of the principal partners do not use the same tax year, and no majority of partners have the same tax year, the partnership must adopt a year that results in the *least aggregate deferral* of income.[7] Under the **least aggregate deferral method**, the different tax years of the principal partners are tested to determine which produces the least aggregate taxable income deferral. This is calculated by first multiplying the combined percentages of the principal partners with the same tax year by the months of deferral for the test year. Once this is done for each set of principal partners with the same tax year, the resulting products are summed to produce the aggregate deferral. After the aggregate deferral is calculated for each of the test years, the year with the smallest total (the least aggregate deferral) becomes the tax year for the partnership.

The Big Picture

Example 3

Return to the facts of *The Big Picture* on p. 16-1. The partnership's tax year must end on November 30 because using that year-end results in the least aggregate deferral of partnership income.

Test for Tax Year Ending December 31

		1	2	1 × 2
	Partner's Year-End	**Profit Percentage**	**Months Income Deferred**	**Aggregate Months of Deferral**
Belinda	12/31	25%	0	0
Pearl, Inc.	11/30	35%	11	3.85
Tweety, Inc.	6/30	40%	6	2.40
				6.25

Test for Tax Year Ending November 30

	Partner's Year-End	Profit Percentage	Months Income Deferred	Aggregate Months of Deferral
Belinda	12/31	25%	1	0.25
Pearl, Inc.	11/30	35%	0	0
Tweety, Inc.	6/30	40%	7	2.80
				3.05

Test for Tax Year Ending June 30

	Partner's Year-End	Profit Percentage	Months Income Deferred	Aggregate Months of Deferral
Belinda	12/31	25%	6	1.50
Pearl, Inc.	11/30	35%	5	1.75
Tweety, Inc.	6/30	40%	0	0
				3.25

[7] Reg. § 1.706–1(b)(3).

Generally, S corporations must adopt a calendar year.[8] However, partnerships and S corporations may *elect* an otherwise impermissible year under either of the following conditions:

- A business purpose for the year can be demonstrated.[9]
- The partnership or S corporation makes a timely election to use a taxable year that results in a deferral of not more than three months' taxable income, and the entity agrees to make required tax payments that relate to this deferral.[10]

Business Purpose

The only business purpose for a fiscal year the IRS has acknowledged is the need to conform the tax year to the natural business year of a company.[11] Generally, only seasonal businesses have a natural business year. For example, the natural business year for a retailer may end on January 31, after holiday sales returns have been processed and clearance sales have been completed.

Required Tax Payments

When required payments are to be made, a tax payment is due from a fiscal year partnership or S corporation by May 15 of each tax year.[12] The amount due is computed by multiplying an estimate of the deferral period income by the highest individual Federal income tax rate plus 1 percentage point. The deferral period runs from the close of the fiscal year to the end of the required year. Estimated income for this period is based on the average monthly earnings for the previous fiscal year. The amount due is reduced by the required tax payment for the previous year.[13]

Example 4

Brown, Inc., an S corporation, timely elected a fiscal year ending September 30. Bob is the only shareholder and is a calendar year taxpayer. The "required" tax year ends on December 31, 2023, the major shareholder's year-end, and the deferral period is the maximum of three months. For the fiscal year ending September 30, 2023, Brown earned $100,000. The required tax payment for the previous year was $5,000. The corporation must pay $4,500 by May 15, 2024.

$$(\$100{,}000 \times 3/12 \times 38\%^*) - \$5{,}000 = \$4{,}500$$

*Maximum individual tax rate 37% + 1%.

Ethics & Equity **Who Benefits from the Change in Tax Year?**

Ajit, a public accounting sole practitioner, has reached a breaking point. All of his clients use the calendar year to report income. Many of the clients are S corporations and partnerships. Ajit's workload the first four months of the year is so heavy that it is putting the quality of his work at risk.

Ajit is considering telling his clients that any new partnership or S corporation that is formed must timely elect, under the required tax payments system, to use a fiscal year ending September 30 (assuming that the required year would otherwise be a calendar year). Although the shareholders and partners would be subject to the required tax payments rule, Ajit will sell the plan to them by promising better service. Evaluate the plan proposed by Ajit.

[8] §§ 1378(a) and (b).

[9] §§ 706(b)(1)(C) and 1378(b)(2).

[10] § 444. See Form 8716.

[11] Rev.Proc. 2006–46. Also see the following discussion in text Section 16-1c.

[12] § 444(c) and Reg. § 1.7519–2T(a)(4)(ii). No payment is required if the calculated amount is $500 or less. See Form 8752.

[13] § 7519(b).

Personal Service Corporations

A **personal service corporation (PSC)** is a corporation whose shareholder-employees provide personal services (e.g., medical, dental, legal, accounting, engineering, actuarial, consulting, or performing arts). Generally, a PSC must use a calendar year.[14] However, a PSC can *elect* a fiscal year under either of the following conditions:

- A business purpose for the year can be demonstrated.
- The PSC year results in a deferral of not more than three months' income, the corporation pays the shareholder-employee's salary during the portion of the calendar year after the close of the fiscal year, and the salary for that period is at least proportionate to the shareholder-employee's salary received for the preceding fiscal year.[15]

Nancy's corporation paid her a salary of $120,000 during its tax year ending September 30, 2023. The corporation cannot satisfy the business purpose test for a fiscal year. The corporation can continue to use its non-calendar tax year for Federal income tax purposes, provided Nancy receives at least $30,000 [(3 months ÷ 12 months) × $120,000] of salary during the period October 1 through December 31, 2023.

If the salary test is not satisfied, the PSC can retain the fiscal year, but the corporation's deduction for salary may be limited.[16] Any amount not deductible is carried over to the next year.

16-1b **Selecting the Tax Year**

A taxpayer elects to use a calendar year or, if eligible, a fiscal year by the timely filing of the initial tax return. For all subsequent tax years, the taxpayer must use this same year-end unless approval for change is obtained from the IRS.[17]

16-1c **Changes in the Accounting Period**

A taxpayer must obtain consent from the IRS before changing its tax year.[18] The IRS issues administrative guidelines that must be met by taxpayers who want to change their accounting period. An application for permission to change tax years must be made on Form 1128. Generally, the application must be filed by the due date (including extensions) for the short taxable period that results from the change.[19]

Beginning in 2023, Gold Corporation, a calendar year taxpayer, would like to switch to a tax year ending March 31. This change results in a short-period return encompassing January 1 to March 31, 2023. The extended due date for this short period return is January 15, 2024, which is also the due date for the Form 1128.

[14] § 441(i).
[15] §§ 444 and 280H.
[16] § 280H.
[17] Reg. §§ 1.441–1(b)(3) and 1.441–1(b)(4).
[18] § 442. Under certain conditions, corporations are allowed to change tax years without obtaining IRS approval. See Reg. § 1.442–1(c)(1); Rev.Proc. 2006–45, modified by Rev.Proc. 2007–64.
[19] Reg. § 1.442–1(b)(1), Rev.Proc. 2006–45, and Form 1128 instructions.

The IRS will not grant permission for the change unless the taxpayer can establish a substantial nontax business purpose for the request. One substantial business purpose is to change to a tax year that coincides with the *natural business year* (the completion of an annual business cycle). The IRS applies an objective gross receipts test to determine whether the entity has a natural business year. At least 25 percent of the entity's gross receipts for the 12-month period must be realized in the final two months of the 12-month period for three consecutive years.[20]

Oceanside, a Virginia Beach motel, would like to know if it can move to a tax year that ends on August 31. It reported the following gross receipts:

	2021	2022	2023
July–August receipts	$ 300,000	$250,000	$ 325,000
September 1–August 31 receipts	1,000,000	900,000	1,250,000
Receipts for final 2 months divided by receipts for 12 months	30.0%	27.8%	26.0%

Because it satisfies the natural business year test, Oceanside can use a tax year ending August 31.

16-1d **Taxable Periods of Less Than One Year**

A **short taxable year** (or **short period**) is a period of less than 12 calendar months. A taxpayer may have a short year for its first or last income tax return or when there is a change in the tax year.

If the short period results from a change in the taxpayer's annual accounting period, the taxable income for the period is annualized in calculating tax liability for the short period. With a flat Federal corporate income tax rate, annualization is not needed for C corporations. However, as shown in Example 8, annualization is required to calculate state income taxes if the state has a progressive tax rate structure.

The calculations to determine the annualized tax for a short tax period resulting from change in accounting period follow.

1. Annualize the short-period income.

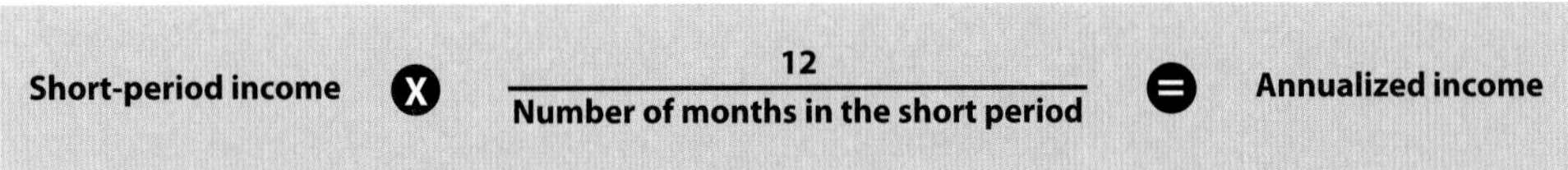

2. Compute the tax on the annualized income.
3. Convert the tax on the annualized income to a short-period tax.

$$\text{Tax on annualized income} \times \frac{\text{Number of months in the short period}}{12} = \text{Short-period tax}$$

[20]Rev.Proc. 2006–46, Rev.Rul. 87–57, and Rev.Proc. 2002–39.

Gray Corporation, a retailer that is not an S corporation, obtained permission to change from a calendar year to a fiscal year ending September 30, beginning in 2024. For the short period January 1 through September 30, 2024, the corporation's taxable income was $48,000. Gray does business in State X. The relevant tax rates in X and the resulting short-period tax are:

Amount of Taxable Income	Tax Rates
$1–$50,000	5% of taxable income
Over $50,000	$2,500 plus 7% of taxable income in excess of $50,000

Calculation of Short-Period Tax

Annualized income: $48,000 × 12/9 = $64,000

Tax on annualized income: $2,500 + 7%($64,000 − $50,000) = $3,480

Short-period tax due to State X: $3,480 × 9/12 = $2,610

Tax with annualizing	$ 2,610
Tax without annualizing (5% × $48,000)	(2,400)
State income tax increase due to annualizing	$ 210

Gray's Federal income tax for the short period is $10,080 (21% × $48,000). Because of the flat corporate rate, no annualization is required to compute Gray's Federal income tax liability for the short tax year.

Some other tax rules require annualization of short-period information. For example, for the average annual gross receipts test explained in text Section 16-2, the gross receipts of any prior short period must be annualized.

Often, the short year counts as a full year for purposes of the carryback and carryforward rules for various losses and credits.[21]

16-1e **Mitigation of the Annual Accounting Period Concept**

Several provisions in the Code are designed to give the taxpayer relief from the seemingly harsh results that may occur due to the combined effects of an arbitrary accounting period and the progressive rate structure that applies to individuals. For example, under the NOL carryover rules, a loss in one year can be carried forward and applied against taxable income in subsequent years.[22] In addition, the Code provides special relief provisions for casualty losses arising from a Federally declared disaster and for the reporting of insurance proceeds from destruction of crops.[23]

[21]Reg. §§ 1.172–4(a)(2), 1.46–2(k), and 1.904–2(e). Certain farm losses can be carried back two years. If one of those carryback years is a short year, it counts as one of the carryback years.

[22]§ 172. Refer to text Section 7-6c.

[23]§§ 165(i) and 451(d).

Farm Relief

Farmers and fishermen often are subject to income fluctuations across years, some of which are due to the weather. Congress has provided these taxpayers with a special method of computing their tax. In the high-income years, these taxpayers can elect to compute their tax on income from farming or fishing as though it were earned equally in the three previous years.[24] Thus, the tax on the farming or fishing income for the year is the sum of the additional tax that would have been due in the three previous years if one-third of the income had been earned in each of those years. This averaging system enables the taxpayer to avoid the higher marginal tax rates associated with a large amount of income received in one year.

The income pattern for farmers also can be disrupted by natural disasters that are covered by insurance. The disaster may occur and the **crop insurance proceeds** may be received in a year before the income from the crop would have been realized. Under these circumstances, the farmer can defer reporting the gross income from the insurance proceeds until the year following the disaster. Similar relief is available when livestock must be sold due to drought or other weather-related conditions.[25]

Restoration of Amounts Received under a Claim of Right

The court-made **claim of right doctrine** applies when the taxpayer receives property as income and it is under the taxpayer's control but a dispute arises over the taxpayer's rights to the income.[26] According to the doctrine, the taxpayer must include the amount as income in the year of receipt. The rationale for the doctrine is that the Federal government cannot await the resolution of all disputes before exacting a tax. As a corollary to the doctrine, if the taxpayer is required to repay the funds later, a deduction generally is allowed in the year of repayment.[27]

In 2023, Pedro received a $5,000 bonus computed as a percentage of profits. In 2024, Pedro's employer determined that the 2023 profits had been computed incorrectly, and Pedro was required to refund the $5,000 in 2024. Pedro must include the $5,000 in his 2023 gross income, but he can claim a $5,000 deduction in 2024.

In Example 9, the transactions were a wash; that is, the income and deduction were the same ($5,000). Suppose, however, that Pedro was in the 35 percent tax bracket in 2023 but in the 22 percent bracket in 2024. Without any kind of relief provision, the mistake would be costly to Pedro. He paid a $1,750 tax in 2023 (35% × $5,000), but the deduction reduced his tax liability in 2024 by only $1,000 (22% × $5,000).

The Code provides relief in such cases. Under § 1341, when income that has been taxed under the claim of right doctrine later must be repaid, the taxpayer can use the tax rate of the year that produces the greatest tax benefit. As a result, in Example 9, the repayment in 2024 would reduce Pedro's 2024 tax liability by $1,750 [the higher 2023 rate (35%) applied to the $5,000 deduction in 2024]. However, relief is provided only in cases where the tax is significantly different (i.e., when the deduction for the amount previously included in income exceeds $3,000).

[24] § 1301. The tax is calculated on Schedule J.

[25] §§ 451(f) and (g). Also see IRS Publication 225.

[26] *North American Consolidated Oil Co. v. Burnet*, 3 USTC ¶943, 11 AFTR 16, 52 S.Ct. 613 (1932).

[27] *U.S. v. Lewis*, 51–1 USTC ¶9211, 40 AFTR 258, 71 S.Ct. 522.

Ethics & Equity **Special Tax Relief**

A taxpayer who reports gross income in one year but must repay the income in a subsequent year is granted special tax relief. If the taxpayer is in a lower marginal tax bracket in the year the income is repaid than in the year it was received, the deduction reduces the tax for the year of repayment by using the higher tax rate that applied to the income when it was received.

In contrast, if a taxpayer takes a deduction in one year and receives a refund of the amount giving rise to the deduction in a subsequent year, the refund is taxed at the marginal tax rate in the year of refund. This is true even though the taxpayer's marginal tax rate in the year of receipt is higher than that in the year of the deduction.

Should adjustments to income and adjustments to deductions receive the same tax relief? Or should neither situation be granted special relief? Discuss.

LO.2

Apply the cash, accrual, and hybrid methods of accounting.

16-2 Accounting Methods

16-2a Permissible Methods

Code § 446 requires the taxpayer to compute taxable income using the method of accounting regularly employed in keeping the corresponding financial accounting records ("the books"), provided the method clearly reflects income. The Code recognizes the following as generally permissible **accounting methods**:

- The cash receipts and disbursements method.
- The accrual method.
- A hybrid method (a combination of cash and accrual).

The Regulations refer to these alternatives as *overall methods* and add that the term *method of accounting* includes not only the taxpayer's overall method of accounting but also the accounting treatment of any item.[28]

Generally, any of the three overall methods of accounting may be used if the method is consistently employed and clearly reflects income. However, certain taxpayers whose average annual gross receipts (computed over the three preceding years) exceed $29 million are required to use the accrual method.

In general, taxpayers that maintain inventory for sale to customers are required to use the accrual method of accounting for determining sales and cost of goods sold. However, taxpayers with average annual gross receipts of $29 million or less for the most recent three-year period can use the cash method to account for inventories, as long as inventories are not a material income-producing factor.[29] No more than 2 percent of all U.S. businesses report average gross receipts in excess of $29 million.

A taxpayer who has more than one trade or business may use a different method of accounting for each trade or business unless the taxpayer is required to use the accrual method. Furthermore, a taxpayer may use one method of accounting to determine income from a trade or business and use another method to compute nonbusiness items of income and deductions.[30]

The Code grants the IRS broad powers to determine whether the taxpayer's accounting method *clearly reflects income*. Thus, if the method employed does not meet this requirement, the IRS can prescribe the method to be used by the taxpayer.[31]

[28]Reg. § 1.446–1(a)(1).

[29]Reg. § 1.446–1(a)(4)(i), Reg. § 1.446–1(c)(2)(i), § 448, and § 471(c). Special methods are permitted for installment sales, long-term construction contracts, and farmers, as discussed in subsequent sections of this chapter.

[30]§ 446(d) and Reg. § 1.446–1(c)(1)(iv)(b).

[31]§ 446(b), as limited by § 471(c)(1)(B).

16-2b Cash Receipts and Disbursements Method

Most individuals and many businesses use the cash basis to report income and deductions. The popularity of this method can largely be attributed to its simplicity and flexibility.

Under the **cash method**, income is not recognized until the taxpayer actually receives, or constructively receives, cash or its equivalent (e.g., the receipt of accounts receivable does not trigger income until collected). Cash is constructively received if it is available to the taxpayer.[32] Generally, a cash equivalent is any asset with a fair market value including any goods or services received in a barter transaction and a note receivable from a customer.

The Big Picture

Example 10

Return to the facts of *The Big Picture* on p. 4-1 in Chapter 4. Recall that Dr. Cliff Payne opened a dental practice as a sole proprietorship and does not accept credit cards. In the second year of business, he adopts a new policy of requiring that his patients either pay cash at the time the services are performed or give him a note receivable with interest at the market rate. Generally, the notes can be sold to the local banks for 95% of their face amount.

At the end of the second year, Dr. Payne holds $60,000 in notes receivable from patients. The notes receivable are a cash equivalent and have a fair market value of $57,000 ($60,000 × 95%). As a result, Dr. Payne must include $57,000 in his gross income for this year.

Deductions generally are permitted in the year of payment under the cash method. Thus, year-end accounts payable and accrued expenses are not deducted in the determination of taxable income.

In many cases, a taxpayer using the cash method can choose the year in which a deduction is claimed simply by postponing or accelerating the payment of expenses. For fixed assets, however, the cash basis taxpayer claims deductions through depreciation or amortization, as does an accrual basis taxpayer. In addition, prepaid expenses must be capitalized and amortized if the life of the asset extends substantially beyond the end of the tax year.[33]

The Regulations provide a **12-month rule for prepaid expenses** that permits the taxpayer to deduct expenditures for benefits that do not extend beyond the earlier of (1) 12 months after the first date on which the taxpayer realizes the benefit or (2) the end of the tax year following the year of payment. Both cash basis and accrual basis taxpayers can use the 12-month rule.[34]

Example 11

On December 1, 2023, Elm Corporation, a calendar year taxpayer, paid $20,000 for a 12-month property insurance policy with coverage starting on February 1, 2024. Elm's benefit under this policy ends on January 31, 2025. Because this date extends beyond the earlier of (1) 12 months after February 1, 2024, or (2) the end of the next tax year (December 31, 2024), the 12-month rule does *not* apply. As a result, Elm must deduct its prepayment over the term of the policy rather than when paid in 2023.

If instead, the policy coverage began on December 15, 2023, and ended on December 14, 2024, the 12-month rule would apply, and Elm would deduct the entire payment in 2023. In this scenario, the benefit of the payment does not extend beyond the earlier of (1) December 14, 2024, or (2) December 31, 2024. Instead, the benefit ends on December 14, 2024.

Restrictions on Use of the Cash Method

The cash method could distort income from a merchandising or manufacturing operation because the cost of goods sold would be a function of when payments for the goods were made rather than when they were sold. Thus, the Regulations require use of the accrual method to measure sales and cost of goods sold if inventories

[32]Reg. § 1.451–1(a). Refer to text Section 4-2c for a discussion of constructive receipt.

[33]Reg. § 1.461–1(a)(1).

[34]Reg. § 1.263(a)–4(f). See text Section 6-2d for additional examples of the 12-month rule.

are material to the business. This targeted prohibition on the use of the cash method for taxpayers with inventories is intended to ensure that annual taxable income is clearly reflected.[35]

The following taxpayers may not use the cash method (and must use the accrual method) for Federal income tax purposes regardless of whether inventories are material: (1) a corporation (other than an S corporation), (2) a partnership with a corporate partner (that is not an S corporation), and (3) a tax shelter. This accrual method requirement of § 448 has three exceptions, each of which allows the cash method to be used.

- A farming business (other than certain corporations).
- A *qualified personal service corporation* (a corporation that performs services in health, law, engineering, architecture, accounting, actuarial science, performing arts, or consulting and whose employees own substantially all of the stock) regardless of gross receipts level.
- A corporation, or a partnership with a corporate partner, whose average annual gross receipts for the prior three-year period do not exceed $29 million.

None of the exceptions apply to an entity that meets the definition of a tax shelter. A tax shelter must use the accrual method regardless of the amount of its gross receipts.[36]

Overall Accounting Method Rules

Estrella and Estrella, CPAs, is a C corporation owned by 10 CPAs that provides accounting and tax services. Its average annual gross receipts are $30,000,000. Because this entity is a qualified personal service corporation and has no inventory, it may use the cash method of accounting.

Fit Corporation is a C corporation that operates several fitness centers. Its average annual gross receipts are $30,000,000. Fit must use the accrual method; it is a C corporation, and its average annual gross receipts for the prior three-year period exceed $29,000,000. If its average annual gross receipts in the prior three-year period were $29,000,000 or less, it could use the cash method.

If Fit were a sole proprietorship, a partnership without a C corporation partner, or an S corporation, it would be allowed to use the cash method regardless of its gross receipts level, because it is not subject to the required accrual method rule of § 448 and has no inventory.

Special Rules for Farmers

The tax accounting rules include several special rules and exceptions for farmers. Generally, farmers with average annual gross receipts in the prior three-year period of $29 million or less may use the cash method.

Farmers with average annual gross receipts greater than $29 million may be required to use the accrual method. However, exceptions exist based on the type of entity.[37] For example, a partnership without a corporate partner generally can use the cash method. In this regard, whether certain costs related to production of products must be capitalized depends on the type of product.[38]

Farmers who produce crops that take more than a year from planting to harvesting (e.g., pineapples) can elect to use the crop method to report the income. Under the **crop method**, the costs of raising the crop are capitalized as those costs are incurred and then deducted in the year the income from the crop is realized.[39] This method is analogous to the completed contract method, discussed in text Section 16-3b.

[35] Reg. § 1.446–1(a)(4)(i).

[36] §§ 448(a) and 448(b). For this purpose, the hybrid method of accounting is considered the same as the cash method. Also see § 447. *Tax shelter* is defined at § 448(d)(3).

[37] See §§ 447(c), 448(b), and 464.

[38] § 263A(d).

[39] Reg. §§ 1.61–4 and 1.162–12(a).

Generally, a cash basis farmer must capitalize the purchase price of an animal, whether it is acquired for sale or for breeding. However, costs to raise the animal generally can be deducted immediately.[40]

16-2c Accrual Method

The tax rules governing when an accrual method taxpayer reports income or claims deductions include an "all events test." The timing rules for deductions also include an "economic performance" requirement. These timing rules for income and deductions of accrual method taxpayers are explained below.

All Events Test for Income

Under the **accrual method**, an item generally is included in gross income for the year in which it is earned, regardless of when the income is collected. An item of income is earned when (1) all of the events have occurred to fix the taxpayer's right to receive the income and (2) the amount of income (the amount the taxpayer has a right to receive) can be determined with reasonable accuracy.[41] However, generally, the income cannot be deferred beyond the tax year in which it is included in the taxpayer's applicable financial statement.[42]

Andre Corporation, a calendar year taxpayer that uses the accrual basis of accounting, was to receive a bonus equal to 6% of Blue Corporation's net income for its fiscal year ending each June 30. For the fiscal year ending June 30, 2023, Blue reported net income of $240,000. For the six months ending December 31, 2023, its net income was $150,000.

Andre includes gross income of $14,400 (6% × $240,000) for 2023 because its right to the amount became fixed when Blue's tax year closed. However, Andre would not accrue income based on Blue's profits for the last six months of 2023, because its right to the income does not accrue until the close of Blue's tax year.

An accrual basis taxpayer's amount of income and the tax year the income is recognized are based on its right to receive the income. Thus, unlike the case of a cash basis taxpayer, the fair market value of a receivable is irrelevant.

Marcey Corporation, an accrual basis taxpayer, has provided services to clients and has the right to receive $60,000. The clients have signed notes receivable to Marcey that have a face value of $60,000 but a fair market value of $57,000. The corporation must include gross income of $60,000, the amount it has the right to receive, rather than the fair market value of the notes of $57,000.

If an accrual basis taxpayer receives advance payments for services, goods, or licensing of software, it should consider adopting a special deferral method.[43] Under this method, in the year the advance payment is received, the taxpayer reports on its tax return the amount reported in its financial statements. In the subsequent year, the balance of the advance payment is included in gross income, regardless of how much is reported in the financial statements for that year (see text Section 4-2d).

[40] Reg. § 1.162–12(a).

[41] § 451(b) and Reg. § 1.451–1(a). Refer to text Section 4-2 for further discussion of the accrual method.

[42] § 451(b). *Applicable financial statement* is defined at § 451(b)(3) and generally is a statement prepared in accordance with Generally Accepted Accounting Principles and certified as such, or per international reporting standards, or is required by a regulatory or government body.

[43] Prior to the change to § 451(c) by the TCJA of 2017, the deferral method for advance payments for services, goods, and licensing of intellectual property was provided at Rev.Proc. 2004–34. For tax years beginning on or after January 1, 2021, Rev.Proc. 2004–34 is obsolete and the new deferral method rules are at Reg. § 1.451–8; they are similar to the 2004 methods.

Troy Corporation is an accrual method, calendar year taxpayer that has adopted the deferral method for advance payments. Troy sells computers and two-year service contracts on the computers. On November 1, 2023, Troy sold a 24-month service contract and received $240. For financial reporting purposes, Troy reports $20 of gross income for 2023, $120 for 2024, and $100 for 2025. For Federal income tax purposes, Troy reports $20 of income for 2023 (same as for financial reporting) and $220 of income for 2024 (the balance of the advance payment).

Prepaid rental income, prepaid interest income, warranty or guarantee contracts, insurance premiums, and payments with respect to certain financial instruments must be recognized in the year of receipt and may not be deferred.[44]

In a situation where the accrual method taxpayer's right to income is contested and the income has not yet been collected, generally, no income is recognized until the dispute has been settled.[45] Before the settlement, "all of the events have not occurred that fix the right to receive the income."

All Events and Economic Performance Tests for Deductions

A three-part test is applied to determine when an accrual method taxpayer considers a liability as either an expense or a capital expenditure: (1) the **all events test**, (2) whether the amount is determinable with reasonable accuracy, and (3) the **economic performance test**. The all events test is met when all events have occurred to establish the fact that a liability exists (that is, the taxpayer legally owes money to another party).[46]

As to when economic performance is met, that depends on the nature of the liability. For example, if an accrual method taxpayer owes money to another entity that provided services to it, economic performance is met as the services are provided. Concept Summary 16.1 lists common types of liabilities covered by the economic performance Regulations and when the test for economic performance is met for each liability.

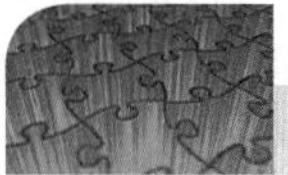

Concept Summary 16.1

Accruals Under the Economic Performance Test (Reg. § 1.461–4)

Event	Example	When Economic Performance Is Satisfied
The taxpayer's use of the owner's property	Rent	Ratably over the period used
Specific property provided to the taxpayer	A company's office supplies are purchased	When the taxpayer receives the supplies
Specific services provided to the taxpayer	The taxpayer contracts for repairs to be made to its equipment	When the repairs are made
Services to be provided for a specific time period	The taxpayer purchases a service contract, such as for cleaning services	Ratably over the contract period
Property or services provided by the taxpayer	A manufacturer provides a warranty on items sold to customers	When the manufacturer incurs costs in fixing the customer's item covered by the warranty
Rebates	Manufacturer rebates based on quantity of purchases	When the rebate is paid
Tort claims	Customers are awarded claims for harm caused by the taxpayer's product	When payment is made to the injured party; not eligible for the recurring item exception
State income tax	Taxes due when filing the return	When payment is made

[44] § 451(c)(4)(B).

[45] *Burnet v. Sanford & Brooks Co.*, 2 USTC ¶636, 9 AFTR 603, 51 S.Ct. 150 (1931).

[46] § 461 and Reg. § 1.461–1(a)(2).

Economic Performance

Example 17

An accrual basis calendar year taxpayer, JAB, Inc., promoted a boxing match held in the company's arena on December 31, 2023. CLN, Inc., was contracted to clean the arena for $5,000 but did not actually perform the work until January 1, 2024. JAB paid the $5,000 on January 3, 2024 (once CLN had completed its work).

Although financial accounting rules would require JAB to accrue the $5,000 cleaning expense in 2023 to match the revenues from the fight, the economic performance test was not satisfied until 2024, when CLN performed the service. Thus, JAB deducts the expense in 2024.

Agmax Corporation farms land owned by an individual. Agmax's contract to use the land is for three years, and, at the end of three years, Agmax agreed to apply lime to the farmland. The contract term expired in 2023, and Agmax applied the lime in 2024. The all events test was satisfied at the end of 2023. However, Agmax did not provide the lime until 2024. Agmax was obligated to provide property (lime) and services. The deduction is not permitted until 2024, when Agmax incurs costs in fulfilling its obligation.[47]

Special rules exist for some expenditures of accrual basis taxpayers. One commonly encountered rule involves certain types of compensation, such as bonuses earned by employees. Bonuses might be tied to whether certain sales or profit goals were met. Since these goals can't be measured until the end of the year, there will be a timing difference between the employer's accrual of the bonus at the end of the year and the payment of the bonus (to the cash basis employee) in the following year. To address this issue, Congress created a special *2½ month rule.* Under this rule, if compensation is paid within 2½ months of the employer's year end, it will *not* be considered deferred compensation and the accrual basis employer may deduct it in the year earned by the employees. If the compensation is paid *more than* 2½ months after year-end, the employer may not deduct the compensation until the year that the employees receive it and report it in their income.[48]

Example 19

Amber Corporation, an accrual basis, calendar year taxpayer, promises all employees a year-end bonus equal to one percent of sales growth compared to the prior year. Amber is not able to measure the bonus amount until it closes its books for the year.

Scenario A: Amber determines the 2023 bonus amounts in early January 2024 and issues the bonus payments to employees on February 12, 2024. Because Amber paid these 2023 bonuses within 2½ months of year end, it takes the compensation deduction on its 2023 income tax return; the employees will report the income on their 2024 income tax returns.

Scenario B: Amber changed its accounting software in 2023 and discovered after year-end that its sales were not all properly reported. The work needed to fix this problem made it impossible for Amber to calculate the 2023 bonus amount until early April 2024. On April 22, 2024, Amber paid the 2023 bonuses to its employees. Because this date is more than 2½ months after December 31, 2023, Amber may not deduct these bonuses in 2023. Instead, Amber will deduct the 2023 bonuses in 2024—the same year that the employees report the bonuses in income.

This 2½ month rule does *not* apply to a cash method employer because that employer may only deduct compensation in the year it is paid. Another special deduction rule for accrual basis taxpayers allows them to make an election to deduct taxes on real property ratably over the period they pertain rather than when they are paid.[49]

The economic performance requirement is accelerated, allowing year-end accruals to be deducted, if the following four conditions are met. This is known as the *recurring item exception.*

1. The all events test is met, and the amount of the liability can be determined with reasonable accuracy.
2. Economic performance occurs on or before the earlier of the date the taxpayer files the return (including extension) or 8½ months after the close of the taxable year.

[47] Reg. § 1.461–4.

[48] § 404; Reg. § 1.404(b)–1T, Q&A 2, Reg. §1.461–4(d)(2)(iii).

[49] § 461(c).

3. The item is recurring in nature.
4. The item either is not material in amount or accruing it results in a better matching of revenues and expenses.

Green Corporation often sells goods that are on hand but cannot be shipped for another week. The all events test for the sale is satisfied; therefore, gross income is recognized although the goods have not been shipped at year-end.

Green is obligated to pay shipping costs. Although the company's obligation for shipping costs can be determined with reasonable accuracy, economic performance is not satisfied until Green (or its agent) actually delivers the goods. However, accruing shipping costs on sold items will better match expenses with revenues for the period. Therefore, the company should accrue the shipping costs on items sold but not shipped at year-end.

The economic performance test detailed in the Code does not address all possible accrued expenses. That is, in some cases, the taxpayer has a liability (owes money for something) even though no property or services were received. In these instances, economic performance generally is not satisfied until the liability is paid. The following liabilities illustrate situations where payment is the only means of satisfying economic performance:[50]

1. Workers' compensation.
2. Torts.
3. Breach of contract.
4. Violation of law.
5. Rebates and refunds.
6. Awards, prizes, and jackpots.
7. Insurance, warranty, and service contracts.[51]
8. Taxes.

Financial Disclosure Insights **Tax Deferrals from Reserves**

The tax law generally applies the all events and economic performance tests in determining when an expense is deductible. Accordingly, the use of reserves for financial accounting purposes does not carry over to the tax return. When a business creates a reserve, for example, to account for warranty obligations to customers or vacation pay for employees, book expenses are allowed, but the corresponding tax deduction usually is delayed until an expenditure is actually incurred. The temporary book-tax difference typically creates or adds to a deferred tax asset on the entity's balance sheet.

On a GAAP balance sheet, all deferred tax assets are deemed to be noncurrent.

Yellow Corporation sold defective merchandise that injured a customer. Yellow admitted liability in 2023 but did not pay the claim until January 2024. The customer's tort claim cannot be deducted by Yellow until it is paid to the customer.

Items (5) through (8) above are eligible for the recurring item exception.

Pelican Corporation, a calendar year taxpayer, filed its 2023 state income tax return in March 2024 and its 2023 Federal return on September 15, 2024. At the time the state return was filed, Pelican was required to pay an additional $5,000. The state taxes are eligible for the recurring item exception. Thus, the $5,000 of state income taxes can be deducted on the corporation's 2023 Federal tax return. The deduction is allowed because all of the events had occurred to fix the liability as of the end of 2023, the payment was made by the earlier of the return filing date or 8½ months after the end of the tax year, the item is recurring in nature, and allowing the deduction in 2023 results in a better matching of revenues and expenses.

Reserves

Generally, the all events and economic performance tests prevent the income tax use of reserves (e.g., for product warranty expense) frequently used in financial accounting to match expenses with revenues. However, small banks can use a bad debt reserve.[52]

[50] Reg. §§ 1.461–4(g)(2)–(6) and 1.461–5(c).

[51] This item applies to contracts that taxpayers enter into for their own protection rather than the taxpayer's liability as insurer, warrantor, or service provider.

[52] § 585.

In addition, an accrual basis taxpayer in a service business may be allowed to not accrue revenue that appears uncollectible based on experience. In effect, this approach indirectly allows a tax reserve.[53]

16-2d Hybrid Method

A **hybrid method** of accounting involves the use of more than one overall method. For example, a taxpayer who uses the accrual basis to report sales and cost of goods sold but uses the cash basis to report other items of income and expense is employing a hybrid method. The Code permits the use of a hybrid tax accounting method provided the taxpayer's income is clearly reflected.[54] A taxpayer who uses the accrual method for business expenses must also use the accrual method for business income.

The Loyal Pet Clinic boards animals, provides veterinarian services, and sells pet supplies and medicines (inventory). The clinic's gross receipts are approximately $4,000,000 per year, and 40% of the receipts are from sales of pet supplies. Under its hybrid method of accounting, the clinic uses the accrual method for the sales of supplies and medicines because inventories are a material income-producing factor. The services income is reported using the cash method.

Businesses with average annual gross receipts in the prior three-year period of $29,000,000 or less are not required to use the accrual method. As a result, Loyal Pet Clinic should consider a change in its method from hybrid to cash and treat its inventory as deductible when purchased (and paid for) or as nonincidental supplies (further discussed in text Section 16-4).

16-2e Change in Accounting Method

LO.3 **Explain the procedure for changing accounting methods.**

The taxpayer, in effect, makes an election to use a particular accounting method when its initial tax return is filed using that method. Once chosen, the taxpayer must obtain the permission of the IRS to change its accounting method. The request for change is made on Form 3115, which should be filed within the taxable year of the desired change.[55]

As previously mentioned, the term *accounting method* encompasses not only the overall accounting method used by the taxpayer (the cash or accrual method) but also the treatment of any material item of income or deduction.[56] For example, a change in the method of deducting property taxes from a cash basis to an accrual basis that results in a deduction for taxes in a different year constitutes a change in an accounting method. Another example of an accounting method change is a change involving the method or basis used in the valuation of inventories.

A change in treatment resulting from a change in the underlying facts does not constitute a change in the taxpayer's method of accounting.[57] For example, a change in employment contracts so that an employee accrues one day of vacation pay for each month of service rather than 12 days of vacation pay for a full year of service is a change in the underlying facts and is not an accounting method change.

Correction of an Error

A change in accounting method is not the same as the *correction of an error*. The taxpayer can correct an error (by filing amended returns) without permission of the IRS, and the IRS simply adjusts the taxpayer's liability if an error is discovered on audit of the return. Some examples of errors are incorrect postings, errors in the calculation of tax liability or tax credits, deductions of business expense items that are actually personal, and omissions of income and deductions.[58] Unless the taxpayer or the IRS corrects the error within the statute of limitations (in general, three years after a tax return is filed), the taxpayer's total lifetime taxable income is overstated or understated by the amount of the error.

---

[53] § 448(d)(5).

[54] § 446(c)(3).

[55] See Rev.Proc. 2015–13 for the method change procedures and Rev.Proc. 2022–14 for the list of automatic method changes. Generally, for an automatic method change, Form 3115 is due when the tax return for the year of change is filed, including extension.

[56] Reg. § 1.446–1(a)(1).

[57] Reg. § 1.446–1(e)(2)(ii).

[58] Reg. § 1.446–1(e)(2)(ii)(b).

Change from an Incorrect Method

An *incorrect accounting method* is the consistent (for at least two tax returns) use of an incorrect rule to report an item of income or expense. The incorrect accounting method will not affect the taxpayer's total lifetime income (unlike the error). That is, an incorrect method has a self-balancing mechanism. For example, deducting freight on inventory in the year the goods are purchased rather than when the inventory is sold is an incorrect accounting method. The total cost of goods sold over the life of the business is not affected, but the year-to-year income is incorrect.[59]

If a taxpayer is employing an incorrect method of accounting, permission must be obtained from the IRS to change to a correct method. An incorrect method cannot be corrected merely by filing an amended tax return.

The tax return preparer as well as the taxpayer will be subject to penalties if the tax return is prepared using an incorrect method of accounting and permission for a change to a correct method was not requested.[60]

Net Adjustments Due to Change in Method of Accounting

In the year of a change in accounting method, an adjustment generally is required to prevent the omission or duplication of income or expense items.

Example 24

White, a C corporation, operates a web platform that allows bookkeepers and accountants to offer their services to companies and individuals. It operates similar to Uber, TaskRabbit, and similar freelancing or gig platforms. Its gross receipts have increased significantly every year since it began operations in 2017.

For 2023, White determines that its average annual gross receipts for the prior three years crossed the $29,000,000 threshold. As a result, White must change its accounting method from cash to accrual starting in 2023 (*the year of change*). It also must calculate a "net § 481(a) adjustment" to be sure that no income or expense is omitted from income (or duplicated) when it makes this method change. White reports the following information:

Accounts receivable at December 31, 2022	$1,100,000
Accounts payable at December 31, 2022	860,000

Because White used the cash method of accounting for tax purposes, the $1,100,000 of receivables was not yet reported in taxable income. Similarly, the $860,000 of payables has not yet been claimed as a deduction. When White changes from the cash method to the accrual method starting with its 2023 tax year, it will behave as if it was always using the accrual method. As a result, when it collects the $1,100,000 of receivables in 2023, White will not report any gross income because, if White had always been using the accrual method, that income would have been reported earlier when earned. Similarly, when White pays the payables in 2023, it will not claim a deduction because, if White had always used the accrual method, the payables would have been deducted earlier when incurred.

To avoid omission of the $1,100,000 of income, White has a positive "§ 481(a) adjustment" of $1,100,000 (meaning it increases White's taxable income). To avoid omission of the $860,000 of deductions, White has a negative "§ 481(a) adjustment" of $860,000. These amounts are combined to yield a "net positive § 481(a) adjustment" of $240,000.

Reporting the Net § 481(a) Adjustment

Required changes in tax accounting methods can result from an IRS examination. Generally, if the IRS finds that a taxpayer is using an incorrect method of accounting, a change is imposed but on less favorable terms than if the taxpayer had corrected the erroneous method on its own. For example, the IRS may require the taxpayer to correct the method for the earliest year open under the statute of limitations and record any positive § 481 adjustment entirely in that year (rather than over four years allowed for a voluntary change in method). Additional tax and interest then may be due.[61]

---

[59] But see *Korn Industries v. U.S.*, 76–1 USTC ¶9354, 37 AFTR 2d 76–1228, 532 F.2d 1352 (Ct.Cls.).

[60] § 446(f).

[61] § 481(b). Guidance on IRS-initiated method changes can be found in Rev.Proc. 2002–18.

To encourage taxpayers to *voluntarily* change from incorrect methods (rather than wait for an IRS audit resulting in a required change) and to facilitate changes from one correct method to another, the IRS generally allows the taxpayer to spread a positive adjustment into future years. One-fourth of the adjustment is applied to the year of the change, and one-fourth of the adjustment is applied to each of the next three taxable years. A negative adjustment is deducted in the year of the change.[62]

White Corporation in Example 24 must add $60,000 (¼ × $240,000 net positive adjustment) to its 2023, 2024, 2025, and 2026 income.

Ethics & Equity **Change in Accounting Method**

The IRS faces a difficult choice when it deals with taxpayers who use incorrect accounting methods. On the one hand, the taxpayer who has used an incorrect accounting method may be just as culpable as a person who has omitted income or taken an improper deduction. On the other hand, it often is difficult to discover that a taxpayer is using an incorrect accounting method.

Therefore, the IRS relies to some extent on self-reporting by taxpayers. The Service encourages voluntary changes in incorrect accounting methods by waiving penalties for an underpayment of prior years' taxes, thus permitting the taxpayer, in effect, to pay the related taxes over a four-year period. Is this equitable treatment? Discuss the reasons underlying your position.

16-3 Special Accounting Methods

LO.4

Determine when the installment method of accounting applies and its effect on taxable income.

The tax law provides special accounting methods for certain installment sales and long-term contracts. These special methods were enacted, in part, to ensure that the tax will be due when the taxpayer is best able to pay the tax.

16-3a Installment Method

Under the general rule for computing the gain or loss from the sale of property, the taxpayer recognizes the entire amount of gain or loss upon the sale or other disposition of the property.

Mark sells property to Pooja for $10,000 cash plus Pooja's note (fair market value and face amount of $90,000). Mark's basis for the property was $15,000. Gain or loss is computed under either the cash or accrual basis as follows:

Selling price	
Cash down payment	$ 10,000
Note receivable	90,000
	$100,000
Basis in the property	(15,000)
Realized gain	$ 85,000

[62]Rev.Proc. 2015–13.

In Example 26, the general rule for recognizing gain or loss requires Mark to pay a substantial amount of tax on the gain in the year of sale even though he received only $10,000 cash. Congress enacted the installment sales provisions to prevent this sort of hardship by allowing the taxpayer to spread the gain from installment sales over time as payments are received, when the taxpayer perhaps is best able to pay the tax. The installment method is an important planning tool because it creates tax deferral possibilities.

Eligibility and Calculations

The **installment method** applies to *gains* (but not losses) from the sale of property by a taxpayer who will receive at least one payment *after* the year of sale. However, the installment method cannot be used for:[63]

- Gains on property held for sale in the ordinary course of business, with limited exceptions.
- Depreciation recapture amounts.
- Gains on stocks or securities traded on an established market.

The Mandatory Aspect

As a general rule, eligible sales *must* be reported by the installment method unless the taxpayer elects not to apply this rule.[64]

Computing the Gain for Each Year Payments Are Received

The gain reported on each sale is computed using the following formula:

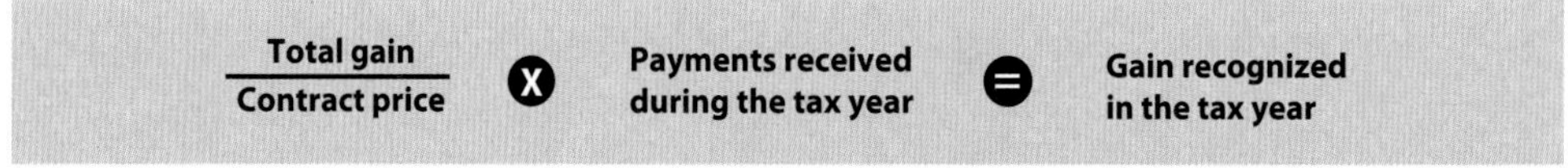

1. *Total gain* is the selling price reduced by selling expenses and the adjusted basis of the property. The selling price is the total consideration received by the seller, including notes receivable from the buyer and the seller's liabilities assumed by the buyer.
2. *Contract price* is the selling price less the seller's liabilities that are assumed by the buyer. Generally, the contract price is the amount, other than interest, the seller will receive from the purchaser.
3. *Payments received* are the collections on the contract price received in each tax year. This generally is equal to the cash received less the interest income collected for the period. If the buyer pays any of the seller's expenses, the seller regards the amount paid as a payment received.[65]

[63] §§ 453(b), (i), and (l).

[64] §§ 453(a) and (d).

[65] The gain is reported on Form 6252.

Example 27

Gonzalo, not a dealer, reports the following for a sale of investment land:

Sales price		
Cash down payment	$ 1,000	
Seller's mortgage assumed by the buyer	3,000	
Notes payable to the seller	13,000	$ 17,000
Selling expenses		(500)
Seller's basis		(10,000)
Total gain		$ 6,500

The contract price is $14,000 ($17,000 − $3,000). Assuming that the $1,000 is the only payment in the year of sale, the recognized gain in that year is:

$$\frac{\$6{,}500 \text{ (total gain)}}{\$14{,}000 \text{ (contract price)}} \times \$1{,}000 = \$464 \text{ (gain recognized in year of sale)}$$

As previously noted, any depreciation recapture amounts generate gain recognized in the year of sale, and the installment sale gain is any remaining amount.

Example 28

Olaf sold equipment for $50,000 cash and a $75,000 note due in two years. Olaf's cost of the property was $90,000, and he had deducted depreciation of $65,000. Thus, the basis in the property was $25,000 ($90,000 − $65,000).

Olaf's realized gain is $100,000 ($125,000 − $25,000), and the $65,000 depreciation recapture gain must be recognized in the year of sale. Of the $35,000 remaining § 1231 gain, $14,000 must be recognized in the year of sale.

$$\frac{\text{§ 1231 gain}}{\text{Contract price}} \times \text{Payment received} = \frac{\$125{,}000 - \$25{,}000 - \$65{,}000}{\$125{,}000} \times \$50{,}000$$

$$= \frac{\$35{,}000}{\$125{,}000} \times \$50{,}000 = \$14{,}000$$

The remaining § 1231 gain of $21,000 ($35,000 − $14,000) is recognized as the $75,000 note is collected.

Imputed Interest

If a deferred payment contract for the sale of property with a selling price greater than $3,000 does not contain a reasonable interest rate, a reasonable rate is imputed by the tax law.[66] The imputing of interest effectively restates the selling price of the property to the sum of the payments at the date of the sale and the discounted present value of the future payments. The difference between the present value of a future payment and the payment's face amount is taxed as interest income.

In this way, the **imputed interest** rules prevent sellers of capital assets from increasing the selling price to reflect the equivalent of unstated interest on deferred payments, thereby converting ordinary (interest) income into long-term capital gains. The imputed interest rules create gross income for every tax year when there is deferred tax liability from installment sales.

Generally, if the contract does not charge at least the Federal rate, interest is imputed at that rate. The Federal rate is the interest rate the Federal government pays on new borrowing and is published monthly by the IRS.[67]

[66] §§ 483 and 1274.

[67] § 1274(d)(1). There are three pertinent Federal rates: short-term (not over three years), midterm (over three years but not over nine years), and long-term (over nine years). For example, see Rev.Rul. 2022–20.

As a general rule, the buyer and seller must account for interest on the accrual basis with semiannual compounding.[68] The use of the accrual method ensures that the seller's interest income and the buyer's interest expense are reported in the same tax year.

Peggy, a cash basis taxpayer, sold land on January 1, 2023, for $200,000 cash and $6,000,000 due on December 31, 2024, with 2% interest payable December 31, 2023, and December 31, 2024. At the time of the sale, the applicable Federal rate was 4% (compounded semiannually). Because Peggy did not charge interest at least equal to the Federal rate, interest is imputed at 4%.

Date	Payment	Present Value (at 4%) on 1/1/2023	Imputed Interest
12/31/2023	$ 120,000	$ 115,384	$ 4,616
12/31/2024	6,120,000	5,658,284	461,716
	$6,240,000	$5,773,668	$466,332

As a result, the selling price is restated to $5,973,668 ($200,000 + $5,773,668) rather than $6,200,000 ($200,000 + $6,000,000). Peggy will recognize interest income, computed as follows:

	Beginning Balance	Interest (at 4%)*	Received	Ending Balance
2023	$5,773,668	$230,947	$ 120,000	$5,884,615
2024	5,884,615	235,385	6,120,000	–0–

*Compounded semiannually.

Related-Party Sales of Nondepreciable Property

If the Code did not contain special rules, a taxpayer could make an installment sale of property to a related party (e.g., a family member) as part of a tax deferral plan. Then the purchasing family member could immediately sell the property to an unrelated party for cash with no recognized gain or loss (because the amount realized would equal the basis in the sold asset). The related-party purchaser would not pay the installment note to the selling family member until a later year. The net result would be that the family has the cash, but no taxable gain is recognized until the purchasing family member makes payments on the installment note.

Under special rules designed to address the scheme described above, the proceeds from the subsequent sale (the second sale) by the purchasing family member are treated as though they were used to pay the installment note due the selling family member (the first sale). As a result, the recognition of gain from the original sale between the related parties is accelerated.[69]

However, even with these special rules, Congress did not eliminate the benefits of all related-party installment sales.

- Related parties include only the first seller's brothers, sisters, ancestors, lineal descendants, controlled corporations, and partnerships, trusts, and estates in which the seller has an interest.[70]
- There is no acceleration if the second disposition occurs more than two years after the first sale.[71]

As a result, if the taxpayer can sell the property to an "unrelated" family member (like a cousin) or a "patient" family member, the intrafamily installment sale still is a powerful tax planning tool.[72]

[68] §§ 1274(a), 1273(a), and 1272(a).

[69] § 453(e).

[70] § 453(f)(1), cross-referencing §§ 267(b) and 318(a). Although spouses are related parties, the exclusion of gains between spouses (§ 1041) overrides the second-disposition rules when the first sale was between spouses.

[71] § 453(e)(2). But see § 453(e)(2)(B) for extensions of the two-year period.

[72] Other exceptions also can be applied in some circumstances. See §§ 453(e)(6) and (7).

Related-Party Sales of Depreciable Property

The installment method cannot be used to report a gain on the sale of depreciable property to a controlled entity. The purpose of this rule is to prevent the seller from deferring gain (until collections are received) while the related purchaser is enjoying a stepped-up basis for depreciation purposes.[73]

The prohibition on the use of the installment method applies to sales between the taxpayer and a partnership or corporation in which the taxpayer holds a more-than-50-percent interest. Constructive ownership rules are used in applying the ownership test (e.g., the taxpayer is considered to own stock owned by a spouse and certain other family members).[74] However, if the taxpayer can establish that tax avoidance was not a principal purpose of the transaction, the installment method can be used to report the gain.

Alan purchased an apartment building from his controlled corporation, Emerald Corporation. Alan was short of cash at the time of the purchase (December 2023) but was to collect a large cash payment in January 2024. The agreement required Alan to pay the entire arm's length price in January 2024. Alan had nontax business reasons for acquiring the building.

Emerald should be able to show that tax avoidance was not a principal purpose for the installment sale, because of Alan's cash flow issues. Emerald reports all of the gain in the year following the year of sale, and Alan depreciates the building over 27.5 years (the cost recovery period for residential real estate).

Interest on Deferred Tax

The installment method allows the seller to defer the payment of taxes on the gain from the sale of property until payments are received from the buyer (borrower). Congress was concerned that this deferral in addition to the seller earning interest on the receivable was too significant of a benefit. To address this concern, sellers are required to pay interest on the deferred taxes if *both* of the following requirements are met:

- The installment obligation arises from the sale of property (other than farming property) for more than $150,000.
- The taxpayer's total installment obligations outstanding at the close of the tax year exceed $5 million.[75]

Disposition of Installment Obligations

Generally, a taxpayer must recognize the deferred profit from an installment sale when the obligation is transferred to another party or is otherwise relinquished. The rationale for accelerating the gain is that the deferral should continue for no longer than the taxpayer owns the installment obligation.[76]

The gift or cancellation of an installment note is treated as a taxable disposition by the donor. This discourages attempts to shift income among family members. The amount realized from the cancellation is the face amount of the note if the parties (obligor and obligee) are related to each other.[77]

[73] § 453(g).

[74] §§ 1239(b) and (c).

[75] § 453A and IRS Publication 537. This amount is not indexed for inflation.

[76] § 453B(a).

[77] § 453B(f)(2).

Liz cancels a note issued by Ting (Liz's daughter) that arose in connection with the sale of property. At the time of the cancellation, the note had a basis to Liz of $10,000, a face amount of $25,000, and a fair market value of $20,000. Presuming that the initial sale by Liz qualified as an installment sale, the cancellation results in gain of $15,000 ($25,000 − $10,000) to Liz.

Certain exceptions to the recognition of gain provisions are provided for transfers of installment obligations to the transferor's 80 percent controlled corporation, contributions of capital to a partnership, certain corporate liquidations, transfers due to the taxpayer's death, and transfers between spouses or incident to divorce.[78] In such situations, the deferred profit is shifted to the transferee, who is responsible for the payment of tax on the subsequent collections of the installment obligations. But in the case of a transfer of installment obligations to a partnership by a partner, the transferor partner is taxed on the income when the partnership collects on the installment receivables.

The Big Picture

Example 32

Return to the facts of *The Big Picture* on p. 16-1. Assume that Belinda's capital contribution to the partnership in 2023 was an installment obligation with a basis of $40,000 and a face amount of $100,000. In 2024, the partnership collected the $100,000. The transfer in 2023 was not a taxable disposition, but in 2024 when the receivable is collected, Belinda recognizes a gain of $60,000.

Electing Out of the Installment Method

While the installment method is mandatory when it applies, a taxpayer can *elect not to use* it. The election is made by reporting the entire recognized gain on the seller's timely filed return.[79] Taxpayers and their tax advisers must be careful not to report the entire gain in the year of sale if the taxpayer did not want to elect out of installment sale treatment.

The election frequently is applied to year-end sales by taxpayers who expect to be in a higher tax bracket in the following year. Permission of the IRS is required to revoke an election not to use the installment method.[80]

Example 33

On December 31, 2023, Kurt sold investment land to Jodie for $20,000 (fair market value). He had owned the land for seven years. Jodie will pay Kurt $20,000 in cash on January 4, 2024. Kurt is a cash basis taxpayer, and his basis in the land is $8,000. As a result, he realizes a $12,000 capital gain from the sale. Kurt has a marginal tax rate of 12% in 2023. He expects his tax rate to increase to 35% in 2024.

The transaction constitutes an installment sale because a payment will be received in a tax year after the tax year of disposition. Jodie's promise to pay Kurt is an installment obligation, and under the Regulations, the value of the installment obligation is equal to the value of the property sold ($20,000). If Kurt elects out of the installment method, he will shift the $12,000 capital gain from the expected higher capital gains rate in 2024 of 15% to the 0% rate for long-term capital gains in 2023. The expected tax savings based on the rate differential may exceed the benefit of the tax deferral available with the installment method.

[78] §§ 453B(c), (d), and (g).

[79] § 453(d) and Reg. § 15a.453–1(d).

[80] § 453(d)(3) and Reg. § 15a.453–1(d)(4).

16-3b **Long-Term Contracts**

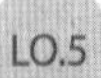

Recognize the methods of accounting for long-term contracts.

A **long-term contract** is a building, installation, construction, or manufacturing contract that is entered into but not completed within the same tax year.[81] However, a *manufacturing* contract is long term *only* if the contract is to manufacture (1) a unique item not normally carried in finished goods inventory or (2) items that normally require more than 12 calendar months to complete.[82] An item is *unique* if it is designed to meet the customer's needs and is not suitable for use by others. A contract to perform services (e.g., auditing or legal services) cannot qualify as a long-term contract.

Rocky, a calendar year taxpayer, entered into two contracts during the year.

One contract was to construct a building foundation. Work was to begin in October 2023 and was to be completed by June 2024. The contract is long term because it will not be entered into and completed in the same tax year. The fact that the contract requires fewer than 12 calendar months to complete is not relevant because the contract is not for manufacturing.

The second contract was for architectural services to be performed over two years. Payments for these services do not qualify for long-term contract treatment.

Generally, the taxpayer must accumulate all of the direct and indirect costs incurred under a contract. This means that the production costs must be accumulated and allocated to individual contracts. Furthermore, mixed services costs (costs that benefit contracts as well as the general administrative operations of the business) must be allocated between production and general administration on a rational basis. Exhibit 16.1 lists the types of costs that must be accumulated and allocated to contracts.[83]

Example 35

Falcon, Inc., uses detailed cost accumulation records to assign labor and materials to its contracts in progress. The total cost of fringe benefits is allocated to a contract on the following basis:

$$\frac{\text{Labor on the contract}}{\text{Total salaries and labor}} \times \text{Total cost of fringe benefits}$$

Similarly, storage and handling costs for materials are allocated to contracts on the following basis:

$$\frac{\text{Contract materials}}{\text{Material purchases}} \times \text{Storage and handling costs}$$

The cost of the personnel operations, a mixed services cost, is allocated between production and general administration based on the number of employees in each function. The personnel cost allocated to production is allocated to individual contracts on the basis of the formula used to allocate fringe benefits.

The accumulated costs are deducted when the revenue from the contract is recognized. Generally, two methods of accounting are used in varying circumstances to determine when the revenue from a contract is recognized.[84]

- The completed contract method.
- The percentage of completion method.

[81] Special rules apply when the Federal government is a party to the contract. §§ 460(c) and (d).

[82] § 460(f) and Reg. § 1.460–2(a).

[83] Reg. §§ 1.460–5(b) and 1.263A–1(e).

[84] § 460.

Exhibit 16.1 **Contract Costs, Mixed Services Costs, and Current Expense Items for Contracts**

	Contracts Eligible for the Completed Contract Method	Other Contracts
Contract costs:		
Direct materials (a part of the finished product).	Capitalize	Capitalize
Indirect materials [consumed in production but not in the finished product (e.g., grease and oil for equipment)].	Capitalize	Capitalize
Storage, handling, and insurance on materials.	Expense	Capitalize
Direct labor (worked on the product).	Capitalize	Capitalize
Indirect labor [worked in the production process but not directly on the product (e.g., a construction supervisor)].	Capitalize	Capitalize
Fringe benefits for direct and indirect labor (e.g., vacation, sick pay, unemployment, and other insurance).	Capitalize	Capitalize
Depreciation on production facilities:		
For financial statements.	Capitalize	Capitalize
Tax depreciation in excess of financial statements.	Expense	Capitalize
Depreciation on idle facilities.	Expense	Expense
Property taxes, insurance, rent, and maintenance on production facilities.	Capitalize	Capitalize
Interest to finance real estate construction.	Capitalize	Capitalize
Interest to finance personal property:		
Production period of one year or less.	Expense	Expense
Production period exceeds one year, and costs exceed $1 million.*	Capitalize	Capitalize
Production period exceeds two years.*	Capitalize	Capitalize
Mixed services costs:		
Personnel operations.	Expense	Allocate
Data processing.	Expense	Allocate
Selling, general, and administrative expenses (including an allocated share of mixed services).	Expense	Expense

*The production period does not include the aging period for beer, wine, and certain distilled spirits, for interest paid or accrued before 2020.

The *completed contract method may be used* for (1) home construction contracts (contracts in which at least 80 percent of the estimated costs are for dwelling units in buildings with four or fewer units) and (2) certain other real estate construction contracts. Other real estate contracts can qualify for the completed contract method if both of the following requirements are satisfied:

- The contract is expected to be completed within the two-year period beginning on the commencement date of the contract.
- The contract is performed by a taxpayer whose average annual gross receipts for the three taxable years preceding the taxable year in which the contract is entered into do not exceed $29 million.

The percentage of completion method must be used for all other contracts.

Completed Contract Method

Under the **completed contract method**, no revenue from the contract is recognized until the contract is completed and accepted. Generally, the contract is completed when it is accepted by the customer as finished or when the customer begins using the subject of the contract.[85]

In some situations, the original contract price may be disputed, or the buyer may want additional work to be done on a long-term contract. If the disputed amount is substantial (it is not possible to determine whether a profit or loss will ultimately be realized on the contract), no amount of income or loss is recognized until the dispute is resolved. In all other cases, the profit or loss (reduced by the amount in dispute) is recognized in the current period upon completion of the contract. However, additional work may need to be performed with respect to the disputed contract. When the amount in dispute is less than the net profit on the contract before the estimated additional cost, the taxpayer must report in the year of completion the applicable profit, reduced by the estimated additional cost.[86]

Ted, a calendar year taxpayer using the completed contract method of accounting, constructed a building for Brad under a long-term contract. The gross contract price was $500,000. Ted finished construction in 2023 at a cost of $475,000. When Brad examined the building, he insisted that the building be repainted or that the contract price be reduced. The estimated cost of repainting is $10,000.

Under the terms of the contract, Ted is assured a profit of at least $15,000 ($500,000 − $475,000 − $10,000) even if the dispute is ultimately resolved in Brad's favor. As a result, Ted must include $490,000 ($500,000 − $10,000) in gross income and is allowed deductions of $475,000 for 2023.

In 2024, Ted and Brad resolve the dispute, and Ted repaints certain portions of the building at a cost of $6,000. Ted must include $10,000 in 2024 gross income and may deduct the $6,000 expense in that year.

If the net profit less the estimated additional cost results in a loss, the loss is deferred until the dispute is resolved.

Assume the same facts as in the previous example, except that the estimated cost of repainting the building is $50,000. Because the resolution of the dispute completely in Brad's favor would mean a net loss on the contract for Ted ($500,000 − $475,000 − $50,000 = $25,000 loss), Ted does not recognize any income or loss until the year the dispute is resolved.

Percentage of Completion Method

Under the **percentage of completion method**, a portion of the gross contract price is included in income during each period as the work progresses. The revenue accrued each period (except for the final period) is:[87]

$$\frac{C}{T} \times P$$

Where C = Contract costs incurred during the period
T = Estimated total cost of the contract
P = Contract price

[85] Reg. § 1.460–1(c)(3).
[86] Reg. §§ 1.451–3(d)(2)(ii)–(vii), Example 2.
[87] § 460(b)(1)(A).

All of the costs allocated to the contract during the period are deductible from the accrued revenue.[88] The revenue reported in the final period is any remaining revenue from the contract. Because T in this formula is an estimate that frequently differs from total actual costs (which are not known until the contract has been completed), the profit on a contract for a particular period may be overstated or understated (such that related income taxes may be overpaid or underpaid).

Tan, Inc., entered into a contract that was to take two years to complete, with an estimated cost of $2,250,000. The contract price was $3,000,000. Costs of the contract for 2022, the first year, totaled $1,350,000. The gross profit reported by the percentage of completion method for 2022 was $450,000 {[($1,350,000 ÷ $2,250,000) × $3,000,000] − $1,350,000}.

The contract was completed at the end of 2023 at a total cost of $2,700,000. In retrospect, the 2022 profit should have been $150,000 {[($1,350,000 ÷ $2,700,000) × $3,000,000] − $1,350,000}. As a result, taxes were overpaid for 2022.

Under a *de minimis* rule, if less than 10 percent of the estimated contract costs have been incurred by the end of the taxable year, the taxpayer can elect to defer the recognition of income and the related costs until the taxable year in which at least 10 percent of total costs are incurred.[89]

Lookback Provision

In the year a contract is completed, a *lookback* provision requires the recalculation of annual profits reported on the contract under the percentage of completion method. Interest is paid to the taxpayer if taxes were overpaid, and interest is payable by the taxpayer if there was an underpayment.[90] For a corporate taxpayer, the lookback interest paid by the taxpayer is deductible, but for an individual taxpayer, it is nondeductible personal interest associated with a tax liability.

Assume that Tan, Inc., in Example 38, was in the 21% tax bracket in both years and the relevant interest rate was 5%. For 2022, the company paid excess taxes of $63,000 [($450,000 − $150,000) × 21%]. When the contract is completed at the end of 2023, Tan should receive interest of $3,150 ($63,000 × 5%) for one year on the tax overpayment.

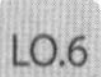

Recognize when accounting for inventories must occur and the key tax accounting methods for inventory.

16-4 Inventories

The use of inventories is necessary to clearly reflect income of any business engaged in the production, purchase, or sale of merchandise. Inventories might not be required for small taxpayers, defined for this purpose as those with average annual gross receipts for the prior three-year period of $29 million or less.[91] Generally, when a taxpayer is required to account for inventories for Federal income tax purposes, tax accounting and financial accounting for inventories are much the same.

- The use of inventories is necessary to clearly reflect the income of any business engaged in the production and sale or purchase and sale of goods.[92]
- The inventories should include all finished goods, goods in process, and raw materials and supplies that will become part of the product (including containers).

[88] Reg. § 1.451–3(c)(3).

[89] § 460(b)(5).

[90] §§ 460(b)(2) and (6). The taxpayer can elect not to apply the lookback method in situations where the cumulative taxable income as of the close of each prior year is within 10% of the correct income for each prior year.

[91] Reg. § 1.471–1.

[92] § 471(a) and Reg. §§ 1.471–1 and −2.

- Inventory rules must give effect to the *best accounting practice* of a particular trade or business, and the taxpayer's method should be followed consistently from year to year.
- All items included in inventory should be valued at either (1) cost or (2) the lower of cost or market value.

The reason for the similarities between tax and financial accounting for inventories is that § 471 establishes a two-prong test. Under this provision, "inventories shall be taken . . . on such basis . . . as conforming as nearly as may be to the *best accounting practice* in the trade or business and as most *clearly reflecting the income*." The best accounting practice is synonymous with generally accepted accounting principles (GAAP). However, the IRS determines whether an inventory method clearly reflects income.

In *Thor Power Tool Co. v. Comm.*, there was a conflict between the two tests.[93] The taxpayer's method of valuing obsolete parts was in conformity with GAAP. The IRS, however, successfully argued that the clear reflection of income test was not satisfied because the taxpayer's procedures for valuing its inventories were contrary to the Regulations. Under the taxpayer's method, inventories for parts in excess of estimated future sales were expensed, although the parts were kept on hand and their asking prices were not reduced. [Under Reg. § 1.471–4(b), inventories cannot be written down unless the selling prices also are reduced.] The taxpayer contended that conformity to GAAP creates a presumption that the method clearly reflects income.

The Supreme Court disagreed, concluding that the clear reflection of income test was paramount. Moreover, the Court indicated that the IRS position controls in determining whether the method of inventory clearly reflects income. As a result, the best accounting practice test was rendered meaningless by this decision: the taxpayer's method of inventory must strictly conform to the Regulations, regardless of what GAAP may require.

16-4a **Determining Inventory Cost**

For merchandise purchased, cost is the invoice price less trade discounts plus freight and other handling charges.[94] Cash discounts approximating a fair interest rate can be deducted or capitalized as the taxpayer elects, provided the method used is consistently applied.

Uniform Capitalization (UNICAP)

For inventory and property produced by the taxpayer, "(A) the direct cost of such property, and (B) such property's share of those indirect costs (including taxes) part or all of which are allocable to such property" must be capitalized. The UNICAP rules apply to all types of businesses: contractors, manufacturers, farmers, wholesalers, and retailers.[95] The procedures are known as the **uniform capitalization (UNICAP) rules**, and many practitioners refer to the rules as a *super-full absorption costing system*.

Taxpayers with average annual gross receipts of $29 million or less (for the previous three years) are not required to apply the UNICAP rules. Special rules exempt certain farming property as well as deductible research expenditures from UNICAP.[96]

The UNICAP rules may result in some costs being capitalized for Federal income tax purposes but not for financial accounting purposes. For example, a wholesaler's or manufacturer's storage costs generally are expensed for financial reporting purposes but are capitalized for tax purposes. The taxpayer may capitalize straight-line depreciation of production equipment for financial accounting purposes, but tax depreciation amounts are capitalized for UNICAP.

---

[93] 79–1 USTC ¶9139, 43 AFTR 2d 79–362, 99 S.Ct. 773. See text Section 4-1d for the Court's discussion of the differences between tax and financial accounting.

[94] Reg. § 1.471–3(b).

[95] § 263A. H. Rep. 99–841, 99th Cong., 2nd Sess., 1986, pp. 302–309. See also Reg. § 1.263A–1(a).

[96] §§ 263A(d) and (e)(3).

To value inventory under the UNICAP rules, a *producer* must first classify all of its costs into three categories:[97]

(1) production,
(2) general administration (nonproduction), and
(3) mixed services [activities that benefit both category (1) and (2) activities, such as the legal and human resources departments].

Next, the producer needs to perform two allocations using the methods of accounting it has adopted for these purposes.

(1) Separate mixed services costs between production and general administration (nonproduction).
(2) Allocate the production costs (that now include the mixed service costs allocated to production) between the cost of goods sold and the ending inventory.

Exhibit 16.1 (see the "Other Contracts" column) lists typical items that are included in the three classes of costs. The mixed services costs should be allocated to production on a rational basis. For example, the costs of operating the human resources department may be allocated between production and general administration (e.g., based on the number of applications processed or the number of employees). In lieu of allocating each mixed services cost, the taxpayer can elect a *simplified method* whereby the total of all mixed services costs is allocated to production in this manner.[98]

$$MSP = \frac{TP}{TC} \times TMS$$

Where MSP = Mixed services costs allocated to production
TP = Total production costs other than interest and mixed services
TC = Total costs other than interest; state, local, or foreign income taxes; and mixed services costs
TMS = Total mixed services costs

Traditional cost accounting techniques (e.g., average cost per equivalent unit) can be used to allocate the costs between the cost of goods sold and the ending inventory. Alternatively, the producer can elect to allocate mixed services costs to production on the basis of labor charges only (production labor as a percentage of total labor costs).

The costs included in the inventory of *wholesalers and retailers* are comparable to those of the producer. However, many of these costs are captured in the price these taxpayers pay for the goods. The following additional costs are capitalized by these taxpayers:

- All storage costs for wholesalers.
- Off-site storage costs for retailers.
- Purchasing costs (e.g., buyers' wages or salaries).
- Handling, processing, assembly, and repackaging.
- The portion of mixed services costs allocable to these functions.
- Interest expense on loans related to production of inventory must be capitalized if (1) the estimated production period exceeds one year and the costs exceed $1 million or (2) the estimated production period exceeds two years.[99]

Mixed services costs are allocated to off-site storage, purchasing, and packaging on the basis of direct labor costs of these departments pro rata to total payroll.

[97] Reg. § 1.263A–1(c).
[98] Reg. § 1.263A–1(h)(5).
[99] § 263A(f). The $1 million amount is not indexed for inflation.

Lower of Cost or Market

Except for those taxpayers who use the LIFO method, inventories may be valued at the **lower of cost or market (replacement cost)**.[100] Any write-down of damaged or shopworn merchandise and goods that otherwise are unsalable at normal prices is not considered to be an application of the lower of cost or market method. Such items are valued at bona fide selling price less direct cost of disposal.[101]

In the case of excess inventories (as in *Thor Power Tool Co.*, discussed previously), the goods can be written down only to the taxpayer's offering price. If the offering price on the goods is not reduced, the goods are valued at cost.

Cardinal Publishing Company invested $50,000 in printing 10,000 copies of a book. Although only 7,000 copies were sold in the first three years and none in the next five years, management is convinced that the book will become a classic in 20 years. Cardinal leaves the cover price the same as it was when the book was first distributed ($38 per copy). The remaining 3,000 books are valued at cost ($15,000). In this way, the tax law provides an incentive for the taxpayer to destroy or abandon its excess inventory and obtain an immediate deduction rather than wait for the event of future sales.

In applying the lower of cost or market method, *each* item included in the inventory must be valued at the lower of its cost or market value.[102]

Information related to a taxpayer's ending inventory follows. Under the lower of cost or market method, the inventory is valued at $7,500 rather than $9,500.

Item	Cost	Market	Lower of Cost or Market
A	$5,000	$ 4,000	$4,000
B	3,000	2,000	2,000
C	1,500	6,000	1,500
	$9,500	$12,000	$7,500

Inventory Shrinkage

The difference between the inventory per physical count and the company's records is referred to as *inventory shrinkage*. Inventory shrinkage usually is the result of accidents, theft, and errors in recording. Many companies take physical inventories at times other than the last day of the tax year and adjust their inventory per books to agree with the physical count. In addition, companies often adjust the ending inventory, to be used in deriving cost of goods sold, for the estimated shrinkage that has occurred between the date of the physical inventory and the last day of the tax year. The adjustment often is based on the historical relationship between inventory shrinkage and sales.[103]

[100] Reg. § 1.472–4.
[101] Reg. § 1.471–2(c).
[102] Reg. § 1.471–4(c).
[103] § 471(b).

Determining Cost—Specific Identification, FIFO, and LIFO

In some cases, it is feasible to determine the cost of the particular item sold. For example, an automobile dealer can determine the specific cost of each automobile that has been sold. However, in most businesses, it is necessary to resort to a flow of goods assumption such as *first in, first out (FIFO), last in, first out (LIFO)*, or an *average cost* method. A taxpayer may use any of these methods provided the method selected is consistently applied from year to year.

During a period of rising prices, LIFO generally produces a lower ending inventory valuation, resulting in a greater cost of goods sold than would be obtained under the FIFO method and lower gross income amounts.

On January 1, 2023, the taxpayer opened a retail store to sell refrigerators. At least 10 refrigerators must be carried in inventory to satisfy customer demands. The initial investment in the 10 refrigerators is $5,000. During the year, 10 refrigerators were sold at $750 each and were replaced at a cost of $6,000 ($600 each). Gross profit under the LIFO and FIFO methods is computed as follows:

		FIFO		LIFO
Sales 10 × $750		$ 7,500		$ 7,500
Beginning inventory	$ 5,000		$ 5,000	
Purchases	6,000		6,000	
	$11,000		$11,000	
Ending inventory				
10 × $600	(6,000)			
10 × $500			(5,000)	
Cost of goods sold		(5,000)		(6,000)
Gross profit		$ 2,500		$ 1,500

Dollar-Value LIFO

In the previous example, the taxpayer was buying and selling a single product, a particular model of a refrigerator. The taxpayer employed the specific goods LIFO technique. Under the specific goods approach, if the identical items are not on hand at the end of the period, the LIFO inventory is depleted and all of the deferred profit is recognized. Thus, taxpayers who frequently change the items carried in inventory might realize little benefit from LIFO. The dollar-value LIFO technique can address this problem.

Under **dollar-value LIFO**, each inventory item is assigned to a pool. A *pool* is a collection of similar items and is treated as a separate inventory. Determining whether items are similar involves considerable judgment. In general, however, the taxpayer would prefer broad pools so that when a particular item is sold out, it can be replaced with increases in other items in the same pool. Generally, all products manufactured at a particular plant can be treated as a pool.[104] An automobile dealer may have separate pools for new cars, lightweight trucks, heavy-duty trucks, and car and truck parts.

At the end of the period, ending inventory is valued at the current-year prices and then at the LIFO base period (the year LIFO was adopted). The ratio of the ending inventory at current prices to the ending inventory at base period prices is the *LIFO index*. If the total current inventory at base period prices is greater than the base period inventory at base period prices, a LIFO layer must be added. The LIFO index is applied to the LIFO layer to convert it to current prices.

[104]See, generally, Reg. § 1.472–8.

Example 43

Black Company adopted LIFO effective January 1, 2023. The base LIFO inventory (from December 31, 2022) was $1,000,000. On December 31, 2023, the inventory was $1,320,000 at end-of-2023 prices and $1,200,000 at end-of-2022 (the base period) prices. As a result, Black must add a LIFO layer of $200,000 ($1,200,000 − $1,000,000) to its inventory. The layer must be converted to 2023 prices.

LIFO index = $1,320,000 ÷ $1,200,000 = 1.10

LIFO layer × LIFO index = $200,000 × 1.10 = $220,000

Therefore, the 2023 ending inventory is $1,000,000 + $220,000 = $1,220,000.

The inventory on December 31, 2024, is $1,325,000 using 2023 prices and $1,250,000 using base period prices. The 2024 LIFO layer is $50,000 ($1,250,000 − $1,200,000), and the 2024 LIFO index is $1,325,000 ÷ $1,250,000 = 1.06. The LIFO inventory on December 31, 2024, is computed as follows:

	Base Period Cost	LIFO Index	LIFO Layers
Base inventory	$1,000,000	1.00	$1,000,000
2023 layer	200,000	1.10	220,000
2024 layer	50,000	1.06	53,000
	$1,250,000		$1,273,000

Ethics & Equity **Preserving the LIFO Reserve**

Blanch Corporation has been using the dollar-value LIFO inventory method for 20 years. The company maintains one inventory pool that includes raw materials, goods in process, and finished goods. The LIFO deferral is several million dollars. At the end of the current year, the corporation's inventory of finished goods was almost depleted because the company's major competitor had to recall a substantial portion of its products.

Blanch's management is aware that if the inventory is not replenished, the corporation will recognize gross income that has been deferred for 20 years. Blanch's controller has suggested that the company buy sufficient raw materials to substitute for the depleted finished goods. This will require having on hand at the end of the year the raw materials required for the next 18 months; ordinarily the company has only a three-month supply on hand. The controller argues that the cost of carrying the additional inventory is much less than the additional taxes that will be due if the inventories are allowed to decrease.

The operations manager has suggested that the company buy the raw materials before the end of the year and have the supplier store the materials. Furthermore, the supplier would act as Blanch's agent to sell the excess materials. This would minimize the actual investment in inventory. Do you think the corporation should follow either proposal? Explain.

16-4b **The LIFO Election**

A taxpayer may adopt LIFO by merely using the method for the year of the change and attaching Form 970 to the tax return (i.e., a taxpayer is assured IRS approval for the change). Once the election is made, it cannot be revoked. A change from LIFO to any other inventory method can be made only if the consent of the IRS is obtained.[105] In making the election, the taxpayer must establish that it is using no inventory method other than LIFO.

The beginning inventory valuation for the first LIFO year is computed by the costing method used in the preceding year. As a result, the beginning LIFO inventory generally equals the closing inventory for the preceding year. Because lower of cost or market methods cannot be used in conjunction with LIFO, previous write-downs to market for items included in the beginning inventory must be restored to income. The amount by which the inventories are written up is an adjustment due to a change in accounting method.[106] The taxpayer can spread the adjustment ratably over the year of the change and the two succeeding years.[107]

[105]Reg. §§ 1.472–3(a) and 1.472–5.

[106]Reg. § 1.472–2(c). In Rev.Rul. 76–282, the IRS required the restoration of write-downs for damaged and shopworn goods when the taxpayer switched to LIFO.

[107]§ 472(d).

Example 44

In 2022, Pablo used the lower of cost or market FIFO inventory method. The FIFO cost of his ending inventory was $30,000, and the market value of the inventory was $24,000. As a result, the ending inventory for 2022 was $24,000.

Pablo switched to LIFO in 2023 and was required to write up the beginning inventory to $30,000. Pablo must add $2,000 ($6,000 ÷ 3) to his gross income in 2023, 2024, and 2025.

Once the LIFO election is made for tax purposes, the taxpayer's financial reports to owners and creditors also must be prepared using LIFO.[108] The *LIFO conformity rule* matching financial reports to tax returns is strictly enforced by the IRS; the LIFO election is lost if a different method is used in financial reporting.

16-4c Special Inventory Methods Relating to Farming and Ranching

Farmers who do not use the cash method may elect to account for inventories using the **farm price method** or the **unit-livestock-price method** rather than one of the inventory methods discussed previously. Under the farm price method, the inventory is valued at its market price less disposition costs (e.g., transportation and selling expenses).[109] If the taxpayer uses the unit-livestock-price method, the animals are valued at a standard cost, which is based on the average cost of raising an animal that is similar to those included in the ending inventory.[110]

16-4d Inventory of Small Taxpayers

Small taxpayers, defined as those with average annual gross receipts of $29 million or less in the prior three-year period, may use the cash method of accounting, and they can choose one of three methods to account for inventory:[111]

1. Treat inventory as nonincidental materials and supplies. Under this method, the taxpayer deducts the cost of the inventory when it is used (i.e., when it is sold to the customer). Because the taxpayer is using the cash method, it may only deduct the inventory if it has not only sold it but also paid for it.
2. If the taxpayer has an *applicable financial statement* (generally a certified GAAP financial statement), it may treat the inventory as it does in the financial statements.
3. If the taxpayer does not have an applicable financial statement, it may deduct the inventory in the same manner as it reports the inventory on its internal books and records.

Example 45

Jain is a sole proprietor selling widgets online. Her gross receipts average $2,700,000 per year. She buys her goods on credit, usually paying the bills when received (about 30 days after purchase). Jain uses the cash method and treats her inventory as nonincidental supplies.

In 2023, Jain recorded beginning inventory of $30,000 (cost), purchases of $1,800,000, and ending inventory of $20,000 (cost). She held outstanding payables for inventory purchases of $50,000 (including for the ending inventory). Jain's records show that all of the beginning inventory was paid for in 2022 and sold in 2023.

The 2023 inventory deduction is:

Beginning inventory paid for in 2022 but not sold until 2023	$ 30,000
Inventory purchased during the year less $50,000 not paid by year-end (including the ending inventory)	1,750,000
Inventory deduction for 2023	$1,780,000

[108] § 472(d).
[109] Reg. § 1.471–6(d).
[110] Reg. § 1.471–6(e). See also IRS Publication 225, p. 8.
[111] § 471(c) and Reg. § 1.471–1(b).

16-5 Tax Planning

LO.7

Identify tax planning opportunities related to accounting periods and accounting methods.

16-5a Taxable Year

Under the general rules for tax years, partnerships and S corporations frequently must use a calendar year. However, if the partnership or S corporation can demonstrate a business purpose for a fiscal year, it can use that year. The advantage to a fiscal year is that the calendar year partners and S corporation shareholders may be able to defer from tax the income earned from the close of the fiscal year until the end of the calendar year. Tax advisers for these entities should apply the IRS's gross receipts test to determine whether permission for the fiscal year will be granted.[112]

16-5b Cash Method of Accounting

The cash method of accounting gives the taxpayer considerable control over the recognition of expenses and some control over the recognition of income. This method can be used by proprietorships, partnerships without a C corporation partner, S corporations, qualified personal service corporations, small C corporations, and small partnerships with a C corporation partner (annual gross receipts of $29 million or less over the prior three-year period). Most farmers also can use the cash method.

16-5c Installment Method

Unlike the cash and accrual methods, the installment method often results in an interest-free loan (i.e., of deferred taxes) from the government. When eligible property is sold, the installment method can allow the seller to defer gain and attain a higher interest rate than from alternative investments. These benefits must be weighed against the risks of nonpayment by the buyer.

Advance Payments from Customers

If a business receives a significant amount of advance payments from customers, it should consider using the accrual method even if it is a small taxpayer allowed to use the cash method. An accrual method taxpayer receiving advance payments can adopt the deferral method of § 451(c) and Reg. § 1.451–8 to obtain limited deferral of all or a portion of each advance payment received from customers.

Electing Out of the Installment Method

While deferral of the reporting of gain from an installment sale generally produces favorable after-tax results, electing out of such treatment can be advantageous under circumstances such as the following:

- The seller expects tax rates to increase in future years.
- The seller has tax credits that will expire soon.
- The seller has a loss carryforward equal to or greater than the gain from the property sale.
- The installment note causes the seller to have installment obligations at year-end greater than $5 million, making the seller subject to interest payments on the deferred tax amount.

Related Parties

Intrafamily installment sales can be a useful family tax planning tool. If the related party holds the property more than two years, a subsequent sale will not accelerate the gain from the first disposition. Patience and forethought are rewarded with this tax planning device.

---

[112]Rev.Proc. 2006–46.

Disposition of Installment Obligations

A disposition of an installment obligation can produce disadvantageous income tax results, accelerating the recognition of gross income to the seller. In each instance where transfers of installment obligations are contemplated, the tax adviser should analyze thoroughly the related tax and nontax consequences.

16-5d Inventories

An ending inventory valuation can be minimized and thus taxable income reduced by electing advantageous accounting methods.

- Purchase prices can be stated net of cash discounts (the net invoice method).
- The lower of cost or market method may be applied.
- The LIFO method can be adopted during periods of significantly rising prices.

Refocus on The Big Picture

Accounting Period and Method

TETRA IMAGES/GETTY IMAGES

Selection of a Tax Year

An entity's tax form will govern the rules for determining the entity's tax year. Because Silver is a partnership, Tweety's 40 percent ownership interest in Silver is not sufficient to enable it to control the selection of the partnership's tax year. Likewise, Belinda and Pearl's collective controlling interest will not allow them to control the selection of the tax year for the partnership.

The partnership applies rules in the following sequence to determine its tax year-end.

- *Majority interest tax year.* The tax year of the partners who have a common year-end and collectively own a greater-than-50-percent interest in the partnership capital and profits.
- *Principal partners' tax year.* The common tax year of all of the principal partners (5 percent or greater interest in capital or profits).
- *Least aggregate deferral tax year.* The tax year of the principal partners (grouped by a common year-end) that produces the least aggregate deferral of gross income.

Alternatively, the partnership can select its tax year based on a business purpose for the tax year selected. However, this requires the approval of the IRS, which is unlikely to be granted. The only business purpose the IRS has acknowledged is the need to conform the tax year to the entity's natural business year.

Therefore, Silver will determine its Federal income tax year by using the least aggregate deferral method. Based on this method, Silver's tax year ends on November 30 (as in Example 3).

Short Tax Year

Silver's short tax year begins on April 1, 2023, and ends on November 30, 2023, as determined by the least aggregate deferral method.

continued

What If?

If Silver Partnership's average annual gross receipts for the prior three-year period exceed $29 million, it must use the accrual method to compute its taxable income because one of the partners is a C corporation. Belinda is a cash basis taxpayer, but her share of the partnership income is computed using the accrual method.

Key Terms

Accounting methods, 16-10
Accounting period, 16-2
Accrual method, 16-13
All events test, 16-14
Cash method, 16-11
Claim of right doctrine, 16-9
Completed contract method, 16-27
Crop insurance proceeds, 16-9
Crop method, 16-12
Dollar-value LIFO, 16-32
Economic performance test, 16-14
Farm price method, 16-34
Fiscal year, 16-2
Hybrid method, 16-17
Imputed interest, 16-21
Installment method, 16-20
Least aggregate deferral method, 16-4
Long-term contract, 16-25
Lower of cost or market (replacement cost), 16-31
Majority interest partners, 16-3
Percentage of completion method, 16-27
Personal service corporation (PSC), 16-6
Principal partner, 16-3
Short period, 16-7
Short taxable year, 16-7
12-month rule for prepaid expenses, 16-11
Uniform capitalization (UNICAP) rules, 16-29
Unit-livestock-price method, 16-34

Discussion Questions

1. **LO.1** Would a calendar or fiscal year be more suitable for a ski lodge? Why?

2. **LO.1** Assume that a partnership is profitable and that its tax year ends on December 31, but one of the partners' tax year ends on September 30. Does the partner enjoy a tax benefit or detriment from the partnership's use of a December 31 tax year-end? Explain. Critical Thinking

3. **LO.1** This year on January 1, Shonda set up a corporation for her catering business and owns 100% of the stock. She expects to earn $25,000 per month before deducting her salary. The corporation and Shonda both use the cash method of accounting. The corporation does not need to retain any of the earnings in the business; thus, the salary of Shonda (a calendar year taxpayer) is the corporation's net income before salary expense. Critical Thinking

   If the corporation could choose any tax year and pay Shonda's salary at the time that would be most tax-efficient (but at least once every 12 months), what tax year should the corporation choose? When should the salary be paid each year? Be specific.

4. **LO.1** Art Funkel started his incorporated medical practice on June 1 of the current year. He immediately made an S election for the corporation. Art would like the corporation to adopt a tax year ending May 31 so that a full 12 months of income would be included in the first tax year. Can the corporation elect a fiscal year ending May 31? Explain.

5. **LO.1** Fred, a cash basis taxpayer, received a $15,000 bonus from his employer in 2023. The bonus was based on the company's profits for 2022. In 2024, the company discovered that its 2022 profits were computed incorrectly. As a result, Fred received an additional $10,000 with respect to 2022 profits. Fred's marginal tax rate in 2023 was 12%, and it was 35% in 2024.

   Sue, also a cash basis taxpayer, received a $35,000 bonus in 2023 that was based on 2022 profits. In 2024, the company discovered that it had overstated its profits in 2023. As a result, Sue was required to repay $10,000 of her bonus in 2024. Sue was in the 35% marginal tax bracket in 2023 and in the 12% marginal bracket in 2024.

   What special tax treatment is available to Fred and Sue as a result of their employer's errors?

Planning

6. **LO.2** Under what conditions would the cash method of accounting be preferred to the accrual basis?

7. **LO.2** In December 2023, Nell, Inc., an accrual basis taxpayer, paid $12,000 for insurance premiums for the 2024 calendar year. How much of the premiums can Nell, Inc., deduct in 2023?

8. **LO.2** In 2023, the taxpayer became ineligible to use the cash method of accounting. At the beginning of the year, accounts receivable totaled $240,000, accounts payable for merchandise totaled $80,000, and inventory on hand totaled $320,000. What is the Federal income tax adjustment due to the change in accounting method?

9. **LO.2** Osprey Corporation, an accrual basis taxpayer, reported taxable income for 2023 and paid $40,000 on its estimated state income tax for the year. During 2023, the company received a $4,000 refund upon filing its 2022 state income tax return. The company filed its 2023 state income tax return in August 2024 and paid the $7,000 state income tax due for 2023.

   In December 2023, Osprey received a notice from the state tax commission that an additional $6,000 of income tax was due for 2021 because of an error on the return. The company acknowledged the error in December 2023 and paid the additional $6,000 tax in February 2024. What is Osprey's 2023 Federal income tax deduction for state income taxes?

10. **LO.2** Compare the results of using cash and accrual methods of accounting for the following events:
    a. Purchased new equipment, paying $50,000 cash and giving a note payable for $30,000 due next year.
    b. Paid $3,600 for a three-year service contract on the new equipment.
    c. Collected $1,800 for services to be provided in the current and following years.
    d. Received a $3,000 note from a customer for services provided in the current year. The market value of the note was $2,400.
    e. A bonus earned by the CEO in the current year was paid to her one month after year end.

Critical Thinking

11. **LO.2** Edgar uses the cash method to report the income from his software consulting business. A publicly held corporation has offered to invest in Edgar's business as a limited partner. What tax accounting complications would be created if Edgar and the corporation became partners?

12. **LO.2** Samantha, a cash basis taxpayer, subscribes to a service that updates a database used in her business. In December 2023, Samantha paid the $120,000 subscription fee for the period January 2024 through December 2024. What is Samantha's deduction for 2023?

13. **LO.2** Findley Motors is an automobile dealer. The controller consults with you about the type of accounting used for a special offer to its new car customers. Findley has offered to provide at no charge to the customer the first four recommended service visits (i.e., at 3,000, 6,000, 9,000, and 12,000 miles). It is a virtual certainty that all customers will exercise their rights to the service, and the cost of the services can be estimated accurately. The controller reasons that the estimated cost should be accrued when the sale of an automobile is made, so that all of the costs of the sale can be matched with the revenue. How would you respond to the controller?

14. **LO.4, 7** Irene has made Sari an offer on the purchase of a capital asset. Irene will pay (1) $200,000 cash or (2) $50,000 cash and a 6% installment note for $150,000 guaranteed by City Bank of New York. If Sari sells for $200,000 cash, she will invest the after-tax proceeds in certificates of deposit yielding 6% interest. Sari's cost of the asset is $25,000. Why would Sari prefer the installment sale? Decision Making Planning

15. **LO.4** Arnold gave land to his son, Bruce. Arnold's basis in the land was $100,000, and its fair market value at the date of the gift was $150,000. Bruce borrowed $130,000 from a bank; he used the funds to improve the property. He sold the property to Della for $360,000. Della paid Bruce $90,000 in cash, assumed his $120,000 mortgage, and agreed to pay $150,000 in two years. Bruce's selling expenses were $10,000. Della is going to pay adequate interest. What is Bruce's installment sale gain in the year of sale?

16. **LO.4, 7** On June 1, 2021, Father sold land to Son for $300,000. Father reported the gain by the installment method, with the gain to be spread over five years. In May 2023, Son received an offer of $400,000 for the land, to be paid over three years. What would be the tax consequences of Son's sale? How could the tax consequences be improved? Critical Thinking

17. **LO.4, 7** In December 2023, Soraya Corporation sold land it held as an investment. The corporation received $50,000 in 2023 and a note payable (with adequate interest) for $150,000 to be paid in 2025. Soraya's cost of the land was $80,000. The corporation has a $90,000 net capital loss carryover that will expire in 2023. Should Soraya report the sale in 2023 or use the installment method to report the income as payments are received? Planning

18. **LO.2, 5** What are the similarities between the crop method used for farming and the completed contract method used for long-term construction? Critical Thinking

19. **LO.5** Nathan uses the percentage of completion method to report income from his real estate construction contracts. A contract was begun in 2023 and completed in 2024. In 2023, Nathan reported gross income from the partial completion of the contract. In 2024, however, costs had increased above the original estimate. The contract was completed with the actual profit on the contract being less than the income from the contract reported in 2023. What mechanism should be used to correct for the overpayment of tax in 2023? Be specific.

20. **LO.5** Neal uses the percentage of completion method to report his gross income from long-term contracts that were to begin in 2023. In 2024, he completes a contract for more than the estimate of total costs that was used in the prior year. What are the tax accounting implications of the incorrect estimate?

21. **LO.5** The Hawk Corporation builds yachts. The vessels it currently produces are practically identical and are completed in approximately eight months. A customer has approached Hawk about constructing a larger yacht that would take approximately 15 months to complete. What are the tax implications of accepting the contract proposal? Critical Thinking

Critical Thinking

22. LO.6 Largo Company is an engineering consulting business that uses the accrual method of accounting for its services. Mango Company is a manufacturer of nuts and bolts that also uses the accrual method to account for its sales. Each company has a personnel department. How should the cost of personnel operations be treated by each of the two companies? *Hint:* Consider whether the UNICAP rules apply.

Critical Thinking

23. LO.6 Amber Auto Parts adopted the dollar-value LIFO inventory method. The company has consistently used a retail price index when it should have used a producer's index. As a result, its LIFO layers have been consistently undervalued. Why is the company's error exacerbated by the fact that the company uses the LIFO method instead of the FIFO method?

Critical Thinking

24. LO.6 Opal, Inc., is about to make its first attempt to borrow from a local bank. The company uses LIFO for tax purposes, solely to defer taxes, and it believes that income computed using the FIFO method would better reflect its income. The company also uses the double-declining balance method of depreciation for tax purposes even though the straight-line method better reflects the actual depreciation.

The company would like to present its financial position in the most favorable light. Therefore, Opal's CEO intends to provide the bank with an income statement prepared using the FIFO inventory method and straight-line depreciation. What problems will presenting the income statement to the bank in this fashion cause for Opal?

Critical Thinking

25. LO.6 Blue is a retailer that uses the FIFO inventory method. Blue always takes its physical inventory at the end of the last day of its tax year, December 31. This practice is very unpopular with its employees, who do not like working on New Year's Eve. The company is considering taking the inventory at the end of November and adjusting for sales and purchases in the last month of the year. However, the CFO has raised the issue that by taking the inventory at the end of November, loss from theft and breakage in December will not be taken into account until the physical inventory is taken in the following year. Is the CFO's concern valid? Explain.

Computational Exercises

26. LO.2 Gaffney Corporation is a wholesale distributor of auto parts and uses the cash method of accounting. The company's sales have been about $20,000,000 per year for the last few years. However, Gaffney has the opportunity to acquire an unincorporated competitor with annual sales of $10,000,000. What would be the tax accounting implications of acquiring the competitor?

27. LO.1 In 2023, Aurora received a $25,000 bonus computed as a percentage of profits. In 2024, Aurora's employer determined that the 2023 profits had been incorrectly computed, and Aurora had to refund the $8,000 in 2024. Assume that Aurora was in the 35% tax bracket in 2023 but in the 12% bracket in 2024.

a. In 2023, how much is Aurora required to include in gross income?

b. In 2024, what is the amount of the deduction Aurora can claim? What is the reduction in taxes for 2024 as a result of the deduction?

28. LO.2 In 2023, Chaya Corporation, an accrual basis, calendar year taxpayer, provided services to clients and earned $25,000. The clients signed notes receivable to Chaya that have a fair market value of $22,000 at year-end. In addition, Chaya sold a 36-month service contract on June 1, 2023, and received payment in full of $12,000.

How much gross income does Chaya report from these transactions in 2023?

29. **LO.3** For 2023, Essence Company, a calendar year taxpayer, will change from the cash method for tax purposes to the accrual method. At the end of 2022, Essence showed the following items.

Accounts receivable	$200,000
Accounts payable	135,000
Bank loan	100,000

What is the § 481(a) adjustment for this change in accounting method? Be sure to state whether it is positive or negative.

30. **LO.4** On December 30, 2023, Whitney sold a piece of property for $85,000. Her basis in the property was $40,000, and she incurred $1,200 in selling expenses. The buyer paid $5,000 down with the balance payable in $10,000 installments over the next eight years. In addition, the buyer assumed a $15,000 mortgage on the property.

Under the installment sales method, what is the total contract price, the total gain on the sale, and the amount of gain reported in 2023? Round any division to four decimal places, and use that amount in subsequent computations.

31. **LO.4** In 2023, Skylar sold equipment for $20,000 cash and a $300,000 note due in two years. Skylar's cost of the property was $250,000, and he had deducted depreciation of $150,000.
   a. Under the installment sales method, what is Skylar's total realized gain?
   b. In the year of sale, how much § 1245 gain does Skylar recognize? How much gain can be deferred under the installment sale method?

32. **LO.4** Farhad canceled a note issued by Emma (Farhad's niece) that arose in connection with the sale of property. At the time of the cancellation, the note had a basis to Farhad of $30,000, a face amount of $55,000, and a fair market value of $42,000. Presuming that the initial sale by Farhad qualified as an installment sale, how much gain does the cancellation result in for Farhad?

33. **LO.5** Jebali Corporation, a calendar year taxpayer utilizing the completed contract method of accounting, constructed a building for Samson, Inc., under a long-term contract. The gross contract price was $2,300,000. Jebali finished construction in 2023 at a cost of $2,100,000. However, Samson insisted that Jebali redo the doorway; otherwise, the contract price would be reduced. The estimated cost of redoing the doorway is $80,000. In 2024, the dispute is settled and Jebali fixed the doorway at a cost of $65,000.
   a. How much must Jebali include in gross income for these items? What amount of deductions is Jebali allowed for 2023?
   b. In 2024, how much must Jebali include in gross income? What expenses can Jebali deduct in that year?

34. **LO.5** Shumpert, Inc., entered into a contract that was to take two years to complete, with an estimated cost of $900,000. The contract price was $1,300,000. Costs of the contract for 2022, the first year, totaled $675,000.
   a. What was the gross profit reported by the percentage of completion method for 2022?
   b. After the contract was completed at the end of 2023 at a total cost of $950,000, what was the gross profit reported by the percentage of completion method for 2023?

35. LO.6 Lakota's ending inventory is stated as follows. Under the lower of cost or market method, what is the Federal income tax value of Lakota's inventory?

Item	Cost	Market
Rakes	$8,100	$7,900
Shovels	$3,800	$4,300
Hoes	$6,000	$6,250

36. LO.6 Shondee Corporation uses the lower of cost or market and FIFO inventory methods. At the end of 2022, the FIFO cost of the ending inventory was $181,000, and the market value of the inventory was $160,000. The corporation switched to LIFO in 2023. As a result, how much must Shondee add to its gross income for each of the years 2023, 2024, and 2025?

Problems

37. LO.1 Red, White, and Blue are unrelated corporations engaged in real estate development. The three corporations formed a joint venture (treated as a partnership) to develop a tract of land. Assuming that the venture does not have a natural business year, what tax year must the joint venture adopt under the following circumstances?

		Tax Year Ending	Interest in Joint Venture
a.	Red	March 31	60%
	Blue	June 30	20%
	White	October 31	20%
b.	Red	October 31	30%
	White	September 30	40%
	Blue	January 31	30%

Decision Making
Planning

38. LO.1, 7 The Cardinal Wholesale Company is an S corporation that began business on March 1, 2023. Robert, a calendar year taxpayer, owns 100% of the Cardinal stock. He has $400,000 taxable income from other sources each year. Robert will work approximately 30 hours a week for the corporation. Cardinal sells swimming pool supplies, and its natural business year ends in September. Approximately 80% of Cardinal's gross receipts occur in June through September.

a. What tax year should Cardinal elect, assuming that Robert anticipates the company producing a net profit for all years?

b. What tax year should Cardinal elect, assuming that it will lose $10,000 a month for the first 12 months and an average of $5,000 a month for the next 12 months? In the third year, the corporation will earn taxable income.

39. LO.1 In 2022, Juan entered into a contract to write a book. The publisher advanced Juan $50,000, which was to be recovered out of future royalties. If the book was not completed by the end of 2023, however, Juan would be required to repay the publisher for the advance. Juan did not complete the book in 2023, and in accordance with the agreement, he repaid the $50,000 to the publisher in 2024. Juan is a cash basis taxpayer. What are the tax consequences to Juan of the repayment under the following assumptions?

a. Juan's marginal tax rate was 15% in 2022 and 35% in 2024.

b. Juan's marginal tax rate was 35% in 2022 and 12% in 2024.

40. **LO.2** Gold, Inc., is an accrual basis taxpayer. In 2023, an employee accidentally spilled hazardous chemicals on leased property. The chemicals destroyed trees on neighboring property, resulting in $30,000 of damages. In 2023, the owner of the property sued Gold, Inc., for the $30,000. Gold's attorney believes that it is liable and that the only issue is whether the neighbor will seek punitive damages that could be as much as three times the actual damages. Communications

In addition, as a result of the spill, Gold was in violation of its lease and was therefore required to pay the landlord $15,000. However, the amount due for the lease violation is not payable until the termination of the lease in 2025. None of these costs were covered by insurance.

Jeff Stuart, the president of Gold, Inc., is generally familiar with the accrual basis tax accounting rules and is concerned about when the company can deduct the amounts the company is required to pay as a result of this environmental disaster. Write Mr. Stuart a letter explaining these issues. Gold's address is 200 Elm Avenue, San Jose, CA 95192.

41. **LO.2** Compute Mary's income or deductions for 2023 using (1) the cash basis and (2) the accrual basis for each of the following.
    a. In May 2023, Mary paid a license fee of $1,200 for the period June 1, 2023, through May 31, 2024.
    b. In December 2023, Mary collected $10,000 for January 2024 rents. In January 2023, Mary collected $2,000 for December 2023 rents.
    c. In June 2023, Mary paid $7,200 for an office equipment service contract for the period July 1, 2023, through December 31, 2024.
    d. In June 2023, Mary purchased office furniture for $273,000. She paid $131,000 in cash and gave a $142,000 interest-bearing note for the balance. The office furniture has a MACRS cost recovery period of seven years. Mary did not make the § 179 election and elected not to take additional first-year depreciation.

42. **LO.2, 5** Which accounting method (cash or accrual) would you recommend for the following businesses? Critical Thinking
    a. A gift shop with average annual gross receipts of $900,000.
    b. An accounting partnership with average annual gross receipts of $12,000,000.
    c. A drywall subcontractor who works on residences and records annual gross receipts of $3,000,000.
    d. An incorporated insurance agency with average annual gross receipts of $30,000,000.
    e. A sole proprietor operating a retail clothing store with average annual gross receipts of $12,000,000.
    f. A sole proprietor operating a widget manufacturing plant with average annual gross receipts of $30,000,000.

43. **LO.2** Blue Company, an architectural firm, maintains a cash receipts and disbursements journal. At the end of the year (2023), the company hires you to convert the cash receipts and disbursements into accrual basis revenues and expenses. The total cash receipts are summarized as follows. Critical Thinking

Cash sales	$150,000
Collections on accounts receivable	350,000
Bank loan	90,000
Total cash receipts	$590,000

The accounts receivable from customers at the end of the year are $120,000. You note that the accounts receivable at the beginning of the year were $190,000. The cash sales included $30,000 of prepayments for services to be provided over the period January 1, 2023, through December 31, 2025.

a. Compute the company's accrual basis gross income for 2023.

b. Would you recommend that Blue use the cash method or the accrual method for Federal income tax reporting? Why?

c. The company does not maintain an allowance for uncollectible accounts. Would you recommend that such an allowance be established for Federal income tax purposes? Explain.

44. **LO.2** How do the all events and economic performance requirements apply to the following transactions by an accrual basis taxpayer?

a. The company guarantees its products for six months. At the end of 2023, customers had made valid claims under the guarantee for $600,000 that were not paid until 2024. The company estimates that another $400,000 in claims from 2023 sales will be filed and paid in 2024.

b. The accrual basis taxpayer reported $200,000 in corporate taxable income for 2023. The state income tax rate was 6%. The corporation paid $7,000 in estimated state income taxes in 2023 and paid $2,000 on 2022 state income taxes when it filed its 2022 state income tax return in March 2023. The company filed its 2023 state income tax return in March 2024 and paid the remaining $5,000 of its 2023 state income tax liability.

c. An employee was involved in an accident while making a sales call. The company paid the employee $15,000 in 2023 and agreed to pay her $15,000 a year for each of the next nine years.

45. **LO.3** Ross Company is a C corporation providing property management services. Ross has used the cash method since inception because its gross receipts did not exceed $29,000,000. This year its average annual gross receipts for the prior three years crossed the $29,000,000 mark, requiring Ross to change from the cash method to the accrual method. At the end of its prior year, Ross had accounts receivable of $850,000 and accounts payable of $540,000.

a. Compute and explain the adjustment to taxable income that Ross must make due to the change in accounting method.

b. When must Ross include this adjustment in its income?

Decision Making

46. **LO.2, 3** Raven Finance Company experiences bad debts of about 3% of its outstanding loans. At the end of the year, the company had outstanding receivables of $18,000,000. This balance included $2,000,000 of accrued interest receivable. Raven's loan loss reserve for the year was computed as follows:

Balance, January 1, 2023	$500,000
Accounts written off as uncollectible	
Loans made in 2023	(20,000)
Loans made in prior years	(40,000)
Collections on loans previously written off	15,000
Adjustment to required balance	85,000
Balance, December 31, 2023	$540,000

a. Determine the effects of the above on Raven's taxable income for 2023.

b. Assume that Raven has used bad debt reserves in computing its taxable income for the 10 years the company has been in existence. In 2023, you begin preparing Raven's tax return. What should be done on the return with regard to the reserve?

Communications

47. **LO.2, 3, 6** Jeffrey Boyd, the president of Eagle Furniture Company (average annual gross receipts of $30,000,000), has prepared the company's financial statements and income tax returns for the past 15 years. In July 2024, however,

he hires you to prepare the 2023 corporate income tax return because he has not studied taxes for over 20 years and suspects that the rules may have changed. Eagle uses the accrual method of accounting. Based on an initial examination of Eagle's trial balance and some account analyses, you have determined that the following items may require adjustments.

- The company uses the FIFO inventory method, as valued at cost. However, all freight expenses on incoming merchandise have been expensed for the 15 years the company has been in business.
- The company experiences inventory shrinkage (due to breakage and theft) of about 1% of sales each year. The shrinkage is not taken into account until the company takes a physical inventory each October, but the corporation's fiscal year ends January 31.
- The company has used an allowance for uncollectible accounts, which has a balance of $60,000. In the past, the company has been able to predict its actual bad debt expense accurately.
- The company sells a three-year service contract on its appliances. The company treats $\frac{1}{36}$ of the contract price as earned each month. At the beginning of the year, the company had $120,000 in its account for unearned revenues from the service contracts.
- The company deducts its state income tax in the year paid. Thus, the 2023 state income tax expense includes the estimated taxes paid in 2023 and the additional amount paid in 2023 on 2022 taxes.

Write a letter to Mr. Boyd, explaining what adjustments will be required and how they will be implemented. The address of Eagle Furniture Company is 1000 East Maryland Street, Evansville, IL 47722.

48. **LO.4, 7** Floyd, a cash basis taxpayer, has received an offer to purchase his land. The cash basis buyer will pay him either $100,000 at closing or $50,000 at closing and $56,000 two years after the date of closing. If Floyd recognizes the entire gain in the current year, his marginal tax rate will be 25% (combined Federal and state rates). However, if he spreads the gain over the two years, his combined marginal tax rate on the gain will be only 20%. Floyd does not consider the buyer a credit risk, and he understands that shifting the gain to next year with an installment sale will save taxes. Still, he realizes that the deferred payment will, in effect, earn only $6,000 for waiting two years for the other $50,000. *Decision Making* *Planning*

Floyd believes he can earn a 10% before-tax rate of return on his after-tax cash. Floyd's adjusted basis for the land is $25,000, the buyer also is a cash basis taxpayer, and the short-term Federal rate is 4%. Floyd has asked you to evaluate the two alternatives on an after-tax basis.

49. **LO.4, 7** Jamal purchased equipment and used materials to develop a patent. The development costs were deducted on prior returns. The bases and fair market values of the assets are presented below. *Decision Making*

Assets	Fair Market Value		Basis
Equipment	$350,000	Cost	$ 350,000
		Less: Depreciation	(250,000)
Patent	250,000		–0–
	$600,000		$ 100,000

Sarah has made an offer to purchase the assets. Under one plan, she would pay $200,000 now and $400,000 plus interest at 5% (the Federal rate) in one year. Alternatively, Jamal would incorporate the assets and then sell the stock to Sarah.

Incorporating the assets would not be a taxable event to Jamal, and his basis in the stock would equal his basis in the assets of $100,000. The corporation's basis in the assets also would be $100,000, the same as Jamal's basis for the stock.

Because the corporation would have a basis in the assets of less than the fair market value (and therefore, there would be less depreciation and amortization than with an asset sale by Jamal), Sarah would pay $200,000 in the current year but only $350,000, plus interest at 5%, in one year. Jamal's combined Federal and state marginal tax rate is 35% and his combined capital gain tax rate is 20%.

a. What is Jamal's gain in the year of sale from the installment sale of his assets?
b. Assuming that Jamal's time value of money is 5%, would he prefer the sale of the assets or the sale of the stock? Why?

50. **LO.4** Kay, who is not a real estate dealer, sold an apartment house to Parra during the current year (2023). The closing statement for the sale is as follows.

Total selling price		$ 190,000
Add: Parra's share of property taxes (six months) paid by Kay		3,000
Less: Kay's 8% mortgage assumed by Parra	$55,000	
Parra's refundable binder ("earnest money") paid in 2022	1,000	
Parra's 8% installment note given to Kay	99,000	
Kay's real estate commissions and attorney's fees	8,000	(163,000)
Cash paid to Kay at closing		$ 30,000
Cash due from Parra = $30,000 + $8,000 expenses		$ 38,000

During 2023, Kay collected $9,000 in principal on the installment note and $2,000 of interest. Kay's basis in the property was $110,000 [$125,000 − $15,000 (depreciation)]. The Federal rate is 6%.

a. Compute the following:
   1. Total gain.
   2. Contract price.
   3. Payments received in the year of sale.
   4. Recognized gain in the year of sale and the character of such gain.

   (*Hint:* Before you begin your computations, think about the manner in which the property taxes are handled.)
b. Same as parts (a)(2) and (3), except that Kay's basis in the property was $35,000.

Critical Thinking
Planning

51. **LO.4** On June 30, 2023, Kelly sold property for $240,000 cash and a $960,000 note due on September 30, 2024. The note pays 6% interest, which is equal to the Federal rate. Kelly's cost of the property was $400,000. She is concerned that Congress may increase the tax rate that will apply for the year when the note is collected. Kelly's after-tax rate of return on investments is 6%.

a. What can Kelly do to avoid the expected higher tax rate?
b. Assuming that Kelly's marginal combined Federal and state tax rate is 25% in 2023, how much would the tax rates need to increase to make the option identified in part (a) advisable?

Planning

52. **LO.4** On December 30, 2022, Maud sold land to her son, Charles, for $50,000 cash and a 7% installment note for $350,000, payable over 10 years. Maud's cost of the land was $150,000. In October 2024, after Charles had paid $60,000 on the principal of the note, he received an offer to sell the land for $500,000 cash. How can Charles minimize the present value of the tax liability for himself and Maud?

53. **LO.4** George sold land to an unrelated party in 2022. His basis in the land was $45,000, and the selling price was $120,000—$30,000 payable at closing and $30,000 (plus 10% interest) due January 1, 2023, 2024, and 2025. What would be the tax consequences of the following? [Treat each part independently, and assume that (1) George did not elect out of the installment method and (2) the installment obligations have values equal to their face amounts. Ignore interest rates in your calculations.]
   a. In 2023, George borrowed $40,000 from the bank. The loan was partially secured by the installment notes, but George was personally liable for the loan.
   b. In 2023, George gave to his daughter the right to collect all future payments on the installment obligations.
   c. On December 31, 2023, George received the payment due on January 1, 2024. On December 15, 2024, George died, and the remaining installment obligation was transferred to his estate. The estate collected the amount due on January 1, 2025.

54. **LO.5** The Wren Construction Company reports its Federal taxable income by the completed contract method. At the end of 2023, the company completed a contract to construct a building at a total cost of $800,000. The contract price was $1,200,000, and the customer paid Wren $900,000. However, the customer refused to accept the work and would not pay anything else on the contract because they claimed that the roof did not meet specifications. Wren's engineers estimated that it would cost $140,000 to bring the roof up to the customer's standards.

   In 2024, the dispute was settled in the customer's favor; the roof was improved at a cost of $150,000, and the customer accepted the building and paid the remaining $300,000.
   a. What would be the effects of the above on Wren's taxable income for 2023 and 2024?
   b. Same as part (a), except that Wren had incurred $1,100,000 of accumulated costs under the contract at the end of 2023.

55. **LO.5** Rust Company is a real estate construction company. Rust uses the completed contract method, and the contracts require 18 months to complete. Communications
   a. Which of the following costs would be allocated to construction in progress by Rust?
      1. The payroll taxes on direct labor.
      2. The current services pension costs for employees whose wages are included in direct labor.
      3. Accelerated depreciation on equipment used on contracts.
      4. Freight charges on materials assigned to contracts.
      5. The past service costs for employees whose wages are included in direct labor.
      6. Bidding expenses for contracts awarded.
   b. Assume that Rust generally builds commercial buildings under contracts with the owners and reports the income using the completed contract method. The company is considering building a series of similar stores for a retail chain. The gross profit margin would be a low percentage, but the company's gross receipts would triple. Write a letter to your client, Rust Company, explaining the tax accounting implications of entering into these contracts. Rust's mailing address is P.O. Box 1000, Harrisonburg, VA 22807.

56. **LO.5** On March 31, 2021, Big Boats Company entered into a contract with Vacations Unlimited to produce a state-of-the-art cruise ship to be completed within three years. Big Boats estimated the total cost of building the ship at $300,000,000. The contract price was $400,000,000. The ship was completed on February 15, 2024.

a. What tax accounting method must Big Boats use for the contract? Why?

b. Using the financial data provided relating to the contract's performance, complete the following schedule.

Date	Total Costs Incurred to Date	Total Percentage of Contract Completed	Current-Year Revenue Accrued	Current-Year Costs Deductible
12/31/21	$ 90,000,000	______	______	______
12/31/22	150,000,000	______	______	______
12/31/23	270,000,000	______	______	______
12/31/24	360,000,000	N/A	______	______

c. What are the consequences of the total cost of $360,000,000 exceeding the estimated total cost of $300,000,000?

57. **LO.5** Ostrich Company makes gasoline storage tanks. Everything produced is under contract (that is, the company does not produce any tanks until it gets a contract for a product). Ostrich makes three basic models. However, the tanks must be adapted to each individual customer's location and needs (e.g., the location of the valves and the quality of the materials and insulation). Discuss the following issues relative to Ostrich's operations.

a. An examining IRS agent contends that each of the company's contracts is to produce a "unique product." What difference does it make whether the product is unique or an "off-the-shelf item"?

b. Producing one of the tanks takes over one year from start to completion, and the total cost is in excess of $1,000,000. What costs must be capitalized for this contract that are not subject to capitalization for a contract with a shorter duration and lower cost?

c. What must Ostrich do with the costs of bidding on contracts?

d. Ostrich frequently makes several cost estimates for a contract, using various estimates of materials costs. These costs fluctuate almost daily. Assuming that Ostrich must use the percentage of completion method to report the income from the contract, what will be the Federal income tax consequence if the company uses the highest estimate of a contract's cost and the actual cost is closer to the lowest estimated cost?

Communications
Planning

58. **LO.5, 7** Swallow Company is a large real estate construction company that has made an S election. The company reports its income using the percentage of completion method. In 2024, the company completed a contract at a total cost of $4,800,000. The contract price was $7,200,000. At the end of 2023, the year the contract was begun, Swallow estimated that the total cost of the contract would be $5,400,000. Total accumulated cost on the contract at the end of 2023 was $1,800,000. The relevant tax rate is 35%, and the relevant Federal interest rate is 5%. Assume that all income tax returns were filed and taxes were paid on March 15 following the end of the calendar tax year.

a. Compute the gross profit on the contract for 2023 and 2024.

b. Compute the lookback interest due or receivable with the 2024 tax return. Assume the relevant interest rate is 5%.

c. Before bidding on a contract, Swallow generally makes three estimates of total contract costs: (1) optimistic, (2) pessimistic, and (3) most likely (based on a blending of optimistic and pessimistic assumptions). The company has asked you to write a letter explaining which of these estimates should be used for percentage of completion purposes.

In writing your letter, you should consider the fact that Swallow is incorporated and has made an S election. Therefore, the income and deductions flow through to the shareholders, who all are individuals in the 35% marginal tax bracket. The relevant Federal interest rate is 5%. Swallow's mailing address is 400 Front Avenue, Ashland, OR 97520.

59. **LO.6** Grouse Company is a furniture retailer whose average annual gross receipts for the three preceding years exceeded $29,000,000. In the current tax year, the company purchased merchandise with an invoice price of $15,000,000, less a 2% discount for early payment. However, the company had to borrow on a bank line of credit and paid $150,000 interest to take advantage of the discount for early payment. Freight on the merchandise purchased totaled $360,000. For September, Grouse agreed to pay the customer's freight on goods sold. The total cost of this freight-out was $70,000.

The company has three stores and operates a warehouse where it stores goods. The cost of operating the warehouse was $240,000, including labor, depreciation, taxes, and insurance on the building. The cost of the purchasing operations totaled $420,000. The jurisdiction where the company operates imposes a tax on inventories on hand as of January 1. The inventory tax for this year is $24,000. The invoice cost of goods on hand at the end of the year is $3,000,000.

Compute Grouse's ending inventory using the FIFO method.

60. **LO.6, 7** Lavender Manufacturing Company began business in the current year. The company uses the simplified method to allocate mixed services costs to production. The company's costs and expenses for the year were as follows: Decision Making

Direct labor	$ 3,000,000
Direct materials	4,000,000
Factory supervision	800,000
Property tax on factory	100,000
Personnel department	400,000
Computer operations	250,000
General administration	550,000
Marketing	800,000
State income tax	200,000
	$10,100,000

a. Determine Lavender's total production costs for the year.

b. Assume that the hourly pay for direct labor is much lower than the hourly pay for employees in general administration. Moreover, employee turnover is much higher for production employees than for general administration employees. How should these facts affect the company's decision to use the simplified mixed services method to allocate mixed services costs to production?

61. **LO.3, 6** In 2023, Gail changed from the lower of cost or market FIFO method to the LIFO inventory method. The ending inventory for 2022 was:

Item	FIFO Cost	Replacement Cost	Lower of Cost or Market
A	$26,000	$15,000	$15,000
B	52,000	55,000	52,000
C	30,000	7,000	7,000
			$74,000

Item C was damaged goods, and the replacement cost used was actually the estimated selling price of the goods. The actual cost to replace item C was $32,000.

a. What is the correct beginning inventory for 2023 under the LIFO method?

b. What immediate tax consequences (if any) will result from the switch to LIFO?

Communications
Planning

62. **LO.4, 7** Your client, Bob Garcia, is negotiating a sale of investment real estate for $12,000,000. Bob believes that the buyer would pay cash of $8,000,000 and a note for $4,000,000 or $3,000,000 cash and a note for $9,000,000. The notes will pay interest at slightly above the market rate. Bob realizes that the second option involves more risks of collection, but he is willing to accept that risk if the tax benefits of the installment sale are substantial.

Write a letter to Bob advising him of the tax consequences of choosing the lower down payment and larger note balance, assuming that he has no other installment receivables. Bob's address is 200 Jerdone, Gettysburg, PA 17325.

63. **LO.2, 4** Ven Company is a retailer. In 2023, its before-tax net income for financial reporting purposes was $600,000. This included a $150,000 gain from the sale of land held for several years as a possible plant site. The cost of the land was $100,000, the contract price for the sale was $250,000, and the company collected $120,000 in the year of sale. The income per books also included $90,000 from a 24-month service contract entered into in July 2022 (the customer paid $180,000 in advance for this contract). The addition to the allowance for uncollectible accounts for the year was $70,000, and the actual accounts written off totaled $40,000.

Make the necessary adjustments to the before-tax net income per books to compute Ven's taxable income for the year.

Research Problems

Note: Solutions to the Research Problems can be prepared by using the Thomson Reuters Checkpoint™ online tax research database, which accompanies this textbook. Solutions can also be prepared by using research materials found in a typical tax library.

Research Problem 1. You recently engaged with a new client that operates a chain of convenience stores that sell food and vehicle fuel. You notice that the company uses a customer card program where customer purchases of fuel are entered on the card. For each gallon purchased, the customer is allowed a $0.05 discount per gallon purchased within the next three months. The client treats the $0.05 discount as "earned" by the customer (and deductible by the store) when the purchase is made, which gives the customer the right to the discount. The client justifies this as clearly reflecting the company's income because an obligation arises when the gasoline is purchased and the right to the future discount is earned. Is the client's tax accounting method correct? Explain.

Research Problem 2. Your client, Vernon Jones, is a self-employed attorney. Vernon uses the cash method of accounting. In reviewing his accounting records to get ready to prepare his tax return for the current year, you find an entry in December about a lost check. In discussing this with Vernon, you learn that a client wrote him a check for $82,000 for services Vernon provided. Unfortunately, Vernon lost the check and still is waiting for a replacement check from the client. Communications

Is the $82,000 gross income in the year Vernon received the check that he lost, or is it taxed in the subsequent year when he receives the replacement check? Summarize your findings in an e-mail to your instructor.

Research Problem 3. In 2023, your client, Clear Corporation, changed from the cash to the accrual method of accounting for its radio stations. The company had a positive § 481 adjustment of $2,400,000 as a result of the change and began amortizing the adjustment in 2023.

In 2024, Clear received an offer to purchase the assets of the radio station business (this would be considered a sale of a trade or business under § 1060). If the offer is accepted, Clear plans to use the proceeds to purchase a satellite television business. Clear has asked you to explain the consequences of the sale of the radio station operation on the amortization of the § 481 adjustment.

Use internet tax resources to address the following questions. Look for reliable websites and blogs of the IRS and other government agencies, media outlets, businesses, tax professionals, academics, think tanks, and political outlets.

Research Problem 4. The U.S. tax system allows many businesses to use the cash method of accounting. Find another country that allows some businesses to use the cash method, and explain how that system compares to the U.S. system. E-mail your answer to your instructor, also noting the country and the references you used. Communications

Research Problem 5. More than one U.S. president and others have called for repeal of the LIFO method for Federal income tax purposes. Find technical arguments for and against such legislation. Summarize these arguments and e-mail this document to your instructor. Provide citations for the items that you found. Communications

Becker CPA Review Question

Becker

1. Paula has sales that qualify to be reported on the installment basis. In year 2, installment sales were $40,000 with a cost of $30,000. In year 3, installment sales were $50,000 with a cost of $25,000. Collections in year 2 were in the amount of $30,000. Collections in year 3 were $10,000 on the year 2 sales and $30,000 on the year 3 sales. How much deferred gross profit exists as of the end of year 2?

   a. $2,500
   b. $5,000
   c. $7,500
   d. $10,000

Part 6 Corporations

A business must choose the legal and tax form in which it will operate. Part 6 of this text examines the operating rules that apply to C corporations and the effects of various transactions on the entity and its shareholders. Part 6 also discusses the Federal income tax effects of changes in the corporation's capital structure.

Chapter 17

Corporations: Introduction and Operating Rules

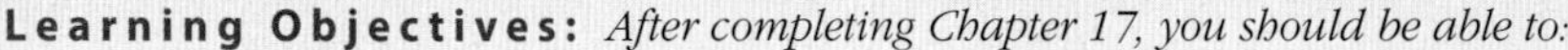

Learning Objectives: *After completing Chapter 17, you should be able to:*

- **LO.1** Compare the taxation of individuals and corporations.
- **LO.2** List and apply the tax rules unique to corporations.
- **LO.3** Compute the corporate income tax.
- **LO.4** Describe the application of the corporate alternative minimum tax.
- **LO.5** Explain the operation of the accumulated earnings and personal holding company taxes.
- **LO.6** Describe the reporting process for corporations.
- **LO.7** Evaluate corporations as an entity form for minimizing income taxes on businesses.

Chapter Outline

PHOONLAMAI PHOTO/SHUTTERSTOCK.COM

The Big Picture

A Half-Baked Idea?

Samantha owns Skylark Bakery. Currently, the bakery is operated as a sole proprietorship and generates an annual operating profit of $100,000. In addition, the bakery earns annual dividends of $5,000 from investing excess working capital in the stock of publicly traded corporations. These stock investments typically are held for a minimum of three to four months before funds are required for the business. As a result of earning income from other business ventures and investments, Samantha is in the 37 percent marginal tax bracket before considering bakery operations. In the past, Samantha has withdrawn $50,000 annually from the bakery, which she regards as reasonable payment for her services.

Samantha has asked you about the tax consequences of conducting the business as a regular (C) corporation. Based on the information given, what would be the annual income tax savings (or cost) of operating the bakery as a corporation? For purposes of this analysis, use the 2023 tax rates and ignore any employment tax or state tax considerations.

Read the chapter and formulate your response.

As discussed in Chapter 15, the distinctions among forms of business organizations are important. Chapter 17 begins a sequence of chapters focusing on corporations. Subchapter C of the Internal Revenue Code is devoted to the tax treatment of **regular corporations** (or **C corporations**). The chapter begins with an introduction to the income taxation of corporations, including the determination of taxable income. We then discuss calculating the tax liability of a corporation and special rules designed to prevent corporations and their shareholders from avoiding the double tax on dividend distributions. Finally, we discuss various procedural matters that a corporate taxpayer faces, including tax return filing requirements, estimated tax payments, reconciling book income to taxable income, and special disclosure schedules on the tax return.

LO.1

Compare the taxation of individuals and corporations.

17-1 An Introduction to the Income Taxation of Corporations

When examining how corporations are treated under the Federal income tax law, a useful approach is to compare their treatment with that applicable to individual taxpayers. In addition, tax provisions that are unique to corporations must be addressed.

17-1a An Overview of Corporate versus Individual Income Tax Treatment

The corporate and individual tax formulas appear in Exhibit 17.1, and the following discussion highlights similarities and differences between the two formulas.

Similarities

Gross income of a corporation is determined in much the same manner as it is for individuals. As a result, gross income includes compensation for services rendered, business income, gains from selling property, interest, rents, royalties, and dividends. Although both individuals and corporations are entitled to exclusions from gross income, fewer exclusions are available to corporate taxpayers. Interest on municipal bonds and life insurance proceeds are exclusions that apply to both individual and corporate taxpayers.

Gains and losses from property transactions are handled similarly. For example, whether a gain or loss is capital or ordinary depends on the nature of the asset in the

Exhibit 17.1 Tax Formulas

Corporations	Individuals
Income (broadly defined)	Income (broadly defined)
(Exclusions)	(Exclusions)
Gross income	Gross income
(Deductions except for NOL and DRD*)	(Deductions *for* AGI**)
Taxable income before NOL and DRD	Adjusted gross income
(Net operating loss deduction)	(Greater of itemized or standard deductions)
(Dividends received deduction)	(Deduction for qualified business income)
Taxable income	Taxable income
Tax on taxable income	Tax on taxable income
(Tax credits)	(Tax credits)
Tax due (or refund)	Tax due (or refund)

*NOL = net operating loss; DRD = dividends received deduction.

**AGI = adjusted gross income.

hands of the taxpayer. In defining what is *not* a capital asset, § 1221 makes no distinction between corporate and noncorporate taxpayers.

In the area of nontaxable exchanges, both corporations and individuals do not recognize gain or loss on a like-kind exchange and may defer realized gain on an involuntary conversion. The disallowance of losses on property sales to related parties (e.g., a corporation and a more-than-50% shareholder) and on wash sales of securities apply to both individual and corporate taxpayers. The exclusion of gain from the sale of a personal residence does not apply to corporations.

Business deductions are allowed for both corporations and individuals. Business deductions include interest (subject to the limitations discussed in text Section 17-1f), certain taxes, losses (including casualty and theft losses), bad debts, cost recovery, charitable contributions, net operating losses, research and experimental expenditures, and some other less common deductions. For corporations, there is no distinction between business and nonbusiness bad debts. Like individuals, corporations are not allowed an interest expense deduction if tax-exempt securities are purchased with borrowed funds. The same holds true for entertainment expenses, expenses contrary to public policy, certain accrued expenses between related parties, and lobbying expenses.

Some of the tax credits available to individuals, such as the foreign tax credit, can also be claimed by corporations. Not available to corporations are certain credits that are personal in nature, such as the child and dependent tax credits, the credit for elderly or disabled taxpayers, and the earned income credit.

Differences

The income taxation of corporations and individuals also differs significantly. Individuals are subject to a progressive tax rate structure; a flat tax rate applies to corporations. The corporate tax rate is discussed in more detail later in the chapter (see Examples 24 and 25). In addition, the computation of the alternative minimum tax for corporations and individuals is significantly different.

All allowable corporate deductions are treated as business deductions. As a result, the determination of adjusted gross income (AGI), so essential for individual taxpayers, has no relevance to corporations. Taxable income is computed simply by subtracting all allowable deductions from gross income. Itemized deductions (and the related limitations), the standard deduction, and the deduction for qualified business income do not apply to corporations. In addition, individuals are subject to a limitation on "excess business losses" (which does not apply to corporations).[1]

17-1b **Specific Provisions Compared**

A comparison of the income taxation of individuals and corporations appears in Concept Summary 17.2 (located at the end of text Section 17-1). Some of the key differences include:

- Accounting periods and methods.
- Capital gains and losses.
- Recapture of depreciation.
- Business interest expense limitation.
- Passive activity losses.
- Charitable contributions.
- Executive compensation.
- Net operating losses.
- Special deductions available only to corporations.

---

[1] § 461(l).

17-1c Accounting Periods and Methods

Accounting Periods

Corporations generally have the same choices of accounting periods as do individual taxpayers. A corporation may choose a calendar year or a fiscal year for reporting purposes, but corporations normally can have different tax years from those of their shareholders. Newly formed corporations (as new taxpayers) usually can choose an accounting period (IRS consent is not needed). **Personal service corporations (PSCs)** and S corporations, however, are restricted in the use of fiscal years. The rules applicable to S corporations are discussed in Chapter 23.

A PSC is a corporation:[2]

- Formed to provide "personal services" (services in the fields of health, law, engineering, architecture, accounting, actuarial science, performing arts, or consulting);
- Where the services are substantially performed by shareholder-employees; and
- Where more than 10 percent of the stock (in value) is held by shareholder-employees.

To limit deferral of income possibilities, PSCs generally must adopt a calendar year.[3] The exceptions that permit the use of a fiscal year are discussed in Chapter 16.

Accounting Methods

As a general rule, the cash method of accounting is unavailable to corporations.[4] However, several important exceptions apply in the case of the following types of corporations:

- S corporations.
- Corporations engaged in the trade or business of farming or timber.
- Qualified PSCs.
- Corporations with average annual gross receipts of $29 million or less for the most recent three-year period.

In general, entities that maintain inventory for sale to customers are required to use the accrual method of accounting for determining sales and cost of goods sold. However, entities with average annual gross receipts of $29 million or less for the most recent three-year period can use the cash method to account for inventories.[5] See Chapter 16 for additional discussion of this exception.

A corporation using the accrual method of accounting must observe a special rule in dealing with cash basis-related parties. If the corporation has an accrual outstanding at the end of any taxable year with a related party, it cannot claim a deduction until the related party reports the amount as income.[6] This rule is most often encountered when an accrual method corporation deals with a cash method individual who owns (directly or indirectly) more than 50 percent of the corporation's stock. However, in the case of a personal service corporation, *any* shareholder-employee is treated as a related party for purposes of this limitation.

The Big Picture

Return to the facts of *The Big Picture* on p. 17-1. Assume that Samantha incorporates her business as Skylark Bakery, Inc., a calendar year, accrual method C corporation. Samantha, a cash method taxpayer, owns 100% of the corporation's stock at the end of 2023. On December 31, 2023, Skylark Bakery has accrued a $10,000 bonus to Samantha. Samantha receives the bonus in 2024 and reports it on her 2024 tax return. Skylark Bakery cannot claim a deduction for the $10,000 until 2024.

---

[2] § 448(d)(2)(A) and Reg. § 1.441–3(d)(1). Any stock held by an employee on any *one day* causes the employee to be a shareholder-employee.

[3] § 441(i). In some cases, a PSC was able to retain the same year as its fiscal year ending in 1987. See § 444(b)(3).

[4] § 448(a).

[5] Such an entity can account for inventory as non-incidental materials and supplies or as conforms to its financial accounting for inventories. The average annual gross receipts test amount is subject to adjustment for inflation each year. In 2022, the amount was $27 million.

[6] § 267(a)(2).

Accrual basis taxpayers generally must recognize gross income no later than the tax year in which the income is included as income for financial statement purposes. In addition, accrual taxpayers can elect to defer income inclusion of advance payments for goods and services to the end of the tax year following the tax year of receipt.[7]

17-1d **Capital Gains and Losses**

Capital gains and losses result from the taxable sales or exchanges of capital assets.[8] These gains and losses are classified as long term or short term depending on the holding period. Each year, a taxpayer's short-term gains and losses are combined, and long-term gains and losses are combined. The result is a net short-term capital gain or loss and a net long-term capital gain or loss. If gains *and* losses result (e.g., net short-term capital gain and net long-term capital loss), these amounts are further netted against each other. If instead the results are *all* gains or *all* losses (e.g., net short-term capital loss and net long-term capital loss), no further combination is necessary.

Capital Gains

Individuals pay the required tax using a preferential rate of 0, 15, or 20 percent on net capital gains (i.e., excess of net long-term capital gain over net short-term capital loss).[9] Corporations, however, receive no favorable tax rate on long-term capital gains; this income is taxed at the normal corporate tax rate.

Capital Losses

Net capital losses of corporate and individual taxpayers receive different income tax treatment. Generally, individual taxpayers can deduct up to $3,000 of net capital losses against other income. Any remaining capital losses are carried forward to future years until absorbed by capital gains or by the $3,000 annual deduction. Loss carryovers retain their identity as either long term or short term.[10]

Example 2

Robin, an individual, incurs a net long-term capital loss of $7,500 for calendar year 2023. Assuming adequate taxable income, Robin may deduct $3,000 of this loss on her 2023 return. The remaining $4,500 ($7,500 − $3,000) of the loss is carried forward to 2024 and years thereafter until completely deducted. The $4,500 will be carried forward as a long-term capital loss.

Unlike individuals, corporate taxpayers are not permitted to deduct any net capital losses against ordinary income. Capital losses, therefore, can be used only as an offset against capital gains. Corporations, however, carry back net capital losses three years, applying them first to the earliest year. Carryforwards then are allowed for a period of five years from the year of the loss. When carried back or forward, a long-term capital loss is treated as a short-term capital loss.[11]

Assume the same facts as in Example 2, except that Robin is a corporation. None of the $7,500 long-term capital loss incurred in 2023 can be deducted that year. Robin Corporation may, however, carry back the loss to 2020, 2021, and 2022 (in this order) and offset it against any capital gains recognized in these years.

If the carryback does not exhaust the loss, it may be carried forward to 2024, 2025, 2026, 2027, and 2028 (in this order). The long-term capital loss is treated as short term in any carryover year.

[7] This deferral applies only if the advance payment is similarly deferred for financial statement purposes. See Chapter 16 for a detailed discussion of accounting periods and methods.

[8] See Chapter 14 for a detailed discussion of capital gains and losses.

[9] In 2023, the 0% rate applies when taxable income does not exceed $89,250 (married, filing jointly), $59,750 (head of household), and $44,625 (single and married, filing separately). The 20% rate applies only when the taxpayer's taxable income exceeds $553,850 (married, filing jointly), $276,900 (married, filing separately), $523,050 (head of household), and $492,300 (single).

[10] §§ 1211(b) and 1212(b).

[11] §§ 1211(a) and 1212(a).

17-1e **Recapture of Depreciation**

The §§ 1245 and 1250 depreciation recapture rules apply to both individual and corporate taxpayers (see Chapter 14). However, corporations may have more depreciation recapture (ordinary income) on the disposition of § 1250 property than do individuals because of § 291 recapture.

Under § 291, a corporation has additional ordinary income equal to *20 percent* of the excess of (1) the amount of depreciation recapture that would be required *if* § 1245 applied to the disposition (i.e., § 1245 recapture potential) over (2) the amount of depreciation recapture computed under § 1250 (without regard to § 291). As a result, the § 1231 portion of the corporation's gain on the disposition is reduced by the additional recapture.

Under § 1250, recapture is limited to the excess of accelerated depreciation over straight-line depreciation. In general, only straight-line depreciation is allowed for real property placed in service after 1986; thus, there usually will be no § 1250 depreciation recapture. In contrast, all depreciation taken on § 1245 property is subject to recapture.

Example 4

Red Corporation purchases nonresidential real property on May 1, 2008, for $800,000. Straight-line depreciation is taken in the amount of $316,239 before the property is sold on October 7, 2023, for $1,200,000.

First, determine the recognized gain:

Sales price		$1,200,000
Less: Adjusted basis—		
Cost of property	$ 800,000	
Less: Cost recovery	(316,239)	(483,761)
Recognized gain		$ 716,239

Second, determine the § 1245 recapture potential. This is the lesser of $716,239 (recognized gain) or $316,239 (cost recovery claimed).

Third, determine the normal § 1250 recapture amount:

Cost recovery taken	$ 316,239
Less: Straight-line cost recovery	(316,239)
§ 1250 ordinary income	$ –0–

Fourth, because the taxpayer is a corporation, determine the ordinary income recognized under § 291:

§ 1245 recapture potential	$ 316,239
Less: § 1250 recapture amount	(–0–)
Excess § 1245 recapture potential	$ 316,239
Apply § 291 percentage	× 20%
Additional ordinary income under § 291	$ 63,248

Red Corporation's recognized gain of $716,239 is accounted for as follows:

Ordinary income under § 1250	$ –0–
Ordinary income under § 291	63,248
§ 1231 gain	652,991
Total recognized gain	$ 716,239

17-1f **Business Interest Expense Limitation**

A limitation on the deduction for business interest applies to all taxpayers.[12] Business interest is interest paid or accrued on trade or business debt. Although the limitation applies to *any* business, the rules are most likely to affect large corporations and flow-through entities due to a small business exception.

[12] § 163(j); the limitation applies to tax years beginning after 2017.

Under § 163(j), the deduction for business interest for any year is limited to the sum of:

1. The taxpayer's *business interest income* for the year,
2. 30 percent of the taxpayer's *adjusted taxable income* for the year, and
3. The taxpayer's *floor plan financing interest* for the year.[13]

Any business interest deduction disallowed by reason of the limitation is treated as business interest paid or accrued in the succeeding tax year. The carryforward period is unlimited.

The business interest deduction limitation does not apply to certain small businesses. In general, the small business exception applies to taxpayers with average gross receipts for the prior three-year period of $29 million or less.[14]

Business Interest Income

"Business interest income" is the amount of interest income includible in gross income for the year that is related to a trade or business. Congress believes that a corporation typically will have neither investment interest income nor investment interest expense; instead, all interest income and interest expense of a corporation is assumed to be part of the corporation's trade or business.[15]

Adjusted Taxable Income

"Adjusted taxable income" is taxable income computed without regard to any:

1. Nonbusiness income, gain, deduction, or loss,
2. Business interest or business interest income,
3. Net operating loss (NOL) deduction, and
4. Deduction for qualified business income (§ 199A).[16]

The Treasury Department and the IRS are authorized to provide other adjustments to the computation of adjusted taxable income.[17] The 30 percent of adjusted taxable income amount cannot be less than zero (see Example 5).[18]

Floor Plan Financing Interest

Virtually all auto dealers acquire their inventory via debt (known as "floor plan" financing), with the debt being secured by the inventory. Interest on this debt ("floor plan financing interest") is deductible without limitation.

Business Interest Expense Limitation

Example 5

In 2023, Tangerine, a calendar year C corporation, has $2,000,000 of adjusted taxable income, $75,000 of business interest income, and $950,000 of business interest expense (it has no floor plan financing interest).

Tangerine's deduction for business interest is limited to $675,000 [$75,000 (business interest income) + $600,000 (30% × $2,000,000 adjusted taxable income)]. The disallowed amount of $275,000 ($950,000 − $675,000) is carried forward to next year and treated as business interest in that year.

If Tangerine satisfies the small business exception (i.e., had average gross receipts for the prior three-year period of $29,000,000 or less), the limitation on business interest does not apply and the entire $950,000 of business interest is deductible in the current year.

---

[13] § 163(j)(1).

[14] § 163(j)(3). This amount is subject to adjustment for inflation each year. In 2022, the amount was $27 million.

[15] TCJA of 2017 Joint Explanatory Statement, p. 288. The Joint Explanatory Statement relies on the rationale that since § 163(d)—the investment interest expense limitation—does not apply to corporations, then any interest income and interest expense should be related to the corporation's trade or business activities (not investment activities).

[16] § 163(j)(8)(A).

[17] § 163(j)(8)(B). See, for example, Reg. § 1.163(j)–1(b)(1).

[18] § 163(j)(1), flush text.

Business Interest Expense Limitation

Example 6

In 2023, Eagle Corporation, a calendar year C corporation, has ($1,000,000) of adjusted taxable income, $40,000 of business interest income, zero floor plan financing interest, and $100,000 of business interest expense.

Eagle's business interest deduction limitation is $40,000 [$40,000 (business interest income) + $0 (30% × adjusted taxable income amount, but not less than zero)]. As a result, Eagle's current-year deduction for business interest is limited to $40,000, and the disallowed amount of $60,000 ($100,000 − $40,000) is carried forward to next year and treated as business interest in that year.

If Eagle satisfies the small business exception (i.e., had average gross receipts for the prior three-year period of $29,000,000 or less), the limitation on business interest does not apply and the entire $100,000 of business interest is deductible in the current year.

Other Rules

Flow-Through Entities In the case of a partnership or an S corporation, the business interest deduction limitation applies at the entity level. The general carryforward rule for disallowed business interest does not apply to partnerships (or S corporations); rather, a partner (or an S corporation shareholder) can deduct the disallowed interest under a special carryforward rule. A partner's (or S corporation shareholder's) adjusted taxable income is determined without regard to the partner's (or shareholder's) distributive share of the partnership's (or S corporation's) items of income, gain, deduction, or loss.[19]

Trade or Business The term *trade or business* does not include performing services as an employee.[20] As a result, an individual cannot include W–2 wages in adjusted taxable income for purposes of computing the interest deduction limitation. The term also does not include certain real property trades or businesses and certain farming businesses.

17-1g Passive Activity Losses

The **passive activity loss** rules apply to individual taxpayers, closely held C corporations, and personal service corporations (PSCs; see definition in text Section 17-1c).[21] These rules prevent taxpayers from incorporating to avoid the passive activity loss limitations (refer to Chapter 11). A corporation is *closely held* if, at any time during the last half of the taxable year, more than 50 percent of the value of the corporation's outstanding stock is owned, directly or indirectly, by five or fewer individuals.

PSCs generally cannot deduct passive activity losses against either active income or portfolio income. However, the application of the passive activity loss rules is not as harsh for closely held C corporations (that are not PSCs). They may offset passive activity losses against *net active income*, but not against portfolio income. The special rules applicable to PSCs are recapped in Concept Summary 17.1.

Brown, a closely held C corporation that is *not* a PSC, has $300,000 of passive activity losses from a rental activity, $200,000 of net active income, and $100,000 of portfolio income. The corporation may offset $200,000 of the $300,000 passive activity loss against the $200,000 of net active income but may not offset the remainder against the $100,000 of portfolio income.

If Brown is a PSC, then none of the $300,000 of passive activity losses is deductible in the current year.

[19] § 163(j)(4).

[20] § 163(j)(7).

[21] § 469(a). For S corporations and partnerships, passive activity income or loss flows through to the owners, and the passive activity loss rules are applied at the owner level. For definitions, see § 469(j)(1) (closely held) and § 469(j)(2) (PSC).

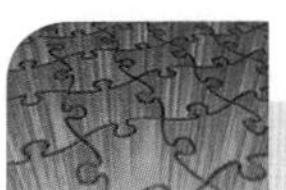

Concept Summary 17.1

Special Rules Applicable to Personal Service Corporations (PSCs)

Item	PSC Treatment
Accounting periods	Calendar year is generally required. Fiscal year exceptions are available for a business purpose or under a § 444 election.
Accounting methods	Both cash and accrual methods are generally available. Any PSC shareholder-employee is treated as a related party for purposes of the accrued expenditure limitation.
Passive activity losses	Passive activity loss rules apply.

17-1h **Charitable Contributions**

Both corporate and individual taxpayers may deduct charitable contributions for the year in which the payment is made. However, an *accrual basis corporation* may claim the deduction in the year *preceding* payment if two requirements are met. First, the contribution must be authorized by the board of directors by the end of that year. Second, it must be paid on or before the due date of the corporation's tax return (i.e., the fifteenth day of the fourth month following the close of its taxable year).[22]

On December 28, 2023, Peach Company, a calendar year, accrual basis partnership, authorizes a $5,000 donation to the Atlanta Symphony Association (a qualified charitable organization). The donation is made on April 12, 2024.

If Peach Company is a corporation and the December 28, 2023 authorization was made by its board of directors, Peach may claim the $5,000 donation as a deduction for calendar year 2023.

However, if Peach Company is a partnership, the contribution cannot be deducted until 2024.[23]

Property Contributions

Generally, a charitable contribution of property results in a deduction equal to the property's fair market value at the date of the gift. As a result, a contribution of loss property (fair market value less than basis) should be avoided. Instead, the loss property should be sold (allowing the loss to be recognized) and the proceeds contributed to the charity.

Heron Corporation owns inventory with a basis of $10,000 and a fair market value of $8,000. A charitable contribution of the inventory results in a deductible amount of $8,000, the inventory's fair market value.

However, a sale of the inventory, for a recognized loss of $2,000 ($8,000 amount realized − $10,000 basis), and donation of the sale proceeds, for a charitable deduction of $8,000, results in a combined deduction of $10,000.

Fair market value also is the valuation amount for most charitable contributions of capital gain property. *Capital gain property* is property that, if sold, would result in long-term capital gain or § 1231 gain for the taxpayer.

[22] § 170(a)(2).

[23] Each calendar year partner will report an allocable portion of the charitable contribution deduction as of December 31, 2024 (the end of the partnership's tax year). See Chapter 21.

During the current year, Mallard Corporation donates a parcel of land (a capital asset) to Oakland Community College. Mallard acquired the land five years ago for $60,000, and the fair market value on the date of the contribution is $100,000.

The corporation's charitable contribution deduction (subject to a percentage limitation discussed later) is measured by the asset's fair market value of $100,000, even though the $40,000 appreciation on the land has never been included in Mallard's income.

In two situations, a charitable contribution of capital gain property is measured by the basis of the property rather than fair market value. First, if the taxpayer contributes *tangible personal property* and the charitable organization puts the property to an *unrelated use*, the deduction is limited to the basis of the property. If the use is related to the charity's exempt purpose, the contribution deduction will be based on the property's fair market value. Second, the deduction for charitable contributions of capital gain property to certain private foundations is also limited to the basis of the property.

Contributions of Tangible Personal Property

During the current year, White Corporation donates a painting worth $200,000 to Western States Art Museum (a qualified organization), which exhibits the painting. White had acquired the painting in 2000 for $90,000. Because the museum put the painting to a related use, White is allowed to deduct $200,000, the fair market value of the painting.

Assume the same facts as in the previous example, except that White Corporation donates the painting to the American Cancer Society, which sells the painting and deposits the $200,000 proceeds in the organization's general fund.

Here, White's deduction is limited to the $90,000 basis because it contributed tangible personal property that was put to an unrelated use by the charitable organization.

As a general rule, the deduction for a contribution of ordinary income property also is limited to the *basis* of the property. *Ordinary income property* is appreciated property that, if sold, would not result in long-term capital gain (inventory and stock held for 12 months or less are common examples).[24] On certain contributions of inventory by *corporations*, however, the amount of the deduction is equal to the *lesser of* (1) the sum of the property's basis plus 50 percent of the appreciation on the property or (2) twice the property's basis. The following inventory contributions qualify for this increased contribution amount:

- A contribution of property to a charitable organization whose exempt purpose includes the care of the ill, the needy, or infants.
- A contribution of tangible personal research property constructed by the corporation to a qualified educational or scientific organization that uses the property for research or experimentation or for research training.[25]

Lark Corporation, a clothing retailer, donates children's clothing to the Salvation Army to be used to clothe homeless children. Lark's basis in the clothes is $2,000, and the fair market value is $3,000. Lark's deduction is $2,500 [$2,000 basis + 50%($3,000 − $2,000)].

If, instead, the fair market value is $7,000, Lark's deduction is limited to $4,000 (2 × $2,000 basis).

[24] In addition, § 1231 property (depreciable property used in a trade or business) is treated as ordinary income property to the extent of any depreciation recaptured under § 1245 or § 1250 (as adjusted under § 291).

[25] The property must be contributed within two years from the date of its construction by the donor, and its original use must begin with the donee. S corporations do not qualify for the increased contribution amount for inventory. These conditions are identified in §§ 170(e)(3) and (4).

Limitations Imposed on Charitable Contribution Deductions

Like individuals, corporations are subject to percentage limits on the charitable contribution deduction. For any tax year, a corporate taxpayer's contribution deduction generally is limited to 10 percent of taxable income (15 percent of taxable income for contributions of *food inventory*).[26] For this purpose, taxable income is computed without regard to the charitable contribution deduction, any net operating loss carryback or capital loss carryback, and dividends received deduction.

Any contributions in excess of the 10 percent limitation may be carried forward to the five succeeding tax years. Any carryforward is combined with contributions in those years and then subject to the 10 percent limitation. The current year's contributions are always deducted first, with carryover amounts from previous years deducted in order of time.[27]

Annual Limitation and Carryover Rules Illustrated

Example 14

During 2023, Orange Corporation (a calendar year taxpayer) had the following income and expenses:

Income from operations	$140,000
Expenses from operations	110,000
Dividends received	10,000
Charitable contributions made in May 2023	6,000

For purposes of the 10% limitation *only*, Orange Corporation's taxable income is $40,000 ($140,000 − $110,000 + $10,000). Consequently, the allowable charitable contribution deduction for 2023 is $4,000 (10% × $40,000). The $2,000 unused portion of the contribution can be carried forward to 2024, 2025, 2026, 2027, and 2028 (in that order) until exhausted.

Example 15

Assume the same facts as in Example 14. In 2024, Orange Corporation has taxable income (for purposes of the 10% limitation) of $50,000 and makes a charitable contribution of $4,500. The maximum deduction allowed for 2024 is $5,000 (10% × $50,000).

The $5,000 deduction allowed is made up of the 2024 $4,500 contribution and $500 of the carryforward from 2023. Current-year contributions are always used first. The remaining $1,500 of the 2023 contribution may be carried over until it is used (or until the five-year carryfoward period ends).

17-1i Excessive Executive Compensation

A closely held corporation's deduction for shareholder-employee compensation is subject to the reasonableness standard of § 162(a)(1). A second limitation applies to *publicly held corporations*. In general, § 162(m) limits the deductible amount of a publicly held corporation's compensation to any covered employee to $1 million annually. Covered employees are the principal executive officer, the principal financial officer, and the three other most highly compensated officers.[28]

The $1 million maximum applies to compensation, commissions based on individual performance, and performance-based compensation tied to overall company performance.[29] The limitation does not apply to retirement plan contributions or

[26] The percentage limitations applicable to individuals and corporations are identified in §§ 170(b) and (e)(3)(C) (food inventory).

[27] The carryover rules relating to all taxpayers are in § 170(d).

[28] An individual is a covered employee if the individual holds one of the principal officer positions at any time during the taxable year. Further, an individual who is a covered employee for any tax year beginning after 2016 remains a covered employee for all future years, including years during which the individual is no longer employed by the corporation and years after the individual has died. For example, the limitation would apply to deferred compensation payments to a covered employee after the individual's departure from the corporation. For taxable years beginning after December 31, 2026, this provision will apply to the principal executive officer, the principal financial officer, and the *eight* other most highly compensated executives.

[29] Before 2018, the $1 million limit *excluded* commissions and performance-based compensation. Contracts in place on November 2, 2017, are grandfathered under pre-2018 law as long as there are no material changes to the contract.

employer-provided benefits that are excludible from gross income by the employee (e.g., health care benefits).

Dora is the newly hired chief executive officer of White Corporation, a publicly traded corporation. For the current year, her compensation package consists of:

Cash compensation	$2,700,000
Taxable fringe benefits	200,000
Bonus tied to company performance	5,000,000
Nontaxable fringe benefits	100,000

White Corporation can deduct $1,100,000 of Dora's compensation package ($1,000,000 of the cash compensation, taxable fringe benefits, and bonus) plus the nontaxable fringe benefits of $100,000.

17-1j **Net Operating Losses**

In computing the amount of a corporation's net operating loss (NOL), some differences apply. Unlike individual taxpayers, a corporation:[30]

- Does not adjust its tax loss for the year for any capital losses (since a corporation cannot deduct net capital losses).
- Does not make adjustments for any nonbusiness deductions (as individual taxpayers do).
- Is allowed to include the dividends received deduction (discussed below) in computing its NOL.

In 2023, Green Corporation has gross income (including dividends) of $200,000 and deductions of $300,000 excluding the dividends received deduction. Green Corporation had received $100,000 of dividends from Fox, Inc., in which Green holds a 5% stock interest. Green has an NOL computed as follows:

Gross income (including dividends)		$ 200,000
Less: Business deductions	$300,000	
Dividends received deduction (50% × $100,000)*	50,000	(350,000)
Taxable income (or loss)		($ 150,000)

*See the discussion of the dividends received deduction in text Section 17-1k.

The NOL is carried forward to 2024 and future years until it is used up. In addition, the NOL can offset no more than 80% of taxable income (computed without regard to the NOL) in those years.

The NOL carryover rules are similar for both individuals and corporations. For instance, an NOL may be carried forward indefinitely to offset taxable income in those future years. In addition, the NOL deduction for any carryover year after 2020 is limited to 80 percent of taxable income (determined without regard to the NOL deduction).[31]

List and apply the tax rules unique to corporations.

17-1k **Deductions Available Only to Corporations**

Certain deductions are specific to corporate taxpayers, including the dividends received deduction and the organizational expenditures deduction.

[30] The modifications required to arrive at the amount of NOL that can be carried forward are in § 172(d).

[31] For NOLs arising in 2018, 2019, and 2020, a 5-year carryback and indefinite carryforward apply. For NOLs arising before 2018, a 2-year carryback and 20-year carryforward apply, and there is no taxable income limitation on the deductibility of the NOL carryovers. §§ 172(a) and (b)(1).

Exhibit 17.2 **Dividends Received Deduction**

Percentage of Ownership by Corporate Shareholder	Deduction Percentage
Less than 20%	50%
20% or more (but less than 80%)	65%
80% or more*	100%

*The payor corporation must be a member of an affiliated group with the recipient corporation.

Dividends Received Deduction

The purpose of the **dividends received deduction** is to mitigate multiple taxation of corporate income. Without the deduction, dividend income paid to a corporation would be taxed to the recipient corporation, with no corresponding deduction to the distributing corporation. Later, when the recipient corporation distributed the income to its shareholders, the income would *again* be subject to taxation, with no corresponding deduction to the corporation. The dividends received deduction alleviates this inequity.

As Exhibit 17.2 illustrates, the amount of the dividends received deduction depends on the percentage of ownership (voting power and value) the recipient corporate shareholder holds in a *domestic corporation* making the dividend distribution.[32]

The dividends received deduction cannot exceed the taxable income limitation. This limitation is equal to the corporation's taxable income multiplied by the same percentage used to compute the deduction. As a result, if a corporate shareholder owns less than 20 percent of the stock in the distributing corporation, the dividends received deduction is limited to 50 percent of taxable income. For this purpose, taxable income is computed without regard to the NOL deduction, the dividends received deduction, and any capital loss carryback. However, the taxable income limitation does not apply if the corporation has an NOL for the current taxable year.[33]

The following steps are useful in applying these rules:

1. Multiply the dividends received by the deduction percentage.
2. Multiply the taxable income by the deduction percentage.
3. Limit the deduction to the lesser of Step 1 or Step 2, unless deducting the amount derived in Step 1 results in an NOL. If so, the amount derived in Step 1 is used. This sometimes is referred to as the *NOL rule*.

Example 18

Red, White, and Blue corporations are three unrelated calendar year corporations. During the year, they report the following information:

	Red Corporation	White Corporation	Blue Corporation
Gross income from operations	$ 400,000	$ 320,000	$ 230,000
Expenses from operations	(340,000)	(340,000)	(340,000)
Dividends received from domestic corporations (less than 20% ownership)	200,000	200,000	200,000
Taxable income before the dividends received deduction	$ 260,000	$ 180,000	$ 90,000

continued

[32]§ 243(a). Dividends from foreign corporations generally do not qualify for a dividends received deduction. But see §§ 245 and 245A.

[33]Further, the limitation does not apply in the case of the 100% deduction available to members of an affiliated group. § 246(b).

In determining the dividends received deduction, use the three-step procedure described previously.

	Red Corporation	White Corporation	Blue Corporation
Step 1 (50% × $200,000)	$100,000	$100,000	$100,000
Step 2			
50% × $260,000 (taxable income)	$130,000		
50% × $180,000 (taxable income)		$ 90,000	
50% × $90,000 (taxable income)			$ 45,000
Step 3			
Lesser of Step 1 or Step 2	$100,000	$ 90,000	
Deduction results in an NOL (use Step 1)			$100,000

White Corporation is subject to the 50% of taxable income limitation (Step 2). The NOL rule does not apply because subtracting $100,000 (Step 1) from $180,000 (taxable income before the dividends received deduction) does not yield a negative figure. Blue Corporation qualifies for NOL rule treatment because subtracting $100,000 (Step 1) from $90,000 (taxable income before the dividends received deduction) yields a negative figure.

In summary, each corporation has a dividends received deduction for the year: $100,000 for Red Corporation, $90,000 for White Corporation, and $100,000 for Blue Corporation.

In those cases where the taxable income limitation applies, the taxpayer should consider the proper timing of income and deductions to bring the NOL rule into play. This can result in a significant increase in the amount of a corporation's dividends received deduction.

Example 19

Pearl Corporation, a calendar year C corporation, has the following information for the year:

Gross income from operations	$ 200,000
Expenses from operations	(245,000)
Dividends received from domestic corporations (less than 20% ownership)	100,000
Taxable income before dividends received deduction	$ 55,000

Pearl's dividends received deduction is $27,500 [50% × $55,000 (taxable income limitation)].

If, however, Pearl incurs additional expenses of $5,001 (or defers $5,001 of income), its taxable income before the dividends received deduction will be reduced to $49,999. If this occurs, the NOL rule applies and Pearl's dividends received deduction is $50,000 [50% × $100,000 (dividends received)].

No dividends received deduction is allowed unless the corporation has held the stock for more than 45 days.[34] This restriction was enacted to close a tax loophole involving dividends on stock that is held only briefly. When stock is purchased shortly before a dividend record date and soon thereafter sold ex-dividend, a capital loss corresponding to the amount of the dividend often results (ignoring other market valuation changes). If the dividends received deduction was allowed in such cases, the capital loss resulting from the stock sale would exceed the taxable portion of the related dividend income.

[34] The stock must be held more than 45 days during the 91-day period beginning on the date that is 45 days before the ex-dividend date (or in the case of preferred stock, more than 90 days during the 181-day period beginning on the date that is 90 days before the ex-dividend date). § 246(c).

On October 1, 2023, Pink Corporation declares a $1-per-share dividend for shareholders of record as of November 1, 2023. The dividend is payable on December 1, 2023. Black Corporation purchases 10,000 shares of Pink stock on October 30, 2023, for $25,000 and sells those 10,000 shares ex-dividend on November 6, 2023, for $15,000. (It is assumed that there is no fluctuation in the market price of the Pink stock other than the dividend element.) The sale results in a short-term capital loss of $10,000 ($15,000 amount realized − $25,000 basis). On December 1, Black receives a $10,000 dividend from Pink.

Without the holding period restriction, Black Corporation would recognize a $10,000 capital loss deduction (subject to the capital loss limitation) but only $5,000 of income [$10,000 dividend − $5,000 dividends received deduction ($10,000 × 50%)], or a $5,000 net loss. However, because Black did not hold the Pink stock for more than 45 days, no dividends received deduction is allowed.

Ethics & Equity **Pushing the Envelope on Year-End Planning**

As of December of the current year, Larson Corporation (a calendar year taxpayer) has gross income from operations of $497,000, expenses from operations of $596,000, and dividends received from domestic corporations (less than 20 percent ownership) of $200,000.

Currently, Larson does not expect any more income or expenses to be realized by year-end. However, Larson's tax department has suggested that the corporation incur another $1,001 of deductible expenditures before year-end. What is the motivation behind the tax department's recommendation, and is such year-end planning ethical?

Organizational Expenditures Deduction

Expenses incurred in connection with the organization of a corporation normally are capitalized. That they benefit the corporation during its existence seems clear. But how can they be amortized when most corporations possess unlimited life? If a useful life cannot be determined, no deduction is allowed. Code § 248 was enacted to solve this problem.

Under § 248, a corporation may *elect* to amortize **organizational expenditures** over the 180-month period beginning with the month in which the corporation begins business.[35] Organizational expenditures include the following:

- Legal services related to organization (e.g., drafting the corporate charter, bylaws, minutes of organizational meetings, and terms of original stock certificates).
- Necessary accounting services.
- Expenses of temporary directors and of organizational meetings of directors or shareholders.
- Fees paid to the state of incorporation.

Expenses that *do not qualify* as organizational expenditures include those connected with issuing or selling shares of stock or other securities (e.g., commissions, professional fees, and printing costs) or with transferring assets to a corporation. These expenses must be capitalized.

The first $5,000 of organizational costs is immediately expensed, with any remaining costs amortized over a 180-month period. However, the $5,000 expensing amount is phased out on a dollar-for-dollar basis when these costs exceed $50,000.

[35]The month in which a corporation begins business may not be immediately apparent. Ordinarily, a corporation begins business when it starts the business operations for which it was organized. Reg. § 1.248–1(d). For a similar problem in the Subchapter S area, see Chapter 23.

Example 21

Stork Corporation (a calendar year C corporation) began business on July 1 of the current year and incurred $52,000 of organizational expenditures. Stork wants to expense as much of these expenditures as possible, electing to amortize any amount it cannot expense. Stork's current-year deduction is $4,633, determined as follows:

Immediate expense [$5,000 − ($52,000 − $50,000)]	$3,000
Amortization [($52,000 − $3,000) ÷ 180] × 6 months in tax year	1,633
Total	$4,633

To qualify for the election, the expenditures must be *incurred* before the end of the tax year in which the corporation begins business. The corporation's method of accounting is of no consequence; an expense incurred by a cash basis corporation in its first tax year qualifies even though it is not paid until a subsequent year. However, this rule could prove to be an unfortunate trap for corporations formed late in the first taxable year. Consider the following example.

Example 22

Thrush Corporation is formed in December 2023. Qualified organizational expenditures are incurred as follows: $62,000 in December 2023 and $30,000 in January 2024. If Thrush uses the calendar year for tax purposes, only $62,000 of the organizational expenditures can be written off over a period of 180 months.

Being aware of the rule and planning appropriately can solve this problem. One option is to make sure that all of the expenditures are incurred in December. Another option is to adopt a different year-end. If Thrush Corporation adopts a fiscal year that ends at or beyond January 31, all organizational expenditures will then have been incurred before the close of the first tax year. With either of these options, $92,000 ($62,000 + $30,000) of organizational expenditures can be amortized over 180 months.

A corporation is deemed to have made the election to amortize organizational expenditures for the taxable year in which it begins business. A corporation can elect to forgo the election by capitalizing organizational expenditures on its first tax return.

Example 23

Black Corporation (an accrual method, calendar year C corporation) was formed and began operations on April 1, 2023. The following expenses were incurred during its first year of operations (April 1 through December 31, 2023):

Expenses of temporary directors and of organizational meetings	$15,500
Fee paid to the state of incorporation	2,000
Accounting services incident to organization	18,000
Legal services for drafting the corporate charter and bylaws	32,000
Expenses incident to the printing and sale of stock certificates	48,000

Black Corporation elects to amortize organizational costs under § 248. Because of the dollar cap (i.e., dollar-for-dollar reduction for amounts in excess of $50,000), none of the $5,000 expensing allowance is available. The monthly amortization is $375 [($15,500 + $2,000 + $18,000 + $32,000) ÷ 180 months], and $3,375 ($375 × 9 months) is deductible for tax year 2023.

Note that the $48,000 of expenses incident to the printing and sale of stock certificates does not qualify for the election. These expenses must be capitalized.

Organizational expenditures are different from *startup expenditures*.[36] Startup expenditures include various investigation expenses involved in entering a new business (e.g., travel, market surveys, financial audits, and legal fees) and operating expenses such as rent and payroll that are incurred by a corporation before it actually begins to produce any gross income. In general, startup expenditures must be capitalized. However, at the election of the taxpayer, startup expenditures are deductible in the same manner as

[36]§ 195. The deduction for startup expenditures is also available to noncorporate taxpayers.

organizational expenditures. So up to $5,000 can be immediately expensed (subject to the phaseout) and any remaining amounts amortized over a period of 180 months. The same rules that apply to the deemed election (and election to forgo the election) for organizational expenditures also apply to startup expenditures.

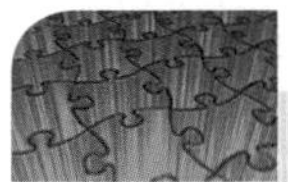

Concept Summary 17.2

Income Taxation of Individuals and Corporations Compared

	Individuals	Corporations
Computation of gross income	§ 61.	§ 61.
Computation of taxable income	§ 62 and §§ 63(b) through (g).	§ 63(a). Concept of AGI has no relevance.
Deductions	Trade or business (§ 162); nonbusiness (§ 212); deduction for qualified business income (§ 199A); reimbursed employee business expenses; some personal expenses (generally deductible as itemized deductions).	Trade or business (§ 162).
Charitable contributions	Limited in any tax year to 50% of AGI (60% of AGI for cash contributions); generally limited to 30% of AGI for capital gain property.	Limited in any tax year to 10% of taxable income (15% of taxable income for food inventory contributions) computed without regard to the charitable contribution deduction, net operating loss carryback, capital loss carryback, and dividends received deduction.
	Excess charitable contributions carried over for five years.	Same as for individuals.
	Amount of deduction is the fair market value of capital gain property; ordinary income property is limited to adjusted basis; capital gain property is treated as ordinary income property if tangible personalty is donated to a nonuse charity or the donation is to certain private foundations.	Same as for individuals, but exceptions allowed for certain inventory and for research property where one-half of the appreciation also is allowed as a deduction.
	Time of deduction is the year in which payment is made.	Time of deduction is the year in which payment is made unless accrual basis taxpayer. Accrual basis corporation can take deduction in year preceding payment if contribution was authorized by board of directors by end of year and contribution is paid by fifteenth day of fourth month of following year.
Casualty losses	Personal casualty losses limited to losses attributable to a Federally declared disaster; $100 floor on losses; total personal casualty losses deductible only to extent losses exceed 10% of AGI.	Deductible in full.
Net operating loss	Adjusted for several items, including nonbusiness deductions over nonbusiness income.	Generally no adjustments.
	Indefinite carryforward; carryforward deduction limited to 80% of taxable income.	Same as for individuals.
Dividends received deduction	None.	50%, 65%, or 100% of dividends received depending on percentage of ownership by corporate shareholder.
Net capital gains	Taxed in full. Tax rate is 0%, 15%, or 20% on net capital gains.	Taxed in full. No preferential tax rate.
Capital losses	Only $3,000 of capital loss per year can offset ordinary income; unused loss is carried forward indefinitely to offset capital gains or ordinary income up to $3,000; short- and long-term carryovers retain their character.	Can offset only capital gains; unused loss is carried back three years and forward five; carryovers and carrybacks are characterized as short-term losses.

continued

Income Taxation of Individuals and Corporations Compared—(Continued)

	Individuals	Corporations
Passive activity losses	In general, passive activity losses cannot offset either active income or portfolio income.	Passive activity loss rules apply to closely held C corporations and personal service corporations. For personal service corporations, passive activity losses cannot offset either active income or portfolio income. For closely held C corporations, passive activity losses may offset active income but not portfolio income.
Tax rates	Progressive with seven rates (10%, 12%, 22%, 24%, 32%, 35%, and 37%).	Flat rate of 21%.
Alternative minimum tax	Applied at a graduated rate schedule of 26% and 28%. Exemption allowed depending on filing status (e.g., $126,500 for married filing jointly in 2023); phaseout begins when AMTI reaches a certain amount (e.g., $1,156,300 in 2023 for married filing jointly).	Flat rate of 15%. Applies to corporations having more than $1 billion in average annual adjusted financial statement income for any 3-year period.

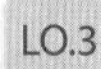
LO.3

Compute the corporate income tax.

17-2 Determining the Corporate Income Tax Liability

17-2a Corporate Income Tax Rates

Corporate income tax rates have fluctuated over the years. The top corporate income tax rate was reduced from 46 percent to 34 percent in 1986, and then raised to a top rate of 35 percent a few years later. This rate was the highest of all the developed countries in the world prior to 2018. The U.S. corporate tax rate was reduced to a flat rate of 21 percent for tax years beginning after 2017.[37]

Example 24

Agile Corporation, a calendar year C corporation, reports taxable income in 2023 of $20,000,000. Agile Corporation's tax liability is $4,200,000 ($20,000,000 × 21%).

The Big Picture

Example 25

Return to the facts of *The Big Picture* on p. 17-1. Assume that Samantha incorporates her business as Skylark Bakery, Inc., a calendar year C corporation. The corporation pays Samantha a salary of $50,000 for the current year. Therefore, Skylark Bakery has taxable income of $52,500 [$100,000 operating profit + $5,000 dividends − $50,000 salary deduction − $2,500 dividends received deduction ($5,000 × 50%)]. Its income tax liability is $11,025 ($52,500 × 21%).

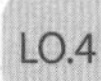
LO.4

Describe the application of the corporate alternative minimum tax.

17-2b Alternative Minimum Tax

Prior to 2018, corporations were subject to an alternative minimum tax (AMT) that was structured similarly to the individual AMT. However, that corporate AMT was repealed for tax years beginning after 2017.

[37] § 11(b). For 2017, the corporate tax rate structure was progressive, with rates ranging from 15% to 35%. However, personal service corporations (PSCs) did not receive the benefit of the lower marginal tax rates; instead, PSCs were taxed at a flat rate of 35%.

"Book Income" Alternative Minimum Tax

In an effort to ensure that corporations with significant economic income pay some minimum amount of Federal income tax, a new corporate **alternative minimum tax (AMT)** was enacted as part of the Inflation Reduction Act of 2022.[38] Unlike the calculation of the individual AMT, which begins with taxable income, the calculation of the new corporate AMT begins with a corporation's financial statement income.[39] Thus, the new corporate AMT could be described as a "book minimum tax."

In general, the new corporate AMT applies to any corporation (other than an S corporation) with more than $1 billion in average annual *adjusted financial statement income* (AFSI) for the three-year period ending with the tax year.[40] As a result, the corporate AMT will impact only a small number of corporate taxpayers.[41] Effective for taxable years beginning after 2022, the corporate AMT is equal to the excess of any applicable corporation's tentative minimum tax over its regular tax including any base erosion and anti-abuse tax (BEAT).[42] Tentative minimum tax is equal to 15 percent of the AFSI for the year, less any corporate AMT foreign tax credit for the year.[43]

"Adjusted financial statement income" is defined as the net income (or loss) reported on the corporation's applicable financial statement[44] for the tax year, as modified by certain adjustments. The statute identifies a number of adjustments that must be made to the financial statement net income (or loss) to arrive at AFSI, but the most commonly applied adjustment is likely to be the one for depreciation. AFSI is computed by deducting the amount of depreciation allowed for tax purposes (including MACRS, § 179 expensing, and bonus depreciation), rather than the amount of financial statement depreciation.[45] In determining AFSI, an adjustment to financial statement income is therefore required to reflect the difference between tax depreciation and financial statement depreciation (see Example 26).

Bramble Corporation, a calendar year C corporation, reports net income of $1,500,000,000 on its 2023 financial statements, including financial statement depreciation of $100,000,000. Also, for 2023, Bramble reports taxable income of $600,000,000, including tax depreciation of $300,000,000. Assume that Bramble's average annual AFSI for the 3-year period ending December 31, 2023, is in excess of $1,000,000,000. Also assume that Bramble has no AMT foreign tax credit for 2023. Bramble has a 2023 corporate AMT of $69,000,000, computed as follows:

1. Compute AFSI (financial statement net income plus/minus adjustments).

   $1,500,000,000 − $200,000,000 ($300,000,000 tax depreciation − $100,000,000 financial statement depreciation) = $1,300,000,000

2. Compute tentative minimum tax [(AFSI × 15%) − AMT foreign tax credit].

   $195,000,000 ($1,300,000,000 × 15%) − $0 (AMT foreign tax credit) = $195,000,000

3. Compute corporate AMT (tentative minimum tax − regular tax).

   $195,000,000 − $126,000,000 ($600,000,000 taxable income × 21%) = $69,000,000

---

[38] An Act to Provide for Reconciliation Pursuant to Title II of S. Con. Res. 14 (commonly referred to as the "Inflation Reduction Act of 2022"), P.L. 117-169; 8/16/22, § 10101.

[39] The former corporate AMT had, as its starting point, a corporation's taxable income. See Chapter 12 of *South-Western Federal Taxation: Individual Income Taxes* for a detailed discussion of the individual AMT.

[40] The corporate AMT also does not apply to a regulated investment company or a real estate investment trust. Special rules apply for corporations in existence for less than three years and for short years. In addition, special rules apply in the case of a corporation that is a member of a foreign-parented multinational group. See §§ 55(b)(2) and 59(k).

[41] The Joint Committee on Taxation estimates that about 150 corporations, comprising about 30% of the Fortune 500, could be subject to the corporate AMT annually. See, e.g., **crsreports.congress.gov/product/pdf/IF/IF12179**. Similarly, see J. L. Hoopes and C. Kindt, "Estimating the Minimum Tax on Book Income Liability using Public Data," (September 21, 2022) at  **tax.unc.edu/wp-content/uploads/2022/09/CAMT-estimate.pdf**. Using publicly reported data, the authors concluded that approximately 78 corporations would have had an AMT liability had the tax applied to 2021.

[42] § 55(a)(2). A corporation may carry forward a credit for the net AMT for all prior taxable years beginning after 2022 to reduce its regular tax including any base erosion and anti-abuse tax (BEAT). § 53(e). The base erosion and anti-abuse tax (BEAT) is discussed in Chapter 27.

[43] For a definition of the corporate AMT foreign tax credit, see § 59(l).

[44] § 56A(a). In most cases, the applicable financial statement will be a corporation's audited financial statements prepared under GAAP or IFRS. See §§ 56A(b) and 451(b)(3).

[45] The adjustments required in the computation of AFSI are identified in § 56A(c). Also, § 56A(d) provides for a reduction in AFSI for a financial statement net operating loss.

Note that the corporate AMT generally applies for all taxable years after the average annual AFSI test is initially satisfied, even if the $1 billion threshold is not exceeded with respect to the three-year period ending with the current tax year.[46] For instance, in Example 26, the AMT still would be applicable to Bramble Corporation in tax year 2024, even if Bramble's average annual AFSI for the three-year period ending December 31, 2024 did not exceed $1 billion.

LO.5

Explain the operation of the accumulated earnings and personal holding company taxes.

17-2c Restrictions on Corporate Accumulations

Over the past several decades, there has been little difference between the top individual and corporate marginal tax rates. For instance, prior to 2018, there was less than a 5 percent difference between those rates (39.6 percent individual rate versus 35 percent corporate rate). This nominal differential in top rates limited the tax savings opportunities that could be achieved by individuals shifting income to a corporation. However, this landscape changed dramatically with the enactment of the corporate 21 percent flat tax rate. Consequently, a high-income individual now can achieve up to a 16 percent reduction in tax rate by shifting income to a corporation (37 percent individual rate versus 21 percent corporate rate). As a result, high-income individuals might consider the corporate entity form as a means to reduce their tax burdens.

The taxation of dividend distributions to shareholders will reduce the tax savings that can be achieved through the shifting of income to a corporation and the arbitraging of tax rates. However, what if the double taxation of corporate earnings could be deferred or possibly avoided entirely? Double taxation is deferred to the extent earnings are accumulated within the corporation instead of being distributed to shareholders. The present value of any tax liability on dividends is reduced the longer distributions are deferred. Also, a corporation's accumulation of earnings should cause its stock to appreciate in value. If a shareholder dies with such appreciated stock, all of the appreciation would avoid income taxation due to the step-up in basis under § 1014 (see Chapter 29). In addition, for most taxpayers, no estate tax would be assessed on the appreciated stock due to the high estate exclusion amount. Thus, double taxation could be avoided entirely by accumulating earnings within the corporation and a subsequent transfer of the stock by death.

Two provisions of the Code are designed to prevent corporations and their shareholders from avoiding the double tax on dividend distributions. Both provisions impose a penalty tax on undistributed income retained by the corporation. The rules underlying these provisions are complex and beyond the scope of this text. However, a brief description is provided as an introduction.

Accumulated Earnings Tax

The **accumulated earnings tax** (described in §§ 531–537) imposes a 20 percent tax on the current year's corporate earnings that have been accumulated without a reasonable business need. The burden of proving what constitutes a reasonable need is borne by the taxpayer. In determining accumulated income, businesses are allowed a $250,000 ($150,000 for service corporations) minimum credit. As a result, most corporations can accumulate $250,000 in earnings over a series of years without fear of an accumulated earnings tax. Beyond the minimum credit, earnings can be accumulated for **reasonable needs of the business**, such as expansion of the business, replacement of plant and equipment, working capital needs, product liability losses, debt retirement, self-insurance, and loans to suppliers and customers. Reasonable needs do *not* include loans to shareholders, investments in unrelated properties or businesses, and unrealistic hazards and contingencies. Finally, the accumulated earnings tax can be further reduced or eliminated by distributing dividends.

[46]Exceptions are available for a corporation that has a change in ownership and for a corporation that has, in the IRS's determination, failed the average annual AFSI test for "a specified number" of consecutive tax years (including the most recent tax year). § 59(k)(1).

Personal Holding Company Tax

The **personal holding company (PHC) tax** (described in §§ 541–547) was enacted to discourage the sheltering of certain kinds of passive income in corporations owned by individuals with high marginal tax rates. Historically, the tax was aimed at "incorporated pocketbooks" that were frequently found in the entertainment and construction industries. For example, a taxpayer could shelter income from securities in a corporation, which would pay no dividends, and allow the corporation's stock to increase in value. Like the accumulated earnings tax, the PHC tax employs a 20 percent rate and is designed to force a corporation to distribute earnings to shareholders.

In any single year, the IRS cannot impose both the PHC tax and the accumulated earnings tax. Generally, a company is considered a PHC and may be subject to the tax if:

- More than 50 percent of the value of the outstanding stock is owned by five or fewer individuals at any time during the last half of the year, and
- A substantial portion (60 percent or more) of the corporation's income is comprised of passive types of income including dividends, interest, rents, royalties, or certain personal service income.

Similar to the accumulated earnings tax, the PHC tax can be further reduced or eliminated by distributing dividends.

17-2d **Consolidated Returns**

The privilege of filing a consolidated return is based on the concept that an affiliated group of corporations constitutes a single taxable entity despite the existence of technically separate businesses (e.g., a parent and its subsidiary). By filing a consolidated return, the corporation can eliminate intercompany profits and losses on the principle that its tax liability should be based on transactions with outsiders rather than on intragroup affairs.

Advantages and Disadvantages of Filing Consolidated Returns

There are several tax advantages for group members in filing consolidated returns.

- Elimination of all intercompany dividends from consolidated taxable income.
- Use of shares held by all group members to meet certain other statutory requirements. For example, the 80 percent corporate control requirement of § 351.
- The ability of group members to offset income with losses from other members. This applies to operating, capital, and other losses.

Consolidation also eliminates any intercompany pricing problems among related corporations that might arise under § 482.[47]

Rust Corporation leases a building to Crimson Corporation for $6,000 a month. If the IRS determines that the market value is really $9,000 per month, a § 482 allocation would increase Rust Corporation's monthly rent income by $3,000. If, however, Rust and Crimson are members of an affiliated group that files a consolidated return, the § 482 adjustment would not be made. Increasing Rust Corporation's rent income by $3,000 is meaningless as it is offset by a $3,000 increase in Crimson Corporation's deduction for rent expense.

However, filing consolidated returns also imposes several tax disadvantages on group members.

- The election to consolidate is binding on the group members for future tax years unless a group member leaves the group (in which case the election is still binding on the remaining members) or the IRS consents to an election revocation.

[47] § 482 (Allocation of Income and Deductions Among Taxpayers) is further discussed in Chapter 27 in regard to international situations.

- The requirement that all group members use the parent's tax year may create short tax periods for subsidiaries when they join the group. As a result, a subsidiary could have to bunch its income, accelerate its tax return due date, and use up a valuable carryforward year with a tax year of less than 12 months.
- Consolidated groups incur additional administrative costs in computing consolidated tax liabilities and in complying with the consolidated return Regulations generally.

In addition, there are tax considerations that could be advantageous *or* disadvantageous, depending on the situation.

- Certain consolidated deductions and credits can be either higher or lower due to using consolidated limitations instead of the separate company limits (e.g., the deductions for charitable contributions and dividends received).
- The tax basis of investments in the stock of subsidiaries increases by the members' contribution to consolidated taxable income, perhaps reducing future investor gains. Conversely, subsidiary tax basis decreases by the member's operating losses and by dividend distributions the member makes to its shareholder/parent. Thus, the basis that parent corporations have in their subsidiaries can be either higher or lower than the original purchase prices.
- The consolidated group must defer recognizing gains and losses arising from intercompany property sales. Ordinarily, this is an advantage when deferring gains and a disadvantage when deferring losses.

Eligibility and the Election

The election to file a consolidated return is available only to an **affiliated group**.[48] An affiliated group exists when one corporation owns at least 80 percent of the voting power *and* stock value of another corporation. The stock ownership test must be met on every day of the tax year. In addition, the group can include other corporations as long as one *or more* of the corporations in the group meet the 80 percent ownership test. So affiliated groups can include multiple tiers and chains of corporations as long as the group has an identifiable parent corporation (i.e., at least 80 percent of one corporation must be owned by another).

Members of an affiliated group need not file a consolidated return, and absent an election to consolidate, each corporation files its own Form 1120. If and when an election is made, all of the transactions for the group are combined and reported on one Form 1120. A Form 1122 (Authorization and Consent of Subsidiary Corporation to Be Included in a Consolidated Income Tax Return) should be attached to the first consolidated Form 1120 for every subsidiary included in the group. Each subsequent consolidated Form 1120 must include a Form 851 (Affiliation Schedule) that provides pertinent information about the members of the group.

Computing Consolidated Taxable Income

Several categories of transactions do not enter into the determination of taxable income.

- Some intercompany transactions are disregarded. Examples would be dividends paid by one group member to another. See also the situation presented in Example 27.
- Gains and losses from certain intercompany sales are not recognized until the sold asset leaves the affiliated group (e.g., disposition of the property to an outside party). See Examples 31 and 32.

In computing the taxable income for any consolidated return year, several items are computed on a group basis. These include net capital (and § 1231) gain or loss, casualty gain or loss, charitable contributions, the dividends received deduction, and net operating loss. The importance of this grouping is illustrated below.

[48] § 1504(a). Most of the tax rules governing consolidated returns are contained in the Regulations. The delegation of this rule-making authority is contained in § 1502.

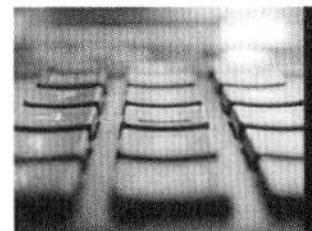

Financial Disclosure Insights — GAAP and Tax Treatment of Consolidations

Both U.S. financial accounting and tax rules use the term *consolidation*, but there is only a slight resemblance in the content of those rules. Here are some of the key similarities and differences between the book and tax treatment of conglomerates.

- GAAP consolidations for the most part are *mandatory* when specified ownership levels are met. Federal income tax consolidation is an *election* by the affiliates to join the parent's tax return.
- GAAP consolidations can include entities such as partnerships and non-U.S. entities. Federal income tax rules generally limit the consolidated return only to U.S. C corporations.
- Ownership levels required for a U.S. subsidiary to consolidate with a parent differ between the book and tax rules. For example, not only does GAAP set a lower maximum for consolidation (50 percent versus 80 percent) but consolidation may not be elective (see above). Furthermore, the categorization and treatment of minority interests may vary.
- Tax rules treat a merger or an acquisition of a target corporation by a parent as a nontaxable transaction (similar to a like-kind exchange), assuming that the requirements of a tax-favored reorganization are met (see Chapter 20). Under GAAP, the transaction usually is reported as a purchase of the target's identifiable assets and liabilities.
- After a takeover occurs, book cost amounts are "stepped up" or "down" to fair market value and any excess purchase price is deemed to be goodwill. For Federal income tax purposes, if reorganization treatment is available, the target's basis in its assets carries over to the parent's accounts.
- Goodwill is treated differently under book and tax rules. Financial accounting goodwill cannot be amortized, but impairments to its value are reported as operating losses. Book income results if that impairment of the goodwill is reversed, for example, because the value of the goodwill has increased. For Federal income tax purposes, purchased goodwill is amortized over 15 years.

Computing Various Items on a Group Basis

Example 28

Maize Corporation owns 100% of the stock of Ecru Corporation, and both use a calendar year for tax purposes. For 2023, they had the following transactions and filed *separate* returns:

	Maize	Ecru
Income from operations	$300,000	$170,000
Capital gain	50,000	
Capital loss of $45,000		(–0–)*
Charitable contribution of $40,000	(35,000)**	
Taxable income	$315,000	$170,000

*No deduction is allowed to a corporation for a net capital loss.
**The charitable deduction is limited to 10% of taxable income, as computed prior to the charitable contribution deduction. In this example, 10% × $350,000 ($300,000 + $50,000) = $35,000.

Example 29

Assume the same facts as in Example 28, except that a consolidated return is filed for 2023. The results are:

Income from operations ($300,000 + $170,000)		$470,000
Capital transactions—		
Capital gain	$ 50,000	
Capital loss	(45,000)*	5,000
Charitable contribution		(40,000)**
Taxable income		$435,000

*A capital loss can be used to offset a capital gain.
**The 10% of taxable income limitation now becomes 10% × $475,000 = $47,500. As a result, the full charitable deduction is allowed.

One of the advantages of filing a consolidated return can be seen by comparing the results reached in Examples 28 and 29. Note that in Example 28, the combined taxable income is $485,000 ($315,000 + $170,000), while in Example 29, taxable income is $435,000, or $50,000 less ($485,000 – $435,000).

The consolidated return rules allow the group to make use of the losses of one (or more) of its members. Because this possibility could lead to major tax avoidance (e.g., a profitable corporation acquires a loss corporation to take advantage of its loss carryovers), multiple safeguards have been enacted by Congress to preclude (or curtail) such potential abuse.

One such safeguard protects against the use of losses and deductions that arose in a separate return year.[49]

For calendar year 2023, Kingfisher Corporation and Starling Corporation first elect to file a consolidated return. As of January 1, 2023, Starling owned land (held as an investment) with a basis of $300,000 and a fair market value of $280,000. During 2023, the land is sold for $270,000. On a consolidated return, only $10,000 of the loss can be claimed. The other $20,000 loss comes from a separate return year(s) and relates only to Starling Corporation. It cannot be used by the affiliated group.

A further safeguard limits the use of losses and deductions when ownership changes within the affiliated group have taken place.[50]

Deferral Treatment for Intercompany Sales

As noted previously, the deferral of certain intercompany sales can be advantageous (if gains are involved) or disadvantageous (if losses are involved). The realized gain or loss from the intercompany sale is not recognized but is deferred.

In 2023, Peach Corporation sells land (basis of $100,000) to Beige Corporation for its fair market value of $180,000. Both Peach and Beige are members of the same affiliated group that files a consolidated return for 2023. None of the $80,000 realized gain is recognized on this return.

The deferred gain or loss may be recognized in a later year when the property ultimately is sold to outsiders.

Assume the same facts as in Example 31. In 2025, Beige Corporation sells the land to an unrelated real estate developer for $210,000. A consolidated return for 2025 should report a recognized gain of $110,000 ($80,000 of which was previously deferred).

Describe the reporting process for corporations.

17-3 Procedural Matters

This section covers various aspects of the corporate income tax return, including filing requirements, estimated tax payments, and special disclosure schedules on the return.

17-3a Filing Requirements for Corporations

A corporation must file a Federal income tax return whether it has taxable income or not. If a corporation began (or ceased) operations during a year, a short-period return (less than 12 months) must be filed for that year.[51]

The corporate income tax return is Form 1120. Corporations electing under Subchapter S (see Chapter 23) use Form 1120S. Forms 1120 and 1120S are reproduced in Appendix B. Corporations with assets of $10 million or more generally are required to file returns electronically.[52]

[49] Aside from the Regulations issued by the Treasury Department, the separate return limitation year (SRLY) safeguards can be invoked pursuant to § 269 (Acquisitions Made to Evade or Avoid Income Tax) and § 482 (Allocation of Income and Deductions Among Taxpayers).

[50] The major statutory weapons available to the IRS are § 381 (Carryovers in Certain Corporate Acquisitions) and § 382 (Limitation on Net Operating Loss Carryforwards and Certain Built-in Losses Following Ownership Change).

[51] § 6012(a)(2) and Reg. § 1.6012–2(a). A corporation must file a return even though it has ceased to do business if it has valuable claims for which it will bring suit. A corporation is relieved of filing income tax returns only when it ceases to do business and retains no assets.

[52] Reg. §§ 1.6012–2(a)(3) (Form 1120), 1.6012–2(h) (Form 1120S), and 301.6011–5 (electronic filing).

A Form 1120 must be filed on or before the fifteenth day of the fourth month following the close of a corporation's tax year.[53] A regular corporation, other than a PSC, can use either a calendar year or a fiscal year to report its taxable income. A Form 1120S must be filed on or before the fifteenth day of the third month following the close of an S corporation's tax year.[54]

A corporation that needs more time to prepare and file its tax return can receive an automatic six-month extension of its tax return due date if it files Form 7004 (and pays the related tax liability) by the due date of its return.[55] The IRS may terminate an extension by mailing a 10-day notice to the corporation.

17-3b **Estimated Tax Payments**

A corporation must make estimated tax payments unless its tax liability can reasonably be expected to be less than $500. The required annual payment is the *lesser* of:

1. 100 percent of the corporation's tax for the current year, or
2. 100 percent of the tax for the preceding year (if that was a 12-month tax year, the return filed showed a tax liability, and the corporation involved is not a *large corporation*).

Estimated payments can be made in four installments due on or before the fifteenth day of the fourth month, the sixth month, the ninth month, and the twelfth month of the corporate taxable year.[56]

Failure to make the required estimated tax prepayments results in a nondeductible penalty being imposed on the corporation. The penalty is avoided, however, if any of various exceptions apply.

17-3c **Schedule M–1—Reconciliation of Income (Loss) per Books with Income per Return**

Schedule M–1 of Form 1120 is used to *reconcile* net income as computed for financial accounting purposes [i.e., using **generally accepted accounting principles (GAAP)**] with taxable income reported on the corporation's income tax return (commonly referred to as book-tax differences). Schedule M–1 is required of corporations with less than $10 million of total assets.

The starting point on Schedule M–1 is net income (or loss) per books. Additions and subtractions are entered for items that affect financial accounting net income and taxable income differently. The following items are entered as additions (see lines 2 through 5 of Schedule M–1):

- Federal income tax expense per books (deducted in computing net income per books but not deductible in computing taxable income).
- The excess of capital losses over capital gains (deducted for financial accounting purposes but not deductible by corporations for income tax purposes).
- Income that is reported in the current year for tax purposes but is not reported in computing net income per books (e.g., prepaid income).
- Various expenses that are deducted in computing net income per books but are not allowed in computing taxable income (e.g., charitable contributions in excess of the 10 percent ceiling applicable to corporations).

The following subtractions are entered on lines 7 and 8 of Schedule M–1:

- Income reported for financial accounting purposes but not included in taxable income (e.g., tax-exempt interest).
- Deductions taken on the tax return but not expensed in computing net income per books (e.g., tax depreciation in excess of financial accounting depreciation).

[53]§ 6072(a). A corporation with a June 30 year-end must file a Form 1120 by the fifteenth day of the *third* month following the close of its fiscal year through 2025 [P.L. 114–41, § 2006(a)(3)(B)]. If the due date falls on a Saturday, Sunday, or legal holiday, the due date is the next business day.

[54]§ 6072(b).

[55]Reg. § 1.6081–3. An extension of seven months applies for C corporations with a June 30 year-end through 2025. § 6081(b).

[56]§ 6655. If the due date falls on Saturday, Sunday, or a legal holiday, the due date is the next business day. See § 6655(g)(2) for the definition of a *large corporation*.

The result is taxable income (before the NOL deduction and the dividends received deduction). Concept Summary 17.3 provides a conceptual diagram of Schedule M–1.

Example 33

During the current year, Tern Corporation had the following transactions:

Net income per books (after tax)	$89,400
Taxable income	50,000
Federal income tax expense per books (21% × $50,000)	10,500
Interest income from tax-exempt bonds	5,000
Interest paid on a loan, the proceeds of which were used to purchase the tax-exempt bonds	500
Life insurance proceeds received as a result of the death of a key employee	50,000
Premiums paid on the key employee life insurance policy	2,600
Excess of capital losses over capital gains	2,000

For book and tax purposes, Tern determines depreciation under the straight-line method. Tern's Schedule M–1 for the current year follows:

Schedule M-1 Reconciliation of Income (Loss) per Books With Income per Return
Note: The corporation may be required to file Schedule M-3 (see instructions).

1	Net income (loss) per books	89,400	7	Income recorded on books this year not included on this return (itemize):	
2	Federal income tax per books	10,500			
3	Excess of capital losses over capital gains	2,000	a	Tax-exempt interest $ 5,000	
4	Income subject to tax not recorded on books this year (itemize):		b	Other (itemize): Life insurance proceeds on key employee $50,000	55,000
			8	Deductions on this return not charged against book income this year (itemize):	
5	Expenses recorded on books this year not deducted on this return (itemize):		a	Depreciation $	
a	Depreciation $		b	Charitable contributions $	
b	Charitable contributions $		c	Other (itemize):	
c	Travel and entertainment $				
d	Other (itemize): Prem.–life ins. $2,600; Int.–tax-exempt bonds $500	3,100	9	Add lines 7 and 8	55,000
6	Add lines 1 through 5	105,000	10	Income—line 6 less line 9	50,000

17-3d Schedule M–2—Analysis of Unappropriated Retained Earnings per Books

Schedule M–2 reconciles unappropriated retained earnings at the beginning of the year with unappropriated retained earnings at year-end. In general, this financial statement reconciliation is done by adding net income per books to the beginning balance of retained earnings and subtracting distributions made during the year. Other sources of increases or decreases in retained earnings are also listed on Schedule M–2.

Assume the same facts as in Example 33. Tern Corporation's beginning balance in unappropriated retained earnings is $125,000. During the year, Tern distributed a cash dividend of $30,000 to its shareholders. Based on this additional information, Tern's Schedule M–2 for the current year is constructed as follows:

Schedule M-2 Analysis of Unappropriated Retained Earnings per Books (Schedule L, Line 25)

1	Balance at beginning of year	125,000	5	Distributions: a Cash	30,000
2	Net income (loss) per books	89,400		b Stock	
3	Other increases (itemize):			c Property	
			6	Other decreases (itemize):	
			7	Add lines 5 and 6	30,000
4	Add lines 1, 2, and 3	214,400	8	Balance at end of year (line 4 less line 7)	184,400

Corporations with less than $250,000 of gross receipts and less than $250,000 in assets do not have to complete Schedule L (balance sheet) and Schedules M–1 and M–2 of Form 1120. Similar rules apply to Form 1120S (used by S corporations). These rules are intended to ease the compliance burden on small business.

Concept Summary 17.3

Conceptual Diagram of Schedule M-1 (Form 1120)

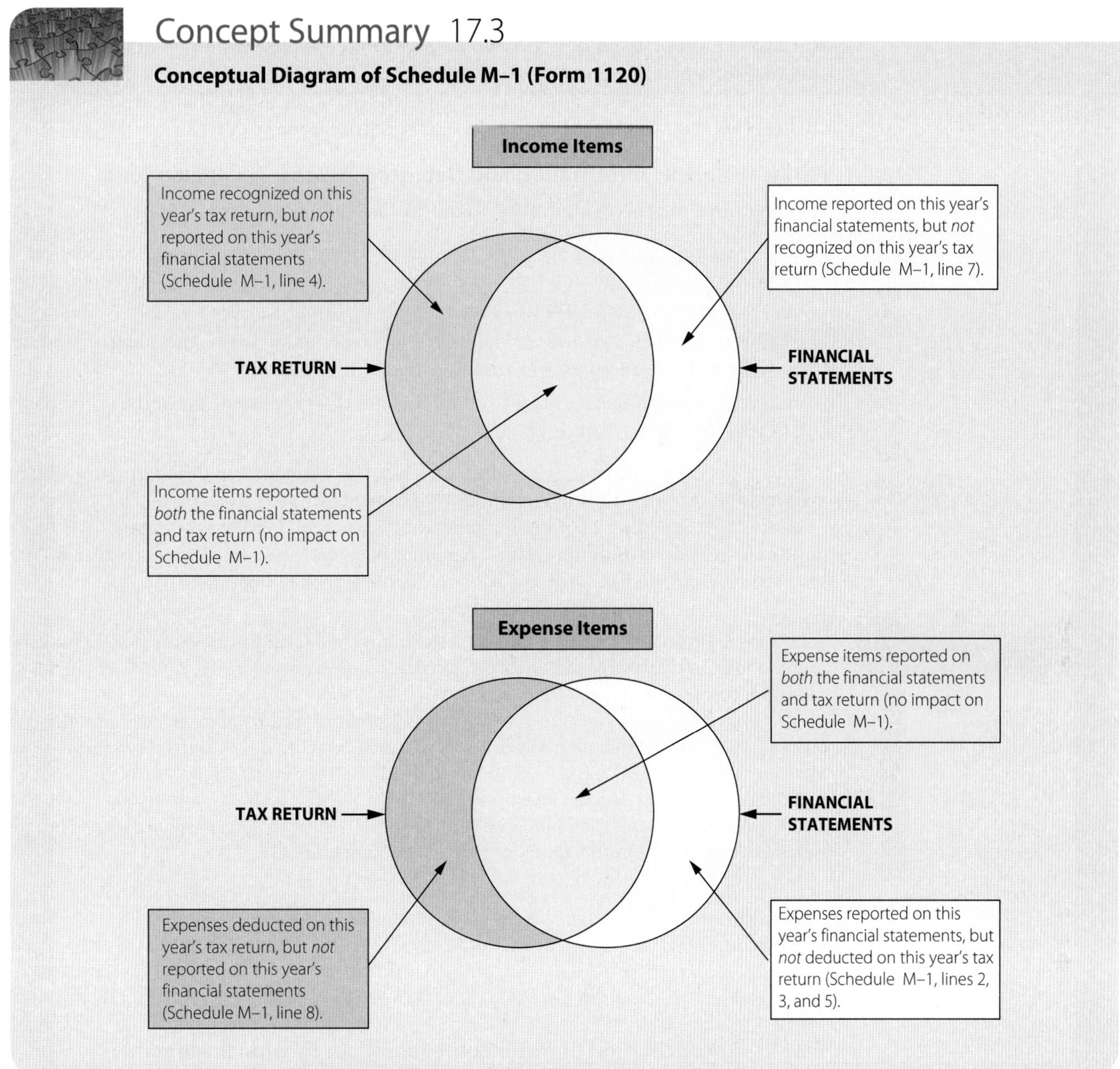

17-3e Schedule M-3—Net Income (Loss) Reconciliation for Corporations with Total Assets of $10 Million or More

Corporate taxpayers with total assets of $10 million or more are required to report much greater detail relative to differences between income (loss) reported for financial purposes and income (loss) reported for tax purposes. This expanded reconciliation of book and taxable income (loss) is reported on **Schedule M-3**.[57] Schedule M-3 is reproduced in Appendix B.

[57]Corporations that are not required to file Schedule M-3 may do so voluntarily. Any corporation that files Schedule M-3 is not allowed to file Schedule M-1. Corporations (and partnerships) with $10 million to $50 million of total assets may elect to file Schedule M-1 in lieu of Schedule M-3, Parts II and III. Electing entities must still file Schedule M-3, Part I (lines 1-12). Entities with less than $10 million of assets that voluntarily file Schedule M-3 also may elect the reduced Schedule M-3 filing requirements.

Schedule M–3 is a response, at least in part, to a variety of financial reporting scandals. One objective of Schedule M–3 is to create greater transparency between corporate financial statements and tax returns. Another objective is to identify corporations that engage in aggressive tax practices by requiring that transactions that create book-tax differences be disclosed on corporate tax returns.

Part I—Financial Information and Net Income (Loss) Reconciliation

Part I requires the following financial information about the corporation:

- The source of the financial net income (loss) amount used in the reconciliation—SEC Form 10–K, audited financial statements, prepared financial statements, or the corporation's books and records.
- Any restatements of the corporation's income statement for the filing period, as well as any restatements for the past five filing periods.
- Any required adjustments to the net income (loss) amount referred to previously (see Part I, lines 5 through 10).

The adjusted net income (loss) amount must be reconciled with the amount of taxable income reported on the corporation's Form 1120.

Because of Schedule M–3's complexity, our coverage is limited to some of the more important concepts underlying the schedule. A series of examples adapted from the instructions for Schedule M–3 are used to illustrate these concepts.

Southwest Sportsman's Corporation (SSC) sells hunting and fishing equipment. SSC has several stores in Texas, New Mexico, and Arizona. It also has a subsidiary in Mexico, which is organized as a Mexican corporation.

SSC, which does not file a Form 10–K with the SEC, reports income from its Mexican subsidiary on its audited financial statements, which show net income of $45,000,000 in the current year. The Mexican corporation, which is not consolidated by SSC for tax purposes (and, as a result, is not an includible corporation), had net income of $7,000,000.

SSC will enter $7,000,000 on Part I, line 5a, of Schedule M–3, resulting in "net income per income statement of includible corporations" of $38,000,000 (Part I, line 11).

A situation similar to that described in Example 35 could result in additional entries in Part I of Schedule M–3. For example, if SSC engaged in transactions with its nonincludible Mexican subsidiary, an entry would be required on line 8 (adjustment to eliminations of transactions between includible corporations and nonincludible entities).

Part II—Reconciliation of Net Income (Loss) per Income Statement of Includible Corporations with Taxable Income per Return

Part II reconciles income and loss items of includible corporations (Part III reconciles expenses and deductions). As indicated in Example 35, corporations included in a financial reporting group may differ from corporations in a tax reporting group. Corporations may also be partners in a partnership, which is a flow-through entity. The following example illustrates the adjustments that are required in this situation.

Southwest Sportsman's Corporation also owns an interest in a U.S. partnership, Southwest Hunting Lodges (SHL). On its audited financial statements, SSC treats the difference between financial statement net income and taxable income from its investment in SHL as a permanent difference. During the year, SSC reported net income of $10,000,000 as its distributive share from SHL. (See Chapters 21 and 22 for a complete discussion of partnership taxation.) SSC's Schedule K–1 from SHL reports the following amounts:

Ordinary income	$5,000,000
Long-term capital gain	7,000,000
Charitable contributions	4,000,000
Section 179 expense	100,000

continued

To adjust for the flow-through items from the partnership, SSC must report these items on Schedule M–3, Part II, line 9 [Income (loss) from U.S. partnerships]. The corporation reports $10,000,000 (book income) on line 9, column (a). SSC reports income per tax return of $7,900,000 ($5,000,000 + $7,000,000 − $4,000,000 − $100,000) in column (d) of line 9 and a permanent difference of $2,100,000 in column (c).

Part III—Reconciliation of Expense/Deduction Items

Part III lists 37 reconciling items relating to expenses and deductions. For these items, taxpayers must reconcile differences between income statement amounts (column a) and tax return amounts (column d) and then classify these differences as temporary (column b) or permanent (column c) differences. The totals of the reconciling items from Part III are transferred to Part II, line 27 and are included with other items required to reconcile financial statement net income (loss) to tax return net income (loss).

Book-Tax Differences Reconciled

Southwest Sportsman's Corporation acquired intellectual property in the current year and expensed amortization of $20,000 on its financial statements, which were prepared according to GAAP. For Federal income tax purposes, SSC deducted $30,000.

The corporation must report the amortization on line 28, Part III as follows: $20,000 book amortization in column (a), $10,000 temporary difference in column (b), and $30,000 tax return amortization in column (d).

In January of the current year, Southwest Sportsman's Corporation established an allowance for uncollectible accounts (bad debt reserve) of $35,000 on its books and increased the allowance by $65,000 during the year. As a result of a client's bankruptcy, SSC decreased the allowance by $25,000 later in the year. The corporation expensed the $100,000 of increases to the allowance on its income statement but was not allowed to deduct that amount on its tax return. On its tax return, the corporation was allowed to deduct the $25,000 actual loss sustained because of its client's bankruptcy.

These amounts must be reported on line 32, Part III as follows: $100,000 book bad debt expense in column (a), $75,000 temporary difference in column (b), and $25,000 tax return bad debt deduction in column (d).

Example 37 illustrates the Schedule M–3 reporting when book expenses are less than tax return deductions. Example 38 illustrates reporting procedures when book expenses are greater than tax return deductions. Both examples illustrate the reporting of temporary differences. The amounts from both examples are included in the totals derived in Part III and are carried to Part II, line 27. The reconciliation of book income and taxable income occurs in lines 26 through 30. The reconciled amount on Part II, line 30, column (a) must be equal to the net income per income statement of includible corporations on Part I, line 11. The reconciled amount on Part II, line 30, column (d) must be equal to the taxable income reported on Form 1120.

17-4 Tax Planning

Evaluate corporations as an entity form for minimizing income taxes on businesses.

17-4a Corporate versus Noncorporate Forms of Business Organization

The decision to use the corporate form in conducting a trade or business must be weighed carefully. Besides the nontax considerations of the corporate form (limited liability, continuity of life, free transferability of interests, centralized management), tax ramifications will play an important role in any such decision. Close attention should be paid to the following:

1. Operating as a regular corporate entity (C corporation) results in the imposition of the corporate income tax. Corporate taxable income will be taxed twice—once as earned by the corporation and again when distributed to the shareholders. Because dividends are not deductible, a closely held corporation may have a strong incentive to structure corporate distributions in a deductible form. With the preferential rates on qualified dividends, shareholders may save taxes by having the corporation pay dividends rather than salaries, rent, or interest, which could be taxed at an individual marginal rate as high as 37 percent. The decision should be made only after comparing the tax cost of the two alternatives. The 3.8 percent additional tax on net investment income (including dividend and net capital gain income) also must be considered in this analysis.
2. The differences in Federal income tax brackets between an individual and a corporation can be substantial. The potential for a 16 percent difference between the top individual rate and the corporate rate (i.e., 37 percent less 21 percent) presents opportunities for significant tax savings. However, several state and local governments impose higher taxes on corporations than on individuals. In these jurisdictions, the combined Federal, state, and local tax rates on the two types of taxpayers must be evaluated. In addition, the deduction for qualified business income must be considered in any tax savings determination. The savings associated with incorporating is enhanced to the extent double taxation of corporate earnings can be deferred or avoided completely. The estate tax exemption ($12,920,000 for 2023), creates greater opportunities for the complete avoidance of double taxation. This complete tax avoidance can be achieved by never distributing corporate earnings and obtaining a stepped-up basis for the corporate stock upon a shareholder's death. However, the accumulated earnings tax and the personal holding company tax may limit opportunities for corporate accumulations and must be factored into any analysis. Consequently, the tax ramifications of incorporating can be determined *only* on a case-by-case basis.
3. Corporate-source income loses its identity as it passes through the corporation to the shareholders. Thus, preferential tax treatment of certain items by the corporation (e.g., interest on municipal bonds) does not carry over to the shareholders.
4. As noted in Chapter 19, it may be difficult for shareholders to recover some or all of their investment in the corporation without an ordinary income result. Most corporate distributions are treated as dividends to the extent of the corporation's earnings and profits. However, the preferential rate on qualified dividends reduces the impact of such a result.
5. Corporate losses cannot be passed through to the shareholders.[58]
6. The liquidation of a corporation will normally generate tax consequences to both the corporation and its shareholders (see Chapter 20).
7. The corporate form provides shareholders with the opportunity to be treated as employees for tax purposes if the shareholders render services to the corporation. Such status makes a number of attractive tax-sheltered fringe benefits available. They include, but are not limited to, group term life insurance and excludible meals and lodging. One of the most attractive benefits of incorporation is the ability of the business to provide accident and health insurance to its employees, including shareholder-employees. Such benefits are not included in the employee's gross income. Similar rules apply to other medical costs paid by the employer. These benefits are not available to partners, sole proprietors, and more-than-2% shareholder-employees of S corporations.

[58]Points 1, 2, and 5 could be resolved by making a Subchapter S election (see Chapter 23), assuming that the corporation qualifies for the election. In part, the same can be said for point 3.

17-4b **Operating the Corporation**

Tax planning to reduce corporate income taxes should occur before the end of the tax year. Effective planning can cause income to be shifted to the next tax year and can produce large deductions by incurring expenses before year-end. Particular attention should be focused on the following.

Timing of Capital Gains and Losses

A corporation should consider offsetting gains on the sale of capital assets by selling some of the depreciated securities in the corporate portfolio. In addition, any already realized capital losses should be carefully monitored. Recall that corporate taxpayers are not permitted to claim any net capital losses as deductions against ordinary income. Capital losses can be used only as an offset against capital gains. Further, net capital losses can only be carried back three years and forward five. Gains from the sales of capital assets should be timed to offset any capital losses. The expiration of the carryover period for any net capital losses should be watched carefully so that sales of appreciated capital assets occur before that date.

Planning for the Business Interest Expense Limitation

Initially, some business sectors (e.g., health care) were more exposed to the limitation than others due to a greater reliance on debt financing, but the limitation's reach expanded in 2022. Beginning in 2022, depreciation, amortization, and depletion must be deducted in arriving at "adjusted taxable income," thus reducing the allowable business interest deduction. The clearest path for reducing the limitation's impact is to pay down debt, such as issuing stock to replace debt. Other alternatives might include forgoing stock buybacks and/or dividends in favor of debt reduction and issuing new debt to replace existing higher interest rate debt.

Charitable Contributions

Recall that accrual basis corporations may claim a deduction for charitable contributions in the year preceding payment. The contribution must be authorized by the board of directors by the end of the tax year and paid on or before the fifteenth day of the fourth month of the following year. It might be useful to authorize a contribution even though it may not ultimately be made. A deduction cannot be thrown back to the previous year (even if paid within the three and a half months) if it has not been authorized.

The enhanced deduction amount for contributions of qualified inventory can produce significant tax savings. Gifts of inventory should be designed to take advantage of this provision whenever feasible, particularly food inventory, which is subject to a higher (15 percent) taxable income limitation. Effort should be taken to properly document the type of inventory donated and each recipient charitable organization, since the statutory provisions that allow for an enhanced deduction have very specific requirements for qualification. Further, a corporation's cost of goods sold must be reduced to reflect any charitable contribution of inventory.

Executive Compensation

A written binding contract in effect on November 2, 2017, is grandfathered under the old executive compensation rules, but only if the contract is not "materially modified" after such date. The renewal of a contract in effect on November 2, 2017, will be treated as a new contract that is not grandfathered. Since performance-based compensation is excluded from the $1 million limitation under prior law, material modifications of grandfathered contracts with such incentives should be avoided. For example, a material modification generally results if a contract is amended to increase or accelerate payment of an employee's compensation.[59]

---

[59]See Reg. § 1.162–33(g)(2) and Notice 2018–68.

Net Operating Losses

The 80%-of-taxable-income limitation applies to NOL deductions for years after 2020. NOLs arising before 2018 and carried over to years after 2020 are not subject to the taxable income limitation. (NOLs arising in 2018, 2019, and 2020 and carried over to years *after* 2020 are subject to the taxable income limitation.)

In 2023, Ruby Corporation has a $10,000,000 carryover of an NOL that originated in 2017. Ruby has 2023 taxable income (before the NOL deduction) of $11,000,000. Since the $10,000,000 NOL carryover arose prior to 2018, the taxable income limitation does not apply and the full amount is deductible in 2023.

For a tax year in which the taxable income limitation is applicable, a corporation might consider taking steps to increase the deductible amount. These steps might include accelerating income into the current tax year or deferring deductions to a subsequent tax year.

Shareholder-Employee Payment of Corporate Expenses

In a closely held corporate setting, shareholder-employees often pay corporate expenses (e.g., office supplies) for which they are not reimbursed by the corporation. Prior to 2018, unreimbursed employee expenses were deductible by an employee (subject to certain limitations). However, from 2018 through 2025, miscellaneous itemized deductions (which includes unreimbursed employee expenses) are not deductible. To preserve the deduction of corporate expenses incurred by shareholder-employees, corporate policy should provide for the reimbursement of these items. The issue can be avoided entirely by having the corporation directly incur the related expenses (e.g., providing a corporate credit card to the shareholder-employee for corporate expenditures).

Avoiding the Accumulated Earnings Tax

The 21 percent flat corporate tax rate will encourage high-income individual taxpayers to shift income to C corporations to obtain a potential 16 percent reduction in their current tax rate (a maximum 37 percent individual tax rate). This tax savings is enhanced the longer dividend distributions can be deferred, thus increasing the possible imposition of the accumulated earnings tax (AET). However, $250,000 ($150,000 for service corporations) of earnings can be accumulated without imposition of the penalty tax.

Accumulations for reasonable needs of the business in excess of the minimum credit amount should be specific, definite, and feasible (see Reg. § 1.537 for further insight into what constitutes reasonable needs of the business). Dividends reduce the impact of the AET, and if the corporation lacks liquidity to make a distribution, a consent dividend (under § 565) should be considered (here, a dividend is deemed distributed by the corporation to the shareholder, then an equal amount is deemed contributed to the capital of the corporation by the shareholder). The lack of liquidity to make dividend distributions is not a defense against the imposition of the AET.

Refocus on The Big Picture

Cooked to Perfection

Conducting Skylark Bakery as a C corporation could save Samantha $8,475 ($38,000 − $29,525) in income taxes annually, computed as follows:

Bakery Operated as Sole Proprietorship	
Operating profit of $100,000:	
Tax on $100,000 × 37%	$37,000
Dividends of $5,000:	
Tax on $5,000 × 20%	1,000
Withdrawals of $50,000:	
No tax	–0–
Total income tax when operated as sole proprietorship	$38,000

Bakery Operated as Regular (C) Corporation	
Corporate taxable income of $52,500*:	
Tax on $52,500 × 21%	$11,025
Samantha's salary of $50,000:	
Tax on $50,000 × 37%	18,500
Total income tax when operated as C corporation	$29,525

*Computation of corporate taxable income:

Operating profit	$ 100,000
Dividend income	5,000
Less: Salary to Samantha	(50,000)
Dividends received deduction (50%)	(2,500)
Taxable income	$ 52,500

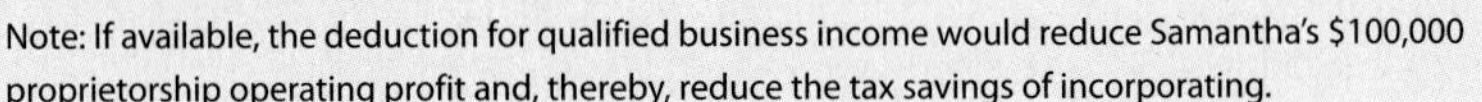

Note: If available, the deduction for qualified business income would reduce Samantha's $100,000 proprietorship operating profit and, thereby, reduce the tax savings of incorporating.

The example illustrates the tax savings available when a high-income individual taxpayer takes advantage of the lower corporate tax rate. However, other issues such as employment tax considerations, the deduction for qualified business income, and the taxation of dividend distributions (i.e., additional Medicare tax on wages and tax on net investment income) also should be considered. Further, other potential entity options, such as the LLC and S corporation, also should be evaluated.

What If?

What if the bakery in the first year it becomes a corporation generates a $10,000 short-term capital loss (STCL) on the disposition of some of its stock investments? Regular corporations can only deduct capital losses against capital gains; thus, the $10,000 STCL would not be deductible currently by the corporation and, instead, would be carried forward for up to five years. If the bakery is operated as a sole proprietorship, Samantha would report the capital loss on her individual return. She could use the $10,000 STCL to offset any capital gains she may have and deduct up to $3,000 of the loss against ordinary income.

Key Terms

Accumulated earnings tax, 17-20
Affiliated group, 17-22
Alternative minimum tax, 17-19
C corporations, 17-2
Dividends received deduction, 17-13
Generally accepted accounting principles (GAAP), 17-25
Organizational expenditures, 17-15
Passive activity loss, 17-8
Personal holding company (PHC) tax, 17-21
Personal service corporations (PSCs), 17-4
Reasonable needs of the business, 17-20
Regular corporations, 17-2
Schedule M–1, 17-25
Schedule M–3, 17-27

Discussion Questions

1. **LO.1** Janice is the sole owner of Catbird Company. In the current year, Catbird had operating income of $100,000, a long-term capital gain of $15,000, and a charitable contribution of $5,000. Janice withdrew $70,000 of profit from Catbird. How should Janice report this information on her individual tax return if Catbird Company is:
   a. An LLC?
   b. An S corporation?
   c. A C corporation?

Critical Thinking
Planning

2. **LO.1** Joel is the sole shareholder of Manatee Corporation, a C corporation. Because Manatee's sales have increased significantly over the last several years, Joel has determined that the corporation needs a new distribution warehouse. Joel has asked your advice as to whether (1) Manatee should purchase the warehouse or (2) he should purchase the warehouse and lease it to Manatee. What relevant tax issues will you discuss with Joel?

3. **LO.1** In the current year, Jeanette, an individual in the 24% marginal tax bracket, recognized a $20,000 long-term capital gain. Also in the current year, Parrot Corporation, a calendar year C corporation, recognized a $20,000 long-term capital gain. Neither taxpayer had any other property transactions in the year. What tax rates are applicable to these capital gains?

4. **LO.1** John (a sole proprietor) and Eagle Corporation (a C corporation) each recognize a long-term capital gain of $10,000 and a short-term capital loss of $18,000 on the sale of capital assets. Neither taxpayer had any other property transactions during the year. Describe the tax consequences of these gains and losses for John and for Eagle.

5. **LO.1** A taxpayer sells a warehouse for a recognized gain. Depreciation had been properly claimed on the property based on the straight-line method over a 39-year recovery period. Will the same amount of depreciation recapture result whether the taxpayer is an individual or a C corporation? Explain.

6. **LO.1** In general, what is the limitation on the deductibility of business interest expense? What happens to any business interest deduction disallowed under the limitation?

7. **LO.1** Osprey Corporation, a closely held corporation, has $100,000 of net active income, $25,000 of portfolio income, and a $120,000 loss from a passive activity.
   a. How much of the passive activity loss can Osprey deduct in the current year if it is a PSC?
   b. If it is not a PSC?

8. **LO.1** On December 28, 2023, the directors of Partridge Corporation, an accrual basis calendar year taxpayer, authorized a cash contribution of $10,000 to the American Cancer Association. The payment is made on April 13, 2024. Can Partridge deduct the charitable contribution in 2023? Explain.

9. **LO.1, 7** The board of directors of Orange Corporation, a calendar year taxpayer, is holding its year-end meeting on December 28, 2023. One topic on the board's agenda is the approval of a $25,000 gift to a qualified charitable organization. Orange has a $20,000 charitable contribution carryover to 2023 from a prior year. Identify the tax issues the board should consider regarding the proposed contribution. Critical Thinking Planning

10. **LO.1, 2, 7** Gold Corporation, a calendar year C corporation, was formed several years ago and has been profitable until the current year. In the current year, Gold incurs a net operating loss. Identify the issues that Gold Corporation should consider regarding its NOL. Critical Thinking Planning

11. **LO.2** Marmot Corporation pays a dividend of $100,000 in the current year. Otter Corporation, a calendar year C corporation, owns 15% of Marmot's stock. Gerald, an individual taxpayer in the 24% marginal bracket, also owns 15% of Marmot's stock. Compare and contrast the treatment of the dividend by Otter Corporation and Gerald.

12. **LO.2** Determine whether the following expenditures by Cuckoo Corporation are organizational expenditures, startup expenditures, or neither.
    a. Legal expenses incurred for drafting the corporate charter and bylaws.
    b. Accounting fees incurred in organization.
    c. Expenses of temporary board of directors' organizational meetings.
    d. Employee salaries incurred during the training period before opening for business.
    e. Brokerage fees incurred in initial stock sales.

13. **LO.4** Megan, the sole shareholder of a calendar year C corporation that operates several fast food restaurants, is concerned that her corporation may have an alternative minimum tax (AMT) liability for 2023. Should Megan be concerned? Explain.

14. **LO.5** Omar, an individual in the 37% tax bracket, wants to shift some of his income to a new corporation in order to take advantage of the 21% corporate tax rate. Omar plans to avoid any tax on dividends by retaining all earnings within the corporation. Will Omar's plan work? Discuss.

15. **LO.6** When are C corporations required to make estimated tax payments? How are these payments calculated?

16. **LO.6** Schedule M–1 of Form 1120 is used to reconcile financial accounting net income with taxable income reported on the corporation's income tax return as follows: Net income per books + Additions − Subtractions = Taxable income. Classify the following items as additions or subtractions in the Schedule M–1 reconciliation.
    a. Life insurance proceeds received upon death of covered executive.
    b. Tax depreciation in excess of book depreciation.
    c. Federal income tax per books.
    d. Capital loss in excess of capital gain.
    e. Charitable contributions in excess of taxable income limitation.
    f. Premiums paid on life insurance policies covering executives (corporation is beneficiary).

17. **LO.6** In the current year, Woodpecker, Inc., a C corporation with $8,500,000 in assets, reported amortization of $40,000 on its financial statements and deducted amortization of $55,000 on its Federal tax return. Is Woodpecker required to file Schedule M–3? If a Schedule M–3 is filed by Woodpecker, how is the difference in amortization amounts treated on that schedule?

Computational Exercises

18. **LO.1** Goose Corporation, a C corporation, incurs a net capital loss of $12,000 for 2023. It also has ordinary income of $10,000 in 2023. Goose had net capital gains of $2,500 in 2019 and $5,000 in 2022.
    a. Determine the amount, if any, of the net capital loss of $12,000 that is deductible in 2023.
    b. Determine the amount, if any, of the net capital loss of $12,000 that is carried forward to 2024.

19. **LO.1** Aqua Corporation purchases nonresidential real property on May 8, 2020, for $1,000,000. Straight-line cost recovery is taken in the amount of $89,765 before the property is sold on November 27, 2023, for $1,500,000.
    a. Compute the amount of Aqua's recognized gain on the sale of the realty.
    b. Determine the amount of the recognized gain that is treated as § 1231 gain and the amount that is treated as § 1250 recapture (ordinary income).

20. **LO.1** In the current year, Nighthawk Corporation, a calendar year C corporation, has $3,700,000 of adjusted taxable income, $125,000 of business interest income, zero floor plan financing interest, and $1,400,000 of business interest expense.
    a. Assume that Nighthawk has average gross receipts for the prior three-year period of $33,000,000. Determine Nighthawk's current-year deduction for business interest.
    b. Assume that Nighthawk has average gross receipts for the prior three-year period of $23,000,000. Determine Nighthawk's current-year deduction for business interest.

21. **LO.1** Hummingbird Corporation, a closely held C corporation that is not a PSC, has $40,000 of net active income, $15,000 of portfolio income, and a $45,000 loss from a passive activity. Compute Hummingbird's taxable income for the year.

22. **LO.1** Compute the charitable contribution deduction (ignoring the percentage limitation) for each of the following C corporations.
    a. Amber Corporation donated inventory of clothing (basis of $24,000, fair market value of $30,000) to a qualified charitable organization that operates homeless shelters.
    b. Brass Corporation donated stock held as an investment to Western College (a qualified organization). Brass acquired the stock three years ago for $18,000, and the fair market value on the date of the contribution is $32,000. Western College plans on selling the stock.
    c. Ruby Corporation donates a sculpture held as an investment and worth $130,000 to a local museum (a qualified organization), which exhibits the sculpture. Ruby acquired the sculpture four years ago for $55,000.

23. **LO.2** Crane and Loon corporations, two unrelated calendar year C corporations, have the following transactions for the current year:

	Crane	Loon
Gross income from operations	$180,000	$300,000
Expenses from operations	255,000	310,000
Dividends received from domestic corporations (15% ownership)	100,000	230,000

    a. Compute the dividends received deduction for Crane Corporation.
    b. Compute the dividends received deduction for Loon Corporation.

24. **LO.2** Cherry Corporation, a calendar year C corporation, is formed and begins business on April 1 of the current year. In connection with its formation, Cherry incurs organizational expenditures of $54,000. Determine Cherry Corporation's deduction for organizational expenditures for the current year.

25. **LO.3** Compute the current-year income tax liability for each of the following unrelated calendar year C corporations.
    a. Darter Corporation has taxable income of $68,000.
    b. Owl Corporation has taxable income of $10,800,000.
    c. Toucan Corporation, a personal service corporation, has taxable income of $170,000.

Problems

26. **LO.1** In the current year, Riflebird Company had operating income of $220,000, operating expenses of $175,000, and a long-term capital loss of $10,000. How do Riflebird Company and Roger, the sole owner of Riflebird, report this information on their respective Federal income tax returns for the current year under the following assumptions?
    a. Riflebird Company is a proprietorship (Roger did not make any withdrawals from the business).
    b. Riflebird Company is a C corporation (no dividends were paid during the year).

27. **LO.1** In the current year, Azure Company has $350,000 of net operating income before deducting any compensation or other payment to its sole owner, Sasha. In addition, Azure has interest on municipal bonds of $25,000. Sasha has significant income from other sources and is in the 37% marginal tax bracket. Based on this information, determine the income tax consequences to Azure Company and to Sasha during the year for each of the following independent situations. (Ignore the deduction for qualified business income and the 3.8% Medicare surtax on net investment income.)
    a. Azure is a C corporation and pays no dividends or salary to Sasha.
    b. Azure is a C corporation and distributes $75,000 of dividends to Sasha.
    c. Azure is a C corporation and pays $75,000 of salary to Sasha.
    d. Azure is a sole proprietorship, and Sasha withdraws $0.
    e. Azure is a sole proprietorship, and Sasha withdraws $75,000.

28. **LO.1** In the current year, Wilson Enterprises, a calendar year taxpayer, suffers a casualty loss of $90,000. The casualty was attributable to a Federally declared disaster. How much of the casualty loss will be deductible by Wilson under the following circumstances?
    a. Wilson is an individual proprietor and has AGI of $225,000. The casualty loss was a personal loss, and the insurance recovered was $50,000.
    b. Wilson is a corporation, and the insurance recovered was $50,000.

29. **LO.3, 7** Genesis Company (GC), a calendar year entity, has one owner, who is in the 37% Federal income tax bracket (any net capital gains or dividends would be taxed at a 20% rate). GC's gross income is $395,000, and its ordinary trade or business deductions are $245,000. Compute the Federal income tax liability on GC's income for the current year under the following assumptions. Ignore the standard deduction (or itemized deductions) and the deduction for qualified business income.

    Communications
    Critical Thinking
    Decision Making
    Planning

    a. GC is operated as a proprietorship, and the owner withdraws $100,000 for personal use.
    b. GC is operated as a corporation, pays out $100,000 as salary, and pays no dividends to its shareholder.
    c. GC is operated as a corporation and pays out no salary or dividends to its shareholder.
    d. GC is operated as a corporation, pays out $100,000 as salary to its shareholder, and pays out the remainder of its earnings as dividends.

e. Assume that Raphael Genesis of 1121 Monroe Street, Ironton, OH 45638 is the owner of GC, which was operated as a proprietorship. Raphael is thinking about incorporating the business for next year and asks your advice. He expects about the same amounts of income and expenses and plans to take $100,000 per year out of the company whether he incorporates or not. Based on your analysis in parts (a) and (b), write a letter to Raphael containing your recommendations.

30. **LO.1, 3** In the current year, Tanager Corporation (a calendar year C corporation) had operating income of $480,000 and operating expenses of $390,000. In addition, Tanager had a long-term capital gain of $55,000 and a short-term capital loss of $40,000.

a. Compute Tanager's taxable income and tax for the year.

b. Assume instead that Tanager's long-term capital gain was $15,000 (not $55,000). Compute Tanager's taxable income and tax for the year.

31. **LO.1** Virginia owns 100% of Goshawk Company. In the current year, Goshawk Company sells a capital asset (held for three years) at a loss of $40,000. In addition, Goshawk has a short-term capital gain of $18,000 and net operating income of $90,000 during the year. Virginia has no recognized capital gain (or loss) before considering her ownership in Goshawk. How much of the capital loss may be deducted for the year, and how much is carried back or forward if Goshawk is:

a. A proprietorship?

b. A C corporation?

Critical Thinking
Planning

32. **LO.1** During 2023, Gorilla Corporation, a calendar year C corporation, has net short-term capital gains of $15,000, net long-term capital losses of $105,000, and taxable income from other sources of $460,000. Prior years' transactions included the following:

2019 net short-term capital gains	$40,000
2020 net long-term capital gains	18,000
2021 net short-term capital gains	25,000
2022 net long-term capital gains	20,000

a. How are the capital gains and losses treated on Gorilla's 2023 tax return?

b. Determine the amount of the 2023 capital loss that is carried back to each of the previous years.

c. Compute the amount of capital loss carryforward, if any, and indicate the years to which the loss may be carried.

d. If Gorilla is a sole proprietorship rather than a corporation, how would these transactions be reported in the proprietor's 2023 tax return?

e. Assume that Gorilla Corporation's capital loss carryforward in part (c) is $27,000 and that Gorilla will be able to use $11,000 of the carryover to offset capital gains in 2024 and the remaining $16,000 to offset capital gains in 2025. In present value terms, determine the tax savings of the $105,000 long-term capital loss recognized in 2023. Assume a discount rate of 5% (present value factors are in Appendix E). Create a spreadsheet using Microsoft Excel (or a similar software program) that summarizes your analysis.

33. **LO.1** Heron Company purchases commercial realty on November 13, 2005, for $650,000. Straight-line depreciation of $287,492 is claimed before the property is sold on February 22, 2023, for $850,000. What are the tax consequences of the sale of realty if Heron is:

a. A C corporation?

b. A sole proprietorship?

34. **LO.1** In the current year, Plum, Inc., a closely held C corporation, has $410,000 of net active income, $20,000 of portfolio income, and a $75,000 passive activity loss. What is Plum's taxable income for the current year under the following circumstances?

a. Plum is a personal service corporation.

b. Plum is not a personal service corporation.

35. **LO.1** Aquamarine Corporation, a calendar year C corporation, makes the following donations to qualified charitable organizations during the current year:

	Adjusted Basis	Fair Market Value
Painting held four years as an investment, to a church, which sold it immediately	$15,000	$25,000
Apple stock held two years as an investment, to United Way, which sold it immediately	40,000	90,000
Canned groceries held one month as inventory, to Catholic Meals for the Poor	10,000	17,000

Determine the amount of Aquamarine Corporation's charitable deduction for the current year. (Ignore the taxable income limitation.)

36. **LO.1, 7** Joseph Thompson is president and sole shareholder of Jay Corporation (a cash method, calendar year C corporation). In December of the current year, Joe asks your advice regarding a charitable contribution he plans to have the corporation make to the University of Maine, a qualified public charity. Joe is considering the following alternatives as charitable contributions in December:

Communications
Critical Thinking
Decision Making
Planning

	Fair Market Value
(1) Cash donation	$200,000
(2) Unimproved land held for six years ($110,000 basis)	200,000
(3) Maize Corporation stock held for eight months ($140,000 basis)	200,000
(4) Brown Corporation stock held for nine years ($360,000 basis)	200,000

Joe has asked you to help him decide which of these potential contributions will be most advantageous taxwise. Jay's taxable income is $3,500,000 before considering the contribution. Rank the four alternatives, and write a letter to Joe communicating your advice. The corporation's address is 1442 Main Street, Freeport, ME 04032.

37. **LO.1, 7** In 2023, Gray Corporation, a calendar year C corporation, has a $75,000 charitable contribution carryover from a gift made in 2018. Gray is contemplating a gift of land to a qualified charity in either 2023 or 2024. Gray purchased the land as an investment five years ago for $100,000 (current fair market value is $250,000). Before considering any charitable deduction, Gray projects taxable income of $1,000,000 for 2023 and $1,200,000 for 2024. Should Gray make the gift of the land to charity in 2023 or in 2024? Provide support for your answer.

Critical Thinking
Decision Making
Planning

38. **LO.1, 7** Julieta Simms is the president and sole shareholder of Simms Corporation (a cash method, calendar year C corporation), 1121 Madison Street, Seattle, WA 98121. Julieta plans for the corporation to make a charitable contribution to the University of Washington, a qualified public charity. She will have the corporation donate Jaybird Corporation stock, held for five years, with a basis of $11,000 and a fair market value of $25,000. Julieta projects a $310,000 net profit for Simms Corporation in 2023 and a $100,000 net profit in 2024. Julieta calls you on December 10, 2023, and asks whether she should make the contribution in 2023 or 2024. Write a letter advising Julieta about the timing of the contribution.

Decision Making
Critical Thinking
Communications
Planning

39. **LO.1** Florence is the newly hired chief financial officer of Hazel Corporation, a publicly traded, calendar year C corporation. For the current year, her compensation package consists of:

Cash compensation	$1,500,000
Bonus tied to company performance	700,000
Taxable fringe benefits	250,000
Nontaxable fringe benefits	75,000

How much of Florence's compensation is deductible by Hazel Corporation?

40. **LO.1, 2** During the current year, Swallow Corporation, a calendar year C corporation, has the following transactions:

Income from operations	$660,000
Expenses from operations	760,000
Dividends received from Brown Corporation	240,000

a. Swallow Corporation owns 12% of Brown Corporation's stock. How much is Swallow's taxable income or NOL for the year?

b. Assume instead that Swallow Corporation owns 26% of Brown Corporation's stock. How much is Swallow's taxable income or NOL for the year?

41. **LO.2** In each of the following *independent* situations, determine the dividends received deduction for the calendar year C corporation. Assume that none of the corporate shareholders owns 20% or more of the stock in the corporations paying the dividends.

	Almond Corporation	Banana Corporation	Cherry Corporation
Income from operations	$ 700,000	$ 800,000	$ 900,000
Expenses from operations	(600,000)	(860,000)	(910,000)
Qualifying dividends	100,000	100,000	100,000

42. **LO.2** Gull Corporation, a cash method, calendar year C corporation, was formed and began business on November 1, 2023. Gull incurred the following expenses during its first year of operations (November 1, 2023–December 31, 2023):

Expenses of temporary directors and organizational meetings	$21,000
Fee paid to state of incorporation	3,000
Expenses for printing and sale of stock certificates	11,000
Legal services for drafting the corporate charter and bylaws (not paid until January 2024)	19,000

a. Assuming that Gull Corporation elects under § 248 to expense and amortize organizational expenditures, what amount may be deducted in 2023?

b. Assume the same facts as above, except that the amount paid for the legal services was $28,000 (instead of $19,000). What amount may be deducted as organizational expenditures in 2023?

43. **LO.2** Egret Corporation, a calendar year C corporation, was formed on March 6, 2023, and opened for business on July 1, 2023. After its formation but prior to opening for business, Egret incurred the following expenditures:

Accounting	$ 7,000
Advertising	14,500
Employee payroll	11,000
Rent	8,000
Utilities	1,000

What is the maximum amount of these expenditures that Egret can deduct in 2023?

44. **LO.3** In each of the following *independent* situations, determine the corporation's income tax liability. Assume that all corporations use a calendar year for tax purposes and that the tax year involved is 2023.

	Taxable Income
Purple Corporation	$ 65,000
Azul Corporation	290,000
Pink Corporation	12,350,000
Turquoise Corporation	19,000,000
Teal Corporation (a personal service corporation)	130,000

45. **LO.4** Crockett Corporation, a calendar year C corporation, reports net income of $2,000,000,000 on its 2023 audited financial statements (including financial statement depreciation of $250,000,000). Also, for 2023, Crockett reports taxable income of $900,000,000 (including tax depreciation of $400,000,000). Assume that Crockett's average annual AFSI for the three-year period ending December 31, 2023, is in excess of $1,000,000,000. Also assume that Crockett has no AMT foreign tax credit for 2023. Compute Crockett's 2023 corporate AMT.

46. **LO.6** Emerald Corporation, a calendar year and accrual method taxpayer, provides the following information and asks you to prepare Schedule M–1 for 2023:

Net income per books (after-tax)	$268,200
Federal income tax per books	31,500
Tax-exempt interest income	15,000
Life insurance proceeds received as a result of death of corporate president	150,000
Interest on loan to purchase tax-exempt bonds	1,500
Excess of capital loss over capital gains	6,000
Premiums paid on life insurance policy on life of Emerald's president	7,800

47. **LO.6** The following information for 2023 relates to Sparrow Corporation, a calendar year, accrual method taxpayer:

Net income per books (after-tax)	$205,050
Federal income tax expense per books	55,650
Tax-exempt interest income	4,500
MACRS depreciation in excess of straight-line depreciation used for financial statement purposes	7,200
Excess of capital loss over capital gains	9,400
Nondeductible meals and entertainment	5,500
Interest on loan to purchase tax-exempt bonds	1,100

Based on the above information, use Schedule M–1 of Form 1120, which is available on the IRS website, to determine Sparrow's taxable income for 2023.

48. **LO.6** Dove Corporation, a calendar year C corporation, had the following information for 2023:

Net income per books (after-tax)	$386,250
Taxable income	120,000
Federal income tax per books	25,200
Cash dividend distributions	150,000
Unappropriated retained earnings, as of January 1, 2023	796,010

Based on the above information, use Schedule M–2 of Form 1120 (see Example 34 in the text) to determine Dove's unappropriated retained earnings balance as of December 31, 2023.

49. **LO.6** In the current year, Pelican, Inc., a calendar year C corporation, incurs $10,000 of meals and entertainment expenses that it deducts in computing net income per the corporation's financial statements. All of the meals and entertainment expenditures are subject to the 100% disallowance rule applicable to such expenditures. How is this information reported on Schedule M–3?

50. **LO.6** In January 2023, Pelican, Inc., established an allowance for uncollectible accounts (bad debt reserve) of $70,000 on its books and increased the allowance by $120,000 during the year. As a result of a client's bankruptcy, Pelican, Inc., decreased the allowance by $60,000 in November 2023. Pelican, Inc., expensed the $190,000 of increases to the allowance on its 2023 income statement but was not allowed to deduct that amount on its tax return. On its 2023 tax return, the corporation was allowed to deduct the $60,000 actual loss sustained because of its client's bankruptcy. On its financial statements, Pelican, Inc., treated the $190,000 increase in the bad debt reserve as an expense that gave rise to a temporary difference. On its 2023 tax return, Pelican, Inc., took a $60,000 deduction for bad debt expense. How is this information reported on Schedule M–3?

Tax Return Problems

Tax Forms Problem

ProConnect™ Tax

51. On November 1, 2011, Janet Morton and Kim Wong formed Pet Kingdom, Inc., to sell pets and pet supplies. Pertinent information regarding Pet Kingdom is summarized as follows:

- Pet Kingdom's business address is 1010 Northwest Parkway, Dallas, TX 75225; its telephone number is (214) 555-2211; and its e-mail address is petkingdom@pki.com.
- The employer identification number is 11-1111112, and the principal business activity code is 453910.
- Janet and Kim each own 50% of the common stock; Janet is president and Kim is vice president of the company. No other class of stock is authorized.
- Both Janet and Kim are full-time employees of Pet Kingdom. Janet's Social Security number is 123-45-6788, and Kim's Social Security number is 123-45-6787.
- Pet Kingdom is an accrual method, calendar year taxpayer. Inventories are determined using FIFO and the lower of cost or market method. Pet Kingdom uses the straight-line method of depreciation for book purposes and accelerated depreciation (MACRS) for tax purposes.
- During 2022, the corporation distributed cash dividends of $250,000.

Pet Kingdom's financial statements for 2022 are shown below.

Income Statement

Income			
Gross sales			$ 5,750,000
Sales returns and allowances			(200,000)
Net sales			$ 5,550,000
Cost of goods sold			(2,300,000)
Gross profit			$ 3,250,000
Dividends received from stock investments in less-than-20%-owned U.S. corporations			43,750
Interest income:			
State bonds	$ 15,000		
Certificates of deposit	20,000		35,000
Total income			$ 3,328,750
Expenses			
Salaries—officers:			
Janet Morton	$262,500		
Kim Wong	262,500	$525,000	
Salaries—clerical and sales		725,000	
Taxes (state, local, and payroll)		238,000	
Repairs and maintenance		140,000	
Interest expense:			
Loan to purchase state bonds	$ 9,000		
Other business loans	207,000	216,000	
Advertising		58,000	
Rental expense		109,000	
Depreciation*		106,000	
Charitable contributions (cash)		38,000	
Employee benefit programs		60,000	
Premiums on term life insurance policies on lives of Janet Morton and Kim Wong; Pet Kingdom is the designated beneficiary		40,000	
Total expenses			(2,255,000)

continued

Net income before taxes	$ 1,073,750
Federal income tax	(221,734)
Net income per books	$ 852,016

*Depreciation for tax purposes is $136,000. You are not provided enough detailed data to complete a Form 4562 (depreciation). If you solve this problem using Intuit ProConnect, enter the amount of depreciation on line 20 of Form 1120.

Balance Sheet

Assets	January 1, 2022	December 31, 2022
Cash	$ 1,200,000	$ 1,039,461
Trade notes and accounts receivable	2,062,500	2,147,000
Inventories	2,750,000	3,030,000
Stock investment	1,125,000	1,125,000
State bonds	375,000	375,000
Certificates of deposit	400,000	400,000
Prepaid Federal tax	-0-	2,266
Buildings and other depreciable assets	5,455,000	5,455,000
Accumulated depreciation	(606,000)	(712,000)
Land	812,500	812,500
Other assets	140,000	128,500
Total assets	$13,714,000	$13,802,727

Liabilities and Equity	January 1, 2022	December 31, 2022
Accounts payable	$ 2,284,000	$ 1,840,711
Other current liabilities	175,000	155,000
Mortgages	4,625,000	4,575,000
Capital stock	2,500,000	2,500,000
Retained earnings	4,130,000	4,732,016
Total liabilities and equity	$13,714,000	$13,802,727

During 2022, Pet Kingdom made estimated tax payments of $56,000 each quarter to the IRS. Prepare Pet Kingdom's corporate tax return for tax year 2022 using Form 1120 (and any other appropriate forms and schedules). Suggested software: ProConnect Tax.

Tax Forms Problem

ProConnect™ Tax

52. On February 12, 2008, Nancy Trout and Delores Lake formed Kingfisher Corporation to sell fishing tackle. Pertinent information regarding Kingfisher is summarized as follows:
    - Kingfisher's business address is 1717 Main Street, Ely, MN 55731; its telephone number is (218) 555-2211; and its e-mail address is kingfisher@kf.com.
    - The employer identification number is 11-1111113, and the principal business activity code is 451110.
    - Nancy owns 50% of the common stock and is president of the company, and Delores owns 50% of the common stock and is vice president of the company. No other class of stock is authorized.
    - Both Nancy and Delores are full-time employees of Kingfisher. Nancy's Social Security number is 123-45-6788, and Delores's Social Security number is 123-45-6787.
    - Kingfisher is an accrual method, calendar year taxpayer. Inventories are determined using FIFO and the lower of cost or market method. Kingfisher uses the straight-line method of deprecation for book purposes and accelerated depreciation (MACRS) for tax purposes.
    - During 2022, the corporation distributed cash dividends of $80,000.

    Kingfisher's financial statements for 2022 are shown below.

Income Statement

Income			
Gross sales			$2,408,000
Sales returns and allowances			(80,000)
Net sales			$2,328,000
Cost of goods sold			(920,000)
Gross profit			$1,408,000
Dividends received from stock investments in less-than-20%-owned U.S. corporations			12,000
Interest income:			
State bonds	$ 14,000		
Certificates of deposit	10,000		24,000
Total income			$1,444,000
Expenses			
Salaries—officers:			
Nancy Trout	$160,000		
Delores Lake	160,000	$320,000	
Salaries—clerical and sales		290,000	
Taxes (state, local, and payroll)		85,000	
Repairs and maintenance		56,000	
Interest expense:			
Business loans	$ 12,000		
Loan to purchase state bonds	8,000	20,000	
Advertising		6,000	
Rental expense		68,000	
Depreciation*		40,000	
Charitable contributions (cash)		15,000	
Employee benefit programs		24,000	
Premiums on term life insurance policies on lives of Nancy Trout and Delores Lake; Kingfisher is the designated beneficiary		16,000	
Total expenses			(940,000)
Net income before taxes			$ 504,000
Federal income tax			(106,680)
Net income per books			$ 397,320

*You are not provided enough detailed information to complete a Form 4562 (depreciation). If you solve this problem using Intuit ProConnect, enter the amount of deprecation on line 20 of Form 1120.

Balance Sheet

Assets	January 1, 2022	December 31, 2022
Cash	$ 380,000	$ 337,300
Trade notes and accounts receivable	308,400	480,280
Inventories	900,000	1,012,000
State bonds	160,000	160,000
Federal income tax refund	-0-	1,320
Certificates of deposit	140,000	140,000
Stock investments	300,000	300,000
Building and other depreciable assets	240,000	240,000
Accumulated depreciation	(88,800)	(128,800)
Land	20,000	20,000
Other assets	3,600	2,000
Total assets	$2,363,200	$2,564,100

Liabilities and Equity	January 1, 2022	December 31, 2022
Accounts payable	$ 300,000	$ 233,880
Other current liabilities	80,300	40,000
Mortgages	210,000	200,000
Capital stock	500,000	500,000
Retained earnings	1,272,900	1,590,220
Total liabilities and equity	$2,363,200	$2,564,100

During 2022, Kingfisher made estimated tax payments of $27,000 each quarter to the IRS. Prepare Kingfisher's corporate tax return for tax year 2022 using Form 1120 (and any other appropriate forms and schedules). Suggested software: ProConnect Tax.

Research Problems

Note: Solutions to the Research Problems can be prepared by using the Thomson Reuters Checkpoint™ online tax research database, which accompanies this textbook. Solutions can also be prepared by using research materials found in a typical tax library.

Research Problem 1. A personal service corporation (PSC) generally is limited to the calendar year for reporting purposes. One exception to this rule is when the PSC can demonstrate a business purpose for a fiscal year-end. Discuss the business purpose exception, including examples of when the standard is and is not satisfied. Support your research with proper citations of tax authority.

Partial list of research aids:
§ 441(i).
Reg. § 1.441–3.

Communications

Research Problem 2. A new client, Southwest Grocers, is a calendar year C corporation that owns and operates a chain of grocery stores. Southwest Grocers is interested in donating food inventory to one or more charitable organizations that will use the food as part of their exempt purpose (e.g., a food bank or homeless shelter). In some cases, the donated items may consist of dented canned food and fungible food items (e.g., baked goods) nearing their freshness expiration dates. Inedible food or food past its expiration date would not be included in any donation. Prepare an outline detailing the information you would provide to Southwest Grocers regarding charitable contributions of food inventory. Make sure to include support for the content of your outline.

Partial list of research aids:
§ 170(e)(3).
Reg. § 1.170A–4A.
Lucky Stores, Inc., 105 T.C. 420 (1995).

Communications

Research Problem 3. A new client, John Dobson, recently formed John's Premium Steakhouse, Inc., to operate a new restaurant. The restaurant will be a first-time business venture for John, who recently retired after 30 years of military service. John transferred cash to the corporation in exchange for 100% of its stock, and the corporation has leased a building and restaurant equipment. John has asked you for guidance on the tax treatment of various expenses (e.g., licensing, training, advertising) he expects the corporation to incur during the restaurant's preopening period. Research the tax treatment of startup expenditures, including the point at which a business begins for purposes of determining what expenses are included. Prepare a memo for the client files describing the results of your research.

Partial list of research aids:
§ 195.
Reg. § 1.195–1.

Use internet tax resources to address the following questions. Look for reliable websites and blogs of the IRS and other government agencies, media outlets, businesses, tax professionals, academics, think tanks, and political outlets.

Communications

Research Problem 4. A significant percentage of U.S. corporations are closely held corporations, with the stock of such corporations often owned predominantly or exclusively by family members. Using the internet as your sole research source, prepare an outline describing the tax implications and planning opportunities unique to family-owned, closely held corporations.

Communications
Data Analytics

Research Problem 5. Find the most recent *IRS Tax Statistics* (**irs.gov/statistics**) for the Corporation Income Tax Returns Complete Report (Publication 16). Use the data from Figure E of this report to prepare a pie chart highlighting the number and percentage of corporate tax returns by return type (e.g., Form 1120, Form 1120S, etc.) for the most recently reported tax year. E-mail your visual to your instructor along with a brief summary of your findings..

Becker CPA Review Questions

Becker

1. In year 6, Garland Corp. contributed $40,000 to a qualified charitable organization. Garland's year 6 taxable income before the deduction for charitable contributions was $410,000. Included in that amount is a $20,000 dividends received deduction. Garland also had carryover contributions of $5,000 from the prior year. In year 6, what amount can Garland deduct as charitable contributions?

   a. $40,000 c. $43,000
   b. $41,000 d. $45,000

2. Tapper Corp., an accrual basis calendar year corporation, was organized on January 2, year 1. During year 1, revenue was exclusively from sales proceeds and interest income. The following information pertains to Tapper:

Taxable income before charitable contributions for the year ended December 31, year 1	$500,000
Tapper's matching contribution to employee-designated qualified universities made during year 1	10,000
Board of Directors' authorized contribution to a qualified charity (authorized December 1, year 1, made February 1, year 2)	30,000

   What is the maximum allowable deduction that Tapper may take as a charitable contribution on its tax return for the year ended December 31, year 1?

   a. $0 c. $30,000
   b. $10,000 d. $40,000

3. In the current year, Acorn, Inc., had the following items of income and expense:

Sales	$500,000
Cost of sales	250,000
Dividends received	25,000

   The dividends were received from a corporation of which Acorn owns 30%. In Acorn's current-year corporate income tax return, what amount should be reported as income before special deductions?

   a. $525,000 c. $275,000
   b. $505,000 d. $250,000

4. Before the provision for Federal income tax, Karas Corporation had book income of $400,000 for the current year. The book income included $100,000 of dividends

received from a 15% owned domestic corporation. What was Karas Corporation's taxable income for the current year?

a. $300,000
b. $335,000
c. $350,000
d. $400,000

5. Campbell Corporation, an accrual basis calendar year corporation, had income of $450,000 for financial statement purposes in year 7. This amount included book depreciation of $50,000. The related tax depreciation was $65,000. Further, the financial statements reported $100,000 of municipal bond interest income, an expense of $2,000 for life insurance premiums on the corporation's president, charitable contributions of $5,000, excess capital losses over capital gains of $3,000, income tax penalties of $10,000, state income tax of $40,000, and Federal income tax expense of $175,000. What is the amount of Campbell's taxable income for year 7?

   a. $522,000
   b. $525,000
   c. $530,000
   d. $565,000

6. Hirsch Incorporated, is a calendar year corporation that has had revenues of less than $500,000 since inception. In year 12, Hirsch had a net operating loss of $50,000 that was able to be used in full in year 13. For year 13, Hirsch expects to have taxable income prior to NOL deduction of $100,000. How will Hirsch avoid a penalty for underpayment of estimated Federal taxes in year 13?

   a. Hirsch must pay 100% of the tax shown on its year 13 return via estimated taxes to avoid an underpayment penalty.
   b. Hirsch must pay the amount of taxes owed on its year 12 return via estimated taxes to avoid an underpayment penalty.
   c. Hirsch must pay 90% of the tax shown on its year 13 return via estimated taxes to avoid an underpayment penalty.
   d. Hirsch may pay the lower of the amount of taxes owed in year 12 or 100% of the tax shown on the return for year 13 via estimated taxes to avoid an underpayment penalty.

7. The dividends received deduction (DRD) is a tax deduction that may be taken by which of the following?

   a. An individual
   b. An S corporation
   c. A partnership
   d. A C corporation

8. Which of the following statements is *not* true for tax years beginning after 2017?

   a. Affiliated corporations that file consolidated returns can take a 100% dividends received deduction.
   b. The dividends received deduction for a small investment in an unrelated corporation is 50%.
   c. The dividends received deduction for a large investment in a corporation is 65%.
   d. There is no income limitation on the dividends received deduction.

9. Parent Corp. owns 40% of Sub Corp. In the current year, Parent has gross income of $43,000 and allowable deductions of $30,000 before considering any dividends received deduction (DRD). Included in the $43,000 gross income is $8,000 of dividends from Sub. What is the maximum DRD available to Parent?

   a. $4,000
   b. $5,200
   c. $8,000
   d. $8,450

10. Parent Corp. owns 15% of Sub Corp. Parent has gross income of $43,000 and allowable deductions of $40,000 before considering any dividends received deduction (DRD). Included in the $43,000 gross income is $8,000 in dividends from Sub. What is the maximum DRD available to Parent?

    a. $1,500
    b. $1,950
    c. $4,000
    d. $8,000

Chapter

18 Corporations: Organization and Capital Structure

Learning Objectives: *After completing Chapter 18, you should be able to:*

LO.1 **Explain the tax consequences of incorporating a business.**

LO.2 **Identify the basis issues relevant to the shareholder and the corporation.**

LO.3 **Determine the consequences when corporations assume shareholder liabilities.**

LO.4 **Explain the tax aspects of the capital structure of a corporation.**

LO.5 **Characterize the tax differences between debt and equity investments.**

LO.6 **Determine the tax treatment of shareholder debt and stock gains and losses.**

LO.7 **Identify tax planning opportunities associated with organizing and financing a corporation.**

Chapter Outline

GOODLUZ/SHUTTERSTOCK.COM

The Vehicle for Business Growth Is the Corporate Form

Emily has operated her startup venture as a sole proprietorship since launching the business two years ago. Marco, a friend from college, has been collaborating with Emily. Together they have developed an innovative software app. They were overjoyed when, as soon as they introduced the app into the market, it was an immediate hit—and it has gained increasing recognition and market traction as sales continue to rise. After only a short period of success though, Emily becomes convinced that the upside potential for even more growth is significant. However, she realizes that a leap to that level of growth and market penetration can only be achieved with a large infusion of capital that she is unable to fund from her resources.

Fortunately, Emily's friend Ethan, who is a venture capitalist, is enthusiastic about making a large investment in the business in exchange for an equity stake. Ethan agrees that Emily's startup easily will enjoy remarkable success once it has the necessary additional resources. To integrate Ethan's capital into the venture, Emily and Ethan will create Transformation, Inc. Emily will contribute her sole proprietorship assets, and Ethan will contribute cash for Transformation, Inc. stock. Emily also has asked Marco, an invaluable employee and a major contributor to the app's development, if he would be interested in becoming a shareholder in Transformation. He was given the option of transferring either property or services in exchange for stock. However, at this point, Marco is not sure what he will do.

Emily will receive 200 shares of Transformation stock in exchange for transferring the following sole proprietorship assets to the new corporation:

	Adjusted Basis	Fair Market Value
Accounts receivable	$ –0–	$ 50,000
Building	100,000	400,000
Proprietary information—app	300,000	1,550,000
	$400,000	$2,000,000

Ethan will contribute $48,000,000 of cash for 4,800 shares of Transformation stock.

What will be the tax and nontax implications relating to the formation of Transformation, Inc.?

Read the chapter and formulate your response.

Chapter 17 dealt with four principal areas fundamental to working with corporations: (1) understanding the treatment that applies to entities treated as corporations for Federal income tax purposes, (2) recognizing specific income tax rules that apply only to corporations, (3) identifying filing and reporting procedures, and (4) considering special situations involving corporations.

Chapter 18 continues this approach by addressing issues involving corporate formations, capital structure, and special corporate investor rules:

- The tax consequences to shareholders and the corporation when shareholders transfer property to form a new corporation.
- The tax results when shareholders transfer property to an already-existing corporation.
- The capital structure of a corporation, including equity and debt financing.
- The special tax treatment afforded to certain corporate investor gains and losses.
- The special treatment given to gain realized from the disposition of qualified small business stock.

LO.1

Explain the tax consequences of incorporating a business.

18-1 Organization of and Transfers to Controlled Corporations

Property transactions normally result in recognized gain or loss when taxpayers realize gain or loss. As a result, unless special provisions in the Code apply, a transfer of property to a corporation in exchange for stock is a taxable transaction. Realized and recognized gain or loss equals the difference between the fair market value of the stock received and the tax basis of the property transferred.

18-1a Section 351 Rationale and General Rules

In contrast to the typical result of full gain or loss recognition, the Code permits nonrecognition of gain or loss in limited circumstances. For example, both § 1031 (like-kind exchanges) and § 351 (transfers of property to controlled corporations) postpone gain or loss recognition until a substantive change in the taxpayer's investment occurs (e.g., a sale of property or ownership shares to outsiders). Code § 1031 provides for gain or loss deferral when a taxpayer exchanges certain property for "like-kind property." The rules accomplish this deferral by reducing the basis of the property received by the deferred gain or increasing the basis by the deferred loss. This substituted basis results in the taxpayer recognizing the gain or loss when the taxpayer sells the new property for cash or non-like-kind property.[1]

Similarly, Example 1 below illustrates that § 351 defers shareholder gain or loss when they transfer property to a controlled corporation (defined in text Section 18-1d) in exchange for the corporation's own stock. There are at least three reasons why Congress granted this tax deferral treatment. First, contributing property to a corporation leaves an owner's economic status unchanged; the contribution changes only the *form* of the investment. That is, the shareholder owned the property outright before the transfer and now owns stock of the corporation that owns the property after the transfer. Second, when a shareholder receives only stock in the corporation, the shareholder lacks the cash to pay a tax on any realized gain. Thus, the *wherewithal to pay concept* discussed in Chapter 1 justifies this approach. As noted later, however, when the taxpayer receives property other than stock (i.e., cash or other "boot") from the corporation, the shareholder recognizes some or all of the realized gain. A third justification for the nonrecognition of gain or loss provisions under § 351 is that Congress believes tax rules should not impede a taxpayer's judgment about the best choice of entity form for conducting business.

[1]For a complete discussion of the rationale and rules pertaining to like-kind exchanges under § 1031, see Chapter 13.

Global Tax Issues — Tax Reform Adds a New Wrinkle to the Choice of Organizational Form When Operating Overseas

When the management of a corporation decides to expand its business by establishing a presence in a foreign market, the new business venture may take one of several organizational forms. As each form comes with its respective advantages and disadvantages, making the best choice can be difficult. And the choice is even more challenging now because a new set of rules applies to the taxation of international operations with the enactment of the Tax Cuts and Jobs Act (TCJA) of 2017.

One common approach is to conduct the foreign activity as a *branch* operation of the U.S. corporation. The foreign branch is not a separate legal entity, but a division of the U.S. corporation established overseas. As a result, the U.S. corporation includes in its financial results any gains and losses that the foreign branch produces.

Another common approach to foreign expansion is to organize the foreign operations as a *subsidiary* of the U.S. parent corporation. The subsidiary may be either a *domestic* subsidiary (i.e., organized in the United States) or a *foreign* subsidiary (organized under the laws of a foreign country).

One fundamental tax difference between these two approaches is that parent corporations can elect to consolidate the gains and losses of a domestic subsidiary with the operations of the U.S. parent, but not with the operations of a foreign subsidiary. Thus, the use of a domestic subsidiary to conduct foreign operations generally yields the same final result as the use of a branch. With both approaches, the financial statements of the U.S. parent reflect the results of its worldwide operations.

The TCJA of 2017 changed many of the tax rules associated with international operations and their impact on organizational forms. Now the United States uses a "territorial system" when taxing foreign earnings from a foreign subsidiary. These rules generally require U.S. corporations to pay U.S. tax only on their domestic income. Given the complexity of the organizational form decisions and the significance of the changes to international taxation rules in the TCJA of 2017, it will take time for tax professionals to determine the most tax-effective ways of structuring foreign operations of U.S. corporations. See Chapter 27 for additional discussion of the taxation of international operations.

Example 1

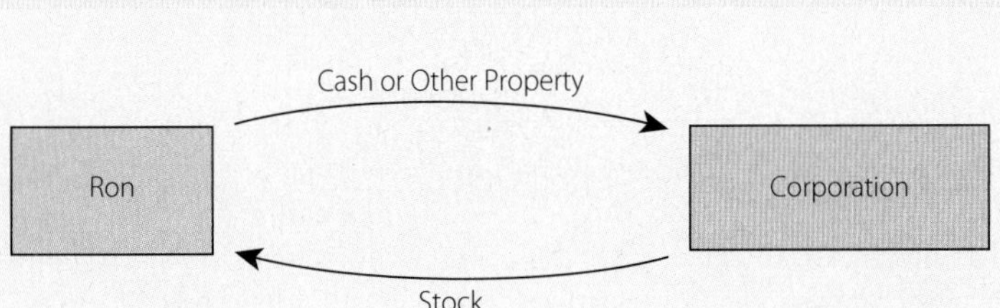

Ron is considering incorporating his sole proprietorship to obtain the limited liability of the corporate form. Ron realizes that if he incorporates, depending on state law, he will be personally liable only for the debts of the business that he personally guarantees.

If Ron incorporates his business, he will transfer the following assets to the corporation:

	Tax Basis	Fair Market Value
Cash	$ 10,000	$ 10,000
Furniture and fixtures	20,000	60,000
Land and building	240,000	300,000
	$270,000	$370,000

Ron will receive the corporation's stock worth $370,000 in exchange for the assets he transfers. Without the deferral provisions of § 351, Ron would recognize a taxable gain of $100,000 on the transfer ($370,000 value of the stock received − $270,000 basis of the assets transferred).

Under § 351, however, Ron recognizes no gain because his economic status has not really changed. Ron's ownership of stock in the corporation now represents his investment in the assets of his sole proprietorship. Ron will take a $270,000 basis in his stock and *not* a $370,000 cost basis. This adjustment to his stock basis results in a $100,000 gain *deferral* and not gain *exemption*. As a result, § 351 provides for tax neutrality on the incorporation decision because there is no immediate tax cost of incorporating his business. If Ron's basis in the assets was $450,000 instead of $270,000, then § 351 would result in Ron deferring the $80,000 loss ($370,000 – $450,000) by not recognizing the loss and taking a $450,000 basis in the stock he received.

In a manner similar to a like-kind exchange, gain and loss deferral is not absolute. If a taxpayer transfers property to a corporation and receives "boot" (cash or property other than stock), the taxpayer recognizes gain (but not loss) to the extent of the lesser of the gain realized or the value of the boot received. The tax character of the gain (e.g., ordinary, capital) depends on the type of assets transferred.[2] As discussed in more detail later, a substituted basis in the shareholder's stock accomplishes gain or loss deferral by reducing basis by the deferred gain or increasing basis by the deferred loss.[3] Example 2 illustrates this gain recognition rule.

Example 2

Amanda and Calvin form Quail Corporation. Amanda transfers equipment with an adjusted basis of $30,000, fair market value of $60,000, for 50% of the stock, worth $60,000. Calvin transfers equipment with an adjusted basis of $70,000, fair market value of $60,000, for the remaining 50% of the stock. The transfers qualify under § 351.

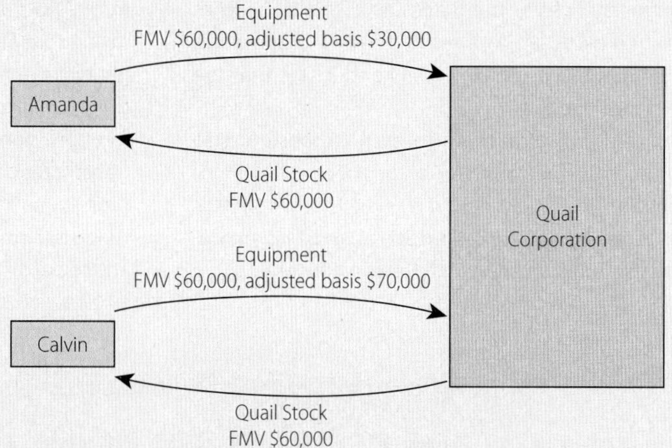

Amanda has an unrecognized gain of $30,000, and Calvin has an unrecognized loss of $10,000. Both have a substituted basis in the stock in Quail Corporation. Amanda has a basis of $30,000 in her stock, and Calvin has a basis of $70,000 in his stock. Therefore, if either Amanda or Calvin later disposes of the Quail stock in a taxable transaction (e.g., a sale), this deferred gain/loss will then be fully recognized—a $30,000 gain to Amanda and a $10,000 loss to Calvin.

Alternatively, suppose that Amanda and Calvin each received Quail stock worth $50,000 and cash of $10,000. In this case, Amanda would recognize $10,000 of the $30,000 realized gain because she received boot of $10,000. In contrast, Calvin's receipt of boot would not trigger the recognition of a loss because receiving boot can only trigger gain recognition. This rule means that a shareholder cannot recognize a loss if § 351 applies to a transaction. Additional discussion of gain/loss recognition and the basis of stock received appears later in the chapter.

Concept Summary 18.1 summarizes the major shareholder consequences of a taxable property transaction versus a tax-deferred transaction.

Code § 351 is *mandatory* if a transaction satisfies the provision's requirements. As explained in the following sections, the three requirements for nonrecognition of gain or loss under § 351 are that (1) *property is transferred* (2) in exchange for *stock* and (3) the property transferors are in *control* of the corporation after the exchange. Therefore, if recognition of gain or loss is *desired*, the taxpayer must plan to fail to meet at least one of these requirements.

[2] § 351(b) and Rev.Rul. 68–55.

[3] § 358(a). See the discussion preceding Example 22.

Concept Summary 18.1

Shareholder Consequences: Taxable Corporate Formation versus Tax-Deferred § 351 Transaction

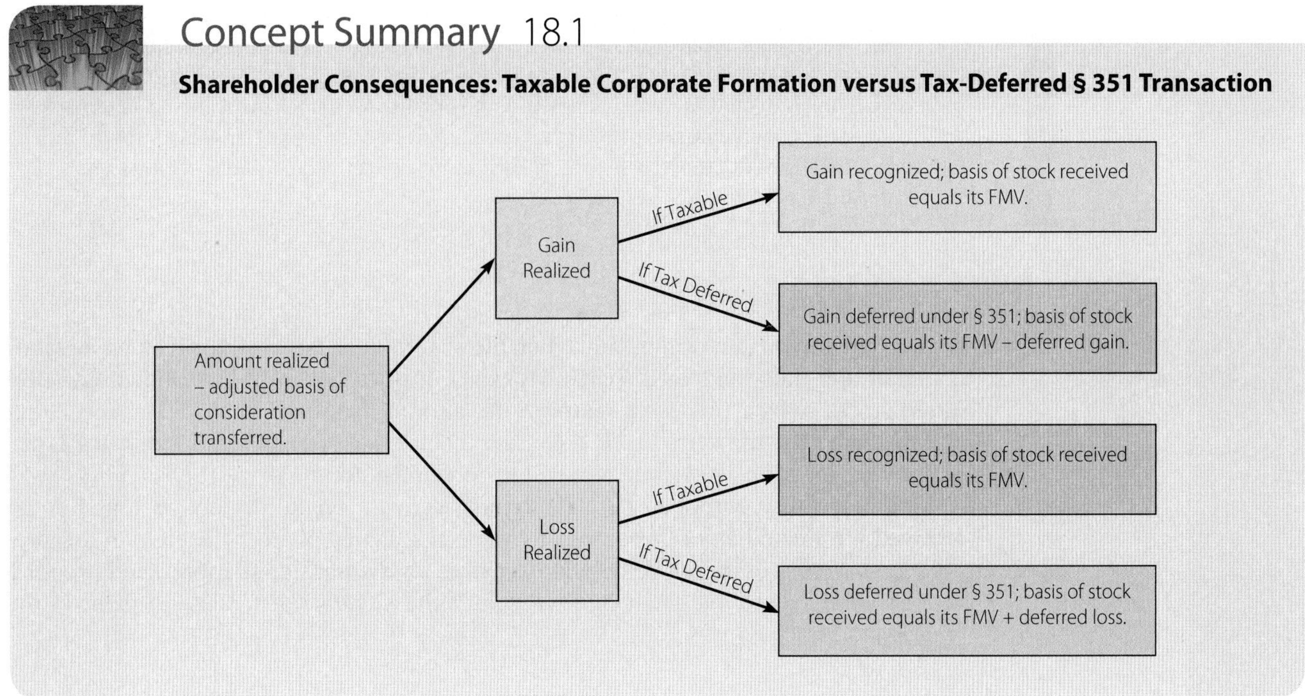

18-1b **Property Defined**

The definition of **property** for § 351 purposes is broad. For example, along with plant and equipment, intangible assets like unrealized receivables of a cash basis taxpayer and installment notes are considered property.[4] Proprietary processes and formulas as well as proprietary information in the general nature of a patentable invention similarly qualify as property under § 351.[5]

Code § 351 specifically excludes services from the definition of property. So a taxpayer must always report as income the fair market value of stock and any other consideration as compensation for services.[6] Consequently, when a taxpayer receives stock as consideration for rendering services to the corporation, the income the taxpayer recognizes equals the fair market value of the stock received. This immediate taxation results in a fair market value stock basis for the taxpayer.

Example 3

Ann and Bob form Olive Corporation with the transfer of the following consideration:

	Consideration Transferred		
	Basis to Transferor	**Fair Market Value**	**Number of Shares Issued**
From Ann:			
Personal services rendered to Olive Corporation	$ -0-	$20,000	200
From Bob:			
Installment note receivable	5,000	40,000	
Inventory	10,000	30,000	800
Proprietary process	-0-	10,000	

continued

[4]*Hempt Brothers, Inc. v. U.S.*, 74–1 USTC ¶9188, 33 AFTR 2d 74–570, 490 F.2d 1172 (CA–3), and Reg. § 1.453–9(c)(2).

[5]Rev.Rul. 64–56; Rev.Rul. 71–564.

[6]§§ 61 and 83.

The value of each share in Olive Corporation is $100.[7] Ann recognizes $20,000 of ordinary income on the transfer because services do not qualify as "property." She has a basis of $20,000 in her 200 shares of Olive (i.e., Ann is treated as having purchased some of the Olive stock by rendering services).

In contrast, Bob recognizes no gain on the receipt of stock because he transfers "property" and he has "control" of Olive after the transfer; see the discussion concerning control that follows. Bob has a substituted basis of $15,000 in the Olive stock.

18-1c **Stock Transferred**

Nonrecognition of gain occurs only when the shareholder receives stock. Stock includes common and most preferred shares. However, it does not include "nonqualified preferred stock," which possesses many of the attributes of debt. In addition, the Regulations state that the term *stock* does not include stock rights and stock warrants. Otherwise, the term *stock* generally needs no clarification.[8]

As a result, any corporate debt or **securities** (e.g., long-term debt such as bonds) received are treated as boot because they are not shares of stock. Therefore, a shareholder who receives corporate debt in exchange for the transfer of appreciated property to a controlled corporation recognizes gain if the shareholder realizes a gain on the contribution.

The Big Picture

Example 4

Return to the facts of *The Big Picture* on p. 18-1. Assume that the proposed transaction involving Emily and Ethan qualifies under § 351, but Emily decides to receive some corporate debt along with the stock.

If she receives Transformation stock worth $1,900,000 and Transformation debt of $100,000 in exchange for the property transferred, Emily realizes gain of $1,600,000 [$2,000,000 (value of consideration received) − $400,000 (basis in the transferred property)]. However, because the transaction qualifies under § 351, she recognizes only $100,000 of gain—the $100,000 of Transformation debt is treated as boot. Emily defers the remaining realized gain of $1,500,000.

18-1d **Control of the Corporation**

For the transaction to qualify as nontaxable under § 351, the property transferors must **control** the corporation immediately after the exchange. Specifically, the property transferors must own stock possessing at least 80 percent of the total combined *voting power* of all classes of stock entitled to vote *and* at least 80 percent of the total *number of shares* of all other classes of stock.[9]

Control Immediately after the Transfer

Control after the exchange can apply to a single person or to several taxpayers if they are all parties in an integrated transaction. To satisfy the timing requirement, when more than one person is involved, the exchange does not necessarily require simultaneous exchanges by those persons. However, the rights of those transferring property to the corporation must be previously set out and determined. Also, the shareholders should execute the agreement to transfer property "with an expedition consistent with orderly procedure," and the transfers should occur close together in time.[10]

[7] The value of closely held stock normally is presumed to equal the value of the property transferred.

[8] § 351(g). Examples of nonqualified preferred stock include preferred stock that is redeemable within 20 years of issuance or has a dividend rate that depends on factors other than corporate performance. See also Reg. § 1.351–1(a)(1)(ii).

[9] § 368(c). Nonqualified preferred stock is treated as stock, not boot, for purposes of this control test.

[10] Reg. § 1.351–1(a)(1).

Jack exchanges property with a basis of $60,000 and fair market value of $100,000 for 70% of the stock of Gray Corporation. The other 30% of the stock is owned by Jane, who acquired it several years ago. The fair market value of Jack's stock is $100,000.

Jack recognizes a taxable gain of $40,000 on the transfer because he does not control the corporation after his transfer, and his transaction cannot be integrated with Jane's for purposes of the control requirement.

The Big Picture

Return to the facts of *The Big Picture* on p. 18-1. Assume that the proposed transaction involving Emily and Ethan occurs as described. However, in addition, Marco decides to contribute property to the new corporation in exchange for an equity interest.

As a result, Emily exchanges her property for 200 shares of Transformation, Inc. stock on January 7, 2023, Marco exchanges his property for 10 shares of Transformation stock on January 14, 2023, and Ethan exchanges his property for 4,800 shares in Transformation on March 5, 2023.

Because the three exchanges are part of a prearranged plan and the control test is met, the nonrecognition provisions of § 351 apply to all of the exchanges.

Once control has been achieved, it is not necessarily lost if, shortly after the transaction, stock received by shareholders is sold or given to persons who are not parties to the exchange.[11]

Naomi and Eric form Eagle Corporation. They transfer appreciated property to the corporation with each receiving 50 shares of Eagle stock. Shortly after the formation, Naomi gives 25 shares to her son.

Because Naomi was not committed to making the gift, she met the control test "immediately after the exchange." Therefore, Naomi and Eric meet the requirements of § 351, and neither recognizes gain on the exchange.

The following two examples show that a different result occurs if a plan for the ultimate disposition of the stock existed *before* the exchange. In other words, momentary control on the part of the transferor may not suffice if loss of control is required by a prearranged agreement.[12]

The Impact of a Preconceived Plan on the Control Requirement

Example 8

Assume the same facts as in Example 7, except that Naomi immediately gives 25 shares to a business associate pursuant to a plan to satisfy an outstanding obligation.

In this case, Naomi fails the "immediately" condition and so the control test calculation excludes her shares. Accordingly, the formation of Eagle is taxable to Naomi and Eric because they jointly own only 75% of the stock.

For many years, Paula operated a business as a sole proprietor employing Brooke as manager. To dissuade Brooke from quitting and going out on her own, Paula promised her a 30% interest in the business. To fulfill this promise, Paula transfers the business to newly formed Green Corporation in return for all of its stock. Immediately thereafter, Paula transfers 30% of the stock to Brooke.

Code § 351 probably does not apply to Paula's transfer to Green Corporation because it appears that Paula was under an obligation to relinquish control. If this preexisting obligation exists, § 351 will not be available to Paula because, as the sole property transferor, she does not have 80% control of Green Corporation.

However, if there is no obligation and the loss of control was voluntary on Paula's part, momentary control would suffice.[13]

[11] *Wilgard Realty Co. v. Comm.*, 42–1 USTC ¶9452, 29 AFTR 325, 127 F.2d 514 (CA–2).

[12] Rev.Rul. 54–96.

[13] Compare *Fahs v. Florida Machine and Foundry Co.*, 48–2 USTC ¶9329, 36 AFTR 1161, 168 F.2d 957 (CA–5), with *John C. O'Connor*, 16 TCM 213, T.C.Memo. 1957–50, *aff'd* in 58-2 USTC ¶9913, 2 AFTR 2d 6011, 260 F.2d 358 (CA–6).

Stock need not be issued to the property transferors in the same proportion as the relative value of the property transferred by each. However, when stock received is not proportionate to the value of the property transferred, the taxpayers must properly recognize the economic effects of the transactions. For example, in such situations, one transferor may actually be making a gift to another transferor.

Noah and Sydney, father and daughter, form Oak Corporation. Noah transfers property worth $50,000 in exchange for 100 shares of stock, and Sydney transfers property worth $50,000 for 400 shares of stock.

The transfers qualify under § 351 because Noah and Sydney have control of the Oak stock immediately after the transfers of property. However, Noah and Sydney must recognize and properly characterize Noah's implicit gift of 150 shares to Sydney. As such, the value of the gift might be subject to the gift tax (see Chapter 29).

Transfers for Property and Services

Examples 5, 8, and 9 show that taxpayers can lose § 351 treatment if persons who do not transfer property own "too much" stock. Example 11 shows how a service contributor also can cause a property contributor to fail the control test and thus have to recognize gain.

Sarah transfers property with a basis of $400,000 and fair market value of $1,000,000 to Garden, Inc., and receives 50% of its stock. Tiffany receives the other 50% of the stock for services rendered (worth $1,000,000).

Tiffany has ordinary income of $1,000,000 because she contributes only services. She must recognize compensation income for services rendered.

Sarah contributes property, but she receives only 50% of Garden's stock. Because Sarah does not own at least 80% of Garden's stock, she has a taxable gain of $600,000 [$1,000,000 (fair market value of the stock in Garden) − $400,000 (basis in the transferred property)].

As noted earlier, a person contributing both services and property in exchange for corporate stock must include in taxable income the value of the stock received for the services but not the value of the stock received for the property, assuming the property transferors control the corporation. In addition, the law allows treating such a person as a "property transferor." In these situations, all stock received by the person transferring property and services counts toward whether the transferors control the corporation.[14]

Assume the same facts as in Example 11, except that Tiffany transfers property worth $800,000 (basis of $260,000) in addition to services rendered to Garden, Inc. (valued at $200,000).

Now Tiffany becomes a part of the control group. Sarah and Tiffany, as property transferors, together own 100% of the corporation's stock. Consequently, § 351 applies to the exchanges. Note that the control test calculation includes all of Tiffany's shares and not just the shares that relate to her property contribution.

As a result, Sarah recognizes no gain. Tiffany does not recognize gain on the transfer of the property, but she recognizes ordinary income to the extent of the value of the shares issued for services rendered. Thus, Tiffany recognizes $200,000 of ordinary income currently.

Transfers for Services and Nominal Property

Note that to be part of the group meeting the 80 percent control test, the person contributing services must transfer property having more than a "relatively small value" compared with the services performed. When the primary purpose of the transfer is to qualify the transaction under § 351, the Regulations provide that the control test

[14]Reg. § 1.351–1(a)(2), Ex. 3.

calculation will ignore stock issued for property whose value is relatively small compared with the value of services rendered.[15]

The regulations do not define a "relatively small" property contribution. The IRS has stated that the control group includes a person who contributes both property and services only if the value of the property equals or exceeds 10 percent of the value of the services provided. If the value of the property transferred is less than this amount, the IRS is likely to treat the property contributed as having a relatively small value and disregard it in applying the control test.[16] A similar 10 percent rule applies when an existing shareholder contributes property so that another person meets the control test. That is, the new stock issued for the newly-contributed property must equal or exceed 10 percent of the value of the old stock already owned. Example 15 illustrates this rule.

Determining Control Group Membership When Services Are Rendered

Example 13

Ava and Rick form Grouse Corporation. Ava transfers land worth $100,000 with a basis of $20,000. Rick transfers equipment worth $50,000 with an adjusted basis of $10,000 and provides services worth $50,000. Ava and Rick each receive 50% of the Grouse stock.

Because the value of the property Rick transfers is not small relative to the value of the services he renders, his stock in Grouse Corporation is counted in determining control under § 351; thus, Ava and Rick jointly own 100% of the stock in Grouse. In addition, all of Rick's stock, not just the shares received for the equipment, counts in determining control.

As a result, Ava does not recognize gain on the transfer of the land. Rick similarly does not recognize the gain on his equipment; however, he must recognize income of $50,000 on the transfer of services. Even though the transfer of the equipment qualifies Rick as a property contributor under § 351, his transfer of services for stock is still taxable compensation income.

Example 14

Assume the same facts as in Example 13, except that the value of Rick's property is $2,000 and the value of his services is $98,000.

In this situation, the value of the property is small relative to the value of the services (and well below the 10% IRS threshold); therefore, Rick does not qualify as a property transferor. Consequently, the transaction is fully taxable to both Ava and Rick. In this situation, Ava, the sole property transferor, lacks at least 80% control of Grouse Corporation following the transfer.

As a result, she will fully recognize her realized gain. Further, because the control test ignores Rick's shares, the § 351 deferral is not available to him. He will recognize income of $98,000 relating to the services provided along with any realized gain or loss on the transfer of the additional $2,000 of property.

Transfers to Existing Corporations

Once a corporation is operational, § 351 also applies to any later transfers of property for stock by either new or existing shareholders. That is, § 351 does not apply solely at the time of corporate formation.

Example 15

Tyrone and Andrew formed Blue Corporation three years ago. Both Tyrone and Andrew transferred appreciated property to Blue in exchange for 50 shares each in the corporation. The original transfers qualified under § 351, and neither Tyrone nor Andrew recognizes gain or loss on the exchange. In the current year, Tyrone transfers property (worth $90,000, adjusted basis of $5,000) for 50 additional Blue shares.

Tyrone has a taxable gain of $85,000 on the transfer. The exchange does not qualify under § 351 because Tyrone does not have 80% control of Blue Corporation immediately after the transfer—he owns 100 shares of the 150 shares outstanding, or a 66⅔% interest.

But what if Tyrone asked Andrew also to contribute property? In this case, Tyrone and Andrew would own 100% of the stock and both would qualify again for tax deferral. This "accommodation transfer" result holds only if Andrew's new stock value exceeds 10% of the value of his old stock.

[15] Reg. § 1.351–1(a)(1)(ii).

[16] Rev.Proc. 77–37.

LO.2

Identify the basis issues relevant to the shareholder and the corporation.

18-1e Basis Determination and Related Issues

Recall that § 351(a) postpones gain or loss until the transferor-shareholder disposes of the stock in a taxable transaction. The postponement of shareholder gain or loss has a corollary effect on the basis of the stock received by the shareholder and the basis of the property received by the corporation. This basis adjustment procedure ensures that the corporation recognizes the gain or loss postponed under § 351 when it sells the contributed asset in a taxable transaction.

Basis of Stock to Shareholder

A shareholder that transfers property to a corporation in a § 351 transaction takes a *substituted basis* in the corporate stock instead of a fair market value basis. Specifically, the stock basis equals the taxpayer's basis in the property transferred plus any gain recognized on the exchange of property minus the fair value of boot received (see Exhibit 18.1). Recall that the value of all boot in any form (cash, other property, or shareholder debt that the corporation assumes) reduces the stock basis because the boot is an economic benefit to the shareholder. In addition, because boot triggers gain recognition, a shareholder takes a fair market value basis in boot received.[17]

Exhibit 18.1 Shareholder's Basis of Stock Received in Exchange for Property

Adjusted basis of property transferred	$xx,xxx
Plus: Gain recognized	xxx
Minus: Boot received (including any liabilities transferred)	(xxx)
Minus: Adjustment for loss property (if elected)	(xxx)
Equals: Basis of stock received	$xx,xxx

Basis of Property to Corporation

Just as a shareholder's stock embeds deferred gain or loss into the stock basis, a similar *carryover* basis rule exists for computing the basis of the corporation's property. This rule provides that the property's basis to the corporation equals the basis in the hands of the transferor plus any gain recognized on the transfer by the transferor-shareholder.[18]

Exhibit 18.2 summarizes the basis calculation for property received by a corporation.

Exhibit 18.2 Corporation's Basis in Property Received

Adjusted basis of property transferred	$xx,xxx
Plus: Gain recognized by transferor-shareholder	xxx
Minus: Adjustment for loss property (if required)	(xxx)
Equals: Basis of property to corporation	$xx,xxx

Examples 16 and 17 illustrate these basis rules.

Calculating Basis: Shareholder Stock and Corporate Property

Example 16

Kesha and Ned form Brown Corporation. Kesha transfers land (basis of $30,000 and fair market value of $70,000); Ned invests cash ($60,000). They each receive 50 shares in Brown Corporation worth $60,000, but Kesha also receives $10,000 in cash from Brown.

The transfers of property, the realized and recognized gain on the transfers, and the basis of the stock in Brown Corporation to Kesha and Ned are as follows:

continued

[17] § 358(a). Recall from earlier discussions that the basis of stock received for services rendered equals its fair market value.

[18] § 362(a).

	A	B	C	D	E	F
	Basis of Property Transferred	**FMV of Stock Received**	**FMV of Boot Received**	**Realized Gain (B + C − A)**	**Recognized Gain (Lesser of C or D)**	**Basis of Stock in Brown (A + E − C)**
From Kesha:						
Land	$30,000	$60,000	$10,000	$40,000	$10,000	$30,000
From Ned:						
Cash	60,000	60,000	-0-	-0-	-0-	60,000

Brown Corporation has a basis of $40,000 in the land (Kesha's basis of $30,000 plus her recognized gain of $10,000).

Example 17

Assume the same facts as in Example 16, except that Kesha's basis in the land is $68,000 (instead of $30,000). Because recognized gain cannot exceed realized gain, the transfer generates only $2,000 of gain to Kesha. The realized and recognized gain and the basis of the stock in Brown Corporation to Kesha are as follows:

	A	B	C	D	E	F
	Basis of Property Transferred	**FMV of Stock Received**	**FMV of Boot Received**	**Realized Gain (B + C − A)**	**Recognized Gain (Lesser of C or D)**	**Basis of Stock in Brown (A + E − C)**
Land	$68,000	$60,000	$10,000	$2,000	$2,000	$60,000

Brown's basis in the land is $70,000 ($68,000 basis to Kesha + $2,000 gain recognized by Kesha).

Concept Summary 18.2 shows the shareholder and corporate consequences of a transfer of property to a corporation for stock, with and without the application of § 351. The facts applicable to shareholder Kesha's transfer in Example 16 are used to illustrate the differences between tax-deferred and taxable transactions.

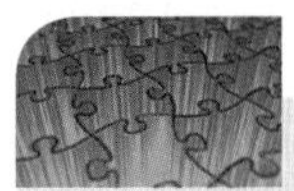

Concept Summary 18.2

Tax Consequences to the Shareholders and Corporation: With and Without the Application of § 351 (Based on the Facts of Example 16)

	With § 351			Without § 351		
Shareholder	**Gain/Loss Recognized**	**Stock Basis**	**Other Property Basis**	**Gain/Loss Recognized**	**Stock Basis**	**Other Property Basis**
Kesha	Realized gain recognized to extent of boot received; loss not recognized.	Substituted (see Exhibit 18.1).	FMV	All realized gain or loss recognized.	FMV	FMV
	$10,000	$30,000	$10,000	$40,000	$60,000	$10,000

	With § 351		Without § 351	
Corporation	**Gain/Loss Recognized**	**Property Basis**	**Gain/Loss Recognized**	**Property Basis**
Brown	No gain or loss recognized on the transfer of corporate stock for property.	Carryover (see Exhibit 18.2).	No gain or loss recognized on the transfer of corporate stock for property.	FMV
	$0	$40,000	$0	$70,000

Note that the benefit to Kesha of deferring $30,000 of gain under § 351 comes with a cost: her stock basis is $30,000 (rather than $60,000), and the corporation's basis in the property received is $40,000 (rather than $70,000). In this sense, the deferred gain reduces the basis of the stock for Kesha ($30,000 stock basis = $60,000 FMV − $30,000 deferred gain) and the basis of the land for Brown Corporation ($40,000 land basis = $70,000 FMV − $30,000 deferred gain).

Basis Adjustment for Loss Property

Concept Summary 18.2 shows that when Kesha contributes property in a § 351 transaction, Kesha and the corporation reduce the basis of Kesha's stock and the basis of the contributed assets. This *duplicates* the gain potential for the two entities. Despite this, the government does not allow taxpayers to duplicate losses in a similar manner. Accordingly, when a taxpayer contributes **built-in loss property** to a corporation, the aggregate basis of the assets transferred by a shareholder can exceed their fair market value. When this built-in loss situation exists, an anti-loss duplication rule requires the basis in the loss properties to be stepped down by allocating the built-in loss proportionately among the assets that included a built-in loss.[19]

Example 18

In a transaction qualifying under § 351, Charles transfers the following assets to Gold Corporation in exchange for all of its stock:

	Tax Basis	Fair Market Value	Built-In Gain/(Loss)
Equipment	$100,000	$ 90,000	($10,000)
Land	200,000	230,000	30,000
Building	150,000	100,000	(50,000)
	$450,000	$420,000	($30,000)

Charles's stock basis is $450,000 [$450,000 (basis of the property transferred) + $0 (gain recognized) − $0 (boot received)]. However, Gold Corporation must reduce its basis in the loss assets transferred by the amount of the net built-in loss ($30,000) in proportion to each asset's share of the loss.

	Unadjusted Tax Basis	Adjustment	Adjusted Tax Basis
Equipment	$100,000	($ 5,000)*	$ 95,000
Land	200,000		200,000
Building	150,000	(25,000)**	125,000
	$450,000	($30,000)	$420,000

* $\frac{\$10,000 \text{ (loss attributable to equipment)}}{\$60,000 \text{ (\textit{total} built-in loss)}} \times \$30,000 \text{ (\textit{net} built-in loss)}$

= $5,000 (adjustment to basis in equipment)

** $\frac{\$50,000 \text{ (loss attributable to building)}}{\$60,000 \text{ (\textit{total} built-in loss)}} \times \$30,000 \text{ (\textit{net} built-in loss)}$

= $25,000 (adjustment to basis in building)

Note the end result for Example 18:

- Charles still has a built-in loss in his stock basis. As a result, if he sells the Gold Corporation stock, he will recognize a loss of $30,000 [$420,000 (presumed selling price of the stock) − $450,000 (basis in the stock)].
- Gold Corporation can no longer recognize a loss on the sale of *all* of its assets [$420,000 (selling price based on value of assets) − $420,000 (adjusted basis in assets) = $0 (gain or loss)].

If a corporation is subject to the built-in loss adjustment, an alternative approach is available. If *both* the shareholder and the corporation elect, the shareholder reduces the basis in the corporate stock rather than the corporation's property. Given capital gain rates that generally are lower than the corporate tax rate, it is frequently desirable for the corporation and individual shareholders to elect this treatment.

Assume the same facts as in the previous example. If Charles and Gold elect, Charles can reduce his stock basis to $420,000 ($450,000 − $30,000). As a result, Gold's aggregate basis in the assets is $450,000.

continued

[19] § 362(e)(2). This adjustment is determined separately for each property transferor. This adjustment also is required in the case of a contribution to capital by a shareholder.

If Charles has no intention of selling his stock, this election could be desirable since it benefits Gold by giving the corporation a higher depreciable basis in the equipment and building. In addition, reducing a capital loss or increasing a capital gain can impose lower tax costs on the shareholder than adjusting a corporation's asset bases.

Note the end result for Example 19:

- Charles has no built-in loss. As a result, if he sells the Gold Corporation stock, he will recognize no gain or loss [$420,000 (presumed value of the stock) − $420,000 (basis in the stock)].
- Gold Corporation has a built-in loss. As a result, if it sells *all* of its assets [$420,000 (presumed value of assets) − $450,000 (basis in assets)], Gold Corporation recognizes a loss of $30,000.

Consequently, as shown in the two previous examples, the built-in loss adjustment places the loss with *either* the shareholder or the corporation but not both.

Corporate Treatment When Issuing Stock for Services

A corporation's transfer of its stock for property is not a taxable exchange. A transfer of shares for services also is not a taxable transaction to a corporation.[20] But another issue arises: can a corporation deduct as a business expense the fair market value of the stock it issues in consideration of services? Yes, unless the services are a capital expenditure.[21]

The Big Picture

Example 20

Return to the facts of *The Big Picture* on p. 18-1. Emily transfers her $2,000,000 of property to Transformation, Inc., and receives 200 shares of stock, and Ethan transfers $48,000,000 of cash for 4,800 shares of stock. In the same transaction, Marco transfers property worth $800,000 (basis of $260,000) and agrees to serve as manager of the corporation for one year (services worth $200,000) for 100 shares of the stock.

Emily's, Ethan's, and Marco's transfers qualify under § 351. None of them is taxed on their property transfers. However, Marco has ordinary income of $200,000, the value of the stock received for the services he will render to Transformation, Inc.

Transformation has a basis of $260,000 in the property it acquired from Marco, and it may claim a compensation expense deduction under § 162 for $200,000. Marco's stock basis is $460,000 [$260,000 (basis of property transferred) + $200,000 (income recognized for services rendered)].

The Big Picture

Example 21

Assume the same facts as in the prior example, except that Marco provides legal services (instead of management services) in organizing the corporation. The value of Marco's legal services is $200,000.

Marco has no gain on the transfer of the property but has income of $200,000 for the value of the stock received for the services rendered. Transformation, Inc., has a basis of $260,000 in the property it acquired from Marco and must capitalize the $200,000 as an organizational expenditure. Marco's stock basis is $460,000 [$260,000 (basis of property transferred) + $200,000 (income recognized for services rendered)].

Holding Period for Shareholder and Transferee Corporation

In a § 351 transfer, the shareholder's holding period for stock received in exchange for a capital asset or § 1231 property includes the holding period of the property transferred to the corporation. That is, the holding period of the property is "tacked on" to the holding period of the stock. The holding period for stock received for any other property (e.g., cash or inventory) begins on the day after the exchange.

[20] Reg. § 1.1032–1(a).

[21] Rev.Rul. 62–217, modified by Rev.Rul. 74–503.

The corporation's holding period for property acquired in a § 351 transfer is the holding period of the transferor-shareholder regardless of the character of the property in the transferor's hands. For instance, whether the property transferred is an ordinary asset (e.g., inventory), a § 1231 asset, or a capital asset, the corporation's holding period is the same as the transferor's.[22]

Recapture Considerations

Sales of depreciable assets with a value that exceeds their basis result in ordinary gain up to the accumulated depreciation deducted. The rest of the gain usually is § 1231 gain. Because § 351 defers the gain when a shareholder contributes depreciable property to a corporation, the depreciation recapture potential also transfers to the corporation.[23] That is, any recapture potential associated with the property carries over to the corporation. This rule prevents taxpayers from converting ordinary income into § 1231 gain by transferring the property to a controlled corporation.

Example 22

Paul transfers equipment (adjusted basis of $30,000, original cost of $120,000, and fair market value of $100,000) to a controlled corporation in return for stock. If Paul had sold the equipment, it would have yielded a gain of $70,000, all of which would have been treated as ordinary income under the § 1245 depreciation recapture rules.

Because the transfer qualifies under § 351, Paul has no recognized gain and no depreciation to recapture. However, if the corporation later disposes of the equipment in a taxable transaction, it must take into account the § 1245 recapture potential originating with Paul.

For example, if the corporation were to sell the asset shortly after incorporation for $100,000, all of the $70,000 gain recognized would be given ordinary treatment because of the depreciation recapture rules.

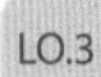

LO.3

Determine the consequences when corporations assume shareholder liabilities.

18-1f Assumption of Liabilities—§ 357

It is not uncommon to form a corporation by transferring assets *and* liabilities of an unincorporated business. Absent a special rule, the party that enjoys the debt relief treats it as cash received equal to the debt relief. Without a provision to the contrary, the transfer of mortgaged property to a controlled corporation could trigger gain to the property transferor if the corporation took over the mortgage. Paying tax on this "gain" could discourage corporate formations. For this reason, § 357(a) provides that when a corporation assumes a liability in a § 351 transaction, the liability is not boot received for gain recognition purposes. (However, liabilities assumed by the corporation are treated as boot in determining the basis of the stock received by the shareholder.) As a result, the liabilities the corporation assumes reduce the basis of the shareholder's stock.

The Big Picture

Example 23

Return to the facts of *The Big Picture* on p. 18-1. Assume that you learn that Marco is not interested in becoming a stockholder in Transformation, Inc., and that Emily and Ethan will transfer their property for 100% of the stock. In addition, you learn that Emily's building is subject to a liability of $70,000 that Transformation assumes. Consequently, Emily receives her Transformation stock, is relieved of the $70,000 liability, and contributes property with an adjusted basis of $400,000 and fair market value of $2,000,000.

The exchange is tax-free to Emily under § 351 because § 357(a) precludes treating the debt relief as boot for determining recognized gain. However, the basis to Emily of the Transformation stock is $330,000 [$400,000 (basis of property transferred) − $70,000 (amount of the liability Transformation assumes)]. This basis reduction reflects the economic benefit that Emily enjoys by transferring her mortgage to the corporation.

---

[22] §§ 1223(1) and (2).

[23] §§ 1245(b)(3), 1250(d)(3), and § 291(a)(1).

While treating contributed debt as something other than boot seems like it should be an easy rule to apply, it creates two potential problems. The first is that shareholders might contribute debt that they only recently incurred and "pocket the cash." The shareholder might have done this innocently or might have done it deliberately to get some cash without recognizing gain. The second problem arises from the stock basis calculation discussed previously: reducing the stock basis by the debt relief can result in a stock basis that is less than zero, which makes little sense. The paragraphs below discuss each of these problems and the tax law's solutions in detail.

Exception (1): Tax Avoidance or No Bona Fide Business Purpose

Code § 357(b) provides that if the principal purpose of the assumption of the liabilities is to avoid tax *or* if there is no bona fide business purpose behind the exchange, the liabilities are treated as boot for determining recognized gain. Satisfying the bona fide business purpose under § 357(b) is not difficult if the shareholder incurs the liabilities in the normal course of conducting a trade or business. But what if the shareholder borrows money shortly before transferring the property and uses the proceeds for personal purposes?[24] This type of situation is economically equivalent to the corporation transferring both stock and cash to the shareholder, resulting in boot treatment for the liabilities assumed.

Example 24

Dan transfers real estate with a basis of $140,000 and fair market value of $190,000 to a controlled corporation in return for stock in the corporation. However, shortly before the transfer, Dan mortgages the real estate and uses the $20,000 of proceeds to meet personal obligations.

In this case, the assumption of the mortgage lacks a bona fide business purpose. Consequently, § 357(b) treats the debt relief as boot received, and Dan has a taxable gain of $20,000 on the transfer.[25]

Amount realized:	
Stock	$ 170,000
Release of liability—treated as boot	20,000
Total amount realized	$ 190,000
Less: Basis of real estate	(140,000)
Realized gain	$ 50,000
Recognized gain	$ 20,000

The effect of the application of § 357(b) is to taint *all* liabilities transferred even if *some* have a bona fide business purpose.

Tim, an accrual basis taxpayer, incorporates his sole proprietorship. Among the liabilities transferred to the new corporation are trade accounts payable of $100,000 and a credit card bill of $5,000. Tim had used the credit card to purchase an anniversary gift for his spouse.

Under these circumstances, § 357(b) treats *all* of the $105,000 of liabilities as boot and triggers gain recognition up to the amount of realized gain.

Exception (2): Liabilities in Excess of Basis

The second exception in § 357(c) provides that if the corporation assumes shareholder liabilities that exceed the shareholder's adjusted basis of contributed property, the difference is taxable gain. Without this provision, when there are **liabilities in excess of basis** in a property exchange, a taxpayer would have a negative basis in the stock received in the controlled corporation.[26] Code § 357(c) precludes the negative basis possibility by treating the excess over basis as gain to the transferor.

[24] See, for example, *Campbell, Jr. v. Wheeler*, 65–1 USTC ¶9294, 15 AFTR 2d 578, 342 F.2d 837 (CA–5).

[25] § 351(b).

[26] *Jack L. Easson*, 33 T.C. 963 (1960), *rev'd* in 61–2 USTC ¶9654, 8 AFTR 2d 5448, 294 F.2d 653 (CA–9).

Andre transfers land and equipment with adjusted bases of $350,000 and $50,000, respectively, to a newly formed corporation in exchange for 100% of the stock. The corporation assumes a $500,000 liability on the transferred land.

Without § 357(c), Andre's basis in the stock of the new corporation would be negative $100,000 [$400,000 (bases of properties transferred) + $0 (gain recognized) − $0 (boot received) − $500,000 (liability assumed)]. Code § 357(c), however, requires Andre to recognize gain of $100,000 ($500,000 liability assumed − $400,000 total bases of assets transferred).

As a result, the stock has a zero basis in Andre's hands, determined as follows:

Bases in the properties transferred ($350,000 + $50,000)	$ 400,000
Plus: Gain recognized	100,000
Less: Boot received	–0–
Less: Liability assumed	(500,000)
Basis in the stock received	$ –0–

Consequently, Andre recognizes $100,000 of gain and avoids a negative stock basis.

The definition of liabilities under § 357(c) *excludes* obligations that would have been deductible to the transferor had those obligations been paid before the transfer. Therefore, accounts payable of a cash basis taxpayer are ignored when applying § 357(c) and in computing the shareholder's stock basis.

Tina, a cash basis taxpayer, incorporates her sole proprietorship. In return for all of the stock of the new corporation, she transfers the following items:

	Adjusted Basis	Fair Market Value
Cash	$10,000	$10,000
Unrealized accounts receivable (amounts due to Tina but not yet received by her)	–0–	40,000
Trade accounts payable	–0–	30,000
Note payable	5,000	5,000

Because uncollected accounts receivable and unpaid trade accounts payable have a zero basis for cash basis taxpayers, they recognize no income until they collect the receivables and no deduction until they pay the accounts payable. In contrast, the note payable has a basis because it was issued for cash or other consideration.

In this situation, Tina disregards the accounts payable for determining her recognized gain and for determining her stock basis. Thus, for purposes of § 357(c), because the balance of the note payable does not exceed the basis of the assets transferred, Tina does not face the situation of liabilities in excess of basis (i.e., the note payable of $5,000 does not exceed the aggregate basis in the cash and accounts receivable of $10,000).

Finally, it is possible that §§ 357(b) and (c) could both apply to the same transfer. In this case, § 357(b) predominates.[27] This could be significant because § 357(b) does not automatically create gain on the transfer, as does § 357(c), but merely converts the liability to boot. On the other hand, the realized gain limitation applies to § 357(b) transactions. So, depending on the facts, either provision would result in more or less gain than the other, as Example 28 illustrates.

Seo-Yeon forms Robin Corporation by transferring land with a basis of $100,000 and a fair market value of $1,000,000. The land is subject to a mortgage of $300,000. One month before incorporating Robin, Seo-Yeon borrows $200,000 for personal purposes and gives the lender a second mortgage on the land. Therefore, on the incorporation, Robin issues stock worth $500,000 to Seo-Yeon and assumes the two mortgages on the land.

continued

[27] § 357(c)(2)(A).

Code § 357(c) seems to apply to the transfer, given that the mortgages on the property exceed the basis of the property. As a result, Seo-Yeon would have a gain of $400,000 under § 357(c).

Code § 357(b), however, also applies to the transfer because Seo-Yeon borrowed $200,000 just prior to the transfer and used the loan proceeds for personal purposes. Thus, under § 357(b), Seo-Yeon has boot of $500,000 in the amount of the liabilities, which triggers $500,000 of recognized gain. Note that *all* of the liabilities are treated as boot, not just the tainted $200,000 liability.

	§ 357(b) Result	**§ 357(c) Result**
Amount realized:		
Robin Corporation stock	$ 500,000	$ 500,000
Release of mortgage on land	300,000	300,000
Release of second mortgage—personal purposes	200,000	200,000
Total amount realized	$1,000,000	$1,000,000
Basis of land	(100,000)	(100,000)
Realized gain	$ 900,000	$ 900,000
Gain recognized under § 357(b) ($300,000 + $200,000)	$ 500,000	
Gain recognized under § 357(c) [($300,000 + $200,000) − $100,000]		$ 400,000

Unfortunately for Seo-Yeon, § 357(b) predominates over § 357(c), requiring the recognition of $500,000 of gain instead of only $400,000 of gain.

Concept Summary 18.3 summarizes the tax rules that apply when liabilities are transferred in property transactions, including the special rules that apply in § 351 transactions.

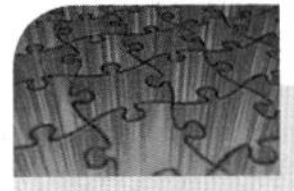

Concept Summary 18.3

Tax Consequences of Liability Assumption

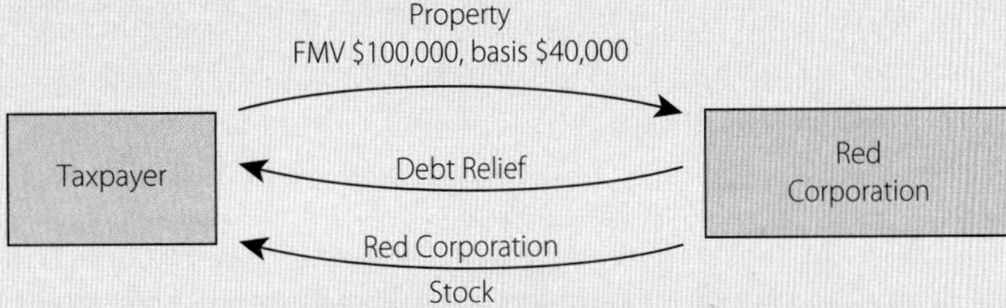

General rule: (§ 1001)	If Red Corporation takes property subject to Taxpayer's liability or assumes Taxpayer's liability, Taxpayer is treated as having received cash due to the debt relief. Therefore, if the liability is $20,000, Taxpayer is treated as receiving Red stock of $80,000 and cash of $20,000 in a fully taxable transaction. Gain realized and recognized is $60,000.
Special rule in a § 351 transaction: [§ 357(a)]	Assume the same facts as above, except that the transfer is a § 351 transaction. Taxpayer is not treated as receiving cash of $20,000 for gain recognition purposes (the debt relief is *not* treated as boot). Therefore, gain recognition is avoided. The debt relief will, however, reduce the Taxpayer's basis in Red Corporation stock.
Exception to § 351 transaction rule—Tax avoidance or no bona fide business purpose: [§ 357(b)]	Assume the same facts as above, except that the transfer is a § 351 transaction and the liability does not have a business purpose. Taxpayer is treated as receiving cash of $20,000 for gain recognition purposes (the debt relief *is* treated as boot). Therefore, $20,000 of the realized gain is recognized.
Exception to § 351 transaction rule—Liabilities in excess of basis: [§ 357(c)]	Assume the same facts as above, except that the transfer is a § 351 transaction, the liability is $45,000, the Red stock is worth $55,000, and § 357(b) does not apply. Taxpayer recognizes $5,000 of gain (excess of $45,000 liability over $40,000 property basis).

LO.4

Explain the tax aspects of the capital structure of a corporation.

18-2 Capital Structure of a Corporation

Shareholders can form or expand a corporation using equity financing, debt financing, or a combination of the two. Evaluating the relative tax and nontax advantages and disadvantages of these two basic elements in the capital structure of a corporation can help the corporation decide how to finance its activities.

18-2a Capital Contributions

Corporations recognize no gain or loss when they issue shares of stock (including treasury stock) for money or property.[28] This is also true for voluntary or required shareholder contributions of money or property when the corporation issues no shares in return. The contributions represent an additional price paid for the shares held by the shareholders and are treated as additions to the capital of the corporation.[29]

In addition, corporations sometimes receive assets from *nonshareholders*. If a civic or government entity contributes property to a corporation to induce the corporation to locate in a particular community, the contributions are not tax-free capital contributions. Instead, the corporation includes these contributions in the corporation's gross income and takes a fair market value basis in the assets.[30] However, a governmental tax abatement granted to a corporation for locating in the jurisdiction is not taxable. The abatement just reduces future payments and related deductions for state and local taxes and is therefore ignored when granted.

A city donates land worth $400,000 to Teal Corporation as an inducement for Teal to locate in the city. The city also agreed to reduce the standard real estate tax rate for Teal by 50% on newly constructed property in the city. Teal expects this tax abatement to save it $350,000 in real estate taxes.

The receipt of the land produces $400,000 of gross income to Teal, and the land's basis to the corporation is $400,000. However, the real estate tax abatement is not taxable to Teal; instead, Teal's real estate tax deductions will be $350,000 lower.

A corporation recognizes income if a nonshareholder (a customer or potential customer) contributes assets to a corporation, even if the corporation labels these as contributions to aid construction or other capital expenditures.[31] Further, a corporation must recognize income if a nonshareholder transfers property to a corporation in exchange for goods or services.

A cable television company charges its customers an initial fee to hook up to a new cable system installed in the area. These payments help to finance the total cost of constructing the cable company's infrastructure. Customers also will make monthly payments for the cable service.

The initial payments are used for capital expenditures, but they represent payments for services to be rendered by the cable company. As such, they are taxable income to the cable company and are not contributions to capital.

The basis of property a shareholder transfers to a corporation as a **capital contribution** equals the shareholder's basis in the property on the contribution date. However, the corporation must reduce this basis if the entire contribution has a built-in loss on the contribution date. This reduction is the same as that illustrated in Example 18.[32] The basis of property transferred to a corporation that is not a capital contribution (e.g., by a governmental entity) equals the property's fair market value.

LO.5

Characterize the tax differences between debt and equity investments.

18-2b Debt in the Capital Structure

Various tax and nontax characteristics of debt and equity are relevant when developing the capital structure of a corporation. The relative amounts of debt and equity are a strategic variable for the corporation.

[28] § 1032.

[29] § 118(a) and Reg. § 1.118–1.

[30] § 118(b)(2).

[31] § 118(b)(1).

[32] §§ 362(a) and 362(e).

Advantages of Debt

The advantages of issuing long-term debt instead of stock are numerous. Interest on debt is deductible by the corporation, but dividend payments are not. Further, loan repayments are not taxable to investors unless the repayments exceed basis. In contrast, property distributions from a corporation to its shareholders are not tax-free if the corporation has earnings and profits (see Chapter 19). The government taxes these distributions as dividends to the extent of the corporation's earnings and profits.

Another distinction between debt and equity relates to the taxation of dividend and interest income. Shareholders enjoy preferential tax treatment on dividend income but not on interest income, which is taxed at the shareholder's ordinary income tax rates.

Example 31

Wade transfers cash of $100,000 to a newly formed corporation for 100% of its stock. In its initial year, the corporation has net income and "earnings and profits" of $40,000. If the corporation distributes $7,500 to Wade, the distribution is a taxable dividend to Wade with no corresponding deduction to the corporation.

Assume, instead, that Wade transfers to the corporation cash of $50,000 for stock and cash of $50,000 for a note of the same amount. The note is payable in equal annual installments of $5,000 and bears interest at the rate of 5%. At the end of the year, the corporation pays Wade interest of $2,500 ($50,000 × 5%) and a note repayment of $5,000. The interest payment is a deductible expense to the corporation and taxable to Wade. The $5,000 principal repayment on the note is neither deducted by the corporation nor taxed to Wade.

Based on current tax rates, the table below computes the after-tax impact to Wade and the corporation under each alternative. For both Wade and the corporation, the better outcome occurs when the distribution is comprised of a note repayment and interest. That is, the after-tax income to Wade is higher and the after-tax cost to the corporation is lower under the debt scenario.

	If the Distribution Is	
	$7,500 Dividend	**$5,000 Note Repayment and $2,500 Interest**
*After-tax benefit to Wade**		
[$7,500 × (1 − 15%)]	$6,375	
{$5,000 + [$2,500 × (1 − 35%)]}		$6,625
After-tax cost to corporation		
No deduction to corporation	$7,500	
{$5,000 + [$2,500 × (1 − 21%)]}		$6,975

*Assumes that Wade's dividend income is taxed at the 15% capital gains rate and that his interest income is taxed at the 35% ordinary income rate.

Reclassification of Debt as Equity (the Thin Capitalization Problem)

The tax and nontax advantages of debt create incentives for taxpayers to classify equity as debt. It is unlikely that a bank would loan money to a corporation that has little or no shareholder investment. However, shareholders could make it look like they are "loaning" money to the corporation instead of contributing additional equity just to obtain the tax advantages of debt. This is called a **thin capitalization** problem in which a corporation appears to have artificially low equity and high debt.

When the IRS concludes that a corporation is thinly capitalized, the IRS reclassifies some or all debt as equity and denies the corporation the tax advantages of debt financing. That is, the government can treat the debt as stock for tax purposes if the debt has too many equity-like features. This will result in treating principal and deductible interest payments as nondeductible dividends. However, now that individual rates are higher (up to 37 percent) than corporate rates (21 percent), the IRS may be less inclined to raise this issue because the conversion of interest income to dividend income could produce a tax benefit to individual investors that outweighs the tax cost of nondeductible dividends.

Code § 385 lists several factors that the IRS uses to determine whether a debtor-creditor relationship or a shareholder-corporation relationship exists. Until recently, taxpayers have had to rely solely on numerous judicial decisions to determine whether a true debtor-creditor relationship exists. In late 2016, the Treasury Department released regulations under § 385 that seek to curb thin capitalization of closely held corporations.[33] However, some tax professionals assert that these rules have not answered important questions. As a result, the long line of judicial decisions establishing key guidelines and principles are likely to have continuing relevance. Together, Congress, the Treasury Department, and the courts identify the following factors as important characteristics in distinguishing between debt and equity:

- Whether the debt instrument is in proper form. The IRS is more likely to treat a verbal, unwritten debt agreement as a contribution to capital than a loan evidenced by a properly written note.[34]
- Whether the debt instrument bears a reasonable rate of interest and has a definite maturity date. When a shareholder advance does not provide for interest, the return expected may appear to be a share of the profits or an increase in the value of the shares.[35] Likewise, an unrelated lender will usually be unwilling to commit funds to the corporation without a definite due date.
- Whether the corporation repays the debt on a timely basis. A lender's failure to insist upon timely repayment or satisfactory renegotiation indicates that the return sought does not depend upon interest income and the repayment of principal.
- Whether payments are contingent upon earnings. A lender ordinarily will not advance funds that are likely to be repaid only if the venture is successful.
- Whether the debt is subordinated to other liabilities. Subordination tends to reduce a significant characteristic of the creditor-debtor relationship. Creditors should have the right to share with other general creditors in the event of the corporation's dissolution or liquidation. Subordination also weakens another basic attribute of creditor status—the power to demand payment at a fixed maturity date.[36]
- Whether holdings of debt are proportionate to shares owned (e.g., each shareholder owns the same percentage of debt as stock). When debt and equity obligations are held in the same proportion, shareholders are, apart from tax considerations, indifferent as to whether corporate distributions are in the form of interest or dividends.
- Whether funds loaned to the corporation are used to finance initial operations or capital asset acquisitions. Funds used to finance initial operations or to acquire capital assets the corporation needs are generally obtained through equity investments.
- Whether the corporation has a high ratio of shareholder debt to shareholder equity. Thin capitalization implies that the corporation lacks reserves to pay interest and principal on debt when corporate income is insufficient to meet current needs.[37] In determining a corporation's debt-equity ratio, courts look at the relation of the debt both to the book value of the corporation's assets and to their fair market value.[38]

Code § 385 gives the IRS the authority to classify an instrument either as *wholly* debt or equity or as *part* debt and *part* equity. This flexible approach is important because it is sometimes difficult to classify some instruments either wholly as stock or wholly as debt. Because the principles above are relevant mainly for closely held corporations, a partial debt, partial equity approach also provides the IRS with a better avenue to address these issues in publicly traded corporations.

[33]See Final and Temporary Reg. §§ 1.385–1 to –4T (T.D. 9790).

[34]*Estate of Mixon, Jr. v. U.S.*, 72–2 USTC ¶9537, 30 AFTR 2d 72–5094, 464 F.2d 394 (CA–5).

[35]*Slappey Drive Industrial Park v. U.S.*, 77–2 USTC ¶9696, 40 AFTR 2d 77–5940, 561 F.2d 572 (CA–5).

[36]*Fin Hay Realty Co. v. U.S.*, 68–2 USTC ¶9438, 22 AFTR 2d 5004, 398 F.2d 694 (CA–3).

[37]A court held that a debt-equity ratio of approximately 14.6:1 was not excessive. See *Tomlinson v. 1661 Corp.*, 67–1 USTC ¶9438, 19 AFTR 2d 1413, 377 F.2d 291 (CA–5). A 26:1 ratio was found acceptable in *Delta Plastics, Inc.*, 85 TCM 940, T.C.Memo. 2003–54.

[38]In *Bauer v. Comm.*, 84–2 USTC ¶9996, 55 AFTR 2d 85–433, 748 F.2d 1365 (CA–9), a debt-equity ratio of 92:1 resulted when book value was used. But the ratio ranged from 2:1 to 8:1 when equity included both paid-in capital and accumulated earnings.

18-3 Investor Losses

LO.6

Determine the tax treatment of shareholder debt and stock gains and losses.

The tax law provides some special rules for recognizing gains and losses from investing in corporate stock and debt. This section describes the general rules for investor losses and then describes some special rules for losses. The next section describes the general rules for investor gains and then some special rules that apply to investor gains.

18-3a Stock and Security Losses

Normally, corporate stock and bonds are capital assets in the hands of investors because they are investments. Investors cannot deduct a mere decline in value because there is no realization event. However, worthlessness can be a realization event if the taxpayer can document it. One way to recognize partial worthlessness is to dispose of the stock or bonds in a taxable sale or exchange.[39]

Code § 165(g)(1) governs losses from worthlessness. This section provides for capital loss treatment as of the last day of the taxable year in which the stock or bonds become worthless. When they are not capital assets (such as when they are held by a broker for resale to customers), worthlessness yields an ordinary loss.[40] However, the **investor loss** is disallowed if the sale or exchange is to a related party as defined under § 267(b). This rule includes parents, siblings, and children as related parties but excludes aunts, uncles, and cousins.

Under certain circumstances involving stock and bonds of affiliated corporations, an ordinary loss is allowed upon worthlessness.[41] The reason for this is that an affiliated corporation that conducts a trade or business would generate ordinary losses if it were not a separate corporation. A corporation is an affiliate of another corporation if the corporate shareholder owns at least 80 percent of the voting power of all classes of stock entitled to vote and 80 percent of each class of nonvoting stock. Further, to be considered affiliated, the worthless corporation must have derived more than 90 percent of its aggregate gross receipts for all taxable years from sources other than passive income. Passive income for this purpose includes items such as rents, royalties, dividends, and interest. The reason for this latter requirement is to prevent a corporation from creating a subsidiary corporation by contributing capital assets and then taking an ordinary loss instead of capital losses from the capital assets.

Ethics & Equity Can a Loss Produce a Double Benefit?

In late 2008, Leticia invested $100,000 in TechCo, a startup high-tech venture. Although she had great expectations of financial gain, TechCo's efforts were not well received in the market, and the value of its stock plummeted. Four years ago when TechCo declared bankruptcy, Leticia wrote off her $100,000 stock investment as worthless securities.

To Leticia's surprise, this year she receives $40,000 from the bankruptcy trustee as a final settlement for her TechCo stock. Leticia now realizes that she probably should not have claimed the loss four years ago because the stock was not *completely* worthless.

However, since the statute of limitations has passed, she does not plan to amend her tax return from four years ago. She also decides that the $40,000 is not income but is merely a recovery of some of her original investment. How do you react to Leticia's plans?

18-3b Business versus Nonbusiness Bad Debts

In addition to worthlessness of stock and bonds, the financial demise of a corporation can result in bad debt deductions to those who have extended credit to the corporation. These deductions can be either business bad debts or **nonbusiness bad debts**. The distinction between the two types of deductions is important for tax purposes in the following respects:

- Business bad debts result in ordinary losses, while nonbusiness bad debts result in short-term capital losses.[42] Thus, a business bad debt also can result in (or increase) a net operating loss, but a nonbusiness bad debt can only create or increase a capital loss.[43]

[39] Reg. § 1.165–4(a).

[40] § 165(a) and Reg. § 1.165–5(b).

[41] § 165(g)(3).

[42] Compare § 166(a) with § 166(d)(1)(B).

[43] Note the modification required by § 172(d)(2).

- An ordinary loss deduction is allowed for the partial worthlessness of a business debt, but investors can deduct nonbusiness debts only when they become entirely worthless.[44]
- Because corporations do not engage in personal transactions, all of their bad debts qualify as business bad debts and are never given nonbusiness bad debt treatment.[45]

When is a debt business or nonbusiness? Because the Code does not define these terms, Congress has left the distinction to the courts.[46] In a leading decision, the Supreme Court somewhat clarified the picture when it held that if individual shareholders lend money to a corporation in their capacity as investors, any resulting bad debt is classified as nonbusiness.[47] Nevertheless, the Court did not preclude the possibility of a shareholder-creditor incurring a business bad debt.

Loss on shareholder loans can avoid nonbusiness bad debt treatment if the loan relates to their trade or business instead of their investment in the corporation. For example, if an employee who is also a shareholder makes a loan to preserve employment status, the loan qualifies for business bad debt treatment.[48] Shareholders also receive business bad debt treatment if they are in the trade or business of lending money or of buying, promoting, and selling corporations. If the shareholder has multiple motives for making the loan, according to the Supreme Court, the "dominant" or "primary" motive for making the loan controls the classification of the loss.[49]

Example 32

Juwon owns 48% of the stock of Lark Corporation, which he acquired several years ago at a cost of $600,000. Juwon is also employed by the corporation at an annual salary of $240,000.

At a time when Lark Corporation experienced financial problems, Juwon loaned it $300,000. Later, the corporation declared bankruptcy, and both Juwon's stock investment and his loan became worthless.

Juwon's stock investment results in a long-term capital loss (assuming that § 1244 does not apply, as discussed below). But how is the bad debt classified? If Juwon can prove that his dominant or primary reason for making the loan was to protect his salary, a business bad debt deduction results. If not, it is likely that Juwon was trying to protect his stock investment, and nonbusiness bad debt treatment results.

Factors in resolving the matter of business versus nonbusiness bad debts include the following:

- A comparison of the amount of the stock investment with the trade or business benefit derived. In Example 32, the stock investment of $600,000 is compared with the annual salary of $240,000. In this regard, the salary should be considered as a recurring item and not viewed in isolation. A salary of $240,000 each year means a great deal to a person who has no other means of support and may have difficulty obtaining similar employment elsewhere.
- A comparison of the amount of the loan with the stock investment and the trade or business benefit derived.
- The percentage of stock ownership held by the shareholder. A minority shareholder, for example, has a greater incentive to lend the corporation money to protect a job than a person who controls corporate decision making.

In summary, without additional facts, it is impossible to conclude whether Juwon in Example 32 suffered a business or nonbusiness bad debt. Even with such facts, the guidelines are vague. Recall that a taxpayer's intent or motivation is at issue. For this reason, the problem is frequently the subject of litigation.[50]

---

[44] Compare § 166(a)(2) with § 166(d)(1)(A).

[45] § 166(d)(1).

[46] For definitional purposes, § 166(d)(2) is almost as worthless as the debt it purports to describe.

[47] *Whipple v. Comm.*, 63–1 USTC ¶9466, 11 AFTR 2d 1454, 83 S.Ct. 1168 (USSC).

[48] *Trent v. Comm.*, 61–2 USTC ¶9506, 7 AFTR 2d 1599, 291 F.2d 669 (CA–2).

[49] *U.S. v. Generes*, 72–1 USTC ¶9259, 29 AFTR 2d 72–609, 92 S.Ct. 827 (USSC).

[50] See, for example, *Kelson v. U.S.*, 74–2 USTC ¶9714, 34 AFTR 2d 74–6007, 503 F.2d 1291 (CA–10), *Kenneth W. Graves*, 87 TCM 1409, T.C.Memo. 2004–140, and *Harry Robert Haury*, 104 TCM 121, T.C.Memo. 2012–215.

18-3c **Section 1244 Stock**

In an exception to the capital loss treatment that generally results, § 1244 permits ordinary loss treatment for losses on the sale or worthlessness of stock of so-called small business corporations. By placing shareholders on a more nearly equal basis with proprietors and partners in terms of the tax treatment of losses, the provision encourages investment of capital in small corporations. Because ordinary loss treatment avoids the capital loss limits that frequently prevent deduction of losses, the shareholder has nothing to lose and everything to gain by complying with § 1244.

Qualification for § 1244

Ordinary loss treatment for **§ 1244 stock** applies only to losses on the first $1 million of stock the corporation issues at its creation. If the corporation issues more than $1 million of stock, the corporation designates which shares qualify for § 1244 treatment.[51] The corporation measures the value of stock on the date issued at its adjusted basis minus any liabilities assumed by the corporation. The fair market value of the property is not considered, presumably because determining fair market value is costly and sometimes difficult, especially for small businesses. Note that these rules mean that stock qualifying for ordinary loss treatment does not lose that status if the stock issued increases past the $1 million limit later.

Mechanics of the Loss Deduction

The ordinary loss deduction limit in any one year from the disposition of § 1244 stock is $50,000 (or $100,000 for spouses filing a joint return). Any loss sustained in the taxable year exceeding the limit receives capital loss treatment. However, because the limit is an annual limit, it is possible to use this provision in two tax years to increase the total ordinary loss.

Example 33

Several years ago, Chao acquired § 1244 stock at a cost of $100,000. He sells the stock for $10,000 in the current year. He has an ordinary loss of $50,000 and a capital loss of $40,000. If Chao instead files a joint return, the entire $90,000 loss is ordinary.

Alternatively, if Chao is single, he can sell half of his stock in one tax year and the other half of his stock in the next tax year. In that case, § 1244 converts both losses to ordinary.

Only the original holder of § 1244 stock, whether an individual or a partnership, qualifies for ordinary loss treatment. If the stock is sold or donated, it loses its § 1244 status.

Shareholders must apply a special basis reduction if they receive § 1244 stock for property with an adjusted basis above its fair market value immediately before the exchange. These shareholders must reduce their stock basis to the fair market value of the property on the date of the exchange when they compute the ordinary loss from a later sale. This rule is another effort to prevent taxpayers from converting capital losses into ordinary losses. Note, however, that this rule applies even if shareholders contribute ordinary income property to the corporation.

Dana transfers property with a basis of $10,000 and a fair market value of $5,000 to a corporation in exchange for shares of § 1244 stock. Assuming that the transfer qualifies under § 351, the basis of the stock under the general rule is $10,000, the same as Dana's basis in the property.

However, for purposes of § 1244 and measuring the amount of ordinary loss, the stock basis is only $5,000. If the stock is later sold for $3,000, the total loss sustained is $7,000 ($3,000 − $10,000); however, only $2,000 of the loss is ordinary ($3,000 − $5,000). The remaining portion of the loss, $5,000, is a capital loss.

Recall the advantages of issuing some debt to shareholders in exchange for cash contributions to a corporation. A *disadvantage* of issuing debt is that it does not qualify under § 1244. If the debt become worthless, the taxpayer generally has a short-term capital loss rather than the ordinary loss for § 1244 stock.

[51] Reg. § 1.1244(c)–2(b)(2).

18-4 Gain from Qualified Small Business Stock

To further encourage certain corporate small businesses formations, § 1202 gives noncorporate shareholders special tax relief for gains recognized on the sale or exchange of stock they acquire from a **qualified small business corporation**. The holder of **qualified small business stock** excludes a portion of gain from the sale or exchange of such stock. The exclusion percentage varies, depending on when the shareholder acquired the qualified small business stock. Shareholders exclude 100 percent of the gain for qualified stock they acquired after September 27, 2010, but can exclude only either 75 percent or 50 percent for earlier acquisitions of stock.[52]

Both the corporation and its shareholder must meet certain conditions to qualify for the exclusion. The noncorporate shareholder must have held the stock for more than five years and must have acquired the stock as part of an original issue.[53] The C corporation must have had an adjusted basis in its gross assets that did not exceed $50 million on the stock issuance date.[54] In addition, the corporation must use at least 80 percent of its assets in the active conduct of one or more qualified trades or businesses.

Each individual shareholder can exclude gain up to the *greater* of (1) $10 million or (2) 10 times the shareholder's aggregate adjusted basis in the qualified stock disposed of during a taxable year.[55]

Example 35

Star Corporation originally issued stock in January 2012 to Jenna and Hao for capital contributions of $3,000,000 each. Star manufactures pipe fittings and other plumbing materials that are much less prone to failure and require much less maintenance than standard fittings. All Star assets contribute to the production and distribution of its products. The corporation performed extremely well, rising in value to $100,000,000. Unfortunately, Hao resigned from the corporation after several heated and unpleasant arguments with Jenna over the future direction of the company. In the middle of the current year, Hao sold his investment in Star to a private equity investment firm for $50,000,000.

Hao's sale qualifies for a 100% § 1202 gain exclusion. Hao is an original individual investor, he has held the stock for over five years, Star's initial assets amounted to far less than $50,000,000, and Star uses all of its assets in a business. The results of the sale are:

- Realized gain = $50,000,000 amount realized − $3,000,000 basis = $47,000,000.
- § 1202 exclusion = greater of $10,000,000 or ($3,000,000 × 10) = $30,000,000.
- Long-term capital gain = $47,000,000 − $30,000,000 = $17,000,000.
- Hao's expected tax cost = $17,000,000 × 23.8% = $4,000,000 (rounded).

The tax rate applied to this gain equals the top 20% net long-term capital gain rate plus the 3.8% net investment income tax rate. Note that if § 1202 did not exist, Hao's expected tax liability would be $11,200,000 ($47,000,000 × 23.8%, rounded). Thus, the § 1202 gain exclusion resulted in a tax savings to Hao of over $7,000,000.

LO.7

Identify tax planning opportunities associated with organizing and financing a corporation.

18-5 Tax Planning

With any provision in the tax law affording special treatment, taxpayers must consider whether they qualify or *could* qualify for the special treatment and whether they *should* take advantage of the treatment. Code § 351 provides one such provision that requires careful planning.

18-5a Qualifying (or Not Qualifying) for § 351 Treatment

Effective tax planning with transfers of property to corporations requires a clear understanding of § 351 and its related Code provisions. The most important question in planning is simply this: does the *desired* tax result come from complying with § 351 or from avoiding it? The following discussion reviews key requirements to meet as well as traps to avoid when planning a § 351 transaction.

[52] § 1202(a).

[53] The stock must have been issued after August 10, 1993, which is the original effective date of § 1202.

[54] § 1202(d). Its aggregate assets may not exceed this amount at any time between August 10, 1993, and the date the stock was issued.

[55] § 1202(b). The amount is $5 million for married taxpayers filing separately.

Qualifying under § 351

If shareholders want § 351 tax deferral, they should ensure that the parties transferring property (which includes cash) receive control of the corporation. Simultaneous transfers are not necessary, but a long period of time between transfers can create problems if the transfers are not properly documented as part of a single plan. The parties should document and preserve written evidence of their intentions. Also, it is helpful to have some reasonable explanation for any delay in the transfers.

The control requirement can be especially difficult to meet for exchanges of property for stock of a mature corporation. In these situations, gain deferral might require a larger contribution of assets than the new shareholders can afford. This provides an incentive to convince existing shareholders to make an "accommodation transfer" so that their shares count toward the control requirement. However, the Regulations make clear that an existing shareholder's previously acquired shares do not count toward meeting the control test if (a) the primary purpose of the transfer is to qualify other transferors for § 351 treatment, and (b) the value of the "new stock" received is relatively small compared to the value of stock already owned.[56] Therefore, if a transferring shareholder who does not meet the 80 percent control test desires tax-deferred treatment of § 351, then the other shareholders should contribute property that equals at least 10 percent of the fair market value of the stock already owned.[57]

Avoiding § 351

Although § 351 frequently benefits shareholders by deferring gain, in some situations shareholders benefit from avoiding § 351. This can occur if the transferors prefer to recognize gain now on the transfer of property. Shareholders might prefer current taxation of gains if they are in low tax brackets or if they have losses available to offset gains. The corporation will then have a fair market value basis in the transferred property at a low or no tax cost.

A transferor also might prefer to avoid § 351 to allow for immediate recognition of a loss. Recall that § 351 provides for the nonrecognition of both gains and losses. A transferor who wants to recognize loss has several alternatives:

- Sell the property to the corporation for its stock. The IRS could attempt to disregard the "sale," however, by taking the approach that the transfer really falls under § 351.[58] A disregarded sale will result in a realized but unrecognized loss that yields no tax savings.
- Sell the property to the corporation for cash or other property. Because the transferor receives no stock, § 351 is inapplicable.
- Transfer the property to the corporation in return for its debt or nonqualified preferred stock. Recall that § 351 does not apply to a transferor that receives only securities or nonqualified preferred stock. In both this and the previous alternatives, watch for the possible disallowance of the loss under the related-party rules.

18-5b Selecting Assets and Liabilities to Transfer in § 351 Transactions

To obtain an optimal result when planning to incorporate a business, the organizers must determine which assets and liabilities shareholders should transfer to the corporation and which they should retain. A transfer of assets that produce passive income (rents, royalties, dividends, and interest) can cause the corporation to be a personal holding company in a tax year when operating income is low. Thus, the corporation could be subject to the § 541 personal holding company penalty tax in addition to the regular income tax.

Leasing property to the corporation sometimes is a more attractive alternative than transferring ownership. Leasing provides the taxpayer with the opportunity to withdraw money from the corporation in a deductible form instead of receiving a nondeductible dividend. If the property is given to a family member in a lower tax bracket, the lease income can be shifted as well. If the tax savings from depreciation and other deductions available in connection with the property exceed the tax on the lease income, the parties could benefit from a leasing arrangement instead of a sale or a capital contribution.

---

[56] Reg. § 1.351–1(a)(1)(ii).

[57] Rev.Proc. 77–37.

[58] *U.S. v. Hertwig*, 68–2 USTC ¶9495, 22 AFTR 2d 5249, 398 F.2d 452 (CA–5).

When an existing cash basis business is incorporated, the business owner must consider whether to contribute the business's accounts receivable and accounts payable to the new corporation or keep them. This decision will determine whether the new corporation or the owner of the old unincorporated business will recognize the income from collecting the cash basis receivables. Paying cash basis accounts payable raises the corresponding issue of who will claim the deduction.

The Big Picture

Example 36

Return to the facts of *The Big Picture* on p. 18-1. If Emily decides to retain the $50,000 of cash basis accounts receivable rather than transfer them to the newly formed Transformation, Inc., she will recognize $50,000 of ordinary income upon their collection.

Alternatively, if she contributes the receivables to Transformation as the facts suggest, the corporation will recognize the ordinary income when they are collected. However, a subsequent corporate distribution to Emily of the cash collected could be subject to double taxation as a dividend (see Chapter 19 for further discussion). Given the alternatives available, Emily needs to evaluate which approach is better for the parties involved.

In addition to asset selection, shareholders should consider the appropriate liabilities to transfer to the corporation. For example, a shareholder should consider avoiding debt transfers that are likely to trigger boot treatment under § 357(b). Retaining one tainted liability could result in no debt characterized as boot. In addition, shareholders should consider retaining debt if they are contributing debt that triggers a § 357(c) gain. In this setting, the amount of debt and not the type of debt is likely to be important.

18-5c Negotiating Shares in § 351 Transactions

The deferral provisions in § 351 effectively transfer gains and some losses from shareholders to the corporation. This can increase or decrease future corporate tax liabilities. That is, transferring a gain asset creates a deferred tax liability for the corporation, but transferring a loss asset creates a deferred tax asset. Shareholders could justifiably consider this in determining the number of shares granted, even if the properties transferred have the same fair market value.

Example 37

Iris and Lamont form Wren Corporation with the following investments: property by Iris (basis of $40,000 and fair market value of $50,000) and property by Lamont (basis of $60,000 and fair market value of $50,000). Each receives 50% of the Wren stock. Has Lamont acted wisely in settling for only 50% of the stock?

At first, it would appear so because Iris and Lamont each invested property of the same value ($50,000). But what about tax considerations? By applying the general carryover basis rules, the corporation now has a basis of $40,000 in Iris's property and $60,000 in Lamont's property. In essence, Iris transferred a possible $10,000 gain to the corporation, while Lamont transferred a $10,000 potential loss. Thus, an equitable allocation of the Wren stock would call for Lamont to receive a greater percentage interest than Iris would receive.

This issue is further complicated by the special basis adjustment required when a shareholder such as Lamont contributes property with a built-in loss to a corporation. In this situation, if Wren is to take a carryover basis in Lamont's property, Lamont must reduce his stock basis by the $10,000 built-in loss. This reduced stock basis, of course, could impose a greater tax burden on Lamont when he sells the Wren stock. This may suggest additional support for Lamont having a greater percentage interest than Iris.

18-5d Debt in the Capital Structure

Another way to shift income to other taxpayers is by using corporate debt. Shareholders who also own corporate debt can give the debt to family members in a lower tax bracket. This gift will shift the interest income without losing control of the corporation.

An earlier section of this chapter discussed the advantages and disadvantages of debt and equity. To increase debt without incurring the thin capitalization problem, consider the following tax planning strategies:

- Preserve the formalities of the debt. This includes providing for written instruments, realistic interest rates, and specified due dates.

- If possible, have the corporation repay the debt when it comes due. If this is not possible, have the parties renegotiate the arrangement. Try to proceed as a nonshareholder creditor would. It is not unusual, for example, for bondholders of publicly held corporations to extend due dates when default occurs. The alternative is to foreclose and perhaps reduce the amount the creditors will recover.
- Avoid provisions in the debt instrument that make the debt convertible to equity in the event of default. These provisions are standard practice when nonshareholder creditors are involved. They serve no purpose if the shareholders are also the creditors and hold debt in proportion to ownership shares.

Gail, Cliff, and Ruth are equal shareholders in Magenta Corporation. Each transfers cash of $100,000 to Magenta in return for its bonds. The bond agreement provides that the holders will receive additional voting rights in the event Magenta Corporation defaults on its bonds.

The voting rights provision is worthless and merely raises the issue of thin capitalization. Gail, Cliff, and Ruth already control Magenta Corporation, so what purpose is served by increasing their voting rights? The parties probably used a boilerplate bond agreement that was designed for third-party lenders (e.g., banks and other financial institutions).

- Shareholders holding debt in proportion to their shareholding invite IRS reclassification of debt as equity. However, tax planning can avoid pro rata holding of debt, as Example 39 illustrates.

Assume the same facts as Example 38, except that only Gail and Cliff acquire the bonds. Ruth leases property to Magenta Corporation at an annual rent that approximates the yield on the bonds.

Presuming the rent passes the arm's length test (i.e., what unrelated parties would charge), all parties reach the desired result. Gail and Cliff withdraw corporate profits in the form of interest income, and Ruth is provided for with rent income. Magenta Corporation can deduct both the interest and the rent payments.

- Try to keep the debt-equity ratio within reasonable proportions. A problem frequently arises when the parties form the corporation. Often, the amount invested in capital stock is the minimum required by state law. For example, if the state of incorporation permits a minimum of $1,000, limiting the investment to this amount does not provide much safety for later debt financing by the shareholders.
- The nature of the business can affect what is an acceptable debt-equity ratio. Capital-intensive industries (e.g., manufacturing and transportation) characteristically rely heavily on debt financing. Consequently, it is easier for shareholders to justify higher debt levels for corporations in these industries.
- A strategy to respond to an IRS assertion of thin capitalization based on book values could be to recompute the debt-equity ratio using fair market values. This presumes that the corporation can credibly measure these values, but the result should better measure the economic debt-equity ratio than the use of book values, which might be very old.

Annika, Josh, and Jun form Black Corporation with the following capital investments: cash of $200,000 from Annika, land worth $200,000 (basis of $20,000) from Josh, and a patent worth $200,000 (basis of $0) from Jun. To state that the equity of Black Corporation is $220,000 (the tax basis to the corporation) does not reflect reality. The equity account is more properly stated at $600,000 ($200,000 + $200,000 + $200,000).

18-5e **Investor Gains and Losses**

Code § 1244 can provide beneficial treatment to qualifying taxpayers. However, careful planning can avoid the risk of losing potential benefits of the provision. Only the original holder of § 1244 stock is entitled to ordinary loss treatment. Shareholders lose the benefits of § 1244 if they transfer shares of stock to family members.

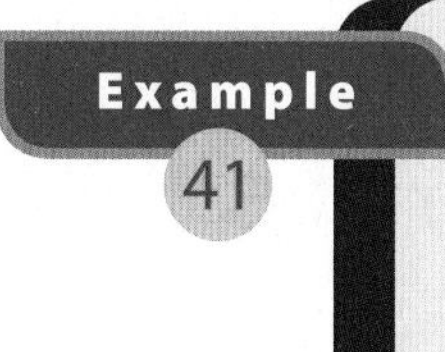
Example 41

Norm incorporates his business by transferring property with a basis of $100,000 for 100 shares of stock. The stock qualifies as § 1244 stock. Norm later gives 50 shares each to his children, Susan and Paul. Eventually, the business fails, and the shares of stock become worthless.

If Norm had retained the stock, he would have had an ordinary loss deduction of $100,000 (assuming that he filed a joint return). Susan and Paul, however, have a capital loss of $50,000 each because the § 1244 attributes are lost as a result of the gift (i.e., neither Susan nor Paul was an original holder of the stock).

A similar result occurs with § 1202 small business stock. The exclusion of capital gain is available only to the original shareholder, not later holders of the stock.

18-5f Corporations versus Flow-Through Entities

Corporations have certain advantages over unincorporated businesses, such as easier capital formation, unlimited life, and limited liability. However, double taxation presents a potentially sizable tax disadvantage. The TCJA of 2017 changed the extent of this disadvantage in two ways. First, it reduced the corporate tax rate from 35 percent to 21 percent. Second, it created a new 20 percent deduction under § 199A for qualified business income of flow-through entities (see Chapter 15). The example below illustrates the effects of these offsetting changes.

Example 42

Albert owns 100% of A Corporation, Betty is the sole proprietor of B Company, and Cai is the sole proprietor of C Company. Each business generated $500,000 of taxable income and before-tax cash flow. A Corporation and B Company produce a product, but C Company provides accounting services. A Corporation will distribute $200,000 of its after-tax income to Albert. All three owners face a 37% marginal tax rate on ordinary income. What is the after-tax cash flow and effective tax rate for each business?

B Company qualifies for the § 199A deduction, but C Company does not because it provides accounting services and its taxable income exceeds the threshold for that deduction. The table below compares the tax and cash flow consequences for each business.

	A Corporation	B Company	C Company
Taxable income and before-tax cash flow	$ 500,000	$500,000	$500,000
Corporate tax @ 21%	(105,000)	–0–	–0–
Cash available to owners	$ 395,000	$500,000	$500,000
§ 199A deduction @ 20%	–0–	(100,000)	–0–
Taxable income to owners	$ 395,000	$400,000	$500,000
Shareholder tax on $200,000 dividend income @ 23.8%	($ 47,600)	$ –0–	$ –0–
Individual tax on ordinary income @ 37%	$ –0–	($148,000)	($185,000)
Before-tax cash flow	$ 500,000	$500,000	$500,000
Corporate tax	(105,000)	–0–	–0–
Shareholder tax on dividend income	(47,600)	–0–	–0–
Individual tax on ordinary income	–0–	(148,000)	(185,000)
After-tax cash flow	$ 347,400	$352,000	$315,000
Effective tax rate	30.5%	29.6%	37.0%

The effective tax rate equals the total tax paid divided by the before-tax cash flow. Note that the 20 percent § 199A qualified business income deduction results in a slightly higher after-tax cash flow for B Company than for the corporation. In contrast, the after-tax cash flow for C Company is lower than for the corporation. Thus, the § 199A deduction results in rough parity between qualifying flow-through entities and corporations for reasonable corporate payout ratios. However, the greater the dividend distributions, the lower the after-tax cash flow and the higher the effective tax rate. The "tax-optimal" strategy is to eliminate dividend payments, but this may be inconsistent with the cash needs of the shareholders.

Refocus on The Big Picture

The Vehicle for Business Growth Is the Corporate Form

Emily and Ethan, the sole property transferors, must acquire at least 80 percent of the stock issued by Transformation, Inc., for the transaction to receive tax-deferred treatment under § 351. This stock ownership threshold is easily achieved under the facts as presented. Otherwise, Emily will recognize a tremendous amount of gain (up to $1,600,000). Because Ethan transfers cash, he will not recognize gain even if the transaction fails to qualify under § 351 (i.e., the fair market value and basis of the cash are identical). However, even if § 351 is available, any debt issued by the corporation is boot and will trigger gain recognition to Emily (see Example 4). Therefore, Emily must evaluate the cost of recognizing gain now versus the benefit of Transformation obtaining an interest deduction later.

If Marco decides to transfer property to Transformation in exchange for stock, § 351 also is available to him as long as his transfer is considered part of a prearranged plan that involves Emily, Ethan, and himself (see Example 6). In addition, if Marco's transaction involves transferring property *and* services in return for stock, § 351 shelters gain recognition only for the property—he will recognize ordinary income for the value of the services rendered (see Examples 20 and 21).

As a result of the incorporation, in addition to being able to raise significant capital with Ethan's equity investment, Emily also benefits from another significant corporate nontax advantage: state law protects her personal assets from unlimited liability exposure.

Another benefit of Transformation operating as a corporation is that Emily and Ethan could easily admit Marco as a shareholder later (assuming he does not participate at the time of incorporation). They could offer him outright stock ownership in exchange for services rendered or establish a stock incentive plan as a reward for his outstanding service and longevity with the business. Further, Emily and Ethan can use similar techniques to entice into the business new employees who may possess unique talents needed to support future expansion. Finally, conversion to a corporation will permit the original shareholders to use § 1202 to exclude potentially large gains from their taxable income (see Example 35).

What If?

Can Emily and Ethan change the terms of the § 351 transaction to further reduce personal and business tax costs, both at the time of formation and in future years? They might consider several modifications.

- Emily might retain certain assets. If the building is not transferred, for example, she can instead lease it to the corporation. The resulting rent payment would mitigate the double tax problem by producing a tax deduction for Transformation.
- An additional benefit results if Emily does not transfer the cash basis receivables to Transformation. This approach avoids an income tax at the corporate level and a further income tax when the receipts are distributed in the form of a dividend. Only Emily will pay tax on the receivables income if she retains those assets (see Example 36).
- The Transformation case facts do not mention any accounts payable outstanding at the time of corporate formation. If they exist, which is likely, it might be wise for Emily to transfer them to Transformation. The subsequent corporate payment of the liability produces a corporate deduction that will reduce any corporate income tax.
- Emily will receive only a small portion of the stock despite having invented the app with Marco. If the app proves to scale successfully, adding financial leverage (i.e., debt) and reducing Ethan's cash contribution would increase Emily's and Marco's ownership percentage and introduce interest deductions that will reduce the corporate tax.

Key Terms

Built-in loss property, 18-12
Capital contribution, 18-18
Control, 18-6
Investor loss, 18-21
Liabilities in excess of basis, 18-15
Nonbusiness bad debts, 18-21
Property, 18-5
Qualified small business corporation, 18-24
Qualified small business stock, 18-24
Section 1244 stock, 18-23
Securities, 18-6
Thin capitalization, 18-19

Discussion Questions

1. LO.1 In terms of justification and effect, § 351 (transfers to a controlled corporation) and § 1031 (like-kind exchanges) are much alike. Explain.

2. LO.1, 3 Under what circumstances will a realized gain and/or loss be recognized on a § 351 transfer?

3. LO.1 What does "property" include for purposes of § 351?

4. LO.3 Can gain ever be recognized in a § 351 transfer if boot is not received? Explain.

5. LO.1 Does the receipt of securities in exchange for the transfer of appreciated property to a controlled corporation cause recognition of gain? Explain.

6. LO.1 What is the control requirement of § 351? Describe the effect of the following in satisfying this requirement:
   a. A shareholder renders only services to the corporation for stock.
   b. A shareholder renders services and transfers property to the corporation for stock.
   c. A shareholder has only momentary control after the transfer.
   d. A long period of time elapses between the transfers of property by different shareholders.

Critical Thinking
Planning

7. LO.1 Nancy and her daughter, Kathleen, have been working together in a cattery called "The Perfect Cat." Nancy formed the business several years ago as a sole proprietorship, and it has been very successful. Assets currently have a fair market value of $450,000 and a basis of $180,000. On the advice of their tax accountant, Nancy decides to incorporate "The Perfect Cat." Because of Kathleen's participation, Nancy would like her to receive shares in the corporation. What are the relevant tax issues?

Critical Thinking
Decision Making
Planning

8. LO.1, 3, 7 Four friends plan to form a corporation for purposes of constructing a shopping center. Charlie will contribute the land for the project and wants more security than shareholder status provides. He is contemplating two possibilities: receive corporate bonds for his land or take out a mortgage on the land before transferring it to the corporation. Comment on the choices Charlie is considering. What alternatives can you suggest?

Critical Thinking

9. LO.1 At a point when Robin Corporation has been in existence for six years, shareholder Ted transfers real estate (adjusted basis of $20,000 and fair market value of $100,000) to the corporation for additional stock. At the same time, Peggy, the other shareholder, acquires one share of stock for cash. After the two transfers, the percentages of stock ownership are as follows: 79% by Ted and 21% by Peggy.
   a. What were the parties trying to accomplish?
   b. Will it work? Explain.

10. LO.2, 3 How does the transfer of mortgaged property to a controlled corporation affect the transferor-shareholder's basis in stock received? Assume that no one recognizes gain on the transfer.

11. **LO.1, 2, 3** Discuss how each of the following affects the calculation of the basis of stock received by a shareholder in a § 351 transfer.
    a. The transfer of a liability to the corporation along with property.
    b. The basis in the property transferred to the corporation.
    c. Property that has been transferred to the corporation has built-in losses.
    d. The receipt of "other property" (i.e., boot) in addition to stock.

12. **LO.2** In a § 351 transfer, Grebe Corporation receives property in exchange for stock. Will Grebe's holding period for the property be the same as the shareholder's holding period for the stock? Explain.

13. **LO.2, 4** A corporation acquires property as a contribution to capital from a shareholder. Describe the rules pertaining to the property's basis.

14. **LO.5** In structuring the capitalization of a corporation, what are the advantages and disadvantages of utilizing debt rather than equity?

15. **LO.6** Hai, a single taxpayer, invested $75,000 in the stock of Penguin Corporation, which recently declared bankruptcy. Although distressed over the loss of her investment, Hai is relieved that she can claim a $75,000 ordinary (rather than capital) loss deduction. Comment on Hai's expectations.

16. **LO.6** Under what circumstances, if any, may a shareholder deduct a business bad debt on a loan made to the corporation?

17. **LO.1, 7** Keith's sole proprietorship holds assets that, if sold, would yield a gain of $100,000. It also owns assets that would yield a loss of $30,000. Keith incorporates his business using only the gain assets. Two days later, Keith sells the loss assets to the newly formed corporation. What is Keith trying to accomplish? Will he be successful? Explain. Critical Thinking

18. **LO.1, 7** Sarah incorporates her small business but does not transfer the machinery and equipment the business uses to the corporation. Subsequently, she leases machinery and equipment to the corporation for an annual rent. What tax reasons might Sarah have for not transferring the machinery and equipment to the corporation when the business was incorporated? Critical Thinking Planning

Computational Exercises

19. **LO.1, 2** Marie and Ramesh form Roundtree Corporation with the transfer of the following. Marie performs personal services for the corporation with a fair market value of $80,000 in exchange for 400 shares of stock. Ramesh contributes an installment note receivable (basis $25,000; fair market value $30,000), land (basis $50,000; fair market value $170,000), and inventory (basis $100,000; fair market value $120,000) in exchange for 1,600 shares. Determine Marie and Ramesh's current income, gain, or loss; calculate the basis that each takes in the Roundtree stock.

20. **LO.1, 2** Grady exchanges property with a basis of $12,000 and fair market value of $18,000 for 60% of the stock of Eadie Corporation. Pedro acquired the other 40% of the stock five years ago. Calculate Grady's current income, gain, or loss and the basis he takes in his shares of Eadie stock as a result of this transaction.

21. **LO.1, 2, 3** Jocelyn contributes land with a basis of $60,000 and fair market value of $90,000 and inventory with a basis of $5,000 and fair market value of $8,000 in exchange for 100% of Zion Corporation stock. The land is subject to a $15,000 mortgage. Determine Jocelyn's recognized gain or loss and the basis in the Zion stock received.

22. **LO.1, 2, 3** Diego transfers real estate with an adjusted basis of $260,000 and fair market value of $350,000 to a newly formed corporation in exchange for 100% of the stock. The corporation assumes the liability on the transferred real estate in the amount of $300,000. Determine Diego's recognized gain on the transfer and the basis for his stock.

23. **LO.1, 2** Yvonne and Simon form Ion Corporation. Yvonne transfers equipment with a basis of $110,000 and fair market value of $165,000 to Ion Corporation. Simon invests $130,000 of cash. They each receive 100 shares in Ion Corporation worth $130,000, but Yvonne also receives $35,000 in cash from Ion. Calculate Ion Corporation's basis in the equipment. In addition, determine Yvonne and Simon's basis in the Ion stock.

24. **LO.5** Chaz transfers cash of $60,000 to a newly formed corporation for 100% of the stock. In its initial year, the corporation has net income of $15,000. The income is credited to its earnings and profits account. The corporation distributes $5,000 to Chaz.

  a. How do Chaz and the corporation treat the $5,000 distribution?
  b. Assume instead that Chaz transfers to the corporation cash of $30,000 for stock and cash of $30,000 for a note of the same amount. The note is payable in equal annual installments of $3,000 each (beginning at the end of the corporation's initial year of operations) and bears interest at the rate of 6%. At the end of the year, the corporation pays an amount to meet this obligation (i.e., the annual $3,000 principal payment plus the interest due). Determine the total amount of the payment and its tax treatment to Chaz and the corporation.

25. **LO.6** Several years ago, Minjun, who is single, acquired § 1244 stock in Blue Corporation at a cost of $60,000. He sells the Blue stock for $5,000 in the current year. Determine the amount and nature of Minjun's gain or loss recognized this year.

Problems

26. **LO.1, 2** Seth, Pete, Cara, and Jen form Kingfisher Corporation with the following consideration:

	Consideration Transferred		
	Basis to Transferor	**Fair Market Value**	**Number of Shares Issued**
From Seth—			
Inventory	$30,000	$96,000	30*
From Pete—			
Equipment ($30,000 of depreciation taken by Pete in prior years)	45,000	99,000	30**
From Cara—			
Proprietary process	15,000	90,000	30
From Jen—			
Cash	30,000	30,000	10

* Seth receives $6,000 in cash in addition to the 30 shares.
** Pete receives $9,000 in cash in addition to the 30 shares.

Assume that the value of each share of Kingfisher stock is $3,000. As to these transactions, provide the following information:

  a. Seth's recognized gain or loss. Identify the nature of any such gain or loss.
  b. Seth's basis in the Kingfisher Corporation stock.

c. Kingfisher Corporation's basis in the inventory.
d. Pete's recognized gain or loss. Identify the nature of any such gain or loss.
e. Pete's basis in the Kingfisher Corporation stock.
f. Kingfisher Corporation's basis in the equipment.
g. Cara's recognized gain or loss.
h. Cara's basis in the Kingfisher Corporation stock.
i. Kingfisher Corporation's basis in the proprietary process.
j. Jen's recognized gain or loss.
k. Jen's basis in the Kingfisher stock.
l. During discussions relating to the formation of Kingfisher, Seth mentions that he may be interested in either (1) just selling all of his inventory in the current year for its fair market value of $96,000 or (2) proceeding with his involvement in Kingfisher's formation as shown above but followed by a sale of his stock five years later for $90,000. What would be the tax cost of these alternative plans stated in present value terms? Referring to Appendix E, assume a discount rate of 6%. Further, assume Seth's marginal income tax rate is 35% and his capital gains rate is 15%.
m. Prepare your solution to part (l) using spreadsheet software such as Microsoft Excel.

27. **LO.1, 2** Tom and Gail form Owl Corporation with the following consideration: Planning

	Consideration Transferred		
	Basis to Transferor	**Fair Market Value**	**Number of Shares Issued**
From Tom—			
Cash	$ 50,000	$ 50,000	
Installment note	240,000	350,000	40
From Gail—			
Inventory	60,000	50,000	
Equipment	125,000	250,000	
Patentable invention	15,000	300,000	60

Tom purchased the $350,000 face value installment note last year for $240,000. As to these transactions, provide the following information:

a. Tom's recognized gain or loss.
b. Tom's basis in the Owl Corporation stock.
c. Owl Corporation's basis in the installment note.
d. Gail's recognized gain or loss.
e. Gail's basis in the Owl Corporation stock.
f. Owl Corporation's basis in the inventory, equipment, and patentable invention.
g. How would your answers to the preceding questions change if Tom received common stock and Gail received preferred stock?
h. How would your answers change if Gail was a partnership?
i. Gail is considering an alternative to the plan as presented above. She is considering selling the inventory to an unrelated third party for $50,000 in the current year instead of contributing it to Owl. After the sale, she will transfer the $50,000 sales proceeds along with the equipment and patentable invention to Owl for 60 shares of Owl stock. Whether or not she pursues the alternative, she plans to sell her Owl stock in six years for an anticipated sales price of $700,000. In present value terms and assuming she later sells her Owl stock, determine the tax cost of (1) contributing the property as originally planned or (2) pursuing

the alternative she has identified. Referring to Appendix E, assume a discount rate of 6%. Further, assume Gail's marginal income tax rate is 32% and her capital gains rate is 15%.

j. Prepare your solution to part (i) using spreadsheet software such as Microsoft Excel.

Decision Making

28. **LO.1, 7** Luciana, Jon, and Clyde incorporate their respective businesses and form Starling Corporation. On March 1 of the current year, Luciana exchanges her property (basis of $50,000 and value of $150,000) for 150 shares in Starling Corporation. On April 15, Jon exchanges his property (basis of $70,000 and value of $500,000) for 500 shares in Starling. On May 10, Clyde transfers his property (basis of $90,000 and value of $350,000) for 350 shares in Starling.

a. If the three exchanges are part of a prearranged plan, what gain will each of the parties recognize on the exchanges?

b. Assume that Luciana and Jon exchanged their property for stock four years ago, while Clyde transfers his property for 350 shares in the current year. Clyde's transfer is not part of a prearranged plan with Luciana and Jon to incorporate their businesses. What gain will Clyde recognize on the transfer?

c. Returning to the original facts, if the property that Clyde contributes has a basis of $490,000 (instead of $90,000), how might the parties otherwise structure the transaction?

Communications

29. **LO.1** Troy Kennedy (1635 Maple Street, Syracuse, NY 13201) exchanges property with a basis of $200,000 and fair market value of $850,000 for 75% of the stock of Red Corporation. Sarah Mitchell acquired the other 25% of the stock several years ago. You represent Troy, who asks whether he must report gain on the transfer. Prepare a letter to Troy and a memorandum for the tax files documenting your response.

30. **LO.1, 2** Dan Knight and Patricia Chen, who are good friends, form Crane Corporation. Dan transfers land (worth $200,000, basis of $60,000) for 50% of the stock in Crane. Patricia transfers machinery (worth $150,000, adjusted basis of $30,000) and provides services worth $50,000 for 50% of the stock.

a. Will the transfers qualify under § 351? Explain.

b. What are the tax consequences to Dan and Patricia?

c. What is Crane Corporation's basis in the land and the machinery?

d. Enter the results of this transaction to Patricia on her Form 1040 (use the most current form available). Assume Patricia is single, has no other income, and claims the standard deduction ($13,850 for 2023; $12,950 for 2022). Complete the Form 1040 to the taxable income line.

31. **LO.1** John organized Toucan Corporation 10 years ago. He contributed property worth $1,000,000 (basis of $200,000) for 2,000 shares of stock in Toucan (representing 100% ownership). John later gave each of his children, Julie and Rachel, 500 shares of the stock. In the current year, John transfers property worth $350,000 (basis of $170,000) to Toucan for 1,000 more of its shares. What gain, if any, will John recognize on the transfer?

32. **LO.1, 2** María and Bob form Robin Corporation. María transfers property worth $420,000 with a basis of $150,000 for 70 shares in Robin Corporation. Bob receives 30 shares for property worth $165,000 with a basis of $30,000 and legal services worth $15,000 in organizing the corporation.

a. What gain or income, if any, will the parties recognize on the transfer?

b. What basis do María and Bob have in the Robin Corporation stock?

c. What is Robin Corporation's basis in the property and services it received from María and Bob?

33. **LO.1, 2** Assume in Problem 32 that the property Bob transfers to Robin Corporation is worth $15,000 with a basis of $3,000 and that his services in organizing the corporation are worth $165,000. What are the tax consequences to María, Bob, and Robin Corporation?

34. **LO.1, 2** Kim is an employee of Azure Corporation. In the current year, she receives a cash salary of $30,000 and also is given 10 shares of Azure stock for services she renders to the corporation. The shares in Azure Corporation are worth $1,000 each. For tax purposes, how will Kim treat the receipt of the 10 shares? What is Azure Corporation's total compensation deduction for Kim's services?

35. **LO.1, 7** Rhonda owns 50% of the stock of Peach Corporation. She and the other 50% shareholder, Rachel, have decided that additional contributions of capital are needed if Peach is to remain successful in its competitive industry. The two shareholders have agreed that Rhonda will contribute assets having a value of $200,000 (adjusted basis of $15,000) in exchange for additional shares of stock. After the transaction, Rhonda will hold 75% of Peach Corporation and Rachel's interest will fall to 25%.

Communications
Decision Making

a. What gain is realized on the transaction? How much of the gain will be recognized?
b. Rhonda is not satisfied with the transaction as proposed. How will the consequences change if Rachel agrees to transfer $1,000 of cash in exchange for additional stock? In this case, Rhonda will own slightly less than 75% of Peach and Rachel's interest will be slightly more than 25%.
c. If Rhonda still is not satisfied with the result, what should be done to avoid any gain recognition?
d. Summarize your solution in an e-mail, and send it to your instructor.

36. **LO.1, 2, 3** Adam transfers property with an adjusted basis of $50,000 and a fair market value of $400,000 to Swift Corporation for 90% of the stock. The property is subject to a liability of $60,000, which Swift assumes.

a. What is the basis of the Swift stock to Adam?
b. What is the basis of the property to Swift Corporation?

37. **LO.1, 2, 3** Cynthia, a sole proprietor, was engaged in a service business and reported her income on the cash basis. In February of the current year, she incorporates her business as Dove Corporation and transfers the assets of the business to the corporation in return for all of the stock in addition to the corporation's assumption of her proprietorship's liabilities. All of the receivables and the unpaid trade payables are transferred to the newly formed corporation. The balance sheet of the corporation immediately after its formation is as follows:

Assets		
	Basis to Dove	**Fair Market Value**
Cash	$ 80,000	$ 80,000
Accounts receivable	-0-	240,000
Equipment (cost $180,000; depreciation previously claimed $60,000)	120,000	320,000
Building (straight-line depreciation)	160,000	400,000
Land	40,000	160,000
Total	$400,000	$1,200,000

Liabilities and Stockholders' Equity	
Liabilities:	
Accounts payable—trade	$ 120,000
Notes payable—bank	360,000
Stockholders' equity:	
Common stock	720,000
Total	$1,200,000

Discuss the tax consequences of the incorporation of the business to Cynthia and to Dove Corporation.

38. **LO.1, 2, 3** Allie forms Broadbill Corporation by transferring land (basis of $125,000, fair market value of $775,000), which is subject to a mortgage of $375,000. One month prior to incorporating Broadbill, Allie borrows $100,000 for personal reasons and gives the lender a second mortgage on the land. Broadbill Corporation issues stock worth $300,000 to Allie and assumes the mortgages on the land.

a. What are the tax consequences to Allie and to Broadbill Corporation?

b. How would the tax consequences to Allie differ if she had not borrowed the $100,000?

Decision Making

39. **LO.1, 2** Rafael transfers the following assets to Crane Corporation in exchange for all of its stock. (Assume that neither Rafael nor Crane plans to make any special tax elections at the time of incorporation.)

Assets	Rafael's Adjusted Basis	Fair Market Value
Inventory	$ 60,000	$100,000
Equipment	150,000	105,000
Shelving	80,000	65,000

a. What is Rafael's recognized gain or loss?

b. What is Rafael's basis in the stock?

c. What is Crane's basis in the inventory, equipment, and shelving?

d. If Rafael has no intentions of selling his Crane stock for at least 15 years, what action would you recommend that Rafael and Crane Corporation consider? How does this change the previous answers?

40. **LO.1, 2, 3** Kesha, a sole proprietor, is engaged in a cash basis service business. In the current year, she incorporates the business to form Kiwi Corporation. She transfers assets with a basis of $500,000 and worth $1,200,000, a bank loan of $450,000 that Kiwi assumes, and $80,000 in trade payables in return for all of Kiwi's stock. What are the tax consequences of the incorporation of the business?

41. **LO.1, 2** Rasa and Jane form Osprey Corporation. Rasa transfers property with a basis of $25,000 and value of $200,000 for 50 shares in Osprey Corporation. Jane transfers property with a basis of $50,000 and value of $165,000 and agrees to serve as manager of Osprey for one year; in return, Jane receives 50 shares in Osprey. The value of Jane's services to Osprey is $35,000.

a. What gain or income do Rasa and Jane recognize on the exchange?

b. What is Osprey Corporation's basis in the property transferred by Rasa and Jane? How does Osprey treat the value of the services that Jane renders?

42. **LO.1, 2** Assume in Problem 41 that Jane receives the 50 shares of Osprey Corporation stock in consideration for the appreciated property and for the provision of accounting services in organizing the corporation. The value of Jane's services is $35,000.

a. What gain or income does Jane recognize?

b. What is Osprey Corporation's basis in the property transferred by Jane? How does Osprey treat the value of the services that Jane renders?

Critical Thinking

43. **LO.1, 2** In January of the current year, Wanda transferred machinery worth $200,000 (basis of $30,000) to a controlled corporation, Oriole, Inc., in a transfer that qualified under § 351. Wanda had deducted depreciation on the machinery in the amount of $165,000 when she held the machinery for use in her proprietorship. Later during the year, Oriole sells the machinery for $190,000. What are the tax consequences to Wanda and to Oriole on the sale of the machinery?

44. **LO.4** Red Corporation wants to set up a manufacturing facility in a midwestern state. After considerable negotiations with a small town in Ohio, Red accepts the following offer of land with a fair market value of $3,000,000 and cash of $1,000,000.
    a. How much income, if any, must Red Corporation recognize?
    b. What basis will Red Corporation have in the land?
    c. Assume that in addition to the facts given, the small town offers to reduce the established property tax rate by 40% on new assets acquired by Red during the two-year period after locating in the town. What are the Federal income tax consequences of the property tax abatement?

45. **LO.5, 6** Emily Patrick (36 Paradise Road, Northampton, MA 01060) formed Teal Corporation a number of years ago with an investment of $200,000 cash, for which she received $20,000 in stock and $180,000 in bonds bearing interest of 8% and maturing in nine years. Several years later Emily lent the corporation an additional $50,000 on open account. In the current year, Teal Corporation becomes insolvent and is declared bankrupt. During the corporation's existence, Emily was paid an annual salary of $60,000. Write a letter to Emily in which you explain how she would treat her losses for tax purposes.

Communications
Critical Thinking

46. **LO.5** Vera, Wade, and Wes hold equal amounts of stock in Jaybird Corporation (555 Industry Lane, Pueblo, CO 81001). Jaybird seeks additional capital of $900,000 to construct a building. Vera, Wade, and Wes each propose to lend Jaybird Corporation $300,000, taking from Jaybird a $300,000 four-year note with interest payable annually at two points below the prime rate. Jaybird Corporation has current taxable income of $2,000,000. You represent Jaybird Corporation. Jaybird's president, Steve Ferguson, asks you how to treat the payments on the notes for tax purposes. Prepare a letter to Ferguson and a memo for your tax files in which you document your conclusions.

Communications
Critical Thinking

47. **LO.6** Sam Upchurch, a single taxpayer, acquired stock in Hummer Corporation that qualified as a small business corporation under § 1244 at a cost of $100,000 three years ago. He sells the stock for $10,000 in the current tax year.
    a. What is the tax treatment of Sam's loss?
    b. Assume instead that Sam sold the stock to his sister, Kara Upchurch, a few months after it was acquired for $100,000 (its fair market value). If Kara sells the Hummer stock for $60,000 in the current year, how should she treat the loss for tax purposes?
    c. Enter the results of this transaction to Kara on Form 1040, Schedule D (p. 1) (use the most current form available). Her Social Security number is 123-45-6789. Assume that relevant facts from the transaction initially had been shown on Form 8949 with Box F checked.

Critical Thinking

48. **LO.6, 7** Three years ago, at a cost of $40,000, Paul Sanchez acquired stock in a corporation that qualified as a small business corporation under § 1244. A few months after he acquired the stock, when it was still worth $40,000, he gave it to his brother, Mike Sanchez. Mike, who is married and files a joint return, sells the stock for $25,000 in the current tax year. Mike asks you, his tax adviser, how to treat the sale for tax purposes. Prepare a letter to your client and a memo for the file. Mike's address is 10 Hunt Wood Drive, Hadley, PA 16130.

Communications

49. **LO.6** Gigi transfers real estate with a basis of $60,000 and a fair market value of $40,000 to Monarch Corporation in exchange for shares of § 1244 stock. Assume that the transfer qualifies under § 351.
    a. What is the basis of the stock to Gigi? Gigi and Monarch do not make an election to reduce her stock basis.
    b. What is the basis of the stock to Gigi for purposes of applying § 1244?
    c. If Gigi sells the stock for $38,000 two years later, how will she treat the loss for tax purposes?

Critical Thinking

Critical Thinking
Decision Making

50. LO.5, 7 Frank, Cora, and Mitch are equal shareholders in Purple Corporation. The corporation's assets have a tax basis of $50,000 and a fair market value of $600,000. In the current year, Frank and Cora each loan Purple Corporation $150,000. The notes to Frank and Cora bear interest of 8% per annum. Mitch leases equipment to Purple Corporation for an annual rental of $12,000. Discuss whether the shareholder loans from Frank and Cora might be reclassified as equity. What other information related to this situation would you want to know before drawing a definitive conclusion?

51. LO.6, 7 Julio sold his corporation to a competitor, Exeter LLC, for $100,000,000. Julio incorporated his business seven years ago by investing $500,000 plus his proprietary know-how. There have been no other corporate shareholders. Compute Julio's after-tax cash flow from the sale, assuming he is in the 37% tax bracket and has no other property sales during the year.

Planning

52. LO.7 Refer to Example 42 in text Section 18-5f. What will be the values of A Corporation, B Company, and C Company after three years? Assume that each business (a) required a $5,000,000 initial investment, (b) earns an annual 10% before-tax rate of return on the beginning-of-the-year investment, (c) can reinvest its after-tax cash flow back into the business, and (d) there is no unrealized appreciation of their assets. Use spreadsheet software such as Microsoft Excel to prepare your answer.

Research Problems

Note: Solutions to the Research Problems can be prepared by using the Thomson Reuters Checkpoint™ online tax research database, which accompanies this textbook. Solutions can also be prepared by using research materials found in a typical tax library.

Communications
Decision Making

Research Problem 1. Lynn Jones, along with Shawn, Walt, and Donna, are deciding whether they should organize a corporation and transfer their shares of stock in several corporations to this new corporation. All of their shares are listed on the New York Stock Exchange and are readily marketable. Lynn would transfer shares in Brown Corporation, Shawn would transfer stock in Rust Corporation, Walt would transfer stock in White Corporation, and Donna would transfer stock in several corporations. The stock would be held by the newly formed corporation for investment purposes. Lynn asks you, her tax adviser, whether she would have gain on the transfer of her substantially appreciated shares in Brown Corporation if she transferred the shares to a newly formed corporation. Your input will be critical as they make their decision. Prepare a letter to your client, Lynn Jones, and a memo for the firm's files. Lynn's address is 1540 Maxwell Avenue, Highland, KY 41099.

Research Problem 2. Mateo is a real estate broker who specializes in commercial real estate. Although he usually buys and sells on behalf of others, he also maintains a portfolio of property of his own. He holds this property, mainly unimproved land, either as an investment or for sale to others.

In early 2018, Irene and Al contact Mateo regarding a tract of land located just outside the city limits. Mateo bought the property, which is known as the Moore farm, several years ago for $600,000. At that time, no one knew that it was located on a geological fault line. Irene, a well-known architect, and Al, a building contractor, want Mateo to join them in developing the property for residential use. They are aware of the fault line but believe that they can circumvent the problem by using newly developed design and construction technology. Because of the geological flaw, however, they regard the Moore farm as being worth only $450,000. Their intent is to organize a corporation to build the housing project, and each party will receive stock commensurate to the property or services contributed.

After consulting his tax adviser, Mateo agrees to join the venture if certain modifications to the proposed arrangement are made. The transfer of the land would be structured as a sale to the corporation. Instead of receiving stock, Mateo would receive a note from the corporation. The note would be interest-bearing and be due in five years. The maturity value of the note would be $450,000—the amount that even Mateo concedes is the fair market value of the Moore farm.

Your tax senior has asked you to determine the income tax consequences that will result from Mateo's suggested approach. You should compare this result with what would happen if Mateo merely transferred the Moore farm in return for stock in the new corporation.

Research Problem 3. Sarah is the sole owner of Bluegrass Corporation. The basis and value of her stock investment in Bluegrass are approximately $100,000. In addition, she manages Bluegrass's operations on a full-time basis and pays herself an annual salary of $40,000. Because of a recent downturn in business, she needs to put an additional $80,000 into her corporation to help meet short-term cash-flow needs (e.g., inventory costs, salaries, and administrative expenses). Sarah believes that the $80,000 transfer can be structured in one of three ways: as a capital contribution, as a loan made to protect her stock investment, or as a loan intended to protect her job. From a tax perspective, which alternative would be preferable in the event that Bluegrass's economic slide worsens and bankruptcy results? Explain your answer.

Partial list of research aids:
Kenneth W. Graves, 87 TCM 1409, T.C.Memo. 2004–140.

Use internet tax resources to address the following questions. Look for reliable websites and blogs of the IRS and other government agencies, media outlets, businesses, tax professionals, academics, think tanks, and political outlets.

Research Problem 4. Find an SEC offering that involves a corporation that originally was established as other than a C corporation (e.g., an S corporation). Describe the particular circumstances that justified the original non-C status and the rationale for subsequently converting to a C corporation.

Research Problem 5. Limited liability company (LLC) status has become a popular form of operating a business in the United States. Investigate how the growth of LLC status has affected the relative number of new businesses that have chosen to operate as corporations.

Research Problem 6. Has § 1202, which relates to qualified small business stock, been widely used since its enactment? What leads you to this conclusion? What rationale did Congress provide as a justification for the provision's enactment? Do you believe that such rationale still is valid in today's environment?

Research Problem 7. Many newly created businesses are established using a tax status that avoids the double tax that applies to C corporations and their owners. Calculate the percentage of entities that filed income tax returns as C corporations (Form 1120), S corporations (Form 1120S), and partnerships and other flow-through entities (Form 706) for the most recent year for which data are available. Use data from the *IRS Tax Statistics* as the basis for your calculations. Compare your findings with comparable percentages for the third and fifth prior years. Using a spreadsheet software such as Microsoft Excel, create graphs that illustrate the results of your research. Be sure the graphs have proper labels and explanations. Data Analytics

Becker CPA Review Questions

Becker

1. Gearty and Olinto organized The Worthington Corp., which issued voting common stock with a fair market value of $240,000. They each transferred property in exchange for stock as follows:

	Property	Adjusted Basis	Fair Market Value	Percentage of The Worthington Corp. Stock Acquired
Gearty	Building	$80,000	$164,000	60%
Olinto	Land	10,000	96,000	40%

The building was subject to a $20,000 mortgage that was assumed by The Worthington Corp. What was The Worthington Corp.'s basis in the building?

a. $60,000
b. $80,000
c. $144,000
d. $164,000

2. Angie and Brad form Cats Are Us, Inc. Angie contributes $120,000 cash for 60% of the stock. Brad contributes an asset with an FMV of $90,000 and an adjusted basis of $30,000 for 40% of the stock. Brad also receives $10,000 cash from the corporation. What is the corporation's basis in the asset received from Brad?
   a. $10,000
   b. $30,000
   c. $40,000
   d. $90,000

3. Gearty and Olinto organized The Worthington Corp., which issued voting common stock with a fair market value of $240,000. They each transferred property in exchange for stock as follows:

	Property	Adjusted Basis	Fair Market Value	Percentage of The Worthington Corp. Stock Acquired
Gearty	Building	$80,000	$164,000	60%
Olinto	Land	10,000	96,000	40%

   The building was subject to a $20,000 mortgage that was assumed by The Worthington Corp. What was Gearty's basis in The Worthington Corp. stock?
   a. $164,000
   b. $80,000
   c. $60,000
   d. $0

4. Gearty and Olinto organized The Worthington Corp., which issued voting common stock with a fair market value of $240,000. They each transferred property in exchange for stock as follows:

	Property	Adjusted Basis	Fair Market Value	Percentage of The Worthington Corp. Stock Acquired
Gearty	Building	$80,000	$164,000	60%
Olinto	Land	10,000	96,000	40%

   The building was subject to a $20,000 mortgage that was assumed by The Worthington Corp. What amount of gain did Gearty recognize on the exchange?
   a. $0
   b. $20,000
   c. $84,000
   d. $104,000

5. Ron, David, and Mary formed Widget, Inc. Ron and David each received 40% of the stock, and Mary received the remaining 20%. Ron contributed land with an FMV of $70,000 and an adjusted basis of $20,000. The corporation also assumed a $30,000 liability on the property. David contributed land with an FMV of $30,000 and an adjusted basis of $15,000. David also contributed $10,000 in cash. Mary received her stock for services rendered. She would normally bill $20,000 for these services. What is Ron's basis in the corporate stock received?
   a. $0
   b. $20,000
   c. $40,000
   d. $70,000

6. Ron, David, and Mary formed Widget, Inc. Ron and David each received 40% of the stock, and Mary received the remaining 20%. Ron contributed land with an FMV of $70,000 and an adjusted basis of $20,000. The corporation also assumed a $30,000 liability on the property. David contributed land with an FMV of $30,000 and an adjusted basis of $15,000. David also contributed $10,000 in cash. Mary received her stock for services rendered. She normally would bill $20,000 for these services. What is Mary's basis in the corporate stock received?
   a. $0
   b. $10,000
   c. $15,000
   d. $20,000

7. Ron, David, and Mary formed Widget, Inc. Ron and David each received 40% of the stock, and Mary received the remaining 20%. Ron contributed land with an FMV of $70,000 and an adjusted basis of $20,000. The corporation also assumed a $30,000 liability on the property. David contributed land with an FMV of $30,000 and an adjusted basis of $15,000. David also contributed $10,000 in cash. Mary received

her stock for services rendered. She normally would bill $20,000 for these services. What is Ron's taxable gain as a result of this transaction?

a. $0
b. $10,000
c. $20,000
d. $30,000

8. In year 1, Stone, a cash basis taxpayer, incorporated her CPA practice. No liabilities were transferred. The following assets were transferred to the corporation:

Cash (checking account)	$ 500
Computer equipment:	
Adjusted basis	30,000
Fair market value	34,000
Cost	40,000

Immediately after the transfer, Stone owned 100% of the corporation's stock. The corporation's total basis for the transferred assets is:

a. $30,000
b. $30,500
c. $34,500
d. $40,500

9. Adams, Beck, and Carr organized Flexo Corp. with authorized voting common stock of $100,000. Adams received 10% of the capital stock in payment for the organizational services that he rendered for the benefit of the newly formed corporation. Adams did not contribute property to Flexo and was under no obligation to be paid by Beck or Carr. Beck and Carr transferred property in exchange for stock as follows:

	Adjusted Basis	Fair Market Value	Percentage of Flexo Stock Acquired
Beck	$ 5,000	$20,000	20%
Carr	60,000	70,000	70%

What amount of gain did Carr recognize from this transaction?

a. $40,000
b. $15,000
c. $10,000
d. $0

10. Clark and Hunt organized Jet Corp. with authorized voting common stock of $400,000. Clark contributed $60,000 cash. Both Clark and Hunt transferred other property in exchange for Jet stock as follows:

	Adjusted Basis	Fair Market Value	Percentage of Jet Stock Acquired
Clark	$ 50,000	$100,000	40%
Hunt	120,000	240,000	60%

What was Clark's basis in Jet stock?

a. $0
b. $100,000
c. $110,000
d. $160,000

11. Ron, David, and Mary formed Widget, Inc. Ron and David each received 40% of the stock, and Mary received the remaining 20%. Ron contributed land with an FMV of $70,000 and an adjusted basis of $20,000. The corporation also assumed a $30,000 liability on the property. David contributed land with an FMV of $30,000 and an adjusted basis of $15,000. David also contributed $10,000 in cash. Mary received her stock for services rendered. She normally would bill $20,000 for these services. What is David's basis in the corporate stock received?

a. $0
b. $10,000
c. $25,000
d. $40,000

12. Which of the following is *not* a requirement about the exclusion of gain for small business stock?

a. The corporation must be a C corporation.
b. The stock must be issued after August 10, 1993.
c. As of the date of the stock issuance, the capital must be less than $50,000,000.
d. The stockholder does not have to be an original stockholder of the corporation.

Chapter 19

Corporations: Distributions Not in Complete Liquidation

Learning Objectives: *After completing Chapter 19, you should be able to:*

LO.1 Explain the role that earnings and profits play in determining the tax treatment of distributions.

LO.2 Compute a corporation's earnings and profits (E & P).

LO.3 Determine taxable dividends paid during the year by correctly allocating current and accumulated E & P to corporate distributions.

LO.4 Describe the tax treatment of dividends for individual shareholders.

LO.5 Evaluate the tax impact of property dividends by computing the shareholder's dividend income, basis in the property received, and the effect on the distributing corporation's E & P and taxable income.

LO.6 Recognize situations when constructive dividends exist, and compute the tax resulting from such dividends.

LO.7 Determine the tax implications arising from receipt of stock dividends and stock rights and the shareholder's basis in the stock and stock rights received.

LO.8 Identify the stock redemptions that qualify for sale or exchange treatment.

LO.9 Determine the tax impact of stock redemptions on the distributing corporation.

LO.10 Identify planning opportunities available to minimize the tax impacts of corporate distributions, constructive dividends, and stock redemptions.

Chapter Outline

The Big Picture

ALEXANDER RATHS/SHUTTERSTOCK.COM

Taxing Corporate Distributions

Plainwell Ice Cream Corporation (Plainwell), a premium ice cream manufacturer, has had a very profitable year. To share its profits with its two shareholders, Waffle Cone Corporation and Luis, it distributes cash of $200,000 to Waffle Cone and real estate worth $300,000 (adjusted basis of $20,000) to Luis (a married taxpayer filing a joint return). The real estate is subject to a mortgage of $100,000, which Luis assumes. The distribution is made on December 31, Plainwell's year-end.

Plainwell has had both good and bad years in the past. More often than not, however, it has lost money. Despite this year's record profits, the GAAP-based balance sheet for Plainwell indicates a year-end deficit in retained earnings. Consequently, the distribution of cash and land is treated as a liquidating distribution for financial reporting purposes, resulting in a reduction of Plainwell's paid-in capital account.

The tax consequences of the distributions to the corporation and its shareholders depend on a variety of factors that are not directly related to the financial reporting treatment. Identify these factors, and explain the tax effects of the distributions to both Plainwell Ice Cream Corporation and its two shareholders.

Read the chapter and formulate your response.

Chapter 18 examines the tax consequences of corporate formation. In Chapters 19 and 20, the focus shifts to the tax treatment of corporate distributions, a topic that plays a leading role in tax planning. The importance of corporate distributions comes from the variety of tax treatments that may apply.

From the *shareholder's perspective*, distributions received from the corporation may be treated as ordinary income, preferentially taxed dividend income, capital gain, or a nontaxable return of capital.

From the *corporation's perspective*, distributions made to shareholders are generally not deductible. However, a corporation may recognize losses in liquidating distributions (see Chapter 20), and gains may be recognized at the corporate level on distributions of appreciated property.

In the most common scenario, a corporate distribution is dividend income to the shareholder and provides no deduction to the corporation, resulting in a double tax (at both the corporate and shareholder levels). The effects of this double tax may be reduced by the corporate dividends received deduction and preferential tax rates on qualified dividends paid to individuals.

The tax treatment of corporate distributions can be affected by a number of items:

- The availability of earnings to be distributed.
- The basis of the shareholder's stock.
- The character of the property being distributed.
- Whether the distribution is a "qualified dividend."
- Whether the distribution is nonliquidating or liquidating.
- Whether the shareholder gives up ownership in return for the distribution.
- Whether the shareholder is an individual or another kind of taxpaying entity.

This chapter discusses the tax rules related to nonliquidating distributions of cash and property. Distributions of stock and stock rights also are discussed along with the tax treatment of stock redemptions (a nonliquidating distribution where the shareholder gives up stock). Corporate liquidations are discussed in Chapter 20.

LO.1

Explain the role that earnings and profits play in determining the tax treatment of distributions.

19-1 Corporate Distributions—Overview

When a distribution is made from corporate earnings and profits (E & P), the shareholder is deemed to receive a dividend, which is taxed either as ordinary income or as preferentially taxed dividend income.[1] Generally, corporate distributions are presumed to be paid out of E & P (discussed in text Section 19-2) and are treated as dividends *unless* the parties to the transaction can show otherwise. Distributions not treated as dividends (because of insufficient E & P) are treated as a nontaxable return of capital to the extent of the shareholder's stock basis, which is reduced accordingly. If the distribution exceeds the shareholder's basis, the excess is treated as a gain from sale or exchange of the stock.[2]

At the beginning of the year, Amber Corporation (a calendar year taxpayer) has E & P of $15,000. The corporation generates no additional E & P during the year. On July 1, the corporation distributes $20,000 to its sole shareholder, Bonnie, whose stock basis is $4,000.

In this situation, Bonnie recognizes dividend income of $15,000 (the amount of E & P distributed). Of the remaining $5,000 distributed, $4,000 reduces her stock basis to zero and Bonnie recognizes a taxable gain of $1,000.

[1] §§ 301(c)(1), 316, and 1(h)(11).

[2] §§ 301(c)(2) and (3).

19-2 Earnings and Profits (E & P)—§ 312

The notion of **earnings and profits (E & P)** is similar in many respects to the accounting concept of retained earnings. Both are measures of the firm's accumulated capital. E & P includes both the accumulated E & P of the corporation since its incorporation date (or February 28, 1913, if later) and the current year's E & P. A difference exists, however, in the way these figures are calculated. The computation of retained earnings is based on financial accounting rules, while E & P is determined using rules specified in the tax law.

Congress has not provided a specific calculation of *earnings and profits* in the Internal Revenue Code. Rather, in § 312, it has provided adjustments that must be made to a corporation's taxable income to arrive at E & P. The Treasury Department (through regulations), the IRS (through rulings), and the courts (through case law) have provided additional guidance. All of these must be taken into account when calculating E & P.

E & P is a measure of the dividend-paying capacity of a corporation (i.e., a measure of *economic income*). As a result, when a corporation makes a distribution to a shareholder, E & P represents the maximum amount of dividend income that shareholders must recognize. As a result, the effect of a specific transaction on E & P often can be determined by assessing whether the transaction increases or decreases the corporation's ability to pay a dividend.

19-2a Computation of E & P

LO.2

Compute a corporation's earnings and profits (E & P).

The Code, regulations, rulings, and court cases provide a series of adjustments to taxable income that result in a measure of the corporation's dividend-paying capacity (or economic income). Both cash basis and accrual basis corporations use the same approach when determining E & P.[3]

Additions to Taxable Income

To determine current E & P, *all* excluded income items are added back to taxable income. These positive adjustments include tax-exempt interest, life insurance proceeds (in excess of cash surrender value), and Federal income tax refunds from tax paid in prior years.

The dividends received deduction also is added back to taxable income to determine E & P since it does not impair a corporation's ability to pay dividends. Effectively, the dividends received deduction is a partial *exclusion* for a specific type of income (dividend income).

Subtractions from Taxable Income

When calculating current E & P, certain nondeductible expenses are subtracted from taxable income. These negative adjustments include the nondeductible portion of meals, entertainment expenses, related-party losses, expenses incurred to produce tax-exempt income, Federal income taxes paid, nondeductible key employee life insurance premiums (net of increases in cash surrender value), and nondeductible fines, penalties, and lobbying expenses.

E & P Calculations

Example 2

Eagle Corporation paid $120,000 of Federal income taxes this year. Eagle also received $6,000 of tax-exempt interest on State of Pennsylvania bonds.

In calculating taxable income for Eagle, the $120,000 is not deductible, and the $6,000 is not taxable. The Federal taxes are subtracted from taxable income to compute Eagle's E & P because this is an amount not available for distribution to shareholders. In contrast, the tax-exempt interest is added to taxable income to compute Eagle's E & P because it represents funds available for distribution.

[3] § 312 describes many of the adjustments to taxable income necessary to determine E & P. Regulations addressing the effect of accounting methods on E & P are at Reg. § 1.312–6.

E & P Calculations

Herron Corporation sells property with a basis of $10,000 to its sole shareholder for $8,000. Because of § 267 (disallowance of losses on sales between related parties), Herron cannot deduct the $2,000 loss when calculating its taxable income.

However, because the overall economic effect of the transaction is a decrease in its assets by $2,000, the loss reduces Herron's current E & P for the year of sale.

Crane Corporation pays a $10,000 premium on a key employee life insurance policy covering the life of its president. As a result of the payment, the cash surrender value of the policy is increased by $7,000.

Although none of the $10,000 premium is deductible for tax purposes, current E & P is reduced by $3,000. The $7,000 increase in cash surrender value is not subtracted because it does not represent a decrease in Crane's ability to pay a dividend. Instead, it represents a shift in Crane's assets from cash to life insurance.

Timing Adjustments

Some E & P adjustments shift the effect of a transaction from the year of its inclusion in the computation of taxable income to the year in which it has an economic effect on the corporation. Charitable contributions, net operating losses, and capital losses all necessitate this kind of adjustment.

Example 5

During 2023, Hawk Corporation makes charitable contributions, $12,000 of which cannot be deducted when calculating its taxable income for the year because of the 10% of taxable income limitation. Consequently, the $12,000 is carried forward to 2024 and fully deducted in that year.

The excess charitable contribution reduces Hawk's current E & P for 2023 by $12,000 and increases its current E & P for 2024 (when the deduction is allowed) by the same amount. The increase in E & P in 2024 is necessary because the charitable contribution carryover reduces the taxable income for that year (the starting point for computing E & P) but already has been taken into account in determining Hawk's E & P for 2023.

Gains and losses from property transactions generally affect the determination of E & P only to the extent they are recognized for tax purposes. As a result, gains and losses deferred under the like-kind exchange provision and gains deferred under the involuntary conversion provision do not affect E & P until recognized.

Accounting Method Adjustments

In addition to the above adjustments, accounting methods used for determining E & P generally are more conservative than those allowed for calculating taxable income. For example, the installment method is not permitted for E & P purposes.[4] As a result, an adjustment is required for the deferred gain from property sales made during the year under the installment method. All principal payments are treated as having been received in the year of sale.

In 2023, Cardinal Corporation, a calendar year taxpayer, sells unimproved real estate for $100,000; its basis in the land is $20,000. Under the terms of the sale, Cardinal will receive two payments, $60,000 in 2024 and $40,000 in 2025, along with interest of 4%. Cardinal Corporation does not elect out of the installment method.

Because Cardinal's taxable income for 2023 will not reflect any of the gain from the sale, the corporation must make an $80,000 positive adjustment for 2023 (the deferred gain from the sale). Then negative adjustments of $48,000 in 2024 and $32,000 in 2025 will be required when the deferred gain is recognized under the installment method.

continued

[4] § 312(n)(5).

Treatment of the gain for regular tax and E & P purposes is summarized as follows:

Tax Year	Regular Tax Treatment	E & P Treatment	E & P Adjustment
2023	$ -0-	$80,000	$ 80,000
2024	48,000	-0-	(48,000)
2025	32,000	-0-	(32,000)

A similar analysis can be used for most of the timing and accounting method adjustments.

The alternative depreciation system (ADS) must be used for purposes of computing E & P.[5] This method requires straight-line depreciation with a half-year convention over a recovery period equal to the Asset Depreciation Range (ADR) midpoint life of an asset.[6] Also, ADS prohibits additional first-year (bonus) depreciation.[7] If MACRS cost recovery is used for income tax purposes, a positive or negative adjustment equal to the difference between MACRS and ADS must be made each year. Likewise, when assets are sold, an additional adjustment to taxable income is required to account for the difference in gain or loss between income tax basis and E & P basis.[8] The adjustments arising from depreciation are illustrated in the following example.

Example 7

On January 2, 2021, White Corporation paid $30,000 to purchase equipment with an ADR midpoint life of 10 years and a MACRS class life of 7 years. The equipment was depreciated under MACRS. The asset was sold on July 2, 2023, for $27,000. For purposes of determining taxable income and E & P, cost recovery claimed on the equipment is summarized below. Assume that White elected not to claim § 179 expense or additional first-year depreciation on the property.

Year	Cost Recovery Computation	MACRS	ADS	E & P Adjustment
2021	$30,000 × 14.29%	$ 4,287		
	$30,000 ÷ 10-year ADR recovery period × ½ (half-year for first year of service)		$1,500	$2,787
2022	$30,000 × 24.49%	7,347		
	$30,000 ÷ 10-year ADR recovery period		3,000	4,347
2023	$30,000 × 17.49% × ½ (half-year for year of disposal)	2,624		
	$30,000 ÷ 10-year ADR recovery period × ½ (half-year for year of disposal)		1,500	1,124
Total cost recovery		$14,258	$6,000	$8,258

Each year, White Corporation will increase taxable income by the adjustment amount indicated above to determine E & P. In addition, when computing E & P for 2023, White will reduce taxable income by $8,258 to account for the excess gain recognized for income tax purposes.

	Income Tax	E & P
Amount realized	$27,000	$ 27,000
Adjusted basis for income tax ($30,000 cost − $14,258 MACRS)	(15,742)	
Adjusted basis for E & P ($30,000 cost − $6,000 ADS)		(24,000)
Gain on sale	$11,258	$ 3,000
E & P adjustment ($3,000 − $11,258)	($ 8,258)	

[5] § 312(k)(3)(A).

[6] See § 168(g)(2). The ADR midpoint lives for most assets are set out in Rev.Proc. 87–56. The recovery period is 5 years for automobiles and light-duty trucks and 40 years for real property. For assets with no class life, the recovery period is 12 years.

[7] § 168(k)(2)(D). In general, additional first-year depreciation (also called "bonus depreciation") is allowed for qualified property placed in service after 2011 and before 2027. No bonus depreciation is scheduled for tax years after 2026. Different rules applied between 2008 and 2011 and prior to 2005.

[8] § 312(f)(1).

In addition to more conservative depreciation methods, the E & P rules impose limitations on the deductibility of § 179 expense. Specifically, any § 179 expense must be deducted over a period of five years (20 percent per year).[9] As a result, in any year that § 179 is elected, 80 percent of the resulting expense must be added back to taxable income to determine current E & P. In each of the following four years, a subtraction from taxable income equal to 20 percent of the § 179 expense must be made.

On January 2, 2022, Blue Corporation placed in service a five-year depreciable asset. The acquisition price of the asset was $25,000, and Blue Corporation claimed a § 179 deduction for the full amount. Treatment of the § 179 deduction for regular tax and E & P purposes is summarized as follows:

Tax Year	Regular Tax Treatment	E & P Treatment	E & P Adjustment
2022	($25,000)	($5,000)	$20,000
2023	–0–	(5,000)	(5,000)
2024	–0–	(5,000)	(5,000)
2025	–0–	(5,000)	(5,000)
2026	–0–	(5,000)	(5,000)

The E & P rules also require specific accounting methods in various situations. For example:

- E & P requires cost depletion rather than percentage depletion.[10]
- When accounting for long-term contracts, E & P requires the percentage of completion method rather than the completed contract method.[11]
- E & P does not allow for the amortization of organizational expenses. As a result, any expense deducted when computing taxable income must be added back to determine E & P.[12]
- If a corporation is using the LIFO inventory method, E & P requires an adjustment for changes in the LIFO recapture amount (the excess of FIFO over LIFO inventory value) during the year. Increases in LIFO recapture are added to taxable income, and decreases are subtracted.[13]
- E & P requires that intangible drilling costs and mine exploration and development costs be amortized over a period of 60 months and 120 months, respectively.[14]

19-2b **Summary of E & P Adjustments**

E & P serves as a measure of a corporation's dividend-paying capacity. Concept Summary 19.1 summarizes the required adjustments to the corporation's taxable income to arrive at current E & P. Other items that affect E & P, such as property dividends and stock redemptions, are covered later in the chapter.

[9] § 312(k)(3)(B).
[10] Reg. § 1.316–2(e).
[11] § 312(n)(6).
[12] § 312(n)(3).
[13] § 312(n)(4).
[14] § 312(n)(2).

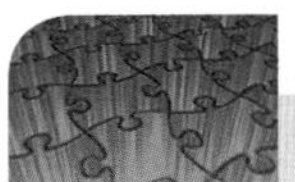

Concept Summary 19.1

E & P Adjustments

Nature of the Transaction	Adjustment to Taxable Income to Determine Current E & P	
	Addition	**Subtraction**
Tax-exempt income	X	
Dividends received deduction	X	
Collection of proceeds from insurance policy on life of corporate employee (in excess of cash surrender value)	X	
Deferred gain on installment sale (all gain is added to E & P in year of sale)	X	
Future recognition of installment sale gross profit		X
Excess charitable contribution (over 10% limitation) and excess capital loss in year incurred		X
Deduction of charitable contribution, NOL, or capital loss carryovers in succeeding taxable year (increase E & P because deduction reduces taxable income while E & P was reduced in a prior year)	X	
Federal income taxes paid		X
Federal income tax refund	X	
Loss on sale between related parties		X
Nondeductible fines, penalties, entertainment, and lobbying expenses		X
Nondeductible portion of meal expenses*		X
Payment of premiums on insurance policy on life of corporate employee (in excess of increase in cash surrender value of policy)		X
Realized gain (not recognized) on an involuntary conversion	No effect	
Realized gain or loss (not recognized) on a like-kind exchange	No effect	
Excess percentage depletion (only cost depletion can reduce E & P)	X	
Accelerated depreciation (E & P is reduced only by straight-line, units-of-production, or machine hours depreciation)	X	X
Additional first-year (bonus) depreciation	X	
Section 179 expense in year elected (80%)	X	
Section 179 expense in four years following election (20% each year)		X
Increase (decrease) in LIFO recapture amount	X	X
Intangible drilling costs deducted currently (reduce E & P in future years by amortizing costs over 60 months)	X	
Mine exploration and development costs (reduce E & P in future years by amortizing costs over 120 months)	X	

* For 2021 and 2022, business meals provided by a restaurant are not subject to the 50% disallowance rule.

Example 9

Crimson Corporation (a calendar year, accrual basis taxpayer) reports taxable income of $429,000 in 2023. In addition, it provides the following information:

Federal income tax liability paid	$ 90,090
Tax-exempt interest income	6,250
Meal expenses (total)	10,000
Entertainment expenses	3,000
Premiums paid on key employee life insurance*	8,500
Life insurance proceeds from key employee life insurance policy*	250,000
Excess of capital losses over capital gains	22,000
MACRS cost recovery deduction	82,000
E & P depreciation (straight-line depreciation using ADS)	64,000
Section 179 expense elected and deducted during 2020 for regular tax purposes	120,000
Dividends received from domestic corporations (less than 20% owned)	35,000

*Term policy; no cash surrender value.

continued

Crimson sold property on installment during 2021. The property was sold for $120,000 and had an $84,000 adjusted basis when sold. During 2023, Crimson received a $30,000 payment on the installment sale. Finally, assume that Crimson did not claim any § 179 expense or bonus depreciation in 2023. What is Crimson's current E & P?

Taxable income	$429,000
Federal income tax liability paid	(90,090)
Tax-exempt interest income	6,250
Disallowed portion of meal expenses	(5,000)
Entertainment expenses	(3,000)
Life insurance premiums paid	(8,500)
Proceeds from life insurance policy	250,000
Excess capital losses	(22,000)
Excess of MACRS cost recovery over E & P (ADS) depreciation	18,000**
Allowable portion of 2020 § 179 expenses (20% × $120,000)	(24,000)
Dividends received deduction (50% × $35,000)	17,500
Installment sale gain	(9,000)***
Current E & P	$559,160

**$82,000 − $64,000
***[($120,000 sales price − $84,000 adjusted basis) ÷ $120,000 sales price] × $30,000

How would your answer change if Crimson told you that the $82,000 MACRS cost recovery deduction was entirely a § 179 expense election?

For E & P purposes, the $82,000 § 179 expense must be deducted over five years (20% per year). So 80% of the $82,000 (or $65,600) would be an addition to taxable income in 2023, and there would be no need to compute E & P depreciation on these items (so the $18,000 E & P depreciation add-back would be eliminated). As a result, Crimson's current E & P would be $606,760 ($559,160 + $65,600 − $18,000). Over each of the next four taxable years, Crimson would have a $16,400 current E & P deduction to account for the § 179 expense taken in 2023 for regular tax purposes ($82,000 × 20%).

19-2c Current versus Accumulated E & P

Accumulated E & P is the total of all previous years' current E & P (since February 28, 1913) reduced by distributions made from E & P in previous years. It is important to distinguish between **current E & P** and **accumulated E & P** because the taxability of corporate distributions depends on how these two accounts are allocated to each distribution made during the year. A complex set of rules governs the allocation process.[15] These rules are described in the following section and summarized in Concept Summary 19.2.

LO.3

Determine taxable dividends paid during the year by correctly allocating current and accumulated E & P to corporate distributions.

19-2d Allocating E & P to Distributions

When a positive balance exists in both the current and accumulated E & P accounts, corporate distributions are deemed to be made first from current E & P and then from accumulated E & P. If there is only one distribution during the year and the distribution is less than total E & P (both current and accumulated), the distribution will be classified as a dividend.

When there are multiple distributions and total distributions exceed the amount of current E & P, it becomes necessary to allocate current and accumulated E & P to each distribution made during the year. First, current E & P is prorated among the distributions using the following formula:[16]

Current E & P  $\frac{\textbf{Amount of distribution}}{\textbf{Total distributions}}$  **Current E & P allocated to a distribution**

[15]Regulations relating to the source of a distribution are at Reg. § 1.316–2.

[16]Reg. §§ 1.316–2(b) and (c).

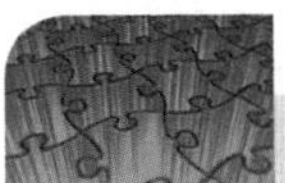

Concept Summary 19.2

Allocating E & P to Distributions

Current E & P at Time of Distribution	Accumulated E & P at Time of Distribution	Outcome	Illustration
Positive	**Positive**	Current E & P is applied first to distributions on a pro rata basis; then accumulated E & P is applied (as necessary) in chronological order beginning with the earliest distribution.	Example 10
		Unless the parties can show otherwise, it is presumed that current E & P covers all distributions.	Example 11
Positive	**Deficit**	Current and accumulated E & P are *not* netted. Distributions are dividends to the extent of current E & P. If the distribution exceeds the current E & P, the excess first reduces the stock basis to zero and then generates a taxable gain.	Example 12
Deficit	**Positive**	Current and accumulated E & P are netted. Any loss in current E & P is deemed to accrue ratably throughout the year unless the corporation can show otherwise.	
		(1) If net amount is *positive:* Distribution is a dividend to the extent of the balance. If the distribution exceeds the net E & P, the excess first reduces the stock basis to zero and then generates a taxable gain.	Example 13
		(2) If net amount is *negative:* Distribution is treated as a return of capital, first reducing the stock basis to zero, then generating taxable gain.	Example 14
Deficit	**Deficit**	Distribution is treated as a return of capital, first reducing the basis of the stock to zero, then generating taxable gain.	Example 15

Then accumulated E & P is applied in chronological order, beginning with the earliest distribution (i.e., on a "first-come, first-served" basis).[17] As shown in the following example, this allocation is important if any shareholder sells stock during the year.

Example 10

On January 1 of the current year, Black Corporation has accumulated E & P of $10,000. Current E & P for the year amounts to $30,000, earned evenly throughout the year. Megan and Matt are sole *equal* shareholders of Black from January 1 to July 31.

On August 1, Megan sells all of her stock to Sundra. Black makes two distributions to shareholders during the year: $40,000 to Megan and Matt ($20,000 to each) on July 1 and $40,000 to Matt and Sundra ($20,000 to each) on December 1. Current and accumulated E & P are applied to the two distributions as follows:

	Source of Distribution		
	Current E & P	**Accumulated E & P**	**Return of Capital**
July 1 distribution ($40,000)	$15,000	$10,000	$15,000
December 1 distribution ($40,000)	15,000	—	25,000

Because 50% of the total distributions are made on July 1 and December 1, respectively, one-half of current E & P is applied to each of the two distributions. Accumulated E & P is applied in chronological order, so the entire amount attaches to the July 1 distribution. The tax consequences to the shareholders are presented on the next page.

continued

[17]Ibid.

	Shareholder		
	Megan	**Matt**	**Sundra**
July distribution ($40,000)			
Dividend income—			
From current E & P ($15,000)	$ 7,500	$ 7,500	$ -0-
From accumulated E & P ($10,000)	5,000	5,000	-0-
Return of capital ($15,000)	7,500	7,500	-0-
December distribution ($40,000)			
Dividend income—			
From current E & P ($15,000)	-0-	7,500	7,500
From accumulated E & P ($0)	-0-	-0-	-0-
Return of capital ($25,000)	-0-	12,500	12,500
Total distribution	$20,000	$40,000	$20,000
Total dividend income	$12,500	$20,000	$ 7,500
Nontaxable return of capital (assuming sufficient basis in the stock investment)	$ 7,500	$20,000	$12,500

Because the balance in the accumulated E & P account is exhausted when it is applied to the July 1 distribution, Megan has more dividend income than Sundra, even though both receive equal distributions during the year. In addition, each shareholder's basis is reduced by the nontaxable return of capital; any excess over basis results in taxable gain.

When the tax years of the corporation and its shareholders are not the same, it may be impossible to determine the amount of current E & P on a timely basis. For example, if shareholders use a calendar year and the corporation uses a fiscal year, then current E & P may not be known until after the shareholders' returns have been filed. To address this timing issue, the allocation rules presume that current E & P is sufficient to cover every distribution made during the year until the parties can show otherwise.

Example 11

Griffen Corporation uses a June 30 fiscal year for tax purposes. Kayla, Griffen's only shareholder, uses a calendar year. On July 1, 2023, Griffen Corporation has a zero balance in its accumulated E & P account. On August 1, 2023, Griffen distributes $10,000 to Kayla. For fiscal year 2023–2024, the corporation determines that it has a $5,000 deficit in current E & P.

Because Kayla cannot prove until June 30, 2024, that the corporation has a current E & P deficit for the 2023–2024 fiscal year, she must assume that current E & P is sufficient to cover the $10,000 distribution. As a result, the distribution will be dividend income to Kayla and reported as such when she files her tax return for the 2023 calendar year. When Kayla learns of the deficit, she can file an amended return for 2023 showing the $10,000 as a return of capital.

Additional difficulties arise when either the current or the accumulated E & P account has a deficit balance. When current E & P is positive and accumulated E & P has a deficit balance, accumulated E & P is *not* netted against current E & P. Instead, the distribution is deemed to be a taxable dividend to the extent of the positive current E & P balance.

The Big Picture

Example 12

Return to the facts of *The Big Picture* on p. 19-1. Recall that Plainwell Ice Cream Corporation had a deficit in GAAP-based retained earnings at the start of the year and record profits during the year. Assume that these financial results translate into an $800,000 deficit in accumulated E & P at the start of the year and current E & P of $600,000.

In this case, current E & P would exceed the total cash and property distributed to the shareholders. The distributions are treated as taxable dividends; they are deemed to be paid from current E & P even though Plainwell still has a deficit in accumulated E & P at the end of the year.

Alternatively, when a deficit exists in current E & P and a positive balance exists in accumulated E & P, the accounts are *netted* at the date of distribution. If the resulting balance is zero or negative, the distribution is a return of capital to the extent of basis; any excess over basis results in a taxable gain. If a positive balance results, the distribution is a dividend to the extent of the balance. A deficit in current E & P is deemed to accrue ratably throughout the year unless the parties can show otherwise.

Distributions with E & P Deficits

Example 13

At the beginning of the current year, Gray Corporation (a calendar year taxpayer) has accumulated E & P of $10,000. During the year, the corporation incurs a $15,000 deficit in current E & P that accrues ratably. On July 1, Gray Corporation distributes $6,000 in cash to Jennifer, its sole shareholder. Jennifer has a $7,500 basis in her Gray Corporation stock.

To determine how much of the $6,000 cash distribution represents dividend income to Jennifer, the balances of both accumulated and current E & P as of July 1 are determined and netted. This is necessary because of the deficit in current E & P.

	Source of Distribution	
	Current E & P	**Accumulated E & P**
January 1		$10,000
July 1 (½ of $15,000 current E & P deficit)	($7,500)	2,500
Outcome: July 1 distribution of $6,000:		
Dividend: $2,500		
Return of capital: $3,500		

The balance in E & P just before the July 1 distribution is $2,500. As a result, of the $6,000 distribution, $2,500 is taxed as a dividend and $3,500 represents a return of capital. After the distribution, Jennifer's stock basis is $4,000 ($7,500 − $3,500).

Example 14

Assume the same facts as Example 13, except that Gray Corporation's current E & P deficit amounts to $30,000 and Jennifer's stock basis is $5,000.

	Source of Distribution	
	Current E & P	**Accumulated E & P**
January 1		$10,000
July 1 (½ of $30,000 current E & P deficit)	($15,000)	(5,000)
Outcome: July 1 distribution of $6,000:		
Return of capital: $5,000		
Taxable gain: $1,000		

The balance in E & P just before the July 1 distribution is ($5,000). As a result, the distribution is first treated as a return of capital (to the extent of Jennifer's stock basis) and then as a taxable gain. Here, Jennifer's basis is reduced to zero and she has a taxable (capital) gain of $1,000.

Assume the same facts as Example 14, except that Gray Corporation began the year with an accumulated E & P deficit of $10,000.

Because Gray has deficits in both accumulated and current E & P, the outcome is the same as in Example 14: a $5,000 return of capital and a $1,000 taxable (capital) gain.

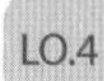

Ethics & Equity **Shifting E & P**

Ten years ago, Leon began a new business venture with Robert. Leon owns 70 percent of the outstanding stock, and Robert owns 30 percent. The business has had some difficult times, but current prospects are favorable.

On November 15, Robert decides to quit the venture and plans to sell all of his stock to Leon's sister, Heidi, a longtime employee of the business. Robert will sell his stock to Heidi after the company pays out the current-year shareholder distribution of about $100,000. Leon is looking forward to working with his sister, but he now faces a terrible dilemma.

The corporation has a $300,000 deficit in accumulated E & P and only about $20,000 of current E & P to date. Within the next two months, however, Leon expects to sign a major deal with a large client. If Leon signs the contract before the end of the year, the corporation will have a large increase in current E & P, causing the upcoming distribution to be fully taxable to Robert as a dividend.

Since a similar contract is not expected next year, most of next year's distribution will be treated as a tax-free return of capital for Heidi. Alternatively, if Leon waits until January, both he and Robert will receive a nontaxable distribution this year. However, next year's annual distribution will be fully taxable to his sister as a dividend. What should Leon do?

LO.4

Describe the tax treatment of dividends for individual shareholders.

19-3 **Dividends**

Distributions by a corporation from its E & P are treated as dividends. The tax treatment of dividends varies, depending on whether the shareholder receiving them is a corporation or an individual. All corporations treat dividends as ordinary income and are permitted a dividends received deduction (see Chapter 17). Qualified dividend income received by individuals is taxed at reduced tax rates.

19-3a **Rationale for Reduced Tax Rates on Dividends**

The double tax on corporate income has always been controversial. Arguably, taxing dividends twice creates several undesirable economic distortions, including:

- An incentive to invest in noncorporate rather than corporate entities.
- An incentive for corporations to finance operations with debt rather than with equity because interest payments are deductible. Notably, this behavior increases the vulnerability of corporations in economic downturns because of higher leverage.
- An incentive for corporations to retain earnings and structure distributions of profits to avoid the double tax.

Collectively, these distortions raise the cost of capital for corporate investments. Estimates are that eliminating the double tax would increase capital stock in the corporate sector by as much as $500 billion.[18] In addition, some argue that elimination of the double tax would make the United States more competitive globally since a majority of our trading partners assess only one tax on corporate income.

Although many support a reduced or no tax rate on dividends, others contend that the double tax should remain in place because of the concentration of economic power held by publicly traded corporations. And many of the distortions noted above can be avoided through the use of deductible payments by C corporations (e.g., by employing, renting property from, or borrowing money from shareholders) or the use of other entity types (e.g., partnerships, limited liability companies, and Subchapter S corporations). Those favoring retention of the double tax also note that the benefits of reduced tax rates on dividends flow disproportionately to the wealthy.[19]

[18] Integration of Individual and Corporate Tax Systems, Report of the Department of the Treasury (January 1992); "Eliminating Double Taxation Through Corporate Integration," Tax Foundation, February 23, 2015.

[19] The Urban Institute–Brookings Institution Tax Policy Center estimates that more than half of the benefits from the reduced tax rate on dividends go to the 0.2% of households with incomes over $1 million.

Because of these differing opinions, the taxation of dividends in the United States has varied through the years. The reduced tax rate on **qualified dividends** for individuals reflects a compromise between the complete elimination of tax on dividends and the treatment of dividends as ordinary income.

19-3b Qualified Dividends

Qualified Dividends—Application and Effect

For most individual taxpayers, dividends that meet certain requirements (called "qualified dividends") are subject to a 15 percent tax rate. High-income taxpayers are subject to a 20 percent rate; a zero percent rate applies to lower-income taxpayers.[20]

Qualified Dividends—Requirements

To be taxed at the lower rates, dividends must be paid by either domestic or certain qualified foreign corporations. Qualified foreign corporations include those traded on a U.S. stock exchange or any corporation located in a country that (1) has a comprehensive income tax treaty with the United States, (2) has an information-sharing agreement with the United States, and (3) is approved by the Treasury.[21]

Two other requirements must be met for dividends to qualify for the favorable rates. First, dividends paid to shareholders who hold both long and short positions in the stock do not qualify. Second, the stock on which the dividend is paid must be held for more than 60 days during the 121-day period beginning 60 days before the ex-dividend date.[22] To allow for settlement delays, the ex-dividend date is typically two days before the date of record on a dividend. This holding period rule parallels the rule applied to corporations that claim the dividends received deduction.[23]

Example 16

In June of the current year, Green Corporation announces that a dividend of $1.50 will be paid on each share of its common stock to shareholders of record on July 15. The ex-dividend date is July 13. Amy and Caleb, two unrelated shareholders, own 1,000 shares of the stock on the record date (July 15). Consequently, each receives $1,500 (1,000 shares × $1.50). Assume that Amy purchased her stock on January 15 of this year and that Caleb purchased his stock on July 1. Both shareholders sell their stock on July 20.

To qualify for the lower dividend rate, stock must be held for more than 60 days during the 121-day period beginning 60 days prior to July 13 (the ex-dividend date). In this case, the 121-day period runs from May 14 to September 11. The $1,500 Amy receives is subject to preferential tax treatment since she held the stock for more than 60 days during this 121-day period. The $1,500 Caleb receives, however, is not. Caleb did not meet the 60-day holding requirement, so his dividend will be taxed as ordinary income.

Qualified dividends are *not* considered investment income when determining the investment interest expense deduction. Taxpayers can, however, elect to treat qualified dividends as ordinary income (taxed at regular rates) and include them in investment interest income. As a result, taxpayers subject to an investment interest expense limitation must evaluate the relative benefits of taxing qualified dividends at reduced rates versus using the dividends as investment income to increase the amount of deductible investment interest expense.

---

[20] See §§ 1(h)(1) and (11). In 2023, the 20% rate applies to married taxpayers filing jointly with taxable income greater than $553,850 ($492,300 for single taxpayers); the 0% rate applies to married taxpayers filing jointly with taxable income of $89,250 or less ($44,625 for single taxpayers). In 2022, these amounts were $517,200, $459,750, $83,350, and $41,675, respectively.

[21] In Notice 2011–64, the Treasury identified 57 qualifying countries (among those included in the list are the members of the European Union, the Russian Federation, Canada, and Mexico). Nonqualifying countries not on the list include most of the former Soviet republics (except Kazakhstan), Bermuda, and the Netherlands Antilles.

[22] § 1(h)(11)(B)(iii)(I).

[23] See § 246(c) and Chapter 17.

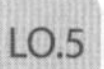

Evaluate the tax impact of property dividends by computing the shareholder's dividend income, basis in the property received, and the effect on the distributing corporation's E & P and taxable income.

19-3c Property Dividends

Although most corporate distributions are cash, a corporation may distribute a **property dividend** for various reasons. For example, shareholders might want a particular property that is held by the corporation. Similarly, a corporation with low cash reserves may still want to distribute a dividend to its shareholders.

Property distributions have the same impact as cash distributions except for effects related to any difference between the basis and the fair market value of the distributed property. In most situations, distributed property is appreciated, so its sale would result in a gain to the corporation. Distributions of property with a basis that differs from fair market value raise several tax questions.

- *For the shareholder:*
  - What is the amount of the distribution?
  - What is the basis of the property in the shareholder's hands?
- *For the corporation:*
  - Is a gain or loss recognized as a result of the distribution?
  - What is the effect of the distribution on E & P?

Property Dividends—Effect on the Shareholder

When a corporation distributes property rather than cash to a shareholder, the amount distributed is measured by the fair market value of the property on the date of distribution.[24] As with a cash distribution, the portion of a property distribution covered by existing E & P is a dividend, with any excess treated as a return of capital. If the fair market value of the property distributed exceeds *both* the corporation's E & P and the shareholder's stock basis, a taxable (capital) gain usually results.

If, as part of the distribution, the shareholder assumes a liability of the corporation or if the property the shareholder receives is subject to a liability (both immediately before and immediately after the distribution), the amount of the distribution is reduced by the liability, but not below zero. The basis of the distributed property for the shareholder is the fair market value of the property on the date of the distribution.

The Big Picture

Example 17

Return to the facts of *The Big Picture* on p. 19-1. Plainwell Ice Cream Corporation distributed property with a $300,000 fair market value and $20,000 adjusted basis to Luis, one of its shareholders. The property was subject to a $100,000 mortgage, which Luis assumed.

As a result, Luis has a distribution of $200,000 [$300,000 (fair market value) − $100,000 (liability)] that is treated as a taxable dividend. The basis of the property to Luis is $300,000.

Example 18

Red Corporation owns 10% of Tan Corporation. Tan has ample E & P to cover any distributions made during the year. One distribution made to Red Corporation consists of a vacant lot with an adjusted basis of $80,000 and a fair market value of $50,000. Red has a taxable dividend of $50,000 (before the dividends received deduction), and its basis in the lot becomes $50,000.

As discussed in the following section, distributing depreciated property is not wise from a tax perspective.

Property Dividends—Effect on the Corporation

All distributions of appreciated property generate gain to the distributing corporation.[25] In effect, a corporation that distributes gain property is treated as if it had sold the property to the shareholder for its fair market value. However, the distributing corporation does *not* recognize loss on distributions of property.

[24] § 301 describes the tax treatment of corporate distributions to shareholders.

[25] § 311 describes how corporations are taxed on distributions.

Refer back to the facts of Example 18. Tan Corporation is not allowed to recognize the $30,000 loss on the property distribution. The $30,000 basis disappears ($50,000 fair market value less $80,000 adjusted basis).

As an alternative, Tan Corporation could sell the vacant lot for $50,000 and use the related $30,000 loss to reduce its taxes. Then Tan could distribute the $50,000 of sales proceeds to its shareholders. Either way, the shareholders end up with property worth $50,000. But by selling the vacant lot and distributing the cash, Tan Corporation benefits by being able to use the $30,000 loss.

The Big Picture

Example 20

Return to the facts of *The Big Picture* on p. 19-1. Plainwell Ice Cream Corporation distributed property with a fair market value of $300,000 and an adjusted basis of $20,000 to Luis, one of its shareholders. As a result, Plainwell recognizes a $280,000 gain on the distribution.

If the distributed property is subject to a liability in excess of basis or the shareholder assumes the liability, a special rule applies. For purposes of determining gain on the distribution, the fair market value of the property is treated as being at least the amount of the liability.[26]

Assume that the land in Example 18 is subject to a liability of $85,000. Tan Corporation recognizes gain of $5,000 on the distribution [$85,000 (liability) − $80,000 (basis of the land)]. Red Corporation has no dividend income (the liability assumed exceeds the fair market value of the land), and its basis in the land is $85,000 (the land's deemed fair market value based on the liability assumed).

Corporate distributions reduce E & P by the amount of money distributed or by the greater of the fair market value or the adjusted basis of property distributed, less the amount of any liability on the property.[27] E & P is increased by gain recognized on appreciated property distributed as a property dividend.

Property Distributions—E & P Impacts

Example 22

Crimson Corporation distributes property (basis of $10,000 and fair market value of $20,000) to Lei, its shareholder. Crimson Corporation recognizes a gain of $10,000. Crimson's E & P is increased by the $10,000 gain and decreased by the $20,000 fair market value of the distribution. Lei has dividend income of $20,000 (presuming sufficient E & P).

Example 23

Assume the same facts as in Example 22, except that Crimson's adjusted basis of the property is $25,000. Because loss is not recognized and the adjusted basis is greater than fair market value, E & P is reduced by $25,000, which is greater than the property's fair market value. Lei reports dividend income of $20,000.

Example 24

Assume the same facts as in Example 23, except that the property is subject to a liability of $6,000, which Lei assumes. E & P is now reduced by $19,000 [$25,000 (adjusted basis) − $6,000 (liability)]. Lei has a dividend of $14,000 [$20,000 (amount of the distribution) − $6,000 (liability)], and her basis in the property is $20,000.

---

[26] §§ 311(b)(2) and 336(b).

[27] §§ 312(a), (b), and (c).

Under no circumstances can a distribution, whether cash or property, either generate a deficit in E & P or add to a deficit in E & P. Deficits can arise only through corporate operations.

Teal Corporation has accumulated E & P of $10,000 at the beginning of the current tax year. During the year, it has current E & P of $15,000. At the end of the year, it distributes cash of $30,000 to Walter, its sole shareholder. Walter's basis in his Teal stock is $18,000.

Teal's E & P at the end of the year is reduced to zero in the following manner: first, the accumulated E & P of $10,000 is increased by current E & P of $15,000, and then this amount is reduced by $25,000 (the amount of the distribution treated as a dividend).

The remaining $5,000 of the distribution to Walter does not reduce E & P because a distribution cannot generate a deficit in E & P. It is treated as a return of capital and reduces Walt's stock basis to $13,000 ($18,000 − $5,000).

The noncash property distribution rules are summarized in Concept Summary 19.3.

Concept Summary 19.3

Noncash Property Distributions

Appreciated Property	Depreciated Property
1. **Regular Tax:** Increase regular taxable income by regular tax gain (difference between FMV and regular tax adjusted basis).	1. **Regular Tax:** No impact on regular taxable income (regular tax loss not recognized).
2. **Current E & P:** Increase current earnings and profits by E & P gain (difference between FMV and E & P adjusted basis).	2. **Current E & P:** Generally, no change in current earnings and profits.
3. **Shareholder(s):** Determine impact of distribution on the shareholder(s).	3. **Shareholder(s):** Determine impact of distribution on the shareholder(s).
4. **End-of-Year E & P:** Decrease earnings and profits by the *fair market value* of property (net of liabilities assumed by the shareholder). As with cash distributions, property distributions cannot create an E & P deficit.	4. **End-of-Year E & P:** Decrease earnings and profits by the *E & P adjusted basis* of property (net of liabilities assumed by the shareholder). As with cash distributions, property distributions cannot create an E & P deficit.
Note: The Internal Revenue Code puts the corporation in the same position as if it had sold the property and distributed the cash.	**Note:** Earnings and profits will reflect the "loss" on the distribution of depreciated property (via the adjusted basis decrease to E & P), but the regular tax loss vanishes.

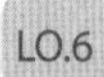

LO.6

Recognize situations when constructive dividends exist, and compute the tax resulting from such dividends.

19-3d Constructive Dividends

An economic benefit provided by a corporation to a shareholder can be treated as a dividend for Federal income tax purposes even though it is not formally declared or identified as a dividend. **Constructive dividends** need not be issued pro rata to all shareholders[28] or satisfy the legal requirements of a dividend.

For tax purposes, constructive distributions are treated the same as actual distributions.[29] As a result, the corporation providing the constructive dividend is not allowed a deduction, corporate shareholders can use the dividends received deduction (see Chapter 17), and noncorporate shareholders receive preferential tax rates (0, 15, or 20 percent) on qualified constructive dividends. The constructive distribution is taxable as a dividend only to the extent of the corporation's current and accumulated E & P; constructive distributions in excess of E & P are treated as a return of capital and then a taxable (capital) gain.

Constructive dividend situations usually arise in closely held corporations. Here, the dealings between the parties are less structured and may not be well documented. The constructive dividend often is intended to convert a nondeductible dividend into some

[28]See *Lengsfield v. Comm.*, 57–1 USTC ¶9437, 50 AFTR 1683, 241 F.2d 508 (CA–5).

[29]*Simon v. Comm.*, 57–2 USTC ¶9989, 52 AFTR 698, 248 F.2d 869 (CA–8).

type of corporate deduction.[30] Alternatively, the shareholders may be seeking benefits for themselves while avoiding the recognition of income.

Although some constructive dividends are disguised dividends, not all are deliberate attempts to avoid dividends; many are inadvertent. As a result, being aware of the most common types of constructive dividends is important; these are summarized briefly below.

Shareholder Use of Corporate-Owned Property

A constructive dividend can occur when a shareholder uses corporation property for personal purposes at no cost. Personal use of corporate-owned automobiles, airplanes, yachts, and facilities used for entertainment (e.g., a lake house that is used for entertaining clients) is commonplace in some closely held corporations. In these situations, the shareholder has dividend income equal to the fair rental value of the property for the period of its personal use.[31]

Bargain Sale of Corporate Property to a Shareholder

Shareholders often purchase property from a corporation at a cost below the fair market value. These bargain sales produce dividend income equal to the difference between the property's fair market value on the date of sale and the amount the shareholder paid for the property.[32]

Bargain Rental of Corporate Property

A bargain rental of corporate property by a shareholder also produces dividend income. Here, the measure of the constructive dividend is the excess of the property's fair rental value over the rent actually paid.

Payments for the Benefit of a Shareholder

If a corporation pays a shareholder's personal expenses (or obligations), these payments are treated as a constructive dividend. Forgiveness of shareholder debt by the corporation also results in a constructive dividend.[33] Excessive rentals paid by a corporation for the use of shareholder property are treated as constructive dividends.

Constructive Dividends—Shareholder Benefit

Example 26

Libby, the president and sole shareholder of Taylor Corporation, is paid an annual salary of $400,000 by the corporation. She is always looking for ways to receive additional benefits from the corporation. However, Libby wants to avoid dividends (because of the effects of double taxation) and has no desire to increase her compensation because she is concerned that additional salary payments might cause the IRS to contend that her salary is unreasonable (see discussion that follows).

Libby has been considering donating $50,000 to her alma mater to establish scholarships for needy students. Taylor Corporation could make the contribution instead of Libby. The payment clearly benefits Libby, but the amount of the contribution is not taxed to her.[34] Taylor Corporation claims a charitable contribution deduction for the payment.

Assume in Example 26 that Libby has made an individual pledge to the university to provide $50,000 for scholarships for needy students. Taylor Corporation satisfies Libby's obligation by paying the $50,000 to the university. The $50,000 will be taxed to Libby.[35] In this context, the $50,000 payment to the university may be treated as indirect compensation to Libby.

continued

[30] Recall that dividend distributions do not provide the distributing corporation with an income tax deduction, although they do reduce E & P.

[31] See *Daniel L. Reeves*, 94 TCM 287, T.C.Memo. 2007–273.

[32] Reg. § 1.301–1(j).

[33] Reg. § 1.301–1(m).

[34] *Henry J. Knott*, 67 T.C. 681 (1977), *acq.* 1979–2 C.B. 2.

[35] *Schalk Chemical Co. v. Comm.*, 62–1 USTC ¶9496, 9 AFTR 2d 1579, 304 F.2d 48 (CA–9).

In determining whether Libby's salary is unreasonable, both the *direct* salary payment of $400,000 and the *indirect* $50,000 payment are considered. Libby's total compensation package is $450,000. Libby may be eligible for a charitable contribution deduction of up to 50% of her adjusted gross income.

Unreasonable Compensation

A salary payment to a shareholder-employee that is determined to be **unreasonable compensation** is frequently treated as a constructive dividend and, as a result, is not deductible by the corporation. Whether compensation is reasonable or not depends on all the facts and circumstances. In determining the reasonableness of salary payments, the following factors have been used by courts:[36]

- The employee's qualifications.
- A comparison of salaries with dividend distributions.
- The prevailing rates of compensation for comparable positions in comparable business concerns.
- The nature and scope of the employee's work.
- The size and complexity of the business.
- A comparison of salaries paid with both gross and net income.
- The taxpayer's salary policy toward all employees.
- For small corporations with a limited number of officers, the amount of compensation paid to the employee in question in previous years.
- Whether a shareholder, acting in the best interests of the corporation, would have agreed to the level of compensation paid.

The last factor above, known as the "reasonable investor test," has been used in different ways by different courts.[37] In some cases, the Seventh Circuit Court of Appeals has relied solely on the reasonable investor test in determining reasonableness. On the other hand, the Tenth Circuit Court of Appeals has largely ignored this factor. Other Federal circuits have used an approach that considers all of the factors in the list.[38]

Ultimately, this is a challenging area. Taxpayers, the IRS, and the courts apply these factors in different ways to support conclusions that often differ. Taxpayers should keep good records and be prepared to defend their conclusions.

Loans to Shareholders

Advances to shareholders that are not bona fide loans usually are reclassified as constructive dividends. As with the reasonableness of compensation, whether an advance qualifies as a bona fide loan depends on all the facts and circumstances. Factors considered in determining whether an advance is a bona fide loan include the following:[39]

- Whether the advance is on open account or is evidenced by a written instrument.
- Whether the shareholder furnished collateral or other security for the advance.
- How long the advance has been outstanding.
- Whether any repayments have been made.
- The shareholder's ability to repay the advance.
- The shareholder's use of the funds (e.g., payment of routine bills versus nonrecurring, extraordinary expenses).

---

[36]All but the final factor in this list are identified in *Mayson Manufacturing Co. v. Comm.*, 49–2 USTC ¶9467, 38 AFTR 1028, 178 F.2d 115 (CA–6).

[37]For example, see *Alpha Medical, Inc. v. Comm.*, 99–1 USTC ¶50,461, 83 AFTR 2d 99–1922, 172 F.3d 942 (CA–6).

[38]See *Vitamin Village, Inc.*, 94 TCM 278, T.C.Memo. 2007–272, for an example of a case that uses the reasonable investor test and other factors.

[39]*Fin Hay Realty Co. v. U.S.*, 68–2 USTC ¶9438, 22 AFTR 2d 5004, 398 F.2d 694 (CA–3). But see *Nariman Teymourian*, 90 TCM 352, T.C.Memo. 2005–232, for an example of how planning can avoid constructive dividends in the shareholder loan context.

- The regularity of the advances.
- The dividend-paying history of the corporation.

Even when a corporation makes a bona fide loan to a shareholder, a constructive dividend may be triggered if the loan is interest-free (or carries a very low rate of interest). In this case, the constructive dividend is equal to the amount of imputed (forgone) interest on the loan.[40] Imputed interest equals the amount by which the interest paid by the Federal government on new borrowings, compounded semiannually, exceeds the interest charged on the loan.

When the imputed interest provision applies, the shareholder is deemed to have made an interest payment to the corporation equal to the amount of imputed interest and the corporation is deemed to have repaid the imputed interest to the shareholder through a constructive dividend. As a result, the corporation receives interest income and makes a nondeductible dividend payment, and the shareholder has taxable dividend income that might be offset with an interest deduction.

Example 28

Mallard Corporation lends its principal shareholder, Henry, $100,000 on January 2 of the current year. The loan is interest-free and payable on demand. On December 31, the imputed interest rules are applied. Assuming that the Federal rate is 2%, compounded semiannually, the amount of imputed interest for the year is $2,010. This amount is deemed paid by Henry to Mallard in the form of interest. Mallard then is deemed to return the amount to Henry as a constructive dividend.

As a result, Henry has dividend income of $2,010, which might be offset with a deduction for the interest paid to Mallard. Mallard has interest income of $2,010 for the interest received, with no offsetting deduction for the dividend payment.

Loans to a Corporation by Shareholders

Shareholder loans to a corporation may be reclassified as equity because the debt has too many features of stock. Any interest and principal payments made by the corporation to the shareholder are then treated as constructive dividends. This topic is covered more thoroughly in Chapter 18 (see text Section 18-2b and the discussion of "the thin capitalization problem").

19-3e Stock Dividends and Stock Rights

LO.7

Determine the tax implications arising from receipt of stock dividends and stock rights and the shareholder's basis in the stock and stock rights received.

Stock Dividends—§ 305

In general, **stock dividends** are excluded from income on the theory that the ownership interest of the shareholder is unchanged as a result of the distribution.[41]

When a stock dividend is declared, the shareholder ends up with additional shares of stock but retains the same total stock basis. As a result, the shareholder's basis is reallocated across both the original shares and the new shares.[42] In total, the basis remains the same, but the *per-share* basis decreases.

Example 29

Green Corporation declares a 10% stock dividend when its stock is selling for $100 per share. As a result of the stock dividend, the per-share stock value declines to $90.91 (Green's market capitalization remains the same, but it is spread over 10% more shares). Jennifer owns 100 shares of Green and has a basis of $1,100 for those shares. Jennifer receives 10 shares as a result of the stock dividend. How does the stock dividend affect Jennifer?

1. The stock dividend does not generate gross income to Jennifer (and has no impact on Green Corporation's taxable income or E & P).
2. Before the stock dividend, Jennifer had 100 shares and a basis of $11 per share ($1,100 ÷ 100).
3. After the stock dividend, Jennifer has the same total basis ($1,100), but it is now allocated over the original shares plus the shares received in the stock dividend.
4. Each share of Jennifer's stock now has a basis of $10 ($1,100 ÷ 110 shares).

---

[40]See § 7872.

[41]§ 305(a). See *Eisner v. Macomber*, 1 USTC ¶32, 3 AFTR 3020, 40 S.Ct. 189 (1920).

[42]§ 307(a).

Stock splits—a more common occurrence—are treated in the same way as a stock dividend. So a 4-for-1 stock split provides a shareholder with three additional shares for each share held before the split. Total basis of the original shares is reallocated across all shares after the split. This means that each share carries one-quarter the per-share basis of the original shares.

Assume the same information as in Example 29, except that Green Corporation declares a 4-for-1 stock split. After the split, Jennifer will own 400 shares, but her total basis remains $1,100. So her per-share basis is $2.75 ($1,100 ÷ 400 shares).

If the dividend stock is not identical to the underlying shares (e.g., a stock dividend of preferred on common), basis is determined by allocating the basis of the formerly held shares between the old and new stock according to the fair market value of each. The holding period includes the holding period of the formerly held stock.[43]

Gail bought 1,000 shares of common stock two years ago for $10,000. In the current tax year, Gail receives a nontaxable preferred stock dividend of 100 shares. The preferred stock has a fair market value of $1,000, and the common stock, on which the preferred is distributed, has a fair market value of $19,000.

After the receipt of the stock dividend, the basis of the common stock is $9,500 and the basis of the preferred is $500, computed as follows:

Fair market value of common	$19,000
Fair market value of preferred	1,000
	$20,000
Basis of common: $\frac{19}{20}$ × $10,000	$ 9,500
Basis of preferred: $\frac{1}{20}$ × $10,000	$ 500

Recognizing that some distributions of stock could affect ownership interests, Congress added rules that tax stock dividends in certain situations.[44] The § 305 rules are based on the proportionate interest concept. Under the general rule, illustrated above, stock dividends are excluded from income if they are pro rata stock distributions paid on common stock.

If the stock dividend is a disproportionate distribution, the stock dividend is taxable. For example, a stock dividend where some common shareholders receive common stock and other common shareholders receive preferred stock would be a disproportionate distribution. The same is true if preferred shareholders received a common stock dividend.

If a stock dividend is determined to be taxable, the fair market value of the shares received is included in the shareholder's gross income. The shareholder's basis for the newly received shares is fair market value, and the holding period starts on the date of receipt. Since taxable stock dividends are rarely encountered in practice, we have chosen not to discuss the technical intricacies of § 305(b).

If stock dividends are not taxable, the corporation's E & P is not reduced.[45] If the stock dividends are taxable, the distributing corporation treats the distribution in the same manner as any other taxable property dividend.

Stock Rights

The rules for determining taxability of **stock rights** are identical to those for determining taxability of stock dividends. If the rights are taxable, the recipient has income equal to the fair market value of the rights. The fair market value then becomes the shareholder-distributee's basis in the rights.[46] If the rights are exercised, the holding period for the new stock begins on the date the rights (whether taxable or nontaxable) are exercised. The basis of the new stock is the basis of the rights plus the amount of any other consideration given.

If stock rights are not taxable and the value of the rights is less than 15 percent of the value of the old stock, the basis of the rights is zero. However, the shareholder may elect to have some of the basis in the formerly held stock allocated to the rights.[47] The

[43] § 1223(5).
[44] § 305(b); see "Stock Dividends," Senate Report 91–552 (H.R. 13270).
[45] § 312(d)(1).
[46] Reg. § 1.305–1(b).
[47] § 307(b)(1).

election is made by attaching a statement to the shareholder's return for the year in which the rights are received.[48] If the fair market value of the rights is 15 percent or more of the value of the old stock and the rights are exercised or sold, the shareholder *must* allocate some of the basis in the formerly held stock to the rights.

Example 32

A corporation with common stock outstanding declares a nontaxable dividend payable in rights to subscribe to common stock. Each right entitles the holder to purchase one share of stock for $90. One right is issued for every two shares of stock owned. Fred owns 400 shares of stock purchased two years ago for $15,000. At the time of the distribution of the rights, the market value of the common stock is $100 per share, and the market value of the rights is $8 per right. Fred receives 200 rights. He exercises 100 rights and sells the remaining 100 rights three months later for $9 per right.

Fred need not allocate the cost of the original stock to the rights because the value of the rights is less than 15% of the value of the stock ($1,600 ÷ $40,000 = 4%). If Fred does not allocate his original stock basis to the rights, the tax consequences are as follows:

- Basis of the new stock is $9,000 [$90 (exercise price) × 100 (shares)]. The holding period of the new stock begins on the date the stock was purchased.
- Sale of the rights produces long-term capital gain of $900 [$9 (sales price) × 100 (rights)]. The holding period of the rights starts with the date the original 400 shares of stock were acquired.

If Fred elects to allocate basis to the rights, the tax consequences are as follows:

- Basis of the stock is $14,423 [$40,000 (value of stock) ÷ $41,600 (value of rights and stock) × $15,000 (cost of stock)].
- Basis of the rights is $577 [$1,600 (value of rights) ÷ $41,600 (value of rights and stock) × $15,000 (cost of stock)].
- When Fred exercises the rights, his basis for the new stock will be $9,288.50 [$9,000 (cost) + $288.50 (basis for 100 rights)].
- Sale of the rights would produce a long-term capital gain of $611.50 [$900 (sales price) − $288.50 (basis in the remaining 100 rights)].

19-4 Stock Redemptions

LO.8

Identify the stock redemptions that qualify for sale or exchange treatment.

19-4a Overview

When a shareholder sells stock to an unrelated third party, the transaction typically is treated as a sale or exchange. Here, the amount realized is offset by the shareholder's stock basis and a capital gain (or loss) results. Effectively, the Code treats the proceeds as a return *of* the shareholder's stock investment.

The Big Picture

Example 33

Return to the facts of *The Big Picture* on p. 19-1. Assume that Luis sells some of his shares of Plainwell Ice Cream Corporation stock (basis of $80,000) to a third party for $1,200,000.

If the transaction is treated as a sale or exchange (a return *of* the owner's stock investment), Luis has a long-term capital gain of $1,120,000 [$1,200,000 (amount realized) − $80,000 (stock basis)].

In a **stock redemption**, where a shareholder sells stock back to the issuing corporation, the transaction can have the *effect* of a dividend distribution (rather than a sale or exchange). This is particularly the case when the stock of the corporation is closely held. For instance, consider a redemption of stock from a sole shareholder. Here, the shareholder's ownership interest is not affected by the stock redemption (the shareholder owns 100 percent of the corporation's outstanding shares before *and* after the transaction). If these redemptions were granted sale or exchange treatment, dividend distributions could be avoided entirely. Instead of formally distributing dividends, the corporation could redeem stock whenever corporate cash was desired by shareholders. Nontaxable stock dividends then could be used to replenish shares as needed.

[48] § 307(b)(2) and Reg. § 1.307–2.

The key distinction between a sale of stock to an unrelated third party and some stock redemptions is the effect of the transaction on the shareholder's ownership interest in the corporation. In a sale of stock to an unrelated third party, the shareholder's ownership interest in the corporation is reduced ("diminished"). In the case of many stock redemptions, however, there is little or no change to the shareholder's ownership interest. In general, if a shareholder's ownership interest is *not* reduced as a result of a stock redemption, the Code will treat the transaction as a dividend distribution (a return *from* the shareholder's stock investment).

The Big Picture

Example 34

Return to the facts of *The Big Picture* on p. 19-1. Assume that Plainwell Ice Cream Corporation redeems some of Luis's shares in the corporation (basis of $80,000) for $1,200,000.

If the transaction is treated as a sale or exchange (a return *of* the owner's stock investment), Luis has a long-term capital gain of $1,120,000 [$1,200,000 (amount realized) − $80,000 (stock basis)].

However, if the redemption is treated as a dividend distribution (a return *from* the owner's stock investment), Luis has $1,200,000 of dividend income (assuming adequate E & P).

The Code does allow sale or exchange treatment for *certain* kinds of stock redemptions. In these transactions, as a general rule, the shareholder's ownership interest is reduced as a result of the redemption. (The requirements for qualifying stock redemptions are provided later in this chapter.)

Stock redemptions occur for a variety of reasons. Publicly traded corporations often reacquire their shares in order to increase shareholder value. For corporations where the stock is closely held, redemptions frequently occur to achieve shareholder objectives. For instance, a closely held corporation might use a redemption to acquire the stock of a deceased shareholder. Using corporate funds to purchase the stock from the decedent's estate means that the remaining shareholders do not need to use their own money to acquire the stock. Stock redemptions also occur as a result of property settlements when a divorce occurs. When spouses jointly own a controlling stock interest in a corporation, a divorce decree may require that the interest of one spouse be bought out. A redemption accomplishes this without using the other spouse's personal assets. Stock redemptions also are frequently incorporated into buy-sell agreements between shareholders. This allows a corporation to redeem (purchase) the stock of a shareholder who wants to end their ownership in the corporation.

Noncorporate shareholders generally prefer to have a stock redemption treated as a sale or exchange rather than as a dividend distribution. As Examples 35 and 36 illustrate, a stock redemption that qualifies for sale or exchange treatment is preferred because it results in *both* the tax-free recovery of the redeemed stock's basis and the ability to offset any capital gain against capital losses. In a nonqualified stock redemption, the *entire* distribution (assuming adequate E & P) is taxed as dividend income and cannot be offset by capital losses. For individual taxpayers, the tax rate for long-term capital gains and qualified dividend income is 0, 15, or 20 percent depending on the taxpayer's taxable income.[49]

Qualifying and Nonqualified Redemptions Compared

Example 35

Abby, an individual in the 32% tax bracket, acquired stock in Quail Corporation four years ago for $80,000. In the current year, Quail Corporation (E & P of $1,000,000) redeems her shares for $170,000. If the redemption qualifies for sale or exchange treatment, Abby will have a long-term capital gain of $90,000 [$170,000 (redemption amount) − $80,000 (basis)]. Her income tax liability on the $90,000 gain will be $13,500 ($90,000 × 15%).

If the stock redemption does not qualify as a sale or exchange, the entire distribution will be treated as a dividend and her income tax liability will be $25,500 ($170,000 × 15%). Thus, Abby will save $12,000 ($25,500 − $13,500) in income taxes if the transaction is a qualifying stock redemption.

[49] A 3.8% additional tax on net investment income of certain high-income taxpayers applies to capital gains and dividend income.

Global Tax Issues **Foreign Shareholders Prefer Sale or Exchange Treatment in Stock Redemptions**

As a general rule, foreign shareholders are subject to U.S. tax on dividend income from U.S. corporations but not on capital gains from the sale of U.S. stock.

In some situations, a nonresident alien is taxed on a capital gain from the disposition of stock in a U.S. corporation, but only if the stock was effectively connected with the conduct of a U.S. trade or business of the individual. Foreign corporations are similarly taxed on gains from the sale of U.S. stock investments.

Whether a stock redemption qualifies for sale or exchange treatment therefore takes on added significance for foreign shareholders. If one of the qualifying stock redemption rules can be satisfied, the foreign shareholder typically will avoid U.S. tax on the transaction. If, instead, dividend income is the result, a 30 percent withholding tax typically applies. For further details, see Chapter 27.

Qualifying and Nonqualified Redemptions Compared

Example 36

Assume in Example 35 that Abby has a capital loss carryover of $60,000 in the current tax year. If the transaction is a qualifying stock redemption, Abby can offset the entire $60,000 capital loss carryover against her $90,000 long-term capital gain. As a result, only $30,000 of the gain will be taxed and her income tax liability will be only $4,500 ($30,000 × 15%).

On the other hand, if the transaction does not qualify for sale or exchange treatment, the entire $170,000 will be taxed as a dividend at 15%. In addition, assuming that she has no capital gains in the current year, Abby will be able to deduct only $3,000 of the $60,000 capital loss carryover to offset her ordinary income.

In contrast, *corporate* shareholders normally receive more favorable tax treatment from a dividend distribution. As a result, most corporations would prefer a *nonqualifying* stock redemption. Corporate taxpayers typically report only a portion of a dividend distribution as taxable income because of the dividends received deduction (see Chapter 17). In addition, corporations do not have a preferential tax rate on dividend and long-term capital gain income. As a result, tax planning for stock redemptions must consider the different preferences of corporate and noncorporate shareholders.

Example 37

Assume in Example 35 that Abby is a calendar year C corporation, that the stock represents a 40% ownership interest in Quail Corporation, and that in the current year Abby has corporate taxable income of $850,000 before the redemption transaction. If the transaction is a qualifying stock redemption, Abby will have a long-term capital gain of $90,000 that will be subject to tax at 21%, or $18,900.

On the other hand, if the $170,000 distribution is treated as a dividend, Abby will have a dividends received deduction of $110,500 ($170,000 × 65%); so only $59,500 of the payment will be taxed. Consequently, Abby's tax liability on the transaction will be only $12,495 ($59,500 × 21%).

When a qualifying stock redemption results in a *loss* to a shareholder rather than a gain, § 267 disallows loss recognition if the shareholder owns (directly or indirectly) more than 50 percent of the corporation's stock.

A shareholder's basis in any property received in a stock redemption, qualifying or nonqualified, generally will be the property's fair market value on the date of the redemption. The holding period of the property also begins on that date.

The Code establishes the criteria for determining whether a transaction is a qualifying stock redemption for tax purposes. Code § 302(b) provides four types of qualifying stock redemptions. In addition, § 303 allows certain distributions of property to an estate in exchange for a deceased shareholder's stock to be treated as a qualifying stock redemption. Each of these five types of qualifying redemptions is discussed later in this section.

19-4b **Historical Background**

Under prior law, the *dividend equivalency rule* was used to determine which stock redemptions qualified for sale or exchange treatment. Under that rule, if the facts and circumstances of a redemption indicated that it was essentially equivalent to a dividend, the redemption did not qualify for sale or exchange treatment. Instead, the amount received by the shareholder was taxed as dividend income to the extent of the corporation's E & P.

The uncertainty and subjectivity surrounding the dividend equivalency rule led Congress to enact several objective tests for determining the status of a redemption. Five types of stock redemptions qualify for sale or exchange treatment:

- Distributions not essentially equivalent to a dividend ("not essentially equivalent redemptions"; see text Section 19-4d).
- Distributions substantially disproportionate in terms of shareholder effect ("disproportionate redemptions"; see text Section 19-4e).
- Distributions in complete termination of a shareholder's interest ("complete termination redemptions"; see text Section 19-4f).
- Distributions to noncorporate shareholders in partial liquidation of a corporation ("partial liquidations"; see text Section 19-4g).
- Distributions to pay a shareholder's death taxes ("redemptions to pay death taxes"; see text Section 19-4h).

Concept Summary 19.4 summarizes the requirements for each of the qualifying stock redemptions.

Concept Summary 19.4

Summary of the Qualifying Stock Redemption Rules

Type of Redemption	Requirements to Qualify
Not essentially equivalent to a dividend [§ 302(b)(1)]	Meaningful reduction in the shareholder's voting interest. Reduction in the shareholder's right to share in earnings or in assets upon liquidation also is considered. Stock attribution rules apply.
Substantially disproportionate [§ 302(b)(2)]	Shareholder's interest in the corporation, after the redemption, must be less than 80% of interest before the redemption *and* less than 50% of the total combined voting power of all classes of stock entitled to vote. Stock attribution rules apply.
Complete termination [§ 302(b)(3)]	Entire stock ownership terminated. In general, stock attribution rules apply. However, *family* attribution rules are waived when the former shareholder has no interest, other than as a creditor, in the corporation for at least 10 years after the redemption and files an agreement to notify the IRS of any prohibited interest acquired during the 10-year period. Shareholder must retain all necessary records during the 10-year period.
Partial liquidation [§ 302(b)(4)]	Not essentially equivalent to a dividend. • Genuine contraction of corporation's business. • Termination of a business. ➤ Corporation has two or more qualified trades or businesses. ➤ Corporation terminates one qualified trade or business while continuing another qualified trade or business. Distribution may be in form of cash or property. Redemption may be pro rata. Stock attribution rules do not apply.
Redemption to pay death taxes [§ 303]	Value of the stock of one corporation in the gross estate exceeds 35% of the value of the adjusted gross estate. Redemption limited to the sum of death taxes and funeral and administration expenses. Generally tax-free because the estate's tax basis of stock is FMV on the date of the decedent's death and the value is unchanged at redemption. Stock attribution rules do not apply.

19-4c Stock Attribution Rules

As explained earlier, to qualify for sale or exchange treatment, a stock redemption generally must result in a reduction in the shareholder's ownership interest in the corporation. In determining whether a stock redemption has sufficiently reduced a shareholder's interest, the stock owned by certain related parties is attributed to the redeeming shareholder.[50]

Congress created stock **attribution** rules to serve this purpose. Under these rules, related parties are defined to include the following family members: spouses, children, grandchildren, and parents. Attribution also takes place *from* and *to* partnerships, estates, trusts, and corporations (50 percent or more ownership required in the case of regular corporations). Exhibit 19.1 summarizes the stock attribution rules.

The Big Picture

Return to the facts of *The Big Picture* on p. 19-1. Assume instead that Luis owns 30% (rather than 50%) of the stock in Plainwell Ice Cream Corporation and his two children own 20% of the Plainwell stock. For purposes of the stock attribution rules, Luis is treated as owning 50% of the stock in Plainwell Ice Cream Corporation. He owns 30% directly and, because of the family attribution rules, 20% indirectly through his children.

Chris owns 40% of the stock in Gray Corporation. The other 60% is owned by a partnership in which Chris has a 20% interest. Chris is deemed to own 52% of Gray Corporation: 40% directly and, because of the partnership interest, 12% indirectly (20% × 60%).

As discussed later, the *family* attribution rules (refer to Example 38) can be waived in the case of some complete termination redemptions. In addition, the stock attribution rules do not apply to partial liquidations or redemptions to pay death taxes.

When a redemption *fails* to satisfy any of the qualifying stock redemption rules, the basis of the redeemed shares does not disappear. Typically, the basis will attach to the basis of the redeeming shareholder's remaining shares in the corporation. If, however, the redeeming shareholder has terminated their direct stock ownership and the redemption is nonqualified due to the attribution rules, the basis of the redeemed shares will attach to the basis of the constructively owned stock.[51] In this manner, a nonqualified stock redemption can result in stock basis being shifted from one taxpayer (the redeeming shareholder) to another taxpayer (the shareholder related under the attribution rules).

Exhibit 19.1 Stock Attribution Rules

	Deemed or Constructive Ownership
• Family	An individual is deemed to own the stock owned by their spouse, children, grandchildren, and parents (not siblings or grandparents).
• Partnership	A partner is deemed to own the stock owned by a partnership to the extent of the partner's proportionate interest in the partnership.
	Stock owned by a partner is deemed to be owned in full by a partnership.
• Estate or trust	A beneficiary or an heir is deemed to own the stock owned by an estate or a trust to the extent of the beneficiary's or heir's proportionate interest in the estate or trust.
	Stock owned by a beneficiary or an heir is deemed to be owned in full by an estate or a trust.
• Corporation	Stock owned by a regular corporation is deemed to be owned proportionately by any shareholder owning 50% or more of the corporation's stock.
	Stock owned by a shareholder who owns 50% or more of a regular corporation is deemed to be owned in full by the corporation.

[50] § 318.

[51] Reg. § 1.302–2(c).

Sanjay and Kiran, a married couple, each own 50 shares in Grouse Corporation, representing 100% of the corporation's stock. All of the stock was purchased for $50,000. Both Sanjay and Kiran serve as directors of the corporation. The corporation redeems Sanjay's 50 shares, but he continues to serve as a director of the corporation. The redemption is treated as a dividend distribution (assuming adequate E & P) because Sanjay constructively owns Kiran's stock, or 100% of the Grouse stock outstanding. Sanjay's $25,000 basis in the 50 shares redeemed attaches to Kiran's stock; as a result, Kiran now has a basis of $50,000 in the 50 shares she owns in Grouse.

Concept Summary 19.5 reviews the major tax consequences of stock redemptions to shareholders.

Concept Summary 19.5

Tax Consequences of Stock Redemptions to Shareholders

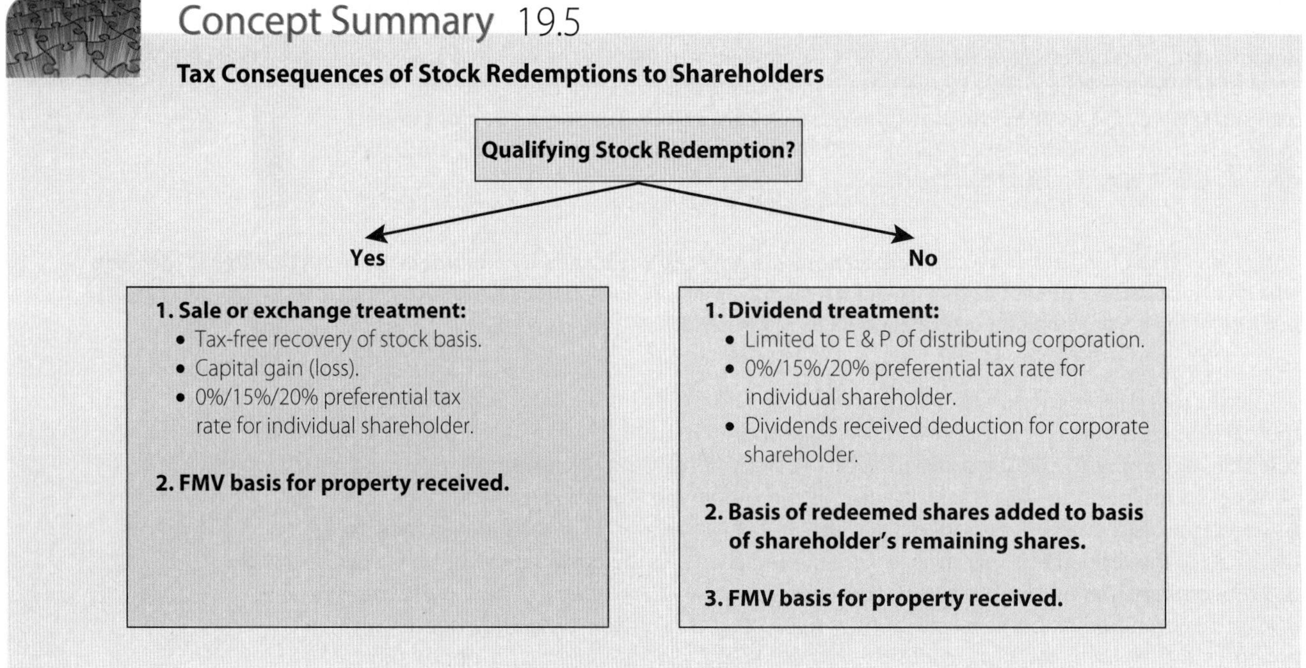

19-4d **Not Essentially Equivalent Redemptions**

Under § 302(b)(1), a redemption qualifies for sale or exchange treatment if it is "not essentially equivalent to a dividend." This is a continuation of the dividend equivalency rule. It was retained principally for redemptions of preferred stock because preferred shareholders often have no control over when corporations redeem preferred stock.[52] Like its predecessor, the **not essentially equivalent redemption** is a subjective test. Each case must be resolved based on all the facts and circumstances.[53]

Based upon the Supreme Court's decision in *U.S. v. Davis*,[54] a redemption will qualify as a not essentially equivalent redemption only when the shareholder's interest in the redeeming corporation has been meaningfully reduced. In determining whether the **meaningful reduction test** has been met, the stock attribution rules apply. A decrease in the redeeming shareholder's voting control appears to be the most significant indicator of a meaningful reduction,[55] but reductions in the rights of the shareholders to share in corporate earnings or to receive corporate assets on liquidation also are considered.[56]

[52] See S.Rept. No. 1622, 83d Cong., 2d Sess. 44 (1954).

[53] Reg. § 1.302–2(b)(1).

[54] 70–1 USTC ¶9289, 25 AFTR 2d 70–827, 90 S.Ct. 1041.

[55] See, for example, *Jack Paparo*, 71 T.C. 692 (1979).

[56] See, for example, *Grabowski Trust*, 58 T.C. 650 (1972).

Meaningful Reduction Test

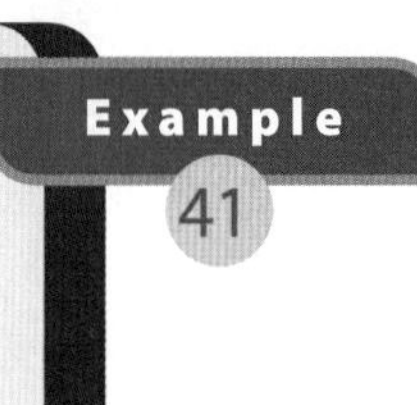

Pat owns 58% of the common stock of Falcon Corporation. As a result of a redemption of some of his stock, Pat's ownership interest in Falcon is reduced to 51%.

Because Pat continues to have voting control over Falcon after the redemption, the distribution is treated as essentially equivalent to a dividend. As a result, the entire amount of the distribution is treated as a dividend (assuming adequate E & P).

Maroon Corporation redeems 2% of its stock from Maria. Before the redemption, Maria owned 10% of Maroon Corporation. In this case, the redemption *may* qualify as a not essentially equivalent redemption. Maria experiences a reduction in her voting rights, her right to participate in current earnings and accumulated surplus, and her right to share in net assets upon liquidation.

19-4e **Disproportionate Redemptions**

A stock redemption qualifies for sale or exchange treatment under § 302(b)(2) as a **disproportionate redemption** if *both* of the following conditions are met:

- After the distribution, the shareholder owns *less than* 80 percent of the interest owned in the corporation before the redemption.
- After the distribution, the shareholder owns *less than* 50 percent of the total combined voting power of all classes of stock entitled to vote.

In determining a shareholder's ownership interest before and after a redemption, the attribution rules apply. Compare Examples 43 and 44.

Disproportionate Redemption Tests

Example 43

Paulina, Carl, and Dan, unrelated individuals, own 30 shares, 30 shares, and 40 shares, respectively, in Wren Corporation. Wren has 100 shares outstanding and E & P of $200,000. The corporation redeems 20 shares of Dan's stock for $30,000. Dan paid $200 a share for the stock two years ago. Dan's ownership in Wren Corporation before and after the redemption is as follows:

	Total Shares	Dan's Ownership	Ownership Percentage	80% of Original Ownership
Before redemption	100	40	40% (40 ÷ 100)	32% (80% × 40%)
After redemption	80	20	25% (20 ÷ 80)*	

*Note that the denominator of the fraction is reduced after the redemption (from 100 to 80).

Dan's 25% ownership after the redemption meets both tests of § 302(b)(2). It is less than 80% of his original ownership and less than 50% of the total voting power. The distribution qualifies as a disproportionate redemption and receives sale or exchange treatment. As a result, Dan has a long-term capital gain of $26,000 [$30,000 − $4,000 (20 shares × $200)].

Example 44

Assume in Example 43 that Carl and Dan are father and son. In this case, the redemption would *not* qualify for sale or exchange treatment because of the *attribution rules*. Dan is deemed to own Carl's stock before and after the redemption. Dan's ownership in Wren Corporation before and after the redemption is as follows:

	Total Shares	Dan's Direct Ownership	Carl's Ownership	Dan's Direct and Indirect Ownership	Ownership Percentage	80% of Original Ownership
Before redemption	100	40	30	70	70% (70 ÷ 100)	56% (80% × 70%)
After redemption	80	20	30	50	62.5% (50 ÷ 80)	

continued

Dan's direct and indirect ownership of 62.5% fails to meet either of the tests of § 302(b)(2). After the redemption, Dan owns more than 80% of his original ownership and more than 50% of the voting stock. As a result, the redemption does not qualify for sale or exchange treatment and results in a dividend distribution of $30,000 to Dan. The basis in the 20 shares redeemed is added to Dan's basis in his remaining 20 shares.

A redemption that does not qualify as a disproportionate redemption may still qualify as a not essentially equivalent redemption if it meets the meaningful reduction test (see Example 42).

19-4f Complete Termination Redemptions

A redemption that terminates a shareholder's *entire* stock ownership in a corporation qualifies for sale or exchange treatment under § 302(b)(3). The attribution rules generally apply in determining whether the shareholder's stock ownership has been completely terminated. However, the *family* attribution rules do not apply to a **complete termination redemption** if *both* of the following conditions are met:

- The former shareholder does not hold or acquire any interest, other than that of a creditor, in the corporation for at least 10 years after the redemption (including an interest as an officer, a director, or an employee). This is called a "prohibited interest."
- The former shareholder files a statement agreeing to notify the IRS within 30 days if a prohibited interest is acquired in the 10-year postredemption period and retains all records related to the redemption during this time period.

The acquisition of stock in the corporation by bequest or inheritance is not a prohibited interest. The required statement must be signed by the former shareholder and attached to the tax return for the year in which the redemption occurs.[57]

Family Attribution Waiver

Example 45

Kevin owns 50% of the stock in Green Corporation, and the remaining interests in Green are held as follows: 40% by Jennifer (Kevin's spouse) and 10% by Carmen (a key employee). Green redeems all of Kevin's stock for its fair market value. As a result, Jennifer and Carmen are the only remaining shareholders, now owning 80% and 20%, respectively.

If the two requirements for the family attribution waiver are met, the transaction will qualify as a complete termination redemption and will result in sale or exchange treatment. If the waiver requirements are not satisfied, Kevin will be deemed to own Jennifer's (his spouse's) stock and the entire distribution will be taxed as a dividend (assuming adequate E & P).

Assume in Example 45 that Kevin qualifies for the family attribution waiver for the redemption. In the year of the redemption, Kevin treats the transaction as a sale or exchange. However, if he purchases Carmen's stock seven years after the redemption, he has acquired a prohibited interest and the redemption distribution is reclassified as a dividend. Kevin must notify the IRS and will owe additional taxes due to this revised treatment.

19-4g Partial Liquidations

Under § 302(b)(4), a *noncorporate* shareholder receives sale or exchange treatment for a distribution that qualifies as a **partial liquidation**. A partial liquidation is a distribution that (1) is *not essentially equivalent to a dividend* and (2) is both pursuant to a plan and made within the plan year or within the succeeding taxable year. A stock redemption pursuant to a partial liquidation may be pro rata with respect to the shareholders. In the case of a pro rata distribution, an actual surrender of stock is not required to qualify the transaction as a partial liquidation.[58]

[57] Reg. § 1.302–4(a).

[58] See *Fowler Hosiery Co. v. Comm.*, 62–1 USTC ¶9407, 9 AFTR 2d 1252, 301 F.2d 394 (CA–7); and Rev.Rul. 90–13.

In determining whether a distribution is not essentially equivalent to a dividend, the effect of the distribution on the *corporation* is examined.[59] Consequently, to qualify as a partial liquidation, the distribution must result in a *genuine contraction* of the business of the corporation.

Dove Corporation owned a building with seven floors. Part of the building was rented, and part was used directly in Dove's business. A fire destroyed the two top floors, and Dove received insurance proceeds in reimbursement for the damage sustained. For business reasons, Dove did not rebuild the two floors and, instead, chose to operate on a smaller scale than before the fire.

Pursuant to a plan adopted in the current year, Dove uses the insurance proceeds to redeem some stock from its noncorporate shareholders. Because a genuine contraction of the business occurs, the distribution is not essentially equivalent to a dividend and qualifies as a partial liquidation.[60]

Applying the genuine contraction of a corporate business concept has proved difficult due to the lack of objective tests. The IRS has ruled that neither the sale of investments nor the sale of excess inventory will satisfy the genuine contraction test.[61] Because the genuine contraction test is subjective, taxpayers should seek a favorable ruling from the IRS before proceeding.

A safe-harbor rule, the *termination of a business* test, will satisfy the "not essentially equivalent to a dividend" requirement. A distribution will qualify under the termination of a business test if all of the following conditions are met:

- The corporation has two or more qualified trades or businesses. A qualified trade or business is any trade or business that (1) has been actively conducted for the five-year period ending on the date of the distribution and (2) was not acquired in a taxable transaction during that five-year period.
- The distribution consists of the assets of a qualified trade or business or the proceeds from the sale of such assets.
- The corporation is actively engaged in the conduct of a qualified trade or business immediately after the distribution.

Swan Corporation, the owner and operator of a wholesale grocery business with a substantial amount of excess cash, purchased a freight-hauling concern. Six years later, Swan distributes the freight-hauling assets in kind on a pro rata basis to its shareholders.

The distribution satisfies the termination of a business test. Swan had conducted both businesses for at least five years and continues to conduct the wholesale grocery business.

As a result, for noncorporate shareholders, the distribution qualifies as a partial liquidation and is treated as a sale or exchange. For Swan's corporate shareholders, the distribution will be taxed as dividend income (assuming adequate E & P).

19-4h **Redemptions to Pay Death Taxes**

Code § 303 provides sale or exchange treatment to a redemption of stock included in, and representing a substantial part of, a decedent's gross estate. This provision provides an estate with liquidity to pay death-related expenses when a significant portion of the estate consists of stock in a closely held corporation.

Because closely held corporation stock is not easily marketable, a stock redemption often represents the only way to dispose of the stock. The redemption might not satisfy any of the other qualifying stock redemption provisions because of the attribution rules (e.g., attribution to estate from beneficiaries). A **redemption to pay death taxes** provides sale or exchange treatment without regard to the attribution rules. However, this treatment is limited to the sum of the death taxes and funeral and administration expenses. A redemption in excess of these expenses may qualify for sale or exchange treatment under one of the § 302 provisions.

[59] § 302(e)(1)(A).

[60] See *Joseph W. Imler*, 11 T.C. 836 (1948), *acq.* 1949–1 C.B. 2; and Reg. § 1.346–1(a).

[61] Rev.Rul. 60–322. The IRS generally will not rule on whether a distribution satisfies the genuine contraction of a business test unless it results in a 20 percent or greater reduction in (1) gross revenue, (2) net fair market value of assets, and (3) employees. Rev.Proc. 2023–3.

An estate's basis in property acquired from a decedent is generally the property's fair market value on the date of death.[62] Typically, there is little change in the fair market value of stock from the date of a decedent's death to the date of a redemption to pay death taxes. When the redemption price is the same as the estate's basis in the stock, a redemption to pay death taxes results in no gain (or loss) to the estate.

Code § 303 applies only to a distribution made with respect to stock of a corporation that is included in the gross estate of a decedent and whose value *exceeds* 35 percent of the value of the adjusted gross estate.[63] (For definitions of *gross estate* and *adjusted gross estate*, see the Glossary in Appendix C.)

Juan's adjusted gross estate is $15,000,000. The death taxes and funeral and administration expenses of the estate total $1,440,000. Included in the gross estate is stock of Yellow Corporation valued at $5,600,000. Juan had acquired the stock nine years ago at a cost of $600,000. Yellow redeems $1,440,000 of the stock from Juan's estate.

Because the value of the Yellow stock in Juan's estate exceeds the 35% threshold ($5,600,000 ÷ $15,000,000 = 37.3%), the redemption qualifies under § 303 as a sale or exchange to Juan's estate. Assuming that the value of the stock has remained unchanged since the date of Juan's death, there is no recognized gain (or loss) on the redemption [$1,440,000 (amount realized) − $1,440,000 (estate's stock basis)].

LO.9

Determine the tax impact of stock redemptions on the distributing corporation.

19-5 Stock Redemptions—Effect on the Corporation

Thus far, the discussion has focused on the tax consequences of stock redemptions to the *shareholder*. There are also several tax issues surrounding the redeeming *corporation* that must be addressed including:

- The recognition of gain or loss on property distributed pursuant to a redemption.
- The effect of a qualifying stock redemption on a corporation's E & P.
- The deductibility of expenditures incurred in connection with a redemption.

These issues are discussed in the following paragraphs.

19-5a Recognition of Gain or Loss

Distributions in redemption of stock, qualifying or not, are nonliquidating distributions. Under § 311, corporations recognize *gain* on all nonliquidating distributions of appreciated property as if the property had been sold for its fair market value. When distributed property is subject to a corporate liability and that liability is greater than the property's fair market value, the liability amount is used to determine the recognized gain.

Losses are not recognized on nonliquidating distributions of property. Therefore, a corporation should avoid distributing loss property (fair market value less than basis) in a stock redemption. However, the corporation could sell the property in a taxable transaction, recognize a loss, and then distribute the proceeds.

To carry out a stock redemption, Blackbird Corporation distributes land (basis of $80,000, fair market value of $300,000) to a shareholder. Blackbird has a recognized gain of $220,000 ($300,000 − $80,000). If the land is subject to a liability of $330,000, Blackbird has a recognized gain of $250,000 ($330,000 − $80,000). If the value of the property distributed was less than its adjusted basis, the realized loss would not be recognized.

[62] If available and elected, an alternate valuation date would apply. § 1014(a).

[63] § 303(b)(2)(A). For purposes of this test, the stock of two or more corporations in which the decedent held a 20% or more interest (by value) is treated as the stock of one corporation. § 303(b)(2)(B).

19-5b Effect on Earnings and Profits

In a qualifying stock redemption, the E & P of the distributing corporation is reduced by no more than the percentage of the corporation's stock redeemed.[64]

Navy Corporation has 100 shares of stock outstanding. In a qualifying stock redemption, Navy distributes $200,000 in exchange for 30 of its shares. At the time of the redemption, Navy has paid-in capital of $120,000 and E & P of $450,000. Navy's E & P is reduced by $135,000 (30% of the corporation's E & P). The remainder of the redemption price ($65,000) is a reduction of the Navy paid-in capital account.

If, instead, the 30 shares were redeemed for $80,000, E & P would be reduced by $80,000, the amount paid by the corporation to carry out the stock redemption.

19-5c Redemption Expenditures

In redeeming its shares, a corporation may incur certain expenses such as accounting, brokerage, legal, and loan fees. Code § 162(k) specifically denies a deduction for expenditures incurred in connection with a stock redemption. The disallowance does not apply to amounts otherwise deductible as interest under § 163, such as interest from debt-financed redemptions.

19-5d Excise Tax on Stock Repurchases

For any *covered corporation*, the Inflation Reduction Act of 2022 includes a 1 percent excise tax that applies to the fair market value of stock repurchases (redemptions) after December 31, 2022.[65] The excise tax is nondeductible.[66] A "covered corporation" is any domestic corporation with stock traded on an established securities market.[67] There are several exceptions to the buyback tax; for instance, the following stock repurchases are *not* subject to the tax:[68]

- Where the total value of the stock repurchased during the tax year does not exceed $1 million.
- Where the repurchase is part of a reorganization and no gain or loss is recognized on the repurchase by shareholder by reason of the reorganization.
- Where the stock repurchased is contributed to an employer-sponsored retirement plan, employee stock ownership plan (ESOP), or similar plan.

In addition, the amount of repurchases subject to tax is reduced by the value of any stock issued during the tax year, including the value of any stock issued (or provided) to employees of the corporation during the tax year.[69]

In 2023, Walnut Inc., a publicly traded corporation, purchased 600,000 shares of its common stock on the open market for a total value of $100 million. Assuming that none of the exceptions to the buyback tax apply, Walnut has a nondeductible excise tax of $1 million (1% × $100 million) for 2023.

19-6 Other Corporate Distributions

Other corporate distributions also can have the effect of a dividend distribution. For instance, the sale (or redemption) of preferred stock received in a tax-free stock dividend ("§ 306 stock") can have the equivalent effect of a dividend distribution. As a result, the sale (or redemption) of § 306 stock generally results in ordinary income to the shareholder. Also, distributions of stock and securities of a controlled corporation to the shareholders of the parent corporation under § 355 can resemble either a dividend, a stock redemption, or a liquidation. The rules surrounding these transactions are not discussed here because of their limited applicability.

[64] § 312(n)(7).

[65] § 4501, as enacted by An Act to Provide for Reconciliation Pursuant to Title II of S. Con. Res. 14 (commonly referred to as the "Inflation Reduction Act of 2022"), P.L. 117–169; 8/16/22, § 10201.

[66] § 275(a)(6).

[67] § 4501(b). Stock repurchases by "specified affiliates" of a covered corporation are treated as repurchases by the covered corporation. See § 4501(c)(2).

[68] Repurchases treated as dividends to the shareholder also are not subject to the excise tax. § 4501(e).

[69] § 4501(c)(3).

LO.10

Identify planning opportunities available to minimize the tax impacts of corporate distributions, constructive dividends, and stock redemptions.

19-7 Tax Planning

19-7a Corporate Distributions

The following points are especially important when planning for corporate distributions:

- Because E & P is the pool of funds from which dividends may be distributed, its computation is essential to corporate planning. However, many corporations do not calculate E & P on a regular basis. Some firms view the financial accounting concept of "retained earnings" as a surrogate; if there are sufficient retained earnings, they assume there is sufficient E & P. And in many instances, this is a fairly safe assumption. But if retained earnings is reduced (or low), the corporation may be at risk for making a distribution that is not a dividend for tax purposes (and, instead, a return of capital). Thus, an E & P account should be established and maintained.
- Accumulated E & P is the sum of all past years' current E & P. Because there is no statute of limitations on the computation of E & P, the IRS can redetermine a corporation's current E & P for a tax year long since passed. Any changes made will affect accumulated E & P and have a direct impact on the taxability of current distributions to shareholders.
- Distributions can be planned to avoid or minimize dividend exposure.

Corporate Distributions—Tax Planning

Example 53

Flicker Corporation has accumulated E & P of $100,000 as of January 1 of the current year. During the year, it expects to have earnings from operations of $80,000 and to sell an asset for a loss of $100,000. As a result, it anticipates a current E & P deficit of $20,000. Flicker Corporation also expects to make a cash distribution of $60,000.

If the shareholders would prefer *not* to have dividend income, the best approach is to recognize the loss as soon as possible and, immediately thereafter, make the cash distribution to the shareholders. Suppose these two steps take place on January 1. Because there is a $100,000 deficit in current E & P at the time of the distribution, the accumulated E & P account comes into play (refer to Example 13 in this chapter).

As a result, at the time of the distribution, the combined E & P balance is zero [$100,000 (beginning balance in accumulated E & P) − $100,000 (existing deficit in current E & P)], and the $60,000 distribution to the shareholders constitutes a return of capital. Current deficits are deemed to accrue pro rata throughout the year unless the parties can prove otherwise; here, they can.

Example 54

After several unprofitable years, Darter Corporation has a deficit in accumulated E & P of $100,000 as of January 1, 2023. Starting in 2023, Darter expects to generate annual E & P of $50,000 for the next four years and would like to distribute this amount to its shareholders. The corporation's cash position (for dividend purposes) will correspond to the current E & P generated. Consider the following two distribution schedules:

1. On December 31 of 2023, 2024, 2025, and 2026, Darter Corporation distributes cash of $50,000.
2. On December 31 of 2024 and 2026, Darter Corporation distributes cash of $100,000.

The two alternatives are illustrated below.

Year	Accumulated E & P (First of Year)	Current E & P	Distribution	Amount of Dividend
		Alternative 1		
2023	($100,000)	$50,000	$ 50,000	$50,000
2024	(100,000)	50,000	50,000	50,000
2025	(100,000)	50,000	50,000	50,000
2026	(100,000)	50,000	50,000	50,000

continued

Alternative 2

2023	($100,000)	$50,000	$ -0-	$ -0-
2024	(50,000)	50,000	100,000	50,000
2025	(50,000)	50,000	-0-	-0-
2026	-0-	50,000	100,000	50,000

Alternative 1 produces $200,000 of dividend income because each $50,000 distribution is fully covered by current E & P. Alternative 2, however, produces only $100,000 of dividend income for the shareholders. The remaining $100,000 is a return of capital. Why?

At the time Darter Corporation made its first distribution of $100,000 on December 31, 2024, it had a deficit of $50,000 in accumulated E & P (the original deficit of $100,000 is reduced by the $50,000 of current E & P from 2023). Consequently, the $100,000 distribution yields a $50,000 dividend (the current E & P for 2024), and $50,000 is treated as a return of capital.

As of January 1, 2025, Darter's accumulated E & P now has a deficit balance of $50,000 because a distribution cannot increase a deficit in E & P. After adding the remaining $50,000 of current E & P from 2025, the balance on January 1, 2026, is zero. As a result, the second distribution of $100,000, made on December 31, 2026, also yields $50,000 of dividends (the current E & P for 2026) and a $50,000 return of capital.

19-7b **Planning for Qualified Dividends**

Retirement Plans

The reduced tax rates available to individual taxpayers on net capital gain and qualified dividend income are not available when stock is held in retirement accounts. Because income in § 401(k) plans and IRAs is not taxed when earned, the benefits of the lower tax rates on these forms of income are lost. Instead, distributions from these plans (other than Roth IRAs) are taxed at ordinary income tax rates.

Individual Alternative Minimum Tax

The lower rates on dividends and long-term capital gains apply under both the regular income tax and the alternative minimum tax. This increases the exposure of many individuals to the alternative minimum tax, particularly those with significant income from dividends or long-term capital gain. As a result, individual taxpayers who pay the alternative minimum tax should consider modifying their investment strategies. Appropriately managing the mix of ordinary income, dividend income, and capital gain can minimize the alternative minimum tax.

Closely Held Corporations

Closely held corporations have considerable discretion regarding their dividend policies. In the past, the double tax result provided strong motivation to avoid the payment of dividends. Instead, the incentive was to bail out corporate profits in a manner that provided tax benefits to the corporation. As a result, liberal use was made of compensation, loan, and lease arrangements because salaries, interest, and rent are deductible. Under current law, however, shareholders might prefer dividends because salaries, interest, and rent are taxed at ordinary rates while dividends receive preferential treatment. As a result, the question becomes this: *Should the corporation or the shareholders benefit?* In general, the best strategy considers the tax consequences to *both parties*.

Example 55

Consider a corporation paying tax at the 21% rate and an individual shareholder in the 32% tax bracket. A deductible $10,000 payment to the shareholder will *save* the corporation $2,100 in tax, resulting in an after-tax cost of $7,900. The shareholder will pay $3,200 in tax, resulting in after-tax income of $6,800. This creates a joint tax burden of $1,100 ($3,200 tax paid by the shareholder − $2,100 tax saved by the corporation).

continued

If, instead, the corporation paid a $10,000 qualified dividend (subject to a 15% tax rate) to the shareholder, no tax savings would be realized by the corporation, resulting in an after-tax cost of $10,000. The shareholder would owe $1,500 in taxes, leaving $8,500 of income. Considering both the corporation and the shareholder, a dividend creates $400 more tax liability than a deductible payment, so the deductible payment is more tax-efficient.

In Example 55, when the deductible payment is made, the shareholder bears an increased tax burden of $1,700 ($3,200 tax due from the deductible payment − $1,500 tax due from the dividend) while the corporation saves $2,100 ($2,100 tax saved because of the deductible payment − $0 tax saved because of the dividend). Both parties could actually benefit if the corporation transferred part of its benefit to the shareholder through a larger deductible payment.

Example 56

Assume the same facts as in Example 55, except that the corporation pays a $12,600 deductible payment to the shareholder. In this case, the corporation will save $2,646 ($12,600 × 21%) in tax, resulting in an after-tax cost of $9,954.

From the corporation's perspective, this is preferable to a $10,000 dividend because it costs $46 less after tax ($10,000 dividend cost − $9,954 after-tax cost of a $12,600 deductible payment). The shareholder will pay taxes of $4,032 on the deductible payment, resulting in after-tax income of $8,568. The shareholder also will prefer this payment to a $10,000 dividend because it generates $68 more after-tax income ($8,568 − $8,500 from a dividend).

As a result, if properly structured, deductible payments by the corporation to the shareholder can be preferable to dividends in many situations. The benefit of this strategy will be even greater if the shareholder is paying alternative minimum tax.

19-7c **Constructive Dividends**

Tax planning can be particularly effective in avoiding constructive dividend situations. Shareholders should try to structure their dealings with the corporation on an arm's length basis. For example, reasonable rent should be paid for the use of corporate property, and a fair price should be paid by a shareholder for its purchase. The parties should support the amount involved with appraisal data or market information obtained from reliable sources at or near the time of the transaction. In the case of loans to shareholders, the parties should provide for an adequate rate of interest and written evidence of the debt. Shareholders also should establish and follow a realistic repayment schedule.

If shareholders want to bail out corporate profits in a form deductible to the corporation, a balanced mix of the possible alternatives lessens the risk of constructive dividend treatment. Rent for the use of shareholder property, interest on amounts borrowed from shareholders, or salaries for services rendered by shareholders are all feasible substitutes for dividend distributions. Overdoing any one approach, however, may attract the attention of the IRS. Too much interest, for example, may mean that the corporation is thinly capitalized, and some of the debt may be reclassified as equity investment.

Much can be done to protect against the disallowance of unreasonable compensation. Example 57 is an illustration, all too common in a family corporation, of what *not* to do.

Example 57

Rebecca Cole wholly owns Eagle Corporation. Corporate employees and annual salaries include Bob, Rebecca's husband ($120,000); Sam, Rebecca's son ($80,000); Rebecca ($640,000); and Tanuja, Rebecca's longtime friend who is unrelated to the Cole family ($320,000). The operation of Eagle Corporation is shared about equally between Rebecca and Tanuja.

Bob performed significant services for Eagle during its formative years, but now merely attends the annual meeting of the board of directors. Sam is a full-time student and occasionally signs papers for the corporation in his capacity as treasurer. Eagle Corporation has not distributed a

continued

dividend for 10 years although it has accumulated substantial E & P. Bob, Sam, and Rebecca run the risk of a finding of unreasonable compensation based on the following factors:

- Bob's salary is vulnerable unless proof is available that some or all of his $120,000 annual salary is payment for services rendered to the corporation in prior years and that he was underpaid for those years.[70]
- Sam's salary is also vulnerable; he does not appear to earn the $80,000 paid to him by the corporation. Neither Sam nor Bob is a shareholder, but each one's relationship to Rebecca is enough of a tie-in to raise the unreasonable compensation issue.
- Rebecca's salary could be challenged by the IRS. Why is Rebecca receiving $320,000 more than Tanuja when they share equally in the operation of the corporation?
- The fact that Eagle Corporation has not distributed dividends over the past 10 years, even though it is capable of doing so, also increases the likelihood of a constructive dividend.

What could have been done to improve the tax position of the parties in Example 57? Bob and Sam are not entitled to a salary since neither seems to be performing any services for the corporation. Paying them a salary simply aggravates the problem. The IRS is more apt to consider *all* the family members' salaries excessive under the circumstances. Rebecca should probably reduce her compensation to correspond with that paid to Tanuja. She can then attempt to distribute corporate earnings to herself in some other form.

Paying some dividends to Rebecca also would help alleviate the problem raised in Example 57. The IRS has been successful in denying a deduction for salary paid to a shareholder-employee, even when the payment was reasonable, in a situation where the corporation had not distributed any dividends.[71] Most courts, however, have not denied deductions for compensation solely because a dividend was not paid. A better approach is to compare an employee's compensation with the level of compensation prevalent in the particular industry.

The corporation can provide *indirect* compensation to Rebecca by paying expenses that benefit her personally but are nevertheless deductible to the corporation. For example, premiums paid by the corporation for sickness, accident, and hospitalization insurance for Rebecca are deductible to the corporation and nontaxable to her.[72] Any payments under the policy are not taxable to Rebecca unless they exceed her medical expenses.[73] The corporation also can pay for travel and entertainment expenses incurred by Rebecca on behalf of the corporation. If these expenses are primarily for the benefit of the corporation, Rebecca will not recognize any taxable income and the corporation will receive a deduction.[74] However, when testing for reasonableness, the IRS looks at the total compensation package, including indirect compensation payments to a shareholder-employee.

Here are some examples of indirect compensation:

- Corporate payment of the shareholder's personal expenses that are not related to the business (e.g., vacations, rent, medical bills, legal fees, country club dues, and/or other living expenses).
- Corporate reimbursements (e.g., excessive expense allowances and moving allowances).
- Shareholder use of company-owned property for personal purposes without fair payment by the shareholder (e.g., automobiles, boats, and office space).
- Purchase (or rental) of shareholder property in excess of fair market (rental) value.
- Shareholder purchase (or lease) of corporate property at a bargain price (rental).

[70]See, for example, *R.J. Nicoll* Co., 59 T.C. 37 (1972), *acq.* 1973–2 C.B. 3.

[71]*Charles McCandless Tile Service v. U.S.*, 70–1 USTC ¶9284, 25 AFTR 2d 70–870, 422 F.2d 1336 (Ct.Cls.). The court in *McCandless* concluded that a return on equity of 15% of net profits was reasonable.

[72]Reg. § 1.162–10.

[73]The medical reimbursement plan must meet certain nondiscrimination requirements of § 105(h)(2).

[74]Reg. § 1.62–2(c)(4).

- Corporate payment of a shareholder's debt or obligation.
- Corporate loan to a shareholder where there is no expectation or demand for repayment (or with a below-market interest rate).
- Corporate loans to finance a shareholder's purchase of personal items (e.g., a house, a vacation, and/or personal investments).
- Shareholder loans to the corporation at an interest rate in excess of market rate.

As with many things in life, indirect compensation is a "gray area" with no single set of standards to be applied. Certain activities can combine both business and personal dimensions (e.g., a business trip to Hawaii). A country club membership can generate both business and personal use. Disentangling the business and personal use of business assets can also be a challenge. In fact, many companies have policies that allow for the "limited personal use" of certain corporate assets (such as computers, mobile devices, copy machines, conference rooms, and vehicles). This "limited personal use" exception is normally provided as long as the use is occasional, is not for outside employment, does not result in excessive costs, and does not interfere with work responsibilities. Ultimately, whether there is "indirect compensation" (and a constructive dividend) will depend on taxpayer policies and related documentation substantiating business justification for the usage.

19-7d **Stock Redemptions**

Stock redemptions offer several possibilities for tax planning:

- Stock redemptions are particularly well suited for purchasing the interest of a retiring or deceased shareholder. Rather than the remaining shareholders buying the stock of the retiring or deceased shareholder, corporate funds are used to redeem these shares. A life insurance policy held by the corporation on a shareholder can be used to fund a redemption. Upon the shareholder's death, the corporation receives tax-free life insurance proceeds that are used to redeem the stock of the deceased shareholder. The ability to use the corporation's funds to buy out a shareholder's interest is also advantageous in property settlements between divorcing taxpayers.
- A third party who wants to purchase all of the stock of a corporation can utilize a stock redemption to finance some of the stock acquisition cost. This technique is referred to as a "bootstrap acquisition." The third party first purchases a small amount of stock from the shareholders. The corporation then redeems all of its outstanding stock except that of the third party. The third party becomes the sole shareholder of the corporation, but corporate funds finance most of the acquisition. Some leveraged buyouts (LBOs) are structured like a bootstrap acquisition.
- The timing and sequence of a redemption should be considered carefully, because a series of redemptions may have the effect of a dividend distribution. The following example illustrates this point.

Sparrow Corporation's stock is held by three unrelated shareholders: Alma (60 shares), Antonio (20 shares), and Ali (20 shares). The corporation redeems 24 of Alma's shares. Shortly thereafter, it redeems 5 of Antonio's shares. Does Alma's redemption qualify as a disproportionate redemption?

Taken in isolation, Alma's redemption satisfies the 80% and 50% tests. Yet, if the IRS takes into account the later redemption of Antonio's shares, Alma has not satisfied the 50% test; she still owns $^{36}/_{71}$ of the corporation after the two redemptions. A greater time lag between the redemptions places Alma in a better position to argue against collapsing the two redemptions as parts of one integrated plan.

- For family-owned corporations, a complete termination redemption is often the only viable option to attain sale or exchange treatment. However, with proper planning, the complete termination redemption can be an integral tool in succession planning for a family-owned corporation, providing sale or exchange treatment to the retiring shareholder and retaining family ownership of the entity. Here, strict compliance with the requirements for the family attribution waiver is critical (e.g., the withdrawing shareholder does not acquire a prohibited interest in the corporation within 10 years).

- The attribution rules do not apply to partial liquidations. This presents another opportunity for sale or exchange treatment for some family-owned corporations. The termination of a business safe-harbor rule and the ability for pro rata distributions make the partial liquidation a unique opportunity for family-owned multi-business corporations to contract the entity while providing favorable tax results to the shareholders.
- In a redemption to pay death taxes, the amount sheltered from dividend treatment is limited to the sum of death taxes and funeral and administration expenses. The estate tax exemption amount was nearly doubled in 2018, and far fewer taxpayers will incur Federal estate tax as a result. This further limits the applicability of qualified redemption treatment under § 303. However, a redemption in excess of the limitation can qualify for sale or exchange treatment under one of the other qualifying stock redemption rules.
- A qualifying stock redemption financed by installment notes can provide tax benefits to both the corporation and the shareholder. For the corporation, the related interest expense is deductible (subject to the business interest expense limitation; see Chapter 17), while the shareholder can use the installment method to defer to the point of collection the gain that is attributable to the notes.

Refocus on The Big Picture

Taxing Corporate Distributions

A number of factors affect the tax treatment of Plainwell Ice Cream Corporation's distributions. The amount of current and accumulated E & P (which differ from the financial reporting concept of retained earnings) partially determines the tax effect on the shareholders. Given that Plainwell Ice Cream Corporation has had a highly profitable year (see Example 12), it is likely that there is sufficient current E & P to cover the distributions. If so, they are dividends to the shareholders rather than a return of capital. Waffle Cone Corporation receives $200,000 of dividend income that is offset by the dividends received deduction.* Luis has $200,000 of dividend income (i.e., $300,000 value of the land less the $100,000 mortgage). Assuming that Plainwell is a domestic corporation and that Luis has held his stock for the entire year, the land is a qualified dividend. As a result, the tax depends on Luis's taxable income.** Luis's basis in the land is its fair market value at distribution, or $300,000 (see Example 17).

From Plainwell Ice Cream Corporation's perspective, the distribution of appreciated property creates a deemed gain (see Example 20). As a result, a $280,000 gain results ($300,000 fair market value of the land less its adjusted basis of $20,000). Although the gain increases Plainwell's E & P, the distributions to the shareholders reduce it by $200,000 for the cash and $200,000 for the land ($300,000 fair market value reduced by the $100,000 mortgage).

What If?

What if current E & P is less than the cash and land distributed to the shareholders? Current E & P is applied pro rata to the cash and the land. Because the amounts received by the two shareholders are equal ($200,000 each), the current E & P applied is taxed as a dividend and is treated as described above. To the extent the distributions are not covered by current E & P, accumulated E & P is then applied in a pro rata fashion (because both distributions were made on December 31). However, Plainwell probably has a deficit in accumulated E & P. As a result, the remaining amounts distributed to the two shareholders are first a tax-free recovery of stock basis, and any excess is taxed as a sale of the stock (likely classified as capital gain).

* Because both shareholders received equal distributions ($200,000), it would appear that each is a 50% shareholder. As a result, Waffle Cone's dividends would be offset by a 65% dividends received deduction.

** Because Luis is married filing jointly in 2023, there will be no tax on the dividend if taxable income is $89,250 or less, a 20% tax if taxable income is greater than $553,850, and a 15% tax if taxable income is between these two figures.

Key Terms

Accumulated E & P, 19-8
Attribution, 19-25
Complete termination redemption, 19-28
Constructive dividends, 19-16
Current E & P, 19-8
Disproportionate redemption, 19-27
Earnings and profits (E & P), 19-3
Meaningful reduction test, 19-26
Not essentially equivalent redemption, 19-26
Partial liquidation, 19-28
Property dividend, 19-14
Qualified dividends, 19-13
Redemption to pay death taxes, 19-29
Stock dividends, 19-19
Stock redemption, 19-21
Stock rights, 19-20
Unreasonable compensation, 19-18

Discussion Questions

1. **LO.2** In determining Blue Corporation's current E & P for 2023, how should taxable income be adjusted as a result of the following transactions?
   a. A capital loss carryover from 2022, fully used in 2023.
   b. Nondeductible meal expenses in 2023.
   c. Interest on municipal bonds received in 2023.
   d. Nondeductible lobbying expenses in 2023.
   e. Loss on a sale between related parties in 2023.
   f. Federal income tax refund received in 2023.

2. **LO.3** Describe the effect of a distribution in a year when the distributing corporation has:
   a. A deficit in accumulated E & P and a positive amount in current E & P.
   b. A positive amount in accumulated E & P and a deficit in current E & P.
   c. A deficit in both current and accumulated E & P.
   d. A positive amount in both current and accumulated E & P.

3. **LO.3** A calendar year corporation has substantial accumulated E & P, but it expects to incur a deficit in current E & P for the year due to significant losses in the last half of the year. A cash distribution to its shareholders on January 1 should result in a return of capital. Comment on the validity of this statement.

4. **LO.4** Discuss the rationale for the reduced tax rates on dividends paid to individuals.

Critical Thinking

5. **LO.1, 2, 3, 4, 5** Orange Corporation distributes $200,000 in cash to each of its three shareholders: Sandy, Byron, and Fuchsia Corporation. What factors must be considered when determining how the distribution is treated for tax purposes by the shareholders?

Critical Thinking

6. **LO.5** Assume the same facts as in Question 5, except that property is distributed. What factors must be considered when determining how the distribution is treated for tax purposes by Orange Corporation?

7. **LO.5** Orion Corporation's board of directors decides to distribute property to its shareholders rather than pay a cash dividend. Why might Orion's board make this decision?

Decision Making
Planning

8. **LO.5** Raven Corporation owns three machines that it uses in its business. It no longer needs two of these machines and is considering distributing them to its two shareholders as a property dividend. All three machines have a fair market value of $20,000 each. The basis of each machine is as follows: Machine A, $27,000; Machine B, $20,000; and Machine C, $12,000. The corporation has asked you for advice. What do you recommend?

9. **LO.5** Tangerine Corporation is considering a property distribution to its shareholders. If appreciated property is to be used, does it matter to Tangerine whether the property distributed is a long-term capital asset or depreciable property subject to recapture? Would your answer differ if the property distributed has a fair market value less than the adjusted basis? Explain. Critical Thinking

10. **LO.6** Samantha is the president and sole shareholder of Toucan Corporation. She is paid an annual salary of $500,000, and her son, Aaron, the company's chief financial officer, is paid a salary of $290,000. Aaron works for Toucan on a part-time basis and spends most of his time training for triathlons. Toucan advances $85,000 to Samantha as an interest-free loan. What are the tax issues? Critical Thinking

11. **LO.6** Whether compensation paid to a corporate employee is reasonable is a question of fact to be determined from the surrounding circumstances. How would the resolution of this problem be affected by each of the following factors? Planning
    a. The employee owns no stock but is the mother-in-law of the sole shareholder.
    b. The shareholder-employee does not have a college degree.
    c. The shareholder-employee works 40 hours per week for another unrelated employer.
    d. The shareholder-employee was underpaid for services during the formative period of the corporation.
    e. The corporation has never paid a dividend.
    f. Year-end bonuses are paid to all employees, but officer-shareholders receive disproportionately larger bonuses.

12. **LO.6, 10** Pink Corporation has several employees. Their names and salaries are listed below.

Judy	$470,000
Holly (Judy's daughter)	100,000
Terry (Judy's son)	100,000
John (an unrelated third party)	320,000

Holly and Terry are the only shareholders of Pink Corporation. Judy and John share equally in the management of the company's operations. Holly and Terry are both full-time college students at a university 200 miles away. Pink has substantial E & P and has never distributed a dividend. Discuss any problems related to Pink's salary arrangement.

13. **LO.8, 9, 10** Chao, Louis, and Mari, unrelated individuals, own all of the shares of Cerise Corporation. All three shareholders have been active in the management of Cerise since its inception. In the current year, Chao wants to retire and sell all of her shares in the corporation. What issues should be considered in determining whether Chao should sell her stock to one of the other shareholders, to Cerise Corporation, or to a third party? Critical Thinking Planning

14. **LO.8** Corporate shareholders typically prefer dividend treatment on a stock redemption. Why?

15. **LO.8** Do the stock attribution rules apply to all stock redemptions? Explain.

16. **LO.8** Briefly discuss the requirements for a redemption to qualify as a not essentially equivalent redemption.

17. **LO.8** If a redemption is treated as a dividend ("nonqualified stock redemption"), what happens to the basis of the stock redeemed?

18. **LO.8, 9** Tammy and Barry formed Pheasant Corporation several years ago in a transaction that qualified under § 351. Both shareholders serve as officers and on the board of directors of Pheasant. In the current year, Pheasant Corporation redeemed all of Barry's shares in the corporation with a property distribution. What are the tax issues for Barry and Pheasant? Critical Thinking Planning

19. **LO.8** To qualify as a partial liquidation, a distribution must not be essentially equivalent to a dividend. Discuss how this requirement is satisfied.

Critical Thinking
Planning

20. **LO.8, 9** Brown Corporation operates several trades and businesses. In the current year, Brown discontinues the operation of one of its trades and businesses. Brown is considering distributing to its shareholders either the assets of the discontinued business or the proceeds from the sale of such assets. Considering both of these alternatives, what are the tax issues for Brown Corporation and its shareholders?

21. **LO.8, 9** Explain the requirements for a redemption to pay death taxes. What are the tax consequences of a redemption to pay death taxes for the shareholder and the corporation?

Critical Thinking
Planning

22. **LO.8, 9, 10** Angie and her daughter, Ann, who are the only shareholders of Bluebird Corporation, each paid $200,000 four years ago for their shares in Bluebird. Angie also owns 20% of the stock in Redbird Corporation. The Redbird stock is worth $1,000,000, and Angie's basis in the stock is $100,000. Angie dies in the current year leaving all of her property to her spouse, Mary, but Ann wants to be the sole shareholder of Bluebird Corporation. Bluebird has assets worth $8,000,000 (basis of $1,400,000) and E & P of $2,000,000. Angie's estate is worth approximately $16,000,000. Angie has made gifts during her lifetime to Ann. What are the tax issues for Angie's estate, Ann, and Bluebird?

23. **LO.9** What are the general rules surrounding the excise tax on stock repurchases?

Computational Exercises

24. **LO.1** At the beginning of the year, Myrna Corporation (a calendar year taxpayer) has E & P of $32,000. The corporation generates no additional E & P during the year. On December 31, the corporation distributes $50,000 to its sole shareholder, Abby, whose stock basis is $10,000. How is the distribution treated for tax purposes?

25. **LO.3** On January 1 of the current year, Rhondell Corporation has accumulated E & P of $13,000. Current E & P for the year is $84,000, earned evenly throughout the year. Elizabeth and Jonathan are sole equal shareholders of Rhondell from January 1 to April 30. On May 1, Elizabeth sells all of her stock to Marshall. Rhondell makes two distributions to shareholders during the year: a total of $42,000 ($21,000 to Elizabeth and $21,000 to Jonathan) on April 30 and a total of $58,000 ($29,000 to Jonathan and $29,000 to Marshall) on December 31.

Determine the allocation of the distributions by completing the table below. Assume that the shareholders have sufficient basis in their stock for any amount that is treated as return of capital.

	From Current E & P	From Accumulated E & P	Treated as Return of Capital
April 30 distribution of $42,000	______	______	______
December 31 distribution of $58,000	______	______	______

Decision Making
Planning

26. **LO.4, 10** Rover Corporation would like to transfer excess cash to its sole shareholder, Aleshia, who is also an employee. Aleshia is in the 24% tax bracket, and Rover is subject to a 21% rate. Because Aleshia's contribution to the business is substantial, Rover believes that a $25,000 bonus in the current year is

reasonable compensation and should be deductible by the corporation. However, Rover is considering paying Aleshia a $25,000 dividend because the tax rate on dividends is lower than the tax rate on compensation. Is Rover correct in believing that a dividend is the better choice? Why or why not?

27. **LO.5** Global Corporation distributed property with an $850,000 fair market value and a $415,000 adjusted basis to one of its shareholders. The property was subject to a $230,000 mortgage, which the shareholder assumed. Global has ample E & P to cover any distribution made during the year. What is the amount of the shareholder's dividend income on the distribution? What is the shareholder's basis in the property received?

28. **LO.5** Quinlan has ample E & P to cover any distributions made during the year. One distribution made to a shareholder consists of property with an adjusted basis of $150,000 and a fair market value of $90,000. What are the tax consequences of this distribution to Quinlan?

29. **LO.6** Deerwood Corporation lends its principal shareholder, Lafayette, $500,000 on July 1 of the current year. The loan is interest-free and payable on demand. On December 31, the imputed interest rules are applied. Assume that the Federal rate is 3%, compounded semiannually. What are the tax consequences of this loan to Lafayette?

30. **LO.7** What are the tax consequences to Euclid from the following independent events?
    a. Euclid bought 500 shares of common stock five years ago for $50,000. This year, Euclid receives 20 shares of common stock as a nontaxable stock dividend. What is Euclid's basis per share after this event?
    b. Assume instead that Euclid received a nontaxable preferred stock dividend of 20 shares. The preferred stock has a fair market value of $5,000, and the common stock, on which the preferred is distributed, has a fair market value of $75,000.

31. **LO.8** During the current year, Gnatcatcher, Inc., (E & P of $1,000,000) distributed $200,000 each to Brandi and Yuen in redemption of some of their Gnatcatcher stock. The two shareholders acquired their shares five years ago. Each shareholder is in the 32% tax bracket, and each had a $45,000 basis in her redeemed stock.
    a. Assume that the distribution to Brandi is a qualifying stock redemption. Determine Brandi's tax liability on the distribution.
    b. Assume that the distribution to Yuen is a nonqualified stock redemption. Determine Yuen's tax liability on the distribution.

32. **LO.8** Rosalie owns 50% of the outstanding stock of Salmon Corporation. In a qualifying stock redemption, Salmon distributes $80,000 to Rosalie in exchange for one-half of her shares, which have a basis of $100,000. Compute Rosalie's recognized loss, if any, on the redemption.

33. **LO.8** Derk owns 250 shares of stock in Rose Corporation. The remaining 750 shares of Rose are owned as follows: 150 by Derk's daughter, 200 by Derk's aunt, and 400 by a partnership in which Derk has an 80% interest. Determine the number of shares Derk owns (directly and indirectly) in Rose Corporation.

34. **LO.9** Caramel Corporation has 5,000 shares of stock outstanding. In a qualifying stock redemption, Caramel distributes $145,000 in exchange for 1,000 of its shares. At the time of the redemption, Caramel has paid-in capital of $800,000 and E & P of $300,000. Calculate the reduction to Caramel's E & P as a result of the distribution.

Problems

35. **LO.1, 4** At the start of the current year, Blue Corporation (a calendar year taxpayer) has accumulated E & P of $100,000. Blue's current E & P is $60,000, and at the end of the year, it distributes $200,000 ($100,000 each) to its equal shareholders, Pooja and Jon. Pooja's stock basis is $11,000; Jon's stock basis is $26,000. How is the distribution treated for tax purposes?

36. **LO.1, 2** Cardinal Corporation, a calendar year taxpayer, receives dividend income of $250,000 from a corporation in which it holds a 10% interest. Cardinal also receives interest income of $35,000 from municipal bonds. (The municipality used the proceeds from the bond issue to construct a library.) Cardinal borrowed funds to purchase the municipal bonds and pays $20,000 of interest on the loan. Excluding these three items, Cardinal's taxable income is $500,000. Cardinal has $150,000 of accumulated E & P at the end of the prior year, and it paid Federal income taxes of $131,250 during the year.
    a. What is Cardinal Corporation's taxable income after these three items are taken into account?
    b. What is Cardinal Corporation's accumulated E & P at the start of next year?

37. **LO.1, 2, 3** On September 30, Silver Corporation, a calendar year taxpayer, sold a parcel of land (basis of $400,000) for a $1,000,000 note. The note is payable in five installments, with the first payment due next year. Because Silver did not elect out of the installment method, none of the $600,000 gain is taxed this year.

    Silver Corporation had a $300,000 deficit in accumulated E & P at the beginning of the year. Before considering the effect of the land sale, Silver had a deficit in current E & P of $50,000.

    Javiera, the sole shareholder of Silver, has a basis of $200,000 in her stock. If Silver distributes $900,000 to Javiera on December 31, how much income must she report for tax purposes?

38. **LO.2** Sparrow Corporation (a calendar year, accrual basis taxpayer) had the following transactions in 2023, its second year of operation:

Taxable income	$330,000
Federal income tax liability paid	69,300
Tax-exempt interest income	5,000
Meals expense (total)	3,000
Premiums paid on key employee life insurance	3,500
Increase in cash surrender value attributable to life insurance premiums	700
Proceeds from key employee life insurance policy	130,000
Cash surrender value of life insurance policy at distribution	20,000
Excess of capital losses over capital gains	13,000
MACRS deduction	26,000
Straight-line depreciation using ADS lives	16,000
Section 179 expense elected during 2022	25,000
Dividends received from domestic corporations (less than 20% owned)	35,000

Sparrow uses the LIFO inventory method, and its LIFO recapture amount increased by $10,000 during 2023. In addition, Sparrow sold property on installment during 2022. The property was sold for $40,000 and had an adjusted basis at sale of $32,000. During 2023, Sparrow received a $15,000 payment on the installment sale. Finally, assume that no additional first-year depreciation was claimed. Compute Sparrow's current E & P.

39. **LO.1, 2** In each of the following independent situations, indicate the effect on taxable income and E & P, stating the amount of any increase (or decrease) in each as a result of the transaction. Assume that E & P has already been increased by taxable income. Critical Thinking

	Transaction	Taxable Income Increase (Decrease)	E & P Increase (Decrease)
a.	Realized gain of $80,000 on involuntary conversion of building ($10,000 of gain is recognized).	________	________
b.	Mining exploration costs incurred on May 1 of current year; $24,000 is deductible from current-year taxable income.	________	________
c.	Sale of equipment to unrelated third party for $240,000; basis is $120,000 (no election out of installment method; no payments are received in current year).	________	________
d.	Dividends of $20,000 received from 5% owned corporation, together with dividends received deduction (assume that taxable income limit does not apply).	________	________
e.	Additional first-year (bonus) depreciation of $45,000 claimed in current year.	________	________
f.	Section 179 expense deduction of $25,000 in current year.	________	________
g.	Impact of current-year § 179 expense deduction in succeeding year.	________	________
h.	MACRS depreciation of $80,000. ADS depreciation would have been $90,000.	________	________
i.	Federal income taxes of $80,000 paid in current year.	________	________

40. **LO.1, 3** Black Corporation and Tom each own 50% of Tan Corporation's common stock. On January 1, Tan has a deficit in accumulated E & P of $200,000. Its current E & P is $90,000. During the year, Tan makes cash distributions of $40,000 each to Black and Tom.

a. How are the two shareholders taxed on the distribution?

b. What is Tan Corporation's accumulated E & P at the end of the year?

41. **LO.1, 3** Complete the following schedule for each case. Unless otherwise indicated, assume that the shareholders have ample basis in the stock investment.

	Accumulated E & P Beginning of Year	Current E & P	Cash Distributions (All on Last Day of Year)	Dividend Income	Return of Capital
a.	($200,000)	$ 70,000	$130,000	______	______
b.	150,000	(120,000)	210,000	______	______
c.	90,000	70,000	150,000	______	______
d.	120,000	(60,000)	130,000	______	______
e.	Same as part (d), except that the distribution of $130,000 is made on June 30 and the corporation uses the calendar year for tax purposes.			______	______

42. **LO.1, 3** YiLing, the sole shareholder of Brown Corporation, sold her Brown stock to Calvin on July 30 for $270,000. YiLing's basis in the stock was $200,000 at the beginning of the year. Brown had accumulated E & P of $120,000 on January 1 and has current E & P of $240,000. During the year, Brown made the following distributions: $450,000 cash to YiLing on July 1 and $150,000 cash to Calvin on December 30. How will YiLing and Calvin be taxed on the distributions? How much gain will YiLing recognize on the sale of her stock to Calvin?

43. **LO.4** In November of the current year, Emerald Corporation declared a dividend of $2 per share (the shareholder record date is December 15). Assume that Emerald has sufficient current E & P to cover the dividend payment. If Judy purchases 500 shares of Emerald stock on December 5 and sells the stock on December 25, how is she taxed on the $1,000 dividend?

Critical Thinking

44. **LO.1, 5** Heather, an individual, owns all of the outstanding stock in Silver Corporation. Heather purchased her stock in Silver nine years ago, and her basis is $56,000. At the beginning of this year, the corporation has $76,000 of accumulated E & P and no current E & P (before considering the effect of the distributions as noted below). What are the tax consequences to Heather (amount and type of income and basis in property received) and Silver Corporation (gain or loss and effect on E & P) in each of the following situations?

a. Silver distributes land to Heather. The land was held as an investment and has a fair market value of $54,000 and an adjusted basis of $42,000.

b. Assume that Silver Corporation has no current or accumulated E & P prior to the distribution. How would your answer to part (a) change?

c. Assume that the land distributed in part (a) is subject to a $46,000 mortgage (which Heather assumes). How would your answer change?

d. Assume that the land has a fair market value of $54,000 and an adjusted basis of $62,000 on the date of the distribution. How would your answer to part (a) change?

e. Instead of distributing land in part (a), assume that Silver decides to distribute equipment used in its business. The equipment has a $14,000 market value, a $1,200 adjusted basis for income tax purposes, and a $5,200 adjusted basis for E & P purposes. When the equipment was purchased four years ago, its original fair market value was $18,000.

45. **LO.1, 5** Lime Corporation, with E & P of $500,000, distributes land (worth $300,000, adjusted basis of $350,000) to Harry, its sole shareholder. The land is subject to a liability of $120,000, which Harry assumes. What are the tax consequences to Lime and to Harry?

46. **LO.1, 3** At the beginning of the year, Penguin Corporation (a calendar year taxpayer) has accumulated E & P of $55,000. During the year, Penguin incurs a $36,000 loss from operations that accrues ratably. On October 1, Penguin distributes $40,000 in cash to Holly, its sole shareholder. How is Holly taxed on the distribution?

Critical Thinking

47. **LO.1, 2, 3, 4, 5** Cerulean Corporation has two equal shareholders, Marco and Avery. Marco acquired his Cerulean stock three years ago by transferring property worth $700,000, basis of $300,000, for 70 shares of the stock. Avery acquired 70 shares in Cerulean Corporation two years ago by transferring property worth $660,000, basis of $110,000. Cerulean Corporation's accumulated E & P as of January 1 of the current year is $350,000. On March 1 of the current year, the corporation distributed to Marco property worth $120,000, basis to Cerulean of $50,000. It distributed cash of $220,000 to Avery. On July 1 of the current year, Avery sold her stock to Harpreet for $820,000. On December 1 of the current year, Cerulean distributed cash of $90,000 each to Harpreet and Marco. What are the tax issues?

48. **LO.5** Iris Corporation owns 30% of Fresia Corporation's stock. On November 15, Fresia Corporation, with current E & P of $320,000, distributes land (fair market value of $100,000; basis of $160,000) to Iris. The land is subject to a liability of $80,000, which Iris assumes.

    a. How is Iris Corporation taxed on the distribution?

    b. What is Fresia Corporation's E & P after the distribution?

49. **LO.6** Parrot Corporation is a closely held company with accumulated E & P of $300,000 and current E & P of $350,000. Tom and Jerry are brothers; each owns a 50% share in Parrot, and they share management responsibilities equally. What are the tax consequences of each of the following independent transactions involving Parrot, Tom, and Jerry? How does each transaction affect Parrot's E & P? Critical Thinking

    a. Parrot sells an office building (adjusted basis of $350,000; fair market value of $300,000) to Tom for $275,000.

    b. Parrot lends Jerry $250,000 on March 31 of this year. The loan is evidenced by a note and is payable on demand. No interest is charged on the loan (the current applicable Federal interest rate is 3%).

    c. Parrot owns an airplane that it leases to others for a specified rental rate. Tom and Jerry also use the airplane for personal use and pay no rent. During the year, Tom used the airplane for 120 hours and Jerry used it for 160 hours. The rental value of the airplane is $350 per hour, and its maintenance costs average $80 per hour.

    d. Tom leases equipment to Parrot for $20,000 per year. The same equipment can be leased from another company for $9,000 per year.

50. **LO.7** Your client, Jacob Corcoran, bought 10,000 shares of Grebe Corporation stock two years ago for $24,000. Last year, Jacob received a nontaxable stock dividend of 2,000 shares in Grebe Corporation. In the current tax year, Jacob sold all of the stock received as a dividend for $18,000. Prepare a letter to Jacob and a memo for the file describing the tax consequences of the stock sale. Jacob's address is 925 Arapahoe Street, Boulder, CO 80304. Communications

51. **LO.4, 10** Kristen, the president and sole shareholder of Egret Corporation, has earned a salary bonus of $30,000 for the current year. Because of the lower tax rates on qualifying dividends, Kristen is considering substituting a dividend for the bonus. Assume that the tax rates are 24% for Kristen and 21% for Egret Corporation. Communications Critical Thinking Decision Making Planning

    a. How much better off would Kristen be if she were paid a dividend rather than salary?

    b. How much better off would Egret Corporation be if it paid Kristen a salary rather than a dividend?

    c. If Egret Corporation paid Kristen a salary bonus of $35,000 instead of a $30,000 dividend, how would your answers to parts (a) and (b) change?

    d. What should Kristen do? Summarize your conclusion in a two- to three-paragraph e-mail to your instructor.

52. **LO.8** Julio Gonzales is in the 32% tax bracket. He acquired 2,000 shares of stock in Gray Corporation seven years ago at a cost of $50 per share. In the current year, Julio received a payment of $150,000 from Gray Corporation in exchange for 1,000 of his shares in Gray. Gray has E & P of $1,000,000. What income tax liability would Julio incur on the $150,000 payment in each of the following situations? Assume that Julio has no capital losses.

    a. The stock redemption qualifies for sale or exchange treatment.

    b. The stock redemption does not qualify for sale or exchange treatment.

    c. For part (b), prepare Julio's Schedule B (Form 1040) to reflect the tax reporting required of the transaction. Julio's Social Security number is 123-45-6789. Assume that Julio did not have an interest in or signature authority over any financial account in a foreign country; in addition, he did not have any relationship with a foreign trust.

53. **LO.8** How would your answer to parts (a) and (b) of Problem 52 differ if Julio were a corporate shareholder rather than an individual shareholder and the stock ownership in Gray Corporation represented a 25% interest?

54. **LO.8** Silver Corporation has 2,000 shares of common stock outstanding. Howard owns 600 shares, Howard's grandfather owns 300 shares, Howard's mother owns 300 shares, and Howard's son owns 100 shares. In addition, Maroon Corporation owns 500 shares. Howard owns 70% of the stock in Maroon Corporation.

a. Applying the § 318 stock attribution rules, how many shares does Howard own in Silver Corporation?

b. Assume that Howard owns only 40% of the stock in Maroon Corporation. How many shares does Howard own, directly and indirectly, in Silver Corporation?

c. Assume the same facts as in part (a) above, but in addition, Howard owns a 25% interest in Yellow Partnership. Yellow owns 200 shares in Silver Corporation. How many shares does Howard own, directly and indirectly, in Silver Corporation?

55. **LO.8** Shonda owns 1,000 of the 1,500 shares outstanding in Rook Corporation (E & P of $1,000,000). Shonda paid $50 per share for the stock seven years ago. The remaining stock in Rook is owned by unrelated individuals. What are the tax consequences to Shonda in the following independent situations?

a. Rook Corporation redeems 450 shares of Shonda's stock for $225,000.

b. Rook Corporation redeems 600 shares of Shonda's stock for $300,000.

Communications
Critical Thinking
Planning

56. **LO.8, 9** Stork Corporation (E & P of $850,000) has 1,000 shares of common stock outstanding. The shares are owned by the following individuals: Lana Johnson, 400 shares; Lori Jones (Lana's mother), 200 shares; and Leo Jones (Lana's brother), 400 shares. Lana paid $200 per share for the Stork stock eight years ago. Lana is interested in reducing her stock ownership in Stork via a stock redemption for $1,000 per share, the fair market value of the stock. Stork Corporation would distribute cash for the entire redemption transaction. In late October, Lana inquired as to the minimum number of shares she would have to redeem to obtain favorable long-term capital gain treatment and the overall tax consequences of such a redemption to both her and Stork Corporation.

a. Prepare a letter to Lana (1000 Main Street, St. Paul, MN 55166) and a memo for the file in which you explain your conclusions.

b. Using Microsoft Excel (or a similar software program), create a spreadsheet template that computes the minimum shares that must be redeemed to qualify for a disproportionate redemption. For Microsoft Excel, use the Solver Add-in in your template.

57. **LO.8** Cyan Corporation (E & P of $700,000) has 4,000 shares of common stock outstanding. The shares are owned as follows: Angelica, 2,000 shares; Dean (Angelica's son), 1,500 shares; and Walter (Angelica's uncle), 500 shares. In the current year, Cyan redeems all of Angelica's shares. Determine whether the redemption can qualify for sale or exchange treatment under the complete termination redemption rules in each of the following independent circumstances.

a. Angelica remains as a director of Cyan Corporation.

b. Three years after the redemption, Angelica loans $100,000 to Cyan Corporation and receives in return a two-year note receivable.

c. Dean replaces Angelica as president of Cyan Corporation.

d. Six years after the redemption, Angelica receives 250 shares in Cyan as a gift from Walter.

58. **LO.8, 9** Robert and Lori (Robert's sister) own all of the stock in Swan Corporation (E & P of $1,000,000). Each owns 500 shares and has a basis of $85,000 in the shares. Robert wants to sell his stock for $600,000, the fair market value, but he will continue to be employed as an officer of Swan Corporation after the sale. Lori would like to purchase Robert's shares, becoming the sole shareholder in Swan, but Lori is short of funds. What are the tax consequences to Robert, Lori, and Swan Corporation under the following circumstances?

    a. Swan Corporation distributes cash of $600,000 to Lori, and she uses the cash to purchase Robert's shares.
    b. Swan Corporation redeems all of Robert's shares for $600,000.

59. **LO.8, 9** For the last 11 years, Lime Corporation has owned and operated four different trades or businesses. Lime also owns stock in several corporations that it purchased for investment purposes. The stock in Lime Corporation is held equally by Sultan, an individual, and by Turquoise Corporation. Both Sultan and Turquoise own 1,000 shares in Lime that were purchased nine years ago at a cost of $200 per share. Determine whether the following independent transactions qualify as partial liquidations under § 302(b)(4). In each transaction, determine the tax consequences to Lime Corporation, to Turquoise Corporation, and to Sultan.

    a. Lime Corporation sells one of its trades or businesses (basis of $500,000, fair market value of $700,000) and distributes the proceeds equally to Sultan and Turquoise Corporation in redemption of 250 shares from each shareholder. Lime Corporation has E & P of $2,100,000 as of the date of the distribution.
    b. Lime Corporation distributes the stock investments (basis of $425,000, fair market value of $700,000) it holds in other corporations to Sultan and Turquoise Corporation equally in redemption of 250 shares from each shareholder. Lime Corporation has E & P of $2,100,000 as of the date of the distribution.

60. **LO.8** The gross estate of Raul, decedent, includes stock in Iris Corporation (E & P of $8,000,000) valued at $6,000,000. At the time of his death, Raul owned 60% of the Iris stock outstanding and he had a basis of $840,000 in the stock. The death taxes and funeral and administration expenses related to Raul's estate amount to $2,000,000, and the adjusted gross estate is $16,000,000. The remainder of the Iris stock is owned by Monica, Raul's daughter and sole heir of his estate. What are the tax consequences to Raul's estate if Iris Corporation distributes $6,000,000 to the estate in redemption of all of its stock in the corporation?

61. **LO.8, 9** Broadbill Corporation (E & P of $650,000) has 1,000 shares of common stock outstanding. The shares are owned by the following individuals: Tammy, 300 shares; Yvette, 400 shares; and Jeremy, 300 shares. Each of the shareholders paid $50 per share for the Broadbill stock four years ago. In the current year, Broadbill Corporation distributes $75,000 to Tammy in redemption of 150 of her shares. Determine the tax consequences of the redemption to Tammy and to Broadbill under the following independent circumstances.

    a. Tammy and Jeremy are grandmother and grandson.
    b. The three shareholders are siblings.

62. **LO.9** Crane Corporation has 2,000 shares of stock outstanding. It redeems 500 shares for $370,000 when it has paid-in capital of $300,000 and E & P of $1,200,000. The redemption qualifies for sale or exchange treatment for the shareholder. Crane incurred $13,000 of accounting and legal fees in connection with the redemption transaction and $18,500 of interest expense on debt incurred to finance the redemption. What is the effect of the distribution on Crane Corporation's E & P? Also, what is the proper tax treatment of the redemption expenditures? Prepare a letter to the president of Crane Corporation (506 Wall Street, Winona, MN 55987) and a memo for the file in which you explain your conclusions. Communications

Research Problems

Note: Solutions to the Research Problems can be prepared by using the Thomson Reuters Checkpoint™ online tax research database, which accompanies this textbook. Solutions can also be prepared by using research materials found in a typical tax library.

Communications

Research Problem 1. Kenny Merinoff and his daughter, Mia, own all outstanding stock of Flamingo Corporation. Both Mia and Kenny are officers in the corporation and, together with Kenny's uncle, Ira, comprise the entire board of directors. Flamingo uses the cash method of accounting and has a calendar year-end. In late 2015, the board of directors adopted the following legally enforceable resolution (agreed to in writing by each of the officers):

> Salary payments made to an officer of the corporation that shall be disallowed in whole or in part as a deductible expense for Federal income tax purposes shall be reimbursed by such officer to the corporation to the full extent of the disallowance. It shall be the duty of the board of directors to enforce payment of each such amount.

In 2021, Flamingo paid Kenny $800,000 in compensation. Mia received $650,000. On an audit in late 2022, the IRS found the compensation of both officers to be excessive. It disallowed deductions for $400,000 of the payment to Kenny and $350,000 of the payment to Mia. The IRS recharacterized the disallowed payments as constructive dividends. Complying with the resolution by the board of directors, both Kenny and Mia repaid the disallowed compensation to Flamingo Corporation in 2023. Mia and Kenny have asked you to determine how their repayments should be treated for tax purposes. Mia is still working as a highly compensated executive for Flamingo, while Kenny is retired and living off his savings. Prepare a memo for your firm's client files describing the results of your research.

Partial list of research aids:
§ 1341.
Vincent E. Oswald, 49 T.C. 645 (1968).

Communications

Research Problem 2. Emerald Corporation is required to change its method of accounting for Federal income tax purposes. The change will require an adjustment to income to be made over three tax periods. Jonas, the sole shareholder of Emerald Corporation, wants to better understand the implications of this adjustment for E & P purposes, because he anticipates a distribution from Emerald in the current year. Prepare a memo for your firm's client files describing the results of your research.

Partial list of research aids:
§ 481(a).
Rev.Proc. 97–27.

Communications
Critical Thinking

Research Problem 3. Your firm has a new individual client, Carla Navarro, who has been assigned to you for preparation of the current year's tax return. Upon review of Carla's tax returns from prior years, you notice that she reported a large capital gain from a stock redemption in 2022. Upon further investigation, you determine that stock in the corporation was owned by some of Carla's family members at the time of the redemption and that the only way the redemption would have qualified for sale or exchange treatment would have been if Carla had availed herself of the family attribution waiver for a complete termination redemption. You establish that the redemption terminated Carla's direct stock ownership in the corporation, that she had no interest in the corporation since the redemption, and that she retained all records pertaining to the redemption. However, you cannot find any evidence that the notification agreement required of a family attribution waiver was properly filed. When asked about the missing agreement, Carla indicated that she knew nothing about any required agreement and that if such an agreement was required, her previous CPA should have taken care of it. Your partner has asked you to research whether it is still possible to file an effective family attribution waiver agreement for Carla. In a memo for the tax file, summarize the results of your research.

Use internet tax resources to address the following questions. Look for reliable websites and blogs of the IRS and other government agencies, media outlets, businesses, tax professionals, academics, think tanks, and political outlets.

Research Problem 4. Just how common are dividend distributions? Are dividends concentrated in the companies traded on the New York Stock Exchange, or do closely held corporations pay dividends in a similar manner? Did dividends decrease during the Great Recession of 2008 and 2009? Search for answers to these questions on the internet and/or in academic journal articles.

Communications
Data Analytics

In addition, using data from the IRS Tax Statistics website (**irs.gov/statistics**), find and analyze corporate balance sheet data (overall and by size of total assets) to provide answers to the questions above. Summarize the data you find in a Microsoft Excel spreadsheet, and report your findings to your instructor in a three-paragraph e-mail.

Research Problem 5. Code § 197 requires a 15-year amortization of certain intangibles incurred in the acquisition of a business, including covenants not to compete. Using the Thomson Reuters Checkpoint™ online tax research database, search *Frontier Chevrolet Co. v. Comm.* [2003–1 USTC ¶50490, 91 AFTR 2d 2003–2338, 329 F.3d 1131 (CA–9)] and determine if § 197 applies to a covenant not to compete incurred in connection with a stock redemption. Summarize your conclusion in an e-mail to your instructor.

Communications

Becker CPA Review Questions

Becker

1. On January 1, year 5, Olinto Corp., an accrual basis, calendar year C corporation, had $35,000 in accumulated earnings and profits. For year 5, Olinto had current earnings and profits of $15,000 and made two $40,000 cash distributions to its shareholders, one in April and one in September of year 5. What amount of the year 5 distributions is classified as dividend income to Olinto's shareholders?

   a. $15,000
   b. $35,000
   c. $50,000
   d. $80,000

2. Fox Corp. owned 2,000 shares of Duffy Corp. stock that it bought in year 0 for $9 per share. In year 8, when the fair market value of the Duffy stock was $20 per share, Fox distributed this stock to a noncorporate shareholder. Fox's recognized gain on this distribution was:

   a. $40,000
   b. $22,000
   c. $18,000
   d. $0

3. Ridge Corp., a calendar year C corporation, made a nonliquidating cash distribution to its shareholders of $1,000,000 with respect to its stock. At that time, Ridge's current and accumulated earnings and profits totaled $750,000 and its total paid-in capital for tax purposes was $10,000,000. Ridge had no corporate shareholders. Ridge's cash distribution:

   I. Was taxable as $750,000 in dividend income to its shareholders.
   II. Reduced its shareholders' adjusted bases in Ridge stock by $250,000.

   a. I only.
   b. II only.
   c. Both I and II.
   d. Neither I nor II.

4. Which of the following statements is *not* true?

   a. Affiliated corporations that file consolidated returns can take a 100% dividends received deduction.
   b. The dividends received deduction for a small investment in an unrelated corporation is 50%.
   c. The dividends received deduction for a large investment in a corporation is 65%.
   d. There is no income limitation on the dividends received deduction.

5. Jane is the sole shareholder of Buttons, Inc. Buttons has a deficit of $60,000 in accumulated earnings and profits (E & P) at the beginning of the current year. Current E & P is $35,000. If Buttons pays out a cash distribution to Jane during the current year of $50,000, how much is a taxable dividend to Jane?

   a. $0
   b. $35,000
   c. $50,000
   d. $85,000

6. Jane is the sole shareholder of Buttons, Inc. Buttons has accumulated earnings and profits (E & P) of $65,000 at the beginning of the current year. The current E & P is $35,000. Buttons pays out a property distribution to Jane during the current year with an FMV of $150,000 and an adjusted basis of $130,000. How much is a taxable dividend to Jane?

   a. $35,000
   b. $100,000
   c. $120,000
   d. $150,000

7. ABC Corp. paid two cash distributions during year 5. The first was $42,000, and the second was $33,000. Accumulated earnings and profits (E & P) at the end of year 4 were $80,000. Current E & P for year 5 is $30,000. How will the second distribution be allocated between current E & P and accumulated E & P?

	Current E & P	**Accumulated E & P**
a.	$13,200	$19,800
b.	$16,500	$16,500
c.	$19,800	$13,200
d.	$30,000	$30,000

8. ABC Corp. paid two cash distributions during year 5. The first was $42,000, and the second was $33,000. Accumulated earnings and profits (E & P) at the end of year 4 were $10,000. Current E & P for year 5 is $30,000. How will the first distribution be allocated between current E & P and accumulated E & P?

	Current E & P	**Accumulated E & P**
a.	$16,800	$25,200
b.	$16,800	$10,000
c.	$25,200	$16,800
d.	$30,000	$10,000

Chapter 20

Corporations: Distributions in Complete Liquidation and an Overview of Reorganizations

Learning Objectives: *After completing Chapter 20, you should be able to:*

LO.1 **Determine the tax consequences of complete liquidations for both the corporation and its shareholders.**

LO.2 **Determine the tax consequences of subsidiary liquidations for both the parent and the subsidiary corporations.**

LO.3 **Explain the general requirements and tax consequences of corporate reorganizations.**

LO.4 **Identify planning opportunities available to minimize the tax impact in complete liquidations and corporate reorganizations.**

Chapter Outline

The Options for Transitioning to Retirement

Mr. and Mrs. Albert Smithson have experienced great pride in Orange Corporation, the successful business that they built over their careers, but they believe the time has come for them to think seriously about retirement. They own all of the stock in Orange, a C corporation, and their stock investment has a basis of $200,000. The business, which pays Federal income tax at the 21 percent rate, owns net assets that are worth $4,000,000 and have a basis of $1,500,000.

Unfortunately, the Smithsons have no family members who are interested in carrying on the business, so they must resort to liquidating Orange Corporation. Their strategy, in general, is to convert the value of their business into a diversified portfolio of marketable securities and to live off the earnings generated by the portfolio during their retirement years. The Smithsons realize that such a plan will be taxable, so they would like to know the amount that will be available after all Federal taxes are paid. It is important that they have a realistic idea of the amount of the after-tax proceeds so that they can determine whether retiring at this point is even feasible. After working for their entire lives, they are eager to live comfortably off their retirement nest egg.

Read the chapter and formulate your response.

Like individuals, corporations sometimes can be personified as being in a particular stage of life. It may be early in a corporation's life, struggling for direction, or it could be later in life, thriving and enjoying continually higher levels of success. Alternatively, the corporation could be at a stage where its viability as a going concern does not seem feasible any longer, or the shareholders may believe the entity's future could be brighter if it were to reshape itself. This chapter discusses the tax implications if the shareholders decide to terminate the existence of the corporation by complete liquidation. In addition, corporate reorganizations are discussed, which essentially are business realignments where the business of the entity operates in a new form. In the case of a complete liquidation, both the shareholders and the corporation face tax consequences, unless a subsidiary corporation is liquidated by its parent. In contrast, a reorganization can produce tax-deferred treatment to both the shareholders and the corporations if the transaction takes one of several forms specified in the Code.

LO.1

Determine the tax consequences of complete liquidations for both the corporation and its shareholders.

20-1 Liquidations—In General

When a corporation makes a nonliquidating distribution (e.g., stock redemption), the entity continues as a going concern. With a complete liquidation, however, corporate existence terminates, as does each shareholder's ownership interest. A complete liquidation, like a qualifying stock redemption, produces sale or exchange treatment to the *shareholder*. However, the tax effects of a liquidation to the *corporation* vary somewhat from those of a redemption. Sale or exchange treatment is the general rule for the liquidating corporation, although some losses are disallowed.

20-1a The Liquidation Process

A **corporate liquidation** occurs when a corporation ceases to be a going concern. The corporation continues solely to wind up affairs, pay debts, and distribute any remaining assets to its shareholders. A legal dissolution under state law is not required. Further, a corporation can retain a nominal amount of assets to pay remaining debts and/or preserve its legal status and still liquidate for tax purposes.[1]

Shareholders may decide to liquidate a corporation for one or more reasons, including:

- The corporate business has been unsuccessful.
- The shareholders want to acquire the corporation's assets.
- Another person or entity wants to purchase the corporation's assets. The purchaser may buy the shareholders' stock and then liquidate the corporation to acquire the assets. Alternatively, the purchaser may buy the assets directly from the corporation. After the assets are sold, the corporation distributes the sales proceeds to its shareholders and liquidates.

As one might expect, the different means used to liquidate a corporation produce varying tax results.

20-1b Liquidating and Nonliquidating Distributions Compared

As discussed in Chapter 19, a *nonliquidating* distribution of noncash property produces gain (but not loss) recognition to the distributing corporation. For the shareholder, the receipt of cash or other property produces dividend income to the extent of the corporation's E & P or, in the case of a qualifying stock redemption, results in sale or exchange treatment.

Like a qualifying stock redemption, a *liquidation* produces sale or exchange treatment for the shareholders. E & P has no impact on the gain or loss recognized.[2] However, in a liquidation, a corporation generally recognizes gain *and* loss on any assets distributed.

[1] Reg. § 1.332–2(c).

[2] § 331.

Goose Corporation, with E & P of $40,000, makes a cash distribution of $50,000 to a shareholder. The shareholder's basis in the Goose stock is $20,000. If the distribution is not a qualifying stock redemption or in complete liquidation, the shareholder recognizes dividend income of $40,000 (the amount of Goose's E & P) and treats the remaining $10,000 of the distribution as a return of capital (i.e., stock basis is reduced to $10,000).

If the distribution is a qualifying stock redemption or is pursuant to a complete liquidation, the shareholder has a capital gain of $30,000 ($50,000 distribution − $20,000 stock basis). In the case of these distributions, Goose's E & P does not affect the shareholder's tax result.

In the event a corporate distribution results in a *loss* to the shareholder, another distinction exists between nonliquidating distributions and liquidations. Code § 267 (a) disallows recognition of losses between related parties in nonliquidating distributions but not in liquidating distributions.

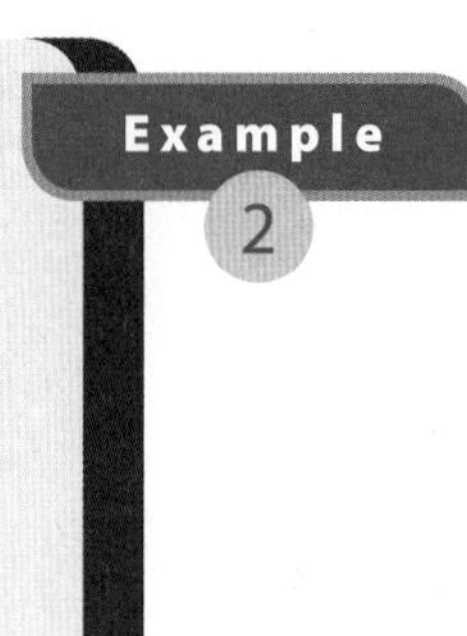

The stock of Tern Corporation is owned equally by three sisters, Pam, Meghann, and Natalie. When Natalie's basis in her stock is $40,000, the corporation distributes $30,000 to her in cancellation of all of her shares.

If the distribution is a qualifying stock redemption, the $10,000 realized loss is not recognized because Natalie and Tern Corporation are related parties. Under § 267, Natalie is deemed to own more than 50% in value of the corporation's outstanding stock. Natalie's direct ownership is 33⅓%, but through her sisters, she owns indirectly another 66⅔% for a total of 100%.

On the other hand, if the distribution is pursuant to a complete liquidation, Natalie's $10,000 realized loss is recognized.

The rules governing the basis of property received from a corporation are identical for both nonliquidating and liquidating distributions. Under § 301(d), the basis of property received in a *nonliquidating distribution* is its fair market value on the date of distribution, while § 334(a) provides the same treatment for property received in a *liquidating distribution*.

Text Section 20-2 discusses the tax consequences of a complete liquidation for the distributing corporation, and text Section 20-3 discusses the shareholder impacts. Because the tax rules differ when a subsidiary corporation is liquidated, these rules are discussed separately in text Section 20-4.

20-2 Liquidations—Effect on the Distributing Corporation

A corporation generally recognizes gain or loss on the distribution of property in a complete liquidation, but there are several exceptions to this rule.

20-2a The General Rule

Under § 336(a), a corporation recognizes *gain or loss* on the distribution of property in a complete liquidation as if the property were sold at its fair market value. This treatment is consistent with the notion of double taxation that is inherent in operating a business as a C corporation—once at the corporate level and again at the shareholder level.

As in the case of a nonliquidating distribution, if distributed property is subject to a corporate liability that is greater than the fair market value of the property, the liability amount is used to calculate gain or loss.

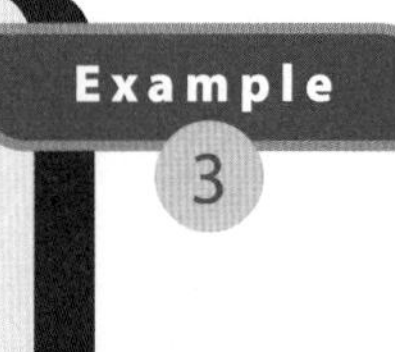

As part of a complete liquidation, Warbler Corporation distributes to its shareholders land held as an investment (basis of $200,000, fair market value of $300,000).

If no liability is involved, Warbler has a gain of $100,000 on the distribution ($300,000 − $200,000). The same result occurs (a gain of $100,000) if the land is subject to a liability of $250,000.

If, instead, the liability were $350,000, Warbler's gain on the distribution would be $150,000 ($350,000 − $200,000).

Liquidation expenses incurred by a corporation are deductible as trade or business expenses under § 162. Examples include accounting and legal costs of drafting and implementing a plan of liquidation, the cost of revoking the corporation's charter, and the basis of abandoned assets. Expenses related to the sale of property (e.g., brokerage commissions and legal costs incurred in title transfers) reduce the amount realized on the sale.

There are four exceptions to the general rule of gain and loss recognition by a liquidating corporation:

- *Losses* are not recognized on certain liquidating distributions to related-party shareholders.
- *Losses* are not recognized on certain sales and liquidating distributions of property that was contributed to the corporation with a built-in loss shortly before the adoption of a plan of liquidation.
- A subsidiary corporation does not recognize *gains or losses* on liquidating distributions to its parent corporation.
- A subsidiary corporation does not recognize *losses* on liquidating distributions to its minority shareholders.

The first two exceptions, referred to as the "antistuffing rules," are discussed in detail in text Section 20-2b and are summarized in Concept Summary 20.1. The last two exceptions, dealing with the liquidation of a subsidiary corporation, are discussed in text Section 20-4.

20-2b **Antistuffing Rules**

When property is transferred to a corporation in a § 351 transaction or as a contribution to capital, carryover basis rules generally apply (see Chapter 18). Usually, the transferee corporation takes a basis in the property equal to that of the transferor-shareholder, and the shareholder takes an equal basis in the stock received in the exchange (or adds this amount to existing stock basis in the case of a capital contribution). Without special limitations, a transfer of loss property (fair market value less than basis) in a carryover basis transaction would present opportunities for the duplication of losses.

The Big Picture

Example 4

Return to the facts of *The Big Picture* on p. 20-1. Assume that Mr. and Mrs. Smithson transfers property (basis of $100,000, fair market value of $55,000) to Orange Corporation in exchange for additional stock. The exchange qualifies under § 351. Absent any exceptions to the contrary, the general rule of carryover basis would apply and Orange would take a carryover basis of $100,000 in the property while the Smithsons would take a $100,000 basis in the additional stock.

A sale or liquidating distribution of the property by Orange Corporation would produce a $45,000 loss [$55,000 (fair market value of property) − $100,000 (property basis)]. Similarly, a sale by the Smithsons of the stock acquired in the § 351 exchange would also generate a $45,000 loss [$55,000 (fair market value of stock) − $100,000 (stock basis)].

Congress addressed this loss duplication issue by enacting two loss limitation ("antistuffing") rules under § 336(d) that apply to corporations on liquidation—loss property distributed to related parties and certain loss property distributed or sold that had been contributed with a built-in loss. The effect of these rules is to disallow some or all of a loss realized by a corporation in liquidating distributions (and, in some cases, sales) of certain property. Each of these rules is discussed below.

These two antistuffing rules limited the duplication of losses realized on a corporation's liquidation, but loss duplication was still possible in other situations (e.g., if the corporation sold high-basis property in the normal course of business rather than in a liquidation).

As a result, Congress enacted § 362(e)(2), which requires a corporation to reduce ("step down") the basis of property acquired in a § 351 or contribution to capital transaction by the amount of any net built-in loss embodied in such property. The basis step-down is required when a shareholder transfers properties having an aggregate basis in excess of their aggregate fair market value ("net built-in loss"), and it is allocated proportionately among the properties having built-in losses. Alternatively, the transferor-shareholder can elect to reduce their stock basis by the amount of net built-in loss. (See Chapter 18 for a complete discussion of the basis step-down rules.)

Although the antistuffing rules of § 336(d) continue to apply in the case of liquidating distributions (and certain sales) of loss property, their bite has been lessened somewhat by the § 362(e)(2) basis step-down rules.

Related-Party Loss Limitation

Losses are disallowed on liquidating distributions to *related parties* in either of the following cases:[3]

- The distribution is *not* pro rata, or
- The property distributed is disqualified property.

A corporation and a shareholder are considered related if the shareholder owns (directly or indirectly) more than 50 percent in value of the corporation's outstanding stock.[4]

A *pro rata distribution* is a distribution where *each* shareholder receives their proportionate share of the corporate asset distributed. Examples 5 and 6 illustrate a non pro rata distribution. *Disqualified property* is property that is acquired by the liquidating corporation in a § 351 or contribution to capital transaction during the five-year period ending on the date of the distribution. The related-party loss limitation can apply even if the property was appreciated (fair market value greater than basis) when it was transferred to the corporation. See Examples 7 and 8.

Related-Party Loss Limitations

Example 5

Bluebird Corporation stock is owned by Ana and Sanjay, who are unrelated. Ana owns 80% and Sanjay owns 20% of the stock in the corporation. Bluebird has the following assets (none of which were acquired in a § 351 or contribution to capital transaction); all are distributed in complete liquidation of the corporation.

	Adjusted Basis	Fair Market Value
Cash	$600,000	$600,000
Equipment	150,000	200,000
Building	400,000	200,000

Assume that Bluebird Corporation distributes the equipment to Sanjay and the cash and the building to Ana. Bluebird recognizes a gain of $50,000 on the distribution of the equipment. The loss of $200,000 on the building is disallowed because the property is distributed to a related party and the distribution is not pro rata (i.e., the building is not distributed 80% to Ana and 20% to Sanjay).

Example 6

Assume in Example 5 that Bluebird Corporation distributes the cash and equipment to Ana and the building to Sanjay.

As in Example 5, Bluebird recognizes the $50,000 gain on the equipment. However, it now recognizes the $200,000 loss on the building because the property is not distributed to a related party (i.e., Sanjay does not own more than 50% of the stock in Bluebird Corporation).

Example 7

Wren Corporation's stock is held equally by three brothers. Four years before Wren's liquidation, the shareholders transfer jointly owned property (basis of $150,000, fair market value of $200,000) to the corporation in return for stock in a § 351 transaction. When the property is worth $100,000, it is distributed pro rata to the brothers in a liquidating distribution.

Because disqualified property is involved and each brother owns directly and indirectly more than 50% of the stock (each owns 100% in this situation), none of the $50,000 realized loss [$100,000 (fair market value) − $150,000 (basis)] is recognized by Wren Corporation.

---

[3] § 336(d)(1).

[4] Code § 267 provides the definition of a related party for purposes of this provision. The rules are similar to the stock attribution rules discussed in Chapter 19; one exception, however, is that stock owned by a sibling is treated as owned by the taxpayer under § 267.

Related-Party Loss Limitations

Example 8

Assume in Example 7 that the property's fair market value is $100,000 at the time of the § 351 transfer and $75,000 at the time of the liquidating distribution to the brothers. As a result of the § 362(e)(2) basis step-down rules, Wren Corporation's basis in the property is $100,000 [$150,000 (basis to brothers) − $50,000 (net built-in loss of property transferred)].

In a liquidating distribution of the property to the brothers, Wren would realize a loss of $25,000 [$75,000 (fair market value of property at distribution) − $100,000 (Wren's stepped-down basis in property)]. Because this is a distribution of disqualified property to related parties, none of the $25,000 loss is recognized by Wren.

Built-In Loss Limitation

A second loss limitation applies to sales, exchanges, or distributions of built-in loss property (fair market value less than basis) that is transferred to a corporation shortly before the corporation is liquidated. The *built-in loss limitation* applies when *both* of the following conditions are met:

- The property was acquired by the corporation in a § 351 (or contribution to capital) transaction.
- This acquisition was part of a plan whose principal purpose was to recognize a loss on that property by the liquidating corporation. A tax avoidance purpose is presumed in the case of transfers occurring *within two years* of a liquidation plan being adopted.

This disallowance rule applies only to the extent that a property's built-in loss at transfer is not eliminated by a § 362(e)(2) stepped-down basis. Some built-in losses on property transfers will avoid the basis step-down either because built-in gain properties also were transferred by the shareholder (see Example 9) or because the shareholder elected to step down the basis of their stock instead. Any loss related to a decline in a property's value *after* its transfer to the corporation is not subject to the built-in loss limitation.[5]

Example 9

In the current year, Brown Corporation acquires two properties from a shareholder in a transaction that qualifies under § 351.

	Shareholder's Basis	Fair Market Value	Built-In Gain/(Loss)
Land	$100,000	$50,000	($50,000)
Securities	10,000	35,000	25,000
			($25,000)

The net built-in loss of $25,000 results in a stepped-down basis of $75,000 in the land for Brown Corporation [$100,000 (shareholder's basis) − $25,000 (step-down equal to net built-in loss)]. Later in the year, Brown adopts a plan of liquidation and distributes the land to an unrelated shareholder when the land is worth $30,000.

Of the $45,000 loss realized by Brown on the distribution [$30,000 (value of land on date of distribution) − $75,000 (basis in land)], $25,000 is disallowed by the built-in loss limitation [$50,000 (value of land when acquired by Brown) − $75,000 (stepped-down basis in land)] and $20,000 is recognized (equal to the decline in value occurring after acquisition by Brown).

The built-in loss limitation applies to a broader range of transactions than the related-party exception, which disallows losses only on certain *distributions* to related parties (i.e., more-than-50 percent shareholders). The built-in loss limitation can apply to distributions of property to any shareholder, including an unrelated party, and to a *sale or exchange* of property by a liquidating corporation. However, the limitation is narrower than the related-party exception in that it applies only to property that had a built-in loss upon its acquisition by the corporation (as adjusted by the basis step-down rules).

[5] § 336(d)(2).

Example 10

Assume in Example 9 that the land was worth $120,000 on the date Brown Corporation acquired the property. Since there is no net built-in loss on the transfer, Brown will have a basis of $100,000 in the land. If the distribution is to an unrelated shareholder, Brown Corporation will recognize the entire $70,000 loss [$30,000 (fair market value on date of distribution) − $100,000 (basis)].

However, if the distribution is to a related party, Brown cannot recognize any of the loss under the related-party loss limitation because the property is disqualified property. When the distribution is to a related party, the loss is disallowed even though the entire decline in value occurred during the period the corporation held the property.

Property held by the corporation for more than two years prior to the liquidation is usually not subject to the built-in loss limitation. Further, the presumption of a tax avoidance purpose for property transferred to a corporation in the "two years prior to liquidation" window can be contested if there is a clear and substantial business purpose for the transfer. When there is a business reason for the transfer, the built-in loss limitation will not apply. Compare Examples 11 and 12.

Presumption of Tax Avoidance Purpose

Example 11

Cardinal Corporation's stock is held by two unrelated individuals: 60% by Manuel and 40% by Jack. One year before Cardinal's liquidation, Manuel transfers land (basis of $150,000, fair market value of $100,000) and equipment (basis of $10,000, fair market value of $70,000) to the corporation as a contribution to capital. Since there is no net built-in loss on the transfer, Cardinal will have a basis of $150,000 in the land. There is no business reason for the transfer.

In liquidation, Cardinal distributes the land (now worth $90,000) to Jack. Even though the distribution is to an unrelated party, the built-in loss of $50,000 is not recognized. However, Cardinal Corporation can recognize the loss of $10,000 ($90,000 − $100,000) that occurred while it held the land.

If, instead, the land is distributed to Manuel, a related party, the entire $60,000 loss is disallowed under the related-party loss limitation.

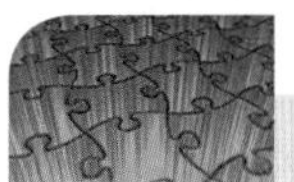

Concept Summary 20.1

Summary of Antistuffing Loss Disallowance Rules

Related-Party Loss Limitation

Distribution of loss property to a related party *and* distribution is not pro rata *or* property is disqualified property.

- Related party if shareholder owns directly or indirectly *more than* 50% in value of the stock.
  - Code § 267 attribution rules apply. Similar to § 318 attribution rules but includes stock owned by siblings.
- Distribution is pro rata if each shareholder receives proportional interest in property.
- Disqualified property is property acquired by the corporation within five years of the distribution date in a § 351 or contribution to capital transaction.

Limitation can apply even if a corporation acquired property by purchase or in a carryover basis transaction with no built-in loss (i.e., fair market greater than basis).

Limitation does not apply to *sales* of loss property.

Built-In Loss Limitation

Distribution, sale, or exchange of certain built-in loss property (fair market value less than basis).

- Property was acquired in a § 351 or contribution to capital transaction.
- Acquisition was part of a plan whose principal purpose was to recognize a loss on the property by the corporation upon liquidation.
  - Presumption of tax avoidance purpose if property was acquired within two years of the date of the plan of liquidation.
  - Clear and substantial business purpose for a transfer of property to a corporation can rebut the presumption.
  - Transfers occurring more than two years before liquidation are rarely subject to the loss limitation.

Loss limitation applies only to amount of the built-in loss at the time of transfer to a corporation (excess of corporation's basis in property over fair market value of property).

- Basis step-down rules will eliminate many built-in losses. However, loss limitation remains applicable where built-in loss is not entirely eliminated by the basis step-down (i.e., built-in gain property transferred with built-in loss property) or where the shareholder elected to step down basis of stock.

Presumption of Tax Avoidance Purpose

Example 12

Assume in Example 11 that the land and equipment are transferred to Cardinal Corporation because a bank required the additional capital investment as a condition to making a loan to the corporation.

Because there is a business purpose for the transfer, all of the $60,000 loss is recognized if the land is distributed to Jack in liquidation.

If, instead, the land is distributed to Manuel, a related party, the entire loss is still disallowed under the related-party loss limitation.

20-3 Liquidations—Effect on the Shareholder

The tax consequences to the shareholders of a corporation in the process of liquidation are generally governed by § 331. The exception to this rule, § 332, applies in the liquidation of a subsidiary (discussed in text Section 20-4).

Under § 331(a), a liquidating distribution results in sale or exchange treatment for the shareholders. As a result, the difference between the fair market value of the assets received from the corporation and the adjusted basis of the stock surrendered is the gain or loss recognized by the shareholder. The fair market value of property received subject to a corporate liability is reduced by the amount of the liability. Typically, the stock is a capital asset in the hands of the shareholder, and capital gain or loss results. The taxpayer must be able to document the adjusted basis of the stock. Without documentation, the stock is deemed to have a zero basis.[6] The basis of property received in a liquidation is the property's fair market value on the date of distribution.[7] If installment notes are distributed in liquidation, shareholders can use the installment method to defer to the point of collection the portion of their gain that is attributable to the notes.[8]

Any taxes paid by a corporation as a result of liquidation gains will reduce the proceeds available to be distributed to the shareholders. This will reduce the amount realized by the shareholders, which will then reduce their gain (or increase the loss) recognized.

The Big Picture

Example 13

Return to the facts of *The Big Picture* on p. 20-1. At the point when the Smithsons are contemplating retirement, their business, Orange Corporation, has net assets worth $4,000,000. This valuation is after the payment of all of Orange's corporate debts except for taxes it would pay on net gains recognized if it liquidates. Assuming that the Smithsons decide to liquidate the corporation and the taxes the corporation pays total $525,000, the amount realized by the Smithsons is $3,475,000 ($4,000,000 − $525,000).

The Big Picture

Example 14

Return to the facts of *The Big Picture* on p. 20-1. Continuing with the preceding example, if Orange Corporation liquidates and the Smithsons receive a liquidating distribution of $3,475,000, they will recognize a capital gain of $3,275,000 ($3,475,000 amount realized − $200,000 stock basis). The basis of any property the Smithsons receive will be its fair market value.

[6] See *John Calderazzo*, 34 TCM 1, T.C.Memo. 1975–1; and *Coloman v. Comm.*, 76–2 USTC ¶9581, 38 AFTR 2d 5523, 540 F.2d 427 (CA–9).

[7] § 334(a).

[8] § 453(h). Shareholders must allocate their stock basis between the notes and the other assets received in the liquidation. Upon distribution, the corporation generally recognizes gain (or loss) equal to the difference between the fair market value of the notes and the corporation's basis in the notes. § 453B(a).

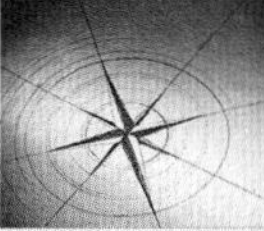

Ethics & Equity **Transferee Liability for Tax Deficiency of Liquidated Corporation**

In 2021, Loon Corporation distributed all of its remaining assets to two equal shareholders in a complete liquidation. The two shareholders, Gloria and Roger, each received a distribution of $250,000 for their stock in Loon.

In 2023, the IRS audited Loon Corporation and assessed additional income tax of $175,000 (plus penalties and interest) against the corporation. Since Loon was defunct and without assets, the IRS then assessed the entire deficiency against Gloria, based on transferee liability. The IRS did not attempt to collect any of the deficiency from Roger.

Is this an equitable solution to the collection of Loon's tax liability? Explain.

20-4 Liquidations—Parent–Subsidiary Situations

LO.2

Determine the tax consequences of subsidiary liquidations for both the parent and the subsidiary corporations.

An exception to the general rule of § 331, § 332 provides that a parent corporation does *not* recognize gain or loss on a liquidation of a subsidiary. In addition, the subsidiary corporation recognizes *neither gain nor loss* on liquidating distributions of property to its parent.[9]

There are three requirements for applying § 332:

- The parent must own at least 80 percent of the subsidiary's stock (both voting power and value).
- All of the subsidiary's property must be distributed in complete cancellation of all of its stock within the taxable year or within three years from the close of the tax year in which the first distribution occurred.
- The subsidiary must be solvent.[10]

If these requirements are met, nonrecognition of gains and losses is *mandatory*. However, if the subsidiary is insolvent, the parent corporation will have an ordinary loss deduction under § 165(g) equal to its basis in the subsidiary stock.

If the liquidation involves several distributions, the 80 percent test must be met on the date the plan of liquidation is adopted and maintained until the final liquidating distribution is received by the parent.[11] If the parent fails the 80 percent test at any time, the provisions for nonrecognition of gain or loss do not apply to any distribution.[12]

Concept Summary 20.2 (presented later in the chapter) contrasts the parent-subsidiary rules with other liquidation rules.

20-4a Minority Shareholder Interests

In a § 332 parent-subsidiary liquidation, up to 20 percent of the subsidiary's stock can be owned by minority shareholders. In such liquidations, a distribution of property to a minority shareholder is treated in the same manner as a *nonliquidating* distribution. That is, the subsidiary corporation recognizes gain (but not loss) on the property distributed to the minority shareholder.[13]

The stock of Tan Corporation is held by Mustard Corporation (80%) and by Arethia, an individual (20%). Tan Corporation is liquidated pursuant to a plan adopted earlier in the year. At the time of its liquidation, Tan Corporation has assets with a basis of $100,000 and fair market value of $500,000. Tan Corporation distributes the property pro rata to Mustard Corporation and to Arethia.

Tan must recognize a gain of $80,000 [($500,000 fair market value − $100,000 basis) × 20% minority interest]. The remaining gain of $320,000 is not recognized because it relates to property being distributed to Mustard, the parent corporation.

[9] § 337(a). This is an exception to the general rule of § 336.

[10] § 332(b) and Reg. §§ 1.332–2(a) and (b).

[11] Establishing the date of the adoption of a plan of complete liquidation could be crucial in determining whether § 332 applies. See, for example, *George L. Riggs, Inc.*, 64 T.C. 474 (1975).

[12] § 332(b)(3) and Reg. § 1.332–2(a).

[13] §§ 336(a) and (d)(3).

Global Tax Issues **Basis Rules for Liquidations of Foreign Subsidiaries**

The basis of property acquired by a parent corporation in the liquidation of a subsidiary corporation is generally equal to the basis the subsidiary had in such property. However, legislation a number of years ago modified the basis rules regarding property acquired by a U.S. parent in certain § 332 liquidations of foreign subsidiaries.

In general, if the aggregate basis in a foreign subsidiary's assets exceeds their aggregate fair market value, the U.S. parent will take a fair market value basis in the property acquired. The purpose of this amendment is to deny the importation of built-in losses (excess of basis over fair market value). [See §§ 334(b)(1)(B) and 362(e)(1)(B).]

A minority shareholder is subject to the general rule requiring the recognition of gain or loss in a liquidation. As a result, the difference between the fair market value of the assets received and the basis of the minority shareholder's stock is the amount of gain or loss recognized. The basis of property received by the minority shareholder is the property's fair market value on the date of distribution.[14]

20-4b **Indebtedness of the Subsidiary to the Parent**

If a subsidiary transfers appreciated property to its parent to satisfy a debt, it must recognize gain on the transaction unless the subsidiary is liquidating and the conditions of § 332 apply. When § 332 applies, the subsidiary does not recognize gain or loss upon the transfer of property to the parent in satisfaction of indebtedness.[15]

Eagle Corporation owes its parent, Finch Corporation, $20,000. It satisfies the obligation by transferring land (basis of $8,000, fair market value of $20,000) to Finch. Normally, Eagle would recognize a gain of $12,000 on the transaction. However, if the transfer relates to a liquidation under § 332, Eagle does not recognize a gain.

This nonrecognition provision does not apply to the parent corporation. The parent corporation recognizes gain or loss on the receipt of property in satisfaction of indebtedness even if the property is received during liquidation of the subsidiary.

Pelican Corporation owns bonds (basis of $95,000) of its subsidiary, Crow Corporation, that were acquired at a discount. Upon liquidation of Crow pursuant to § 332, Pelican receives a distribution of $100,000, the face amount of the bonds. The transaction has no tax effect on Crow. However, Pelican Corporation recognizes a gain of $5,000 [$100,000 (amount realized) − $95,000 (basis in bonds)].

20-4c **Basis of Property Received by the Parent Corporation—The General Rule**

Property received by the parent corporation in the complete liquidation of a subsidiary has the same basis it had in the hands of the subsidiary.[16] Unless the parent corporation makes a § 338 election (discussed in text Section 20-4d), this carryover basis in the assets generally will differ from the parent's basis in the stock of the subsidiary. Because the liquidation is a nontaxable exchange, the parent's gain or loss on the difference in basis is not recognized. Further, the parent's basis in the stock of the subsidiary disappears.

Basis Issues in Subsidiary Liquidations

Lark Corporation has a basis of $200,000 in the stock of Heron Corporation, a subsidiary in which it owns 85% of all classes of stock. Lark purchased the Heron stock 10 years ago. In the current year, Lark liquidates Heron and acquires assets that are worth $800,000 and have a tax basis to Heron of $500,000.

Lark Corporation takes a basis of $500,000 in the assets, with a potential gain on their sale of $300,000. Lark's $200,000 basis in Heron's stock disappears.

[14] § 334(a).

[15] § 337(b)(1).

[16] § 334(b)(1) and Reg. § 1.334–1(b). But see § 334(b)(1)(B) (exception for property acquired in some liquidations of foreign subsidiaries).

Basis Issues in Subsidiary Liquidations

Indigo Corporation has a basis of $600,000 in the stock of Kackie Corporation, a wholly owned subsidiary acquired 10 years ago. It liquidates Kackie Corporation and receives assets that are worth $400,000 and have a tax basis to Kackie of $300,000.

Indigo Corporation takes a basis of $300,000 in the assets it acquires from Kackie. If Indigo sells the assets, it has a gain of $100,000 even though its basis in the Kackie stock was $600,000. Indigo's loss on its stock investment in Kackie will never be recognized.

In addition to the parent corporation taking the subsidiary's basis in its assets, the parent's holding period for the assets includes that of the subsidiary.[17] Further, the carryover rules of § 381 apply. As a result, the parent acquires other tax attributes of the subsidiary, including the subsidiary's net operating loss carryover, business credit carryover, capital loss carryover, and E & P.

20-4d **Basis of Property Received by the Parent Corporation—§ 338 Election**

As discussed above, the liquidation of a subsidiary generally is a nontaxable transaction resulting in the nonrecognition of gain or loss for both the parent and the subsidiary corporations and the carryover of the subsidiary's asset bases (and other tax attributes). This treatment reflects the fact that such a liquidation often is merely a change in corporate structure and not a change in substance. This is particularly the case when the parent has owned the stock of the subsidiary since the subsidiary's inception. In these cases, the carried-over bases are comparable to what the parent would have if it, and not the subsidiary, had originally acquired the assets.

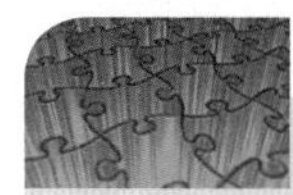

Concept Summary 20.2

Summary of Liquidation Rules

Effect on the Shareholder	Basis of Property Received	Effect on the Corporation
§ 331—The general rule provides for gain or loss treatment on the difference between the FMV of property received and the basis of the stock in the corporation. Gain allocable to installment notes received can be deferred to the point of collection.	§ 334(a)—Basis of assets received by the shareholder will be the FMV on the date of distribution (except for installment obligations on which gain is deferred to the point of collection).	§ 336—Gain or loss is recognized for distributions in kind and for sales by the liquidating corporation. Losses are not recognized for distributions to related parties if the distribution is not pro rata or if disqualified property is distributed. Losses may be disallowed on sales and distributions of built-in loss property even if made to unrelated parties.
§ 332—In liquidation of a subsidiary, no gain or loss is recognized by the parent. Subsidiary must distribute all of its property within the taxable year or within three years from the close of the taxable year in which the first distribution occurs. Minority shareholders are taxed under the general rule of § 331.	§ 334(b)(1)—Property has the same basis that it had in the hands of the subsidiary. Parent's basis in the stock disappears. Carryover rules of § 381 apply. Minority shareholders get FMV basis under § 334(a).	§ 337—No gain or loss is recognized by the subsidiary on distributions to the parent. Gain (but not loss) is recognized on distributions to minority shareholders.
	§ 338—Subsidiary need not be liquidated. If subsidiary is liquidated, parent's basis in the assets is the new stepped-up (or -down) basis. Parent's basis in the stock disappears. Carryover rules of § 381 apply, but such amounts are likely to be nominal.	§ 338—Gain or loss is recognized by the subsidiary. Subsidiary is treated as a new corporation, and its basis in the assets is stepped up (or down) to reflect the parent's basis in the subsidiary stock plus subsidiary's liabilities. New basis is allocated among various asset classes.

[17] § 1223(2).

The carryover basis rule for § 332 liquidations can result in some inequities when the subsidiary has been in existence for some time prior to the parent's acquisition of the subsidiary's stock. The parent's basis in the stock of the subsidiary will reflect the fair market value of the subsidiary's assets (and goodwill) at the time of the stock purchase. As a result, the parent's basis in the stock of the subsidiary will usually be greater than the subsidiary's basis in its assets. In this case, a subsidiary liquidation under § 332 would result in the parent taking a basis in the subsidiary's assets that is less than the parent's basis in the stock of the subsidiary. This is the case even if the parent acquired the subsidiary stock solely to obtain the subsidiary's assets.

If the parent could treat the purchase of the subsidiary stock as a purchase of its assets, the parent could take a basis in the assets equal to the acquisition cost of the stock. In most cases, this would mean a higher asset basis and, as a result, larger depreciation deductions and lower gains upon disposition for the parent. To obtain this stock-basis-for-asset-basis result, taxpayers successfully devised stock purchase/subsidiary liquidation transactions that fell outside § 332.[18] Congress codified this treatment by enacting § 338, which permits the purchase of a controlling interest of stock to be treated as a purchase of the subsidiary's assets.

Requirements for Application

A corporation (the "parent") may *elect* the provisions of § 338 if it acquires at least 80 percent of the stock (both voting power and value) of another corporation (the "subsidiary") within a 12-month period (*"qualified stock purchase"*). The stock must be acquired in a *taxable* transaction (i.e., a transaction where § 351 and other nonrecognition provisions do not apply). An acquisition of stock by any member of an affiliated group that includes the parent corporation is considered to be an acquisition by the parent. The **§ 338 election** must be made by the fifteenth day of the ninth month beginning after the month in which a qualified stock purchase occurs. If made, the election is irrevocable.

Tax Consequences

If § 338 is elected, the subsidiary is treated as having sold its assets on the qualified stock purchase date for a value that is determined with reference to the parent's basis in the subsidiary stock plus any liabilities of the subsidiary ("aggregate deemed sale price").[19] The subsidiary is then treated as a new corporation that purchased those assets for a similarly computed amount ("adjusted grossed-up basis") on the day following the qualified stock purchase date.[20] The deemed sale results in gain (or loss) recognition by the subsidiary, and the deemed purchase results in a stepped-up (or -down) basis for the subsidiary's assets.[21] The subsidiary may, but need not, be liquidated. If the subsidiary is liquidated, the parent will obtain a carryover of the stepped-up (or -down) basis of the subsidiary's assets.

A Comparison of the General Rule and the § 338 Election

Under § 332, the liquidation of a subsidiary is tax-free to both the subsidiary (except for any minority interest) and the parent corporation. Under § 338, the subsidiary recognizes gain (or loss) on the deemed disposition of its assets, while the liquidation of the subsidiary remains tax-free to the parent. Although a carryover basis rule applies in both cases, the subsidiary's assets generally will have a stepped-up basis as a result of the § 338 election and a liquidation of the subsidiary will result in a carryover of the stepped-up basis to the parent. Regardless of whether a § 338 election is made, a liquidation of the subsidiary results in a carryover of its other tax attributes (e.g., E & P) to the parent. However, when the election is made, the subsidiary is treated as a new corporation as of the day following the qualified stock purchase date; as a result, any tax attributes acquired by the parent are likely to be nominal (or zero) in amount.

---

[18] See, for example, *U.S. v. M.O.J. Corp.*, 60–1 USTC ¶9209, 5 AFTR 2d 535, 274 F.2d 713 (CA–5). See also *Kimbell-Diamond Milling Co.*, 14 T.C. 74 (1950), *aff'd* 51–1 USTC ¶9201, 40 AFTR 328, 187 F.2d 718 (CA–5), *cert. den.* 72 S.Ct. 50 (1951) (IRS argued stock-for-asset basis).

[19] See §§ 338(a)(1) and (b) and Reg. § 1.338–4.

[20] See §§ 338(a)(2) and (b) and Reg. § 1.338–5.

[21] For the rules governing the allocation of the purchase price to the assets, see § 338(b)(5) and Reg. § 1.338–6.

The holding period of the subsidiary's assets is determined with reference to the substance of the transaction. When the subsidiary is liquidated and there is no § 338 election, the subsidiary's historical holding period in its assets carries over to the parent. This is the typical carryover rule found in other nonrecognition provisions. A § 338 election, however, assumes a sale and repurchase of the subsidiary's assets. As a result of these deemed transactions, the holding period starts anew. If there is a § 338 election and the subsidiary is liquidated, the holding period of the property received by the parent begins on the date of the qualified stock purchase. On the other hand, if there is a § 338 election and the subsidiary is not liquidated, the holding period of the assets begins on the day *after* the qualified stock acquisition date. Exhibit 20.1 illustrates the consequences of a § 338 election to both the parent and subsidiary corporations.

Exhibit 20.1 **Consequences of a Section 338 Election**

Assume the following:

- Parent acquires 100% of Subsidiary's stock for $750,000 on August 5, 2023.
- Subsidiary (E & P of $400,000) has only one asset, land (fair market value of $1,000,000, basis of $504,000), no liabilities, and no loss or tax credit carryovers.
- Parent files a timely § 338 election, and both aggregate deemed sale price (ADSP) and adjusted grossed-up basis (AGUB) are $815,392.

Subsidiary Is Liquidated

Consequences to Subsidiary:

Deemed to have sold the land for ADSP of $815,392, which results in a recognized gain of $311,392 [$815,392 (ADSP) − $504,000 (basis)], and tax of $65,392 ($311,392 × 21%). The land's new basis is $815,392 (AGUB). No gain or loss recognized on distribution of land to Parent.

Consequences to Parent:

No gain or loss recognized on receipt of land from Subsidiary. Basis in land is $815,392; holding period for the land begins on August 5, 2023; and basis in Subsidiary stock disappears. Acquires Subsidiary's E & P, but that amount is $0 as a result of the § 338 election.

Subsidiary Is *Not* Liquidated

Consequences to Subsidiary:

Deemed to have sold the land for ADSP of $815,392, which results in a recognized gain of $311,392 [$815,392 (ADSP) − $504,000 (basis)], and tax of $65,392 ($311,392 × 21%).
Treated as a new corporation (e.g., E & P of $0) as of August 6, 2023; land's new basis is $815,392 (AGUB); and holding period for the land begins on August 6, 2023.

Consequences to Parent:

No tax consequences. Basis in Subsidiary stock remains unchanged at $750,000.

20-5 **Corporate Reorganizations**

LO.3

Explain the general requirements and tax consequences of corporate reorganizations.

In the context of Federal income taxation, a reorganization is a change in the legal or economic structure of a business entity. It may be a process of combining two or more corporations into one entity, but it may also be the spin-off or split-up of one large corporation into multiple separate entities. Corporations may engage in reorganizations to improve efficiency, consolidate management functions, or enhance operations. No matter the outcome, a reorganization can significantly change the structure and appearance of the business.

Carrying out corporate reorganizations can be expensive and chaotic. Because the dollar value of most reorganizations is substantial, the tax implications can be significant. Shareholders and corporations generally avoid transaction-year gain or loss recognition if they plan and execute a reorganization that is classified under one of seven major types identified in the Code.

Tax planning is essential to reducing the present value of Federal income taxes for events involving corporate reorganizations. When feasible, parties contemplating a corporate reorganization should obtain a letter ruling from the IRS to determine the anticipated income tax effect of the reorganization. Such a letter acts as a form of insurance that the transaction qualifies for elimination or reduction of the possible current-period taxes for the corporations and their shareholders.

20-5a **In General**

Although the term **reorganization** commonly is associated with a corporation in financial difficulty, for tax purposes the term refers to any corporate restructuring that may be currently tax-free under § 368.[22] To qualify as a tax-free reorganization, a corporate restructuring must meet not only the specific requirements of the tax Code but also several general requirements. These requirements include the following:

1. There must be a *plan of reorganization.*
2. The reorganization must meet the *continuity of interest* and the *continuity of business enterprise* tests provided in the Regulations.
3. The judicial doctrine of having a *sound business purpose* must be met.
4. The court-imposed *step transaction* doctrine should not be applicable.

All of these concepts are discussed in this chapter. The initial and most important consideration, however, is whether the reorganization qualifies for nonrecognition status under § 368.

20-5b **Different Types of Reorganizations**

The tax law specifies seven corporate restructurings or *reorganizations* that qualify as nontaxable exchanges. If the transaction fails to qualify as a reorganization, it will not receive the special tax-favored treatment. Therefore, a corporation considering a business reorganization must determine in advance whether the proposed transaction specifically falls within one of these seven types.

The Code states, in § 368(a)(1), that the term *reorganization* applies to any of the following:

A. A statutory merger or consolidation.
B. The acquisition by a corporation of another using solely stock of each corporation (voting-stock-for-stock exchange).
C. The acquisition by a corporation of substantially all of the property of another corporation in exchange for voting stock (voting-stock-for-asset exchange).
D. The transfer of all or part of a corporation's assets to another corporation when the original corporation's shareholders are in control of the new corporation immediately after the transfer (divisive exchange: spin-off, split-off, or split-up).
E. A recapitalization.
F. A mere change in identity, form, or place of organization.
G. A transfer by a corporation of all or a part of its assets to another corporation in a bankruptcy or receivership proceeding.

These seven types of tax-free reorganizations typically are designated by their identifying letters: "Type A," "Type B," "Type C," etc. Each will be described in more detail later in the chapter.

20-5c **Tax Consequences in a Tax-Free Reorganization**

The tax treatment for the parties involved in a tax-free reorganization almost parallels the treatment under the like-kind exchange provisions of § 1031 (see Chapter 13); however, those rules apply only to real estate and not to the exchange of stock or securities.[23]

---

[22] Code § 368 does not allow taxpayers to permanently avoid recognition of a realized gain as a result of a reorganization. Instead, it provides opportunities for taxpayers to defer recognition of gain until a later date.

[23] § 1031(a)(2).

When an investor exchanges stock in one corporation for another, the exchange generally constitutes a taxable transaction. A qualifying reorganization avoids such treatment by creating a nontaxable exchange under § 368. Concept Summary 20.3 is useful in computing the gain or loss recognized and the basis in the new stock received in a corporate reorganization.

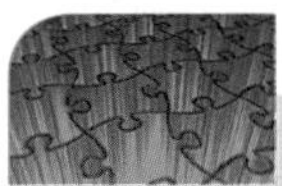

Concept Summary 20.3

Gain and Basis Rules for Nontaxable Exchanges

(1) Realized Gain/Loss	(2) Recognized Gain (Not Loss)	(3) Postponed Gain/Loss	(4) Basis of New Asset
Amount realized − Basis of asset(s) surrendered	Lesser of boot received or gain realized	Realized gain/loss (column 1) − Recognized gain (column 2)	FMV of asset (stock) received − Postponed gain (column 3) or + Postponed loss (column 3)
Realized gain/loss	Recognized gain	Postponed gain/loss	Basis in new asset (stock)

Example 20

Castel holds 1,000 shares of Lotus stock that were purchased for $6,000 several years ago. In a merger of Lotus into Blossom, Inc., Castel exchanges these 1,000 Lotus shares for 500 Blossom shares. The Lotus stock and the Blossom stock both are valued at $10,000. Assuming that this exchange qualifies for tax-free treatment under § 368, Castel's recognized gain and basis in the Blossom stock are computed as follows, using the template of Concept Summary 20.3.

Realized Gain	Recognized Gain	Postponed Gain	Basis in Blossom Stock
$10,000	$-0-	$4,000	$10,000
−6,000			−4,000
$ 4,000			$ 6,000

The exchange of Castel's stock produces no Federal income tax consequences for Lotus or Blossom.

Gain or Loss

Corporations meeting the § 368 requirements do not recognize current gains or losses on reorganizations. However, gain recognition may occur when other property is transferred by the acquiring corporation in the reorganization. **Other property**, also called **boot**, is any asset other than stock or securities exchanged in the reorganization.[24] If boot is transferred, gain but not loss may be recognized.

In a qualifying reorganization, Acquiring exchanges $800,000 of stock and land valued at $200,000 ($150,000 basis) for all of Target's assets, which have a value of $1,000,000 and a $600,000 basis. Due to the boot (land) it used in the transfer, Acquiring recognizes a $50,000 gain ($200,000 − $150,000) on the reorganization. If Target distributes the land to its shareholders, it does not recognize gain on the boot received. If Target retains the land, however, it recognizes a gain to the extent of the *boot* received, $200,000.

[24] §§ 361(a) and (b).

Generally, the shareholders of corporations involved in a tax-free reorganization do not recognize gain or loss when exchanging their stock unless they receive boot in addition to stock. As demonstrated in Concept Summary 20.3, the gain recognized by the stockholder is the lesser of the boot received or the realized gain. This is analogous to the treatment of boot in a real estate like-kind exchange. The only instance when shareholders may recognize (deduct) losses in reorganizations is when they receive solely boot and no stock.

Example 22

Kalla, the sole shareholder of Target in Example 21, has a $700,000 basis in her stock. She exchanges her Target stock for the $800,000 of Acquiring stock plus the land ($200,000) transferred by Acquiring to Target. The recognized gain for Kalla is the lesser of boot received (land, $200,000) or realized gain ($300,000). Thus, Kalla incurs a $200,000 recognized gain on the reorganization.

Realized Gain	Recognized Gain	Postponed Gain	Basis in Acquiring Stock
$1,000,000*	$200,000	$ 300,000	$800,000
−700,000	Boot	−200,000	−100,000
$ 300,000		$ 100,000	$700,000

*$800,000 Acquiring stock + $200,000 land.

Once gain is recognized, its tax character must be determined. The following are the possibilities for gain characterization.

- The gain is taxed as a dividend to the extent of the shareholder's proportionate share of earnings and profits (E & P). The remaining gain generally is capital gain.
- If the requirements of § 302(b) can be met, the transaction is treated similarly to a stock redemption, receiving capital gain treatment (see text Section 19-4).

Sam Adams acquired his 5% interest in Target 15 years ago for $55,000. He exchanges his Target stock for $50,000 cash and 2% of Acquiring's outstanding stock worth $100,000. At the time of the reorganization, Target's E & P is $60,000. Sam's recognized gain and basis in the Acquiring stock are computed as follows.

Realized Gain	Recognized Gain	Postponed Gain	Basis in Acquiring Stock
$150,000*	$50,000	$95,000	$100,000
−55,000	Boot	−50,000	−45,000
$ 95,000		$45,000	$ 55,000

*$100,000 Acquiring stock + $50,000 cash.

The first $3,000 ($60,000 Target E & P × 5% ownership) of the $50,000 gain recognized by Sam is taxed as a dividend, and the remaining $47,000 is treated as a long-term capital gain.

Debt security holders receive treatment similar to shareholders. They recognize gain only when the principal (face) amount of the debt received is greater than the principal (face) amount of the debt surrendered. Gain is recognized when debt instruments are received and none are relinquished.

The term **security** is not defined in the Code or the Regulations. Generally, however, debt instruments with terms longer than 10 years (e.g., bonds) are treated as securities, and those with terms of five years or less (e.g., notes) are not. An exception to this general rule occurs when the debt instrument issued by the acquiring corporation is exchanged for target obligations having the same term and/or maturity date.[25]

[25]Rev.Rul. 2004–78.

Financial Disclosure Insights

Digital Transformation Drives M&A Activity

While 2022 saw a reduction in global M&A activity, access to new technology, increased efficiencies, and access to new capabilities will drive interest in mergers and acquisitions according to KPMG. Deals where a non-tech firm purchased a tech firm jumped 68 percent according to their study. Increasing inflation and recession headwinds may not be strong enough to overcome the need to stay competitive. Want to learn more? Read about it at **https://tinyurl.com/4he64tkp**.

Example 24

Addison holds a debt instrument from Hibiscus with a principal value of $10,000 and a maturity date of December 31, 2022. In connection with the merger of Hibiscus and Tea, Addison exchanges Hibiscus debt for a $10,000 Tea note that also matures on December 31, 2022. Even though the Tea notes do not have a term remaining of more than five years, they qualify for tax-free reorganization treatment because they have the same term as the Hibiscus security.

Assume, instead, that in exchange for the $10,000 debt instrument, Addison receives a note from Tea with a $15,000 principal value. Addison recognizes a $5,000 capital gain on the exchange. The basis in the Tea bond is $15,000 ($10,000 original basis + $5,000 gain recognized).

Basis

The assets transferred from the target corporation to the acquiring corporation retain their basis (called carryover basis). The acquiring corporation's carryover basis is increased by any gain recognized by the target corporation on the reorganization, as shown in Concept Summary 20.4.

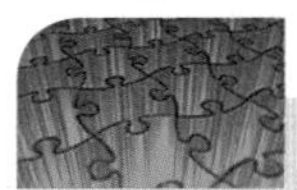

Concept Summary 20.4

Basis to Acquiring Corporation of Property Received

Target's basis in property transferred	$xx,xxx
Plus: Gain recognized by Target on the transaction	x,xxx
Equals: Basis of property to Acquiring corporation	$xx,xxx

Example 25

Target exchanges its assets with a value of $5,000,000 and a $3,000,000 basis for $4,500,000 of Acquiring stock and $500,000 of land. Target does not distribute the land to its shareholders. Target recognizes a $500,000 gain on the reorganization due to the boot (land) not being distributed. Acquiring's basis in the assets received from Target is $3,500,000 [$3,000,000 (Target's basis) + $500,000 (Target's gain recognized)].

In a tax-free reorganization, the shareholder/bondholder starts with a tax basis in the stock and securities received that is equal to the basis of the stock and securities surrendered (called substituted basis). This basis is decreased by the fair market value of boot received and increased by the gain and/or dividend income recognized on the transaction.

Basis also may be computed using the Concept Summary 20.3 template. Using the template, the fair market value of the stock and securities received is reduced by the gain (or increased by the loss) postponed. This basis computation ensures that the postponed gain or loss is recognized when the new stock or securities are disposed of in a future taxable transaction.

Basis Computations

Example 26

All of Quinn's Target stock is exchanged for Acquiring stock plus $3,000 cash. The exchange is pursuant to a tax-free reorganization. Quinn paid $10,000 for the Target stock two years ago. The Acquiring stock received by Quinn has a $12,000 fair market value. Quinn has a $5,000 realized gain, which is recognized to the extent of the boot received, $3,000. The basis in the Acquiring stock is $10,000.

Realized Gain	Recognized Gain	Postponed Gain	Basis in Acquiring Stock
$15,000*	$3,000	$5,000	$12,000
−10,000	Boot	−3,000	−2,000
$ 5,000		$2,000	$10,000

*$12,000 Acquiring stock + $3,000 cash.

Example 27

Assume the same facts as in Example 26, except that Quinn's Target stock basis was $16,000. Quinn realizes a $1,000 loss on the exchange, none of which is recognized. The basis in the Acquiring stock is computed as follows.

Realized Gain	Recognized Loss	Postponed Loss	Basis in Acquiring Stock
$15,000*	$-0-	($1,000)	$12,000
−16,000		− 0	+ 1,000
($ 1,000)		($1,000)	$13,000

*$12,000 Acquiring stock + $3,000 cash.

LO.4

Identify planning opportunities available to minimize the tax impact in complete liquidations and corporate reorganizations.

20-6 Tax Planning

20-6a Effect of a Liquidating Distribution on the Corporation

With the exception of parent-subsidiary liquidations, liquidating distributions are taxed at both the corporate level and the shareholder level. When a corporation liquidates, it can, as a general rule, claim losses on assets that have depreciated in value. These assets should not be distributed in the form of a property dividend or stock redemption because losses are not recognized on nonliquidating distributions.

20-6b Effect of a Liquidating Distribution on the Shareholder

Shareholders faced with large prospective gains in a liquidation may consider shifting part or all of that gain to other taxpayers. One approach is to donate stock to charity. A charitable contribution of the stock produces a deduction equal to the stock's fair market value (see Chapter 10). Alternatively, the stock may be given to family members in the 10 or 12 percent marginal tax bracket. Here, some or all of the gain on liquidation could be taxed at the 0 percent preferential rate on long-term capital gains. However, there is a risk that the donor may be deemed to have made an anticipatory assignment of income. If so, the gain is still taxed to the donor. In addition, any gift tax issues on the stock transfer must be considered (see Chapter 29). Advance planning of stock transfers, therefore, is crucial in arriving at the desired tax result.

The installment sale rules might also provide some relief. Rather than distributing assets to its shareholders, a sale of the liquidating corporation's assets in exchange for installment notes should be considered. Shareholders receiving the notes in a liquidation can then report their gain on the installment method as payments on the notes are collected. Gain deferred under the installment method is subject to the tax rates applicable in each year of collection. Taxpayers may be able to reduce the tax consequences of an installment sale by directing collections to a year in which a lower rate applies to the capital gain.

20-6c **Parent–Subsidiary Liquidations**

The nonrecognition provision applicable to the liquidation of a subsidiary, § 332, is not elective. Nevertheless, some flexibility may be available.

- Whether § 332 applies depends on the 80 percent stock ownership test. A parent corporation may be able to avoid § 332 by reducing its stock ownership in the subsidiary below this percentage to allow for recognition of a loss. On the other hand, the opposite approach may be desirable to avoid gain recognition. A corporate shareholder possessing less than the required 80 percent ownership may want to acquire additional stock to qualify for § 332 treatment.
- Once § 332 becomes effective, less latitude is allowed in determining the parent's basis in the subsidiary's assets. Generally, the subsidiary's existing basis in its assets carries over to the parent. If a timely § 338 election is made, the subsidiary's basis in its assets is stepped up to reflect, in part, the parent's basis in the subsidiary stock. If the subsidiary also is liquidated, the parent obtains assets with the stepped-up basis.
- An election to have the § 338 rules apply should be carefully weighed since the election can be detrimental. The income tax liability on the subsidiary's recognized gain that results from the deemed sale of its assets is the cost under § 338 for obtaining the stepped-up basis. As a result, a § 338 election may be a viable option only when the subsidiary possesses loss and/or credit carryovers that can be used to offset the associated tax.

20-6d **Asset Purchase versus Stock Purchase**

The acquisition of a corporation's assets generally takes one of two forms. In one form, the acquirer purchases the stock of the target corporation from its shareholders and then the target (subsidiary) is liquidated. In the other form, the acquirer purchases the assets of the target corporation and then the target distributes the proceeds to its shareholders in liquidation. Nontax considerations may affect the form of acquisition, with each form having both favorable and unfavorable aspects.

An asset purchase requires that title be transferred and that creditors be notified. Further, an asset purchase may not be feasible if valuable nontransferable trademarks, contracts, or licenses are involved. Alternatively, an asset purchase may be preferable to a stock purchase if the target's shareholders refuse to sell their stock. In addition, an asset purchase avoids the transfer of liabilities (including unknown liabilities) generally inherent in stock acquisitions. An asset purchase also has the advantage of allowing the purchaser to avoid the acquisition of unwanted assets, whereas a stock purchase would involve all of a target's assets.

Refocus on The Big Picture

The Transition to Retirement Is Subject to Double Taxation

© BIKERIDERLONDON/SHUTTERSTOCK.COM

The Smithsons are wise to evaluate the affordability of their retirement plan *before* they sell or liquidate their business. Nonetheless, after payment of income tax at both the corporate and shareholder levels, they will net only $2,820,000 from the sale of their $4,000,000 business.

Specifically, in the event the corporation is able to sell the business assets for $4,000,000, the realized gain of $2,500,000 will give rise to Federal income tax of $525,000 ($2,500,000 × 21%). Following the payment of the corporate income tax, the net proceeds to the Smithsons will be $3,475,000. After offsetting the amount realized from the liquidation by their stock basis of $200,000, their capital gain of $3,275,000 will be subject to capital gains tax of $655,000 ($3,275,000 × 20%). Therefore, the net after-tax cash available for investment will be $2,820,000 ($3,475,000 proceeds – capital gains tax of $655,000). (To simplify this analysis, the 3.8 percent additional tax on net investment income is not considered.) Now the question for the Smithsons is whether this amount will likely be sufficient to fund the type of retirement they desire.

continued

What If?

Instead of the complete liquidation transaction just described, the Smithsons should consider alternatives that could produce a better tax result such as the following:

- If the Smithsons are able to find a buyer who is interested in maintaining the business in the current corporate form, they should try to sell their stock in the business rather than selling the business assets in liquidation. If the buyer is willing to pay $4,000,000 for the corporation's stock, the Smithsons would recognize a capital gain of $3,800,000 and net $3,240,000 after tax ($4,000,000 proceeds – capital gains tax of $760,000). This approach would increase the net after-tax amount available to fund their retirement portfolio by $420,000 due to the fact that the corporate-level tax is avoided. Again, the 3.8 percent additional tax on net investment income is not considered in this analysis.
- Another approach would be to attempt to market the corporation as a potential takeover target in a tax-free reorganization. With this approach, the Smithsons would receive stock in the acquiring corporation without having to recognize any gain from the transaction. This strategy could enable the Smithsons to live off the subsequent dividend distributions made by the acquiring corporation. Further, if they needed additional cash flow to meet living expenses, they could sell shares of stock in the acquiring corporation as needed, and any resulting gain would be subject to the capital gains rates at that time. An obvious advantage of this approach is that gain from the disposition of their stock would be deferred until the stock in the acquiring corporation is sold in a taxable transaction. However, a disadvantage the Smithsons would need to evaluate is that they would not be able to build a diversified portfolio, given that their investment holdings would largely, if not completely, consist of the stock of the acquiring corporation.

Key Terms

Boot, 20-15
Corporate liquidation, 20-2
Other property, 20-15
Reorganization, 20-14
Section 338 election, 20-12
Security, 20-16

Discussion Questions

1. **LO.1** Under what circumstances are losses disallowed to a corporation in liquidation?
2. **LO.1** For purposes of the related-party loss limitation within the context of a complete liquidation of a corporation, what is the definition of *disqualified property*?
3. **LO.1** For the built-in loss limitation to apply, the property must have been acquired by the corporation as part of a plan whose principal purpose was to recognize a loss on the property by the liquidating corporation. Explain.
4. **LO.1** Explain the tax consequences to a shareholder of a corporation in the process of liquidation under the general rule of § 331.
5. **LO.2** Discuss the tax consequences to the parent corporation in a § 332 liquidation of a subsidiary.
6. **LO.2** In terms of the rules applying to a § 332 parent-subsidiary liquidation, comment on each of the following:
   a. The parent corporation's ownership interest in the subsidiary.
   b. The period of time in which the subsidiary must liquidate.
   c. The solvency of the subsidiary.

7. **LO.2** A subsidiary corporation is liquidated under § 332. Pursuant to its liquidation, the subsidiary distributed property to a minority shareholder. With respect to this distribution, what are the tax consequences to the subsidiary corporation and to the minority shareholder?

8. **LO.2** In general, what are the tax consequences of a § 338 election?

9. **LO.2** From the perspective of the parent corporation, contrast the tax consequences of a subsidiary liquidation under the general nonrecognition rules with a subsidiary liquidation that follows a § 338 election.

10. **LO.3** For each reorganization, provide the letter of its most likely type.

Reorganization	Type
Example: The acquisition by one corporation of another in a stock-for-stock exchange	Type B
a. A recapitalization	
b. A transfer by a corporation of all or part of its assets because of a bankruptcy	
c. A consolidation	
d. A spin-off	
e. The acquisition by a corporation of another in a stock-for-asset exchange	
f. A change in the state of incorporation from Nevada to Delaware	

11. **LO.3** Explain why a private letter ruling from the IRS is like an insurance policy for a corporate reorganization.

12. **LO.3** Along with specific requirements in the Code, what four general requirements (coming from court decisions) must be met for a reorganization to receive tax-free status?

13. **LO.3** How does the receipt of boot affect the taxation of shareholders in a transaction that qualifies under § 368?

14. **LO.3** How is the four-column template in Concept Summary 20.3 used to determine a shareholder's basis in the stock received in a corporate restructuring?

Computational Exercises

15. **LO.1** Sunset Corporation, with E & P of $400,000, makes a cash distribution of $120,000 to a shareholder. The shareholder's basis in the Sunset stock involved is $50,000.
    a. Determine the tax consequences to the shareholder if the distribution is a nonqualified stock redemption.
    b. Determine the tax consequences to the shareholder if the distribution is a qualifying stock redemption.
    c. Determine the tax consequences to the shareholder if the distribution is pursuant to a complete liquidation of Sunset.

16. **LO.1** Pursuant to a complete liquidation, Carrot Corporation distributes to its shareholders real estate held as an investment (basis of $650,000, fair market value of $880,000).
    a. Determine the gain or loss recognized by Carrot on the distribution if no liability is involved.
    b. Determine the gain or loss recognized by Carrot on the distribution if the real estate is subject to a liability of $690,000.
    c. Determine the gain or loss recognized by Carrot on the distribution if the real estate is subject to a liability of $885,000.

17. **LO.1** Osprey Corporation stock is owned by Pedro and Pittro, who are unrelated. Pedro and Pittro each own 50% of the stock in the corporation. Osprey has the following assets (none of which were acquired in a § 351 or contribution to capital transaction) that are distributed in complete liquidation of the corporation.

	Adjusted Basis	Fair Market Value
Cash	$300,000	$300,000
Land	200,000	440,000
Equipment	250,000	140,000

Assume that Osprey Corporation distributes the land to Pedro and the cash and equipment to Pittro.

a. Determine Osprey's recognized gain or loss on the distribution of land.
b. Determine Osprey's recognized gain or loss on the distribution of the equipment.

18. **LO.1** On January 7, 2023, Martin Corporation acquires two properties from a shareholder solely in exchange for stock in a transaction that qualifies under § 351. The shareholder's basis, the fair market value, and the built-in gain (loss) of each property are:

	Shareholder's Basis	Fair Market Value	Built-In Gain (Loss)
Property 1	$300,000	$375,000	$ 75,000
Property 2	525,000	400,000	(125,000)
Net built-in loss			($ 50,000)

Martin adopts a plan of liquidation later in the year and distributes Property 2 to a 30% shareholder when the property is worth $350,000.

a. Compute Martin's basis in Property 1 and in Property 2 as of January 7, 2023.
b. Compute Martin's realized and recognized loss on the liquidating distribution of Property 2.

19. **LO.1** Green Corporation's assets are valued at $920,000 after payment of all corporate debts, except for $134,000 of taxes payable on net gains it recognized on the liquidation. Bruno, an individual and the sole shareholder of Green, has a basis of $280,000 in his stock. Compute the gain or loss recognized by Bruno on the liquidation of Green Corporation.

20. **LO.2** The stock of Quail Corporation is held as follows: 85% by Pheasant Corporation and 15% by Gisela, an individual. Quail Corporation is liquidated in December of the current year pursuant to a plan adopted earlier in the year. At the time of its liquidation, Quail Corporation has assets with a basis of $730,000 and fair market value of $1,000,000. Quail Corporation distributes the property pro rata to Pheasant Corporation and to Gisela.

a. Compute Quail's recognized gain or loss on the distribution of property to Pheasant.
b. Compute Quail's recognized gain or loss on the distribution of property to Gisela.

21. **LO.2** Blush Corporation owns long-term bonds (basis of $1,300,000) of its subsidiary, Brass Corporation, that were acquired at a discount. Upon liquidation of Brass pursuant to § 332, Blush receives a distribution of $1,500,000, the face amount of the bonds. Determine Blush Corporation's recognized gain or loss on the distribution.

22. **LO.2** Goose Corporation has a basis of $2,400,000 in the stock of Swift Corporation, a wholly owned subsidiary acquired 30 years ago. Goose liquidates Swift Corporation and receives assets that are worth $2,000,000 and have a basis to Swift of $1,700,000.
    a. Determine Goose Corporation's recognized gain or loss on the liquidation.
    b. Determine Goose Corporation's basis in the assets received in liquidation.

23. **LO.3** Rebecca holds 100 shares of Gotchas stock that she purchased for $1,000 several years ago. In a merger of Gotchas into Solis, Inc., Rebecca exchanges her 100 Gotchas shares for 1,000 Solis shares and $500. Gotchas is valued at $40.00 per share and Solis at $3.50 per share. Prepare your solution using spreadsheet software such as Microsoft Excel.
    a. What is Rebecca's realized and recognized gain/loss from the reorganization?
    b. What is Rebecca's basis in her Solis stock?

24. **LO.3** In a qualifying reorganization, Cato Corporation exchanges $1,200,000 worth of stock and property valued at $500,000 ($245,000 basis) for all of Firestar Corporation's assets, which have a value of $1,700,000 and a $500,000 basis. Firestar distributes the property received from Cato. The exchange meets all Code requirements.
    a. What is Cato's recognized gain/loss from the reorganization?
    b. What is Firestar's recognized gain/loss from the reorganization?

25. **LO.3** Townsend, the sole shareholder of Pruett Corporation, has a $480,000 basis in his stock. He exchanges all of his Pruett stock for $600,000 of Rogers voting common stock plus land with a fair market value of $100,000 and basis of $25,000. Pruett distributed the land to Townsend. This exchange meets all Code requirements. Prepare your solution using spreadsheet software such as Microsoft Excel.
    a. What is Townsend's recognized gain/loss from the reorganization?
    b. What is the gain/loss recognized by Pruett Corporation and Rogers Corporation on the reorganization?
    c. What is Townsend's basis in the Rogers stock and the land received?

Problems

26. **LO.1, 4** Dove Corporation (E & P of $800,000) has 1,000 shares of stock outstanding. The shares are owned as follows: Julia, 600 shares; Maxine (Julia's sister), 300 shares; and Janine (Julia's daughter), 100 shares. Dove Corporation owns land (basis of $300,000, fair market value of $260,000) that it purchased as an investment seven years ago. Dove distributes the land to Julia in exchange for all of her shares in the corporation. Julia had a basis of $275,000 in the shares. What are the tax consequences for both Dove Corporation and Julia if the distribution is:
    a. A qualifying stock redemption?
    b. A liquidating distribution?

27. **LO.1** Pursuant to a complete liquidation, Oriole Corporation distributes to its shareholders land held for three years as an investment (adjusted basis of $250,000, fair market value of $490,000). The land is subject to a liability of $520,000.
    a. What are the tax consequences to Oriole Corporation on the distribution of the land?
    b. If the land is, instead, subject to a liability of $400,000, what are the tax consequences to Oriole on the distribution?

28. LO.1 The stock of Mulberry Corporation is owned by Archana (60%) and Anar (40%), who are mother and daughter. Pursuant to a plan of complete liquidation adopted earlier in the current year, Mulberry distributes land worth $575,000 to Anar (basis of $100,000 in Mulberry stock). The land was purchased by Mulberry Corporation three years ago for $650,000, and it is distributed subject to a liability of $425,000. What amount of gain or loss is recognized by Mulberry Corporation and by Anar with respect to the distribution of the land?

29. LO.1 Last year Lory Corporation, a land development company, acquired land and construction equipment from its sole shareholder in a § 351 transaction. At the time, the land had a basis of $790,000 and a fair market value of $650,000 and the equipment had a basis of $130,000 and a fair market value of $300,000. The assets were transferred to Lory Corporation for the purpose of developing the land and constructing a residential home community. However, the residential housing market suffered a steep decline in the current year, and as a result of financial difficulties, Lory Corporation was forced to sell its assets and liquidate. Pursuant to a plan of liquidation adopted during the year, Lory sold the land to an unrelated party for its current fair market value of $500,000. What amount of loss, if any, is recognized by Lory Corporation on the sale of the land?

30. LO.1 Last year a shareholder transferred land (basis of $650,000, fair market value of $575,000) to Roadrunner Corporation in a § 351 transaction. This was the only property transferred to Roadrunner at that time. During the current year, Roadrunner Corporation adopted a plan of liquidation and distributed the land to Rhonda, a 15% shareholder. On the date of the distribution, the land had a fair market value of $400,000. Roadrunner Corporation never used the land for business purposes during the time it owned the property. What amount of loss may Roadrunner recognize on the distribution of the land?

Decision Making

31. LO.1, 4 Last year Pink Corporation acquired land and securities in a § 351 tax-free exchange. On the date of the transfer, the land had a basis of $720,000 and a fair market value of $1,000,000 and the securities had a basis of $110,000 and a fair market value of $250,000. Pink Corporation has two shareholders, Maria and Paul, unrelated individuals. Maria owns 85% of the stock in Pink Corporation, and Paul owns 15%. The corporation adopts a plan of liquidation in the current year. On this date, the value of the land has decreased to $500,000. What is the effect of each of the following on Pink Corporation? Which option should be selected?

a. Distribute all of the land to Maria.
b. Distribute all of the land to Paul.
c. Distribute 85% of the land to Maria and 15% to Paul.
d. Distribute 50% of the land to Maria and 50% to Paul.
e. Sell the land and distribute the proceeds of $500,000 proportionately to Maria and to Paul.

Decision Making

32. LO. 1, 4 Assume in Problem 31 that the land had a fair market value of $630,000 on the date of its transfer to Pink Corporation. On the date of the liquidation, the land's fair market value has decreased to $500,000. How would your answers to Problem 31 change if:

a. All of the land is distributed to Maria?
b. All of the land is distributed to Paul?
c. The land is distributed 85% to Maria and 15% to Paul?
d. The land is distributed 50% to Maria and 50% to Paul?
e. The land is sold and the proceeds of $500,000 are distributed proportionately to Maria and to Paul?

33. **LO.1** Pursuant to a complete liquidation in the current year, Scarlet Corporation distributes to Jake land (basis of $425,000, fair market value of $390,000) that was purchased three years ago and held as an investment. The land is subject to a liability of $250,000. Jake, who owned 35% of the Scarlet Corporation shares outstanding, had a basis of $60,000 in the stock. What are the tax consequences of the liquidating distribution to Scarlet Corporation and to Jake?

34. **LO.2** The stock of Magenta Corporation is owned by Fuchsia Corporation (95%) and Marta (5%). Magenta is liquidated in the current year, pursuant to a plan of liquidation adopted earlier in the year. In the liquidation, Magenta distributes various assets worth $950,000 (basis of $620,000) to Fuchsia (basis of $700,000 in Magenta stock) and a parcel of land worth $50,000 (basis of $75,000) to Marta (basis of $30,000 in Magenta stock). Assuming that the § 338 election is not made, what are the tax consequences of the liquidation to Magenta, Fuchsia, and Marta?

35. **LO.2** The stock in Ivory Corporation is owned by Gold Corporation (80%) and Imelda (20%). Gold Corporation purchased its shares in Ivory nine years ago at a cost of $650,000, and Imelda purchased her shares in Ivory four years ago at a cost of $175,000. Ivory Corporation has the following assets that are distributed in complete liquidation:

	Adjusted Basis	Fair Market Value
Cash	$600,000	$600,000
Inventory	80,000	200,000
Equipment	350,000	200,000

a. Assume that Ivory Corporation distributes the cash and inventory to Gold Corporation and the equipment to Imelda. What are the tax consequences of the distributions to Ivory Corporation, to Gold Corporation, and to Imelda?

b. Assume that Ivory Corporation distributes the cash and equipment to Gold Corporation and the inventory to Imelda. What are the tax consequences of the distributions to Ivory Corporation, to Gold Corporation, and to Imelda?

36. **LO.2** Orange Corporation purchased bonds (basis of $350,000) of its wholly owned subsidiary, Green Corporation, at a discount. Upon liquidation of Green pursuant to § 332, Orange receives payment in the form of land worth $400,000, the face amount of the bonds. Green Corporation had a basis of $320,000 in the land. What are the tax consequences of this land transfer to Green Corporation and to Orange Corporation?

37. **LO.2** On July 15, 2022, Lilac Corporation purchased 25% of the Coffee Corporation stock outstanding. Lilac Corporation purchased an additional 40% of the stock in Coffee on March 24, 2023, and an additional 20% on May 5, 2023. On September 24, 2023, Lilac Corporation purchased the remaining 15% of Coffee Corporation stock outstanding. For purposes of the § 338 election, on what date does a qualified stock purchase occur? What is the due date for making the § 338 election?

38. **LO.2** On April 23, 2023, Auk Corporation acquires 100% of the outstanding stock of Amazon Corporation (E & P of $750,000) for $1,200,000. Amazon Corporation has assets with a fair market value of $1,400,000 (basis of $800,000), no liabilities, and no loss or tax credit carryovers. Auk Corporation files a timely

§ 338 election. Assume that both the aggregate deemed sale price (ADSP) and adjusted grossed-up basis (AGUB) are $1,306,329.

a. What are the tax consequences of the § 338 election to Amazon Corporation and to Auk Corporation?

b. Assume that Amazon Corporation is liquidated immediately following the § 338 election. What are the tax consequences of the liquidation to Amazon Corporation and to Auk Corporation?

39. **LO.3** Quail Corporation was created six years ago through contributions from Kasha ($900,000) and Frank ($100,000). In a transaction qualifying as a reorganization, Quail exchanges all of its assets currently valued at $1,800,000 (basis of $1,200,000) for Covey Corporation stock valued at $1,700,000 plus $100,000 in Covey bonds. Quail distributes the Covey stock and bonds proportionately to Frank and Kasha in exchange for their stock in Quail. Quail's current and accumulated E & P before the reorganization amounts to $70,000.

a. How do Kasha and Frank treat this transaction for income tax purposes? What is Kasha's and Frank's basis in their Covey stock? Prepare your solution using spreadsheet software such as Microsoft Excel.

b. How do Quail and Covey treat this transaction for income tax purposes? What is Covey's basis in the assets it receives from Quail?

Communications

40. **LO.3** Jed acquired 25% of the stock of Alpha (basis of $100,000) 12 years ago, and the other 75% was purchased by Manny (basis of $400,000) three years ago.

Alpha enters into a tax-free consolidation with Beta, in which Jed will receive an 8% interest in the new AlphaBeta (value $90,000) plus $36,000 cash, and Manny will receive a 28% interest (value $315,000) plus land worth $63,000. Alpha's basis in the land is $35,000.

Before the reorganization or distributions to its shareholders, Alpha's value is $504,000, and Beta's value is $720,000.

a. What is Jed's and Manny's recognized gain or loss on the reorganization? What is each shareholder's basis in their AlphaBeta stock? Prepare your solution using spreadsheet software such as Microsoft Excel.

b. What is Alpha's and Beta's recognized gain or loss on the reorganization?

c. Draft a detailed diagram of the consolidation of Alpha and Beta.

41. **LO.3** Target Corporation holds assets with a fair market value of $4,000,000 (adjusted basis of $2,200,000) and liabilities of $1,500,000. It transfers assets worth $3,700,000 to Acquiring Corporation in a "Type C" reorganization, in exchange for Acquiring voting stock and the assumption of $1,400,000 of Target's liabilities.

Target retained a building worth $300,000 (adjusted basis of $225,000). Target distributes the Acquiring voting stock and the building with its $100,000 mortgage to Wei, its sole shareholder, for all of her stock in Target. Wei's basis in her stock is $2,100,000. Prepare your solution using spreadsheet software such as Microsoft Excel.

a. What is the value of the stock transferred from Acquiring to Target?

b. What is the amount of gain (loss) recognized by Wei, Target, and Acquiring on the reorganization?

c. What is Wei's basis in the stock and building she received?

Research Problems

Note: Solutions to the Research Problems can be prepared by using the Thomson Reuters Checkpoint™ online tax research database, which accompanies this textbook. Solutions can also be prepared by using research materials found in a typical tax library.

Communications
Critical Thinking

Research Problem 1. Shelly Zumaya (2220 East Hennepin Avenue, Minneapolis, MN 55413) is the president and sole shareholder of Kiwi Corporation (stock basis of $400,000). Incorporated in 2010, Kiwi Corporation's sole business has consisted of the purchase and resale of used farming equipment. In December 2021, Kiwi transferred its entire inventory (basis of $1,200,000) to Shelly in a transaction described by the parties as a sale. According to Shelly and collaborated by the minutes of the board of directors, the inventory was sold to her for the sum of $2,000,000, the fair market value of the inventory. The terms of the sale provided that Shelly would pay Kiwi Corporation the $2,000,000 at some future date. This debt obligation was not evidenced by a promissory note, and to date, Shelly has made no payments (principal or interest) on the obligation. The inventory transfer was not reported on Kiwi's 2021 tax return as either a sale or a distribution. After the transfer of the inventory to Shelly, Kiwi Corporation had no remaining assets and ceased to conduct any business. Kiwi did not formally liquidate under state law. On an audit of Kiwi Corporation's 2021 tax return, the IRS asserted that the transfer of inventory constituted a liquidation of Kiwi; as a result, the corporation recognized a gain on the liquidating distribution in the amount of $800,000 [$2,000,000 (fair market value) – $1,200,000 (inventory basis)]. Further, because Kiwi Corporation is devoid of assets, the IRS assessed the entire tax liability against Shelly, based on transferee liability. Finally, the IRS assessed a tax due from Shelly for her gain recognized in the purported liquidating distribution. Shelly has contacted you regarding the IRS's determination. Prepare a letter to Shelly Zumaya and a memo for the file, documenting your research.

Research Problem 2. On December 1, year 1, Ash Co. and Leigh Co. entered into a merger agreement under which Ash Co. agreed to acquire Leigh Co. in a "Type A" reorganization. The purpose of the merger was to benefit the business operations of both organizations. The merger was successful and was completed on March 15, year 2.

On June 1, year 2, a lawsuit was filed against Ash Co. and its shareholders by current and former shareholders related to misrepresentations made by Leigh Co. management during the merger process. The lawsuit alleges that the Board of Directors of Ash Co. was aware of material facts regarding the merger that were not properly disclosed to Ash Co. shareholders. It alleges further that Ash Co. management made statements and claims to facilitate the merger in securities filings that were unsubstantiated or in error.

The lawsuit does not challenge the validity of the merger or the price paid for Leigh Co. stock. As a result of these facts, the post-merger price of Ash Co. shares declined substantially. To avoid further negative publicity and stem the slide in stock price, Ash Co. paid $50,000,000 to settle all of the claims made in the lawsuit.

Is Ash Co. legally obligated to satisfy this liability that was due to conduct that occurred prior to the merger of Ash Co. and Leigh Co? Justify your answer. Is the payment deductible?

Use internet tax resources to address the following questions. Look for reliable websites and blogs of the IRS and other government agencies, media outlets, businesses, tax professionals, academics, think tanks, and political outlets.

Communications

Research Problem 3. The requirements for effectively liquidating a corporate entity under state law vary from state to state. Using the internet as your sole research source, prepare an outline discussing how an entity incorporated in your home state is liquidated, including any reporting requirements associated with such liquidation.

Communications

Research Problem 4. Although the requirements for a § 332 parent-subsidiary liquidation are fairly straightforward, some planning and reporting issues must be addressed to ensure the proper outcome. Using the internet as your sole research source, prepare an outline discussing the general requirements for a § 332 parent-subsidiary liquidation, including any associated planning and reporting considerations.

Communications
Critical Thinking
Data Analytics

Research Problem 5. Corporate executives engage in reorganizations to improve shareholder value. If shareholder value increases, the reorganization often is deemed a success. If shareholder value falls, corporate executives may take the blame.

Pick a reorganization of a publicly traded company that occurred between three and seven years ago. Obtain the monthly stock price for the parent company for the three-year period before and the three-year period after the reorganization (six years total). Then obtain the monthly stock price of an S&P 500 Index mutual fund, as well as the monthly stock price of a major competitor of your company over the same period.

Pick two performance metrics (e.g., return on assets, return on equity), and calculate those ratios for the merged company for the three years following the reorganization. Compare those performance metrics to the same metrics for the firm's major competitor for the same period.

Use Microsoft Excel, or a data visualization software package, to create no more than five appropriate tables or charts that show how the reorganization added to or diminished shareholder value. Place those visuals into Microsoft PowerPoint, along with two other slides that provide your arguments for or against the success of the merger. Your slides should be visually appealing, easy to interpret, and concise.

Communications

Research Problem 6. Browse the internet sites of several public accounting firms, and find discussions comparing stock purchases with asset purchases when acquiring a business. Based solely on your findings, prepare an outline of the advantages and disadvantages of each form of acquisition.

Becker CPA Review Questions

Becker

1. Krol Corp. distributed marketable securities in redemption of its stock in a complete liquidation. On the date of distribution, these securities had a basis of $100,000 and a fair market value of $150,000. What gain does Krol have as a result of the distribution?

   a. $0
   b. $50,000 capital gain
   c. $50,000 § 1231 gain
   d. $50,000 ordinary gain

2. A corporation was completely liquidated and dissolved during year 14. The filing fees, professional fees, and other expenditures incurred in connection with the liquidation and dissolution are:

   a. Deductible in full by the dissolved corporation.
   b. Deductible by the shareholders and *not* by the corporation.
   c. Treated as capital losses by the corporation.
   d. Not deductible either by the corporation or shareholders.

3. Generally, in a direct distribution of assets to the shareholders that results in a complete corporate liquidation:

   a. There is no taxable event.

   b. The corporation recognizes no gain or loss because it transfers the assets to the shareholders at the corporation's basis immediately before the distribution.

   c. The shareholders recognize dividend income in the amount of the fair market value of property received.

   d. The shareholders recognize gain or loss to the extent the fair market value of the distributed assets differs from the adjusted basis of the stock.

4. Olinto Corp., an accrual basis calendar year C corporation, had no corporate shareholders when it liquidated in year 12. In cancellation of all their Olinto Corp. stock, each Olinto Corp. shareholder received in year 12 a liquidating distribution of $12,000 cash and land with a corporate tax basis of $15,000 and a fair market value of $20,500. Before the distribution, each shareholder's tax basis in Olinto Corp. stock was $16,500. What amount of gain should each Olinto Corp. shareholder recognize on the liquidating distribution?

   a. $0

   b. $10,500

   c. $4,000

   d. $16,000

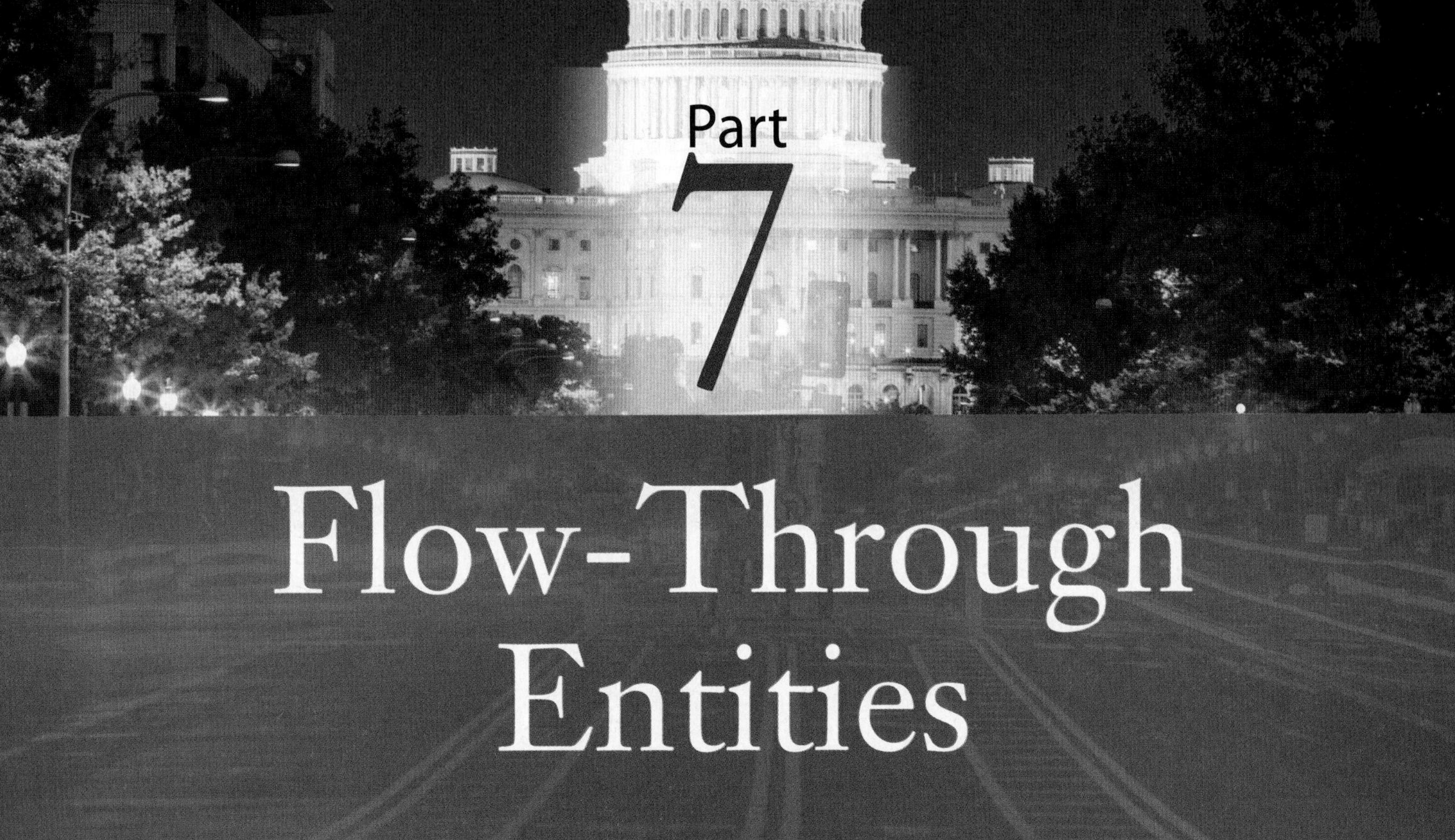

Flow-Through Entities

Unlike C corporations, some business entities are taxed under the conduit perspective. Generally, this means the tax attributes of various transactions are retained as they flow through the entity directly to the owners. Usually, no Federal income tax is imposed at the entity level. Part 7 of this text discusses two types of flow-through entities—partnerships and S corporations. Similarities and differences in the taxing systems for the two types of entities are highlighted.

Chapter 21

Partnerships: Formation, Operation, and Basis

Learning Objectives: *After completing Chapter 21, you should be able to:*

- **LO.1** Define "partnership," and distinguish among the various types of entities treated as partnerships for tax purposes.
- **LO.2** Describe the conceptual framework for partnership taxation and reporting.
- **LO.3** Determine the tax effects (and special rules) when forming a partnership with cash and property contributions.
- **LO.4** Specify the elections available to a new partnership and the treatment of its expenditures.
- **LO.5** Specify the accounting methods and taxable years available to a partnership.
- **LO.6** Report a partnership's taxable income and separately stated items on Form 1065.
- **LO.7** Report information on a partner's Schedule K–1 and the partner's tax return.
- **LO.8** Discuss the requirements for allocating income, gains, losses, deductions, and credits among the partners.
- **LO.9** Determine a partner's basis in the partnership interest.
- **LO.10** Explain how liabilities affect a partner's basis.
- **LO.11** Illustrate a partner's capital account roll forward, and explain why the year-end balance might differ from the partner's year-end basis in the partnership interest.
- **LO.12** Apply the limitations on deducting partnership losses.
- **LO.13** Describe how a partner calculates self-employment tax and net investment income tax on partnership income.
- **LO.14** Provide insights regarding advantageous use of a partnership.

Chapter Outline

RODERICK PAUL WALKER/ALAMY STOCK PHOTO

The Big Picture

Why Use a Partnership, Anyway?

For 15 years, Maria has owned and operated a seaside bakery and café called The Beachsider. Each morning, customers line up on the boardwalk in front of the building and enjoy fresh coffee and croissants while waiting for a table. "The building is too small," Maria commented to her landlord, Kyler. "Is there any way we can expand?" The Beachsider occupies one of several buildings on three acres of a 10-acre parcel that Kyler inherited several years ago. The remaining seven acres are undeveloped.

Kyler and Maria talked to Josh, a real estate developer, and he proposed an expansion to The Beachsider and upgrades to the other buildings. The improvements would preserve the character of the original retail center, and the remaining acreage would be available for future expansion.

They liked his ideas, so Kyler, Maria, and Josh agreed to form a partnership to own and operate The Beachsider and to improve and lease the other buildings. Josh summarized the plan as follows: "Kyler and Maria will each contribute one-half of the capital we need. Kyler's real estate is valued at about $2,000,000. Maria's bakery equipment and the café furnishings are valued at about $500,000. The improvements will cost about $1,500,000 of cash, which Maria has agreed to contribute to the partnership."

Josh continued, "You have agreed that I do not need to contribute any capital to the partnership. I will oversee the construction, and when it is complete, I will vest in a 5 percent interest in the partnership's capital. On an ongoing basis, I will oversee the partnership's operations in exchange for a fixed salary and 20 percent of the partnership's ongoing profits. The construction should be completed in June of this year, and my capital interest is estimated to be valued at $200,000 at that time."

What are the tax consequences if the trio forms Beachside Properties as a partnership to own and operate the retail center? What issues might arise later in the life of the entity?

Read the chapter and formulate your response.

Partnerships are the focus of this chapter and Chapter 22, and Subchapter S corporations are discussed in Chapter 23. Both partnerships and Subchapter S corporations are called *flow-through* or *pass-through* entities because the entity's income, gains, losses, deductions, credits, and general tax information flow through the entity and are taxed or attributed to its owners. As we'll discuss, a pass-through entity is flexible and has a single level of taxation. This can result in significant tax and business advantages over a Subchapter C corporation. However, distinct differences between partnerships and S corporations demand that taxpayers choose the best entity for their particular business.

This chapter addresses partnership formation and operations. Chapter 22 focuses on partnership distributions, dispositions of partnership interests, and optional basis adjustments. Chapter 23 discusses the taxation of S corporations.

21-1 Overview of Partnership Taxation

Let's look at some of the general concepts that apply to all partnerships.

LO.1

Define "partnership," and distinguish among the various types of entities treated as partnerships for tax purposes.

21-1a What Is a Partnership?

Partnerships are governed by Subchapter K of the Internal Revenue Code. A partnership is defined as an association formed by two or more persons to carry on a trade or business, with each contributing money, property, labor, or skill, and with all expecting to share in profits and losses. A "person" can be an individual, trust, estate, corporation, association, or another partnership.[1] The entity must be unincorporated and cannot be otherwise classified as a corporation, trust, or estate.

Example 1

Andrew and Ashleigh, unrelated individuals, want to mine and stake some cryptocurrencies as a side hustle to get rich quick. They decide to pool their resources and purchase a powerful computer and related equipment. They both contribute $4,000 cash and use the funds to buy equipment which they immediately put to use. Their plan is to split profits and losses equally. Andrew and Ashleigh have formed a partnership.

Types of Partnerships

You'll see several types of partnerships, each suited for different situations. Partnership entities are defined and formed under state law. They are typically distinguished based on the classification of the partners as **general partners** or **limited partners** and the types of business permitted to be conducted.

- General partners can participate in managing the entity. A general partner can be legally required to repay a partnership's "recourse" debt (described later).
- Limited partners are typically *not* permitted to participate in entity management, and they are *not* liable for partnership debts (except to the extent the partner owes unpaid contributions to the partnership).

Some of the more common types of entities treated as partnerships include the following:

- A **general partnership (GP)** consists of two or more general partners who may participate in management; there are no limited partners. General partnerships often are used for operating activities (e.g., product manufacturing or sales) and corporate joint ventures.

[1] §§ 7701(a)(1) and (2).

- A **limited partnership (LP)** is a partnership with at least one general partner and one or more limited partners.[2] These partnerships often have numerous limited partners and are used to raise capital for real estate development, oil and gas exploration, research and development, and various financial product investment vehicles. To reduce exposure to the entity's liabilities, the general partners are often entities that, themselves, have limited liability, such as a C corporation (or a limited liability company, discussed next).
- In a **limited liability company (LLC)**, the owners (termed "members") are a hybrid type of partner. With respect to the LLC's debts, members are treated as limited partners. However, LLC members generally participate in management of the LLC. Therefore, an LLC combines the corporate benefit of limited liability for the owners with the benefits of partnership taxation, including the single level of tax. A properly structured multiowner[3] LLC is generally treated as a partnership for all Federal tax purposes.[4]
- In most states, a **limited liability partnership (LLP)** is treated similarly to a general partnership; however, an LLP partner is not personally liable for any malpractice committed by other partners. The LLP is currently the organizational form of choice for the large accounting firms and many other service-providing entities.

A **partnership agreement** is signed by each partner. This document outlines the rights and obligations of the partners; the allocation of income, deductions, and cash flows; initial and future capital contribution requirements; conditions for terminating the partnership; and other matters. The agreement will typically include information the tax preparer needs to complete the tax return, such as whether allocations are intended to follow the § 704(b) regulations, whether guaranteed payments will be made, and other issues discussed in this chapter. The governing agreement of an LLC is known as an **operating agreement**.

Concept Summary 21.1 summarizes characteristics of the various entities treated as partnerships.

The Big Picture

Example 2

Return to the facts of *The Big Picture* on p. 21-1. When Beachside Properties is formed, Kyler, Maria, and Josh must first decide which type of entity to form. They've narrowed the decision to a C corporation or a partnership. Assume that all three owners are single individuals in the highest tax brackets before considering Beachside's income.

The owners compared (1) tax rates on pass-through income, including ordinary income and capital gains, if the entity was a partnership, to (2) corporate tax rates plus capital gains tax on dividends distributed if the entity was a C corporation. For both entities, they also considered special taxes (such as employment taxes and the net investment income tax), and special benefits (such as the qualified business income deduction). They completed their analysis for a 10-year time period to take time value of money issues into account.

After completing their analysis, Kyler, Maria, and Josh decided to form a partnership. They must next decide which type of partnership to utilize.

With a GP, Kyler, Maria, and Josh would each be jointly and severally liable for all entity debts. With an LP, one of the partners would be designated as a general partner and would be liable for all entity debts. Neither of these is ideal if there's a way all three owners can have limited liability.

An LLP is not considered because LLPs are typically reserved for service-providing entities.

With an LLC, each partner's losses will be limited to the partner's contributed capital. Therefore, Kyler, Maria, and Josh decide to form Beachside Properties as an LLC.

---

[2]A limited liability limited partnership (LLLP) is an extension of the limited partnership form in which all partners, whether general or limited, are accorded limited liability. At this writing, approximately 30 U.S. states permit formation of LLLPs or recognize LLLPs formed in another state. LLLPs are not discussed further in this chapter.

[3]Note that an LLC might have only one owner. Single-member LLCs (SMLLCs) are treated as sole proprietorships or disregarded entities rather than partnerships.

[4]In most of the examples in Chapters 21 and 22, the entities are structured as LLCs for state law purposes. Unless otherwise indicated, assume that these entities are treated as partnerships for Federal income tax purposes.

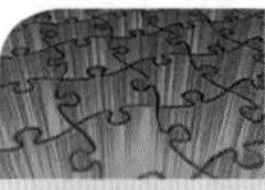

Concept Summary 21.1

Comparison of Partnership Types

The following table summarizes information about the types of partnerships and limited liability entities discussed in this chapter.

Type of entity	Types of owners	Are owners liable for entity debts?	May owners participate in entity management?	Types of businesses operated by entity*
General partnership (GP)	General partners only	Yes, recourse to GP No, debt secured only by property	Yes	Operating businesses and joint ventures formed by other operating businesses
Limited partnership (LP)	Limited partners plus at least one general partner**	Yes, for general partners No, for limited partners	Yes, for general partners No, for limited partners	Entities raising capital from investors
Limited liability company (LLC)	"Members" have some general and some limited characteristics	No	Yes, generally	Generally, operating businesses and non-professional service businesses
Limited liability partnership (LLP)	General partners with limited liability for malpractice committed by other partners	Yes, for partner's own malpractice	Yes	Professional service entities such as accounting and law firms

* In general; permitted business operations depend on state law.
** The general partner is often a C corporation or LLC, to minimize exposure to entity liabilities.

LO.2

Describe the conceptual framework for partnership taxation and reporting.

21-1b Key Concepts in Taxation of Partnership Income

A partnership is not a taxable entity.[5] Rather, the taxable income or loss of the partnership flows through to the partners at the end of the partnership's tax year.[6]

Flow-Through Status of Entity

The partnership itself pays no Federal income tax.[7] Instead, the partners report their **distributive share** of the partnership's income or loss on their tax returns and pay any tax due.

A partnership files Form 1065, U.S. Return of Partnership Income. This return includes a **Schedule K–1** for each partner (with a copy provided to the partner) that shows that partner's share of partnership items. If the partnership has foreign operations or income, it will also prepare Schedules K–2 (partnership foreign activities) and K–3 (partner's share of Schedule K–2 items) (foreign activities are beyond our scope). The partners use Schedules K–1 and K–3 in preparing their tax returns and paying tax on the entity's income. See text Sections 21-3c and 21-4a later in the chapter.

As discussed in Chapter 22, a partner's withdrawals generally are not taxable (unless they exceed the partner's basis in the partnership interest).

Adam contributes land with a basis and value of $60,000 in exchange for a 40% share of the profits and losses of the calendar year ABC LLC. In 2022, ABC generates $200,000 of ordinary taxable income and distributes cash of $5,000 to Adam. Adam is taxed on his $80,000 allocable share of income. He is not separately taxed on the $5,000 distribution.

The same result would arise if ABC reported a loss: 40% of the loss would be allocated to Adam, and he would deduct the loss, subject to the loss limitation rules discussed later.

[5] § 701.
[6] § 702.
[7] However, as discussed in text Section 21-3, the partnership may be required to pay employment taxes for its employees (not partners) or certain U.S. state franchise taxes or fees.

Conceptual Framework for Partnership Taxation

The unique tax treatment of partners and partnerships can be traced to two legal concepts: the **aggregate** (or **conduit**) **concept** and the **entity concept**.

Aggregate (or Conduit) Concept The aggregate concept treats the partnership as a channel through which income, credits, deductions, and other items flow to the partners. The partnership is regarded as a collection of taxpayers joined in an agency relationship. For example, the income tax is imposed on the partners rather than the partnership.

Entity Concept The entity concept treats partners and partnerships as separate units and gives the partnership its own tax "personality." For example, the partnership must file an information return that summarizes its activities for the tax year.

Combined Concepts The "aggregate" concept governs most of the "general rules" for partnerships; the "entity" concept governs many of the exceptions to those general rules. Some rules are governed by both aggregate and entity concepts.

Inside and Outside Basis

The partnership basis rules are the key reason single taxation of partnership income is possible. A partnership has an **inside basis** for each asset it owns, and each partner has an **outside basis** in the partnership interest. In general, the partnership basis rules—an aggregate concept—ensure that the partnership's total inside bases in all assets equals the sum of the outside bases of all partners' partnership interests. In Chapter 21, you can assume that inside basis equals outside basis. In Chapter 22, we'll discuss situations that can result in inside/outside basis differences.

When income or gain flows through to a partner from the partnership, the partner's outside basis in the partnership interest is increased. When a deduction or loss flows through to a partner, the outside basis is reduced. These adjustments ensure that partnership items are taxed only once.

In Example 3, Adam's outside basis in the LLC interest is $60,000 after his contribution of land in exchange for the LLC interest. The LLC's inside basis in the land is also $60,000. When Adam reports his $80,000 share of the LLC's income, his outside basis is increased to $140,000.

If Adam sold his interest at the beginning of 2024 for its presumed value of $140,000, he would have no gain or loss. If, instead, there were no adjustments to basis, Adam's outside basis would be only $60,000 and he would be taxed on an $80,000 gain in addition to paying tax on his $80,000 share of ABC's income. Without the basis adjustment, the LLC's income would be subject to double taxation.

Partners' Ownership and Allocation of Partnership Items

Another "aggregate" concept is that each partner typically owns both a **capital interest** and a **profits (loss) interest** in the partnership. A capital interest is measured by a partner's **capital sharing ratio**, which is the partner's percentage ownership of the capital of the partnership. Generally, this is the share of capital the partner would receive if the entity was liquidated.

A profits (loss) interest is the partner's share of the partnership's current operating results. **Profit and loss sharing ratios** are usually specified in the partnership agreement and are used to determine each partner's allocation of the partnership's ordinary taxable income and loss items.[8]

A key advantage of partnerships is that these ratios and allocations can differ for a given partner, provided the **capital account maintenance** rules discussed later in the chapter are followed. These rules generally work to ensure that everything evens out over time—at the latest, by the time the partnership liquidates.

[8]§ 704(a).

Later in the chapter, we will also discuss **separately stated items** (items that could differently affect two partners' tax situations) and **special allocations** (items that the partnership does not allocate using profit or loss interests).

In Example 3, Adam contributed $60,000 of cash in exchange for a 40% share of ABC LLC's profits. Assume that the other LLC members, Beth and Carl, only contributed capital of $20,000 each for their 30% share of profits, for a total of $100,000 of contributed capital. When the partnership is formed, Adam's capital sharing ratio is 60%, because he would be entitled to 60% of the partnership's $100,000 of capital if the partnership was liquidated immediately.

Adam's profit sharing ratio is 40%, per Example 3. In addition, the LLC's operating agreement could easily allocate 30% of losses to Adam and provide a special allocation of 100% of depreciation deductions to him.

Because of the capital account maintenance rules, by the time the partnership liquidates, Adam will receive the capital he deserves. Each year, his capital sharing ratio will be adjusted to reflect his percentage ownership.

LO.3

Determine the tax effects (and special rules) when forming a partnership with cash and property contributions.

21-2 Formation of a Partnership: Tax Effects

When a partnership is formed, the partners contribute cash and other property in exchange for the partnership interest. This transaction has implications for both the partners and the partnership. Are any gains or losses recognized? What is the basis for each property and the basis of each partnership interest? How does the partnership recover (depreciate, deduct, amortize) the basis of contributed property? What issues must the partnership address in its initial year?

21-2a Contributions to the Partnership

Congress intended the partnership formation transaction to be tax-neutral, so partnerships can be formed without (generally) prohibitive tax consequences.

Gain or Loss Recognition

As a general rule, neither the partner nor the partnership recognizes any realized gain or loss arising on contribution of property to a partnership. This applies upon formation of the entity or if the contribution occurs at some later date. The realized gain or loss is deferred rather than forgiven.[9]

Alicia (a U.S. person) transfers assets to the Wren LLC on the day the entity is created in exchange for a 60% profit and loss interest worth $60,000. She contributes cash of $40,000 and retail display fixtures (basis to her as a sole proprietor, $8,000; fair market value, $20,000). Alicia *realizes* a $12,000 gain [$60,000 fair market value of LLC interest less $48,000 basis ($40,000 cash plus $8,000 basis in fixtures)].

Alicia *does not recognize* the $12,000 realized gain in the year of contribution. She received only a nonliquid LLC interest; she received no cash with which to pay any resulting tax liability.

Similarly, if Alicia's basis had been $25,000 in the contributed assets, § 721 would have disallowed the $5,000 realized loss [$60,000 − ($40,000 + $25,000)].

Basis Issues

When a partner makes a tax-deferred contribution of an asset to the capital of a partnership, any potential gain or loss recognition is merely postponed instead of being permanently excluded.

Partnership's Basis in Assets The partnership takes a *carryover basis* in the contributed assets it receives. This means that the partner's basis in the asset carries over to become the partnership's inside basis in the asset.[10]

[9] § 721.

[10] § 723.

Partner's Basis in the Partnership Interest The partner takes a *substituted basis* in the partnership interest. This means that the partner's basis in the contributed assets transfers over to become the partner's outside basis in the partnership interest.[11]

Holding Period

Partnership's Holding Period in Assets The partnership's holding period for the contributed assets includes the period during which the partner owned the asset.

Partner's Holding Period in the Partnership Interest The partner's holding period in the partnership interest depends on the type of contributed assets. To the extent a partner contributes capital and § 1231 assets, the partner's holding period in the partnership interest is the same as that partner's holding period for these assets. To the extent the partner contributes cash or noncapital/§ 1231 assets, the holding period in the partnership interest begins on the date the partnership interest is acquired.

Luis transfers a capital asset in exchange for a one-third interest in JKL LLC. The asset has an adjusted basis to Luis of $10,000 and a fair market value of $30,000. Luis has a $20,000 realized gain on the exchange ($30,000 − $10,000), but, under § 721, he does not recognize any of the gain.

Luis's outside basis for his LLC interest is a substituted basis of $10,000. This rule ensures that Luis's $20,000 deferred gain would be recognized on a subsequent sale at its $30,000 fair market value. Because Luis contributed a capital asset, his holding period "tacks" and becomes his holding period for the partnership interest.

The LLC's inside basis for the contributed property is a carryover basis of $10,000. This basis ensures that Luis's $20,000 deferred gain would be recognized if the LLC sold the property for its $30,000 fair market value. Luis's holding period for the capital asset becomes the partnership's holding period for the asset.

Note that if Luis had contributed cash for the interest, both his and the partnership's holding periods would begin on the date the cash was contributed.

21-2b Exceptions to the General Rule of § 721

In certain situations, the nonrecognition provisions do not apply and any realized gain or loss will be recognized. The most widely applicable situations are when:

- Appreciated stocks are contributed to an investment partnership.
- The transaction is essentially a disguised sale or exchange of properties.
- The partnership interest is received in exchange for services rendered to the partnership by the partner.
- § 721(c) applies.[12]

Investment Partnership

If the transfer consists of appreciated stocks and securities and the partnership is an investment partnership, it is possible that the contributing partner will recognize the inherent realized gain at the time of the contribution.[13] This rule prevents investors from using the partnership form to diversify their investment portfolios on a tax-free basis.

Disguised Sale or Exchange

If a transaction appears to be a sale or exchange of property rather than a contribution, it is deemed a **disguised sale** and § 721 cannot be used to defer a gain or loss. For example, if a partner contributes appreciated property to a partnership and soon thereafter receives a distribution of cash or other property from the partnership, the distribution could be viewed as a payment to purchase the contributed property.[14]

---

[11] § 722.

[12] § 721(c) prohibits U.S. taxpayers from using a partnership to transfer property with substantial unrealized gains to a non-U.S. taxing authority.

[13] § 721(b).

[14] § 707(a)(2)(B) and related Regulations.

Kim's basis in her KLM partnership interest was $50,000. She transfers to the partnership a property with an adjusted basis of $20,000 (and a fair market value of $50,000), resulting in a basis of $70,000 in her partnership interest. Two weeks later, the partnership distributes $25,000 cash to Kim (this is one-half of the value of the property Kim contributed). Under the general rule, the distribution would not be taxable to Kim but instead reduces her basis in the partnership interest to $45,000 ($70,000 basis − $25,000 cash distribution). However, the transaction appears to be a disguised purchase-sale transaction. Therefore, Kim must recognize gain of $15,000 on the deemed sale of one-half of the property [$25,000 cash "payment" (distribution) − ($20,000 basis × 50%)], and the partnership is deemed to have purchased that half of the property for $25,000. The partnership's basis in the property becomes $35,000 ($10,000 basis in 50% portion that is "contributed" property + $25,000 amount deemed paid for 50% portion that is "purchased" property).

Extensive Regulations outline situations in which (1) assumption of liabilities "other than a qualified liability" by the partnership can trigger disguised sale treatment and (2) the IRS may presume that a disguised sale has occurred. For example, a disguised sale is presumed to exist if both of the following occur:

- A contractual agreement requires a contribution by one partner to be followed within two years by a specified distribution from the partnership.
- The distribution is to be made without regard to partnership profits. In other words, the forthcoming distribution is not subject to significant "entrepreneurial risk."

If the distribution occurs more than two years after the property contribution or if it is deemed "reasonable" in relation to the partner's invested capital, the distribution is *not* presumed to be a disguised sale.

Services

A partner may receive an interest in partnership capital or profits in exchange for services rendered to the partnership. In certain circumstances, special rules will apply.

Capital Interest Received in Exchange for Services When a partner receives a fully vested interest in partnership capital (i.e., unrestricted liquidation rights) in exchange for services, the value of the interest is generally taxable to the partner as ordinary compensation income. Services are not treated as "property" that can be transferred to a partnership on a tax-free basis. Generally, the partner's ordinary income equals the amount the partner would receive if the partnership was liquidated immediately following the contribution of services, less any amount the partner paid for the interest.[15]

The partnership may deduct any amount included in the service partner's income if the services are of a deductible nature.[16] Otherwise, the amount must be capitalized. Any deduction related to the service partners' interest is generally allocated to the other partners in the partnership.

Profits Interest Received in Exchange for Services Transfer of a partnership *profits* interest in exchange for services is generally taxed to the recipient partner as the profits are earned. The amount of the partnership's future profits cannot typically be determined, so there is no current value to the interest.[17]

If the future profits interest is classified as a **carried interest**, special rules apply.[18] The effect of these rules is that for certain types of interests received in exchange for services, future capital gains related to the interest (whether pass-through gains on Schedule K–1 or gains on the partner's sale of the interest) are recharacterized and treated as short-term capital gains, which are generally taxed as ordinary income to the partner. This recharacterization applies unless a three-year holding period is met. This holding period requirement and gain character reclassification do not apply to other Schedule K–1 items, such as interest income or qualified dividends.

[15]§ 83(a); for treatment when there is a "substantial risk of forfeiture," also see Reg. § 1.83–3, Prop.Reg. § 1.83–3(l), and Notice 2005–43.

[16]§ 83(h).

[17]For situations in which the future interest might be taxable, see Rev.Proc. 93–27, as clarified by Rev.Proc. 2001–43.

[18]The IRS has released a substantial regulation project and FAQs offering guidance on calculation and treatment of carried interests.

A partnership interest is a carried interest if (1) it was received in exchange for performance of services, (2) the partnership's business relates to raising capital or investing in or developing assets such as stocks, commodities, rental or investment real estate, or similar assets, and (3) the income or gain relates to assets held for portfolio investment on behalf of third-party investors.[19] An interest is not a carried interest if the partner "pays" for it, either with contributed cash or other assets, or through income recognition under § 83.

Dave receives his one-third capital and profits interest in BCD LLC (valued at $20,000) as compensation for tax planning services he provided before the LLC was formed.

Dave recognizes $20,000 of compensation income, and he takes a $20,000 basis in his LLC interest. The interest is not a carried interest because Dave "pays" for the capital interest by recognizing the value as compensation income.

The same result would occur if the LLC had paid Dave $20,000 for his services and he immediately contributed that amount to the entity for a one-third ownership interest. The LLC will probably treat the $20,000 as an amortizable startup expense.

21-2c **Other Issues Related to Contributed Property**

When property is contributed to a partnership, other issues arise, including cost recovery, allocations related to the property, and subsequent dispositions of the property.

Depreciation Method and Period

If a partner contributes depreciable property, the partnership generally "steps into the shoes" of the contributing partner and continues to use the depreciation schedule and calculations the partner used. The partnership may not claim a § 179 deduction with respect to contributed property.[20]

Amortization of Intangible Assets

Similarly, if a partner contributes an existing intangible asset to the partnership, the partnership generally will "step into the shoes" of the partner in determining future amortization deductions. Code § 197 intangible assets are amortized over 15 years and include purchased goodwill, going-concern value, information systems, customer- or supplier-related intangible assets, patents, licenses obtained from a governmental unit, franchises, trademarks, covenants not to compete, and other items. Other intangible assets (i.e., not addressed in § 197) are amortized over their useful life, if any.[21]

On January 1 of the current year, Jan contributed the assets of a sole proprietorship in exchange for a 50% interest in the JK LLC. One of the assets was a commercial property (depreciable over 39 years) that had been purchased seven years ago. For that property, JK will claim the year 8 depreciation and continue with the remainder of Jan's 39-year schedule.

A second property was a § 197 intangible asset that Jan had acquired three years earlier. That property was being amortized over 15 years. Again, JK will continue Jan's amortization schedule for years 4 to 15.

Character of Gain or Loss on Disposition of Receivables, Inventory, and Built-In Loss Properties

When a partner contributes certain types of property to a partnership, the aggregate theory comes into play if the partnership later sells the property. In three situations, the character of the partnership's gain or loss is not the capital gain or ordinary loss you might expect under general tax rules.[22]

[19] § 1061 and related Regulations.
[20] §§ 168(i)(7) and 179(d)(2)(C).
[21] Reg. § 1.167(a)-3.
[22] § 724.

Ordinary Income Property If the partner contributes either of the following types of property, the partnership's later sale of the property results in ordinary income for:

- Accounts receivable where the contributing partner has not yet recognized the related income (e.g., cash basis accounts receivable).
- Inventory (in the contributing partner's hands) that would have resulted in ordinary income if the partner had sold it *if* the partnership sells the inventory *within five years of the contribution date.*

Capital Loss Property Similarly, if the partner contributes property with a "built-in" capital loss at the contribution date, the partnership's later sale of that property *within five years of the contribution date* results in a capital loss. The capital loss is limited to the "built-in" loss at the contribution date.

Example 11

Deon contributed accounts receivable, inventory, and land to DR LLC as follows.

	Adjusted Basis	Fair Market Value
Receivables	$ -0-	$20,000
Inventory	25,000	50,000
Land (investment property to Deon)	12,000	9,000

Soon after formation, DR collects $20,000 cash for the receivables and sells the inventory for $50,000 cash. The LLC recognizes ordinary income of $20,000 for the receivables and $25,000 for the inventory, even if the property is not an ordinary trade receivable or inventory in the LLC's hands.

DR uses the land as a parking lot for a year (§ 1231 property) and then sells it for $7,000. The LLC's loss on the land is $5,000 ($12,000 adjusted basis − $7,000 selling price). DR classifies the $3,000 precontribution loss ($12,000 − $9,000) as a capital loss because it would have been a capital loss to Deon. The remaining $2,000 loss ($9,000 − $7,000) is a § 1231 loss based on DR's use of the land.

Allocations Related to Contributed Property

As discussed later in the chapter, special allocations must be made relative to contributed property that is appreciated or depreciated. The partnership's income and losses must be allocated to ensure that the inherent gain or loss is not shifted away from the contributing partner. So, in Example 11, the precontribution portion of the income, gains, and losses would be allocated to Deon.

The Big Picture

Example 12

Return to the facts of *The Big Picture* on p. 21-1. Assume that Kyler's $2,000,000 of contributed real estate consists of land with a $600,000 basis and a fully depreciated building and fixtures ($0 basis). Maria has fully depreciated the $500,000 of bakery equipment and café furnishings that she contributed and so has a $0 basis in those assets.

When Beachside Properties LLC is formed, no tax arises for the LLC or for Kyler or Maria. Kyler does not recognize his $1,400,000 realized gain, nor does Maria recognize her $500,000 realized gain.

Kyler takes a substituted basis of $600,000 for his interest, and Maria takes a substituted basis of $1,500,000 ($1,500,000 of contributed cash + $0 basis in contributed property). Beachside Properties assumes a carryover basis of $600,000 for the real estate contributed by Kyler and $0 for the property contributed by Maria. If there had been a remaining depreciable basis for any of the contributed property, the LLC would have "stepped into the member's shoes" in calculating depreciation deductions. Any future income related to the precontribution gains will be allocated to the contributing partner.

continued

When Josh vests in his 5% *capital interest* in the LLC, the $200,000 value of the interest is taxable to him because he received it in exchange for services. Beachside Properties will capitalize this amount and allocate it to the building expansion and new fixtures. Josh's 20% interest in the *future profits* of the LLC will be taxed to him as profits are earned by the LLC.[23]

Concept Summary 21.2 reviews the rules that apply to partnership asset contribution and basis adjustments.

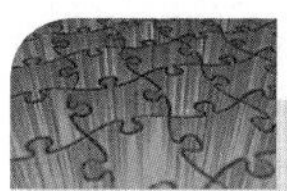

Concept Summary 21.2

Partnership Formation and Initial Basis Computation

1. Under the general rule of § 721, partners or partnerships do not recognize gain or loss when property is contributed in exchange for capital interests.
2. Partners take a substituted basis in their partnership interest *(outside basis)* equal to the basis of the property contributed to the partnership.
3. The partnership takes a carryover basis in assets received *(inside basis)* equal to the partner's basis in those assets.
4. The partner's holding period in the partnership interest begins when the interest is acquired (for cash or "other" property contributions) and/or on the date the contributed property was acquired (for contributions of capital or § 1231 property).
5. The partnership's holding period for contributed property includes the contributing partner's holding period.
6. The partnership "steps into the partner's shoes" in calculating depreciation and amortization of contributed property.
7. Rules prevent the recharacterization of ordinary income as capital gains for inventory and accounts receivable and prevent conversion of capital losses to ordinary losses.
8. The general rule of § 721 does not apply to partnership interests received upon formation of certain investment partnerships, as a disguised sale or exchange, or as a fully vested capital interest received in exchange for services.

21-2d Tax Accounting Elections

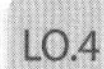
LO.4

Specify the elections available to a new partnership and the treatment of its expenditures.

A newly formed partnership must make numerous tax accounting elections stating how certain transactions or tax attributes should be handled. In general, these elections must be made by the partnership rather than by the partners individually.[24] For example, as discussed later in the chapter, the partnership selects its taxable year and accounting method and elects the treatment of organizational and startup expenditures. As discussed in text Section 22-5, the partnership also makes any optional basis adjustment election and calculations under § 754 (available only to partnerships).

The partnership, rather than the partners, makes other elections and calculations under general tax accounting rules, including the following:

- Cost recovery methods and assumptions.
- § 179 deductions for certain tangible personal property.
- Inventory method.
- Calculation of the partnership's allowable business interest expense deduction.
- Calculation of all partnership tax credits except foreign tax credit.
- Cost or percentage depletion method, excluding oil and gas wells.
- Amounts and treatment of research and experimental expenditures.

Each partner is bound by the decisions made by the partnership relative to these items. If the partnership fails to make an election, a partner cannot make the election individually.

There are three rather narrow exceptions to this general rule. Each *partner* is required to make a specific election for the following tax issues:

- Whether to reduce the basis of depreciable property first when excluding income from discharge of indebtedness.
- Whether to claim cost or percentage depletion for oil and gas wells.
- Whether to take a deduction or credit for taxes paid to non-U.S. jurisdictions.

---

[23]Note that the 15% difference between the "paid for" capital interest and the future services interest *might* be considered a "carried interest" to the extent the underlying partnership interest is deemed to be engaged in rental or investment real estate activities. As such, a portion of future capital gains allocated to Josh from the LLC *might* be recharacterized as ordinary income under the rules of § 1061.

[24]§ 703(b).

21-2e Initial Costs of a Partnership

In its initial stages, a partnership incurs expenses related to some or all of the following activities: forming the partnership (organizational costs), starting business operations (startup costs), admitting partners to the partnership, marketing and selling partnership units to prospective partners (syndication costs), and acquiring assets.

Organizational and Startup Costs

A partnership's organizational costs and startup costs parallel the rules illustrated in text Section 17-1k for corporations. Refer to Examples 21 to 23 in that discussion. Each type of cost is considered separately, so for each category, a partnership can deduct up to $5,000 immediately (subject to phaseout) with the excess amortized over 180 months, beginning with the month in which the partnership begins business.[25]

This treatment is elected simply by deducting the proper amounts on the tax return.[26]

Syndication Costs

Syndication costs are capitalized, but no amortization election is available.[27] Syndication costs include expenditures incurred for promoting and marketing partnership interests such as brokerage fees, registration fees, certain legal fees, accounting fees related to the offering materials, and printing costs of the prospectus and other selling materials. As with organizational and startup costs, this parallels the corporate tax treatment of stock marketing, issuance, and brokerage costs.

Acquisition Costs of Depreciable Assets

As mentioned earlier, the partnership typically determines its depreciation deductions by "stepping into the shoes" of the contributing partner. If additional costs are incurred, though, the additional basis is treated as a new MACRS asset, placed in service on the date the partnership places the asset in service, with the same tax treatment as any other newly acquired capital asset. For example, legal fees and transfer taxes incurred in transferring assets to a partnership must be capitalized. Cost recovery for the new costs commences when the partnership places the underlying property in service (not when the partner originally placed the asset in service).

LO.5

Specify the accounting methods and taxable years available to a partnership.

21-2f Method of Accounting

A newly formed partnership may adopt either the cash or accrual method of accounting or a hybrid of these two methods.

If a partnership uses the accrual method of accounting, its income must be reported no later than the date that income would be reported on the partnership's "applicable financial statement" (e.g., an audited financial statement) or other similar financial statement.[28] This rule is designed to ensure that any advance payments (i.e., cash receipts) received by the taxpayer are reported in taxable income at least as quickly as they are reported in book income.

Two exceptions limit use of the cash method of accounting by partnerships. The cash method may *not* be adopted by a partnership that:

- Has one or more C corporation partners.
- Is a tax shelter.

As an "exception to the exception," a partnership that is not a tax shelter and that has a C corporation partner may still elect to use the cash method if:

- The partnership meets the $29 million gross receipts (small business) test described below.[29]

[25] § 709(b) and § 195(b)(1).

[26] Reg. § 1.709–1 and Reg. § 1.195–1.

[27] § 709(a).

[28] §§ 451(a) and (b).

[29] § 448. The $29 million threshold is indexed for inflation; in the Code, you will see the initial amount of $25 million. A $26 million threshold applied in 2020 and 2021. A $27 million threshold applied in 2022.

- The C corporation partner(s) is a qualified personal service corporation, such as an incorporated attorney.
- The partnership is engaged in the business of farming.

A partnership meets the $29 million gross receipts test if its average annual gross receipts are $29 million or less for 2023. "Average annual gross receipts" is the average of gross receipts for the three tax years (or the number of prior years the partnership has been in existence, if fewer) ending with the tax period *prior to* the tax year in question. If the gross receipts test is not met, the partnership must change to the accrual method the next tax year.

A tax shelter is a partnership whose interests have been sold in a registered offering, a partnership in which 35 percent of the losses are allocated to limited partners, or a partnership with a significant purpose to avoid or evade Federal income tax.

Jason and Julia are both attorneys. In 2020, each of them formed a professional personal service corporation to operate their separate law practices. In 2023, the two attorneys form the JJ Partnership, which consists of the two professional corporations. In 2023, JJ's gross receipts are $30 million.

Because JJ's two corporate partners are both personal service corporations, JJ may adopt the cash method in 2023. It may continue to use the cash method in 2024 and future years even though its average annual gross receipts are greater than $29 million. [In this case, average annual gross receipts would be calculated considering only JJ's one year (2023) prior history.] Alternatively, JJ may adopt the accrual method of accounting or a hybrid of the cash and accrual methods.

21-2g Taxable Year of the Partnership

Partnership taxable income (and any separately stated items) flows through to each partner at the end of the *partnership's* taxable year. A *partner's* taxable income, then, includes the distributive share of partnership income for any *partnership* taxable year that ends during the partner's tax year. A partnership must use either the **required taxable year** or one of three alternate taxable years, as shown in Exhibit 21.1.

Deferral of Partnership Income

The required taxable year rules prevent excess deferral of tax on the partnership's income. How might deferral arise?

Exhibit 21.1 Permitted Taxable Years of Partnerships

Required Taxable Year	
In Order, Partnership Must Use	**Requirements**
Majority partners' tax year	• More than 50% of capital *and* profits is owned by partners who have the same taxable year.
Principal partners' tax year	• All partners who own 5% or more of capital *or* profits are principal partners. • All principal partners must have the same tax year.
Year with smallest amount of income deferred	• "Least aggregate deferral rule" per IRS regulations.
Alternative Tax Years	
Business purpose year	• Use an IRS-approved year-end for which there is a business purpose.
Three-month deferral year	• Use a year-end with not more than a three-month deferral of income, compared to the required taxable year, and pay an interest deposit on the deferred tax.
52–53 week fiscal year	• Use a year ending on a specific day of the week rather than the last day of a month.

Suppose Partners A, B, and C use a calendar year. What if their partnership, ABC, could use a February 28 fiscal year-end? ABC's income through February 2023 (including income earned since March 2022) would not be taxed to Partners A, B, and C until December 31, 2023. This would allow taxation of ABC's income to be deferred ten months.

Instead of this result, you'll see that the permitted year-end rules result in partnership income being taxed sooner rather than later. In our example, Partnership ABC would be required to use a calendar year or certain alternative permitted years.

Required Taxable Year

The partnership's required taxable year is determined under the first of three rules that applies.[30] The rules are evaluated in order. First, the partnership uses the tax year of the "majority partners" if partners owning more than 50 percent of partnership capital and profits have the same tax year.

If there are no "majority partners" (e.g., if there are two 50 percent partners with different tax years), we go to the second rule. Under this rule, the partnership uses the tax year of the "principal partners" if all partners who own 5 percent or more of capital or profits have the same tax year.

If no year-end can be determined under the first two rules, the partnership determines a year under the **least aggregate deferral rule** as outlined in the Regulations for § 706.

Alternative Tax Years

If the required tax year is undesirable to the entity, three alternative tax years may be available. (1) The taxpayer can establish a business purpose for a different taxable year.[31] (2) The taxpayer can elect a year-end with not more than a three-month deferral of income, relative to the required taxable year, under § 444. (3) The taxpayer can use a 52–53 week taxable year.[32]

Crimson, Inc., and Indigo, Inc., (both subchapter C corporations) are equal partners in the CI Partnership. Crimson uses the calendar year, and Indigo uses a fiscal year ending August 31. Neither Crimson nor Indigo is a majority partner as neither owns more than 50%. Although Crimson and Indigo are both principal partners (i.e., each owns at least 5%), they do not have the same tax year. Therefore, the general rules indicate that the partnership's required tax year must be determined by the "least aggregate deferral rule."

Assume that the least aggregate deferral rule yields a required taxable year of August 31. In 2023, CI closes its books and files a Form 1065 as of August 31. Indigo reports its share of CI's income (from the Schedule K–1 received from CI) in its tax return for the year ending August 31, 2023. Crimson reports its share of CI's income in its 2023 calendar year return.

If August 31 is not a desirable year-end, CI can use a 52- to 53-week year ending around August 31; establish a business purpose tax year; or select May, June, or July as the year-end under § 444.

Report a partnership's taxable income and separately stated items on Form 1065.

21-3 Partnership Operations and Reporting

As a business entity, a partnership is just like any other enterprise. It produces and sells products and/or services, it owns property and pays employees, and it distributes profits to owners or holds those profits for reinvestment in the company. For income tax purposes, a partnership is a tax-reporting, rather than a taxpaying, entity.

21-3a Partnership Reporting

As mentioned, the partnership prepares Form 1065 to report information from its operations. The partners receive a Schedule K–1 for use in preparing their returns.

[30] § 706(b).

[31] Rev.Proc. 2006–46, § 5.07.

[32] § 441(f). This typically is elected when the tax year always ends on the same day of the week.

Partnership Reporting and Form 1065

The partnership's Form 1065 organizes and reports the transactions of the entity for the tax year. Form 1065 and Schedule K–1 are included in Appendix B, and all tax forms can be downloaded at **irs.gov**. Find a copy of Form 1065, and follow along. Form 1065 consists of five pages and is organized as follows.

- Page 1 summarizes the partnership's ordinary income and loss from trade or business activities. Cost of goods sold (line 2) is calculated on Form 1125–A and carried to this page.[33]
- Pages 2 and 3 provide information about the partnership's activities and general information about the partners.
- Page 4 (Schedule K) summarizes the partnership's ordinary income or loss, separately stated items, and other items that will be allocated among the partners on Schedules K–1. Schedule K, line 1, shows the ordinary income/loss from page 1.
- Page 5 provides several schedules, including a balance sheet (Schedule L), a reconciliation of book and "taxable" income [Schedules M–1 and the Analysis of Net Income (Loss)], and a reconciliation of partners' beginning and ending capital (Schedule M–2).

Form 1065 is due by the fifteenth day of the third month following the end of the tax year. For a calendar year partnership, this deadline is March 15. The partnership may request (by the original due date) an automatic six-month extension of time for filing (to September 15 for a calendar year partnership). Note that these due dates are one month earlier than the due date and extended deadline for individual taxpayers.

Partner Reporting and Schedule K–1

Almost any type of entity can be a partner: individuals, corporations, trusts, estates, or another partnership, for example. Consequently, the partnership's income, deductions, credits, and alternative minimum tax (AMT) preferences and adjustments can ultimately be reported and taxed on any of a number of income tax returns [e.g., Forms 1040 (individuals), 1041 (fiduciaries, see Chapter 30), 1120 (C corporations), and 1120S (S corporations)].

These partners must be informed of their shares of partnership income, expenses, gains, losses, and other information they must report. The partnership allocates each item from Schedule K [including the partnership's ordinary income (loss) from line 1] among all the partners on Schedules K–1. One copy of each Schedule K–1 is filed with the Form 1065, and another copy is provided to the respective partner.

Other Partnership Taxes

A partnership is subject to all taxes (other than income taxes) in the same manner as any other business. Thus, the partnership files returns and pays appropriate sales taxes and property taxes. For employees (not partners), the partnership files returns and pays Social Security, unemployment, and other payroll taxes. In some states, franchise taxes are assessed based on partnership net income or gross receipts, or capital or asset values.

21-3b Measuring Partnership Income

A partnership measures and reports two general kinds of income: ordinary business income (Form 1065, page 1, shown on p. 21-19) and separately stated items (Form 1065, Schedule K, shown on p. 21-20).

[33] A "Tax and Payment" section is completed in unusual situations where the partnership must pay interest related to certain permitted tax deferral situations (e.g., certain long-term contracts).

Ordinary Business Income

A partnership's ordinary business income consists of any income or expenses that are not required to be separately stated. For example, the partnership's sales revenues, utilities, rent expense, depreciation expense related to business assets, and other ordinary and necessary business expenses under § 162 are reported on Form 1065, page 1. As mentioned earlier, the partnership makes elections related to inventory, depreciation, research and experimentation expenses, and similar business-related amounts, so it makes sense that the partners don't need separate information about these calculations. The partnership also calculates and claims the allowable business interest expense deduction, but any disallowed interest expense is treated as a separately stated item, as discussed later.

Separately Stated Items

A separately stated item is any item with tax attributes that *might* affect any two partner's tax liabilities in different ways.[34] For example, charitable contributions are separately stated because partners need to compute their own deductions for charitable contributions. Other income and deduction items passed through separately include the following:

- Net short-term and net long-term capital gains or losses. (Note that the partnership reports both a net long-term and a net short-term gain or loss. The final short- and/or long-term netting is done at the partner level.)
- § 1231 gains and losses.
- Portfolio income items (qualified and ordinary dividends, interest, and royalties).
- Expenses related to portfolio income.
- Disallowed business interest expense and related information.
- Immediately expensed tangible personal property (§ 179).
- Guaranteed payments for capital and services, discussed later in this section.
- Passive activity items such as rental real estate income or loss.
- Intangible drilling and development costs.
- General business tax credits (the partnership calculates the credit and allocates the credit to the partners so they can apply their limitations).
- Taxes paid to non-U.S. countries and to U.S. possessions and related information (the partners decide whether to claim a foreign tax credit or a deduction and determine any limitations).[35]

The reason for separately reporting the preceding items is rooted in the aggregate or conduit concept. These items affect various exclusions, deductions, and credits at the partner level and must pass through without loss of identity so that the proper tax for each partner may be determined.[36]

A partnership is not allowed to claim the following deductions:

- Net operating losses (NOLs).
- Depletion of oil and gas interests.
- Dividends received deduction.

Deductions taken by individuals, such as standard deductions, are not available to the partnership. If a partnership makes a payment on behalf of a partner, such as for alimony, medical expenses, or items that might constitute deductions to individuals, the partnership treats the payment as a distribution or guaranteed payment to the partner, and the partner determines whether any deduction is permitted.

[34] § 703(a)(1).

[35] § 702(a).

[36] § 702(b).

The Big Picture

Example 15

Return to the facts of *The Big Picture* on p. 21-1. In its second year of operations, Beachside Properties LLC reports income and expenses from operating the café; rent income and expenses from leasing the other buildings; and contributions, distributions, and other information as follows.

Sales revenue	$2,000,000
Cost of sales	800,000
W–2 wages paid to employees (no employment credits)	500,000
Cost recovery deductions (related to the Beachsider café business only)	91,984
Utilities, supplies, and other ordinary business expenses	128,016
Taxes and licenses (including payroll taxes)	60,000
Guaranteed payments to LLC members for services	120,000
Guaranteed payments to LLC members for use of partners' capital	120,000
Charitable contributions	6,000
Short-term capital gain	12,000
Net income from rental real estate (net of all expenses, including depreciation)	300,000
Qualified dividends received	4,000
Exempt income (bond interest)	2,100
Alternative minimum tax (AMT) adjustment (cost recovery)	18,224
Payment of medical expenses on behalf of Kyler	4,000
Contribution of additional cash from Maria	110,000
Contribution of other property from Maria (basis $0)	50,000
Distribution of cash to Maria	30,000

Beachside will determine its ordinary income or loss for the year, along with its separately stated items. Beachside has elected not to claim bonus depreciation or § 179 deductions. As discussed next, the guaranteed payments are either deducted or capitalized by the LLC; they are reported as ordinary income by the member who receives them. Beachside also reports any additional information the partners might need to prepare their individual income tax returns.

The LLC cannot deduct the payment for Kyler's medical expenses. This payment is probably handled as a distribution to Kyler, who may report it as a medical expense on his Schedule A in determining his itemized deductions. Similarly, the LLC cannot deduct the distribution to Maria (distributions are discussed in Chapter 22). The AMT adjustment is not a separate component of the LLC's income. However, it must be reported to Beachside's members so that they can properly calculate any AMT liability. Other information also will be passed through, including information for business interest deduction carryovers, qualified business income (the § 199A deduction), and self-employment and other taxes. These topics are discussed later.

Last year (the first year of operations), the LLC reported a $250,000 net loss from operations. Beachside could not deduct that loss; instead, it was passed through to the LLC members. Loss deduction limitations might have applied at the member level. These limitations are discussed later in the chapter.

Guaranteed Payments Paid by the Partnership

A **guaranteed payment** is a payment to a partner for services performed by the partner or for the use of the partner's capital. These payments resemble the salary or interest payments of other businesses.[37] The partnership either deducts or capitalizes the payment, depending on its nature. As discussed later, regardless of the partnership's treatment, the partner reports the payment as ordinary income.

Guaranteed payments are usually expressed as a fixed-dollar amount or as a percentage of capital the partner has invested in the partnership. By definition, a guaranteed payment cannot be calculated based on partnership income (e.g., as a percentage of annual income).

[37] § 707(c).

The Big Picture

Example 16

Return to the facts of *The Big Picture* as updated in Example 15. Assume that Josh was elected as managing member of Beachside Properties LLC; he has the sole authority to contract for the LLC and works 1,000 hours per year in the business. Maria works 1,000 hours per year in the café. After transferring his land to Beachside, Kyler has generally not been involved in the LLC's operations. In addition, recall that the LLC uses capital contributed by Maria and Kyler ($2,000,000 each in year 1).

Josh and Maria both receive guaranteed payments of $5,000 per month for services to the LLC. In addition, Maria and Kyler both receive guaranteed payments of $5,000 per month for the LLC's use of their capital. The guaranteed payments total $120,000 for partners' services (12 months × $5,000 × 2 payments) and $120,000 for use of the partners' capital (12 months × $5,000 × 2 payments). Beachside may deduct these payments.

Deductible guaranteed payments, like any other deductible expenses of a partnership, can create an ordinary loss for the entity.[38]

Partnership Interest Expense

A partnership's interest expense also is subject to special reporting rules: it must be allocated among the partnership's various activities, generally based on how and why the underlying debt arose. Regulations prescribe that interest expense of a Subchapter C corporation is generally treated as business interest expense; however, this is not true for partnership interest expense. For example, some interest expense might relate to funds borrowed for investment purposes. In that case, it is classified as investment interest expense and must be separately stated on Schedule K, line 13b.

Business interest expense is subject to the rules discussed in text Section 17-1f. For a partnership or an S corporation, in the year the interest expense arises, the entity determines the amount that can be deducted.[39] If the entity is defined as a small business (using the $29 million gross receipts test described in text Section 21-2f) or if it is an electing business in certain fields (e.g., real estate or farming), the business interest expense limitation does not apply. For other businesses, the 30 percent limitation described in Chapter 17 applies. The entity deduction is an ordinary business deduction (i.e., not a separately stated item), so it would be deducted on page 1 of the partnership or S corporation return.

Any disallowed business interest expense is passed through to the partners (reducing their basis in the partnership interest) and can be used to offset the partner's share of the partnership's "excess taxable income" in future years.

21-3c Form 1065 Example

Let's look at an example. Pages 1, 4, and 5 of the Beachside Form 1065 for its second tax year are constructed on the following pages.

Beachside's Form 1065

Beachside's Form 1065, page 1, includes general information, ordinary business income (loss), information related to certain (rare) taxes that might apply to the partnership, and signatures of officers and tax return preparers.

Schedule K includes "Partners' Distributive Share Items." The Schedule K shows subheadings down the left side of the form for the various types of information provided. These subheadings include separately stated income and deductions and then additional information the partners would need related to self-employment taxes, tax credits, international transactions, alternative minimum taxes, and other information.

Form 1065, page 5, includes an "Analysis of Net Income (Loss)," a balance sheet (book method), a reconciliation of book and tax income, and an analysis of partners' capital accounts.

[38] Per Rev.Rul. 2007–40, if the partnership distributes appreciated property to pay a guaranteed payment, the partnership recognizes any gain on the transfer.

[39] § 163(j)(4).

Form **1065** Department of the Treasury Internal Revenue Service

U.S. Return of Partnership Income

For calendar year 2022, or tax year beginning ____________, 2022, ending ____________, 20 ____.

Go to *www.irs.gov/Form1065* for instructions and the latest information.

OMB No. 1545-0123 — **2022**

A Principal business activity: *Restaurant/Commercial Rental*	Name of partnership: *Beachside Properties LLC*	**D** Employer identification number: *11-1111112*
B Principal product or service: *Food service*	**Type or Print** — Number, street, and room or suite no. If a P.O. box, see instructions.: *1600 Ocean Vista Way*	**E** Date business started: *1/1/2020*
C Business code number: *722110*	City or town, state or province, country, and ZIP or foreign postal code: *Surfside*	**F** Total assets (see instructions): $ *3,218,100*

G Check applicable boxes: (1) ☐ Initial return (2) ☐ Final return (3) ☐ Name change (4) ☐ Address change (5) ☐ Amended return

H Check accounting method: (1) ☐ Cash (2) ☒ Accrual (3) ☐ Other (specify): ____________

I Number of Schedules K-1. Attach one for each person who was a partner at any time during the tax year: *3*

J Check if Schedules C and M-3 are attached . . . ☐

K Check if partnership: (1) ☐ Aggregated activities for section 465 at-risk purposes (2) ☐ Grouped activities for section 469 passive activity purposes

Caution: Include **only** trade or business income and expenses on lines 1a through 22 below. See instructions for more information.

Section	Line	Description			Line	Amount
Income	1a	Gross receipts or sales	1a	*2,000,000*		
	b	Returns and allowances	1b			
	c	Balance. Subtract line 1b from line 1a			1c	*2,000,000*
	2	Cost of goods sold (attach Form 1125-A)			2	*800,000*
	3	Gross profit. Subtract line 2 from line 1c			3	*1,200,000*
	4	Ordinary income (loss) from other partnerships, estates, and trusts (attach statement)			4	
	5	Net farm profit (loss) (attach Schedule F (Form 1040))			5	
	6	Net gain (loss) from Form 4797, Part II, line 17 (attach Form 4797)			6	
	7	Other income (loss) (attach statement)			7	
	8	**Total income (loss).** Combine lines 3 through 7			8	*1,200,000*
Deductions (see instructions for limitations)	9	Salaries and wages (other than to partners) (less employment credits)			9	*500,000*
	10	Guaranteed payments to partners			10	*240,000*
	11	Repairs and maintenance			11	
	12	Bad debts			12	
	13	Rent			13	
	14	Taxes and licenses			14	*60,000*
	15	Interest (see instructions)			15	
	16a	Depreciation (if required, attach Form 4562)	16a	*91,984*		
	b	Less depreciation reported on Form 1125-A and elsewhere on return	16b		16c	*91,984*
	17	Depletion **(Do not deduct oil and gas depletion.)**			17	
	18	Retirement plans, etc.			18	
	19	Employee benefit programs			19	
	20	Other deductions (attach statement)			20	*128,016*
	21	**Total deductions.** Add the amounts shown in the far right column for lines 9 through 20			21	*1,020,000*
	22	**Ordinary business income (loss).** Subtract line 21 from line 8			22	*180,000*
Tax and Payment	23	Interest due under the look-back method—completed long-term contracts (attach Form 8697)			23	
	24	Interest due under the look-back method—income forecast method (attach Form 8866)			24	
	25	BBA AAR imputed underpayment (see instructions)			25	
	26	Other taxes (see instructions)			26	
	27	**Total balance due.** Add lines 23 through 26			27	
	28	Payment (see instructions)			28	
	29	**Amount owed.** If line 28 is smaller than line 27, enter amount owed			29	
	30	**Overpayment.** If line 28 is larger than line 27, enter overpayment			30	

Sign Here

Under penalties of perjury, I declare that I have examined this return, including accompanying schedules and statements, and to the best of my knowledge and belief, it is true, correct, and complete. Declaration of preparer (other than partner or limited liability company member) is based on all information of which preparer has any knowledge.

Signature of partner or limited liability company member ____________ Date ____________

May the IRS discuss this return with the preparer shown below? See instructions. ☐ Yes ☐ No

Paid Preparer Use Only

Print/Type preparer's name	Preparer's signature	Date	Check ☐ if self-employed	PTIN
Firm's name			Firm's EIN	
Firm's address			Phone no.	

Form 1065 (2022) 11-1111112 Page **4**

		Schedule K Partners' Distributive Share Items		**Total amount**
Income (Loss)	1	Ordinary business income (loss) (page 1, line 22)	1	*180,000*
	2	Net rental real estate income (loss) (attach Form 8825)	2	*300,000*
	3a	Other gross rental income (loss) . . . **3a**		
	b	Expenses from other rental activities (attach statement) . . . **3b**		
	c	Other net rental income (loss). Subtract line 3b from line 3a	3c	*0*
	4	Guaranteed payments: **a** Services **4a** *120,000* **b** Capital **4b** *120,000*		
		c Total. Add lines 4a and 4b	4c	*240,000*
	5	Interest income	5	
	6	Dividends and dividend equivalents: **a** Ordinary dividends	6a	*4,000*
		b Qualified dividends **6b** *4,000* **c** Dividend equivalents **6c**		
	7	Royalties	7	
	8	Net short-term capital gain (loss) (attach Schedule D (Form 1065))	8	*12,000*
	9a	Net long-term capital gain (loss) (attach Schedule D (Form 1065))	9a	
	b	Collectibles (28%) gain (loss) . . . **9b**		
	c	Unrecaptured section 1250 gain (attach statement) . . . **9c**		
	10	Net section 1231 gain (loss) (attach Form 4797)	10	
	11	Other income (loss) (see instructions) Type:	11	
Deductions	12	Section 179 deduction (attach Form 4562)	12	
	13a	Contributions	13a	*6,000*
	b	Investment interest expense	13b	
	c	Section 59(e)(2) expenditures: **(1)** Type: **(2)** Amount:	13c(2)	
	d	Other deductions (see instructions) Type:	13d	
Self-Employment	14a	Net earnings (loss) from self-employment	14a	*150,000**
	b	Gross farming or fishing income	14b	
	c	Gross nonfarm income	14c	*720,000***
Credits	15a	Low-income housing credit (section 42(j)(5))	15a	
	b	Low-income housing credit (other)	15b	
	c	Qualified rehabilitation expenditures (rental real estate) (attach Form 3468, if applicable)	15c	
	d	Other rental real estate credits (see instructions) Type:	15d	
	e	Other rental credits (see instructions) Type:	15e	
	f	Other credits (see instructions) Type:	15f	
International	16	Attach Schedule K-2 (Form 1065), Partners' Distributive Share Items—International, and check this box to indicate that you are reporting items of international tax relevance . . . ☐		
Alternative Minimum Tax (AMT) Items	17a	Post-1986 depreciation adjustment	17a	*18,224*
	b	Adjusted gain or loss	17b	
	c	Depletion (other than oil and gas)	17c	
	d	Oil, gas, and geothermal properties—gross income	17d	
	e	Oil, gas, and geothermal properties—deductions	17e	
	f	Other AMT items (attach statement)	17f	
Other Information	18a	Tax-exempt interest income	18a	*2,100*
	b	Other tax-exempt income	18b	
	c	Nondeductible expenses	18c	
	19a	Distributions of cash and marketable securities	19a	*34,000*
	b	Distributions of other property	19b	
	20a	Investment income	20a	*12,000*
	b	Investment expenses	20b	
	c	Other items and amounts (attach statement)		***
	21	Total foreign taxes paid or accrued	21	

Form **1065** (2022)

* See Example 33 later in the chapter. This amount includes Maria's guaranteed payment for services, Josh's guaranteed payment for services, and Josh's allocable share of the LLC's income. Include only the amounts subject to self-employment tax.

** This amount is the partnership's gross nonfarm income (Form 1065, page 1, line 8) allocated to Josh and Maria (the LLC members subject to SE tax on earnings from the LLC).

*** As shown in Example 25 later in the chapter, a supporting schedule will show the partnership's totals for additional information related to the partners' qualified business income deduction.

Form 1065 (2022) *Beachside Properties LLC* *11-1111112* Page **5**

Analysis of Net Income (Loss) per Return

1	Net income (loss). Combine Schedule K, lines 1 through 11. From the result, subtract the sum of Schedule K, lines 12 through 13d, and 21 . . .					1	*730,000*
2	Analysis by partner type:	**(i)** Corporate	**(ii)** Individual (active)	**(iii)** Individual (passive)	**(iv)** Partnership	**(v)** Exempt Organization	**(vi)** Nominee/Other
a	General partners						
b	Limited partners		*486,000*	*244,000*			

Schedule L Balance Sheets per Books

		Beginning of tax year (a)	Beginning of tax year (b)	End of tax year (c)	End of tax year (d)
	Assets				
1	Cash . . .		*97,503*		*123,740*
2a	Trade notes and accounts receivable . . .				
b	Less allowance for bad debts . . .		*0*		*0*
3	Inventories . . .		*60,000*		*80,000*
4	U.S. Government obligations . . .				
5	Tax-exempt securities . . .		*40,000*		*40,000*
6	Other current assets (attach statement) . . .				
7a	Loans to partners (or persons related to partners) .				
b	Mortgage and real estate loans . . .				
8	Other investments (attach statement) . . .		*120,000*		*860,000*
9a	Buildings and other depreciable assets . . .	*3,400,000*		*3,400,000*	
b	Less accumulated depreciation . . .	*1,767,503*	*1,632,497*	*1,885,640*	*1,514,360*
10a	Depletable assets . . .				
b	Less accumulated depletion . . .		*0*		*0*
11	Land (net of any amortization) . . .		*600,000*		*600,000*
12a	Intangible assets (amortizable only) . . .	*10,000*		*10,000*	
b	Less accumulated amortization . . .	*10,000*	*0*	*10,000*	*0*
13	Other assets (attach statement) . . .				
14	Total assets . . .		*2,550,000*		*3,218,100*
	Liabilities and Capital				
15	Accounts payable . . .				
16	Mortgages, notes, bonds payable in less than 1 year				
17	Other current liabilities (attach statement) . . .				
18	All nonrecourse loans . . .		*500,000*		*600,000*
19a	Loans from partners (or persons related to partners) .				
b	Mortgages, notes, bonds payable in 1 year or more .				
20	Other liabilities (attach statement) . . .				
21	Partners' capital accounts . . .		*2,050,000*		*2,618,100*
22	Total liabilities and capital . . .		*2,550,000*		*3,218,100*

Schedule M-1 Reconciliation of Income (Loss) per Books With Analysis of Net Income (Loss) per Return

Note: The partnership may be required to file Schedule M-3. See instructions.

1	Net income (loss) per books . . .	*492,100*	6	Income recorded on books this year not included on Schedule K, lines 1 through 11 (itemize):	
2	Income included on Schedule K, lines 1, 2, 3c, 5, 6a, 7, 8, 9a, 10, and 11, not recorded on books this year (itemize):	*0*	a	Tax-exempt interest $ *2,100*	*2,100*
3	Guaranteed payments (other than health insurance) . . .	*240,000*	7	Deductions included on Schedule K, lines 1 through 13d, and 21, not charged against book income this year (itemize):	
4	Expenses recorded on books this year not included on Schedule K, lines 1 through 13d, and 21 (itemize):		a	Depreciation $	*0*
a	Depreciation $		8	Add lines 6 and 7 . . .	*2,100*
b	Travel and entertainment $	*0*	9	Income (loss) (Analysis of Net Income (Loss), line 1). Subtract line 8 from line 5	*730,000*
5	Add lines 1 through 4 . . .	*732,100*			

Schedule M-2 Analysis of Partners' Capital Accounts

1	Balance at beginning of year . . .	*2,050,000*	6	Distributions: **a** Cash . . .	*34,000*
2	Capital contributed: **a** Cash . . .	*110,000*		**b** Property . . .	
	b Property . .		7	Other decreases (itemize):	
3	Net income (loss) (see instructions) .	*492,100*			
4	Other increases (itemize):	*0*	8	Add lines 6 and 7 . . .	*34,000*
5	Add lines 1 through 4 . . .	*2,652,100*	9	Balance at end of year. Subtract line 8 from line 5	*2,618,100*

Form **1065** (2022)

The Big Picture

Example 17

Continue with the facts of Examples 15 and 16, and refer to pages 1, 4, and 5 of Beachside's Form 1065 on the three prior pages. Beachside's ordinary income on Form 1065, page 1, is $180,000 after considering the sales revenue, cost of sales, guaranteed payments, and other operating expenses.

On Schedule K (Form 1065, page 4), Beachside's separately stated income and deduction items (lines 1 to 13a) include net income from rental real estate, guaranteed payments (reported as income by the members), qualified dividends received, short-term capital gain, and charitable contributions.

Beachside's real estate rental operations are reported separately from the bakery's income on a Form 8825 (not shown) and included with Beachside's tax return. Beachside's *deduction* for guaranteed payments is shown on Form 1065, page 1, and the amount the LLC members must report as *income* (from capital and services) is shown on Schedule K, line 4.

Other Items Reported on Schedules K and K–2

As mentioned, the partnership must report any information the partners might need to prepare a complete and accurate income tax return. Separately stated income and deductions are reported on Schedule K, lines 1 to 13. Other information reported on Schedules K and K–2 includes the following:

- The partner's share of tax credits that are calculated at the partnership level.
- Information the partner uses to make various tax or credit calculations (e.g., self-employment tax, net investment income tax, alternative minimum tax).
- Foreign taxes paid or accrued (line 21) and information the partner needs to calculate the foreign tax credit or deduction and for other tax issues related to U.S. taxation of foreign income (Schedule K–2).
- Information the partner needs for other calculations and limitations [e.g., information for the qualified business income (QBI) deduction or interest expense deductions discussed elsewhere in the chapter].
- Information the partner needs to calculate the basis in the partnership interest (e.g., cash and property distributions received, tax-exempt/nondeductible items).
- Any additional information (e.g., summary schedules for each partnership activity or state tax information) the partners might need in preparing their tax returns.

The Big Picture

Example 18

Continue with the information in Examples 15 to 17. In addition to the business income and separately stated items described in Example 17, the LLC also reports the following information that the LLC members will use in preparing their tax returns.

Additional Information (Schedule K)	
Net earnings (loss) from self-employment (line 14a)	$150,000[40]
AMT adjustment—cost recovery (line 17a)	18,224
Tax-exempt income—bond interest (line 18a)	2,100
Distributions (line 19a)	34,000
Investment income (line 20a)	12,000
Other information for LLC member-level calculations	

Investment income on line 20a (used to calculate any allowable investment interest expense deduction) includes Beachside's short-term capital gains but does not include favorably taxed qualified dividends.

Other information for LLC member-level calculations is reported on supporting schedules and includes net investment income (for calculating the net investment income tax), excess taxable income (for calculating business interest expense carryover deductions), and information the members need for qualified business income calculations.

---

[40]This only includes net earnings for partners who are subject to the SE tax. See Example 33 later in this chapter.

Financial Disclosure Insights **Financial Reporting for Partnerships**

Partnerships might be required to prepare GAAP-basis financial statements so they can be provided to a lender, to the Securities and Exchange Commission, or for the partners themselves.

A partnership's financial statements look quite similar to GAAP-basis corporate financial statements, with two major exceptions. First, a partnership will prepare a "Statement of Changes in Partners' Capital" rather than a "Statement of Shareholders' Equity." Second, a partnership will *not* record a Federal income tax liability/tax provision, because the income taxes are paid by the partners.

In the statements themselves, calculations are made using financial reporting methods rather than tax methods. For example, GAAP methods are used to calculate depreciation expense recorded on the partnership's books; you won't see bonus depreciation or § 179 deductions.

A partnership's footnotes to the financial statements describe various *accounting* methods, but they don't typically describe any *tax* elections the partnership has made. A tax footnote will generally be included, but its main function is to clarify why an income tax provision is not recorded. An interested partner would need to examine the partnership's tax return, especially Schedule M–1 or Schedule M–3, to see the nature of any book-tax differences.

The tax footnote also explains whether any tax returns are under examination by the IRS or other tax authority (e.g., state tax agencies) and if any potential partnership-level tax liability might exist (e.g., if state franchise taxes are due or if it is likely that a penalty might be assessed at the partnership level because the partnership made aggressive elections regarding certain tax matters).

A partnership's financial statements will also outline the rights and obligations of the general and limited (if any) partner groups, including any requirements the partners might face for guaranteeing entity debt.

The partnership might use the GAAP basis balance sheet in reporting Schedule L on the tax return, and it is required to do so if the partnership is required to file Schedule M–3 (book to tax reconciliation for larger partnerships). However, Schedule M–2 (Analysis of Partners' Capital Accounts) and the Partner's Capital Account Analysis on the partners' Schedules K–1 must be prepared using tax basis capital accounts. Therefore, capital account totals might differ between the GAAP-basis financial statements and Schedule L and the tax basis capital accounts reported on Schedules K–1 and Schedule M–2.

Reconciling Taxable Income

The partnership reconciles "book" income with income reported on the return. Refer to pages 4 and 5 of Beachside's Form 1065.

The partnership calculates "taxable income"—the net of the partnership's ordinary and separately stated income and expense amounts on Schedule K (generally, lines 1 to 13 less any foreign tax payments shown on line 21). It reports that amount on line 1 of the Analysis of Net Income (Loss) (page 5 of Form 1065). Note that because guaranteed payments are shown separately on Schedule K, line 4, the partnership's "taxable income" is calculated *before* the deduction for guaranteed payments.

Book income is reconciled to this "taxable income" on either Schedule M–1 or Schedule M–3. Schedule M–1 is found on page 5 of Form 1065. Schedule M–3 is a separate three-page form and is often required (in lieu of Schedule M–1) for larger partnerships. The Schedule M–1 or Schedule M–3 is completed similarly to the forms shown for a C corporation; see text Sections 17-3c and 17-3e.

The Big Picture

Example 19

Continue with the facts in Examples 15 to 18, and follow along on Beachside's Form 1065, page 5. To calculate Beachside's "taxable income" on the Analysis of Net Income (Loss) schedule, we combine the ordinary income of $180,000, guaranteed payments of $240,000, and the four separately stated income and deduction amounts [lines 2, 6a, 8, and 13a (negative)] from Beachside's Schedule K. This net amount is $730,000 and is the amount to which the $492,100 (assumed) of book income is reconciled on Schedule M–1, line 9.

Reconciling Partners' Capital

Schedule M–2 reconciles partners' beginning and ending capital accounts, considering contributions to and distributions from the partnership as well as the partnership's income, gains, losses, and deductions. For tax years 2020 and beyond, partnerships must report partners' capital on Schedule M–2 using tax basis capital accounts. In prior tax years, capital might have been prepared using other methods, such as GAAP or § 704(b) book information. (See Concept Summary 21.4 later in the chapter.)

Partners' capital on Schedule M–2 will generally equal the totals of the partner's capital shown on Schedule L (balance sheet) if Schedule L is also prepared on a tax basis. However, larger partnerships might report GAAP basis information as discussed in Financial Reporting for Partnerships on the prior page.

The Big Picture

Example 20

Continue with Examples 15 to 19 and the Beachside Properties Form 1065 excerpts. Beachside prepares its Schedule L and Schedule M–2 using the same ("tax") method, so Beachside's beginning and ending capital accounts have the same balances on both Schedule L and Schedule M–2.

In addition to Beachside's book income, Schedule M–2 also reflects the $30,000 cash distribution to Maria, payment of medical expenses of $4,000 to Kyler, and a $110,000 cash contribution from Maria. Because this is tax method reporting, Maria's property contribution (valued at $50,000) is not shown; that property has a $0 basis to Maria and, as such, has a $0 carryover basis to Beachside.

LO.7

Report information on a partner's Schedule K–1 and the partner's tax return.

21-4 Partner Calculations and Reporting

Once partnership items are calculated on Schedules K and K–2, they are allocated among the partners on their Schedules K–1 and K–3 and reported on their personal income tax returns. Schedules K–2 and K–3 are beyond our scope.

21-4a Partner Reporting of Partnership Income

Schedule K summarizes the tax-related items for the entire partnership. Schedule K–1 summarizes the tax-related items for each partner after considering the allocation conventions outlined in the partnership agreement or required under the Code and Regulations. For each partnership item, the sum of the amounts allocated to all the partners on Schedules K–1 should equal the partnership's total amount per Schedule K.

We'll discuss the information on Maria's Schedule K–1 later in this section. For now, refer to the form on the next page and compare it to the partnership's Schedule K. As you can see, the lines in Part III of a partner's Schedule K–1 correspond to the same lines in the partnership's Schedule K, as shown on p. 21-20. In addition, the partners might need additional information not shown on the face of Schedule K–1.

Other Schedule K–1 Information

Often, the person (or firm) that prepares a *partnership* return is different from the person (or firm) that prepares a given *partner's* tax return. Therefore, Schedule K–1 is designed to include any information the partner might need in preparing the tax return, including some information not summarized on Schedule K.

Line 20 is designated for "Other Information" and could include several lines of additional details. The last several pages of the instructions for Schedule K–1 list "codes" that can be used to identify the type of information being provided, such as information needed to calculate the QBI deduction. You can download the Schedule K–1 instructions at **irs.gov**.

Guaranteed Payments on Schedule K–1

A partner who receives guaranteed payments during a partnership year must include the payments in income as if they were received on the last day of the partnership year. Guaranteed payments are not "allocated" among the partners; instead, they are attributed to the partner who actually received the payment. Guaranteed payments are always taxable as ordinary income to the recipient partner.

651121

☐ Final K-1 ☐ Amended K-1 OMB No. 1545-0123

Schedule K-1 (Form 1065) 2022

Department of the Treasury
Internal Revenue Service

For calendar year 2022, or tax year beginning / / 2022 ending / /

Partner's Share of Income, Deductions, Credits, etc.

See separate instructions.

Part I Information About the Partnership

A Partnership's employer identification number
11-1111112

B Partnership's name, address, city, state, and ZIP code
Beachside Properties LLC
1600 Ocean Vista Way
Surfside

C IRS center where partnership filed return: *P.O. Box 409101, Ogden, UT 84409*

D ☐ Check if this is a publicly traded partnership (PTP)

Part II Information About the Partner

E Partner's SSN or TIN (Do not use TIN of a disregarded entity. See instructions.)
111-11-1112

F Name, address, city, state, and ZIP code for partner entered in E. See instructions.
Maria LeClerc
1600 Ocean Vista Way
Surfside

G ☐ General partner or LLC member-manager ☒ Limited partner or other LLC member

H1 ☒ Domestic partner ☐ Foreign partner

H2 ☐ If the partner is a disregarded entity (DE), enter the partner's:
TIN ______ Name ______

I1 What type of entity is this partner? *Active Individual*

I2 If this partner is a retirement plan (IRA/SEP/Keogh/etc.), check here ☐

J Partner's share of profit, loss, and capital (see instructions):

	Beginning	Ending
Profit	*40.000000* %	*40.000000* %
Loss	*40.000000* %	*40.000000* %
Capital	*47.500000* %	*47.500000* %

Check if decrease is due to sale or exchange of partnership interest ☐

K Partner's share of liabilities:

	Beginning	Ending
Nonrecourse	$ *200,000*	$ *240,000*
Qualified nonrecourse financing	$	$
Recourse	$	$

Check this box if item K includes liability amounts from lower-tier partnerships ☐

L **Partner's Capital Account Analysis**

Beginning capital account	$ *1,400,000*
Capital contributed during the year	$ *110,000*
Current year net income (loss)	$ *214,840*
Other increase (decrease) (attach explanation)	$
Withdrawals and distributions	$ (*30,000*)
Ending capital account	$ *1,694,840*

M Did the partner contribute property with a built-in gain (loss)?
☒ **Yes** ☐ **No** If "Yes," attach statement. See instructions.

N **Partner's Share of Net Unrecognized Section 704(c) Gain or (Loss)**
Beginning $ *500,000*
Ending $ *550,000*^

Part III Partner's Share of Current Year Income, Deductions, Credits, and Other Items

Line	Item	Amount
1	Ordinary business income (loss)	*90,000*
2	Net rental real estate income (loss)	*120,000*
3	Other net rental income (loss)	
4a	Guaranteed payments for services	*60,000*
4b	Guaranteed payments for capital	*60,000*
4c	Total guaranteed payments	*120,000*
5	Interest income	
6a	Ordinary dividends	*1,600*
6b	Qualified dividends	*1,600*
6c	Dividend equivalents	
7	Royalties	
8	Net short-term capital gain (loss)	*4,800*
9a	Net long-term capital gain (loss)	
9b	Collectibles (28%) gain (loss)	
9c	Unrecaptured section 1250 gain	
10	Net section 1231 gain (loss)	
11	Other income (loss)	
12	Section 179 deduction	
13	Other deductions	*A* *2,400*
14	Self-employment earnings (loss)	*A* *60,000*** ; *C* *480,000****
15	Credits	
16	Schedule K-3 is attached if checked ☐	
17	Alternative minimum tax (AMT) items	*A* *7,290*
18	Tax-exempt income and nondeductible expenses	*A* *840*
19	Distributions	*A* *30,000*
20	Other information	*A* *4,800*; *Z** STMT (amounts follow for convenience): Section 199A income *210,000*; W–2 wages *200,000*; UBIA *600,000*
21	Foreign taxes paid or accrued	

22 ☒ More than one activity for at-risk purposes*
23 ☒ More than one activity for passive activity purposes*

*See attached statement for additional information.

For IRS Use Only

For Paperwork Reduction Act Notice, see the Instructions for Form 1065. www.irs.gov/Form1065 Cat. No. 11394R **Schedule K-1 (Form 1065) 2022**

** See Example 33 later in the chapter. This amount equals Maria's guaranteed payment for services, which is Maria's only SE income from this LLC.
*** This amount is 40% of gross nonfarm income from Form 1065, page 1, line 8 (Maria's allocable share).
^ As indicated in Example 29, Maria contributed $0 basis property valued at $50,000 during the tax year. This unrecognized § 704(c) gain is allocated to Maria.

The guaranteed payments the partner receives for capital and/or services are reported on Schedule K–1, lines 4a and 4b, with the total guaranteed payments shown on line 4c. The partner uses this information (in lieu of a Form W–2 or 1099) to report the income on the partner's tax return. A guaranteed payment often is subject to self-employment tax and, potentially, other additional taxes, as discussed later in the chapter.

LO.8

Discuss the requirements for allocating income, gains, losses, deductions, and credits among the partners.

21-4b Partner Allocations

Once the partnership's overall information is determined (including any additional information the partners might need), the total amounts for each item must be allocated among the partners (or, in the case of guaranteed payments, attributed to the partner receiving the payment). These allocations must have economic effect and substantiality, and they must take into account any precontribution gains and losses.[41]

Economic Effect

Partnership allocations are made in accordance with the partnership agreement or an LLC's operating agreement. These allocations can be flexible. Profits, losses, and cash flows are not required to be allocated in accordance with capital ownership, as is the case under state law for most corporate entities. Partnership allocations have, at times, been used to manipulate the allocation of tax benefits among partners. Extensive Regulations[42] are designed to ensure that allocations do not result in undue tax revenue losses to the Treasury. The rules are complex, but the primary general rule—the **economic effect test**—has three general requirements.

1. **§ 704(b) book capital accounts** must be maintained as described in the Regulations.[43] These capital accounts reflect contributions and distributions at their fair market values. An allocation of income or gain to a partner must increase the partner's capital account, and an allocation of deduction or loss must decrease the partner's capital account. These capital accounts are for the partnership's information and are not generally reported on the tax return.
2. When the partnership interest is liquidated, if a partner has a *positive* balance in the capital account, the partner must receive net assets with a fair market value equal to that positive balance.
3. When the partnership interest is liquidated, if a partner has a *negative* balance in the capital account, the partner must "restore" that account, generally by contributing cash. Alternative tests may also be used to meet this requirement.

These capital account maintenance requirements are designed to ensure that a partner bears the economic burden of a loss or deduction allocation and receives the economic benefit of an income or gain allocation.

The Big Picture

Example 21

Continue with Examples 15 to 17 and the Beachside Properties Form 1065 excerpts. Maria arrives at the bakery at 4 A.M. (or earlier) six days a week to make sure her cinnamon rolls and croissants are ready when the café opens at 7. Consequently, the other LLC members have agreed with Maria that she should be allocated the first $30,000 of gross revenues (and cash flows) from bakery operations each year, starting in year 2. All other revenues and expenses (including W–2 wages and depreciation expense) are allocated in the expected 40%/40%/20% ratios to Kyler, Maria, and Josh, respectively.

Beachside's Form 1065, page 1, for the LLC's second year of operations includes only the bakery's retail operations. To simplify the illustration, assume that the § 704(b) book income and taxable income are the same amount. Maria is entitled to the first $30,000 shown on page 1. The remaining

continued

[41]§§ 704(a), (b), and (c).

[42]Reg. § 1.704–1(b)(2)(ii).

[43]Reg. § 1.704–1(b)(2)(iv).

$150,000 of ordinary income and all other items of partnership income, gain, loss, or deduction are allocated based on the members' profit sharing percentages.

Assume *for this example only* that the bakery operations are the only item impacting the § 704(b) book capital accounts this year and that the initial § 704(b) book capital amounts are as follows.

	Maria	Kyler	Josh
Beginning § 704(b) book capital	$1,900,000	$1,900,000	$150,000
Special allocation of gross income	30,000	–0–	–0–
Allocation of remaining net income	60,000	60,000	30,000
Ending § 704(b) book capital	$1,990,000	$1,960,000	$180,000

This allocation will be respected as long as the members eventually (i.e., any time on or before liquidation) receive cash and property that reflects their ending § 704(b) book capital account values.

Substantiality

Partnership allocations must also have "substantial" effect.[44] In general, an allocation does not meet the "substantial" test unless it has economic consequences in addition to tax consequences that might benefit a subset of the partners. Allocations are not generally permitted if they are for tax reasons only or if an allocation in one tax year is required to be offset by an equal allocation in a future tax year.

The Big Picture

Example 22

In Example 21, assume instead (for this example only) that the $30,000 special allocation of net income was awarded to Maria in year 2 simply to allow Maria to utilize her personal expiring net operating loss carryover and that an offsetting $30,000 special allocation of deductions would be made to Maria the following tax year.

Even though the LLC's allocations meet the "economic effect" tests, they would not be permitted because there is no substantial nontax economic reason for the allocations. The allocations over the two-year period are intended only to reduce the LLC members' combined income tax liability.

Precontribution Gain or Loss

For property contributed to a partnership, the difference between fair market value and basis at the contribution date is a **precontribution gain or loss**. The partnership keeps track of these gains and losses in its § 704(b) book accounting records. Allocated income, gain, loss, or deduction related to such property takes the precontribution amount into account.[45] Certain § 704(c) information must be reported on the partners' Schedules K–1.

An easy example occurs when a gain or loss is recognized when a nondepreciable contributed property is later sold by the partnership. The precontribution portion of the gain or loss is allocated to the contributing partner.

As you can imagine, allocations are more challenging when depreciable property is involved. Regulations describe several permitted depreciation allocation methods.[46]

The Big Picture

Example 23

Return to the facts of *The Big Picture* on p. 21-1. When Beachside Properties LLC was formed, Kyler contributed land (value of $800,000 and basis of $600,000) and buildings (value of $1,200,000 and basis of $0). Maria contributed $1,500,000 of cash, plus equipment and furnishings (value of $500,000 and basis of $0). For § 704(b) book capital account purposes, Beachside records the land

continued

[44] Reg. § 1.704–1(b)(2)(iii).

[45] §§ 704(c)(1)(A) and (C).

[46] Reg. § 1.704–3.

and other properties at their fair market values. For tax purposes, the LLC takes carryover bases in the properties. The LLC must keep track of the differences between the basis in each property and the value at the contribution date. If any of this property is sold, the gain must be allocated to the contributing partner to the extent of any previously unrecognized built-in gain.

For example, if Beachside sells the land contributed by Kyler for $1,100,000, the gain will be calculated and allocated as follows.

	§ 704(b) Book	Tax
Amount realized	$1,100,000	$1,100,000
Less: Adjusted basis	800,000	600,000
Gain realized	$ 300,000	$ 500,000
Built-in gain to Kyler	–0–	200,000
Remaining gain (allocated proportionately)	$ 300,000	$ 300,000

For tax purposes, Kyler would recognize $320,000 of the gain [($300,000 × 40%) + $200,000 built-in gain], Maria would recognize $120,000 ($300,000 × 40%), and Josh would recognize $60,000 ($300,000 × 20%).

21-4c **Schedule K–1 Example**

Let's look in detail at Maria's Schedule K–1 from Beachside Properties on p. 21-25. Part I includes information about the partnership. Part II includes information about the partner, including the partner's profit, loss, and capital sharing percentages; share of partnership liabilities at the beginning and end of the year; and changes in the partner's capital account during the year.

Part III includes information the partners use in completing their tax return. As a parallel to Schedule K, you'll find that, in general, Schedule K–1, lines 1 to 13 and line 21 reflect the partner's distributive share of the partnership's income and deductions, including any amounts specially allocated to that partner; lines 14 to 17 include information the partner needs for other tax calculations (e.g., self-employment tax, tax credits passed through from the partnership, alternative minimum tax); lines 18 and 19 help the partner calculate the outside basis in the partnership interest; and line 20 provides additional information the partner might need (e.g., information for the QBI deduction, discussed next).

The Big Picture

Example 24

Continue with the Beachside Properties examples and the Form 1065 excerpts. Also refer to Maria's Schedule K–1. Maria, a 40% owner, will receive a Schedule K–1 from Beachside Properties. Part III, line 1, of Maria's Schedule K–1 reflects her $30,000 special allocation of ordinary income, plus her normal allocation of 40% of the remaining ordinary income, for a total of $90,000 (calculated in Example 21). She is also allocated 40% of all separately stated items.

On her Form 1040, Maria includes $90,000 of ordinary income, a $2,400 charitable contribution, a $4,800 short-term capital gain, $120,000 of passive rental income, and $1,600 of qualified dividend income. On the first page of Form 1040, Maria lists her $840 share of tax-exempt interest. She must also report as ordinary income the $120,000 guaranteed payment she received.

Therefore, Maria's taxable income is increased by $336,400 from the LLC ($90,000 + $4,800 + $120,000 + $1,600 + $120,000) and she can deduct $2,400 if she itemizes deductions. As discussed next, she might also be able to claim a deduction related to her "qualified business income" from the LLC. In determining her AMT liability (if any), Maria takes into account a $7,290 positive adjustment.

Note that the specially allocated income simply increases Maria's amount on line 1 and decreases the amounts allocated to the other members. Kyler's and Josh's allocations on line 1 will be $60,000 and $30,000, respectively. The total remains $180,000, as shown on Form 1065, page 1, and Schedule K, line 1.

continued

In her personal tax return, Maria combines the partnership's amounts with similar items from sources other than Beachside. For example, if Maria has a $3,000 long-term capital loss from a stock transaction, the overall net short-term capital gain calculated on Schedule D of her Form1040 is $1,800.

For each LLC item, the sum of the allocated amounts on Josh's, Kyler's, and Maria's K–1s will equal the totals on Beachside Properties' Schedule K.

Qualified Business Income

As discussed in Chapter 15, under § 199A, a noncorporate taxpayer can deduct up to 20 percent of "the combined qualified business income amount" as the qualified business income deduction (QBID). The 20 percent QBID is based on qualified business income (QBI), which reflects income from the business, less related deductions, including the self-employment tax deduction on QBI. The QBID is limited by the taxpayer's modified taxable income and the entity's wages/capital investment. Further, the QBID might be limited if the business is a "specified service trade or business" ("SSTB") (e.g., certain service-oriented businesses). There is no cash outflow related to this deduction; it just works to lower the noncorporate party's effective tax rate on this income. For more information on the QBID, the wages/capital investment limitations, SSTBs, and specific calculations, see text Section 15-5.

For a partner, QBI does not include guaranteed payments received for *services* provided to the partnership or payments from the partnership under § 707(a) for *services* unrelated to the partnership's business (e.g., payments by a restaurant LLC to a member for providing accounting services). In addition, the regulations provide that guaranteed payments for use of the partner's *capital* do not constitute QBI as it is more in the nature of investment income to the partner.[47]

The QBID is calculated at the partner level. The partnership determines its QBI and reports, on Schedules K–1 (and supporting schedules), any information the partners need to complete their tax returns.[48] The partner's QBI generally equals the share of business income on Schedule K–1 Part III, line 1 and possibly lines 2 and 3, reduced by business expenses on lines 12 and 13. (SE taxes at the personal level also reduce QBI.)

Per the instructions to Form 1065, the partnership reports "Z* STMT" on line 20 of the Schedule K–1 and provides a supporting schedule with all information the partner needs to calculate the § 199A deduction. For example, the statement will report the partnership's QBI, W–2 wages, and the "unadjusted basis immediately after acquisition of qualified property" (termed UBIA in the regulations). The W–2 wages and UBIA are allocated among the partners in the same manner as the related wage and depreciation deductions are allocated to the partners or shareholders. If the entity has multiple trades or businesses and/or income from SSTBs, additional schedules should be provided with allocated amounts for each business.[49]

The Big Picture

Example 25

Continue with the Beachside Properties examples and the Form 1065 excerpts. Beachside has income from real estate and from a restaurant. Neither business is an SSTB. The income from the café is a qualified trade or business, and Beachside meets the rental real estate safe harbor (see text Section 15-5d) and has elected to treat the real estate rental activity as QBI. On Maria's Schedule K–1, Beachside reports ordinary business income of $90,000 (line 1, per Example 24) and net rental real estate income of $120,000 (line 2).

The LLC prepares a supporting schedule for code Z, which includes any information the partner might need to calculate the QBI deduction. Per Example 15, the LLC pays W–2 wages of $500,000; guaranteed payments and other payments to partners are not included in this amount. Per Example 12, the property contributed by Kyler and Maria is either land (ineligible) or fully depreciated property. Immediately after formation, the LLC spent $1,500,000 on improvements, so this is the

continued

[47] Reg. § 1.199A–3(b)(1)(ii).

[48] § 199A(f)(1).

[49] See Reg. § 1.199A–6 for complete information related to computational and reporting rules.

LLC's UBIA. The LLC allocates these amounts to Kyler, Maria, and Josh in the 40%/40%/20% proportions, respectively, in which the related wage expense and depreciation deductions are allocated. Maria's allocated amounts are $200,000 for W–2 Wages and $600,000 for UBIA. These amounts are included in the code Z statement, but for convenience, this chapter shows the information directly on Maria's Schedule K–1. Additional information would be provided for the rental and sales activities.

In her personal QBI deduction calculation, Maria considers the $210,000 of QBI from the partnership, less her personal deductions related to this income, such as her self-employment tax deduction. (See text Section 15-5c.)

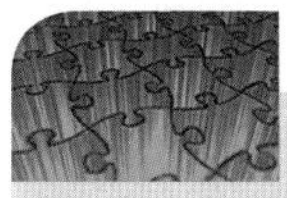

Concept Summary 21.3

Tax Reporting of Partnership Items

Item	Partnership reports on Form 1065	Partner's share reported on Schedule K–1, Part III
1. Partnership ordinary income or loss.	Page 1, line 22. Schedule K, line 1.	Line 1. Special allocations, basis adjustments, and loss limitations may apply.
2. Guaranteed payments to partners for capital or services.	Page 1, line 10, if deductible; otherwise capitalized. All amounts on Schedule K, line 4, for partner reporting.	Line 4. Partner reports as ordinary income; no basis adjustment.
3. Separately stated income and deduction items such as portfolio income, capital gain and loss, and § 179 deductions.	Schedule K, lines 2, 3, and 5 to 13.	Lines 2, 3, and 5 to 13. Special allocations, basis adjustments, and loss limitations may apply.
4. Net earnings from self-employment.	Schedule K, line 14a.	Line 14, code A.
5. Additional information so that the partner can make various calculations (e.g., AMT, foreign tax credits, net investment income tax, and the partner's outside basis).	Schedule K, lines 15 to 21.	Lines 15 to 21. Each partner's share of each item is passed through and considered in various calculations.
6. Qualified business income.	Schedule K, line 20 supporting schedule.	Line 20, supporting statement for code Z.

Ethics & Equity **Built-In Appreciation on Contributed Property**

In the "old days," one partner could contribute cash and another partner could contribute an equal value of appreciated property with no subsequent record-keeping requirements. Future depreciation deductions and gains on sale of the property could be allocated to both partners equally, thereby shifting income from one taxpayer to another. A partner in a lower tax bracket (or with expiring net operating losses and the like) could report the share of the gain on sale of the asset with a relatively low corresponding tax burden.

Code § 704(c)(1)(A) was enacted to ensure that the partner contributing the property pays tax on any built-in gain. This prevents income shifting among taxpayers and loss of revenue to the U.S. Treasury.

There is no corresponding provision for S corporations—gains and losses and depreciation expense are allocated among the shareholders without regard to any built-in appreciation on contributed property.

Assume that a new partner or shareholder owns land valued at $100,000 in which the tax basis is $60,000. How would the "incidence of taxation" differ for the entities and owners if (1) the owner (partner or shareholder) sold the property and contributed the $100,000 proceeds versus (2) the owner (partner or shareholder) contributed that same property with the entity selling it for $100,000? What theory of partnership taxation supports this difference in treatment?

21-4d **Partner's Basis**

LO.9

Determine a partner's basis in the partnership interest.

Each partner has an outside basis in the partnership interest. That basis is increased/(decreased) over time for the partner's share of income/(deductions), contributions/(distributions), and increases/(decreases) in the partner's share of partnership liabilities.

Relevance of Partner's Basis

The partner's basis is important for determining the treatment of distributions from the partnership to the partner and establishing the deductibility of partnership losses. When a partnership interest is sold (or liquidated by the partnership), the partner's gain or loss is determined by reference to the adjusted basis of the partnership interest (see Chapter 22).

Generally, the total of the partners' outside bases equals the partnership's inside basis in its assets. However, as noted in Chapter 22, certain transactions can throw this parity out of balance.

A partner's basis is not reflected anywhere on the Schedule K–1. Instead, each partner should maintain a personal record of the basis in the partnership interest. Under no circumstances can the partner's adjusted basis in the partnership be reduced below zero.

Adjustments to Basis

As discussed earlier, the partner's initial outside basis generally equals the partner's basis in contributed assets. This could be a cost basis (plus any amount recognized as income on contribution of services) or a basis determined under the gift or inheritance rules. After the partner is admitted to the partnership, the partner's basis is adjusted for numerous items. The following items *increase* a partner's adjusted basis:

- The partner's proportionate share of partnership income (including capital gains and tax-exempt income).
- The partner's proportionate share of any increase in partnership liabilities (as discussed in text Section 21-4e).
- Contributions of cash or property from the partner to the partnership after the partnership is formed.

The following items *decrease* the partner's adjusted basis in the partnership:

- The partner's proportionate share of partnership deductions and losses [including capital losses, foreign taxes, charitable contributions (including the allocable basis of donated property), and suspended business interest expense that will be available for future tax years].
- The partner's proportionate share of nondeductible expenses.
- The partner's proportionate share of any reduction in partnership liabilities (as discussed in text Section 21-4e).[50]
- Distributions of cash or property from the partnership to the partner after the partnership is formed.

As shown in Example 4 earlier in the chapter, increasing the adjusted basis for the partner's share of partnership taxable income is logical because the partner has already been taxed on the income. By increasing the partner's basis, the partner is not taxed again on the income when the interest is sold or the partner receives a distribution from the partnership.

Using the same logic, tax-exempt income (or noncapitalizable, nondeductible expenditures) should increase (decrease) the partner's basis. If the income is exempt in the current period, it should not contribute to the recognition of gain when the partner either sells the interest or receives a distribution from the partnership. For example, forgiveness of Covid-related program loans (such as Payroll Protection Program loans) is tax-exempt to the partnership, and the forgiven debt is added to the partners' bases in the partnership interests.

---

[50] §§ 705 and 752.

LO.10

Explain how liabilities affect a partner's basis.

21-4e Effect of Partnership Liabilities

All partnership debt is allocated among the partners and included in the partners' bases.[51] [In contrast, the liabilities of an S corporation are generally *not* included in the shareholder's bases (see text Section 23-3f).] Partnership debt includes any partnership obligation that creates an asset; results in an expense to the partnership; or results in a nondeductible, noncapitalizable item at the partnership level. This definition includes certain contingent liabilities.[52] The definition also includes most debt that is considered a liability under financial accounting rules. However, partnership debt does *not* include accounts payable of a cash basis partnership.

Allocation of Partnership Liabilities—In General

An increase in a partner's share of partnership debt is treated as a cash contribution by the partner to the partnership and increases the partner's basis. A decrease in a partner's share of partnership debt is treated as a cash distribution from the partnership to the partner and decreases the partner's basis.

Example 26

Jim and Becky contribute property to form the JB Partnership. Jim contributes cash of $30,000. Becky contributes land with an adjusted basis and fair market value of $45,000, subject to a liability of $15,000; the partnership assumes the debt (treated as a distribution to Becky). The partnership borrows $50,000 to finance construction of a building on the contributed land.

At the end of the first year, the accrual basis partnership owes $3,500 in trade accounts payable to various vendors. Disregard any operating activities and deductions related to these debts. *If Jim and Becky share equally in liabilities*, the partners' bases in their partnership interests are determined as follows.

Jim's Basis		Becky's Basis	
Contributed cash	$30,000	Basis in contributed land	$ 45,000
		Less: Debt assumed by partnership	(15,000)
Share of debt on land	7,500	Share of debt on land	7,500
Initial basis	$37,500	Initial basis	$ 37,500
Share of construction loan	25,000	Share of construction loan	25,000
Share of trade accounts payable (accrual basis)	1,750	Share of trade accounts payable (accrual basis)	1,750
Basis, end of first year	$64,250	Basis, end of first year	$ 64,250

Assume in the following year that the partnership pays off its accounts payable, debt on land, and construction loan. The partners' bases would be correspondingly decreased and (disregarding any other operating activities) would become $30,000 each at the end of that second year.

In the above example, liabilities were allocated equally between the two partners. In addition, each partner contributed an asset with an identical $30,000 net basis (basis less related debt), so the partners' ending bases were the same.

However, it's not always that simple. Look at Maria's Schedule K–1 on p. 21-25. In Part II, item K, you can see that partnership debt, at the beginning and end of the partnership's tax year, is allocated based on whether it is recourse, nonrecourse, or qualified nonrecourse financing. **Recourse debt** is partnership debt for which the partnership or at least one of the partners is personally liable. This personal liability can exist, for example, through the operation of state law or through personal guarantees that a partner makes to the creditor. **Nonrecourse debt** is debt for which no partner is personally liable.

[51] § 752.

[52] Reg. § 1.752–1(a)(4)(ii).

Lenders of nonrecourse debt generally require that collateral be pledged against the loan. Upon default, the lender can claim only the collateral, not the partners' personal assets. **Qualified nonrecourse financing** is a subset of nonrecourse debt that applies for purposes of the at-risk limitation discussed later in the chapter. Qualified nonrecourse financing is generally bank debt (or similar third-party debt) on real estate.

In general (disregarding any personal guarantees of any partnership debt), recourse debt is allocated among *general partners only*, and nonrecourse debt is allocated among *all partners*. If any partner or LLC member personally guarantees a debt, it is treated as a recourse debt with respect to that partner. For an LLC, most debt will, by default, be treated as nonrecourse debt because the LLC members, by definition, have no liability for entity debts.

Recourse Debt Rules

Recourse debt is allocated based on each partner's "economic risk of loss." For a partnership in which all contributions and allocations have been proportionate to the capital contributions, recourse debt is allocated among the general partners in proportion to their *loss sharing* ratios. In more complex situations, the partner's economic risk of loss is determined under a **constructive liquidation scenario** outlined in the Regulations.[53]

Hill, Inc., and Dart, Inc., own the newly created HD Partnership, where both entities are treated as general partners. Assume that all contributions and allocations are equal (50%/50%). At the end of the year, HD has $40,000 of recourse accounts payable and a $100,000 personal property loan that is guaranteed by Dart.

Because recourse debt is allocated according to *loss* sharing ratios, each partner is allocated 50% of the accounts payable. Dart is allocated 100% of the debt it guaranteed. Hill's share of recourse debt is $20,000, and Dart's share is $120,000.

Nonrecourse Debt Rules

Nonrecourse debt (including qualified nonrecourse financing) is allocated among all the partners. For our purposes, it is allocated to the partners in accordance with their *profit sharing* ratios.[54]

In Example 27, assume instead that HD is an LLC instead of a general partnership. Also assume that 40% of profits are allocated to Hill and 60% are allocated to Dart. (Losses are still allocated equally.)

In an LLC, accounts payable are treated as *nonrecourse* debt and are allocated according to *profit* sharing ratios. Therefore, the $40,000 of accounts payable are allocated $16,000 (40%) to Hill and $24,000 (60%) to Dart. The debt guaranteed by Dart remains a recourse debt allocated 100% to Dart. Therefore, Hill's Schedule K–1 will show $16,000 of nonrecourse debt, and Dart's will show $24,000 of nonrecourse debt and $100,000 of recourse debt.

Exhibit 21.2 summarizes the rules for computing a partner's basis in a partnership interest and the order in which the rules are applied.

[53]See Reg. § 1.752–2 and related Regulations and Proposed Regulations. Under the constructive liquidation scenario, debts are allocated based on which partner would be required to pay the debt in the event of a hypothetical catastrophic event that left all of the partnership's assets worthless. The assumed losses are allocated among the partners, and the debt is allocated in proportion to the partners' negative capital accounts after this deemed allocation.

[54]Reg. § 1.752–3. This Regulation outlines a first stage allocation of minimum gain and a second stage allocation where liabilities on contributed property exceed the tax basis of the contributed property.

Exhibit 21.2 Partner's Basis in Partnership Interest

Basis is generally adjusted in the following order every tax year.

Initial basis or beginning basis for the taxable year.

+ Partner's contributions, including increases in the partner's share of partnership debt.

+ Partner's share of the partnership's
  - Taxable income items.
  - Exempt income items.
  - Excess of depletion deductions over adjusted basis of property subject to depletion.

− Partner's distributions and withdrawals, including decreases in the partner's share of partnership debt.

− Partner's share of the partnership's
  - Separately stated foreign taxes, charitable contributions (limited to the basis of contributed property), and other deductions.
  - Nondeductible items not chargeable to a capital account.
  - Special depletion deduction for oil and gas wells.
  - Other loss items.

The basis of a partner's interest can never be negative.

The Big Picture

Example 29

Return to the facts of *The Big Picture* on p. 21-1. Example 24 described how the income and deduction items of Beachside Properties LLC are allocated to Maria on her Schedule K–1. But how is Maria's basis affected by those items?

Assume that at the beginning of that tax year (Beachside's second year of operations), Maria's basis in her LLC interest was $1,600,000, including a $200,000 share of the LLC's $500,000 of nonrecourse debt. At the end of the year, Beachside had $600,000 of debt, which was again treated as nonrecourse to all of the LLC members.

During the year, Maria contributes to the LLC cash of $110,000 and additional property (basis of $0 and fair market value of $50,000). Maria also received a cash distribution equal to her $30,000 special allocation of the LLC's gross income. Maria's share of Beachside's income, gain, and deductions is as described in Example 24 and on her Schedule K–1.

Maria's basis can be calculated using the ordering rules shown in Exhibit 21.2. The $120,000 guaranteed payment Maria received does not directly affect Maria's basis even though it affects her taxable income. It's cash she received that is taxable as if it was salary or interest revenue to her.

The $840 of tax-exempt income increases Maria's basis even though it is not taxed to Maria. Similarly, the charitable contribution reduces her basis even though it might not be deductible to her. Maria's QBI deduction does not affect her basis.

Beginning basis (including beginning liability share)	$1,600,000
Contributions, including increase in share of liabilities	
Share of net increase in LLC liabilities [40% × ($600,000 − $500,000)]	40,000
Cash contribution to LLC capital	110,000
Maria's basis in noncash capital contribution	-0-
Share of LLC income items	
Ordinary LLC income	90,000
LLC's net passive activity income from rental real estate	120,000
Tax-exempt income	840
Short-term capital gain	4,800
Qualified dividend income	1,600
Distributions and withdrawals	
Capital withdrawal (distribution related to special allocation of income)	(30,000)
Share of LLC deduction items	
Charitable contribution	(2,400)
Ending basis (including ending liability share)	$1,934,840

21-4f Partner's Capital Account

LO.11

Illustrate a partner's capital account roll forward, and explain why the year-end balance might differ from the partner's year-end basis in the partnership interest.

As mentioned earlier in the chapter, the partner's tax basis is not the same as the partner's capital account.

The partner's *capital account* is an accounting calculation that measures the partner's ownership of the entity. It is the partner's share of the net partnership assets (partnership equity, or assets less liabilities). A partner's *tax basis* measures the assets the partner can receive relative to the partnership interest without paying additional tax (e.g., as a cash distribution or if the partner were to sell the partnership interest).

A capital account analysis (sometimes called a "roll forward" or "reconciliation") shows the change in the partner's capital account from the beginning to the end of the tax year. This analysis can be prepared using any of several methods, depending upon the purpose of the analysis and the needs of the user. The methods include the **tax basis capital account**, GAAP, or the § 704(b) book capital methods. The GAAP and § 704(b) book capital method calculations incorporate, respectively, GAAP accounting rules or asset values. The tax method corresponds to the tax calculations made by the partnership.

The tax basis capital account is required to be used to prepare Schedule M–2 (as well as the partners' Schedules K–1) in the partnership return.[55] The sum of the partners' ending capital accounts on Schedules K–1 should equal ending capital on Schedule M–2.

The GAAP method capital account might be used if the partnership has financial reporting requirements to partners or lenders. The § 704(b) book capital account method must be used by any partnership that has contributions or distributions of appreciated or depreciated property; § 704(b) book capital account calculations are used to ensure that liquidating distributions are in accordance with those capital accounts.

A partner's tax basis capital account (on Schedule K–1) can sometimes be negative. This can be for legitimate reasons, or it can indicate to the IRS that allocations to the negative capital partner might be excessive and could warrant an examination. If negative tax basis capital accounts are reported, then additional information (beyond our scope) must be reported to the IRS by the partnership.

The partner's ending capital account balance is rarely the same amount as the partner's tax basis, largely because the tax basis capital account does not include the partner's share of partnership liabilities (and, as we know, liabilities *are* included in tax basis). The partner's share of partnership liabilities is shown separately in Part II of Schedule K–1. Therefore, the partner's ending tax basis in the partnership interest can be estimated by adding the partner's tax basis ending capital account and the partner's share of liabilities.[56]

Concept Summary 21.4 compares a partner's tax basis and capital accounts.

The Big Picture

Example 30

Please follow along on Maria's Schedule K–1 on p. 21-25. Her Schedule K–1 shows her tax basis capital account roll forward from the prior year to the current year. Her beginning capital account balance was $1,400,000. The roll forward shows the $110,000 of cash Maria contributed, the $0 basis of other contributed property, and the $30,000 distribution related to the special allocation of cash to Maria.

The current-year increase (decrease) of $214,840 is the combination (additions and subtractions) of Maria's amounts shown on Schedule K–1, Part III, lines 1 to 13 (excluding the guaranteed payment), plus the tax-exempt income shown on line 18. (Note that the ordinary/qualified dividends are included only one time.)

Maria's ending tax basis capital account on Schedule K–1 is $1,694,840. Her Schedule K–1 shows a $240,000 share of nonrecourse liabilities. The sum of these amounts equals her ending tax basis of $1,934,840 as calculated in Example 29.

---

[55] State tax law can vary widely based on jurisdiction. Starting in 2022, California requires all partners to report tax basis capital accounts using the tax basis method under California law. Other states are silent on this issue. As a result, tax basis capital accounts may vary across Federal and state Schedules K–1 for the same taxpayer.

[56] This tax basis calculation shortcut will not be correct for a partner whose outside basis differs from their share of the partnership's inside basis. This could happen when, for example, a partner acquires a partnership interest and the partnership does not make a § 754 election. See Chapter 22.

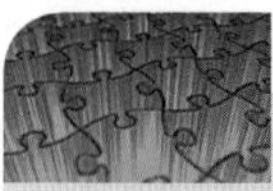

Concept Summary 21.4

Comparing a Partner's Tax Basis and Capital Account

- A partner's **tax basis** in the partnership interest represents the partner's investment in the entity for tax purposes. It is used as the benchmark against which gain or loss is calculated [e.g., when (1) a partnership interest is sold or (2) the partnership distributes property to the partner]. Tax basis includes the partner's share of partnership debts and is calculated as shown in Exhibit 21.2. The tax basis can *never* be negative.
- A partner's **capital account** represents the partner's share of *net* partnership assets. It might be used to determine (1) whether the partnership can allocate certain income, gain, or loss items to the partner or (2) the partner's allocation of partnership assets upon liquidation of the partnership. Capital accounts generally *do not* include the partner's share of partnership debts, and they can be negative (although additional reporting might be required).
- The partners could have several **capital accounts.** The most common are (1) tax basis capital account, (2) § 704(b) book capital account, and (3) GAAP-basis capital account. Note that "tax basis" refers to the first bullet above and "tax basis capital account" refers to the second bullet.
- **Tax basis capital accounts** are calculated starting with contributions the partner made (using the contributing partner's tax basis for the contribution), less distributions to the partner (at tax basis), plus and minus the partner's distributive shares of income and expense items reported on Part III of Schedule K–1.
- **The § 704(b) book capital accounts** must reflect allocations in accordance with the "substantial economic effect" (SEE) rules as described in text Section 21-4c. In this calculation, partners' contributions and the partnership's distributions of property are considered at their fair market values rather than their tax bases. Otherwise, contributions and distributions of cash, and most allocations of income, gains, losses, and deductions generally are considered as reported in the tax return.
- **GAAP-basis capital accounts** might be used when the partnership must report GAAP-basis financial information to third parties, such as lenders or even the partners themselves. The accounting methods used to reflect assets, liabilities, income, and expenses are reflected in the partners' capital account balances.
- The **partner** maintains records of the **partner's basis.** It is not shown on Schedule K–1, although the partner's tax basis (bullet 1 above) often equals the sum of the partner's tax basis capital account (bullet 2) and the partner's share of partnership liabilities (both amounts per Schedule K–1).
- The **partnership** maintains records of **partners' capital.** Only the tax basis account analysis is shown on Schedule K–1 even if different methods are used for different purposes.

LO.12

Apply the limitations on deducting partnership losses.

21-4g Loss Limitations

Partnership losses flow through to the partners to be reported on their tax returns. However, the loss deduction might be limited at the partner level. When limitations apply, all or a portion of the losses are suspended until a triggering event occurs. No time limit is imposed on such loss carryforwards.

The following different limitations might apply, in the order shown.

1. **Basis limitation [§ 704(d)].** This limitation allows a loss deduction only to the extent of the partner's adjusted outside basis.
2. **At-risk limitation (§ 465).** Losses that are deductible under the basis limitation are deductible only to the extent the partner is at risk for the partnership interest.
3. **Passive activity loss limitation (§ 469).** Any losses that survive this second limitation may be subject to the passive activity loss rules.
4. **Excess business losses [§ 461(l)].** If a loss passes the above three limitations, a noncorporate taxpayer must consider whether the excess business loss limitation applies.

The partner can only deduct losses that make it through all of the hurdles. Special rules apply to losses from real estate activities.

Megan is a 50% partner in Green LLC, which does not invest in real estate. On January 1, 2023, Megan's adjusted basis for her LLC interest is $50,000, and her at-risk amount is $35,000. Her share of losses from Green is $60,000, all of which is passive. She has another investment that produced $25,000 of passive activity income. She has no other passive or active losses. Megan can deduct $25,000 of Green's losses on her Form 1040 for 2023, calculated as follows.

continued

Applicable Provision	Deductible Loss	Suspended Loss
§ 704(d) basis limitation	$50,000	$10,000
At-risk limitation	35,000	15,000
Passive activity loss limitation	25,000	10,000
Excess business loss limitation	25,000	–0–

Megan can deduct only $50,000 under the basis limitation. Of this $50,000, only $35,000 is deductible under the at-risk limitation. Under the passive activity loss limitation, passive losses can be deducted only against passive income. The net passive income/loss from the two investments is $0, so the excess business loss limitation does not apply. Thus, Megan can deduct $25,000. This amount, plus the three suspended loss amounts, equals the original $60,000 loss.

Basis Limitation

For the first limitation, basis (including the partner's share of partnership liabilities) is determined at the end of the partnership's taxable year. It is adjusted for any partnership income and gain items and contributions and distributions made during the year, but it is determined *before considering any loss or deduction items for the year*. (In Exhibit 21.2, basis would be calculated through "partner's distributions and withdrawals.")

Losses that cannot be deducted because of this rule are suspended and carried forward (never back) for use against future increases in the partner's adjusted basis. Such increases might result from additional capital contributions, from sharing in additional partnership debts, or from future partnership income.

At-Risk Limitation

Under the at-risk rules, certain loss deductions are limited to amounts that are economically invested in the partnership. Limited losses are those from business and income-producing activities allocated to individual partners and closely held C corporation partners. Suspended losses are carried forward until a partner has a sufficient amount at risk in the activity to absorb them.[57]

Invested amounts include cash, the adjusted basis of property contributed by the partner, and the partner's share of partnership earnings that have not been withdrawn.[58]

Recourse debt generally is included in the amount at risk, but nonrecourse debt is not. As an exception, qualified recourse financing is deemed to be at risk.[59] In general terms, qualified nonrecourse financing is nonrecourse financing provided by a bank, retirement plan, or similar party or by a Federal, state, or local government for the purchase of real estate.

Example 32

In Example 31, Megan's amount at risk was $35,000, and $15,000 was suspended under the at-risk limitation. Assume that this limitation applied because Megan's basis in her partnership interest included a $15,000 nonrecourse debt that could not be included in her amount at risk.

If, instead, the activity was a real estate activity and the debt was qualified nonrecourse financing, Megan's basis and at-risk amounts would have been the same ($50,000), and no additional loss deduction would have been suspended under the at-risk rules.

Passive Activity Loss Limitation

The third loss limitation is that passive activity losses can generally only be deducted to the extent they offset passive activity income.[60] These rules apply to partners who are individuals, estates, trusts, closely held C corporations, or personal service corporations.

Passive activity income is income from a trade or business activity in which the partner does not materially participate on a regular, continuous, and substantial basis,[61] or income from many rental activities.

[57] § 465(a)(2).

[58] § 465(a).

[59] § 465(b)(6).

[60] § 469(a)(1).

[61] §§ 469(c)(1) and (2).

Global Tax Issues — Withholding Requirements for non-U.S. Partners

A U.S. partnership may have non-U.S. partners subject to U.S. tax on their partnership income. The Code provides tax withholding rules to counter the challenge of collecting tax from parties not physically present in the United States. The rules differ depending on whether the income is "effectively connected with a U.S. trade or business," derived from investment property, or related to real estate transactions.

If the partnership purchases real property from a non-U.S. seller, for example, the partnership generally must withhold 10 percent of the purchase price. If a partnership sells a U.S. real property interest, it typically withholds tax at the partner's highest tax rate applied to the gain allocated to a foreign partner. Further, if the partnership receives dividends, interest, rents, or other income described in § 1441(b), it typically withholds 30 percent of the non-U.S. partner's distributive share of such income.

Finally, if the partnership generates U.S. business income, it must withhold and pay an amount equal to the highest U.S. tax rate applicable to the non-U.S. taxpayer's allocable share of partnership income.

Many of these withholding requirements can be reduced or eliminated through various alternative procedures available in the Regulations (designed to ensure that the withholding does not exceed the actual tax that might be due, while still protecting the U.S. revenue) or through tax treaties between the United States and the foreign jurisdiction.

If amounts withheld exceed the actual tax liability (e.g., because the partner's U.S. tax rate is lower than the withholding rate), the partner can obtain a refund by filing a tax return that calculates and reports the actual tax due.

For tax years beginning after 2020, the partnership prepares Schedules K–2 and K–3 to assist the partners in reporting foreign amounts from the partnership.

Source: See IRC §§ 1441(b), 1445(a) and (e), and 1446(a) and related Regulations.

Material participation means that the partner should have substantial involvement in daily operations of the activity. By definition, a partner treated as a limited partner is typically considered *not* to materially participate in partnership activities.[62]

Rent income from real or personal property generally is passive activity income, regardless of the partner's level of participation. The primary exception is that rental real estate is not treated as a passive activity for a person who qualifies as a real estate professional and meets a material participation test for the rental.

As a special allowance, individuals can offset up to $25,000 of passive activity losses from rental real estate against active and portfolio income.[63] (This amount is phased out at a rate of $0.50 for every excess dollar, starting at $100,000 of modified adjusted gross income.) This deduction is available to those who actively (rather than materially) participate in rental real estate activities.

For additional information regarding loss limitations, the passive activity loss rules, and the rental real estate exception, refer to *Individual Income Taxes* (South-Western Federal Taxation), Chapter 11.

Excess Business Losses of Noncorporate Taxpayers

If a noncorporate taxpayer has net trade or business losses that (1) pass the above three tests and (2) exceed a threshold amount, the excess loss is carried forward as part of the taxpayer's net operating loss carryover.[64] The threshold is $289,000 (2023) for single taxpayers and $578,000 (2023) for married taxpayers filing a joint tax return. These amounts are adjusted for inflation each year.

The limitation is applied at the partner or S corporation shareholder level. As examples, losses from farming, active business losses, or losses of a real estate professional might be subject to this rule.

LO.13

Describe how a partner calculates self-employment tax and net investment income tax on partnership income.

21-5 Other Taxes on Partnership Income

A partner is not treated as an employee for Federal income tax purposes. Thus, certain types of partnership income allocated to an individual taxpayer may be considered "net earnings from self-employment" [subject to self-employment (SE) tax] or "net investment income" [subject to the tax on net investment income (NII)].

[62] § 469(h)(2).

[63] § 469(i).

[64] §§ 461(l)(1) and (4).

21-5a Self-Employment Tax

Self-employed individuals may be liable for an SE tax, consisting of a 12.4 percent tax for old-age, survivors, and disability insurance (on up to $160,200 of SE income in 2023, less any wages on which the tax is withheld) and a 2.9 percent tax for hospital insurance (on all SE income).[65] An additional Medicare tax of 0.9 percent applies to SE income in excess of $250,000 for married taxpayers filing joint tax returns (half that amount if a separate return is filed, or $200,000 for other taxpayers).[66] The taxpayer calculates the SE tax on Schedule SE and the additional Medicare tax on Form 8959.

SE Treatment of Distributive Shares versus Guaranteed Payments

With a total potential tax rate of 15.3 percent (or 16.2 percent), the partners have an incentive to exclude their income shares from SE income.

Distributive Shares SE income includes a general partner's distributive share of income from a partnership's trade or business, whether or not that income is distributed (e.g., income reported on line 1 of Schedule K–1). It also includes the distributive share allocated to a limited partner that is in the nature of compensation for services performed for or on behalf of the partnership.[67] However, SE income does not include the distributive share allocated to a limited partner who merely is an investor in the entity.

Guaranteed Payments For both general and limited partners, any guaranteed payments for *services* are subject to the SE tax. Guaranteed payments for use of the partner's *capital* are not subject to the SE tax.

SE Treatment of General versus Limited Partners

Because of the rules above, for SE tax purposes, a taxpayer might take extra measures to be classified as a *limited* partner. As a result, this has been a contentious area for the IRS. According to Proposed Regulations dating from 1997, a partner or an LLC member will be treated as a *general* partner if:

- The partner has personal liability for partnership debts by virtue of status as a partner.
- The partner can enter into contractual relationships on behalf of the partnership.
- The partner works more than 500 hours in the partnership's trade or business during the tax year.

The Big Picture

Example 33

Return to the facts of *The Big Picture* in Examples 16 and 24. Beachside's Schedule K and Schedules K–1 were prepared in accordance with these Proposed Regulations, with the members' distributive shares and guaranteed payments being treated as follows.

	Distributive Share (Proposed Regulations)	Guaranteed Payments [§ 1402(a)(13)]
Kyler	$60,000—not SE income	$60,000—not SE income (capital)
Maria	$90,000—not SE income*	$60,000—SE income (services) and $60,000—not SE income (capital)
Josh	$30,000—SE income	$60,000—SE income (services)

*See Prop.Reg. § 1.1402(a)–2(i), Example (iii). Maria works more than 500 hours in the business, but because she has identical management rights and obligations as Kyler, her distributive share is not subject to SE tax.

21-5b Net Investment Income Tax

An individual taxpayer's "net investment income" (NII) is subject to an additional tax of 3.8 percent to the extent the taxpayer's modified adjusted gross income (MAGI) exceeds $250,000 for married taxpayers filing joint returns (or half that amount if a separate return

[65] §§ 1401(a) and (b)(1).

[66] § 1401(b)(2).

[67] § 1402(a)(13). See also Prop.Reg. § 1.1402(a)–2(h).

is filed) or $200,000 for other taxpayers.[68] MAGI equals the taxpayer's adjusted gross income increased by any foreign earned income exclusion.[69] This tax is calculated on Form 8960.

Certain types of income allocated from a partnership are treated as net investment income (NII), including dividends, interest, passive activity income, and gains from property not used in a trade or business. In addition, the partner's distributive share is considered NII if the partner is a "passive" investor, as defined under the passive activity loss rules. The tax also applies to "income on investment of working capital," which includes guaranteed payments for use of a partner's capital. Tax-exempt income is not subject to this tax.

The Big Picture

Example 34

Refer to Maria's Schedule K–1 on p. 21-25. Maria's NII includes the $60,000 guaranteed payment she received in exchange for capital plus her distributive share of the partnership's qualified dividends ($1,600) and net short-term capital gains ($4,800). It does not include the $840 of tax-exempt interest reported to her on line 18.

Maria will prepare Form 8960 to calculate her net investment income tax. Assuming that Maria has no net investment income from other sources and files as a single taxpayer, she will pay a tax of 3.8% on the lesser of $66,400 ($60,000 + $1,600 + $4,800) or the excess of her modified AGI over $200,000.

21-6 Tax Planning

Proper Federal tax planning should be used at all stages of entity formation and operations to ensure that the results match the partners' expectations.

21-6a Choosing Partnership Taxation

LO.14 **Provide insights regarding advantageous use of a partnership.**

A partnership often provides tax advantages over a C or S corporation. Partnership income is subject to only a single level of taxation; for partners who are individual taxpayers, the rate can be as high as 37 percent (or 40.8 percent if subject to the net investment income tax). Individual partners can deduct up to 20 percent of QBI passed through from a partnership; the maximum effective tax rate on this income is 29.6 percent. Corporate income, however, is taxed at the entity level (at 21 percent) and upon distribution to shareholders as dividends (at up to 23.8 percent for qualified dividends paid to individual shareholders). Partnership income may be subject to high tax rates at the partner level, but (especially for QBI) this tax will generally be lower than the combined layers of tax on corporate income (about 40 percent).

Income tax rates, however, don't tell the full story. Self-employment tax or the net investment income tax might also apply. An active "general" partner might be subject to self-employment tax (up to 15.3 percent of income, plus additional Medicare tax of up to 0.9 percent) on the entire distributive share from the partnership, as well as on any guaranteed payments for services. A C or S corporation shareholder, however, will only be subject to employment taxes to the extent the shareholder receives wages from the entity. Distributions from a C corporation (dividends) might be subject to net investment income tax, but for partners or S corporation shareholders, this tax only applies to distributive shares of the entity's actual investment income.

When selecting a legal form in which to conduct business, a complete analysis, then, must consider the expected types and amounts of income for both the entity and the owners, plans to distribute cash flows (i.e., present value considerations), differences between actual salaries or wages that might be paid versus the amounts a partner would be required to report as self-employment income, and whether additional taxes might apply.

The chief disadvantage of partnerships is that any general partners might be liable for entity debts (which only occurs with C or S corporations if the debt is guaranteed). However, if the partnership can operate as an LLC or LLP, the owners' liability is minimized. In addition, any general partners (for example in a GP or LP) could be structured as LLCs or corporate entities to minimize the general partners' liability.

[68] § 1411.

[69] § 911.

For both C and S corporations, income or loss allocations or distributions are required to be proportionate to ownership interests. A partnership, though, may adjust its allocations of income and cash flow among the partners each year according to their needs, as long as the allocation meets the substantial economic effect and capital account maintenance rules discussed in the chapter.

For smaller business operations, a partnership enables several owners to combine their resources at low cost. It offers simple filing requirements, the taxation of income only once, and the ability to discontinue operations relatively inexpensively.

For larger businesses, a partnership offers a unique ability to raise capital with low filing and reporting costs compared to corporate stock or bond issuances.

Concept Summary 21.5 outlines considerations in choosing to use a C corporation, an S corporation, or a partnership as a means of doing business.

21-6b Formation and Operation of a Partnership

Potential partners should ensure that they will not be taxed on gains realized when transferring assets to create the entity. A partner can make a tax-deferred contribution of assets to the entity either at the inception of the partnership or later. This possibility is not available to less-than-controlling shareholders in a corporation.

Partnership allocation rules should be used to the partners' best advantage. Special allocations of income, expense, or credit items must satisfy certain requirements to be acceptable to the IRS.

21-6c Basis Considerations and Loss Deduction Limitations

If a partnership incurs a loss for the taxable year, careful planning will help ensure that the partners can claim the deduction.

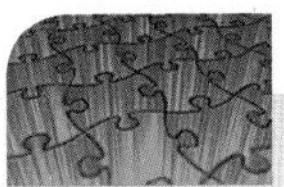

Concept Summary 21.5

Major Advantages and Disadvantages of the Partnership Form

The partnership form may be attractive when one or more of the following factors is present.

- The entity will generate net taxable losses and/or valuable tax credits, which will be of use to the owners (subject to loss limitation rules).
- The entity will have individual partners and will generate qualified business income, of which up to 20% can be deducted.
- The partners' distributive shares of income will be taxed at lower individual tax rates (e.g., 10%, 12%, 22%, 24%, etc.).
- Any individual partners will be passive or will have sufficient wages from other sources, so self-employment taxes will be minimized.
- The owners want to avoid complex corporate administrative and filing requirements.
- The owners want to make special allocations of certain income or deduction items.
- Other means of reducing the effects of corporate double taxation (e.g., compensation to owners, interest, and rental payments) have been exhausted.
- The owners anticipate liquidating the entity within a short period of time. Liquidation of a C or S corporation would generate entity-level recognized gains on appreciated property distributed.

The partnership form may be less attractive when one or more of the following factors is present.

- The tax paid by the individual owners of a partnership is greater than the tax the entity would pay if it were a C corporation. [An individual partner in a partnership could pay Federal tax at up to 40.8% if the income is not QBI (37% top rate plus a potential 3.8% net investment income tax) plus potential self-employment taxes.]
- The entity is generating net taxable income without distributing any cash to the owners. The owners may not have sufficient cash with which to pay the tax on the entity's earnings. (Federal tax on corporate income is only 21% until that income is distributed to the shareholders.)
- The entity is in a high-exposure business, and the owners want protection from personal liability. An LLC or LLP, however, would limit personal liability.
- The entity has already been formed as a corporation, and conversion to partnership status could result in significant liquidation taxes.

A partner can contribute capital to the partnership before the end of the tax year to ensure that there is adequate basis to absorb the loss. If economic conditions warrant, the partnership could incur additional debt. The partner's cash contribution or share of debt increases the partner's basis in the partnership interest. If the loss also meets the "at-risk," "passive," and "excess business loss" hurdles, the loss can be deducted.

In the following year, if the partnership is expected to report adequate taxable income, the partner could withdraw cash or the partnership could pay off debt, without triggering gain recognition.

21-6d **Partners' Capital Considerations**

For tax returns prepared for years beginning after 2019, the partnership must report tax basis capital accounts on the partners' Schedules K–1 and on the partnership's Schedule M–2. The sum of the amounts on each capital account line on the K–1s (e.g., beginning and ending capital) should equal the totals shown on Schedule M–2.

A partner can have a negative tax basis capital account balance, but the tax preparer should be able to explain the reason for the negative amount. The IRS is concerned that allocations to a partner might exceed allowable limits. For example, if the sum of the partner's *tax basis* plus the *tax basis capital account balance* on Schedule K–1 is a negative amount, it indicates that the partner has a negative tax basis—which is not permitted. If this happens, the partner might have received a cash distribution or a loss allocation that exceeds the partner's tax basis in the partnership interest, triggering gain recognition or a loss disallowance to the partner.

If a negative tax basis capital account balance that should be reported on the partnership's return is calculated, then (1) determine the reason, (2) verify that allocations to the partner are within the limitations under §§ 704(b) and (c), (3) verify that allocations follow the guidelines set forth in the partnership agreement, (4) review distributions to determine whether they exceed the partner's tax basis in the partnership interest (if possible), (5) prepare the additional documentation required by the IRS, and (6) notify the partnership and (if feasible) the partner if there is an error or a potential IRS investigation issue.

21-6e **Partnership Reporting Requirements**

The partnership return is generally due by the fifteenth day of the third month following the tax year-end (March 15 for a calendar year partnership).

The partners cannot file an accurate return until they receive the Schedule K–1 (and possibly Schedule K–3) from the partnership. If a partnership return is filed (and Schedules K–1 and K–3 are provided to the partners) near this filing deadline, individual partners will have only limited time in which to complete their tax returns, and corporate partners will need to file an extension.

If a partner needs to file a return before the partnership prepares the partner's Schedule K–1, the partner can estimate income from the partnership and then file an amended return when the Schedule K–1 is received.

21-6f **Transactions between Partners and Partnerships**

If both a partner and a partnership are involved in a single transaction, pay attention to how the transaction is structured. Consider the impact of related party rules, and restructure the transaction, if necessary, to avoid unanticipated adverse tax results.

Under § 707(a), certain transactions between a partner and the partnership are treated as if the partner were an outsider, dealing with the partnership at arm's length. This includes loan transactions, rental payments, sales of property between the partner and the partnership, and payments for services when the services are short-term technical services the partner also provides for parties other than the partnership.

On the other hand, for some transactions, the partner and partnership are treated as related parties, and the tax treatment is adjusted accordingly. For example, § 707(b)(1) provides that no loss is recognized on a sale of property between a person and a partnership when the person owns, directly or indirectly, more than 50 percent of partnership capital or profits. (Note that the disallowed loss might not vanish entirely, however. If the transferee eventually sells the property at a gain, the disallowed loss reduces any gain on subsequent sale of the property.)

Similarly, under § 707(b)(2), gain is treated as ordinary income (rather than capital gain) if the sale or exchange is between a partnership and a more-than-50% partner, unless the property is a capital asset to both parties. Note that this provision recharacterizes the gain from capital gain to ordinary income, whereas the above provision disallows a realized loss.

One option is for the partner to consider leasing, rather than selling, property to a partnership. The partner recognizes rent income (which might be qualified business income, eligible for up to a 20 percent deduction), and the partnership has a rent expense. Alternatively, the partner can sell the property to an outside third party; then the third party can lease the property to the partnership for a fair rental.

21-6g **Drafting the Partnership Agreement**

A partner's distributive share of income, gain, loss, deduction, or credit is determined in accordance with the partnership agreement. In addition, the partner's status as a limited or general partner is often determined by reference to the rights the partner has in managing the entity. While a formal agreement is not always required, an agreement that sets forth the obligations, rights, and powers of the partners would provide some certainty as to the tax consequences of the partners' actions.

Refocus on The Big Picture

Why Use a Partnership, Anyway?

After considering the various types of partnerships, Kyler, Maria, and Josh decided to form Beachside Properties as an LLC (see Example 2). On formation of the entity, there was no tax to the LLC or to any of its members (see Example 12). Beachside Properties computes its income as shown in Examples 15 and 17. Beachside determines additional information the members will need (Example 18) and reconciles book and tax income and members' capital (Examples 19 and 20). Payments to the members for services or for the use of their capital are treated as guaranteed payments; the amounts are deducted by the LLC and reported as income by the LLC members (see Examples 16 and 24). The LLC members can claim a qualified business income deduction related to Beachside's operating income and rental income; the LLC will report additional information the members need to calculate their deduction limitations (see Example 25).

A portion of ordinary income was specially allocated to Maria under the substantial economic effect rules; precontribution gains will eventually be specially allocated under § 704(c); the remaining income is allocated according to profit sharing ratios (Examples 21 to 24). The LLC's income affects the members' bases and capital accounts as shown in Examples 29 and 30.

An important consideration for the LLC members is whether their distributive shares and guaranteed payments will be treated as self-employment income or subject to net investment income tax (Examples 33 and 34).

What If?

What happens in the future when the LLC members decide to expand or renovate Beachside's facilities? At that time, the existing members can contribute additional funds, the LLC can obtain new members, or the entity can solicit third-party financing. An LLC is not subject to the 80 percent control requirement applicable to the formation of and subsequent transfers to a corporation. Therefore, new investors can contribute cash or other property in exchange for interests in the LLC—and the transaction will qualify for tax-deferred treatment.

RODERICK PAUL WALKER/ALAMY STOCK PHOTO

Key Terms

Aggregate concept, 21-5
Capital account maintenance, 21-5
Capital interest, 21-5
Capital sharing ratio, 21-5
Carried interest, 21-8
Conduit concept, 21-5
Constructive liquidation scenario, 21-33
Disguised sale, 21-7
Distributive share, 21-4
Economic effect test, 21-26
Entity concept, 21-5
General partners, 21-2
General partnership (GP), 21-2
Guaranteed payment, 21-17
Inside basis, 21-5
Least aggregate deferral rule, 21-14
Limited liability company (LLC), 21-3
Limited liability partnership (LLP), 21-3
Limited partners, 21-2
Limited partnership (LP), 21-3
Nonrecourse debt, 21-32
Operating agreement, 21-3
Outside basis, 21-5
Partnership agreement, 21-3
Precontribution gain or loss, 21-27
Profit and loss sharing ratios, 21-5
Profits (loss) interest, 21-5
Qualified nonrecourse financing, 21-33
Recourse debt, 21-32
Required taxable year, 21-13
Schedule K–1, 21-4
Section 704(b) book capital accounts, 21-26
Separately stated items, 21-6
Special allocations, 21-6
Syndication costs, 21-12
Tax basis capital account, 21-35

Discussion Questions

1. **LO.1** What is a partnership agreement? What types of provisions does it include?

2. **LO.1** What is the difference between a general partnership and a limited liability company? When might each type of entity be used? Why?

Critical Thinking

3. **LO.2, 4, 6, 7, 8** Describe how a partnership reports its income for tax purposes. Who makes most elections related to partnership income and deductions? What two theories underlie most partnership tax rules? As an example, contrast the theories underlying the treatments of (1) the business interest expense limitation and (2) the qualified business income deduction.

4. **LO.3** Compare the provision for the nonrecognition of gain or loss on contributions to a partnership (i.e., § 721) with the similar provision related to corporate formation (i.e., § 351). What are the major differences and similarities?

Communications
Practice

5. **LO.4** If a partner contributes depreciable or amortizable property to the partnership, how is the basis of those properties recovered? In addition, what types of expenditures might a new partnership incur? How are those costs treated for Federal tax purposes? Create a job aid you could use in practice to determine tax treatment of expenditures of a new partnership. Describe each type of property or expenditure, the treatment, and the Code section requiring this treatment. At the beginning of the document, include a title and a statement describing how your firm should use this chart in practice.

6. **LO.5** When can a partnership use the cash method of accounting?

Critical Thinking
Practice

7. **LO.6, 7, 13** What is a guaranteed payment? How is it reported on Form 1065 and its various schedules? How is it reported and taxed to the partner (including taxes other than income taxes)? Describe ways in which the tax treatment of a guaranteed payment for services differs from guaranteed payments for use of the partner's capital. When preparing a partnership return for a client, how do you think you could determine the classification of its guaranteed payments (services or capital)?

Practice

8. **LO.6, 7, 8** What is the purpose of the qualified business income deduction under § 199A? With respect to partnership activities, how is the deduction calculated? What information does the partner need to make this calculation?

9. **LO.8** What is the purpose of the three rules that implement the economic effect test? What is one way you might be able to ensure a partnership intends to follow these rules? Practice

10. **LO.9, 10** Discuss the adjustments that must be made to a partner's basis in the partnership interest. When are such adjustments made? Why? Where can you find a partner's basis calculation? Practice

11. **LO.11** What is a partner's capital account? What methods can be used to determine the capital account, and when might these methods be used? Describe how a partner's ending capital account balance is determined. Where can you find the partner's capital account information? Practice

12. **LO.12** Describe the limitations that apply to the deductibility of a loss from a partnership. In what order are these limitations applied? Why do these rules exist?

13. **LO.13** When is partnership income subject to self-employment tax or the net investment income tax by an individual partner?

14. **LO.10, 12, 13, 14** Write an e-mail to a client describing situations in which the partnership entity form might be more advantageous (or disadvantageous) than operating as a C corporation. Use subheadings and bullet points to highlight your major thoughts. Communications Critical Thinking

15. **LO.6** Penguin LLC operates a large automobile showroom with several employees and substantial debt. Each LLC member is active in the business and receives compensation from the LLC. The LLC invests its excess cash in government and corporate bonds, blue chip stocks, and a global mutual fund. It owns property that is subject to accelerated depreciation. What types of information might Penguin report (and allocate to the partners) on its Schedule K and related schedules? Refer to Form 1065 and the instructions if necessary. Critical Thinking

Computational Exercises

16. **LO.2, 6, 7, 9** Enercio contributes $100,000 in exchange for a 40% interest in the calendar year ABC LLC, which is taxed as a partnership. This year, the LLC generates $80,000 of ordinary taxable income and has no separately stated income or expenses. Enercio withdrew $10,000 from the partnership during the year.

    Enercio is taxed on what amount of ABC's income? On how much of the $10,000 distribution will Enercio be taxed?

17. **LO.3** Henrietta transfers cash of $75,000 and equipment with a fair market value of $25,000 (basis to her as a sole proprietor, $10,000) in exchange for a 40% profit and loss interest worth $100,000.
    a. How much are Henrietta's realized and recognized gains?
    b. What is the amount of Henrietta's basis in her partnership interest?
    c. What is the partnership's basis in the contributed equipment?

18. **LO.3** Wozniacki and Wilcox form Jewel LLC, with each receiving a one-half interest in the capital and profits of the LLC. Wozniacki receives the one-half interest as compensation for tax planning services rendered prior to the formation of the LLC. Wilcox contributes $50,000 cash. The value of a one-half capital interest in the LLC (for each of the parties) is $50,000.
    a. How much income does Wozniacki recognize as a result of this transaction, and what is its character?
    b. How much is Wozniacki's basis in the LLC interest? How will Jewel LLC treat this amount?

19. **LO.3** On January 2 of the current year, Fenton and Myers form the FM LLC. Their contributions to the LLC are as follows.

	Adjusted Basis	Fair Market Value
From Fenton:		
Cash	$ 50,000	$ 50,000
Accounts receivable	–0–	90,000
Inventory	25,000	60,000
From Myers:		
Land	250,000	200,000

FM originally intended to hold the inventory as investment property. Myers held the land as long-term investment property, but FM will use it in its business as a § 1231 asset.

Within 30 days of formation, FM collects the receivables. Two years later, FM sells the inventory contributed by Fenton for $60,000 cash. After three years, FM sells the land for $200,000. How much income does FM recognize from these transactions, and what is its character? Why does this result apply?

20. **LO.4** Candlewood LLC started business on September 1, and it adopted a calendar tax year. During the year, Candlewood incurred $6,500 in legal fees for drafting the LLC's operating agreement and $3,000 in accounting fees for tax advice of an organizational nature, for a total of $9,500 of organizational costs. Candlewood also incurred $30,000 of preopening advertising expenses and $24,500 of salaries and training costs for new employees before opening for business, for a total of $54,500 of startup costs. The LLC wants to take the largest deduction available for these costs.

How much can Candlewood deduct as organizational expenses? As startup expenses? Refer to Chapter 17 if necessary.

21. **LO.6, 7** This year, the Tastee Partnership reported income before guaranteed payments of $92,000. Stella owns a 90% profits interest and works 1,600 hours per year in the business. Euclid owns a 10% profits interest (with a basis of $30,000 at the beginning of the tax year) and performs no services for the partnership during the year. For services performed during the year, Stella receives a "salary" of $6,000 per month. Euclid withdrew $10,000 from the partnership during the year as a normal distribution of cash from Tastee (i.e., not for services).

a. What is the amount of guaranteed payments made by the partnership this year?

b. How much is the partnership's ordinary income after any permitted deduction for guaranteed payments?

c. How much income will Stella report?

d. How much income will Euclid report?

22. **LO.8** When Padgett Properties LLC was formed, Nova contributed land (value of $200,000 and basis of $50,000) and $100,000 cash, and Oscar contributed cash of $300,000. Both partners received a 50% interest in partnership profits and capital.

a. How is the land recorded for § 704(b) book capital account purposes?

b. What is Padgett's tax basis in the land?

c. If Padgett sells the land several years later for $300,000, how much tax gain will Nova and Oscar report?

23. **LO.9** At the beginning of the tax year, Barnaby's basis in the BBB Partnership was $50,000, including his $5,000 share of partnership debt. At the end of the tax year, his share of debt was $8,000. His share of the partnership's income for the year was $20,000, and he received cash distributions totaling $12,000. In addition, his share of the partnership's nontaxable income was $1,000. How much is Barnaby's basis at the end of the tax year? Show your calculations.

24. **LO.10** Jokan contributes a nondepreciable asset to the Mahali LLC in exchange for a one-fourth (25%) interest in the LLC's capital and profits and a 30% interest in the LLC's losses. The asset has an adjusted tax basis to Jokan and the LLC of $60,000 and a fair market value and § 704(b) "book" basis on the contribution date of $150,000. The asset is encumbered by a nonrecourse note of $40,000 that has not been guaranteed by any of the LLC members.

    How much of the nonrecourse debt is allocated to Jokan, and what is the amount of Jokan's basis in the LLC interest following the contribution?

25. **LO.12** Tobias is a 50% partner in Solomon LLC, which does not invest in real estate. On January 1, Tobias's adjusted basis for his LLC interest is $130,000, and his at-risk amount is $105,000. His share of losses from Solomon for the current year is $150,000, all of which is passive. Tobias owns another investment that produced $90,000 of passive activity income during the year. (Assume that Tobias is a single taxpayer, there were no distributions or changes in liabilities during the year, and the Solomon loss is Tobias's only loss for the year from any activity.)

    How much of Solomon's losses may Tobias deduct on his Form 1040? How much of the loss is suspended, and what Code provisions cause the suspensions?

26. **LO.14** Heather sells land (adjusted basis, $75,000; fair market value, $85,000) to a partnership in which she controls an 80% capital interest. The partnership pays her only $50,000 for the land.
    a. How much loss does Heather realize and recognize?
    b. If the partnership later sells the land to a third party for $80,000, how much gain does that partnership realize and recognize?

Problems

27. **LO.3, 9, 14** Kenisha and Shawna form the equal KS LLC with a cash contribution of $360,000 from Kenisha and a property contribution (adjusted basis of $380,000, fair market value of $360,000) from Shawna. Critical Thinking Planning
    a. How much gain or loss, if any, does Shawna realize on the transfer? Does Shawna recognize any gain or loss? If so, how much?
    b. What is Kenisha's tax basis in her LLC interest? The § 704(b) book basis?
    c. What is Shawna's tax basis in her LLC interest? The § 704(b) book basis?
    d. What tax basis does the LLC take in the property transferred by Shawna?
    e. How could the transaction be restructured to maximize the tax benefits to Shawna?

28. **LO.3, 8, 9, 14** Liz and John formed the equal LJ Partnership on January 1 of the current year. Liz contributed $80,000 of cash and land with a fair market value of $90,000 and an adjusted basis of $75,000. John contributed equipment with a fair market value of $170,000 and an adjusted basis of $20,000. John had used the equipment in his sole proprietorship. Critical Thinking
    a. How much gain or loss will Liz, John, and the partnership realize?
    b. How much gain or loss will Liz, John, and the partnership recognize?
    c. What tax bases will Liz and John take in their partnership interests?
    d. What § 704(b) book basis will Liz and John take in their partnership interests?
    e. What bases will LJ take in the assets it receives?
    f. Are there any differences between inside basis and outside basis? Explain.
    g. How will the partnership depreciate any assets it receives from the partners?
    h. Do additional considerations arise because of the difference between the basis and fair market values of the properties Liz and John contributed? Explain.

Critical Thinking
Decision Making
Planning

29. **LO.3, 8, 14** Manuel and Melissa want to form the equal MM Partnership. Melissa will contribute cash of $140,000. Manuel has cash of $40,000 and land (fair market value of $100,000, adjusted basis of $136,000). Manuel purchased the land several years ago as an investment (capital) asset. Manuel and MM LLC are trying to decide between two alternatives for Manuel's contribution.

   - In Alternative 1, Manuel will contribute the land to the LLC. MM will use the property as a § 1231 asset (a parking lot) and then sell it in six years at an estimated $100,000 price. (Disregard any potential improvements to the land.)
   - In Alternative 2, Manuel will sell the land immediately to a third party and contribute to MM the $100,000 cash proceeds from the sale. MM will use that cash to purchase similar land for $100,000 (also to be used as a parking lot).

   Use the following additional assumptions: (1) neither Manuel nor MM will realize other capital or § 1231 gains or losses now or in the future, (2) Manuel's marginal tax rate is 35%, (3) a reasonable annual discount rate is 5%, and (4) the tax treatment of capital and § 1231 gains and losses does not change in the foreseeable future.

   a. For each alternative, when would the $36,000 loss be recognized, to whom would the loss be allocated, what is the character of the loss, and over what time period can the loss be deducted?
   b. In these two alternatives, calculate Manuel's tax savings each year from deducting his share of any loss allocated to him that year. Use the tables in Appendix E (or Microsoft Excel) to calculate the present value of these savings. Considering only tax savings, as Manuel's tax adviser, would you recommend Alternative 1 or Alternative 2? Why? What other issues should Manuel consider?
   c. How would the results in parts (a) and (b) change if MM were to sell the property in Alternative 1 after only four years? Answer conceptually; do not make calculations.

Decision Making
Planning

30. **LO.3, 14** During the current tax year, Dave and Stu formed the DS LLC with Dave contributing land with a basis of $360,000 and a fair market value of $600,000 at the contribution date. At the end of the year, the LLC distributes $300,000 of cash to Dave. The LLC made no distributions to Stu. Assume that there were no other income or loss transactions for the year that would affect Dave's basis in his LLC interest.

   a. Under general tax rules, how would the payment to Dave be treated?
   b. Under general tax rules, how much income or gain would Dave recognize as a result of the contribution and distribution?
   c. Under general tax rules, what basis would the LLC take in the land Dave contributed?
   d. What alternative treatment might the IRS try to impose?
   e. Under the alternative treatment, how much income or gain would Dave recognize?
   f. Under the alternative treatment, what basis would the LLC take in the land contributed by Dave?
   g. How can the transaction be restructured to minimize risk of IRS recharacterization?

Critical Thinking

31. **LO.5** Browne and Red, both C corporations, formed the BR Partnership on January 1, 2023. Neither Browne nor Red is a personal service corporation, and BR is not a tax shelter. BR's gross receipts were $23,000,000, $29,000,000, $38,000,000, and $39,000,000, respectively, for 2023 to 2026. Describe the methods of accounting available to BR in each tax year.

Critical Thinking

32. **LO.4** The Parakeet Partnership was formed on August 1 of the current year and admitted Morlan and Merriman as equal partners on that date. The partners both contributed $300,000 of cash to establish a children's clothing store in a local shopping mall. The partners spent August and September buying inventory, equipment, supplies, and advertising for their "Grand Opening" on October 1. Following are some of the costs the partnership incurred during its first year of operations.

Legal fees to form partnership	$ 8,000
Advertising for "Grand Opening"	18,000
Advertising after opening	30,000
Consulting fees for establishing accounting system	20,000
Rent, five months at $2,000/month	10,000
Utilities at $1,000 per month	5,000
Salaries to salesclerks (beginning in October)	50,000
Payments to Morlan and Merriman for services ($6,000/month each for three months, beginning in October)	36,000
Tax return preparation expense	12,000

In addition, on October 1, the partnership purchased all of the assets of Granny Newcombs, Inc. Of the total purchase price for these assets, $252,000 was allocated to the trade name and logo.

Determine how each of these costs is treated by the partnership, and identify the period over which the costs can be deducted, if any. Refer to Chapter 17 if necessary.

33. **LO.5** Cerulean, Inc., Coral, Inc., and Crimson, Inc., form the Three Cs Partnership on January 1 of the current year. Cerulean is a 50% partner, and Crimson and Coral are 25% partners. For reporting purposes, Crimson uses a fiscal year with an October 31 year-end, Coral uses the calendar year, and Cerulean uses a fiscal year with a February 28/29 year-end. In general terms, how is the required taxable year determined (no calculations required)? Explain. If the *required* taxable year is, for example, October 31, what alternative tax years could the new partnership consider?

34. **LO.6** CL LLC is a manufacturing business and reported "adjusted taxable income" in 2023 of $40,000,000, plus $1,500,000 of separately stated investment income. CL incurred interest expense of $1,000,000 in connection with this investment income and $14,000,000 in connection with its trade or business. Decision Making

 a. How much interest expense can CL deduct? What happens to any additional interest expense?
 b. How is the interest expense reported on CL's Schedules K–1?
 c. What action, if any, is needed by the LLC members?
 d. How would your answers to parts (a) through (c) change if CL's adjusted taxable income was $4,000,000 (plus $150,000 of investment income), its average annual gross receipts for all prior tax years was $10,000,000 or less, and the interest expense amounts were $100,000 (investment) and $1,400,000 (business)?

35. **LO.3, 6, 7, 8, 9** Phoebe and Parker are equal members of Phoenix Investors LLC. They are real estate investors who formed the LLC several years ago with equal cash contributions. Phoenix then purchased a parcel of land.

On January 1 of the current year, to acquire a one-third interest in the entity, Reece contributed to the LLC some land she had held for investment. Reece purchased the land five years ago for $75,000; its fair market value at the contribution date was $90,000. No special allocation agreements were in effect before or after Reece was admitted to the LLC. Phoenix holds all land for investment.

Immediately before Reece's property contribution, the balance sheet of Phoenix Investors LLC was as follows.

	Basis	FMV		Basis	FMV
Land	$30,000	$180,000	Phoebe, capital	$15,000	$ 90,000
			Parker, capital	15,000	90,000
	$30,000	$180,000		$30,000	$180,000

 a. At the contribution date, what is Reece's basis in her interest in the LLC?
 b. When does the LLC's holding period begin for the contributed land?

c. On June 30 of the current year, the LLC sold the land contributed by Reece for $90,000. What is the LLC's recognized gain or loss? How is it allocated among the LLC members?

d. Prepare a balance sheet reflecting basis and fair market value for the LLC immediately after the land sale described in part (c). No other transactions occurred during the tax year.

36. **LO.3, 6, 7, 8, 9, 11** Marcus and Madison are equal members of an LLC. On January 1 of the current year, to acquire a one-third interest in the entity, Nora contributed a parcel of land she had held for investment. (At this time, the entity was renamed MMN, LLC.) Nora had purchased the land for $120,000; its fair market value was $90,000 at the contribution date.

A few years later, the LLC sells Nora's land for $84,000. At the beginning of that year, Nora's tax basis capital account was $200,000 and Marcus and Madison's tax basis capital accounts were $170,000.

a. What is the LLC's recognized gain or loss? How is it allocated among the LLC members?

b. Use Microsoft Excel to prepare schedules that compute the partners' tax basis capital accounts immediately after the sale. Use variables to input the amount allocated to each LLC member and the total *not* specially allocated.

37. **LO.6, 7, 8, 9, 10, 11** Amy and Mitchell share equally (50%) in the profits, losses, and capital of the accrual basis AM Products LLC. Amy is a managing member of the LLC (treated as a general partner) and is a U.S. person.

At the beginning of the current tax year, Amy's *tax basis capital account* has a balance of $300,000, and the LLC has debts of $200,000 payable to unrelated parties. All debts are recourse to the LLC, but neither of the LLC members has personally guaranteed them. The following information about AM's operations for the current year is obtained from the LLC's records.

Sales revenues	$1,400,000
Other "ordinary and necessary" operating expenses (e.g., utilities, repairs, and rent)	500,000
W–2 wages to employees	200,000
Depreciation expense	300,000
Interest income	4,000
Long-term capital gain	6,000
Charitable contribution (cash)	4,000
Cash distribution to Amy	20,000
Unadjusted basis of partnership property immediately after acquisition	1,600,000

Year-end LLC debt payable to unrelated parties is $140,000. All transactions are reflected in Amy's beginning capital account and tax basis in the same manner. All AM Products' activities are eligible for the qualified business income deduction.

a. Calculate Amy's tax basis in her LLC interest at the beginning and end of the tax year. Use her capital account as a starting point.

b. What income, gains, losses, and deductions does Amy report on her income tax return?

c. What other calculations is Amy required to make?

d. Prepare Amy's tax basis capital account roll forward from the beginning to the end of the tax year. How does her ending capital account differ from her ending tax basis in the LLC interest as calculated in part (a)?

e. Using the information from parts (a) to (d), prepare Amy's Schedule K–1 as if you were the preparer of AM Products LLC's tax return. Provide all information that Amy needs to the extent you can. For Parts I and II (items A to F), omit any missing information (e.g., last names, addresses, EINs).

f. Using the Schedule K–1, how much would you estimate as Amy's ending tax basis in the partnership interest? How did you arrive at this amount?

38. **LO.7, 8, 9, 11** Barney is a managing LLC member (treated as a general partner) of BG LLC and is allocated qualified business income (QBI) from BG of $800,000. (BG is not a "specified service trade or business.") Barney's Schedule K–1 reflects a $300,000 share of BG's W–2 wages and a $1,200,000 share of BG's UBIA (unadjusted basis immediately after acquisition). Barney's taxable income excluding capital gains is $600,000; and Barney has no income from REITs, publicly traded partnerships, or other qualified businesses. Refer to the QBI discussion in this chapter, the discussion in text Section 15-5, and the flowchart in Concept Summary 15.2. For simplification, disregard any SE tax or other deductions related to Barney's QBI from BG LLC (assume these amounts equal $0).

a. Calculate Barney's deduction under § 199A for qualified business income. Show your work, and show how any limitations are calculated.

b. How does Barney's § 199A deduction affect his (1) cash flow, (2) basis in the LLC interest, and (3) capital account?

39. **LO.6, 7, 8, 9, 12** The KL Partnership is owned equally by Kayla and Lisa. At the beginning of the year, Kayla's tax basis in her KL interest is $20,000 and Lisa's tax basis is $16,000. Partnership debt did not change from the beginning to the end of the tax year. KL reported the following income and expenses for the current tax year. Decision Making

Sales revenue	$150,000
Cost of sales	80,000
Distribution to Lisa	15,000
Depreciation expense	20,000
Utilities	14,000
Rent expense	18,000
Long-term capital gain	6,000
Payment to Mercy Hospital for Kayla's medical expenses	12,000

a. Prepare a Microsoft Excel spreadsheet that could be used to accumulate KL's information to be reported on Form 1065, page 1 [Ordinary business income (loss)] and page 4 (Schedule K). Include calculations and subtotals to ensure that the spreadsheet will update if the information changes.

How much is the partnership's ordinary income on page 1? What information is shown on Schedule K?

b. Use the information in part (a) to prepare Form 1065, pages 1 and 4 (Schedule K) for the KL Partnership. On page 1, omit items A to J at the top if the facts do not provide that information. For Schedule K, line 14, assume that both partners are active in the partnership.

c. Add columns to your spreadsheet to allocate amounts to Kayla and Lisa. (For this requirement, disregard the information related to the qualified business income deduction.) Show the partners' allocation percentages at the top of their columns, and use those percentages in formulas to allocate any separately stated items that should be allocated. (Note that some items are directly assigned to a partner.)

What information will be shown on Kayla's and Lisa's Schedules K–1, Part III? What items will Kayla and Lisa report on their Federal income tax returns?

d. Expand your spreadsheet. Add rows for beginning basis and ending basis below Kayla's and Lisa's columns, and calculate each partner's ending basis in the partnership interest. How do you make this calculation? What is each partner's basis in her partnership interest at the end of the tax year?

e. Consider the results if the partnership's revenues were $100,000 instead of $150,000. What happens if you update the revenues line on your spreadsheet? Are your new amounts correct for the Form 1065/Schedule K information, Schedule K–1 information, and partners' bases? Why or why not? What conclusions can you draw?

Critical Thinking
Planning

40. **LO.3, 6, 7, 9, 10, 11** Suzy contributed assets valued at $360,000 (basis of $200,000) in exchange for her 40% interest in Suz-Anna GP (a general partnership in which both partners are active owners). Anna contributed land and a building valued at $640,000 (basis of $380,000) in exchange for the remaining 60% interest. Anna's property was encumbered by qualified nonrecourse financing of $100,000, which was assumed by the partnership.

The partnership reports the following income and expenses for the current tax year.

Sales	$560,000
Utilities, salaries, depreciation, and other operating expenses	360,000
Short-term capital gain	10,000
Tax-exempt interest income	4,000
Charitable contributions (cash)	8,000
Distribution to Suzy	10,000
Distribution to Anna	20,000

During the current tax year, Suz-Anna refinanced the land and building. In doing so, they took out new qualified nonrecourse financing of $200,000 and used $100,000 of the proceeds to repay the original $100,000 debt (with $100,000 of cash left over for business use). At the end of the year, Suz-Anna held recourse debt of $100,000 for partnership accounts payable (recourse to the partnership but not personally guaranteed by either of the partners) and the new $200,000 debt.

a. What is Suzy's basis in Suz-Anna after formation of the partnership? Anna's basis?

b. What income and separately stated items does the partnership report on Suzy's Schedule K–1? What income, deduction, and taxes does Suzy report on her tax return? What additional information is needed?

c. Assume that all partnership debts are shared proportionately. At the end of the tax year, what are Suzy's basis and amount at risk in her partnership interest?

d. What are Suzy's tax basis capital account balances (i.e., amounts reported on Schedule K–1) at the beginning and end of the tax year? What accounts for the difference between Suzy's ending tax basis capital account and her ending tax basis in the partnership interest?

e. Back up in time to when Suzy and Anna first came to you for advice. How would the results have changed if Suz-Anna were formed as an LLC instead of a general partnership? How would Suz-Anna's ending liabilities be treated? How would Suzy's basis and amount at risk be different?

41. **LO.6, 7** Burgundy, Inc., and Violet are equal partners in the calendar year BV LLC. Burgundy uses a fiscal year ending April 30, and Violet uses a calendar year. Burgundy receives an annual guaranteed payment of $100,000 for use of capital contributed by Burgundy. BV's taxable income (after deducting the payment to Burgundy, Inc.) is $80,000 for 2023 and $90,000 for 2024.

a. What is the amount of income from the LLC that Burgundy must report for its tax year ending April 30, 2024?

b. What is the amount of income from the LLC that Violet must report for her tax year ending December 31, 2024?

c. Now assume that Burgundy, Inc.'s annual guaranteed payment is increased to $120,000 starting on January 1, 2024, and the LLC's taxable income for 2023 and 2024 (after deducting Burgundy's guaranteed payment) is the same (i.e., $80,000 and $90,000, respectively). What is the amount of income from the LLC that Burgundy, Inc., must report for its tax year ending April 30, 2024?

Critical Thinking

42. **LO.3, 6, 7, 9, 12** Bryan and Cody each contributed $120,000 to the newly formed BC Partnership in exchange for a 50% interest. The partnership used the available funds to acquire equipment costing $200,000 and to fund current operating expenses. The partnership agreement provides that depreciation will be allocated 80% to Bryan and 20% to Cody. All other items of income and loss will be allocated equally between the partners.

Upon liquidation of the partnership, property will be distributed to the partners in accordance with their § 704(b) book capital account balances. Any partner with a negative capital account must contribute cash in the amount of the negative balance to restore the capital account to $0.

In its first year, the partnership reported an ordinary loss (before depreciation) of $80,000 and depreciation expense of $36,000. In its second year, the partnership reported $40,000 of income from operations (before depreciation), and it reported depreciation expense of $57,600.

a. Calculate the partners' bases in their partnership interests at the end of the first and second tax years. Are any losses suspended? Explain.

b. Does the allocation provided in the partnership agreement have economic effect? Explain.

c. Now assume that on the first day of the third tax year, the partnership sells the equipment for $150,000. The gain on the sale is allocated equally to the partners. The partnership distributes all cash in accordance with the partners' capital account balances, and the partnership liquidates. How will partnership cash balances be distributed to the partners upon liquidation? (*Hint:* First, calculate the partners' bases in their partnership interests after reflecting any gain or loss on disposal of the equipment. Disregard any depreciation in year 3.) What observations can you make regarding the value of a deduction to each partner?

43. **LO. 9, 10** This year, Callie and Neil formed CN LLC. Callie contributed $300,000 of cash, and Neil contributed real estate valued at $450,000 (basis of $200,000). The property was subject to a recourse liability of $150,000 that was assumed by the LLC but is not guaranteed by either LLC member. Callie and Neil's profit sharing ratios are 40%/60%, respectively, but the loss sharing ratios are 50%/50%. Is the debt treated as a recourse debt or a nonrecourse debt to the LLC members? How is the debt allocated between Callie and Neil? What are Neil's and Callie's bases in the LLC interest immediately after the LLC was formed? Show your calculations.

44. **LO.3, 9, 10, 12** Pedro and Anna plan to form the PA LLC by the end of 2022 to produce and sell specialty athletic apparel. Pedro and Anna will both serve as member-managers of the LLC and will be active in its operations. The members will each contribute $80,000 cash, and in addition, the LLC will borrow $440,000 from First State Bank. The $600,000 will be used to buy equipment and to lease a property they can use as a small manufacturing facility and a storefront.

Communications
Decision Making
Planning

The bank has stated that the debt must be guaranteed, and Anna has agreed to guarantee the entire amount. At the end of the year, the LLC also expects to have accounts payable of $40,000 for inventory and supplies.

The LLC's operating agreement provides that all LLC items will be allocated equally. The agreement also provides that capital accounts will be properly maintained and that each member must restore any deficit in the capital account upon the LLC's liquidation.

If the LLC claims 100% bonus depreciation, it will report a loss of about $580,000 in 2022, which the LLC members would like to deduct.

Pedro and Anna would like to know how the debt ($440,000 loan and $40,000 of accounts payable) will be allocated between them and how that allocation affects their ability to deduct the losses. Pedro and Anna are single individual taxpayers. If limitations arise, can any adjustments be made to ensure that the losses can be deducted? Consider all potential loss limitations, and assume that neither Pedro nor Anna will have business income or losses from other sources. Using the format (1) facts, (2) issues, (3) conclusion and recommendations, and (4) law and analysis, draft a memo to the PA LLC tax planning file for your manager's review that describes how the debt will be shared between Pedro and Anna for purposes of computing the adjusted basis of each LLC interest. Include any planning ideas that could be addressed to improve the results.

Critical Thinking
Planning

45. **LO.9, 10, 12, 14** The BCD Partnership plans to distribute cash of $20,000 to partner Brad at the end of the tax year. The partnership reported a loss for the year, and Brad's share of the loss is $10,000. At the beginning of the tax year, Brad's basis in his partnership interest, including his share of partnership liabilities, was $15,000. The partnership expects to report substantial income in future years.
    a. What ordering rules are used to calculate Brad's ending basis in his partnership interest?
    b. How much gain or loss will Brad report for the tax year?
    c. Will the deduction for the $10,000 loss be suspended? Why or why not?
    d. Could any planning opportunities be used to minimize any negative tax ramifications of the distribution? Explain.

Tax Return Problem

Tax Forms Problem

ProConnect™ Tax

1. Ryan Ross (111-11-1112), Oscar Omega (222-22-2223), Clark Carey (333-33-3334), and Kim Kardigan (444-44-4445) are equal active members in ROCK the Ages LLC. ROCK serves as agent and manager for prominent musicians in the Los Angeles area. The LLC's Federal ID number is 55-5555556. It uses the cash basis and the calendar year and began operations on January 1, 2010. Its current address is 6102 Wilshire Boulevard, Suite 2100, Los Angeles, CA 90036. ROCK was the force behind such music icons as Adrianna Venti, Drake Malone, Elena Gomez, Tyler Quick, Queen Bey, and Bruno Mercury and has had a very profitable year. The following information was taken from the LLC's income statement for the current year.

Revenues	
Fees and commissions	$4,800,000
Taxable interest income from bank deposits	1,600
Tax-exempt interest	3,200
Net gain on stock sales	4,000
Total revenues	$4,808,800
Expenses	
Advertising and public relations	$ 380,000
Charitable contributions	28,000
§ 179 expense	20,000
Employee W–2 wages	1,000,000
Guaranteed payment (services), Ryan Ross, office manager	800,000
Guaranteed payment (services), other members	600,000
Business meals subject to 50% disallowance	200,000
Business restaurant meals and travel (100% deductible)	320,000
Legal and accounting fees	132,000
Office rentals paid	80,000
Interest expense on operating line of credit	10,000
Insurance premiums	52,000
Office expense	200,000
Payroll taxes	92,000
Utilities	54,800
Total expenses	$3,968,800

Recently, ROCK has taken advantage of bonus depreciation and § 179 deductions and fully remodeled the premises and upgraded its leasehold improvements. This year, ROCK wrapped up its remodel with the purchase of $20,000 of office furniture for which it will claim a § 179 deduction. (For simplicity, assume that ROCK uses the same cost recovery methods for both tax and financial purposes.) There is no depreciation adjustment for alternative minimum tax purposes.

ROCK invests much of its excess cash in non-dividend-paying growth stocks and tax-exempt securities. During the year, the LLC sold two securities. On June 15, ROCK purchased 1,000 shares of Tech, Inc. stock for $100,000; it sold those shares on December 15 for $80,000. On March 15 of last year, ROCK purchased 2,000 shares of BioLabs, Inc. stock for $136,000; it sold those shares for $160,000 on December 15 of the current year. These transactions were reported to the IRS on Forms 1099–B; ROCK's basis in these shares *was* reported.

Net income per books is $840,000. On January 1, the members' tax basis capital accounts equaled $200,000 each. No additional capital contributions were made this year. In addition to their guaranteed payments, each member withdrew $250,000 cash during the year. All contributions and distributions have been in cash, so the LLC has no net unrecognized § 704(c) gain or loss. The LLC's balance sheet as of December 31 of this year is as follows.

	Beginning	Ending
Cash	$ 444,000	$??
Tax-exempt securities	120,000	120,000
Marketable securities	436,000	300,000
Leasehold improvements, furniture, and equipment	960,000	980,000
Accumulated depreciation	(960,000)	(980,000)
Total assets	$1,000,000	$??

	Beginning	Ending
Operating line of credit	$ 200,000	$ 160,000
Capital, Ross	200,000	??
Capital, Omega	200,000	??
Capital, Carey	200,000	??
Capital, Kardigan	200,000	??
Total liabilities and capital	$1,000,000	$??

All debt is shared equally by the members. Each member has personally guaranteed the debt of the LLC. All members are active in LLC operations.

For our purposes, assume the LLC is not considered an SSTB, and ROCK's operations constitute one active trade or business for purposes of the passive activity and at-risk limitations. (Note that the § 179 deduction is a business-related expense.) The LLC's UBIA (unadjusted basis immediately after acquisition) equals the total original cost of all leasehold improvements, or $980,000.

The appropriate business code for the entity is 711410. For the Form 1065, page 5, Analysis of Net Income, put all partners' allocations in cell 2(b)(ii), per IRS instructions for an LLC.

a. Complete the 2022 Form 1065 for ROCK the Ages LLC with appropriate forms and schedules. Suggested software: ProConnect Tax. Use tax-basis information for Schedules L and M–2. Provide any special information the LLC members might need, including net income from self-employment and information for the § 199A calculation. Attach additional statements if needed, and leave information blank if not available.

b. Continue by preparing Schedules K–1 for ROCK's members. Pay attention to any special allocation required for Ryan Ross. Ross's address is 15520 W. Earlson Street, Pacific Palisades, CA 90272. (Leave other addresses blank.)

Research Problems

Note: Solutions to the Research Problems can be prepared by using the Thomson Reuters Checkpoint™ online tax research database, which accompanies this textbook. Solutions can also be prepared by using research materials found in a typical tax library.

Planning

Research Problem 1. Barry, an individual, and Aldrin, Inc., a domestic C corporation, have decided to form BA LLC. The new LLC will produce a product that Barry recently developed and patented. Barry and Aldrin, Inc., will each own a 50% capital and profits interest in the LLC. Barry is a calendar year U.S. taxpayer, while Aldrin, Inc., uses a July 1–June 30 fiscal year. The LLC does not have a "natural business year" and elects to be taxed as a partnership.

a. BA LLC, your client, would like to know what taxable year it must use under the Code and Regulations.

b. The partners would also like to know what would happen in various hypothetical situations. For example, what would happen if two years after formation of the LLC Barry were to sell half of his interest (25%) to Aldrin, Inc.? Could the LLC retain the taxable year determined in part (a)? Why or why not?

Communications
Critical Thinking
Planning

Research Problem 2. Your clients, Grayson Investments, Inc. (Ana Marks, President), and Blake Caldwell, each contributed $200,000 of cash to form the Realty Management Partnership, a limited partnership. Grayson is the general partner, and Blake is the limited partner. The partnership used the $400,000 cash to make a down payment on a building. The rest of the building's $4,000,000 purchase price was financed with an interest-only nonrecourse loan of $3,600,000, which was obtained from an independent third-party bank.

The partnership allocates all partnership items equally between the partners except for the MACRS deductions and building maintenance, which are allocated 70% to Blake and 30% to Grayson. The partnership wants to satisfy the "economic effect" requirements of Reg. §§ 1.704–1 and 1.704–2 and will reallocate MACRS, if necessary, to satisfy the requirements of the Regulations.

Under the partnership agreement, liquidation distributions will be paid in proportion to the partners' positive capital account balances. Capital accounts are maintained as required in the Regulations. Grayson Investments has an unlimited obligation to restore its capital account, while Blake is subject to a qualified income offset provision under Reg. § 1.704–1(b)(2)(ii)(d).

Assume that all partnership items, except for MACRS, will net to zero throughout the first three years of the partnership operations. Also assume that each year's MACRS deduction will be $200,000 (to simplify the calculations).

Draft a letter to the partnership evaluating the allocation of MACRS in each of the three years under Reg. §§ 1.704–1 and –2. The partnership's address is 53 East Marsh Ave., Smyrna, GA 30082. Do not address the "substantial" test.

Critical Thinking

Research Problem 3. Texas Land, Inc., wanted to acquire and develop 100 acres of property in west Texas at a cost of $10,000,000 ($4,000,000 to purchase the land from ABC, Inc., plus $6,000,000 for development costs). However, Texas Land had only $2,000,000 of cash available for the land purchase and no funds to put toward the development costs.

Texas Land approached Gateway Savings & Loan, an S&L with significant tax losses but available cash. Gateway agreed to contribute the remaining $2,000,000 (for the land purchase) to a partnership (TG Partners) that would acquire and develop the property. Gateway would also make additional funds available for the development as needed. (Gateway's additional contributions would never total the remaining $6,000,000 cost because portions of the property were intended to be sold as they were completed, and those sales proceeds would fund future phases of the improvements.)

In return, Gateway will receive a guaranteed payment of 6% of its capital each year, plus Gateway and Texas Land will share (50%/50%) any profits on the development and sale of the property. The parties also agreed that Texas Land would manage the property and oversee its development and would receive a fixed guaranteed payment related to those services. No partnership agreement was drafted or signed.

As it turned out, Texas Land located another party (DEF, Inc.) that wanted to purchase "the best" 30 acres of the property for $5,000,000. Texas Land and Gateway arranged that the closing on the 100-acre purchase from ABC would occur the same day as the closing on the 30-acre sale to DEF. The $5,000,000 sales proceeds were enough to pay the entire purchase price to ABC, with $1,000,000 left over to begin improvements on the remaining 70-acre parcel. That first $4,000,000 of sales proceeds essentially funded the $2,000,000 capital contributions for both Texas Land and Gateway, so neither partner needed to immediately contribute cash to TG Partners.

Even though neither Texas Land nor Gateway invested cash upon formation, they intend to carry on as if TG Partners was established and is the entity completing the development activities. However, they are concerned that the IRS might contend that no partnership was formed and that the arrangement was simply designed to shift a tax liability (gain on the land sale to DEF, Inc., and on future development) from Texas Land to Gateway, which has no current tax liability.

a. All of these events happened in the prior year, and now it's February and TG Partners is your client. Review the rules of § 761. Under these rules, make your best case that TG Partners is, indeed, a partnership. (TG will operate on the calendar year.)

b. Consider the effect of the Check-the-box Regulations under Reg. § 301.7701 and your knowledge, in general, of partnership taxation. What can you do to ensure that partnership treatment is assured?

Use internet tax resources to address the following questions. Look for reliable websites and blogs of the IRS and other government agencies, media outlets, businesses, tax professionals, academics, think tanks, and political outlets.

Research Problem 4. CityDAO (**www.citydao.io**) is a decentralized autonomous organization (DAO), which is defined as a collectively owned community that is established under a blockchain and works toward some communal goal or vision. CityDAO purchased a 40 acre parcel in Wyoming (Parcel Zero) and is considering purchasing two other parcels (The Baby Parcel and The Big Parcel). Their goal is to create a community-governed futuristic crypto city. Communications

Please go to CityDAO's website and read more about this organization. Assume you have been asked to provide guidance regarding the type of business entity best suited for their Wyoming operations. Which entity would you suggest? Why do you think Wyoming was chosen as the state in which the first land purchase was made? Are there any other U.S. jurisdictions that have laws similar to Wyoming where CityDAO could make future purchases? Prepare a 1-page memorandum describing the results of your research and send it to your instructor.

Research Problem 5. Search for news or current reports related to partnerships, LLCs, or limited partnerships. What entities did you find that are taking advantage of the partnership entity form? In what industries do they operate? What are their gross receipts and asset holdings?

Research Problem 6. The IRS Statistics on Income division accumulates information each year on the various types of businesses operating as partnerships. Go to **irs.gov/taxstats**, click "Partnerships," and then click "By Sector or Industry." Open the Microsoft Excel file for one of the tables (e.g., Table 1) for the most recent tax year available. For that year, sort and evaluate the data various ways to "dig deeper" into the various ways in which partnerships are used. Communications Data Analytics

Write a memo to your instructor that describes some of the things you learned. For example, in which industries do you find the largest numbers of partnerships, the largest numbers of partners, and/or the largest concentration of gross and net assets? Which industries tend to produce the highest profits? Losses? What conclusions can you draw? Support your findings with at least one graphic or chart prepared in Microsoft Excel.

Becker CPA Review Questions

Becker

1. Gray is a 50% partner in Fabco Partnership. Gray's tax basis in Fabco on January 1, year 4, was $5,000. Fabco made no distributions to the partners during year 4 and recorded the following.

Ordinary income	$20,000
Tax-exempt income	8,000
Portfolio income	4,000

What is Gray's tax basis in Fabco on December 31, year 4?

a. $21,000 c. $12,000
b. $16,000 d. $10,000

2. Nick, Chris, Stacey, and Mike are each 25% partners in Liberty Partnership, a general partnership. During the current year, the partnership had revenues of $300,000 and nonseparately stated business expenses of $100,000, including a guaranteed payment of $30,000 to Nick for services provided to the partnership. Also, during the current year, the partnership had interest income of $10,000 and charitable contributions of $16,000. With regard to activity in the partnership, what should Stacey report on her income tax return for the current year?

	Ordinary Income	Interest Income	Charitable Contributions
a.	$200,000	$10,000	$16,000
b.	80,000	2,500	4,000
c.	57,500	2,500	4,000
d.	50,000	2,500	4,000

3. Duffy Associates is a partnership engaged in real estate development. Olinto, a civil engineer, billed Duffy $40,000 in the current year for consulting services rendered. In full settlement of this invoice, Olinto accepted $15,000 cash payment plus the following:

	Fair Market Value	Carrying Amount on Duffy's Books
10% partnership interest in Duffy	$10,000	N/A
Automobile	7,000	$3,000

What amount should Olinto, a cash basis taxpayer, report in his current-year return as income for the services rendered to Duffy?

a. $15,000 c. $32,000
b. $28,000 d. $40,000

4. On January 2 of the current year, Black acquired a 50% interest in New Partnership by contributing property with an adjusted basis of $7,000 and a fair market value of $9,000, subject to a mortgage of $3,000. What was Black's basis in New at January 2 of the current year?

a. $3,500 c. $5,500
b. $4,000 d. $7,500

5. At partnership inception, Black acquires a 50% interest in Decorators Partnership by contributing property with an adjusted basis of $250,000. Black recognizes a gain if:

   I. The fair market value of the contributed property exceeds its adjusted basis.
   II. The property is encumbered by a mortgage with a balance of $100,000.

   a. I only.
   b. II only.
   c. Both I and II.
   d. Neither I nor II.

6. When a partner's share of partnership liabilities increases, that partner's basis in the partnership interest:
   a. Increases by the partner's share of the liabilities.
   b. Decreases by the partner's share of the liabilities.
   c. Decreases, but not to less than zero.
   d. Is not affected.

7. Peter, a 25% partner in Gold & Stein Partnership, received a $20,000 guaranteed payment in the current year for deductible services rendered to the partnership. Guaranteed payments were not made to any other partner. Gold & Stein's current-year partnership income consisted of:

Net business income before guaranteed payments	$80,000
Net long-term capital gains	10,000

   What amount of income should Peter report from Gold & Stein Partnership on his current-year tax return? (Disregard the character of the income and just calculate the total increase to Peter's income.)

   a. $37,500
   b. $27,500
   c. $22,500
   d. $20,000

Chapter 22

Partnerships: Distributions, Transfer of Interests, and Terminations

Learning Objectives: *After completing Chapter 22, you should be able to:*

- **LO.1** Define terms related to distributions from a partnership.
- **LO.2** Describe hot assets and their significance.
- **LO.3** Determine the tax treatment of proportionate current distributions from a partnership to a partner.
- **LO.4** Determine the tax treatment of proportionate distributions that liquidate a partnership.
- **LO.5** Describe the rules that apply to property distributions with special tax treatment.
- **LO.6** Explain the general concepts governing tax treatment of disproportionate distributions.
- **LO.7** Determine the tax treatment under § 736 of payments from a partnership to a retiring or deceased partner.
- **LO.8** Calculate the selling partner's amount and character of gain or loss on the sale or exchange of a partnership interest.
- **LO.9** Describe tax issues related to other dispositions of partnership interests.
- **LO.10** Calculate the optional adjustments to basis under § 754.
- **LO.11** Outline the events that could terminate a partnership.
- **LO.12** Identify the special considerations of a family partnership.
- **LO.13** Describe the application of partnership provisions to limited liability companies (LLCs) and limited liability partnerships (LLPs).
- **LO.14** Evaluate various tax planning considerations related to partnership distributions and sales of partnership interests.

Chapter Outline

PETER TITMUSS/ALAMY STOCK PHOTO

The Big Picture

The Life Cycle of a Partnership

In the previous chapter, Josh, Kyler, and Maria created Beachside Properties LLC to own and operate the Beachsider Café and to own, manage, and lease the remaining properties in the Shorefront Center. The 10-acre center includes three developed acres (including the Beachsider Café) and seven acres being held for expansion. Josh, Kyler, and Maria own, respectively, 20 percent, 40 percent, and 40 percent shares in the LLC's profits and losses and 5 percent, 47.5 percent, and 47.5 percent interests in its capital. The entity was formed as an LLC to limit the members' liability for claims against the LLC (see text Section 21-1a).

In the years since the LLC was formed, it's been business as usual: income each year and regular cash and property distributions to the LLC members. Meanwhile, property values have skyrocketed. The LLC interests and the net underlying assets are currently valued at approximately $10 million (including $1 million of goodwill for the Beachsider Café).

Josh wants to develop the remaining seven acres at an estimated cost of $15 million. However, Kyler and Maria are ready to retire. Their interests are valued at $9.5 million, or 95 percent of the current $10 million net LLC value. Josh has found a group of developers who are willing to invest the $24.5 million necessary for improvements and to purchase Kyler's and Maria's interests.

There are two ways to accomplish the transition and make everyone happy. First, the LLC could admit the new members for $24.5 million of cash and use $9.5 million to redeem Kyler's and Maria's interests (with the remaining $15 million of cash being used for property improvements). Alternatively, Kyler and Maria could sell their LLC interests directly to the new members for $9.5 million; the new members then would contribute the additional $15 million of cash to the LLC for the expansion. Although the two alternatives have identical economic effects, the tax results could differ substantially.

We'll look at several issues related to ongoing operations as well as the buyout. First, on an annual basis, how are the cash and property distributions treated by the LLC? For future planning, what are the tax consequences of admitting the new members to the LLC and *redeeming* Kyler's and Maria's interests? What are the results if the new members *buy* Kyler's and Maria's interests directly and contribute additional cash for development? Which alternative is best for Josh, the new owners, and the LLC? Which alternative is best for Kyler and Maria?

Read the chapter and formulate your response.

In Chapter 21, we looked at forming and operating a partnership. In this chapter, we look at "life cycle" issues for these entities, such as:

- Routine ("current") distributions of cash or property.
- Distributions that liquidate the partnership or buy out a partner's interest.
- Sale of a partnership interest.

We also discuss the § 754 election (a special election a partnership can make to help keep inside and outside bases in balance), as well as partnership terminations, and we introduce family partnerships. At the end of the chapter, we take a deeper look at limited liability companies (LLCs) and limited liability partnerships (LLPs).

22-1 Distributions from a Partnership

Distributions don't typically cause the partner to recognize income or gain. Instead, the partner's outside basis is reduced by the amount of cash received. The partnership's inside basis in assets is also reduced. This reflects the aggregate theory, which holds that the partner essentially owns a share of the partnership's underlying assets.

The Big Picture

Example 1

Return to the facts of *The Big Picture* on p. 22-1. Assume that Josh's outside basis in his Beachside Properties LLC interest is $300,000. The LLC distributes $50,000 cash to Josh. Josh does not recognize any current gain; instead, he reduces his basis in the entity to $250,000 ($300,000 original basis − $50,000 distribution).

This result applies whether or not Kyler and Maria, Beachside's other members, receive a similar distribution.

As discussed in text Section 21-4b, the capital account maintenance rules ensure that each partner eventually receives a "fair share" of assets from the partnership. At the end of the day (i.e., when the partnership liquidates, at the latest), distributions are in accordance with the partners' ending § 704(b) book capital accounts.

LO.1

Define terms related to distributions from a partnership.

22-1a Distributions in General

First, consider a few definitions. A *distribution* is a payment from a partnership to a partner with respect to the partner's ownership interest in the partnership.

Not all payments from a partnership to a partner are treated as distributions. For example, as discussed in text Section 21-6f, a partnership may pay rent to a partner for use of the partner's property, make a guaranteed payment to a partner for services or for use of the partner's capital, or purchase property from a partner.

In addition, the general rules for distributions (and other partnership transaction rules) can be affected by changes in the partners' shares of ordinary income-producing assets (so-called "**hot assets**") and **disproportionate distributions**. We'll discuss these overarching concepts first, at a definitional level, and then we'll see how everything fits together.

Current versus Liquidating Distributions

If a payment *is* treated as a distribution from the partnership to the partner, it falls into one of two categories.

- Current (or nonliquidating) distributions.
- Liquidating distributions.

These distributions may consist of cash or partnership property. Whether a distribution is a **current distribution** or a **liquidating distribution** depends solely on whether the partner remains a partner in the partnership after the distribution is made.

Liquidating Distributions A *liquidating* distribution occurs either (1) when a partnership itself liquidates and distributes all of its property to its partners or (2) when an ongoing partnership redeems the interest of one of its partners.

Current Distributions A *current* distribution (sometimes called a "nonliquidating distribution") is any other distribution from a continuing partnership to a continuing partner—that is, any distribution that is not a liquidating distribution.

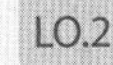

Kate buys a 25% interest in the KLM LLC by contributing $40,000 cash. Her distributive share of the LLC's income that year is $25,000. Assume that the LLC distributes $65,000 ($25,000 share of profits + $40,000 initial capital contribution) to Kate on the last day of the LLC's tax year. Even though Kate's capital account and basis are reduced to $0, the distribution is a current distribution if Kate continues to be a member of the LLC. If the LLC liquidates or if Kate's interest is liquidated, it is a liquidating distribution.

Ordinary Income-Producing (Hot) Assets

LO.2

Describe hot assets and their significance.

One aspect of partnership taxation creates much of the complexity of Subchapter K: the idea that ordinary income treatment must be preserved and allocated to the partner to whom that income accrued. This ordinary income preservation concept applies to all three of the main topics discussed in this chapter: (1) distribution of assets from a partnership, (2) liquidation of a partnership interest under § 736 (discussed in text Section 22-2), and (3) sale of a partnership interest under § 741 (discussed in text Section 22-3).

Under the aggregate theory discussed in Chapter 21, each partner is deemed to own a respective share of each underlying partnership asset.[1] When a transaction would change a partner's interest in the partnership's underlying hot assets, an accounting must be made, and the related ordinary income is recognized by the affected partner. For example, as discussed under Disproportionate Distributions later in the chapter, if a partnership distributes cash to one partner and a hot asset to another, both partners' share of the partnership's ordinary income-producing assets is changed. The actual ramifications are discussed later; at this point, just recognize the definitions.

Hot assets include **unrealized receivables** and **inventory**, as defined in §§ 751(c) and (d). The definitions of these two types of hot assets differ, depending on whether the triggering transaction is a sale or a distribution.

Unrealized receivables Code § 751(c) defines unrealized receivables as any amount not previously reported as income by the partnership under its normal methods of accounting to the extent it would arise from (1) "goods delivered or to be delivered... other than [from disposition of] a capital asset," or (2) "services rendered or to be rendered." So, for example, for either sales or distributions, hot assets include ordinary income potential from cash basis accounts receivable and other sales or services that would result in ordinary income, if recognized (e.g., an installment sale of ordinary income-producing property).

As discussed later, potential depreciation recapture income (and similar items, as defined) is treated as a hot asset for purposes of sales of a partnership interest or normal distributions, but it is not treated as a hot asset for purposes of § 736.

Inventory Code § 751(d) defines inventory so broadly that it basically includes any asset that would yield ordinary income if the asset were sold either *by the partner* or *by the partnership*. It includes traditional inventory [as defined in § 1221(a)(1), or (2)] as well as property that, if sold, would not be treated as a capital or §1231 asset.

For distributions (including distributions under §736), only **substantially appreciated inventory** is considered a hot asset, meaning its fair market value must be more than 120 percent of its basis. However, for sales of a partnership interest, any inventory (whether or not appreciated) is treated as a hot asset; if the inventory (overall) is **appreciated inventory**, the sale results in ordinary income to the selling partner.

Concept Summary 22.1 summarizes some of the items that may be treated as hot assets for each of the three situations in which they might trigger ordinary income. Refer to this chart as you progress through the chapter.

---

[1]§ 751.

Concept Summary 22.1

Hot Assets

- Hot assets are ordinary income-producing assets of the partnership and include inventory and unrealized receivables, as defined.
- Hot assets can trigger ordinary income recognition if an underlying transaction changes a partner's ownership interest in the partnership's hot assets.
- Whether or not an asset is "hot" depends on the underlying transaction.
- For a **distribution**, inventory must be substantially appreciated (value is more than 120% of basis) and "unrealized receivables" includes depreciation recapture.
- For a **§ 736 payment** in liquidation of a partner's interest in a continuing partnership, inventory must (again) be substantially appreciated, but "unrealized receivables" does *not* include depreciation recapture.
- For **sale of a partnership interest,** *any* ordinary income on the partner's share of "inventory" (as broadly defined and whether or not substantially appreciated) must be recognized as ordinary income; "unrealized receivables" includes the potential depreciation recapture.
- The following table summarizes treatment of common partnership assets in each scenario.

Hot asset for purposes of a(n):	Distribution	Liquidation under § 736	Sale of a partnership interest
Cash basis accounts receivable	Yes	Yes	Yes
Accrual method accounts receivable	No (not substantially appreciated)	No (not substantially appreciated)	Yes (broad inventory definition)
Inventory that is 120% appreciated	Yes	Yes	Yes
Inventory that is not appreciated	No	No	Yes
Depreciation recapture	Yes	No	Yes
Land held for investment	No	No	No
Land held as inventory	Only if 120% appreciated	Only if 120% appreciated	Yes

Example 3

IDK, LLC is a consulting business owned equally by Ida, Derek, and Kevin. It owns cash, cash basis accounts receivable, and land. As shown in Concept Summary 22.1, the cash basis accounts receivable are hot assets for all three types of partnership transactions.

If the LLC distributes cash to Ida and equivalent land shares to Derek and Kevin, there is no change in the LLC members' shares of ordinary income-producing property, so normal tax consequences for a distribution will apply. The members' bases will be reduced, and none of the LLC members will recognize ordinary income related to the hot assets.

If, however, IDK distributes a portion of cash basis accounts receivable to Derek and distributes equivalent land values each to Kevin and Ida, the transaction is disproportionate to the LLC members. Kevin and Ida's shares of the partnership's hot assets have decreased, and Derek's share (including receivables received in the distribution) has increased. One or more partners will be required to recognize ordinary income under the hot assets rules.

The amount of recognized ordinary income will be determined by the disproportionate distribution rules discussed in text Section 22-1e.

Proportionate versus Disproportionate Distributions

Each distribution is also classified based on whether it is proportionate or disproportionate. In a **proportionate distribution**, a partner receives the appropriate share of the partnership's hot assets (or no hot assets are distributed). A disproportionate distribution occurs when the distribution increases or decreases the distributee partner's interest in these assets. In Example 3, the distribution of cash and land is proportionate (paragraph 2). The distribution of land and cash basis accounts receivable is disproportionate (paragraph 3).

We'll start by discussing *proportionate* current and liquidating distributions. Then we'll give a brief overview of special rules and disproportionate distributions.

22-1b Proportionate Current Distributions

LO.3

Determine the tax treatment of proportionate current distributions from a partnership to a partner.

In general, neither the partner nor the partnership recognizes gain or loss when a proportionate current distribution occurs.[2] The partner usually takes a carryover basis for the assets distributed.[3] The distributee partner's outside basis is reduced (but not below zero) by the amount of cash and the adjusted basis of property distributed to the partner by the partnership.[4] As the following example illustrates, a distribution does not change a partner's overall economic position.

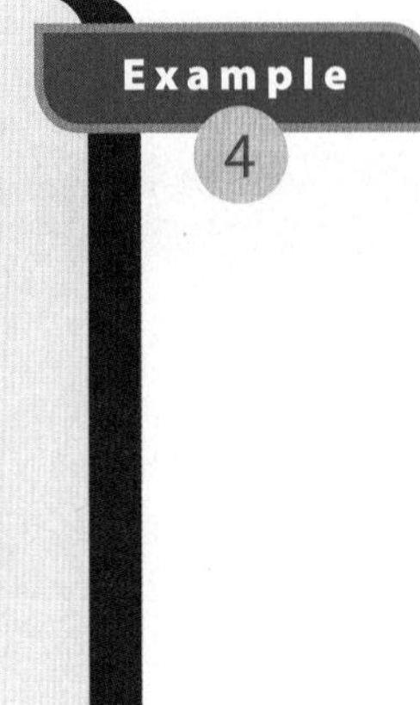

Payton owns a 25% interest in the SP LLC. On the last day of the current tax year, Payton's basis in the LLC interest is $40,000, and its fair market value is $70,000. On that date, the LLC distributes $25,000 of cash plus a parcel of land (adjusted basis to the LLC is $13,000; fair market value is $30,000). The distribution is not taxable to Payton or the LLC. Payton's $40,000 basis is reduced by the $25,000 cash and the LLC's $13,000 basis in the land. After the distribution, Payton's basis in the LLC interest is $2,000, the basis in the land is a carryover basis of $13,000, and Payton has $25,000 of cash—for a before and after total basis of $40,000. Similarly, the fair market value of Payton's remaining interest in the LLC interest is (arguably) reduced to $15,000 [$70,000 – ($25,000 cash + $30,000 value of land)].

If Payton sells the land and remaining LLC interest on the first day of the next year (the day after the distribution), Payton realizes and recognizes gains of $17,000 ($30,000 – $13,000) on the land and $13,000 ($15,000 – $2,000) on the LLC interest. These gains total $30,000, which is the amount of the original deferred gain.

Partnership distributions are governed by the aggregate theory; C corporation distributions are governed by the entity theory. In a C corporation, a distribution from current or accumulated earnings and profits (E & P) is taxable as a dividend to the shareholder, and the corporation does not receive a deduction for the amount distributed. This results in corporate income being subject to double taxation. In a partnership, a partner pays tax when the share of income is earned by the partnership; this income is not taxed again when distributed, so only a single level of taxation occurs.

Cash Distributions

Gain Recognition A proportionate current distribution of cash is taxable to the partner to the extent the distributed cash exceeds the partner's outside basis.[5]

Angelica's basis in her partnership interest is $50,000 on December 31, after accounting for the calendar year LLC's current-year operations. On that date, the LLC distributes $60,000 of cash to Angelica. She recognizes a $10,000 gain from this distribution ($60,000 cash received – $50,000 basis in her LLC interest). Most likely, this gain is taxed as a capital gain.[6]

Liability Reduction Treated as Cash Distribution Recall from text Section 21-4e that the reduction of a partner's share of partnership debt is treated as a distribution of cash from the partnership to the partner. A reduction of a partner's share of partnership debt, then, first reduces the partner's basis in the partnership. Any reduction of a share of debt in excess of a partner's basis in the partnership is taxable to the partner as a gain.

Return to the facts of Example 5, except rather than a cash distribution, assume the LLC repaid all its liabilities. If Angelica's $50,000 basis in her LLC interest included a $60,000 share of the LLC's liabilities, Angelica is treated as receiving a $60,000 cash distribution. The first $50,000 reduces her basis to $0. The last $10,000 creates a taxable gain to Angelica of $10,000.

[2] §§ 731(a) and (b).

[3] § 732(a)(1).

[4] § 733.

[5] § 731(a)(1).

[6] § 731(a). If the partnership holds any "hot assets," however, Angelica may recognize some ordinary income. See the discussion of disproportionate distributions later in this chapter.

Marketable Security Distributions Treated as Cash A distribution of marketable securities also can be treated as a distribution of cash. The rationale for this rule is discussed later in text Section 22-1d.

Loss Recognition Disallowed The distributee partner cannot recognize a loss on a proportionate current distribution of cash or property. This loss is deferred because tax law typically does not permit losses to be recognized until the loss is certain to occur and the amount is known—which does not happen until the final liquidating distribution is received.

Henry has a $50,000 basis in his partnership interest. On December 31, he receives a $10,000 cash distribution, and his partnership interest basis is reduced to $40,000.

The partnership has fallen on hard times, and Henry knows that future distributions will be minimal and the partnership interest has no real value. However, he cannot recognize a current loss even though a loss in the value of the partnership probably exists. The amount of the loss is not fixed and determinable because he still owns the partnership interest.

Property Distributions

In general, a distributee partner does not recognize gain from a property distribution whether the distribution is current or liquidating. If the partnership's basis in the property is greater than the partner's basis in the partnership interest, the distributed asset takes the lower substituted basis. This ensures that the partner does not receive asset basis that is not "paid for."

Amanda holds a $50,000 basis in her LLC interest. The LLC distributes land that had a partnership basis of $60,000 and a fair market value of $100,000. Amanda does not recognize any gain on this distribution because it is a distribution of property, not cash. Amanda takes a substituted basis of $50,000 in the land. Her basis in her LLC interest is reduced by the basis she takes in the asset received, or $50,000. Therefore, Amanda has a $50,000 basis in the land and a $0 basis in her LLC interest, and she recognizes no gain on this distribution.

If she later sells the land for its $100,000 value, she will recognize a $50,000 gain, which includes the partnership's $40,000 inherent gain at the distribution date, plus the $10,000 excess value of the land over Amanda's basis in the partnership interest.

There are several exceptions to the general "no gain or loss" rules for property distributions. This discussion is deferred until text Section 22-1d.

Ordering Rules

When multiple properties are distributed, the assets are deemed distributed in the following order.

- Step 1. Cash is distributed first.
- Step 2. Unrealized receivables and inventory ("hot assets") are distributed second.
- Step 3. All other assets are distributed last.

Basis in Distributed Property and Partnership Interest (Steps 2 and 3) In a current distribution, the partner cannot **step up** (increase) the basis in distributed property beyond the partnership's basis. This applies to distributions of both hot assets and other assets. As illustrated in Example 8, however, a current distribution *can* result in a **step down** (reduction to the property's basis). These potential decreases to basis are determined at each step of the asset distribution. For example, after a cash distribution (step 1), the partner's basis in the interest is recomputed. Then we can determine the effect of a distribution of unrealized receivables or inventory (step 2). If the remaining outside basis at the end of any step is insufficient to cover the entire inside basis of the assets in the next step, the basis in the remaining assets (step 3) is stepped down to equal the partner's remaining basis in the partnership interest.[7]

As shown in Concept Summary 22.1, hot assets, for purposes of the distribution rules, include cash basis accounts receivable and depreciation recapture (unrealized receivables) and substantially appreciated inventory (which might include land held as inventory or other substantially appreciated assets that are not capital or § 1231 assets). Recall that in this discussion, we are talking about distributions that are proportionate with respect to hot assets, so the distribution would not trigger ordinary income recognition by either the partner or the partnership.

Effect of Ordering Rules

Lindsey holds a $48,000 basis in her partnership interest. On October 10, Lindsey receives a proportionate current distribution from the partnership of (1) cash of $12,000, (2) cash basis receivables (inside basis $0; fair market value $10,000), and (3) land (inside basis and fair market value $60,000). Lindsey has a realized gain of $34,000 [$12,000 + $10,000 + $60,000 (values) − $48,000 (basis)].

However, none of that gain is recognized yet. The cash distribution (step 1) is considered first. Since the cash distributed does not exceed Lindsey's basis in the partnership interest before the distribution ($12,000 cash < $48,000 basis in interest), no gain is currently recognized on the proportionate current distribution. The distributed cash reduces her basis in the partnership interest to $36,000 ($48,000 − $12,000). The receivables (step 2) are distributed next, taking a $0 carryover basis to Lindsey. Her partnership basis remains $36,000. The land is distributed last, (step 3). Lindsey's remaining $36,000 basis in the partnership interest is less than the partnership's basis in the land ($60,000), so Lindsey takes a substituted basis of $36,000 in the land and reduces the basis for her partnership interest to $0.

Assume the same facts as in Example 9 and that Lindsey sells the parcel of land early the following year for its fair market value of $60,000. She also collects $10,000 from the cash basis receivables. Now she recognizes all of the previously deferred $34,000 gain ($70,000 amount realized and collected − $36,000 basis for the land − $0 basis for the receivables).

In Examples 9 and 10, although Lindsey does not recognize any of the gain she realizes from the distribution, she has a zero outside basis for her partnership interest. If the partnership generates net losses in the following year, she will not be able to deduct them.

When more than one asset in a particular class is distributed, special rules apply, as discussed in text Section 22-1c.

Ethics & Equity **Arranging Tax-Advantaged Distributions**

The Sparrow Partnership plans to distribute $200,000 cash to its partners at the end of the year. Marjorie is a 40 percent partner and would receive $80,000. Her basis in the partnership is only $10,000, however, so she would be required to recognize a $70,000 gain if she received a cash distribution. She has asked the partnership instead to purchase a parcel of land that she has found, on which she will build her retirement residence. The partnership then will distribute that land to her. Under the partnership distribution rules, Marjorie would take a $10,000 basis in land worth $80,000. Her basis in the partnership would be reduced to $0, and the $70,000 gain is deferred. Discuss whether this is an appropriate result.

[7] § 732.

Concept Summary 22.2 reviews the general rules that apply to proportionate current partnership distributions.

Concept Summary 22.2

Proportionate Current Distributions (General Rules)

Gains and Losses

- Generally, neither the distributee partner nor the partnership recognizes any gain or loss on a proportionate current distribution of cash or property.
- Exception: Gain is recognized if *cash* (and deemed cash) distributions exceed the distributee partner's basis.

Basis in Partnership Interest and Property Received

- The partner's basis in the partnership interest is reduced by the partner's basis in distributed property received.
- General rule: Partner's basis in distributed property equals partnership's basis before distribution (carryover basis).
- Exception: Where the partner's *outside* basis is less than the partnership's *inside* (property) basis, partner's *outside* basis is assigned to distributed property (substituted basis; basis in the property is reduced in the partner's hands).

Other Issues

- If the partner recognizes gain on a *proportionate* current distribution, the gain is a capital gain.
- Neither the partner nor the partnership recognizes loss on a *proportionate* current distribution of cash or property.

Proportionate Current Distribution Inputs and Calculations

Input the following information and complete the Calculations chart to determine the partner's (1) gain or loss and (2) basis in distributed property on a proportionate current distribution.

Inputs

Line 1 below	Partner's outside basis before distribution.	______
Line 2 below	*Step 1.* Cash and deemed cash distributed.	______
Line 5 below	*Step 2.* Partnership's basis in distributed hot assets.	______
Line 8 below	*Step 3.* Partnership's basis in other distributed property.	______

Calculations

1. Partner's outside basis (input above).	______
2. Step 1. Cash and deemed cash distributed (input above).	______
3. **Gain recognized by partner (excess of line 2 over line 1, if any).**	______
4. Partner's remaining outside basis (line 1 − line 2). If less than $0, enter $0.	______
5. Step 2. Partnership's basis in distributed hot assets (input above).	______
6. **Partner's basis in distributed hot assets (lesser of line 4 or line 5).**	______
7. Partner's remaining outside basis (line 4 − line 6). Cannot be < $0.	______
8. Step 3. Partnership's basis in other distributed property (input above).	______
9. **Partner's basis in other distributed property (lesser of line 7 or line 8).**	______
10. Partner's remaining outside basis (line 7 − line 9). Cannot be < $0.	______

LO.4

Determine the tax treatment of proportionate distributions that liquidate a partnership.

22-1c Proportionate Liquidating Distributions

Proportionate liquidating distributions consist of a single distribution or a series of distributions that result in the termination of the partner's entire interest in the partnership. This section examines the rules for liquidating distributions that arise when the partnership itself is liquidating. If the partnership continues in existence but the partner's interest is liquidated, the rules of § 736 (discussed in text Section 22-2) apply.

No Partnership Level Gain or Loss

In a proportionate liquidating distribution where the partnership liquidates, the partnership does not recognize either gain or loss. In contrast, if a corporation distributes property in a complete liquidation, the corporation recognizes gain or loss as if it sold all of its property at fair market value. This is another example of how the aggregate theory applies to partnerships and the entity theory applies to corporations.

Gain Recognition and Ordering Rules

When a partnership liquidates, the liquidating distributions to a partner usually consist of an interest in several or all of the partnership's assets. The ordering rules parallel those for current distributions except that the partner's *entire* basis in the partnership interest is allocated to the assets received in the liquidating distribution, *unless* the partner is required to recognize a loss (see the discussion that follows).

The general ordering and gain recognition rules for a proportionate liquidating distribution are summarized as follows. The first two rules are similar to the previous discussion.

- Step 1. Cash is distributed first. As with a proportionate current distribution, the cash distribution results in a capital gain if the amount distributed exceeds the partner's basis in the partnership interest. The cash distributed (including "deemed cash," such as relief of the partner's share of partnership debt) reduces the liquidated partner's outside basis dollar for dollar, except that the partner's basis cannot be reduced below zero.
- Step 2. Unrealized receivables and inventory are distributed second. As with proportionate nonliquidating distributions, these assets take a basis equal to the lesser of the *partnership's* inside basis in those assets or the *partner's* remaining outside basis. The partner's outside basis is reduced by the amount of basis assigned to these ordinary income-producing assets.
- Step 3. Here's where proportionate liquidating and nonliquidating distributions differ: for a liquidating distribution, if the liquidating partner has any remaining outside basis (after the step 2 distribution), the entire remaining basis is allocated to the assets received in step 3.[8]

Example 11

When Tara's basis in her LLC interest is $70,000, she receives a proportionate liquidating distribution of cash of $15,000 (step 1), inventory (basis to LLC $20,000; fair market value $30,000) (step 2), and land (basis to LLC $8,000; fair market value $12,000) (step 3). The distribution liquidates both the LLC and Tara's entire LLC interest.

Tara recognizes no gain or loss. Tara's $70,000 basis is reduced to $55,000 by the $15,000 cash received (step 1). The inventory (step 2) takes a basis to Tara of $20,000 and reduces her basis in the LLC interest to $35,000. The land (step 3) absorbs Tara's remaining LLC basis of $35,000, even though the value of the land is only $12,000.

Multiple Properties in an Asset Class

When more than one asset in a particular class is distributed in either a proportionate current distribution or a proportionate liquidating distribution, special rules may apply. If a step-*down* is needed (i.e., the partner's remaining basis for the partnership interest is *less than* the partnership's basis for the distributed assets in the particular class), the partner's basis for each distributed asset is proportionately reduced so as to reduce the differences between each asset's basis and its fair market value.

[8] §§ 731 and 732.

If, however, in a liquidating distribution, a step-*up* is needed (i.e., the partner's remaining basis for the partnership interest is *greater than* the partnership's basis for the distributed assets in the "other assets" class), the partner's basis for the assets in the class is determined such that the basis amounts ultimately are in proportion to the fair market values of the distributed assets in that class.

Example 12

Assume the same facts as in Example 11, except that Tara receives two parcels of land instead of one. The LLC's basis for the parcels is $2,000 for Parcel 1 and $6,000 for Parcel 2. Each parcel has a fair market value of $6,000.

Tara again takes a $15,000 basis for the cash and a $20,000 carryover basis for the inventory. Now Tara has a $35,000 remaining basis that must be allocated to the two parcels of land (step 3). The partnership's inside basis for the land of $8,000 is stepped up by $27,000.

Without going through the detailed rules, the remaining $35,000 basis is allocated $17,500 to each parcel of land. In this specific situation, the step-up allocation and ending basis follows the intuitive result because the properties' fair market values are equal.

Loss Recognition

The distributee partner recognizes a *loss* on a liquidating distribution *only if both* of the following are true:

1. The partner receives *only* cash, unrealized receivables, or inventory. The word *only* is important. A distribution of any other property precludes recognition of the loss.
2. The partner's outside basis exceeds the partnership's inside basis for the distributed cash and hot assets.

The basis of hot assets cannot be increased. Therefore, the step 2 assets take a carryover basis, and the partner claims a loss for any remaining basis in the partnership interest.[9]

Liquidating Distributions with Potential Losses

When Ramon's outside basis is $40,000, he receives a liquidating distribution of $7,000 cash and a proportionate share of inventory having a partnership basis of $3,000 and a fair market value of $10,000. Ramon is not allowed to "step up" the basis in the inventory, so it is allocated a $3,000 carryover basis. Ramon's unutilized outside basis is $30,000 ($40,000 − $7,000 − $3,000). Because he received a liquidating distribution of *only* cash and inventory, he recognizes a capital loss of $30,000 on the liquidation.

Example 14

Assume the same facts as in Example 13, except that in addition to the cash and inventory, Ramon receives an antique desk he used while working at the partnership. The desk originally was purchased at a flea market for $100. Later, it was discovered that the desk was valued at $2,000, but because the desk was held as a § 1231 asset rather than an investment, it was depreciable. By the time the partnership liquidated, the desk was fully depreciated, with a basis of $0 and potential depreciation recapture (a "hot asset" for distribution purposes) of $100.

The $100 of potential depreciation recapture (with a $0 basis) is added to the hot assets in step 2. Therefore, Ramon's step 2 assets include inventory (basis $3,000, value $10,000) and depreciation recapture (basis $0, value $100).

As with the previous example, Ramon's basis is $30,000 after the step 2 allocation. Because the desk is not cash, an unrealized receivable, or inventory, he cannot recognize a loss. Therefore, Ramon's remaining basis of $30,000 in his partnership interest is allocated to the desk.

[9] § 731(a)(2).

What can Ramon do with a $30,000 antique desk (valued at $2,000)? If he continues to use it in a trade or business, he can depreciate it. Once he has established his business use of the desk, he could sell it and recognize a large § 1231 loss, which would be treated as an ordinary loss if it is the only § 1231 loss of Ramon's tax year. (Because depreciation recapture is not recognized on a loss, the $100 of potential ordinary income from prior depreciation deductions simply disappears.)

If the antique desk, however, is held as an investment asset, it will generate a $28,000 *capital* loss if it is sold at its $2,000 value. With proper planning, no liquidated partner should be forced to recognize a capital loss instead of an ordinary loss.

If the withdrawing partner later sells distributed inventory, gain on the sale is ordinary income unless the sale occurs more than five years after the distribution.[10] The withdrawing partner's holding period for all other property received in a liquidating distribution includes the partnership's related holding period.

Concept Summary 22.3 outlines the general rules that apply to proportionate liquidating partnership distributions.

22-1d Property Distributions with Special Tax Treatment

LO.5

Describe the rules that apply to property distributions with special tax treatment.

This section discusses exceptions in which a *proportionate* distribution, either liquidating or nonliquidating, may result in gain to the partner.

Disguised Sales

As discussed in text Section 21-2b, a disguised sale is a transaction in which a partner contributes appreciated property to a partnership and, soon thereafter, receives a distribution of cash or property from the partnership. If the IRS determines that the payment is part of a "purchase" of the property, the partner must report a gain on the deemed sale, and the partnership takes a cost basis in the "purchased" property.

Marketable Securities

A portion of a marketable security distribution might be treated as a cash distribution, resulting in a gain to the distributee partner if the partnership's basis in the security is greater than the partner's basis in the partnership interest.[11]

The primary purpose of this rule is to stop the tax avoidance that otherwise would occur if a partnership purchased marketable securities with the intent of immediately distributing them to the partner. As the "Ethics & Equity" feature earlier in this chapter indicated, a partnership can purchase property desired by a partner, distribute that property to the partner, and allow the partner to defer tax on any appreciation inherent in the partnership interest. Because of the marketable security rule, the partner and partnership cannot arrange such a transaction with marketable securities.

However, if the securities are *appreciated*, they probably have been held by the partnership for some time and, therefore, were not acquired in anticipation of being distributed to a partner. Therefore, under a complex set of rules, a portion of the marketable security value is reclassified as a property distribution (no gain) rather than a cash distribution (potential gain).

Unless otherwise indicated, the remaining examples in this chapter assume that the partnership is not distributing marketable securities.

[10] § 735(a)(2).

[11] § 731(c).

Concept Summary 22.3

Proportionate Liquidating Distributions When the Partnership Also Liquidates (General Rules)

Gains and Losses

- Generally, neither the partner nor the partnership recognizes gain or loss when a partnership liquidates with a proportionate distribution of hot assets. This general rule applies to both cash and property distributions.
- Exception: Gain is recognized if cash (and deemed cash) distributions exceed the distributee partner's basis.
- Exception: A partner recognizes loss when (a) the partner receives only cash, unrealized receivables, or inventory and (b) the partner's outside basis is greater than the partnership's inside basis of the assets distributed.

Basis in Property Received

- A partner's basis in distributed assets must be determined in a certain order. Cash is distributed first, inventory and unrealized receivables second, and all other assets last.
- Assets in step 3 take a substituted basis equal to the distributee partner's remaining outside basis.

Other Issues

- For a *proportionate* liquidating distribution, any gain or loss recognized by the partner is usually capital in nature.

Proportionate Liquidating Distribution Inputs and Calculations

Input the following information and complete the Calculations chart to determine the partner's (1) gain or loss and (2) basis in distributed property on a proportionate liquidating distribution.

Inputs

Line 1 below	Partner's outside basis before distribution.	
Line 2 below	Step 1. Cash and deemed cash distributed.	
Line 5 below	Step 2. Partnership's basis in distributed hot assets.	
Line 8 below	Step 3. Partnership's basis in other distributed property (N/A if no step 3 property was distributed).	

Calculations

1. Partner's outside basis (input above).	
2. Step 1. Cash and deemed cash distributed (input above).	
3. **Gain recognized by partner (excess of line 2 over line 1, if any).**	
4. Partner's remaining outside basis (line 1 − line 2). If less than \$0, enter \$0.	
5. Step 2. Partnership's basis in distributed hot assets (input above).	
6. **Partner's basis in distributed hot assets (lesser of line 4 or line 5).**	
7. Partner's remaining outside basis (line 4 − line 6). Cannot be < \$0.	
8. Step 3. Partnership's basis in other distributed property (input above).	
9. **Partner's basis in other distributed property (If the line 8 input is \$0 or positive, enter the amount from line 7; if it is "N/A," enter \$0).**	
10. **Loss recognized by partner (If the line 8 input is "N/A," enter amount from line 7; otherwise, enter \$0).**	
11. Partner's remaining outside basis. Check: line 7 − line 9 − line 10 = \$0.	\$0

Precontribution Gain

Taxable gains may arise on a distribution of property to a partner where precontribution (built-in) gains exist. Specifically, if a partner contributes appreciated property to a partnership, the contributing partner recognizes gain in two situations.

1. The contributed appreciated property is distributed to another partner within seven years of the contribution date.[12]
2. The partnership distributes *any* property other than cash to a contributing partner within seven years after that partner contributed appreciated property to the partnership.[13]

[12]§ 704(c)(1)(B).

[13]§ 737.

These situations result in gain recognition to the contributing partner, as well as adjustments to that partner's basis in the partnership interest and/or the basis in the precontribution gain property.

Example 15

In 2023, Rick contributes nondepreciable property with an adjusted basis of $10,000 and a fair market value of $40,000 to the RTCO Partnership in exchange for a one-fourth interest in profits and capital. In 2024, when the property's fair market value is $50,000, the partnership distributes the property to Tom, another one-fourth partner. This is situation 1 above.

Because the precontribution gain property [$30,000 potential gain ($40,000 value at contribution date − $10,000 basis)] was contributed to the partnership less than seven years before it was distributed to another partner, the built-in gain on the property is taxable to Rick. Therefore, in 2024, when the property is distributed to Tom, *Rick* must pay tax on the $30,000 built-in gain. Rick increases his basis in his partnership interest by the $30,000 gain recognized, and Tom increases his basis in the property received by $30,000.

Note that if the partnership were to sell the property to an unrelated third party for $40,000 in 2024, the result would be the same for Rick. Recognized built-in gains are allocated to the partner who contributed the property, and the partner's outside basis is increased accordingly. See text Section 21-4b.

Situation 2 would arise if a different property were distributed to Rick (the contributing partner) within seven years after the property was contributed. The tax calculations would be slightly different. Rick's gain would be the lesser of (1) his (remaining) precontribution gain ($30,000) or (2) the excess of the property's fair market value over Rick's basis in the partnership. Exact calculations of Rick's basis in the property and the remaining basis in the partnership interest are beyond the scope of this text.

22-1e **Disproportionate Distributions**

LO.6

Explain the general concepts governing tax treatment of disproportionate distributions.

Disproportionate distributions are another exception to the general nonrecognition rules for partnership distributions. A disproportionate distribution occurs when a partnership distributes cash or property to a partner, and that distribution increases or decreases the distributee partner's proportionate interest in hot assets. For example, a distribution is disproportionate if a partnership distributes cash to one partner and hot assets to another partner. (Note that the partnership *can* distribute cash and *nonhot* assets at the same time to different partners as a proportionate distribution. For example, in a two-person partnership, Partner A could receive $10,000 cash and Partner B could receive $10,000 of investment property and the normal proportionate distribution rules would apply.)

As shown in Concept Summary 22.1, for the disproportionate distribution rules, hot assets include unrealized receivables and substantially appreciated inventory. Substantially appreciated inventory is inventory that has a fair market value in excess of 120 percent of the partnership's adjusted basis for the inventory.[14]

The taxation of disproportionate distributions is based on the aggregate theory of taxation. Each partner is deemed to own a proportionate share of the underlying assets of the partnership, and each partner is responsible for recognizing and reporting the proportionate share of ordinary income related to substantially appreciated inventory and cash basis receivables.

Code § 751(b) maintains each partner's proportionate share of ordinary income by recasting any transaction in which a disproportionate distribution of hot assets is made. If the distributee partner receives less than a proportionate share of hot assets, the transaction is treated as if two separate events occurred: (1) the partnership made a distribution of some of the hot assets to the distributee partner, and (2) that partner immediately sold these hot assets back to the partnership. The partner recognizes ordinary income on the sale of the hot assets, and the partnership takes a cost basis for the hot assets purchased.

[14] § 751(b)(3).

Example 16

The balance sheet of the AB LLP is as follows on December 31 of the current tax year.

	Basis	FMV		Basis	FMV
Cash	$26,000	$26,000	Abby, capital	$13,000	$26,000
Unrealized receivables	-0-	26,000	Baahir, capital	13,000	26,000
Total	$26,000	$52,000	Total	$26,000	$52,000

Abby and Baahir are equal partners in the partnership. The partnership makes a liquidating distribution of the unrealized receivables to Abby and the cash to Baahir. Because the unrealized receivables are a hot asset, Abby has received more than her proportionate share of the hot asset, and Baahir has received less than his proportionate share. Code § 751 recasts the transaction into two separate events. First, Baahir is deemed to receive a current distribution of his 50% share of hot assets (basis $0; fair market value $13,000), which he then immediately sells back to the partnership for $13,000 of the cash. Baahir recognizes $13,000 ordinary income on the sale, and the partnership takes a $13,000 basis in the receivables purchased. The remaining $13,000 cash received by Baahir reduces his adjusted basis for his partnership interest to $0 ($13,000 cash distributed − $13,000 adjusted basis).

Abby receives receivables of $26,000 which are composed of her share of the partnership's unrealized receivables (basis $0; fair market value $13,000) and the receivables the partnership purchased from Baahir (basis $13,000; fair market value $13,000). She takes a substituted basis of $13,000 in the receivables and reduces her adjusted basis for her partnership interest to $0. When she collects all $26,000 of the receivables, she will recognize $13,000 of ordinary income ($26,000 cash collected − $13,000 basis for receivables).

Although the mechanical rules of § 751(b) are complicated, the application of the rules in this example has ensured that each partner eventually recognizes their $13,000 share of ordinary income. Baahir holds the cash and recognizes his share of the income at the time the partnership is liquidated. Abby recognizes her share of the income when she collects the unrealized receivables.

Although most of the problems and examples in Chapters 21 and 22 involve proportionate distributions, be aware that disproportionate distributions occur frequently in practice. The calculation of ordinary income in disproportionate distributions can become extremely complex. These more difficult calculations are not discussed in this text.

LO.7

Determine the tax treatment under § 736 of payments from a partnership to a retiring or deceased partner.

22-2 Section 736—Liquidating Distributions to Retiring or Deceased Partners

In text Sections 22-2, 22-3, and 22-4, we'll discuss special situations in which a partner leaves the partnership and the partnership (or a successor entity) continues in existence. Section 22-2 covers the situation where a partnership "redeems" the partner's interest. Section 22-3 covers the sale of a partnership interest between a partner and a third party. Section 22-4 covers special situations.

Code § 736 applies when a partner's interest is liquidated by an ongoing partnership. For example, in *The Big Picture* at the beginning of the chapter, one alternative is for Beachside LLC to buy out Kyler's and Maria's LLC interests. Code § 736 also applies when the partnership must buy out the interest of a successor who inherited an interest from a deceased partner.[15]

For both situations, the buy-out by the partnership is similar in concept to the redemption of a corporate shareholder's stock by the corporation. See text Section 19-1.

22-2a General Partners in Service-Providing Partnerships

Code § 736 generally is most relevant when the retiring or deceased partner was treated as a *general* partner in a *service-providing* partnership.

[15]A successor typically is the estate of the deceased or the party who inherits the decedent's interest.

- You'll see § 736 when the deceased or retiring partner was a *general* partner or a partner *treated* as a general partner. For example, a member of an LLP might be treated as a general partner if that partner has the right, under the partnership agreement, to enter contractual relationships on behalf of the LLP.
- The partnership must also be "service providing," which happens if "capital is *not* a material income-producing factor for the partnership."[16] For our purposes, we'll label partnerships as either "service providing" or "capital intensive." (Note that an LLP would likely be "service providing" and an LLC more likely is "capital intensive.")
- The deceased or retiring partner *for purposes of text Section 22-2a* will generally be a person—an individual taxpayer—rather than a corporation, trust, or other entity.[17]

From a practical standpoint, if the service-providing partnership redeems the individual general partner's or successor's interest, the two parties (partner and partnership) negotiate a buyout package. The payments under the buyout package are classified as either § 736(a) income payments or § 736(b) property payments. It is critical to note that § 736 only *classifies* the payments between these two categories. Other rules determine the *tax effects* of that classification.

For our purposes, *assume that all payments from the partnership are in* ***cash***. However, you should realize that the payments could be in the form of cash and/or other property, in which case the analysis can become sticky. We'll discuss specific tax treatment in greater detail later, but for now, let's look at income and property payments.

Income Payments

"Income" payments under § 736(a) typically represent compensation for the partner's share of the partnership's going-concern value. Code § 736(a) payments result (generally) in a deduction to the partnership and ordinary income to the deceased or retiring partner.

Payments by a service-providing partnership to a general partner are § 736(a) income payments if they fall into the following categories:

- Payments for the partner's pro rata share of unrealized receivables. For purposes of this rule, unrealized receivables are as defined previously for other distributions, except that they do *not* include potential depreciation recapture (see Concept Summary 22.1).
- Payments for the partner's pro rata share of partnership goodwill *if* the payment is "unstated" (not provided in the partnership agreement). If the payment is "stated" (outlined in the partnership agreement), it is a § 736(b) payment.
- Certain annuities and lump-sum payments to the partner.

Property Payments

Any payments that are not § 736(a) payments are treated as § 736(b) property payments. These payments are just what they sound like: the partnership pays the retiring partner for the value of the partnership's underlying assets.

Code § 736(b) payments result in no deduction to the partnership; the partner might have a capital gain or loss and/or ordinary income to the extent the § 736(b) payment relates to underlying hot assets. Code § 736(b) payments, therefore, include payments to the partner for the partnership's:

- Fixed assets and equipment.
- Inventory, whether or not it is classified as a hot asset.
- Accrual basis accounts receivable.
- Goodwill, if it is stated in the partnership agreement.

---

[16] Capital is a material income-producing factor if a partnership derives a substantial portion of its gross income from the use of capital, such as inventories or investments in plant, machinery, or equipment. Ordinarily, capital is not a material income-producing factor if the partnership's income consists principally of fees, commissions, or other compensation for personal services performed by partners or employees.

[17] Although not specifically required in the Code or Regulations, this convention makes sense given that § 736(a) payments (discussed next) must be made to a service-providing general partner.

22-2b Limited Partners or Capital-Intensive Partnerships

In contrast, if the payment is from a *capital-intensive* partnership to *any* partner or from a *service-providing* partnership to a partner treated as a *limited partner*, the entire payment is treated as a § 736(b) property payment, again, with no deduction to the partnership and capital/ordinary gain or loss to the partner.

Similarly, if the redeemed partner is any entity other than an individual taxpayer, the entire payment generally is a § 736(b) payment. For example, if a joint venture with three corporate partners redeems the interest of one of the partners, the entire liquidation payment probably is a § 736(b) property payment because the partnership is not likely to be considered a service-providing entity.

Example 17

The ABC LLP reports the following balance sheet at the end of the current tax year. ABC pays partner Anne $32,000 cash in exchange for her interest in the LLC. None of the cash is stated in the partnership agreement to be in exchange for partnership goodwill.

	Basis	FMV		Basis	FMV
Cash	$36,000	$36,000	Anne, capital	$15,000	$27,000
Unrealized receivables	-0-	18,000	Bonnie, capital	15,000	27,000
Land	9,000	27,000	Cindy, capital	15,000	27,000
Total	$45,000	$81,000	Total	$45,000	$81,000

General partner in a service-providing partnership. Anne is an active (i.e., "general") partner retiring from the service-providing partnership. Because the fair market value of Anne's share of the three recorded assets is only $27,000 (⅓ × $81,000), the $5,000 excess payment ($32,000 − $27,000) is for unstated goodwill.

The payment Anne receives for her interest in the cash and land is a § 736(b) property payment. This payment is $21,000, consisting of $12,000 paid for the cash (⅓ × $36,000 FMV) and $9,000 paid for Anne's share of the fair market value of the land (⅓ × $27,000 FMV).

The remaining $11,000 distribution [$32,000 total − $21,000 § 736(b) payment] is a § 736(a) payment, consisting of the $6,000 Anne receives for her share of the LLP's unrealized receivables, and the $5,000 payment for unstated goodwill.

Limited partner in any partnership or any partner in a capital-intensive partnership. If, instead, Anne was a limited partner in (service-providing) ABC LLP, the entire cash payment of $32,000 would be treated as a § 736(b) property payment.

22-2c Tax Treatment of § 736 Payments

Again, § 736 only *classifies* the liquidation payment from the partnership; other provisions govern the *tax treatment*.

Tax Treatment of § 736(b) Property Payments

Code § 736(b) property payments (including "stated" goodwill) may *not* be deducted by the *partnership*. Code § 736(b) payments to the partner for "nonhot" assets are treated first as a return of the partner's outside basis in the partnership.[18] Once the entire basis is returned, any additional amounts are taxed to the partner as capital gain. If the cash distributions are not sufficient to return the partner's entire outside basis, the shortfall is treated by the partner as a capital loss.[19]

Example 18

In Example 17, if Anne is a general partner in a service-providing partnership, the property payment of $21,000 cash includes amounts for Anne's share of land and cash only, neither of which is a hot asset.

- If Anne's outside basis is $15,000, she recognizes capital gain of $6,000 {($12,000 + $9,000) [§ 736(b) payment] − $15,000 (basis)} on the distribution.
- If Anne's outside basis is $25,000 (e.g., because when the partnership was formed, she contributed property with a higher basis than her proportionate share), she recognizes a $4,000 capital loss on the distribution [($12,000 + $9,000) − $25,000].
- The partnership cannot deduct any part of the $21,000 property payment.

[18] §§ 736(b) and 731(a)(1).

[19] § 731(a)(2).

As a corollary (and an easy-to-follow general rule), if the partnership has *no* "hot assets," and if the liquidation payment is in cash (as assumed for our purposes), the partner's treatment of § 736(b) payments follows the proportionate liquidating distribution rules discussed in text Section 22-1c: the distribution results in a capital gain to the partner to the extent it exceeds the partner's basis and a capital loss to the extent it is less than the partner's basis.

To keep things simpler, we won't discuss situations where the partnership has hot assets treated as § 736(b) payments. You can probably see, though, that a cash payment under § 736(b) in exchange for a retiring partner's share of hot assets would be a disproportionate distribution as shown in Example 16.

Tax Treatment of § 736(a) Income Payments

All payments that are not § 736(b) payments are § 736(a) payments. Code § 736(a) income payments are treated either as (1) a partner's distributive share of partnership income or (2) a guaranteed payment to the retiring partner.

Code § 736(a) income payments are treated as a distributive share of partnership income (i.e., an allocation of the partnership's income for the year) if the partnership agreement or buy-out agreement states that they are determined by reference to the total amount of partnership income. For example, if the § 736(a) payment must equal 10 percent of ordinary income (or capital gain), then 10 percent of the partnership's total ordinary income (or capital gain) is allocated to the retiring partner, and the remaining 90 percent is allocated to the partners remaining in the partnership. These amounts are taxed to the retiring partner according to their character to the partnership (as shown on the partner's Schedule K–1).[20] These payments simply reduce the amount of income/gain of a specific character that is allocated to the remaining partners.[21]

The payments treated as guaranteed payments are fully taxable as ordinary income to the distributee partner and are fully deductible by the continuing partnership. See text Sections 21-3b and 21-4a. [Note that the partner's income *character* might change depending on whether the payments are treated as guaranteed payments or distributive share/special allocations, but the total *amount* of the § 736(a) payment would not change.] The examples in this chapter are structured such that all § 736(a) payments are treated as guaranteed payments and result in an ordinary deduction to the partnership and ordinary income to the retiring partner.

Example 19

Continue with the same facts as in Example 17 where the LLP is service-oriented and Anne is an active general partner. Anne's § 736(a) payment is $11,000, consisting of a $6,000 cash payment ($18,000 × ⅓) for Anne's pro rata share of the unrealized receivables and the $5,000 payment for unstated goodwill.

Because the $11,000 § 736(a) income payment is not determined by reference to partnership income, the payment is classified as a guaranteed payment. It is included as ordinary income on Anne's tax return and is deductible by the partnership.

Exhibit 22.1 summarizes the taxation results of Examples 17 through 19 for situations where capital is or is not a material income-producing factor (or where the partner is a limited partner). In both cases, assume that Anne's basis in her partnership interest was $15,000 before the distribution.

Conceptually, you should recognize that the characterization under § 736 does not change the partner's overall gain: whether Anne was a general or limited partner (or whether the partnership was service-oriented or capital-intensive), Anne would recognize a total gain of $17,000. This is appropriate because she receives $32,000 cash against a basis of $15,000. However, the character of Anne's income (ordinary income or capital gain/loss) could differ as a result of the characterization of goodwill.

From the partnership's perspective, the classification will determine whether it can deduct any portion of the payment to the retiring partner. The partnership can deduct § 736(a) payments for unstated goodwill or hot assets if the partnership is

---

[20] § 702(b).

[21] Reg. § 1.736–1(a)(4).

Exhibit 22.1 Summary of Tax Results—Examples 17 to 19

	Tax Character to Anne	Deduction to ABC
General partner in service-oriented partnership.		
§ 736(b) (Example 18)	$ 6,000 capital gain	None
§ 736(a) (Example 19)	11,000 ordinary income	$11,000 deduction
Total gain	$17,000	

Limited partner OR capital-intensive partnership. Entire payment is a § 736(b) payment. The partnership cannot deduct the payment. Anne would have a total gain of $17,000 ($32,000 cash received in exchange for partnership interest basis of $15,000). A portion of the gain ($6,000) would be treated as ordinary income under the disproportionate distribution rules. (The partnership would be deemed to distribute the $6,000 share of receivables to Anne and then buy them back for cash.) The remaining $11,000 gain ($17,000 total – $6,000 ordinary income) would be a capital gain.

service-oriented and the payment is to a general partner. It cannot deduct those payments if the goodwill payment is stated in the partnership agreement *or* if the partner is limited *or* the partnership is capital-intensive.

The Big Picture

Example 20

Return to the facts of *The Big Picture* on p. 22-1. Assume that the members of Beachside Properties LLC decide to admit new partners for $24,500,000 and use $9,500,000 of the cash to redeem the interests of Kyler and Maria.

Because the LLC itself is not liquidating, the distribution to Kyler and Maria is classified under § 736. The current balance sheet for Beachside Properties LLC is as follows.

	Basis	Fair Market Value
Cash	$1,000,000	$ 1,000,000
Accounts receivable and inventory	500,000	1,000,000
Land	500,000	6,000,000
Buildings and other § 1231 property	2,000,000	3,000,000
Goodwill	–0–	1,000,000
Total assets	$4,000,000	$12,000,000
Debt	$2,000,000	$ 2,000,000
Capital, Josh	300,000*	500,000
Capital, Kyler	400,000*	4,750,000
Capital, Maria	1,300,000*	4,750,000
Net assets	$4,000,000	$12,000,000

*The LLC members' tax basis capital accounts correspond to their bases, excluding their shares of the LLC's liabilities. The members' bases are not proportionate because the bases of the contributed properties (and Josh's services) were not proportionate and because distributions over time have not always been proportionate.

Capital is a "material income-producing factor" for Beachside Properties LLC. Therefore, in this redemption scenario, the entire $9,500,000 distribution from the LLC to Kyler and Maria is a § 736(b) payment for their interests in the partnership's property regardless of whether Kyler and Maria are "active" members of the LLC and whether the LLC's operating agreement provides for partnership goodwill payments. Kyler and Maria recognize a gain to the extent that this cash distribution (including forgiveness of their shares of the LLC's debt) exceeds their bases in the LLC interests.

Because Kyler and Maria receive cash in lieu of their shares of the LLC's unrealized receivables (including potential depreciation recapture) and inventory, this is a disproportionate distribution. They recognize ordinary income to the extent that their gain relates to these receivables and inventory. The remaining gain is a capital gain.

Because there are no § 736(a) payments, the LLC cannot claim any deductions. Absent a § 754 election (discussed later), the basis of the LLC's property is not affected.

Concept Summary 22.4 reviews the rules for liquidating distributions under § 736.

Concept Summary 22.4

Liquidating Distributions of Cash When the Partnership Continues

1. Payments made by an ongoing partnership to a liquidating partner are classified as § 736(a) income payments or as § 736(b) property payments.
2. Code § 736(b) property payments are payments for the liquidated partner's share of partnership assets.
3. Code § 736(a) classification is required for certain payments if the partnership is a service provider and the partner is a general partner. These payments include amounts paid for the liquidated partner's share of certain unrealized receivables, certain goodwill that is not stated in the partnership agreement, and certain annuity payments.
4. Code § 736(a) income payments are the payments mentioned in item 3 above and any other payments that are not classified as § 736(b) property payments [e.g., a payment that is negotiated to be a § 736(a) payment].
5. To the extent that the § 736(b) property payment is for the partner's share of partnership hot assets, the disproportionate distribution rules apply. That individual partner is deemed to have received and sold their share of such assets to the partnership.
6. Code § 736(b) payments that are for the partner's share of "nonhot" assets are taxed as a return of the partner's outside basis. Any excess cash received over the partner's outside basis is taxed as capital gain; any shortfall results in a capital loss.
7. Code § 736(a) income payments are further classified as either guaranteed payments or distributive shares. In this chapter, the examples reflect guaranteed payment treatment (ordinary income to the partner; ordinary deduction to the partnership).
8. The partnership cannot deduct § 736(b) payments.

22-3 Sale of a Partnership Interest

LO.8

Calculate the selling partner's amount and character of gain or loss on the sale or exchange of a partnership interest.

A partner can sell or exchange all or part of a partnership interest. For example, in *The Big Picture* at the beginning of the chapter, one alternative is for Kyler and Maria to sell their LLC interests directly to the new developer. A sale of a partnership interest to a third party is similar in concept to a sale of corporate stock. However, because both the entity and aggregate theories are at work, the partner might be required to split the gain or loss on disposition of the partnership interest into ordinary and capital gains or losses.

22-3a General Rules

Generally, the sale or exchange of a partnership interest results in gain or loss, measured by the difference between the amount realized and the selling partner's basis in the partnership interest.[22]

Liabilities

In computing the amount realized and the basis of the interest sold, the selling partner's share of partnership liabilities must be considered, as discussed in text Section 21-4e. The purchasing partner includes any assumed indebtedness as a part of the consideration paid for the partnership interest, just as the selling partner includes the share of liabilities in the basis in the partnership interest. The concern is that the liabilities will be incorrectly excluded from either the selling price or basis when they should be included in both amounts.[23]

Cole originally contributed $50,000 in cash for a one-third interest in the CDE LLC. During the time Cole was a member of the LLC, his share of the LLC's income was $90,000 and he withdrew $60,000 cash. Cole's tax method capital account balance is now $80,000, and the LLC's liabilities are $45,000, of which Cole's share is $15,000. Cole's outside basis is $95,000 ($80,000 capital account + $15,000 share of the LLC's debts).

Cole sells his LLC interest to Stephanie for $110,000 cash, with Stephanie also assuming Cole's share of the LLC's liabilities. The total amount realized by Cole is $125,000 ($110,000 cash received + $15,000 of the LLC's debts transferred to Stephanie). Cole's gain on the sale is $30,000 ($125,000 amount realized − $95,000 outside basis).

Stephanie's adjusted basis for her LLC interest is the purchase price of $125,000 ($110,000 cash paid + $15,000 assumed LLC debt).

[22] § 741.

[23] § 742.

Income Allocation

When a partner sells an entire interest in the partnership:

- Income for the partnership interest for the tax year is allocated between the buying partner and the selling partner (discussed next).
- The partnership's tax year "closes" with respect to the selling partner.

The closing of the tax year causes the selling partner to report the share of income on the sale date rather than at the end of the partnership's tax year.

The selling partner's basis is adjusted for the allocated income or loss before the partner calculates the gain or loss on the sale of the interest.

Example 22

On September 30, 2023, Erica sells her 20% interest in Evergreen LLC to Aarav for $25,000. Erica is a calendar year taxpayer. Evergreen owns no hot assets, and its tax year ends on June 30.

On January 1, 2023, Erica's basis in Evergreen is $5,000. Here's what happens to Erica in calendar year 2023. First, on June 30, 2023, Evergreen's fiscal tax year closes, and Erica is allocated $3,000 of the LLC's income for that year.

Immediately before the sale of her LLC interest on September 30, 2023, Erica's basis in the LLC is $8,000 ($5,000 beginning basis + $3,000 fiscal year 2022–2023 allocation). Evergreen determines that Erica's share of LLC income is $10,000 for the additional period she owned the LLC interest (July 1 to September 30, 2023). Because the LLC's tax year closes with respect to Erica, she must also report that $10,000 of income on her 2023 tax return. Her basis in the LLC interest is increased to $18,000, and she recognizes a $7,000 capital gain on the sale ($25,000 − $18,000).

In her calendar year 2023 tax return, Erica reports income from two Schedules K–1 ($3,000 and $10,000), plus her gain on the sale ($7,000). This $20,000 of reported income accounts for the difference between her $5,000 basis at the beginning of the year and the $25,000 she received from Aarav.

In general, the partnership may use the interim closing method or the proration method to allocate income among the partners when ownership interests vary during the year.[24] Under the *proration method*, the variation in the partnership interest is deemed to occur on a given day, and partnership income is prorated and allocated on a daily basis to the time before and after the change. Under the *interim closing method*, the partnership's books are actually closed, and income is attributed to the before and after time periods. (Simplifying cutoff points such as mid-month can be used.) Under either method, income for each period is allocated among the partners who owned interests during that period. If partnership earnings are seasonal, the two methods can produce vastly different results.

Example 23

Cardinal, Inc., sold its 40% interest in the Owl Partnership to Sparrow, Inc., exactly halfway through the current tax year. Under the *interim closing method*, the partnership's income was $60,000 for the first half of the year, and its income for the last half of the year was $2,000. Cardinal is allocated 40% of $60,000, or $24,000, and Sparrow is allocated 40% of $2,000, or $800 of partnership income.

Under the *proration method*, the partnership's income for the year is $62,000, of which 40%, or $24,800, is allocated to the 40% interest. Based on the number of days each was a partner, both Cardinal and Sparrow report income of $12,400 for the current year.

The partnership must allocate certain items, such as interest, taxes, rent, or other amounts that accrue over time, to each day in the tax year over which they economically accrue. The interim closing method must be used for these items.[25] Similarly, extraordinary items, as defined, are allocated to the exact time at which they occurred.

Tax Reporting

The partnership is not required to issue a Schedule K–1 to the selling partner until the normal filing of its tax return. The partner, though, is required to include the share of partnership income as of the sale date. Consequently, selling partners may have to obtain an extension for filing their returns until the partnership provides the Schedules K–1. As you saw in Example 22, the partner may be required to report income from two partnership years in one tax return. The partners are required to report the sale to the partnership, and the partnership may be required to file an information statement with the IRS.

[24] § 706(d)(1) and Reg. § 1.706–4.

[25] § 706(d)(2).

22-3b **Hot Assets and Carried Interests**

Special rules apply if the partnership owns hot assets (as defined in text Section 22-1a) or if the partnership interest is a "carried interest" (as defined in text Section 21-2b).

Sale of Partnership Interests with Hot Assets

If the partnership holds hot assets, the selling partner will incur both ordinary income (loss) and capital gain (loss) on the sale of the interest. The sale is treated as if the partner sold the underlying share of the partnership's ordinary income (loss) assets. The primary purpose of this rule is to prevent a partner from converting ordinary income into capital gain through the sale of a partnership interest.[26] The partner's § 751 gain or loss is reported on the selling partner's Schedule K–1.

Unrealized Receivables As shown in Concept Summary 22.1, the term *unrealized receivables* generally includes the accounts receivable of a cash basis partnership and, for sale or exchange purposes, depreciation recapture potential.[27]

Example 24

The cash basis Canary LLP owns only a $10,000 receivable for rendering health care advice. Its basis in the receivable is zero because no income has been recognized. This item is a hot asset because ordinary income is not generated until Canary collects on the account.

Jacob, a 50% partner, sells his interest to Mark for $5,000. If Jacob's basis in his partnership interest is $0, his total gain is $5,000. The entire gain is attributable to Jacob's 50% share of the unrealized receivable, so his gain is taxed as ordinary income.

Depreciation recapture represents ordinary income the partnership would recognize if it sold depreciable property. Under the aggregate theory, the selling partner's share of depreciation recapture potential is treated as an unrealized receivable and is taxed to the selling partner as ordinary income rather than capital gain.

Andrew sells his 40% interest in the accrual basis Wren Partnership. The partnership's only asset is a depreciable business asset that it originally purchased for $25,000. The asset now has an adjusted basis of $15,000 and a market value of $30,000. Depreciation recapture potential is $10,000 ($25,000 − $15,000). If Wren sold the asset for $30,000, it would recognize $10,000 of ordinary income and $5,000 of § 1231 gain. If Andrew sells his partnership interest for a $6,000 gain, he recognizes $4,000 ($10,000 × 40%) of ordinary income and a $2,000 capital gain ($6,000 total gain less $4,000 ordinary income).

The partner selling an interest in a partnership with hot assets usually recognizes both ordinary income (loss) and capital gain (loss).

Sale of Partnership Interest with Hot Assets

Example 26

Ahmad sells his one-third interest in the equal ABC LLP to Dave for $17,000 cash. On the sale date, the partnership's cash basis balance sheet reflects the following.

	Basis	FMV		Basis	FMV
Cash	$10,000	$10,000	Liabilities	$ 9,000	$ 9,000
Accounts receivables (for services)	-0-	30,000	Capital accounts		
Nonhot assets	14,000	20,000	Ahmad	5,000	17,000
			Beth	5,000	17,000
			Chris	5,000	17,000
Total	$24,000	$60,000	Total	$24,000	$60,000

For this fact pattern, assume that liabilities are shared equally and that the capital account plus liability share equals the partner's tax basis. The total amount realized by Ahmad is $20,000 ($17,000 cash price + $3,000 of debt assumed by Dave). Ahmad's basis for his partnership interest is $8,000 ($5,000 capital account + $3,000 debt share), and Ahmad's total gain recognized on the sale is $12,000 ($20,000 − $8,000).

Because the partnership has unrealized receivables, the hot asset rule applies. If ABC collected the $30,000 of accounts receivable, Ahmad's proportionate share of ABC's ordinary income would

continued

[26] § 751(a).

[27] § 751(a)(1).

be $10,000 ($30,000 × ⅓). Consequently, $10,000 of the $12,000 recognized gain on the sale of the partnership interest relates to Ahmad's interest in the unrealized receivables and is taxed to him as ordinary income. The remaining gain of $2,000 is taxed to him as a capital gain.

Note that Ahmad still reports a total of $12,000 of income and gain; the hot asset rule merely reclassifies part of the gain as ordinary income. The effect of the rule is that the partnership's inherent ordinary income is allocated to the partner who earned it.

Example 27

Assume the same facts as in Example 26, except that Ahmad's basis in his partnership interest is $10,000. Under these circumstances, Ahmad still has $10,000 of ordinary income because of the unrealized receivables, but his capital gain or loss is zero ($20,000 sales proceeds including liabilities – $10,000 basis – $10,000 ordinary income).

Taking this to the next level, if Ahmad's basis in his partnership interest had been $15,000, he would have the same $10,000 of ordinary income, but he would have a capital *loss* of $5,000 ($20,000 sales proceeds –$15,000 basis –$10,000 ordinary income). The partner's share of ordinary income potential must always be recognized.

Inventory For a sale or exchange of a partnership interest, the term *inventory* includes all partnership property except cash, capital assets, and § 1231 assets. Receivables of an accrual basis partnership are included in the definition of inventory because they are not cash, capital assets, or § 1231 assets.[28] This definition also is broad enough to include all items considered to be unrealized receivables. For sales of a partnership interest, the inventory is not required to be substantially appreciated. (See Concept Summary 22.1.)

Example 28

Jan sells her one-third interest in the JKL LLC to Matt for $20,000 cash when her basis was $15,000. On the sale date, the LLC's balance sheet reflects the following.

	Basis	FMV		Basis	FMV
Cash	$10,000	$10,000	Jan, capital	$15,000	$20,000
Inventory	21,000	30,000	Kelly, capital	15,000	20,000
Capital assets	14,000	20,000	Luis, capital	15,000	20,000
Total	$45,000	$60,000	Total	$45,000	$60,000

The overall gain on the sale is $5,000 ($20,000 – $15,000). Jan's share of the appreciation in the inventory is $3,000 [($30,000 – $21,000) × ⅓]. Therefore, she recognizes $3,000 of ordinary income because of the inventory and $2,000 of capital gain from the rest of the sale.

Sale of Carried Interests

As a further exception, if the partnership interest being sold is classified as a "carried interest," any gain on the sale of that interest is treated as a short-term capital gain unless the interest has been held for more than three years.[29] Carried interests were introduced in text Section 21-2b.

Concept Summary 22.5 outlines the rules that apply to sales of partnership interests.

Concept Summary 22.5

Sale of a Partnership Interest

1. A partnership interest is a capital asset and generally results in capital gain or loss when it is sold.
2. The outside bases of the selling and buying partners, as well as the pertinent selling price and purchase price, include an appropriate share of partnership debt. (The debt amount is the same on both sides of the transaction: buying and selling.)
3. Partnership income or loss for the year of the sale is allocated between the selling and buying partners. The selling partner's basis is adjusted before the gain or loss on the sale is calculated.
4. The partnership's tax year closes with respect to the selling partner on the sale date; the seller reports partnership income at that time, and income "bunching" may occur.
5. When the partnership owns hot assets, the selling partner's overall gain or loss is reclassified into ordinary income or loss and a capital gain or loss. The ordinary portion equals the partner's share of the partnership's potential ordinary income.
6. If the interest is a carried interest, gain on the sale is treated as a short-term capital gain (ordinary income) to the extent the holding period is three years or less.

[28] § 751(d).

[29] § 1061(a).

The Big Picture

Example 29

Return to the facts of *The Big Picture* on p. 22-1. Recall that the second restructuring option for Beachside Properties LLC is for Kyler and Maria to sell their interests directly to the new members of the LLC. The new members will pay $4,750,000 each to Kyler and Maria in exchange for their interests in the LLC. The new members then will contribute an additional $15,000,000 of cash to Beachside Properties for the expansion.

Refer to the balance sheet in Example 20. Kyler and Maria receive cash of $9,500,000 (total) plus relief of their shares of the LLC's debt. Assume their bases in the LLC interests equal their capital account balances plus their shares of the LLC's liabilities. The difference must be recognized as a gain.

The gain is ordinary income to the extent that it relates to Kyler's and Maria's 95% total share of the LLC's $500,000 potential gain on receivables and inventory, plus 95% of potential depreciation recapture. The remaining gain is a capital gain. Absent a § 754 election (discussed later), the basis of the LLC's property is not affected.

Global Tax Issues — A Partnership Isn't Always a Partnership—Complications of State and International Taxes

State tax issues. Entities are treated differently by the various U.S. states. For example, each state has its own requirements for establishing LLCs and LLPs. Also, about a dozen states require a partnership or LLC to pay some sort of franchise, "gross receipts," or "business privilege" tax. Each state has its own calculation and definition of these entity-level taxes. Some entities operate across state lines, so tax preparers have to address multi-state partnership taxation, as well as the taxation of owners who live outside the main state in which the partnership operates.

A new entity-level partnership tax is gaining ground across the country, but this time it's designed to help the partners—at no cost to the state taxing authority. A few years ago, Congress enacted a $10,000 cap on an individual taxpayer's ability to deduct itemized state taxes on the Federal return. This cap covers property taxes as well as state and local income taxes. And, (drumroll), this limitation includes the state tax that an individual partner pays on their share of partnership taxable income—even though that tax generally is a tax on *business* income.

When the state tax deduction limitation first arose, pass-through entity owners approached state legislatures to allow a partnership's income to be taxed at the state level. The partnership pays and deducts the state tax for Federal purposes and passes through a lower level of income to its partners. From the state's perspective, the result is generally no different from allowing the partners to deduct the state tax directly. So far, 22 states have either required or permitted a partnership to pay the partners' taxes, and several other states are considering similar legislation.

The IRS has even signed off on this result: Notice 2020–75 specifically states that, for a state permitting a partnership-level payment of state income taxes, the entity may deduct the payment, and the amount is not required to be separately stated and passed through to the partners.

Foreign tax issues. You'll also find differences in tax treatment in the global arena. A "hybrid" entity might be treated as a partnership or a disregarded entity (DRE) for U.S. tax purposes and as a corporation in the foreign country in which it does business. A "reverse-hybrid" entity is treated as a corporation for U.S. tax purposes; a partnership or DRE, for foreign purposes.

Complications can arise because the United States generally imposes its tax on worldwide income, which is offset by a credit for foreign taxes paid (or deemed paid) in other countries. As you can imagine, entities had incentive to create situations that allowed foreign taxes to be credited against U.S. income before the related foreign income was actually taxed in the United States. For 2010 and later years, § 909 prevents this result: the credit cannot be claimed until the income is taxed.

Even though U.S. corporate income tax rates are now more in line with maximum rates in many Asian and European countries, potential disparities can exist. The rules of § 909 likely will be needed until the United States discontinues its taxation of worldwide income. Under a territorial tax system, the United States would only tax income earned within its borders and (after a transition period) the foreign tax credit—and its massive complications—would no longer be necessary.

Sources: IRC § 909; T.D. 9710.

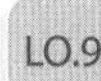

LO.9

Describe tax issues related to other dispositions of partnership interests.

22-4 Other Dispositions of Partnership Interests

There are various other ways to terminate a partnership interest, including:

- Transfer of the interest to a corporation.
- Death of a partner.
- Gifts.

22-4a Transfers to a Corporation

A partnership might incorporate to secure some of the advantages of a C corporation, to raise capital or to more easily retain capital for expansion, or when one or all partners are ready to retire from the business.

Recall the controlled corporation rules of § 351 from text Section 18-1. These rules provide that gain or loss is not recognized on the transfer of property to a corporation solely in exchange for stock in that corporation if, immediately after the exchange, the stockholders are in control of the corporation.

Incorporation of a partnership can be structured in various ways, depending on the manner in which partnership assets are deemed to be transferred and whether the corporate stock is deemed to be issued in exchange for partnership assets or partnership interests. Specifics are beyond the scope of this text, but you should recognize that different incorporation methods could have different tax results. In most situations in which an existing partnership is incorporated and continues to operate, § 351 conditions are met, and the incorporation is a nontaxable exchange. If § 351 conditions are not met, the partners recognize gain or loss on the transfer according to standard rules for sales or exchanges.

22-4b Death of a Partner

If a partner in a partnership dies, several issues must be addressed.

- **Allocation of income.** The partnership's income is allocated between the decedent and the successor in interest just as with a sale or exchange.
- **Successor's basis and capital account.** The successor takes a basis in the partnership interest as determined under estate tax rules (generally a fair market value basis). That basis likely differs from the underlying basis of the partner's share of partnership assets. The successor accedes to the decedent partner's capital account immediately prior to the decedent's death. To account for this, the successor partner's capital account roll forward should include an "other increase" equal to the decedent's ending capital account.
- **Automatic liquidation or sale.** The partnership might have a buy-sell agreement in effect that triggers liquidation or sale of the interest on death of the partner. That agreement will govern the tax treatment: if the transfer is structured as a liquidation, § 736 (discussed in text Section 22-2) will apply, and if the transfer is structured as a sale between the partners, § 741 (discussed in text Section 22-3) will apply.
- **Section 754 election.** As discussed in the next section, a § 754 election can remove the disparity that might arise between the successor's basis in the partnership interest and the successor's share of the partnership's basis in its assets.

22-4c Gifts

Generally, the donor of a partnership interest recognizes neither gain nor loss. If the donor's entire interest is transferred, all items of partnership income, loss, deduction, or credit attributable to the interest are prorated between the donor and donee.

The taxable year of the partnership does not close with respect to the donor, however, so the donor reports their share of partnership income or loss at the end of the partnership's tax year.

22-5 Section 754—Optional Adjustments to Property Basis

LO.10

Calculate the optional adjustments to basis under § 754.

A potential § 754 adjustment arises any time a transaction could change the balance between the (total) partners' outside bases in their partnership interests and the partnership's inside basis in its assets. The transactions that could trigger an out-of-balance situation fall into two general categories: (1) sale or transfer of a partnership interest or (2) certain distributions of partnership property.

When one of these situations arises, the partnership can make an **optional adjustment election**, or **§ 754 election**. If this election is made, the inside basis of the partnership's property is adjusted to bring inside basis and outside basis back into balance.

For example, when a partner purchases an existing partnership interest (as in text Section 22-3), the purchase price reflects what the acquiring partner believes the interest in the partnership—and the partnership's underlying assets—is worth. Because the value of the assets probably differs from their inside bases, a discrepancy exists between the purchasing partner's outside basis and that partner's share of the inside basis of partnership assets. (As a comparison, think of the difference between the price a purchaser pays for corporate stock versus the inside tax basis of the corporation's assets.)

If the § 754 election is made, the partnership's basis in its assets can be adjusted to reflect the purchase price paid by the new partner. If the election is not made, the statute produces some inequitable results.

A partnership's sole asset is a building with an adjusted basis of $450,000 and a fair market value of $900,000. George buys a one-third interest in the partnership for $300,000 (one-third of the value of the building). The partnership does not make an election under § 754. Although the price George paid for the interest was based on fair market value, the building's depreciation continues to be determined on the partnership's adjusted basis of $450,000, of which George's share is only $150,000 rather than the $300,000 paid for the interest.

A result similar to that in Example 30 can take place if certain conditions arise when a partnership distributes property to a partner (as in text Section 22-1) or redeems a retiring partner's interest (as in text Section 22-2). Without a § 754 election, the partnership cannot increase the adjusted basis of its assets.[30]

The partnership (not the partner) makes the § 754 election. The election is made by attaching a statement to a timely filed partnership return (including extensions).[31] The election applies to basis increases as well as basis decreases. An election is binding in the year for which it is made and for all subsequent years, unless the IRS consents to its revocation. Permission to revoke is granted for business reasons, such as a substantial change in the nature of the business or a significant increase in the frequency of interest transfers. Permission is not granted if it appears the primary purpose is to avoid downward adjustments to basis otherwise required under the election.

A basis adjustment is generally *required* if a sale or distribution occurs and the partnership has a **substantial built-in loss** or a **substantial basis reduction**—even if the partnership does not make (or have) a § 754 election. A substantial built-in loss arises from a sale of a partnership interest when the partnership's adjusted basis for all partnership property exceeds the fair market value of the property by more than $250,000, or if the partner would be allocated more than a $250,000 loss if all partnership assets were sold. A substantial basis reduction arises when the partnership distributes assets and the distributee partner recognizes a loss (or basis reduction) of at least $250,000.[32]

[30] §§ 743(a) and 734(a), respectively.

[31] § 754.

[32] §§ 743(d) and 734(d), respectively. The $250,000 threshold is not indexed for inflation.

Example 31

Refer to Example 30, but assume, instead, that the building had an adjusted basis of $300,000 and a fair market value of $150,000. Assume also that George purchased the one-third interest for $50,000 (an amount equal to one-third of the value of the building). Although the purchase price was based on fair market value, George obtains the benefit of *double* depreciation deductions because these deductions are calculated on the adjusted basis of the depreciable property ($300,000), which is twice the property's market value.

If the partnership has a § 754 election in effect, the downward basis adjustment is required. If there is no § 754 election in effect, it is unlikely the partnership would make one because the result is disadvantageous. There is no substantial built-in loss, so the mandatory adjustment does not apply: the overall depreciation in the partnership's property is only $150,000 ($300,000 adjusted basis − $150,000 fair market value) rather than $250,000.

22-5a Adjustment: Sale or Exchange of an Interest

If the § 754 optional adjustment-to-basis election is in effect and a partner's interest is sold, exchanged, or inherited, the partnership adjusts the basis of its assets as follows.[33]

Purchaser's (transferee's) outside basis in the partnership	$ xxx
Less: Purchaser's (transferee's) share of the inside basis of all partnership property	(xxx)
Adjustment	$ xxx

The step-up or step-down is allocated among all of the partnership's assets (except cash). The basis adjustments apply only to the transferee partner, and all subsequent income, deductions, gains, and losses related to the step-up or step-down are allocated to that partner. For example, any portion of the step-up that relates to depreciable property is depreciated as if it were a newly acquired asset. The transferee partner, therefore, shares in the depreciation taken by the partnership on the original asset and, in addition, reports *all* of the depreciation taken on the step-up basis created by the optional adjustment.

Example 32

Trevon is a member of the TLM LLC, and all members have equal interests in capital and profits. The LLC has made an optional adjustment-to-basis election. Trevon sells his interest to Tark for $76,000. The balance sheet of the LLC immediately before the sale shows the following.

	Basis	FMV		Basis	FMV
Cash	$ 15,000	$ 15,000	Capital accounts		
Depreciable assets	150,000	213,000	Trevon	$ 55,000	$ 76,000
			Leah	55,000	76,000
			Morgan	55,000	76,000
Total	$165,000	$228,000	Total	$165,000	$228,000

The adjustment is the difference between the basis of Tark's interest in the LLC (the $76,000 paid) and his share of the adjusted basis of the LLC's property ($55,000, or $165,000 × ⅓). Therefore, the optional adjustment that is added to the basis of the LLC's property is $21,000.

The $21,000 basis increase is allocated to the LLC's assets (except cash). In this case, TLM owns only fixed assets, so the step-up is treated as a new depreciable asset. Depreciation on the step-up is allocated to Tark.

If the LLC were to immediately sell the depreciable property for $213,000, the gain allocated to Leah and Morgan would be $21,000 ($71,000 share of sales price less $50,000 basis), but the gain allocated to Tark would be $0 [$71,000 share of sales price less $71,000 basis ($50,000 original basis + $21,000 step-up)].

[33] §§ 743(b) and 755.

22-5b Adjustment: Partnership Distributions

Optional adjustments to basis are also available to the partnership when property is distributed to a partner. If a § 754 optional adjustment-to-basis election is in effect, the basis of partnership property is *increased* by:[34]

- Any gain recognized by a distributee partner (e.g., when a cash distribution exceeds the partner's basis).
- Any *step-down* in the basis of property received by the distributee partner (i.e., the excess of the partnership's adjusted basis for any distributed property over the adjusted basis of that property in the hands of the distributee partner).

Conversely, the basis of partnership property is *decreased* by:

- Any loss recognized by a distributee partner in a liquidating distribution (e.g., under § 736).
- Any *step-up* in the basis of property received by the distributee partner (i.e., the excess of the distributee partner's adjusted basis of any nonhot assets received in a distribution over the basis of that property to the partnership).

The basis adjustments created by distributions affect the bases of all remaining partnership properties. Therefore, any depreciation deductions taken on such basis adjustments are allocated to all partners remaining in the partnership after the distribution. The *partnership* also takes these basis adjustments into account in determining any gains or losses on subsequent sales of partnership properties.

Basis Adjustments Related to Partnership Distributions

Example 33

Ryan has a basis of $50,000 in his partnership interest and receives a building with an adjusted basis to the partnership of $120,000 in termination of his interest. (Assume that the partnership has no hot assets.) The building's basis in Ryan's hands is a substituted basis of $50,000 under the proportionate liquidating distribution rules. If an optional adjustment-to-basis election is in effect, the partnership increases the basis of its remaining property by $70,000, and the depreciation expense related to this step-up is allocated to all remaining partners in the partnership.

Partnership's adjusted basis in distributed property	$120,000
Less: Distributee's basis in distributed property	(50,000)
Increase	$ 70,000

Example 34

Assume the same facts as in Example 33, except that the partnership's basis in the building was $40,000. Ryan's basis in the building is still $50,000, and the partnership reduces the basis of its remaining property by $10,000.

Distributee's basis in distributed property	$ 50,000
Less: Partnership's adjusted basis in distributed property	(40,000)
Decrease	$ 10,000

Although these rules may seem confusing at first reading, understanding the theory on which they are based helps to clarify the situation. Code § 734(b) assumes that the inside basis for all partnership assets equals the outside basis for all of the partners' interests immediately before the distribution. When this equality exists both before and after a distribution, no adjustment to the basis of partnership property

[34] § 734(b).

is necessary. However, when the equality does not exist after the distribution, an adjustment can bring the inside and outside bases back into equality. This is the adjustment that is made by the two increases and the two decreases described in the bulleted lists on the previous page.

Example 35

Assume that the Mockingbird LLC has an inside basis of $12,000 for its assets, which have a fair market value of $15,000. Aaron, Bill, and Chelsea each have outside bases of $4,000 for their LLC interests. If the LLC liquidates Aaron's interest with a $5,000 cash distribution (1/3 of the $15,000 value of assets), the resulting balance sheet is unbalanced.

	Inside (Assets)		Outside (Capital)
Before	$12,000	=	$12,000
Distribution	(5,000)	≠	(4,000)
After	$ 7,000	≠	$ 8,000

This unbalanced situation can be eliminated by adding $1,000 to the inside basis. Note that this is the same amount as the gain that Aaron recognizes on the distribution ($5,000 cash − $4,000 outside basis = $1,000 gain). Therefore, by adding the amount of Aaron's gain to the inside basis of the LLC's assets, the inside basis = outside basis formula is back in balance for the remaining LLC members.

Inside (Assets)		Outside (Capital)
$7,000	≠	$8,000
+1,000		
$8,000	=	$8,000

If the LLC liquidates Aaron's interest with a distribution of land having a $5,000 inside basis, the same unbalanced situation occurs. Although this transaction does not create any recognized gain for Aaron, the $1,000 optional adjustment is the excess of the $5,000 inside basis of the distributed property over the $4,000 substituted basis of that property to Aaron.

The Big Picture

Example 36

Return to the facts of *The Big Picture* on p. 22-1 and Beachside's balance sheet in Example 20. Recall that the members of Beachside Properties LLC are considering two restructuring options. For either option, Beachside Properties could make a § 754 election and record an adjustment to the basis of the LLC's property.

- *Step-up related to sale of interests.* On a sale of the interests to the new LLC members, the step-up would equal the difference between the $9,500,000 purchase price and Kyler's and Maria's share of the inside basis of the LLC's property. This step-up of approximately $7,600,000 [$9,500,000 − (95% × $2,000,000 net assets)] would be allocated to the various LLC properties under the rules of § 755 (not discussed in this chapter). Deductions related to the step-up, such as depreciation, would be allocated to the new developer group.
- *Step-up related to distribution in liquidation of the LLC members' interests.* If the LLC redeems the interests of Kyler and Maria, the LLC can step up the bases of its remaining assets by the amount of gain recognized by Kyler and Maria. This step-up is approximately $7,800,000 [$9,500,000 distribution − $1,700,000 total basis in LLC interests (Kyler's basis of $400,000 + Maria's basis of $1,300,000)] and benefits all of the remaining members of the LLC (Josh and the new developer group).

continued

Note that the step-up and treatment differ depending on whether there is a sale or redemption because Kyler's and Maria's share of the basis of the assets differs from their basis in the LLC interests and because of the difference in makeup of the member group to whom the resulting adjustments are allocated.

Concept Summary 22.6 outlines the rules related to basis adjustments under § 754.

Concept Summary 22.6

Basis Adjustments under § 754

1. A partnership can make a § 754 election if a transaction would cause the partnership's inside basis in assets to differ from the sum of the partners' outside bases in their partnership interests.
2. This situation could arise upon the sale of a partnership interest, the death of a partner, or a distribution of cash or property to a partner.
3. The § 754 election adjusts the partnership's basis in its assets to rebalance inside basis and outside basis.
4. A step-up in the partnership's asset basis arises when a purchasing partner pays more for an interest than the selling partner's share of the partnership's basis in its assets, when a distributee partner recognizes gain, or when a distributee partner takes a lower basis than the partnership had in distributed property.
5. A step-down in the partnership's asset basis arises when a purchasing partner pays less for the interest than the selling partner's share of the partnership's basis in its assets, when a distributee partner recognizes loss, or when a distributee partner takes a higher basis than the partnership had in distributed property.
6. An adjustment might be *required* (whether or not a § 754 election is in effect):
   - Upon sale of a partnership interest if the partnership has a "substantial built-in loss" (e.g., the partnership's basis in its assets exceeds their value by more than $250,000 or the partner would be allocated a loss of more than $250,000).
   - Upon distribution of property if there is a "substantial basis reduction" (i.e., a distributee partner recognizes more than a $250,000 loss or a distribution results in the partner having more than a $250,000 increase in the basis of distributed assets).
7. For a § 754 adjustment arising from sale of an interest, the resulting step-up or step-down is allocated to the acquiring partner.
8. For a § 754 election arising from a distribution of property, the resulting step-up or step-down is allocated to all remaining partners.
9. The partnership (not the partner) makes the election. It is binding for that year and all future years for which such transactions arise, unless the IRS consents to a revocation.

22-6 Other Issues

This section examines termination of a partnership as well as the special considerations that apply to family partnerships, LLCs, and LLPs.[35]

22-6a Termination of a Partnership

LO.11

Outline the events that could terminate a partnership.

When does a partnership's final tax year end? Technically, it ends when no part of the business continues to be carried on by any of the partners in a partnership.

The partnership terminates and its tax year closes when the partnership incorporates or when one partner in a two-party partnership buys out the other partner, thereby creating a sole proprietorship. A termination also occurs when the partnership ceases operations and liquidates.

The partnership taxable year usually does not close upon the death of a partner or upon the liquidation of a partner's interest, unless there is only one partner remaining.[36]

---

[35] See § 704(e) for rules related to family partnerships.

[36] § 706(c)(1).

The partnership year does not close upon the entry of a new partner to the partnership. It also does not close upon the sale or exchange of an existing partnership interest.

When the partnership terminates, it distributes its assets as described in text Section 22-1c (Proportionate Liquidating Distributions) or 22-1e (Disproportionate Distributions).

The Big Picture

Example 37

Return to the facts of *The Big Picture* on p. 22-1. Before the sale or redemption, Kyler's and Maria's combined interests equal 95% of the LLC's capital and 80% of the LLC's profits interests. Whether the interests are sold to the new developer group or Beachside redeems the interests under § 736, the partnership continues in existence after the transaction.

22-6b Family Partnerships

LO.12

Identify the special considerations of a family partnership.

Family partnerships are owned and controlled primarily by members of the same family. For this purpose, "family" includes the individual's spouse, ancestors, lineal descendants, and trusts established for the benefit of any of those parties; it does not include siblings. Often, one primary reason for establishing a family partnership is the desire to save taxes. For example, parents might want to reallocate partnership income to children in a lower tax bracket. However, rules are in place to limit such opportunities for tax avoidance.

Capital versus Services

A family member is recognized as a partner (to receive pass-through income and loss) only in the following cases:

- Capital is a material income-producing factor in the partnership,[37] and the family member's capital interest is acquired in a bona fide transaction (even if by gift or purchase from another family member) in which the partner receives both ownership and control over the interest.
- Capital is not a material income-producing factor, but the family member contributes substantial or vital services.

Gift of Capital Interest

If a family member receives a gift of a capital interest in a family partnership in which capital is a material income-producing factor, only part of the income may be allocated to this interest. First, the donor of the interest is allocated an amount of partnership income that represents reasonable compensation for services to the partnership. Then the remaining income is divided among the partners in accordance with their capital interests in the partnership. An interest purchased by one family member from another is considered to be created by gift for this purpose.[38]

Note that allocations to younger partners might be subject to the "kiddie tax rules," which could require the income to be taxed at higher tax rates, except to the extent the child performs services for the partnership and is compensated for them.

[37]See footnote 16 for the definition of capital as a material income-producing factor.

[38]§ 704(e)(3).

Global Tax Issues **Sale of Global Partnership Interests**

In the past, the IRS and the Tax Court differed on whether partnership property sited in the United States but owned by a foreign partnership was "effectively connected with a U.S. trade or business." The issue is whether taxation is determined at the entity level (based on the domicile of the partnership) or at the property level (based on the underlying assets owned by the partnership). If the asset (either the partnership interest or underlying property) is "effectively connected," then income from the sale of the asset is subject to U.S. taxation and U.S. withholding.

A new provision in the tax law solves the issue by adopting a property-level analysis. It requires that, if a partnership interest owned by a foreign partner is sold, a portion of the gain or loss on the sale is treated as "effectively connected" income. The partnership determines the selling partner's distributive share of the gain or loss that would arise if all partnership assets were sold at fair market value. The portion of the gain or loss arising from U.S. assets is effectively connected with a U.S. trade or business.

The buyer of a partnership interest must ascertain that the seller is a U.S. taxpayer or must withhold 10 percent of the selling price as prepayment of the non-U.S. seller's estimated tax on the sale.

Sources: IRC §§ 864(c)(8) and 1446(f).

A partnership in which a parent transferred a 50% interest by gift to a child (with the parent retaining 50%) generated a profit of $90,000. Capital is a material income-producing factor. The parent performed services valued at $20,000. The child performed no services. Under these circumstances, $20,000 is allocated to the parent as compensation. Of the remaining $70,000 of income attributable to capital, at least 50%, or $35,000, is allocated to the parent. Depending on the child's age, income allocated to the child (e.g., $35,000) might be taxed at "kiddie tax" rates (currently estate and gift tax rates) because the child performed no services.

22-6c **Limited Liability Companies**

LO.13

Describe the application of partnership provisions to limited liability companies (LLCs) and limited liability partnerships (LLPs).

The limited liability company was introduced in Chapter 21, and it is discussed in more detail here. The LLC combines partnership taxation with limited personal liability for all owners of the entity.

Taxation of LLCs

A properly structured LLC with two or more owners is generally taxed as a partnership. Because none of the LLC members are personally liable for any debts of the entity, the LLC is effectively treated as a limited partnership with no general partners. As described in Chapter 21, this results in unusual application of partnership taxation rules in areas such as allocation of liabilities to the LLC members, inclusion or exclusion of debt for at-risk purposes, passive or active status of a member for passive activity loss purposes, and determination of a member's liability for self-employment tax.

Converting to an LLC

A partnership can convert to an LLC with few, if any, tax ramifications: the old elections of the partnership continue, and the partners retain their bases and ownership interests in the new entity. However, a C or S corporation that reorganizes as an LLC is treated as having liquidated prior to forming the new entity. The transaction is taxable to both the corporation and the shareholders.

Advantages of an LLC

An LLC offers certain advantages over a limited partnership, including the following:

- Generally, none of the owners of an LLC are personally liable for the entity's debts. General partners in a limited partnership have personal liability for partnership recourse debts.
- Limited partners cannot participate in the management of the partnership. All owners of an LLC have the legal right to participate in the entity's management.

Disadvantages of an LLC

The disadvantages of an LLC stem primarily from the lack of Final Regulations in certain areas. There is only a limited body of case law interpreting the various state statutes, so the application of some provisions is uncertain. An additional uncertainty for LLCs that operate in more than one jurisdiction is which state's law will prevail and how it will be applied.

22-6d **Limited Liability Partnerships**

A limited liability partnership (LLP) is similar to a general partnership. The differences between the two entities are small but very significant. Recall that general partners are jointly and severally liable for all partnership debts. In some states, partners in a registered LLP are jointly and severally liable for contractual liabilities (i.e., they are treated as general partners for commercial debt). They are also always personally liable for their own malpractice or other torts. They are not, however, personally liable for the malpractice and torts of their partners. As a result, the exposure of their personal assets to lawsuits filed against other partners and the partnership is considerably reduced.

LLPs are treated as partnerships under Federal income tax statutes. They are most similar to general partnerships. An LLP must have formal documents of organization and register with the state. Because the LLP is a general partnership in other respects, it does not have to pay any state franchise taxes on its operations—an important difference between LLPs and LLCs in states that impose franchise taxes on LLCs.

When a general partnership converts to an LLP, it generally is treated as a continuation of the old partnership for tax purposes. This means that all of the old partnership's elections continue in the LLP, including accounting methods, the taxable year-end, and the § 754 election.

22-6e **Partnership Administration and Anti-Abuse**

Most larger partners will designate a "tax matters partner" who oversees the partnership's relationship with the IRS.

A partner's share of each partnership item should be reported on the partner's tax return in the same manner as presented on the partner's Schedule K–1. If a partner treats an item differently, the IRS should be notified of the inconsistent treatment.[39] If a partner fails to notify the IRS, a penalty may be added to the tax due.

Partnership taxation allows flexibility, which leaves the doors open for potential abuse. Regulations allow the IRS to disregard the form of a partnership transaction when it believes that the transaction (or series of transactions) is abusive.[40]

LO.14

Evaluate various tax planning considerations related to partnership distributions and sales of partnership interests.

22-7 Tax Planning

22-7a **Planning Partnership Distributions**

In planning for any partnership distributions, be alert to the following possibilities:

- When gain recognition is undesirable, make sure that cash distributions from a partnership, including any debt assumptions or repayments, do not exceed the basis of the receiving partner's interest.
- When a partner is to receive a liquidating distribution and the full basis of the interest will not be recovered, the partner's capital loss can be ensured by providing that the only assets received by the partner are cash, unrealized receivables, and inventory. If a capital loss is undesirable, however, the partnership should also distribute a capital or § 1231 asset that will take the partner's remaining basis in the interest. A capital asset would defer the loss, and a § 1231 asset could yield a more favorable ordinary deduction or loss in the future.

[39] See § 6222.

[40] Reg. § 1.701–2.

- Current and liquidating distributions may result in ordinary income recognition for either the receiving partner or the partnership if hot assets are present. When such income is undesirable, consider making a proportionate distribution.
- If precontribution gain property is contributed to a partnership, gain to the contributing partner can be further deferred if the partnership waits seven years before (1) distributing the precontribution gain property to another partner or (2) distributing other partnership property to the precontribution gain partner if the value of the other property exceeds the partner's basis in the partnership.
- When the partnership agreement initially is drafted, consider including provisions that govern liquidating distributions of partnership income and property for purposes of § 736. The specifics of the agreement generally will be followed by the IRS, especially if these and other relevant points are addressed early in the life of the entity.

22-7b **Sales and Exchanges of Partnership Interests**

Delaying Income for the Seller

A partner planning to dispose of a partnership interest in a taxable transaction might consider receiving a pro rata distribution of hot assets, followed by a sale of the remaining interest in the partnership. Although the partner will realize ordinary income when these hot assets are collected or sold, the partner can spread the income over more than one tax year by controlling the collection or disposal dates.

Providing Basis for the Buyer

If a partnership interest is acquired by purchase, the purchaser may want to condition the acquisition on the partnership's promise to make an election to adjust the basis of partnership assets. Making the election under § 754 results in the basis in the partner's ratable share of partnership assets being adjusted to reflect the purchase price. Failure to do so could result in the loss of future depreciation deductions or could convert ordinary losses into capital losses.

22-7c **Comparing Sales to Liquidations**

The *before-tax* result is the same for (1) a sale of a partnership interest to another party or (2) the liquidation of the partnership interest under § 736. Because the two transactions would result in the partner receiving the same amount of pretax dollars, the partner should be ambivalent about which form the transaction takes, unless one form offers tax savings that the other does not. The *after-tax* result of a sale of a partnership interest and a liquidation of a partner's interest by an ongoing partnership may differ considerably.

Payments over Time

One difference occurs when the payment for that interest is extended over several years. When a partner sells the partnership interest to another partner, the selling partner can postpone the recognition of income under the installment sale rules. These rules are very restrictive and require that gain and income be recognized at least as quickly as the proportionate share of the receivable is collected. However, in a liquidation, more flexibility may be available. Under § 736, the partners can agree that the § 736(b) payments for partnership property can be made before the income payments under § 736(a). Furthermore, the § 736(b) payments can be treated as a return of basis first, with gain recognized only after the distributee partner has received amounts equal to the basis. This treatment results in a deferral of gain and income recognition under § 736 that is not available under the installment sale provisions.

Payments for Goodwill

Sale The partner who purchases a partnership interest often pays an amount that can be attributed, in part, to partnership goodwill. Purchased goodwill is included in a purchasing partner's outside basis for the partnership interest. The partner cannot amortize the goodwill unless the asset qualifies as a § 197 intangible, amortizable over 15 years, *and* the partnership makes an election under § 754 to adjust the basis of partnership assets to reflect the purchase price paid. Absent these conditions, the purchasing partner will not obtain a tax benefit from the goodwill until the partnership interest is sold, exchanged, or liquidated.

Liquidation Amounts paid by a service partnership in liquidation of a general partner's share of partnership goodwill can be treated as a § 736(a) payment, provided it is *not* required by the partnership agreement ("unstated goodwill"). If this constitutes a guaranteed payment, it is deductible by the partnership. If (1) capital is a material income-producing factor of the partnership or (2) the distributee partner was a limited partner, payments for goodwill constitute § 736(b) property payments. These payments are not deductible by the partnership; they result in increased capital gain (or decreased capital loss) to the retiring partner.

Valuation Problems

Both the IRS and the courts usually consider the value of a partner's interest or any partnership assets agreed upon by all partners to be correct. Thus, when planning the sale or liquidation of a partnership interest, the results of the bargaining process should be documented. To avoid valuation problems on liquidation, the documentation should include a formula or agreed-upon valuation procedure in the partnership agreement or in a related buy-sell agreement. The adviser should determine whether the parties want § 736(a) or (b) treatment for partnership goodwill and provide appropriate documentation to achieve that goal.

22-7d **Other Partnership Issues**

Liquidating the Entity

The partnership liquidation rules demonstrate the tax advantages of the partnership form over the C corporation in the final stage of the business's life.

- A service partnership can effectively claim deductions for its payment to a retiring general partner for goodwill.
- The partnership liquidation itself is not a taxable event. Under corporate rules, however, liquidating distributions and sales in preparation for a distribution are fully taxable.
- Tax liability relative to the liquidation is generated at the partner level but only upon a recognition event (such as receipt of cash in excess of basis, sale of an asset received in a distribution, or a disproportionate distribution of hot assets). If the (ex)partner can control the timing of the recognition event, the tax obligations can be placed in the most beneficial tax year and rate bracket.

Family Partnerships

If possible, make certain that very young and older members of a family partnership contribute services to the entity so that you can justify making income allocations to them.

Because there is no equivalent of the kiddie tax for taxpayers who are 65 years and older, retention of the founding members of the partnership past the usual retirement age can facilitate the income-shifting goals of a family where the founding members are not independently wealthy.

Refocus on The Big Picture

The Life Cycle of a Partnership

PETER TITMUSS/ALAMY STOCK PHOTO

Two things are happening when the new developers become members of Beachside Properties LLC. The developers are buying out the interests of two existing LLC members, and they are providing cash with which to expand the LLC's operations.

The expansion itself raises no specific tax problems. An LLC can admit new members with no immediate tax consequences. In addition to the issues addressed earlier in the chapter, the LLC's operating agreement should be modified to ensure that there is no shift in ownership rights between Josh and the new LLC members.

What If?

Changing the facts, assume that the developers have only $5 million in cash, with good prospects for receiving an additional $10 million over the next two years and the remaining $9.5 million in the third year. The LLC has found a bridge loan and temporary financing of $12 million to cover costs during this interim period. This loan, though, is not large enough to fund the new development and to completely buy out Kyler's and Maria's interests. Thus, Kyler and Maria have agreed to accept installment payments for the sale or redemption of their interests.

Now the buyout of Kyler and Maria can be treated either as an installment sale or as a redemption under § 736 requiring a series of payments. Although the specific results of these arrangements are beyond the scope of this chapter, different tax consequences might arise as to the timing and character of Kyler's and Maria's gain recognition.

Key Terms

Appreciated inventory, 22-3
Current distribution, 22-2
Disproportionate distributions, 22-2
Hot assets, 22-2
Inventory, 22-3
Liquidating distribution, 22-2
Optional adjustment election, 22-25
Proportionate distribution, 22-4
Section 754 election, 22-25
Step down, 22-6
Step up, 22-6
Substantial basis reduction, 22-25
Substantial built-in loss, 22-25
Substantially appreciated inventory, 22-3
Unrealized receivables, 22-3

Discussion Questions

1. **LO.1, 2, 3, 4, 6** What is the difference between the definition of a proportionate current distribution and a proportionate liquidating distribution? What is the significance of the word *proportionate*?

2. **LO.1, 3** How does a proportionate current distribution of cash from a partnership to a partner compare with one from a Subchapter C corporation to a shareholder?

3. **LO.5** What issues arise if a partner contributes appreciated property to a partnership and other property is later distributed to that partner? Examine Form 1065 and Schedule K–1. What is the partnership's reporting obligation with respect to appreciated or depreciated partnership property (in general) and distributions of precontribution gain property specifically? Critical Thinking Practice

4. **LO.7** Distinguish between the treatment of § 736 income and property payments. What are the tax consequences of such payments to the retiring partner, the remaining partners, and the partnership?

Practice

5. **LO.8** When a partnership interest is sold during the partnership's taxable year, how is the income allocated between the buying partner and selling partner? When is the income reported? What documentation will the selling partner's tax preparer require?

6. **LO.9** What tax consequences result from the death of a partner? What collateral issues might arise?

7. **LO.10** Who makes the optional adjustment-to-basis election? How is the election made? What is its effect on future years? In what situations might the partnership *not* make the election?

8. **LO.11** Describe how a partnership is terminated.

Communications
Critical Thinking

9. **LO.13, 14** To what extent are the personal assets of a general partner, limited partner, or member of an LLC subject to (a) contractual liability claims such as trade accounts payable and (b) malpractice claims against the entity? Prepare a chart summarizing your findings. Provide answers for partners or members in a general partnership, an LLP, a nonprofessional LLC, and both general and limited partners in a limited partnership.

Computational Exercises

10. **LO.3** Franco owns a 60% interest in the Dulera LLC. On December 31 of the current tax year, his basis in the LLC interest is $128,000. The fair market value of the interest is $140,000. In a proportionate current distribution, the LLC distributes $30,000 cash and equipment with an adjusted basis of $5,000 and a fair market value of $8,000 to him on that date.

    How much is Franco's adjusted basis in the LLC interest after the distribution, and what is the amount of his basis in the equipment received?

11. **LO.3** Lola owns a one-half interest in the Lenax LLC. Her basis in this ownership interest is $22,000 at the end of the year, after accounting for the calendar year LLC's current operations. On that date, the LLC distributes $25,000 cash to Lola in a proportionate current distribution.

    What is the amount of any gain or loss Lola recognizes as a result of this distribution? What is her basis in the LLC interest?

12. **LO.3** Pablo has a $63,000 basis in his partnership interest. On May 9 of the current tax year, the partnership distributes to him, in a proportionate current distribution, cash of $25,000, cash basis receivables with an inside basis of $0 and a fair market value of $16,000, and land with a basis and fair market value to the partnership of $80,000.

    a. How much is Pablo's realized and recognized gain on the distribution?

    b. What is Pablo's basis in the receivables, land, and partnership interest following the distribution?

13. **LO.4** When Bruno's basis in his LLC interest is $150,000, he receives cash of $55,000, a proportionate share of inventory, and land in a distribution that liquidates both the LLC and his entire LLC interest. The inventory has a basis to the LLC of $45,000 and a fair market value of $48,000. The land's basis is $70,000, and the fair market value is $60,000.

    How much gain or loss does Bruno recognize, and what is his basis in the inventory and land received in the distribution?

14. **LO.4** When Magdalena's outside basis is $58,000, she receives a liquidating distribution of $15,000 cash and a proportionate share of inventory having a partnership basis of $20,000 and a fair market value of $24,000. The distribution results in a liquidation of both the partnership and her interest.

    a. How much is Magdalena's basis in the inventory received?

    b. What is the amount of any gain or loss recognized on the liquidation?

15. **LO.5** Ryce contributes nondepreciable property with an adjusted basis of $60,000 and a fair market value of $95,000 to the Montgomery Partnership in exchange for a one-half interest in profits and capital. In the next tax year, when the property's fair market value is $100,000, the partnership distributes the property to Jarvis, the other one-half partner. Jarvis's basis in the partnership interest was $100,000 immediately before the distribution.

    Which partner must recognize a gain, what is the amount recognized, and what is the effect on that partner's basis in the partnership interest? What is the effect on Jarvis's basis in the nondepreciable property received?

16. **LO.7** Wylie is a general partner in a service-providing partnership and receives cash of $145,000 in liquidation of his partnership interest, in which he has a basis of $110,000. The partnership owns no hot assets and continues in existence. After following all of the classification requirements of § 736, $100,000 of this amount is classified as a property payment [§ 736(b)] and $45,000 is classified as a guaranteed payment [§ 736(a)] (assume that this payment is for unstated partnership goodwill).

    As a result of the liquidation proceeds, how much will Wylie recognize as a capital gain or loss, and how much will be ordinary income? How much can the partnership likely deduct?

17. **LO.7** The Whitewater LLP is equally owned by three partners and shows the following balance sheet at the end of the current tax year.

	Basis	FMV
Cash	$60,000	$ 60,000
Unrealized receivables	–0–	15,000
Land	15,000	45,000
	$75,000	$120,000
Petula, capital	$25,000	$ 40,000
Prudence, capital	25,000	40,000
Primrose, capital	25,000	40,000
	$75,000	$120,000

    Partner Petula is an active (i.e., "general") partner retiring from the service-oriented partnership. She receives $60,000 cash, none of which is stated to be for goodwill.

    a. How much of the payment is for "unstated goodwill"?
    b. How is the $60,000 allocated between a § 736(a) income payment and a § 736(b) property payment?

18. **LO.2, 8** Sweeney originally contributed $175,000 in cash for a one-fourth interest in the Gilbert LLC. During the several years that Sweeney was a member of the LLC, his share of the LLC's income was $90,000 and he withdrew $75,000 cash. The LLC's liabilities are $80,000, of which Sweeney's share is $20,000. The LLC has $40,000 of hot assets, of which Sweeney's share is $10,000.

    Sweeney sells his LLC interest to Jana for $225,000 cash, with Jana also assuming Sweeney's share of the LLC's liabilities.

    How much is Sweeney's gain on the sale, and what is its character? How much is Jana's adjusted basis for her LLC interest?

19. **LO.8** On December 31, Yong sells his 10% interest in Catawissa LLC to Mei for $17,500. Yong is a calendar year taxpayer. Catawissa owns no hot assets, and its tax year ends on September 30. On October 1, Yong's basis in the LLC interest was $11,000. His share of current LLC income is $4,000 for the period in which he owned the LLC interest (October 1 to December 31).

    How much capital gain does Yong recognize on the sale?

20. **LO.8** The Lexington Partnership has a depreciable business asset (personal property) that it originally purchased for $60,000. The asset now has an adjusted basis of $36,000 and a market value of $70,000. The partnership has no other potential hot assets. Ambroz sells his 25% interest in the partnership.

    a. How much is Lexington's depreciation recapture potential?

    b. How much ordinary income does Ambroz recognize when he sells this partnership interest?

21. **LO.10** Dušan is a member of the Tonda LLC, and all members have equal interests in capital and profits. The LLC has made an optional adjustment-to-basis election. Dušan's interest is sold to Adele for $35,000. The balance sheet of the LLC immediately before the sale shows the following.

	Basis	FMV
Cash	$ 40,000	$ 40,000
Depreciable assets	80,000	100,000
	$120,000	$140,000
Dušan, capital	$ 30,000	$ 35,000
Randal, capital	30,000	35,000
Thom, capital	30,000	35,000
Erim, capital	30,000	35,000
	$120,000	$140,000

    a. How much is the § 754 adjustment?

    b. What is the amount of Adele's basis in the acquired interest?

    c. Which partners receive deductions related to the step-up?

22. **LO.10** Berdine has a basis of $32,000 in her partnership interest and receives land with an adjusted basis to the partnership of $78,000 in termination of her interest. [Assume the partnership holds no hot assets and the entire payment is a § 736(b) payment with the tax treatment determined under the proportionate liquidating distribution rules.]

    a. What is Berdine's basis in the distributed land?

    b. If an optional § 754 adjustment-to-basis election is in effect, by what amount does the partnership adjust the basis of its remaining property? If that adjustment is allocated to depreciable property, to whom does the partnership allocate the resulting depreciation deductions?

23. **LO.12** A partnership in which a parent transferred a 40% interest by gift to a child generated a profit of $130,000. Capital is a material income-producing factor. The parent performed services valued at $44,000; the child performed no services.

    How much income is allocated to the parent for services and for use of capital?

Problems

24. **LO.3** When Teri's outside basis in the TMF Partnership is $80,000, the partnership distributes to her $30,000 cash, an account receivable (fair market value of $60,000, inside basis to the partnership of $0), and a parcel of land (fair market value of $60,000, inside basis to the partnership of $80,000). Teri remains a partner in the partnership, and the distribution is proportionate to the partners.

    a. Use the format of Concept Summary 22.2 to create a spreadsheet to calculate the effects of the distribution. Set up an Input area for the amounts on lines 1, 2, 5, and 8. Code the formulas shown in the Calculations section of the concept summary to calculate the amounts in the remaining lines. You will use "sum," "min," and "max" formulas. Enter Teri's relevant facts in the input section of your spreadsheet.

b. Based on the information in your spreadsheet, how much gain or loss will Teri recognize as a result of the distribution? Explain your answer.

c. How much is Teri's basis in the land, account receivable, and TMF Partnership after the distribution? What can you conclude regarding Teri's basis in the assets and the fair market value she received?

d. How would your answer to part (c) change if, instead, the partnership's basis in the land was $10,000 and its fair market value was $30,000 (and the cash and unrealized receivable distributions do not change)? Adjust the input section of your spreadsheet, and explain your findings.

25. **LO.3, 10** Consider each of the following independent situations, and answer the following questions.

Decision Making
Planning

a. For each fact pattern, indicate:

- Whether the partner recognizes gain or loss.
- Whether the partnership recognizes gain or loss.
- The partner's adjusted basis for the property distributed.
- The partner's outside basis in the partnership after the distribution.

In each case, assume that the partnership owns no hot assets. Show your calculations in a spreadsheet using a template similar to the format shown in Concept Summary 22.2. You will use "sum," "min," and "max" formulas. Enter a partner's relevant facts in the Input section of your spreadsheet, and simply adjust the input numbers to address the next situation.

(1) Kim receives $20,000 cash in partial liquidation of her interest in the partnership. Kim's outside basis for her partnership interest immediately before the distribution is $3,000.

(2) Kourtni receives $40,000 cash and land with an inside basis to the partnership of $30,000 (value of $50,000) in partial liquidation of her interest. Kourtni's outside basis for her partnership interest immediately before the distribution is $80,000.

(3) Assume the same facts as in part (2), except that Kourtni's outside basis for her partnership interest immediately before the distribution is $60,000.

(4) Klois receives $50,000 cash and inventory with a basis of $30,000 and a fair market value of $50,000 in partial liquidation of her partnership interest. Her basis was $90,000 before the distribution. All partners received proportionate distributions.

b. For fact patterns (1) to (4) in part (a) above, are additional planning opportunities available to the partnership to maximize its inside basis in its assets? If so, by how much can the basis be increased? What is the effect of any basis increase to the distributee partner or the other partners?

26. **LO.3** Cari Hawkins is a 50% partner in the calendar year Hawkins-Lopez Partnership. On January 1, 2023, her basis in her partnership interest is $160,000. The partnership has no taxable income or loss for the current year. In a current distribution on December 15, the partnership distributes $120,000 cash to Cari and inventory proportionately to all partners. Cari's share of the inventory has an inside basis of $50,000 (fair market value of $60,000).

Communications
Planning

In January 2024, Cari asks your advice regarding treatment of 2023 operations and distributions. Using the format (1) facts, (2) issues, and (3) conclusion and analysis, draft a letter to Cari at the Hawkins-Lopez Partnership (1622 E. Henry Street, St. Paul, MN 55118). Without including specific citations, your letter should address the following points and provide enough information for the client to understand the applicable tax provisions.

a. How much gain or loss does the partnership recognize as a result of 2023 activities?
b. How much gain or loss must Cari recognize in 2023?
c. What is Cari's basis in inventory received?
d. What is Cari's basis in her partnership interest at the end of 2023?
e. What other considerations should Cari and/or the partnership address? Explain.

27. **LO.3, 4** At the beginning of the tax year, Melodie's basis in the MIP LLC was $60,000, including her $40,000 share of the LLC's liabilities. At the end of the year, MIP distributed to Melodie cash of $10,000 and inventory (basis of $6,000, fair market value of $10,000). In addition, MIP repaid all of its liabilities by the end of the year.
   a. If this is a proportionate current distribution, what is the tax effect of the distribution to Melodie and MIP? After the distribution, what is Melodie's basis in the inventory and in her MIP interest?
   b. Would your answers to part (a) change if this had been a proportionate liquidating distribution? Explain.

Critical Thinking
Planning

28. **LO.2, 3, 4, 5, 6, 14** Vincent is a 50% partner in the TAV Partnership. He became a partner three years ago when he contributed land with a value of $60,000 and a basis of $30,000 (current value is $100,000). Tyler and Anita each contributed $30,000 cash for a 25% interest. Vincent's basis in his partnership interest is currently $135,000; the other partners' bases are each $82,500. The partnership holds the following assets.

	Basis	FMV
Cash	$200,000	$200,000
Accounts receivable	–0–	200,000
Marketable securities	70,000	100,000
Land	30,000	100,000
Total	$300,000	$600,000

   a. In general terms (i.e., no calculations are required), describe the tax results to the partners and the partnership in each of the following independent scenarios where the partnership distributes the assets indicated in a current nonliquidating distribution at the end of its tax year. *Hint:* You should first determine whether the distributions are proportionate.
      (1) TAV distributes a $50,000 (FMV) plot of land each to Tyler and Anita and $100,000 of accounts receivable to Vincent.
      (2) TAV distributes $100,000 of cash to Vincent, $50,000 (FMV) of marketable securities to Tyler, and $50,000 (FMV) of accounts receivable to Anita.
      (3) TAV distributes a $50,000 (FMV) interest in the land and $50,000 (FMV) of accounts receivable to Vincent and $25,000 of cash and $25,000 (FMV) of accounts receivable each to Anita and Tyler.
   b. Now consider what would happen if the partnership distributed all of its assets in a liquidating distribution. In deciding the allocation of assets, what issues should the partnership consider to minimize each partner's taxable gains?

Critical Thinking
Planning

29. **LO.3, 4, 10** Answer the following questions regarding four independent liquidating distributions in which the partnership also liquidates.
   a. Prepare a spreadsheet to determine the amount and character of any gain or loss to be recognized by each partner and the basis of each asset (other than cash) received. In each case, assume that distributions of hot assets are proportionate to the partners (or there are no hot assets). You can use the format in Concept Summary 22.3, or you can create your own. In either case, be sure you can explain your rationale.

If you use the format in Concept Summary 22.3, set up an Inputs section for the amounts on lines 1, 2, 5, and 8. Code the formulas shown in the Calculations section to determine the amounts in the remaining lines. You will use "sum," "min," "max," and "if/then/else" formulas. Enter a partner's relevant facts in the Inputs section of your spreadsheet, and simply adjust the input numbers to address the remaining situations.

(1) Rafael has a partnership basis of $40,000 and receives a distribution of $50,000 in cash.

(2) Mark has a partnership basis of $50,000 and receives $20,000 cash and a capital asset with a basis to the partnership of $25,000 and a fair market value of $40,000.

(3) Neil has a partnership basis of $100,000 and receives $40,000 cash, inventory with a basis to the partnership of $30,000, and a capital asset with a partnership basis of $20,000. The inventory and capital asset have fair market values of $20,000 and $30,000, respectively.

(4) Oscar has a partnership basis of $40,000 and receives a distribution of $10,000 cash and an account receivable with a basis of $0 to the partnership (value is $15,000).

b. In each of the four situations in part (a), are any planning techniques available to the partnership to avoid any "lost basis" results? Explain.

c. In the four situations in part (a), would your answers change if the transaction had been a current distribution? Explain.

30. **LO.4, 14** Paula's basis in her partnership interest is $60,000. In liquidation of her interest, the partnership makes a proportionate distribution to Paula of $20,000 of cash and inventory (basis of $5,000 and value of $7,000). No "other property" was distributed. (Assume that the partnership then liquidates.)

Decision Making
Planning

a. Use the format of Concept Summary 22.3 to create a spreadsheet to calculate the effects of the distribution. Set up an Inputs area for the amounts on lines 1, 2, 5, and 8. Code the formulas shown in the Calculations section to determine the amounts in the remaining lines. You will use "sum," "min," "max," and "if/then/else" formulas. Enter Paula's relevant facts in the Inputs section of your spreadsheet.

b. Based on the information in your spreadsheet, how much gain or loss, if any, will Paula recognize on the distribution?

c. What basis will Paula take in the inventory?

d. What happens if the partnership also distributes artwork to Paula with a basis of $1,000 and a fair market value of $30,000? Adjust the Inputs section of your spreadsheet, and explain your findings.

e. Return to the original facts. Conceptually, how would your answer to part (b) or (c) change if this had been a current distribution? (You do not need to create a spreadsheet for the current distribution rules.) Explain.

31. **LO.4** Jamie's basis in her partnership interest is $52,000. In a proportionate distribution in liquidation of the partnership, Jamie receives $2,000 cash and two parcels of land with bases of $10,000 and $18,000, respectively, to the partnership. The partnership holds both parcels of land for investment, and the parcels have fair market values of $20,000 each.

a. How much gain or loss, if any, must Jamie recognize on the distribution?

b. What basis will Jamie take in each parcel?

c. If the land had been held as inventory by the partnership, what effect, if any, would it have on your responses to parts (a) and (b)?

Decision Making
Planning

32. **LO.4, 14** Ebony has a basis in her partnership interest of $85,000. In a proportionate liquidating distribution of the partnership, Ebony receives $5,000 cash and a car (a § 1231 asset to the partnership) having a basis of $20,000 to the partnership and a fair market value of $30,000. Disregard any potential depreciation recapture on the car.

    a. How much loss, if any, may Ebony recognize on the distribution?
    b. What basis will Ebony take in the car?
    c. Suppose Ebony's 18-year-old son uses the car for his personal use for one year before Ebony sells it for $28,000. How much loss may Ebony recognize on the sale of the car? What tax planning procedures should be considered?

Critical Thinking

33. **LO.5** In 2019, Adrianna contributed land with a basis of $16,000 and a fair market value of $25,000 to the A&I Partnership in exchange for a 25% interest in capital and profits. In 2022, the partnership distributes this property to Isabel, also a 25% partner, in a current distribution. The fair market value had increased to $30,000 at the time the property was distributed. Isabel's and Adrianna's bases in their partnership interests were each $40,000 at the time of the distribution.

    a. How much gain or loss, if any, does Adrianna recognize on the distribution to Isabel? What is Adrianna's basis in her partnership interest following the distribution?
    b. What is Isabel's basis in the land she received in the distribution?
    c. How much gain or loss, if any, does Isabel recognize on the distribution? What is Isabel's basis in her partnership interest following the distribution?
    d. How much gain or loss would Isabel recognize if she later sells the land for its $30,000 fair market value? Is this result equitable?
    e. How would your answers to parts (a) and (b) change if Adrianna originally contributed the property to the partnership in 2011? Explain.

Critical Thinking

34. **LO.7, 14** Damon owns a 20% interest as a general partner in the Vermillion Partnership, which provides consulting services. The partnership distributes $60,000 cash to Damon in complete liquidation of his partnership interest. Damon's share of partnership unrealized receivables immediately before the distribution is $20,000. The partnership has no other hot assets. None of the cash payment is for goodwill. Damon's basis for his partnership interest immediately before the distribution is $30,000.

    a. How is the cash payment treated under § 736?
    b. How much gain or loss must Damon recognize on the distribution? What is the character of these amounts?
    c. How does the partnership treat the distribution to Damon?
    d. What planning opportunities might the partnership want to consider?
    e. How would your answers to parts (a), (b), and (c) change if Damon had been a limited partner? Would the partnership be more likely to prefer Damon's treatment as a general or limited partner? Which type of partner classification would Damon likely prefer?

35. **LO.2, 7, 8, 10** The December 31 balance sheet of the GAB LLP reads as follows.

	Adjusted Basis	FMV
Cash	$300,000	$300,000
Receivables	–0–	100,000
Capital assets	60,000	80,000
Total	$360,000	$480,000

	Adjusted Basis	FMV
Gina, capital	$ 90,000	$120,000
Adelle, capital	180,000	240,000
Britney, capital	90,000	120,000
Total	$360,000	$480,000

Capital is not a material income-producing factor for the LLP. Gina is an active (general) partner and owner of a 25% interest in the LLP's profits and capital.

a. On December 31, Gina receives a distribution of $140,000 cash in liquidation of her partnership interest. Nothing is stated in the partnership agreement about goodwill. Gina's outside basis for the partnership interest immediately before the distribution is $90,000.

(1) How much is Gina's recognized gain from the distribution? What is the character of the gain?

(2) How much can GAB claim as a deduction?

(3) What action might the partnership want to take?

b. Now assume instead that Gina sells her partnership interest to Jess for $140,000 of cash.

(1) What is the amount and character of Gina's gain?

(2) What deductions can be claimed by the LLP?

(3) What action might Jess request of the partnership?

36. **LO.7, 8** Skylar is ready to retire and wants your professional opinion on the most advantageous way to dispose of a 40% limited ownership interest in the three-member STU LLC. *Communications, Critical Thinking, Decision Making, Planning*

Option 1. Skylar will immediately sell the LLC interest to Partner Tameeka for $300,000 cash. Skylar will then invest the after-tax proceeds in a tax-exempt (Federal and state) municipal bond paying 4% interest per year, compounded at the end of each year. (Assume that there are no Federal or state income taxes on the interest earned on the bond.)

Option 2. STU will distribute a parcel of land (investment property) to Skylar in complete redemption of the 40% interest. STU's land was recently appraised for $260,000. The appraiser estimated that Skylar could sell the land for $400,000 (before taxes) at the end of eight years. For simplicity, determine the tax results of the land distribution under the proportionate liquidating distribution rules. [The proportionate liquidating distribution rules yield the correct result because Skylar is a limited partner and the entire distribution is treated as a § 736(b) payment.]

Other information. In either scenario, at the end of the eighth year, Skylar will convert the asset (bond or land) to cash to help cover living expenses. If needed, use the Present and Future Value Tables in Appendix E.

Assumptions:

- STU owns no hot assets and has no stated or unstated goodwill.
- Skylar's basis in the LLC interest is $100,000.
- The LLC's basis in the land is $80,000.
- Skylar's tax rate is 20% on capital gains.

Draft a memo to Skylar describing how each option would be treated for tax purposes and the after-tax amount of cash Skylar would have on hand after cashing the bond or selling the land at the end of year 8. Based solely on this analysis, recommend one of these options to Skylar.

Communications
Critical Thinking
Practice

37. **LO.2, 8** BDD Partnership is a service-oriented partnership that has three equal general partners. One of them, Barry Evans, sells his interest to another partner, Dale Allen, on December 31 (the last day of the current tax year) for $90,000 cash and the assumption of Barry's share of partnership liabilities. (Liabilities are shared equally by the partners.)

Immediately before the sale (after reflecting operations for the year), the partnership's cash basis balance sheet was presented as shown below. Assume that the capital accounts *before* the sale reflect the partners' bases in their partnership interests, excluding liabilities. The payment exceeds the stated fair market value of the assets because of goodwill that is not recorded on the books.

	Basis	FMV		Basis	FMV
Cash	$120,000	$120,000	Note payable	$ 30,000	$ 30,000
Accounts receivable	–0–	90,000	Capital accounts		
Capital assets	30,000	75,000	Barry	40,000	85,000
			David	40,000	85,000
			Dale	40,000	85,000
Total	$150,000	$285,000	Total	$150,000	$285,000

a. What is the total amount realized by Barry on the sale?

b. How much, if any, ordinary income must Barry recognize on the sale?

c. How much capital gain must Barry report?

d. What is Dale's basis in the partnership interest acquired?

e. Refer to Reg. § 1.751–1(a)(3). What information is the seller required to provide? Draft a statement that meets these requirements.

f. How would Barry's tax result differ if, instead, BDD distributed $90,000 of its cash in liquidation of Barry's interest (with the remaining partners assuming Barry's share of partnership debt)? Why is this result different from Barry's result when the interest is sold? The LLC's operating agreement does not address payment of goodwill to the partner.

Critical Thinking

38. **LO.2, 8, 10** Diana, a partner in the cash basis HDA Partnership, has a one-third interest in partnership profits and losses. The partnership's balance sheet at the end of the current year is as follows.

	Basis	FMV		Basis	FMV
Cash	$120,000	$120,000	Hannah, capital	$ 90,000	$250,000
Receivables	–0–	240,000	Diana, capital	90,000	250,000
Land	150,000	390,000	Alexis, capital	90,000	250,000
Total	$270,000	$750,000	Total	$270,000	$750,000

Diana sells her interest in the HDA Partnership to Kenneth at the end of the current year for cash of $250,000.

a. How much income must Diana report on her tax return for the current year from the sale? What is its nature?

b. If the partnership does not make an optional adjustment-to-basis election, what are the type and amount of income that Kenneth must report in the next year when the receivables are collected?

c. Refer to Example 35. Describe how an out-of-balance situation arises and is resolved for Diana's *sale* of a partnership interest. (Note that Example 35 relates to a *distribution* that causes an out-of-balance situation.) Prepare a spreadsheet that illustrates the out-of-balance situation and how a § 754 adjustment can restore balance. Allocate any basis step-up to partnership assets. *Hint:* You'll need to significantly modify the format for this situation.

d. If the partnership did make an optional adjustment-to-basis election, what are the type and amount of income that Kenneth would report in the next year when the receivables are collected? If the land (which is used in the HDA Partnership's business) was sold for $420,000? Assume that no other transactions occurred that year.

39. **LO.8, 9, 11** At the end of last year, June, a 30% partner in the four-person BJJM Partnership, had an outside basis of $75,000 in the partnership, including a $60,000 share of partnership debt. June's share of the partnership's § 1245 recapture potential was $40,000. All parties use the calendar year. Describe the income tax consequences to June in both of the following independent situations that take place in the current year. In both situations, also explain whether the partnership continues in existence.

a. On the first day of the tax year, June sells her partnership interest to Marilyn for $120,000 cash plus the assumption by Marilyn of the appropriate share of partnership liabilities.

b. June dies on April 1 of the current year. June's brother immediately takes June's place in the partnership.

40. **LO.12** Ming and Denise, mother and daughter, operate a local restaurant as an LLC. The MD LLC earned a profit of $200,000 in the current year. Denise's equal partnership interest was acquired by gift from Ming. Assume that capital is a material income-producing factor and that Ming manages the day-to-day operations of the restaurant without any help from Denise. Reasonable compensation for Ming's services is $50,000.

a. How much of the LLC's income is allocated to Ming?

b. What is the maximum amount of the LLC's income that can be allocated to Denise?

c. Assuming that Denise is 15 years old, has no other income, and is a dependent of Ming, how is Denise's income from the LLC taxed?

Research Problems

Note: Solutions to the Research Problems can be prepared by using the Thomson Reuters Checkpoint™ online tax research database, which accompanies this textbook. Solutions can also be prepared by using research materials found in a typical tax library.

Decision Making

Research Problem 1. Your client, Paul, owns a one-third interest as a managing (general) partner in the service-oriented PRE LLP. He would like to retire from the limited liability partnership at the end of 2024 and asks your help in structuring the buyout transaction. He expects that his basis in the LLP interest will be about $60,000 at that time.

Based on interim financial data and revenue projections, the LLP's balance sheet is expected to approximate the following at the end of the year.

	Basis	FMV		Basis	FMV
Cash	$ 60,000	$ 60,000	Paul, capital	$ 60,000	$150,000
Accounts receivable	–0–	180,000	Rachel, capital	60,000	150,000
Land (capital asset)	120,000	210,000	Erik, capital	60,000	150,000
Total assets	$180,000	$450,000	Total capital	$180,000	$450,000

Although the LLP has some cash, the amount is not adequate to purchase Paul's entire interest in the current year. The LLP has proposed to pay Paul, in liquidation of his interest, according to the following schedule.

December 31, 2024	$50,000
December 31, 2025	$50,000
December 31, 2026	$50,000

Paul has agreed to this payment schedule, but the parties are not sure of the tax consequences of the buyout and have temporarily halted negotiations to consult with their tax advisers. Paul has retained you to determine the income tax ramifications of the buyout and to make sure he secures the most advantageous result available.

a. If the buyout agreement between Paul and PRE is silent as to the treatment of each payment, how will each payment be treated by Paul and the partnership?

b. As Paul's adviser, what payment schedule would you recommend that Paul negotiate to minimize his current tax liability?

c. Regarding the LLP, what payment schedule would ensure that the remaining partners receive the earliest possible deductions?

d. Under the three alternatives in parts (a) to (c), what is the present value of Paul's after-tax cash received from the buyout? Which alternative do you recommend to your client, Paul? Does this change your recommendations in parts (a) through (c)? Paul's Federal and state tax rate for capital gains is 25%, and his marginal combined state and Federal rate for ordinary income is 40%. Paul typically earns 6% on his investments (after-tax discount rate); the first payment will be received one year from now (with the other payments one year apart). Use the present value tables in Appendix E. Each year's after-tax cash flow differs, so discount each year's net after-tax proceeds separately and then sum the totals.

   Create a spreadsheet that summarizes the after-tax cash flows, and present values of the three alternatives. You might use the format shown at the end of this problem for part (a), where the partnership agreement is silent, and then copy and modify the format for parts (b) and (c).

e. What additional planning opportunities might be available to the partnership?

Partnership Agreement Silent

	§ 736(a)	§ 736(b)	Basis Recovery	Taxable Gain	Tax on Ordinary Income	Tax on Taxable Gain	Total Tax on Distribution	Net After-Tax Proceeds	Discount Factor for Year	Discounted Proceeds
2024										
2025										
2026										

Critical Thinking **Research Problem 2.** The Get It Done LLC (GIDL) was originally formed several years ago by Gina, Ignacio, Dani, and Larry. At that time, each LLC member contributed $1,000,000 of cash in exchange for a 25% interest in the LLC. GIDL now owns and leases heavy-duty construction equipment in the Tri-State area.

At the beginning of the current tax year, Dani sold her 25% interest in GIDL to Denique (an unrelated party) for $3,000,000. At that time the basis and fair market values of the assets recorded on the partnership's books was as follows (the LLC has no debt):

	Basis	Fair Market Value
Cash	$1,500,000	$ 1,500,000
Accounts receivable	500,000	500,000
Land	2,000,000	1,000,000
Seven-year equipment	–0–	9,000,000
Total	$4,000,000	$12,000,000

You advised your client, Denique, to get assurance from the LLC that a § 754 election and adjustment would be made. GIDL agreed to make the election and plans to allocate any step-up to the equipment and recover the cost using a seven-year depreciation schedule. Denique wants to know if this is the correct treatment and if a more favorable treatment is possible. GIDL told Denique that the equipment was originally purchased several years ago for about $12,000,000 and that GIDL claimed the 100% bonus depreciation deduction that was permitted in that tax year.

a. Calculate the amount of Denique's § 754 basis adjustment.

b. Prepare a spreadsheet to allocate Denique's § 754 basis adjustment among GIDL's assets. Use the rules outlined in Reg. § 1.755–1(b). Refer especially to Example 1 in (b)(2) and as continued in (b)(3). [Note that depreciation recapture is not relevant for this calculation, as the seller (Dani) would recognize any necessary ordinary recapture income on sale of the LLC interest.]

c. Can Denique make a case that any step up allocated to the equipment is eligible for an immediate bonus depreciation deduction rather than seven-year cost recovery? See Reg. § 1.168(k)–2(b)(3)(iv)(D). You can also refer to Examples 13 to 17 in Reg. § 1.168(k)–2(b)(3)(vii).

d. How would your answer to part (c) change if Dani was Denique's mother?

e. Denique wants to know if she has any exposure if the IRS questions the step-up allocation. What might you caution her about the equipment valuation? For example, how would Denique's result change if the IRS contended the equipment should only be valued at $4,000,000?

Research Problem 3. The IRS is auditing your client, Artis, on the tax treatment of disposition of an interest in the ABC Partnership. Here's the background: Partner Artis received $100,000 of cash from ABC Partnership on July 1, 2023, to retire her entire interest in ABC (ABC continues to operate). ABC is a service provider (consulting services), and Artis was a general partner. The ABC General Partnership agreement, which was drafted in 2018, did not explain how a retiring partner would be paid for their share of partnership goodwill. In 2022, the partnership executed an "Amendment of General Partnership Agreement," which provided that Partner Artis was to receive $100,000 cash from the partnership on July 1, 2023, to retire the partnership interest. It continued to state that $30,000 of that amount was "in return for Artis's one-third interest in the fair market value of the net assets of the partnership, and the other $70,000 was a guaranteed payment or a payment for goodwill."

Saying that the "Amendment of General Partnership Agreement" is not clear, the IRS wants to treat the payment for goodwill as ordinary income to Artis and deductible by the partnership. (This approach maximizes the tax revenue for the government.) Your manager recalls that a Tax Court case from several years ago addresses partnership agreements and goodwill. (The manager said "maybe it's 'Jordan' or 'Jackson' or something.") Use Checkpoint to research this issue. Can you find such a case? If so, does it help Artis's position that she should receive a return of basis and capital gain treatment for the "goodwill" portion of the payment? Describe whether and how any subsequent cases have modified this ruling.

Use internet tax resources to address the following questions. Look for reliable websites and blogs of the IRS and other government agencies, media outlets, businesses, tax professionals, academics, think tanks, and political outlets.

Research Problem 4. On what form or attachment does a partnership report that it has made a § 754 election? Prepare such a form using the facts of Example 30 in the text.

Research Problem 5. Over the years, Congress has considered (several times) various "partnership simplification" plans. For example, imagine how much less complex partnership taxation would be if § 751 was repealed—the whole idea of "hot assets" would disappear. Try different searches in Checkpoint to see if any such changes

Communications
Critical Thinking

are in the works. For example, is there any "News" in the area? If you look at "Bill Tracker" for § 751, do you see any pending legislation that might repeal it? Write a memo to your instructor outlining your ideas for simplifying partnership taxation. Include your findings on any potential changes to "hot assets" and the ramifications if § 751 was repealed as well as other ideas you come up with on your own or through your research.

Communications
Data Analytics

Research Problem 6. For the most recent year available, what types of partnerships are most commonly used in various industries? Consider general and limited partnerships and LLCs; disregard LLPs and foreign partnerships. Which types of industries/partnerships account for the largest numbers of partners? Profits (or losses)? Why do you think these results might arise? In other words, why do you think the partnership entity form "works" for these industries?

Use the partnership information "by entity type" at **irs.gov/taxstats** to help you discover these data. For each situation, evaluate the industry total compared to "All Industries." Consider only "main categories." For example, consider "Finance and insurance" and "Real estate and rental and leasing" rather than subcategories such as "Securities and commodity contracts" or "Lessors of residential buildings and dwellings." *Hint:* Your total (for a given category) for separate industries should equal the total for "all industries."

In an e-mail to your instructor, describe your results. Support your findings with pie charts, line charts, and/or "stacked" area charts.

Becker CPA Review Questions

Becker

1. Hart's adjusted basis of his interest in a partnership was $30,000. He received a nonliquidating distribution of $24,000 cash plus a parcel of land with a fair market value and partnership basis of $9,000. Hart's basis for the land is:

   a. $9,000
   b. $6,000
   c. $3,000
   d. $0

2. Gearty's adjusted basis in Worthington Company, a partnership, was $18,000 at the time Gearty received the following nonliquidating distributions of partnership property:

Cash	$10,000
Land	
Adjusted basis	14,000
Fair market value	20,000

   What is Gearty's tax basis in the land received from the partnership?

   a. $0
   b. $8,000
   c. $14,000
   d. $20,000

3. Desi's adjusted basis of her partnership interest was $40,000 immediately before she received a distribution in full liquidation of her Makris partnership interest. The distribution consisted of $25,000 in cash and land with a fair market value of $30,000. Makris's basis in the land was $28,000 immediately prior to the distribution. During the year, Desi sold the land for $50,000. How will Desi report the liquidating distribution and the sale on her income tax return?

	Liquidating Distribution	Sale of the Land
a.	No gain or loss	$35,000 capital gain
b.	No gain or loss	$22,000 capital gain
c.	$15,000 gain	$20,000 capital gain
d.	$25,000 loss	$10,000 capital gain

4. On December 31 of the current year, Fox sold his interest in a limited partnership for $50,000 cash and relief of all partnership liabilities. On that date, the adjusted basis of Fox's partnership interest, after the increase for his share of current year partnership income, was $60,000 consisting of his capital account of $35,000 and his share of the partnership liabilities of $25,000. The partnership has no unrealized receivables or substantially appreciated inventory. What is Fox's gain or loss on the sale of his partnership interest?

   a. Ordinary loss of $10,000
   b. Ordinary gain of $15,000
   c. Capital loss of $10,000
   d. Capital gain of $15,000

Chapter 23

S Corporations

Learning Objectives: *After completing Chapter 23, you should be able to:*

- **LO.1** Explain the tax effects of S corporation status on shareholders.
- **LO.2** Identify corporations that qualify for the S election.
- **LO.3** Explain how to make an S election.
- **LO.4** Explain how an S election can be terminated.
- **LO.5** Compute nonseparately stated income, and identify separately stated items.
- **LO.6** Allocate income, deductions, and credits to shareholders.
- **LO.7** Determine how distributions to S corporation shareholders are taxed.
- **LO.8** Calculate a shareholder's basis in S corporation stock.
- **LO.9** Explain the tax effects of losses on shareholders.
- **LO.10** Compute the various S corporation penalty taxes.
- **LO.11** Describe other tax issues applicable to S corporations.
- **LO.12** Engage in tax planning for S corporations.

Chapter Outline

LISA S./SHUTTERSTOCK.COM

Deductibility of Losses and the Choice of Business Entity

Cane, Inc., has been a C corporation for a number of years, earning taxable income of less than $100,000 per year. Thus, the business has been subject to the lower C corporation tax rates, but, due to competitors' sales of cheap products from China, Cane's two owners, Smith and Jones, expect operating losses for the next two or three years. They hope to outsource some of the manufacturing to Vietnam and turn the company around. How can they deduct these anticipated future losses in the earliest tax years possible?

The corporation receives some tax-exempt income, generates a small amount of passive investment income, and holds some C corporation earnings and profits. Each owner draws a salary of $92,000. Cane has issued two classes of stock, voting and nonvoting common. Cane is located in Texarkana, Texas. Smith lives in Texas, and Jones lives in Arkansas. Both are married to Mexican citizens who live outside the United States.

Should Smith and Jones elect to have Cane treated as an S corporation?

Read the chapter and formulate your response.

An individual establishing a business has a number of choices as to the form of business entity under which to operate. One alternative, the **S corporation**, provides many of the benefits of partnership taxation and, at the same time, gives the owners limited liability protection from creditors. The S corporation rules, which are contained in **Subchapter S** of the Internal Revenue Code (§§ 1361–1379), were enacted to allow flexibility in the entity choice that businesspeople face. Exhibit 23.1 compares the number and operations of the various entity choices.

Exhibit 23.1 Comparison of Business Entity Choices

	Returns	Receipts	Income	Assets
Sole Proprietorships (non-farm) (2019)	27.8M	$ 1.6T	$355.2B	Unknown
Partnerships (2019)	3.8M[1]	8.1T	760.6B	$ 36T
Corporations (2019)[2]	6.5M	35.9T	2.9T[3]	114.8T

[1]71% LLCs; 13% GPs; 11% LPs; 3% LLPs; 2% other.
[2]4.9M Forms 1120S; $511B pretax profits.
[3]Income subject to Federal income tax.
Source: irs.gov/statistics.

LO.1

Explain the tax effects of S corporation status on shareholders.

23-1 Choice of Business Entity

S corporations (like C corporations) are organized under state law. Similar to C corporations, S corporations are recognized as separate legal entities and generally provide shareholders with limited liability protection. However, as a general rule, S corporations are exempt from Federal income taxes, including the corporate income tax and the corporate alternative minimum tax.[1] Otherwise, as a rule, where the S corporation provisions are silent, C corporation rules apply.

The S corporation rules should be seen as supplementary to the Federal income tax rules for all C corporations (see Chapters 17 through 20) and to those for partnerships and limited liability entities (contained in Code Subchapter K; see Chapters 21 and 22). Some provisions apply only to electing S corporations (addressed throughout this chapter), but S corporations also must apply certain tax rules of Subchapters C and K.

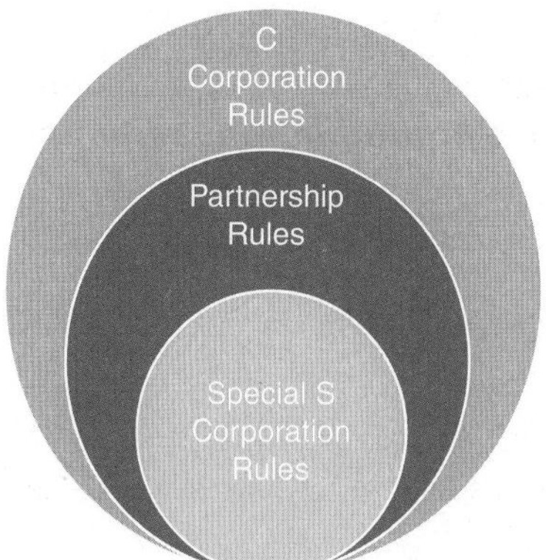

Today the choice of a flow-through entity for a closely held business often is between an S corporation (a Federal tax entity) and an LLC (a state tax entity). Both are flowthrough entities for Federal income tax purposes and provide limited liability for the owners under nontax state law. In this way, income, deductions, and tax credits of an S corporation flow through to shareholders annually, regardless of whether distributions of wealth (like cash) are made to the shareholders. Thus, income is taxed only once at the shareholder level and not at the corporate level, a highly attractive tax planning result.

[1]§ 1363(a). See also §§ 55(b)(2) and 59(k)(1)(A) (AMT).

23-1a An Overview of S Corporations

S corporations can be advantageous even when the individual tax rate exceeds the corporate tax rate.

S Corporation Advantages

Example 1

An S corporation earns $300,000 for the tax year. The marginal individual tax rate applicable to the entity's shareholders is 37% on ordinary income and 20% on dividends (ignoring the 3.8% net investment income tax). The corporate tax rate is 21%, and the S corporation shareholders receive the full 20% qualified business income deduction (see text Section 23-3b). All after-tax income is distributed currently.

	C Corporation	S Corporation
Earnings	$300,000	$300,000
Less: Corporate Federal income tax	(63,000)	(-0-)
Available for distribution	$237,000	$300,000
Less: Tax at owner level	(47,400)*	(88,800)**
Available after-tax earnings	$189,600	$211,200

The S corporation generates an extra $21,600 of after-tax earnings ($211,200 – $189,600) when compared with a similar C corporation. The C corporation might be able to reduce this disadvantage by paying out its earnings as deductible compensation, rents, or interest expense. Tax at the owner level also can be deferred or avoided by not distributing after-tax earnings.

*20% (tax rate on dividend income) × $237,000 = $47,400.

**37% × [$300,000 – $60,000 (qualified business income deduction)] = $88,800.

A new corporation elects S status and incurs a net operating loss (NOL) of $300,000. The shareholders may use their proportionate shares of the NOL to offset other taxable income in the current year, providing an immediate tax savings. In contrast, a newly formed C corporation is required to carry the NOL forward and does not receive any tax benefit in the current year. Hence, an S corporation can accelerate NOL deductions and thereby provide a greater present value for tax savings generated by the loss.

23-2 Qualifying for S Corporation Status

Identify corporations that qualify for the S election.

23-2a Defining an S Corporation

To achieve S corporation status, a corporation *first* must qualify as a **small business corporation**. If each of the following requirements is met, then the entity can elect S corporation status:

- Is a domestic corporation (incorporated and organized in the United States).
- Is an eligible corporation (see the following section for ineligible types).
- Issues only one class of stock.
- Is limited to a theoretical maximum of 100 shareholders.
- Has only individuals, estates, and certain trusts and exempt organizations as shareholders.
- Has no nonresident alien shareholders.[2]

No maximum or minimum dollar sales or capitalization restrictions apply to small business corporations.

Ineligible Corporations

Small business corporation status is not permitted for non-U.S. corporations or for certain banks and insurance companies.

[2]Federal tax law uses the term "alien" to describe a person who is not a U.S. citizen. § 7701(b).

Any domestic corporation that is not an ineligible corporation can be a qualified Subchapter S corporation subsidiary (QSSS) if another S corporation holds 100 percent of its stock and elects to treat the subsidiary as a QSSS.[3] QSSSs are separate entities for legal purposes, but they are treated as a division of the parent for Federal income tax purposes.

One Class of Stock

An S corporation may have only one class of stock issued and outstanding. This restriction permits differences in voting rights but not differences in distribution or liquidation rights.[4] Thus, two classes of common stock that are identical, except that one class is voting and the other is nonvoting, are treated as a single class of stock for S corporation purposes. In contrast, voting common stock and voting preferred stock (with a preference on dividends) are treated as two classes of stock. Authorized and unissued stock or treasury stock of another class do not count as a second class of stock. Likewise, unexercised stock options, warrants, and convertible debt usually do not constitute a second class of stock.[5]

The Big Picture

Example 3

Return to the facts of *The Big Picture* on p. 23-1. Cane, Inc., could elect S status as long as the two classes of common stock are identical except for differences in voting rights. In this situation, one class of common stock is voting and the other class is nonvoting. This situation does not violate the one-class-of-stock rule.

You learn that both shareholders have binding employment contracts with Cane, Inc. The amount of compensation paid by the corporation to Jones under her contract is reasonable, but the amount paid to Smith under his contract is excessive, resulting in a constructive dividend. Smith's employment contract was not designed to circumvent the one-class-of-stock requirement.

Because employment contracts are not considered governing provisions, Cane still is treated as though it has only one class of stock if an S election is made.

Number of Shareholders

An S corporation theoretically is limited to 100 shareholders. However, a group of family members is treated as one shareholder in meeting the 100-shareholder limit. For this purpose, a family includes any common ancestor, the lineal descendants of the common ancestor, and the spouses (or former spouses) of the lineal descendants or common ancestor.[6] This rule allows the entity stock to be held by more than 100 shareholders. Note, though, that over 99 percent of all S corporations have 10 or fewer shareholders.

Fred and Wilma (husband and wife) jointly own 10 shares in Marlins, Inc., an S corporation, with the remaining 290 shares outstanding owned by 99 other unrelated shareholders. Fred and Wilma are divorced; pursuant to the property settlement approved by the court, the 10 shares held by Fred and Wilma are divided between them, five shares to each.

Before the divorce settlement, Marlins had 100 shareholders under the S corporation rules. After the settlement, it still has 100 shareholders and continues to qualify for S treatment. A former spouse is treated as being in the same family as the individual to whom they were married.

[3] § 1361(b)(3)(B).

[4] §§ 1361(b)(1)(D) and (c)(4).

[5] Reg. § 1.1361–1(l).

[6] § 1361(c)(1).

Type of Shareholder Limitation

S corporation shares may be held by U.S. citizens or residents, estates, certain trusts, charities, and certain other tax-exempt organizations.[7] Qualified retirement plans other than IRAs and one-person LLCs also can qualify as shareholders of an S corporation. This limitation prevents partnerships, corporations, limited liability partnerships, and most LLCs from owning S corporation stock. The 100-shareholder limitation could be circumvented if partnerships and corporations were to own S stock.

Saul and 105 of his friends want to form an S corporation. Saul reasons that if he and his friends form a partnership, the partnership can then form an S corporation and act as a single shareholder, thereby avoiding the 100-shareholder rule. Saul's plan will not work because partnerships cannot own stock in an S corporation.

Although partnerships and corporations cannot own S corporation stock, S corporations can be partners in a partnership, members in an LLC, or shareholders in another corporation. As a result, the 100-shareholder requirement can be bypassed in a limited sense. For example, if two S corporations, both with 80 shareholders, form a partnership, then all 160 shareholders can enjoy the limited liability conferred by S status and a single level of tax on the S corporation and partnership profits.

Nonresident Aliens

Individuals who are not U.S. citizens *must live in the United States* if they are to own S corporation stock.[8] One who is neither a U.S. citizen nor a U.S. resident is termed a nonresident alien (NRA). Therefore, shareholders with NRA spouses in community property states[9] cannot own S corporation stock because the spouse would be treated as owning half of the community property.[10] Similarly, if a resident alien shareholder moves outside the United States, the S election is terminated.

The Big Picture

Return to the facts of *The Big Picture* on p. 23-1. Because Jones lives in Arkansas, a common law property state, the fact that she is married to an NRA spouse would not affect an S election. However, because Smith lives in Texas, a community property state, his spouse is treated as owning half of his community property stock, and an S election would not be allowed. To qualify for S status, Smith could move to Arkansas or his wife could move to Texas (becoming a resident alien).

23-2b **Making the Election**

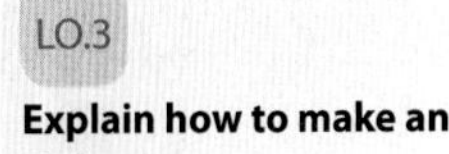

Explain how to make an S election.

To become an S corporation, the entity must file a valid election with the IRS. The election is made on Form 2553. For the election to be valid, it should be filed on a timely basis and all shareholders must consent.

[7] §§ 1361(b)(1)(B) and (c)(2); Reg. § 1.1361–1(h). When an S shareholder dies, a trust created by their will can hold S stock for no more than two years.

[8] § 1362(b)(1)(C).

[9] Assets acquired by a married couple generally constitute community property in these states: Arizona, California, Idaho, Louisiana, Nevada, New Mexico, Texas, Washington, Wisconsin, and (if elected) Alaska.

[10] Reg. § 1.1361–1(g). See, for example, *Ward v. U.S.*, 81–2 USTC ¶9674, 48 AFTR 2d 81–5942, 661 F.2d 226 (Ct.Cl.). Because the taxpayer-shareholder (a U.S. citizen) was married to a citizen and resident of Mexico, the nonresident alien prohibition was violated. If the taxpayer-shareholder had held all of the stock as separate property, the S election would have been valid.

For S corporation status to apply in the current tax year, the election must be filed either in the previous year or on or before the fifteenth day of the third month of the current year.

The Big Picture

Return to the facts of *The Big Picture* on p. 23-1. Suppose that in 2023, shareholders Smith and Jones decide to become an S corporation beginning January 1, 2024. Because the C corporation uses a calendar tax year, the S election can be made at any time in 2023 or by March 15, 2024. An election after March 15, 2024, is not effective until the 2025 calendar tax year.

Even if the 2½-month deadline is met, an S election is not valid unless the entity qualifies under the S rules for the *entire* tax year. Otherwise, the election is not effective until the following tax year.

A corporation that does not yet exist cannot make an S corporation election.[11] Thus, for new corporations, a premature election may not be effective. A new corporation's 2½-month election period begins at the earliest occurrence of any of the following events:

- When the corporation has shareholders.
- When it acquires assets.
- When it begins doing business.[12]

Several individuals acquire assets on behalf of Rock Corporation on June 29, 2023, and they begin doing business on July 6, 2023. They subscribe to shares of stock; file articles of incorporation for Rock; and become shareholders on July 8, 2023. The S election must be filed no later than 2½ months after June 29, 2023 (i.e., on or before September 12), to be effective for 2023.

23-2c **Shareholder Consent**

A qualifying election requires the consent of all of the corporation's shareholders.[13] Consent must be in writing, and it generally must be filed by the election deadline. A consent extension is available only if Form 2553 is filed on a timely basis, reasonable cause is given, and the interests of the government are not jeopardized.[14]

Vern and Yvonne decide to convert their C corporation into a calendar year S corporation for 2023. At the end of February 2023 (before the election is filed), Yvonne travels to Ukraine and forgets to sign a consent to the election. Yvonne will not return to the United States until June, and she cannot be reached by fax or e-mail.

Vern files the S election on Form 2553 and requests an extension of time to file Yvonne's consent to the election. Vern indicates that there is a reasonable cause for the extension: a shareholder is out of the country. Because the government's interest is not jeopardized, the IRS probably will grant Yvonne an extension of time to file the consent. Vern must file the election on Form 2553 on or before March 15, 2023, for the election to be effective for the 2023 calendar year.

[11] See, for example, *T.H. Campbell & Bros., Inc.*, 34 TCM 695, T.C.Memo. 1975–149; Ltr.Rul. 8807070.

[12] Reg. § 1.1362–6(a)(2)(ii)(C). Also see, for example, *Nick A. Artukovich*, 61 T.C. 100 (1973).

[13] § 1362(a)(2).

[14] § 1362(b)(5) and Reg. § 1.1362–6(b)(3)(iii).

Both husband and wife must consent if they own their stock jointly (as joint tenants, tenants in common, tenants by the entirety, or community property), even though they count as one shareholder for purposes of the 100-shareholder limitation.

Three shareholders, Amy, Monty, and Dianne, incorporate in January and file Form 2553. Amy is married and lives in California. Monty is single, and Dianne is married; both live in South Carolina. Because Amy is married and lives in a community property state, her husband also must consent to the S election. South Carolina is not a community property state, so Dianne's husband need not consent.

For current-year S elections, persons who were shareholders during any part of the taxable year before the election date but were not shareholders when the election was made also must consent to the election.[15]

On January 17, 2023, the stock of Columbus Corporation (a calendar year C corporation) was held equally by three individual shareholders: Jim, Sally, and LuEllen. On that date, LuEllen sells her interest to Jim and Sally. On March 13, 2023, Columbus Corporation files Form 2553. Jim and Sally indicate their consent by signing the form. Columbus cannot become an S corporation until 2024 because LuEllen did not indicate consent. Had all three shareholders consented by signing Form 2553, S status would have taken effect as of January 1, 2023.

23-2d Loss of the Election

LO.4

Explain how an S election can be terminated.

An S election remains in force until it is revoked or lost. Election or consent forms are not required for future years. However, an S election can terminate if any of the following occurs:

- Shareholders owning a majority of shares (voting and nonvoting) voluntarily revoke the election.
- A new shareholder owning more than one-half of the stock affirmatively refuses to consent to the election.
- The corporation no longer qualifies as an S corporation.
- The corporation fails the passive investment income test.

Voluntary Revocation

A **voluntary revocation** of the S election requires the consent of shareholders owning a majority of shares on the day the revocation is to be made.[16] A revocation filed up to and including the fifteenth day of the third month of the tax year is effective for the entire tax year unless a later date is specified. Similarly, unless an effective date is specified, revocation made after the first 2½ months of the current tax year is effective for the following tax year.

The shareholders of Petunia Corporation, a calendar year S corporation, voluntarily revoke the S election on January 5 of the current year (not a leap year). They do not specify a future effective date in the revocation. If the revocation is properly executed and timely filed, Petunia will be a C corporation for the entire current tax year. If the election is not made until June, though, Petunia remains an S corporation for this year; it becomes a C corporation at the beginning of the next year.

[15] § 1362(b)(2)(B)(ii).

[16] § 1362(d)(1).

A corporation can revoke its S status *prospectively* by specifying a future date when the revocation is to be effective. A revocation that designates a future effective date splits the corporation's tax year into a short S corporation year and a short C corporation year. The day on which the revocation occurs is treated as the first day of the C corporation year. The corporation allocates income or loss for the entire year on a pro rata basis, using the number of days in each short year.

Assume the same facts as in the preceding example, except that Petunia designates July 1 as the revocation date. Accordingly, June 30 is the last day of the S corporation's tax year. The C corporation's tax year runs from July 1 to December 31 of the current year. Income or loss for the 12-month period is allocated between the two short years (i.e., 184/365 to the C corporation year).

Rather than allocating on a pro rata basis, the corporation can elect to compute actual income or loss attributable to the two short years. This election requires the consent of everyone who was a shareholder at any time during the S corporation's short year and everyone who owns stock on the first day of the C corporation's year.[17]

Assume the same facts as in the preceding example, except that all of Petunia's shareholders consent to allocate the income or loss to the two short tax years based on its actual realization. Assume further that Petunia experiences a loss of $102,000 for the year, of which $72,000 is incurred in the first half of the year. Because $72,000 of the loss occurs before July 1, this amount is allocated to the S corporation short year, and only $30,000 of the loss is allocated to the C corporation year.

Loss of S Corporation Status

If an entity fails to qualify as an S corporation at any time after the election has become effective, its status as an S corporation ends. The termination occurs on the day that an S requirement is violated.[18] Thus, if the corporation ever has more than 100 qualified shareholders, has a second class of stock, has a nonqualifying shareholder, or otherwise fails one of the S qualification rules, the S election is terminated immediately.

Peony Corporation has been a calendar year S corporation for three years. On August 13, one of its 100 shareholders sells *some* of her stock to an outsider. Peony now has 101 shareholders, and it ceases to be an S corporation. For the tax year, Peony is an S corporation through August 12 and a C corporation from August 13 to December 31.

Passive Investment Income Limitation

The Code provides a **passive investment income (PII)** limitation for a few S corporations. If an S corporation holds C corporation E & P and it generates passive investment income in excess of 25 percent of its gross receipts for three consecutive tax years, the S election is terminated as of the beginning of the fourth year.[19]

For 2021, 2022, and 2023, Diapason Corporation, a calendar year S corporation, received passive investment income in excess of 25% of its gross receipts. If Diapason holds accumulated E & P from years in which it was a C corporation, its S election is terminated as of January 1, 2024.

[17] § 1362(e)(3).

[18] § 1362(d)(2)(B).

[19] § 1362(d)(3)(A)(ii).

PII includes dividends, interest, rents, gains and losses from sales of capital assets, and royalties net of investment deductions. Rents are not considered PII if the corporation renders significant personal services to the occupant.

Violet Corporation owns and operates an apartment building. The corporation provides utilities for the building, maintains the lobby, and furnishes trash collection for tenants. These activities are not considered significant personal services, so any rent income earned by the corporation will be considered PII.

Alternatively, if Violet also furnishes maid services to its tenants (personal services beyond what normally would be expected from a landlord in an apartment building), the rent income would no longer be PII.

Reelection after Termination

After an S election has been terminated, the corporation must wait five years before reelecting S corporation status. The five-year waiting period is waived if:

- There is a more-than-50% change in ownership of the corporation after the first year for which the termination is applicable.
- The event causing the termination was not reasonably within the control of the S corporation or its majority shareholders.[20]

Conditions that a corporation must meet before S corporation status is available are illustrated in Exhibit 23.2.

23-3 Operational Rules

S corporations are treated much like partnerships for tax purposes. With a few exceptions,[21] S corporations generally make tax accounting and other elections at the corporate level. Each year, the S corporation determines nonseparately stated income or loss and separately stated income, deductions, and credits. These items are taxed only once, at the shareholder level. All items are allocated to each shareholder based on average ownership of stock throughout the year. The *flow-through* of each item of income, deduction, and credit from the corporation to the shareholder is illustrated in Exhibit 23.3.

23-3a Taxable Income

LO.5

Compute nonseparately stated income, and identify separately stated items.

An S corporation's taxable income or loss is determined in a manner similar to the tax rules that apply to partnerships, except that S corporations amortize organizational expenditures under the C corporation rules[22] and must recognize gains, *but not losses*, on distributions of appreciated property to shareholders.[23] Other provisions affecting only the computation of C corporation income, such as the dividends received deduction, do not extend to S corporations. Finally, as with partnerships, certain items designed for individuals are not permitted, such as the standard deduction.[24]

In general, S corporation items are divided into (1) nonseparately stated income or loss and (2) separately stated income, losses, deductions, and credits that could affect the tax liability of any shareholder in a different manner, depending on other factors in the shareholder's tax situation.

[20] § 1362(g) and Reg. § 1.1362–5(a).

[21] A few elections can be made at the shareholder level (e.g., the choice between a foreign tax deduction or credit). But shareholders cannot make these accounting method elections; only the entity can do so. *Ronald A. Caselli*, 115 TCM 1448, T.C.Memo. 2018–81.

[22] §§ 248 and 1363(b)(3).

[23] § 311(b).

[24] §§ 703(a)(2) and 1363(b)(2).

Exhibit 23.2 **Conditions Required to Elect S Corporation Status**

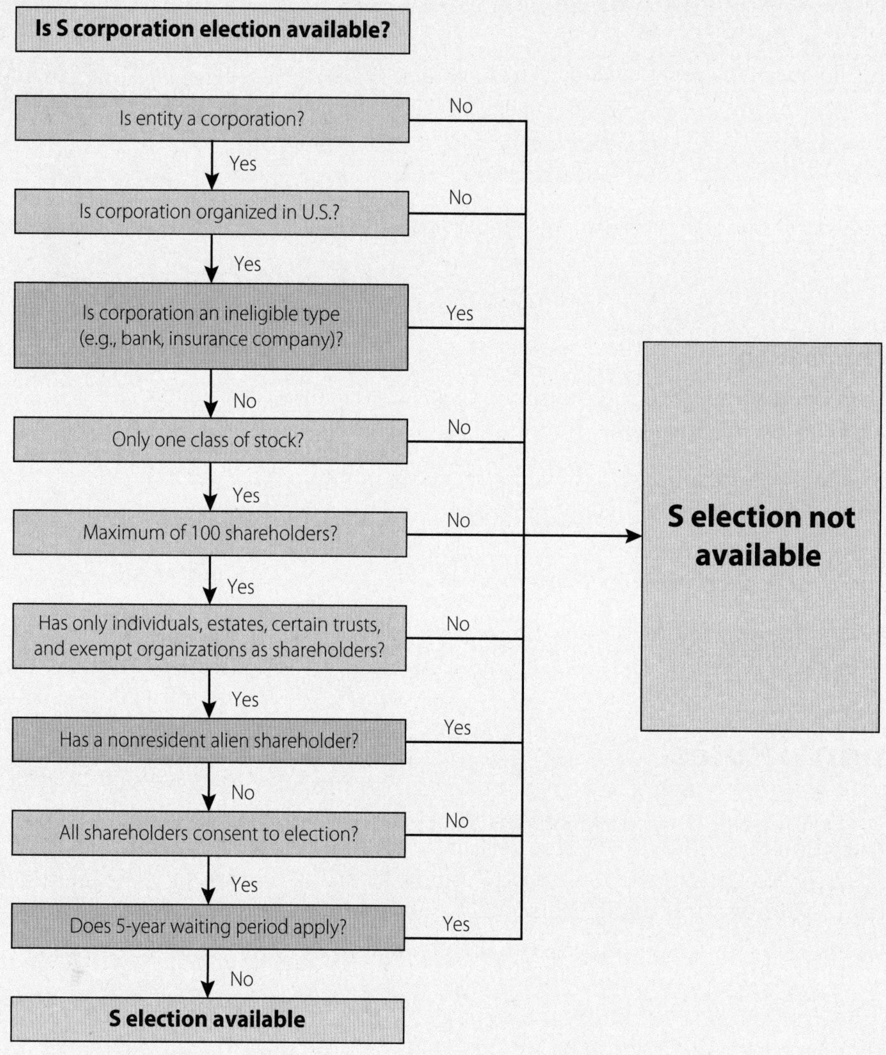

Nonseparate items are aggregated into an undifferentiated amount that constitutes S corporation ordinary income or loss. An S corporation's separately stated items are identical to those separately stated by partnerships. These items retain their tax attributes on the shareholder's return. Separately stated items are listed on Schedule K of the 1120S. They include the following:

- Tax-exempt income.
- Long-term and short-term capital gains and losses.
- § 1231 gains and losses.
- Charitable contributions.
- Passive activity gains, losses, and credits.
- Data used to compute the qualified business income deduction.
- § 179 depreciation.
- Tax preferences and adjustments for the shareholders' potential alternative minimum tax.
- Depletion computations.
- Foreign income or loss.
- Recoveries of tax benefit items.
- Intangible drilling costs.
- Investment interest, income, and expenses.

Exhibit 23.3 **Flow-Through of Separate Items (Selected) to S Corporation Shareholders**

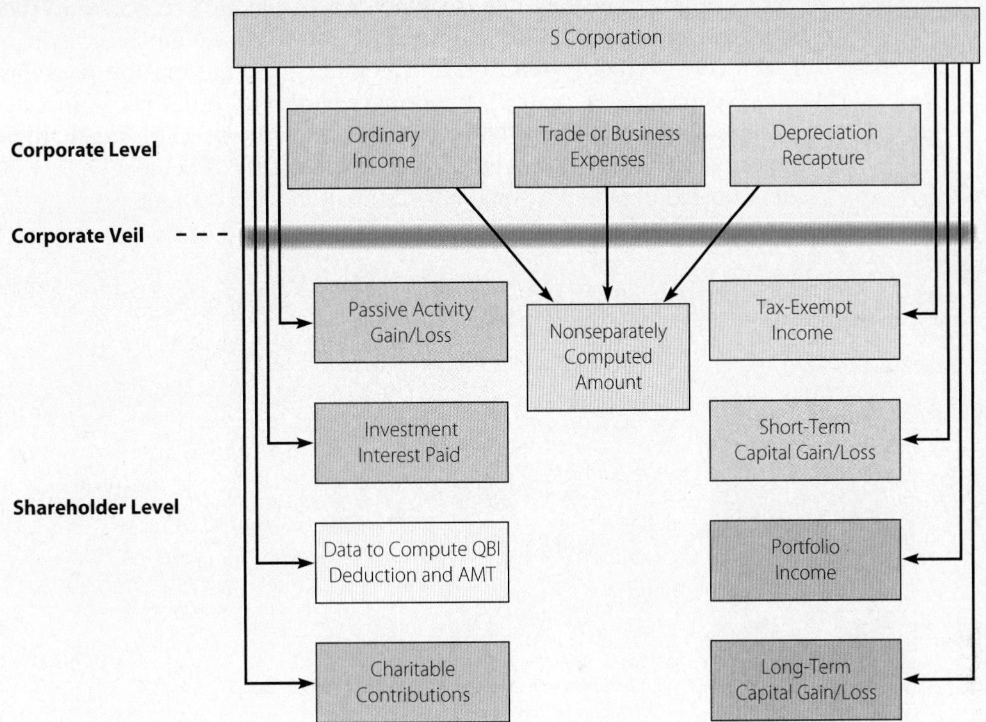

Example 18

The following is the income statement for Jersey, Inc., an S corporation:

Sales		$ 40,000
Less cost of sales		(23,000)
Gross profit on sales		$ 17,000
Less: Interest expense	$1,200	
Charitable contributions	400	
Advertising expenses	1,500	
Other operating expenses	2,000	(5,100)
Book income from operations		$ 11,900
Add: Tax-exempt interest	$ 300	
Dividend income	200	
Long-term capital gain	500	1,000
Less: Short-term capital loss		(150)
Net income per books		$ 12,750

Jersey's ordinary income is calculated as follows, using net income for book purposes as the starting point:

Net income per books		$ 12,750
Separately stated items		
Subtract: Tax-exempt interest	$ 300	
Dividend income	200	
Long-term capital gain	500	(1,000)
Add: Charitable contributions	$ 400	
Short-term capital loss	150	550
Ordinary income		$ 12,300

The $12,300 of Jersey's ordinary income, as well as each of the five separately stated items, are divided among the shareholders based upon their stock ownership.

23-3b Qualified Business Income Deduction

To bring the taxation of flow-through entities such as S corporations closer to the C corporation 21 percent rate, shareholders of certain S corporations (and other qualified flow-through entities) may deduct up to 20 percent of certain qualified business income (QBI).[25] With the full 20 percent deduction, the pass-through top rate is 29.6 percent (0.80 × 0.37), ignoring payroll and other taxes. Income earned by a C corporation that is distributed after-tax as a dividend to the shareholders may be subject to a maximum Federal income tax rate of 39.8 percent [0.21 + (0.79 × 0.238)] after considering the 3.8 percent investment income tax rate.

The **qualified business income deduction (QBID)** is:

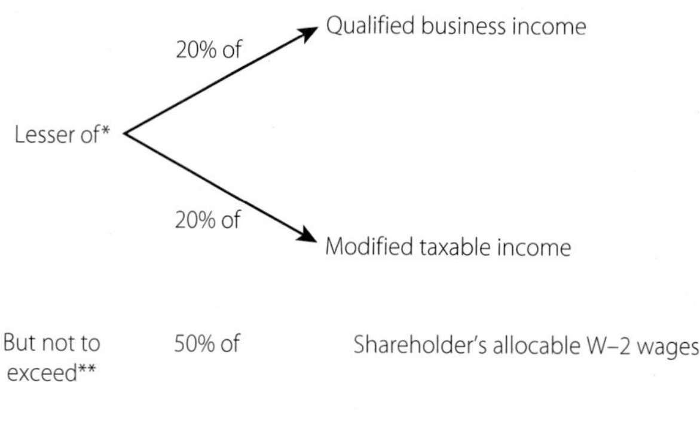

This deduction has no effect on AAA or the shareholder's stock basis. If the S corporation is a specified service trade or business and the owner's income exceeds a maximum amount, the QBID is zero. See text Section 15-5g.

LO.6

Allocate income, deductions, and credits to shareholders.

23-3c Allocation of Income and Loss

Each shareholder is allocated a pro rata portion of nonseparately stated income or loss and all separately stated items. The pro rata allocation method assigns an equal amount of each of the S items to each day of the year. If a shareholder's stock holding changes during the year, this allocation assigns the shareholder a pro rata share of each item for *each* day the stock is owned. On the date of transfer, the transferor (and not the transferee) is considered to own the stock.[26]

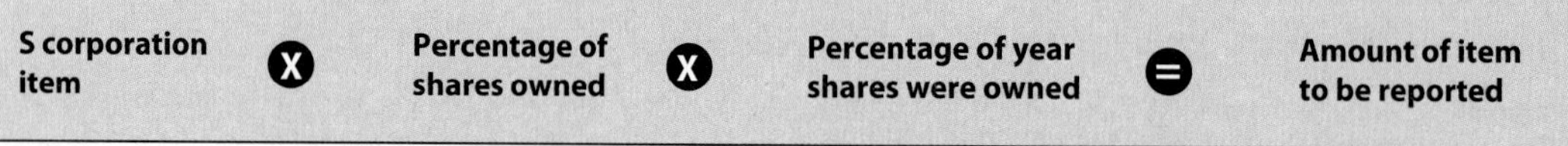

The per-day allocation must be used unless the shareholder disposes of their entire interest in the entity.[27]

[25] § 199A. See also text Section 15-5.

[26] Reg. § 1.1377–1(a)(2)(ii).

[27] §§ 1366(a)(1) and 1377(a)(1).

Example 19

Assume in the previous example that Pat, a shareholder, owned 10% of Jersey's stock for 100 days and 12% for the remaining 265 days of the tax year (not a leap year). Using the required per-day allocation method, Pat's share of the S corporation items is determined as follows.

	Schedule K Totals	Pat's Share 10%	Pat's Share 12%	Pat's Schedule K–1 Totals
Ordinary income	$12,300	$337	$1,072	$1,409
Tax-exempt interest	300	8	26	34
Dividend income	200	5	17	22
Long-term capital gain	500	14	44	58
Charitable contributions	400	11	35	46
Short-term capital loss	150	4	13	17

Pat's share of Jersey's ordinary income is the total of $12,300 × [0.10 × (100/365)] plus $12,300 × [0.12 × (265/365)], or $1,409. Each of the Schedule K–1 totals from the right column flows through to the appropriate lines on Pat's individual income tax return (Form 1040).

The Short-Year Election

If a shareholder's interest is completely terminated by a sale or by a disposition following death during the tax year, all shareholders owning stock during the year and the corporation may elect to treat the S taxable year as two taxable years. The first year ends on the date of the termination. Under this election, an interim closing of the books is undertaken, and the shareholders report their shares of the S corporation items as they occurred during the short tax year.[28]

The short-year election provides an opportunity to shift income, losses, and credits among shareholders. The election is desirable in circumstances where more loss can be allocated to taxpayers with higher marginal rates.

Alicia, the owner of all of the shares of an S corporation, transfers her stock to Cindy halfway through the tax year. There is a $100,000 NOL for the entire tax year, but $30,000 of the loss occurs during the first half of the year. Without a short-year election, $50,000 of the loss is allocated to Alicia, and $50,000 is allocated to Cindy. If the corporation makes the short-year election, Cindy is allocated $70,000 of the loss. Note that the sales price of the stock would probably be increased to recognize the tax benefits being transferred from Alicia to Cindy.

23-3d Distributions to Shareholders

Determine how distributions to S corporation shareholders are taxed.

The amount of any actual distribution of wealth (like cash) to an S corporation shareholder is equal to the cash plus the fair market value of any other property distributed. How the distribution is taxed depends upon whether the S corporation has C corporation accumulated earnings and profits (AEP) (described in text Section 19-2).

No C Corporation AEP

If the S corporation never has been a C corporation or if it holds no C corporation AEP, the distribution is a tax-free recovery of capital to the extent that it does not exceed the shareholder's basis in the stock of the S corporation. When the amount of the

[28] § 1377(a)(2).

distribution exceeds the basis of the stock, the excess is treated as a gain from the sale or exchange of property (capital gain in most cases). The vast majority of S corporations fall into this easy-to-apply category.

Example 21

Twirl, Inc., a calendar year S corporation, has no AEP. During the year, Juan, an individual shareholder of the corporation, receives a cash distribution of $12,200 from Twirl. Juan's basis in his stock is $9,700. Juan recognizes a capital gain of $2,500, the excess of the distribution over the stock basis ($12,200 − $9,700). The remaining $9,700 is tax-free, but it reduces Juan's basis in his stock to zero.

C Corporation AEP Exists

S corporations that hold AEP, a rare occurrence, treat distributions of pre-election (C corporation) and post-election (S corporation) earnings differently. An S corporation can hold AEP if the entity previously was a C corporation, or if a C corporation was merged into it.

In such a case, distributions of AEP are taxed as dividends, while distributions of previously taxed S corporation earnings are tax-free to the extent of the shareholder's basis in the stock.

Concept Summary 23.1 outlines the taxation of distributions in these circumstances. These rules are intended to prevent two problems that result when a profitable C corporation (i.e., one holding C corporation accumulated E & P) has been converted to an S corporation.

- Manipulation in the shareholders' favor could result because the AEP would not be taxed when an S distribution is made; S corporation shareholders are taxed on income, not on distributions.
- On the other hand, double taxation could occur if the rules acted to tax as dividend income any AEP that exists when a distribution is made to the S shareholders; S distributions usually are free of income tax.

The Accumulated Adjustments Account A special account is required to track undistributed earnings of an S corporation that have been taxed to shareholders previously. Distributions from this account, known as the **accumulated adjustments account (AAA)**,

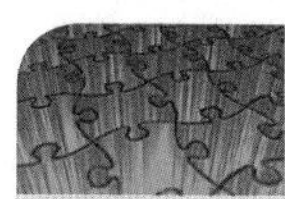

Concept Summary 23.1

Classification Procedures for Distributions from an S Corporation

Where No Earnings and Profits Exist	Where Earnings and Profits Exist
	1. Distributions are tax-free to the extent of the AAA.*
	2. Distributions from AEP constitute dividend income.†
	3. Distributions are tax-free to the extent of the other adjustments account (OAA).*
1. Distributions are nontaxable to the extent of shareholder's basis of stock.*	4. Any residual distribution amount is nontaxable to the extent of shareholder's basis of stock.*
2. Excess is treated as gain from a sale or exchange of stock (capital gain in virtually all cases).	5. Excess is treated as gain from a sale or exchange of stock (capital gain in virtually all cases).

*The distribution reduces the stock basis. Once stock basis reaches zero, any distribution from the AAA is treated as a gain from the sale or exchange of stock. Thus, the shareholder's stock basis is an upper limit on what a shareholder may receive tax-free.

†The AAA bypass election is available to pay out AEP before reducing the AAA [§ 1368(e)(3)].

are tax-free. The AAA begins with a zero balance on the first day of an S corporation's first tax year. Essentially, the AAA is the cumulative total of undistributed nonseparately and separately stated items for S corporation tax years. Calculation of the AAA should be made by all S corporations, but the AAA is most important to those that have been C corporations. The AAA provides a mechanism to ensure that the earnings of an S corporation are taxed to shareholders only once.

The AAA is computed by making adjustments in the order specified in Exhibit 23.4. Its balance typically is determined at the end of each year, rather than on the date of the distribution. When more than one distribution occurs in the same year, a pro rata portion of each payment is treated as having been made out of the AAA.

In calculating the amount in the AAA for purposes of determining the tax treatment of current-year distributions, the net negative adjustments (e.g., the excess of losses and deductions over income) for that tax year are ignored. Tax-exempt income and related expenses (e.g., insurance proceeds and premiums paid for life insurance) do not affect the AAA.

A shareholder has a proportionate interest in the AAA, regardless of the size of their stock basis.[29] However, because the AAA is a corporate account, no connection exists between the prior accumulated S corporation income and any specific shareholder.[30] When shares are transferred, the benefits of the AAA are shifted from one shareholder to another.

The AAA can have a negative balance. All losses decrease the AAA balance, even those in excess of the shareholder's stock basis. However, *distributions* may not make the AAA negative or increase a negative balance.

Distribution Ordering Rules A cash distribution from an S corporation with AEP comes first from the AAA.[31] A distribution from the AAA is a tax-free recovery of capital and reduces the shareholder's stock basis. The remaining distribution is taxed as a dividend to the extent of AEP. After AEP is fully distributed, any residual amount reduces the other adjustments account (OAA, discussed in the next section) (but not below zero) and is a tax-free recovery of capital to the extent of the shareholder's stock basis. Any distributions in excess of the stock basis typically are taxed as capital gains.[32]

Exhibit 23.4 Adjustments to the Corporate AAA

Increase by:

1. Schedule K income items other than tax-exempt income.
2. Nonseparately computed income.
3. Depletion in excess of basis in the property.

Decrease by:

4. Negative Schedule K adjustments other than distributions (e.g., losses and deductions).
5. Any portion of a distribution that is considered to be tax-free from the AAA (but not below zero).

Note: When the combination of items 1 through 4 results in a negative number, the AAA is adjusted first for the distribution and then for the adjustments in items 1 through 4.

[29] § 1368(c).

[30] § 1368(e)(1)(A).

[31] §§ 1368(c)(1) and (e)(1).

[32] §§ 1368(c)(2) and (3).

Ordering Rules for Distributions

Example 22

Short, a calendar year S corporation, distributes $1,300 cash to its only shareholder, Otis, on December 31. Otis's basis in his stock is $1,400, Short's AAA balance is $500, and Short holds $750 AEP before the distribution.

According to the distribution ordering rules, the first $500 is a tax-free recovery of basis from the AAA. The next $750 is a taxable dividend distribution from AEP. The remaining $50 distributed is a tax-free recovery of basis. Short now holds a zero balance in its AAA and AEP. Otis's stock basis now is $850.

	Corporate AAA	Corporate AEP	Otis's Stock Basis*
Balance before the distribution	$ 500	$ 750	$1,400
Distribution ($1,300)			
From AAA	(500)		(500)
From AEP		(750)	
From stock basis			(50)
Balance after the distribution	$ -0-	$ -0-	$ 850

*Details of basis adjustments are discussed later in the chapter.

Assume the same facts as in the preceding example. During the following year, Short reports zero ordinary income and distributes $1,000 to Otis. Of the distribution, $850 is a tax-free recovery of basis, and $150 is taxed to Otis as a capital gain.

With the consent of all of its shareholders, an S corporation can elect to have a distribution treated as if it were made from AEP rather than from the AAA. This mechanism is known as an AAA **bypass election**. This election may be desirable as a simple means by which to eliminate a small AEP balance and simplify the taxation of future distributions.

Collett, a calendar year S corporation, has AEP of $12,000 and a balance of $20,000 in the AAA. Collett Corporation may elect to distribute the AEP first, creating a $12,000 dividend for its shareholders, before using the AAA. Afterward, any distribution from Collett merely reduces stock basis.

Other Aspects of the AAA

Schedule M–2. S corporations report changes in the AAA on Schedule M–2 of Form 1120S. Schedule M–2 contains a column labeled **other adjustments account (OAA)**. This account includes items that affect basis but not the AAA, such as tax-exempt income and any related nondeductible expenses. For example, life insurance proceeds received and insurance premiums paid are traced through the OAA. Distributions are made from the OAA after AEP and the AAA are depleted to zero. Distributions from the OAA generally are tax-free.

Example 25

Sparrow, an S corporation, records the following items:

AAA, beginning of the year	$ 8,500
Ordinary income	25,000
Tax-exempt interest	4,000
Key employee life insurance proceeds received	5,000
Payroll penalty expense	2,000
Charitable contributions	3,000
Unreasonable compensation	5,000
Premiums on key employee life insurance	2,100
Distributions to shareholders	16,000

Sparrow's Schedule M–2 for the current year appears as follows.

Schedule M-2 **Analysis of Accumulated Adjustments Account, Shareholders' Undistributed Taxable Income Previously Taxed, Accumulated Earnings and Profits, and Other Adjustments Account** (see instructions)

		(a) Accumulated adjustments account	(b) Shareholders' undistributed taxable income previously taxed	(c) Accumulated earnings and profits	(d) Other adjustments account
1	Balance at beginning of tax year	8,500			
2	Ordinary income from page 1, line 21	25,000			
3	Other additions				9,000**
4	Loss from page 1, line 21	( )			
5	Other reductions	(10,000*)			(2,100)
6	Combine lines 1 through 5	23,500			6,900
7	Distributions	16,000			
8	Balance at end of tax year. Subtract line 7 from line 6	7,500			6,900

**$2,000 (payroll penalty) + $3,000 (charitable contributions) + $5,000 (unreasonable compensation).*
***$4,000 (tax-exempt interest) + $5,000 (life insurance proceeds).*

Schedule M–3: Net Income or Loss Reconciliation. S corporations that have total assets on Schedule L at the end of the tax year that equal or exceed $10 million must file Schedule M–3 in lieu of Schedule M–1. Only a few large S corporations must file a Schedule M–3. The schedule provides detailed information about the entity's book-tax differences, and it can be used by the IRS to target specific items that will be subjected to an audit.

Effect of Terminating the S Election. Normally, distributions to shareholders from a C corporation are taxed as dividends to the extent of E & P. However, any distribution of *cash* by a corporation to shareholders during a one-year period[33] following S election termination receives a different treatment. Such a distribution is treated as a tax-free recovery of stock basis to the extent that it does not exceed the AAA.[34] To take advantage of post-termination benefits, an S corporation must know the amount of both the AAA and the OAA as of the date the election terminates.

Example 26

Quinn, the sole shareholder of Roman, Inc., a calendar year S corporation, elects during 2023 to terminate the S election, effective January 1, 2024. As of the end of 2023, Roman holds an AAA of $1,300. Quinn can receive a nontaxable distribution of cash during a post-termination period of approximately one year to the extent of Roman's AAA. Although a cash distribution of $1,300 during 2024 would be nontaxable to Quinn, it would reduce the basis of his stock.

[33] The period is approximately one year in length. The post-termination transition period is discussed later in the chapter.

[34] §§ 1371(e) and 1377(b).

23-3e Noncash Property Distributions

An S corporation recognizes a gain on any distribution of appreciated property in the same manner as if the asset were sold to the shareholder at its fair market value.[35] The corporate gain is passed through to the shareholders. The character of the gain—capital gain or ordinary income—depends upon the type of asset being distributed.

The S corporation does not recognize a loss when distributing assets that are worth less than their basis. As with gain property, the shareholder's basis in the asset is equal to its fair market value. Thus, the potential loss is postponed until the shareholder sells the stock of the S corporation. Because loss property receives a step-down in basis without any loss recognition by the S corporation, distributions of loss property should be avoided. Concept Summary 23.2 summarizes the tax treatment of noncash distributions for various entities.

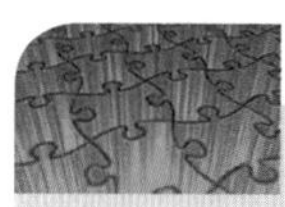

Concept Summary 23.2

Consequences of Noncash Distributions

	Appreciated Property	Depreciated Property
S corporation	Realized gain is recognized by the corporation, which passes it through to the shareholders. Such gain increases a shareholder's stock basis, generating a basis in the property equal to FMV. On the distribution, the shareholder's stock basis is reduced by the FMV of the property (but not below zero).	Realized loss is not recognized. The shareholder takes an FMV basis in the property. On the distribution, the shareholder's stock basis is reduced by the FMV of the property (but not below zero).
C corporation	Realized gain is recognized under § 311(b) and increases E & P (net of tax). The shareholder reports a taxable dividend to the extent of corporate E & P equal to the property's FMV. The shareholder takes an asset basis equal to its FMV.	Realized loss is not recognized. The shareholder takes an FMV basis in the property.
Partnership	No gain to the partnership or partner. The partner takes a carryover basis in the asset, but the asset basis is limited to the partner's basis in the partnership.	Realized loss is not recognized. The partner takes a carryover basis in the asset, but the asset basis is limited to the partner's basis in the partnership.

Noncash Distributions

Example 27

Turnip, Inc., an S corporation for 10 years, distributes a tract of land held as an investment to Chang, its majority shareholder. The land was purchased for $22,000 many years ago and currently is worth $82,000. Turnip recognizes a capital gain of $60,000, which increases the AAA by $60,000. The gain appears on Turnip's Schedule K, and a proportionate share of it passes through to the shareholders' tax returns. Then the property distribution reduces the AAA by $82,000 (the fair market value). The tax consequences are the same for appreciated property, whether it is distributed to the shareholders and they dispose of it or the corporation sells the property and distributes the proceeds to the shareholders.

If the land had been purchased for $82,000 and was currently worth $22,000, Chang would take a $22,000 basis in the land. The $60,000 realized loss is not recognized at the corporate level. The loss does reduce Turnip's AAA, though not an attractive result for Turnip shareholders.

[35] § 311(b).

Noncash Distributions

Example 28

Assume the same facts as in the previous example, except that Turnip is a C corporation ($1,000,000 E & P balance) or a partnership. The partner's basis in the partnership interest is $100,000.

	Appreciated Property		
	S Corporation	C Corporation	Partnership
Entity gain/loss	$60,000	$60,000	$ -0-
Owner's gain/loss/dividend	60,000	82,000	-0-
Owner's basis in land	82,000	82,000	22,000
	Property That Has Declined in Value		
	S Corporation	**C Corporation**	**Partnership**
Entity gain/loss	$ -0-	$ -0-	$ -0-
Owner's gain/loss/dividend	-0-	22,000	-0-
Owner's basis in land	22,000	22,000	82,000

23-3f Shareholder's Basis in S Stock

LO.8 **Calculate a shareholder's basis in S corporation stock.**

The calculation of the initial tax basis of stock in an S corporation is similar to that for the basis of stock in a C corporation and depends upon the manner in which the shares are acquired (e.g., gift, inheritance, purchase, or exchange under § 351). Once the initial tax basis is determined, various transactions during the life of the corporation affect the shareholder's basis in the stock.

A shareholder's basis in S stock is required for determining gain (or loss) upon disposition, determining the deductibility of loss pass-throughs (see text Section 23-3g), and determining the treatment of distributions (see text Section 23-3d). Further, a shareholder's basis in loans to an S corporation can impact the deductibility of loss pass-throughs (see text Section 23-3g), as well as the treatment of loan repayments. Form 7203, *S Corporation Shareholder Stock and Debt Basis Limitations*, is required to be filed by an S corporation shareholder with their individual tax return when the shareholder:

- Claims a deduction for their share of an aggregate loss of an S corporation.
- Receives a non-dividend distribution from an S corporation.
- Disposes of stock in an S corporation.
- Receives a loan repayment from an S corporation.

Stock Basis Adjustments

A shareholder's basis in S stock is increased by stock purchases and capital contributions. Operations during the year cause the following upward adjustments to basis:

- Nonseparately computed income.
- Separately stated income items (e.g., nontaxable income).
- Depletion in excess of basis in the property.

Basis then is reduced by distributions not reported as income by the shareholder (e.g., an AAA distribution). Next, the following items reduce basis (*but not below zero*):

- Nondeductible expenses of the corporation (e.g., fines, penalties, and illegal kickbacks).
- Nonseparately computed loss.
- Separately stated loss and deduction items.

As for partnerships, basis first is increased by income items; then it is decreased by distributions and finally by losses. In most cases, this *losses last* rule is advantageous to the S shareholder.

In its first year of operation, Iris, Inc., a calendar year S corporation, earns income of $2,000. On February 2 in its second year of operation, Iris distributes $2,000 to Ebony, its sole shareholder. During the remainder of the second year, the corporation incurs a $2,000 loss.

Before accounting for the entity's operating results, Ebony's stock basis is zero. Under the S corporation ordering rules, the $2,000 distribution is tax-free AAA to Ebony, and the $2,000 loss is suspended until Ebony generates additional stock basis (e.g., from capital contributions or future entity profits).

Shareholder Loans to S Corporations

A shareholder's basis in S stock never can be reduced below zero. Once stock basis reaches zero, any additional basis reductions from losses or deductions, but *not* distributions, decrease (but not below zero) the shareholder's basis in loans made to the S corporation. Any excess of losses or deductions over both bases is *suspended* until there are subsequent bases.

Once the basis of any debt is reduced, it later is increased (up to the original amount) by the subsequent *net increase* resulting from all positive and negative basis adjustments. The debt basis is adjusted before any increase is made in the stock basis.[36]

A distribution in excess of stock basis does not reduce any debt basis. If a loss and a distribution occur in the same year, the loss reduces the stock basis *after* the distribution.[37]

Sofia, a sole shareholder, has a $7,000 stock basis and a $2,000 basis in a loan that she made to Romulus, a calendar year S corporation with no AEP. At the beginning of the tax year, the corporation's AAA and OAA balances are zero. Ordinary income for the year is $8,200, during which Romulus received $2,000 of tax-exempt interest income.

Cash of $17,300 is distributed to Sofia on November 15. Sofia recognizes a $100 capital gain from the distribution.

	Corporate AAA	Corporate OAA	Sofia's Stock Basis	Sofia's Loan Basis
Beginning balance	$ -0-	$ -0-	$ 7,000	$2,000
Ordinary income	8,200		8,200	
Tax-exempt income		2,000	2,000	
Subtotal	$ 8,200	$ 2,000	$17,200	$2,000
Distribution ($17,300)				
From AAA	(8,200)		(8,200)	
From OAA		(2,000)	(2,000)	
From stock basis			(7,000)	
Ending balance	$ -0-	$ -0-	$ -0-	$2,000
Distribution in excess of basis = Capital gain			$ 100	

Pass-through losses can reduce loan basis, but distributions do not. Stock basis cannot be reduced below zero, so the $100 excess distribution does not reduce Sofia's loan basis.

The basis rules for an S corporation are similar to the rules for determining a partner's interest basis in a partnership. However, a partner's basis in the partnership interest includes the partner's direct investment plus a *ratable share* of any partnership liabilities.[38] In contrast, except for loans from the shareholder to the corporation, corporate borrowing has no effect on S corporation shareholder basis.

The fact that a shareholder has guaranteed a loan made to the corporation by a third party has no effect on the shareholder's loan basis, unless payments actually have been made as a result of that guarantee.[39]

[36] § 1367(b)(2)(B) and Reg. § 1.1367–2(c)(1).

[37] Reg. § 1.1367–1(f).

[38] § 752(a).

[39] Reg. § 1.1366–2(a)(2)(ii). See, for example, *Estate of Leavitt*, 90 T.C. 206 (1988), *aff'd* 89–1 USTC ¶9332, 63 AFTR 2d 89–1437, 875 F.2d 420 (CA–4); *Selfe v. U.S.*, 86–1 USTC ¶9115, 57 AFTR 2d 86–464, 778 F.2d 769 (CA–11, 1985); *James K. Calcutt*, 91 T.C. 14 (1988).

Effects of Debt

Bree owns 40% of Triangle, in which she holds a basis of $100,000. Triangle has borrowed funds to finance its operations, and Bree's share of this loan is $40,000. If Triangle is a partnership, Bree's basis in her ownership interest is $140,000. If Triangle is an S corporation, Bree's basis in her stock is $100,000.

Khalid is a shareholder in Octagon, an S corporation. Khalid's basis in his Octagon stock is zero, due to a series of pass-through operating losses. Khalid loaned Octagon $50,000 to cover payroll; after accounting for operating losses, his basis in the loan is $30,000. This year, Octagon generates an operating profit, and Khalid's share of the income is $25,000. The income first restores Khalid's loan basis to $50,000, and it then increases his stock basis to $5,000.

23-3g **Treatment of Losses**

Explain the tax effects of losses on shareholders.

Net Operating Loss

One major advantage of an S election is the ability to pass through any net operating loss of the corporation directly to the shareholders. A shareholder can deduct its share of the entity's operating loss on its own tax return for the year in which the S corporation's tax year ends. The corporation does not deduct the NOL. A shareholder's basis in the stock is reduced to the extent of any pass-through of the NOL, and the entity's AAA is reduced by the same deductible amount.[40]

The Big Picture

Return to the facts of *The Big Picture* on p. 23-1. If Smith and Jones make the S election for Cane, Inc., Cane's NOLs will pass through to the shareholders to the extent of their stock basis. If the new S corporation incurs an NOL of $84,000 for the tax year, both shareholders are entitled to deduct $42,000 against other income for the tax year in which Cane's tax year ends. Any NOL incurred before the S election is in effect does not flow through to the two shareholders.

Deductions for an S corporation's loss pass-throughs (e.g., NOL, capital loss, and charitable contributions) cannot exceed a shareholder's adjusted basis in the stock *plus* the basis of any loans made by the shareholder to the corporation. If a taxpayer is unable to prove the tax basis, the loss pass-through can be denied.

Distributions made by an S corporation are taken into account *before* applying the loss limitations for the year.

Pylon, Inc., a calendar year S corporation, is partly owned by Doris, who has a beginning stock basis of $10,000. The basis in a loan that Doris made to Pylon is $4,000.

Doris's share of Pylon's current-year operating loss is $11,000. She deducts this amount on her Form 1040. Doris's stock now has a basis of zero, and her basis in the loan is now $3,000.

A shareholder's share of an NOL may be greater than both stock basis and loan basis. A shareholder can carry forward a loss to the extent that the loss for the year exceeds basis. Any loss carried forward may be deducted *only* by the *same* shareholder if and when the basis in the stock or loans to the corporation is restored.[41]

Example 35

Dana has a stock basis of $4,000 in an S corporation. He has loaned $2,000 to the corporation and has guaranteed another $4,000 loan made to the corporation by a local bank. Although his share of the S corporation's NOL for the current year is $9,500, Dana may deduct only $6,000 of the NOL on his Form 1040; the loan guarantee had no effect on Dana's stock or loan basis.

continued

[40] §§ 1367(a)2)(C) and 1368(e)(1)(A).

[41] § 1366(d).

Dana may carry forward $3,500 of the NOL to be deducted when the basis in his stock or loan to the corporation is restored. Dana has a zero basis in both the stock and the loan after the flow-through of the $6,000 NOL.

Any loss carryover due to insufficient basis remaining at the end of an approximately one-year post-termination transition period is *lost forever*. The post-termination period usually begins when the shareholder disposes of S stock or the S election is terminated.[42] Thus, if a shareholder has a loss carryover, they should increase the stock or loan basis and flow through the loss before disposing of the stock.

Net operating losses from C corporation years cannot be utilized at the corporate level (except with respect to built-in gains, discussed in text Section 23-3h), nor can they be passed through to the shareholders. When a corporation is expecting losses in the future, an S election should be made *before* the loss years occur.

At-Risk Rules

S corporation shareholders, like partners, are limited in the amount of loss they may deduct by their "at-risk" amounts; see text Section 21-4g. These rules apply to the shareholders but not to the corporation. An amount at risk is determined separately for each shareholder.

Example 36

Shareholder Ricketts has a basis of $35,000 in his S corporation stock. His share of this year's S corporation loss is $40,000.

Ricketts takes a $15,000 nonrecourse loan from a local bank and lends the proceeds to the S corporation. Ricketts now has a stock basis of $35,000 and a loan basis of $15,000. However, a nonrecourse loan does not place Ricketts "at risk," so he can deduct only $35,000 of S corporation losses, reducing his stock basis to $0.

Passive Activity Losses and Credits

S corporations are not directly subject to the passive activity limits, but corporate rental activities are inherently passive, and other activities of an S corporation may be passive unless the shareholder materially participates in operating the business. If the corporate activity involves rentals or the shareholder does not materially participate, any loss or credit that flows through is passive. The shareholder can apply such losses or credits only against income from other passive activities.

LO.10

Compute the various S corporation penalty taxes.

23-3h Tax on Pre-Election Built-In Gain

In almost all cases, an S corporation does *not* pay an income tax because all items flow through to the shareholders. But a few S corporations are required to pay a built-in gains tax, LIFO recapture tax, general business credit recapture, or passive investment income tax.

Without the **built-in gains tax** (§ 1374), it would be possible to avoid the corporate double tax on a disposition of appreciated property by electing S corporation status.

The built-in gains tax generally applies to C corporations converting to S status. It is a *corporate-level* tax on any built-in gain recognized when the S corporation disposes of an asset in a taxable disposition within five calendar years after the date on which the S election took effect.[43] The holding period begins on the date of the S election.

General Rules

The base for the built-in gains tax includes any unrealized gain on appreciated assets (e.g., real estate, cash basis receivables, and goodwill) held by a corporation on the day it elects S status. The highest corporate tax rate (currently 21 percent) is applied to the unrealized gain when any of the assets are sold. Furthermore, the gain on the sale (net of the tax itself)[44] passes through as a taxable gain to shareholders.

[42] § 1377(b)(1)(A).

[43] § 1374(d)(7)(A).

[44] § 1366(f)(2).

Zinnia, Inc., a C corporation, owns a single asset with a basis of $100,000 and a fair market value of $500,000. Zinnia elects S corporation status. A corporate-level tax must be paid by Zinnia if it sells the asset within five years after electing S status.

Assume Zinnia sells the asset three years later for $500,000. In that case, the corporation owes a tax of $84,000 ($400,000 × 21%). The shareholders report a $316,000 taxable gain ($400,000 − $84,000). In this manner, the built-in gains tax effectively imposes a double tax on Zinnia and its shareholders.

The gain that is subject to the tax is limited to the *aggregate net* built-in gain of the corporation at the time it converted to S status. Recognized built-in losses and built-in gains are netted each year to determine the built-in gains tax base. The tax base then is limited to the entity's taxable income for the year.[45]

An S corporation can offset built-in gains with NOLs or unexpired capital losses from C corporation years.

The Big Picture

Example 38

Return to the facts of *The Big Picture* on p. 23-1. If Cane, Inc., becomes an S corporation, a built-in gain may be recognized. Assume that Cane has a net built-in gain of $50,000 on conversion and that it holds a $20,000 NOL carryforward for C corporation years before the S election. If the built-in gain is recognized, Cane's built-in gains tax applies only to $30,000 ($50,000 – $20,000 deduction for the NOL carryforward).

23-3i LIFO Recapture Tax

To preclude deferral of gain recognition by a C corporation that is electing S status, any LIFO recapture amount at the time of the S election is subject to a corporate-level tax.

The taxable LIFO recapture amount equals the excess of the inventory's value under FIFO over the LIFO value. No tax refund is allowed if the LIFO value is higher than the FIFO value.

The resulting tax is payable in four equal installments, with the first payment due on or before the due date for the corporate return for the last C corporation year (without regard to any extensions). The remaining three installments are paid on or before the due dates of the succeeding corporate returns.

No interest is due if payments are made by the due dates, and no estimated taxes are due on the four tax installments. The basis of the LIFO inventory is adjusted to account for this LIFO recapture amount, but the AAA is not decreased by payment of the tax.

23-3j Passive Investment Income Penalty Tax

A tax is imposed on the excess passive income of S corporations that possess C corporation AEP. The tax rate is the highest corporate rate for the year (21 percent). The rate is applied to excess net passive income (ENPI), which is determined using the following formula:

$$\frac{\text{Passive investment income in excess of 25\% of gross receipts for the year}}{\text{Passive investment income for the year}} \times \text{Net passive investment income for the year} = \text{Excess net passive income}$$

Passive investment income (PII) includes gross receipts derived from royalties, passive rents, dividends, interest, and annuities. Only the net gain from the disposition of capital assets is taken into account in computing PII gross receipts.[46] Net passive income is PII reduced by any deductions directly connected with the production of that income. Any PII tax reduces the gross income that flows through to the shareholders.

[45] §§ 1374(c)(2), (d)(1), and (d)(2)(A).

[46] §§ 1362(d)(3)(B) and (C).

The excess net passive income cannot exceed the S corporation's taxable income for the year, calculated as if it were a C corporation.[47]

Barnhardt Corporation, an S corporation, generates gross receipts for the year totaling \$264,000 (of which \$110,000 is PII). Expenditures directly connected to the production of the PII total \$30,000. Therefore, Barnhardt reports net PII of \$80,000 (\$110,000 − \$30,000), and its PII for the tax year exceeds 25% of its gross receipts by \$44,000 [\$110,000 PII − (25% × \$264,000)]. Excess net passive income (ENPI) is \$32,000, calculated as follows:

$$\text{ENPI} = \frac{\$44,000}{\$110,000} \times \$80,000 = \$32,000$$

Barnhardt's PII tax is \$6,720 (\$32,000 × 21%).

LO.11

Describe other tax issues applicable to S corporations.

23-4 Other Tax Issues

Several other points may be made about the possible effects of various Code provisions on S corporations.

- An S corporation must make estimated tax payments with respect to any tax on a net recognized built-in gain and excess passive investment income.
- An S corporation is *not* subject to the 10 percent of taxable income limitation applicable to charitable contributions made by a C corporation.
- Any family member who renders services or furnishes capital to an S corporation must be paid reasonable compensation. Otherwise, the IRS can make adjustments to reflect the value of the services or capital.[48] This rule may make it more difficult for related parties to shift Subchapter S taxable income to children or other family members.
- The flow-through of S items does not create self-employment income to the shareholder, nor is it subject to the additional Medicare tax on upper-income taxpayers.[49] This treatment is attractive compared to the treatment of a proprietorship or a partnership whose income is taxed as self-employment income to the owners.
- The \$10,000 limitation on the deduction for state and local taxes ("SALT cap") can be minimized for S shareholders in a number of states that have adopted a pass-through entity tax (PTET) election. The PTET election allows a resident S corporation to pay state income taxes and treat such payment as an entity-level tax, even if a shareholder receives a deduction or credit for the tax for state income tax purposes. Under these "SALT cap workarounds," state income taxes are treated as deductions in computing non-separately stated income (or loss), instead of as separately stated items, thus avoiding the \$10,000 SALT cap for S shareholders.[50]
- In most cases, an LLC will be taxed as a sole proprietorship (in the case of a single-member LLC) or as a partnership (in the case of a multi-member LLC). However, under the Check-the-box Regulations, an LLC can file Form 8832 and elect to be taxed as a corporation. See text Section 15–3d. An LLC electing to be taxed as a corporation and meeting the S corporation eligibility requirements can elect to be treated as an S corporation by timely filing Form 2553.[51]

S Corporations and SE Income

Mickey and Dana each own one-third of a fast-food restaurant, and their 14-year-old son owns the other shares. Both parents work full-time in the restaurant operations, but the son works infrequently. Neither parent receives a salary this year when the taxable income of the S corporation is \$160,000. The IRS can require that reasonable compensation be paid to the parents to prevent the full one-third of the \$160,000 from being taxed to the son. Otherwise, this would be an effective technique to shift earned income to a family member to reduce the total family tax burden. Furthermore, low or zero salaries can reduce FICA taxes.

[47] § 1375(b)(1)(B).

[48] § 1366(e).

[49] Rev.Rul. 59–221.

[50] See Notice 2020–75.

[51] But see Ltr.Rul. 202110010 (S election terminated when LLC's operating agreement contained terms causing the entity to have more than one class of stock).

S Corporations and SE Income

Example 41

Dave is a professor at a southeastern university earning a salary of $180,000. He also generates consulting income of $80,000. If the consulting business is organized as an S corporation, Dave should withdraw a reasonable salary from the S corporation for his services. The S corporation pays payroll and withholding tax on the salary.

If the business is operated as a proprietorship, Dave is exempt from the Social Security portion of the self-employment tax because his university salary exceeds the annual FICA ceiling. Here, operating as a proprietorship offers a tax advantage over an S corporation.

- Some or all of the entity's income may be subject to a state-level income tax (e.g., a gross receipts tax or a "sting tax" on large S corporations in Massachusetts).
- An S corporation may issue § 1244 stock to its shareholders to obtain ordinary loss treatment. Review text Section 18-3c for the Federal income tax effects of such stock.
- The exclusion of gain on disposition of small business stock is *not* available for S stock.[52]
- Losses may be disallowed due to a lack of a profit motive. If the activities at the corporate level are not profit-motivated, the losses may be disallowed under the hobby loss rules.[53]
- A penalty is imposed for failure to file (including extensions) timely S corporation returns. The minimum penalty for returns filed in 2024 is $235 per month times the number of S corporation shareholders. The penalty is assessed against the corporation for a maximum of 12 months.[54]
- Partnership treatment applies for certain fringe benefits to more-than-2% shareholder-employees of S corporations. Thus, these shareholders are not entitled to exclude certain fringe benefits from gross income. A more-than-2% shareholder-employee is allowed an above-the-line (*for* AGI) deduction on Form 1040 for accident and health insurance premiums.[55]

23-5 Tax Planning

LO.12 **Engage in tax planning for S corporations.**

23-5a When the Election Is Advisable

Effective tax planning with S corporations begins with the determination of whether the election is appropriate. In this context, one should consider the following factors:

- Are losses from the business anticipated? If so, the S election may be highly attractive because these losses pass through to the shareholders.
- What are the tax brackets of the shareholders? If the shareholders are in high individual income tax brackets, it may be desirable to avoid S corporation status and have profits taxed to the entity at the lower C corporation rate (21 percent). However, the income still is not in the owners' hands and the income tax on dividend distributions also must be considered.
- When the shareholders are in low individual income tax brackets, the pass-through of corporate profits is attractive, and reducing the combined income tax becomes the paramount consideration.
- Does a C corporation hold an NOL carryforward? Such a loss cannot be used in an S year (except for purposes of the built-in gains tax).
- S corporations generally use a calendar tax year.[56]

[52] § 1202.

[53] § 183; *Michael J. Houston*, 69 TCM 2360, T.C.Memo. 1995–159; *Mario G. De Mendoza, III*, 68 TCM 42, T.C.Memo. 1994–314.

[54] § 6699. For returns required to be filed in 2023, the penalty is $220 per month.

[55] § 1372(a); Notice 2008–1.

[56] Entity tax-year constraints parallel those pertaining to partnerships, as discussed in text Section 21-2g. But the least aggregate deferral method is not used by S corporations.

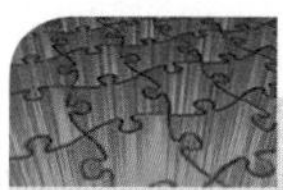

Concept Summary 23.3

Making an S Election

Various considerations will affect a decision to make an S election.

- Avoid the S election if shareholders have high marginal income tax rates relative to the C corporation rate.
- If corporate losses are anticipated and there is unlikely to be corporate taxable income soon, S corporation status is advisable.
- If a C corporation holds an NOL carryover from prior years, the losses cannot be used in an S corporation year (except with respect to built-in gains).
- There may be tax advantages to the S shareholder who receives a flow-through of passive activity income.
- Tax-exempt income at the S level does not lose its special tax treatment for shareholders.

23-5b **Making a Proper Election**

Once the parties have decided the election is appropriate, it becomes essential to ensure that the election is made properly.

- Make sure that all shareholders timely file a proper consent. If any doubt exists concerning the shareholder status of an individual, it would be wise to have that party issue a consent anyway.[57] Too few consents are fatal to the election; the same cannot be said for too many consents.
- Make sure the election is timely and properly filed, using certified or registered mail or a commercial delivery service. A copy of the election should become part of the corporation's permanent files.
- Ascertain when the election period begins to run for a newly formed corporation. An election made too soon (before the corporation is in existence) is ineffective.
- An S election can be lost in several ways, and a five-year waiting period generally is imposed before another S election is available, so the S election must be preserved once it is made.

23-5c **Operation of the S Corporation**

Accumulated Adjustments Account

Although the corporate-level accumulated adjustments account (AAA) is used primarily by an S corporation with AEP, all S corporations should maintain an accurate record of the AAA. Because there is a grace period for distributing the AAA after termination of the S election, the parties must be in a position to determine the balance of the account.

The AAA bypass election may be used to eliminate a small E & P balance and pay a small current tax, but then to avoid future exposure to taxable dividend distributions and the passive investment income penalty tax and S election termination.

Salary Structure

The salary paid to a shareholder-employee of an S corporation can have varying tax consequences and should be considered carefully. Larger amounts might be advantageous if the maximum contribution allowed for the shareholder-employee under the corporation's retirement plan has not been reached. Smaller amounts may be beneficial if the parties are trying to shift taxable income to lower-bracket shareholders, reduce payroll taxes, curtail a reduction of Social Security benefits, or restrict losses that do not pass through because of the stock basis limitation.[58]

A strategy of decreasing compensation and correspondingly increasing distributions to shareholder-employees often results in substantial savings in employment taxes. This technique also may increase the QBID for shareholders.

[57] See *Wilson v. Comm.*, 77–2 USTC ¶9684, 40 AFTR 2d 77–5883, 560 F.2d 687 (CA–5).

[58] Rev.Rul. 74–44; *Spicer Accounting, Inc. v. U.S.*, 91–1 USTC ¶50,103, 66 AFTR 2d 90–5806, 918 F.2d 90 (CA–9, 1990); *Radtke v. U.S.*, 90–1 USTC ¶50,113, 65 AFTR 2d 90–1155, 895 F.2d 1196 (CA–7); *Joseph M. Grey Public Accountant, P.C.*, 119 T.C. 121 (2002), *aff'd* 2004–1 USTC ¶50,214, 93 AFTR 2d 2004–1626, 93 Fed.Appx. 473 (CA–3); *David E. Watson, P.C., v. U.S.*, 2012–2 USTC ¶50,203, 109 AFTR 2d 2012–1059, 668 F.3d 1008 (CA–8). The IRS uses salary surveys and other data to determine the appropriate compensation level.

The Big Picture

Example 42

Return to the facts of *The Big Picture* on p. 23-1. The two shareholders should consider reducing their $92,000 salary, instead receiving a larger undistributed share of the S corporation income. A shareholder's share of pass-through S corporation income is not treated as self-employment income, whereas traditional compensation is subject to the Social Security and Medicare taxes for the corporation and both employees. In addition, the larger amount of S corporation income may result in an increased qualified business income deduction for the shareholders.

The IRS can require that reasonable compensation be paid to family members who render services or provide capital to the S corporation. The IRS also can adjust the items taken into account by family-member shareholders to reflect the value of services or capital they provided (refer to Example 40).

Deductions for various tax-free fringe benefits are denied to a more-than-2% shareholder-employee of an S corporation. Such benefits include group term life insurance, medical insurance, and meals and lodging furnished for the convenience of the employer. These items are treated as wages and are subject to most payroll taxes. The employee can deduct medical insurance premiums on their tax return.

The choice between a salary and pass-through income is not clear-cut.

- Although a salary is subject to payroll tax and pass-through income is not, pass-through income does not accrue Social Security benefits for its recipient.
- S corporation income distributions do not count as compensation for computing an employee's contribution formula for a qualified retirement plan.
- The IRS and the courts require an S shareholder to take a reasonable salary (see footnote 58).
- If a partner or proprietor reports salary income from other sources and the aggregate salaries exceed the annual FICA ceiling, a partnership or proprietorship entity may provide tax savings over an S corporation.

Form 7203

It is recommended that S shareholders complete and retain Form 7203 for all tax years, even for years in which the form is not required to be filed. This will ensure that the S stock (and loan) basis is maintained and accurate for any years in which Form 7203 is required, as well as for general planning purposes (e.g., the donor's basis in a gift of S stock).

Loss Considerations

A net loss in excess of tax basis may be carried forward and deducted only by the same shareholder in succeeding years. Thus, before disposing of the stock, a shareholder should increase the basis of such stock/loan to flow through the loss. The next shareholder does not obtain the loss carryover.

Any unused loss carryover in existence upon the termination of the S election may be deducted only in the next tax year and is limited to the individual's *stock* basis (not loan basis) in the post-termination year.[59] The shareholder may want to purchase more stock before the termination date to increase the tax basis to absorb the loss.

Avoiding the Passive Investment Income Tax

Too much passive investment income (PII) may cause an S corporation to incur a penalty tax on excessive passive investment income and/or terminate the S election. Several planning techniques can be used to avoid both of these unfavorable events. The corporation might reduce taxable income below the excess net passive income; similarly, PII might be accelerated into years in which there is an offsetting NOL. The passive investment income penalty tax and S election termination apply only if accumulated E & P exists. The AAA bypass election can be used to eliminate E & P.

[59] § 1366(d)(3).

23-6 Overall Comparison of Forms of Doing Business

See Concept Summary 23.4 for a detailed comparison of the tax consequences of the following forms of doing business: sole proprietorship, partnership, limited liability company, S corporation, and C corporation.

Concept Summary 23.4

Tax Attributes of Different Forms of Business (Assuming That Partners and Shareholders Are All Individuals)

	Sole Proprietorship	Partnership/Limited Liability Company*	S Corporation	Regular (C) Corporation**
Basic Tax Treatment				
Incidence of tax	Sole proprietorship's income and deductions are reported on Schedule C of the individual's Form 1040. A separate Schedule C is prepared for each business.	Entity not subject to tax. Owners in their separate capacity subject to tax on their distributive share of income. Entity files Form 1065.	Except for certain built-in gains and passive investment income when earnings and profits are present from C corporation tax years, entity not subject to Federal income tax. S corporation files Form 1120S. Shareholders are subject to tax on income attributable to their stock ownership.	Income subject to double taxation. Entity subject to tax, and shareholder subject to tax on any corporate dividends received. Corporation files Form 1120.
Highest tax rate	37% at individual level.	37% at owner level.	37% at shareholder level.	21% at corporate level plus 0%/15%/20% on any corporate dividends at shareholder level (if qualified dividends; otherwise 37%). NIIT of 3.8% may apply to dividend income.
Qualified business income deduction (QBID) (§ 199A)	Applicable.	Applicable. Eligible partners (noncorporate) need data from the entity to compute the deduction amount.	Applicable. Eligible shareholders need data from the entity to compute the deduction amount.	Deduction not applicable to C corporations.
Built-in gains	Not applicable.	Not applicable.	Possible corporate-level tax.	Not applicable.
Alternative minimum tax	Applies at owner level. AMT rates are 26% and 28%.	Applies at the owner level rather than at the entity level. AMT preferences and adjustments are passed through from the entity to the owners.	Applies at the shareholder level rather than at the corporate level. AMT preferences and adjustments are passed through from the S corporation to the shareholders.	Only very large C corporations (generally those with average annual adjusted financial statement income over a 3-year period in excess of $1 billion) are subject to the 15% AMT.
AMT preference and adjustment items	Apply at owner level in determining AMT.	Conduit—passed through to owners who must account for such items in their separate capacities.	Conduit—passed through to shareholders who must account for such items in their separate capacities.	Corporate AMT is based on financial reporting income rather than specific preferences and adjustments.

continued

Tax Attributes of Different Forms of Business—(Continued)

	Sole Proprietorship	Partnership/Limited Liability Company*	S Corporation	Regular (C) Corporation**
Self-employment (SE) tax on owner	Schedule C income subject to SE tax. Owner not treated as employee.	Guaranteed payment for services and distributive share of net earnings of general partner subject to SE tax. Partners not treated as employees.	Not applicable. Payroll taxes owed on reasonable compensation paid to shareholder/employee; no SE tax on shareholder's distributive share of earnings.	Not applicable. Payroll taxes owed on wages of shareholder/employee.
Foreign tax credits	Available at owner level.	Conduit—passed through to owners.	Generally conduit—passed through to shareholders.	Available at corporate level only.
Operational Tax Rules				
Choice of tax year	Same tax year as owner.	Selection generally restricted to coincide with tax year of majority owners or principal owners or to tax year determined under the least aggregate deferral method.	Generally restricted to a calendar year unless IRS approves a different year for business purposes.	Generally unrestricted selection allowed at time of filing first tax return (special rules apply for personal service corporations).
Return due date (normal and extended) for a calendar year entity	April 15 October 15	March 15 September 15	March 15 September 15	April 15 October 15
Timing of taxation	Based on owner's tax year.	Owners report their share of income in their tax year with or within which the entity's tax year ends. Owners in their separate capacities are subject to payment of estimated taxes.	Shareholders report their shares of income in their tax year with or within which the corporation's tax year ends. Shareholders may be subject to payment of estimated taxes.	Corporation subject to tax at close of its tax year. May be subject to payment of estimated taxes. Dividends will be subject to tax at the shareholder level in the tax year received.
Organizational costs	Startup expenditures are eligible for $5,000 limited expensing (subject to phaseout) and amortizing balance over 180 months.	Organizational costs are eligible for $5,000 limited expensing (subject to phaseout) and amortizing balance over 180 months.	Same as partnership.	Same as partnership.
Charitable contributions	Limitations apply at owner level.	Conduit—owners are subject to deduction limitations in their own capacities.	Conduit—shareholders are subject to deduction limitations in their own capacities.	Limited to 10% of taxable income before certain deductions.
Capital gains	Taxed at owner level with net long-term gains taxed at preferential rates.	Conduit—owners must account for their respective shares.	Conduit, except for certain built-in gains—shareholders must account for their respective shares.	Taxed at corporate level at a flat 21% rate. No other benefits.
Capital losses	May offset capital gains plus no more than $3,000 of ordinary income. Indefinite carryover.	Conduit—owners must account for their respective shares.	Conduit—shareholders must account for their respective shares.	Recognizable to extent of capital gains. Excess losses may be carried back three years and forward five.
§ 1231 gains and losses	Taxable or deductible at owner level. Five-year lookback rule for § 1231 losses.	Conduit—owners must account for their respective shares.	Conduit—shareholders must account for their respective shares.	Taxable or deductible at corporate level only. Five-year lookback rule for § 1231 losses.

continued

Tax Attributes of Different Forms of Business—(Continued)

	Sole Proprietorship	Partnership/Limited Liability Company*	S Corporation	Regular (C) Corporation**
Entity Tax Rules				
Restrictions on type or number of owners	One owner. The owner must be an individual.	Must have at least two owners.	Only individuals, estates, certain trusts, and certain tax-exempt entities can be owners. Maximum number of shareholders limited to 100.***	None, except that some states require a minimum of two shareholders.
Contribution of property to the entity	Not a taxable transaction.	Generally not a taxable transaction.	Taxable transaction unless the § 351 requirements are satisfied.	Taxable transaction unless the § 351 requirements are satisfied.
Character of income taxed to owners	Retains source characteristics.	Conduit—retains source characteristics.	Conduit—retains source characteristics.	All source characteristics are lost when income is distributed to owners.
Basis for allocating income to owners	Not applicable (only one owner).	Profit and loss sharing agreement. Cash basis items of cash basis entities are allocated on a daily basis. Other entity items are allocated after considering varying interests of owners.	Pro rata share based on stock ownership. Shareholder's pro rata share is determined on a daily basis, according to the number of shares of stock held on each day of the corporation's tax year.	Not applicable.
Basis for allocating a net operating loss to owners	Not applicable (only one owner).	Profit and loss sharing agreement. Cash basis items of cash basis entities are allocated on a daily basis. Other entity items are allocated after considering varying interests of owners.	Prorated among shareholders on a daily basis.	Not applicable.
Special allocations to owners	Not applicable (only one owner).	Available if supported by substantial economic effect.	Not available.	Not applicable.
Entity deduction for fringe benefits of owners	None.	None.	None unless a 2%-or-less shareholder.	Available within antidiscrimination rules.
Basis treatment of entity liabilities	Includible in interest basis.	Includible in interest basis.	Not includible in stock basis.	Not includible in stock basis.
Limitation on losses deductible by owners	Investment plus liabilities.	Owner's investment plus share of liabilities.	Shareholder's investment plus loans made by shareholder to corporation.	Not applicable.
Subject to at-risk rules	Yes, at the owner level. Indefinite carryover of excess loss.	Yes, at the owner level. Indefinite carryover of excess loss.	Yes, at the shareholder level. Indefinite carryover of excess loss.	Yes, for closely held corporations. Indefinite carryover of excess loss.
Subject to passive activity loss rules	Yes, at the owner level. Indefinite carryover of excess loss.	Yes, at the owner level. Indefinite carryover of excess loss.	Yes, at the shareholder level. Indefinite carryover of excess loss.	Yes, for closely held corporations and personal service corporations. Indefinite carryover of excess loss.
Subject to limitation on excess business losses	Yes, at the owner level.	Yes, at the owner level (unless partner is a corporation).	Yes, at the shareholder level.	No. Limitation does not apply to corporate taxpayers.

continued

Tax Attributes of Different Forms of Business—(Continued)

	Sole Proprietorship	Partnership/Limited Liability Company*	S Corporation	Regular (C) Corporation**
Tax consequences of earnings retained by entity	Taxed to owner when earned and increases their investment in the sole proprietorship.	Taxed to owners when earned and increases their respective basis in the entity.	Taxed to shareholders when earned and increases their respective bases in stock.	Taxed to corporation as earned and may be subject to penalty tax if accumulated unreasonably.
Sale of ownership interest	Treated as the sale of individual assets. Classification of recognized gain or loss depends on the nature of the individual assets.	Treated as the sale of an entity interest. Recognized gain or loss is classified as capital under § 741, subject to ordinary income treatment under § 751.	Treated as the sale of corporate stock. Recognized gain is classified as capital gain. Recognized loss is classified as capital loss, or as ordinary loss under § 1244.	Treated as the sale of corporate stock. Recognized gain is classified as capital gain. Recognized loss is classified as capital loss, or as ordinary loss under § 1244. Gain could be excluded if noncorporate owner held the stock over 5 years and § 1202 applies.
Distribution of appreciated property	Not taxable.	No recognition at the entity level.	Recognition at the corporate level to the extent of the appreciation. Gain then is passed through to shareholders.	Taxable at the corporate level to the extent of the appreciation.
Splitting of income among family members	Not applicable (only one owner). Spouses running a business together can elect "qualified joint venture" status where earnings are split and identical Schedule Cs are filed for each spouse rather than a partnership return [§ 761(f)].	IRS will not recognize a family member as an owner unless certain requirements are met.	IRS can make adjustments to reflect adequate compensation for services.	Other than by asserting unreasonable compensation, IRS generally cannot make adjustments to reflect adequate compensation for services and capital.
Nonliquidating distributions to owners	Not taxable.	Not taxable unless cash received exceeds recipient owner's basis in entity interest. Existence of § 751 assets may cause recognition of ordinary income.	Generally not taxable unless the distribution exceeds stock basis. Existence of accumulated earnings and profits could cause some distributions to be dividends.	Taxable in year of receipt to extent of earnings and profits or if exceeds basis in stock.
Effect of liquidation/ redemption/ reorganization on basis of entity assets	Not applicable.	Usually carried over from entity to owner unless a § 754 election is made, excessive cash is distributed, or more than 50% of the capital interests are transferred within 12 months.	Taxable step-up to fair market value.	Taxable step-up to fair market value.
§ 1244 treatment of loss on sale of interest	Not applicable.	Not applicable.	Available.	Available.

*Refer to Chapters 21 and 22 for additional details on partnerships and limited liability companies.
**Refer to Chapters 17 through 20 for additional details on regular (C) corporations.
***Spouses and family members are treated as one shareholder.

Refocus on The Big Picture

Using a Pass-Through Entity to Achieve Deductibility of Losses

LISA S./SHUTTERSTOCK.COM

As long as Smith and Jones, the owners of Cane, Inc., maintain C corporation status, they cannot deduct on their individual tax returns any NOLs the business incurs. For the owners to deduct any future NOLs on their Forms 1040, Cane should be operated as a flow-through entity. The most logical alternatives are to make an S election or to become a limited liability company.

An S election may be appropriate for Cane. Cane should make a timely election on Form 2553, and both shareholders must consent to the election. The owners should make the election on or before the fifteenth day of the third month of the current year to claim losses for the current year. Otherwise, the S election becomes effective only at the beginning of the next tax year.

Normally, an S corporation does not pay any income tax because all items (including NOLs) flow through to the shareholders. A C corporation making an S election may be required to pay a corporate-level built-in gains tax or a LIFO recapture tax.

An S corporation can issue both voting and nonvoting common stock, provided that all shares have the same economic rights to corporate income or loss.

Cane might sell off the bonds that generate its tax-exempt income, which will not be reflected in the AAA. Although it is reflected in stock basis, tax-exempt income (as part of the OAA) is distributed to the shareholders only after the S corporation has distributed all of its C corporation earnings and profits.

What If?

An individual who is neither a citizen nor a resident of the United States cannot own S stock, so if joint ownership of Cane shares is desired among all of the spouses, a change in the spouses' residency must occur. When Cane begins to turn a profit, the S election will be less attractive, and termination of the S election should be considered by the parties.

Key Terms

Accumulated adjustments account (AAA), 23-14
Built-in gains tax, 23-22
Bypass election, 23-16
Other adjustments account (OAA), 23-16
Passive investment income (PII), 23-8
Qualified business income deduction (QBID), 23-12
S corporation, 23-2
Small business corporation, 23-3
Subchapter S, 23-2
Voluntary revocation, 23-7

Discussion Questions

1. **LO.1, 10** Which of these taxes may be incurred by an S corporation?
   a. Corporate income tax.
   b. Tax on certain built-in gains.
   c. Property tax assessed by the county.
   d. Corporate minimum tax.

2. **LO.2** Which of the following are requirements to be an S corporation?
   a. Is limited to an absolute maximum of 100 shareholders.
   b. Has no resident alien shareholders.
   c. Has only one class of stock.
   d. Cannot have any C corporation earnings and profits (E & P).

3. **LO.2** Which of the following can be shareholders of an S corporation?
   a. Partnership.
   b. Limited liability partnership.
   c. Corporation.
   d. One-member limited liability company.

4. **LO.2** Joey lives in North Carolina, a common law state. He is a shareholder in an S corporation. If he marries a citizen and resident of Germany, will the S election terminate? Would your answer change if he lived in Louisiana? Explain.

5. **LO.2** Bob Roman, the majority owner of an S corporation, approaches you for some tax planning help. He would like to exchange some real estate in a like-kind transaction under § 1031 for real estate that may have some environmental liabilities. Prepare a letter to Bob outlining your suggestion. Bob's address is 8411 Huron Boulevard, West Chester, PA 19382. *Communications Critical Thinking Planning*

6. **LO.2, 3** On March 7, 2023, the two 50% shareholders of a calendar year corporation decide to elect S status. Shareholder Mila purchased her stock from a previous shareholder (a nonresident alien) on January 18, 2023. Identify any potential problems for Mila and the corporation. *Critical Thinking Planning*

7. **LO.4** Caleb calls you and says that his two-person S corporation was involuntarily terminated in February 2022. He asks you if they can make a new S election now, in November 2023. Draft a memo for your firm's tax research file outlining what you told Caleb. *Communications*

8. **LO.6** Using the categories in the following legend, classify each transaction as a plus (+) or minus (−) on Schedule M–2 of Form 1120S. An answer might look like one of these: +AAA or −OAA.

Legend
AAA = Accumulated adjustments account
OAA = Other adjustments account
NA = No direct effect on Schedule M–2

   a. Receipt of tax-exempt interest income.
   b. Administrative expenses.
   c. Depreciation recapture income.
   d. Nontaxable life insurance proceeds.
   e. Expenses related to tax-exempt securities.
   f. Charitable contributions.
   g. Business gifts in excess of $25.
   h. Nondeductible fines and penalties.

9. **LO.6, 8** Scott Tierney owns 21% of an S corporation. He is confused with respect to the amounts of the corporate AAA and his stock basis. Write a memo to Scott identifying the key differences between AAA and an S shareholder's stock basis. *Communications*

10. **LO.8** For each of the following independent statements, indicate whether the transaction will increase (+), decrease (−), or have no effect (*NE*) on the basis of a shareholder's stock in an S corporation.
    a. Expenses related to tax-exempt income.
    b. Short-term capital gain.
    c. Nonseparately computed loss.
    d. Section 1231 gain.
    e. Depletion *not* in excess of basis.
    f. Separately computed income.
    g. Nontaxable return-of-capital distribution by the corporation.
    h. Advertising expenses.
    i. Business gifts in excess of $25.
    j. Depreciation recapture income.
    k. Dividend income received by the S corporation.
    l. LIFO recapture tax paid.
    m. Collection of a bad debt previously deducted.
    n. Long-term capital loss.
    o. Cash distribution to shareholder out of AAA (with positive stock basis).

Critical Thinking

11. **LO.9** Sheila Jackson is a 50% shareholder in Washington, Inc., an S corporation. This year, Jackson's share of the Washington loss is $100,000. Jackson reports income from several other sources. Identify at least four tax issues related to the effects of the S corporation loss on Jackson's tax return.

Decision Making
Planning

12. **LO.1, 12** One of your clients is considering electing S status. Texas, Inc., is a six-year-old manufacturing company with two equal shareholders, both of whom paid $30,000 for their stock. Going into 2023, Texas holds a $110,000 NOL carryforward. Estimated income is $40,000 for 2023 and $25,000 for each of the next three years. Should Texas make an S election for 2023? Why or why not?

Critical Thinking

13. **LO.7, 12** Collette's S corporation holds a small amount of accumulated earnings and profits (AEP), thereby requiring the use of a more complex set of distribution rules. Collette's accountant tells her that this AEP requires the maintenance of the AAA figure each year. Discuss the issues that arise with respect to distributions when an S corporation holds AEP.

Computational Exercises

14. **LO.6** Dion, an S shareholder, owned 20% of MeadowBrook's stock for 292 days and 25% for the remaining 73 days in the year. Using the per-day allocation method, compute Dion's share of the following S corporation items.

	Schedule K Totals	Dion's Schedule K–1 Totals
Ordinary income	$60,000	________
Tax-exempt interest	1,000	________
Charitable contributions	3,400	________

15. **LO.6** Noelle, the owner of all of the shares of ClockCo, an S corporation, transfers her stock to Grayson on April 1. ClockCo reports a $70,000 NOL for the entire tax year, but only $10,000 of the loss occurs during January–March. Without a short-year election, how much of the loss is allocated to Noelle and how much is allocated to Grayson? If the corporation makes the short-year election, how much of the loss is allocated to Grayson? The tax year is not a leap year.

16. **LO.7** Holbrook, a calendar year S corporation, distributes $15,000 cash to its only shareholder, Cody, on December 31. Cody's basis in his stock is $20,000, Holbrook's AAA balance is $8,000, and Holbrook holds $2,500 AEP before the distribution. Complete the chart below using spreadsheet software such as Microsoft Excel.

	Basis in Stock	Distribution from Account	Effect on Stock Basis
From AAA account	______	______	______
From AEP account	______	______	______
From Cody's stock basis	______	______	______

17. **LO.7** Vogel, Inc., an S corporation for five years, distributes a tract of land held as an investment to Jamari, its majority shareholder. The land was purchased for $45,000 ten years ago and is currently worth $120,000.

   a. As a result of the distribution, what is Vogel's recognized capital gain? How much is reported as a distribution to shareholders?

   b. What is the net effect of the distribution on Vogel's AAA?

   c. Assume instead that the land had been purchased for $120,000 and was currently worth $45,000. How much would Vogel recognize as a loss? What would be the net effect on Vogel's AAA? What would be Jamari's basis in the land?

18. **LO.8** Jonas is a 60% owner of Ard, an S corporation. At the beginning of the year, his stock basis is zero. Jonas's basis in a $20,000 loan made to Ard and evidenced by Ard's note has been reduced to $0 by prior losses.

   During the year, Jonas's net share of Ard's taxable income is $10,000. At the end of the year, Ard makes a $15,000 cash distribution to Jonas. After these transactions, what is Jonas's basis in his stock, and what is his basis in the debt? What is Jonas's recognized capital gain?

19. **LO.9** Kaiwan, Inc., a calendar year S corporation, is partly owned by Sharrod, whose beginning stock basis is $32,000. During the year, Sharrod's share of a Kaiwan long-term capital gain (LTCG) is $5,000, and his share of an ordinary loss is $18,000. Sharrod then receives a $20,000 cash distribution. Compute the following.

   a. Sharrod's deductible loss.

   b. Sharrod's suspended loss.

   c. Sharrod's new basis in the Kaiwan stock.

Problems

20. **LO.5, 6** The profit and loss statement of Kitsch Ltd., an S corporation, shows $100,000 book income. Kitsch is owned equally by four shareholders. From supplemental data, you obtain the following information about items that are included in book income.

Selling expenses	($21,200)
Tax-exempt interest income	3,000
Dividends received	9,000
§ 1231 gain	7,000
Depreciation recapture income	11,000
Net income from passive real estate rentals	5,000
Long-term capital loss	(6,000)
Salary paid to owners (each)	(12,000)
Cost of goods sold	(91,000)

a. Compute Kitsch's nonseparately stated income or loss for the tax year.

b. What would be the share of this year's nonseparately stated income or loss items for James Billings, one of the Kitsch shareholders?

c. What is James Billings's share of tax-exempt interest income, if any? Is the income taxable to him this year?

21. **LO.5, 6** Zebra, Inc., a calendar year S corporation, incurred the following items this year. Sammy is a 40% Zebra shareholder throughout the year.

Sales	$100,000
Cost of goods sold	(40,000)
Depreciation expense (MACRS)	(10,000)
Administrative expenses	(5,000)
§ 1231 gain	21,000
Depreciation recapture income	25,000
Short-term capital loss from stock sale	(6,000)
Long-term capital loss from stock sale	(4,000)
Long-term capital gain from stock sale	15,000
Charitable contributions	(4,500)

a. Calculate Sammy's share of Zebra's nonseparately computed income or loss.

b. Calculate Sammy's share of any Zebra long-term capital gain, if any.

c. Calculate Sammy's share of charitable contributions, if any.

22. **LO.7** Lonergan, Inc., a calendar year S corporation in Athens, Georgia, had a balance in AAA of $200,000 and AEP of $110,000 on December 31, 2023. During 2024, Lonergan, Inc., distributes $140,000 to its shareholders, while sustaining an ordinary loss of $120,000. Calculate the balance in Lonergan's AAA and AEP accounts at the end of 2024.

23. **LO.7** If the beginning balance in Swan, Inc.'s OAA is $6,700 and the following transactions occur, what is Swan's ending OAA balance?

Depreciation recapture income	$ 21,600
Payroll tax penalty	(4,200)
Tax-exempt interest income	4,012
Nontaxable life insurance proceeds	100,000
Life insurance premiums paid (nondeductible)	(3,007)

24. **LO.7** Based upon the following facts about Aqua, Inc., a calendar year S corporation, prepare the entity's Schedule M-2.

AAA, beginning of the year	$ 9,400
Ordinary income	24,600
Tax-exempt income	3,000
Key employee life insurance proceeds received	4,900
Payroll penalty expense	2,200
Charitable contributions	3,000
Unreasonable compensation	4,000
Premiums on key employee life insurance	2,300
Distribution to shareholders	17,000

Critical Thinking

25. **LO.5, 6, 7** McLin, Inc., is a calendar year S corporation. Its AAA balance is zero.

a. McLin holds $90,000 of AEP. Tobias, the sole shareholder, has an adjusted basis of $80,000 in his stock. Determine the tax aspects if a $90,000 salary is paid to Tobias. Ignore the 20% QBI deduction.

b. Same as part (a), except that McLin pays Tobias a $90,000 cash distribution from AEP.

26. **LO.6, 7** On January 1, Kinney, Inc., an S corporation, reports $4,000 of accumulated E & P and a balance of $10,000 in AAA. Kinney has two shareholders, Erin and Frank, each of whom owns 500 shares of Kinney's stock. Kinney's nonseparately stated ordinary income for the year is $5,000.

    Kinney distributes $6,000 to each shareholder on July 1, and it distributes another $3,000 to each shareholder on December 21. How are the shareholders taxed on the distributions? Ignore the 20% QBI deduction.

27. **LO.6, 7, 8** Tiger, Inc., a calendar year S corporation, is owned equally by four shareholders: Ann, Becky, Chris, and David. Tiger owns investment land that was purchased for $160,000 four years ago. On September 14, when the land is worth $240,000, it is distributed to David. Assuming that David's basis in his S corporation stock is $270,000 on the distribution date, discuss any Federal income tax ramifications. Ignore the 20% QBI deduction.

28. **LO.6, 7, 8** Cougar, Inc., is a calendar year S corporation. Cougar's Form 1120S shows nonseparately stated ordinary income of $80,000 for the year. Johnny owns 40% of the Cougar stock throughout the year. The following information is obtained from the corporate records.

Tax-exempt interest income	$ 3,000
Salary paid to Johnny	(52,000)
Charitable contributions	(6,000)
Dividends received from a non-U.S. corporation	5,000
Short-term capital loss	(6,000)
Depreciation recapture income	11,000
Interest income from certificate of deposit	5,000
Cost of goods sold	(72,000)
Long-term capital loss	(7,000)
Administrative expenses	(18,000)
Long-term capital gain	14,000
Selling expenses	(11,000)
Johnny's beginning stock basis	32,000
Johnny's additional stock purchases	9,000
Beginning AAA	31,000
Johnny's loan to corporation	20,000

    a. Compute Cougar's book income or loss.
    b. Compute Johnny's ending stock basis.
    c. Calculate Cougar's ending AAA balance.

29. **LO.6, 7, 8** Money, Inc., a calendar year S corporation in Denton, Texas, has two unrelated shareholders, each owning 50% of the stock. Both shareholders record a $400,000 stock basis as of January 1. At the beginning of the tax year, Money reports balances in AAA of $300,000 and AEP of $600,000. During the year, Money generates operating income of $100,000. At the end of the year, Money distributes securities worth $1,000,000, with an adjusted basis of $800,000. Determine the Federal income tax effects of these transactions.

30. **LO.6, 7, 8** Assume the same facts as in Problem 29, except that the two shareholders consent to an AAA bypass election.

31. **LO.7, 8** Jeff, a 52% owner of an S corporation, has a stock basis of zero at the beginning of the year. Jeff's basis in a $10,000 loan made to the corporation and evidenced by a corporate note has been reduced to zero by pass-through losses. During the year, his net share of the entity's taxable income is $11,000. At the end of the year, Jeff receives a $15,000 cash distribution. Discuss the tax effects of the distribution.

32. **LO.7, 8, 9** Mary is a shareholder in CarrollCo, a calendar year S corporation. At the beginning of the year, her stock basis is $10,000, her share of the AAA is $2,000, and her share of corporate AEP is $6,000.

At the end of the year, Mary receives from CarrollCo a $6,000 cash distribution. Mary's share of S corporation items includes a $2,000 long-term capital gain and a $10,000 ordinary loss. Determine the effects of these events on Mary's share of the entity's AAA, her stock basis, and CarrollCo's AEP using spreadsheet software such as Microsoft Excel.

33. **LO.7, 8, 9** Drop, Inc., a calendar year S corporation, distributes $16,000 cash to its only shareholder, Luetta, on December 31. Luetta's basis in her stock is $20,000. Drop's AAA balance is $9,000, and Drop holds $3,000 of AEP and $1,000 of OAA before the distribution. Complete the following chart using spreadsheet software such as Microsoft Excel.

	Distribution from Account	Effect on Stock Basis	Balance after Distribution
From AAA account	________	________	________
From AEP account	________	________	________
From OAA account	________	________	________
From Luetta's stock basis	________	________	________

34. **LO.7, 8, 9** Liang, a calendar year S corporation, distributes $13,000 cash to its only shareholder, Aaron, on December 31. Aaron's basis in his stock is $15,000. Liang's AAA balance is $5,000; Liang holds $7,500 of AEP before this distribution. There is a zero OAA balance. Complete the following chart using spreadsheet software such as Microsoft Excel.

	Distribution from AAA	Distribution from AEP	Aaron's Stock Basis
Beginning balance	________	________	________
Distribution ($13,000)	________	________	________
From AAA	________	________	________
From AEP	________	________	________
From stock basis	________	________	________
Ending balance	________	________	________

35. **LO.7, 8, 9** At the beginning of the tax year, Lizzie holds a $10,000 stock basis as the sole shareholder of Spike, Inc., an S corporation. During the year, Spike reports the following. Determine Lizzie's stock basis at the end of the year and the treatment of her cash distribution.

Net taxable income from sales	$ 25,000
Net short-term capital loss	(18,000)
Cash distribution to Lizzie, 12/31	15,000

36. **LO.7, 8, 9** Assume the same facts as in Problem 35, except that the cash distribution to Lizzie amounts to $40,000. Determine Lizzie's stock basis at the end of the year and the treatment of her cash distribution.

37. **LO.6, 9** At the beginning of the year, Ann and Becky own equally all of the stock of Whitman, Inc., an S corporation. Whitman generates a $120,000 loss for the year (not a leap year). On the 219th day of the year, Ann sells her half of the Whitman stock to her son, Scott. How much of the $120,000 loss, if any, belongs to Scott?

38. **LO.6, 9** In Problem 37, how much of the Whitman loss belongs to Ann and Becky? Becky's stock basis is $41,300.

39. **LO.5, 6, 8, 9** A calendar year S corporation reports an ordinary loss of $80,000 and a capital loss of $20,000. Mei Freiberg owns 30% of the entity's stock and holds a $24,000 basis in her stock. Determine the amounts of the ordinary loss and capital loss, if any, that flow through to Freiberg. Prepare a tax memo for the files, explaining your computations. Communications

40. **LO.10** Whindy Corporation, an S corporation, reports a recognized built-in gain of $80,000 and a recognized built-in loss of $10,000 this year. Whindy holds an $8,000 unexpired NOL carryforward from a C corporation year. Whindy's ordinary income for the year is $65,000. Calculate any built-in gains tax.

41. **LO.10** Matulis, Inc., a calendar year C corporation, owns a single asset with a basis of $325,000 and a fair market value of $800,000. Matulis holds a positive E & P balance. The entity elects S corporation status for 2024 and then sells the asset. Compute the corporate-level built-in gains tax that must be paid by Matulis.

42. **LO.10** TyroneCo, an S corporation with a positive E & P balance, reports gross receipts for the year totaling $400,000 (of which $200,000 is PII). Expenditures directly connected to the production of the PII total $80,000. Compute Tyrone's PII tax.

43. **LO.10** Flint, an S corporation with substantial AEP, reports operating gross receipts of $410,000, taxable interest income of $390,000, operating expenses of $260,000, and deductions attributable to the interest of $150,000. Calculate any passive investment income penalty tax payable.

44. **LO.11** Samuel sold 1,000 shares of his stock in Maroon, Inc., an S corporation. He sold the stock for $15,700 after he had owned it for six years. Samuel had a basis of $141,250 in the stock, which was issued under § 1244. Samuel is married and is the owner of the 1,000 shares. Determine the appropriate treatment of any gain or loss on the stock sale. Critical Thinking

45. **LO.5, 6, 11, 12** Bonnie and Clyde each own one-third of a fast-food restaurant, and their 13-year-old daughter owns all of the other shares. Both parents work full-time in the restaurant, but the daughter works infrequently. Neither Bonnie nor Clyde receives a salary during the year when the ordinary income of the S corporation is $180,000. Critical Thinking

An IRS agent estimates that reasonable salaries for Bonnie, Clyde, and the daughter are $30,000, $35,000, and $10,000, respectively. What adjustments would you expect the IRS to impose upon these taxpayers?

46. **LO.7, 12** Blue is the owner of all of the shares of an S corporation, and Blue is considering receiving a salary of $110,000 from the business. She will pay the 7.65% FICA taxes on the salary, and the S corporation will pay the same amount of FICA tax. If Blue reduced her salary to $50,000 and took an additional $60,000 as a cash distribution, how would her Federal income tax liabilities change? Critical Thinking Planning

47. **LO.7, 8, 9, 12** Spence, Inc., a calendar year S corporation, generates an ordinary loss of $110,000 and makes a distribution of $140,000 to its sole shareholder, Storm Nelson. Nelson's stock basis and AAA at the beginning of the year are $200,000. Write a memo to your senior manager, Ahmad McMullin, discussing the tax treatment of Spence's activities. Communications

48. **LO.1, 6, 8, 9, 12** Orange, Inc., a calendar year corporation, elects S corporation status for 2023. The company generated a $74,000 NOL in 2022 and another NOL of $43,000 in 2023. Orange recorded no other transactions for the year. Critical Thinking Planning

At all times in 2022 and 2023, the stock of the corporation is owned by the same four shareholders, each owning 25% of the stock. Pete, one of the shareholders, holds a $6,020 basis in the Orange stock at the beginning of 2023. Identify the Federal income tax issues that Pete faces.

Tax Return Problem

Tax Forms Problem

ProConnect™ Tax

1. John Parsons (123-45-6781) and George Smith (123-45-6782) are 70% and 30% owners, respectively, of Premium, Inc. (11-1111120), a candy company located at 1005 16th Street, Cut and Shoot, TX 77303. Premium's S election was made on January 15, 2013, its date of incorporation. The following information was taken from the company's 2022 income statement.

Interest income	$ 100,000
Gross sales receipts	2,410,000
Beginning inventory	9,607
Direct labor	(203,102)
Direct materials purchased	(278,143)
Direct other costs	(249,356)
Ending inventory	3,467
Salaries and wages	(442,103)
Officers' salaries ($75,000 each to Parsons and Smith)	(150,000)
Repairs	(206,106)
Depreciation expense, tax and book	(15,254)
Interest expense	(35,222)
Rent expense (operating)	(40,000)
Taxes	(65,101)
Charitable contributions (cash)	(20,000)
Advertising expenses	(20,000)
Payroll penalties	(15,000)
Other deductions	(59,899)
Book income	704,574

A comparative balance sheet appears below.

	January 1, 2022	December 31, 2022
Cash	$ 47,840	$?
Accounts receivable	93,100	123,104
Inventories	9,607	3,467
Prepaid expenses	8,333	17,582
Building and equipment	138,203	185,348
Accumulated depreciation	(84,235)	(?)
Land	2,000	2,000
Total assets	$214,848	$844,422
Accounts payable	$ 42,500	$ 72,300
Notes payable (less than 1 year)	4,500	2,100
Notes payable (more than 1 year)	26,700	24,300
Capital stock (100 shares outstanding)	30,000	30,000
Retained earnings	111,148	?
Total liabilities and capital	$214,848	$844,422

Premium's accounting firm provides the following additional information.

Distributions to shareholders	$100,000
Beginning balance, Accumulated adjustments account	111,148
Ordinary business income for QBI	639,574
W-2 wages for QBI	795,205
UBIA of qualified property	125,000

Complete the 2022 Form 1120S for Premium, Inc., and Schedule K–1s for John Parsons and George Smith, 5607 20th Street, Cut and Shoot, TX 77303. Suggested software: ProConnect Tax.

Research Problems

Note: Solutions to the Research Problems can be prepared by using the Thomson Reuters Checkpoint™ online tax research database, which accompanies this textbook. Solutions can also be prepared by using research materials found in a typical tax library.

Research Problem 1. A new client comes to you in June 2023 and indicates that she instructed her previous accountant in a letter dated January 2022 to file an S election for 2022. It now appears that the prior accountant failed to follow through and make the election. What can you tell this new client about the availability of S corporation status?

Research Problem 2. Sean Moon is president, secretary, treasurer, sole director, and sole shareholder of Streetz, an S corporation real estate company. He manages all aspects of the company's operations, and he is the only person working at the company that holds a real estate broker's license. Sean works 12-hour days and takes few days off. Streetz's gross receipts and net income figures were reported as follows.

Year	Gross Receipts	Net Income
1	$376,453	$122,605
2	405,244	161,660
3	518,189	231,454

Sean and his wife, Kim, filed joint Federal income tax returns, but they did not report any wages or salaries on line 7 of their Forms 1040. During year 3, Sean transferred $240,000 from the S corporation to his personal account.

You are an expert witness for the IRS. Identify the items you would present to the U.S. Tax Court with respect to the amount of Sean's compensation that is subject to employment taxes and any other taxes due for year 3 (especially the Medicare net investment income tax). *Hint:* This is a reasonable compensation issue.

Research Problem 3. The 2020 Coronavirus Aid, Relief, and Economic Security Act (CARES Act) created the Paycheck Protection Program (PPP) allowing S corporations and others to receive loans that may be forgiven. Is the forgiveness of PPP indebtedness taxable? Are expenses paid from PPP borrowed funds deductible? For S corporations and their shareholders, how are PPP loan forgiveness and related expenditures treated? Prepare a brief outline summarizing your answers to these questions. Communications

Partial list of research aids:
Rev. Rul. 2021–2.
Consolidated Appropriations Act of 2021 (P.L. 116–260), § 276(a).

Use internet tax resources to address the following questions. Look for reliable websites and blogs of the IRS and other government agencies, media outlets, businesses, tax professionals, academics, think tanks, and political outlets.

Research Problem 4. Prepare a graph of the growth in the number of S elections since 1980, using increments of no more than five years. On the same graph, show the maximum Federal income tax rates for those years as they applied to individuals and to C corporations. Send your graph and other observations in an e-mail to your instructor with some explanatory comments as to what you found. You might use the IRS Data Book and other items at **irs.gov/taxstats**. Communications Data Analytics

Communications
Data Analytics

Research Problem 5. Based on the most recent data from **irs.gov/taxstats** or the *IRS Data Book*, use Microsoft Excel to prepare a pie chart showing the total number of business tax returns filed, including sole proprietorships (nonfarm), partnerships, C corporations, S corporations, and Forms 1120–RIC and 1120–REIT.

Communications

Research Problem 6. A client forwards Field Service Advice 200230030 to you and inquires how the government can force an S corporation shareholder to have a negative basis in their stock. Using the Thomson Reuters Checkpoint™ online tax research database, search FSA 200230030 and prepare an outline summarizing the Field Service Advice. E-mail the outline to your instructor.

Becker CPA Review Questions

Becker

1. Village Corp., a calendar year corporation, began business in year 1. Village made a valid S corporation election on December 5, year 4, with the unanimous consent of its shareholders. The eligibility requirements for S status continued to be met throughout year 5. On what date did Village's S status become effective?

   a. January 1, year 4
   b. January 1, year 5
   c. December 5, year 4
   d. December 5, year 5

2. Fox Corp., an S corporation, had an ordinary loss of $36,500 for the year ended December 31, year 2. At January 1, year 2, Duffy owned 50% of Fox's stock. Duffy held the stock for 40 days in year 2 before selling the entire 50% interest to an unrelated third party. Duffy's basis for the stock was $10,000. Duffy was a full-time employee of Fox until the stock was sold. Duffy's share of Fox's loss was:

   a. $0
   b. $2,000
   c. $10,000
   d. $18,250

3. An S corporation has 30,000 shares of voting common stock and 20,000 shares of nonvoting common stock issued and outstanding. The S election can be revoked voluntarily with the consent of the shareholders holding, on the day of the revocation, the following number of outstanding shares.

	Shares of Voting Stock	Shares of Nonvoting Stock
a.	0	20,000
b.	7,500	5,000
c.	10,000	16,000
d.	20,000	0

4. The Haas Corp., a calendar year S corporation, has two equal shareholders. For the year ended December 31, year 6, Haas had net income of $60,000, which included $50,000 from operations and $10,000 from investment interest income. There were no other transactions that year. Each shareholder's basis in the stock of Haas will increase by:

   a. $50,000
   b. $30,000
   c. $25,000
   d. $0

5. Zinco Corp. was a calendar year S corporation. Zinco's S status terminated on April 1, year 6, when Case Corp. became a shareholder. During year 6 (365-day calendar year), Zinco had nonseparately computed income of $310,250. If no election was made by Zinco, what amount of the income, if any, was allocated to the S short year for year 6?

   a. $233,750
   b. $155,125
   c. $76,500
   d. $0

6. The Matthew Corporation, an S corporation, is equally owned by three shareholders—Emily, Alejandra, and Kristina. The corporation is on the calendar year basis for tax and financial purposes. On April 1 of the current year, Emily sold her one-third interest in the Matthew Corporation equally to the other two shareholders. For the current year, the corporation had nonseparately stated ordinary income of $900,000. For the current year, how much ordinary income should be allocated to Kristina on her Schedule K–1?

   a. $25,000
   b. $75,000
   c. $337,500
   d. $412,500

7. After a corporation's status as an S corporation is revoked or terminated, how many years is the corporation required to wait before making a new S election in the absence of IRS consent to an earlier election?

   a. 1
   b. 3
   c. 5
   d. 10

8. An S corporation may deduct:

   a. Charitable contributions within the percentage of income limitation applicable to corporations
   b. Net operating loss carryovers
   c. Foreign income taxes
   d. Compensation of officers

9. XYZ Inc. was a C corporation through the end of year 6. Starting at the beginning of year 7, XYZ elected S corporation status. At the end of year 6, XYZ had accumulated earnings and profits (E & P) of $53,700. At the end of year 7, XYZ had a balance of $32,000 in its accumulated adjustments account (AAA). During year 8, XYZ had ordinary income of $15,300 and made distributions of $100,000. What amount of the distribution will be a nontaxable distribution out of S corporation earnings to the shareholders of XYZ at the end of year 8?

   a. $1,000
   b. $47,300
   c. $52,700
   d. $53,700

10. On March 4, year 1, Miqdadi Corporation, a calendar year corporation, elected S status, and all of its shareholders consented to the election. All of the eligibility requirements had been met by the corporation for S status during the portion of the year that was pre-election. On which date is the earliest that Miqdadi Corporation can be recognized as an S corporation?

    a. January 1, year 1
    b. March 4, year 1
    c. January 1, year 2
    d. March 4, year 2

11. As of January 1, year 6, Kane owned all the 100 issued shares of Manning Corp., a calendar year S corporation. On the 41st day of year 6, Kane sold 25 of the Manning shares to Rodgers. For the year ended December 31, year 6 (a 365-day calendar year), Manning had $73,000 in nonseparately stated income and made no distributions to its shareholders. What amount of nonseparately stated income from Manning should be reported on Kane's year 6 tax return?

    a. $56,750
    b. $54,750
    c. $16,250
    d. $0

Advanced Tax Practice Considerations

Chapter 24
Taxes in the Financial Statements

Chapter 25
Exempt Entities

Chapter 26
Multistate Corporate Taxation

Chapter 27
Taxation of International Transactions

Chapter 28
Tax Practice and Ethics

In this part of the text, we discuss some of the more complex issues that regularly are addressed by tax professionals. A tax professional must understand how taxes are treated under GAAP in the reconciliation and reporting of tax and accounting information. When the taxpayer is exempt from Federal income taxation, disclosure and operating requirements often differ from those applicable to corporations. Many businesses operate in more than one U.S. state and must account for the taxable activities in each. This Part also discusses additional rules that apply when a U.S. taxpayer does business outside the United States. Finally, the conduct of a tax professional's practice is bound by ethical and operational constraints. An understanding of these constraints helps guide effective tax practice to avoid penalties, interest, and other sanctions that can apply to both taxpayers and tax professionals.

Chapter 24

Taxes in the Financial Statements

Learning Objectives: *After completing Chapter 24, you should be able to:*

- **LO.1** **Identify and characterize common book-tax differences.**
- **LO.2** **Explain the basic principles of Accounting Standards Codification (ASC) 740.**
- **LO.3** **Determine current tax expense.**
- **LO.4** **Determine deferred tax expense.**
- **LO.5** **Describe the purpose of the valuation allowance, when it is used, and its impact on tax expense.**
- **LO.6** **Identify and interpret the tax-related information disclosed in the financial statement footnotes.**
- **LO.7** **Apply the GAAP standards concerning tax uncertainties and tax law changes.**
- **LO.8** **Use financial statement income tax information to benchmark a company's tax position.**

Chapter Outline

WAVEBREAKMEDIA/SHUTTERSTOCK.COM

Taxes in the Financial Statements

Raymond Jones, the CEO of Arctic Corporation, would like some help reconciling the amount of income tax expense on Arctic's financial statements with the amount of income tax reported on the company's corporate income tax return for its first year of operations. Mr. Jones does not understand why he can't simply multiply the financial statement income by the Federal 21 percent income tax rate to get the tax expense recognized in the income statement. Although the financial statements show book income before tax of $21.5 million, the reported income tax expense is only $5 million. In addition, the corporate Federal income tax return reports taxable income of $19 million and Federal income taxes payable of $3.99 million ($19 million × 21%).

Without knowing the specifics of the company's financial statements, do the seeming discrepancies noted by Mr. Jones seem plausible? What might cause the difference between the taxes shown in the financial statements and the taxes due on the tax return?

Read the chapter and formulate your response.

Taxes are not a direct operating cost of producing the goods or services sold by a business enterprise. Nonetheless, taxes can significantly affect the income available to the owners of a business, and businesses may engage in significant tax planning activities to minimize the taxes owed. In addition, an entity's tax liability can convey much more to interested parties than simply the tax costs of conducting its business. For example, depending on one's perspective, a corporation's tax expense may indicate the extent to which the corporation engages in activities Congress has chosen to encourage through the tax law, how much effort they have devoted to aggressive tax planning, how good a corporate citizen they are, or how efficiently the business is managed. As a result, a number of parties (including investors and policymakers) are interested in the amount of income taxes incurred by corporations. However, because tax returns are not available to the general public, the primary source of information about a corporation's income tax liability is its financial statements. Because of their nature and significance, income taxes are reported separately in a corporation's income statement immediately following operating income.

However, due to the different goals underlying financial reporting and the tax law, the income tax expense reported in a corporation's financial statements will seldom equal the income tax liability reported on its tax return for the same reporting period. Interpreting the expense reported in the financial statements can be difficult for those not well versed in both financial accounting and tax law. Further, because of the complexities that arise in trying to provide tax-related information that achieves the goals of financial reporting, and the limited number of professionals well versed in both financial accounting and tax law, the income tax expense reported in the financial statements may not always be reliable. Misreported income tax expense regularly accounts for a significant portion of financial statement restatements. In addition, the process of determining the reported income tax expense is among the top sources of material weaknesses in financial reporting systems. An understanding of the income tax expense reported in financial statements is important for financial statement preparers as well as users. Because accounting for income taxes requires an understanding of both financial reporting and tax law, those with a deep understanding of tax accounting are in high demand. This chapter covers the basics of income tax accounting that should be relevant for most accounting professionals, including those engaged in financial reporting, auditing, and tax planning, as well as for finance professionals, investors, and policymakers who must interpret the income tax expense reported in financial statements.

24-1 Accounting for Income Taxes—Basic Principles

Although both the financial reporting and tax systems focus heavily on the measurement of income, the systems serve very different purposes. Financial statements, prepared using **generally accepted accounting principles (GAAP)**, are intended to provide readers with information regarding the future cash flows expected to be generated by a business. Alternatively, the taxable income and tax liability reported by taxpayers, as determined by the tax law, are primarily intended to capture taxpayers' relative abilities to pay tax based on their current and past financial activities within the context of economic and social goals established by Congress. As a result, it is not unreasonable for the income tax expense reported in an entity's financial statements to differ from the income tax liability reported to the Federal government for the same time period covered by those financial statements.

24-1a Book-Tax Differences

LO.1

Identify and characterize common book-tax differences.

As a general rule, taxable income and pretax income reported in the financial statements (i.e., pretax "book" income) are determined in a similar manner. However, recall that the concept of income serves different purposes for tax and financial reporting purposes. Because of these different purposes, many items impact taxable income and pretax book income differently. From a tax perspective, these differences may be viewed as either *favorable* or *unfavorable*. Favorable book-tax differences cause taxable income to be *lower* than book income, reducing a corporation's current tax liability. Conversely, unfavorable book-tax differences cause taxable income to be *greater* than book income, increasing a corporation's current tax liability.

In addition to their impact on current taxable income, book-tax differences also can be considered in terms of their impact on future taxable income. Some items included in the determination of book income are never included in the determination of taxable income and vice versa. For example, although interest income on state and municipal bonds and fines and penalties are included in the determination of book income, they are neither includible in gross income (state and municipal bond interest) nor deductible (fines and penalties) for tax purposes. These differences in the determination of financial accounting and taxable income are referred to as book-tax **permanent differences**.

Other items are included in both financial and taxable income, but because they are accounted for using different accounting methods or by different applications of the accrual method of accounting, they are taken into account in different accounting periods. Although these items cause differences in current book and taxable income, over time these differences will *reverse*, resulting in the same cumulative amount of income being recognized for both book and taxable income purposes. These differences are referred to as book-tax **temporary differences**. Sources of temporary differences include the use of different accounting methods required for specific items [e.g., using cost recovery (MACRS) for tax purposes versus straight-line depreciation for book purposes and determining bad debt expense using the direct write-off method for tax purposes versus the allowance method for book purposes] as well as differences in the general application of the accrual accounting method for book and tax (e.g., the economic performance requirement that must be met for expenses to be deductible for tax purposes).

Diff, Inc., has $1,000,000 of pretax book income in both 2023 and 2024 before considering the following:

- $2,000 of nondeductible lobbying expenses incurred in 2023.
- A $10,000 lawsuit filed against it in 2023. The company's attorneys decided in 2023 that the company would probably be found liable for the full $10,000, but the suit was not settled and the $10,000 not paid until 2024. Although the settlement reduces book income in 2023, it is not deductible for tax purposes until 2024.

Diff's 2023 and 2024 book and taxable income would be computed as follows:

2023	**Book Income**	**Taxable Income**	**Book-Tax Difference Favorable/(Unfavorable)**
Preliminary pretax book income	$1,000,000	$1,000,000	$ –0–
Lobbying expenses	(2,000)	–0–	(2,000)
Lawsuit settlement	(10,000)	–0–	(10,000)
Net income	$ 988,000	$1,000,000	($12,000)

2024	**Book Income**	**Taxable Income**	**Book-Tax Difference Favorable/(Unfavorable)**
Preliminary pretax book income	$1,000,000	$1,000,000	$ –0–
Lobbying expenses	–0–	–0–	–0–
Lawsuit settlement	–0–	(10,000)	10,000
Net income	$1,000,000	$ 990,000	$10,000

The lobbying expenses represent a permanent, unfavorable book-tax difference, increasing Diff's 2023 taxable income relative to its book income but having no future impact on either. The lawsuit settlement also represents an unfavorable book-tax difference in 2023, increasing taxable income relative to book income. However, it is a temporary difference since it reverses in 2024 when the payment is deducted, creating a favorable book-tax difference in 2024.

The Big Picture

Example 2

Return to the facts of *The Big Picture* on p. 24-1. Arctic, Inc., has pretax book income of $25,000,000, but it reports taxable income of only $19,000,000 on its tax return. Arctic has net positive book-tax differences of $6,000,000 for the year. Such a difference should not be a surprise given the different purposes for which book income and taxable income are used.

Given the differing goals of financial reporting and income taxation, many book-tax differences exist. A few of the more prominent differences are described below. Temporary differences include the following:

- *Accrued income and expenses.* Although most income and expense items are recognized for tax and book purposes in the same period, a number of items potentially appear in different periods. In general, the tax law does not allow the use of estimates or reserves, as is common under GAAP. For example, the future costs of honoring warranties on products sold by a taxpayer must be estimated and expensed in the year the product is sold. This means the GAAP financial statements will reflect the estimated warranty costs in the same period as revenue from the sale of the product. However, due to the economic performance test, these costs are not deductible for tax purposes until the services are provided. As a result, the taxpayer will recognize income from the sale of the product in a period before it recognizes any expense associated with honoring any warranties on that product. A similar idea applies to bad debts, which are expensed using the reserve method for financial reporting purposes but cannot be deducted for tax purposes until actually written off. Similarly, different methods regarding the timing of income recognition may create temporary differences. For instance, changes in the value of investments (i.e., unrealized gains and losses) are often recognized in the financial statements in the year of the change but are only recognized for tax purposes on the sale or other disposition of the investments.[1]
- *Depreciation on fixed assets.* Taxpayers may use an accelerated depreciation method for tax purposes [e.g., the modified accelerated cost recovery system (MACRS)] but adopt the straight-line method for book purposes. Even if identical methods are used, the period over which the asset is depreciated is likely to differ between book and tax (with tax recovery periods often shorter than an asset's estimated useful life used to calculate book depreciation). As a result, tax rules can allow the acceleration of the deductions over the asset's life.
- *Net operating losses.* For tax purposes, operating losses from one tax year may be "carried over" (i.e., used to offset taxable income in another tax year).[2] No such loss carryovers are used in determining book income for the year. As a result, the losses incurred in one year for book purposes may be used as a deduction for tax purposes in a different year.
- *Intangible assets.* For tax purposes, many intangibles (including goodwill) can be amortized over 15 years.[3] Rather than periodic amortization, GAAP requires an annual determination of whether the intangible asset has suffered a reduction in value (i.e., impairment).[4] If an intangible has suffered an impairment, a current expense is required to reduce the asset's book value to its economic value.

Permanent differences include the following:

- *Nontaxable income.* Due to social or economic reasons, some types of income are never included in gross income. A common example is municipal bond interest, which is included in income for book purposes even though it is nontaxable.

[1] Other examples of these differences include additional inventory costs that must be capitalized under the uniform capitalization rules for tax purposes, nonqualified stock option compensation expenses that are recorded at the grant date for financial reporting purposes but are not deductible for tax purposes until the options are exercised, and certain accrued compensation and vacation pay.

[2] § 172; see text Section 17-1j.

[3] § 197.

[4] *Intangibles—Goodwill and Other*, ASC 350.

- *Nondeductible expenses.* Due to various policy or political concerns, some expenses are never deductible. For example, a portion of business meals, all entertainment expenses, and certain penalties, though fully expensed in determining book income, are not deductible for tax purposes.
- *Special tax deductions.* The tax law allows certain deductions that are not associated with any expenditures and, therefore, are not reported as expenses in determining pretax book income. A common example is the dividends received deduction.
- *Tax credits.* Although credits such as the research activities credit do not reduce taxable income, they do reduce a company's tax liability directly. Because they have no corresponding impact on pretax book income, they are considered to be permanent book-tax differences.

Concept Summary 24.1 summarizes the sources of typical corporate book-tax differences.

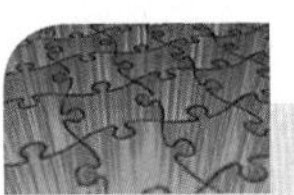

Concept Summary 24.1

Common Book-Tax Differences

Temporary Differences	Permanent Differences

• Accelerated recognition of unearned revenues.
• Expenses failing the *all events* or *economic performance* tests.
• Accelerated depreciation of fixed assets.
• Amortization of goodwill.
	• Nontaxable income (e.g., state/municipal bond interest; life insurance proceeds).
	• Nondeductible expenses:
	  ○ Meals and entertainment.
	  ○ Fines and penalties.
	  ○ Political contributions and lobbying expenses.
	  ○ Federal income taxes.
	• Special deductions:
	  ○ Dividends received deduction.
	• Credits:
	  ○ Research activities credit.

24-1b Generally Accepted Accounting Principles and ASC 740

LO.2

Explain the basic principles of Accounting Standards Codification (ASC) 740.

Accounting for income taxes under GAAP is governed by Accounting Standards Codification (ASC) 740. Consistent with most financial accounting principles, **ASC 740** emphasizes the balance sheet, taking a **balance sheet approach** to the accounting for income taxes. Specifically, it requires that the balance sheet reflect both a current liability related to all income taxes (Federal, state and local, and foreign) reflected on its tax returns for the year as well as a **deferred tax liability** or **deferred tax asset** for the future tax effects of items included in its current and prior financial statements but not in taxable income (i.e., temporary book-tax differences). That is, ASC 740 adopts a comprehensive inter-period allocation approach to income taxes, requiring that all income taxes that relate to the income reported in the current financial statements be reported in those same financial statements regardless of when they might be legally due under the tax law. The sum of the liabilities reflected on the current tax returns represents a corporation's **current tax expense** while the future tax effects related to its temporary book-tax differences lead to the recognition of either a **deferred tax expense** or **deferred tax benefit**.

Example 3

In 2023, PanCo, Inc., earns $100,000 in pretax book income before considering a $30,000 gain realized on an installment sale. This gain represents a favorable, temporary book-tax difference. For financial reporting purposes, the entire $30,000 gain is recognized in current-year income. However, for tax purposes, the gain can be recognized over the periods in which the sales proceeds are collected. Assuming that the proceeds will be collected evenly over three years, beginning in 2023, PanCo will report the installment sale gain as follows:

	Book Income	Taxable Income
2023	$30,000	$10,000
2024	-0-	10,000
2025	-0-	10,000
	$30,000	$30,000

In 2023, PanCo will report $130,000 ($100,000 + $30,000 gain) of pretax book income. However, it will report only $110,000 ($100,000 + $10,000 gain) of taxable income and pay $23,100 ($110,000 × 21%) of income taxes for the year. Therefore, its financial statements will reflect a current tax liability and current tax expense, of $23,100.

However, PanCo also will report a deferred tax liability, and deferred tax expense, of $4,200 ($20,000 deferred gain × 21%). The total tax expense reported in the financial statements, $27,300 ($23,100 current tax expense + $4,200 deferred tax expense), captures the total income tax that will be paid on the $130,000 of pretax book income even though some of that tax expense is not yet due.

Note that, in Example 3, the total tax expense reported in the financial statements is equal to the tax related to pretax book income. This is the intended result of ASC 740, which requires the recognition of the deferred tax liability and related expense. Due to the recording of the deferred tax expense, temporary differences will never cause the tax expense reported on the books to differ from what might be expected based on pretax book income. Even with a temporary difference, the total tax expense in the financial statements reflects taxes on the entire pretax book income, although some of that tax is deferred.

However, the same is not true for permanent book-tax differences. As a result, if there are permanent book-tax differences, tax expense cannot be determined simply by multiplying pretax book income by the tax rate.

Example 4

Referring back to Example 3, assume that PanCo's pretax book income included a $5,000 nondeductible fine. Its pretax book income would remain $130,000. However, its taxable income and related tax expense would be calculated as follows:

Pretax book income	$130,000
Book-tax permanent differences:	
Fines	5,000
Book-tax temporary differences:	
Gain deferred on installment sale	(20,000)
Taxable income	$115,000
Tax rate	× 21%
Current tax payable/expense	$ 24,150
Deferred tax expense (from Example 3)	4,200
Total tax expense	$ 28,350

Notice that, in Example 4, total tax expense ($28,350) is greater than one might have expected based on pretax book income [$27,300 ($130,000 × 21%)]. This is due to the unfavorable, permanent book-tax difference ($5,000 × 21% = $1,050).

The Big Picture

Return to the facts of *The Big Picture* on p. 24-1. Mr. Jones is using Arctic's Federal tax rate to try to understand Arctic's tax expense. However, if Arctic operates in a state that imposes an income tax, the reported income tax expense will reflect state taxes as well.

The Big Picture

Return to the facts of *The Big Picture* on p. 24-1. Assume that Arctic's combined Federal and state tax rate is 25%. The tax expense reported in Arctic's income statement includes both current and deferred tax expense. Arctic's current tax expense is likely equal to the amount reported on both its Federal and state tax returns, or $4,750,000 ($19,000,000 3 25%). The remaining $250,000 of tax expense is likely due to deferred taxes that relate to current-year pretax book income that is not yet includible in Federal taxable income. Mr. Jones should find a liability on the balance sheet for these deferred taxes.

The Big Picture

Example 7

Return to the facts of *The Big Picture* on p. 24-1. If the difference between Arctic's pretax book income and taxable income were due only to temporary book-tax differences, one might expect its total reported tax expense to be $5,375,000 ($21,500,000 pretax book income × 25%). Given that total reported income tax expense is only $5,000,000, some of Arctic's book-tax differences must be permanent differences.

Finally, ASC 740 also requires an intra-period allocation of income taxes. That is, any tax expense or benefit attributable to items included in comprehensive income other than income from continuing operations must be netted with those items rather than be included in tax expense. For example, any tax expense or benefit related to discontinued operations must be included with the income or loss from discontinued operations reported in the income statement. Although intra-period allocation will not by itself cause reported tax expense to differ from what might be expected based on pretax book income, it will cause reported tax expense to differ from what is reported on a company's tax return.

24-2 Capturing, Measuring, and Recording Tax Expense—The Provision Process

The process used to capture, measure, and record the tax expense reported in the financial statements, as well as the expense itself, is often referred to as the **tax provision**. As discussed previously, ASC 740 requires the reporting on the balance sheet of both a current tax liability (related to the liability reflected in a corporation's current tax returns) and a deferred asset or liability (related to the future tax consequences of items reported in the current or prior financial statements). However, while a corporation may have to issue its financial statements, including the tax provision, soon after year end, its tax returns may not be filed until much later.[5] In this case, estimates of book-tax differences and the current and deferred tax liabilities must be made as part of the tax provision process before the tax return is filed.

[5]Although the due date for a Federal corporate tax return is three and one-half months after year-end (April 15 for a calendar year corporation), many corporations request an extension of time to file the tax return (using Form 7004). This six-month extension request is automatically approved by the IRS. While the due date for filing the tax return is extended, any taxes due must be paid by the original due date of the return.

LO.3

Determine current tax expense.

24-2a Current Tax Expense

Determining current tax expense begins with estimating the current tax liabilities to be reflected on the corporation's tax returns. This includes three steps:

1. Identifying (and adjusting pretax book income for) all permanent and temporary book-tax differences related to items included in current pretax book income.
2. Identifying carryovers that may impact current taxable income (e.g., capital losses, charitable contributions, NOLs).
3. Identifying (and reducing the current tax liability for) any tax credits that may be available but have no impact on either book or taxable income.

Exhibit 24.1 illustrates the process for determining current tax expense. Note that the book-tax differences captured in steps 1 and 2 above (with the exception of an NOL carryover) are the same items that are expected to appear in Schedule M–1 (see Exhibit 24.2) or Schedule M–3 (reproduced in Appendix B) of the corporation's Federal tax return when it is eventually filed.

Exhibit 24.1 Current Tax Expense (Provision) (Simplified)

	Pretax book income
±	Permanent and temporary book-tax differences
	Taxable income before NOLs
−	Carryovers
	Taxable income
×	Applicable tax rate
	Current tax expense (provision) before tax credits
−	Tax credits
	Current tax expense (provision)

Exhibit 24.2 Form 1120, Schedule M–1

Schedule M-1 Reconciliation of Income (Loss) per Books With Income per Return

Note: The corporation may be required to file Schedule M-3. See instructions.

1	Net income (loss) per books		7	Income recorded on books this year not included on this return (itemize):	
2	Federal income tax per books			Tax-exempt interest $	
3	Excess of capital losses over capital gains .				
4	Income subject to tax not recorded on books this year (itemize):				
5	Expenses recorded on books this year not deducted on this return (itemize):		8	Deductions on this return not charged against book income this year (itemize):	
a	Depreciation . . . . $		a	Depreciation . . $	
b	Charitable contributions . $		b	Charitable contributions $	
c	Travel and entertainment . $				
			9	Add lines 7 and 8	
6	Add lines 1 through 5		10	Income (page 1, line 28)—line 6 less line 9	

Financial Disclosure Insights **The Book-Tax Income Gap**

According to a recent study by the Institute on Taxation and Economic Policy, 55 Fortune 500 companies reported profits to their shareholders in 2020 yet paid zero or negative Federal corporate income taxes over the same period. These companies include FedEx, Nike, and Dish Network. Thirty-nine profitable Fortune 500 companies paid no taxes from 2018–2020, the first three years following the Tax Cuts and Jobs Act of 2017. Another 73 reported effective tax rates less than half that of the 21 percent U.S. statutory rate.

The study concluded that the companies were using a diverse array of legal means to eliminate their tax liabilities, including the following:

- Various forms of accelerated depreciation.
- Stock options.
- Alternative energy subsidies (e.g., subsidies for pursuing renewable energy).
- The research and development tax credit.

Source: *Corporate Tax Avoidance Under the Tax Cuts and Jobs Act* (**itep.org/corporate-tax-avoidance-under-the-tax-cuts-and-jobs-act/**).

The Big Picture

Example 8

Return to the facts of *The Big Picture* on p. 24-1. To better understand Arctic's current tax expense, Mr. Jones should refer to Arctic's state tax return as well as its Federal return. To learn why the taxes reported on those returns are not equal to Arctic's pretax book income times 25% (Arctic's combined Federal and state tax rate), Mr. Jones can refer to Schedule M–1 or Schedule M–3 of Form 1120 to find the temporary and permanent book-tax differences. Any tax credits claimed by Arctic also will have to be factored into his analysis.

24-2b **Deferred Tax Expense**

LO.4

Determine deferred tax expense.

Companies may report either a deferred tax expense or a deferred tax benefit in their income statement. A deferred tax expense is the result of a deferred tax liability (a future tax liability related to transactions already reflected in the financial statements). Similarly, a deferred tax benefit is the result of a deferred tax asset (future tax savings related to transactions already reflected in the financial statements).

Deferred tax assets and liabilities can be generated in several ways. The most common way is the use of different accounting methods for financial reporting and taxable income. For most large corporations, the accrual method generally is required for both financial reporting and tax purposes. However, in several situations, the accrual method is applied differently in determining book and taxable income. Further, different accounting methods may be used for specific transactions (e.g., the installment method is available for tax purposes in certain situations).

Generally, a *deferred tax asset* is produced when:

- The recognition of revenue is accelerated for tax purposes relative to book (e.g., the recognition of unearned revenues for tax earlier than book), or
- The deductibility of an expense reported in the financial statements is deferred for tax purposes (e.g., an expense reported in the financial statements has not yet met the economic performance test for tax).

Global Tax Issues **Accounting for Income Taxes under International Standards**

The Financial Accounting Standards Board (FASB) and international accounting standard setters have worked for decades to enhance the comparability of financial statements prepared under U.S. GAAP and those prepared under international accounting standards. Currently, the FASB is a member of the Accounting Standards Advisory Forum (ASAF), which advises the International Accounting Standards Board (IASB) as it sets international standards.

Over time, accounting for income taxes under U.S. GAAP and International Financial Reporting Standards (IFRS) have converged. Nevertheless, several significant differences exist between ASC 740 and International Accounting Standards (IAS) 12. These include the thresholds for recognition and approach to valuation allowances and the measurement of uncertain tax positions.

Generally, a *deferred tax liability* is produced when:

- The recognition of revenue is deferred for tax purposes relative to book (e.g., when installment sale treatment is available for tax purposes), or
- The deductibility of an expense reported in the financial statements is accelerated for tax purposes (e.g., the use of accelerated cost recovery methods for tax purposes).

Identifying and Measuring Deferred Tax Assets and Liabilities

As discussed above, an accounting method difference that causes current book and taxable income to differ will produce both a deferred tax asset or liability on the balance sheet and a deferred tax benefit or expense on the income statement. Recall that a deferred tax benefit or expense relates to the *future* tax consequences attributable to events reported in the current or prior financial statements, not the current consequences of book-tax differences. As you will see, not all future tax benefits and expenses related to transactions already recorded in the financial statements are the result of accounting method differences. As a result, successfully identifying all deferred tax assets and liabilities requires more than the identification of current differences in book and taxable income.

A review of financial accounting principles may help at this point. Recall the basic accounting equation:

$$\text{Assets} = \text{Liabilities} + \text{Owners' Equity}$$

The equation suggests that income (which represents a change in owners' equity) must be accompanied by a similar change in assets or liabilities.

Imagine that we simultaneously maintain an accounting equation (or a set of double-entry books and records) for tax purposes using tax accounting methods rather than GAAP. In this system, assets and liabilities would be measured by their tax adjusted bases (AB) rather than their net book value (NBV). Any taxable income would similarly correspond to a change in the bases of assets and liabilities.[6] If the same accounting methods were used for financial reporting and tax purposes, assets, liabilities, and income would be the same in both equations (i.e., there would be no book-tax differences). However, the use of different methods results not only in book-tax differences in income but also differences in the tax ABs and the NBVs of assets and liabilities. Since it is the use of assets and the incurrence of liabilities that produce future income, it is these differences in the current NBV and tax ABs of assets and liabilities that will cause differences in future financial reporting and taxable income and, therefore, related deferred tax assets and liabilities.

[6]Note that, although we typically do not consider a liability to have a tax basis, the idea is to capture what would be on the balance sheet if the taxpayer were using a double-entry accounting system for tax purposes.

Deferred Tax Assets and Liabilities

Orange, Inc., acquired an asset during the current year. Current-year book depreciation, using the straight-line method over the asset's useful life, is $100. However, MACRS produces a $500 cost recovery deduction for tax purposes. The impact of the asset's depreciation for book and tax purposes would be reflected in journal entries as follows:

	Debit	Credit
Book		
Depreciation expense	$100	
Net book value (NBV) of asset		$100
Tax		
Cost recovery deduction	$500	
Tax adjusted basis (AB) of asset		$500
Difference between NBV and AB of asset		$400

The $400 difference in the current net book value and tax adjusted basis of the asset will result in future taxable income being $400 higher than future book income. This will lead to a tax liability higher than what would relate to future book income, creating a *deferred tax liability.*

Blue, Inc., sells products subject to a two-year warranty. Blue estimates that it will spend $10,000 in the future to make repairs pursuant to warranties on products it sold in the current year. For book purposes, it accrues this $10,000 as a current-year expense. However, because there has been no economic performance, the estimated expenses are not currently deductible. This would be reflected in book and tax journal entries as follows:

	Debit	Credit
Book		
Warranty expense	$10,000	
Warranty liability (NBV)		$10,000
Tax		
Warranty expense	$ 0	
Warranty liability (AB)		$ 0
Difference between NBV and AB of liability		$10,000

The $10,000 difference in the net book value and tax adjusted basis of the liability reflects the $10,000 tax deduction available to Blue in the future for the expense reflected on the books currently. This future deduction represents a *deferred tax asset.*

Although accounting method differences produce NBV–AB differences (and, as a result, deferred tax assets and liabilities), not all deferred tax assets and liabilities are the result of accounting method differences. As a result, ASC 740 defines *temporary differences*, to which deferred tax assets and liabilities relate, as differences in the net book value and tax adjusted basis of a corporation's assets and liabilities (not as differences in current book and taxable income and expenses). Accordingly, the tax provision process requires the identification and measurement of these differences between net book value and tax adjusted basis. ASC 740 refers to temporary differences that lead to deferred tax assets as *deductible differences* while those that lead to deferred tax liabilities are referred to as *taxable differences.*

Of course, although the differences in the net book value and tax adjusted bases of a company's assets and liabilities lead to deferred tax assets and liabilities, these temporary differences do not accurately capture those deferred tax assets and liabilities. Rather, we are interested in the future tax consequences of these differences. As a result, these differences must be multiplied by the appropriate tax rate to capture a corporation's deferred tax assets and liabilities.

The appropriate tax rate is the one that, based on current tax law at the balance sheet date, is expected to apply when the tax consequences will be realized or when the temporary difference reverses. If no future changes in tax rates have been enacted as of the balance sheet date, this is the tax rate currently in effect. If, however, on the balance sheet date, legislation has been adopted that will modify the tax rate that will be in effect when a deferred tax asset or liability is realized, then the modified future tax rate should be used in measuring deferred tax assets and liabilities.

Example 11

Assume that in November 2024, Congress passes a law that increases the Federal corporate income tax rate from 21% to 25% for all taxable years beginning after December 31, 2024. AM, Inc., uses a calendar year for tax and financial reporting purposes. It will apply a tax rate of 21% to its 2024 taxable income to determine its 2024 tax liability, which will be reported as its current tax expense in its financial statements.

However, it will use a 25% rate to measure any deferred tax assets and liabilities reported in its 2024 financial statements, since that will be the rate applied to its temporary book-tax differences when they are eventually realized.

Finally, realize the deferred tax asset or liability that is identified exists as of the current balance sheet date. Recall that income and expenses are the result of *changes* in assets and liabilities during the year. As a result, a company's deferred tax benefit or expense for the year is the *change* in its deferred tax assets and liabilities from the beginning of the year to the end of the year. Examples 12 and 13 illustrate the determination of deferred tax expense.

Deferred Tax Expense

Example 12

PJ Enterprises began operations in 2023 and earned pretax book income of $500,000 in its first year of operations. In performing its 2023 tax provision, PJ noted the following temporary differences:

- In January 2023, PJ purchased equipment at a cost of $800,000. For book purposes, PJ depreciated the asset on a straight-line basis over 10 years, resulting in $80,000 of depreciation expense in 2023. For tax purposes, PJ was able to use a combination of accelerated cost recovery methods and deducted $720,000 in 2023.
- Most of PJ's sales are on account. At the end of 2023, it had established an allowance for uncollectible accounts of $30,000. For tax purposes, PJ must use the direct write-off method to account for uncollectible accounts. No write-offs occurred during 2023.

PJ operates in a state with an income tax, making its combined Federal and state tax rate equal to 25%. No laws have been passed that will change the tax rates faced by PJ in the future. The provision for PJ's 2023 deferred tax expense was determined as follows:

Partial Balance Sheet (December 31, 2023)

	Net Book Value	Tax Adjusted Basis	Temporary Difference	Combined Tax Rate	Deferred Tax Asset/(Liability)
Accounts receivable (net of allowance for uncollectible accounts)	$100,000	$130,000	$ 30,000	25%	$ 7,500
Equipment	720,000	80,000	640,000	25%	(160,000)
Net deferred tax liability					($152,500)

At the end of 2023, PJ had a net deferred tax liability of $152,500, consisting of a $7,500 deferred tax asset (for the NBV–AB difference related to the accounts receivable) and a $160,000 deferred tax liability (for the NBV–AB difference related to the equipment). PJ made the following journal entry to record its 2023 deferred tax expense:

Deferred tax expense (income statement)	$152,500	
Deferred tax liability (balance sheet)		$152,500

Deferred Tax Expense

Example 13

PJ Enterprises, from Example 12, earned pretax book income of $600,000 in 2024. PJ continues to use the equipment it acquired in 2023 and to depreciate it on a straight-line basis over 10 years. For tax purposes, PJ can recover $32,000 of the equipment's cost in 2024. At the end of 2024, it estimates that $45,000 of its accounts receivable will be uncollectible. The provision for PJ's 2024 deferred income tax expense is determined as follows:

Partial Balance Sheet (December 31, 2024)

	Net Book Value	Tax Adjusted Basis	Temporary Difference	Combined Tax Rate	Deferred Tax Asset/(Liability)
Accounts receivable (net of allowance for uncollectible accounts)	$150,000	$195,000	$ 45,000	25%	$ 11,250
Equipment	640,000	48,000	592,000	25%	(148,000)
Net deferred tax liability					($136,750)

At the end of 2024, PJ has a net deferred tax liability of $136,750, consisting of a $11,250 deferred tax asset (for the NBV–AB difference related to the accounts receivable) and a $148,000 deferred tax liability (for the NBV–AB difference related to the equipment).

PJ must reduce the $152,500 deferred tax liability recorded in 2023 to $136,750, with the $15,750 liability reduction representing a deferred tax benefit. PJ would make the following journal entry to record its 2023 deferred taxes:

Deferred tax liability (balance sheet)	$15,750	
Deferred tax benefit (income statement)		$15,750

After the above journal entry, PJ's 2024 balance sheet will reflect a deferred tax liability of $136,750.

There are those who would argue that recognizing deferred taxes makes little sense. After all, unlike most liabilities recorded in the financial statements, they are not legally enforceable. Should a corporation discontinue its operations, it would not be required to pay its deferred tax liability. Similarly, even if the business continues, the liability may never be settled. For example, a deferred tax liability related to accelerated cost recovery will continue to grow as long as a company continues to grow or its costs continue to rise.

However, failure to recognize deferred taxes can be misleading for financial statement users for at least two reasons. First, it would overstate a corporation's net assets. Recall that a basic premise of financial accounting is that an entity is a going concern and that its assets represent benefits that will be realized at some time in the future. If the adjusted basis of those assets is lower than their net book value, the benefit ultimately realized will be lower than what is reflected on the books.

Example 14

Assume that Living the Life (LtL), Inc.'s only noncash asset is an apartment building. The fair market value and net book value of the building is $1,000,000. LtL has no liabilities. LtL faces a combined Federal and state tax rate of 25%. Its balance sheet reflects the following:

Assets		Liabilities and Owners' Equity	
Cash	$ 250,000	Liabilities	$ -0-
Real estate	1,000,000	Owners' equity	1,250,000
Total assets	$1,250,000	Total liabilities and owners' equity	$1,250,000

continued

A private investment group purchases all of the stock of LtL for $1,250,000 (the fair market value of its assets). When the building is sold, they learn that its tax adjusted basis is $0, resulting in a $1,000,000 taxable gain. After paying Federal and state taxes on the sale at a combined rate of 25%, LtL is left with only $1,000,000 of cash (rather than the $1,250,000 expected based on the fair market value of the assets). The failure to record the deferred tax liability related to the property resulted in an overstatement of LtL's assets.

The failure to record deferred taxes also will provide an unreliable depiction of a corporation's current income and, therefore, its future income and cash flows.

Example 15

Current, Inc., reported $1,000,000 of pretax operating income in 2023, its first year of operations. Current operated in a state with a 4% income tax, making its combined Federal and state tax rate 25%. However, because of several tax incentives available to businesses in its industry (all temporary book-tax differences), Current was able to reduce its 2023 taxable income to $600,000 and its combined Federal and state tax liability to $150,000. Ignoring deferred taxes, Current reported $850,000 of after-tax net income in its financial statements ($1,000,000 book income − $150,000 current tax expense).

This income was higher than potential investors had anticipated, and several purchased Current stock. In 2024, Current's business grew 25% and it earned $1,250,000 of pretax operating income. However, the $400,000 of temporary book-tax differences that had reduced its 2023 tax liability reversed in 2024. As a result, Current paid taxes of $412,500 [($1,250,000 2024 pretax book income + $400,000) × 25%], much more than investors had anticipated. Investors were surprised and disappointed when Current's net income fell to $837,500 ($1,250,000 − $412,500 current tax expense).

LO.5

Describe the purpose of the valuation allowance, when it is used, and its impact on tax expense.

24-2c The Valuation Allowance

As discussed previously, a corporation may have deferred tax assets as well as deferred tax liabilities. Although a future benefit need not be certain for it to be recognized as an asset in the financial statements, recognition requires a reasonable expectation that a future benefit will be realized. ASC 740 specifically requires that a deferred tax asset not be recognized unless it is *more likely than not* (a greater than 50 percent likelihood) that a future tax benefit will eventually be realized.[7]

Recognizing Deferred Tax Assets

Example 16

Pear, Inc., reported pretax book income and taxable income of $2,000,000 in 2023 (i.e., there are no temporary or permanent differences) and a current Federal income tax liability for the year of $420,000 before tax credits ($2,000,000 × 21%). During the year, Pear earned $100,000 in general business credits that it is not able to use on its 2023 tax return.

Pear's management believes it is *more likely than not* that Pear will be able to use the $100,000 of tax credits before they expire. Consequently, the future tax benefit of the tax credits is accounted for in the current-year book tax expense as a $100,000 deferred tax benefit.

The current and deferred tax expense are calculated as follows:

	Book Tax Expense
Current tax expense (benefit)	$420,000
Deferred tax expense (benefit)	(100,000)
Total tax expense	$320,000

[7] ASC 740–10–30–5(e).

Global Tax Issues Tax Losses and the Deferred Tax Asset

Although a current-year net operating loss (NOL) represents a failure of an entity's business model to some, others see it as a potential tax refund. But when an NOL hits the balance sheet as a deferred tax asset, the story is not over. The NOL creates or increases a deferred tax asset that may or may not be realizable in future periods: the key question for a financial analyst is whether the entity will generate enough taxable income in future years to create a positive tax liability that can be offset by the NOL carryover amount.

Both International Financial Reporting Standards (IFRS) and U.S. GAAP preclude recognizing a deferred tax asset when the asset is unlikely to be realized. However, unlike U.S. GAAP, IFRS does not make use of a valuation allowance. Rather, under IAS 12, a deferred tax asset is recorded only when it is "probable" (interpreted as "more likely than not") that the deferred tax amount will be realized, and then only to the extent of that probable amount. Thus, no offsetting valuation allowance is needed.

Recognizing Deferred Tax Assets

Example 17

Continue with the facts of Example 16. Pear records the following journal entry for the book income tax expense and deferred tax asset related to the expected use of the credits:

Income tax expense (provision)	$320,000	
Deferred tax asset	100,000	
Income tax payable		$420,000

Because the future benefits of the tax credit carryovers are considered more likely than not to be realized, they are recognized as a deferred tax asset and reduce Pear's current-year tax expense.

When a deferred tax asset does not meet the *more likely than not* threshold for recognition, ASC 740 requires that a valuation allowance be created. The **valuation allowance** is a contra-asset account that offsets all or a portion of the deferred tax asset (similar to the way an allowance for uncollectible accounts is used to reflect the net realizable value of accounts receivable).

Example 18

Returning to Example 16, assume that Pear's management believes it is more likely than not that Pear will be able to use only $40,000 of the 2023 general business credits in any tax year, with the remaining $60,000 expiring unused. Pear will use a valuation allowance to reflect the realizability of the deferred tax asset, making the following journal entry in addition to the one made in Example 17:

Deferred tax expense	$60,000	
Valuation allowance		$60,000

As a result of recording the valuation allowance, Pear's tax expense will be increased to $380,000 as follows:

		Book Tax Expense
Current tax expense (benefit)		$420,000
Deferred tax expense (benefit)		
Deferred tax asset	($100,000)	
Less: Valuation allowance	60,000	(40,000)
Total tax expense		$380,000

When evaluating the realizability of a deferred tax asset and the need for a valuation allowance, all relevant negative and positive evidence must be considered. Negative evidence (i.e., evidence suggesting that the deferred tax asset will not be realized) includes the following:[8]

- Cumulative losses in recent years.
- A history of loss or credit carryovers expiring unused.
- A carryback or carryforward period so brief as to practically preclude realization.
- An expectation of losses in upcoming years.
- Uncertainties that could adversely affect future profits on a continuing basis.

Given the existence of any negative evidence, offsetting positive evidence should be considered. Positive evidence (i.e., evidence that supports the realizability of the deferred tax asset) includes the following:[9]

- Existing contracts that will produce sufficient taxable income to allow realization of the deferred tax asset.
- Unrealized appreciation of assets.
- A strong earnings history exclusive of the loss that created the deferred tax asset.

ASC 740 requires that deferred tax assets be evaluated for realizability even if an entity reports an overall net deferred tax liability. In other words, although deferred tax assets and liabilities from different temporary differences may result in an overall net deferred tax liability, *the realizability of the deferred tax asset resulting from each temporary difference must be evaluated separately.*

The need for a valuation allowance is considered at each balance sheet date, including the one at the end of the period in which the deferred tax asset is first created as well as each subsequent period. An allowance is established whenever the deferred tax asset fails to meet the more likely than not test. Conversely, the allowance may be reduced or released when a deferred tax asset that had formerly failed to meet the recognition requirement is subsequently judged more likely than not to be realized.

Referring back to Example 18, assume that in 2026, Pear signs sales contracts with several new customers. Based on the profits expected from the new contracts, Pear determines that it will generate enough income to fully utilize its general business credit carryforward before the end of the carryover period (i.e., Pear determines that it is *more likely than not*—a greater than 50% likelihood—that the general business credit carryforward will be used before it expires).

As a result, in 2026, Pear will release the valuation allowance it created in 2023, increasing its deferred tax assets and reducing its tax expense.

Valuation allowance	$60,000	
Deferred tax expense		$60,000

Notice that Pear is decreasing its tax expense in 2026 for tax credits that relate to transactions that occurred and were reported in the financial statements in 2023.

Exhibit 24.3 summarizes the computation of deferred tax expense or benefit.

[8] ASC 740–10–30–21.

[9] ASC 740–10–30–22.

Exhibit 24.3 Deferred Tax Expense (Benefit)

	NBV in excess of AB of assets at the balance sheet date
+	AB in excess of NBV of liabilities at the balance sheet date
	Cumulative net temporary book-tax differences
×	Applicable tax rate
	Net deferred tax liability (asset) at balance sheet date
–	Net deferred tax liability (asset) at prior balance sheet date
	Tentative deferred tax expense (benefit)
±	Change in valuation allowance
	Deferred tax expense (benefit)

24-3 Tax Disclosures in the Financial Statements

LO.6

Identify and interpret the tax-related information disclosed in the financial statement footnotes.

As discussed previously, several tax-related items are recognized throughout the financial statements. Additional details regarding these items must be disclosed in the footnotes to those financial statements.

24-3a Presentation of Amounts Recognized in the Financial Statements

Deferred tax asset and liability accounts are treated as noncurrent items on the GAAP balance sheet.[10] A corporation with both deferred tax assets and liabilities should report the *net* deferred tax assets or liabilities related to any particular tax jurisdiction [e.g., the United States, state(s), and foreign jurisdiction(s)] as a single line item on the balance sheet. However, it should not offset assets and liabilities that relate to different jurisdictions. Therefore, a corporation operating in multiple taxing jurisdictions may report both a deferred tax asset and a deferred tax liability on its balance sheet.[11]

In its GAAP income statement, a corporation generally reports its total income tax expense, including both its current tax expense (or benefit) and the deferred tax expense, (or benefit) as a single line item. However, its total tax expense must be allocated among income from continuing operations, discontinued operations, other comprehensive income, and items directly impacting shareholders' equity. Amounts other than those relating to continuing operations generally are presented in the financial statements net of tax (i.e., without the related tax expense or benefit stated separately).

The Big Picture

Example 20

Return to the facts of *The Big Picture* on p 24-1. Even if Arctic has no permanent book-tax differences, the tax expense reported on its income statement may not equal 25% (Arctic's combined Federal and state tax rate) of its pretax book income because part of that expense, or benefit, is netted with other items. Mr. Jones should determine whether Arctic is reporting sources of comprehensive income that appear below net income from continuing operations in the income statement (e.g., income from discontinued operations or other comprehensive income) or other items that relate directly to shareholders' equity. If so, the tax attributed to these items should be disclosed in the related footnotes.

24-3b The Financial Statement Footnotes

The income tax footnote contains a wealth of information, including the following:[12]

- A breakdown of income between domestic and foreign sources.
- A breakdown of total tax expense by its current and deferred components.

[10] ASC 740–10–45–4.

[11] ASC 740–10–45–6. FASB is currently conducting a project examining the possibility of requiring disclosure of the amount of taxes paid in each jurisdiction in which the corporation conducts business. For more information, see **fasb.org/Page/ProjectPage?metadata=fasb-Targeted%20Improvements%20to%20Income%20Tax%20Disclosures&isPrintView=true**.

[12] ASC 740–10–50. The disclosures listed here apply to public entities. Nonpublic entities sometimes have fewer disclosure requirements.

- The deferred tax asset and liability associated with each source of temporary difference.
- The total valuation allowance applied against the deferred tax assets and the change in the allowance during the year.
- The amount and expiration date of loss and tax credit carryovers.
- A reconciliation of the reported tax expense (or effective tax rate) to the amount that would be expected based on pretax book income and the Federal statutory rate.
- A discussion of significant tax matters.

Other financial statement footnotes may also contain information related to a company's taxes. For example, the amount of income taxes actually paid during the year must be disclosed either on the face of the Statement of Cash Flows or in the related footnotes.[13]

24-3c The Effective Tax Rate Reconciliation

To provide readers of the financial statements more information about the reported tax expense, companies are required to disclose a reconciliation of the tax expense reported in the income statement to what might be expected by a reader. Although this is often described as the tax **rate reconciliation**, a company may present a reconciliation of either:[14]

1. The tax expense it reports to the expense that would be expected based on its pretax income and the statutory rate of the country in which it is located, or
2. Its effective tax rate to its home country statutory rate.

For financial statement purposes, the *effective tax rate* refers to the total tax expense reported in the financial statements, whether currently payable or not, as a percentage of pretax book income. Reporting the deferred tax expense and deferred tax assets and liabilities related to temporary book-tax differences ensures that the tax related to all income reported in the financial statements is included in tax expense. Therefore, temporary book-tax differences will not cause the reported tax expense to differ from what might otherwise be expected and will not be included in the rate reconciliation. In addition to permanent book-tax differences, items that will cause the reported tax expense to differ from the expected tax expense, and the effective tax rate to differ from the statutory rate, include the following:

- Any change in the valuation allowance.
- Any change in deferred tax assets and liabilities due to a tax rate change.
- Any tax benefits resulting from available credits.
- Any non-U.S. income tax expense or benefit (e.g., foreign and state income taxes).

Example 21

BoxCo, Inc., a domestic corporation, owns 100% of PaperCo, Ltd., a Macedonian corporation. The U.S. corporate tax rate is 21%; the Macedonian corporate tax rate is 10%. Book income, permanent and temporary differences, and current tax expense are computed as follows:

	BoxCo	PaperCo
Book income before tax	$300,000	$200,000
Permanent differences:		
Business meals expense	20,000	—
Municipal bond interest income	(50,000)	—
Book income after permanent differences	$270,000	$200,000
Temporary differences:		
Tax > book depreciation	(50,000)	—
Book > tax bad debt expense	10,000	—
Taxable income	$230,000	$200,000
Tax rate	× 21%	× 10%
Current tax expense	$ 48,300	$ 20,000

BoxCo will report current tax expense of $68,300 ($48,300 + $20,000).

continued

[13]ASC 230–10–50–2.

[14]ASC 740–10–50–12.

BoxCo's deferred tax expense is determined by evaluating the change in its net deferred tax asset/liability during the year. To determine its deferred tax assets and liabilities, it identifies its temporary book-tax differences and determines the tax consequences of each. At the beginning of the year, BoxCo's deferred tax assets and liabilities were as follows:

	Net Book Value	Tax Adjusted Basis	Temporary Difference	Combined Tax Rate	Deferred Tax Asset/ (Liability)
Depreciable assets	$900,000	$750,000	($150,000)	21%	($31,500)
Accounts receivable	800,000	850,000	50,000	21%	10,500
Net deferred tax liability					($21,000)

At the end of the year, BoxCo's deferred tax asset and liabilities are as follows:

	Net Book Value	Tax Adjusted Basis	Temporary Difference	Combined Tax Rate	Deferred Tax Asset/ (Liability)
Depreciable assets	$860,000	$660,000	($200,000)	21%	($42,000)
Accounts receivable	785,000	845,000	60,000	21%	12,600
Net deferred tax liability					($29,400)

BoxCo's deferred tax expense for the year is the $8,400 increase in its deferred tax liability ($29,400 − $21,000). Its total tax expense of $76,700 ($68,300 + $8,400) would be recognized in its income statement. The following details would be disclosed in its footnotes:

	Total Income
Domestic	$300,000
Foreign	200,000
	$500,000

	Tax Expense		
	Domestic	Foreign	Total
Current	$48,300	$20,000	$68,300
Deferred	8,400	–0–	8,400
	$56,700	$20,000	$76,700

	Deferred Tax Assets and Liabilities		
	Beginning of Year	End of Year	Change
Depreciable assets	($31,500)	($42,000)	($10,500)
Accounts receivable	10,500	12,600	2,100
Less: Valuation allowance	–0–	–0–	–0–
	($21,000)	($29,400)	($ 8,400)

continued

	Effective Tax Rate Reconciliation	
	$	%
Expected tax at U.S. statutory tax rate	$105,000	21.0%**
Disallowed meals expense	4,200	0.8
Municipal bond interest	(10,500)	(2.1)
Foreign income taxed at less than U.S. rate	(22,000)*	(4.4)
Income tax expense (provision)	$ 76,700	15.3%

*$200,000 × (21% − 10%).

**The expected effective tax rate, rate changes attributable to permanent differences, and the actual effective tax rate are all determined by dividing the amount of tax shown by book income of $500,000.

Only permanent differences appear in the rate reconciliation. Temporary differences do not affect the *total* book income tax expense; they simply affect the amount of the tax expense that is current versus deferred.

The Big Picture

Example

22

Return to the facts of *The Big Picture* on p. 24-1. Arctic's total reported tax expense, $5,000,000, is not equal to what might be expected by applying the Federal tax rate of 21% to its pretax book income, or $4,515,000 ($21,500,000 × 21%). And given that Arctic's combined Federal and state income tax rate is 25%, one might expect to find book tax expense of $5,375,000.

Arctic's effective tax rate of 23.26% ($5,000,000 total tax expense ÷ $21,500,000 pretax book income) does not equal the Federal statutory rate of 21% or the combined Federal and state tax rate of 25%. This suggests that Arctic has some combination of permanent book-tax differences and/or available credits. Mr. Jones should be able to find these in Arctic's tax rate reconciliation in its tax footnote.

Because Arctic operates in a state that imposes an income tax, Mr. Jones should expect to find state taxes in the reconciliation as an item that increases Arctic's effective tax rate relative to the Federal statutory rate of 21% and its tax expense over what would be expected based on multiplying its pretax book income by the statutory rate. Because state income taxes increase Arctic's effective tax rate, Mr. Jones should expect to find other reconciling items that reduce Arctic's effective tax rate.

24-4 Special Issues

LO.7

Apply the GAAP standards concerning tax uncertainties and tax law changes.

24-4a The Financial Accounting for Tax Uncertainties

Applying the tax law to a complex business transaction can be challenging. The law may be unclear as to a taxpayer's unique business situation, or facts about a taxpayer's potential tax liability may be uncertain or incomplete. Financial Accounting Standards Interpretation (FIN) 48, incorporated into ASC 740–10,[15] addresses how this uncertainty should impact the accounting for income taxes. FIN 48 requires a two-step analysis to determine whether, and how much of, the tax savings (or tax benefits) related to an uncertain tax position taken by a taxpayer may reduce the tax expense reported in the taxpayer's financial statements. The two-step analysis, requiring consideration of whether the benefits are recognizable at all and, if so, the measurement of those benefits, is described below (see Concept Summary 24.2). Technically, FIN 48 requires this analysis of all tax positions taken by a company, although materiality typically limits the number of tax positions considered.

[15]ASC 740–10–25–5 through –17.

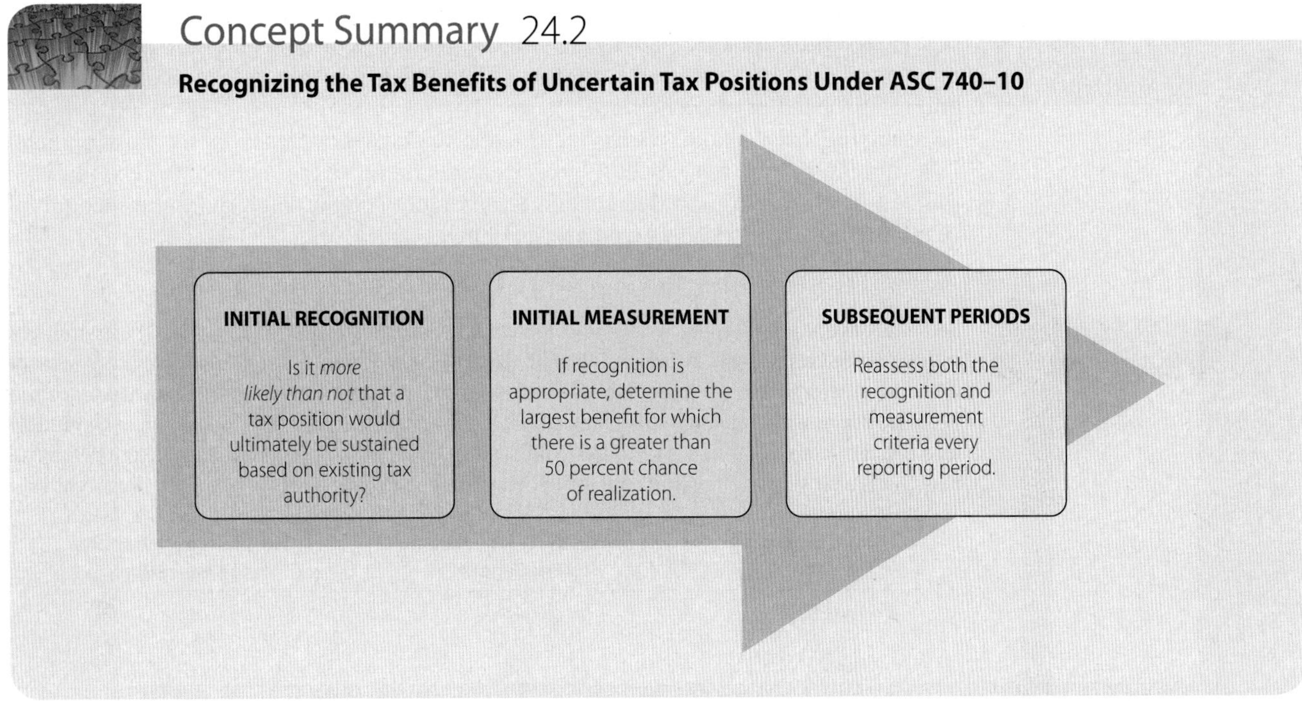

Initial Recognition

Whether the tax benefits of an uncertain position may be *recognized* at all depends on the strength of the tax authority supporting the position. For tax purposes, taxpayers may take a tax position as long as there is *substantial authority* for the position. Although the substantial authority standard can be challenging to interpret and apply, the Regulations provide that a position may meet the standard as long as it has a reasonable basis, even if its probability of being upheld fails to exceed 50 percent.[16] Positions with much lower probabilities of success may be taken if a taxpayer discloses on the tax return the relevant facts surrounding the position.[17]

For financial reporting purposes, however, ASC 740 prohibits the recognition of any tax benefits related to an uncertain tax position unless it is *more likely than not* (i.e., a greater than 50 percent likelihood) that the position would ultimately be sustained based only on existing tax authority.[18] When applying this test, it must be assumed that the position is identified by the relevant tax enforcement agency; the possibility that the position is not detected by the authorities is irrelevant. As a result, it is possible that a corporation may legally take an uncertain tax position, and reduce its tax liability, but be unable to reduce the tax expense reported in its financial statements.

Initial Measurement

If the uncertain tax position meets the *more likely than not* threshold, the second step is to determine the amount of the tax benefit that may be recognized (the *measurement* process). The amount of the benefit that may be recognized is limited to the largest amount that is *more likely than not* (a greater than 50 percent probability) to be realized taking into account all relevant factors, including the probability the position is detected by the enforcement agency and the possible outcomes of any negotiated settlements

[16] Reg. § 1.6662–4(d)(2).

[17] § 6662(d)(2)(B).

[18] ASC 740–10–25–5 through –7.

between the taxpayer and the agency.[19] One approach to measuring the benefit to be recognized is to use a probability outcome table that considers all of the possible post-audit and post-settlement outcomes that might result from taking the uncertain position and the probability of each.

Assuming that the taxpayer has recorded its tax provision based on the position taken in its tax return, failure to meet the recognition criteria or the inability to recognize the full benefit of the position due to the measurement criteria will require the recognition of additional tax expense as well as a liability.

Example 23

StarksCo has adopted certain transfer pricing strategies with related parties overseas. These strategies reduce StarksCo's Federal income tax liability by $100,000. However, the IRS is likely to challenge the pricing structure in an audit. StarksCo estimates that, although it is more likely than not that these positions would be upheld if taken to court after an IRS audit, the tax benefit may be reduced as a result of compromises it may make with the IRS to avoid the costs of going to court. StarksCo constructs a table of the potential outcomes from this negotiation process and their probabilities.

Resulting Estimated Tax Benefit	Probability of Realizing Tax Benefit	Cumulative Probability of Realization
$100,000	40%	40%
80,000	35%	75%
45,000	20%	95%
-0-	5%	100%

Assume that StarksCo recorded a book tax provision of $250,000, *including* the $100,000 tax benefit from the transfer pricing positions. In light of the requirements of ASC 740–10, StarksCo instead should recognize only an $80,000 tax benefit for this item, the largest amount for which there is at least a 50% cumulative probability of being realized (here, a 75% chance of acceptance exists).

As a result, StarksCo should increase its current tax expense, and recognize a related liability, for $20,000 ($100,000 benefit initially recognized – $80,000 recognizable per ASC 740–10). The journal entry to record the unrecognizable tax benefit would be as follows:

Current income tax expense (provision)	$20,000	
ASC 740–10 liability		$20,000

Subsequent Events

Once an entity takes an uncertain tax position, the recognition and measurement criteria must be reassessed at each reporting date.[20] If there is a change in the tax authority on which the initial recognition judgment was based (e.g., a new Regulation is issued related to the tax position), a previously unrecognized tax benefit may become recognizable. Conversely, a previously recognized benefit may need to be reversed (derecognized).

Revisit the facts in Example 23. StarksCo previously recognized an $80,000 tax benefit related to its transfer pricing strategies. Assume in the subsequent year that the U.S. Tax Court rejects the use of a strategy that is similar to the one used by StarksCo. As a result, StarksCo reduces its belief that its strategy would be upheld in court to 45%.

StarksCo is no longer allowed to recognize any tax benefit from its transfer pricing strategy. In the year the court case is settled, StarksCo must recognize $80,000 of additional tax expense as follows:

Income tax expense	$80,000	
ASC 740–10 liability		$80,000

[19] ASC 740–10–30–7.

[20] ASC 740–10–35.

Similarly, any change in the facts surrounding the initial measurement of a tax benefit will result in the recognition of a tax expense or benefit in the year of the change.

Finally, ultimate resolution of the tax position must also be accounted for. Eventually, the position will be examined by the taxing authority and resolved, or the statute of limitations will expire without the position ever being examined. If the position is examined, any amounts to be paid to the taxing authority are considered first to be payments on the existing liability with no impact on current year tax expense or net income. Any payments less than or greater than the previously established liability will impact tax expense in the year the position is settled.

Example 25

Revisit the facts in Example 23. Two years after recognizing the $20,000 liability for uncertain tax positions, Starks is audited by the IRS. Starks agrees to pay $25,000 in additional taxes to settle the matter. As a result, Starks records the following journal entry:

Income tax expense	$ 5,000	
ASC 740–10 liability	20,000	
Cash		$25,000

Notice that Starks is recognizing $5,000 in tax expense related to income it included in its financial statements two years ago.

If the statute of limitations expires without the position being examined, the liability for unrecognized tax benefits as well as the tax expense are reduced by the amount of the previously unrecognized benefit in the year in which the statute lapses.

Example 26

Revisit the facts of Example 23. Assume that the statute of limitations for the year in which Starks took the uncertain tax position lapses and the taxing authority can no longer challenge the position. Starks will reduce its liability and its tax expense as follows:

ASC 740–10 liability	$20,000	
Income tax expense		$20,000

Notice that Starks is recognizing a tax benefit in the current year related to income it reported three years ago.

ASC 740 requires public companies to provide, in its footnotes, a reconciliation of its unrecognized tax benefits at the beginning and end of the year.[21] The reconciliation must include the following:

- Any increase or decrease related to tax positions taken in prior years;
- Any increase related to tax positions taken during the current year;
- Any decreases related to settlements with the taxing authorities; and
- Any decreases due to the lapse of the applicable statute of limitations.

Companies also are required to disclose the following:

- The nature and amount of any changes in unrecognized tax benefits that are reasonably possible over the 12 months following the date of the financial statements;
- The tax years that remain subject to examination by major tax jurisdictions; and
- The amount of unrecognized tax benefits that, if recognized, would impact the effective tax rate.

[21]ASC 740–10–50–15A.

Ethics & Equity **How Much Uncertainty?**

While the only things certain in life may be death and taxes, how much taxes is certainly uncertain. In order for the tax benefits of an uncertain tax position to be recognized for financial reporting purposes, it must be more likely than not that the position will ultimately be upheld based solely on its technical merits. However, making such a judgment can be filled with, well, uncertainty. The basis for such a judgment may include judicial as well as legislative and administrative authority including court cases addressing positions similar to that taken by the taxpayer. But when a court has already ruled against the taxpayer, can it still be more likely than not that the taxpayer's position will be upheld? Several companies, including Whirlpool and Newell Brands, Inc. (the makers of Krazy Glue), after losing a case in Tax Court, have recently continued to recognize tax benefits related to the overturned positions.

Another of those companies is Coca-Cola. In 2020, Coca-Cola lost a case concerning its transfer pricing practices for the years 2007 to 2009. After the Tax Court ordered Coca-Cola to pay $3.3 billion in tax, the company announced that it could potentially be liable for up to $12 billion in additional taxes as a result of its use of the same practices since the years in question. This would exceed the annual pretax profits reported by the company for the last several years. However, Coca-Cola announced its intention to continue defending its position and recognized only an additional $438 million in tax expense as a result of the Tax Court's ruling.

Is Coca-Cola's decision to recognize the tax benefits of their position, even after the Tax Court's ruling, problematic? How relevant and reliable is the reporting of uncertain tax positions under ASC 740–10 given its reliance on judgments about the probability of future judgments? What alternatives might there be for dealing with tax uncertainty?

For more information, see **wsj.com/articles/coke-whirlpool-keep-tax-court-losses-off-the-books-1614168007**.

24-4b **Effects of Statutory Tax Rate Changes**

As discussed earlier, deferred tax expense is the change in an entity's deferred tax assets and deferred tax liabilities from the beginning to the end of the year. Usually, that change is due to changes in cumulative book-tax differences. However, even with no changes in cumulative book-tax differences, deferred tax assets and liabilities will change if there is a change during the year in the tax rate that will apply when those differences are expected to reverse.

For example, if future tax rates increase from 21 percent to 25 percent, the tax benefit of deferred tax assets generated by temporary differences also will increase because, when they are realized, they will reduce income taxed at 25 percent (rather than 21 percent). Conversely, an increase in future tax rates from 21 percent to 25 percent will increase the tax cost of deferred tax liabilities since they will generate taxable income taxed at 25 percent (rather than 21 percent when they are realized).

Although tax rate changes are uncommon, they can be significant when they do occur. For example, the Tax Cuts and Jobs Act (TCJA) of 2017 reduced Federal corporate tax rates from as much as 35 percent to 21 percent—significantly reducing the value of deferred tax assets but also reducing the cost of deferred tax liabilities (and impacting the financial statements of many corporations).

Effects of Change in Corporate Tax Rate

Example 27

Alpha Corporation had accumulated a net temporary book-tax difference of $1,000,000 as of January 1, 2017, due primarily to the use of accelerated cost recovery. Accordingly, its deferred tax liability account on January 1, 2017, was $350,000 ($1,000,000 × 35%).

When the TCJA of 2017 reduced the applicable Federal corporate income tax rate to 21%, the balance of the deferred tax liability account was adjusted to $210,000 ($1,000,000 × 21%), reducing its deferred tax expense and increasing its 2017 book income by $140,000.

Financial Disclosure Insights — The Impact of Tax Rate Changes

As illustrated in Examples 27 and 28, the effect of tax rate changes can vary significantly across corporations. In 2017, AT&T recorded a $20.2 billion tax benefit as a result of the tax rate reductions included in TCJA, mostly from revaluing its significant net deferred tax liability. The benefit reduced its effective tax rate for the year from 36.7 percent to (97.2) percent. Conversely, given its significant net deferred tax asset, Citigroup recorded an additional $22.6 billion tax expense as a result of the Act, increasing its effective tax rate from 29.8 percent to 129.1 percent.

Beta Corporation had accumulated a net temporary book-tax difference of $1,000,000 as of January 1, 2017, due primarily to a net operating loss. Accordingly, its deferred tax asset account on January 1, 2017, was $350,000.

When the TCJA of 2017 reduced the applicable Federal corporate income tax rate to 21%, the balance of the deferred tax asset account was adjusted to $210,000 ($1,000,000 × 21%), reducing its deferred tax asset and decreasing its 2017 book income by $140,000.

24-4c The Corporate Tax Department

The corporate tax department often is charged with shaping and implementing the entity's tax strategies (*tax planning*) and filing all required tax returns (*tax compliance*) while preparing for subsequent audit and litigation activity (*tax controversy*). Tax professionals often work closely with those who prepare the entity's financial statements, especially concerning the tax footnote, tax deferral accounts, and tax rate reconciliations. Professional tax and accounting research underlies all of this work.

The functions of a modern tax department are illustrated in Exhibit 24.4. Tax professionals must be proficient in all of the indicated areas to meet the demands of the entity and its shareholders, regulators, and taxing agencies.

Information related to tax expense and its related balance sheet effects is required for SEC taxpayers long before the corporate income tax return is due. Tax professionals must work with those charged with completing financial reporting requirements so that these SEC deadlines are met (e.g., in filing a Form 10–K for a calendar year corporation in February or March of the following year, even though the extended due date of the Form 1120 is not until mid-October).

If the tax professional grasps both the tax and financial statement effects of various tax planning and compliance activities, the tax professional brings great value to the entity through the tax department.

Exhibit 24.4 **Functions of a Tax Department (by Percent of Time Spent)**

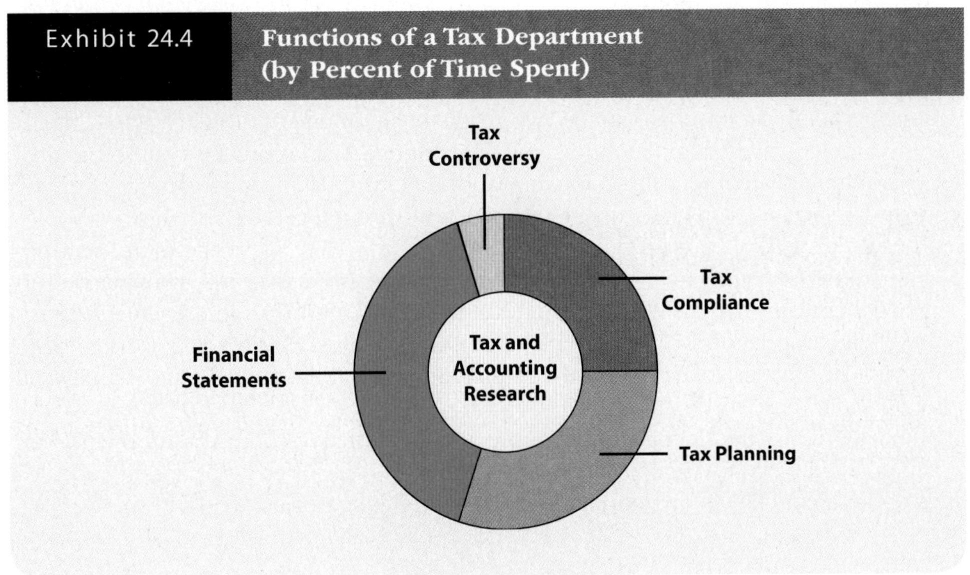

The steps in determining a corporation's income tax expense for book purposes are summarized in Concept Summary 24.3.

Concept Summary 24.3

The Income Tax Provision Process

Expense (Benefit) Recognized in the Financial Statements

Current Tax Expense (Benefit)		**Deferred Tax Expense (Benefit)**
Sum of all liabilities expected to be reported on all (Federal, state, and foreign) current-year tax returns		Change in deferred tax assets and liabilities during the reporting period (including that due to tax rate changes)
± Change in unrecognized tax benefits		± Change in valuation allowance
± Amounts attributable to items not included in income from continuing operations (i.e., intra-period allocation)	+	± Change in unrecognized tax benefits
Current tax expense (benefit)		± Amounts attributable to items not included in income from continuing operations (i.e., intra-period allocation)
		Deferred tax expense (benefit)

Footnote Disclosures

- Breakdown of income between domestic and foreign sources
- Breakdown of tax expense between current and deferred
- Tax assets and liabilities attributable to individual temporary book-tax differences
- Amount of any valuation allowance
- Tax rate reconciliation
- Breakdown of changes in unrecognized tax benefits during the year

LO.8

Use financial statement income tax information to benchmark a company's tax position.

24-5 Benchmarking

As discussed earlier, an entity's tax expense can convey many things about the entity to a wide array of interested parties (e.g., shareholders, creditors, policymakers, and potential investors). A company's income tax expense is one of the single largest expense items on its income statement, and understanding the components of this expense is a critical activity for tax professionals, as well as for readers of the financial statements.

Consider a typical baseball game. Two teams meet, interact following a specific set of rules, and ultimately complete the game, generating a final score. Of course, the final score is of immediate interest to the teams and the fans, but once the game is over, the score and associated statistics (runs, hits, and errors) are relegated to the history books. Yet these statistics still can be quite useful. A team coach may use the game statistics to evaluate the strengths and weaknesses of the players to assist in improving performance. Other teams may use the data to develop strategies for upcoming games. Players can use this information to "benchmark" themselves against their own performance in prior games or against players on other teams. In short, there is a wealth of analytical possibilities in these historical data.

A taxpayer's reported income tax expense also is a valuable source of information for the company, its tax advisers, and its competitors. The reported information provides clues about a company's operational and tax planning strategies.

Companies may benchmark their tax situation to other years' results or to other companies in the same industry. The starting point for a **benchmarking** exercise usually is the data from the income tax note rate reconciliation.

24-5a Methods of Analysis

In addition to comparing effective tax rates, one can analyze entities' levels of deferred tax assets and liabilities.

Example 29

Akiko Enterprises reports a net deferred tax liability of $280,000. Erde, Inc., a company in the same industry, reports a net deferred tax liability of $860,000. The presence of deferred tax liabilities on the balance sheet indicates that both companies are benefiting from deferring actual tax payments (essentially, an interest-free loan from the government).

At first glance, it may appear that Erde is doing better in this regard. However, what if Akiko holds total assets of $2,600,000 and Erde's assets total $19,200,000? This information indicates that Akiko has 10.8% ($280,000 ÷ $2,600,000) of its total assets "financed" with an interest-free loan from the government; Erde has only 4.5% ($860,000 ÷ $19,200,000) of its assets "financed" with its deferred tax liabilities.

One may do a more refined benchmarking analysis by examining each component of an entity's deferred tax assets and liabilities as a percentage of total assets. For example, an observer can examine how the deferred tax assets or liabilities related to property, plant, and equipment compare with those of its competitors. The nature of the components of deferred tax liabilities and deferred tax assets becomes important in a benchmarking analysis.

Benchmarking Financial Results

Example 30

LinCo reports total book income before taxes of $10,000,000 and a total tax provision of $1,600,000, producing a 16% effective tax rate. TuckCo also reports book income before taxes of $10,000,000. TuckCo's total tax expense is $1,500,000, producing an effective tax rate of 15%. At first glance, it appears that the entities are similar based on their effective tax rates. The total tax expense divided between current and deferred is as follows:

	LinCo	TuckCo
Current tax expense	$2,500,000	$2,600,000
Deferred tax benefit	(900,000)	(1,100,000)
Total tax expense	$1,600,000	$1,500,000

Again, it appears that both companies have created deferred tax assets in the current year that are expected to produce tax savings in the future. Knowing the nature of the underlying deferred tax assets will add greatly to one's interpretation of the effective tax rates.

With additional investigation, you determine that the deferred tax asset generating LinCo's expected future tax savings is due to an NOL carryover. The deferred tax asset generating TuckCo's expected future tax savings is generated by the use of different book and tax methods in accounting for warranty expense. This additional information reveals that LinCo previously has incurred losses; to use the NOLs in the coming years, it will be critical for LinCo to generate future taxable income.

This is quite different from TuckCo's situation, which reveals only that common differences in accounting methods exist and that the future deductions likely will be used fully. Although the tax positions of LinCo and TuckCo seem very similar on the surface, a closer look reveals a striking difference.

Benchmarking Financial Results

Example 31

WageCo and SalaryCo operate in the same industry. Their book income and current, deferred, and total tax expense were reported as follows:

	WageCo	SalaryCo
Book income before tax	$1,500,000	$2,300,000
Current tax expense	$ 680,000	$ 24,000
Deferred tax expense (benefit)	(410,000)	390,000
Total tax expense	$ 270,000	$ 414,000
Effective tax rate	18%	18%

Although the companies have the same effective tax rate, WageCo is paying a significant amount of taxes currently, with a large portion of the tax benefits related to its operations deferred. SalaryCo appears to be deferring a substantial portion of its tax expense to future years. Although both companies report the same effective tax rate, the details indicate that the two companies face very different tax situations. By looking more closely at the financial statements, an analyst should be able to determine why these differences exist.

24-5b Tax Rate Sustainability

It is important in benchmarking exercises to remove the effect of nonrecurring items to evaluate the sustainability of effective tax rates across time or companies. Examples of nonrecurring items include restructuring costs, legal settlements, and IRS or other tax liability settlements. A nonrecurring item may significantly impact a company's current year effective tax rate. However, the very nature of this item implies that it has little to do with the company's *long-term* sustainable tax costs.

Example 32

MetalCo and IronCo operate in the same industry, and they report the following tax rate reconciliations in their tax footnotes:

	MetalCo	IronCo
Hypothetical tax at U.S. statutory tax rate	21.0%	21.0%
State and local taxes	2.2	2.1
Foreign income taxed at less than U.S. rate	(6.2)	(6.1)
Tax Court settlement on disputed tax issue	(18.6)	—
Effective tax rate	(1.6)%	17.0%

Although it appears that MetalCo has a significantly lower effective tax rate than IronCo's effective tax rate, removing MetalCo's Tax Court settlement, a nonrecurring item, indicates that both companies may regularly face a similar 17% effective tax rate [(1.6)% + 18.6% = 17%].

24-5c Uses of Benchmarking Analysis

Benchmarking is part science and part art. A useful analysis requires both an accountant's knowledge of how the underlying financial statements are constructed, including arriving at the appropriate tax expense, and a detective's sense of where to look and what questions to ask.

In addition to benchmarking, financial analysts perform an important function for the capital markets in their detailed analyses of companies. The analyst combs through both the financial reports and other information about a company to produce an informed opinion on how a company is performing. Analysts' earnings forecasts often constitute an important metric to examine when making decisions about investing in companies.

An experienced financial analyst typically will have a good handle on interpreting financial statement information. However, even experienced analysts will often "punt" when it comes to interpreting the tax information contained in a financial statement, preferring to look at net income before taxes (or even EBITDA, earnings before interest, taxes, depreciation, and amortization). A great deal of useful information about a business is contained in its tax footnote, and analysts might have an edge if they work at understanding the mysteries of taxes in the financial statements. Some typical uses of benchmarking in an analysis of an entity's financial results are summarized in Concept Summary 24.4.

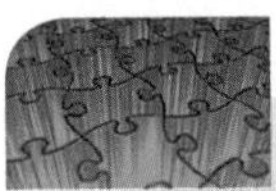

Concept Summary 24.4

Benchmarking Analysis

A benchmarking analysis can be helpful in comparing the tax positions of two or more business entities. One might consider the following aspects of the taxpayers' financial disclosures in this regard. This list is not all-inclusive; benchmarking also includes the judgment and experience of the parties conducting the analysis.

- Compare the effective tax rates of the entities.
- Explain the differences in effective rates. Are these differences sustainable over time?
- Apply the analysis to both the tax dollars involved and the underlying net assets of the entities.
- Discount (but do not ignore) any one-time tax benefits/detriments that are observed.
- Include in your analysis any knowledge of the nontax, competitive strategy and tactics employed and planned by the entity.

24-6 Tax Planning

24-6a Releasing Valuation Allowances

A valuation allowance must be established if it is *more likely than not* that the tax benefits of a deferred tax asset will never be realized. By recording a valuation allowance (a contra-asset), the corporation offsets all (or a portion) of the deferred tax asset and increases reported tax expense. For example, if a taxpayer generates an NOL, it records a deferred tax asset for the future tax savings related to using the NOL. However, if the evidence suggests that it is *more likely than not* that all or a portion of the NOL never will be used, a valuation allowance must be recorded.

However, in a future accounting period, the valuation allowance may be reduced or eliminated, reducing reported tax expense and increasing book income. To do this, however, the taxpayer must demonstrate that the facts and circumstances that led to the establishment of the valuation allowance have changed. For example, to reduce the valuation allowance related to the NOL, the taxpayer must demonstrate that there will be enough future taxable income to absorb the NOL in the future. Sources of future taxable income include reversals of temporary differences that will produce future taxable income, demonstrated efficiencies that will reduce future expenses, documented expected increases in sales (and capacity), and any other sources of future profits.

Taxpayers also may demonstrate that the adoption of new tax planning strategies will allow the use of deferred tax assets. The proposed tax strategies must be prudent and feasible in their execution, and the taxpayer must be willing to execute the strategy in a manner that will use the deferred tax assets. Such strategies might include the following:

- Slow down cost recovery deductions (e.g., by using straight-line methods or electing to capitalize expenditures).
- Sell off appreciated assets.
- Convert tax-exempt investments into taxable holdings.
- Change tax accounting methods (e.g., moving from LIFO to FIFO for inventories).

The Big Picture

Example 33

Return to the facts of *The Big Picture* on p. 24-1. Arctic Corporation's $3,000,000 deferred tax asset for an NOL carryforward has been offset by a $1,000,000 valuation allowance due to doubts over the levels of future sales and profitability.

This year Arctic completed improvements to its inventory management system that are likely to increase the contribution margin of every product that Arctic sells. In addition, two of Arctic's largest customers have secured financing that will relieve the financial difficulties that have restricted them. In fact, Arctic just received purchase orders from those customers that will increase unit sales by 20% over the next 18 months. As a result, Arctic's management determines that a release of $200,000 of the valuation allowance in the current quarter can be supported.

Example 34

Pear, Inc., from Example 18, adopts new planning strategies in 2024 that it's management believes will allow it ultimately to use the $60,000 of general business credits against which it had previously established a valuation allowance. Pear earns $2,300,000 in book income before tax and reports $2,300,000 in taxable income in 2024 (i.e., there are no permanent or temporary differences). The current Federal income tax expense is $483,000 ($2,300,000 × 21%).

In light of the new strategy, the $60,000 valuation allowance from 2023 is "released," and the tax benefit of this release affects the 2024 financial results as follows:

	Book Tax Expense
Current tax expense (benefit)	$483,000
Deferred tax expense (benefit)	
Release of valuation allowance	(60,000)
Total tax expense	$423,000

Pear makes the following 2024 journal entry to record the book income tax expense and valuation allowance release related to the expected use of the credits:

Income tax expense (provision)	$423,000	
Valuation allowance	60,000	
Income tax payable		$483,000

Pear's effective tax rate for 2024 is 18.4% ($423,000 ÷ $2,300,000). Without the valuation allowance release, Pear's effective tax rate would have been 21% ($483,000 ÷ $2,300,000). This tax rate benefit is realized even though the $100,000 in credit carryforwards has yet to be used in Pear's tax return.

24-6b Comparing Tax Savings

Many different types of tax planning strategies can produce tax savings. Yet even when planning ideas produce identical current cash-flow effects, some ideas may have an edge. CEOs and CFOs of public companies are focused on the bottom line—the company's net income after tax and related earnings per share. A CFO is likely to be just as interested in an idea's effect on the company's bottom line income as on the cash tax savings.

For example, consider two tax planning ideas that each produce $420,000 of current Federal income tax savings. The first idea generates its $420,000 in tax savings by increasing tax depreciation relative to book depreciation by $2,000,000 ($420,000 = $2,000,000 × 21%). The second idea produces research activities tax credits of $420,000, thus reducing current-year tax by $420,000.

Idea 1 produces its current tax savings via a temporary difference. Accordingly, the book tax expense will not reflect the related tax savings. Instead, this strategy simply reclassifies $420,000 from current to deferred tax expense. Even if the book-tax difference is not expected to reverse for 30 years (effectively generating "permanent" savings), the book tax expense does not reflect this savings.

In contrast, idea 2 is based on a permanent difference. As a result, the credit positively impacts reported net income, as well as current tax expense and cash flow.

Refocus on The Big Picture

Taxes in the Financial Statements

Raymond Jones should understand that the tax expense reported on the company's financial statements and the tax payable on the company's income tax returns often differ as a result of both temporary and permanent differences in financial statement income and taxable income. Examples of permanent differences include nontaxable income such as municipal bond interest and tax credits. Temporary differences include depreciation differences and other amounts that are affected by the timing of a deduction or an inclusion, but they ultimately result in the same amount being reflected in the financial statements and income tax returns.

Temporary differences will cause pretax book income to differ from taxable income. However, because a corporation must report its deferred as well as its current tax expense, temporary differences will not cause the tax expense, or the effective tax rate, reported in the financial statements to differ from what might be expected given the corporation's pretax book income and the statutory tax rate. However, permanent differences will impact both a corporation's reported tax expense and effective tax rate.

In this case, Arctic's income tax expense of $5 million is higher than the current Federal income tax payable. This results from timing differences that lead to the recognition of a deferred tax liability as well as permanent differences that do not.

What If?

Mr. Jones is concerned about a newspaper article that said that companies reporting less tax on their tax returns than on their financial statements were cheating the IRS. Is this an accurate assessment?

Although differences in income taxes payable to the IRS and financial tax expense can result from aggressive and illegal tax shelters, differences also result from different methods of accounting that are required for financial statement reporting using GAAP and tax laws enacted by Congress.

WAVEBREAKMEDIA/SHUTTERSTOCK.COM

Key Terms

ASC 740, 24-5
Balance sheet approach, 24-5
Benchmarking, 24-27
Current tax expense, 24-5
Deferred tax asset, 24-5
Deferred tax benefit, 24-5
Deferred tax expense, 24-5
Deferred tax liability, 24-5
Generally accepted accounting principles (GAAP), 24-2
Permanent differences, 24-3
Rate reconciliation, 24-18
Tax provision, 24-7
Temporary differences, 24-3
Valuation allowance, 24-15

Discussion Questions

1. **LO.1** Evaluate the following statement: For most business entities, book income differs from taxable income because "income" is meant to capture different constructs for book and tax purposes.

2. **LO.1** Define the terms *temporary difference* and *permanent difference* as they pertain to the financial reporting of income tax expenses. Describe how these two book-tax differences affect the gap between book and taxable income. How are permanent and temporary differences alike? How are they different? Critical Thinking

Communications 3. **LO.1** In no more than three PowerPoint slides, list several commonly encountered temporary and permanent book-tax differences. The slides will be used in your presentation next week to your school's Future CPAs Club.

Communications 4. **LO.2** Marcellus Jackson, the CFO of Mac, Inc., notices that the tax liability reported on Mac's tax return is less than the tax expense reported on Mac's financial statements. Provide a letter to Marcellus outlining why these two tax expense numbers differ. Mac's address is 482 Linden Road, Paris, KY 40362.

5. **LO.5** While viewing the Business News Channel, you heard that YoungCo has "released one-third of its valuation allowances because of an upbeat forecast for sales of its tablet computers over the next 30 months." What effect does such a release likely have on YoungCo's current-year book effective tax rate? Be specific.

6. **LO.5** Identify whether each of the following items typically constitutes *positive* or *negative* evidence when a manufacturing entity assesses whether a valuation allowance is required or should be adjusted for its net operating losses.
   a. Product orders are increasing.
   b. Book income for the past three years totals to a negative amount.
   c. Investment assets held by the taxpayer show an unrealized gain.
   d. The industry in which the taxpayer operates is in a down cycle.
   e. The entity's tax plan includes a switch from MACRS accelerated depreciation to straight-line for future equipment purchases.

7. **LO.6, 7** While performing a financial statement audit for a client, you notice that its current tax expense does not equal the tax liability that is reflected on the client's tax return for the year. Provide at least two possible explanations for the difference and where you might look to see if those explanations are relevant.

8. **LO.7** DraftJacks, Inc., took an uncertain tax position in 2021, recording an unrecognized tax benefit of $100,000. In 2023, the IRS challenged the position and DraftJacks agreed to pay $120,000 to settle it. What impact does the settlement have on DraftJacks's 2023 book tax expense and book income? Explain.

Decision Making 9. **LO.8** Jill is the CFO of Portech, Inc. Portech's tax advisers have recommended two tax planning ideas, each providing $5,000,000 of current-year cash tax savings. One idea is based on a timing difference and is expected to reverse in full 10 years in the future. The other idea creates a permanent difference that never will reverse.

   Determine whether these ideas will allow Portech to reduce its reported book income tax expense for the current year. Illustrate in a table or timeline your preference for one planning strategy over the other. Which idea will you recommend to Jill?

10. **LO.7** U.S. corporate income tax law changed dramatically at the end of 2017. What impact did it have on corporate tax rates and how did this affect the current and deferred tax expense reported in 2017 financial statements?

11. **LO.8** RoofCo reports total book income before taxes of $32,000,000 and a total tax expense of $8,000,000. FloorCo reports book income before taxes of $48,000,000 and a total tax expense of $12,000,000. The companies' breakdown between current and deferred tax expense (benefit) is as follows:

	RoofCo	FloorCo
Current tax expense	$10.0	$13.0
Deferred tax benefit	(2.0)	(1.0)
Total tax expense	$ 8.0	$12.0

RoofCo's deferred tax benefit is created by the expected future use of a capital loss carryforward. FloorCo's deferred tax benefit is related to a lawsuit that will not be settled until early next year. FloorCo's lawyers predict that the company will probably lose the lawsuit. Compare and contrast these two companies' effective tax rates. How are they similar? How are they different?

12. **LO.8** LawnCo and TreeCo operate in the same industry, and both report a 25% effective tax rate (combined Federal, state, and global). Their book income and current, deferred, and total tax expense are reported below.

Communications
Critical Thinking

	LawnCo	TreeCo
Book income before tax	$600,000	$780,000
Current tax expense	$200,000	$ 20,000
Deferred tax expense (benefit)	(50,000)	175,000
Total Federal, state, and global tax expense	$150,000	$195,000
Effective tax rate	25%	25%

ShrubCo is a competitor of both of these companies. Prepare a letter to Laura Collins, VP-Taxation of ShrubCo, outlining your analysis of the other two companies' effective tax rates, using only the preceding information. ShrubCo's address is 9979 West Third Street, Peru, IN 46970.

13. **LO.8** HippCo and HoppCo operate in the same industry and report the following tax rate reconciliations in their tax footnotes:

	HippCo	HoppCo
Hypothetical tax at U.S. statutory tax rate	21.0%	21.0%
State and local taxes	2.7	3.9
Municipal bond interest	(12.5)	(7.8)
Tax Court settlement on disputed tax issue	6.0	—
Effective tax rate	17.2%	17.1%

Compare and contrast the effective tax rates of these two companies.

Computational Exercises

14. **LO.1, 3** Prance, Inc., earned pretax book net income of $800,000 in 2022. Prance acquired a depreciable asset that year, and first-year tax depreciation exceeded book depreciation by $80,000. Prance reported no other temporary or permanent book-tax differences. The pertinent U.S. tax rate is 21%, and Prance earned an after-tax rate of return on capital of 4%. Compute Prance's current income tax benefit or expense for the year.

15. **LO.1, 4** Using the facts of Problem 14, determine Prance's 2022 deferred tax benefit or expense, total tax expense, and any deferred tax asset or liability.

16. **LO.1, 3** Prance reports $600,000 of pretax book net income in 2023. Prance's book depreciation exceeds tax depreciation that year by $20,000. Prance reports no other temporary or permanent book-tax differences. Assuming that the pertinent U.S. tax rate is 21%, compute Prance's current income tax benefit or expense for the year.

17. **LO.1, 4** Using the facts of Problem 16, determine Prance's 2023 deferred tax benefit or expense and any deferred tax asset or liability that should be reported on its 2022 balance sheet. In net present value terms, what has been the value to Prance of accelerating $20,000 of 2023 book depreciation to 2022? Use text Appendix E to calculate your answer.

18. **LO.1, 3** Mini, Inc., earns pretax book net income of $750,000 in 2022, its first year of operations. Mini recognized $20,000 in bad debt expense for book purposes. This expense is not yet deductible for tax purposes. Mini reports no other

temporary or permanent book-tax differences. The applicable U.S. tax rate is 21%, and Mini earns an after-tax rate of return on capital of 4%. Compute Mini's current income tax benefit or expense.

19. **LO.1, 4** Using the facts of Problem 18, determine Mini's 2022 deferred tax assets and liabilities, deferred tax benefit or expense, and total tax benefit or expense.

20. **LO.1, 3** Mini, in Problem 18, reports $800,000 of pretax book net income in 2023. For that year, Mini did not recognize any bad debt expense for book purposes but did deduct $15,000 in bad debt expense for tax purposes. Mini reports no other temporary or permanent differences. Assuming that the U.S. tax rate is 21%, compute Mini's current income tax benefit or expense.

21. **LO.1, 4** Using the facts of Problem 20, determine Mini's deferred tax asset or liability at the end of 2023 and its deferred tax benefit or expense and total tax benefit or expense for the year. In net present value terms, what has been the cost to Mini of the deferred tax deduction for bad debts? Use text Appendix E to calculate your answer.

22. **LO.1, 4** Ovate, Inc., earns $140,000 in book income before tax and is subject to a 21% marginal Federal income tax rate in its first year of operations. Ovate estimates it will incur $6,000 over the next two years to honor warranties on products it sold during the current year and recorded the appropriate liability on its balance sheet at the end of the year.
    a. Determine the amount of Ovate's deferred tax assets and liabilities, if any, as of the end of the year.
    b. Express your computation as a Microsoft Excel formula.

23. **LO.4, 6** Facegram, Inc., reported net cumulative favorable book-tax temporary differences of $1,000,000 at the end of 2022. During 2023, legislation was passed that will increase Facegram's tax rate from 21% to 25% beginning in 2024. Facegram expects to report $500,000 of 2023 pre-tax book and taxable income with no change to its net cumulative book-tax temporary differences.
    a. What will Facegram report as its deferred tax benefit or expense for 2023?
    b. What, if any, effect will the above information have on Facegram's 2023 tax rate reconciliation?
    c. (How) would the answers to parts (a) and (b) change if Facegram's $1,000,000 net cumulative book-tax temporary difference at the end of 2022 had been unfavorable rather than favorable?

24. **LO.5** In its books, Ion Corporation reports income tax expense and income tax payable of $200,000 and $250,000, respectively. Assume that Ion will be able to use only $30,000 of any deferred tax asset, with the balance expiring unused. Determine the amount of Ion's deferred tax asset and any necessary valuation allowance, and construct the appropriate journal entry that Ion would record.

25. **LO.6** RadioCo, a domestic corporation, reports a deferred tax asset relating to receivables of $100,000 and a deferred tax liability relating to cost recovery of $165,000. Identify all of the places in RadioCo's financial statements where these items will be reported. When relevant, indicate how they will be classified.

Problems

26. **LO.1, 3, 4** Britton, Inc., an accrual basis C corporation, sells widgets on credit. Its pretax book income in its first year of operations is $50,000. Britton's book allowance for uncollectible accounts at the end of the year is $10,000. The applicable income tax rate (combined Federal, state, and global) for year 1 and thereafter is 30%. Compute Britton's year 1 current and deferred income tax benefit or expense.

27. **LO.1, 3, 4** Continue with the results of Problem 26. Prepare the GAAP journal entries for Britton's year 1 income tax expense.

28. **LO.1, 3** Rubio, Inc., an accrual basis C corporation, reports the following amounts for the tax year. The applicable income tax rate is 30% (combined Federal, state, and global). Compute Rubio's current income tax benefit or expense.

Book income, including the items below	$80,000
Interest income from City of Westerville bonds	10,000
Bribes paid to Federal inspectors	17,000
Liability for anticipated warranty costs (beginning of year)	20,000
Liability for anticipated warranty costs (end of year)	25,000

29. **LO.1, 4** Continue with the results of Problem 28.

    a. Determine Rubio's deferred income tax benefit or expense and GAAP income for the year.

    b. Express your calculation of Rubio's tax provision using Microsoft Excel commands.

30. **LO.1, 3, 4** Willingham, Inc., an accrual basis C corporation, reports pretax book income of $1,600,000. At the beginning of the year, Willingham reported no deferred tax assets or liabilities on its balance sheet. At the end of the year, Willingham's depreciable assets had a net book value of $15,000,000. It is subject to a 21% U.S. income tax rate in the current year and for the foreseeable future.

    Willingham's book-tax differences include the following. Compute the corporation's current and deferred Federal income tax benefit or expense for the year.

Estimate of uncollectible accounts at year-end	$4,000,000
Tax depreciation in excess of book	3,000,000
Book gain from installment sale of nonbusiness asset, deferred for tax	2,000,000
Interest income from school district bonds	200,000

31. **LO.1, 3, 4** Continue with the results of Problem 30. Prepare the GAAP journal entries for Willingham's income tax expense.

32. **LO.1, 4** Relix, Inc., is a domestic corporation with $4,800 of book income before taxes. Included in its book income are $2,375 of tax-exempt interest and $780 of nondeductible entertainment expenses. It's balance sheets at the end of the year for book and tax purposes are as follows:

	Tax Debit/(Credit)	Book Debit/(Credit)
Assets		
Cash	$ 500	$ 500
Accounts receivable	8,000	8,000
Buildings	750,000	750,000
Accumulated depreciation	(450,000)	(380,000)
Furniture & fixtures	70,000	70,000
Accumulated depreciation	(46,000)	(38,000)
Total assets	$332,500	$410,500

	Tax Debit/(Credit)	Book Debit/(Credit)
Liabilities		
Accrued litigation expense	$ -0-	($ 50,000)
Note payable	(78,000)	(78,000)
Total liabilities	($ 78,000)	($128,000)
Stockholders' Equity		
Paid-in capital	($ 10,000)	($ 10,000)
Retained earnings	(244,500)	(272,500)
Total liabilities and stockholders' equity	($332,500)	($410,500)

Based on this information, determine Relix's Federal net deferred tax asset or net deferred tax liability at year-end. Assume a 21% Federal corporate tax rate, no state or foreign taxes, and no need for a valuation allowance.

33. **LO.1, 4** Based on the facts and results of Problem 32 and the partial beginning-of-the-year tax and book balance sheet information below, determine Relix's deferred tax benefit or expense for the year. Provide the journal entry necessary to record this amount.

	Tax Debit/(Credit)	Book Debit/(Credit)
Assets		
Accumulated depreciation—Buildings	($417,000)	($360,000)
Accumulated depreciation—Furniture & fixtures	(35,200)	(31,000)
Liabilities		
Accrued litigation expense	$ -0-	($ 34,000)

34. **LO.1, 3** Based on the information in Problems 32 and 33, calculate Relix's current tax benefit or expense.

35. **LO.1, 3** Provide the journal entry to record Relix's current tax benefit or expense as determined in Problem 34.

36. **LO.1, 3, 4** Based on the facts and results of Problems 32–35, calculate Relix's total provision for income tax reported in its financial statements, and determine its book net income after tax.

37. **LO.6** Based on the facts and results of Problems 32–36, prepare the rate reconciliation, using both tax amounts and rates, Relix must include in its financial statement footnotes. Round calculations off to the nearest dollar or one tenth of one percent (e.g., 13.9%) as appropriate.

38. **LO.1, 4** Kantner, Inc., is a domestic corporation with the $50,000 of pretax book income. Included in that income are $7,800 of tax-exempt municipal bond interest and $1,700 of entertainment expenses. It's balance sheets for book and tax purposes at the end of the year are as follows:

	Tax Debit/(Credit)	Book Debit/(Credit)
Assets		
Cash	$ 1,000	$ 1,000
Accounts receivable	9,000	9,000
Buildings	850,000	850,000
Accumulated depreciation	(685,000)	(620,000)
Furniture & fixtures	40,000	40,000
Accumulated depreciation	(10,000)	(8,000)
Total assets	$205,000	$272,000
Liabilities		
Accrued warranty expense	$ -0-	($ 40,000)
Note payable	(16,000)	(16,000)
Total liabilities	($ 16,000)	($ 56,000)
Stockholders' Equity		
Paid-in capital	($ 50,000)	($ 50,000)
Retained earnings	(139,000)	(166,000)
Total liabilities and stockholders' equity	($205,000)	($272,000)

Based on this information, determine Kantner's net Federal deferred tax asset or net deferred tax liability at year-end. Assume a 21% Federal corporate tax rate, no state or foreign taxes, and no need for a valuation allowance.

39. **LO.1, 4** Based on the facts and results of Problem 38 and the partial beginning-of-the-year tax and book balance sheet information below, determine Kantner's deferred tax benefit or expense for the current year. Provide the journal entry necessary to record this amount.

	Tax Debit/(Credit)	Book Debit/(Credit)
Assets		
Accumulated depreciation—Buildings	($662,000)	($600,000)
Accumulated depreciation—Furniture & fixtures	(4,400)	(4,000)
Liabilities		
Accrued warranty expense	$ –0–	($ 30,000)

40. **LO.1, 3** Based on the information in Problems 38 and 39, calculate Kantner's current tax benefit or expense.

41. **LO.3** Provide the journal entry to record Kantner's current tax benefit or expense as determined in Problem 40.

42. **LO.1, 3, 4** Based on the facts and results of Problems 38–41, calculate Kantner's total provision for income tax expense reported on its financial statement and its book net income after tax.

43. **LO.6** Based on the facts and results of Problems 38–42, provide the income tax footnote rate reconciliation for Kantner. Round calculations off to the nearest dollar or one tenth of one percent (e.g., 13.9%) as appropriate.

44. **LO.1, 3, 4, 6** Refer back to Problems 38 through 43. Assume that you are a tax accountant with Kantner, Inc. Your supervisor has asked you to develop a Microsoft Excel workbook to automate as much as possible the current-year provision. She also would like the workbook to be structured so that it can be used for the provision every year going forward with minimal input required. She has suggested using separate worksheets to determine current tax expense, deferred tax expense, and the rate reconciliation. The worksheets should require as little numerical input as possible and be linked to avoid requiring the entry of the same information more than once. Create the workbook including this year's provision and e-mail it to your instructor.

45. **LO.5** GinnyCo has pretax book and taxable income of $400,000 and reports a $100,000 income tax payable in the current year. GinnyCo's activities generated a general business tax credit of $40,000 that it cannot use this year, and its management believes it is more likely than not that one-fourth of the credit carryforward will expire unused. What is GinnyCo's book tax expense (provision) for the year?

46. **LO.7** In 2020, LaceCo engaged in activities that it believes qualified for the research activities credit. The credit reduced its Federal income tax liability by $400,000, but LaceCo believed that the IRS would likely challenge the credit in an audit.

LaceCo estimated that the tax benefit ultimately realized would be less than the immediate tax savings. The estimated potential benefits and related probabilities are presented in the following table.

Resulting Estimated Tax Benefit	Probability of Realizing Tax Benefit	Cumulative Probability of Realization
$400,000	10%	10%
300,000	35%	45%
250,000	40%	85%
–0–	15%	100%

a. Determine the amount that LaceCo should have recognized in 2020 for the tax benefit from this item under GAAP rules and ASC 740–10.

b. Assuming that LaceCo initially recorded a book tax provision of $600,000, including the $400,000 tax benefit from this tax uncertainty, provide the journal entry that LaceCo should have also recorded to account for the uncertainty surrounding the research activities credit.

c. By the end of 2023, LaceCo has not been audited and the statute of limitations regarding its 2020 research activities credit expired. Assuming LaceCo recorded the journal entries described in part b. what, if anything, should the company recognize related to the research credit in 2023?

47. **LO.7** Jazz, Inc., claimed $100,000 of rehabilitation credits on its 2023 tax return. There was sufficient tax authority to take the credits. However, due to uncertainty regarding the eligibility of some of the expenditures, Jazz only recognized $70,000 of the benefits in its 2023 financial statements. When its tax return was audited in 2024, the IRS challenged the eligibility of some of the expenditures and Jazz agreed to pay $20,000 additional tax to settle the dispute.

a. By how much does the settlement impact Jazz's 2024 book tax expense?

b. Provide the journal entry necessary to record the 2024 tax payment.

Research Problems

Use internet tax resources to address the following questions. Look for reliable websites and blogs of the IRS and other government agencies, media outlets, businesses, tax professionals, academics, think tanks, and political outlets.

Communications

Research Problem 1. Locate the most recent financial statements of two companies in the same industry using the companies' websites or the SEC's website (**sec.gov**). Perform a benchmarking analysis of the two companies' effective tax rates, using the effective tax rate reconciliation, levels of deferred tax assets and liabilities, and other relevant data. Summarize this information in an e-mail to your instructor.

Communications
Critical Thinking

Research Problem 2. Metro builds and operates traditional shopping malls. It reports a $25,000,000 deferred tax asset relating to credit carryforwards at the state, local, and Federal levels. No valuation allowances exist.

The shopping mall industry finds itself in hard times due to the loss of anchor stores and the increase in online shopping activity by consumers. Review various sources in the press that discuss how these problems arose and what some proposed solutions might be.

Metro's business plan for the next three years includes:

- The conversion of store space by new tenants (e.g., theaters, gyms, religious groups), none of which are likely to produce the profit levels lost from the stores they replace, and
- The sale of several malls at depressed prices.

In no more than three PowerPoint slides, summarize your thoughts as to the need for Metro to establish a valuation allowance against its deferred tax assets. Be specific in listing the indicators of future activity that support your conclusions.

Communications

Research Problem 3. Locate the financial statements of three different companies that report information in the income tax footnote regarding uncertain tax positions under ASC 740–10. Create a schedule that identifies the changes reported, and then compare and contrast the apparent tax strategies employed by the three companies. E-mail the schedule and analysis to your instructor.

Communications
Critical Thinking

Research Problem 4. Locate summary financial information for two companies in the same industry. Compare and contrast their effective tax rates. In your comparison, include the Federal, state/local, and international effective rates for the entities. Summarize in one paragraph the key reasons that make you believe the effective tax rates are so similar (or different).

Research Problem 5. Choose one of the so-called FAANG stocks (i.e., Facebook/Meta, Apple, Amazon, Netflix, Google/Alphabet). Using data that you find at EDGAR or the company website, provide the following information for the latest full reporting year, and indicate where in the financial statements you found this data. E-mail your findings to your instructor. Communications

- Effective tax rate.
- Tax rate on international income.
- Total deferred tax assets.
- The largest single deferred tax asset.
- Total deferred tax liabilities.
- The largest single deferred tax liability.

What is your best estimate of the total tax reported by the company on its tax returns for the period?

Becker CPA Review Questions

1. Two independent situations are described below. Each involves future deductible amounts and/or future taxable amounts produced by temporary differences.

Situation	1	2
Taxable income	$40,000	$80,000
Amounts at year-end:		
Future deductible amounts	5,000	10,000
Future taxable amounts	–0–	5,000
Balances at beginning of year:		
Deferred tax asset	1,000	4,000
Deferred tax liability	–0–	1,000

The enacted state and Federal tax rate is 25% for both situations. Determine the change in the deferred tax asset balance for the year.

	Situation 1	Situation 2
a.	$5,000	$10,000
b.	$250	$1,500
c.	$1,250	$2,500
d.	$0	$0

2. Two independent situations are described below. Each situation has future deductible amounts and/or future taxable amounts produced by temporary differences.

Situation	1	2
Taxable income	$40,000	$80,000
Amounts at year-end:		
Future deductible amounts	5,000	10,000
Future taxable amounts	–0–	5,000
Balances at beginning of year:		
Deferred tax asset	1,000	4,000
Deferred tax liability	–0–	1,000

The enacted state and Federal tax rate is 25% for both situations. Determine the income tax expense for the year.

	Situation 1	Situation 2
a.	$10,000	$20,000
b.	$9,750	$21,750
c.	$250	$500
d.	$0	$0

3. At the end of year 6, the cumulative tax effects of Tortoise Company's temporary differences were as follows:

	Deferred Tax Assets (Liabilities)
Accelerated tax depreciation	($120,000)
Warranty expense	80,000
NOL carryforward	200,000
Total	$160,000

A valuation allowance was not considered necessary. Tortoise anticipates that $40,000 of the deferred tax liability will reverse in year 7, that actual warranty costs will be incurred evenly in year 8 and year 9, and that the NOL carryforward will be used in year 7. On Tortoise's December 31, year 6 balance sheet, what amount should Tortoise report as its net deferred tax asset under U.S. GAAP?

a. $160,000
b. $200,000
c. $240,000
d. $280,000

4. Cavan Company prepared the following reconciliation between book income and taxable income for the current year ended December 31, year 1.

Pretax accounting income	$1,000,000
Taxable income	(600,000)
Difference	$ 400,000
Book-tax differences:	
Interest on municipal income	$ 100,000
Tax depreciation in excess of book	300,000
Total	$ 400,000

Cavan's effective Federal and state income tax rate for year 1 is 30%. The depreciation difference will reverse equally over the next three years at enacted tax rates as follows:

Year	Tax Rate
Year 2	30%
Year 3	25%
Year 4	25%

In Cavan's year 1 income statement, the deferred portion of its provision for income taxes should be:

a. $120,000
b. $80,000
c. $100,000
d. $90,000

Chapter

25 Exempt Entities

Learning Objectives: *After completing Chapter 25, you should be able to:*

LO.1 **Identify the different types of exempt organizations.**

LO.2 **List additional requirements for exempt status.**

LO.3 **Apply the tax consequences of exempt status, including certain restrictions on public charities and private foundations.**

LO.4 **Determine which exempt organizations are classified as a private foundation or public charity.**

LO.5 **Identify the taxes imposed on private foundations and calculate the related initial tax and additional tax amounts.**

LO.6 **Determine when an exempt organization is subject to the unrelated business income tax and calculate the amount of the tax.**

LO.7 **List the tax forms that exempt organizations must file with the IRS and the related due dates.**

LO.8 **Identify tax planning opportunities for exempt organizations.**

Chapter Outline

DRAGANA GORDIC/SHUTTERSTOCK.COM

The Big Picture

Effect of a For-Profit Business on a Tax-Exempt Entity

Hopeful, Inc., is a tax-exempt organization under § 501(c)(3) that provides temporary lodging and psychological services for abused women and children. Its annual operating budget is $12 million. More than two decades ago, Jennifer Abbott was a recipient of the services provided by Hopeful. Now Hopeful's administrator has been notified by the attorney for Jennifer's estate that her will transfers to Hopeful her shares in the outstanding stock of Taste Good Ice Cream, a chain of 40 gourmet ice cream shops located in Virginia, North Carolina, and South Carolina. The business has existed for eight years and has produced substantially higher profits each year.

Hopeful's board is considering the following options regarding the bequest from Jennifer and has hired you to provide an analysis of the tax consequences of each option:

- Sell the stock of Taste Good Ice Cream, and add the net proceeds to Hopeful's endowment.
- Continue to conduct the Taste Good Ice Cream business as a *division* of Hopeful.
- Continue to conduct the business as a *wholly owned subsidiary* of Hopeful.

With the second and the third options, the existing Taste Good management team will remain in place. After-tax profits not needed to expand the ice cream shop chain will be transferred to Hopeful, to be used in carrying out its exempt purpose.

Read the chapter and formulate your response.

The Federal income tax falls on most individuals and business entities. However, in 1938 Congress exempted certain entities from income taxation. Subchapter F (Exempt Organizations) of the Code (§§ 501–530) provides the authority for this exemption. The related House Committee Report provides the rationale for this exemption:

> The exemption from taxation of money or property devoted to charitable and other purposes is based upon the theory that the Government is compensated for the loss of revenue by its relief from the financial burden which would otherwise have to be met by appropriations from public funds, and by the benefits resulting from the promotion of the general welfare.[1]

Entities that the Code classifies as **exempt organizations** may escape Federal income taxation. For example, a private school enjoys tax exemption because the government now may not need to build and operate an extra educational facility of its own. In addition, tax exemption allows charities to devote more resources to their charitable purpose. As we will see, however, tax-exempt entities include non-charities as well. For example, a water plant operated jointly by several unrelated companies qualifies for tax exemption because it is merely a cost-sharing arrangement that reduces costs but produces no revenue. So there are several categories of entities that Congress affords tax exemption because they lack a profit motive.

Despite this limited income tax exemption, qualifying entities nevertheless may be subject to some Federal taxes:

- The Federal income tax may fall on some of its operations.[2]
- The organization may be subject to taxes that are designed to encourage or discourage certain activities.[3]
- Other Federal taxes may apply (e.g., payroll and excise taxes).

Even though tax exemption is not absolute, limited exemption from Federal income taxation is an extremely valuable alternative by which altruistic and other qualifying business and investment entities can conduct their operations.

Benefits of Exempt Status

Governments support exempt entities in ways that far exceed the mere exemption from Federal income taxation. For instance, consider these Federal tax benefits that a university sports team enjoys in addition to the university's exemption from income taxes:

- *Charitable Contributions.* Donors can claim charitable contribution deductions for gifts to support the team and (to a limited extent) for assessments associated with obtaining and keeping "good seats" at games. Thus, contributions by supporters are deductible and the contributions are not taxable to charities.
- *Interest Income Exclusion.* Bondholders do not pay Federal income tax on interest earned from purchases of university- or state-level debt that is used to build stadiums, workout facilities, and other permanent sports structures.
- *Business Deductions.* Businesses can claim advertising deductions for costs incurred to promote goods and services at sports facilities and in websites and publications.
- *Payroll Tax Exemption.* College athletes are not employees of the university, so they are exempt from payroll taxes, unemployment insurance, workers' compensation benefits, contributions to retirement plans, and the like.
- *Postage Benefits.* Exempt organizations may receive postal rate discounts.

In addition to being exempt from Federal income tax, states may also exempt these organizations from state and local income tax, sales tax, or property tax. The extent of these exemptions depends on each state's law.

[1] House Committee Report, Revenue Act of 1938, 1939–1 (Part 2) C.B. 742.

[2] See the subsequent discussion of Unrelated Business Income Tax (text Section 25-5).

[3] See the subsequent discussions of Taxable Transactions (text Section 25-3a) and Taxes Imposed on Private Foundations (text Section 25-4b).

The Exempt Economy

The tax-exempt sector is an important component of the U.S. economy. About 1.5 million entities hold Federal income tax exempt status. These entities employ over 12 million workers, representing about 10 percent of the nongovernment U.S. workforce and wages paid. Nonprofits control about $6 trillion in assets, the majority held by health care and education institutions. Exempt entities generate over $1 trillion in economic activity every year, accounting for about 5 percent of annual GDP.

About 75 percent of public charities are "small" (i.e., they hold assets of less than $500,000). Only about 5 percent of public charities hold more than $10 million of assets, but they account for 93 percent of the assets held and 88 percent of the expenditures reported. About 3.8 percent of tax-exempt entities hold assets exceeding $50 million. The IRS audits about 0.13 percent of these entities every tax year.

The Federal government gives up perhaps $100 billion per year in tax revenues by granting exempt status to these entities, due to the exemption from income tax and the charitable contribution deductions of donors to the organizations. Because most state and local governments also grant exemptions to public charities from income, sales, and property taxes, those jurisdictions suffer significant revenue losses when the entity is located or operates in the jurisdiction. Some local jurisdictions attempt to recoup some of this revenue by charging fees for specific services, like police protection and garbage collection, in lieu of tax assessments.

A typical exempt organization uses a dual budgeting and reporting system:

- An *operating fund* is used to make expenditures in support of the entity's exempt purpose (e.g., providing hospital services or offering educational programs). Revenues are raised from donors, sales of goods and services, and contracts with governmental bodies or other exempt entities.
- An *endowment* holds long-term funds contributed by donors or accumulated from operating surpluses; these amounts are used to provide support over time for the organization's mission. Most endowments require that the principal of the endowment be invested for the entity's security and growth, and that the operating budget can spend only the current income earned by the endowment fund.

25-1 Types of Exempt Organizations

LO.1

Identify the different types of exempt organizations.

An organization qualifies for exempt status *only* if it fits into one of the categories provided in the Code. Examples of qualifying exempt organizations and the specific statutory authority for their exempt status are listed in Exhibit 25.1.[4]

Not all exempt organizations are "charities" (i.e., qualifying their donors for tax deductions). For instance, a taxpayer can claim a charitable contribution deduction for a gift to the Dallas Museum of Art, but not for a gift to the LPGA, the Teachers' Retirement Fund, or the Tempe Chamber of Commerce.

Generally, only contributions to § 501(c)(3) organizations qualify for a charitable contribution deduction. Payments to other exempt entities may be deductible as business expenses (e.g., advertising or membership dues).

25-2 Characteristics of Exempt Entities

LO.2

List additional requirements for exempt status.

Many of the organizations that qualify for exempt status also must demonstrate the following characteristics:

- The organization serves some type of *common good*.[5]
- The organization is *not* a *for-profit* entity.[6]
- The organization can *influence legislation* to only a limited extent.[7] See Section 25-3a for a discussion of this issue.
- *Net earnings* do not benefit the members of the organization.[8] See Section 25-3b for a discussion of this issue.

[4]Certain other entities (e.g., qualified retirement plans) are exempt from Federal income tax but are not discussed in this chapter.

[5]See, for example, §§ 501(c)(3) and (4).

[6]See, for example, §§ 501(c)(3), (4), (6), (13), and (14).

[7]§ 501(h).

[8]See, for example, §§ 501(c)(3), (6), (7), (9), (10), (11), and (19).

Exhibit 25.1 **Types of Exempt Organizations, Selected**[9]

Statutory Authority	Brief Description	Examples or Comments
§ 501(c)(1)	Federal and related agencies.	Commodity Credit Corporation, Federal Deposit Insurance Corporation, Federal Land Bank.
§ 501(c)(2)	Corporations holding title to property for and paying income to exempt organizations.	Owns assets, such as a building or a patent, for the benefit of another exempt entity. Usually does not conduct other business.
§ 501(c)(3)	Religious, charitable, educational, scientific, literary, etc., organizations.	Boy Scouts of America, Red Cross, Salvation Army, Episcopal Church, PTA, United Fund, University of Richmond.
§ 501(c)(4)	Civic leagues and employee unions.	Garden club, tenants' association promoting tenants' legal rights in entire community, League of Women Voters.
§ 501(c)(5)	Labor, agricultural, and horticultural organizations.	Teachers' association, organization formed to promote effective agricultural pest control, garden club.
§ 501(c)(6)	Business leagues, chambers of commerce, real estate boards, etc.	American Plywood Association, National Hockey League (NHL), Ladies Professional Golfers Association (LPGA) Tour, organization promoting acceptance of women in business and professions.
§ 501(c)(7)	Social clubs.	Country club, rodeo club, press club, bowling club, college fraternities.
§ 501(c)(8)	Fraternal beneficiary societies.	Other clubs and associations. Must provide for the payment of life, sickness, accident, or other benefits to members or their dependents.
§ 501(c)(9)	Voluntary employees' beneficiary associations.	Provide for the payment of life, sickness, accident, or other benefits to members, their dependents, or their designated beneficiaries.
§ 501(c)(10)	Domestic fraternal societies.	Other clubs and associations. Must devote any net earnings exclusively to religious, charitable, scientific, literary, educational, and fraternal purposes.
§ 501(c)(11)	Local teachers' retirement fund associations.	Can receive income only from (1) public taxation, (2) assessments on teaching salaries of members, and (3) income from investments.
§ 501(c)(12)	Benevolent life insurance associations, mutual or cooperative utilities, etc.	Local cooperative telephone company, local mutual water company, local mutual electric company.
§ 501(c)(13)	Cemetery companies.	Must be operated exclusively for the benefit of lot owners who hold the lots for burial purposes.
§ 501(c)(14)	Credit unions.	Other than credit unions exempt under § 501(c)(1).
§ 501(c)(15)	Mutual insurance companies.	Mutual fire insurance company, mutual automobile insurance company.
§ 501(c)(19)	Armed forces members' posts or organizations.	Veterans of Foreign Wars (VFW), Reserve Officers Association.
§ 501(d)	Religious and apostolic organizations.	Communal organization that pools its member churches' finances into a common treasury.
§ 501(e)	Cooperative hospital service organizations.	Centralized purchasing organization for exempt hospitals.
§ 501(f)	Cooperative service organization of educational institutions.	Organization formed to manage universities' endowment funds.
§ 529	Qualified tuition programs.	Prepaid tuition and educational savings programs.
§ 530	Coverdell education savings accounts.	Qualified education savings accounts.

[9]About 1.7 million entities are exempt under one of the paragraphs of § 501(c), with about 1.4 million entities classified under § 501(c)(3).

25-2a **Serving the Common Good**

The underlying rationale for all exempt organizations is that they serve some type of *common good*. Qualifying organizations can meet this test broadly or narrowly. That is, the common good can apply to the general public, a large subset of it, or a specific interest group. For example, a large public charity can benefit many different communities in many different ways. In contrast, a social club or a credit union provides benefits primarily to their members.

25-2b **Not-for-Profit Entity**

The organization may not be organized or operated for the purpose of making a profit. For some types of exempt organizations, the *for-profit prohibition* appears in the statutory language. For other types, the prohibition is implied.

Despite this for-profit prohibition, a "not-for-profit" entity still may generate more revenue than the expenses it incurs. The net earnings of the entity should be used to accomplish the exempt purposes of the entity and not benefit any of its patrons or other related parties.[10]

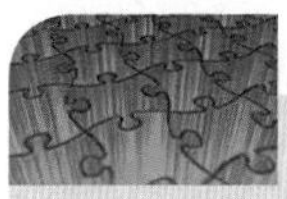

Concept Summary 25.1

Consequences of Exempt Status

General

Exempt from Federal income tax.

Exempt from most state and local income, franchise, sales, and property taxes.

Qualify for reductions in postage rates.

Contributions to the organization often can be deducted by donor.

Exceptions

May be subject to Federal income and excise taxes associated with other activities, including the following:

- Engaging in a lobbying transaction (text Section 25-3a).
- Being a private foundation (text Section 25-4).
- Generating unrelated business taxable income (text Section 25-5).
- Being a feeder organization (text Section 25-5c).

25-3 **Excise Taxes and Loss of Tax Exemption**

LO.3

Apply the tax consequences of exempt status, including certain restrictions on public charities and private foundations.

The advantage of Federal income tax exemption for exempt entities is not absolute. This section describes the major exceptions to tax exemption that apply to exempt entities. In addition to these exceptions, exempt entities that violate one or more of the exemption requirements risk losing their exempt status. In this case, the normal income tax rules apply to the formerly-exempt entity.

The exceptions to tax exemption include the following:

- An exempt organization that engages in a *prohibited transaction*.
- If the organization is classified as a *private foundation*, it may be partially subject to tax.
- An exempt organization can be subject to tax on its *unrelated business taxable income*. A so-called *feeder organization* is also subject to the normal income tax rules, even if its net profits support a tax-exempt entity.

25-3a **Political and Lobbying Transactions**

Legislative Framework

Congress intended for a public charity (i.e., religious, charitable, educational, etc., organization)[11] largely to refrain from *substantial* political lobbying efforts or any efforts to influence elections of public officials.[12]

---

[10] § 501(c)(6).

[11] § 501(c)(3). Public charities are discussed in text Section 25-4a.

[12] § 4912(a).

Congress enacted a two-prong approach to discouraging these efforts:

- First, Congress enacted excise taxes on lobbying and election influencing expenditures. Taken together, these excise taxes amount to penalties on charities that pursue these activities. Congress created these sanctions as excise taxes because the tax base is not *income* but rather on *expenditures* for these activities. Three of these excise tax provisions are discussed below.
- Second, Congress enacted rules that will result in revocation of the charity's tax exemption if it engages in "too much" lobbying efforts or virtually any efforts to influence elections. To implement this policy, Congress set limits on permissible lobbying expenditures.[13] Public charities that exceed this limit, aggregated over the current and three prior years, no longer enjoy tax exemption.[14] That is, these entities become taxable just like any business entity.

Excise Tax on Expenditures to Influence Elections

The first excise tax is a tax on expenditures relating to efforts to influence elections.[15] The public charity's tax equals 10 percent of these expenditures. In addition, the manager who authorized the expenditures is also subject to a 2.5 percent excise tax.

However, there is another "second level" tax that applies if the charity and its managers do not correct these expenditures. Correction means that they must try to reclaim the amounts paid toward influencing elections (if possible), and they must enact controls to prevent future expenditures of this type.

Absent these corrections, the charity's tax equals 100 percent of these expenditures. In addition, a manager of the charity who refuses to take these corrective measures is subject to a 50 percent penalty. Clearly, Congress intends for the excise tax provisions in § 4955 to dissuade public charities from attempting to influence elections of public officials!

Excise Tax on Lobbying and Grass Roots Expenditures

The second excise tax equals 5 percent of the public charity's **lobbying expenditures**.[16] These are expenditures relating to efforts to influence legislation (as opposed to influencing the outcome of elections). There is also a 5 percent tax on the public charity's management that applies if the IRS proves that they knew that these expenditures were likely to jeopardize the organization's exempt status.

This provision does not apply to private foundations or to public charities that elect an alternative excise tax discussed after Example 1.

Tan, Inc. is a qualifying § 501(c)(3) public charity. During the year, Tan spends $525,000 on lobbying activities. Tan's § 4912 excise tax equals $26,250 ($525,000 × 5%). If the manager knew or should have known that these activities can jeopardize the charity's exempt status, the manager is also subject to an excise tax equaling $26,250.

Alternative Excise Tax on Lobbying Expenditures

The Tax Reform Act of 1976 added an alternative excise tax on lobbying expenditures in § 501(h). Charities must *elect* this alternative excise tax, and most do. This election is not available to churches. The effect of the election is to allow limited lobbying expenditures with no chance of the IRS revoking the entity's tax exemption.

---

[13] § 4911.

[14] Reg. § 1.501(h)-3.

[15] § 4955.

[16] § 4912.

The "price" of making this election is a different excise tax that replaces the 5 percent excise tax described above (§ 4911). This alternative provision levies a 25 percent excise tax, but only on **excess lobbying expenditures** instead of on *all* lobbying expenditures. Computing this tax requires three steps:

1. Determine the charity's total lobbying expenditures that relate to influencing legislation through direct contact with lawmakers or their staff.
2. Compute the charity's lobbying nontaxable amount. Exhibit 25.2 presents this computation, which equals a percentage of the charity's "exempt purpose expenditures" (expenditures that are the reason for the charity's existence). This amount of lobbying is not subject to the excise tax, but this nontaxable amount cannot exceed $1,000,000.
3. The difference between (1) and (2) above equals the charity's excess lobbying expenditures. The excise tax equals 25% of this difference.

There is a similar required computation for **grass roots expenditures**. These are expenditures relating to efforts to influence legislation by affecting the opinions of the general public or a segment of it. This type of lobbying excise tax has a different nontaxable amount that equals 25 percent of the direct lobbying nontaxable amount described above. Otherwise, the excise tax computation is the same as the three steps identified above.

Example 2

Tan, Inc., a qualifying § 501(c)(3) organization, makes a § 501(h) election. Its exempt purpose expenditures for the taxable year are $5,000,000 and, during the year, it incurs lobbying expenditures of $525,000 and grass roots expenditures of $0.

Applying the table in Exhibit 25.2, the lobbying nontaxable amount is $400,000 [$225,000 + 5%($5,000,000 − $1,500,000)]. The ceiling on lobbying expenditures is $600,000 (150% × $400,000).

Tan's $525,000 of lobbying expenditures are under the ceiling of $600,000. However, the election results in a tax on the excess lobbying expenditures of $125,000 ($525,000 lobbying expenditures − $400,000 lobbying nontaxable amount). The resulting tax liability is $31,250 ($125,000 × 25%).

Note that the amount of this excise tax exceeds the earlier excise tax. Thus, Tan's election resulted in a $5,000 increase in tax ($31,250 − $26,250). However, the election means that this level of lobbying cannot jeopardize Tan's exemption status.

Loss of Tax Exemption

Code § 501(c)(3) states that a public charity will lose its exempt status if a substantial part of its activities involves influencing legislation. Congress was concerned that this standard was too subjective and arbitrary. Consequently, Congress added an objective standard that relies on the alternative excise tax discussed above [§ 503(h)]. This rule allows public charities to engage in lobbying activities on a limited basis without jeopardizing their exempt status.

Under this standard, tax exemption is revoked if lobbying (or grass roots) expenditures exceed 150 percent of the nontaxable amount described above. The test period for this computation is the current tax year and the three prior tax years. If the actual

Exhibit 25.2 Calculation of Lobbying Nontaxable Amount

Exempt Purpose Expenditures	Lobbying Nontaxable Amount Is
Not over $500,000	20% of exempt purpose expenditures*
Over $500,000 but not over $1 million	$100,000 + 15% of the excess of exempt purpose expenditures over $500,000
Over $1 million but not over $1.5 million	$175,000 + 10% of the excess of exempt purpose expenditures over $1 million
Over $1.5 million	$225,000 + 5% of the excess of exempt purpose expenditures over $1.5 million

*Exempt purpose expenditures generally are the amounts paid or incurred for the taxable year for the following uses: religious, charitable, scientific, literary, educational, fostering of national or international amateur sports competition, or the prevention of cruelty to children or animals.

aggregate lobbying expenditures exceed the aggregate limit computed over this four-year window, then the charity loses its tax exemption immediately. It is possible for such a charity to reapply for tax exemption later.

Summary of Provisions

Taken together, these three excise taxes, coupled with the loss of tax exemption rules, create three tiers of lobbying activities for public charities that elect § 503(h) treatment:

- The first tier involves expenditures that do not exceed their computed nontaxable amounts. This level of lobbying expenditures escapes excise taxes and cannot result in loss of tax exemption.
- The second tier involves expenditures that exceed their computed nontaxable amounts but are less than the 150 percent limits. This level of lobbying expenditures results in excise tax but cannot result in loss of tax exemption.
- The third tier involves expenditures that exceed their computed nontaxable amounts and exceed the 150 percent limits. This level of lobbying expenditures results in excise tax and can result in loss of tax exemption if sustained over time. Exhibit 25.3 illustrates this choice.

25-3b **Excess Benefit Transactions and Intermediate Sanctions**

When an individual who is related to a public charity receives inappropriate benefits from the charity, the Code applies **intermediate sanctions** rather than revoking the entity's exempt status immediately. The intermediate sanctions consist of excise taxes imposed on disqualified persons (individuals who can exercise substantial influence over the affairs of the organization) who engage in *excess benefit transactions.*[17]

In a typical benefit transaction, a disqualified person engages in a non-fair-market-value transaction with the exempt organization (e.g., the purchase of property from the exempt entity at a large discount) or receives unreasonable compensation. The excise tax on the disqualified person is 25 percent of the excess benefit.

Exhibit 25.3 Taxes on Lobbying Expenditures by Public Charities

- **Without § 501(h) election:** A 5% tax is assessed on all lobbying expenditures; any substantial lobbying expenditures jeopardize the organization's exempt status.
- **With § 501(h) election:** A tax is assessed. Exempt status is not jeopardized unless the lobbying or grass roots expenditures ceiling is exceeded repeatedly.

Expenditures *below* lobbying/grass roots nontaxable amount ➡ **No Tax**	OR	Expenditures *between* lobbying/grass roots nontaxable amount and ceiling amount ➡ **25% tax**	OR	Expenditures *above* lobbying/grass roots expenditures ceiling ➡ **25% tax on such lobbying expenditures; exempt status is jeopardized**

[17] § 4958. A disqualified person can be an officer or manager of the entity, a substantial donor, or a legislator who directs funds to the organization. See *Vincent J. Fumo*, T.C.Memo 2021–61.

The tax also can be assessed on exempt organization managers who participate in such a transaction, knowing that it is improper. For the exempt organization's management, the excise tax is 10 percent of the excess benefit (with a maximum of $20,000 for each excess benefit transaction), unless the participation is not willful and is due to reasonable cause. These excise taxes are referred to as first-level taxes.

A second-level tax applies to the disqualified person if the excess benefit transaction is not corrected (e.g., if the excess amount is *not* paid back to the charity) before the first-level tax is due. This excise tax is 200 percent of the excess benefit. Thus, the person receiving the benefit and the exempt organization's managers pay this tax, *not* the exempt organization.

Excess Benefit Transactions

The compensation committee of an exempt organization is deciding what to pay Carter, its new president. Reyes, a member of the organization's board of directors, is on the committee and knows that the fair market value of the president's services is no more than $150,000. However, Reyes votes to approve setting the new president's compensation at $250,000.

Reyes is subject to an excise tax of $10,000 (10% × $100,000 excess benefit) as an organization manager. In addition, Carter is subject to an excise tax of $25,000 (25% × $100,000 excess benefit) and should repay the $100,000 excess benefit, plus interest, to the organization. If Carter does not repay this amount, he could be subject to a second-level tax of $200,000 (200% × $100,000 excess benefit).

An exempt organization rents office space to Willoughby, a member of its board of directors, for $100,000 per year. It later is determined that fair rental value is $140,000 per year.

Willoughby is subject to a first-level tax of $10,000 (25% × $40,000 excess benefit), and she should repay the $40,000 excess benefit, plus interest, to the organization. Failure to repay may result in a second-level tax for Willoughby of $80,000 (200% × $40,000 excess benefit).

25-3c **Other Excise Taxes**

Certain large private colleges and universities are subject to a 1.4 percent excise tax on their net investment income for the tax year. The tax is meant to encourage these institutions to use the investment income derived from these "excessive" endowment funds to increase student financial aid and to decrease tuition levels. The tax applies if the fair market value of the school's endowment fund divided by the number of tuition-paying full-time equivalent students at the school exceeds $500,000.[18] Fewer than 50 schools appear to be liable for this tax.

In addition, a 21 percent excise tax is applied to compensation paid to or vested for certain highly paid employees of public charities. In general, the tax applies to compensation in excess of $1 million for the tax year and can be assessed only on the five highest-paid employees of the organization.[19] This tax might apply to a hospital administrator, a symphony conductor, or a private university's president or basketball coach. Those providing medical services are exempt from the tax. About 400 charities incur this tax every year, with total payments of about $125 million.

[18]§ 4968. There must be at least 500 such students, more than half of whom are located in the United States. "Tuition" includes payments made through scholarships and financial aid. Harvard University's endowment is about $53 billion. Yale, Princeton, and Stanford each control endowments of $25 billion to $45 billion. Each of these institutions pays a tax of about $40 million per year under this provision.

[19]§ 4960. The $1 million amount is not indexed for inflation. Once an individual is a top-five paid employee, the excise tax applies for the duration of his or her employment with the organization. As a result, more than five individuals may be subject to the tax in a single year; § 4960(c)(2).

Determine which exempt organizations are classified as a private foundation or public charity.

25-4 Private Foundations and Public Charities

Certain exempt organizations are **private foundations**. These are usually charitable organizations established by a small number of donors (e.g., a family) to accomplish a particular charitable purpose. The Bill and Melinda Gates Foundation is the largest private foundation, with assets of $50 billion and charitable expenditures of about $5.8 billion during fiscal 2020. The Gates' funded this foundation with a large grant of Microsoft common stock in 1994.

25-4a Tax Consequences of Private Foundation Status

Classifying an exempt organization as a private foundation produces two negative consequences compared to those for public charities. First, the classification may have an adverse effect on the contributions it receives, because the tax consequences for donors generally are less favorable than those given to other exempt organizations.[20] Second, the private foundation may be subject to additional Federal excise taxes. The reason for this less beneficial tax treatment is that private foundations seem to define *common good* more narrowly and are not seen as being supported sufficiently by, and operated for the good of, the public.

Definition of a Private Foundation

All § 501(c)(3) organizations are private foundations by default, unless one of the statutory exceptions applies. The following entities are *not* private foundations:[21]

1. Churches, educational institutions, hospitals and medical research organizations, and governmental units (*favored activities* category).
2. Organizations that are broadly supported by the general public, by governmental units, or by organizations described in (1) above.
3. Entities organized and operated exclusively for the benefit of organizations described in (1) or (2) above (i.e., a *supporting organization*, like an entity holding a university's endowment funds or patents).

Public Charities

A *public charity* is either an organization listed in (1) above, or one that meets the "broadly supported" requirement in (2) above. To be a public charity and avoid private foundation status, *both* an *external support test* and an *internal support test* must be satisfied.[22] In general, these tests are computed using data from the four preceding tax years.

The intent of the two tests is to grant the more favorable public charity status to those organizations that are responsive to the general public, rather than to the private interests of a limited number of donors or other persons.

Under the *external support test*, more than one-third of the organization's support each taxable year *normally* must come in the following forms:

- Gifts, grants, contributions, and membership fees.
- Gross receipts from admissions, sales of merchandise, performance of services, or the furnishing of facilities in an activity that is not an unrelated trade or business for purposes of the unrelated business income tax (discussed subsequently).
  - Gross receipts of this type from any person or governmental agency in excess of the greater of $5,000 or 1 percent of the organization's support for the taxable year are not counted in the numerator of the support fraction.

[20] § 170(e)(1)(B)(ii).

[21] § 509(a).

[22] § 509(a)(2). An alternative means by which to qualify as a public charity, designed for organizations that operate largely using donations from third parties, is found at § 509(a)(1). When the external and internal support tests are met, public charity status is granted for the current year and for the subsequent year. Reg. §§ 1.509(a)–3(c) and 1.170A–9(e)(4)(i).

Amounts received from disqualified persons are not included in the numerator of the support fraction. For this purpose, disqualified persons include, among others:

- Substantial contributors whose cumulative gifts and bequests to the exempt entity exceed both 2 percent of aggregate contributions received by the entity and $5,000.
- Significant members of the governing body of the exempt entity, including officers, directors, trustees, and their families.

The *internal support test* limits the amount of support *normally* received from the sum of the following sources to one-third of the organization's support for the taxable year:

- Gross investment income (gross income from interest, dividends, rents, and royalties).
- Unrelated business taxable income (discussed in text Section 25-5) minus any related tax.

Support does not include *unusual grants* received or gain/loss from the sale of the entity's investment assets (e.g., a one-time $100 million gift to build a new hospital wing); it would be difficult for an organization to meet the external support test if unusual grants were included in the analysis.

Example 5

Lion, Inc., a § 501(c)(3) organization, received the following support amounts, averaged for the last four tax years. Lion wants to be classified as a public charity, not as a private foundation.

Governmental unit A for services rendered	$ 30,000
Governmental unit B for services rendered	20,000
General public for services rendered	20,000
Gross investment income	15,000
Contributions from individual substantial contributors (disqualified persons)	15,000
Total support	$100,000

The *internal support test* is satisfied for the taxable year.

Internal Support Test	
Gross investment income	$15,000
Unrelated business taxable income	–0–
Total countable support	$15,000

$\frac{\$15,000}{\$100,000} = 15\%$ **Passes internal support test**

For purposes of the *external support test*, the support from A and B is counted only to the extent of $5,000 (greater of $5,000 or 1% of $100,000 support). The $15,000 received from disqualified persons is excluded from the numerator but is included in the denominator. As a result, Lion fails the test for the taxable year.

External Support Test	
Governmental unit A for services rendered	$ 5,000
Governmental unit B for services rendered	5,000
General public for services rendered	20,000
Total countable support	$30,000

$\frac{\$30,000}{\$100,000} = 30\%$ **Fails external support test**

Because Lion did not satisfy both tests, it does *not* qualify as an organization that is broadly supported. As a result, it is a private foundation.

Concept Summary 25.2 shows the classifications of exempt organizations and indicates the potential negative consequences of classification as a private foundation.

Concept Summary 25.2

Exempt Organizations: Classification

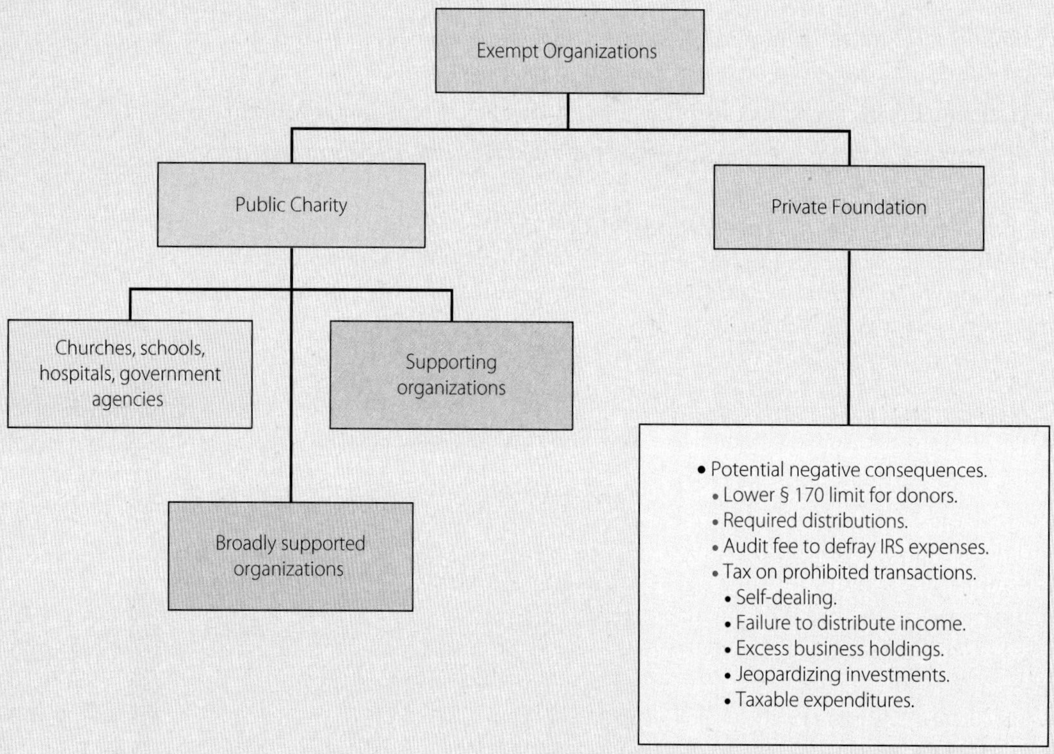

Exempt Organizations

- Public Charity
  - Churches, schools, hospitals, government agencies
  - Supporting organizations
  - Broadly supported organizations
- Private Foundation
  - Potential negative consequences.
    - Lower § 170 limit for donors.
    - Required distributions.
    - Audit fee to defray IRS expenses.
    - Tax on prohibited transactions.
      - Self-dealing.
      - Failure to distribute income.
      - Excess business holdings.
      - Jeopardizing investments.
      - Taxable expenditures.

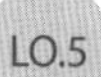
LO.5

Identify the taxes imposed on private foundations and calculate the related initial tax and additional tax amounts.

25-4b Taxes Imposed on Private Foundations

About 100,000 private foundations file returns annually with the IRS. These entities largely hold investment assets and make annual grants to third parties. Private foundations control about $1 trillion in assets, but most of them are family-controlled organizations that hold no more than $10 million of investable assets.

Distributions of more than $80 billion are made each tax year by private foundations of all sizes. Most of these distributions are made to other charitable entities. Foundation operating expenses generally amount to 10 percent of total assets.

In general, a private foundation is exempt from Federal income tax. However, it is potentially subject to several Federal excise taxes.[23] Exhibit 25.4 lists and describes these taxes.

The intent of these excise taxes is to restrict the permitted activities of private foundations. They operate by imposing two levels of tax on the private foundation and the foundation manager: an initial "first level" tax and an additional "second level" tax. Except for the tax based on investment income, the Code imposes first-level taxes because the private foundation engages in an undesirable activity, called a *prohibited transaction*. Foundations pay second-level taxes only if they fail to correct the prohibited transaction within a statutory time period.[24]

Annually, about 1,000 private foundations incur an excise tax of this type. The IRS collects about $10 million in taxes under these provisions, more than half of which are collected for failing to distribute adequate amounts of the private foundation's income.

[23] §§ 4940–4945.

[24] § 4961.

Exhibit 25.4 Taxes Imposed on Private Foundations

Type of Tax	Code Section	Purpose	Private Foundation		Foundation Manager	
			Initial Tax	Additional Tax	Initial Tax	Additional Tax
On investment income	§ 4940	Audit fee to defray IRS expenses.	1.39%*			
On self-dealing	§ 4941	Engaging in transactions with disqualified persons.	10%**	200%**	5%†	50%†
On undistributed income	§ 4942	Failing to distribute adequate amount of income for exempt purposes, usually 5% of the foundation's net asset value.	30%	100%		
On excess business holdings	§ 4943	Investments that enable the private foundation to control unrelated businesses (usually by owning >20% of outstanding shares).	10%	200%		
On jeopardizing investments	§ 4944	Speculative investments that put the private foundation's assets at an excessive amount of risk.	10%	25%	10%‡	5%†

*An exempt operating foundation [see §§ 4940(d)(2) and 4942(j)(3)] is not subject to the tax.
**Imposed on the disqualified person rather than the foundation.
†Subject to a statutory ceiling of $20,000.
‡Subject to a statutory ceiling of $10,000.

The tax on undistributed income illustrates how expensive these taxes can be (and why foundations should avoid them). The first-level tax is 30 percent on the undistributed income for the taxable year that is not distributed by the end of the following taxable year. The tax applies on this undistributed income for each year until the tax is assessed by the IRS.

The second-level tax is 100 percent on the remaining amount of the inadequate distribution. Distributing the previously undistributed income within 90 days after the IRS issues a deficiency notice waives this additional tax.

Undistributed income is the excess of the amount that should have been distributed over qualifying distributions made by the entity. The tax applies if the entity did not distribute its minimum investment return (i.e., typically 5 percent of the fair market value of the foundation's assets, net of any outstanding debt).[25] The undistributed amount is reduced by related salaries and administrative expenses, so the actual required distribution usually is less than 5 percent of asset value.

The 5 percent rule was designed to provide a minimum amount that private foundations would distribute every year, but it acts more as a ceiling amount; most private foundations make distributions of 6 percent of their assets or less per year.

Example 6

Gold, Inc., a private foundation, records undistributed income of $80,000 for the 2021 taxable year. It distributes $15,000 of this amount during 2022 and an additional $45,000 during 2023. An IRS deficiency notice is mailed to Gold on August 5, 2024. The initial tax is $25,500 [($65,000* × 30%) + ($20,000** × 30%)].

As of the date of the deficiency notice, Gold has made no additional distributions from the 2021 undistributed income. Therefore, because the remaining undistributed income of $20,000 has not been distributed by August 5, 2024, an additional tax of $20,000 ($20,000 × 100%) is imposed.

If Gold distributes the $20,000 of 2021 undistributed income within 90 days of the deficiency notice, the additional tax is waived. Without this distribution, however, the foundation will owe $45,500 in taxes ($25,500 + $20,000).

*$80,000 − $15,000. **$80,000 − $15,000 − $45,000.

[25] § 4942(e)(1).

LO.6

Determine when an exempt organization is subject to the unrelated business income tax and calculate the amount of the tax.

25-5 Unrelated Business Income Tax

Federal income tax exemption applies to certain entities to reduce the cost of their pursuing a socially desirable exempt purpose. However, this creates a strong incentive to "disguise" a for-profit business as a not-for-profit entity. This tax exemption would provide such entities with a substantial competitive advantage compared to taxable businesses. For this reason, exempt entities are subject to Federal income tax on income unrelated to their exempt purpose. Text Section 25-3 described the excise taxes that apply to public and private foundations. This section discusses income tax on the business operations of an exempt organization. About 300,000 exempt entities file a tax return with the IRS every year, and more than 20 percent of those report a tax liability on business income. Tax collections in a typical year equal about $600 million.

The **unrelated business income tax (UBIT)** is designed to treat charitable entities as if they were subject to the corporate income tax, chiefly because they compete with taxable enterprises. The corporate income tax rate is used for this purpose.[26]

In general, **unrelated business income (UBI)** is derived from activities not related to the exempt purpose of the exempt organization. The UBIT applies because the organization is engaging in substantial commercial activities.[27] Thus, the UBIT mitigates the exempt entity's tax advantage.[28]

It is the source of the business profits that triggers the UBIT, not their use. UBI is subject to income tax even if the otherwise exempt entity uses the profits to further its exempt purpose. Fortunately for exempt entities, unrelated business taxable income (UBTI) does not by itself jeopardize the entity's exempt status.

The Big Picture

Example 7

Return to the facts of *The Big Picture* on p. 25-1. Recall that Hopeful, Inc., an exempt organization under § 501(c)(3), has received Taste Good Ice Cream, a chain of gourmet ice cream shops, as a bequest.

Assume that Hopeful has decided to operate Taste Good as a *division*. Although the income from Taste Good's shops will be used to support Hopeful's exempt purpose, the net revenue constitutes unrelated business income; therefore, it is subject to the UBIT.

The UBIT applies to all organizations that are exempt from Federal income tax under § 501(c), except Federal agencies. In addition, the tax applies to state colleges and universities.[29]

A materiality exception generally exempts an entity from being subject to the UBIT if such income is insignificant. This $1,000 "standard deduction" generally available to all exempt organizations is discussed in text Section 25-5b.

25-5a Unrelated Trade or Business

An exempt organization is subject to the UBIT when all of the following conditions are met:[30]

- The organization conducts a trade or business.
- The trade or business is *not* substantially related to the exempt purpose of the organization.
- The trade or business is regularly carried on by the organization.

However, the Code specifically excludes the following activities from classification as an unrelated trade or business:

- A trade or business where the individuals performing substantially all of its work do so without compensation (e.g., an orphanage operates a retail store for sales to the general public, and all of the work is done by volunteers).

[26] § 511(a)(1).
[27] § 512(a)(1).
[28] Reg. § 1.513–1(b).
[29] § 511(a)(2) and Reg. § 1.511–2(a)(2).
[30] § 513(a) and Reg. § 1.513–2(a).

- The trade or business consists of selling merchandise, and substantially all of the merchandise has been received as contributions (e.g., thrift shops).
- For § 501(c)(3) organizations and for state colleges or universities, the trade or business is conducted primarily for the convenience of the organization's members, students, patients, officers, or employees (e.g., a college bookstore and a laundry operated by the college for laundering dormitory linens and students' clothing).
- For most employee unions, the trade or business consists of selling to members, at their usual place of employment, work-related clothing and equipment and items normally sold through vending machines, snack bars, or food-dispensing facilities.

Conducting a Trade or Business

Trade or business, for this purpose, is broadly defined. It includes any activity conducted for the production of income through the sale of merchandise or the performance of services. An activity need not generate a profit to be treated as a trade or business.[31]

Health, Inc., is an exempt hospital that operates a pharmacy. The pharmacy provides medicines and supplies to the patients in the hospital (i.e., it contributes to the conduct of the hospital's exempt purpose). In addition, the pharmacy sells medicines and supplies to the general public.

The activity of selling to the general public constitutes a trade or business for purposes of the UBIT.

An organization with more than one unrelated trade or business must compute unrelated business taxable income separately for each. Losses from one unrelated trade or business cannot offset income derived from a different activity. NOLs can be carried forward indefinitely, but not back.[32] Deductible expenses are allocated among the separate unrelated businesses using any reasonable computational method. The entity's investment activities are treated as one business under this rule.

Not Substantially Related to the Exempt Purpose

Exempt organizations frequently conduct unrelated trades or businesses to provide income to help defray their costs. If the activity is related to its exempt purpose, it is not subject to the UBIT. To be related to the accomplishment of the exempt purpose, the business activities must contribute importantly to the exempt purpose.[33]

Is It an Unrelated Trade or Business?

Art, Inc., an exempt organization, operates a school for training children in the performing arts. As an essential part of that training, the children perform for the general public once a month. The children are paid for their performances, and Art receives income by charging admission to the performances.

The income from admissions is *not* income from an unrelated trade or business. The performances by the children contribute importantly to the accomplishment of the exempt purpose of providing training in the performing arts.

Assume the same facts as in Example 9, except that four performances are conducted each weekend of the year; each child must appear in three of the performances every week. Further, assume that this number of performances far exceeds that required for training the children.

Here, the income derived from admissions for any *excess* performances is income from an unrelated trade or business.

[31] Reg. § 1.513–1(b).

[32] §§ 172(a)(2)(B)(ii), 172(b)(1)(A)(ii)(II), and 512(a)(6). An NOL deduction can offset no more than 80 percent of UBTI. The first unrelated trade or business is reported on the Form 990–T, and each additional business is reported on its own Schedule M (Form 990–T).

[33] Reg. § 1.513–1(d).

The trade or business may sell merchandise that has been produced as part of the accomplishment of the exempt purpose.[34] Income derived by the organization from use of its property for a nonexempt purpose is UBI.[35]

Unrelated Business Income

Help-Self, Inc., an exempt organization, conducts programs for the rehabilitation of the handicapped. One of the programs includes training in radio and television repair. Help-Self derives gross income by selling the repaired items.

The income is substantially related to the accomplishment of the exempt purpose and, therefore, is not UBI.

Example 12

Civil, Inc., an exempt organization, operates a museum. As part of the exempt purpose of the museum, educational lectures are given in the museum's theater during the operating hours of the museum. In the evening, when the museum is closed, the theater is leased to an LLC that sells tickets and shows current movies to the general public. The lease income is UBI.

Corporate Sponsorship Payments The term *unrelated trade or business* does not include the soliciting and receiving of qualified sponsorship payments.[36] A qualified sponsorship payment must meet all of the following requirements:

- The trade or business making the payment expects no substantial benefit other than the use or acknowledgment of its name, logo, or product lines in connection with the activities of the exempt organization.
- The exempt organization does not advertise or endorse the payor's products or services.
- The payment does not include any amount that is contingent on the degree of public exposure that results (e.g., the level of attendance at one or more events, the number of website hits, or streaming hours).

Sponsorship Payments

Pets, Inc., a manufacturer of cat food, contributes $25,000 to Feline Care, Inc., an exempt organization that cares for abandoned cats. In return for the contribution, Feline agrees to put Pets' corporate logo in its monthly newsletter to donors. The $25,000 payment is a qualified sponsorship payment and is not subject to the UBIT.

Assume the same facts as in Example 13, except that Feline agrees to endorse Pets' cat food in its monthly newsletter by stating that it feeds only Pets' cat food to its cats. The $25,000 payment is not a qualified sponsorship payment and is subject to the UBIT.

Bingo Games A *qualified bingo game* is not an unrelated trade or business if both of the following requirements are met:[37]

- The bingo game is legal under both state and local law.
- Commercial bingo games (conducted for a profit motive) ordinarily are not allowed in the pertinent jurisdiction.

[34] Reg. § 1.513–1(d)(4)(ii). If the merchandise is not sold in substantially the same state it was in at the completion of the exempt purpose (e.g., it has been converted into another product), the gross income subsequently derived from the sale of the merchandise *is* unrelated business income (UBI).

[35] Reg. § 1.513–1(d)(4)(iii) addresses the allocation of expenses to exempt and nonexempt activities.

[36] § 513(i).

[37] § 513(f).

Play, Inc., an exempt organization, conducts weekly bingo games. The town in which Play conducts the games allows exempt organizations to conduct bingo games, but they do not permit profit-oriented entities to do so.

Because both of the requirements for bingo games are satisfied, the bingo games conducted by Play are not an unrelated trade or business.

Distribution of Low-Cost Articles When a donor receives a product, like a briefcase, in exchange for a gift to a charity, it appears that a sale has occurred, and the entity has generated UBI. But where an exempt organization distributes low-cost items as an incidental part of its solicitation for charitable contributions, the activity is not considered an unrelated trade or business.

A low-cost article is an item that costs $12.50 or less in 2023 (indexed annually). Examples of such items are pens, tote bags, and address labels. If more than one item is distributed to a person during the calendar year, the costs of the items are combined.[38]

Rental or Exchange of Membership Lists If an exempt organization sells or rents its donor or membership list (i.e., its mailing list) to other exempt organizations, the activity is *not* an unrelated trade or business.[39]

Regularly Carried on by the Organization

Requiring the activity to be one that is regularly carried on by the exempt organization ensures that only activities that are actually competing with taxable organizations are subject to the UBIT. The factors considered in applying the *regularly carried on* test include the frequency of the activity, the continuity of the activity, and the manner in which the exempt entity pursues the activity.[40]

Activity Regularly Carried On

Silver, Inc., an exempt organization, owns land that is located next to the state fairgrounds. During the 10 days of the state fair, Silver uses the land as a parking lot and allows attendees to park on its land for a fee. The activity is not regularly carried on.

Black, Inc., an exempt organization, has its offices in the downtown area. It owns a parking lot adjacent to its offices on which its employees park during the week. On Saturdays, it rents the spaces in the parking lot to individuals shopping or working in the downtown area. Black is conducting a business activity on a year-round basis even though it is only for one day per week. Thus, an activity is regularly being carried on.

25-5b **Unrelated Business Taxable Income**

General Tax Model

A template for computing unrelated business taxable income (UBTI) appears in Exhibit 25.5. In computing UBTI, several adjustments are made to the entity's net UBI for the year, including the following.[41]

Positive adjustments—Add to UBI

1. A deduction is allowed for gifts to another charity, but it is limited to 10 percent of UBTI (without regard to the charitable contribution deduction). Amounts in excess of this limit are added back to UBI as a positive adjustment.

[38] § 513(h)(1)(A).

[39] § 513(h)(1)(B).

[40] § 512(a)(1) and Reg. § 1.513–1(c).

[41] § 512(b) and Reg. § 1.512(b)–1. Other adjustments are required (e.g., concerning net operating losses, research expenditures, and related party transactions).

Exhibit 25.5 Tax Formula for Unrelated Business Taxable Income

Gross unrelated business income
− Deductions related to the business income
= Net unrelated business income (Net UBI)
± Adjustments (positive and negative)
− $1,000 "standard deduction"
= Unrelated business taxable income (UBTI)

Brown, Inc., an exempt organization, records UBTI of $87,000 after deducting the entity's $13,000 of charitable contributions. As a result, UBTI before any charitable contribution deduction is $100,000.

Because Brown's accounting practice is to deduct all $13,000 of contributions in calculating UBTI, $3,000 [$13,000 − 10%($100,000)] is a positive adjustment (i.e., an "add back" to reduce the deduction) in calculating UBTI. The 10% charitable contribution deduction limit for corporations causes this adjustment.

2. Unrelated debt-financed income net of the unrelated debt-financed deductions (see later discussion).

Negative adjustments—Subtract from UBI

1. Income from dividends, interest, and annuities, net of all directly related deductions. This enables exempt entities to use investment-related income to finance their exempt purpose without incurring income tax.
2. Royalty income, regardless of whether it is measured by production, gross income, or taxable income from the property, net of all directly related deductions.
3. Rent income from real property and from certain personal property, net of all directly related deductions.
    - Personal property rents are included in the negative adjustment only if the personal property is leased with the real property. The personal property rent income must not exceed 10 percent of the gross rent income under the lease.
    - None of rents are a negative adjustment if more than 50 percent of the rent income under the lease is derived from personal property.

Rentals as UBI

Example 19

Beaver, Inc., an exempt organization, leases land and a building (realty) and computers (personalty) housed in the building. Under the lease, $46,000 of the rent is for the land and building and $4,000 is for the computers. Expenses incurred for the land and building are $10,000.

Here, the personal property rent ($4,000) does not exceed 10 percent of the gross rental income ($5,000 = $50,000 × 10%). As a result, the net rent income from both the land and building of $36,000 ($46,000 − $10,000) and the income from the computers of $4,000 are negative adjustments in computing UBTI.

Example 20

Assume the same facts as in Example 19, except that the rent income is $35,000 from the land and building and $15,000 from the computers.

Because the rent income from the computers exceeds $5,000 and is not incidental, it is *not* a negative adjustment; it is a business activity and is included in UBTI. The $35,000 rent income from the real property remains a negative adjustment.

Assume the same facts as in Example 19, except that the rent income is $20,000 from the land and building and $30,000 from the computers.

Because more than 50% of the rent income under the lease is from the computers, neither the rent income from the land and building nor that from the computers is a negative adjustment. Both amounts remain in UBTI.

These three examples show that, depending on the relative amounts involved, the exempt entity can exclude all, some, or none of its rental income from UBI.

4. Gains and losses from the sale, exchange, or other disposition of property *except for* inventory.

Beaver, the owner of the land, building, and computers in Example 19, sells these assets for $450,000. Their adjusted basis is $300,000.

Beaver's recognized gain of $150,000 is removed from UBTI as a negative adjustment.

In determining UBTI, a "standard deduction" of $1,000 is allowed.[42]

Petit Care, Inc., an exempt organization, reports net unrelated business income of $800. Because Petit claims a $1,000 "standard deduction," its UBTI is $0. Therefore, its income tax liability is $0.

The calculated UBTI is subject to tax using the appropriate Federal income tax rate.[43]

Patient, Inc., an exempt organization, generates UBTI of $500,000. Patient's income tax liability is $105,000 ($500,000 UBTI × 21% corporate tax rate).

Concept Summary 25.3 provides a summary of the UBIT rules.

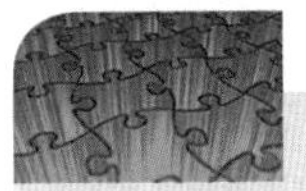

Concept Summary 25.3

Unrelated Business Income Tax

Purpose	To tax the entity on unrelated business income as if it were subject to the corporate income tax.
Applicable tax rates	Corporate (or sometimes, trust) income tax rates. In addition, the entity may be required to pay the newly-enacted 15 percent corporate alternative minimum tax on its UBI.
Exempt organizations to which applicable	All organizations exempt under § 501(c), except Federal agencies.
Entities subject to the tax	The organization conducts a trade or business, the trade or business is not substantially related to the exempt purpose of the organization, and the organization conducts the trade or business regularly.
Exceptions to the tax	• Substantially all of the work is performed by volunteers. • Substantially all of the merchandise being sold has been received by gift. • For § 501(c)(3) organizations, the business is conducted primarily for the benefit of the organization's members, students, patients, officers, or employees. • For most employee unions, the trade or business consists of selling to members work-related clothing and equipment and items normally sold through vending machines, snack bars, or food-dispensing facilities. • Other items relating to bingo games, corporate sponsorships, list rentals, and the like.
$1,000 "standard deduction"	If gross income from an unrelated trade or business is less than $1,000, no tax results, and it is not necessary to file a return associated with the unrelated business income tax.

[42] § 512(b)(12). For an association of churches, each parish or congregation is allowed its own standard deduction.

[43] If the charity is organized as a trust, the rates under Subchapter J are used; see Exhibit 30.3.

Unrelated Debt-Financed Income

In calculating UBTI (see Exhibit 25.5), unrelated debt-financed income is one of the positive adjustments. Examples of income from debt-financed property include rent income from real estate or tangible personal property (e.g., a church that owns and leases space in a leveraged office building) and gains from the disposition of debt-financed property.

Without this provision, a tax-exempt organization could use borrowed funds to acquire unrelated business or investment property and use the resulting exempt income to pay for the property.

Definition of Debt-Financed Income **Debt-financed income** is the gross income generated from debt-financed property. *Debt-financed property* is all property of the exempt organization that is held to produce income and on which debt has been incurred, *except* for the following:[44]

- Property where substantially all (at least 85 percent) of the use is devoted to the organization's exempt purpose.[45]
- Property whose gross income otherwise is treated as unrelated business income.
- Property whose gross income is related to various research activities and otherwise is not treated as unrelated business income.

If the 85 percent test is not satisfied, only the portion of the property that is *not* used for the exempt purpose is debt-financed property.

Example 25

Deer, Inc., an exempt organization, owns a five-story office building on which it has a mortgage liability. Three of the floors are used for Deer's exempt purpose. The two other floors are leased to Purple Corporation, an unrelated taxable data analytics entity. Ordinarily, UBI does not include rent from real property. However, the mortgage on the property makes it debt-financed, which triggers the 85% test. In this case, the *substantially all* test is not satisfied. Therefore, 40% of the office building is debt-financed property and 60% is not.

What if Deer used all but one-half of one floor for its exempt purpose (with Purple leasing the half floor)? Now the "substantially all" test is met, and the rent income is not UBI (i.e., there is no positive adjustment).

Certain land that is acquired by an exempt organization for later exempt use is excluded from debt-financed property if the following requirements are satisfied:[46]

- The principal purpose of acquiring the land is for use (substantially all) in achieving the organization's exempt purpose.
- This use will begin within 10 years of the acquisition date.
- The land, on its acquisition date, is located in the *neighborhood* of other property of the organization for which substantially all of the use is for achieving the organization's exempt purpose.

If the exempt organization is a church, the 10-year period becomes a 15-year period, and the neighborhood requirement is waived.[47]

25-5c Feeder Organizations

A **feeder organization** carries on a trade or business for the benefit of an exempt organization and remits its profits to the exempt organization. Feeder organizations are *not* exempt from Federal income tax.[48] This treatment prevents an entity, whose primary purpose is to conduct a profitable trade or business, from escaping taxation merely because its profits are given to one or more exempt organizations. In addition, this rule means that an exempt entity faces the same tax whether it operates a business directly or through a subsidiary corporation.

[44] § 514(b).
[45] Reg. § 1.514(b)–1(b)(1)(ii).
[46] § 514(b)(3).
[47] § 514(b)(3)(E).
[48] § 502(a).

The Big Picture

Example 26

Return to the facts of *The Big Picture* on p. 25-1. Recall that Hopeful, Inc., an exempt organization under § 501(c)(3) that provides temporary lodging and psychological services to abused women and children, is trying to decide what it should do with Taste Good Ice Cream, a chain of gourmet ice cream shops it received as a bequest.

Assume that Hopeful decides to operate Taste Good as a *subsidiary*, with the profits going to Hopeful to support its tax-exempt operations. The subsidiary is a feeder organization, and its profits will be subject to the Federal corporate income tax.

25-6 Reporting Requirements

LO.7

List the tax forms that exempt organizations must file with the IRS and the related due dates.

25-6a Obtaining Exempt Organization Status

Not all exempt organizations are required to obtain IRS approval to ensure their exempt status. Churches, and entities with typical annual gross receipts of up to $5,000, need not apply for exempt status.[49]

Organizations exempt under § 501(c)(3) use Form 1023 to apply for exempt status; small organizations file Form 1023–EZ, which requires a smaller application fee.[50] Form 1024 is used by most other types of exempt organizations. All applications are filed electronically.

25-6b Annual Filing Requirements

Most exempt organizations must file one of four annual information returns:

- Exempt organizations with gross receipts that exceed $200,000 or assets that exceed $500,000 must file Form 990 (Return of Organization Exempt from Income Tax). Religious groups and Federal agencies are exempt from filing a Form 990.[51]
- Small exempt organizations, whose annual gross receipts normally are $50,000 or less, must file a Form 990–N, known as the e-Postcard.[52] The e-Postcard is designed to be a simpler version of the full Form 990.
- The Form 990–EZ, another abbreviated version of the Form 990, can be used by exempt organizations with gross receipts of less than $200,000 and total assets of less than $500,000.
- Private foundations must file Form 990–PF (Return of Private Foundation). Form 990–PF requires more information than does Form 990. Form 4720 is used to compute any excise tax liabilities of the private foundation. The return is filed with the private foundation's Form 990–PF.

Failure to file required returns for three consecutive tax years results in revocation of tax exemption. The IRS notifies the entity after the second consecutive year of non-filing.[53] Once an exemption is lost in this way, the entity must reapply for exempt status. A revoked exemption can be restored retroactively if it was lost due to reasonable cause.

[49] § 508(c)(1).

[50] A small organization is defined as one that holds assets not in excess of $250,000, and its annual gross receipts for the last three years have not exceeded $50,000. More than one-half of all new applications for exempt status are received on Form 1023-EZ.

[51] §§ 6033(a)(1) and (3). For public charities, the form includes the names and addresses of significant donors. Other exempt entities can omit this information from the form, but they must keep the names and addresses in their private records. This data can facilitate a later IRS audit. TD 9898, 5/28/2020.

[52] Supporting organizations and private foundations cannot use the Form 990–N.

[53] § 6033(j).

The due date for Form 990 or Form 990–PF is the fifteenth day of the fifth month after the end of the taxable year. An automatic six-month extension of the filing deadline is available. In 2023, a $20-per-day penalty is assessed when the entity fails to file a required return, subject to a $12,000 maximum amount; a $120-per-day penalty with a $60,000 maximum amount applies to large charities.[54]

Green, Inc., a § 501(c)(3) organization, has a fiscal year that ends June 30, 2023. The due date for the annual return is November 15, 2023.

If Green were a calendar year entity, the due date for its 2023 return would be May 15, 2024, with an extension available to November 15, 2024.

In addition to the annual reporting forms, exempt organizations that receive at least $1,000 from an unrelated trade or business must file Form 990–T. The purpose of this form is to compute the entity's Federal tax liability. This form is due on the same day as the entity's Form 990. The IRS requires electronic filing of the Form 990–T.

Here are some illustrations of the annual filing requirements faced by exempt organizations:

- During the year, the First Church of Kentwood receives parishioner contributions of $450,000. Of this amount, $125,000 is designated for the church building fund. None of its receipts constitute unrelated business income. First Church is not required to file an annual return (Form 990) because churches are exempt from doing so. In addition, it is not required to file Form 990–T.
- Colonial, Inc., is a private foundation. Gross receipts for the year total $800,000, of which 40% is from admission fees paid by members of the general public who visit Colonial's museum of eighteenth-century life. The balance is endowment income and contributions from the founding donor. Because Colonial is a private foundation, it files Form 990–PF.
- Orange, Inc., is an exempt organization and is not a private foundation. Gross receipts for the year are $20,000. None of this amount is unrelated business income. Orange files an e-Postcard Form 990–N instead of Form 990 because its annual gross receipts do not exceed $50,000.
- Restoration, Inc., is an exempt organization with $400,000 of assets. Gross receipts for the year are $100,000. None of this amount is unrelated business income. Restoration files Form 990–EZ because its gross receipts are between $50,000 and $200,000 and its assets are less than $500,000.
- During the year, the Second Church of Port Allen receives parishioner contributions of $300,000. In addition, the church has unrelated business income of $5,000. Second Church is not required to file Form 990 because churches are exempt from doing so. Form 990–T must be filed, however, because churches are not exempt from the UBIT, and Second Church's earnings exceed the $1,000 "standard deduction."

25-6c **Public Disclosure Requirements**

Unlike tax returns of individuals and businesses, the information returns of exempt entities are public information. As such, exempt entities must make copies of the following forms available to the general public:[55]

- Form 990.
- Form 990–PF.
- Form 1023 (or Form 1024).

Copies of the three most recent Forms 990 must be made available. If an individual requests the entity's tax form in person, the exempt entity must provide a copy immediately. If the request is received in writing or by e-mail, the copy must be provided within 30 days. The copy must be provided without charge, except for a reasonable fee for copying and distribution costs.

[54] §§ 6652(c)(1)(A) and (B). Additional penalties may be assessed of the organization's management.

[55] § 6104(d). Penalties apply if the entity does not make these disclosures. §§ 6652(c)(1)(C) and (D). One valuable source of Forms 990 and 990–PF and other relevant materials concerning exempt entities is **guidestar.org**.

If the exempt entity has made the forms widely available to the general public, it is not required to fill individual requests.[56] Putting the forms on the organization's website meets this requirement. Individual inquiries can be disregarded if the exempt entity can show that the request is part of a harassment campaign.[57]

25-7 Tax Planning

LO.8

Identify tax planning opportunities for exempt organizations.

25-7a Choosing an Exempt Classification

An organization is exempt from taxation only if it fits into one of the categories enumerated in the Code. Thus, particular attention must be given to the entity's qualification requirements. These requirements must continue to be satisfied to avoid termination of exempt status (in effect, they become maintenance requirements).

Organizations that want to engage in political activities beyond the elective lobbying limits cannot use the § 501(c)(3) classification. A § 501(c)(4) social welfare organization might be used instead. Such an entity can engage in partisan political work and promote specific candidates, as long as these activities do not reach 50 percent of its annual expenditures. However, payments to a § 501(c)(4) entity are not deductible as charitable contributions because these entities are not charities.

25-7b Maintaining Exempt Status

To maintain exempt status, most organizations must satisfy both an organizational test and an operational test. The organizational test requires that the entity satisfy the statutory requirements for exempt status based on its legal structure. The operational test ensures that the entity satisfies the statutory requirements for exempt status through its mission and operations.

King Shipping Consum., Inc. (Zion Coptic Church, Inc.) illustrates that it is usually much easier to satisfy the organizational test than the operational test.[58] Zion's stated purpose was to engage in activities usually and normally associated with churches. Based on this, the IRS approved Zion's exempt status as a § 501(c)(3) organization.

Zion's real intent, however, was to smuggle illegal drugs into the country and to distribute them for profit. The church's justification for the drugs was that it used marijuana in its sacraments. During a four-month period, however, the police confiscated 33 tons of marijuana from church members. The IRS calculated that even assuming the maximum alleged church membership of several thousand, each member would have had to consume over 33 pounds of marijuana during the four-month period to justify those inventory levels.

The court concluded that Zion's real purpose was to hide a large commercial drug smuggling operation. Because this activity was inconsistent with the religious purpose for exempt status, the court upheld the IRS's revocation of Zion's exempt status and the related tax assessment of approximately $1.6 million.

25-7c Private Foundations

Exempt organizations that can qualify as public charities receive more beneficial tax treatment than do those that qualify as private foundations. If possible, the organization should be structured to qualify as a public charity. One important difference in this treatment is that donors value contributions to public charities at fair market value but only at adjusted basis for private foundations.

[56] Reg. § 301.6104(d)-2.

[57] § 6104(d)(4).

[58] 58 TCM 574, T.C.Memo. 1989–593.

David has owned undeveloped land since 2010 ($25,000 adjusted basis, $100,000 fair market value) that he is going to contribute to one of the following exempt organizations: Blue, Inc., a public charity, or Teal, Inc., a private foundation.

David asks the manager of each organization to describe the tax benefits of contributing the land to that organization. He tells them that his marginal income tax rate (Federal and state combined) is 35%.

Based on the data provided by the managers, David decides to contribute the land to Blue, Inc. He calculates the amount of the charitable contribution under each option as follows.[59]

Donee	David's Contribution Deduction	David's Tax Rate	Contribution Borne by U.S. Government
Blue	$100,000	35%	$35,000
Teal	25,000	35%	8,750

If the organization is a private foundation, care must be exercised to avoid the assessment of a tax liability on a prohibited transaction. Foundations can best avoid these taxes by establishing board-level and administrative controls that prevent the entity from engaging in transactions that trigger them. If an initial tax is assessed, the foundation should quickly implement corrective actions to avoid the assessment of an additional tax.

25-7d Unrelated Business Income Tax

If the exempt organization conducts an unrelated trade or business, it may be subject to Federal income tax on the unrelated business income. Further, the unrelated trade or business could result in the loss of exempt status if the IRS determines that the activity is the primary purpose of the organization. In addition, land and buildings used to produce unrelated business income may be subject to state and local property taxes.

One approach that can be used to avoid the UBIT is for the organization to establish a taxable subsidiary to conduct the unrelated trade or business. Using such a feeder organization, the revenues and expenses of the exempt organization can be separated from those of the unrelated business. In addition, recall that an exempt entity *cannot* net together unrelated business income from one activity with unrelated business loss from another activity. However, a fully-taxable subsidiary *can* net the income or loss from different activities. When the subsidiary remits its after-tax profits to the exempt organization in the form of dividends, the dividends will not be taxable to the exempt organization; dividends are eliminated from UBTI as a negative adjustment. These results frequently make creating a taxable feeder subsidiary advantageous for exempt entities.

Another approach to avoiding the UBIT is purposely to fail the definition of an unrelated trade or business. This is accomplished if:

- The activities do *not* constitute a trade or business.
- The activities are substantially related to the exempt purpose of the organization.
- The trade or business is *not* regularly carried on by the organization.

[59]Charitable contribution deductions for gifts of capital gain property made to private nonoperating foundations are limited to asset basis; § 170(e)(1)(B)(ii).

Refocus on The Big Picture

Effect of a For-Profit Business on a Tax-Exempt Entity

A § 501(c)(3) entity is exempt from Federal income tax only on the conduct of its charitable activities. However, if an exempt entity generates income from the conduct of a trade or business that is not related to the organization's exempt purpose, this income generally is subject to Federal income tax. These principles can be used in analyzing Hopeful's options for the ice cream business it inherited:

- *Sell the stock of Taste Good Ice Cream.* A sale of the Taste Good Ice Cream stock is unlikely to result in much realized gain because the fair market value probably has not changed very much in the limited time between the date of Jennifer's death and the present. In any case, a realized gain on the sale of the stock is tax-exempt under § 501(c)(3).
- *Conduct the ice cream business as a division of Hopeful.* Under this option, the taxable income of the ice cream chain is classified as unrelated business income. Because the ice cream division is competing with for-profit entities, it is subject to the Federal income tax that applies to corporate entities. In essence, the tax is levied because the exempt organization is engaging in substantial commercial activities.
- *Conduct the ice cream business as a wholly owned subsidiary of Hopeful.* Under this option, the ice cream chain subsidiary is classified as a feeder organization (i.e., carries on a trade or business for the benefit of an exempt organization and remits its profits to that entity). As a result, the subsidiary pays Federal income tax on its profits.

What If?

Hopeful's board of directors must be careful that an acceptance of the Taste Good stock does not change the exempt status of the entity. If Hopeful owns "too much" of the Taste Good shares, Hopeful could lose its status as a § 501(c)(3) entity and be reclassified as a private foundation. Then an excise tax could apply if Hopeful is found to have "excess business holdings" in the form of the stock.

Key Terms

Debt-financed income, 25-20
Excess lobbying expenditures, 25-7
Exempt organizations, 25-2
Feeder organization, 25-20
Grass roots expenditures, 25-7
Intermediate sanctions, 25-8
Lobbying expenditures, 25-6
Private foundations, 25-10
Unrelated business income (UBI), 25-14
Unrelated business income tax (UBIT), 25-14

Discussion Questions

1. **LO.3** An exempt organization makes the § 501(h) election to lobby on a limited basis. The amount of its lobbying expenditures is less than its lobbying expenditures ceiling, yet it is subject to a tax at a 25% rate. Explain.

2. **LO.5** Sunset, Inc., a § 501(c)(3) exempt organization that is classified as a private foundation, generates investment income of $500,000 for the current tax year. This amount represents 18% of Sunset's total income.
   a. What type of tax imposed on Sunset is associated with its investment income?
   b. Is the receipt of this investment income likely to result in Sunset losing its exempt status? Why or why not?
   c. Would your answers in parts (a) and (b) change if the $500,000 represented greater than 50% of Sunset's total income? Explain.

Critical Thinking

3. **LO.4, 5** Really Welcome, Inc., a tax-exempt organization, receives 30% of its support from disqualified persons. Another disqualified person has agreed to match this support if Really Welcome will appoint him to the organization's board of directors. What tax issues are relevant to Really Welcome as it makes this decision?

4. **LO.6** Winston recently became the treasurer of Homeless, Inc., a § 501(c)(3) organization that feeds individuals who are in challenging circumstances. One of the entity's directors has proposed that Homeless purchase and operate a fast-food franchise to raise additional revenue (a projected annual increase of 45%) for its charitable mission. Because the earnings generated by the fast-food franchise would be tax-exempt, substantial additional net revenues would be provided. How should Winston respond?

5. **LO.6** An exempt hospital operates a pharmacy that is staffed by a pharmacist 24 hours per day. The pharmacy serves only hospital patients. Is the pharmacy likely an unrelated trade or business? Explain.

Critical Thinking

6. **LO.6** An exempt organization is considering conducting bingo games on Thursday nights as a way of generating additional revenue to support its exempt purpose. Before doing so, however, the president of the organization asks you for advice regarding the effect on the organization's exempt status and whether the net income from the bingo games will be taxable. Identify the relevant tax issues.

7. **LO.1, 7** Sofía is the treasurer of the Chestnut City Garden Club, a new entity in the community. A friend who is the treasurer of the garden club in a neighboring community tells Sofía that Chestnut need not file a request for exempt status with the IRS. Has Sofía received correct advice? Explain.

Critical Thinking

8. **LO.1, 7** Abby Wang recently became the treasurer of First Point Church. The church has existed for three years and never has filed any documents with the IRS. Identify any Federal income tax reporting responsibilities that Abby might have as church treasurer.

9. **LO.7** Shane is the treasurer for Jain Clinics, and Brittany is the treasurer for EmPowerMentors, both of which are § 501(c)(3) exempt organizations. Each year Jain files a Form 990, while EmPowerMentors files a Form 990–PF. Discuss the public disclosure requirements for each exempt entity.

Computational Exercises

10. **LO.3** Helpers, Inc., a qualifying § 501(c)(3) organization, incurs lobbying expenditures of $250,000 for the taxable year and grass roots expenditures of $0. Exempt purpose expenditures for the taxable year are $1,200,000. Helpers elects to make limited lobbying expenditures.
    a. What amount of lobbying expenditures is Helpers allowed to make tax-free under the terms of the election?

b. What is its tax liability as a result of the election?

c. Express your answer to part (b) as a Microsoft Excel formula. Use the variable names "LOBBYTAX" for the final tax, "LOBBYEXPEND" for the organization's lobbying expenditures, and "LOBBYNONTAX" for the organization's nontaxable lobbying expenditures.

11. **LO.3** Davis, an officer for a § 501(c)(3) organization, receives benefits in the form of an overly generous health insurance plan; these benefits are inappropriate in the context of a charitable entity of its type. The excess benefits are determined to be $35,000. Davis does not pay back the excess benefits to the organization before the first-level tax is due.

    a. Apply the rules for the appropriate excise tax intermediate sanction. What amount of first-level taxes are imposed on Davis? On the exempt organization management?

    b. What amount of second-level taxes are imposed on Davis?

12. **LO.5** Rejoice, Inc., a private foundation, has existed for 10 years. Rejoice held undistributed income of $160,000 at the end of its 2021 tax year. Of this amount, $90,000 was distributed in 2022, and $70,000 was distributed during the first quarter of 2023. The IRS mailed a deficiency notice to Rejoice on August 1, 2024, relating to the entity's undistributed income.

    a. What is Rejoice's initial tax on the 2021 undistributed taxable income for 2022? For 2023?

    b. Express the 2022 tax computation as a Microsoft Excel formula. Use the variable names "2022TAX" for the final tax amount, "21UNDISTRIB" for 2021 undistributed income, and "22DISTRIB" for 2022 distributed income.

    c. What is Rejoice's additional tax for 2024 relative to the 2021 income?

13. **LO.6** Harmony, Inc., an exempt organization, reports unrelated business income of $7,500 and unrelated business expenses of $4,000. Calculate Harmony's UBIT.

Problems

14. **LO.1** Match the following exempt organizations with the statutory authority under which exempt status is granted. The statutory authority may apply to more than one exempt organization. Not all of the authority citations are used.

Exempt Organizations	Statutory Authority
Girl Scouts	§ 501(c)(1)
St. Óscar Romero Catholic Church	§ 501(c)(2)
American Red Cross	§ 501(c)(3)
Salvation Army	§ 501(c)(4)
United Fund	§ 501(c)(5)
Lilly Foundation	§ 501(c)(6)
Pomona College	§ 501(c)(7)
Association of Women Engineers	§ 501(c)(8)
Ladies PGA Tour	§ 501(c)(9)
Veterans of Foreign Wars (VFW)	§ 501(c)(10)
Dallas Rodeo Club	§ 501(c)(11)
Township School's Parent-Teacher Association (PTA)	§ 501(c)(12)
Toano Cemetery Association	§ 501(c)(13)
Alpha Chi Omega Sorority	§ 501(c)(14)
National Press Club	§ 501(c)(15)
Federal Deposit Insurance Corporation (FDIC)	§ 501(c)(19)
League of Women Voters	§ 501(d)

15. **LO.1, 3** Wellness, Inc., a § 501(c)(3) organization, makes lobbying expenditures of $340,000 this year. Exempt-purpose expenditures by Wellness were $600,000 for the first six months of the year and $950,000 for the last six months of the year. Determine the Federal income tax consequences to Wellness if:
   a. It does not make the § 501(h) lobbying election.
   b. It makes the § 501(h) lobbying election.

16. **LO.3** Wish, Inc., a § 501(c)(3) organization, pays unreasonable compensation to Renata, the treasurer of Wish. Renata's compensation is $600,000. Assume that reasonable compensation would be $500,000.
   a. Apply the rules for the appropriate excise tax intermediate sanction. Determine any tax consequences for Wish, Inc.
   b. Determine any tax consequences for Renata.

Communications
Critical Thinking
Planning

17. **LO.3, 6, 8** Roadrunner, Inc., is an exempt medical organization. Quail, Inc., a sporting goods retailer, is a wholly owned subsidiary of Roadrunner. Roadrunner inherited the Quail stock last year from a major benefactor. Quail's taxable income is $550,000. Quail remits all of its earnings, net of any taxes, to Roadrunner every year to support the exempt purpose of the parent.
   a. Is Quail subject to Federal income tax? If so, calculate the liability.
   b. Ling Zhao, the treasurer of Roadrunner, has contacted you regarding minimizing or eliminating Quail's Federal income tax liability. She would like to know if the tax consequences would be better if Quail were liquidated into Roadrunner. Write a letter to Ms. Zhao that contains your advice. Roadrunner's address is 500 Rouse Tower, Rochester, NY 14627.

18. **LO.3** Initiate, Inc., is a § 501(c)(3) organization. Landscaping, Inc., is a wholly owned for-profit subsidiary of Initiate, Inc., and it remits all of its after-tax profits each year to Initiate. Based on the following information, calculate the amount of Federal income tax, if any, for Initiate and for Landscaping.

Grant from Oprah Winfrey Foundation	$ 70,000
Charitable contributions received	625,000
Expenses in carrying out its exempt urban gardening projects	500,000
Net income before taxes of Landscaping, Inc.	400,000

Communications

19. **LO.4** Pigeon, Inc., a § 501(c)(3) organization, received support from the following sources.

Governmental unit A for services rendered	$ 6,300
Governmental unit B for services rendered	4,500
Fees from the general public for services rendered (Each payment was of $100)	75,000
Gross investment income	39,000
Contributions from disqualified persons	26,000
Contributions from other persons (Each gift was of $50 or less)	160,000
Total support	$310,800

   a. Does Pigeon satisfy the test for receiving broad public support? Why or why not?
   b. Is Pigeon a private foundation? Be specific in your answer.
   c. Elena Mariñez, Pigeon's treasurer, has asked you for advice on whether Pigeon is a private foundation. Write a letter to Elena in which you address the issue. Her address is 250 Bristol Road, Phoenix, AZ 85264.

20. **LO.5** Gray, Inc., a private foundation, reports the following.

Interest income	$ 29,000
Rent income	61,000
Dividend income	15,000
Royalty income	22,000
Unrelated business income	80,000
Rent expenses	(26,000)
Unrelated business expenses	(12,000)

a. Calculate Gray's net investment income.
b. Calculate Gray's tax on net investment income.

21. **LO.5, 8** Otis is the CEO of Rectify, Inc., a private foundation. Otis invests $500,000 (80%) of the foundation's investment portfolio in high-risk derivatives. Previously, the $500,000 had been invested in corporate bonds with an AA rating that earned 4% per annum. If the derivatives investment works as Otis's investment adviser claims, the annual earnings could be as high as 20%. Critical Thinking

a. Determine whether Rectify is subject to any of the taxes imposed on private foundations.
b. If so, calculate the amount of the initial tax.
c. If so, calculate the amount of the additional tax if the act causing the imposition of the tax is not addressed within the correction period.
d. Are Otis and the foundation better off financially if the prohibited transaction, if any, is addressed within the correction period? Explain.

22. **LO.5** The board of directors of Teton Pearl, Inc., a private foundation, consists of Charlyne, Beth, and Carlos. They vote unanimously to provide a $500,000 grant to Carlos. The grant is to be used for travel and education and does not qualify as a permitted grant to individuals (i.e., it is an act of self-dealing).

a. Calculate the initial tax imposed on Teton Pearl.
b. Calculate the initial tax imposed on the foundation manager (i.e., board of directors).
c. Express the computation in part (b) as a Microsoft Excel formula. Use the variable names "MGRINITAX" for the initial self-dealing tax and "SELFDEALAMT" for the amount of self-dealing expenditures.

23. **LO.6** The Open Museum is an exempt organization that operates a gift shop. The museum's annual operations budget is $3,200,000. Gift shop sales generate a profit of $900,000. Another $600,000 of investment income is generated by the museum's endowment fund. Communications

Both the gift shop and the endowment income support the exempt purpose of the museum. Admission fees of $1,700,000 make up the balance of the annual operating budget.

Wayne Hsu, a new board member, does not understand why the museum is subject to tax at all, particularly because all of the entity's profits are used in carrying out the mission of the museum. The museum's address is 250 Oak Avenue, Peoria, IL 61625.

a. Calculate the amount of unrelated business income.
b. Assume instead that the investment income is reinvested in the endowment fund, rather than used to support annual operations. Calculate the amount of unrelated business income.
c. As the museum treasurer, write a letter to Wayne explaining the reason for these results. Wayne's address is 45 Pine Avenue, Peoria, IL 61625.

24. **LO.6** Upward and Onward, Inc., a § 501(c)(3) organization that provides training programs for government assistance recipients, reports the following income and expenses from the sale of products associated with the training program. Calculate Upward and Onward's UBIT.

Gross income from sales	$425,000
Cost of goods sold	106,000
Advertising and selling expenses	26,000
Administrative expenses	112,500

   a. Assume that the sale of the training program products is substantially related to Upward and Onward's exempt purpose.
   b. Assume that the sale of the training program products is not substantially related to Upward and Onward's exempt purpose.
   c. Express the computation in part (b) as a Microsoft Excel formula. Use the variable names "UBIT" for the unrelated business income tax amount, "UBI" for unrelated business income, and "NETADJS" for net adjustments to UBI.

Communications

25. **LO.6** Perch, Inc., an exempt organization, records unrelated business taxable income of $4,000,000.
   a. Calculate Perch's UBIT.
   b. Prepare an outline of a presentation you are going to give to the new members of Perch's board on why Perch is subject to the UBIT even though it is an exempt organization.

26. **LO.6** For each of the following organizations, determine its UBTI and any related UBIT.
   a. AIDS Relief, Inc., an exempt charitable organization that provides support for individuals with AIDS, operates a retail medical supply store open to the general public. The net income of the store, before any Federal income taxes, is $305,000.
   b. St. Andrew Episcopal Church operates a retail gift shop. The inventory consists of the typical items sold by commercial gift shops in the city. The director of the gift shop estimates that 80% of the gift shop sales are to tourists and 20% are to church members. The net income of the gift shop, before the salaries of the three gift shop employees and any Federal income taxes, is $300,000. The salaries of the employees total $80,000.
   c. Innovation University, Inc., a private institution, has placed vending machines in the student dormitories and academic buildings on campus. In recognition of recent tuition increases, the university has adopted a policy of merely trying to recover its costs associated with the vending machine activity. For the current year, however, the net income of the activity, before any Federal income taxes, is $75,000.

27. **LO.6** For each of the following organizations, determine its UBTI and any related UBIT.
   a. Connect, Inc., an exempt organization, provides food for the homeless. It operates a thrift store that sells used clothing to the general public. The thrift shop is staffed solely by four salaried employees. All of the clothes it sells are received as contributions. The $100,000 profit generated for the year by the thrift shop is used in Connect's mission of providing food to the homeless.
   b. Small, Inc., an exempt organization, recorded gross unrelated business income of $900 and unrelated business expenses of $400.
   c. In Care, Inc., is a § 501(c)(3) exempt organization. It owns a convenience store and gas pumps, which it received as a bequest from a patron. The store/gas pumps entity is operated as StopBy, a C corporation. Because StopBy is profitable, In Care hires a manager and several employees to run the entity. For the current year, StopBy's profit is $640,000. All of this amount is distributed by StopBy to In Care to use in carrying out its exempt purpose.

28. **LO.6** Falcon Basketball League, an exempt organization, is a youth basketball league for children ages 12 through 14. The league has existed for 30 years. In the past, revenue for operations has been provided through community fund-raising and the sale of snacks at the games by the parents. Due to a projected revenue shortfall of approximately $5,000, the governing board has decided to charge admission to the basketball games of $1.00 for adults and $0.50 for children. Communications

a. Will the admission charge affect Falcon's exempt status? Explain.

b. What are the tax consequences to Falcon of the net income from snack sales and the new admission fee?

c. As the volunteer treasurer of the Falcon League, prepare a memo for the entity's board in which you explain the effect, if any, of the admission fee policy on Falcon's exempt status.

29. **LO.6** Forward, Inc., is an exempt organization that assists disabled individuals by training them in digital TV repair. Used digital TVs are donated to Forward, Inc., by both organizations and individuals. Some of the donated digital TVs are operational, but others are in disrepair. After being used in the training program, the digital TVs, all of which are now operational, are sold to the general public. Forward's revenues and expenses for the current period are reported as follows.

Contributions	$ 700,000
Revenues from digital TV sales	3,600,000
Administrative expenses	500,000
Materials and supplies for digital TV repairs	800,000
Utilities	25,000
Wages paid to disabled individuals in the training program (at minimum-wage rate)	1,200,000
Rent for building and equipment	250,000

Any revenues not expended during the current period are deposited in a reserve fund to finance future activities.

a. Is the digital TV repair and sales activity an unrelated trade or business? Explain.

b. Calculate the net income of Forward, Inc., and the related Federal income tax liability, if any.

30. **LO.6** Save the Squirrels, Inc., a § 501(c)(3) organization that feeds squirrels in municipal parks, receives a $250,000 contribution from Animal Feed, Inc., a for-profit entity that sells animal feed. In exchange for the contribution, Save the Squirrels will identify Animal Feed as a major supporter in its monthly newsletter. Determine Save the Squirrels's UBTI and any related UBIT under the following independent assumptions.

a. Save the Squirrels receives no other similar payments.

b. Save the Squirrels agrees to identify Animal Feed as a major supporter and to include a half-page advertisement for Animal Feed products in its monthly newsletter as a result of the contribution.

31. **LO.6** Faith Community Church is exempt from Federal income taxation under § 501(c)(3). To supplement its contribution revenue, it holds bingo games on Saturday nights. It holds all of the licenses and permits required to do so. Critical Thinking

The net income from the bingo games is $90,000. Of these funds, $60,000 is used to support the ministry of the church. The balance of $30,000 is invested in Faith's endowment fund for church music.

Faith Community Church is located in a resort city where bingo games can be conducted by churches, charities, and for-profit entities.

a. Will conducting the bingo games affect the exempt status of the church? Explain.

b. Calculate the Federal tax liability, if any, associated with the bingo games.

32. **LO.6** Fish, Inc., an exempt organization, reports unrelated business income of $500,000 (before any charitable contribution deduction). Fish makes charitable contributions to other organizations of $54,000, of which $38,000 is associated with the unrelated trade or business.

a. Calculate Fish's unrelated business taxable income (UBTI).

b. Express your computation in part (a) as a Microsoft Excel formula. Use the variable names "UBTI" for unrelated business taxable income, "UBI_BEFORE" for UBI before the contribution deduction, and "CHAR" for the amount of charitable contributions before the 10% limit.

c. Assume instead that the charitable contributions are $41,000. Calculate any UBTI.

33. **LO.6** Save, Inc., an exempt organization, sells the following assets during the tax year. Determine the effect of these transactions on Save's unrelated business taxable income.

Asset	Gain (Loss)	Use
Land and building	$100,000	In exempt purpose
Land	25,000	In exempt purpose
Equipment	(12,000)	Leased to a taxable entity
Automobile	(9,000)	Leased to a taxable entity

34. **LO.7** Seagull, Inc., a § 501(c)(3) exempt organization, uses a tax year that ends on October 31. Seagull's gross receipts are $600,000, and related expenses are $580,000.

a. Is Seagull required to file an annual Form 990?

b. If so, what is the due date?

35. **LO.7** Wong, Inc., a § 501(c)(3) organization, is a private foundation with a tax year that ends on May 31. Gross receipts for the fiscal year are $180,000, and the related expenses are $160,000.

a. Is the entity required to file an annual information return?

b. If so, what form is used?

c. If so, what is the due date?

d. How would your answers in parts (a), (b), and (c) change if Wong were an exempt organization that was not a private foundation?

Research Problems

Note: Solutions to the Research Problems can be prepared by using the Thomson Reuters Checkpoint™ online tax research database, which accompanies this textbook. Solutions can also be prepared by using research materials found in a typical tax library.

Communications

Research Problem 1. Wonderful Wilderness, Inc., is a tax-exempt organization. Its mission is to "make the world a greener place through education, research, exploration, and restoration."

Martín Morales, the chief financial officer, presents you with the following information. Wonderful Wilderness raises funds to support its mission in a variety of ways, including contributions and membership fees. As part of this effort, Wonderful Wilderness develops and maintains mailing lists of its members, donors, catalog purchasers, and other supporters.

Wonderful Wilderness holds exclusive ownership rights to its mailing lists. To acquire the names of additional prospective members and supporters, Wonderful Wilderness occasionally exchanges membership lists with other organizations. In addition, Wonderful Wilderness permits other tax-exempt organizations and commercial entities to pay a fee, identified in an annually updated schedule, to use its mailing lists on a one-time basis per transaction.

Martín is aware that the Federal income tax law applies a UBIT. He is also aware of the § 512(b)(2) provision that excludes royalties from the UBIT. An IRS agent has raised the issue that the revenue from the use of the mailing lists by other entities may be taxable as unrelated business income. Martín wants you to research this issue.

Write a letter to Martín that contains your findings, and prepare a memo for the tax research files. Wonderful Wilderness's address is 100 Wilderness Way, Pocatello, ID 83209.

Use internet tax resources to address the following questions. Look for reliable websites and blogs of the IRS and other government agencies, media outlets, businesses, tax professionals, academics, think tanks, and political outlets.

Research Problem 2. Send your instructor a table of the number of recognized tax-exempt organizations under § 501(c). Organize your list by paragraph number [e.g., § 501(c)(7)]. Show only the paragraphs with the five largest numbers of qualifying entities [i.e., starting with § 501(c)(3)]. The most recent *IRS Data Book* will be useful in your research.

Communications

Research Problem 3. With respect to the constitutionality of a church to engage in political activities, submit to your instructor a two-page paper defining and tracing the history of the so-called *Johnson Amendment*.

Communications
Critical Thinking

Research Problem 4. Send your instructor a graph of the number of tax returns reporting UBI, and the UBIT collected from those returns, for the last 20 years. Use five-year intervals in your analysis.

Data Analytics

Research Problem 5. Verify the exempt status of the symphony orchestra that performs closest to your home. Who are its three highest-paid individuals? Send an e-mail to your instructor summarizing your results and explaining how you found this information. *Hint:* At **irs.gov**, use the query Tax Exempt Organization Search.

Communications

Research Problem 6. Obtain the following information concerning the Denver Zoo:

Data Analytics

- Locate the entity's website.
- Under what paragraph of § 501(c) do you believe the organization is exempt from Federal income tax?
- Use the organization's Form 990 to determine the entity's total budget, its expenditures for educational programs, and the amount of compensation paid to officers and directors.

Research Problem 7. With respect to § 501(c)(3) exempt organizations, send your instructor a table showing information about the unrelated business income that the entities generated for the latest reported tax year. The most recent *IRS Data Book* will be useful in your research. Stratifying the data by the source of UBI (e.g., health care, rental operations), indicate for any five sources of this income:

Communications
Data Analytics

- The number of entities that report this type of UBI.
- The UBI and UBTI amounts reported.
- The UBIT assessed.

Communications **Research Problem 8.** The Fiscal Year 2022 priorities for the Tax Exempt & Government Entities (TE/GE) Division of the IRS are available on the IRS website (**irs.gov/pub/irs-pdf/p5313.pdf**). One of the priorities for the year is to "Leverage Technology and Data Analytics" (including to detect emerging issues using data analytics and to deploy robotic process automation to improve efficiency).

Read this section of the report and discuss at least two specific actions the TE/GE division might take to meet this priority. Submit your answer in an email to your instructor.

Becker CPA Review Questions

Becker

1. Unrelated business income (UBI):
   a. includes unrelated income from an activity where all the work is performed by volunteers.
   b. is not created if the activity results in a loss.
   c. includes proceeds from the sale of merchandise received as gifts or contributions.
   d. excludes income from research by a college or hospital.

2. Which of the following is a false statement?
   a. An annual information return (Form 990) stating gross income, receipts, contributions, and disbursements is required of many exempt organizations that are exempt from tax.
   b. For organizations that normally have less than $50,000 in annual gross receipts, a Form 990 or 990–EZ is not required; however, an "electronic postcard" (Form 990–N) is filed with the IRS and provides only limited information.
   c. An organization operated primarily for the purposes of carrying on a trade or business for profit can claim exemption from tax if all of its profits are payable to exempt organizations.
   d. If an organization fails to file the required return for three consecutive years, the tax-exempt status of the organization will be revoked.

3. Which of the following organizations does not qualify as a § 501(c)(3) tax-exempt organization?
   a. Churches.
   b. Schools.
   c. Charitable hospitals.
   d. Political parties.

4. For which of the following types of tax-exempt organizations are contributions deductible on the donor's Federal income tax return?
   a. A § 501(c)(1) Federal credit union.
   b. A § 501(c)(2) title-holding corporation for an exempt organization.
   c. A § 501(c)(3) organization.
   d. A § 501(c)(7) social club.

Chapter 26

Multistate Corporate Taxation

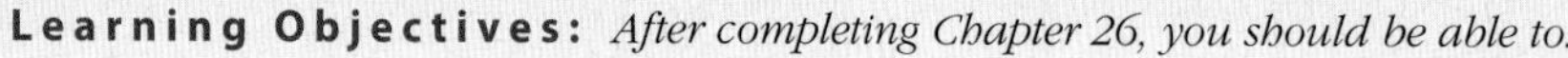

Learning Objectives: *After completing Chapter 26, you should be able to:*

- **LO.1** Explain the computation of a multistate corporation's state income tax liability.
- **LO.2** Explain nexus and its role in state income taxation.
- **LO.3** Distinguish between allocation and apportionment of a multistate corporation's taxable income.
- **LO.4** Describe the nature and treatment of business and nonbusiness income.
- **LO.5** Discuss the sales, payroll, and property apportionment factors.
- **LO.6** Apply the unitary method of state income taxation.
- **LO.7** Discuss the states' income tax treatment of S corporations, partnerships, and LLCs.
- **LO.8** Describe other commonly encountered state and local taxes on businesses.
- **LO.9** Recognize tax planning opportunities available to minimize a corporation's state and local tax liability.

Chapter Outline

Making a Multistate Location Decision

LocalCo has customers in most U.S. states. It does not employ a traditional sales force. Instead, it sells its products exclusively through internet solicitations and its elaborate website.

LocalCo has two product lines: smartphone accessories, which it manufactures in Alabama, and various sports-themed apparel items, all of which are produced in California. LocalCo has been quite profitable in the past, and it holds a sizable investment portfolio made up chiefly of U.S. Treasury securities. Banking, payroll, and other administrative operations are located in rural New York State, where the entity is incorporated. LocalCo's rank-and-file employees receive compensation packages that are below the national median, but its top 10 executives are highly paid.

In an effort to "go green," LocalCo wants to hold down its costs for shipping raw materials to its manufacturing facilities and for sending its sold goods to customers. As a result, it is considering the construction of a sizable new multifunction building. Ideally, the new facility would have access to both interstate highways and a reliable airport with excess capacity for freight operations.

How will LocalCo's expansion decision be affected by state and local tax considerations?

Read the chapter and formulate your response.

Although most of this textbook concentrates on the effects of the Federal income tax law upon the computation of a taxpayer's annual tax liability, a variety of taxes apply to most business taxpayers. For instance, a multinational corporation may be subject to tax in a number of different countries (see Chapter 27). Furthermore, estimates are that at least 40 percent of the income tax dollars paid by business taxpayers go to state and local authorities.

U.S. state and local governments collect more than $6 trillion in taxes each year; this comes to more than $18,000 per individual citizen. Individual income taxes account for about 30 percent of state and local tax collections. Local property taxes bring in about one-third of all revenues, and corporate income taxes bring in about 5 percent.

State/Local Taxes in Context

Businesses operate in a multistate environment for a variety of reasons. Nontax motivations are the key drivers of location decisions about where to build new plants or distribution centers or whether to move communications and data processing facilities and corporate headquarters. For instance, a business typically wants to be close to its largest markets and to operate in a positive private- and public-sector business climate where it has access to well-trained and reasonably priced labor, suppliers and support operations, sources of natural resources, communication facilities, and transportation networks.

Location decisions are sometimes motivated by multistate tax considerations, including the following:

- Tax credits and other incentives that encourage businesses to relocate, expand, or retain jobs in the area. Some of the incentives include *clawback* provisions where the tax savings granted must be returned to the state by the business if new job targets are not met or construction projects not completed.
- The compliance burdens created by each new level of tax compliance. For instance, how many tax returns must be filed by a three-shareholder S corporation operating in 15 states?
- The extent to which a local political climate encourages tax burdens on visitors and others who have no direct say in the election of local politicians.

This chapter reviews the basic concepts of state and multistate income taxation, and it discusses the major areas in which tax planning can reduce a corporation's overall state tax burden.[1] The chapter concludes with a review of other types of taxes used by the U.S. states, with a special focus on sales and use taxes.

26-1 Corporate State Income Taxation

Forty-six states and the District of Columbia impose a tax based on a C corporation's taxable income. Because each state is free to create its own tax rules, the taxpayer could be faced with 47 entirely different sets of state tax provisions.[2] All of the states require separate filing of tax returns (rather than linking their filings with other states and/or with the IRS).

26-1a Computing State Income Tax

LO.1

Explain the computation of a multistate corporation's state income tax liability.

In more than 40 of the states that impose a corporate income tax, the starting point in computing the tax base is taxable income as reflected on the Federal corporate income tax return (Form 1120). Those states whose computation of state taxable income is not coupled to the Federal tax return have their own state-specific definitions of gross and taxable income. Nonetheless, even these states typically adopt most Federal income and deduction provisions.

[1]Some states refer to their tax on corporate income as a franchise tax, a business tax, a license tax, or a business profits tax.

[2]The District of Columbia operates in much the same manner as a state and imposes a tax based on income. Four states impose no corporate income tax at all: Nevada, South Dakota, Washington, and Wyoming. Corporations, however, are subject to a business and occupation tax in Washington. A few states base the tax on the entity's gross receipts, not on net income.

Although Federal tax law plays a significant role in the computation of state taxable income, there is a wide disparity in both the methods used to determine a state's taxable income and the tax rates imposed on that income. Only a few states apply more than one or two tax rates to taxable income, so there is little progressivity to these tax systems.

State tax credits typically are designed to encourage increased hiring and investment in local facilities. Cities and states often use targeted tax credits to entice businesses to expand or relocate within their borders. For instance, a state might offer a $50,000 credit for each new job created by the taxpayer or a 15 percent credit for taxpayers who purchase automobiles that were assembled in the state.

Generally, the accounting period and methods used by a corporation for state tax purposes must be consistent with those used on the Federal return. States often apply different rules, however, in identifying the members of a group filing a consolidated return and the income of each group member that is subject to tax.

Virtually all of the states that levy an income tax require notification of the final settlement of a Federal income tax audit. In addition, some states share their audit results with other states. State authorities then adjust the originally calculated state tax liability to account for these out-of-state audit changes.

The formula used by a multistate corporation to determine its tax liability in a typical state is illustrated in Exhibit 26.1.

26-1b **State Modifications**

Federal taxable income is generally the starting point in computing the state's income tax base, but state adjustments or modifications often are made to Federal taxable income to:

- Reflect differences between state and Federal tax statutes.
- Remove income that a state is constitutionally prohibited from taxing.

Exhibit 26.2 lists the most frequently encountered state income tax modifications. In computing the taxable income for a given state, only some of these modifications may apply.

26-1c **The UDITPA and the Multistate Tax Commission**

The Multistate Tax Compact is a model law designed to promote uniformity in administering state income tax laws among the states. Part of the Compact includes the Uniform Division of Income for Tax Purposes Act (**UDITPA**), last revised in 2015, which relates to the assignment of income among the states for corporations that maintain operations in

Exhibit 26.1 **Computing Corporate State Income Tax Liability**

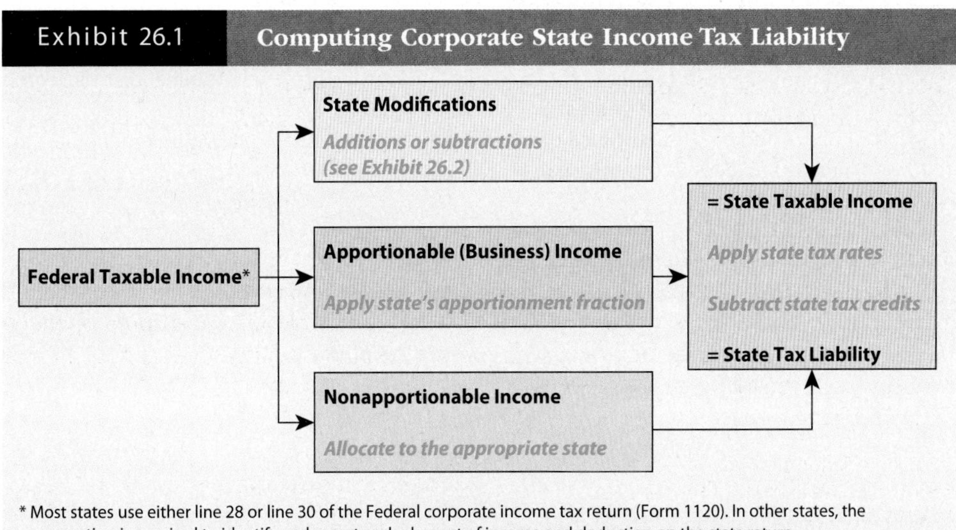

* Most states use either line 28 or line 30 of the Federal corporate income tax return (Form 1120). In other states, the corporation is required to identify and report each element of income and deduction on the state return.

Exhibit 26.2 **Common State Corporate Income Tax Modifications**

Addition Modifications

- Interest income received on state and municipal obligations and any other interest income that is exempt from Federal income tax. For this purpose, some states exempt interest earned on their own obligations.
- Expenses deducted in computing Federal taxable income that are directly or indirectly related to U.S. obligations.
- Income-based franchise and income taxes imposed by any state and the District of Columbia that were deducted in computing Federal taxable income.
- The amount by which the Federal deductions for depreciation, amortization, or depletion exceed those permitted by the state.
- The amount by which the state gain or loss from the disposal of assets differs from the Federal gain or loss. Due to the difference in permitted depreciation methods and other adjustments, a corporation's assets may have different Federal and state tax bases. This adjustment is not necessary if the state and Federal basis provisions are identical.
- Adjustments required as a result of different elections being made for state and Federal purposes. Examples of such elections include the methods under which income from installment sales or long-term contracts is determined.
- Federal net operating loss deduction, if the starting point in the computation of taxable income is Federal taxable income after special deductions.

Subtraction Modifications

- Interest on U.S. obligations or obligations of Federal agencies to the extent included in Federal taxable income but exempt from state income taxes under U.S. law.
- Expenses that are directly or indirectly related to the state and municipal interest that is taxable for state purposes.
- Refunds of franchise and income taxes imposed by any state and the District of Columbia, to the extent included in Federal taxable income.
- The amount by which the state deductions for depreciation, amortization, or depletion exceed the deductions permitted for Federal tax purposes.
- Adjustments required as a result of different elections being made for state and Federal purposes, as above.
- Dividends received from other U.S. corporations, to the extent included in Federal taxable income.
- Net operating loss deduction as determined for state tax purposes.

more than one state (multistate corporations). Many states have adopted the provisions of the UDITPA, either by adopting in full the Multistate Tax Compact or by modeling their laws after the provisions of the UDITPA.

Computing State Taxable Income

Example 1

Blue Corporation is subject to tax only in State A. The starting point in computing Blue's taxable income in State A is Federal taxable income. Modifications then are made to reflect, among other provisions, the exempt status of interest on State B obligations, all dividends received from other U.S. corporations, and the disallowance of a deduction for state income taxes. Blue generated the following income and deductions this year.

Sales	$1,500,000
Interest on Federal obligations	50,000
Interest on municipal obligations of State B	100,000
Dividends received from 30% owned U.S. corporations	200,000
Total income	$1,850,000
Expenses related to Federal obligations	$ 1,000
Expenses related to municipal obligations of State B	5,000
State income tax expense	50,000
Depreciation allowed for Federal tax purposes (the deduction allowed for state purposes is $300,000)	400,000
Other allowable deductions	1,000,000
Total deductions	$1,456,000

continued

Blue's taxable income for Federal and state purposes is computed as follows.

Federal Taxable Income	
Sales	$1,500,000
Interest on Federal obligations	50,000
Dividends received from U.S. corporations	200,000
Total income	$1,750,000
Expenses related to Federal obligations	$ 1,000
State income tax expense	50,000
Depreciation	400,000
Other allowable deductions	1,000,000
Total deductions	$1,451,000
Taxable income before special deductions	$ 299,000
Less: Dividends received deduction (65% × $200,000)	(130,000)
Federal taxable income	$ 169,000

State A Taxable Income	
Federal taxable income	$169,000
Addition Modifications	
Interest on State B obligations	100,000
State income tax expense	50,000
Excess depreciation deduction allowed for Federal purposes ($400,000 − $300,000)	100,000
Expenses related to Federal obligations	1,000
Subtraction Modifications	
Expenses related to State B obligations	(5,000)
Dividends from other corporations, to extent included in Federal taxable income ($200,000 − $130,000)	(70,000)
Interest on Federal obligations	(50,000)
State A taxable income	$295,000

Example 2

Continue with the facts of Example 1, but assume that the $100,000 of municipal bond interest (and related expenses) are related to obligations issued by State A (rather than State B). The computation of Federal taxable income is unaffected by this change. Because State A exempts interest on its own obligations from taxation, Blue's State A taxable income now is $200,000.

State A Taxable Income	
Federal taxable income	$169,000
Addition Modifications	
State income tax expense	50,000
Excess depreciation deduction allowed for Federal purposes ($400,000 − $300,000)	100,000
Expenses related to Federal obligations	1,000
Subtraction Modifications	
Dividends from other U.S. corporations, to extent included in Federal taxable income ($200,000 − $130,000)	(70,000)
Interest on Federal obligations	(50,000)
State A taxable income	$200,000

The **Multistate Tax Commission (MTC)** is an agency created by the Multistate Tax Compact, made up of tax administrators from many of the states. As states enacted the Multistate Tax Compact, first drafted in 1966, they became members of the MTC. The MTC promotes uniformity in tax administration procedures, advocates for the equitable apportionment of tax bases, and facilitates joint audits of taxpayers. When the MTC drafts model legislation or a position statement, the member states propose its adoption to their respective legislatures or tax authorities. The majority of MTC member states adopt the proposals with no exceptions or only minor changes.[3]

LO.2

Explain nexus and its role in state income taxation.

26-1d Jurisdiction to Impose Tax: Nexus and Public Law 86–272

The state in which a business is incorporated (i.e., its state of *legal domicile*) has the jurisdiction to tax the corporation regardless of the volume of its business activity within the state. Whether a state can tax the income of a business that operates within its borders but is incorporated in a different state (i.e., the state in which the business has a *commercial domicile*) usually depends on the level of activity of the taxpayer in the state and on state law and principles of the U.S. Constitution.

The term **nexus** describes the degree of business activity that must be present before a taxing jurisdiction has the right to impose a tax on an out-of-state entity's income. Generally, each state defines nexus differently. Typically, sufficient nexus is present when a corporation derives income from sources within the state, owns or leases property in the state, employs personnel in the state, or has physical or financial capital there.

Public Law 86–272 (P.L. 86–272) limits the states' right to impose an income tax on certain interstate activities.[4] This Federal law prohibits a state from taxing a business whose only connection with the state is to solicit orders for sales of tangible personal property that are sent outside the state for approval or rejection. If approved, the orders must be filled and shipped by the business from a point outside the state.

Only sales of tangible personal property are immune from taxation under this law, however. Leases, rentals, and other dispositions of tangible personal property are not protected activities. Moreover, dispositions of real property and intangible property, as well as sales of services, are not protected by P.L. 86–272.

Business activity that involves tangible personal property and consists merely of solicitation is immune from taxation. The statute does not define the term *solicitation*, but the Supreme Court has held that *solicitation of orders* includes any explicit verbal request for orders and any speech or conduct that implicitly invites an order.[5] The Court also created a *de minimis* rule, allowing immunity from nexus where a limited amount of solicitation occurs.

P.L. 86–272 was enacted by Congress in 1959. Technology changes since 1959 allow for business practices not imagined when P.L. 86–272 was drafted. For example, today customers normally have a choice between tangible books and intangible digital books. Many other transactions and activities that could occur only in person before the internet existed can now be completed online. These changes raised new questions including what solicitation means and what types of activities handled by a seller's website are not protected by P.L. 86–272. In 2021, the Multistate Tax Commission released an updated version of its *Statement of Information Concerning Practices of Multistate Tax Commission and Signatory States Under Public Law 86–272* to address activities conducted via the internet including the implications of providing a set of frequently asked questions (FAQs) on a vendor's website and the placement of "cookies" on customer computers.[6]

Under the revised Statement, if a seller's website provides merely a set of static FAQs, P.L. 86–272 protection exists. If instead, the vendor places internet "cookies" on the customer's website that enable promotion of new products and gathering of information to update production schedules, P.L. 86–272 protection no longer exists.

Exhibit 26.3 summarizes the activities the MTC has identified as directly related to solicitation (protected activities) and activities unrelated to solicitation (which establish income tax nexus for the entity).

[3] Many of the states that are not members of the Multistate Tax Compact still model their laws after the UDITPA and the MTC regulations. See **mtc.gov** and **tinyurl.com/uditpa**.

[4] 15 U.S.C. §§ 381–385.

[5] *Wisconsin Department of Revenue v. William Wrigley, Jr., Co.*, 505 U.S. 214 (1992).

[6] MTC, P.L. 86–272 Statement revised and adopted August 4, 2021; **mtc.gov/Uniformity/Project-Teams/Statement-on-PL-86-272-Adopted.aspx**.

Exhibit 26.3 Common Nexus Definitions under P.L. 86–272

General Rule P.L. 86–272 immunity from income tax nexus applies for sales of tangible personal property, where the seller's activities are ancillary to the order-solicitation process.

Activities That Usually Do Not Create Nexus

- Advertising campaigns.
- Carrying free samples only for display or distribution.
- Owning or furnishing automobiles, phones, and computers to salespersons.
- Passing inquiries or complaints on to the home office.
- Maintaining a sample or display room for two weeks or less during the year.
- Maintaining a website to solicit orders of tangible personal property that are sent outside the state for approval or rejection and, if approved, are shipped from a point outside of that state.
- Posting of static FAQs on the seller's website.

Activities Usually Sufficient to Establish Nexus

- Approving or rejecting orders.
- Making repairs or providing maintenance.
- Collecting delinquent accounts; investigating creditworthiness.
- Conducting installation or supervising installation.
- Conducting training classes, seminars, or lectures for persons other than sales personnel.
- Picking up or replacing damaged or returned property.
- Hiring, training, or supervising personnel other than sales employees.
- Providing shipping information and coordinating deliveries.
- Owning, leasing, maintaining, or otherwise using any of the following facilities or property in the state.
  - Real estate.
  - Parts department.
  - Employment office.
  - Meeting place for directors, officers, or employees.
  - Purchasing office.
  - Warehouse.
  - Call center.
  - Mobile retailing (e.g., trucks with driver-salespersons).
- Maintaining a website where interactions with in-state customers extend beyond solicitation of orders of tangible personal property (e.g., by providing post-sale assistance to in-state customers via either electronic chat or e-mail that customers initiate by clicking on an icon on the business's website).
- Remotely fixing or upgrading products previously purchased by in-state customers by directly transmitting code or other electronic instructions to those products via the Internet.

26-1e **Nexus in Today's Economy**

States and the MTC have issued regulations and interpretations of P.L. 86–272, but the law is not robust enough to account for many of today's economic transactions (e.g., sales of realty and intangible assets, net income from services, and some e-commerce sales). As a result, many states contend that a broader definition of income tax nexus is needed. This alternative approach often is referred to as *economic nexus* because it is triggered by business and other activities, not by more traditional legal connections or physical presence.

Several states, following an MTC model statute, automatically assign nexus to a taxpayer that exceeds at least one of the following thresholds for the tax year:

- $50,000 of property.
- $50,000 of payroll.
- $500,000 of sales.
- 25% of total property.
- 25% of total payroll.
- 25% of total sales.

These "factor presence nexus" standards provide a measure of the sales or solicitation activity in the state that indicates a "sufficient" economic presence to trigger income taxation there, even if the business has little or no physical presence in the state. The "factor presence nexus" standard provides some uniformity among the states as to measuring the taxpayer's business activities.

Concept Summary 26.1

Multitaxate Taxation

1. For a profitable business entity that operates in multiple U.S. states, at least 40 percent of the total tax expense may be made up of levies by state and local governments.
2. State and local tax incentives might be used to accomplish political goals or to provide incentives for businesses to remain in, or relocate to, the taxing jurisdiction.
3. A U.S. state can apply an income tax only on a business that has a sufficient presence ("nexus") with the state.
4. Multistate income tax planning involves the reduction of the overall state and local tax burden. This may be the result of being subject to tax in the fewest number of states or of reducing the tax burden in a particular state.

LO.3

Distinguish between allocation and apportionment of a multistate corporation's taxable income.

26-2 Apportionment and Allocation of Income

A corporation that conducts business activities in more than one state must determine the portion of its net income that is subject to tax by each state. A corporation that has established sufficient nexus with another state generally must both **apportion** and **allocate** its income.

Apportionment is a means by which a corporation's taxable income is divided among the states in which it conducts business. Under an apportionment procedure, a corporation determines allowable income and deductions for the company as a whole and then apportions its income among the states in which it has nexus, according to an approved formula.

Allocation is a method under which specific components of a corporation's income, net of related expenses, are directly assigned to a certain state. Allocable income is assigned to a single state, whereas apportionable income is divided among several states. Nonapportionable (nonbusiness) income generally includes either:

- Income or losses derived from the sale of nonbusiness real or tangible property, or
- Income or losses in the form of rentals and royalties from nonbusiness real or tangible personal property. Rentals and royalties constituting a business are apportioned.

Nonapportionable income is allocated to the state where the property that generated the income or loss is located.

Example 3

Green Corporation conducts business in States N, O, P, and Q. Green's $900,000 taxable income consists of $800,000 apportionable income and $100,000 allocable income generated from transactions conducted in State Q. Green's sales, property, and payroll are evenly divided among the four states, and the states all employ an identical apportionment formula. As a result, $200,000 of Green's income is taxable in each of States N, O, and P. Green is subject to income tax on $300,000 of income in State Q.

Apportionable income	$800,000
Apportionment percentage (apportionable income is divided equally among the four states)	× 25%
Income apportioned to each state	$200,000

	State N	State O	State P	State Q
Income apportioned	$200,000	$200,000	$200,000	$200,000
Income allocated	–0–	–0–	–0–	100,000
Taxable income	$200,000	$200,000	$200,000	$300,000

26-2a The Apportionment Procedure

Apportionment assumes that the production of the taxpayer's income is linked to business activity, and the laws of each state define one or more factors believed to indicate the amount of corporate activity conducted within the state. However, apportionment often does not provide a uniform division of an organization's income based on its business activity because each state is free to choose the type and number of factors it believes are indicative of the business activity conducted within its borders. As a result, a business may be subject to state income tax on more or less than 100 percent of its Federal taxable income.

An equally incongruous consequence of apportionment may occur when the operations in a state result in a loss.

Red Corporation's operations include two manufacturing facilities, one in State A and one in State B. The plant located in State A generated $500,000 of income, and the plant located in State B generated a loss of $200,000. Based on this information, Red's total taxable income is $300,000.

Applying the statutes of each state, Red determines that its apportionment factors for States A and B are 65% and 35%, respectively. As a result, Red's income is apportioned to the states as follows.

$$\text{Income apportioned to State A}: \ 65\% \times \$300,000 = \$195,000$$

$$\text{Income apportioned to State B}: \ 35\% \times \$300,000 = \$105,000$$

Red is subject to tax in State B on $105,000 of income, even though the operations conducted in that state resulted in a loss.

26-2b Apportionable Income

LO.4

Describe the nature and treatment of business and nonbusiness income.

Apportionable income is assigned among the states by using an apportionment formula. In contrast, *nonapportionable income* is allocated to the state where the income-producing asset is located. For instance, income derived from the rental of nonbusiness real property generally is allocated to the state where the property is located.

Example 5

Jupiter Corporation, a manufacturer of various automobile parts, is a multistate taxpayer that has nexus with States P and Q. During the taxable year, Jupiter's net sales of parts were $900,000; $600,000 of these sales were made in State P, and $300,000 were made in State Q. The corporation also received $90,000 from the rental of nonbusiness real property located in State P. As a result, Jupiter's Federal taxable income is $990,000.

Applying the statutes of each state, Jupiter determines that its apportionment factors for States P and Q are 65% and 42%, respectively. Jupiter's taxable income for each state is determined as follows.

Income apportioned to State P	65% × $900,000 =	$585,000	
Income allocated to State P		90,000	
P taxable income			$ 675,000
Income apportioned to State Q	42% × $900,000 = Q taxable income		378,000
Aggregate state taxable income			$1,053,000

Jupiter's aggregate state taxable income exceeds its Federal taxable income. Tax rules in the two states differed, such that the apportionment factors totaled to more than 100%.

Apportionable income arises from the taxpayer's regular course of business or constitutes an integral part of the taxpayer's regular business.[7] In determining whether an

[7] MTC Reg. IV.1.(a).

item of income is apportionable (business) income, state courts have developed a variety of approaches to determine a taxpayer's "regular course of business."[8]

Nonapportionable income is "all income other than apportionable income."[9] Usually, nonapportionable income comprises passive and portfolio income, such as dividends, interest, rents, royalties, and certain capital gains. However, passive activity or portfolio income may be apportionable when the acquisition, management, and disposition of the underlying property constitute an integral part of the taxpayer's regular business operation.[10]

A few states fail to distinguish between apportionable and nonapportionable income. In these states, all of a corporation's income is deemed to be subject to apportionment.

Apportionable Income

Example 6

Scarlet Corporation is subject to income tax in several states. Scarlet earned $2,500,000 from the sales of its products and $1,000,000 from the sale of assets that were unrelated to its regular business operations.

In the states that distinguish between business and nonbusiness income, $2,500,000 of Scarlet's income is apportioned to the state according to the state's apportionment formula. The gain on the sale of the nonbusiness assets is allocated to the state where the assets were located. In the states that subject a corporation's entire income to apportionment, $3,500,000 ($2,500,000 + $1,000,000) is apportioned among the states in which the taxpayer conducts business.

Example 7

Gray Corporation owns and operates two manufacturing facilities, one in State A and the other in State B. Due to a temporary decline in sales, Gray has rented 10% of its State A facility to an unaffiliated corporation. Gray generated $100,000 net rent income and $900,000 income from manufacturing.

Both States A and B classify the rent income as allocable income. By applying the statutes of each state, Gray determines that its apportionment factors are 40% for State A and 60% for State B.

Income Subject to Tax in State A	
Taxable income	$1,000,000
Less: Allocable income	(100,000)
Apportionable income	$ 900,000
Times: Apportionment factor	× 40%
Income apportioned to State A	$ 360,000
Plus: Income allocated to State A	100,000
Income subject to tax in State A	$ 460,000

Income Subject to Tax in State B	
Taxable income	$1,000,000
Less: Allocable income	(100,000)
Apportionable income	$ 900,000
Times: Apportionment factor	× 60%
Income apportioned to State B	$ 540,000
Plus: Income allocated to State B	–0–
Income subject to tax in State B	$ 540,000

[8] *Atlantic Richfield Co. v. State of Colorado and Joseph F. Dolan*, 601 P.2d 628 (Colo.S.Ct., 1979); *Appeal of A. Epstein and Sons, Inc.* (Cal.State Bd. of Equalization, 1984).

[9] UDITPA § 1(e).

[10] MTC Reg. IV.1.(a)(5).

Apportionable Income

Continue with the facts of Example 7, but assume that B does not distinguish between apportionable and nonapportionable income. As a result, all of Gray's income is apportionable in State B.

Gray properly determines that its apportionment factors are 40% for A and 58% for B. In this situation, Gray's income that is subject to tax is greater than $1,000,000.

Income Subject to Tax in State A, computed in Example 7	$ 460,000
Income Subject to Tax in State B	
Apportionable income	$1,000,000
Times: Apportionment factor	× 58%
Income apportioned to State B	$ 580,000

26-2c Apportionment Factors: Elements and Planning

LO.5

Discuss the sales, payroll, and property apportionment factors.

Apportionable income is divided among the states by determining the appropriate apportionment percentage for each state that has a right to tax the entity. To determine the apportionment percentage for each state, a ratio is established for each of the factors included in the state's apportionment formula. Each ratio is calculated by comparing the level of a specific business activity within a state to the total corporate activity of that type. The ratios then are summed, averaged, and appropriately weighted to determine the taxpayer's apportionment percentage for a specific state.

The traditional three-factor formula equally weights sales, property, and payroll.[11] However, fewer than 10 states use an equal three-factor formula; in all other states, the sales factor receives more than a one-third weight.

The use of a higher-weighted sales factor tends to pull a larger percentage of an out-of-state corporation's income into the taxing jurisdiction of the state because the corporation's major activity within the state—the sales of its goods and services—is weighted more heavily than are its payroll and property activities. Overweighting the sales factor, accordingly, provides income tax relief for corporations that are headquartered in the state. Those corporations generally own significantly more property and incur more payroll costs (factors that are given less weight in the apportionment formula) within the state than do out-of-state corporations.

Example 9

Luna Corporation realized $500,000 of taxable income from the sales of its products in States A and B. Luna's activities in both states establish nexus for income tax purposes. Luna reports the following sales, payroll, and property in two states.

	State A	State B	Total
Sales	$1,250,000	$750,000	$2,000,000
Property	2,500,000	-0-	2,500,000
Payroll	1,500,000	-0-	1,500,000

continued

[11] Certain industries, such as financial services institutions, insurance companies, air and motor carriers, pipeline companies, and communications providers, typically are required to use apportionment formulas with different factors and weightings.

If State B uses an *equally weighted three-factor* apportionment formula, $62,500 of Luna's taxable income is apportioned to State B.

Sales ($750,000 ÷ $2,000,000)	=	37.5%
Property ($0 ÷ $2,500,000)	=	-0-
Payroll ($0 ÷ $1,500,000)	=	-0-
Sum of apportionment factors		37.5%
Average	÷	3
Apportionment factor for State B		12.5%
Taxable income	×	$500,000
Income apportioned to State B		$ 62,500

If State B uses a *double-weighted sales factor* in its three-factor apportionment formula, $93,750 of Luna's taxable income is apportioned to State B.

Sales ($750,000 ÷ $2,000,000)	=	37.5% × 2	=	75%
Property ($0 ÷ $2,500,000)	=			-0-
Payroll ($0 ÷ $1,500,000)	=			-0-
Sum of apportionment factors				75%
Average			÷	4
Apportionment factor for State B				18.75%
Taxable income			×	$500,000
Income apportioned to State B				$ 93,750

When a state uses a double-weighted sales factor, typically a larger percentage of an out-of-state corporation's income is subject to tax in the state. Here, an additional $31,250 ($93,750 − $62,500) of Luna's income is subject to tax in State B.

A single-factor apportionment formula consisting solely of a sales factor is even more detrimental to an out-of-state corporation than an apportionment factor that double-weights the sales factor. About 25 states use or allow a sales-factor-only apportionment formula.

Continue with the facts of Example 9. If State B uses a *sales-factor-only* apportionment formula, Luna's income apportionable to State B becomes $187,500.

Sales ($750,000 ÷ $2,000,000)	=	37.5%
Sum of apportionment factors		37.5%
Average	÷	1
Apportionment factor for State B		37.5%
Taxable income	×	$500,000
Income apportioned to State B		$187,500

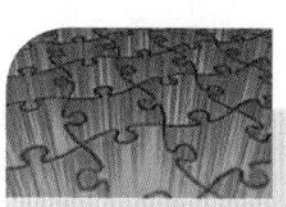

Concept Summary 26.2

Apportionable Income

1. In most states, an apportionment procedure is used to assign the income of a multistate taxpayer to the various states in which business is conducted. Generally, nonapportionable income is allocated, rather than apportioned, directly to the state in which the nonbusiness income-generating assets are located.
2. Variations in state apportionment factors and formulas offer planning opportunities for businesses, in that more or less than 100% of the taxpayer's income may be subjected to state income tax.
3. A few states employ an equally weighted three-factor apportionment formula. In some states, the sales factor is doubled; in other states, only the sales factor is used in apportioning multistate taxable income. Generally, the greater the relative weight assigned to the sales factor, the greater the tax burden on out-of-state taxpayers.

26-2d The Sales Factor

The **sales factor** is a fraction whose numerator is the corporation's total receipts in the state during the tax period. The denominator is the corporation's total receipts generated everywhere during the tax period. Gross receipts for this purpose generally are determined net of returns, allowances, and discounts.

Because the sales factor is a component in the formula used to apportion a corporation's business income to a state, only receipts that generate apportionable income are includible in the fraction. The sales factor generally includes business income from the sale of inventory or services, interest, dividends, rentals, royalties, sales of assets, and other business income. Income on Federal obligations, however, is not included in the sales factor.

These rules work best when the object of the sale is tangible property. Different rules may be needed when the taxpayer sells services, conducting work in one state for a customer in another. UDITPA sources service transactions to the location where the taxpayer incurred costs in conducting its work. About 20 states, though, have adopted *market-sourcing* rules, where a sale of services is sourced to the customer's state or states. The states do not apply uniform rules in this area, so aggregate state taxable income from service transactions may be greater or less than the corresponding Federal taxable income amount.

When the sale involves capital assets, some states require that the gross proceeds, rather than the net gain or loss, be included in the fraction. Most states allow incidental or occasional asset sales and sales of certain intangible assets to be excluded from gross receipts.[12]

In determining the numerator of the sales factor, most states follow the UDITPA's "ultimate destination concept," under which tangible asset sales are assumed to take place at the point of delivery, not at the location at which the shipment originates.

Olive Corporation, whose only manufacturing plant is located in State A, sells its products to residents of State A through its local retail store. Olive also ships its products to customers in States B and C. The products that are sold to residents of State A are assigned to State A, and the products that are delivered to States B and C are assigned to States B and C, respectively, even though all goods are manufactured in and shipped from State A.

Several exceptions exist concerning the ultimate destination concept. The most important of these exceptions include the following:

- Because the U.S. government is present in every state, sales to the Federal government are assigned to the sales factor numerator of the state from which the sale occurs.
- **Dock sales** occur where a purchaser uses its owned or rented vehicles, or a common carrier with which it has made arrangements, to take delivery of the product at the seller's shipping dock. In most states, if the seller makes dock sales to a purchaser that has an out-of-state location to which it returns with the product, the sale is assigned to the purchaser's state.
- Out-of-state sales that are not subject to tax in the destination state are pulled back into the origination state if that state has adopted a **throwback rule**. About half of the states apply this exception to the destination test. States that adopt a throwback rule attempt to make sure that a sale does not escape income taxation because it is made to a customer in a state in which the seller is not taxable. Such a case would place the sale in neither state's sales factor numerator (i.e., it could be called a "nowhere sale").

  Throwback sales are treated as in-state receipts of the origination state, and the actual destination of the product is disregarded. Consequently, when the

[12]MTC Reg. IV.18.(c).

seller is immune from tax in the destination state under P.L. 86–272, the sales are considered to be in-state receipts of the origination state if that state has a throwback rule.

Example 12

Braun Corporation's entire operations are located in State A. Seventy percent ($700,000) of Braun's sales are made in State A, and the remaining 30% ($300,000) are made in State B. Braun's solicitation of sales in State B is limited to mailing a monthly catalog to its customers in that state. However, Braun employees do pick up and replace damaged merchandise in State B.

Under State A's rules, the pickup and replacement of damaged goods establishes nexus with State B. Braun's activities in State B are sufficient (as determined by State A's law) to subject Braun to a positive tax, based on its income. As a result, Braun is permitted to apportion its income between States A and B (70% and 30%, respectively). However, State B's definition of activities necessary to create nexus is less strict than that imposed by State A; in State B, the mere pickup and replacement of damaged goods does not establish income tax nexus.

Braun's taxable income is $900,000. Both States A and B impose a 10% corporate income tax and include only the sales factor in their apportionment formulas. If State A has *not* adopted a throwback rule, Braun's effective state income tax rate is 7%.

	Apportionment Factors	Taxable Income	Tax Rate	Tax
State A	70%	$900,000	10%	$63,000
State B	*	900,000	10%	–0–
Total tax liability				$63,000
Effective state income tax rate:	$63,000 ÷ $900,000			7%

*As determined under State B's laws, Braun's income is not apportionable to State B, because of insufficient nexus.

If State A has adopted a throwback rule, Braun does not benefit from its lack of nexus with State B because the sales in State B are considered to be in-state receipts of State A. State A's throwback rule increases Braun's effective state income tax rate to 10%.

	Apportionment Factors	Taxable Income	Tax Rate	Tax
State A	100%	$900,000	10%	$90,000
State B	–0–	900,000	10%	–0–
Total tax liability				$90,000
Effective state income tax rate:	$90,000 ÷ $900,000			10%
Tax increase due to throwback provision ($90,000 – $63,000)				$27,000

26-2e The Payroll Factor

The **payroll factor** is determined by comparing the compensation paid for services rendered within a state to the total compensation paid by the corporation. Generally, the payroll factor is a fraction whose numerator is the total amount a corporation paid or accrued for compensation in a state during the tax period. The denominator is the total amount paid or accrued by the corporation for compensation during the tax period.

For purposes of the payroll factor, compensation includes wages, salaries, commissions, and any other form of remuneration paid or accrued to employees for personal services. Compensation also may include the value of board, rent, housing, lodging, and other benefits or services furnished to employees by the taxpayer in return for personal services, if these amounts constitute Federal gross income.

Payments made to an independent contractor or any other person who is not properly classifiable as an employee generally are excluded from the numerator and denominator of the payroll factor. A few states, including Delaware, New York, and North Carolina, exclude from the payroll factor the compensation paid to corporate officers. Most states exclude from the payroll factor any compensation made to corporate directors.

More than half of the states provide that earnings paid to a cash or deferred compensation plan, excluded from Federal gross income under § 401(k), are to be included in the numerator and the denominator of the payroll factor. As a result, the total compensation that is included in the denominator of a corporation's payroll factor may vary among the states in which the corporation's income is apportioned.

Example 13

Mice Corporation's sales office and manufacturing plant are located in State A. Mice also maintains a manufacturing plant and sales office in State C. For purposes of apportionment, State A defines payroll as all compensation paid to employees, including contributions to § 401(k) deferred compensation plans. Under the statutes of State C, neither compensation paid to officers nor contributions to § 401(k) plans are included in the payroll factor. Mice incurred the following personnel costs.

	State A	State C	Total
Wages and salaries for employees other than officers	$350,000	$250,000	$600,000
Salaries for officers	150,000	100,000	250,000
Contributions to § 401(k) plans	30,000	20,000	50,000
Total	$530,000	$370,000	$900,000

The payroll factor for State A is computed as follows:

$$\frac{\$530,000}{\$900,000} = 58.89\%$$

Because C excludes from the payroll factor any compensation paid to officers and contributions to § 401(k) plans, C's factor is computed as follows:

$$\frac{\$250,000}{\$600,000} = 41.67\%$$

The aggregate of Mice's payroll factors is 100.56% (58.89% + 41.67%).

Typically, the compensation of an employee is not split between two or more states during the year unless the employee is transferred or changes positions during the year. Instead, each employee's entire compensation is assigned to only one state. Under the UDITPA, compensation is treated as being paid in the state (i.e., it is included in the numerator of the payroll factor) in which the services primarily are performed.

When an employee's services are performed in more than one state, the employee's entire compensation is attributed to the employee's base of operations or, if there is no base of operations in any state in which some part of the service is performed, to the place from which the services are directed or controlled. When no services are performed in the state that serves as the base of operations or the place from which the services are directed, the employee's compensation is attributed to the employee's state of residency.[13]

Example 14

Geese Corporation has its headquarters and a manufacturing plant in State A. Reggie, a resident of State Y, works at the State A manufacturing plant. His compensation is included in the numerator of State A's payroll factor because the service is performed entirely in State A. None of Reggie's compensation is included in the payroll factor of State Y, Reggie's "home" state.

Only compensation that is related to the production of apportionable income is included in the payroll factor.

[13]UDITPA § 14.

Example 15

Dog Corporation, a manufacturer of appliance parts, is subject to tax in States X and Y. Dog incurred the following payroll costs.

	State X	State Y	Total
Wages and salaries for officers and personnel of manufacturing facilities	$450,000	$350,000	$800,000
Wages and salaries for personnel involved in nonapportionable rental activities	50,000	-0-	50,000

Dog's payroll factors are computed as follows:

Payroll factor for State X: $450,000 ÷ $800,000 = 56.25%
Payroll factor for State Y: $350,000 ÷ $800,000 = 43.75%

26-2f The Property Factor

The **property factor** generally is a fraction whose numerator is the average value of the corporation's real property and its tangible personal property owned and used or rented and used in the state during the taxable year. The denominator is the average value of all of the corporation's real property and its tangible personal property owned or rented and used during the taxable year, wherever it is located. In this manner, a state's property factor reflects the extent of total property usage by the taxpayer in the state.

For this purpose, property includes land, buildings, machinery, inventory, equipment, and other real and tangible personal property.[14] Other types of property that may be included in the factor are offshore property, outer space property (satellites), and partnership property.

In the case of property that is in transit between locations of the taxpayer or between a buyer and seller, the assets are included in the numerator of the destination state. With respect to mobile or movable property such as construction equipment, trucks, and leased equipment, which is both in- and outside the state during the tax period, the numerator of a state's property factor generally is determined on the basis of the total time the property was within the state.

Property owned by the corporation typically is valued at its average original or historical cost plus the cost of additions and improvements but without adjusting for depreciation. Some states allow property to be included at net book value or adjusted tax basis. The value of the property usually is determined by averaging the values at the beginning and end of the tax period. Alternatively, some states allow or require the amount to be calculated on a monthly basis if annual computation results in substantial distortions.

Example 16

Blond Corporation, a calendar year taxpayer, owns property in States A and B. Both States A and B require that the average value of assets be included in the property factor. State A requires that the property be valued at its historical cost, and State B requires that the property be included in the property factor at its net book value.

Account Balances at January 1

	State A	State B	Total
Inventories	$ 150,000	$100,000	$ 250,000
Building and machinery (cost)	200,000	400,000	600,000
Accumulated depreciation for building and machinery	(150,000)	(50,000)	(200,000)
Land	50,000	100,000	150,000
Total	$ 250,000	$550,000	$ 800,000

continued

[14] MTC Reg. IV.10.(a).

Account Balances at December 31	State A	State B	Total
Inventories	$ 250,000	$ 200,000	$ 450,000
Building and machinery (cost)	200,000	400,000	600,000
Accumulated depreciation for building and machinery	(175,000)	(100,000)	(275,000)
Land	50,000	100,000	150,000
Total	$ 325,000	$ 600,000	$ 925,000

State A Property Factor

Historical Cost	January 1	December 31	Average
Property in State A	$ 400,000*	$ 500,000**	$ 450,000
Total property	1,000,000†	1,200,000‡	1,100,000

*$150,000 + $200,000 + $50,000.
**$250,000 + $200,000 + $50,000.
†$250,000 + $600,000 + $150,000.
‡$450,000 + $600,000 + $150,000.

$$\text{Property factor for State A: } \frac{\$450{,}000}{\$1{,}100{,}000} = 40.91\%$$

State B Property Factor

Net Book Value	January 1	December 31	Average
Property in State B	$550,000	$600,000	$575,000
Total property	800,000	925,000	862,500

$$\text{Property factor for State B: } \frac{\$575{,}000}{\$862{,}500} = 66.67\%$$

Due to the variations in the property factor rules, the aggregate of Blond's property factors equals 107.58% (40.91% + 66.67%).

Leased property, when included in the property factor, is valued at eight times its annual rental. Annual rentals may include payments such as real estate taxes and insurance made by the lessee in lieu of rent.

Financial Disclosure Insights — State/Local Taxes and the Tax Expense

In applying GAAP principles for a business entity, state and local tax expenses are found in several places in the taxpayer's financial reports. In the tax footnote, the state/local tax costs often are reported in dollar and/or percentage terms, in both current and deferred components. The following are examples of state/local tax expenses that were reported for 2021.

	Current State/ Local Tax Expenses ($ million)	Deferred State/ Local Tax Expenses ($ million)
Eli Lilly	$(28.4)	$ 0.6
eBay	128.0	(125.0)
Netflix	109.6	(2.7)
Ford Motor	26.0	108.0

Example 17

Jasper Corporation is subject to tax in States D and G. Both states require that leased or rented property be included in the property factor at eight times the annual rental costs and that the average historical cost be used for other assets. Information regarding Jasper's property and rental expenses follows.

Average Historical Cost	
Property located in State D	$ 750,000
Property located in State G	450,000
Total property	$1,200,000

Lease and Rental Expenses	
State D	$ 50,000
State G	150,000
Total	$200,000

Property factor for State D

$$\frac{\$750{,}000 + 8(\$50{,}000)}{\$1{,}200{,}000 + 8(\$200{,}000)} = \frac{\$1{,}150{,}000}{\$2{,}800{,}000} = 41.07\%$$

Property factor for State G

$$\frac{\$450{,}000 + 8(\$150{,}000)}{\$1{,}200{,}000 + 8(\$200{,}000)} = \frac{\$1{,}650{,}000}{\$2{,}800{,}000} = 58.93\%$$

Only property that is used in the production of apportionable income is includible in the numerator and denominator of the property factor. In this regard, idle property, property under construction, and property that is used in producing nonapportionable income generally are excluded.

LO.6

Apply the unitary method of state income taxation.

26-3 The Unitary Theory

When two affiliated corporations are subject to tax in different states, each entity must file a return and report its income in the state in which it conducts business. Each entity reports its income separately from that of its affiliated corporations. In an effort to minimize overall state income tax, multistate entities have attempted to separate the parts of the business that are carried on in the various states.

Arts Corporation owns a chain of retail stores located in several states. To enable each store to file and report the income earned only in that state, each store was organized as a separate subsidiary in the state in which it did business. In this manner, each store is separately subject to tax only in the state in which it is located.

Most states attempt to assign as much of an entity's income to in-state sources as possible, so the **unitary theory** for computing state taxable income is attractive to them. Under this method, a corporation is required to file a **combined return** that includes the results from all of the operations of the related corporations, not just from those that transacted business in the state. In this manner, the unitary method allows a state to apply the apportionment formula to a firm's nationwide or worldwide unitary income. To include the activities of the corporation's subsidiaries in the apportionment formula, the state must determine that the subsidiaries' activities are an integral part of a unitary business and, as a result, are subject to apportionment.

26-3a What Is a Unitary Business?

A unitary business operates as a unit and cannot be segregated into independently operating divisions. The operations are integrated, and each division depends on or contributes to the operation of the business as a whole. It is not necessary that each unit operating within a state contribute to the activities of all divisions outside the state.

The unitary theory ignores the separate legal existence of the entities and focuses instead on practical business realities. As a result, the separate entities are treated as a single business for state income tax purposes, and the apportionment formula is applied to the combined income of the unitary business.

What Is a Unitary Business?

Example 19

Continue with the facts of Example 18. Arts manufactured no goods, but it housed the central management, purchasing, distribution, advertising, and administrative departments. Each of the subsidiaries carried on a purely intrastate business, and they paid for the goods and services received at the parent company's cost plus overhead.

Arts and the subsidiaries constitute a unitary business due to their unitary operations (purchasing, distribution, advertising, and administrative functions). As a result, in states that have adopted the unitary method, the income and apportionment factors of the entire unitary group are combined and apportioned to the states in which at least one member of the group has nexus.

Example 20

Crafts Corporation organized its departments as separate corporations on the basis of function: mining copper ore, refining the ore, and fabricating the refined copper into consumer products. Even though the various steps in the process are operated substantially independently of each other with only general supervision from Crafts' executive offices, Crafts is engaged in a single unitary business. Its various divisions are part of a large, vertically structured enterprise in which each business segment needs the products or raw materials provided by another. The flow of products among the affiliates also provides evidence of functional integration, which generally requires some form of central decision or policy making, another characteristic of a unitary business.

More than half of the states require or allow unitary reporting. Notice that the application of the unitary theory is based on a series of subjective observations about the organization and operation of the taxpayer's businesses, while the availability of Federal affiliated group status (see text Section 17-2d) is based on objective, mechanical ownership tests.

26-3b Tax Effects of the Unitary Theory

Use of the unitary approach by a state eliminates several of the planning techniques that could be used to shift income between corporate segments to avoid or minimize state taxes. In addition, the unitary approach usually results in a larger portion of the corporation's income being taxable in states where the compensation, property values, and sales prices are high relative to other states. This occurs because the larger in-state costs (numerators in the apportionment formula) include in the tax base a larger portion of the taxable income within the state's taxing jurisdiction. This has an adverse effect on the corporation's overall state tax burden if the states in which the larger portions are allocated impose a high tax rate relative to the other states in which the business is conducted.

The presence of a unitary business is favorable when losses of unprofitable affiliates may be offset against the earnings of profitable affiliates. It also is favorable when income earned in a high-tax state may be shifted to low-tax states due to the use of combined apportionment factors.

Effects of Unitary Computations

Example 21

Rita Corporation owns two subsidiaries, Brown and Tan. Brown, located in State K, generated taxable income of $700,000 in the current year. During this same period, Tan, located in State M, generated a loss of $400,000. If the subsidiaries are independent corporations, Brown is required to pay State K tax on $700,000 of income.

However, if the corporations constitute a unitary business, the incomes, as well as the apportionment factors, of the two entities are combined. As a result, the combined income of $300,000 ($700,000 − $400,000) is apportioned to unitary States K and M.

Example 22

Eve Corporation, a wholly owned subsidiary of Dan Corporation, generated $1,000,000 of taxable income in the current year. Eve's activities and sales are restricted to State P, which imposes a 10% income tax. Dan's taxable income for the current year is $1,500,000. Dan's activities and sales are restricted to State Q, which imposes a 5% income tax. Both states use a three-factor apportionment formula that equally weights sales, payroll, and property. Sales, payroll, and average property for each of the corporations are as follows.

	Eve Corporation	Dan Corporation	Total
Sales	$3,000,000	$7,000,000	$10,000,000
Payroll	2,000,000	3,500,000	5,500,000
Property	2,500,000	4,500,000	7,000,000

If the corporations are *independent entities*, the overall state income tax liability is $175,000.

Eve: State P (10% × $1,000,000)	=	$100,000
Dan: State Q (5% × $1,500,000)	=	75,000
Total state income tax		$175,000

If the corporations are *members of a unitary business*, the income and apportionment factors are combined in determining the income tax liability in unitary States P and Q. As a result of the combined reporting, the overall state income tax liability is reduced.

State P Income Tax				
Total apportionable income			$2,500,000	
Apportionment formula				
Sales ($3,000,000 ÷ $10,000,000)	=	30.00%		
Payroll ($2,000,000 ÷ $5,500,000)	=	36.36%		
Property ($2,500,000 ÷ $7,000,000)	=	35.71%		
Total		102.07%		
Average (102.07% ÷ 3)			× 34.02%	
State P taxable income			$ 850,500	
Tax rate			× 10%	
State P tax liability				$85,050

State Q Income Tax				
Total apportionable income			$2,500,000	
Apportionment formula				
Sales ($7,000,000 ÷ $10,000,000)	=	70.00%		
Payroll ($3,500,000 ÷ $5,500,000)	=	63.64%		
Property ($4,500,000 ÷ $7,000,000)	=	64.29%		
Total		197.93%		
Average (197.93% ÷ 3)			× 65.98%	
State Q taxable income			$1,649,500	
Tax rate			× 5%	
State Q tax liability				$82,475

continued

Total State Income Tax	
Total state income tax if nonunitary	$175,000
Total state income tax if unitary ($85,050 + $82,475)	(167,525)
Tax reduction from unitary combined reporting	$ 7,475

The results of unitary reporting would have been detrimental if Q had imposed a higher rate of tax than P, because a larger percentage of the corporation's income is attributable to Q when the apportionment factors are combined.

26-3c Consolidated and Combined Returns

As discussed in Chapter 17, an affiliated group of corporations may file a consolidated Federal return if all members of the group consent. Once such a return has been filed, the group must continue to file on a consolidated basis as long as it remains in existence or until permission to file separate returns has been obtained. The consolidated return essentially treats the controlled corporations as a single taxable entity. As a result, the affiliated group pays only one tax, based on the combined income of its members after certain adjustments (e.g., net operating losses) and eliminations (e.g., intercompany dividends and inventory profits).

Several states permit affiliated corporations to file a consolidated return if such a return has been filed for Federal purposes. The filing of a consolidated return is mandatory in only a few states.

Usually, only corporations that are subject to tax in the state can be included in a consolidated return, unless specific requirements are met or the state permits the inclusion of corporations that do not have in-state nexus.

Do not confuse elective consolidated returns with required combined returns in unitary states. A combined return is filed in every unitary state in which one or more of the affiliates have nexus. A consolidated return often includes an election for affiliates to join in a return-filing group as initiated by the taxpayers; most states apply rules similar to those presented in text Section 17-2d.

Global Tax Issues — Water's Edge Is Not a Day at the Beach

As a result of pressure from the business community, the Federal government, and foreign countries, most of the states that impose an income tax on a unitary business's worldwide operations permit a multinational business to elect **water's edge** unitary reporting as an alternative to worldwide unitary filing.

The water's edge provision permits a multinational corporation to elect to limit the reach of the state's taxing jurisdiction over out-of-state affiliates to activities occurring within the boundaries of the United States. The decision to make a water's edge election may have a substantial effect on the apportionment computations and the tax liability of a multinational corporation. A water's edge election usually cannot be revoked for a number of years without permission from the appropriate tax authority.

Corporations making this election may be assessed an additional tax or fee for the privilege of excluding out-of-state entities from the combined report.

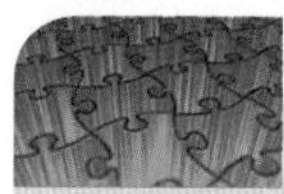

Concept Summary 26.3

Using Apportionment Formulas

1. The sales factor is based on the ultimate destination concept for sales of tangible personal property. Other rules apply when a sale of services is involved and when other exceptions are available.
2. The payroll factor generally includes compensation that is included in Federal gross income, but some states include excludible fringe benefits. An employee's compensation usually is not divided among states.
3. The property factor generally is derived using the average undepreciated historical costs for the assets and eight times the rental value of the assets.
4. The unitary theory may require the taxpayer to include worldwide activities and holdings in the apportionment factors. A *water's edge election* can limit these amounts to U.S. transactions.
5. When the unitary theory applies, a combined return is filed. This is different from the consolidated return that an affiliated group of corporations would file for Federal income tax purposes.

LO.7

Discuss the states' income tax treatment of S corporations, partnerships, and LLCs.

26-4 Taxation of S Corporations

The majority of the states that impose a corporate income tax apply special provisions, similar to the Federal law, that govern the taxation of S corporations. Only a few states—including New Hampshire and Tennessee—and the District of Columbia do not provide pass-through (no corporate-level tax) treatment for Federal S corporations.

In the non-S election states, a Federal S corporation generally is subject to tax in the same manner as a C corporation. As a result, if a multistate S corporation operates in any of these states, it is subject to state income tax and does not realize one of the primary benefits of S status—the avoidance of double taxation. Other potential tax-related benefits of the S election, such as the immediate deduction of net operating losses, may not be allowed.

Example 23

Horizon, an S corporation, has established nexus in States A and B. State A recognizes S status; State B does not. Horizon generated \$600,000 of ordinary business income and \$100,000 of dividends that were received from corporations in which Horizon owns 5% of the stock. Horizon's State B apportionment percentage is 50%.

For State B tax purposes, Horizon first computes its income as though it were a C corporation. It then apportions the resulting income to State B. Assuming that State B has adopted the Federal provisions governing the dividends received deduction, Horizon's income, determined as though it were a C corporation, is \$650,000 {\$600,000 + [(100% − 50%) × \$100,000]}. Accordingly, Horizon may be subject to State B corporate income tax on \$325,000 (\$650,000 × 50% apportionment percentage) of taxable income.

26-4a Eligibility

All of the states that recognize S status permit a corporation to be treated as an S corporation for state purposes only if the corporation has a valid Federal S election in place. Generally, the filing of a Federal S election is sufficient to render the corporation an S corporation for state tax purposes. In most states, an entity that is an S corporation for Federal tax purposes automatically is treated as an S corporation for state tax purposes. New Jersey and New York require a separate state-level S election.

26-4b State Tax Filing Requirements

About half of the states require the corporation to withhold taxes on the nonresident shareholders' portions of the entity's income.

Maple, an S corporation, is subject to income tax only in Vermont. On the last day of its taxable year, 40% of Maple's stock is held by nonresident shareholders. Maple withholds Vermont income tax for its nonresident shareholders.

In an effort to decrease compliance burdens and simplify the filing process for nonresident shareholders of S corporations, several states allow an S corporation to file a single income tax return and pay the resulting tax on behalf of some or all of its nonresident shareholders. State requirements for the filing of a "block" or **composite return** vary substantially.

26-5 Taxation of Partnerships and LLCs

Most states apply income tax provisions to partnerships, limited liability companies (LLCs), and limited liability partnerships (LLPs) in a manner that parallels Federal treatment. For income tax purposes, the entity is a tax-reporting, not a taxpaying, entity. Income, loss, and credit items are allocated and apportioned among the partners according to the terms of the partnership agreement and state income tax law.

Some states require that the entity make estimated tax payments on behalf of out-of-state partners. This approach helps to ensure that nonresident partners file appropriate forms and pay any resulting tax to the state. As is the case with S corporations, some states allow composite returns to be filed relative to out-of-state partners.

A few states impose a minimum income tax on flow-through entities, including S corporations, LLCs, and partnerships. Such a tax might be computed, for instance, as the greater of $800 or 1.5 percent of net revenues.

26-6 Other State and Local Taxes

LO.8

Describe other commonly encountered state and local taxes on businesses.

26-6a State and Local Sales and Use Taxes

Forty-five states and the District of Columbia impose a sales tax on retail sales of tangible personal property for use or consumption. In many of these states, in-state localities, including cities, towns, school districts, and counties, also have the power to levy a sales tax; likely 10,000 such taxing jurisdictions exist in the United States. A sales tax is imposed directly on the purchaser who acquires the asset at retail; the tax is measured by the price of the sale. The vendor or retailer merely acts as a collection agent for the government.

A use tax is designed to complement the sales tax. A use tax arises when the product in a taxable sale is sold in or shipped to another jurisdiction, one with which the seller has no sales tax nexus. The resulting use tax is the obligation of the purchaser and is payable to the purchaser's state. Since most taxpayers are unaware of the use tax, states have implemented a variety of methods to collect this tax (including requesting information on out-of-state purchases when the taxpayer's income tax return is filed). See Exhibit 26.4.

The use tax has two purposes: to prevent consumers from evading sales tax by purchasing goods outside the state for in-state use and to provide an equitable sales environment between in-state and out-of-state retailers.

Generally, sales of tangible personal property are subject to tax. In several states, selected services and digital goods also are subject to tax.

Each jurisdiction that applies a sales/use tax defines its own tax base (i.e., which items are taxable and to whom). For a multistate business, complying with the thousands of sets of sales/use tax statutes and regulations can be a difficult burden. In an effort to ease this confusion, state and local government officials in about half of the states developed the Streamlined Sales Tax Project (SSTP). Members working in conjunction with the SSTP wrote a model law for taxing jurisdictions to adopt, thereby allowing for a more uniform application of the rules and for a more efficient exchange of information among revenue agencies. However, little interest has been shown in having identical sales/use tax rates among all the taxing jurisdictions.

To date, the most commonly adopted SSTP rules are those defining which products and services are subject to sales/use tax. For instance, SSTP rules set out the items of clothing that would be subject to tax, but each jurisdiction decides on its own whether to include clothing in the tax base and whether to allow "back-to-school" clothing amnesties (or holidays) during specific weeks of the year.

Sales/Use Tax Exemptions

A majority of the states exempt sales of certain items from the sales/use tax base. The most common exemptions and exclusions include the following:

- *Sales for resale* are exempt because the purchaser is not the ultimate user of the sold property. For instance, meat purchased by a grocer and a garment purchased by a retailer are not subject to sales/use tax under the resale rule.
- *Casual or occasional sales* that occur infrequently are exempt from the sales/use tax base chiefly for administrative convenience. Most states exclude rummage sales, the transfer of an entire business, and the like under this rule.
- Most *purchases by exempt organizations* are excluded from taxable sales. Charities, governments and their agencies, and other organizations qualifying for Federal income tax exemption (see text Section 25-2) are relieved of sales/use tax liabilities in all of the states.
- *Sales of necessities* such as groceries and medical prescriptions and equipment. Restaurant and other prepared meals typically are subject to tax, though.
- *Sales of targeted items* can be exempt to improve the equity of the sales/use tax system or support particular industries. Special exemptions for sales of farm, industrial, and computing equipment are allowed by several states.

Exhibit 26.4 **Sales and Use Taxes**

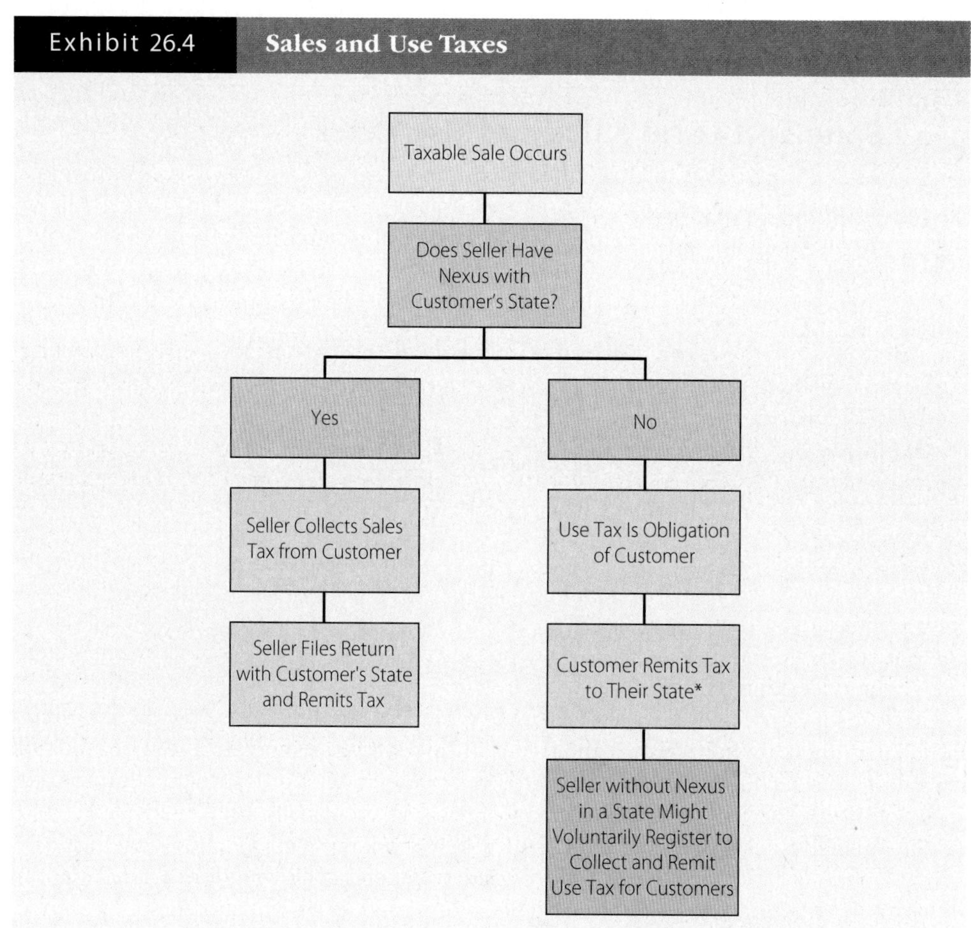

*Many states include a line on the personal income tax form for individuals to pay use tax. Otherwise, a use tax form is usually required.

- *Economic development concerns* A state or local government might waive the tax for a period of time to encourage a business to move to or remain in the jurisdiction.
- Certain *sales to manufacturers, producers, and processors* also may be exempt. Exemptions usually include one or more of the following:
  - Containers and other packing, packaging, and shipping materials actually used to transfer merchandise to customers of the purchaser.
  - Machines and specific processing equipment and repair parts or replacements exclusively and directly used in manufacturing tangible personal property.

Sales/Use Tax Nexus

Rules governing nexus for sales/use taxes are different from those used for income taxes. The regular solicitation of sales by independent brokers establishes sufficient nexus to require a nonresident seller to register and collect the use tax, even though the seller does not have regular employees, agents, and an office or other place of business in the state.[15] As a result, a corporation may be required to collect sales and use taxes in a state even though it is not subject to income tax in the state because it is has protection under P.L. 86–272.

The states have a great degree of freedom to define sales/use tax nexus in their jurisdictions.[16] Nexus definitions for this purpose range from having a physical presence in the state to having customers in the jurisdiction (e.g., where the seller's only contact with the jurisdiction is through online sales).[17]

One common economic nexus rule, adopted by many states, makes the seller taxable in the state for the year if at least $100,000 in sales or 200 sales transactions are found. Some states use higher thresholds or may only consider sales rather than also the number of transactions. For example, the threshold is over $500,000 of sales in California in the preceding year or the current year to date regardless of the number of transactions. Pennsylvania only requires at least $100,000 of sales in the year. Sales/use tax nexus also is established in most states for a seller who uses affiliated vendors to take orders and process sales (e.g., Amazon and eBay are such *marketplace facilitators* and must collect the sales/use tax with respect to sales made by its affiliates).

Sales/Use Tax on Services

Some states have added specific service transactions to their sales/use tax base. The services most commonly subjected to tax include transactions involving hotels and restaurants, hair and beauty salons, entertainment events, cable and satellite television subscriptions, and lawn care. To date, extension of the tax base for legal/accounting, medical, education, and advertising services largely has been blocked in most legislatures by the providers of these services.

Revenue shortfalls at the state and local levels and shifts in the general economy to the sales of services and goods other than tangible personal property, however, have led some legislatures to expand the sales/use tax base to include a broader array of consumption. For instance, some states tax the transfer of digital goods, such as downloads of songs, books, software, and games.

26-6b **Local Property Taxes**

Property taxes, a major source of revenue at the city and county levels, often are designated as *ad valorem* taxes because they are based on the value of property that is located in the state on a specific date. Generally, that date fixes taxable ownership, situs (location), and the valuation of the property.

Property taxes can take the form of either real property taxes or personal property taxes. States apply different tax rates and means of assessment to the two classes of property.

[15] *Scripto, Inc., v. Carson*, 362 U.S. 207 (1960).

[16] These privileges were confirmed in *South Dakota v. Wayfair, Inc.*, 138 S.Ct. 2080 (2018).

[17] Most taxing jurisdictions establish a *de minimis* rule, providing relief for sellers with only a limited amount of sales in the state.

Although a personal property tax may be imposed on both intangible and tangible property, most states limit the tax to tangible property. The distinction between the various items of personal property is important because special rates, computations, or exemptions may apply. For instance, inventory constitutes tangible personal property, but it is exempt from property taxation in most states.

26-6c **Other Taxes**

States may impose a variety of other state and local taxes on corporations, including incorporation or entrance fees or taxes, gross receipt taxes, stock transfer taxes, realty transfer and mortgage recording taxes, license taxes, and franchise taxes based on net worth or capital stock outstanding.

Administrative Taxes

An *incorporation tax* is an excise tax for the corporate privilege conferred on the business. At the time the business is incorporated, the state generally imposes a fee or tax for the privilege of conducting business as a corporation within the state. Similarly, an out-of-state corporation usually must pay an entrance fee or tax before it can transact business in a state other than its state of incorporation.

A *license tax* is an excise tax on the privilege of engaging in a certain business, occupation, or profession. A jurisdiction may impose business, occupational, or professional license taxes as a means of generating revenue or regulating the activities of the business, occupation, or profession for the public welfare.

Taxes on nonresident visitors to a state are common, since the one who pays the tax lives somewhere else and cannot vote against it. Examples are taxes on hotel rooms (such as a *transient occupancy tax*), rental cars, and other transient arrangements, like house sharing or swapping.

Stock and realty transfer and mortgage recording taxes are nonrecurring taxes that are imposed at the time of recording or transfer. *Stock transfer taxes* are imposed on the transfer of shares or certificates of stock of domestic and foreign corporations. The tax typically is based on the number of shares transferred and the par or market value of the stock.

The base of the *realty transfer tax* usually is measured by the consideration paid or to be paid for the realty. The *mortgage recording tax* may be based on the actual consideration given, the value of the property, or the debt to be secured by the instrument.

Collections of Unclaimed Property

All of the U.S. states enforce rules that allow them to take possession of certain unclaimed property. In essence, this procedure acts like a tax on businesses with large consumer operations.

Unclaimed property might take the form of an unused gift card or a paycheck the employee has not yet cashed. On the balance sheet, these amounts are reported as payables by the business. After a stated period of time passes (usually five or more years) and an effort is made to contact the holder of the business's obligation, the value of the property reverts to the state. These rights of the states often are referred to as *escheat* laws.

Because unclaimed property rules are not enacted as a taxing statute, the usual nexus and apportionment tests do not apply. Instead, the property is taken by the state in which the business is incorporated.[18]

Capital Stock and Franchise Taxes

Typically, a *capital stock tax* is an excise tax imposed on a domestic corporation for the privilege of existing as a corporation or imposed on an out-of-state corporation, either for the privilege of doing business or for the actual transaction of business within the state. This annual tax usually is based on the book value of the corporation's net worth, including capital, surplus, and retained earnings.

[18] *Texas v. New Jersey*, 379 U.S. 674 (1965).

The majority of capital stock taxes are apportioned if the corporation does business or maintains an office in another state. In some states, however, the tax is levied on the entire authorized or issued capital stock of a domestic corporation, even though the corporation may be engaged in business in other states.

State Franchise Tax on Net Worth

Example 25

The balance sheet of Bull, a domestic corporation of State A, at the end of its taxable year is as follows.

Cash	$100,000
Equipment (net of $50,000 accumulated depreciation)	150,000
Building (net of $75,000 accumulated depreciation)	225,000
Land	125,000
Total assets	$600,000
Accounts payable and other short-term liabilities	$100,000
Long-term liabilities	200,000
Capital stock	50,000
Paid-in capital in excess of par value	50,000
Retained earnings	200,000
Total liabilities and equity	$600,000

State A imposes a 2% franchise tax based on the entire net worth of a domestic corporation. Bull is subject to a franchise tax in State A of $6,000 ($600,000 assets − $300,000 liabilities = $300,000 net worth × 2% rate).

Continue with the facts of Example 25, except that State A subjects a domestic corporation to tax only on the capital that is employed in the state. Bull properly determines that its State A apportionment percentage is 20%. In this case, Bull's State A franchise tax liability is $1,200 ($300,000 net worth × 20% apportionment percentage = $60,000 capital employed in State A × 2% rate).

Ethics & Equity **Encouraging Economic Development through Tax Concessions**

The tax professional occasionally is in a position to negotiate with a state or city taxing jurisdiction to garner tax relief for a client as an incentive to locate a plant or distribution center in that geographic area. In times when construction budgets are high and interstate competition is fierce to attract or retain businesses that are making location decisions, such tax concessions can be significant.

For instance, to encourage a business to build a large distribution center in the area, community leaders might be agreeable to (1) paying for roads, sewer, water, and other improvements after issuing bonds; (2) reducing property taxes by 50 percent for the first 10 years of the center's operations; or (3) offering interest rate discounts or cash grants for the construction of new facilities. For corporate taxpayers, cash incentive payments received from a government or civic group constitute gross income.[19]

An incentive-granting community provides the concessions even though the influx of new workers may place a strain on public school facilities and likely necessitate improvements in traffic patterns and other infrastructure.

Consider the position of a large employer that has been located in the area for more than 50 years. By how much should it be willing to absorb the tax increases that result when economic development concessions are used to attract new, perhaps temporary, businesses to the area? Should the employer challenge the constitutionality of the grant of such sizable tax breaks to some, but not all, business taxpayers in the jurisdiction?

What should be the rate of "impact fees" assessed on new developments? Does your analysis change if the new business competes with the longtime resident for sales? For employees? For political power?

[19] § 118(b)(2). See also CCA 20085201F.

Recognize tax planning opportunities available to minimize a corporation's state and local tax liability.

26-7 Tax Planning

The inconsistencies in the tax laws and rates among the states not only complicate state tax planning, but also provide the nucleus of pertinent planning opportunities. Although several income tax planning devices are available to a corporation that does business in only one state, most planning techniques are directed toward corporations that do business or maintain property in more than one state. All suggested tax planning strategies should be reviewed in light of practical business considerations and the additional administrative and other costs that may be incurred because simply minimizing state taxes may not be prudent from a business perspective.

26-7a Selecting the Optimal State in Which to Operate

Because the states employ different definitions of the amount and type of activity necessary to establish nexus, a company has some latitude in selecting the states by which it will be taxed. When a corporation has only a limited connection with a high-tax state, it may abandon that activity by electing an alternative means of accomplishing the same result. For example, if providing a sales representative with a company-owned iPad constitutes nexus in an undesired state, the company could eliminate its connection with that state by reimbursing sales personnel for equipment expenses instead of providing a company communications device. Similarly, when nexus is caused by conducting customer training sessions or seminars in the state, the corporation could conduct the meetings in another way. This can be done by sending the personnel to a nearby state in which nexus clearly has been established or in which the activity would not constitute nexus or by meeting electronically.

In addition, when sufficient activity originates from the repair and maintenance of the corporation's products or the activities performed by the sales representatives within the state, the organization could incorporate the service or sales divisions. This would invalidate a nonunitary state's right to tax the parent corporation's income; only the income of the service or sales divisions would be subject to tax. However, this technique is successful only if the incorporated division is a *bona fide* business operation. Therefore, the pricing of any sales or services between the new subsidiary and the parent corporation must be at arm's length, and the operations of the new corporation preferably should result in a profit.

Although planning techniques often are employed to disconnect a corporation's activities from an undesirable state, they also can be utilized to create nexus in a desirable state. For example, when the presence of a company-owned computer creates nexus in a desirable state, the corporation could provide its sales representatives in that state with company-owned equipment, rather than reimbursing or providing increased compensation for equipment costs.

Establishing nexus in a state is advantageous, for instance, when that state has a lower tax rate than the state in which the income currently is taxed or when losses or credits become available to reduce tax liabilities in the state.

Example 27

Bird Corporation generates $500,000 of taxable income from selling goods; specifically, 40% of its product is sold in State A and 60% in State B. Both states levy a corporate income tax and include only the sales factor in their apportionment formulas. The tax rate in State A is 10%; State B's rate is only 3%. Bird's manufacturing operation is located in State A; therefore, the corporation's income is subject to tax in that state. Currently, Bird is immune from tax under P.L. 86–272 in State B. Because State A has adopted a throwback provision, Bird incurs $50,000 of state income taxes.

	Apportionment Formula	Net Income	Tax Rate	Tax
State A	100 ÷ 100	$500,000	10%	$50,000
State B	0 ÷ 100	500,000	3%	–0–
Total tax liability				$50,000

continued

Because State B imposes a lower tax rate than State A does, Bird substantially reduces its state tax liability if sufficient nexus is created with State B.

	Apportionment Formula	Net Income	Tax Rate	Tax
State A	40 ÷ 100	$500,000	10%	$20,000
State B	60 ÷ 100	500,000	3%	9,000
Total tax liability				$29,000

26-7b Restructuring Corporate Entities

One of the major objectives of state tax planning is to design the proper mix of corporate entities. An optimal mix of entities often generates the lowest combined state income tax for the corporation. The goal of designing a good corporate combination often is to situate the highly profitable entities in states that impose a low (or no) income tax.

Matching Tax Rates and Corporate Income

When the corporation must operate in a high-tax state, divisions that generate losses also should be located there. Alternatively, unprofitable or less profitable operations can be merged into profitable operations to reduce the overall income subject to tax in the state. An ideal candidate for this type of merger may be a research and development subsidiary that is only marginally profitable but is vital to the parent corporation's strategic goals and that may attract research credits and incentives for the taxpayer. By using simulation models, a variety of different combinations can be tested to determine the optimal corporate structure.

Unitary Operations

By identifying the states that have adopted the unitary method and the criteria under which a particular state defines a unitary business, a taxpayer may reduce its overall state tax by restructuring its corporate relationships to create or guard against a unitary relationship. For instance, an independent business enterprise can be made unitary by exercising day-to-day operational control and by centralizing functions such as marketing, financing, accounting, and legal services.

The Big Picture

Example 28

Return to the facts of *The Big Picture* on p. 26-1. Assume that LocalCo already operates in both unitary and nonunitary states. Application of unitary corporate income tax rules can make tax planning more difficult. Subjecting certain LocalCo activities to the unitary theory could either increase or decrease the combined corporate income tax liability of the affiliates, depending especially on the apportionment formulas applied in the unitary states.

LocalCo needs to make projections of the profitability of its operations in the new multifunction building. Then LocalCo should determine the income tax effects of expanding its operations into several target states, including both unitary and nonunitary jurisdictions, and compare how the unitary rules (and all associated compliance costs) affect its after-tax profits.

Passive Investment Companies

The creation of a **passive investment company** is another restructuring technique utilized to minimize a nonunitary corporation's state tax burden. Nonbusiness or passive/portfolio income generally is allocated to the state in which the income-producing asset is located, rather than being apportioned among the states in which the corporation does business. Therefore, significant tax savings may be realized when nonbusiness assets are located in a state that either does not levy an income tax or provides favorable tax treatment for passive/portfolio income.

The corporation need not be domiciled in the state to benefit from these favorable provisions. Instead, the tax savings can be realized by forming a passive investment subsidiary to hold the intangible assets and handle the corporation's investment activities.

The passive investment subsidiary technique usually produces the desired result in any no-tax state. Delaware, however, often is selected for this purpose due to its other corporate statutory provisions and favorable political, business, and legal climate.

Delaware does not impose an income tax upon a corporation whose only activity within the state is the maintenance and management of intangible investments and the collection and distribution of income from such investments or from tangible property physically located in another state. Consequently, trademarks, patents, stock, and other intangible property can be transferred to a Delaware corporation whose activity is limited to collecting such income. The assets can be transferred to the subsidiary without incurring a current Federal income tax on the exchange (see text Section 18-1).

However, to receive the desired preferential state tax treatment, the holding company's activities within the state must be sufficient to establish income tax nexus in the state. The passive investment company should avoid performing any activity outside the state that may result in establishing nexus with another state. In addition, the formation of the subsidiary must be properly implemented to ensure the legal substance of the operation. The passive investment company must have a physical office, and it must function as an independent operation.

Because the subsidiary's activities are confined to Delaware (or some other no- or low-tax state) and its operations generate only passive/portfolio income, its income will not be taxed in any nonunitary state. Moreover, most states exclude dividends from taxation or otherwise treat them favorably; therefore, the earnings of a passive investment subsidiary can be distributed as a dividend to the parent at a minimal tax cost. If the state in which the parent is located does not levy the full income tax on dividends received, the entire measure of passive/portfolio income may escape taxation.

Example 29

Purple Corporation generates $800,000 of taxable income; $600,000 is income from its manufacturing operations, and $200,000 is dividend income from passive investments. All of Purple's sales are made and assets are kept in State A, which imposes a 10% corporate income tax and permits a 100% deduction for dividends received from subsidiaries. The corporation is not subject to tax in any other state. Consequently, Purple incurs $80,000 of income tax (tax base $800,000 × tax rate 10%).

If Purple creates a passive investment subsidiary in State B, which does not impose an income tax upon a corporation whose only activity within the state is the maintenance and management of passive investments, Purple's tax liability is reduced by $20,000 (a 25% decrease). Because such income is nonapportionable (allocated for state tax purposes to the state in which it is located), the income earned from its passive investments is not subject to tax in State A.

	State A (Purple Corporation)	State B (Passive Investment Company)
Taxable income	$600,000	$200,000
Tax rate	× 10%	× –0–*
Tax liability	$ 60,000	$ –0–
Tax liability without restructuring		$ 80,000
Tax liability with restructuring		(60,000)
Tax reduction due to use of subsidiary		$ 20,000

*B does not impose an income tax on a passive investment corporation.

The income earned by the subsidiary from its passive investments can be distributed to Purple as a dividend without incurring a tax liability because A allows a 100% deduction for dividends that are received from subsidiary corporations.

These desired results, however, will not be fully available in states that view the entire corporate operation as being unitary. Because those states require combined reporting, the income earned by the passive investment subsidiary is included in the corporation's apportionable or allocable income. Other states may levy gross receipts taxes or restrict interest and dividend deductions, or legislatively include in the income tax base any income resulting from credit card usage by customers or the use of intangible or digital assets in the state,[20] to limit the effectiveness of the passive investment subsidiary.

26-7c Subjecting the Corporation's Income to Apportionment

When a multistate organization is domiciled in a high-tax state, some of its apportionable income is eliminated from the tax base in that state. In light of the high tax rate, this may result in significant tax savings. Apportioning income will be especially effective where the income that is attributed to the other states is not subject to income tax. The income removed from the taxing jurisdiction of the domicile state entirely escapes state income taxation when the state to which the income is attributed (1) does not levy a corporate income tax, (2) requires a higher level of activity necessary to subject an out-of-state company to taxation than that adopted by the state of domicile, or (3) is prohibited under P.L. 86–272 from taxing the income (assuming that the domicile state has not adopted a throwback provision). As a result, the right to apportion income may provide substantial benefits because the out-of-state sales are excluded from the numerator of the sales factor and may not be taxed in another state.

However, to acquire the right to apportion its income, the organization must have sufficient activities in or contacts with one or more other states. Whether the type and amount of activities and/or contacts are considered adequate is determined by the other state's nexus rules. Therefore, a corporation should analyze its current activities in and contacts with other states to determine which, if any, activities or contacts could be redirected so that the corporation gains the right to apportion its income.

The Big Picture

Example 30

Return to the facts of *The Big Picture* on p. 26-1. Most corporate taxpayers consist of a parent corporation and perhaps one or more existing subsidiaries. Given its expansion plans, LocalCo has the opportunity to determine "from scratch" in which states it wants to create nexus for the operations in the multifunction building.

The tax professional needs to offer advice to LocalCo's board of directors as to where the building might be situated and how the operations of any related sales and administrative personnel might be structured in an effort to provide optimal tax consequences. Nexus issues to be considered include the following:

- Is income tax nexus created with the target state?
- Is sales/use tax nexus created with the target state?
- How are the income tax apportionment factors affected by the expansion plans (e.g., whether the target state uses a property factor in the apportionment formula and, if so, how it is weighted)?
- Would a building such as that planned by LocalCo receive any special computational treatment for the target state's property factor (e.g., in averaging the building's costs or applying accumulated depreciation)?

[20] These laws often are rooted in *Geoffrey, Inc. v. South Carolina Tax Commission*, 437 SE2d 13 (SC S.Ct., 1993).

Ethics & Equity Can You Be a Nowhere Adviser?

The intent of much of today's multistate income tax planning is to create so-called *nowhere sales*, such that the income from the transaction is not subject to tax in any state. Suppose, for instance, that a sale is made from Georgia (a state with no throwback rule) into Nevada (the place of ultimate destination but a state with no income tax). No state-level income tax liability is generated.

Is it ethical for a tax adviser to suggest such a strategy? Could you ethically propose the establishment of a sales office in a nonthrowback state, thereby avoiding state income tax on a transaction that is fully taxable under Federal rules?

26-7d Planning with Apportionment Factors

Sales Factor

Working with the sales factor often yields the greatest planning opportunities for a multistate corporation. In-state receipts include sales to purchasers with a destination point in that state; sales delivered to out-of-state purchasers are included in the numerator of the sales factor of the destination state. However, to be permitted to exclude out-of-state sales from the sales factor of the origination state, the seller generally must substantiate the shipment of goods to an out-of-state location. Therefore, the destinations of sales that a corporation makes and the means by which the goods are shipped must be carefully reviewed.

The corporation's overall state tax possibly can be reduced by establishing a better record-keeping system or by affecting the numerator of the sales factor by changing the delivery location or method.

For example, a corporation may substantially reduce its state income tax if the delivery location of its sales is changed from a state in which the company is taxed to one in which it is not. This technique may not benefit the corporation if the state in which the sales originate has adopted the throwback rule.

Property Factor

Because most fixed assets are physically stationary in nature, the property factor is not so easily manipulated in the short term. Nonetheless, significant tax savings can be realized by establishing a leasing subsidiary in a low- or no-tax state. If the property is located in a state that does not include leased assets in the property factor, the establishment of a subsidiary from which to lease the property eliminates the assets from the property factor in the parent's state.

Permanently idle property generally is excluded from the property factor. As a result, a corporation should identify and remove such assets from the property factor to ensure that the factor is not distorted.

Example 31

The property factor valuations of Quake Corporation's holdings are as follows:

	State A	Total
Equipment (average historical cost)	$1,200,000	$2,000,000
Accumulated depreciation (average)	800,000	1,000,000

Twenty percent of the equipment in State A is fully depreciated and is idle. Assuming that State A includes property in the factor at historical cost, Quake's property factor is 54.55% [($1,200,000 − $240,000 idle property) ÷ ($2,000,000 − $240,000)]. If the idle property is not removed from the property factor, Quake's property factor in State A is incorrectly computed as 60% ($1,200,000 ÷ $2,000,000).

Payroll Factor

The payroll factor provides income tax planning potential where several corporate employees spend substantial periods of time outside their state of employment or the corporation is able to relocate highly paid employees to low- or no-tax states.

Because the commissions paid to independent contractors are excluded from the payroll factor, the taxpayer may reduce its payroll factor in a high-tax state.

Yellow Corporation's total payroll costs are $1,400,000. Of this amount, $1,000,000 was attributable to State A, a high-tax state. Yellow's payroll factor in State A is 71.43% ($1,000,000 ÷ $1,400,000).

Assuming that $200,000 of the State A compensation had been paid to sales representatives and that Yellow replaced its sales force with independent contractors, Yellow's payroll factor in State A would be reduced to 66.67% [($1,000,000 − $200,000) ÷ ($1,400,000 − $200,000)].

26-7e Sales/Use Tax Compliance

A seller conceivably must deal with thousands of different sales/use taxing jurisdictions, each with its own forms and filing deadlines, rates of applicable tax, and definitions of what is taxable or exempt. Examples of issues on which jurisdictions may disagree, presenting compliance problems for sellers, include the following:

- Are snack foods exempt groceries or taxable candy?
- Are therapeutic stockings exempt medical supplies or taxable clothing?
- Which types of software are subject to tax?

26-7f Capital Stock Taxation

Capital stock tax liabilities can be significant for capital-intensive taxpayers to the extent they reinvest a large portion of retained earnings (the tax base) in productive assets. If all nontax factors are equal, a taxpayer with sizable exposure to a capital stock tax should consider the following techniques:

- Funding expansion with debt rather than retained earnings.
- Funding subsidiary operations with debt rather than direct capital contributions.
- Regularly paying dividends to parent companies that are domiciled in tax-favored states such as Delaware and Nevada.

Refocus on The Big Picture

Making a Multistate Location Decision

LocalCo holds a competitive advantage with the states and localities in negotiating where its new facility should be located. Politicians like to attract new facilities to their jurisdictions as a way to create construction jobs and to expand the income and sales/use tax base. LocalCo's top management should work with the governors and development executives of the states that are final candidates for the location of the proposed new building.

LocalCo's agenda for these negotiations should include the following items:

- Many states offer targeted tax incentives to attract and retain "clean" businesses such as LocalCo. These incentives might include property tax abatements, research and investment credits, and tax waivers for the state and local income and payroll taxes on new jobs. The company should determine whether it qualifies for any existing incentives and how to structure such incentives so as to

FOXY BURROW/SHUTTERSTOCK.COM

continued

avoid any inclusion in the gross income of the business. Government incentives such as tax abatements and infrastructure improvements are to be preferred for this purpose over upfront cash transfers.

- Currently, LocalCo's manufacturing operations are split between a low-tax state (Alabama) and a high-tax state (California). Under a relocation plan that does not jeopardize LocalCo's customer base, nexus might be eliminated with California and shifted to a low-tax jurisdiction. Nevada is a good candidate, given its proximity to California (the current sportswear location). But economic nexus thresholds might prevent this technique from working effectively.
- California applies the unitary theory of income taxation. LocalCo should determine whether unitary rules increase or decrease its total tax burden.
- Corporate headquarters currently are located in New York, another high-tax jurisdiction. If the new facility is located in a corporation-favorable, low-tax state, the company should consider moving its headquarters there.
- Relocating the corporate headquarters also could benefit the entity's highly paid executives. The individual income and sales/use tax burden of employees should be a factor in LocalCo's decision.
- States often assess special taxes on trucking and airport functions and might apply different income tax apportionment formulas to these operations. LocalCo's tax department and its outside advisers should research these features of the various relevant tax systems to avoid any unexpected surprises.

What If?

If LocalCo did not have a history of strong profitability, some of these state and local tax recommendations might be different. In that case, the company would consider issues such as how a state allows loss and credit carryovers. In addition, if there is no state income tax liability to pay, income tax credits and deductions would be less attractive, so the negotiations might focus on property and payroll taxes instead.

LocalCo's tax plans might be exposed to tax law changes that will work to its detriment. Its locations include some of the most aggressive legislatures and taxing agencies in the country, so the taxpayer must watch for changes in those states' rules concerning nexus, income sourcing, apportionment, and incentives. Tax planning ideas that work currently might be undone by the adoption of gross receipts taxes, a unitary approach, market-based income sourcing, or economic income and sales/use nexus provisions.

Key Terms

Allocate, 26-8
Apportion, 26-8
Combined return, 26-18
Composite return, 26-23
Dock sales, 26-13
Multistate Tax Commission (MTC), 26-6
Nexus, 26-6
Passive investment company, 26-29
Payroll factor, 26-14
Property factor, 26-16
Public Law 86–272, 26-6
Sales factor, 26-13
Throwback rule, 26-13
UDITPA, 26-3
Unclaimed property, 26-26
Unitary theory, 26-18
Water's edge, 26-21

Discussion Questions

1. **LO.1** You are working with the top management of one of your clients in selecting the U.S. location for a new manufacturing operation. Craft a plan for the CEO to use in discussions with the economic development representatives of several candidate states. In no more than three PowerPoint slides, list some of the tax incentives the CEO should request from a particular state during the negotiations. Be both creative and aggressive in the requests. Communications Critical Thinking

2. **LO.1** Complete the following chart by indicating whether each item is true or false. Explain your answers by referencing the overlap of rules appearing in Federal and most state income tax laws.

	Item	True or False
a.	Most of the states start with Federal taxable income in computing state taxable income.	________
b.	The states use a wide variety of rules to compute corporate taxable income; as a result, there is no "typical" state income tax computation.	________
c.	Aggregate state taxable incomes always equal Federal taxable income; tax rules merely split the income among the states.	________
d.	The corporate income tax systems of most states can be described as applying progressive rate structures.	________
e.	A typical state income tax credit would equal 10% of the costs incurred to purchase and install solar energy panels for an existing factory.	________

3. **LO.2** In no more than three PowerPoint slides, list some general guidelines that a taxpayer can use to determine whether it has an obligation to file an income tax return with a particular state. (Include the terms *nexus* and *domicile* in your answer.) Communications

4. **LO.2** Josie is a sales representative for Talk2Me, a communications retailer based in Fort Smith, Arkansas. Josie's sales territory is Oklahoma, and she regularly takes day trips to Tulsa to meet with customers.

   During a typical sales call, Josie takes the customers' current orders for phones, cases, and attachments and, using an app on her wireless phone, sends the orders to headquarters in Fort Smith for immediate action. Approved orders are shipped from the Little Rock warehouse.

   Are Josie's sales subject to the Oklahoma corporate income tax? Explain.

5. **LO.2** Continue with the facts of Question 4. CheapPhones, one of Josie's customers who is facing tight cash-flow problems, wants to return about 100 defective cell phones. Talk2Me tells Josie to bring the phones back to headquarters. Fearing that she will lose CheapPhones as a customer if she does not comply with the request, Josie says, "Let me save you the time and cost of packing and shipping the defective phones. Put them in the trunk of my car, and I'll take them back." Does Josie's action change the answer to Question 4? Why or why not?

6. **LO.3, 4** Indicate whether each of the following items should be *allocated* or *apportioned* by the taxpayer in computing state corporate taxable income. Assume that the state follows the general rules of UDITPA.
   a. Profits from sales activities.
   b. Profits from consulting and other service activities.
   c. Losses from sales activities.
   d. Profits from managing the stock portfolio of a client.
   e. Profits from managing one's own stock portfolio.
   f. Gain on the sale of a plot of land held by a real estate developer.

g. Gain on the sale of a plot of land held by a manufacturer, on which it may expand its factory.

h. Rent income received by a manufacturer from the leasing of space to a supplier.

Critical Thinking 7. **LO.3, 5** Regarding the apportionment formula used to compute state taxable income, does each of the following independent characterizations describe a taxpayer that likely is based in state or out of state? Explain.

a. The sales factor is positively correlated with the payroll, but not the property, factor.

b. The sales factor is much higher than the property and payroll factors.

c. The property and payroll factors are much higher than those for other nexus states.

d. The sales and payroll factors are low, but the property factor is very high.

e. The sales factor is remaining constant, but the payroll factor is decreasing.

Critical Thinking 8. **LO.5** The trend in state income taxation is to adopt an apportionment formula that places extra weight on the sales factor. Many states now use sales-factor-only apportionment. Explain why this development is attractive to the taxing states.

9. **LO.5** Megan is an accountant for KnoxCo. She is a telecommuter and works most days from her home in Tennessee. Twice a month, she travels to Georgia for a staff meeting at the employer's Atlanta headquarters. In which state's payroll factor should Megan's compensation be included if:

a. Megan is an employee and is covered by the qualified retirement plan of her Atlanta employer?

b. Megan works as an independent contractor for several clients, including the Atlanta-based firm?

c. Megan is an employee and, for one day each month, she provides accounting services for KnoxCo's Memphis rental properties?

Critical Thinking 10. **LO.5** Keystone, your tax consulting client, is considering an expansion program that would entail the construction of a new logistics center in State Q. List at least five questions you should ask in determining whether an asset that is owned by Keystone is to be included in State Q's property factor numerator.

11. **LO.6** The trend in state income taxation is for states to adopt a version of the unitary theory of multijurisdictional taxation in their statutes and regulations.

a. Explain why some states are attracted to the unitary theory and a combined reporting scheme of multistate income taxation.

b. Is the application of the unitary theory a help or a detriment to the taxpayer? Why?

Critical Thinking 12. **LO.6** State A enjoys a prosperous economy, with high real estate values and compensation levels. State B's economy has seen better days—property values are depressed, and unemployment is higher than in other states. Most consumer goods are priced at about 10% less in State B than in State A. Both States A and B apply unitary income taxation to businesses that operate within the state. Does unitary taxation distort the assignment of taxable income between States A and B? Explain.

13. **LO.7** Evaluate this statement: An S corporation can facilitate the meeting of its state income tax filing obligations by developing a common spreadsheet that allocates and apportions income among the states with which it has nexus. This spreadsheet is attached to each of the state returns to be filed. (*Hint:* Use the term *composite return* in your answer.)

Communications 14. **LO.8** Create an outline describing the major exemptions and exclusions from the sales/use tax base of most states. The outline should be suitable for creating a presentation to classmates.

15. **LO.8** Your client, HillTop, is a retailer of women's clothing. It has increased sales during the holiday season by advertising gift cards for in-store and online use. HillTop has found that gift card holders who come into the store tend to purchase goods that total more than the amount of the gift card. Further, about one-third of the gift cards never are redeemed, thereby yielding cash to the company without a reduction of inventory. What are the tax issues confronting HillTop related to the gift cards? Critical Thinking

16. **LO.2, 9** Your client, Ecru Limited, uses a small sales force to solicit sales of its wholesale restaurant supplies. Ecru is based in State W, and the sales representatives are assigned territories in States X, Y, and Z. Ecru owns no property and employs no other personnel outside of State W. Communications Planning

    As Ecru's tax adviser, you are to write a policy manual listing various "do's and don'ts" for the sales personnel so that Ecru does not create income tax nexus with States X, Y, and Z.

    To prepare for your assignment, write a memo for the tax research file, summarizing the rules as to the ability of a corporation to terminate or create income tax nexus. Make certain that you discuss the *Wrigley* case [505 U.S. 214 (1992)] in your analysis.

17. **LO.9** Your client, Royal Corporation, generates significant interest income from its working capital liquid investments. Write a memo for the tax research file, discussing the planning opportunities presented by establishing a passive investment company. Support your memo with a diagram of the resulting flow of assets and income. Communications Planning

18. **LO.2, 5, 9** As the director of the multistate tax planning department of a consulting firm, you are developing a brochure to highlight the services it can provide. Part of the brochure is a list of five or so key techniques that clients can use to reduce state income tax liabilities. Develop this list for the brochure. Consider only income tax consequences in your analysis.

Computational Exercises

19. **LO.3, 4, 5** Castle Corporation conducts business in States 1, 2, and 3. Castle's $630,000 taxable income consists of $555,000 apportionable income and $75,000 allocable income generated from transactions conducted in State 3. Castle's sales, property, and payroll are evenly divided among the three states, and the states all employ a three-equal-factors apportionment formula. How much of Castle's income is taxable in:
    a. State 1?
    b. State 2?
    c. State 3?
    d. Express your computation as a Microsoft Excel formula that will provide the correct solution for all three states.

20. **LO.3, 4, 5** Fillon Corporation's operations include two manufacturing facilities, one in State A and one in State B. The plant located in State A generated $200,000 of income, and the plant located in State B generated a loss of $50,000. Therefore, Fillon's total taxable income is $150,000. By applying the statutes of each state, Fillon determines that its apportionment factors for States A and B are 70% and 30%, respectively.

    How much of Fillon's income is apportioned to:
    a. State A?
    b. State B?

21. **LO.1, 3, 4** Legends Corporation owns and operates two manufacturing facilities, one in State A and the other in State B. Due to a temporary decline in sales, Legends has rented 25% of its State A facility to an unaffiliated corporation. Legends generated $200,000 net rent income and $1,400,000 income from manufacturing. Both states classify the rent income as allocable (nonapportionable) income. By applying the statutes of each state, Legends determines that its apportionment factors are 70% for State A and 30% for State B.

    How much income is subject to tax in:

    a. State A?

    b. State B?

22. **LO.5** Beckett Corporation realized $800,000 of taxable income from the sales of its products in States A and B. Beckett's activities establish nexus for income tax purposes in both states. Beckett's sales, payroll, and property in the states include the following:

	State A	State B	Total
Sales	$960,000	$640,000	$1,600,000
Property	180,000	–0–	180,000
Payroll	220,000	–0–	220,000

    State B uses a double-weighted sales factor in its three-factor apportionment formula. How much of Beckett's taxable income is apportioned to State B?

23. **LO.5** Alvarez Corporation operates in two states, as indicated below. This year's operations generated $400,000 of apportionable income.

	State A	State B	Total
Sales	$800,000	$200,000	$1,000,000
Property	300,000	300,000	600,000
Payroll	200,000	50,000	250,000

    Compute Alvarez's State A taxable income assuming that State A apportions income based on a:

    a. Three-factor formula, equally weighted.

    b. Three-factor formula, with a double-weighted sales factor.

    c. Sales factor only.

24. **LO.5** Isle Corporation's entire operations are located in State A. Of Isle's $600,000 sales, 60% are made in State A and 40% are made in State B. Isle's solicitation of sales in State B is limited to mailing a monthly catalog to its customers in that state. However, Isle's employees pick up and replace damaged merchandise in State B. The pickup and replacement of damaged goods establish nexus with State A.

    However, State B's definition of activities necessary to create income-tax nexus is less strict than that imposed by State A; in State B, the mere pickup and replacement of damaged goods does not create nexus there. Isle's taxable income is $60,000. Both states impose a 10% corporate income tax and include only the sales factor in their apportionment formulas.

    Determine Isle's effective state income tax rate if:

    a. State A *has not* adopted a throwback rule.

    b. State A *has* adopted a throwback rule.

    c. Create a Microsoft Excel formula that will compute correctly the State A taxable income regardless of whether a throwback rule has been adopted.

25. **LO.5** Sante Fe Corporation's sales office and manufacturing plant are located in State A. Sante Fe also maintains a manufacturing plant and sales office in State B. For purposes of apportionment, State A defines payroll as all compensation paid to employees, including contributions to § 401(k) deferred compensation plans. Under the statutes of State B, neither compensation paid to officers nor contributions to § 401(k) plans are included in the payroll factor. Sante Fe incurred the following personnel costs.

	State A	State B	Total
Wages and salaries for employees other than officers	$ 60,000	$40,000	$100,000
Salaries for officers	40,000	20,000	60,000
Contributions to § 401(k) plans	20,000	10,000	30,000
Total	$120,000	$70,000	$190,000

What is the payroll factor for:

a. State A?

b. State B?

26. **LO.6** Vogel Corporation owns two subsidiaries, Song and Bird. Song, located in State A, generated taxable income of $500,000. During this same period, Bird, located in State B, generated a loss of $100,000.

a. Determine Song's taxable income in States A and B, assuming that the subsidiaries constitute independent corporations under the tax law.

b. How does your answer change if the corporations constitute a unitary business?

Problems

27. **LO.1** Use Exhibit 26.1 to compute Balboa Corporation's State F taxable income for the year.

Addition modifications	$29,000
Allocated income (total)	25,000
Allocated income (State F)	3,000
Allocated income (State G)	22,000
Apportionment percentage	40%
Credits	800
Federal taxable income	90,000
Subtraction modifications	15,000
Tax rate	5%

28. **LO.1, 3, 4** Use Exhibit 26.1 to provide the required information for Warbler Corporation, whose Federal taxable income totals $10,000,000.

Warbler apportions 70% of its manufacturing income to State C. Warbler generates $4,000,000 of nonapportionable income each year, and 30% of that income is allocated to State C. Applying the state income tax modifications, Warbler's total business income from the manufacturing operation this year is $12,000,000.

a. How much of Warbler's manufacturing income does State C tax?

b. How much of Warbler's allocable income does State C tax?

c. Explain your results.

29. **LO.1** For each of the following items considered independently, indicate whether the circumstances call for an addition modification (*A*), a subtraction modification (*S*), or no modification (*N*) in computing state taxable income. Then indicate the amount of any modification. The starting point in computing State Q taxable income is the year's Federal taxable income before any deduction for net operating losses.
   a. Federal cost recovery = $10,000, and State Q cost recovery = $15,000.
   b. Federal cost recovery = $15,000, and State Q cost recovery = $10,000.
   c. Federal income taxes paid = $30,000.
   d. Refund received from last year's State Q income taxes = $3,000.
   e. Local property taxes, deducted on the Federal return as a business expense = $80,000.
   f. Interest income from holding U.S. Treasury bonds = $5,000.
   g. Interest income from holding State Q revenue anticipation bonds = $3,000.
   h. Interest income from State P school district bonds = $10,000.
   i. Change in the excess of FIFO inventory valuation over the Federal LIFO amount = $6,000. State Q does not allow the LIFO method.
   j. An asset was sold for $18,000; its purchase price was $20,000. Accumulated Federal cost recovery = $15,000, and accumulated State Q cost recovery = $8,000.
   k. Dividend income received from State R corporation = $30,000, subject to a Federal dividends received deduction of 70%.

30. **LO.1** Perk Corporation is subject to tax only in State A. Perk generated the following income and deductions.

Federal taxable income	$300,000
State A income tax expense	15,000
Refund of State A income tax	3,000
Depreciation allowed for Federal tax purposes	200,000
Depreciation allowed for state tax purposes	120,000

Federal taxable income is the starting point in computing State A taxable income. State income taxes are not deductible for State A tax purposes. Determine Perk's State A taxable income.

31. **LO.1** Fallow Corporation is subject to tax only in State X. Fallow generated the following income and deductions. State income taxes are not deductible for State X income tax purposes.

Sales	$4,000,000
Cost of sales	2,800,000
State X income tax expense	200,000
Depreciation allowed for Federal tax purposes	400,000
Depreciation allowed for state tax purposes	250,000
Interest income on Federal obligations	40,000
Interest income on State X obligations	30,000
Expenses related to carrying State X obligations	2,000

   a. The starting point in computing the State X income tax base is Federal taxable income. Derive this amount.
   b. Determine Fallow's State X taxable income assuming that interest on State X obligations is exempt from State X income tax.
   c. Determine Fallow's State X taxable income assuming that interest on State X obligations is subject to State X income tax.

32. **LO.5** Dillman Corporation has nexus in States A and B. Dillman's activities for the year are summarized below.

	State A	State B	Total
Sales	$1,200,000	$ 400,000	$1,600,000
Property			
Average historical cost	500,000	300,000	800,000
Average accumulated depreciation	(300,000)	(100,000)	(400,000)
Payroll	2,500,000	500,000	3,000,000
Rent expense	–0–	35,000	35,000

Determine the apportionment factors for States A and B assuming that State A uses a three-factor apportionment formula under which sales, property (net depreciated basis), and payroll are equally weighted and State B employs a single-factor formula that consists solely of sales. State A has adopted the UDITPA with respect to the inclusion of rent payments in the property factor.

33. **LO.5** Assume the same facts as in Problem 32, except that State A uses a single-factor apportionment formula that consists solely of sales and State B uses a three-factor apportionment formula that equally weights sales, property (at historical cost), and payroll. State B does not include rent payments in the property factor.

34. **LO.5** Assume the same facts as in Problem 32, except that both states employ a three-factor formula, under which sales are double-weighted. The property factor in State A is computed using historical cost; this factor in State B is computed using the net depreciated basis. Neither State A nor State B includes rent payments in the property factor.

35. **LO.5** Jung Corporation operates in States A and B as indicated below. All goods are manufactured in State A. Determine the sales to be assigned to both states in computing Jung's sales factor for the year. Both states follow the UDITPA and the MTC regulations in this regard.

Sales shipped to State A locations	$300,000
Sales shipped to State B locations	500,000
Interest income from Jung's State B business checking accounts	5,000
Rent income from excess space in State A warehouse	40,000
Interest income from Treasury bills in Jung's State B brokerage account, holding only idle cash from operations	65,000
One-time sale of display equipment to State B purchaser (tax basis $90,000)	75,000
Royalty received from holding patent, licensed to State B user	90,000

36. **LO.5, 9** State E applies a throwback rule to sales, but State F does not. State G has not adopted an income tax to date. Clay Corporation, headquartered in State E, reported the following sales for the year. All of the goods were shipped from Clay's State E manufacturing facilities.

Critical Thinking
Planning

Customer	Customer's Location	This Year's Sales
ShellTell, Inc.	State E	$ 75,000,000
Tourists, Ltd.	State F	40,000,000
PageToo Corp.	State G	100,000,000
Total		$215,000,000

a. Determine Clay's sales factor in these states.

b. Comment on Clay's location strategy using only your tax computations.

Critical Thinking

37. **LO.5, 9** Quinn Corporation is subject to tax in States G, H, and I. Quinn's compensation expense includes the following.

	State G	State H	State I	Total
Salaries and wages for nonofficers	$200,000	$400,000	$400,000	$1,000,000
Officers' salaries	–0–	–0–	500,000	500,000
Total				$1,500,000

Officers' salaries are included in the payroll factor for States G and I, but not for State H. Compute Quinn's payroll factors for States G, H, and I. Comment on your results.

38. **LO.5** Fiona, a regional sales manager, works from her office in State U. Her region includes several states, as indicated in the sales report below. Fiona is compensated through straight commissions on the sales in her region and a fully excludible cafeteria plan conveying various fringe benefits to her. Determine how much of Fiona's $250,000 commissions and $75,000 fringe benefit package is assigned to the payroll factor of State U.

State	Sales Generated	Fiona's Time Spent There
U	$3,000,000	20%
V	4,000,000	50%
X	8,000,000	30%

39. **LO.5** Kim Corporation, a calendar year taxpayer, operates manufacturing facilities in States A and B. A summary of Kim's property holdings follows.

	Beginning of Year		
	State A	State B	Total
Inventory	$ 300,000	$ 200,000	$ 500,000
Plant and equipment	2,500,000	1,500,000	4,000,000
Accumulated depreciation: plant and equipment	(1,000,000)	(600,000)	(1,600,000)
Land	600,000	1,000,000	1,600,000
Rental property*	900,000	300,000	1,200,000
Accumulated depreciation: rental property	(200,000)	(90,000)	(290,000)

	End of Year		
	State A	State B	Total
Inventory	$ 400,000	$ 200,000	$ 600,000
Plant and equipment	2,800,000	1,200,000	4,000,000
Accumulated depreciation: plant and equipment	(1,200,000)	(650,000)	(1,850,000)
Land	600,000	1,200,000	1,800,000
Rental property*	1,000,000	300,000	1,300,000
Accumulated depreciation: rental property	(250,000)	(100,000)	(350,000)

*Unrelated to regular business operations.

Determine Kim's property factors for the two states. The statutes of both States A and B provide that average historical cost of business property is to be included in the property factor.

40. **LO.6, 9** True Corporation, a wholly owned subsidiary of Trumaine Corporation, generated a $400,000 taxable loss in its first year of operations. True's activities and sales are restricted to State A, which imposes an 8% income tax.

Communications
Decision Making
Planning

In the same year, Trumaine's taxable income is $1,000,000. Trumaine's activities and sales are restricted to State B, which imposes an 11% income tax. Both states use a three-factor apportionment formula that equally weights sales, payroll, and property, and both require a unitary group to file on a combined basis. Sales, payroll, and average property for each corporation are as follows.

	True Corporation	Trumaine Corporation	Total
Sales	$2,500,000	$4,000,000	$6,500,000
Property	1,000,000	2,500,000	3,500,000
Payroll	500,000	1,500,000	2,000,000

True and Trumaine have been found to be members of a unitary business.

a. Determine the overall state income tax for the unitary group.

b. Determine aggregate state income tax for the entities as if they were nonunitary.

c. Compare your results, and comment on the desirability of True's arrangement. Incorporate this analysis in a letter to Trumaine's board of directors. Corporate offices are located at 1234 Mulberry Lane, Birmingham, AL 35298.

41. **LO.6** Chang Corporation is part of a three-corporation unitary business. The group has a water's edge election in effect with respect to unitary State Q. State B does not apply the unitary concept with respect to its corporate income tax laws. Nor does Despina, a European country to which Saldez paid a $7,000,000 value added tax this year.

Saldez was organized in Despina and conducts all of its business there. Given the summary of operations that follows, determine Chang's and Elena's sales factors in States B and Q.

Corporation	Customer's Location	Sales
Chang	State B	$20,000,000
	State Q	60,000,000
Elena	State Q	70,000,000
Saldez	Despina	50,000,000

42. **LO.8** Using the following information from the books and records of Grande Corporation, determine Grande's total sales that are subject to State C's sales tax. Grande operates a retail general store.

Sales to State C consumers, general merchandise	$1,100,000
Sales to State C consumers, crutches and other medical supplies	245,000
Sales to consumers in State D, via mail order	80,000
Purchases from suppliers	55,000

43. **LO.8** As a retailer, Zertan Corporation sells software programs manufactured and packaged by other parties. Zertan also purchases computer parts, assembles them as specified by a customer in a purchase order, and sells them as operating stand-alone computers. All of Zertan's operations take place in State F, which levies a 9% sales tax. Results for the current year are as follows.

Sales of software	$2,500,000
Purchases of computer parts	1,600,000
Sales of computer systems	8,500,000
Purchases of office supplies	60,000
Purchases of packaging materials for the computer systems	20,000
Purchases of tools used by computer assemblers	50,000

a. What is Zertan's own sales tax expense for the year?

b. How much State F sales tax must Zertan collect and pay to the state on behalf of other taxpayers subject to the tax?

44. **LO.8** Indicate for each transaction whether a sales (*S*) or use (*U*) tax applies or whether the transaction is nontaxable (*N*). Assume that the most common definitional rules apply in both states. All taxpayers are individuals.

a. A resident of State A purchases an automobile in State A.

b. A resident of State A purchases groceries in State A.

c. A resident of State B purchases an automobile in State A.

d. A charity purchases office suppiies in State A.

e. A State A resident purchases an item in State B that will be in the inventory of her business.

45. **LO.5, 8** Wayne Corporation is subject to State A's franchise tax. The tax is imposed at a rate of 1.2% of the corporation's net worth, as apportioned to the state by use of a two-factor formula (sales and property factors, equally weighted). The property factor includes real and tangible personal property valued at historical cost as of the end of the taxable year.

Forty percent of Wayne's sales are attributable to State A, and $600,000 of the cost of Wayne's tangible personal property is located in State A.

Determine the State A franchise tax payable by Wayne this year given the following end-of-the-year balance sheet.

Cash		$ 200,000
Equipment	$1,000,000	
Accumulated depreciation	(300,000)	700,000
Furniture and fixtures	$ 800,000	
Accumulated depreciation	(50,000)	750,000
Intangible assets		450,000
Total assets		$2,100,000
Accounts and taxes payable		$ 600,000
Long-term debt		750,000
Common stock		1,000
Additional paid-in capital		249,000
Retained earnings		500,000
Total liabilities and equity		$2,100,000

Decision Making

46. **LO.5, 9** Dread Corporation operates in a high-tax state. The firm asks you for advice on a plan to outsource administrative work done in its home state to independent contractors. This work now costs the company $750,000 in wages and benefits. Dread's total payroll for the year is $8,000,000, of which $6,000,000 is for work currently done in the home state.

Communications
Critical Thinking
Planning

47. **LO.2, 5, 9** Prepare a PowerPoint presentation (maximum of six slides) entitled "Planning Principles for Our Multistate Clients." The slides will be used to lead a 20-minute discussion with colleagues in the corporate tax department. Keep the outline general, but assume that your colleagues have clients among them operating in at least 15 states. Address only income tax issues.

Research Problems

Use internet tax resources to address the following questions. Look for reliable websites and blogs of the IRS and other government agencies, media outlets, businesses, tax professionals, academics, think tanks, and political outlets.

Research Problem 1. Pick two of the following provisions that currently do not exist in your state. If your state does not levy a sales/use tax or an income tax on corporations, review the rules of a neighboring state. Send an e-mail to your instructor, listing pro and con arguments for the state to adopt the provisions.

Communications
Critical Thinking

a. Exempt "green" technology from the apportionment weight for the property factor.
b. Subject song and movie downloads to the sales/use tax.
c. Allow an income tax credit for 20% of the cost of in-state construction projects that are substantially completed within the next 18 months.
d. Establish income tax nexus using the factor presence nexus standards of the Multistate Tax Commission.
e. Add an income-tax "nexus team" to find the taxpayers operating in your state but based in Ohio, Illinois, or Arizona.
f. Adopt the definitions and other rules of the Streamlined Sales Tax Project.
g. Allow an income tax credit for 25% of the wages paid to newly hired employees and contractors who work in the tech and pharma industries.
h. Apply a tax on S corporations operating in the state equal to 2% of the entity's gross receipts.
i. Convert the corporate income tax to a tax on gross receipts in an effort to tax the profits of passive investment companies owned by in-state parent entities.
j. Broaden the definition of sales/use tax nexus so as to force sellers or marketplace facilitators to remit the tax for online sales.

Research Problem 2. For your state and one of its neighbors, find the following income tax rules. Place your data in a chart, and e-mail your findings to your instructor.

Communications

a. To what extent does each state follow the rulings of the Multistate Tax Commission?
b. Does the state adopt pertinent changes to the Internal Revenue Code? If so, as of what date?
c. What is the highest income tax rate for corporations?
d. Is the tax effectiveness of a passive investment company limited in some way? Has the state adopted the *Geoffrey* approach (see footnote 20) to the taxation of income from intangibles? Explain.
e. Does the state apply entity-level income taxes for S corporations, partnerships, and LLCs? If so, what are the terms of those taxes?

Research Problem 3. For your state and one of its neighbors, find the following sales/use tax rules. Place your data in a chart, and e-mail your findings to your instructor.

Communications
Data Analytics

a. What are the dollar amounts for sales and the number of sales transactions that trigger economic nexus with the state?
b. Describe any exemptions from the sales/use tax base that are allowed for transactions involving groceries, school clothing and supplies, religious goods, and legal services.
c. What is the discount allowed, if any, when a vendor remits sales/use tax to the state in a timely manner?
d. Is manufacturing equipment exempt from the sales/use tax? Medical devices for a clinic? Medical devices for a consumer?

e. Can a vendor use an electronic funds transfer system to remit its sales/use tax collections? If so, when is it required to do so?

f. Has the state joined the Streamlined Sales Tax Project? If yes, what is the effective date?

Communications
Data Analytics

Research Problem 4. Identify three states considered to be in the same economic region as your own. For each of the three states, answer the following questions. Answers to most can be found at **taxadmin.org**.

- What is the overall tax burden per capita, and where does it rank among all states?
- What is the overall tax burden as a percentage of personal income, and where does it rank among all states?
- From what source(s) does it raise most of its revenues (e.g., sales/use tax, highway tolls)? In what proportions?
- What is the highest marginal tax rate on corporate income?
- What is its apportionment formula, including factors and weights?

Summarize your findings in a Microsoft Excel spreadsheet, and submit it to your instructor.

Communications
Data Analytics

Research Problem 5. Read the "tax footnote" of five publicly traded U.S. corporations. Find the effective state/local income tax rates of each. Create a PowerPoint presentation (maximum of three slides) for your instructor, summarizing the search and reporting your findings.

Communications

Research Problem 6. Conduct a web search to find a recent state tax newsletter of a large CPA firm. Find one item of interest that pertains to how a state taxes a business. Write a summary of it and how it relates to a topic covered in this chapter; submit the summary to your instructor.

Becker CPA Review Questions

Becker

1. Olinto, Inc., has taxable income (before special deductions and the net operating loss deduction) of $92,000. Included in that amount is $12,000 of interest and dividend income. Forty percent of Olinto's property, payroll, and sales are in its home state. What amount of this taxable income will be taxed by Olinto, Inc.'s home state?

   a. $12,000 c. $44,000
   b. $36,800 d. $90,000

2. In which of the following cases will Federal law prohibit a state from imposing an income tax on net income?

   a. The business has a retail outlet store in the state.
   b. The business has its corporate headquarters in the state and generates sales from there.
   c. Orders are taken within the state and accepted at corporate headquarters outside of the state and shipped from a location outside of the state.
   d. Orders are taken within the state and accepted at corporate headquarters outside of the state and shipped from a location inside the state.

3. Which of the following activities will not trigger nexus in a state in which a company operates?

   a. Providing installation services with the purchase of tangible personal property.
   b. Acceptance of an order within the state.
   c. Delivery by a common carrier.
   d. Collection of delinquent accounts.

4. Which of the following statements best describes a multistate corporation's approach to the apportionment and allocation of its income?

   I. The corporation will allocate its nonbusiness income.
   II. The corporation will apportion its business income.

   a. I only.
   b. II only.
   c. Both I and II.
   d. Neither I nor II.

5. Reiki, Inc., operates stores in Massachusetts and Vermont. Reiki's payroll, property, and sales by state are as follows:

State	Payroll	Property (Ending)	Property (Average)	Sales
Massachusetts	$200,000	$175,000	$195,000	$ 750,000
Vermont	350,000	225,000	200,000	900,000
Total	550,000	400,000	395,000	1,650,000

   What is Reiki's apportionment factor for Massachusetts (round to two decimal places)?

   a. 41.86%
   b. 44.12%
   c. 45.45%
   d. 43.73%

Chapter 27

Taxation of International Transactions

Learning Objectives: *After completing Chapter 27, you should be able to:*

- **LO.1** Explain the framework underlying the U.S. taxation of cross-border transactions.
- **LO.2** Describe the interaction between Internal Revenue Code provisions and tax treaties.
- **LO.3** Determine whether income is U.S.- or foreign-sourced.
- **LO.4** Apply foreign currency exchange rules as they affect the tax consequences of international transactions.
- **LO.5** Work with the U.S. tax provisions affecting U.S. persons earning foreign-source income, including antideferral provisions and the foreign tax credit.
- **LO.6** Apply the U.S. tax provisions concerning nonresident alien individuals and foreign corporations.

Chapter Outline

MONKEY BUSINESS IMAGES/SHUTTERSTOCK.COM

The Big Picture

Going International

VoiceCo, a domestic corporation, designs, manufactures, and sells specialty microphones for use in theaters. All of its activities take place in Florida, although it ships products to customers all over the United States. When it receives inquiries about its products from potential non-U.S. customers, VoiceCo decides to test the overseas market and places ads in various trade journals that have an international focus. Soon it is taking orders from offshore customers.

VoiceCo is concerned about its potential worldwide income tax exposure. Although it has no assets or employees outside the United States, it now is involved in international commerce. Is VoiceCo subject to income taxes in any other countries? Must it pay U.S. income taxes on the profits from its overseas sales? What if VoiceCo pays taxes to other countries? Does it receive any benefit from these payments on its U.S. tax return?

Later, VoiceCo establishes a manufacturing plant in Ireland to meet the European demand for its products. VoiceCo incorporates the Irish operation as VoiceCo-Ireland, an Irish corporation. Ireland imposes only a 12.5 percent tax on VoiceCo-Ireland's profits. How does U.S. corporate income tax law affect these activities?

Read the chapter and formulate your response.

In today's global business environment, most large businesses are truly international in scope. Large U.S. corporations earn on average more than 20 percent of their profits overseas, with offshore sales by "all-American" companies Coca-Cola and Apple exceeding two-thirds of their total sales for a typical year. "Offshore" companies like Honda and Toyota operate large manufacturing plants in the United States, with as much as one-third of their total sales taking place in the United States.

Global trade is an integral part of the U.S. economy. In 2021, U.S. exports and imports of goods and services totaled $2.5 trillion and $3.4 trillion, respectively. The largest dollar volume of U.S. exports consists of petroleum products, pharmaceuticals, and semiconductors. The top U.S. export partners are Mexico, Canada, and China.[1]

Cross-border transactions create special tax considerations for both the United States and its trading partners. Tax planning opportunities can arise as different countries raise revenue through income and other taxes, applying various tax bases and tax rates. Exhibit 27.1 includes data about the top statutory tax rates that various countries apply to corporate taxable income.

From a U.S. perspective, international tax laws should promote the global competitiveness of U.S. enterprises while protecting the tax revenue base of the United States. These two objectives sometimes conflict, however. The need to deal with both contributes to the complexity of the rules governing the U.S. taxation of cross-border transactions.

U.S. persons engage in activities outside the United States for many different reasons. Consider two U.S. corporations that have established sales subsidiaries in foreign countries. Dedalus, Inc., operates in Germany, a high-tax country, because customers demand local attention from sales agents. Mulligan, Inc., operates in the Cayman Islands, a low-tax country, simply to shift income outside the United States. U.S. tax law must fairly address both situations with the same law.

Exhibit 27.1 Top Statutory Corporate Income Tax Rates for Selected OECD Countries, 2022

Country	Rate
Ireland	12.5%
United Kingdom	19.0%
Sweden	20.6%
United States	25.8%
France	25.8%
Japan	29.7%
Germany	29.8%
Mexico	30.0%
OECD average	23.1%

Note: Tax rates include additional taxes on corporate taxable income levied by states, cities, provinces, cantons, and other smaller jurisdictions. Deductions, exemptions, and credits can reduce an entity's effective tax rate below the top statutory rate. Some countries outside of the OECD, such as Bermuda, have a 0% corporate tax rate.

Source: OECD 2022 Statutory Corporate Income Tax Rates (**stats.oecd.org/Index.aspx?DataSetCode=TABLE_II1#**).

[1] U.S. Census Bureau; see **https://www.census.gov/foreign-trade/Press-Release/current_press_release/index.html**, Exhibits 1, 7, and 19.

U.S. multinational taxpayers—and tax professionals—must understand the Federal tax rules related to international business, so that these rules can be incorporated into their overall tax plans. Generally, this involves reducing the exposure to double taxation of business profits, locating cash and other assets where they will be the most productive, and decreasing the present value of income tax liabilities (e.g., by accelerating losses and deductions and deferring taxable income recognition).

27-1 Overview of International Taxation

LO.1

Explain the framework underlying the U.S. taxation of cross-border transactions.

The U.S. taxation of cross-border transactions can be organized in terms of "outbound" and "inbound" taxation. **Outbound taxation** refers to the U.S. taxation of foreign-source income earned by U.S. taxpayers. **Inbound taxation** refers to the U.S. taxation of U.S.-source income earned by non-U.S. taxpayers.[2]

U.S. persons[3] earning U.S.-source income are taxed using only the domestic provisions of the Internal Revenue Code. Non-U.S. persons earning foreign-source income are not within the taxing jurisdiction of the United States unless this income is connected to a U.S. trade or business. Exhibit 27.2 illustrates this categorization.

Most countries in the developed world use a *territorial* taxing system under which only the taxable income generated within the country's borders is subject to tax there, regardless of who the taxpayer is. By taxing all events for all taxpayers that occur within their borders and nothing else, most business income generated in those countries is subject to tax only at one time and in one place. For the most part, U.S. corporate income tax law applies a territorial system for transactions entered into by non-U.S. persons.

In addition, most countries have been cutting their business income tax rates over the last two decades. According to the Organization for Economic Cooperation and Development (OECD), the average corporate tax rate for member countries has fallen from 32.3% in 2000 to 23.1% in 2021.[4] Taxes have become a significant device by which countries compete for business, capital, and jobs.

U.S. business income tax provisions generally constitute a *worldwide* system. Under these rules, the United States assesses income tax on all domestic and foreign income of U.S. taxpayers, from whatever source derived. This means that the income of a U.S. person could be subject to income tax in the United States and, simultaneously, in the non-U.S. country where it arises. Strict worldwide taxation systems are rare today throughout the developed world.

This potential for the *double taxation* of business income for a U.S. taxpayer under a worldwide system is addressed in the Code in several ways. Historically, the most important of these is the **foreign tax credit (FTC)**. U.S. taxpayers are allowed a credit against their U.S. income tax for income taxes paid on income generated in another country, up to the amount of U.S. income tax that would result from the same income.[5]

Although the worldwide taxing system still undergirds the income taxation of U.S. persons' cross-border transactions, recent tax law changes overlay these rules, especially for corporations. These changes:

- Move the United States closer to a territorial system of taxation for U.S. businesses.
- Provide incentives for U.S. businesses to locate jobs in the United States and repatriate foreign profits back to the United States.
- Prevent U.S. entities from shifting taxable income outside the United States into low-tax-rate countries.

[2]The terms *domestic* and *foreign* are defined in §§ 7701(a)(4) and (5).

[3]The term *person* includes an individual, corporation, partnership, trust, estate, or association. § 7701(a)(1).

[4]**https://stats.oecd.org/index.aspx?DataSetCode=Table_II1**.

[5]A carryback or carryforward of an FTC arose when the foreign tax paid exceeded the amount of the corresponding Federal income tax liability for the tax year.

Exhibit 27.2 U.S. Taxation of Cross-Border Transactions

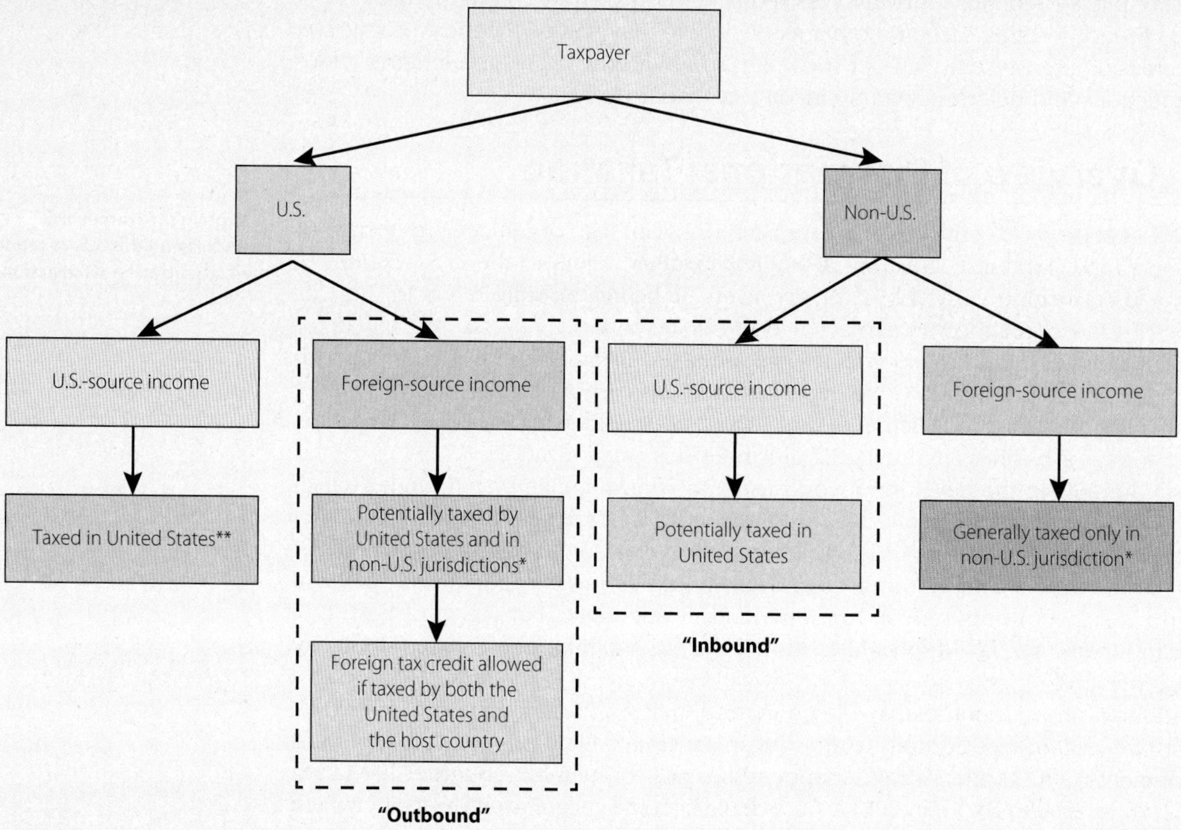

Taxpayer

U.S.

U.S.-source income

Taxed in United States**

Foreign-source income

Potentially taxed by United States and in non-U.S. jurisdictions*

Foreign tax credit allowed if taxed by both the United States and the host country

"Outbound"

Non-U.S.

U.S.-source income

Potentially taxed in United States

"Inbound"

Foreign-source income

Generally taxed only in non-U.S. jurisdiction*

*Depends on local country tax law.
**Worldwide tax rules may apply.

The Big Picture

Example 2

Return to the facts of *The Big Picture* on p. 27-1. Assume that VoiceCo operates an unincorporated manufacturing branch in Singapore to take advantage of local materials and low labor costs. This branch income is taxed in the United States as part of VoiceCo's worldwide income, but it also is taxed in Singapore. Without the availability of a foreign tax credit to mitigate this double taxation, VoiceCo would face a tax burden higher than both its domestic and foreign competitors.

The Big Picture

Return to the facts of *The Big Picture* on p. 27-1. VoiceCo's major competitor is a Swiss-based foreign corporation with operations in the United States. Although not a U.S. person, the Swiss competitor is taxed in the United States on its U.S.-source business income. If the Swiss competitor could operate free of U.S. tax, VoiceCo would face a serious competitive disadvantage.

LO.2

Describe the interaction between Internal Revenue Code provisions and tax treaties.

27-2 Tax Treaties

Without **tax treaties**, countries where income is sourced ("source countries") would enjoy significant advantages over countries where taxpayers reside ("residence countries"). Absent economic consequences, source countries could create their own definition of income and impose any rate of tax. Residence countries would have little ability to tax the foreign profits of their citizens.

Tax treaties demonstrate a compromise between residence and source countries to bifurcate primary taxing responsibility between the two jurisdictions. Treaties generally stipulate which country has primary taxing authority over certain types of income. When source countries have primary taxing responsibility, residence countries provide a credit, deduction, or exclusion from tax for source country income. Tax treaties also promote the exchange of information between countries to reduce fiscal evasion and provide a degree of income tax certainty for complex international business ventures.

The United States has almost 70 bilateral tax treaties in effect (see Exhibit 27.3). Tax treaties do not interfere with a country's ability to tax its own citizens within its own borders and do not obligate a country to enforce the tax laws of other countries. In its own tax treaties, the United States provides that it will treat similarly situated foreign and domestic taxpayers comparably and requires other nations to pledge the same. U.S. tax treaties with other countries are also limited in scope to U.S. income taxation and not to the tax laws and regulations of individual states or localities. Tax treaty provisions must be harmonized with the treatment otherwise called for under the Internal Revenue Code or foreign tax statutes.[6] If there is a conflict, preference is given to whichever is newer, the treaty or the law; this is known as the "later in time" rule.[7]

Treaty language, in general, reserves for a taxpayer's country of residence the right to tax passive income (e.g., dividends, interest, and royalties). Source countries are generally granted taxing authority over income earned within their borders when a business creates a *permanent establishment*, or a fixed place of business, within the country.

Example 4

ForCo, Ltd., a resident of a country with which the United States has an income tax treaty, earns income attributable to a permanent establishment (e.g., a fixed place of business) in the United States.

Under the treaty, the United States has primary taxing rights related to this income. The other country can require that the income be included in gross income and can subject the income to its income tax, but it must allow a credit, an exemption, or some other offset for the taxes paid to the United States on the income.

Exhibit 27.3 U.S. Income Tax Treaties in Force as of 2022

Armenia	France	Lithuania	South Africa
Australia	Georgia	Luxembourg	Spain
Austria	Germany	Malta	Sri Lanka
Azerbaijan	Greece	Mexico	Sweden
Bangladesh	Hungary	Moldova	Switzerland
Barbados	Iceland	Morocco	Tajikistan
Belarus	India	Netherlands	Thailand
Belgium	Indonesia	New Zealand	Trinidad
Bulgaria	Ireland	Norway	Tunisia
Canada	Israel	Pakistan	Turkey
China	Italy	Philippines	Turkmenistan
Cyprus	Jamaica	Poland	Ukraine
Czech Republic	Japan	Portugal	United Kingdom
Denmark	Kazakhstan	Romania	Uzbekistan
Egypt	Korea	Russia	Venezuela
Estonia	Kyrgyzstan	Slovak Republic	Vietnam
Finland	Latvia	Slovenia	

Source: Internal Revenue Service (**https://www.irs.gov/businesses/international-businesses/united-states-income-tax-treaties-a-to-z**).

[6]§ 7852(d)(1).

[7]§ *Cook v. U.S.*, 288 U.S. 102 (1933).

The United States has developed a Model Income Tax Convention as the starting point for negotiating income tax treaties with other countries.[8] To help ensure that non-U.S. parties pay any Federal income tax they may owe on income generated in the United States, U.S. taxpayers are required to withhold taxes on payments made to non-U.S. parties. Most U.S. income tax treaties reduce the withholding tax rate on certain items of investment income, such as interest and dividends. Exhibit 27.4 summarizes the treaty-based withholding rates for selected countries. Lacking a treaty provision, the withholding rate likely would be 30 percent.[9]

Exhibit 27.4 Selected Tax Treaty Withholding Rates, Income Paid by U.S. Entity

	Interest	Dividends (in General)	Dividends Paid by U.S. Subsidiary to a Foreign Parent Corporation
Australia	10%	15%	5%
Canada	0%	15%	5%
China	10%	10%	10%
Ireland	0%	15%	5%
Japan	0%	10%	5%
Mexico	15%	10%	5%
Philippines	15%	25%	20%
United Kingdom	0%	15%	5%
Non-treaty countries	30%	30%	30%

Source: Internal Revenue Service (**https://www.irs.gov/pub/irs-utl/Tax_Treaty_Table_1_2019_Feb.pdf**).

LO.3

Determine whether income is U.S.- or foreign-sourced.

27-3 Sourcing of Income and Deductions

The *sourcing* of income and deductions inside and outside the United States has a direct bearing on a number of tax provisions affecting both U.S. and offshore taxpayers. For example, non-U.S. taxpayers generally are taxed only on U.S.-source income, and U.S. taxpayers apply the sourcing rules in making several income, credit, and deduction computations. Sourcing is very important to U.S. taxpayers, since only foreign-sourced income is eligible for the foreign tax credit.

27-3a Income Sourcing Rules

The determination of the source of income depends on the type of income realized (e.g., income from the sale of property versus income for the use of property).[10] An item is determined to be either "U.S.-source" or "foreign-source" under the following rules.

Interest

Interest income received from the U.S. government, from the District of Columbia, and from noncorporate U.S. residents or domestic corporations is U.S.-source income.[11]

There are a few exceptions to this rule. Certain interest received from a U.S. corporation that earned 80 percent or more of its active business income from offshore sources over the prior three-year period is treated as foreign-source income. Interest received on amounts deposited with an overseas branch of a U.S. corporation also is treated as foreign-source income if the branch is engaged in the commercial banking business.

John holds a bond issued by Alpha, a domestic corporation. For the immediately preceding three tax years, 82% of Alpha's gross income has been active foreign business income. The interest income that John receives for the current tax year from Alpha is foreign-source income.

[8] Treasury Department Model Income Tax Convention (November 17, 2016). See **irs.gov/businesses/international-businesses/united-states-model-tax-treaty-documents**.

[9] § 871(a).

[10] Rules pertaining to the sourcing of income are found in §§ 861 through 865.

[11] § 861(a)(1).

Dividends

Dividends received from domestic corporations generally are U.S.-source income.[12] Typically, dividends paid by a non-U.S. corporation are foreign-source income. However, if 25 percent or more of an offshore corporation's gross income is effectively connected with a U.S. trade or business during the three-year period immediately preceding the year of the dividend payment, that percentage of the dividend is treated as U.S.-source income.

Annika receives dividend income from the following corporations during the current tax year:

Amount	Corporation	Effectively Connected U.S. Income for Past Three Years	U.S.-Source Income
$500	Green, domestic	85%	$500
600	Brown, domestic	13%	600
300	Orange, foreign	92%	276

Because Green Corporation and Brown Corporation are domestic corporations, the dividends they pay are U.S.-source income. Orange Corporation is a non-U.S. corporation that earned 92% of its business income over the prior three years from income effectively connected with a U.S. trade or business. Because Orange meets the 25% threshold, 92% of its dividend is U.S.-source.

Personal Services Income

The source of income from personal services generally is determined by the location in which the services are performed (inside or outside the United States). However, a limited *commercial traveler* exception is available for non-U.S. persons. Under this exception, personal services income that meets *all* of the following requirements will not be classified as U.S.-source income:

- The services must be performed by a nonresident alien[13] who is in the United States for 90 days or less during the taxable year.
- The compensation may not exceed $3,000 in total for the services performed in the United States.
- The services must be performed on behalf of:
  - A nonresident alien, non-U.S. partnership, or non-U.S. corporation that is not engaged in a U.S. trade or business, or
  - An office or place of business maintained in a country outside the United States by an individual who is a citizen or resident of the United States, a domestic partnership, or a domestic corporation.

Global Tax Issues — Agreement on Global Minimum Corporate Tax Rate Reached

In October 2021, almost 140 countries agreed to set a minimum corporate tax rate of 15% to curb incentives for corporations to shift profits from high to low marginal tax rate countries. These nations have all agreed in principle, but the details are more problematic. For example, one proposal in the United States is to raise the minimum tax rate on global intangible income to 16.6% and apply it on a country-by-country basis. Another proposal is to change the rules governing where income is sourced, which would require renegotiation of bilateral income tax treaties. The original agreement called for countries to implement the minimum tax beginning in 2023. A handful of countries have signaled they intend to meet this target date, meaning some multinationals may soon be required to comply. Others have been slower to act. For example, in November 2022, the U.K. said it would start collecting the tax in 2024. In December 2022, all EU countries agreed to a standard approach of changing national laws to allow for collection of the tax.

[12] § 861(a)(2)(A).

[13] Tax law uses the term *alien* to describe a person who is not a citizen or national of the United States.

Global Tax Issues

Meet Your Fast-Food Restaurant Cashier—From 2,500 Miles Away

Labor costs are one of the largest expenses for fast-food restaurants–sometimes up to 30 percent of gross sales. Managing labor costs effectively can mean using labor from other countries, such as call centers in India and Malaysia. Fast-food seemed immune to this trend–until now. A Canadian fast-food franchise uses an in-store system to connect customers to employees based in Nicaragua. The customer, who is in the store, communicates with the Nicaraguan employee through "Percy," a computer screen with a headset. The customer's order is then communicated to in-store employees who make and deliver the food to the customer. If this happened in the United States, would the Nicaraguan employee have U.S.-source or Nicaragua-source income?

Example 7

Mark, a nonresident alien, is an engineer employed by a foreign oil company. He spent four weeks in the United States arranging the purchase of field equipment for his company. His salary for the four weeks was $3,500.

Even though the oil company is not engaged in a U.S. trade or business, and Mark was in the United States for less than 90 days during the taxable year, the income is U.S.-source income because it exceeds $3,000.

Rents and Royalties

Income received for the use of tangible property is sourced to the country in which the property is located. The source of income received for the use of intangible property (e.g., patents, copyrights, processes, and formulas) is the country where the property is used.

Sale or Exchange of Property

Generally, the location of *real property* determines the source of any income derived from the sale of that property. Income from the disposition of U.S. real property interests is U.S.-source income.

The source of income from the sale of *personal property* (assets other than real property) depends on several factors, including the following:

- Whether the property was produced by the seller.
- What type of property was sold (e.g., inventory or a capital asset).
- Where the residence of the seller was.

Generally, income or gain from the sale of personal property is sourced according to the residence of the seller. Income from the sale of inventory, however, is sourced differently depending on whether the taxpayer *purchased* or *produced* the inventory.[14] When the seller has *produced* the inventory, the income is sourced to the country where the inventory was produced. Income from the sale of *purchased* inventory is sourced where the sale takes place.

The following exceptions apply to the sale of personal property other than inventory:

- Gain on the sale of depreciable personal property is sourced according to prior depreciation deductions to the extent of the deductions. Any excess gain is sourced the same as the sale of inventory.
- Gain on the sale of intangibles is sourced according to prior amortization deductions to the extent of the deductions.
- Gain attributable to an office or a fixed place of business maintained outside the United States by a U.S. resident is foreign-source income.
- Income or gain attributable to an office or a fixed place of business maintained in the United States by a nonresident is U.S.-source income.

Losses are sourced depending on the nature of the property. Different rules exist for the disposition of stock versus other personal property.[15]

[14] §§ 861(a)(6) and 865. The sale is deemed to take place where title passes. Reg. § 1.861–7(c). There has been considerable conflict in this area. See, for example, *Liggett Group, Inc.*, 58 TCM 1167, T.C.Memo. 1990–18.

[15] See Reg. § 1.861–8(e)(7) and Reg. § 1.865–1(a)(1). See Reg. §§ 1.865–2)(a)(1) and (2) regarding the source of losses on the disposition of stock.

Transportation and Communication Income

Income derived from providing transportation services is U.S.-source income if the transportation begins and ends in the United States. Fifty percent of the income from transportation services beginning *or* ending in the United States is U.S.-source income, unless the U.S. point is only an intermediate stop. Income from space and ocean activities conducted outside the jurisdiction of any country is sourced according to the residence of the person conducting the activity.

International communication income derived by a U.S. person is one-half U.S.-source when transmission is between the United States and another country. International communication income derived by non-U.S. persons is foreign-source income unless it is attributable to an office or another fixed place of business in the United States. In that case, it is U.S.-source income.

Software Income

Income from the sale or license of software is sourced depending on how the income is classified. A transfer of software is classified as either the transfer of a copyright (e.g., the right to the computer program itself) or the transfer of a copyrighted article (the right to use a copy of the computer program).[16] If the transfer is considered a transfer of a copyright, the income is sourced using the royalty income rules. If the transfer is considered a transfer of a copyrighted article, the income is treated as resulting from a sale of the article and is sourced based on the personal property sales rules.[17]

27-3b Allocation and Apportionment of Deductions

The United States levies a tax on *taxable income* (gross income minus deductions). Deductions and losses, therefore, also must be *allocated* and *apportioned* between U.S.- and foreign-source gross income to determine U.S.- and foreign-source taxable income. Deductions directly related to an activity or property are first *allocated* to classes of income. Then these deductions are *apportioned* between U.S.- and foreign-source on a reasonable basis.[18]

Ace, Inc., a domestic corporation, reports $2,000,000 of gross income and $50,000 of expenses related to real estate sales and rental activities. The expenses can be *allocated* and then *apportioned* using gross income as a basis in the following way:

	Gross Income		Expense	Expense Apportionment	
	Foreign	U.S.	Allocation	Foreign	U.S.
Sales	$1,000,000	$500,000	$37,500*	$25,000	$12,500**
Rentals	400,000	100,000	12,500	10,000	2,500***
Totals			$50,000	$35,000	$15,000

*$50,000 × ($1,500,000 ÷ $2,000,000).

**$37,500 × ($500,000 ÷ $1,500,000).

***$12,500 × ($100,000 ÷ $500,000).

If, instead, Ace could show that $45,000 of the expenses were directly related to sales income, the $45,000 would be allocated specifically to that class of gross income, with the remainder allocated and apportioned ratably based on gross income.

Interest expense is allocated and apportioned based on the theory that borrowed money can be raised and spent in any country without being earmarked to any specific location or use (i.e., it is *fungible*). With limited exceptions, interest expense is attributable to all of the activities and property of the taxpayer, regardless of the specific purpose for incurring the debt on which interest is paid. Taxpayers allocate and apportion interest expense on the basis of the tax book value of the leveraged assets.[19]

16 Reg. § 1.861–18.

17 Reg. §§ 1.861–18(f)(1) and (2).

18 Reg. § 1.861–8.

19 Reg. § 1.861–9T. Reg. § 1.861–10T(b) describes circumstances in which interest expense can be directly allocated to specific debt. This exception to the fungibility concept is limited to cases in which specific property is purchased or improved with nonrecourse debt.

The Big Picture

Example 9

Return to the facts of *The Big Picture* on p. 27-1. Assume that VoiceCo generates U.S.-source and foreign-source gross income for the current year. VoiceCo's assets (measured at tax book value) are as follows:

Assets generating U.S.-source income	$18,000,000
Assets generating foreign-source income	5,000,000
	$23,000,000

VoiceCo incurs interest expense of $800,000 for the current year. Interest expense is apportioned to foreign-source income as follows:

$$\frac{\$5{,}000{,}000 \text{ (foreign assets)}}{\$23{,}000{,}000 \text{ (total assets)}} \times \$800{,}000 = \$173{,}913$$

Different rules apply to research and development (R&D) expenditures, certain costs of day-to-day management, legal and accounting fees and expenses, income taxes, and losses. Although U.S. companies incur about 90 percent of their R&D expenditures at U.S. facilities, several billion dollars are spent on offshore R&D each year. If the R&D relates to offshore product sales, a portion of a U.S. company's R&D expense is treated as foreign-source.

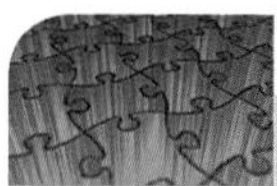

Concept Summary 27.1

The Sourcing Rules

The Code and Regulations include rules that designate income and deduction items as U.S.-source or foreign-source. These rules are important for several purposes.

- A U.S. taxpayer uses U.S.- and foreign-source amounts in computing various income, credits, and deductions.
- A non-U.S. taxpayer is subject to U.S. Federal income taxes only on U.S.-source taxable income.
- An expatriate from the United States (e.g., an employee of a U.S. business entity who temporarily is stationed overseas) can claim a foreign earned income exclusion only on foreign-source income (§ 911; not otherwise discussed in this chapter).

27-3c **Transfer Pricing**

Income Shifting

A **transfer pricing** arrangement sets the internal prices at which goods and services are sold between related parties (e.g., a parent corporation and its subsidiary). Transfer pricing also can refer to the use of charges, such as fees for management services and database access, that are assessed on one related party by another. Through transfer pricing, net profits can be shifted from one entity to a different entity, thereby achieving a tax advantage. For instance, an entity in a high-tax country might pay a management fee to its parent in a low-tax country. Doing so creates a valuable deduction in a high-tax jurisdiction, with the related income (the management fee received) subject to a lower tax rate.

The IRS uses § 482 to counter a taxpayer's use of transfer pricing to manipulate taxable income within a group of entities. This provision gives the IRS the power to reallocate gross income, deductions, credits, or allowances between or among organizations, trades, or businesses owned or controlled directly or indirectly by the same interests. This very powerful tool can be used whenever the IRS determines that reallocation is necessary to prevent the evasion of taxes or to reflect income more clearly. A variety of methods can be used to determine the best transfer price. No one method is favored over another or deemed more reliable than another by the Treasury Department.

Ultimately, the *best method*, according to the Treasury Department, is the one that most accurately reflects the economic reality of the transaction.[20]

Code § 482 is a "one-edged sword" available only to the IRS. A taxpayer generally cannot invoke § 482 to reallocate income and expenses.[21]

Ethics & Equity **The Costs of Good Tax Planning**

High Tech Tops (HTT), a C corporation based in California, manufactures resilient cases and covers for laptops, smartphones, and tablets. Its sales and profits have more than doubled in each of the last five years (i.e., the company is growth-oriented and recession-proof). Its employees and contractors make above-average wages, so they make important contributions to the local individual income, sales, and property tax collections.

But the Federal and state corporate income tax is another story. Using legal and effective transfer pricing techniques, HTT shifts most of its operating profits to low-tax subsidiaries in Ireland and Singapore. Most of the firm's executives, engineers, and designers are based in the United States, but almost all of the sales operations are run from overseas. HTT's customers live around the world, but its tax liabilities are concentrated in the low-tax jurisdictions.

You are the president of State University, across town from HTT's headquarters. The company sends hundreds of its employees to take graduate and professional courses on your campus, and several of the corporate leaders are frequent guest speakers and adjunct lecturers in classes.

Still, the state income tax the company avoids through its transfer pricing plans would fund millions of dollars of campus growth and improvements for State University.

Should you become involved in the politics of the matter and lobby at your statehouse for tighter rules on transfer pricing? Such an action might result in tax increases that would improve your university's situation, but it also might force HTT to consider moving its headquarters to another location.

Example 10

Consider the transaction depicted in Exhibit 27.5. A U.S. corporation manufactures and sells inventory to an unrelated foreign customer. The sales price for the inventory is $1,000, and the related cost of goods sold (COGS) is $600. All of the resulting profit of $400 is taxed to the U.S. corporation, resulting in an $84 U.S. income tax liability ($400 × 21%). If the U.S. corporation has no business presence in the foreign jurisdiction and is merely selling to a customer located there, the foreign government is unlikely to impose any local income tax on the U.S. corporation. Consequently, the total tax burden imposed on the inventory sale is $84.

Suppose instead that the U.S. corporation attempts to reduce its total tax expense by channeling the inventory sale through a subsidiary in the same country as the foreign customer. In this case, because the U.S. corporation controls the foreign subsidiary, it chooses an intercompany sales price (the transfer price) that effectively moves a portion of the profits from the United States to the non-U.S. country.

By selling the inventory it manufactured to its 100%-owned foreign subsidiary for $700, the U.S. corporation reports only $100 of profits and an associated U.S. tax liability of $21. The subsidiary then sells the inventory to the ultimate customer for $1,000 and, with a $700 COGS, earns a $300 profit. In this example, the non-U.S. country imposes only a 10% tax on corporate profits, resulting in an income tax there of $30 ($300 × 10%). By using a related offshore entity in a lower-tax jurisdiction, the U.S. corporation has lowered its overall tax liability on the sale from $84 (all U.S.) to $51 ($21 U.S. and $30 foreign).

Will the IRS agree to $700 as the appropriate transfer price in considering whether to apply § 482? The IRS may question why the subsidiary deserved to earn $300 of the total $400 profit related to the manufacture and sale of the inventory. In general, the U.S. corporation must document the functions performed by its subsidiary, the assets it owns that assist in producing the income, or the risks it takes (e.g., credit risk) to justify its profit assignment.

If the IRS does not consider the $300 profit earned by the subsidiary to be appropriate, it will use § 482 to adjust the transfer price upward. If the IRS determines that the transfer price should have been, for example, $990, then the U.S. corporation reports a $390 profit (with $82 of U.S. income tax) and the non-U.S. corporation earns a $10 profit (with $1 of the other country's income tax). With this change in transfer price, the U.S. corporation reduces its tax liability, but only by $1 [$84 − ($82 + $1)].

[20] Reg. § 1.482–1(c).

[21] Reg. § 1.482–1(a)(3).

Exhibit 27.5 Transfer Pricing Example

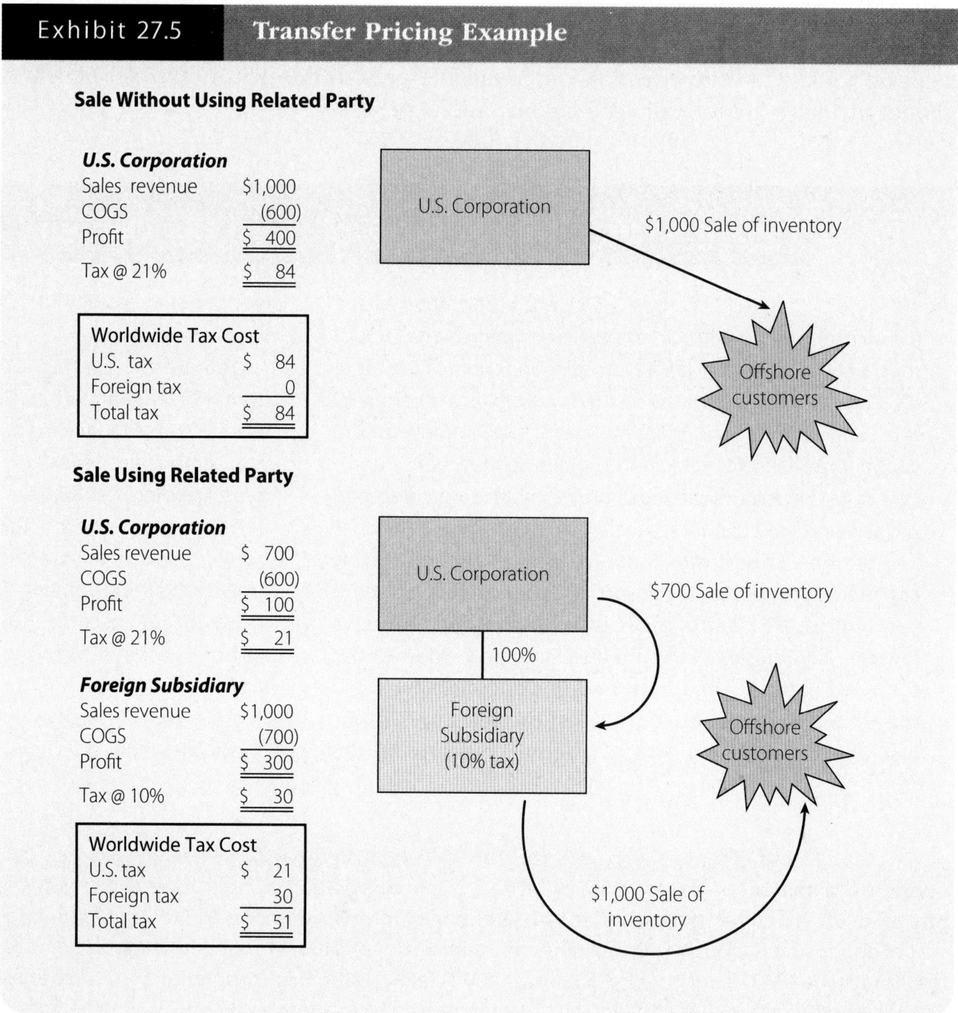

In addition to any tax that might be assessed as a result of the IRS invoking § 482, the IRS also may impose a penalty on the taxpayer. The 20 percent accuracy penalty is imposed when:

1. The § 482 adjustment exceeds the *lesser* of $5 million or 10 percent of the taxpayer's gross receipts, or
2. The transfer price is either *overstated* by 200 percent or more or *understated* by 50 percent or less.

The penalty is doubled for "gross misstatements" of taxable income. This is defined as a net transfer price adjustment that:[22]

1. Exceeds the *lesser* of $20 million or 20 percent of the taxpayer's gross receipts, or
2. Occurs when a transfer price is *overstated* by 400 percent or more, or *understated* by 25 percent or less, due to transfer pricing arrangements.

Preemptive Transfer Pricing Arrangements

As an aid to reducing pricing disputes, the IRS initiated the Advance Pricing Agreement (APA) program, where the taxpayer can propose a transfer pricing method for certain future cross-border transactions.[23] The taxpayer provides relevant data, which then are evaluated by the IRS. If accepted, the APA provides a safe-harbor transfer pricing result for the taxpayer, preempting most later IRS adjustments. This safe-harbor comes at a cost, however, since a significant amount of data must be disclosed to the IRS without assurance that the agreement will be made.

[22] §§ 6662(e)(1)(B) and (h)(2)(A)(ii).

[23] Rev.Proc. 2015–41, 2015–35 I.R.B. 263. The IRS offers an application template based on this document.

APAs can be complex in their application, and they may take three or four years to negotiate fully. About 350 APAs were filed between 2019 and 2021, with almost 3,000 filed since 1991.[24] About 60 percent of the APAs affect transfer pricing between the United States and Japan, Canada, and India. In 2021, the manufacturing and wholesale/retail trade industries made up 75 percent of APA filings.[25] Most APAs are effective for five years.

Additional Tax for Base Erosion Payments

The Code provides another sanction for large C corporations that appear to shift "too much" taxable income to other countries where a lower income tax rate may be available. A *base erosion and anti-abuse* provision applies to C corporations with average annual gross receipts of at least $500 million for the prior three tax years.

An alternative tax computation applies to the entity when "excessive" deductions result from payments made to a related (25 percent ownership) non-U.S. person. If these deductions, or base erosion items, total at least 3 percent of total deductible expenses for the year, the entity pays a Federal corporate income tax equal to the *greater of*:[26]

1. The corporation's regular tax liability, or
2. 10% × modified taxable income (taxable income after adding back the base erosion items).

The **Base Erosion and Anti-Abuse Tax (BEAT)** is similar in nature to provisions adopted in the last decade by other developed countries that want to keep the income tax base indicative of where multinational profits are earned. The BEAT provisions effectively act as a minimum tax to keep a taxpayer from unduly reducing its U.S. taxable income to zero (or close to it) by using income-shifting deductions and other devices with a related party.

Base erosion items do not include those related to cost of goods sold or those where a withholding tax already applies.

Example 11

GiantCo is a U.S. corporation with a subsidiary, RogersCo, operating in Xanadu (a country with a corporate income tax rate of 15%). GiantCo, whose average annual gross receipts over the last three years is $685 million, reports the following for the current year:

Gross Income		$750,000,000
Royalties paid to RogersCo for use of its intellectual property	$250,000,000	
Other deductible expenses	380,000,000	(630,000,000)
Taxable Income		$120,000,000

GiantCo is subject to the base erosion tax as:

- Its average annual gross receipts over the last three years is at least $500 million, and
- Its base erosion items (the royalties paid to RogersCo) are at least 3% of deductible items for the year ($250 million royalties ÷ $630 million total deductions = 40%).

As a result, GiantCo's U.S. income tax is the *greater of*:

- Regular U.S. income tax: $25.2 million ($120 million taxable income × 21%), or
- Base erosion tax: $37 million [$370 million modified taxable income ($120 million taxable income + $250 million base erosion items) × 10%].

27-4 Foreign Currency Gain/Loss

LO.4

Apply foreign currency exchange rules as they affect the tax consequences of international transactions.

An exchange rate provides the relative value of a foreign currency to the U.S. dollar. Changes in this rate affect the dollar value of overseas property held by the taxpayer, the dollar value of non-U.S. debts, and the dollar amount of gain or loss on a transaction denominated in a foreign currency.[27] Almost every international tax issue requires consideration of currency exchange implications.

[24]Part II: APMA Program Statistical Data, Table 1: APA Applications Filed, available at: **https://www.irs.gov/pub/irs-apa/po70328-announcement-2022-7-apa-report.pdf**.

[25]U.S. Department of Treasury, Announcement and Report Concerning Advance Pricing Agreements, March 22, 2022.

[26]§ 59A. The 10% tax rate becomes 12.5% after 2025. The BEAT may apply if base erosion items are 2% of total deductible expenses for some financial institutions. The BEAT rate is not used for book purposes in deriving the deferred tax accounts.

[27]§ 988(b).

Dress, Inc., a domestic corporation, purchases merchandise for resale from Fiesta, Inc., a non-U.S. corporation, for 50,000K (a foreign currency). On the date of purchase, 1K is equal to $1 U.S. (1K:$1). At this time, the account payable is $50,000.

On the date of payment by Dress (the foreign exchange date), the exchange rate is 1.25K:$1. In other words, the foreign currency has been devalued in relation to the U.S. dollar, and Dress will pay Fiesta 50,000K, which will cost Dress only $40,000. Dress must record the purchase of the merchandise at $50,000 and recognize a foreign currency gain of $10,000 ($50,000 − $40,000).

The foreign currency exchange rates, however, have no effect on the transactions of a U.S. person who arranges all international transactions in U.S. dollars.

Sellers, Inc., a domestic corporation, purchases goods from Rose, Ltd., a foreign corporation, and pays for these goods in U.S. dollars. Rose then exchanges the U.S. dollars for the currency of the country in which it operates. Sellers has no foreign exchange considerations with which to contend.

If, instead, Rose required Sellers to pay for the goods in a foreign currency, Sellers would have to exchange U.S. dollars to obtain the foreign currency to make payment. If the exchange rate changed from the date of purchase to the date of payment, Sellers would have a foreign currency gain or loss on the currency exchange.

In recent years, U.S. currency abroad has amounted to more than 60 percent of the U.S. currency in circulation. Taxpayers may find it necessary to translate amounts denominated in foreign currency into U.S. dollars for any of the following purposes:

- Purchase of goods, services, and property.
- Sale of goods, services, and property.
- Collection of foreign receivables.
- Payment of foreign payables.
- Foreign tax credit calculations.

The IRS maintains that transactions involving virtual currencies and cryptocurrencies do not create foreign currency gain or loss.[28]

The Code generally adopts the **functional currency** approach. For book and tax purposes, the currency of the economic environment in which the non-U.S. entity operates generally is used as the monetary unit to measure gains and losses.

All income tax determinations are made in the taxpayer's functional currency.[29] A U.S. taxpayer's default functional currency is the U.S. dollar. In most cases, however, a **qualified business unit (QBU)** operating in another country uses that country's currency as its functional currency. A QBU is a separate and clearly identified unit of a taxpayer's trade or business (e.g., a foreign branch).[30] When a QBU uses something other than the U.S. dollar as its functional currency, its profits and losses need to be converted to U.S. dollars for the U.S. parent to determine its U.S. tax liability.[31] While the specific mechanisms underlying this conversion are beyond the scope of this text, the general conversion must be applied separately to each item of income and deduction (e.g., sales, COGS, etc.), rather than to the overall net income of the QBU.

LO.5

Work with the U.S. tax provisions affecting U.S. persons earning foreign-source income, including antideferral provisions and the foreign tax credit.

27-5 U.S. Persons with Offshore Income

U.S. taxpayers often "internationalize" gradually over time. For example, a U.S. business may operate on a strictly domestic basis for several years, then explore offshore markets by exporting its products abroad, and later license its products to an overseas manufacturer or enter into a joint venture with a non-U.S. partner. If its forays into these markets are successful, the U.S. business may create a foreign branch and then a subsidiary, moving a portion of its operations abroad by establishing a sales or manufacturing facility.

[28]Notice 2014–21, 2014–16 I.R.B. 938.

[29]§ 985. These rules are similar to those of ASC 830.

[30]Reg. § 1.989(a)–1(b). An individual is not a QBU; however, a trade or business conducted by an individual may be a QBU.

[31]§ 987.

Exhibit 27.6 shows a typical timeline for "going global." Both U.S. and offshore entities generally move into international markets in this manner. Each step in this process generates increasingly significant international income tax consequences.

The Big Picture

Return to the facts of *The Big Picture* on p. 27-1. It appears that VoiceCo has moved along the Global Activities Timeline (see Exhibit 27.6), since it is making export sales, and it has a manufacturing plant in Ireland.

27-5a Export Property, Licenses, Foreign Branches

The easiest way for a U.S. business to engage in global commerce is simply to sell U.S.-produced goods and services abroad. These sales can be conducted with little or no foreign presence and allow the business to explore offshore markets without making costly financial commitments to overseas operations. Under the worldwide provisions of the U.S. tax law, a U.S. person immediately includes income from export sales in gross income.

Whether foreign taxes must be paid on this export income depends on the laws of the non-U.S. jurisdiction, the terms of any bilateral tax treaty between the jurisdiction and the U.S. that might exist, and whether the U.S. taxpayer is deemed to have a business presence there (i.e., a "permanent establishment"). In many cases, this export income is not taxed by the receiving country.

Like export sales, fees from licensing arrangements generally are recognized by the U.S. taxpayer when earned or collected; these usually entail royalties and profit sharing payments. Whether fees from licensing products to a non-U.S. party triggers foreign taxes will also depend on the laws of the non-U.S. jurisdiction, the terms of any bilateral tax treaty between the jurisdiction and the U.S. that might exist, and whether the U.S. taxpayer is deemed to have a permanent establishment in the country. However, as with exporting, fees from licensing agreements typically will not trigger foreign income taxes.

A U.S. person's *foreign branch* typically is an offshore office or other operating facility owned by the U.S. business (and not a corporation, partnership, or other legal entity in the other country). Profits and losses from branch operations are recognized immediately (i.e., the operating results flow through to the U.S. parent's taxable income in the same tax year). This often means that entities that generate current operating losses should remain branches of the U.S. parent. On the other hand, a profitable foreign branch can create a cash-flow problem if the U.S. tax liability is due before the cash related to those profits is repatriated to the U.S. parent. Further, given branch operations require a permanent establishment, a foreign branch will likely trigger foreign income taxes.

The final step in our global activities timeline is the incorporation of the foreign branch into a separate legal entity. Generally, when a U.S. person transfers property to a controlled corporation in exchange for stock, any realized gains or losses are deferred under § 351. In the context of the creation of a *foreign corporation*, however, § 367 overrides the non-recognition provision of § 351. As a result, if property is transferred to a foreign corporation in exchange for stock, any realized gains, but not losses, are generally recognized.

Exhibit 27.6 **Global Activities Timeline**

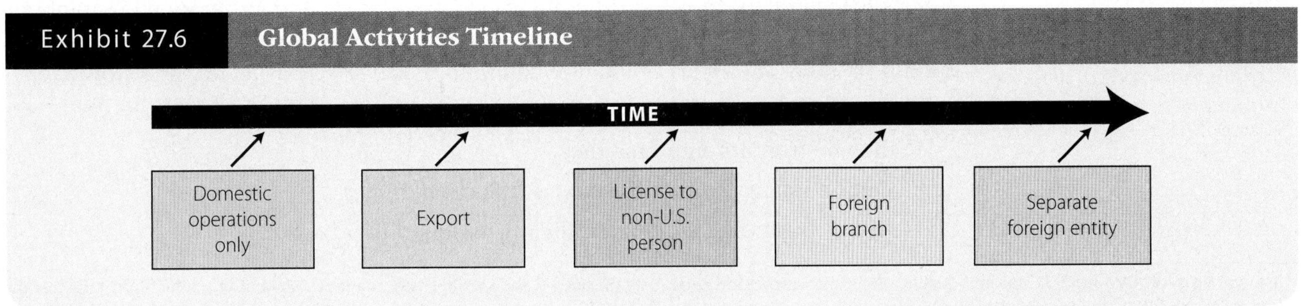

Foreign Tax Credit

Income and loss from the export, licensing, and branch operations of a U.S. person are taxed under the worldwide system of business taxation. If the non-U.S. country also imposes an income tax on such income, the possibility of double taxation arises. Problems associated with double taxation include the stacking of tax rates for the various countries upon each other, resulting in high effective tax rates on the dual-taxed income, and the lack of harmonization of the tax rules of the various countries to the taxpayer's detriment.

Concerns involving double taxation most often are addressed through language in applicable tax treaties, ideally assigning taxable income to only one of the countries involved, and through tax credits and exemptions in the taxpayer's home country. The United States long has allowed a foreign tax credit (FTC) for this purpose, typically for use when the dual-taxed transaction occurs in a non-treaty country.[32] The FTC is an annual taxpayer election; lacking an FTC election, the tax payments are claimed as deductions against gross income.

The FTC is allowed against the taxpayer's regular tax liability, such that only the non-U.S. tax obligation is paid on the dual-taxed income. The FTC is limited, though, to the U.S. tax that would be incurred on the dual-taxed income. As a result, the credit equals the *lesser of* (1) the foreign tax actually paid or (2) the corresponding U.S. income tax,[33] using the sourcing rules discussed in text Section 27-3, computed using the following formula:

$$\frac{\text{Foreign-source taxable income}}{\text{Total (worldwide) taxable income}} \times \text{U.S. tax before FTC}$$

Where a foreign tax payment is not allowed as a current-year credit because it exceeds the U.S. tax allocable to the income, the disallowed amount is allowed in another tax year as a carryover. FTCs are carried back one year and forward 10 years. FTC carryovers tend to occur when the effective tax rate that applies to the dual-taxed income is lower in the United States than it is in the other country.

BlueCo, a U.S. corporation, manufactures and sells most of its products in the United States. It also conducts some business in the European Union through various branches. During the current year, BlueCo reports taxable income of $700,000, of which $500,000 is U.S.-source and $200,000 is foreign-source. Foreign income taxes paid amounted to $45,000. BlueCo's U.S. income tax liability before any foreign tax credit (FTC) is $147,000. What is its allowable FTC?

(1) Foreign taxes paid	$45,000
(2) U.S. tax associated with dual-taxed income	
$\frac{\$200{,}000 \text{ (Foreign-source TI)}}{\$700{,}000 \text{ (Total TI)}} \times \$147{,}000 \text{ (U.S. tax)}$	$42,000
(3) FTC allowed [lesser of (1) or (2)]	$42,000
(4) FTC carryforward [(1) − (2), but not below $0]	$ 3,000

A separate FTC is computed for each of four types of taxable income. These FTC "baskets" were devised so that a taxpayer could not use low-taxed types of income (like portfolio income, perhaps under treaty language) to take a credit for taxes paid on higher-taxed types of income that might otherwise be subject to the limit. The taxpayer's FTC for the year is the sum of the separately computed amounts; there might be a carryforward in one basket and none in another, but the FTCs cannot be combined among baskets. The types of income falling into each FTC basket are as follows:

- Portfolio income, like dividends and capital gains.
- Income from foreign branches.
- Certain intangible income (see text Section 27-5e).
- Active, business income not already assigned to a basket.

[32]The credit is allowed via § 27, but the qualifications and calculation procedure for the FTC are contained in §§ 901–908. Although taxpayers can claim a deduction for the foreign taxes paid instead of a credit, in most instances, the credit is advantageous since it is a direct offset against the tax liability.

[33]§ 904.

Financial Disclosure Insights — Overseas Operations and Book-Tax Differences

Non-U.S. operations account for a large portion of the permanent book-tax differences of U.S. business entities. These differences may relate to different tax bases, different tax rate structures, or special provisions concerning tax-based financing with the other country.

Tax planning strategies using non-U.S. operations also are found in the deferred tax asset and liability accounts. Tax deferrals allowed under current U.S. tax rules and carryforwards of the foreign tax credit can be substantial for some businesses. For example, IBM recently reported a deferred tax asset relating to delays in using its FTCs amounting to about $900 million. For the operating arm of General Electric, that amount was about $1.5 billion. For Microsoft, there were no FTC carryovers.

To qualify for the FTC, the foreign levy must resemble a tax on net income, like the Federal income tax. For instance, it cannot be a tax on gross receipts, on the right to extract minerals, or on property values.[34] However, these tax payments can be deducted by the taxpayer. A tax is eligible for the FTC when it is paid or accrued, according to the taxpayer's method of tax accounting. Concept Summary 27.2 summarizes the FTC rules.

Concept Summary 27.2

The Foreign Tax Credit

The foreign tax credit (FTC) is related to the worldwide system of income taxation that applies under U.S. income tax law to many cross-border transactions. The credit works to eliminate the exposure of a taxpayer to the double taxation of income that is generated in another country. In effect, foreign income taxes are used to reduce the Federal income tax liability, in a form of "revenue sharing" by the governments involved.

- The FTC is available to C corporations and individuals.
- The FTC is an annual taxpayer election. If the FTC is not elected, a deduction may be claimed for foreign taxes paid or accrued.
- The FTC is allowed for taxes paid by the taxpayer directly or through a foreign withholding procedure.
- An FTC is allowed only for income taxes on net taxable income that are levied by the host country. Other forms of fees or non-income taxes can be claimed by the taxpayer as a deduction.
- The taxpayer's taxable income and foreign tax payments are split among four income "baskets" (i.e., among portfolio, intangible, foreign branch, and other business income).
- The FTC then is allowed in each income basket.
  - The FTC for the year in each basket equals the lesser of (1) the foreign taxes paid or accrued or (2) the share of the U.S. tax liability that corresponds to the foreign-source income of the taxpayer as a percentage of worldwide taxable income.
  - In this way, if the taxpayer is operating in a jurisdiction that applies an income tax rate that is higher than that of the United States, the credit cannot be used to offset income tax that relates to other types of income.
- If the FTC otherwise available in a year is not allowed because of the above limitation, the credit is carried back one year and then forward 10 years.

Special Effective Tax Rate for Foreign-Derived Intangible Income (FDII)

The FTC mitigates the double taxation of income earned by U.S. taxpayers from foreign operations. The U.S. tax law also provides an incentive for taxpayers to generate income from foreign customers through operations conducted in the United States.[35] The incentive was designed to provide a lower effective tax rate on income derived from the development of intangible assets (e.g., intellectual property) easily moved across jurisdictions with the goal of encouraging U.S. corporations to maintain these assets (and the related business activities) within the United States. This income is called **Foreign-Derived Intangible Income (FDII)**. However, the incentive is not limited to such income.

The income to which the lower rate applies is derived by first determining intangible income, the excess of the corporation's deduction-eligible income, if any, over 10 percent of its tangible assets. Deduction-eligible income excludes certain types and sources

[34] § 904(c).

[35] § 250.

of income including income from foreign branches and financial services income. It also excludes income taxable under Subpart F and global intangible low-taxed income (see text Sections 27-5c and 27-5e, respectively). A deduction is then allowed for 37.5 percent of the portion of this intangible income that is derived from sales to foreign customers. The deduction results in an effective tax rate of 13.125 percent ([1 − 0.375] × 0.21) on the foreign-derived intangible income.[36]

27-5b Tax Havens

Many outbound transfers of assets to foreign corporations are to countries with tax rates higher than or equal to the U.S. rate; tax avoidance is not the motive for these transfers. Some U.S. corporations, however, make their offshore investment in (or through) a tax haven. A **tax haven** is a country where either locally sourced income or residents are subject to zero or very low levels of local income taxation. The Bahamas, Ireland, the Netherlands, the Cayman Islands, and Bermuda, among other countries, are seen as tax havens. U.S. corporations shift sizable amounts of taxable income annually to these countries.

A tax haven usually has adopted rules that allow taxpayers to establish residency with a minimal presence. Tax haven countries also may have in effect provisions limiting the exchange of financial and commercial information.[37]

Exhibit 27.7 illustrates this use of a tax haven by a U.S. corporation. The U.S. corporation uses a foreign subsidiary in a low- or no-tax country to earn either investment income or a portion of income from business activities (as illustrated previously in the transfer pricing discussion). Because the foreign subsidiary cannot be consolidated with the domestic parent under U.S. tax law and is not itself engaged in any U.S. trade or business, the subsidiary is not subject to U.S. taxation. Without the application of the transfer pricing rules, the base-erosion tax, or the Subpart F rules (discussed in text Section 27-5c), the subsidiary's income escapes U.S. taxation.

A tax haven also can, in effect, be created by an income tax treaty. For example, under an income tax treaty between Country A and Country B, residents of Country A are subject to a withholding tax of only 5 percent on dividend and interest income sourced in Country B. The United States and Country A have a similar treaty. The United States does not have a treaty with Country B, and the withholding tax is 30 percent. A U.S. corporation can create a foreign subsidiary in Country A and use that subsidiary to make investments in Country B.

Exhibit 27.7 Use of a Tax Haven Corporation

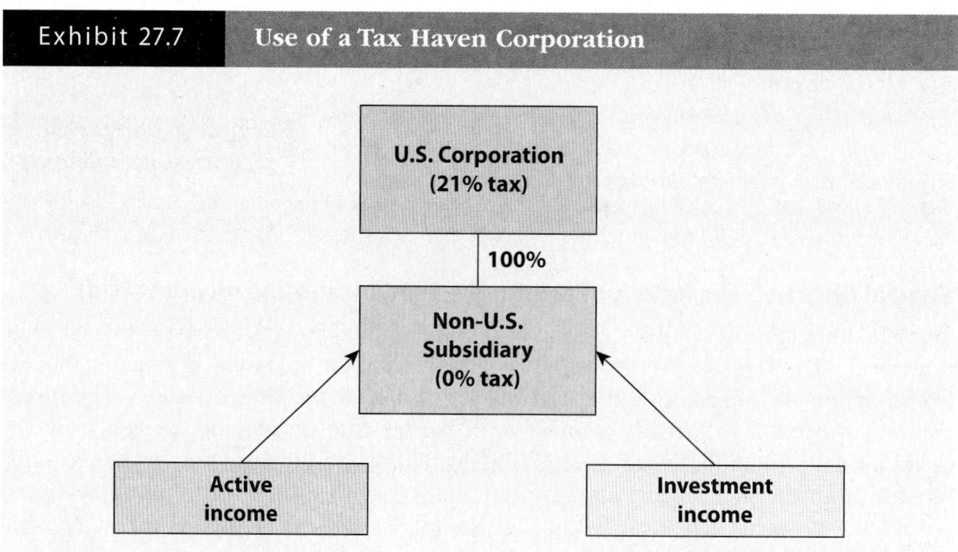

Without the use of a subsidiary in the tax haven, all of the investment and shifted active income would be taxed at the U.S. tax rate of 21 percent. This tax can be reduced or eliminated by shifting some of the taxpayer's assets and operations to the tax haven country.

[36] § 250(b)(2)(A). The deduction will be reduced to 21.875 percent of foreign-derived intangible income after 2025.

[37] § 894(c) contains additional limitations on the use of treaty benefits.

This practice often is referred to as **treaty shopping**. If the Country B investment income had been earned directly by the U.S. corporation, it would have been subject to a 30 percent withholding tax. As a result of investing through the foreign subsidiary created in Country A, the U.S. parent corporation pays only 10 percent in foreign taxes on the income earned (i.e., 5 percent to Country B and 5 percent to Country A).

27-5c **Offshore (Foreign) Corporations Controlled by U.S. Persons**

To minimize current tax liability, taxpayers often shift an income-generating activity to an entity that is not within the U.S. taxing jurisdiction. When a foreign corporation is used in this manner, its offshore taxable income may be subject to lower income tax rates, and it may attract certain treaty benefits. U.S. tax law extends a worldwide approach to some of this income, treating such items on a pass-through basis that triggers immediate U.S. income taxation, even though the income is earned by a separate foreign corporation.

Controlled Foreign Corporations

An elaborate antideferral system is in place that attempts to keep U.S. taxpayers from sheltering current taxable income by using foreign subsidiaries. Subpart F of the Code provides that certain types of income generated by controlled foreign corporations (CFCs) are included in current-year gross income by the U.S. shareholders, without regard to actual distributions.[38] Subpart F and CFC rules thus create an immediate "flow-through" of taxable income from the foreign subsidiary to its U.S. shareholders.

A **controlled foreign corporation (CFC)** is any non-U.S. corporation in which U.S. shareholders own on *any day* during the foreign corporation's taxable year more than 50 percent of (1) the total combined voting power of all classes of stock entitled to vote or (2) the total value of the stock of the corporation. The offshore subsidiaries of most multinational U.S. parent corporations are CFCs. The latest data available indicates there are approximately 95,000 U.S.-owned CFCs located largely in Europe and Asia.[39]

For this purpose, a **U.S. shareholder** is defined as a U.S. person who owns, or is considered to own, 10 percent or more of the total combined voting power of all classes of voting stock of the non-U.S. corporation. All stock owned directly by, or attributed to (see text Section 19-4c), a person is considered when determining whether the person is a U.S. shareholder.

Does Subpart F Apply?

Beetle Company is a French corporation. It is equally owned by 11 unrelated U.S. citizens. How many U.S. shareholders exist [as defined under § 951(b) and other Internal Revenue Code sections], and is Beetle Company a CFC?

No U.S. person owns 10% or more of the total combined voting power or value of Beetle shares. As a result, there are *no* § 951(b) U.S. shareholders, and the corporation is *not* a CFC.

Bailey Company is a French corporation. It is owned by Annie Partnership, a U.S. partnership with 15 unrelated U.S. partners. How many U.S. shareholders exist [as defined under § 951(b) and other Internal Revenue Code sections], and is Bailey Company a CFC?

There is one § 951(b) U.S. shareholder (the partnership), and it owns 100% of Bailey. As a result, the corporation *is* a CFC.

[38] §§ 951 through 964.

[39] **irs.gov/statistics/soi-tax-stats-controlled-foreign-corporations**.

Does Subpart F Apply?

Example 18

Rochelle Corporation is a French corporation. It owns 100% of the stock of Andrew Corporation, also a French corporation. Rochelle Corporation also owns 100% of the stock of Ashleigh Corporation, a U.S. corporation. How many U.S. shareholders exist [as defined under § 951(b) and other Internal Revenue Code sections], and is either Rochelle Corporation or Andrew Corporation a CFC?

Without a U.S. shareholder, Rochelle Corporation cannot be a CFC. However, the attribution rules of § 318(a)(3) cause Ashleigh Corporation to own the stock that its shareholder owns. As a result, Ashleigh Corporation constructively owns 100% of the stock of Andrew Corporation, making Andrew Corporation a CFC.

When Subpart F applies, U.S. shareholders include in gross income their pro rata share of Subpart F income. The Subpart F income is includable in the U.S. shareholder's gross income in the year in which the CFC's taxable year ends.

Gray, Inc., a calendar year corporation, is a CFC for the entire tax year. Chance Company, a U.S. corporation, owns 60% of Gray's one class of stock for the entire year. Subpart F income is $100,000, and no distributions have been made during the year.

Chance, a calendar year taxpayer, includes $60,000 in gross income as a constructive dividend from Gray for the tax year.

Subpart F Income Only certain income earned by the CFC triggers immediate U.S. taxation as a constructive dividend. This **Subpart F income** can generally be thought of as income with little or no economic connection with the CFC's country of incorporation. Subpart F income typically includes foreign base company income (FBCI), including:

- Foreign personal holding company income.
- Foreign base company sales income.
- Foreign base company services income.

Foreign personal holding company (FPHC) income commonly includes:

- Dividends, interest, royalties, rents, and annuities.
- Excess gains over losses from the sale or exchange of property that gives rise to FPHC income.
- Excess of foreign currency gains over foreign currency losses (other than amounts directly related to the business needs of the CFC).

Foreign base company (FBC) sales income is income derived by a CFC where the CFC has very little connection with the process that generates the income and a related party is involved. If (1) the property being sold is neither manufactured, produced, grown, or extracted, nor consumed, in the CFC's country of incorporation and (2) either the supplier or the customer is related to the CFC, this typically constitutes FBC sales income. FBC sales income usually involves three different countries in the arrangement, as illustrated in Concept Summary 27.3.

Ulysses, Ltd., is a CFC organized in Ireland and owned 100% by Joyce, Inc., a U.S. corporation. Ulysses purchases finished inventory from Joyce and sells the inventory to customers in the European Union. This sales income constitutes FBC sales income.

Concept Summary 27.3

Subpart F Income and a CFC

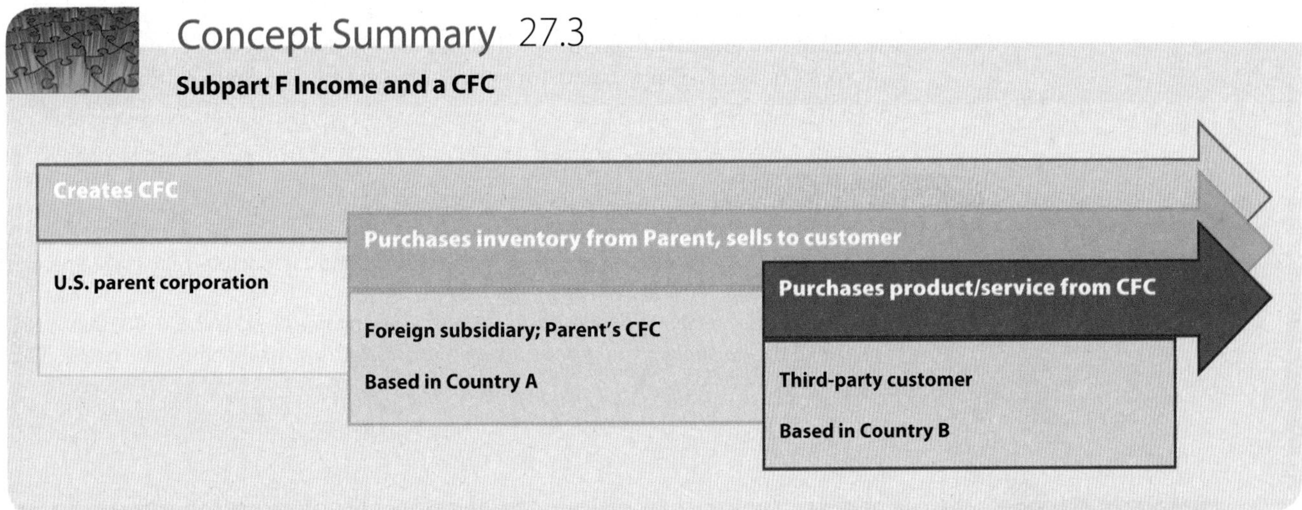

If Ulysses, from Example 20, purchases raw materials from Joyce and performs substantial manufacturing activity in Ireland before selling the inventory to customers in the EU, the income is not FBC sales income.

Even without the manufacturing activity, sales to customers within Ireland would not produce FBC sales income.

FBC services income is income derived from the performance of services for or on behalf of a related person and performed outside the country in which the CFC was created or organized. Income from services performed in connection with the sale of property by a CFC that has manufactured, produced, grown, or extracted such property is *not* FBC services income.

Redden Co. is a U.S. corporation that owns 100% of Mubiru Co., a Ugandan Corporation. Mubiru Co. services computers throughout Africa, earning $5,000,000 of services income during the year. Of that income, $1,000,000 was earned from servicing computers in Uganda.

Mubiru Co. would have FBC services income of $4,000,000, the amount of income earned from servicing computers outside of its country of incorporation (Uganda).

Subpart F Income Exceptions Potentially large amounts of offshore profits (e.g., active trade or business income not involving related persons) escape the definition of Subpart F income, resulting in no immediate U.S. income taxation. Other exceptions also apply to the Subpart F rules.

- A *de minimis* rule provides that if the total amount of a foreign corporation's FBCI for the taxable year is less than the smaller of 5 percent of the CFC's gross income or $1 million, *none* of its gross income is treated as FBCI for the tax year.
- A *full inclusion* rule applies if a foreign corporation's FBCI exceeds 70 percent of total gross income. In this case, *all* of the corporation's gross income for the tax year is treated as Subpart F income.
- FBCI subject to high foreign taxes is not included under Subpart F. The taxpayer must establish that the income was taxed by the other country at an effective rate of more than 90 percent of the Federal corporate income tax rate. For example, the other country's effective income tax rate must be greater than 18.9 percent (90% × 21%, where 21 percent is the current U.S. corporate rate).

- Subpart F income includible in gross income by a U.S. shareholder may not exceed the CFC's current earnings and profits (CE & P) for the year. Subpart F income in excess of CE & P is carried forward and recaptured when sufficient CE & P becomes available.

Subpart F Income

Example 23

USP, Inc., is the sole U.S. shareholder of Gaelic, Inc., a CFC. During the taxable year, Gaelic reports gross income of $12,000,000 and FBCI of $521,000.

Since Gaelic's FBCI is less than the smaller of (1) 5% of gross income ($600,000; $12,000,000 × 5%) or (2) $1,000,000, the *de minimis* rule applies and *none* of Gaelic's gross income is treated as FBCI for the year.

Example 24

Assume the same facts as in the previous example, except that Gaelic's FBCI is $8,500,000. Here, FBCI is 70.8% of gross income ($8,500,000 ÷ $12,000,000).

Under the *full inclusion* rule, *all* of Gaelic's gross income is treated as Subpart F income.

Last year, Clover Co. had $12,000,000 of Subpart F income and a $3,000,000 non-Subpart F loss for the year. As a result, Clover's CE & P was $9,000,000. Clover's Subpart F income cannot exceed its $9,000,000 CE & P, so it has a $3,000,000 Subpart F income carryforward.

This year, Clover has $2,000,000 of Subpart F income and $15,000,000 of non-Subpart F income. This would give Clover $17,000,000 of CE & P. As a result, Clover recaptures its $3,000,000 of Subpart F income from the prior year, giving it $5,000,000 of Subpart F income ($3,000,000 from the prior year and $2,000,000 from the current year).

Other Tax Consequences of Being a CFC The Subpart F and CFC rules create an immediate flow-through of taxable income, regardless of distributions received by the taxpayer. This works in a manner similar to that of the income taxation of partnerships, S corporations, and similar entities (see Chapters 21 through 23). A foreign tax credit is allowed with respect to a Subpart F income inclusion.[40]

A U.S. shareholder's basis in CFC stock is increased by the constructive dividend and decreased by subsequent distributions of previously taxed income.[41]

CFC Tax Consequences

Singh, a U.S. shareholder in the CFC Bombay United, records a $100,000 constructive dividend from the entity as foreign base company services income under Subpart F rules. Singh's basis in the Bombay United stock increases correspondingly by $100,000.

Continue with the facts of Example 26. When Bombay United makes a $40,000 cash distribution to Singh from the prior constructive dividend, Singh's basis in the Bombay United stock is reduced by $40,000. The payment does not constitute gross income.

[40] § 960.

[41] § 961.

The various components of Subpart F income are illustrated in Concept Summary 27.4.

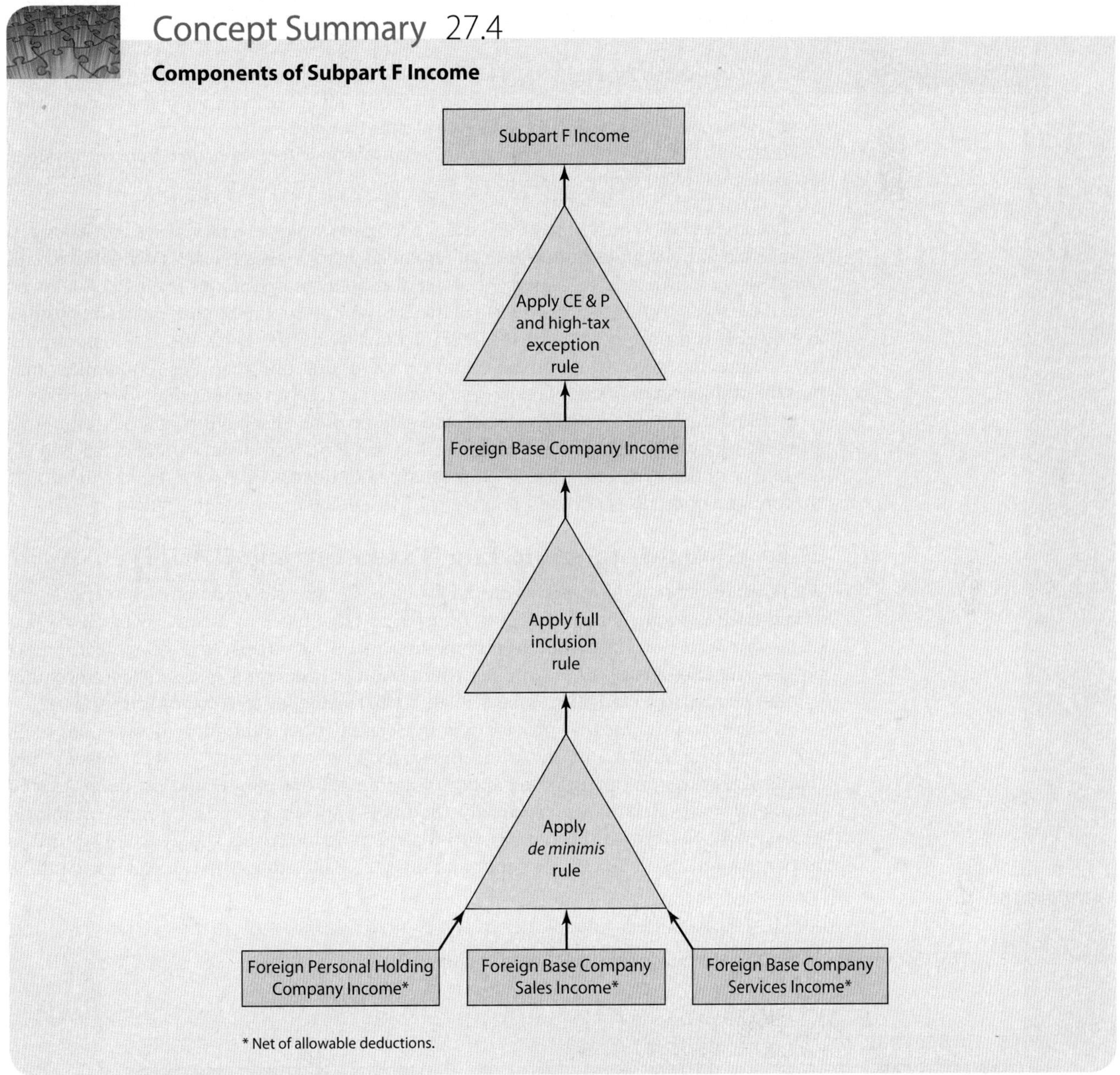

27-5d Movement Toward a More Territorial System

As discussed earlier, U.S. income tax law generally applies a worldwide system with respect to the cross-border activities of U.S. persons, but most of the rest of the developed world uses a territorial approach. Congress believes that moving toward a territorial system will increase the competitiveness of U.S. businesses in the global marketplace, and has taken steps to adopt some territorial aspects within current law, although the worldwide system still undergirds the taxation of outbound transactions.

Historically, the income earned by a foreign subsidiary of a U.S. corporation was not taxable to the U.S. parent until it was distributed to the U.S. taxpayer, or "repatriated." While the income was eligible for the FTC, income earned in low-tax countries still triggered U.S. tax when it was distributed. This created an incentive for U.S. corporations to generate income in foreign subsidiaries and to defer the repatriation of that income as long as possible. To alleviate these concerns, U.S. corporations are now allowed a dividends received deduction (DRD) equal to 100 percent of the dividends received from a "10%-owned" foreign subsidiary.[42] This rule fully exempts from U.S. taxation the foreign-source profits that underlie the dividend payment (thereby resembling a territorial taxing system), and removes any barriers to repatriating the profits to the U.S. economy (perhaps in large amounts).

OffCo, a 100%-owned Nigerian subsidiary of the U.S. C corporation BossCo, earned a current-year profit of $10,000,000, and it immediately paid all of this amount to its parent in the form of a dividend. The income did not represent Subpart F income for BossCo.

BossCo reports zero gross income for OffCo's current activities; its income from the dividend received is fully offset by the 100% DRD.

Though the DRD causes the U.S. system to look more like a territorial system, its impact is limited: it only excludes from U.S. taxation foreign income distributed as dividends to corporations who own at least 10 percent of the distributing corporation. The DRD is allowed even if the foreign affiliate is not a CFC of the U.S. parent. Subpart F pass-through constructive dividends do not qualify for the DRD. To qualify for the DRD, the U.S. parent must have owned the stock of the offshore affiliate for at least one year; this requirement may present problems when the entities were involved in recent merger or takeover activity.

In addition, any recognized gain on the sale or other disposition of stock of a 10%-owned CFC by a U.S. shareholder is treated as dividend income and triggers the DRD to the extent of the transferor's share of unrepatriated, untaxed E & P of the corporation.[43] No foreign tax credit is allowed relative to dividends eligible for the DRD.

27-5e **Global Intangible Low-Taxed Income (GILTI)**

With the adoption of a form of territorial taxation, Congress feared that U.S. corporations would have even greater incentives to transfer portable types of income overseas to permanently avoid Federal corporate income taxation. To counter these possibilities, a tax on U.S. shareholders of a CFC applies when that CFC generates a significant amount of income relative to its tangible assets [called **Global Intangible Low-Taxed Income (GILTI)**].

Income taxed under this provision is not classified as Subpart F income, although it is taxed in a similar manner (i.e., immediately when earned).[44] GILTI results in a shareholder level tax intended to apply to earnings from intellectual property located outside of the United States. Practically, the tax is imposed on most foreign earnings in excess of 10 percent of the foreign subsidiary's tangible assets (i.e., earnings above a 10 percent return on assets). Concept Summary 27.5 illustrates the calculation of GILTI.

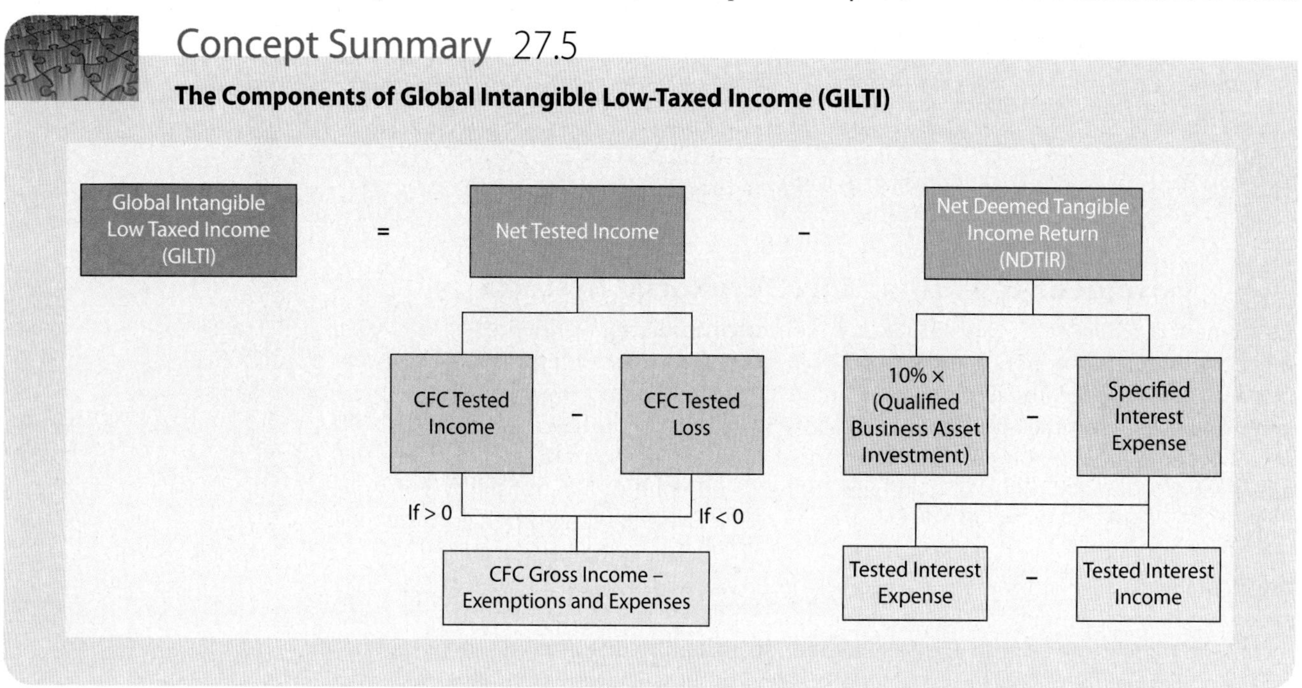

[42] § 245A; "10%-owned" means owning 10% or more of the voting stock of the foreign corporation.

[43] § 1248.

[44] § 951A(f).

CFC Gross and Net Tested Income or Loss

Computing GILTI begins with each CFC of the U.S. shareholder computing a base amount, called *gross tested income.* As the computation in Exhibit 27.8 demonstrates, gross tested income excludes income effectively connected with a U.S. trade or business, Subpart F income, gross income excluded from Subpart F due to the high-tax exception, and certain other income.

Exhibit 27.8 CFC Net Tested Income or (Loss)

	CFC Tested Income	$ x,xxx
Less:	Income effectively connected with a trade or business	(xxx)
Less:	Subpart F income	(xxx)
Less:	Other income[45]	(xxx)
	Gross Tested Income	$ x,xxx
Less:	Allowable deductions	(xxx)
	CFC Net Tested Income (Loss)	$ x,xxx

CFCs are then allowed to subtract deductions allocable to gross tested income to arrive at *net tested income or (loss).*[46] These allocations can be very complicated and generally are beyond the scope of this text.[47] For our purposes, we will allocate deductions to gross tested income or (loss) according to the following ratio:

$$\frac{\text{Gross tested income}}{\text{CFC income}} \times \text{Total deductions} = \text{Allocable deductions}$$

Once net tested income or (loss) is computed for each CFC, the U.S. shareholder aggregates these together to determine net tested income used in the GILTI calculation.

Rochelle Co., a U.S. Corporation, owns 100% of Redden Co., a CFC. An analysis of Redden reveals the following:

Redden Co. gross income	$500,000
Redden Co. subpart F income	200,000
Redden Co. deductions	400,000

Redden Co.	CFC Gross Income	Subpart F Income	Tested Income
Gross Income	$ 500,000	$ 200,000	$300,000
Deductions	(400,000)	(160,000)*	(240,000)**
Net Income	$ 100,000	$ 40,000	$ 60,000

* ($200,000 ÷ $500,000) × $400,000.
** ($300,000 ÷ $500,000) × $400,000.

Redden's gross tested income is its CFC gross income less its Subpart F income, which equals $300,000. The deduction amount of $400,000 is allocated based on the proportion of Redden's tested income to its total income, ($300,000 ÷ $500,000). As a result, the net tested income of Redden would be $60,000.

In this example, Redden would be classified as a "tested income CFC." If the allocated deductions would have exceeded gross tested income, Redden would have been classified as a "tested loss CFC." If Rochelle had multiple CFCs, tested income or loss would have been calculated separately for each entity.

[45] §§ 951(A)(c)(2)(A)(i)(IV) and (V).

[46] Reg. § 1.951A-2.

[47] § 951A(c)(2)(A)(ii) and Reg. § 1.951A-2(c)(3).

Net Deemed Tangible Income Return (NDTIR)

U.S. shareholders must include in their taxable income only net tested income that exceeds an allowed return on the CFC's tangible assets. This return, called **Net Deemed Tangible Income Return (NDTIR)**, is equal to 10 percent of the CFC's U.S. tax basis in their foreign assets, or their *Qualified Business Asset Investment* (QBAI). Assets from CFCs that have tested income increase QBAI; however, assets from CFCs with a tested loss are ignored (and these assets will have no impact on the computation of QBAI).[48] The formula below illustrates how NDTIR is calculated:

$$\text{NDTIR} = (\text{QBAI} \times 10\%) - \text{Specified interest expense}$$

To prevent CFCs from acquiring assets with a principal purpose of increasing NDTIR, certain assets held only temporarily must be disregarded in the calculation of NDTIR.[49]

Continuing with Example 29, assume that Rochelle Co. owns a 100% interest in three CFCs, with the following income, loss, and business assets:

CFC	CFC Net Tested Income (Loss)	CFC Qualified Business Asset Investment (QBAI)	10% QBAI
Redden Co.	$ 60,000	$500,000	$50,000
Andrew Co.	(100,000)	–	–
Ashleigh Co.	500,000	300,000	30,000
Total	$460,000	$800,000	$80,000

Rochelle's net tested income from these three entities is $460,000 ($60,000 − $100,000 + $500,000), and its QBAI is $800,000 ($500,000 + $300,000). Since Andrew Co. is reporting a net tested loss, its assets have no effect on the computation of QBAI for the year.

NDTIR must also be reduced by the net interest expense included in tested income.[50]

Orange Co., a U.S. corporation, owns all the stock in CFC1 and CFC2 (both tested income CFCs). Operating results from the two CFCs indicates that Orange has net tested income of $300,000 and QBAI of $250,000. Further information indicates that CFC1 has tested interest income of $40,000, while CFC2 has tested interest expense of $60,000.

As a result, Orange has specified interest expense of $20,000 ($40,000 − $60,000). NDTIR would be $5,000 ([$250,000 QBAI × 10%] − $20,000 net interest expense).

Calculating GILTI and the Related Tax

Once net tested income and NDTIR are known, GILTI can be calculated as follows:

$$\text{GILTI} = \text{Net tested income} - \text{NDTIR}$$

If the aggregation of CFC net tested income or loss results in an overall net tested loss or if the GILTI calculation results in a negative amount, the U.S. taxpayer has GILTI of zero for the year. The U.S. taxpayer cannot use a negative GILTI amount to offset positive GILTI in past or future tax years.

[48] § 951A(d)(2)(A).

[49] Reg. § 1.951A-3(h)(1).

[50] § 951A(b)(2)(B).

Example 32

Continuing with Example 31, Orange Co., a U.S. Corporation with 100% ownership in two CFCs, is using the following information to calculate GILTI:

Net tested income	$300,000
QBAI	$250,000
Net deemed tangible income return	$ 5,000

Orange Co.'s GILTI would be $295,000 (Net tested income of $300,000 − NDTIR of $5,000).

U.S. corporate shareholders subject to GILTI have an advantage that individual shareholders subject to GILTI do not have. A U.S. corporate CFC shareholder is allowed a deduction equal to 50 percent of GILTI included in the gross income of that U.S. corporation.[51] In Example 32, Orange Co.'s GILTI is $295,000. After subtracting the 50 percent deduction, Orange Co.'s net GILTI is $147,500 ($295,000 – $147,500). Given a U.S. corporate tax rate of 21 percent, Orange Co.'s U.S. income tax on its GILTI would be $30,975 ($147,500 × 21 percent). As a result of the allowed deduction, the effective GILTI tax rate for corporations is 10.5 percent ($30,975 ÷ $295,000). The full $295,000 of GILTI would be included in the taxable income of an individual U.S. shareholder (i.e., no 50 percent deduction is available).[52]

27-6 U.S. Taxation of Nonresident Aliens and Foreign Corporations

LO.6

Apply the U.S. tax provisions concerning nonresident alien individuals and foreign corporations.

Generally, only the U.S.-source income of nonresident alien individuals and foreign corporations is subject to U.S. taxation. This reflects the reach of the U.S. tax jurisdiction. The constraint, however, does not prevent the United States from also taxing the foreign-source income of nonresident alien individuals and non-U.S. corporations when that income is effectively connected with the conduct of a U.S. trade or business, in the manner of territorial taxation.[53]

27-6a Nonresident Alien Individuals

A **nonresident alien (NRA)** is an individual who is neither a citizen nor a resident of the United States. Citizenship is determined under the immigration and naturalization laws of the United States.[54] Usually, citizenship statutes are broken down into two categories: nationality at birth or through naturalization.

Residency

An individual is a resident of the United States for income tax purposes if either the green card test or the substantial presence test is met.[55] If either of these tests is met for the calendar year, the individual is deemed a U.S. resident for the year.

A non-U.S. person issued a green card is considered a U.S. resident on the first day the person is physically present in the United States after issuance. The green card is Immigration Form I–551. Newly issued cards no longer are green, but the form still is referred to as the "green card." Status as a U.S. resident remains in effect until the green card has been revoked or the individual has abandoned lawful permanent resident status.

The *substantial presence* test is applied to an alien without a green card. It is a mathematical test involving physical presence in the United States. An individual who is physically present in the United States for at least 183 days during the calendar year is a U.S. resident for income tax purposes.

[51]§ 250. The deduction is reduced to 37.5 percent after 2025.

[52]Depending upon facts and circumstances, an individual taxpayer may elect to be treated as a corporation under § 962 with respect to GILTI and/or Subpart F income. This would allow the individual taxpayer to take advantage of the 50% GILTI deduction and possibly other foreign tax credits available only to corporations.

[53]§§ 871, 881, and 882.

[54]Title 8, Aliens and Nationality, *United States Code.*

[55]§ 7701(b).

This 183-day requirement also can be met over a three-year period that includes the two immediately preceding years and the current year, as long as the individual is present in the United States at least 31 days during the current year.[56] For this purpose, each day of the current calendar year is counted as a full day, each day of the first preceding year as one-third day, and each day of the second preceding year as one-sixth day. A nominal presence of 10 days or less can be ignored in determining whether the substantial presence test is met.

Li, who is not a U.S. citizen, was present in the United States for 90 days in 2020, 180 days in 2021, and 110 days in 2022. For Federal income tax purposes, Li is a U.S. resident for 2022, because she was physically present for 185 days [(90 days × ⅙) + (180 days × ⅓) + (110 days × 1)] during the three-year period.

When counting days of physical presence in the United States, there are several exceptions. Commuters from Mexico and Canada who are employed in the United States but return home each day do not count those work days as days of physical presence. The same is true for individuals who are prevented from leaving the United States by medical conditions that arose while the individuals were in the United States. Some individuals are exempt altogether from the substantial presence test, including foreign government-related individuals (e.g., diplomats), qualified teachers, trainees and students, and certain professional athletes.

Nonresident Aliens Not Engaged in a U.S. Trade or Business

Certain U.S.-source income that is *not* effectively connected with the conduct of a U.S. trade or business is subject to a flat 30 percent tax. This income includes dividends, certain interest, rents, royalties, certain compensation, premiums, annuities, and other similar income. This tax generally requires the payors of the income to withhold 30 percent of gross amounts.[57] The withholding procedures work to eliminate the problems of ensuring payment by nonresidents and determining allowable deductions as well as, in most instances, the filing of tax returns by nonresidents.

Interest received from certain portfolio debt investments, even though U.S. sourced, is exempt from taxation when earned by non-U.S. persons. Interest earned on bank deposits also is exempt as long as it is not effectively connected with the conduct of a U.S. trade or business. These rules encourage offshore investors to purchase U.S. Treasury bonds and notes and to deposit U.S. currency in domestic bank accounts.

Capital gains *not* effectively connected with the conduct of a U.S. trade or business are exempt from this tax, as long as the NRA was not present in the United States for 183 days or more during the taxable year. If an NRA has not established a taxable year, the calendar year is used. NRAs are not permitted to carry forward capital losses.[58]

Nonresident Aliens Engaged in a U.S. Trade or Business

Two important definitions determine the U.S. tax consequences to NRAs with U.S.-source income: "the conduct of a **U.S. trade or business**" and "**effectively connected income**." Specifically, for an NRA's noninvestment income to be subject to U.S. taxation, the NRA must be considered engaged in a U.S. trade or business and must earn income effectively connected with that business.

General criteria for determining whether a U.S. trade or business exists include the location of production activities, management, distribution activities, and other business functions. Trading in commodities and securities ordinarily does not constitute a trade or business. Dealers, however, need to avoid maintaining a U.S. trading office and trading for their own accounts.

[56] § 7701(b)(3)(A).

[57] §§ 871 and 1441. Tax treaty provisions can change these rates. See Exhibit 27.4.

[58] § 871(a)(2).

The Code does not explicitly define a U.S. trade or business, but case law looks for activities carried on in the United States that are regular, substantial, and continuous.[59] Once an NRA is considered engaged in a U.S. trade or business, all U.S.-source income other than investment and capital gain income is considered effectively connected to that trade or business and is therefore subject to U.S. taxation.

Example 34

Vito, an NRA, produces wine for export. During the current year, Vito earns $500,000 from exporting wine to unrelated wholesalers in the United States. The title to the wine passes to the U.S. wholesalers in New York. Vito has no offices or employees in the United States. The income from wine sales is U.S.-source income, but, because Vito is not engaged in a U.S. trade or business, the income is not subject to taxation in the United States.

Vito begins operating a hot dog cart in New York City. This activity constitutes a U.S. trade or business. Consequently, all U.S.-source income other than investment or capital gain income is taxed in the United States as income effectively connected with a U.S. trade or business. As a result, both the hot dog cart profits and the $500,000 in wine income are subject to U.S. income tax.

Effectively connected income is taxed at the same rates that apply to U.S. citizens and residents, and deductions for expenses attributable to that income are allowed. NRAs with income effectively connected with the conduct of a U.S. trade or business also are subject to the alternative minimum tax.

27-6b Foreign Corporations

A corporation created or organized in the United States is a domestic corporation. A foreign corporation is one that is not domestic. Although McDonald's is a global corporation, it is considered a domestic corporation for U.S. tax purposes, solely because it was organized in the United States.

Foreign corporations are taxed very much like NRAs. Capital gain income is exempt from tax, and a flat 30 percent tax rate is applied to U.S.-source investment income items if they are not effectively connected with a U.S. trade or business. Foreign corporations conducting a trade or business in the United States are subject to Federal income taxation on any U.S.-source income effectively connected with the trade or business.

27-6c Foreign Investment in Real Property Tax Act

At one time, NRAs and foreign corporations could avoid U.S. taxation on gains from the sale of U.S. real estate if the gains were treated as capital gains and were not effectively connected with the conduct of a U.S. trade or business. In the mid-1970s, midwestern farmers pressured Congress to eliminate what they saw as a tax advantage that would allow nonresidents to bid up the price of farmland. This and other concerns about foreign ownership of U.S. real estate led to the enactment of the **Foreign Investment in Real Property Tax Act (FIRPTA)**.

Under FIRPTA, gains and losses realized by NRAs and foreign corporations from the sale or other disposition of U.S. real property interests (USRPIs) are treated as effectively connected with the conduct of a U.S. trade or business, even when those individuals or corporations are not actually so engaged. Any direct interest in real property situated in the United States and any interest in a domestic corporation (other than solely as a creditor) are U.S. real property interests.

NRA individuals must pay a tax equal to the *lesser of*:

- The applicable tax on their alternative minimum taxable income, or
- Regular U.S. rates on the net U.S. real property gain for the taxable year.[60]

Any purchaser acquiring a USRPI from a foreign person must withhold 10 percent of the amount realized on the disposition.[61]

[59] See, for example, *Higgins v. Comm.*, 41–1 USTC ¶9233, 25 AFTR 1160, 61 S.Ct. 475 and *Continental Trading, Inc. v. Comm.*, 59–1 USTC ¶9316, 3 AFTR 2d 923, 265 F.2d 40 (CA–9).

[60] § 897.

[61] § 1445. This amount increases to 15% when the amount realized by the foreign person exceeds $1,000,000.

27-6d Expatriation to Avoid U.S. Taxation

U.S. taxation of U.S.-source income is required of individuals who relinquished their U.S. citizenship within 10 years of deriving that income if they gave up their citizenship to avoid U.S. taxation. Furthermore, NRAs who lost U.S. citizenship within a 10-year period immediately preceding the close of the tax year must pay taxes on their U.S.-source income as though they were still U.S. citizens. This provision applies only if the expatriation had as one of its principal purposes the avoidance of U.S. taxes. Individuals are presumed to have a tax avoidance purpose if they meet either of the following criteria:[62]

- Average annual net income tax for the five taxable years ending before the date of loss of U.S. citizenship is more than $190,000 for 2023 ($178,000 for 2022).
- Net worth as of that date is at least $2 million.

These provisions also apply to "long-term lawful permanent residents" who cease to be taxed as U.S. residents. A long-term permanent resident is an individual (other than a citizen of the United States) who is a lawful permanent resident of the United States in at least eight taxable years during the previous 15-year period. An exception applies to certain individuals with dual citizenship.

The United States continues to treat individuals as U.S. citizens or residents until the taxpayers provide required information and an expatriation notice. Expatriates who are subject to the 10-year rule outlined previously must file an information disclosure statement annually. If an expatriate is physically present in the United States for more than 30 days during a calendar year during the 10-year period, the individual is taxed as a U.S. citizen or resident.[63] These expatriation rules, taken as a whole, make it difficult to give up U.S. citizenship or residency simply to avoid U.S. taxation.

27-7 Reporting Requirements

The U.S. tax provisions involving cross-border transactions include numerous reporting requirements. Significant civil and criminal penalties exist for failure to comply with these requirements.

With respect to outbound activities, U.S. owners of foreign branches or foreign disregarded entities are required to file Form 8858, *Information Return of U.S. Persons With Respect to Foreign Disregarded Entities (FDEs) and Foreign Branches (FBs).*[64] The purpose of this form, aside from reporting the income of the branch or entity, is to provide the IRS with additional information about the relationship between the entity and any foreign corporation or partnership, as well as the relationship between the entity or branch and its owners.

Generally, U.S. persons who own a 10 percent or more interest in a foreign corporation are among those who must complete Form 5471, *Information Return of U.S. Persons with Respect to Certain Foreign Corporations.* The form provides various information about the corporation including the nature of the corporation's business, the country in which it is organized, its principle shareholders, and transactions involving related parties. Similarly, U.S. persons who own a 10 percent or more interest in a foreign partnership must file Form 8865, *Return of U.S. Persons With Respect to Certain Foreign Partnerships.*

U.S. partnerships with foreign operations also must report their foreign-source income. For tax years beginning after 2020, new Schedules K–2 and K–3 are required to be filed by U.S. partnerships with foreign-source income and partners with certain ownership interests in foreign partnerships. These schedules are designed to provide additional information necessary for partners to calculate U.S. tax liability on foreign-source partnership income.

[62] § 877(a)(2). The average annual net income tax dollar amount is adjusted for inflation each year.

[63] § 877(g)(1).

[64] Reg. § 1.367(a)–6T(g).

With respect to inbound activities, non-U.S. corporations with a U.S. income tax liability file Form 1120–F. In addition to reporting the U.S. income and tax liability of the foreign corporation, the return provides the IRS with information about the type and scope of the corporation's business operations, the extent to which those operations involve other U.S. persons, the effect of treaties on the corporation's U.S. tax liability, and the corporation's compliance with withholding rules on U.S.-source income paid to foreign persons. Foreign corporations engaged in a U.S. trade or business, as well as 25 percent foreign-owned U.S. corporations, who had certain reportable transactions with a related party also must file Form 5472, *Information Return of a 25% Foreign-Owned U.S. Corporation or a Foreign Corporation Engaged in a U.S. Trade or Business.*

Huskie Corporation, a domestic corporation, operates a foreign branch in Italy. It also is the sole owner of a disregarded entity that operates in Germany, and Poodle corporation, organized and operating in France.

Huskie Corporation is required to file separate Forms 8858 relating to its Italian branch and its German disregarded entity. It also must file Form 5471 related to its ownership of Poodle corporation.

Toyanda, a Japanese corporation, conducts business in the United States through a branch. Toyanda must report its U.S. income using Form 1120–F. BenzWagon, a German corporation, conducts business in the United States through a wholly owned subsidiary, BenzWagon, U.S. BenzWagon, U.S. reports its U.S. income using Form 1120–F. It also files Form 5472 to report, among other things, its transactions with its parent, BenzWagon.

27-8 **Tax Planning**

Tax planning techniques for the multinational taxpayer are effective when they combine opportunities presented by Federal income tax law, the tax provisions and economic incentives offered by the overseas jurisdictions in which business is conducted, income-shifting devices, and the use of tax treaties and tax havens.

Return to the timeline of Exhibit 27.6, and consider the decision to operate a multinational business entity as a branch and when to convert the structure of the business to an overseas subsidiary. Exhibit 27.9 identifies the major advantages and disadvantages for each of these decisions from a Federal income tax standpoint.

Additional tax planning opportunities and considerations are discussed below.

27-8a **The Foreign Tax Credit Limitation and Sourcing Provisions**

The FTC limitation is partially based on the amount of foreign-source taxable income in the numerator of the limitation formula. Consequently, the sourcing of income is extremely important. Generally, in this regard, the U.S. taxpayer benefits when the sourcing rules work to:

- Generate *income* items that are *foreign-source*, to maximize net foreign-source income (the numerator of the FTC fraction).
- Realize *deduction* items as *U.S.-source*, to minimize any reduction in net foreign-source income (the numerator of the FTC fraction).

Exhibit 27.9 Foreign Branch vs. Separate Overseas Entity: Tax Considerations

U.S. Income Tax Considerations	Operate as a Branch of the U.S. Corporation	Operate Through a Separate Overseas Entity (e.g., Subsidiary)
Advantages	• Current U.S. deduction for foreign losses (i.e., flow-through treatment) • If permanent establishment tests are met, treaty benefits are available	• Exemption for U.S. income taxation on profits repatriated as dividends (except for GILTI and Subpart F income) • Availability of income shifting by transfer pricing strategies (e.g., by paying management fees or setting internal pricing levels) • Liability protection for U.S. net assets from overseas operations
Disadvantages	• Current profits are subject to immediate U.S. taxation (i.e., flow-through treatment, even without cash repatriations) • Local tax and financial incentives may not be available (i.e., to an "outside" entity)	• The transfer of assets to the new entity may trigger the recognition of gains by the U.S. taxpayer. • Operating losses are not available to offset U.S. taxable income.

Income that is taxed by an overseas tax jurisdiction benefits from the FTC only to the extent that it is classified as foreign-source income under U.S. tax law. As a result, elements that affect the sourcing of income, such as the place of title passage, should be considered carefully before a transaction is undertaken.

It further may be possible for a U.S. corporation to alleviate the problem of excess foreign taxes by using the following techniques:

- Generate "same basket" foreign-source income that is subject to a tax rate lower than the U.S. tax rate.
- Reduce, by relocating operations, highly taxed foreign-source income in favor of foreign-source income that is taxed at a lower rate.
- Deduct foreign taxes for years when the deduction benefit would exceed the FTC benefit.

Example 37

Donohoe, Inc., a U.S. corporation, reports total U.S. taxable income of $100,000, classified as follows:

	Total	U.S.-Source Income	Foreign-Source Income—Active Basket
Gross income	$150,000	$100,000	$ 50,000
Deductions	(50,000)	(40,000)	(10,000)
Taxable income	$100,000	$ 60,000	$ 40,000

U.S. income tax before the FTC is $21,000, and Donohoe's FTC limitation is $8,400 [($40,000 ÷ $100,000) × $21,000]. If, through planning and analysis, Donohoe is able to convert $5,000 of the deductions related to foreign-source income to U.S. source, the total taxable income would remain the same, but the FTC limitation would increase to $9,450 [($45,000 ÷ $100,000) × $21,000].

27-8b Transfer Pricing

U.S. multinational companies earn income across many different jurisdictions and operate through several different types of entities (e.g., subsidiary corporations, joint ventures, and partnerships). With proper planning and documentation, a U.S. corporation can organize its intercompany payments for goods and services, interest on debt, and royalties for use of intangible property in such a way as to minimize its worldwide tax burden. For example, a U.S. multinational may choose to borrow in high-tax jurisdictions (where the interest deduction will be more valuable) and earn royalty income in low-tax jurisdictions (where the income escapes heavy taxation). The anti-base-erosion tax might restrict these arrangements.

Refocus on The Big Picture

Going International

Now you can address the questions about VoiceCo's activities that were posed at the beginning of the chapter. Simply selling assets overseas may not trigger any host country income tax consequences, but such income is taxed currently to VoiceCo in the United States. When VoiceCo sets up an Irish corporation as a manufacturer, it can avoid deemed dividends under Subpart F.

VoiceCo must file Form 5471 to report the activities of its foreign subsidiary. If VoiceCo receives dividends from such a subsidiary, it can claim exemption from U.S. taxation.

What If?

Suppose that although VoiceCo's European sales become a substantial part of its total revenues, it decides not to create a foreign subsidiary. Instead, because shipping costs are high and customers demand quick turnaround on product orders, VoiceCo decides to license its design and manufacturing process to a local European musical instruments company for sales in Europe. The European company pays VoiceCo a royalty equal to 25 percent of the sales price on all of its sales of microphones based on VoiceCo's design. The royalty income is foreign-source, because the underlying intangible property is exploited outside the United States.

The European country imposes a 5 percent withholding tax on all royalty payments to VoiceCo. The royalties are part of its worldwide income and so are currently taxed to VoiceCo in the United States. Will VoiceCo receive a foreign tax credit for the withholding tax?

MONKEY BUSINESS IMAGES/SHUTTERSTOCK.COM

Key Terms

Base Erosion and Anti-Abuse Tax (BEAT), 27-13
Controlled foreign corporation (CFC), 27-19
Effectively connected income, 27-28
Foreign-Derived Intangible Income (FDII), 27-17
Foreign Investment in Real Property Tax Act (FIRPTA), 27-29
Foreign tax credit (FTC), 27-3
Functional currency, 27-14
Global Intangible Low-Taxed Income (GILTI), 27-24
Inbound taxation, 27-3
Net Deemed Tangible Income Return (NDTIR), 27-26
Nonresident alien (NRA), 27-27
Outbound taxation, 27-3
Qualified business unit (QBU), 27-14
Subpart F income, 27-20
Tax haven, 27-18
Tax treaties, 27-4
Transfer pricing, 27-10
Treaty shopping, 27-19
U.S. shareholder, 27-19
U.S. trade or business, 27-28

Discussion Questions

1. **LO.1** "U.S. persons are taxed on their worldwide income." Explain.
2. **LO.1, 5** Liang Corporation, a U.S. entity, owns 100% of ForCo, a non-U.S. corporation not engaged in a U.S. trade or business. Is Liang subject to any U.S. income tax on its dealings with ForCo? Explain.
3. **LO.5** Randall operates his distribution business in several countries. He wants to move some equipment to a new corporation with an office in South Africa. This equipment includes assets with a large acquisition price and accumulated MACRS depreciation. The assets to be transferred would generate a $1,000,000 realized gain if sold. Advise Randall on the tax effects of his proposed asset transfer. Critical Thinking

Communications

4. **LO.5** Joy Marcus owns several income-producing assets, including a stock portfolio and a small consulting services proprietorship. She wants to start up a new corporation in the country Molto, where the income tax rates are about one-third of those in the United States, and transfer all of her assets and operations there.

   How tax-effective is Joy's plan in shifting the income from her activities when they are placed in the Molto corporation? Write a memo for the tax research file highlighting the Federal income tax rules that apply.

5. **LO.5** Five unrelated U.S. individuals own all of the shares of Popping, a corporation organized and operating fully in the country Vivace. Mariam, one of the shareholders, asks you whether the income from Popping will be taxed to her immediately as earned; she believes the entity is classified as "a controlled foreign corporation (CFC)." Explain how the Federal income tax law applies to the profits earned by Popping. Use the correct Federal income tax terminology in your comments.

6. **LO.5** QuinnCo could not claim all of the income taxes it paid to Japan as a foreign tax credit (FTC) this year. What computational limit probably kept QuinnCo from taking its full FTC? Explain.

7. **LO.5** FoldIt, a U.S. business, paid income taxes to Mexico relative to profitable sales of shipping boxes it made in that country. Can it claim a deduction for these taxes in computing U.S. taxable income? A tax credit? Both? Explain.

Critical Thinking

8. **LO.5** Molly, Inc., a domestic corporation, generates income from the receipt of royalty income from patents that it owns. Molly wants to avoid U.S. income tax on these royalties, so it has its 100%-owned subsidiary, based in Nigeria, hold the patents and collect the royalties.

   What U.S. income tax issues must be considered in assessing this arrangement by Molly, Inc.?

9. **LO.5** HiramCo, a U.S. entity, wholly owns corporations that operate manufacturing businesses in both Mexico and Costa Rica, and it holds its investment portfolio in Sweden. How many foreign tax credit computations must HiramCo make? Be specific, and use the term *basket* in your answer.

Communications

10. **LO.1, 6** Write a memo for the tax research file on the difference between "inbound" and "outbound" activities in the context of U.S. taxation of international income.

Communications

11. **LO.1, 3, 5** Draft a short speech that you will give to your university's Business Club. The title of your talk is "What Is Worldwide Taxation and How Can I Avoid It?" Be certain to include the term *territorial taxing system* in your presentation.

12. **LO.1, 3, 5** Explain how GILTI reduces the incentive for U.S. multinational corporations to shift profits outside of the United States.

13. **LO.1, 6** Who is responsible for filing Forms 5471 and 5472?

Computational Exercises

14. **LO.3** Shonda receives dividend income from the following foreign and domestic corporations in the current tax year:

Corporation	Dividends Received	Percentage of U.S. Income for Past 3 Years
Silver (foreign)	$1,500	35%
Bronze (domestic)	1,000	20%
Copper (domestic)	2,000	80%

Determine the amount of U.S.-source income for each corporation.

15. **LO.5** Cordeio, Inc., is a CFC for the entire tax year (not a leap year). Yancy Company, a U.S. corporation, owns 75% of Cordeio's one class of stock for the entire year. Cordeio's Subpart F income is $450,000, and no distributions have been made during the year. Both entities use the calendar tax year.
    a. What amount does Yancy include in gross income as a constructive dividend for the tax year?
    b. Assume that Cordeio is a CFC until March 1 of the calendar tax year. What amount does Yancy include in gross income as a constructive dividend for the tax year? Use Microsoft Excel to compute your answer.

16. **LO.5** Enders, Inc., a domestic corporation that invests in foreign securities, reports total taxable income for the tax year of $290,000, consisting of $208,800 in U.S.-source business profits and $81,200 of Subpart F income from foreign sources. Income taxes of $24,000 were withheld by foreign tax authorities. Enders's U.S. tax before the FTC is $60,900. Compute Enders' FTC for the tax year using Microsoft Excel.

17. **LO.5** Rogers Co., a U.S. multinational corporation, owns 100% of Orange Co., a CFC. Orange Co. has net tested income of $200,000, qualified business asset investments of $400,000, and no specified business interest expense.
    a. What is Rogers Co.'s GILTI for the year?
    b. By how much do Orange Co.'s operations impact Rogers Co.'s U.S. taxable income?

18. **LO.6** Velocity, Inc., a non-U.S. corporation, earned $500,000 U.S.-source income from royalties that it collected and $400,000 interest from its investment in U.S. Treasury bonds. Compute Velocity's U.S. income tax on these amounts.

Problems

19. **LO.3, 5** BlueCo, a domestic corporation, incorporates GreenCo, a new wholly owned entity, in Germany. Under both German and U.S. legal principles, this entity is a corporation. BlueCo faces a 21% U.S. tax rate.

    GreenCo earns $1,500,000 in net profits from its German manufacturing activities and makes no dividend distributions to BlueCo. How much U.S. income tax must BlueCo pay for the current year as a result of GreenCo's earnings, assuming that it triggers no constructive dividend under Subpart F?

20. **LO.3** Emma, a U.S. resident, received the following income items for the current tax year. Identify the sourcing of each item as either U.S. or foreign.
    a. $600 interest from a savings account at a Florida bank.
    b. $5,000 dividend from U.S. Flower Company, a U.S. corporation that operates solely in the eastern United States.
    c. $7,000 dividend from Stern Corporation, a U.S. corporation that generated total gross income of $4,000,000 from the active conduct of a foreign trade or business for the immediately preceding three tax years. Stern's total gross income for the same period was $5,000,000.
    d. $10,000 dividend from International Consolidated, Inc., a foreign corporation that reported gross income of $4,000,000 effectively connected with the conduct of a U.S. trade or business for the immediately preceding three tax years. International's total gross income for the same period was $12,000,000.
    e. $5,000 interest on Warren Corporation bonds. Warren is a U.S. corporation that derived $6,000,000 of its gross income for the immediately preceding three tax years from operation of an active foreign business. Warren's total gross income for this same period was $7,200,000.

Communications

21. **LO.3, 6** Gloria Martinez, an NRA, is a professional golfer. She played in seven tournaments in the United States in the current year and earned $250,000 in prizes from these tournaments. She deposited the winnings in a bank account she opened in Mexico City after her first tournament win.

    Gloria played a total of 30 tournaments for the year and earned $800,000 in total prize money. She spent 40 days in the United States, 60 days in England, 20 days in Scotland, and the rest of the time in South America. Write a letter to Gloria explaining how much U.S.-source income she will generate, if any, from her participation in these tournaments and whether any of her winnings are subject to U.S. taxation. Gloria's address is AV Rio Branco, 149-4#, Rio de Janeiro, RJ 20180, Brazil.

22. **LO.3, 6** Determine whether the sourcing of income for the following transactions is U.S. or foreign.
    a. Suarez, an NRA, sells stock in Home Depot, a U.S. corporation, through a broker in San Antonio.
    b. Chris sells stock in IBM, a U.S. corporation, to her brother, Rich. Both Chris and Rich are NRAs, and the sale takes place outside the United States.
    c. Crows, Inc., sells inventory produced in the United States to customers in Europe. Title passes in the international waters of the Atlantic Ocean.
    d. Doubles, Inc., a U.S. corporation, manufactures equipment in Malaysia and sells the equipment to customers in the United States.

23. **LO.3, 6** Determine whether the sourcing of income in each of the following situations is U.S. or foreign.
    a. USCo sells depreciable personal property (produced in the United States) that it has been using in its foreign branch operations. The property sells for $180,000, has a tax basis of $75,000, and has been depreciated for tax purposes to the extent of $90,000. The property is located in a foreign country but is sold to another domestic corporation. The sales transaction takes place in the United States.
    b. Jacques, an NRA, sells an apartment building to Julie, a U.S. resident, at a $200,000 gain. The building is located in Denver. The closing takes place in Jacques's country of residence.
    c. Carla, an NRA, is an employee of a non-U.S. corporation. During the tax year, she spends 80 days in the United States purchasing cloth for her employer, a clothing manufacturer. Her yearly salary is $150,000 (translated into U.S. dollars). Carla spends a total of 200 days working during the year. Her employer has no other business contacts with the United States.
    d. Development, Inc., a U.S. corporation, earns $1,100,000 in royalty income from Far East, Ltd., a foreign corporation, for the use of several patented processes in Far East's manufacturing business located in Singapore.

24. **LO.3** Chock, a U.S. corporation, purchases inventory for resale from distributors within the United States and resells this inventory at a $1,000,000 profit to customers outside the United States. Title to the goods passes outside the United States. What is the sourcing of Chock's inventory sales income?

25. **LO.3** Willa, a U.S. corporation, owns the rights to a patent related to a medical device. Willa licenses the rights to use the patent to IrishCo, which uses the patent in its manufacturing facility located in Ireland. What is the sourcing of the $1,000,000 royalty income Willa received from IrishCo for the use of the patent?

26. **LO.3** USCo incurred $100,000 in interest expense for the current year. The tax book value of USCo's assets generating foreign-source income is $5,000,000. The tax book value of USCo's assets generating U.S.-source income is $45,000,000. How much of the interest expense is allocated and apportioned to foreign-source income?

27. **LO.3** LearCo, a non-U.S. conglomerate, generates $4,000,000,000 in gross receipts annually. Its U.S. subsidiary, KingCo, accounts for $750,000,000 of the annual gross receipts; KingCo's average annual gross receipts for the last three years is $820,000,000. KingCo generates U.S. taxable income of $180,000,000 after deducting a $350,000,000 management fee that it pays to LearCo. KingCo reports no U.S. tax credits. The corporate income tax rate in LearCo's country is 14%. What are the tax implications (if any) of this arrangement? Critical Thinking

28. **LO.4** Honk, Inc., a U.S. corporation, purchases weight-lifting equipment for resale from HiDisu, a Japanese corporation, for 60,000,000 yen. On the date of purchase, 110 yen is equal to $1 U.S. (¥110:$1). The purchase is made on December 15, 2023, with payment due in 90 days. Honk is a calendar year taxpayer. On December 31, 2023, the foreign exchange rate is ¥112:$1.

    On February 2, 2024, the invoice is paid when the exchange rate is ¥115:$1. What amount of foreign currency gain or loss, if any, must Honk recognize for 2023 as a result of this transaction? For 2024?

29. **LO.5** Locket, a U.S. C corporation, makes a sale to a customer in Sustainia, a country that applies a 25% income tax to business profits. The customer found out about Locket through an internet search. Locket has no facilities or employees outside the United States. Locket's profit on the sale totals $25,000. Where is the tax levied on this profit?

30. **LO.5** USCo incorporated its foreign branch operations in Italy by transferring the branch's assets to a foreign corporation in return solely for stock in the new corporation. All of the branch's assets are located outside the United States and are used in the active conduct of a foreign trade or business. Is this transaction eligible for tax deferral under § 351? Explain.

31. **LO.5** Brutus Corporation transferred inventory (basis of $10, fair market value of $30) and machinery used in a U.S. factory (adjusted basis of $50, fair market value of $75) to MapleLeaf, a newly formed corporation in Canada, in exchange for all of MapleLeaf's stock. Brutus previously deducted $30 of depreciation related to the machinery on its U.S. tax return.

    How much gain, if any, must Brutus recognize on the transfers of the property to MapleLeaf?

32. **LO.5** Packard, Inc., a domestic corporation, operates a branch in Mexico. Over the last 10 years, this branch has generated $30,000,000 in losses. For the last three years, however, the branch has been profitable and has earned enough income to offset the prior losses in full. Most of the assets are fully depreciated, and a net gain would be recognized if the assets were sold. Communications Critical Thinking

    Packard's CFO believes that Packard should incorporate the branch now so that this potential gain can be transferred to a foreign corporation, deferring the realized gain on the transfer under § 351. Draft a memo to Akiko Henderson, the CFO, addressing the tax issues involved in the proposed transaction.

33. **LO.5** USCo owns 65% of the voting stock of LandCo, a Country X corporation. Terra, an unrelated Country Y corporation, owns the other 35% of LandCo. LandCo owns 100% of the voting stock of OceanCo, a Country Z corporation. Assuming that USCo is a U.S. shareholder, do LandCo and OceanCo meet the definition of a CFC? Explain.

34. **LO.5** Hart Enterprises, a U.S. corporation, owns 100% of OK, Ltd., an Irish corporation. OK's gross income for the year is $10,000,000. Determine OK's Subpart F income (before any expenses) from the transactions that it reported this year.
    a. OK received $600,000 from sales of products purchased from Hart and sold to customers outside Ireland.

b. OK received $1,000,000 from sales of products purchased from Hart and sold to customers in Ireland.

c. OK received $400,000 from sales of products purchased from unrelated suppliers and sold to customers in Germany.

d. OK purchased raw materials from Hart, used these materials to manufacture finished goods, and sold these goods to customers in Italy. OK earned $300,000 from these sales.

e. OK received $100,000 for the performance of warranty services on behalf of Hart. These services were performed in Japan for customers located in Japan.

f. OK received $50,000 in dividend income from investments in Canada and Mexico.

35. **LO.5** Brandy, a U.S. corporation, operates a manufacturing branch in Chad, which does not have an income tax treaty with the United States. Brandy's worldwide Federal taxable income is $30,000,000; it is subject to a 21% marginal tax rate. Profits and taxes in Chad for the current year are summarized as follows. Compute Brandy's foreign tax credit associated with its operations in Chad.

Income Item	Chad Income This Year	Chad Tax Rate	Chad Tax Paid
Manufacturing profits	$2,500,000	20%	$500,000
Dividend	300,000	5%	15,000

36. **LO.5** Weather, Inc., a domestic corporation, operates in both Fredonia and the United States. This year, the business generated taxable income of $600,000 from foreign sources and $900,000 from U.S. sources. All of Weather's foreign-source income is in the general limitation basket. Weather's total taxable income is $1,500,000. Weather pays Fredonia taxes of $228,000. What is Weather's FTC for the tax year? Assume a 21% U.S. income tax rate.

37. **LO.5** Blunt, Inc., a U.S. corporation, earned $600,000 in total taxable income, including $80,000 in foreign-source taxable income from its German branch's manufacturing operations and $30,000 in foreign-source taxable income from its Swiss branch's engineering services operations. Blunt paid $20,000 in German income taxes and $1,800 in Swiss income taxes. Compute Blunt's U.S. tax liability after any available FTCs. Blunt's Federal income tax rate is 21%.

38. **LO.5** Dunne, Inc., a U.S. corporation, earned $500,000 in total taxable income, including $50,000 in foreign-source taxable income from its branch manufacturing operations in Brazil and $20,000 in foreign-source income from interest earned on bonds issued by Dutch corporations. Dunne paid $25,000 in Brazilian income taxes and $3,000 in Dutch income taxes. Compute Dunne's U.S. tax liability after any available FTCs. Dunne's U.S. tax rate is 21%.

39. **LO.5** ABC, Inc., a domestic corporation, reports $50,000,000 of taxable income, including $15,000,000 of foreign-source taxable income from services rendered, on which ABC paid $2,500,000 in foreign income taxes. The U.S. tax rate is 21%. What is ABC's foreign tax credit?

Critical Thinking

40. **LO.1, 5** Indeco, a U.S. C corporation, operates Grange, a sales branch in Staccato. Indeco's U.S. marginal income tax rate is 21%; it is 15% for Staccato. Grange's pretax profit for the year is $1,000,000. There is no income tax treaty between the United States and Staccato. Staccato's currency is the U.S. dollar. Compute Indeco's combined U.S. and foreign income tax on the Grange profits under each of the following assumptions.

	U.S. Income Tax	Staccato Income Tax	Combined Tax Liability
a. U.S. income tax law allows no deduction or credit for foreign income taxes paid.	_____	_____	_____
b. U.S. income tax law allows only a deduction for foreign income taxes paid.	_____	_____	_____
c. U.S. income tax law allows only an exclusion of foreign branch profits.	_____	_____	_____
d. U.S. income tax law allows only a credit for the full amount of foreign income taxes paid.	_____	_____	_____
e. U.S. income tax law allows only a credit for the full amount of foreign income taxes paid. The applicable Staccato tax rate is now 30%.	_____	_____	_____
f. U.S. income tax law allows only a credit for the full amount of foreign income taxes paid, but limited currently to the corresponding tax on this income at U.S. rates. The applicable Staccato tax rate is now 30%.	_____	_____	_____

41. **LO.5** Night, Inc., a domestic corporation, earned $300,000 from offshore manufacturing activities on which it paid $36,000 of foreign income taxes. Night's foreign sales income is taxed at a 50% income tax rate. What amount of foreign sales income can Night earn without generating any excess FTCs for the current year? Assume a 21% U.S. tax rate. Critical Thinking

42. **LO.3, 4, 5** You are the head tax accountant for Venture Company, a U.S. corporation. The board of directors is considering expansion overseas and asks you to present a summary of the U.S. tax consequences of investing overseas through an offshore subsidiary. Prepare a detailed outline of the presentation you will make to the board. Communications

43. **LO.1, 3, 5** Oasis Co., a U.S. shareholder, owns 100% of Shack Co. and 100% of Studio Co., both CFCs. Shack Co. has $300,000 of gross income, of which $50,000 is effectively connected income, and $30,000 is interest expense without any allocable interest income. Shack Co. has $500,000 of machinery used in its trade or business. Studio Co. has a $150,000 loss and machinery worth $1,000,000 used in its operations.
    a. What is GILTI for Oasis Co.?
    b. What impact do the operations of Shack Co. and Studio Co. have on Oasis Co.'s U.S. taxable income?

44. **LO.2, 6** IrishCo, a manufacturing corporation resident in Ireland, distributes products through a U.S. office. Current-year taxable income from such sales in the United States is $12,000,000. IrishCo's U.S. office deposits working capital funds in short-term certificates of deposit with U.S. banks. Current-year interest income from these deposits is $150,000.

    IrishCo also invests in U.S. securities traded on the New York Stock Exchange. This investing is done by the home office. For the current year, IrishCo records realized capital gains of $300,000 and dividend income of $50,000 from these stock investments. Compute IrishCo's U.S. tax liability using Microsoft Excel, assuming that the U.S.-Ireland income tax treaty reduces withholding on dividends to 15% and on interest to 5%. Use formulas whenever possible.

45. **LO.6** Calabra, S.A., a Peruvian corporation, manufactures inventory in Peru. The inventory is sold to independent distributors in the United States; title passes to the purchaser in the United States. Calabra has no employees or operations within the United States. All sales activities are conducted via telephone and internet communication between Calabra's home office and its U.S. customers. Explain whether Calabra incurs any income effectively connected with a U.S. trade or business.

46. **LO.6** Clario, S.A., a Peruvian corporation, manufactures furniture in Peru. It sells the furniture to independent distributors in the United States. Because title to the furniture passes to the purchasers in the United States, Clario reports $2,000,000 in U.S.-source income. Clario has no employees or operations in the United States related to its furniture business.

    As a separate line of business, Clario buys and sells antique toys. Clario has a single employee operating a booth on weekends at a flea market in Waldo, Florida. The antique toy business generated $85,000 in net profits from U.S. sources during the current year.

    What is Clario's effectively connected income for the current year?

47. **LO.3, 6** Carter, Ltd., a Bohemia corporation, operates a sales branch in the United States that constitutes a U.S. trade or business. Rather than return the profits from the sales branch to the Bohemia home office, Carter invests the profits in certificates of deposit at U.S. banks. Explain whether the interest earned on these CDs is considered effectively connected with Carter's U.S. trade or business.

48. **LO.6** Martinho is a citizen of Brazil and lives there year-round. He has invested in a plot of Illinois farmland with a tax basis to him of $1,000,000. Martinho has no other business or investment activities in the United States. He is not subject to the alternative minimum tax.

    a. Upon sale of the land for $1,500,000 to Emma, an Illinois individual, what are the Federal income tax consequences to Martinho?

    b. What are the Federal income tax withholding requirements with respect to Martinho's sale? Who pays the withheld amount to the U.S. Treasury?

Communications
Critical Thinking

49. **LO.6** Sarah Liu is single, an attorney, and a U.S. citizen. Sarah's net worth is $5,000,000. Sarah recently attended a seminar where she heard that she could give up her U.S. citizenship, move to Bermuda (where she would pay no income tax), and operate a law practice long distance via the internet with no U.S. tax consequences. Write a letter informing Sarah of the tax consequences of the proposed actions. Her address is 1005 NE Farwell Street, Gainesville, GA 32612.

50. **LO.6** ForCo, a foreign corporation not engaged in a U.S. trade or business, received a $600,000 dividend from USCo, a domestic corporation. ForCo incurred $45,000 in expenses related to earning the dividend. All of USCo's income is from U.S. sources. ForCo is not eligible for any treaty benefits. What is the withholding tax on the dividend paid to ForCo?

51. **LO.6** ForCo, a foreign corporation not engaged in a U.S. trade or business, received a $250,000 dividend from USCo, a domestic corporation. ForCo incurred $40,000 in expenses related to earning the dividend. All of USCo's income is from U.S. sources. ForCo is not eligible for any treaty benefits. What is the withholding tax on the dividend paid to ForCo?

52. **LO.6** ForCo, a foreign corporation not engaged in a U.S. trade or business, received an $800,000 dividend from USCo, a domestic corporation. ForCo incurred $75,000 in expenses related to earning the dividend. All of USCo's income is from U.S. sources. ForCo is eligible for an income tax treaty that limits withholding on dividends to 10%. What is the withholding tax on the dividend paid to ForCo?

Research Problems

Note: Solutions to the Research Problems can be prepared by using the Thomson Reuters Checkpoint™ online tax research database, which accompanies this textbook. Solutions can also be prepared by using research materials found in a typical tax library.

Communications
Critical Thinking

Research Problem 1. Jerry Jeff Keen, the CFO of Boots Unlimited, a Texas corporation, has come to you regarding a potential restructuring of business operations. Boots has long manufactured its western boots in plants in Texas and Oklahoma. Recently, Boots has explored the possibility of setting up a manufacturing subsidiary in Ireland, where manufacturing profits are taxed at 12.5%. Jerry Jeff sees this as a great idea, given that the alternative is to continue all manufacturing in the United States, where profits are taxed at 21%.

Boots plans to continue all of the cutting, sizing, and hand tooling of leather in its U.S. plants. This material will be shipped to Ireland for final assembly, with the finished product shipped to retail outlets all over Europe and Asia.

Your initial concern is whether the income generated by the Irish subsidiary will be considered foreign base company income. Address this issue in a research memo, along with any planning suggestions.

Partial list of research aids:
§ 954(d).
Reg. § 1.954–3(a).
Bausch & Lomb, 71 TCM 2031, T.C.Memo. 1996–57.

Research Problem 2. Polly Ling is a successful professional golfer. She is a resident of a country that does not have a tax treaty with the United States. Ling plays matches around the world, about one-half of which are in the United States. Ling's reputation is without blemish; in fact, she is known as being exceedingly honest and upright, and many articles discuss how she is a role model for young golfers due to her tenacious and successful playing style and her favorable character traits. Every year, she reports the most penalty strokes on herself among the participants in women's matches, and this is seen as reinforcing her image as an honest and respectful competitor.

This combination of quality play and laudable reputation has brought many riches to Ling. She comes to you with several Federal income tax questions. She knows that as a non-U.S. resident, any of her winnings from tournament play that occur in the United States are subject to U.S. income taxation. But what about each of the following items? How does U.S. tax law affect Ling? Apply the sourcing rules in this regard, and determine whether the graduated U.S. Federal income Tax Rate Schedules apply.

- Endorsement income from YourGolf for wearing clothing during matches with its logo prominently displayed. Ling must play in at least 10 tournaments per year that are televised around the world. She also must participate in photo sessions and in blogs and tweets associated with the tournaments. Payment to Ling is structured as a flat fee, with bonuses paid if she finishes in the top five competitors for each match. This is known as an *on-court endorsement.*
- Endorsement income from GolfZone for letting the company use her likeness in a video game that simulates golf tournaments among known golfers and other players that the (usually middle-aged men and women) gamers identify. In this way, the gamer seems to be playing against Ling on famous golf courses. Two-thirds of all dollar sales of the game licenses are to U.S. customers.
- Endorsement income from Eliteness for appearing in print and internet ads that feature Ling wearing the company's high-end watches. One-fifth of all dollar sales of the watches are to U.S. customers. The latter two items are known as *off-court endorsements.*

Partial list of research aids:
Goosen, 136 T.C. (2011).

Use internet tax resources to address the following questions. Look for reliable websites and blogs of the IRS and other government agencies, media outlets, businesses, tax professionals, academics, think tanks, and political outlets.

Communications
Data Analytics

Research Problem 3. Locate data on the size of the international economy, including data on international trade, foreign direct investment by U.S. firms, and investment in the United States by foreign firms. Useful web locations include **census.gov** and **bea.gov**. Prepare an analysis of the data for a three-year period using spreadsheet and graphing software, and e-mail the results to your instructor.

Communications

Research Problem 4. Choose 10 countries, one of which is the United States. Create a table showing whether each country applies a worldwide or territorial approach to international income taxation. Then list the country's top income tax rate on business profits. Send a copy of this table to your instructor.

Communications

Research Problem 5. Find the text of various tax treaties currently in force in the United States. In an e-mail to your instructor, address the following items.

a. How does the U.S. income tax treaty with Germany define "business profits" for multinational businesses?
b. How does the U.S. income tax treaty with Japan treat the FIRPTA provisions?
c. List five countries with which the United States has entered into an estate tax treaty.
d. What is the effective date of the latest income tax treaty with the United Kingdom?
e. List three countries with which the United States does not have in force a bilateral income tax treaty.

Communications

Research Problem 6. Technology has upended the way consumers purchase and receive goods and services. The digital age has resulted in increased opportunities for multinational companies (MNCs) to shift profits from high-tax to low-tax jurisdictions. The Organization for Economic Co-operation and Development (OECD), a collection of 137 countries, is responding by drafting a set of rules that will reduce the opportunity for base erosion and ensure that MNCs pay a minimum amount of tax.

There is considerable debate in the United States about the OECD proposal. Some believe that the United States needs a 21% or higher minimum tax on corporate earnings, while others believe that GILTI serves as the appropriate minimum tax on global profits. Still others contend that no tax on the corporate profits of U.S. multinational corporations should exist until those profits are repatriated to the United States.

Go to **oecd.org/tax/beps** and read about the OECD/G20 framework. Write a one-page summary with three arguments in favor of or against a U.S. corporate minimum tax on global profits. Send a copy to your instructor.

Becker CPA Review Questions

Becker

1. A binding contract between the IRS and the taxpayer by which the IRS agrees not to seek a transfer pricing adjustment for a covered transaction if the taxpayer files its return for a covered year consistent with the agreed transfer pricing method is called a(n):

   a. Section 482 study.
   b. Advance Pricing Agreement Program.
   c. Request for competent authority.
   d. Controlled transaction analysis agreement.

2. Bangle Supplies, Inc. (a U.S. corporation), is a wholesale distributor of office supplies. In year 3, Bangle sells office supplies to Go Green Ltd. (a Canada corporation). Bangle ships $300,000 in office supplies to Go Green's headquarters in Quebec, Canada, and $250,000 in office supplies to Go Green's warehouse in Detroit, Michigan (with title passing upon delivery). In addition, Go Green pays Bangle $35,000 to provide environmental consulting services at its headquarters in Quebec. What is Bangle's U.S.-source and foreign-source income in year 3?
   a. U.S. source, $585,000; foreign source, $0
   b. U.S. source, $250,000; foreign source, $335,000
   c. U.S. source, $0; foreign source, $585,000
   d. U.S. source, $285,000; foreign source, $300,000
3. DomCo (a domestic corporation) owns 100% of ForCo (a foreign corporation), which operates outside of the United States. Which of the following statements is correct?
   a. ForCo is not considered a controlled foreign corporation (CFC).
   b. ForCo's Subpart F income will generally be treated as deemed dividend subject to immediate recognition by DomCo.
   c. ForCo's income will be subject to current taxation in the United States because ForCo is a foreign subsidiary.
   d. ForCo is considered a foreign branch of DomCo.
4. Which of the following is not a category of income for foreign tax credit limitation purposes?
   a. General category income
   b. Foreign-derived intangible income
   c. Passive category income
   d. Foreign branch income
5. The base erosion and anti-abuse tax (BEAT) may apply to corporations:
   a. Taxed as S corporations.
   b. With any deductible payments to non-U.S. persons.
   c. With net assets of $500 million or more in any of the three preceding tax years.
   d. With average annual gross receipts of $500 million or more for the three preceding tax years.
6. In which of the following situations will a foreign person not be treated as a U.S. resident?
   a. A foreign person who holds a permanent resident visa ("green card") and is present in the United States for more than 30 days during the current year.
   b. A foreign person who holds a permanent resident visa ("green card") and is present in the United States for less than 30 days during the current year.
   c. A foreign person who is present in the United States for 30 days during the current year and 350 days in each of the two preceding tax years.
   d. A foreign person who is present in the United States for 40 days during the current year and 300 days in each of the two preceding tax years.

Chapter

28 Tax Practice and Ethics

Learning Objectives: *After completing Chapter 28, you should be able to:*

- **LO.1** Illustrate the organization and structure of the IRS.
- **LO.2** Identify administrative pronouncements issued by the IRS, and explain how they can be used in tax practice.
- **LO.3** Describe the audit process, including how tax returns are selected for audit and the various types of audits.
- **LO.4** Explain the taxpayer appeal process, including various settlement options available.
- **LO.5** Determine the amount of interest on a deficiency or a refund and when it is due.
- **LO.6** Explain penalties imposed on acts of noncompliance by taxpayers and return preparers.
- **LO.7** Apply the rules governing the statute of limitations on assessments and on refunds.
- **LO.8** Summarize the legal and ethical guidelines that apply to those engaged in tax practice.

Chapter Outline

Martin Barraud/Ojo Images/Getty Images

The Big Picture

A Tax Adviser's Dilemma

Campbell Corporation is preparing its Form 1120 for the tax year. The corporation develops and manufactures a number of clean-energy products including solar panels, inverters, and batteries. The advanced manufacturing production credit provided by § 45X is available for many of the components produced by Campbell if sold to an unrelated person. For components to be eligible for the credit, they must meet certain specifications. For example, photovoltaic wafers must be at least 240 square centimeters in size and their production must take place in the United States. Additionally, taxpayers can make an election for sales to a related person to count as if they were sales to an unrelated person. The IRS intends to issue guidance regarding this election to prevent improper use or an excessive amount of the credit.

Some of the components produced by Campbell clearly qualify for the advanced manufacturing production Federal income tax credit, but for some other items, the availability of the credit is not so certain. Because § 45X is new, the IRS has not yet published Regulations or other guidance on which taxpayers can rely when claiming the credit.

You are Campbell's tax adviser. This situation presents you with several levels of difficulty. How aggressive should you advise Campbell to be in reporting items on its Form 1120 that qualify for the advanced manufacturing production credit? Will an overly aggressive position on the credit trigger a tax preparer penalty for your tax consulting firm? What level of diligence should you exercise in advising Campbell as to whether specific components qualify for the credit, given that your expertise regarding clean energy components is limited?

Read the chapter and formulate your response.

Few events arouse so much fear in the typical individual taxpayer or corporate tax department as the receipt of a letter from the Internal Revenue Service (IRS) notifying the taxpayer that prior years' tax returns are the subject of an audit. Almost immediately, calls are made to the tax adviser. Advice is sought as to what to reveal (or not reveal) in the course of the audit, how to delay or avoid the audit, and how friendly one should be with the auditor during the audit process.

The tax professional can render valuable services to the taxpayer in an audit context, thereby ensuring that tax payments for the disputed years are neither under- nor over-reported as part of an ongoing tax practice. In this regard, the adviser must appreciate the following, each of which is addressed in this chapter:

- The elements of the Treasury's tax administration process and opportunities for appeal within the structure of the IRS.
- The extent of the negative sanctions that can be brought to bear against taxpayers whose returns are found to have been inaccurate.
- The ethical and professional constraints on the advice tax advisers can give and the actions they can take on behalf of their clients within the context of an adversarial relationship with the IRS.

28-1 **Tax Administration**

The Treasury has delegated the administration and enforcement of the Federal laws to its subsidiary agency, the IRS. The Service is responsible for working with taxpayers through its website (**irs.gov**), printed materials, and personal interaction, so that the U.S. tax laws can be applied with integrity and fairness. The IRS collects current and delinquent taxes through voluntary taxpayer compliance and with audits and litigation under the restrictions of due process and other constitutional guarantees. The IRS also is called on to administer special tax or payment programs. For example, the IRS administered several COVID-19-related stimulus programs during the pandemic. The annual *IRS Data Book* provides data on IRS activities (including revenue collections and refunds, enforcing the law, assisting taxpayers, and information on its workforce and budget).[1]

The IRS employs more than 78,000 individuals, about two-thirds of whom are women; more than half of the staff entail ethnic minorities, and 9 percent are veterans. About 45 percent of the IRS workforce is dedicated to enforcement, and about 40 percent is dedicated to taxpayer service.

The total agency budget is about $13.7 billion. In meeting its responsibilities, the Service conducts audits of selected tax returns. For 2021, the IRS reported that less than 0.55 percent of individual income tax returns were subjected to audit. However, high-income individuals and large corporations are subject to higher probabilities of audit. The audit rate for corporations with at least $5 billion in assets is about 35 percent, but it is only about 0.3 percent for businesses with less than $1 million in assets.

From 2010 to 2021, the number of individual taxpayers the IRS served increased by about 19 percent while the IRS's baseline budget was reduced by about 20 percent and its workforce shrunk by about 17 percent. This imbalance left the IRS without enough resources to meet taxpayer needs and set the stage for a perfect storm during the COVID-19 pandemic. Taxpayer service in 2021 was historically poor. For example, the IRS finished the 2021 filing season with a backlog of 35.3 million returns that required manual processing. When taxpayers called the IRS for assistance, only about 11 percent reached a representative, with hold times for taxpayers who got through averaging about 23 minutes (the IRS experienced a tremendous increase in calls during the pandemic).[2]

[1] **irs.gov/pub/irs-pdf/p55b.pdf**.

[2] See information at **taxpayeradvocate.irs.gov/reports/2021-annual-report-to-congress/**.

The Inflation Reduction Act of 2022 (PL 117–169) included $80 billion in additional IRS funding for the next decade. The IRS plans to clear its backlog, improve taxpayer service, modernize technology, and hire thousands of new employees (although thousands are expected to retire over the next few years).

Paid tax return preparers also play an important role in tax administration; they prepare the majority of individual tax returns. Penalties may be assessed on those who prepared a tax return where the IRS's interpretation of applicable law conflicts with that of the preparer.

Taxes Collected and the Tax Gap

The IRS processes about 260 million Federal tax returns and over 4.7 billion information returns every year. **Information returns** are filed by third parties, such as employers, banks, and brokers; they provide information about payments or transactions. Fifty unique types of information returns provide information on individual taxpayers. The IRS matches information returns and tax returns to identify potential noncompliance. Taxpayers misreport about 1 percent of wage income where substantial third-party information reporting and withholding exits but misrepresent 55 percent of income when there is little or no third-party information reporting.

The difference between how much tax *is* collected and how much *should be* collected is the "tax gap." The IRS uses results from random audits to periodically estimate the tax gap. Based on data for tax years 2011, 2012, and 2013, the IRS estimated the tax gap to be $441 billion per year. The Treasury recently estimated the tax gap to be around $600 billion. In testimony to Congress in 2021, IRS Commissioner Charles Rettig said the tax gap is approximately $1 trillion each year.[3]

Estimates of the tax gap vary because it is difficult to identify and measure all forms of possible tax evasion as well as unintentional errors. Random audits detect many ways individuals cheat on taxes, such as underreporting self-employment income and overstating deductions, but do not detect all sophisticated forms of tax evasion. Tax evasion through foreign intermediaries (e.g., undeclared foreign bank accounts) and pass-through businesses (e.g., partnerships) go almost entirely undetected in random audits. An academic study that adjusts data for sophisticated tax evasion techniques estimated that 36 percent of unpaid Federal income taxes are owed by the top 1 percent of the income distribution and that collecting all unpaid Federal income tax from this group would increase Federal revenues by about $175 billion annually.[4] Part of the tax gap also is due to unintentional errors and failure or inability to pay what is owed.

28-1a Organizational Structure of the IRS

LO.1 **Illustrate the organization and structure of the IRS.**

The structure of the IRS is illustrated in Exhibit 28.1. The Commissioner of Internal Revenue is appointed by the President for a five-year renewable term.[5] Eight executives report directly to the Commissioner, four of whom oversee significant direct interactions with taxpayers.

The Chief Counsel, another Presidential appointee, is the head legal officer of the IRS. The Chief Counsel's office provides legal advice to the IRS and guidance to the public on matters pertaining to the administration and enforcement of the tax laws. For instance, the Chief Counsel's duties include establishing uniform nationwide interpretive positions on the law, drafting tax guide material for taxpayers and IRS personnel, issuing technical rulings to taxpayers, and providing advice and technical assistance to IRS personnel. The Chief Counsel represents the IRS in all litigation before the Tax Court.

[3]Rappaport, Alan, "Tax Cheats Cost the U.S. $1 Trillion Per Year, IRS Chief Says," *New York Times*, Apr 13, 2021 (**du.idm.oclc.org/login?url=https://www.proquest.com/newspapers/tax-cheats-cost-u-s-1-trillion-per-year-irs-chief/docview/2512141802/se-2**). Also see IRS tax gap information at **irs.gov/newsroom/the-tax-gap**.

[4]Guyton, John, et al. *Tax evasion at the top of the income distribution: theory and evidence*. No. w28542. National Bureau of Economic Research, 2021.

[5]§ 7803 specifies appointment procedures for the Commissioner, the Chief Counsel for the IRS, the National Taxpayer Advocate, the Chief of Appeals, and the Chief Information Officer.

Exhibit 28.1 **IRS National Office Organization**

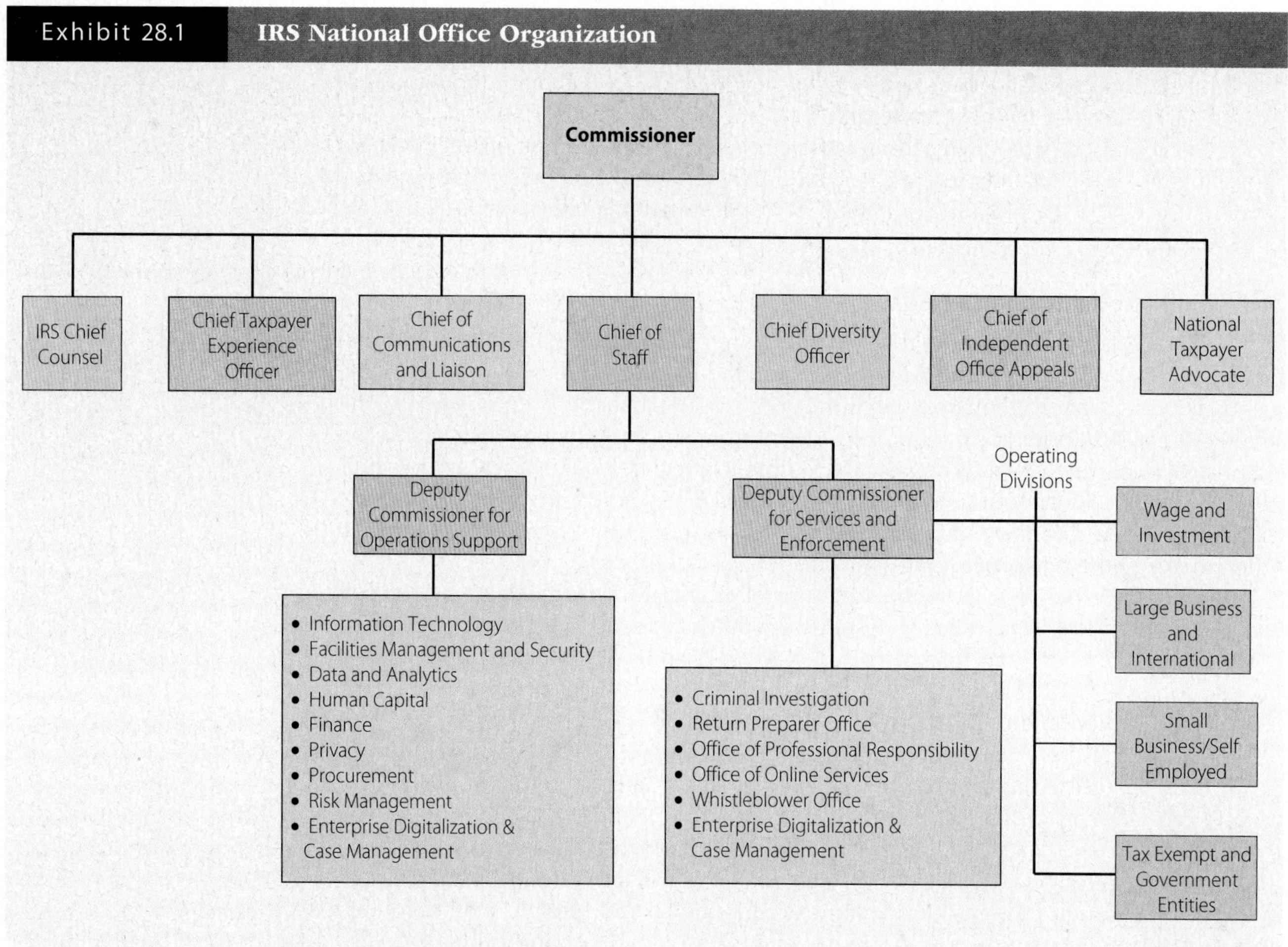

The National Taxpayer Advocate is appointed by the Secretary of the Treasury, reports to the Commissioner, and must also report to Congress each year. The Taxpayer Advocate Service is an independent organization within the IRS that assists taxpayers who are experiencing financial hardship, have been unable to resolve problems they are having with the IRS, or believe an IRS system or procedure is not working as it should. There is at least one Taxpayer Advocate for each state and the organization has approximately 1,700 employees. One indicator of a systemic problem at the IRS is a delay of 30 days beyond normal processing time for an issue to be resolved. The National Taxpayer Advocate's annual report to Congress summarizes the ten most serious problems encountered by taxpayers and recommends administrative and legislative action that may help resolve problems.

The Independent Office of Appeals is led by the Chief of Appeals. The office is charged with resolving Federal tax controversies without litigation in a manner that is fair, consistent, and that enhances public confidence in the IRS. The Office of Appeals may call upon the Office of Chief Counsel for legal assistance and advice.

The fourth executive that leads significant interactions with taxpayers is the Chief of Staff, to whom two Deputy Commissioners report. The Deputy Commissioner for Operations Support oversees administrative functions that are organized around a shared-services model. The Deputy Commissioner for Services and Enforcement oversees four major operating divisions and several other functions. Each operating division is assigned a particular group of taxpayers. For example, the Small Business/Self-Employed (SB/SE) Division focuses on individuals who file Schedule C (self-employed) and partnerships with under $10 million in assets. About 57 million taxpayers meet this profile. The Large Business and International Division focuses on all Form 1120 and 1120–S filers, partnerships with more than $10 million in assets, and individuals with global high wealth.

28-1b IRS Procedure—Letter Rulings

LO.2

Identify administrative pronouncements issued by the IRS, and explain how they can be used in tax practice.

When a tax issue is controversial or a transaction involves considerable tax dollars, the taxpayer often wants to obtain either assurance or direction from the IRS as to the treatment of the event. The **letter ruling** process is an effective means of dealing directly with the IRS while in the planning stages of a large or otherwise important transaction.

Rulings issued by the National Office provide a written statement of the position of the IRS concerning the tax consequences of a course of action contemplated by the taxpayer. Letter rulings do not have the force and effect of law, but they do provide guidance and support for taxpayers in similar transactions. The IRS issues rulings only on uncompleted, actual (rather than hypothetical) transactions or on transactions that have been completed before the filing of the tax return for the year in question.

In certain circumstances, the IRS will not issue a ruling. It ordinarily will not rule in cases that essentially involve a question of fact.[6] For example, no ruling will be issued to determine whether compensation paid to employees is reasonable in amount and therefore allowable as a deduction.

A letter ruling represents the current opinion of the IRS on the tax consequences of a transaction with a given set of facts. IRS rulings are not unchangeable. They can be declared obsolete or superseded by new rulings in response to tax law changes.

A ruling may be relied upon only by the taxpayer who requested and received it. It must be attached to the tax return for the year in question.

Letter rulings benefit both the IRS and the taxpayer. They not only help promote uniform application of the tax laws but also may reduce the potential for litigation or disputes with IRS agents. In addition, they make the IRS aware of significant transactions being consummated by taxpayers. A fee of $38,000 is charged for processing most ruling requests; the fee is reduced to $3,000 if the taxpayer's gross income is less than $250,000.

28-1c IRS Procedure—Other Issuances

In addition to issuing unpublished letter rulings and published rulings and procedures, the IRS issues determination letters and technical advice memoranda.

A group of physicians plans to form an entity to construct and operate a hospital. The determination letter procedure is appropriate to ascertain whether the group is subject to the Federal income tax or is tax-exempt.

Ethics & Equity **Tax Compliance Costs**

By one estimate, the cost of compliance with Federal tax laws exceeds *$338 billion* per year, equivalent to more than 6 billion hours of taxpayers' time devoted to tax compliance efforts. This amount equals about 1.7 percent of the U.S. gross domestic product.

In this estimate, the following items were counted as costs of tax compliance:[7]

- The value of taxpayers' time spent record keeping, filing, planning, and otherwise complying with the tax laws.
- Tax collection costs (chiefly wages and benefits) of IRS employees.
- Expenditures made to professional tax preparers, consultants, and other preparers.

Comment on the appropriateness of Congress and the Treasury passing along to taxpayers the costs of its revenue collection operation.

[6]Rev.Proc. 2023–1.

[7]**ntu.org/foundation/detail/increasing-complexity-brings-back-bigger-compliance-burdens**.

A **determination letter** relates to a completed transaction when the issue involved is covered by judicial or statutory authority, Regulations, or rulings. Determination letters are issued for various estate, gift, income, excise, and employment tax matters.

A **technical advice memorandum (TAM)** is issued by the National Office to IRS personnel in response to a technical or procedural request by an agent, Appellate Conferee, or IRS executive. The taxpayer may request a TAM if an issue in dispute is not treated by the law or precedent and/or published rulings or Regulations. Technical advice requests arise from the audit or appeals process, whereas letter ruling requests typically are issued as part of the filing of an original tax return (i.e., before any IRS audit).

28-1d **Administrative Powers of the IRS**

Examination of Records

The IRS can examine the taxpayer's books and records as part of the process of determining the correct amount of tax due. The IRS also can require the persons responsible for the return to appear and to produce any necessary books and records.[8] Taxpayers are required to maintain certain record-keeping procedures and retain the records necessary to facilitate the audit.

Burden of Proof

If the taxpayer meets the record-keeping requirement and substantiates income and deductions properly, the IRS bears the burden of proof in establishing a tax deficiency during litigation. The taxpayer must have cooperated with the IRS regarding reasonable requests for information, documents, meetings, and interviews. For individual taxpayers, the IRS's burden of proof also extends to penalties and interest amounts that it assesses in a court proceeding with the taxpayer.[9]

Assessment and Demand

The Code permits the IRS to assess a deficiency and to demand payment for the tax. However, no assessment or effort to collect the tax may be made until 90 days after a statutory notice of a deficiency (a *90-day letter*) is issued. The taxpayer then has 90 days to pay the indicated tax or file a petition to the U.S. Tax Court, effectively preventing the deficiency from being assessed or collected pending the outcome of the case.[10]

Following assessment of the tax, the IRS issues a notice and demand for payment. The taxpayer can be given as little as 10 days to pay the tax after the demand for payment is issued. If the IRS believes the assessment or collection of a deficiency is in jeopardy, it may assess the deficiency and demand immediate payment.[11]

Collection

If the taxpayer refuses to pay the tax after receiving the demand for payment, a lien in favor of the IRS is placed on all property (realty and personalty, tangible and intangible) belonging to the taxpayer.

The levy power of the IRS is very broad. It allows the IRS to garnish (*attach*) wages and salary and to seize and sell all nonexempt property by any means. After a notice period, the IRS can make successive seizures on any property owned by the taxpayer until the levy is satisfied. A taxpayer's principal residence and certain business assets are exempt from the levy process, unless the disputed tax, interest, and penalty exceed $5,000 and a U.S. District Court judge approves of the seizure.[12]

[8] § 7602.

[9] § 7491.

[10] §§ 6212 and 6213.

[11] § 6861. A jeopardy assessment is appropriate, for instance, when the IRS fears that the taxpayer will flee the country or destroy valuable property.

[12] § 6334. Taxpayers can keep certain personal and business property and a minimal amount of their income as a subsistence allowance, even if a lien is outstanding.

28-1e The Audit Process

LO.3

Describe the audit process, including how tax returns are selected for audit and the various types of audits.

Selection of Returns for Audit

The IRS continually adapts its tools and processes to identify errors, detect fraudulent activity, and allocate resources efficiently and effectively. The IRS does not disclose all of its audit selection techniques. However, the IRS reports results of some of its automated programs in the annual *IRS Data Book*.

- The Automated Underreporter Program matches information returns to tax returns and contacts taxpayers to resolve discrepancies. In 2021, the IRS closed over 2 million cases and collected over $10 billion in additional assessments under this program.

Example 2

Kristina prepares her own tax return. She forgets to include $130 of dividend income from an online investment account, even though she received a Form 1099–DIV reporting this income (and the issuer sent the form to the IRS as well). Approximately a year after filing her tax return she receives a notice from the IRS. The notice computes the tax and interest due on the unreported dividend income and tells Kristina how to either pay the amount due, make payment arrangements, or reply if she does not agree with the adjustment made by the IRS. The IRS matched its copy of Kristina's Form 1099–DIV with her reported income and found the error.

- The Substitute for Return (SFR) Program uses information returns to identify nonfilers; construct tax returns for certain nonfilers based on that third-party information; and assess tax, interest, and penalties based on the substitute returns. The IRS closed over 400,000 cases and assessed nearly $4 billion of revenue under this program in 2021.
- During 2021, the IRS sent more than 12.3 million notices to taxpayers for more than 12.9 million math errors identified on their returns.
- Certain individual income tax returns identified as containing potentially unallowable items are examined through correspondence. About 78 percent of audits are conducted via correspondence; the remainder are conducted in the field.

Roberto is age 44, employed by MetaVerse, and covered by its medical insurance plan. Last year Roberto contracted a rare disease and opted for experimental medical treatment that was not covered by his insurance plan. He deducted $95,000 of medical expenses on his tax return. His tax return was selected for examination. The IRS sent Roberto a letter and asked him to submit documentation to support his medical expense deduction.

The IRS provides guidelines regarding procedures and techniques for IRS auditors to follow when examining returns in the **Internal Revenue Manual (IRM)**. The IRM describes several compliance programs including the National Research Program. Under the National Research Program, returns are selected for audit using scientific sampling techniques. The IRS uses results to construct Discriminant Function (DIF) methods that score tax returns and identify those most likely to yield substantial amounts of additional tax revenue upon audit.

The IRS also conducts audits targeted to certain industries or taxpayers. For example, the Large Business and International Division periodically announces additions to its compliance campaigns. One campaign targets taxpayers who engage in transactions involving virtual currency. It is not illegal for taxpayers to hold or exchange virtual currency. However, taxpayers must comply with income tax and information reporting requirements associated with these activities.

Khaled is a freelance programmer. He designed and built a website for a client who paid Khaled's fee in a virtual currency. At the time Khaled received the virtual currency its value was $25,000, the fee Khaled charged for his service. Khaled must report gross income of $25,000. When Khaled sells or exchanges the virtual currency in a later transaction, he will have capital gain or loss to the extent its value increases or decreases (his basis in this virtual currency is $25,000).

Another method the IRS uses to obtain information relevant to tax investigations is the issuance of a **John Doe summons** to financial service providers such as banks. A John Doe summons does not identify the taxpayer or group about whom records are requested because they are not yet known. In 2016, the IRS started using John Doe summonses to obtain information about owners of digital assets. A court ultimately ordered Coinbase to produce identifying information for over 10,000 account holders. Since then, similar enforcement actions have been taken against other virtual asset service providers.[13]

The IRS also obtains information through information exchange agreements with other agencies or governments, both domestic and foreign.

Eitan's 2021 tax return was selected for audit by the State of New York. The New York Department of Taxation and Finance determined that Eitan had understated the income of his sole proprietorship by $250,000. At the conclusion of the proceedings, New York reported the adjustment to the IRS.

Ethics & Equity Can the IRS Pretend to Be Your Friend?

Should IRS agents be allowed to identify audit subjects by reading the society page of the newspaper, looking for indicators of wealth? What if the agency subscribes to Facebook and seeks comments from its "friends" as to income windfalls and stock market dealings?

In the past, some state and local taxing agencies have used social networking sites for audit selection purposes. State and local revenue agents have used the sites to find self-employed individuals who advertise their business and report about upcoming income-producing events. The sites also have been used to determine whether a taxpayer who has requested an extension of time to pay a delinquent tax actually is strapped for cash.

Some state tax officials claim that looking for a taxpayer's self-declarations on a website is a much more efficient way to find income understatements than searching through most other sources of nonstatistical data. Should taxing agencies be using Instagram, Facebook, and other public-domain online sources of taxpayer information to help find nonfilers and identify tax returns for audit?

Role of Informants

Since 1867, the Treasury Department has had authority to pay awards for information related to violations of internal revenue laws. Awards paid under this general authority are at the discretion of the IRS and the maximum award is 15 percent of collected taxes and penalties. The claimant initiates the process with Form 211.[14]

Betty is discharged by her employer of 15 years, Franklin, who owns a chain of restaurants. Shortly thereafter, the IRS receives a Form 211 from Betty stating that Franklin keeps two sets of books, one of which substantially understates his cash receipts. Using information Betty supplies, the IRS audit results in the collection of $400,000 in taxes, interest, and penalties. The IRS pays Betty a whistle-blower award of $60,000 (which is taxable income for Betty).

Code § 7623(b), added in 2006, enhanced the IRS **Whistleblower Program**. Awards of at least 15 percent but not more than 30 percent are paid to informants when the amount in dispute exceeds $2 million and, if the taxpayer is an individual, their gross income exceeds $200,000. The amount of the award depends on the degree to which the information provided by the whistleblower contributed to the collection of unpaid tax, penalties, interest, additions to tax, and additional amounts provided under the internal revenue laws. If the whistleblower is not the original source of the information, the award may not be more than 10 percent of the collected proceeds.[15]

[13] *U.S. v. Coinbase, Inc., et al.*, 2017–2 USTC ¶50,423, 120 AFTR 2d 2017–6671 (ND CA).

[14] § 7623(a) and Reg. § 301.7623–1.

[15] The informant's information must lead directly to a recovery of tax. See *Lissack*, 157 T.C. 63 (2021).

An award is paid after the final determination of tax has been made with respect to IRS actions undertaken based on the whistleblower's allegations, the IRS has determined the amount of the award, and either appeals of the IRS's determination have been concluded or the whistleblower signs a waiver agreeing to the determination.[16]

The year in which an award is paid generally is not the year in which collections occur because the IRS must wait until the taxpayer has exhausted all appeal rights and the taxpayer no longer can seek to recover the proceeds from the government. In fiscal year 2021, the IRS made 179 whistleblower awards totaling over $36 million. On average, more than 8 years pass between the filing of a Form 211 and payment of an award under the discretionary authority of § 7623(a); more than 11 years lapse before the payment of a § 7623(b) award.[17]

Verification and Audit Procedures

The filed tax return is reviewed for mathematical accuracy when the IRS receives it. A check is also made for deductions, exclusions, etc., that are clearly erroneous. One obvious error would be the failure to comply with the AGI limitation on the deduction for medical expenses. When a math or clerical error occurs, the IRS sends the taxpayer revised computations and a bill or refund as appropriate, usually within one year of the filing date.

Taxpayers usually are able to settle routine tax disputes (e.g., queries involving the documentation of deductions) through a by-mail-only *correspondence audit* with the IRS, without the necessity of a formal meeting. For example, when a tax return's information does not match a third-party information return, the IRS will send a letter to the taxpayer (see Example 2). The letter is a **Notice CP 2000**, and it gives detailed information about the issue the IRS identified and provides steps the taxpayer should take to resolve the issue.

Office audits are rare today; they are conducted in an office of the IRS. In most instances, the taxpayer is required to substantiate a deduction, a credit, or an item of income that appears on the return. The taxpayer presents documentation in the form of canceled checks, invoices, etc., for the items in question.

The *field audit* procedure commonly is used for corporate returns and for returns of individuals engaged in business or professional activities. This type of audit generally involves a more complete examination of a taxpayer's transactions.

A field audit is conducted by an IRS agent at the office or home of the taxpayer, by video conference, or at the office of the taxpayer's representative. The agent's work may be facilitated by a review of certain tax workpapers and discussions with the taxpayer's representative about items appearing on the tax return.

Prior to or at the initial interview, the IRS must provide the taxpayer with an explanation of the audit process that is the subject of the interview and describe the taxpayer's rights under that process. If the taxpayer clearly states at any time during the interview the desire to consult with an attorney, a CPA, or an enrolled agent or any other person permitted to represent the taxpayer before the IRS, then the IRS representative must suspend the interview.[18]

Any officer or employee of the IRS must, upon advance request, allow a taxpayer to make an audio recording of any in-person interview with the officer or employee concerning the determination and collection of any tax.[19]

Settlement with the Revenue Agent

Following an audit, the IRS agent may either accept the return as filed or recommend certain adjustments. The **Revenue Agent's Report (RAR)** is reviewed within the IRS. In most instances, the agent's proposed adjustments are approved.

[16] *Reg. § 301.7623–4(d).*

[17] IRS, Fiscal Year 2021 Annual Report – IRS Whistleblower Office, **irs.gov/pub/irs-pdf/p5241.pdf**.

[18] § 7521(b).

[19] § 7521(a).

Agents must adhere strictly to IRS policy as reflected in published rulings, Regulations, and other releases. The agent cannot settle an unresolved issue based upon the probability of winning the case in court. Usually, issues involving factual questions can be settled at the agent level, and it may be advantageous for both the taxpayer and the IRS to reach agreement at the earliest point in the settlement process. For example, it may be best for the taxpayer to reach agreement at the agent level and avoid any further opportunity for the IRS to raise new issues.

If agreement is reached upon the proposed deficiency, the taxpayer signs Form 870. One advantage to the taxpayer of signing Form 870 at this point is that if the IRS does not timely issue notice and demand for payment, interest stops accumulating on the deficiency 30 days after the form is filed.[20] When this form is signed, the taxpayer effectively waives the right to receive the 90-day letter and to subsequently petition the Tax Court. In addition, it is no longer possible for the taxpayer later to go to the IRS Independent Office of Appeals.

LO.4

Explain the taxpayer appeal process, including various settlement options available.

28-1f The Taxpayer Appeal Process

If agreement cannot be reached at the agent level, the taxpayer receives a copy of the Revenue Agent's Report and a **30-day letter**. The taxpayer has 30 days to request an administrative appeal. If an appeal is not requested, a **90-day letter** is issued. Exhibit 28.2 illustrates the taxpayer's alternatives when a disagreement with the IRS persists.

Exhibit 28.2 **Income Tax Appeal Procedure**

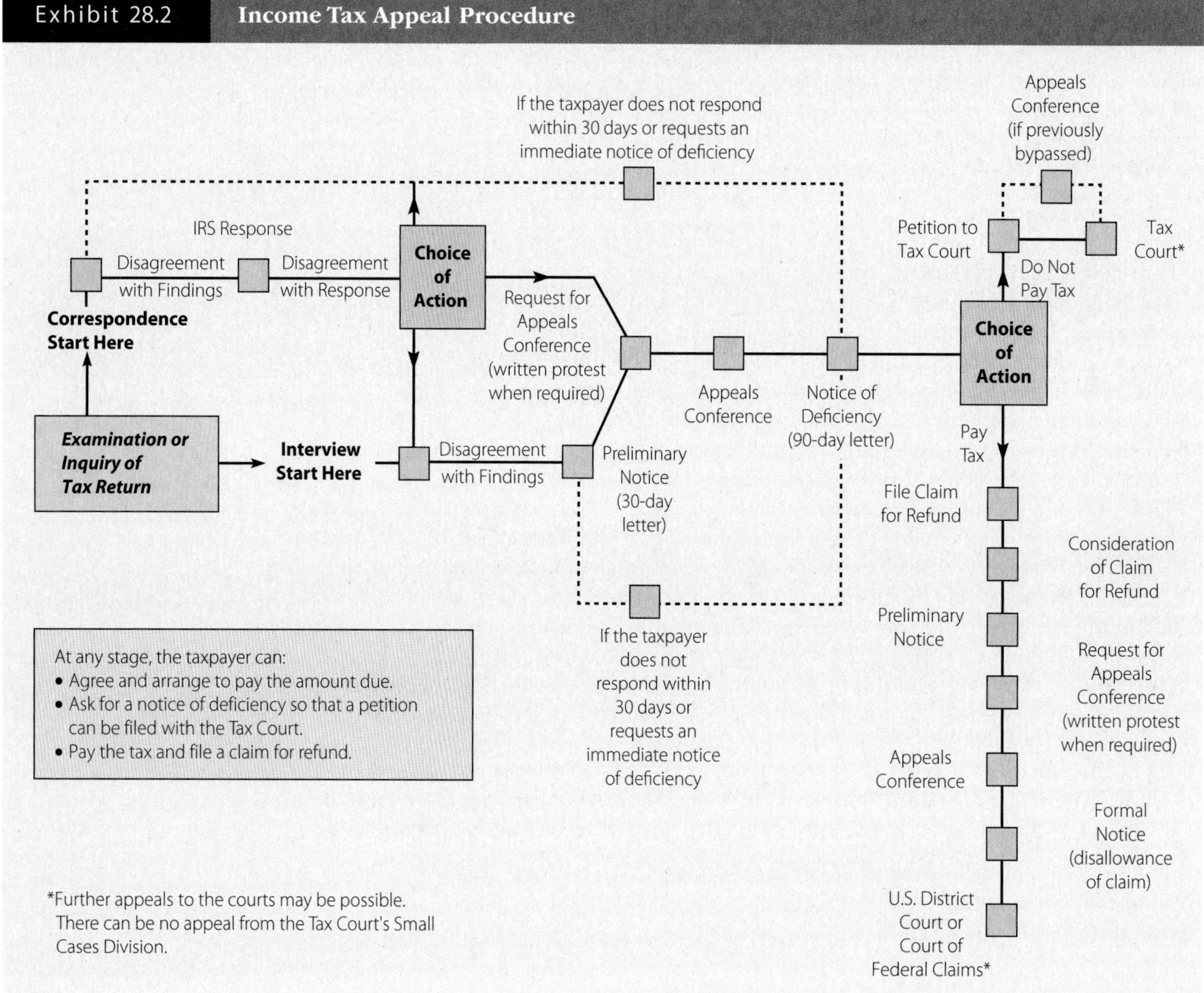

[20] § 6601(c).

A taxpayer must make an appropriate request to the Independent Office of Appeals. The request must be accompanied by a written protest, except when:

- The proposed tax deficiency does not exceed $25,000 for any of the tax periods involved in the audit, and
- The deficiency resulted from a correspondence or office audit (i.e., not as a result of a field audit).

The Appeals Office is authorized to settle all tax disputes based on the hazards of litigation (the chances of winning in court). Because the Appeals Office has final settlement authority until a 90-day letter has been issued, the taxpayer may be able to negotiate a settlement. In addition, an overall favorable settlement may be reached by "trading" disputed issues.

Example 7

At the time Maria is audited, the corporation that she controls had advances outstanding to her in the amount of $80,000. The IRS field agent held that these advances were constructive dividends to her (refer to the discussion in text Section 19-3d). Some facts point toward this result (e.g., the corporation is closely held, Maria has made no repayments, and the loan balance has increased over several years). Other facts, however, appear to indicate that these advances are bona fide loans (e.g., a written instrument provides for interest, Maria has the independent means of repayment, and the corporation has a good dividend-paying record).

Maria's representative assesses the hazards of litigation as being 50% for each side. As a result, if Maria chooses to take the issue to court, she would have an even chance of winning or losing her case. Based on this assessment, both sides agree to treat $40,000 of the advance as a dividend and $40,000 as a bona fide loan. The agreement enables Maria to avoid $40,000 of dividend income (the loan portion) and saves her the cost of litigating the issue.

By going to the Appeals Office, Maria obtained a satisfactory settlement otherwise unobtainable from the agent.

Taxpayers who file a petition with the U.S. Tax Court have the option of having the case heard before the more informal Small Cases Division if the amount of tax in dispute does not exceed $50,000.[21] If the Small Cases Division is used, neither party may appeal the decision.

28-1g **Offers in Compromise, Installment Agreements, and Closing Agreements**

The IRS can negotiate a compromise if the taxpayer's ability to pay the tax is doubtful. If the taxpayer is financially unable to pay the total amount of the tax, a Form 656 (Offer in Compromise) is filed. An **offer in compromise** is appropriate in the following circumstances:[22]

- There is doubt as to the taxpayer's liability for the tax (i.e., disputed issues still exist).
- There is doubt as to the collectibility of the tax (i.e., the taxpayer's net worth and earnings capacity are low).
- Payment of the disputed amount would constitute an economic hardship for the taxpayer (e.g., the taxpayer is incapable of earning a living because of a long-term illness or disability, or liquidation of the taxpayer's assets to pay the amount due would leave the taxpayer unable to meet basic living expenses).

---

[21] § 7463(a).

[22] § 7122 and Reg. § 301.7122–1(b).

Ethics & Equity **Our Taxing System of Self-Assessment**

The United States is a large country of diverse taxpayers and businesses. Perhaps the only way the massive dollar amounts of Federal income taxes can be collected on a timely basis is through a *self-assessment* process, whereby the taxpayer is charged with disclosing a full picture of the tax year's results and the corresponding computation of taxable income. But a system of self-assessment depends heavily on the honesty and integrity of the taxpayers and their ability to know and comply with the pertinent tax rules.

A recent survey of taxpayer attitudes by the IRS revealed the results shown to the right.

Given the results of this survey, do you think the current self-assessment system is satisfactory? If not, should Congress create additional enforcement procedures to ensure taxpayer compliance? What sort of new reporting rules might be useful?

Why Do You Report and Pay Your Taxes Honestly? (more than one answer allowed)

Taxpayer Responses	**Taxpayers for Whom This Reason Is Key (Percent)**
My own personal integrity	90%
I want to pay my fair share to support the government	60%
A third party reported my information to the IRS (e.g., through a Form W–2 or Form 1099)	61%
Fear of an audit	60%
My neighbors report and pay their taxes honestly, so I will too	37%

	Taxpayers Agreeing (Percent)
What Is an Acceptable Amount by Which to Cheat on Your Income Taxes?	
Not at all	88%
Would you report to the IRS a neighbor who cheats on taxes?	
Yes	44%

Sources: *2021 IRS Comprehensive Taxpayer Attitude Survey* at **irs.gov/pub/irs-pdf/p5296.pdf**.

The IRS investigates the offer by evaluating the taxpayer's financial ability to pay the tax. In some instances, the compromise settlement includes an agreement for final settlement of the tax through payments of a specified percentage of the taxpayer's future earnings. This settlement procedure usually entails lengthy negotiations with the IRS, but the presumption is that the IRS will be able to compromise with the taxpayer.

To settle their obligation, taxpayers can select either a "lump-sum" option (payments over no more than 5 months with 20 percent down) or a "periodic payment" option (equal payments over no more than 24 months). Either option requires a $205 filing fee. Low-income individuals generally receive a waiver of the fee and of the 20 percent down payment required under the lump-sum option.[23]

Every year, the IRS accepts about 15,000 offers in compromise out of about 50,000 applications, involving about $200 million in unpaid taxes, interest, and penalties.

The IRS can agree to allow taxes to be paid on an installment basis if that arrangement facilitates the tax collection. An individual who has filed timely tax returns for five years is guaranteed the right to use an **installment agreement** when the amount in dispute does not exceed $10,000. The taxpayer uses Form 9465 to initiate an installment plan. If the tax owed does not exceed $50,000, a taxpayer can use an online application for an installment agreement.

A user fee is assessed with the application for the installment plan. The fee is between $31 and $225, depending on the taxpayer's income level and the form of payment (e.g., credit card, e-check, or funds transfer).

[23]Reg. § 300.3(b)(1)(ii). "Low-income" is defined as less than 250% of the Federal poverty level. A preliminary check as to the taxpayer's qualifications for an offer in compromise, and the construction of an initial application, is found at **irs.treasury.gov/oic_pre_qualifier/**.

The IRS provides an annual statement accounting for the status of the agreement. The agreement may later be modified or terminated because of (1) inadequate information, (2) subsequent change in financial condition, or (3) failure to pay an installment when due or to provide requested information.[24]

A **closing agreement** is binding on both the taxpayer and the IRS except upon a subsequent showing of fraud, malfeasance, or misrepresentation of a material fact.[25] The closing agreement may be used when disputed issues carry over to future years. It also may be employed to dispose of a dispute involving a specific issue for a prior year or a proposed transaction involving future years. If, for example, the IRS is willing to make substantial concessions in the valuation of assets for estate tax purposes, it may require a closing agreement from the recipient of the property to establish the income tax basis of the assets.

28-1h Interest

LO.5

Determine the amount of interest on a deficiency or a refund and when it is due.

Determination of the Interest Rate

Congress sets the interest rates applicable to Federal tax underpayments (deficiencies) and overpayments (refunds) close to the rates available in financial markets. The Code provides for the rates to be determined quarterly.[26] As a result, the rates that are determined during March are effective for the following April through June.

For tax purposes, interest is based on the Federal short-term rates published periodically by the IRS in Revenue Rulings. They are based on the average market yield on outstanding marketable obligations of the United States with remaining maturity of three years or less.

For noncorporate taxpayers, the interest rate applicable to *both* overpayments and underpayments is 3 percent plus the Federal short-term rate. For most corporate taxpayers, the rate is the Federal short-term rate plus 2 percent for overpayments and 3 percent for underpayments. Corporations with large overpayments receive only 0.5 percent over the Federal short-term rate for the portion of the overpayment exceeding $10,000. Corporations with large underpayments are charged interest at 5 percent over the Federal short-term rate. IRS interest is compounded daily.[27]

Refund of Taxpayer's Overpayments

The period of interest generally begins on the date of the overpayment. However, if an overpayment is refunded to the taxpayer within 45 days after the date the return is filed or is due, no interest is paid. When the taxpayer files an amended return that results in a refund of a prior year's tax (e.g., when an amended return is filed to claim a previously overlooked deduction), however, interest is authorized from the original due date of the return through the date when the amended return is filed. In general, taxpayers applying for refunds receive interest as follows:

- When a return is filed after the due date, interest on any overpayment accrues from the date of filing. However, no interest is due if the IRS makes the refund within 45 days of the date of filing.

IRS Interest Payments

Example 8

Naomi, a calendar year taxpayer, files her 2023 return on December 1, 2024. The return reflects an overwithholding of $2,500. On June 8, 2025, Naomi receives a refund of her 2023 overpayment. Interest on the refund began to accrue on December 1, 2024 (not April 15, 2024).

[24] § 6159.

[25] § 7121.

[26] § 6621.

[27] § 6622. See, e.g., Rev.Rul. 2022–23.

IRS Interest Payments

Example 9

Assume the same facts as in Example 8, except that the refund is paid to Naomi on January 5, 2025 (rather than June 8, 2025). No interest is payable by the IRS because the refund was made within 45 days of the filing of the return.

- In no event will interest accrue on an overpayment unless the return that is filed is in "processible form." Generally, this means that the return must be signed and contain enough information in a readable format to enable the IRS to identify the taxpayer and to determine the tax (and overpayment) involved.[28]
- In the case of a carryback (e.g., capital loss or tax credit), interest on any refund begins to accrue on the due date of the return (disregarding extensions) for the year in which the carryback arises. Even then, however, no interest accrues until a return is filed or, if the return has been filed, if the IRS pays the refund within 45 days.

Example 10

Top Corporation, a calendar year taxpayer, incurs a net capital loss during 2023 that it can carry back to tax year 2020 and obtain a refund. On December 28, 2024, Top files a claim for refund. The earliest that interest begins to accrue in this situation is April 15, 2024, the due date of the Form 1120, but because the return was not filed until December 28, 2024, the later date controls. If the IRS pays the refund within 45 days of December 28, 2024, no interest need be paid.

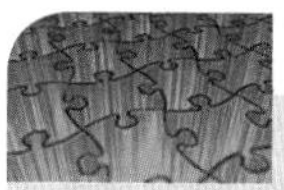

Concept Summary 28.1

Working with the IRS

1. The Internal Revenue Service (IRS) enforces the tax laws of the United States. Its size and form of organization reflect its various responsibilities relative to taxpayer interaction, litigation, and collection, as well as its internal functions.
2. The IRS issues various pronouncements in communicating its position on certain tax issues. These pronouncements promote the uniform enforcement of the tax law among taxpayers and among the internal divisions of the IRS. Taxpayers should seek such rulings and memoranda when the nature or magnitude of a pending transaction requires a high degree of certainty in the planning process.
3. IRS audits can take several forms. Taxpayers are usually selected for audit based on the probable net dollar return to the Treasury from the process. Offers in compromise and closing agreements can be a useful means of completing an audit without resorting to litigation.
4. Certain IRS personnel are empowered to consider the hazards of litigation in developing a settlement with the taxpayer during the audit process.
5. The IRS pays interest to taxpayers on overpayments when it is unable to process a refund request within 45 days in amounts tied to the Federal short-term rate. Interest paid to the IRS on underpayments is similarly based on the Federal rate, starting essentially on the date taxes were due. Interest for both purposes is compounded daily.

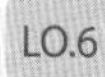

LO.6

Explain penalties imposed on acts of noncompliance by taxpayers and return preparers.

28-1i Taxpayer Penalties

Congress has enacted a comprehensive array of penalties for improper actions by taxpayers. In the typical year, about 40 million penalties are assessed, totaling about $24 billion in payments received.

Tax penalties may involve both criminal and civil offenses. Criminal tax penalties are imposed only after the usual criminal process in which the taxpayer is entitled to the same constitutional guarantees as nontax criminal defendants. Normally, a criminal penalty provides for fines and imprisonment. Civil tax penalties are collected in the same manner as other taxes and usually provide only for monetary fines. Criminal and civil penalties are not mutually exclusive; both types of sanctions may be imposed on a taxpayer.

The Code characterizes tax penalties as additions to tax; as a result, the taxpayer cannot subsequently deduct them.

Ad valorem penalties are additions to tax that are based upon a percentage of the owed tax. *Assessable penalties*, on the other hand, typically include a flat dollar amount.

[28]Both taxpayers must sign on a Form 1040 joint return. *Reifler*, 106 TCM 554, T.C.Memo. 2015–199.

Failure to File and Failure to Pay

For a *failure to file a tax return* by the due date (including extensions), a penalty of 5 percent per month (up to a maximum of 25 percent) is imposed on the amount of tax shown as due on the return, with a minimum penalty amount of $485.[29] If the failure to file is attributable to fraud, the penalty becomes 15 percent per month, to a maximum of 75 percent of the tax.[30]

For a *failure to pay the tax due* as shown on the return, a penalty of 0.5 percent per month (up to a maximum of 25 percent) is imposed on the amount of the tax. The penalty is doubled if the taxpayer fails to pay the tax after receiving a deficiency assessment.

In all of these cases, a fraction of a month counts as a full month. These penalties relate to the net amount of the tax due.

Obtaining an extension for filing a tax return does not by itself extend the date by which the taxes due must be paid. As a result, virtually all applications requesting an extension of time to file a tax return are accompanied by the taxpayer's payment of a good faith estimate of the taxes that will be owed when the return is ultimately filed (i.e., by the extended due date). If the taxpayer does not make a good faith estimate and payment, the extension itself may be voided by the IRS (e.g., when the return is filed by the extended due date with a much larger amount due than had been estimated).

Conchita uses an automatic six-month extension for the filing of her Federal income tax return. As a result, the return is due on October 15, not on April 15. Conchita's application for the extension includes a $5,000 check, the amount that she estimates her return will show as owing for the year when she files it in October.

During any month in which both the failure to file penalty and the failure to pay penalty apply, the failure to file penalty is reduced by the amount of the failure to pay penalty.

Example 12

Jason files his tax return 10 days after the due date. Along with the return, he remits a check for $5,000, which is the balance of the tax he owes. Disregarding any interest liabilities, Jason's total penalties are as follows:

Failure to pay penalty (0.5% × $5,000)		$ 25
Failure to file penalty (5% × $5,000)	$250	
Less: Failure to pay penalty for the same period	(25)	
Failure to file penalty		225
Total penalties		$250

The penalties for one full month are imposed even though Jason was delinquent by only 10 days. Unlike the method used to compute interest, any part of a month is treated as a whole month.

These penalties can be avoided if the taxpayer shows that the failure to file and/or failure to pay was due to reasonable cause and not due to willful neglect. The Code is silent as to what constitutes reasonable cause, and the Regulations do little to clarify this important concept.[31] Reasonable cause for failure to pay is presumed under the automatic six-month extension (Form 4868) when the additional tax due is not more than 10 percent of the tax liability shown on the return. In addition, the courts have ruled on some aspects of **reasonable cause**.

[29]§ 6651(a). The minimum penalty is waived if the tax is paid within 60 days of the due date of the return. The $485 minimum penalty cannot exceed the amount of tax due on the return. As a result, if no tax is due, the penalty is zero.

[30]§ 6651(f).

[31]Reg. § 301.6651–1(c)(1) likens reasonable cause to the exercise of "ordinary business care and prudence" on the part of the taxpayer.

- Reasonable cause was found where the taxpayer worked with a competent tax adviser in good faith, the facts were fully disclosed to the adviser, and the taxpayer actually relied on the adviser's judgment in filing the return.[32] No reasonable cause was found, however, where the taxpayer delegated the filing task to another, even when that person was an accountant or an attorney.[33]
- Among the reasons not qualifying as reasonable cause were lack of information on the due date of the return,[34] illness that did not incapacitate a taxpayer from completing a return,[35] refusal of the taxpayer's spouse to cooperate for a joint return,[36] and ignorance or misunderstanding of the tax law.[37]

Accuracy-Related Penalties

Major civil penalties relating to the accuracy of tax return data, including misstatements stemming from taxpayer negligence and improper valuation of income and deductions, are coordinated under the umbrella term **accuracy-related penalties**.[38] This consolidation of related penalties into a single levy eliminates the possibility that multiple penalties will apply to a single understatement of tax.

The accuracy-related penalties each amount to 20 percent of the portion of the tax underpayment that is attributable to one or more of the following infractions:

- Negligence or disregard of rules and Regulations.
- Substantial understatement of tax liability.
- Substantial valuation overstatement.
- Substantial valuation understatement.

The penalties apply only where the taxpayer fails to show a *reasonable basis* for the position taken on the return.[39]

Negligence

For purposes of this accuracy-related penalty, **negligence** includes any failure to make a reasonable attempt to comply with the provisions of the tax law. The penalty also applies to taxpayer disregard (whether careless, reckless, or intentional) of rules and Regulations.[40] The penalty can be avoided upon a showing of reasonable cause and the fact that the taxpayer acted in good faith.[41]

The negligence penalty applies to *all* taxes, except when fraud is involved. A negligence penalty may be assessed when the taxpayer fails to report gross income, overstates deductions, or fails to keep adequate records. When the taxpayer takes a nonnegligent position on the return that is contrary to a judicial precedent or published pronouncement of the IRS, the penalty is waived if the taxpayer has a reasonable basis for the interpretation and has disclosed the disputed position on Form 8275.

[32]*Neonatology Assoc., PC*, 115 T.C. 43 (2000).

[33]*U.S. v. Boyle*, 85–1 USTC ¶13,602, 55 AFTR 2d 85–1535, 105 S.Ct. 687. This rule appears to apply to electronic as well as paper-based return filings, to employment as well as income taxes, and to returns where the tax preparer is the one committing a fraudulent act. *Brandon R. Ballantyne*, 99 TCM 1523, T.C.Memo. 2010–125; *McNair Eye Center, Inc.*, 99 TCM 1345, T.C.Memo. 2010–81. Knowledgeable taxpayers such as a tax attorney are held to a higher standard in determining negligence. *Pelton & Gunther P.C.*, 78 TCM 578, T.C.Memo. 1999–339. A taxpayer might be negligent if, when a complicated tax issue is involved, a tax expert is *not* consulted. *Zmuda v. Comm.*, 84–1 USTC ¶9,442, 53 AFTR 2d 84–1269, 731 F.2d 1417 (CA–9).

[34]*Beck Chemical Equipment Co.*, 27 T.C. 840 (1957).

[35]*Joel Rappaport*, 91 TCM 1079, T.C.Memo. 2006–87, and *Babetta Schmidt*, 28 T.C. 367 (1957). Compare *Estate of Kirchner*, 46 B.T.A. 578 (1942).

[36]*Electric and Neon, Inc.*, 56 T.C. 1324 (1971).

[37]*Stevens Brothers Foundation, Inc.*, 39 T.C. 93 (1965).

[38]§ 6662.

[39]Reg. § 1.6662–3(b)(3). Most tax professionals measure this standard as a 20% probability of prevailing in court.

[40]§ 6662(c). There can be no intentional disregard of the rules where the underlying law is unclear, complex, or subject to disagreement. *Simonsen*, 150 T.C. 201 (2018), and *Lansdown v. Comm.*, 96–1 USTC ¶50,025, 77 AFTR 2d 96–491, 73 F.3d 373 (CA–10).

[41]§ 6664(c)(1).

Substantial Understatement of Tax Liability

The understatement penalty is designed to strike at middle- and high-income taxpayers who fail to apply the law correctly or take overly aggressive tax return filing positions.[42]

A substantial understatement of a tax liability transpires when the understatement exceeds the larger of 10 percent of the tax due or $5,000. For a C corporation, a substantial understatement is the lesser of the following:[43]

- 10 percent of the tax due, but at least $10,000.
- $10 million.

The understatement to which the penalty applies is the difference between the amount of tax required to be paid and the amount of tax actually shown on the return. The penalty is avoided under any of the following circumstances:[44]

- The taxpayer has **substantial authority** for the treatment. Substantial authority exists when it is perhaps 40 percent likely that a court would find in favor of the taxpayer's position. This conclusion might be reached with an examination of pertinent statutory, administrative, and judicial tax law.
- There is a *reasonable basis* for the tax return position, which is adequately disclosed in the return by attaching Form 8275 or as otherwise allowed by the IRS.[45]

Penalty for Overvaluation

The overvaluation penalty is meant to deter taxpayers from inflating values (or basis), usually of charitable contributions of property, to reduce income taxes.[46]

- The penalty applies only when the valuation used by the taxpayer is 150 percent or more of the correct valuation.
- The penalty is 20 percent of the additional tax that would have been paid had the correct valuation been used.
- The penalty is doubled if the valuation error is overstated by 200 percent or more (i.e., the valuation is *grossly* misstated).
- The penalty applies only when the resulting income tax underpayment exceeds $5,000 ($10,000 for C corporations).

Example 13

Gretchen (a calendar year taxpayer) purchased a painting for $10,000. When the painting is worth $18,000 (as later determined by the IRS), Gretchen donates it to an art museum. Based on the appraisal by a cousin who is an amateur artist, she deducts $40,000 for the donation. Because Gretchen was in the 32% tax bracket, overstating the deduction by $22,000 results in a tax underpayment of $7,040.

Gretchen's penalty for overvaluation is $2,816, or *double* the regular penalty of $1,408 (20% × $7,040 underpayment) because the $40,000 deduction constitutes a gross overvaluation.

The substantial valuation overstatement penalty is avoided if the taxpayer can show reasonable cause and good faith. However, when the overvaluation involves *charitable deduction property*, the taxpayer must substantiate both of the following:

- The claimed value of the property is based on a qualified appraisal made by a qualified appraiser.
- The taxpayer made a good faith investigation of the value of the contributed property.

Based on these criteria, Gretchen in Example 13 would find it difficult to avoid the penalty. A cousin who is an amateur artist does not meet the definition of a qualified appraiser. Likewise, Gretchen apparently has not made her own good faith investigation of the value of the contributed property.[47]

---

[42] § 6662(b)(2).

[43] § 6662(d)(1). For noncorporate taxpayers claiming the qualified business income deduction of § 199A, 5% is substituted for 10%. § 6662(d)(1)(C).

[44] § 6662(d)(2)(B). Substantial authority is measured as of either the last day of the tax year to which the return relates or the date the return was filed. Reg. § 1.6662–4(d)(3)(iv)(C).

[45] See, for example, Rev.Proc. 2016–13 and Rev.Proc. 2019–9.

[46] §§ 6662(b)(3), (e), and (h).

[47] §§ 6664(c)(2) and (3). If the donor has been dishonest in valuing the property, the IRS may use a "correct valuation" of zero, increasing the penalty amount. *Fakiris*, T.C.Memo. 2020–157.

Penalty for Undervaluation

When attempting to minimize the income tax, it is to the benefit of taxpayers to *overvalue* deductions. When attempting to minimize transfer taxes (estate and gift taxes), however, executors and donors may be inclined to *undervalue* the assets transferred. A lower valuation reduces estate and gift taxes. An accuracy-related penalty is imposed for substantial estate or gift tax valuation understatements.[48] As with other accuracy-related penalties, reasonable cause and good faith on the part of the taxpayer can result in a waiver of the penalty.

- The penalty is 20 percent of the additional transfer tax that would have been due had the correct valuation been used on Form 706 (estate and generation-skipping tax return) or Form 709 (gift and generation-skipping tax return).
- The penalty applies only if the value of the property claimed on the return is 65 percent or less than the amount determined to be correct. The penalty is doubled if the reported valuation error is *gross* (reported value is 40 percent or less than the correct determination).
- The penalty applies only to an additional transfer tax liability in excess of $5,000.

Appraiser's Penalty

When a valuation penalty arises because of the taxpayer's reliance on an appraisal, a further penalty can apply.[49] If the appraiser knew or reasonably should have known that the appraisal would be used as part of a tax or refund computation and that the appraised value more likely than not was improper, then the appraiser pays a penalty equal to the lesser of:

- 10 percent of the tax understatement but at least $1,000, or
- 125 percent of the gross income received by the appraiser from the engagement (e.g., the appraisal fee collected).

Penalty for Improper Refund Claim

Whenever a taxpayer files a claim for a tax refund and the refund claim later is found to exceed the final amount allowed by the IRS or a court, a penalty of 20 percent of the disallowed refund results.[50] The penalty is waived if the taxpayer can show a *reasonable cause* for the refund claim (i.e., probably a one-third chance that a court would allow the refund). This penalty is meant to discourage the taxpayer from overstating the amount of the refund requested from the IRS. It does not apply to claims for the earned income tax credit.

Civil Fraud Penalty

A 75 percent civil penalty is imposed on any underpayment resulting from **fraud** by the taxpayer who has filed a return.[51] For this penalty, the burden of proof *is on the IRS* to show that the taxpayer acted with a specific intent to evade a tax.

Once the IRS initially has established that fraud occurred, the taxpayer then bears the burden of proof to show by a preponderance of the evidence the portion of the underpayment that is not attributable to fraud.

Although the Code and Regulations do not provide any assistance in ascertaining what constitutes civil fraud, fraud can be described as actual, intentional wrongdoing, usually occurring over several tax years. Fraud has been found in cases of manipulations of the books, substantial omissions from income, and erroneous deductions.[52]

[48] §§ 6662(b)(5), (g), and (h).

[49] § 6695A.

[50] § 6676.

[51] § 6663. As noted later in the chapter, underpayments traceable to fraudulent acts are not subject to a statute of limitations.

[52] *Dogget v. Comm.*, 60–1 USTC ¶9342, 5 AFTR 2d 1034, 275 F.2d 823 (CA–4); *George Maciel*, 87 TCM 881, T.C.Memo. 2004–28; and *John A. Hatling*, 104 TCM 475, T.C.Memo. 2012–293.

Frank underpaid his income tax by $90,000. The IRS can prove that $60,000 of the underpayment was due to fraud. The civil fraud penalty is $45,000 (75% × $60,000).

Failure to Pay Estimated Taxes

A penalty is imposed for a failure to pay estimated income taxes. The penalty applies to individuals and corporations and is based on the rate of interest in effect for deficiency assessments.[53] The penalty also applies to trusts and certain estates that are required to make estimated tax payments. The penalty is not imposed if the tax due for the year (less amounts withheld and credits) is less than $500 for corporations, $1,000 for all others. For employees, an equal part of withholding is deemed paid on each due date.

Quarterly payments are made on or before the fifteenth day of the fourth month (April 15 for a calendar year taxpayer), sixth month, ninth month, and the first month of the following year. Corporations must make the last quarterly payment by the twelfth month of the same year. Generally, the payment is one-fourth of the tax expected to be due.

Ethics & Equity **First-Time Tax Violators Can Get Off with Just a Warning**

Tax penalties can be a harsh wake-up call when a taxpayer understates a tax liability, and there appears to be "no mercy" when a penalty is applied. Often, a tax penalty arises when the taxpayer has undergone a change in life/business circumstances (e.g., as the consequence of a divorce, retirement, or merger). The taxpayer may not have prepared adequately for the resulting tax increase and a penalty results, but the taxpayer's legitimate response might be "I didn't mean to do it; I just didn't know the rules."

The Federal income tax law does allow a measure of mercy, though. A procedure exists under which the taxpayer can apply for an abatement (waiver) of certain tax penalties if all of the following circumstances are met:

- The penalty relates to a single tax year.
- The taxpayer shows *reasonable cause* for the understatement of tax, such as serious illness, inability to obtain records, or reliance on erroneous tax advice.
- The taxpayer otherwise is current as to tax filings and payment compliance.
- The taxpayer has not been assessed any other penalties of a significant amount on similar tax returns within the last three years.

Often, the IRS includes a flyer with a taxpayer notice of deficiency, providing information about how to apply for the penalty waiver.[54] Comment on how the IRS benefits from this procedure.

An individual's underpayment of estimated tax is the difference between the estimates that were paid and the least of:

- 90 percent of the current-year tax,
- 100 percent of the prior-year tax (the tax year must have been a full 12 months, and a return must have been filed), and
- 90 percent of the tax that would be due on an annualized income computation for the period running through the end of the quarter.

If the taxpayer's prior-year AGI exceeds $150,000, the 100 percent requirement becomes 110 percent.

A corporation's underpayment of estimated tax is the difference between the estimates that were paid and the least of:

- The current-year tax,
- The prior-year tax, and
- The tax on an annualized income computation using one of three methods of computation sanctioned by the Code.

[53] §§ 6655 (corporations) and 6654 (other taxpayers). Other computations can avoid the penalty. See §§ 6654(d)(2) and (k), 6655(e) and (i).

[54] IRM 20.1.1.3.3.2.1 (10/2020). The waiver applies to the failure to pay, failure to file, and failure to deposit penalties, among others.

For the prior-year alternative, (1) the prior tax year must have been a full 12 months, (2) a nonzero tax amount must have been generated for that year, and (3) large corporations (taxable income of $1 million or more in any of the three immediately preceding tax years) can use the alternative only for the first installment of a year.

In computing the penalty, Form 2210 (Underpayment of Estimated Tax by Individuals) or Form 2220 (Underpayment of Estimated Tax by Corporations) is used.

False Information with Respect to Withholding

Withholding from wages is an important element of the Federal income tax system, which is based on a pay-as-you-go approach. One way employees might hope to avoid this withholding would be to falsify the information provided to the employer on Form W–4 (Employee Withholding Allowance Certificate). For example, by overstating the number of exemptions, income tax withholdings could be reduced or completely eliminated.

To encourage compliance, a civil penalty of $500 applies when a taxpayer claims withholding allowances based on false information. The criminal penalty for willfully failing to supply information or for willfully supplying false or fraudulent information in connection with wage withholding is an additional fine of up to $1,000 and/or up to one year of imprisonment.[55]

Failure to Make Deposits of Taxes and Overstatements of Deposits

When a business is not doing well or cash-flow problems develop, employers have a great temptation to "borrow" from Uncle Sam. One way this can be done is to fail to pay to the IRS the amounts that have been withheld from the wages of employees for FICA and income tax purposes. The IRS can apply a number of weapons to discourage the practice.

- A penalty of up to 15 percent of any underdeposited amount not paid, unless the employer can show that the failure is due to reasonable cause and not to willful neglect.[56]
- Various criminal penalties.[57]
- A 100 percent penalty if the employer's actions are willful.[58] The penalty is based on the amount of the tax evaded (i.e., not collected or not accounted for or paid over). Because the penalty is assessable against the "responsible person" of the business, more than one party may be vulnerable (e.g., the president and treasurer of a corporation, the third-party payroll service of the entity). Although the IRS may assess the penalty against several persons, it cannot collect more than 100 percent of the tax that is due.

In addition to these penalties, the actual tax due must be remitted. For instance, an employer remains liable for the employees' income and payroll taxes that should have been paid.

Failure to Provide Information Regarding Tax Shelters

The IRS has identified numerous transactions that it regards as improper in determining one's tax liability, usually because the transaction lacks economic substance beyond the resulting tax reduction. These arrangements are termed "reportable transactions" or "tax shelters," and they often involve leveraged financing and accelerated interest and cost recovery deductions.

A tax shelter organizer must inform the IRS of the arrangement before any sales are made to investors.[59] A penalty of $50,000 is assessed if the required information is not filed with the IRS, using Form 8918. The disclosure includes a description of the shelter and the tax benefits that are being used to attract investors.

[55] §§ 6682 and 7205.

[56] § 6656.

[57] See, for example, § 7202 (willful failure to collect or pay over a tax).

[58] § 6672.

[59] § 6111. The penalty amount increases if the failure to disclose relates to a listed transaction or is intentional by the taxpayer.

Criminal Penalties

In addition to civil fraud penalties, the Code contains numerous criminal sanctions that carry various monetary fines and/or imprisonment. The IRS annually attains about 1,300 convictions. Almost 80 percent of criminal tax convictions result in incarceration, home confinement, or electronic monitoring.

The difference between civil and criminal fraud often is one of degree. Code § 7201, dealing with attempts to evade or defeat a tax, contains the following language:

> Any person who *willfully* attempts in any manner to evade or defeat any tax imposed by this title or the payment thereof shall, in addition to other penalties provided by law, be guilty of a felony and, upon conviction thereof, shall be fined not more than $100,000 ($500,000 in the case of a corporation), or imprisoned not more than five years, or both, together with the costs of prosecution. [Emphasis added.]

As to the burden of proof, the IRS must show that the taxpayer was guilty of willful evasion "beyond the shadow of any reasonable doubt." As a result, to avoid a criminal tax penalty, the taxpayer needs to create a degree of reasonable doubt as to guilt. To do so, the taxpayer might assert that they were confused or ignorant about the application of the tax law or relied on the erroneous advice of a competent tax adviser. Another defense against a criminal tax penalty is the lack of capacity to plan and carry out tax evasion (e.g., mental limitations or other medical disorder).

Violations of the Federal criminal code in the context of filing tax returns also may arise from other crimes that are not provided for in the Internal Revenue Code. Examples include:

- Making a false claim against the Federal government.
- Participating in a conspiracy to evade Federal taxes (i.e., in addition to the tax understatement).
- Making a false statement to the Federal government or filing a false document (i.e., perjury).

28-1j Statute of Limitations

LO.7

Apply the rules governing the statute of limitations on assessments and on refunds.

A **statute of limitations** defines the period of time during which one party may pursue against another party a cause of action or other suit allowed under the governing law. Failure to satisfy any requirement provides the other party with an absolute defense should the statute be invoked.

Inequities could result if no limits were placed on such suits. Permitting an extended period of time to elapse between the initiation of a claim and its pursuit could place the defense at a serious disadvantage. Witnesses may have died or disappeared; records or other evidence may have been discarded or destroyed.

Assessment and the Statute of Limitations

In general, any tax that is imposed must be assessed within three years of the later of (a) the filing date of the return or (b) the unextended due date of the return.[60] Some exceptions to this three-year limitation exist.

- If no return is filed or a fraudulent return is filed, assessments can be made at any time. The statute of limitations, in effect, never expires in these cases.
- If a taxpayer omits an amount of gross income in excess of 25 percent of the gross income stated on the return, the statute of limitations is increased to six years. The courts have interpreted this rule as including only items affecting income and not the omission of items affecting deductions, operating losses, or cost of sales.[61] *Gross income* here includes capital gains, but not reduced by capital losses. It also includes any gross income that results from an overstatement of tax basis (e.g., in an asset sale).[62]

[60] §§ 6501(a) and (b)(1).

[61] *The Colony, Inc. v. Comm.*, 58–2 USTC ¶9593, 1 AFTR 2d 1894, 78 S.Ct. 1033.

[62] § 6501(e)(1)(B)(ii).

Example 15

During 2019, Jamar recorded the following income transactions (all of which were duly reported on his timely filed return):

Gross receipts		$ 480,000
Cost of sales		(400,000)
Net business income		$ 80,000
Capital gains and losses		
Capital gain	$ 36,000	
Capital loss	(12,000)	24,000
Total income		$ 104,000

Jamar retains your services in 2024 as a tax consultant. It seems that he inadvertently omitted some income on his 2019 return, and he wants to know if he is "safe" under the statute of limitations. The three-year statute of limitations has expired, but the six-year statute of limitations still applies, putting Jamar in a vulnerable position only if he omitted more than $129,000 on his 2019 return [($480,000 + $36,000) × 25%].

- The statute of limitations may be extended for a fixed period of time by mutual consent of the IRS and the taxpayer. This extension covers a definite period and is made by signing Form 872. The extension frequently is requested by the IRS when the lapse of the statutory period is imminent and the audit has not been completed. This practice often is applied to audits of corporate taxpayers and explains why many corporations have more than three "open years."[63]

The statute also is suspended when the taxpayer is "financially disabled"; that is, the taxpayer has been rendered unable to manage financial affairs by a physical or mental impairment that is likely to last for a year or more or to cause the taxpayer's death.[64]

Refund Claims and the Statute of Limitations

The IRS accepts refund claims electronically on Form 1040X for individuals and Form 1120X for corporations. If the refund claim does not meet certain procedural requirements, the IRS may reject the claim with no consideration of its merit.

- A separate claim must be filed for each taxable period.
- The grounds for the claim must be stated in sufficient detail.
- The statement of facts must be sufficient to permit the IRS to evaluate the merits of the claim.

The refund claim must be filed within three years of the filing of the tax return or within two years following the payment of the tax if this period expires on a later date.[65]

Example 16

On March 10, 2021, Louise filed her 2020 income tax return reflecting a tax of $10,500. On July 11, 2022, she filed an amended 2020 return showing an additional $3,000 of tax that was then paid. On May 19, 2024, she filed a claim for refund of $4,500.

Assuming that Louise is correct in claiming a refund, how much tax can she recover? Because the claim was not filed within the three-year statute of limitations period, Louise is limited to $3,000, the amount she actually paid during the last two years.

Special rules are available for claims relating to bad debts and worthless securities. A seven-year period of limitations applies in lieu of the normal three-year rule.[66] The extended period is provided in recognition of the inherent difficulty of identifying the exact year in which a bad debt or security becomes worthless.

[63] § 6501(c)(4).
[64] § 6511(h).
[65] §§ 6511(a) and 6513(a).
[66] § 6511(d)(1).

28-2 The Tax Profession and Tax Ethics

LO.8

Summarize the legal and ethical guidelines that apply to those engaged in tax practice.

Society and its governments expect taxpayers to comply with the letter and the spirit of the tax laws. Tax audits and penalties encourage a high degree of technical tax conformity, but the proper functioning of a voluntary tax compliance system also depends on the ethics of the taxpayer and the tax adviser.

The Treasury and various professional organizations have issued ethical guidelines that are relevant to the tax profession. Professional licensing agencies also are likely to require tax professionals to receive training in ethics to obtain initial certification and to remain in good standing over time.

28-2a The Tax Professional

Who is a tax professional? What services does a tax professional perform? A number of different groups apply constraints on the way a tax professional conducts a practice.

Generally, practice before the IRS is limited to CPAs, attorneys, and persons who have been enrolled to practice before the IRS [**enrolled agents (EAs)**]. In most cases, EAs are admitted to practice only if they pass an examination administered by the IRS. CPAs and attorneys are not required to take this examination and are automatically admitted to practice if they are in good standing with the appropriate licensing board regulating their profession.

Persons other than CPAs, attorneys, and EAs may be allowed to practice before the IRS in limited situations. **Circular 230** ("Regulations Governing Practice before the Internal Revenue Service") issued by the Treasury Department permits certain notable exceptions.

- A taxpayer always may represent oneself. A person also may represent a member of the immediate family if no compensation is received for such services.
- Full-time employees may represent their employers.
- Corporations may be represented by any of their officers.
- Partnerships may be represented by any of the partners.
- Trusts, receiverships, guardianships, or estates may be represented by their trustees, receivers, guardians, or administrators or executors, respectively.
- A taxpayer may be represented by the individual or entity who prepared the return for the year in question. Preparers who are not a CPA, an EA, or an attorney can represent a taxpayer in an audit only if they prepared and signed the return and completed a voluntary IRS continuing education program.

All nonattorney tax professionals should avoid becoming engaged in activities that constitute the *unauthorized practice of law*. If they engage in this practice (e.g., by drafting legal documents for a third party), action could be instituted against them in the appropriate state court by the local or state bar association or state Attorney General's office. To avoid these charges, nonattorney tax professionals should not give advice about matters that that go beyond the tax law (e.g., the status of an individual as an employee or contractor, or the application of health insurance provisions).

28-2b Regulating Tax Preparers

There are no minimum education or experience requirements for those who are paid to file Federal tax returns for others. But the IRS does require that all paid tax return preparers, including CPAs and attorneys, obtain with the Form W–12 or renew online a Preparer Tax Identification Number (PTIN) before they assist taxpayers with returns for a new filing season.

A PTIN holder must confirm to the IRS that it has a written plan that puts a system in place with which to protect taxpayer data and all pertinent operating and storage systems from security breaches. In recent years, tax professionals have been targeted by identity thieves and others who want access to confidential client financial and personal data. Such safeguards are required under the Gramm-Leach-Bliley Act (GLBA). Failure to comply can subject the tax professional to jail time and a fine of up to $100,000.

The IRS may use PTIN data to identify preparers who commit a pattern of errors or who participate in fraudulent actions. With more than 700,000 paid preparers at work in any filing season,[67] the IRS uses an outside consultant to manage the registration process, charging an annual fee of less than $35 to obtain a PTIN.

28-2c **IRS Rules Governing Tax Practice**

Circular 230 prescribes the rules governing practice before the IRS. Following are some of the most important rules imposed on CPAs, attorneys, EAs, and a few others specified in Circular 230.

- A requirement that the tax practitioner be competent in the matters involved in the engagement with the taxpayer (i.e., the practitioner can show appropriate levels of knowledge, skill, thoroughness, and preparation for the assigned tasks).

The Big Picture

Example 17

Return to the facts of *The Big Picture* on p. 28-1. Campbell has developed a superior material for solar panel backsheets and has started producing backsheets with this material. The material did not exist when Congress passed the advanced manufacturing production credit (§ 45X). Based on their tax research on this issue, the members of your firm's tax department have severe doubts about taking the § 45X credit for this product. Your firm's position is that there is a one-in-six chance that the courts will allow Campbell's credit.

Claiming the credit fails the standard of Circular 230 because there is no reasonable basis (roughly 20% probability of prevailing if challenged by the government) for the position.

- A prohibition against willful or reckless behavior in signing a return that includes a position that could subject the practitioner to the preparer penalty because, for example, the position lacks a reasonable basis (see text Section 28-2d).
- A requirement to inform clients of penalties likely to apply to return positions and of ways such penalties can be avoided.
- A requirement to make known to a client any error or omission the client may have made on any return or other document submitted to the IRS.
- A duty to submit, in a timely fashion, records or information lawfully requested by the IRS.
- An obligation to exercise *due diligence* and to use the *best practices* of the tax profession in preparing, reviewing, and filing tax returns accurately.

Example 18

Your niece, Selma, plans to start a tax return preparation service. She seeks advice on what procedures and practices to establish in order to develop and maintain a successful business. As a starting point, Selma should set up a standardized procedure for receiving, processing, and reviewing client tax returns. A key to achieving a high-quality product would be an appropriate choice of tax accounting software. She should be sure that all client data are kept confidential, and that the digital files holding such data are secure and properly backed up.

Any employees who are hired should be technically competent and properly trained as to office procedure. All hires should be subject to a background check and be made aware that they are expected to participate in continuing education covering developments in tax law changes. In addition, Selma should formulate adequate disclaiming language so that e-mail and text recipients do not assume that the content represents technical advice upon which they can rely.

[67]Included in this number are about 202,000 CPAs, 58,000 EAs, and 28,000 attorneys.

- A restriction against unreasonably delaying the prompt disposition of any matter before the IRS.
- A restriction against charging the client a contingent fee for preparing an original return. Such a fee can be charged when the tax professional deals with an audited return and assists the taxpayer in filing certain refund claims.
- A restriction against charging the client "an unconscionable fee" for representation before the IRS.
- A restriction against representing clients with conflicting interests.

In a firm that prepares tax returns for compensation, personnel supervisors must ensure that the work of staff members complies with Circular 230 rules. This usually entails education programs and other means by which the current Circular 230 rules are conveyed to all affected employees.

Circular 230 is administered by the IRS Office of Professional Responsibility (OPR). Among other duties, the OPR carries out disciplinary hearings and issues penalties, such as fines and licensing restrictions and retractions, relative to tax preparers. Information about Circular 230 violations is published in the Internal Revenue Bulletin. A Circular 230 violation could lead to the loss or suspension of a CPA's license at the state level as well.

28-2d **Preparer Penalties**

The Code provides penalties to discourage improper actions by tax professionals. **Tax preparer** penalties are assessed on any person who prepares for compensation, or engages employees to prepare, a substantial portion of any Federal tax return or refund claim.[68] The following individuals are exempt from the preparer penalties:[69]

- An IRS employee.
- A volunteer who prepares tax returns in a government assistance effort such as Tax Counseling for the Elderly (TCE) or the Volunteer Income Tax Assistance (VITA) program.
- An employee preparing a return for the employer.
- A fiduciary preparing a return for a trust or an estate.
- An individual who provides only data processing, reproduction, or similar assistance in preparing a return.

The preparer penalties can compound quickly in a tax practice that has many professionals. Some of the most important tax preparer penalties include the following:

1. A penalty for understatements due to taking an **unreasonable position** on a tax return.[70] The penalty is imposed if the tax position:
   - Is not disclosed on the return and there was no *substantial authority* (i.e., a greater than 40 percent chance) that the tax position would be sustained by its merits on a final court review, or
   - Is disclosed on the return and there was not a *reasonable basis* (i.e., at least a 20 percent chance of success) for the position.

   The penalty is computed as the greater of $1,000 or one-half of the income of the practitioner that is attributable to the return or claim that violated the conduct standard. The penalty can be avoided by showing reasonable cause and by showing that the preparer acted in good faith.

[68] § 7701(a)(36); Reg. § 301.7701–15(a).

[69] Reg. § 301.7701–15(f).

[70] § 6694(a). For the most part, these standards match those that apply to the taxpayer penalties of § 6662(d). Stricter disclosure standards apply for tax shelter items and reportable transactions. § 6662A.

Josie is the tax return preparer for Hal's Form 1040. The return includes a deduction that has a 60% chance of being sustained on its merits; it is contrary to an applicable tax Regulation but a taxpayer won a court case with similar facts. If a court denies the deduction, Josie is not assessed a penalty for taking an unreasonable position on the tax return.

Now assume that Hal's deduction has a 30% chance of being sustained on its merits. If a court denies the deduction, Josie is assessed the penalty (unless the disputed position was disclosed on the return with a Form 8275–R). The amount of the penalty is the greater of $1,000 or one-half of Josie's fees for preparing Hal's Form 1040.

What if Hal's deduction has a 15% chance of being sustained on its merits? If a court denies the deduction, Josie is assessed a penalty for taking an unreasonable tax return position (even if the disputed position was disclosed on the return with a Form 8275–R). The amount of the penalty is the greater of $1,000 or one-half of Josie's fees for preparing Hal's Form 1040.

2. A penalty for willful and reckless conduct.[71] The penalty applies if any part of the understatement of a taxpayer's liability on a return or claim for refund is due to:
   - The preparer's willful attempt to understate the taxpayer's tax liability in any manner.
   - Any reckless or intentional disregard of IRS rules or Regulations by the preparer.

   The penalty is computed as the greater of $5,000 or 75 percent of the income of the practitioner that is attributable to the return or claim that violated the conduct standard. Adequate disclosure can avoid the penalty. If both this penalty and the unreasonable position penalty (see item 1) apply to the same return, the reckless conduct penalty is reduced by the amount of the penalty for unreasonable positions.
3. A $1,000 ($10,000 for the tax returns of corporations) penalty per return or document is imposed against persons who aid in the preparation of returns or other documents they know (or have reason to believe) would result in an understatement of the tax liability of another person.[72] As a result, this penalty also applies to those other than the preparer of the actual tax return (e.g., advisers, attorneys, corporate officers and executives, and tax shelter promoters). Administrative assistance in the return preparation process does not incur the penalty.

   If this penalty applies, neither the unreasonable position penalty (item 1) nor the willful and reckless conduct penalty (item 2) is assessed.
4. A $250 penalty for each third-party disclosure or improper use of tax return data, up to a $10,000 annual maximum per practitioner.[73] These amounts become $1,000 and $50,000 when criminal identity theft of a taxpayer's data is involved.
5. A $60 penalty is assessed against the preparer for failure to sign a return or furnish the preparer's PTIN.[74]
6. A $60 penalty is assessed if the preparer fails to furnish a copy of the return or claim for refund to the taxpayer, and if the preparer fails to keeps its own copy thereof.
7. A $600 penalty may be assessed if a preparer endorses or otherwise negotiates a check for refund of tax issued to the taxpayer.
8. A $600 penalty for each instance of failure to be diligent in determining the taxpayer's eligibility for the earned income tax credit, child tax credit, other dependent credit, American Opportunity tax credit, and head-of-household filing status.

[71] § 6694(b).

[72] § 6701.

[73] § 6713.

[74] § 6695. The penalty amounts for the rest of this list are adjusted annually for inflation. Items 5. and 6. cannot exceed $30,000 per year for the preparer or firm. See § 6695(h) and Rev.Proc. 2022–38.

Other parts of the Code provide additional constraints to govern all parties engaged in rendering tax returns for the general public.

- A person who claims to the general public to possess tax expertise can be liable to the client if services are performed in a negligent manner. At a minimum, the practitioner is liable for any interest and penalties the client incurs because of the practitioner's failure to exercise due professional care.
- If a practitioner agrees to perform a service (e.g., prepare a tax return) and subsequently fails to do so, the aggrieved party may be in a position to obtain damages for breach of contract.
- All persons who prepare tax returns or refund claims for a fee must sign as preparer of the return.[75] Failure to comply with this requirement could result in a penalty assessment against the preparer.
- Various penalties apply concerning the deliberate filing of false or fraudulent returns. These felonies apply to a tax practitioner who either was aware of the situation or actually perpetrated the false information or the fraud.[76]
- A criminal penalty applies to tax practitioners who recklessly disclose to third parties information they have received from clients in connection with the preparation of tax returns or the rendering of tax advice.[77] The penalty is $1,000 per violation, or $100,000 if identity theft is involved, or potential imprisonment.

Sarah operates a tax return preparation service. Her brother-in-law, Andre, has just taken a job as a life insurance salesperson. To help Andre find contacts, Sarah furnishes him with a list of the names and addresses of all of her clients who report AGI of $50,000 or more. Sarah is subject to the $1,000 reckless disclosure penalty.

28-2e **Privileged Communications**

Communications between an attorney and a client long have been protected from disclosure to other parties (such as the IRS and the courts). A similar privilege of confidentiality extends to tax advice between a taxpayer and a Federally authorized tax practitioner (attorney, CPA, EA). The privilege is not available for matters involving criminal charges or questions brought by other agencies, such as the Securities and Exchange Commission. Nor is it allowed in matters involving promoting or participating in tax shelters.[78]

A taxpayer likely will want to protect documents such as the tax adviser's research memo detailing the strengths and weaknesses of a tax return position or a conversation about an appeals strategy. The confidentiality privilege should be interpreted in the following manner:

- The privilege for certain communications between a client and a CPA or EA applies only to certain tax advice. The attorney-client privilege applies to most legal advice and communications (tax and non-tax legal matters).
- The privilege is not available for tax accrual workpapers prepared as part of an independent financial audit.
- Generally, there is no privilege as to taxpayer information that is intended to be disclosed on a tax return (including no attorney-client privilege).

[75] Reg. § 1.6065–1(b)(1). Rev.Rul. 84–3 contains a series of examples illustrating when a person is deemed to be a preparer of the return.

[76] § 7206.

[77] § 7216.

[78] § 7525.

28-2f AICPA Statements on Standards for Tax Services

Tax practitioners who are CPAs, attorneys, or EAs must abide by the codes or canons of professional ethics applicable to their respective professions. The various codes and canons have much in common with and parallel the standards of conduct set forth in Circular 230.[79]

The AICPA has issued a series of **Statements on Standards for Tax Services (SSTS)**.[80] The Statements are enforceable standards of professional practice for AICPA members working in state or Federal tax practice. The SSTSs comprise part of the AICPA's Code of Professional Conduct. Together with the provisions of Circular 230 and the penalty provisions of the Code, the SSTSs make up a set of guidelines for the conduct of the tax practitioner who is also a CPA. Other sources of professional ethics are issued by state bar associations and CPA societies, the American Bar Association, and the associations of enrolled agents.

Statement No. 1: Tax Return Positions

Under certain circumstances, a CPA may take a position that is contrary to that taken by the IRS. To do so, however, the CPA must have a good faith belief that the position has a realistic possibility (i.e., probably a one-in-three chance) of being sustained administratively or judicially on its merits if challenged. If the taxing authority (e.g., a state revenue statute) uses a lower standard than that of a *realistic possibility*, this higher standard still applies. But where the taxing authority applies a higher standard, such as one of *substantial authority*, that standard is in effect.

The client should be fully advised of the risks involved and the penalties that may result if the position taken on the tax return is not successful. The client also should be informed that disclosure on the return may avoid some or all of these penalties.

In no case, though, should the CPA exploit the audit lottery. That is, the CPA should not take a questionable position based on the probabilities that the client's return will not be chosen by the IRS for audit. Furthermore, the CPA should not "load" the return with questionable items in the hope that they might aid the client in a later settlement negotiation with the IRS.

The Big Picture

Example 21

Return to the facts of *The Big Picture* on p. 28-1. Campbell's new marketing program solicits the opinions of a focus group regarding the attractiveness of various solar panel prototypes. Campbell's engineers consider the opinions when selecting prototypes to put into production. Based on your tax research, you believe that the costs of designing and building all prototypes, including those not selected, and the costs of the focus groups could be considered production costs and, therefore, eligible for the advanced manufacturing production credit (§ 45X). Still, you believe that there is only a 30% chance the courts would allow the credit.

You meet with Seung Watkins, Campbell's tax director, to convey the results of your research. Watkins agrees that the § 45X credit would be turned down by an IRS auditor, but she says that Campbell never has been audited and that it is not likely to be audited as long as its legal structure and income levels do not significantly change. Watkins believes that Campbell's corporate officers will sign off on the credit, given both the firm's weak cash position and the low chances that the item will be discovered.

continued

[79] For an additional discussion of tax ethics, see Sawyers and Gill, *Federal Tax Research*, 12th ed. (Cengage, 2021), especially Chapters 1 and 13.

[80] In 2022, the AICPA released an exposure draft for comment of revisions to the SSTSs. After comment, revision, and approval, they are expected to become effective in 2024. See Susan C. Allen, "Proposed revisions to the AICPA tax standards," *Journal of Accountancy*, Aug. 29, 2022; **journalofaccountancy.com/news/2022/aug/proposed-revisions-to-aicpa-tax-standards.html**.

As a CPA, you must inform Campbell that claiming the credit for this activity is a position that lacks substantial authority. The 30% chance of being upheld indicates that it may have a reasonable basis, though. In that case, the position needs to be disclosed on the return to avoid a taxpayer penalty.

Whether the credit is claimed is the decision of your client, the taxpayer. But if Campbell wants to claim the credit without the required additional disclosures, you must terminate your engagement with Campbell, under the SSTS and other AICPA provisions.

Statement No. 2: Questions on Returns

A CPA should make a reasonable effort to obtain from the client and provide appropriate answers to all questions on a tax return before signing as preparer. Reasonable grounds may exist for omitting an answer.

- The information is not readily available, and the answer is not significant in amount in computing the tax.
- The meaning of the question as it applies to a particular situation is genuinely uncertain.
- The answer to the question is voluminous.

The fact that an answer to a question could prove disadvantageous to the client does not justify omitting the answer.

Statement No. 3: Procedural Aspects of Preparing Returns

In preparing a return, a CPA may in good faith rely without verification on information furnished by the client or by third parties. However, the CPA should make reasonable inquiries if the information appears to be incorrect, incomplete, or inconsistent. In this regard, the CPA should refer to the client's returns for prior years whenever appropriate.

Example 22

While preparing Sunni's income tax return, you review her prior year's income tax return. In comparing the dividend income reported on the Schedule B for the two years, you note a significant decrease from last year's amounts. Further investigation reveals that the variation is due to a stock sale this year that was unknown to you until now. As a result, the review of the prior year's return has unearthed a transaction that should be reported on this year's return.

If the Code or Regulations require certain types of verification (as is the case with business travel expenditures), the CPA must advise the client of these rules. In addition, the CPA must determine whether the client has complied with the verification requirements.

Statement No. 4: Estimates

A CPA may prepare a tax return using estimates received from a taxpayer if it is impracticable to obtain exact data. The estimates must be reasonable under the facts and circumstances as known to the CPA. When estimates are used, they should avoid the impression of greater accuracy than exists.

Statement No. 5: Recognition of Administrative Proceeding or Court Decision

As facts may vary from year to year, so may the position taken by a CPA. In these situations, the CPA is not bound by an administrative or judicial proceeding for a prior year.

As part of a prior year's audit of Ramon Corporation's income tax return, the IRS disallowed $78,000 of the $600,000 salary paid to its president and sole shareholder on the grounds that it is unreasonable. You are the CPA who has been engaged to prepare Ramon's income tax return for the current year. Again this year, the corporation paid its president a salary of $600,000 and chose to deduct this amount.

Because you are not bound for this year's return by what the IRS deemed reasonable for the prior tax year, the full $600,000 can be claimed as a salary deduction, assuming that you and Ramon both believe that the entire salary represents reasonable compensation.

Statement No. 6: Knowledge of Error

A CPA should advise a client promptly upon learning of an error in a previously filed return or upon learning of a client's failure to file a required return, where the error has a significant (material in amount) effect on the tax liability. The advice can be oral or written and should include a recommendation of the corrective measures, if any, to be taken. The error or other omission should not be disclosed to the IRS without the client's consent.

If the past error is material in amount and is not corrected by the client, the CPA may be unable to prepare the current year's tax return. The CPA must consider the cumulative effects of the error on the taxpayer's liabilities for all tax years, including those in the future.

In preparing a client's year 2 income tax return, you discover that final inventory for year 1 was materially understated. First, you should advise the client to file an amended return for year 1 reflecting the correct amount in final inventory. Second, if the client refuses to make this adjustment, you should consider whether the error will preclude you from preparing a substantially correct return for year 2. Because this probably is the case (last year's closing inventory becomes this year's beginning inventory), you should withdraw from the engagement.

If the client corrects the error, you may proceed with the preparation of the year 2 tax return. You must assure yourself that the error is not repeated on the return that you are preparing.

Statement No. 7: Advice to Clients

In providing tax advice to a client, the CPA must use judgment to ensure that the advice reflects professional competence and appropriately serves the client's needs. No standard format or guidelines can cover all situations and circumstances involving written or oral advice by the CPA.

The CPA may communicate with the client when subsequent developments affect previous advice on significant matters. However, the CPA need not initiate the communication unless they have agreed to do so in the engagement letter with the client.

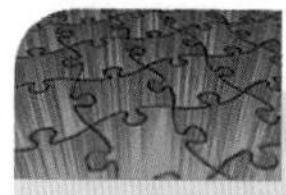

Concept Summary 28.2

Tax Profession and Ethics

1. The Treasury assesses penalties when the taxpayer fails to file a required tax return or pay a tax. Penalties also are assessed when an inaccurate return is filed due to negligence or other disregard of tax rules. Tax preparers are subject to penalties for assisting a taxpayer in filing an inaccurate return, failing to follow IRS rules in an appropriate manner, or mishandling taxpayer data or funds.
2. Statutes of limitations place outer boundaries on the timing and amounts of proposed amendments to completed tax returns that can be made by the taxpayer or the IRS.
3. Tax practitioners must operate under constraints imposed on them by codes of ethics or pertinent professional societies and by Treasury Circular 230. These rules also define the parties who can represent others in an IRS proceeding.
4. A limited privilege of confidentiality exists between the taxpayer and tax preparer who also is a CPA, an EA, or an attorney.

28-3 Tax Planning

28-3a Strategies in Seeking a Letter Ruling

In some cases, it may not be necessary or desirable to request an advance ruling from the IRS. For example, it generally is not desirable to request a ruling if the tax results are doubtful and the company is committed to completing the transaction in any event. If a ruling is requested and negotiations with the IRS indicate that an adverse determination will be forthcoming, it usually is possible to have the ruling request withdrawn before the IRS issues it. In determining the advisability of a ruling request, the taxpayer should consider the potential exposure of other items in the tax returns of all "open years."

28-3b Considerations in Handling an IRS Audit

As a general rule, a taxpayer should attempt to settle disputes at the earliest possible stage of the administrative appeal process. It usually is possible to limit the scope of the examination by furnishing pertinent information requested by the agent. Extraneous information or fortuitous comments may result in the opening of new issues and should be avoided. Agents usually appreciate prompt and efficient responses to inquiries, because their performance may in part be judged by their ability to close or settle assigned cases.

To the extent possible, it is advisable to conduct the investigation of field audits in the practitioner's office, not the client's office. This permits greater control over the audit investigation and facilitates the agent's review and prompt closure of the case.

Many practitioners believe that it is generally not advisable to have clients present at the scheduled conferences with the agent, because the client may give emotional or gratuitous comments that impair prompt settlement. If the client is not present, however, they should be advised of the status of negotiations. The client makes the final decision on any proposed settlement.

Preparing for the Audit

The tax professional must prepare thoroughly for the audit or Appeals proceeding. Practitioners often cite the following steps as critical to such preparations. Carrying out a level of due diligence in preparing for the proceeding is part of the tax professional's responsibility in representing the client.

- Make certain that both sides agree on the issues to be resolved in the audit. The goal here is to limit the IRS agent's list of open issues to defensible items.
- Identify all of the facts underlying the issues in dispute, including those favorable to the IRS. Gather evidence to support the taxpayer's position, and evaluate the evidence supporting the other side.
- Conduct research with current tax law authorities as they relate to the facts and open issues, within the parameters of the audit to which the tax professional and the IRS have agreed. The IRS agent is bound only by U.S. Supreme Court cases and IRS pronouncements. Determine the degree of discretion that the IRS is likely to have in settling the case.
- Prepare a list of points supporting and contradicting the taxpayer's case. Include both minor points bearing little weight and core principles. Short research memos also will be useful in the discussion with the agent. Points favoring the taxpayer should be mentioned during the discussion and "entered into the record."
- Prepare tax and interest computations showing the effects of points that are in dispute so that the consequences of closing or compromising an issue can be determined accurately.

- Determine a "litigation point" (i.e., at which the taxpayer will withdraw from further audit or appeals negotiation and pursue the case in the courts). This position should be based on the dollars of tax, interest, and penalty involved; the chances of prevailing in various trial-level courts; and other strategies discussed with the taxpayer. One must have an "end game" strategy for the audit, and in rare cases, litigation may present a possible resolution.

Documentation Issues

The tax practitioner's workpapers should include all research memoranda, and a list of resolved and unresolved issues should be continually updated during the course of the IRS audit. Occasionally, agents request access to excessive amounts of accounting data to engage in a so-called fishing expedition. Providing blanket access to working papers should be avoided. Workpapers should be reviewed carefully to minimize opportunities for the agent to raise new issues not otherwise apparent. It generally is advisable to provide the agent with copies of specific workpapers only upon request.

In unusual situations, a Special Agent may be brought in by the government to gather evidence in the investigation of possible criminal fraud. When this occurs, the tax professional should seek one's own separate legal counsel to determine the extent of any cooperation in providing information to the agent, and to measure the tax professional's own exposure to sanctions.

If the taxpayer receives a Revenue Agent's Report, it generally indicates that the IRS has decided not to initiate criminal proceedings. The IRS usually does not take any action on a tax deficiency until any related criminal matter has been resolved.

28-3c **Statute of Limitations**

The IRS requests an extension of the statute of limitations when it finds that there is insufficient time to complete an audit or appellate review. The taxpayer is not compelled to agree to the extension request and may be averse to giving the IRS more time. But denying the IRS request may make matters worse.

Although the statute of limitations governing Thornton's tax return is scheduled to expire in 15 days, the IRS has requested an extension for another 60 days. It wants to complete a more thorough investigation into a disputed $500,000 deduction. If Thornton refuses to agree to the extension, the IRS likely will disallow the entire deduction and issue a 90-day letter. However, if Thornton agrees to the extension, all or part of the deduction may be salvaged.

A disadvantage of extending the statute is that the IRS sometimes can raise new issues during the extension period. Moreover, any extension of the statute further extends the period for which the return is subject to audit in subsequent years. However, the taxpayer should attempt to take the following protective measures as a condition to agreeing to the extension:

- Shorten the extension period requested before signing the Form 872. This will reduce the chance that the IRS will find and investigate new issues.
- Restrict the scope of the issues covered by the extension (e.g., extend the period only as to the computation of cost of goods sold).

28-3d **Litigation Considerations**

During the process of settlement with the IRS, the taxpayer must assess the economic consequences of possible litigation. Specifically, the probability of winning in court should be weighed against the costs of litigating the dispute (legal, support, and court costs). In some instances, taxpayers become overly emotional and do not adequately consider the economic and psychological costs of litigation.

The taxpayer also should consider the effects of the settlement upon the tax liability for future periods (i.e., in addition to the years under audit). If the taxpayer litigates the tax dispute, personal information may become public in a published court decision or in related media releases.

In selecting a proper tax forum, consideration should be given to the decisions of the various courts in related cases. The Tax Court follows the decisions of U.S. Courts of Appeals if the court is one to which the taxpayer may appeal.[81] For example, if an individual is in the jurisdiction of the Fifth Circuit Court of Appeals and that court has issued a favorable opinion on the same issue that currently confronts the taxpayer, the Tax Court will follow this opinion in deciding the taxpayer's case, even if previous Tax Court decisions have led to contrary results.

If the issue involves a question in which some special consideration is needed, an effective strategy may dictate the choice of the Court of Federal Claims, which is seen by some observers as on occasion giving greater weight to equity considerations than to strict legal precedent, or of a Federal District Court, where a jury trial is available.

28-3e **Penalties**

The failure to file and failure to pay penalties are not a threat for most individual taxpayers. Those penalties are computed as a percentage of the unpaid tax liability; because most taxpayers receive a refund on the Form 1040, the penalty as computed would be zero.

The penalty for failure to pay estimated taxes can become quite severe. Often trapped by the provision are employed taxpayers with outside income. They may forget about the outside income and assume that the amount withheld from wages and salaries is adequate to cover their liability, thereby triggering a penalty.

28-3f **Ethics in the Tax Practice**

Committed to working within the ethical standards that apply, tax professionals must carry out a number of quality control measures within the practice.

- Adopt a "tone at the top" that stresses ethical tax practice, emphasizing at all times the importance of integrity and objectivity in the context of client advocacy. Stress the importance of all employees to stay current with the requirements of Circular 230 and the tax preparer penalty rules.
- Establish and follow ethical guidelines with respect to all forms of client communication and documentation, including tax returns and written, spoken, and digital tax advice.
- Prepare an engagement letter to lay out the responsibilities of all parties in complying with the tax law when taking on a new client, or whenever the scope of the work to be performed for a client changes. The firm should use the engagement letter to make certain that the client provides all documents needed to avoid penalties and compute the tax liability correctly, and to establish the high levels of tax ethics that will be met in the engagement. The client should be aware of, and participate in, this dedication to ethical behavior.
- The firm and its staff must ascertain at all times that none of its clients or engagements present an unacceptable conflict of interest necessitating corrective measures. Such conflicts might occur when the firm represents two or more parties in the same transaction where competing goals are present (e.g., in the context of divorce, corporate liquidation, estate settlement, or innocent spouse claim).
- Conduct annual reviews to ascertain that all tax preparers in the firm are current as to their PTIN registration and CPA or other licenses and certifications held, including currency with continuing education requirements.

---

[81] *Jack E. Golsen*, 54 T.C. 742 (1970). A recent application of the *Golsen* rule by the U.S. Tax Court can be found in *Thompson*, 124 TCM 51, T.C.Memo. 2022–80. See text Sections 2-1c and 2-3d.

- Emphasize to all who handle tax return data the importance of data security and confidentiality, as well as other aspects of the firm's best practices. Confidentiality of data extends to files that relate to both present and former clients, following the firm's data retention policies.
- Monitor the compliance of all members of the firm with its established ethical guidelines. Use a peer review process periodically to confirm that the system is working as designed and to bring third-party suggestions into the process.

28-3g **Privileged Communications**

CPAs need to exercise care to ensure that the privilege of confidentiality will apply to their tax work. Taking the following steps can help:

- Segregate the time spent and documents produced in rendering services for tax compliance from that devoted to tax advice. Doing this will protect the privilege from being waived as to the tax advice.
- Explain the extent of the privilege to the client—specify what will and will not be protected from the IRS in a dispute.
- Do not inadvertently waive the privilege, for example, by telling "too much" to the IRS or to a third party who is not protected by the privilege.

Refocus on The Big Picture

A Tax Adviser's Dilemma

Martin Barraud/Ojo Images/Getty Images

Your work with Campbell Corporation and its advanced manufacturing production credit may prove troublesome. To avoid the taxpayer and tax preparer penalties, substantial authority must exist for claiming the credit, but there is little guidance regarding the new credit. How does one craft a tax return position when the tax law largely is silent as to the particulars of the facts of the taxpayer's situation? How much risk of incurring a tax penalty are the taxpayer and your firm willing to assume in deciding how and whether to report these expenditures?

Beyond the monetary effects of claiming the credit, you and the client must consider the publicity aspects of taking this issue to court: Does Campbell want to be the "test case" in the Tax Court on this matter? What would be the effects on your consulting firm if a preparer penalty or even loss of professional certification were to result? If the credit is to be claimed, what degree of "disclosure" does the law require?

At a minimum, your firm and Campbell's tax department must conduct thorough research of analogous situations in the law. Due diligence in this regard would require that you examine how other technological innovations, probably having nothing to do with the type of product Campbell manufactures, were treated for tax credit purposes. Your firm should also discuss with Campbell whether a private letter ruling can be requested (see text Section 28-1b). Constrained only by the budget dollars that Campbell is willing to dedicate to this task, your research is likely to be both interesting and frustrating, as no "on point" resolution is likely to be found prior to a later audit of the Form 1120 and its disclosures.

What If?

The risk profiles of the tax adviser and a client seldom are identical. What position should your firm take if Campbell's tax department decides to claim the full credit for an item on which the tax law is unclear, but your firm recommends that a special disclosure be made on the return concerning the item? A disclosure of this sort would

continued

protect the parties from later assessment of tax penalties, but Campbell believes that drawing attention to the credit item would increase the likelihood of a targeted audit of the expenditures by the IRS.

Although you are certain that tax fraud is not a problem on the Campbell return, you are concerned about the ramifications of Campbell's desire to omit the recommended disclosure. Your firm might decide to leave the Campbell engagement altogether if it is especially sensitive to exposure to penalties, or if it is not certain that your tax research has established and documented that there is substantial authority or a reasonable basis for the tax return position. Charges of a lack of appropriate competence or due diligence by your firm might be brought by the IRS, the firm's professional ethics or certification bodies, or the issuer of its malpractice insurance. Clearly, none of these results is attractive to your firm.

Key Terms

30-day letter, 28-10
90-day letter, 28-10
Accuracy-related penalties, 28-16
Circular 230, 28-23
Closing agreement, 28-13
Determination letter, 28-6
Enrolled agents (EAs), 28-23
Fraud, 28-18
Information returns, 28-3
Installment agreement, 28-12
Internal Revenue Manual (IRM), 28-7
John Doe summons, 28-8
Letter ruling, 28-5
Negligence, 28-16
Notice CP 2000, 28-9
Offer in compromise, 28-11
Reasonable cause, 28-15
Revenue Agent's Report (RAR), 28-9
Statements on Standards for Tax Services (SSTS), 28-28
Statute of limitations, 28-21
Substantial authority, 28-17
Tax preparer, 28-25
Technical advice memorandum (TAM), 28-6
Unreasonable position, 28-25
Whistleblower Program, 28-8

Discussion Questions

1. **LO.1** As a tax professional with a diverse group of clients and tax issues, why is it important that you understand how the IRS is organized and how its personnel are deployed?

2. **LO.1, 8** Your tax client Chen asks whether it is likely that her Form 1040 will be audited this year. You suspect that Chen might modify the information she reports on her return based on your answer. Address Chen's question, and provide her with a justification to comply fully with the tax law's reporting requirements.

3. **LO.1** Recently, a politician was interviewed about fiscal policy, and she mentioned reducing the "tax gap." Explain what this term means. What are some of the pertinent political and economic issues relative to the tax gap? *Critical Thinking*

4. **LO.1** Review Exhibit 28.1, and identify the following.
   a. The title of the IRS's chief executive officer.
   b. The title of the "IRS's attorney."
   c. The names of the four major operating divisions of the IRS.
   d. The titles of the two deputy commissioners.
   e. The function that reports to both deputy commissioners.

Critical Thinking

5. **LO.3** During an interview with an IRS official on a news show, the interviewer asks, "So how do you decide which Forms 1040 get audited and which do not?" How should the IRS official respond, taking into account that only some of the audit selection process is public information?

6. **LO.3** On June 10, Ming states, "I filed my Form 1040 on April 5 and haven't heard from the IRS since then, so I know I will not be audited!" Evaluate Ming's assumption.

7. **LO.3** You overhear Matheus say, "I am so glad to be divorced from my cheating wife Larissa. She keeps two sets of books in her coding business, and I wish the IRS would find out about it." Is Matheus a candidate for the informant award program that is operated by the IRS? Explain how the program works and how an award might be paid to Matheus.

8. **LO.6** Which of the valuation penalties is likely to arise when an aggressive taxpayer reports:
   a. A charitable contribution?
   b. A business deduction?
   c. A taxable gift to a friend?

9. **LO.4, 5** Indicate whether each of the following statements is true or false.
   a. The government never pays a taxpayer interest on an overpayment of tax.
   b. The IRS can compromise on the amount of tax liability if there is doubt as to the taxpayer's ability to pay.
   c. Once a taxpayer receives the Revenue Agent's Report, the taxpayer has no choice but to pay the assessed tax.
   d. The IRS is required to accept an application for an installment plan that delays the payment of the taxpayer's $6,000 outstanding tax liability as long as the taxpayer has a history of filing timely tax returns.
   e. The offer in compromise program attempts to allow upper-income taxpayers additional time in which to pay delinquent tax amounts.

Critical Thinking

10. **LO.7** Discuss the concept of statutes of limitations in the context of the Federal income tax law.
    a. Who benefits when the statute applies—the government, the taxpayer, or both?
    b. What happens when the statute is scheduled to expire within two weeks but the IRS audit will not be completed by then?

11. **LO.8** Consider the ethical standards under which the tax profession operates. Who regulates the behavior of tax return preparers? What documents provide the major constraints on the conduct of the tax profession?

12. **LO.8** Give the Circular 230 position concerning each of the following situations sometimes encountered in the tax profession.
    a. Taking an aggressive pro-taxpayer position on a tax return.
    b. Not having a quality review process for a return completed by a partner of the tax firm.
    c. Purposely delaying compliance with a document request received from the IRS.
    d. Not keeping up with changes in the tax law.
    e. Charging $4,500 to complete a simple Form 1040 with no supporting schedules.
    f. When representing a taxpayer in a Federal income tax audit, charging a fee equal to one-third of the reduction of the tax proposed by the IRS agent.

g. Representing both spouses when negotiating tax matters pertinent to their divorce.

h. Advertising on the Web for new tax clients and including *Se habla español* in the text of the ads.

13. **LO.8** Indicate whether each of the following parties could be subject to the tax preparer penalties.

a. Tom prepared Sally's return for $250.

b. Theresa prepared her grandmother's return for no charge.

c. Georgia prepared her church's return for $500 (she would have charged an unrelated party $3,000 for the same work).

d. Miguel prepared returns for low-income taxpayers under his college's VITA program.

e. Hildy prepared the return of her corporate employer.

f. Heejeo, an administrative assistant for an accounting firm, processed a client's return through TurboTax.

14. **LO.8** Using no more than five PowerPoint slides, create a presentation for your Advanced Accounting Capstone class, listing at least three of the Statements on Standards for Tax Services that apply to CPAs. For each standard you choose, provide a short explanation of its content. Communications

Computational Exercises

15. **LO.6** Alexi files her tax return 20 days after the due date. Along with the return, she remits a check for $3,000, which is the balance of the tax she owes. Disregarding any interest liabilities, compute Alexi's total penalties for this period.

16. **LO.6** Marcella (a calendar year taxpayer) purchased a sculpture for $5,000. When the sculpture is worth $12,000 (as later determined by the IRS), Marcella donates it to the Peoria Museum of Art, a public charity. Based on the appraisal of a friend, Marcella deducts $38,000 for the donation. Because Marcella was in the 24% marginal Federal income tax bracket, overstating the deduction by $26,000 results in a tax underpayment of $6,240.

a. Compute Marcella's overvaluation penalty.

b. Construct a Microsoft Excel formula that will compute the penalty for all noncorporate taxpayers.

17. **LO.6** Rivera underpaid her income tax by $45,000. The IRS can prove that $40,000 of the underpayment was due to fraud.

a. Determine Rivera's civil fraud penalty.

b. Rivera pays the penalty five years after committing the fraudulent act. Her after-tax rate of return on available cash is 9%. Construct a Microsoft Excel formula that generates the present value of Rivera's penalty.

18. **LO.7** On June 15, 2021, Sheridan filed his 2020 income tax return, paying a tax of $10,500. On October 5, 2022, he filed an amended 2020 return showing an additional $6,400 of tax, which he paid with the amended return. On August 22, 2024, he filed a claim for a refund of $7,000. How much Federal income tax can Sheridan recover on the amended return?

Problems

19. **LO.5** Gordon paid the $10,000 balance of his Federal income tax three months late. Ignore daily compounding of interest. Determine the interest rate that applies relative to this amount if the Federal short-term rate for the relevant period is 3%, assuming that:
    a. Gordon is an individual.
    b. Gordon is a calendar year C corporation.
    c. The $10,000 is not a tax that is due, but is a refund payable by the IRS to Gordon (an individual).
    d. The $10,000 is not a tax that is due, but is a refund payable by the IRS to Gordon (a calendar year C corporation).

20. **LO.6** Rita forgot to pay her Federal income tax on time. When she actually filed, she reported a balance due. Compute Rita's failure to file penalty in each of the following cases.
    a. Two months late, $1,000 additional tax due.
    b. Five months late, $3,000 additional tax due.
    c. Eight months late, $4,000 additional tax due.
    d. Three and a half months late, $3,000 additional tax due.
    e. Five months late due to fraud by Rita, $4,000 additional tax due.
    f. Ten months late due to fraud by Rita, $15,000 additional tax due.

21. **LO.6** Wade filed his Federal income tax return on time but did not remit the balance due. Compute Wade's failure to pay penalty in each of the following cases.
    a. Four months late, $3,000 additional tax due.
    b. Ten months late, $4,000 additional tax due.
    c. Five years late, $5,000 additional tax due.

22. **LO.6** Compute the failure to pay and failure to file penalties for John, who filed his 2022 income tax return on December 20, 2023, paying the $10,000 amount due at that time. On April 1, 2023, John received a six-month extension of time in which to file his return. He has no reasonable cause for failing to file his return by October 15 or for failing to pay the tax that was due on April 15. John's failure to comply with the tax laws was not fraudulent.

23. **LO.6** Olivia, a calendar year taxpayer, does not file her 2022 Form 1040 until December 12, 2023. At this point, she pays the $40,000 balance due on her 2022 tax liability of $70,000. Olivia did not apply for and obtain any extension of time for filing the 2022 return. When questioned by the IRS on her delinquency, Olivia asserts: "If I was too busy to file my regular tax return, I was too busy to request an extension."
    a. Is Olivia liable for any penalties for failure to file and for failure to pay?
    b. If so, compute the penalty amounts.

24. **LO.6** Baez, a cash basis, calendar year taxpayer, filed his Federal income tax return 48 days after the due date. Baez never extended his return, and he paid the taxes that were due when he filed the return. What penalty will Baez incur, and how much will he have to pay if his additional tax is $10,000? Disregard any interest he must pay.

25. **LO.6** Maureen, a calendar year individual taxpayer, files her 2021 return on November 4, 2023. She did not obtain an extension for filing her return, and the return reflects additional income tax due of $15,000.
    a. What are Maureen's penalties for failure to file and to pay?
    b. Would your answer to part (a) change if Maureen, before the due date of the return, had retained a CPA to prepare and e-file the return, and it was the CPA's negligence that caused the delay? Explain.

26. **LO.6** Blair underpaid her taxes by $250,000. A portion of the underpayment was shown to be attributable to Blair's negligence ($100,000). A court found that the rest of the deficiency constituted civil fraud ($150,000).
    a. Compute the total fraud and negligence penalties incurred.
    b. Construct a Microsoft Excel formula that computes the penalties incurred in part (a).
    c. Blair pays the penalties four years after committing the improper acts. Her after-tax rate of return on available cash is 7%. Construct a Microsoft Excel formula that generates the present value of Blair's penalty obligations.

27. **LO.6** Compute the overvaluation penalty for each of the following independent cases involving the fair market value of charitable contribution property.

	Taxpayer	Corrected IRS Value	Reported Valuation	Applicable Tax Rate
a.	Individual	$ 40,000	$ 50,000	35%
b.	C corporation	30,000	50,000	21
c.	S corporation	40,000	50,000	35
d.	Individual	150,000	200,000	35
e.	Individual	150,000	250,000	35
f.	C corporation	150,000	750,000	21

28. **LO.6** Compute the undervaluation penalty for each of the following independent cases involving the value of a closely held business in the decedent's gross estate. In each case, assume a marginal Federal estate tax rate of 40%.

	Reported Value	Corrected IRS Valuation
a.	$ 20,000	$ 25,000
b.	100,000	150,000
c.	150,000	250,000
d.	150,000	500,000

29. **LO.6** Singh, a qualified appraiser of fine art and other collectibles, was advising Colleen when she was determining the amount of the charitable contribution deduction for a gift of a sculpture to a museum. Singh sanctioned a $900,000 appraisal, even though he knew the market value of the piece was only $300,000. Colleen assured Singh that she had never been audited by the IRS and that the risk of the government questioning his appraisal was negligible.

    But Colleen was wrong, and her return was audited. The IRS used its own appraisers to set the value of the sculpture at $400,000. Colleen is in the 32% Federal income tax bracket. Singh's fee for preparing the appraisal was $20,000.
    a. Compute the penalty the IRS can assess against Singh. (Do not consider the valuation penalty as to Colleen's return.)
    b. What is the penalty if Singh's appraisal fee was $7,500 (not $20,000)?
    c. Construct a Microsoft Excel formula that generates the correct answer for parts (a) and (b).

30. **LO.6** Eggers Corporation filed an amended Form 1120, claiming an additional $400,000 deduction for payments to a contractor for a prior tax year, in which a 21% tax rate applied. The amended return was based on the entity's interpretation of a Regulation that defined deductible advance payment expenditures. The nature of Eggers's activity with the contractor did not exactly fit the language of the Regulation. Nevertheless, because so much tax was at stake, Eggers's tax department decided to claim the deduction.

    Eggers's tax department estimated that there was only a 15% chance that Eggers's interpretation would stand up to a Tax Court review.

a. What is the amount of tax penalty that Eggers is risking by taking this position?
b. What would be the result if there was a 45% chance that Eggers's interpretation of the Regulation was correct?
c. Construct a Microsoft Excel formula that generates the correct answer for parts (a) and (b).

31. **LO.6** Kaitlin donated a painting to the local art museum. Because she is subject to a 35% marginal income tax rate, she is looking for a large charitable contribution deduction for the year. She engaged Vargas (who was referred to her by the museum) to provide an appraisal of the painting before she filed her Form 1040 for the year. Kaitlin told Vargas, "Be kind to me on this appraisal, and I'll send several more clients to you in the future." Kaitlin paid Vargas a $45,000 fee for his services.

Vargas completed his appraisal and determined that the painting was worth $500,000 under current market conditions. Still, in light of Kaitlin's promise of future business, Vargas sent Kaitlin an official appraisal reporting a $900,000 value for the artwork. Vargas had never compromised his integrity, but this time the temptation was too much.

Kaitlin used the appraisal to claim a $900,000 deduction for her charitable gift. Kaitlin will incur a valuation penalty now that her Form 1040 has been audited and the IRS has determined that the correct amount of the deduction is $500,000.

a. Compute any appraiser's penalty to which Vargas might be exposed.
b. Express the computation of this penalty as a Microsoft Excel formula.

32. **LO.6** Wan's AGI last year was $260,000. Her Federal income tax came to $65,000, paid through both withholding and estimated payments. This year, her AGI will be $220,000, with a projected tax liability of $50,000, all to be paid through estimates. Wan wants to pay the least amount of tax during the year that does not incur a Federal tax penalty.

a. Compute Wan's quarterly estimated tax payment schedule for this year.
b. Assume instead that Wan's AGI last year was $110,000 and resulted in a Federal income tax of $20,000. Determine her quarterly estimated tax payment schedule for this year.

33. **LO.6** Kold Services Corporation estimates that its current-year taxable income will be $500,000. Assuming a 21% Federal corporate income tax rate, it will incur a $105,000 liability. For each of the following independent cases, compute Kold's minimum quarterly estimated tax payments that will avoid an underpayment penalty.

a. Last year, taxable income was ($200,000). As a result, Kold generated a zero Federal income tax liability.
b. Last year, taxable income was $450,000, and the Federal income tax liability was $94,500.
c. Two years ago, taxable income was $2,000,000, and tax liability was $680,000. Last year, taxable income was $400,000, and tax liability was $84,000.

Communications
Critical Thinking

34. **LO.6** Leake Company, owned equally by Jacquie (chair of the board of directors) and Jeff (company president), is in very difficult financial straits. Last month, Jeff used the $300,000 withheld from employee paychecks for Federal payroll and income taxes to pay a creditor who threatened to cut off all supplies. To keep the company afloat, Jeff used these government funds willfully for the operations of the business, but even that effort was not enough. The company missed the next two payrolls, and today other creditors took action to shut down Leake altogether.

How much will the IRS assess in taxes and penalties in this matter and from whom? How can you as a tax professional best offer service to Jacquie, Jeff, and Leake? Address these matters in a memo for the tax research file.

35. **LO.7** Linn filed her 2022 Form 1040 on April 4, 2023. What is the date on which the applicable statute of limitations expires in each of the following independent situations?

a. Linn incurred a bad debt loss that she failed to claim.
b. Linn inadvertently omitted one-third of the correct gross income.

c. Same as part (b), except that the omission was deliberate.

d. Linn innocently overstated her deductions by a large amount.

e. No return was filed by Linn.

36. **LO.7** Loraine (a calendar year taxpayer) reported the following transactions, all of which were properly included in a timely filed return. Critical Thinking

Gross receipts		$ 975,000
Cost of sales		(850,000)
Gross profit		$ 125,000
Capital gain	$ 40,000	
Capital loss	(25,000)	15,000
Total income		$ 140,000

a. Presuming the absence of fraud, how much of an omission from gross income would trigger the six-year statute of limitations?

b. Would it matter if cost of sales had been inadvertently overstated by $150,000?

c. How does the situation change in the context of fraud by Loraine?

37. **LO.5, 7** On April 3, 2022, Luis filed his 2021 income tax return, which showed a tax due of $75,000. On June 1, 2024, he filed an amended return for 2021 that showed an additional tax of $10,000. Luis paid the additional amount. On May 18, 2025, Luis filed a claim for a 2021 refund of $25,000. Critical Thinking

a. If Luis's claim for a refund is correct in amount, how much tax will he recover?

b. What is the period that government-paid interest runs with respect to Luis's claim for a refund?

c. How would you have advised him differently?

38. **LO.8** Rod's Federal income tax returns (Form 1040) for the indicated years were prepared by the following persons.

Year	Preparer
1	Rod
2	Ann
3	Salma

Ann is Rod's next-door neighbor and owns and operates a pharmacy. Salma is a licensed CPA and is engaged in private practice. In the event Rod is audited and all three returns are examined, who may represent him before the IRS in an audit?

39. **LO.8** Christie is the preparer of the Form 1120 for Yostern Corporation. On the return, Yostern claimed a deduction that the IRS later disallowed on audit. Compute the tax preparer penalty that could be assessed against Christie in each of the following independent situations.

	Form 8275 Disclosure on the Return of the Disputed Deduction?	Tax Reduction Resulting from the Deduction	Probability That the Courts Would Approve the Deduction	Christie's Fee to Complete Yostern's Return
a.	No	$40,000	65%	$7,000
b.	No	40,000	35	7,000
c.	No	40,000	35	1,500
d.	Yes	40,000	35	7,000
e.	Yes	40,000	15	4,000

40. **LO.8** Discuss which penalties, if any, might be imposed on the tax adviser in each of the following independent circumstances. In this regard, assume that the tax adviser:

    a. Suggested to the client various means by which to generate excludible income.
    b. Suggested to the client various means by which to conceal cash receipts from gross income.
    c. Suggested to the client means by which to improve her cash flow by delaying for six months or more the deposit of the employees' share of Federal employment taxes.
    d. Failed, because of pressing time conflicts, to conduct the usual review of the client's tax return after his associate prepared it. The IRS later discovered that the return included fraudulent data.
    e. Failed, because of pressing time conflicts, to conduct the usual review of the client's tax return after his associate prepared it. The IRS later discovered a math error in the computation of the business mileage deduction.

41. **LO.8** Compute the preparer penalty the IRS could assess on Gerry in each of the following independent cases.

    a. On March 21, the copy machine was not working, so Gerry gave original returns that day to her 20 clients, without providing any duplicates for them. Copies for Gerry's records and for use in preparing state tax returns had been made on March 20.
    b. Because Gerry extended her vacation a few days, she missed the Annual Tax Update seminar that she usually attends. As a result, she was unaware that Congress had changed a law affecting limited partnerships. The change affected the transactions of 25 of Gerry's clients, all of whom understated their tax as a result.
    c. Gerry heard that the IRS was increasing its audits of corporations that hold assets in a foreign trust. As a result, Gerry instructed Hulan, the intern who prepared the initial drafts of the returns for five corporate clients, to leave blank the question about such trusts. Not wanting to lose her position, Hulan, a senior accounting major at State University, complied with Gerry's instructions.

Critical Thinking

42. **LO.8** You are the chair of the Ethics Committee of your state's CPA Licensing Commission. Interpret controlling AICPA authority in addressing the following assertions by your membership.

    a. When a CPA has reasonable grounds for not answering an applicable question on a client's return, a brief explanation of the reason for the omission should not be provided, because it would flag the return for audit by the IRS.
    b. If a CPA discovers during an IRS audit that the client has a material error in the return under examination, he should immediately withdraw from the engagement.
    c. If the client tells you that she paid $500 for office supplies but has lost the receipts, you should deduct an odd amount on her return (e.g., $499), because an even amount ($500) would indicate to the IRS that her deduction was based on an estimate.
    d. If a CPA knows that the client has a material error in a prior year's return, he should not, without the client's consent, disclose the error to the IRS.
    e. If a CPA's client will not correct a material error in a prior year's return, the CPA should not prepare the current year's return for the client.

Research Problems

Note: Solutions to the Research Problems can be prepared by using the Thomson Reuters Checkpoint™ online tax research database, which accompanies this textbook. Solutions can also be prepared by using research materials found in a typical tax library.

Research Problem 1. Lopez always had taken his Form 1040 data to the national brand tax preparers in a local mall, but this year, his friend Cheryl asked to prepare his return. Cheryl quoted a reasonable fee, and Lopez reasoned that, with finances especially tight in Cheryl's household, she could use the money. — Communications, Critical Thinking

Lopez delivered his Forms W–2, 1099, and other documentation and said, "I'll pick up the finished return from you on Monday." Cheryl completed the return by that deadline, and without signing and reviewing the forms, Lopez allowed Cheryl to e-file it that day. The arrangement was that Cheryl would receive the refund through a special bank account and write Lopez a check for that amount, minus her fee. When the refund came through about three weeks later, Cheryl wrote Lopez a check for $2,400, and all parties were satisfied. Lopez gladly used Cheryl to e-file the next year's return using the same procedures.

To his surprise, Lopez received a letter from the IRS about 18 months later. The auditor had found that the return Cheryl had e-filed vastly overstated deductions and wrongly calculated the earned income tax credit. According to the audit report, the refund issued was $4,500—Cheryl had pocketed the difference. As a result, the corrected tax liability meant that Lopez now owed $7,000 in tax, before considering interest and penalties.

Lopez contends that he relied on Cheryl's expertise in the tax law and e-filing procedures. Consequently, there was reasonable cause for the underpayment of tax, and the IRS should waive the understatement and negligence penalties. The IRS has expressed sympathy for Lopez's position, but it maintains that the penalty should stand. What do you think? Summarize your findings in a memo for the tax research file.

Research Problem 2. Blanche Young Eagle (111 Elm Avenue, Plymouth, IN 46563) has engaged your firm because she has been charged with failure to file her 2020 Federal Form 1040. Blanche maintains that the "reasonable cause" exception should apply. During the entire tax filing season in 2021, she was under a great deal of stress at work and in her personal life. As a result, Blanche developed a sleep disorder, which was treated through a combination of pills and counseling. — Communications

Your firm ultimately prepared the 2020 tax return for Blanche, but it was filed far beyond the due date. Blanche is willing to pay the delinquent tax and related interest. However, she believes that the failure to pay penalty is unfair, because she was ill. Consequently, she could not be expected to keep to the usual deadlines for filing.

Write a letter to Blanche concerning these matters.

Research Problem 3. Several taxpayer and preparer penalties depend on whether a tax return has been filed by its due date. Send to your instructor a discussion of no more than two pages about how the Code and Regulations determine whether a return has been filed on a timely basis. Include in your review aspects of this issue in filing a return using the postal service, TurboTax, and FedEx. — Communications

Use internet tax resources to address the following questions. Look for reliable websites and blogs of the IRS and other government agencies, media outlets, businesses, tax professionals, academics, think tanks, and political outlets.

Research Problem 4. Make a list of the individuals currently serving in the following tax-related positions. Identify the website address where you found this information. Send this list to your instructor. — Communications

a. IRS Commissioner.

b. IRS Chief Counsel.

c. Heads of the four major operating divisions of the IRS.
d. Heads of the IRS Appeals and Criminal Investigation divisions.
e. Chair of the House Ways and Means Committee.
f. Chair of the Senate Finance Committee.
g. President of the Tax Foundation.
h. Chair of the AICPA Tax Executive Committee.

Communications
Data Analytics

Research Problem 5. Taxpayers generally "go to jail" on tax charges only when criminal activities have been involved. Find information about the criminal tax prosecutions the Treasury undertakes. Compare data for the last year of information available from the IRS and for five years prior to that.

How many criminal tax charges are initiated in a year? How much time does a criminal tax case take from the filing of charges to disposition by the IRS or a court? What issues tend to be the focus of a criminal tax prosecution? How much additional tax, interest, and penalty revenue does the Treasury collect due to its criminal prosecutions? Summarize your findings for your classmates in no more than four PowerPoint slides.

Research Problem 6. Corporations with large estimated tax overpayments and underpayments are subject to special interest rates.

a. Find in the Code how these rates are determined.
b. List the rates that have been in effect for the last six calendar quarters.
c. Find and subscribe to a feed that will alert you automatically when the interest rate changes.

Communications

Research Problem 7. Every year toward the end of the Form 1040 filing season, suggestions are offered to taxpayers about how to pay their taxes if they lack the funds to do so. The discussions address filing extensions, installment plans, and credit card payments. Find two online videos of this sort. Summarize the videoclips, and develop a speech outline and no more than four PowerPoint slides for a presentation you will make to your town's Young Executives Club.

Communications

Research Problem 8. Find a website that lists suggestions on how to deal with an IRS auditor during your first meeting. You might start at **irs.gov** by reading Publication 556. Then find at least three sites offered by tax professionals with different credentials and certifications. Summarize and evaluate each of the key points in an e-mail to your instructor.

Communications
Data Analytics

Research Problem 9. Construct a chart for a specific tax year, showing the audit rate for high-income tax returns, broken down by income ranges such as $200,000 to $500,000 of total positive income, $500,000 to $1,000,000, and so on. Indicate in your chart how many Forms 1040 were filed in each income range for the tax year and how many of those were audited by the IRS.

Communications
Data Analytics

Research Problem 10. Fraudulent claims relative to the earned income tax credit appear to be significant in frequency, so the IRS audits at a higher rate the Forms 1040 that include the credit. This leaves the agency open to charges that it targets its audits to people of color and to those who live in southern states. Review audit data in the *IRS Data Book* and related discussions at **propublica.org** and similar forums. Send a two-page analysis of these issues to your instructor. Include at least one graphic in your paper, such as a chart or a map.

Communications

Research Problem 11. Your client Ellie, a single U.S. individual, owes the IRS $84,000 in income taxes that relate to her tax year 2021. This year, Ellie submits a renewal request for her U.S. passport. In a research memo to your instructor, explain what is likely to happen concerning Ellie's passport. *Hint*: Search using the phrase "seriously delinquent tax debt."

Research Problem 12. Security breaches occur with regularity in today's world, and the IRS offers tips with which a tax professional can safeguard a client's data. Find the documents (a) IRS Data Security Resource Guide for Tax Professionals and (b) Safeguarding Taxpayer Data. In a two-page memo, highlight the IRS's suggestions to better secure the data that a tax firm deals with. Identify some of the indicators that tax data may have been breached, including signs of phishing activity that may have occurred. List five specific internal controls that a tax firm can adopt to strengthen its data security. Submit your memo to your instructor. Communications

Becker CPA Review Questions

Becker

1. A taxpayer presented her tax return preparer, Dev Powell, with documentation supporting income she had earned as an independent contractor. Although Powell knew that the taxpayer's income should be reported on the taxpayer's Form 1040 (U.S. individual income tax return), he intentionally did not report the income on the taxpayer's tax return. Powell understated the taxpayer's liability because he believed keeping the tax liability low would help retain the taxpayer as a client. In this situation, Powell may be subject to which of the following penalties?
   a. Understatement of taxpayer's liability due to failure to follow substantial authority by the tax return preparer.
   b. Failure to file correct information returns by a tax return preparer.
   c. Wrongful disclosure or use of tax return information by the tax return preparer.
   d. Understatement of taxpayer's liability due to willful or reckless conduct of the tax return preparer.

2. Treasury Department Circular 230 provides guidance for doing which of the following activities?
   a. Practicing before the IRS.
   b. Practicing before the U.S. Tax Court.
   c. Presenting before state boards of accountancy.
   d. Reporting income taxes in financial statements.

3. Which of the following is *not* required conduct for a preparer of an income tax return, under AICPA Tax Standards?
   a. Abide by the tax Code and legally minimize the taxpayer's tax liability.
   b. Verify that the information the client provides is correct.
   c. Notify the client if the preparer becomes aware of an error in a tax return.
   d. Inform the taxpayer about how to correct the situation of the taxpayer's failure to file an income tax return.

4. Various defenses to penalties based on the Internal Revenue Code standards of compliance are available to taxpayers. One of these is the reasonable basis standard. Which of the following statements is *true* regarding the reasonable basis standard?
   a. It is a position that has more than a 50 percent chance of succeeding.
   b. It is a position that has more than a 40 percent chance of succeeding but less than a more-than-50 percent chance of succeeding.
   c. It is a position that has at least a 20 percent chance of succeeding, one that is arguable but fairly unlikely to prevail in court.
   d. It applies only to tax shelters.

Part 9

Family Tax Planning

Family tax planning has as its objective the minimization of the present value of income and transfer taxes imposed on the family unit. Carrying out this objective requires a familiarity with the rules applicable to transfers by gift and at death. Entities often created as a result of these transfers (trusts and estates) are subject to unique income tax rules, as discussed in this part of the text.

Chapter

29

The Federal Gift and Estate Taxes

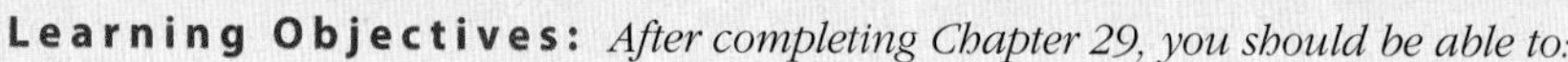

Learning Objectives: *After completing Chapter 29, you should be able to:*

- **LO.1** Explain the nature of the Federal asset transfer taxes.
- **LO.2** Describe and analyze the Federal gift tax formula.
- **LO.3** Describe and analyze the Federal estate tax formula.
- **LO.4** Illustrate the operation of the Federal gift tax.
- **LO.5** Calculate the Federal gift tax liability.
- **LO.6** Identify the components of the gross estate.
- **LO.7** Describe the components of the taxable estate.
- **LO.8** Calculate the Federal estate tax liability.
- **LO.9** Review and demonstrate the role of the generation-skipping transfer tax.
- **LO.10** Recognize strategies to minimize Federal gift and estate taxes.

Chapter Outline

KELENY/SHUTTERSTOCK.COM

The Big Picture

An Eventful and Final Year

Over his lifetime, Peter Hood started and purchased numerous automobile dealerships that he eventually transferred to a newly formed entity, Hood Corporation. Upon his death in a previous year, the stock in Hood Corporation passed in equal shares to Peter's surviving spouse, Martha, and their adult children, John and Helen.

For John Hood, 2023 proved to be an eventful and final tax year. Among the major happenings were the following:

- In January, John's divorce from his first wife, Hannah, became final.
- In February, he married Ashley, the manager of one of the Hood car dealerships.
- He made various gifts to family members.
- In July, John's mother Martha died of a heart condition, and John served as executor of her estate.
- In late November, he was seriously injured in a car accident (caused by another motorist).
- In early December, John worked with professional advisers to carry out some pre-death tax and estate planning.
- John died of his injuries in mid-December.

What are some of the tax problems (e.g., income, gift, and estate taxes) that the parties might encounter as a result of these events?

Read the chapter and formulate your response.

Until now, this text has dealt primarily with various applications of the Federal income tax. We now add to the discussion the Federal excise taxes on an individual's right to transfer property to another party. The Federal estate, gift, and generation-skipping taxes constitute the central focus of this chapter.

LO.1

Explain the nature of the Federal asset transfer taxes.

29-1 Transfer Taxes—In General

For more than 100 years, Congress has applied a gift and estate tax on the right of individuals (rather than the government) to determine who will receive their assets as the result of a legal transfer of title during life or at death. The chief purposes of these taxes are to keep well-endowed families from retaining "too much" wealth over the generations such that competition in the marketplace would become unfair and to increase the chances that all individuals pay a "fair share" of taxes to the government to support annual Federal expenditures.

In the typical year, about 3.5 million U.S. individuals die. At the same time, almost 2,600 estates file a Federal estate tax return showing an estate tax liability. About half of these returns are filed for residents of New York, Florida, Texas, and California. Likewise, about 500 Federal gift tax returns are filed each year showing a gift tax liability. Total collections of Federal estate and gift tax revenues in 2021 were about $27 billion. This represents less than one percent of total Federal tax collections.

29-1a Nature of the Taxes

The Code imposes a tax on an individual's gratuitous transfer of property. If the transfer occurs during the owner's life (e.g., by a cash transfer or the use of a trust), it is subject to the Federal gift tax. If the property passes by virtue of the death of the owner (e.g., under the terms of a will or life insurance policy), the Federal estate tax applies. If the recipient (i.e., the donee, heir, or beneficiary) of the transfer is two or more generations younger than the person making the transfer, the separate generation-skipping transfer tax also applies.[1]

A **unified transfer tax** applies to all gratuitous transfers of assets by an individual, regardless of how or when the transfers are made.

The gift, estate, and generation-skipping transfer taxes operate as a single, cumulative tax over the course of one's lifetime. In general, planning techniques relative to transfer taxes attempt to avoid or defer the payment of any estate and gift tax liabilities and to avoid the payment of the tax on generation-skipping transfers, which acts as a tax penalty on aggressive family wealth transfers.

Persons Subject to the Tax

The Federal gift tax is imposed on the right to transfer property by one person (the donor) to another (the donee) for less than full and adequate consideration. The tax is payable by the donor.[2] If the donor fails to pay the tax when due, the donee may be held liable for the tax to the extent of the value of the property received.[3]

Upon the death of an individual, the Federal estate tax is imposed on the taxable estate.[4] The executor (or administrator) of the estate pays any estate tax that may be due.

The Federal gift, estate, and generation-skipping taxes apply to a resident or citizen of the United States, regardless of where the transferred property is located. Someone who is not a U.S. citizen or resident (a non-resident alien, or NRA) is subject to the taxes only if the transferred property is located in the United States.[5]

[1]The estate tax was enacted in 1916. Because the estate tax then could be avoided by making transfers just prior to dying (i.e., "deathbed gifts"), a gift tax was added in 1932.

[2]§ 2502(c).

[3]§ 6324(b); known as the doctrine of transferee liability.

[4]§ 2001(a). Subchapter A (§§ 2001 through 2058) relates to the estate tax treatment of those who are U.S. residents or citizens. Subchapter B (§§ 2101 through 2108) addresses the estate tax applicable to NRAs, where different exemption and exclusion amounts apply.

[5]§§ 2001(a), 2511(a), and 2801.

Global Tax Issues — U.S. Transfer Taxes and NRAs

For individuals who are NRAs, the Federal gift tax applies only to gifts of property situated within the United States. Exempted, however, are gifts of intangibles, such as stocks and bonds.

For decedents who are NRAs, the Federal estate tax is imposed on the value of property located within the United States. Unlike the gift tax, however, the estate tax applies to stock in U.S. corporations.

Types of Tax at Death

Taxes payable by virtue of a person's death fall into two categories: estate and inheritance. The U.S. government, some states, and several other countries impose estate taxes. Inheritance taxes are imposed by some states and other countries. A few U.S. states and countries use both types of taxes.

The Federal estate tax differs in several respects from the typical inheritance tax. First, the estate tax is levied on the decedent's taxable estate. It is a tax on the right to pass property at death. Inheritance taxes apply to the right to receive property at death and are therefore levied on the heirs. Second, the relationship of the heirs to the decedent usually affects the amount of the inheritance tax. In general, the more closely related the parties, the larger the exemptions and the lower the applicable rates. Except for transfers to surviving spouses that may result in a marital deduction, the relationship of the heirs to the decedent has no effect on the Federal estate tax.

Formula for the Gift Tax

LO.2

Describe and analyze the Federal gift tax formula.

The Federal gift tax is reported annually on Form 709. Like the income tax, which uses taxable income (not gross income) as a tax base, the gift tax usually does not apply to the full amount of the gift. Deductions and the annual exclusion may be allowed to arrive at the **taxable gift**.[6] Concept Summary 29.1 outlines the formula for the gift tax and its chief deductions and exclusions. For this discussion, we assume that the gift tax is applied at a flat 40 percent rate on the taxable gifts for the year.[7]

Because Congress did not intend for the gift tax to apply to smaller transfers, it provided for an annual exclusion, which reduces the taxable gift to zero when a small amount is involved. The exclusion amount periodically is adjusted for *significant* inflation. For 2023, the exclusion is $17,000 ($16,000 in 2022).[8]

Formula for the Federal Estate Tax

LO.3

Describe and analyze the Federal estate tax formula.

When a decedent transfers property as a result of death, the Federal estate tax can apply. As a simplifying assumption, a flat 40 percent tax rate applies to the taxable estate—the fair market value of property owned or controlled by the decedent at the date of death, minus various deductions. The unified transfer tax credit applies against this tax. More deductions are allowed against the estate tax than can be used in computing the gift tax, as illustrated in Concept Summary 29.2.

The tax on generation-skipping transfers (GSTT)[9] acts as a penalty for passing assets to certain younger individuals. It applies to both lifetime and deathtime transfers, and the GSTT is added to the gift or estate tax that is computed above. Such a transfer thus can become quite expensive from a Federal transfer tax standpoint.

---

[6] § 2503(a).

[7] The flat rate assumption is made throughout Chapters 29 and 30 to simplify the tax computations. The complete § 2001 tax rate schedule for gifts and estates is reproduced on the inside back cover of this text. It shows some progressivity for taxable amounts under $1 million.

[8] § 2503(b)(2).

[9] § 2601.

Concept Summary 29.1

Formula for the Federal Gift Tax

Sum of fair market values of transfers that are subject to the Federal gift tax; this includes any "gift splitting" with a spouse		$xxx,xxx
Claim the annual exclusion (per donee) as available	$17,000 each	
Determine the charitable and marital deductions	xx,xxx	(xx,xxx)
Taxable gifts for the current period		$ xx,xxx
This year's gift tax, 40% of taxable gifts		$ x,xxx
Unified transfer tax credit		(xxx)
Gift tax due		$ xxx

Concept Summary 29.2

Formula for the Federal Estate Tax

Gross estate, sum of fair market values of property owned and controlled on the date of death		$xxx,xxx
Subtract:		
Expenses, indebtedness, and taxes	$xx	
Losses	xx	
Charitable bequests	xx	
Marital deduction	xx	
State-level estate or inheritance taxes	xx	(x,xxx)
Taxable estate		$ xx,xxx
Estate tax, 40% of taxable estate		$ xx,xxx
Subtract:		
Unified transfer tax credit, minus amount used against lifetime gifts	$xx	
Other tax credits (e.g., for non-U.S. taxes paid at death)	xx	(x,xxx)
Estate tax due		$ xxx

The chief purpose of the GSTT is to prevent families from transferring assets to much younger members, so as to reduce the present value of the transfer tax on the older generation's asset accumulations. The GSTT aims to apply a transfer tax to the family assets at least once every other generation.

The Unified Transfer Tax Credit

The purpose of the **unified transfer tax credit** is to allow donors and decedents to transfer specified amounts of wealth without being subject to current gift, estate, and GST taxes. The unified credit offsets the tax on a specified value of transferred assets, referred to as the exclusion amount.

Exhibit 29.1 shows the exclusion amount applicable to taxable asset transfers for the past several years. The exclusion amount is subject to annual indexation from its statutory amount of $10 million.[10]

[10]§ 2010.

Exhibit 29.1 **Unified Transfer Tax Exclusion Amount**

Year of Transfer	Exclusion Amount
2021	$11,700,000
2022	12,060,000
2023	12,920,000

The **exclusion amount** (also termed the **exemption equivalent** and the **bypass amount**) is the amount of the transfer that passes free of the gift or estate tax by virtue of the credit. Because the Federal transfer taxes are unified and cumulative in effect, these amounts are available to an individual only once during their lifetime.

Unified Transfer Tax Credit

In 2023, Janet makes a taxable gift of $6 million, the first taxable gift that she ever has made. Janet does not owe any Federal gift tax for the year. The taxable gift is less than the exclusion amount.

Example 2

In 2023, Sanjay makes a taxable gift of $3,500,000. In prior years, Sanjay's taxable gifts totaled $10,000,000. The exclusion amount applies to Sanjay in a cumulative manner, such that his lifetime taxable gifts amount to $13,500,000, and a Federal gift tax is due for 2023 on $580,000 ($13,500,000 − $12,920,000).

Example 3

In 2023, Dulcea dies reporting a taxable estate of $3,500,000. In prior years, Dulcea's taxable gifts totaled $10,000,000. The exclusion amount applies to Dulcea in a cumulative manner, such that her lifetime and at-death taxable asset transfers amount to $13,500,000, and a Federal estate tax is due on $580,000 ($13,500,000 − $12,920,000).

A married couple can make taxable transfers of $12,920,000 each and pay no tax by using their unified credit. If a spouse dies without using all of their unified credit, the executor of the estate can make an election to transfer any unused exemption from gift or estate taxes of the deceased spouse to the surviving spouse. The **"deceased spousal unused exclusion" (DSUE) election**, also known as the "portability" election must be made on a timely filed estate tax return for the first spouse to die.[11]

29-1b **Valuation Issues**

The value of the property on the date of its transfer generally determines the amount that is subject to the Federal gift, GST, or estate tax. For this purpose, fair market value is used. Under certain conditions, however, an executor can elect to value estate assets on the **alternate valuation date**. The election is made by the executor of the estate and is irrevocable. No alternate valuation date election is available for the gift tax.

The alternate valuation date election was designed as a relief provision to ease the economic hardship that could result when estate assets decline in value between the date of death and the payment of the estate tax liability. If the election is made, all assets of the estate are valued six months after death *or* on the date of disposition if this occurs earlier.[12] The election covers *all* assets in the gross estate and cannot be applied to only a portion of the property.

[11]§§ 2010(c)(4) and (5).

[12]§ 2032(a)(1).

Roberto's gross estate consists of the following property.

	Value on Date of Death	Value Six Months Later
Land	$14,800,000	$14,840,000
Stock in Brown Corporation	900,000	700,000
Stock in Green Corporation	500,000	460,000
Total	$16,200,000	$16,000,000

If Roberto's executor elects the alternate valuation date, the estate is valued at $16,000,000. The estate cannot value the land at its date of death value ($14,800,000) and choose the alternate valuation date for the rest of the gross estate, so as to reduce the tax base further.

The election of the alternate valuation date must decrease the value of the gross estate *and* decrease the estate tax liability. The reason for this last requirement is that the income tax basis of property acquired from a decedent will be the value used for estate tax purposes. Without a special limitation, the alternate valuation date could be elected solely to add to income tax basis, at a zero estate tax cost.

Al's gross estate consists of assets with a date of death value of $16,000,000 and an alternate valuation date value of $17,100,000. Under Al's will, all of his property passes outright to Jean (Al's wife). Because of the marital deduction (see text Section 29-3b), no estate tax results regardless of which value is used. But if the alternate valuation date could be elected (which it cannot because the tax liability is zero with and without the election), Jean would take a stepped-up income tax basis of $17,100,000 in the property acquired from Al, without incurring any Federal transfer tax liability.

29-1c **Key Property Concepts**

Separate and Joint Asset Ownership

Most property is owned by one individual who holds title to the asset and perhaps to a liability associated with it. When that individual passes the title to the asset to another party, during lifetime or at death, a gift or bequest may occur, and a Federal transfer tax may apply.

Now assume that Dan and Vicky jointly own equal interests in a tract of land. Such ownership can fall into any of four categories, originating in common law statutes of the states: joint tenancy, tenancy by the entirety, tenancy in common, or community property. Estate tax consequences that arise when jointly owned property like this transfers on account of death are discussed in text Section 29-3a. During lifetime, one of the joint owners can make a gift of their "share" of the property, and a gift tax may apply at that time.

If Dan and Vicky hold ownership as **joint tenants** or **tenants by the entirety**, the right of survivorship exists. This means that the tenant(s) who survive another owner's death then receive full ownership of the property. Thus, if Dan predeceases Vicky, the land belongs entirely to Vicky. None of the land will pass to Dan's heirs or will be subject to provisions in Dan's will or other documents. A tenancy by the entirety is a joint tenancy between only a married couple.[13]

If Dan and Vicky hold ownership as **tenants in common** or as community property, no right of survivorship exists. Thus, if Dan predeceases Vicky, Dan's one-half interest in the land will pass to his estate or heirs, as determined under his will or other arrangements. Vicky continues to own her share outright.

Community property interests work such that all income earned during the marriage and any property acquired after marriage, except by gift or inheritance, are owned by the spouses "50-50". The following states operate under the community property system: Arizona, California, Idaho, Louisiana, Nevada, New Mexico, Texas, Washington, Wisconsin, and (by election of the spouses) Alaska. All other states follow the common law system of ascertaining a spouse's rights to property acquired after marriage, usually assigning full property rights to the income earner or asset owner.

[13]Some state laws do not use the term *tenancy by the entirety* but, nevertheless, recognize a joint tenancy between spouses.

Marisol owns a building in an equal joint tenancy with Jada. While both individuals are living, Marisol can make a gift of her half of the property to Willie. But if Marisol dies and Jada survives, Marisol's one-half interest in the building passes to Jada automatically under state law, in the form of the survivorship feature of the joint tenancy. At that point, Marisol no longer can pass "her half" of the building to Willie, and a clause in Marisol's will that transfers a half interest to Willie is invalid.

If Marisol and Jada own the building as tenants in common or as community property, Marisol can pass her half of the asset to Willie as a lifetime gift or as a bequest at death. No right of survivorship exists under state property law.

29-2 The Federal Gift Tax

Illustrate the operation of the Federal gift tax.

29-2a General Considerations

In working with the gift tax, one determines whether and when a gift has taken place. In the typical situation, a gift occurs when one party takes ownership of an asset without providing full and adequate consideration to the other party. Most reported gifts involve transfers of cash, stock, bonds, and similar liquid assets.

Requirements for a Gift

For a gift to be complete under state law, the following elements typically must be present:

- A donor competent to make the gift.
- A donee capable of receiving and possessing the property.
- Donative intent on behalf of the donor.
- Actual or constructive delivery of the property to the donee or the donee's representative.
- Acceptance of the gift by the donee.

The Federal gift tax does not apply to transfers that are incomplete. Thus, if the transferor retains the right to reclaim the property or has not really parted with the possession of the property, a taxable event has not taken place.

In a business setting, full and adequate consideration for an exchange is apt to exist; thus, gifts in a business setting are rare. If the parties are acting in a personal setting, however, a gift usually is the result.

Valuable consideration does not include a payment or transfer based on "love and affection" and the like.[14] Property settlements in consideration of marriage (i.e., pre- or antenuptial agreements) are regarded as gifts.

Ethics & Equity It's the Thought That Counts

Joe (age 86) and Nicole (age 22) are married on Saturday. Two days later, they exchange wedding gifts. Joe's gift to Nicole is stock in Tesla (valued at $2 million), and Nicole's gift to Joe is a bottle of cologne (value of $32). What tax goals are they trying to accomplish? Will their plan work?

[14] Reg. § 25.2512–8.

Defining a Gift

Example 7

Grace makes a gift of a grand piano to Carlos. The piano is packed and sent to Carlos in December year 1. It arrives at Carlos's studio in January year 2, due to extra precautions taken by the movers as directed by Grace. The gift of the piano occurs in year 2, when Carlos accepts the gift.

Example 8

Motivated by respect and admiration, Julie transfers some shares of stock to Pattie and receives nothing in return. Julie has made a gift to Pattie in the amount of the fair market value of the stock. Julie is the *donor*, and Pattie is the *donee*.

Similarly, if the stock is worth $50,000 and Pattie pays Julie $12,000 to take ownership of it, Julie has made a $38,000 gift to Pattie.

Example 9

Peter sells Bob some real estate for $40,000. Unknown to Peter, the property contains valuable mineral deposits and is really worth $200,000. Peter may have made a bad business deal, but he has not made a gift of $160,000 to Bob.

Excluded Transfers

Transfers to political organizations are exempt from the application of the Federal gift tax.[15] This provision includes gifts to political parties, candidates, committees, and the like.

The Federal gift tax does not apply to tuition payments made to an educational organization (e.g., a college) on another's behalf. Nor does it apply to amounts paid on another's behalf for medical care.[16] In this regard, the law is realistic because it is unlikely that most donors would make such transfers when motivated solely by tax planning concerns. The payments, however, must be made directly to the provider (e.g., physician, hospital, or school). There is no requirement that the patient or student qualify as a relative or dependent of the person making the payment.

The Big Picture

Example 10

Return to the facts of *The Big Picture* on p. 29-1. After Peter died, his widow, Martha, continued to live in the family home and refused to move in with either of her children (John or Helen). As Martha's health and mental condition deteriorated, her children did everything possible to keep Claudia, the family housekeeper, from quitting. In fact, Helen paid for Claudia's gallbladder operation, and John paid the college tuition of her oldest son.

Neither Helen nor John has made gifts to Claudia or her son that are subject to taxation. Gifts would have occurred, however, if Helen and John had reimbursed Claudia for such amounts after she paid them rather than paying the providers (i.e., physician, hospital, and college) directly.

Satisfying an obligation of support is not subject to the gift tax. Thus, no gift takes place when parents pay for their children's elementary education, because one of the state-level obligations of parents is to educate their children.

What constitutes an obligation of support is determined by applicable state law. In many states, for example, an adult may have an obligation of support to provide for indigent parents, or a wealthy parent may have an obligation to support the law school tuition of a child. Similarly, payment of alimony or child support to an ex-spouse satisfies a legal obligation and does not constitute a gift to the recipient.

Lifetime versus Deathtime Transfers

One must distinguish between lifetime *(inter vivos)* and deathtime (testamentary) transfers.

[15] § 2501(a)(4).

[16] § 2503(e).

Example 11

Dudley buys a 12-month certificate of deposit (CD) from State Bank and lists ownership as follows: "Dudley, payable on proof of death to Faye." Nine months later, Dudley dies. When the CD matures, Faye collects the proceeds from State Bank.

No gift takes place when Dudley invests in the CD; Faye has received a mere expectancy (i.e., to obtain ownership of the CD upon Dudley's death). At any time before his death, Dudley may withdraw the funds or delete Faye's name from the account, thereby eliminating her rights. Furthermore, no gift occurs upon Dudley's death; the CD passes to Faye as a deathtime bequest instead.

A payable on death (POD) designation is a form of ownership frequently used in a family setting when investments are involved (e.g., stocks and bonds and savings accounts). The POD designation can be simpler to use than a will or trust arrangement.

29-2b **Transfers Subject to the Gift Tax**

Property Settlements in Divorce

Transfers of property interests made under the terms of a written agreement between spouses in settlement of their marital or property rights are deemed to be for adequate consideration.[17] These transfers are exempt from the Federal gift tax if a final decree of divorce is obtained within the three-year period beginning on the date one year before the parties entered into the agreement. Likewise excluded are child support arrangements. Such an agreement need not be approved by the divorce decree.

The Big Picture

Example 12

Return to the facts of *The Big Picture* on p. 29-1. Recall that John and Hannah's divorce became final in January. After extended but amicable negotiations, in September, John and Hannah agreed on a property settlement. In return for the receipt of $200,000 and title to their home, Hannah released all of her rights to future claims. Shortly thereafter, John made the transfer. The property settlement resulted in no gift tax consequences to John.

Disclaimers

A **disclaimer** is a refusal by a person to accept property that is designated to pass to them. The effect of the disclaimer is to pass the property to someone else, for instance, under the terms of the will. Assume that Julio dies and passes an asset to Maria. Maria does not want the asset, so she disclaims it back to Julio's estate, and the will directs that the asset now passes to Eva. If the disclaimer is executed properly, Maria *has not* made a gift of her own to Eva, and no gift tax is due from Maria.

The Big Picture

Example 13

Return to the facts of *The Big Picture* on p. 29-1. Recall that Martha died of a heart condition in July. Under her will, her estate passes in equal parts to her son and daughter or, if they disclaim, to their children. Helen disclaims her share of the inheritance, and the assets pass to her children.

Why might Helen disclaim her inheritance and have the property pass directly from Martha to the children? By doing so, an extra transfer tax may be avoided. If the disclaimer does not take place (i.e., Helen accepts the inheritance) and the property eventually passes to the children (either by gift or at death), the later transfer is subject to the application of either the gift tax or the estate tax.

The Federal gift tax also can be avoided in cases of a partial disclaimer of assets.

[17] § 2516.

The Big Picture

Assume the same facts as in Example 13. John's share of his inheritance from Martha also includes the family hunting lodge. Except for the hunting lodge, John disclaims his share of the inheritance, and the remaining assets pass to his children.

To be effective, the disclaimer must be in writing and timely made. Generally, this means that a statement must be executed no later than nine months after the right to the property arose. Furthermore, the person making the disclaimer must not have accepted any benefits or interest in the property during the nine-month period.

Other Transfers Subject to Gift Tax

Other transfers that may carry gift tax consequences (e.g., the creation of joint ownership) are discussed and illustrated in connection with the Federal estate tax.

Income Tax Considerations

Generally, a donor incurs no Federal income tax consequences on making a gift.[18] A donee recognizes no income on the receipt of a gift.[19] A donee's income tax basis in the property received depends on a number of factors (e.g., donor's basis, fair market value of the asset on the transfer date).[20]

29-2c Annual Gift Tax Exclusion

The first $17,000 of gifts made to any one person during any calendar year is excluded in determining the total amount of taxable gifts for the year.[21] This provision allows most "everyday" gratuitous transfers of assets to avoid the Federal gift tax.

The **annual exclusion** applies to all gifts of a *present interest* made during the calendar year in the order in which they are made, until the amount of the exclusion per donee is exhausted. For a gift in trust, each beneficiary of the trust is treated as a separate person for purposes of the exclusion.

Laura makes the following cash gifts: $10,000 to Rita and $20,000 to Maureen. Laura may claim an annual exclusion of $10,000 with respect to Rita and $17,000 with respect to Maureen.

A **future interest** is defined as an interest that will come into being (as to use, possession, or enjoyment) at some future date. Examples of future interests include deferred gifts to minors and remainder interests that are commonly encountered when property is transferred to a trust.[22] A *present interest* is an unrestricted right to the immediate use, possession, or enjoyment of property or of the income.

By a lifetime gift, Ron transfers property to a trust with income payable annually to June and the trust's assets remaining upon June's death to Albert. Ron has made two gifts when the trust was created: one to June of a life estate and one to Albert of a remainder interest. The life estate is a present interest and qualifies for the annual exclusion. Albert's remainder is a future interest and does not qualify for the exclusion.

[18] Gifts of installment notes receivable can result in gain recognition [see § 453B(a)] and deferred interest income on U.S. savings bonds is taxable at redemption.

[19] Both gifts and inheritances are excluded from the recipient's gross income under § 103.

[20] See text Section 13-2.

[21] § 2503(b). In 2022 the annual exclusion was $16,000.

[22] Trust terms are explained and trust arrangements are illustrated in text Exhibit 30.2.

If a possibility exists that the income beneficiary may not receive the immediate enjoyment of the property, the transfer is of a future interest.

Assume the same facts as in Example 16, except that the income from the trust need not be payable annually to June. It may, at the trustee's discretion, be accumulated and added to the underlying trust assets. Because June's right to receive the income from the trust is conditioned on the trustee's discretion, it is not a present interest. No annual exclusion is allowed.

The mere possibility of diversion is enough. It would not matter if the trustee never exercised the discretion to accumulate and did, in fact, distribute the trust income to June annually.

Contributions to Qualified Tuition Programs

For income tax purposes, § 529 plans possess attributes that reflect the best of all possible worlds. Although no up-front Federal income tax deduction is allowed, income earned by the fund accumulates free of income tax and distributions are not taxed if they are used for educational purposes. A special provision allows a donor to enjoy a gift tax advantage by using five years of annual exclusions (e.g., for a large one-time gift) but only once in a five-year period. Moreover, these college plans are not included in the gross estate of the transferor.[23]

Trevor and Audrey would like to start building a college education fund for their 10-year-old granddaughter Loni. Trevor contributes $170,000 to the designated carrier of their state's § 529 plan. By electing to split the gift and using five annual exclusions [2 (number of donors) × $17,000 (annual exclusion) × 5 years = $170,000], no taxable gift results. (The gift-splitting election is discussed in detail in text Section 29-2e.) Making the five-year election precludes Trevor and Audrey from using an annual exclusion on gifts to Loni for the next four years.

29-2d Deductions

In arriving at taxable gifts, a deduction is allowed for transfers to certain qualified charitable organizations. On transfers between spouses, a marital deduction may be available. Because both the charitable and marital deductions also apply in determining the Federal estate tax, these deductions are discussed in text Section 29-3.

29-2e Computing the Federal Gift Tax

LO.5 **Calculate the Federal gift tax liability.**

The gift tax rate is a flat 40 percent for most transfers made by U.S. citizens and residents.[24]

The Election to Split Gifts by Married Persons

To understand the reason for the gift-splitting election, consider the following situations.

[23] § 529(c)(4).

[24] § 2001(c). Cf. footnote 7.

Effect of Splitting Gifts

Example 19

Kong and Margaret are married and reside in Michigan, a common law property state. Kong has been the only breadwinner in the family, and Margaret has no significant property of her own. Neither has made any prior taxable gifts. Kong makes a gift to Gita of $17,017,000. Presuming that the election to split gifts did not exist, Kong's gift tax is computed as follows:

Amount of gift	$17,017,000
Subtract: Annual exclusion	(17,000)
Taxable gift	$17,000,000
Taxable gift after exemption equivalent ($17,000,000 − $12,920,000)	$ 4,080,000
Gift tax due at assumed 40% rate	$ 1,632,000

Example 20

Assume the same facts as in Example 19, except that Kong and Margaret always have resided in California (a community property state). Generally, income from personal services is community property. Consequently, the gift to Gita probably involves community property. If this is the case, the gift tax is computed as follows:

	Kong	Margaret
Amount of gift	$8,508,500	$8,508,500
Subtract: Annual exclusion	(17,000)	(17,000)
Taxable gift	$8,491,500	$8,491,500
Taxable gift after exemption equivalent	$ –0–	$ –0–
Gift tax due	$ –0–	$ –0–

As the results of Examples 19 and 20 indicate, married donors residing in community property jurisdictions could possess a significant Federal gift tax advantage over those residing in common law states. To rectify this inequity, when a gift-splitting election is made, a gift made by a person to someone other than their spouse may be considered as having been made one-half by each spouse.[25]

Returning to Example 19, Kong and Margaret could treat the gift passing to Gita as being made one-half by each of them. They may do this even though all of the gifted cash came from Kong. As a result, the parties can achieve the same tax consequences as in Example 20. There is no such thing as a "joint return" for Federal gift tax purposes, but the gift-splitting election achieves the same result; both spouses must file a gift tax return making the election and assigning the "two halves" of the gift separately.

To split gifts, the spouses must be legally married to each other at the time of the gift. A gift-splitting election means that all gifts made in that calendar year are split between them. In addition, both must be citizens or residents of the United States on the date of the gift.

29-2f **Procedural Matters**

The Federal Gift Tax Return

For transfers by gift, a Form 709 (U.S. Gift Tax Return) must be filed whenever the gifts for any one calendar year exceed the annual exclusion or involve a gift of a future

[25] § 2513.

interest. The Form 709 also must be filed when the election to split gifts is made by the nonowner spouse (see Example 22). A Form 709 need not be filed, however, for transfers between spouses that are offset by the unlimited marital deduction, regardless of the amount of the transfer.[26]

When Must a Form 709 Be Filed?

Example 21

This year, Larry makes five gifts, each in the amount of $17,000, to his five children. If the gifts do not involve future interests, a Form 709 need not be filed to report the transfers.

Example 22

Esther makes a gift of $34,000 cash of her separate property to her daughter. To double the amount of the annual exclusion allowed, Jerry (Esther's husband) is willing to split the gift. To make the gift-splitting election, a Form 709 must be filed, even though no gift tax will be due as a result of the transfer.

If a gift tax return is due, it must be filed on or before the fifteenth day of April following the year of the gift.[27] As is the case with other Federal taxes, when the due date falls on Saturday, Sunday, or a legal holiday, the date for filing the return is the next business day. If sufficient reason is shown, the IRS is authorized to grant reasonable extensions of time for filing the return.[28]

Concept Summary 29.3

Federal Gift Tax Provisions

1. The Federal gift tax applies to all gratuitous transfers of property made by U.S. citizens or residents, wherever the property is located. Different rules apply to gifts by NRAs.
2. A gratuitous transfer is one not supported by full and adequate consideration. If the parties are acting in a business setting, full consideration is presumed.
3. Property settlements can escape the gift tax if a divorce occurs within a prescribed period of time.
4. A disclaimer is a refusal by a person to accept property designated to pass to that person. The effect of a disclaimer is to pass the property to someone else. If certain conditions are satisfied, the issuance of a disclaimer will not subject to the Federal gift tax the party making the disclaimer.
5. The donor is allowed an annual exclusion for a gift of a present interest to a donee.
6. The election to split a gift enables a married couple to be treated as two donors. The election doubles the annual exclusion and makes the nonowner spouse's exemption equivalent available to the owner spouse.
7. The Federal gift tax generally applies at a flat 40% rate on cumulative taxable gifts in excess of the exemption equivalent amount.
8. Taxable gifts are reported on Form 709. The return is due on April 15 following the year of the gift.

29-3 The Federal Estate Tax

The following discussion of the estate tax applies the formula that appeared earlier in the chapter in Concept Summary 29.2. The key components in the formula are the gross estate, the taxable estate, and the credits allowed against the tentative tax. This formula can be summarized as follows.

[26] § 6019(a)(2).

[27] § 6075(b)(1).

[28] § 6081. Under § 6075(b)(2), an extension of time granted to a calendar year taxpayer for filing an income tax return automatically extends the due date of a gift tax return.

Gross estate − **Deductions allowed** = **Taxable estate** − **Exemption equivalent** × **40% tax rate** − **Tax credits*** = **Estate tax due**

*** Other than unified transfer tax credit**

LO.6

Identify the components of the gross estate.

29-3a Gross Estate

Simply stated, the **gross estate** includes the net assets owned and controlled by the decedent as of the date of death.

In contrast to the gross estate, one's **probate estate** is determined by state (rather than Federal) law. The probate estate consists of all of a decedent's property subject to the terms of the will. The administration is supervised by a local court (usually designated as a probate court). An executor is the decedent's personal representative appointed under the decedent's will. When a decedent dies without a will or fails to name an executor in the will (or that person refuses to serve), the local probate court appoints an administrator.

The probate estate frequently is smaller than the gross estate. Certain items like the proceeds of many life insurance policies and distributions from retirement plans are controlled by contracts outside of the will; they become part of the gross estate, as controlled by the decedent, but are not included in the probate estate.

All U.S. states provide for an order of distribution in the event someone dies *intestate* (i.e., without a will). After the surviving spouse, who receives some or all of the estate, the preference is usually in the following order: down to lineal descendants (e.g., children and grandchildren), then up to lineal ascendants (e.g., parents and grandparents), and out to collateral relations (e.g., brothers, sisters, aunts, and uncles).

Property Owned by the Decedent

Property owned by the decedent at the time of death is included in the gross estate. The nature of the property or the use to which it was put during the decedent-owner's lifetime has no significance as far as the estate tax is concerned. Thus, personal effects (such as clothing), stocks, bonds, mutual funds, furniture, jewelry, bank accounts, and certificates of deposit are included in the deceased owner's gross estate. No distinction is made between tangible and intangible, depreciable and nondepreciable, or business and personal assets.

Property Owned at Death

Example 23

Rani dies owning some City of Denver bonds. The fair market value of the bonds plus any interest accrued to the date of Rani's death is included in her gross estate. Although interest on municipal bonds usually is not taxable under the Federal income tax, it is property owned by Rani at the time of death and is subject to the estate tax. Any interest accrued after death is not part of the gross estate.

Sharon dies on April 7, when she owns stock in Robin Corporation and Wren Corporation. On March 2, both corporations authorized a cash dividend payable on May 4. Robin's dividend is payable to shareholders of record as of April 2. Wren's date of record is April 9. Sharon's gross estate includes the following: the stock in Robin, the stock in Wren, and the dividend on the Robin stock. It does not include the dividend on the Wren stock.

Ray dies holding some notes relating to a loan to his son. In his will, Ray forgives these notes, relieving the son of the obligation to make any more payments. The fair market value of these notes is included in Ray's gross estate.

The Big Picture

Return to the facts of *The Big Picture* on p. 29-1. At the time of his death, John was the president of Hood Corporation. John's estate receives a distribution from Hood's qualified pension plan of $1,100,000 consisting of the following:

Hood's contributions	$450,000
John's after-tax contributions	350,000
Income earned by the plan over the years	300,000

John's estate also receives $150,000 from Hawk Insurance Company. The payment represents the maturity value of term life insurance from a group plan that Hood maintains for its employees. As to these amounts, John's gross estate includes $1,250,000 ($1,100,000 + $150,000).

In most cases, retirement plan benefits are subject to estate tax. Besides the conventional qualified pension and profit sharing plans involved in Example 26, retirement plans include those under § 401(k) and similar arrangements for employees, various plans for self-employed persons, and traditional and Roth IRAs.

The gross estate also includes other assets that can be of significant value. Examples include:

- Real estate holdings.
- Present value of future royalty rights (e.g., patents, copyrights, and mineral interests).
- Interests in a business (e.g., sole proprietorship and partnership).
- Collectibles (e.g., works of art and coin collections).
- Unmatured insurance policies on the lives of others.
- Present value of settlements receivable from pending and potential lawsuits.
- Certain transfers that occur in the three years before death, or are made during lifetime but are effective only at death.[29]

Revocable Transfers

The gross estate includes the value of property interests transferred by the decedent if the enjoyment of the property transferred was subject, at the date of the decedent's death, to any power of the decedent to *alter, amend, revoke, or terminate* the transfer (i.e., it is more like a promise to pay). Transfers of this sort typically occur because the donor is not able or ready to part with the asset without qualifications (e.g., due to reservations about future events or about how the donee will use the transferred asset).

Joint Interests

The Federal *estate tax treatment* of tenancies in common or of community property follows the logical approach of taxing only the portion of the property that was controlled by the deceased owner's will.

[29]§§ 2035–2037 and 2041.

Homer, Wilma, and Thelma acquire a tract of land, ownership listed as tenants in common, each party furnishing $200,000 of the $600,000 purchase price. When the property is worth $900,000, Homer dies. If Homer's undivided interest in the property is 33⅓%, the gross estate includes $300,000. This one-third interest is the same amount that passes to Homer's heirs.

Unless the parties have provided otherwise, each tenant is deemed to own an interest equal to the portion of the original consideration they furnished. The parties in Example 27 could have provided that Homer would receive an undivided half interest in the property although he contributed only one-third of the purchase price. In that case, Wilma and Thelma have made a gift to Homer when the tenancy was created, and Homer's gross estate includes $450,000.

For certain joint tenancies, the tax consequences are different. All of the property is included in the deceased co-owner's gross estate unless it can be proved that the surviving co-owners contributed to the cost of the property.[30] If a contribution can be shown, the amount to be *excluded* is calculated by the following formula.

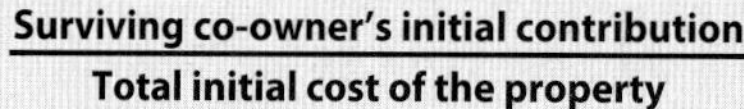

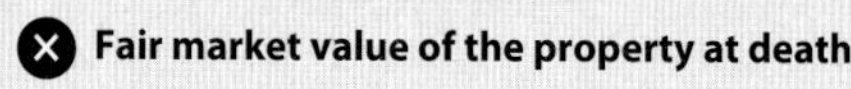

In computing a survivor's contribution, any funds received as a gift *from the deceased co-owner* and applied to the cost of the property are counted as zero.

Example 28

Keith and Steve (father and son) acquire a tract of land, ownership listed as joint tenancy with right of survivorship. Keith furnished $400,000 and Steve $200,000 of the $600,000 purchase price. Of the $200,000 provided by Steve, $100,000 had previously been received as a gift from Keith. When the property is worth $900,000, Keith dies. Because only $100,000 of Steve's contribution can be counted (the other $100,000 was received as a gift from Keith), Steve has furnished only one-sixth ($100,000 ÷ $600,000) of the cost. Thus, Keith's gross estate must include five-sixths of $900,000, or $750,000.

This result presumes that Steve can prove that he did in fact make the $100,000 contribution. In the absence of such proof, the full value of the property is included in Keith's gross estate. Keith's death makes Steve the immediate owner of the property by virtue of the right of survivorship.

If the co-owners receive the property as a gift or bequest *from another*, each donee owner is deemed to have contributed to the cost (or value on date of death) of their own interest.

The Big Picture

Example 29

Return to the facts of *The Big Picture* on p. 29-1. During his lifetime, Peter Hood purchased timberland listing title as follows: "John and Helen Hood as equal tenants in common." John's basis in the property is one-half of Peter's cost. Upon John's death, one-half of the value of the timberland is included in his gross estate.

The Big Picture

Example 30

Return to the facts of *The Big Picture* on p. 29-1. In her will, Martha leaves the Hood family residence to her children (John and Helen) as joint tenants with right of survivorship. John's income tax basis in the residence is one-half of the value on Martha's death. Upon John's later death, one-half of the value at that time is included in his gross estate. Under the right of survivorship, outright ownership of the residence goes to Helen and none of the property passes to John's heirs.

---

[30] § 2040(a).

To simplify the joint ownership rules for *married persons*, an automatic inclusion rule applies upon the death of the first joint-owner spouse to die. Regardless of the amount contributed by each spouse, one-half of the value of the property is included in the gross estate of the spouse who dies first. The special rule eliminates the need to trace the source of contributions and recognizes that any inclusion in the gross estate likely is neutralized by the marital deduction.

The Big Picture

Example 31

Return to the facts of *The Big Picture* on p. 29-1. Recall that after his divorce from Hannah, John married Ashley. Because Hannah kept John's prior home as part of the property settlement (see Example 12), he purchased a new residence. He listed title to the property as "John and Ashley Hood, tenancy by the entirety with right of survivorship." Upon John's death, only one-half of the value of the property is included in his gross estate.

If Ashley had died first, one-half of the value of the residence would have been included in her gross estate, even though she made no contribution to its cost.

Whether a *gift* results when property is transferred into some form of joint ownership depends on the consideration furnished by each of the contributing parties for the ownership interest acquired.

Joint Ownership and the Gift Tax

Example 32

Brenda and Sarah purchase real estate as tenants in common. Of the $800,000 purchase price, Brenda furnishes $600,000, and Sarah furnishes $200,000. If each is an equal owner in the property, Brenda has made a gift to Sarah of $200,000.

Example 33

Ava purchases real estate for $900,000, the title to the property being listed as follows: "Ava, Sylvia, and Dan as joint tenants with the right of survivorship." If under state law the parties are deemed to be equal owners in the property, Ava is treated as having made gifts of $300,000 to Sylvia and $300,000 to Dan.

Several important exceptions exist to the general rule that gift treatment is triggered by the creation of a joint ownership with disproportionate interests resulting from unequal consideration. First, if the transfer involves a joint bank account, there is no gift at the time of the contribution. A gift occurs when a noncontributing party withdraws funds provided by the other joint tenant. Second, the same rule applies to the purchase of U.S. savings bonds.[31]

When a Gift Occurs

Example 34

Cynthia deposits $400,000 in a bank account under the names of Cynthia and Carla as joint tenants. Both Cynthia and Carla have the right to withdraw funds from the account without the other's consent. Cynthia has not made a gift to Carla when the account is established.

Example 35

Assume the same facts as in Example 34. At some later date, Carla withdraws $100,000 from the account for her own use. At this point, Cynthia has made a gift to Carla of $100,000.

---

[31]Reg. § 25.2511–1(h)(4).

When a Gift Occurs

Example 36

Wesley purchases a U.S. savings bond that he registers in the names of Wesley and Harriet. No gift takes place when Wesley buys the bond. If Harriet redeems the bond and takes the proceeds as her own, a gift from Wesley occurs at that time. If Harriet does not redeem the bond and Wesley dies, the fair market value of the bond is included in Wesley's gross estate.

Life Insurance

Life insurance includes policies of various forms, group life insurance, and travel and accident insurance.[32]

Merely purchasing a life insurance contract with someone else designated as the beneficiary does not constitute a gift to the beneficiary. As long as the purchaser still owns the policy, nothing yet has passed to the beneficiary.

The gross estate includes life insurance on the decedent's life if:

- The policy's proceeds are receivable by the estate, or
- The decedent possessed any of the incidents of ownership in the policy.

In this connection, *incidents of ownership* means not only the ownership of the policy but also the right of the insured or their estate to the economic benefits of the policy. Thus, it includes the power to change beneficiaries, pledge the policy for a loan, or surrender or cancel the policy.[33]

Life Insurance in the Gross Estate

Example 37

At the time of death, Broderick was the insured under a policy (face amount of $1,000,000) owned by Gregory with Demi as the designated beneficiary. Broderick took out the policy five years ago and immediately transferred it as a gift to Gregory. Under the assignment, Broderick transferred all rights in the policy except the right to change beneficiaries.

Broderick died without having exercised this right, and the policy proceeds are paid to Demi. Broderick's retention of an incident of ownership in the policy (i.e., the right to change beneficiaries) causes $1,000,000 to be included in his gross estate, even though he never exercised the right.

Example 38

Kurt purchases an insurance policy on his own life that he transfers to Olga. Kurt retains no control over the policy (such as the power to change beneficiaries). In these circumstances, Kurt has made a gift to Olga. Furthermore, if Kurt continues to pay the premiums on the transferred policy, each payment constitutes a separate gift.

Life insurance on the life of another individual owned by a decedent at the time of death is included in the gross estate as an asset owned by the decedent. The amount includible is the replacement value of the policy.[34] Inclusion of the face amount of the policy is inappropriate; the policy has not yet matured.

[32]Reg. § 20.2042–1(a)(1). As to travel and accident insurance, see *Comm. v. Estate of Noel*, 65–1 USTC ¶12,311, 15 AFTR 2d 1397, 85 S.Ct. 1238.

[33]Reg. § 20.2042–1(c)(2).

[34]Reg. § 20.2031–8(a)(1).

At the time of his death, Luigi owned a life insurance policy on the life of Benito, face amount of $500,000 and replacement value of $50,000, with Sofia as the designated beneficiary. Because the policy had not matured before Luigi's death, only $50,000 (the policy's replacement value) is included in Luigi's gross estate.

Under certain conditions, the death of the insured may constitute a gift to the beneficiary of the proceeds. This typically occurs when the owner of the policy is not the insured.

Miguel owns an insurance policy on the life of Frank, with Tracy as the designated beneficiary. Up until the time of Frank's death, Miguel retained the right to change the beneficiary of the policy. The proceeds paid to Tracy by the insurance company by reason of Frank's death constitute a gift from Miguel to Tracy.[35]

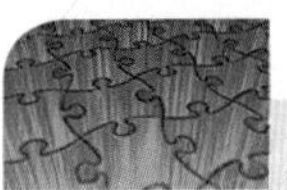

Concept Summary 29.4

Federal Estate Tax Provisions—Gross Estate

1. The starting point for applying the Federal estate tax is to determine which assets are subject to tax. Such assets comprise a decedent's gross estate.
2. The gross estate includes all assets owned by the decedent, regardless of where they are located.
3. Upon the death of a joint tenant, the full value of the property is included in the gross estate unless the survivor(s) made a contribution toward the cost of the property. Spouses include half of the value of the property in the gross estate of the first tenant to die.
4. The creation of joint ownership is subject to the gift tax when a tenant receives a lesser interest in the property than is warranted by the consideration furnished.
5. If the decedent is the insured, life insurance proceeds are included in the gross estate if the proceeds are paid to the estate, or if the decedent possessed incidents of ownership (e.g., the right to change beneficiaries) in the policy.

29-3b **Taxable Estate**

LO.7 **Describe the components of the taxable estate.**

After the gross estate has been determined, the next step is to compute the taxable estate. The **taxable estate** is the gross estate minus a number of available deductions. Almost 90 percent of all estate tax deductions relate to asset transfers to a charity or surviving spouse.

Expenses, Indebtedness, and Taxes

A deduction is allowed for funeral expenses, expenses incurred in administering property, claims against the estate, and unpaid mortgages and other charges against property included in the gross estate.

Administration expenses include commissions of the executor or administrator, attorney's fees of the estate, accountant's fees, court costs, and certain selling expenses for disposition of estate property.[36]

Claims against the estate include property taxes accrued before the decedent's death, unpaid income taxes on income received by the decedent before they died, and unpaid gift taxes on gifts made by the decedent before death.

[35] *Goodman v. Comm.*, 46–1 USTC ¶10,275, 34 AFTR 1534, 156 F.2d 218 (CA–2).

[36] The estate deducts one-half of expenses incurred in administering community property. *U.S. v. Stapf*, 63–2 USTC ¶12,192, 12 AFTR 2d 6326, 84 S.Ct. 248.

The decedent's unpaid pledge or subscription in favor of a charitable, religious, or educational organization is deductible to the extent that it would have been a deductible bequest.[37]

Deductible funeral expenses include the cost of interment or inurnment, the burial plot or vault, a gravestone, perpetual care of the grave site, and the transportation expense of the person bringing the body to the place of burial. No deduction is allowed for cemetery lots the decedent acquired before death, but the lots are not included in the decedent's gross estate as an asset of the decedent.

Losses

An estate tax deduction is allowed for losses from a casualty or theft incurred during the period when the estate is being settled. Any anticipated insurance recovery is taken into account in arriving at the amount of the deductible loss. Unlike the income tax, however, the deduction is not limited by a dollar or a percentage amount.

As is true of certain administration expenses, a casualty or theft loss of estate property can be claimed as an income tax deduction on the fiduciary return of the estate (Form 1041; see text Sections 30-3c and 30-3d). But a double deduction prohibition applies, and claiming the income tax deduction eliminates any estate tax deduction.[38]

Transfers to Charity

A transfer tax deduction is allowed for the value of the decedent's gross estate property that is transferred by the decedent through testamentary disposition to (or for the use of) organizations that would qualify a donor for an income tax deduction, with the following chief exceptions:[39]

- Certain nonprofit cemetery associations qualify for income tax but not transfer tax purposes.
- Non-U.S. charities may qualify under the transfer tax but not for the income tax.

No deduction is allowed unless the charitable bequest is specified by a provision in the decedent's will or the transfer was made before death and the property is subsequently included in the gross estate. Generally, a deduction does not materialize when an individual dies without a will.

The amount of the bequest to charity must be mandatory and cannot be left to someone else's discretion. It is, however, permissible to allow another person—such as the executor of the estate—to choose which specific charity will receive the donation.

The Big Picture

Example 41

Return to the facts of *The Big Picture* on p. 29-1. After John's accident, he was in the intensive care unit at a local hospital. Although physically incapacitated, he was mentally alert. In early December, he reviewed his financial affairs with his attorney and CPA and executed a new will. His prior will, drawn up several years ago, contained a bequest to the Hood Scholarship Foundation (HSF), an organization created by Peter (John's father) to provide financial assistance to community college students. HSF never applied for a tax exemption as a charity.

John's new will kept the bequest, but only if the IRS approved HSF as a charity. John's CPA arranged to have all of John's medical expenses (e.g., hospital and physicians) paid as incurred. He also advised John to make a substantial payment on his property taxes and state income taxes. All of these provisions would reduce John's taxable estate.

[37] § 2053(c)(1)(A) and Reg. § 20.2053–5.

[38] §§ 642(g) and 2054.

[39] §§ 170, 2055, and 2522.

Marital Deduction

The **marital deduction** allows spouses to arrange their financial affairs without Federal gift or estate tax consequences. Assets can pass between them without any immediate gift or estate tax liability, with a deduction allowed to offset an otherwise taxable gift or estate amount. Used well, the marital deduction can be seen as a means by which to reduce the present value of the couple's transfer tax liability: the gift or bequest places the asset into the hands of (perhaps) a younger or healthier spouse, such that the Federal transfer tax on the asset is deferred until the survivor dies, at a later date.

The marital deduction is available to all married couples. Registered domestic partnerships, civil unions, and similar formal relationships *are not* marriages, so no marital deduction can be claimed.

Passing Requirement The marital deduction is allowed only for property that is included in the deceased spouse's gross estate *and* that passes or has passed to the surviving spouse.[40]

The Big Picture

Example 42

Return to the facts of *The Big Picture* on p. 29-1 and Example 41. In reviewing John's prior will, the parties discovered that one of the main beneficiaries was Hannah, John's first wife. The new will substituted Ashley (John's present wife) for Hannah, thereby preserving the marital deduction.

Property that *passes* from the decedent to the surviving spouse includes any interest received as, for example, (1) the decedent's heir or donee, (2) the decedent's surviving tenant by the entirety or joint tenant, or (3) the beneficiary of insurance on the life of the decedent.

At the time of his death in the current year, Tao owned an insurance policy on his own life (face amount of $500,000) with Ella (his spouse) as the designated beneficiary. Tao and Ella also owned real estate (worth $600,000) as tenants by the entirety (Tao had furnished all of the purchase price). As to these transfers, $800,000 ($500,000 + $300,000) is included in Tao's gross estate, and this amount represents the property that passes to Ella for purposes of the marital deduction, under the terms of the insurance contract and the state law survivorship feature.

When a property interest passing to the surviving spouse is subject to a mortgage or other debt, only the net value of the interest after reduction by the amount of the debt qualifies for the marital deduction.

In his will, Jacob leaves real estate (fair market value of $500,000) to Martin, his spouse. If the real estate is subject to a mortgage of $100,000 (upon which Jacob was personally liable), the marital deduction is limited to $400,000 ($500,000 − $100,000). The $100,000 mortgage is deductible as an obligation of the decedent (Jacob).

---

[40]§§ 2056 and 2523.

Disclaimers can affect the amount passing to the surviving spouse. If, for example, the surviving spouse receives the remainder of the estate after all other obligations have been met, a disclaimer by another heir increases the amount passing to the surviving spouse. This, in turn, increases the amount of the marital deduction allowed.

Terminable Interest Limitation Certain interests in property passing from the deceased spouse to the surviving spouse are referred to as **terminable interests**. Such an interest will terminate or fail after the passage of time, upon the happening of some contingency, or upon the failure of some event to occur. Examples are life estates, annuities, receivables for terms of years, and patents. A terminable interest does not qualify for the marital deduction.[41]

The marital deduction merely postpones the transfer tax upon the death of the first spouse, and it operates to shift any such tax to the surviving spouse. Thus, it is appropriate that the marital deduction is not available where the surviving spouse can enjoy the property and still pass it to another with zero Federal estate tax consequences.

Olivia's gross estate includes an installment note receivable with payments scheduled to occur for five more years, as of the date of her death. Under Olivia's will, the note passes to her spouse Ethan, whose life expectancy is 17 years. The note is a terminable interest, and no marital deduction is allowed in computing Olivia's taxable estate. Because it appears that no asset will be placed in Ethan's gross estate as to the note, the marital deduction for Olivia's estate is disallowed.

Consistent with the objective of the terminable interest rule, the marital deduction is allowed for transfers of **qualified terminable interest property (QTIP)**. Such property passes from one spouse to another by gift or at death; the transferee-spouse holds an income interest for life in the QTIP assets.[42]

If these conditions are met, an election can be made to claim a marital deduction as to the QTIP assets. The election is irrevocable.[43] Then the fair market value of the property on the date of death (or alternate valuation date) is included in the gross estate of the second spouse to die.[44]

In this manner, the QTIP election "plays fair" with the transferred income interest: a marital deduction is claimed on the first death, and the asset is included in the gross estate of the second death.[45]

Clyde dies and provides in his will that certain assets (fair market value of $3,000,000) are to be transferred to a trust under which Lily (Clyde's spouse) receives the income of the trust for her life, with the remainder passing to their children upon Lily's death. Presuming that all of the preceding requirements are satisfied and Clyde's executor so elects, his estate receives a marital deduction of $3,000,000.

Lily dies when the trust assets are worth $8,400,000. This amount is included in her gross estate.

[41] §§ 2056(b)(1) and 2523(b)(1).

[42] §§ 2523(f) and 2056(b)(7).

[43] § 2056(b)(7)(B)(v).

[44] § 2044.

[45] If the surviving spouse disposes of the property before death, a Federal gift tax applies. § 2519.

Citizenship and Residency of Spouses Property passing to a surviving spouse who is not a U.S. citizen is not eligible for the estate tax marital deduction.[46] Similarly, no gift tax marital deduction is allowed where the spouse is not a U.S. citizen.[47] However, the annual exclusion for these gift transfers is $175,000 for 2023.[48]

State Taxes at Death

About a dozen states, and a number of cities, counties, and similar jurisdictions, levy taxes when property passes to another party because of the death of a decedent. These taxes can be assessed at marginal rates of almost 20 percent, and the applicable exemption amounts typically are less than that for the Federal estate tax. A deduction is allowed against the decedent's Federal taxable estate for estate and inheritance taxes paid to such jurisdictions.[49]

The deduction for taxes paid to a state at death mitigates the effect of subjecting property to multiple taxes payable because of a death.

29-3c Estate Tax Credits

LO.8

Calculate the Federal estate tax liability.

Other credits are allowed in computing the Federal estate tax liability.

Credit for Tax on Prior Transfers

Suppose that Nancy owns some property that she passes at death to Lisa. Shortly thereafter, Lisa dies and passes the property to Rita. Assuming that both estates are subject to the Federal estate tax, the successive deaths result in an expensive and undesirable double taxation of the same asset.

To mitigate the multiple taxation that might result from successive unanticipated deaths, a credit is allowed for Federal estate tax paid on prior, overlapping transfers.[50] Here, Lisa's estate may be able to claim as a credit some of the taxes paid by Nancy's estate.

The credit is limited to the lesser of the following amounts:

1. The amount of the Federal estate tax attributable to the transferred property in the transferor's estate.
2. The amount of the Federal estate tax attributable to the transferred property in the decedent's estate.

The credit is allowed when the property is subjected to Federal estate taxation "too soon" after it was taxed at the first death. Exhibit 29.2 shows the relationship between the credit allowed and the time interval between the two deaths.

Exhibit 29.2 Credit for Tax on Prior Transfers

Interval between Deaths	Credit Allowed
Within 2 years	100%
Within 3 to 4 years	80%
Within 5 to 6 years	60%
Within 7 to 8 years	40%
Within 9 to 10 years	20%

[46] § 2056(d)(1).

[47] § 2523(i).

[48] § 2523(i)(2).

[49] § 2058.

[50] § 2013.

Time Interval between Successive Deaths

Example 47

Under Nancy's will, Lisa inherits property. One year later, Lisa dies. Assume that the estate tax attributable to the inclusion of the property in Nancy's gross estate was $160,000 and that the estate tax attributable to the inclusion of the property in Lisa's gross estate is $120,000. Under these circumstances, Lisa's estate claims a credit against the estate tax of $120,000 (refer to limitation 2).

Example 48

Assume the same facts as in Example 47, except that Lisa dies three years after Nancy. The credit now is 80% of $120,000, or $96,000 (see Exhibit 29.2).

Credit for Foreign Taxes Paid at Death

A credit is allowed against the estate tax for any estate, inheritance, legacy, or succession tax paid to another country.[51] The credit is allowed for taxable estate property that is situated outside the United States. The credit is limited to the lesser of the following amounts:

- The amount of the foreign tax paid at death, attributable to the property situated in the country imposing the tax and included in the decedent's gross estate.
- The amount of the Federal estate tax attributable to property situated in the other country, subject to estate or inheritance tax in that country, and included in the decedent's gross estate.

Similar credits are allowable under estate/gift tax treaties with a number of countries. If a credit is allowed under either the provisions of the Code or the provisions of a treaty, the credit that is most beneficial to the estate should be claimed.[52]

Global Tax Issues — Treaty Relief Is Not Abundant!

One means of mitigating double taxation at the international level is to take advantage of treaty provisions. A treaty will determine which country has primary taxing rights, and this may depend on such factors as the domicile of the decedent or the nature of the property involved (e.g., personalty or realty). Unfortunately, the United States has estate tax conventions with only these countries: Australia*, Austria*, Canada, Denmark*, Finland, France*, Germany*, Greece, Ireland, Italy, Japan*, the Netherlands, South Africa, Switzerland, and the United Kingdom*. In contrast, almost 70 countries have income tax treaties with the United States. Thus, treaty relief in the estate tax area is not as widespread as it is with income taxes.

*Indicates the existence of a gift tax treaty as well.

[51] § 2014.

[52] Reg. § 20.2014–4 illustrates the selection process when both the § 2014 credit and an estate tax treaty are involved.

29-3d **Procedural Matters**

A Federal estate tax return, if required, is due nine months after the date of the decedent's death.[53] The time limit applies to all estates regardless of the nationality or residence of the decedent. Not infrequently, an executor will request and obtain from the IRS an extension of time for filing the Form 706 (estate tax return).[54] An *automatic* six-month extension of time to file the estate tax return can be claimed.

Concept Summary 29.5

Federal Estate Tax Provisions—Taxable Estate and Procedural Matters

1. In computing the taxable estate, certain deductions are allowed.
2. Deductions are permitted for various administration expenses (e.g., executor's commissions), professional fees (appraisal, accounting, and legal), debts of the decedent, certain unpaid taxes, and funeral expenses.
3. Casualty and theft losses occurring during the settlement of the estate and not compensated for by insurance can be deducted.
4. Charitable transfers are deductible if the designated organization holds qualified status with the IRS at the time of death.
5. Transfers to a surviving spouse yield a marital deduction if they do not violate the terminable interest rule. The terminable interest rule can be avoided by making a QTIP election.
6. A deduction is allowed for certain state and local taxes paid on account of a death.
7. If required, a Federal estate tax return (Form 706) must be filed within nine months of the date of the decedent's death. An extension for filing beyond this date is available.

29-4 **The Generation-Skipping Transfer Tax**

LO.9

Review and demonstrate the role of the generation-skipping transfer tax.

To discourage families from deferring Federal gift and estate taxes by transferring assets to very young beneficiaries, the tax law imposes an additional generation-skipping transfer tax (GSTT). The tax is added to any gift or estate tax that may be due. The GSTT attempts to collect a Federal transfer tax from a family at least once *every other* generation, by blood or marriage.

29-4a **Inter-Generational Transfers**

Previously, by structuring the transaction carefully, it was possible to bypass a generation or more of Federal gift and estate taxes.

Types of Generation-Skipping Transfers

Under his will, Edward creates a trust, life estate to Stephen (Edward's son) and remainder to Ava (Edward's granddaughter) upon Stephen's death. Edward is subject to the Federal estate tax, but no tax results upon Stephen's death. The result is that the property in trust skips a generation of transfer taxes.

[53] § 6075(a).

[54] § 6081.

Types of Generation-Skipping Transfers

Elena gives assets directly to Rodrigo (her grandson). The gift would circumvent any transfer taxes that would have resulted had the assets been channeled through Rodrigo's parents.

29-4b The Tax on Generation-Skipping Transfers

The GSTT is designed to preclude the avoidance of either the estate tax or the gift tax by making transfers that bypass the next lower generation. In the typical family setting, this involves transfers to grandchildren or younger individuals.

The GSTT is triggered by any of these three events: a taxable *termination* occurs, a taxable *distribution* takes place, or a *direct skip* is made.[55] Example 49 illustrates a termination event. Upon Stephen's death, the fair market value of the trust property that passes to Ava is subject to the GSTT (imposed on the trust). The GSTT will have the effect of reducing the amount Ava receives from the trust.

Example 50 illustrates a lifetime version of the direct skip event.[56] In this situation, the GSTT is imposed upon Elena when the gift is made to Rodrigo, because the gift skips over the generation of Rodrigo's parents.

The GSTT rate is the highest rate under the gift and estate tax schedules (i.e., 40 percent). The GSTT base is reduced by the same exemption equivalent amount that is available against the Federal estate and gift tax (see Exhibit 29.1).[57] For a donor who is married, the election to split the gift (as under § 2513) can double the amount of the GSTT exemption.[58]

The tax base also is reduced by the annual gift tax exclusion and the charitable and marital deductions. The GSTT does not apply to gifts made for political, medical, and educational purposes, if the corresponding gift tax exemption applies. A credit is allowed for certain state-level GST taxes paid.

Generations are assigned by birth or marriage. For other parties, a generation is 25 years long. Individuals born within 12½ years are in the same generation. Individuals born more than 12½ years but not more than 37½ years after the transferor are in the first generation below the transferor, and each succeeding 25 years is a later generation. The GSTT computation is made on a schedule that is part of Form 706 or 709 (i.e., the gift or estate tax return to which it relates).

Mother Anna (age 60) and son Barry (age 40) are in two successive GSTT generations. Father Carl (age 60) and daughter Denny (age 15) are in two successive generations.

Spouses E'Toin (age 60) and Fantasia (age 58) are in the same generation. Spouses Gerardo (age 60) and Hermosa (age 20) are in the same generation.

Unrelated individuals Ishu (age 60) and Jiva (age 50) are in the same generation. Unrelated individuals Kong (age 60) and Lian (age 12) are two generations apart.

LO.10

Recognize strategies to minimize Federal gift and estate taxes.

29-5 Tax Planning

29-5a The Federal Gift Tax

For gifts that generate a tax, consideration must be given to the present value to the donor of the gift taxes paid. Because the donor loses the use of these funds, the expected interval between a gift (the imposition of the gift tax) and death (the imposition of the estate tax) may make the gift less attractive from an economic standpoint.

[55] § 2611.

[56] § 2612(c)(1).

[57] § 2631(c).

[58] § 2652(a)(2).

On the plus side, however, are the estate tax savings that result from any gift tax paid. Because these funds are no longer in the gross estate of the donor (except for certain gifts within three years of death), the estate tax thereon is avoided.

Gifts possess distinct advantages over transfers made at death. First, and often most important, income from the property is generally shifted to the donee. If the donee is in a lower bracket than the donor, the family unit will save on income taxes. Second, the proper pacing of gifts can further cut down the Federal gift tax by maximizing the number of annual exclusions available. Third, many states impose some type of tax at death, but only a relatively few impose a gift tax. Thus, a gift may completely avoid a state transfer tax.

In minimizing gift tax liability in lifetime asset transfers, the optimum use of the annual exclusion can have significant results. Because a new annual exclusion is available each year, spacing gifts over multiple years increases the amount that can be transferred free of gift tax.

Example 52

Starting in 2014, Cora makes gifts in the amount of the annual exclusion to each of her five grandchildren. Taking into account the changes in the amount of the annual exclusion allowed, Cora will have transferred $745,000 through 2023 with no Federal gift tax consequences.

Years		Amount of Exclusion
2023	$17,000 (annual exclusion) × 5 (number of donees) × 1 (number of years)	$85,000
2022	$16,000 (annual exclusion) × 5 (number of donees) × 1 (number of years)	$80,000
2018–2021	$15,000 (annual exclusion) × 5 (number of donees) × 4 (number of years)	$300,000
2014–2017	$14,000 (annual exclusion) × 5 (number of donees) × 4 (number of years)	$280,000

For married donors, the election to split gifts can double the amount of a tax-free transfer; see text Section 29-2e. Referring to Example 52, if Cora is married and her husband Julio makes the gift-splitting election for each year, $1.49 million [$745,000 (amount allowed Cora) × 2 (number of donors)] can be transferred with no gift tax consequences.

29-5b The Federal Estate Tax

Controlling the Amount of the Gross Estate

Presuming that an estate tax problem is anticipated, the starting point for planning purposes is to reduce the size of the potential gross estate. Aside from initiating a program of lifetime giving, as described next, several other possibilities exist.

Estate taxes can be reduced either by decreasing the size of the gross estate or by increasing the total allowable deductions. The lower the taxable estate, the less estate tax is generated. Planning with deductions includes:

- Making proper use of the marital deduction.
- Working effectively with the charitable deduction.
- Taking advantage of the bypass amount.
- Optimizing other deductions and losses allowed (discussed in text Section 18-3b).

The Marital Deduction

When planning for the estate tax marital deduction, both tax and nontax factors are taken into account. As to the present value of taxes deferred, taxpayers should try to postpone estate taxation as long as possible. Usually, by maximizing the marital deduction on the death of the first spouse to die, taxes are saved and the surviving spouse can reduce the future estate by entering into a program of lifetime gifts. By making optimum use of the annual gift tax exclusion, considerable amounts can be shifted without incurring *any* transfer tax.

The Charitable Deduction

As a general guide to obtaining overall tax savings, contributions to charities during a taxpayer's life are preferred over a charitable bequest (a transfer via a will). For example, an individual who gives $200,000 to a qualified charity during their life secures an income tax deduction, uses the gift tax deduction to avoid any gift tax, and reduces the gross estate by the amount of the gift. On the other hand, if the $200,000 is transferred by will after the donor's death to the charity, no individual income tax deduction is available, and the amount of the gift is includible in the decedent's gross estate (although later deducted for estate tax purposes). In short, the lifetime contribution provides a double tax benefit (income tax deduction plus reduced estate taxes) at no gift tax cost.

An individual may be able to accelerate an income and gift tax charitable deduction with the use of a *donor-advised fund* (DAF). Many banks and mutual fund companies offer the ability to create a DAF. The donor makes an irrevocable gift to the DAF, claiming an immediate income tax deduction for the amount of the cash or the fair market value of any securities transferred. The DAF holds the gift property; it must distribute the assets to qualified charities, but it will do so only when the donor later advises the fund as to how much to contribute and to which charity. In this way, the donor claims a charitable deduction (perhaps long) before the charity receives the gift; as a result, the present value of the deduction is increased. The donor cannot reclaim the gifted assets, but retains control over their disposition while held by the DAF.

DAFs constitute over 10 percent of annual charitable giving. They hold over $230 billion in assets and typically pay out about 23 percent of that amount every year. The National Philanthropic Trust reports that the number of individual DAF accounts in the United States is now above 1.2 million.[59] A donor may find that a DAF simplifies the execution of a plan that involves gifts to several charities every year, without incurring the legal and administrative fees typical of a private foundation (see text Section 25-4).

On occasion, a charitable bequest depends on the issuance of a disclaimer by a noncharitable heir.[60] Usually this involves special types of property or collections where the decedent allows a noncharitable heir to choose whether to receive the property or allow it to transfer to the charity.

Use of Disclaimers in Charitable Bequests

Example 53

Megan specified in her will that her valuable art collection is to pass to her son Teddy. If Teddy refuses the gift, the collection passes to the local art museum. At the time the will was drawn, Megan knew that Teddy was not interested in owning the collection. If, after Megan's death, Teddy issues a timely disclaimer, the collection passes to the museum, and Megan's estate takes a charitable deduction for its estate tax value.

Paresh's will specifies that one-half of his disposable estate is to pass to his wife, Amanda. The remainder of his property passes to a specified qualified charitable organization. If Amanda issues a timely disclaimer after Paresh's death, all of the property passes to the charity and qualifies for the charitable deduction.

[59] See **nptrust.org/reports/daf-report/**.

[60] As noted in text Section 29-2b, a disclaimer is a refusal to accept the property. If the disclaimer is timely made, the property is not treated as having passed through the person issuing the disclaimer, and a gift tax is avoided.

Has Teddy in Example 53 acted wisely if he issues the disclaimer in favor of the museum? Although the disclaimer will provide Megan's estate with a deduction for the value of the art collection, consider the income tax deduction alternative. If Teddy accepts the bequest, he still can dispose of the collection (and fulfill his mother's philanthropic objectives) through a donation to the museum. As a result, he obtains an income tax deduction of his own. Whether this plan reduces taxes for the family depends on a comparison of Megan's and Teddy's marginal income tax rates.

The use of a disclaimer in Example 54 would be sheer folly. It would not reduce Paresh's estate tax; it would merely substitute a charitable deduction for the marital deduction. Whether or not Amanda issues a disclaimer, no estate taxes will be due. Amanda should accept her bequest and, if she is so inclined, make lifetime gifts of it to a qualified charity. In so doing, she could generate an income tax deduction for herself.

Taking Advantage of the Bypass Amount

The bypass amount, also known as the exclusion amount or the exemption equivalent, is the amount that can pass free of a transfer tax due to the unified credit. Generally, this amount of property should be transferred to children or other parties for whom the transfer does not produce an estate or gift tax deduction.

Year	Bypass Amount
2021	$11,700,000
2022	12,060,000
2023	12,920,000

Spousal Transfers In the past, a bypass amount frequently was wasted when the first spouse died. Love, affection, and obligation often compel a spouse to leave all of their assets to the survivor.

Ethan and Hope are married, and each has a net worth of $3,500,000. Upon Ethan's prior death in 2009, his will passed his entire net worth to Hope; this often is called an "I Love You" will. Although Ethan avoided any Federal estate tax due to the marital deduction, he wasted his bypass amount and concentrated additional assets in Hope's potential estate.

Under current Federal estate tax law, the bypass amount is "portable," meaning that the deceased spousal unused exclusion (DSUE) amount is available to the surviving spouse.[61] This provision effectively treats a married couple as a single unit for estate tax purposes; lifetime transfers between spouses are not necessary to make use of the combined bypass amounts. Portability is not allowed for the exemption in computing the tax on generation-skipping transfers.

Assume the same facts as in Example 55, except that Ethan dies in 2021 with a net worth of $15,000,000, all of which he passes to Hope. Presuming a proper election was made on his return, Ethan's DSUE amount transfers to his wife. Should Hope die in 2023, her exclusion amount would be $24,620,000 [$11,700,000 (Ethan's DSUE amount) + $12,920,000 (her own exclusion amount)].

[61] § 2010(c). Portability is available for those who die after 2010.

If a surviving spouse is predeceased by more than one spouse, the DSUE amount that is available for the surviving spouse is limited to the unused exclusion of the last surviving spouse.

Use of Disclaimers to Maximize the Benefits of the Bypass Amount In some cases, it may be possible to control the bypass amount by the careful use of disclaimers.

Using Disclaimers

Deepak dies in 2023, leaving an estate of $19,000,000. He is survived by his wife, Emma, and an adult daughter, Riya. Deepak's will passes $10,000,000 to Emma and the remainder ($9,000,000) to Riya. Emma disclaims $3,920,000 of her inheritance, increasing the amount passing to Riya to $12,920,000. This delays the payment of Federal estate tax on the bypass amount until Riya's death, decreasing the present value of the tax.

Assume the same facts as in Example 57, except that Deepak's will passes $14,000,000 to his daughter (Riya) and the remainder to his wife (Emma). Riya disclaims $1,080,000 of her inheritance, thereby transferring to Riya only the bypass amount ($12,920,000); the disclaimed amount passes to Emma and qualifies for the marital deduction, eliminating all of the current-year transfer tax.

Both examples reflect the wise use of disclaimers. In Example 57, Emma's disclaimer has the effect of increasing Riya's inheritance from Deepak to $12.92 million, fully using the allowable bypass amount for the year. If the disclaimer is not desired and only $9 million passes to Riya, the $3.92 million unused bypass amount still passes to Emma as a DSUE.

In Example 58, Riya eliminates any estate tax on $1.08 million (the excess over the $12.92 million bypass amount) by shifting it to Emma, the remainder beneficiary. Because that party is the surviving spouse, the $1.08 million is sheltered from current estate tax by the marital deduction.

Proper Handling of Other Deductions and Losses under §§ 2053 and 2054

Many estate-related deductions and losses may be claimed either as estate tax deductions or as income tax deductions by the estate on the fiduciary return (Form 1041), but not both.[62] The income tax deduction is not allowed unless the estate tax deduction is waived. It is possible for these deductions to be divided between the two returns.

In situations where the taxpayer has a terminal illness (i.e., death is imminent), it may be possible to shift some upcoming expenses to obtain a lifetime income tax benefit. For example, accrued medical expenses can be paid prior to death if they will be deductible on the decedent's final income tax return. The funds used to pay these expenses are not part of the gross estate, so the taxable estate is correspondingly reduced, and the estate tax savings still exist. Rate differentials and a present value analysis should be considered before these techniques are carried out.

[62] § 642(g) and Reg. § 20.2053–1(d).

Refocus on The Big Picture

An Eventful and Final Year

KELENY/SHUTTERSTOCK.COM

As to their divorce, John was able to carry out a property settlement with Hannah without incurring any gift tax consequences (see Example 12). Both Helen and John acted wisely when they chose to disclaim most of their inheritance from their mother. By making the disclaimers, they were able to pass the property to their children without a transfer tax being imposed (see Examples 13 and 14).

John's retirement plan benefits and any proceeds paid under his life insurance policy are included in his gross estate (see Example 26).

John's pre-death planning was highly advantageous in several respects.

- By drawing up a new will, the charitable and marital deductions were retained (see Examples 41 and 42).
- By prepaying state and local property and income taxes and staying current on medical expenses, John improved his Federal income tax position (see Example 41). He also avoided any estate taxes on the amounts used to pay these expenses.

Key Terms

Alternate valuation date, 29-5
Annual exclusion, 29-10
Bypass amount, 29-5
Community property, 29-6
Deceased spousal unused exclusion (DSUE) election, 29-5
Disclaimer, 29-9
Exclusion amount, 29-5
Exemption equivalent, 29-5
Future interest, 29-10
Gross estate, 29-14
Joint tenants, 29-6
Marital deduction, 29-21
Probate estate, 29-14
Qualified terminable interest property (QTIP), 29-22
Taxable estate, 29-19
Taxable gift, 29-3
Tenants by the entirety, 29-6
Tenants in common, 29-6
Terminable interests, 29-22
Unified transfer tax, 29-2
Unified transfer tax credit, 29-4

Discussion Questions

1. **LO.1** How does the Federal unified transfer tax differ from an income tax?

2. **LO.1** Kim, a wealthy Korean national, is advised by his physicians to have an operation performed at the Mayo Clinic in Minnesota. Kim is hesitant to come to the United States because of the possible tax consequences. If the procedure is not successful, Kim does not want his wealth in Korea to be subject to the Federal estate tax. Are Kim's concerns justified? Explain. *Critical Thinking*

3. **LO.1** Felipe will incur a $1,000,000 Federal transfer tax when he passes a plot of land to Barbara, an unrelated friend. Felipe's after-tax rate of return on his real estate investments is 3%. Compute the present value of the transfer tax if:
   a. Felipe transfers the land to Barbara as a lifetime taxable gift today.
   b. Felipe transfers the land to Barbara through his will after his death 20 years from now, as a gross estate asset.

Communications 4. **LO.1, 2, 3, 4** Prepare a list of points to guide a discussion about how the time value of money affects the application of the Federal unified transfer taxes.

Critical Thinking 5. **LO.2, 4, 5** Regarding the formula for the Federal gift tax (see Concept Summary 29.1), comment on the following observations:

a. The annual exclusion is adjusted each year for inflation.

b. The charitable and marital deductions play an important role.

c. Some gratuitous transfers might not be subject to the gift tax.

6. **LO.3, 6** Regarding the formula for the Federal estate tax (see Concept Summary 29.2), comment on the following:

a. The gross estate includes only property interests owned by the decedent at the time of death.

b. The gross estate is not the same as the probate estate.

c. Taxable estate × Applicable unified transfer tax rate = Estate tax due.

7. **LO.3** As to the alternate valuation date for asset transfers at death, comment on the following:

a. The justification for the election.

b. The main heir prefers the date of death value.

c. An estate asset is sold seven months after the decedent's death.

d. Effect of the election on the income tax basis in the property received by the heir.

Critical Thinking 8. **LO.4, 6** At a local bank, Jack purchases for $100,000 a five-year CD listing title as follows: "Meredith, payable on death to Briana." Four years later, Meredith dies. Briana, Meredith's daughter, then redeems the CD when it matures. Discuss the transfer tax consequences if Meredith is:

a. Jack's spouse.

b. Jack's ex-spouse.

c. Jack's girlfriend.

Critical Thinking 9. **LO.4** Derek dies intestate (i.e., without a will) and is survived by a daughter, Ruth, and a grandson, Ted (Ruth's son). Derek's assets include a large portfolio of stocks and bonds and a beach house. Ruth has considerable wealth of her own; Ted just finished college and is unemployed. Under applicable state law, children have first priority as to bequests, and then grandchildren.

a. To minimize future transfer taxes, what action might Ruth take? *Hint:* Use the term *disclaimer* in your answer, and consider the time value of money in your analysis.

b. What if Ruth wants only the beach house?

10. **LO.4** Qualified tuition programs under § 529 enjoy significant tax advantages. Describe these advantages with regard to the Federal:

a. Income tax.

b. Gift tax.

c. Estate tax.

11. **LO.5** Regarding the gift-splitting election, comment on the following:

a. What it is designed to accomplish.

b. How the election is made.

12. **LO.5** In connection with the filing of a Federal gift tax return, comment on the following:
    a. No Federal gift tax is due.
    b. The gift is between spouses.
    c. The donor obtained from the IRS an extension of time for filing their Federal income tax return.

13. **LO.4, 6** In each of the following independent situations, indicate whether the transfer is subject to the Federal gift tax.
    a. Asa contributes to his mayor's reelection campaign fund. The mayor has promised to get some of Asa's property rezoned from residential to commercial use.
    b. Mary Ann inherits her father's collection of guns and mounted animals. Five months later, she disclaims any interest in the mounted animals.
    c. Same as part (b). Ten months later, Mary Ann disclaims any interest in the guns.
    d. Haydon pays an orthodontist for the dental work performed on Michele, his cousin.
    e. Florence purchases a U.S. savings bond listing herself and Taylor (her daughter) as joint owners.
    f. Same as part (e). One year later, Taylor predeceases Florence.
    g. Same as part (e). One year later, Florence predeceases Taylor.

14. **LO.6** At the time of Emile's death, he was a joint tenant with Colette in a parcel of real estate. With regard to the inclusion of the realty in Emile's gross estate, comment on the following independent assumptions:
    a. Emile and Colette received the property as a gift from Douglas.
    b. Colette provided the entire purchase price of the property.
    c. Colette's contribution was received as a gift from Emile.
    d. Emile's contribution was derived from income generated by property he received as a gift from Colette.

15. **LO.6** With regard to "life insurance" in the context of the Federal estate tax, comment on the following:
    a. What the term includes (i.e., types of policies).
    b. The meaning of "incidents of ownership."
    c. When a gift occurs upon maturity of the policy.
    d. The tax consequences when the owner of the policy predeceases the insured and the beneficiary.

16. **LO.7** Troy predeceases his wife, Nell. Under his will, his estate is placed in trust, income for her life to Nell, remainder to his children. Regarding any marital deduction allowed to Troy's estate, comment on the effect of the following independent cases: Critical Thinking
    a. Troy's executor makes a QTIP election.
    b. Nell issues a timely disclaimer that rejects her income interest.

17. **LO.7** Bernice dies and, under a valid will, passes real estate to her surviving spouse. The real estate is subject to a mortgage. For estate tax purposes, how is any marital deduction determined? Can Bernice's estate deduct the mortgage in computing the taxable estate? Explain.

18. **LO.8** Three unmarried and childless sisters live together. All are of advanced age and in poor health, and each owns a significant amount of wealth. Each has a will that passes her property to her surviving sister(s) or, if no survivor, to their church. Within a period of two years and on different dates, all three sisters die. Discuss the Federal estate tax consequences of these deaths. Critical Thinking

Computational Exercises

19. **LO.3** Elizabeth made taxable gifts of $3,000,000 in 2021 and $14,000,000 in 2023. She paid no gift tax on the 2021 transfer. On what amount is the Federal gift tax computed for the 2023 gift?

20. **LO.3** Included in Mary's gross estate are the following assets:

	Fair Market Value	
	Date of Death	**Six Months Later**
Stock in Orange Corporation	$13,000,000	$13,100,000
Stock in Crimson Corporation	6,100,000	5,900,000

a. How much is included in her gross estate if the alternate valuation date is elected?

b. Instead, what if all of Mary's assets pass to her surviving spouse?

21. **LO.4** During the year, Rajeev makes the following transfers:

- $1,000 to his mayor's reelection campaign.
- $21,000 to his aunt, Ava, to reimburse her for what she paid the hospital for her gallbladder operation.
- $18,000 paid directly to the surgeon who performed Ava's gallbladder operation.
- $22,000 to purchase a used car for his son to use at college.

Which of these transfers are subject to the Federal gift tax? (Include the total amount, and disregard the annual exclusion.)

22. **LO.4** In 2016 and with $200,000, Alice purchases a CD at State Bank listing title as follows: "Alice, payable on proof of death to Clark." Alice dies in 2023, and Clark (Alice's nephew) redeems the CD (now worth $205,000). Disregarding the annual exclusion, what is Alice's gift to Clark in:

a. 2016?

b. 2023?

Critical Thinking

23. **LO.5** Christian wants to transfer as much as possible to his four adult married children (including spouses) and eight minor grandchildren without using any unified transfer tax credit.

a. What amount should Christian transfer to accomplish his tax goal?

b. What if Christian's spouse, Mia, joins in the gifts?

24. **LO.5** Noah and Sophia want to make a maximum contribution to their state's qualified tuition program (§ 529 plan) on behalf of their minor granddaughter, Amanda, without exceeding the annual Federal gift tax exclusion. How much can they transfer to the plan for Amanda without incurring a current Federal gift tax?

25. **LO.6, 7** At his death, Andrew was a participant in his employer's contributory qualified pension plan. His account reflects the following:

Employer's contribution	$1,000,000
Andrew's contribution	800,000
Income earned and accumulated by the plan	900,000

a. As to this plan, how much is included in Andrew's gross estate?

b. If the account balance is paid to Andrew's surviving spouse as the designated beneficiary, how much qualifies for the marital deduction?

26. **LO.6** Mason buys real estate for $1,500,000 and lists ownership as follows: "Mason and Dana, joint tenants with the right of survivorship." Mason dies first, when the real estate is valued at $2,000,000. How much is included in Mason's gross estate if Mason and Dana are:
   a. Brother and sister?
   b. Spouses?

27. **LO.6** Matthew owns an insurance policy (face amount of $500,000) on the life of Emily with Uma listed as the designated beneficiary. If Emily dies first and the $500,000 is paid to Uma, how much as to this policy is included in:
   a. Matthew's gross estate?
   b. Emily's gross estate?

28. **LO.7** Donald dies this year, and under his will, a trust is created in the amount of $6,000,000 with the following provisions: life estate to Cindy (Donald's spouse) and remainder to their children. His will also passes land (cost basis of $1,000,000 and fair market value of $3,000,000) to the Salvation Army for the site of a new homeless housing project.
   a. If a QTIP election is made, how much will these transactions reduce Donald's gross estate to arrive at the taxable estate?
   b. If a QTIP election is not made?

29. **LO.8** Under Emma's will, Addison inherits property that generates an estate tax of $800,000. Three years later, Addison dies and the property triggers an estate tax of $700,000. What is the credit for estate tax on prior transfers claimed by Addison's estate?

30. **LO.9** With $15,000,000, Paul's will creates a trust with the following provisions: life estate to Jacob (Paul's son) and remainder to Anastasia (Paul's granddaughter and Jacob's daughter). Jacob dies when the value of the trust is $28,000,000.
   a. Does a generation-skipping transfer result?
   b. If so, when and to what amount?

31. **LO.10** During 2023, Vasu wants to take advantage of the annual exclusion and make gifts to his 6 married children (plus their spouses) and his 12 minor grandchildren.
   a. How much property can Vasu give away this year without creating a taxable gift?
   b. How does your answer change if Vasu's spouse, Coleen, elects to join in making the gifts?

Problems

32. **LO.3** In each of the following independent situations, indicate whether the alternate valuation date can be elected. Explain why or why not.

	Value of Gross Estate		Estate Tax Liability	
Decedent	**Date of Death**	**Six Months Later**	**Date of Death**	**Six Months Later**
Jayden	$26,000,000	$25,900,000	$5,040,000	$5,039,000
Isabella	26,100,000	26,000,000	5,065,000	5,060,000
Liam	26,100,000	26,000,000	5,000,000	5,010,000
Lily	26,500,000	26,400,000	5,005,000	5,004,000

33. **LO.4, 6** Carl made the following transfers during the current year. What are Carl's taxable gifts for the current year? Disregard the annual exclusion.

- Transferred $900,000 in cash and securities to a trust, income to himself for life, and remainder to his three adult children by a former spouse. Carl can revoke the trust at any time.
- In consideration of their upcoming marriage, gave Maria a $90,000 convertible.
- Purchased a $100,000 certificate of deposit listing title as "Carl, payable on proof of death to Maria."
- Established a joint checking account with his now-spouse, Maria, in December of the current year with $30,000 of funds he inherited from his parents. In January of the following year, Maria withdrew $18,000 of the funds.
- Purchased for $80,000 a paid-up insurance policy on his life (maturity value of $500,000). Carl designated Maria as the beneficiary.
- Paid $23,400 to a college for his niece Mindy's tuition and $11,000 for her room and board.
- Gave his aunt Betty $152,000 for her heart bypass operation.

Critical Thinking

34. **LO.4, 7** In May year 1, Dudley and Eva enter into a property settlement in anticipation of the dissolution of their marriage. Under the agreement, Dudley is to pay Eva $6,000,000 in full satisfaction of her marital rights. Of this amount, Dudley pays $2,500,000 immediately, and the balance is due one year later. The parties are divorced in July. Dudley dies in December, and his estate pays Eva the remaining $3,500,000 in May year 2. Discuss the Federal estate and gift tax ramifications of these transactions to the parties involved.

Critical Thinking

35. **LO.4** Jesse dies intestate (i.e., without a will) in May year 1. Jesse's major asset is a tract of land. Under applicable state law, Jesse's property will pass to Lorena, who is his only child. In December year 1, Lorena disclaims one-half of the property. In June year 2, Lorena disclaims the other half interest. Under state law, Lorena's disclaimer results in the property passing to Arnold (Lorena's only child).

The value of the land (in its entirety) is as follows: $2,000,000 in May year 1, $2,100,000 in December year 1, and $2,200,000 in June year 2. Discuss the transfer tax ramifications of these transactions.

Critical Thinking

36. **LO.5** Using property she inherited, Lei makes a 2023 gift of $16,200,000 to her adult daughter, Doris. Neither Lei nor her spouse, Greg, have made any prior taxable gifts. Assuming that a flat 40% tax rate applies, determine the Federal gift tax liability if:

a. The election to split gifts is not made.
b. The election to split gifts is made.
c. What are the tax savings from making the election?

37. **LO.6** At the time of his death this year on September 4, Kenneth owned the following assets, among others:

	Fair Market Value
City of Boston bonds	$2,500,000
Stock in Brown Corporation	900,000
Promissory note issued by Brad (Kenneth's son)	600,000

In October, the executor of Kenneth's estate received the following: $120,000 interest on the City of Boston bonds ($10,000 accrued since September 4) and a $7,000 cash dividend on the Brown stock (date of record was September 5). The declaration date on the dividend was August 12.

The $600,000 loan was made to Brad in late 2019, and he used the money to create a very successful business. The note was forgiven by Kenneth in his will.

What are the estate tax consequences of these transactions?

38. **LO.6** Assume the same facts as in Problem 37 with the following modifications. What amount is included in Kenneth's gross estate?

- The bonds were issued by the Houston (TX) Independent School District.
- The dividend record date was September 3 (not September 5).
- Kenneth's will does not forgive Brad's note. The business that Brad started with the loan funds was not successful, and the note has a zero value.

39. **LO.6** At the time of her death on September 4, Alicia held the following assets:

	Fair Market Value
Bonds of Emerald Tool Corporation	$ 900,000
Stock in Drab Corporation	1,100,000
Insurance policy (face amount of $400,000) on the life of her brother, Mitch	80,000*
Traditional IRAs	300,000

*Cash surrender value.

Alicia also held a lifetime income interest in a trust (fair market value of trust assets $2,000,000) created by her late spouse Bert. (The executor of Bert's estate had made a QTIP election.)

In October, Alicia's estate received an interest payment of $11,500 ($6,000 accrued before September 4) paid by Emerald and a cash dividend of $9,000 from Drab. The Drab dividend was declared on August 19 and was payable to date of record shareholders on September 3.

Although Mitch survives Alicia, she is the designated beneficiary of the insurance policy. The IRAs are distributed to Alicia's children.

What amount is included in Alicia's gross estate for these items?

40. **LO.6** Assume the same facts as in Problem 39 with the following modifications. What amount is included in Alicia's gross estate for these items?

- Mitch is killed by a rockslide while mountain climbing in November, and the insurer pays Alicia's estate $400,000 before the end of the year.
- Bert's executor did not make a QTIP election.
- Alicia's IRAs were the Roth type (not traditional).
- The record date for the Drab Corporation dividend is September 5 (not September 3).
- On November 7, Alicia's estate receives from the IRS an $8,000 income tax refund, a receivable amount at her death relating to the taxes she paid for the preceding calendar year.

41. **LO.6, 7** At the time of Mateo's death, he was involved in the transactions described below.

- Mateo was a participant in his employer's contributory qualified pension plan. The plan balance of $2,000,000 is paid to Olivia, Mateo's daughter and beneficiary. The distribution consists of the following:

Employer contributions	$900,000
Mateo's after-tax contributions	600,000
Income earned and accumulated by the plan	500,000

- Mateo was covered by his employer's group term life insurance plan for employees. The $200,000 proceeds are paid to Olivia, as designated beneficiary.

a. What are the Federal estate tax consequences of these events?

b. Would the answer to part (a) change if Olivia was Mateo's surviving spouse (not his daughter)? Explain.

Critical Thinking 42. **LO.6** At the time of his death on July 9, Aiden held rights in the following real estate:

	Fair Market Value (on July 9)
Apartment building	$2,100,000
Tree farm	1,500,000
Pastureland	750,000
Residence	900,000

The apartment building was purchased by Chloe, Aiden's mother, and is owned in a joint tenancy with her. The tree farm and pastureland were gifts from Chloe to Aiden and his two sisters. The tree farm is held in joint tenancy, and the pastureland is owned as tenants in common. Aiden purchased the residence and owns it with his spouse Katrine, as tenants by the entirety. How much is included in Aiden's gross estate based on the following assumptions?

a. Aiden dies first and is survived by Chloe, his sisters, and Katrine.

b. Aiden dies after Chloe but before his sisters and Katrine.

c. Aiden dies after Chloe and his sisters but before Katrine.

d. Aiden dies last (i.e., he survives Chloe, his sisters, and Katrine).

43. **LO.4, 6** Gordon purchased real estate for $900,000 and listed title to the property as "Gordon and Fawn, joint tenants with right of survivorship." Gordon predeceases Fawn when the real estate is worth $2,900,000. Gordon and Fawn are brother and sister.

a. Did a gift occur when the real estate was purchased? Explain.

b. What, if any, are the estate tax consequences upon Gordon's death?

c. Under part (b), would your answer change if it was Fawn (not Gordon) who died? Explain.

44. **LO.4, 6, 7** Assume the same facts as in Problem 43, except that Gordon and Fawn are married to each other (not brother and sister).

a. What are the gift tax consequences when the real estate was purchased?

b. What are the estate tax consequences upon Gordon's death?

c. Under part (b), would your answer change if it was Fawn (not Gordon) who died? Explain.

45. **LO.5, 6, 7** In each of the independent situations below, determine the Federal estate and gift tax consequences of what has occurred. (In all cases, assume that Gene and Mary are married and that Tanisha is their daughter.)

a. Mary purchases an insurance policy on Gene's life and designates Tanisha as the beneficiary. Mary dies first, and under her will, the policy passes to Gene.

b. Gene purchases an insurance policy on Mary's life and designates Tanisha as the beneficiary. Tanisha dies first one year later.

c. Gene purchases an insurance policy on his life and designates Mary as the beneficiary. Gene dies first, and the policy proceeds are paid to Mary.

46. **LO.7** While vacationing in Florida in November, Sally was seriously injured in an automobile accident. Sally died several days later. Apply the Federal estate tax rules to each of these items.
    a. Bruce, Sally's son and executor, incurred $6,200 in travel expenses in flying to Florida, retrieving the body, and returning it to Frankfort, Kentucky, for burial.
    b. Sally had pledged $50,000 to the building fund of her church. Bruce paid this pledge from the assets of the estate.
    c. Prior to her death, Sally had promised to give her nephew, Gary, $20,000 when he passed the bar exam. Gary passed the exam late in the year, and Bruce kept Sally's promise by paying him $20,000 from estate assets.
    d. At the scene of the accident and before the ambulance arrived, someone took Sally's jewelry (i.e., Rolex watch and wedding ring) and money. The property (valued at $33,000) was not insured and was never recovered.
    e. As a result of the accident, Sally's auto was totally destroyed. The auto had a basis of $52,000 and a fair market value of $28,000. In January of the next year, the insurance company pays Sally's estate $27,000.

47. **LO.6, 7** Tavon dies and is survived by his spouse, Marge. Under Tavon's will, all of his otherwise uncommitted assets pass to Marge. For each of the property interests listed below, determine the marital deduction allowed to Tavon's estate.
    a. Timberland worth $1,200,000 owned by Tavon, Marge, and Amber (Marge's sister) as equal tenants in common. Amber furnished the original purchase price.
    b. Residence of Tavon and Marge worth $900,000 owned by them as tenants by the entirety with right of survivorship. Tavon provided the original purchase price.
    c. Insurance policy on Tavon's life (maturity value of $1,000,000) owned by Marge and payable to her as the beneficiary.
    d. Insurance policy on Tavon's life (maturity value of $500,000) owned by Tavon with Marge as the designated beneficiary.
    e. Lump-sum distribution from a qualified pension plan of $1,600,000 (Tavon had contributed $500,000 to his account), with Marge as the beneficiary.

48. **LO.8** Under Rowena's will, Mandy (Rowena's sister) inherits her property. One year later, Mandy dies. Based on the following independent assumptions, what is Mandy's credit for the tax on prior transfers?
    a. The estate tax attributable to the inclusion of the property in Rowena's gross estate is $700,000, and the estate tax attributable to the inclusion of the property in Mandy's gross estate is $800,000.
    b. The estate tax attributable to the inclusion of the property in Rowena's gross estate is $1,200,000, and the estate tax attributable to the inclusion of the property in Mandy's gross estate is $1,100,000.
    c. Would your answers to parts (a) and (b) change if Mandy died seven years (rather than one year) after Rowena?

Tax Return Problems

1. James A. and Ella R. Polk, ages 70 and 65, respectively, are retired physicians who live at 3319 Taylorcrest Street, Houston, Texas 77079. Their three adult children (Benjamin Polk, Michael Polk, and Olivia Turner) are mature and responsible professionals.

   The Polks have heard that some in Congress have proposed lowering the Federal gift tax exclusion to $3,000,000. Although this change likely will not occur, the Polks believe that they should take advantage of the more generous exclusion amount available under existing law. Thus, the Polks make gifts during the current year, as summarized below.

	Donor	
Asset Transfer	**James**	**Ella**
Condominium located in Conroe (TX) acquired in 2015, cost $1,200,000, to Benjamin, Michael, and Olivia as equal tenants in common.	$1,900,000	$1,900,000
Office building, located in Round Rock (TX) built in 2017, cost $1,800,000, to Benjamin, Michael, and Olivia as equal tenants in common.	2,300,000	2,300,000
Vacation ranch in Bandera (TX) inherited by James from his father in 2006, value then $900,000, to Benjamin, Michael, and Olivia as equal joint tenants with right of survivorship.	2,600,000	–0–
Separate property reimbursing Ella's father (Alan Roberts) for his heart bypass operation.	–0–	82,000
Paid for daughter's (Olivia's) wedding to John Turner, a state-law obligation of support	20,000	20,000
Separate property to purchase a new automobile as a graduation present (from medical school) for James's favorite niece (Carol Polk)	42,000	–0–

   Prepare 2022 gift tax returns (Form 709) for both of the Polks to compute the total taxable gifts (line 3) for James and Ella; stop with line 3 of page 1, but complete pages 2 and 3 of the return.

   An election to split gifts is made. The Polks made no taxable gifts in prior years. Relevant Social Security numbers are 123-45-6789 (James) and 123-45-6788 (Ella).

2. Natalie Bryan, a single adult who lives at 425 Flathead Way, Kalispell, Montana 59901, has three adult children (Daniel Bryan, Amanda Green, and Samantha Cruz). During the year, Natalie makes the following gifts to the children:

   - **To Daniel.** Office building in Helena acquired in 2012 at a cost of $900,000, current value $1,900,000.
   - **To Amanda.** Rental cabins in Whitefish inherited in 2010 (value $1,000,000) from her father, current value $1,800,000.
   - **To Samantha.** Vacation lodge on Flathead Lake acquired in 2016 at a cost of $800,000, current value $1,900,000.

   Prepare a 2022 gift tax return (Form 709) for Natalie (Social Security number 123-45-6787) to compute the total taxable gifts (line 3) for her; stop with line 3 of page 1, but complete pages 2 and 3 of the return. Natalie made no taxable gifts in prior years.

Research Problems

Note: Solutions to the Research Problems can be prepared by using the Thomson Reuters Checkpoint™ online tax research database, which accompanies this textbook. Solutions can also be prepared by using research materials found in a typical tax library.

Research Problem 1. Before her death, Lucy entered into the following transactions. Discuss the estate and income tax ramifications of each of these transactions.

a. Lucy borrowed $600,000 from her brother, Irwin, so that Lucy could start a business. The loan was on open account, and no interest or due date was provided for. Under applicable state law, collection on the loan was barred by the statute of limitations before Lucy died. Because the family thought that Irwin should recover his funds, the executor of the estate paid him $600,000.

b. Lucy promised her sister, Ida, a bequest of $500,000 if Ida would move in with her and care for her during an illness (which eventually proved to be terminal). Ida moved in and became a caregiver, but Lucy did not keep her promise; her will was silent on any bequest to Ida. After Lucy's death, Ida sued the estate and eventually recovered $600,000 for breach of contract.

Partial list of research aids:
§ 2053.
Reg. §§ 20.2053–4(d)(4) and (7).
Estate of Allie W. Pittard, 69 T.C. 391 (1977).
Joseph F. Kenefic, 36 TCM 1226, T.C.Memo. 1977–310.
Hibernia Bank v. U.S., 78–2 USTC ¶13,261, 42 AFTR 2d 78–6510, 581 F.2d 741 (CA–9).

Use internet tax resources to address the following questions. Look for reliable websites and blogs of the IRS and other government agencies, media outlets, businesses, tax professionals, academics, think tanks, and political outlets.

Research Problem 2. What type of transfer tax, if any, does your home state impose? What about the state(s) contiguous to your home state? (For Alaska, use Washington; for Hawaii, use California.) Make a chart relating your findings, and send it to your instructor. Communications

Research Problem 3. For the same states that you used in Research Problem 3, list the number of Federal estate tax returns filed and the estate tax liabilities collected, for the latest year with figures available. Use **irs.gov/statistics/soi-tax-stats-estate-tax-statistics** in your work. Send your data table to your instructor. Communications Data Analytics

Research Problem 4. Make a graph showing the number of Forms 706 and 709 that have been filed for every third year starting with 2005. On the same graph, indicate the revenue collected by the Treasury from these taxes for each year. Communications Data Analytics

Research Problem 5. In 2021, some members of Congress proposed the Ultra-Millionaire Tax Act (H.R. 1459 and S.510). Make a list of three arguments in favor and three arguments against the proposed legislation.

Becker CPA Review Questions

Becker

1. Fred and Amy Kehl, both U.S. citizens, are married. All of their real and personal property is owned by them as tenants by the entirety or as joint tenants with right of survivorship. The gross estate of the first spouse to die:
   a. Includes 50% of the value of all property owned by the couple, regardless of which spouse furnished the original consideration.
   b. Includes only the property that had been acquired with the funds of the deceased spouse.
   c. Does not include any of the value of the property held as joint tenancy with right of survivorship (or tenancy by the entirety) because of the unlimited marital deduction.
   d. Includes one-third of the value of all real estate owned by the Kehls as the dower right in the case of the wife or curtesy right in the case of the husband.

2. Which of the following requires filing a gift tax return if the transfer exceeds the available annual gift tax exclusion?
   a. Medical expenses paid directly to a physician on behalf of an individual unrelated to the donor.
   b. Tuition paid directly to an accredited university on behalf of an individual unrelated to the donor.
   c. Payments for college books, supplies, and dormitory fees on behalf of an individual unrelated to the donor.
   d. Campaign expenses paid to a political organization.

3. Steve and Kay Briar, U.S. citizens, were married for the entire calendar year. During 2023, Steve gave a $36,000 cash gift to his sister. The Briars made no other gifts in the year. They each signed a timely election to treat the $36,000 gift as made one-half by each spouse. Disregarding the applicable credit and estate tax consequences, what amount of the current-year gift is taxable to the Briars?
   a. $32,000
   b. $30,000
   c. $2,000
   d. $0

4. Larry plans to gift his daughter $25,000 during the current taxable year. Further, provided she graduates from a four-year accredited college, he will also gift her $100,000. Which of the following is correct with regard to these gifts during the current year, assuming the cash is given to his daughter in the current year and she does not graduate from a four-year accredited college in the current year?

	$25,000	**$100,000**
a.	Completed Gift	Incomplete Gift
b.	Completed Gift	Completed Gift
c.	Incomplete Gift	Incomplete Gift
d.	Incomplete Gift	Completed Gift

5. Which of the following statements about the estate tax is *not* correct?
   a. The estate tax return, Form 706, is due nine months after the date of death.
   b. The alternate valuation date for an estate, if elected, is six months after the date of death.
   c. The estate may not deduct outstanding debts of the decedent.
   d. An estate is allowed an unlimited marital deduction.

6. Bob died in year 3. His gross estate consisted of assets with a fair market value of $13,500,000. In his will, Bob leaves $1,000,000 to his spouse, $500,000 to his only daughter, and $250,000 to his favorite charity. Prior to Bob's death, he was involved in a lawsuit when one of his tenants slipped and fell at one of the rental properties owned by Bob. After his death, the personal representative settled the lawsuit for $750,000. The expenses to close Bob's estate were $50,000. In year 3, the Federal estate exclusion amount is $11,000,000. By what amount, if any, does Bob's taxable estate exceed the $11,000,000 exclusion amount?

   a. $450,000
   b. $500,000
   c. $1,200,000
   d. $0

7. David Collins died during the current year. The personal representative of David's estate identified the following assets:

Stocks in David's name only	$ 2,000,000
Investment property in a trust that David has the right to revoke	1,500,000
Primary home owned jointly with his spouse (spouse did not contribute to the purchase)	1,000,000
Insurance policy owned by and insuring David with the proceeds payable to his daughter	800,000
Vacation home owned jointly with his son (son did not contribute to the purchase)	500,000
Cash placed in an irrevocable trust by David eight years ago with David's friend as trustee	600,000

   What is the value of David's gross estate for estate tax purposes?

   a. $3,500,000
   b. $4,250,000
   c. $5,300,000
   d. $6,400,000

Chapter 30

Income Taxation of Trusts and Estates

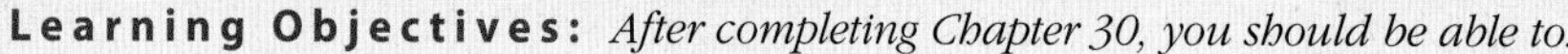

Learning Objectives: *After completing Chapter 30, you should be able to:*

LO.1 Define and use terminology with respect to trusts, estates, beneficiaries, and other parties.

LO.2 Identify the steps in determining the accounting and taxable income of a trust or an estate and the related taxable income of the beneficiaries.

LO.3 Illustrate the uses and implications of distributable net income.

LO.4 Use the special rules that apply to trusts where the creator (grantor) of the trust retains certain rights.

LO.5 Apply the fiduciary income tax rules in a manner that minimizes the income taxation of trusts and estates and still accomplishes the intended objectives of the grantor or decedent.

Chapter Outline

The Big Picture

Setting Up a Trust to Protect a Family

Anna Jiang is the main breadwinner in her family, which includes her husband Tom, a social worker, and two children, Bobby, age 6, and Sally, age 8. Anna has accumulated about $2 million in after-tax investment accounts, largely made up of growth stocks that do not regularly pay dividends; she inherited most of these securities when her grandmother died about five years ago. Anna reduced her exposure to probate costs through joint property ownership, life insurance policies, and beneficiary arrangements for her retirement plans. She and Tom update their wills every five years or so.

Because there is a history of Alzheimer's disease in her family, Anna wants to make certain that, if she becomes unable to work and cannot manage her financial assets, Tom and the children will have adequate cash flow from the investment assets. In addition, one of Anna's colleagues at the office suggests that Anna should set up a trust to take care of her family in case a medical problem ever arises.

Read the chapter and formulate your response.

Taxpayers create trusts for a variety of reasons. Some trusts are established primarily for tax purposes, but most are designed to accomplish a broader financial goal or to provide for the orderly management of assets in case of an emergency.

Because a trust is a separate tax entity, its gross income and deductions must be measured and an annual tax return must be filed. Similarly, when an individual dies, a legal and tax entity is created in the form of the individual's estate. This chapter examines the rules related to the income taxation of trusts and estates.

30-1 Fiduciary Income Taxation

When a trust or an estate is involved, a taxpayer has put a third party into a **fiduciary** relationship, where the third party (i.e., the trustee or executor) is required to act on behalf (and for the benefit) of the taxpayer who assigned the duties to them. The fiduciary essentially acts in the place of the decedent or the creator of the trust, for instance, in making investment decisions and meeting financial obligations.

The income taxation of trusts and estates is governed by Subchapter J of Chapter 1 of the Internal Revenue Code, §§ 641 through 692. Certain similarities are apparent between Subchapter J and the income taxation of individuals (e.g., the definitions of gross income and deductible expenditures), partnerships and limited liability entities (e.g., the pass-through principle), and S corporations (e.g., the pass-through principle and the trust or estate as a separate taxable entity). Trusts also involve several important new concepts, however, including the determination of *distributable net income* and the *tier system* of distributions to beneficiaries.

Exhibit 30.1 lists some of the more common reasons that might prompt an individual to create a trust, and Exhibit 30.2 illustrates the structure of a typical trust and estate.

LO.1

Define and use terminology with respect to trusts, estates, beneficiaries, and other parties.

30-1a What Is a Trust?

The Code does not contain a definition of a trust; instead, trusts are defined and governed by state law. However, the term usually refers to an arrangement created by a will or by an *inter vivos* (lifetime) declaration through which trustees take title to property for the purpose of protecting or conserving it for the beneficiaries.[1] Usually, trust operations are controlled by the trust document and by the fiduciary laws of the state in which the trust documents are executed.

Exhibit 30.1 Common Motivations for Creating a Trust

Type of Trust	Financial and Other Goals
Life insurance trust	Holds life insurance policies on the insured, removes the proceeds of the policies from the gross estate (if an irrevocable trust), and safeguards against receipt of the proceeds by a young or inexperienced beneficiary.
"Living" (revocable) trust	Manages assets, reduces probate costs, provides privacy for asset disposition, protects against medical or other emergencies, and provides relief from the day-to-day management of the underlying assets. No estate tax savings: trust assets remain in the gross estate.
Trust for minors	Provides funds for a college education or other needs of the minor and transfers accumulated income without permanently parting with the underlying assets.
Divorce trust	Manages the assets of an ex-spouse and ensures that they are distributed in a timely fashion to specified beneficiaries (e.g., as child support).

[1]Reg. § 301.7701-4(a).

Exhibit 30.2 **Structure of a Typical Trust and Estate**

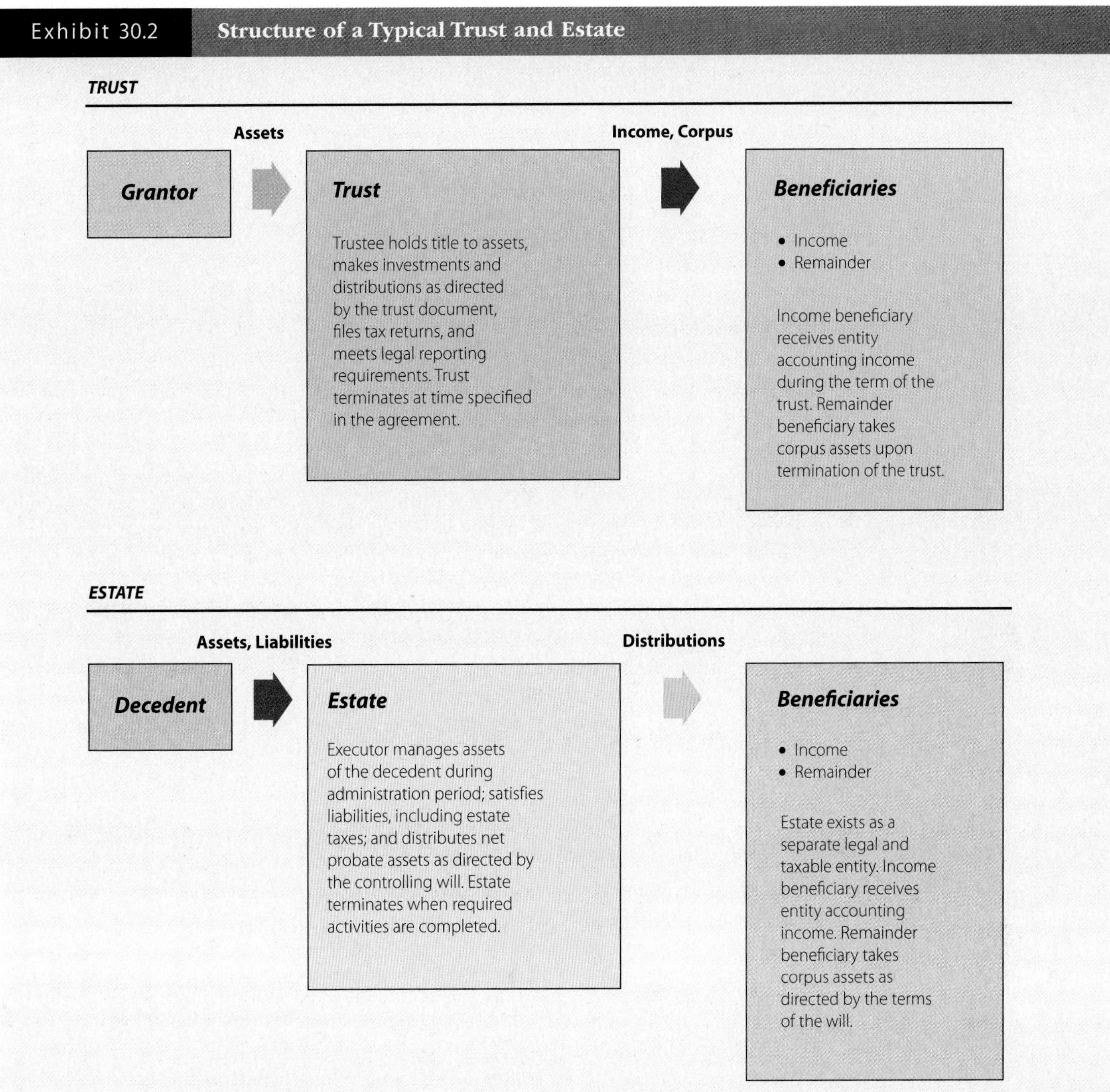

Typically, the creation of a trust involves at least three parties.

1. The **grantor** (sometimes referred to as the settlor or donor) transfers selected assets to the trust entity.
2. The trustee, who usually is either an individual or a corporation, is charged with the fiduciary duties associated with the trust.
3. The beneficiary is designated to receive income or property from the trust.

In some situations, fewer than three persons may be involved, as specified by the trust agreement. For instance, an elderly individual who no longer can manage their own property (e.g., because of ill health) may create a trust under which the individual is both the grantor and the income beneficiary. In this case, a family member or corporate trustee is charged with the management of the grantor's assets until their death.

In another situation, the grantor might be named the trustee of the entity. For example, one who wants to transfer selected assets to a minor child or elderly parent could use a trust entity to ensure that the beneficiary does not misuse or waste the property. As the trustee, the grantor retains virtual control over the property that is transferred.

When only one party is involved (when the same individual is grantor, trustee, and sole beneficiary of the trust), Subchapter J rules do not apply and the entity is ignored for Federal income tax purposes; the grantor is liable for Federal income taxes on the entity's taxable income. This might occur, for instance, when the grantor desires protection of the assets and/or income from creditors or an ex-spouse.

Other Definitions

When the grantor transfers title of selected assets to a trust, those assets become the **corpus** (body), or principal, of the trust. Trust corpus, in most situations, earns *income*, which may be distributed to the beneficiaries or accumulated for the future by the trustee, as the trust instrument directs.

In a typical trust, the grantor creates two types of beneficiaries: one who receives the accounting income of the trust (defined in text Section 30-3a), and one who receives the trust corpus that remains at the termination of the trust as a legal entity. Beneficiaries in the former category hold an *income interest* in the trust, and those in the latter category hold a *remainder interest* in the trust's assets. If the grantor retains the remainder interest (e.g., for a trust for a minor beneficiary's education), the interest is known as a **reversionary interest** (corpus reverts to the grantor when the trust entity terminates).

The trust document establishes the term of the trust. The term may be for a specific number of years (*term certain*) or until the occurrence of a specified event. For instance, a trust might exist:

- For the life of the income beneficiary, in which case the income beneficiary is known as a *life tenant* in the trust corpus.
- For the life of some other individual (e.g., one's spouse).
- Until the income or remainder beneficiary reaches the age of majority.
- Until the beneficiary, or another individual, marries, graduates, or reaches some specified age.

The trustee may be required to distribute the accounting income of the entity according to a distribution schedule specified in the agreement. Usually, though, the trustee is given more discretion with respect to the timing and nature of the distributions. If the trustee can determine, within guidelines found in the trust document, either the timing of the income or corpus distributions or the specific beneficiaries who will receive them (from among those identified in the agreement), the trust is called a discretionary or **sprinkling trust**. Here, the trustee can "sprinkle" the distributions among the various beneficiaries. As discussed in Chapter 29, family-wide income taxes can be reduced by directing income to those who are subject to lower marginal tax rates. Thus, by giving the trustee a sprinkling power, the income tax liability of the family unit can be manipulated by applying the terms of the trust agreement.

For purposes of certain provisions of Subchapter J, a trust is classified as either a **simple trust** or a **complex trust**. A simple trust:

- Is required to distribute its entire accounting income to designated beneficiaries every year,
- Has no beneficiaries that are qualifying charitable organizations, and
- Makes no distributions of trust corpus during the year.

A complex trust is any trust that is not a simple trust.[2] These criteria are applied to the trust every year. Thus, every trust is classified as a complex trust in the year in which it terminates (because it distributes all of its corpus during that year).

30-1b **What Is an Estate?**

An estate is created upon the death of an individual. The entity is charged with collecting and conserving all of the individual's assets, satisfying all liabilities, and distributing the remaining assets to the heirs identified by state law or the will.

Typically, the creation of an estate involves at least three parties: the decedent, all of whose probate assets are transferred to the estate for disposition; the executor, who is appointed under the decedent's valid will (or the administrator, if no valid will exists); and the beneficiaries of the estate, who are to receive assets or income from the entity, as the decedent has indicated in the will. Refer to Exhibit 30.2 for an illustration of these relationships.

An estate's operations are controlled by the probate laws of the decedent's state of residence and by the terms of the will as interpreted by the probate court. If the decedent did not execute a valid will, state law dictates who will carry out the executor's duties and which beneficiaries will receive which of the decedent's net assets.

An estate is a separate legal and taxable entity. The termination date of the estate is somewhat discretionary, since it occurs when all of the assets and income of the decedent have been distributed, all estate and decedent liabilities have been satisfied, and all other business of the entity is completed. Thus, there may be an incentive to use the estate as part of an income-shifting strategy (e.g., where the income beneficiaries are subject to low marginal tax rates).

Maria dies, and her estate holds a high-yield investment portfolio. Paulo, the income beneficiary, is subject to a 15% marginal state and Federal income tax rate, and Julia, the remainder beneficiary, is subject to a 30% marginal rate. The tax adviser might suggest that Maria's estate delay its final distribution of assets by a year or more to take advantage of the income tax savings that are available from Paulo's low rates and extend the date upon which the entity terminates.

If an estate's existence is unduly prolonged, however, the IRS can terminate it for Federal income tax purposes after the expiration of a reasonable period for completing the duties of administration.[3]

30-2 **Nature of Trust and Estate Taxation**

Subchapter J produces a significant amount of income tax revenue. More than 3.1 million Forms 1041 are filed every year, and these returns reflect the following approximate aggregate amounts:

- Gross income of over $140 billion.
- Taxable income of about $70 billion on about 1 million returns.
- Tax liability of almost $24 billion on about 860,000 returns.

For most fiduciaries, almost 70 percent of income is in the form of capital gains and dividends. Other gross income tends to be interest, rents and royalties, and pass-through amounts from partnerships and other fiduciaries.

In general, the taxable income of a trust or an estate is taxed to the entity or to its beneficiaries to the extent that each has received the accounting income of the entity. Thus, the Federal income tax law creates a modified pass-through principle relative to the income taxation of trusts, estates, and their beneficiaries. Whoever receives the accounting income of the entity, or some portion of it, is liable for the income tax that results.

[2]Reg. § 1.651(a)–1.

[3]Reg. § 1.641(b)–3(a).

Adam receives 80% of the accounting income of the Zero Trust. The trustee accumulated the other 20% of the income at her discretion under the trust agreement and added it to trust corpus. Adam is liable for income tax only on the amount of the distribution, and Zero is liable for the income tax on the accumulated portion of the income.

Concept Summary 30.1 summarizes the major similarities and differences between the taxation of trusts and estates and that of other **pass-through entities**—partnerships, limited liability entities, and S corporations.

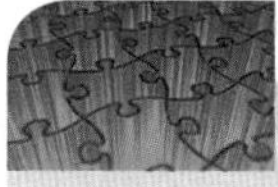

Concept Summary 30.1

Tax Characteristics of Major Pass-Through Entities

Tax Treatment	Subchapter K (Partnerships, LLCs)	Subchapter S (S Corporations)	Subchapter J (Trusts, Estates)
Controlling documents	Partnership agreement, LLC operating agreement.	Corporate charter and bylaws.	Trust document or will, state fiduciary or probate law.
Taxing structure	Pure pass-through, only one level of Federal income tax.	Chiefly pass-through, one level of Federal income tax.	Modified pass-through, Federal income tax falls on the recipient(s) of entity accounting income.
Entity-level Federal income tax?	Never.	Rarely. See text Sections 23-3h, i, and j.	Yes, if the entity retains any net taxable income amounts.
Form for reporting income and expense pass-through	Schedules K and K–1, Form 1065.	Schedules K and K–1, Form 1120S.	Schedules K and K–1, Form 1041.
Subject to entity-level AMT?	No, but preferences and adjustments pass through to owners.	No, but preferences and adjustments pass through to owners.	Yes, if the entity retains any AMT-related accounting income amounts.
Subject to entity-level NIIT?	No, but amounts and types of income are reported to owners.	No, but amounts and types of income are reported to shareholders.	Yes, on income items retained by the entity (i.e., not distributed to beneficiaries).

30-2a Tax Accounting Periods and Methods

An estate or a trust may use many of the tax accounting methods available to individuals. The method of accounting used by the grantor of a trust or the decedent of an estate need not carry over to the entity.

An estate has the same options for choosing a tax year as any new taxpayer. Thus, the estate of a calendar year decedent dying on March 3 can select any fiscal year or report on a calendar year basis. To eliminate the possibility of deferring the taxation of fiduciary-source income simply by using a fiscal tax year, virtually all trusts (other than tax-exempt trusts) are required to use a calendar tax year.[4]

30-2b Tax Rates and Personal Exemption

Congress's desire to stop trusts from being used as income-shifting devices has made the fiduciary entity the highest-taxed taxpayer in the Code. The entity reaches the 37 percent marginal Federal income tax rate in 2023 once taxable income exceeds $14,450, so the grantor's ability to shift income in a tax-effective manner is nearly eliminated. Exhibit 30.3, which lists the 2023 Federal income taxes paid by various entities on taxable income of $80,000, shows how different the applicable marginal tax

[4] § 644.

Exhibit 30.3 Comparative Tax Liabilities

Filing Status/Entity	Taxable Income	Marginal Income Tax Rate (%)	2023 Federal Income Tax Liability
Single	$80,000	22	$12,908
Married, filing jointly	80,000	12	9,160
C corporation	80,000	21	16,800
Trust or estate	80,000	37	27,745

rates are and how expensive the taxes on an accumulation of income within an estate or a trust can be. Given the lower tax rates for individuals, tax-motivated income shifting usually moves assets *out of* the estate or trust and into the hands of the lower-bracket grantor or beneficiary.

A fiduciary's dividend income and net long-term capital gain are taxed for 2023 at a zero rate if taxable income is no more than $3,000, at 15 percent up to $14,650 of taxable income, and at 20 percent thereafter. These amounts for 2022 were $2,800 and $13,700, respectively.

In addition to the regular income tax, an estate or a trust may be subject to the alternative minimum tax and the additional tax on net investment income (discussed in text Sections 30-2c and 30-2d). Estimated tax payments must take into account any liabilities for these taxes.

Both trusts and estates are allowed a personal exemption in computing the fiduciary tax liability. All estates are allowed a personal exemption of $600. The exemption available to a trust depends upon the type of trust involved. A trust that is required to distribute all of its income currently is allowed an exemption of $300. All other trusts are allowed an exemption of $100 per year.[5]

The classification of trusts as to the appropriate personal exemption is similar but not identical to the distinction between simple and complex trusts.

Example 3

Three trusts appear to operate in a similar fashion, but they are subject to different Subchapter J classifications and exemptions.

Trust Alpha is required to distribute all of its current accounting income to Susan. Thus, it is allowed a $300 personal exemption. No corpus distributions or charitable contributions are made during the year. Accordingly, Alpha is a simple trust.

Trust Beta is required to distribute all of its current accounting income; it is allowed a $300 personal exemption. The beneficiaries of these distributions are specified in the trust instrument: one-half of accounting income is to be distributed to Tyrone, and one-half is to be distributed to State University, a qualifying charitable organization. Because Beta has made a charitable distribution for the tax year, it is a complex trust.

The trustee of Trust Gamma can, at her discretion, distribute the current-year accounting income or corpus of the trust to Dr. Chapman. Because the trustee is not required to distribute current accounting income, only a $100 personal exemption is allowed. Because it lacks the current-year income distribution requirement, Gamma is a complex trust, even in a year that accounting income is fully distributed.

30-2c **Alternative Minimum Tax**

The alternative minimum tax (AMT) may apply to a trust or an estate in any tax year. Given the types of income that such an entity tends to recognize, and the nature and magnitude of the tax preferences, adjustments, and exemptions that determine alternative minimum taxable income (AMTI), however, most trusts and estates are unlikely to incur the tax.

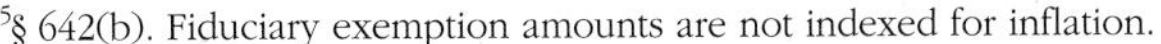

[5] § 642(b). Fiduciary exemption amounts are not indexed for inflation.

In general, derivation of AMTI for the entity follows the rules that apply to individual taxpayers. AMTI may be created through the application of most of the AMT preference and adjustment items.

The fiduciary's AMT is computed using Schedule I of Form 1041. Two full pages of the Form 1041 are dedicated to the computation of taxable income and other items when the AMT applies to the trust or estate. A minimum tax credit might be available in future years through these computations.

The entity claims a $28,400 annual AMT exemption for the 2023 tax year. The exemption phases out at a rate of one-fourth of the amount by which AMTI exceeds $94,600. These amounts are indexed annually.

A 26 percent AMT rate is applied to 2023 AMTI, increasing to 28 percent when AMTI in excess of the exemption reaches $220,700.

30-2d Additional Tax on Net Investment Income

Trusts and estates that are subject to the highest Federal income tax rate for the tax year must pay an additional tax to support the Medicare system, using Form 8960. This tax is 3.8 percent of the lesser of (1) the undistributed net investment income (NII) of the trust, or (2) the excess (if any) of adjusted gross income (AGI) over $14,450 for 2023 ($13,450 for 2022).[6]

NII includes gross income (less deductions) from interest, dividends, royalties, rents, and passive activities. NII also includes net recognized gains from the disposition of assets producing such income (e.g., capital gains). NII items make up about 90 percent of income items for many investment-oriented fiduciary entities. The NII tax (NIIT) is in addition to the entity's ordinary income tax (maximum rate 37 percent) and net capital gains tax (maximum rate 20 percent).

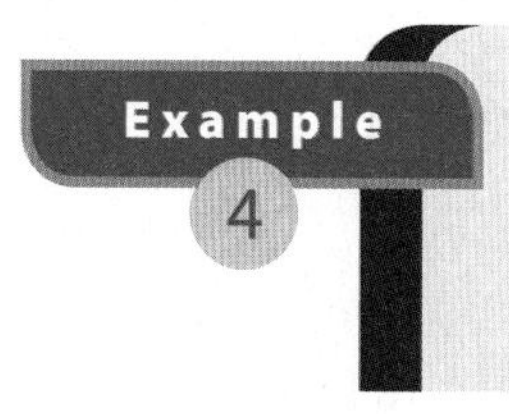

The Zeta Trust reports $20,000 of net investment income (NII) and $30,000 in net profits from an active business operation for 2023. Zeta retains all of the business profits but, under the terms of the trust agreement, distributes $5,000 cash from the NII to its sole beneficiary Victoria. Zeta's liability under the additional tax on NII is $570 (3.8% × $15,000 undistributed NII). Undistributed NII ($15,000) is less than the excess of Zeta's AGI over $14,450 ($50,000 − $14,450 = $35,550).

Identify the steps in determining the accounting and taxable income of a trust or an estate and the related taxable income of the beneficiaries.

30-3 Taxable Income of Trusts and Estates

Generally, the taxable income of an estate or a trust is computed similarly to that for an individual. Fiduciary income tax rules, however, include several important exceptions and provisions that make it necessary to use a systematic approach to calculate the taxable income of these entities. Exhibit 30.4 illustrates the procedure implied by the Code, and Exhibit 30.5 presents a systematic computation method followed in this chapter.

30-3a Entity Accounting Income

Step 1 in determining the taxable income of a trust or an estate is to compute the entity's accounting income for the period. Although this prerequisite is not apparent from a cursory reading of Subchapter J, a closer look at the Code reveals a number of references to the *income* of the entity.[7] Wherever the term *income* is used in this part of the Code without some modifier (e.g., *gross* income or *taxable* income), the statute is referring to the accounting income of the trust or estate for the tax year.

A definition of **entity accounting income** is critical to understanding the computation of fiduciary taxable income. Usually, entity accounting income is the amount the income beneficiary of the trust or estate is eligible to receive from the entity. More importantly, the calculation of accounting income is virtually under the control of the grantor or decedent (through a properly drafted trust agreement or will). If the document has been drafted at arm's length, a court will enforce a fiduciary's good faith efforts to carry out the computation of accounting income, as specified in the agreement.

[6]This dollar amount is indexed annually. The "AGI" of a trust is similar to the AGI of an individual with a few variations, such as a deduction for certain administrative expenses. See § 67(e).

[7]For example, see §§ 651(a)(1), 652(a), and 661(a)(1).

Exhibit 30.4 Accounting Income, Distributable Net Income, and Taxable Income of the Entity and Its Beneficiaries—The Five-Step Procedure

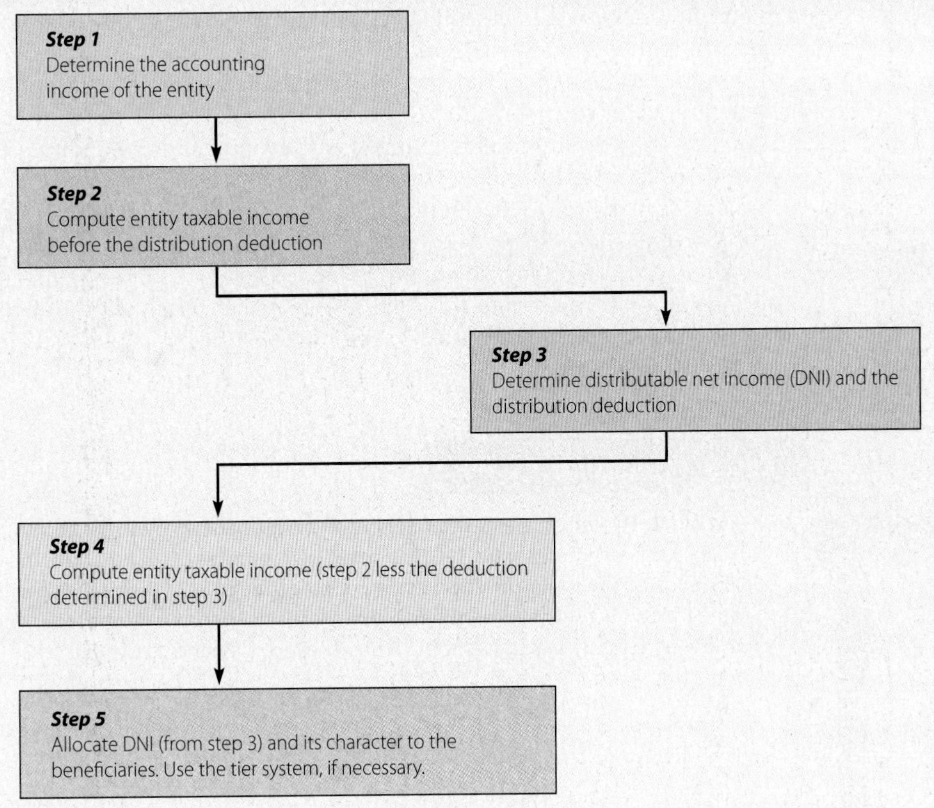

Exhibit 30.5 Computational Template Applying the Five-Step Procedure

Item	Totals	Accounting Income	Taxable Income	Distributable Net Income/Distribution Deduction
Income	____	____	____	
Income	____	____	____	
Expense	____	____	____	
Expense	____	____	____	
Personal exemption			____	
Accounting income/taxable income before the distribution deduction		____	____	____
		Step 1	***Step 2***	
Personal exemption				____
Corpus capital gain/loss				____
Net tax-exempt income				____
Distributable net income				____
Distribution deduction			____	***Step 3***
Entity taxable income			____	***Step 4***

Beneficiary taxable income is addressed in ***step 5***.

Entity accounting income generally is defined by state laws that are derived from the Uniform Fiduciary Income and Principal Act (UFIPA). The UFIPA is a revision of the former Uniform Principal and Income Act, which was originally completed in 1931 and most recently revised and retitled in 2018. Nearly every state has adopted some form of the Uniform Act, which essentially constitutes generally accepted accounting principles (GAAP) in the fiduciary tax setting.

When specific items of income and expenditure are allocated either to the income beneficiaries or to corpus, the desires of the grantor or decedent are put into effect. Exhibit 30.6 shows typical assignments of revenue and expenditure items to fiduciary income or corpus. Examples 5 through 7 illustrate that the amounts received by beneficiaries can vary widely due to changes in these allocations under the terms of the trust agreement.

Where the controlling document is silent as to whether an item should be assigned to income or corpus, state fiduciary law prevails. These allocations are an important determinant of the benefits received from the entity by its beneficiaries and the timing of those benefits.

Entity Accounting Income

Example 5

The Arnold Trust is a simple trust. Mrs. Bennett is its sole beneficiary. In the current year, the trust earns $20,000 in taxable interest and $15,000 in tax-exempt interest. In addition, the trust recognizes an $8,000 long-term capital gain. The trustee assesses a fee of $11,000 for the year.

If the trust agreement allocates fees and capital gains to corpus, trust accounting income is $35,000 and Mrs. Bennett receives that amount. Thus, the income beneficiary receives no immediate benefit from the trust's capital gain, and she bears none of the financial burden of the trustee's fees.

Interest income	$35,000
Long-term capital gain	+ -0-*
Trustee's fees	− -0-*
Trust accounting income	$35,000

*Allocable to corpus.

Example 6

Assume the same facts as in Example 5, except that the trust agreement allocates the trustee's fees to income. The trust accounting income is $24,000, and Mrs. Bennett receives that amount.

Interest income	$35,000
Long-term capital gain	+ -0-*
Trustee's fees	−11,000
Trust accounting income	$24,000

*Allocable to corpus.

Example 7

Assume the same facts as in Example 5, except that the trust agreement allocates to income all capital gains and losses and one-half of the trustee's fees. The trust accounting income is $37,500, and Mrs. Bennett receives that amount.

Interest income	$35,000
Long-term capital gain	+8,000
Trustee's fees	−5,500*
Trust accounting income	$37,500

*One-half allocable to corpus.

Exhibit 30.6 Common Allocations of Items to Income or Corpus

Allocable to Income	Allocable to Corpus
Ordinary and operating net income from trust assets	Depreciation on business assets
	Casualty gain/loss on income-producing assets
Interest, dividend, rent, and royalty income	Insurance recoveries on income-producing assets
	Capital gain/loss on investment assets
One-half of administrative fees/commissions	Adjustments due to stock splits
	One-half of administrative fees/commissions

30-3b Gross Income

The gross income of an estate or a trust is similar to that of an individual. In determining the gain or loss to be recognized by an estate or a trust upon the sale or other taxable disposition of assets, the rules for basis determination are similar to those applicable to other taxpayers. Thus, an estate's basis for property received from a decedent is stepped up or stepped down to the gross estate valuation (refer to Chapters 13 and 29 for a more detailed discussion). Property received as a gift during the donor's lifetime (e.g., in irrevocable trust arrangements) usually takes the donor's basis. Property purchased by the trust from a third party is assigned a basis equal to the purchase price.

Noncash Property Distributions

In general, the fiduciary entity does not recognize gain or loss upon its distribution of property to a beneficiary under the provisions of the will or trust document. The distributed property has the same basis to the beneficiary of the distribution as it did to the estate or trust. Moreover, the distribution absorbs distributable net income (DNI) and qualifies for a distribution deduction (both of which are explained in text Sections 30-3f and 30-4) to the extent of the lesser of the distributed asset's basis to the beneficiary or the asset's fair market value as of the distribution date.[8]

The Big Picture

Example 8

Return to the facts of *The Big Picture* on p. 30-1. Assume that Anna has established the Jiang Family Trust. The trust distributes a painting (basis of $40,000 and fair market value of $90,000) to beneficiary Sally. Sally's basis in the painting is $40,000. The distribution absorbs $40,000 of the Jiang Family Trust's DNI, and the trust claims a $40,000 distribution deduction relative to the transaction.

A trustee or an executor can elect for the entity to recognize gain or loss with respect to all of its in-kind property distributions for the year. If the election is made, the beneficiary's basis in the asset is equal to the asset's fair market value as of the distribution date. The distribution absorbs DNI and qualifies for a distribution deduction to the extent of the asset's fair market value. However, the related-party rules can restrict an estate's or trust's deduction for such losses. Generally, related parties include (1) a trust, its trustee, its grantor, and its beneficiaries and (2) an estate, its executor, and its beneficiaries.

Distributing Property

Example 9

The Green Estate distributes an antique piano, basis to Green of $10,000 and fair market value of $15,000, to beneficiary Kyle. The executor elects that Green recognize the related $5,000 gain on the distribution. Accordingly, Kyle's basis in the piano is $15,000 ($10,000 basis to Green + $5,000 gain recognized). The election likely increased the Federal income tax paid related to the gain: Green almost certainly is subject to a higher marginal income tax rate than is Kyle. Without the election, Green would not recognize any gain, and Kyle's basis in the piano would be $10,000.

[8] § 643(e).

Distributing Property

Example 10

Assume the same facts as in Example 9, except that Green's basis in the piano is $18,000. The executor elects that Green be assigned the related $3,000 loss on the distribution. Accordingly, Kyle's basis in the piano is $15,000 ($18,000 – $3,000). Without the election, Kyle's basis in the piano would be $18,000.

The estate cannot deduct this loss, however. Because an estate and its beneficiaries are related parties, realized losses cannot be recognized immediately.[9] Instead, the disallowed loss can be recognized if Kyle later sells the piano to an unrelated party.

Income in Respect of a Decedent

The gross income of a trust or an estate includes **income in respect of a decedent (IRD)** that the entity received.[10] For a cash basis decedent, IRD typically includes accrued salary, interest, rent, and other income items that were not constructively received before death. For both cash and accrual basis decedents, IRD includes, for instance, distributions from qualified retirement plans and deferred compensation contracts.

The tax consequences of IRD can be summarized as follows:

- The fair market value of the right to IRD on the appropriate valuation date is included in the decedent's gross estate. Thus, it is subject to the Federal estate tax.[11]
- The decedent's basis in the property carries over to the recipient (the estate or heirs). There is no step-up or step-down in the basis of IRD items.
- The recipient of the income recognizes gain or loss, measured by the difference between the amount realized and the adjusted basis of the IRD in the hands of the decedent. The character of the gain or loss matches the treatment that it would have received had it been realized by the decedent before death. Thus, if the decedent would have realized capital gain, the recipient must do likewise.
- Expenses related to the IRD (such as interest, taxes, and depletion) that were not deducted on the final income tax return of the decedent may be claimed by the recipient of the IRD. These items are known as **deductions in respect of a decedent**. Typically, such deductions also include administrative fees, commissions paid to dispose of estate assets, and state income taxes payable. They are deductible on the estate tax return *and* on the IRD recipient's income tax return, *for* or *from* adjusted gross income (AGI) as would have been the case for the decedent.

Working with IRD

Amanda died on July 13 of the current year. On August 2, the estate received a check (before withholdings) for $1,200 from Amanda's former employer; this was Amanda's compensation for the last pay period of her life. On November 23, the estate received a $45,000 distribution from the qualified pension plan of Amanda's employer, the full amount to which Amanda was entitled under the plan. Both Amanda and the estate are calendar year, cash basis taxpayers.

The last salary payment and the retirement plan distribution constitute IRD to the estate. Amanda had earned these items during her lifetime, and the estate was to receive each of them after Amanda's death. Consequently, the gross estate includes $46,200 with respect to these two items. However, the income tax basis to the estate for these items is not stepped up (from zero to $1,200 and $45,000, respectively) upon distribution to the estate.

The estate reports gross income of $46,200 for the current tax year with respect to the IRD items [($1,200 + $45,000 amounts realized) – $0 adjusted bases].

---

[9] § 267(b)(13).

[10] See § 691 and the Regulations thereunder. The concept of IRD was introduced in Chapter 29.

[11] To mitigate the effect of double taxation (imposition of both the estate tax and the income tax), § 691(c) allows the recipient an income tax deduction for the incremental estate tax attributable to the net IRD.

Working with IRD

Assume the same facts as in Example 11. Amanda's last paycheck was reduced by $165 for state income taxes that were withheld by the employer. The $165 tax payment is a deduction in respect of a decedent and is available as a deduction on *both* Amanda's estate tax return *and* the estate's income tax return.

Including the IRD in both the taxpayer's gross estate and the gross income of the estate may seem harsh. Nevertheless, the tax consequences of IRD are similar to the treatment that applies to all of a taxpayer's earned income. The item is subject to income tax upon receipt, and to the extent it is not consumed by the taxpayer before death, it is included in the gross estate.

Ethics & Equity **To Whom Can I Trust My Pet?**

Humane societies encourage the general public to care for their own pets and to adopt those who need owners. It is not uncommon to find provisions in a will to establish a trust or an endowment to care for the pets that the deceased leaves behind. After all, over 65 percent of all individuals live with a pet and more than $120 billion is spent each year in caring for these companions.

Boilerplate legal language is available to establish a pet-assistance trust. The trust should provide a guaranteed distribution for pet care, including the costs of pet sitters, kennels, and veterinary fees. Typically, the trust must terminate after 21 years or upon the earlier death of the pet.

When decedents establish permanent funds to provide for a favorite pet, the surviving (human) family members may not be so enthused. In a few cases, the survivors challenge the terms of the will or trust, often requesting that a judge downsize the principal amount involved or reduce the specified annual distributions. In this way, the human heirs benefit from any adjustment that is made.

How would you advise a client who wants to establish a well-funded trust to care for Fifi when the family members have income and asset needs of their own?

30-3c **Ordinary Deductions**

As a general rule, the taxable income of an estate or a trust is similar to that of an individual.[12] Deductions are allowed for ordinary and necessary expenses paid or incurred in carrying on a trade or business; for the production or collection of income; for the management, conservation, or maintenance of property; and in connection with the determination, collection, or refund of any tax.

Reasonable administration expenses, including trustee/executor fees, tax preparation costs, appraisal fees, investment advisory fees for services beyond what an individual investor would need, and legal costs relative to entity administration, also can be deducted. Business interest deductions are deductible up to 30 percent of related taxable income. State and local taxes not related to a business are deductible up to $10,000.[13]

Expenses attributable to the production or collection of tax-exempt income are not deductible.[14] The amount of the disallowed deduction is proportionate to the income elements of entity accounting income for the year of the deduction. The deductibility of the fees is determined by the usual Federal income tax rules, and the allocation of expenditures to income and to corpus is controlled by the trust agreement or will or by state law.

The Silver Trust operates a business and invests idle cash in marketable securities. Its sales proceeds for the current year are $180,000. Expenses for wages, cost of sales, and office administration are $80,000. Interest income recognized is $20,000 from taxable bonds and $50,000 from tax-exempt bonds. The trustee claims a $35,000 fee for its activities. According to the trust agreement, $30,000 of this amount is allocated to the income beneficiaries, and $5,000 is allocated to corpus. Entity accounting income is computed as follows.

continued

[12] § 641(b).

[13] For example, see §§ 162, 163(j), 164(b)(6)(B), and 212, and Reg. § 1.67–4(b).

[14] § 265.

Sales proceeds	$180,000
Business expenses	(80,000)
Interest income (from all sources)	70,000
Trustee's fees, as allocated	(30,000)
Trust accounting income	$140,000

In computing the trust's taxable income, the sales proceeds are included in gross income under § 61. The costs associated with the business are deductible in full under § 162. The taxable interest income is included in Silver's gross income under § 61, but the tax-exempt interest is excluded under § 103. The trustee's fees are deductible by Silver under § 212, but a portion of the deduction is lost because § 265 prohibits deductions for expenses incurred in the generation of tax-exempt income.

As shown below, 50/250 of the fees of $35,000 can be traced to tax-exempt income, so $7,000 of the fees is nondeductible. For purposes of the computation, only the income elements of the year's trust accounting income are included in the denominator. Moreover, the allocation of portions of the fees to income and to corpus is irrelevant in the calculation. The disallowed deduction for the trustee's fees is computed in the following manner:

$$\$35{,}000^{*}\text{(total fees paid)} \times \frac{\$50{,}000^{**}\ \text{(}\textit{tax-exempt}\text{ income elements of trust accounting income)}}{\$250{,}000^{**}\ \text{(}\textit{all}\text{ income elements of trust accounting income)}}$$

$$= \$7{,}000 \text{ (amount disallowed)}$$

*All fees, and not just those that are allocated to income, are deductible by the trust under § 212.
**The numerator and denominator of this fraction are *not* reduced by expense items allocable to income (e.g., cost of sales).

Silver is a complex trust and makes no distributions to beneficiaries for the year. Silver's taxable income for the year is computed as follows:

Sales proceeds	$180,000
Deductible expenses	(80,000)
Taxable interest income	20,000
Trustee's fees, as reduced	(28,000)
Personal exemption	(100)
Taxable income	$ 91,900

Amounts deductible as administration expenses or losses for estate tax purposes cannot be claimed by the estate for income tax purposes unless the estate waives the estate tax deduction. Although these expenses cannot be deducted twice, they may be allocated as the fiduciary sees fit between Forms 706 and 1041; they need not be claimed in their entirety on either return.[15]

Trusts and estates are allowed cost recovery deductions. Such deductions are assigned proportionately among the recipients of the entity accounting income.[16]

Cost Recovery Deductions

Example 14

Lisa and Martin are the equal income beneficiaries of the Needle Trust. Under the terms of the trust agreement, the trustee has complete discretion as to the timing of the distributions from Needle's current accounting income. The trust agreement allocates all depreciation expense to income. In the current year, the trustee distributes 40% of the current trust accounting income to Lisa and 40% to Martin; thus, 20% of the income is accumulated. The depreciation deduction allowable to Needle is $100,000. This deduction is allocated among the trust and its beneficiaries on the basis of the distribution of current accounting income: Lisa and Martin each claim a $40,000 deduction, and the trust can deduct $20,000.

Assume the same facts as in Example 14, except that the trust agreement allocates all depreciation expense to corpus. There is no change in the tax result; Lisa and Martin both still claim a $40,000 depreciation deduction, and Needle retains its $20,000 deduction. The Code assigns the depreciation deduction proportionately to the recipients of entity accounting income. Allocation of depreciation to income or to corpus is irrelevant in determining which party can properly claim the deduction.

[15]Reg. § 1.642(g)–2.

[16]§§ 167(d) and 611(b)(3) and (4).

If the entity operates a trade or business, the income beneficiaries of a fiduciary entity may qualify for the 20 percent deduction for qualified business income (QBI); see text Section 15-3. The trust or estate will report to the beneficiaries all information necessary for those parties to compute the deduction, such as QBI and W–2 wages. Such items are allocated to the beneficiaries proportionate to the amount of distributable net income (see text Section 30-3f) that they receive.[17] This means that the entity will claim its own QBI deduction if it retains some of the DNI for the tax year.

30-3d **Deductions for Losses**

An estate or a trust is allowed an income tax deduction for casualty or theft losses related to its assets that are not reimbursed by insurance or other arrangements. Such losses may also be deductible on a Federal estate tax return.[18] An estate is not allowed an income tax deduction unless the estate tax deduction is waived.

The net operating loss (NOL) deduction is available for estates and trusts (i.e., where trade or business income is generated). No more than 80 percent of entity taxable income can be offset by the NOL after 2020; see text Section 17-1j. The net capital losses of an estate or a trust can be claimed by the fiduciary. The tax treatment of these losses is the same as for individual taxpayers.

Fiduciary entities are subject to the passive activity loss limitations; passive activity losses can be deducted by the trust or estate only against income from passive activities. Excess business losses are not currently deductible to the extent they exceed $289,000 (for 2023).

30-3e **Charitable Contributions**

An estate or a complex trust is allowed a deduction for contributions from the gross income of the current tax year to charitable organizations under certain conditions.[19]

- The contribution is made pursuant to the will or trust instrument, and its amount is determinable using the language of that document.
- The recipient is a qualified organization. For this purpose, qualified organizations include the same charities for which individual and corporate donors are allowed deductions, except that estates and trusts also are permitted a deduction for contributions to certain foreign charitable organizations.
- Generally, the contribution is claimed in the tax year it is paid, but a fiduciary can treat amounts paid in the year immediately following as a deduction for the preceding year. Under this rule, estates and complex trusts may receive more favorable treatment than do individuals or C corporations.

Example 16

Chisum, a calendar year taxpayer, wants to claim a deduction for a gift to a charity on its year 1 Federal income tax return. Such a gift must be made by the following date, depending on the type of taxpayer Chisum is:

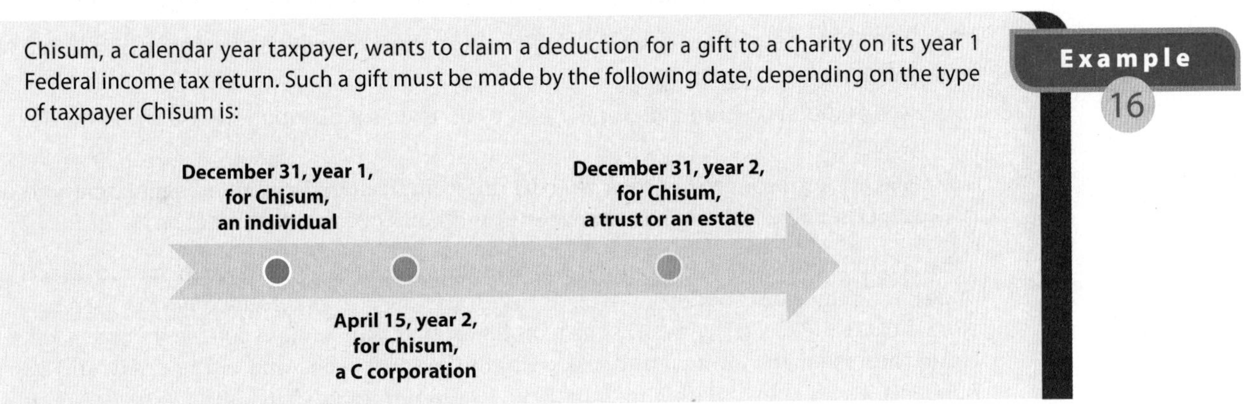

Unlike the charitable contribution deductions of individuals and corporations, the deductions of estates and complex trusts are not limited in amount (e.g., to a percentage of taxable or adjusted gross income). Nonetheless, the deduction is limited to amounts that have been included in the gross income of the entity.

[17] Reg. § 1.199A–6(d).
[18] § 2054.
[19] § 642(c)(1) and Reg. §§ 1.642(c)–1 and –3. But see *Green v. U.S.*, 121 AFTR 2d 2018–427, 2018–1 USTC ¶50,126, 880 F.3d 519 (CA–10).

The deduction for a gift of a noncash asset is limited to that asset's basis to the fiduciary. A contribution is deemed to be made proportionately from each of the income elements of entity accounting income. However, if the will or trust agreement requires that the contribution be made from a specific type of income, or from income from a specified asset, the allocation of the contribution to taxable and tax-exempt income is not required.

The Big Picture

Return to the facts of *The Big Picture* on p. 30-1. Again assume that Anna has established the Jiang Family Trust. The trust reports gross rent income of $80,000, expenses attributable to the rents of $60,000, and tax-exempt interest from state bonds of $20,000. Under the trust agreement, the trustee is to pay 30% of the annual trust accounting income to the United Way, a qualifying organization. Accordingly, the trustee pays $12,000 to the charity (i.e., 30% × $40,000). The charitable contribution deduction allowed is $9,600 [($80,000 ÷ $100,000) × $12,000], even if the payment to the charity is not made until the following tax year.

The Big Picture

Assume the same facts as in Example 17, except that the trust instrument also requires that the contribution be paid from the net rent income. The agreement controls, and the contribution deduction is not reduced. The entire $12,000 is deductible for the year.

LO.3

Illustrate the uses and implications of distributable net income.

30-3f Deduction for Distributions to Beneficiaries

The modified pass-through approach of Subchapter J is embodied in the deduction allowed to trusts and estates for the distributions made to beneficiaries during the year. Some portion of any distribution that a beneficiary receives from a trust may be subject to income tax on the beneficiary's own return. At the same time, the distributing entity is allowed a deduction for some or all of the distribution.

An analogy for this treatment is to the taxability of corporate profits distributed to employees as wages. The corporation pays wages from its otherwise taxable income and deducts the payment, but the employee receives gross income in the form of compensation.

Distributable Net Income

A critical value that is used in computing the amount of the entity's distribution deduction is **distributable net income (DNI)**. As it is defined in Subchapter J, DNI serves several functions. Concept Summary 30.2 illustrates these critical roles of DNI.

- DNI is the maximum amount of the distribution on which the beneficiaries can be taxed.[20]
- DNI is the maximum amount the entity can use as a distribution deduction for the year.[21]
- The makeup of DNI carries over to the beneficiaries (the items of income and expenses retain their DNI character in the hands of the distributees).[22]

Subchapter J defines DNI in a circular manner. The DNI value is necessary to determine the entity's distribution deduction and therefore its taxable income for the year. Nonetheless, the Code defines DNI as a modification of the entity's taxable income itself. Using the systematic approach to determining the taxable income of the entity and its beneficiaries, as shown earlier in Exhibit 30.4, compute *taxable income before the distribution deduction*, modify that amount to determine DNI and the distribution deduction, return to the calculation of *taxable income*, and apply the deduction that has resulted.

[20] §§ 652(a) and 662(a).

[21] §§ 651(b) and 661(c).

[22] §§ 652(b) and 662(b).

Concept Summary 30.2

Uses of the DNI Amount

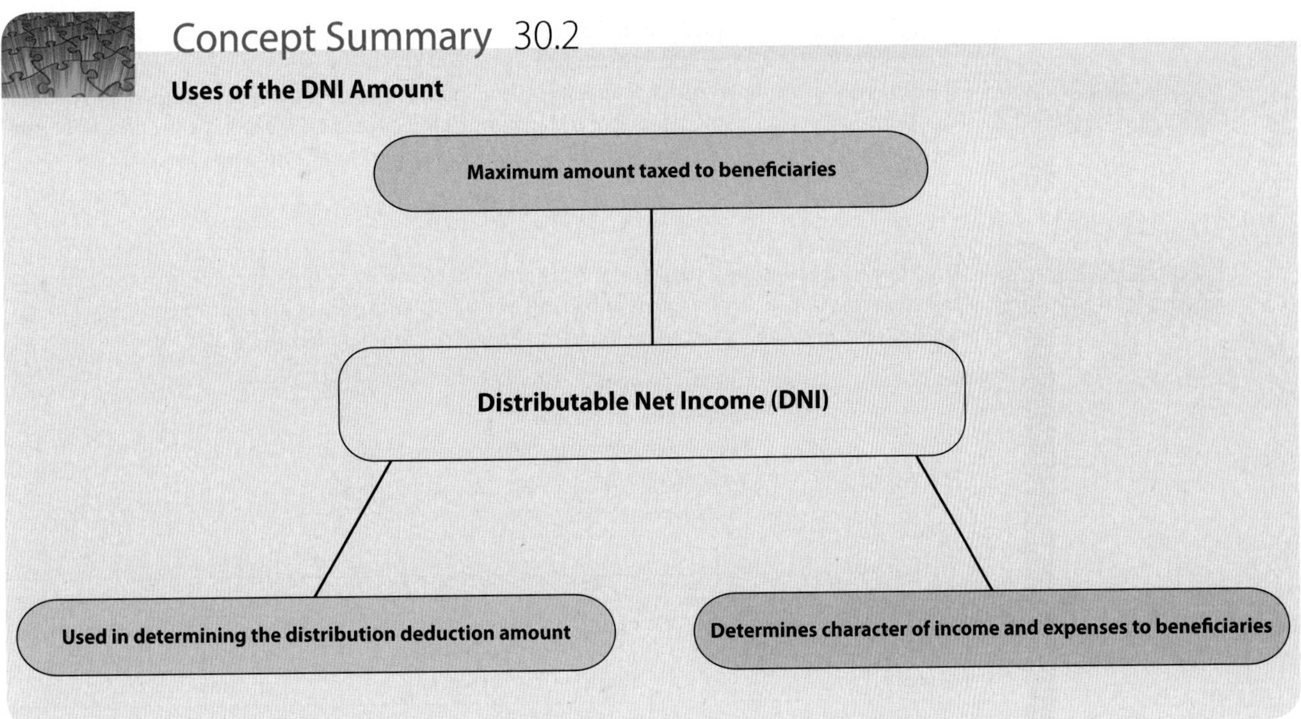

Taxable income before the distribution deduction (step 2) includes all of the entity's items of gross income, deductions, gains, losses, and exemptions for the year.

Therefore, to compute this amount, (1) determine the appropriate personal exemption for the year and (2) account for all of the other gross income and deductions of the entity.

Step 3 in Exhibit 30.4 is the determination of *distributable net income*, computed by making the following adjustments to the entity's *taxable income before the distribution deduction*:[23]

- Add back the entity's personal exemption.
- Add back *net* tax-exempt interest; reduce the total tax-exempt interest by charitable contributions and by related expenses that are not deductible.
- Add back the entity's net capital losses.
- Subtract any net capital gains allocable to corpus. The only net capital gains included in DNI are those attributable to income beneficiaries or to charitable contributions.[24]

Distribution Deduction

DNI includes the net tax-exempt interest income of the entity, so that amount must be removed from DNI in computing the distribution deduction. Moreover, for estates and complex trusts, DNI and the distribution amount might not be the same; the amount actually distributed during the year may include discretionary distributions of income or corpus permissible under the will or trust instrument.

The distribution deduction for estates and complex trusts is computed as the lesser of (1) the deductible portion of DNI or (2) the taxable amount actually distributed to the beneficiaries during the year. For a simple trust, however, full distribution is always assumed, relative to both the entity and its beneficiaries, in a manner similar to the pass-through entities.

DNI and the distribution deduction are computed on the entity's Form 1041. The beneficiaries' Schedules K–1 report the allocations of income, deduction, and credit items to them.

[23]These and other (less common) adjustments are detailed in § 643.

[24]§ 643(a)(3).

DNI and Distribution Deduction

Example 19

The Zinc Trust is a simple trust. Because of severe liquidity problems, its year 1 accounting income is not distributed to its sole beneficiary, Mark, until early in year 2. Zinc still is allowed a full distribution deduction for, and Mark still is taxed upon, the entity's year 1 income in year 1.

The Pork Trust is required to distribute its current accounting income annually to its sole income beneficiary, Barbosa. Capital gains and losses and all other expenses are allocable to corpus. In the current year, Pork incurs the following items. Apply the template of Exhibit 30.5.

Dividend income	$25,000
Taxable interest income	15,000
Tax-exempt interest income	20,000
Net long-term capital gain	10,000
Trustee fees	6,000

Item	Totals	Accounting Income		Taxable Income	Distributable Net Income/ Distribution Deduction
Dividend income	$25,000	$25,000		$ 25,000	
Taxable interest income	15,000	15,000		15,000	
Tax-exempt interest income	20,000	20,000			
Net long-term capital gain	10,000			10,000	
Trustee fees	6,000			(4,000)	
Personal exemption				(300)	
Accounting income/taxable income before the distribution deduction		$60,000		$ 45,700	$ 45,700
		Step 1		*Step 2*	
Personal exemption					300
Corpus capital gain/loss					(10,000)
Net tax-exempt income					18,000
Distributable net income					$ 54,000
Distribution deduction			*Step 3*	(36,000)	
Entity taxable income			*Step 4*	$ 9,700	

Step 1. Trust accounting income is $60,000; this includes the tax-exempt interest income, but not the fees or the capital gains, pursuant to the trust document. Barbosa receives $60,000 from the trust for the current year.

Step 2. Taxable income before the distribution deduction is computed as directed by the Code. The tax-exempt interest is excluded under § 103. Only a portion of the fees is deductible {[($60,000 − $20,000) ÷ $60,000] × $6,000 = $4,000} because some of the fees are traceable to the tax-exempt income. The trust claims a $300 personal exemption because it is required to distribute its annual trust accounting income.

Step 3. DNI and the distribution deduction reflect the required adjustments. The distribution deduction is the lesser of the distributed amount ($60,000) or the deductible portion of DNI [$54,000 − $18,000 (net tax-exempt income)].

Step 4. Finally, return to the computation of the taxable income of the Pork Trust. A simple test should be applied at this point to ensure that the proper figure for the trust's taxable income has been determined. On what is Pork to be taxed? Pork has distributed to Barbosa $60,000, which is all of its gross income except the $10,000 net long-term capital gain. The $300 personal exemption reduces Pork's taxable income to $9,700.

DNI and Distribution Deduction

Example 21

The Quick Trust is required to distribute all of its current accounting income equally to its two beneficiaries, Faith Gonzalez and the Universal Church, a qualifying charitable organization. Capital gains and losses and depreciation expenses are allocable to income. Trustee fees are allocable to corpus. In the current year, Quick incurs various items as indicated. Apply the template of Exhibit 30.5.

Item	Totals	Accounting Income		Taxable Income	Distributable Net Income/ Distribution Deduction
Rent income	$100,000	$100,000		$100,000	
Expenses—rent income	30,000	(30,000)		(30,000)	
Depreciation—rent income	15,000	(15,000)			
Net long-term capital gain	20,000	20,000		20,000	
Charitable contribution				(37,500)	
Trustee fees	18,000			(18,000)	
Personal exemption				(300)	
Accounting income/taxable income before the distribution deduction		$ 75,000		$ 34,200	$34,200
		Step 1		***Step 2***	
Personal exemption					300
Corpus capital gain/loss					
Net tax-exempt income					
Distributable net income					$34,500
Distribution deduction			***Step 3***	(34,500)	
Entity taxable income			***Step 4***	($ 300)	

Step 1. Trust accounting income of $75,000 reflects the indicated allocations of items to income and to corpus. Each income beneficiary receives $37,500.

Step 2. In the absence of tax-exempt income, a deduction is allowed for the full amount of the trustee's fees. Quick is a complex trust, but because it is required to distribute its full accounting income annually, a $300 exemption is allowed. Properly, the trust does not deduct any depreciation for the rental property. The depreciation deduction is available only to the recipients of the entity's accounting income for the period. Thus, the deduction is split equally between Faith and the church. The deduction probably is of no direct value to the church, a tax-exempt organization. The trust's charitable contribution deduction equals the $37,500 the charity actually received (one-half of trust accounting income).

Step 3. Because there is no tax-exempt income, the only adjustment needed to compute DNI is to add back the trust's personal exemption. Subchapter J requires no adjustment for the charitable contribution. DNI is computed only from the perspective of Faith, who also received $37,500 from the trust.

Step 4. Now check that the proper taxable income for the Quick Trust has been computed. All of the trust's gross income has been distributed to Faith and the charity. As is the case with most trusts that distribute all of their accounting income, the Quick Trust "wastes" the personal exemption, and taxable income is ($300).

30-3g Tax Credits

Available tax credits are apportioned between the estate or trust and the beneficiaries on the basis of the entity accounting income allocable to each.

Concept Summary 30.3 outlines the principles underlying the Federal taxation of estates and trusts.

Concept Summary 30.3

Principles of Fiduciary Income Taxation

1. Estates and trusts are temporary entities created to locate, maintain, and distribute assets and to satisfy liabilities according to the wishes of the decedent or grantor as expressed in the will or trust document.
2. Generally, the estate or trust acts as a conduit of the taxable income that it receives. To the extent the income is distributed by the entity, it is taxed to the beneficiary. Taxable income retained by the entity is taxed to the entity itself.
3. The entity's accounting income first must be determined. Accounting conventions that are stated in the controlling document or, lacking such provisions, in state law allocate specific items of receipt and expenditure either to income or to corpus. Income beneficiaries typically receive payments from the entity equal to the entity's accounting income.
4. The taxable income of the entity is computed using the template in Exhibit 30.5. The entity usually recognizes income in respect of a decedent.
5. Deductions for administrative fees and for charitable contributions may be reduced if the entity received any tax-exempt income during the year.
6. Business deductions are allowed, including the QBI and NOL deductions, if the entity operates a trade or business. Deductions may be limited for business losses, business interest, passive activity losses, and state and local taxes. Cost recovery deductions are assigned proportionately to the recipients of accounting income.
7. Upon election, realized gain or loss on assets that are properly distributed in kind can be recognized by the entity.

30-4 Taxation of Beneficiaries

The beneficiaries of an estate or a trust receive taxable income from the entity under the modified pass-through principle of fiduciary income taxation. Distributable net income determines the maximum amount that can be taxed to the beneficiaries for any tax year. The constitution of DNI carries over to the beneficiaries (e.g., net long-term capital gains and dividends retain their character when they are distributed from the entity).

A beneficiary includes in gross income an amount based upon the DNI of the trust for any taxable year or years of the entity ending with or within the beneficiary's taxable year.[25] These amounts are reported to the beneficiary on the Form 1041, Schedule K–1.

30-4a Distributions by Simple Trusts

The amount taxable to the beneficiaries of a trust is limited by the trust's DNI. However, because DNI includes net tax-exempt income, the amount included in the gross income of the beneficiaries could be less than DNI. When there is more than one income beneficiary, the elements of DNI are apportioned ratably according to the amount required to be distributed currently to each.

A simple trust has ordinary income of $40,000, a long-term capital gain of $15,000 (allocable to corpus), and a trustee administrative expense of $4,000 (payable from corpus). The two income beneficiaries, Allie and Bart, receive distributions of the trust's annual accounting income, equal to 75% and 25%, respectively.

Although Allie receives $30,000 as her share (75% × trust accounting income of $40,000), she is allocated DNI of only $27,000 (75% × $36,000). Similarly, Bart's distribution is $10,000 (25% × $40,000), but he is allocated DNI of only $9,000 (25% × $36,000). The $15,000 capital gain is taxed to the trust.

30-4b Distributions by Estates and Complex Trusts

Typically, an estate or a complex trust makes only discretionary distributions. In those cases, the DNI is apportioned ratably according to the distributed amounts, as seen in Example 22.

A computational problem arises with estates and complex trusts when more than one beneficiary receives a distribution from the entity and the controlling document does not require a distribution of the entire accounting income of the entity.

[25]§§ 652(c) and 662(c).

The trustee of the Wilson Trust has the discretion to distribute the income or corpus of the trust in any proportion between the two beneficiaries of the trust, Wong and Washington. Under the trust instrument, Wong must receive $15,000 from the trust every year. In the current year, the trust's accounting income is $50,000, and its DNI is $40,000. The trustee pays $15,000 to Wong and $25,000 to Washington.

How is Wilson's DNI to be divided between Wong and Washington? Several arbitrary methods of allocating DNI between the beneficiaries could be devised. Subchapter J resolves the problem by creating a two-tier system to govern the taxation of beneficiaries in such situations.[26] The tier system determines which distributions will be included in the gross income of the beneficiaries in full, which will be included in part, and which will not be included at all.

First and Second Tiers

Income that is required to be distributed currently, whether or not it is distributed, is categorized as a *first-tier distribution*. All other discretionary amounts paid, credited, or distributed are *second-tier distributions*.[27] A formula is used to allocate DNI among the appropriate beneficiaries when only first-tier distributions are made and those amounts exceed DNI.

When both first-tier and second-tier distributions are made and the first-tier distributions exceed DNI, the above formula is applied to the first-tier distributions. In this case, none of the second-tier distributions are taxed because all of the DNI has been allocated to the first-tier beneficiaries.

If both first-tier and second-tier distributions are made and the first-tier distributions do not exceed DNI, but the total of both first-tier and second-tier distributions does exceed DNI, the second-tier beneficiaries recognize income as shown below.

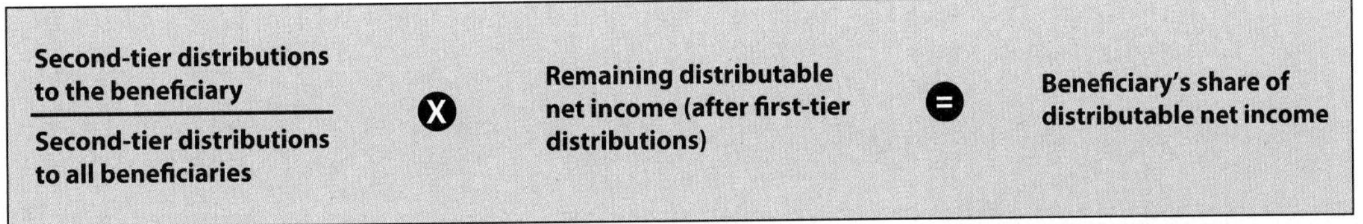

Distributing DNI

Example 24

The trustee of the Gray Trust is required annually to distribute $10,000 each to Harriet and Wally, the two beneficiaries of the entity. In addition, the trustee can distribute other amounts of trust income or corpus at its sole discretion. In the current year, the trust reports accounting income of $60,000 and DNI of $50,000. However, the trustee distributes only the required $10,000 each to Harriet and to Wally. The balance of the income is accumulated and added to trust corpus.

In this case, only first-tier distributions have been made, but the total amount of the distributions does not exceed DNI for the year. Although DNI is the maximum amount included by the beneficiaries for the year, they can include no more in gross income than is distributed by the entity. Thus, both Harriet and Wally may be subject to tax on $10,000 as their proportionate shares of DNI.

[26] §§ 662(a)(1) and (2).

[27] Reg. §§ 1.662(a)–2 and –3.

Distributing DNI

Example 25

Assume the same facts as in Example 24, except that DNI is $12,000. Harriet and Wally each receive $10,000, but they cannot be taxed in total on more than DNI. Each is taxed on $6,000 [DNI $12,000 × ($10,000 ÷ $20,000 of the first-tier distributions)].

Example 26

Return to the facts in Example 23. Wong receives a first-tier distribution of $15,000. Now assume that second-tier distributions include $20,000 to Wong and $25,000 to Washington. Wilson's DNI is $40,000, so total distributions exceed DNI. The DNI is allocated as follows:

(1)	**First-tier distributions**	
	To Wong	$15,000 DNI
	To Washington	–0–
	Remaining DNI = $25,000	
(2)	**Second-tier distributions**	
	To Wong	$11,111 DNI [($20,000 ÷ $45,000) × $25,000]
	To Washington	$13,889 DNI [($25,000 ÷ $45,000) × $25,000]

Example 27

Assume the same facts as in Example 26, except that accounting income is $80,000 and DNI is $70,000. Now, total distributions are less than DNI.

(1)	**First-tier distributions**	
	To Wong	$15,000 DNI
	To Washington	–0–
	Remaining DNI = $55,000	
(2)	**Second-tier distributions**	
	To Wong	$20,000 DNI
	To Washington	$25,000 DNI

30-4c Character of Income

Consistent with the modified pass-through principle of Subchapter J, various classes of income (e.g., dividends, passive activity or portfolio gain and loss, AMT adjustments and preferences, tax-exempt interest) retain the same character for the beneficiaries that they had when they were received by the entity. If there are multiple beneficiaries *and* if all of the DNI is distributed, a problem arises in allocating the various classes of income among the beneficiaries.

Distributions are treated as consisting of the same proportion as the items that enter into the computation of DNI.

$$\frac{\text{Beneficiary's total share of DNI distributed}}{\text{Total DNI distributed}} \times \text{Total of DNI element deemed distributed (e.g., tax-exempt interest)} = \text{Beneficiary's share of the DNI element}$$

If the entity distributes only a part of its DNI, the amount of a specific class of DNI that is deemed distributed first must be determined.[28]

$$\frac{\text{Total distribution}}{\text{Total distributable net income}} \times \text{Total of a particular class of distributable net income (e.g., tax-exempt interest)} = \text{Total of the DNI element deemed distributed}$$

[28]Reg. § 1.662(b)−1.

DNI Flow-Throughs

Example 28

The Baron Trust has DNI of $40,000, including $10,000 of taxable interest, $10,000 of tax-exempt interest, and $20,000 of passive activity income. The trustee distributes only one-half of DNI, at her discretion, $8,000 to Mai and $12,000 to Nancy.

		Income Type		
Beneficiary	**Amount Received**	**Taxable Interest**	**Tax-Exempt Interest**	**Passive Activity Income**
Mai	$ 8,000	$2,000*	$2,000	$4,000
Nancy	12,000	3,000	3,000	6,000

*($8,000 distribution ÷ $40,000 total DNI) × $10,000 taxable interest in DNI.

Continue with the facts of Example 28. The character of the income that flows through to Mai and Nancy is effective for all other tax purposes. For instance, the $4,000 passive activity income that is allocated to Mai is available for offset against passive activity losses that she incurred from limited partnerships and rental activities for the year. Similarly, the $3,000 taxable interest income allocated to Nancy may be subject to the net investment income tax. Each item is treated as if it had been received directly by the taxpayer.

Special Allocations

Under limited circumstances, the parties may modify the character-of-income allocation method set forth above. A modification is permitted only to the extent the allocation is required in the trust instrument and only to the extent it has an economic effect independent of the cash-flow and income tax consequences of the allocation.[29]

Return to the facts in Example 28. Assume that the beneficiaries are elderly individuals who have pooled their investment portfolios to avail themselves of the trustee's professional asset management skills. The trustee has the discretion to allocate different classes of income to different beneficiaries, and she designates $10,000 of Nancy's $12,000 distribution as being from the tax-exempt income. Such a designation *would not be recognized* for tax purposes, and the allocation method of Example 28 must be used.

Suppose, however, the trust instrument stipulated that Nancy was to receive all of the income from the tax-exempt securities because Nancy alone contributed the exempt securities to trust corpus. Under this provision, the $10,000 of the nontaxable interest is paid to Nancy. This allocation *is recognized*, and $10,000 of Nancy's distribution is tax-exempt.

30-5 Grantor Trusts

LO.4

Use the special rules that apply to trusts where the creator (grantor) of the trust retains certain rights.

A series of special provisions applies when the grantor of the trust retains beneficial enjoyment or substantial control over the trust property or income.[30] Such an entity is known as a **grantor trust**. The grantor is taxed on the trust's net income, and the trust is disregarded for income tax purposes.

Such taxes restrict the grantor's ability to redirect the income recognized from trust corpus to the trust or its beneficiaries. The trustee still files a Form 1041, but no dollar amounts are included on the mostly "blank" return. All income and deduction items are reported on the grantor's Form 1040.[31]

[29]Reg. § 1.652(b)–2(b). This is similar to the § 704(b)(2) requirement for partnerships. See text Section 21-4b.

[30]§§ 671–679.

[31]Reg § 1.671–4(a).

The grantor is taxed on the income if they retain (1) control of the corpus or (2) the power to dispose of the trust income without the approval or consent of any adverse party. An *adverse party* is any person having a substantial beneficial interest in the trust who could be affected negatively by the grantor's action.[32]

A number of important powers, including the following, will *not* cause such income to be taxed to the grantor:[33]

- To apply the income toward the support of the grantor's dependents.[34]
- To allocate trust income or corpus among charitable beneficiaries.
- To invade corpus on behalf of a designated beneficiary.
- To withhold income from a beneficiary during their minority or disability.
- To allocate receipts and disbursements between income and corpus.

The retention by the grantor of certain administrative powers over the trust causes the income to be taxed to the grantor. Such powers include those to deal with trust income or corpus for less than full and adequate consideration and to borrow from the trust without providing adequate interest or security.[35]

The grantor of a trust is taxed on the trust's income if they can revoke the trust.[36] In addition, a grantor is taxed on all or part of the income of a trust when, without the consent of any adverse party, the income may be:

- Distributed to the grantor or the grantor's spouse.
- Held or accumulated for future distribution to the grantor or the grantor's spouse.
- Applied to the payment of premiums on insurance policies on the life of the grantor or the grantor's spouse.[37]

Frank creates an irrevocable trust for his children with a transfer of income-producing property and an insurance policy on the life of Marion, his wife. During the year, the trustee uses $3,000 of the entity's $40,000 accounting income to pay the premiums on the policy covering Marion's life. Frank is taxed on $3,000 under the grantor trust rules.

Moreover, trust income accumulated for the benefit of someone whom the grantor is *legally obligated* to support is taxed to the grantor, but only to the extent it is applied for that purpose.[38] In these cases, the beneficiary often is a child or an ex-spouse.

Melanie creates an irrevocable family trust. Her son, Sean, is the life beneficiary, and the remainder goes to any grandchildren. During the year, the trust income of $8,000 is applied as follows: $5,000 toward Sean's college tuition and other related educational expenses and $3,000 accumulated on Sean's behalf. If, under state law, Melanie has an obligation to support Sean and, if this obligation includes providing a college education, Melanie is taxed on the $5,000 that is so applied.

[32] §§ 672(a) and 674. See Reg. § 1.672(a)–1 for examples of adverse party situations.

[33] § 674(b).

[34] § 677(b). However, when the income actually is applied for this purpose, the grantor is subject to income tax on that amount.

[35] See Reg. § 1.675–1(b) for a further discussion of this matter.

[36] § 676.

[37] § 677(a).

[38] § 677(b). The taxpayer's legal obligations vary according to state law, financial resources, and family expectations. See *Frederick C. Braun, Jr.*, 48 TCM 210, T.C.Memo. 1984–285, and *Cristopher Stone*, 54 TCM 462, T.C.Memo. 1987–454.

30-6 **Procedural Matters**

The fiduciary is required to file a Form 1041 (U.S. Income Tax Return for Estates and Trusts) in the following situations:[39]

- For an estate that has gross income of $600 or more for the year.
- For a trust that either has any taxable income or, if there is no taxable income, has gross income of $600 or more.

The fiduciary return (and any related tax liability) is due no later than the fifteenth day of the fourth month following the close of the entity's taxable year. A filing extension is available to the last day of the ninth month after the end of the tax year. For calendar year entities, these dates are April 15 and September 30.

Many fiduciary entities recognize capital gains during the year, through sales of assets that are part of corpus. In that event, a Schedule D is filed with the Form 1041, and the fiduciary entity or its beneficiaries can qualify for the lower tax rates on long-term capital gains.

The pass-through of income and deduction items to the beneficiary is accomplished through Schedule K–1 to Form 1041. This form is similar in format and function to the Schedule K–1 for partners and S corporation shareholders (see Chapters 21 and 23).

Trusts and estates must make estimated Federal income tax payments using the same quarterly schedule that applies to individual taxpayers. This requirement applies to estates only for tax years that end two or more years after the date of the decedent's death.[40]

Fiduciary entities also must determine filing requirements that must be met for each of the U.S. states. These matters may turn on the location of the entity, the trustee/executor, and the beneficiaries.

30-7 **Tax Planning**

LO.5

Apply the fiduciary income tax rules in a manner that minimizes the income taxation of trusts and estates and still accomplishes the intended objectives of the grantor or decedent.

Many of the tax planning possibilities for estates and trusts were discussed in Chapter 29. However, several specific tax planning possibilities are available to help minimize the present value of any income tax liabilities on estates and trusts and their beneficiaries.

30-7a **A Trust or an Estate as an Income-Shifting Device**

Opportunities to use fiduciary entities for effective income shifting from one individual to another are limited, because the kiddie tax might apply to the amounts received by the beneficiary, and the fiduciary is likely to be subject to a marginal tax rate that is equal to or higher than that of the grantor/decedent. Other strategies still should be considered by the parties.

- Trust corpus should be invested in growth assets that are low on yield but high on appreciation so that the trustee can determine the timing of the gain and somewhat control the effective tax rate that applies.
- Trust corpus should be invested in tax-exempt securities such as municipal bonds and mutual funds that invest in them, to reduce entity tax liabilities.
- The grantor should retain high-yield assets, rather than contribute them to a fiduciary entity (i.e., where the income tax marginal rates are high).
- Use of trust vehicles should be reserved for cases where professional management of the assets is necessary for portfolio growth and the additional tax costs can be justified.

[39]§§ 6012(a)(3) and (4).

[40]§ 6654(l)(2)(A).

30-7b **Income Tax Planning for Estates**

As a separate taxable entity, an estate can select its own tax year and accounting methods. The executor of an estate should consider selecting a fiscal year because this will determine when beneficiaries include income distributions from the estate in their own tax returns. Beneficiaries include the income for their tax year with or within which the estate's tax year ends. Proper selection of the estate's tax year can result in a smoothing out of income and a reduction of the income taxes for all parties involved.

The timing and amounts of income distributions to the beneficiaries present important tax planning opportunities. If the executor can make discretionary income distributions, they should evaluate the relative marginal income tax rates of the estate and its beneficiaries. By timing the distributions properly, the overall income tax liability can be minimized. Care should be taken, however, to time the distributions in light of the estate's DNI.

Distribution Strategies

Example 33

For several years before his death on March 7, Don had entered into annual deferred compensation agreements with his employer. These agreements collectively called for the payment of $200,000 six months after Don's retirement or death. To provide a maximum 12-month period within which to generate deductions to offset this large item of income in respect of a decedent, the executor or administrator of the estate should elect a fiscal year ending August 31. The election is made simply by filing the estate's first tax return for the short period of March 7 to August 31.

Carol, the sole beneficiary of an estate, is a calendar year, cash basis taxpayer. If the estate elects a fiscal year ending January 31, all distributions during the period of February 1 to December 31, 2022, are reported on Carol's tax return for calendar year 2023 (due April 15, 2024). Thus, assuming that estimated tax requirements otherwise have been met, any income taxes that result from a $50,000 distribution made by the estate on February 20, 2022, may be deferred until April 15, 2024.

Assume the same facts as in Example 34. If the estate is closed on December 15, 2023, the DNI for both the fiscal year ending January 31, 2023 and the final tax year ending December 15, 2023 is included in Carol's tax return for the same calendar year. To avoid the effect of this bunching of income, the estate should not be closed until early in 2024.

In general, those beneficiaries who are subject to high income tax rates should be made beneficiaries of second-tier (but not IRD) distributions of the estate. Most likely, these individuals will have less need for an additional steady stream of (taxable) income while their income tax savings can be relatively large. Moreover, a special allocation of tax-favored types of income and expenses should be considered. For example, tax-exempt income can be directed more easily to beneficiaries in higher income tax brackets.

Review Examples 26 and 27 carefully. Note, for instance, the flexibility that is available to the executor or administrator in timing the second-tier distributions of income and corpus of the estate. To illustrate, if Washington is subject to a high tax rate, distributions to him should be minimized except in years when DNI is low. In this manner, Washington's exposure to gross income from the distributions can be controlled so that most of the distributions he receives will be free of income tax.

30-7c Distributions of In-Kind Property

The ability of the trustee or executor to elect to recognize the realized gain or loss relative to a distributed noncash asset allows the gain or loss to be allocated to the optimal taxpayer.

Example 37

The Yorba Linda Estate distributed some inventory, basis of $40,000 and fair market value of $41,500, to beneficiary Larry. Yorba Linda is subject to a 24% marginal income tax rate, and Larry is subject to a 35% marginal rate. The executor of Yorba Linda should elect that the entity recognize the related $1,500 realized gain, thereby subjecting the gain to the estate's lower marginal tax rate.

Tax without election, at Larry's 35% rate	$525
Tax with election, at estate's 24% rate	360

Ethics & Equity Who Should Be a Trustee?

Often, grantors choose a family member to be the trustee of the family savings, the children's education fund, or whatever other assets are placed into management by the trust. The relative chosen often is the most trusted member of the family, but this person may not have the appropriate business, tax, and financial skills. Moreover, as the financial world has become more complex, with stock market fluctuations, increased fiduciary standards, and potential conflicts of interest, some question the wisdom of using a family member as the trustee in any case.

Using a trust company or other financial institution as a trustee usually results in more stable (if lower) investment returns, eliminating both the highs and the lows of the stock market cycle. Institutions also can bring other advantages.

- They do not die, run away, become mentally or physically incapacitated, or otherwise unexpectedly become unqualified for the position.
- They are not easily swayed by emotional appeals; nor do they react to family jealousies.
- They are prohibited by law from acting under a conflict of interest, such as might exist between family members when the related trustee is also a trust beneficiary.

On the other hand, human trustees often waive or discount their fiduciary fee, but institutions do not. Especially for trusts with a small corpus, institutional trustees can be prohibitively expensive.

How would you advise a client to address this delicate issue? Compromise solutions might be to:

- Appoint co-trustees. Aunt Grace or Uncle Roberto can provide the personal touch and ensure that trust decisions recognize family needs, and the trust company maximizes investment returns and furnishes professional management.
- Keep the family trustee but hire professionals at an hourly rate to provide advice only when needed. This approach avoids the fees based on asset values that trust companies usually charge and can be expensive when incurred every year.

30-7d Deductibility of Administrative Expenses

Some deductions and losses may be claimed either on the estate tax return or as income tax deductions of the estate on the fiduciary return, at the taxpayer's choice.[41] In such a case, the deduction for income tax purposes is not allowed unless the estate tax deduction is waived. These deductions can be apportioned between the two returns.

[41] § 642(g) and Reg. § 20.2053–1(d).

Don's will named his surviving spouse, Donna, as the executor of his estate. The estate's assets total $25,000,000. The will includes bequests to pay various debts, make gifts to certain charities, and provide for the grandchildren through trusts. The will also allows for the payment of an executor's fee equal to 2% of the assets ($500,000).

Should Donna pay herself an executor's fee? If Donna also is the estate's remainder beneficiary, a common occurrence, payment of the fee would result in the following:

- A deduction by the estate on the Form 706 (e.g., at the 40% marginal rate) or the estate's Form 1041 (at the 37% marginal rate).
- Gross income for services to Donna (e.g., at her individual 32% marginal tax rate).

If Donna waives the executor's fee, she will receive the $500,000 as the remainder beneficiary of the estate. Then the results would be:

- An increased marital deduction on the Form 706 (deductible at the 40% tax rate).
- No gross income to Donna, because the receipt of a bequest is excludible.

Almost certainly, a remainder beneficiary who is a surviving spouse would waive the fee.

An expense deductible for estate tax purposes may not qualify as an income tax deduction because of differences in the tax base. The expenses likely should be claimed for estate tax purposes; otherwise, the deduction will be completely lost.

The executor of Dana's estate pays $15,000 in burial expenses (authorized under local law and approved by the probate court) from estate assets. The $15,000 expense should be claimed on the estate tax return, because it is not deductible at all for income tax purposes.

30-7e **Duties of an Executor**

One of the duties of an estate's executor is to file the last income tax return of the decedent.[42] That Form 1040 is due on April 15 of the year following the date of death, regardless of when during the year death occurs.[43] Several planning considerations are apparent in this regard.

The executor must be aware that the decedent's tax year ends on the date of death, but the standard deduction is not reduced even though a short tax year results.

The final Form 1040 may be filed simply to claim a refund of the decedent's estimated tax payments or withholdings. If the decedent was married on the date of death, a joint return can be filed with signatures of both the executor and the surviving spouse.[44]

30-7f **Additional Taxes on Capital Gains and Net Investment Income**

Aggressive income shifting among a fiduciary entity and its beneficiaries may be prompted by the fiduciary's exposure to the liabilities for additional Federal income taxes on capital gains and net investment income (NII). These additional taxes apply only to "high-income" taxpayers, but the income level at which the tax applies is much lower for fiduciaries than it is for individuals.

Thus, investment income and capital gains might best be distributed to individual beneficiaries, removing the items from the NII of the fiduciary, perhaps without creating an additional tax liability for the beneficiary.

[42] § 6012(b)(1).

[43] Reg. § 1.6072–1(b).

[44] § 6013(a). This also might occur for the prior year (when the spouse was alive) if the return for that year has not yet been filed.

The entity's NII tax can be reduced if the fiduciary invests in securities that produce tax-exempt or tax-deferred income or meets the material participation requirement for otherwise passive activities. In addition, the tax liability can be minimized if the entity invests in assets that produce a low yield (like growth stocks or funds) and if it arranges its portfolio to produce a low turnover rate.

Refocus on The Big Picture

Setting Up a Trust to Protect a Family

Anna Jiang and her family should consider the creation of one or more trusts to provide security in case Anna is incapacitated by medical problems and unable to manage the family's finances. Some suggestions for the family might be:

- Anna transfers some or all of the $2 million in assets to the Jiang Family Trust, with quarterly income payable to Tom and the children. Recipients would be designated by the trustee, but all of the entity's accounting income must be distributed. In this way, the income could be directed to the beneficiary most in need (e.g., to pay for education expenses or to start a new business). The children could be named first-tier beneficiaries, with Tom as a second-tier income beneficiary.
- While Anna is still healthy and earning a regular salary, the trustee could accumulate the accounting income and allow the corpus to grow. Alternatively, the trustee could make gifts to charity or fund education plans for Bobby and Sally.
- Anna should provide clear instructions to the trustee as to her preferences on how the trust corpus should be invested and specify which of Tom's and the children's expenses should and should not be covered.
- The children should be named as remainder beneficiaries of the Jiang Family Trust. In case the trust corpus exceeds the estate tax bypass amount, other remainder beneficiaries could be named, ideally while avoiding any generation-skipping tax (see Chapter 29).
- Amendments to the trust document should be considered whenever Tom and Anna update their wills.

What If?

If Anna remains healthy, the Jiang Family Trust might be terminated when the children reach the age of majority, as their need for financial support will have diminished. However, if Tom is unable or unwilling to take over management of the assets, the trust should continue. In this event, the trustee should be chosen from family members or business associates who know Anna and Tom well and are familiar with the couple's objectives. Then the trustee might shift the focus to funding long-term care for the couple, making charitable gifts, or financing the education needs of grandchildren.

Key Terms

Complex trust, 30-4
Corpus, 30-4
Deductions in respect of a decedent, 30-12
Distributable net income (DNI), 30-16
Entity accounting income, 30-8
Fiduciary, 30-2
Grantor, 30-3
Grantor trust, 30-23
Income in respect of a decedent (IRD), 30-12
Pass-through entities, 30-6
Reversionary interest, 30-4
Simple trust, 30-4
Sprinkling trust, 30-4

Discussion Questions

Communications

1. **LO.1** A local bank has asked you to speak at its Building Personal Wealth Conference on the topic of "What Should Your Trust Do for You?" Develop at least four talking points, each one identifying a function that a trust might be able to accomplish for an individual who has more than a modest level of financial resources.

2. **LO.1** In general terms, describe how the following entities are subject to the Federal income tax. (Answer only for the entity, not for its owners, beneficiaries, etc.)
   a. C corporations (Subchapter C).
   b. Partnerships (Subchapter K).
   c. S corporations (Subchapter S).
   d. Trusts and estates (Subchapter J).

3. **LO.1** Create a fact pattern that illustrates each of the following tax situations. Be specific.
   a. A simple trust.
   b. A complex trust with a $300 personal exemption.
   c. A complex trust with a $100 personal exemption.

4. **LO.2** The Liu Trust is short of cash. It is required to distribute $100,000 to Yang every year, and that payment is due in six weeks. In its asset corpus, Liu holds a number of investments that are valued at $100,000. One of them is a plot of land with a tax basis to the trust of $80,000. What are the alternative Federal income tax consequences if Liu distributes this land to Yang? *Hint:* You should consider a trustee election in your answer.

Critical Thinking

5. **LO.2** In its first tax year, the Vasquez Estate generated $50,000 of taxable interest income and $30,000 of tax-exempt interest income. It paid $8,000 in fees to the executor. The estate is subject to a 40% marginal estate tax rate and a 37% marginal income tax rate. How much should the executor assign as an estate tax deduction for the payment of the fees?

6. **LO.2** The Sterling Trust owns a business and generated $100,000 in depreciation deductions for the tax year. Mona is one of the income beneficiaries of the entity.
   a. Given the following information, compute Mona's deduction, if any, for the Sterling depreciation.
   b. Express your solution as a Microsoft Excel command.

Sterling's taxable income from the business	$ 800,000
Sterling's gross income from the business	4,000,000
Mona's share of trust accounting income	500,000
Total trust accounting income	2,500,000
Mona's share of distributable net income	1,200,000
Total distributable net income	1,600,000

7. **LO.2** In year 1, the Helpful Trust agreed to make a $50,000 cash contribution to Local Soup Kitchen, a charitable organization. Helpful's board agreed to the gift at a November year 1 meeting, but the check was not issued until February 20, year 2 (i.e., during the next tax year).
   a. For which tax year can the trust claim a charitable contribution deduction?
   b. Would the answer to part (a) change if the check was issued on May 1, year 2? If so, how?

8. **LO.3** One of the key concepts in fiduciary income taxation is that of *distributable net income* (DNI). List the major functions of DNI. Just review the uses of DNI in Subchapter J, and do not discuss its computation.

9. **LO.4** Jada wants to transfer some assets to a trust this year; the income beneficiaries will be her two grandchildren. The trust income and assets will be used to pay the grandchildren's tuition to private high schools and universities. Upon the younger grandchild's graduation, the trust assets will return to Jada's ownership. Identify tax issues related to Jada's plan to use a temporary fiduciary entity. Critical Thinking

10. **LO.4** Carol has been promoted several times, and she may be named a partner in her consulting firm next year. Thus, she will be subject to higher marginal income tax rates than in the past. Carol's colleague Isaiah has told her about a "college education trust" from which he pays tuition and fees for his children. He has implied that there are sizable tax advantages to setting up a trust for this purpose. Communications Decision Making

    Carol is considering establishing a similar trust to pay tuition for her own children. She believes that the trust will be able to deduct the tuition payments, something that she cannot currently do on her Form 1040. Write a memo for the tax research file addressing Carol's ideas and recommending a tax-effective course of action.

11. **LO. 3, 5** Comment on the following items relative to tax planning strategies of a fiduciary entity. Decision Making

    a. To reduce taxes for a typical family, should income be shifted *to* a trust or *from* a trust? Why?

    b. From a tax planning standpoint, who should invest in tax-exempt bonds, the trust or its beneficiaries?

    c. To reduce overall taxes, should a high-income, wealthy beneficiary be assigned to the first or second tier of trust distributions? Why?

Computational Exercises

12. **LO.1** Compute the Federal income tax liability for the Valerio Trust. The entity reports the following transactions for the 2023 tax year. The trustee accumulates all accounting income for the year.

Operating income from a business	$ 500,000
Dividend income, all from U.S. corporations (20% tax rate)	30,000
Interest income, City of San Antonio bonds	40,000
Trustee fees, deductible portion	(15,000)
Net rental losses, passive activity	(100,000)

13. **LO.1** The Wes Trust reports $140,000 of AMT income before the annual exemption. Compute the entity's AMT for 2023.

14. LO.1 For 2023, the Guess Trust retains all of its income items, which include only $100,000 of net investment income and $140,000 of profits from an active business operation. Guess incurs an additional tax on net investment income (NIIT) of:
   a. $9,120.
   b. $5,320.
   c. $3,800.
   d. $0.

15. LO.2 The Bildge Trust is a simple trust. Crawford is its sole beneficiary. In the current year, the trust earns $3,200 in taxable interest and $8,000 in tax-exempt interest. In addition, the trust recognizes a $2,500 long-term capital gain. The trustee charges a fee of $1,800 for the year.
   a. Compute trust accounting income, where the trust agreement allocates fees and capital gains to corpus.
   b. Same as part (a), except that fees are allocated to income.

16. LO.2 The Hosta Trust reports gross rent income of $72,000, expenses attributable to the rents of $55,000, and tax-exempt interest from state bonds of $18,000. Under the trust agreement, the trustee is to pay 20% of the annual trust accounting income to the American Red Cross, a qualifying charitable organization.
   a. Compute Hosta's charitable contribution deduction.
   b. Express the solution as a Microsoft Excel command.

Problems

17. LO.1 Complete the following chart, indicating the comparative attributes of the typical simple trust and complex trust by answering yes/no or explaining the differences between the entities where appropriate.

Attribute	Simple Trust	Complex Trust
Trust could incur its own tax liability for the year	________	________
Trust generally distributes all of the DNI	________	________
Maximum tax rate on net long-term capital gains = 20%	________	________
Trust can adopt the FIFO method for its inventory assets; the grantor had been using lower of cost or market	________	________
Trust can use a tax year other than the calendar year	________	________
Amount of personal exemption	________	________

Decision Making

18. LO.2 The Polozzi Trust will incur the following items in the next tax year, its first year of existence:

Interest income	$ 25,000
Rent income	100,000
Cost recovery deductions for the rental activity	35,000
Capital gain income	40,000
Trustee and tax preparation fees	7,000

Betty, the grantor of the trust, is working with you on the language in the trust instrument relative to the derivation of annual accounting income for the entity. She will name Shirley as the sole income beneficiary and Benny as the remainder beneficiary.

a. Suggest language to Betty that will maximize the annual income distribution to Shirley.

b. Suggest language to Betty that will minimize the annual distribution to Shirley and maximize the accumulation on Benny's behalf.

19. **LO.2** Complete the chart below, indicating the Calvet Trust's entity accounting income for each of the alternatives. For this purpose, use the following information:

Interest income, taxable	$300,000
Interest income, tax-exempt	30,000
Interest income, tax-exempt but AMT preference item	20,000
Long-term capital gain	40,000
Trustee fee	10,000

Trust Agreement Provisions	Trust Accounting Income
Fees and capital gains allocable to corpus	______
Capital gains allocable to corpus, one-half of fees allocable to income	______
Capital gains allocable to income, silent concerning allocation of fees	______
Fees and exempt income allocable to corpus, silent concerning allocation of capital gain/loss	______

20. **LO.1, 2, 3** Complete the following chart, indicating the comparative attributes of the typical trust and estate by answering yes/no or explaining the differences between the entities where appropriate.

Attribute	Estate	Trust
Separate income tax entity	______	______
Controlling document	______	______
Can have both income and remainder beneficiaries	______	______
Termination date is determinable from controlling document	______	______
Document identifies both income and remainder beneficiaries	______	______
Generally must use calendar tax year	______	______

21. **LO.2** Roberto is one of the income beneficiaries of the Carol LeMans Estate. This year, as directed by the will, Roberto received all of the sales commissions that were earned and payable to Carol (cash basis) at her death, as well as one of three remaining installment payments. Compute Roberto's gross income attributable to Carol's activities for the current year, given the following financial data:

Sales commissions receivable	$40,000
Ordinary gain, $60,000, on installment sale; first of three payments received this year	20,000

22. **LO.2** Sanchez incurred the following items:

Business income, exclusive of the following items	$80,000
Tax-exempt interest income	40,000
Payment to charity from 2023 Sanchez gross income, paid 3/1/24	20,000

Complete the following chart, indicating the charitable contributions deduction under the various assumptions. See also text Section 17-1h.

Assumption	2023 Deduction for Contribution
Sanchez is a cash basis individual.	________
Sanchez is an accrual basis corporation.	________
Sanchez is a trust.	________

23. **LO.2** The Twist Trust has generated $60,000 in depreciation deductions for the year. Its accounting income is $75,000. In computing this amount, pursuant to the trust document, depreciation was allocated to corpus. Accounting income was distributed at the trustee's discretion: $25,000 to Hernandez and $50,000 to Jackson.
    a. Compute the depreciation deductions that Hernandez, Jackson, and Twist may claim.
    b. Same as part (a), except that depreciation was allocated to income.
    c. Same as part (a), except that the trustee distributed $15,000 each to Hernandez and to Jackson and retained the remaining accounting income.

24. **LO.2, 3** The Allwardt Trust is a simple trust that correctly uses the calendar year for tax purposes. Its income beneficiaries (Lucy and Ethel) are entitled to the trust's annual accounting income in shares of one-half each.

    For the current tax year, Allwardt reports the following:

Ordinary income	$100,000
Long-term capital gains, allocable to corpus	30,000
Legal and accounting fees, allocable to corpus	5,000

Use the format of Exhibit 30.5 to address the following items:

    a. How much income is each beneficiary entitled to receive?
    b. What is the trust's DNI?
    c. What is the trust's taxable income?
    d. How much gross income is reported by each of the beneficiaries?

25. **LO.2, 3** The Allwardt Trust is a simple trust that correctly uses the calendar year for tax purposes. Its income beneficiaries (Lucy and Ethel) are entitled to the trust's annual accounting income in shares of one-half each.

    For the current tax year, Allwardt reports the following:

Ordinary income	$100,000
Long-term capital gains, allocable to income	30,000
Legal and accounting fees, allocable to corpus	5,000

    a. How much income is each beneficiary entitled to receive?
    b. What is the trust's DNI?
    c. What is the trust's taxable income?
    d. How much gross income is reported by each of the beneficiaries?

26. **LO.3** The Kilp Sisters Trust is required to distribute $60,000 annually equally to its two income beneficiaries, Clare and Renee. If trust income is not sufficient to pay these amounts, the trustee can invade corpus to the extent necessary.

    During the current year, the trust generates only taxable interest income and records DNI of $160,000; the trustee distributes $30,000 to Clare and $150,000 to Renee.

    a. Are these distributions first-tier or second-tier distributions?
    b. How much of the $150,000 distributed to Renee is included in her gross income?
    c. How much of the $30,000 distributed to Clare is included in her gross income?

27. **LO.3** The Dolce Estate reports the following items for the current tax year:

Dividend income	$ 50,000
Taxable interest income	8,000
Passive activity income	30,000
Tax-exempt interest income	12,000
Distributable net income	$100,000

Dolce's two noncharitable income beneficiaries, Brenda and Dev, receive cash distributions of $20,000 each. How much of each class of income is deemed to have been distributed to Brenda? To Dev?

28. **LO.2, 3** The trustee of the Pieper Trust can distribute any amount of accounting income and corpus to the trust's beneficiaries, Lydia and Avi. This year, the trust incurred the following:

Taxable interest income	$40,000
Tax-exempt interest income	20,000
Long-term capital gains—allocable to corpus	80,000
Legal and accounting fees—allocable to corpus	9,000

The trustee distributed $26,000 to Lydia and $13,000 to Avi.

a. What is Pieper's trust accounting income?

b. What is Pieper's DNI?

c. What is Pieper's taxable income?

d. What amounts are taxed to each of the beneficiaries?

29. **LO.4** In each of the following independent cases, write a memo for the tax research file in preparation for a meeting with Marques. In each memo, explain whether the proposed plan meets his objective of shifting income and avoiding the grantor trust rules.

Communications
Decision Making

a. Marques transfers property in trust, income payable to Wayne (his spouse) for life, remainder to his grandson. Marques's son is designated as the trustee.

b. Marques transfers income-producing assets and a life insurance policy to a trust, life estate to his children, remainder to his grandchildren. The policy is on Wayne's life, and the trustee (an independent trust company) is instructed to pay the premiums with income from the income-producing assets. The trust is designated as the beneficiary of the policy.

c. Marques transfers property in trust, income payable to Wayne (Marques's ex-spouse), remainder to Marques or his estate upon Wayne's death. The transfer was made in accord with the couple's divorce agreement. An independent trust company is designated as the trustee.

30. **LO.4** Woody wants to transfer some of the income from his investment portfolio to his daughter Wendy, age 12. Woody wants the trust to be able to accumulate income on Wendy's behalf and to meet any excessive expenses associated with her chronic medical conditions. Furthermore, Woody wants the trust to protect Wendy against his premature death without increasing his Federal gross estate. Thus, Woody provides the trustee with the powers to purchase insurance on his life and to meet any medical expenses that Wendy incurs.

Decision Making
Planning

The trust is created in 2021. A whole life insurance policy with five annual premium payments is purchased during that year. The trustee spends $30,000 for Wendy's medical expenses in 2024 (but in no other year). Woody dies in 2025. Has the trust been tax-effective? Explain.

Tax Return Problems

Tax Forms Problem
ProConnect™ Tax

1. Compute the 2022 fiduciary income and Federal income tax for the Blue Trust. Prepare a spreadsheet solution to make your computations. Then complete a Form 1041 for the entity.

   In addition, determine the amount and character of the income and expense items that each beneficiary must report for the year. Omit any alternative minimum tax computations. The year's activities of the trust include the following:

Dividend income, all qualified U.S. stocks	$50,000
Taxable interest income	10,000
Tax-exempt interest income	15,000
Trustee's fees	4,000

   The trust and Betty both use the calendar tax year. Under the terms of the trust instrument, administrative fees are allocated to income. The trustee must distribute all of the entity's accounting income to Betty Blue by February 15 of the following year. The trustee followed this charge and made no other distributions during the year. Administrative fees were assigned properly as an offset to taxable interest income.

   The trust was created on July 8, 2003. There are no tax credits for the year, and none of the entity's income was derived from a personal services contract. Blue has no economic interest in any foreign trust, and it is not subject to the AMT. Its Federal identification number is 11-1111121.

   The trustee, Hoover State Federal Bank, is located at 49599 Cold Harbor Boulevard, Mountain Brook, AL 35223. Betty lives at 67671 Crestline Road, Birmingham, AL 35212. Her Social Security number is 123-45-6788.

Tax Forms Problem
ProConnect™ Tax

2. Compute the 2022 fiduciary income tax return (Form 1041) and Federal income tax for the Green Trust. Prepare a spreadsheet solution to make your computations. Round to four digits. Then complete a Form 1041 for the entity and a Schedule K–1 for beneficiary Marcus.

   In addition, determine the amount and character of the income and expense items that each beneficiary must report for the year. The trust is not subject to the AMT. The year's activities of the trust include the following:

Dividend income, all qualified U.S. stocks	$10,000
Taxable interest income	50,000
Tax-exempt interest income	20,000
Net long-term capital gain, incurred 11/1	25,000
Trustee's fees	6,000

   Under the terms of the trust instrument, cost recovery, net capital gains and losses, and administrative fees are allocable to corpus. The trustee is required to distribute $25,000 to Marcus every year. For the year, the trustee distributed $40,000 to Marcus and $40,000 to Marcus's sister, Ellen Hayes. No other distributions were made.

   In computing DNI, the trustee properly assigned all of the deductible trustee fees to the taxable interest income.

   The trustee paid $4,000 in estimated taxes for the year on behalf of the trust. Any resulting refund is to be credited to the next tax year. The exempt income was not derived from private activity bonds.

   The trust was created on December 14, 1993. It is not subject to any recapture taxes, nor can it claim any tax credits. None of its income was derived under a personal services contract. The trust has no economic interest in any foreign trust. Its Federal identification number is 11-1111122.

   The trustee, Wisconsin State National Bank, is located at 3100 East Wisconsin Avenue, Milwaukee, WI 53201. Marcus lives at 9880 East North Avenue, Shorewood, WI 53211. His Social Security number is 123-45-6788. Ellen lives at 6772 East Oklahoma Avenue, Milwaukee, WI 53204. Her Social Security number is 987-65-4321.

Research Problems

Note: Solutions to the Research Problems can be prepared by using the Thomson Reuters Checkpoint™ online tax research database, which accompanies this textbook. Solutions can also be prepared by using research materials found in a typical tax library.

Research Problem 1. For three generations, the Dexter family has sent its children to Private University, preparing them for successful professional careers. The Edna Dexter Trust was established in the 1970s by LaKeisha's late grandmother and has accumulated a sizable corpus. It makes distributions to Edna's descendants rarely, and then only when they need large amounts of capital. For example, two years ago, the trust distributed $500,000 to DuJuan Dexter to aid him in starting a practice in retirement and elder law. In most years, the trust's income is donated to a single charity. Critical Thinking

Under the terms of the trust, Bigby Dexter, LaKeisha's uncle and legal guardian, can specify the trust beneficiaries and the amounts to be distributed to them. He also can replace the trustee and designate the charity that will receive the year's contribution. Accordingly, the trust falls under the grantor trust rules, and Bigby reports the trust's transactions on his own Form 1040.

LaKeisha wants to attend the prestigious local Academy High School, which will require a four-year expenditure for tuition and fees of $250,000, payable in advance. She approaches the Dexter trustee and requests a current-year distribution of this amount, payable directly to the Academy. Under the laws of the state, the parent or guardian must provide a child with a public school education (no tuition charge) until age 16.

If the payment to the Academy is made by the trust, how is it treated under the Subchapter J rules: as a charitable contribution to the Academy, as a corpus distribution to LaKeisha, or in some other manner? Be specific.

Use internet tax resources to address the following questions. Look for reliable websites and blogs of the IRS and other government agencies, media outlets, businesses, tax professionals, academics, think tanks, and political outlets.

Research Problem 2. Use the latest *IRS Data Book* to determine how many Forms 1041 were filed in the two most recent years. How much Federal income tax was collected on Forms 1041 over those tax years? Summarize your findings in bullet points to share with your classmates.

Research Problem 3. Send a chart to your instructor concerning three of the last five years for which data are available. Use the latest *IRS Data Book* to determine the IRS audit rate for estate and trust income tax returns for each period, the number of audited Forms 1041 for the year, the dollar amount of additional tax assessed from such audits, and the number of the audited returns with a zero recommended tax liability change. Communications Data Analytics

Research Problem 4. Under the income tax laws of your state applicable to fiduciary entities, how are the following items allocated among the entity and the beneficiaries? Put your findings in a PowerPoint presentation for your classmates. Communications

- Capital gain.
- Cost recovery.
- Exempt interest income.
- QBI deduction.

Research Problem 5. Find the website of a law firm that seems to specialize in fiduciary entities, preferably a firm located in your state. Ask the firm to quote you a fee for (1) establishing a simple trust and (2) filing the annual Form 1041. Summarize your findings and your communications with the firm in an e-mail to your instructor. Communications

Becker CPA Review Questions

Becker

1. Which of the following distributions meets the qualifications of a simple trust?
   a. The trust distributes all of the current year's income to the beneficiaries.
   b. The trust distributes part of the trust principal to the beneficiaries.
   c. The trust distributes all of the current year's income to a charitable organization.
   d. The trust distributes part of the trust principal to a charitable organization.

2. Which of the following is a characteristic of a complex trust, rather than a simple trust?
   a. A complex trust must distribute all of the income earned by trust assets to the beneficiaries each year.
   b. A complex trust is required to make distributions to beneficiaries every year.
   c. A complex trust is not allowed to make distributions to a charitable organization.
   d. A complex trust is allowed to distribute trust principal to the beneficiaries.

3. On January 1, year 1, Olinto created a $650,000 trust that provided his mother with a lifetime income interest starting on January 1, year 1, with the remainder interest to go to his son. Olinto expressly retained the power to revoke both the income interest and the remainder interest at any time. Who is taxed on the trust's year 1 income?
   a. Olinto's mother
   b. Olinto's son
   c. Olinto
   d. The trust

4. A distribution from estate income *currently* required was made to the estate's sole beneficiary during its calendar year. The maximum amount of the distribution to be included in the beneficiary's gross income is limited to the estate's:
   a. Capital gain income.
   b. Ordinary gross income.
   c. Distributable net income.
   d. Net investment income.

5. Lyon, a cash basis taxpayer, died on January 15 of the current year. During the current year, the estate executor made the required periodic distribution of $9,000 from estate income to Lyon's sole heir. The following information pertains to the estate's income and disbursements for the year. For the current calendar year, what was the estate's distributable net income (DNI)?

Estate Income	
Taxable interest	$20,000
Net long-term capital gains allocable to corpus	10,000

Estate Disbursements	
Administrative expenses attributable to taxable income	$5,000

   a. $15,000
   b. $20,000
   c. $25,000
   d. $30,000

6. Reinus, a cash basis taxpayer, died on February 3. During the year, the estate's executor made a distribution of $12,000 from estate income to Reinus's sole heir and adopted a calendar year to determine the estate's taxable income. The following additional information pertains to the estate's income and disbursements for the year. For the calendar year, what was the estate's distributable net income (DNI)?

Estate Income	
Taxable interest	$85,000
Net long-term capital gains allocable to corpus	10,000

Estate Disbursements	
Administrative expenses attributable to taxable income	$24,000
Charitable contributions from gross income to a public charity, made under the terms of the will	19,000

a. $39,000
b. $42,000
c. $58,000
d. $65,000

7. A distribution to an estate's sole beneficiary for the calendar year equaled $15,000, the amount currently required to be distributed by the will. The estate's records showed the following. What amount of the distribution was taxable to the beneficiary?

Estate Income	
Taxable interest	$40,000

Estate Disbursements	
Expenses attributable to taxable interest	$34,000

a. $40,000
b. $15,000
c. $6,000
d. $0

8. Peyton Trust, which is a simple trust, distributed $45,000 to its sole beneficiary, Brooke, in the current year. Further, it had the following items of income and expense for the current year:

Interest income from municipal bonds	$10,000
Gross income from rental properties	30,000
Operating expenses for the rental properties	5,000
Trust fees allocable to the rental properties	2,000

What is Peyton's income distribution deduction for the current year?

a. $23,000
b. $33,000
c. $40,000
d. $45,000

Appendix A

Tax Formulas, Tax Rate Schedules, and Tables

(The 2023 Individual Income Tax Tables and the 2023 Individual Optional Sales Tax Tables can be accessed at the IRS website when released: **irs.gov**)

Tax Formula for Individuals

Income (broadly defined)............	$xx,xxx
Less: Exclusions............	(x,xxx)
Gross income............	$xx,xxx
Less: Deductions *for* adjusted gross income............	(x,xxx)
Adjusted gross income............	$xx,xxx
Less: The greater of—	
Total itemized deductions	
or standard deduction............	(x,xxx)
Less: Personal and dependency exemptions*............	(x,xxx)
Deduction for qualified business income**............	(x,xxx)
Taxable income............	$xx,xxx
Tax on taxable income............	$ x,xxx
Less: Tax credits (including Federal income tax	
withheld and prepaid)............	(xxx)
Tax due (or refund)............	$ xxx

*Exemption deductions are not allowed from 2018 through 2025.
**Only applies from 2018 through 2025.

Basic Standard Deduction Amounts

Filing Status	2022	2023
Single	$12,950	$13,850
Married, filing jointly	25,900	27,700
Surviving spouse	25,900	27,700
Head of household	19,400	20,800
Married, filing separately	12,950	13,850

Amount of Each Additional Standard Deduction

Filing Status	2022	2023
Single	$1,750	$1,850
Married, filing jointly	1,400	1,500
Surviving spouse	1,400	1,500
Head of household	1,750	1,850
Married, filing separately	1,400	1,500

Personal and Dependency Exemption

2022	2023
$4,400	$4,700

Note: Exemption deductions have been suspended from 2018 through 2025. However, the personal and dependency exemption amount is used for other purposes (including determining whether a "qualifying relative" is a taxpayer's dependent).

2022 Tax Rate Schedules

Single—Schedule X

If taxable income is: Over—	But not over—	The tax is:	of the amount over—
$ 0	$ 10,275	.........10%	$ 0
10,275	41,775	$ 1,027.50 + 12%	10,275
41,775	89,075	4,807.50 + 22%	41,775
89,075	170,050	15,213.50 + 24%	89,075
170,050	215,950	34,647.50 + 32%	170,050
215,950	539,900	49,335.50 + 35%	215,950
539,900	....	162,718.00 + 37%	539,900

Head of household—Schedule Z

If taxable income is: Over—	But not over—	The tax is:	of the amount over—
$ 0	$ 14,650	.........10%	$ 0
14,650	55,900	$ 1,465.00 + 12%	14,650
55,900	89,050	6,415.00 + 22%	55,900
89,050	170,050	13,708.00 + 24%	89,050
170,050	215,950	33,148.00 + 32%	170,050
215,950	539,900	47,836.00 + 35%	215,950
539,900	....	161,218.50 + 37%	539,900

Married filing jointly or Qualifying widow(er)—Schedule Y-1

If taxable income is: Over—	But not over—	The tax is:	of the amount over—
$ 0	$ 20,550	.........10%	$ 0
20,550	83,550	$ 2,055.00 + 12%	20,550
83,550	178,150	9,615.00 + 22%	83,550
178,150	340,100	30,427.00 + 24%	178,150
340,100	431,900	69,295.00 + 32%	340,100
431,900	647,850	98,671.00 + 35%	431,900
647,850	....	174,253.50 + 37%	647,850

Married filing separately—Schedule Y-2

If taxable income is: Over—	But not over—	The tax is:	of the amount over—
$ 0	$ 10,275	.........10%	$ 0
10,275	41,775	$ 1,027.50 + 12%	10,275
41,775	89,075	4,807.50 + 22%	41,775
89,075	170,050	15,213.50 + 24%	89,075
170,050	215,950	34,647.50 + 32%	170,050
215,950	323,925	49,335.50 + 35%	215,950
323,925	....	87,126.75 + 37%	323,925

2023 Tax Rate Schedules

Single—Schedule X

If taxable income is: Over—	But not over—	The tax is:	of the amount over—
$ 0	$ 11,000	.........10%	$ 0
11,000	44,725	$ 1,100.00 + 12%	11,000
44,725	95,375	5,147.00 + 22%	44,725
95,375	182,100	16,290.00 + 24%	95,375
182,100	231,250	37,104.00 + 32%	182,100
231,250	578,125	52,832.00 + 35%	231,250
578,125	....	174,238.25 + 37%	578,125

Head of household—Schedule Z

If taxable income is: Over—	But not over—	The tax is:	of the amount over—
$ 0	$ 15,700	.........10%	$ 0
15,700	59,850	$ 1,570.00 + 12%	15,700
59,850	95,350	6,868.00 + 22%	59,850
95,350	182,100	14,678.00 + 24%	95,350
182,100	231,250	35,498.00 + 32%	182,100
231,250	578,100	51,226.00 + 35%	231,250
578,100	....	172,623.50 + 37%	578,100

Married filing jointly or Qualifying widow(er)—Schedule Y-1

If taxable income is: Over—	But not over—	The tax is:	of the amount over—
$ 0	$ 22,000	.........10%	$ 0
22,000	89,450	$ 2,200.00 + 12%	22,000
89,450	190,750	10,294.00 + 22%	89,450
190,750	364,200	32,580.00 + 24%	190,750
364,200	462,500	74,208.00 + 32%	364,200
462,500	693,750	105,664.00 + 35%	462,500
693,750	....	186,601.50 + 37%	693,750

Married filing separately—Schedule Y-2

If taxable income is: Over—	But not over—	The tax is:	of the amount over—
$ 0	$ 11,000	.........10%	$ 0
11,000	44,725	$ 1,100.00 + 12%	11,000
44,725	95,375	5,147.00 + 22%	44,725
95,375	182,100	16,290.00 + 24%	95,375
182,100	231,250	37,104.00 + 32%	182,100
231,250	346,875	52,832.00 + 35%	231,250
346,875	....	93,300.75 + 37%	346,875

2022 Tax Table

See the instructions for line 16 to see if you must use the Tax Table below to figure your tax.

Example. A married couple are filing a joint return. Their taxable income on Form 1040, line 15, is $25,300. First, they find the $25,300-25,350 taxable income line. Next, they find the column for married filing jointly and read down the column. The amount shown where the taxable income line and filing status column meet is $2,628. This is the tax amount they should enter in the entry space on Form 1040, line 16.

Sample Table

At Least	But Less Than	Single	Married filing jointly*	Married filing sepa-rately	Head of a house-hold
			Your tax is—		
25,200	**25,250**	2,822	2,616	2,822	2,734
25,250	**25,300**	2,828	2,622	2,828	2,740
25,300	**25,350**	2,834	(2,628)	2,834	2,746
25,350	**25,400**	2,840	2,634	2,840	2,752

If line 15 (taxable income) is—		And you are—			
At least	But less than	Single	Married filing jointly *	Married filing sepa-rately	Head of a house-hold
		Your tax is—			
0	**5**	0	0	0	0
5	**15**	1	1	1	1
15	**25**	2	2	2	2
25	**50**	4	4	4	4
50	**75**	6	6	6	6
75	**100**	9	9	9	9
100	**125**	11	11	11	11
125	**150**	14	14	14	14
150	**175**	16	16	16	16
175	**200**	19	19	19	19
200	**225**	21	21	21	21
225	**250**	24	24	24	24
250	**275**	26	26	26	26
275	**300**	29	29	29	29
300	**325**	31	31	31	31
325	**350**	34	34	34	34
350	**375**	36	36	36	36
375	**400**	39	39	39	39
400	**425**	41	41	41	41
425	**450**	44	44	44	44
450	**475**	46	46	46	46
475	**500**	49	49	49	49
500	**525**	51	51	51	51
525	**550**	54	54	54	54
550	**575**	56	56	56	56
575	**600**	59	59	59	59
600	**625**	61	61	61	61
625	**650**	64	64	64	64
650	**675**	66	66	66	66
675	**700**	69	69	69	69
700	**725**	71	71	71	71
725	**750**	74	74	74	74
750	**775**	76	76	76	76
775	**800**	79	79	79	79
800	**825**	81	81	81	81
825	**850**	84	84	84	84
850	**875**	86	86	86	86
875	**900**	89	89	89	89
900	**925**	91	91	91	91
925	**950**	94	94	94	94
950	**975**	96	96	96	96
975	**1,000**	99	99	99	99

If line 15 (taxable income) is—		And you are—			
At least	But less than	Single	Married filing jointly *	Married filing sepa-rately	Head of a house-hold
		Your tax is—			
1,000					
1,000	**1,025**	101	101	101	101
1,025	**1,050**	104	104	104	104
1,050	**1,075**	106	106	106	106
1,075	**1,100**	109	109	109	109
1,100	**1,125**	111	111	111	111
1,125	**1,150**	114	114	114	114
1,150	**1,175**	116	116	116	116
1,175	**1,200**	119	119	119	119
1,200	**1,225**	121	121	121	121
1,225	**1,250**	124	124	124	124
1,250	**1,275**	126	126	126	126
1,275	**1,300**	129	129	129	129
1,300	**1,325**	131	131	131	131
1,325	**1,350**	134	134	134	134
1,350	**1,375**	136	136	136	136
1,375	**1,400**	139	139	139	139
1,400	**1,425**	141	141	141	141
1,425	**1,450**	144	144	144	144
1,450	**1,475**	146	146	146	146
1,475	**1,500**	149	149	149	149
1,500	**1,525**	151	151	151	151
1,525	**1,550**	154	154	154	154
1,550	**1,575**	156	156	156	156
1,575	**1,600**	159	159	159	159
1,600	**1,625**	161	161	161	161
1,625	**1,650**	164	164	164	164
1,650	**1,675**	166	166	166	166
1,675	**1,700**	169	169	169	169
1,700	**1,725**	171	171	171	171
1,725	**1,750**	174	174	174	174
1,750	**1,775**	176	176	176	176
1,775	**1,800**	179	179	179	179
1,800	**1,825**	181	181	181	181
1,825	**1,850**	184	184	184	184
1,850	**1,875**	186	186	186	186
1,875	**1,900**	189	189	189	189
1,900	**1,925**	191	191	191	191
1,925	**1,950**	194	194	194	194
1,950	**1,975**	196	196	196	196
1,975	**2,000**	199	199	199	199

If line 15 (taxable income) is—		And you are—			
At least	But less than	Single	Married filing jointly *	Married filing sepa-rately	Head of a house-hold
		Your tax is—			
2,000					
2,000	**2,025**	201	201	201	201
2,025	**2,050**	204	204	204	204
2,050	**2,075**	206	206	206	206
2,075	**2,100**	209	209	209	209
2,100	**2,125**	211	211	211	211
2,125	**2,150**	214	214	214	214
2,150	**2,175**	216	216	216	216
2,175	**2,200**	219	219	219	219
2,200	**2,225**	221	221	221	221
2,225	**2,250**	224	224	224	224
2,250	**2,275**	226	226	226	226
2,275	**2,300**	229	229	229	229
2,300	**2,325**	231	231	231	231
2,325	**2,350**	234	234	234	234
2,350	**2,375**	236	236	236	236
2,375	**2,400**	239	239	239	239
2,400	**2,425**	241	241	241	241
2,425	**2,450**	244	244	244	244
2,450	**2,475**	246	246	246	246
2,475	**2,500**	249	249	249	249
2,500	**2,525**	251	251	251	251
2,525	**2,550**	254	254	254	254
2,550	**2,575**	256	256	256	256
2,575	**2,600**	259	259	259	259
2,600	**2,625**	261	261	261	261
2,625	**2,650**	264	264	264	264
2,650	**2,675**	266	266	266	266
2,675	**2,700**	269	269	269	269
2,700	**2,725**	271	271	271	271
2,725	**2,750**	274	274	274	274
2,750	**2,775**	276	276	276	276
2,775	**2,800**	279	279	279	279
2,800	**2,825**	281	281	281	281
2,825	**2,850**	284	284	284	284
2,850	**2,875**	286	286	286	286
2,875	**2,900**	289	289	289	289
2,900	**2,925**	291	291	291	291
2,925	**2,950**	294	294	294	294
2,950	**2,975**	296	296	296	296
2,975	**3,000**	299	299	299	299

(Continued)

* This column must also be used by a qualifying surviving spouse.

2022 Tax Table — *Continued*

If line 15 (taxable income) is—		And you are—			
At least	But less than	Single	Married filing jointly *	Married filing separately	Head of a household
		Your tax is—			
3,000					
3,000	3,050	303	303	303	303
3,050	3,100	308	308	308	308
3,100	3,150	313	313	313	313
3,150	3,200	318	318	318	318
3,200	3,250	323	323	323	323
3,250	3,300	328	328	328	328
3,300	3,350	333	333	333	333
3,350	3,400	338	338	338	338
3,400	3,450	343	343	343	343
3,450	3,500	348	348	348	348
3,500	3,550	353	353	353	353
3,550	3,600	358	358	358	358
3,600	3,650	363	363	363	363
3,650	3,700	368	368	368	368
3,700	3,750	373	373	373	373
3,750	3,800	378	378	378	378
3,800	3,850	383	383	383	383
3,850	3,900	388	388	388	388
3,900	3,950	393	393	393	393
3,950	4,000	398	398	398	398
4,000					
4,000	4,050	403	403	403	403
4,050	4,100	408	408	408	408
4,100	4,150	413	413	413	413
4,150	4,200	418	418	418	418
4,200	4,250	423	423	423	423
4,250	4,300	428	428	428	428
4,300	4,350	433	433	433	433
4,350	4,400	438	438	438	438
4,400	4,450	443	443	443	443
4,450	4,500	448	448	448	448
4,500	4,550	453	453	453	453
4,550	4,600	458	458	458	458
4,600	4,650	463	463	463	463
4,650	4,700	468	468	468	468
4,700	4,750	473	473	473	473
4,750	4,800	478	478	478	478
4,800	4,850	483	483	483	483
4,850	4,900	488	488	488	488
4,900	4,950	493	493	493	493
4,950	5,000	498	498	498	498
5,000					
5,000	5,050	503	503	503	503
5,050	5,100	508	508	508	508
5,100	5,150	513	513	513	513
5,150	5,200	518	518	518	518
5,200	5,250	523	523	523	523
5,250	5,300	528	528	528	528
5,300	5,350	533	533	533	533
5,350	5,400	538	538	538	538
5,400	5,450	543	543	543	543
5,450	5,500	548	548	548	548
5,500	5,550	553	553	553	553
5,550	5,600	558	558	558	558
5,600	5,650	563	563	563	563
5,650	5,700	568	568	568	568
5,700	5,750	573	573	573	573
5,750	5,800	578	578	578	578
5,800	5,850	583	583	583	583
5,850	5,900	588	588	588	588
5,900	5,950	593	593	593	593
5,950	6,000	598	598	598	598
6,000					
6,000	6,050	603	603	603	603
6,050	6,100	608	608	608	608
6,100	6,150	613	613	613	613
6,150	6,200	618	618	618	618
6,200	6,250	623	623	623	623
6,250	6,300	628	628	628	628
6,300	6,350	633	633	633	633
6,350	6,400	638	638	638	638
6,400	6,450	643	643	643	643
6,450	6,500	648	648	648	648
6,500	6,550	653	653	653	653
6,550	6,600	658	658	658	658
6,600	6,650	663	663	663	663
6,650	6,700	668	668	668	668
6,700	6,750	673	673	673	673
6,750	6,800	678	678	678	678
6,800	6,850	683	683	683	683
6,850	6,900	688	688	688	688
6,900	6,950	693	693	693	693
6,950	7,000	698	698	698	698
7,000					
7,000	7,050	703	703	703	703
7,050	7,100	708	708	708	708
7,100	7,150	713	713	713	713
7,150	7,200	718	718	718	718
7,200	7,250	723	723	723	723
7,250	7,300	728	728	728	728
7,300	7,350	733	733	733	733
7,350	7,400	738	738	738	738
7,400	7,450	743	743	743	743
7,450	7,500	748	748	748	748
7,500	7,550	753	753	753	753
7,550	7,600	758	758	758	758
7,600	7,650	763	763	763	763
7,650	7,700	768	768	768	768
7,700	7,750	773	773	773	773
7,750	7,800	778	778	778	778
7,800	7,850	783	783	783	783
7,850	7,900	788	788	788	788
7,900	7,950	793	793	793	793
7,950	8,000	798	798	798	798
8,000					
8,000	8,050	803	803	803	803
8,050	8,100	808	808	808	808
8,100	8,150	813	813	813	813
8,150	8,200	818	818	818	818
8,200	8,250	823	823	823	823
8,250	8,300	828	828	828	828
8,300	8,350	833	833	833	833
8,350	8,400	838	838	838	838
8,400	8,450	843	843	843	843
8,450	8,500	848	848	848	848
8,500	8,550	853	853	853	853
8,550	8,600	858	858	858	858
8,600	8,650	863	863	863	863
8,650	8,700	868	868	868	868
8,700	8,750	873	873	873	873
8,750	8,800	878	878	878	878
8,800	8,850	883	883	883	883
8,850	8,900	888	888	888	888
8,900	8,950	893	893	893	893
8,950	9,000	898	898	898	898
9,000					
9,000	9,050	903	903	903	903
9,050	9,100	908	908	908	908
9,100	9,150	913	913	913	913
9,150	9,200	918	918	918	918
9,200	9,250	923	923	923	923
9,250	9,300	928	928	928	928
9,300	9,350	933	933	933	933
9,350	9,400	938	938	938	938
9,400	9,450	943	943	943	943
9,450	9,500	948	948	948	948
9,500	9,550	953	953	953	953
9,550	9,600	958	958	958	958
9,600	9,650	963	963	963	963
9,650	9,700	968	968	968	968
9,700	9,750	973	973	973	973
9,750	9,800	978	978	978	978
9,800	9,850	983	983	983	983
9,850	9,900	988	988	988	988
9,900	9,950	993	993	993	993
9,950	10,000	998	998	998	998
10,000					
10,000	10,050	1,003	1,003	1,003	1,003
10,050	10,100	1,008	1,008	1,008	1,008
10,100	10,150	1,013	1,013	1,013	1,013
10,150	10,200	1,018	1,018	1,018	1,018
10,200	10,250	1,023	1,023	1,023	1,023
10,250	10,300	1,028	1,028	1,028	1,028
10,300	10,350	1,034	1,033	1,034	1,033
10,350	10,400	1,040	1,038	1,040	1,038
10,400	10,450	1,046	1,043	1,046	1,043
10,450	10,500	1,052	1,048	1,052	1,048
10,500	10,550	1,058	1,053	1,058	1,053
10,550	10,600	1,064	1,058	1,064	1,058
10,600	10,650	1,070	1,063	1,070	1,063
10,650	10,700	1,076	1,068	1,076	1,068
10,700	10,750	1,082	1,073	1,082	1,073
10,750	10,800	1,088	1,078	1,088	1,078
10,800	10,850	1,094	1,083	1,094	1,083
10,850	10,900	1,100	1,088	1,100	1,088
10,900	10,950	1,106	1,093	1,106	1,093
10,950	11,000	1,112	1,098	1,112	1,098
11,000					
11,000	11,050	1,118	1,103	1,118	1,103
11,050	11,100	1,124	1,108	1,124	1,108
11,100	11,150	1,130	1,113	1,130	1,113
11,150	11,200	1,136	1,118	1,136	1,118
11,200	11,250	1,142	1,123	1,142	1,123
11,250	11,300	1,148	1,128	1,148	1,128
11,300	11,350	1,154	1,133	1,154	1,133
11,350	11,400	1,160	1,138	1,160	1,138
11,400	11,450	1,166	1,143	1,166	1,143
11,450	11,500	1,172	1,148	1,172	1,148
11,500	11,550	1,178	1,153	1,178	1,153
11,550	11,600	1,184	1,158	1,184	1,158
11,600	11,650	1,190	1,163	1,190	1,163
11,650	11,700	1,196	1,168	1,196	1,168
11,700	11,750	1,202	1,173	1,202	1,173
11,750	11,800	1,208	1,178	1,208	1,178
11,800	11,850	1,214	1,183	1,214	1,183
11,850	11,900	1,220	1,188	1,220	1,188
11,900	11,950	1,226	1,193	1,226	1,193
11,950	12,000	1,232	1,198	1,232	1,198

(Continued)

* This column must also be used by a qualifying surviving spouse.

2022 Tax Table — *Continued*

If line 15 (taxable income) is—		And you are—			
At least	But less than	Single	Married filing jointly *	Married filing separately	Head of a household
		Your tax is—			
12,000					
12,000	12,050	1,238	1,203	1,238	1,203
12,050	12,100	1,244	1,208	1,244	1,208
12,100	12,150	1,250	1,213	1,250	1,213
12,150	12,200	1,256	1,218	1,256	1,218
12,200	12,250	1,262	1,223	1,262	1,223
12,250	12,300	1,268	1,228	1,268	1,228
12,300	12,350	1,274	1,233	1,274	1,233
12,350	12,400	1,280	1,238	1,280	1,238
12,400	12,450	1,286	1,243	1,286	1,243
12,450	12,500	1,292	1,248	1,292	1,248
12,500	12,550	1,298	1,253	1,298	1,253
12,550	12,600	1,304	1,258	1,304	1,258
12,600	12,650	1,310	1,263	1,310	1,263
12,650	12,700	1,316	1,268	1,316	1,268
12,700	12,750	1,322	1,273	1,322	1,273
12,750	12,800	1,328	1,278	1,328	1,278
12,800	12,850	1,334	1,283	1,334	1,283
12,850	12,900	1,340	1,288	1,340	1,288
12,900	12,950	1,346	1,293	1,346	1,293
12,950	13,000	1,352	1,298	1,352	1,298
13,000					
13,000	13,050	1,358	1,303	1,358	1,303
13,050	13,100	1,364	1,308	1,364	1,308
13,100	13,150	1,370	1,313	1,370	1,313
13,150	13,200	1,376	1,318	1,376	1,318
13,200	13,250	1,382	1,323	1,382	1,323
13,250	13,300	1,388	1,328	1,388	1,328
13,300	13,350	1,394	1,333	1,394	1,333
13,350	13,400	1,400	1,338	1,400	1,338
13,400	13,450	1,406	1,343	1,406	1,343
13,450	13,500	1,412	1,348	1,412	1,348
13,500	13,550	1,418	1,353	1,418	1,353
13,550	13,600	1,424	1,358	1,424	1,358
13,600	13,650	1,430	1,363	1,430	1,363
13,650	13,700	1,436	1,368	1,436	1,368
13,700	13,750	1,442	1,373	1,442	1,373
13,750	13,800	1,448	1,378	1,448	1,378
13,800	13,850	1,454	1,383	1,454	1,383
13,850	13,900	1,460	1,388	1,460	1,388
13,900	13,950	1,466	1,393	1,466	1,393
13,950	14,000	1,472	1,398	1,472	1,398
14,000					
14,000	14,050	1,478	1,403	1,478	1,403
14,050	14,100	1,484	1,408	1,484	1,408
14,100	14,150	1,490	1,413	1,490	1,413
14,150	14,200	1,496	1,418	1,496	1,418
14,200	14,250	1,502	1,423	1,502	1,423
14,250	14,300	1,508	1,428	1,508	1,428
14,300	14,350	1,514	1,433	1,514	1,433
14,350	14,400	1,520	1,438	1,520	1,438
14,400	14,450	1,526	1,443	1,526	1,443
14,450	14,500	1,532	1,448	1,532	1,448
14,500	14,550	1,538	1,453	1,538	1,453
14,550	14,600	1,544	1,458	1,544	1,458
14,600	14,650	1,550	1,463	1,550	1,463
14,650	14,700	1,556	1,468	1,556	1,468
14,700	14,750	1,562	1,473	1,562	1,474
14,750	14,800	1,568	1,478	1,568	1,480
14,800	14,850	1,574	1,483	1,574	1,486
14,850	14,900	1,580	1,488	1,580	1,492
14,900	14,950	1,586	1,493	1,586	1,498
14,950	15,000	1,592	1,498	1,592	1,504
15,000					
15,000	15,050	1,598	1,503	1,598	1,510
15,050	15,100	1,604	1,508	1,604	1,516
15,100	15,150	1,610	1,513	1,610	1,522
15,150	15,200	1,616	1,518	1,616	1,528
15,200	15,250	1,622	1,523	1,622	1,534
15,250	15,300	1,628	1,528	1,628	1,540
15,300	15,350	1,634	1,533	1,634	1,546
15,350	15,400	1,640	1,538	1,640	1,552
15,400	15,450	1,646	1,543	1,646	1,558
15,450	15,500	1,652	1,548	1,652	1,564
15,500	15,550	1,658	1,553	1,658	1,570
15,550	15,600	1,664	1,558	1,664	1,576
15,600	15,650	1,670	1,563	1,670	1,582
15,650	15,700	1,676	1,568	1,676	1,588
15,700	15,750	1,682	1,573	1,682	1,594
15,750	15,800	1,688	1,578	1,688	1,600
15,800	15,850	1,694	1,583	1,694	1,606
15,850	15,900	1,700	1,588	1,700	1,612
15,900	15,950	1,706	1,593	1,706	1,618
15,950	16,000	1,712	1,598	1,712	1,624
16,000					
16,000	16,050	1,718	1,603	1,718	1,630
16,050	16,100	1,724	1,608	1,724	1,636
16,100	16,150	1,730	1,613	1,730	1,642
16,150	16,200	1,736	1,618	1,736	1,648
16,200	16,250	1,742	1,623	1,742	1,654
16,250	16,300	1,748	1,628	1,748	1,660
16,300	16,350	1,754	1,633	1,754	1,666
16,350	16,400	1,760	1,638	1,760	1,672
16,400	16,450	1,766	1,643	1,766	1,678
16,450	16,500	1,772	1,648	1,772	1,684
16,500	16,550	1,778	1,653	1,778	1,690
16,550	16,600	1,784	1,658	1,784	1,696
16,600	16,650	1,790	1,663	1,790	1,702
16,650	16,700	1,796	1,668	1,796	1,708
16,700	16,750	1,802	1,673	1,802	1,714
16,750	16,800	1,808	1,678	1,808	1,720
16,800	16,850	1,814	1,683	1,814	1,726
16,850	16,900	1,820	1,688	1,820	1,732
16,900	16,950	1,826	1,693	1,826	1,738
16,950	17,000	1,832	1,698	1,832	1,744
17,000					
17,000	17,050	1,838	1,703	1,838	1,750
17,050	17,100	1,844	1,708	1,844	1,756
17,100	17,150	1,850	1,713	1,850	1,762
17,150	17,200	1,856	1,718	1,856	1,768
17,200	17,250	1,862	1,723	1,862	1,774
17,250	17,300	1,868	1,728	1,868	1,780
17,300	17,350	1,874	1,733	1,874	1,786
17,350	17,400	1,880	1,738	1,880	1,792
17,400	17,450	1,886	1,743	1,886	1,798
17,450	17,500	1,892	1,748	1,892	1,804
17,500	17,550	1,898	1,753	1,898	1,810
17,550	17,600	1,904	1,758	1,904	1,816
17,600	17,650	1,910	1,763	1,910	1,822
17,650	17,700	1,916	1,768	1,916	1,828
17,700	17,750	1,922	1,773	1,922	1,834
17,750	17,800	1,928	1,778	1,928	1,840
17,800	17,850	1,934	1,783	1,934	1,846
17,850	17,900	1,940	1,788	1,940	1,852
17,900	17,950	1,946	1,793	1,946	1,858
17,950	18,000	1,952	1,798	1,952	1,864
18,000					
18,000	18,050	1,958	1,803	1,958	1,870
18,050	18,100	1,964	1,808	1,964	1,876
18,100	18,150	1,970	1,813	1,970	1,882
18,150	18,200	1,976	1,818	1,976	1,888
18,200	18,250	1,982	1,823	1,982	1,894
18,250	18,300	1,988	1,828	1,988	1,900
18,300	18,350	1,994	1,833	1,994	1,906
18,350	18,400	2,000	1,838	2,000	1,912
18,400	18,450	2,006	1,843	2,006	1,918
18,450	18,500	2,012	1,848	2,012	1,924
18,500	18,550	2,018	1,853	2,018	1,930
18,550	18,600	2,024	1,858	2,024	1,936
18,600	18,650	2,030	1,863	2,030	1,942
18,650	18,700	2,036	1,868	2,036	1,948
18,700	18,750	2,042	1,873	2,042	1,954
18,750	18,800	2,048	1,878	2,048	1,960
18,800	18,850	2,054	1,883	2,054	1,966
18,850	18,900	2,060	1,888	2,060	1,972
18,900	18,950	2,066	1,893	2,066	1,978
18,950	19,000	2,072	1,898	2,072	1,984
19,000					
19,000	19,050	2,078	1,903	2,078	1,990
19,050	19,100	2,084	1,908	2,084	1,996
19,100	19,150	2,090	1,913	2,090	2,002
19,150	19,200	2,096	1,918	2,096	2,008
19,200	19,250	2,102	1,923	2,102	2,014
19,250	19,300	2,108	1,928	2,108	2,020
19,300	19,350	2,114	1,933	2,114	2,026
19,350	19,400	2,120	1,938	2,120	2,032
19,400	19,450	2,126	1,943	2,126	2,038
19,450	19,500	2,132	1,948	2,132	2,044
19,500	19,550	2,138	1,953	2,138	2,050
19,550	19,600	2,144	1,958	2,144	2,056
19,600	19,650	2,150	1,963	2,150	2,062
19,650	19,700	2,156	1,968	2,156	2,068
19,700	19,750	2,162	1,973	2,162	2,074
19,750	19,800	2,168	1,978	2,168	2,080
19,800	19,850	2,174	1,983	2,174	2,086
19,850	19,900	2,180	1,988	2,180	2,092
19,900	19,950	2,186	1,993	2,186	2,098
19,950	20,000	2,192	1,998	2,192	2,104
20,000					
20,000	20,050	2,198	2,003	2,198	2,110
20,050	20,100	2,204	2,008	2,204	2,116
20,100	20,150	2,210	2,013	2,210	2,122
20,150	20,200	2,216	2,018	2,216	2,128
20,200	20,250	2,222	2,023	2,222	2,134
20,250	20,300	2,228	2,028	2,228	2,140
20,300	20,350	2,234	2,033	2,234	2,146
20,350	20,400	2,240	2,038	2,240	2,152
20,400	20,450	2,246	2,043	2,246	2,158
20,450	20,500	2,252	2,048	2,252	2,164
20,500	20,550	2,258	2,053	2,258	2,170
20,550	20,600	2,264	2,058	2,264	2,176
20,600	20,650	2,270	2,064	2,270	2,182
20,650	20,700	2,276	2,070	2,276	2,188
20,700	20,750	2,282	2,076	2,282	2,194
20,750	20,800	2,288	2,082	2,288	2,200
20,800	20,850	2,294	2,088	2,294	2,206
20,850	20,900	2,300	2,094	2,300	2,212
20,900	20,950	2,306	2,100	2,306	2,218
20,950	21,000	2,312	2,106	2,312	2,224

(Continued)

* This column must also be used by a qualifying surviving spouse.

2022 Tax Table — *Continued*

If line 15 (taxable income) is—		And you are—			
At least	But less than	Single	Married filing jointly *	Married filing sepa-rately	Head of a house-hold
		Your tax is—			
21,000					
21,000	21,050	2,318	2,112	2,318	2,230
21,050	21,100	2,324	2,118	2,324	2,236
21,100	21,150	2,330	2,124	2,330	2,242
21,150	21,200	2,336	2,130	2,336	2,248
21,200	21,250	2,342	2,136	2,342	2,254
21,250	21,300	2,348	2,142	2,348	2,260
21,300	21,350	2,354	2,148	2,354	2,266
21,350	21,400	2,360	2,154	2,360	2,272
21,400	21,450	2,366	2,160	2,366	2,278
21,450	21,500	2,372	2,166	2,372	2,284
21,500	21,550	2,378	2,172	2,378	2,290
21,550	21,600	2,384	2,178	2,384	2,296
21,600	21,650	2,390	2,184	2,390	2,302
21,650	21,700	2,396	2,190	2,396	2,308
21,700	21,750	2,402	2,196	2,402	2,314
21,750	21,800	2,408	2,202	2,408	2,320
21,800	21,850	2,414	2,208	2,414	2,326
21,850	21,900	2,420	2,214	2,420	2,332
21,900	21,950	2,426	2,220	2,426	2,338
21,950	22,000	2,432	2,226	2,432	2,344
22,000					
22,000	22,050	2,438	2,232	2,438	2,350
22,050	22,100	2,444	2,238	2,444	2,356
22,100	22,150	2,450	2,244	2,450	2,362
22,150	22,200	2,456	2,250	2,456	2,368
22,200	22,250	2,462	2,256	2,462	2,374
22,250	22,300	2,468	2,262	2,468	2,380
22,300	22,350	2,474	2,268	2,474	2,386
22,350	22,400	2,480	2,274	2,480	2,392
22,400	22,450	2,486	2,280	2,486	2,398
22,450	22,500	2,492	2,286	2,492	2,404
22,500	22,550	2,498	2,292	2,498	2,410
22,550	22,600	2,504	2,298	2,504	2,416
22,600	22,650	2,510	2,304	2,510	2,422
22,650	22,700	2,516	2,310	2,516	2,428
22,700	22,750	2,522	2,316	2,522	2,434
22,750	22,800	2,528	2,322	2,528	2,440
22,800	22,850	2,534	2,328	2,534	2,446
22,850	22,900	2,540	2,334	2,540	2,452
22,900	22,950	2,546	2,340	2,546	2,458
22,950	23,000	2,552	2,346	2,552	2,464
23,000					
23,000	23,050	2,558	2,352	2,558	2,470
23,050	23,100	2,564	2,358	2,564	2,476
23,100	23,150	2,570	2,364	2,570	2,482
23,150	23,200	2,576	2,370	2,576	2,488
23,200	23,250	2,582	2,376	2,582	2,494
23,250	23,300	2,588	2,382	2,588	2,500
23,300	23,350	2,594	2,388	2,594	2,506
23,350	23,400	2,600	2,394	2,600	2,512
23,400	23,450	2,606	2,400	2,606	2,518
23,450	23,500	2,612	2,406	2,612	2,524
23,500	23,550	2,618	2,412	2,618	2,530
23,550	23,600	2,624	2,418	2,624	2,536
23,600	23,650	2,630	2,424	2,630	2,542
23,650	23,700	2,636	2,430	2,636	2,548
23,700	23,750	2,642	2,436	2,642	2,554
23,750	23,800	2,648	2,442	2,648	2,560
23,800	23,850	2,654	2,448	2,654	2,566
23,850	23,900	2,660	2,454	2,660	2,572
23,900	23,950	2,666	2,460	2,666	2,578
23,950	24,000	2,672	2,466	2,672	2,584

If line 15 (taxable income) is—		And you are—			
At least	But less than	Single	Married filing jointly *	Married filing sepa-rately	Head of a house-hold
		Your tax is—			
24,000					
24,000	24,050	2,678	2,472	2,678	2,590
24,050	24,100	2,684	2,478	2,684	2,596
24,100	24,150	2,690	2,484	2,690	2,602
24,150	24,200	2,696	2,490	2,696	2,608
24,200	24,250	2,702	2,496	2,702	2,614
24,250	24,300	2,708	2,502	2,708	2,620
24,300	24,350	2,714	2,508	2,714	2,626
24,350	24,400	2,720	2,514	2,720	2,632
24,400	24,450	2,726	2,520	2,726	2,638
24,450	24,500	2,732	2,526	2,732	2,644
24,500	24,550	2,738	2,532	2,738	2,650
24,550	24,600	2,744	2,538	2,744	2,656
24,600	24,650	2,750	2,544	2,750	2,662
24,650	24,700	2,756	2,550	2,756	2,668
24,700	24,750	2,762	2,556	2,762	2,674
24,750	24,800	2,768	2,562	2,768	2,680
24,800	24,850	2,774	2,568	2,774	2,686
24,850	24,900	2,780	2,574	2,780	2,692
24,900	24,950	2,786	2,580	2,786	2,698
24,950	25,000	2,792	2,586	2,792	2,704
25,000					
25,000	25,050	2,798	2,592	2,798	2,710
25,050	25,100	2,804	2,598	2,804	2,716
25,100	25,150	2,810	2,604	2,810	2,722
25,150	25,200	2,816	2,610	2,816	2,728
25,200	25,250	2,822	2,616	2,822	2,734
25,250	25,300	2,828	2,622	2,828	2,740
25,300	25,350	2,834	2,628	2,834	2,746
25,350	25,400	2,840	2,634	2,840	2,752
25,400	25,450	2,846	2,640	2,846	2,758
25,450	25,500	2,852	2,646	2,852	2,764
25,500	25,550	2,858	2,652	2,858	2,770
25,550	25,600	2,864	2,658	2,864	2,776
25,600	25,650	2,870	2,664	2,870	2,782
25,650	25,700	2,876	2,670	2,876	2,788
25,700	25,750	2,882	2,676	2,882	2,794
25,750	25,800	2,888	2,682	2,888	2,800
25,800	25,850	2,894	2,688	2,894	2,806
25,850	25,900	2,900	2,694	2,900	2,812
25,900	25,950	2,906	2,700	2,906	2,818
25,950	26,000	2,912	2,706	2,912	2,824
26,000					
26,000	26,050	2,918	2,712	2,918	2,830
26,050	26,100	2,924	2,718	2,924	2,836
26,100	26,150	2,930	2,724	2,930	2,842
26,150	26,200	2,936	2,730	2,936	2,848
26,200	26,250	2,942	2,736	2,942	2,854
26,250	26,300	2,948	2,742	2,948	2,860
26,300	26,350	2,954	2,748	2,954	2,866
26,350	26,400	2,960	2,754	2,960	2,872
26,400	26,450	2,966	2,760	2,966	2,878
26,450	26,500	2,972	2,766	2,972	2,884
26,500	26,550	2,978	2,772	2,978	2,890
26,550	26,600	2,984	2,778	2,984	2,896
26,600	26,650	2,990	2,784	2,990	2,902
26,650	26,700	2,996	2,790	2,996	2,908
26,700	26,750	3,002	2,796	3,002	2,914
26,750	26,800	3,008	2,802	3,008	2,920
26,800	26,850	3,014	2,808	3,014	2,926
26,850	26,900	3,020	2,814	3,020	2,932
26,900	26,950	3,026	2,820	3,026	2,938
26,950	27,000	3,032	2,826	3,032	2,944

If line 15 (taxable income) is—		And you are—			
At least	But less than	Single	Married filing jointly *	Married filing sepa-rately	Head of a house-hold
		Your tax is—			
27,000					
27,000	27,050	3,038	2,832	3,038	2,950
27,050	27,100	3,044	2,838	3,044	2,956
27,100	27,150	3,050	2,844	3,050	2,962
27,150	27,200	3,056	2,850	3,056	2,968
27,200	27,250	3,062	2,856	3,062	2,974
27,250	27,300	3,068	2,862	3,068	2,980
27,300	27,350	3,074	2,868	3,074	2,986
27,350	27,400	3,080	2,874	3,080	2,992
27,400	27,450	3,086	2,880	3,086	2,998
27,450	27,500	3,092	2,886	3,092	3,004
27,500	27,550	3,098	2,892	3,098	3,010
27,550	27,600	3,104	2,898	3,104	3,016
27,600	27,650	3,110	2,904	3,110	3,022
27,650	27,700	3,116	2,910	3,116	3,028
27,700	27,750	3,122	2,916	3,122	3,034
27,750	27,800	3,128	2,922	3,128	3,040
27,800	27,850	3,134	2,928	3,134	3,046
27,850	27,900	3,140	2,934	3,140	3,052
27,900	27,950	3,146	2,940	3,146	3,058
27,950	28,000	3,152	2,946	3,152	3,064
28,000					
28,000	28,050	3,158	2,952	3,158	3,070
28,050	28,100	3,164	2,958	3,164	3,076
28,100	28,150	3,170	2,964	3,170	3,082
28,150	28,200	3,176	2,970	3,176	3,088
28,200	28,250	3,182	2,976	3,182	3,094
28,250	28,300	3,188	2,982	3,188	3,100
28,300	28,350	3,194	2,988	3,194	3,106
28,350	28,400	3,200	2,994	3,200	3,112
28,400	28,450	3,206	3,000	3,206	3,118
28,450	28,500	3,212	3,006	3,212	3,124
28,500	28,550	3,218	3,012	3,218	3,130
28,550	28,600	3,224	3,018	3,224	3,136
28,600	28,650	3,230	3,024	3,230	3,142
28,650	28,700	3,236	3,030	3,236	3,148
28,700	28,750	3,242	3,036	3,242	3,154
28,750	28,800	3,248	3,042	3,248	3,160
28,800	28,850	3,254	3,048	3,254	3,166
28,850	28,900	3,260	3,054	3,260	3,172
28,900	28,950	3,266	3,060	3,266	3,178
28,950	29,000	3,272	3,066	3,272	3,184
29,000					
29,000	29,050	3,278	3,072	3,278	3,190
29,050	29,100	3,284	3,078	3,284	3,196
29,100	29,150	3,290	3,084	3,290	3,202
29,150	29,200	3,296	3,090	3,296	3,208
29,200	29,250	3,302	3,096	3,302	3,214
29,250	29,300	3,308	3,102	3,308	3,220
29,300	29,350	3,314	3,108	3,314	3,226
29,350	29,400	3,320	3,114	3,320	3,232
29,400	29,450	3,326	3,120	3,326	3,238
29,450	29,500	3,332	3,126	3,332	3,244
29,500	29,550	3,338	3,132	3,338	3,250
29,550	29,600	3,344	3,138	3,344	3,256
29,600	29,650	3,350	3,144	3,350	3,262
29,650	29,700	3,356	3,150	3,356	3,268
29,700	29,750	3,362	3,156	3,362	3,274
29,750	29,800	3,368	3,162	3,368	3,280
29,800	29,850	3,374	3,168	3,374	3,286
29,850	29,900	3,380	3,174	3,380	3,292
29,900	29,950	3,386	3,180	3,386	3,298
29,950	30,000	3,392	3,186	3,392	3,304

(Continued)

* This column must also be used by a qualifying surviving spouse.

2022 Tax Table — *Continued*

If line 15 (taxable income) is—		And you are—			
At least	But less than	Single	Married filing jointly *	Married filing sepa-rately	Head of a house-hold
		Your tax is—			
30,000					
30,000	30,050	3,398	3,192	3,398	3,310
30,050	30,100	3,404	3,198	3,404	3,316
30,100	30,150	3,410	3,204	3,410	3,322
30,150	30,200	3,416	3,210	3,416	3,328
30,200	30,250	3,422	3,216	3,422	3,334
30,250	30,300	3,428	3,222	3,428	3,340
30,300	30,350	3,434	3,228	3,434	3,346
30,350	30,400	3,440	3,234	3,440	3,352
30,400	30,450	3,446	3,240	3,446	3,358
30,450	30,500	3,452	3,246	3,452	3,364
30,500	30,550	3,458	3,252	3,458	3,370
30,550	30,600	3,464	3,258	3,464	3,376
30,600	30,650	3,470	3,264	3,470	3,382
30,650	30,700	3,476	3,270	3,476	3,388
30,700	30,750	3,482	3,276	3,482	3,394
30,750	30,800	3,488	3,282	3,488	3,400
30,800	30,850	3,494	3,288	3,494	3,406
30,850	30,900	3,500	3,294	3,500	3,412
30,900	30,950	3,506	3,300	3,506	3,418
30,950	31,000	3,512	3,306	3,512	3,424
31,000					
31,000	31,050	3,518	3,312	3,518	3,430
31,050	31,100	3,524	3,318	3,524	3,436
31,100	31,150	3,530	3,324	3,530	3,442
31,150	31,200	3,536	3,330	3,536	3,448
31,200	31,250	3,542	3,336	3,542	3,454
31,250	31,300	3,548	3,342	3,548	3,460
31,300	31,350	3,554	3,348	3,554	3,466
31,350	31,400	3,560	3,354	3,560	3,472
31,400	31,450	3,566	3,360	3,566	3,478
31,450	31,500	3,572	3,366	3,572	3,484
31,500	31,550	3,578	3,372	3,578	3,490
31,550	31,600	3,584	3,378	3,584	3,496
31,600	31,650	3,590	3,384	3,590	3,502
31,650	31,700	3,596	3,390	3,596	3,508
31,700	31,750	3,602	3,396	3,602	3,514
31,750	31,800	3,608	3,402	3,608	3,520
31,800	31,850	3,614	3,408	3,614	3,526
31,850	31,900	3,620	3,414	3,620	3,532
31,900	31,950	3,626	3,420	3,626	3,538
31,950	32,000	3,632	3,426	3,632	3,544
32,000					
32,000	32,050	3,638	3,432	3,638	3,550
32,050	32,100	3,644	3,438	3,644	3,556
32,100	32,150	3,650	3,444	3,650	3,562
32,150	32,200	3,656	3,450	3,656	3,568
32,200	32,250	3,662	3,456	3,662	3,574
32,250	32,300	3,668	3,462	3,668	3,580
32,300	32,350	3,674	3,468	3,674	3,586
32,350	32,400	3,680	3,474	3,680	3,592
32,400	32,450	3,686	3,480	3,686	3,598
32,450	32,500	3,692	3,486	3,692	3,604
32,500	32,550	3,698	3,492	3,698	3,610
32,550	32,600	3,704	3,498	3,704	3,616
32,600	32,650	3,710	3,504	3,710	3,622
32,650	32,700	3,716	3,510	3,716	3,628
32,700	32,750	3,722	3,516	3,722	3,634
32,750	32,800	3,728	3,522	3,728	3,640
32,800	32,850	3,734	3,528	3,734	3,646
32,850	32,900	3,740	3,534	3,740	3,652
32,900	32,950	3,746	3,540	3,746	3,658
32,950	33,000	3,752	3,546	3,752	3,664
33,000					
33,000	33,050	3,758	3,552	3,758	3,670
33,050	33,100	3,764	3,558	3,764	3,676
33,100	33,150	3,770	3,564	3,770	3,682
33,150	33,200	3,776	3,570	3,776	3,688
33,200	33,250	3,782	3,576	3,782	3,694
33,250	33,300	3,788	3,582	3,788	3,700
33,300	33,350	3,794	3,588	3,794	3,706
33,350	33,400	3,800	3,594	3,800	3,712
33,400	33,450	3,806	3,600	3,806	3,718
33,450	33,500	3,812	3,606	3,812	3,724
33,500	33,550	3,818	3,612	3,818	3,730
33,550	33,600	3,824	3,618	3,824	3,736
33,600	33,650	3,830	3,624	3,830	3,742
33,650	33,700	3,836	3,630	3,836	3,748
33,700	33,750	3,842	3,636	3,842	3,754
33,750	33,800	3,848	3,642	3,848	3,760
33,800	33,850	3,854	3,648	3,854	3,766
33,850	33,900	3,860	3,654	3,860	3,772
33,900	33,950	3,866	3,660	3,866	3,778
33,950	34,000	3,872	3,666	3,872	3,784
34,000					
34,000	34,050	3,878	3,672	3,878	3,790
34,050	34,100	3,884	3,678	3,884	3,796
34,100	34,150	3,890	3,684	3,890	3,802
34,150	34,200	3,896	3,690	3,896	3,808
34,200	34,250	3,902	3,696	3,902	3,814
34,250	34,300	3,908	3,702	3,908	3,820
34,300	34,350	3,914	3,708	3,914	3,826
34,350	34,400	3,920	3,714	3,920	3,832
34,400	34,450	3,926	3,720	3,926	3,838
34,450	34,500	3,932	3,726	3,932	3,844
34,500	34,550	3,938	3,732	3,938	3,850
34,550	34,600	3,944	3,738	3,944	3,856
34,600	34,650	3,950	3,744	3,950	3,862
34,650	34,700	3,956	3,750	3,956	3,868
34,700	34,750	3,962	3,756	3,962	3,874
34,750	34,800	3,968	3,762	3,968	3,880
34,800	34,850	3,974	3,768	3,974	3,886
34,850	34,900	3,980	3,774	3,980	3,892
34,900	34,950	3,986	3,780	3,986	3,898
34,950	35,000	3,992	3,786	3,992	3,904
35,000					
35,000	35,050	3,998	3,792	3,998	3,910
35,050	35,100	4,004	3,798	4,004	3,916
35,100	35,150	4,010	3,804	4,010	3,922
35,150	35,200	4,016	3,810	4,016	3,928
35,200	35,250	4,022	3,816	4,022	3,934
35,250	35,300	4,028	3,822	4,028	3,940
35,300	35,350	4,034	3,828	4,034	3,946
35,350	35,400	4,040	3,834	4,040	3,952
35,400	35,450	4,046	3,840	4,046	3,958
35,450	35,500	4,052	3,846	4,052	3,964
35,500	35,550	4,058	3,852	4,058	3,970
35,550	35,600	4,064	3,858	4,064	3,976
35,600	35,650	4,070	3,864	4,070	3,982
35,650	35,700	4,076	3,870	4,076	3,988
35,700	35,750	4,082	3,876	4,082	3,994
35,750	35,800	4,088	3,882	4,088	4,000
35,800	35,850	4,094	3,888	4,094	4,006
35,850	35,900	4,100	3,894	4,100	4,012
35,900	35,950	4,106	3,900	4,106	4,018
35,950	36,000	4,112	3,906	4,112	4,024
36,000					
36,000	36,050	4,118	3,912	4,118	4,030
36,050	36,100	4,124	3,918	4,124	4,036
36,100	36,150	4,130	3,924	4,130	4,042
36,150	36,200	4,136	3,930	4,136	4,048
36,200	36,250	4,142	3,936	4,142	4,054
36,250	36,300	4,148	3,942	4,148	4,060
36,300	36,350	4,154	3,948	4,154	4,066
36,350	36,400	4,160	3,954	4,160	4,072
36,400	36,450	4,166	3,960	4,166	4,078
36,450	36,500	4,172	3,966	4,172	4,084
36,500	36,550	4,178	3,972	4,178	4,090
36,550	36,600	4,184	3,978	4,184	4,096
36,600	36,650	4,190	3,984	4,190	4,102
36,650	36,700	4,196	3,990	4,196	4,108
36,700	36,750	4,202	3,996	4,202	4,114
36,750	36,800	4,208	4,002	4,208	4,120
36,800	36,850	4,214	4,008	4,214	4,126
36,850	36,900	4,220	4,014	4,220	4,132
36,900	36,950	4,226	4,020	4,226	4,138
36,950	37,000	4,232	4,026	4,232	4,144
37,000					
37,000	37,050	4,238	4,032	4,238	4,150
37,050	37,100	4,244	4,038	4,244	4,156
37,100	37,150	4,250	4,044	4,250	4,162
37,150	37,200	4,256	4,050	4,256	4,168
37,200	37,250	4,262	4,056	4,262	4,174
37,250	37,300	4,268	4,062	4,268	4,180
37,300	37,350	4,274	4,068	4,274	4,186
37,350	37,400	4,280	4,074	4,280	4,192
37,400	37,450	4,286	4,080	4,286	4,198
37,450	37,500	4,292	4,086	4,292	4,204
37,500	37,550	4,298	4,092	4,298	4,210
37,550	37,600	4,304	4,098	4,304	4,216
37,600	37,650	4,310	4,104	4,310	4,222
37,650	37,700	4,316	4,110	4,316	4,228
37,700	37,750	4,322	4,116	4,322	4,234
37,750	37,800	4,328	4,122	4,328	4,240
37,800	37,850	4,334	4,128	4,334	4,246
37,850	37,900	4,340	4,134	4,340	4,252
37,900	37,950	4,346	4,140	4,346	4,258
37,950	38,000	4,352	4,146	4,352	4,264
38,000					
38,000	38,050	4,358	4,152	4,358	4,270
38,050	38,100	4,364	4,158	4,364	4,276
38,100	38,150	4,370	4,164	4,370	4,282
38,150	38,200	4,376	4,170	4,376	4,288
38,200	38,250	4,382	4,176	4,382	4,294
38,250	38,300	4,388	4,182	4,388	4,300
38,300	38,350	4,394	4,188	4,394	4,306
38,350	38,400	4,400	4,194	4,400	4,312
38,400	38,450	4,406	4,200	4,406	4,318
38,450	38,500	4,412	4,206	4,412	4,324
38,500	38,550	4,418	4,212	4,418	4,330
38,550	38,600	4,424	4,218	4,424	4,336
38,600	38,650	4,430	4,224	4,430	4,342
38,650	38,700	4,436	4,230	4,436	4,348
38,700	38,750	4,442	4,236	4,442	4,354
38,750	38,800	4,448	4,242	4,448	4,360
38,800	38,850	4,454	4,248	4,454	4,366
38,850	38,900	4,460	4,254	4,460	4,372
38,900	38,950	4,466	4,260	4,466	4,378
38,950	39,000	4,472	4,266	4,472	4,384

(Continued)

* This column must also be used by a qualifying surviving spouse.

2022 Tax Table — *Continued*

If line 15 (taxable income) is—		And you are—			
At least	But less than	Single	Married filing jointly *	Married filing separately	Head of a household
		Your tax is—			
39,000					
39,000	39,050	4,478	4,272	4,478	4,390
39,050	39,100	4,484	4,278	4,484	4,396
39,100	39,150	4,490	4,284	4,490	4,402
39,150	39,200	4,496	4,290	4,496	4,408
39,200	39,250	4,502	4,296	4,502	4,414
39,250	39,300	4,508	4,302	4,508	4,420
39,300	39,350	4,514	4,308	4,514	4,426
39,350	39,400	4,520	4,314	4,520	4,432
39,400	39,450	4,526	4,320	4,526	4,438
39,450	39,500	4,532	4,326	4,532	4,444
39,500	39,550	4,538	4,332	4,538	4,450
39,550	39,600	4,544	4,338	4,544	4,456
39,600	39,650	4,550	4,344	4,550	4,462
39,650	39,700	4,556	4,350	4,556	4,468
39,700	39,750	4,562	4,356	4,562	4,474
39,750	39,800	4,568	4,362	4,568	4,480
39,800	39,850	4,574	4,368	4,574	4,486
39,850	39,900	4,580	4,374	4,580	4,492
39,900	39,950	4,586	4,380	4,586	4,498
39,950	40,000	4,592	4,386	4,592	4,504
40,000					
40,000	40,050	4,598	4,392	4,598	4,510
40,050	40,100	4,604	4,398	4,604	4,516
40,100	40,150	4,610	4,404	4,610	4,522
40,150	40,200	4,616	4,410	4,616	4,528
40,200	40,250	4,622	4,416	4,622	4,534
40,250	40,300	4,628	4,422	4,628	4,540
40,300	40,350	4,634	4,428	4,634	4,546
40,350	40,400	4,640	4,434	4,640	4,552
40,400	40,450	4,646	4,440	4,646	4,558
40,450	40,500	4,652	4,446	4,652	4,564
40,500	40,550	4,658	4,452	4,658	4,570
40,550	40,600	4,664	4,458	4,664	4,576
40,600	40,650	4,670	4,464	4,670	4,582
40,650	40,700	4,676	4,470	4,676	4,588
40,700	40,750	4,682	4,476	4,682	4,594
40,750	40,800	4,688	4,482	4,688	4,600
40,800	40,850	4,694	4,488	4,694	4,606
40,850	40,900	4,700	4,494	4,700	4,612
40,900	40,950	4,706	4,500	4,706	4,618
40,950	41,000	4,712	4,506	4,712	4,624
41,000					
41,000	41,050	4,718	4,512	4,718	4,630
41,050	41,100	4,724	4,518	4,724	4,636
41,100	41,150	4,730	4,524	4,730	4,642
41,150	41,200	4,736	4,530	4,736	4,648
41,200	41,250	4,742	4,536	4,742	4,654
41,250	41,300	4,748	4,542	4,748	4,660
41,300	41,350	4,754	4,548	4,754	4,666
41,350	41,400	4,760	4,554	4,760	4,672
41,400	41,450	4,766	4,560	4,766	4,678
41,450	41,500	4,772	4,566	4,772	4,684
41,500	41,550	4,778	4,572	4,778	4,690
41,550	41,600	4,784	4,578	4,784	4,696
41,600	41,650	4,790	4,584	4,790	4,702
41,650	41,700	4,796	4,590	4,796	4,708
41,700	41,750	4,802	4,596	4,802	4,714
41,750	41,800	4,808	4,602	4,808	4,720
41,800	41,850	4,819	4,608	4,819	4,726
41,850	41,900	4,830	4,614	4,830	4,732
41,900	41,950	4,841	4,620	4,841	4,738
41,950	42,000	4,852	4,626	4,852	4,744

If line 15 (taxable income) is—		And you are—			
At least	But less than	Single	Married filing jointly *	Married filing separately	Head of a household
		Your tax is—			
42,000					
42,000	42,050	4,863	4,632	4,863	4,750
42,050	42,100	4,874	4,638	4,874	4,756
42,100	42,150	4,885	4,644	4,885	4,762
42,150	42,200	4,896	4,650	4,896	4,768
42,200	42,250	4,907	4,656	4,907	4,774
42,250	42,300	4,918	4,662	4,918	4,780
42,300	42,350	4,929	4,668	4,929	4,786
42,350	42,400	4,940	4,674	4,940	4,792
42,400	42,450	4,951	4,680	4,951	4,798
42,450	42,500	4,962	4,686	4,962	4,804
42,500	42,550	4,973	4,692	4,973	4,810
42,550	42,600	4,984	4,698	4,984	4,816
42,600	42,650	4,995	4,704	4,995	4,822
42,650	42,700	5,006	4,710	5,006	4,828
42,700	42,750	5,017	4,716	5,017	4,834
42,750	42,800	5,028	4,722	5,028	4,840
42,800	42,850	5,039	4,728	5,039	4,846
42,850	42,900	5,050	4,734	5,050	4,852
42,900	42,950	5,061	4,740	5,061	4,858
42,950	43,000	5,072	4,746	5,072	4,864
43,000					
43,000	43,050	5,083	4,752	5,083	4,870
43,050	43,100	5,094	4,758	5,094	4,876
43,100	43,150	5,105	4,764	5,105	4,882
43,150	43,200	5,116	4,770	5,116	4,888
43,200	43,250	5,127	4,776	5,127	4,894
43,250	43,300	5,138	4,782	5,138	4,900
43,300	43,350	5,149	4,788	5,149	4,906
43,350	43,400	5,160	4,794	5,160	4,912
43,400	43,450	5,171	4,800	5,171	4,918
43,450	43,500	5,182	4,806	5,182	4,924
43,500	43,550	5,193	4,812	5,193	4,930
43,550	43,600	5,204	4,818	5,204	4,936
43,600	43,650	5,215	4,824	5,215	4,942
43,650	43,700	5,226	4,830	5,226	4,948
43,700	43,750	5,237	4,836	5,237	4,954
43,750	43,800	5,248	4,842	5,248	4,960
43,800	43,850	5,259	4,848	5,259	4,966
43,850	43,900	5,270	4,854	5,270	4,972
43,900	43,950	5,281	4,860	5,281	4,978
43,950	44,000	5,292	4,866	5,292	4,984
44,000					
44,000	44,050	5,303	4,872	5,303	4,990
44,050	44,100	5,314	4,878	5,314	4,996
44,100	44,150	5,325	4,884	5,325	5,002
44,150	44,200	5,336	4,890	5,336	5,008
44,200	44,250	5,347	4,896	5,347	5,014
44,250	44,300	5,358	4,902	5,358	5,020
44,300	44,350	5,369	4,908	5,369	5,026
44,350	44,400	5,380	4,914	5,380	5,032
44,400	44,450	5,391	4,920	5,391	5,038
44,450	44,500	5,402	4,926	5,402	5,044
44,500	44,550	5,413	4,932	5,413	5,050
44,550	44,600	5,424	4,938	5,424	5,056
44,600	44,650	5,435	4,944	5,435	5,062
44,650	44,700	5,446	4,950	5,446	5,068
44,700	44,750	5,457	4,956	5,457	5,074
44,750	44,800	5,468	4,962	5,468	5,080
44,800	44,850	5,479	4,968	5,479	5,086
44,850	44,900	5,490	4,974	5,490	5,092
44,900	44,950	5,501	4,980	5,501	5,098
44,950	45,000	5,512	4,986	5,512	5,104

If line 15 (taxable income) is—		And you are—			
At least	But less than	Single	Married filing jointly *	Married filing separately	Head of a household
		Your tax is—			
45,000					
45,000	45,050	5,523	4,992	5,523	5,110
45,050	45,100	5,534	4,998	5,534	5,116
45,100	45,150	5,545	5,004	5,545	5,122
45,150	45,200	5,556	5,010	5,556	5,128
45,200	45,250	5,567	5,016	5,567	5,134
45,250	45,300	5,578	5,022	5,578	5,140
45,300	45,350	5,589	5,028	5,589	5,146
45,350	45,400	5,600	5,034	5,600	5,152
45,400	45,450	5,611	5,040	5,611	5,158
45,450	45,500	5,622	5,046	5,622	5,164
45,500	45,550	5,633	5,052	5,633	5,170
45,550	45,600	5,644	5,058	5,644	5,176
45,600	45,650	5,655	5,064	5,655	5,182
45,650	45,700	5,666	5,070	5,666	5,188
45,700	45,750	5,677	5,076	5,677	5,194
45,750	45,800	5,688	5,082	5,688	5,200
45,800	45,850	5,699	5,088	5,699	5,206
45,850	45,900	5,710	5,094	5,710	5,212
45,900	45,950	5,721	5,100	5,721	5,218
45,950	46,000	5,732	5,106	5,732	5,224
46,000					
46,000	46,050	5,743	5,112	5,743	5,230
46,050	46,100	5,754	5,118	5,754	5,236
46,100	46,150	5,765	5,124	5,765	5,242
46,150	46,200	5,776	5,130	5,776	5,248
46,200	46,250	5,787	5,136	5,787	5,254
46,250	46,300	5,798	5,142	5,798	5,260
46,300	46,350	5,809	5,148	5,809	5,266
46,350	46,400	5,820	5,154	5,820	5,272
46,400	46,450	5,831	5,160	5,831	5,278
46,450	46,500	5,842	5,166	5,842	5,284
46,500	46,550	5,853	5,172	5,853	5,290
46,550	46,600	5,864	5,178	5,864	5,296
46,600	46,650	5,875	5,184	5,875	5,302
46,650	46,700	5,886	5,190	5,886	5,308
46,700	46,750	5,897	5,196	5,897	5,314
46,750	46,800	5,908	5,202	5,908	5,320
46,800	46,850	5,919	5,208	5,919	5,326
46,850	46,900	5,930	5,214	5,930	5,332
46,900	46,950	5,941	5,220	5,941	5,338
46,950	47,000	5,952	5,226	5,952	5,344
47,000					
47,000	47,050	5,963	5,232	5,963	5,350
47,050	47,100	5,974	5,238	5,974	5,356
47,100	47,150	5,985	5,244	5,985	5,362
47,150	47,200	5,996	5,250	5,996	5,368
47,200	47,250	6,007	5,256	6,007	5,374
47,250	47,300	6,018	5,262	6,018	5,380
47,300	47,350	6,029	5,268	6,029	5,386
47,350	47,400	6,040	5,274	6,040	5,392
47,400	47,450	6,051	5,280	6,051	5,398
47,450	47,500	6,062	5,286	6,062	5,404
47,500	47,550	6,073	5,292	6,073	5,410
47,550	47,600	6,084	5,298	6,084	5,416
47,600	47,650	6,095	5,304	6,095	5,422
47,650	47,700	6,106	5,310	6,106	5,428
47,700	47,750	6,117	5,316	6,117	5,434
47,750	47,800	6,128	5,322	6,128	5,440
47,800	47,850	6,139	5,328	6,139	5,446
47,850	47,900	6,150	5,334	6,150	5,452
47,900	47,950	6,161	5,340	6,161	5,458
47,950	48,000	6,172	5,346	6,172	5,464

(Continued)

* This column must also be used by a qualifying surviving spouse.

2022 Tax Table — *Continued*

If line 15 (taxable income) is—		And you are—			
At least	But less than	Single	Married filing jointly *	Married filing separately	Head of a household
		Your tax is—			
48,000					
48,000	**48,050**	6,183	5,352	6,183	5,470
48,050	**48,100**	6,194	5,358	6,194	5,476
48,100	**48,150**	6,205	5,364	6,205	5,482
48,150	**48,200**	6,216	5,370	6,216	5,488
48,200	**48,250**	6,227	5,376	6,227	5,494
48,250	**48,300**	6,238	5,382	6,238	5,500
48,300	**48,350**	6,249	5,388	6,249	5,506
48,350	**48,400**	6,260	5,394	6,260	5,512
48,400	**48,450**	6,271	5,400	6,271	5,518
48,450	**48,500**	6,282	5,406	6,282	5,524
48,500	**48,550**	6,293	5,412	6,293	5,530
48,550	**48,600**	6,304	5,418	6,304	5,536
48,600	**48,650**	6,315	5,424	6,315	5,542
48,650	**48,700**	6,326	5,430	6,326	5,548
48,700	**48,750**	6,337	5,436	6,337	5,554
48,750	**48,800**	6,348	5,442	6,348	5,560
48,800	**48,850**	6,359	5,448	6,359	5,566
48,850	**48,900**	6,370	5,454	6,370	5,572
48,900	**48,950**	6,381	5,460	6,381	5,578
48,950	**49,000**	6,392	5,466	6,392	5,584
49,000					
49,000	**49,050**	6,403	5,472	6,403	5,590
49,050	**49,100**	6,414	5,478	6,414	5,596
49,100	**49,150**	6,425	5,484	6,425	5,602
49,150	**49,200**	6,436	5,490	6,436	5,608
49,200	**49,250**	6,447	5,496	6,447	5,614
49,250	**49,300**	6,458	5,502	6,458	5,620
49,300	**49,350**	6,469	5,508	6,469	5,626
49,350	**49,400**	6,480	5,514	6,480	5,632
49,400	**49,450**	6,491	5,520	6,491	5,638
49,450	**49,500**	6,502	5,526	6,502	5,644
49,500	**49,550**	6,513	5,532	6,513	5,650
49,550	**49,600**	6,524	5,538	6,524	5,656
49,600	**49,650**	6,535	5,544	6,535	5,662
49,650	**49,700**	6,546	5,550	6,546	5,668
49,700	**49,750**	6,557	5,556	6,557	5,674
49,750	**49,800**	6,568	5,562	6,568	5,680
49,800	**49,850**	6,579	5,568	6,579	5,686
49,850	**49,900**	6,590	5,574	6,590	5,692
49,900	**49,950**	6,601	5,580	6,601	5,698
49,950	**50,000**	6,612	5,586	6,612	5,704
50,000					
50,000	**50,050**	6,623	5,592	6,623	5,710
50,050	**50,100**	6,634	5,598	6,634	5,716
50,100	**50,150**	6,645	5,604	6,645	5,722
50,150	**50,200**	6,656	5,610	6,656	5,728
50,200	**50,250**	6,667	5,616	6,667	5,734
50,250	**50,300**	6,678	5,622	6,678	5,740
50,300	**50,350**	6,689	5,628	6,689	5,746
50,350	**50,400**	6,700	5,634	6,700	5,752
50,400	**50,450**	6,711	5,640	6,711	5,758
50,450	**50,500**	6,722	5,646	6,722	5,764
50,500	**50,550**	6,733	5,652	6,733	5,770
50,550	**50,600**	6,744	5,658	6,744	5,776
50,600	**50,650**	6,755	5,664	6,755	5,782
50,650	**50,700**	6,766	5,670	6,766	5,788
50,700	**50,750**	6,777	5,676	6,777	5,794
50,750	**50,800**	6,788	5,682	6,788	5,800
50,800	**50,850**	6,799	5,688	6,799	5,806
50,850	**50,900**	6,810	5,694	6,810	5,812
50,900	**50,950**	6,821	5,700	6,821	5,818
50,950	**51,000**	6,832	5,706	6,832	5,824

If line 15 (taxable income) is—		And you are—			
At least	But less than	Single	Married filing jointly *	Married filing separately	Head of a household
		Your tax is—			
51,000					
51,000	**51,050**	6,843	5,712	6,843	5,830
51,050	**51,100**	6,854	5,718	6,854	5,836
51,100	**51,150**	6,865	5,724	6,865	5,842
51,150	**51,200**	6,876	5,730	6,876	5,848
51,200	**51,250**	6,887	5,736	6,887	5,854
51,250	**51,300**	6,898	5,742	6,898	5,860
51,300	**51,350**	6,909	5,748	6,909	5,866
51,350	**51,400**	6,920	5,754	6,920	5,872
51,400	**51,450**	6,931	5,760	6,931	5,878
51,450	**51,500**	6,942	5,766	6,942	5,884
51,500	**51,550**	6,953	5,772	6,953	5,890
51,550	**51,600**	6,964	5,778	6,964	5,896
51,600	**51,650**	6,975	5,784	6,975	5,902
51,650	**51,700**	6,986	5,790	6,986	5,908
51,700	**51,750**	6,997	5,796	6,997	5,914
51,750	**51,800**	7,008	5,802	7,008	5,920
51,800	**51,850**	7,019	5,808	7,019	5,926
51,850	**51,900**	7,030	5,814	7,030	5,932
51,900	**51,950**	7,041	5,820	7,041	5,938
51,950	**52,000**	7,052	5,826	7,052	5,944
52,000					
52,000	**52,050**	7,063	5,832	7,063	5,950
52,050	**52,100**	7,074	5,838	7,074	5,956
52,100	**52,150**	7,085	5,844	7,085	5,962
52,150	**52,200**	7,096	5,850	7,096	5,968
52,200	**52,250**	7,107	5,856	7,107	5,974
52,250	**52,300**	7,118	5,862	7,118	5,980
52,300	**52,350**	7,129	5,868	7,129	5,986
52,350	**52,400**	7,140	5,874	7,140	5,992
52,400	**52,450**	7,151	5,880	7,151	5,998
52,450	**52,500**	7,162	5,886	7,162	6,004
52,500	**52,550**	7,173	5,892	7,173	6,010
52,550	**52,600**	7,184	5,898	7,184	6,016
52,600	**52,650**	7,195	5,904	7,195	6,022
52,650	**52,700**	7,206	5,910	7,206	6,028
52,700	**52,750**	7,217	5,916	7,217	6,034
52,750	**52,800**	7,228	5,922	7,228	6,040
52,800	**52,850**	7,239	5,928	7,239	6,046
52,850	**52,900**	7,250	5,934	7,250	6,052
52,900	**52,950**	7,261	5,940	7,261	6,058
52,950	**53,000**	7,272	5,946	7,272	6,064
53,000					
53,000	**53,050**	7,283	5,952	7,283	6,070
53,050	**53,100**	7,294	5,958	7,294	6,076
53,100	**53,150**	7,305	5,964	7,305	6,082
53,150	**53,200**	7,316	5,970	7,316	6,088
53,200	**53,250**	7,327	5,976	7,327	6,094
53,250	**53,300**	7,338	5,982	7,338	6,100
53,300	**53,350**	7,349	5,988	7,349	6,106
53,350	**53,400**	7,360	5,994	7,360	6,112
53,400	**53,450**	7,371	6,000	7,371	6,118
53,450	**53,500**	7,382	6,006	7,382	6,124
53,500	**53,550**	7,393	6,012	7,393	6,130
53,550	**53,600**	7,404	6,018	7,404	6,136
53,600	**53,650**	7,415	6,024	7,415	6,142
53,650	**53,700**	7,426	6,030	7,426	6,148
53,700	**53,750**	7,437	6,036	7,437	6,154
53,750	**53,800**	7,448	6,042	7,448	6,160
53,800	**53,850**	7,459	6,048	7,459	6,166
53,850	**53,900**	7,470	6,054	7,470	6,172
53,900	**53,950**	7,481	6,060	7,481	6,178
53,950	**54,000**	7,492	6,066	7,492	6,184

If line 15 (taxable income) is—		And you are—			
At least	But less than	Single	Married filing jointly *	Married filing separately	Head of a household
		Your tax is—			
54,000					
54,000	**54,050**	7,503	6,072	7,503	6,190
54,050	**54,100**	7,514	6,078	7,514	6,196
54,100	**54,150**	7,525	6,084	7,525	6,202
54,150	**54,200**	7,536	6,090	7,536	6,208
54,200	**54,250**	7,547	6,096	7,547	6,214
54,250	**54,300**	7,558	6,102	7,558	6,220
54,300	**54,350**	7,569	6,108	7,569	6,226
54,350	**54,400**	7,580	6,114	7,580	6,232
54,400	**54,450**	7,591	6,120	7,591	6,238
54,450	**54,500**	7,602	6,126	7,602	6,244
54,500	**54,550**	7,613	6,132	7,613	6,250
54,550	**54,600**	7,624	6,138	7,624	6,256
54,600	**54,650**	7,635	6,144	7,635	6,262
54,650	**54,700**	7,646	6,150	7,646	6,268
54,700	**54,750**	7,657	6,156	7,657	6,274
54,750	**54,800**	7,668	6,162	7,668	6,280
54,800	**54,850**	7,679	6,168	7,679	6,286
54,850	**54,900**	7,690	6,174	7,690	6,292
54,900	**54,950**	7,701	6,180	7,701	6,298
54,950	**55,000**	7,712	6,186	7,712	6,304
55,000					
55,000	**55,050**	7,723	6,192	7,723	6,310
55,050	**55,100**	7,734	6,198	7,734	6,316
55,100	**55,150**	7,745	6,204	7,745	6,322
55,150	**55,200**	7,756	6,210	7,756	6,328
55,200	**55,250**	7,767	6,216	7,767	6,334
55,250	**55,300**	7,778	6,222	7,778	6,340
55,300	**55,350**	7,789	6,228	7,789	6,346
55,350	**55,400**	7,800	6,234	7,800	6,352
55,400	**55,450**	7,811	6,240	7,811	6,358
55,450	**55,500**	7,822	6,246	7,822	6,364
55,500	**55,550**	7,833	6,252	7,833	6,370
55,550	**55,600**	7,844	6,258	7,844	6,376
55,600	**55,650**	7,855	6,264	7,855	6,382
55,650	**55,700**	7,866	6,270	7,866	6,388
55,700	**55,750**	7,877	6,276	7,877	6,394
55,750	**55,800**	7,888	6,282	7,888	6,400
55,800	**55,850**	7,899	6,288	7,899	6,406
55,850	**55,900**	7,910	6,294	7,910	6,412
55,900	**55,950**	7,921	6,300	7,921	6,421
55,950	**56,000**	7,932	6,306	7,932	6,432
56,000					
56,000	**56,050**	7,943	6,312	7,943	6,443
56,050	**56,100**	7,954	6,318	7,954	6,454
56,100	**56,150**	7,965	6,324	7,965	6,465
56,150	**56,200**	7,976	6,330	7,976	6,476
56,200	**56,250**	7,987	6,336	7,987	6,487
56,250	**56,300**	7,998	6,342	7,998	6,498
56,300	**56,350**	8,009	6,348	8,009	6,509
56,350	**56,400**	8,020	6,354	8,020	6,520
56,400	**56,450**	8,031	6,360	8,031	6,531
56,450	**56,500**	8,042	6,366	8,042	6,542
56,500	**56,550**	8,053	6,372	8,053	6,553
56,550	**56,600**	8,064	6,378	8,064	6,564
56,600	**56,650**	8,075	6,384	8,075	6,575
56,650	**56,700**	8,086	6,390	8,086	6,586
56,700	**56,750**	8,097	6,396	8,097	6,597
56,750	**56,800**	8,108	6,402	8,108	6,608
56,800	**56,850**	8,119	6,408	8,119	6,619
56,850	**56,900**	8,130	6,414	8,130	6,630
56,900	**56,950**	8,141	6,420	8,141	6,641
56,950	**57,000**	8,152	6,426	8,152	6,652

* This column must also be used by a qualifying surviving spouse.

(Continued)

2022 Tax Table — *Continued*

If line 15 (taxable income) is—		And you are—			
At least	But less than	Single	Married filing jointly *	Married filing sepa-rately	Head of a house-hold
		Your tax is—			
57,000					
57,000	57,050	8,163	6,432	8,163	6,663
57,050	57,100	8,174	6,438	8,174	6,674
57,100	57,150	8,185	6,444	8,185	6,685
57,150	57,200	8,196	6,450	8,196	6,696
57,200	57,250	8,207	6,456	8,207	6,707
57,250	57,300	8,218	6,462	8,218	6,718
57,300	57,350	8,229	6,468	8,229	6,729
57,350	57,400	8,240	6,474	8,240	6,740
57,400	57,450	8,251	6,480	8,251	6,751
57,450	57,500	8,262	6,486	8,262	6,762
57,500	57,550	8,273	6,492	8,273	6,773
57,550	57,600	8,284	6,498	8,284	6,784
57,600	57,650	8,295	6,504	8,295	6,795
57,650	57,700	8,306	6,510	8,306	6,806
57,700	57,750	8,317	6,516	8,317	6,817
57,750	57,800	8,328	6,522	8,328	6,828
57,800	57,850	8,339	6,528	8,339	6,839
57,850	57,900	8,350	6,534	8,350	6,850
57,900	57,950	8,361	6,540	8,361	6,861
57,950	58,000	8,372	6,546	8,372	6,872
58,000					
58,000	58,050	8,383	6,552	8,383	6,883
58,050	58,100	8,394	6,558	8,394	6,894
58,100	58,150	8,405	6,564	8,405	6,905
58,150	58,200	8,416	6,570	8,416	6,916
58,200	58,250	8,427	6,576	8,427	6,927
58,250	58,300	8,438	6,582	8,438	6,938
58,300	58,350	8,449	6,588	8,449	6,949
58,350	58,400	8,460	6,594	8,460	6,960
58,400	58,450	8,471	6,600	8,471	6,971
58,450	58,500	8,482	6,606	8,482	6,982
58,500	58,550	8,493	6,612	8,493	6,993
58,550	58,600	8,504	6,618	8,504	7,004
58,600	58,650	8,515	6,624	8,515	7,015
58,650	58,700	8,526	6,630	8,526	7,026
58,700	58,750	8,537	6,636	8,537	7,037
58,750	58,800	8,548	6,642	8,548	7,048
58,800	58,850	8,559	6,648	8,559	7,059
58,850	58,900	8,570	6,654	8,570	7,070
58,900	58,950	8,581	6,660	8,581	7,081
58,950	59,000	8,592	6,666	8,592	7,092
59,000					
59,000	59,050	8,603	6,672	8,603	7,103
59,050	59,100	8,614	6,678	8,614	7,114
59,100	59,150	8,625	6,684	8,625	7,125
59,150	59,200	8,636	6,690	8,636	7,136
59,200	59,250	8,647	6,696	8,647	7,147
59,250	59,300	8,658	6,702	8,658	7,158
59,300	59,350	8,669	6,708	8,669	7,169
59,350	59,400	8,680	6,714	8,680	7,180
59,400	59,450	8,691	6,720	8,691	7,191
59,450	59,500	8,702	6,726	8,702	7,202
59,500	59,550	8,713	6,732	8,713	7,213
59,550	59,600	8,724	6,738	8,724	7,224
59,600	59,650	8,735	6,744	8,735	7,235
59,650	59,700	8,746	6,750	8,746	7,246
59,700	59,750	8,757	6,756	8,757	7,257
59,750	59,800	8,768	6,762	8,768	7,268
59,800	59,850	8,779	6,768	8,779	7,279
59,850	59,900	8,790	6,774	8,790	7,290
59,900	59,950	8,801	6,780	8,801	7,301
59,950	60,000	8,812	6,786	8,812	7,312
60,000					
60,000	60,050	8,823	6,792	8,823	7,323
60,050	60,100	8,834	6,798	8,834	7,334
60,100	60,150	8,845	6,804	8,845	7,345
60,150	60,200	8,856	6,810	8,856	7,356
60,200	60,250	8,867	6,816	8,867	7,367
60,250	60,300	8,878	6,822	8,878	7,378
60,300	60,350	8,889	6,828	8,889	7,389
60,350	60,400	8,900	6,834	8,900	7,400
60,400	60,450	8,911	6,840	8,911	7,411
60,450	60,500	8,922	6,846	8,922	7,422
60,500	60,550	8,933	6,852	8,933	7,433
60,550	60,600	8,944	6,858	8,944	7,444
60,600	60,650	8,955	6,864	8,955	7,455
60,650	60,700	8,966	6,870	8,966	7,466
60,700	60,750	8,977	6,876	8,977	7,477
60,750	60,800	8,988	6,882	8,988	7,488
60,800	60,850	8,999	6,888	8,999	7,499
60,850	60,900	9,010	6,894	9,010	7,510
60,900	60,950	9,021	6,900	9,021	7,521
60,950	61,000	9,032	6,906	9,032	7,532
61,000					
61,000	61,050	9,043	6,912	9,043	7,543
61,050	61,100	9,054	6,918	9,054	7,554
61,100	61,150	9,065	6,924	9,065	7,565
61,150	61,200	9,076	6,930	9,076	7,576
61,200	61,250	9,087	6,936	9,087	7,587
61,250	61,300	9,098	6,942	9,098	7,598
61,300	61,350	9,109	6,948	9,109	7,609
61,350	61,400	9,120	6,954	9,120	7,620
61,400	61,450	9,131	6,960	9,131	7,631
61,450	61,500	9,142	6,966	9,142	7,642
61,500	61,550	9,153	6,972	9,153	7,653
61,550	61,600	9,164	6,978	9,164	7,664
61,600	61,650	9,175	6,984	9,175	7,675
61,650	61,700	9,186	6,990	9,186	7,686
61,700	61,750	9,197	6,996	9,197	7,697
61,750	61,800	9,208	7,002	9,208	7,708
61,800	61,850	9,219	7,008	9,219	7,719
61,850	61,900	9,230	7,014	9,230	7,730
61,900	61,950	9,241	7,020	9,241	7,741
61,950	62,000	9,252	7,026	9,252	7,752
62,000					
62,000	62,050	9,263	7,032	9,263	7,763
62,050	62,100	9,274	7,038	9,274	7,774
62,100	62,150	9,285	7,044	9,285	7,785
62,150	62,200	9,296	7,050	9,296	7,796
62,200	62,250	9,307	7,056	9,307	7,807
62,250	62,300	9,318	7,062	9,318	7,818
62,300	62,350	9,329	7,068	9,329	7,829
62,350	62,400	9,340	7,074	9,340	7,840
62,400	62,450	9,351	7,080	9,351	7,851
62,450	62,500	9,362	7,086	9,362	7,862
62,500	62,550	9,373	7,092	9,373	7,873
62,550	62,600	9,384	7,098	9,384	7,884
62,600	62,650	9,395	7,104	9,395	7,895
62,650	62,700	9,406	7,110	9,406	7,906
62,700	62,750	9,417	7,116	9,417	7,917
62,750	62,800	9,428	7,122	9,428	7,928
62,800	62,850	9,439	7,128	9,439	7,939
62,850	62,900	9,450	7,134	9,450	7,950
62,900	62,950	9,461	7,140	9,461	7,961
62,950	63,000	9,472	7,146	9,472	7,972
63,000					
63,000	63,050	9,483	7,152	9,483	7,983
63,050	63,100	9,494	7,158	9,494	7,994
63,100	63,150	9,505	7,164	9,505	8,005
63,150	63,200	9,516	7,170	9,516	8,016
63,200	63,250	9,527	7,176	9,527	8,027
63,250	63,300	9,538	7,182	9,538	8,038
63,300	63,350	9,549	7,188	9,549	8,049
63,350	63,400	9,560	7,194	9,560	8,060
63,400	63,450	9,571	7,200	9,571	8,071
63,450	63,500	9,582	7,206	9,582	8,082
63,500	63,550	9,593	7,212	9,593	8,093
63,550	63,600	9,604	7,218	9,604	8,104
63,600	63,650	9,615	7,224	9,615	8,115
63,650	63,700	9,626	7,230	9,626	8,126
63,700	63,750	9,637	7,236	9,637	8,137
63,750	63,800	9,648	7,242	9,648	8,148
63,800	63,850	9,659	7,248	9,659	8,159
63,850	63,900	9,670	7,254	9,670	8,170
63,900	63,950	9,681	7,260	9,681	8,181
63,950	64,000	9,692	7,266	9,692	8,192
64,000					
64,000	64,050	9,703	7,272	9,703	8,203
64,050	64,100	9,714	7,278	9,714	8,214
64,100	64,150	9,725	7,284	9,725	8,225
64,150	64,200	9,736	7,290	9,736	8,236
64,200	64,250	9,747	7,296	9,747	8,247
64,250	64,300	9,758	7,302	9,758	8,258
64,300	64,350	9,769	7,308	9,769	8,269
64,350	64,400	9,780	7,314	9,780	8,280
64,400	64,450	9,791	7,320	9,791	8,291
64,450	64,500	9,802	7,326	9,802	8,302
64,500	64,550	9,813	7,332	9,813	8,313
64,550	64,600	9,824	7,338	9,824	8,324
64,600	64,650	9,835	7,344	9,835	8,335
64,650	64,700	9,846	7,350	9,846	8,346
64,700	64,750	9,857	7,356	9,857	8,357
64,750	64,800	9,868	7,362	9,868	8,368
64,800	64,850	9,879	7,368	9,879	8,379
64,850	64,900	9,890	7,374	9,890	8,390
64,900	64,950	9,901	7,380	9,901	8,401
64,950	65,000	9,912	7,386	9,912	8,412
65,000					
65,000	65,050	9,923	7,392	9,923	8,423
65,050	65,100	9,934	7,398	9,934	8,434
65,100	65,150	9,945	7,404	9,945	8,445
65,150	65,200	9,956	7,410	9,956	8,456
65,200	65,250	9,967	7,416	9,967	8,467
65,250	65,300	9,978	7,422	9,978	8,478
65,300	65,350	9,989	7,428	9,989	8,489
65,350	65,400	10,000	7,434	10,000	8,500
65,400	65,450	10,011	7,440	10,011	8,511
65,450	65,500	10,022	7,446	10,022	8,522
65,500	65,550	10,033	7,452	10,033	8,533
65,550	65,600	10,044	7,458	10,044	8,544
65,600	65,650	10,055	7,464	10,055	8,555
65,650	65,700	10,066	7,470	10,066	8,566
65,700	65,750	10,077	7,476	10,077	8,577
65,750	65,800	10,088	7,482	10,088	8,588
65,800	65,850	10,099	7,488	10,099	8,599
65,850	65,900	10,110	7,494	10,110	8,610
65,900	65,950	10,121	7,500	10,121	8,621
65,950	66,000	10,132	7,506	10,132	8,632

(Continued)

* This column must also be used by a qualifying surviving spouse.

2022 Tax Table — *Continued*

If line 15 (taxable income) is— At least	But less than	And you are— Single	Married filing jointly *	Married filing sepa-rately	Head of a house-hold
		Your tax is—			
66,000					
66,000	**66,050**	10,143	7,512	10,143	8,643
66,050	**66,100**	10,154	7,518	10,154	8,654
66,100	**66,150**	10,165	7,524	10,165	8,665
66,150	**66,200**	10,176	7,530	10,176	8,676
66,200	**66,250**	10,187	7,536	10,187	8,687
66,250	**66,300**	10,198	7,542	10,198	8,698
66,300	**66,350**	10,209	7,548	10,209	8,709
66,350	**66,400**	10,220	7,554	10,220	8,720
66,400	**66,450**	10,231	7,560	10,231	8,731
66,450	**66,500**	10,242	7,566	10,242	8,742
66,500	**66,550**	10,253	7,572	10,253	8,753
66,550	**66,600**	10,264	7,578	10,264	8,764
66,600	**66,650**	10,275	7,584	10,275	8,775
66,650	**66,700**	10,286	7,590	10,286	8,786
66,700	**66,750**	10,297	7,596	10,297	8,797
66,750	**66,800**	10,308	7,602	10,308	8,808
66,800	**66,850**	10,319	7,608	10,319	8,819
66,850	**66,900**	10,330	7,614	10,330	8,830
66,900	**66,950**	10,341	7,620	10,341	8,841
66,950	**67,000**	10,352	7,626	10,352	8,852
67,000					
67,000	**67,050**	10,363	7,632	10,363	8,863
67,050	**67,100**	10,374	7,638	10,374	8,874
67,100	**67,150**	10,385	7,644	10,385	8,885
67,150	**67,200**	10,396	7,650	10,396	8,896
67,200	**67,250**	10,407	7,656	10,407	8,907
67,250	**67,300**	10,418	7,662	10,418	8,918
67,300	**67,350**	10,429	7,668	10,429	8,929
67,350	**67,400**	10,440	7,674	10,440	8,940
67,400	**67,450**	10,451	7,680	10,451	8,951
67,450	**67,500**	10,462	7,686	10,462	8,962
67,500	**67,550**	10,473	7,692	10,473	8,973
67,550	**67,600**	10,484	7,698	10,484	8,984
67,600	**67,650**	10,495	7,704	10,495	8,995
67,650	**67,700**	10,506	7,710	10,506	9,006
67,700	**67,750**	10,517	7,716	10,517	9,017
67,750	**67,800**	10,528	7,722	10,528	9,028
67,800	**67,850**	10,539	7,728	10,539	9,039
67,850	**67,900**	10,550	7,734	10,550	9,050
67,900	**67,950**	10,561	7,740	10,561	9,061
67,950	**68,000**	10,572	7,746	10,572	9,072
68,000					
68,000	**68,050**	10,583	7,752	10,583	9,083
68,050	**68,100**	10,594	7,758	10,594	9,094
68,100	**68,150**	10,605	7,764	10,605	9,105
68,150	**68,200**	10,616	7,770	10,616	9,116
68,200	**68,250**	10,627	7,776	10,627	9,127
68,250	**68,300**	10,638	7,782	10,638	9,138
68,300	**68,350**	10,649	7,788	10,649	9,149
68,350	**68,400**	10,660	7,794	10,660	9,160
68,400	**68,450**	10,671	7,800	10,671	9,171
68,450	**68,500**	10,682	7,806	10,682	9,182
68,500	**68,550**	10,693	7,812	10,693	9,193
68,550	**68,600**	10,704	7,818	10,704	9,204
68,600	**68,650**	10,715	7,824	10,715	9,215
68,650	**68,700**	10,726	7,830	10,726	9,226
68,700	**68,750**	10,737	7,836	10,737	9,237
68,750	**68,800**	10,748	7,842	10,748	9,248
68,800	**68,850**	10,759	7,848	10,759	9,259
68,850	**68,900**	10,770	7,854	10,770	9,270
68,900	**68,950**	10,781	7,860	10,781	9,281
68,950	**69,000**	10,792	7,866	10,792	9,292

If line 15 (taxable income) is— At least	But less than	And you are— Single	Married filing jointly *	Married filing sepa-rately	Head of a house-hold
		Your tax is—			
69,000					
69,000	**69,050**	10,803	7,872	10,803	9,303
69,050	**69,100**	10,814	7,878	10,814	9,314
69,100	**69,150**	10,825	7,884	10,825	9,325
69,150	**69,200**	10,836	7,890	10,836	9,336
69,200	**69,250**	10,847	7,896	10,847	9,347
69,250	**69,300**	10,858	7,902	10,858	9,358
69,300	**69,350**	10,869	7,908	10,869	9,369
69,350	**69,400**	10,880	7,914	10,880	9,380
69,400	**69,450**	10,891	7,920	10,891	9,391
69,450	**69,500**	10,902	7,926	10,902	9,402
69,500	**69,550**	10,913	7,932	10,913	9,413
69,550	**69,600**	10,924	7,938	10,924	9,424
69,600	**69,650**	10,935	7,944	10,935	9,435
69,650	**69,700**	10,946	7,950	10,946	9,446
69,700	**69,750**	10,957	7,956	10,957	9,457
69,750	**69,800**	10,968	7,962	10,968	9,468
69,800	**69,850**	10,979	7,968	10,979	9,479
69,850	**69,900**	10,990	7,974	10,990	9,490
69,900	**69,950**	11,001	7,980	11,001	9,501
69,950	**70,000**	11,012	7,986	11,012	9,512
70,000					
70,000	**70,050**	11,023	7,992	11,023	9,523
70,050	**70,100**	11,034	7,998	11,034	9,534
70,100	**70,150**	11,045	8,004	11,045	9,545
70,150	**70,200**	11,056	8,010	11,056	9,556
70,200	**70,250**	11,067	8,016	11,067	9,567
70,250	**70,300**	11,078	8,022	11,078	9,578
70,300	**70,350**	11,089	8,028	11,089	9,589
70,350	**70,400**	11,100	8,034	11,100	9,600
70,400	**70,450**	11,111	8,040	11,111	9,611
70,450	**70,500**	11,122	8,046	11,122	9,622
70,500	**70,550**	11,133	8,052	11,133	9,633
70,550	**70,600**	11,144	8,058	11,144	9,644
70,600	**70,650**	11,155	8,064	11,155	9,655
70,650	**70,700**	11,166	8,070	11,166	9,666
70,700	**70,750**	11,177	8,076	11,177	9,677
70,750	**70,800**	11,188	8,082	11,188	9,688
70,800	**70,850**	11,199	8,088	11,199	9,699
70,850	**70,900**	11,210	8,094	11,210	9,710
70,900	**70,950**	11,221	8,100	11,221	9,721
70,950	**71,000**	11,232	8,106	11,232	9,732
71,000					
71,000	**71,050**	11,243	8,112	11,243	9,743
71,050	**71,100**	11,254	8,118	11,254	9,754
71,100	**71,150**	11,265	8,124	11,265	9,765
71,150	**71,200**	11,276	8,130	11,276	9,776
71,200	**71,250**	11,287	8,136	11,287	9,787
71,250	**71,300**	11,298	8,142	11,298	9,798
71,300	**71,350**	11,309	8,148	11,309	9,809
71,350	**71,400**	11,320	8,154	11,320	9,820
71,400	**71,450**	11,331	8,160	11,331	9,831
71,450	**71,500**	11,342	8,166	11,342	9,842
71,500	**71,550**	11,353	8,172	11,353	9,853
71,550	**71,600**	11,364	8,178	11,364	9,864
71,600	**71,650**	11,375	8,184	11,375	9,875
71,650	**71,700**	11,386	8,190	11,386	9,886
71,700	**71,750**	11,397	8,196	11,397	9,897
71,750	**71,800**	11,408	8,202	11,408	9,908
71,800	**71,850**	11,419	8,208	11,419	9,919
71,850	**71,900**	11,430	8,214	11,430	9,930
71,900	**71,950**	11,441	8,220	11,441	9,941
71,950	**72,000**	11,452	8,226	11,452	9,952

If line 15 (taxable income) is— At least	But less than	And you are— Single	Married filing jointly *	Married filing sepa-rately	Head of a house-hold
		Your tax is—			
72,000					
72,000	**72,050**	11,463	8,232	11,463	9,963
72,050	**72,100**	11,474	8,238	11,474	9,974
72,100	**72,150**	11,485	8,244	11,485	9,985
72,150	**72,200**	11,496	8,250	11,496	9,996
72,200	**72,250**	11,507	8,256	11,507	10,007
72,250	**72,300**	11,518	8,262	11,518	10,018
72,300	**72,350**	11,529	8,268	11,529	10,029
72,350	**72,400**	11,540	8,274	11,540	10,040
72,400	**72,450**	11,551	8,280	11,551	10,051
72,450	**72,500**	11,562	8,286	11,562	10,062
72,500	**72,550**	11,573	8,292	11,573	10,073
72,550	**72,600**	11,584	8,298	11,584	10,084
72,600	**72,650**	11,595	8,304	11,595	10,095
72,650	**72,700**	11,606	8,310	11,606	10,106
72,700	**72,750**	11,617	8,316	11,617	10,117
72,750	**72,800**	11,628	8,322	11,628	10,128
72,800	**72,850**	11,639	8,328	11,639	10,139
72,850	**72,900**	11,650	8,334	11,650	10,150
72,900	**72,950**	11,661	8,340	11,661	10,161
72,950	**73,000**	11,672	8,346	11,672	10,172
73,000					
73,000	**73,050**	11,683	8,352	11,683	10,183
73,050	**73,100**	11,694	8,358	11,694	10,194
73,100	**73,150**	11,705	8,364	11,705	10,205
73,150	**73,200**	11,716	8,370	11,716	10,216
73,200	**73,250**	11,727	8,376	11,727	10,227
73,250	**73,300**	11,738	8,382	11,738	10,238
73,300	**73,350**	11,749	8,388	11,749	10,249
73,350	**73,400**	11,760	8,394	11,760	10,260
73,400	**73,450**	11,771	8,400	11,771	10,271
73,450	**73,500**	11,782	8,406	11,782	10,282
73,500	**73,550**	11,793	8,412	11,793	10,293
73,550	**73,600**	11,804	8,418	11,804	10,304
73,600	**73,650**	11,815	8,424	11,815	10,315
73,650	**73,700**	11,826	8,430	11,826	10,326
73,700	**73,750**	11,837	8,436	11,837	10,337
73,750	**73,800**	11,848	8,442	11,848	10,348
73,800	**73,850**	11,859	8,448	11,859	10,359
73,850	**73,900**	11,870	8,454	11,870	10,370
73,900	**73,950**	11,881	8,460	11,881	10,381
73,950	**74,000**	11,892	8,466	11,892	10,392
74,000					
74,000	**74,050**	11,903	8,472	11,903	10,403
74,050	**74,100**	11,914	8,478	11,914	10,414
74,100	**74,150**	11,925	8,484	11,925	10,425
74,150	**74,200**	11,936	8,490	11,936	10,436
74,200	**74,250**	11,947	8,496	11,947	10,447
74,250	**74,300**	11,958	8,502	11,958	10,458
74,300	**74,350**	11,969	8,508	11,969	10,469
74,350	**74,400**	11,980	8,514	11,980	10,480
74,400	**74,450**	11,991	8,520	11,991	10,491
74,450	**74,500**	12,002	8,526	12,002	10,502
74,500	**74,550**	12,013	8,532	12,013	10,513
74,550	**74,600**	12,024	8,538	12,024	10,524
74,600	**74,650**	12,035	8,544	12,035	10,535
74,650	**74,700**	12,046	8,550	12,046	10,546
74,700	**74,750**	12,057	8,556	12,057	10,557
74,750	**74,800**	12,068	8,562	12,068	10,568
74,800	**74,850**	12,079	8,568	12,079	10,579
74,850	**74,900**	12,090	8,574	12,090	10,590
74,900	**74,950**	12,101	8,580	12,101	10,601
74,950	**75,000**	12,112	8,586	12,112	10,612

(Continued)

* This column must also be used by a qualifying surviving spouse.

2022 Tax Table — *Continued*

If line 15 (taxable income) is—		And you are—			
At least	But less than	Single	Married filing jointly *	Married filing separately	Head of a household
		Your tax is—			
75,000					
75,000	75,050	12,123	8,592	12,123	10,623
75,050	75,100	12,134	8,598	12,134	10,634
75,100	75,150	12,145	8,604	12,145	10,645
75,150	75,200	12,156	8,610	12,156	10,656
75,200	75,250	12,167	8,616	12,167	10,667
75,250	75,300	12,178	8,622	12,178	10,678
75,300	75,350	12,189	8,628	12,189	10,689
75,350	75,400	12,200	8,634	12,200	10,700
75,400	75,450	12,211	8,640	12,211	10,711
75,450	75,500	12,222	8,646	12,222	10,722
75,500	75,550	12,233	8,652	12,233	10,733
75,550	75,600	12,244	8,658	12,244	10,744
75,600	75,650	12,255	8,664	12,255	10,755
75,650	75,700	12,266	8,670	12,266	10,766
75,700	75,750	12,277	8,676	12,277	10,777
75,750	75,800	12,288	8,682	12,288	10,788
75,800	75,850	12,299	8,688	12,299	10,799
75,850	75,900	12,310	8,694	12,310	10,810
75,900	75,950	12,321	8,700	12,321	10,821
75,950	76,000	12,332	8,706	12,332	10,832
76,000					
76,000	76,050	12,343	8,712	12,343	10,843
76,050	76,100	12,354	8,718	12,354	10,854
76,100	76,150	12,365	8,724	12,365	10,865
76,150	76,200	12,376	8,730	12,376	10,876
76,200	76,250	12,387	8,736	12,387	10,887
76,250	76,300	12,398	8,742	12,398	10,898
76,300	76,350	12,409	8,748	12,409	10,909
76,350	76,400	12,420	8,754	12,420	10,920
76,400	76,450	12,431	8,760	12,431	10,931
76,450	76,500	12,442	8,766	12,442	10,942
76,500	76,550	12,453	8,772	12,453	10,953
76,550	76,600	12,464	8,778	12,464	10,964
76,600	76,650	12,475	8,784	12,475	10,975
76,650	76,700	12,486	8,790	12,486	10,986
76,700	76,750	12,497	8,796	12,497	10,997
76,750	76,800	12,508	8,802	12,508	11,008
76,800	76,850	12,519	8,808	12,519	11,019
76,850	76,900	12,530	8,814	12,530	11,030
76,900	76,950	12,541	8,820	12,541	11,041
76,950	77,000	12,552	8,826	12,552	11,052
77,000					
77,000	77,050	12,563	8,832	12,563	11,063
77,050	77,100	12,574	8,838	12,574	11,074
77,100	77,150	12,585	8,844	12,585	11,085
77,150	77,200	12,596	8,850	12,596	11,096
77,200	77,250	12,607	8,856	12,607	11,107
77,250	77,300	12,618	8,862	12,618	11,118
77,300	77,350	12,629	8,868	12,629	11,129
77,350	77,400	12,640	8,874	12,640	11,140
77,400	77,450	12,651	8,880	12,651	11,151
77,450	77,500	12,662	8,886	12,662	11,162
77,500	77,550	12,673	8,892	12,673	11,173
77,550	77,600	12,684	8,898	12,684	11,184
77,600	77,650	12,695	8,904	12,695	11,195
77,650	77,700	12,706	8,910	12,706	11,206
77,700	77,750	12,717	8,916	12,717	11,217
77,750	77,800	12,728	8,922	12,728	11,228
77,800	77,850	12,739	8,928	12,739	11,239
77,850	77,900	12,750	8,934	12,750	11,250
77,900	77,950	12,761	8,940	12,761	11,261
77,950	78,000	12,772	8,946	12,772	11,272
78,000					
78,000	78,050	12,783	8,952	12,783	11,283
78,050	78,100	12,794	8,958	12,794	11,294
78,100	78,150	12,805	8,964	12,805	11,305
78,150	78,200	12,816	8,970	12,816	11,316
78,200	78,250	12,827	8,976	12,827	11,327
78,250	78,300	12,838	8,982	12,838	11,338
78,300	78,350	12,849	8,988	12,849	11,349
78,350	78,400	12,860	8,994	12,860	11,360
78,400	78,450	12,871	9,000	12,871	11,371
78,450	78,500	12,882	9,006	12,882	11,382
78,500	78,550	12,893	9,012	12,893	11,393
78,550	78,600	12,904	9,018	12,904	11,404
78,600	78,650	12,915	9,024	12,915	11,415
78,650	78,700	12,926	9,030	12,926	11,426
78,700	78,750	12,937	9,036	12,937	11,437
78,750	78,800	12,948	9,042	12,948	11,448
78,800	78,850	12,959	9,048	12,959	11,459
78,850	78,900	12,970	9,054	12,970	11,470
78,900	78,950	12,981	9,060	12,981	11,481
78,950	79,000	12,992	9,066	12,992	11,492
79,000					
79,000	79,050	13,003	9,072	13,003	11,503
79,050	79,100	13,014	9,078	13,014	11,514
79,100	79,150	13,025	9,084	13,025	11,525
79,150	79,200	13,036	9,090	13,036	11,536
79,200	79,250	13,047	9,096	13,047	11,547
79,250	79,300	13,058	9,102	13,058	11,558
79,300	79,350	13,069	9,108	13,069	11,569
79,350	79,400	13,080	9,114	13,080	11,580
79,400	79,450	13,091	9,120	13,091	11,591
79,450	79,500	13,102	9,126	13,102	11,602
79,500	79,550	13,113	9,132	13,113	11,613
79,550	79,600	13,124	9,138	13,124	11,624
79,600	79,650	13,135	9,144	13,135	11,635
79,650	79,700	13,146	9,150	13,146	11,646
79,700	79,750	13,157	9,156	13,157	11,657
79,750	79,800	13,168	9,162	13,168	11,668
79,800	79,850	13,179	9,168	13,179	11,679
79,850	79,900	13,190	9,174	13,190	11,690
79,900	79,950	13,201	9,180	13,201	11,701
79,950	80,000	13,212	9,186	13,212	11,712
80,000					
80,000	80,050	13,223	9,192	13,223	11,723
80,050	80,100	13,234	9,198	13,234	11,734
80,100	80,150	13,245	9,204	13,245	11,745
80,150	80,200	13,256	9,210	13,256	11,756
80,200	80,250	13,267	9,216	13,267	11,767
80,250	80,300	13,278	9,222	13,278	11,778
80,300	80,350	13,289	9,228	13,289	11,789
80,350	80,400	13,300	9,234	13,300	11,800
80,400	80,450	13,311	9,240	13,311	11,811
80,450	80,500	13,322	9,246	13,322	11,822
80,500	80,550	13,333	9,252	13,333	11,833
80,550	80,600	13,344	9,258	13,344	11,844
80,600	80,650	13,355	9,264	13,355	11,855
80,650	80,700	13,366	9,270	13,366	11,866
80,700	80,750	13,377	9,276	13,377	11,877
80,750	80,800	13,388	9,282	13,388	11,888
80,800	80,850	13,399	9,288	13,399	11,899
80,850	80,900	13,410	9,294	13,410	11,910
80,900	80,950	13,421	9,300	13,421	11,921
80,950	81,000	13,432	9,306	13,432	11,932
81,000					
81,000	81,050	13,443	9,312	13,443	11,943
81,050	81,100	13,454	9,318	13,454	11,954
81,100	81,150	13,465	9,324	13,465	11,965
81,150	81,200	13,476	9,330	13,476	11,976
81,200	81,250	13,487	9,336	13,487	11,987
81,250	81,300	13,498	9,342	13,498	11,998
81,300	81,350	13,509	9,348	13,509	12,009
81,350	81,400	13,520	9,354	13,520	12,020
81,400	81,450	13,531	9,360	13,531	12,031
81,450	81,500	13,542	9,366	13,542	12,042
81,500	81,550	13,553	9,372	13,553	12,053
81,550	81,600	13,564	9,378	13,564	12,064
81,600	81,650	13,575	9,384	13,575	12,075
81,650	81,700	13,586	9,390	13,586	12,086
81,700	81,750	13,597	9,396	13,597	12,097
81,750	81,800	13,608	9,402	13,608	12,108
81,800	81,850	13,619	9,408	13,619	12,119
81,850	81,900	13,630	9,414	13,630	12,130
81,900	81,950	13,641	9,420	13,641	12,141
81,950	82,000	13,652	9,426	13,652	12,152
82,000					
82,000	82,050	13,663	9,432	13,663	12,163
82,050	82,100	13,674	9,438	13,674	12,174
82,100	82,150	13,685	9,444	13,685	12,185
82,150	82,200	13,696	9,450	13,696	12,196
82,200	82,250	13,707	9,456	13,707	12,207
82,250	82,300	13,718	9,462	13,718	12,218
82,300	82,350	13,729	9,468	13,729	12,229
82,350	82,400	13,740	9,474	13,740	12,240
82,400	82,450	13,751	9,480	13,751	12,251
82,450	82,500	13,762	9,486	13,762	12,262
82,500	82,550	13,773	9,492	13,773	12,273
82,550	82,600	13,784	9,498	13,784	12,284
82,600	82,650	13,795	9,504	13,795	12,295
82,650	82,700	13,806	9,510	13,806	12,306
82,700	82,750	13,817	9,516	13,817	12,317
82,750	82,800	13,828	9,522	13,828	12,328
82,800	82,850	13,839	9,528	13,839	12,339
82,850	82,900	13,850	9,534	13,850	12,350
82,900	82,950	13,861	9,540	13,861	12,361
82,950	83,000	13,872	9,546	13,872	12,372
83,000					
83,000	83,050	13,883	9,552	13,883	12,383
83,050	83,100	13,894	9,558	13,894	12,394
83,100	83,150	13,905	9,564	13,905	12,405
83,150	83,200	13,916	9,570	13,916	12,416
83,200	83,250	13,927	9,576	13,927	12,427
83,250	83,300	13,938	9,582	13,938	12,438
83,300	83,350	13,949	9,588	13,949	12,449
83,350	83,400	13,960	9,594	13,960	12,460
83,400	83,450	13,971	9,600	13,971	12,471
83,450	83,500	13,982	9,606	13,982	12,482
83,500	83,550	13,993	9,612	13,993	12,493
83,550	83,600	14,004	9,621	14,004	12,504
83,600	83,650	14,015	9,632	14,015	12,515
83,650	83,700	14,026	9,643	14,026	12,526
83,700	83,750	14,037	9,654	14,037	12,537
83,750	83,800	14,048	9,665	14,048	12,548
83,800	83,850	14,059	9,676	14,059	12,559
83,850	83,900	14,070	9,687	14,070	12,570
83,900	83,950	14,081	9,698	14,081	12,581
83,950	84,000	14,092	9,709	14,092	12,592

(Continued)

* This column must also be used by a qualifying surviving spouse.

2022 Tax Table — *Continued*

If line 15 (taxable income) is—		And you are—			
At least	But less than	Single	Married filing jointly *	Married filing sepa-rately	Head of a house-hold
		Your tax is—			
84,000					
84,000	84,050	14,103	9,720	14,103	12,603
84,050	84,100	14,114	9,731	14,114	12,614
84,100	84,150	14,125	9,742	14,125	12,625
84,150	84,200	14,136	9,753	14,136	12,636
84,200	84,250	14,147	9,764	14,147	12,647
84,250	84,300	14,158	9,775	14,158	12,658
84,300	84,350	14,169	9,786	14,169	12,669
84,350	84,400	14,180	9,797	14,180	12,680
84,400	84,450	14,191	9,808	14,191	12,691
84,450	84,500	14,202	9,819	14,202	12,702
84,500	84,550	14,213	9,830	14,213	12,713
84,550	84,600	14,224	9,841	14,224	12,724
84,600	84,650	14,235	9,852	14,235	12,735
84,650	84,700	14,246	9,863	14,246	12,746
84,700	84,750	14,257	9,874	14,257	12,757
84,750	84,800	14,268	9,885	14,268	12,768
84,800	84,850	14,279	9,896	14,279	12,779
84,850	84,900	14,290	9,907	14,290	12,790
84,900	84,950	14,301	9,918	14,301	12,801
84,950	85,000	14,312	9,929	14,312	12,812
85,000					
85,000	85,050	14,323	9,940	14,323	12,823
85,050	85,100	14,334	9,951	14,334	12,834
85,100	85,150	14,345	9,962	14,345	12,845
85,150	85,200	14,356	9,973	14,356	12,856
85,200	85,250	14,367	9,984	14,367	12,867
85,250	85,300	14,378	9,995	14,378	12,878
85,300	85,350	14,389	10,006	14,389	12,889
85,350	85,400	14,400	10,017	14,400	12,900
85,400	85,450	14,411	10,028	14,411	12,911
85,450	85,500	14,422	10,039	14,422	12,922
85,500	85,550	14,433	10,050	14,433	12,933
85,550	85,600	14,444	10,061	14,444	12,944
85,600	85,650	14,455	10,072	14,455	12,955
85,650	85,700	14,466	10,083	14,466	12,966
85,700	85,750	14,477	10,094	14,477	12,977
85,750	85,800	14,488	10,105	14,488	12,988
85,800	85,850	14,499	10,116	14,499	12,999
85,850	85,900	14,510	10,127	14,510	13,010
85,900	85,950	14,521	10,138	14,521	13,021
85,950	86,000	14,532	10,149	14,532	13,032
86,000					
86,000	86,050	14,543	10,160	14,543	13,043
86,050	86,100	14,554	10,171	14,554	13,054
86,100	86,150	14,565	10,182	14,565	13,065
86,150	86,200	14,576	10,193	14,576	13,076
86,200	86,250	14,587	10,204	14,587	13,087
86,250	86,300	14,598	10,215	14,598	13,098
86,300	86,350	14,609	10,226	14,609	13,109
86,350	86,400	14,620	10,237	14,620	13,120
86,400	86,450	14,631	10,248	14,631	13,131
86,450	86,500	14,642	10,259	14,642	13,142
86,500	86,550	14,653	10,270	14,653	13,153
86,550	86,600	14,664	10,281	14,664	13,164
86,600	86,650	14,675	10,292	14,675	13,175
86,650	86,700	14,686	10,303	14,686	13,186
86,700	86,750	14,697	10,314	14,697	13,197
86,750	86,800	14,708	10,325	14,708	13,208
86,800	86,850	14,719	10,336	14,719	13,219
86,850	86,900	14,730	10,347	14,730	13,230
86,900	86,950	14,741	10,358	14,741	13,241
86,950	87,000	14,752	10,369	14,752	13,252
87,000					
87,000	87,050	14,763	10,380	14,763	13,263
87,050	87,100	14,774	10,391	14,774	13,274
87,100	87,150	14,785	10,402	14,785	13,285
87,150	87,200	14,796	10,413	14,796	13,296
87,200	87,250	14,807	10,424	14,807	13,307
87,250	87,300	14,818	10,435	14,818	13,318
87,300	87,350	14,829	10,446	14,829	13,329
87,350	87,400	14,840	10,457	14,840	13,340
87,400	87,450	14,851	10,468	14,851	13,351
87,450	87,500	14,862	10,479	14,862	13,362
87,500	87,550	14,873	10,490	14,873	13,373
87,550	87,600	14,884	10,501	14,884	13,384
87,600	87,650	14,895	10,512	14,895	13,395
87,650	87,700	14,906	10,523	14,906	13,406
87,700	87,750	14,917	10,534	14,917	13,417
87,750	87,800	14,928	10,545	14,928	13,428
87,800	87,850	14,939	10,556	14,939	13,439
87,850	87,900	14,950	10,567	14,950	13,450
87,900	87,950	14,961	10,578	14,961	13,461
87,950	88,000	14,972	10,589	14,972	13,472
88,000					
88,000	88,050	14,983	10,600	14,983	13,483
88,050	88,100	14,994	10,611	14,994	13,494
88,100	88,150	15,005	10,622	15,005	13,505
88,150	88,200	15,016	10,633	15,016	13,516
88,200	88,250	15,027	10,644	15,027	13,527
88,250	88,300	15,038	10,655	15,038	13,538
88,300	88,350	15,049	10,666	15,049	13,549
88,350	88,400	15,060	10,677	15,060	13,560
88,400	88,450	15,071	10,688	15,071	13,571
88,450	88,500	15,082	10,699	15,082	13,582
88,500	88,550	15,093	10,710	15,093	13,593
88,550	88,600	15,104	10,721	15,104	13,604
88,600	88,650	15,115	10,732	15,115	13,615
88,650	88,700	15,126	10,743	15,126	13,626
88,700	88,750	15,137	10,754	15,137	13,637
88,750	88,800	15,148	10,765	15,148	13,648
88,800	88,850	15,159	10,776	15,159	13,659
88,850	88,900	15,170	10,787	15,170	13,670
88,900	88,950	15,181	10,798	15,181	13,681
88,950	89,000	15,192	10,809	15,192	13,692
89,000					
89,000	89,050	15,203	10,820	15,203	13,703
89,050	89,100	15,214	10,831	15,214	13,714
89,100	89,150	15,226	10,842	15,226	13,726
89,150	89,200	15,238	10,853	15,238	13,738
89,200	89,250	15,250	10,864	15,250	13,750
89,250	89,300	15,262	10,875	15,262	13,762
89,300	89,350	15,274	10,886	15,274	13,774
89,350	89,400	15,286	10,897	15,286	13,786
89,400	89,450	15,298	10,908	15,298	13,798
89,450	89,500	15,310	10,919	15,310	13,810
89,500	89,550	15,322	10,930	15,322	13,822
89,550	89,600	15,334	10,941	15,334	13,834
89,600	89,650	15,346	10,952	15,346	13,846
89,650	89,700	15,358	10,963	15,358	13,858
89,700	89,750	15,370	10,974	15,370	13,870
89,750	89,800	15,382	10,985	15,382	13,882
89,800	89,850	15,394	10,996	15,394	13,894
89,850	89,900	15,406	11,007	15,406	13,906
89,900	89,950	15,418	11,018	15,418	13,918
89,950	90,000	15,430	11,029	15,430	13,930
90,000					
90,000	90,050	15,442	11,040	15,442	13,942
90,050	90,100	15,454	11,051	15,454	13,954
90,100	90,150	15,466	11,062	15,466	13,966
90,150	90,200	15,478	11,073	15,478	13,978
90,200	90,250	15,490	11,084	15,490	13,990
90,250	90,300	15,502	11,095	15,502	14,002
90,300	90,350	15,514	11,106	15,514	14,014
90,350	90,400	15,526	11,117	15,526	14,026
90,400	90,450	15,538	11,128	15,538	14,038
90,450	90,500	15,550	11,139	15,550	14,050
90,500	90,550	15,562	11,150	15,562	14,062
90,550	90,600	15,574	11,161	15,574	14,074
90,600	90,650	15,586	11,172	15,586	14,086
90,650	90,700	15,598	11,183	15,598	14,098
90,700	90,750	15,610	11,194	15,610	14,110
90,750	90,800	15,622	11,205	15,622	14,122
90,800	90,850	15,634	11,216	15,634	14,134
90,850	90,900	15,646	11,227	15,646	14,146
90,900	90,950	15,658	11,238	15,658	14,158
90,950	91,000	15,670	11,249	15,670	14,170
91,000					
91,000	91,050	15,682	11,260	15,682	14,182
91,050	91,100	15,694	11,271	15,694	14,194
91,100	91,150	15,706	11,282	15,706	14,206
91,150	91,200	15,718	11,293	15,718	14,218
91,200	91,250	15,730	11,304	15,730	14,230
91,250	91,300	15,742	11,315	15,742	14,242
91,300	91,350	15,754	11,326	15,754	14,254
91,350	91,400	15,766	11,337	15,766	14,266
91,400	91,450	15,778	11,348	15,778	14,278
91,450	91,500	15,790	11,359	15,790	14,290
91,500	91,550	15,802	11,370	15,802	14,302
91,550	91,600	15,814	11,381	15,814	14,314
91,600	91,650	15,826	11,392	15,826	14,326
91,650	91,700	15,838	11,403	15,838	14,338
91,700	91,750	15,850	11,414	15,850	14,350
91,750	91,800	15,862	11,425	15,862	14,362
91,800	91,850	15,874	11,436	15,874	14,374
91,850	91,900	15,886	11,447	15,886	14,386
91,900	91,950	15,898	11,458	15,898	14,398
91,950	92,000	15,910	11,469	15,910	14,410
92,000					
92,000	92,050	15,922	11,480	15,922	14,422
92,050	92,100	15,934	11,491	15,934	14,434
92,100	92,150	15,946	11,502	15,946	14,446
92,150	92,200	15,958	11,513	15,958	14,458
92,200	92,250	15,970	11,524	15,970	14,470
92,250	92,300	15,982	11,535	15,982	14,482
92,300	92,350	15,994	11,546	15,994	14,494
92,350	92,400	16,006	11,557	16,006	14,506
92,400	92,450	16,018	11,568	16,018	14,518
92,450	92,500	16,030	11,579	16,030	14,530
92,500	92,550	16,042	11,590	16,042	14,542
92,550	92,600	16,054	11,601	16,054	14,554
92,600	92,650	16,066	11,612	16,066	14,566
92,650	92,700	16,078	11,623	16,078	14,578
92,700	92,750	16,090	11,634	16,090	14,590
92,750	92,800	16,102	11,645	16,102	14,602
92,800	92,850	16,114	11,656	16,114	14,614
92,850	92,900	16,126	11,667	16,126	14,626
92,900	92,950	16,138	11,678	16,138	14,638
92,950	93,000	16,150	11,689	16,150	14,650

(Continued)

* This column must also be used by a qualifying surviving spouse.

2022 Tax Table — *Continued*

If line 15 (taxable income) is—		And you are—			
At least	But less than	Single	Married filing jointly *	Married filing sepa-rately	Head of a house-hold
		Your tax is—			
93,000					
93,000	93,050	16,162	11,700	16,162	14,662
93,050	93,100	16,174	11,711	16,174	14,674
93,100	93,150	16,186	11,722	16,186	14,686
93,150	93,200	16,198	11,733	16,198	14,698
93,200	93,250	16,210	11,744	16,210	14,710
93,250	93,300	16,222	11,755	16,222	14,722
93,300	93,350	16,234	11,766	16,234	14,734
93,350	93,400	16,246	11,777	16,246	14,746
93,400	93,450	16,258	11,788	16,258	14,758
93,450	93,500	16,270	11,799	16,270	14,770
93,500	93,550	16,282	11,810	16,282	14,782
93,550	93,600	16,294	11,821	16,294	14,794
93,600	93,650	16,306	11,832	16,306	14,806
93,650	93,700	16,318	11,843	16,318	14,818
93,700	93,750	16,330	11,854	16,330	14,830
93,750	93,800	16,342	11,865	16,342	14,842
93,800	93,850	16,354	11,876	16,354	14,854
93,850	93,900	16,366	11,887	16,366	14,866
93,900	93,950	16,378	11,898	16,378	14,878
93,950	94,000	16,390	11,909	16,390	14,890
94,000					
94,000	94,050	16,402	11,920	16,402	14,902
94,050	94,100	16,414	11,931	16,414	14,914
94,100	94,150	16,426	11,942	16,426	14,926
94,150	94,200	16,438	11,953	16,438	14,938
94,200	94,250	16,450	11,964	16,450	14,950
94,250	94,300	16,462	11,975	16,462	14,962
94,300	94,350	16,474	11,986	16,474	14,974
94,350	94,400	16,486	11,997	16,486	14,986
94,400	94,450	16,498	12,008	16,498	14,998
94,450	94,500	16,510	12,019	16,510	15,010
94,500	94,550	16,522	12,030	16,522	15,022
94,550	94,600	16,534	12,041	16,534	15,034
94,600	94,650	16,546	12,052	16,546	15,046
94,650	94,700	16,558	12,063	16,558	15,058
94,700	94,750	16,570	12,074	16,570	15,070
94,750	94,800	16,582	12,085	16,582	15,082
94,800	94,850	16,594	12,096	16,594	15,094
94,850	94,900	16,606	12,107	16,606	15,106
94,900	94,950	16,618	12,118	16,618	15,118
94,950	95,000	16,630	12,129	16,630	15,130
95,000					
95,000	95,050	16,642	12,140	16,642	15,142
95,050	95,100	16,654	12,151	16,654	15,154
95,100	95,150	16,666	12,162	16,666	15,166
95,150	95,200	16,678	12,173	16,678	15,178
95,200	95,250	16,690	12,184	16,690	15,190
95,250	95,300	16,702	12,195	16,702	15,202
95,300	95,350	16,714	12,206	16,714	15,214
95,350	95,400	16,726	12,217	16,726	15,226
95,400	95,450	16,738	12,228	16,738	15,238
95,450	95,500	16,750	12,239	16,750	15,250
95,500	95,550	16,762	12,250	16,762	15,262
95,550	95,600	16,774	12,261	16,774	15,274
95,600	95,650	16,786	12,272	16,786	15,286
95,650	95,700	16,798	12,283	16,798	15,298
95,700	95,750	16,810	12,294	16,810	15,310
95,750	95,800	16,822	12,305	16,822	15,322
95,800	95,850	16,834	12,316	16,834	15,334
95,850	95,900	16,846	12,327	16,846	15,346
95,900	95,950	16,858	12,338	16,858	15,358
95,950	96,000	16,870	12,349	16,870	15,370
96,000					
96,000	96,050	16,882	12,360	16,882	15,382
96,050	96,100	16,894	12,371	16,894	15,394
96,100	96,150	16,906	12,382	16,906	15,406
96,150	96,200	16,918	12,393	16,918	15,418
96,200	96,250	16,930	12,404	16,930	15,430
96,250	96,300	16,942	12,415	16,942	15,442
96,300	96,350	16,954	12,426	16,954	15,454
96,350	96,400	16,966	12,437	16,966	15,466
96,400	96,450	16,978	12,448	16,978	15,478
96,450	96,500	16,990	12,459	16,990	15,490
96,500	96,550	17,002	12,470	17,002	15,502
96,550	96,600	17,014	12,481	17,014	15,514
96,600	96,650	17,026	12,492	17,026	15,526
96,650	96,700	17,038	12,503	17,038	15,538
96,700	96,750	17,050	12,514	17,050	15,550
96,750	96,800	17,062	12,525	17,062	15,562
96,800	96,850	17,074	12,536	17,074	15,574
96,850	96,900	17,086	12,547	17,086	15,586
96,900	96,950	17,098	12,558	17,098	15,598
96,950	97,000	17,110	12,569	17,110	15,610
97,000					
97,000	97,050	17,122	12,580	17,122	15,622
97,050	97,100	17,134	12,591	17,134	15,634
97,100	97,150	17,146	12,602	17,146	15,646
97,150	97,200	17,158	12,613	17,158	15,658
97,200	97,250	17,170	12,624	17,170	15,670
97,250	97,300	17,182	12,635	17,182	15,682
97,300	97,350	17,194	12,646	17,194	15,694
97,350	97,400	17,206	12,657	17,206	15,706
97,400	97,450	17,218	12,668	17,218	15,718
97,450	97,500	17,230	12,679	17,230	15,730
97,500	97,550	17,242	12,690	17,242	15,742
97,550	97,600	17,254	12,701	17,254	15,754
97,600	97,650	17,266	12,712	17,266	15,766
97,650	97,700	17,278	12,723	17,278	15,778
97,700	97,750	17,290	12,734	17,290	15,790
97,750	97,800	17,302	12,745	17,302	15,802
97,800	97,850	17,314	12,756	17,314	15,814
97,850	97,900	17,326	12,767	17,326	15,826
97,900	97,950	17,338	12,778	17,338	15,838
97,950	98,000	17,350	12,789	17,350	15,850
98,000					
98,000	98,050	17,362	12,800	17,362	15,862
98,050	98,100	17,374	12,811	17,374	15,874
98,100	98,150	17,386	12,822	17,386	15,886
98,150	98,200	17,398	12,833	17,398	15,898
98,200	98,250	17,410	12,844	17,410	15,910
98,250	98,300	17,422	12,855	17,422	15,922
98,300	98,350	17,434	12,866	17,434	15,934
98,350	98,400	17,446	12,877	17,446	15,946
98,400	98,450	17,458	12,888	17,458	15,958
98,450	98,500	17,470	12,899	17,470	15,970
98,500	98,550	17,482	12,910	17,482	15,982
98,550	98,600	17,494	12,921	17,494	15,994
98,600	98,650	17,506	12,932	17,506	16,006
98,650	98,700	17,518	12,943	17,518	16,018
98,700	98,750	17,530	12,954	17,530	16,030
98,750	98,800	17,542	12,965	17,542	16,042
98,800	98,850	17,554	12,976	17,554	16,054
98,850	98,900	17,566	12,987	17,566	16,066
98,900	98,950	17,578	12,998	17,578	16,078
98,950	99,000	17,590	13,009	17,590	16,090
99,000					
99,000	99,050	17,602	13,020	17,602	16,102
99,050	99,100	17,614	13,031	17,614	16,114
99,100	99,150	17,626	13,042	17,626	16,126
99,150	99,200	17,638	13,053	17,638	16,138
99,200	99,250	17,650	13,064	17,650	16,150
99,250	99,300	17,662	13,075	17,662	16,162
99,300	99,350	17,674	13,086	17,674	16,174
99,350	99,400	17,686	13,097	17,686	16,186
99,400	99,450	17,698	13,108	17,698	16,198
99,450	99,500	17,710	13,119	17,710	16,210
99,500	99,550	17,722	13,130	17,722	16,222
99,550	99,600	17,734	13,141	17,734	16,234
99,600	99,650	17,746	13,152	17,746	16,246
99,650	99,700	17,758	13,163	17,758	16,258
99,700	99,750	17,770	13,174	17,770	16,270
99,750	99,800	17,782	13,185	17,782	16,282
99,800	99,850	17,794	13,196	17,794	16,294
99,850	99,900	17,806	13,207	17,806	16,306
99,900	99,950	17,818	13,218	17,818	16,318
99,950	100,000	17,830	13,229	17,830	16,330

$100,000 or over
use the Tax Computation Worksheet

* This column must also be used by a qualifying surviving spouse.

2022 Optional Sales Tax Tables

When Used

The election to deduct state and local general sales taxes requires that the taxpayer give up any deduction for state and local income taxes. Whether this is advisable or not depends on a comparison of the amounts involved. In making the choice, however, the outcome could be influenced by the additional sales tax incurred due to certain "big ticket" purchases that were made. For example, a taxpayer who chose to deduct state and local income taxes for 2021 might well prefer the sales tax deduction in 2022 if a new boat was purchased or home improvements were made during the year. To make the sales tax election, the taxpayer must enter the amount on Schedule A, line 5a, and check the related box.

If the sales tax election is made, the amount of the deduction can be determined by use of the *actual expense method* or *the optional sales tax tables* issued by the IRS. The actual expense method can be used only when the taxpayer has actual receipts to support the deduction claimed. In the absence of receipts (the usual case with most taxpayers), the optional sales tax tables must be used. Sales taxes related to the purchase of items used in a taxpayer's trade or business are determined separately, with this amount deducted on Schedule C (Form 1040).

Adjustments Necessary

The optional sales tax tables are based on a number of assumptions that require adjustments to be made. As the starting point for the use of the tables is AGI, nontaxable receipts have not been included. Examples of receipts that should be added include: tax-exempt interest, veterans' benefits, nontaxable combat pay, public assistance payments, workers' compensation, nontaxable Social Security, and other retirement benefits. They do not include any large nontaxable items that are not likely to be spent. For example, a $100,000 inheritance should not be added if it was invested in a certificate of deposit.

The tables represent the sales tax on the average (and recurring) expenditures based on level of income by family size and do not include exceptional purchases. Therefore, add to the table amount any sales taxes on major purchases (such as motor vehicles, aircraft, boats, and home building materials, etc.).

When the optional sales tax tables are used, special adjustments may be needed when a taxpayer has lived in more than one taxing jurisdiction (e.g., state, county, city) during the year. The adjustments involve apportionment of taxes based on days involved and are illustrated in Instructions for Schedule A (Form 1040), pages A-3 to A-7.

Local Sales Taxes

Local sales taxes (i.e., those imposed by counties, cities, transit authorities) may or may not require a separate determination. In those states where they are not imposed, no further computations are necessary. This is also the case where the local taxes are uniform and are incorporated into the state sales tax table. In other situations, another step is necessary to arrive at the optional sales tax table deduction. Depending on where the taxpayer lives, one of two procedures needs to be used. In one procedure, the local sales tax is determined by using the **state table** amount—see Example 1 and the related worksheet. In the other procedure, special **local tables** issued by the IRS for specified state and local jurisdictions are modified (if necessary) and used—see Example 2 and the related worksheet.

IRS Sales Tax Deduction Calculator

The IRS has created an online Sales Tax Deduction Calculator to assist taxpayers in making this calculation (**apps.irs.gov/app/stdc/**). The calculator includes the ability to make adjustments for large purchases and includes a local sales tax calculation.

Use Illustrated

Example 1 The Archers file a joint return for 2022 reflecting AGI of $88,000 and have three dependents. They have tax-exempt interest of $3,000, and during the year they incurred sales tax of $1,650 on the purchase of an automobile for their dependent teenage son. They live in Bellaire, Texas, where the general sales tax rates are 6.25% for state and 2% for local. Since the IRS *has not issued* optional local sales tax tables for Texas, use the Worksheet below to arrive at the Archers' general sales tax deduction of $3,305.

Sales Tax Deduction Worksheet
(To be used when *no* IRS Optional Local Sales Tax Table Available)

Adjusted Gross Income (AGI) as listed on line 11 of Form 1040		$88,000
Add nontaxable items		3,000
Table income to be used for purposes of line 1 below		$91,000
1. Use table income to determine table amount—go to state of residence and find applicable range of table income and family size column for *state* sales tax		$ 1,254
2a. Enter local general sales tax rate	2.00	
2b. Enter state general sales tax rate	6.25	
2c. Divide 2a by 2b	0.32	
2d. Multiply line 1 by line 2c for the local sales tax		401
3. Enter general sales tax on large purchases		1,650
4. Deduction for general sales tax (add lines 1 + 2d + 3) and report on line 5a of Schedule A of Form 1040		$ 3,305

Example 2 The Hardys file a joint return for 2022, reporting AGI of $42,000 and have two dependents. They received $30,000 in nontaxable pension benefits. Although the Hardys do not keep sales tax receipts, they can prove that they paid $1,185 in sales tax on the purchase of a new boat in 2022. The Hardys are residents of Georgia and live in a jurisdiction that imposes a 2% local sales tax. Since the IRS *has issued* optional local sales tax tables for Georgia, use the Worksheet below to arrive at the Hardys' general sales tax deduction of $2,315.

Sales Tax Deduction Worksheet
(To be used for Alaska, Arizona, Arkansas, Colorado, Georgia, Illinois, Louisiana, Mississippi, Missouri, New York, North Carolina, South Carolina, Tennessee, Utah, and Virginia)

Adjusted Gross Income (AGI) as listed on line 11 of Form 1040		$42,000
Add nontaxable income		30,000
Table income to be used for purposes of line 1 below		$72,000
1. Use the table income to determine *state* sales tax amount—go to table for state of residence and find applicable income range and family size column		$ 660
2a. Enter local general sales tax rate	2.0	
2b. Enter IRS *local* sales tax table amount (based on a 1% tax rate)	$235	
2c. Multiply line 2b by 2a for the local sales tax		470
3. Enter general sales tax on large purchases		1,185
4. Deduction for general sales tax (add lines 1 + 2c + 3) and report on line 5a of Schedule A of Form 1040		$ 2,315

Assume that the Hardys live in Lawrenceville, GA 30045. Use the IRS Sales Tax Deduction Calculator to confirm the calculated amount (**apps.irs.gov/app/stdc/**).

2022 Optional State Sales Tax Tables

Income		Family Size						Family Size						Family Size					
At least	But less than	1	2	3	4	5	Over 5	1	2	3	4	5	Over 5	1	2	3	4	5	Over 5
		Alabama			1		4.0000%	**Arizona**			2		5.6000%	**Arkansas**			2		6.5000%
$0	$20,000	310	372	415	448	476	515	321	367	397	419	438	464	385	440	476	504	526	557
$20,000	$30,000	422	507	564	609	647	700	457	522	565	597	624	661	555	634	686	726	758	803
$30,000	$40,000	477	572	637	688	730	790	525	600	649	687	717	759	640	732	793	838	876	927
$40,000	$50,000	523	627	698	753	800	865	583	666	721	762	796	843	713	816	883	934	975	1033
$50,000	$60,000	563	674	751	810	860	930	634	724	783	829	865	916	777	889	962	1018	1063	1125
$60,000	$70,000	598	716	797	860	913	988	679	776	839	888	927	982	834	955	1033	1093	1141	1208
$70,000	$80,000	630	754	839	906	961	1039	720	823	890	941	983	1041	887	1014	1098	1161	1213	1284
$80,000	$90,000	659	789	878	947	1005	1087	758	866	937	991	1035	1096	935	1070	1158	1224	1279	1354
$90,000	$100,000	686	821	913	986	1046	1131	794	907	981	1037	1083	1147	980	1121	1213	1283	1341	1420
$100,000	$120,000	721	863	960	1036	1099	1189	840	960	1039	1098	1147	1215	1040	1189	1287	1362	1422	1506
$120,000	$140,000	767	917	1020	1100	1168	1262	900	1029	1113	1177	1229	1301	1116	1277	1382	1462	1528	1618
$140,000	$160,000	808	966	1075	1159	1230	1330	956	1092	1181	1249	1305	1381	1187	1358	1470	1555	1625	1720
$160,000	$180,000	846	1011	1124	1213	1286	1391	1006	1150	1244	1315	1374	1454	1252	1433	1551	1640	1713	1815
$180,000	$200,000	880	1053	1170	1262	1339	1447	1054	1204	1302	1377	1438	1523	1313	1502	1626	1720	1797	1903
$200,000	$225,000	916	1096	1218	1313	1393	1506	1103	1260	1363	1441	1505	1594	1376	1574	1704	1803	1883	1994
$225,000	$250,000	954	1141	1268	1367	1450	1568	1155	1319	1427	1509	1576	1669	1443	1651	1787	1891	1975	2092
$250,000	$275,000	990	1183	1315	1418	1504	1625	1203	1375	1487	1573	1643	1739	1506	1723	1865	1973	2061	2183
$275,000	$300,000	1023	1223	1359	1465	1554	1679	1249	1428	1544	1633	1706	1806	1565	1791	1939	2051	2143	2270
$300,000	or more	1215	1450	1611	1736	1841	1989	1517	1734	1875	1983	2071	2193	1913	2189	2370	2507	2619	2774
Income		**California**			3		7.2500%	**Colorado**			2		2.9000%	**Connecticut**			4		6.3500%
$0	$20,000	402	459	496	524	547	578	163	187	202	214	224	237	318	355	379	397	411	431
$20,000	$30,000	565	645	697	736	768	813	231	264	286	303	317	336	446	498	532	557	577	605
$30,000	$40,000	647	738	797	842	878	929	265	303	329	348	364	386	509	569	607	636	659	691
$40,000	$50,000	715	815	881	930	971	1027	293	336	364	386	403	428	563	629	671	703	729	764
$50,000	$60,000	775	884	954	1008	1052	1113	319	365	396	419	438	464	610	681	727	761	789	827
$60,000	$70,000	828	944	1020	1077	1124	1189	341	391	423	448	469	497	651	728	777	813	843	883
$70,000	$80,000	877	999	1079	1140	1190	1258	361	414	449	475	497	526	689	770	822	860	892	935
$80,000	$90,000	921	1050	1134	1198	1250	1322	380	436	472	500	522	554	724	809	863	904	937	982
$90,000	$100,000	963	1097	1185	1252	1306	1381	398	456	494	523	546	579	756	845	902	944	979	1026
$100,000	$120,000	1017	1159	1252	1322	1380	1460	421	482	522	553	578	613	799	892	952	997	1034	1083
$120,000	$140,000	1087	1239	1338	1413	1475	1560	451	516	559	592	619	656	853	953	1017	1066	1104	1157
$140,000	$160,000	1151	1312	1417	1497	1562	1652	478	547	593	628	656	696	903	1009	1077	1128	1169	1225
$160,000	$180,000	1210	1379	1489	1573	1641	1736	503	576	624	661	691	732	949	1060	1132	1185	1228	1287
$180,000	$200,000	1265	1441	1557	1644	1716	1814	526	603	653	691	723	766	992	1108	1183	1239	1284	1345
$200,000	$225,000	1322	1506	1626	1718	1792	1895	550	630	683	723	756	801	1036	1158	1235	1294	1341	1405
$225,000	$250,000	1382	1574	1700	1795	1874	1981	576	660	715	757	791	838	1083	1210	1291	1352	1401	1469
$250,000	$275,000	1438	1638	1769	1868	1949	2062	600	687	744	788	824	873	1126	1259	1343	1406	1458	1528
$275,000	$300,000	1491	1699	1834	1937	2021	2138	622	713	773	818	855	906	1168	1305	1392	1458	1511	1584
$300,000	or more	1798	2048	2211	2335	2437	2577	754	864	936	990	1035	1097	1406	1571	1677	1756	1820	1907
Income		**District of Columbia**			4		6.0000%	**Florida**			1		6.0000%	**Georgia**			2		4.0000%
$0	$20,000	306	343	367	385	399	419	345	392	423	446	465	491	227	259	280	296	309	327
$20,000	$30,000	426	477	510	534	554	582	494	561	605	639	666	704	323	368	398	421	439	464
$30,000	$40,000	485	543	580	608	631	662	569	647	698	736	768	811	371	423	457	483	504	533
$40,000	$50,000	535	599	640	670	695	730	632	719	776	818	853	902	411	469	507	536	559	591
$50,000	$60,000	578	647	691	724	751	788	688	783	844	891	929	982	447	509	551	582	607	642
$60,000	$70,000	616	690	737	772	801	840	738	839	905	955	996	1053	478	545	589	623	650	688
$70,000	$80,000	651	729	778	816	846	888	783	891	961	1014	1058	1118	507	578	625	660	689	729
$80,000	$90,000	683	764	817	856	888	931	825	939	1013	1069	1115	1178	533	609	658	695	725	767
$90,000	$100,000	712	797	852	893	926	972	864	983	1061	1120	1167	1234	558	637	688	727	759	803
$100,000	$120,000	751	841	899	942	977	1025	916	1042	1124	1187	1237	1307	591	674	728	770	803	850
$120,000	$140,000	801	897	958	1004	1042	1093	982	1118	1206	1273	1327	1403	633	722	780	824	860	910
$140,000	$160,000	847	948	1013	1062	1101	1155	1044	1188	1281	1352	1410	1490	671	766	827	874	913	966
$160,000	$180,000	889	995	1063	1114	1155	1212	1100	1251	1350	1425	1486	1570	706	806	871	920	960	1016
$180,000	$200,000	928	1038	1109	1163	1206	1265	1152	1311	1415	1493	1557	1646	739	844	911	963	1005	1064
$200,000	$225,000	968	1083	1157	1213	1258	1319	1207	1373	1482	1564	1631	1723	774	882	953	1008	1052	1113
$225,000	$250,000	1010	1131	1208	1266	1313	1377	1265	1439	1553	1639	1709	1806	810	924	998	1055	1101	1165
$250,000	$275,000	1050	1175	1255	1316	1364	1431	1319	1501	1619	1709	1782	1884	844	962	1040	1099	1147	1213
$275,000	$300,000	1088	1217	1300	1363	1413	1482	1370	1559	1682	1776	1852	1957	876	999	1079	1141	1191	1260
$300,000	or more	1304	1459	1558	1633	1693	1776	1669	1899	2049	2163	2256	2384	1062	1211	1309	1383	1443	1527
Income		**Hawaii**			1,6		4.0000%	**Idaho**			1		6.0000%	**Illinois**			2		6.2500%
$0	$20,000	349	406	443	472	495	528	466	555	615	662	701	756	330	382	418	445	467	498
$20,000	$30,000	497	578	631	672	706	753	644	766	849	914	968	1044	467	541	591	629	660	704
$30,000	$40,000	572	665	726	773	812	865	731	870	964	1038	1099	1185	535	620	677	721	757	807
$40,000	$50,000	635	738	806	858	901	960	805	957	1061	1141	1208	1303	593	687	750	798	838	894
$50,000	$60,000	690	802	876	933	979	1044	868	1033	1145	1232	1304	1406	643	746	814	866	909	970
$60,000	$70,000	739	859	938	999	1049	1119	925	1100	1219	1311	1388	1497	688	798	870	927	973	1037
$70,000	$80,000	784	911	995	1060	1113	1187	976	1161	1286	1384	1465	1579	730	845	922	982	1030	1099
$80,000	$90,000	825	959	1048	1116	1172	1249	1023	1217	1348	1450	1535	1655	767	889	970	1032	1084	1155
$90,000	$100,000	864	1004	1097	1168	1226	1308	1067	1269	1405	1512	1600	1725	803	930	1014	1079	1133	1208
$100,000	$120,000	915	1063	1162	1237	1299	1385	1125	1337	1481	1593	1686	1817	849	983	1073	1142	1198	1277
$120,000	$140,000	980	1140	1245	1325	1392	1484	1198	1424	1577	1696	1796	1935	909	1052	1148	1222	1282	1367
$140,000	$160,000	1041	1210	1321	1407	1477	1575	1266	1504	1665	1791	1896	2043	963	1116	1217	1295	1359	1449
$160,000	$180,000	1096	1274	1391	1481	1556	1659	1327	1577	1746	1878	1987	2141	1014	1174	1280	1362	1430	1524
$180,000	$200,000	1147	1334	1457	1551	1629	1737	1384	1644	1821	1958	2072	2233	1060	1228	1339	1425	1496	1594
$200,000	$225,000	1201	1396	1525	1623	1705	1817	1443	1714	1898	2041	2160	2328	1109	1284	1400	1490	1564	1667
$225,000	$250,000	1257	1462	1597	1700	1785	1903	1505	1788	1980	2129	2253	2427	1160	1343	1465	1559	1636	1744
$250,000	$275,000	1310	1523	1664	1772	1860	1984	1563	1857	2056	2211	2339	2521	1209	1399	1526	1623	1703	1815
$275,000	$300,000	1361	1582	1728	1840	1932	2060	1618	1922	2128	2288	2421	2609	1254	1452	1583	1684	1767	1884
$300,000	or more	1653	1921	2099	2235	2346	2502	1934	2296	2541	2732	2891	3114	1518	1757	1915	2037	2138	2278

Income		Family Size						Family Size						Family Size					
At least	But less than	1	2	3	4	5	Over 5	1	2	3	4	5	Over 5	1	2	3	4	5	Over 5
		Indiana			4		7.0000%	**Iowa**			1		6.0000%	**Kansas**			1		6.5000%
$0	$20,000	398	457	496	525	550	583	368	419	453	478	499	528	506	609	680	735	781	847
$20,000	$30,000	565	649	703	745	780	827	524	598	646	682	712	752	695	836	932	1007	1071	1160
$30,000	$40,000	648	744	807	855	895	949	603	687	742	784	818	865	787	946	1055	1141	1212	1313
$40,000	$50,000	719	825	895	948	992	1052	669	763	824	870	908	960	864	1039	1158	1252	1330	1440
$50,000	$60,000	780	896	972	1030	1077	1142	727	830	896	946	987	1044	931	1119	1248	1348	1432	1551
$60,000	$70,000	835	959	1040	1102	1153	1223	779	889	960	1014	1058	1119	990	1190	1327	1434	1523	1649
$70,000	$80,000	885	1017	1103	1168	1222	1296	827	943	1018	1076	1122	1187	1044	1254	1398	1511	1605	1738
$80,000	$90,000	932	1070	1160	1229	1285	1364	870	993	1072	1132	1182	1250	1093	1313	1464	1582	1680	1819
$90,000	$100,000	974	1119	1213	1286	1345	1426	911	1039	1122	1185	1237	1308	1139	1368	1525	1647	1750	1895
$100,000	$120,000	1031	1184	1284	1360	1423	1509	965	1100	1188	1255	1310	1385	1199	1440	1604	1734	1841	1993
$120,000	$140,000	1104	1267	1375	1456	1523	1616	1034	1179	1273	1345	1404	1484	1275	1532	1707	1844	1958	2120
$140,000	$160,000	1171	1344	1458	1545	1616	1714	1097	1252	1352	1428	1490	1576	1345	1615	1800	1944	2065	2235
$160,000	$180,000	1232	1415	1534	1625	1700	1803	1155	1318	1423	1504	1569	1659	1409	1692	1885	2036	2162	2340
$180,000	$200,000	1289	1480	1605	1701	1779	1887	1210	1380	1491	1575	1643	1738	1468	1763	1964	2121	2253	2438
$200,000	$225,000	1348	1548	1679	1779	1861	1974	1266	1444	1560	1648	1720	1818	1529	1836	2045	2209	2346	2539
$225,000	$250,000	1411	1620	1757	1862	1947	2066	1326	1512	1634	1726	1801	1904	1594	1913	2131	2302	2444	2645
$250,000	$275,000	1470	1688	1831	1939	2028	2152	1382	1576	1703	1799	1877	1985	1654	1985	2211	2388	2536	2745
$275,000	$300,000	1526	1752	1900	2013	2105	2233	1435	1637	1768	1868	1949	2061	1711	2053	2287	2470	2622	2838
$300,000	or more	1848	2122	2302	2438	2550	2705	1743	1988	2148	2269	2368	2504	2037	2443	2720	2937	3118	3374

Income		**Kentucky**			4		6.0000%	**Louisiana**			2		4.4500%	**Maine**			4		5.5000%
$0	$20,000	355	401	431	454	473	498	258	291	313	329	343	361	273	313	339	359	376	399
$20,000	$30,000	512	579	623	655	682	719	370	418	449	473	492	518	376	431	468	495	518	549
$30,000	$40,000	591	669	719	758	789	831	426	482	518	545	567	597	427	490	531	562	588	623
$40,000	$50,000	659	746	802	844	879	926	474	536	576	606	631	664	470	539	583	618	646	685
$50,000	$60,000	718	813	874	920	958	1010	516	584	627	660	687	723	507	581	629	666	697	739
$60,000	$70,000	771	873	939	989	1029	1085	554	626	673	708	737	776	540	619	670	709	742	786
$70,000	$80,000	820	928	998	1051	1094	1153	588	665	714	752	782	824	570	653	707	748	782	829
$80,000	$90,000	865	979	1053	1109	1154	1217	620	701	753	792	825	869	598	684	741	784	820	869
$90,000	$100,000	907	1026	1104	1162	1210	1276	649	734	789	830	864	910	623	713	772	817	854	906
$100,000	$120,000	962	1089	1171	1233	1284	1354	688	778	836	880	916	965	657	751	814	861	900	954
$120,000	$140,000	1034	1170	1258	1325	1379	1454	738	835	897	944	983	1035	699	800	866	917	958	1016
$140,000	$160,000	1100	1245	1339	1410	1468	1547	785	887	953	1004	1044	1100	739	845	915	968	1012	1072
$160,000	$180,000	1160	1313	1412	1487	1548	1632	827	935	1005	1058	1101	1160	774	886	959	1015	1060	1124
$180,000	$200,000	1217	1377	1481	1560	1624	1712	867	980	1053	1109	1154	1216	808	924	1000	1058	1106	1172
$200,000	$225,000	1275	1444	1553	1635	1702	1795	908	1026	1103	1161	1208	1273	842	963	1042	1103	1152	1221
$225,000	$250,000	1338	1514	1629	1715	1786	1883	951	1076	1156	1217	1267	1335	878	1004	1087	1150	1202	1273
$250,000	$275,000	1396	1581	1700	1791	1864	1965	992	1122	1206	1270	1321	1392	912	1043	1129	1194	1248	1322
$275,000	$300,000	1452	1644	1768	1862	1938	2044	1031	1166	1253	1319	1373	1447	944	1080	1168	1236	1291	1368
$300,000	or more	1776	2011	2163	2278	2371	2500	1257	1422	1528	1609	1674	1764	1128	1289	1395	1475	1541	1633

Income		**Maryland**			4		6.0000%	**Massachusetts**			4		6.2500%	**Michigan**			4		6.0000%
$0	$20,000	308	361	397	425	448	481	307	345	370	389	404	425	330	377	408	432	451	478
$20,000	$30,000	432	506	556	595	627	673	433	487	522	549	570	599	468	535	579	613	640	678
$30,000	$40,000	494	578	635	680	716	768	496	558	598	628	653	687	537	614	665	703	735	778
$40,000	$50,000	545	639	702	750	791	848	549	617	662	695	723	760	595	681	737	779	814	862
$50,000	$60,000	591	692	760	812	856	917	595	670	718	754	784	824	646	739	800	846	884	936
$60,000	$70,000	631	739	811	868	914	979	636	716	768	807	838	881	692	791	856	906	946	1002
$70,000	$80,000	668	782	858	918	967	1036	674	758	813	854	887	933	733	838	907	960	1003	1062
$80,000	$90,000	702	821	901	964	1015	1088	709	797	855	898	933	981	771	882	955	1010	1055	1118
$90,000	$100,000	733	857	941	1006	1060	1136	741	834	893	939	975	1026	807	923	999	1056	1104	1169
$100,000	$120,000	774	906	994	1063	1120	1199	783	881	945	992	1031	1084	854	976	1057	1118	1168	1237
$120,000	$140,000	827	967	1062	1135	1196	1281	838	943	1010	1061	1103	1160	914	1045	1131	1197	1250	1324
$140,000	$160,000	876	1024	1124	1201	1265	1355	888	999	1071	1125	1169	1229	969	1109	1200	1269	1326	1405
$160,000	$180,000	920	1076	1181	1262	1329	1423	933	1050	1126	1183	1229	1292	1020	1167	1262	1336	1395	1478
$180,000	$200,000	962	1124	1234	1318	1389	1487	976	1099	1177	1237	1285	1351	1068	1221	1321	1398	1460	1547
$200,000	$225,000	1005	1174	1288	1377	1450	1553	1020	1148	1231	1293	1343	1413	1117	1277	1382	1462	1527	1618
$225,000	$250,000	1050	1227	1346	1439	1515	1622	1067	1201	1287	1352	1405	1477	1169	1336	1446	1530	1598	1693
$250,000	$275,000	1093	1277	1400	1496	1576	1687	1111	1250	1340	1408	1462	1538	1217	1392	1506	1594	1665	1763
$275,000	$300,000	1133	1323	1452	1551	1633	1749	1152	1297	1390	1460	1517	1595	1263	1445	1563	1654	1728	1830
$300,000	or more	1365	1594	1747	1867	1965	2104	1392	1567	1679	1764	1833	1927	1530	1750	1894	2003	2093	2217

Income		**Minnesota**			1		6.8750%	**Mississippi**			2		7.0000%	**Missouri**			2		4.2250%
$0	$20,000	357	396	422	441	456	477	562	668	739	795	841	905	251	289	315	334	350	373
$20,000	$30,000	520	578	615	643	665	695	777	922	1020	1096	1159	1248	357	412	448	476	499	531
$30,000	$40,000	603	671	714	746	772	807	882	1047	1158	1244	1316	1417	411	474	516	547	574	610
$40,000	$50,000	674	750	798	834	863	902	970	1151	1273	1368	1447	1557	456	526	572	608	637	677
$50,000	$60,000	737	820	872	911	943	986	1047	1242	1373	1476	1561	1680	495	572	622	660	692	736
$60,000	$70,000	793	882	939	981	1015	1061	1115	1322	1462	1571	1662	1788	531	612	666	707	741	788
$70,000	$80,000	845	940	1000	1045	1081	1130	1176	1395	1543	1658	1753	1887	563	649	707	750	786	836
$80,000	$90,000	893	993	1056	1104	1142	1194	1233	1462	1617	1737	1837	1977	593	684	744	790	828	880
$90,000	$100,000	937	1042	1109	1159	1199	1254	1285	1524	1685	1811	1915	2061	620	716	778	827	866	921
$100,000	$120,000	996	1108	1179	1232	1275	1333	1354	1606	1775	1907	2017	2170	657	758	824	875	917	975
$120,000	$140,000	1073	1193	1269	1326	1372	1435	1442	1710	1891	2031	2148	2311	704	812	883	938	983	1045
$140,000	$160,000	1143	1271	1353	1414	1463	1530	1523	1805	1996	2144	2267	2440	747	862	937	995	1043	1109
$160,000	$180,000	1208	1343	1429	1494	1546	1617	1596	1892	2092	2247	2376	2557	786	907	987	1048	1098	1168
$180,000	$200,000	1269	1411	1501	1569	1624	1698	1665	1973	2182	2343	2478	2666	823	950	1033	1097	1150	1223
$200,000	$225,000	1332	1481	1576	1647	1705	1783	1735	2057	2274	2442	2582	2778	862	994	1081	1148	1203	1279
$225,000	$250,000	1399	1556	1656	1731	1791	1873	1810	2145	2371	2547	2693	2897	902	1041	1132	1202	1260	1340
$250,000	$275,000	1463	1627	1731	1809	1872	1958	1879	2227	2462	2645	2796	3008	940	1085	1180	1253	1313	1396
$275,000	$300,000	1523	1693	1802	1883	1949	2038	1945	2305	2548	2737	2893	3113	976	1126	1225	1301	1363	1450
$300,000	or more	1875	2085	2218	2319	2399	2509	2323	2752	3041	3266	3452	3714	1185	1367	1488	1580	1655	1760

Income		Family Size						Family Size						Family Size					
At least	But less than	1	2	3	4	5	Over 5	1	2	3	4	5	Over 5	1	2	3	4	5	Over 5
		Nebraska			1		5.5000%	**Nevada**			5		6.8500%	**New Jersey**			4		6.6250%
$0	$20,000	320	361	388	408	425	447	382	436	471	498	520	550	365	403	427	445	460	479
$20,000	$30,000	461	521	560	589	613	645	539	615	664	702	732	775	529	584	619	645	666	694
$30,000	$40,000	533	602	647	681	708	746	617	704	760	803	839	887	612	676	716	746	770	803
$40,000	$50,000	594	671	721	758	789	831	683	779	841	889	928	981	682	753	798	832	859	895
$50,000	$60,000	647	732	786	827	860	906	740	844	912	964	1006	1064	744	822	871	908	937	977
$60,000	$70,000	695	786	844	888	924	973	791	903	975	1030	1075	1138	800	883	936	975	1007	1050
$70,000	$80,000	739	835	897	944	982	1034	838	956	1033	1091	1139	1205	851	939	996	1037	1071	1117
$80,000	$90,000	779	881	946	996	1036	1091	881	1005	1085	1147	1197	1266	898	991	1051	1095	1130	1178
$90,000	$100,000	817	923	992	1044	1086	1144	921	1050	1134	1199	1251	1323	942	1040	1102	1148	1185	1236
$100,000	$120,000	867	980	1053	1108	1152	1214	973	1110	1199	1267	1322	1399	1000	1104	1170	1219	1258	1312
$120,000	$140,000	931	1053	1131	1190	1238	1304	1041	1187	1282	1355	1414	1496	1075	1187	1257	1310	1353	1411
$140,000	$160,000	991	1120	1203	1266	1317	1387	1103	1258	1359	1435	1498	1585	1144	1263	1338	1395	1440	1501
$160,000	$180,000	1045	1181	1269	1336	1390	1464	1160	1322	1428	1509	1575	1666	1207	1333	1412	1472	1520	1584
$180,000	$200,000	1096	1239	1331	1401	1457	1535	1213	1383	1494	1578	1647	1742	1267	1399	1482	1544	1594	1663
$200,000	$225,000	1149	1299	1395	1469	1528	1609	1267	1445	1561	1649	1721	1820	1328	1467	1554	1620	1672	1744
$225,000	$250,000	1205	1362	1464	1541	1603	1688	1325	1511	1632	1724	1800	1904	1394	1539	1631	1700	1755	1830
$250,000	$275,000	1258	1422	1528	1608	1673	1762	1380	1573	1699	1795	1873	1981	1455	1607	1703	1775	1832	1911
$275,000	$300,000	1308	1479	1589	1672	1740	1833	1431	1632	1762	1862	1943	2055	1514	1672	1772	1846	1906	1987
$300,000	or more	1600	1809	1944	2046	2128	2242	1728	1970	2128	2248	2346	2481	1855	2048	2171	2262	2335	2435
Income		**New Mexico**			1		5.0620%	**New York**			2		4.0000%	**North Carolina**			2		4.7500%
$0	$20,000	346	379	400	416	428	445	220	244	260	272	281	294	310	365	401	429	452	485
$20,000	$30,000	508	556	587	610	628	653	318	354	376	393	407	426	434	510	561	600	632	678
$30,000	$40,000	590	647	683	710	731	760	368	409	435	455	471	493	495	582	640	684	722	774
$40,000	$50,000	661	725	765	795	818	851	410	456	485	507	525	549	547	642	706	755	796	854
$50,000	$60,000	724	793	837	870	896	931	447	498	530	554	573	599	592	695	764	818	862	924
$60,000	$70,000	780	855	902	937	965	1004	481	535	569	595	616	644	632	742	816	873	920	986
$70,000	$80,000	831	911	962	999	1029	1070	511	569	605	633	655	685	668	784	862	923	973	1042
$80,000	$90,000	879	964	1017	1056	1088	1131	539	600	639	668	691	723	702	824	905	969	1021	1094
$90,000	$100,000	924	1013	1068	1110	1143	1189	566	629	670	700	725	758	733	860	945	1011	1066	1143
$100,000	$120,000	983	1077	1137	1181	1217	1265	600	668	711	743	769	805	774	908	998	1068	1125	1206
$120,000	$140,000	1059	1161	1225	1273	1311	1363	645	718	764	799	827	865	826	969	1065	1140	1201	1288
$140,000	$160,000	1130	1239	1307	1358	1399	1454	687	764	814	851	880	921	874	1026	1127	1206	1271	1362
$160,000	$180,000	1195	1310	1383	1436	1479	1538	725	807	859	898	929	972	918	1077	1184	1266	1335	1430
$180,000	$200,000	1257	1377	1453	1510	1555	1617	760	846	901	942	975	1020	959	1125	1237	1323	1394	1494
$200,000	$225,000	1320	1447	1527	1586	1634	1698	797	887	945	988	1022	1070	1001	1175	1291	1381	1455	1560
$225,000	$250,000	1388	1521	1605	1668	1718	1786	837	931	991	1036	1073	1122	1046	1227	1349	1443	1520	1629
$250,000	$275,000	1452	1591	1679	1744	1797	1868	874	972	1035	1082	1120	1172	1088	1276	1402	1500	1581	1694
$275,000	$300,000	1512	1658	1749	1817	1872	1946	909	1011	1077	1126	1165	1219	1127	1322	1453	1555	1638	1756
$300,000	or more	1868	2047	2160	2244	2311	2402	1113	1239	1319	1379	1428	1494	1355	1590	1747	1868	1969	2110
Income		**North Dakota**			1		5.0000%	**Ohio**			1		5.7500%	**Oklahoma**			1		4.5000%
$0	$20,000	268	309	336	357	374	398	341	385	413	435	452	476	341	405	449	483	511	551
$20,000	$30,000	380	438	477	506	530	564	487	549	590	620	645	679	472	560	621	668	707	762
$30,000	$40,000	437	503	547	581	609	647	560	632	678	714	742	781	537	637	705	759	803	865
$40,000	$50,000	484	558	607	644	675	718	622	702	753	792	824	867	591	701	776	835	883	952
$50,000	$60,000	526	606	659	699	733	779	676	763	819	862	896	943	638	757	838	901	953	1027
$60,000	$70,000	563	648	705	749	784	834	725	818	878	924	960	1011	680	807	893	960	1016	1094
$70,000	$80,000	597	687	747	793	831	884	769	868	932	980	1019	1073	718	851	942	1013	1072	1155
$80,000	$90,000	628	723	786	835	875	930	810	914	981	1032	1073	1130	753	893	988	1062	1124	1210
$90,000	$100,000	657	756	823	873	915	973	848	957	1027	1080	1123	1183	785	931	1030	1107	1172	1262
$100,000	$120,000	695	801	870	924	968	1030	898	1013	1088	1144	1190	1253	827	981	1086	1167	1235	1330
$120,000	$140,000	744	857	932	989	1037	1102	962	1086	1166	1226	1275	1343	882	1046	1157	1243	1315	1417
$140,000	$160,000	789	909	988	1049	1099	1169	1022	1153	1238	1302	1354	1426	932	1105	1222	1313	1389	1496
$160,000	$180,000	831	957	1040	1104	1157	1230	1076	1215	1304	1371	1426	1501	977	1158	1281	1377	1456	1569
$180,000	$200,000	869	1001	1089	1156	1211	1287	1127	1272	1366	1436	1494	1572	1020	1208	1336	1436	1519	1636
$200,000	$225,000	909	1047	1139	1209	1266	1346	1180	1332	1430	1503	1563	1646	1063	1260	1393	1497	1584	1706
$225,000	$250,000	952	1096	1192	1265	1325	1409	1236	1395	1497	1575	1638	1724	1110	1315	1454	1562	1652	1779
$250,000	$275,000	992	1142	1241	1318	1380	1468	1288	1454	1561	1642	1707	1797	1153	1366	1510	1623	1716	1848
$275,000	$300,000	1029	1185	1288	1368	1433	1523	1338	1510	1621	1705	1773	1866	1193	1414	1563	1680	1777	1913
$300,000	or more	1247	1436	1561	1657	1736	1845	1626	1835	1970	2072	2155	2269	1428	1691	1869	2008	2123	2286
Income		**Pennsylvania**			1		6.0000%	**Rhode Island**			4		7.0000%	**South Carolina**			2		6.0000%
$0	$20,000	316	355	380	399	415	436	358	406	436	459	478	504	344	394	426	450	470	498
$20,000	$30,000	446	501	536	563	584	614	508	575	619	652	678	715	487	557	602	637	665	704
$30,000	$40,000	510	573	614	644	669	703	583	660	710	748	778	821	558	638	690	730	762	807
$40,000	$50,000	565	634	679	713	740	778	647	732	787	829	863	909	618	706	764	808	844	893
$50,000	$60,000	612	688	736	773	802	843	702	795	855	900	937	988	670	766	829	877	916	969
$60,000	$70,000	655	735	787	826	858	901	752	851	915	963	1003	1057	717	820	887	938	979	1037
$70,000	$80,000	693	778	833	875	908	954	797	902	970	1021	1063	1120	760	868	939	993	1037	1098
$80,000	$90,000	728	818	876	919	955	1003	838	949	1020	1074	1118	1179	799	913	988	1045	1091	1155
$90,000	$100,000	761	855	916	961	998	1048	877	992	1067	1124	1170	1233	835	955	1033	1092	1141	1208
$100,000	$120,000	805	904	968	1016	1055	1108	928	1050	1129	1189	1238	1305	883	1010	1092	1155	1206	1277
$120,000	$140,000	861	967	1035	1086	1128	1185	993	1124	1209	1273	1325	1397	945	1080	1169	1236	1291	1366
$140,000	$160,000	912	1024	1096	1151	1195	1256	1053	1192	1282	1350	1405	1481	1002	1145	1239	1310	1368	1448
$160,000	$180,000	959	1077	1153	1210	1256	1320	1108	1255	1349	1421	1479	1559	1054	1205	1303	1378	1439	1523
$180,000	$200,000	1002	1126	1205	1265	1314	1380	1160	1313	1412	1487	1547	1631	1102	1260	1363	1441	1505	1593
$200,000	$225,000	1047	1177	1260	1322	1373	1442	1213	1373	1477	1555	1618	1706	1152	1317	1425	1506	1573	1665
$225,000	$250,000	1095	1230	1317	1383	1436	1508	1269	1437	1545	1627	1694	1785	1206	1378	1490	1576	1646	1742
$250,000	$275,000	1140	1281	1371	1439	1494	1570	1322	1497	1610	1695	1764	1860	1255	1435	1552	1641	1714	1814
$275,000	$300,000	1183	1328	1422	1493	1550	1628	1372	1554	1671	1759	1831	1930	1302	1489	1610	1702	1778	1882
$300,000	or more	1428	1604	1717	1802	1871	1965	1662	1882	2024	2131	2218	2338	1575	1800	1947	2058	2150	2275

Income		Family Size						Family Size						Family Size					
At least	But less than	1	2	3	4	5	Over 5	1	2	3	4	5	Over 5	1	2	3	4	5	Over 5
		South Dakota			**1**		**4.5000%**	**Tennessee**			**2**		**7.0000%**	**Texas**			**1**		**6.2500%**
$0	$20,000	374	440	484	519	547	586	481	561	614	655	689	736	369	423	458	484	506	536
$20,000	$30,000	527	620	683	731	770	826	676	788	863	921	969	1035	526	602	652	690	721	764
$30,000	$40,000	604	710	782	836	882	945	773	902	987	1053	1108	1184	605	693	750	794	830	879
$40,000	$50,000	668	786	865	925	976	1046	855	997	1091	1164	1224	1308	672	769	833	881	921	976
$50,000	$60,000	724	852	937	1003	1058	1134	926	1080	1183	1262	1327	1418	730	836	905	958	1001	1061
$60,000	$70,000	775	911	1002	1073	1131	1212	990	1154	1264	1348	1418	1515	782	896	970	1027	1073	1137
$70,000	$80,000	820	964	1061	1136	1197	1283	1048	1222	1338	1427	1501	1603	830	950	1029	1089	1138	1206
$80,000	$90,000	862	1014	1115	1194	1258	1349	1101	1284	1406	1499	1577	1684	874	1001	1083	1147	1198	1269
$90,000	$100,000	901	1060	1166	1248	1315	1410	1150	1341	1469	1567	1647	1760	914	1047	1134	1200	1254	1329
$100,000	$120,000	952	1120	1232	1319	1390	1490	1215	1417	1552	1655	1741	1860	968	1109	1201	1271	1328	1407
$120,000	$140,000	1018	1198	1317	1410	1486	1593	1299	1515	1658	1769	1860	1987	1038	1189	1287	1362	1423	1508
$140,000	$160,000	1079	1269	1396	1494	1575	1688	1376	1604	1756	1874	1970	2105	1102	1262	1366	1446	1511	1601
$160,000	$180,000	1134	1334	1467	1570	1655	1774	1446	1686	1846	1969	2070	2212	1160	1329	1439	1523	1591	1686
$180,000	$200,000	1186	1395	1534	1642	1731	1855	1511	1762	1929	2058	2164	2312	1215	1391	1507	1595	1666	1766
$200,000	$225,000	1240	1458	1603	1716	1809	1939	1579	1841	2016	2150	2261	2415	1271	1456	1577	1669	1744	1848
$225,000	$250,000	1296	1524	1677	1794	1891	2027	1651	1925	2107	2247	2363	2525	1331	1525	1651	1748	1826	1935
$250,000	$275,000	1349	1587	1745	1867	1969	2110	1718	2003	2193	2339	2459	2627	1387	1589	1721	1822	1904	2017
$275,000	$300,000	1400	1646	1810	1937	2042	2188	1781	2077	2273	2425	2550	2724	1441	1650	1787	1892	1977	2095
$300,000	or more	1690	1986	2185	2338	2464	2641	2148	2504	2741	2923	3074	3283	1750	2005	2171	2298	2402	2545
Income		**Utah**			**2**		**4.8500%**	**Vermont**			**1**		**6.0000%**	**Virginia**			**2**		**4.3000%**
$0	$20,000	342	397	435	463	487	519	253	275	289	300	308	319	251	295	324	346	365	391
$20,000	$30,000	481	560	612	652	685	731	354	385	404	419	430	446	355	416	457	489	515	552
$30,000	$40,000	550	640	700	746	783	836	404	439	462	478	491	509	407	477	524	560	590	632
$40,000	$50,000	609	708	774	825	866	925	446	485	510	528	542	562	450	528	580	620	653	700
$50,000	$60,000	660	768	839	894	939	1002	482	525	551	571	587	608	489	573	629	673	709	759
$60,000	$70,000	705	820	897	955	1004	1071	515	560	589	610	627	649	523	612	673	719	758	812
$70,000	$80,000	747	868	949	1011	1062	1134	544	592	623	645	663	687	554	649	712	762	803	860
$80,000	$90,000	785	913	998	1063	1117	1191	572	622	654	677	696	721	582	682	749	801	844	904
$90,000	$100,000	820	954	1042	1111	1167	1245	597	650	682	707	726	753	609	713	783	837	882	945
$100,000	$120,000	867	1008	1102	1174	1233	1316	630	686	721	746	767	795	644	754	828	885	933	999
$120,000	$140,000	927	1077	1178	1255	1318	1406	673	732	769	797	819	849	689	807	886	947	998	1068
$140,000	$160,000	981	1141	1247	1329	1396	1490	712	775	814	843	867	898	730	855	939	1004	1057	1132
$160,000	$180,000	1032	1200	1311	1397	1467	1566	748	814	855	885	910	943	768	899	987	1055	1112	1191
$180,000	$200,000	1079	1254	1371	1460	1534	1637	781	850	893	925	951	985	803	940	1033	1104	1163	1245
$200,000	$225,000	1127	1310	1432	1526	1603	1710	815	887	932	966	992	1029	839	983	1079	1154	1215	1301
$225,000	$250,000	1178	1370	1497	1595	1676	1788	852	927	974	1009	1037	1075	878	1028	1129	1207	1271	1361
$250,000	$275,000	1226	1426	1558	1660	1744	1861	886	964	1013	1049	1078	1118	914	1071	1175	1256	1323	1417
$275,000	$300,000	1272	1479	1616	1722	1809	1930	918	999	1050	1087	1118	1158	949	1111	1219	1303	1373	1470
$300,000	or more	1534	1784	1950	2077	2182	2328	1103	1201	1262	1307	1344	1393	1147	1343	1474	1575	1659	1776
Income		**Washington**			**1**		**6.5000%**	**West Virginia**			**1**		**6.0000%**	**Wisconsin**			**1**		**5.0000%**
$0	$20,000	397	452	487	514	536	566	351	399	430	453	472	498	304	346	373	393	410	433
$20,000	$30,000	569	647	698	736	768	811	513	583	628	662	690	729	436	495	534	564	587	620
$30,000	$40,000	656	746	804	848	885	934	596	677	730	769	802	847	502	571	616	649	677	715
$40,000	$50,000	729	829	894	943	983	1039	666	757	816	861	897	947	558	635	684	722	753	795
$50,000	$60,000	793	902	973	1026	1070	1130	729	828	892	941	981	1036	608	691	745	786	819	865
$60,000	$70,000	850	967	1043	1100	1147	1212	784	891	961	1014	1056	1115	652	741	799	843	879	928
$70,000	$80,000	903	1027	1107	1168	1218	1287	836	950	1024	1080	1125	1188	692	787	848	895	933	985
$80,000	$90,000	951	1082	1166	1231	1283	1356	883	1004	1082	1141	1189	1256	729	829	894	943	983	1038
$90,000	$100,000	996	1133	1222	1289	1344	1420	927	1054	1136	1199	1249	1319	764	868	936	988	1030	1088
$100,000	$120,000	1055	1200	1295	1366	1424	1504	986	1121	1208	1275	1329	1403	809	920	993	1047	1092	1153
$120,000	$140,000	1132	1287	1388	1465	1528	1614	1062	1207	1302	1373	1431	1511	868	987	1065	1123	1171	1237
$140,000	$160,000	1202	1368	1475	1556	1623	1714	1132	1287	1388	1464	1526	1611	923	1049	1131	1194	1244	1314
$160,000	$180,000	1267	1441	1554	1640	1710	1806	1197	1360	1467	1547	1613	1703	972	1106	1192	1258	1311	1385
$180,000	$200,000	1327	1510	1628	1718	1792	1893	1257	1429	1541	1626	1695	1790	1019	1159	1249	1318	1374	1451
$200,000	$225,000	1390	1581	1705	1799	1876	1982	1320	1501	1618	1707	1780	1879	1067	1213	1308	1380	1439	1520
$225,000	$250,000	1456	1657	1787	1885	1966	2077	1387	1577	1701	1794	1870	1975	1118	1272	1371	1447	1508	1593
$250,000	$275,000	1519	1728	1863	1966	2050	2165	1450	1649	1778	1876	1955	2065	1166	1326	1430	1509	1573	1661
$275,000	$300,000	1578	1795	1936	2043	2130	2250	1510	1717	1851	1953	2036	2150	1212	1378	1486	1568	1634	1726
$300,000	or more	1921	2185	2357	2487	2593	2739	1860	2116	2282	2407	2510	2651	1476	1679	1810	1910	1991	2103

Income		**Wyoming**			**1**		**4.0000%**
$0	$20,000	239	270	289	304	316	333
$20,000	$30,000	341	384	412	433	450	474
$30,000	$40,000	392	442	474	498	518	545
$40,000	$50,000	435	490	526	553	575	605
$50,000	$60,000	473	533	572	601	625	658
$60,000	$70,000	507	571	613	644	670	705
$70,000	$80,000	537	606	650	683	711	748
$80,000	$90,000	566	638	684	720	748	787
$90,000	$100,000	592	668	716	753	783	824
$100,000	$120,000	627	707	759	798	829	873
$120,000	$140,000	672	758	813	855	889	935
$140,000	$160,000	713	804	863	907	943	993
$160,000	$180,000	751	847	909	955	993	1045
$180,000	$200,000	787	887	952	1000	1040	1095
$200,000	$225,000	823	928	996	1047	1089	1146
$225,000	$250,000	862	972	1043	1097	1140	1200
$250,000	$275,000	899	1013	1087	1143	1188	1250
$275,000	$300,000	933	1052	1129	1187	1234	1298
$300,000	or more	1133	1278	1371	1442	1499	1577

Note: Residents of **Alaska** do not have a state sales tax, but should follow the instructions on the next page to determine their local sales tax amount.

1. Use the Ratio Method to determine your local sales tax deduction. Your state sales tax rate is provided next to the state name.
2. Follow the instructions on the next page to determine your local sales tax deduction.
3. The California table includes the 1.25% uniform local sales tax rate in addition to the 6.00% state sales tax rate for a total of 7.25%. Some California localities impose a larger local sales tax. Taxpayers who reside in those jurisdictions should use the Ratio Method to determine their local sales tax deduction. The denominator of the correct ratio is 7.25%, and the numerator is the total sales tax rate minus 7.25%.
4. This state does not have a local general sales tax, so the amount in the state table is the only amount to be deducted.
5. The Nevada table includes the 2.25% uniform local sales tax rate in addition to the 4.6000% state sales tax rate for a total of 6.85%. Some Nevada localities impose a larger local sales tax. Taxpayers who reside in those jurisdictions should use the Ratio Method to determine their local sales tax deduction. The denominator of the correct ratio is 6.85%, and the numerator is the total sales tax rate minus 6.85%.
6. The 4.0% rate for Hawaii is actually an excise tax but is treated as a sales tax for purpose of this deduction.

Which Optional Local Sales Tax Table Should I Use?

IF you live in the state of...	AND you live in...	THEN use Local Table...
Alaska	Juneau, Kenai, Ketchikan, Kodiak, Sitka, Wasilla or any locality that imposes a local sales tax	C
Arizona	Tempe	C
	Chandler, Gilbert, Glendale, Mesa, Peoria, Phoenix, Scottsdale, Tucson, Yuma or any other locality that imposes a local sales tax	B
Arkansas	Any Locality that imposes a local sales tax	C
Colorado	Adams County, Boulder County, Centennial, Colorado Springs, Denver City, El Paso County, Larimer County, Pueblo City, Pueblo County or any other locality that imposes a local sales tax	A
	Arapahoe County, Arvada, Aurora, Boulder, Fort Collins, Greeley, Jefferson County, Lakewood, Longmont, Thornton or Westminster	B
Georgia	Dekalb County (excluding Atlanta)	B
	Any other locality that imposes a local sales tax	C
Illinois	Arlington Heights, Bloomington, Champaign, Chicago, Cicero, Decatur, Evanston, Palatine, Peoria, Schaumburg, Skokie, Springfield or any other locality that imposes a local sales tax	A
	Aurora, Elgin, Joliet, Waukegan	B
Louisiana	East Baton Rouge Parish	B
	Ascension Parish, Bossier Parish, Caddo Parish, Calcasieu Parish, Iberia Parish, Jefferson Parish, Lafayette Parish, Lafourche Parish, Livingston Parish, Orleans Parish, Ouachita Parish, Rapides Parish, St. Bernard Parish, St. Landry Parish, St. Tammany Parish, Tangipahoa Parish, Terrebonne Parish or any other locality that imposes a local sales tax	C
Mississippi	City of Jackson only	A
	City of Tupelo only	C
Missouri	Any locality that imposes a local sales tax	C
New York	Counties: Chautauqua, Chenango, Columbia, Delaware, Dutchess, Greene, Hamilton, Tioga Cities: New York, Norwich (Chenango County)	A
	Counties: Albany, Allegany, Broome, Cattaraugus, Cayuga, Chemung, Clinton, Cortland, Erie, Essex, Franklin, Fulton, Genesee, Herkimer, Jefferson, Lewis, Livingston, Madison, Monroe, Montgomery, Nassau, Niagara, Oneida, Onondaga, Ontario, Orange, Orleans, Oswego, Otsego, Putnam, Rensselaer, Rockland, St. Lawrence, Saratoga, Schenectady, Schoharie, Schuyler, Seneca, Steuben, Suffolk, Sullivan, Tompkins, Ulster, Warren, Washington, Wayne, Westchester, Wyoming or Yates Cities: Auburn, Glens Falls, Gloversville, Ithaca, Johnstown, Mount Vernon, New Rochelle, Ogdensburg, Olean, Oneida (Madison County), Oswego, Rome, Salamanca, Saratoga Springs, Utica, White Plains, Yonkers	B
	Any other locality that imposes a local sales tax	D*
North Carolina	Any locality that imposes a local sales tax	B
South Carolina	Aiken County, Anderson County, Greenwood County, Horry County, Lexington County, Myrtle Beach, Newberry County, Orangeburg County, Spartanburg County and York County	A
	Allendale County, Bamberg County, Barnwell County, Calhoun County, Charleston County, Cherokee County, Chester County, Chesterfield County, Colleton County, Darlington County, Dillon County, Edgefield County, Florence County, Jasper County, Kershaw County, Lancaster County, Laurens County, Lee County, Marion County, Marlboro County, McCormick County, Saluda County, Sumter County and Williamsburg County	B
	Abbeville County, Berkeley County, Clarendon County, Dorchester County, Fairfield County, Hampton County, Pickens County, Richland County, Union County or any other locality that imposes a local sales tax	C
Tennessee	Any locality that imposes a local sales tax	C
Utah	Any locality that imposes a local sales tax	A
Virginia	Any locality that imposes a local sales tax	C

*** Note: Local Table D is just 25% of the NY State table.**

2022 Optional Local Sales Tax Tables

Income		Family Size						Family Size						Family Size						Family Size					
At least	But less than	1	2	3	4	5	Over 5	1	2	3	4	5	Over 5	1	2	3	4	5	Over 5	1	2	3	4	5	Over 5
		Local Table A						Local Table B						Local Table C						Local Table D					
$0	$20,000	54	61	66	70	73	78	63	74	81	86	91	98	79	94	104	112	118	127	55	61	65	68	70	74
20,000	30,000	76	87	94	99	103	110	88	103	113	121	127	136	110	130	144	155	164	176	80	89	94	98	102	107
30,000	40,000	87	99	107	114	119	126	100	117	129	138	145	155	125	148	164	176	186	200	92	102	109	114	118	123
40,000	50,000	96	110	119	126	131	139	111	130	142	152	160	171	138	163	180	194	205	220	103	114	121	127	131	137
50,000	60,000	104	119	129	136	142	151	120	140	154	165	173	186	149	176	195	209	221	238	112	125	133	139	143	150
60,000	70,000	112	128	138	146	152	161	128	150	164	176	185	198	158	188	207	223	235	253	120	134	142	149	154	161
70,000	80,000	118	135	146	155	161	171	135	158	174	186	195	209	167	198	219	235	248	267	128	142	151	158	164	171
80,000	90,000	124	142	154	163	170	180	142	166	182	195	205	220	175	208	229	246	260	280	135	150	160	167	173	181
90,000	100,000	130	149	161	170	178	188	148	174	190	203	214	229	183	216	239	257	271	292	142	157	168	175	181	190
100,000	120,000	138	157	170	180	188	199	157	183	201	215	226	242	193	228	252	271	286	308	150	167	178	186	192	201
120,000	140,000	147	168	182	192	201	213	167	196	215	229	241	258	205	243	269	288	305	328	161	180	191	200	207	216
140,000	160,000	156	178	193	204	213	226	177	207	227	243	255	273	217	257	284	305	322	346	172	191	204	213	220	230
160,000	180,000	164	187	203	214	224	237	186	217	238	255	268	287	227	269	297	319	337	363	181	202	215	225	232	243
180,000	200,000	172	196	212	224	234	248	194	227	249	266	280	300	237	281	310	333	352	378	190	212	225	236	244	255
200,000	225,000	179	205	222	235	245	259	203	237	260	278	292	313	247	293	323	347	367	395	199	222	236	247	256	268
225,000	250,000	188	215	232	245	256	271	212	248	272	290	305	327	258	305	337	362	383	412	209	233	248	259	268	281
250,000	275,000	196	223	242	255	267	283	220	257	282	302	318	340	268	317	350	376	397	427	219	243	259	271	280	293
275,000	300,000	203	232	251	265	277	293	228	267	293	313	329	352	278	328	363	389	411	442	227	253	269	282	291	305
300,000	or more	245	280	303	321	335	354	274	321	352	376	395	423	332	393	434	465	492	529	278	310	330	345	357	374

Tax Formula for Corporations

Income *(from whatever source)*	$ xxx,xxx
Less: Exclusions from gross income	− xx,xxx
Gross Income	$ xxx,xxx
Less: Deductions	− xx,xxx
Taxable Income	$ xxx,xxx
Applicable tax rate	× 21%
Gross Tax	$ xx,xxx
Less: Tax credits and prepayments	− x,xxx
Tax Due *(or refund)*	$ xx,xxx

Income Tax Rates—C Corporations, 2018 and After

For all taxable income levels, the tax rate is 21%.

Income Tax Rates—Estates and Trusts

Tax Year 2022

Taxable Income		The Tax Is:	
Over—	But not Over—		Of the Amount Over—
$ 0	$ 2,750	10%	$ 0
2,750	9,850	$ 275.00 + 24%	2,750
9,850	13,450	1,979.00 + 35%	9,850
13,450	....	3,239.00 + 37%	13,450

Tax Year 2023

Taxable Income		The Tax Is:	
Over—	But not Over—		Of the Amount Over—
$ 0	$ 2,900	10%	$ 0
2,900	10,550	$ 290.00 + 24%	2,900
10,550	14,450	2,126.00 + 35%	10,550
14,450	....	3,491.00 + 37%	14,450

Unified Transfer Tax Rates

For Gifts Made and for Deaths After 2012

If the Amount with Respect to Which the Tentative Tax to Be Computed Is:	The Tentative Tax Is:
Not over $10,000	18 percent of such amount.
Over $10,000 but not over $20,000	$1,800, plus 20 percent of the excess of such amount over $10,000.
Over $20,000 but not over $40,000	$3,800, plus 22 percent of the excess of such amount over $20,000.
Over $40,000 but not over $60,000	$8,200, plus 24 percent of the excess of such amount over $40,000.
Over $60,000 but not over $80,000	$13,000, plus 26 percent of the excess of such amount over $60,000.
Over $80,000 but not over $100,000	$18,200, plus 28 percent of the excess of such amount over $80,000.
Over $100,000 but not over $150,000	$23,800, plus 30 percent of the excess of such amount over $100,000.
Over $150,000 but not over $250,000	$38,800, plus 32 percent of the excess of such amount over $150,000.
Over $250,000 but not over $500,000	$70,800, plus 34 percent of the excess of such amount over $250,000.
Over $500,000 but not over $750,000	$155,800, plus 37 percent of the excess of such amount over $500,000.
Over $750,000 but not over $1,000,000	$248,300, plus 39 percent of the excess of such amount over $750,000.
Over $1,000,000	$345,800, plus 40 percent of the excess of such amount over $1,000,000.

Valuation Tables, Excerpts

Table S: Single Life Remainder Factors Interest Rate

AGE	4.2%	4.4%	4.6%	4.8%	5.0%	5.2%	5.4%	5.6%
0	.06083	.05483	.04959	.04501	.04101	.03749	.03441	.03170
1	.05668	.05049	.04507	.04034	.03618	.03254	.02934	.02652
2	.05858	.05222	.04665	.04178	.03750	.03373	.03042	.02750
3	.06072	.05420	.04848	.04346	.03904	.03516	.03173	.02871
4	.06303	.05634	.05046	.04530	.04075	.03674	.03319	.03006
5	.06547	.05861	.05258	.04726	.04258	.03844	.03478	.03153
6	.06805	.06102	.05482	.04935	.04453	.04026	.03647	.03312
7	.07074	.06353	.05717	.05155	.04658	.04217	.03826	.03479
8	.07356	.06617	.05964	.05386	.04875	.04421	.04017	.03658
9	.07651	.06895	.06225	.05631	.05105	.04637	.04220	.03849
10	.07960	.07185	.06499	.05889	.05347	.04865	.04435	.04052
11	.08283	.07490	.06786	.06160	.05603	.05106	.04663	.04267
12	.08620	.07808	.07087	.06444	.05871	.05360	.04903	.04494
13	.08967	.08137	.07397	.06738	.06149	.05623	.05152	.04729
14	.09321	.08472	.07715	.07038	.06433	.05892	.05406	.04971
15	.09680	.08812	.08036	.07342	.06721	.06164	.05664	.05214
16	.10041	.09154	.08360	.07649	.07011	.06438	.05923	.05459
17	.10409	.09502	.08689	.07960	.07305	.06716	.06185	.05707
18	.10782	.09855	.09024	.08276	.07604	.06998	.06452	.05959
19	.11164	.10217	.09366	.08600	.07910	.07288	.06726	.06218
20	.11559	.10592	.09721	.08937	.08228	.07589	.07010	.06487
21	.11965	.10977	.10087	.09283	.08557	.07900	.07305	.06765
22	.12383	.11376	.10465	.09642	.08897	.08223	.07610	.07055
23	.12817	.11789	.10859	.10016	.09252	.08559	.07930	.07358
24	.13270	.12221	.11270	.10408	.09625	.08914	.08267	.07678
25	.13744	.12674	.11703	.10821	.10019	.09289	.08625	.08018
26	.14239	.13149	.12158	.11256	.10435	.09686	.09003	.08380
27	.14758	.13647	.12636	.11714	.10873	.10106	.09405	.08764
28	.15300	.14169	.13137	.12195	.11335	.10549	.09829	.09171
29	.15864	.14712	.13660	.12698	.11819	.11013	.10275	.09598
30	.16448	.15275	.14203	.13222	.12323	.11498	.10742	.10047
31	.17053	.15861	.14769	.13768	.12849	.12006	.11230	.10517
32	.17680	.16468	.15357	.14336	.13398	.12535	.11741	.11009
33	.18330	.17099	.15968	.14927	.13970	.13088	.12275	.11525
34	.19000	.17750	.16599	.15539	.14562	.13661	.12829	.12061

continued

Valuation Tables, Excerpts

Table S: Single Life Remainder Factors Interest Rate

AGE	4.2%	4.4%	4.6%	4.8%	5.0%	5.2%	5.4%	5.6%
35	.19692	.18423	.17253	.16174	.15178	.14258	.13408	.12621
36	.20407	.19119	.17931	.16833	.15818	.14879	.14009	.13204
37	.21144	.19838	.18631	.17515	.16481	.15523	.14635	.13811
38	.21904	.20582	.19357	.18222	.17170	.16193	.15287	.14444
39	.22687	.21348	.20105	.18952	.17882	.16887	.15962	.15102
40	.23493	.22137	.20878	.19707	.18619	.17606	.16663	.15784
41	.24322	.22950	.21674	.20487	.19381	.18350	.17390	.16493
42	.25173	.23786	.22494	.21290	.20168	.19120	.18141	.17227
43	.26049	.24648	.23342	.22122	.20982	.19918	.18922	.17990
44	.26950	.25535	.24214	.22979	.21824	.20742	.19730	.18781
45	.27874	.26447	.25112	.23862	.22692	.21595	.20566	.19600
46	.28824	.27385	.26038	.24774	.23589	.22476	.21431	.20450
47	.29798	.28349	.26989	.25712	.24513	.23386	.22326	.21328
48	.30797	.29338	.27967	.26678	.25466	.24325	.23250	.22238
49	.31822	.30355	.28974	.27674	.26449	.25294	.24206	.23179
50	.32876	.31401	.30011	.28701	.27465	.26298	.25196	.24156
51	.33958	.32477	.31079	.29759	.28513	.27335	.26221	.25168
52	.35068	.33582	.32178	.30851	.29595	.28407	.27282	.26216
53	.36206	.34717	.33308	.31974	.30710	.29513	.28378	.27301
54	.37371	.35880	.34467	.33127	.31857	.30651	.29507	.28420
55	.38559	.37067	.35652	.34308	.33032	.31820	.30668	.29572
56	.39765	.38275	.36859	.35512	.34232	.33014	.31855	.30751
57	.40990	.39502	.38086	.36739	.35455	.34233	.33068	.31957
58	.42231	.40747	.39333	.37985	.36700	.35474	.34304	.33188
59	.43490	.42011	.40600	.39253	.37968	.36740	.35567	.34446
60	.44768	.43296	.41890	.40546	.39261	.38033	.36858	.35733
61	.46064	.44600	.43200	.41860	.40578	.39351	.38175	.37048
62	.47373	.45920	.44527	.43194	.41915	.40690	.39514	.38387
63	.48696	.47253	.45870	.44544	.43271	.42049	.40876	.39749
64	.50030	.48601	.47229	.45911	.44645	.43428	.42258	.41133
65	.51377	.49963	.48603	.47295	.46037	.44827	.43662	.42540
66	.52750	.51352	.50007	.48711	.47464	.46262	.45103	.43987
67	.54144	.52765	.51436	.50154	.48919	.47727	.46578	.45468
68	.55554	.54196	.52885	.51619	.50398	.49218	.48079	.46978
69	.56976	.55640	.54349	.53102	.51896	.50731	.49603	.48513

Valuation Tables, Excerpts

Table B: Term Certain Remainder Factors Interest Rate

YEARS	4.2%	4.4%	4.6%	4.8%	5.0%	5.2%	5.4%	5.6%
1	.959693	.957854	.956023	.954198	.952381	.950570	.948767	.946970
2	.921010	.917485	.913980	.910495	.907029	.903584	.900158	.896752
3	.883887	.878817	.873786	.868793	.863838	.858920	.854040	.849197
4	.848260	.841779	.835359	.829001	.822702	.816464	.810285	.804163
5	.814069	.806302	.798623	.791031	.783526	.776106	.768771	.761518
6	.781257	.772320	.763501	.754801	.746215	.737744	.729384	.721135
7	.749766	.739770	.729925	.720230	.710681	.701277	.692015	.682893
8	.719545	.708592	.697825	.687242	.676839	.666613	.656561	.646679
9	.690543	.678728	.667137	.655765	.644609	.633663	.622923	.612385
10	.662709	.650122	.637798	.625730	.613913	.602341	.591009	.579910
11	.635997	.622722	.609750	.597071	.584679	.572568	.560729	.549157
12	.610362	.596477	.582935	.569724	.556837	.544266	.532001	.520035
13	.585760	.571339	.557299	.543630	.530321	.517363	.504745	.492458
14	.562150	.547259	.532790	.518731	.505068	.491790	.478885	.466343
15	.539491	.524195	.509360	.494972	.481017	.467481	.454350	.441612
16	.517746	.502102	.486960	.472302	.458112	.444374	.431072	.418194
17	.496877	.480941	.465545	.450670	.436297	.422408	.408987	.396017
18	.476849	.460671	.445071	.430028	.415521	.401529	.388033	.375016
19	.457629	.441256	.425498	.410332	.395734	.381681	.368153	.355129
20	.439183	.422659	.406786	.391538	.376889	.362815	.349291	.336296
21	.421481	.404846	.388897	.373605	.358942	.344881	.331396	.318462
22	.404492	.387783	.371794	.356494	.341850	.327834	.314417	.301574
23	.388188	.371440	.355444	.340166	.325571	.311629	.298309	.285581
24	.372542	.355785	.339813	.324586	.310068	.296225	.283025	.270437
25	.357526	.340791	.324869	.309719	.295303	.281583	.268525	.256096
26	.343115	.326428	.310582	.295533	.281241	.267664	.254768	.242515
27	.329285	.312670	.296923	.281998	.267848	.254434	.241715	.229654
28	.316012	.299493	.283866	.269082	.255094	.241857	.229331	.217475
29	.303275	.286870	.271382	.256757	.242946	.229902	.217582	.205943
30	.291051	.274780	.259447	.244997	.231377	.218538	.206434	.195021
31	.279319	.263199	.248038	.233776	.220359	.207736	.195858	.184679
32	.268061	.252106	.237130	.223069	.209866	.197468	.185823	.174886
33	.257256	.241481	.226702	.212852	.199873	.187707	.176303	.165612
34	.246887	.231304	.216732	.203103	.190355	.178429	.167270	.156829
35	.236935	.221556	.207201	.193801	.181290	.169609	.158701	.148512

AMT Formula for Individuals

Taxable income (increased by any standard deduction taken)
Plus or minus: Adjustments
Plus: Preferences
Equals: Alternative minimum taxable income (AMTI)
Minus: Exemption
Equals: Alternative minimum tax (AMT) base
Multiplied by: 26% or 28% rate
Equals: Tentative minimum tax before foreign tax credit
Minus: AMT foreign tax credit
Equals: Tentative minimum tax (TMT)
Minus: Regular tax liability (less any foreign tax credit)
Equals: AMT (if TMT > regular tax liability)

2022 AMT Exemption and Phaseout for Individuals

		Phaseout	
Filing Status	**Exemption**	**Begins at**	**Ends at**
Married, filing jointly	$118,100	$1,079,800	$1,552,200
Single or Head of household	75,900	539,900	843,500
Married, filing separately	59,050	539,900	776,100

2023 AMT Exemption and Phaseout for Individuals

		Phaseout	
Filing Status	**Exemption**	**Begins at**	**Ends at**
Married, filing jointly	$126,500	$1,156,300	$1,662,300
Single or Head of household	81,300	578,150	903,350
Married, filing separately	63,250	578,150	831,150

Appendix B

Tax Forms

(More forms are available at **irs.gov/forms-instructions**. Go to the tax agency website for any state to find comparable state tax forms.)

Form **709**

Department of the Treasury
Internal Revenue Service

United States Gift (and Generation-Skipping Transfer) Tax Return

Go to *www.irs.gov/Form709* for instructions and the latest information.
(For gifts made during calendar year 2022)
See instructions.

OMB No. 1545-0020

2022

Part 1—General Information

1 Donor's first name and middle initial	2 Donor's last name	3 Donor's social security number
4 Address (number, street, and apartment number)		5 Legal residence (domicile)
6 City or town, state or province, country, and ZIP or foreign postal code		7 Citizenship (see instructions)

		Yes	No
8	If the donor died during the year, check here ☐ and enter date of death ______________, ______ .		
9	If you extended the time to file this Form 709, check here ☐		
10	Enter the total number of donees listed on Schedule A. Count each person only once:		
11a	Have you (the donor) previously filed a Form 709 (or 709-A) for any other year? If "No," skip line 11b		
b	Has your address changed since you last filed Form 709 (or 709-A)?		
12	**Gifts by husband or wife to third parties.** Do you consent to have the gifts (including generation-skipping transfers) made by you and by your spouse to third parties during the calendar year considered as made one-half by each of you? (See instructions.) (If the answer is "Yes," the following information must be furnished and your spouse must sign the consent shown below. **If the answer is "No," skip lines 13–18.**)		
13	Name of consenting spouse ____________ **14** SSN		
15	Were you married to one another during the entire calendar year? See instructions		
16	If line 15 is "No," check whether ☐ married ☐ divorced or ☐ widowed/deceased, and give date. See instructions:		
17	Will a gift tax return for this year be filed by your spouse? If "Yes," mail both returns in the same envelope		
18	**Consent of Spouse.** I consent to have the gifts (and generation-skipping transfers) made by me and by my spouse to third parties during the calendar year considered as made one-half by each of us. We are both aware of the joint and several liability for tax created by the execution of this consent.		
	Consenting spouse's signature: **Date:**		
19	Have you applied a DSUE amount received from a predeceased spouse to a gift or gifts reported on this or a previous Form 709? If "Yes," complete Schedule C		

Part 2—Tax Computation

1	Enter the amount from Schedule A, Part 4, line 11	1	
2	Enter the amount from Schedule B, line 3	2	
3	Total taxable gifts. Add lines 1 and 2	3	
4	Tax computed on amount on line 3 (see *Table for Computing Gift Tax* in instructions)	4	
5	Tax computed on amount on line 2 (see *Table for Computing Gift Tax* in instructions)	5	
6	Balance. Subtract line 5 from line 4	6	
7	Applicable credit amount. If donor has DSUE amount from predeceased spouse(s) or Restored Exclusion Amount, enter amount from Schedule C, line 5; otherwise, see instructions	7	
8	Enter the applicable credit against tax allowable for all prior periods (from Sch. B, line 1, col. C) . . .	8	
9	Balance. Subtract line 8 from line 7. Do not enter less than zero	9	
10	Enter 20% (0.20) of the amount allowed as a specific exemption for gifts made after September 8, 1976, and before January 1, 1977. See instructions	10	
11	Balance. Subtract line 10 from line 9. Do not enter less than zero	11	
12	Applicable credit. Enter the smaller of line 6 or line 11	12	
13	Credit for foreign gift taxes (see instructions)	13	
14	Total credits. Add lines 12 and 13	14	
15	Balance. Subtract line 14 from line 6. Do not enter less than zero	15	
16	Generation-skipping transfer taxes (from Schedule D, Part 3, col. G, total)	16	
17	Total tax. Add lines 15 and 16	17	
18	Gift and generation-skipping transfer taxes prepaid with extension of time to file	18	
19	If line 18 is less than line 17, enter **balance due**. See instructions	19	
20	If line 18 is greater than line 17, enter **amount to be refunded**	20	

Attach check or money order here.

Sign Here

Under penalties of perjury, I declare that I have examined this return, including any accompanying schedules and statements, and to the best of my knowledge and belief, it is true, correct, and complete. Declaration of preparer (other than donor) is based on all information of which preparer has any knowledge.

May the IRS discuss this return with the preparer shown below? See instructions. ☐ **Yes** ☐ **No**

Signature of donor | Date

Paid Preparer Use Only

Print/Type preparer's name	Preparer's signature	Date	Check ☐ if self-employed	PTIN
Firm's name			Firm's EIN	
Firm's address			Phone no.	

Form **1040** Department of the Treasury—Internal Revenue Service
U.S. Individual Income Tax Return **2022** OMB No. 1545-0074 IRS Use Only—Do not write or staple in this space.

Filing Status Check only one box. ☐ Single ☐ Married filing jointly ☐ Married filing separately (MFS) ☐ Head of household (HOH) ☐ Qualifying surviving spouse (QSS)

If you checked the MFS box, enter the name of your spouse. If you checked the HOH or QSS box, enter the child's name if the qualifying person is a child but not your dependent:

Your first name and middle initial	Last name			Your social security number
If joint return, spouse's first name and middle initial	Last name			Spouse's social security number
Home address (number and street). If you have a P.O. box, see instructions.			Apt. no.	**Presidential Election Campaign** Check here if you, or your spouse if filing jointly, want $3 to go to this fund. Checking a box below will not change your tax or refund. ☐ You ☐ Spouse
City, town, or post office. If you have a foreign address, also complete spaces below.		State	ZIP code	
Foreign country name	Foreign province/state/county		Foreign postal code	

Digital Assets At any time during 2022, did you: (a) receive (as a reward, award, or payment for property or services); or (b) sell, exchange, gift, or otherwise dispose of a digital asset (or a financial interest in a digital asset)? (See instructions.) ☐ **Yes** ☐ **No**

Standard Deduction **Someone can claim:** ☐ You as a dependent ☐ Your spouse as a dependent
☐ Spouse itemizes on a separate return or you were a dual-status alien

Age/Blindness **You:** ☐ Were born before January 2, 1958 ☐ Are blind **Spouse:** ☐ Was born before January 2, 1958 ☐ Is blind

Dependents (see instructions): If more than four dependents, see instructions and check here . . ☐

(1) First name Last name	(2) Social security number	(3) Relationship to you	(4) Check the box if qualifies for (see instructions): Child tax credit	Credit for other dependents
			☐	☐
			☐	☐
			☐	☐
			☐	☐

Income

Attach Form(s) W-2 here. Also attach Forms W-2G and 1099-R if tax was withheld.

If you did not get a Form W-2, see instructions.

1a	Total amount from Form(s) W-2, box 1 (see instructions)	1a	
b	Household employee wages not reported on Form(s) W-2	1b	
c	Tip income not reported on line 1a (see instructions)	1c	
d	Medicaid waiver payments not reported on Form(s) W-2 (see instructions)	1d	
e	Taxable dependent care benefits from Form 2441, line 26	1e	
f	Employer-provided adoption benefits from Form 8839, line 29	1f	
g	Wages from Form 8919, line 6	1g	
h	Other earned income (see instructions)	1h	
i	Nontaxable combat pay election (see instructions) 1i		
z	Add lines 1a through 1h	1z	
2a	Tax-exempt interest . . . 2a ___ **b** Taxable interest	2b	
3a	Qualified dividends . . . 3a ___ **b** Ordinary dividends	3b	
4a	IRA distributions . . . 4a ___ **b** Taxable amount	4b	
5a	Pensions and annuities . . 5a ___ **b** Taxable amount	5b	
6a	Social security benefits . . 6a ___ **b** Taxable amount	6b	
c	If you elect to use the lump-sum election method, check here (see instructions) ☐		
7	Capital gain or (loss). Attach Schedule D if required. If not required, check here ☐	7	
8	Other income from Schedule 1, line 10	8	
9	Add lines 1z, 2b, 3b, 4b, 5b, 6b, 7, and 8. This is your **total income**	9	
10	Adjustments to income from Schedule 1, line 26	10	
11	Subtract line 10 from line 9. This is your **adjusted gross income**	11	
12	**Standard deduction or itemized deductions** (from Schedule A)	12	
13	Qualified business income deduction from Form 8995 or Form 8995-A	13	
14	Add lines 12 and 13	14	
15	Subtract line 14 from line 11. If zero or less, enter -0-. This is your **taxable income**	15	

Attach Sch. B if required.

Standard Deduction for—
- Single or Married filing separately, $12,950
- Married filing jointly or Qualifying surviving spouse, $25,900
- Head of household, $19,400
- If you checked any box under *Standard Deduction*, see instructions.

For Disclosure, Privacy Act, and Paperwork Reduction Act Notice, see separate instructions. Cat. No. 11320B Form **1040** (2022)

Form 1040 (2022) Page 2

Tax and Credits	16	**Tax** (see instructions). Check if any from Form(s): 1 ☐ 8814 2 ☐ 4972 3 ☐ ______		16
	17	Amount from Schedule 2, line 3		17
	18	Add lines 16 and 17		18
	19	Child tax credit or credit for other dependents from Schedule 8812		19
	20	Amount from Schedule 3, line 8		20
	21	Add lines 19 and 20		21
	22	Subtract line 21 from line 18. If zero or less, enter -0-		22
	23	Other taxes, including self-employment tax, from Schedule 2, line 21		23
	24	Add lines 22 and 23. This is your **total tax**		24
Payments	25	Federal income tax withheld from:		
	a	Form(s) W-2	25a	
	b	Form(s) 1099	25b	
	c	Other forms (see instructions)	25c	
	d	Add lines 25a through 25c		25d
If you have a qualifying child, attach Sch. EIC.	26	2022 estimated tax payments and amount applied from 2021 return		26
	27	Earned income credit (EIC)	27	
	28	Additional child tax credit from Schedule 8812	28	
	29	American opportunity credit from Form 8863, line 8	29	
	30	Reserved for future use	30	
	31	Amount from Schedule 3, line 15	31	
	32	Add lines 27, 28, 29, and 31. These are your **total other payments and refundable credits**		32
	33	Add lines 25d, 26, and 32. These are your **total payments**		33
Refund	34	If line 33 is more than line 24, subtract line 24 from line 33. This is the amount you **overpaid**		34
	35a	Amount of line 34 you want **refunded to you**. If Form 8888 is attached, check here ☐		35a
Direct deposit? See instructions.	b	Routing number ______ **c** Type: ☐ Checking ☐ Savings		
	d	Account number ______		
	36	Amount of line 34 you want **applied to your 2023 estimated tax**	36	
Amount You Owe	37	Subtract line 33 from line 24. This is the **amount you owe**. For details on how to pay, go to *www.irs.gov/Payments* or see instructions		37
	38	Estimated tax penalty (see instructions)	38	

Third Party Designee

Do you want to allow another person to discuss this return with the IRS? See instructions ☐ **Yes.** Complete below. ☐ **No**

Designee's name | Phone no. | Personal identification number (PIN)

Sign Here

Under penalties of perjury, I declare that I have examined this return and accompanying schedules and statements, and to the best of my knowledge and belief, they are true, correct, and complete. Declaration of preparer (other than taxpayer) is based on all information of which preparer has any knowledge.

Your signature	Date	Your occupation	If the IRS sent you an Identity Protection PIN, enter it here (see inst.)
Spouse's signature. If a joint return, **both** must sign.	Date	Spouse's occupation	If the IRS sent your spouse an Identity Protection PIN, enter it here (see inst.)
Phone no.	Email address		

Joint return? See instructions. Keep a copy for your records.

Paid Preparer Use Only

Preparer's name	Preparer's signature	Date	PTIN	Check if: ☐ Self-employed
Firm's name				Phone no.
Firm's address				Firm's EIN

Go to *www.irs.gov/Form1040* for instructions and the latest information. Form **1040** (2022)

SCHEDULE 1
(Form 1040)

Department of the Treasury
Internal Revenue Service

Additional Income and Adjustments to Income

Attach to Form 1040, 1040-SR, or 1040-NR.
Go to *www.irs.gov/Form1040* for instructions and the latest information.

OMB No. 1545-0074
2022
Attachment Sequence No. **01**

Name(s) shown on Form 1040, 1040-SR, or 1040-NR | **Your social security number**

Part I Additional Income

Line	Description			
1	Taxable refunds, credits, or offsets of state and local income taxes		1	
2a	Alimony received		2a	
b	Date of original divorce or separation agreement (see instructions): ______			
3	Business income or (loss). Attach Schedule C		3	
4	Other gains or (losses). Attach Form 4797		4	
5	Rental real estate, royalties, partnerships, S corporations, trusts, etc. Attach Schedule E		5	
6	Farm income or (loss). Attach Schedule F		6	
7	Unemployment compensation		7	
8	Other income:			
a	Net operating loss	8a ( )		
b	Gambling	8b		
c	Cancellation of debt	8c		
d	Foreign earned income exclusion from Form 2555	8d ( )		
e	Income from Form 8853	8e		
f	Income from Form 8889	8f		
g	Alaska Permanent Fund dividends	8g		
h	Jury duty pay	8h		
i	Prizes and awards	8i		
j	Activity not engaged in for profit income	8j		
k	Stock options	8k		
l	Income from the rental of personal property if you engaged in the rental for profit but were not in the business of renting such property	8l		
m	Olympic and Paralympic medals and USOC prize money (see instructions)	8m		
n	Section 951(a) inclusion (see instructions)	8n		
o	Section 951A(a) inclusion (see instructions)	8o		
p	Section 461(l) excess business loss adjustment	8p		
q	Taxable distributions from an ABLE account (see instructions)	8q		
r	Scholarship and fellowship grants not reported on Form W-2	8r		
s	Nontaxable amount of Medicaid waiver payments included on Form 1040, line 1a or 1d	8s ( )		
t	Pension or annuity from a nonqualifed deferred compensation plan or a nongovernmental section 457 plan	8t		
u	Wages earned while incarcerated	8u		
z	Other income. List type and amount: ______	8z		
9	Total other income. Add lines 8a through 8z		9	
10	Combine lines 1 through 7 and 9. Enter here and on Form 1040, 1040-SR, or 1040-NR, line 8		10	

Part II Adjustments to Income

11	Educator expenses			11	
12	Certain business expenses of reservists, performing artists, and fee-basis government officials. Attach Form 2106			12	
13	Health savings account deduction. Attach Form 8889			13	
14	Moving expenses for members of the Armed Forces. Attach Form 3903			14	
15	Deductible part of self-employment tax. Attach Schedule SE			15	
16	Self-employed SEP, SIMPLE, and qualified plans			16	
17	Self-employed health insurance deduction			17	
18	Penalty on early withdrawal of savings			18	
19a	Alimony paid			19a	
b	Recipient's SSN				
c	Date of original divorce or separation agreement (see instructions):				
20	IRA deduction			20	
21	Student loan interest deduction			21	
22	Reserved for future use			22	
23	Archer MSA deduction			23	
24	Other adjustments:				
a	Jury duty pay (see instructions)	24a			
b	Deductible expenses related to income reported on line 8l from the rental of personal property engaged in for profit	24b			
c	Nontaxable amount of the value of Olympic and Paralympic medals and USOC prize money reported on line 8m	24c			
d	Reforestation amortization and expenses	24d			
e	Repayment of supplemental unemployment benefits under the Trade Act of 1974	24e			
f	Contributions to section 501(c)(18)(D) pension plans	24f			
g	Contributions by certain chaplains to section 403(b) plans	24g			
h	Attorney fees and court costs for actions involving certain unlawful discrimination claims (see instructions)	24h			
i	Attorney fees and court costs you paid in connection with an award from the IRS for information you provided that helped the IRS detect tax law violations	24i			
j	Housing deduction from Form 2555	24j			
k	Excess deductions of section 67(e) expenses from Schedule K-1 (Form 1041)	24k			
z	Other adjustments. List type and amount:	24z			
25	Total other adjustments. Add lines 24a through 24z			25	
26	Add lines 11 through 23 and 25. These are your **adjustments to income**. Enter here and on Form 1040 or 1040-SR, line 10, or Form 1040-NR, line 10a			26	

SCHEDULE 2 (Form 1040)

Department of the Treasury Internal Revenue Service

Additional Taxes

Attach to Form 1040, 1040-SR, or 1040-NR.
Go to *www.irs.gov/Form1040* for instructions and the latest information.

OMB No. 1545-0074
2022
Attachment Sequence No. **02**

Name(s) shown on Form 1040, 1040-SR, or 1040-NR	**Your social security number**

Part I Tax

1	Alternative minimum tax. Attach Form 6251			1	
2	Excess advance premium tax credit repayment. Attach Form 8962			2	
3	Add lines 1 and 2. Enter here and on Form 1040, 1040-SR, or 1040-NR, line 17			3	

Part II Other Taxes

4	Self-employment tax. Attach Schedule SE			4	
5	Social security and Medicare tax on unreported tip income. Attach Form 4137	5			
6	Uncollected social security and Medicare tax on wages. Attach Form 8919	6			
7	Total additional social security and Medicare tax. Add lines 5 and 6			7	
8	Additional tax on IRAs or other tax-favored accounts. Attach Form 5329 if required. If not required, check here ☐			8	
9	Household employment taxes. Attach Schedule H			9	
10	Repayment of first-time homebuyer credit. Attach Form 5405 if required			10	
11	Additional Medicare Tax. Attach Form 8959			11	
12	Net investment income tax. Attach Form 8960			12	
13	Uncollected social security and Medicare or RRTA tax on tips or group-term life insurance from Form W-2, box 12			13	
14	Interest on tax due on installment income from the sale of certain residential lots and timeshares			14	
15	Interest on the deferred tax on gain from certain installment sales with a sales price over $150,000			15	
16	Recapture of low-income housing credit. Attach Form 8611			16	

(continued on page 2)

Schedule 2 (Form 1040) 2022 Page 2

Part II Other Taxes *(continued)*

17	Other additional taxes:				
a	Recapture of other credits. List type, form number, and amount:	**17a**			
b	Recapture of federal mortgage subsidy, if you sold your home see instructions	**17b**			
c	Additional tax on HSA distributions. Attach Form 8889	**17c**			
d	Additional tax on an HSA because you didn't remain an eligible individual. Attach Form 8889	**17d**			
e	Additional tax on Archer MSA distributions. Attach Form 8853	**17e**			
f	Additional tax on Medicare Advantage MSA distributions. Attach Form 8853	**17f**			
g	Recapture of a charitable contribution deduction related to a fractional interest in tangible personal property	**17g**			
h	Income you received from a nonqualified deferred compensation plan that fails to meet the requirements of section 409A	**17h**			
i	Compensation you received from a nonqualified deferred compensation plan described in section 457A	**17i**			
j	Section 72(m)(5) excess benefits tax	**17j**			
k	Golden parachute payments	**17k**			
l	Tax on accumulation distribution of trusts	**17l**			
m	Excise tax on insider stock compensation from an expatriated corporation	**17m**			
n	Look-back interest under section 167(g) or 460(b) from Form 8697 or 8866	**17n**			
o	Tax on non-effectively connected income for any part of the year you were a nonresident alien from Form 1040-NR	**17o**			
p	Any interest from Form 8621, line 16f, relating to distributions from, and dispositions of, stock of a section 1291 fund	**17p**			
q	Any interest from Form 8621, line 24	**17q**			
z	Any other taxes. List type and amount:	**17z**			
18	Total additional taxes. Add lines 17a through 17z			**18**	
19	Reserved for future use			**19**	
20	Section 965 net tax liability installment from Form 965-A	**20**			
21	Add lines 4, 7 through 16, and 18. These are your **total other taxes**. Enter here and on Form 1040 or 1040-SR, line 23, or Form 1040-NR, line 23b			**21**	

SCHEDULE 3 (Form 1040)

Department of the Treasury
Internal Revenue Service

Additional Credits and Payments

Attach to Form 1040, 1040-SR, or 1040-NR.
Go to *www.irs.gov/Form1040* for instructions and the latest information.

OMB No. 1545-0074
2022
Attachment Sequence No. 03

Name(s) shown on Form 1040, 1040-SR, or 1040-NR	**Your social security number**

Part I Nonrefundable Credits

1	Foreign tax credit. Attach Form 1116 if required			1	
2	Credit for child and dependent care expenses from Form 2441, line 11. Attach Form 2441			2	
3	Education credits from Form 8863, line 19			3	
4	Retirement savings contributions credit. Attach Form 8880			4	
5	Residential energy credits. Attach Form 5695			5	
6	Other nonrefundable credits:				
a	General business credit. Attach Form 3800	6a			
b	Credit for prior year minimum tax. Attach Form 8801	6b			
c	Adoption credit. Attach Form 8839	6c			
d	Credit for the elderly or disabled. Attach Schedule R	6d			
e	Alternative motor vehicle credit. Attach Form 8910	6e			
f	Qualified plug-in motor vehicle credit. Attach Form 8936	6f			
g	Mortgage interest credit. Attach Form 8396	6g			
h	District of Columbia first-time homebuyer credit. Attach Form 8859	6h			
i	Qualified electric vehicle credit. Attach Form 8834	6i			
j	Alternative fuel vehicle refueling property credit. Attach Form 8911	6j			
k	Credit to holders of tax credit bonds. Attach Form 8912	6k			
l	Amount on Form 8978, line 14. See instructions	6l			
z	Other nonrefundable credits. List type and amount: ____________	6z			
7	Total other nonrefundable credits. Add lines 6a through 6z			7	
8	Add lines 1 through 5 and 7. Enter here and on Form 1040, 1040-SR, or 1040-NR, line 20			8	

(continued on page 2)

Part II Other Payments and Refundable Credits

9	Net premium tax credit. Attach Form 8962			9	
10	Amount paid with request for extension to file (see instructions)			10	
11	Excess social security and tier 1 RRTA tax withheld			11	
12	Credit for federal tax on fuels. Attach Form 4136			12	
13	Other payments or refundable credits:				
a	Form 2439	13a			
b	Credit for qualified sick and family leave wages paid in 2022 from Schedule(s) H for leave taken before April 1, 2021	13b			
c	Reserved for future use	13c			
d	Credit for repayment of amounts included in income from earlier years	13d			
e	Reserved for future use	13e			
f	Deferred amount of net 965 tax liability (see instructions)	13f			
g	Reserved for future use	13g			
h	Credit for qualified sick and family leave wages paid in 2022 from Schedule(s) H for leave taken after March 31, 2021, and before October 1, 2021	13h			
z	Other payments or refundable credits. List type and amount:	13z			
14	Total other payments or refundable credits. Add lines 13a through 13z			14	
15	Add lines 9 through 12 and 14. Enter here and on Form 1040, 1040-SR, or 1040-NR, line 31			15	

SCHEDULE A (Form 1040)

Department of the Treasury Internal Revenue Service

Itemized Deductions

Go to *www.irs.gov/ScheduleA* for instructions and the latest information.
Attach to Form 1040 or 1040-SR.

Caution: If you are claiming a net qualified disaster loss on Form 4684, see the instructions for line 16.

OMB No. 1545-0074

2022

Attachment Sequence No. **07**

Name(s) shown on Form 1040 or 1040-SR | **Your social security number**

Section	Line	Description	Box	Amount	Box	Amount
Medical and Dental Expenses		**Caution:** Do not include expenses reimbursed or paid by others.				
	1	Medical and dental expenses (see instructions)	1			
	2	Enter amount from Form 1040 or 1040-SR, line 11 [2]				
	3	Multiply line 2 by 7.5% (0.075)	3			
	4	Subtract line 3 from line 1. If line 3 is more than line 1, enter -0-			4	
Taxes You Paid	5	State and local taxes.				
	a	State and local income taxes or general sales taxes. You may include either income taxes or general sales taxes on line 5a, but not both. If you elect to include general sales taxes instead of income taxes, check this box . . . . ☐	5a			
	b	State and local real estate taxes (see instructions)	5b			
	c	State and local personal property taxes	5c			
	d	Add lines 5a through 5c	5d			
	e	Enter the smaller of line 5d or $10,000 ($5,000 if married filing separately)	5e			
	6	Other taxes. List type and amount: ----------	6			
	7	Add lines 5e and 6			7	
Interest You Paid Caution: Your mortgage interest deduction may be limited. See instructions.	8	Home mortgage interest and points. If you didn't use all of your home mortgage loan(s) to buy, build, or improve your home, see instructions and check this box . . . . ☐				
	a	Home mortgage interest and points reported to you on Form 1098. See instructions if limited	8a			
	b	Home mortgage interest not reported to you on Form 1098. See instructions if limited. If paid to the person from whom you bought the home, see instructions and show that person's name, identifying no., and address . . . . ---------- ----------	8b			
	c	Points not reported to you on Form 1098. See instructions for special rules	8c			
	d	Reserved for future use	8d			
	e	Add lines 8a through 8c	8e			
	9	Investment interest. Attach Form 4952 if required. See instructions .	9			
	10	Add lines 8e and 9			10	
Gifts to Charity Caution: If you made a gift and got a benefit for it, see instructions.	11	Gifts by cash or check. If you made any gift of $250 or more, see instructions	11			
	12	Other than by cash or check. If you made any gift of $250 or more, see instructions. You **must** attach Form 8283 if over $500	12			
	13	Carryover from prior year	13			
	14	Add lines 11 through 13			14	
Casualty and Theft Losses	15	Casualty and theft loss(es) from a federally declared disaster (other than net qualified disaster losses). Attach Form 4684 and enter the amount from line 18 of that form. See instructions			15	
Other Itemized Deductions	16	Other—from list in instructions. List type and amount: ---------- ----------			16	
Total Itemized Deductions	17	Add the amounts in the far right column for lines 4 through 16. Also, enter this amount on Form 1040 or 1040-SR, line 12			17	
	18	If you elect to itemize deductions even though they are less than your standard deduction, check this box . . . . ☐				

SCHEDULE B (Form 1040)

Department of the Treasury
Internal Revenue Service

Interest and Ordinary Dividends

Go to *www.irs.gov/ScheduleB* for instructions and the latest information.
Attach to Form 1040 or 1040-SR.

OMB No. 1545-0074

2022

Attachment Sequence No. **08**

Name(s) shown on return | **Your social security number**

Part I Interest

(See instructions and the Instructions for Form 1040, line 2b.)

Note: If you received a Form 1099-INT, Form 1099-OID, or substitute statement from a brokerage firm, list the firm's name as the payer and enter the total interest shown on that form.

			Amount
1	List name of payer. If any interest is from a seller-financed mortgage and the buyer used the property as a personal residence, see the instructions and list this interest first. Also, show that buyer's social security number and address:	**1**	
2	Add the amounts on line 1	**2**	
3	Excludable interest on series EE and I U.S. savings bonds issued after 1989. Attach Form 8815	**3**	
4	Subtract line 3 from line 2. Enter the result here and on Form 1040 or 1040-SR, line 2b	**4**	

Note: If line 4 is over $1,500, you must complete Part III.

Part II Ordinary Dividends

(See instructions and the Instructions for Form 1040, line 3b.)

Note: If you received a Form 1099-DIV or substitute statement from a brokerage firm, list the firm's name as the payer and enter the ordinary dividends shown on that form.

			Amount
5	List name of payer:	**5**	
6	Add the amounts on line 5. Enter the total here and on Form 1040 or 1040-SR, line 3b	**6**	

Note: If line 6 is over $1,500, you must complete Part III.

Part III Foreign Accounts and Trusts

Caution: If required, failure to file FinCEN Form 114 may result in substantial penalties. Additionally, you may be required to file Form 8938, Statement of Specified Foreign Financial Assets. See instructions.

You must complete this part if you (**a**) had over $1,500 of taxable interest or ordinary dividends; (**b**) had a foreign account; or (**c**) received a distribution from, or were a grantor of, or a transferor to, a foreign trust.

		Yes	**No**
7a	At any time during 2022, did you have a financial interest in or signature authority over a financial account (such as a bank account, securities account, or brokerage account) located in a foreign country? See instructions		
	If "Yes," are you required to file FinCEN Form 114, Report of Foreign Bank and Financial Accounts (FBAR), to report that financial interest or signature authority? See FinCEN Form 114 and its instructions for filing requirements and exceptions to those requirements		
b	If you are required to file FinCEN Form 114, list the name(s) of the foreign country(-ies) where the financial account(s) are located:		
8	During 2022, did you receive a distribution from, or were you the grantor of, or transferor to, a foreign trust? If "Yes," you may have to file Form 3520. See instructions		

SCHEDULE C (Form 1040)

Department of the Treasury Internal Revenue Service

Profit or Loss From Business
(Sole Proprietorship)

Go to *www.irs.gov/ScheduleC* for instructions and the latest information.

Attach to Form 1040, 1040-SR, 1040-NR, or 1041; partnerships must generally file Form 1065.

OMB No. 1545-0074

2022

Attachment Sequence No. **09**

Name of proprietor | **Social security number (SSN)**

A Principal business or profession, including product or service (see instructions) | **B Enter code from instructions**

C Business name. If no separate business name, leave blank. | **D Employer ID number (EIN)** (see instr.)

E Business address (including suite or room no.)

City, town or post office, state, and ZIP code

F Accounting method: **(1)** ☐ Cash **(2)** ☐ Accrual **(3)** ☐ Other (specify)

G Did you "materially participate" in the operation of this business during 2022? If "No," see instructions for limit on losses . ☐ **Yes** ☐ **No**

H If you started or acquired this business during 2022, check here . . . ☐

I Did you make any payments in 2022 that would require you to file Form(s) 1099? See instructions . . . ☐ **Yes** ☐ **No**

J If "Yes," did you or will you file required Form(s) 1099? . . . ☐ **Yes** ☐ **No**

Part I Income

1	Gross receipts or sales. See instructions for line 1 and check the box if this income was reported to you on Form W-2 and the "Statutory employee" box on that form was checked . . . ☐	1	
2	Returns and allowances . . .	2	
3	Subtract line 2 from line 1 . . .	3	
4	Cost of goods sold (from line 42) . . .	4	
5	**Gross profit.** Subtract line 4 from line 3 . . .	5	
6	Other income, including federal and state gasoline or fuel tax credit or refund (see instructions) . . .	6	
7	**Gross income.** Add lines 5 and 6 . . .	7	

Part II Expenses. Enter expenses for business use of your home **only** on line 30.

8	Advertising . . .	8		18	Office expense (see instructions) .	18	
9	Car and truck expenses (see instructions) . . .	9		19	Pension and profit-sharing plans .	19	
10	Commissions and fees .	10		20	Rent or lease (see instructions):		
11	Contract labor (see instructions)	11		a	Vehicles, machinery, and equipment	20a	
12	Depletion . . .	12		b	Other business property . . .	20b	
13	Depreciation and section 179 expense deduction (not included in Part III) (see instructions) . . .	13		21	Repairs and maintenance . . .	21	
				22	Supplies (not included in Part III) .	22	
				23	Taxes and licenses . . .	23	
				24	Travel and meals:		
14	Employee benefit programs (other than on line 19) .	14		a	Travel . . .	24a	
15	Insurance (other than health)	15		b	Deductible meals (see instructions) . . .	24b	
16	Interest (see instructions):			25	Utilities . . .	25	
a	Mortgage (paid to banks, etc.)	16a		26	Wages (less employment credits)	26	
b	Other . . .	16b		27a	Other expenses (from line 48) . .	27a	
17	Legal and professional services	17		b	**Reserved for future use** . . .	27b	

28	**Total expenses** before expenses for business use of home. Add lines 8 through 27a . . .	28	
29	Tentative profit or (loss). Subtract line 28 from line 7 . . .	29	
30	Expenses for business use of your home. Do not report these expenses elsewhere. Attach Form 8829 unless using the simplified method. See instructions. **Simplified method filers only:** Enter the total square footage of (a) your home: ______ and (b) the part of your home used for business: ______ . Use the Simplified Method Worksheet in the instructions to figure the amount to enter on line 30 . . .	30	
31	**Net profit or (loss).** Subtract line 30 from line 29. • If a profit, enter on both **Schedule 1 (Form 1040), line 3,** and on **Schedule SE, line 2.** (If you checked the box on line 1, see instructions.) Estates and trusts, enter on **Form 1041, line 3.** • If a loss, you **must** go to line 32.	31	
32	If you have a loss, check the box that describes your investment in this activity. See instructions. • If you checked 32a, enter the loss on both **Schedule 1 (Form 1040), line 3,** and on **Schedule SE, line 2.** (If you checked the box on line 1, see the line 31 instructions.) Estates and trusts, enter on **Form 1041, line 3.** • If you checked 32b, you **must** attach **Form 6198.** Your loss may be limited.	**32a** ☐ All investment is at risk. **32b** ☐ Some investment is not at risk.	

Schedule C (Form 1040) 2022 Page 2

Part III Cost of Goods Sold (see instructions)

33 Method(s) used to value closing inventory: a ☐ Cost b ☐ Lower of cost or market c ☐ Other (attach explanation)

34 Was there any change in determining quantities, costs, or valuations between opening and closing inventory? If "Yes," attach explanation . . . ☐ Yes ☐ No

35	Inventory at beginning of year. If different from last year's closing inventory, attach explanation	35	
36	Purchases less cost of items withdrawn for personal use	36	
37	Cost of labor. Do not include any amounts paid to yourself	37	
38	Materials and supplies	38	
39	Other costs	39	
40	Add lines 35 through 39	40	
41	Inventory at end of year	41	
42	**Cost of goods sold.** Subtract line 41 from line 40. Enter the result here and on line 4	42	

Part IV Information on Your Vehicle.

Complete this part **only** if you are claiming car or truck expenses on line 9 and are not required to file Form 4562 for this business. See the instructions for line 13 to find out if you must file Form 4562.

43 When did you place your vehicle in service for business purposes? (month/day/year) ____/____/____

44 Of the total number of miles you drove your vehicle during 2022, enter the number of miles you used your vehicle for:

a Business ____________ b Commuting (see instructions) ____________ c Other ____________

45 Was your vehicle available for personal use during off-duty hours? . . . ☐ Yes ☐ No

46 Do you (or your spouse) have another vehicle available for personal use? . . . ☐ Yes ☐ No

47a Do you have evidence to support your deduction? . . . ☐ Yes ☐ No

b If "Yes," is the evidence written? . . . ☐ Yes ☐ No

Part V Other Expenses.

List below business expenses not included on lines 8–26 or line 30.

48 Total other expenses. Enter here and on line 27a . . . 48	

Schedule C (Form 1040) 2022

SCHEDULE D (Form 1040)

Department of the Treasury
Internal Revenue Service

Capital Gains and Losses

Attach to Form 1040, 1040-SR, or 1040-NR.
Go to *www.irs.gov/ScheduleD* for instructions and the latest information.
Use Form 8949 to list your transactions for lines 1b, 2, 3, 8b, 9, and 10.

OMB No. 1545-0074
2022
Attachment Sequence No. **12**

Name(s) shown on return	**Your social security number**

Did you dispose of any investment(s) in a qualified opportunity fund during the tax year? ☐ **Yes** ☐ **No**
If "Yes," attach Form 8949 and see its instructions for additional requirements for reporting your gain or loss.

Part I Short-Term Capital Gains and Losses—Generally Assets Held One Year or Less (see instructions)

See instructions for how to figure the amounts to enter on the lines below. This form may be easier to complete if you round off cents to whole dollars.	**(d)** Proceeds (sales price)	**(e)** Cost (or other basis)	**(g)** Adjustments to gain or loss from Form(s) 8949, Part I, line 2, column (g)	**(h) Gain or (loss)** Subtract column (e) from column (d) and combine the result with column (g)
1a Totals for all short-term transactions reported on Form 1099-B for which basis was reported to the IRS and for which you have no adjustments (see instructions). However, if you choose to report all these transactions on Form 8949, leave this line blank and go to line 1b .				
1b Totals for all transactions reported on Form(s) 8949 with **Box A** checked				
2 Totals for all transactions reported on Form(s) 8949 with **Box B** checked				
3 Totals for all transactions reported on Form(s) 8949 with **Box C** checked				

4 Short-term gain from Form 6252 and short-term gain or (loss) from Forms 4684, 6781, and 8824 . .	4	
5 Net short-term gain or (loss) from partnerships, S corporations, estates, and trusts from Schedule(s) K-1	5	
6 Short-term capital loss carryover. Enter the amount, if any, from line 8 of your **Capital Loss Carryover Worksheet** in the instructions	6	( )
7 **Net short-term capital gain or (loss).** Combine lines 1a through 6 in column (h). If you have any long-term capital gains or losses, go to Part II below. Otherwise, go to Part III on the back	7	

Part II Long-Term Capital Gains and Losses—Generally Assets Held More Than One Year (see instructions)

See instructions for how to figure the amounts to enter on the lines below. This form may be easier to complete if you round off cents to whole dollars.	**(d)** Proceeds (sales price)	**(e)** Cost (or other basis)	**(g)** Adjustments to gain or loss from Form(s) 8949, Part II, line 2, column (g)	**(h) Gain or (loss)** Subtract column (e) from column (d) and combine the result with column (g)
8a Totals for all long-term transactions reported on Form 1099-B for which basis was reported to the IRS and for which you have no adjustments (see instructions). However, if you choose to report all these transactions on Form 8949, leave this line blank and go to line 8b .				
8b Totals for all transactions reported on Form(s) 8949 with **Box D** checked				
9 Totals for all transactions reported on Form(s) 8949 with **Box E** checked				
10 Totals for all transactions reported on Form(s) 8949 with **Box F** checked.				

11 Gain from Form 4797, Part I; long-term gain from Forms 2439 and 6252; and long-term gain or (loss) from Forms 4684, 6781, and 8824	11	
12 Net long-term gain or (loss) from partnerships, S corporations, estates, and trusts from Schedule(s) K-1	12	
13 Capital gain distributions. See the instructions	13	
14 Long-term capital loss carryover. Enter the amount, if any, from line 13 of your **Capital Loss Carryover Worksheet** in the instructions	14	( )
15 **Net long-term capital gain or (loss).** Combine lines 8a through 14 in column (h). Then, go to Part III on the back	15	

Part III **Summary**

16 Combine lines 7 and 15 and enter the result **16**

- If line 16 is a **gain**, enter the amount from line 16 on Form 1040, 1040-SR, or 1040-NR, line 7. Then, go to line 17 below.
- If line 16 is a **loss**, skip lines 17 through 20 below. Then, go to line 21. Also be sure to complete line 22.
- If line 16 is **zero**, skip lines 17 through 21 below and enter -0- on Form 1040, 1040-SR, or 1040-NR, line 7. Then, go to line 22.

17 Are lines 15 and 16 **both** gains?

☐ **Yes.** Go to line 18.

☐ **No.** Skip lines 18 through 21, and go to line 22.

18 If you are required to complete the **28% Rate Gain Worksheet** (see instructions), enter the amount, if any, from line 7 of that worksheet **18**

19 If you are required to complete the **Unrecaptured Section 1250 Gain Worksheet** (see instructions), enter the amount, if any, from line 18 of that worksheet **19**

20 Are lines 18 and 19 both zero or blank and you are not filing Form 4952?

☐ **Yes.** Complete the **Qualified Dividends and Capital Gain Tax Worksheet** in the instructions for Form 1040, line 16. **Don't** complete lines 21 and 22 below.

☐ **No.** Complete the **Schedule D Tax Worksheet** in the instructions. **Don't** complete lines 21 and 22 below.

21 If line 16 is a loss, enter here and on Form 1040, 1040-SR, or 1040-NR, line 7, the **smaller** of:

- The loss on line 16; or
- ($3,000), or if married filing separately, ($1,500)

} . . . . **21** (   )

Note: When figuring which amount is smaller, treat both amounts as positive numbers.

22 Do you have qualified dividends on Form 1040, 1040-SR, or 1040-NR, line 3a?

☐ **Yes.** Complete the **Qualified Dividends and Capital Gain Tax Worksheet** in the instructions for Form 1040, line 16.

☐ **No.** Complete the rest of Form 1040, 1040-SR, or 1040-NR.

SCHEDULE E (Form 1040)
Department of the Treasury Internal Revenue Service

Supplemental Income and Loss

(From rental real estate, royalties, partnerships, S corporations, estates, trusts, REMICs, etc.)

Attach to Form 1040, 1040-SR, 1040-NR, or 1041.
Go to *www.irs.gov/ScheduleE* for instructions and the latest information.

OMB No. 1545-0074
2022
Attachment Sequence No. **13**

Name(s) shown on return | **Your social security number**

Part I Income or Loss From Rental Real Estate and Royalties

Note: If you are in the business of renting personal property, use **Schedule C**. See instructions. If you are an individual, report farm rental income or loss from **Form 4835** on page 2, line 40.

A Did you make any payments in 2022 that would require you to file Form(s) 1099? See instructions . . . . . ☐ **Yes** ☐ **No**
B If "Yes," did you or will you file required Form(s) 1099? . . . . . ☐ **Yes** ☐ **No**

1a	Physical address of each property (street, city, state, ZIP code)
A	
B	
C	

1b	Type of Property (from list below)
A	
B	
C	

2 For each rental real estate property listed above, report the number of fair rental and personal use days. Check the QJV box only if you meet the requirements to file as a qualified joint venture. See instructions.

	Fair Rental Days	**Personal Use Days**	**QJV**
A			☐
B			☐
C			☐

Type of Property:
1 Single Family Residence
2 Multi-Family Residence
3 Vacation/Short-Term Rental
4 Commercial
5 Land
6 Royalties
7 Self-Rental
8 Other (describe) ____________

			Properties: A	B	C
Income:					
3	Rents received	3			
4	Royalties received	4			
Expenses:					
5	Advertising	5			
6	Auto and travel (see instructions)	6			
7	Cleaning and maintenance	7			
8	Commissions	8			
9	Insurance	9			
10	Legal and other professional fees	10			
11	Management fees	11			
12	Mortgage interest paid to banks, etc. (see instructions)	12			
13	Other interest	13			
14	Repairs	14			
15	Supplies	15			
16	Taxes	16			
17	Utilities	17			
18	Depreciation expense or depletion	18			
19	Other (list) ____________	19			
20	Total expenses. Add lines 5 through 19	20			
21	Subtract line 20 from line 3 (rents) and/or 4 (royalties). If result is a (loss), see instructions to find out if you must file **Form 6198**	21			
22	Deductible rental real estate loss after limitation, if any, on **Form 8582** (see instructions)	22	( )	( )	( )

23a	Total of all amounts reported on line 3 for all rental properties	23a	
b	Total of all amounts reported on line 4 for all royalty properties	23b	
c	Total of all amounts reported on line 12 for all properties	23c	
d	Total of all amounts reported on line 18 for all properties	23d	
e	Total of all amounts reported on line 20 for all properties	23e	
24	**Income.** Add positive amounts shown on line 21. **Do not** include any losses	24	
25	**Losses.** Add royalty losses from line 21 and rental real estate losses from line 22. Enter total losses here	25	( )
26	**Total rental real estate and royalty income or (loss).** Combine lines 24 and 25. Enter the result here. If Parts II, III, IV, and line 40 on page 2 do not apply to you, also enter this amount on Schedule 1 (Form 1040), line 5. Otherwise, include this amount in the total on line 41 on page 2 .	26	

Schedule E (Form 1040) 2022 — Attachment Sequence No. 13 — Page 2

Name(s) shown on return. Do not enter name and social security number if shown on other side.	Your social security number

Caution: The IRS compares amounts reported on your tax return with amounts shown on Schedule(s) K-1.

Part II Income or Loss From Partnerships and S Corporations

Note: If you report a loss, receive a distribution, dispose of stock, or receive a loan repayment from an S corporation, you **must** check the box in column **(e)** on line 28 and attach the required basis computation. If you report a loss from an at-risk activity for which **any** amount is **not** at risk, you **must** check the box in column **(f)** on line 28 and attach **Form 6198**. See instructions.

27 Are you reporting any loss not allowed in a prior year due to the at-risk or basis limitations, a prior year unallowed loss from a passive activity (if that loss was not reported on Form 8582), or unreimbursed partnership expenses? If you answered "Yes," see instructions before completing this section . . . ☐ **Yes** ☐ **No**

28	**(a)** Name	**(b)** Enter **P** for partnership; **S** for S corporation	**(c)** Check if foreign partnership	**(d)** Employer identification number	**(e)** Check if basis computation is required	**(f)** Check if any amount is not at risk
A			☐		☐	☐
B			☐		☐	☐
C			☐		☐	☐
D			☐		☐	☐

	Passive Income and Loss		**Nonpassive Income and Loss**		
	(g) Passive loss allowed (attach **Form 8582** if required)	**(h)** Passive income from **Schedule K-1**	**(i)** Nonpassive loss allowed (see **Schedule K-1**)	**(j)** Section 179 expense deduction from **Form 4562**	**(k)** Nonpassive income from **Schedule K-1**
A					
B					
C					
D					
29a Totals					
b Totals					

30	Add columns (h) and (k) of line 29a . . .	30	
31	Add columns (g), (i), and (j) of line 29b . . .	31	( )
32	**Total partnership and S corporation income or (loss).** Combine lines 30 and 31 . . .	32	

Part III Income or Loss From Estates and Trusts

33	**(a)** Name	**(b)** Employer identification number
A		
B		

	Passive Income and Loss		**Nonpassive Income and Loss**	
	(c) Passive deduction or loss allowed (attach **Form 8582** if required)	**(d)** Passive income from **Schedule K-1**	**(e)** Deduction or loss from **Schedule K-1**	**(f)** Other income from **Schedule K-1**
A				
B				
34a Totals				
b Totals				

35	Add columns (d) and (f) of line 34a . . .	35	
36	Add columns (c) and (e) of line 34b . . .	36	( )
37	**Total estate and trust income or (loss).** Combine lines 35 and 36 . . .	37	

Part IV Income or Loss From Real Estate Mortgage Investment Conduits (REMICs)—Residual Holder

38	**(a)** Name	**(b)** Employer identification number	**(c)** Excess inclusion from **Schedules Q**, line 2c (see instructions)	**(d)** Taxable income (net loss) from **Schedules Q**, line 1b	**(e)** Income from **Schedules Q**, line 3b

39	Combine columns (d) and (e) only. Enter the result here and include in the total on line 41 below .	39	

Part V Summary

40	Net farm rental income or (loss) from **Form 4835**. Also, complete line 42 below . . .			40	
41	**Total income or (loss).** Combine lines 26, 32, 37, 39, and 40. Enter the result here and on Schedule 1 (Form 1040), line 5 . . .			41	
42	**Reconciliation of farming and fishing income.** Enter your **gross** farming and fishing income reported on Form 4835, line 7; Schedule K-1 (Form 1065), box 14, code B; Schedule K-1 (Form 1120-S), box 17, code AD; and Schedule K-1 (Form 1041), box 14, code F. See instructions .	42			
43	**Reconciliation for real estate professionals.** If you were a real estate professional (see instructions), enter the net income or (loss) you reported anywhere on Form 1040, Form 1040-SR, or Form 1040-NR from all rental real estate activities in which you materially participated under the passive activity loss rules . . .	43			

SCHEDULE SE (Form 1040)

Department of the Treasury
Internal Revenue Service

Self-Employment Tax

Go to *www.irs.gov/ScheduleSE* for instructions and the latest information.
Attach to Form 1040, 1040-SR, or 1040-NR.

OMB No. 1545-0074
2022
Attachment Sequence No. **17**

Name of person with self-employment income (as shown on Form 1040, 1040-SR, or 1040-NR)	Social security number of person with **self-employment** income

Part I Self-Employment Tax

Note: If your only income subject to self-employment tax is **church employee income**, see instructions for how to report your income and the definition of church employee income.

A If you are a minister, member of a religious order, or Christian Science practitioner **and** you filed Form 4361, but you had $400 or more of **other** net earnings from self-employment, check here and continue with Part I . . . . ☐

Skip lines 1a and 1b if you use the farm optional method in Part II. See instructions.

1a	Net farm profit or (loss) from Schedule F, line 34, and farm partnerships, Schedule K-1 (Form 1065), box 14, code A . . .		**1a**	
b	If you received social security retirement or disability benefits, enter the amount of Conservation Reserve Program payments included on Schedule F, line 4b, or listed on Schedule K-1 (Form 1065), box 20, code AH		**1b**	( )
	Skip line 2 if you use the nonfarm optional method in Part II. See instructions.			
2	Net profit or (loss) from Schedule C, line 31; and Schedule K-1 (Form 1065), box 14, code A (other than farming). See instructions for other income to report or if you are a minister or member of a religious order		**2**	
3	Combine lines 1a, 1b, and 2 . . .		**3**	
4a	If line 3 is more than zero, multiply line 3 by 92.35% (0.9235). Otherwise, enter amount from line 3		**4a**	
	Note: If line 4a is less than $400 due to Conservation Reserve Program payments on line 1b, see instructions.			
b	If you elect one or both of the optional methods, enter the total of lines 15 and 17 here . . .		**4b**	
c	Combine lines 4a and 4b. If less than $400, **stop**; you don't owe self-employment tax. **Exception:** If less than $400 and you had **church employee income**, enter -0- and continue . . .		**4c**	
5a	Enter your **church employee income** from Form W-2. See instructions for definition of church employee income . . .	**5a**		
b	Multiply line 5a by 92.35% (0.9235). If less than $100, enter -0- . . .		**5b**	
6	Add lines 4c and 5b . . .		**6**	
7	Maximum amount of combined wages and self-employment earnings subject to social security tax or the 6.2% portion of the 7.65% railroad retirement (tier 1) tax for 2022 . . .		**7**	147,000
8a	Total social security wages and tips (total of boxes 3 and 7 on Form(s) W-2) and railroad retirement (tier 1) compensation. If $147,000 or more, skip lines 8b through 10, and go to line 11 . . .	**8a**		
b	Unreported tips subject to social security tax from Form 4137, line 10 . . .	**8b**		
c	Wages subject to social security tax from Form 8919, line 10 . . .	**8c**		
d	Add lines 8a, 8b, and 8c . . .		**8d**	
9	Subtract line 8d from line 7. If zero or less, enter -0- here and on line 10 and go to line 11 . . .		**9**	
10	Multiply the **smaller** of line 6 or line 9 by 12.4% (0.124) . . .		**10**	
11	Multiply line 6 by 2.9% (0.029) . . .		**11**	
12	**Self-employment tax.** Add lines 10 and 11. Enter here and on **Schedule 2 (Form 1040), line 4** . .		**12**	
13	**Deduction for one-half of self-employment tax.** Multiply line 12 by 50% (0.50). Enter here and on **Schedule 1 (Form 1040), line 15** . . .	**13**		

Part II Optional Methods To Figure Net Earnings (see instructions)

Farm Optional Method. You may use this method **only** if **(a)** your gross farm income[1] wasn't more than $9,060, **or (b)** your net farm profits[2] were less than $6,540.

14	Maximum income for optional methods . . .	**14**	6,040
15	Enter the **smaller** of: two-thirds (2/3) of gross farm income[1] (not less than zero) **or** $6,040. Also, include this amount on line 4b above . . .	**15**	

Nonfarm Optional Method. You may use this method **only** if **(a)** your net nonfarm profits[3] were less than $6,540 and also less than 72.189% of your gross nonfarm income,[4] **and (b)** you had net earnings from self-employment of at least $400 in 2 of the prior 3 years. **Caution:** You may use this method no more than five times.

16	Subtract line 15 from line 14 . . .	**16**	
17	Enter the **smaller** of: two-thirds (2/3) of gross nonfarm income[4] (not less than zero) **or** the amount on line 16. Also, include this amount on line 4b above . . .	**17**	

[1] From Sch. F, line 9; and Sch. K-1 (Form 1065), box 14, code B.
[2] From Sch. F, line 34; and Sch. K-1 (Form 1065), box 14, code A—minus the amount you would have entered on line 1b had you not used the optional method.
[3] From Sch. C, line 31; and Sch. K-1 (Form 1065), box 14, code A.
[4] From Sch. C, line 7; and Sch. K-1 (Form 1065), box 14, code C.

Form **1041** Department of the Treasury—Internal Revenue Service

U.S. Income Tax Return for Estates and Trusts

Go to *www.irs.gov/Form1041* for instructions and the latest information.

2022 OMB No. 1545-0092

For calendar year 2022 or fiscal year beginning , 2022, and ending , 20

A Check all that apply:
- ☐ Decedent's estate
- ☐ Simple trust
- ☐ Complex trust
- ☐ Qualified disability trust
- ☐ ESBT (S portion only)
- ☐ Grantor type trust
- ☐ Bankruptcy estate—Ch. 7
- ☐ Bankruptcy estate—Ch. 11
- ☐ Pooled income fund

Name of estate or trust (If a grantor type trust, see the instructions.)

Name and title of fiduciary

Number, street, and room or suite no. (If a P.O. box, see the instructions.)

City or town, state or province, country, and ZIP or foreign postal code

C Employer identification number

D Date entity created

E Nonexempt charitable and split-interest trusts, check applicable box(es). See instructions.
- ☐ Described in sec. 4947(a)(1). Check here if not a private foundation . . . ☐
- ☐ Described in sec. 4947(a)(2)

B Number of Schedules K-1 attached (see instructions)

F Check applicable boxes: ☐ Initial return ☐ Final return ☐ Amended return ☐ Net operating loss carryback ☐ Change in trust's name ☐ Change in fiduciary ☐ Change in fiduciary's name ☐ Change in fiduciary's address

G Check here if the estate or filing trust made a section 645 election . . . . ☐ Trust TIN

Income	1	Interest income	1	
	2a	Total ordinary dividends	2a	
	b	Qualified dividends allocable to: (1) Beneficiaries ______ (2) Estate or trust ______		
	3	Business income or (loss). Attach Schedule C (Form 1040)	3	
	4	Capital gain or (loss). Attach Schedule D (Form 1041)	4	
	5	Rents, royalties, partnerships, other estates and trusts, etc. Attach Schedule E (Form 1040)	5	
	6	Farm income or (loss). Attach Schedule F (Form 1040)	6	
	7	Ordinary gain or (loss). Attach Form 4797	7	
	8	Other income. List type and amount ______	8	
	9	**Total income.** Combine lines 1, 2a, and 3 through 8	9	
Deductions	10	Interest. Check if Form 4952 is attached ☐	10	
	11	Taxes	11	
	12	Fiduciary fees. If only a portion is deductible under section 67(e), see instructions	12	
	13	Charitable deduction (from Schedule A, line 7)	13	
	14	Attorney, accountant, and return preparer fees. If only a portion is deductible under section 67(e), see instructions	14	
	15a	Other deductions (attach schedule). See instructions for deductions allowable under section 67(e)	15a	
	b	Net operating loss deduction. See instructions	15b	
	16	Add lines 10 through 15b	16	
	17	Adjusted total income or (loss). Subtract line 16 from line 9 17		
	18	Income distribution deduction (from Schedule B, line 15). Attach Schedules K-1 (Form 1041)	18	
	19	Estate tax deduction including certain generation-skipping taxes (attach computation)	19	
	20	Qualified business income deduction. Attach Form 8995 or 8995-A	20	
	21	Exemption	21	
	22	Add lines 18 through 21	22	
Tax and Payments	23	Taxable income. Subtract line 22 from line 17. If a loss, see instructions	23	
	24	**Total tax** (from Schedule G, Part I, line 9)	24	
	25	Current year net 965 tax liability paid from Form 965-A, Part II, column (k) (see instructions)	25	
	26	**Total payments** (from Schedule G, Part II, line 19)	26	
	27	Estimated tax penalty. See instructions	27	
	28	**Tax due.** If line 26 is smaller than the total of lines 24, 25, and 27, enter amount owed	28	
	29	**Overpayment.** If line 26 is larger than the total of lines 24, 25, and 27, enter amount overpaid	29	
	30	Amount of line 29 to be: **a Credited to 2023** ; **b Refunded**	30	

Sign Here

Under penalties of perjury, I declare that I have examined this return, including accompanying schedules and statements, and to the best of my knowledge and belief, it is true, correct, and complete. Declaration of preparer (other than taxpayer) is based on all information of which preparer has any knowledge.

Signature of fiduciary or officer representing fiduciary | Date | EIN of fiduciary if a financial institution

May the IRS discuss this return with the preparer shown below? See instructions. ☐ **Yes** ☐ **No**

Paid Preparer Use Only

Print/Type preparer's name	Preparer's signature	Date	Check ☐ if self-employed	PTIN
Firm's name			Firm's EIN	
Firm's address			Phone no.	

For Paperwork Reduction Act Notice, see the separate instructions. Cat. No. 11370H Form **1041** (2022)

Form 1041 (2022) Page **2**

Schedule A — Charitable Deduction. Don't complete for a simple trust or a pooled income fund.

1	Amounts paid or permanently set aside for charitable purposes from gross income. See instructions	1	
2	Tax-exempt income allocable to charitable contributions. See instructions	2	
3	Subtract line 2 from line 1	3	
4	Capital gains for the tax year allocated to corpus and paid or permanently set aside for charitable purposes	4	
5	Add lines 3 and 4	5	
6	Section 1202 exclusion allocable to capital gains paid or permanently set aside for charitable purposes. See instructions	6	
7	**Charitable deduction.** Subtract line 6 from line 5. Enter here and on page 1, line 13	7	

Schedule B — Income Distribution Deduction

1	Adjusted total income. See instructions	1	
2	Adjusted tax-exempt interest	2	
3	Total net gain from Schedule D (Form 1041), line 19, column (1). See instructions	3	
4	Enter amount from Schedule A, line 4 (minus any allocable section 1202 exclusion)	4	
5	Capital gains for the tax year included on Schedule A, line 1. See instructions	5	
6	Enter any gain from page 1, line 4, as a negative number. If page 1, line 4, is a loss, enter the loss as a positive number	6	
7	**Distributable net income.** Combine lines 1 through 6. If zero or less, enter -0-	7	
8	If a complex trust, enter accounting income for the tax year as determined under the governing instrument and applicable local law — 8		
9	Income required to be distributed currently	9	
10	Other amounts paid, credited, or otherwise required to be distributed	10	
11	Total distributions. Add lines 9 and 10. If greater than line 8, see instructions	11	
12	Enter the amount of tax-exempt income included on line 11	12	
13	Tentative income distribution deduction. Subtract line 12 from line 11	13	
14	Tentative income distribution deduction. Subtract line 2 from line 7. If zero or less, enter -0-	14	
15	**Income distribution deduction.** Enter the smaller of line 13 or line 14 here and on page 1, line 18	15	

Schedule G — Tax Computation and Payments (see instructions)

Part I — Tax Computation

1	**Tax:**				
a	Tax on taxable income. See instructions	1a			
b	Tax on lump-sum distributions. Attach Form 4972	1b			
c	Alternative minimum tax (from Schedule I (Form 1041), line 54)	1c			
d	**Total.** Add lines 1a through 1c			1d	
2a	Foreign tax credit. Attach Form 1116	2a			
b	General business credit. Attach Form 3800	2b			
c	Credit for prior year minimum tax. Attach Form 8801	2c			
d	Bond credits. Attach Form 8912	2d			
e	**Total credits.** Add lines 2a through 2d			2e	
3	Subtract line 2e from line 1d. If zero or less, enter -0-			3	
4	Tax on the ESBT portion of the trust (from ESBT Tax Worksheet, line 17). See instructions			4	
5	Net investment income tax from Form 8960, line 21			5	
6	Recapture taxes. Check if from: ☐ Form 4255 ☐ Form 8611			6	
7	Household employment taxes. Attach Schedule H (Form 1040)			7	
8	Other taxes and amounts due			8	
9	**Total tax.** Add lines 3 through 8. Enter here and on page 1, line 24			9	

Part II — Payments

10	2022 estimated tax payments and amount applied from 2021 return	10	
11	Estimated tax payments allocated to beneficiaries (from Form 1041-T)	11	
12	Subtract line 11 from line 10	12	
13	Tax paid with Form 7004. See instructions	13	
14	Federal income tax withheld. If any is from Form(s) 1099, check here ☐	14	
15	Current year net 965 tax liability from Form 965-A, Part I, column (f) (see instructions)	15	
16	Other payments: **a** Form 2439 ______ ; **b** Form 4136 ______ ; **Total**	16c	
17	Credit for qualified sick and family leave wages for leave taken before April 1, 2021	17	
18	Credit for qualified sick and family leave wages for leave taken after March 31, 2021, and before October 1, 2021	18	
19	**Total payments.** Add lines 12 through 15 and 16c through 18. Enter here and on page 1, line 26	19	

Form 1041 (2022) Page **3**

Other Information		Yes	No
1	Did the estate or trust receive tax-exempt income? If "Yes," attach a computation of the allocation of expenses. Enter the amount of tax-exempt interest income and exempt-interest dividends . . . . . $		
2	Did the estate or trust receive all or any part of the earnings (salary, wages, and other compensation) of any individual by reason of a contract assignment or similar arrangement? . . .		
3	At any time during calendar year 2022, did the estate or trust have an interest in or a signature or other authority over a bank, securities, or other financial account in a foreign country? . . . See the instructions for exceptions and filing requirements for FinCEN Form 114. If "Yes," enter the name of the foreign country		
4	During the tax year, did the estate or trust receive a distribution from, or was it the grantor of, or transferor to, a foreign trust? If "Yes," the estate or trust may have to file Form 3520. See instructions . . .		
5	Did the estate or trust receive, or pay, any qualified residence interest on seller-provided financing? If "Yes," see the instructions for the required attachment . . .		
6	If this is an estate or a complex trust making the section 663(b) election, check here. See instructions . . . ☐		
7	To make a section 643(e)(3) election, attach Schedule D (Form 1041), and check here. See instructions . . . ☐		
8	If the decedent's estate has been open for more than 2 years, attach an explanation for the delay in closing the estate, and check here . . . ☐		
9	Are any present or future trust beneficiaries skip persons? See instructions . . .		
10	Was the trust a specified domestic entity required to file Form 8938 for the tax year? See the Instructions for Form 8938 . . .		
11a	Did the estate or trust distribute S corporation stock for which it made a section 965(i) election? . . .		
b	If "Yes," did each beneficiary enter into an agreement to be liable for the net tax liability? See instructions . . .		
12	Did the estate or trust either make a section 965(i) election or enter into a transfer agreement as an eligible 965(i) transferee for S corporation stock held on the last day of the tax year? See instructions . . .		
13	**ESBTs only.** Does the ESBT have a nonresident alien grantor? If "Yes," see instructions . . .		
14	**ESBTs only.** Did the S portion of the trust claim a qualified business income deduction? If "Yes," see instructions		

Form **1041** (2022)

661117

☐ Final K-1 ☐ Amended K-1 OMB No. 1545-0092

Schedule K-1 (Form 1041)

Department of the Treasury
Internal Revenue Service

2022

For calendar year 2022, or tax year

beginning / / ending / /

Beneficiary's Share of Income, Deductions, Credits, etc.

See back of form and instructions.

Part I Information About the Estate or Trust

A Estate's or trust's employer identification number

B Estate's or trust's name

C Fiduciary's name, address, city, state, and ZIP code

D ☐ Check if Form 1041-T was filed and enter the date it was filed

E ☐ Check if this is the final Form 1041 for the estate or trust

Part II Information About the Beneficiary

F Beneficiary's identifying number

G Beneficiary's name, address, city, state, and ZIP code

H ☐ Domestic beneficiary ☐ Foreign beneficiary

Part III Beneficiary's Share of Current Year Income, Deductions, Credits, and Other Items

1	Interest income	11	Final year deductions
2a	Ordinary dividends		
2b	Qualified dividends		
3	Net short-term capital gain		
4a	Net long-term capital gain		
4b	28% rate gain	12	Alternative minimum tax adjustment
4c	Unrecaptured section 1250 gain		
5	Other portfolio and nonbusiness income		
6	Ordinary business income		
7	Net rental real estate income	13	Credits and credit recapture
8	Other rental income		
9	Directly apportioned deductions		
		14	Other information
10	Estate tax deduction		

*See attached statement for additional information.

Note: A statement must be attached showing the beneficiary's share of income and directly apportioned deductions from each business, rental real estate, and other rental activity.

For IRS Use Only

Schedule K-1 (Form 1041) 2022 Page **2**

This list identifies the codes used on Schedule K-1 for beneficiaries and provides summarized reporting information for beneficiaries who file Form 1040 or 1040-SR. For detailed reporting and filing information, see the Instructions for Schedule K-1 (Form 1041) for a Beneficiary Filing Form 1040 or 1040-SR and the instructions for your income tax return.

	Report on
1. Interest income	Form 1040 or 1040-SR, line 2b
2a. Ordinary dividends	Form 1040 or 1040-SR, line 3b
2b. Qualified dividends	Form 1040 or 1040-SR, line 3a
3. Net short-term capital gain	Schedule D, line 5
4a. Net long-term capital gain	Schedule D, line 12
4b. 28% rate gain	28% Rate Gain Worksheet, line 4 (Schedule D Instructions)
4c. Unrecaptured section 1250 gain	Unrecaptured Section 1250 Gain Worksheet, line 11 (Schedule D Instructions)
5. Other portfolio and nonbusiness income	Schedule E, line 33, column (f)
6. Ordinary business income	Schedule E, line 33, column (d) or (f)
7. Net rental real estate income	Schedule E, line 33, column (d) or (f)
8. Other rental income	Schedule E, line 33, column (d) or (f)
9. Directly apportioned deductions	
Code	
A Depreciation	Form 8582 or Schedule E, line 33, column (c) or (e)
B Depletion	Form 8582 or Schedule E, line 33, column (c) or (e)
C Amortization	Form 8582 or Schedule E, line 33, column (c) or (e)
10. Estate tax deduction	Schedule A, line 16
11. Final year deductions	
A Excess deductions – Section 67(e) expenses	Schedule 1 (Form 1040), line 24k (also see the beneficiary's instructions)
B Excess deductions – Non–miscellaneous itemized deductions	See the beneficiary's instructions
C Short-term capital loss carryover	Schedule D, line 5
D Long-term capital loss carryover	Schedule D, line 12; line 5 of the wksht. for Sch. D, line 18; and line 16 of the wksht. for Sch. D, line 19
E Net operating loss carryover — regular tax	Schedule 1 (Form 1040), line 8a
F Net operating loss carryover — minimum tax	Form 6251, line 2f
12. Alternative minimum tax (AMT) items	
A Adjustment for minimum tax purposes	Form 6251, line 2j
B AMT adjustment attributable to qualified dividends	See the beneficiary's instructions and the Instructions for Form 6251
C AMT adjustment attributable to net short-term capital gain	See the beneficiary's instructions and the Instructions for Form 6251
D AMT adjustment attributable to net long-term capital gain	See the beneficiary's instructions and the Instructions for Form 6251
E AMT adjustment attributable to unrecaptured section 1250 gain	See the beneficiary's instructions and the Instructions for Form 6251
F AMT adjustment attributable to 28% rate gain	See the beneficiary's instructions and the Instructions for Form 6251
G Accelerated depreciation	See the beneficiary's instructions and the Instructions for Form 6251
H Depletion	See the beneficiary's instructions and the Instructions for Form 6251
I Amortization	See the beneficiary's instructions and the Instructions for Form 6251
J Exclusion items	2023 Form 8801

13. Credits and credit recapture	
Code	*Report on*
A Credit for estimated taxes	Form 1040 or 1040-SR, line 26
B Credit for backup withholding	Form 1040 or 1040-SR, line 25c
C Low-income housing credit	See the beneficiary's instructions
D Rehabilitation credit and energy credit	See the beneficiary's instructions
E Other qualifying investment credit	See the beneficiary's instructions
F Work opportunity credit	See the beneficiary's instructions
G Credit for small employer health insurance premiums	See the beneficiary's instructions
H Biofuel producer credit	See the beneficiary's instructions
I Credit for increasing research activities	See the beneficiary's instructions
J Renewable electricity, refined coal, and Indian coal production credit	See the beneficiary's instructions
K Empowerment zone employment credit	See the beneficiary's instructions
L Indian employment credit	See the beneficiary's instructions
M Orphan drug credit	See the beneficiary's instructions
N Credit for employer-provided child care and facilities	See the beneficiary's instructions
O Biodiesel and renewable diesel fuels credit	See the beneficiary's instructions
P Credit to holders of tax credit bonds	See the beneficiary's instructions
Q Credit for employer differential wage payments	See the beneficiary's instructions
R Recapture of credits	See the beneficiary's instructions
Z Other credits	See the beneficiary's instructions
14. Other information	
A Tax-exempt interest	Form 1040 or 1040-SR, line 2a
B Foreign taxes	Schedule 3 (Form 1040), line 1 or Schedule A, line 6
C Reserved for future use	
D Reserved for future use	
E Net investment income	Form 4952, line 4a
F Gross farm and fishing income	Schedule E, line 42
G Foreign trading gross receipts (IRC 942(a))	See the Instructions for Form 8873
H Adjustment for section 1411 net investment income or deductions	Form 8960, line 7 (also see the beneficiary's instructions)
I Section 199A information	See the beneficiary's instructions
Z Other information	See the beneficiary's instructions

Note: If you are a beneficiary who does not file a Form 1040 or 1040-SR, see instructions for the type of income tax return you are filing.

Form **1065**

Department of the Treasury
Internal Revenue Service

U.S. Return of Partnership Income

For calendar year 2022, or tax year beginning ________, 2022, ending ________, 20 ____.

Go to *www.irs.gov/Form1065* for instructions and the latest information.

OMB No. 1545-0123

2022

A Principal business activity	Type or Print	Name of partnership	D Employer identification number
B Principal product or service		Number, street, and room or suite no. If a P.O. box, see instructions.	E Date business started
C Business code number		City or town, state or province, country, and ZIP or foreign postal code	F Total assets (see instructions) $

G Check applicable boxes: (1) ☐ Initial return (2) ☐ Final return (3) ☐ Name change (4) ☐ Address change (5) ☐ Amended return

H Check accounting method: (1) ☐ Cash (2) ☐ Accrual (3) ☐ Other (specify): ________

I Number of Schedules K-1. Attach one for each person who was a partner at any time during the tax year: ________

J Check if Schedules C and M-3 are attached . . . ☐

K Check if partnership: (1) ☐ Aggregated activities for section 465 at-risk purposes (2) ☐ Grouped activities for section 469 passive activity purposes

Caution: Include **only** trade or business income and expenses on lines 1a through 22 below. See instructions for more information.

Income	1a	Gross receipts or sales	1a			
	b	Returns and allowances	1b			
	c	Balance. Subtract line 1b from line 1a			1c	
	2	Cost of goods sold (attach Form 1125-A)			2	
	3	Gross profit. Subtract line 2 from line 1c			3	
	4	Ordinary income (loss) from other partnerships, estates, and trusts (attach statement)			4	
	5	Net farm profit (loss) (attach Schedule F (Form 1040))			5	
	6	Net gain (loss) from Form 4797, Part II, line 17 (attach Form 4797)			6	
	7	Other income (loss) (attach statement)			7	
	8	**Total income (loss).** Combine lines 3 through 7			8	
Deductions (see instructions for limitations)	9	Salaries and wages (other than to partners) (less employment credits)			9	
	10	Guaranteed payments to partners			10	
	11	Repairs and maintenance			11	
	12	Bad debts			12	
	13	Rent			13	
	14	Taxes and licenses			14	
	15	Interest (see instructions)			15	
	16a	Depreciation (if required, attach Form 4562)	16a			
	b	Less depreciation reported on Form 1125-A and elsewhere on return	16b		16c	
	17	Depletion **(Do not deduct oil and gas depletion.)**			17	
	18	Retirement plans, etc.			18	
	19	Employee benefit programs			19	
	20	Other deductions (attach statement)			20	
	21	**Total deductions.** Add the amounts shown in the far right column for lines 9 through 20			21	
	22	**Ordinary business income (loss).** Subtract line 21 from line 8			22	
Tax and Payment	23	Interest due under the look-back method—completed long-term contracts (attach Form 8697)			23	
	24	Interest due under the look-back method—income forecast method (attach Form 8866)			24	
	25	BBA AAR imputed underpayment (see instructions)			25	
	26	Other taxes (see instructions)			26	
	27	**Total balance due.** Add lines 23 through 26			27	
	28	Payment (see instructions)			28	
	29	**Amount owed.** If line 28 is smaller than line 27, enter amount owed			29	
	30	**Overpayment.** If line 28 is larger than line 27, enter overpayment			30	

Sign Here

Under penalties of perjury, I declare that I have examined this return, including accompanying schedules and statements, and to the best of my knowledge and belief, it is true, correct, and complete. Declaration of preparer (other than partner or limited liability company member) is based on all information of which preparer has any knowledge.

Signature of partner or limited liability company member — Date

May the IRS discuss this return with the preparer shown below? See instructions. ☐ **Yes** ☐ **No**

Paid Preparer Use Only

Print/Type preparer's name	Preparer's signature	Date	Check ☐ if self-employed	PTIN
Firm's name			Firm's EIN	
Firm's address			Phone no.	

Schedule B Other Information

		Yes	No
1	What type of entity is filing this return? Check the applicable box:		
a	☐ Domestic general partnership **b** ☐ Domestic limited partnership		
c	☐ Domestic limited liability company **d** ☐ Domestic limited liability partnership		
e	☐ Foreign partnership **f** ☐ Other:		
2	At the end of the tax year:		
a	Did any foreign or domestic corporation, partnership (including any entity treated as a partnership), trust, or tax-exempt organization, or any foreign government own, directly or indirectly, an interest of 50% or more in the profit, loss, or capital of the partnership? For rules of constructive ownership, see instructions. If "Yes," attach Schedule B-1, Information on Partners Owning 50% or More of the Partnership		
b	Did any individual or estate own, directly or indirectly, an interest of 50% or more in the profit, loss, or capital of the partnership? For rules of constructive ownership, see instructions. If "Yes," attach Schedule B-1, Information on Partners Owning 50% or More of the Partnership		
3	At the end of the tax year, did the partnership:		
a	Own directly 20% or more, or own, directly or indirectly, 50% or more of the total voting power of all classes of stock entitled to vote of any foreign or domestic corporation? For rules of constructive ownership, see instructions. If "Yes," complete (i) through (iv) below		

(i) Name of Corporation	**(ii)** Employer Identification Number (if any)	**(iii)** Country of Incorporation	**(iv)** Percentage Owned in Voting Stock

		Yes	No
b	Own directly an interest of 20% or more, or own, directly or indirectly, an interest of 50% or more in the profit, loss, or capital in any foreign or domestic partnership (including an entity treated as a partnership) or in the beneficial interest of a trust? For rules of constructive ownership, see instructions. If "Yes," complete (i) through (v) below		

(i) Name of Entity	**(ii)** Employer Identification Number (if any)	**(iii)** Type of Entity	**(iv)** Country of Organization	**(v)** Maximum Percentage Owned in Profit, Loss, or Capital

		Yes	No
4	Does the partnership satisfy **all four** of the following conditions?		
a	The partnership's total receipts for the tax year were less than $250,000.		
b	The partnership's total assets at the end of the tax year were less than $1 million.		
c	Schedules K-1 are filed with the return and furnished to the partners on or before the due date (including extensions) for the partnership return.		
d	The partnership is not filing and is not required to file Schedule M-3		
	If "Yes," the partnership is not required to complete Schedules L, M-1, and M-2; item F on page 1 of Form 1065; or item L on Schedule K-1.		
5	Is this partnership a publicly traded partnership, as defined in section 469(k)(2)?		
6	During the tax year, did the partnership have any debt that was canceled, was forgiven, or had the terms modified so as to reduce the principal amount of the debt?		
7	Has this partnership filed, or is it required to file, Form 8918, Material Advisor Disclosure Statement, to provide information on any reportable transaction?		
8	At any time during calendar year 2022, did the partnership have an interest in or a signature or other authority over a financial account in a foreign country (such as a bank account, securities account, or other financial account)? See instructions for exceptions and filing requirements for FinCEN Form 114, Report of Foreign Bank and Financial Accounts (FBAR). If "Yes," enter the name of the foreign country		
9	At any time during the tax year, did the partnership receive a distribution from, or was it the grantor of, or transferor to, a foreign trust? If "Yes," the partnership may have to file Form 3520, Annual Return To Report Transactions With Foreign Trusts and Receipt of Certain Foreign Gifts. See instructions		
10a	Is the partnership making, or had it previously made (and not revoked), a section 754 election? See instructions for details regarding a section 754 election.		
b	Did the partnership make for this tax year an optional basis adjustment under section 743(b) or 734(b)? If "Yes," attach a statement showing the computation and allocation of the basis adjustment. See instructions		
c	Is the partnership required to adjust the basis of partnership assets under section 743(b) or 734(b) because of a substantial built-in loss (as defined under section 743(d)) or substantial basis reduction (as defined under section 734(d))? If "Yes," attach a statement showing the computation and allocation of the basis adjustment. See instructions		

Form 1065 (2022) Page **3**

Schedule B **Other Information** *(continued)*

		Yes	No
11	Check this box if, during the current or prior tax year, the partnership distributed any property received in a like-kind exchange or contributed such property to another entity (other than disregarded entities wholly owned by the partnership throughout the tax year) . . . ☐		
12	At any time during the tax year, did the partnership distribute to any partner a tenancy-in-common or other undivided interest in partnership property? . . .		
13	If the partnership is required to file Form 8858, Information Return of U.S. Persons With Respect to Foreign Disregarded Entities (FDEs) and Foreign Branches (FBs), enter the number of Forms 8858 attached. See instructions . . . ________		
14	Does the partnership have any foreign partners? If "Yes," enter the number of Forms 8805, Foreign Partner's Information Statement of Section 1446 Withholding Tax, filed for this partnership . . . ________		
15	Enter the number of Forms 8865, Return of U.S. Persons With Respect to Certain Foreign Partnerships, attached to this return . . . ________		
16a	Did you make any payments in 2022 that would require you to file Form(s) 1099? See instructions . . .		
b	If "Yes," did you or will you file required Form(s) 1099? . . .		
17	Enter the number of Forms 5471, Information Return of U.S. Persons With Respect to Certain Foreign Corporations, attached to this return . . . ________		
18	Enter the number of partners that are foreign governments under section 892 . . . ________		
19	During the partnership's tax year, did the partnership make any payments that would require it to file Forms 1042 and 1042-S under chapter 3 (sections 1441 through 1464) or chapter 4 (sections 1471 through 1474)? . . .		
20	Was the partnership a specified domestic entity required to file Form 8938 for the tax year? See the Instructions for Form 8938 . . .		
21	Is the partnership a section 721(c) partnership, as defined in Regulations section 1.721(c)-1(b)(14)? . . .		
22	During the tax year, did the partnership pay or accrue any interest or royalty for which one or more partners are not allowed a deduction under section 267A? See instructions . . . If "Yes," enter the total amount of the disallowed deductions . . . $________		
23	Did the partnership have an election under section 163(j) for any real property trade or business or any farming business in effect during the tax year? See instructions . . .		
24	Does the partnership satisfy one or more of the following? See instructions . . .		
a	The partnership owns a pass-through entity with current, or prior year carryover, excess business interest expense.		
b	The partnership's aggregate average annual gross receipts (determined under section 448(c)) for the 3 tax years preceding the current tax year are more than $27 million and the partnership has business interest expense.		
c	The partnership is a tax shelter (see instructions) and the partnership has business interest expense. If "Yes" to any, complete and attach Form 8990.		
25	Is the partnership attaching Form 8996 to certify as a Qualified Opportunity Fund? . . . If "Yes," enter the amount from Form 8996, line 15 . . . $________		
26	Enter the number of foreign partners subject to section 864(c)(8) as a result of transferring all or a portion of an interest in the partnership or of receiving a distribution from the partnership . . . ________ Complete Schedule K-3 (Form 1065), Part XIII, for each foreign partner subject to section 864(c)(8) on a transfer or distribution.		
27	At any time during the tax year, were there any transfers between the partnership and its partners subject to the disclosure requirements of Regulations section 1.707-8? . . .		
28	Since December 22, 2017, did a foreign corporation directly or indirectly acquire substantially all of the properties constituting a trade or business of your partnership, and was the ownership percentage (by vote or value) for purposes of section 7874 greater than 50% (for example, the partners held more than 50% of the stock of the foreign corporation)? If "Yes," list the ownership percentage by vote and by value. See instructions. Percentage: By vote: ________ By value: ________		
29	Reserved for future use . . .		
30	Is the partnership electing out of the centralized partnership audit regime under section 6221(b)? See instructions. If "Yes," the partnership must complete Schedule B-2 (Form 1065). Enter the total from Schedule B-2, Part III, line 3 . . . ________ If "No," complete Designation of Partnership Representative below.		

Designation of Partnership Representative (see instructions)

Enter below the information for the partnership representative (PR) for the tax year covered by this return.

Name of PR	
U.S. address of PR ________	U.S. phone number of PR
If the PR is an entity, name of the designated individual for the PR	
U.S. address of designated individual ________	U.S. phone number of designated individual

Form **1065** (2022)

Form 1065 (2022) Page 4

Schedule K		Partners' Distributive Share Items		Total amount
Income (Loss)	1	Ordinary business income (loss) (page 1, line 22)	1	
	2	Net rental real estate income (loss) (attach Form 8825)	2	
	3a	Other gross rental income (loss) . . . 3a		
	b	Expenses from other rental activities (attach statement) . . . 3b		
	c	Other net rental income (loss). Subtract line 3b from line 3a	3c	
	4	Guaranteed payments: a Services 4a b Capital 4b		
		c Total. Add lines 4a and 4b	4c	
	5	Interest income	5	
	6	Dividends and dividend equivalents: a Ordinary dividends	6a	
		b Qualified dividends 6b c Dividend equivalents 6c		
	7	Royalties	7	
	8	Net short-term capital gain (loss) (attach Schedule D (Form 1065))	8	
	9a	Net long-term capital gain (loss) (attach Schedule D (Form 1065))	9a	
	b	Collectibles (28%) gain (loss) . . . 9b		
	c	Unrecaptured section 1250 gain (attach statement) . . . 9c		
	10	Net section 1231 gain (loss) (attach Form 4797)	10	
	11	Other income (loss) (see instructions) Type:	11	
Deductions	12	Section 179 deduction (attach Form 4562)	12	
	13a	Contributions	13a	
	b	Investment interest expense	13b	
	c	Section 59(e)(2) expenditures: (1) Type: (2) Amount:	13c(2)	
	d	Other deductions (see instructions) Type:	13d	
Self-Employ-ment	14a	Net earnings (loss) from self-employment	14a	
	b	Gross farming or fishing income	14b	
	c	Gross nonfarm income	14c	
Credits	15a	Low-income housing credit (section 42(j)(5))	15a	
	b	Low-income housing credit (other)	15b	
	c	Qualified rehabilitation expenditures (rental real estate) (attach Form 3468, if applicable)	15c	
	d	Other rental real estate credits (see instructions) Type:	15d	
	e	Other rental credits (see instructions) Type:	15e	
	f	Other credits (see instructions) Type:	15f	
International	16	Attach Schedule K-2 (Form 1065), Partners' Distributive Share Items—International, and check this box to indicate that you are reporting items of international tax relevance ☐		
Alternative Minimum Tax (AMT) Items	17a	Post-1986 depreciation adjustment	17a	
	b	Adjusted gain or loss	17b	
	c	Depletion (other than oil and gas)	17c	
	d	Oil, gas, and geothermal properties—gross income	17d	
	e	Oil, gas, and geothermal properties—deductions	17e	
	f	Other AMT items (attach statement)	17f	
Other Information	18a	Tax-exempt interest income	18a	
	b	Other tax-exempt income	18b	
	c	Nondeductible expenses	18c	
	19a	Distributions of cash and marketable securities	19a	
	b	Distributions of other property	19b	
	20a	Investment income	20a	
	b	Investment expenses	20b	
	c	Other items and amounts (attach statement)		
	21	Total foreign taxes paid or accrued	21	

Form **1065** (2022)

Analysis of Net Income (Loss) per Return

1	Net income (loss). Combine Schedule K, lines 1 through 11. From the result, subtract the sum of Schedule K, lines 12 through 13d, and 21					1	
2	Analysis by partner type:	**(i)** Corporate	**(ii)** Individual (active)	**(iii)** Individual (passive)	**(iv)** Partnership	**(v)** Exempt Organization	**(vi)** Nominee/Other
a	General partners						
b	Limited partners						

Schedule L Balance Sheets per Books

		Beginning of tax year		End of tax year	
	Assets	**(a)**	**(b)**	**(c)**	**(d)**
1	Cash				
2a	Trade notes and accounts receivable				
b	Less allowance for bad debts				
3	Inventories				
4	U.S. Government obligations				
5	Tax-exempt securities				
6	Other current assets (attach statement)				
7a	Loans to partners (or persons related to partners)				
b	Mortgage and real estate loans				
8	Other investments (attach statement)				
9a	Buildings and other depreciable assets				
b	Less accumulated depreciation				
10a	Depletable assets				
b	Less accumulated depletion				
11	Land (net of any amortization)				
12a	Intangible assets (amortizable only)				
b	Less accumulated amortization				
13	Other assets (attach statement)				
14	Total assets				
	Liabilities and Capital				
15	Accounts payable				
16	Mortgages, notes, bonds payable in less than 1 year				
17	Other current liabilities (attach statement)				
18	All nonrecourse loans				
19a	Loans from partners (or persons related to partners)				
b	Mortgages, notes, bonds payable in 1 year or more				
20	Other liabilities (attach statement)				
21	Partners' capital accounts				
22	Total liabilities and capital				

Schedule M-1 Reconciliation of Income (Loss) per Books With Analysis of Net Income (Loss) per Return

Note: The partnership may be required to file Schedule M-3. See instructions.

1	Net income (loss) per books		6	Income recorded on books this year not included on Schedule K, lines 1 through 11 (itemize):	
2	Income included on Schedule K, lines 1, 2, 3c, 5, 6a, 7, 8, 9a, 10, and 11, not recorded on books this year (itemize):		a	Tax-exempt interest $	
3	Guaranteed payments (other than health insurance)		7	Deductions included on Schedule K, lines 1 through 13d, and 21, not charged against book income this year (itemize):	
4	Expenses recorded on books this year not included on Schedule K, lines 1 through 13d, and 21 (itemize):		a	Depreciation $	
a	Depreciation $		8	Add lines 6 and 7	
b	Travel and entertainment $		9	Income (loss) (Analysis of Net Income (Loss), line 1). Subtract line 8 from line 5	
5	Add lines 1 through 4				

Schedule M-2 Analysis of Partners' Capital Accounts

1	Balance at beginning of year		6	Distributions: **a** Cash	
2	Capital contributed: **a** Cash			**b** Property	
	b Property		7	Other decreases (itemize):	
3	Net income (loss) (see instructions)				
4	Other increases (itemize):		8	Add lines 6 and 7	
5	Add lines 1 through 4		9	Balance at end of year. Subtract line 8 from line 5	

651121

☐ Final K-1 ☐ Amended K-1 OMB No. 1545-0123

Schedule K-1 (Form 1065) **2022**

Department of the Treasury
Internal Revenue Service

For calendar year 2022, or tax year

beginning ___/___/ 2022 ending ___/___/___

Partner's Share of Income, Deductions, Credits, etc.

See separate instructions.

Part I Information About the Partnership

A Partnership's employer identification number

B Partnership's name, address, city, state, and ZIP code

C IRS center where partnership filed return:

D ☐ Check if this is a publicly traded partnership (PTP)

Part II Information About the Partner

E Partner's SSN or TIN (Do not use TIN of a disregarded entity. See instructions.)

F Name, address, city, state, and ZIP code for partner entered in E. See instructions.

G ☐ General partner or LLC member-manager ☐ Limited partner or other LLC member

H1 ☐ Domestic partner ☐ Foreign partner

H2 ☐ If the partner is a disregarded entity (DE), enter the partner's:

TIN ________ Name ________

I1 What type of entity is this partner? ________

I2 If this partner is a retirement plan (IRA/SEP/Keogh/etc.), check here . ☐

J Partner's share of profit, loss, and capital (see instructions):

	Beginning	Ending
Profit	%	%
Loss	%	%
Capital	%	%

Check if decrease is due to sale or exchange of partnership interest . . ☐

K Partner's share of liabilities:

	Beginning	Ending
Nonrecourse . .	$	$
Qualified nonrecourse financing . . .	$	$
Recourse . . .	$	$

Check this box if item K includes liability amounts from lower-tier partnerships ☐

L **Partner's Capital Account Analysis**

Beginning capital account . . . $________

Capital contributed during the year . . $________

Current year net income (loss) . . . $________

Other increase (decrease) (attach explanation) $________

Withdrawals and distributions . . . $ (________)

Ending capital account . . . . $________

M Did the partner contribute property with a built-in gain (loss)?

☐ **Yes** ☐ **No** If "Yes," attach statement. See instructions.

N **Partner's Share of Net Unrecognized Section 704(c) Gain or (Loss)**

Beginning . . . . $________

Ending . . . . $________

Part III Partner's Share of Current Year Income, Deductions, Credits, and Other Items

1	Ordinary business income (loss)	14	Self-employment earnings (loss)
2	Net rental real estate income (loss)		
3	Other net rental income (loss)	15	Credits
4a	Guaranteed payments for services		
4b	Guaranteed payments for capital	16	Schedule K-3 is attached if checked . . . . . ☐
4c	Total guaranteed payments	17	Alternative minimum tax (AMT) items
5	Interest income		
6a	Ordinary dividends		
6b	Qualified dividends	18	Tax-exempt income and nondeductible expenses
6c	Dividend equivalents		
7	Royalties		
8	Net short-term capital gain (loss)	19	Distributions
9a	Net long-term capital gain (loss)		
9b	Collectibles (28%) gain (loss)	20	Other information
9c	Unrecaptured section 1250 gain		
10	Net section 1231 gain (loss)		
11	Other income (loss)		
12	Section 179 deduction	21	Foreign taxes paid or accrued
13	Other deductions		

22 ☐ More than one activity for at-risk purposes*

23 ☐ More than one activity for passive activity purposes*

*See attached statement for additional information.

For IRS Use Only

For Paperwork Reduction Act Notice, see the Instructions for Form 1065. www.irs.gov/Form1065 Cat. No. 11394R **Schedule K-1 (Form 1065) 2022**

Form **1120**
Department of the Treasury
Internal Revenue Service

U.S. Corporation Income Tax Return

For calendar year 2022 or tax year beginning ________, 2022, ending ________, 20 ___

Go to *www.irs.gov/Form1120* for instructions and the latest information.

OMB No. 1545-0123

2022

A Check if:	TYPE OR PRINT		
1a Consolidated return (attach Form 851) ☐		Name	**B Employer identification number**
b Life/nonlife consolidated return . . ☐		Number, street, and room or suite no. If a P.O. box, see instructions.	**C** Date incorporated
2 Personal holding co. (attach Sch. PH) . ☐		City or town, state or province, country, and ZIP or foreign postal code	**D** Total assets (see instructions)
3 Personal service corp. (see instructions) . ☐			$
4 Schedule M-3 attached ☐	**E** Check if: **(1)** ☐ Initial return **(2)** ☐ Final return **(3)** ☐ Name change **(4)** ☐ Address change		

Income	1a	Gross receipts or sales	1a	
	b	Returns and allowances	1b	
	c	Balance. Subtract line 1b from line 1a		1c
	2	Cost of goods sold (attach Form 1125-A)		2
	3	Gross profit. Subtract line 2 from line 1c		3
	4	Dividends and inclusions (Schedule C, line 23)		4
	5	Interest		5
	6	Gross rents		6
	7	Gross royalties		7
	8	Capital gain net income (attach Schedule D (Form 1120))		8
	9	Net gain or (loss) from Form 4797, Part II, line 17 (attach Form 4797)		9
	10	Other income (see instructions—attach statement)		10
	11	**Total income.** Add lines 3 through 10		11
Deductions (See instructions for limitations on deductions.)	12	Compensation of officers (see instructions—attach Form 1125-E)		12
	13	Salaries and wages (less employment credits)		13
	14	Repairs and maintenance		14
	15	Bad debts		15
	16	Rents		16
	17	Taxes and licenses		17
	18	Interest (see instructions)		18
	19	Charitable contributions		19
	20	Depreciation from Form 4562 not claimed on Form 1125-A or elsewhere on return (attach Form 4562)		20
	21	Depletion		21
	22	Advertising		22
	23	Pension, profit-sharing, etc., plans		23
	24	Employee benefit programs		24
	25	Reserved for future use		25
	26	Other deductions (attach statement)		26
	27	**Total deductions.** Add lines 12 through 26		27
	28	Taxable income before net operating loss deduction and special deductions. Subtract line 27 from line 11		28
	29a	Net operating loss deduction (see instructions)	29a	
	b	Special deductions (Schedule C, line 24)	29b	
	c	Add lines 29a and 29b		29c
Tax, Refundable Credits, and Payments	30	**Taxable income.** Subtract line 29c from line 28. See instructions		30
	31	Total tax (Schedule J, Part I, line 11)		31
	32	Reserved for future use		32
	33	Total payments and credits (Schedule J, Part III, line 23)		33
	34	Estimated tax penalty. See instructions. Check if Form 2220 is attached ☐		34
	35	**Amount owed.** If line 33 is smaller than the total of lines 31 and 34, enter amount owed		35
	36	**Overpayment.** If line 33 is larger than the total of lines 31 and 34, enter amount overpaid		36
	37	Enter amount from line 36 you want: **Credited to 2023 estimated tax**	**Refunded**	37

Sign Here

Under penalties of perjury, I declare that I have examined this return, including accompanying schedules and statements, and to the best of my knowledge and belief, it is true, correct, and complete. Declaration of preparer (other than taxpayer) is based on all information of which preparer has any knowledge.

Signature of officer | Date | Title

May the IRS discuss this return with the preparer shown below? See instructions. ☐ **Yes** ☐ **No**

Paid Preparer Use Only	Print/Type preparer's name	Preparer's signature	Date	Check ☐ if self-employed	PTIN
	Firm's name			Firm's EIN	
	Firm's address			Phone no.	

For Paperwork Reduction Act Notice, see separate instructions. Cat. No. 11450Q Form **1120** (2022)

Form 1120 (2022) Page 2

Schedule C Dividends, Inclusions, and Special Deductions (see instructions)

		(a) Dividends and inclusions	(b) %	(c) Special deductions (a) × (b)
1	Dividends from less-than-20%-owned domestic corporations (other than debt-financed stock)		50	
2	Dividends from 20%-or-more-owned domestic corporations (other than debt-financed stock)		65	
3	Dividends on certain debt-financed stock of domestic and foreign corporations		See instructions	
4	Dividends on certain preferred stock of less-than-20%-owned public utilities		23.3	
5	Dividends on certain preferred stock of 20%-or-more-owned public utilities		26.7	
6	Dividends from less-than-20%-owned foreign corporations and certain FSCs		50	
7	Dividends from 20%-or-more-owned foreign corporations and certain FSCs		65	
8	Dividends from wholly owned foreign subsidiaries		100	
9	**Subtotal.** Add lines 1 through 8. See instructions for limitations		See instructions	
10	Dividends from domestic corporations received by a small business investment company operating under the Small Business Investment Act of 1958		100	
11	Dividends from affiliated group members		100	
12	Dividends from certain FSCs		100	
13	Foreign-source portion of dividends received from a specified 10%-owned foreign corporation (excluding hybrid dividends) (see instructions)		100	
14	Dividends from foreign corporations not included on line 3, 6, 7, 8, 11, 12, or 13 (including any hybrid dividends)			
15	Reserved for future use			
16a	Subpart F inclusions derived from the sale by a controlled foreign corporation (CFC) of the stock of a lower-tier foreign corporation treated as a dividend (attach Form(s) 5471) (see instructions)		100	
b	Subpart F inclusions derived from hybrid dividends of tiered corporations (attach Form(s) 5471) (see instructions)			
c	Other inclusions from CFCs under subpart F not included on line 16a, 16b, or 17 (attach Form(s) 5471) (see instructions)			
17	Global Intangible Low-Taxed Income (GILTI) (attach Form(s) 5471 and Form 8992)			
18	Gross-up for foreign taxes deemed paid			
19	IC-DISC and former DISC dividends not included on line 1, 2, or 3			
20	Other dividends			
21	Deduction for dividends paid on certain preferred stock of public utilities			
22	Section 250 deduction (attach Form 8993)			
23	**Total dividends and inclusions.** Add column (a), lines 9 through 20. Enter here and on page 1, line 4			
24	**Total special deductions.** Add column (c), lines 9 through 22. Enter here and on page 1, line 29b			

Form **1120** (2022)

Form 1120 (2022) Page **3**

Schedule J Tax Computation and Payment (see instructions)

Part I—Tax Computation

1	Check if the corporation is a member of a controlled group (attach Schedule O (Form 1120)). See instructions ☐				
2	Income tax. See instructions			2	
3	Base erosion minimum tax amount (attach Form 8991)			3	
4	Add lines 2 and 3			4	
5a	Foreign tax credit (attach Form 1118)	5a			
b	Credit from Form 8834 (see instructions)	5b			
c	General business credit (attach Form 3800)	5c			
d	Credit for prior year minimum tax (attach Form 8827)	5d			
e	Bond credits from Form 8912	5e			
6	**Total credits.** Add lines 5a through 5e			6	
7	Subtract line 6 from line 4			7	
8	Personal holding company tax (attach Schedule PH (Form 1120))			8	
9a	Recapture of investment credit (attach Form 4255)	9a			
b	Recapture of low-income housing credit (attach Form 8611)	9b			
c	Interest due under the look-back method—completed long-term contracts (attach Form 8697)	9c			
d	Interest due under the look-back method—income forecast method (attach Form 8866)	9d			
e	Alternative tax on qualifying shipping activities (attach Form 8902)	9e			
f	Interest/tax due under section 453A(c) and/or section 453(l)	9f			
g	Other (see instructions—attach statement)	9g			
10	**Total.** Add lines 9a through 9g			10	
11	**Total tax.** Add lines 7, 8, and 10. Enter here and on page 1, line 31			11	

Part II—Reserved For Future Use

12	Reserved for future use			12	

Part III—Payments and Refundable Credits

13	2021 overpayment credited to 2022			13	
14	2022 estimated tax payments			14	
15	2022 refund applied for on Form 4466			15	( )
16	Combine lines 13, 14, and 15			16	
17	Tax deposited with Form 7004			17	
18	Withholding (see instructions)			18	
19	**Total payments.** Add lines 16, 17, and 18			19	
20	Refundable credits from:				
a	Form 2439	20a			
b	Form 4136	20b			
c	Reserved for future use	20c			
d	Other (attach statement—see instructions)	20d			
21	**Total credits.** Add lines 20a through 20d			21	
22	Reserved for future use			22	
23	**Total payments and credits.** Add lines 19 and 21. Enter here and on page 1, line 33			23	

Form **1120** (2022)

Form 1120 (2022) Page **4**

Schedule K Other Information (see instructions)

		Yes	No
1	Check accounting method: **a** ☐ Cash **b** ☐ Accrual **c** ☐ Other (specify)		
2	See the instructions and enter the:		
a	Business activity code no.		
b	Business activity		
c	Product or service		
3	Is the corporation a subsidiary in an affiliated group or a parent–subsidiary controlled group? . . . . If "Yes," enter name and EIN of the parent corporation		
4	At the end of the tax year:		
a	Did any foreign or domestic corporation, partnership (including any entity treated as a partnership), trust, or tax-exempt organization own directly 20% or more, or own, directly or indirectly, 50% or more of the total voting power of all classes of the corporation's stock entitled to vote? If "Yes," complete Part I of Schedule G (Form 1120) (attach Schedule G)		
b	Did any individual or estate own directly 20% or more, or own, directly or indirectly, 50% or more of the total voting power of all classes of the corporation's stock entitled to vote? If "Yes," complete Part II of Schedule G (Form 1120) (attach Schedule G) .		
5	At the end of the tax year, did the corporation:		
a	Own directly 20% or more, or own, directly or indirectly, 50% or more of the total voting power of all classes of stock entitled to vote of any foreign or domestic corporation not included on **Form 851,** Affiliations Schedule? For rules of constructive ownership, see instructions. If "Yes," complete (i) through (iv) below.		

(i) Name of Corporation	**(ii)** Employer Identification Number (if any)	**(iii)** Country of Incorporation	**(iv)** Percentage Owned in Voting Stock

		Yes	No
b	Own directly an interest of 20% or more, or own, directly or indirectly, an interest of 50% or more in any foreign or domestic partnership (including an entity treated as a partnership) or in the beneficial interest of a trust? For rules of constructive ownership, see instructions. If "Yes," complete (i) through (iv) below.		

(i) Name of Entity	**(ii)** Employer Identification Number (if any)	**(iii)** Country of Organization	**(iv)** Maximum Percentage Owned in Profit, Loss, or Capital

		Yes	No
6	During this tax year, did the corporation pay dividends (other than stock dividends and distributions in exchange for stock) in excess of the corporation's current and accumulated earnings and profits? See sections 301 and 316 . . . . If "Yes," file **Form 5452,** Corporate Report of Nondividend Distributions. See the instructions for Form 5452. If this is a consolidated return, answer here for the parent corporation and on Form 851 for each subsidiary.		
7	At any time during the tax year, did one foreign person own, directly or indirectly, at least 25% of the total voting power of all classes of the corporation's stock entitled to vote or at least 25% of the total value of all classes of the corporation's stock? . For rules of attribution, see section 318. If "Yes," enter: **(a)** Percentage owned ______ and **(b)** Owner's country ______ **(c)** The corporation may have to file **Form 5472,** Information Return of a 25% Foreign-Owned U.S. Corporation or a Foreign Corporation Engaged in a U.S. Trade or Business. Enter the number of Forms 5472 attached		
8	Check this box if the corporation issued publicly offered debt instruments with original issue discount . . . . ☐ If checked, the corporation may have to file **Form 8281,** Information Return for Publicly Offered Original Issue Discount Instruments.		
9	Enter the amount of tax-exempt interest received or accrued during the tax year $		
10	Enter the number of shareholders at the end of the tax year (if 100 or fewer)		
11	If the corporation has an NOL for the tax year and is electing to forego the carryback period, check here (see instructions) ☐ If the corporation is filing a consolidated return, the statement required by Regulations section 1.1502-21(b)(3) must be attached or the election will not be valid.		
12	Enter the available NOL carryover from prior tax years (do not reduce it by any deduction reported on page 1, line 29a.) . . . . $		

Form **1120** (2022)

Schedule K Other Information *(continued from page 4)*

		Yes	No
13	Are the corporation's total receipts (page 1, line 1a, plus lines 4 through 10) for the tax year **and** its total assets at the end of the tax year less than $250,000?		
	If "Yes," the corporation is not required to complete Schedules L, M-1, and M-2. Instead, enter the total amount of cash distributions and the book value of property distributions (other than cash) made during the tax year $		
14	Is the corporation required to file Schedule UTP (Form 1120), Uncertain Tax Position Statement? See instructions		
	If "Yes," complete and attach Schedule UTP.		
15a	Did the corporation make any payments in 2022 that would require it to file Form(s) 1099?		
b	If "Yes," did or will the corporation file required Form(s) 1099?		
16	During this tax year, did the corporation have an 80%-or-more change in ownership, including a change due to redemption of its own stock?		
17	During or subsequent to this tax year, but before the filing of this return, did the corporation dispose of more than 65% (by value) of its assets in a taxable, non-taxable, or tax deferred transaction?		
18	Did the corporation receive assets in a section 351 transfer in which any of the transferred assets had a fair market basis or fair market value of more than $1 million?		
19	During the corporation's tax year, did the corporation make any payments that would require it to file Forms 1042 and 1042-S under chapter 3 (sections 1441 through 1464) or chapter 4 (sections 1471 through 1474) of the Code?		
20	Is the corporation operating on a cooperative basis?		
21	During the tax year, did the corporation pay or accrue any interest or royalty for which the deduction is not allowed under section 267A? See instructions		
	If "Yes," enter the total amount of the disallowed deductions $		
22	Does the corporation have gross receipts of at least $500 million in any of the 3 preceding tax years? (See sections 59A(e)(2) and (3))		
	If "Yes," complete and attach Form 8991.		
23	Did the corporation have an election under section 163(j) for any real property trade or business or any farming business in effect during the tax year? See instructions		
24	Does the corporation satisfy one or more of the following? See instructions		
a	The corporation owns a pass-through entity with current, or prior year carryover, excess business interest expense.		
b	The corporation's aggregate average annual gross receipts (determined under section 448(c)) for the 3 tax years preceding the current tax year are more than $27 million and the corporation has business interest expense.		
c	The corporation is a tax shelter and the corporation has business interest expense.		
	If "Yes," complete and attach Form 8990.		
25	Is the corporation attaching Form 8996 to certify as a Qualified Opportunity Fund?		
	If "Yes," enter amount from Form 8996, line 15 $		
26	Since December 22, 2017, did a foreign corporation directly or indirectly acquire substantially all of the properties held directly or indirectly by the corporation, and was the ownership percentage (by vote or value) for purposes of section 7874 greater than 50% (for example, the shareholders held more than 50% of the stock of the foreign corporation)? If "Yes," list the ownership percentage by vote and by value. See instructions		
	Percentage: By Vote By Value		

Schedule L **Balance Sheets per Books**

	Assets	Beginning of tax year (a)	(b)	End of tax year (c)	(d)
1	Cash				
2a	Trade notes and accounts receivable				
b	Less allowance for bad debts	( )		( )	
3	Inventories				
4	U.S. government obligations				
5	Tax-exempt securities (see instructions)				
6	Other current assets (attach statement)				
7	Loans to shareholders				
8	Mortgage and real estate loans				
9	Other investments (attach statement)				
10a	Buildings and other depreciable assets				
b	Less accumulated depreciation	( )		( )	
11a	Depletable assets				
b	Less accumulated depletion	( )		( )	
12	Land (net of any amortization)				
13a	Intangible assets (amortizable only)				
b	Less accumulated amortization	( )		( )	
14	Other assets (attach statement)				
15	Total assets				
	Liabilities and Shareholders' Equity				
16	Accounts payable				
17	Mortgages, notes, bonds payable in less than 1 year				
18	Other current liabilities (attach statement)				
19	Loans from shareholders				
20	Mortgages, notes, bonds payable in 1 year or more				
21	Other liabilities (attach statement)				
22	Capital stock: **a** Preferred stock				
	b Common stock				
23	Additional paid-in capital				
24	Retained earnings—Appropriated (attach statement)				
25	Retained earnings—Unappropriated				
26	Adjustments to shareholders' equity (attach statement)				
27	Less cost of treasury stock		( )		( )
28	Total liabilities and shareholders' equity				

Schedule M-1 **Reconciliation of Income (Loss) per Books With Income per Return**

Note: The corporation may be required to file Schedule M-3. See instructions.

1	Net income (loss) per books		7	Income recorded on books this year not included on this return (itemize): Tax-exempt interest $	
2	Federal income tax per books				
3	Excess of capital losses over capital gains				
4	Income subject to tax not recorded on books this year (itemize):		8	Deductions on this return not charged against book income this year (itemize):	
5	Expenses recorded on books this year not deducted on this return (itemize):		a	Depreciation $	
a	Depreciation $		b	Charitable contributions $	
b	Charitable contributions $				
c	Travel and entertainment $				
			9	Add lines 7 and 8	
6	Add lines 1 through 5		10	Income (page 1, line 28)—line 6 less line 9	

Schedule M-2 **Analysis of Unappropriated Retained Earnings per Books (Schedule L, Line 25)**

1	Balance at beginning of year		5	Distributions: **a** Cash	
2	Net income (loss) per books			**b** Stock	
3	Other increases (itemize):			**c** Property	
			6	Other decreases (itemize):	
			7	Add lines 5 and 6	
4	Add lines 1, 2, and 3		8	Balance at end of year (line 4 less line 7)	

SCHEDULE M-3 (Form 1120)
(Rev. December 2019)
Department of the Treasury
Internal Revenue Service

Net Income (Loss) Reconciliation for Corporations With Total Assets of $10 Million or More

▶ Attach to Form 1120 or 1120-C.
▶ Go to *www.irs.gov/Form1120* for instructions and the latest information.

OMB No. 1545-0123

Name of corporation (common parent, if consolidated return) | **Employer identification number**

Check applicable box(es): (1) ☐ Non-consolidated return (2) ☐ Consolidated return (Form 1120 only)
(3) ☐ Mixed 1120/L/PC group (4) ☐ Dormant subsidiaries schedule attached

Part I Financial Information and Net Income (Loss) Reconciliation (see instructions)

1a Did the corporation file SEC Form 10-K for its income statement period ending with or within this tax year?
☐ **Yes.** Skip lines 1b and 1c and complete lines 2a through 11 with respect to that SEC Form 10-K.
☐ **No.** Go to line 1b. See instructions if multiple non-tax-basis income statements are prepared.

b Did the corporation prepare a certified audited non-tax-basis income statement for that period?
☐ **Yes.** Skip line 1c and complete lines 2a through 11 with respect to that income statement.
☐ **No.** Go to line 1c.

c Did the corporation prepare a non-tax-basis income statement for that period?
☐ **Yes.** Complete lines 2a through 11 with respect to that income statement.
☐ **No.** Skip lines 2a through 3c and enter the corporation's net income (loss) per its books and records on line 4a.

2a Enter the income statement period: Beginning MM/DD/YYYY Ending MM/DD/YYYY

b Has the corporation's income statement been restated for the income statement period on line 2a?
☐ **Yes.** (If "Yes," attach an explanation and the amount of each item restated.)
☐ **No.**

c Has the corporation's income statement been restated for any of the five income statement periods immediately preceding the period on line 2a?
☐ **Yes.** (If "Yes," attach an explanation and the amount of each item restated.)
☐ **No.**

3a Is any of the corporation's voting common stock publicly traded?
☐ **Yes.**
☐ **No.** If "No," go to line 4a.

b Enter the symbol of the corporation's primary U.S. publicly traded voting common stock . . . .

c Enter the nine-digit CUSIP number of the corporation's primary publicly traded voting common stock . . . .

Line	Description	Box	Amount
4a	Worldwide consolidated net income (loss) from income statement source identified in Part I, line 1 .	4a	
b	Indicate accounting standard used for line 4a (see instructions): (1) ☐ GAAP (2) ☐ IFRS (3) ☐ Statutory (4) ☐ Tax-basis (5) ☐ Other (specify) ______		
5a	Net income from nonincludible foreign entities (attach statement)	5a	( )
b	Net loss from nonincludible foreign entities (attach statement and enter as a positive amount) . . .	5b	
6a	Net income from nonincludible U.S. entities (attach statement)	6a	( )
b	Net loss from nonincludible U.S. entities (attach statement and enter as a positive amount)	6b	
7a	Net income (loss) of other includible foreign disregarded entities (attach statement)	7a	
b	Net income (loss) of other includible U.S. disregarded entities (attach statement)	7b	
c	Net income (loss) of other includible entities (attach statement)	7c	
8	Adjustment to eliminations of transactions between includible entities and nonincludible entities (attach statement)	8	
9	Adjustment to reconcile income statement period to tax year (attach statement)	9	
10a	Intercompany dividend adjustments to reconcile to line 11 (attach statement)	10a	
b	Other statutory accounting adjustments to reconcile to line 11 (attach statement)	10b	
c	Other adjustments to reconcile to amount on line 11 (attach statement)	10c	
11	**Net income (loss) per income statement of includible corporations.** Combine lines 4 through 10 .	11	

Note: Part I, line 11, must equal Part II, line 30, column (a), or Schedule M-1, line 1 (see instructions).

12 Enter the total amount (not just the corporation's share) of the assets and liabilities of all entities included or removed on the following lines.

	Total Assets	Total Liabilities
a Included on Part I, line 4 . . . . ▶		
b Removed on Part I, line 5 . . . . ▶		
c Removed on Part I, line 6 . . . . ▶		
d Included on Part I, line 7 . . . . ▶		

Schedule M-3 (Form 1120) (Rev. 12-2019) Page 2

Name of corporation (common parent, if consolidated return)	Employer identification number

Check applicable box(es): (1) ☐ Consolidated group (2) ☐ Parent corp (3) ☐ Consolidated eliminations (4) ☐ Subsidiary corp (5) ☐ Mixed 1120/L/PC group

Check if a sub-consolidated: (6) ☐ 1120 group (7) ☐ 1120 eliminations

Name of subsidiary (if consolidated return)	Employer identification number

Part II Reconciliation of Net Income (Loss) per Income Statement of Includible Corporations With Taxable Income per Return (see instructions)

Income (Loss) Items (Attach statements for lines 1 through 12)	(a) Income (Loss) per Income Statement	(b) Temporary Difference	(c) Permanent Difference	(d) Income (Loss) per Tax Return
1 Income (loss) from equity method foreign corporations				
2 Gross foreign dividends not previously taxed . . .				
3 Subpart F, QEF, and similar income inclusions . .				
4 Gross-up for foreign taxes deemed paid				
5 Gross foreign distributions previously taxed . . .				
6 Income (loss) from equity method U.S. corporations				
7 U.S. dividends not eliminated in tax consolidation .				
8 Minority interest for includible corporations . . .				
9 Income (loss) from U.S. partnerships				
10 Income (loss) from foreign partnerships				
11 Income (loss) from other pass-through entities . .				
12 Items relating to reportable transactions				
13 Interest income (see instructions)				
14 Total accrual to cash adjustment				
15 Hedging transactions				
16 Mark-to-market income (loss)				
17 Cost of goods sold (see instructions)	( )			( )
18 Sale versus lease (for sellers and/or lessors) . . .				
19 Section 481(a) adjustments				
20 Unearned/deferred revenue				
21 Income recognition from long-term contracts . .				
22 Original issue discount and other imputed interest .				
23a Income statement gain/loss on sale, exchange, abandonment, worthlessness, or other disposition of assets other than inventory and pass-through entities				
b Gross capital gains from Schedule D, excluding amounts from pass-through entities				
c Gross capital losses from Schedule D, excluding amounts from pass-through entities, abandonment losses, and worthless stock losses				
d Net gain/loss reported on Form 4797, line 17, excluding amounts from pass-through entities, abandonment losses, and worthless stock losses .				
e Abandonment losses				
f Worthless stock losses (attach statement)				
g Other gain/loss on disposition of assets other than inventory				
24 Capital loss limitation and carryforward used . . .				
25 Other income (loss) items with differences (attach statement)				
26 **Total income (loss) items.** Combine lines 1 through 25				
27 **Total expense/deduction items** (from Part III, line 39)				
28 Other items with no differences				
29a Mixed groups, see instructions. All others, combine lines 26 through 28				
b PC insurance subgroup reconciliation totals . . .				
c Life insurance subgroup reconciliation totals . . .				
30 **Reconciliation totals.** Combine lines 29a through 29c				

Note: Line 30, column (a), must equal Part I, line 11, and column (d) must equal Form 1120, page 1, line 28.

Schedule M-3 (Form 1120) (Rev. 12-2019) Page **3**

Name of corporation (common parent, if consolidated return)	**Employer identification number**

Check applicable box(es): **(1)** ☐ Consolidated group **(2)** ☐ Parent corp **(3)** ☐ Consolidated eliminations **(4)** ☐ Subsidiary corp **(5)** ☐ Mixed 1120/L/PC group

Check if a sub-consolidated: **(6)** ☐ 1120 group **(7)** ☐ 1120 eliminations

Name of subsidiary (if consolidated return)	**Employer identification number**

Part III Reconciliation of Net Income (Loss) per Income Statement of Includible Corporations With Taxable Income per Return—Expense/Deduction Items (see instructions)

Expense/Deduction Items	(a) Expense per Income Statement	(b) Temporary Difference	(c) Permanent Difference	(d) Deduction per Tax Return
1 U.S. current income tax expense				
2 U.S. deferred income tax expense				
3 State and local current income tax expense				
4 State and local deferred income tax expense				
5 Foreign current income tax expense (other than foreign withholding taxes)				
6 Foreign deferred income tax expense				
7 Foreign withholding taxes				
8 Interest expense (see instructions)				
9 Stock option expense				
10 Other equity-based compensation				
11 Meals and entertainment				
12 Fines and penalties				
13 Judgments, damages, awards, and similar costs				
14 Parachute payments				
15 Compensation with section 162(m) limitation				
16 Pension and profit-sharing				
17 Other post-retirement benefits				
18 Deferred compensation				
19 Charitable contribution of cash and tangible property				
20 Charitable contribution of intangible property				
21 Charitable contribution limitation/carryforward				
22 Domestic production activities deduction (see instructions)				
23 Current year acquisition or reorganization investment banking fees				
24 Current year acquisition or reorganization legal and accounting fees				
25 Current year acquisition/reorganization other costs				
26 Amortization/impairment of goodwill				
27 Amortization of acquisition, reorganization, and start-up costs				
28 Other amortization or impairment write-offs				
29 Reserved				
30 Depletion				
31 Depreciation				
32 Bad debt expense				
33 Corporate owned life insurance premiums				
34 Purchase versus lease (for purchasers and/or lessees)				
35 Research and development costs				
36 Section 118 exclusion (attach statement)				
37 Section 162(r)—FDIC premiums paid by certain large financial institutions (see instructions)				
38 Other expense/deduction items with differences (attach statement)				
39 **Total expense/deduction items.** Combine lines 1 through 38. Enter here and on Part II, line 27, reporting positive amounts as negative and negative amounts as positive				

Form **1120-S**

Department of the Treasury
Internal Revenue Service

U.S. Income Tax Return for an S Corporation

Do not file this form unless the corporation has filed or is attaching Form 2553 to elect to be an S corporation.
Go to *www.irs.gov/Form1120S* for instructions and the latest information.

OMB No. 1545-0123

2022

For calendar year 2022 or tax year beginning , 2022, ending , 20

	TYPE OR PRINT	
A S election effective date	Name	**D Employer identification number**
B Business activity code number (see instructions)	Number, street, and room or suite no. If a P.O. box, see instructions.	**E** Date incorporated
C Check if Sch. M-3 attached ☐	City or town, state or province, country, and ZIP or foreign postal code	**F** Total assets (see instructions) $

G Is the corporation electing to be an S corporation beginning with this tax year? See instructions. ☐ Yes ☐ No

H Check if: **(1)** ☐ Final return **(2)** ☐ Name change **(3)** ☐ Address change **(4)** ☐ Amended return **(5)** ☐ S election termination

I Enter the number of shareholders who were shareholders during any part of the tax year . . . .

J Check if corporation: **(1)** ☐ Aggregated activities for section 465 at-risk purposes **(2)** ☐ Grouped activities for section 469 passive activity purposes

Caution: Include **only** trade or business income and expenses on lines 1a through 21. See the instructions for more information.

Income	1a	Gross receipts or sales	1a			
	b	Returns and allowances	1b			
	c	Balance. Subtract line 1b from line 1a			1c	
	2	Cost of goods sold (attach Form 1125-A)			2	
	3	Gross profit. Subtract line 2 from line 1c			3	
	4	Net gain (loss) from Form 4797, line 17 (attach Form 4797)			4	
	5	Other income (loss) (see instructions—attach statement)			5	
	6	**Total income (loss).** Add lines 3 through 5			6	
Deductions (see instructions for limitations)	7	Compensation of officers (see instructions—attach Form 1125-E)			7	
	8	Salaries and wages (less employment credits)			8	
	9	Repairs and maintenance			9	
	10	Bad debts			10	
	11	Rents			11	
	12	Taxes and licenses			12	
	13	Interest (see instructions)			13	
	14	Depreciation from Form 4562 not claimed on Form 1125-A or elsewhere on return (attach Form 4562)			14	
	15	Depletion **(Do not deduct oil and gas depletion.)**			15	
	16	Advertising			16	
	17	Pension, profit-sharing, etc., plans			17	
	18	Employee benefit programs			18	
	19	Other deductions (attach statement)			19	
	20	**Total deductions.** Add lines 7 through 19			20	
	21	**Ordinary business income (loss).** Subtract line 20 from line 6			21	
Tax and Payments	22a	Excess net passive income or LIFO recapture tax (see instructions)	22a			
	b	Tax from Schedule D (Form 1120-S)	22b			
	c	Add lines 22a and 22b (see instructions for additional taxes)			22c	
	23a	2022 estimated tax payments and 2021 overpayment credited to 2022	23a			
	b	Tax deposited with Form 7004	23b			
	c	Credit for federal tax paid on fuels (attach Form 4136)	23c			
	d	Add lines 23a through 23c			23d	
	24	Estimated tax penalty (see instructions). Check if Form 2220 is attached ☐			24	
	25	**Amount owed.** If line 23d is smaller than the total of lines 22c and 24, enter amount owed			25	
	26	**Overpayment.** If line 23d is larger than the total of lines 22c and 24, enter amount overpaid			26	
	27	Enter amount from line 26: **Credited to 2023 estimated tax** **Refunded**			27	

Sign Here

Under penalties of perjury, I declare that I have examined this return, including accompanying schedules and statements, and to the best of my knowledge and belief, it is true, correct, and complete. Declaration of preparer (other than taxpayer) is based on all information of which preparer has any knowledge.

Signature of officer | Date | Title

May the IRS discuss this return with the preparer shown below? See instructions. ☐ **Yes** ☐ **No**

Paid Preparer Use Only

Print/Type preparer's name	Preparer's signature	Date	Check ☐ if self-employed	PTIN
Firm's name			Firm's EIN	
Firm's address			Phone no.	

Form 1120-S (2022) Page **2**

Schedule B Other Information (see instructions)

		Yes	No
1	Check accounting method: a ☐ Cash b ☐ Accrual c ☐ Other (specify) ________		
2	See the instructions and enter the: **a** Business activity ________ **b** Product or service ________		
3	At any time during the tax year, was any shareholder of the corporation a disregarded entity, a trust, an estate, or a nominee or similar person? If "Yes," attach Schedule B-1, Information on Certain Shareholders of an S Corporation . .		
4	At the end of the tax year, did the corporation:		
a	Own directly 20% or more, or own, directly or indirectly, 50% or more of the total stock issued and outstanding of any foreign or domestic corporation? For rules of constructive ownership, see instructions. If "Yes," complete (i) through (v) below . . .		

(i) Name of Corporation	**(ii)** Employer Identification Number (if any)	**(iii)** Country of Incorporation	**(iv)** Percentage of Stock Owned	**(v)** If Percentage in (iv) Is 100%, Enter the Date (if applicable) a Qualified Subchapter S Subsidiary Election Was Made

		Yes	No
b	Own directly an interest of 20% or more, or own, directly or indirectly, an interest of 50% or more in the profit, loss, or capital in any foreign or domestic partnership (including an entity treated as a partnership) or in the beneficial interest of a trust? For rules of constructive ownership, see instructions. If "Yes," complete (i) through (v) below . . .		

(i) Name of Entity	**(ii)** Employer Identification Number (if any)	**(iii)** Type of Entity	**(iv)** Country of Organization	**(v)** Maximum Percentage Owned in Profit, Loss, or Capital

		Yes	No
5a	At the end of the tax year, did the corporation have any outstanding shares of restricted stock? . . .		
	If "Yes," complete lines (i) and (ii) below.		
	(i) Total shares of restricted stock . . . ________		
	(ii) Total shares of non-restricted stock . . . ________		
b	At the end of the tax year, did the corporation have any outstanding stock options, warrants, or similar instruments? .		
	If "Yes," complete lines (i) and (ii) below.		
	(i) Total shares of stock outstanding at the end of the tax year . . ________		
	(ii) Total shares of stock outstanding if all instruments were executed ________		
6	Has this corporation filed, or is it required to file, **Form 8918,** Material Advisor Disclosure Statement, to provide information on any reportable transaction? . . .		
7	Check this box if the corporation issued publicly offered debt instruments with original issue discount . . . ☐		
	If checked, the corporation may have to file **Form 8281,** Information Return for Publicly Offered Original Issue Discount Instruments.		
8	If the corporation **(a)** was a C corporation before it elected to be an S corporation **or** the corporation acquired an asset with a basis determined by reference to the basis of the asset (or the basis of any other property) in the hands of a C corporation, **and (b)** has net unrealized built-in gain in excess of the net recognized built-in gain from prior years, enter the net unrealized built-in gain reduced by net recognized built-in gain from prior years. See instructions . . . $ ________		
9	Did the corporation have an election under section 163(j) for any real property trade or business or any farming business in effect during the tax year? See instructions . . .		
10	Does the corporation satisfy one or more of the following? See instructions . . .		
a	The corporation owns a pass-through entity with current, or prior year carryover, excess business interest expense.		
b	The corporation's aggregate average annual gross receipts (determined under section 448(c)) for the 3 tax years preceding the current tax year are more than $27 million and the corporation has business interest expense.		
c	The corporation is a tax shelter and the corporation has business interest expense.		
	If "Yes," complete and attach **Form 8990**, Limitation on Business Interest Expense Under Section 163(j).		
11	Does the corporation satisfy **both** of the following conditions? . . .		
a	The corporation's total receipts (see instructions) for the tax year were less than $250,000.		
b	The corporation's total assets at the end of the tax year were less than $250,000.		
	If "Yes," the corporation is not required to complete Schedules L and M-1.		

Form 1120-S (2022) Page 3

Schedule B Other Information (see instructions) *(continued)*

		Yes	No
12	During the tax year, did the corporation have any non-shareholder debt that was canceled, was forgiven, or had the terms modified so as to reduce the principal amount of the debt?		
	If "Yes," enter the amount of principal reduction . . . $		
13	During the tax year, was a qualified subchapter S subsidiary election terminated or revoked? If "Yes," see instructions		
14a	Did the corporation make any payments in 2022 that would require it to file Form(s) 1099?		
b	If "Yes," did or will the corporation file required Form(s) 1099?		
15	Is the corporation attaching Form 8996 to certify as a Qualified Opportunity Fund?		
	If "Yes," enter the amount from Form 8996, line 15 . . . $		

Schedule K Shareholders' Pro Rata Share Items

					Total amount
Income (Loss)	1	Ordinary business income (loss) (page 1, line 21)		1	
	2	Net rental real estate income (loss) (attach Form 8825)		2	
	3a	Other gross rental income (loss)	3a		
	b	Expenses from other rental activities (attach statement)	3b		
	c	Other net rental income (loss). Subtract line 3b from line 3a		3c	
	4	Interest income		4	
	5	Dividends: **a** Ordinary dividends		5a	
		b Qualified dividends	5b		
	6	Royalties		6	
	7	Net short-term capital gain (loss) (attach Schedule D (Form 1120-S))		7	
	8a	Net long-term capital gain (loss) (attach Schedule D (Form 1120-S))		8a	
	b	Collectibles (28%) gain (loss)	8b		
	c	Unrecaptured section 1250 gain (attach statement)	8c		
	9	Net section 1231 gain (loss) (attach Form 4797)		9	
	10	Other income (loss) (see instructions) . . . Type:		10	
Deductions	11	Section 179 deduction (attach Form 4562)		11	
	12a	Charitable contributions		12a	
	b	Investment interest expense		12b	
	c	Section 59(e)(2) expenditures . . . Type:		12c	
	d	Other deductions (see instructions) . . . Type:		12d	
Credits	13a	Low-income housing credit (section 42(j)(5))		13a	
	b	Low-income housing credit (other)		13b	
	c	Qualified rehabilitation expenditures (rental real estate) (attach Form 3468, if applicable)		13c	
	d	Other rental real estate credits (see instructions) Type:		13d	
	e	Other rental credits (see instructions) . . . Type:		13e	
	f	Biofuel producer credit (attach Form 6478)		13f	
	g	Other credits (see instructions) . . . Type:		13g	
International	14	Attach Schedule K-2 (Form 1120-S), Shareholders' Pro Rata Share Items—International, and check this box to indicate you are reporting items of international tax relevance ☐			
Alternative Minimum Tax (AMT) Items	15a	Post-1986 depreciation adjustment		15a	
	b	Adjusted gain or loss		15b	
	c	Depletion (other than oil and gas)		15c	
	d	Oil, gas, and geothermal properties—gross income		15d	
	e	Oil, gas, and geothermal properties—deductions		15e	
	f	Other AMT items (attach statement)		15f	
Items Affecting Shareholder Basis	16a	Tax-exempt interest income		16a	
	b	Other tax-exempt income		16b	
	c	Nondeductible expenses		16c	
	d	Distributions (attach statement if required) (see instructions)		16d	
	e	Repayment of loans from shareholders		16e	
	f	Foreign taxes paid or accrued		16f	

Form **1120-S** (2022)

Form 1120-S (2022) Page **4**

Schedule K		**Shareholders' Pro Rata Share Items** *(continued)*		**Total amount**
Other Information	**17a**	Investment income	**17a**	
	b	Investment expenses	**17b**	
	c	Dividend distributions paid from accumulated earnings and profits	**17c**	
	d	Other items and amounts (attach statement)		
Recon-ciliation	**18**	**Income (loss) reconciliation.** Combine the amounts on lines 1 through 10 in the far right column. From the result, subtract the sum of the amounts on lines 11 through 12d and 16f	**18**	

Schedule L **Balance Sheets per Books**	Beginning of tax year		End of tax year	
Assets	**(a)**	**(b)**	**(c)**	**(d)**
1 Cash				
2a Trade notes and accounts receivable				
b Less allowance for bad debts	( )		( )	
3 Inventories				
4 U.S. government obligations				
5 Tax-exempt securities (see instructions)				
6 Other current assets (attach statement)				
7 Loans to shareholders				
8 Mortgage and real estate loans				
9 Other investments (attach statement)				
10a Buildings and other depreciable assets				
b Less accumulated depreciation	( )		( )	
11a Depletable assets				
b Less accumulated depletion	( )		( )	
12 Land (net of any amortization)				
13a Intangible assets (amortizable only)				
b Less accumulated amortization	( )		( )	
14 Other assets (attach statement)				
15 Total assets				
Liabilities and Shareholders' Equity				
16 Accounts payable				
17 Mortgages, notes, bonds payable in less than 1 year				
18 Other current liabilities (attach statement)				
19 Loans from shareholders				
20 Mortgages, notes, bonds payable in 1 year or more				
21 Other liabilities (attach statement)				
22 Capital stock				
23 Additional paid-in capital				
24 Retained earnings				
25 Adjustments to shareholders' equity (attach statement)				
26 Less cost of treasury stock		( )		( )
27 Total liabilities and shareholders' equity				

Form 1120-S (2022) Page 5

Schedule M-1 Reconciliation of Income (Loss) per Books With Income (Loss) per Return

Note: The corporation may be required to file Schedule M-3. See instructions.

1	Net income (loss) per books		5	Income recorded on books this year not included on Schedule K, lines 1 through 10 (itemize):	
2	Income included on Schedule K, lines 1, 2, 3c, 4, 5a, 6, 7, 8a, 9, and 10, not recorded on books this year (itemize)		a	Tax-exempt interest $	
3	Expenses recorded on books this year not included on Schedule K, lines 1 through 12, and 16f (itemize):		6	Deductions included on Schedule K, lines 1 through 12, and 16f, not charged against book income this year (itemize):	
a	Depreciation $		a	Depreciation $	
b	Travel and entertainment $		7	Add lines 5 and 6	
4	Add lines 1 through 3		8	Income (loss) (Schedule K, line 18). Subtract line 7 from line 4	

Schedule M-2 Analysis of Accumulated Adjustments Account, Shareholders' Undistributed Taxable Income Previously Taxed, Accumulated Earnings and Profits, and Other Adjustments Account (see instructions)

		(a) Accumulated adjustments account	**(b)** Shareholders' undistributed taxable income previously taxed	**(c)** Accumulated earnings and profits	**(d)** Other adjustments account
1	Balance at beginning of tax year				
2	Ordinary income from page 1, line 21				
3	Other additions				
4	Loss from page 1, line 21	( )			
5	Other reductions	( )			( )
6	Combine lines 1 through 5				
7	Distributions				
8	Balance at end of tax year. Subtract line 7 from line 6				

Form **1120-S** (2022)

671121

☐ Final K-1 ☐ Amended K-1 OMB No. 1545-0123

Schedule K-1 (Form 1120-S) **2022**

Department of the Treasury
Internal Revenue Service

For calendar year 2022, or tax year

beginning / / 2022 ending / /

Shareholder's Share of Income, Deductions, Credits, etc.

See separate instructions.

Part I Information About the Corporation

A Corporation's employer identification number

B Corporation's name, address, city, state, and ZIP code

C IRS Center where corporation filed return

D Corporation's total number of shares
Beginning of tax year . . . . . . ______
End of tax year . . . . ______

Part II Information About the Shareholder

E Shareholder's identifying number

F Shareholder's name, address, city, state, and ZIP code

G Current year allocation percentage . . . ______ %

H Shareholder's number of shares
Beginning of tax year . . . . . . ______
End of tax year . . . . ______

I Loans from shareholder
Beginning of tax year . . . . . . $ ______
End of tax year . . . . $ ______

For IRS Use Only

Part III Shareholder's Share of Current Year Income, Deductions, Credits, and Other Items

1	Ordinary business income (loss)	13	Credits
2	Net rental real estate income (loss)		
3	Other net rental income (loss)		
4	Interest income		
5a	Ordinary dividends		
5b	Qualified dividends	14	Schedule K-3 is attached if checked . . . . . ☐
6	Royalties	15	Alternative minimum tax (AMT) items
7	Net short-term capital gain (loss)		
8a	Net long-term capital gain (loss)		
8b	Collectibles (28%) gain (loss)		
8c	Unrecaptured section 1250 gain		
9	Net section 1231 gain (loss)	16	Items affecting shareholder basis
10	Other income (loss)		
		17	Other information
11	Section 179 deduction		
12	Other deductions		

18 ☐ More than one activity for at-risk purposes*
19 ☐ More than one activity for passive activity purposes*

* See attached statement for additional information.

Form **4797**

Department of the Treasury
Internal Revenue Service

Sales of Business Property

(Also Involuntary Conversions and Recapture Amounts Under Sections 179 and 280F(b)(2))

Attach to your tax return.

Go to *www.irs.gov/Form4797* for instructions and the latest information.

OMB No. 1545-0184

2022

Attachment Sequence No. 27

Name(s) shown on return	**Identifying number**

1a	Enter the gross proceeds from sales or exchanges reported to you for 2022 on Form(s) 1099-B or 1099-S (or substitute statement) that you are including on line 2, 10, or 20. See instructions	1a	
b	Enter the total amount of gain that you are including on lines 2, 10, and 24 due to the partial dispositions of MACRS assets	1b	
c	Enter the total amount of loss that you are including on lines 2 and 10 due to the partial dispositions of MACRS assets	1c	

Part I Sales or Exchanges of Property Used in a Trade or Business and Involuntary Conversions From Other Than Casualty or Theft—Most Property Held More Than 1 Year (see instructions)

2 (a) Description of property	(b) Date acquired (mo., day, yr.)	(c) Date sold (mo., day, yr.)	(d) Gross sales price	(e) Depreciation allowed or allowable since acquisition	(f) Cost or other basis, plus improvements and expense of sale	(g) Gain or (loss) Subtract (f) from the sum of (d) and (e)

3	Gain, if any, from Form 4684, line 39	3	
4	Section 1231 gain from installment sales from Form 6252, line 26 or 37	4	
5	Section 1231 gain or (loss) from like-kind exchanges from Form 8824	5	
6	Gain, if any, from line 32, from other than casualty or theft	6	
7	Combine lines 2 through 6. Enter the gain or (loss) here and on the appropriate line as follows	7	
	Partnerships and S corporations. Report the gain or (loss) following the instructions for Form 1065, Schedule K, line 10, or Form 1120-S, Schedule K, line 9. Skip lines 8, 9, 11, and 12 below.		
	Individuals, partners, S corporation shareholders, and all others. If line 7 is zero or a loss, enter the amount from line 7 on line 11 below and skip lines 8 and 9. If line 7 is a gain and you didn't have any prior year section 1231 losses, or they were recaptured in an earlier year, enter the gain from line 7 as a long-term capital gain on the Schedule D filed with your return and skip lines 8, 9, 11, and 12 below.		
8	Nonrecaptured net section 1231 losses from prior years. See instructions	8	
9	Subtract line 8 from line 7. If zero or less, enter -0-. If line 9 is zero, enter the gain from line 7 on line 12 below. If line 9 is more than zero, enter the amount from line 8 on line 12 below and enter the gain from line 9 as a long-term capital gain on the Schedule D filed with your return. See instructions	9	

Part II Ordinary Gains and Losses (see instructions)

10 Ordinary gains and losses not included on lines 11 through 16 (include property held 1 year or less):

11	Loss, if any, from line 7	11	( )
12	Gain, if any, from line 7 or amount from line 8, if applicable	12	
13	Gain, if any, from line 31	13	
14	Net gain or (loss) from Form 4684, lines 31 and 38a	14	
15	Ordinary gain from installment sales from Form 6252, line 25 or 36	15	
16	Ordinary gain or (loss) from like-kind exchanges from Form 8824	16	
17	Combine lines 10 through 16	17	
18	For all except individual returns, enter the amount from line 17 on the appropriate line of your return and skip lines a and b below. For individual returns, complete lines a and b below.		
a	If the loss on line 11 includes a loss from Form 4684, line 35, column (b)(ii), enter that part of the loss here. Enter the loss from income-producing property on Schedule A (Form 1040), line 16. (Do not include any loss on property used as an employee.) Identify as from "Form 4797, line 18a." See instructions	18a	
b	Redetermine the gain or (loss) on line 17 excluding the loss, if any, on line 18a. Enter here and on Schedule 1 (Form 1040), Part I, line 4	18b	

For Paperwork Reduction Act Notice, see separate instructions. Cat. No. 13086I Form **4797** (2022)

Form 4797 (2022) Page **2**

Part III Gain From Disposition of Property Under Sections 1245, 1250, 1252, 1254, and 1255 (see instructions)

19 **(a)** Description of section 1245, 1250, 1252, 1254, or 1255 property:	**(b)** Date acquired (mo., day, yr.)	**(c)** Date sold (mo., day, yr.)
A		
B		
C		
D		

These columns relate to the properties on lines 19A through 19D.		Property A	Property B	Property C	Property D
20 Gross sales price (**Note:** *See line 1a before completing.*) .	20				
21 Cost or other basis plus expense of sale	21				
22 Depreciation (or depletion) allowed or allowable . . .	22				
23 Adjusted basis. Subtract line 22 from line 21	23				
24 Total gain. Subtract line 23 from line 20	24				
25 **If section 1245 property:**					
a Depreciation allowed or allowable from line 22 . . .	25a				
b Enter the **smaller** of line 24 or 25a.	25b				
26 **If section 1250 property:** If straight line depreciation was used, enter -0- on line 26g, except for a corporation subject to section 291.					
a Additional depreciation after 1975. See instructions .	26a				
b Applicable percentage multiplied by the **smaller** of line 24 or line 26a. See instructions.	26b				
c Subtract line 26a from line 24. If residential rental property **or** line 24 isn't more than line 26a, skip lines 26d and 26e	26c				
d Additional depreciation after 1969 and before 1976. .	26d				
e Enter the **smaller** of line 26c or 26d	26e				
f Section 291 amount (corporations only)	26f				
g Add lines 26b, 26e, and 26f	26g				
27 **If section 1252 property:** Skip this section if you didn't dispose of farmland or if this form is being completed for a partnership.					
a Soil, water, and land clearing expenses	27a				
b Line 27a multiplied by applicable percentage. See instructions	27b				
c Enter the **smaller** of line 24 or 27b	27c				
28 **If section 1254 property:**					
a Intangible drilling and development costs, expenditures for development of mines and other natural deposits, mining exploration costs, and depletion. See instructions	28a				
b Enter the **smaller** of line 24 or 28a.	28b				
29 **If section 1255 property:**					
a Applicable percentage of payments excluded from income under section 126. See instructions	29a				
b Enter the **smaller** of line 24 or 29a. See instructions .	29b				

Summary of Part III Gains. Complete property columns A through D through line 29b before going to line 30.

30 Total gains for all properties. Add property columns A through D, line 24	30	
31 Add property columns A through D, lines 25b, 26g, 27c, 28b, and 29b. Enter here and on line 13	31	
32 Subtract line 31 from line 30. Enter the portion from casualty or theft on Form 4684, line 33. Enter the portion from other than casualty or theft on Form 4797, line 6	32	

Part IV Recapture Amounts Under Sections 179 and 280F(b)(2) When Business Use Drops to 50% or Less (see instructions)

		(a) Section 179	(b) Section 280F(b)(2)
33 Section 179 expense deduction or depreciation allowable in prior years.	33		
34 Recomputed depreciation. See instructions	34		
35 Recapture amount. Subtract line 34 from line 33. See the instructions for where to report . .	35		

Form **8949**

Department of the Treasury
Internal Revenue Service

Sales and Other Dispositions of Capital Assets

Go to *www.irs.gov/Form8949* for instructions and the latest information.

File with your Schedule D to list your transactions for lines 1b, 2, 3, 8b, 9, and 10 of Schedule D.

OMB No. 1545-0074

2022

Attachment Sequence No. **12A**

Name(s) shown on return | **Social security number or taxpayer identification number**

Before you check Box A, B, or C below, see whether you received any Form(s) 1099-B or substitute statement(s) from your broker. A substitute statement will have the same information as Form 1099-B. Either will show whether your basis (usually your cost) was reported to the IRS by your broker and may even tell you which box to check.

Part I **Short-Term.** Transactions involving capital assets you held 1 year or less are generally short-term (see instructions). For long-term transactions, see page 2.

Note: You may aggregate all short-term transactions reported on Form(s) 1099-B showing basis was reported to the IRS and for which no adjustments or codes are required. Enter the totals directly on Schedule D, line 1a; you aren't required to report these transactions on Form 8949 (see instructions).

You *must* check Box A, B, *or* C below. Check only one box. If more than one box applies for your short-term transactions, complete a separate Form 8949, page 1, for each applicable box. If you have more short-term transactions than will fit on this page for one or more of the boxes, complete as many forms with the same box checked as you need.

☐ **(A)** Short-term transactions reported on Form(s) 1099-B showing basis was reported to the IRS (see **Note** above)
☐ **(B)** Short-term transactions reported on Form(s) 1099-B showing basis **wasn't** reported to the IRS
☐ **(C)** Short-term transactions not reported to you on Form 1099-B

1 (a) Description of property (Example: 100 sh. XYZ Co.)	(b) Date acquired (Mo., day, yr.)	(c) Date sold or disposed of (Mo., day, yr.)	(d) Proceeds (sales price) (see instructions)	(e) Cost or other basis See the **Note** below and see *Column (e)* in the separate instructions.	Adjustment, if any, to gain or loss If you enter an amount in column (g), enter a code in column (f). **See the separate instructions.** (f) Code(s) from instructions	(g) Amount of adjustment	(h) **Gain or (loss)** Subtract column (e) from column (d) and combine the result with column (g).
2 Totals. Add the amounts in columns (d), (e), (g), and (h) (subtract negative amounts). Enter each total here and include on your Schedule D, **line 1b** (if **Box A** above is checked), **line 2** (if **Box B** above is checked), or **line 3** (if **Box C** above is checked) . .							

Note: If you checked Box A above but the basis reported to the IRS was incorrect, enter in column (e) the basis as reported to the IRS, and enter an adjustment in column (g) to correct the basis. See *Column (g)* in the separate instructions for how to figure the amount of the adjustment.

Form 8949 (2022) Attachment Sequence No. **12A** Page **2**

Name(s) shown on return. Name and SSN or taxpayer identification no. not required if shown on other side	**Social security number or taxpayer identification number**

Before you check Box D, E, or F below, see whether you received any Form(s) 1099-B or substitute statement(s) from your broker. A substitute statement will have the same information as Form 1099-B. Either will show whether your basis (usually your cost) was reported to the IRS by your broker and may even tell you which box to check.

Part II **Long-Term.** Transactions involving capital assets you held more than 1 year are generally long-term (see instructions). For short-term transactions, see page 1.

Note: You may aggregate all long-term transactions reported on Form(s) 1099-B showing basis was reported to the IRS and for which no adjustments or codes are required. Enter the totals directly on Schedule D, line 8a; you aren't required to report these transactions on Form 8949 (see instructions).

You *must* check Box D, E, *or* F below. Check only one box. If more than one box applies for your long-term transactions, complete a separate Form 8949, page 2, for each applicable box. If you have more long-term transactions than will fit on this page for one or more of the boxes, complete as many forms with the same box checked as you need.

☐ **(D)** Long-term transactions reported on Form(s) 1099-B showing basis was reported to the IRS (see **Note** above)
☐ **(E)** Long-term transactions reported on Form(s) 1099-B showing basis **wasn't** reported to the IRS
☐ **(F)** Long-term transactions not reported to you on Form 1099-B

1 (a) Description of property (Example: 100 sh. XYZ Co.)	(b) Date acquired (Mo., day, yr.)	(c) Date sold or disposed of (Mo., day, yr.)	(d) Proceeds (sales price) (see instructions)	(e) Cost or other basis See the **Note** below and see *Column (e)* in the separate instructions.	**Adjustment, if any, to gain or loss** If you enter an amount in column (g), enter a code in column (f). **See the separate instructions.** (f) Code(s) from instructions	(g) Amount of adjustment	(h) **Gain or (loss)** Subtract column (e) from column (d) and combine the result with column (g).
2 Totals. Add the amounts in columns (d), (e), (g), and (h) (subtract negative amounts). Enter each total here and include on your Schedule D, **line 8b** (if **Box D** above is checked), **line 9** (if **Box E** above is checked), or **line 10** (if **Box F** above is checked) . .							

Note: If you checked Box D above but the basis reported to the IRS was incorrect, enter in column (e) the basis as reported to the IRS, and enter an adjustment in column (g) to correct the basis. See *Column (g)* in the separate instructions for how to figure the amount of the adjustment.

Form **8960**

Department of the Treasury
Internal Revenue Service

Net Investment Income Tax— Individuals, Estates, and Trusts

Attach to your tax return.

Go to *www.irs.gov/Form8960* for instructions and the latest information.

OMB No. 1545-2227

2022

Attachment Sequence No. **72**

Name(s) shown on your tax return | **Your social security number or EIN**

Part I Investment Income

☐ Section 6013(g) election (see instructions)
☐ Section 6013(h) election (see instructions)
☐ Regulations section 1.1411-10(g) election (see instructions)

1	Taxable interest (see instructions)			1	
2	Ordinary dividends (see instructions)			2	
3	Annuities (see instructions)			3	
4a	Rental real estate, royalties, partnerships, S corporations, trusts, etc. (see instructions)	4a			
b	Adjustment for net income or loss derived in the ordinary course of a non-section 1411 trade or business (see instructions)	4b			
c	Combine lines 4a and 4b			4c	
5a	Net gain or loss from disposition of property (see instructions)	5a			
b	Net gain or loss from disposition of property that is not subject to net investment income tax (see instructions)	5b			
c	Adjustment from disposition of partnership interest or S corporation stock (see instructions)	5c			
d	Combine lines 5a through 5c			5d	
6	Adjustments to investment income for certain CFCs and PFICs (see instructions)			6	
7	Other modifications to investment income (see instructions)			7	
8	Total investment income. Combine lines 1, 2, 3, 4c, 5d, 6, and 7			8	

Part II Investment Expenses Allocable to Investment Income and Modifications

9a	Investment interest expenses (see instructions)	9a			
b	State, local, and foreign income tax (see instructions)	9b			
c	Miscellaneous investment expenses (see instructions)	9c			
d	Add lines 9a, 9b, and 9c			9d	
10	Additional modifications (see instructions)			10	
11	Total deductions and modifications. Add lines 9d and 10			11	

Part III Tax Computation

12	Net investment income. Subtract Part II, line 11, from Part I, line 8. Individuals, complete lines 13–17. Estates and trusts, complete lines 18a–21. If zero or less, enter -0-			12	
	Individuals:				
13	Modified adjusted gross income (see instructions)	13			
14	Threshold based on filing status (see instructions)	14			
15	Subtract line 14 from line 13. If zero or less, enter -0-	15			
16	Enter the smaller of line 12 or line 15			16	
17	Net investment income tax for individuals. Multiply line 16 by 3.8% (0.038). **Enter here and include on your tax return** (see instructions)			17	
	Estates and Trusts:				
18a	Net investment income (line 12 above)	18a			
b	Deductions for distributions of net investment income and deductions under section 642(c) (see instructions)	18b			
c	Undistributed net investment income. Subtract line 18b from line 18a (see instructions). If zero or less, enter -0-	18c			
19a	Adjusted gross income (see instructions)	19a			
b	Highest tax bracket for estates and trusts for the year (see instructions)	19b			
c	Subtract line 19b from line 19a. If zero or less, enter -0-	19c			
20	Enter the smaller of line 18c or line 19c			20	
21	Net investment income tax for estates and trusts. Multiply line 20 by 3.8% (0.038). **Enter here and include on your tax return** (see instructions)			21	

For Paperwork Reduction Act Notice, see your tax return instructions. Cat. No. 59474M Form **8960** (2022)

Form **8995**

Department of the Treasury
Internal Revenue Service

Qualified Business Income Deduction Simplified Computation

Attach to your tax return.

Go to *www.irs.gov/Form8995* for instructions and the latest information.

OMB No. 1545-2294

2022

Attachment Sequence No. **55**

Name(s) shown on return | **Your taxpayer identification number**

Note. *You can claim the qualified business income deduction* **only** *if you have qualified business income from a qualified trade or business, real estate investment trust dividends, publicly traded partnership income, or a domestic production activities deduction passed through from an agricultural or horticultural cooperative. See instructions.*
Use this form if your taxable income, before your qualified business income deduction, is at or below $170,050 ($340,100 if married filing jointly), and you aren't a patron of an agricultural or horticultural cooperative.

1	**(a)** Trade, business, or aggregation name	**(b)** Taxpayer identification number	**(c)** Qualified business income or (loss)
i			
ii			
iii			
iv			
v			

2	Total qualified business income or (loss). Combine lines 1i through 1v, column (c)	2			
3	Qualified business net (loss) carryforward from the prior year	3	( )		
4	Total qualified business income. Combine lines 2 and 3. If zero or less, enter -0-	4			
5	Qualified business income component. Multiply line 4 by 20% (0.20)			5	
6	Qualified REIT dividends and publicly traded partnership (PTP) income or (loss) (see instructions)	6			
7	Qualified REIT dividends and qualified PTP (loss) carryforward from the prior year	7	( )		
8	Total qualified REIT dividends and PTP income. Combine lines 6 and 7. If zero or less, enter -0-	8			
9	REIT and PTP component. Multiply line 8 by 20% (0.20)			9	
10	Qualified business income deduction before the income limitation. Add lines 5 and 9			10	
11	Taxable income before qualified business income deduction (see instructions)	11			
12	Net capital gain (see instructions)	12			
13	Subtract line 12 from line 11. If zero or less, enter -0-	13			
14	Income limitation. Multiply line 13 by 20% (0.20)			14	
15	Qualified business income deduction. Enter the smaller of line 10 or line 14. Also enter this amount on the applicable line of your return (see instructions)			15	
16	Total qualified business (loss) carryforward. Combine lines 2 and 3. If greater than zero, enter -0-			16	( )
17	Total qualified REIT dividends and PTP (loss) carryforward. Combine lines 6 and 7. If greater than zero, enter -0-			17	( )

For Privacy Act and Paperwork Reduction Act Notice, see instructions. Cat. No. 37806C Form **8995** (2022)

Form **8995-A** Department of the Treasury Internal Revenue Service

Qualified Business Income Deduction

Attach to your tax return.

Go to *www.irs.gov/Form8995A* for instructions and the latest information.

OMB No. 1545-2294 | 2022 | Attachment Sequence No. **55A**

Name(s) shown on return | **Your taxpayer identification number**

Note: *You can claim the qualified business income deduction* ***only*** *if you have qualified business income from a qualified trade or business, real estate investment trust dividends, publicly traded partnership income, or a domestic production activities deduction passed through from an agricultural or horticultural cooperative. See instructions.*

Use this form if your taxable income, before your qualified business income deduction, is above $170,050 ($340,100 if married filing jointly), or you're a patron of an agricultural or horticultural cooperative.

Part I Trade, Business, or Aggregation Information

Complete Schedules A, B, and/or C (Form 8995-A), as applicable, before starting Part I. Attach additional worksheets when needed. See instructions.

1	**(a)** Trade, business, or aggregation name	**(b)** Check if specified service	**(c)** Check if aggregation	**(d)** Taxpayer identification number	**(e)** Check if patron
A		☐	☐		☐
B		☐	☐		☐
C		☐	☐		☐

Part II Determine Your Adjusted Qualified Business Income

			A	B	C
2	Qualified business income from the trade, business, or aggregation. See instructions	2			
3	Multiply line 2 by 20% (0.20). If your taxable income is $170,050 or less ($340,100 if married filing jointly), skip lines 4 through 12 and enter the amount from line 3 on line 13	3			
4	Allocable share of W-2 wages from the trade, business, or aggregation	4			
5	Multiply line 4 by 50% (0.50)	5			
6	Multiply line 4 by 25% (0.25)	6			
7	Allocable share of the unadjusted basis immediately after acquisition (UBIA) of all qualified property	7			
8	Multiply line 7 by 2.5% (0.025)	8			
9	Add lines 6 and 8	9			
10	Enter the greater of line 5 or line 9	10			
11	W-2 wage and UBIA of qualified property limitation. Enter the smaller of line 3 or line 10	11			
12	Phased-in reduction. Enter the amount from line 26, if any	12			
13	Qualified business income deduction before patron reduction. Enter the greater of line 11 or line 12	13			
14	Patron reduction. Enter the amount from Schedule D (Form 8995-A), line 6, if any. See instructions	14			
15	Qualified business income component. Subtract line 14 from line 13	15			
16	Total qualified business income component. Add all amounts reported on line 15	16			

Form 8995-A (2022) Page **2**

Part III Phased-in Reduction

Complete Part III only if your taxable income is more than $170,050 but not $220,050 ($340,100 and $440,100 if married filing jointly) and line 10 is less than line 3. Otherwise, skip Part III.

					A	B	C
17	Enter the amounts from line 3			17			
18	Enter the amounts from line 10			18			
19	Subtract line 18 from line 17			19			
20	Taxable income before qualified business income deduction	20					
21	Threshold. Enter $170,050 ($340,100 if married filing jointly)	21					
22	Subtract line 21 from line 20	22					
23	Phase-in range. Enter $50,000 ($100,000 if married filing jointly)	23					
24	Phase-in percentage. Divide line 22 by line 23	24	%				
25	Total phase-in reduction. Multiply line 19 by line 24			25			
26	Qualified business income after phase-in reduction. Subtract line 25 from line 17. Enter this amount here and on line 12, for the corresponding trade or business			26			

Part IV Determine Your Qualified Business Income Deduction

27	Total qualified business income component from all qualified trades, businesses, or aggregations. Enter the amount from line 16	27			
28	Qualified REIT dividends and publicly traded partnership (PTP) income or (loss). See instructions	28			
29	Qualified REIT dividends and PTP (loss) carryforward from prior years	29	( )		
30	Total qualified REIT dividends and PTP income. Combine lines 28 and 29. If less than zero, enter -0-	30			
31	REIT and PTP component. Multiply line 30 by 20% (0.20)	31			
32	Qualified business income deduction before the income limitation. Add lines 27 and 31			32	
33	Taxable income before qualified business income deduction	33			
34	Net capital gain. See instructions	34			
35	Subtract line 34 from line 33. If zero or less, enter -0-			35	
36	Income limitation. Multiply line 35 by 20% (0.20)			36	
37	Qualified business income deduction before the domestic production activities deduction (DPAD) under section 199A(g). Enter the smaller of line 32 or line 36			37	
38	DPAD under section 199A(g) allocated from an agricultural or horticultural cooperative. Don't enter more than line 33 minus line 37			38	
39	Total qualified business income deduction. Add lines 37 and 38			39	
40	Total qualified REIT dividends and PTP (loss) carryforward. Combine lines 28 and 29. If zero or greater, enter -0-			40	( )

Form **8995-A** (2022)

Appendix C

Glossary

The key terms in this glossary have been defined to reflect their conventional use in the field of taxation. The definitions may therefore be incomplete for other purposes.

A

AAA bypass election. In the context of a distribution by an S corporation, an election made by the entity to designate that the distribution is first from accumulated earnings and profits (AEP) and only then from the accumulated adjustments account (AAA). § 1368(e)(3).

Abandoned spouse. The abandoned spouse provision enables a married taxpayer with a dependent child whose spouse did not live in the taxpayer's home during the last six months of the tax year to file as a head of household rather than as married filing separately. §§ 2(b) and 7703(b).

Accelerated cost recovery system (ACRS). A method in which the cost of tangible property is recovered (depreciated) over a prescribed period of time. This depreciation approach disregards salvage value, imposes a period of cost recovery that depends upon the classification of the asset into one of various recovery periods, and prescribes the applicable percentage of cost that can be deducted each year. A modified system is currently the default cost recovery method; it is referred to as MACRS. § 168.

Accelerated death benefits. The amount received from a life insurance policy by the insured who is terminally ill or chronically ill. Any realized gain may be excluded from the gross income of the insured if the policy is surrendered to the insurer or is sold to a licensed viatical settlement provider. § 101(g).

Acceleration rule. Treatment of an intercompany transaction on a consolidated return, when the corporation that sold an asset leaves the consolidated group.

Accident and health benefits. Employee fringe benefits provided by employers through the payment of health and accident insurance premiums or the establishment of employer-funded medical reimbursement plans. Employers generally are entitled to a deduction for such payments, whereas employees generally exclude such fringe benefits from gross income. §§ 105 and 106.

Accident and health insurance benefits. See *accident and health benefits*.

Accountable plan. A type of expense reimbursement plan that requires an employee to render an adequate accounting to the employer and return any excess reimbursement or allowance. If the expense qualifies, it will be treated as a deduction *for* AGI. §§ 62(a)(2)(A) and (c).

Accounting income. The accountant's concept of income is generally based upon the realization principle. Financial accounting income may differ from taxable income (e.g., accelerated depreciation might be used for Federal income tax and straight-line depreciation for financial accounting purposes). Differences are included in a reconciliation of taxable and accounting income on Schedule M–1 or Schedule M–3 of Form 1120 for corporations.

Accounting method. The method under which income and expenses are determined for tax purposes. Important tax accounting methods include the cash basis and the accrual basis. Special methods are available for the reporting of gain on installment sales, recognition of income on construction projects (the completed contract and percentage of completion methods), and the valuation of inventories (last-in, first-out and first-in, first-out). Accounting methods deal with the timing of *when* income and deductions are reported. §§ 446–474.

Accounting period. The period of time, usually a year, used by a taxpayer for the determination of tax liability. Unless a fiscal year is chosen, taxpayers must determine and pay their income tax liability by using the calendar year (January 1 through December 31) as the period of measurement. An example of a fiscal year is July 1 through June 30. A change in accounting period (e.g., from a calendar year to a fiscal year) generally requires the consent of the IRS. Usually, taxpayers are free to select either an initial calendar or a fiscal year without the consent of the IRS. §§ 441–444.

Accrual method. A method of accounting that recognizes expenses when incurred and income when earned. In contrast to the cash basis of accounting, expenses need not be paid to be deductible, nor need income be received to be taxable. § 446(c)(2).

Accumulated adjustments account (AAA). An account that aggregates an S corporation's post-1982 income, loss, and deductions for the tax year (including nontaxable income and nondeductible losses and expenses). After the year-end income and expense adjustments are made, the account is reduced by distributions made during the tax year.

Accumulated E & P. Net undistributed tax-basis earnings of a corporation aggregated from March 1, 1913, to the end of the prior tax year. Used to determine the amount of dividend income associated with a distribution to shareholders. § 316 and Reg. § 1.316–2.

Accumulated earnings tax. A special 20 percent tax imposed on C corporations that accumulate (rather than distribute) their earnings beyond the reasonable needs of the business. The accumulated earnings tax and related interest are imposed on accumulated taxable income in addition to the corporate income tax. §§ 531–537.

Accuracy-related penalties. Major civil taxpayer penalties relating to the accuracy of tax return data, including misstatements stemming from taxpayer negligence and improper valuation of income and deductions, are coordinated under this umbrella term. The penalty usually equals 20 percent of the understated tax liability. § 6662.

Acquiescence. Agreement by the IRS on the results reached in certain judicial decisions; sometimes abbreviated *Acq.* or *A.*

Acquisition indebtedness. Debt incurred in acquiring, constructing, or substantially improving a qualified residence of the taxpayer. The interest on such loans is deductible as qualified residence interest. However, interest on such debt is deductible only on the portion of the indebtedness that does not exceed $750,000 ($1,000,000 for debt incurred before December 15, 2017). § 163(h)(3).

Active income. Wages, salary, commissions, bonuses, profits from a trade or business in which the taxpayer is a material participant, gain on the sale or other disposition of assets used in an active trade or business, and income from intangible property if the taxpayer's personal efforts significantly contributed to the creation of the property. The passive activity loss rules require classification of income and losses into three categories with active income being one of them.

Ad valorem taxes. A tax imposed on the value of property. The most common ad valorem tax is that imposed by states, counties, and cities on real estate. Ad valorem taxes can be imposed on personal property as well.

Additional first-year depreciation. In general, this provision provides for an additional cost recovery deduction of 100 percent for qualified property acquired and placed in service after September 27, 2017, and before January 1, 2027. The bonus depreciation percentage is reduced by 20 percent for each tax year after 2022. For 2023, the bonus deprecation percentage is 80 percent. Qualified property includes most types of new and used property other than buildings. The taxpayer can elect to forgo this bonus depreciation. Different rules applied between 2008 and September 28, 2017. § 168(k).

Adjusted basis. The cost or other basis of property reduced by depreciation allowed or allowable and increased by capital improvements. Other special adjustments are provided in § 1016 and the related Regulations.

Adjusted gross estate. Used in determining eligibility for deferred payments of Federal estate tax. The gross estate less the sum allowable as deductions under § 2053 (expenses, indebtedness, and taxes) and § 2054 (casualty and theft losses during the administration of the estate). § 6166(b)(6).

Adjustments. In calculating AMTI, certain amounts (i.e., adjustments) are added to or deducted from the taxable income starting point of the AMTI calculation. These adjustments generally reflect timing differences. § 56.

Adoption expenses credit. A provision intended to assist taxpayers who incur nonrecurring costs directly associated with the adoption process, such as legal costs, social service review costs, and transportation costs. Up to $15,950 of costs incurred to adopt an eligible child qualify for the credit (unique rules apply when adopting a special needs child). A taxpayer may claim the credit in the year qualifying expenses are paid or incurred if the expenses are paid during or after the year in which the adoption is finalized. For qualifying expenses paid or incurred in a tax year prior to the year the adoption is finalized, the credit must be claimed in the tax year following the tax year during which the expenses are paid or incurred. § 23.

Affiliated group. A parent-subsidiary group of corporations that is eligible to elect to file on a consolidated basis. Eighty percent ownership of the voting power and value of all of the corporations must be achieved every day of the tax year, and an identifiable parent corporation must exist (i.e., it must own at least 80 percent of another group member without applying attribution rules). § 1504(a).

Aggregate (or conduit) concept. A perspective that regards a venture as an aggregation of its owners joined together in an agency relationship rather than as a separate entity. For tax purposes, this results in the income of the venture being taxable directly to its owners. For example, partnership income and expense, capital gains and losses, tax credits, etc., pass through the partnership (a conduit) and are subject to taxation at the partner level. Also, in an S corporation, certain items pass through and are reported on the returns of the shareholders. See also *entity perspective.*

Alimony and separate maintenance payments. Alimony deductions result from the payment of a legal obligation arising from the termination of a marital relationship. Payments designated as alimony generally are included in the gross income of the recipient and are deductible *for* AGI by the payor. For divorce or separation instruments executed after December 31, 2018, alimony is neither gross income for the recipient nor deductible by the payor. § 71.

All events test. As applied to the recognition of income, the all events test requires that income of an accrual basis taxpayer be recognized when (1) all events have occurred that fix the taxpayer's right to receive the income and (2) the amount can be determined with reasonable accuracy. Under § 451(b), an accrual method taxpayer must include amounts in income no later than for financial reporting purposes (other than for special rules such as the installment method). As applied to the recognition of expenses, the all events test prevents the recognition of a deduction by an accrual basis taxpayer until all the events have occurred that fix the taxpayer's related obligation. This can be contrasted with GAAP under which a fixed or legal obligation is not required before an expense is recognized. Reg. §§ 1.446–1(c)(1)(ii) and 1.461–1(a)(2).

Allocate. The assignment of income for various tax purposes. A multistate corporation's nonbusiness income usually is allocated to the state where the nonbusiness assets are located; it is not apportioned with the rest of the entity's income. The income and expense items of an estate or a trust are allocated between income and corpus components. Specific items of income, expense, gain, loss, and credit can be allocated to specific partners if a substantial economic nontax purpose for the allocation is established.

Alternate valuation date. Property passing from a decedent by death may be valued for estate tax purposes as of the date of death or the alternate valuation date. The alternate valuation date is six months after the date of death or the date the property is disposed of by the estate, whichever comes first. To use the alternate valuation date, the executor or administrator of the estate must make an affirmative election. The election applies to all of the estate's assets. Election of the alternate valuation date is not available unless it decreases the amount of the gross estate and reduces the estate tax liability. § 2032.

Alternative depreciation system (ADS). A cost recovery system in which the cost or other initial basis of an asset is recovered using the straight-line method over recovery periods similar to those used in MACRS. The alternative system must be used in certain instances and can be elected in other instances. § 168(g).

Alternative minimum tax (AMT). For taxpayers other than a corporation, the AMT is a surtax, calculated as a percentage of alternative minimum taxable income (AMTI). AMTI generally starts with the taxpayer's taxable income, prior to any standard deduction taken. To this amount, the taxpayer (1) adds designated preference items (e.g., tax-exempt interest income on private activity bonds), (2) makes other specified adjustments (e.g., to reflect a slower cost recovery method), (3) adjusts certain AMT itemized deductions (e.g., interest incurred on housing), and (4) subtracts an exemption amount. The taxpayer must pay the greater of the resulting AMT or the regular income tax (reduced by all allowable tax credits). AMT preferences and adjustments are assigned to partners, LLC members, and S corporation shareholders. For tax years beginning after 2022, an AMT applies to any corporation (other than an S corporation) with more than $1 billion in average annual adjusted financial statement income (AFSI) for the three-year period ending with the tax year. The AMT is equal to the excess of any applicable corporation's tentative minimum tax over its regular tax including any base erosion and anti-abuse tax (BEAT). Tentative minimum tax is equal to 15 percent of the AFSI for the year, less any corporate AMT foreign tax credit for the year. "Adjusted financial statement income" is the net income (or loss) reported on the corporation's financial statement for the tax year, as modified by certain adjustments. For instance, AFSI is computed by deducting tax depreciation rather than book depreciation. §§ 55–59.

Alternative minimum tax credit. For noncorporate taxpayers, AMT liability can result from timing differences that give rise to positive adjustments in calculating AMTI. To provide equity for the taxpayer when these timing differences reverse, the regular tax liability may be reduced by a tax credit for a prior year's minimum tax liability attributable to timing differences. The corporate AMT also results in a tax credit, regardless of the type of book-tax differences contributing to the tax liability, that can be carried forward to reduce a corporation's regular tax in future tax years. § 53.

Alternative minimum taxable income (AMTI). The base (prior to deducting the exemption amount) for computing a taxpayer's alternative minimum tax. This consists of the taxable income for the year modified for AMT adjustments and AMT preferences. § 55(b)(2).

Alternative tax. An option that is allowed in computing the tax on net capital gain. For noncorporate taxpayers, the rate is usually 15 percent (but is 25 percent for unrecaptured § 1250 gain and 28 percent for collectibles). However, the alternative tax rate is 0 percent (rather than 15 percent) for lower-income taxpayers (e.g., taxable income of $89,250 or less for married persons filing jointly). Certain high-income taxpayers (e.g., taxable income of more than $553,850 for married persons filing jointly) have an alternative tax rate of 20 percent. § 1(h).

Alternative tax NOL deduction (ATNOLD). In calculating the AMT, a noncorporate taxpayer is allowed to deduct NOL carryovers following the regular tax NOL carryover provisions. The AMT NOL amount is referred to as the ATNOLD. The regular income tax NOL is modified for AMT adjustments and preferences to produce the ATNOLD. § 56(d).

Amended tax return. An amended tax return is filed to make corrections to a tax return from a previous year. For example, an amended tax return is filed if there is an error in the reporting of income, deductions, and/or tax credits on the original return.

American Opportunity credit. This credit applies for qualifying expenses for the first four years of postsecondary education. Qualified expenses include tuition and related expenses and books and other course materials. Room and board are ineligible for the credit. The maximum credit available per student is $2,500 (100 percent of the first $2,000 of qualified expenses and 25 percent of the next $2,000 of qualified expenses). Eligible students include the taxpayer, taxpayer's spouse, and taxpayer's dependents. To qualify for the credit, a student must take at least one-half of the full-time course load for at least one academic term at a qualifying educational institution. The credit is phased out for higher-income taxpayers. § 25A.

Amortization. The tax deduction for the cost or other basis of an intangible asset over the asset's estimated useful life. Examples of amortizable intangibles include patents, copyrights, and leasehold interests. Most purchased intangible assets (e.g., goodwill) can be amortized for income tax purposes over a 15-year period. § 197.

Amount realized. The amount received by a taxpayer upon the sale or exchange of property. Amount realized is the sum of the cash and the fair market value of any property or services received by the taxpayer plus any related debt assumed by the buyer. Determining the amount realized is the starting point for arriving at realized gain or loss. § 1001(b).

Annual exclusion. In computing the taxable gifts for the year, each donor excludes the first $17,000 (for 2023) of a gift to each donee. Usually, the annual exclusion is not available for gifts of future interests. § 2503(b).

Annuity. A fixed sum of money payable to a person at specified times for a specified period of time or for life. If the party making the payment (i.e., the obligor) is regularly engaged in this type of business (e.g., an insurance company), the arrangement is classified as a commercial annuity. A so-called private annuity involves an obligor that is not regularly engaged in selling annuities (e.g., a charity or family member).

Apportion. The assignment of the business income of a multistate corporation to specific states for income taxation. Usually, the apportionment procedure accounts for the property, payroll, and sales activity levels of the various states, and a proportionate assignment of the entity's total income is made using a statutory apportionment formula. Most states exclude nonbusiness income from the apportionment procedure; they allocate nonbusiness income to the states where the nonbusiness assets are located.

Appreciated inventory. In partnership taxation, appreciated inventory is a hot asset, and a partner's share of its ordinary income potential must be allocated to that partner. If a partner sells an interest in the partnership, ordinary income is recognized to the extent of the partner's share of the partnership's inventory and unrealized receivables. The definition of "inventory" here is broad enough to include any accounts receivable, including unrealized receivables. See also *substantially appreciated inventory*. § 751.

Arm's length. See *arm's length price*.

Arm's length price. The standard under which unrelated parties would determine an exchange price for a transaction. Suppose, for example, Cardinal Corporation sells property to its sole shareholder for $10,000. In testing whether the $10,000 is an "arm's length" price, one would ascertain the price that would have been negotiated between the corporation and an unrelated party in a bargained exchange.

ASC 740. Accounting Standards Codification 740 governs how companies report the effects of income taxes on their financial statements under U.S. generally accepted accounting principles (GAAP). The Standard generally requires the recognition of a liability for any income tax related to the income reported in the financial statements regardless of when that tax is legally due and payable.

Asset Depreciation Range (ADR) system. A system of estimated useful lives for categories of tangible assets prescribed by the IRS. The system provides a range for each category that extends from 20 percent above to 20 percent below the guideline class lives prescribed by the IRS.

Asset use test. In the context of a corporate reorganization, a means by which to determine if the continuity of business enterprise requirement is met. The acquiring corporation must continue to use the target entity's assets in the acquiror's business going forward; if this is not the case, the requirement is failed.

Assignment of income. A taxpayer attempts to avoid the recognition of income by assigning to another the property that generates the income. Such a procedure will not avoid income recognition by the taxpayer making the assignment if the income was earned at the point of the transfer. In this case, the income is taxed to the person who earns it.

At-risk limitation. Generally, a taxpayer can deduct losses related to a trade or business, S corporation, partnership, or investment asset only to the extent of the at-risk amount. The taxpayer has an amount at risk in a business or investment venture to the extent that personal assets have been subjected to the risks of the business. Typically, the taxpayer's at-risk amount includes (1) the amount of money or other property that the investor contributed to the venture for the investment, (2) the amount of any of the entity's liabilities for which the taxpayer personally is liable and that relate to the investment, and (3) an allocable share of nonrecourse debts incurred by the venture from third parties in arm's length transactions for real estate investments. § 465.

Attribution. Under certain circumstances, the tax law applies attribution (constructive ownership) rules to assign to one taxpayer the ownership interest of another taxpayer. If, for example, the stock of Gold Corporation is held 60 percent by Marsha and 40 percent by Sidney, Marsha may be deemed to own 100 percent of Gold Corporation if Marsha and Sidney are mother and child. In that case, the stock owned by Sidney is attributed to Marsha. Stated differently, Marsha has a 60 percent direct and a 40 percent indirect interest in Gold Corporation. It can also be said that Marsha is the constructive owner of Sidney's interest.

Automatic mileage method. Automobile expenses are generally deductible only to the extent the automobile is used in business or for the production of income. Personal commuting expenses are not deductible. The taxpayer may deduct actual expenses (including depreciation and insurance), or the standard (automatic) mileage rate may be used. For 2023, the rate is 65.5 cents per mile (58.5 cents per mile for first six months of 2022 and 62.5 cents per mile for final six months of 2022). Automobile expenses incurred for medical purposes are deductible to the extent of actual out-of-pocket expenses or at the rate of 22 cents per mile for 2023 (18 cents per mile for first six months of 2022 and 22 cents per mile for final six months of 2022). For charitable activities, the rate is 14 cents per mile.

Average tax rate. The average tax rate is equal to the tax liability divided by taxable income. This rate can be useful in comparing taxpayers or a taxpayer's changed tax picture from one year to another.

B

Bad debt. A deduction is permitted if a business account receivable subsequently becomes partially or completely worthless, providing the income arising from the debt previously was included in income. Available methods are the specific charge-off method and the reserve method. However, except for certain financial institutions, the reserve method may not be used for tax purposes. A nonbusiness bad debt deduction is allowed as a short-term capital loss if the loan did not arise in connection with the creditor's trade or business activities. Loans between related parties (family members) generally are classified as nonbusiness. § 166.

Balance sheet approach. The process under ASC 740 by which an entity's deferred tax expense or deferred tax benefit is determined as a result of the reporting period's changes in the balance sheet's deferred tax asset and deferred tax liability accounts.

Base Erosion and Anti-Abuse Tax (BEAT). A 10 percent minimum tax designed to prevent multinational corporations from shifting profits out of the United States to a foreign subsidiary located in a low-tax jurisdiction. § 59A.

Basis in partnership interest. Initially, the acquisition cost of the partner's ownership interest in the partnership. Includes purchase price and associated debt acquired from other partners and in the course of the entity's trade or business.

The basis is adjusted to reflect the partner's distributive share of partnership income, gain, deductions, losses, and distributions. §§ 705, 722, and 742.

Benchmarking. The tax professional's use of two or more entities' effective tax rates and deferred tax balance sheet accounts. Used chiefly to compare the effectiveness of the entities' tax planning techniques and to suggest future tax-motivated courses of action.

Blockage rule. A factor to be considered in valuing a large block of corporate stock. Application of this rule generally justifies a discount in the asset's fair market value, because the disposition of a large amount of stock at any one time may depress the value of the shares in the marketplace.

Boot. Cash or property of a type not included in the definition of a tax-deferred exchange. The receipt of boot causes an otherwise tax-deferred transfer to become immediately taxable to the extent of the lesser of the fair market value of the boot or the realized gain on the transfer. For example, see transfers to controlled corporations under § 351(b), reorganizations under § 368, and like-kind exchanges under § 1031(b).

Built-in gains tax. A penalty tax designed to discourage a shift of the incidence of taxation on unrealized gains from a C corporation to its shareholders, via an S election. Under this provision, any recognized gain during the first five years of S status generates a corporate-level tax on a base not to exceed the aggregate untaxed built-in gains brought into the S corporation upon its election from C corporation taxable years. § 1374.

Built-in loss property. Property contributed to a corporation under § 351 or as a contribution to capital that has a basis in excess of its fair market value. An adjustment is necessary to step down the basis of the property to its fair market value. The adjustment prevents the corporation and the contributing shareholder from obtaining a double tax benefit. The corporation allocates the adjustment proportionately among the assets with the built-in loss. As an alternative to the corporate adjustment, the shareholder may elect to reduce the basis in the stock. § 362(e).

Business bad debt. A tax deduction allowed for obligations obtained in connection with a trade or business that have become either partially or completely worthless. In contrast to nonbusiness bad debts, business bad debts are deductible as business expenses. § 166.

Business purpose. A justifiable business reason for carrying out a transaction. Mere tax avoidance is not an acceptable business purpose. The presence of a business purpose is crucial in the area of corporate reorganizations and certain liquidations.

Buy-sell agreement. An arrangement, particularly appropriate in the case of a closely held corporation or a partnership, whereby the surviving owners (shareholders or partners) or the entity agrees to purchase the interest of a withdrawing owner. The buy-sell agreement provides for an orderly disposition of an interest in a business and may aid in setting the value of the interest for estate tax purposes.

Bypass amount. The amount that can be transferred by gift or at death free of any unified transfer tax. For 2023, the bypass amount is $12,920,000 for estate tax and $12,920,000 for gift tax. §§ 2010 and 2505.

Bypass election. In the context of a distribution by an S corporation, an election made by the entity to designate that the distribution is first from accumulated earnings and profits and only then from the accumulated adjustments account (AAA). § 1368(e)(3).

C

C corporation. A separate taxable entity subject to the rules of Subchapter C of the Code. This business form may create a double taxation effect relative to its shareholders. The entity is subject to the regular corporate tax and a number of penalty taxes at the Federal level.

Cafeteria plan. An employee benefit plan under which an employee is allowed to select from among a variety of employer-provided fringe benefits. Some of the benefits may be taxable, and some may be statutory nontaxable benefits (e.g., health and accident insurance and group term life insurance). The employee is taxed only on the taxable benefits selected. A cafeteria benefit plan is also referred to as a flexible benefit plan. § 125.

Capital account. The financial accounting analog of a partner's tax basis in the entity.

Capital account maintenance. Under the § 704(b) Regulations, partnership allocations will be respected only if capital accounts are maintained in accordance with those Regulations. These so-called "§ 704(b) book capital accounts" are properly maintained if they reflect the partner's contributions and distributions of cash; increases and decreases for the fair market value of contributed/distributed property; and adjustments for the partner's share of income, gains, losses, and deductions. Certain other adjustments are also required. See also *economic effect test* and *Section 704(b) book capital accounts.*

Capital asset. Broadly speaking, all assets are capital except those specifically excluded from that definition by the Code. Major categories of noncapital assets include property held for resale in the normal course of business (inventory), trade accounts and notes receivable, and depreciable property and real estate used in a trade or business (§ 1231 assets). § 1221.

Capital contribution. Various means by which a shareholder makes additional funds available to the corporation (placed at the risk of the business), sometimes without the receipt of additional stock. If no stock is received, the contributions are added to the basis of the shareholder's existing stock investment and do not generate gross income to the corporation. § 118.

Capital gain property. Property contributed to a charitable organization that, if sold rather than contributed, would have resulted in long-term capital gain to the donor. § 170(e).

Capital gains. The gain from the sale or exchange of a capital asset.

Capital interest. Usually, the percentage of the entity's net assets that a partner would receive on liquidation. Typically determined by the partner's capital sharing ratio.

Capital losses. The loss from the sale or exchange of a capital asset.

Capital sharing ratio. A partner's percentage ownership of the entity's capital.

Carbon tax. A tax on fossil fuels to help reduce greenhouse gas emissions.

Carried interest. A "partnership interest held in connection with performance of services," as defined under § 1061. Long-term capital gains from such an interest are reclassified as short-term capital gains (with potential ordinary income treatment) unless the underlying asset that triggered the gain had more than a three-year holding period. This provision only applies to income and gains arising from managing portfolio investments on behalf of third-party investors, including publicly traded securities, commodities, certain real estate, or options to buy/sell such assets. Section 1061 was enacted in the TCJA of 2017 in an effort to curtail an industry practice that resulted in fund managers receiving partnership profits interests in exchange for services: these "profits partners" received long-term capital gain allocations from the fund, rather than ordinary income for the services provided in managing the fund's assets. In addition to § 1061, the IRS has, from time to time, announced that it might issue Regulations (under its general "anti-abuse" authority) to expand the scope of the carried interest rules.

Cash balance plan. A hybrid form of pension plan similar in some aspects to a defined benefit plan. Such a plan is funded by the employer, and the employer bears the investment risks and rewards. But like defined contribution plans, a cash balance plan establishes allocations to individual employee accounts, and the payout for an employee depends on investment performance.

Cash method. A method of accounting that reflects deductions as paid and income as received in any one tax year. However, deductions for prepaid expenses that benefit more than one tax year (e.g., prepaid rent and prepaid interest) usually are spread over the period benefited rather than deducted in the year paid. § 446(c)(1).

Casualty loss. A casualty is defined as "the complete or partial destruction of property resulting from an identifiable event of a sudden, unexpected, or unusual nature" (e.g., floods, storms, fires, auto accidents). Individuals may deduct a casualty loss only if the loss is incurred in a trade or business or in a transaction entered into for profit or arises from fire, storm, shipwreck, or other casualty or from theft. Individuals usually deduct personal casualty losses as itemized deductions subject to a $100 nondeductible amount and to an annual floor equal to 10 percent of adjusted gross income that applies after the $100 per casualty floor has been applied. Special rules are provided for the netting of certain casualty gains and losses. For tax years beginning after 2017 (and before 2026), personal casualty losses are limited to those sustained in an area designated as a disaster area by the President of the United States. §§ 165(c)(3) and (h).

Charitable contribution. Contributions made to qualified nonprofit organizations. Taxpayers, regardless of their accounting method, are generally allowed to deduct (subject to various restrictions and limitations) contributions in the year of payment. Accrual basis corporations may accrue contributions at year-end if payment is properly authorized before the end of the year and payment is made within three and one-half months after the end of the year. § 170.

Check-the-box Regulations. By using the check-the-box rules prudently, an entity can select the most attractive tax results offered by the Code, without being bound by legal forms. By default, an unincorporated entity with more than one owner is taxed as a partnership; an unincorporated entity with one owner is a disregarded entity, taxed as a sole proprietorship or corporate division. No action is necessary by the taxpayer if the legal form or default status is desired. Form 8832 is used to "check a box" and change the tax status. Not available if the entity is incorporated under state law.

Child tax credit. A tax credit based solely on the number of qualifying children under age 17. The maximum credit available is $2,000 per qualifying child. (In addition, a $500 nonrefundable credit is available for qualifying dependents other than qualifying children.) A qualifying child must be claimed as a dependent on a parent's tax return and have a Social Security number to qualify for the credit. Taxpayers who qualify for the child tax credit may also qualify for a supplemental credit. The supplemental credit is treated as a component of the earned income credit and is therefore refundable. The credit is phased out for higher-income taxpayers. § 24. See also *dependent tax credit*.

Circuit Court of Appeals. Any of 13 Federal courts that consider tax matters appealed from the U.S. Tax Court, a U.S. District Court, or the U.S. Court of Federal Claims. Appeal from a U.S. Court of Appeals is to the U.S. Supreme Court by Certiorari.

Circular 230. A portion of the Federal tax Regulations that describes the levels of conduct at which a tax preparer must operate. Circular 230 dictates, for instance, that a tax preparer may not charge an unconscionable fee or delay the execution of a tax audit with inappropriate delays. Circular 230 requires that there be a reasonable basis for a tax return position and that no frivolous returns be filed.

Citator. A tax research resource that presents the judicial history of a court case and traces the subsequent references to the case. When these references include the citating cases' evaluations of the cited case's precedents, the research can obtain some measure of the efficacy and reliability of the original holding.

Claim of right doctrine. A judicially imposed doctrine applicable to both cash and accrual basis taxpayers that holds that an amount is includible in income upon actual or constructive receipt even if the payment is subject to an unsettled dispute. For the tax treatment of amounts repaid when previously included in income under the claim of right doctrine, see § 1341.

Closely held C corporation. A regular corporation (i.e., the S election is not in effect) for which more than 50 percent of the value of its outstanding stock is owned, directly or indirectly, by five or fewer individuals at any time during the tax year. The term is relevant in identifying C corporations that are subject to the passive activity loss provisions. § 469.

Closely held corporation. A corporation where stock ownership is not widely dispersed. Rather, a few shareholders are in control of corporate policy and are in a position to benefit personally from that policy.

Closing agreement. In a tax dispute, the parties sign a closing agreement to spell out the terms under which the matters are settled. The agreement is binding on both the Service and the taxpayer. § 7121.

Collectibles. A special type of capital asset, the gain from which is taxed at a maximum rate of 28 percent if the holding period is more than one year. Examples include art, rugs, antiques, gems, metals, stamps, some coins and bullion, and alcoholic beverages held for investment. §§ 1(h)(5) and 408(m).

Combined return. In multistate taxation, a group of unitary corporations may elect or be required to file an income tax return that includes operating results for all of the affiliates, not just those with nexus in the state. Thus, apportionment data are reported for the group's worldwide or waters'-edge operations.

Community property. Arizona, California, Idaho, Louisiana, Nevada, New Mexico, Texas, Washington, and Wisconsin have community property systems. Alaska residents can elect community property status for assets. The rest of the states are common law property jurisdictions. The difference between common law and community property systems centers around the property rights possessed by married persons. In a common law system, each spouse owns whatever he or she earns. Under a community property system, one-half of the earnings of each spouse is considered owned by the other spouse. Assume, for example, that Jeff and Alice are husband and wife and that their only income is the $50,000 annual salary Jeff receives. If they live in New York (a common law state), the $50,000 salary belongs to Jeff. If, however, they live in Texas (a community property state), the $50,000 salary is owned one-half each by Jeff and Alice.

Compensatory damages. Damages received or paid by the taxpayer can be classified as compensatory damages or as punitive damages. Compensatory damages are paid to compensate one for harm caused by another. Compensatory damages received on account of physical injuries are excludible from the recipient's gross income. § 104(a)(2).

Complete termination redemption. Sale or exchange treatment is available relative to this type of redemption. The shareholder must retire all of his or her outstanding shares in the corporation (ignoring family attribution rules) and cannot hold an interest, other than that of a creditor, for the 10 years following the redemption. § 302(b)(3).

Completed contract method. A method of reporting gain or loss on certain long-term contracts. Under this method of accounting, all gross income and expenses are recognized in the tax year in which the contract is completed. Reg. § 1.451–3.

Complex trust. Not a simple trust. Such trusts may have charitable beneficiaries, accumulate income, and distribute corpus. §§ 661–663.

Composite return. In multistate taxation, an S corporation may be allowed to file a single income tax return that assigns pass-through items to resident and nonresident shareholders. The composite or "block" return allows the entity to remit any tax that is attributable to the nonresident shareholders.

Conduit concept. See *conduit perspective.*

Conduit perspective. A perspective taken toward a venture that regards the venture as an aggregation of its owners joined together in an agency relationship rather than as a separate entity. For tax purposes, this results in the income of the venture being taxable directly to its owners. For example, items of income and expense, capital gains and losses, tax credits, etc., realized by a partnership pass through the partnership (a conduit) and are subject to taxation at the partner level. Also, in an S corporation, certain items pass through and are reported on the returns of the shareholders.

Consolidated returns. A procedure whereby certain affiliated corporations may file a single return, combine the tax transactions of each corporation, and arrive at a single income tax liability for the group. The election to file a consolidated return usually is binding on future years. §§ 1501–1505 and related Regulations.

Consolidation. The combination of two or more corporations into a newly created corporation. Thus, Black Corporation and White Corporation combine to form Gray Corporation. A consolidation may qualify as a nontaxable reorganization if certain conditions are satisfied. §§ 354 and 368(a)(1)(A).

Constructive dividends. A taxable benefit derived by a shareholder from his or her corporation that is not actually initiated by the board of directors as a dividend. Examples include unreasonable compensation, excessive rent payments, bargain purchases of corporate property, and shareholder use of corporate property. Constructive dividends generally are found in closely held corporations.

Constructive liquidation scenario. The means by which recourse debt is shared among partners in basis determination. Reg. § 1.752–2.

Constructive receipt. If income is unqualifiedly available although not physically in the taxpayer's possession, it still is subject to the income tax. An example is accrued interest on a savings account. Under the constructive receipt concept, the interest is taxed to a depositor in the year available, rather than the year actually withdrawn. The fact that the depositor uses the cash basis of accounting for tax purposes is irrelevant. See Reg. § 1.451–2.

Continuity of business enterprise. In a tax-favored reorganization, the acquiring corporation must continue the historic business of the target or use a significant portion of the target's assets in the new business.

Continuity of interest. In a tax-favored reorganization, a shareholder or corporation that has substantially the same investment after an exchange as before should not be taxed on the transaction. Specifically, the target shareholders must acquire an equity interest in the acquiring corporation equal in value to at least 40 percent of all the outstanding stock of the target entity.

Control. Holding a specified level of stock ownership in a corporation. For § 351, the new shareholder(s) must hold at least 80 percent of the total combined voting power of all voting classes of stock and at least 80 percent of the shares of all nonvoting classes. Other tax provisions require different levels of control to bring about desired effects, such as 50 or 100 percent.

Controlled foreign corporation (CFC). A non-U.S. corporation in which more than 50 percent of the total combined voting power of all classes of stock entitled to vote or the total value of the stock of the corporation is owned by U.S. shareholders on any day during the taxable year of the foreign corporation. For purposes of this definition, a U.S. shareholder is any U.S. person who owns, or is considered to own, 10 percent or more of the total combined voting power of all classes of voting stock of the foreign corporation. Stock owned directly, indirectly, and constructively is used in this measure. See *U.S. shareholder.* §§ 951–965.

Controlled group. Controlled groups include parent-subsidiary groups, brother-sister groups, combined groups, and certain insurance companies. Controlled groups are required to share certain elements of tax calculations (e.g., $250,000 accumulated earnings credit) or tax credits (e.g., research credit). §§ 1561 and 1563.

Corporate liquidation. Occurs when a corporation distributes its net assets to its shareholders and ceases to be a going concern. Generally, a shareholder recognizes capital gain or loss upon the liquidation of the entity, regardless of the corporation's balance in its earnings and profits account. The liquidating corporation recognizes gain and loss on assets that it sells during the liquidation period and on assets that it distributes to shareholders in kind.

Corpus. The body or principal of a trust. Suppose, for example, Grant transfers an apartment building into a trust, income payable to Ruth for life, remainder to Shawn upon Ruth's death. Corpus of the trust is the apartment building.

Correspondence audit. An audit conducted by the IRS by the U.S. mail. Typically, the IRS writes to the taxpayer requesting the verification of a particular deduction or exemption. The remittance of copies of records or other support is requested of the taxpayer.

Cost depletion. Depletion that is calculated based on the adjusted basis of the asset. The adjusted basis is divided by the expected recoverable units to determine the depletion per unit. The depletion per unit is multiplied by the units sold during the tax year to calculate cost depletion. §§ 611 and 612.

Cost recovery. The system by which taxpayers are allowed to recover their investment in an asset by reducing their taxable income by the asset's cost or initial basis. Cost recovery methods include MACRS, § 179 expense, additional first-year deprecation, amortization, and depletion. §§ 168, 179, and 611.

Court of original jurisdiction. The Federal courts are divided into courts of original jurisdiction and appellate courts. A dispute between a taxpayer and the IRS is first considered by a court of original jurisdiction (i.e., a trial court). The four Federal courts of original jurisdiction are the U.S. Tax Court, the U.S. District Court, the U.S. Court of Federal Claims, and the Small Cases Division of the U.S. Tax Court.

Coverdell education savings account (§ 530 plan). Coverdell education savings account exempts from tax the earnings on amounts placed in a qualified account for the education expenses of a named beneficiary. Contributions are limited to $2,000 per year per beneficiary, and the proceeds can be withdrawn without tax provided the funds are used to pay qualified educational expenses for primary, secondary, or higher education. (There is an annual $10,000 per student limitation on distributions for tuition expenses for primary and secondary education.) Qualified educational expenses also include certain homeschooling expenses. The account is named for the late Senator Paul Coverdell (R-GA), who sponsored the legislation in Congress. § 530.

Credit for certain retirement plan contributions. A nonrefundable credit is available based on eligible contributions of up to $2,000 to certain qualified retirement plans, such as traditional and Roth IRAs and § 401(k) plans. The benefit provided by this credit is in addition to any deduction or exclusion that otherwise is available resulting from the qualifying contribution. The amount of the credit depends on the taxpayer's AGI and filing status. § 25B.

Credit for child and dependent care expenses. A nonrefundable tax credit ranging from 20 percent to 35 percent of employment-related expenses (child and dependent care expenses) for amounts of up to $6,000 is available to individuals who are employed (or deemed to be employed) and maintain a household for a dependent child under age 13, disabled spouse, or disabled dependent. § 21.

Credit for employer-provided child care. A nonrefundable credit is available to employers who provide child care facilities to their employees during normal working hours. The credit, limited to $150,000, is comprised of two components. The portion of the credit for qualified child care expenses is equal to 25 percent of these expenses, while the portion of the credit for qualified child care resource and referral services is equal to 10 percent of these expenses. Any qualifying expenses otherwise deductible by the taxpayer must be reduced by the amount of the credit. In addition, the taxpayer's basis for any property used for qualifying purposes is reduced by the amount of the credit. § 45F.

Credit for employer-provided family and medical leave. A nonrefundable credit is available to employers who pay wages to employees while they are on family and medical leave. The credit is equal to 12.5 percent of wages paid to qualifying employees (limited to 12 weeks per employee per year). Employers must pay a minimum of 50 percent of the wages normally paid; if wages paid during the leave *exceed* 50 percent of normal wages, the credit is increased by 0.25 percent for each percentage point above 50 percent to a maximum of 25 percent of wages paid. The credit does not apply to wages paid in taxable years beginning after 2025. § 45S.

Credit for small employer pension plan startup costs. A nonrefundable credit available to small businesses based on administrative costs associated with establishing and maintaining certain qualified plans. While such qualifying costs generally are deductible as ordinary and necessary business expenses, the availability of the credit is intended to lower the costs of starting a qualified retirement program and therefore encourage qualifying businesses to establish retirement plans for their employees. The credit is available for eligible employers at the rate of 50 percent of qualified startup costs. The maximum credit is $500 (based on a maximum $1,000 of qualifying expenses). § 45E.

Crop insurance proceeds. The proceeds received when an insured crop is destroyed. Section 451(f) permits the farmer to defer reporting the income from the insurance proceeds until the tax year following the taxable year of the destruction.

Crop method. A method of accounting for agricultural crops that are planted in one year but harvested in a subsequent year. Under this method, the costs of raising the crop are accumulated as inventory and are deducted when the income from the crop is realized.

Cross-purchase buy-sell agreement. Under this arrangement, the surviving owners of the business agree to buy out the withdrawing owner. Assume, for example, Ron and Sara are equal shareholders in Tip Corporation. Under a cross-purchase buy-sell agreement, Ron and Sara would contract to purchase the other's interest, should that person decide to withdraw from the business.

Current distribution. A payment made by a partnership to a partner when the partnership's legal existence does not cease thereafter. The partner usually assigns a basis in the distributed property that is equal to the lesser of the partner's basis in the partnership interest (substituted basis) or the basis of the distributed asset to the partnership (carryover basis). The partner first assigns basis to any cash that he or she receives in the distribution. A cash distribution in excess of the partner's basis triggers a gain. The partner's remaining basis, if any, is assigned to the noncash assets according to their relative bases to the partnership.

Current E & P. Net tax-basis earnings of a corporation aggregated during the current tax year. A corporate distribution is deemed to be first from the entity's current earnings and profits and then from accumulated earnings and profits. Shareholders recognize dividend income to the extent of the earnings and profits of the corporation. A dividend results to the extent of current earnings and profits, even if there is a larger negative balance in accumulated earnings and profits.

Current tax expense. Under ASC 740, the book tax expense that relates to the current reporting period's net income and is actually payable (or creditable) to the appropriate governmental agencies for the current period. Also known as "cash tax" or "tax payable."

D

***De minimis* fringe.** Benefits provided to employees that are too insignificant to warrant the time and effort required to account for the benefits received by each employee and the value of those benefits. Such amounts are excludible from the employee's gross income. § 132.

***De minimis* fringe benefits.** See *de minimis fringe.*

Death benefits. A payment made by an employer to the beneficiary or beneficiaries of a deceased employee on account of the death of the employee.

Debt-financed income. Included in computations of the unrelated business income of an exempt organization, the gross income generated from debt-financed property.

Deceased spousal unused exclusion (DSUE). In computing the Federal estate tax, the decedent uses the exclusion amount to shelter an amount of the gross estate from taxation. When the first spouse to die fails to use a portion of his/her exclusion amount, the unused portion is "portable" and becomes available to the surviving spouse. The surviving spouse can use the DSUE only of his/her last spouse to predecease. § 2010(c)(4).

Deceased spousal unused exclusion (DSUE) election. The process used by a surviving spouse to transfer any unused exemption from gift or estate taxes of their deceased spouse to themselves. See *deceased spousal unused exclusion (DSUE).* § 2010(c)(5)(A).

Deduction for qualified business income. A deduction allowed for noncorporate taxpayers based on the qualified business income of a qualified trade or business. In general, the deduction is limited to the lesser of 20 percent of qualified business income, or 20 percent of taxable income before the qualified business income deduction less any net capital gain. There are *three limitations* on the deduction—an overall limitation (based on modified taxable income), another that applies to high-income taxpayers, and a third that applies to certain types of services businesses. § 199A.

Deductions *for* adjusted gross income. The Federal income tax is not imposed upon gross income. Rather, it is imposed upon taxable income. Congressionally identified deductions for individual taxpayers are subtracted either from gross income to arrive at adjusted gross income or from adjusted gross income to arrive at the tax base, taxable income. § 62(a).

Deductions *from* adjusted gross income. See *deductions for adjusted gross income.*

Deductions in respect of a decedent. Deductions accrued at the moment of death but not recognizable on the final income tax return of a decedent because of the method of accounting used. Such items are allowed as deductions on the estate tax return and on the income tax return of the estate (Form 1041) or the heir (Form 1040). An example of a deduction in respect of a decedent is interest expense accrued to the date of death by a cash basis debtor. § 691(b).

Deferred compensation. Compensation that will be taxed when received or upon the removal of certain restrictions on receipt and not when earned. Contributions by an employer to a qualified pension or profit sharing plan on behalf of an employee are an example. The contributions will not be taxed to the employee until the funds are made available or distributed to the employee (e.g., upon retirement).

Deferred tax asset. Under ASC 740, an asset recorded on the balance sheet to reflect the future tax benefits related to a transaction or activity which has already been reflected in the financial statements. A deferred tax asset is often the result of the deferral of a deduction or the acceleration of income for tax purposes relative to Generally Accepted Accounting Principles.

Deferred tax benefit. Under ASC 740, a reduction in the book tax expense that relates to the current reporting period's net income but will not be realized until a future reporting period. Creates or adds to the entity's deferred tax asset balance sheet account. For instance, an NOL will result in a deferred tax benefit and a deferred tax asset.

Deferred tax expense. Under ASC 740, a book tax expense that relates to the current reporting period's net income but will not be realized until a future reporting period. Creates or adds to the entity's deferred tax liability balance sheet account. For instance, a deferred tax expense is created when tax depreciation deductions for the period are "accelerated" and exceed the corresponding book depreciation expense.

Deferred tax liability. Under ASC 740, a liability recorded on the balance sheet to reflect the future tax costs of a transaction or activity which has already been reflected in the financial statements. A deferred tax liability is often the result of the deferral of the recognition of income or the acceleration of a deduction for tax purposes relative to Generally Accepted Accounting Principles.

Defined benefit plan. Qualified plans can be dichotomized into defined benefit plans and defined contribution plans. Under a defined benefit plan, a formula defines the benefits employees are to receive. The formula usually includes years of service, employee compensation, and some stated percentage. The employer must make annual contributions based on actuarial computations that will be sufficient to pay the vested retirement benefits.

Defined contribution pension plan. Qualified plans can be dichotomized into defined benefit plans and defined contribution plans. Under a defined contribution plan, a separate account is maintained for each covered employee. The employee's benefits under the plan are based solely on (1) the amount contributed and (2) income from the fund that accrues to the employee's account. The plan defines the amount the employer is required to contribute (e.g., a flat dollar amount, an amount based on a special formula, or an amount equal to a certain percentage of compensation).

Dependency exemptions. See *personal and dependency exemptions.*

Dependent tax credit. For 2018 through 2025, the TCJA of 2017 replaced the dependency exemption with a $500 nonrefundable credit. This credit can be claimed for dependents who are not a qualifying child or under the age of 17. The dependent must be a citizen or resident of the United States. § 24(h).

Depletion. The process by which the cost or other basis of a natural resource (e.g., an oil or gas interest) is recovered upon extraction and sale of the resource. The two ways to determine the depletion allowance are the cost and percentage (or statutory) methods. Under cost depletion, each unit of production sold is assigned a portion of the cost or other basis of the interest. This is determined by dividing the cost or other basis by the total units expected to be recovered. Under percentage (or statutory) depletion, the tax law provides a special percentage factor for different types of minerals and other natural resources. This percentage is multiplied by the gross income from the interest to arrive at the depletion allowance. §§ 611–613A.

Depreciation. The system by which a taxpayer allocates for financial reporting purposes the cost of an asset to periods benefited by the asset.

Determination letter. Upon the request of a taxpayer, the IRS will comment on the tax status of a completed transaction. Determination letters frequently are used to determine whether a retirement or profit sharing plan qualifies under the Code and to determine the tax-exempt status of certain nonprofit organizations.

Disabled access credit. A tax credit designed to encourage small businesses to make their facilities more accessible to disabled individuals. The credit is equal to 50 percent of the eligible expenditures that exceed $250 but do not exceed $10,250. Thus, the maximum amount for the credit is $5,000. The adjusted basis for depreciation is reduced by the amount of the credit. To qualify, the facility must have been placed in service before November 6, 1990. § 44.

Disaster area losses. A casualty sustained in an area designated as a disaster area by the President of the United States. In such an event, the disaster loss may be treated as having occurred in the taxable year immediately preceding the year in which the disaster actually occurred. Thus, immediate tax benefits are provided to victims of a disaster. § 165(i).

Disclaimer. Rejections, refusals, or renunciations of claims, powers, or property. Section 2518 sets forth the conditions required to avoid gift tax consequences as the result of a disclaimer.

Disguised sale. When a partner contributes property to the entity and soon thereafter receives a distribution from the partnership, the transactions are collapsed and the distribution is seen as a purchase of the asset by the partnership. § 707(a)(2)(B).

Disproportionate distributions. A distribution from a partnership to one or more of its partners in which at least one partner's interest in partnership hot assets is increased or decreased. For example, a distribution of cash to one partner and hot assets to another changes both partners' interest in hot assets and is disproportionate. The intent of the disproportionate distribution rules is to ensure that each partner eventually recognizes his or her proportionate share of partnership ordinary income.

Disproportionate redemption. Sale or exchange treatment is available relative to this type of redemption. After the exchange, the shareholder owns less than 80 percent of his or her pre-redemption interest in the corporation and only a minority interest in the entity. § 302(b)(2).

Disregarded entity. The Federal income tax treatment of business income usually follows the legal form of the taxpayer (i.e., an individual's sole proprietorship is reported on the Form 1040); a C corporation's taxable income is computed on Form 1120. The check-the-box Regulations are used if the unincorporated taxpayer wants to use a different tax regime. Under these rules, a disregarded entity is taxed as an individual or a corporate division; other tax regimes are not available. For instance, a one-member limited liability company is a disregarded entity.

Distributable net income (DNI). The measure that determines the nature and amount of the distributions from estates and trusts that the beneficiaries must include in income. DNI also limits the amount that estates and trusts can claim as a deduction for such distributions. § 643(a).

Distributive share. In partnership or S corporation taxation, the distributive share is the amount of income, gain, deduction, loss, or credit allocated to a given partner or shareholder. The distributive share is the amount reported on a given line of the owner's Schedule K–1. For example, a partner's distributive share of ordinary income is the amount of income shown on that partner's Schedule K–1, Part III, line 1. For S corporations, the distributive share must be determined based on the shareholder's ownership percentage. For partnerships, the distributive share is generally determined in accordance with the partnership agreement. For both types of entities, amounts can be prorated if the ownership interest is transferred during the tax year.

Dividend. A nondeductible distribution to the shareholders of a corporation. A dividend constitutes gross income to the recipient if it is paid from the current or accumulated earnings and profits of the corporation. § 316.

Dividends received deduction. A deduction allowed a shareholder that is a corporation for dividends received from a domestic corporation. The deduction usually is 50 percent of the dividends received, but it could be 65 or 100 percent depending upon the ownership percentage held by the recipient corporation. §§ 243–246.

Divisive reorganization. A "Type D" spin-off, split-off, or split-up reorganization in which the original corporation divides its active business (in existence for at least five years) assets among two or more corporations. The stock received by the original corporation shareholders must be at least 80 percent of the other corporations.

Dock sales. A purchaser uses its owned or rented vehicles to take possession of the product at the seller's shipping dock. In most states, the sale is apportioned to the operating state of the purchaser, rather than the seller. See also *apportion* and *sales factor*.

Dollar-value LIFO. An inventory technique that focuses on the dollars invested in the inventory rather than the particular items on hand each period. Each inventory item is assigned to a pool. A pool is a collection of similar items and is treated as a separate inventory. At the end of the period, each pool is valued in terms of prices at the time LIFO was adopted (base period prices), whether or not the particular items were actually on hand in the year LIFO was adopted, to compare with current prices to determine if there has been an increase or decrease in inventories.

E

Earned income credit. A tax credit designed to provide assistance to certain low-income individuals who generally have a qualifying child. This is a refundable credit. To receive the most beneficial treatment, the taxpayer must have qualifying children. However, it is possible to qualify for the credit without having a child. See the text chapter on credits for the computation procedure required in order to determine the amount of the credit allowed. § 32.

Earnings and profits (E & P). Measures the economic capacity of a corporation to make a distribution to shareholders that is not a return of capital. Such a distribution results in dividend income to the shareholders to the extent of the corporation's current and accumulated earnings and profits.

Economic effect test. Requirements that must be met before a special allocation may be used by a partnership. The premise behind the test is that each partner who receives an allocation of income or loss from a partnership bears the economic benefit or burden of the allocation.

Economic income. The change in the taxpayer's net worth, as measured in terms of market values, plus the value of the assets the taxpayer consumed during the year. Because of the impracticality of this income model, it is not used for tax purposes.

Economic performance test. One of the requirements that must be satisfied for an accrual basis taxpayer to deduct an expense. Economic performance occurs when property or services are provided to the taxpayer, or in the case in which the taxpayer is required to provide property or services, whenever the property or services are actually provided by the taxpayer.

Education expenses. Taxpayers may deduct education expenses that are incurred either (1) to maintain or improve existing job-related skills or (2) to meet the express requirements of the employer or the requirements imposed by law to retain employment status. The expenses are not deductible if the education is required to meet the minimum educational standards for the taxpayer's job or if the education qualifies the individual for a new trade or business. The TCJA of 2017 suspended the deduction of unreimbursed employee trade or business expenses for tax years after 2017 (and through 2025). Reg. § 1.162–5.

Educational savings bonds. U.S. Series EE bonds whose proceeds are used for qualified higher educational expenses for the taxpayer, the taxpayer's spouse, or a dependent. The interest may be excluded from gross income, provided the taxpayer's adjusted gross income does not exceed certain amounts. § 135.

Effective tax rate. The financial statements for an entity include several footnotes, one of which reconciles the expected (statutory) income tax rate (e.g., 21 percent for a C corporation) with the effective tax rate. The effective tax rate is equal to taxes paid (often the tax liability) divided by the taxpayer's ability to pay (some income measure, like adjusted gross income or disposable income). For financial reporting purposes, effective tax rate generally refers to total tax expense as a percentage of pretax book income. The reconciliation often is done in dollar and/or percentage terms.

Effectively connected income. Income of a nonresident alien or foreign corporation that is attributable to the operation of a U.S. trade or business under either the asset use or the business activities test.

E-file. The electronic filing of a tax return. The filing is either direct or indirect. In direct filing, the taxpayer goes online using a computer and tax return preparation software. Indirect filing occurs when a taxpayer utilizes an authorized IRS e-file provider. The provider often is the *tax preparer*.

Employment taxes. Taxes that an employer must pay on account of its employees. Employment taxes include FICA (Federal Insurance Contributions Act) and FUTA (Federal Unemployment Tax Act) taxes. Employment taxes are paid to the IRS in addition to income tax withholdings at specified intervals. Such taxes can be levied on the employees, the employer, or both.

Energy tax credits. Various tax credits are available to those who produce clean energy or invest in certain energy property. The purpose of the credit is to create incentives for conservation and to develop alternative energy sources.

Enrolled agents (EAs). A tax practitioner who has gained admission to practice before the IRS by passing an IRS examination and maintaining a required level of continuing professional education.

Entity accounting income. Entity accounting income is not identical to the taxable income of a trust or estate, nor is it determined in the same manner as the entity's financial accounting income would be. The trust document or will determines whether certain income, expenses, gains, or losses are allocated to the corpus of the entity or to the entity's income beneficiaries. Only the items that are allocated to the income beneficiaries are included in entity accounting income.

Entity buy-sell agreement. An arrangement whereby the entity is to purchase a withdrawing owner's interest. When the entity is a corporation, the agreement generally involves a stock redemption on the part of the withdrawing shareholder. See also *buy-sell agreement* and *cross-purchase buy-sell agreement.*

Entity concept. See *entity perspective.*

Entity perspective. A perspective that regards a venture as an entity separate and distinct from its owners. For tax purposes, this results in the venture being directly responsible for the tax on the income it generates. The entity perspective taken toward C corporations results in the double taxation of income distributed to the corporation's owners.

Estate tax. A tax imposed on the right to transfer property by death. Thus, an estate tax is levied on the decedent's estate and not on the heir receiving the property. § 2001.

Estimated tax. The amount of tax (including alternative minimum tax and self-employment tax) a taxpayer expects to owe for the year after subtracting tax credits and income tax withheld. The estimated tax must be paid in installments at designated intervals (e.g., for a calendar year individual taxpayer, by April 15, June 15, September 15, and January 15 of the following year).

Excess business loss. The excess of aggregate deductions of the taxpayer attributable to trades or businesses of the taxpayer over the sum of aggregate gross income or gain of the taxpayer plus a threshold amount. In 2023, the threshold amount is $289,000 ($578,000 in the case of a married taxpayer filing a joint return). The threshold amount is adjusted for inflation each year. An excess business loss is not currently deductible; instead, it is carried forward and treated as part of the taxpayer's net operating loss (NOL) carryfoward in subsequent years. This loss limitation applies to taxpayers other than C corporations and applies after the passive activity loss limitation of § 469. The excess business loss limitation applies to tax years beginning before 2029. § 461(l).

Excess lobbying expenditures. An excise tax is applied to otherwise tax-exempt organizations on the excess of total lobbying expenditures over grass roots lobbying expenditures for the year. § 4911.

Excess loss account. When a subsidiary has generated more historical losses than its parent has invested in the entity, the parent's basis in the subsidiary is zero, and the parent records additional losses in an excess loss account. This treatment allows the parent to continue to deduct losses of the subsidiary, even where no basis reduction is possible, while avoiding the need to show a negative stock basis on various financial records. If the subsidiary stock is sold while an excess loss account exists, capital gain income usually is recognized to the extent of the balance in the account.

Excise taxes. A tax on the manufacture, sale, or use of goods; on the carrying on of an occupation or activity; or on the transfer of property. Thus, the Federal estate and gift taxes are, theoretically, excise taxes.

Exclusion amount. The value of assets that is exempt from transfer tax due to the credit allowed for gifts or transfers by death. For gifts and deaths in 2023, the exclusion amount is $12,920,000. An exclusion amount unused by a deceased spouse may be used by the surviving spouse. See also *exemption equivalent amount.*

Exempt organizations. An organization that is either partially or completely exempt from Federal income taxation. § 501.

Exemption amount. For noncorporate taxpayers, an amount deducted from alternative minimum taxable income (AMTI) to determine the alternative minimum tax base. The exemption amount is adjusted for inflation and is phased out when AMTI exceeds specified threshold amounts. § 55(d).

Exemption equivalent. The maximum value of assets that can be transferred to another party without incurring any Federal gift or estate tax. See also *exemption equivalent amount.*

Exemption equivalent amount. The nontaxable amount (in 2023, $12,920,000 for gift tax and estate tax) that is the equivalent of the unified transfer tax credit allowed.

F

Fair market value. The amount at which property would change hands between a willing buyer and a willing seller, neither being under any compulsion to buy or to sell and both having reasonable knowledge of the relevant facts. Reg. §§ 1.1001–1(a) and 20.2031–1(b).

Farm price method. A method of accounting for agricultural crops. The inventory of crops is valued at its market price less the estimated cost of disposition (e.g., freight and selling expense).

Feeder organization. An entity that carries on a trade or business for the benefit of an exempt organization. However, such a relationship does not result in the feeder organization itself being tax-exempt. § 502.

FICA tax. An abbreviation that stands for Federal Insurance Contributions Act, commonly referred to as the Social Security tax. The FICA tax is comprised of the Social Security tax (old age, survivors, and disability insurance) and the Medicare tax (hospital insurance) and is imposed on both employers and employees. The employer is responsible for withholding from the employee's wages the Social Security tax at a rate of 6.2 percent on a maximum wage base and the Medicare tax at a rate of 1.45 percent (no maximum wage base). The maximum Social Security wage base for 2023 is $160,200 and for 2022 is $147,000.

Fiduciary. One who holds a legal obligation to act on another's behalf. A *trustee* and an *executor* take fiduciary relationships relative to the *grantor* and the *decedent,* respectively. The fiduciary is assigned specific duties by the principal party (e.g., to file tax returns, manage assets, satisfy debt and other obligations, and to make investment decisions). The fiduciary often possesses specialized knowledge and experience. A fiduciary must avoid conflicts of interest in which the principal's goals are compromised in some way.

Field audit. An audit conducted by the IRS on the business premises of the taxpayer or in the office of the tax practitioner representing the taxpayer.

Filing status. Individual taxpayers are placed in one of five filing statuses each year (single, married filing jointly, married filing separately, surviving spouse, or head of household). Marital status and household support are key determinants. Filing status is used to determine the taxpayer's filing requirements, standard deduction, eligibility for certain deductions and credits, and tax liability.

Final Regulations. The U.S. Treasury Department Regulations (abbreviated Reg.) represent the position of the IRS as to how the Internal Revenue Code is to be interpreted. Their purpose is to provide taxpayers and IRS personnel with rules of general and specific application to the various provisions of the tax law. Regulations are published in the *Federal Register* and in all tax services.

Financial Accounting Standards Board (FASB). See *Generally Accepted Accounting Principles (GAAP).*

Financial statement income inclusion rule. An accrual basis taxpayer who recognizes income in certified financial statements must also recognize that income for tax purposes if they have an enforceable right to the income, even if the all events test has not otherwise been met. § 451(b).

Financial transaction tax. A tax imposed on some type of financial transaction, such as stock sales.

Fiscal year. A 12-month period ending on the last day of a month other than December. In certain circumstances, a taxpayer is permitted to elect a fiscal year instead of being required to use a calendar year.

Flat tax. A form of consumption tax designed to alleviate the regressivity of a value added tax (VAT). It is imposed on individuals and businesses at the same single (flat) rate.

Flexible spending plans. An employee benefit plan that allows the employee to take a reduction in salary in exchange for the employer paying benefits that can be provided by the employer without the employee being required to recognize income (e.g., medical and child care benefits). Contributions to a flexible spending plan are limited to $3,050 for 2023. § 125(i).

Flow-through entity. The entity is a tax reporter rather than a taxpayer. The owners are subject to tax. Examples are partnerships, S corporations, and limited liability companies.

Foreign-Derived Intangible Income (FDII). Income earned from sales by U.S. corporations to foreign customers from intangible assets held in the United States. § 250(b).

Foreign earned income exclusion. The Code allows exclusions for earned income generated outside the United States to alleviate any tax base and rate disparities among countries. The exclusion is limited to $120,000 for 2023 ($112,000 for 2022). In addition, an exclusion is allowed for housing expenditures incurred by the taxpayer's employer with respect to the non-U.S. assignment, and self-employed individuals can deduct foreign housing expenses incurred in a trade or business. The housing exclusion is limited to $16,800 for 2023 ($15,680 for 2022). § 911.

Foreign Investment in Real Property Tax Act (FIRPTA). Under the Foreign Investment in Real Property Tax Act, gains or losses realized by nonresident aliens and non-U.S. corporations on the disposition of U.S. real estate create U.S.-source income and are subject to U.S. income tax.

Foreign tax credit (FTC). A U.S. citizen or resident who incurs or pays income taxes to a foreign country on income subject to U.S. tax may be able to claim some of these taxes as a credit against the U.S. income tax. §§ 27 and 901–905.

Franchise. An agreement that gives the transferee the right to distribute, sell, or provide goods, services, or facilities within a specified area. The cost of obtaining a franchise may be amortized over a statutory period of 15 years. In general, the franchisor's gain on the sale of franchise rights is an ordinary gain because the franchisor retains a significant power, right, or continuing interest in the subject of the franchise. §§ 197 and 1253.

Franchise tax. A tax levied on the right to do business in a state as a corporation. Although income considerations may come into play, the tax usually is based on the capitalization of the corporation.

Fraud. Tax fraud falls into two categories: civil and criminal. Under civil fraud, the IRS may impose as a penalty an amount equal to as much as 75 percent of the underpayment [§ 6651(f)]. Fines and/or imprisonment are prescribed for conviction of various types of criminal tax fraud (§§ 7201–7207). Both civil and criminal fraud involve a specific intent on the part of the taxpayer to evade the tax; mere negligence is not enough. Criminal fraud requires the additional element of willfulness (i.e., done deliberately and with evil purpose). In practice, it becomes difficult to distinguish between the degree of intent necessary to support criminal, rather than civil, fraud. In either situation, the IRS has the burden of proof to show the taxpayer committed fraud.

Fringe benefits. Compensation or other benefit received by an employee that is not in the form of cash. Some fringe benefits (e.g., accident and health plans, group term life insurance) may be excluded from the employee's gross income and therefore are not subject to the Federal income tax.

Fruit and tree metaphor. The courts have held that an individual who earns income from property or services cannot assign that income to another. For example, a father cannot assign his earnings from commissions to his child and escape income tax on those amounts.

Functional currency. The currency of the economic environment in which the taxpayer carries on most of its activities and in which the taxpayer transacts most of its business.

FUTA tax. An employment tax levied on employers. Jointly administered by the Federal and state governments, the tax provides funding for unemployment benefits. FUTA applies at a rate of 6.0 percent on the first $7,000 of covered wages paid during the year for each employee. The Federal government allows a credit for FUTA paid (or allowed under a merit rating system) to the state. The credit cannot exceed 5.4 percent of the covered wages. §§ 3301–3311.

Future interest. An interest that will come into being at some future time. It is distinguished from a present interest, which already exists. Assume that Dan transfers securities to a newly created trust. Under the terms of the trust instrument, income from the securities is to be paid each year to Wilma for her life, with the securities passing to Sam upon Wilma's death. Wilma has a present interest in the trust because she is entitled to current income distributions. Sam has a future interest because he must wait for Wilma's death to benefit from the trust. The annual exclusion of $17,000 (in 2023) is not allowed for a gift of a future interest. § 2503(b).

G

General business credit. The summation of various nonrefundable business credits, including the tax credit for rehabilitation expenditures, business energy credit, work opportunity credit, research activities credit, low-income housing credit, and disabled access credit. The amount of general business credit that can be used to reduce the tax liability is limited to the taxpayer's net income tax reduced by the greater of (1) the tentative minimum tax or (2) 25 percent of the net regular tax liability that exceeds $25,000. Unused general business credits can be carried back one year and forward 20 years. § 38.

General partners. A partner who is fully liable in an individual capacity for the debts owed by the partnership to third parties. A general partner's liability is not limited to the investment in the partnership. See also *limited partners*.

General partnership (GP). A partnership that is owned by general partners (only). Creditors of a general partnership can collect amounts owed them from both the partnership assets and the assets of the partners individually.

Generally Accepted Accounting Principles (GAAP). Guidelines relating to how to construct the financial statements of enterprises doing business in the United States. Promulgated chiefly by the Financial Accounting Standards Board (FASB).

Gift tax. A tax imposed on the transfer of property by gift. The tax is imposed upon the donor of a gift and is based on the fair market value of the property on the date of the gift. § 2501.

Global Intangible Low-Taxed Income (GILTI). Income earned by a controlled foreign corporation in excess of a predefined rate of return on tangible assets, the tax on which being designed to limit the shifting of intangible assets to countries with tax rates below the U.S. corporate rate. § 951A.

Golden parachute payments. A severance payment to employees that meets the following requirements: (1) the payment is contingent on a change of ownership of a corporation through a stock or asset acquisition and (2) the aggregate present value of the payment equals or exceeds three times the employee's average annual compensation. To the extent the severance payment meets these conditions, a deduction is disallowed to the employer for the excess of the payment over a statutory base amount (a five-year average of compensation if the taxpayer was an employee for the entire five-year period). In addition, a 20 percent excise tax is imposed on the employee who receives the excess severance pay. §§ 280G and 4999.

Goodwill. The reputation and other unidentifiable intangible assets of a company. For accounting purposes, goodwill has no basis unless it is purchased. In the purchase of a business, goodwill generally is the difference between the purchase price and the fair market value of the assets acquired. The intangible asset goodwill can be amortized for tax purposes over a 15-year period. § 197 and Reg. § 1.167(a)–3.

Grantor. A transferor of property. The creator of a trust is usually referred to as the grantor of the entity.

Grantor trust. A trust under which the grantor retains control over the income or corpus (or both) to such an extent that he or she is treated as the owner of the property and its income for income tax purposes. Income from a grantor trust is taxable to the grantor and not to the beneficiary who receives it. §§ 671–679.

Grass roots expenditures. Exempt organizations are prohibited from engaging in political activities, but spending incurred to influence the opinions of the general public relative to specific legislation is permitted by the law. § 4911.

Gross estate. The property owned or previously transferred by a decedent that is subject to the Federal estate tax. The gross estate can be distinguished from the probate estate, which is property actually subject to administration by the administrator or executor of an estate. §§ 2031–2046.

Gross income. Income subject to the Federal income tax. Gross income does not include all economic income. That is, certain exclusions are allowed (e.g., interest on municipal bonds). For a manufacturing or merchandising business, gross income usually means gross profit (gross sales or gross receipts less cost of goods sold). § 61 and Reg. § 1.61–3(a).

Group term life insurance. Life insurance coverage provided by an employer for a group of employees. Such insurance is renewable on a year-to-year basis, and typically no cash surrender value is built up. The premiums paid by the employer on the insurance are not taxed to the employees on coverage of up to $50,000 per person. § 79 and Reg. § 1.79–1(b).

Guaranteed payments. Payments made by a partnership to a partner for services rendered or for the use of capital to the extent the payments are determined without regard to the income of the partnership. The payments are treated as though they were made to a nonpartner and thus are deducted by the entity. On the partnership's Schedule K and the partners' Schedules K–1, guaranteed payments are distinguished between those payments for use of the partners' capital and those paid for services provided by the partners to the partnership. The partners report the amounts as ordinary income based on the timing and amounts reported on their respective Schedules K–1. In addition to being subject to the income tax, a guaranteed payment might be subject to self-employment tax (guaranteed payment for services) or net investment income tax (guaranteed payment for capital). Guaranteed payments are not eligible for the qualified business income deduction. § 707(c).

H

Half-year convention. A cost recovery convention that assumes that property is placed in service at mid-year and thus provides for a half-year's cost recovery for that year. § 168(d).

Head of household. An unmarried individual who maintains a household for another and satisfies certain conditions set forth in § 2(b). This status enables the taxpayer to use a set of income tax rates that are lower than those applicable to other unmarried individuals but higher than those applicable to surviving spouses and married persons filing a joint return.

Health Savings Account (HSA). A medical savings account created in legislation enacted in December 2003 that is designed to replace and expand Archer Medical Savings Accounts. § 223.

Highly compensated employee. The employee group is generally divided into two categories for fringe benefit (including pension and profit sharing plans) purposes. These are (1) highly compensated employees and (2) non-highly compensated employees. For most fringe benefits, if the fringe benefit plan discriminates in favor of highly compensated employees, it will not be a qualified plan with respect, at a minimum, to the highly compensated employees.

Historic business test. In a corporate reorganization, a means by which to determine if the continuity of business enterprise requirement is met. The acquiring corporation must continue to operate the target entity's existing business(es) going forward; if this is not the case, the requirement is failed.

Hobby losses. Losses from an activity not engaged in for profit. The Code restricts the amount of losses that an individual can deduct for hobby activities so that these transactions cannot be used to offset income from other sources. The TCJA of 2017 suspended the deduction of hobby expenses for tax years after 2017 (and through 2025). § 183.

Holding period. The period of time during which property has been held for income tax purposes. The holding period is significant in determining whether gain or loss from the sale or exchange of a capital asset is long or short term. § 1223.

Home equity loans. Loans that utilize the personal residence of the taxpayer as security. The interest on such loans is deductible as qualified residence interest. However, interest is deductible only on the portion of the loan that does not exceed the lesser of (1) the fair market value of the residence, reduced by the acquisition indebtedness, or (2) $100,000 ($50,000 for married persons filing separate returns). A major benefit of a home equity loan is that there are no tracing rules regarding the use of the loan proceeds. The TCJA of 2017 suspended the deduction of interest on home equity indebtedness for tax years after 2017 (and through 2025). § 163(h)(3).

Hot assets. Unrealized receivables and substantially appreciated inventory under § 751. [For a sale of a partnership interest, "inventory" (as defined) need not be appreciated.] When hot assets are present, the sale of a partnership interest or the disproportionate distribution of the assets can cause ordinary income to be recognized.

Hybrid method. A combination of the accrual and cash methods of accounting. That is, the taxpayer may account for some items of income on the accrual method (e.g., sales and cost of goods sold) and other items (e.g., interest income) on the cash method.

I

Imputed interest. If certain loans have a stated rate of interest below a minimum threshold, or call for no interest at all, both the lender and borrower must nonetheless determine their taxable income as if interest had been paid. The requirement to impute interest mitigates the use of below-market rate loans to re-characterize interest as part of the gain when the loan relates to a property sale, and to shift income across taxpayers in other contexts. §§ 483, 1274, and 7872.

Inbound taxation. U.S. tax effects when a non-U.S. person begins an investment or business activity in the United States.

Incentive stock options (ISOs). A type of stock option that receives favorable tax treatment. If various qualification requirements can be satisfied, stock option grants do not create taxable income for the recipient. However, the spread (the excess of the fair market value at the date of exercise over the option price) is an adjustment item for purposes of the alternative minimum tax (AMT). The gain on disposition of the stock resulting from the exercise of the stock option will be classified as long-term capital gain if certain holding period requirements are met (the employee must not dispose of the stock within two years after the option is granted or within one year after acquiring the stock). § 422.

Income. For tax purposes, an increase in wealth that has been realized.

Income in respect of a decedent (IRD). Income earned by a decedent at the time of death but not reportable on the final income tax return because of the method of accounting that appropriately is utilized. Such income is included in the gross estate and is taxed to the eventual recipient (either the estate or heirs). The recipient is, however, allowed an income tax deduction for the estate tax attributable to the income. § 691.

Income tax provision. Under ASC 740, a synonym for the tax expense reported by a company in its financial statements for the period. Following the "matching principle," all income taxes that relate to the net income for the reporting period is reported on that period's financial statements, including not only the current tax expense but also any deferred tax expense and deferred tax benefit.

Income tax treaties. See *tax treaties*.

Independent contractor. A self-employed person as distinguished from one who is employed as an employee.

Indexation. A procedure whereby adjustments are made by the IRS to key tax components (e.g., standard deduction, tax brackets, personal and dependency exemptions) to reflect inflation. The adjustments usually are made annually and are based on the change in the consumer price index.

Individual Retirement Accounts (IRAs). A type of retirement plan to which an individual with earned income can contribute a statutory maximum of $6,500 ($7,500 if age 50 or above) in 2023. IRAs can be classified as traditional IRAs or Roth IRAs. With a traditional IRA, an individual can contribute and deduct a maximum of $6,500 ($7,500 if age 50 or above) per tax year in 2023. The deduction is a deduction *for* AGI. However, if the individual is an active participant in another qualified retirement plan, the deduction is phased out proportionally between certain AGI ranges (note that the phaseout limits the amount of the deduction and not the amount of the contribution). With a Roth IRA, an individual can contribute a maximum of $6,500 ($7,500 if age 50 or above) per tax year in 2023. No deduction is permitted. However, if a five-year holding period requirement is satisfied and if the distribution is a qualified distribution, the taxpayer can make tax-free withdrawals from a Roth IRA. The maximum annual contribution is phased out proportionally between certain AGI ranges. §§ 219 and 408A.

Information returns. Forms filed by third parties, such as employers, banks, and brokers that provide information about payments or transactions, including Forms W–2 and 1099.

Inheritance tax. A tax imposed on the right to receive property from a decedent. Thus, theoretically, an inheritance tax is imposed on the heir. The Federal estate tax is imposed on the estate.

Inside basis. A partnership's basis in the assets it owns.

Installment agreement. A written agreement under which a taxpayer pays taxes with periodic payments over time.

Installment method. A method of accounting enabling certain taxpayers to spread the recognition of gain on the sale of property over the collection period. Under this procedure, the seller arrives at the gain to be recognized by computing the gross profit percentage from the sale (the gain divided by the contract price) and applying it to each payment received. § 453.

Intangible drilling and development costs (IDCs). Taxpayers may elect to expense or capitalize (subject to amortization) intangible drilling and development costs. However, ordinary income recapture provisions apply to oil and gas properties on a sale or other disposition if the expense method is elected. §§ 263(c) and 1254(a).

Intercompany transactions. A sale or exchange of goods or services between members of an *affiliated group* that files a *consolidated return*. Generally, the results of the transaction are recorded by both affiliates under general Federal income tax rules, but certain gains, losses, income, or deductions may be deferred until a later tax year.

Intermediate sanctions. The IRS can assess excise taxes on disqualified persons and organization management associated with so-called public charities engaging in excess benefit transactions. An excess benefit transaction is one in which a disqualified person engages in a non-fair market value transaction with the exempt organization or receives unreasonable compensation. Prior to the enactment of intermediate sanctions, the only option available to the IRS was to revoke the organization's exempt status.

Internal Revenue Manual (IRM). The primary, official source of instructions to IRS employees relating to the organization, administration, and operation of the IRS.

International Accounting Standards Board (IASB). The body that promulgates International Financial Reporting Standards (IFRS). Based in London, representing accounting standard setting bodies in over 100 countries, the IASB develops accounting standards that can serve as the basis for harmonizing conflicting reporting standards among nations.

International Financial Reporting Standards (IFRS). Produced by the International Accounting Standards Board (IASB), guidelines developed since 2001 as to revenue recognition, accounting for business combinations, and a conceptual framework for financial reporting. IFRS provisions are designed so that they can be used by all entities, regardless of where they are based or conduct business. IFRS have gained widespread acceptance throughout the world, and the SEC is considering how to require U.S. entities to use IFRS in addition to, or in lieu of, the accounting rules of the Financial Accounting Standards Board.

Interpretive Regulations. A Regulation issued by the Treasury Department that purports to explain the meaning of a particular Code Section. An interpretive Regulation is given less deference than a legislative Regulation.

Inventory. Under § 1221(a)(1), a taxpayer's stock in trade or property held for resale. For partnership tax purposes, inventory is defined in § 751(d) as inventory (per the above definition) or any partnership asset other than capital or § 1231 assets. See also *appreciated inventory*.

Investment income. Consisting of virtually the same elements as portfolio income, a measure by which to justify a deduction for interest on investment indebtedness.

Investment interest. Payment for the use of funds used to acquire assets that produce investment income. The deduction for investment interest is limited to net investment income for the tax year.

Investor loss. Losses on stock and securities. If stocks and bonds are capital assets in the hands of the holder, a capital loss materializes as of the last day of the taxable year in which the stocks or bonds become worthless. Under certain circumstances involving stocks and bonds of affiliated corporations, an ordinary loss is permitted upon worthlessness.

Involuntary conversion. The loss or destruction of property through theft, casualty, or condemnation. Gain realized on an involuntary conversion can, at the taxpayer's election, be deferred for Federal income tax purposes if the owner reinvests the proceeds within a prescribed period of time in property that is similar or related in service or use. § 1033.

Itemized deductions. Personal expenditures allowed by the Code as deductions from adjusted gross income. Examples include certain medical expenses, interest on home mortgages, state income taxes, and charitable contributions. Itemized deductions are reported on Schedule A of Form 1040.

J

John Doe summons. An order to compel the production of records or testimony of a third party that does not identify the taxpayer or group about whom records are sought because they are not yet known. A court order is required before the summons is issued.

Joint tenants. Two or more persons having undivided ownership of property with the right of survivorship. Right of survivorship gives the surviving owner full ownership of the property. Suppose Bob and Tami are joint tenants of a tract of land. Upon Bob's death, Tami becomes the sole owner of the property. For the estate tax consequences upon the death of a joint tenant, see § 2040.

K

Keogh plans. Retirement plans available to self-employed taxpayers. They are also referred to as H.R. 10 plans. Under such plans, a taxpayer may deduct each year up to 100 percent of net earnings from self-employment or $66,000 for 2023, whichever is less. If the plan is a profit sharing plan, the percentage is 25 percent.

Kiddie tax. Passive income, such as interest and dividends, that is recognized by a child under age 19 (or under age 24 if a full-time student) is taxed according to the brackets applicable to the child's parent(s), generally to the extent the income exceeds $2,500 for 2023. The additional tax is assessed regardless of the source of the income or the income's underlying property. § 1(g).

L

Least aggregate deferral method. An algorithm set forth in the Regulations to determine the tax year for a partnership or limited liability entity with owners whose tax years differ. The tax year selected is the one that produces the least aggregate deferral of income for the owners.

Least aggregate deferral rule. See *least aggregate deferral method*.

Legislative Regulations. Some Code Sections give the Secretary of the Treasury or his delegate the authority to prescribe Regulations to carry out the details of administration or to otherwise complete the operating rules. Regulations issued pursuant to this type of authority truly possess the force and effect of law. In effect, Congress is almost delegating its legislative powers to the Treasury Department.

Lessee. One who rents property from another. In the case of real estate, the lessee is also known as the tenant.

Lessor. One who rents property to another. In the case of real estate, the lessor is also known as the landlord.

Letter ruling. The written response of the IRS to a taxpayer's request for interpretation of the revenue laws with respect to a proposed transaction (e.g., concerning the tax-free status of a reorganization). Not to be relied on as precedent by other than the party who requested the ruling.

Liabilities in excess of basis. On the contribution of capital to a corporation, an investor recognizes gain on the exchange to the extent contributed assets carry liabilities with a face amount in excess of the tax basis of the contributed assets. This rule keeps the investor from holding the investment asset received with a negative basis. § 357(c).

Life insurance proceeds. A specified sum (the face value or maturity value of the policy) paid to the designated beneficiary of the policy by the life insurance company upon the death of the insured.

Lifetime learning credit. A tax credit for qualifying expenses for taxpayers pursuing education beyond the first two years of postsecondary education. Individuals who are completing their last two years of undergraduate studies, pursuing graduate or professional degrees, or otherwise seeking new job skills or maintaining existing job skills are all eligible for the credit. Eligible individuals include the taxpayer, taxpayer's spouse, and taxpayer's dependents. The maximum credit is 20 percent of the first $10,000 of qualifying expenses and is computed per taxpayer. The credit is phased out for higher-income taxpayers. § 25A.

Like-kind exchanges. An exchange of real property held for productive use in a trade or business or for investment for other investment or trade or business real property. Unless non-like-kind property (boot) is received, the exchange is fully tax-deferred. § 1031.

Limited liability company (LLC). A legal entity in which all owners are protected from the entity's debts but which may lack other characteristics of a corporation (i.e., centralized management, unlimited life, free transferability of interests). LLCs generally are treated as partnerships (or disregarded entities if they have only one owner) for tax purposes.

Limited liability partnership (LLP). A legal entity allowed by many of the states, where a general partnership registers with the state as an LLP. All partners are at risk with respect to any liabilities arising from their own malpractice or torts or those of their subordinates. However, all partners are protected from any liabilities resulting from the malpractice or torts of other partners.

Limited partners. A partner whose liability to third-party creditors of the partnership is limited to the amounts invested in the partnership. See also *general partners* and *limited partnership (LP)*.

Limited partnership (LP). A partnership in which some of the partners are limited partners. At least one of the partners in a limited partnership must be a general partner.

Liquidating distribution. A distribution by a partnership that is in complete liquidation of the partnership trade or business activities or in complete liquidation of a partner's interest in the partnership. A liquidating distribution is generally a tax-deferred transaction if it is proportionate with respect to the partnership's hot assets. In a proportionate liquidating distribution, the partnership recognizes no gain or loss. The partner only recognizes gain if the distributed cash (and cash equivalents, such as debt relief or certain marketable securities) exceeds the partner's basis in the partnership. The partner recognizes a loss if *only* cash and hot assets are distributed and their combined inside (partnership) basis is less than the partner's basis in the partnership interest. In any case where no gain or loss is recognized, the partner's basis in the partnership interest is fully assigned to the basis of the assets received in the distribution.

Listed property. Property that includes (1) any passenger automobile; (2) any other property used as a means of transportation; (3) any property of a type generally used for purposes of entertainment, recreation, or amusement; and (4) any other property of a type specified in the Regulations. If listed property is predominantly used for business, the taxpayer is allowed to use the statutory percentage method of cost recovery. Otherwise, the straight-line cost recovery method must be used. § 280F.

Lobbying expenditures. An expenditure made for the purpose of influencing legislation. Such payments can result in the loss of the exempt status of, and the imposition of Federal income tax on, an exempt organization. Lobby expenditures are not deductible. § 162(e).

Long-term care insurance. Insurance that helps pay the cost of care when the insured is unable to care for himself or herself. Such insurance is generally thought of as insurance against the cost of an aged person entering a nursing home. The employer can provide the insurance, and the premiums may be excluded from the employee's gross income. § 7702B.

Long-term contract. A building, installation, construction, or manufacturing contract that is entered into but not completed within the same tax year. A manufacturing contract is a long-term contract only if the contract is to manufacture (1) a unique item not normally carried in finished goods inventory or (2) items that normally require more than 12 calendar months to complete. The two available methods to account for long-term contracts are the percentage of completion method and the completed contract method. The completed contract method can be used only in limited circumstances. § 460.

Long-term nonpersonal use capital assets. Includes investment property with a long-term holding period. Such property disposed of by casualty or theft may receive § 1231 treatment.

Long-term tax-exempt rate. Used in deriving the yearly limitation on net operating loss and other tax benefits that carry over from the target to the acquiring when there is a more than 50-percentage-point ownership change (by value). The highest of the Federal long-term interest rates in effect for any of the last three months. § 382.

Lower of cost or market (replacement cost). An elective inventory method, whereby the taxpayer may value inventories at the lower of the taxpayer's actual cost or the current replacement cost of the goods. This method cannot be used in conjunction with the LIFO inventory method.

Low-income housing credit. Beneficial treatment to owners of low-income housing is provided in the form of a tax credit. The calculated credit is claimed in the year the building is placed in service and in the following nine years. § 42.

Lump-sum distribution. Payment of the entire amount due at one time rather than in installments. Such distributions often occur from qualified pension or profit sharing plans upon the retirement or death of a covered employee. The recipient of a lump-sum distribution may recognize both long-term capital gain and ordinary income upon the receipt of the distribution. The ordinary income portion may be subject to a special 10-year income averaging provision. § 402(e).

M

Majority interest partners. Partners who have more than a 50 percent interest in partnership profits and capital, counting only those partners who have the same taxable year. The term is of significance in determining the appropriate taxable year of a partnership. § 706(b).

Marginal tax rate. The tax rate applicable to the next dollar of income (if describing an income tax).

Marital deduction. A deduction allowed against the taxable estate or taxable gifts upon the transfer of property from one spouse to another. §§ 2056 and 2523.

Marriage penalty. The additional tax liability that results for a married couple when compared with what their tax liability would be if they were not married and filed separate returns.

Matching rule. Deferral treatment on a consolidated return for an intercompany sale as long as a sold asset remains in the consolidated group.

Material participation. If an individual taxpayer materially participates in a nonrental trade or business activity, any loss from that activity is treated as an active loss that can be offset against active income. Material participation is achieved by meeting any one of seven tests provided in the Regulations. § 469(h).

Meaningful reduction test. A decrease in the shareholder's voting control. Used to determine whether a stock redemption qualifies for sale or exchange treatment.

Medical expenses. Medical expenses of an individual, a spouse, and dependents are allowed as an itemized deduction to the extent such amounts (less insurance reimbursements) exceed 7.5 percent of adjusted gross income. § 213.

Merger. The absorption of one corporation by another with the corporation being absorbed losing its legal identity. Flow Corporation is merged into Jobs Corporation, and the shareholders of Flow receive stock in Jobs in exchange for their stock in Flow. After the merger, Flow ceases to exist as a separate legal entity. If a merger meets certain conditions, it is not currently taxable to the parties involved. § 368(a)(1).

Mid-month convention. A cost recovery convention that assumes that property is placed in service in the middle of the month that it is actually placed in service. § 168(d).

Mid-quarter convention. A cost recovery convention that assumes that property placed in service during the year is placed in service at the middle of the quarter in which it is actually placed in service. The mid-quarter convention applies if more than 40 percent of the value of property (other than eligible real estate) is placed in service during the last quarter of the year. § 168(d).

Miscellaneous itemized deductions. A special category of itemized deductions that includes expenses such as professional dues, tax return preparation fees, job-hunting costs, unreimbursed employee business expenses, and certain investment expenses. Such expenses are deductible only to the extent they exceed 2 percent of adjusted gross income. The TCJA of 2017 suspended the deduction for these items for tax years after 2017 (and through 2025). § 67.

Modified accelerated cost recovery system (MACRS). A method in which the cost of tangible property is recovered over a prescribed period of time. Enacted by the Economic Recovery Tax Act (ERTA) of 1981 and substantially modified by the Tax Reform Act (TRA) of 1986, the method disregards salvage value, imposes a period of cost recovery that depends upon the classification of the asset into one of various recovery periods, and prescribes the applicable percentage of cost that can be deducted each year. § 168.

Multiple support agreement. To qualify for a dependency exemption, the support test must be satisfied. This requires that over 50 percent of the support of the potential dependent be provided by the taxpayer. Where no one person provides more than 50 percent of the support, a multiple support agreement enables a taxpayer to still qualify for the dependency exemption. Any person who contributed more than 10 percent of the support is entitled to claim the exemption if each person in the group who contributed more than 10 percent files a written consent (Form 2120). Each person who is a party to the multiple support agreement must meet all of the other requirements for claiming the dependency exemption. § 152(c).

Multistate Tax Commission (MTC). A regulatory body of the states that develops operating rules and regulations for the implementation of the UDITPA and other provisions that assign the total taxable income of a multistate corporation to specific states.

N

National sales tax. Intended as a replacement for the current Federal income tax. Unlike a value added tax (VAT), which is levied on the manufacturer, it would be imposed on the consumer upon the final sale of goods and services. To reduce regressivity, individuals would receive a rebate to offset a portion of the tax.

Negligence. Failure to exercise the reasonable or ordinary degree of care of a prudent person in a situation that results in harm or damage to another. A penalty is assessed on taxpayers who exhibit negligence or intentional disregard of rules and Regulations with respect to the underpayment of certain taxes. § 6662(c).

Net capital gain (NCG). The excess of the net long-term capital gain for the tax year over the net short-term capital loss. The net capital gain of an individual taxpayer is eligible for the alternative tax. § 1222(11).

Net capital loss (NCL). The excess of the losses from sales or exchanges of capital assets over the gains from sales or exchanges of such assets. Up to $3,000 per year of the net capital loss may be deductible by noncorporate taxpayers against ordinary income. The excess net capital loss carries over to future tax years. For corporate taxpayers, the net capital loss cannot be offset against ordinary income, but it can be carried back three years and forward five years to offset net capital gains. §§ 1211, 1212, and 1221(10).

Net Deemed Tangible Income Return (NDTIR). The excess of 10 percent of a controlled foreign corporation shareholder's qualified business asset investment over the amount of interest expense considered in determining net tested income of such corporation. § 951A(b)(2).

Net investment income. The excess of investment income over investment expenses. Investment expenses are those deductible expenses directly connected with the production of investment income. Investment expenses do not include investment interest. The deduction for investment interest for the tax year is limited to net investment income. § 163(d).

Net operating loss (NOL). To mitigate the effect of the annual accounting period concept, § 172 allows taxpayers to use an excess loss of one year as a deduction for certain past or future years. For NOLs incurred after 2020, an indefinite carryforward period applies, and such NOLs are subject to an 80 percent of taxable income limitation in any carryforward year. (Different carryover rules apply for NOLs incurred before 2021, and there is no limitation on an NOL deduction in such years.)

Nexus. The degree of activity that must be present before a taxing jurisdiction has the right to impose a tax on an out-of-state entity. The rules for income tax nexus are not the same as for sales tax nexus.

Ninety-day (90-day) letter. This notice is sent to a taxpayer upon request, upon the expiration of the 30-day letter, or upon exhaustion by the taxpayer of his or her administrative remedies before the IRS. The notice gives the taxpayer 90 days in which to file a petition with the U.S. Tax Court. If a petition is not filed, the IRS will demand payment of the assessed deficiency. §§ 6211–6216.

No-additional-cost service. Services the employer may provide the employee at no additional cost to the employer. Generally, the benefit is the ability to utilize the employer's excess capacity (e.g., vacant seats on an airliner). Such amounts are excludible from the recipient's gross income. § 132(b).

Nonaccountable plan. An expense reimbursement plan that does not have an accountability feature. The result is that employee expenses are not deductible.

Nonacquiescence. Disagreement by the IRS on the result reached in certain judicial decisions. *Nonacq.* or *NA*.

Nonbusiness bad debt. A bad debt loss that is not incurred in connection with a creditor's trade or business. The loss is classified as a short-term capital loss and is allowed only in the year the debt becomes entirely worthless. In addition to family loans, many investor losses are nonbusiness bad debts. § 166(d).

Nonqualified deferred compensation (NQDC). Compensation arrangements that are frequently offered to executives. Such plans may include stock options or annuities upon separation, for example. Often, an executive may defer the recognition of taxable income. The employer, however, does not receive a tax deduction until the employee is required to include the compensation in income. § 409A.

Nonqualified stock option (NQSO). A type of stock option that does not satisfy the statutory requirements of an incentive stock option. If the NQSO has a readily ascertainable fair market value (e.g., the option is traded on an established exchange), the value of the option must be included in the employee's gross income at the date of the grant. Otherwise, the employee does not recognize income at the grant date. Instead, ordinary income is recognized in the year of exercise of the option.

Nonrecourse debt. Debt secured by the property that it is used to purchase. The purchaser of the property is not personally liable for the debt upon default. Rather, the creditor's recourse is to repossess the related property. Nonrecourse debt generally does not increase the purchaser's at-risk amount.

Nonrefundable credits. A credit that is not paid if it exceeds the taxpayer's tax liability. Some nonrefundable credits qualify for carryback and carryover treatment.

Nonresident alien (NRA). An individual who is neither a citizen nor a resident of the United States. Citizenship is determined under the immigration and naturalization laws of the United States. Residency is determined under § 7701(b) of the Internal Revenue Code.

Nontaxable exchange. A transaction in which realized gains or losses are not recognized. The recognition of gain or loss is postponed (deferred) until the property received in the nontaxable exchange is subsequently disposed of in a taxable transaction. Examples are § 1031 like-kind exchanges and § 1033 involuntary conversions.

Not essentially equivalent redemption. Sale or exchange treatment is given to this type of redemption. Although various safe-harbor tests are failed, the nature of the redemption is such that dividend treatment is avoided, because it represents a meaningful reduction in the shareholder's interest in the corporation. § 302(b)(1).

Notice CP 2000. A letter the IRS sends to a taxpayer with a proposed change to a tax return. The letter identifies the issue and explains what taxpayers need to do to resolve the issue.

Notices. A Notice is issued by the National Office of the IRS as official guidance when such information is needed before the time it takes to issue a Final Regulation. Such guidance is typically transitional until final guidance is issued. A Notice is published in an *Internal Revenue Bulletin* (I.R.B.).

Occupational fee. A tax imposed on various trades or businesses. A license fee that enables a taxpayer to engage in a particular occupation.

Occupational taxes. See *occupational fee*.

Offer in compromise. A settlement agreement offered by the IRS in a tax dispute, especially where there is doubt as to the collectibility of the full deficiency. Offers in compromise can include installment payment schedules as well as reductions in the tax and penalties owed by the taxpayer. § 7122.

Office audit. An audit conducted by the IRS in the agent's office.

Office in the home expenses. Employment and business-related expenses attributable to the use of a residence (e.g., den or office) are allowed only if the portion of the residence is exclusively used on a regular basis as a principal place of business of the taxpayer or as a place of business that is used by patients, clients, or customers. In computing the office in the home expenses, a taxpayer can use either the regular method or simplified method. As a general rule, the regular method requires more effort and recordkeeping but results in a larger deduction. Office in home expenses incurred by an employee are not deductible for tax years after 2017 (and through 2025). § 280A.

Operating agreement. The governing document of a limited liability company. This document is similar in structure, function, and purpose to a partnership agreement.

Optional adjustment election. See *Section 754 election*.

Options. The sale or exchange of an option to buy or sell property results in capital gain or loss if the property is a capital asset. Generally, the closing of an option transaction results in short-term capital gain or loss to the writer of the call and the purchaser of the call option. § 1234.

Ordinary and necessary. Two tests for the deductibility of expenses incurred or paid in connection with a trade or business; for the production or collection of income; for the management, conservation, or maintenance of property held for the production of income; or in connection with the determination, collection, or refund of any tax. An expense is ordinary if it is common and accepted in the general industry or type of activity in which the taxpayer is engaged. An expense is necessary if it is appropriate and helpful in furthering the taxpayer's business or income-producing activity. §§ 162(a) and 212.

Ordinary income property. Property contributed to a charitable organization that, if sold rather than contributed, would have resulted in other than long-term capital gain to the donor (i.e., ordinary income property and short-term capital gain property). Examples are inventory and capital assets held for less than the long-term holding period. A contribution of ordinary income property must generally be valued at its fair market value less the gain, if any, that would have been realized if sold. § 170(e).

Organizational expenditures. Expenditures related to the creation of a corporation or partnership. Common organizational expenditures include legal and accounting fees and state incorporation payments. Organizational expenditures exclude those incurred to obtain capital (underwriting fees) or assets (subject to cost recovery). Such expenditures incurred by the end of the entity's first year are eligible for a $5,000 limited expensing (subject to phaseout) and an amortization of the balance over 180 months. §§ 248 and 709(b).

Original issue discount (OID). The difference between the issue price of a debt obligation (e.g., a corporate bond) and the maturity value of the obligation when the issue price is less than the maturity value. OID represents interest and must be amortized and recognized as interest income over the life of the debt obligation using the effective interest method. The difference is not considered to be original issue discount for tax purposes when it is less than one-fourth of 1 percent of the redemption price at maturity multiplied by the number of years to maturity. §§ 1272 and 1273(a)(3).

Other adjustments account (OAA). Used in the context of a distribution from an S corporation. The net accumulation of the entity's exempt income (e.g., municipal bond interest), net of related nondeductible expenses. See § 1368(e)(1)(A).

Other property. In a corporate reorganization, any property in the exchange that is not stock or securities, such as cash or land. This amount constitutes boot. This treatment is similar to that in a like-kind exchange.

Outbound taxation. U.S. tax effects when a U.S. person begins an investment or business activity outside the United States.

Outside basis. A partner's basis in his or her partnership interest.

Ownership change. An event that triggers a § 382 limitation for the acquiring corporation.

P

Partial liquidation. A stock redemption where noncorporate shareholders are permitted sale or exchange treatment. In certain cases, an active business must have existed for at least five years. Only a portion of the outstanding stock in the entity is retired. §§ 302(b)(4) and (e).

Partnership. For income tax purposes, a partnership includes a syndicate, group, pool, or joint venture as well as ordinary partnerships. In an ordinary partnership, two or more parties combine capital and/or services to carry on a business for profit as co-owners. § 7701(a)(2).

Partnership agreement. The governing document of a partnership. A partnership agreement should describe the rights and obligations of the partners; the allocation of entity income, deductions, and cash flows; initial and future capital contribution requirements; conditions for terminating the partnership; and other matters.

Passive activity loss. Any loss from (1) activities in which the taxpayer does not materially participate or (2) rental activities (subject to certain exceptions). Net passive activity losses cannot be used to offset income from nonpassive activity sources. Rather, they are suspended until the taxpayer either generates net passive activity income (and a deduction of such losses is allowed) or disposes of the underlying property (at which time the loss deductions are allowed in full). One relief provision allows landlords who actively participate in the rental activities to deduct up to $25,000 of passive activity losses annually. However, a phaseout of the $25,000 amount commences when the landlord's AGI exceeds $100,000. Another relief provision applies for material participation in a real estate trade or business. § 469.

Passive investment company. A means by which a multistate corporation can reduce the overall effective tax rate by isolating investment income in a low- or no-tax state.

Passive investment income (PII). Gross receipts from royalties, certain rents, dividends, interest, annuities, and gains from the sale or exchange of stock and securities. When earnings and profits (E & P) also exist, if the passive investment income of an S corporation exceeds 25 percent of the corporation's gross receipts for three consecutive years, S status is lost. § 1362(d)(3)(C).

Pass-through entities. A form of business structure for which the income and other tax items are attributed directly to the owners and generally no separate tax is levied upon the entity itself. Examples include sole proprietorships, partnerships, and S corporations. Also referred to as a flow-through entity.

Patent. An intangible asset that may be amortized over a statutory 15-year period as a § 197 intangible. The sale of a patent usually results in favorable long-term capital gain treatment. §§ 197 and 1235.

Payroll factor. The proportion of a multistate corporation's total payroll that is traceable to a specific state. Used in determining the taxable income that is to be apportioned to that state.

Pension plan. A type of deferred compensation arrangement that provides for systematic payments of definitely determinable retirement benefits to employees who meet the requirements set forth in the plan.

Percentage depletion. Depletion based on a statutory percentage applied to the gross income from the property. The taxpayer deducts the greater of cost depletion or percentage depletion. § 613.

Percentage of completion method. A method of reporting gain or loss on certain long-term contracts. Under this method of accounting, the gross contract price is included in income as the contract is completed. Reg. § 1.451–3.

Permanent differences. Under ASC 740, tax-related items that appear in the entity's financial statements or its tax return but not both. For instance, interest income from a municipal bond is a permanent book-tax difference.

Permanent establishment (PE). A level of business activity, as defined under an income tax treaty, that subjects the taxpayer to taxation in a country other than that in which the taxpayer is based. Often evidenced by the presence of a plant, an office, or other fixed place of business. Inventory storage and temporary activities do not rise to the level of a PE. PE is the treaty's equivalent to nexus.

Personal and dependency exemptions. The tax law provides an exemption for each individual taxpayer and an additional exemption for the taxpayer's spouse if a joint return is filed. An individual may also claim a dependency exemption for each dependent, provided certain tests are met. The TCJA of 2017 suspended the deduction for exemptions for tax years after 2017 (and through 2025).

Personal exemptions. See *personal and dependency exemptions.*

Personal holding company (PHC) tax. A penalty tax imposed on certain closely held corporations with excessive investment income. Assessed at a 20 percent tax rate on personal holding company income, reduced by dividends paid and other adjustments. § 541.

Personal residence. If a residence has been owned and used by the taxpayer as the principal residence for at least two years during the five-year period ending on the date of sale, up to $250,000 of realized gain is excluded from gross income. For a married couple filing a joint return, the $250,000 is increased to $500,000 if either spouse satisfies the ownership requirement and both spouses satisfy the use requirement. § 121.

Personal service corporation (PSC). A corporation whose principal activity is the performance of personal services (e.g., health, law, engineering, architecture, accounting, actuarial science, performing arts, or consulting) and where such services are substantially performed by the employee-owners. § 269A(b).

Personalty. All property that is not attached to real estate (realty) and is movable. Examples of personalty are machinery, automobiles, clothing, household furnishings, and personal effects.

Points. Loan origination fees that may be deductible as interest by a buyer of property. A seller of property who pays points reduces the selling price by the amount of the points paid for the buyer. While the seller is not permitted to deduct this amount as interest, the buyer may do so.

Portfolio income. Income from interest, dividends, rentals, royalties, capital gains, or other investment sources. Net passive activity losses cannot be used to offset net portfolio income.

Precedents. A previously decided court decision that is recognized as authority for the disposition of future decisions.

Precontribution gain or loss. Partnerships allow for a variety of special allocations of gain or loss among the partners, but gain or loss that is "built in" on an asset contributed to the partnership is assigned specifically to the contributing partner. § 704(c)(1)(A).

Preferences. In calculating alternative minimum taxable income (AMTI), preference items are added to the taxable income starting point of the AMT calculation. AMT preferences are amounts allowed in the calculation of regular taxable income but not allowed in the calculation of AMTI. For instance, interest income from certain state and local bonds (i.e., private activity bonds) is an AMT preference item. § 57.

Preferred stock bailout. A process where a shareholder used the issuance and sale, or later redemption, of a preferred stock dividend to obtain long-term capital gains, without any loss of voting control over the corporation. In effect, the shareholder received corporate profits without suffering the consequences of dividend income treatment. This procedure led Congress to enact § 306, which, if applicable, converts the prior long-term capital gain on the sale or redemption of the tainted stock to dividend income.

Premium Tax Credit (PTC). A tax credit that is refundable and available in advance of filing a return for the year. The PTC serves to reduce the cost of health coverage obtained on the Marketplace (Exchange). A PTC is available to individuals who purchase coverage on the Exchange and have household income equal to or greater than 100 percent of the Federal poverty line (FPL) and no greater than 400 percent of the FPL. Also, an individual must not have been able to obtain affordable coverage from his or her employer. If obtained in advance, the PTC is given to the insurance provider to lower the monthly premium cost to the individual. The PTC is reconciled on Form 8962 (Premium Tax Credit) filed with Form 1040 or 1040-A (not Form 1040-EZ). Individuals who obtain insurance through the Marketplace receive Form 1095-A (Health Insurance Marketplace Statement) by January 31 of the following year. This form provides information necessary to claim or reconcile the PTC, including the monthly cost of premiums and the amount of PTC received in advance each month. § 36B.

Preparer Tax Identification Number (PTIN). This number is required for individuals who are compensated for preparing or assisting in the preparation of all or substantially all of most Federal tax returns. The number must be renewed annually and reported along with the preparer's signature on the tax return to avoid imposition of a penalty. §§ 6109 and 6695.

Principal partner. A partner with a 5 percent or greater interest in partnership capital or profits. § 706(b)(3).

Private activity bonds. Interest on state and local bonds is excludible from gross income. Certain such bonds are labeled private activity bonds. Although the interest on such bonds is excludible for regular tax purposes, it is treated as a tax preference in calculating the AMT. §§ 57(a)(5) and 103.

Private foundations. An exempt organization that is subject to additional statutory restrictions on its activities and on contributions made to it, because it is not sufficiently supported by the public. Excise taxes may be levied on certain prohibited transactions, and the Code places more stringent restrictions on the deductibility of contributions to private foundations. § 509.

Probate costs. The costs incurred in administering a decedent's estate.

Probate estate. The property of a decedent that is subject to administration by the executor or administrator of an estate.

Procedural Regulations. A Regulation issued by the Treasury Department that is a housekeeping-type instruction indicating information that taxpayers should provide the IRS as well as information about the internal management and conduct of the IRS itself.

Profit and loss sharing ratios. Specified in the partnership agreement and used to determine each partner's allocation of ordinary taxable income and separately stated items. Profits and losses can be shared in different ratios. The ratios can be changed by amending the partnership agreement or by using a special allocation. § 704(a).

Profit sharing plan. A deferred compensation plan established and maintained by an employer to provide for employee participation in the company's profits. Contributions are paid from the employer's current or accumulated profits to a trustee. Separate accounts are maintained for each participant employee. The plan must provide a definite, predetermined formula for allocating the contributions among the participants. It also must include a definite, predetermined formula for distributing the accumulated funds after a fixed number of years, on the attainment of a stated age, or on the occurrence of certain events such as illness, layoff, or retirement.

Profits (loss) interest. The extent of a partner's entitlement to an allocation of the partnership's operating results. This interest is measured by the profit and loss sharing ratios.

Property. Assets defined in the broadest legal sense. Property includes the unrealized receivables of a cash basis taxpayer, but not services rendered. § 351.

Property dividend. Generally treated in the same manner as a cash distribution, measured by the fair market value of the property on the date of distribution. Distribution of appreciated property causes the distributing C or S corporation to recognize gain. The distributing corporation does not recognize loss on property that has depreciated in value. §§ 311 and 1371(a).

Property factor. The proportion of a multistate corporation's total property that is traceable to a specific state. Used in determining the taxable income that is to be apportioned to that state.

Proportionate distribution. A distribution in which the partners' interests in hot assets does not change. This can happen, for instance, when no hot assets are distributed (e.g., a proportionate cash distribution) or when each partner in a partnership receives a pro rata share of hot assets being distributed. For example, a distribution of $10,000 of hot assets equally to two 50 percent partners is a proportionate distribution.

Proposed Regulations. A Regulation issued by the Treasury Department in proposed, rather than final, form. The interval between the proposal of a Regulation and its finalization permits taxpayers and other interested parties to comment on the propriety of the proposal.

Proprietorship. A business entity for which there is a single owner. The net profit of the entity is reported on the owner's Federal income tax return (Schedule C of Form 1040).

Public Law 86–272. A congressional limit on the ability of the state to force a multistate corporation to assign taxable income to that state. Under P.L. 86–272, where orders for tangible personal property are both filled and delivered outside the state, the entity must establish more than the mere solicitation of such orders before any income can be apportioned to the state.

Publicly traded partnership. A partnership the interests in which are traded on an established securities market or are readily tradable on a secondary market. Publicly traded partnerships are generally treated as corporations for tax purposes unless substantially all of their income is passive or is derived in connection with any mineral or natural resource or certain fuels. § 7704.

Punitive damages. Damages received or paid by the taxpayer can be classified as compensatory damages or as punitive damages. Punitive damages are those awarded to punish the defendant for gross negligence or the intentional infliction of harm. Such damages are includible in gross income. § 104(a)(2).

Q

QBI deduction. See *deduction for qualified business income.*

Qualified ABLE program. A state program that allows funds to be set aside for the benefit of an individual who became disabled or blind before age 26. Cash may be put into the fund annually up to the annual gift tax exclusion amount. Distributions to the designated beneficiary are not taxable provided they do not exceed qualified disability expenses for the year. § 529A.

Qualified business income (QBI). For purposes of the qualified business income deduction, it is the ordinary income less ordinary deductions a taxpayer earns from a qualified trade or business conducted in the United States by the taxpayer. Includes the distributive share of these amounts from each partnership or S corporation interest held by the taxpayer. Does not include certain types of investment income (e.g., capital gains or losses and dividends), "reasonable compensation" paid to a taxpayer with respect to any qualified trade or business, or guaranteed payments made to a partner for services rendered. § 199A(c).

Qualified business income deduction (QBID). See *deduction for qualified business income.*

Qualified business unit (QBU). A subsidiary, branch, or other business entity that conducts business using a currency other than the U.S. dollar.

Qualified dividend income (QDI). See *qualified dividends.*

Qualified dividends. Distributions made by domestic (and certain non-U.S.) corporations to noncorporate shareholders that are subject to tax at the same rates as those applicable to net long-term capital gains (i.e., 0 percent, 15 percent, or 20 percent). The 20 percent rate applies to certain high-income taxpayers. The dividend must be paid out of earnings and profits, and the shareholders must meet certain holding period requirements as to the stock. §§ 1(h)(1) and (11).

Qualified employee discount. Discounts offered employees on merchandise or services that the employer ordinarily sells or provides to customers. The discounts must be generally available to all employees. In the case of property, the discount cannot exceed the employer's gross profit (the sales price cannot be less than the employer's cost). In the case of services, the discounts cannot exceed 20 percent of the normal sales price. § 132(c).

Qualified improvement property. Any improvement to an interior portion of nonresidential real property made after the property is placed in service, including leasehold improvements. § 168(e)(6).

Qualified joint venture. At the election of the taxpayers, certain joint ventures between spouses can avoid partnership classification. Known as a qualified joint venture, the spouses generally report their share of the business activities from the venture as sole proprietors (using two Schedule C forms). This would be reported on Schedule E if the venture relates to a rental property. § 761(f).

Qualified nonrecourse financing. Debt issued on realty by a bank, retirement plan, or governmental agency. Included in the at-risk amount by the investor. In a partnership tax return, the partners' shares of qualified nonrecourse financing are reported on their Schedules K–1. § 465(b)(6).

Qualified real property business indebtedness. Indebtedness that was incurred or assumed by the taxpayer in connection with real property used in a trade or business and is secured by such real property. The taxpayer must not be a C corporation. For qualified real property business indebtedness, the taxpayer may elect to exclude some or all of the income realized from cancellation of debt on qualified real property. If the election is made, the basis of the property must be reduced by the amount excluded. The amount excluded cannot be greater than the excess of the principal amount of the outstanding debt over the fair market value (net of any other debt outstanding on the property) of the property securing the debt. § 108(c).

Qualified residence interest. A term relevant in determining the amount of interest expense the individual taxpayer may deduct as an itemized deduction for what otherwise would be disallowed as a component of personal interest (consumer interest). Qualified residence interest consists of interest paid on qualified residences (principal residence and one other residence) of the taxpayer. Debt that qualifies as qualified residence interest is limited to $1,000,000 of debt to acquire, construct, or substantially improve qualified residences (acquisition indebtedness). For acquisition indebtedness incurred after December 15, 2017, the limit is reduced to $750,000. § 163(h)(3).

Qualified small business corporation. For purposes of computing an exclusion upon the sale of *qualified small business stock,* a C corporation that has aggregate gross assets not exceeding $50 million and that is conducting an active trade or business. § 1202.

Qualified small business stock. Stock in a qualified small business corporation, purchased as part of an original issue after August 10, 1993. The shareholder may exclude from gross income 100 (or 50 or 75) percent of the realized gain on the sale of the stock if he or she held the stock for more than five years. The exclusion percentage depends on when the stock was acquired. § 1202.

Qualified terminable interest property (QTIP). Generally, the marital deduction (for gift and estate tax purposes) is not available if the interest transferred will terminate upon the death of the transferee spouse and pass to someone else. Thus, if Jim (the husband) places property in trust, life estate to Mary (the wife), and remainder to their children upon Mary's death, this is a terminable interest that will not provide Jim (or Jim's estate) with a marital deduction. If, however, the transfer in trust is treated as qualified terminable interest property (the QTIP election is made), the terminable interest restriction is waived and the marital deduction becomes available. In exchange for this deduction, the surviving spouse's gross estate must include the value of the QTIP election assets, even though he or she has no control over the ultimate disposition of the asset. Terminable interest property qualifies for this election if the donee (or heir) is the only beneficiary of the asset during his or her lifetime and receives income distributions relative to the property at least annually. For gifts, the donor spouse is the one who makes the QTIP election. For property transferred by death, the executor of the estate of the deceased spouse makes the election. §§ 2056(b)(7) and 2523(f).

Qualified trade or business. Used in determining the deduction for qualified business income (§ 199A). In general, it includes any trade or business other than providing services as an employee. In addition, a "specified services trade or business" is not a qualified trade or business. § 199A(d)(1)(B).

Qualified transportation fringes. Transportation benefits provided by the employer to the employee. If these benefits are reimbursed by the employer, they are excludible from gross income by the employee, but not deductible by the employer after 2017. Such benefits include (1) transportation in a commuter highway vehicle between the employee's residence and the place of employment, (2) a transit pass, and (3) qualified parking. Qualified transportation fringes are excludible from the employee's gross income to the extent categories (1) and (2) above do not exceed $300 per month in 2023 and category (3) does not exceed $300 per month in 2023. These amounts are indexed annually for inflation. § 132(f).

Qualified tuition program (§ 529 plan). A program that allows college tuition to be prepaid for a beneficiary. When amounts in the plan are used, nothing is included in gross income provided they are used for qualified higher education expenses. § 529.

Qualifying child. An individual who, as to the taxpayer, satisfies the relationship, abode, and age tests. To be claimed as a dependent, such individual must also meet the citizenship and joint return tests and not be self-supporting. §§ 152(a)(1) and (c).

Qualifying relative. An individual who, as to the taxpayer, satisfies the relationship, gross income, and support tests. To be claimed as a dependent, such individual must also meet the citizenship and joint return tests. §§ 152(a)(2) and (d).

R

Rate reconciliation. Under Generally Accepted Accounting Principles, a footnote to the financial statements often includes a table that accounts for differences in the statutory income tax rate that applies to the entity (e.g., 21 percent) and the higher or lower effective tax rate that the entity realized for the reporting period. The rate reconciliation includes only permanent differences between the pre-tax income reported in the financial statements (book income) and taxable income (including credits which have no book equivalent). The rate reconciliation table often is expressed in dollar and/or percentage terms.

Realized gain. See *realized gain or loss.*

Realized gain or loss. The difference between the amount realized upon the sale or other disposition of property and the adjusted basis of the property. § 1001.

Realized loss. See *realized gain or loss.*

Realty. Real estate.

Reasonable cause. Relief from taxpayer and preparer penalties often is allowed where reasonable cause is found for the taxpayer's actions. For example, reasonable cause for the late filing of a tax return might be a flood that damaged the taxpayer's record-keeping systems and made a timely completion of the return difficult.

Reasonable needs of the business. A means of avoiding the penalty tax on an unreasonable accumulation of earnings. In determining the base for this tax (accumulated taxable income), § 535 allows a deduction for "such part of earnings and profits for the taxable year as are retained for the reasonable needs of the business." § 537.

Reasonableness. See *reasonableness requirement.*

Reasonableness requirement. The Code includes a reasonableness requirement with respect to the deduction of salaries and other compensation for services. The courts have expanded this requirement to all business expenses, ruling that an expense must be reasonable in order to be ordinary and necessary. What constitutes reasonableness is a question of fact. If an expense is unreasonable, the amount that is classified as unreasonable is not allowed as a deduction. The question of reasonableness generally arises with respect to closely held corporations where there is no separation of ownership and management. § 162(a)(1).

Recapitalization. A "Type E" reorganization, constituting a major change in the character and amount of outstanding equity of a corporation. Tax-free exchanges are stock for stock, bonds for bonds, and bonds for stock. For example, common stock exchanged for preferred stock can qualify as a tax-free "Type E" reorganization.

Recognized gain. See *recognized gain or loss.*

Recognized gain or loss. The portion of realized gain or loss subject to income taxation.

Recognized loss. See *recognized gain or loss.*

Recourse debt. Debt for which the lender may both foreclose on the property and assess a guarantor for any payments due under the loan. A lender also may make a claim against the assets of any general partner in a partnership to which debt is issued, without regard to whether the partner has guaranteed the debt.

Recovery of capital doctrine. When a taxable sale or exchange occurs, the seller may be permitted to recover his or her investment (or other adjusted basis) in the property before gain or loss is recognized.

Redemption to pay death taxes. Sale or exchange treatment is available relative to this type of stock redemption, to the extent of the proceeds up to the total amount paid by the estate or heir for estate/inheritance taxes and administration expenses. The stock value must exceed 35 percent of the value of the decedent's adjusted gross estate. In meeting this test, shareholdings in corporations where the decedent held at least 20 percent of the outstanding shares are combined. § 303.

Refundable credits. A credit that is paid to the taxpayer even if the amount of the credit (or credits) exceeds the taxpayer's tax liability.

Regular corporations. See *C corporation.*

Rehabilitation expenditures credit. A credit that is based on expenditures incurred to rehabilitate industrial and commercial buildings and certified historic structures. The credit is intended to discourage businesses from moving from older, economically distressed areas to newer locations and to encourage the preservation of historic structures. § 47.

Related party. Various Code Sections define related parties and often include a variety of persons within this (usually detrimental) category. Generally, related parties are accorded different tax treatment from that applicable to other taxpayers who enter into similar transactions. For instance, realized losses that are generated between related parties are not recognized in the year of the loss. However, these deferred losses can be used to offset recognized gains that occur upon the subsequent sale of the asset to a nonrelated party. Other uses of a related-party definition include the conversion of gain upon the sale of a depreciable asset into all ordinary income (§ 1239) and the identification of constructive ownership of stock relative to corporate distributions, redemptions, liquidations, reorganizations, and compensation.

Related-party transactions. The tax law places restrictions upon the recognition of gains and losses between related parties because of the potential for abuse. For example, restrictions are placed on the deduction of losses from the sale or exchange of property between related parties. In addition, under certain circumstances, related-party gains that would otherwise be classified as capital gain are classified as ordinary income. §§ 267, 707(b), and 1239.

Rental activity. Any activity where payments are received principally for the use of tangible property is a rental activity. Temporary Regulations provide that in certain circumstances, activities involving rentals of real and personal property are not to be treated as rental activities. The Temporary Regulations list six exceptions.

Reorganization. Any corporate restructuring, including when one corporation acquires another, a single corporation divides into two or more entities, a corporation makes a substantial change in its capital structure, a corporation undertakes a change in its legal name or domicile, or a corporation goes through a bankruptcy proceeding and continues to exist. The exchange of stock and other securities in a corporate reorganization can be effected favorably for tax purposes if certain statutory requirements are followed strictly. Tax consequences include the nonrecognition of any gain that is realized by the shareholders except to the extent of boot received. § 368.

Report of Foreign Bank and Financial Accounts (FBAR). FinCEN Form 114, Report of Foreign Bank and Financial Accounts (FBAR), must be filed by individuals and some businesses if they have foreign bank, brokerage, or similar accounts where at any time during the calendar year the aggregate balance exceeds $10,000. The form is filed electronically with the U.S. Department of the Treasury and is due by April 15 with an automatic extension to October 15. Significant penalties apply for failure to file the FBAR. The form is not attached to the income tax return (it is separately filed), but any interest earned by the foreign accounts is generally included in the account holder's U.S. taxable income.

Required taxable year. A partnership or limited liability company must use a required tax year as its tax accounting period, or one of three allowable alternative tax year-ends. If there is a common tax year used by owners holding a majority of the entity's capital or profits interests or if the same year-end is used by all "principal partners" (partners who hold 5 percent or more of the capital or profits interests), then that tax year-end is used by the entity. If neither of the first tests results in an allowable year-end (e.g., because there is no majority partner or because the principal partners do not have the same tax year), then the partnership uses the least aggregate deferral method to determine its tax year. § 706.

Research activities credit. A tax credit whose purpose is to encourage research and development. It consists of three components: the incremental research activities credit, the basic research credit, and the energy credit. The incremental research activities credit is equal to 20 percent of the excess qualified research expenditures over the base amount. The basic research credit is equal to 20 percent of the excess of basic research payments over the base amount. § 41.

Research and experimental expenditures. Costs incurred to develop a product or process for which there exists uncertainty regarding its viability. The Code provides three alternatives for the tax treatment of research and experimentation expenditures. They may be expensed in the year paid or incurred, deferred subject to amortization, or capitalized. If the taxpayer does not elect to expense such costs or to defer them subject to amortization (over 60 months), the expenditures must be capitalized. § 174. In general, research and experimentation expenditures paid or incurred after 2021 must be capitalized and amortized over a five-year period. Some of these expenditures may also qualify the taxpayer for the credit for increasing research activities. § 41.

Reserve method. A method of accounting whereby an allowance is permitted for estimated uncollectible accounts. Actual write-offs are charged to the reserve, and recoveries of amounts previously written off are credited to the reserve. The Code permits only certain financial institutions to use the reserve method. § 166.

Residential rental real estate. Buildings for which at least 80 percent of the gross rents are from dwelling units (e.g., an apartment building). This type of building is distinguished from nonresidential (commercial or industrial) buildings in applying the recapture of depreciation provisions. The term also is relevant in distinguishing between buildings that are eligible for a 27.5-year life versus a 39-year life for MACRS purposes. Generally, residential buildings receive preferential treatment. § 168(e)(2)(A).

Revenue Agent's Report (RAR). A Revenue Agent's Report (RAR) reflects any adjustments made by the agent as a result of an audit of the taxpayer. The RAR is mailed to the taxpayer along with the 30-day letter, which outlines the appellate procedures available to the taxpayer.

Revenue neutrality. A description that characterizes tax legislation when it neither increases nor decreases the total revenue collected by the taxing jurisdiction. Thus, any tax revenue losses are offset by tax revenue gains.

Revenue Procedures. A matter of procedural importance to both taxpayers and the IRS concerning the administration of the tax laws is issued as a Revenue Procedure (abbreviated Rev.Proc.). A Revenue Procedure is published in an *Internal Revenue Bulletin* (I.R.B.).

Revenue Rulings. A Revenue Ruling (abbreviated Rev.Rul.) is issued by the National Office of the IRS to express an official interpretation of the tax law as applied to specific transactions. It is more limited in application than a Regulation. A Revenue Ruling is published in an *Internal Revenue Bulletin* (I.R.B.).

Reversionary interest. The trust property that reverts to the grantor after the expiration of an intervening income interest. Assume that Phil places real estate in trust with income to Junior for 11 years and that upon the expiration of this term, the property returns to Phil. Under these circumstances, Phil holds a reversionary interest in the property. A reversionary interest is the same as a remainder interest, except that, in the latter case, the property passes to someone other than the original owner (e.g., the grantor of a trust) upon the expiration of the intervening interest.

Roth IRA. See *Individual Retirement Accounts (IRAs)*.

S

S corporation. The designation for a corporation that elects to be taxed similarly to a partnership. See also *Subchapter S.*

Sale or exchange. A requirement for the recognition of capital gain or loss. Generally, the seller of property must receive money or relief from debt to have sold the property. An exchange involves the transfer of property for other property. Thus, collection of a debt is neither a sale nor an exchange. The term *sale or exchange* is not defined by the Code.

Sales factor. The proportion of a multistate corporation's total sales that is traceable to a specific state. Used in determining the taxable income that is to be apportioned to that state.

Sales tax. A state- or local-level tax on the retail sale of specified property. Generally, the purchaser pays the tax, but the seller collects it, as an agent for the government. Various taxing jurisdictions allow exemptions for purchases of specific items, including certain food, services, and manufacturing equipment. If the purchaser and seller are in different states, a use tax usually applies.

Salvage value. The estimated amount a taxpayer will receive upon the disposition of an asset used in the taxpayer's trade or business. Salvage value is relevant in calculating depreciation under § 167, but is not relevant in calculating cost recovery under § 168.

Schedule K–1. A tax information form prepared for each partner in a partnership, each shareholder of an S corporation, and some beneficiaries of certain trusts. The Schedule K–1 reports the owner's share of the entity's ordinary income or loss from operations as well as the owner's share of separately stated items, along with any other information the partner, shareholder, or beneficiary needs to prepare the return.

Schedule M–1. On the Form 1120, a reconciliation of book net income with Federal taxable income. Accounts for temporary and permanent differences in the two computations, such as depreciation differences, exempt income, and nondeductible items. On Forms 1120S and 1065, the Schedule M–1 reconciles book income with the owners' aggregate taxable income.

Schedule M–3. An *expanded* reconciliation of book net income with Federal taxable income (see *Schedule M–1*). Required of C and S corporations and partnerships/LLCs with total assets of $10 million or more.

Scholarship. Scholarships are generally excluded from the gross income of the recipient unless the payments are a disguised form of compensation for services rendered. However, the Code imposes restrictions on the exclusion. The recipient must be a degree candidate. The excluded amount is limited to amounts used for tuition, fees, books, supplies, and equipment required for courses of instruction. Amounts received for room and board are not eligible for the exclusion. § 117.

Section 121 exclusion. If a residence has been owned and used by the taxpayer as the principal residence for at least two years during the five-year period ending on the date of sale, up to $250,000 of realized gain is excluded from gross income. For a married couple filing a joint return, the $250,000 is increased to $500,000 if either spouse satisfies the ownership requirement and both spouses satisfy the use requirement.

Section 179 expensing. The ability to deduct the cost of qualified property in the year the property is placed in service rather than over the asset's useful life or cost recovery period. The annual ceiling on the deduction is $1,160,000 in 2023 ($1,080,000 in 2022). However, the deduction is reduced dollar for dollar when § 179 property placed in service during the taxable year exceeds $2,890,000 ($2,700,000 in 2022). In addition, the amount expensed under § 179 cannot exceed the aggregate amount of taxable income derived from the conduct of any trade or business by the taxpayer. In the case of a § 179 deduction for a sport-utility vehicle, a $28,900 limitation applies for 2023 ($27,000 for 2022).

Section 179 expensing election. See *Section 179 expensing.*

Section 338 election. When a corporation acquires at least 80 percent of a subsidiary within a 12-month period, it can elect to treat the acquisition of such stock as an asset purchase. The acquiring corporation's basis in the subsidiary's assets then is the cost of the stock. The subsidiary is deemed to have sold its assets for an amount equal to the grossed-up basis in its stock.

Section 382 limitation. When one corporation acquires another, the acquiring corporation's ability to use the loss and credit carryovers of the target may be limited by this anti-abuse provision. For instance, the maximum NOL deduction available to the acquiring is the value of the target when acquired times the long-term tax-exempt interest rate on that date.

Section 401(k) plan. A cash or deferred arrangement plan that allows participants to elect to receive up to $22,500 ($30,000 if age 50 or above) in 2023 in cash (taxed currently) or to have a contribution made on their behalf to a qualified retirement plan (excludible from gross income). The plan may be in the form of a salary reduction agreement between the participant and the employer.

Section 704(b) book capital accounts. Capital accounts calculated as described under Reg. § 1.704–1(b)(2)(iv). All partnerships must maintain § 704(b) book capital accounts for the partners with the intent that final liquidating distributions are in accordance with these capital account balances. Partnership allocations will not be accepted unless they are properly reflected in the partners' § 704(b) book capital accounts. These capital accounts are a hybrid of book and tax accounting methods. They reflect contributions and distributions of property at their fair market values, but the capital accounts are otherwise generally increased by the partnership's tax-basis income and decreased by tax-basis deductions (as reported on the partner's Schedule K–1). Liabilities are only reflected in these capital accounts to the extent the partnership assumes a partner's liability [reduces that partner's § 704(b) book capital account] or a partner assumes a partnership liability [increases that partner's § 704(b) book capital account]. See also *capital account maintenance* and *economic effect test.*

Section 754 election. An election that may be made by a partnership to adjust the basis of partnership assets to reflect a purchasing partner's outside basis in interest or to reflect a gain, loss, or basis adjustment of a partner receiving a distribution from a partnership. The intent of the election is to maintain the equivalence between outside and inside bases for the purchasing partner (in the case of a sale of a partnership interest) or the remaining partners in the partnership (in the case of a distribution that changes the balance of inside and outside bases). Once the election is made, the partnership must make basis adjustments for all future transactions, unless the IRS consents to revoke the election.

Section 1231 gains and losses. If the combined gains and losses from the taxable dispositions of § 1231 assets plus the net gain from business involuntary conversions (of both § 1231 assets and long-term capital assets) result in a gain, the gains and losses are treated as long-term capital gains and losses. In arriving at § 1231 gains, however, the depreciation recapture provisions (e.g., § 1245) are applied first to produce ordinary income. If the net result of the combination is a loss, the gains and losses from § 1231 assets are treated as ordinary gains and losses. § 1231(a).

Section 1231 lookback. For gain to be classified as § 1231 gain, the gain must survive the § 1231 lookback. To the extent of nonrecaptured § 1231 losses for the five prior tax years, the gain is classified as ordinary income. § 1231(c).

Section 1231 property. Depreciable assets and real estate used in trade or business and held for the required long-term holding period. § 1231(b).

Section 1244 stock. Stock issued under § 1244 by qualifying small business corporations. If § 1244 stock becomes worthless, the shareholders may claim an ordinary loss rather than the usual capital loss, within statutory limitations.

Section 1245 property. Property that is subject to the recapture of depreciation under § 1245. For a definition of § 1245 property, see § 1245(a)(3).

Section 1245 recapture. Upon a taxable disposition of § 1245 property, all depreciation claimed on the property is recaptured as ordinary income (but not to exceed any recognized gain from the disposition).

Section 1250 property. Real estate that is subject to the recapture of depreciation under § 1250. For a definition of § 1250 property, see § 1250(c).

Section 1250 recapture. Upon a taxable disposition of § 1250 property, accelerated depreciation claimed in excess of straight-line depreciation on the property is recaptured as ordinary income.

Securities. Stock, debt, and other financial assets. To the extent securities other than the stock of the transferee corporation are received in a § 351 exchange, the new shareholder recognizes a gain. For purposes of corporate reorganizations, securities are generally debt with terms longer than 10 years. To the extent stock and securities are transferred in a corporate reorganization under § 368, no gain or loss is recognized.

Self-employment tax. A tax of 12.4 percent is levied on individuals with net earnings from self-employment (up to $160,200 in 2023) to provide Social Security benefits (i.e., the old age, survivors, and disability insurance portion) for such individuals. In addition, a tax of 2.9 percent is levied on individuals with net earnings from self-employment (with no statutory ceiling) to provide Medicare benefits (i.e., the hospital insurance portion) for such individuals. If a self-employed individual also receives wages from an employer that are subject to FICA, the self-employment tax will be reduced. A partial deduction is allowed in calculating the self-employment tax. Individuals with net earnings of $400 or more from self-employment are subject to this tax. §§ 1401 and 1402.

Separate foreign tax credit income categories. The foreign tax credit of a taxpayer is computed for each of several types of income sources, as specified by the Code to limit the results of tax planning. FTC income "baskets" include general and passive. The FTC for the year is the sum of the credits as computed within all of the taxpayer's separate FTC baskets used for the tax year.

Separate return limitation year (SRLY). A series of rules limits the amount of an acquired corporation's net operating loss carryforwards that can be used by the acquiror. Generally, a consolidated return can include the acquiree's net operating loss carryforward only to the extent of the lesser of the subsidiary's (1) current-year or (2) cumulative positive contribution to consolidated taxable income.

Separately stated items. Any item of a partnership or an S corporation that might be taxed differently to any two owners of the entity. These amounts are not included in the ordinary income of the entity, but are instead reported separately to the owners; tax consequences are determined at the owner level.

Severance taxes. A tax imposed upon the extraction of natural resources.

Short period. See *short taxable year*.

Short sale. A sale that occurs when a taxpayer sells borrowed property (usually stock) and repays the lender with substantially identical property either held on the date of the short sale or purchased after the sale. No gain or loss is recognized until the short sale is closed, and such gain or loss is generally short term. § 1233.

Short taxable year. A tax year that is less than 12 months. A short taxable year may occur in the initial reporting period, in the final tax year, or when the taxpayer changes tax years. Special income tax computations may be required.

Significant participation activity. Seven tests determine whether an individual has achieved material participation in an activity, one of which is based on more than 500 hours of participation in significant participation activities. A significant participation activity is one in which the individual's participation exceeds 100 hours during the year. Temp.Reg. § 1.469–5T.

Simple trust. Trusts that are not complex trusts. Such trusts may not have a charitable beneficiary, accumulate income, or distribute corpus.

Simplified employee pension (SEP) plans. An employer may make contributions to an employee's IRA in amounts not exceeding the lesser of 15 percent of compensation or $66,000 per individual in 2023. These employer-sponsored simplified employee pensions are permitted only if the contributions are nondiscriminatory and are made on behalf of all employees who have attained age 21 and have worked for the employer during at least three of the five preceding calendar years. § 219(b).

Small business corporation. A corporation that satisfies the definition of § 1361(b), § 1244(c), or both. Satisfaction of § 1361(b) permits an S election, and satisfaction of § 1244 enables the shareholders of the corporation to claim an ordinary loss on the worthlessness of stock.

Small business stock (§ 1244 stock). See *Section 1244 stock.*

Small Cases Division. A division within the U.S. Tax Court where jurisdiction is limited to claims of $50,000 or less. There is no appeal from this court.

Solicitation of orders. A level of activity brought about by the taxpayer within a specific state. Under Public Law 86–272, certain types of solicitation activities do not create nexus with the state. Exceeding mere solicitation, though, creates nexus.

Special allocation. Any amount for which an agreement exists among the partners of a partnership outlining the method used for spreading the item among the partners.

Special use value. Permits the executor of an estate to value, for estate tax purposes, real estate used in a farming activity or in connection with a closely held business at its current use value rather than at its most suitable or optimal use value. Under this option, a farm is valued for farming purposes even though, for example, the property might have a higher potential value as a shopping center. For the executor of an estate to elect special use valuation, the conditions of § 2032A must be satisfied.

Specific charge-off method. A method of accounting for bad debts in which a deduction is permitted only when an account becomes partially or completely worthless.

Specified service trade or business. For purposes of the deduction for qualified business income, a specified service trade or business includes those involving the performance of services in certain fields, including health, law, accounting, actuarial science, performing arts, consulting, athletics, financial services, and brokerage services; services consisting of investing and investment management, trading or dealing in securities, partnership interests, or commodities; and any trade or business where the business's principal asset is the reputation of one or more of its employees or owners. § 199A(d)(2).

Spin-off. A type of reorganization where, for example, Apple Corporation transfers some assets to Core Corporation in exchange for Core stock representing control. Apple then distributes the Core stock to its shareholders.

Split-off. A type of reorganization where, for example, Apple Corporation transfers some assets to Core Corporation in exchange for Core stock representing control. Apple then distributes the Core stock to its shareholders in exchange for some of their Apple stock. Not all shareholders need to exchange stock.

Split-up. A type of reorganization where, for example, Firefly Corporation transfers some assets to Fire Corporation and the remainder to Fly Corporation. In return, Firefly receives enough Fire and Fly stock representing control of each corporation. Firefly then distributes the Fire and Fly stock to its shareholders in return for all of their Firefly stock. Firefly then liquidates, and its shareholders now have control of Fire and Fly.

Sprinkling trust. When a trustee has the discretion to either distribute or accumulate the entity accounting income of the trust and to distribute it among the trust's income beneficiaries in varying magnitudes. The trustee can "sprinkle" the income of the trust.

Standard deduction. The individual taxpayer can either itemize deductions or take the standard deduction. The amount of the standard deduction is equal to the sum of the basic standard deduction and any additional standard deduction, and it depends on the taxpayer's filing status (single, head of household, married filing jointly, surviving spouse, or married filing separately). For 2023, the amount of the basic standard deduction ranges from $13,850 (for single) to $27,700 (for married, filing jointly). Additional standard deductions of either $1,500 (for married taxpayers) or $1,850 (for single taxpayers) are available if the taxpayer is blind or age 65 or over. Limitations exist on the amount of the basic standard deduction of a taxpayer who is another taxpayer's dependent. The standard deduction amounts are adjusted for inflation each year. § 63(c).

Startup expenditures. Expenditures paid or incurred prior to the beginning of the business that would have been deductible as an ordinary and necessary business expense if business operations had begun. Examples of such expenditures include advertising; salaries and wages; travel and other expenses incurred in lining up prospective distributors, suppliers, or customers; and salaries and fees to executives, consultants, and professional service providers. A taxpayer will immediately expense the first $5,000 (subject to phaseout) of startup expenditures and amortize the balance over a period of 180 months, unless the taxpayer elects not to do so. § 195.

Statements on Standards for Tax Services (SSTS). Ethical standards for tax practice applicable to members of the AICPA.

Statute of limitations. Provisions of the law that specify the maximum period of time in which action may be taken concerning a past event. Code §§ 6501–6504 contain the limitation periods applicable to the IRS for additional assessments, and §§ 6511–6515 relate to refund claims by taxpayers.

Statutory employees. Statutory employees are considered self-employed independent contractors for purposes of reporting income and expenses on their tax returns. Generally, a statutory employee must meet three tests:

- It is understood from a service contract that the services will be performed by the person.
- The person does not have a substantial investment in facilities (other than transportation used to perform the services).
- The services involve a continuing relationship with the person for whom they are performed.

For further information on statutory employees, see Circular E, *Employer's Tax Guide* (IRS Publication 15).

Statutory tax rate. The statutory tax rate is the tax rate (or rates) specified in the law. For example, § 11 provides that the income tax rate for corporations is 21 percent.

Step down. See *step-down in basis.*

Step transaction. Disregarding one or more transactions to arrive at the final result. Assume, for example, Beta Corporation creates Alpha Corporation by transferring assets desired by Beta's sole shareholder, Carl. Carl then causes Alpha to liquidate to obtain the assets. Under these circumstances, the IRS may contend that the creation and liquidation of Alpha be disregarded. What really happened was a dividend distribution from Beta to Carl.

Step up. See *step-up in basis.*

Step-down in basis. A reduction in the tax basis of property. See also *step-up in basis.*

Step-up in basis. An increase in the income tax basis of property. In an estate context, a step-up in basis occurs when a decedent dies owning appreciated property. Because the estate or heir acquires a basis in the property equal to the property's fair market value on the date of death (or alternate valuation date if available and elected), any appreciation is not subject to the income tax. Thus, a step-up in basis is the result, with no immediate income tax consequences. In the partnership context, a step-up arises when a § 754 election is in effect and when one of several transactions arises: (1) a partner purchases a partnership interest for an amount that exceeds the partner's share of the partnership's inside basis, (2) the partner recognizes a gain on a distribution of cash from the partnership, or (3) a partner takes a basis in a distributed asset that is less than the partnership's basis in that asset. In the opposite situations (e.g., loss recognition or where a partner takes a basis in a distributed asset that exceeds the partnership's basis in that asset), a step-down can arise. See also *step-down in basis.*

Stock bonus plan. A type of deferred compensation plan in which the employer establishes and maintains the plan and contributes employer stock to the plan for the benefit of employees. The contributions need not be dependent on the employer's profits. Any benefits of the plan are distributable in the form of employer stock, except that distributable fractional shares may be paid in cash.

Stock dividend. Not taxable if pro rata distributions of stock or stock rights on common stock. Section 305 governs the taxability of stock dividends and sets out five exceptions to the general rule that stock dividends are nontaxable.

Stock option. The right to purchase a stated number of shares of stock from a corporation at a certain price within a specified period of time. §§ 421 and 422.

Stock redemption. A corporation buys back its own stock from a specified shareholder. Typically, the corporation recognizes any realized gain on the noncash assets that it uses to effect a redemption, and the shareholder obtains a capital gain or loss upon receipt of the purchase price.

Stock rights. Assets that convey to the holder the power to purchase corporate stock at a specified price, often for a limited period of time. Stock rights received may be taxed as a distribution of earnings and profits. After the right is exercised, the basis of the acquired share includes the investor's purchase price or gross income, if any, to obtain the right. Disposition of the right also can be taxable.

Subchapter S. Sections 1361–1379 of the Internal Revenue Code. An elective provision permitting certain small business corporations (§ 1361) and their shareholders (§ 1362) to elect to be treated for income tax purposes in accordance with the operating rules of §§ 1363–1379. S corporations usually avoid the corporate income tax, and corporate losses can be claimed by the shareholders.

Subpart F income. Certain types of income earned by a controlled foreign corporation that are included in U.S. gross income by U.S. shareholders of such an entity as they are generated, not when they are repatriated. See § 951.

Substance over form. A standard used when one must ascertain the true reality of what has occurred. Suppose, for example, a father sells stock to his daughter for $1,000. If the stock is really worth $50,000 at the time of the transfer, the substance of the transaction is probably a gift to her of $49,000.

Substantial authority. Taxpayer and tax preparer understatement penalties are waived where substantial authority existed for the disputed position taken on the return.

Substantial basis reduction. Arises when the partnership makes a liquidating distribution to a partner (under § 736) and the distributee partner recognizes a loss (or has a basis increase for the distributed assets) of at least $250,000. (The second situation would arise when the basis of the assets the liquidated partner receives must be stepped up to absorb all remaining partnership interest basis.) If there is a substantial basis reduction, the partnership is required to make a downward adjustment to the basis of its assets, even if the partnership does not have a § 754 election in effect. This adjustment is treated as a § 754 adjustment related to a distribution and so is allocated to the basis of all remaining partnership assets (except for cash). See also *substantial built-in loss* and *§ 754 election.*

Substantial built-in loss. Arises when a partner sells a partnership interest (under § 741) and the selling partner recognizes a loss on the sale of at least $250,000. In addition, a substantial built-in loss arises if the selling partner would be allocated more than a $250,000 loss if all partnership assets were sold (after considering special allocations). If there is a substantial built-in loss, the partnership is required to make a downward adjustment in the basis of its assets, even if the partnership does not have a § 754 election in effect. This adjustment is treated as a § 754 adjustment related to a sale of a partnership interest and so is allocated to the purchasing partner. See also *substantial basis reduction* and *§ 754 election.*

Substantially appreciated inventory. In partnership taxation, for purposes of the regular distribution rules and distributions under § 736, a distribution of inventory is only treated as a hot asset if it is substantially appreciated, meaning the fair market value of the inventory exceeds 120 percent of its basis. See *appreciated inventory.*

Sunset provision. A provision attached to new tax legislation that will cause such legislation to expire at a specified date. Sunset provisions are attached to tax cut bills for long-term budgetary reasons to make their effect temporary. Once the sunset provision comes into play, the tax cut is rescinded and former law is reinstated. An example of a sunset provision is contained in the Tax Relief Reconciliation Act of 2001 that related to the estate tax. After the estate tax was phased out in 2010, a sunset provision called for the reinstatement of the estate tax as of January 1, 2011.

Surviving spouse. When a husband or wife predeceases the other spouse, the survivor is known as a surviving spouse. Under certain conditions, a surviving spouse may be entitled to use the income tax rates in § 1(a) (those applicable to married persons filing a joint return) for the two years after the year of death of his or her spouse. § 2(a).

Syndication costs. Incurred in promoting and marketing partnership interests for sale to investors. Examples include legal and accounting fees, printing costs for prospectus and placement documents, and state registration fees. These items are capitalized by the partnership as incurred, with no amortization thereof allowed.

T

Tax avoidance. The minimization of one's tax liability by taking advantage of legally available tax planning opportunities. Tax avoidance can be contrasted with tax evasion, which entails the reduction of tax liability by illegal means.

Tax basis capital account. Capital accounts calculated using the tax rules by which the Form 1065 income, expenses, gains, and losses are reported. Beginning in tax year 2020, all partnerships must report partners' capital on Schedules K–1 using the tax method. These capital accounts reflect contributions and distributions of property at their tax (generally carryover) basis. Capital accounts are otherwise generally increased by the partnership's tax-basis income and decreased by tax-basis deductions. Liabilities are not included in the partners' tax basis capital accounts. See also *§ 704(b) book capital accounts.*

Tax benefit rule. A provision that limits the recognition of income from the recovery of an expense or a loss properly deducted in a prior tax year to the amount of the deduction that generated a tax saving.

Tax credits. Amounts that directly reduce a taxpayer's tax liability. The tax benefit received from a tax credit is not dependent on the taxpayer's marginal tax rate, whereas the benefit of a tax deduction or exclusion is dependent on the taxpayer's tax bracket.

Tax evasion. The reduction of taxes by the use of subterfuge or fraud or other nonlegal means. For example, a cash basis taxpayer tries to increase his or her charitable contribution deduction by prepaying next year's church pledge with a pre-dated check issued in the following year.

Tax haven. A country in which either locally sourced income or residents of the country are subject to a low rate of taxation.

Tax preparer. One who prepares tax returns for compensation. A tax preparer must register with the IRS and receive a special ID number to practice before the IRS and represent taxpayers before the agency in tax audit actions. The conduct of a tax preparer is regulated under Circular 230. Tax preparers also are subject to penalties for inappropriate conduct when working in the tax profession.

Tax provision. Used interchangeably to (1) describe the total amount of income tax expense (benefit) recognized by a corporation in its financial statements and (2) the process of determining that amount. The tax provision includes both a current amount (composed primarily of the income taxes related to the corporation's current taxable income) and a deferred amount [the tax consequences of income reported in the current-year financial statements but not yet due (realizable) under the tax law].

Tax Rate Schedules. Rate schedules that are used by upper-income taxpayers and those not permitted to use the tax table. Separate rate schedules are provided for married individuals filing jointly, heads of households, single taxpayers, estates and trusts, and married individuals filing separate returns. § 1.

Tax research. The method used to determine the best available solution to a situation that possesses tax consequences. Both tax and nontax factors are considered.

Tax shelters. The typical tax shelter generated large losses in the early years of the activity. Investors would offset these losses against other types of income and therefore avoid paying income taxes on this income. These tax shelter investments could then be sold after a few years and produce capital gain income, which is taxed at a lower rate compared to ordinary income. The passive activity loss rules and the at-risk rules now limit tax shelter deductions.

Tax Table. A table that is provided for taxpayers with less than $100,000 of taxable income. Separate columns are provided for single taxpayers, married taxpayers filing jointly, heads of households, and married taxpayers filing separately. § 3.

Tax treaties. An agreement between the U.S. Department of State and another country designed to alleviate double taxation of income and asset transfers, and to share administrative information useful to tax agencies in both countries. The United States has income tax treaties with almost 70 countries.

Taxable estate. The taxable estate is the gross estate of a decedent reduced by the deductions allowed by §§ 2053–2057 (e.g., administration expenses, marital and charitable deductions). The taxable estate is subject to the unified transfer tax at death. § 2051.

Taxable gift. The amount of a gift that is subject to the unified transfer tax. Thus, a taxable gift has been adjusted by the annual exclusion and other appropriate deductions (e.g., marital and charitable). § 2053.

Taxable year. The annual period over which income is measured for income tax purposes. Most individuals use a calendar year, but many businesses use a fiscal year based on the natural business year. Certain entities, including S corporations, have a required taxable year. §§ 441, 706, and 1378.

Technical Advice Memoranda (TAM). TAMs are issued by the IRS in response to questions raised by IRS field personnel during audits. They deal with completed rather than proposed transactions and are often requested for questions related to exempt organizations and employee plans.

Temporary differences. Under ASC 740 (SFAS 109), tax-related items that appear in the entity's financial statements and its tax return, but in different time periods. For instance, doubtful accounts receivable often create a temporary book-tax difference, as a bad debt reserve is used to compute an expense for financial reporting purposes, but a bad debt often is deductible only under the specific write-off rule for tax purposes, and the difference observed for the current period creates a temporary difference.

Temporary Regulations. A Regulation issued by the Treasury Department in temporary form. When speed is critical, the Treasury Department issues Temporary Regulations that take effect immediately. These Regulations have the same authoritative value as Final Regulations and may be cited as precedent for three years. Temporary Regulations are also issued as proposed Regulations.

Tenants by the entirety. Essentially, a joint tenancy between husband and wife.

Tenants in common. A form of ownership where each tenant (owner) holds an undivided interest in property. Unlike a joint tenancy or a tenancy by the entirety, the interest of a tenant in common does not terminate upon that individual's death (there is no right of survivorship). Assume that Tim and Cindy acquire real estate as equal tenants in common. Upon Tim's death, his one-half interest in the property passes to his estate or heirs, not automatically to Cindy.

Terminable interests. An interest in property that terminates upon the death of the holder or upon the occurrence of some other specified event. The transfer of a terminable interest by one spouse to the other may not qualify for the marital deduction. §§ 2056(b) and 2523(b).

Theft losses. A loss from larceny, embezzlement, or robbery. It does not include misplacement of items.

Thin capitalization. When debt owed by a corporation to the shareholders becomes too large in relation to the corporation's capital structure (i.e., stock and shareholder equity), the IRS may contend that the corporation is thinly capitalized. In effect, some or all of the debt is reclassified as equity. The immediate result is to disallow any interest deduction to the corporation on the reclassified debt. To the extent of the corporation's earnings and profits, interest payments and loan repayments on the reclassified debt are treated as dividends to the shareholders.

Thirty-day (30-day) letter. A letter that accompanies an RAR (Revenue Agent's Report) issued as a result of an IRS audit of a taxpayer (or the rejection of a taxpayer's claim for refund). The letter outlines the taxpayer's appeal procedure before the IRS. If the taxpayer does not request any such procedures within the 30-day period, the IRS issues a statutory notice of deficiency (the 90-day letter).

Throwback rule. If there is no income tax in the state to which a sale otherwise would be apportioned, the sale essentially is exempt from state income tax, even though the seller is domiciled in a state that levies an income tax. Nonetheless, if the seller's state has adopted a throwback rule, the sale is attributed to the seller's state and the transaction is subjected to a state-level tax.

Traditional IRA. See *Individual Retirement Accounts (IRAs)*.

Transfer pricing. The process of setting internal prices for transfers of goods and services among related taxpayers. For example, what price should be used when Subsidiary purchases management services from Parent? The IRS can adjust transfer prices when it can show that the taxpayers were attempting to avoid tax by, for example, shifting losses, deductions, or credits from low-tax to high-tax entities or jurisdictions.

Transportation expenses. Expenses that include the cost of transporting the self-employed taxpayer (or employee) from one place to another in the course of business when the taxpayer is not in travel status. For tax years beginning after 2017 and before 2026, only reimbursed transportation expenses are deductible by employees. Commuting expenses are not deductible.

Travel expenses. Expenses that include meals (generally subject to a 50 percent disallowance) and lodging and transportation expenses while away from home in the pursuit of a trade or business (including that of an employee). For tax years beginning after 2017 and before 2026, only reimbursed travel expenses are deductible by employees.

Treaty shopping. An international investor attempts to use the favorable aspects of a tax treaty to his or her advantage, often elevating the form of the transaction over its substance (e.g., by establishing only a nominal presence in the country offering the favorable treaty terms).

Twelve-month (12-month) rule for prepaid expenses. Taxpayers who use the cash method are required to use the accrual method for deducting certain prepaid expenses (i.e., must capitalize the item and can deduct only when used). If a prepayment will not be consumed or expire by the end of the tax year following the year of payment, the prepayment must be capitalized and prorated over the benefit period. Conversely, if the prepayment will be consumed by the end of the tax year following the year of payment, it can be expensed when paid. To obtain the current deduction under the one-year rule, the payment must be a required payment rather than a voluntary payment.

U

UDITPA. The Uniform Division of Income for Tax Purposes Act has been adopted in some form by many of the states. The Act develops criteria by which the total taxable income of a multistate corporation can be assigned to specific states.

Unclaimed property. A U.S. state may have the right to acquire property that has been made available to an individual or legal entity for a fixed period of time, where the claimant has not taken possession of the property after a notice period. Examples of such property that a state could acquire are an uncashed payroll check or an unused gift card.

Unearned income. Income received but not yet earned. Normally, such income is taxed when received, even for accrual basis taxpayers.

Unified transfer tax. Rates applicable to transfers by gift and death made after 1976. § 2001(c).

Unified transfer tax credit. A credit allowed against any unified transfer tax. §§ 2010 and 2505.

Uniform capitalization (UNICAP) rules. Under § 263A, the Regulations provide a set of rules that all taxpayers (regardless of the particular industry) can use to determine the items of cost (and means of allocating those costs) that must be capitalized with respect to the production of tangible property. Small businesses, defined as those with average annual gross receipts in the prior three-year period of $29 million or less, that are not a tax shelter, are not required to use the UNICAP rules.

Unitary approach. See *unitary theory*.

Unitary theory. Sales, property, and payroll of related corporations are combined for nexus and apportionment purposes, and the worldwide income of the unitary entity is apportioned to the state. Subsidiaries and other affiliated corporations found to be part of the corporation's unitary business (because they are subject to overlapping ownership, operation, or management) are included in the apportionment procedure. This approach can be limited if a waters'-edge election is in effect.

Unit-livestock-price method. A method of accounting for the cost of livestock. The livestock are valued using a standard cost of raising an animal with the characteristics of the animals on hand to the same age as those animals.

Unrealized receivables. Amounts earned by a cash basis taxpayer but not yet received. Because of the method of accounting used by the taxpayer, these amounts have a zero income tax basis. When unrealized receivables are distributed to a partner, they generally convert a transaction from nontaxable to taxable or an otherwise capital gain to ordinary income (i.e., as a "hot asset").

Unreasonable compensation. A deduction is allowed for "reasonable" salaries or other compensation for personal services actually rendered. The issue of unreasonable compensation usually is limited to closely held corporations, where the motivation is to pay out profits in some form that is deductible to the corporation. To the extent compensation is "excessive" ("unreasonable"), the distribution could be treated as a dividend, such that no deduction is allowed.

Unreasonable position. A tax preparer penalty is assessed regarding the understatement of a client's tax liability due to a tax return position that is found to be too aggressive. The penalty is avoided if there is substantial authority for the position or if the position is disclosed adequately on the tax return. The penalty equals the greater of $1,000 or one-half of the tax preparer's fee that is traceable to the aggressive position.

Unrecaptured § 1250 gain. Gain from the sale of depreciable real estate held more than one year. The gain is equal to or less than the depreciation taken on such property and is reduced by § 1245 and § 1250 gain. § 1(h)(6).

Unrelated business income (UBI). Income recognized by an exempt organization that is generated from activities not related to the exempt purpose of the entity. For instance, the gift shop located in a hospital may generate unrelated business income. §§ 511 and 512.

Unrelated business income tax (UBIT). Levied on the unrelated business income of an exempt organization.

U.S. Court of Federal Claims. A trial court (court of original jurisdiction) that decides litigation involving Federal tax matters. Appeal from this court is to the Court of Appeals for the Federal Circuit.

U.S. District Court. A trial court for purposes of litigating Federal tax matters. This court allows a jury trial.

U.S. shareholder. For purposes of classification of an entity as a controlled foreign corporation, a U.S. person who owns, or is considered to own, 10 percent or more of the total combined voting power of all classes of voting stock of a foreign corporation. Stock owned directly, indirectly, and constructively is counted for this purpose. § 951(b).

U.S. Supreme Court. The highest appellate court or the court of last resort in the Federal court system and in most states. Only a small number of tax decisions of the U.S. Courts of Appeal are reviewed by the U.S. Supreme Court under its certiorari procedure. The Supreme Court usually grants certiorari to resolve a conflict among the Courts of Appeal (e.g., two or more appellate courts have assumed opposing positions on a particular issue) or when the tax issue is extremely important (e.g., due to the size of the revenue loss to the Federal government).

U.S. Tax Court. One of four trial courts of original jurisdiction that decides litigation involving Federal income, death, or gift taxes. The only trial court where the taxpayer must not first pay the deficiency assessed by the IRS. The Tax Court does not have jurisdiction over a case unless a statutory notice of deficiency (90-day letter) has been issued by the IRS and the taxpayer files the petition for hearing within the time prescribed.

U.S. trade or business. A set of activities that is carried on in a regular, continuous, and substantial manner. A non-U.S. taxpayer is subject to U.S. tax on the taxable income that is effectively connected with a U.S. trade or business.

Use tax. A use tax is designed to complement the sales tax. The use tax has two purposes: to prevent consumers from evading sales tax by purchasing goods outside the state for in-state use, and to provide an equitable taxing environment between in-state and out-of-state retailers. Purchasers of taxable goods or services who were not charged sales tax because the seller did not have *nexus* with the purchaser's state may owe use tax on the purchase.

V

Vacation homes. The Code places restrictions upon taxpayers who rent their residences or vacation homes for part of the tax year. The restrictions may result in a scaling down of expense deductions for the taxpayers. § 280A.

Valuation allowance. Under ASC 740 (SFAS 109), a tax-related item is reported for book purposes only when it is more likely than not that the item actually will be realized. When the "more likely than not" test is failed, a contra-asset account is created to offset some or all of the related deferred tax asset. For instance, if the entity projects that it will not be able to use all of its net operating loss carryforward due to a lack of future taxable income, a valuation allowance is created to reduce the net deferred tax asset that corresponds to the carryforward. If income projections later change and it appears that the carryforward will be used, the valuation allowance is reversed or "released." Creation of a valuation allowance usually increases the current tax expense and thereby reduces current book income, and its release often increases book income in the later reporting period.

Value added tax (VAT). A national sales tax that taxes the increment in value as goods move through the production process. A VAT is much used in the majority of countries but has not yet been incorporated as part of the U.S. Federal tax structure.

Vesting requirements. A qualified deferred compensation arrangement must satisfy a vesting requirement. Under this provision, an employee's right to accrued plan benefits derived from employer contributions must be nonforfeitable in accordance with one of two vesting time period schedules (or two required alternate vesting schedules for certain employer matching contributions).

Voluntary revocation. The owners of a majority of shares in an S corporation elect to terminate the S status of the entity as of a specified date. The day on which the revocation is effective is the first day of the C corporation's tax year.

W

W–2 Wages/Capital Investment Limit. A limitation on the deduction for qualified business income that caps the deduction at the greater of (1) 50 percent of the wages paid by a qualified trade or business or (2) 25 percent of the wages paid by the qualified trade or business plus 2.5 percent of the taxpayer's share of the unadjusted basis of property used in the business that has not been fully depreciated prior to the close of the taxable year. § 199A(b)(2)(B).

Wash sale. A loss from the sale of stock or securities that is disallowed because the taxpayer, within 30 days before or after the sale, has acquired stock or securities substantially identical to those sold. § 1091.

Waters' edge. A limitation on the worldwide scope of the unitary theory. If a corporate waters'-edge election is in effect, the state can consider in the apportionment procedure only the activities that occur within the boundaries of the United States.

Waters'-edge election. See *waters' edge.*

Wherewithal to pay. This concept recognizes the inequity of taxing a transaction when the taxpayer lacks the means with which to pay the tax. Under it, there is a correlation between the imposition of the tax and the ability to pay the tax. It is particularly suited to situations in which the taxpayer's economic position has not changed significantly as a result of the transaction.

Whistleblower Program. An IRS initiative that offers special rewards to informants who provide evidence regarding tax evasion activities of businesses or high-income individuals. More than $2 million of tax, interest, and penalty must be at stake. The reward can reach 30 percent of the tax recovery that is attributable to the whistleblower's information.

Work opportunity tax credit. Employers are allowed a tax credit equal to 40 percent of the first $6,000 of wages (per eligible employee) for the first year of employment. Eligible employees include certain hard-to-employ individuals (e.g., qualified ex-felons, high-risk youth, food stamp recipients, and veterans). The employer's deduction for wages is reduced by the amount of the credit taken. For qualified summer youth employees, the 40 percent rate is applied to the first $3,000 of qualified wages. The credit does not apply to any amount paid to an individual who begins work for the employer after 2025. §§ 51 and 52.

Working condition fringes. A type of fringe benefit received by the employee that is excludible from the employee's gross income. It consists of property or services provided (paid or reimbursed) by the employer for which the employee could take a tax deduction if the employee had paid for them. § 132(d).

Worthless securities. A loss (usually capital) is allowed for a security that becomes worthless during the year. The loss is deemed to have occurred on the last day of the year. Special rules apply to securities of affiliated companies and small business stock. § 165.

Writ of Certiorari. Appeal from a U.S. Court of Appeals to the U.S. Supreme Court is by Writ of Certiorari. The Supreme Court need not accept the appeal and usually does not (*cert. den.*) unless a conflict exists among the lower courts that must be resolved or a constitutional issue is involved.

Appendix D

Table of Code Sections Cited

Appendix E

Present Value and Future Value Tables

Present Value of $1

N/R	1%	2%	3%	4%	5%	6%	7%	8%	9%	10%	11%	12%
1	0.9901	0.9804	0.9709	0.9615	0.9524	0.9434	0.9346	0.9259	0.9174	0.9091	0.9009	0.8929
2	0.9803	0.9612	0.9426	0.9246	0.9070	0.8900	0.8734	0.8573	0.8417	0.8264	0.8116	0.7972
3	0.9706	0.9423	0.9151	0.8890	0.8638	0.8396	0.8163	0.7938	0.7722	0.7513	0.7312	0.7118
4	0.9610	0.9238	0.8885	0.8548	0.8227	0.7921	0.7629	0.7350	0.7084	0.6830	0.6587	0.6355
5	0.9515	0.9057	0.8626	0.8219	0.7835	0.7473	0.7130	0.6806	0.6499	0.6209	0.5935	0.5674
6	0.9420	0.8880	0.8375	0.7903	0.7462	0.7050	0.6663	0.6302	0.5963	0.5645	0.5346	0.5066
7	0.9327	0.8706	0.8131	0.7599	0.7107	0.6651	0.6227	0.5835	0.5470	0.5132	0.4817	0.4523
8	0.9235	0.8535	0.7894	0.7307	0.6768	0.6274	0.5820	0.5403	0.5019	0.4665	0.4339	0.4039
9	0.9143	0.8368	0.7664	0.7026	0.6446	0.5919	0.5439	0.5002	0.4604	0.4241	0.3909	0.3606
10	0.9053	0.8203	0.7441	0.6756	0.6139	0.5584	0.5083	0.4632	0.4224	0.3855	0.3522	0.3220
11	0.8963	0.8043	0.7224	0.6496	0.5847	0.5268	0.4751	0.4289	0.3875	0.3505	0.3173	0.2875
12	0.8874	0.7885	0.7014	0.6246	0.5568	0.4970	0.4440	0.3971	0.3555	0.3186	0.2858	0.2567
13	0.8787	0.7730	0.6810	0.6006	0.5303	0.4688	0.4150	0.3677	0.3262	0.2897	0.2575	0.2292
14	0.8700	0.7579	0.6611	0.5775	0.5051	0.4423	0.3878	0.3405	0.2992	0.2633	0.2320	0.2046
15	0.8613	0.7430	0.6419	0.5553	0.4810	0.4173	0.3624	0.3152	0.2745	0.2394	0.2090	0.1827
16	0.8528	0.7284	0.6232	0.5339	0.4581	0.3936	0.3387	0.2919	0.2519	0.2176	0.1883	0.1631
17	0.8444	0.7142	0.6050	0.5134	0.4363	0.3714	0.3166	0.2703	0.2311	0.1978	0.1696	0.1456
18	0.8360	0.7002	0.5874	0.4936	0.4155	0.3503	0.2959	0.2502	0.2120	0.1799	0.1528	0.1300
19	0.8277	0.6864	0.5703	0.4746	0.3957	0.3305	0.2765	0.2317	0.1945	0.1635	0.1377	0.1161
20	0.8195	0.6730	0.5537	0.4564	0.3769	0.3118	0.2584	0.2145	0.1784	0.1486	0.1240	0.1037

Present Value of an Ordinary Annuity of $1

N/R	1%	2%	3%	4%	5%	6%	7%	8%	9%	10%	11%	12%
1	0.9901	0.9804	0.9709	0.9615	0.9524	0.9434	0.9346	0.9259	0.9174	0.9091	0.9009	0.8929
2	1.9704	1.9416	1.9135	1.8861	1.8594	1.8334	1.8080	1.7833	1.7591	1.7355	1.7125	1.6901
3	2.9410	2.8839	2.8286	2.7751	2.7232	2.6730	2.6243	2.5771	2.5313	2.4869	2.4437	2.4018
4	3.9020	3.8077	3.7171	3.6299	3.5460	3.4651	3.3872	3.3121	3.2397	3.1699	3.1024	3.0373
5	4.8534	4.7135	4.5797	4.4518	4.3295	4.2124	4.1002	3.9927	3.8897	3.7908	3.6959	3.6048
6	5.7955	5.6014	5.4172	5.2421	5.0757	4.9173	4.7665	4.6229	4.4859	4.3553	4.2305	4.1114
7	6.7282	6.4720	6.2303	6.0021	5.7864	5.5824	5.3893	5.2064	5.0330	4.8684	4.7122	4.5638
8	7.6517	7.3255	7.0197	6.7327	6.4632	6.2098	5.9713	5.7466	5.5348	5.3349	5.1461	4.9676
9	8.5660	8.1622	7.7861	7.4353	7.1078	6.8017	6.5152	6.2469	5.9952	5.7590	5.5370	5.3282
10	9.4713	8.9826	8.5302	8.1109	7.7217	7.3601	7.0236	6.7101	6.4177	6.1446	5.8892	5.6502
11	10.3676	9.7868	9.2526	8.7605	8.3064	7.8869	7.4987	7.1390	6.8052	6.4951	6.2065	5.9377
12	11.2551	10.5753	9.9540	9.3851	8.8633	8.3838	7.9427	7.5361	7.1607	6.8137	6.4924	6.1944
13	12.1337	11.3484	10.6350	9.9856	9.3936	8.8527	8.3577	7.9038	7.4869	7.1034	6.7499	6.4235
14	13.0037	12.1062	11.2961	10.5631	9.8986	9.2950	8.7455	8.2442	7.7862	7.3667	6.9819	6.6282
15	13.8651	12.8493	11.9379	11.1184	10.3797	9.7122	9.1079	8.5595	8.0607	7.6061	7.1909	6.8109
16	14.7179	13.5777	12.5611	11.6523	10.8378	10.1059	9.4466	8.8514	8.3126	7.8237	7.3792	6.9740
17	15.5623	14.2919	13.1661	12.1657	11.2741	10.4773	9.7632	9.1216	8.5436	8.0216	7.5488	7.1196
18	16.3983	14.9920	13.7535	12.6593	11.6896	10.8276	10.0591	9.3719	8.7556	8.2014	7.7016	7.2497
19	17.2260	15.6785	14.3238	13.1339	12.0853	11.1581	10.3356	9.6036	8.9501	8.3649	7.8393	7.3658
20	18.0456	16.3514	14.8775	13.5903	12.4622	11.4699	10.5940	9.8181	9.1285	8.5136	7.9633	7.4694

Future Value of $1

N/R	1%	2%	3%	4%	5%	6%	7%	8%	9%	10%	11%	12%
1	1.0100	1.0200	1.0300	1.0400	1.0500	1.0600	1.0700	1.0800	1.0900	1.1000	1.1100	1.1200
2	1.0201	1.0404	1.0609	1.0816	1.1025	1.1236	1.1449	1.1664	1.1881	1.2100	1.2321	1.2544
3	1.0303	1.0612	1.0927	1.1249	1.1576	1.1910	1.2250	1.2597	1.2950	1.3310	1.3676	1.4049
4	1.0406	1.0824	1.1255	1.1699	1.2155	1.2625	1.3108	1.3605	1.4116	1.4641	1.5181	1.5735
5	1.0510	1.1041	1.1593	1.2167	1.2763	1.3382	1.4026	1.4693	1.5386	1.6105	1.6851	1.7623
6	1.0615	1.1262	1.1941	1.2653	1.3401	1.4185	1.5007	1.5869	1.6771	1.7716	1.8704	1.9738
7	1.0721	1.1487	1.2299	1.3159	1.4071	1.5036	1.6058	1.7138	1.8280	1.9487	2.0762	2.2107
8	1.0829	1.1717	1.2668	1.3686	1.4775	1.5938	1.7182	1.8509	1.9926	2.1436	2.3045	2.4760
9	1.0937	1.1951	1.3048	1.4233	1.5513	1.6895	1.8385	1.9990	2.1719	2.3579	2.5580	2.7731
10	1.1046	1.2190	1.3439	1.4802	1.6289	1.7908	1.9672	2.1589	2.3674	2.5937	2.8394	3.1058
11	1.1157	1.2434	1.3842	1.5395	1.7103	1.8983	2.1049	2.3316	2.5804	2.8531	3.1518	3.4785
12	1.1268	1.2682	1.4258	1.6010	1.7959	2.0122	2.2522	2.5182	2.8127	3.1384	3.4985	3.8960
13	1.1381	1.2936	1.4685	1.6651	1.8856	2.1329	2.4098	2.7196	3.0658	3.4523	3.8833	4.3635
14	1.1495	1.3195	1.5126	1.7317	1.9799	2.2609	2.5785	2.9372	3.3417	3.7975	4.3104	4.8871
15	1.1610	1.3459	1.5580	1.8009	2.0789	2.3966	2.7590	3.1722	3.6425	4.1772	4.7846	5.4736
16	1.1726	1.3728	1.6047	1.8730	2.1829	2.5404	2.9522	3.4259	3.9703	4.5950	5.3109	6.1304
17	1.1843	1.4002	1.6528	1.9479	2.2920	2.6928	3.1588	3.7000	4.3276	5.0545	5.8951	6.8660
18	1.1961	1.4282	1.7024	2.0258	2.4066	2.8543	3.3799	3.9960	4.7171	5.5599	6.5436	7.6900
19	1.2081	1.4568	1.7535	2.1068	2.5270	3.0256	3.6165	4.3157	5.1417	6.1159	7.2633	8.6128
20	1.2202	1.4859	1.8061	2.1911	2.6533	3.2071	3.8697	4.6610	5.6044	6.7275	8.0623	9.6463

Future Value of an Ordinary Annuity of $1

N/R	1%	2%	3%	4%	5%	6%	7%	8%	9%	10%	11%	12%
1	1.0000	1.0000	1.0000	1.0000	1.0000	1.0000	1.0000	1.0000	1.0000	1.0000	1.0000	1.0000
2	2.0100	2.0200	2.0300	2.0400	2.0500	2.0600	2.0700	2.0800	2.0900	2.1000	2.1100	2.1200
3	3.0301	3.0604	3.0909	3.1216	3.1525	3.1836	3.2149	3.2464	3.2781	3.3100	3.3421	3.3744
4	4.0604	4.1216	4.1836	4.2465	4.3101	4.3746	4.4399	4.5061	4.5731	4.6410	4.7097	4.7793
5	5.1010	5.2040	5.3091	5.4163	5.5256	5.6371	5.7507	5.8666	5.9847	6.1051	6.2278	6.3528
6	6.1520	6.3081	6.4684	6.6330	6.8019	6.9753	7.1533	7.3359	7.5233	7.7156	7.9129	8.1152
7	7.2135	7.4343	7.6625	7.8983	8.1420	8.3938	8.6540	8.9228	9.2004	9.4872	9.7833	10.0890
8	8.2857	8.5830	8.8923	9.2142	9.5491	9.8975	10.2598	10.6366	11.0285	11.4359	11.8594	12.2997
9	9.3685	9.7546	10.1591	10.5828	11.0266	11.4913	11.9780	12.4876	13.0210	13.5795	14.1640	14.7757
10	10.4622	10.9497	11.4639	12.0061	12.5779	13.1808	13.8164	14.4866	15.1929	15.9374	16.7220	17.5487
11	11.5668	12.1687	12.8078	13.4864	14.2068	14.9716	15.7836	16.6455	17.5603	18.5312	19.5614	20.6546
12	12.6825	13.4121	14.1920	15.0258	15.9171	16.8699	17.8885	18.9771	20.1407	21.3843	22.7132	24.1331
13	13.8093	14.6803	15.6178	16.6268	17.7130	18.8821	20.1406	21.4953	22.9534	24.5227	26.2116	28.0291
14	14.9474	15.9739	17.0863	18.2919	19.5986	21.0151	22.5505	24.2149	26.0192	27.9750	30.0949	32.3926
15	16.0969	17.2934	18.5989	20.0236	21.5786	23.2760	25.1290	27.1521	29.3609	31.7725	34.4054	37.2797
16	17.2579	18.6393	20.1569	21.8245	23.6575	25.6725	27.8881	30.3243	33.0034	35.9497	39.1899	42.7533
17	18.4304	20.0121	21.7616	23.6975	25.8404	28.2129	30.8402	33.7502	36.9737	40.5447	44.5008	48.8837
18	19.6147	21.4123	23.4144	25.6454	28.1324	30.9057	33.9990	37.4502	41.3013	45.5992	50.3959	55.7497
19	20.8109	22.8406	25.1169	27.6712	30.5390	33.7600	37.3790	41.4463	46.0185	51.1591	56.9395	63.4397
20	22.0190	24.2974	26.8704	29.7781	33.0660	36.7856	40.9955	45.7620	51.1601	57.2750	64.2028	72.0524

Appendix F

Practice Set Assignments—Comprehensive Tax Return Problems

Problem 1

Diego B. (age 42) and Isabel S. (age 41) Castillo are married and live at 11426 W. Antelope Drive, Grapevine, TX 76092. Diego is the manager for Escondite, a popular restaurant in Grapevine. Isabel is a self-employed architect. They are calendar-year, cash-basis taxpayers.

1. Diego's annual salary from Escondite is $98,000. He also earns an annual bonus. The amount is determined in late December based on performance during the year and is paid in January of the following year. Diego's 2021 bonus was $6,000 (received in 2022), and his 2022 bonus was $7,000 (received in 2023). Diego participates in his employer's group health insurance plan to which he contributed $7,200 in 2022 for medical coverage. These contributions are made with after-tax dollars. The health plan covers Diego, Isabel, and their two dependent children. Escondite does not provide any retirement benefits, but it has established a § 401(k) plan to enable its employees to save for retirement. Diego contributed $19,000 to the plan in 2022. Diego's Form W–2 from Escondite shows $15,800 of Federal income tax was withheld during the year. Diego commutes to and from work six days a week (a roundtrip of 18 miles) in the family SUV. During 2022, Diego drove the SUV a total of 12,700 miles ratably throughout the year.

2. Isabel is a licensed architect who works part time as an architectural consultant. Her professional activity code is 541310. Her major clients are real estate developers (both residential and commercial) for whom she prepares structural designs and construction plans. She also advises on building code requirements regarding the renovation and remodeling of existing structures. Isabel does some of her work at client locations and the remainder in her office at home (see item 3).

   Isabel collected $72,000 in consulting fees during 2022. This total includes a $3,000 payment for work she performed in 2021 and does not include $5,000 she billed in December for work performed in late 2022. In addition, Isabel has a $6,400 unpaid invoice for work done in 2020. This client was convicted of arson in August 2019 and is now serving a five-year sentence in state prison. Isabel feels certain that she will never collect the $6,400 she is owed.

Isabel's business expenses for 2022 are:

Drafting supplies	$4,800
Reproduction materials (e.g., molds, models, photos, blueprints, copies)	3,200
On-site work clothing (e.g., hip boots, safety glasses, safety helmet)	860
Professional license fee	400
Subscriptions to professional journals	250
Dues to professional organizations	240

In addition, Isabel drove the family Acura (purchased on June 7, 2021) 940 miles on her job assignments. She uses the standard mileage method to deduct business costs related to the Acura. During 2022, Isabel drove the car a total of 10,000 miles. Both business and total mileage occurred ratably throughout the year.

3. When the Castillos purchased their home on February 2, 2020, they set aside 300 square feet (out of a total of 2,400 square feet) of living space for Isabel's office. The Castillos do not use the simplified method for computing the home office deduction. As of January 1, 2022, the home had an adjusted basis of $240,000 ($40,000 of which is attributable to the land) for purposes of line 37 of Form 8829. The fair market value of the property was $282,000. Relevant information concerning the residence for all of 2022 appears below.

Homeowner's insurance	$3,200
Repairs and maintenance	1,800
Utilities	6,200
Painting (office area only)	1,250

The cost of Isabel's office furniture and equipment was previously deducted under § 179 in the years these assets were acquired. On June 29, 2022, she purchased a fireproof file cabinet for $800 to safeguard the blueprints of her structural designs and construction plans. Whenever possible, Isabel prefers to avoid depreciating capital expenditures over time.

4. One of Isabel's clients was interested in building a shopping center on a tract of land she owned in Ector County. Isabel inherited the property from her uncle when he died on June 6, 1999. At that time, the land was valued at $40,000. It has since been rezoned for commercial use and has a current value of $200,000. On February 10, 2022, Isabel exchanged the Ector parcel for a similar tract in McLennan County worth $190,000 plus cash of $10,000.
5. On September 2, 2022, Isabel sold a tract of land in Hansford County to a farmer who owned the adjoining property. The land was inherited from the same uncle who died in 1999 and was valued at $30,000 on June 6, 1999. Under the terms of the sale, Isabel received cash of $20,000 and a note receivable to be paid in four equal installments at one-year intervals from the date of sale. Each note calls for the payment of $25,000 plus simple interest of 8%. To the extent allowed by law, Isabel wants to defer recognition of gain for as long as possible.
6. In early 2021, Diego learned that one of the restaurant's best servers, Alexis Garcia, was suffering domestic abuse at the hands of her husband Robert. When Robert started to abuse their five-year-old daughter as well, Alexis decided it was time to leave. Before they left on April 14, 2021, Diego loaned Alexis $5,500 to help her relocate with her daughter. Diego had her sign an interest-free note due in one year. Diego never heard from Alexis again. In late 2022, Diego learned that Alexis and her daughter had left the United States with no plans to ever return. Based on this information, Diego has no expectation the loan will ever be repaid.
7. On August 5, 2017, Diego purchased 1,000 shares of Farmers' Markets America (FMA) common stock for $16 a share as part of its initial public offering. The corporation was formed to establish and operate farmers' markets in mid-size cities

throughout the United States. Although some market locations were profitable, the venture as a whole proved to be a failure. In April 2022, FMA's remaining assets were seized by its creditors, and FMA stock became worthless.

8. In addition to the items previously noted, the Castillos had the following receipts for 2022:

Interest income from:		
General Motors corporate bonds	$1,900	
City of Grapevine, TX, bonds	1,400	
Castle Bank certificate of deposit	210	$ 3,510
Qualified dividends from MG&E Inc.		3,100
Refund from HomeStuff		430
Loan repayment by Elle Castillo-Anderson		4,500
Cash gift from Isabel's parents		32,000
2021 Federal income tax refund		290

In December 2021, the Castillos made a major purchase of household items (e.g., appliances, furniture, etc.) at HomeStuff. They called the manager when they realized they did not receive the advertised sale price. Consequently, the store corrected the mistake and sent a $430 refund that the Castillos received in January 2022.

In December 2018, Diego lent his sister Elle $4,000 to help pay for a honeymoon trip following her wedding to John Anderson. At that time, Elle signed a note payable that stated she would pay Diego the loan's principal amount plus 2.5% simple interest within five years. Diego was pleasantly surprised when Elle paid him back (plus interest of $500) on December 20, 2022.

On March 20 of each year, Isabel's parents send a generous gift of cash as a birthday present. Just as she has done for the past seven years, Isabel immediately contributed half of the gift to each of her kids' § 529 college savings plans.

9. The Castillos had the following expenditures for 2022:

Isabel's contribution to her traditional IRA		$ 6,000
Net gambling loss		1,000
Life insurance premiums		2,700
Medical and dental expenses not covered by insurance		16,612
Taxes:		
Ad valorem taxes on personal residence	$4,100	
State and local sales taxes from receipts	2,800	6,900
Interest on home mortgage reported on Form 1098		4,000
Cash contributions:		
Feeding Texas (EIN 74-2762542)	$1,750	
Texas governor's election campaign fund	300	2,050
Federal estimated tax payments		4,000

The $1,000 net gambling loss for 2022 is the difference between the Castillos' gambling winnings of $1,200 and losses of $2,200. The life insurance premiums relate to the universal life insurance policies that Diego and Isabel own. The first beneficiary on both policies is the other spouse, with the second beneficiaries being the children. Included in the medical expenses is $1,200, which was incurred in 2021 and paid in early February 2022. The Castillos can substantiate the $2,800 in sales taxes paid based on their purchase receipts for the year. The local sales tax rate in Grapevine is 2%. (*Hint*: Be sure to check to see if the Optional Sales Tax Tables provide the Castillos with a greater deduction.) Isabel contributed to the governor's campaign fund because she thinks his influence was key in getting the McLennan County land rezoned for commercial use (see item 4).

10. The Castillos maintain a household that includes their two children, Nico (age 16) and Rosa (age 19). Nico is a junior in high school and a talented wrestler. In hopes of competing at the state tournament, all of his free time is consumed with weight training and wrestling practices. Rosa graduated from high school on June 7, 2022, and decided to take a gap year. She is an accomplished vocalist and during 2022 earned $7,200 performing at various events (e.g., weddings, funerals). Rosa placed most of her earnings in a savings account for future use and kept only a small amount to spend on herself. Rosa plans to start college in fall of 2023.

11. Relevant Social Security numbers are noted below.

Name	Social Security Number
Diego B. Castillo	123-45-6876
Isabel S. Castillo	123-45-6877
Rosa J. Castillo	123-45-6878
Nico W. Castillo	123-45-6879

Requirements

Prepare a 2022 Federal income tax return (with all appropriate forms and schedules) for the Castillos following these guidelines:

- Diego and Isabel choose to file a joint income tax return.
- They do not wish to contribute to the Presidential Election Campaign Fund.
- They do not own any foreign bank accounts or other foreign investments.
- They had no transactions in digital assets during the tax year.
- They prefer to receive a refund of any overpaid taxes.
- The taxpayers are preparing their own return (i.e., no preparer is involved).
- For the past several years, the Castillos have itemized their deductions *from* AGI.
- The taxpayers have the necessary substantiation (e.g., records, receipts) to support all transactions reported in their tax return.
- Make necessary assumptions for information not given in the problem but needed to complete the return.

Problem 2

Gunnar B. (age 42) and Hannah R. (age 48) Ferguson are married and live at 5944 Overhill Road, Council Bluffs, IA 51503 (a suburb of Omaha). Gunnar is a chemist employed by BAC Pharmaceuticals, Inc., and Hannah is a self-employed doctor of anesthesiology. They are calendar-year, cash-basis taxpayers.

1. BAC Pharmaceuticals develops and produces injectable medicines used in chemotherapy treatments for cancer patients. Gunnar's Form W–2 from BAC reports taxable wages of $91,180 which is comprised of the following items. Gunnar manages the Omaha facility for an annual salary of $95,000. BAC makes contributions to a qualified defined contribution pension plan for all its full-time employees which are not included in current compensation. Although Gunnar could make contributions into the plan, he chose not to do so in 2022. Gunnar participates in his employer's group health insurance plan to which he contributed $4,000 in 2022 for medical coverage. These contributions are made with pre-tax dollars, so his taxable salary is reduced by $4,000. The health plan covers Gunnar, Hannah, and their two dependent children. Because of the risk associated with Gunnar's work (i.e., processing of chemotherapy drugs), BAC

provides all its employees with $200,000 of group term life insurance coverage. An additional $180 of income is included in Gunnar's Form W–2 to report the taxable value of this insurance. Gunnar's Form W–2 from BAC also reflects income tax withholding of $6,500 for Federal income taxes and $4,000 for state of Iowa income taxes.

2. BAC generally reimburses Gunnar for expenses related to his work for the company. However, as a matter of policy, BAC does not reimburse for the following:

Monthly dinner meetings of the Midwestern Chemists Association (MCA)	$825
Dues to professional organizations	240
Subscriptions to professional journals	180
MIA correspondence study course	230

Gunnar attended 11 MCA dinner meetings in 2022. The cost of each dinner included the following: $40 fee for speaker, $25 price of meal, and $10 parking fee. Gunnar goes to the meetings from work and returns home the same night. The Management Institute of America (MIA) charge was for an online home study course on ways to improve safety measures and avoid accidents in the industrial workplace.

3. Hannah Ferguson is a board-certified doctor of anesthesiology. She provides anesthesiology services at several hospitals and surgical centers in the greater Omaha area. Hannah is well-respected by the surgeons with whom she works. She uses her home as her business address. She keeps her records there, dictates notes to patient files, participates in conference calls regarding upcoming surgeries and postoperative surgical care, answers work-related phone calls, and compiles and sends patient bills. Because Hannah does not maintain a specific area for exclusive business use, she does not claim a tax deduction for a home office. Hannah's receipts from her practice during 2022 were $185,000, $16,000 of which was for services performed in 2021. Not included in these amounts is $17,500 she received in January 2023 for services rendered in December 2022. Hannah's professional activity code is 621111.

Hannah had the following business expenses in 2022:

Medical clothing (e.g., lab coats, surgical scrubs)	$2,200
Medical malpractice insurance	9,500
State medical license fee	450
Dues to professional organizations	350
Subscriptions to professional journals	340

In addition, she drove the family Suburban (purchased on March 2, 2021) 2,900 miles in connection with her work. She uses the standard mileage method for computing deductible vehicle costs. Total mileage for the Suburban is 9,000 miles for the year. Both business and total mileage occurred ratably throughout the year.

4. Gunnar's widowed mother, Astrid, endured a few different medical challenges in late 2021. On December 30, 2021, she suffered a massive stroke and died in the hospital on January 16, 2022. Some of Astrid's medical expenses were covered by Medicare, with the remainder being paid by the Fergusons. On February 18, 2022, Gunnar paid $39,800 to the hospital, $28,000 of which was attributable to expenses incurred in 2021. At the same time, Gunnar also paid the funeral expenses of $16,000. Although Astrid lived in her own home prior to the stroke, Gunnar and Hannah have properly claimed her as a dependent for the past few years.

5. As Astrid's sole heir, Gunnar inherited her home and its furnishings (located at 5422 Turnbury Court, Carson, IA 51525). The costs and values involved are as follows:

	Cost Basis	FMV on 1/16/22
Lot	$ 10,000	$ 30,000
House	110,000	250,000
Furnishings	55,000	25,000

Because the home was located in an attractive rental area, Gunnar decided not to sell. Instead, he rented the property fully furnished on May 1, 2022. The terms of the lease (executed on April 30) provide for the following: one-year lease at $2,500 per month (payable on the first of each month), last month's rent payable in advance, and damage deposit of $1,500. In total, Gunnar received $24,000 from the tenants in 2022 for their use of the property. Besides depreciation, his expenses were as follows:

Property taxes	$4,800
Insurance	3,900
Repairs	2,100
Tenant locator service	400

For MACRS depreciation purposes, Gunnar plans to use the straight-line method with the mid-month convention to compute the deduction for the realty and the 200%-declining-balance method with a half-year convention for the personalty.

6. While walking the family dogs in late July, Gunnar was struck by a delivery van and seriously injured. After being hospitalized for a week, he returned home, bruised and sore, but with no permanent injuries. The driver of the van was arrested and ticketed by the police for reckless operation of a vehicle and was later prosecuted for drug use. To prevent adverse publicity related to a lawsuit, the owner of the delivery service paid for Gunnar's medical expenses and sent him a check on August 16, 2022, for $90,000. The check was accompanied by a letter that stated: "This $90,000 is a settlement for physical injuries sustained by Gunnar Ferguson." Gunnar was represented in the negotiations with the delivery company by his brother, a practicing attorney. He did not charge the Fergusons for his services.

7. The Fergusons had the following property transactions during 2022:
   a. On May 5, the City Council condemned unimproved land owned by Gunnar for the construction of a new fire station. He purchased the land (two vacant lots at 3400 and 3402 Maple Lane) as an investment on May 25, 2012, for $14,000. In exchange for the lots, the city gave Gunnar a large unimproved lot at 440 Washington Street that was valued at $20,000. All in all, he was satisfied with the exchange because the Washington Street property is in a better neighborhood and has a greater potential for appreciation.
   b. On August 22, Gunnar sold a gun collection for $32,000 to an avid collector. The collection was a gift from Gunnar's father on December 25, 2014, when it was worth $22,000. His father bought the collection in 1997 for $14,000. Gunnar's sale of the collection was documented by a bill of sale, signed by both Gunnar and the buyer.
   c. On September 9, the Fergusons sold 3,000 shares of Raptor Pharmaceuticals for $2,000. The couple purchased the stock on December 4, 2021, for $25,000. The investment was motivated by the rumor that Raptor was developing a new drug for infertility. On September 7, the FDA announced that it would not approve the drug due to adverse side effects, and the price of Raptor stock plummeted. The Fergusons' broker provided them with a Form 1099–B, which reported the gross proceeds from the sale and their basis in the stock.

8. The Fergusons have a long-term capital loss carryover of $1,500 from 2021.

9. In March 2022, the Fergusons were audited by the Iowa Department of Revenue for tax years 2019 and 2020. The audit proposed no changes for the 2019 tax return. However, the Fergusons were assessed $2,250 additional income tax for 2020 (no interest or penalties were assessed). The Fergusons agreed with the assessment and paid the $2,250 immediately.

10. During 2022, Gunnar served on a jury for a civil case that was litigated at the county courthouse. As a result of the service, he was paid $700 and incurred unreimbursed parking expenses of $60. In conformance with company policy, Gunnar remitted the $700 of jury duty fees to BAC.

11. In addition to the items already noted, the Fergusons had the following receipts in 2022:

Life insurance proceeds		$50,000
2021 Iowa state income tax refund		450
Proceeds from garage sale		2,600
Interest income:		
City of Omaha bonds	$480	
CitiBank certificate of deposit	600	1,080

The insurance proceeds were paid to Gunnar as the designated beneficiary of Astrid's life insurance policy. At the garage sale, the Fergusons sold personal items (e.g., camper, furniture, hunting and fishing equipment) that belonged to Gunnar's father and mother (i.e., Astrid). Gunnar and Hannah estimated the items they sold originally cost $7,100. The garage sale proceeds were donated to the Alzheimers Research Association (EIN 23-7438025) in memory of Gunnar's father. The Fergusons had an overpayment of tax on their 2021 Federal income tax return. Instead of receiving a refund, they applied the $3,000 overpayment toward their 2022 income tax liability.

12. The Fergusons had the following additional expenditures for 2022:

Dentist bills not covered by insurance	$ 3,100
Federal estimated income tax payments	36,000
Iowa estimated income tax payments	20,000
Ad valorem property taxes on personal residence	14,100
Interest on home mortgage reported on Form 1098	2,600
Contributions to Philadelphia Church in Council Bluffs (EIN 42-1301970)	23,600

As part of a program sponsored by their church (a qualified charity), the Fergusons used the family Suburban to transport senior citizens to religious services for a total of 900 miles during 2022. The Suburban also was used for numerous visits to an orthodontist for both the Fergusons' children for a total of 480 miles. Both the charitable and medical mileage occurred ratably throughout the year.

13. The Fergusons' household includes two dependent children, Eric (age 15) and Olivia (age 14), both of whom are full-time students in high school. Relevant Social Security numbers appear below.

Name	**Social Security Number**
Gunnar B. Ferguson	123-45-6575
Hannah R. Ferguson	123-45-6576
Astrid E. Ferguson	123-45-6577
Eric M. Ferguson	123-45-6578
Olivia A. Ferguson	123-45-6579

Requirements

Prepare a 2022 Federal income tax return (with all appropriate forms and schedules) for the Fergusons, following these guidelines:

- Gunnar and Hannah choose to file a joint income tax return.
- They do not wish to contribute to the Presidential Election Campaign Fund.
- They do not own any foreign bank accounts or other foreign investments.
- They had no transactions in digital assets during the tax year.
- They prefer to receive a refund of any overpaid taxes.
- The taxpayers are preparing their own return (i.e., no preparer is involved).
- For the past several years, the Fergusons have itemized their deductions *from* AGI instead of using the standard deduction. In addition, the Fergusons have deducted state income taxes (not sales taxes) for the past several years.
- The taxpayers have the necessary substantiation (e.g., records, receipts) to support all transactions reported in their tax return.
- Make necessary assumptions for information not given in the problem but needed to complete the return.

Index

A

B

C

E

F

G

H

I

J

K

L

M

N

Q

R

S

T

U

V

W

Y

Z

CNOWv2

Closing the Gap Between the Classroom and the Real World

Career Prep Tools

Students gain access to powerful Business, Tax and Accounting tools they'll use in the real world, including Excel Online, Tax Forms, Data Analytics and General Ledger Software.

Student Support

Give students the tools and feedback they need to succeed when working on their own, including question tutorial videos, lecture videos, study plans and Check My Work question feedback.

Real-Time Analytics

Track progress and know where students stand in class at all times with the easy-to-use gradebook and robust analytics reports.

LMS Integration

Enhanced features such as grade sync are available to help manage every aspect of your class in one place, from practice and graded assignments to quizzes and tests.

cengage.com/cnowv2

Student Reviews

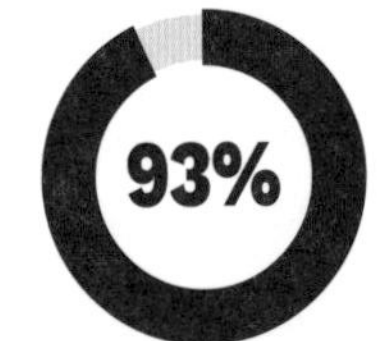

"*CNOWv2* helped me understand course materials better."

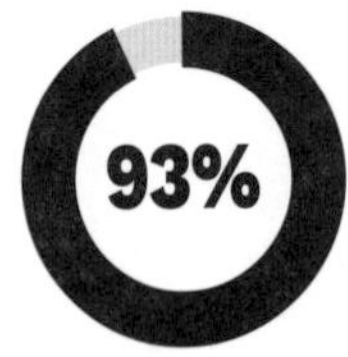

"Using *CNOWv2* allowed me to better track my progress in this course."

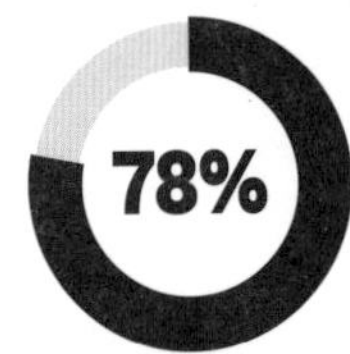

"The feedback and explanations in *CNOWv2* helped me learn the material."

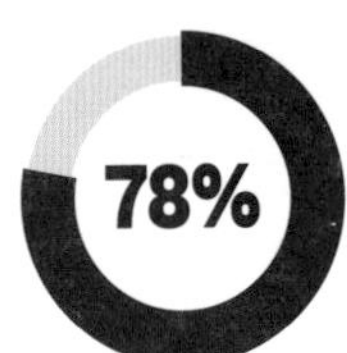

"*CNOWv2* helped me better understand the expectations of my instructor."

Cengage Unlimited

With Cengage Unlimited, a student receives access to an entire library of eTextbooks, online learning platforms, at least four free hardcopy rentals and hundreds of student success and career readiness skill-building activities. Only assigning textbooks for your course? Ask about Cengage Unlimited eTextbooks.

Available to all higher education and career students in the U.S., in bookstores and online. For customers outside the U.S., contact your local sales partner.

cengage.com/unlimited/instructor

Cengage

AMT Formula for Individuals

Taxable income (increased by any standard deduction taken)
Plus or minus: Adjustments
Plus: Preferences
Equals: Alternative minimum taxable income (AMTI)
Minus: Exemption
Equals: Alternative minimum tax (AMT) base
Multiplied by: 26% or 28% rate
Equals: Tentative minimum tax before foreign tax credit
Minus: AMT foreign tax credit
Equals: Tentative minimum tax (TMT)
Minus: Regular tax liability (less any foreign tax credit)
Equals: AMT (if TMT > regular tax liability)